D1453632

# THE
# COMPUTER
# ENGINEERING
# HANDBOOK

# The Electrical Engineering Handbook Series

*Series Editor*
**Richard C. Dorf**
University of California, Davis

## Titles Included in the Series

*The Avionics Handbook*, Cary R. Spitzer
*The Biomedical Engineering Handbook, 2nd Edition*, Joseph D. Bronzino
*The Circuits and Filters Handbook*, Wai-Kai Chen
*The Communications Handbook*, Jerry D. Gibson
*The Control Handbook*, William S. Levine
*The Digital Signal Processing Handbook*, Vijay K. Madisetti & Douglas Williams
*The Electrical Engineering Handbook, 2nd Edition*, Richard C. Dorf
*The Electric Power Engineering Handbook*, Leo L. Grigsby
*The Electronics Handbook*, Jerry C. Whitaker
*The Engineering Handbook*, Richard C. Dorf
*The Handbook of Formulas and Tables for Signal Processing*, Alexander D. Poularikas
*The Industrial Electronics Handbook*, J. David Irwin
*The Measurement, Instrumentation, and Sensors Handbook*, John G. Webster
*The Mechanical Systems Design Handbook*, Osita D.I. Nwokah and Yidirim Hurmuzlu
*The RF and Microwave Handbook*, Mike Golio
*The Mobile Communications Handbook, 2nd Edition*, Jerry D. Gibson
*The Ocean Engineering Handbook*, Ferial El-Hawary
*The Technology Management Handbook*, Richard C. Dorf
*The Transforms and Applications Handbook, 2nd Edition*, Alexander D. Poularikas
*The VLSI Handbook*, Wai-Kai Chen
*The Mechatronics Handbook*, Robert H. Bishop
*The Computer Engineering Handbook*, Vojin G. Oklobdzija

## Forthcoming Titles

*The Circuits and Filters Handbook, 2nd Edition*, Wai-Kai Chen
*The Handbook of Ad hoc Wireless Networks*, Mohammad Ilyas
*The Handbook of Optical Communication Networks*, Mohammad Ilyas
*The Handbook of Nanoscience, Engineering, and Technology*, William A. Goddard,
   Donald W. Brenner, Sergey E. Lyshevski, and Gerald J. Iafrate
*The Communications Handbook, 2nd Edition*, Jerry Gibson and Daniel Blumenthal

# THE
# COMPUTER
# ENGINEERING
# HANDBOOK

Edited by
VOJIN G. OKLOBDZIJA

# CRC PRESS

Boca Raton   London   New York   Washington, D.C.

Cover photos from Molecular Expressions Website (www.microscopy.fsu.edu), National High Magnetic Field Laboratory, Optical Microscopy Division, The Florida State University, Tallahassee, FL. ©1995–2001 Michael W. Davidson and The Florida State University. With permission.

**Library of Congress Cataloging-in-Publication Data**

The computer engineering handbook / Vojin G. Oklobdzija, editor-in-chief.
     p.  cm.--(Electrical engineering handbook series)
  Includes bibliographical references and index.
  ISBN 0-8493-0885-2 (alk. paper)
    1. Computer engineering. 2. Electronic digital computers. I. Oklobdzija, Vojin G. II.
Series.

TK7885 .C645 2001
004—dc21
                                         2001043891

**Visit the CRC Press Web site at www.crcpress.com**

© 2002 by CRC Press LLC

No claim to original U.S. Government works
International Standard Book Number 0-8493-0885-2
Library of Congress Card Number 2001043891
Printed in the United States of America 1 2 3 4 5 6 7 8 9 0
Printed on acid-free paper

**Fernanda**
por tu orgullo
coraje y dignidad
de una mujer luchadora

# Preface

## Purpose and Background

Computer engineering is such a vast field that it is difficult and almost impossible to present everything in a single book. This problem is also exaggerated by the fact that the field of computers and computer design has been changing so rapidly that by the time this book is introduced some of the issues may already be obsolete. However, we have tried to capture what is fundamental and therefore will be of lasting value. Also, we tried to capture the trends, new directions, and new developments. This book could easily fill thousands of pages because there are so many issues in computer design and so many new fields that are popping out daily. We hope that in the future CRC Press will come with new editions covering some of the more specialized topics in more details. Given that, and many other limitations, we are aware that some areas were not given sufficient attention and some others were not covered at all. However, we hope that the areas covered are covered very well given that they are written by specialists that are recognized as leading experts in their fields. We are thankful for their valuable time and effort.

## Organization

This book contains a dozen sections. First, we start with the fabrication and technology that has been a driving factor for the electronic industry. No sector of the industry has experienced such tremendous growth. The progress has surpassed what we thought to be possible, and limits that were once thought of as fundamental were broken several times. When the first 256 kbit DRAM chips were introduced the "alpha particle scare" (the problem encountered with alpha particles discharging the memory cell) predicted that radiation effects would limit further scaling in dimensions of memory chips. Twenty years later, we have reached 256 Mbit DRAM chips—a thousand times improvement in density—and we see no limit to further scaling. In fact, the memory capacity has been tripling every two years while the number of transistors on the processor chip has been doubling every two years.

The next section deals with computer architecture and computer system organization, a top-level view. Several architectural concepts and organizations of computer systems are described. The section ends with description of performance evaluation measures, which are the bottom line from the user's point of view.

Important design techniques are described in two separate sections, one of which deals exclusively with power consumed by the system. Power consumption is becoming the most important issue as computers are starting to penetrate large consumer product markets, and in several cases low-power consumption is more important than the performance that the system can deliver.

Penetration of computer systems into the consumer's market is described in the sections dealing with signal processing, embedded applications, and future directions in computing.

Finally, reliability and testability of computer systems is described in the last section.

## Locating Your Topic

Several avenues are available to access desired information. A complete table of contents is presented at the front of the book. Each of the sections is preceded with an individual table of contents. Finally, each chapter begins with its own table of contents. Each contributed article contains comprehensive references. Some of them contain a "To Probe Further" section where a general discussion of various sources such as books, journals, magazines, and periodicals are discussed. To be in tune with the modern times, some of the authors have also included Web pointers to valuable resources and information. We hope our readers will find this to be appropriate and of much use.

A subject index has been compiled to provide a means of accessing information. It can also be used to locate definitions. The page on which the definition appears for each key defining term is given in the index.

*The Computer Engineering Handbook* is designed to provide answers to most inquiries and to direct inquirers to further sources and references. We trust that it will meet the needs of our readership.

## Acknowledgments

The value of this book is completely based on the work of many experts and their excellent contributions. I am grateful to them. They spent hours of their valuable time without any compensation and with a sole motivation to provide learning material and help enhance the profession. I would like to thank Prof. Saburo Muroga, who provided editorial advice, reviewed the content of the book, made numerous suggestions, and encouraged me to do it. I am indebted to him as well as to other members of the advisory board. I would like to thank my colleague and friend Prof. Richard Dorf for asking me to edit this book and trusting me with this project. Kristen Maus worked tirelessly to put all of this material in a decent shape and so did Nora Konopka of CRC Press. My son, Stanisha, helped me with my English. It is their work that made this book.

# Editor-in-Chief

**Vojin G. Oklobdzija** is a Fellow of the Institute of Electrical and Electronics Engineers and Distinguished Lecturer of IEEE Solid-State Circuits and IEEE Circuits and Systems Societies. He received his Ph.D. and M.Sc. degrees from the University of California, Los Angeles in 1978 and 1982, as well as a Dipl. Ing. (MScEE) from the Electrical Engineering Department, University of Belgrade, Yugoslavia in 1971.

From 1982 to 1991 he was at the IBM T. J. Watson Research Center in New York where he made contributions to the development of RISC architecture and processors. In the course of this work he obtained a patent on Register-Renaming, which enabled an entire new generation of super-scalar processors.

From 1988–90 he was a visiting faculty at the University of California, Berkeley, while on leave from IBM. Since 1991, Prof. Oklobdzija has held various consulting positions. He was a consultant to Sun Microsystems Laboratories, AT&T Bell Laboratories, Hitachi Research Laboratories, Silicon Systems/Texas Instruments Inc., and Siemens Corp. where he was principal architect of the Siemens/Infineon's TriCore processor. Currently he serves as an advisor to SONY and Fujitsu Laboratories.

In 1988 he started Integration, which was incorporated in 1996. Integration Corp. delivered several successful processor and encryption processor designs (see: www.integration-corp.com).

Prof. Oklobdzija has held various academic appointments, besides the current one at the University of California. In 1991, as a Fulbright professor, he helped to develop programs at universities in South America. From 1996–98 he taught courses in the Silicon Valley through the University of California, Berkeley Extension, and at Hewlett-Packard.

He holds seven U.S., four European, one Japanese, and one Taiwanese patents in the area of computer design and seven others are currently pending.

Prof. Oklobdzija is a member of the American Association for the Advancement of Science, and the American Association of University Professors. He serves on the editorial boards of the *IEEE Transactions on VLSI Systems* and the *Journal of VLSI Signal Processing*. He served on the program committees of the International Conference on Computer Design, the International Symposium on VLSI Technology and the Symposium on Computer Arithmetic. In 1997, he was a General Chair of the 13th Symposium on Computer Arithmetic and has served as a program committee member of the International Solid-State Circuits Conference (ISSCC) since 1996. He has published over 120 papers in the areas of circuits and technology, computer arithmetic and computer architecture, and has given over 100 invited talks and short courses in the USA, Europe, Latin America, Australia, China, and Japan.

# Editorial Board

# Contributors

**Cyrus (Morteza) Afghahi**
Broadcom Corporation
Irvine, California

**Chouki Aktouf**
Institute Universitaire de
Technologie
Valex Cedex, France

**John F. Alexander**
University of North Florida
Jacksonville, Florida

**Krste Asanovic**
Massachusetts Institute of
Technology
Cambridge, Massachusetts

**William Athas**
Apple Computer Inc.
Sunnyvale, California

**Ming Au-Yeung**
San Francisco State University
San Francisco, California

**Pervez M. Aziz**
Agere Systems
Allentown, Pennsylvania

**Raymond Barrett**
University of North Florida
Jacksonville, Florida

**Mario Blaum**
IBM Alamaden Research Center
San Jose, California

**Shekhar Borkar**
Intel Corporation
Hillsboro, Oregon

**Pradip Bose**
IBM T.J. Watson Research Center
Yorktown Heights, New York

**Don Bouldin**
University of Tennessee
Knoxville, Tennessee

**E. Bozorgzadeh**
University of California
Los Angeles, California

**Thomas D. Burd**
University of California
Berkeley, California

**R. Chandramouli**
Synopsys Inc.
Mountain View, California

**Tzi-cker Chiueh**
State University of New York at Stony
Brook
Stony Brook, New York

**K. Wayne Current**
University of California
Davis, California

**Adam Dabrowski**
Poznan University of Technology
Poznan, Poland

**Babak Daneshrad**
University of California
Los Angeles, California

**Vivek De**
Intel Corporation
Hillsboro, Oregon

**Miroslav Despotović**
Technical University of Novi Sad
Novi Sad, Yugoslavia

**Jozo J. Dujmović**
San Francisco State University
San Francisco, California

**Manoj Franklin**
University of Maryland
College Park, Maryland

**Matt Franklin**
University of California at Davis
Davis, California

**Borko Furht**
Florida Atlantic University
Boca Raton, Florida

**Jean-Luc Gaudiot**
University of Southern California
City of Commerce, California

**U. Glaeser**
Halstenbach ACT GmbH
Paderborn, Germany

**Ricardo Gonzalez**
Tensilica, Inc.
Santa Clara, California

**Gensuke Goto**
Yamagata University
Yamagata, Japan

**Anna Hać**
University of Hawaii
Honolulu, Hawaii

**Siamack Haghighi**
Intel Corporation
Santa Clara, California

**Yoshiaki Hagiwara**
Sony Corporation
Tokyo, Japan

**James O. Hamblen**
Georgia Institute of Technology
Atlanta, Georgia

**Mohammad Ilyas**
Florida Atlantic University
Boca Raton, Florida

**Hiroshi Iwai**
Tokyo Institute of Technology
Yokohama, Japan

**Bruce Jacob**
University of Maryland
College Park, Maryland

**Shahram Jamshidi**
Intel Corporation
Santa Clara, California

**Snehal Jariwala**
Intel Corporation
Santa Clara, California

**Wenjie Jiang**
Intel Corporation
Santa Clara, California

**Eugene John**
The University of Texas
San Antonio, Texas

**Lizy Kurian John**
University of Texas at Austin
Austin, Texas

**Yuichi Kado**
NIT Telecommunications
   Technology Laboratories
Kanagawa, Japan

**James Kao**
Intel Corporation
Hillsboro, Oregon

**R. Kastner**
University of California
Los Angeles, California

**Ali Keshavarzi**
Intel Corporation
Hillsboro, Oregon

**Fabian Klass**
Sun Microsystems, Inc.
Palo Alto, California

**Tadahiro Kuroda**
Keio University
Keio, Japan

**Ruby Lee**
Princeton University
Princeton, New Jersey

**Worayot Lertniphonphun**
Georgia Institute of Technology
Atlanta, Georgia

**John George Maneatis**
True Circuits, Inc.
Los Altos, California

**Tomasz Marciniak**
Poznan University of Technology
Poznan, Poland

**Brian Marcus**
IBM Almaden Research Center
San Jose, California

**Dejan Marković**
University of California
Berkeley, California

**Daniel Martin**
Infineon
Mountain View, California

**Binu Matthew**
University of Utah
Salt Lake City, Utah

**John C. McCallum**
National University of Singapore
Singapore, Singapore

**James H. McClellan**
Georgia Institute of Technology
Atlanta, Georgia

**S.O. Memik**
University of California
Los Angeles, California

**Masayuki Miyazaki**
Hitachi, Ltd.
Tokyo, Japan

**John Morris**
University of Western Australia
Perth, Australia

**Samiha Mourad**
Santa Clara University
Santa Clara, California

**Raj Nair**
Intel Corporation
Hillsboro, Oregon

**Siva Narendra**
Intel Corporation
Hillsboro, Oregon

**Danny F. Newport**
University of Tennessee
Knoxville, Tennessee

**Kevin J. Nowka**
IBM Austin Research Laboratory
Austin, Texas

**Shun-ichiro Ohmi**
Tokyo Institute of Technology
Yokohama, Japan

**Garrett Okamoto**
Santa Clara University
Santa Clara, California

**Ara Patapoutian**
Maxtor
Shrewsbury, Massachusetts

**Rakesh Patel**
Intel Corporation
Santa Clara, California

**Gerald G. Pechanek**
BOPS, Inc.
Chapel Hill, North Carolina

**Christian Piguet**
CSEM: Centre Suisse d'Electronique
et de Microtechnique SA and
LAP-EPFL
Neuchatel, Switzerland

**Donna Quammen**
George Mason University
Fairfax, Virginia

**Hema Ramamurthy**
Intel Corporation
Santa Clara, California

**Todd R. Reed**
University of California at Davis
Davis, California

**Peter Reiher**
University of California
Los Angeles, California

**Eric Rotenberg**
North Carolina State University
Raleigh, North Carolina

**Kaushik Roy**
Purdue University
West Lafayette, Indiana

**Abdul Sadka**
University of Surrey
Surrey, England

**Sadiq M. Sait**
King Fahd University
Dhahran, Saudi Arabia

**M. Sarrafzadeh**
University of California
Los Angeles, California

**Thomas C. Savell**
Creative Advanced Technology
Center
Santa Cruz, California

**Necip Sayiner**
Agere Systems
Allentown, Pennsylvania

**Giovanni Seni**
Motorola Human Interface Labs
Palo Alto, California

**Vojin Šenk**
University of Novi Sad
Novi Sad, Yugoslavia

**Katsunori Seno**
Sony Corporation
Tokyo, Japan

**Dezsö Sima**
Budapest Polytechnic
Budapest, Hungary

**Kevin Skadron**
University of Virginia
Charlottesville, Virginia

**Mark Smotherman**
Clemson University
Clemson, South Carolina

**Hendrawan Soeleman**
Purdue University
West Lafayette, Indiana

**Emina Šoljanin**
Lucent Technologies
New Vernon, New Jersey

**Dinesh Somasekhar**
Intel Corporation
Hillsboro, Oregon

**Z. Stamenković**
University of Nis
Nis, Yugoslavia

**N. Stojadinović**
University of Nis
Nis, Yugoslavia

**Jayashree Subrahmonia**
IBM Thomas J. Watson Research
Center
Yorktown Heights, New York

**Earl E. Swartzlander, Jr.**
University of Texas at Austin
Austin, Texas

**Fred J. Taylor**
University of Florida
Gainesville, Florida

**Vivek Tiwari**
Intel Corporation
Santa Clara, California

**Daniel Tomasevich**
San Francisco State University
San Francisco, California

**Nestoras Tzartzanis**
Fujitsu Laboratories of America
Sunnyvale, California

**Jonathan W. Valvano**
University of Texas at Austin
Austin, Texas

**Hemmige Varadarajan**
Intel Corporation
Santa Clara, California

**Peter J. Varman**
Rice University
Houston, Texas

**Bane Vasić**
University of Arizona
Tucson, Arizona

**Ingrid Verbauwhede**
University of California
Los Angeles, California

**H. T. Vierhaus**
Bradenburgische Technische
Universitat
Cottbus, Germany

**Jeffrey Scott Vitter**
Duke University
Durham, North Carolina

**Albert Wang**
Tensilica, Inc.
Santa Clara, California

**Shoichi Washino**
Tottori University
Tottori City, Japan

**Wayne Wolf**
Princeton University
Princeton, New Jersey

**Thucydides Xanthopoulos**
Caveo Networks, Inc.
Marlboro, Massachusetts

**Shunzo Yamashita**
Hitachi, Ltd.
Tokyo, Japan

**Chik-Kong Ken Yang**
University of California
Los Angeles, California

**Yibin Ye**
Intel Corporation
Hillsboro, Oregon

**Habib Youssef**
King Fahd University
Dharan, Saudi Arabia

# Contents

## SECTION III   Design Techniques

## SECTION IV   Design for Low Power

## SECTION V   Embedded Applications

## SECTION VI   Signal Processing

# SECTION VII  Communications and Networks

# SECTION VIII  Input/Output

# SECTION IX  Operating System

# SECTION X  New Directions in Computing

# I

# Fabrication and Technology

# 1

# Trends and Projections for the Future of Scaling and Future Integration Trends

Hiroshi Iwai
*Tokyo Institute of Technology*

Shun-ichiro Ohmi
*Tokyo Institute of Technology*

## 1.1 Introduction

Recently, information technology (IT)—such as Internet, i-mode, cellular phone, and car navigation—has spread very rapidly all over of the world. IT is expected to dramatically raise the efficiency of our society and greatly improve the quality of our life. It should be noted that the progress of IT entirely owes to that of semiconductor technology, especially Silicon LSIs (Large Scale Integrated Circuits). Silicon LSIs provide us high speed/frequency operation of tremendously many functions with low cost, low power, small size, small weight, and high reliability. In these 30 years, the gate length of the metal oxide semiconductor field effect transistors (MOSFETs) has reduced 100 times, the density of DRAM increased 500,000 times, and clock frequency of MPU increased 2,500 times, as shown in Table 1.1. Without such a marvelous progress of LSI technologies, today's great success in information technology would not be realized at all.

The origin of the concept for solid-state circuit can be traced back to the beginning of last century, as shown in Fig. 1.1. It was more than 70 years ago, when J. Lilienfeld using $Al/Al_2O_3/Cu_2S$ as an MOS structure invented a concept of MOSFETs. Then, 54 years ago, first transistor (bipolar) was realized using germanium. In 1960, 2 years after the invention of integrated circuits (IC), the first MOSFET was realized by using the Si substrate and $SiO_2$ gate insulator [1]. Since then Si and $SiO_2$ became the key materials for electronic circuits. It takes, however, more than several years until the Silicon MOSFET evolved to Silicon ICs and further grew up to Silicon LSIs. The Silicon LSIs became popular in the market from the beginning of 1970s as a 1 kbit DRAM and a 4 bit MPU (microprocessor). In the early 1970s, LSIs started

**TABLE 1.1**    Past and Current Status of Advanced LSI Products

| Year | Min. $L_g$ ($\mu$m) | Ratio | DRAM | Ratio | MPU | Ratio |
|------|------|-------|------|-------|-----|-------|
| 1970/72 | 10 | 1 | 1 k | 1 | 750 k | 1 |
| 2001 | 0.1 | 1/100 | 512 M | 256,000 | 1.7 G | 2,300 |

## Year 2001    New Century for Solid-State Circuit

|  | 73 years since the concept of MOSFET |
|--|--|
| 20th C | 1928, J. Lilienfeld, MOSFET patent |
|  | 54 years since the 1st Transistor |
|  | 1947, J. Bardeen, W. Bratten, bipolar Tr |
|  | 43-42 years since the 1st Integrated Circuits |
|  | 1958, J. Kilby, IC |
|  | 1959, R. Noice, Planar Technolgy |
|  | 41 years since the 1st Si-MOSFET |
|  | 1960, D. Kahng, Si-MOSFET |
|  | 38 years since the 1st CMOS |
|  | 1963, CMOS, by F. Wanlass, C. T. Sah |
|  | 31 years since the 1st 1 kbit DRAM (or LSI) |
|  | 1970 Intel 1103 |
|  | 16 years since CMOS became the major technology |
|  | 1985, Toshiba 1 Mbit CMOS DRAM |

**FIGURE 1.1**    History of LSI in 20th century.

by using PMOS technology in which threshold voltage control was easier, but soon the PMOS was replaced by NMOS, which was suitable for high speed operation. It was the middle of 1980s when CMOS became the main stream of Silicon LSI technology because of its capability for low power consumption. Now CMOS technology has realized 512 Mbit DRAMs and 1.7 GHz clock MPUs, and the gate length of MOSFETs in such LSIs becomes as small as 100 nm.

Figure 1.2 shows the cross sections of NMOS LSIs in the early 1970s and those of present CMOS LSIs. The old NMOS LSI technology contains only several film layers made of Si, $SiO_2$, and Al, which are basically composed of only five elements: Si, O, Al, B, and P. Now, the structure becomes very complicated, and so many layers and so many elements have been involved.

In the past 30 years, transistors have been miniaturized significantly. Thanks to the miniaturization, the number of components and performance of LSIs have increased significantly. Figures 1.3 and 1.4 show the microphotographs of 1 kbit and 256 Mbit DRAM chips, respectively. Individual tiny rectangle units barely recognized in the 16 large rectangle units of the 256 M DRAM correspond to 64 kbit DRAM. It can be said that the downsizing of the components has driven the tremendous development of LSIs.

Figure 1.5 shows the past and future trends of the downsizing of MOSFET's parameters and LSI chip properties mainly used for high performance MPUs. Future trend was taken from ITRS'99 (International Technology Roadmap for Semiconductors) [2]. In order to maintain the continuous progress of LSIs for future, every parameter has to be shrunk continuously with almost the same rate as before. However, it was anticipated that shrinking the parameters beyond the 0.1 $\mu$m generation would face severe difficulties due to various kinds of expected limitations. It was expected that huge effort would be required in research and development level in order to overcome the difficulties.

In this chapter, silicon technology from past to future is reviewed for advanced CMOS LSIs.

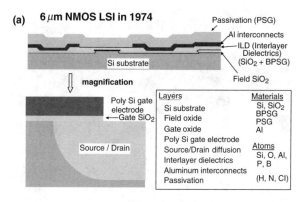

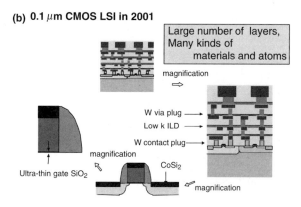

**FIGURE 1.2**    Cross-sections of (a) NMOS LSI in 1974 and (b) CMOS LSI in 2001.

**FIGURE 1.3**    1 kbit DRAM (TOSHIBA).

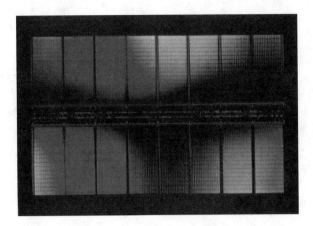

**FIGURE 1.4**   256 Mbit DRAM (TOSHIBA).

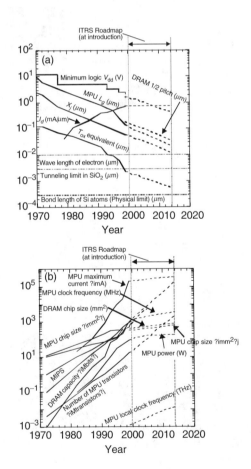

**FIGURE 1.5**   Trends of CPU and DRAM parameters.

## 1.2 Downsizing below 0.1 μm

In digital circuit applications, a MOSFET functions as a switch. Thus, complete cut-off of leakage current in the "off" state, and low resistance or high current drive in the "on" state are required. In addition, small capacitances are required for the switch to rapidly turn on and off. When making the gate length small, even in the "off" state, the space charge region near the drain—the high potential region near the drain—touches the source in a deeper place where the gate bias cannot control the potential, resulting in a leakage current from source to drain via the space charge region, as shown in Fig. 1.6. This is the well-known, short-channel effect of MOSFETs. The short-channel effect is often measured as the threshold voltage reduction of MOSFETs when it is not severe. In order for a MOSFET to work as a component of an LSI, the capability of switching-off or the suppression of the short-channel effects is the first priority in the designing of the MOSFETs. In other words, the suppression of the short-channel effects limits the downsizing of MOSFETs.

In the "on" state, reduction of the gate length is desirable because it decreases the channel resistance of MOSFETs. However, when the channel resistance becomes as small as source and drain resistance, further improvement in the drain current or the MOSFET performance cannot be expected. Moreover, in the short-channel MOSFET design, the source and drain resistance often tends to even increase in order to suppress the short-channel effects. Thus, it is important to consider ways for reducing the total resistance of MOSFETs with keeping the suppression of the short-channel effects. The capacitances of MOSFETs usually decreases with the downsizing, but care should be taken when the fringing portion is dominant or when impurity concentration of the substrate is large in the short-channel transistor design.

Thus, the suppression of the short-channel effects, with the improvement of the total resistance and capacitances, are required for the MOSFET downsizing. In other words, without the improvements of the MOSFET performance, the downsizing becomes almost meaningless even if the short-channel effect is completely suppressed.

To suppress the short-channel effects and thus to secure good switching-off characteristics of MOSFETs, the scaling method was proposed by Dennard et al. [3], where the parameters of MOSFETs are shrunk or increased by the same factor $K$, as shown in Figs. 1.7 and 1.8, resulting in the reduction of the space charge region by the same factor $K$ and suppression of the short-channel effects.

In the scaling method, drain current, $I_d$ $(= W/L \times V^2/t_{ox})$, is reduced to $1/K$. Even the drain current is reduced to $1/K$, the propagation delay time of the circuit reduces to $1/K$, because the gate charge reduces to $1/K^2$. Thus, scaling is advantageous for high-speed operation of LSI circuits.

If the increase in the number of transistors is kept at $K^2$, the power consumption of the LSI—which is calculated as $1/2fnCV^2$ as shown in Fig. 1.7—stays constant and does not increase with the scaling. Thus, in the ideal scaling, power increase will not occur.

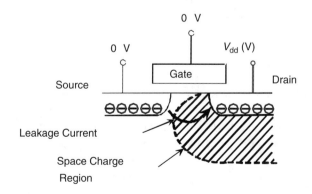

**FIGURE 1.6**  Short channel effect at downsizing.

**TABLE 1.2**   Real Scaling (Research Level)

|  | 1972 | 2001 | Ratio | Limiting Factor |
|---|---|---|---|---|
| Gate length | 6 $\mu$m | 0.1 $\mu$m | 1/60 | |
| Gate oxide | 100 nm | 2 nm | 1/50 | Gate leakage TDDB |
| Junction depth | 700 nm | 35 nm | 1/20 | Resistance |
| Supply voltage | 5 V | 1.3 V | 1/3.8 | $V_{th}$ |
| Threshold voltage | 0.8 V | 0.35 V | 1/2 | Subthreshold leakage |
| Electric field ($V_d/t_{ox}$) | 0.5 MV/cm | 6.5 MV/cm | 13 | TDDB |

Drain Current: $I_d \rightarrow 1/K$
Gate area: $S_g = L_g \cdot W_g \rightarrow 1/K^2$
Gate capacitance: $C_g = a \cdot S_g/tox \rightarrow 1/K$
Gate charge: $Q_g = C_g \cdot V_g \rightarrow 1/K^2$
Propagation delay time: tpd $= a \cdot Q_g/I_d \rightarrow 1/K$
Clock frequency: $f = 1/tpd \rightarrow K$
Chip area: Sc: set const. $\rightarrow 1$
Number of Tr. in a chip: $n \rightarrow K^2$
Power consumption: $P = (1/2) \cdot f \cdot n \cdot C_g \cdot V_d^2 \rightarrow 1$
$\qquad\qquad\qquad\qquad$ K K$^2$ 1/k 1/k$^2$

**FIGURE 1.7**   Parameters change by ideal scaling.

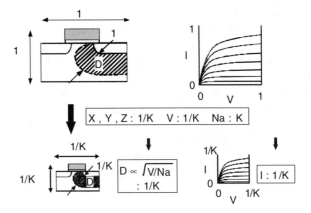

**FIGURE 1.8**   Ideal scaling method.

However, the actual scaling of the parameters has been different from that originally proposed as the ideal scaling, as shown in Table 1.2 and also shown in Fig. 1.5(a). The major difference is the supply voltage reduction. The supply voltage was not reduced in the early phase of LSI generations in order to keep a compatibility with the supply voltage of conventional systems and also in order to obtain higher operation speed under higher electric field. The supply voltage started to decrease from the 0.5 $\mu$m generation because the electric field across the gate oxide would have exceeded 4 MV/cm, which had been regarded as the limitation in terms of TDDB (time-dependent break down)—recently the maximum field is going to be raised to high values, and because hot carrier induced degradation for the short-channel MOSFETs would have been above the allowable level; however, now, it is not easy to reduce the

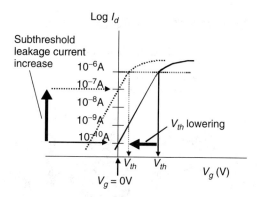

**FIGURE 1.9**    Subthreshold leakage current at low $V_{th}$.

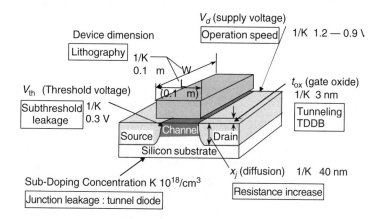

**FIGURE 1.10**    Scaling limitation factor for Si MOSFET below 0.1 $\mu$m.

supply voltage because of difficulties in reducing the threshold voltage of the MOSFETs. Too small threshold voltage leads to significantly large subthreshold leakage current even at the gate voltage of 0 V, as shown in Fig. 1.9. If it had been necessary to reduce the supply voltage of 0.1 $\mu$m MOSFETs at the same ratio as the dimension reduction, the supply voltage would have been 0.08 V (=5 V/60) and the threshold voltage would have been 0.0013 V (=0.8 V/60), and thus the scaling method would have been broken down. The voltage higher than that expected from the original scaling is one of the reasons for the increase of the power. Increase of the number of transistors in a chip by more than the factor $K^2$ is another reason for the power increase. In fact, the transistor size decreases by factor 0.7 and the transistor area decreases by factor 0.5 (=0.7 × 0.7) for every generation, and thus the number of transistors is expected to increase by a factor of 2. In reality, however, the increase cannot wait for the downsizing and the actual increase is by a factor of 4. The insufficient area for obtaining another factor 2 is earned by increasing the chip area by a factor of 1.5 and further by extending the area in the vertical direction introducing multilayer interconnects, double polysilicon, and trench/stack DRAM capacitor cells.

In order to downsizing MOSFETs down to sub-0.1 $\mu$m, further modification of the scaling method is required because some of the parameters have already reached their scaling limit in the 0.1 $\mu$m generation, as shown in Fig. 1.10. In the 0.1 $\mu$m generation, the gate oxide thickness is already below the direct-tunneling leakage limit of 3 nm. The substrate impurity concentration (or the channel impurity concentration) has already reached $10^{18}$ cm$^{-3}$. If the concentration is further increased, the source-substrate and drain-substrate junctions become highly doped pn junctions and act as tunnel diodes. Thus, the isolation of source and drains with substrate cannot be maintained. The threshold voltage has already

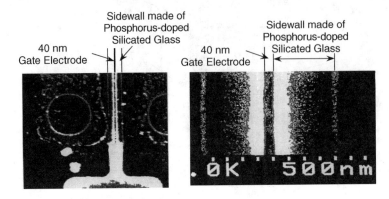

**FIGURE 1.11**    Top view of 40 nm gate length MOSFETs [4].

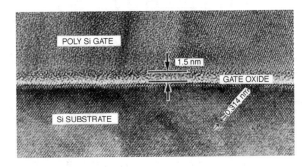

**FIGURE 1.12**    Cross-sectional TEM image of 1.5 nm gate oxide [5].

decreased to 0.3–0.25 V and further reduction causes significant increase in subthreshold leakage current. Further reduction of the threshold voltage and thus the further reduction of the supply voltage are difficult.

In 1990s, fortunately, those difficulties were shown to be solved somehow by invention of new techniques, further modification of the scaling, and some new findings for short gate length MOSFET operation. In the following, examples of the solutions for the front end of line are described. In 1993, first successful operation of sub-50 nm n-MOSFETs was reported [4], as shown in Fig. 1.11. In the fabrication of the MOSFETs, 40 nm length gate electrodes were realized by introducing resist-thinning technique using oxygen plasma. In the scaling, substrate (or channel doping) concentration was not increased any more, and the gate oxide thickness was not decreased (because it was not believed that MOSFETs with direct-tunnelling gate leakage operates normally), but instead, decreasing the junction depth more aggressively (in this case) than ordinary scaling was found to be somehow effective to suppress the short-channel effect and thus to obtain good operation of sub-50 nm region. Thus, 10-nm depth S/D junction was realized by introduction of solid-phase diffusion by RTA from PSG gate sidewall. In 1994, it was found that MOSFETs with gate $SiO_2$ less than 3 nm thick—for example 1.5 nm as shown in Fig. 1.12 [5]—operate quite normally when

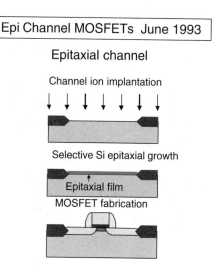

**FIGURE 1.13**  Epitaxial channel [9].

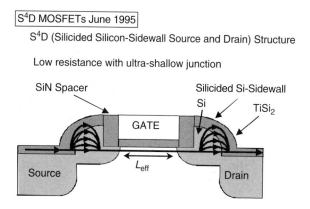

**FIGURE 1.14**  S⁴D MOSFETs [9].

the gate length is small. This is because the gate leakage current decreases in proportion with the gate length while the drain current increases in inverse proportion with the gate length. As a result, the gate leakage current can be negligibly small in the normal operation of MOSFETs. The performance of 1.5 nm was record breaking even at low supply voltage.

In 1993, it was proposed that ultrathin-epitaxial layer shown in Fig. 1.13 is very effective to realize super retrograde channel impurity profiles for suppressing the short-channel effects. It was confirmed that 25 nm gate length MOSFETs operate well by using simulation [6]. In 1993 and 1995, epitaxial channel MOSFETs with buried [7] and surface [8] channels, respectively, were fabricated and high drain current drive with excellent suppression of the short-channel effects were experimentally confirmed. In 1995, new raised (or elevated) S/D structure was proposed, as shown in Fig. 1.14 [10]. In the structure, extension portion of the S/D is elevated with self-aligned to the gate electrode by using silicided silicon sidewall. With minimizing the $Si_3N_4$ spacer width, the extension S/D resistance was dramatically reduced. In 1991, NiSi salicide were presented for the first time, as shown in Fig. 1.15 [10]. NiSi has several advantages over $TiSi_2$ and $CoSi_2$ salicides, especially in use for sub-50 nm regime. Because NiSi is a monosilicide, silicon consumption during the silicidation is small. Silicidation can be accomplished at low temperature. These features are suitable for ultra-shallow junction formation. For NiSi salicide, there

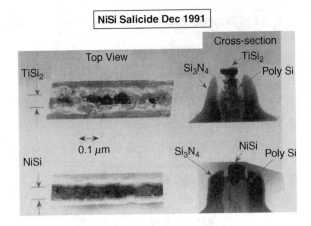

**FIGURE 1.15**    NiSi Salicide [10].

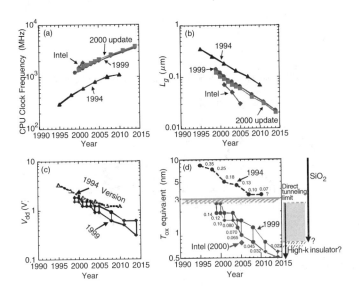

**FIGURE 1.16**    ITRS'99. (a) CPU clock frequency, (b) gate length, (c) supply voltage, and (d) gate insulator thickness.

was no narrow line effect—increase in the sheet resistance in narrow silicide line—and bridging failure by the formation of silicide path on the gate sidewall between the gate and S/D. NiSi-contact resistances to both $n^+$ and $p^+$ Si are small. These properties are suitable for reducing the source, drain, and gate resistance for sub-50 nm MOSFETs.

The previous discussion provides examples of possible solutions, which the authors found in the 1990s for sub-50 nm gate length generation. Also, many solutions have been found by others. In any case, with the possible solutions demonstrated for sub-50 nm generation as well as the keen competitions among semiconductor chipmakers for high performance, the downsizing trend or roadmap has been significantly accelerated since the late 1990s, as shown in Fig. 1.16. The first roadmap for downsizing was published in 1994 by SIA (Semiconductor Industry Association, USA) as NTRS'94 (National Technology Roadmap for Semiconductors) [11]—at that time, the roadmap was not an international version. On NTRS'94, the clock frequency was expected to stay at 600 MHz in year 2001 and expected to exceed 1 GHz in 2007. However, it has already reached 2.1 GHz for 2001 in ITRS 2000 [12]. In order to realize high clock frequencies, the gate length reduction was accelerated. In fact, in the NTRS'94, gate length was expected to stay at 180 nm in year 2001 and expected to reach 100 nm only in 2007, but the gate length is 90 nm in 2001 on ITRS 2000, as shown in Fig. 1.16(b).

The real world is much more aggressive. As shown in Fig. 1.16(a), the clock frequency of Intel's MPU already reached 1.7 GHz [12] in April 2001, and its roadmap for gate length reduction is unbelievably aggressive, as shown in Fig. 1.16(b) [13,14]. In the roadmap, 30-nm gate length CMOS MPU with 70-nm node technology is to be sold in the market in year 2005. It is even several years in advance compared with the ITRS 2000 prediction.

With the increase in clock frequency and the decrease in gate length, together with the increase in number of transistors in a chip, the tremendous increase in power consumption becomes the main issue. In order to suppress the power consumption, supply voltage should be reduced aggressively, as shown in Fig. 1.16(c). In order to maintain high performance under the low supply voltage, gate insulator thickness should be reduced very tremendously. On NTRS'94, the gate insulator thickness was not expected to exceed 3 nm throughout the period described in the roadmap, but it is already 1.7 nm in products in 2001 and expected to be 1.0 nm in 2005 on ITRS'99 and 0.8 nm in Intel's roadmap, as shown in Fig. 1.16(d). In terms of total gate leakage current of an entire LSI chip for use for mobile cellular phone, 2 nm is already too thin, in which standby power consumption should be minimized. Thus, high $K$ materials, which were assumed to be introduced after year 2010 at the earliest on NTRS'94, are now very seriously investigated in order to replace the $SiO_2$ and to extend the limitation of gate insulator thinning.

Introduction of new materials is considered not only for the gate insulator, but also almost for every portion of the CMOS structures. More detailed explanations of new technology for future CMOS will be given in the following sections.

## 1.3   Gate Insulator

Figure 1.17 shows gate length ($L_g$) versus gate oxide thickness ($t_{ox}$) published in recent conferences [4,5,14–19]. The x-axis in the bottom represents corresponding year of the production to the gate length according to ITRS 2000. The solid curve in the figure is $L_g$ versus $t_{ox}$ relation according to the ITRS 2000 [12]. It should be noted that most of the published MOSFETs maintain the scaling relationship between $L_g$ and $t_{ox}$ predicted by ITRS 2000. Figures 1.18 and 1.19 are $V_d$ versus $L_g$, and $I_d$ (or $I_{on}$) versus $L_g$ curves, respectively obtained from the published data at the conferences. From the data, it can be estimated that MOSFETs will operate quite well with satisfaction of $I_{on}$ value specified by the roadmap until the generation

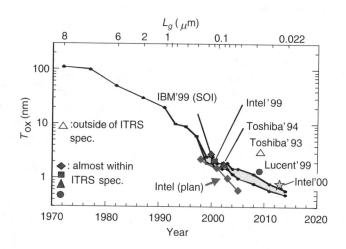

**FIGURE 1.17**   Trend of $T_{ox}$.

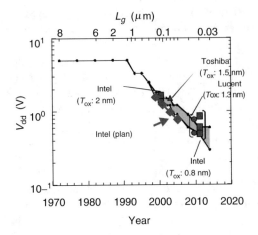

**FIGURE 1.18**   Trend of $V_{dd}$.

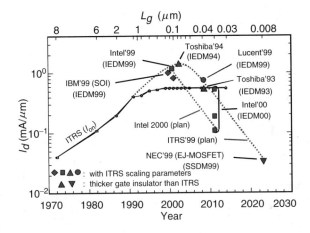

**FIGURE 1.19**   Trend of drain current.

around $L_g = 30$ nm. One small concern is that the $I_{on}$ starts to reduce from $L_g = 100$ nm and could be smaller than the value specified by the roadmap from $L_g = 30$ nm. This is due to the increase in the S/D extension resistance in the small gate length MOSFETs. In order to suppress the short-channel effects, the junction depth of S/D extension needs to be reduced aggressively, resulting in high sheet resistance. This should be solved by the raised (or elevated) S/D structures. This effect is more significantly observed in the operation of an 8-nm gate length EJ-MOSFET [20], as shown in Fig. 1.19. In the structure, S/D extension consists of inversion layer created by high positive bias applied on a 2nd gate electrode, which is placed to cover the 8-nm, 1st gate electrode and S/D extension area. Thus, reduction of S/D extension resistance will be another limiting factor of CMOS downsizing, which will come next to the limit in thinning the gate $SiO_2$.

In any case, it seems at this moment that $SiO_2$ gate insulator could be used until the sub-1 nm thickness with sufficient MOSFET performance. There was a concern proposed in 1998 that TDDB (Time Dependent Dielectric Breakdown) will limit the $SiO_2$ gate insulator reduction at $t_{ox} = 2.2$ nm [21]; however, recent results suggest that TDDB would be OK until $t_{ox} = 1.5 - 1.0$ nm [22–25]. Thus, $SiO_2$ gate insulator would be used until the 30 nm gate length generation for high-speed MPUs. This is a big change of the prediction. Until only several years ago, most of the people did not believe the possibility of gate $SiO_2$ thinning below 3 nm because of the direct-tunnelling leakage current, and until only 2 years ago, many people are sceptical about the use of sub-2 nm gate $SiO_2$ because of the TDDB concern.

However, even excellent characteristics of MOSFETs with high reliability was confirmed, total gate leakage current in the entire LSI chip would become the limiting factor. It should be noted that 10 A/cm$^2$ gate leakage current flows across the gate $SiO_2$ at $t_{ox} = 1.2$ nm and 100 A/cm$^2$ leakage current flows at $t_{ox} = 1.0$ nm. However, AMD has claimed that 1.2 nm gate $SiO_2$ (actually oxynitrided) can be used for high end MPUs [26]. Furthermore, Intel has announced that total-chip gate leakage current of even 100 A/cm$^2$ is allowable for their MPUs [14], and that even 0.8 nm gate $SiO_2$ (actually oxynitrided) can be used for product in 2005 [15].

Total gate leakage current could be minimized by providing plural gate oxide thicknesses in a chip, and by limiting the number of the ultra-thin transistors; however, in any case, such high gate leakage current density is a big burden for mobile devices, in which reduction of standby power consumption is critically important. In the cellular phone application, even the leakage current at $t_{ox} = 2.5$ nm would be a concern. Thus, development of high dielectric constant (or high-k) gate insulator with small gate leakage current is strongly demanded; however, intensive study and development of the high-k gate dielectrics have started only a few years ago, and it is expected that we have to wait at least another few years until the high-k insulator becomes mature for use of the production.

The necessary conditions for the dielectrics are as follows [27]: (i) the dielectrics remain in the solid-phase at the process temperature of up to about 1000 K, (ii) the dielectrics are not radio-active, (iii) the dielectrics are chemically stable at the Si interface at high process temperature. This means that no barrier film is necessary between the Si and the dielectrics. Considering the conditions, white columns in the periodic law of the elements shown in Fig. 1.20 remained as metals whose oxide could be used as the high-k gate insulators [27]. It should be noted that $Ta_2O_5$ is now regarded as not very much suitable for use as the gate insulator of MOSFET from this point of view.

Figure 1.21 shows the statistics of high-k dielectrics—excluding $Si_3N_4$—and its formation method published recently [28–43]. In most of the cases, 0.8–2.0 nm capacitance equivalent thicknesses to $SiO_2$ (CET) were tested for the gate insulator of MOS diodes and MOSFETs and leakage current of several orders of magnitude lower value than that of $SiO_2$ film was confirmed. Also, high TDDB reliability than that of the $SiO_2$ case was reported.

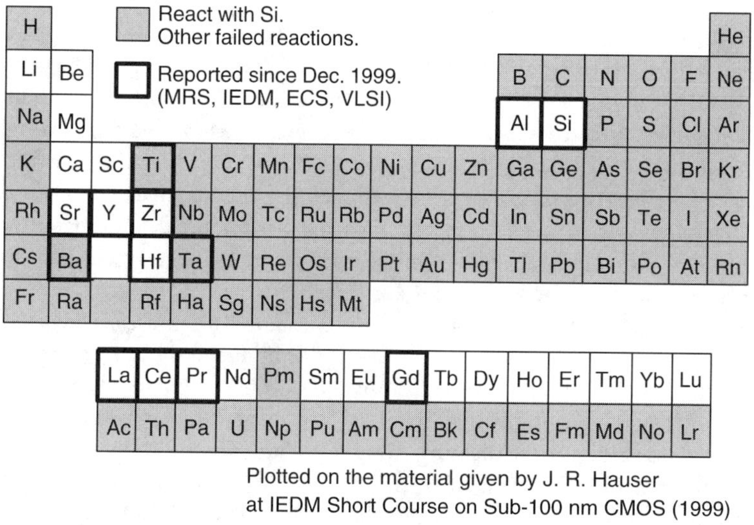

Plotted on the material given by J. R. Hauser
at IEDM Short Course on Sub-100 nm CMOS (1999)

**FIGURE 1.20**   Metal oxide gate insulators reported since Dec. 1998 [27].

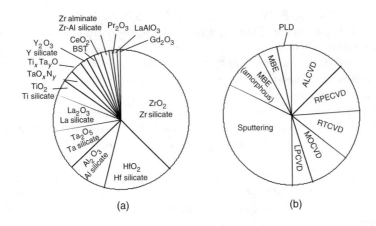

**FIGURE 1.21**    Recently reported (a) high-k materials and (b) deposition methods.

Among the candidates, $ZrO_2$ [29–31,34–37] and $HfO_2$ [28,32,34,36,38–40] become popular because their dielectric constant is relatively high and because $ZrO_2$ and $HfO_2$ were believed to be stable at the Si interface. However, in reality, formation and growth of interfacial layer made of silicate ($ZrSi_xO_y$, $HfSi_xO_y$) or $SiO_2$ at the Si interface during the MOSFET fabrication process has been a serious problem. This interfacial layer acts to reduce the total capacitance and is thought to be undesirable for obtaining high performance of MOSFETs. Ultrathin nitride barrier layer seems to be effective to suppress the interfacial layer formation [37]. There is a report that mobility of MOSFETs with $ZrO_2$ even with these interfacial layers were significantly degraded by several tens of percent, while with entire Zr silicate gate dielectrics is the same as that of $SiO_2$ gate film [31]. Thus, there is an argument that the thicker interfacial silicate layer would help the mobility improvement as well as the gate leakage current suppression; however, in other experiment, there is a report that $HfO_2$ gate oxide MOSFETs mobility was not degraded [38]. For another problem, it was reported that $ZrO_2$ and $HfO_2$, easily form micro-crystals during the heat process [31,33].

Comparing with the cases of $ZrO_2$ and $HfO_2$, $La_2O_3$ film was reported to have better characteristics at this moment [33]. There was no interfacial silicate layer formed, and mobility was not degraded at all. The dielectric constant was 20–30. Another merit of the $La_2O_3$ insulator is that no micro-crystal formation was found in high temperature process of MOSFET fabrication [33]. There is a strong concern for its hygroscopic property, although it was reported that the property was not observed in the paper [33]. However, there is a different paper published [34], in which $La_2O_3$ film is reported to very easily form a silicate during the thermal process. Thus, we have to watch the next report of the $La_2O_3$ experiments. Crystal $Pr_2O_3$ film grown on silicon substrate with epitaxy is reported to have small leakage current [42]. However, it was shown that significant film volume expansion by absorbing the moisture of the air was observed. La and Pr are just two of the 15 elements in lanthanoids series. There might be a possibility that any other lanthanoid oxide has even better characteristics for the gate insulator. Fortunately, the atomic content of the lanthanoids, Zr, and Hf in the earth's crust is much larger than that of Ir, Bi, Sb, In, Hg, Ag, Se, Pt, Te, Ru, Au, as shown in Fig. 1.22.

$Al_2O_3$ [41,43] is another candidate, though dielectric constant is around 10. The biggest problem for the $Al_2O_3$ is that film thickness dependence of the flatband shift due to the fixed charge is so strong that controllability of the flatband voltage is very difficult. This problem should be solved before it is used for the production. There is a possibility that Zr, Hf, La, and Pr silicates are used for the next generation gate insulator with the sacrifice of the dielectric constant to around 10 [31,35,37]. It was reported that the silicate prevent from the formation of micro-crystals and from the degradation in mobility as described before. Furthermore, there is a possibility that stacked $Si_3N_4$ and $SiO_2$ layers are used for mobile device application. $Si_3N_4$ material could be introduced soon even though its dielectric constant is not very high [44–46], because it is relatively mature for use for silicon LSIs.

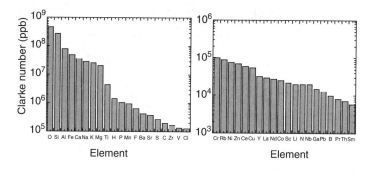

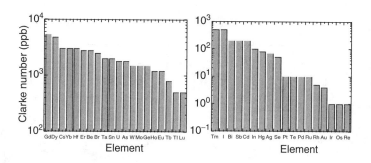

**FIGURE 1.22** Clarke number of elements.

# 1.4 Gate Electrode

Figure 1.23 shows the changes of the gate electrode of MOSFETs. Originally, Al gate was used for the MOSFETs, but soon poly Si gate replaced it because of the adaptability to the high temperature process and to the acid solution cleaning process of MOSFET fabrication. Especially, poly gate formation step can be put before the S/D (source and drain) formation. This enables the easy self-alignment of S/D to the gate electrode as shown in the figure. In the metal gate case, the gate electrode formation should come to the final part of the process to avoid the high temperature and acid processes, and thus self-alignment is difficult. In the case of damascene gate process, the self-alignment is possible, but process becomes complicated as shown in the figure [47]. Refractory metal gate with conventional gate electrode process and structure would be another solution, but RIE (Reactive Ion Etching) of such metals with good selectivity to the gate dielectric film is very difficult at this moment.

As shown in Fig. 1.24, poly Si gate has a big problem of depletion layer formation. This effect would not be ignored when the gate insulator becomes thin. Thus, despite the above difficulties, metal gate is desirable and assumed to be necessary for future CMOS devices. However, there is another difficulty for the introduction of metal gate to CMOS. For advance CMOS, work function of gate electrode should be selected differently for n- and p-MOSFETs to adjust the threshold voltages to the optimum values. Channel doping could shift the threshold voltage, but cannot adjust it to the right value with good control of the short-channel effects. Thus, $n^+$-doped poly Si gate is used for NMOS and $p^+$-doped poly Si gate is used for PMOS. In the metal gate case, it is assumed that two different metals should be used for N- and PMOS in the same manner as shown in Table 1.3. This makes the process further complicated and makes the device engineer to hesitate to introduce the metal gate. Thus, for the short-range—probably to 70 or 50 nm node, heavily doped poly Si or poly SiGe gate electrode will be used. But in the long range, metal gate should be seriously considered.

**TABLE 1.3**  Candidates for Metal Gate
Electrodes (unit: eV)

| Midgap | | Dual Gate | | | |
|---|---|---|---|---|---|
| | | NMOS | | PMOS | |
| W | 4.52 | Hf | 3.9 | $RuO_2$ | 4.9 |
| | | Zr | 4.05 | WN | 5.0 |
| Ru | 4.71 | Al | 4.08 | Ni | 5.15 |
| | | Ti | 4.17 | Ir | 5.27 |
| TiN | 4.7 | Ta | 4.19 | $Mo_2N$ | 5.33 |
| | | Mo | 4.2 | TaN | 5.41 |
| | | | | Pt | 5.65 |

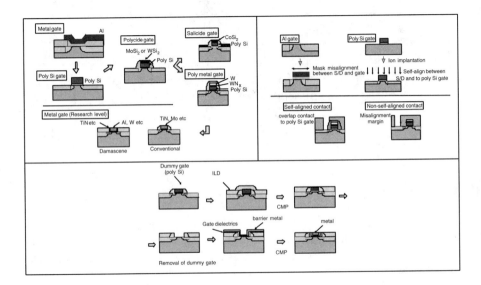

**FIGURE 1.23**  Gate electrode formation change.

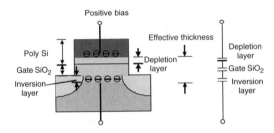

**FIGURE 1.24**  Depletion in poly-Si gate.

## 1.5 Source and Drain

Figure 1.25 shows the changes of S/D (source and drain) formation process and structure. S/D becomes shallower for every new generation in order to suppress the short-channel effects. Before, the extension part of the S/D was called as LDD (Lightly Doped Drain) region and low doping concentration was required in order to suppress electric field at the drain edge and hence to suppress the hot-carrier effect. Structure of the source side becomes symmetrical as the drain side because of process simplicity. Recently, major concern of the S/D formation is how to realize ultra-shallow extension with low resistance. Thus, the doping of the extension should be done as heavily as possible and the activation of the impurity should be as high as possible. Table 1.4 shows the trends of the junction depth and sheet resistance of the extension requested by ITRS 2000. As the generation proceeds, junction depth becomes shallower, but at the same time, the sheet resistance should be reduced. This is extremely difficult. In order to satisfy this request, various doping and activation methods are being investigated. As the doping method, low energy implantation at 2–0.5 keV [48] and plasma doping with low energy [49] are thought to be the most promising at this moment. The problem of the low energy doping is lower retain dose and lower activation rate of the implanted species [48]. As the activation method, high temperature spike lamp anneal [48] is the best way at this moment. In order to suppress the diffusion of the dopant, and to keep the over-saturated activation of the dopant, the spike should be as steep as possible. Laser anneal [50] can realize very high activation, but very high temperature above the melting point at the silicon surface is a concern. Usually laser can anneal only the surface of the doping layer, and thus deeper portion may be necessary to be annealed by the combination of the spike lamp anneal.

**TABLE 1.4**  Trend of S/D Extension by ITRS

|  | 1999 | 2000 | 2001 | 2002 | 2003 | 2004 | 2005 | 2008 | 2011 | 2014 |
|---|---|---|---|---|---|---|---|---|---|---|
| Technology node (nm) | 180 |  |  | 130 |  |  | 100 | 70 | 50 | 35 |
| Gate length (nm) | 140 | 120 | 100 | 85 | 80 | 70 | 65 | 45 | 32 | 22 |
| Extension $X_j$ (nm) | 42–70 | 36–60 | 30–50 | 25–43 | 24–40 | 20–35 | 20–33 | 16–26 | 11–19 | 8–13 |
| Extension sheet resistance ($\Omega/\square$) | 350–800 | 310–760 | 280–730 | 250–700 | 240–675 | 220–650 | 200–625 | 150–525 | 120–450 | 100–400 |

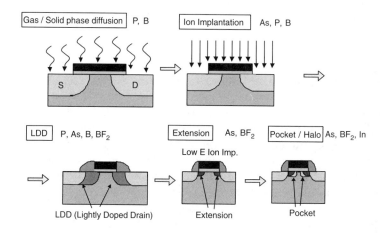

**FIGURE 1.25**  Source and drain change.

**TABLE 1.5**   Physical Properties of Silicides

|                           | MoSi$_2$ | WSi$_2$ | C54–TiSi$_2$ | CoSi$_2$ | NiSi  |
|---------------------------|----------|---------|--------------|----------|-------|
| Resistivity ($\mu\Omega$ cm) | 100      | 70      | 10~15        | 18~25    | 30~40 |
| Forming temperature (°C)  | 1000     | 950     | 750~900      | 550~900  | 400   |
| Diffusion species         | Si       | Si      | Si           | Co*      | Ni    |

*Si(CoSi), Co(Co$_2$Si).

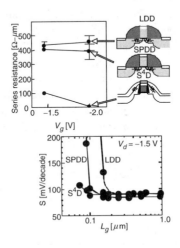

**FIGURE 1.26**   Elevated source and drain.

In order to further reduce the sheet resistance, elevated S/D structure of the extension is necessary, as shown in Fig. 1.26 [6]. Elevated S/D will be introduced at the latest from the generation of sub-30 nm gate length generation, because sheet resistance of S/D will be the major limiting factor of the device performance in that generation.

Salicide is a very important technique to reduce the resistance of the extrinsic part of S/D—resistance of deep S/D part and contact resistance between S/D and metal. Table 1.5 shows the changes of the salicide/silicide materials. Now CoSi$_2$ is the material used for the salicide. In future, NiSi is regarded as promising because of its superior nature of smaller silicon consumption at the silicidation reaction [10].

# 1.6   Channel Doping

Channel doping is an important technique not only for adjusting the threshold voltage of MOSFETs but also for suppressing the short-channel effects. As described in the explanation of the scaling method, the doping of the substrate or the doping of the channel region should be increased with the downsizing of the device dimensions; however, too heavily doping into the entire substrate causes several problems, such as too high threshold voltage and too low breakdown voltage of the S/D junctions. Thus, the heavily doping portion should be limited to the place where the suppression of the depletion layer is necessary, as shown in Fig. 1.27. Thus, retrograde doping profile in which only some deep portion is heavily doped is requested. To realize the extremely sharp retrograde profile, undoped-epitaxial-silicon growth on the heavily doped channel region is the most suitable method, as shown in the figure [7–9]. This is called as epitaxial channel technique. The epitaxial channel will be necessary from sub-50 nm gate length generations.

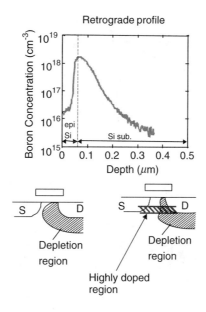

**FIGURE 1.27**    Retrograde profile.

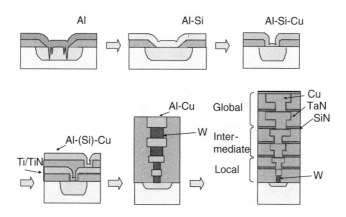

**FIGURE 1.28**    Interconnect change.

## 1.7   Interconnects

Figure 1.28 shows the changes of interconnect structures and materials. Aluminium has been used for many years as the interconnect metal material, but now it is being replaced by cupper with the combination of dual damascene process shown in Fig. 1.29, because of its superior characteristics on the resistivity and electromigration [51,52]. Figure 1.30 shows some problems for the CMP process used for the copper damascene, which is being solved. The major problem for future copper interconnects is the necessity of diffusion barrier layer, as shown in Fig. 1.31. The thickness of the barrier layer will consume major part of the cross-section area of copper interconnects with the reduction of the dimension, because it is very difficult to thin the barrier films less than several nanometers. This leads to significant increase in the resistance of the interconnects. Thus, in 10 years, diffusion-barrier-free copper interconnects process should be developed.

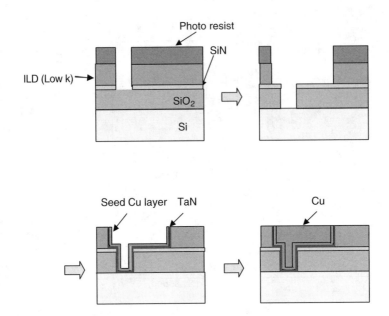

**FIGURE 1.29** Dual damascene for Cu.

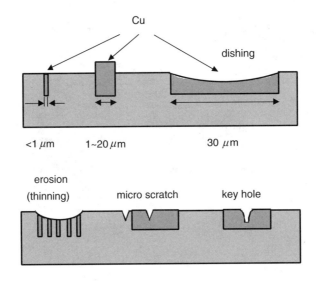

**FIGURE 1.30** Dual damascene for Cu.

Reducing the interconnect capacitance is very important for obtaining high-speed circuit operation. Thus, development of low-k inter-deposition layer (IDL) is essential for the future interconnects shown in Table 1.6. Various materials as shown in Table 1.7 are being developed at this moment. Unfortunately, however, only the dielectric constant of 3.2–4.0 has been used for the products. Originally, low-k material with dielectric constant of less than 3.0 was scheduled to be introduced much earlier. However, because of the technological difficulty, the schedule was delayed in ITRS 2000, as shown in Table 1.6.

**TABLE 1.6**     Trend of Interconnect by ITRS

|  | 1999 | 2000 | 2001 | 2002 | 2003 | 2004 | 2005 | 2008 | 2011 | 2014 |
|---|---|---|---|---|---|---|---|---|---|---|
| Technology node (nm) | 180 | | | 130 | | | 100 | 70 | 50 | 35 |
| Gate length (nm) | 140 | 120 | 100 | 85 | 80 | 70 | 65 | 45 | 32 | 22 |
| Number of metal levels | 6–7 | 6–7 | 7 | 7–8 | 8 | 8 | 8–9 | 9 | 9–10 | 9–10 |
| Local (AI or Cu) (nm) | 500 | 450 | 405 | 365 | 330 | 295 | 265 | 185 | 130 | 95 |
| Intermediate (AI or Cu) (nm) | 640 | 575 | 520 | 465 | 420 | 375 | 340 | 240 | 165 | 115 |
| Global (AI or Cu) (nm) | 1050 | 945 | 850 | 765 | 690 | 620 | 560 | 390 | 275 | 190 |
| Dielectric constant ($\kappa$) | 3.5–4.0 | 3.5–4.0 | 2.7–3.5 | 2.7–3.5 | 2.2–2.7 | 2.2–2.7 | 1.6–2.2 | 1.5 | <1.5 | <1.5 |
| Interlevel metal insulator | Fluorinated silicate glass | | Hydrogen silsesqioxane-type | | Organic polymer Inorganic dielectrics | | Xerogel Fluoropolymer Porous SiO$_2$ | | Porous dielectrics and air gap | |
| Dielectric constant ($\kappa$) for DRAM | 4.1 | 4.1 | 4.1 | 3.0–4.1 | 3.0–4.1 | 3.0–4.1 | 2.5–3.0 | 2.5–3.0 | 2.0–2.5 | 2.0–2.3 |

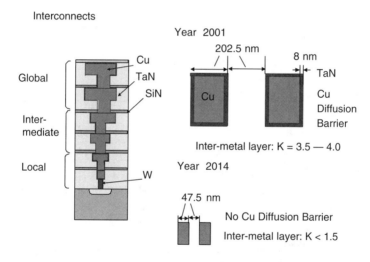

**FIGURE 1.31**     Interconnects.

# 1.8   Memory Technology

Memory device requires some special technologies. Figure 1.32, and Tables 1.8 and 1.9 show the change of DRAM cells. The cell structure becomes too complicated in order to secure the capacitor area in the small dimensions. To solve this problem, new high-k dielectrics and related metal electrode as shown in Table 1.8 have been already developed for production and new materials are also being investigated for future [53]. New dielectric materials are being developed not only for DRAM, but also for other memories such as FERAMs (Ferro-electric RAM) [54].

Although, the structure becomes very complicated, embedded DRAM logic LSIs [55] are attractive and necessary for the SOC (Silicon On a Chip) application. In the future, chip module technology will solve the complexity problem in which different functional chips are made separately and finally assembled on a chip.

**TABLE 1.7**    Candidates of Low-k Materials for Next Generation Interconnects

| Low $\kappa$ Materials | Chemical Formula | $\kappa$ | Deposition Method |
|---|---|---|---|
| Silicon dioxide | $SiO_2$ | 3.9–4.5 | PECVD |
| Fluorinated silicate glass | $(SiO_2)_x \cdot (SiO_3F_2)_{1-x}$ | 3.2–4.0 | PECVD |
| Polyimide | 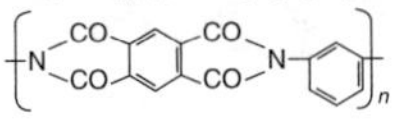  | 3.1–3.4 | Spin on |
| HSQ | $SiO_{1.5}H_{0.5}$ | 2.9–3.2 | Spin on |
| Diamond-like carbon | C | 2.7–3.4 | PECVD |
| Parylene-N | 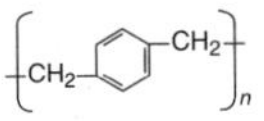  | 2.7 | CVD |
| DVS-BCB | (1) | 2.6–2.7 | Spin on |
| Fluorinated polyimide | (2) | 2.5–2.9 | Spin on |
| MSQ | $SiO_{1.5}(CH_3)_{0.5}$ | 2.6–2.8 | Spin on |
| Aromatic thermoset | 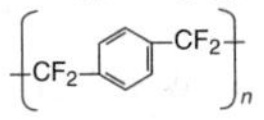  | 2.6–2.8 | Spin on |
| Parylene-F | a-C:F | 2.4–2.5 | CVD |
| Teflon AF | $(CF_2CF_2)_n$ | 2.1 | Spin on |
| Mesoporous silica | $SiO_2$ | 2.0 | Spin on |
| Porous HSQ | $SiO_{1.5}H_{0.5}$ | 2.0 | Spin on |
| Porous aero gel | $SiO_2$ | 1.8–2.2 | Spin on |
| Porous PTFE | $(CF_2CF_2)_n$ | 1.8–2.2 | Spin on |
| Porous MSQ | $SiO_{1.5}(CH_3)_{0.5}$ | 1.7–2.2 | Spin on |
| Xerogels (porous silica) | $SiO_2$ | 1.1–2.2 | Spin on |

HSQ : Hydrogen Silsesquioxane
BCB : Benzocyclobutene
MSQ : Methyl Silsesquioxane
Teflon : (PTFE+2,2 bis-trifluromethyl-4,5 difluoro-1,3 dioxole)
PTFE : Polytetrafluoroethylene

(1)

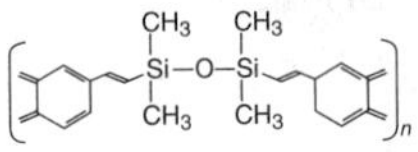

(2)

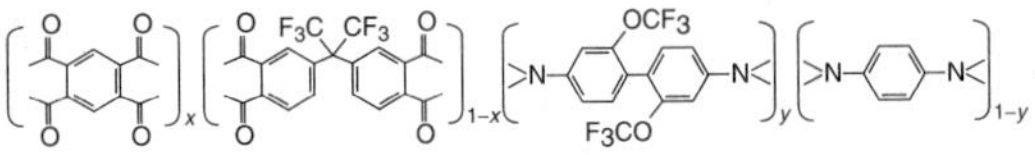

**TABLE 1.8**    Trend of DRAM Cell

| Generation | Year | Ground | $V_d$ (V) | Device | $T_{ox}$ (nm) | $x_j$ ($\mu$m) | Cell | Dielectrics |
|---|---|---|---|---|---|---|---|---|
| 1K | 1971 | 10 | 20 | PMOS | 120 | 1.5 | 3 Tr | |
| 4K | 1975 | 8 | 12 |  | 100 | 0.8 | 1 Tr | |
| 16K | 1979 | 5 |  | NMOS | 75 | 0.5 |  | $SiO_2$ |
| 64K | 1982 | 3 |  |  | 50 | 0.35 | Planar Capacitor | |
| 256K | 1985 | 2 | 5 |  | 35 | 0.3 | | |
| 1M | 1988 | 1 |  |  | 25 | 0.25 | | |
| 4M | 1991 | 0.8 |  |  | 20 | 0.2 | | |
| 16M | 1994 | 0.5 |  |  | 15 | 0.15 | | NO |
| 64M | 1997 | 0.3 | 3.3–2.5 |  | 12 | 0.12 | | |
| 256M | 1999 | 0.18 |  | CMOS | 6 | 0.1 | 3D Capacitor | |
| 1G | 2002 | 0.13 | 1.8–1.2 |  | 5 | 0.08 | (Stack or Trench) | |
| 4G | 2005 | 0.10 |  |  | 4 | 0.05 | | |
| 16G | 2008 | 0.07 | 0.9 |  | 3 | 0.03 | | High-$\kappa$ |
| 64G | 2011 | 0.05 | 0.6 |  | 2 | 0.02 | | |
| 256G | 2014 | 0.035 | 0.5 |  | 1.5 | 0.01 | | |

**TABLE 1.9a**   Trend of DRAM Cell: Stack

| Year | Technology Node (nm) | Cell Size ($\mu m^2$) | Capacitor Structure | Dielectric Material | Dielectric Constant | Upper Electrode | Bottom Electrode |
|------|------|------|------|------|------|------|------|
| 1999 | 180 | 0.26 | Cylinder MIS | $Ta_2O_5$ | 22 | poly-Si | poly-Si |
| 2002 | 130 | 0.10 | Pedestal MIM | $Ta_2O_5$ | 50 | TiON TiN | |
| 2005 | 100 | 0.044 | Pedestal MIM | BST | 250 | W, Pt, Ru, | W, Pt, Ru, |
| 2008 | 70 | 0.018 | Pedestal MIM | epi-BST | 700 | $RuO_2$, $IrO_2$ | $RuO_2$, $IrO_2$ |
| 2011 | 50 | 0.0075 | Pedestal MIM | ??? | 1500 | | $SrRuO_3$ |
| 2014 | 35 | 0.0031 | Pedestal MIM | ??? | 1500 | | |

**TABLE 1.9b**   Trend of DRAM Cell: Trench

| Year | Technology node (nm) | Aspect Ratio (trench depth/trench width) | Trench Depth ($\mu m$) (at 35 fF) | Dielectric Material |
|------|------|------|------|------|
| 1999 | 180 | 30–40 | 6–7 | NO |
| 2002 | 130 | 40–45 | 5–6 | NO |
| 2005 | 100 | 50–60 | 5–6 | NO |
| 2008 | 70 | 60–70 | 4–5 | High $\kappa$ |
| 2011 | 50 | >70 | 4–5 | High $\kappa$ |
| 2014 | 35 | >70 | 5–6 | High $\kappa$ |

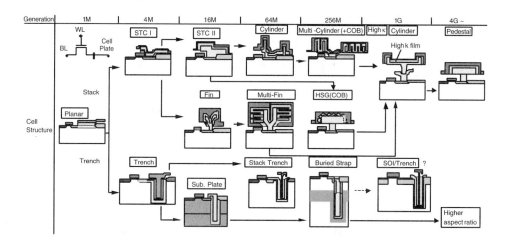

**FIGURE 1.32**   DRAM cell structure change.

# 1.9   Future Prospects

Figures 1.33 and 1.34 show future trends of parameters for 2005 and 2014, respectively, according to the ITRS 2000. Cost of next generation lithography tool is a concern, but it looks that there are solutions for 2005; however, we cannot see obvious solutions for 2014 when gate length becomes 20 nm. Despite the unknown status 10 years from now, the near-term roadmap of high performance LSI makers is too aggressive, as shown in Fig. 1.35. With this tremendously rapid downsizing trend, we might reach the possible downsizing limit in 5 years, as shown in Fig. 1.36. What will happen after that? It should be noted that not all the devices follow the aggressive trends. For example, gate oxide thickness of the mobile devices would not reduce so aggressively. Even using high-k gate insulator, gate leakage current of 1 mA/cm$^2$ flows through 1 nm (CET) film at $V_d = 1$ V at this moment, as shown in Fig. 1.37. Thus, rapid pace of the downsizing will not become a merit. According to the device purpose, the pace of the downsizing will

Year 2001  →   2005 According to ITRS2000 update
              X 2/3

$L_g$ = 90 nm                          60 nm          Lithography is critical.
$t_{ox}$ = 1.9–1.5 nm                 1.5–1.0 nm
$x_j$ = 25–43 nm                       20–33 nm

                                                      Others could be realized by
Wire 1/2 pitch = 180 nm               115 nm         conventional way.
Total interconnect length = 12.6 km   31.6 km
ILD k = 3.5–2.9                        2.2–1.6

$f$ = 2.1 GHz                          4.15 GHz (Local)
$V_d$ = 1.5–1.2 V                      1.1–0.8 V
$V_{th}$ = 0.3 V?                      0.2 V?

**FIGURE 1.33**    ITRS 2000 update.

Year 2001  →   2014       According to ITRS2000 update
              X 1/4

$L_g$ = 90 nm                          20 nm
$t_{ox}$ = 1.9–1.5 nm                 0.5–0.6 nm
$x_j$ = 25–43 nm                       8–13 nm

Wire 1/2 pitch = 180 nm               40 nm
Total interconnect length = 12.6 km   150 km
ILD k = 3.5–2.9                        1.5–1

$f$ = 2.1 GHz                          15 GHz (Local)
$V_d$ = 1.5–1.2 V                      0.6–0.3 V
$V_{th}$ = 0.3 V?                      ??

**FIGURE 1.34**    ITRS 2000 update.

Year 2001  →   2005

|                        | ITRS 2000  | Intel2000  | (IEDM2000)           |
|------------------------|------------|------------|----------------------|
|                        | 2001       | 2005       | 2005                 | Intel's Demonstration |
| $L_g$ = 90 nm          | 60 nm      | 35 nm      | (30 nm)              |
| $t_{ox}$ = 1.9–1.5 nm  | 1.5–1.0 nm | 0.6 nm     | (0.8 nm)             |
| $x_j$ = 25–43 nm       | 20–33 nm   | 17 nm      |                      |
| $V_d$ = 1.5–1.2 V      | 1.1–0.8 V  | 0.8 V      | (0.85 V)             |

**FIGURE 1.35**    ITRS 2000 vs. Intel 2000.

become different and some of the devices will not reach the downsizing limit for a long time. Even if we reach the downsizing limit, we have still many things to do for integration of the devices in multi-chip mode, as shown in Figs. 1.38 and 1.39. For deep twenty-first century, still the device and hardware technology will be important, as shown in Fig. 1.40, and in order to overcome the expected limitations, development of technologies for ultra-small dimensions, for new structures, and for new materials will become important, as shown in Figs. 1.40 and 1.41.

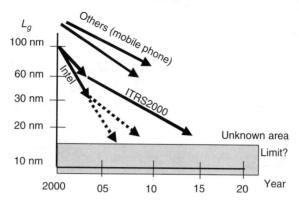

**FIGURE 1.36** Trend of gate length.

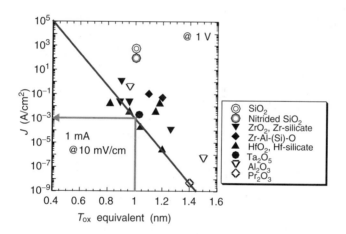

**FIGURE 1.37** Reported leakage current density as a function of $T_{ox}$ equivalent.

|  | Driver | Requirement | Important items |
|---|---|---|---|
| 1970–1990: |  |  |  |
| M | Memory | High integration | Downsizing |
| 1990–2000: |  |  |  |
| PC | MPU Personal | High Speed | Downsizing Multi-level interconnect |
| 2000–: |  |  |  |
| CMP | Communication Mobile Personal | High frequency Low noise Extremely Low power Very low cost | Downsizing passive elements Low voltage Multi-Chip-Module |

**FIGURE 1.38** Technology drivers in LSI industries.

Chip Embedded Chip (CEC) Technology for SoC

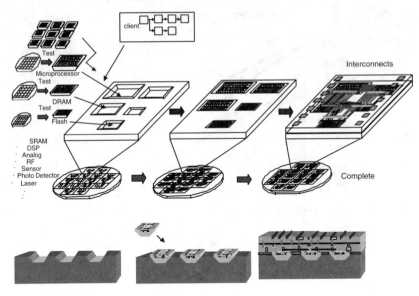

**FIGURE 1.39**   Chip embedded chip technology for SoC.

21st Century

Material, Medicine, Chemical
  →      Biology, New Material
Decive, Hardware

        Hyper LSI, Opt device, New sensor (Ultra-small,
        New Structure, New materials)
  →      We do not know now

Application, Sofware
  →      IT, New algorithm

**FIGURE 1.40**   New technologies in 21st century.

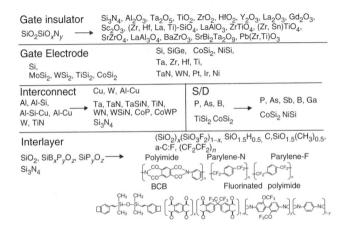

**FIGURE 1.41**   Various new materials to be used for future ULSI.

# References

1. D. Kahng and M. M. Atalla, "Silicon-silicon dioxide field induced durface devices," *IRE Solid-State Device Res. Conf.*, 1960.
2. SIA, EECA, EIAJ, KSIA, and TSIA, "International Technology Road Map for Semiconductors," in 1999 edition.
3. R. H. Dennard, F. H. Gaensslen, H.-N., Yu, V. L. Rideout, E. Bassous, and A. R. LeBlanc, "Design of ion-implanted MOSFET's with very small physical dimensions," *IEEE J. Solid-State Circuits*, SC-9, pp. 256–268, 1974.
4. M. Ono, M. Saito, T. Yoshitomi, C. Fiegna, T. Ohguro, and H. Iwai, "Sub-50 nm gate length n-MOSFETs with 10 nm phosphorus source and drain junctions," *IEDM Tech. Dig.*, pp. 119–122, December, 1993.
5. H. S. Momose, M. Ono, T. Yoshitomi, T. Ohguro, S. Nakamura, M. Saito, and H. Iwai, "Tunnelling gate oxide approach to ultra-high current drive in small-geometry MOSFETs," *IEDM Tech.*, pp. 593–596, 1994.
6. C. Fiegna, H. Iwai, T. Wada, M. Saito, E. Sangiorgi, and B. Ricco, "A new scaling methodology for the 0.1–0.025 $\mu$m MOSFET," *Symp. on VLSI Tech.*, pp. 33–34, 1993.
7. T. Ohguro, K. Yamada, N. Sugiyama, K. Usuda, Y. Akasaka, T. Yoshitomi, C. Fiegna, M. Ono, M. Saito, and H. Iwai, "Tenth micron P-MOSFET's with ultra-thin epitaxial channel layer grown by ultra-high vacuum CVD," *IEDM Tech. Dig.*, pp. 433–436, December, 1993.
8. T. Ohguro, N. Sugiyama, K. Imai, K. Usuda, M. Saito, T. Yoshitomi, M. Ono, H. S. Momose, and H. Iwai, "The influence of oxygen at epitaxial Si/Si substrate interface for 0.1 $\mu$m epitaxial Si channel n-MOSFETs grown by UHV-CVD," *Symp. on VLSI Tech.*, pp. 21–22, 1995.
9. T. Yoshitomi, M. Saito, T. Ohguro, M. Ono, H. S. Momose, and H. Iwai, "Silicided silicon-sidewall source and drain (S4D) structure for high-performance 75-nm gate length p-MOSFETs," *Symp. on VLSI Tech.*, pp. 11–12, 1995.
10. T. Morimoto, H. S. Momose, T. Iinuma, I. Kunishima, K. Suguro, H. Okano, I. Katakabe, H. Nakajima, M. Tsuchiaki, M. Ono, Y. Katsumata, and H. Iwai, "A NiSi salicide technology for advanced logic devices," *IEDM Tech. Dig.*, pp. 653–656, December, 1991.
11. Semiconductor Industry Association, "National Technology Roadmap for Semiconductors," 1994, 1997 editions.
12. SIA, EECA, EIAJ, KSIA, and TSIA, "International Technology Road Map for Semiconductors," in 1998 update, 1999 edition, 2000 update.
13. http://www.intel.com.
14. T. Ghani, K. Mistry, P. Packan, S. Thompson, M. Stettler, S. Tyagi, and M. Bohr, "Scaling challenges and device design requirements for high performance sub-50 nm gate length planar CMOS transistors," *Symp. on VLSI Tech., Dig. Tech.*, pp. 174–175, June, 2000.
15. R. Chau, J. Kavalieros, B. Roberds, R. Schenker, D. Lionberger, D. Barlage, B. Doyle, R. Arghavani, A. Murthy, and G. Dewey, "30 nm physical gate length CMOS transistors with 1.0 ps n-MOS and 1.7 ps p-MOS gate delays," *IEDM Tech. Dig.*, pp. 45–49, December, 2000.
16. E. Leobandung, E. Barth, M. Sherony, S.-H. Lo, R. Schulz, W. Chu, M. Khare, D. Sadana, D. Schepis, R. Bolam, J. Sleight, F. White, F. Assaderaghi, D. Moy, G. Biery, R. Goldblatt, T.-C. Chen, B. Davari, and G. Shahidi, "High Performance 0,18 $\mu$m SOI CMOS Technology," *IEDM Tech. Dig.*, pp. 679–682, December, 1999.
17. T. Ghani, S. Ahtned, P. Aminzadeh, J. Bielefeld, P. Charvat, C. Chu, M. Harper, P. Jacob, C. Jan, J. Kavalieros, C. Kenyon, R. Nagisetty, P. Packan, J. Sebastian, M. Taylor, J. Tsai, S. Tyagi, S. Yang, and M. Bohr, "100 nm gate length high performance/low power CMOS transistor structure," *IEDM Tech. Dig.*, pp. 415–418, December, 1999.
18. G. Timp, J. I. Bude, K. K. Bourdelle, J. Garno, A. Ghetti, H. Gossmann, M. Green, G. Forsyth, Y. Kim, R. Kleiman, F. Klemens, A. Komblit, C. Lochstampfor, W. Mansfield, S. Moccio, T. Sorsch, D. M. Tennant, W. Timp, and R. Tung, "The ballistic nano-transistor," *IEDM Tech. Dig.*, pp. 55–58, December, 1999.

19. H. Iwai and H. S. Momose, "Ultra-thin gate oxide—performance and reliability," *IEDM Tech. Dig.*, pp. 162–166, 1998.

20. H. Kawaura, T. Sakamoto, and T. Baba, "Transport properties in sub-10-nm-gate EJ-MOSFETs," *Ext. Abs. Int. Conf. SSDM*, pp. 20–21, September, 1999.

21. J. H. Stathis and D. J. DiMaria, "Reliability Projection Ultra-Thin at Low Voltage," *IEDM Tech. Dig.*, pp. 167–170, 1998.

22. K. Okada and K. Yoneda, "Consistent model for time dependent dielectric breakdown in ultrathin silicon dioxides," *IEDM Tech. Dig.*, pp. 445–448, 1999.

23. M. A. Alam, J. Bude, and A. Ghetti, "Field acceleration for oxide breakdown—Can an accurate anode hole injection model resolve the E vs. 1/E controversy?," *Proc. IRPS*, pp. 21–26, April, 2000.

24. J. H. Stathis, "Physical and predictable models of ultra thin oxide reliability in CMOS devices and circuits," *Proc. IRPS*, pp. 132–149, May, 2001.

25. M. Takayanagi, S. Takagi, and Y. Toyoshima, "Experimental study of gate voltage scaling for TDDB under direct tunnelling regime," *Proc. IRPS*, pp. 380–385, May, 2001.

26. B. Yu, H. Wang, C. Riccobene, Q. Xiang, and M.-R. Lin, "Limits of gate-oxide scaling in nano-transistors," *Symp. on VLSI Tech., Dig. Tech.*, pp. 90–91, June, 2000.

27. J. R. Hauser et al., "IEDM Short Course on Sub-100 nm CMOS," 1999.

28. B. H. Lee, L. Kang, W.-J. Qi, R. Nieh, Y. Jeon, K. Onishi, and J. C. Lee, "Ultrathin hafnium oxide with low leakage and excellent reliability for alternative gate dielectric application," *IEDM Tech. Dig.*, pp. 133–136, 1999.

29. W.-J. Qi, R. Nieh, B. H. Lee, L. Kang, Y. Jeon, K. Onishi, T. Ngai, S. Banerjee, and J. C. Lee, "MOSCAP and MOSFET characteristics using $ZrO_2$ gate dielectric deposited directly on Si," *IEDM Tech. Dig.*, pp. 145–148, 1999.

30. Y. Ma, Y. Ono, L. Stecker, D. R. Evans, and S. T. Hsu, "Zirconium oxide based gate dielectrics with equivalent oxide thickness of less than 1.0 nm and performance of submicron MOSFET using a nitride gate replacement Process," *IEDM Tech. Dig.*, pp. 149–152, 1999.

31. W.-J. Qi, R. Nieh, B. H. Lee, K. Onishi, L. Kang, Y. Jeon, J. C. Lee, V. Kaushik, B.-Y. Nguyenl, L. Prabhul, K. Eisenbeiser, and J. Finder, "Performance of MOSFETS with ultra thin $ZrO_2$ and Zr-silicate gate dielectrics," *Symp. on VLSI Tech., Dig. Tech.*, pp. 40–41, June, 2000.

32. L. Kang, Y. Jeon, K. Onishi, B. H. Lee, W.-J. Qi, R. Nieh, S. Gopalan, and J. C. Lee, "Single-layer Thin $HfO_2$ Gate Dielectric with $n^+$-Polysilicon Gate," *Symp. on VLSI Tech., Dig. Tech.*, pp. 44–45, June, 2000.

33. A. Chin, Y. H. Wu, S. B. Chen, C. C. Liao, and W. J. Chen, "High quality $La_2O_3$ and $Al_2O_3$ gate dielectrics with equivalent oxide thickness 5–10 Å," *Symp. on VLSI Tech., Dig. Tech.*, pp. 16–17, June, 2000.

34. A. Kingon and J.-P. Maria, "A comparison of $SiO_2$-based alloys as high permittivity gate oxides," *Ex. Abs. SSDM*, pp. 226–227, August, 2000.

35. T. Yamaguchi, H. Satake, N. Fukushima, and A. Toriumi, "Band diagram and carrier conduction mechanism in $ZrO_2$/Zr-silicate/Si MIS dtructure fabricated by pulsed-laser-ablation deposition," *IEDM Tech. Dig.*, pp. 19–22, 2000.

36. L. Manchanda, M. L. Green, R. B. van Dover, M. D. Morris, A. Kerber, Y. Hu, J.-P. Han, P. J. Silverman, T. W. Sorsch, G. Weber, V. Donnelly, K. Pelhos, F. Klemens, N. A. Ciampa, A. Kornblit, Y. O. Kim, J. E. Bower, D. Barr, E. Ferry, D. Jacobson, J. Eng, B. Busch, and H. Schulte, "Si-doped aluminates for high temperature metal-gate CMOS: Zr-Al-Si-O, a Novel gate dielectric for low power applications," *IEDM Tech. Dig.*, pp. 23–26, 2000.

37. C. H. Lee, H. F. Luan, W. P. Bai, S. J. Lee, T. S. Jeon, Y. Senzaki, D. Roberts, and D. L. Kwong, "MOS characteristics of ultra thin rapid thermal CVD $ZrO_2$ and Zr silicate gate dielectrics," *IEDM Tech. Dig.*, pp. 27–30, 2000.

38. S. J. Lee, H. F. Luan, W. P. Bai, C. H. Lee, T. S. Jeon, Y. Senzaki, D. Roberts, and D. L. Kwong, "High quality ultra thin CVD $HfO_2$ gate stack with poly-Si gate electrode," *IEDM Tech. Dig.*, pp. 31–34, 2000.

39. L. Kang, K. Onishi, Y. Jeon, B. H. Lee, C. Kang, W.-J. Qi, R. Nieh, S.r Gopalan, R. Choi, and J. C. Lee, "MOSFET devices with polysilicon on single-layer $HfO_2$ high-k dielectrics," *IEDM Tech. Dig.*, pp. 35–38, 2000.

40. B. H. Lee, R. Choi, L. Kang, S. Gopalan, R. Nieh, K. Onishi, Y. Jeon, W.-J. Qi, C. Kang, and J. C. Lee, "Characteristics of TaN gate MOSFET with ultrathin hafnium oxide (8 Å–12 Å)," *IEDM Tech. Dig.,* pp. 39–42, 2000.

41. J. H. Lee, K. Koh, N. I. Lee, M. H. Cho, Y. K. Kim, J. S. Jeon, K. H. Cho, H. S. Shin, M. H. Kim, K. Fujihara, H. K. Kang, and J. T. Moon, "Effect of polysilicon gate on the flatband voltage shift and mobility degradation for ALD-Al$_2$O$_3$ gate dielectric," *IEDM Tech. Dig.,* pp. 645–648, 2000.

42. H. J. Osten, J. P. Liu, P. Gaworzewski, E. Bugiel, and P. Zaumseil, "High-k gate dielectrics with ultra-low leakage current based on praseodymium oxide," *IEDM Tech. Dig.,* pp. 653–656, 2000.

43. D. A. Buchanan, E. P. Gusev, E. Cartier, H. Okorn-Schmidt, K. Rim, M. A. Gribelyuk, A. Mocuta, A. Ajmera, M. Copel, S. Guha, N. Bojarczuk, A. Callegari, C. D'Emic, P. Kozlowski, K. Chan, R. J. Fleming, P. C. Jamison, J. Brown, and R. Arndt, "80 nm poly-silicon gated n-FETs with ultra-thin Al$_2$O$_3$ gate dielectric for ULSI applications," *IEDM Tech. Dig.,* pp. 223–226, 2000.

44. H. Iwai, H. S. Momose, T. Morimoto, Y. Ozawa, and K. Yamabe, "Stacked-nitrided oxide gate MISFET with high hot-carrier-immunity," *IEDM Tech. Dig.,* pp. 235–238, 1990

45. H. Yang and G. Lucovsky, "Integration of ultrathin (1.6~2.0 nm) RPECVD oxynitride gate dielectrics into dual poly-Si gate submicron CMOSFETs," *IEDM Tech. Dig.,* pp. 245–248, 1999.

46. M. Togo and T. Mogami, "Impact of recoiled-oxygen-free processing on 1.5 nm SiON gate-dielectric in sub-100 nm CMOS technology," *IEDM Tech. Dig.,* pp. 637–640, 2000.

47. K. Matsuo, T. Saito, A. Yagishita, T. Iinuma, A. Murakoshi, K. Nakajima, S. Omoto, and K. Suguro, "Damascene metal gate MOSFETs with Co silicided source/drain and high-k gate dielectrics," *Symp. on VLSI Tech. Dig. Tech.,* pp. 70–71, 2000.

48. D. F. Downey, S. B. Felch, and S. W. Falk, "Doping and annealing requirements to satisfy the 100 nm technology node," *Proc. ECS Symp. on Advances in Rapid Thermal Processing,* vol. PV99-10, pp. 151–162, 1999.

49. B. Mizuno, M. Takase, I. Nakayama, and M. Ogura, "Plasma Doping of Boron for Fabricating the Surface Channel Sub-quarter micron PMOSFET," *Symp. on VLSI Tech.,* pp. 66–67, 1996.

50. H. Takato, "Embedded DRAM Technologies," *Proc. ESSDERC,* pp. 13–18, 2000.

51. S. Venkatesan, A. V. Gelatos, V. Misra, B. Smith, R. Islam, J. Cope, B. Wilson, D. Tuttle, R. Cardwell, S. Anderson, M. Angyal, R. Bajaj, C. Capasso, P. Crabtree, S. Das, J. Farkas, S. Filipiak, B. Fiordalice, M. Freeman, P. V. Gilbert, M. Herrick, A. Jain, H. Kawasaki, C. King, J. Klein, T. Lii, K. Reid, T. Saaranen, C. Simpson, T. Sparks, P. Tsui, R. Venkartraman, D. Watts, E. J. Weitzman, R. Woodruff, I. Yang, N. Bhat, G. Hamilton, and Y. Yu, "A high performance 1.8 V, 0.20 $\mu$m CMOS technology with copper metallization," *IEDM Tech. Dig.,* pp. 769–772, 1997.

52. D. Edelstein, J. Heidenreich, R. Goldblatt, W. Cote, C. Uzoh, N. Lustig, P. Roper, T. McDevitt, W. Motsiff, A. Simon, J. Dukovic, R. Wachnik, H. Rathore, R. Schulz, L. Su, S. Luce, and J. Slattery, "Full copper wiring in a sub-0.25 $\mu$m CMOS ULSI technology," *IEDM Tech. Dig.,* pp. 773–776, 1997.

53. K. N. Kim, D. H. Kwak, Y. S. Hwang, G. T. Jeong, T. Y. Chung, B. J. Park, Y. S. Chun, J. H. Oh, C. Y. Yoo, and B. S. Joo, "A DRAM technology using MIM BST capacitor for 0.15 $\mu$m DRAM generation and beyond," *Symp. on VLSI Tech.,* pp. 33–34, 1999.

54. T. Eshita, K. Nakamura, M. Mushiga, A. Itoh, S. Miyagaki, H. Yamawaki, M. Aoki, S. Kishii, and Y. Arimoto, "Fully functional 0.5-$\mu$m 64-kbit embedded SBT FeRAM using a new low temperature SBT deposition technique," *Symp. on VLSI Tech.,* pp. 139–140, 1999.

55. H. Takato, H. Koike, T. Yoshida, and H. Ishiuchi, "Process integration trends for embedded DRAM," *Proc. ECS Symp.,* "ULSI Process Integration," pp. 107–119, 1999.

# 2

# CMOS Circuits

Eugene John
*The University of Texas at San Antonio*

Shunzo Yamashita
*Hitachi, Ltd.*

Dejan Marković
*University of California at Berkeley*

Yuichi Kado
*NTT Telecommunications Technology Laboratories*

## 2.1 VLSI Circuits

*Eugene John*

### Introduction

The term very large scale integration (VLSI) refers to a technology through which it is possible to implement large circuits consisting of up to or more than a million transistors on semiconductor wafers, primarily silicon. Without the help of VLSI technology the advances made in computers and in the Internet would not have been possible. The VLSI technology has been successfully used to build large digital systems such as microprocessors, digital signal processors (DSPs), systolic arrays, large capacity memories, memory controllers, I/O controllers, and interconnection networks. The number of transistors on a chip, depending on the application can range from tens (an op-amp) to hundreds of millions (a large capacity DRAM). The Intel Pentium III microprocessor with 256 kbyte level two cache contains approximately 28 million transistors while the Pentium III microprocessor with a 2 Mbyte level two cache contains 140 million transistors [1]. Circuit designs, where a very large number of transistors are integrated on a single semiconductor die, are termed VLSI designs.

Complementary metal oxide semiconductor (CMOS) VLSI logic circuits can be mainly classified into two main categories: static logic circuits and dynamic logic circuits. Static logic circuits are circuits in which the output of the logic gate is always a logical function of the inputs and always available on the outputs of the gate regardless of time. A static logic circuit holds its output indefinitely. On the contrary, a dynamic logic circuit produces its output by storing charge in a capacitor. The output thus decays with time unless it is refreshed periodically. Dynamic or clocked logic gates are used to decrease complexity, increase speed, and lower power dissipation. The basic idea behind the dynamic logic is to use the capacitive input of the transistors to store a charge and thus remember a logic level for use later. Logic circuits may also be classified into combinational and sequential logic circuits. Combinational circuits produce outputs which are dependent on inputs only. There is no memory or feedback in the circuit. Circuits with feedback whose outputs depend on the inputs as well as the state of the circuit are called sequential circuits.

The rest of this chapter section is organized as follows. Static CMOS circuits are described, including combinational and sequential circuits in the following subsection. Special circuits, such as Pseudo NMOS logic and pass transistor logic, are also described in the same subsection. Then the next subsection describes dynamic logic circuits. The last subsection describes memory arrays including static RAMs, dynamic RAMs, and ROMs. Section 2.1 concludes with a discussion of VLSI CMOS low power circuits and illustrates a few low power adder circuits. Section 2.1 explains and develops the circuits at the logic level instead of the device level. References [2–10] are excellent sources for detailed analysis.

### The Transistor as a Switch

CMOS logic circuits are made up of n-channel and p-channel metal oxide semiconductor field effect transistors (MOSFETs). The remarkable ability of these transistors to act almost like ideal switches makes CMOS VLSI circuit design practical and interesting. The n-channel MOSFET is often called the NMOS transistor and the p-channel MOSFET is called the PMOS transistor. A PMOS transistor works complementary to an NMOS transistor. Several symbols represent the NMOS and the PMOS transistors. Figure 2.1 shows the simplified circuit symbols of the NMOS and the PMOS transistors. We will assume that a logic 1 (or simply a 1) is a high voltage. In present day VLSI circuit design it could be any value between 1.0 and 5 V. Normally this is equal to the power supply voltage, $V_{DD}$, of the circuit. It is also assumed that a logic 0 (or simply a 0) is zero volt or close to zero volt, which is the typical ground potential and often denoted by $V_{SS}$. It should be noted that unlike bipolar junction transistors, MOSFETs are symmetrical devices, and the drain and the source terminals can be interchanged. For the NMOS transistor, the terminal where $V_{DD}$ is connected is the drain, and for the PMOS transistor, the terminal where $V_{DD}$ is connected is the source. Figure 2.2 illustrates the basic switching action of the NMOS and the PMOS transistors. The NMOS transistor behaves as an open switch when the gate voltage $S = 0$, and when the gate voltage $S = 1$, the transistor behaves as a closed switch (short circuit). For the PMOS transistor, the complement is true. That is, when $S = 0$, the PMOS transistor behaves as a closed switch, and when $S = 1$, the transistor behaves as an open switch. The transistor models presented in Fig. 2.2 are a very simplistic approximation, but it is an adequate model to understand the logic level behavior of VLSI circuits. The way the PMOS and NMOS transistors pass the high and low voltages from drain to source or source to drain for the appropriate gate signal is an interesting and peculiar property of these transistors. It has been observed that n-channel passes "0" very well and the p-channel passes "1" very well. Referring to Fig. 2.2, when $S = 1$, the NMOS acts like a closed switch, but if we connect $V_{DD}$ at the node A, at the node B instead of $V_{DD}$ we will get a voltage slightly less than $V_{DD}$, for this reason we call this sigal a weak 1. But when $V_{SS}$ is connected at node A of the NMOS, at node B we get a strong

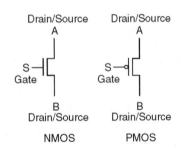

**FIGURE 2.1**  Simplified circuit symbols of NMOS and PMOS transistors.

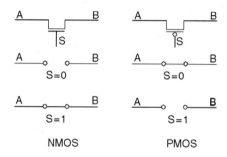

**FIGURE 2.2** The basic switching actions of the NMOS and PMOS transistors.

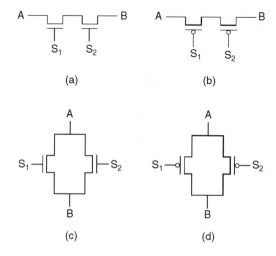

**FIGURE 2.3** Series and parallel switch networks using NMOS and PMOS transistors.

ground and we call this signal a strong 0. Again, for the PMOS transistor, the complement is true. For the PMOS, when the gate signal $S = 0$, if we connect $V_{DD}$ at the node $A$, we get a strong 1 at node $B$, and if we connect $V_{SS}$ at the node $A$, we get a weak 0 at node $B$.

The NMOS and PMOS switches can be combined in various ways to produce desired simple and complex logic operations. For example, by connecting $n$ NMOS or $n$ PMOS transistors in series, one can realize circuits in which the functionality is true only when all the $n$ transistors are ON. For instance, in the circuit in Fig. 2.3(a), the nodes $A$ and $B$ will get connected only when $S_1 = S_2 = 1$. Similarly, in Fig. 2.3(b), $A$ and $B$ will get connected only when $S_1 = S_2 = 0$. Similarly by connecting $n$ PMOS or $n$ NMOS transistors in parallel between two nodes $A$ and $B$, one can realize circuits in which the functionality is true when any one of the $n$ transistors is ON. For instance, in Fig. 2.3(c), if either $S_1$ or $S_2$ is equal to 1, there is a connection between $A$ and $B$. Similarly, in Fig. 2.3(d), if either $S_1$ or $S_2$ is equal to 0, there is a connection between $A$ and $B$.

## Static CMOS Circuit Design

### CMOS Combinational Circuits

Any Boolean function, whether simple or complex, depending on the input combinations can have only two possible output values, a logic high or a logic low. Therefore, to construct a logic circuit that realizes a given Boolean function, all that is required is to conditionally connect the output to $V_{DD}$ for logic high or to $V_{SS}$ for logic low. Therefore, to construct a logic circuit that realizes a given Boolean function, all that is required is to conditionally connect the output to $V_{DD}$ for logic high or to $V_{SS}$ for logic low.

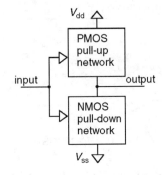

**FIGURE 2.4**   The general structure of a CMOS logic circuit.

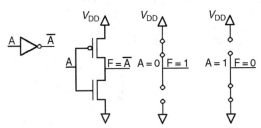

**FIGURE 2.5**   A CMOS inverter: logic symbol, CMOS realization, and the switch level equivalent circuit when the input is equal to 0 and 1.

This is the basic principle behind the realization of CMOS logic circuits. A CMOS logic gate consists of an NMOS pull-down network and a complementary PMOS pull-up network. The NMOS pull-down network is connected between the output and the ground. The PMOS pull-up network is connected between the output and the power supply, $V_{DD}$. The inputs go to both the networks. This is schematically illustrated in Fig. 2.4. The number of transistors in each network is equal to the number of inputs. The NMOS pull-down network can be designed using the series and parallel switches illustrated in Fig. 2.3. The PMOS pull-up network is designed as a dual of NMOS pull-down network. That is, parallel components in NMOS network translate into series components in the PMOS network, and series components in NMOS network translate into parallel components in PMOS network. This procedure is elaborated by design examples later in this section.

For a given combination of inputs, when the output is a logic 0, the NMOS network provides a closed path between the output and ground, thereby pulling the output down to ground (logic 0). This is the reason for the name NMOS pull-down network. When the output is a logic 1, for a given combination of inputs, the PMOS network provides a closed path between the output and $V_{DD}$, thereby pulling the output up to $V_{DD}$ (logic 1). This is the reason for the name PMOS pull-up network. For CMOS logic gates for both the outputs (0 and 1), we get strong signals at the output. If the output is a logic high, we get a strong 1 since the output gets connected to $V_{DD}$ through the PMOS pull-up network, and if the output is a logic low, we get a strong 0 since the output gets connected to $V_{ss}$ through the NMOS pull-down network. It should be clearly noticed that only one of the networks remains closed at a given time for any combination of the inputs. Therefore, at steady state no dc path exists between $V_{DD}$ and ground and hence no power dissipation. This is the primary reason for the inherent low power dissipation of CMOS VLSI circuits.

We now illustrate the CMOS realization of inverters, NAND and NOR logic circuits. An inverter is the simplest possible of all the logic gates. An inverter can be constructed by using a PMOS and an NMOS transistor. Figure 2.5 shows the logic symbol, CMOS realization and switch level equivalent circuits of the inverter for both a 0 input and a 1 input. When the input is 0, the NMOS transistor is open (or OFF) and the PMOS transistor is closed (or ON). Since the P switch is closed, the output is pulled high to $V_{DD}$ (logic 1). When the input is 1, the PMOS transistor is OFF and the NMOS transistor is ON, and the output is pulled down to ground (logic 0), which is the expected result of an inverter circuit.

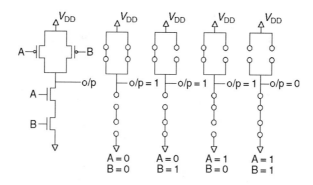

**FIGURE 2.6** A 2-input CMOS NAND gate and the switch-level equivalent circuits for all the possible input combinations.

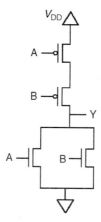

**FIGURE 2.7** A 2-input CMOS NOR gate.

A 2-input CMOS NAND gate and the switch level equivalent circuits for all the possible input combinations are shown in Fig. 2.6. This circuit realizes the function $F = (AB)'$. The generation of the CMOS circuit has the following steps. For the pull-down network, take the non-inverted expression $AB$ (called the n-expression) and realize using NMOS transistors. For the pull-up network, find the dual of the n-expression (called the p-expression) and realize using PMOS transistors. In this example the dual is $A + B$ (p-expression). For the CMOS NAND gate shown in Fig. 2.6, if any of the inputs is a 0, one of the NMOS transistors will be OFF and the pull-down network will be open. At the same time one of the PMOS transistors will be ON and the pull-up network will be closed, and the output will be pulled up to $V_{DD}$ (logic 1). If all the inputs are high (logic 1), the pull-down network will be closed and the pull-up network will be open and the output will be pulled down to ground (logic 0), which is the desired functionality of a NAND gate.

Figure 2.7 illustrates the CMOS realization of a 2-input NOR gate. In Fig. 2.7, the output value is equal to 0 when either $A$ or $B$ is equal to 1 because one of the NMOS transistors will be ON. But if both inputs are equal to 0, the series pair of PMOS transistors between $V_{DD}$ and the output $Y$ will be ON, resulting in a 1 at the output, which is the desired functionality of a NOR gate. Figure 2.8 illustrates a 2-input CMOS OR gate realized in two different fashions. In the first method, an inverter is connected to the output of a NOR circuit to obtain an OR circuit. In the second method, we make use of DeMorgan's theorem, $(A'B')' = A + B$, to realize the OR logic function. It should be noted that the inputs are inverted in the second method. To realize the CMOS AND gate, the same principles can be used.

CMOS compound gates can be realized using a combination of series and parallel switch structures. Figure 2.9 shows the CMOS realization of the logic function $Y = (ABC + D)'$. The pull-down network is realized using the n-expression: $ABC + D$ (the noninverted expression of $Y$). The pull-up network is realized using the dual of the n-expression, which is equal to $(A + B + C)D$. In order to further illustrate

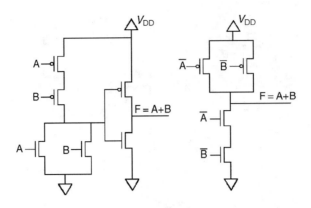

**FIGURE 2.8**    Two different realizations of a 2-input CMOS OR gate.

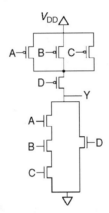

**FIGURE 2.9**    CMOS realization of the compound gate
$Y = (ABC + D)'$.

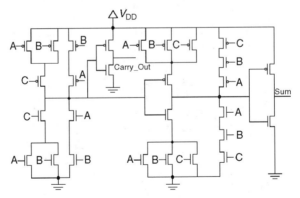

**FIGURE 2.10**    A CMOS 1-bit full adder.

CMOS designs, we show a full adder design in Fig. 2.10. The two 1-bit inputs are $A$ and $B$, and the carry-in is $C$. Two 1-bit outputs are the Sum and the Carry-Out. The outputs can be represented by the equations: Sum $= ABC + AB'C' + A'B'C + A'BC'$ and Carry-Out $= AB + AC + BC = AB + (A + B)C$ [9]. The implementation of this circuit requires 14 NMOS and 14 PMOS transistors.

## Pseudo-NMOS Logic

Pseudo NMOS is a ratioed logic. That is for the correct operation of the circuit the width-to-length ratios (W/L s) of the transistors must be carefully chosen. Instead of a combination of active pull-down and pull-up networks, the ratioed logic consists of a pull-down network and a simple load device.

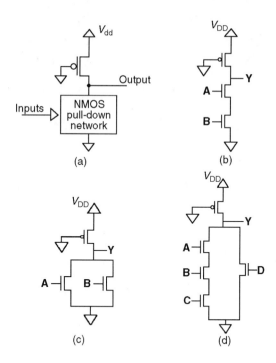

**FIGURE 2.11** (a) The general structure of a Pseudo-NMOS logic; (b) Pseudo-NMOS realization of a 2-input NAND gate; (c) Pseudo-NMOS realization of a 2-input NOR gate; (d) Pseudo-NMOS realization of the logic function $Y = (ABC + D)'$.

The pull-down network realizes the logic function and a PMOS with grounded gate presents the load device, as shown in Fig. 2.11(a). The pseudo-NMOS logic style results in a substantial reduction in gate complexity, by reducing the number of transistors required to realize the logic function by almost half. The speed of the pseudo-NMOS circuit is faster than that of static CMOS realization because of smaller parasitic capacitance. One of the main disadvantages of this design style is the increased static power dissipation. This is due to the fact that, at steady state when the output is 0, pseudo-NMOS circuits provide dc current path from $V_{DD}$ to ground. Figure 2.11(b) shows the realization of a 2-input NAND gate using pseudo-NMOS logic. When the inputs $A = 0$ and $B = 0$, both the transistors in the pull-down network will be OFF and the output will be a logic 1. When $A = 0$ and $B = 1$, or $A = 1$ and $B = 0$, the pull-down network again will be OFF and the output will be logic 1. When $A = 1$ and $B = 1$, both transistors in the pull-down network are ON and the output will be a logic 0, which is the expected result of a NAND gate. Figure 2.11(c) illustrates the pseudo-NMOS realization of a 2-input NOR gate. Another example for the pseudo-NMOS logic realization is given in Fig. 2.11(d). This circuit realizes the function $Y = (ABC + D)'$, and the operation of this logic circuitry can also be explained in a manner explained above.

### Pass Transistor/Transmission Gate Logic

In all the circuits we have discussed so far, the outputs are obtained by closing either the pull-up network to $V_{DD}$ or the pull-down network to ground. The inputs are used essentially to control the condition of the pull-up and the pull-down networks. One may design circuits in which the input signals in addition to $V_{DD}$ and $V_{SS}$ are steered to output, depending on the logic function being realized. Pass transistor logic implements a logic gate as a simple switch network. The pass transistor design methodology has the advantage of being simple and fast. Complex CMOS combinational logic functions can be implemented with minimal number of transistors. This results in reduced parasitic capacitance and hence faster circuits. As a pass transistor design example, Fig. 2.12 shows a Boolean function unit realized using

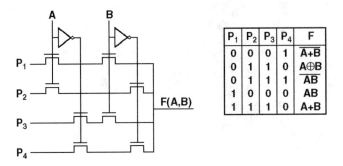

**FIGURE 2.12**   Multifunction circuitry using pass transistor logic and the function table.

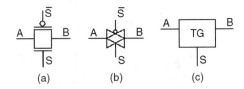

**FIGURE 2.13**   The transmission gate: (a) schematic, (b) logic symbol, and (c) simplified logic symbol.

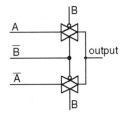

**FIGURE 2.14**   Transmission gate implementation of XOR gate.

pass transistors [3,7]. In this circuit the output is a function of the inputs $A$ and $B$ and the functional inputs $P1$, $P2$, $P3$, and $P4$. Depending on the values of $P1$, $P2$, $P3$, and $P4$, the $F$ output is either the NOR, XOR, NAND, AND, or OR of inputs $A$ and $B$. This is summarized in the table in Fig. 2.12.

The simple pass transistor only passes one logic level well, but if we put NMOS and PMOS in parallel we get a simple circuit that passes both logic levels well. This simple circuit is called the transmission gate (TG). The schematic and logic symbol of the transmission gate are shown in Fig. 2.13(a,b). Figure 2.13(c) shows the simplified logic symbol. The CMOS transmission gate operates as a bi-directional switch between nodes $A$ and $B$, which is controlled by $S$. The transmission gate requires two control signals. The control signal $S$ is applied to the NMOS and the complement of the control signal $S'$ to the PMOS. If the control signal $S$ is high, both transistors are turned ON providing a low resistance path between $A$ and $B$. If the control signal $S$ is low, both transistors will be OFF and the path between the nodes $A$ and $B$ will be an open circuit.

The transmission gate can be used to realize logic gates and functions. Consider the exclusive-OR (XOR) gate shown in Fig. 2.14 [5]. When both inputs $A$ and $B$ are low, the top TG is ON (and the bottom TG is OFF) and its output is connected to $A$, which is low (logic 0). If both the inputs are high, the bottom TG is ON (and the top TG is OFF), and its output is connected to $A'$, which is also a low (logic 0). If $A$ is high and $B$ is low, the top TG is on and the output is connected to $A$, which is a high (logic 1). Similarly, if $A$ is low and $B$ is high, the bottom TG is on and the output gets connected to $A'$, which is a high (logic 1), which is the expected result of a XOR gate. In Fig. 2.14, if we change $B$ to $B'$ and $B'$ to $B$, the circuit will realize the exclusive-NOR (XNOR) function. In the next section we will use transmission gates to realize latches and flip-flops.

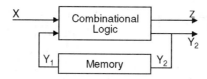

**FIGURE 2.15** A general model of a sequential network.

## Sequential CMOS Logic Circuits

As mentioned earlier, in combinational logic circuits, the outputs are a logic combination of the current input signals. In sequential logic circuits the outputs depend not only on the current values of the inputs, but also on the preceding input values. Therefore, a sequential logic circuit must remember information about its past state. Figure 2.15 shows the schematic of a synchronous sequential logic circuit. The circuit consists of a combinational logic circuit, which accepts inputs $X$ and $Y_1$ and produces outputs $Z$ and $Y_2$. The output $Y_2$ is stored in the memory element as a state variable. The number of bits in the state variable decides the number of available states, and for this reason a sequential circuit is also called a finite state machine. The memory element can be realized using level-triggered latches or edge triggered flip-flops.

For a VLSI circuit designer, a number of different latches and flip-flops are available for the design of the memory element of a sequential circuit. Figure 2.16(a) shows the diagram of a CMOS positive level sensitive $D$ latch realized using transmission gates and inverters and its switch level equivalent circuits for CLK = 0 and CLK = 1. It has a data input $D$ and a clock input CLK. $Q$ is the output and the complement of the output $Q'$ is also available. When CLK = 0, the transmission gate in the inverter loop will be closed and the transmission gate next to the data input will be open. This establishes a feedback path around the inverter pair and this feedback loop is isolated from the input $D$ as shown in Fig. 2.16(a). This causes the current value of $Q$ (and hence $Q'$) to be stored in the inverter loop. When the clock input CLK = 1, the transmission gate in the inverter loop will be open and the transmission gate close to the input will be closed, as shown in Fig. 2.16(a). Now the output $Q = D$, and the data is accepted continuously. That is, any change at the input is reflected at the output after a nominal delay. By inverting the clocking signals to the transmission gates a negative level sensitive latch can be realized.

A negative level sensitive latch and a positive level sensitive latch may be combined to form an edge triggered flip-flop. Figure 2.16(b) shows the circuit diagram of a CMOS positive edge triggered $D$ flip-flop. The first latch, which is the negative level sensitive latch, is called the master and the second latch (positive level sensitive latch) is called the slave. The electrical equivalent circuits for the CMOS positive edge triggered $D$ flip-flop for CLK = 0 and for CLK = 1 are also shown in Fig. 2.16(b). When CLK = 0, both latches will be isolated from each other and the slave latch holds the previous value, and the master latch (negative level sensitive latch) follows the input ($Q_m = D'$). When CLK changes from 0 to 1, the transmission gate closest to data $D$ will become open and the master latch forms a closed loop and holds the value of $D$ at the time of clock transition from 0 to 1. The slave latch feedback loop is now open, and it is now connected to the master latch through a transmission gate. Now the open slave latch passes the value held by the master ($Q_m = D'$) to the output. The output $Q = Q'_m$, which is the value of the input $D$ at the time of the clock transmission from 0 to 1. Since the master is disconnected from the data input $D$, the input $D$ cannot affect the output. When the clock signal changes from 1 to 0, the slave forms a feedback loop, saving the value of the master and the open master start to sampling and following the input data $D$ again. But, as is evident from the Fig. 2.16(b), this will not affect the output. Together with RAM and ROM, which are explained in the section on Memory Circuits, these structures form the basis of most CMOS storage elements and are also used as the memory element in the design of sequential circuits. Figure 2.16(c) shows the CMOS realization of the positive edge triggered $D$ flip-flop, including the transistors required for generating the CLK' signal—18 transistors are required for its implementation.

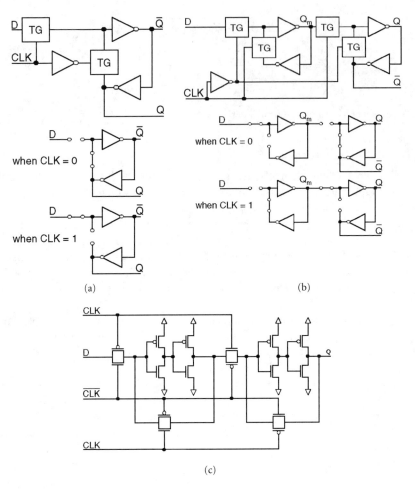

**FIGURE 2.16** (a) CMOS positive-level sensitive $D$ latch and the switch level equivalent circuits for CLK = 0 and CLK = 1; (b) CMOS positive-edge triggered $D$ flip-flop and the switch level equivalent circuits for CLK = 0 and CLK = 1; (c) CMOS implementation of the positive-edge triggered $D$ flip-flop.

## Dynamic Logic Circuits

The basic idea behind the dynamic logic is to use the capacitive input of the MOSFET to store a charge and thus remember a logic level for later use. The output decays with time unless it is refreshed periodically since it is stored in a capacitor. Dynamic logic gates, which are also known as clocked logic gates, are used to decrease complexity, increase speed, and lower power dissipation.

Figure 2.17 shows the basic structure of a dynamic CMOS logic circuit. The dynamic logic design eliminates one of the switch networks from a complementary logic circuit, thus reducing the number of transistors required to realize a logic function by almost 50%. The operation of a dynamic circuit has two phases: a precharge phase and an evaluation phase depending on the state of the clock signal. When clock CLK = 0, the PMOS transistor in the circuit is turned ON and the NMOS transistor in the circuit is turned OFF, and the load capacitance is charged to $V_{DD}$. This is called the precharge phase. The precharge phase should be long enough for the load capacitance to completely charge to $V_{DD}$. During the precharge phase, since the NMOS transistor is turned OFF, no conducting path exists between $V_{DD}$ and ground, thus eliminating static current. The precharging phase ends and the evaluation phase begins when the clock CLK turns 1. Now the PMOS transistor is turned OFF and the NMOS transistor is turned ON. Depending on the values of the inputs and the composition of the pull-down network, a conditional path may exist between the output and the ground. If such a path exists, the capacitor discharges and logic low output

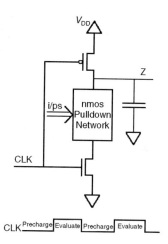

**FIGURE 2.17**   Basic structure of a dynamic CMOS logic circuitry.

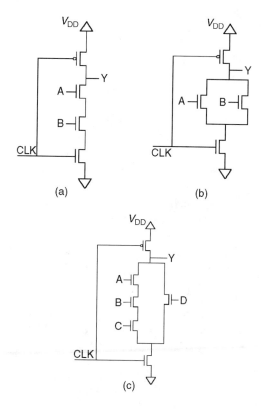

**FIGURE 2.18**   Dynamic logic implementation of (a) 2-input NAND gate, (b) 2-input NOR gate, and (c) the logic function $Y = (ABC + D)'$.

is obtained. If no such path exists between the output and the ground, the capacitor retains its value and a logic high output is obtained. In the evaluate phase, since the PMOS transistor is turned OFF, no path exists between $V_{DD}$ and ground, thus eliminating the static current during that phase also.

Figure 2.18(a) shows the realization of the 2-input NAND gate using dynamic logic. During the precharge phase (CLK = 0), the NMOS transistor is OFF and the PMOS transistor is ON, and the capacitor is precharged to logic 1. During the evaluate phase, if the inputs $A$ and $B$ are both equal to 0, both the transistors in the pull-down network will be OFF, and the output goes into high impedance state and holds the precharged value of logic 1. When $A = 0$ and $B = 1$, or $A = 1$ and $B = 0$, the pull-down network again will be OFF and the output holds the precharged value of logic 1. When $A = 1$ and $B = 1$, both transistors in the pull-down network are ON, and the load capacitor discharges through the low resistance path provided by the NMOS pull-down network, and the output will be a logic 0, which is the expected result of a NAND gate. It should be noted that once the capacitor discharges, it cannot be charged until the next precharge phase. Figure 2.18(b) illustrates the dynamic logic implementation of a 2-input NOR gate. Another example for the dynamic logic realization is given in Fig. 2.18(c). This circuit realizes the function $Y = (ABC + D)'$, and the operation of this dynamic logic circuitry can also be explained in a manner explained earlier.

## Memory Circuits

Semiconductor memory arrays are widely used in many VLSI subsystems, including microprocessors and other digital systems. More than half of the real estate in many state-of-the-art microprocessors is devoted to cache memories, which are essentially memory arrays. Memory circuits belong to different categories; some memories are volatile, i.e., they lose their information when power is switched off, whereas some memories are nonvolatile. Similarly, some memory circuits allow modification of information, whereas some only allow reading of prewritten information. As shown in Fig. 2.19, memories may be classified into two main categories, Read/Write Memories (RWMs) or Read Only Memories (ROMs). Read/Write Memories or memory circuits that allow reading (retrieving) and writing (modification) of information are more popularly referred to as Random Access Memories or RAMs. (Historically, RAMs were referred to by that name to contrast with non-semiconductor memories such as disks which allow only sequential access. Actually, ROMs also allow random access in the way RAMs do; however, they should not be called RAMs. The advent of new RAM chips such as page mode DRAMs and cached DRAMs have rendered RAMs to be strictly not random access memories because latency for random access to any location is not uniform any more.)

In contrast to RAMs, ROMs are nonvolatile, i.e., the data stored in them is not lost when power supply is turned off. The contents of the simple ROM cannot be modified. Some ROMs allow erasing and rewriting of the information (typically, the entire information in the whole chip is erased). The ROMs, which are programmed in the factory and are not reprogrammable anymore, are called mask-programmed ROMs, whereas programmable ROMs (PROMs) allow limited reprogramming, and erasable PROMs (EPROMs), electrically erasable PROMs (EEPROMs), and FLASH memories allow erasing and rewriting of the information in the chip. EPROMs allow erasure of the information using ultraviolet light, whereas EEPROMs and FLASH memories allow erasure by electrical means.

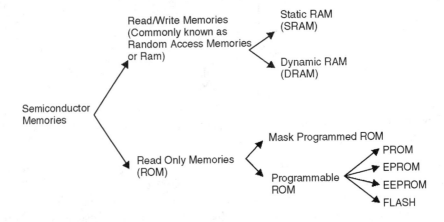

**FIGURE 2.19**  Different types of semiconductor memories.

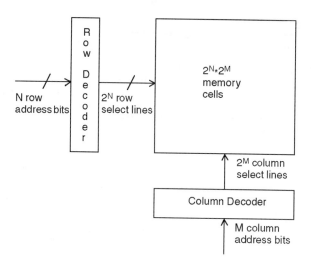

**FIGURE 2.20** Typical memory array organization.

Memory chips are typically organized in the form of a matrix of memory cells. For instance, a 32-kbit memory chip can be organized as 256 rows of 128 cells each. Each cell is capable of storing one bit of binary information, a 0 or a 1. Each cell needs two connections to be selected, a row select signal and a column select signal. All the cells in a row are connected to the same row select signal (also called word-line) and all the cells in a column are connected to the same column select signal (also called bit-line). Only cells that get both the row and column selects activated will get selected. Figure 2.20 shows the structure of a typical memory cell array. A 32-kbit memory chip will have 15 address lines, and if the chip is organized as 256 rows or 128 cells, 8 address lines will be connected to the row address decoder and 7 address lines will be connected to the column address decoder.

## Static RAM Circuits

Static RAMs are static memory circuits in the sense that information can be held indefinitely as long as power supply is on, which is in contrast to DRAMs which need periodic refreshing. A static RAM cell basically consists of a pair of cross-coupled inverters, as shown in Fig. 2.21(a). The cross-coupled latch has two possible stable states, which will be interpreted as the two possible values one wants to store in the cell, the "0" and the "1". To read and write the data contained in the cell, some switches are required. Because the two inverters are cross-coupled, the outputs of the two transistors are complementary to each other. Both outputs are brought out as bit line and complementary bit line. Hence, a pair of switches are provided between the 1-bit cell and the complementary bit lines. Figure 2.21(b) illustrates the structure of a generic MOS static RAM cell, with the two cross-coupled transistors storing the actual data, the two transistors connected to the word line and bit-lines acting as the access switches and two generic loads, which may be active or passive. Figure 2.21(c) illustrates a case where the loads are resistive, whereas Fig. 2.21(d) illustrates the case where the loads are PMOS transistors. A resistive load can be realized using undoped polysilicon. Such a resistive load yields compact cell size and is suitable for high density memory arrays; however, one cannot obtain good noise rejection properties and good energy dissipation properties for passive loads. Low values of the load resistor results in better noise margins and output pull-up times; however, high values of the resistor is better to reduce the amount of standby current drawn by each memory cell. The load can also be realized using an active device, which is the approach in the 6-transistor cell in Fig. 2.21(d). This 6-transistor configuration, often called the full CMOS SRAM, has desirable properties of low power dissipation, high switching speed, and good noise margins. The only disadvantage is that it consumes more area than the cell with the resistive load.

**TABLE 2.1**

| Desired Action | WB | WB' | Operation |
|---|---|---|---|
| WRITE 1 | 0 | 1 | WT1 OFF, WT2 ON, forcing $C'$ low |
| WRITE 0 | 1 | 0 | WT1 ON, WT2 OFF, forcing $C$ low |
| Do not write | 0 | 0 | WT1 and WT2 OFF, forcing $C$ and $C'$ to be high |

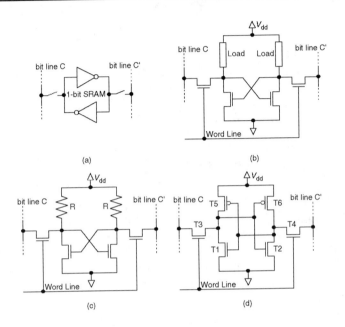

**FIGURE 2.21** Different configurations of the SRAM cell: (a) basic two-inverter latch, (b) generic SRAM cell topology, (c) SRAM cell with resistive load, (d) the 6-transistor CMOS SRAM cell.

In Fig. 2.21(d), the cross-coupled latch formed by transistors T1 and T2 forms the core of the SRAM cell. This transistor pair can be in one of two stable states, with either T1 in the ON state or T2 in the ON state. These two stable states form the one-bit information that one can store in this transistor pair. When T1 is ON (conducting), and T2 is OFF, a "0" is considered to be stored in the cell. When a "1" is stored, T2 will be conducting and T1 will be OFF. The transistors T3 and T4 are used to perform the read and write operations. These transistors are turned ON only when the word line is activated (selected). When the word line is not selected, the two pass transistors T3 and T4 are OFF and the latch formed by T1 and T2 simply "holds" the bit it contains. Once the memory cell is selected by using the word line, one can perform read and write operations on the cell. In order to write a "1" into the cell, the bit line $C'$ must be forced to logic low, which will turn off transistor T1, which leads to a high voltage level at T1's drain, which turns T2 ON and the voltage level at T2's drain goes low. In order to write a "0", voltage level at bit line $C$ is forced low, forcing T2 to turn off and T1 to turn ON. To accomplish forcing the bit-lines to logic low, a write circuitry has to be used. Figure 2.22 illustrates a static RAM cell complete with read and write circuitry [6]. The write circuitry consists of transistors WT1 and WT2 that are used to force $C$ or $C'$ to low-voltage appropriately (Table 2.1). Typically, two NOR gates are used to generate the appropriate gate signals for the transistors WT1 and WT2 (not shown in Fig. 2.22).

The read circuitry is also illustrated in Fig. 2.22. In order to read values contained in a cell, the cell is selected using the word select line. Both transistors T3 and T4 are ON, and one of either T1 or T2 is ON. If T1 is ON, as soon as the row select signal is applied, the voltage level on bit line $C$ drops slightly because it is pulled down by T1 and T3. The data read circuitry detects the small voltage difference between the $C$ and $C'$ lines ($C'$ is higher) and amplifies it as a logic "0" output. If T2 is ON, as soon as

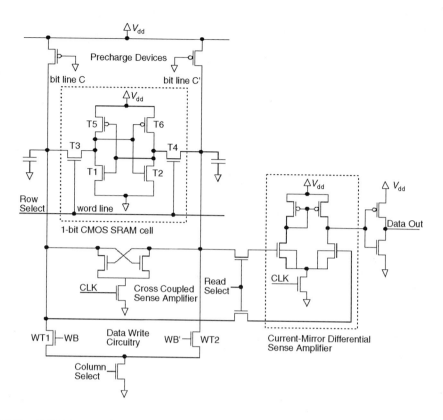

**FIGURE 2.22**   CMOS SRAM cell with read amplifier and data write circuitry [6].

the row select signal is applied, the voltage level on complementary bit line $C'$ drops slightly because it is pulled down by T2 and T4. The data read circuitry detects the small voltage difference between $C$ and $C'$ lines ($C$ is higher) and amplifies it as logic "1" output. The data read circuitry can be constructed as a simple source-coupled differential amplifier or as a differential current-mirror sense amplifier circuit (as indicated in Fig. 2.22). The current-mirror sense amplifier achieves a faster read time than the simple source-coupled read amplifier. The read access speed can be further improved by two- or three-stage current mirror differential sense amplifiers [6].

## Dynamic RAM Circuits

All RAMs lose their contents when power supply is turned off. However, some RAMs gradually lose the information even if power is not turned off, because the information is held in a capacitor. Those RAMs need periodic refreshing of information in order to retain the data. They are called dynamic RAMs or DRAMs.

Static RAM cells require 4–6 transistors per cell and need 4–5 lines connecting to each cell including power, ground, bit lines, and word lines. It is desirable to realize memory cells with fewer transistors and less area, in order to construct high density RAM arrays. The early steps in this direction were to create a 4-transistor cell as in Fig. 2.23(a) by removing the load devices of the 6-transistor SRAM cell. The data is stored in a cross-coupled transistor pair as in the SRAM cells we discussed earlier. But it should be noted that voltage from the storage node is continuously being lost due to parasitic capacitance, and there is no current path from a power supply to the storage node to restore the charge lost due to leakage. Hence, the cell must be refreshed periodically. This 4-transistor cell has some marginal area advantage over the 6-transistor SRAM cell, but not any significant advantage. An improvement over the 4-transistor DRAM cell is the 3-transistor DRAM cell shown in Fig. 2.23(b). Instead of using a cross-coupled transistor pair, this cell uses a single transistor as the storage device. The transistor is turned ON or OFF depending

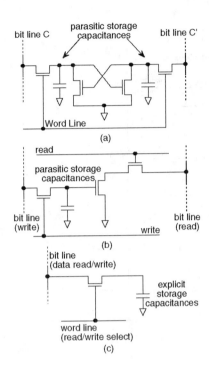

**FIGURE 2.23** Different configurations of a DRAM cell: (a) 4-transistor DRAM cell, (b) 3-transistor DRAM cell, (c) 1-transistor DRAM cell.

on the charge stored on its gate capacitance. Two more transistors are contained in each cell, one used as read access switch and the other used as write access switch. This cell is faster than the 4-transistor DRAM cell; however, every cell needs two control and two I/O (bit) lines making the area advantage insignificant.

The widely popular DRAM cell is the single transistor DRAM cell shown in Fig. 2.23(c). It stores data as charge in an explicit capacitor. There is also one transistor which is used as the access switch. This structure consumes significantly less area than a static RAM cell. The cell has one control line (word line) and one data line (bit line). The cells can be selected using the word line, and the charge in the capacitor can be modified using the bit line.

## Read Only Memories (ROMs)

ROM arrays are simple memory circuits, significantly simpler than the RAMs, which we discussed in the preceding section. A ROM can be viewed as a simple combinational circuit, which produces a specified output value for each input combination. Each input combination corresponds to a unique address or location. Storing binary information at a particular address can be achieved by the presence or absence of a connection from the selected row to the selected column. The presence or absence of the connection can be implemented by a transistor. Figure 2.24 illustrates a 4 × 4 memory array. At any time, only one word line among A1, A2, A3, and A4 is selected by the ROM decoder. If an active transistor exists at the cross point of the selected row and a data line (D1, D2, D3, and D4), the data line is pulled low by that transistor. If no active transistor exists at the cross point, the data line stays high because of the PMOS load device. Thus, absence of an active transistor indicates a "1" whereas the presence of an active transistor indicates a "0".

ROMs are most effectively used in devices, which need a set of fixed values for operation. The set of values are predetermined before fabrication and a transistor is made only at those cross-points where one is desired. If the information that is to be stored in the ROM is not known prior to fabrication, a transistor is made at every cross-point. The resulting chip is a write-once ROM. The ROM is programmed

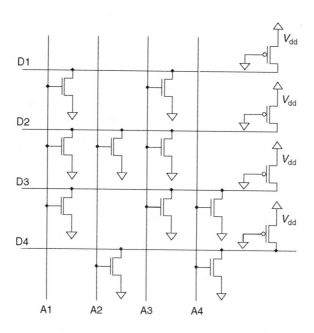

**FIGURE 2.24** Read only memory (ROM) circuit.

by cutting the connection between the drain of the MOSFET and the column (bit) line. ROMs are effective in applications where large volumes are required.

## Low-Power CMOS Circuit Design

The increasing importance and growing popularity of mobile computing and communications systems have made power consumption a critical design parameter in VLSI circuits and systems. The design of portable devices requires consideration of the peak power for reliability and proper circuit operation, but more critical is the time-averaged power consumption to operate the circuits for a given amount of time to perform a certain task [11,12]. There are four sources of power dissipation in digital CMOS VLSI circuits, which are summarized in the following equation:

$$P_{avg} = P_{switching} + P_{short\text{-}circuit} + P_{leakage} + P_{static}$$
$$= C_L V V_{DD} f + I_{sc} V_{DD} + I_{leakage} V_{DD} + I_{static} V_{DD}$$
$$= C_L V^2 f + I_{sc} V_{DD} + I_{leakage} V_{DD} + I_{static} V_{DD}$$

where

$P_{avg}$ = time-averaged power
$P_{switching}$ = switching component of power
$P_{short\text{-}circuit}$ = short circuit power dissipation
$P_{leakage}$ = leakage power
$P_{static}$ = static power
$C_L$ = load capacitance
$V$ = voltage swing (and in most cases this will be the same as the supply voltage $V_{DD}$)
$f$ = clock frequency
$I_{sc}$ = short-circuit current
$I_{leakage}$ = leakage current
$I_{static}$ = static current

In some literature, the authors like to group $P_{\text{leakage}}$ and $P_{\text{static}}$ together and call it as the static component of power.

The switching component of the power occurs when energy is drawn from the power supply to charge parasitic capacitors made up of gate, diffusion, and interconnect capacitance. For properly designed circuits, the switching component will contribute more than 90% of the power consumption, making it the primary target for power reduction [12]. A system level approach, which involves optimizing algorithms, architectures, logic design, circuit design, and physical design, can be used to minimize power. The physical capacitance can be minimized through choice of substrate, layout optimization, device sizing, and choice of logic styles. The choice of supply voltage has the greatest impact on the power-delay product, which is the amount of energy required to perform a given function. From the expression for the switching component of power ($P_{\text{switching}} = C_L V^2 f$), it is clear that if the supply voltage is reduced, the power delay-product will improve quadratically. Unfortunately, a reduction in supply voltage is associated with a reduction in circuit speed. However, if the goal is to increase the MIPS/Watt in general purpose computing for a fixed level, then various architectural schemes can be used for voltage reduction.

The short-circuit power dissipation, $P_{\text{short-circuit}}$, is due to short-circuit current, $I_{\text{sc}}$. Finite rise and fall time of the input waveforms result in a direct current path between supply voltage $V_{\text{DD}}$ and ground, which exists for a short period of time during switching. Such a path never exists in dynamic circuits, as precharge and evaluate transistors should never be ON simultaneously, as this would lead to incorrect evaluation. Short-circuit currents are, therefore, a problem encountered only in static designs. Through proper choices of transistor sizes, the short-circuit component of power dissipation can be kept to less than 10%.

Leakage power, $P_{\text{leakage}}$, is due to the leakage current, $I_{\text{leakage}}$. Two types of leakage currents seen through in CMOS VLSI circuits: reverse biased diode leakage current at the transistor drain, and the subthreshold leakage current through the channel of an "OFF" device. The magnitude of these leakage currents is set predominantly by the processing technology. The sub-threshold leakage occurs due to carrier diffusion between the source and the drain when the gate-source voltage, $V_{\text{gs}}$, has exceeded the weak inversion point, but still below the threshold voltage $V_t$. In this regime, the MOSFET behaves almost like a bipolar transistor, and the subthreshold current is exponentially dependent on $V_{\text{gs}}$. At present $P_{\text{leakage}}$ is a small percentage of total power dissipation, but as the transistor size becomes smaller and smaller and the number of transistors that can be integrated into a single silicon die increases, this component of power dissipation is expected to become more significant.

Static power, $P_{\text{static}}$, is due to constant static current, $I_{\text{static}}$, from $V_{\text{DD}}$ to ground when the circuit is not switching. As we have seen earlier, complementary CMOS combines pull-up and pull-down networks and only one of them is ON at any given time. Therefore, in true complementary CMOS design, there is no static power dissipation. There are times when deviations from the CMOS design style are necessary. For example in special circuits such as ROMs or register files, it may be useful to use pseudo NMOS logic circuit due to its area efficiency. In such a circuit under certain output conditions there is a constant static current flow, $I_{\text{static}}$, from $V_{\text{DD}}$ to ground, which dissipates power.

The power reduction techniques at the circuit level are quite limited when compared with the other techniques at higher abstraction levels. At the circuit level, percentage power reduction in the teens is considered good [11]; however, low-power circuit techniques can have major impact because some circuits are repeated several times to complete the design. For example, adders are one of the most often used arithmetic circuits in digital systems. Adders are used to perform subtraction, multiplication, and division operations. Reducing power consumption in adders will result in reduced power consumption of many digital systems. Various different types of adders have different speeds, areas, power dissipations, and configurations available for the VLSI circuit designer. Adders or subsystems consisting of adder circuits are often in the critical path of microcomputers and digital signal processing circuit; thus a lot of effort has been spent on optimizing them. As shown in Fig. 2.10, the straight forward realization of a CMOS full adder will require 28 transistors. This adder is not optimized for power dissipation. Recently, there has been tremendous research effort in the design and characterization of low-power adders. The 14-transistor (14T) full adder proposed by Abu Shama et al. [13], dual value

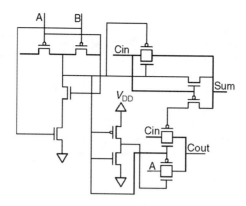

**FIGURE 2.25**   14-transistor full adder.

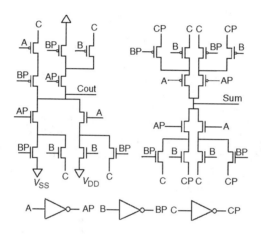

**FIGURE 2.26**   Dual value logic (DVL) full adder.

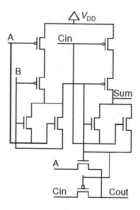

**FIGURE 2.27**   The SERF full adder.

logic (DVL) full adder techniques outlined by Oklobdzija et al. [14], and the static energy recovery full (SERF) adder proposed by Shalem et al. [15,16] are examples of power optimized full adder circuits. More often optimization of one parameter involves the sacrificing of some other parameters. The 14T adder shown in Fig. 2.25, DVL adder shown in Fig. 2.26, and SERF adder shown in Fig. 2.27 are power efficient adders, which also have good delay characteristics [15,16]. Power, area, and delay characteristics of various different low power adder topologies are compared and presented by Shalem et al. [15,16].

## Concluding Remarks

The feature size in the Intel Pentium III microprocessor is 0.18 $\mu$m. Chips with feature size 0.13 $\mu$m are emerging as this chapter section is published. Several hundreds of millions of transistors are being integrated into the same chip. Excellent design automation tools are required in order to handle these large-scale designs. Although automatic synthesis of circuits has improved significantly in the past few years, careful custom hand-designs are done in many high-performance and low-power integrated circuits. Gallium Arsenide (GaAs) and other compound semiconductor-based circuits have been used for very high-speed systems, but the bulk of the circuits will continue to be in silicon, until efficient and high-yield integration techniques can be developed for such technologies.

## References

1. www.sandpile.org.
2. J. M. Rabaey, *Digital Integrated Circuits: A Design Perspective,* Prentice-Hall, 1996.
3. N. H. E. Weste and K. Eshraghian, *Principles of CMOS VLSI Design A Systems Perspective,* Addison Wesley, Reading, MA, 1992.
4. K. Martin, *Digital Integrated Circuit Design,* Oxford University Press, London, 1999.
5. R. J. Baker, H. W. Li, and D. E. Boyce, *CMOS Circuit Design, Layout, and Simulation,* IEEE Press, 1997.
6. S.-M. Kang and Y. Leblebici, *CMOS Digital Integrated Circuits Analysis and Design,* McGraw Hill, New York, 1996.
7. C. A. Mead and L. Conway, *Introduction to VLSI Systems,* Addison-Wesley, Reading, MA, 1980.
8. M. Michael Vai, *VLSI Design,* CRC Press, Boca Raton, FL, 2001.
9. C. H. Roth, *Fundamentals of Logic Design,* 4th ed. PWS, 1992.
10. V. G. Oklobdzija, *High-Performance System Design: Circuits and Logic,* IEEE Press, 1999.
11. G. Yeap, *Practical Low Power Digital VLSI Design,* Kluwer Academic Publishers, 1998.
12. A. Chandrakasan, S. Sheng, and R. Broderson, "Low-Power CMOS Digital Design," IEEE Journal of Solid-State Circuits, vol. 27, no. 4, pp. 473–484, 1992.
13. A. M. Shams and M. A. Bayoumi, "A New Full Adder Cell for low-power Applications," *Proceedings of the IEEE Great Lakes Symposium on VLSI,* pp. 45–49, 1998.
14. V. G. Oklobdzija, M. Soderstrand, and B. Duchene, "Development and Synthesis Method for Pass-Transistor Logic Family for High-Speed and Low Power CMOS," *Proceedings of the 1995 IEEE 38th Midwest Symposium on Circuits and Systems,* Rio de Janeiro, 1995.
15. R. Shalem, Static Energy Recovering Logic for Low Power Adder Design, Masters Thesis, Electrical and Computer Engineering Department, UT Austin, August 1998.
16. R. Shalem, E. John, and L. K. John, Novel Low Power Static Energy recovery Adder, *Proceedings of the 1999 IEEE Great Lakes Symposium on VLSI,* March 1999, Michigan, pp. 380–383.

# 2.2  Pass-Transistor CMOS Circuits

*Shunzo Yamashita*

## Introduction

Complementary metal oxide semiconductor (CMOS) logic circuits are widely used in today's very large scale integration (VLSI) chips. The CMOS circuit performs logic functions through complementary switching of nMOS and pMOS transistors according to their gate voltage, which is controlled by the input signal values "1" or "0". Here, "1" corresponds to a high voltage, namely $V_{dd}$ in the circuit, and "0" corresponds to a low voltage, Gnd. For example, in the case of the inverter shown in Fig. 2.28(a), when input is set to "0", the pMOS transistor becomes conductive and the nMOS transistor becomes nonconductive, so the capacitance Cout is charged and the output is pulled up to $V_{dd}$, resulting in a logic value of "1". Here, Cout is the input capacitance of the circuit in the next stage, the wiring capacitance, or the parasitic

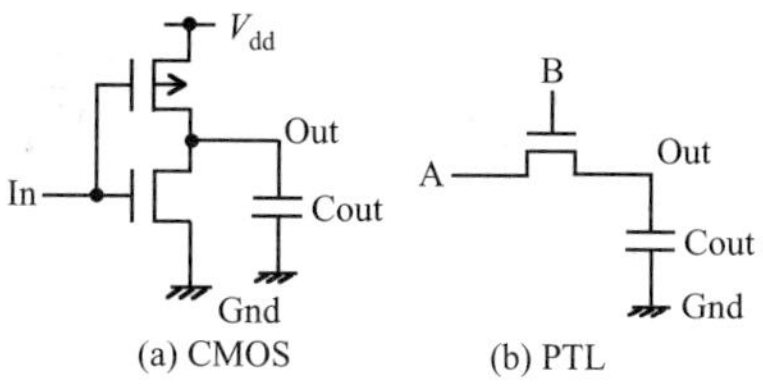

**FIGURE 2.28**   Comparison of CMOS logic with PTL.

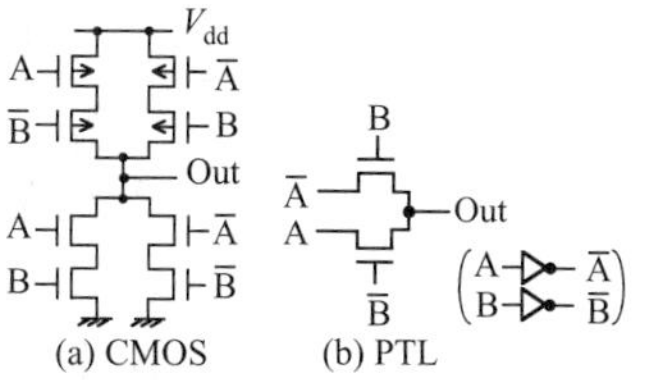

**FIGURE 2.29**   Comparison for 2-input XOR logic.

capacitance, and so on. On the other hand, when "1" is input, the nMOS transistor becomes conductive and the pMOS transistor becomes nonconductive in turn. Cout is then discharged, and the output is pulled down to Gnd. Thus, "0" is output, and inverter operation is achieved. As shown here, in the CMOS circuit nMOS and pMOS transistors complementarily perform the pull-up and pull-down operations, respectively. This complementary operation allows the logic signal to swing fully from $V_{dd}$ to Gnd, resulting in a high noise margin. As a result, CMOS circuits are widely used in VLSI chips, such as microprocessors.

As an alternative to CMOS logic, pass-transistor logic (PTL) has recently been getting much attention. This is because well-constructed PTL can provide a logic circuit with fewer transistors than the corresponding CMOS logic circuit. In the PTL circuit, one nMOS transistor can perform both the pull-up and pull-down operations by utilizing not only the gate but also the drain/source as signal terminals, as shown in Fig. 2.28(b) [1]. Here, the signal connected to the gate of the transistor (*B* in this figure) is called the control signal, and the signal connected to the drain/source (*A* in this figure) is called the pass signal. In PTL, logic operation is performed by connecting and disconnecting the input signal to the output. For example, in this figure, when the control signal is set to "0", the nMOS transistor becomes nonconductive. However, when the control signal is set to "1", the transistor becomes conductive, pulling the output up or down according to the input voltage, and the input signal is then transmitted to the output. Thus, PTL is also called a transmission gate.

PTL is often used to simplify logic functions. For example, Fig. 2.29 shows a comparison of PTL and CMOS circuits for 2-input XOR logic, Out = $A\bar{B} + \bar{A}B$. PTL provides this XOR logic circuit with only two transistors, while the CMOS circuit requires six transistors. (To generate complementary signals for *A* and *B*, an additional four transistors in two inverters are required for both circuits.) This simplification ability of PTL is effective not only for reducing chip size, but also for enhancing operating speed and reducing power consumption. This is because the decrease in the number of transistors reduces the total capacitance in the circuit, which must be charged and discharged for the logic operation, thus wasting power and causing delay. In addition, the pMOS-free structure of the PTL is also advantageous in terms of operating speed and power consumption. This is because the capacitance of a pMOS transistor is twice as large as that of an nMOS transistor due to the wider size required by its inferior current characteristics. The lack of a pMOS transistor thus enables lower capacitance, resulting in both faster speed and lower power.

Because of these advantages, PTL is preferably used in arithmetic units in microprocessors, in which complex logic functions such as XOR are needed to implement adders and multipliers with high-performance [2–8]. PTL is also used to implement *D*-type latches and DRAM memory cell to reduce chip size or the number of transistors, as shown in Fig. 2.30.

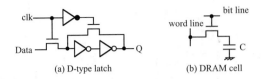

(a) D-type latch      (b) DRAM cell

**FIGURE 2.30**  Other pass-transistor circuits used in VLSI chips.

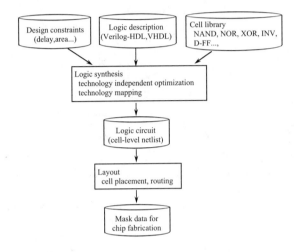

**FIGURE 2.31**  Top-down design flow.

## Problems of PTL

In the 1990s, so-called top-down design, in which logic circuit are automatically synthesized, has been widely applied for random logic such as the control block of a microprocessor, rather than bottom-up design. This is mainly because the size of VLSI chip has been increasing dramatically, and manual design can no longer be used in terms of design period and cost. In top-down design, as shown in Fig. 2.31, logic circuits are designed using a hardware description language (HDL), such as Verilog-HDL or VHDL (Very High Speed Integrated Circuit Hardware Description Language). These HDLs are used to describe the register-transfer-level functionality of logic circuits. The conversion from the HDL to a circuit is performed automatically by a logic synthesis tool, a so-called CAD tool. The logic synthesis tool generates a netlist of the target circuit through the combinations of fundamental circuit elements called cells, which are prepared in a cell library. The netlist represents the logic circuit in the form of connections between cells. Finally, an automatic layout tool generates a mask pattern for fabricating the VLSI chip. Top-down design of LSI is similar to today's software compilation process, so it is often called silicon compilation.

Despite many advantages, however, PTL has not been adapted for such synthesized logic blocks in top-down design. This is mainly because adequate CAD tools that can synthesize PTL have not yet been developed. One of the main reasons for this is the great difference between CMOS and PTL circuits. For example, PTL designed inadequately may contain a sneak path that provides an unintended short-circuit path from $V_{dd}$ to Gnd, causing the circuit not to work correctly. CMOS circuits, on the other hand, have never such paths. For example, the PTL circuit shown in Fig. 2.32(a) seems to work correctly for the logic function: Out = $AB + CD$. Here, $AB$ represents logic AND of two variables, $A$ and $B$, and this boolean equation represents that Out is given by logic OR of $AB$ and $CD$. However, when $A = 1$, $B = 1$, $C = 0$, and $D = 1$, the output is connected to both $V_{dd}$ and Gnd at the same time, resulting in a short-circuit current from $V_{dd}$ to Gnd.

The complex electrical behavior of PTL also makes automatic synthesis of PTL difficult. The $V_{th}$ drop shown in Fig. 2.32(b) is a typical problem [1]. As described before, in PTL, the pull-up and pull-down

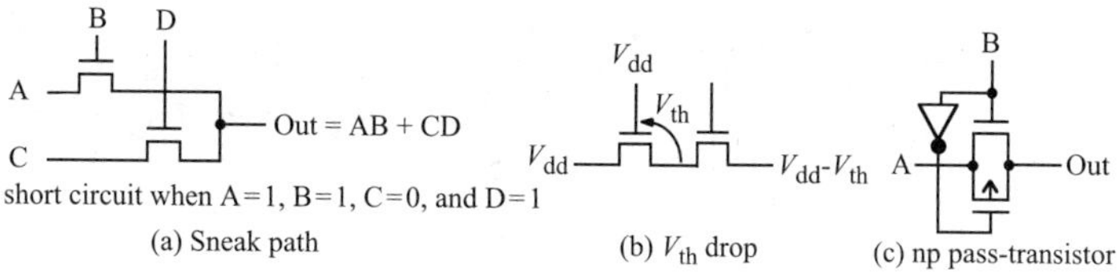

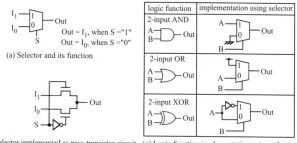

**FIGURE 2.32**   Problem of PTL.

**FIGURE 2.33**   Selector and pass-transistor circuit.

operations are performed by the same nMOS transistor; that is, the pull-up operation is accomplished by a source-follower nMOS transistor. Thus, the maximum pulled-up voltage is limited to $V_{dd} - V_{th}$, where $V_{th}$ is a threshold voltage of the nMOS transistor, and the nMOS transistor does not become conductive when the gate-source voltage is less than $V_{th}$. Such a dropped signal may cause serious problems, such as a short-circuit current from $V_{dd}$ to Gnd, when it drives other CMOS circuits, such as inverter. Moreover, the decreased signal swing due to the $V_{th}$ drop degrades the noise margin. This problem is effectively solved by using a structure combining nMOS and pMOS transistors, as shown in Fig. 2.32(c). However, such a structure loses the advantages of pMOS-free structure of PTL. In addition, in a PTL circuit, the number of serially connected pass-transistors must be carefully considered, because a PTL circuit has quadratic delay characteristics with respect to the number of the stages of pass-transistors [1].

## Top-Down Design of Pass-Transistor Logic Based on BDD

As described in the previous section, PTL has not generally been applied for random logic circuits because of the lack of adequate synthesis techniques. However, the recent increasing demand for LSI chips with enhanced performance, reduced power, and lower cost has been changing this situation, and now many methods for automatically synthesizing PTL circuits for random logic have been proposed [9–20]. Most of them use selector logic and binary decision diagrams (BDDs). This is because BDDs and selector logic are suitable for generating pass-transistor logic circuits, and PTL synthesized from a BDD has many advantages, as described below. BDDs are thus widely used in PTL synthesis [17].

The selector, also called multiplexer, has good correspondence with the pass-transistor circuit. The function of the selector is shown in Fig. 2.33(a). Here, two inputs, I0 and I1, are called data inputs, and input S, which selects one of the two data inputs, is called the control input. The selector is easily implemented as a wired OR structure of two pass-transistors with one inverter, as shown in Fig. 2.33(b). The selector is thus suitable for pass-transistor circuits. In addition, it has an advantage in that by changing the connections of the two data inputs I0 and I1, any kind of logic function can be implemented, as shown in Fig. 2.33(c).

However, the selector shown in Fig. 2.33(b) requires an inverter to generate the selection signal for input I0. Consequently, the delay of the circuit is increased by the delay of the inverter. To overcome this, dual-rail, pass-transistor circuits such as CPL (complementary pass-transistor logic) and SRPL (swing

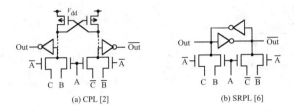

**FIGURE 2.34**  Dual-rail, pass-transistor logic circuits.

$$Out = \overline{A}B + A\overline{B}$$

| A B | Out |
|-----|-----|
| 0 0 | 0   |
| 0 1 | 1   |
| 1 0 | 1   |
| 1 1 | 0   |

(a) Boolean equation            (b) Truth table            (c) BDD

— 1-edge true if node = 1

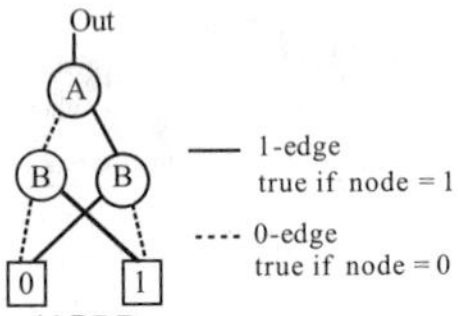

···· 0-edge true if node = 0

**FIGURE 2.35**  BDD and other logic representations for 2-input XOR logic.

restored pass-transistor logic) shown in Fig. 2.34(a,c) [2,3,6] are effective solutions. These circuits have both positive and negative polarities for all signals complementarily, so there is no need for an inverter to generate complementary signals. Thus, high-speed operation becomes possible. Moreover, the differential operation in these dual-rail pass-transistor circuits is also effective in improving the noise-margin characteristics of the pass-transistor circuit. In addition, dual-rail PTL can still provide logic circuits with fewer transistors than their CMOS counterparts [1,2], although it requires twice as many transistors as a single-rail pass-transistor circuit. In this chapter, a method for synthesizing single-rail PTL is described below, because same method can be applied to dual-rail PTL by just changing pass-transistor selector from single-rail to dual-rail PTL.

BDD is one type of logic representation and expresses a logic function in a binary tree [21–23]. For example, Fig. 2.35(a–c) shows three typical logic representations for 2-input XOR logic: (a) boolean equation, (b) truth table, and (c) BDD. As shown in Fig. 2.35(c), the BDD consists of nodes and edges. The nodes are categorized into two types: variable nodes and constant nodes of "0" or "1". A variable node represents a variable of the logic function. For example, node $A$ in the BDD corresponds to the variable $A$ in the logic function shown in Fig. 2.35(a,b). A variable node has one outgoing edge and two incoming edges, a 0-edge and a 1-edge. In this figure, a 0-edge is denoted by a dotted line and a 1-edge by a straight line, although there are other representations used in BDDs. These two incoming edges show the logic functions when the variable of the node is set to "0" and "1", respectively. The logic functions are represented by the connections of these elements. For example, when $(A, B)$ is $(0, 0)$, Out becomes 0 in the truth table. This corresponds to selecting the 0-edge at the nodes $A$ and $B$. The path to node "0" can be traced from the root in the BDD in Fig. 2.35(c). Furthermore, the fact that there are two cases, $(A, B) = (0, 1)$ and $(1, 0)$, for Out = 1 in the truth table corresponds to the fact that in the BDD there are two paths from the root to "1"; that is, $A = 0 \rightarrow B = 1$ and $A = 1 \rightarrow B = 0$.

A BDD can be simplified by using complementary edges. The complementary edges are used to represent the inverted logic of a node, as shown in Fig. 2.36(a). By using complementary edges, two nodes, $B$ and $\overline{B}$, can be combined as one node and the BDD can be simplified. For example, Fig. 2.36(b) shows a simplified BDD with complementary edges for the BDD shown in Fig. 2.35(c).

BDDs have a good correspondence with selector logic and pass-transistor circuits, as shown in Fig. 2.37, because the BDD represents logic functions in a binary tree structure. Thus, it is possible to generate a pass-transistor circuit for a target logic function by replacing the nodes in the BDD with pass-transistor selectors and connecting their control inputs with the input variables related to the nodes [10].

A detailed example how to synthesize PTL from a BDD is shown in Fig. 2.38(a–i). BDD is first constructed for the logic functions shown in Fig. 2.38(a). The BDD can be built by recursively applying

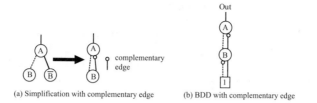

Out
A
B
B̄
complementary
edge
1
(a) Simplification with complementary edge
(b) BDD with complementary edge

**FIGURE 2.36** BDD with complementary edges for function in Fig. 2.35.

BDD
Selector
Pass-transistor circuit
A
0 1
1
0
Gnd $V_{dd}$

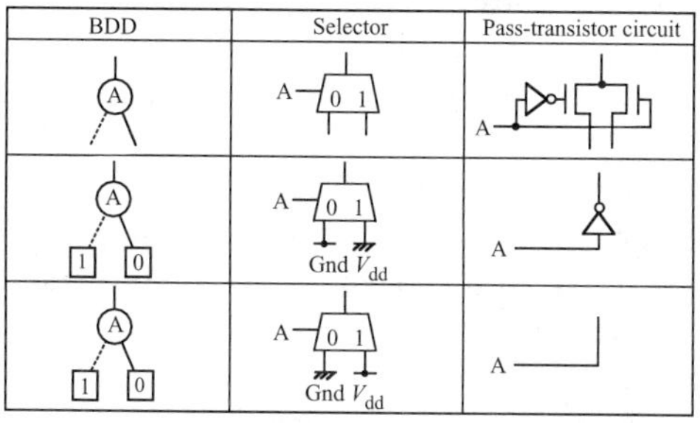

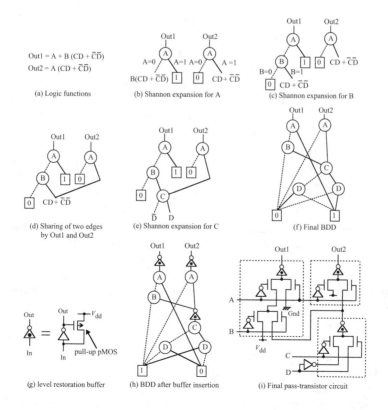

**FIGURE 2.37** Correspondence among BDD, selector, and pass-transistor circuit.

Out1 = A + B (CD + C̄D̄)
Out2 = A (CD + C̄D̄)
(a) Logic functions
Out1
Out2
A=0
A=1
B(CD + C̄D̄)
CD + C̄D̄
(b) Shannon expansion for A
B=0
B=1
(c) Shannon expansion for B
(d) Sharing of two edges by Out1 and Out2
D̄
D
(e) Shannon expansion for C
(f) Final BDD
Out
In
$V_{dd}$
pull-up pMOS
(g) level restoration buffer
(h) BDD after buffer insertion
Gnd
(i) Final pass-transistor circuit

**FIGURE 2.38** Example of PTL synthesis using BDD.

Shannon expansion, as shown below, to the logic function [22]:

$$f = \bar{a} \cdot f(a = 0) + a \cdot f(a = 1)$$

In this example, Shannon expansion is first applied to input variable $A$ (Fig. 2.38(b)), then to input variable $B$ (Fig. 2.38(c)). In Fig. 2.38(c), both the 1-edge of node $B$ of Out1 and the 0-edge of node $A$ of Out2 are equivalent to the logic function $CD + \overline{CD}$, so these two edges are shared, as shown in Fig. 2.38(d). Such a BDD that shares two or more isomorphic sub-graphs among different outputs is called a shared BDD. By applying Shannon expansion to variables $C$ and $D$, as shown in Fig. 2.38(e), the final BDD shown in Fig. 2.38(f) is obtained.

Although a PTL circuit can be obtained by simply replacing all the nodes in a BDD with pass-transistor selectors, such a PTL may not work correctly, or it may have a very long delay because of electrical problems in the pass-transistor circuit, as described in the section on "Problems of PTL". To overcome these problems, buffers like that shown in Fig. 2.38(g) are inserted [1,10]. This buffer consists of an inverter and a pull-up pMOS transistor. It can restore the signal swing with little short-circuit current, because the gate of the pMOS transistor has feedback connection from the output, so the pull-up pMOS transistor forcedly pulls up the inverter input to $V_{dd}$ even if a $V_{th}$-dropped signal is input. The gate width of the pull-up pMOS transistor is set small enough for pull-up operation, because a wide-gate pMOS transistor makes it difficult for the nMOS pass-transistors to pull down the input node of the inverter and can degrade the speed of the pull-down operation.

Level restoration buffers are inserted in the following three types of nodes in a BDD. First, for the primary output node, buffers are inserted to prevent $V_{th}$-dropped signals of the pass-transistor selectors from driving other CMOS circuits. Second, buffers are inserted for nodes with two or more fanouts for current amplification. Finally, for nodes that belong to a series of long-chained nodes, buffers are needed to prevent the relatively long delay due to the quadratic delay characteristics of the pass-transistor circuit. However, using too many buffers adversely increases the overall delay of the circuit because of their intrinsic delay. Thus, buffers are inserted every three stages, in general [10]. In addition, for a node in which a buffer is inserted, inverters should also be inserted in the two incoming edges of the node to adjust the polarity. Inverter propagation is thus performed to remove extra inverters by adjusting the polarity between adjacent nodes. Figure 2.38(h) shows the result of buffer insertion and inverter propagation. In this example, three buffers are inserted without additional inverters, due to inverter propagation.

Finally, by replacing the nodes in the BDD with 2-input pass-transistor selectors and mapping groups of several selectors and a buffer into cells, the target pass-transistor circuit shown in Fig. 2.38(i) is obtained. Here, for the leaf nodes—that is, the two nodes $D$ in Fig. 2.38(h)—selectors whose two inputs $I0$ and $I1$ are connected to $V_{dd}$ or Gnd are generated, so these selectors can be removed or simplified into an inverter, as shown in Fig. 2.37.

These speed-up buffers are not required for all paths. This is because in an actual circuit, a few bottleneck paths called critical paths limit its maximum operating speed, and these buffers are not necessary for other paths, unless their delay do not exceed those of the critical paths. Reducing the total number of the buffers in this way is effective for power and area reduction [16].

The synthesized PTL completely corresponds to the BDD except for the inserted buffers and inverters, as shown in Fig. 2.38. Thus, in PTL synthesis, reducing the size and depth of the BDD is important. This is the greatest difference from CMOS logic synthesis, in which reducing the literal count of boolean equation is essential.

PTL synthesized from a BDD has various advantages. One of the most important advantages is that the synthesized PTL is guaranteed to be sneak-path free [9]. This is because in a BDD, all paths terminate in "1" or "0" and only one of them is activated at a time. Therefore, the synthesized PTL includes no paths that can be connected to both $V_{dd}$ and Gnd at the same time.

Another superior characteristic of PTL synthesized from a BDD is that the synthesized result is independent of the quality of the input HDL description. In other words, even if the input HDL contains some redundancy, the synthesized PTL is free from any redundancy. This excellent characteristic derives

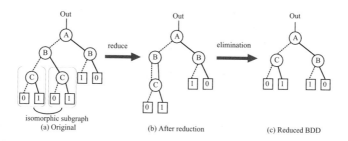

**FIGURE 2.39**  Reduce operation and reduced BDD.

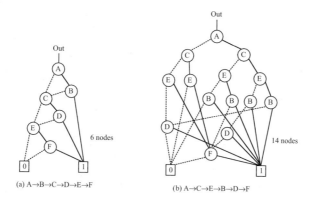

**FIGURE 2.40**  BDD size dependency on variable ordering for Out = $AB + CD + EF$.

from the property of a BDD called canonicity [21]. Canonicity means that after reduce operation that removes isomorphic sub-graphs, as shown in Fig. 2.39(a–c), the final BDD is always identical for the same logic function and the same variable ordering, even if the initial BDDs are different. Here, variable ordering means the order of the input variables in the BDD construction. A BDD for which the redundant sub-graphs have been removed by the reduce operation is called a reduced BDD (RBDD) or reduced ordered BDD (ROBDD). In this chapter, a BDD is assumed to be a ROBDD, unless otherwise stated. Because of this canonicity property of BDDs, the synthesized PTL is independent of the input HDL quality and redundancy free. This is one of the most important advantages of PTL synthesized from a BDD, compared with CMOS logic synthesis, in which the result depends on the quality of the input HDL description. The canonicity of BDDs also plays an important role in other fields in logic synthesis such as formal verification of logic functions [21].

## Variable Ordering of BDDs

As described in the previous section, the BDD has various superior characteristics for PTL synthesis. However, it has a drawback in that its size strongly depends on the input variable ordering. In PTL synthesis, the size of the BDD is directly reflected by the synthesized result. Therefore, finding the variable ordering that generates the minimum-size BDD is important. For example, Fig. 2.40 compares the BDDs for the logic function Out = $AB + CD + EF$ for two different variable orders: (a) $A \rightarrow B \rightarrow C \rightarrow D \rightarrow E \rightarrow F$, and (b) $A \rightarrow C \rightarrow E \rightarrow B \rightarrow D \rightarrow F$. As shown in the figure, for case (a), the node count of the BDD is 6. On the other hand, 14 nodes are required for the same logic function in case (b). In general, an inefficient variable order can increase the size of a BDD by an order of magnitude.

However, the problem of finding appropriate variable ordering for arbitrary logic functions is well known to be an NP-complete problem [23]. For a logic function with a small number of inputs, it is possible to examine all combinations of variable ordering with a practical time. However, such a method

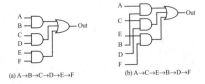

**FIGURE 2.41**    Logic circuit for Out = AB + CD + EF and variable ordering.

| variable order | operation |
|---|---|
| x1,x2,x3,x4,x5,x6,x7 | initial |
| x1,x2,x3,x5,x4,x6,x7 | swap(x4,x5) |
| x1,x2,x3,x5,x6,x4,x7 | swap(x4,x6) |
| x1,x2,x3,x5,x6,x7,x4 | swap(x4,x7) |
| x1,x2,x3,x5,x6,x4,x7 | swap(x7,x4) |
| x1,x2,x3,x5,x4,x6,x7 | swap(x6,x4) |
| x1,x2,x3,x4,x5,x6,x7 | swap(x5,x4) |
| x1,x2,x4,x3,x5,x6,x7 | swap(x3,x4) |
| x1,x4,x2,x3,x5,x6,x7 | swap(x2,x4) |
| x4,x1,x2,x3,x5,x6,x7 | |

(a) sifting

(b) swap operation

**FIGURE 2.42**    Variable ordering by sifting.

cannot be applied to an actual logic function whose inputs exceed 100, because the number of combinations becomes too huge ($100! \approx 10^{157}$). Therefore, heuristic methods for finding an approximate optimal ordering have been developed [24–27]. These methods can be roughly categorized into two types: static methods and the dynamic methods.

One example of a static method is to determine the variable ordering based on information obtained from the circuit structure for the logic function. For example, in the case of the logic function in Fig. 2.40, the corresponding circuit is as shown in Fig. 2.41. Thus, the input pairs *A* and *B*, *C* and *D*, and *E* and *F* should be adjacent in the variable ordering as in Fig. 2.41(a), not as in Fig. 2.41(b). An adequate ordering can be searched for under these constraints.

On the other hand, in a dynamic method, the optimal order is searched for by changing the order of the variables in the BDD. Figure 2.42(a) shows a representative method of this type, called sifting [26]. In sifting, by applying a swap operation, in which the orders of two adjacent variables are swapped as shown in Fig. 2.42(b), and by applying the reduce operation iteratively, an appropriate order for each variable is determined and the size of BDD is minimized. Variations of this method have also been proposed [27].

In practice, these methods can be combined. For example, the initial variable ordering is determined by a static method and the BDD is constructed, then the BDD is minimized using a dynamic method. Another approach that reduces the size of the BDD by changing the local ordering in the BDD has also been proposed [28].

## Multilevel Pass-Transistor Logic

A PTL circuit synthesized by the method described in the section on "Top-Down Design of Pass-Transistor Logic Based on BDD" may not be acceptable in terms of delay. This is because that type of PTL has a flat structure and the selectors are serially connected over *n* stages for a logic function with *n* inputs, since the control input of each selector is connected only to the primary input, as shown in Fig. 2.43(a). To solve this problem, multilevel pass-transistor circuits like that shown in Fig. 2.43(b) are expected to be as effective as multilevel logic in CMOS logic circuits. In this section, the synthesis method for such multilevel pass-transistor logic (MPL) is described. To distinguish it from MPL, the pass-transistor logic described in the previous section is called monolithic PTL.

MPL has a hierarchical structure, in which the control inputs of the pass-transistor selectors are connected not only to the primary inputs but also to the outputs of other pass-transistor selectors, as

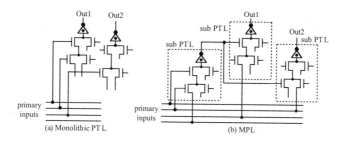

**FIGURE 2.43**   Monolithic PTL and multilevel PTL.

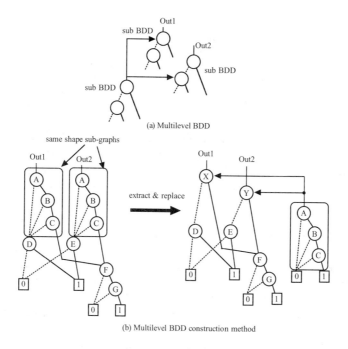

**FIGURE 2.44**   Example of multilevel BDD and its construction method.

shown in Fig. 2.43(b). MPL can be synthesized from a multilevel BDD shown in Fig. 2.44(a). The methods for building a multilevel BDD can be categorized into two types. One is based on conversion from a monolithic BDD described in the section on "Top-Down Design of Pass-Transistor Logic Based on BDD". Figure 2.44(b) shows a representative method in this category [11]. In this method, subgraphs that cannot be shared because at least one of their edges is not equivalent are searched for. Then, the detected sub-graphs are extracted and replaced with new nodes. For these new nodes, new introduced variables are assigned. In Fig. 2.44(b), $X$ and $Y$ are the new introduced variables. These variables are connected to the output of a new BDD, which has the same diagram as the extracted sub-graph except that its 0-edge and 1-edge are terminated to "0" and "1" nodes, respectively. By this extraction, it is possible to convert the monolithic BDD into two or more sub-BDDs, which are multiply connected with one another and have the same logic function as the original. Finally, by replacing the nodes with pass-transistor selectors, as described in the section on "Top-Down Design of Pass-Transistor Logic Based on BDD," the MPL is obtained. Here, in the MPL the outputs of the pass-transistor selectors can be connected to the control inputs of other pass-transistor selectors, so level-restoration buffers are required for these places.

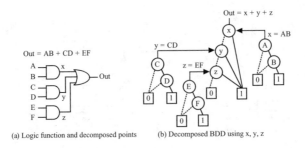

**FIGURE 2.45**   Example decomposed BDD.

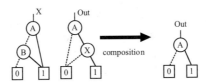

**FIGURE 2.46**   Elimination by composition.

MPL has superior characteristics compared to monolithic PTL, especially in terms of delay, because the depth of sub-BDDs in a multilevel BDD is much less than that of a monolithic BDD. Empirically, the delay can be reduced by a factor of 2 compared to the monolithic PTL [11]. In addition, MPL is effective in simplifying the circuit, because more sub-graphs than in the monolithic BDD can be shared by extraction.

The other method is to directly build hierarchical BDDs simultaneously, without constructing a monolithic BDD [9]. Such a BDD is also called a decomposed BDD. Figure 2.45 shows an example. The decomposed BDD is constructed from input to output according to the structure of the circuit corresponding to the logic function. During the construction, the size and depth of the BDD is monitored and if either value is over a limit, BDD construction is stopped and a new intermediate variable that points to the output of the BDD is introduced. In this example, $x$, $y$, and $z$ are the intermediate variables. BDD construction is then restarted and the decomposed BDD is obtained by repeating this process. Here, a point where a new intermediate variable is introduced is called a decomposed point.

The decomposed BDD has a superior characteristic in that for certain logic functions, such as a multiplier, which cannot be constructed in a practical size from a monolithic BDD [23], it is possible to build a decomposed BDD and synthesize a pass-transistor circuit. Therefore, the decomposed BDD is essential for a practical PTL synthesis, and many methods based on the decomposed BDD have been proposed [12,13,34]. Another merit of the decomposed BDD is that by changing the decomposed points, the characteristics of the synthesized MPL can be flexibly controlled [9,12,13]. However, the decomposed BDD has a drawback, in that canonicity is not guaranteed because of the freedom in selecting decomposed points. This means that the synthesized result depends on the quality of the input logic description, or in other words, it may contain some redundancy. For this reason, in a decomposed BDD, sub-BDDs are simplified by several methods [9,12] such as elimination, shown in Fig. 2.46. Elimination removes the redundancy by composition of two or more sub-BDDs. Moreover, as with multilevel CMOS logic synthesis, BDD simplification based on "don't care" conditions, such as satisfiability don't care (SDC) and observability don't care (ODC), can be applied, as shown in Fig. 2.47 [12,29,30].

## PTL Cell

In practical PTL synthesis several cells, each of which packs one or more selectors, inverters, and a pull-up pMOS transistor, are used, although PTL circuits can be synthesized with only two cells, namely a selector and an inverter. These packed cells of one or more selectors are effective not only

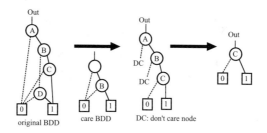

**FIGURE 2.47** BDD simplification with "don't care" conditions.

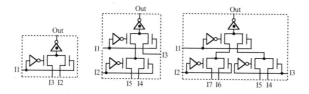

**FIGURE 2.48** Example of pass-transistor cells.

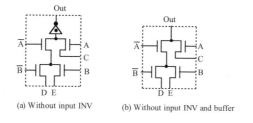

(a) Without input INV      (b) Without input INV and buffer

**FIGURE 2.49** PTL cell configuration.

for reducing the chip size but also for reducing the power and delay, because parasitic capacitance can be reduced.

Figure 2.48 shows an example of a PTL cell-set [31]. In this example, each PTL cell contains an inverter to generate complementary signals for the control input of the selector, although other cell configurations without inverters can also be considered, as shown in Fig. 2.49. This seems wasteful in terms of cell area, but in fact, external inverters adversely increase the final chip size because a large area is required for the wire connecting the external inverters and PTL cells [32].

The structure of a PTL cell is quite different from that of a CMOS cell [31]. This is because the symmetrical layout of pMOS and nMOS transistors as in a CMOS cell results in a large cell size in a PTL cell, where the number of nMOS transistors is much greater than that of pMOS transistors, and at least three sizes of transistors (small for inverters and a pull-up pMOS transistor, mid-size for the nMOS transistors of the selectors, and large for the output buffers) are required. In addition, sharing the diffusion area of the nMOS transistors in a selector is also important, not only to reduce the chip size but also to reduce the parasitic capacitance in the PTL cell. For this purpose, a method based on the Eulerian path is used, as shown in Fig. 2.50 [31].

## PTL and CMOS Mixed Circuit

Although in many cases PTL can provide a superior circuit with fewer transistors than conventional CMOS logic, it is not always superior. For example, as shown in Fig. 2.51 for simple 2-input NAND and 2-input NOR logic, PTL circuits require six transistors, while CMOS circuits only require four. For these cases, a

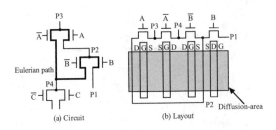

(a) Circuit    (b) Layout

**FIGURE 2.50**  Diffusion-area sharing for better layout.

|  | Pass-transistor circuit | CMOS circuit |
|---|---|---|
| 2-input NAND<br><br>Out = $\overline{AB}$ 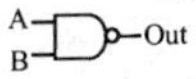<br><br>A, B → Out | 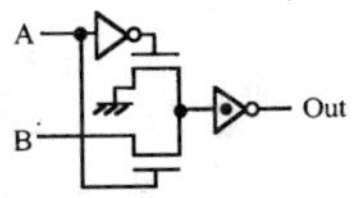 | 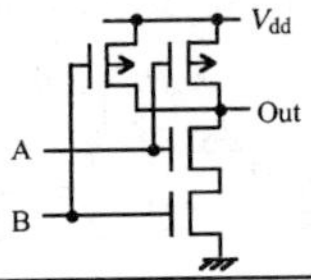 |
| Tr count | 7 | 4 |
| Area ($\mu$m$^2$) | 172 | 129 |
| Delay (ns) | 0.69 | 0.31 |
| Power ($\mu$W/MHz) | 15.9 | 40.0 |
| 2-input NOR<br><br>Out = $\overline{A+B}$ 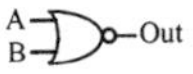<br><br>A, B → Out | 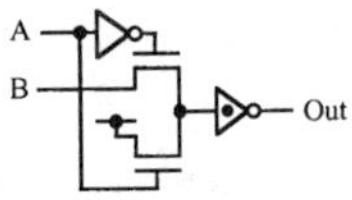 | 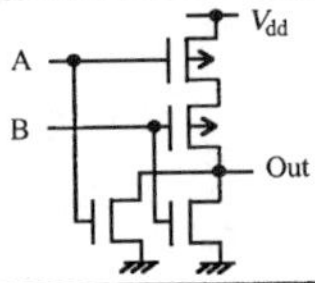 |
| Tr count | 7 | 4 |
| Area ($\mu$m$^2$) | 172 | 129 |
| Delay (ns) | 0.69 | 0.48 |
| Power ($\mu$W/MHz) | 15.9 | 30.0 |

**FIGURE 2.51**  Comparison of pass-transistor circuit and CMOS circuit for 2-input NAND/NOR logic.

CMOS circuit provides better performance in terms of area and delay. However, a PTL circuit still provides lower power consumption because of its pMOS-free structure, which enables small capacitance.

Pass-transistor circuits are more suitable for implementing logic functions in which some signals are selected by other signals. In contrast, CMOS circuits are more suitable for implementing NAND/NOR logic (or AND/OR logic). Thus, PTL and CMOS mixed structures, in which logic corresponding to a selector is implemented with PTL circuits and other logic is implemented with CMOS circuits, are attractive [33,34]. In this section, such mixed-logic circuits called pass-transistor and CMOS collaborated logic (PCCL) are described.

The key to PCCL is finding CMOS-beneficial parts and selector-beneficial parts in the logic functions. To accomplish this, the BDD-based method shown in Fig. 2.52(a) is used, in which first an entire PTL circuit is constructed from a multilevel BDD or decomposed BDD, and then some parts are replaced with CMOS circuits. The key to this procedure is to find CMOS-beneficial functions based on the BDD. This is accomplished as follows: those selectors with one of two inputs fixed to $V_{dd}$ or Gnd operate as AND or OR logic (NAND or NOR logic) rather than as a selector, so they are good candidates to be replaced with CMOS circuits, as shown in Fig. 2.52(b). Using this method, logic functions can be categorized into pro-selector functions and pro-AND/OR functions.

Figure 2.53 shows a detailed example of the PCCL synthesis flow. For the logic function shown in Fig. 2.53(a), the multilevel BDD shown in Fig. 2.53(b) is constructed. The PTL shown in Fig. 2.53(c) is then obtained from the BDD. Then, in the synthesized PTL, selectors in which one of the two data inputs is fixed to $V_{dd}$ or Gnd are searched for. As described before, however, because of the low-power characteristics of the pass-transistor circuits, the power consumption will increase if all these pass-transistor

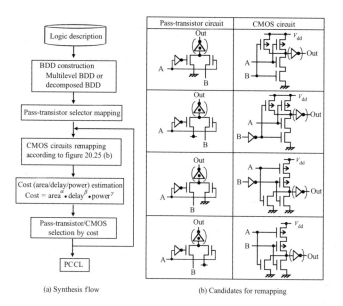

(a) Synthesis flow                    (b) Candidates for remapping

**FIGURE 2.52**    PCCL synthesis flow.

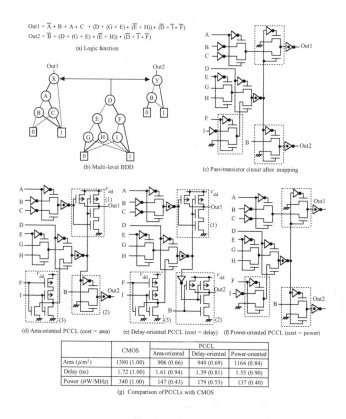

$$Out1 = \overline{A} \cdot B + A \cdot C + (D + (G + E) \cdot (\overline{E} + H)) \cdot (\overline{D} + \overline{T} \cdot \overline{F})$$
$$Out2 = \overline{B} + (D + (G + E) \cdot (\overline{E} + H)) \cdot (\overline{D} + \overline{T} \cdot \overline{F})$$

(a) Logic function

(b) Multi-level BDD

(c) Pass-transistor circuit after mapping

(d) Area-oriented PCCL (cost = area)   (e) Delay-oriented PCCL (cost = delay)   (f) Power-oriented PCCL (cost = power)

|  | CMOS | PCCL | | |
|---|---|---|---|---|
|  |  | Area-oriented | Delay-oriented | Power-oriented |
| Area ($\mu m^2$) | 1380 (1.00) | 906 (0.66) | 949 (0.69) | 1164 (0.84) |
| Delay (ns) | 1.72 (1.00) | 1.61 (0.94) | 1.39 (0.81) | 1.55 (0.90) |
| Power ($\mu$W/MHz) | 340 (1.00) | 147 (0.43) | 179 (0.53) | 137 (0.40) |

(g) Comparison of PCCLs with CMOS

**FIGURE 2.53**    Example of PCCL synthesis.

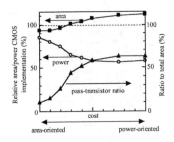

**FIGURE 2.54** Relationship between cost parameter and area, power, and pass-transistor ratio.

selectors are re-mapped to CMOS circuits. Therefore, it is necessary to choose which circuits are suitable for the purpose, rather than simply replacing selectors with CMOS circuits automatically. To accomplish this, a cost function is used, such as this example:

$$\cos t = \text{area}^{\alpha} \times \text{delay}^{\beta} \times \text{power}^{\gamma}$$

where $\alpha$, $\beta$, and $\gamma$ are the weights for the area, delay, and power, respectively.

By changing the parameters of the cost function, the characteristics of the synthesized PCCL can flexibly be controlled for the purpose. Figure 2.53(d–f) shows area-oriented, delay-oriented, and power-oriented PCCLs derived from the PTL in Fig. 2.53(c), by changing the cost parameters. In this figure, there are three pass-transistor selectors (1), (2), and (3) that correspond to the selectors in Fig. 2.52(b). However, in the case of the area-oriented PCCL, only selectors (1) and (3) are converted (to CMOS 2-input NAND and 2-input NOR circuits, respectively), because for pass-transistor selector (2), the inverter needed to adjust the polarity in CMOS implementation resulting in a larger area. In the case of delay-oriented PCCL, all three selectors are converted to CMOS circuits, because the delay can be reduced by replacing selector (2), containing a slow inverter, with a CMOS circuit. On the other hand, in the case of the power-oriented PCCL, CMOS circuits are not adopted because the pass-transistor selectors use less power, as described before. Figure 2.53(g) shows the comparison of the results of these three PCCLs with CMOS counterpart. PCCL is superior to CMOS for all these cases.

This flexible control of the characteristic of the synthesized circuit by changing the cost parameters is possible for large logic function. Figure 2.54 shows an example, in which the cost parameters are continuously changed from area-oriented to power-oriented. The size of the logic function is about 10 k gate in CMOS configuration. By changing the pass-transistor ratio from 10% to 60%, the power is reduced by over 40%, but at the expense of area by 10%. The optimum pass-transistor ratio is usually 10–60%, although it strongly depends of the kind of the logic functions.

## To Probe Further

For MOS transistors and MOS circuits, please read a textbook such as [35]. For logic synthesis, please read a textbook such as [21]. For BDD, please read papers [22,23]. For PTL synthesis, please read papers that are listed in [17].

## References

1. Yano, K. and Muroga, S., Pass Transistors, in *VLSI Handbook*, Chen, W.-K., CRC Press, Boca Raton, FL, 2000, chap. 37.
2. Yano, K., et al., A 3.8-ns CMOS 16 × 16-b Multiplier Using Complementary Pass-Transistor Logic, *IEEE J. Solid-State Circuits*, SC-25, 388–395, 1990.
3. Suzuki, M., et al., 1.5-ns 32-b CMOS ALU in Double Pass-Transistor Logic, *IEEE J. Solid-State Circuits*, SC-28, 1145–1151, 1993.
4. Ohkubo, N., et al., A 4.4-ns CMOS 54 × 54-b Multiplier Using Pass-Transistor Multiplexer, in *Proc. of IEEE Custom Integrated Circuits Conference*, 1994, 599–602.
5. Matsui, M., et al., 200 MHz Video Compression Macrocells Using Low-Swing Differential Logic, in *Proc. of ISSCC Digest of Technical Papers*, 1994, 76–77.

6. Parameswar, A., Hara, H., and Sakurai, T., A High Speed, Low Power, Swing Restored Pass-Transistor Logic Based Multiply and Accurate Circuit for Multimedia Applications, in *Proc. of IEEE Custom Integrated Circuits Conference*, 1994, 278–281.

7. Fuse, T., et al., A 0.5 V 200 MHz 1-Stage 32-b ALU Using a Body Bias Controlled SOI Pass-Gate Logic, in *Proc. of ISSCC Digest of Technical Papers*, 1997, 286–287.

8. Fuse, T., et al., 0.5 V SOI CMOS Pass-Gate Logic, in *Proc. of ISSCC Digest of Technical Papers*, 1996, 88–89.

9. Buch, P., Narayan, A., Newton, R., and Sangiovanni-Vicentelli, A. L., Logic Synthesis for Large Pass Transistor Circuit, in *Proc. of International Conference on Computer-Aided Design*, 1997, 663–670.

10. Yano, K., Sasaki, Y., Rikino, K., and Seki, K., Top-Down Pass-Transistor Logic Design, *IEEE J. Solid-State Circuits*, SC-31, 792–803, 1996.

11. Sasaki, Y., Yano, K., Yamashita, S., Chikata, H., Rikino, K., Uchiyama, K., and Seki, K., Multi-Level Pass-Transistor Logic for Low-Power ULSIs, in *Proc. of IEEE Symp. on Low Power Electronics*, 1995, 14–15.

12. Chaudhry, R., Liu, T.-H., Aziz, A., and Burns, J. L., Area-Oriented Synthesis for Pass-Transistor Logic, in *Proc. of International Conference on Computer-Aided Design*, 1998, 160–167.

13. Liu, T.-H., Ganai, M. K., Aziz, A., and Burns, J. L., Performance Driven Synthesis for Pass-Transistor Logic, in *Proc. of International Conference on Computer-Aided Design*, 1998, 255–259.

14. Cheung, T.-S. and Asada, K., Regenerative Pass-Transistor Logic: A Modular Circuit Technique for High Speed Logic Circuit Design, *IEIEC Trans. on Electronics*, E79-C, No. 9, 1274–1284, 1996.

15. Konishi, K., Kishimoto, S., Lee, B.-Y., Tanaka, H., and Taki, K., A Logic Synthesis System for the Pass-Transistor Logic SPL, in *Proc. of the 6th Workshop on Synthesis and System Integration of Mixed Technology*, 1996, 32–39.

16. Taki, K., Lee, B.-Y., Tanaka, H., and Konishi, K., Super Low Power 8-bit CPU with Pass-Transistor Logic, in *Proc. of the 6th Workshop on Synthesis and System Integration of Mixed Technology*, 1997, 663–664.

17. Taki, K., A Survey for Pass-Transistor Logic Technologies, in *Proc. of the Asia and South Pacific Design Automation Conference*, 1998, 223–226.

18. Karoubalis, T., Alexiou, G. P., and Kanopoulos, N., Optimal Synthesis of Differential Cascode Voltage Switch (DCVS) Logic Circuits Using Ordered Binary Decision Diagrams, in *Proc. of the European Design Automation Conference*, 1995, 282–287.

19. Oklobdzija, V. G., Soderstrand, M., and Duchêne, B., Development and Synthesis Method for Pass-Transistor Logic Family for High-Speed and Low Power CMOS, in *Proc. of the 38th Midwest Symp. on Circuits and Systems*, 1996, 298–301.

20. Scholl, C. and Becker, B., On the Generation of Multiplexer Circuits for Pass Transistor Logic, in *Proc. of Design Automation and Test in Europe Conference*, 2000, 372–379.

21. Hachtel, G. D. and Somenzi, F., *Logic Synthesis and Verification Algorithms*, Kluwer Academic Publishers, 1996.

22. Akers, S. B., Binary Decision Diagrams, *IEEE Trans. on Computers*, C-27, No. 6, 509–518, 1978.

23. Bryant, R. E., Graph-Based Algorithms for Boolean Function Manipulation, *IEEE Trans. on Computers*, C-35, No. 8, 677–691, 1986.

24. Fujita M., Fujisawa, H., and Matsunaga, Y., Variable Ordering Algorithms for Ordered Binary Decision Diagrams and Their Evaluation, *IEEE Trans. on Computer-Aided Design of Integrated Circuits and Systems*, vol. 12, no. 1, 6–12, 1993.

25. Ishiura, N., Sawada, H., and Yajima, S., Minimization of Binary Decision Diagrams Based on Exchanges of Variables, in *Proc. of International Conference on Computer-Aided Design*, 1991, 472–475.

26. Rudell, R., Dynamic Variable Ordering for Ordered Binary Decision Diagrams, in *Proc. of International Conference on Computer-Aided Design*, 1993, 42–47.

27. Meinel, C. and Somenzi, F., Linear Sifting of Decision Diagrams, in *Proc. of Design Automation Conference*, 1997, 202–207.

28. Tachibana, M., Synthesize Pass Transistor Logic Gate by Using Free Binary Decision Diagram, in *Proc. of IEEE ASIC Conference*, 1997, 201–205.

29. Shiple, T. R., Hojati, R., Sangiovanni-Vicentelli, A. L., and Brayton, R. K., Heuristric Minimization of BDDs Using Don't Cares, in *Proc. of Design Automation Conference*, 1994, 225–231.

30. Hong, Y. P., Beeral, A., Burch, J. R., and McMillan, K. L., Safe BDD Minimization Using Don't Cares, in *Proc. of Design Automation Conference*, 1997, 208–213.

31. Sasaki, Y., Rikino, K., and Yano, K., ALPS: An Automatic Layouter for Pass-Transistor Cell Synthesis, in *Proc. of the Asia and South Pacific Design Automation Conference*, 1998, 227–232.

32. Ferrandi, F., Macii, A., Macii, E., Poncino, M., Scarsi, R., and Somenzi, F., Symbolic Algorithms for Layout-Oriented Synthesis of Pass Transistor Logic Circuits, in *Proc. of International Conference on Computer-Aided Design*, 1998, 235–241.

33. Yamashita, S., Yano, K., Sasaki, Y., Akita, Y., Chikata, H., Rikino, K., and Seki, K., Pass-Transistor/CMOS Collaborated Logic: The Best of Both Worlds, in *Proc. of Symp. on VLSI Circuits Digest of Technical Papers*, 1997, 31–32.

34. Yang, C. and Ciesielski, M., Synthesis for Mixed CMOS/PTL Logic, in *Proc. of Design Automation and Test in Europe Conference*, 2000, 750.

35. Weste, N. H. E. and Eshraghian, *Principles of CMOS VLSI Design*, 2nd ed., Addison-Wesley Publishing, Reading, MA, 1994.

# 2.3    Synthesis of CMOS Pass-Transistor Logic

*Dejan Marković*

## Introduction

Pass-transistor logic (PTL) circuits are often superior to standard complementary metal oxide semiconductor (CMOS) circuits in terms of layout density, circuit delay, and power consumption. Lack of sophisticated design automation tools for synthesis of random logic functions limits the usage of PTL networks to the implementation of Boolean functions, comparators, and arithmetic macros—full-adder cells and multipliers. The research over the last 10–15 years [1] has been mainly focused on the development of more efficient circuit techniques and the formalization of synthesis methodologies. Newly introduced PTL circuit techniques were compared to the existing PTL and standard CMOS techniques, but comparison results were not always consistent [2].

The basic element of pass networks is the MOS transistor, in which gate is driven by a control signal, often termed "gate variable." The source of this transistor is connected to a signal, called "pass variable," that can have constant or variable voltage potential which is passed to the output when the transistor is "on." In a case of NMOS, when the gate signal is "high," input is passed to the output, and when the gate is "low," the output is floating (high impedance), Fig. 2.55.

Section 2.3 surveys the existing pass-transistor logic families, including their main characteristics and associated challenges. The main focus is placed on the discussion of different methods for synthesis of PTL circuits. Emphasis is given to a unified method for mapping logic functions into circuit realizations using different pass-transistor logic styles. The method is based on Karnaugh map representation of a logic function, and it is convenient for library-based synthesis, since it can easily generate optimized basic logic gates—the main building blocks in library-based designs.

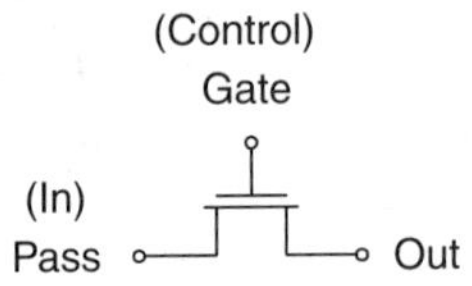

| Gate | Pass | Out |
|------|------|-----|
| 0 | 0 | hi-Z |
| 0 | 1 | hi-Z |
| 1 | 0 | 0 |
| 1 | 1 | 1 |

**FIGURE 2.55**  NMOS pass-transistor [21].

## Pass-Transistor Logic Styles

Various PTL circuits, static or dynamic, can be implemented using two fundamental design styles: the style that uses NMOS pass-transistors only and the style that uses both NMOS and PMOS pass-transistors. Within each of these two styles, there is a further differentiation based on realization of the output stage.

### NMOS Pass-Transistor Logic

Complementary pass-transistor logic (CPL), introduced in [3], consists of an NMOS pass-transistor network, and CMOS output inverters. The circuit function is implemented as a tree consisting of pull-down and pull-up branches. Since the "high" level at the pass-transistor outputs experiences degradation by the threshold voltage drop of NMOS transistors, the outputs are restored to full-swing by CMOS inverters, Fig. 2.56. Conventional CPL [3] uses restoration option (a). It is suitable for driving large output loads because the output load is decoupled from the internal nodes of the PTL network. Subfamily based on restoration option (b) is called differential cascode voltage switch with the pass-gate (DCVSPG), and it is good in driving smaller loads. Restoration option (c) is associated with the logic family called swing-restored pass-transistor logic (SRPL) [4]. Another variation of (b), which employs level restoring circuit shown in Fig. 2.56(d), was introduced in [5] in a logic family called power saved pass-transistor logic (PSPL). Compared to conventional CPL, this technique compromises circuit speed for smaller power consumption, resulting in worse energy-delay product.

Sizing of pass-transistors is an important issue. As discussed in [5], the NMOS transistors closer to the output have smaller size than the transistors farther away from the output because the transistors closer to the output pass smaller swing "high" signals due to the voltage drop across the transistors away from the output. However, this technique has to be carefully applied because small output transistors might not be able to provide sufficient driving strength at the output if the output load is large.

The LEAP pass-transistor library [6], uses two level restoring circuits, one for driving small loads, Fig. 2.57(a), and another for driving very large loads, Fig. 2.58(b). This level restoring technique decouples the true and complementary outputs in conventional CPL (dashed PMOS transistors in Fig. 2.56(a)).

CPL has traditionally been applied to the implementation of arithmetic building blocks [3,6–9], and it has been shown to result in high-speed operation due to its low input capacitance and reduced transistor count. Also, this logic family has smaller noise margins compared to the conventional CMOS.

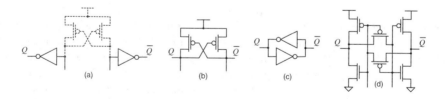

**FIGURE 2.56** NMOS pass-transistor subfamilies: (a) CPL, (b) DCVSPG, (c) SRPL, (d) PSPL.

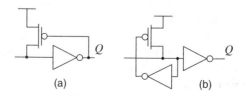

**FIGURE 2.57** The output inverters in LEAP library of driving (a) large and (b) small output capacitance.

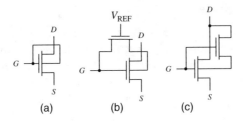

**FIGURE 2.58**   DTMOS devices: (a) standard DTMOS, (b) with limiter device, (c) with augmenting device.

### Technology Scaling of NMOS Pass-Transistor Logic

Technology scaling rules, given by the SIA roadmap, do not work in favor of NMOS-based PTL networks because the threshold voltage is predicted to scale at a slower rate than the supply voltage. This not only incurs speed degradation of the pass-transistor networks, but also slows down the pull-down of the output buffers, causing excessive leakage currents. To overcome this barrier, dynamic threshold MOS (DTMOS) is used. Various DTMOS devices that can be used in PTL networks are analyzed in [10]. Standard DTMOS device shown in Fig. 2.58(a) is suitable for supply voltages below 0.5 V, while for higher supplies the source-to-body junction could become forward-biased, causing excessive gate current. The use of auxiliary minimum-sized devices allows devices shown in Fig. 2.58(b,c), to operate at higher supplies. These two schemes are advantageous especially for driving larger loads when the area penalty for minimum-sized auxiliary devices is smaller, because the driver transistors are large. It is therefore expected that the supply voltage scaling does not impose barrier to the use of NMOS pass-transistor networks.

## CMOS Pass-Transistor Logic

### Double Pass-Transistor Logic (DPL)

To avoid signal swing degradation along the NMOS pass-transistor network, twin PMOS transistor branches are added to N-tree in double pass-transistor logic (DPL) for full-swing operation [9]. DPL logic family was introduced with the idea of overcoming swing degradation problem of CPL, resulting in improved circuit performance and improved noise margins at reduced supply voltages. Additional PMOS transistors in DPL result in increased input capacitance, but the symmetrically arranged and balanced input signals as well as the double-transmission characteristics compensate for the speed degradation arising from increased input loading. As introduced in [9], basic DPL logic gates have the same overall area as CPL gates—the widths of the PMOS transistors in DPL are two-thirds and the width of the NMOS transistors in DPL are one-third of the width of the NMOS transistor in CPL gates, respectively.

Newly introduced DPL was compared to CPL and standard CMOS on the example of a full-adder in 0.25 $\mu$m, loaded with 0.2 pF. It has been shown in [9] that for this load both pass-transistor designs, CPL and DPL, have higher power consumption than CMOS due to their dual-rail structure. When the load capacitance is smaller, then PTL architectures actually dissipate less power. Speed improvement of DPL gates has been demonstrated by AND/NAND and OR/NOR ring oscillators that have shown performance improvement of 15–30% relative to CMOS counterparts [9].

### Dual Value Logic (DVL)

Another logic family that uses both NMOS and PMOS pass-transistors is dual value logic (DVL), introduced in [11,12]. DVL is derived from DPL with the idea to eliminate redundant branches in DPL. This is performed in the following three steps: (1) elimination of redundant branches, (2) signal rearrangement, and (3) the selection of faster halves, as illustrated in Fig. 2.59. DVL preserves the full swing operation of DPL with reduced transistor count.

Elimination of redundant branches can be performed by direct elimination (faster NAND half), or it can be performed by merging functionality of two branches into one (faster AND half), Fig. 2.59.

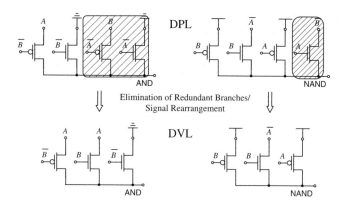

**FIGURE 2.59** DVL: Elimination of redundant branches from DPL.

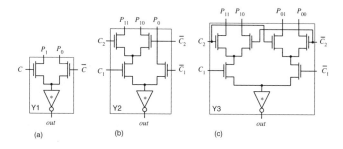

**FIGURE 2.60** Pass-transistor function cells in LEAP library [6].

The final step in synthesizing a DVL gate is the selection of the faster halves obtained in previous two steps. Main benefit of DVL is reduced transistor count relative to DPL. Since DVL gates have inherent asymmetry and imbalance of their inputs, circuit resizing is often required for balanced performance. Original work [11] reported about 20% improvement in speed of AND/NAND gate in DVL compared to equal area gate in DPL. The idea of DVL, extended to synthesis of random logic functions [11] will be discussed in more detail in the section on "Synthesis of Complex Logic Networks."

## Synthesis of Pass-Transistor Networks

The PTL synthesis methodologies can be classified into two categories: (1) binary decision diagram (BDD)-based and (2) other, which are not based on BDDs. Direct synthesis of large pass-transistor networks is difficult because of speed degradation when the signal propagates through long pass-transistor chains. The delay in PTL networks is a quadratic function of the number of PTL cells, while the delay in standard CMOS logic networks is a linear function of the number of cells. Therefore, large PTL networks need to be decomposed into smaller cells to overcome the significant delay degradation. When new pass-transistor families were introduced, the emphasis was usually given on their suitability for block design, and less attention was paid to the tradeoffs in the design of basic logic gates, which are essential blocks in the design of large PTL circuits.

### Binary Decision Diagram-Based Synthesis

Synthesis using pass-transistor cell library was introduced in [6]. The library consists of only seven cells—three function cells (Y1, Y2, and Y3) shown in Fig. 2.60 and four inverters with various drive capability shown in Fig. 2.57. The idea is to partition the BDD into smaller trees that can be mapped to the library cells. Logic design is carried out by a logic/circuit synthesis tool called "circuit inventor," which first converts the design into a BDD representation, then maps it into netlists of library cells. The netlist is then passed to an automatic place-and-route tool which generates the layout. This synthesis method generates PTL layouts superior to automatically generated static CMOS layouts in terms of area, delay, and power consumption, but this was true only for relatively small designs. In larger designs, unnecessary cascading of output inverters proves to be inefficient in terms of area. The reason for this, as pointed out in [13], is the use of primitive BDD approach with static variable ordering and without decomposition, which has been shown to result in bigger BDDs than the BDDs constructed with the approach of dynamic variable ordering and decomposition. A summary of the different types of BDD decompositions can be found in [14].

Pass-transistor mapper (PTM) was presented in [15] as an improvement of the "circuit inventor" tool. PTM technique was based on the same pass-transistor library cells, with the main improvement being the use of optimized reduced-order BDDs (ROBDDs) [16] that allowed for synthesis of large logic functions. Efficiency of PTM was verified in comparison with CMOS-based synthesis algorithms presented in [17]. Although PTM typically generated more compact layout with smaller overall active capacitance, speed of larger blocks was in favor of CMOS implementations. For example, cordic block synthesized by PTM had 30% smaller area, but three times longer delay than the same block in standard CMOS. Smaller blocks averaged a factor of 1.4 reduction in delay and marginal increase in area.

BDD-based optimization of pass-transistor networks guarantees the avoidance of sneak current paths. However, it has been shown that BDDs are not suitable for synthesizing area-efficient pass-transistor networks [18]. As an alternative, 123 decision diagrams (123-DD)—layout driven synthesis—were proposed in [18]. Main feature of this method is that the designs can be directly mapped into layout because the synthesis is driven from layout, including the consideration of interconnect. This synthesis technique utilizes two metal layers, with a set of rules that define geometrical placement and connectivity between transistors. Tested on single output functions, 123-DD synthesis method resulted in about 30% area improvement compared to standard synthesis techniques [19]. More details about these comparisons and the method can be found in [20].

## Synthesis Based on Karnaugh Maps

The method of Karnaugh maps can be effectively applied to the optimization of logic gates. Random logic functions with up to six inputs can be efficiently synthesized from the Karnaugh maps. Synthesis of pass-transistor networks using Karnaugh maps was presented in [21] and demonstrable area savings have been shown for small PTL cells. Approach to synthesis of PTL circuits based on incomplete transmission gates without degrading circuit performance, the idea similar to DVL, was presented in [20]. The focus of this section is on a unified approach to synthesis of basic logic gates in both NMOS and CMOS PTL circuits, developed in [22]. The synthesis method is further enhanced to the generation of circuits with balanced input loads, suitable for library-based designs. The versatility of these circuits is increased by application of complementarity and duality principles.

### Synthesis of NMOS PTL Networks

A general method for translation of Karnaugh maps into circuit realizations is applied to design logic AND/NAND, OR/NOR, and XOR/XNOR gates. The use of complementarity and duality principles simplifies the generation of the entire set of 2-input and 3-input logic gates.

The rules for synthesis of NMOS pass-transistor network in CPL are given below:

1. Cover Karnaugh map with largest possible cubes (overlapping allowed).
2. Derive the value of a function in each cube in terms of input signals.
3. Assign one branch of transistor(s) to each of the cubes and connect all branches to one common node, which is the output of NMOS pass-transistor network.

The generation of complementary and dual functions is simple, by observing the basic properties of these gates as given below.

*Complementarity principle:* The same circuit topology with inverted pass signals produces the complementary logic function.

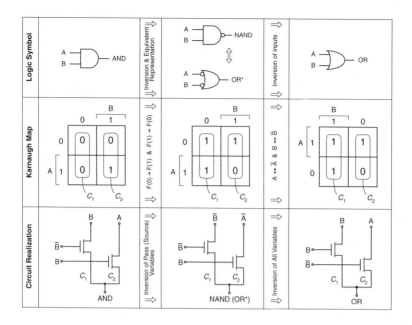

**FIGURE 2.61** Illustration of duality principle in NMOS pass-transistor networks [22].

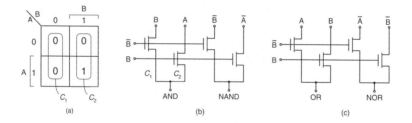

**FIGURE 2.62** Synthesis of 2-input functions: (a) Karnaugh map of AND function, (b) circuit diagram of AND/NAND function, (c) circuit diagram of OR/NOR function [22].

*Duality principle:* The same circuit topology with inverted gate signals gives the dual logic function. The dual logic functions are: AND-OR and NAND-NOR. XOR and XNOR are self-dual.

The duality principle follows from DeMorgan's rules, and it is illustrated by the example of AND to OR transformation, Fig. 2.61. The procedure of a logic gate synthesis is shown using an example of 2-input AND function, Fig. 2.62. The value covered by cube $C_1$ is equal to $B$, which becomes pass signal of the transistor branch driven with $\bar{B}$. Similarly the transistor representing cube $C_2$ passes input signal $A$ when the gate signal $B$ is "high." The NMOS transistor branches corresponding to $C_1$ and $C_2$ implement 2-input AND gate. Complementarity principle applied to AND circuit results in the transistor realization of NAND circuit shown in Fig. 2.62(b). By applying duality principle on AND, two-input OR function is synthesized. NOR gate is then generated from OR (complementarity) or from NAND (duality), Fig. 2.62(c).

### CPL Gates with Balanced Input Loads

The aforementioned synthesis procedure does not guarantee balanced loading of input signals. In AND/NAND circuit of Fig. 2.62(b) loads on input signals $A$, $\bar{A}$, $B$, and $\bar{B}$ are not equal. The gates shown in Fig. 2.62 are commutative with respect to their inputs, and when signals $A$ and $B$ are swapped in the NAND circuit of Fig. 2.62(a), resulting AND/NAND circuit has the balanced input loading, Fig. 2.63,

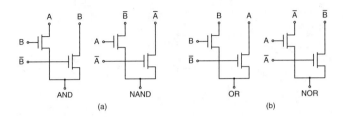

**FIGURE 2.63**    Circuit diagram of 2-input functions with balanced input load [22].

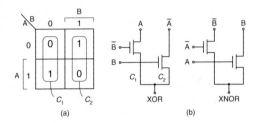

**FIGURE 2.64**    Synthesis of 2-input XOR/XNOR function: (a) Karnaugh map of XOR function, (b) circuit diagram of XOR/XNOR function [22].

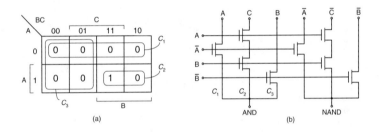

**FIGURE 2.65**    Synthesis of 3-input AND/NAND function: (a) Karnaugh map of AND function, (b) circuit diagram of AND/NAND function [22].

where each input "sees" the load given by Eq. (2.1).

$$C_{in} = C_{drain} + C_{gate} \qquad (2.1)$$

Balanced loading does not come without cost—circuits in Fig. 2.63 would require more layout area due to increased wiring complexity. Balancing also does not guarantee balanced propagation of true and complementary signals because logical transitions of input signals do not experience similar paths in true and complementary circuits. For instance, when $B$ changes from "high" to "low," and $A$ is "high," the output of AND circuit transitions "low"-to-"high" because *gate* signals ($B$, $\bar{B}$) have switched. Complementary signal—the output of the NAND gate—on the other hand, undergoes the "high"-to-"low" transition, affected by the switching of *source* signal $\bar{B}$. The two different paths, gate-to-output and source-to-output, cause different rising/falling delays of true and complementary output signals.

Realization of 2-input XOR/XNOR circuit, with balanced input loads, is shown in Fig. 2.64. The XNOR function is obtained from XOR by applying the complementarity principle and swapping input variables for balanced input loading.

Input loads cannot be balanced for any circuit topology and any number of inputs. To illustrate this, a single-stage 3-input AND/NAND circuit shown in Fig. 2.65 is analyzed. Eight input signals (including complementary signals) are connected to the total of 14 terminals, resulting in imbalanced inputs. If the

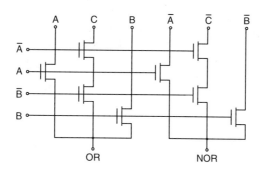

**FIGURE 2.66**   Circuit diagram of 3-input OR/NOR function [22].

3-input AND/NAND gates were implemented as cascade of 2-input gates with balanced loads, the loading would remain balanced.

The example in Fig. 2.65 also illustrates the reduction in transistor count by overlapping cubes $C_1$ and $C_3$. The consequence of the overlapping is that both of the corresponding branches are simultaneously pulling down for those input vectors under which the cubes overlap. Direct realization of 3-input OR/NOR circuit, Fig. 2.66, is straightforward if complementarity and duality are applied to circuit in Fig. 2.65. A three-input XOR/XNOR circuit in CPL is typically composed of 2-input XOR/XNOR modules [3].

### Synthesis of CMOS PTL Networks (DPL and DVL)
#### Synthesis of DPL
DPL has twice as many transistors as CPL for the same logic function. Consequently, the synthesis of double pass-transistor logic is based on covering every input vector in the Karnaugh map twice. The idea is to assure all logic "0"s in the map are passed to the output through at least one NMOS branch and all logic "1"s through at least one PMOS branch.

The rules to synthesize random logic function in DPL from its Karnaugh map are:

1. Two NMOS branches cannot be overlapped on logic "1"s. Similarly, two PMOS branches cannot be overlapped on logic "0"s.
2. Pass signals are expressed in terms of input signals or supply. Every input vector has to be covered with exactly two branches.

*Complementarity principle:*  The complementary logic function in DPL is generated after the following modifications of the true function: (1) swap PMOS and NMOS transistors, and (2) invert all pass and gate signals. Unlike purely NMOS pass-transistor networks, in CMOS networks both pass and gate signals need to be inverted because the PMOS and NMOS transistors are swapped in step (1).

*Duality principle:*  The dual logic function in DPL is generated when PMOS and NMOS transistors are swapped, and $V_{dd}$ and GND are swapped.

The procedure to synthesize DPL circuits is illustrated on the example of 2-input AND circuit shown in Fig. 2.67. Cube $C_1$, Fig. 2.67(a), is mapped to an NMOS transistor, with the source connected to ground and the gate connected to $\bar{B}$. Cube $C_2$ is mapped to a PMOS transistor, which passes $A$, when gate signal $\bar{B}$ is "low." The NMOS transistor of $C_3$ pulls down to ground, when $A$ is "low," and the PMOS transistor of $C_4$ passes $B$, when $A$ is "high." Complementary circuit (NAND), Fig. 2.67(b), is generated from AND, by applying the complementarity principle. Following the duality principle, OR circuit is formed from AND circuit, Fig. 2.68.

Different 2-input XOR/XNOR circuit arrangements are possible, depending on mapping strategy. Fig. 2.69 shows a realization with balanced load on both true and complementary input signals. Three-input functions in DPL are implemented as cascaded combinations of 2-input DPL modules.

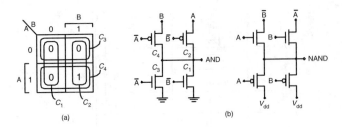

**FIGURE 2.67**  Synthesis of 2-input AND/NAND function: (a) Karnaugh map of AND function, (b) circuit diagram AND/NAND function [22].

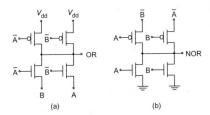

**FIGURE 2.68**  Circuit diagram of OR/NOR function [22].

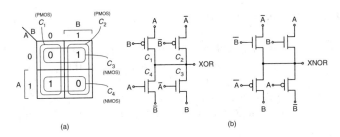

**FIGURE 2.69**  Synthesis of 2-input XOR/XNOR function: (a) Karnaugh map of XOR function, (b) circuit diagram XOR/XNOR function [22].

*Synthesis of DVL*

The rules to synthesize random logic function in DVL from Karnaugh map are outlined below:

1. Cover all input vectors that produce "0" at the output with largest possible cubes (overlapping allowed) and represent those cubes with NMOS devices, in which sources are connected to GND.
2. Repeat step 1 for input vectors that produce "1" at the output and represent those cubes with PMOS devices, in which sources are connected to $V_{dd}$.
3. Finish with mapping of input vectors that are not mapped in steps 1 and 2 (overlapping with cubes from steps 1 and 2 allowed) that produce "0" or "1" at the output. Represent those cubes with parallel NMOS (good pull-down) and PMOS (good pull-up) branches, in which sources are connected to the corresponding input signals.

The complementarity and duality principles are identical as in DPL. Generation of 2-input AND/NAND function is shown in Fig. 2.70. Circuit realizations with balanced loads are not possible in this case. Signals in brackets of Fig. 2.70(b) denote alternative signal arrangement in NAND circuit. The optimal signal arrangement depends on circuit environment and switching probabilities of input signals.

Efficient realization of 2-input OR/NOR circuits is shown in Fig. 2.71. Realization of 2-input XOR/XNOR circuit is identical to DPL, Fig. 2.69. Direct circuit implementation of 3-input DVL gates is shown in Fig. 2.72.

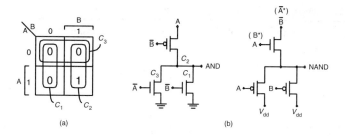

**FIGURE 2.70** Synthesis of 2-input AND/NAND function: (a) Karnaugh map of AND function, (b) circuit diagram of AND/NAND function [22].

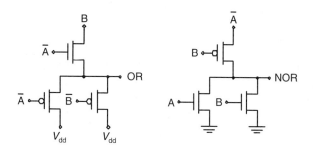

**FIGURE 2.71** Circuit diagram of OR/NOR function [22].

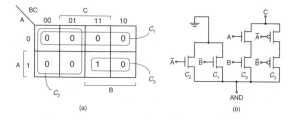

**FIGURE 2.72** Karnaugh map and circuit diagram of 3-input AND function [22].

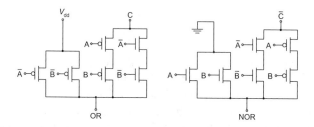

**FIGURE 2.73** Circuit diagram of 3-input OR/NOR function [22].

Overlapping cubes $C_1$ and $C_2$, Fig. 2.72, saves area, which allows for wider transistors for cube $C_3$. The OR/NOR circuit, directly generated from the AND circuit, is shown in Fig. 2.73.

## Synthesis of Complex Logic Networks

Synthesis of large pass-transistor networks is a challenging problem. The method presented in the "Synthesis of Pass-Transistor Networks" section can be extended to synthesize larger functions, as well as to synthesize complementary CMOS circuits. Complementary CMOS logic is essentially a special case of

**TABLE 2.2**   Comparison of Different Realizations of 3-Input Function $F = B'C + ABC'$ [22]

| Realization | No. of Input Signals | Signal Termination | Transistor Count | Output Load |
|---|---|---|---|---|
| CMOS | 9 | 10G | 10 | 4S |
| DVL (e) | 9 | 8G + 6S | 8 | 6S |
| DVL (f) | 9 | 7G + 3S | 7 | 4S |

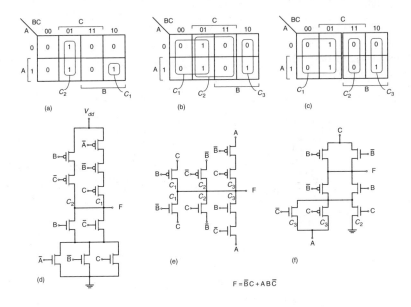

**FIGURE 2.74**   Karnaugh map coverage of 3-input function in (a) complementary CMOS, (b) DVL, (c) DVL and corresponding circuit realizations in (d) complementary CMOS, (e) DVL, and (f) DVL [22].

pass-transistor logic, constrained that all source signals must terminate to $V_{dd}$ or GND. This unnecessary constraint is removed in PTL, but at the same time complexity of designing large PTL circuits is increased. The most area-efficient method to synthesis of large PTL networks is decomposition into fundamental units with small number of inputs, typically two or three. To illustrate this, the synthesis of random logic function using three different mapping techniques is analyzed.

Consider the function

$$F = \bar{B} \cdot C + A \cdot B \cdot \bar{C} \tag{2.2}$$

and its three different realizations shown in Fig. 2.74. All three circuits implement the same function, but have different total active switching capacitance and different energy consumption. This example is extension of the analysis provided in [11] towards generalization of random logic function synthesis. Realization in complementary CMOS, Fig. 2.74(d), has smaller load on input signals and internal output load than the DVL realization in Fig. 2.74(e). Two realizations of DVL show different mapping strategies: the first strategy is to cover the map with largest possible cubes, Fig. 2.74(b), while the second strategy, Fig. 2.74(c), is based on map decomposition and reduction to implementation of basic 2-input functions. The DVL realization in Fig. 2.74(f) has smallest total load on input signals and similar internal output load as complementary CMOS realization, as shown in Table 2.2.

This example illustrates the importance of strategy used to cover Karnaugh map and leads to a conclusion that functional decomposition is the most efficient method in PTL circuit optimization. Straightforward coverage of Karnaugh map with largest cubes, as shown in Fig. 2.74(b) results in a circuit with lower performance, Fig. 2.74(e), while more careful coverage with decomposition of inputs, Fig. 2.74(c), results in a circuit with both smaller transistor stack and smaller transistor count, Fig. 2.74(f).

## Summary

Pass-transistor logic circuits are often more efficient than conventional CMOS circuits in terms of area, speed, and power consumption. This has been particularly the case when PTL is applied to the implementation of adders and multipliers. There are two main PTL design styles: NMOS-only pass-transistor networks, and CMOS pass-transistor networks. The use of DTMOS pass-transistors would allow an NMOS-based pass-transistor networks to operate at scaled supply voltages without significant speed degradation. The CMOS-based pass-transistor networks present the generalization of complementary CMOS where the pass variables could terminate to a variable voltage potential instead of $V_{dd}$ or GND in standard CMOS. This added flexibility of PTL circuits increases complexity of synthesis of large pass-transistor networks. Decomposition of a complex function into its fundamental units, typically gates with two or three inputs, seems to be optimal solution. Finding a correspondence between logic function and these fundamental units can be performed in a systematic way using BDD-based synthesis algorithms or other non-BDD methods. Among the other non-BDD methods, synthesis and optimization based on Karnaugh maps presents systematic approach to synthesis of logic gates with balanced input loads. Further optimization of PTL circuits under multiple and/or variable transistor thresholds or supply voltage is a challenging problem for future research.

## References

1. Taki, K., A Survey for pass-transistor logic technologies—recent researches and developments and future prospects, in *Proc. ASP-DAC '98 Asian and South Pacific Design Automation Conference*, pp. 223–226, Feb. 1998.
2. Zimmermann, R. and Fichtner, W., Low-power logic styles: CMOS versus pass-transistor logic, *IEEE Journal of Solid-State Circuits*, vol. 32, pp. 1079–1090, July 1997.
3. Yano, K. et al., A 3.8 ns CMOS $16 \times 16$-b Multiplier using complementary pass-transistor logic, *IEEE Journal of Solid-State Circuits*, vol. 25, pp. 388–395, April 1990.
4. Parameswar, A., Jara, H., and Sakurai, T., A swing restored pass-transistor logic-based multiply and accumulate circuit for multimedia applications, *IEEE Journal of Solid-State Circuits*, vol. 31, pp. 804–809, June 1996.
5. Song, M. and Asada, K., Design of low power digital VLSI circuits based on a novel pass-transistor logic, *IEICE Trans. Electron.*, vol. E81-C, pp. 1740–1749, Nov. 1998.
6. Yano, K. et al., Top-down pass-transistor logic design, *IEEE Journal of Solid-State Circuits*, vol. 31, pp. 792–803, June 1996.
7. Cheung, P. Y. K. et al., High speed arithmetic design using CPL and DPL logic, in *Proc. 23rd European Solid-State Circuits Conference*, pp. 360–363, Sept. 1997.
8. Abu-Khater, I. S., Bellaouar, A., and Elmashry, M. I., Circuit techniques for CMOS low-power high-performance multipliers, *IEEE Journal of Solid-State Circuits*, vol. 31, pp. 1535–1546, Oct. 1996.
9. Suzuki, M. et al., A 1.5 ns CMOS $16 \times 16$ Multiplier using complementary pass-transistor logic, *IEEE Journal of Solid-State Circuits*, vol. 28, pp. 599–602, Nov. 1993.
10. Landert, N. et al., Dynamic threshold pass-transistor logic for improved delay at lower power supply voltages, *IEEE Journal of Solid-State Circuits*, vol. 34, pp. 85–89, Jan. 1999.
11. Oklobdzija, V. G. and Duchene, B., Pass-transistor dual value logic for low-power CMOS, in *Proc. 1995 Int. Symp. on VLSI Technology, Systems, and Applications*, pp. 341–344, May-June, 1995.
12. Oklobdzija, V. G. and Duchene, B., Synthesis of high-speed pass-transistor logic, *IEEE Trans. CAS II: Analog and Digital Signal Processing*, vol. 44, pp. 974–976, Nov. 1997.
13. Chaudhry, R. et al., Area-oriented synthesis for pass-transistor logic, in *Proc. Int. Conf. Comput. Design*, pp. 160–167, Oct. 1998.
14. Yang, C. and Ciesielski, M., Synthesis for mixed CMOS/PTL logic, —, 2000 IEEE.
15. Zhuang, N., Scotti, M. V., and Cheung, P. Y. K., PTM: Technology mapper for pass-transistor logic, in *Proc. IEE Computers and Digital Techniques*, vol. 146, pp. 13–19, Jan. 1999.

16. Bryant, R., Graph-based algorithms for Boolean function manipulation, *IEEE Trans. Comput.*, vol. C-35, pp. 677–691, Aug. 1986.

17. Sentovich, E. M. et al., SIS: a system for sequential circuit synthesis, *Technical report UCB/ERL M92/41*, University of California, Berkeley, May 1992.

18. Jaekel, A., Bandyopadhyay, S., and Jullien, G. A., Design of dynamic pass-transistor logic using 123 decision diagrams, *IEEE Transactions on Circuits and Systems-I: Fundamental Theory and Applications*, vol. 45, pp. 1172–1181, Nov. 1998.

19. Pedron, C. and Stauffer, A., Analysis and synthesis of combinatorial pass transistor circuits, *IEEE Transactions of Computer-Aided Design of Integrated Circuits and Systems*, vol. 7, pp. 775–786, July 1988.

20. Jaekel, A., Synthesis of multilevel pass transistor logic networks, *Ph.D. dissertation*, University of Windsor, 1995.

21. Radhakrishnan, D., Whitaker, S. R., and Maki, G. K., Formal design procedures for pass transistor switching circuits, *IEEE Journal of Solid-State Circuits*, vol. SC-20, pp. 531–536, April 1985.

22. Markovic, D., Nikolic, B., and Oklobdzija, V. G., A General Method in Synthesis of Pass-Transistor Circuits, *Microelectronics Journal*, vol. 31, pp. 991–998, Nov. 2000.

## 2.4 Silicon on Insulator (SOI)

*Yuichi Kado*

### Background for the Introduction of SOI CMOS

As the popularity of broadband access networks in the home continues to expand and multimedia data such as video and sound are received over high-speed Internet connections, the introduction of electronic commerce is expected to reach a serious stage. For the implementation of such services, there is an urgent need for the development of high-performance terminals and network information processing systems. The key devices for realizing that hardware are high-end microprocessors and digital signal processors that have high performance and low power consumption. The predicted trend for high-performance LSI clock frequencies taken from the 1994 NTRS (National Technology Roadmap for Semiconductors) [1] and the 1999 ITRS (International Technology Roadmap for Semiconductors) [2] is shown in Fig. 2.75.

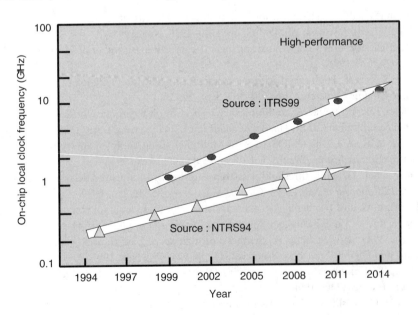

**FIGURE 2.75**  On-chip local clock frequency.

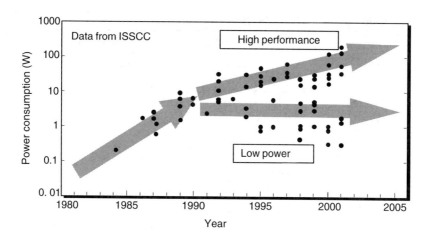

**FIGURE 2.76** Trend in microprocessor power.

The increases in LSI speed that we have seen so far are expected to continue at least until the year 2010, when the clock frequency should reach 10 GHz. Power consumption, on the other hand, is increasing along with processor speed, as we see in the trend in microprocessor power consumption reported by the International Solid-State Circuits Conference (ISSCC) (Fig. 2.76). Recently, high-performance MPUs that operate at gigahertz speeds and consume over 100 W of power have been reported. The calculated power density of these devices is nearly 100 W/cm$^2$, and with further increases in speed, the energy densities may approach those of a nuclear reactor [3]. This situation is recognized as a power crisis for LSI devices, and there is a need for lower power consumption and higher speed than is being obtained through the scaling of bulk Si devices. Furthermore, the market for portable information devices has experienced large growth, especially cell phones. To be conveniently useful, these information devices must be small, light, and have a sufficiently long use time under battery operation. Thus, there is a strong demand for lowering the power consumption of microprocessors, which account for nearly half of the power consumed by these information devices. This situation paves the way for the introduction of SOI (silicon on insulator) CMOS (complementary metal oxide semiconductor) devices, which are suited to low parasitic capacitance and operation on low supply voltage, as well as for the introduction of copper lines in the LSI wiring and a low-permittivity layer between wiring layers. The history of the development of the current SOI devices that employ a thin-film SOI substrate is shown in Table 2.3. The stream of development, which leads to the current SOI CMOS devices that employ an SOI substrate, originated with the forming of CMOS circuits on a SIMOX substrate for the first time in 1978 and the demonstration of the operation of those circuits [4].

## Distinctive Features of SOI CMOS Structures

A cross-section of an SOI CMOS structure is shown in Fig. 2.77. In an SOI CMOS structure, a metal oxide semiconductor field effect transistor (MOSFET) is formed on a thin SOI layer over a buried oxide layer, and the entire MOSFET is enclosed in a silicon oxide layer; the n-MOSFETs and p-MOSFETs are completely separated by an insulator. Furthermore, the process technology that is required for the fabrication of the CMOS devices is similar to the conventional bulk Si-CMOS process technology, and device structures are also simpler than for bulk CMOS. For that reason, compared to CMOS using ordinary bulk Si substrate, the CMOS that employ an SOI substrate have various distinctive features that result from those structures, as shown in Fig. 2.78. Here, in particular, the features of small junction capacitance, no substrate bias effects, and reduced cross-talk are described. These are powerful features for attaining higher LSI performance, lower power consumption, and multifunctionality.

**TABLE 2.3**    Thin-Film SOI History

| Year | Circuits/LSI | SOI Substrates |
|------|--------------|----------------|
| 1978 | First SIMOX circuits (NTT) | SIMOX |
| 1982 | 1 kb SRAM SIMOX (NTT) | |
| 1990 | 21 ps CMOS ring oscillator (NTT) | |
| 1991 | 256 kb SRAM (IBM) | |
| 1992 | 2 GHz prescaler | Low-dose SIMOX |
| 1993 | PLL (0.25 $\mu$m FD) | |
| | 1 Mb SRAM (TI) | |
| | 512 kb SRAM (IBM) | |
| 1994 | 1 M gate array (Mitsubishi) | ITOX-SIMOX |
| | | ELTRAN UNIBOND |
| 1995 | 16 Mb DRAM (Samsung) | |
| 1996 | 300 kg gate array (NTT) | |
| | 0.5 V MTCMOS/SIMOX (NTT) | |
| | 16 Mb DRAM (Mitsubishi) | |
| 1997 | 40 Gb/s ATM switch (NTT) | |
| | 1 Gb DRAM (Hyundai) | |
| 1999 | Power PC (IBM) | |
| | 64 b ALPHA (Samsung) | |
| 2000 | 3.5 Gb/s optical transceiver (NTT) | |
| | 2 GHz 0.5–1 V RF circuits (NTT) | |
| 2001 | 1 GHz PA-RISC MPU (HP) | |

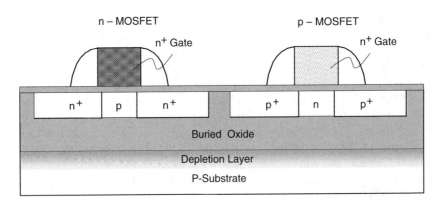

**FIGURE 2.77**    SOI CMOS structure.

As shown in Fig. 2.79, the MOSFET drain junction capacitance consists mainly of the capacitance between the drain and the substrate. In SOI structures, the capacitance between the drain and the substrate comprises a series connection of the buried oxide layer capacitance created by the silicon oxide layer, which has a dielectric constant 1/3 smaller than Si, and the capacitance of the extended depletion layer that is below the buried oxide layer. In SOI structures, the concentration of dopant in the substrate can be $10^{14}$ cm$^3$ or less, and by using the capacitance of the depletion layer that is below the buried oxide layer, the drain contact capacitance can be reduced to about 1/10 that of a MOSFET that employs a bulk Si substrate even if the buried oxide layer is about 100 nm thick. This is true even if we consider that the drain voltage changes in the range between 0 V and the supply voltage in CMOS circuit operation. Furthermore, reduction of the drain voltage $V_d$ decreases the depletion layer width of the drain n$^+$-p junction in proportion to $(V_{bi} + V_d)^{1/2}$ (where $V_d$ is the drain voltage and $V_{bi}$ is the built-in potential), so the drain capacitance is increased. Thus, the fact that lower supply voltages in SOI structures result

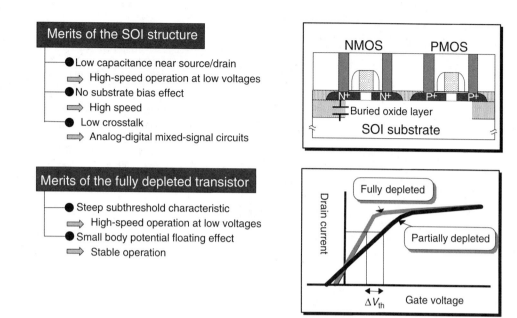

FIGURE 2.78   Features of a fully depleted SOI transistor.

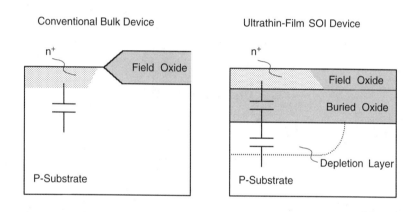

FIGURE 2.79   Small junction capacitance.

in lower junction capacitance due to the SOI structure is a remarkable advantage considering the trend of reducing the LSI supply voltage in order to reduce power consumption.

In SOI structures, there is no MOS reverse body effect, because the body is electrically floating due to the presence of the buried oxide layer, as shown in Fig. 2.80. In MOSFETs on a bulk Si substrate, the body, which is to say the p-well, is connected to ground, so when the circuit is operating, the body potential, $V_{BS}$, is always negative. Thus, if threshold voltage of MOSFETs ($V_{th}$) rises, the drain current decreases. When the supply voltage is 1 V or more in n-MOSFETs on an SOI substrate, holes generated in the high electric field drain region accumulate in the body region and create a positive body bias. Thus the $V_{BS}$ becomes positive, $V_{th}$ is reduced, and the drain current increases. This feature results in better performance than is obtained with MOSFETs on bulk Si substrate in the case of logic gates that consist of stacked MOSFETs and pass transistor logic gates.

For the development of multifunction LSI chips, the implementation of a mixed analog/digital (mixed-signal LSI) chip, which is a single chip on which reside RF circuits and analog-digital conversion circuits rather than just a digital signal processing block, is desired as a step toward realizing the system-on-a-chip.

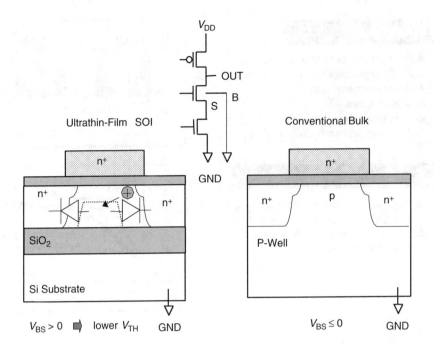

**FIGURE 2.80**  No reverse body effects.

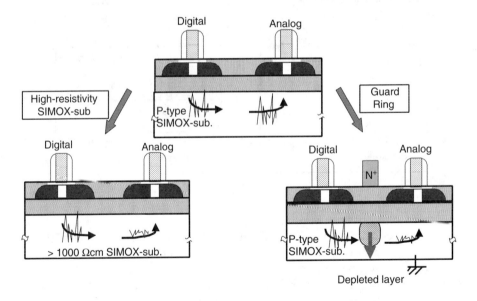

**FIGURE 2.81**  Cross talk suppression.

A problem in such development is cross talk, which is the effect that the switching noise generated by the digital circuit block has on the high precision analog circuit via the substrate. With SOI structures, as shown in Fig. 2.81, it is possible to reduce the effect of this cross talk by using a high-resistance SOI substrate (having a resistivity of 1000 $\Omega$ cm or more, for example) to create a high impedance in the noise propagation path [5]. Furthermore, even with an ordinary SOI substrate, by surrounding the analog circuit with N+ active SOI layer and applying a positive bias to it to form a depletion layer below the buried oxide layer, it is possible to suppress the propagation of the noise [6]. Although guard ring structures and

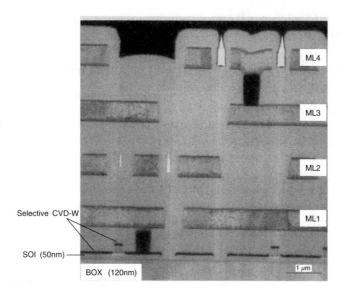

**FIGURE 2.82**  Cross section TEM image of fully depleted SOI CMOS.

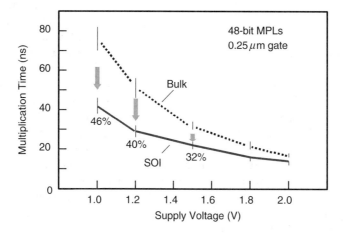

**FIGURE 2.83**  Comparison of a 48-b multiplier performance between SOI and bulk-Si using 0.25-$\mu$m CMOS technology.

double-well structures are employed as measures against cross-talk for CMOS circuits on bulk Si substrates, too, SOI structures are simpler, as described previously, and inexpensive countermeasures are possible.

Here, an example of a trial fabrication of an LSI of the SOI CMOS structures that have the features described above on a SIMOX substrate (described later) and the performance of a multiplier on that LSI are described. A cross-section TEM photograph of a CMOS logic LSI of 0.25 $\mu$m gates formed on a 50-nm SOI layer is shown in Fig. 2.82. In order to reduce the parasitic resistance of the thin Si layer, a tungsten thin-film was formed by selective CVD. A four-layer wiring structure is used. The dependence of the performance of a 48-bit multiplier formed with that structure on the supply voltage is shown in Fig. 2.83. For comparison, the performance of a multiplier fabricated from the same 0.25 $\mu$m gate CMOS form on a bulk Si substrate is also shown. For a proper comparison, the standby leak current levels of the multipliers that were compared were made the same [7]. Clearly, the lower the supply voltage, the more striking is the superiority of the performance of the SOI CMOS multiplier. From 32% higher performance at 1.5 V, the performance advantage increases to 46% at 1.0 V. Thus, the SOI CMOS structures are a powerful solution in the quest for higher LSI performance, lower operating voltage, and lower power consumption.

## Higher Quality and Lower Cost for the SOI Substrate

Against the backdrop of the recognition of SOI CMOS as a key technology for logic LSI of higher performance and lower power consumption, the fact that SOI substrates based on Si substrates have higher quality and lower cost are extremely important. A thin-film SOI substrate that has a surface layer of Si that is less than 0.1 $\mu$m thick serves as the substrate for forming the fine CMOS devices of a logic LSI chip. In addition, various factors of substrate quality, including the quality of the SOI layer, which affects the reliability of the gate oxide layer and the standby leak current, the uniformity of thickness of the SOI layer and the buried oxide layer and controllability in the production process, roughness of the SOI surface, the characteristics of the boundary between the buried oxide layer and the SOI layer, whether or not there are pinholes in the buried oxide layer, and the breakdown voltage, must be cleared [8,9]. Furthermore, for the production of SOI CMOS with the same production line, as is used for CMOS on bulk Si substrate, the absence of metal contamination and a metal contamination gettering capability are needed. Also, adaptability for mass production, cost reduction, and larger wafer diameters must be considered. From this point of view, remarkable progress has been achieved in thin-film SOI substrates for fine CMOS over these past several years. In particular, the SOI substrates that have attracted attention are broadly classified into SIMOX (separation by implanted oxygen) substrates and wafer bonding (WB) substrates, as shown in Fig. 2.84. A SIMOX substrate is formed by oxygen ion implantation and high-temperature annealing. Wafer bonding substrates, on the other hand, are made by bonding together a Si substrate on which an oxide layer is formed, which is called a device wafer (DW) because the devices are formed on it, and another substrate, called the handle wafer (HW), and then thinning down the DW from the surface so as to create an SOI layer of the desired thickness. For fine CMOS, a thin SOI layer of less than 0.1 $\mu$m must be fabricated to a layer thickness accuracy of within ±5–10%. Because that accuracy is difficult to achieve with simple grinding or polishing technology, various methods are being studied. Of those, two methods that are attracting attention are ELTRAN (epitaxial layer transfer) [10] and UNIBOND [11]. ELTRAN involves the use of a porous Si layer formed by anodizing and a Si epitaxial layer to form the separation layer of the DW and HW; the UNIBOND substrate uses hydrogen ion implantation in the formation of the peel-off layer. It has already been demonstrated that the application of these SOI substrates to 300 mm wafers and mass production is technologically feasible, and because this is also considered to be important from the viewpoint of application to logic LSI chips, which are a typical representative of MPUs, an overview of the technology and issues is presented in the next section.

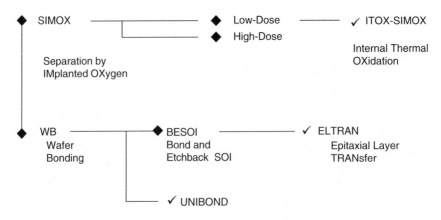

**FIGURE 2.84**   SOI material technologies for production.

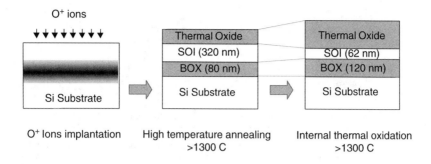

**FIGURE 2.85** Main process steps of ITOX-SIMOX.

## SIMOX Substrates

For SIMOX substrates, the buried oxide (BOX) layer is formed by the implantation of a large quantity of oxygen ions at energies of about 200 keV followed by annealing at high temperatures above 1300°C, as shown in Fig. 2.85 [4]. Because the amount of oxygen implanted and the implantation energy are controlled electronically with high accuracy, there is excellent control of the uniformity of the thickness of the SOI layer and the BOX layer. A substrate obtained by high-dose oxygen implantation in the order of $10^{18} cm^2$ is called a high-dose SIMOX substrate and has a BOX layer thickness of about 400–500 nm. The presence of $10^8 cm^2$ or more dislocation density in the SOI layer and the long period of time required for the high-dose oxygen ion implantation create problems with respect to the quality of the SOI layer and the cost and mass producibility of the substrate. On the other hand, it has been discovered that if the oxygen ion implantation dose is lowered to about $4 \times 10^{17} cm^2$, there are dose regions in which the dislocation density is reduced to below 300 $cm^2$, resulting in high quality of the SOI layer and lower substrate cost [12]. Such a substrate is referred to as a low-dose SIMOX substrate. However, the BOX layer of this substrate is thin (about 90 nm), making it necessary to reduce the number of pinholes and other defects in the BOX layer. In later studies, it was found that a further high-temperature oxidation at over 1300°C after high-temperature annealing results in the formation of a thermal oxide layer at the interface between the SOI layer and BOX layer at the same time as the oxidation of the SOI layer surface [13]. Typically, the BOX layer thickness is increased by about 40 nm. A substrate produced with this internal oxidation processing is referred to as an ITOX-SIMOX substrate. In this way, an SOI layer can be formed over an oxide layer of high quality, even on SIMOX substrates formed by oxygen ion implantation.

## ELTRAN Substrates

Although thin-film SOI substrates for fine CMOS devices are categorized as either SIMOX substrates or wafer bonded substrates, as shown in Fig. 2.84. ELTRAN substrates are classified as BESOI (Bond and Etch-back SOI) substrates, a subdivision of the bonded substrate category. The BESOI substrate is produced by the growth of a two-layer structure that consists of the final layer that remains on the DW as the SOI layer and a layer that has a high etching speed by epitaxial growth followed by the formation of a thermal oxide layer on the surface and subsequent bonding to the HW. After that, most of the substrate is removed from the backside of the DW by grinding and polishing. Finally, the difference in etching speed is used to leave an SOI layer of good uniformity. The fabrication process for an SOI substrate produced by the ELTRAN method is shown in Fig. 2.86 [14]. First, a porous Si layer that comprises two layers of different porosities is formed by anodization near the surface of the Si substrate on which the devices are formed (DW). After smoothening of the wafer surface by annealing in hydrogen to move the surface Si atoms, the layer that is to remain as the SOI layer is formed by epitaxial growth. After forming the layer that is to become the buried oxide layer by oxidation, the DW is bonded to the HW. Next, a water jet is used to separate the DW and HW at the boundary of the two-layer porous Si layer structure. Finally, the porous Si layer is removed by selective chemical etching of the Si layer, hydrogen annealing

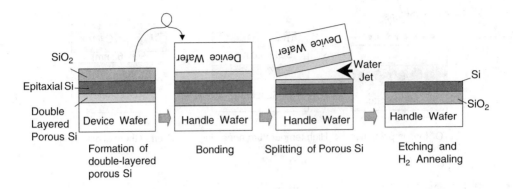

**FIGURE 2.86**　Main process steps of ELTRAN.

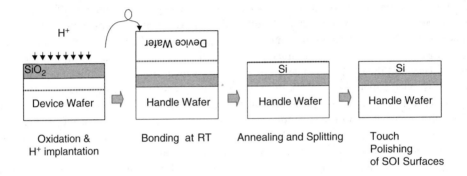

**FIGURE 2.87**　Main process steps of UNIBOND.

is performed, and then the surface of the SOI layer is flattened to the atomic level. The ELTRAN method also uses epitaxial layer forming technology, so layer thickness controllability and uniformity of the layer that will become the SOI layer are obtained.

### UNIBOND Substrates

The UNIBOND method features the introduction of the high controllability of ion implantation technology to wafer-bonded substrate fabrication technology [11]. The process of UNIBOND SOI substrate fabrication is shown in Fig. 2.87. Hydrogen ions are implanted to a concentration of about $10^{16}$ cm$^2$ in a DW on which a thermal oxide layer has previously been formed and then the DW is bonded to the HW. Then, after an additional annealing at low temperatures of about 400–600°C, separation from the hydrogen ion implanted layer occurs. The surface of the SOI layer is smoothened by light polishing to obtain the SOI substrate. By using ion implantation to determine the thickness of the SOI layer, controllability and uniformity are improved.

Here, three types of SOI substrates that have attracted particular attention have been introduced, but it is highly possible that in future, the SOI substrates will undergo further selection on the basis of productivity, cost, LSI yield, adaptability to large wafer diameters, and other such factors.

## SOI MOSFET Operating Modes

SOI MOSFETs have two operating modes: the fully depleted (FD) mode and the partially depleted (PD) mode. The differences between those modes are explained using Fig. 2.88. For each operating mode, the cross-sectional structure of the device and the energy band diagram for the region near the bottom of the body in the source–body–drain direction are shown. For the FD device, the entire body region is depleted, regardless of the gate voltage. Accordingly, FD devices generally have a thinner body region

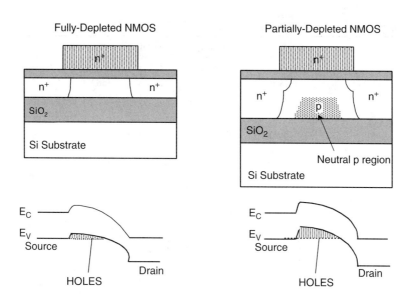

**FIGURE 2.88**   SOI device operation modes.

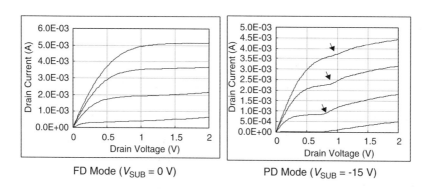

**FIGURE 2.89**   Id-Vd characteristics in FD and PD modes.

than PD devices. For example, the thickness of the body region of a PD device is about 100 nm, but that of an FD device is about 50 nm. In the PD device, on the other hand, the body region is only partly depleted and electrically neutral region exists. The presence of the region, focusing attention on the change in potential in the depth direction of the body region from the gate oxide layer, limits the gate field effect to within the body region, and the neutral region in which there is no potential gradient exists in the lower part of the body. Accordingly, the difference in potential between the surface of the body region and the bottom of the region is greater in a PD device than in an FD device, and the potential barrier corresponding to the holes between the source and body near the bottom of the body region is higher in the PD structure than in the FD structure. This difference in potential barrier height corresponding to the holes creates a difference in the number of holes that can exist within the body region, as shown in Fig. 2.88. These holes are created by impact ionization when the channel electrons pass through the high electric field region near the drain during n-MOSFET operation. The holes flow to the source via the body region. At that time, more holes accumulate in the body region of the PD structure, which has a higher potential barrier than the FD structure. This fact brings about a large difference in the floating body effect of the FD device and the PD device, determines whether or not a kink appears in the drain current-voltage characteristic and creates a difference in the subthreshold characteristic, as shown in Fig. 2.89.

**TABLE 2.4** PD-SOI Activities in ISSCC

| LSIs | Gate Length | Performance | VDD | Company | Year |
|---|---|---|---|---|---|
| Logic | 0.3 $\mu$m | 200 MHz | 0.5 V | Toshiba | '96 |
| 16 b Multiplier | 0.18 $\mu$m | 380 ns | 1.5 V | Intel | '01 |
| ALU | 0.08 $\mu$m | 1 ns | 1.3 V | Fujitsu | '01 |
| 32 b Adder | | | | | |
| DRAM | | | | | |
| 16 Mb | 0.5 $\mu$m | 46 ns | 1 V | Mitsubishi | '97 |
| Microprocessor | | | | | |
| 32 b Power PC | 0.25 $\mu$m | 580 MHz | 2 V | IBM | '99 |
| 64 b Power PC | 0.2 $\mu$m | 550 MHz | 1.8 V | IBM | '99 |
| 64 b Power PC | 0.18 $\mu$m | 660 MHz | 1.5 V | IBM | '00 |
| 64 b PA-RISC | 0.18 $\mu$m | 1 GHz | 1.5 V | HP | '01 |

**TABLE 2.5** FD vs. PD

| | FD | PD |
|---|---|---|
| Manufacturability | | + |
| Kink effect | + | |
| Body contact | + | |
| $V_{th}$ control | | + |
| SCE (scaling ability) | | + |
| Parasitic resistivity | | + |
| Breakdown voltage | | + |
| Subthreshold slope | + | |
| Pass gate leakage | + | |
| History dependence | + | |

## PD-SOI Application to High-Performance MPU

An example of a prototype LSI that employs PD-SOI technology and which was presented at the latest ISSCC is shown in Table 2.4. The year 1999 will be remembered as far as application of SOI to a high-performance MPUs is concerned. In an independently organized session at ISSCC that focused on SOI technology, IBM reported a 32-bit Power PC (chip size of 49 mm$^2$) that employs 0.25 $\mu$m PD-SOI technology [15] and a 64-bit Power PC (chip size of 139 mm$^2$) that employs 0.2 $\mu$m PD-SOI technology [16]. Samsung reported a 64-bit ALPHA microprocessor (chip size of 209 mm$^2$) that employs 0.25 $\mu$m FD-SOI technology [17]. According to IBM, the SOI-MPU attained performance that was 20–35% higher than an MPU fabricated using an ordinary bulk Si substrate. Furthermore, in the year 2000, IBM reported the performance of a 64-bit Power PC microprocessor that was scaled down from 0.22 $\mu$m to 0.18 $\mu$m, confirming a 20% increase in performance [18]. In this way, the scenario that increased performance could be attained for SOI technology through finer design scales in the same way it can be done for bulk Si devices was first established. IBM is attracting attention by applying these high-performance SOI-MPUs to middle-range commercial products, such as servers for e-business etc. and shipping them to market as examples of the commercialization of SOI technology [19]. Also, many manufacturers that are developing high-performance MPUs have recently begun programs for developing SOI-MPU. Currently, PD-SOI technology is becoming the mainstream in the high-performance MPU. The characteristics of PD-SOI and FD-SOI are compared in Table 2.5. In the high-performance MPU, improvement of transistor performance through aggressive increase in integration scale is an essential requirement, and PD-SOI devices have the merit that the extremely fine device design scenario and process technology that have been developed for bulk Si devices can be used without modification. Also, as described previously, because the PD-SOI can have a thicker body region than the FD-SOI (about 100 nm), those devices have the advantage of a greater fabrication margin in the contact forming process and the process for lowering the parasitic resistance of the SOI layer. On the other hand, the PD-SOI devices exhibit a striking floating

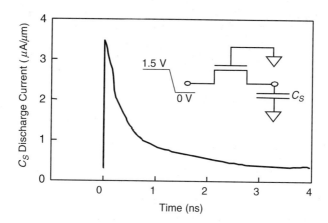

**FIGURE 2.90**  Pass gate leakage.

body effect, so it is necessary to take that characteristic into consideration in the circuit design of a practical MPU.

### Floating Body Effect

PD-SOI structures exhibit the kinking phenomenon, as shown in Fig. 2.89, but IBM has reported that the most important factor in the improvement of MPU performance, in addition to reduction of the junction capacitance and reduction of the back gate effect, is increasing the drain current due to impact ionization. This makes use of the phenomenon in which, if the drain voltage exceeds 1.1 V, the holes that are created by impact ionization (in the case of an n-MOSFET) accumulate in the body region, giving the body a positive potential and thus lowering the $V_{th}$ of the n-MOSFET, and thus increasing the drain current. The increase in drain current due to this effect is taken to be 10–15%. On the other hand, from the viewpoint of devices for application to large-scale LSI, it is necessary to consider the relation between the MOSFET $V_{th}$ and standby leak current. According to IBM, even if there is a drop in $V_{th}$ due to the floating body effect, there is no need to preset the device $V_{th}$ setting for the operating voltage to a higher value than is set for bulk Si devices in the worst case for the increase in the standby leak current, which is to say, transistors that have the shortest gate lengths at high temperatures [15].

Next, consider the pass gate leak problem [15,20], which is shown in Fig. 2.90. In the case of an n-MOSFET on SOI, consider the state in which the source and drain terminals are at the high level and the gate terminal is at the low level. If this state continues longer than 1 $\mu$s, for example, the body potential becomes roughly $V_s - V_{bi}$ (where $V_s$ is the source terminal voltage and $V_{bi}$ is the built-in potential). In this kind of state, the gate voltage is negative in relation to the n-MOSFET source and drain, and holes accumulate on the MOS surface. If, in this state, the source is put into the low level, the holes that have accumulated on the MOS surface become surplus holes, and the body region–source pn junction is biased in the forward direction so that a pulsed current flows, even if the gate is off. Because this phenomenon affects the normal operation of the access transistors of DRAM and SRAM and the dynamic circuits in logic LSIs, circuit design measures such as providing a margin for maintenance of the signal level in SRAM and dynamic logic circuits are required. For DRAM, it is necessary to consider shorter refresh frequencies than are used for bulk Si devices.

Finally, we will describe the dependence of the gate delay time on the operating frequency, which is called the history effect [15,21]. As previously described, the body potential is determined by the balance between charging due to impact ionization and discharging through the body–source pn junction diode, and a change in that produces a change in the MOSFET $V_{th}$ as well. For example, consider the pulse width relationship of the period of a pulse that is input to an inverter chain and the pulse width after passing through the chain, which is shown in Fig. 2.91. The n-MOSFETs of the odd-numbered

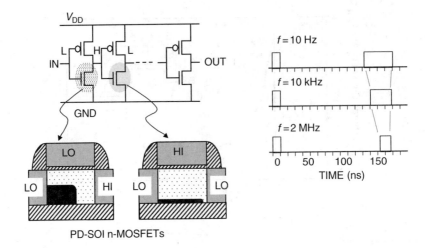

**FIGURE 2.91** History effects.

stages have lower $V_{th}$ than do the n-MOSFETs of the even-numbered stages. The reason for this characteristic is that the odd-stage n-MOSFETs have a high body potential due to impact ionization. This imbalance in $V_{th}$ in the inverter chain results in the longer pulse width after passing through the chain. The time constant for the charging and discharging is relatively long (1 ms or longer, for example), so the shorter the pulse period becomes, the smaller the extension of the pulse width becomes. IBM investigated the effect of changes in the dynamic body potential during the operation of this kind of circuit on various logic gate circuit delay times and found that the maximum change in the delay time was about 8%. Although this variation in delay times is increased by the use of PD-SOI devices, various factors also produce variation when bulk Si devices are used. For example, there is a variation in delay time of 15–20% due to changes in line width within the chip that result from the fabrication process, a variation of 10–20% due to a 10% fluctuation in the on-chip supply voltage, and a variation of between 15% and 20% from the effect of temperature changes (25–85°C). Compared with these, the 8% change due to the floating body is small and permissible in the design [15].

## FD-SOI Application to Low-Power, Mixed-Signal LSI

### Features of FD-SOI Device

As we have already seen in the comparisons of Fig. 2.78 and Table 2.5, in addition to the SOI device features, the special features of the FD-SOI device include a steep subthreshold characteristic and small dynamic instabilities such as changes in $V_{th}$ during circuit operation due to the floating body effect. In particular, the former is an important characteristic with respect to low-voltage applications. The subthreshold characteristics of FD-SOI devices and bulk Si devices are compared in Fig. 2.92. Taking the subthreshold characteristic to be the drain current–gate voltage characteristic in the region of gate voltages below the $V_{th}$, the drain current increases exponentially with respect to the gate voltage ($V_g$). The steeper this characteristic is, the smaller can be made the drain leak current when $V_g = 0$, which is to say the standby leak at the time the LSI was made even if $V_{th}$ is set to a small value. An effective way to realize low-power LSI chips is to lower the voltage. In order to obtain circuit speed performance at low-voltages, it is necessary to set $V_{th}$ to a low value. On the other hand, because there is a trade-off between reduction of the $V_{th}$ and the standby leak current, we can see that the characteristic described above is important [7,22]. As a criterion for steepness, the subthreshold coefficient ($S$) is defined as the change in the gate voltage that is required to change the drain current in the subthreshold region by a factor of 10. This coefficient corresponds to the proportion of the change in channel surface potential with respect to the change in gate voltage. For the FD type structure, the body region is fully depleted, so the channel

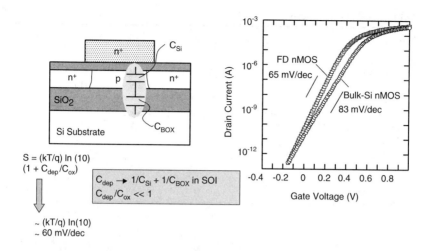

**FIGURE 2.92** Steep subthreshold slope in FD device.

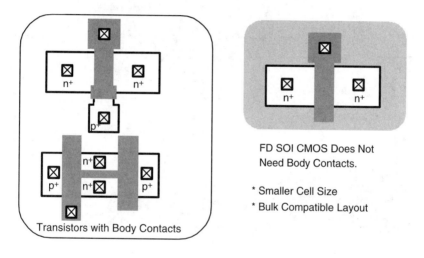

**FIGURE 2.93** No need for body contacts in FD device.

depletion layer capacitance in the bulk Si device, $C_{dep}$, is a series connection of the body depletion layer capacitance, $C_{Si}$, and the buried oxide layer capacitance, $C_{BOX}$, and the controllability of the gate voltage with respect to the channel surface potential is improved.

Furthermore, from the viewpoint of circuit design, the superiority of the FD-SOI device relative to the PD-SOI device is that the kink phenomenon does not appear in the drain voltage current characteristic (Fig. 2.89), and, further, that dynamic instabilities such as changes in $V_{th}$ caused by the floating body effect during circuit operation are small [23]. As a result, there is an advantage in terms of the layout area, because there is no need for body contacts including for analog circuits, and it is also possible for the layoutss and other such design assets that have been used for bulk Si to be used as they are (Fig. 2.93). An example of a prototype FD-SOI device LSI that takes advantage of the features described above that was newly announced at the ISSCC is shown in Table 2.6.

## Low-Power, Mixed-Signal LSI Application

Further advancement of portable systems in the form of wearable information equipment with a wireless interface will enable us to enjoy various multimedia applications anywhere and anytime. The realization of wearable communication devices requires lower power consumption, ultra-compactness, reduced

**TABLE 2.6**    FD-SOI Activities in ISSCC

| LSIs | Gate Length | Performance | VDD | Company | Year |
|---|---|---|---|---|---|
| Communications | | | | | |
| 4:1 MUX | 0.25 $\mu$m | 2.98 GHz | 2.2 V | NTT | '96 |
| 8 ×8 ATM switch | 0.25 $\mu$m | 40 Gb/s | 2 V | NTT | '97 |
| Optical transceiver | 0.25 $\mu$m | 3.5 Gb/s | 2 V | NTT | '00 |
| RF front-end circuits | 0.25 $\mu$m | 2 GHz | 0.5 V | NTT | '00 |
| Receiver front-end | 0.20 $\mu$m | 2 GHz | 1 V | NTT | '01 |
| Logic | | | | | |
| 300 kg gate array | 0.25 $\mu$m | 70 MHz | 2 V | NTT | '96 |
| Adder | 0.25 $\mu$m | 50 MHz | 0.5 V | NTT | '98 |
| Microprocessor | | | | | |
| 64 b ALPHA | 0.25 $\mu$m | 600 MHz | 1.5 V | Samsung | '99 |

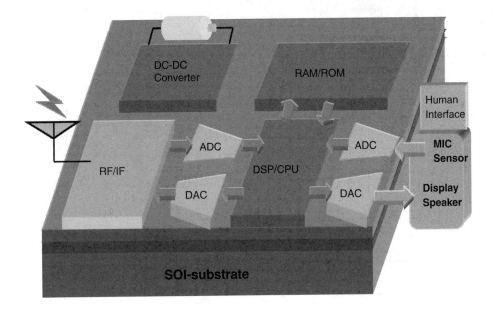

**FIGURE 2.94**    Analog-digital, mixed-signal LSI.

weight, lower cost, a wireless interface function, and a barrier-free human interface function. The key to satisfying those requirements is an analog-digital, mixed-signal LSI that integrates analog-digital conversion circuits, RF circuits, etc., and digital signal processing circuits on a single chip and also operates on ultra-low power supplies of 1 V or less (Fig. 2.94).

However, in the development of mixed-signal system LSI chips, problems arise that need not be considered in efforts to achieve finer design rules and increased integration scales for conventional digital LSIs. Examples include the improvement of analog circuit performance under low supply voltages and the reduction of the effects of cross talk noise from digital circuits on analog circuits. A promising solution for those problems is the use of FD-SOI device technology, which offers the promise of low-voltage, low-power operation.

Considering the digital circuit first, a method of reducing energy consumption by lowering the voltage and employing adiabatic charging is described. The problems associated with lower voltage operation for analog circuits and circuit technology for overcoming those problems is then discussed.

### Digital Circuits

The low-voltage, low-power trend for digital circuits is shown in Fig. 2.95. That figure is based on the supply voltage trend described in the 1999 SIA International Technology Roadmap for Semiconductors [2]

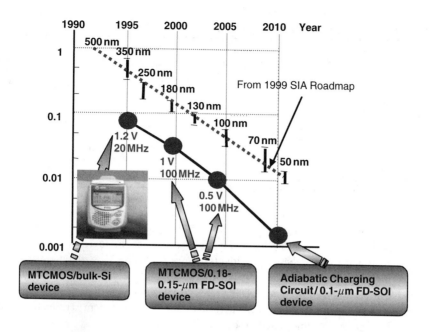

**FIGURE 2.95** Low-voltage trends in digital circuits.

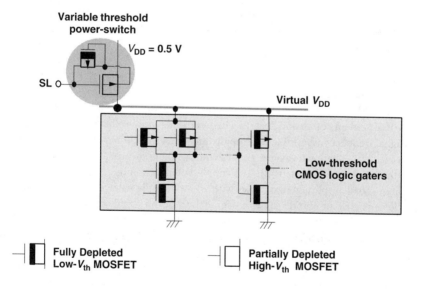

**FIGURE 2.96** MTCMOS circuit scheme.

and shows the trend in power consumption per basic gate, normalized to the power consumption for 5 V operation. The supply voltage for 0.05 $\mu$m generation LSI circuits is predicted to be 0.5 V in the year 2011, a reduction of two orders of magnitude from the 5 V operation of the 0.5 $\mu$m generation. However, it is possible to realize wearable information equipment that requires ultra-low-power-consumption ahead of that low-voltage, low-power consumption time trend, even without waiting for the finer processes of 2011, by using a combination of FD-SOI devices and MTCMOS circuits [24] or adiabatic charging circuits [25]. NTT is proceeding along a low-voltage research roadmap that shows 1 V operation in the year 2000 and 0.5 V operation sometime between 2003 and 2005.

MTCMOS (Multi-Threshold CMOS) circuits [24] are an effective means to achieve lower operating voltages in digital circuits (Fig. 2.96). These circuits are constructed of MOSFETs that have two different

TABLE 2.7    Performance of sub-1 V MTCMOS/SIMOX-LSI

| LSIs | Gate Length | Source Voltage | $V_{th}$ Configuration | Operating Frequency | Power Consumption |
|---|---|---|---|---|---|
| 16-bit ALU | 8 K | 0.5 V | Dual | 40 MHz | 0.35 mW |
| Communication | 8 K | 0.5 V | Dual | 100 MHz | 1.45 mW |
| Coding LSI | 30 K | 0.5 V | Dual | 18 MHz | 2 mW |
| 8-bit CPU | 53 K | 0.5 V | Dual | 30 MHz | 5 mW |
| Communication LSI | 200 K | 1 V | Dual | 60 MHz | 150 mW |
| 16-bit adder | 2 K | 0.5 V | Triple | 50 MHz | 0.16 mW |
| Communication LSI | 8 K | 0.5 V | Triple | 100 MHz | 1.65 mW |
| 54-bit adder | 26 K | 0.5 V | Triple | 30 MHz | 3 mW |

threshold voltages—some have a high $V_{th}$ and others a low one. High-speed operation at low supply voltages can be achieved by using low $V_{th}$ MOSFETs to construct the logic circuits and blocking the standby leak current that arises in these logic circuits because of the low $V_{th}$ with power switch transistors constructed of high $V_{th}$ MOSFETs, making it possible to apply these circuits to battery-driven devices such as wearable information equipment. A DSP (1.2 V, 20 MHz operation) that employs this technology has already been introduced in a wristwatch personal handy-phone system terminal, contributing to lower power consumption in audio signal processing [26].

Using FD SOI devices to construct the MTCMOS circuits even further improves the operation speed under low-voltage conditions [27]. By combining 0.25–0.18 $\mu$m gate FD SOI devices and MTCMOS circuit technology, it is fully possible to implement a digital signal processing chip for a wearable terminal that operates at high speeds (100 MHz or higher) at 1 V. The performance levels of various prototype MTCMOS/SIMOX chips are listed in Table 2.7.

### Analog Circuits

#### Problems associated with low-voltage operations

We will begin with the problems concerning the low-voltage driving of amplifiers and analog switches, which are the basic circuits of analog circuits. The trends in supply voltage ($V_{dd}$), cut-off frequency (fT), and analog signal frequency (fsig) that accompany the increasingly finer scale of bulk-Si CMOS devices are shown in Fig. 2.97. These parameters are drawn from the trends related to mixed-signal LSI circuits predicted in the 1999 SIA Roadmap [2]. The supply voltage exhibits a trend toward portable devices. The reduction in signal amplitude that comes with a lower supply voltage is a critical concern for analog circuits. The lower signal amplitude causes a degradation of the signal-to-noise (S/N) ratio. Because the linear output range of the basic amplifier used in analog circuits extends from ground to $V_{dd}$ minus about twice the $V_{th}$ of the transistor. So, lowering of the $V_{th}$ is essential to realizing a 1-V, operation-mixed signal LSI circuit.

On the other hand, lowering the $V_{th}$ increases the leak current of the analog switch, reduces the accuracy of the A/D converter, generates an offset voltage in the sample-hold circuit, creates high-frequency distortion in switch-type mixer circuits, etc. The relation between the transistor $V_{th}$ and the voltage variation caused by the analog switch leak current and the relation between the transistor $V_{th}$ and the analog signal amplitude, when $V_{dd}$ is 1 V, are shown in Fig. 2.98. The voltage variation values in that figure are the values calculated for an SC integrator (10 MHz sampling frequency and 1 pF integral capacitance) that uses analog switches. For a $V_{th}$ of 200 mV, the voltage variation in the subthreshold characteristics ($S$ = 85–90 mV/dec) of bulk Si devices and PD SOI devices is 3 mV or more, and 8-bit accuracy in an A/D converter cannot be guaranteed with a 1-V amplitude input signal. FD SOI devices, on the other hand, have a steep subthreshold characteristic and the leak current can be suppressed, so the voltage variation is 1 mV or less. This feature can improve the relations among the S/N ratio, signal band, voltage variation due to leak current, etc., which are trade-offs in analog circuit design.

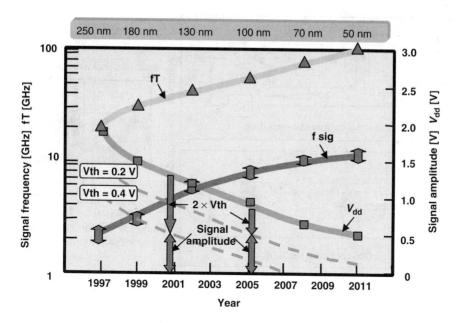

**FIGURE 2.97**  Trends in A-D, mixed signal LSI technology.

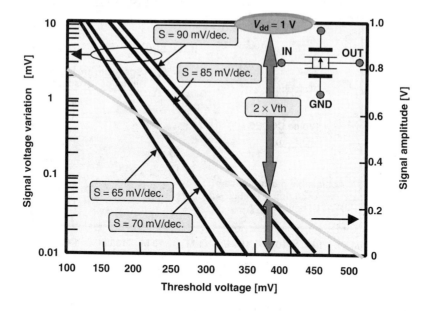

**FIGURE 2.98**  Relation between analog signal amplitude, accuracy, and $V_{th}$.

*1V A/D-D/A conversion circuit*

To solve the analog switch leak current problem described earlier, NTT has developed a 1-V operation noise shaping A/D-D/A converter with an RC integrator that does not employ analog switches. We have also proposed a configuration in which the integrator output is either the input signal only or the quantization noise only (swing-suppression circuit Fig. 2.99) as opposed to the conventional secondary $\Delta\Sigma$ circuit, in which the output of the two-stage integrator is the large-amplitude sum of the input signal and quantization noise [28]. In that way, it is possible to compensate the reduced dynamic range of the

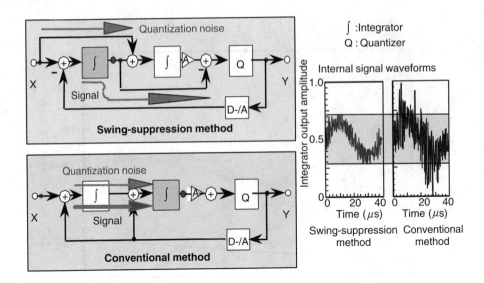

**FIGURE 2.99**   1 V A/D converter using the swing-suppression circuit.

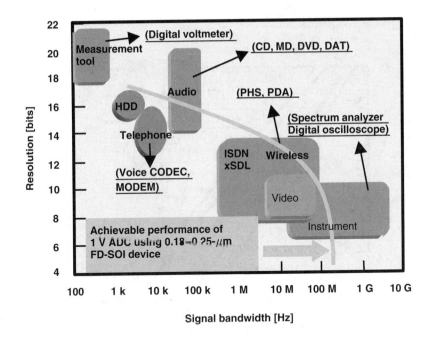

**FIGURE 2.100**   Performance of an SOI-A/D conversion circuit.

amplifier used in the integrator that results from the reduced voltage. Using a prototype that employs 0.5–0.35 $\mu$m gate bulk Si devices, we have already confirmed 16-bit precision conversion operation in the voice band (20 kHz) on a 1-V supply voltage with a power consumption of 3 mW or less.

To handle multimedia data such as audio, still pictures and video, it is necessary to increase the conversion speed and increase the bandwidth of the signal that can be handled. The performance of the A/D converter and an application example are shown in Fig. 2.100, along with the actual performance range for a circuit configured with 0.25–0.18 $\mu$m gate FD-SOI devices. We expect that a broadband A/D converter, which operates on a 1-V supply voltage and can be applied to wireless communication, can be realized.

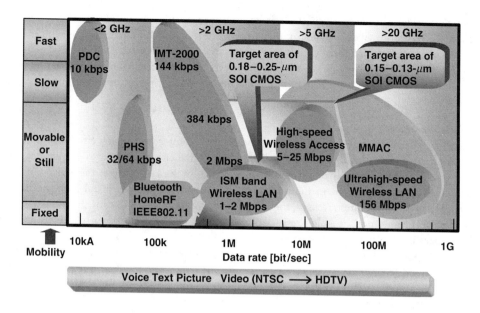

**FIGURE 2.101** Applications for SOI-CMOS RF circuits.

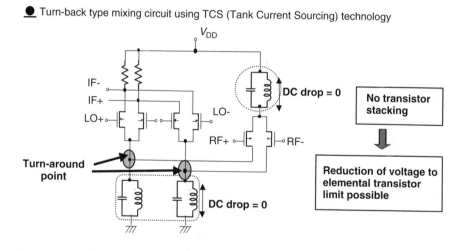

**FIGURE 2.102** RF circuit using TCS technology.

*RF circuit*

Concerning the wireless interface, standardization for the next-generation mobile communications is proceeding, beginning with IMT-2000, which aims for commercial implementation in 2001 (Fig. 2.101). Among those standards, what is attracting attention with respect to the application of CMOS circuits are the wireless communication technology standards for short-range communication in the 2.4 GHz ISM band (Bluetooth and HomeRF).

A prototype 2 GHz band, 1 V, low-noise amplifier that employs 0.25 $\mu$m FD CMOS/SIMOX devices has already been reported [29]. Moreover, RF circuit technology that allows reduction of the voltage to the limit of the elemental transistor by using tank current sourcing (TCS) technology to reduce the number of vertical stages of the transistor to 1 has recently been developed. That has made it possible to realize a 2 GHz band RF front-end circuit that operates on a mere 0.5 V [30] (Fig. 2.102).

When the communication range is 10 m or less and the transmission output is several milliwatts or less, as in the Bluetooth Class 3 standard, the entire 2.4 GHz band RF circuit that is required for the wireless interface can be configured with 0.25–0.18 $\mu$m gate FD-SOI devices. Doing so makes it possible to implement a low-voltage, low-power conssumption wireless interface circuit that operates on from 1 V to 0.5 V, thus providing a powerful wireless interface for implementing future fingertip-size communication devices.

### Cross Talk Immunity

In a mixed-signal LSI circuit (see Fig. 2.94), it is necessary to protect the analog circuit from the effects of the noise generated by the high-speed switching of the digital circuit in order to prevent degradation of the S/N and accuracy of the analog circuit that is formed on the same chip as the digital circuit. This is a particularly important point in the implementation of the RF amplifier and high-precision A/D converter. When SOI structures are used, the insulation separation is effective for suppressing substrate cross talk noise. Furthermore, if a high-resistance SOI substrate is used, the performance of the on-chip inductor that is used in the RF circuit an be improved [31].

The effect of cross talk was evaluated experimentally by designing a circuit in which a TEG is placed near an RF low-noise amplifier and inverter chain [5]. The circuit was test-fabricated by a 0.25 $\mu$m FD CMOS/SIMOX process with an ordinary SIMOX substrate (30–40 $\Omega$ cm) and with a high-resistance SIMOX substrate (1 k$\Omega$ cm or more). The placement of the TEG is shown in Fig. 2.103. The circuit was operated by inputting a 5 MHz rectangular wave to the input pad of the inverter chain ($V_{dd} = 2$ V) and the noise level was measured at the output pad of the low-noise amplifier. The noise level for the ordinary SIMOX substrate was −75 dBm, which cannot be ignored for a highly-sensitive RF circuit. For the high-resistance SIMOX substrate, on the other hand, the noise was clearly reduced to below the measurable level (−85 dBm).

It has also been confirmed that substrate noise from the digital circuit can be sufficiently reduced, even with an ordinary SIMOX substrate, by surrounding the analog circuit with an SOI guard ring and applying a positive bias to it to form a depletion layer below the buried oxide layer (Fig. 2.81). Using this guard ring technique, NTT have made a single-chip 3.5 Gb/s optical transceiver chip on a CMOS/SIMOX process [6].

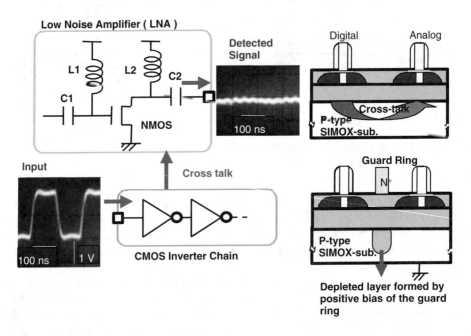

**FIGURE 2.103**   Cross talk evaluation circuit.

# Conclusion

An application example of an LSI chip that employs SOI devices has been described here. Against the backdrop that the SOI CMOS process has been recognized as a key technology for increasing the performance and reducing the power consumption of logic LSI circuits, there is a strong need by information distribution services for LSI chips of higher performance and lower power consumption, improvement of the quality of thin-film SOI substrates based on Si substrates, lower cost, and development of suitability for mass production. Furthermore, progress in explaining the physical phenomena of SOI devices is progressing, and another major factor is the establishment of control technology in both device design and circuit design for the characteristics that bulk Si devices do not have, especially the floating body effect. On the other hand, it is said that future LSI chips will be oriented to the system-on-a-chip era, in which memory circuits, RF circuits, analog circuits, etc., will reside on the same chip, rather than digital logic circuits alone. Although SOI structures are effective in reducing cross talk, as has already been described, problems exist concerning the establishment of a precise circuit model of the devices, which is necessary for application of SOI devices to analog circuits as well as ascertaining the influence of the floating body effect on circuit precision. It is also necessary to continue with studies on countermeasures for memory pass gate leakage in DRAM, SRAM, etc.

In the future, if progress in finer designs leads to the 0.1 $\mu$m era, in which the standard LSI supply voltage will be reduced to about 1 V, we believe that the superiority of SOI CMOS over Si CMOS will become even more remarkable.

# Acknowledgments

The author thanks Y. Sato, Y. Matsuya, T. Douseki, M. Harada, Y. Ohtomo, J. Kodate, and J. Yamada for helpful discussions and advice.

# References

1.  National Technology Roadmap for Semiconductors, 1994 Edition, SIA (Semiconductor Industry Association).
2.  International Technology Roadmap for Semiconductors, 1999 Edition, SIA.
3.  Gelsinger, P. P., Microprocessors for the new millennium, *ISSCC Digest of Technical Papers*, ISSCC, p. 22, Feb. 2001.
4.  Izumi, K., Doken, M., and Ariyoshi, H., CMOS devices fabricated on buried $SiO_2$ layers formed by oxygen implantation into silicon, *Electron. Lett.*, 14, p. 593, 1978.
5.  Kodate, K., et al., Suppression of substrate crosstalk in mixed analog-digital CMOS circuits by using high-resistivity SIMOX wafers, *Ext. Abstracts of the SSDM*, p. 362, 1999.
6.  Ohtomo, Y., et al., A single-chip 3.5 Gb/s CMOS/SIMOX transceiver with automatic-gain-control and automatic-power-control circuits, *ISSCC Digest of Technical Papers,* p. 58, 2000.
7.  Kado, Y., et al., Substantial advantages of fully-depleted CMOS/SIMOX devices as low-power high-performance VLSI components compared with its bulk-CMOS counterpart, *IEDM Technical Digest,* p. 635, 1995.
8.  International Technology Roadmap for Semiconductors, 1999 Edition, Front End Processes, Starting materials technology requirements, SIA.
9.  Maszara, W. P., Silicon-on-insulator material for deep submicron technologies, *Ext. Abstracts of the SSDM*, p. 294, 1998.
10.  Yonehara, T., et al., Epitaxial layer transfer by bond and etch back of porous Si, *Appl. Phys. Lett.*, 64, p. 2108, 1994.
11.  Auberton-Herve, A. J., SOI: Materials to systems, *IEDM Technical Digest,* p. 3, 1996.
12.  Nakashima, S. and Izumi, K., Practical reduction of dislocation density in SIMOX wafers, *Electron. Lett.*, 26, p. 1647, 1990.

13. Nakashima, S., et al., Thickness increment of buried oxide in a SIMOX wafer by high-temperature oxidation, *Proc. Of IEEE Int'l SOI Conf.*, p. 71, 1994.

14. Isaji, H., et al., Volume production in ELTRAN SOI-epi wafers, *ECS Proc. 10th Int. Symp. On SOI Tech. and Devices*, 2001-3, p. 45, 2001.

15. Shahidi, G. G., et al., Partially depleted SOI technology for digital logic, *ISSCC Digest of Technical Papers*, ISSCC, p. 426, Feb. 1999.

16. Allen, D. H., et al., A 0.2 $\mu$m 1.8 V SOI 550 MHz 64b PowerPC microprocessor with copper interconnects, *ISSCC Digest of Technical Papers*, ISSCC, p. 448, Feb. 1999.

17. Kim, Y. W., et al., A 0.25 $\mu$m 600 MHz 1.5 V SOI 64b ALPHA microprocessor, *ISSCC Digest of Technical Papers*, ISSCC, p. 432, Feb. 1999.

18. Buchholtz, T. C., et al., A 660 MHz 64b SOI processor with Cu interconnects, *ISSCC Digest of Technical Papers*, ISSCC, p. 88, Feb. 2000.

19. Shahidi, G. G., Silicon on insulator technology for the pervasive systems' technology, *Digest of COOL Chips, Keynote Presentation 1*, p. 3, April, 2001.

20. Wei, A., et al., Measurement of transient effects in SOI DRAM/SRAM access transistors, *IEEE Electron Device Letters*, vol. 17, pp. 193–195, 1996.

21. Wei, A., et al., Minimizing floating-body-induced threshold voltage variation in partially depleted SOI CMOS, *IEEE Electron Device Letters*, vol. 17, pp. 391–394, 1996.

22. Ito, M., et al., Fully depleted SIMOX SOI process technology for low power digital and RF device, *ECS Proc. 10th Int. Symp. On SOI Tech. and Devices*, 2001-3, p. 331, 2001.

23. Tsuchiya, T., Stability and reliability of fully-depleted SOI MOSFETs, *Proc. SPIE Symp. On Micro-electronic Device and Multilevel Interconnection Tech. II*, p. 16, 1996.

24. Mutoh, S., et al., 1-V high-speed digital circuit technology with 0.5 $\mu$m multi-threshod CMOS, *Proc. of IEEE International ASIC Conf.*, p. 186, 1993.

25. Nakata, S., et al., A low power multiplier using adiabatic charging binary decision diagram circuit, *Ext. Abstracts of the SSDM*, p. 444, 1999.

26. Suzuki, Y., et al., Development of an integrated wristwatch-type PHS telephone, *NTT REVIEW*, 10, 6, p. 86, 1998.

27. Douseki, T., et al., A 0.5 V SIMOX-MTCMOS circuit with 200 ps logic gate, *ISSCC Digest of Technical Papers*, p. 84, Feb. 1996.

28. Matsuya, Y., et al., 1 V power supply, low-power consumption A/D conversion technique with swing-suppression noise shaping, *IEEE Journal of Solid-State Circuits*, 29, p. 1524, 1994.

29. Harada, M., et al., Low dc power Si-MOSFET L- and C-band low noise amplifiers fabricated by SIMOX technology, *IEICE Trans. Electron.*, E82-C, 3, p. 553, 1999.

30. Harada, M., et al., 0.5–1 V 2 GHz RF front-end circuits in CMOS/SIMOX, *ISSCC Digest of Technical Papers*, p. 378, Feb. 2000.

31. Eggert, D., et al., A SOI-RF-CMOS technology on high resistivity SIMOX substrates for microwave applications to 5 GHz, *IEEE Trans. Electron Devices*, 44, 11, p. 1981, 1997.

# 3

# High-Speed, Low-Power Emitter Coupled Logic Circuits

Tadahiro Kuroda

*Keio University*

Emitter-coupled logic (ECL) circuits have often been employed in very high-speed VLSI circuits. However, a passive pull-down scheme in an output stage results in high power dissipation as well as slow pull-down transition. Gate stacking in a current switch logic stage keeps ECL circuits from operating at low power supply voltages. In this section, a high-speed active pull-down scheme in the output stage, as well as a low-voltage series-gating scheme in the logic stage will be presented. The two circuit techniques can be employed together to obtain multiple effects in terms of speed and power.

## 3.1 Active Pull-Down ECL Circuits

An ECL inverter circuit is depicted in Fig. 3.1, together with the simulated output voltage and pull-down current waveforms. As shown in the figure, the pull-down transition time increases much more rapidly than the pull-up transition time as the load capacitance increases. This slow pull-down transition time, and consequently unbalanced pull-up and pull-down switching speed, can cause an erroneous operation of the circuit due to signal skew or because of a racing condition.

The figure also demonstrates the disadvantageous power consumption of the circuit. The circuit requires a constant pull-down current $I_{EF}$. This power is consumed even when the gate output is not being switched. To reduce this power loss, the current $I_{EF}$ must be reduced. However, reducing the current $I_{EF}$ causes the pull-down transition time to increase to an unacceptable level. This high power dissipation and slow pull-down transition of ECL circuits has long been known to limit their VLSI applications. The power-speed limitation comes primarily from the passive pull-down scheme in the emitter-follower stage.

Various active pull-down schemes have been proposed [1–5] where a capacitor is utilized to couple a transient voltage pulse to the base of a pull-down npn transistor. An ac-coupled active-pull-down ECL (AC-APD-ECL) circuit [3] is depicted in Fig. 3.2. The steady-state dc current can be kept an order of magnitude lower than in the conventional ECL gate. As for the transient action, $C_X$ and $R_B$ determine the magnitude of the transient collector current of transistor QD. $C_E$ and $R_E$ determine the time while transistor QD turns on. These capacitors and resistors should be optimized for a specific loading condition, since they determine the dynamic pull-down current. The dynamic pull-down current is predetermined for a given design. In other words, there is a finite range of loading, outside of which proper operation of the circuit cannot be ensured.

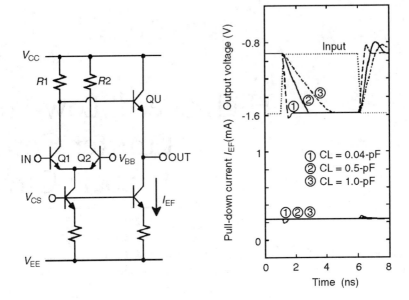

**FIGURE 3.1**   Conventional ECL circuit.

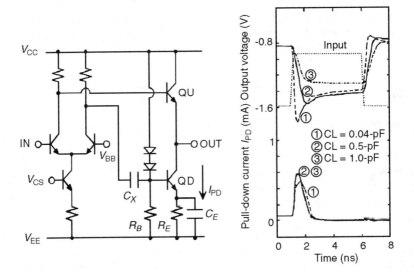

**FIGURE 3.2**   AC-APD-ECL circuit that is optimized to drive a 0.5-pF loading ($C_X = 0.2$ pF, $C_E = 1.0$ pF, $R_B = 170$ kΩ, $R_E = 50$ kΩ).

Simulated output voltage and pull-down current waveforms of the AC-APD-ECL circuit are also shown in Fig. 3.2. The circuit is optimized for a 0.5-pF loading. The simulation is performed under the 0.5-pF loading, as well as under much lighter loading, 0.04 pF, and much heavier loading, 1.0 pF. The dynamic pull-down current does not change according to the loadings. With the smaller loading, the excess pull-down current is consumed as crossover current at the end of the pull-down transition, resulting in waste of power. The excess pull-down current also causes unfavorable undershoot in the output. With the larger loading, a slowly discharging tail results, because the dynamic pull-down current is insufficient for the loading. The slowly discharging tail is dictated by the steady-state current.

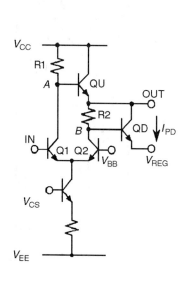
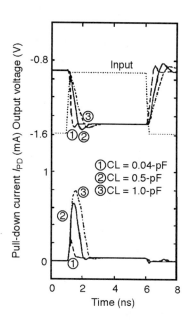

**FIGURE 3.3**    LS-APD-ECL circuit.

Because the circuit loading condition is uncertain with cell library design methodology, large dynamic and steady-state, pull-down current are used in a macrocell to cover wide range of loadings, thus diminishing the overall power savings. The need of additional devices, such as capacitors (typically several hundreds of fF) and large resistors (typically several tens of kilohm), also causes significant area penalty and added process complexity. The increase of the cell size implies increased interconnection delay, thus degrading the chip performance.

Another example of the active pull-down scheme is a level-sensitive active pull-down ECL (LS-APD-ECL) circuit [6], as shown in the circuit schematic depicted in Fig 3.3. No additional device, such as a capacitor or a large resistor, is required. On the contrary, the circuit is a rearrangement of the conventional ECL circuit, using exactly the same devices. Therefore, the circuit can be implemented directly on existing ECL gate arrays with no area penalty. The only addition is a regulated bias voltage $V_{REG}$ that should be biased to one $V_{BE}$ below the "low" level.

Circuit operation is illustrated in Fig. 3.4 when the input signal is switched from "high" to "low" so that the output rises to "high." When "low" input signal is applied, transistor Q1 is turned off and transistor Q2 is turned on, so that the current $I_{CS}$ switches from the left side branch to the right side branch of the current switch logic stage. Consequently, the potential at node $A$ goes up, which turns transistor QU on strongly. This allows a large charging current to flow and causes OUT to rise from "low" to "high". Before QU switches on, the potential at node $B$ is "low," because $I_{CS}$ does not flow on the right side branch initially so the potential at node $B$ is the same as that at OUT. After QU switches on, the portion of the QU charging current corresponding to $I_{CS}$ flows into Q2 . As a result, the potential at node $B$ drops, causing transistor QD to turn off. Once QD switches off, the major part of the charging current, $I_{PULL-UP}$, flows into OUT, so that the potential at OUT rises quickly. When the potential at OUT reaches the "high" level, QU turns off gradually. At the same time, the potential at node $B$ reaches the "low" level again, gradually turning QD on. Accordingly, when the potential at OUT reaches the "high" level, $V_{OH}$, both QU and QD turn on slightly, and a small steady-state current, $I_{SS(H)}$, flows.

Pull-down action is illustrated in Fig. 3.5. In response to the input "high" signal, transistor Q1 is turned on and transistor Q2 is turned off, so that the current $I_{CS}$ flows on the left side branch of the current switch logic stage. As a result, the potential at node $A$ drops, causing QU to turn off initially. As Q2 turns off, the potential at node $B$ goes up to turn QD on strongly. Consequently, a large discharge current,

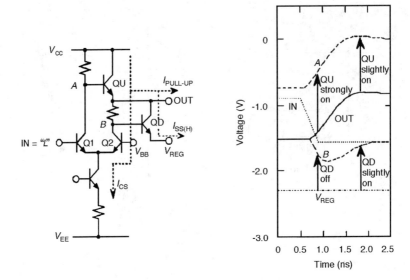

**FIGURE 3.4**    Pull-up action of LS-APD-ECL circuit.

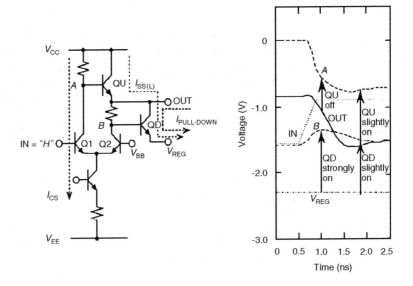

**FIGURE 3.5**    Pull-down action of LS-APD-ECL circuit.

$I_{PULL-DOWN}$, flows through QD into $V_{REG}$, resulting in fast pull-down of the output. As the potential at OUT approaches the "low" level, the potential at node $B$ approaches the "low" level, causing QD to gradually turn off again. At the same time, QU turns on gradually. When OUT reaches the "low" level, $V_{OL}$, both QU and QD turn on slightly, and a small steady-state current, $I_{SS(L)}$, flows.

In this way, the circuit self-terminates the dynamic pull-down action by sensing the output level. By comparing the output voltage and the pull-down current waveforms in Fig. 3.3 with those in Fig. 3.2, it is clear that the LS-APD-ECL circuit consumes less dc current than the AC-APD-ECL circuit and that the LS-APD-ECL circuit offers larger dynamic pull-down current whose level is self-adjusted in accordance with loading conditions. Therefore, proper and balanced output waveforms can be observed in the LS-APD-ECL circuit under a wide range of loading conditions.

The collector-emitter voltage of transistor Q2, $V_{CE.Q2}$, is given by

$$V_{CE.Q2} = (V_{OL} - \alpha V_{sig}) - (V_{BB} - V_{BE})$$

$$= V_{BE} - (0.5 + \alpha) - V_{sig} \tag{3.1}$$

where $V_{sig}$ is the logic voltage swing and $\alpha$ is a constant between $-1$ and $1$. As shown in Fig. 3.4, $\alpha$ is 0 when the output stays and increases when the output is rising. The maximum $\alpha$ is dependent on the output rise time; the slower, the larger. SPICE simulation predicts the maximum $\alpha$ is between 0.2 and 0.4 when $I_{CS} = 70 \ \mu A$ and $C_L$ ranged from 0.1 to 1.25 pF and temperature ranges from 0°C to 80°C. When $V_{sig}$ is 0.6 V, $V_{CE.Q2}$ may become as low as 0.36 V for an instance in switching, but never stays in the saturation region.

Only inverting structures are possible in the LS-APD-ECL circuit. If the input is fed to the base of Q2 to construct noninverting structures, $V_{CE.Q2}$ is given by

$$V_{CE.Q2} = (V_{OL} - \alpha V_{sig}) - (V_{OH} - V_{BE})$$

$$= V_{BE} - (1 + \alpha) - V_{sig} \tag{3.2}$$

In order to keep Q2 out of the saturation region, $V_{sig}$ should be lower than 0.45 V, which is impractical.

Because transistor QD self-terminates at the point where the output reaches $V_{BE}$ above $V_{REG}$, $V_{OL}$ becomes a direct function of $V_{REG}$. On the other hand, as $V_{REG}$ goes lower, both QU and QD turn on more deeply, resulting in larger steady-state current. Simulated $V_{OH}$, $V_{OL}$, $I_{SS(H)}$, and $I_{SS(L)}$ dependence on $V_{REG}$ are shown in Fig. 3.6. In order to keep enough noise margins between $V_{OL}$ and the circuit threshold, $V_{BB}$, $V_{REG}$ should be lower than about $-2.2$ V. At the same time, in order to restrict $I_{SS(L)}$ to an acceptably low level, $V_{REG}$ should be higher than about $-2.4$ V. Accordingly, $V_{REG}$ needs to be controlled very tightly around $-2.3$ V within the small error indicated in the figure.

A $V_{REG}$ voltage regulator circuit for the LS-APD-ECL circuit is presented in Fig. 3.7. An automated bias control (ABC) circuit [7] is employed to automatically adjust $I_{SS(L)}$ constantly even under process deviation, power supply voltage change, and temperature change. A replica circuit of the LS-APD-ECL circuit generates a reference $V_{REG}$ level, $V_R$, when $I_{SS(L)}$ is one-eighth of the current $I_{CS}$. A monitored $V_{REG}$

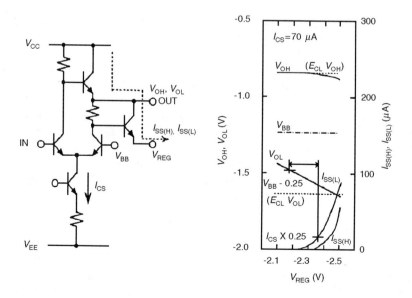

**FIGURE 3.6** Output voltage and crossover current vs. $V_{REG}$ in LS-APD-ECL circuit.

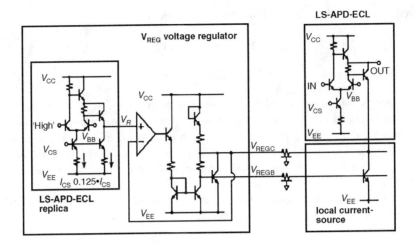

**FIGURE 3.7**   $V_{REG}$ voltage regulator circuit.

level and $V_R$ are compared by an operational amplifier whose output controls $V_{REG}$. When the monitored $V_{REG}$ level is lower than the target level $V_R$, the output potential of the op-amp rises, which increases the current in the $V_{REG}$ voltage regulator and pushes the potential of $V_{REG}$ up. On the contrary, when the monitored $V_{REG}$ level is higher than the target level $V_R$, the potential of $V_{REG}$ is controlled to go down. This way, the op-amp adjusts the $V_{REG}$ level such that the LS-APD-ECL circuits which are hooked up to the $V_{REG}$ lines have the same $I_{SS(L)}$ as that in the replica circuit. The stability of the negative feedback loop in the $V_{REG}$ regulator can be secured by a common method of compensation, narrow banding. A phase margin of 90 degrees is preserved when an external capacitor of 0.1 $\mu F$ is put on the $V_{REG}$ lines.

The voltage regulator can be implemented in an I/O slot of a chip from which $V_{REG}$ lines are provided to internal cells. Parasitic resistance along the $V_{REG}$ lines, however, produces a significant voltage drop when large dynamic pull-down current from all the LS-APD-ECL cells is concentrated in one regulator. Therefore, a local current-source is provided in each LS-APD-ECL gate to distribute the pull-down current. Parasitic capacitance between the two lines, $V_{REGC}$ and $V_{REGB}$, helps improve the transient response of the local current-source.

In Fig. 3.8 are depicted simulated dependence of the output voltages, $V_{OH}$ and $V_{OL}$; the steady-state currents, $I_{SS(H)}$ and $I_{SS(L)}$; and the circuit delays, $T_{pLH}$ and $T_{pHL}$, on power supply voltage, temperature, and the number of the LS-APD-ECL gates. It is assumed in the simulation study that 8 mm by 8 mm chip area is covered by 16 by 16 mesh layout for $V_{REGC}$ lines of 2 $\mu m$ width. The equivalent resistance between two far ends of the meshed $V_{REG}$ lines is estimated to be 20 $\Omega$. Even at the tip of the meshed $V_{REG}$ lines, the tracking error can be controlled within a range of 30 mV, which is small enough to be within the allowed error range. Since the $V_{REG}$ voltage regulator circuit controls the output voltage swing and the bias current of QU and QD constant, variation of the circuit delay can be kept very small even under the large changes in circuit conditions.

Simulated transient response of the LS-APD-ECL circuit with the $V_{REG}$ voltage regulator circuit is depicted in Fig. 3.9 when 1100 LS-APD-ECL gates are hooked up to the $V_{REG}$ voltage regulator, and 100 gates are switching simultaneously. Small bounce noise is observed at the $V_{REG}$ lines, which, however, does not affect $V_{OL}$ nor $V_{OH}$ of staying gates, nor does it degrade the switching speed. The broken line in the figure is the output waveform of a gate placed near the $V_{REG}$ voltage regulator, while the solid line is for a gate placed in the far end of the $V_{REG}$ lines. Very little difference can be observed between them.

Layout of inverter gates with the conventional ECL and the LS-APD-ECL circuits are depicted in Fig. 3.10. They both are implemented on an ECL gate array [8]. The $V_{REG}$ voltage regulator is implemented in an I/O slot from which $V_{REG}$ lines are provided to internal cells. In a 9.6-mm by 9.5-mm chip, 24 types of gate chains are implemented for three loading conditions (fanout one plus metal interconnection of

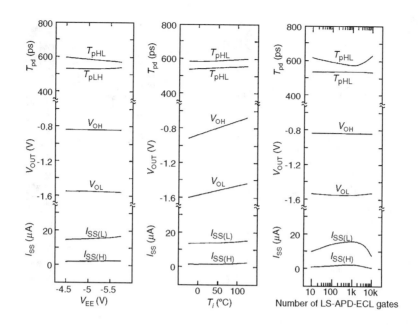

**FIGURE 3.8** Dependence of the output voltage, $V_{OH}$ and $V_{OL}$, the steady-state current, $I_{SS(H)}$ and $I_{SS(L)}$, the circuit delay, and $T_{pLH}$ and $T_{pHL}$ on power supply voltage, temperature, and the number of the LS-APD-ECL gates.

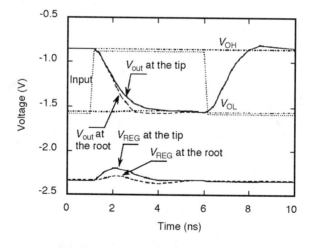

**FIGURE 3.9** Transient response of LS-APD-ECL circuits when 100 out of 1100 gates are switching simultaneously. $V_{REG}$ is provided by $V_{REG}$ voltage regulator through meshed $V_{REG}$ lines whose parasitic resistance is 20 $\Omega$. As a reference, output waveform when $V_{REG} = -2.3$ V is ideally supplied in broken lines ($V_{out'}$).

0.02, 2.5, and 6.4 mm length) and three power options, for both the conventional ECL and the LS-APD-ECL circuits. The 2.5-mm metal interconnection has about 0.55 pF capacitance. The test sites are fabricated using a 1.2-$\mu$m, 17-GHz, double-poly, self-aligned bipolar technology. Twelve wafers are fabricated in every process corner. Totally around 60,000 measurement points are obtained from 200 working samples. The logic voltage swing is 650 mV, and the power supply voltage is −5.2 V.

Measured and simulated power-delay characteristics for the conventional ECL and the LS-APD-ECL circuits are shown in Fig. 3.11. The circles represent measurement data from several process splits. The solid lines represent the SPICE simulation results under a nominal condition. Good agreement is seen between the measurements and simulations.

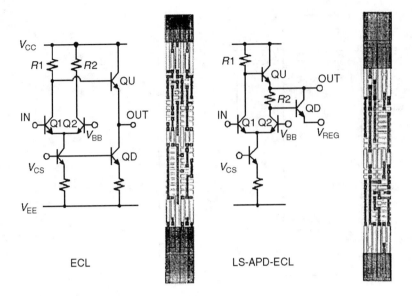

**FIGURE 3.10**    Layout of inverter gate with ECL and LS-APD-ECL circuits.

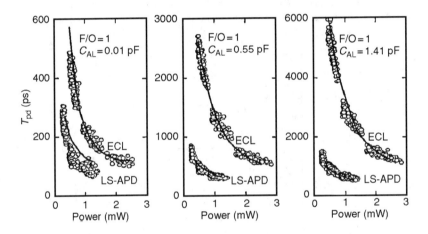

**FIGURE 3.11**    Power-delay characteristics for conventional ECL and LS-APD-ECL circuits.

The circuit under FO = 1 plus $C_L = 0.55$ pF (2.5 mm metal interconnection) loading condition, which is often seen in a typical chip design, offers 300 ps delay at a power consumption of 1 mW/gate. This is a 4.4 times speed improvement over the conventional ECL circuit. Furthermore, the circuit consumes only 0.25 mW for a gate speed of 700 ps/gate, which is a 1/7.8 power reduction compared with the conventional ECL circuit. A better speed improvement and power reduction can be achieved under heavier loading conditions. For example, under FO = 1 plus $C_L = 1.41$ pF (6.4 mm metal interconnection) loading condition, the speed improvement over the conventional ECL circuit is about 5.5 times at 1 mW/gate, and the power reduction is about 1/11 times at 1.2 ns/gate. Even with the lightest loading of FO = 1 plus $C_L = 0.01$ pF (0.02 mm metal interconnection), the LS-APD-ECL circuit outperforms the conventional ECL circuit. The speed improvement is about 2.2 times at 1 mW/gate, and the power reduction is about 1/2.8 times at 120 ps/gate.

In Fig. 3.12, measured and simulated delay versus capacitive loading for the conventional ECL, the AC-APD-ECL, and the LS-APD-ECL circuits are depicted. The AC-APD-ECL circuit is optimized for 0.5 pF loading, and therefore, for loadings heavier than 1.5 pF, the pull-down transition time degrades

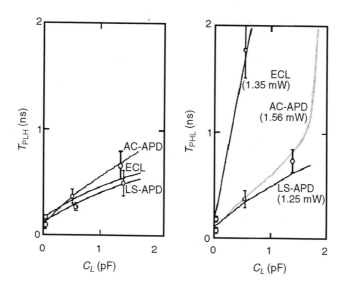

**FIGURE 3.12** Delay vs. capacitive loading for ECL (1.35 mW/gate), AC-APD-ECL (1.56 mW/gate), and LS-APD-ECL (1.25 mW/gate) circuits. AC-APD-ECL circuit is optimized for a 0.5-pF loading. Error bar indicates three times standard deviation.

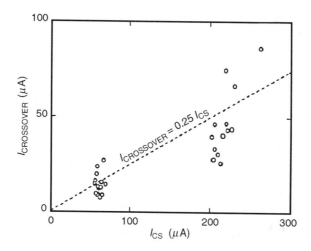

**FIGURE 3.13** Crossover current vs. $I_{CS}$ in LS-APD-ECL circuit.

rapidly. On the contrary, the LS-APD-ECL circuit offers superior load driving capability under a wide range of loading conditions. The LS-APD-ECL circuit also provides balanced pull-up and pull-down switching speed to minimize signal skews.

The measurements of $I_{SS(L)}$ versus $I_{CS}$, as plotted in Fig. 3.13, demonstrate that even under process deviation and parasitic resistance along the $V_{REG}$ lines, the $V_{REG}$ voltage generator keeps the steady-state current of the LS-APD-ECL circuits below one-fourth of $I_{CS}$.

The LS-APD-ECL circuit brings the minimum operating frequency at which ECL consumes less power than CMOS to within a range of frequencies commonly encountered in leading edge designs. Simulated power consumption versus operating frequency of sub-micron CMOS, the conventional ECL, and the LS-APD-ECL circuits are shown in Fig. 3.14. The probability of gate switching used in the simulation is 0.3, which is typically observed in VLSI circuits. The 1.2-$\mu$m LS-APD-ECL under 5 V consumes less power

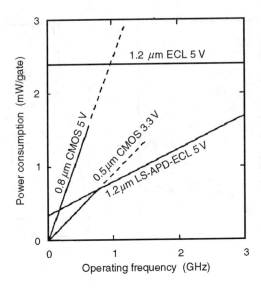

**FIGURE 3.14** Power consumption versus operating frequency of CMOS, ECL, and LS-APD-ECL circuits. The broken lines represent range of toggle frequencies of flip-flop that cannot be reached by the technology.

than 0.5 $\mu$m CMOS under 3.3 V at an operating frequency higher than 780 MHz. In case of applications with higher probability of gate switching or with an advanced bipolar technology, the crossing frequency can further be reduced.

## 3.2 Low-Voltage ECL Circuits

Demand for low-power dissipation has motivated scaling of a supply voltage of digital circuits in many electronic systems. Reducing the supply voltage of ECL circuits is becoming important not only to reduce the power dissipation but also to have ECL and CMOS circuits work and interface together, under a single power supply on a board or on a chip.

Gate stacking in ECL is effective in reducing the power dissipation because complex logic can be implemented in a single gate with fewer current sources. This, however, brings difficulty in reducing the supply voltage. Various design techniques for low-voltage ECL have been reported before [9,10], but none of them allows a use of stacked differential pairs in three levels.

In conventional ECL circuits, input signals to the stacked differential pairs are shifted down by the emitter-follower circuit to keep all the bipolar transistors out of the saturation region. $V_{IH}$ of the differential pairs in the $n$th level from the top is $-n \cdot V_{BE}$, where $V_{BE}$ is the base-emitter voltage of a bipolar transistor in the forward-active region. As illustrated in Fig. 3.15, the minimum operating power supply voltage (minimum $|V_{EE}|$) of a three-level series gating ECL circuit is $4V_{BE} + V_{CS}$, where $V_{CS}$ is the voltage drop across a tail current source. This implies that scaling $V_{BE}$ is the most effective means of reducing the minimum $|V_{EE}|$, but, in practice, $V_{BE}$ does not scale linearly with technology and has remained constant. For $V_{BE} = 0.9$ V and $V_{CS} = 0.4$ V, the minimum $|V_{EE}|$ is 4.0 V. On the other hand, the collector-emitter voltage ($V_{CE}$) of the bipolar transistors is $2V_{BE} - V_S$ ($=1.5$ V) in the top level and $V_{BE}$ ($=0.9$ V) in the second and the third levels, where $V_S$ is the signal voltage swing. $V_{CE}$ can be reduced to 0.4 V without having a transistor enter the saturation region. This $V_{CE}$ voltage headroom comes from the emitter follower circuit, shifting the signal levels down by $V_{BE}$.

Figure 3.16 illustrates a voltage level of signals in three-level series gating in a low-voltage ECL (LV-ECL) circuit [11]. In the LV-ECL circuit, the input signals to the top and the second levels are shifted up by current mode logic (CML) gates, and the input signals to the third level are directly provided. By adjusting the amount of the level shifting for the second level by a resistor $R_S$, $V_{CE}$ of the bipolar transistors is set to

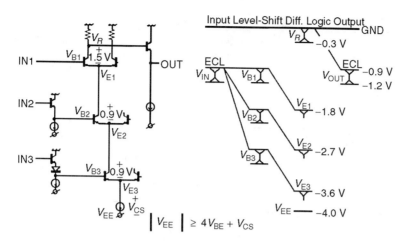

**FIGURE 3.15** Three-level series gating in conventional ECL circuit.

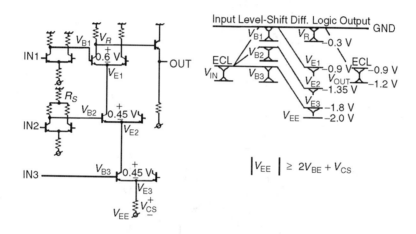

**FIGURE 3.16** Three-level series gating in low-voltage ECL (LV-ECL) circuit.

$V_{BE} - V_S$ ($=0.6$ V) in the top level and $0.5\,V_{BE}$ ($=0.45$ V) in the second and the third levels. The minimum $|V_{EE}|$ is $2V_{BE} + V_{CS}$, the same as that for a single-level ECL gate. By setting $V_{CS} = 0.2$ V, the minimum $|V_{EE}|$ of 2 V is achieved. In reality, $V_{CE}$ may be as low as 0.3 V in switching, but never stays in heavy saturation region.

A schematic of a 4:1 MUX gate and a toggle flip-flop implemented in the LV-ECL circuit is shown in Figs. 3.17 and 3.18, respectively. Since the logic stage in the LV-ECL remains the same as that in the conventional ECL, all ECL circuits can be modified as the LV-ECL circuits.

Table 3.1 compares simulated power dissipation, circuit delay, and element count of the 4:1 MUX gate in LV-ECL with those in conventional ECL. Compared to the conventional ECL, speed and area penalties are very small in the LV-ECL, because level shifting is not required for the third-level inputs, the critical path in the conventional ECL. This compensates for the delay increase in the CML level-shifter.

A number of test circuits, such as a 4:1 multiplexer, a 1:4 demultiplexer, and a 16-bit ripple carry adder, are fabricated in a 1.2 $\mu$m, 15 GHz bipolar technology to demonstrate the feasibility of the LV-ECL. As illustrated in Figs. 3.19 and 3.20, widely used architecture is used in the multiplexer and the demultiplexer. The test circuits are implemented on an existing ECL gate array to demonstrate that the LV-ECL circuit improves performance without design optimization of circuit or layout. Power dissipation, including

**TABLE 3.1**    4:1 MUX Gate Performance Comparison

|  | Min. VEE (V) | Power (mW) | Delay (ps) | PD (pJ) | Element Tran. | Count Res. |
|---|---|---|---|---|---|---|
| Conventional ECL |  |  |  |  |  |  |
|    3-level series gating | −4.0 | 5.6 | 440 | 2.46 | 29 | 9 |
|    2-level series gating | −3.1 | 9.3 | 440 | 4.14 | 45 | 21 |
| LV-ECL | −2.0 | 3.2 | 460 | 1.47 | 26 | 21 |

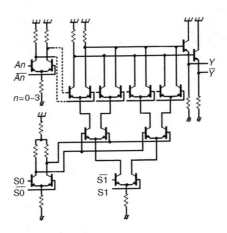

**FIGURE 3.17**    4:1 MUX gate in LV-ECL.

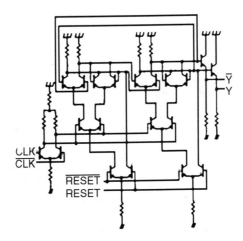

**FIGURE 3.18**    Toggle flip-flop in LV-ECL.

I/O Pads, is 60 mW for the multiplexer and 80 mW for the demultiplexer, both from −2 V power supply. The multiplexer occupies 0.132 mm$^2$, and the demultiplexer occupies 0.163 mm$^2$, both without I/O Pads. Measured eye diagrams at the outputs are also presented in Figs. 3.19 and 3.20. Figure 3.21 shows the error-free maximum operating speed of 1.65 Gb/s for the multiplexer and 1.80 Gb/s for the demultiplexer. The LV-ECL circuit tolerates ±5% variations in supply voltage with no significant degradation in speed. In these tests, a pseudo-random bit sequence of length $2^{23} - 1$ is applied at the input. $V_{OH}$ shows 1.4 mV/°C temperature dependence, the same as that in the conventional ECL. $V_{OL}$ exhibits −0.7 mV/°C over a range of 0–75°C, and 3 mV/°C for the range of 75–125°C. As a consequence, the output voltage swing is 0.17 V

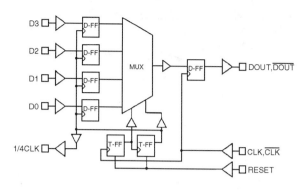

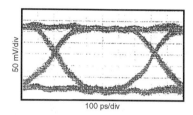

**FIGURE 3.19** 4:1 multiplexer block diagram and output eye diagram.

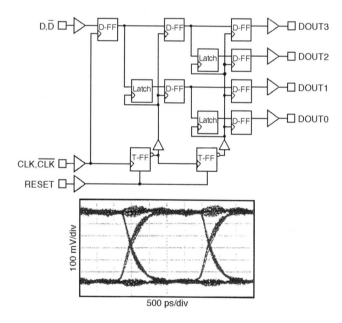

**FIGURE 3.20** 1:4 demultiplexer block diagram and output eye diagram.

at 0°C, 0.28 V at 50°C, and 0.24 V at 125°C. Bipolar transistors in the third level enter the soft saturation region above 75°C.

If minimum $|V_{EE}|$ is 2.2 V, $V_{CS}$ can be 0.4 V and a bipolar current source circuit can be used instead of the resistor to provide much higher immunity to variations in supply voltage and temperature. SPICE simulation indicates tolerance to a ±10% variations in supply voltage can be obtained and the output voltage swing is 0.3 V over the range of 0–125°C.

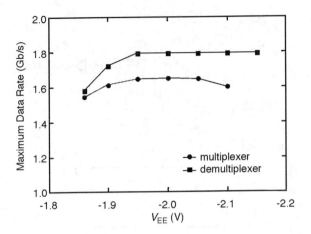

**FIGURE 3.21**    Maximum data rate vs. $V_{EE}$.

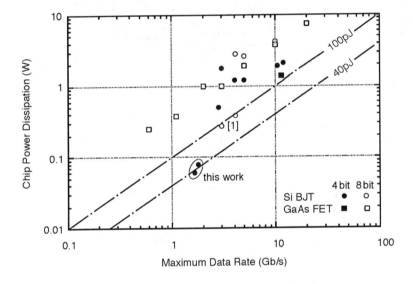

**FIGURE 3.22**    Power-delay products of multiplexers and demultiplexers.

A 8:1 multiplexer and a 1:8 demultiplexer are designed in the same manner. In SPICE simulation, the power dissipation of the 8:1 multiplexer is 84 mW and that of the 1:8 demultiplexer is 136 mW, both from −2 V power supply at the same maximum operating speed. Figure 3.22 shows that the LV-ECL circuit exhibits the lowest reported power-delay products in both 4-bit and 8-bit multiplexers and demultiplexers.

## References

1. C. T. Chuang, "Advanced bipolar circuits," *IEEE Circuits Devices Magazine,* pp. 32–36, Nov. 1992.
2. M. Usami et al., "SPL (Super Push-pull Logic): a bipolar novel low-power high-speed logic circuit," in *Symp. VLSI Circuits Dig. Tech. Papers,* pp. 11–12, May 1989.
3. C. T. Chuang et al., "High-speed low-power ac-coupled complementary push-pull ECL circuit," *IEEE J. Solid-State Circuits,* vol. 27, no. 4, pp. 660–663, Apr. 1992.
4. C. T. Chuang et al., "High-speed low-power ECL circuit with ac-coupled self-biased dynamic current source and active-pull-down emitter-follower stage," *IEEE J. Solid-State Circuits,* vol. 27, no. 8, pp. 1207–1210, Aug. 1992.

5. Y. Idei et al., "Capacitor-coupled complementary emitter-follower for ultra-high-speed low-power bipolar logic circuits," in *Symp. VLSI Circuits Dig. Tech. Papers,* pp. 25–26, May 1993.

6. T. Kuroda et al., "Capacitor-free level-sensitive active pull-down ECL circuit with self-adjusting driving capability," *IEEE J. Solid-State Circuits,* vol. 31, no. 6, pp. 819–827, June 1996.

7. T. Kuroda et al., "Automated bias control (ABC) circuit for high-performance VLSI's," *IEEE J. Solid-State Circuits,* vol. 27, no. 4, pp. 641–648, April 1992.

8. D. Gray et al., "A 51 K gate low power ECL gate array family with metal-compiled and embedded SRAM," in *Proc. IEEE CICC,* pp. 23.4.1–23.4.4., May 1993.

9. B. Razavi et al., "Design techniques for low-voltage high-speed digital bipolar circuits," *IEEE J. Solid-State Circuits,* vol. 29, no. 3, pp. 332–339, March 1994.

10. W. Wihelm and P. Weger, "2 V Low-Power Bipolar Logic," in *ISSCC Dig. of Tech. Papers,* pp. 94–95, Feb. 1994.

11. T. Kuroda et al., "1.65 Gb/s 60 mW 4:1 multiplexer and 1.8 Gb/s 80 mW 1:4 demultiplexer Ics using 2 V 3-level series-gating ECL circuits," in *ISSCC Dig. of Tech. Papers,* pp. 36–37, Feb. 1995.

# 4

# Price-Performance of Computer Technology

John C. McCallum
*National University of Singapore*

## 4.1 Introduction

When you buy a computer, you normally decide what to buy based on what the computer will do (performance) and on the cost of the computer (price). Price-performance is the normal trade-off in buying any computer.

Performance of a computer system is primarily determined by the speed of the processor. But, it may also depend on other features, such as the size of the memory, the size of the disk drives, speed of the graphics adapter, etc. You normally have a limited choice of speeds, sizes, and features that are available within an approximate price budget.

A personal computer (PC) of today is much more powerful than supercomputers of several years ago. The $5 million CRAY-1 supercomputer of 1976 [1,2] was rated at about 100–250 million floating-point operations per second (MFLOPS) in performance. A $1,400 PC in 2001 [3] has a performance of about 200–1000 MFLOPS. The price-performance improvements have been due to better computer manufacturing technologies and the large volume production of PCs, in the order of 100 million PCs compared with only 85 CRAY-1 computers produced.

The incredible improvement in performance of computers over time has meant that the price-performance trade-off normally improves dramatically even in a short period. The improvement trends have been predicted since 1965 by Moore's Law, which originally applied to the number of transistors on an integrated circuit doubling every 18 months [4]. The ability to predict the future price-performance of a computer system is often more important than knowing the current price of a computer, unless you need to buy your computer today. Therefore, the main thrust of this chapter is looking at historical price and performance trends to help predict the future.

Technologies other than processor speed have also been involved in the improving price-performance of computer systems. The capacity and cost of memory (currently using dynamic random access memory, i.e., DRAM), and the capacity and cost of magnetic disk drives are also critical. This chapter will concentrate on the price and performance of processors, memory, and storage.

**TABLE 4.1**  Selected Categories of Computers

| Start Year | Price Level $ | Computer Category | Typical Usage |
|---|---|---|---|
| 1990 | 1.0E+00 | Disposable computer | Smart cards, greeting card music generator, telephone SIMs |
| 1975 | 1.0E+01 | Embedded processor | Disk drive controller, automobile engine controller |
| 1990 | 1.0E+02 | PDA | Contact list, schedule, notes, calculator |
| 1980 | 1.0E+03 | Personal computer | Word processing, spreadsheets, email, web browsing, games |
| 1975 | 1.0E+03 | Workstation | Computer aided design and engineering, animation rendering |
| 1965 | 1.0E+03 | Minicomputer | Dedicated, or general computing for one user |
| 1985 | 1.0E+04 | Workgroup server | General computing support for a small group of people |
| 1955 | 1.0E+05 | Departmental server | Computing support for a large group (about 50–500 people) |
| 1970 | 1.0E+06 | Enterprise server | General computing support, interactive and network services |
| 1960 | 1.0E+06 | Mainframe | Corporate databases, transaction processing |
| 1970 | 1.0E+07 | Supercomputer | Nuclear weapons simulation, global challenge problems |

The changing price-performance is seen in different ways: improved performance at the same price; same performance at a lower price; or, both improved performance and improved price. A ten-fold improvement in price-performance often gives a qualitative change that results in a different product category. For example, computers can be categorized in different ways, such as those given in Table 4.1.

The price-performance of software is not discussed in this chapter. Software creation is mainly a labor-intensive activity. Therefore, the cost of creating software has been related to the cost of manpower, which is related to the rate of inflation. Some companies have outsourced software development to countries with lower labor rates, such as India. The second main factor in the cost of software is the number of people who buy a package. More sales result in lower costs for PC versions of software compared to software used on less common (bigger) computers.

## Price

The price and performance of a computer system appear to be easily definable items. But, neither price nor performance is well defined. Price is often adjusted historically for inflation. Price is often quoted in a specific currency. In global markets, changing currencies can affect pricing of components and products. In this chapter, the prices are given in United States dollars ($) and are not adjusted for inflation.

Pricing is dependant on sales factors, such as discounts, marketing agreements, customer categories, etc. The size of the market for a product is also important for costs. Quantities affect the price based on writing off of development costs over the number of units, cost of setting up production lines, setting up maintenance and training operations, etc. Generally, computers or general technologies that are produced in large quantities are cheaper at the same performance level than less popular items.

A separate but important pricing issue is the difference between the entry price and unit pricing. For example, consider big disk drives versus floppy disk drives. The low entry price of a floppy disk drive opened a new market for low performance, high unit price (dollars per megabyte, or $/MB) floppy drives. Big high-speed hard disk drives were more expensive to purchase, but were much lower in unit costs of $/MB.

Computer systems are a collection of component parts, such as the CPU, memory, storage, power supply, etc. The cost of a computer system depends on the choice of the components, which change with time [5].

## Performance

The performance of computer technology depends on what you want the computer to do. Computers that are used for text processing do not need floating-point operations. Scientific computing needs heavy floating-point computation and typically high memory bandwidth.

Standard benchmark programs often exhibit a 2:1 performance range on a single computer. One comparison of the execution times of different benchmarks run on two specific computers gave performance ratios ranging from 0.54 to 17295 [6]. Performance is also dependent on the quality of the compiler or interpreter, the algorithms used, and the actual source language programs. The sieve of Erasothenes benchmark took between 15.7 and 5115 s to run on various Z80 microprocessor systems [7]. Performance is usually based on processor performance. But, performance may be based on other features: graphics performance, sound quality, physical size, power consumption, main memory size, disk drive speed, or system configuration capability.

Speed of execution on a standard benchmark application is important for a CPU. The size in megabytes is the main measure for disk drives, although access time and data throughput are often important factors for disk drives as well. Also, nonfunctional features are often important performance features for practical computer systems. Typical nonfunctional features are: reliability, compatibility, scalability, and flexibility. These features are not as easy to measure as speed or size.

Generally, there is an upper limit to performance of a technology at any point in time: the fastest processor available, the biggest disk drive, etc. Exceeding this limit requires either the development of new technology, or parallel operation (multiple CPUs, multiple disk drives, etc.). Other constraints, such as physical size or operating power, may place an absolute upper threshold on performance. In practice, the main constraint is usually the price.

The performance of systems may be determined by marketing decisions of vendors. Rather than produce a variety of systems, a vendor may make one fast system, and slow the clock speed to produce a range of slower systems. Recently a computer vendor shipped a computer system with performance on demand—you pay to enable existing processors to be used. Thus, it may not always be possible to use the performance that is possible without paying an additional price.

## Applications

Computers in themselves are of little interest to most people. The importance is what the computer can do—the applications. A "killer app" is a computer program that causes a computer to become popular. VisiCalc, the first electronic spreadsheet program, was a killer app for the Apple II computer. Over the years there have been a number of important applications that have driven the sales of computers. Selected applications are listed in Table 4.2 [8–22].

**TABLE 4.2**  Selected Applications Driving Computer Usage and Sales

| Year | Application Category | Typical Computer | Program | Ref. |
|------|---------------------|------------------|---------|------|
| 1889 | Census tabulation | Hollerith E. T. S. | — | [8] |
| 1943 | Scientific calculations | Harvard Mark 1 | — | [9] |
| 1943 | Cryptography | Collosus | — | [10] |
| 1945 | Ballistic calculations | ENIAC | — | [11] |
| 1950 | Census analysis | UNIVAC 1 | — | [12] |
| 1951 | Real time control | Whirlwind | — | [13] |
| 1955 | Payroll | IBM 650 | — | [14] |
| 1960 | Data processing | UNIVAC II | COBOL | [15] |
| 1961 | Mass billing | IBM 1401 | — | [16] |
| 1964 | Large scale scientific computing | CDC 6600 | — | [17] |
| 1965 | Laboratory equipment control | PDP-8 | — | [18] |
| 1968 | Timeshared interactive computing | PDP-10 | TOPS-10 | [19] |
| 1970 | Email | PDP-10 | mail | — |
| 1971 | Text editing | PDP-11 UNIX | ed, roff | [20] |
| 1974 | Data base management systems | IBM 360 | IMS | [21] |
| 1975 | Video games | Commodore PET | — | — |
| 1980 | Word processing | Z-80 with CP/M | WordStar | — |
| 1980 | Spreadsheet | Apple-II | VisiCalc | — |
| 1985 | CAD/CAM | Apollo workstation | — | — |
| 1986 | Desktop publishing | Macintosh | PageMaker | — |
| 1994 | WWW browser | PC plus servers | Mosaic | [22] |
| 1997 | E-commerce | PC plus servers | Netscape | — |
| 1999 | Realistic rendered 3D games | PC | Quake | — |
| 2000 | Video capture and editing | iMAC | iMovie | — |

Applications normally change with time, as customers demand new features. Adding new features expands the size and usually slows the speed of the application. But, since hardware performance normally improves much more than the loss of speed due to new features, the overall application performance generally improves with time.

The characteristics of the main applications determine the important performance features for the supporting hardware technology. General-purpose computers must be capable of performing well on a variety of applications. Embedded systems may run only a single application. Business systems may require fast storage devices for transaction processing. Generally, however, fast speed, low cost, big memory and storage, and small physical size tend to be important for most applications.

## 4.2 Computer and Integrated Circuit Technology

Computers have used a variety of technologies: mechanics, electrical relays, vacuum tubes, electrostatics, transistors, integrated circuits, magnetic recording, and lasers. Changing technologies have allowed improved price-performance, resulting in faster speed, larger memories, smaller physical size, and lower cost. The main technologies where price-performance has increased dramatically are in processor performance, memory, and storage size.

The driver of current price-performance improvements is complementary metal oxide semiconductor (CMOS) integrated circuit production technology [23]. An integrated circuit starts as a $300 slice of poly-silicon crystal. After processing, a 300 mm wafer is worth about $5000, but may contain several hundred circuits, depending on the size of the circuit. The price of a specific circuit is dependant mainly on the size of the circuit. The size and complexity of the circuit are the main factors determining the yield of the circuit. Many circuits do not function properly due to impurities in the wafer or due to defects in the manufacturing process.

CMOS circuits make up the majority of all circuits for processors. Some special processes are required for producing specific types of circuits, such as memory chips, analog circuits, opto-electronic components, and ultra-high speed circuits. However, CMOS has become the main production technology over the last 20 years [24]. CMOS technology has improved significantly with time and will continue to improve over the next several years with some effort [25,26]. Wafer sizes have grown, and the sizes of features (line widths) on the circuit have been reduced. The speed and cost of CMOS circuits improve with smaller line sizes. As the feature size decreases by the scaling factor $\alpha$, the gate area and chip size decrease by $\alpha^2$, the speed increases (the gate delay decreases) by a factor of $\alpha$, and the power decreases by a factor of $\alpha$ [23]. These scaling rules have been used for some time. However, with the small features sizes used now, other effects also limit the speed. Table 4.3 shows selected features about the improvement of integrated circuits over time [25–36].

**TABLE 4.3** Integrated Circuit Process Improvement with Time

| Year | Process | Chip Size (mm) | Features (microns) | Wafer (mm) | Sample IC | Clock | Metal Layers |
|------|---------|----------------|--------------------|------------|-----------|-------|--------------|
| 1958 | Planar | — | 100 | — | First IC | — | — |
| 1961 | — | 1.5 × 1.5 | 25 | 25 | First silicon IC | — | — |
| 1966 | — | 1.5 × 1.5 | 12 | 25 | SSI | — | — |
| 1971 | pMOS | 2.5 × 2.5 | 10 | 50 | i4004 | .74 MHz | 1 |
| 1975 | pMOS | 5 × 5 | 8 | 75 | i8080 | 2 MHz | 1 |
| 1978 | nMOS | 5 × 5 | 5 | 75 | Z-80 | 4 MHz | 1 |
| 1982 | HMOS | 9 × 9 | 3 | 100 | i8088 | 8 MHz | 1 |
| 1985 | HMOS | 12 × 12 | 1.50 | 125 | i286 | 10 MHz | 2 |
| 1990 | HCMOS | 12 × 12 | 0.80 | 150 | MC68040 | 25 MHz | 3 |
| 1995 | CMOS | 12 × 12 | 0.50 | 150 | Pentium | 100 MHz | 4 |
| 2000 | CMOS | 15 × 15 | 0.25 | 200 | Pentium-III | 1 GHz | 6 |
| 2001 | CMOS | 15 × 15 | 0.18 | 300 | Pentium-4 | 1.5 GHz | 7 |
| 2005 | CMOS | 22 × 22 | 0.10 | 300 | — | 4 GHz | 8 |
| 2010 | CMOS | 25 × 25 | 0.06 | 300 | — | 10 GHz | 9 |
| 2015 | CMOS | 28 × 28 | 0.03 | 450 | — | 25 GHz | 10 |

The improvements in line widths, chip sizes, and speed should continue for several years. The International Roadmap for Semiconductors [36] outlines the expected improvements in technology. Samsung has already demonstrated a 4-GB DRAM chip [37]. Current fast production CMOS integrated circuit processes use line widths of 0.18 $\mu$m and are moving to 0.13 $\mu$m [38].

## 4.3 Processors

Early processors were based on mechanical devices. Later electro-mechanical relays were used to build computing devices [9]. Electronic digital computers were developed using vacuum tubes in the mid 1940s [10,11]. Transistors took over in early 1960s because of higher reliability, smaller size, and lower power consumption [17]. In the late 1960s, standard integrated circuits started to become available and were used in place of discrete transistors [19]. Integrated circuits allowed a high density of transistors, resulting in faster computers with lower price, lower power consumption, and higher reliability due to improved interconnections. The increasing complexity of integrated circuits, as outlined by Moore's Law, allowed building ever increasingly complex microprocessors since the early 1970s [29].

Processors have become categorized by application and particularly by cost and speed. In the 1970s, the main categories were: microcomputers, minicomputers, mainframes, and supercomputers. About 1990, the fastest microprocessors started to overtake the fastest processors in speed. This has meant that new categories are often used, as almost all computer systems are now microprocessors or collections of microprocessors.

The performance of processors is based mainly on the clock speed and the internal architecture. The clock speed depends primarily on the integrated circuit process technology. Internal pipelining [39], superscalar operation [40], and multiprocessor operation [41] are the main architectural improvements. RISC processors simplified the internal processor structure to allow faster clock operation [42,43]. Internal code translation has allowed complex instruction sets to execute as sets of micro-operations with RISC characteristics. The goal of architectural improvements has been to improve performance, measured by the execution time of specific programs. The execution time equals the instruction count times the number of clock cycles per instruction (CPI) divided by the clock speed. RISC processors increased the instruction count, but improved the CPI, and allowed building simpler processors with faster clock speeds. Fast processors became much faster than the memory speed. Cache memory is used to help match the slower main memory with the faster CPU speed. Increased processor performance comes with increased complexity, which is seen as increased number of transistors on the processor chip. In current processor chips, the on-chip cache memory is sometimes larger than the processor core. Future processor chips are likely to have multiple processor cores and share large on-chip caches.

Processors have been designed to operate on various word sizes. Some early computers worked with decimal numbers or variable-sized operands. Most computers used different numbers of binary digits; 4, 8, 12, 18, and 36 bits were used in some computers. Most current computers use either 32 bits or 64 bits word-lengths. The trend is toward 64 bits, to allow a larger addressing range. Comparing the performance of different word-length computers may be difficult. Smaller word-lengths allow faster operation in a cheap processor with a small number of transistors and minimal internal wiring. But, processors with more address bits allow building larger and more complex programs, and allow easy access to large amounts of data. A common pitfall of designing general purpose computers has been to provide too small an address space [43]. Generally, word size and addressing space of processors have been increasing with time, driven roughly by the increasing complexity of integrated circuits.

Early microprocessors had small 4 or 8 bit word-lengths (see Table 4.4). The size of the early integrated circuits limited the number of transistors and thus word-length. The very cheapest current microprocessors use small word-lengths to minimize costs. The most powerful current general purpose microprocessors have 64 bit word-lengths, although the mass market PCs still use 32 bit processors. Table 4.4 shows some of the features of selected Intel microprocessors [32,34,35,44,45].

The fastest processors are now microprocessors. The latest Pentium 4 processor (in March 2001) has a clock speed of 1.5 GHz. The distance that light travels in one clock cycle at 1.5 GHz (667 ps) is about 20 cm.

**TABLE 4.4**   Features of Selected Intel Microprocessors

| Year | Processor | Transistors | Die Size (sq. mm) | Cache on Chip | Bits | Line Width (microns) | Clock (MHz) | Perf. (MIPS) |
|------|-----------|-------------|-------------------|---------------|------|----------------------|-------------|--------------|
| 1971 | i4004 | 2.30E+03 | 12 | 0 | 4 | 10 | 0.108 | 1.5E−03 |
| 1972 | i8008 | 3.50E+03 | — | 0 | 8 | 10 | 0.2 | 3.0E−03 |
| 1975 | i8080A | 6.00E+03 | 14 | 0 | 8 | 6 | 2 | 2.8E−02 |
| 1978 | i8086 | 2.90E+04 | — | 0 | 16 | 3 | 10 | 5.7E−01 |
| 1982 | i286 | 1.34E+05 | — | 0 | 16 | 1.50 | 12 | 1.3E+00 |
| 1985 | i386DX | 2.75E+05 | — | 0 | 32 | 1.00 | 16 | 2.2E+00 |
| 1989 | i486DX | 1.20E+06 | — | 8K | 32 | 1.00 | 25 | 8.7E+00 |
| 1993 | Pentium | 3.10E+06 | 296 | 8KI/8KD | 32 | 0.80 | 66 | 6.4E+01 |
| 1995 | Pentium Pro | 5.50E+06 | 197 | 8KI/8KD | 32 | 0.35 | 200 | 3.2E+02 |
| 1997 | Pentium II | 7.50E+06 | 203 | 16KI/16KD | 32 | 0.35 | 300 | 4.5E+02 |
| 1999 | Pentium III | 9.50E+06 | 125 | 16KI/16KD | 32 | 0.25 | 500 | 7.1E+02 |
| 2000 | Pentium IIIE | 2.80E+07 | 106 | 16KI/16KD+256K | 32 | 0.18 | 933 | 1.7E+03 |
| 2000 | Pentium 4 | 4.20E+07 | 217 | 12KI/8KD+256K | 32 | 0.18 | 1500 | 2.5E+03 |
| 2001 | Itanium | 2.50E+07 | — | 16KI/16KD+96K+4M | 64 | 0.18 | 800 | 2.6E+03 |

Electric signals are slower than light. This means that the dimensions that a signal must travel within a clock cycle are very small, and almost certainly must be within a single integrated circuit package to achieve results within a single cycle.

Computer systems, which exceed the processing performance of the fastest microprocessor, must use multiple processors in parallel. Multiple processors on a single chip are starting to appear [46]. PCs with multiple processors are becoming more frequent, and many operating systems support multiprocessor operation. The largest computers [47] are collections, or clusters of processors.

## Measuring Processor Performance

No single number can accurately represent the performance of a processor. But, there is a need to have such a number for general comparisons [48].

Processor performance was originally measured by the time required to add two numbers [49,50]. In 1966, Knight [51] built a more complex model to compare 225 computers starting with the Harvard Mark I. He generated performance measures for scientific applications and for commercial applications and calculated price-performance information. His plots showed the improving price-performance with time. Other early approaches to measuring performance included benchmarks, synthetic programs, simulation, and the use of hardware monitors [52].

Standard benchmark programs started to become popular for estimating performance with the creation of the Whetstone benchmark in 1976 [53,54]. Other benchmark programs were widely used, such as Dhrystone for integer performance [55] and the sieve of Eratosthenes [7] for simple microprocessor performance.

Computerworld reported computer system performance and prices for many years [56–69]. The company's tables reported performances compared systems with standard computers, such as the IBM 360/50 [56,57] or IBM 370/158-3 [58–66]. The IBM 370/158-3 was roughly a 1 million instructions per second (MIPS) machine. MIPS and MFLOPS were widely used as performance measures. But, MIPS and MFLOPS are not well regarded due to the differences in what one instruction can perform on different systems. Even the conversion between thousands of operations per second (KOPS) and MIPS is fuzzy [70].

The Standard Performance Evaluation Corporation was set up as a nonprofit consortium to develop good benchmarks for computing applications [71]. The initial CPU performance benchmark, the SPECmark89, used the VAX 11/780 performance as the base rating of 1 SPECmark. The benchmark consisted of several integer and floating point oriented application program sections, selected to represent typical CPU usage. The SPECmark was a geometric mean of the ratios of execution time taken on the target machine compared with the base machine (VAX 11/780). This was an excellent quality benchmark for measuring CPU performance. Extensive lists of SPECmark89 results were reported [72]. Over time, people optimized their compilers to get uncharacteristically good performance from some parts of the benchmark. The SPEC consortium then created a new pair of benchmarks, SPECint92 and SPECfp92, using new application program code. The cpu92 benchmarks measured typical integer performance, typical of system programming and office uses of computers, and floating point performance typical of scientific computing. These benchmarks also used the VAX 11/780 = 1 as the base machine. As well, base and rate versions of the cpu92 benchmarks were defined. The base measures required using a single setting for the compilers for running the benchmarks, rather than optimizing the compiler for each component program. The rate benchmarks measured the throughput of the computer by running multiple copies of the programs and measuring the completion time. SPECrate is a good measure of performance for a multiprocessor system. Extensive results are available for SPECint92, SPECfp92, SPECint_base92, SPECfp_base92, SPECint_rate92, SPECfp_rate92, SPECint_rate_base92, and SPECfp_rate_base92 [73].

SPEC released new versions of the CPU benchmarks in 1995 and in 2000 [71]. The new benchmark versions were created for two main reasons: to ensure that compiler optimizations for the older versions did not mask machine performance and to use larger programs that would exercise the cache memory hierarchy better. SPECint95 and SPECfp95 use the Sun SPARCstation 10/40 as the base machine instead of the VAX 11/780. Extensive results have been collected for the SPECcpu95 benchmarks [74]. The SPECcpu2000 benchmarks are relative to a 300-MHz Sun Ultra5_10, which is rated as 100 [71]. SPECcpu2000 results, which include base and peak versions of cint and cfp with the rate results, are listed at the SPEC Web site [75]. The difference in base machines among the SPECcpu benchmarks makes direct comparisons of performance difficult. However, the SPECcpu benchmarks are the best measures available for general processor performance.

Many other benchmarks exist and are used for comparing performance: SPEC has many other benchmarks [76]; LINPAC [77] is used for comparing very large computers; STREAM [79] compares memory hierarchy performance; the Transaction Processing Council [80] has created several benchmarks for commercial applications; etc. The main advice to people buying computers is to use the actual application programs that they will be running to evaluate the performance of computer systems. But, some standard number to describe system performance is always a good starting point. Table 4.5 lists the performance and price for several selected computer systems over time. Note that the performance ratings should only be used as a rough indicator, and should not be used to directly compare specific machines. Similarly, the prices may correspond to very different configurations of machines.

The performance estimates have been normalized to a single comparison number for each computer. The number is a rough MIPS estimate, where a VAX 11/780 is considered to be a 1-MIPS processor. Estimates of prices were available for over 300 systems. Price-performance ratios were calculated in MIPS per dollar. These are plotted against the year and are shown in Fig. 4.1. The data in Fig. 4.1 and Table 4.5 were calculated from many sources [1,12,13,16,17,19,47,49,51,56–75,81–97].

## 4.4 Memory and Storage—The Memory Hierarchy

The memory hierarchy includes the registers internal to the processor, various levels of cache memory, the main memory, virtual memory, disk drives (secondary storage), and tape (tertiary storage). Memory devices are used for a variety of functions. Basically, any computer system needs a place from which a program with its data is executed. There is a need for storing program files and data files. Files need to be backed up, with the ability to move the backup files to another location for safety. A mechanism is needed to support the distribution of programs and data files. Not all devices are suitable for all functions. Some devices are used mainly to get an increase in performance. The remaining functions are generally necessary for general-purpose computer systems, and some device must be selected to implement each function. Table 4.6 lists the storage functions, and several categories of memory and storage device used over time to implement the functions. For example, nonvolatile memory cartridges could be used for all of the storage functions necessary for a computer system, if speed, capacity, and price were satisfactory.

**TABLE 4.5**  Price and Performance of Selected Processors 1945–2001

| Year | Processor | Price $ | Performance (MIPS) | Clock (MHz) | Microprocessor | Bits | Ref. |
|------|-----------|---------|--------------------|-------------|----------------|------|------|
| 1945 | ENIAC | 487,000 | 1.8E−05 | — | | — | [81] |
| 1951 | UNIVAC I | 900,000 | 1.9E−04 | 2.3 | | — | [12,13] |
| 1954 | IBM 650 | 145,000 | 1.8E−04 | — | | — | [49] |
| 1956 | UNIVAC 1103A | 1,260,000 | 1.8E−03 | — | — | 36 | [49] |
| 1960 | IBM 7090 | 2,300,000 | 6.7E−02 | — | — | 36 | [49] |
| 1961 | IBM 1401 | 270,000 | 9.0E−04 | — | — | — | [49] |
| 1964 | CDC 6600 | 2,700,000 | 5.4E+00 | 10.0 | 10 PPU 12 bit | 60 | [17,83] |
| 1965 | IBM 360/50 | 270,000 | 1.4E−01 | 2.0 | — | 32 | [16,97] |
| 1965 | PDP-8 | 18,000 | 1.3E−03 | 0.6 | — | 12 | [19,82] |
| 1968 | PDP-10 (KA10) | 500,000 | 2.0E−01 | 1.0 | — | 36 | [19] |
| 1971 | PDP-11/20 | 5,200 | 5.7E−02 | 3.6 | — | 16 | [19] |
| 1972 | IBM 370/145 | 700,000 | 4.5E−01 | 4.9 | — | 32 | [56,97] |
| 1975 | Altair 8800 | 395 | 2.8E−02 | 2.0 | i8080 | 8 | — |
| 1977 | IBM 370/158-3 | 2,000,000 | 7.3E−01 | 8.7 | — | 32 | [56,97] |
| 1978 | Apple II | 1,445 | 2.3E−02 | 1.0 | MOS 6502 | 8 | [84] |
| 1978 | CRAY-1 | 8,000,000 | 8.6E+01 | 80.0 | — | 64 | [1,83] |
| 1978 | VAX 11/780 | 500,000 | 1.0E+00 | 5.0 | — | 32 | [82] |
| 1980 | IBM 3031 | 1,455,000 | 7.3E−01 | 8.7 | — | 32 | [56] |
| 1981 | OsbornE-1 | 1,795 | 5.7E−02 | 4.0 | Z-80 | 8 | [85] |
| 1981 | IBM 4341 | 288,650 | 6.0E−01 | 33.0 | — | 32 | [60,97] |
| 1983 | IBM PC/XT | 4,995 | 2.5E−01 | 4.8 | i8088 | 16 | [86] |
| 1984 | Apple Macintosh | 2,500 | 5.0E−01 | 8.0 | MC68000 | 16 | [87] |
| 1985 | IBM PC/AT | 4,950 | 6.4E−01 | 6.0 | i286 | 16 | [88] |
| 1985 | VAX 8600 | 350,000 | 4.2E+00 | 12.5 | — | 32 | [82] |
| 1987 | Dell PC Limited 386-16 | 4,499 | 2.2E+00 | 16.0 | i386DX | 32 | [89] |
| 1989 | Sun Sparcstation 1 | 8,995 | 1.0E+01 | 20.0 | SPARC | 32 | — |
| 1990 | DEC VAX 6000-410 | 175,300 | 6.8E+00 | 36.0 | NVAX | 32 | [69] |
| 1990 | DEC VAX 6000-460 | 960,000 | 3.9E+01 | 36.0 | NVAX | 32 | [69] |
| 1990 | Dell System 425E | 7,899 | 8.7E+00 | 25.0 | i486DX | 32 | [90] |
| 1991 | HP 9000/730 | — | 7.8E+01 | 66.0 | HP-PA7000 | 32 | — |
| 1991 | Dell 433P | 2,999 | 1.1E+01 | 33.0 | i486DX | 32 | [91] |
| 1993 | Dell XPS-P60 | 2,999 | 6.2E+01 | 60.0 | Pentium | 32 | [92] |
| 1993 | Digital 7000-610 | 500,000 | 1.6E+02 | 200.0 | Alpha 21064 | 64 | — |
| 1995 | Sun SPARCserver 1000 × 8 | 200,000 | 4.7E+02 | 50.0 | SuperSPARC | 32 | — |
| 1995 | Dell Dimension XPS-P133c | 2,699 | 1.4E+02 | 133.0 | Pentium | 32 | [93] |
| 1995 | Dell Latitude XPi P75D | 2,499 | 1.2E+02 | 100.0 | Pentium | 32 | [93] |
| 1996 | Intel ASCI Red | 46,000,000 | 1.9E+06 | 333.0 | P-II Xeon core | 32 | [47] |
| 1997 | Digital 8400-5/350 × 6 | 600,000 | 2.3E+03 | 350.0 | Alpha 21164 | 64 | — |
| 1997 | Dell Dimension XPS D266 | 2,499 | 3.5E+02 | 266.0 | Pentium-II | 32 | [94] |
| 1998 | Sun Ultra Enterprise 450 × 4 | 50,000 | 2.2E+03 | 300.0 | UltraSPARC-II | 64 | — |
| 1999 | Sun Ultra Enterprise 10000 | 2,000,000 | 4.8E+04 | 400.0 | UltraSPARC-II | 64 | — |
| 1999 | Dell Dimension XPS T | 1,599 | 1.2E+03 | 600.0 | Pentium-IIIE | 32 | [95] |
| 1999 | Compaq DS20 × 1 | 20,000 | 1.7E+03 | 500.0 | Alpha 21264 | 64 | — |
| 2001 | Dell Dimension 8100 | 1,699 | 2.3E+03 | 1,300.0 | Pentium-4 | 32 | [96] |
| 2001 | Dell Dimension 4100 | 1,299 | 1.7E+03 | 933.0 | Pentium-IIIE | 32 | [96] |
| 2001 | Dell Inspiron 3800 | 1,299 | 1.2E+03 | 700.0 | Pentium-IIIE | 32 | [96] |
| 2001 | Sun Blade 1000 × 2 | 10,000 | 4.2E+03 | 900.0 | UltraSPARC-III | 64 | — |
| 2001 | Compaq GS320 × 32 | 1,000,000 | 5.8E+04 | 733.0 | Alpha 21264 | 64 | — |
| 2001 | Itanium | — | 2.6E+03 | 800.0 | Itanium | 64 | est. |

The price-performance characteristics of different memory and storage technologies help determine their roles in computer systems. The main trade-off is between access time and cost (measured in $/MB). Figure 4.2 shows a rough 2001 pricing (in $/MB) of various memory and storage media versus access time. Both the media cost and access times of devices generally improve with time. But, the main improvements are in the cost of storage capacity with time.

**TABLE 4.6**  Functions of Memory and Storage Devices

| Device | Speedup | Program Data | Program Code | Temporary File | File Storage | Program Storage | Off-Site Backup | Distribution |
|---|---|---|---|---|---|---|---|---|
| CPU registers | yes | yes | maybe | no | no | no | no | no |
| Cache memory | yes | yes | yes | no | no | no | no | no |
| Main memory | no | yes | yes | yes | no | no | no | no |
| Nonvolatile RAM | no | yes | yes | yes | maybe | maybe | no | no |
| Disk cache | yes | no | no | maybe | no | no | no | no |
| Hard disk | no | no | no | yes | yes | yes | no | no |
| Solid-state disk | yes | no | no | yes | no | no | no | no |
| RAM disk | yes | no | no | yes | no | no | no | no |
| ROM cartridge | maybe | no | no | no | no | yes | no | yes |
| NVRAM cartridge | no | yes | yes | yes | yes | yes | yes | yes |
| Floppy disk | no | no | no | yes | yes | yes | yes | yes |
| Disk cartridge | no | no | no | yes | yes | yes | yes | yes |
| Tape cartridge | no | no | no | maybe | yes | yes | yes | yes |
| Tape library | yes | no | no | maybe | yes | yes | yes | yes |
| Punch cards | no | no | no | maybe | maybe | maybe | yes | maybe |
| Paper tape | no | no | no | maybe | maybe | maybe | yes | yes |
| Audio cassette | no | no | no | maybe | yes | yes | yes | yes |
| CD-ROM | no | no | no | no | no | no | no | yes |
| CD-R | no | no | no | no | maybe | maybe | yes | yes |
| Optical disk (MO) | no | no | no | yes | yes | yes | yes | yes |

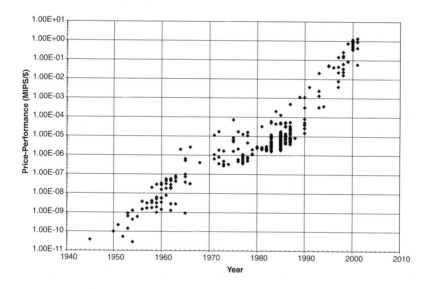

**FIGURE 4.1**  Increasing price-performance with time.

## Primary Memory

Primary memory is made up of the main memory and cache hierarchy. The role of cache memory is to match the fast speed of the processor to the slower main memory. In earlier processors, there was little speed mismatch. Recent microprocessors are much faster than main memory, and the speed mismatch is growing [79]. Cache memory is much more expensive per byte than main memory, but is much faster. In the memory hierarchy, the important speed factor for cache memory is the latency or access time. The cache needs to keep the CPU's instruction queue and data registers filled at the speed of the CPU. For bulk main memory, the important speed factor is bandwidth, to be able to keep the cache memory filled. To accomplish this, the slower main memory normally uses a wide data path to transfer data to the cache. Most recent microprocessors

**TABLE 4.7**   Cost of Selected Memory Devices

| Year | Device | Size (bits) | Cost ($) | Cost ($/MB) | Speed (ns) |
|------|--------|-------------|----------|-------------|------------|
| 1943 | Relay | 1 | — | — | 100,000,000 |
| 1958 | Magnetic drum (IBM650) | 80,000 | 157,400 | 1.7E+07 | 4,800,000 |
| 1959 | Vacuum tube flip-flop | 1 | 8.10 | 6.8E+07 | 10,000 |
| 1960 | Core | 8 | 5.00 | 5.2E+06 | 11,500 |
| 1964 | Transistor flip-flop | 1 | 59.00 | 4.9E+08 | 200 |
| 1966 | I.C. flip-flop | 1 | 6.80 | 5.7E+07 | 200 |
| 1970 | Core | 8 | 0.70 | 7.3E+05 | 770 |
| 1972 | I.C. flip-flop | 1 | 3.30 | 2.8E+07 | 170 |
| 1975 | 256 bit static RAM | 256 | — | — | 1000 |
| 1977 | 1 Kbit static RAM | 1,024 | 1.62 | 1.3E+04 | 500 |
| 1977 | 4 Kbit DRAM | 4,096 | 16.40 | 3.4E+04 | 270 |
| 1979 | 16 Kbit DRAM | 16,384 | 9.95 | 5.1E+03 | 350 |
| 1982 | 64 Kbit DRAM | 65,536 | 6.85 | 8.8E+02 | 200 |
| 1985 | 256 Kbit DRAM | 262,144 | 6.00 | 1.9E+02 | 200 |
| 1989 | 1 Mbit DRAM | 1,048,576 | 20.00 | 1.6E+02 | 120 |
| 1991 | 4 M x 9 DRAM SIMM | 37,748,736 | 165.00 | 3.7E+01 | 80 |
| 1995 | 16 MB ECC DRAM DIMM | 150,994,944 | 489.00 | 2.7E+01 | 70 |
| 1999 | 64 MB PC-100 DIMM | 536,870,912 | 55.00 | 8.6E−01 | 60/10 |
| 2001 | 256 MB PC-133 DIMM | 2,147,483,648 | 88.00 | 3.4E−01 | 45/7 |
| 2002 | 1 Gbit chip | 1,073,741,824 | — | — | — |
| 2005 | 4 Gbit chip | 4,294,967,296 | — | — | — |

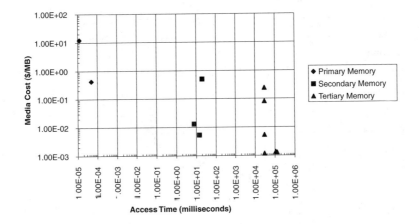

**FIGURE 4.2**   Memory device characteristics.

use multiple levels of cache to smooth the speed mismatch. Memory system design for multiprocessor systems is complicated by needs of coherent cache and memory consistency [43]. Current fast processors can lose in the order of one half of their performance due to the imperfect behavior of the memory system.

Main memory in electronic digital computers began as flip-flops implemented using vacuum tubes. Other early memory devices were mercury ripple tank, electrostatic tube storage, and magnetic drum storage (IBM 650). Magnetic core memory was developed in the Whirlwind project and was cost effective for a long period, until integrated circuit RAM devices replaced core memory in the late 1970s.

Static RAM, which is used for cache memories, normally uses 4–8 transistors to store 1 bit of information. Dynamic RAM, which is used for bulk main memory, normally uses a single transistor and a capacitor for each bit. This results in DRAM being much cheaper than SRAM. SRAM was used in some early microcomputers because the design of small memories was much easier than using DRAM.

The speed of memory has been improving with time. But, the improvements have been much slower. Table 4.7 shows the cost and access times (speed) of selected memory devices over time. New versions

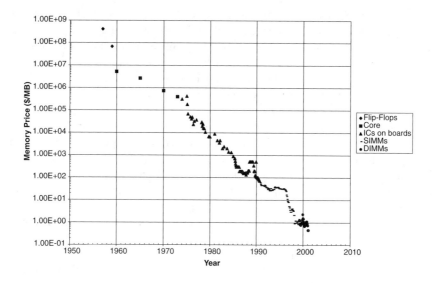

**FIGURE 4.3**   Cost of memory with time.

of DRAM memory devices have been developed to improve on both bandwidth and latency. Standard DRAM has progressed through fast-page mode (FPM) DRAM, to extended-data out (EDO) DRAM, to synchronous SDRAM, RAMBUS, dual-data rate (DDR), DDR2, and quad data rate (QDR). The newer synchronous designs attempt to maximize the bandwidth per pin so that fast high bandwidth transfers of data are possible from main memory to the cache memory.

The price of memory has dropped dramatically with time. At the same time, the size of memory in computer systems has grown. The cost of the memory used in a typical 2001 PC (64 MB) would have cost about $10 million in 1975. Figure 4.3 shows the decreasing cost of memory (in $/MB) over time.

The data for Fig. 4.3 and Table 4.7 come from several sources. Phister [14] gives data for early computers up to the mid 1970s. Memory prices were collected from advertisements in various magazines through different periods: *Radio-Electronics* (1975–78), *Interface Age* (1979–1983), BYTE (1984–1997), and *PC Magazine* (1997–2001). The magazines were scanned to find the lowest price per bit for memory mounted on boards, or SIMMs, or DIMMs for easy installation in a computer system. Summaries of recent data are harder to collect because advertisements with price information have mainly moved to the Internet, where historical information is not retained.

Note the small increases in memory prices in 1988, 1994, and again in 2000 in Fig. 4.3. The short-term rises in the price of memory were unexpected, because in the long term the improvement in integrated circuit technology keeps forcing the price down. Thus, short term memory pricing can be difficult to predict. But, longer term pricing is fairly predictable. It takes several years for new memory chip generations to move from the laboratory to mass production. Currently, 256 Mbit memory chips are production devices. But, a prototype 4 Gbit DRAM memory chip was constructed by Samsung [37], using a 0.10-$\mu$m process with an overall size of 643 mm$^2$. Production 4 Gbit memory chips are likely after 2005.

## Secondary Memory

The size of secondary memory has also increased dramatically, as the price of disk storage dropped. The first hard disk drive was the IBM 305 RAMAC developed in 1956. It held a total of 5 MB on fifty 24-in. disk platters. Fixed disk drives allowed fast access to data and were much cheaper per byte than using fixed head magnetic drum memories. Next, removable pack disk drives were developed. Removable disk packs had low cost per byte based on media cost. But, the high cost of the drive meant that cost of the online files were higher. The relative advantages and disadvantages of removable pack drives versus fixed disk drives meant that removable packs were widely used in the 1960s and 1970s. Fixed disk drives became more common after the mid 1970s, mainly due to their lower cost of storage.

The main performance factor for disk drives is the cost of storage in dollars per megabyte. Data is stored in circular tracks on disk surfaces. The more bits per inch along the track and the more tracks per inch across the surface, the higher the storage capacity of the disk surface [98]. Adding more disk platters, with two surfaces per platter, increases the storage capacity of the drive.

The main measures of speed are: seek time, rotation speed, and data transfer rate. The seek time is the time to move the read/write head to the track. The rotation speed determines the time for the disk to rotate to the start of the data. The maximum media transfer rate is the speed at which the data is read from the disk, which depends on the rotational speed and the density of bits along the track. Several other factors affect the operational speed of a disk drive. These include: head settling time; head switching time; disk controller performance; internal disk cache size, organization, and management; disk controller interface; and data access patterns (random versus sequential access).

Disk drive development currently concentrates on improving the density of information on the disk drive, increasing the rotational speed of the disk platters, speeding up the motion of the read/write heads, improving the disk cache performance, and speeding up the disk transfer rate with faster controllers.

Early large computer disk drive technology improved by a factor of 10 in price per megabyte about every 11 years [5] compared with about five years for main memory. But, the cost of disk drive units was high [99]. Floppy disk drives dramatically reduced the entry level cost for magnetic storage, although the unit cost ($/MB) was high. The development of small hard disk drives for the PC accelerated the rate of improvement in price-performance.

Early disk drives were about 1000 times cheaper per megabyte than main memory. Recent disk drives are about 20–50 times cheaper than main memory. Figure 4.4 shows the improving in the cost of disk capacity with time. Table 4.8 gives characteristics for selected hard disk drives. The data for Fig. 4.4 and Table 4.8 are taken from several sources. Phister [14] provides disk price and performance data for early disk drives. Pricing data for floppy disk drives and more recent hard disk drives were collected from advertisements in *Interface Age* magazine (1979–1984), BYTE (1983–1997), and *PC Magazine* (1997–2001). The advertisements were scanned periodically to find the lowest cost capacity. Technical specification for many drives were taken from the Tech Page Web site [100] and Web sites for Maxtor [101] and IBM [102].

RAID technology improved the number of random input–output operations that could be performed per second (IOPS) [43]. RAID also improved the reliability for collections of small standard disk drives compared with large system disk drives. Large system disk drives have generally been replaced with standard small, high capacity, high performance 3.5 in. disk drives. These are used singly in desktop

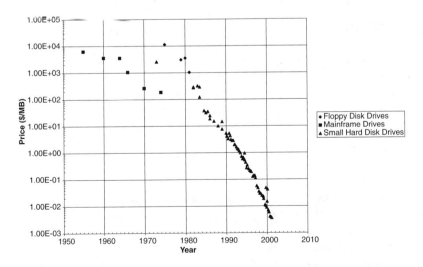

**FIGURE 4.4** Disk drive cost with time.

**TABLE 4.8**  Disk Drive Characteristics over Time

| Year | Device | Interface Type or Feature | Size (MB) | Disk Size (in.) | Heads/ Platters | Rotation Speed (rpm) | Avg. Seek Time (ms) | Max. Transfer Rate (MB/s) | Cost ($) |
|---|---|---|---|---|---|---|---|---|---|
| 1956 | IBM 350 RAMAC | Vacuum tube control | 5 | 24.00 | 1/50 | 1,200 | 475.0 | 0.010 | 57,000 |
| 1960 | IBM 1405-2 | — | 20 | 24.00 | 1/50 | 1,790 | 600.0 | 0.020 | 48,500 |
| 1963 | IBM 1311-2 | Removable | 2 | 14.00 | -/5 | 1,500 | 250.0 | 0.050 | 16,510 |
| 1964 | IBM 2311-1 | Removable | 7 | 14.00 | -/5 | 2,400 | 85.0 | 0.145 | 25,510 |
| 1966 | IBM 2314 | Removable | 29 | 14.00 | 20/10 | 2,400 | 75.0 | 0.292 | 30,555 |
| 1970 | IBM 3330-1 | Removable | 100 | — | 20/10 | 3,600 | 30.0 | 0.782 | 25,970 |
| 1974 | IBM 3330-11 | Removable | 200 | — | 20/10 | 3,600 | 30.0 | 0.782 | 37,000 |
| 1981 | Seagate ST-412 | 5 in. full height MFM | 10 | 5.25 | 4/2 | 3,600 | 85.0 | 0.625 | 369 |
| 1981 | Seagate ST-506 | 5 in. full height MFM | 5 | 5.25 | 4/2 | 3,600 | 85.0 | 0.625 | 1,350 |
| 1982 | Digital RM05 | Removeable | 256 | 14.00 | 19/10 | 3,600 | 30.0 | 1.200 | — |
| 1985 | Seagate ST-225 | 5 in. half height MFM | 20 | 5.25 | 4/2 | 3,600 | 65.0 | 0.625 | 695 |
| 1985 | Digital RA81 | UDA fixed, dual path | 464 | 14.00 | 7/4 | 3,600 | 28.0 | 2.200 | — |
| 1987 | Digital RA82 | UDA fixed, dual path | 622 | 14.00 | — | 3,600 | 20.0 | 2.400 | — |
| 1988 | Seagate ST138 | 3.5 in. MFM | 32 | 3.50 | 6/3 | 3,600 | 40.0 | 0.625 | 429 |
| 1989 | Seagate ST-277 | 5 in. half height RLL | 66 | 5.25 | 6/3 | 3,600 | 40.0 | 0.938 | 449 |
| 1990 | Miniscribe 9380E | 5 in. full height ESDI | 338 | 5.25 | 15/8 | 3,600 | 16.0 | 1.250 | 1,795 |
| 1990 | Digital RA92 | UDA fixed, dual path | 1,500 | 9.00 | — | 3,400 | 16.0 | 2.800 | — |
| 1991 | Maxtor 9380E | 5 in. full height ESDI | 338 | 5.25 | 15/8 | 3,600 | 16.0 | 1.250 | 695 |
| 1993 | Maxtor Panther P117S | 5 in. full height SCSI | 1,503 | 5.25 | 19/10 | 3,600 | 13.0 | 3.613 | 1,459 |
| 1994 | Seagate ST12550 | Barracuda 7200 rpm | 2,139 | 3.50 | 19/10 | 7,200 | 8.5 | 7.063 | 1,999 |
| 1995 | Seagate ST410800N | 5 in. full height SCSI | 9,090 | 5.25 | 27/14 | 5,400 | 11.5 | 8.125 | 2,399 |
| 1999 | Seagate ST317242A | 3.5 in. ATA-4 | 17,245 | 3.50 | 8/4 | 5,400 | 9.8 | 23.500 | 175 |
| 2000 | Maxtor M94098U8 | 3.5 in. Ultra DMA 66 | 39,082 | 3.50 | 16/8 | 5,400 | 9.0 | 36.900 | 279 |
| 2000 | IBM DSCM-11000 | 1 in. 1 GB microdrive | 1,000 | 1.00 | -/1 | 3,600 | 12.0 | 7.488 | 499 |
| 2001 | Maxtor 98196H8 | 3.5 in. Ultra DMA 100 | 81,964 | 3.50 | 16/8 | 5,400 | 9.0 | 46.700 | 295 |
| 2001 | IBM Ultrastart 73LZX | Ultra160 SCSI | 73,400 | 3.50 | 12/6 | 10,000 | 4.9 | 87.125 | — |

personal computers and in multiple drive configurations with RAID controllers in large computer systems. Smaller drives were developed for portable laptop computers, mainly 2.5-in. drives and 1-in. drives for smaller PDA and portable devices. However, solid-state flash memory cartridges are starting to replace small capacity disk drives. Although they are more expensive per megabyte, they have a lower entry price, are physically smaller than disk drives, and are more rugged for portable operation. Currently, 3.5-in. hard disk drives are the main production drives with the best price and performance characteristics.

## Tertiary Memory

Tertiary storage is used mainly for backing up files and for transportation and distribution of programs and data. The major concern here is for storage for file backup and restore. Magnetic tape is the main storage medium used for tertiary storage. However, punched cards, paper tape, removable disk packs, and optical disks have been used. Packaged magnetic tape cartridges are the most popular format of tape for backup.

Backup includes frequently incremental and full backup copies created in a backup pattern [103]. Often there may be 20–40 tapes retained in a backup cycle for a single file system. Media cost is therefore very important. It can take a few hours to read or write one tape cartridge. Therefore, transfer speed of data from the computer to the tape is also important. After creating a backup tape, it is useful to verify that the tape was written correctly. It is necessary to remember that the reason for making a backup is to be able to restore the data at some future time.

IBM created the IBM 701 tape drive in 1952. Reel-to-reel tapes were popular until about 1990. Helical scan cartridges and linear scan tape cartridges became popular about that time. Early QIC tapes had similar storage cost to magnetic tape drives. Later, Exabyte 8-mm tape drives and 4-mm digital audio tape (DAT) cartridges were used for low-cost storage. The digital linear tape (DLT) cartridge became the most popular backup tape format. Similar to 8 mm, DAT, and other tape formats, DLT has undergone a number of revisions to increase the tape capacity and to improve the data throughput rate. The latest SuperDLT has a capacity of 113 GB on one cartridge and a throughput rate of 11 MB/s (about three hours to write one tape). The main consideration is that a backup tape system must keep pace with the increase in storage capacity of disk drives. The other device types listed in Table 4.6 for backup have generally not met the low cost of media required for large-scale backup.

## 4.5   Computer Systems—Small to Large

A typical general-purpose computer system consists of a processor, main memory, disk storage, a backup device, and possibly interface devices such as a keyboard and mouse, graphics adapter and monitor, sound card with microphone and speakers, communications interface, and a printer. The processor speed is normally used to characterize the system—a 1.5 GHz Pentium-4 system, etc. But, the processor is only a portion of the cost of the system [5]. Using a slightly faster processor will likely cause little change in the performance seen by the owner of a personal computer, but is important for a multiuser server.

General-purpose desktop PCs for single users are common. PCs are cheap because millions are produced per year by many competing vendors. Millions of portable laptops, notebooks, and PDA devices are also sold every year. Currently, the laptops and notebooks are more expensive than desktop computers because of a more expensive screen and power management requirements. Workstations are similar to personal computers, but are produced in smaller quantities, with better reliability and packaging. Workstations are more expensive than PCs primarily due to the smaller quantities produced.

Servers have special features for supporting multiple simultaneous users, such as more rugged components, ECC memory, swappable disk and power supplies, and a good backup device. They normally have some method of adding extra processors, memory, storage, and I/O devices. This means more components and more expensive components than in a typical PC. There is extra design work required for the extra features even if not used, and there are fewer servers sold than PCs. Thus, servers of similar capability will be more expensive.

In large servers, reliability and expandability are very important, because several hundred people may be using them at any time. Designing very high-speed interconnect busses to support cache coherence across many processors sharing common memory is expensive. Special bus interconnect circuitry is required for each board connecting to the system. Large servers are sold in small quantities, and the design costs form a large percentage of the selling price. Extensive reliability testing means that the large servers are slower to use the latest, fastest CPUs, which may be the same as are used in PCs and workstations. Additional processors or upgraded processors may directly increase the number of users that can be supported, making the entire system more valuable. Often, chip manufacturers charge double the price for the fastest CPU they produce, compared with a 10% lower speed CPU. People pay the premium for the overall system performance upgrade, particularly in the server market.

Another approach to improving computer system performance is to cluster a few computers [104]. Cooperative sharing and fail-over is one type of cluster that provides enhanced reliability and performance. Other clusters are collections of nodes with fast interconnections to share computations. The TOP500 list [47] ranks the fastest computer systems in the world based on LINPACK benchmarks. The top entries contain many thousand processors.

Beowulf clusters [105] use fairly standard home PCs to form affordable supercomputers. These clusters scale in peak performance roughly with price. But, like most cluster computers, they are difficult to program for obtaining usable performance on real problems.

An interesting approach to low-cost computational power is to use the unused cycles from under-utilized PCs. The SETI@home program distributed client programs to PCs connected to the Internet to allow over 2 million computers to be used for computations that were distributed and collected by the SETI program [106]. SETI@home is likely the largest distributed computation problem in existence and forms the largest computational system.

## 4.6  Summary

The performance of computer systems has increased dramatically over time, and it is likely to continue for many years. The price of computers has dropped in the same period, both generally and for entry-level systems. These price-performance improvements have created new opportunities for low-cost applications of computers, and created a market for millions of PCs per year.

Price and performance are not easy to define except in specific applications. We can generally predict approximate price and performance levels of general-purpose computers and their main components. But, the predictions based on historical trends and current estimates are subject to large variations. The actual performance of a computer depends on what the user wants the computer system to do, and how well, or how fast the computer does that task. The price depends on the circumstances of the purchase.

It is usually possible to trade-off price for performance and vice-versa within ranges. You can buy a faster processor up to a point. Beyond the maximum speed, it is necessary to use multiple processors to obtain more performance. The optimal price-performance for a computer system is likely to be what the majority of people are buying (an entry-level PC), bought only when it is necessary to use it. For bigger systems, use collections of shared memory or distributed microprocessors. Alternatively, for SETI@home, use other people's computers.

## References

1. Russel, R. M., The CRAY-1 Computer System, in *Computer Structures: Principals and Examples,* Siewiorek, D. P., Bell, C. G., and Newell, A., Eds., McGraw-Hill, New York, 1982, Chap. 44.
2. Data General, Cray-1, http://www.dg.com/about/html/cray-1.html, March 2001.
3. Dell, advertisement, *PC Magazine,* 20(8), C4, April 24, 2001.
4. Moore, G. E., The Continuing Silicon Technology Evolution Inside the PC Platform, *Intel Platform Solutions,* 2, 1, October 15, 1997, archived at http://developer.intel.com/update/archive/issue2/feature.htm.
5. Touma, W. R., *The Dynamics of the Computer Industry: Modeling the Supply of Workstations and Their Components,* Kluwer, Boston, 1993.
6. Perkin-Elmer, The benchmarks prove it, *Computerworld,* 66, March 17, 1980.
7. Gilbreath, J., and Gilbreath, G., Eratosthenes Revisited, *Byte,* 283, January, 1983.
8. Hollerith, H., An Electric Tabulating System, in *The Origins of Digital Computers,* 2nd ed., Randell, B., Ed., Springer-Verlag, Berlin, 1973, Chap. 3.1.
9. Aiken, H. H., Proposed Automatic Calculating Machine, in *The Origins of Digital Computers,* 2nd ed., Randell, B., Ed., Springer-Verlag, Berlin, 1973, Chap. 5.1.
10. Michie, D., The Bletchley Machines, in *The Origins of Digital Computers,* 2nd ed., Randell, B., Ed., Springer-Verlag, Berlin, 1973, Chap. 7.3.
11. Mauchly, J. W., The Use of High Speed Vacuum Tube Devices for Calculating, in *The Origins of Digital Computers,* 2nd ed., Randell, B., Ed., Springer-Verlag, Berlin, 1973, Chap. 7.4.
12. Eckert, J. P. Jr., et al., The UNIVAC System, in *Computer Structures: Readings and Examples,* Bell, C. G., and Newell, A., Eds., McGraw-Hill, New York, 1971, Chap. 8.
13. Redmond, K. C., and Smith, T. M., *Project Whirlwind,* Digital Press, Bedford, MA, 1980.
14. Phister, M. Jr., *Data Processing Technology and Economics,* Santa Monica Publishing Co., Santa Monica CA, 1976.
15. Sammet, J. E., *Programming Languages: History and Fundamentals,* Prentice-Hall, Englewood Cliffs, NJ, 1969.
16. Bell, C. G., and Newell, A., The IBM 1401, in *Computer Structures: Readings and Examples,* McGraw-Hill, New York, 1971, Chap. 18.
17. Thornton, J. E., Parallel Operation in the Control Data 6600, in *Computer Structures: Readings and Examples,* Bell, C. G., and Newell, A., Eds., McGraw-Hill, New York, 1971, Chap. 39.
18. Bell, C. G., and Newell, A., The DEC PDP-8, *Computer Structures: Readings and Examples,* McGraw-Hill, New York, 1971, Chap. 5.

19. Bell, C. G., Mudge, J. C., and McNamara, J. E., *Computer Engineering: A DEC View of Hardware Systems Design,* Digital Press, Bedford, MA, 1978.

20. Salus, P. H., *A Quarter Century of UNIX,* Addison-Wesley, Reading, MA, 1994.

21. Martin, J., *Principles of Data-Base Management,* Prentice-Hall, Englewood Cliffs, NJ, 1976.

22. Dougherty, D., Koman, R., and Ferguson, P., *The Mosaic Handbook for the X Window System,* O'Reilly & Associates, Sebastopol, CA, 1994.

23. Weste, N. H. E., and Eshraghian, K., *Principles of CMOS VLSI Design,* Addison-Wesley, Reading, MA, 1985.

24. Taur, Y. The incredible shrinking transistor, *IEEE Spectrum,* 36(7), 25, July 1999.

25. Herrell, D., Power to the package, *IEEE Spectrum,* 36(7), 46, July 1999.

26. Zorain, Y., Testing the monster chip, *IEEE Spectrum,* 36(7), 54, July 1999.

27. Moore, G. E., Progress in Digital Integrated Electronics, in *VLSI Technology Through the 80s and Beyond,* McGreivy, D. J., and Pickar, K. A., Eds., IEEE Computer Society Press, 1982, 41.

28. McGreivy, D. J., VLSI chip trends—size, complexity, cost, in *VLSI Technology Through the 80s and Beyond,* McGreivy, D. J., and Pickar, K. A., Eds., IEEE Computer Society Press, 1982, 31.

29. Bayko, J., Great Microprocessors of the Past and Present (V 11.7.0), in *Computer Information Centre,* http://bwrc.eecs.Berkeley.edu/CIC/archive/cpu_history.html, February 2000.

30. Mukherjee, A., *Introduction to nMOS and CMOS VLSI Systems Design,* Prentice-Hall, Englewoods Cliffs, NJ, 1986.

31. Mead, C., and Conway, L., *Introduction to VLSI Systems,* Addison-Wesley, Reading, MA, 1980.

32. Burd, T., General Processor Information, in *Computer Information Centre,* http://bwrc.eecs.Berkeley.edu/CIC/local/summary.pdf, January 10, 2001.

33. Harned, N., Ultralight lithography, *IEEE Spectrum,* 36(7), 35, July 1999.

34. ChipGeek, Processor specs, http://www.ugeek.com/procspec/procspec.htm, March 2001.

35. Intel, Processor Hall of Fame, http://www.intel.com/intel/museum/25anniv/hof/hof_main.htm.

36. International Technology Roadmap 2000 Update Overall Roadmap Technology Characteristics, http://public.itrs.net/Files/2000UpdateFinal/ORTC2000final.pdf, 2000.

37. Yoon, H., et al., A 4Gb DDR SDRAM, *ISSCC 2001,* 44, 378, 2001.

38. Intel, Intel hits key milestone—yields first silicon from industry's most advanced 0.13 micron, 300 mm wafer fab, Intel press release, http://www.intel.com/pressroom/archive/releases/20010402corp.htm, March 28, 2001.

39. Kogge, P. M., *The Architecture of Pipelined Computers,* Hemisphere Publishing (McGraw-Hill), New York, 1981.

40. Johnson, *Superscalar Microprocessor Design,* Prentice-Hall, Englewood Cliffs, NJ, 1991.

41. Satyanarayan, M., *Multiprocessors. A Comparative Study,* Prentice-Hall, Englewood Cliffs, NJ, 1980.

42. Slater, M., *Understanding RISC Microprocessors,* Ziff-Davis Press, Emeryville, CA, 1993.

43. Hennessy, J. L., and Patterson, D. A., *Computer Architecture A Quantitative Approach,* 2nd. ed., Morgan Kaufmann, San Francisco, CA, 1996.

44. Offerman, A., Chiplist 9.9.5, http://einstein.et.tudelft.nl/~offerman/chiplist.html, July 1998.

45. Intel, Intel Microprocessor Quick Reference Guide, http://www.intel.com/pressroom/kits/processors/quickreffam.htm, 2001.

46. Nishi, N., et al., A 1 GIPS 1W single-chip tightly-coupled four-way multiprocessor with architecture support for multiple control flow execution, *ISSCC 2000,* 43, 418, 2000.

47. TOP500, The top 500 computers, http://www.top500.org, November 2000.

48. Smith, J. E., Characterizing computer performance with a single number, *Communications of the ACM,* 31(10), 1202, 1988.

49. Adams, C. W., A chart for EDP experts, *Datamation,* November/December 1960, 13, 1960.

50. Statland, N., Computer characteristics revisited, *Datamation,* November 1961, 87, 1961.

51. Knight, K. E., Changes in computer performance, *Datamation,* September 1966, 40, 1966.

52. Lucas, H. C., Performance evaluation and monitoring, *Computing Surveys,* 3(3), 79, 1971.

53. Curnow, H. J., and Wichmann, B. A., A synthetic benchmark, *The Computer Journal*, 19(1), 43, February 1976.

54. Price, W. J., A benchmark tutorial, *IEEE Micro*, October 1989, 28, 1989.

55. Weicker, R. P., Dhrystone: a synthetic systems programming benchmark, *Communications of the ACM*, 27(10), 1013, October 1984.

56. Lundell, E. D., Two CPUs stretch IBM 30 series, *Computerworld*, 11(41), 1, October 10, 1977.

57. Computerworld, IBM, Amdahl, Itel: how they stack up now, *Computerworld*, 11(42), 4, October 17, 1977.

58. Rosenberg, M., and Lundell, E. D., IBM and the compatibles: how they measure up, *Computerworld*, January 8, 1979, 10, 1979.

59. Computerworld, After the IBM 4300 announcement, *Computerworld*, July 16, 1979, 10, 1979.

60. Henkel, T., IBM mainframes and the plug compatibles, *Computerworld*, July 13, 1981, 12, 1981.

61. Henkel, T., Other mainframers' systems, *Computerworld*, July 13, 1981, 15, 1981.

62. Henkel, T., Superminis, an alternative, *Computerworld*, July 13, 1981, 17, 1981.

63. A comparison of the IBM Syste/38 and the 4300 line, *Computerworld*, January 11, 1982, 11, 1982.

64. Mainframes and compatibles, *Computerworld*, 17(32), 30, August 8, 1983.

65. Henkel, T., The superminis, *Computerworld*, 17(32), 37, August 8, 1983.

66. IBM mainframes and plug compatibles, *Computerworld*, August 19, 1985, 24, 1985.

67. Hardware roundup: large systems; special purpose systems; medium scale systems, *Computerworld*, September 21, 1987, S8, 1987.

68. Hardware roundup: small systems, *Computerworld*, September 27, 1987, S4, 1987.

69. Late-model minicomputers, *Computerworld*, September 24, 1990, 83, 1990.

70. Lias, E. J., Tracking the elusive KOPS, *Datamation*, November 1980, 99, 1980.

71. Henning, J. L., SPEC CPU2000: measuring CPU performance in the new millennium, *IEEE Computer*, 33(7), 28, July 2000.

72. DiMarco, J., SPECmark table v2.20, ftp://ftp.cdf.toronto.edu/pub/spectable, April 1994.

73. DiMarco, J., SPECmark table v5.26, ftp://ftp.cdf.toronto.edu/pub/spectable, January 1996.

74. DiMarco, J., SPECmark table v5.208, ftp://ftp.cs.toronto.edu/pub/jdd/spectable, December 2000.

75. SPEC, All SPEC cpu2000 results published by SPEC, http://www.spec.org/osg/cpu2000/results/cpu2000.html, March 2001.

76. Standard Performance Evaluation Corporation, http://www.spec.org, March 2001.

77. Dongara, J. J., Performance of Various Computers Using Standard Linear Equations Software, http://www.netlib.org/benchmark/performance.ps, March 12, 2001.

78. The Performance Database Server, http://performance.netlib.org/performance/html/PDStop.html, January 2001.

79. McCalpin, J. D., STREAM: Sustainable memory bandwidth in high performance computers, http://www.cs.virginia.edu/stream, March 2001.

80. Transaction Processing Council, http://www.tpc.org, March 2001.

81. Moye, W. T., ENIAC: The army-sponsored revolution, http://ftp.arl.army.mil/~mike/comphist/96summary/, February, 2001.

82. Bell, C. G., Towards a history of (personal) workstations, pp 4–47, in *A History of Personal Workstations*, Goldberg, A., Ed., ACM Press, New York, 1988.

83. Siewiorek, D. P., Bell, C. G., and Newell, A., *Computer Structures: Principals and Examples*, McGraw-Hill, New York, 1982, part 3 section 4.

84. Apple, advertisement, *Interface Age*, 3(7), 24, July 1978.

85. Fox, T., Challenge for the computer industry, *Interface Age*, 6(7), 6, July 1981.

86. Product highlights, *Interface Age*, 8(7), 16, July 1983.

87. Thompson, C. J., Mac and Lisa, *Interface Age*, 9(7), 86, July 1984.

88. IBM, advertisement, *Byte*, 10(7), 174, July 1985.

89. Dell, PC's Limited advertisement, *Byte,* 12(8), 142, July 1987.

90. Dell, advertisement, *Byte,* 15(7), C2, July 1990.

91. Dell, advertisement, *PC Magazine,* 10(22), C4, December 31, 1991.

92. Dell, advertisement, *PC Magazine,* 12(22), C3, December 21, 1993.

93. Dell, advertisement, *PC Magazine,* 14(22), C4, December 19, 1995.

94. Dell, advertisement, *PC Magazine,* 16(22), C4, December 16, 1997.

95. Dell, advertisement, *PC Magazine,* 18(22), C4, December 14, 1999.

96. Dell, advertisement, *PC Magazine,* 20(5), C3, March 6, 2001.

97. Bell, C. G., et al., The IBM System/360, System/370, 3030, and 4300: A series of planned machines that span a wide performance range, in *Computer Structures: Principals and Examples,* McGraw-Hill, New York, 1982, Chap. 52.

98. Teja, E. R., *The Designer's Guide to Disk Drives,* Reston Publishing, Reston, VA, 1985.

99. Lecht, C. P., *The Waves of Change,* McGraw-Hill, New York, 1977.

100. The Tech Page, http://www.thetechpage.com, March, 2001.

101. Maxtor, http://www.maxtor.com, March, 2001.

102. IBM, Table of all IBM hard disk drives, http://www.storage.ibm.com/techsup/hddtech/table.htm, March, 2001.

103. Preston, W. C., *Unix Backup & Recovery,* O'Reilly & Associates, Sebastopol, CA, 1999.

104. Pfister, G. F., *In search of clusters,* 2nd ed., Prentice-Hall, Englewood Cliffs, NJ, 1998.

105. The Beowulf Project, http://www.beowulf.org, April, 2001.

106. Korpela, E., et al., SETI@home: Massively distributed computing for SETI, *Computing in Science & Engineering,* 3(1), 77, January/February 2001.

# II

# Computer Systems and Architecture

# 5

# Computer Architecture and Design

**Jean-Luc Gaudiot**
*University of Southern California*

**Siamack Haghighi**
*Intel Corporation*

**Binu Matthew**
*University of Utah*

**Krste Asanovic**
*MIT Laboratory for Computer Science*

**Manoj Franklin**
*University of Maryland*

**Donna Quammen**
*George Mason University*

**Bruce Jacob**
*University of Maryland*

## Introduction

### Jean-Luc Gaudiot

It is a truism that computers have become ubiquitous and portable in the modern world: Personal Digital Assistants, as well as many various kinds of mobile computing devices are easily available at low cost. This is also true because of the ever increasing presence of the Wide World Web connectivity. One should not forget, however, that these life changing applications have only been made possible by the phenomenal advances that have been made in device fabrication and more importantly in the architecting of these individual components into powerful systems.

In the 1980s, advances in computer architecture research were most pronounced on two fronts: on the one hand, new architectural techniques such as RISC made their appearance and revolutionized single processor design and allowed high performance for the single chip microprocessors which first came out as system components in the 1970s. At the same time, large-scale parallel processors became mature and could be used by researchers in many high-end, computationally intensive, scientific applications.

In recent times, the appetite of Internet surfers has been fueling the design of architectures for powerful servers: in Section 5.1 "Server Computer Architecture," Siamack Haghighi emphasizes the unique requirements of server design and identifies the characteristics of their applications.

In Section 5.2, Binu Matthew describes the VLIW (Very Long Instruction Word) processor model, compares it to more traditional approaches of Instruction Level Parallelism extraction, and demonstrates the future of VLIW processors, particularly in the context of multimedia applications.

Similarly, multimedia applications have promoted a dual architectural approach. In Section 5.3 "Vector Processing," Krste Asanovic traces the ancestry of vector processors to the supercomputers of the 1980s (Crays, Fujitsu, etc.) and describes the modern applications of this architecture model.

Architectures cannot be evaluated independently of the underlying technology. Indeed, nowadays, while deep-submicron design rules for VLSI circuit are allowing increasing numbers of devices on the same chip, techniques of multiprocessing are seeing additional applications in different forms which range from Networks Of Workstations. Portability, all the way to multiprocessing on a chip, is the topic of Section 5.4 "Multithreading, Multiprocessing," by Manoj Franklin.

Taking concurrent processing to the next level, Donna Quammen surveys parallel systems in Section 5.5 "Survey of Parallel Systems," including large-scale tightly coupled parallel processors.

Finally, in Section 5.6 "Virtual Memory Systems," Bruce Jacob surveys the concepts underlying virtual memory systems and describes the tremendous advances this approach has undergone since first being proposed in the late 1960s.

# 5.1   Server Computer Architecture

*Siamack Haghighi*

## Introduction

Widespread availability of inexpensive Internet access and powerful computers has resulted in considerable business productivity improvement. Electronic automation of business operations and Internet communication has resulted in many profitable electronic or "e" business models such as e commerce. The cost-saving potential has required many modern companies to automate their traditional manual customer interface operations and processing through Web technologies. Businesses rely on enterprise information technology (IT) computing and communication infrastructure as a backbone for their operations. It is estimated that the current e-commerce revenues exceed hundreds of billions of dollars in the U.S. alone.

Availability of robust, reliable, secure, and cost-effective IT infrastructure is one of the key drivers of the new Internet-based businesses. Customer usage models and applications also affect IT infrastructure performance, operation, and cost. IT infrastructure hardware and software requirements can be met cost effectively with client–server computing paradigm. Although not a new idea, availability of inexpensive high performance microprocessors, scalable computing and storage systems, and high bandwidth networks make client–server computing model an ideal fit. Shared data storage and backup, infrastructure cost, reliability, serviceability, and availability are some of the other reasons for adoption of client–server computing. Powerful central processing units (CPU), reliable and available memory system, scalable input/output (I/O), advanced software, and services and packaging are some of the elements of servers. This chapter will highlight some of the architecture, design, deployment, usage model, and application of servers.

## Client–Server Computing

Client–server computing was developed to address cost-effective computing and communication capability. Clients use low cost terminals to make service requests from servers. In this manner, server costs and services are shared between all users and minimized. Figure 5.1 depicts client–server information processing model.

In late 1970s and early 1980s, business computing and communication infrastructure needs were met via one or more centralized mainframes connected to user terminals via networks. Figure 5.2 illustrates this model. In most cases, client low-computing-need program processes are executed on the terminals while mainframe servers execute the more expensive request-handling programs. The mainframe servers provided a centralized resource for most computing needs as well as other tasks such as data storage, external network interfaces, and task management. In late 1980s and early 1990s, the enterprise IT evolved due to advent of personal computers (PCs) fueled by the availability of inexpensive powerful microprocessors. In the new IT infrastructure, many of the tasks previously provided by the servers were processed locally by the PCs.

In late 1990s and now, explosive growth of Internet as the common communication medium has resulted in yet another change to the IT infrastructure. Due to advent of World Wide Web (WWW) and other related technologies, many e-commerce businesses electronically automate customer request processing. Some of the characteristics of the new environment are:

- Simple and robust user interfaces (typically Web-based services) for customer entry request entry and response display
- High-speed networks for data transmission
- Powerful centralized systems to handle data storage, transaction processing, and inventory management

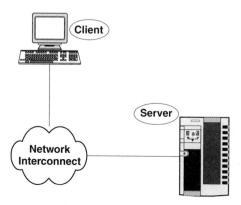

**FIGURE 5.1**  Client and server model.

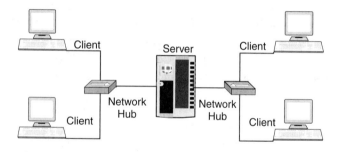

**FIGURE 5.2**  Computing and communication infrastructure.

## Server Types

Servers are optimized for cost, performance, support, and the usage model. An e-commerce transaction-processing server will require fast network interface for quick user response, powerful central processing unit (CPU) to handle database management, and scalable architecture for possible future enhancements. An e-commerce server needs to be reliable and secure, without securing issues such as fraud, to ensure good customer experience. A variety of servers such as proxy, Web cache, data processing, communication, video, file, and compute are used.

A server needs to be optimized for most frequently used applications and the usage model. Typical server configurations have several high performance CPUs, large system memory size, and support for high-speed I/O for storage systems and network interfaces. As an example, a file server is cost-optimized by using several CPUs, high-speed network interface and extensive storage subsystems. Using more powerful CPUs than a file server and large amount of system memory are the optimizations used for a compute server. A compute server may be further optimized to run specific applications such as transaction processing. Configuration of the hardware elements and software tuning are used to ensure peak performance and lowest-cost infrastructure.

## Server Deployment Considerations

Optimal server deployment requires many requirements. For example, Internet service providers' (ISP) servers have extensive communication network capabilities. In this section, some of these issues will be detailed.

### Server Features

A term commonly used to address many of the physical issues in server design is reliability, availability, and serviceability (RAS). RAS and other elements are:

1. Reliability: Customers expect reliable and robust services continually. Providing Internet services to customers such as banking and brokerage services requires special consideration. During business hours, if server goes offline, the revenue loss and potential liability may be significant. The majority of servers include various forms of reliability detecting and enhancing features. Alternatively, multiply redundant server configurations can be used to improve reliability of the infrastructure. Many application and operating system software providers include reliability features for their server products. Failure prevention solutions include:
   - Reducing probability of a failure through additional hardware and software features (some of the techniques used are independent operating system images on each server node and error correcting code (ECC) hardware features)
   - Minimizing the effect of failures by designing hardware and software robustness features such as fault isolation and provisioning
   - ECC memory scrubbing to detect and correct single bit errors that cause system crash due to accumulation of soft memory errors
   - System management interrupts handlers that allow special software to interface with hardware error detection and fault isolation independent of the underlying operating system
   - High performance and fault tolerant storage architectures such as redundant array of independent disks (RAID) are used to ensure data and operational integrity.

2. Availability: With the rapid growth of electronic businesses, companies need to ensure that their systems are running 24 h everyday. Some business server's downtime costs are in the order of millions of dollars. Traffic capacities beyond the system capability and component failures are two of the many sources of system failure. Modern servers are designed to accommodate ever-increasing traffic and system capacity by using more extensive I/O capability, powerful CPUs, and large system memory. Online management systems are also used to ensure system resources are not exhausted or overdriven. Using duplicate resources such as power supplies, CPU, and even multiply redundant

servers can mitigate component failures. Capability to quickly detect and remedy failures need to be included in various server hardware and software elements. Scheduled maintenance and upgrade of hardware and software elements can also ensure availability of servers.

3. Serviceability: Uninterrupted operation of business servers requires frequent and routine services before a fault occurs. Built-in failure prevention mechanisms include real-time diagnostic tools and alerting services to quickly and easily identify and resolve faults. New features such as hot plug and play also improves ease of service. Hot add allows installation of new hardware without interrupting server power. Hot replace allows changing faulty subsystems without needing to power down a server. Other services such as scheduled down time to do off-line enhancement are also used.

4. Scalability: High performance IT infrastructure can be scaled in two ways. One way is to deploy systems with more CPUs and more powerful I/O capability. The second way is to connect multiple servers using clustering technology. A combination of both approaches is also used.

5. Manageability: Issues that need to be addressed are:

   - Monitoring performance and tuning key applications and systems
   - Planning for capacity expansion for new users or services
   - Automatic or manual load balancing, distribution, and task scheduling for efficient operation of the enterprise resources and applications
   - Handling situations requiring increased alerting and management capabilities
   - Installation and configuration of system and services are rapid and easy to do (this is especially important for tasks such as system management, recommendation, and application of software and hardware upgrades)
   - Using notification and preventive action to keep system up and performing optimally
   - Recovering rapidly from service outages
   - Remote or local server management, even when part of the system may not be functioning.

6. Security: In routine and emergency cases, user access to system resources and facilities such as user authentication, intrusion detection, and privileged access needs to be provided. Cryptographic technologies such as encryption and decryption are frequently used to enhance overall system security. In many cases, cooperation with local and government officials may be required as part of intrusion prevention and detection.

## Operation

Additional operational issues also need consideration. Some of these factors are: Space: Many servers are modularly built. A typical server board contains several CPUs, system interconnect chipset, and other peripherals. Data centers, for example, may house several hundred server modules housed in cabinets or racks. Physical sizing of racks as well as maintenance and management of wiring to a server is a major challenge. The proximity of data center to major customer sites also needs to be considered. The overall cost of operating a data service center housing server needs to comprehend all these overheads as part of the economy of the provided service. Other considerations may include packaging of servers based on space requirements such as provision for high-density servers (large number of CPUs and I/O).

1. Power: A typical server board requires several hundred watts of power. Providing power to a server rack containing modular servers is a challenge. Power provisioning includes inclusion of services for proper handling of outage, uninterrupted power supply, or backup battery operation.

2. Thermal: Server modules generate large amounts of heat. Large server installations need to properly plan and accommodate heat generation and dissipation issues. In many cases, thermal constraints are the limiter for server capacity expansion. Other infrastructure costs such as air conditioning services to handle heat dissipation may also be prohibitive. Since thermal issues are rapidly expanding, most new servers have specialized technologies to lower power consumption. Development of low-power CPUs and chipsets that do not require active cooling are examples of technologies that aim to address thermal issues.

### Total Cost of Ownership

Another consideration, in the selection of enterprise servers, is the total cost of ownership or TCO. This metric is used to capture the cost of the IT infrastructure including operation, hardware and software purchases, services and downtimes. It is quite possible that for some enterprise application one or more of these factors becomes dominant. For example, in business critical online brokerage services, downtimes may be in the order of millions of dollars per hour. Evaluation of downtime costs versus other costs may easily justify the cost of additional and backup servers. In such a case, server clustering is used to improve TCO.

### Server Clustering

Many business applications such as manufacturing, financial, healthcare, and telecommunication require mission or business critical servers for their operation. An example is telecommunication billing and record keeping. Mission critical servers are designed with two or more servers physically connected to provide automated fail over. If one server crashes, the other servers can take over, keeping key applications running. Server clustering can be used to mitigate hardware (servers, storage arrays, networking hardware), operating system and cluster software, database, other application and human error failures. A variety of hardware and software automatic fault detection, isolation, and fail-over mechanisms are needed and used by various server manufacturers in the development of mission critical servers.

## Server Architecture

In this section, some of the more generic hardware, software server architecture design issues will be detailed. The hardware and software interaction and usage model issues will also be discussed.

### Hardware Architecture

Even though it is possible to build servers from full custom very large scale integrated (VLSI) devices or chips, economic issues govern use of commodity hardware whenever possible. Figure 5.3 illustrates common server hardware architecture. The main building block components in a server are the CPU, system memory, system bus, system interconnection or bridging devices, and peripheral subsystems.

### *CPU*

Most servers contain several CPUs. For economy reasons, many servers choose to use CPUs readily available such as those used in desktop PCs or workstations. A high performance server CPU contains very fast execution capability. Multiple processors can be built using variety of mechanisms. The most popular multiprocessor (MP) architecture is symmetric multiprocessor (SMP). Figure 5.4 illustrates this architecture. SMP systems use several CPUs interconnected through a common system bus to access shared system resources such as system memory and the peripherals.

Depending on the application of the server, CPUs with different addressing capability can be used. Cost-effective servers can be developed using 32-bit processors. Servers built with 64-bit processors are

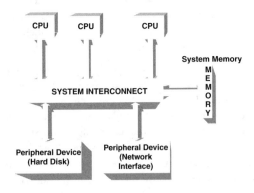

**FIGURE 5.3**   Server hardware architecture.

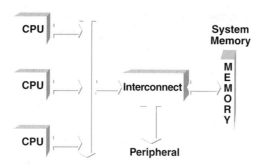

**FIGURE 5.4**   Symmetric multiprocessor architecture.

also available and are used for applications requiring large data sets. Each CPU processing core consists of several arithmetic and logic units (ALU), multi-ported register files, floating point multipliers, and branch execution units. Most widely used CPU architecture can execute instructions out of order (OOO) and several operations at a time (super scalar).

Server applications operate on many instruction and data sets. During program execution, the same instruction and data elements may be repeatedly used. High-performance CPU execution rate requires high instruction and data bandwidth. Caches are used to store and operate on the most frequently used instruction and data as well as provide high bandwidth for fast execution. A high-performance server CPU contains several levels of hardware caches. Each cache may consist of separate instruction and data caches or an integrated instruction and data cache. Caches are numbered in increasing order, starting from one from the processing core toward system memory. The size of each cache in the order of increasing number is several times that of a lower level cache. Current server microprocessors use L3 or L4 caches to achieve highest level of performance. Cache size, associativity, line size, and replacement policy are determined by the characteristics of the desired applications running on the server using performance simulation models. Caches costs are determined by the state-of-the-art VLSI processing technology, implementation, and power dissipation considerations.

The number of CPUs used in a server is determined by the server performance requirement and design limitations. Most server designs contain several sockets for optional future CPU enhancement. Multiple CPUs provide more computing performance. Architecture and design of high performance MP architectures is still an active area of research.

Cost considerations also demand sharing of expensive resources such as system memory or peripheral storage devices. High-performance arbitrated access to common system resources by all CPUs is another topic of current research in server design.

### System Memory
One of the critical subsystems in a server is the system memory. System memory consists of several banks of dynamic random access memory (DRAM) modules. The larger the number of independent memory banks, the larger is the total bandwidth available to system devices requesting memory access (such as CPUs and peripheral devices). There are a variety of DRAM memory configurations such as single in-line memory module (SIMM) or dual in-line memory module (DIMM). Current servers can have several gigabytes of system memory.

Due to need for improved reliability and robustness, server system memory use fault tolerance features such as ECC. Errors can happen for a variety of reasons such as DRAM memory soft error rate (SER) or errors in transmission signaling among various chips. Another robustness measure is the number of error bits than can be detected and corrected. Low-end servers use single error correct double error detect (SECDED). Another robustness feature is chipkill. Chipkill enables isolation and correction of multi-bit faults such as failure of a single memory chip.

Finally, because server system memory may be large, auto-initialization of memory values to known values such as during power up may be required. Other robustness features include memory mirroring, redundant memory-bit steering, and soft-error scrubbing. Depending on the desired level of robustness, a design may include one or several error detection and correction features.

### Peripheral Subsystem

Due to extensive computational capability, servers peripheral subsystem is much more elaborate than their desktop counterparts. Server peripherals include hard disk storage, fast network interface controllers (NIC) and other archival storage devices. Traditional computer interfaces such as boot Flash memory, keyboard, mouse, and graphics interfaces are also available. Example peripheral features are:

- Data storage and retrieval: Server storage and archival systems can be centralized or distributed. High performance and fault tolerant disk storage access is available using redundant array of independent disks (RAID) technology. There are also networked storage systems available.
- Network Interface: High-performance server communication links use gigabit or higher-speed Ethernet technology.
- Clustering interfaces: These interfaces are provided to support server clustering. One type of interface uses switching fabric technologies to enable connection of several server nodes.
- Direct attach interfaces: Proprietary interfaces for connection of servers is also another available technology. This interface is optimized for larger data transfer sizes compared to switched fabric approaches.
- Other peripherals interfaces such as keyboard, mouse, and graphics display device are also provided.
- Interconnection of peripheral subsystems with system memory and CPUs can be accomplished in a variety of ways. Depending on cost considerations, some systems use specialized chips to provide open standard solutions such as peripheral component interface (PCI) bus. PCI bus can be used to accommodate several peripheral devices such as network card and small computer serial interface (SCSI) solutions for hard disk and archival storage. More modern solutions provide open or proprietary switching fabrics that can be used to connect to peripheral devices. One advantage of the use of switching fabrics is the ability to scale servers to larger sizes by expanding switch fabric for additional devices such as storage devices. Figure 5.5 depicts a server configuration using switching fabric components.
- Whatever the solution, the overall solution has to satisfy high throughput, support for large or small data transfer, and low latency access operation. PCI solutions need to account for various

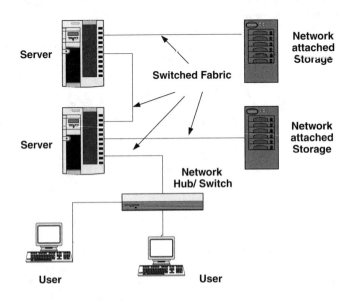

**FIGURE 5.5**    Switching fabric usage.

peripheral packet transfer size differences and shared bandwidth issues. Switching fabric solutions that use technologies, such as virtual connection or circuit switching, need to carefully architect solutions that meet connection channel setup, tear down, and blocking rates as well as quality of service (QOS) for real-time, multimedia data.

- Additional peripheral or system hardware solutions for specialized functions such as encryption and decryption may also be available.

### *System Interconnect*

Design and implementation of system interconnect to support communication between multiple CPUs, system memory, and the peripheral subsystem is a challenging task. The solution has to satisfy several requirements.

System interconnect has to provide high bandwidth, low latency access between CPUs (or system bus) and the system memory. If there is insufficient bandwidth or large memory latency, the overall server performance will degrade. Some of the design choices are multiple fast and wide memory channels, memory interleave, and high-speed pipelined CPU-to-system interconnect bus.

System interconnect has to provide efficient and high bandwidth access between the system memory and the peripheral subsystem. If there is insufficient bandwidth for memory to peripheral subsystems, high performance transfer of pre- or post-processed data to network interface will not be possible. The same issue may plague the storage subsystems. The access latency for peripheral subsystems may not be as critical as that required by CPUs. The main reason for this is that peripheral accesses such as disk storage are typically pre-fetched or scheduled before they are needed.

Because system memory is a shared resource, memory traffic balancing is critical. If the CPU is favored in system memory access, there may not be sufficient bandwidth available from the peripheral subsystem to fill or empty required data. As a result, the CPU will ultimately be data starved. Favoring peripheral access to the main memory may be detrimental to nonstalled CPU operation. To make matters worse, the balancing of the traffic from CPU and the peripheral subsystem to system memory is application dependent and even varying within an application. For example, at boot time large amount of data transfer from peripheral such as hard disk may be needed. On the other hand, high throughput transaction processing may require favoring CPU to memory bandwidth demands. Optimized arbitration policy for access to main memory is determined through extensive computer simulations that include dynamic models of the application, operating system (OS) services and hardware components.

Other issues such as high speed signaling and dissipated power in VLSI components may also be factors. Careful balance of all these factors is critical for optimized system interconnect.

## Software Architecture

High performance server operation is also affected by the server software architecture. Two software components that need optimization are peripheral device drivers and the operating system. Peripheral device drivers need to be optimized for efficient and high performance data transfer to and from system memory. Operating system software may need to be optimized to better utilize the capability of CPUs (such as cache sizes), system memory capacity, and interprocess communication between multiple CPUs. The operating system may also be optimized to efficiently handle scheduling of tasks among multiple CPUs.

Clustered servers use independent OS for each server node. Clustered solutions may also use different OS. Internetworking issues in such heterogeneous environment is another software architecture issue. Many OS and software programs also use advanced caching techniques for high performance data access.

## Applications and Usage Models

A variety of applications are available for servers such as database management, transaction processing, inventory management, and decision support. Many users also use an application differently. For example, a user may be updating the database with recent entries while others are trying to access and use the database. Each usage model and application has a specific system demand characteristics. Robust IT infrastructure ensures that the servers, network, and client architecture are tuned and optimized for the majority of the users. Hardware optimizations include selection of CPU, system memory type and size, VLSI interconnection chips, peripheral storage size, speed and features, and network interface speed and features. Software tuning mechanisms include optimizing compilers supporting multithreading and optimized libraries.

Server applications can be characterized in several ways. Some applications require large communication bandwidth between CPUs, system memory, and storage devices. Other applications require more execution processing capability by the CPUs. Finally, some servers, such as Web cache, may require high-performance network interfaces. Hardware and software tuning mechanism satisfies most of these and other requirements.

### Challenges in Server Design

Many challenges exist in the advancement of server designs. Some of the major issues such as physical and architectural considerations have already been mentioned. Below are several additional challenges that also need to be addressed:

1. Developing scalable solutions that meet the needs of a variety of users cost effectively is an active areas of research and development. Scalable architecture elements, such as CPU and system interconnection, memory, peripheral subsystem, and CPUs, are needed.
2. Development of applications that can benefit more users and take advantage of multiprocessor or clustered systems is another area of active research and development.
3. Development of additional high performance hardware and software technologies to enable large number of users sharing the IT infrastructure for new usage models is another active area. New usage model examples include support for variety of clients such as handheld devices and other information appliances.
4. Development of scalable and high performance networking technology to interconnect server components and clusters is also actively being pursued.
5. Research and development of security solutions that do not affect overall system performance, stop intrusion, and enhance user needs is another area of increasing importance.

### Summary

We reviewed many aspects of server infrastructure planning, selection, system design, and development. Critical requirements such as RAS were described. Server element architecture such as CPU, memory, and peripherals were discussed. Scalable solutions, software architecture, and applications were discussed, and avenues of current and future research and development are also described.

## 5.2  Very Large Instruction Word Architectures

*Binu Matthew*

### What Is a VLIW Processor?

Recent high performance processors have depended on instruction level parallelism (ILP) to achieve high execution speed. ILP processors achieve their high performance by causing multiple operations to execute in parallel, using a combination of compiler and hardware techniques. Very long instruction word (VLIW) is one particular style of processor design that tries to achieve high levels of ILP by executing long instruction words composed of multiple operations. The long instruction word called a "MultiOp," consists of multiple arithmetic, logic, and control operations each of which would probably be an individual operation on a simple RISC processor. The VLIW processor concurrently executes the set of operations within a MultiOp, thereby achieving ILP. The remainder of this article discusses the technology, history, uses, and the future of such processors.

## Different Flavors of Parallelism

Improvements in processor performance come from two main sources: faster semiconductor technology and parallel processing. Parallel processing on multiprocessors, multicomputers, and processor clusters has traditionally involved a high degree of programming effort in mapping an algorithm to a form that can better exploit multiple processors and threads of execution. Such reorganization has often been productively applied, especially for scientific programs. The general-purpose microprocessor industry on the other hand has pursued methods of automatically speeding up existing programs without major restructuring effort. This lead to the development of ILP processors that try to speed up program execution by overlapping the execution of multiple instructions from an otherwise sequential program.

We will call a simple processor that fetches and executes one instruction at a time a simple scalar processor. A processor with multiple functional units has the potential to execute several operations in parallel. If the decision about which operations to execute in an overlapped manner is made at run time by the hardware, it is called a super scalar processor. To a simple scalar processor, a binary program represents a plan of execution. The processor acts as an interpreter that executes the instructions in the program one at a time. From the point of view of a modern super scalar processor, an input program is more like a representation of an algorithm for which several different plans of execution are possible. Each plan of execution specifies when and on which function unit each instruction from instruction stream is to be executed.

The ILP processors differ in the manner in which the plan of execution is derived, but it typically involves both the compiler and the hardware. In the current breed of high performance processors like the Intel Pentium and the Ultra Sparc, the compiler tries to expose parallelism to the processor by means of several optimizations, the net result of which is to place as many independent operations as possible close to each other in the instruction stream. At run time, the processor examines several instructions at a time, analyzes the dependences between instructions, and keeps track of the availability of data and hardware resources for each instruction. It tries to schedule each instruction as soon as the data and functional units it needs are available. The processor's decisions are often further complicated by the fact that operations like memory accesses often have variable latencies that depend on whether a memory access hits in the cache or not. Because such processors decide which functional unit should be allocated to which instruction as execution progresses, they are said to be dynamically scheduled. Often, as a further performance improvement, such processors allow later instructions that are independent to execute ahead of an earlier instruction, which is waiting for data or resources. In that case the processor is said to be out of order.

Branches are common operations in general-purpose code. On encountering a branch, a processor must decide whether or not to take the branch. If the branch is to be taken, the processor must start fetching instructions from the branch target. To avoid delays due to branches, modern processors try to predict the outcome of branches and execute instructions from beyond the branch. If the processor predicted the branch incorrectly, it may need to undo the effects of any instructions it has already executed beyond the branch. If a super scalar processor uses resources that may otherwise go idle to execute operations the result of which may or may not be used, it is said to be speculative.

Out of order speculative execution comes at a significant hardware expense. The complexity and nonscalability of the hardware structures used to implement these features could significantly hinder the performance of future processors. An alternative solution to this problem is to simplify processor hardware and transfer some of the complexity of extracting ILP to the compiler and run time system—the solution explored by VLIW processors.

Joseph Fisher, who coined the acronym VLIW, characterized such machines as architectures that issue one long instruction per cycle, where each long instruction called a MultiOp consists of many tightly coupled independent operations each of which executes in a small and statically predictable number of cycles. In such a system the task of grouping independent operations into a MultiOp is done by a compiler or binary translator. The processor freed from the cumbersome task of dependence analysis has to merely execute in parallel the operations contained within a MultiOp. This leads to simpler and faster processor implementations. In later sections, we will see how VLIW processors try to deal with the problems of branch and memory latencies and implement their own kind of speculation. But, first, we present a brief history of VLIW processors.

## A Brief History of VLIW Processors

For various reasons which were appropriate at that time, early computers were designed to have extremely complicated instructions. These instructions made designing the control circuits for such computers difficult. A solution to this problem was microprogramming, a technique proposed by Maurice Wilkes in 1951. In a microprogrammed CPU, each program instruction is considered a macroinstruction to be executed by a simpler processor inside the CPU. Corresponding to each macroinstruction, there will be a sequence of microinstructions stored in a micro code ROM in the CPU. One particular style of microprogramming where bits in a typically very wide microinstruction are directly used as control signals within the processor is called horizontal microprogramming.

In contrast, vertical microprogramming uses a shorter microinstruction or series of microinstructions in combination with some decoding logic to generate control signals. Microprogramming became popular as a way of implementing the control for a CPU after IBM adopted it for its system/360 series.

Even before the days of the first VLIW machines, several processors and custom computing devices used a single wide instruction word to control several functional units working in parallel. However, these machines were typically hand-coded and the code for such machines could not be generalized to other architectures. The basic problem was that compilers at that time looked only within basic blocks to extract ILP. Basic blocks are often short and contain many dependences and therefore the amount of ILP that can be obtained inside a basic block is quite limited.

Joseph Fisher, a pioneer of VLIW, while working on PUMA, a CDC-6600 emulator, was frustrated by the difficulty of writing and maintaining 64 bit horizontal micro code for that processor. He started investigating a technique for global micro code compaction—a method to generate long horizontal micro code instructions from short sequential ones. Fisher soon realized that the technique he developed in 1979, called trace scheduling, could be used in a compiler to generate code for VLIW like architectures from a sequential source since the style of parallelism available in VLIW is very similar to that of horizontal micro code. His discovery lead to the design of the ELI-512 processor and the Bulldog trace-scheduling compiler.

Two companies were founded in 1984 to build VLIW-based mini supercomputers. One was Multiflow started by Fisher and his colleagues from Yale University. The other was Cydrome founded by Bob Rau, who was another VLIW pioneer, and his colleagues. In 1987, Cydrome delivered its first machine, the 256 bit Cydra 5, which included hardware support for software pipelining. This feature based on Bob Rau's research can be found in Intel Itanium processors today. In the same year, Multiflow delivered the Trace/200 machine, which was followed by the Trace/300 in 1988 and Trace/500 in 1990. The 200 and 300 series used a 256-bit instruction for 7 wide issue, 512 bits for 14 wide issue, and 1024 bits for 28 wide issue. The 500 series only supported 14 and 28 wide issue. Unfortunately, the early VLIW machines failed commercially. Cydrome closed in 1998 and Multiflow closed in 1990.

Since then, VLIW processors have seen a revival and some degree of commercial success. Some of the notable VLIW processors of recent years are IA-64 or Itanium from Intel, the Crusoe processor from Transmeta, the Trimedia media processor from Philips and TMS320C62x DSPs from Texas Instruments. Some important research machines designed during this time include the Playdoh from HP labs, Tinker from North Carolina State University, and the imagine stream and image processor currently being developed at Stanford University.

## Defoe: An Example VLIW Architecture

Rather than describe the properties of a VLIW architecture, we now introduce the Defoe. The Defoe is an example processor used in this section to give the reader a feel for VLIW architecture and programming. Though it does not exist in reality, its features are derived from those of several existing VLIW processors. Later sections that describe IA-64 and Crusoe will contrast those architectures with Defoe.

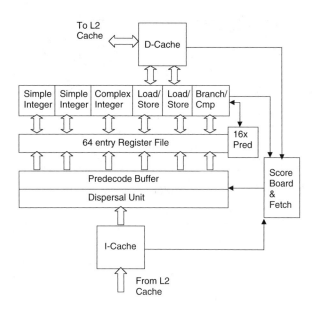

**FIGURE 5.6**   Defoe architecture.

### Functional Units

Defoe is a 64-bit architecture with the following functional units.

- Two load/store units
- Two simple ALUs that perform add, subtract, shift, and logical operations on 64-bit numbers and packed 32-, 16-, and 8-bit numbers; in addition, these units also support multiplication of packed 16 and 8 bit numbers.
- One complex ALU that can perform multiply and divide on 64 bit integers and packed 32-, 16-, and 8-bit integers
- One branch unit that performs branch, call, and comparison operations

There is no support for floating point. Figure 5.6 shows a simplified diagram of the Defoe architecture.

### Registers

Defoe has a set of 64 programmer visible general purpose registers which are 64 bits wide. Register R0 always contains 0. There is no support for register renaming like in a super scalar architecture.

### Predication

Predicate registers are special 1 bit registers that specify a true or false value. There are 16 programmer visible predicate registers in the Defoe named PR0 to PR15. All operations in Defoe are predicated, i.e., each operation specifies a predicate register in the PR field. The instruction is always executed. Logically, if the predicate is false, the results are discarded or the side effects of the instruction do not happen. In practice, for reasons of efficiency, this may be implemented by computing a result, but writing back the old value of the target register. Predicate register 0 always contains the value 1 and cannot be altered. Specifying PR0 as the predicate performs unconditional operations. Comparison operations use predicate registers as their target register.

### Instruction Encoding

Defoe is a 64-bit compressed VLIW architecture. By compressed, we mean that rather than use a fixed size MultiOp and waste slots by filling in NOPs when no suitable operation can be scheduled in a slot within a MultiOp we use variable length MultiOps. Individual operations are encoded as 32-bit words. A special stop bit in the 32-bit word indicates the end of an instruction word (Fig. 5.7). Common arithmetic operations also have an immediate mode, where a sign or zero extended 8 bit constant may be used as

| Stop bit (1 bit) | Predicate (4 bits) | Opcode (9 bits) | Rdest (6) | Rsrc1 (6) | Rscr2 (6) |
|---|---|---|---|---|---|

**FIGURE 5.7**   Instruction encoding.

an operand. For larger constants of say 16, 32, or 64 bits, a special Nop pattern may be written into opcode field of the next operation and the low order bits may be used to store the constant. In that case, the predecoder concatenates the bits from two or more different words to assemble a constant.

### Instruction Dispersal and Issue

A traditional VLIW, with a fixed encoding for MultiOps, has no need to disperse operations. However, when using a compressed format like that of the Defoe, there is a need to expand the operations and insert Nops for functional units to which no operation is to be issued. To make the dispersal task easy we make the following assumptions:

- A few bits in the opcode specify the type of functional unit (i.e. load/store, simple arithmetic, complex arithmetic or branch) the operation needs.
- The compiler ensures that the instructions that comprise a MultiOp are sorted in the same order as the functional units in the processor.
- For example, if a MultiOp consists of a load, a 32-bit divide, and a branch, then the ordering (load, multiply, branch) is legal, but the ordering (load, branch, multiply) is not.
- The compiler ensures that all the operations in the same MultiOp are independent.
- The compiler ensures that the functional units are not over subscribed. For example, two loads in a MultiOp are legal, but three is not.
- It is illegal to not have a stop bit in a sequence of more than six instructions.
- Basic blocks are aligned at 32-byte boundaries.

Apart from reducing wastage of memory, another reason to prefer a compressed format VLIW over an uncompressed one is that the former provides better I-cache utilization. To improve performance, we use a predecode buffer that can hold up to eight uncompressed MultiOps. The dispersal network can use a wide interface (say 512 bits) to the I-cache to uncompress up to 2 MultiOps every cycle and save them in the predecode buffer. Small loops of up to 8 MultiOps (maximum 48 operations) may repeatedly hit in the predecode buffer. It may also help lower the power consumption of a low power VLIW processor. Defoe supports in order issue and out of order completion. Further, all the operations in a MultiOp are issued simultaneously. If even one operation cannot be issued, issue of the whole MultiOp stalls.

### Branch Prediction

Following the VLIW philosophy of enabling the software to communicate its needs to the hardware, branch instructions in Defoe can advise the processor about their expected behavior. A 2-bit hint associated with every branch may be interpreted as follows.

| Opcode Modifier | Meaning |
|---|---|
| Stk | Static prediction. Branch is usually taken. |
| Sntk | Static prediction. Branch is usually not taken. |
| dtk | Dynamic prediction. Assume branch is taken if no history is available. |
| dntk | Dynamic prediction. Assume branch is not taken if no history is available. |

Implementations of the Defoe architecture may provide branch prediction hardware, but are not required to. If branch prediction h/w is provided, static branches need not be entered in the branch history table, thereby freeing up resources for dynamically predicted branches.

## Score Board

To accommodate branch prediction and variable latency of memory because of cache hits and misses, some amount of score boarding is required. Though we will not describe the details of the scoreboard here, it should be emphasized that the scoreboard and control logic for a VLIW processor such as the Defoe are much simpler than that of a modern super scalar processor because of the lack of out of order execution and speculation.

## Assembly Language Syntax

The examples that follow use the following syntax for assembly language instructions.

```
(predicate_reg) opcode.modifier Rdest = Rsource1, Rsource2
```

If the predicate register is omitted, PR0 will be assumed. In addition, a semicolon following an instruction indicates that the stop bit is set for that operation, i.e., that operation is the last one in its MultiOp. The prefix "!" for a predicate implies that the opcode actually depends on the logical not on the value of the predicate register.

## Example 1

This example demonstrates the execution model of the Defoe by computing the following set of expressions:

```
a = x + y - z
b = x + y - 2 * z
c = x + y - 3 * z
```

Register assignments: r1 = x, r2 = y, r3 = z, r32 = a, r33 = b, r34 = c

```
Line #    Code                             Comments
1.  add r4 = r1, r2          // r4 = x + y
2.  shl r5 = r3, 1           // r5 = z << 1, i.e. z * 2
3.  mul r6 = r3, 3 ;         // r6 = z * 3.   Stop bit.

4.  sub r32 = r4, r3         // r5 = a = gets x + y - z
5.  sub r33 = r4, r5 ;       // r33 = b = x + y - 2 * z.
                             // Stop bit.

6.  sub r34 = r4, r6 ;       // r34 = c = x + y - 3 * z.
                             // Stop bit.
```

The first three lines are followed by a stop bit to indicate that those three operations constitute a MultiOp and that they should be executed in parallel. Unlike a super scalar processor where independent operations are detected by the processor, the programmer/compiler has indicated to the processor by means of the stop bit that these three operations are independent. In a real processor, the multiplication will have a greater latency, perhaps four cycles. In that case we have two different ways of scheduling this code. Because Defoe already uses score boarding to deal with variable load latencies, it is only natural for the scoreboard to stall issue for three cycles after issuing the first MultiOp. In a more traditional VLIW, the compiler will insert three MultiOps consisting of just NOP after the first MultiOp. Lines 4–6 illustrate the way scheduling in the presence of structural hazards work on a VLIW. The compiler is aware that Defoe has only two simple integer ALUs. So, even though line 6 is independent of lines 4 and 5, it needs to wait for another cycle and be issued as a separate MultiOp. In a super scalar processor, these actions will be done by the hardware at run time.

## Example 2

This example contrasts the execution of an algorithm on Defoe and a super scalar processor (Intel Pentium). The C language function absdiff computes the sum of absolute difference of two arrays A and B which contain 256 elements each.

```c
int absdiff(int *A, int *B)
{
  int sum, diff, i;
  sum = 0;
  for(i = 0; i<256; i++)
    {
      diff = A[i] - B[i];
      if(A[i] >= B[i])
      sum = sum + diff;
      else
      sum = sum - diff;
    }
    return sum;
}
```

A hand-assembled version of absdiff in Defoe assembly language is shown below. For clarity, it has been left unoptimized. An optimizing compiler will unroll this loop and software schedule it.

Register assignment: On entry, r1 = a, r2 = b. On exit, sum is in r4.

```
Line #   Code                           Comment
1.    add r3 = r1, 2040                 // r3 = End of array A
2.    add r4 = r0, r0  ;                // sum = r4 = 0


.L1:
3.    ld r5 = [r1]                      // load A[i]
4.    ld r6 = [r2]                      // load B[i]
5.    add r1 = r1, 8                    // Increment A address
6.    add r2 = r2, 8                    // Increment B address
7.    cmp.neq pr1 = r1, r3 ;            // pr1 = (i != 255)

8.    sub r7, r5, r6                    // diff = A[i] - B[i]
9.    cmp.gte pr2 = r5, r6 ;            // pr2  = (A[i] >= B[i])
10.   (pr2) add r4 = r4, r7             // if A[i] >= B[i]
                                        // sum = sum + diff
11.   (!pr2) sub r4 = r4, r7            // else sum = sum - diff
12.   (pr1) br.sptk .L1     ;
```

The corresponding code for an Intel processor is shown below. This is a snippet of actual code generated by the GCC compiler.

Stack assignment: On entry, 12(%ebp) = B, 8(%ebp) = A. On exit, sum is in eax.

```
Line #       Code                      Comment
1.           movl   12(%ebp), %edi     // edi = B
2.           xorl   %esi, %esi         // esi sum = 0
3.           xorl   %ebx, %ebx         // ebx = 0
```

```
.p2align 2
.L6:
4.          movl    8(%ebp), %eax          // eax = A
5.          movl    (%eax,%ebx,4), %edx    // edx = A[i]
6.          movl    %edx, %ecx             // ecx = A[i]
7.          movl    (%edi,%ebx,4), %eax    // eax = B[i]
8.          subl    %eax, %ecx           // ecx = diff = A[i] - B[i]
9.          cmpl    %eax, %edx           // A[i] < B[i]
10.         jl      .L7                  // goto .L7 is A[i] < B[i]
11.         addl    %ecx, %esi           // sum = sum + diff
12.         jmp     .L5
.p2align 2
.L7:
13.         subl    %ecx, %esi                // sum = sum - diff
.L5:
14.         incl    %ebx             // i++
15.         cmpl    $255, %ebx       // i <= 255 ?
16.         jle     .L6
17.         popl    %ebx
18.         movl    %esi, %eax
```

The level of parallelism available in the Defoe listing lines 3–7 (5 issue) can be achieved on a super scalar processor only if the processor can successfully isolate the five independent operations fast enough to issue them all during the same cycle. Dependency checking in h/w is extremely complex and adds to the delay of super scalar processors. The x86, which is a register deficient CISC architecture, also incurs additional penalties because of register renaming and CISC to internal RISC format translation.

Another important point is that the Defoe listing contains only one branch on line 12, whereas the x86 listing contains three branches. On a VLIW processor, in some cases, using predicated instructions may eliminate jumps. In both listings, line 9 corresponds to the comparison of A[i] and B[i]. The super scalar had to do a conditional jump based on the result of the comparison. The VLIW on the other hand used the result of the comparison to set a predicate, which selectively executed either an add or a subtract and nullified the other. This technique of converting a control dependence to data dependence is called "if conversion." The benefits go beyond the single cycle saved by not doing a jump like in the case of the super scalar processor. The jumps on lines 10 and 12 in the second listing depend on the condition code which, in turn, depends on the data. Such data dependent branches are difficult to predict. Assuming that A[i] < B[i] and A[i] ≥ B[i] are equally likely, the super scalar processor is likely to experience a branch misprediction and the resulting branch penalty half of the time.

Further, going by the VLIW philosophy of communicating performance critical information from the software to the hardware, the final branch on line 12 uses the opcode modifier "sptk" to inform the processor that the branch is statically predicted to be taken. For that particular loop, a VLIW processor can therefore predict the loop accurately 255 times out of 256 loop iterations without any hardware branch predictor. Even when a hardware branch predictor is available, the instruction advises the processor not to waste a branch history table entry on that branch since its behavior is already known at compile time.

## The Intel Itanium Processor

The Itanium processor is Intel's first implementation of the IA-64 ISA. IA-64 is an ISA for the EPIC (Explicitly Parallel Instruction Computing) style of VLIW developed jointly by Intel and HP. It is a 64-bit, 6 issue VLIW processor with 4 integer units, 4 multimedia units, 2 load/store units, 2 extended precision floating point units, and 2 single precision floating point units. This processor running at 800 MHz on a 0.18-$\mu$m process has a 10-stage deep pipeline.

Unlike the Defoe, the IA-64 architecture uses a fixed bundled instruction format. Each MultiOp consists of one or more 128 bit bundles. Each 128 bit bundle consists of three operations and a template. Unlike the Defoe where the opcode in each operation specifies a type field, the template encodes commonly used combinations of operation types. Allowed operation types are shown in Table x. Since the template field is only 5 bits wide, bundles do not support all possible combinations of instruction types. Much like the Defoe's stop bit, in the IA-64, some template codes specify where in the bundle a MultiOp ends. In IA-64 terminology, MultiOps are called instruction groups. Like Defoe, the IA-64 uses a decoupling buffer to improve its issue rate. Though the IA-64 registers are nominally 64 bits wide, there is a hidden 65th bit called NaT (Not a Thing). This is used to support speculation. There are 128 general purpose registers and another set of 128, 82 bit wide floating point registers. Similar to the Defoe, all operations on the IA-64 are predicated. However, the IA-64 has 64 predicate registers.

The IA-64 register mechanism is more complex than the Defoe's because it implements support for software pipelining using a method similar to the overlapped loop execution support pioneered by Bob Rau and implemented in the Cydra 5. On the IA-64, general-purpose registers GPR0 to GPR31 are fixed. Registers 32–127 can be renamed under program control to support a register stack or to do modulo scheduling for loops. When used to support software pipelining, this feature is called register rotation. Predicate registers 0–15 are fixed, while predicate registers 16–63 can be made to rotate in unison with the general purpose registers. The floating point registers also support rotation.

A modulo scheduled loop is similar to a pipelined functional unit. In a pipelined functional unit, each stage can hold a computation and successive items of data may be applied to the functional unit before previous data is completely processed. In a similar manner, in a modulo scheduled loop, the loop body may be logically split into several stages. The compiler can schedule multiple iterations of a loop in a pipelined manner as long as data outputs of one stage flow into the inputs of the next stage in a pipeline. Traditionally, this required unrolling the loop and renaming the registers used in successive iterations. The IA-64 reduces the overhead of such a loop and avoids the need for register renaming by rotating registers forward. After one rotation, the value that was in register X will be found in register X + 1. When used in conjunction with predication, this allows a natural expression of software pipelines similar to their hardware counterparts.

The IA-64 supports software directed control and data speculation. To do control speculation, the compiler moves loads before its controlling branch. The load is then flagged as a speculative load. The processor does not signal exceptions on a speculative load. If the controlling branch is later taken, the compiler uses a special check operation to see if an exception occurred. If an exception occurred, the check operation transfers control to exception handling code.

To support data speculation, the processor supports a special kind of load called an advance load. If the compiler cannot disambiguate between the addresses of a store and a later load, it can issue an advance load ahead of the store. The processor uses a special hardware structure called the ALAT to keep track of whether a later store wrote to the same location as the advance load. Later, in the original location of the load, the compiler uses a special check operation to see if a store invalidated the result of an advance load. If so, the check operation transfers control to special recovery code.

Similar to the Defoe, the IA-64 also supports both static and dynamic hints for branches. It also makes use of hardware branch prediction. There are also hints in load and store instructions that inform the processor about the cache behavior of a particular memory operation.

The IA-64 also includes SIMD instructions suitable for media processing. Special multimedia instructions similar to the MMX and SSE extensions of 80x86 processors treat the contents of a general purpose register as two 32-bit, four 16-bit, or eight 8-bit operands and operate on them in parallel.

To improve performance, the IA-64 architecture includes several features that are not found in a traditional VLIW architecture. The Intel Itanium processor is probably the most complex VLIW ever designed. It is a matter of debate whether some of the control complexity of the IA-64 is justifiable in a VLIW architecture and whether the enhancements actually improve performance enough to justify their complexity. Next, we will look at a simpler VLIW processor that has been designed with a totally different goal—that of reducing power consumption.

## The Transmeta Crusoe Processor

Even though very little information is publicly available at the time of this writing about the architecture of the Crusoe series of processors from Transmeta Corp., it represents a very interesting point in the history of VLIW processors. Traditionally, VLIW processors have been designed with the goal of maximizing ILP and performance. The designers of the Crusoe on the other hand needed to build a processor with moderate performance compared to current desktop processors, but with the additional restriction that their CPU consume very little power since it is intended for mobile applications and that it should be able to efficiently emulate the ISA of other processors, particularly the 80x86 and the Java virtual machine.

The designers came to the conclusion that features like out of order issue and dynamic scheduling consumed more power than could justify the performance benefits they provided. They set out replace such complex ways of gaining ILP with simpler and more power efficient alternatives. The end result was a simple VLIW architecture. Long instructions on the Crusoe are either 64 or 128 bits. A 128-bit instruction word called a molecule in Transmeta parlance encodes four operations called atoms. The molecule format directly determines how operations get routed to functional units. The Crusoe has two integer units, a floating point unit, a load/store unit, and a branch unit. Similar to the Defoe, the Crusoe has 64 general-purpose registers and supports strictly in order issue. Unlike the Defoe, which uses predication, the Crusoe uses condition flags, which are identical to those of the x86 for ease of emulation.

Binary x86 programs, firmware, and operating systems are emulated with the help of a run time binary translator called code morphing software. This makes VLIW software compatibility a non issue. Only the native code morphing software needs to be changed when the Crusoe architecture or ISA changes. As a power and performance optimization, the hardware and software together maintain a cache of translated code. The translations are instrumented to collect execution frequencies and branch history, and this information is fed back to the code morphing software to guide its optimizations.

To correctly model the precise exception semantics of the x86 processor, the part of the register file that holds x86 register state is duplicated. The duplicate is called a shadow copy. Normal operations only affect the original registers. At the end of a translated section of code, a special commit operation is used to copy the working register values to the shadow registers. If an exception happens while executing a translated unit, the run time software uses the shadow copy to recreate the precise exception state. Store operations are implemented in a similar manner using a store buffer. The Crusoe provides alias detection hardware and data speculation primitives, which are quite similar to those of the IA-64.

## Scheduling Algorithms for VLIW

The difficulty of programming VLIW processors by hand should be evident even from the simple Defoe programming examples. One reason programming VLIWs is more difficult than writing code for a super scalar processor is that the program for a super scalar processor is inherently sequential and it is left to the hardware to extract parallelism from the sequential program. On the other hand, when generating code for a VLIW processor the assembly language programmer or the compiler is faced with the task of extracting parallelism from a sequential algorithm and scheduling independent operations concurrently. For this reason, instruction scheduling algorithms are critical to the performance of a VLIW processor. So, we describe three important scheduling algorithms next starting with the trace scheduling algorithm which started off the VLIW style of architectures.

### Trace Scheduling

Compilers for the first ILP processors used a 3-phase method to generate code. The passes were:

- Generate a sequential program. Analyze each basic block in the sequential program for independent operations.
- Schedule independent operations within the same block in parallel if sufficient hardware resources are available.
- Move operations between blocks when possible.

This 3-phase approach fails to exploit much of the ILP available in the program for two reasons.

- Oftentimes, operations in a basic block are dependent on each other. Therefore, sufficient ILP may not be available within a basic block.
- Arbitrary choices made while scheduling basic blocks make it difficult to move operations between blocks.

Trace scheduling is a profile driven method developed by Joseph Fisher to circumvent this problem. In trace scheduling, a set of commonly executed sequence of blocks is gathered together into a trace and the whole trace is scheduled together.

The trace scheduling algorithm works as follows:

1. Generate a possibly unoptimized version of the program, run it on sample input and collect statistics. Estimate the probability of each conditional branch.
2. From the basic block level data precedence graph of the program (also commonly called DAG for Directed Acylic Graph), select a loop-free linear sequence of basic blocks, which have a high probability of execution. Such a sequence is called a trace. The compiler may use other optimizations like loop unrolling or procedure inlining to generate DAGS from which suitable traces can be selected.
3. Consider the trace as if it were a basic block. Build a DAG for it, considering branches like all other operations. If an operation controlled by a conditional jump could over write a value that is live on the off-trace edge, add an edge that makes the operation dependent on the branch so that the operation cannot be moved ahead of the branch. Also, add edges to preserve the relative order of conditional branches.
4. Schedule the resulting DAG as if it were a basic block doing register allocation and functional unit selection, as each operation is scheduled.
5. Generate compensation codes for mistakes made by considering the trace as a basic block. In particular:
   a. If an operation that used to precede a conditional branch in the sequential code is moved after that branch, then add a copy of that operation preceding the off-trace target of the conditional jump.
   b. If an operation that succeeded a point of entry into the trace from outside the trace is moved ahead of that point of entry, then copy of that operation must be placed outside the trace on the path that leads to that point of entry.
   c. Ensure that rejoins that used to enter the trace enter at the new trace only at a point after which no operation is found in the new trace that were not below the rejoin point in the old trace.
6. Link the new trace back into the old DAG.
7. After scheduling the very first trace, new operations would have been added to the original DAG. Pick a different frequent trace and schedule it. Repeat till the DAG has been covered using disjoint traces, and no unscheduled operations remain.

## Trace Scheduling-2

Trace scheduling-2 goes beyond trace scheduling in that it allows nonlinear code motion, i.e., it allows operations from both sides of a conditional branch to be moved above the branch. Trace scheduling usually misses code motions that are speculative or moves operations from one trace to another. Trace scheduling-2 on the other hand uses an expected value function called speculative yield, to consider the cost of speculative execution and decide whether or not to move operations from one block to another. Unlike trace scheduling, which operates on a linear sequence of blocks, the newer algorithm works by picking clusters of operations where each cluster is a maximal set of operations that are connected without back edges in the flow graph of the program. The actual details of the algorithm are beyond the scope of this section.

## Super Block Scheduling

Super block scheduling is a region-scheduling algorithm developed in conjunction with the Impact compiler at the University of Illinois. Similar to trace scheduling, super block scheduling is based on the premise that to extract ILP from a sequential program, the compiler should perform code motion across multiple basic blocks. Unlike trace scheduling, super block scheduling is driven by static branch analysis, not profile data. A super block is a set of basic blocks in which control may enter only at the top, but may exit at more than one point. Super blocks are identified by first identifying traces and then eliminating side entries into a trace by a process called tail duplication. Tail duplication works by creating a separate off-trace copy of the basic blocks in between a side entrance and the trace exit and redirecting the edge corresponding to the side entry to the copy. Traces are identified using static branch analysis based on loop detection, heuristic hazard avoidance, and heuristics for path selection. Loop detection identifies loops and marks loop back edges as taken and loop exits as not taken. Hazard avoidance uses a set of heuristics to detect situations, such as ambiguous stores and procedure calls, that could cause a compiler to use conservative optimization strategies and then predicts the branches so as to avoid having to optimize hazards. Path-selection heuristics use the opcode of a branch, its operands and the contents of its successor blocks to predict its direction if no other method already predicted the direction of the branch. These are based on common programming patterns like the fact that pointers are unlikely to be NULL, floating point comparisons are unlikely to be equal, etc. Once branch information is available, traces are grown and super blocks created by tail duplication followed by scheduling of the super block. Studies have shown that static analysis based super block scheduling can achieve results that are comparable to profile-based methods.

## The Future of VLIW Processors

VLIW processors have enjoyed moderate commercial success in recent times as exemplified by the Philips Trimedia, TI TMS320C62x DSPs, Intel Itanium, and to a lesser extend the Transmeta Crusoe. The role of VLIW processors, however, has changed since the days of Cydrome and Multiflow. Even though early VLIW processors were developed to be scientific super computers, newer processors have been used mainly for stream, image and digital signal processing, multimedia codec hardware, low-power mobile computers, and for running commercial servers. VLIW compiler technology has made major advances during the last decade; however, most of the compiler techniques developed for VLIW are equally applicable to super scalar processors as well. Stream and media processing applications are typically very regular with predictable branch behavior and large amounts of ILP. They lend themselves easily to VLIW style execution. The ever increasing demand for multimedia applications will continue to fuel development of VLIW technology; however, in the short term, super scalar processors will probably dominate in the role of general-purpose processors. Increasing wire delays in deep sub-micron processes will ultimately force super scalar processors to use simpler and more scalable control structures and seek more help from software. It is reasonable to assume that in the long run, much of the VLIW technology and design philosophy will make its way into main stream processors.

# References

1. Joseph A. Fisher, Global code generation for instruction-level parallelism: Trace Scheduling-2. *Technical Report HPL-93-43,* Hewlett-Packard Laboratories, June 1993.
2. Joseph A. Fischer, Very long instruction word architectures and the ELI-512, in *Proc. 10th Symposium on Computer Architectures,* pp. 140–150, IEEE, June 1983.
3. Joseph A. Fisher, Very long instruction word architectures and the ELI-512. *25 Years ISCA: Retrospectives and Reprints,* 1998: 263–273.
4. M. Schlansker, B. R. Rau, S. Mahlke, V. Kathail, R. Johnson, S. Anik, and S. G. Abraham, Achieving high levels of instruction-level parallelism with reduced hardware complexity. *Technical Report HPL-96-120,* Hewlett Packard Laboratories, Feb. 1997.
5. M. Schlansker and B. R. Rau. Epic: An architecture for instruction level parallel processors. *Technical Report HPL-1999-111,* Hewlett Packard Laboratories, Feb. 2000.

6.  Scott Rixner, William J. Dally, Ujval J. Kapasi, Brucek, Lopez-Lagunas, Abelardo, Peter R. Mattson, and John D. Owens. A bandwidth-efficient architecture for media processing, in *Proc. 31st Annual International Symposium on Microarchitecture*, Dallas, TX, November 1998.
7.  Intel Corporation. *Itanium Processor Microarchitecture Reference for Software Optimization.* Intel Corporation, March 2000.
8.  Intel Corporation. *Intel IA-64 Architecture Software Developer's Manula, Volume 3: Instruction Set Reference.* Intel Corporation, January 2000.
9.  Intel Corporation. *IA-64 Application Developer's Architecture Guide.* Intel Corporation, May 1999.
10. P. G. Lowney, S. M. Freudenberger, T. J. Karzes, W. D. Lichtenstein, R. P. Nix, J. S. O'Donnell, and J. C. Ruttenberg. The multiflow trace scheduling compiler. *Journal of Supercomputing*, 7, 1993.
11. R. E. Hank, S. A. Mahlke, J. C. Gyllenhaal, R. Bringmann, and W. W. Hwu, Superblock formation using static program analysis, in *Proc. 26th Annual International Symposium on Microarchitecture*, Austin, TX, pp. 247–255, Dec. 1993.
12. S. A. Mahlke, D. C. Lin, W. Y. Chen, R. E. Hank, and R. A. Bringmann, Effective compiler support for predicated execution using the hyperblock, in *Proc. 25th International Symposium on Microarchitecture*, pp. 45–54, December 1992.
13. James C. Dehnert, Peter Y. T. Hsu, Joseph P. Bratt, Overlapped loop support in the Cydra 5, in *Proc. ASPLOS 89*, pp. 26–38.
14. Alexander Klaiber, *The Technology Behind Crusoe Processors.* Transmeta Corp., 2000.

## 5.3   Vector Processing

*Krste Asanovic*

### Introduction

For nearly 30 years, vector processing has been used in the world's fastest supercomputers to accelerate applications in scientific and technical computing. More recently vector-like extensions have become popular on desktop and embedded microprocessors to accelerate multimedia applications. In both cases, architects are motivated to include data parallel instructions because they enable large increases in performance at much lower cost than alternative approaches to exploiting application parallelism. This chapter reviews the development of data parallel instruction sets from the early SIMD (single instruction, multiple data) machines, through the vector supercomputers, to the new multimedia instruction sets.

### Data Parallelism

An application is said to contain data parallelism when the same operation can be carried out across arrays of operands, for example, when two vectors are added element by element to produce a result vector. Data parallel operations are usually expressed as loops in sequential programming languages. If each loop iteration is independent of the others, data parallel instructions can be used to execute the code. The following vector add code written in C is a simple example of a data parallel loop:

```
for (i=0; i<N; i++)
    C[i] = A[i] + B[i];
```

Provided that the result array C does not overlap the source arrays A and B, the individual loop iterations can be run in parallel. Many compute-intensive applications are built around such data parallel loop kernels. One of the most important factors in determining the performance of data parallel programs is the range of vector lengths observed for typical data sets. Vector lengths vary depending on the application, how the application is coded, and also on the input data for each run. In general, the longer the vectors, the greater the performance achieved by a data parallel architecture, as any loop startup overheads will be amortized over a larger number of elements.

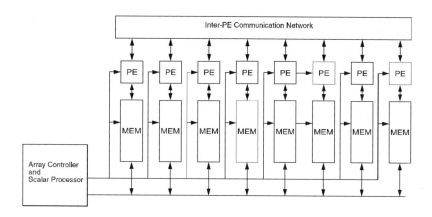

**FIGURE 5.8**   Structure of a distributed memory SIMD (DM-SIMD) processor.

The performance of a piece of vector code running on a data parallel machine can be summarized with a few key parameters. $R_n$ is the rate of execution (for example, in MFLOPS) for a vector of length $n$. $R_\infty$ is the maximum rate of execution achieved assuming infinite length vectors. $N_\_$ is the number of elements at which vector performance reaches one half of $R_\infty$. $N_\_$ indirectly measures startup overhead, as it gives the vector length at which the time lost to overheads is equal to the time taken to execute the vector operation at peak speed ignoring overheads. The larger the $N_\_$ for a code kernel running on a particular machine, the longer the vectors must be to achieve close to peak performance.

## History of Data Parallel Machines

Data parallel architectures were first developed to provide high throughput for supercomputing applications. There are two main classes of data parallel architectures: distributed memory SIMD (single instruction, multiple data [1]) architecture and shared memory vector architecture. An early example of a distributed memory SIMD (DM-SIMD) architecture is the Illiac-IV [2]. A typical DM-SIMD architecture has a general-purpose scalar processor acting as the central controller and an array of processing elements (PEs) each with its own private memory, as shown in Fig. 5.8. The central processor executes arbitrary scalar code and also fetches instructions, and broadcasts them across the array of PEs, which execute the operations in parallel and in lockstep. Usually the local memories of the PE array are mapped into the central processor's address space so that it can read and write any word in the entire machine. PEs can communicate with each other, using a separate parallel inter-PE data network. Many DM-SIMD machines, including the ICL DAP [3] and the Goodyear MPP [4], used single-bit processors connected in a 2-D mesh, providing communication well-matched to image processing or scientific simulations that could be mapped to a regular grid. The later connection machine design [5] added a more flexible router to allow arbitrary communication between single-bit PEs, although at much slower rates than the 2-D mesh connect. One advantage of single-bit PEs is that the number of cycles taken to perform a primitive operation, such as an add can scale with the precision of the operands, making them well suited to tasks such as image processing where low-precision operands are common. An alternative approach was taken in the Illiac-IV where wide 64-bit PEs could be subdivided into multiple 32-bit or 8-bit PEs to give higher performance on reduced precision operands. This approach reduces $N_\_$ for calculations on vectors with wider operands but requires more complex PEs. This same technique of subdividing wide datapaths has been carried over into the new generation of multimedia extensions (referred to as MX in the rest of this chapter) for microprocessors. The main attraction of DM-SIMD machines is that the PEs can be much simpler than the central processor because they do not need to fetch and decode instructions. This allows large arrays of simple PEs to be constructed, for example, up to 65,536 single-bit PEs in the original connection machine design.

Shared-memory vector architectures (henceforth abbreviated to just "vector architectures") also belong to the class of SIMD machines, as they apply a single instruction to multiple data items. The primary difference in the programming model of vector machines versus DM-SIMD machines is that vector machines allow any PE to access any word in the system's main memory. Because it is difficult to construct machines that allow a large number of simple processors to share a large central memory, vector machines typically have a smaller number of highly pipelined PEs.

The two earliest commercial vector architectures were CDC STAR-100 [6] and TI ASC [7]. Both of these machines were vector memory–memory architectures where the vector operands to a vector instruction were streamed in and out of memory. For example, a vector add instruction would specify the start addresses of both source vectors and the destination vector, and during execution elements were fetched from memory before being operated on by the arithmetic unit which produced a set of results to write back to main memory.

The Cray-1 [8] was the first commercially successful vector architecture and introduced the idea of vector registers. A vector register architecture provides vector arithmetic operations that can only take operands from vector registers, with vector load and store instructions that only move data between the vector registers and memory. Vector registers hold short vectors close to the vector functional units, shortening instruction latencies and allowing vector operands to be reused from registers thereby reducing memory bandwidth requirements. These advantages have led to the dominance of vector register architectures and vector memory–memory machines are ignored for the rest of this section.

DM-SIMD machines have two primary disadvantages compared to vector supercomputers when writing applications. The first is that the programmer has to be extremely careful in selecting algorithms and mapping data arrays across the machine to ensure that each PE can satisfy almost all of its data accesses from its local memory, while ensuring the local data set still fits into the limited local memory of each PE. In contrast, the PEs in a vector machine have equal access to all of main memory, and the programmer only has to ensure that data accesses are spread across all the interleaved memory banks in the memory subsystem.

The second disadvantage is that DM-SIMD machines typically have a large number of simple PEs and so to avoid having many PEs sit idle, applications must have long vectors. For the large-scale DM-SIMD machines, $N_-$ can be in the range of tens of thousands of elements. In contrast, the vector supercomputers contain a few highly pipelined PEs and have $N_-$ in the range of tens to hundreds of elements.

To make effective use of a DM-SIMD machine, the programmer has to find a way to restructure code to contain very long vector lengths, while simultaneously mapping data structures to distributed small local memories in each PE. Achieving high performance under these constraints has proven difficult except for a few specialized applications. In contrast, the vector supercomputers do not require data partitioning and provide reasonable performance on much shorter vectors and so require much less effort to port and tune applications. Although DM-SIMD machines can provide much higher peak performances than vector supercomputers, sustained performance was often similar or lower and programming effort was much higher. As a result, although they achieved some popularity in the 1980s, DM-SIMD machines have disappeared from the high-end, general-purpose computing market with no current commercial manufacturers, while there are still several manufacturers of high-end vector supercomputers with sufficient revenue to fund continued development of new implementations. DM-SIMD architectures remain popular in a few niche special-purpose areas, particularly in image processing and in graphics rendering, where the natural application parallelism maps well onto the DM-SIMD array, providing extremely high throughput at low cost.

Although data parallel instructions were originally introduced for high-end supercomputers, they can be applied to many applications outside of scientific and technical supercomputing. Beginning with the Intel i860 released in 1989, microprocessor manufacturers have introduced data parallel instruction set extensions that allow a small number of parallel SIMD operations to be specified in single instruction. These microprocessor SIMD ISA (instruction set architecture) extensions were originally targeted at multimedia applications and supported only limited-precision, fixed-point arithmetic, but now support single and double precision floating-point and hence a much wider range of applications. In this chapter, SIMD ISA extensions are viewed as a form of short vector instruction to allow a unified discussion of design trade-offs.

## Basic Vector Register Architecture

Vector processors contain a conventional scalar processor that executes general-purpose code together with a vector processing unit that handles data parallel code. Figure 5.9 shows the general architecture of a typical vector machine. The vector processing unit includes a set of vector registers and a set of vector functional units that operate on the vector registers. Each vector register contains a set of two or more data elements. A typical vector arithmetic instruction reads source operand vectors from two vector registers, performs an operation pair-wise on all elements in each vector register and writes a result vector to a destination vector register, as shown in Fig. 5.10. Often, versions of vector instructions are provided that replace one vector operand with a scalar value; these are termed vector–scalar instructions. The scalar value is used as one of the operand inputs at each element position.

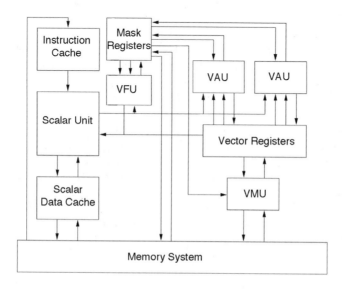

**FIGURE 5.9**   Structure of a vector machine. This example has a central vector register file, two vector arithmetic units (VAU), one vector load/store unit (VMU), and one vector mask unit (VFU) that operates on the mask registers. (Adapted from Asanovic, K., *Vector Microprocessors*, 1998. With permission.)

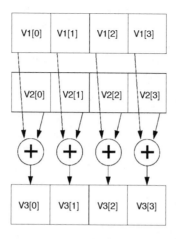

**FIGURE 5.10**   Operation of a vector add instruction. Here, the instruction is adding vector registers 1 and 2 to give a result in vector register 3.

The vector ISA usually fixes the maximum number of elements in each vector register, although some machines such as the IBM vector extension for the 3090 mainframe support implementations with differing numbers of elements per vector register. If the number of elements required by the application is less than the number of elements in a vector register, a separate vector length register (VLR) is set with the desired number of operations to perform. Subsequent vector instructions only perform this number of operations on the first elements of each vector register. If the application requires vectors longer than will fit into a vector register, a process called strip mining is used to construct a vector loop that executes the application code loop in segments that each fit into the machine's vector registers. The MX ISAs have very short vector registers and do not provide any vector length control. Various types of vector load and store instruction can be provided to move vectors between the vector register file and memory. The simplest form of vector load and store transfers a set of elements that are contiguous in memory to successive elements of a vector register. The base address is usually specified by the contents of a register in the scalar processor. This is termed a unit-stride load or store, and is the only type of vector load and store provided in existing MX instruction sets.

Vector supercomputers also include more complex vector load and store instructions. A strided load or store instruction transfers memory elements that are separated by a constant stride, where the stride is specified by the contents of a second scalar register. Upon completion of a strided load, vector elements that were widely scattered in memory are compacted into a dense form in a vector register suitable for subsequent vector arithmetic instructions. After processing, elements can be unpacked from a vector register back to memory using a strided store.

Vector supercomputers also include indexed load and store instructions to allow elements to be collected into a vector register from arbitrary locations in memory. An indexed load or store uses a vector register to supply a set of element indices. For an indexed load or gather, the vector of indices is added to a scalar base register to give a vector of effective addresses from which individual elements are gathered and placed into a densely packed vector register. An indexed store, or scatter, inverts the process and scatters elements from a densely packed vector register into memory locations specified by the vector of effective addresses.

Many applications contain conditionally executed code, for example, the following loop clears values of A[i] smaller than some threshold value:

```
for (i=0; i<N; i++)
    if (A[i] < threshold)
        A[i] = 0;
```

Data parallel instruction sets usually provide some form of conditionally executed instruction to support parallelization of such loops. In vector machines, one approach is to provide a mask register that has a single bit per element position. Vector comparison operations test a predicate at each element and set bits in the mask register at element positions where the condition is true. A subsequent vector instruction takes the mask register as an argument, and at element positions where the mask bit is set, the destination register is updated with the result of the vector operation, otherwise the destination element is left unchanged. The vector loop body for the previous vector loop is shown below (with all stripmining loop code removed).

```
lv va, (ra)           # Load slice of vector A from memory
cmp.lt.vs va, rt      # Set mask where A[i] < threshold
move.vs.m va, r0      # Clear elements of A[i] under mask
sv va, (ra)           # Store updated slice of A to memory
```

## Vector Instruction Set Advantages

Vector instruction set extensions provide a number of advantages over alternative mechanisms for encoding parallel operations. Vector instructions are compact, encoding many parallel operations in a single short instruction, as compared to superscalar or VLIW instruction sets which encode each individual operation using a separate collection of bits.

They are also expressive, relaying much useful information from software to hardware. When a compiler or programmer specifies a vector instruction, they indicate that all of the elemental operations within the instruction are independent, allowing hardware to execute the operations using pipelined execution units, or parallel execution units, or any combination of pipelined and parallel execution units, without requiring dependency checking or operand bypassing for elements within the same vector instruction. Vector ISAs also reduce the dependency checking required between two different vector instructions. Hardware only has to check dependencies once per vector register, not once per elemental operation. This dramatically reduces the complexity of building high throughput execution engines compared with RISC or VLIW scalar cores, which have to perform dependency and interlock checking for every elemental result. Vector memory instructions can also relay much useful information to the memory subsystem by passing a whole stream of memory requests together with the stride between elements in the stream.

Another considerable advantage of a vector ISA is that it simplifies scaling of implementation parallelism. As described in the next section, the degree of parallelism in the vector unit can be increased while maintaining object–code compatibility.

## Lanes: Parallel Execution Units

Figure 5.11(a) shows the execution of a vector add instruction on a single pipelined adder. Results are computed at the rate of one element per cycle. Figure 5.11(b) shows the execution of a vector add instruction using four parallel pipelined adders. Elements are interleaved across the parallel pipelines allowing up to four element results to be computed per cycle. This increase in parallelism is invisible to software except for the increased performance.

Figure 5.12 shows how a typical vector unit can be constructed as a set of replicated lanes, where each lane is a cluster containing a portion of the vector register file and one pipeline from each vector

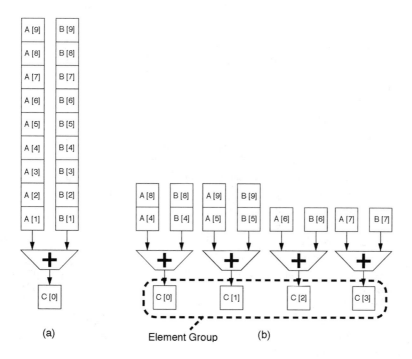

**FIGURE 5.11** Execution of vector add instruction using different numbers of execution units. The machine in (a) has a single adder and completes one result per cycle, while the machine in (b) has four adders and completes four results every cycle. An element group is the set of elements that proceed down the parallel pipelines together. (From Asanovic, K., *Vector Microprocessors*, 1998. With permission.)

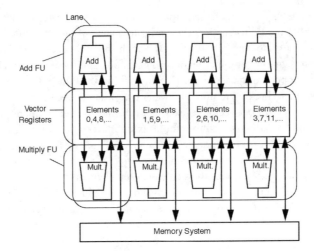

**FIGURE 5.12**   A vector unit constructed from replicated lanes. Each lane holds one adder and one multiplier as well as one portion of the vector register file and a connection to the memory system. The adder functional unit (adder FU) executes add instructions using all four adders in all four lanes.

functional unit. Because of the way the vector ISA is designed, there is no need for communication between the lanes except via the memory system. The vector registers are striped over the lanes, with lane 0 holding all elements 0, $N$, $2N$, etc., lane 1 holding elements 1, $N + 1$, $2N + 1$, etc. In this way, each elemental vector arithmetic operation will find its source and destination operands located within the same lane, which dramatically reduces interconnect costs.

The fastest current vector supercomputers, NEC SX-5 and Fujitsu VPP5000, employ 16 parallel 64-bit lanes in each CPU. The NEC SX-5 can complete 16 loads, 16 64-bit floating-point multiplies, and 16 floating-point adds each clock cycle.

Many data parallel systems, ranging from vector supercomputers, such as the early CDC STAR-100, to the MX ISAs, such as AltiVec, provide variable precision lanes, where a wide 64-bit lane can be subdivided into a larger number of lower precision lanes to give greater performance on reduced precision operands.

## Vector Register File Organization

Vector machines differ widely in the organization of the vector register file. The important software-visible parameters for a vector register file are the number of vector registers, the number of elements in each vector register, and the width of each element. The Cray-1 had eight vector registers each holding sixty-four 64-bit elements (4096 bits total). The AltiVec MX for the PowerPC has 32 vector registers each holding 128-bits that can be divided into four 32-bit elements, eight 16-bit elements, or sixteen 8-bit elements. Some vector supercomputers have extremely large vector register files organized in a vector register hierarchy, e.g., the NEC SX-5 has 72 vector registers (8 foreground plus 64 background) that can each hold five hundred twelve 64-bit elements.

For a fixed vector register storage capacity (measured in elements), an architecture has to choose between few longer vector registers or more shorter vector registers. The primary advantage of lengthening a vector register is that it reduces the instruction bandwidth required to attain a given level of performance because a single instruction can specify a greater number of parallel operations. Increases in vector register length give rapidly diminishing returns, as amortized startup overheads become small and as fewer applications can take advantage of the increased vector register length.

The primary advantage of providing more vector registers is that it allows more temporary values to be held in registers, reducing data memory bandwidth requirements. For machines with only eight vector registers, vector register spills have been shown to consume up to 70% of all vector memory traffic, while increasing the number of vector registers to 32 removes most register spill traffic [9,10]. Adding more vector registers also gives compilers more flexibility in scheduling vector instructions to boost vector instruction-level parallelism.

Some vector machines provide a configurable vector register file to allow software to dynamically choose the optimal configuration. For example, the Fujitsu VPP 5000 allows software to select vector register configurations ranging from 256 vector registers each holding 128 elements to eight vector registers holding 4096 elements each. For loops where few temporary values exist, longer vector registers can be used to reduce instruction bandwidth and stripmining overhead, while for loops where many temporary values exist, the number of shorter vector registers can be increased to reduce the number of vector register spills and, hence, the data memory bandwidth required. The main disadvantage of a configurable vector register file is the increase in control logic complexity and the increase in machine state to hold the configuration information.

## Traditional Vector Computers versus Microprocessor Multimedia Extensions

Traditional vector supercomputers were developed to provide high performance on data parallel code developed in a compiled high level language (almost always a dialect of FORTRAN) while requiring only simple control units. Vector registers were designed with a large number of elements (64 for the Cray-1). This allowed a single vector instruction to occupy each deeply pipelined functional unit for many cycles. Even though only a single instruction could be issued per cycle, by starting separate vector instructions on different vector functional units, multiple vector instructions could overlap in execution at one time. In addition, adding more lanes allows each vector instruction to complete more elements per cycle.

MX ISAs for microprocessors evolved at a time where the base microprocessors were already issuing multiple scalar instructions per cycle. Another distinction is that the MX ISAs were not originally developed as compiler targets, but were intended to be used to write a few key library routines. This helps explain why MX ISAs, although sharing many attributes with earlier vector instructions, have evolved differently. The very short vectors in MX ISAs allow each instruction to only specify one or two cycle's worth of work for the functional units. To keep multiple functional units busy, the superscalar dispatch capability of the base scalar processor is used. To hide functional unit latencies, the multimedia code must be loop unrolled and software pipelined. In effect, the multimedia engine is being programmed in a microcoded style with the base scalar processor providing the microcode sequencer and each MX instruction representing one microcode primitive for the vector engine.

This approach of providing only primitive microcode level operations in the multimedia extensions also explains the lack of other facilities standard in a vector ISA. One example is vector length control. Rather than use long vectors and a VLR register, the MX ISAs provide short vector instructions that are placed in unrolled loops to operate on longer vectors. These unrolled loops can only be used with long vectors that are a multiple of the intrinsic vector length multiplied by the unrolling factor. Extra code is required to check for shorter vectors and to jump to separate code segments to handle short vectors and the remnants of any longer vector that were not handled by the unrolled loop. This overhead is greater than for the stripmining code in traditional vector ISAs, which simply set the VLR appropriately in the last iteration of the stripmined loop.

Vector loads and stores are another place where functionality has been moved into software for the MX ISAs. Most MX ISAs only provide unit-stride loads and stores that have to be aligned on boundaries corresponding to the vector length, not just aligned at element boundaries as in regular scalar code. For example, a unit-stride load of four 16-bit quantities has to be aligned at 64-bit boundaries in most MX instruction sets, although in some cases hardware will handle misaligned loads and stores at a slower rate. To help handle misaligned application vectors, various shift and align instructions have been added to MX ISAs to allow misalignment to be handled as part of the software microcoded loop. This approach simplifies the hardware design, but unfortunately these misaligned vectors are common in application code, and significant slowdown occurs when performing alignment in software. This encourages the use of loops optimized for certain operand alignments, which leads to an increase in code size and also in loop startup time to select the appropriate routine. In certain cases, the application can constrain the layout of the data elements to ensure alignment at the necessary boundaries, but typically this is only possible when the entire application has been optimized for these MX instructions, for example, in a dedicated media player. Strided and indexed operations are also usually coded as scalar loads and stores with a corresponding slowdown over full vector mode.

## Memory System Design

Perhaps the biggest difference between microprocessors and vector supercomputers is in the capabilities of the vector memory system. Vector supercomputers usually forgo data caches and rely on many banks of interleaved main memory to provide high memory bandwidth, while microprocessors rely on multilevel cache hierarchies to isolate the CPU from memory latencies and limited main memory bandwidth. A modern high-end vector supercomputer provides over 50 GB/s of main memory bandwidth per CPU, while high-end microprocessor systems provide only around 1 GB/s per CPU. For applications that require non-unit stride accesses to large data sets, the bandwidth discrepancy is even larger, because microprocessors access memory using long cache lines that waste bandwidth when there is little spatial locality. A modern vector CPU might sustain 16 or 32 non-unit stride memory operations every cycle pipelined out to main memory, with hundreds of outstanding memory accesses, while a microprocessor usually can only have a total of four to eight cache line misses outstanding at any time. This large difference in non-unit stride memory bandwidth is the main reason that vector supercomputers remain popular for certain applications, including car crash simulation and weather forecasting.

Traditional vector ISAs use long vector registers to help hide memory latency. MX ISAs have only very short vector registers and so require a different mechanism to hide memory latency and make better use of available main memory bandwidth. Various forms of hardware and software prefetching schemes have become popular with microprocessor designers to hide memory latency. Hardware prefetching schemes dynamically inspect memory references and attempt to predict which data will be needed next, fetching these into the cache before requested by the application. This approach has the advantage of not requiring changes to software, but can be inaccurate and can consume excessive memory bandwidth on mis-speculated prefetches.

Software prefetching can be very accurate as the compiler knows the reference patterns of each piece of code, but the software prefetch instructions have to be carefully scheduled so that data are not brought in too early, perhaps evicting useful data, or too late, which will leave some memory latency exposed. The optimal schedule depends on the CPU and memory system implementations, which implies that code optimized for one generation of CPU or one particular memory system.

For either hardware or software prefetching schemes, it is essential that the memory controller can support many outstanding requests, otherwise high memory bandwidths cannot be sustained from a typical high latency memory system.

## Future Directions

Microprocessor architects are continually searching for techniques that can take advantage of ever increasing transistor counts to improve application performance. Data parallel ISA extensions have proven effective on a wide range of applications, and hardware designs scale well to more parallel lanes. Existing supercomputers have sixteen 64-bit lanes while microprocessor MX implementations have expanded to two 64-bit lanes. It is likely that there will be further expansion of MX units to four or more 64-bit lanes. At higher lane counts, efficiencies drop, partly because of limited application vector lengths and partly because additional lanes do not help non-data parallel portions of each application.

An alternative approach to attaining high throughput on data parallel applications is to add more CPUs each with vector units and to parallelize loops at the thread level. This technique also allows independent CPUs to run different tasks to improve system throughput. The main disadvantages of this multiprocessor approach compared to simply increasing the number of lanes are the hardware costs of additional scalar processor logic and the additional inter-CPU synchronization costs. The relative cost of adding more CPUs is reduced as lane counts grow, particularly when the cost of providing sufficient main memory bandwidth is considered. The inter-CPU synchronization cost is a more serious issue as it adds to vector startup latencies and can increase $N_\_$ dramatically, reducing the effectiveness of multi-processors on shorter vectors. For this reason, vector supercomputers have added fast inter-CPU synchronization through dedicated shared semaphore registers. The Cray SV1 design makes use of these registers to gang together four 2-lane processors in software to appear as a single 8-lane processor to the user. It should be expected that some form of fast inter-CPU synchronization primitive will be added to ISAs as design move to chip-scale multiprocessors, as these primitives can also be applied to many types of thread-level parallel code.

Increased CPU clock frequencies and increased lane counts combine to dramatically increase the memory bandwidth required by a vector CPU. The cost of a traditional vector style memory system will become prohibitive even for high-end vector supercomputers. Even if the cost could be justified, the high memory latency of a flat memory system will hamper performance for applications that have lower degrees of parallelism and that can fit in caches, and a continued move towards cached memory hierarchies for vector machines is to be expected leading to a merging of vector supercomputer and microprocessor design points.

MX extensions for microprocessors have undergone considerable changes since first introduced. The current designs provide low-level arithmetic and memory system primitives that are intended to be used in hand-microcoded loops. These result in high startup overheads and large code size relative to traditional vector extensions as discussed above. A possible future direction that could merge the benefit of vector ISAs and out-of-order superscalar microprocessors would be to add vector-style ISA extensions, but have these interpreted by microcode sequencers that would produce internal elemental microoperations that would be passed through the regular register renaming and out-of-order dispatch stages of a modern superscalar execution engine. This is similar to the way that legacy CISC string operations are handled by modern implementations.

## Conclusions

Data parallel instructions have appeared in many forms in high-performance computer architectures over the last 30 years. They remain popular because many applications are amenable to data parallel execution, and because data parallel hardware is the simplest and cheapest way to exploit this type of application parallelism. As multimedia extensions evolve, they are likely to adopt more of the characteristics of traditional shared-memory vector ISAs to reduce loop startup overhead and decrease code size. However, these new multimedia vector ISAs will be shaped by the need to coexist with the speculative out-of-order execution engines used by the superscalar processors.

## References

1. Flynn, M. J., Very high-speed computing systems, *Proc. IEEE*, 54, 1901, 1966.
2. Barnes, G. H., et al., The Illiac IV computer, *IEEE Trans. on Computers*, C-17, 46, 1968.
3. Reddaway, S., DAP–A Distributed Array Processor, in *Proc. 1st Annual Symp. Computer Architectures*, Florida, 1973, 61.
4. Batcher, K. E., Architecture of a massively parallel processor, in *Proc. Int. Symp. Computer Architecture*, 1980.
5. Hillis, W. D., *The Connection Machine*, MIT Press, Cambridge, Massachusetts, 1985.
6. Hintz, R. G. and Tate, D. P., Control data STAR-100 processor design, in *Proc. COMPCON*, 1972, 1.
7. Cragon, H. G. and Watson, W. J., A retrospective analysis: the TI advanced scientific computer, *IEEE Computer*, 22, 55, 1989.
8. Russel, R. M., The CRAY-1 computer system, *Communications of the ACM*, 21, 63, 1978.

9.  Espasa, R., *Advanced Vector Architectures*, Ph.D. Thesis, Universitat Politecnica de Catalunya, Barcelona, 1997.

10. Asanovic, K., *Vector Microprocessors*, Ph.D. Thesis, University of California, Berkeley, 1998.

# 5.4  Multithreading, Multiprocessing

## Manoj Franklin

## Introduction

A defining challenge for research in computer science and engineering has been the ongoing quest for faster execution of programs. There is broad consensus that barring the use of novel technologies such as quantum computing and biological computing, the key to further progress in this quest is to do parallel processing of some kind.

The commodity microprocessor industry has been traditionally looking to fine-grained or instruction level parallelism (ILP) for improving performance, with sophisticated microarchitectural techniques (such as pipelining, branch prediction, out-of-order execution, and superscalar execution) and sophisticated compiler optimizations. Such hardware-centered techniques appear to have scalability problems in the sub-micron technology era and are already appearing to run out of steam. According to a recent position paper by Dally and Lacy [4], "Over the past 20 years, the increased density of VLSI chips was applied to close the gap between microprocessors and high-end CPUs. Today this gap is fully closed and adding devices to uniprocessors is well beyond the point of diminishing returns." We view ILP as the main success story form of parallelism thus far, as it was adopted in a big way in the commercial world for reducing the completion time of general purpose applications. The future promises to expand the "parallelism bridgehead" established by ILP with the "ground forces" of thread-level parallelism (TLP), by using multiple processing elements to exploit both fine-grained and coarse-grained parallelism in a natural way.

Current hardware trends are playing a driving role in the development of multiprocessing techniques. Two important hardware trends in this regard are single chip transistor count and clock speed, both of which have been steadily increasing due to advances in sub-micron technology. The Semiconductor Industry Association (SIA) has predicted that by 2012, industry will be manufacturing processors containing 1.4 billion transistors and running at 10 GHz [39]. DRAMs will grow to 4 Gbits in 2003. This increasing transistor budget has opened up new opportunities and challenges for the development of on-chip multiprocessing.

One of the challenges introduced by sub-micron technology is that wire delays become more important than gate delays [39]. This effect is predominant in global wires because their length depends on the die size, which is steadily increasing. An important implication of the physical limits of wire scaling is that, the area that is reachable in a single clock cycle of future processors will be confined to a small portion of the die [39].

A natural way to make use of the additional transistor budget and to deal with the wire delay problem is to use the concept of *multithreading* or *multiprocessing*[1] in the processor microarchitecture. That is, build the processor as a collection of independent *processing elements (PEs)*, each of which executes a separate *thread* or flow of control. By designing the processor as a collection of PEs, (a) the number of global wires reduces, and (b) very little communication occurs through global wires. Thus, much of the communication occurring in the multi-PE processor is *local* in nature and occurs through short wires.

In the recent past, several multithreading proposals have appeared in the literature. A few commercial processors have already started implementing some of these multithreading concepts in a single chip [24,34]. Although the underlying theme behind the different proposals is quite similar, the exact manner in which they perform multithreading is quite different. Each of the methodologies has different hardware

---

[1] In this section, we use the terms *multithreading, multiprocessing*, and *parallel processing* interchangeably. Similarly, we use the generic term *threads* whenever the context is applicable to processes, light-weight processes, and light-weight threads.

and software requirements and trade-offs. The objective of this chapter is to present a common framework for studying different multiprocessing and multithreading techniques, and to discuss existing multi-threaded processors and futuristic proposals in the light of this framework. The following are some of the questions that are specifically addressed in the common framework:

- Parallel programming model
- Nature of threads
- PE Interconnects
- Role of the compiler

The introduction section has highlighted the importance of multithreading and multiprocessing. The rest of this chapter is organized as follows. The section on "Parallel Processing Software Framework" presents a common framework for studying different multithreading and multiprocessing approaches, and highlights software issues that are important to consider while examining them. The section on "Parallel Processing Hardware Framework" presents a common framework for studying parallel processor hardware configurations. The "Concluding Remarks" section provides a survey of existing multithreaded processors and proposals. In particular, it describes how multithreading is employed in the multiscalar processor, the superthreaded processor, the trace processor, the M-machine, and some of the other multithreaded microarchitectures. Finally, "Concluding Remarks" presents a qualitative comparison and discusses future trends.

## Parallel Processing Software Framework

In this section we discuss our framework for studying multithreading and multiprocessing. We also identify three key issues related to multithreading: thread granularity, parallel programming model, and program partitioning into threads. We shall discuss each of these issues in detail. Not all of these issues are entirely orthogonal to each other, and it is our objective to highlight how each issue bears on other related issues.

We define a *thread* as a flow of control through a program and that flow's current state (represented by a current program counter, a call/return stack and, occasionally, some thread-private data). The central idea behind multithreading and multiprocessing is to have multiple flows of control within a process, allowing parts of the process to be executed in parallel. A process can have one or more threads doing its work. Threads that execute in parallel are invariably control-independent, in which case the decision to execute a thread does not depend on the other active threads. Thus, instructions that are control-dependent on a conditional branch invariably belong to the thread to which that branch belongs.

### Parallel Programming Model

An important attribute of any multiprocessing/multithreading system is its parallel programming model, embodied in a parallel language or programming environment. This model specifies the names (such as registers and memory addresses) the thread can access, the operations it can perform on the named data, and the ordering semantics among these operations, particularly those done by distinct threads. (In the simplest case, the model assumes multiprogramming, which has no inter-thread communication and synchronization.) First, we will discuss thread sequencing model, which specifies ordering constraints (if any) on multiple threads. Then, we discuss inter-thread communication, which deals with passing data values among two or more threads. Finally, we discuss synchronization aspects of the programming model, which cause running threads to wait for one another, and waiting threads to resume execution at the proper time. Orchestrating the inter-thread ordering often requires explicit synchronization operations when the ordering implicit in the basic operations is not sufficient.

#### *Thread Granularity and Management*

Thread-level parallelism (TLP) is more coarse-grained than ILP, and has wide variance in granularity. We categorize the TLP granularities into three levels as described below. Depending on the granularity, thread management (including run-time thread scheduling) is done by the operating system or the run-time hardware.

- *Processes:* In this case, a thread is a process itself. Parallel processing then involves executing multiple processes in parallel, which is traditionally known as *multitasking* or *multiprogramming*. This is perhaps the most common form of parallel processing, as even most of the uniprocessor operating systems implement this (by time sharing). Multiple processes can be created using the `fork` system call. Processes can be thought of as heavy-weight threads, as their creation entails duplicating the memory address space, and can take hundreds of thousands of CPU clock cycles. Management and scheduling of processes is done by the operating system. In a multiprogramming environment, parallelly executing processes either do not communicate, or communicate through operating system features such as `pipes`.

- *Light-weight processes or threads:* A light-weight process (also called *thread*) has a granularity somewhat finer than a process. The concept of light-weighted processes has been implemented in a number of operating systems (SUN Solaris, IBM AIX, and Microsoft Windows NT), thread libraries, and parallel programming languages. Such threads are used in today's symmetric multiprocessor workstations and servers. An important characteristic is that these threads share a common memory address space, and are nonspeculative from the control point of view.

- *Fine-grain threads:* These threads are much smaller (of the order a few hundred instructions, at most) and are not generally known to the operating system. Thread management and scheduling are typically done by the run-time hardware. In many cases, such threads share a common register space, besides sharing a common memory address space. Furthermore, the threads are often speculative from the control point of view.

For a particular TLP granularity, the system performance will depend to a large extent on the nature of the application and the level of the memory hierarchy at which the PEs are interconnected.

### Thread Sequencing Model

The commonly used model for control flow among threads is the *parallel threads* model (also called the *control operators based parallel control flow* model). In this model, a *fork* instruction or a variant specifies the creation of new threads and their starting addresses. The parent thread as well as the forked threads are allowed to execute in parallel until they reach a *join* instruction, after which only one of them can continue. Thus, the join operation serves as a synchronizing point. Apart from the join, other explicit synchronization operations can be introduced using *locks* and *barriers*. Computation inside each thread is based on sequential control flow. This thread sequencing model is illustrated in Fig. 5.13.

Compilers and programmers have made significant progress in parallelizing regular numeric applications for the parallel threads model; however, they have had little or no success in doing the same for highly irregular numeric or especially nonnumeric applications [18]. In such applications memory addresses

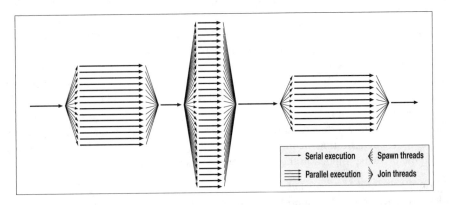

**FIGURE 5.13**   Parallelism profile for a parallel threads model.

are difficult (if not impossible) to statically predict—in part because they often depend on run-time inputs and behavior—that makes it extremely difficult for the compiler to statically prove whether or not potential threads are independent. Given the size and complexity of real non-numeric programs, parallelization appears to be an unrealistic goal if we stick to the parallel threads model. For such applications, we can use a different thread control flow model called *sequential threads* model. This model is closer to sequential control flow, and envisions a strict sequential ordering among the threads. That is, threads are extracted from sequential code and run in parallel, without violating the sequential program semantics. The control flow of the sequential code imposes an order on the threads and, therefore, we can use the terms *predecessor* and *successor* to qualify the relation between any given pair of threads. This means that inter-thread communication between any two threads (if any) is strictly in one direction, as dictated by the sequential thread ordering. Thus, no explicit synchronization operations are necessary, as the sequential semantics of the threads guarantee proper synchronization. This relaxation allows us to "parallelize" nonnumeric applications into threads without explicit synchronization, even if there is a potential inter-thread data dependence. Program correctness will not be violated if at run time there is a true data dependence between two threads. The purpose of identifying threads in such a model is to indicate that those threads are good candidates for parallel execution.

Examples for multithreading proposals using sequential threads are the multiscalar model [8,9,30], the superthreading model [35], the trace processing model [28,36], and the dynamic multithreading model [1]. When using the sequential threads model, we can have threads that are *nonspeculative* from the control point of view, as well as threads that are *speculative* from the control point of view. The latter model is often called *speculative multithreading (SpMT)*. This model is particularly important to deal with the complex control flow present in typical non-numeric programs. The multiscalar architecture [8,9,30] provided a complete design and evaluation of an SpMT architecture. Since then, many other proposals have extended the basic idea of SpMT [5,19,22,28,31,35,36]. One such extension is threaded multipath execution (TME) [38], in which the speculative threads are the alternate paths of hard-to-predict branches. A simple form of the SpMT model uses loop-based threads only [15,22].

### Inter-Thread Communication

Inter-thread communication refers to passing data values between two or more threads. One of the key issues in a parallel programming model is the name levels at which sharing takes place between threads. Communication can take place at the level of register space, memory address space, and I/O space, with the registers being the level closest to the processor. If sharing can happen at a particular level, it can also happen at a more distant level. Parallel programming models can be classified into three categories, based on the sharing level that is closest to the processor:

- Shared register model
- Shared memory model
- Message passing model

In the *shared register model*, multiple threads share the same register space (or a portion of it). Inter-thread communication happens implicitly due to reads and writes to the shared registers (and to shared memory locations). This model typically uses fine-grain threads, because it is difficult to have long threads that communicate at the low level of registers, granularity is small. This class of parallel processors is fairly new and has evolved as an extension of single-threaded ILP processors. Examples are the multiscalar execution model [8,9,30], the trace execution model [28,36], and the dynamic multithreading model (DMT) [1].

In the *shared memory model*, multiple threads share a common memory address space (or a portion of it). Inter-thread communication occurs implicitly as a result of conventional memory access instructions to shared memory locations. That is, writes to a logically shared address by one thread are visible to reads of the other threads, provided there are no other prior writes to that address as per the memory consistency/synchronization model.

In the *message passing model*, inter-thread communication occurs only through explicit I/O operations called messages. That is, the inter-thread communication is integrated at the I/O level rather than at the memory level. The messages are of two kinds—*send* and *receive*—and their variants. The combination of a send and a matching receive accomplishes a pairwise synchronization event. Several variants of the above synchronization event are possible. Message passing has long been used as a means of communication and synchronization among cooperating processes. Operating system functions such as *sockets* serve precisely this function.

### Inter-Thread Synchronization
Synchronization involves coordinating the results of a set of parallel threads into some merged result. An example is waiting for one thread to finish filling a buffer before another begins using the data. Synchronization is achieved in different ways:

- *Control Synchronization:* Control synchronization depends only on the threads' control state and is not affected by the threads' data state. This synchronization method requires a thread to wait until other thread(s) reach a particular control point. Examples for control synchronization operations are *barriers* and *critical sections*. With barrier synchronization, all parallel threads have a common barrier point. Each thread is allowed to proceed after the barrier only after all of the spawned threads have reached the barrier point. This type of synchronization is typically used when the results generated by the spawned threads need to be merged. With critical section type synchronization, only one thread is allowed to enter into the critical section code at a time. Thus, when a thread reaches a critical section, it will wait if another thread is currently executing the same critical section code.
- *Data Synchronization:* Data synchronization depends on the threads' data values. This synchronization method requires a thread to wait at a point until a shared name is updated with a particular value (by another thread). For instance, a thread executing a `wait (x == 0)` statement will be delayed until `x` becomes zero. Data synchronization operations are typically used to implement *locks*, *monitors*, and *events*, which, in turn, can be used to implement *atomic operations* and *critical sections*. When a thread executes a sequence of operations as an atomic operation, other threads cannot access any of the (shared) names updated during the atomic operation until the atomic operation has been completed.

## Coherence and Consistency
The last aspect that we will consider about the parallel programming model is coherence and consistency when threads share a name space. Coherence specifies that the value obtained by a read to a shared location should be the latest value written to that location. Notice that when a read and a write are present in two parallel threads, coherence does not specify any ordering between them. It merely states that if one thread sees an updated value at a particular time, all other threads must also see the updated value from that time onward (until another update happens to the same location).

The consistency model determines the time at which a written value will be made visible to other threads. It specifies constraints on the order in which operations to the shared space must appear to be performed (i.e., become visible to other threads) with respect to one another. This includes operations to the same locations or to different locations, and by the same thread or different threads. Thus, every transaction (or parallel transactions) transfers a collection of threads from one consistent state to another. Exactly what is consistent depends on the consistency model. Several consistency models have been proposed:

- *Sequential Consistency:* This is the most intuitive consistency model. As per sequential consistency, the reads and writes to a shared address space from all threads must appear to execute serially in such a manner as to conform to the program orders in individual threads. This implies that the overall order of memory accesses must preserve the order in each thread, regardless of how instructions from different threads are interleaved. A multiprocessor system is *sequentially consistent* if it always produces results that are same as what could be obtained when the operations of all threads are executed in some sequential order [20]. Sequential consistency is very restrictive and prevents the multiprocessor hardware from performing many optimizations to improve performance.

- *Weak Consistency:* This consistency model [6] relaxes the constraints imposed by sequential consistency by relating memory access order to synchronization points in the program. That is, sequential consistency is maintained among the synchronization accesses. In addition, a synchronization access serves as a barrier by enforcing that all previous memory accesses must be completed before performing a synchronization access, and no subsequent memory accesses can be performed before completing a synchronization access.

In addition to weak consistency, several other relaxed consistency models have been proposed—*release consistency* [12], *processor consistency* [13], etc.

## Partitioning a Program into Threads

Thread selection involves partitioning a control flow graph (CFG) into threads. Given a particular parallel programming model (inter-thread communication model as well as thread sequencing model), how should the parallelizer go about deciding where the thread boundaries should be? Perhaps the most important issue in multiprocessing/multithreading is the basis used for partitioning a program into threads. The criterion used for partitioning is very important, because an improper partitioning could in fact result in high inter-thread communication and synchronization, thereby degrading performance! True multithreading should not only aim to distribute instructions evenly among the threads, but also aim to minimize inter-thread communication by localizing a major share of the inter-instruction communication occurring in the processor to within each PE. In order to achieve this, mutually data dependent instructions are most likely allocated to the same thread. This is somewhat hard, because programs are currently written in control-driven form, which often causes individual strands of data-dependent instructions to be spread over a large segment of code. Thus, the partitioning software has to first construct the data flow graph (DFG), and then do the program partitioning. Notice that if programs were specified in data-driven form as in the dataflow computation model [17], taking data dependences into account would have been simpler.

Thread selection is a difficult problem, because we need to consider many issues such as PE utilization, load balancing, control independence of threads (thread prediction accuracy for SpMT models), and inter-thread data dependences. Often, trying to make optimizations for one area will have a negative effect on another.

### Who Does the Program Partitioning?

Program partitioning can be done by the programmer, compiler, or run-time hardware. Depending on who does the partitioning, the type of analysis that can be done will be different.

- *Programmer:* In this approach, the programmer explicitly represents the threads in the high-level language program. In order to do this, three types of extensions are provided at the high-level language level: (i) multithreading library, (ii) language extensions, and (iii) compiler directives. Examples for this approach are EARTH [21] and XMT [37]. All of these use the parallel threads model. Notice that the compiler has to be modified to handle these extensions. The compiler does not, however, make decisions on where to do the partitioning. It is interesting to note that although conventional multiprocessors have been commercially available for quite some time, only a small fraction of the software has been written so far to exploit parallelism.

- *Compiler:* In this case, the compiler takes a sequential program and partitions it into threads. The main advantage of deferring program partitioning to the compiler is that it frees the programmer from reasoning about parallel threads. Its main advantages with respect to hardware-based partitioning are that it does not add to the complexity of the processor, and that it has the ability to perform complex pre-partitioning and post-partitioning optimizations that are difficult to perform at run-time. Compiler-directed partitioning algorithms are generally insensitive to the number of PEs in the processor, however, its partitioning decisions need to be conveyed to the multithreaded hardware, possibly by making it part of the ISA (at the expense of incompatibility for existing binaries). Parallelizing compilers have been successful in parallelizing many numeric applications for the parallel threads model. As pointed out earlier, their success has not been spectacular when it comes to non-numeric applications and the parallel threads model. Several researchers are currently working on parallelizing compilers that parallelize such applications for the sequential threads model.

- *Hardware:* It is also possible to let the run-time hardware do the program partitioning. If partitioning decisions are taken by the hardware, the multithreaded processor provides object code compatibility to existing sequential code. Furthermore, it has the ability to adapt to run-time behavior. Hardware-based partitioning is typically done only if the thread granularity is small, and if sequential control flow is used. The main limitation is the significant impact it may have on clock cycle time. In order to simplify the dynamic partitioning hardware and to reduce the impact on clock cycle time, the partitioning job is often split into two parts—a static part (which is done by pre-processing hardware) and a dynamic part. The static part collects information that is static in nature (such as register dependences in a straightline piece of code) and stores it in a special i-cache structure, often after performing some additional processing. The dynamic part uses this information while deciding the final partitioning at run-time. Examples of multithreaded processors that use hardware-based partitioning are trace processor [28,36], speculative multi-threading processor [22], and dynamic multithreading processor [1].

### Compiling for Multithreading

Most of the multithreading approaches perform partitioning at compile time, possibly with some help from the programmer; it is somewhat unrealistic at this time to expect programmers to write only parallel programs. The hardware is also limited in its program partitioning capability. Therefore, the compiler has the potential to play a significant role in multithreading. Besides program partitioning, it can schedule threads as well as the instructions within threads.

The task of the compiler is to identify sufficient parallelism to keep the processors busy, while minimizing the effects of synchronization and communication latencies on the execution time of the program. To accomplish this objective, a parallelizing compiler typically performs the following functions:

1. Identify the parallelism inherent in the program. This phase has received the most attention in parallel compiler research to date [25,26]. Many varied program transformations have been developed to unearth parallelism buried in the semantics of sequential programs.
2. Partition the program into multiple threads for parallel execution. This is perhaps the most crucial phase. Many factors must be considered, such as inter-thread dependences, intra-thread locality, thread size, critical path, and deadlock avoidance.
3. Schedule the concurrent execution of threads; the final scheduling is often determined by the run-time environment. The compiler must assign threads to processors in a way that maximizes processor utilization without severely restricting the amount of parallelism to be exploited.
4. After program partitioning, the compiler can schedule the instructions in a thread so as to reduce inter-thread wait times. For instance, if a shared value is produced very late in one thread, but is needed very early in another thread, very little parallelism will be exploited by the hardware. This problem is likely to surface frequently, if the compiler assumed a single-threaded processor in the code generation phase. In such situations, post-partitioning scheduling can help minimize the waiting time of instructions by ensuring that shared values required in other threads are produced as early as possible. Post-partitioning scheduling is especially beneficial if PEs execute their instructions in strict serial order.

### Object Code Compatibility

Another important issue, especially from the commercial point of view, is the level of compatibility that the multithreaded processor provides. We can think of three levels of compatibility in the context of multithreaded processors: full compatibility, family-wide compatibility, and no compatibility.

- *Full Compatibility:* In some multithreaded processors, the multithreading aspect is strictly a microarchitectural phenemenon and is invisible at the ISA level. Such processors provide full compatibility, i.e., both backward compatibility and forward compatibility. Existing executable binaries can be run on them, and their executable binaries can be run on existing processors. Furthermore, these processors also provide compatibility across all multithreading models (of the same ISA) that provide full compatibility. In these processors, the thread partitioning is done by offline hardware or run-time hardware. Fully compatible multithreaded processors have a higher chance for commercial success.

- *Family-Wide Compatibility:* Although full compatibility is desirable, some multithreaded processors opt for ISA-level changes so as to benefit from compiler techniques to extract additional performance. Processors in the family-wide compatibility category provide compatibility within its multithreading family. Thus, they do not require recompilation to be performed when the number of PEs is changed. Generally, these processors also provide limited backward compatibility (albeit at reduced performance). For example, if an existing binary executable is given to the multiscalar processor, it can execute the entire program as a single task. This will not give good performance, but it can run the old binaries.

- *No Compatibility:* In spite of the benefits of object code compatibility, some multithreaded processors, such as the M-machine, go in for significant changes at the ISA-level, which preclude any possibility of backward compatibility or family-wide compatibility. The motivation is to tap into sophisticated compiler techniques to extract performance.

Several techniques for binary translation have been proposed recently to address the object code compatibility problem. These include static approach as in the FX!32 [16], dynamic approach as in the DAISY [7] and hardware-based schemes such as DIF [23]. Object code compatibility may become a less important issue in the future when these techniques become more mature and efficient. This will also open up more opportunities to tap architecture specific optimizations for multithreading in the future.

## Parallel Processing Hardware Framework

The previous section discussed a common framework for parallel programming and compilation. This section discusses a common framework for parallel processing hardware. In our hardware framework, regardless of the specific implementation, a multithreaded processor consists of multiple PEs, possibly along with a few centralized resources such as the thread allocation mechanism and parts of the memory subsystem, as shown in Fig. 5.14. The PEs work independently of each other (subject only to inter-PE

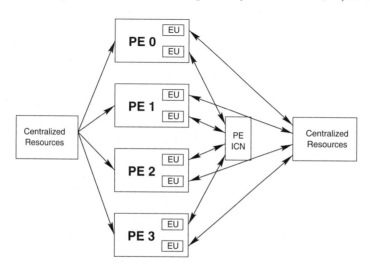

**FIGURE 5.14**  A generic 4-PE multiprocessor.

synchronization) and usually contain multiple execution units (EUs). The PEs are interconnected by some network or through centralized resources such as register file and memory, for inter-PE communication.

Our definition of a PE is somewhat loose. On one extreme, the PEs in some multithreaded processors are separate processor-memory systems with their own instruction cache, decode unit, register file, and execution units; on the other extreme, the PEs in some multithreaded processors even share the execution units, as in the dynamic multithreading processor [1]. Such a loose definition allows us to discuss a wide spectrum of multithreaded processors under a common framework.

## Number of PEs and PE Organization

The number of PEs in a multiprocessor is an important hardware parameter. This number is strongly tied to the perceived parallelism in the targeted application domain, and also the nature of the threads. On one extreme, we have single-PE multithreaded processors that perform time sharing. On the other extreme, we have massively parallel processors (MPPs) consisting of thousands of PEs, which are the most powerful machines available today for many time-critical applications [4]. Because of the sharp increase in the number of transistors integrated in a single chip, there is significant interest in integrating multiple PEs in the same chip. This has been the motivation behind many of the SpMT processing models.

### *Processor Context Interleaving*

When the number of parallel threads exceeds the number of PEs, it is possible to time-share a single PE among multiple threads in a way that minimizes the time required to switch threads. This is accomplished by sharing as much as possible of the program execution environment between the different threads so that very little state needs to be saved and restored when changing threads. This type of low-overhead interleaving is given the name *multithreading* in many circles [2,3,17]. Interleaving-based multithreading differs from conventional multitasking (or multiprogramming) in that the concurrent threads share more of their environment with each other than do concurrent tasks under multitasking. Threads may be distinguished only by the value of their program counters and stack pointers while sharing a single address space and set of global variables. As a result, there is very little protection of one thread from another, in contrast to multitasking. Interleaving-based multithreading can thus be used for very fine-grain multitasking, at the level of a few instructions, and so can hide latency by keeping the processor busy after one thread issues a long-latency instruction on which subsequent instructions in that thread depend.

- *Cycle-level interleaving:* In this scheme, a PE switches to a different thread after each instruction fetch; i.e., an instruction of another thread is fetched and fed into the execution pipeline in the next clock cycle. Cycle level interleaving is typically used for coarse-grain threads—processes or light-weight processes. The motivation for this is that it eliminates control and data dependences between the instructions that are simultaneously active in the pipeline. Thus, there is no need to build complex forwarding paths, permitting a simple and potentially fast pipeline. Furthermore, the context switch latency is zero cycles. Memory latency is tolerated by not scheduling a thread until the memory access has been completed. For this interleaving to work well, there must be as many threads as the worst-case latencies experienced by the instructions. Interleaving the instructions from many threads limits the processing speed of a single thread, thereby degrading single-thread performance. The most well-known examples of cycle-level interleaving processors are HEP [29], Horizon [33], and Tera MTA [2].

- *Block interleaving:* In this scheme, the instructions of a thread are executed successively until a long-latency event occurs, which causes a context switch. A typical long-latency operation is a remote memory access. Compared to the cycle-level interleaving technique, a smaller number of threads is sufficient, and a single thread can execute at full speed until the next context switch. The events that cause a context switch can be determined statically or dynamically.

When hardware technology allows more PEs to be integrated in a processor, PE interleaving becomes less attractive, because computational throughput will clearly improve when multiple threads execute in

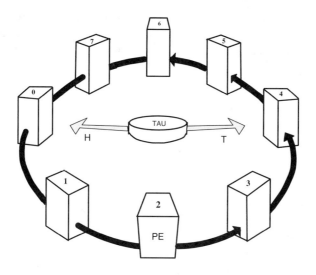

**FIGURE 5.15** Organizing the PEs of a multithreaded processor as a circular queue.

parallel on multiple PEs instead of time-sharing a single PE. As we look into the future, and the prospect of a billion transistors on a single chip, it seems inevitable that microprocessors will have multiple PEs.

### PE Organization

The next issue of importance in a multithreaded processor is the organization of the PEs. This issue is strongly tied to the PE interconnect used. Most of the sequential threads model based processors organize the PEs as a circular queue, as shown in Fig. 5.15. The circular queue imposes a sequential order among the PEs, with the head pointer indicating the oldest active PE. When the tail PE is idle, a thread allocation unit (TAU) invokes the next thread (as per the sequential thread ordering) on the tail PE and advances the tail pointer. Completed threads are retired from the head of the PE queue, enforcing the required sequential ordering. Although this PE organization is tailored for sequential threads (from a sequential program), this multithreaded hardware can also execute multiple threads from different processes, if required.

An important issue that needs to be considered when organizing the PEs as a circular queue is *load balancing*. If some PEs have long threads assigned to them, and the rest have short ones, only modest performance will be obtained. If threads are not close to the same size, a short thread may complete soon and perform no useful computation while it waits for longer predecessor threads to retire. To get good performance, threads should be of uniform length.[1] One option to deal with load balancing, albeit with additional hardware complexity, is to let each physical PE have multiple virtual PEs and assign a thread to each of the virtual PEs.

## Inter-PE Register Communication and Synchronization

As discussed earlier, a few multithreading approaches have a shared register space for all threads, and the rest do not. When threads share a common register space, the thread sequencing model has always been the sequential threads model. Because the semantics of this model are in line with sequential control flow, synchronization happens automatically, once inter-PE register communication is handled properly.

### Register File Implementation

When threads do not share a common register space, it is straightforward to implement the register file (RF)—each PE can have its own register file, thereby providing fast register access. When threads share

---

[1]The actual, more stringent, requirement is that the thread execution times should be matched across all PEs. This is a more difficult problem, because it depends on intra- and inter-PE data dependences as well.

a common register space, it is important that we still provide a separate register file in each PE to support fast register access, as it is difficult for a centralized register file to provide a 1-cycle multi-port access time with today's high clock rates. This decentralization can be achieved in two ways, both of which provide faster register access times due to physical proximity and fewer access ports per physical register file.

- *RF Partitioning:* In this approach, each physical register file implements (or maps) an independent set of ISA-visible registers. Notice that a PE may occasionally need a register value stored in a nonlocal register file, in which case the value is fetched through an interconnection network that interconnects the PEs.

- *RF Replication:* With the replication scheme, a physical copy of the register file is kept in each PE, so that each PE has a local copy of the shared set register space. These register file replica maintain different *versions* of the register space, i.e., the multiple copies of the register file store register values that correspond to the processor state at different points in a sequential execution of the program. In general, replication avoids unnecessary communication; however, if not done carefully, it might increase communication by replicating data that is not used in the future. A multithreaded processor that uses the replication scheme is the multiscalar processor [9].

### PE Interconnect for Register Values

When threads share a common register space, and a distributed RF structure is used, an important hardware attribute is the type of interconnect used to send register values from one PE to another. The interconnects that have been proposed in the context of multithreaded processors are bus, ring (unidirectional and bi-directional), crossbar, mesh, and hypercube; of course, it is possible to use other types of interconnects as well.

**Bus:** The bus is a simple, fully connected network. However, it permits only one data transmission at any time, providing a bandwidth of only O(1). In fact, the bandwidth scaling is worse than O(1) because of reduction in bus operating speed with the number of ports, due to increase in capacitance. Therefore, it may be a poor choice as an interconnect for inter-PE register communication, which may be nontrivial, especially when using a large number of PEs.

**Crossbar:** A crossbar interconnect also provides full connectivity from every PE to every other PE. It provides O($N$) bandwidth, but the cost of the interconnect is proportional to the number of cross-points, or O($N^2$). When using a crossbar, all PEs are of same proximity to each other; hence the thread allocation algorithm becomes straightforward; however, a crossbar may not scale as easily as a ring or mesh. It is important to note that fast crossbars can be built on a single chip. With a crossbar-type interconnect, there is no notion of neighboring PEs, so all PEs become equally far away. Therefore, the cross-chip wire delays begin to dominate the inter-PE communication latency.

**Ring:** With a ring-type interconnect, the PEs are connected as a circular loop, and there is a notion of neighboring PEs and distant PEs. Routing in a ring is trivial because there is exactly one route between any pair of nodes (two routes if it is a bi-directional ring). The ring can be easily laid out with O($N$) space using short wires (as depicted in Fig. 5.15), which can be easily widened. A ring is ideal if most of the inter-PE register communication can be localized to neighboring PEs (which is typically the case in a sequential threads processor that uses the circular queue PE organization [36]), but is a poor choice if a lot of communication happens across distant PEs. An advantage of the ring is that it easily supports the scaling up of the number of PEs, as allowed by technological advances.

**Mesh:** Rings generalize naturally to higher dimensions, including 2D grids and 3D cubes (with end-around connections). The main advantages of mesh are its regular structure and its ability to provide full connectivity between four neighboring PEs (as opposed to two PEs with the ring). Similar to a ring, a mesh can easily support the scaling up of the number of PEs. The mesh suffers from the same disadvantages of a ring in communicating with distant PEs. Moreover, thread allocation for a mesh topology is more complex than that for ring and crossbar.

## Inter-PE Memory Communication and Synchronization

When threads do not share a common memory address space (as in the message passing model), it is straightforward to provide a memory system for each PE, as we do not need to worry about inter-thread memory communication and synchronization.

### Memory System Implementation

When threads do share a common memory address space, the multithreaded processor needs to provide appropriate mechanisms for inter-thread memory communication as well as synchronization. One option is to provide a central memory system, in which all memory accesses roughly take the same amount of time. Such a system is called *uniform memory access (UMA)* system. An important class of UMA systems is the *symmetric multiprocessor (SMP)*.

A UMA system may provide uniformly slow access time for every memory access. Instead of slowing down every access, we can provide fast access time for most of the accesses by distributing the memory system (or at least the top portions of the memory hierarchy system). Shared memory multiprocessors that use partitioning are called *distributed shared memory (DSM)* systems. As with the register file structure, we can use two techniques—partitioning and replication—to distribute the memory.

- *Memory Partitioning:* Partitioning is useful if it is possible to confine most of the memory accesses made in one PE to its partition. Partitioning the top portion of the memory hierarchy may not be attractive, at least for irregular, non-numeric applications, because it may be difficult to do this confinement due to not knowing the addresses of most of the loads and stores at compile time. Partitioning of the lower portion of the memory hierarchy is often done, however, as this portion needs to handle only those accesses that missed in the PEs' local caches.

- *Memory Replication:* It is impractical to replicate the entire memory system. Therefore, only the top part of the memory hierarchy is replicated. The basic motivation behind replicating the top portion of the memory hierarchy among local caches is to satisfy most of the memory accesses made in a PE with its local cache. Notice that a replicated cache structure must maintain proper coherency among all the duplicate copies of data.

DSMs often use a combination of partitioning and replication, i.e., portions of the memory hierarchy are replicated and the rest are partitioned. One type uses replicated cache memories and partitioned main memories. One interesting variation is the *cache only memory architecture (COMA)* system. A COMA multiprocessor partitions the entire memory system across the PEs; however, there is no fixed partition assigned for a particular memory location. Rather, the partition associated with a memory location is dynamically changed based on the PEs that access that location. Several other shared memory organizations are also possible [3,17].

### Inter-PE Data Dependence Speculation

In the parallel threads model, synchronization of threads is carried out with the use of special mechanisms such as locks and barriers. In the sequential threads model, ensuring sequential semantics ensures proper memory synchronization. However, this means that when a load instruction is encountered in a PE, it has to ensure that its producer store has been already executed. This is difficult to determine if the producer store belongs to another thread, as memory addresses are calculated at run-time, and it is possible that the producer store instruction may not have even been fetched. In order to overcome this problem, sequential threads based processors incorporate some form of *thread-level data speculation* [11]. The idea is to speculate if a memory operation has to wait for inter-thread synchronization. This speculation can be as simple as predicting that the producer store has been already executed, or it can be more complex, based on past behavior of the load instruction. Below we discuss some of the hardware schemes proposed for carrying out thread-level data speculation.

- *Address Resolution Buffer (ARB):* The ARB [11] is a hardware buffer for storing different versions of several memory locations as well as information regarding the loads and stores executed from the currently active threads. Each entry in the ARB buffers all versions of the same memory location.

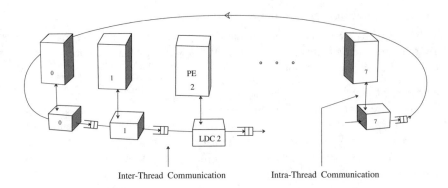

**FIGURE 5.16**    Block diagram of a multi-version cache in a sequential threads based multithreaded processor.

When a load request is issued for a particular memory address, the corresponding ARB entry is checked to see if a prior store has been done to the same address; if so, the value written by the latest store is returned by the ARB; if not, the request is sent to the next lower level of the memory hierarchy. In either case, the state information for that location is updated to reflect the fact that a load has been made by the current thread. When a store operation is performed, the ARB checks if any sequentially successor loads have been prematurely performed. If so, that is an incorrect data dependence speculation, and the ARB hardware initiates a recovery action such as partially re-executing the thread containing the incorrect load (and subsequent threads). A centralized hardware approach such as the ARB has the danger of increasing the load latency due to long latency incurred because of long wires.

- *Multi-Version Cache (MVC):* The MVC uses a decentralized approach by using a local data cache (LDC) for each PE [10]. Each LDC thus stores a different version for each mapped memory location. The local data caches are interconnected by a unidirectional ring, as shown in Fig. 5.16. The loads and stores generated in a PE are serviced directly from its local data cache. When a load request is issued to a local data cache, it provides a value if it has a copy; otherwise, the request is sent to the next lower level of the memory hierarchy. In either case, the state information for that location in the data cache is updated to reflect the fact that a load has been made by the current thread. When a store operation is performed, the value is written in its local data cache. The last updates to each memory location (in a thread) are forwarded to the subsequent LDCs through the ring-type interconnect. When a forwarded value reaches an LDC, it checks for incorrect speculations and takes appropriate recovery actions.

- *Speculative Versioning Cache (SVC):* The speculative versioning cache is similar to the multi-version cache in many respects [14]. It also keeps a separate private cache for each PE. The differences are mainly in the way the caches are connected and in the methodology by which the caches are kept coherent. SVC uses a bus interconnect for the caches a snooping bus based cache coherence protocol.

## Concluding Remarks

Multithreaded processors are the future of computer design. The ease of hardware replication has proven to be an ever-increasing impetus toward parallel processor implementations. The goal is to maintain high levels of parallelism (without increasing hardware complexity and the clock rate) by distributing the dynamic instruction stream among several processing elements. The combined issue rates of several processing elements allow large amounts of parallelism to be exploited.

Multithreading and multiprocessing, as with other complex engineering problems, undergo an ongoing process of reinventing, borrowing, and adapting.

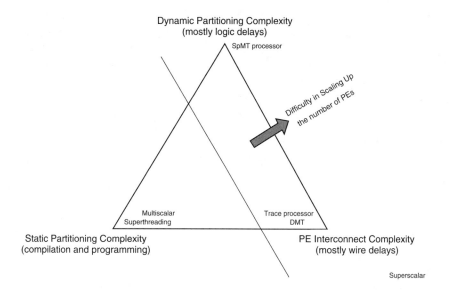

**FIGURE 5.17**  Complexity in multithreading/multiprocessing.

Looking forward to the future of multithreaded processors, the pace of change makes for rich opportunities and also for great challenges. Although it is difficult to precisely predict where this field will go, this final section seeks to outline some of the key areas of development in multithreaded processors. Whatever technological breakthroughs occur and whatever directions the market takes, the fundamental issues addressed in the "Parallel Processing Software Framework" section will still apply. The realization of multithreaded processors will still rest upon good techniques to perform thread selection, inter-PE communication, and synchronization. The core techniques for addressing these issues will remain valid; however, the way that they are employed will surely change as the critical parameters of clock speeds and wire delays continue to change.

It is difficult to obtain good performance without having *complexity* somewhere in the hardware-software multithreaded system! In a high-performance multithreaded processor, the complexity could be at the static partitioning side (programming or compiler), at the dynamic partitioning hardware side, or at the PE interconnect side. Figure 5.17 illustrates this concept. To support hardware scalability, complexity at the dynamic partitioning hardware and the PE interconnect act as hurdles. In the long run, as more transistors are integrated into a processor chip, it can be expected that the number of PEs would be scaled up. However, the trend towards higher clock rates will make it more difficult to support complexity in the dynamic partitioning hardware and in the PE interconnect.[2] Thus, the end result of the trends in high transistor count and high clock rates (which encourage multithreading/multiprocessing) is a shift towards doing more and more things statically, as opposed to dynamically. This means that program partitioning will eventually be done only at compilation time, and perhaps more and more at programming time.

## To Probe Further

Multiprocessing has been around for a long time, and so naturally the computer literature has an overabundance of articles and textbooks on this subject. The multiprocessing community consists of different camps, which often use different terminology for the same concepts. This lack of consensus makes it somewhat difficult to merge the ideas presented in different papers or books. Nevertheless, we

---

[2]Although it is possible to pipeline a crossbar interconnect so that it can accept new requests every cycle, the long inter-PE latency that it causes would increase the number of clock cycles required to execute a program, compared with what is obtained with scalable interconnects [27].

list a few helpful references to which interested readers can refer. Two recent good textbooks on this subject are *Parallel Computer Architecture: A Hardware/Software Approach* [3] and *Scalable Parallel Computing* [17]. Two important journals dealing with parallel processing are *Journal of Parallel and Distributed Computing* and *IEEE Transactions on Parallel and Distributed Systems*. In addition, readers can keep abreast of the latest research developments by reading the yearly proceedings of *International Conference on Parallel Processing, International Conference on Supercomputing,* and *Supercomputing*.

## Acknowledgments

The author thanks U.S. National Science Foundation (NSF grants MIP 9702569, CCR 9711566, and CCR 0073582) for supporting this work.

## References

1. H. Akkary and M. A. Driscoll, "A Dynamic Multithreading Processor," *Proceedings of 31st International Symposium on Microarchitecture,* 1998.
2. R. Alverson, D. Callahan, D. Cummings, B. Koblenz, A. Porterfield, and J. B. Smith, "The Tera Computer System," *Proceedings of International Conference on Supercomputing,* pp. 1–6, 1990.
3. D. E. Culler and J. P. Singh, Parallel Computer Architecture A Hardware/Software Approach. Morgan Kaufmann, 1999.
4. W. J. Dally and S. Lacy, "VLSI Architecture: Past, Present, and Future," *Proceedings of Advanced Research in VLSI Conference,* 1999.
5. P. Dubey, K. O'Brien, K. M. O'Brien, and C. Barton, "Single-Program Speculative Multithreading (SPSM) Architecture: Compiler-assisted Fine-Grained Multithreading," *Proceedings of International Conference on Parallel Architecture and Compilation Techniques (PACT '95),* 1995.
6. M. Dubois, C. Scheurich, and F. A. Briggs, "Memory Access Buffering in Multiprocessors," *Proceedings of the 13th International Symposium on Computer Architecture,* pp. 434–442, 1986.
7. K. Ebcioğlu and E. R. Altman, "DAISY: Dynamic Compilation for 100% Architectural Compatibility," *Proceedings of the 24th Annual International Symposium on Computer Architecture,* pp. 26–37, 1997.
8. M. Franklin and G. S. Sohi, "The Expandable Split Window Paradigm for Exploiting Fine-Grain Parallelism," *Proceedings of 19th International Symposium on Computer Architecture,* pp. 58–67, 1992.
9. M. Franklin, "The Multiscalar Architecture," Ph.D. Thesis, Technical Report TR 1196, Computer Sciences Department, University of Wisconsin, Madison, 1993.
10. M. Franklin, "Multi-Version Caches for Multiscalar Processors," *Proceedings of International Conference on High Performance Computing,* 1995.
11. M. Franklin and G. S. Sohi, "ARB: A Hardware Mechanism for Dynamic Reordering of Memory References," *IEEE Transactions on Computers,* vol. 45, no. 5, pp. 552–571, May 1996.
12. K. Gharachorloo et al., "Memory Consistency and Event Ordering in Scalable Shared-Memory Multiprocessors," *Proceedings of the 17th International Symposium on Computer Architecture,* pp. 15–25, 1990.
13. J. R. Goodman, "Cache Consistency and Sequential Consistency," Technical Report 61, IEEE SCI Committee, 1990.
14. S. Gopal, T. N. Vijaykumar, J. E. Smith, and G. S. Sohi, "Speculative Versioning Cache," *Proceedings of 4th International Symposium on High Performance Computer Architecture (HPCA-4),* 1998.
15. L. Hammond, B. A. Nayfeh, and K. Olukotun, "A Single-Chip Multiprocessor," *IEEE Computer,* September 1997.
16. R. Hookway, "Running 32-bit x86 Applications on Alpha NT," *Proceedings of IEEE COMPCON 97,* pp. 37–42, 1997.
17. K. Hwang and Z. Xu, *Scalable Parallel Computing,* WCB McGraw-Hill, New York, 1998.

18. R. Joy and K. Kennedy. *President's Information Technology Advisory Committee (PITAC)—Interim Report to the President*. National Coordination Office for Computing, Information and Communication, 4201 Wilson Blvd, Suite 690, Arlington, VA 22230, August 10, 1998.

19. V. Krishnan and J. Torellas, "A Chip Multiprocessor Architecture with Speculative Multithreading," *IEEE Transactions on Computers*, September 1999.

20. L. Lamport, "How to Make a Multiprocessor Computer That Correctly Executes Multiprocess Programs," *IEEE Transactions on Computers*, vol. C-28, pp. 690–691, September 1979.

21. O. C. Maquelin, H. H. J. Hum, and G. R. Gao. "Costs and Benefits of Multithreading with Off-the-Shelf RISC Processors," *Proceedings of 1st International EURO-PAR Conference*, 1995.

22. P. Marcuello, A. Gonzalez, and J. Tubella, "Speculative Multithreaded Processors," *Proceedings of International Conference on Supercomputing*, 1998.

23. R. Nair and M. E. Hopkins, "Exploiting Instruction Level Parallelism in Processors by Caching Scheduled Groups," *Proceedings of the 24th Annual International Symposium on Computer Architecture*, pp. 13–25, 1997.

24. N. Nishi et al., "A 1-GIPS 1-W Single-Chip Tightly Coupled Four-Way Multiprocessor with Architecture Support for Multiple Control-Flow Execution," *Proceedings of the 47th International Solid-States Circuits Conference*, pp. 418–475, 2000.

25. D. Padua, "Polaris: An Optimizing Compiler for Parallel Workstations and Scalable Multiprocessors," Technical Report 1475, University of Illinois at Urbana-Champaign, Center for Supercomputing Research & Development, January 1996.

26. C. Polychronopoulos, M. B. Girkar, M. R. Haghighat, C. L. Lee, B. P. Leung, D. A. Schouten, "The Structure of Parafrase-2: An Advanced Parallelizing Compiler for C and Fortran," *Languages and Compilers for Parallel Computing*, MIT Press, Cambridge, MA, 1990.

27. N. Ranganathan and M. Franklin, "An Empirical Study of Decentralized ILP Execution Models," *Proceedings of 8th International Conference on Architectural Support for Programming Languages and Operating Systems (ASPLOS-VIII)*, pp. 272–281, 1998.

28. E. Rotenberg, Q. Jacobson, Y. Sazeides, and J. E. Smith, "Trace Processors," *Proceedings of the 30th International Symposium on Microarchitecture*, pp. 138–148, 1997.

29. B. J. Smith, "The Architecture of HEP," *Parallel MIMD Computation: HEP Supercomputer and Its Applications*, pp. 41–55, MIT Press, Cambridge, MA.

30. G. S. Sohi, S. E. Breach, and T. N. Vijaykumar, "Multiscalar Processors," *Proceedings of the 22nd Annual International Symposium on Computer Architecture*, pp. 414–425, 1995.

31. J. G. Steffan and T. C. Mowry, "The Potential for Using Thread-Level Data Speculation to Facilitate Automatic Parallelization," *Proceedings of 4th International Symposium on High Performance Computer Architecture*, 1998.

32. K. K. Sundararaman and M. Franklin, "Multiscalar Execution along a Single Flow of Control," *Proceedings of International Conference on Parallel Processing (ICPP)*, pp. 106–113, 1997.

33. M. Thistle and B. J. Smith, "A Processor Architecture for Horizon," *Proceedings of Supercomputing '88*, pp. 35–41, 1988.

34. M. Tremblay et al, "The MAJC Architecture: A Synthesis of Parallelism and Scalability," *IEEE MICRO*, pp. 12–25, November/December 2000.

35. J-Y. Tsai and P-C. Yew, "The Superthreaded Architecture: Thread Pipelining with Run-Time Data Dependence Checking and Control Speculation," *Proceedings of the 1996 Conference on Parallel Architectures and Compilation Techniques (PACT '96)*, pp. 35–46, 1996.

36. S. Vajapeyam and T. Mitra, "Improving Superscalar Instruction Dispatch and Issue by Exploiting Dynamic Code Sequences," *Proceedings of the 24th Annual International Symposium on Computer Architecture*, pp. 1–12, 1997.

37. U. Vishkin, S. Dascal, E. Berkovich, and J. Nuzman, "Explicit Multi-threaded (XMT) Bridging Models for Instruction Parallelism," *Proceedings of the 10th ACM Symposium on Parallel Algorithms and Architectures (SPAA)*, pp. 140–151, 1998.

38. S. Wallace, B. Calder, and D. Tullsen, "Threaded Multiple Path Execution," *Proceedings of the 25th Annual International Symposium on Computer Architecture*, pp. 238–249, 1998.

39. "The National Technology Roadmap for Semiconductors," Semiconductor Industry Association, 1997.

## 5.5 Survey of Parallel Systems

*Donna Quammen*

### Introduction

Computers have long been considered "a solution looking for a problem," but because of limits found by *complexity theory* and limits on computing power some problems that were presented could not be solved. Multimedia problems, image processing and recognition, AI application, and weather prediction may not be accomplished unless processing power is increased. There are many varieties of parallel machines, each has the same goal, to complete a task quickly and inexpensively. Modern physics has continually increased the speed and capacity of the media on which modern computer chips are housed, usually VLSI, and at the same time decreased the price. The challenge of the computer engineers is to use the media effectively. Different components may be addressed to accomplish this, such as, but not limited to:

- Functionality of the processors—floating point, integer, or high level function, etc.
- Topology of the network which interconnects the processors
- Instruction scheduling
- Position and capability of any master control units that direct the processors
- Memory address space
- Input/output features
- Compilers and operating systems support to make the parallel system accessible
- Application's suitability to a particular parallel system
- Algorithms to implement the applications

As can be imagined there is an assortment of chooses for each of these components. This provides for the possibility of a large variety of parallel systems. Plus more chooses and variations are continually being developed to utilize the increased capacity of the underlining media.

Mike Flynn, in 1972 [Flynn72], developed a classification for various parallel systems, which has remained authoritative. It is based on the number of instruction streams and the number of data streams active in one cycle. A sequential machine is considered to have *single instruction stream executing on a single data stream*; this is called *SISD*. An *SIMD* machine has a *single instruction stream executing on multiple data streams* in the same cycle. *MIMD* has *multiple instruction streams executing on multiple data streams* simultaneously. All are shown in Fig. 5.18. An *MISD* is not shown but is considered to be a *systolic array*.

Four categories of *MIMD* systems, *dataflow, multithreaded, out of order execution, and very long instruction words (VLIW)*, are of particular interest, and seem to be the tendency for the future. These categories can be applied to a single CPU, providing parallelism by having *multiple functional units*. All four attempt to use fine-grain parallelism to maximize the number of instructions that may be executing in the same cycle. They also use fine-grain parallelism to assist in utilizing cycles, which possibly could be lost due to large *latency* in the execution of an instruction. Latency increases when the execution of one instruction is temporarily staled while waiting for some resource currently not available, such as the results of a cache miss, or even a cache fetch, the results of a floating point instruction (which takes longer than a simpler instruction), or the availability of a needed functional unit. This could cause delays in the execution of other instructions. If there is very fine grain parallelism, other instructions can use available resources while the staled instruction is waiting. This is one area where much computing power has been reclaimed.

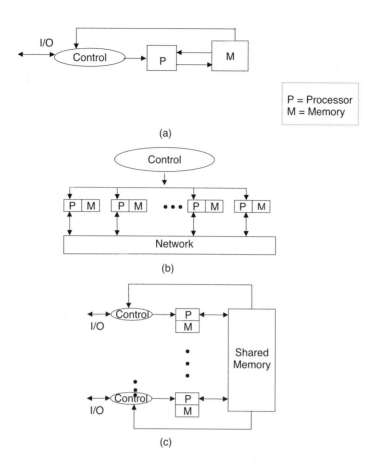

**FIGURE 5.18** (a) SISD uniprocessor architecture. (b) General SIMD with distributed memory. (c) Shared memory MIMD.

Two other compelling issues exist in parallel systems. *Portability*, once a program has been developed it should not need to be recoded to run efficiently on a parallel system, and *scalability*, the performance of a system should increase proportional to the size of the system. This is problematic since unexpected bottlenecks occur when more processors are added to many parallel systems.

## Single Instruction Multiple Processors (SIMD)

Perhaps the simplest parallel system to describe is an SIMD machine. As the name implies all processors execute the same instruction at the same time. There is one master control unit, which issues instructions, and typically each processor also has its own local memory unit. SIMD processors are fun to envision as a school of fish that travel closely together, always in the same direction. Once one turns, they all turn. In most systems, processors communicate only with a set of nearest neighbors; *grids, hypercubes,* or *torus* are popular. In the most generic system, shown in Fig. 5.18(b), no set communication pattern is dictated. Because different algorithms do better on different physical topologies (algorithms for sorting do well on tree structures, but array arithmetic does well on grids), reconfigureable networks are ideal but hard to actually implement. A variety of structures can be built on top of grids if the programmer is resourceful, but some processing power would be lost. It is difficult for a compiler to decide which substructure would be optimal to use. A mixture of a close connections supplemented with longer connections seems to be most advantageous. *MasPar* [MasPar91] has SIMD capability and uses a grid structure supplemented with longer connections. The *Thinking Machines CM-5* has SIMD capability using a *fat-tree* network, also a mix of closer and longer connections. The PEC network also has this quality [Kirkman91, Quammen96].

Of course, SIMD machines have limits. Logical arrays may not meet the physical topology of the processors but require folding or skewing. *If* statements may cause different paths to be followed on different processors, and since it is necessary to always have synchronization, some processing power will be lost. *Masks* are used to inhibit issued instructions on processors on which they should not be executed. A single control unit becomes a bottleneck as an SIMD system expands. If an SIMD system were very large, it would be desirable to be able to use it as a multiprogrammed machine where different programs would be allocated different "farms" of processors for their use as a dedicated array. A large SIMD system should be sub-dividable for disjoint multiuser applications. The operating system would have to handle this allocation.

On an SIMD computer a loop such as the one below can be translated to one SIMD instruction as is shown. The form $A(1:N)$ means array $A$ indexes 1 to $N$:

```
for I = 1 to N do
    A(I) = B(I) + C(I);        A(1:N) = B (I:N) + C(1:N);
endfor;
```

The code below would take four steps:

```
F(0) = 0;
for I = 1 to N do              F(0) = 0;
    A(I) = B(I)/C(I);          A(1:N) = B (I:N)/C(1:N);
    D(I) = A(I) * E(I);        D(1:N) = A(1:N) * E(1:N);
    F(I) = D(I) + F(I - 1);    F(1:N) = D(1:N) + F(0:N - 1);
endfor;
```

Compilers can identify loops such as the ones presented above [Wolfe91]. However, many loops are not capable of executing in an SIMD fashion because of reverse dependencies. Languages have been developed for SIMD programming, which allows the programmer to specify data locations and communication patterns.

## Multiple Instruction Multiple Data (MIMD)

Perhaps the easiest MIMD processor to envision is a shared memory multiprocessor such as shown in Fig. 5.18(c). With this machine, all processors access the same memory bank with the addition of local caches. This allows the processors to communicate by placing data in the shared memory. However, sharing data causes problems. *Data* and *cache coherence* are of major concern. If one processor is altering data that another processor wishes to use, and the first processor is also holding the current updated value for this data in its cache, there is a need to guard access to the stale value which is being held in the shared memory. This creates a need for *locks* and *protocols* to protect communal data. Inefficient algorithms to handle cache coherence can cause delays, or invalidate results. In addition, if more than one processor wishes to access the same locked memory location, a fairness issue occurs as to which processor should be allowed first access after the location becomes unlocked [Hwang93]. Further delays in accessing the shared memory occur due to the use of a single bus. This arrangement is described as a uniform memory access (UMA) time approach and avoids worst-case communication scenarios possible in other memory arrangements.

To reduce contention on the bus as a MIMD memory system scales, a distributed memory organization can be used. Here, clusters of processors share common memories, and the clusters are connected to allow communications between clusters. This is called an NUMA (nonuniform memory access) organization [Gupta91]. If a MIMD machine is to be *scalable*, this approach must be used. Machines within the same cluster will be able to share data with less latency than machines housed on different memory banks. It will be possible to access all data. This creates questions as to which sets of data should be placed on which processor cluster. Compilers can help with this by locating a code that uses common data. If data is poorly placed, the worst-case execution time could be devastating.

Message passing systems, such as the *Transputer* [May87], have no shared memory but handle communications using message passing. This can cause high latency while waiting for requested data; however, each processor can hold multiple threads, and may be able to occupy itself while waiting for remote data. Deadlocks are a problem.

Another variation of memory management is cache only memory access (COMA). Memory is distributed, but only held in cache [Saulsbury95]. The Kendall Square machine [KSR91] has this organization. On the KSM distributed memory is held in the cache of each processor, which is connected by a ring. The caches of remote processors are accessed using this ring.

## Vector Machines

A *vector machine* creates a series of functional units and pumps a stream of data through the series. Each stage of the pipe will store its resulting data in a *vector register*, which will be read by the next stage. In this way the parallelism is equal to the number of stages in the pipeline. This is very efficient if the same functions are to be preformed on a long stream of data. The Cray series computer [Cray92] is famous for this technique. It is becoming popular to make an individual processor of a MIMD system a vector processor.

## Dataflow Machine

The von Neumann approach to computing has one control state in existence at one time. A program counter is used to point to the single next instruction. This approach is used in traditional machines, and is also used in most of the single processors of the multiple processor systems described earlier. A completely different approach was developed at the Massachusetts Institute of Technology [Dennis91, Arvind90, Polychronopoulos89]. They realized that the maximum amount of parallelism could be realized if at any one point *all instructions that are ready to execute* were executed. An instruction is *ready* to execute if the data that is required for its complete execution is available. Therefore, execution of an instruction is not governed by the sequential order, but by its readiness to execute, that is, when both operands are available. A table is kept of the instructions that are *about ready* to execute, that is, one of the two operands needed for the *assembly language level instruction* is available. When the second operand is found, this instruction is executed. The result of the execution is passed to a control unit, which will select a set of new instructions to be *about ready* to execute, or mark an instruction as *ready* (because the second operand needed has arrived).

This approach yields the maximum amount of parallelism. However, it runs into problems with "run away execution." Too many instructions may be *about ready*, and clog the system. It is a fascinating approach, and machines have been developed. It has the advantage that no, or very little, changes need to be made to *old dusty decks* to extract parallelism. Steps can be made to avoid "run away execution."

## Out of Order Execution Concept

An approach similar to the *dataflow* concept is called *out of order execution* [Cintra00]. Here again, program elements that are ready to execute may be executed. It has a big advantage when multiple functional units are available on the same CPU, but the functional units have different latency values. The technique is not completely new but similar to issuing a *load instruction*, which has high latency, well before the result of the *load* is required. By the time the *load* is completed the code has reached the location where it is used. Also a *floating point instruction*, again a class of instructions with high latency, is frequently started before *integer instructions* coded to execute first are executed. By the time the *floating point* is complete, its results are ready to be used. The compiler can make this decision statically. In *out of order execution* the hardware has more of a role in the decision of what to execute. This may include both the *then* and the *else* parts of an *if* statement. They can both be executed, but not be committed to until the correct path is determined. This technique is also called *speculative execution*. Any changes that have been made by a wrong path must be capable of being rolled *back*. Although this may seem to be extra computation, it will decrease execution time if done well. Other areas of the program may also be executed, if it is determined that their execution will not affect the final result or *can be rolled back*. The temporary results may be kept in registers. The Alpha Computer [Kessler99] as well as the Intel Pentium Pro [Intel97] use this technique. This method is becoming popular to fully utilize increasingly powerful computers.

Compiler techniques can be used to try to determine which streams should be chosen for advance execution. If the wrong choice is made, there is a risk of extremely poor performance due to continual rollbacks. Branch prediction, either statically by the compiler, or dynamically by means of architecture prediction flags, is a useful technique for increasing the number of instructions, which may be beneficial to execute prematurely.

Since assembler instructions contain precise register addresses, set by the compiler, and it is unknown which assembler instructions will be caught in partial execution at the same time, a method called *register renaming* is used. A *logical* register address is mapped to a *physical* register chosen from a *free list*. The mapping is then used throughout the execution of the instruction, and released again to the *free list*.

## Multithreading

*Multithreading* [Tullsen95] is another method to hide the latency endured by various instructions. More than one chain, or thread, of execution is active at any one point. The states of different chains are saved simultaneously [Lo97, Miller90] in their own *state space*. Modern programs are being written as a collection of modules, either *threads* or *objects*. Because one of the main advantages of this form of programming is data modulization, many of these modules could be ready to execute concurrently. While the processor is waiting for one thread's data (for example, a cache miss or even a cache access), other threads, which have a full state in their dedicated space, can be executed. The compiler cannot determine which modules will be active at the same time, that will have to be done dynamically. The method is somewhat similar to the *multiprogramming* technique of changing context while waiting for I/O; however, it is at a *finer grain*. Multiple access lines to memory are beneficial since many threads may be waiting for I/O. The *Tera machine* [Smith90] is the prime example of this technique. This approach should help lead to Teraflops performance.

## Very Long Instruction Word (VLIW)

A VLIW will issue an instruction to multiple functional units in parallel. Therefore, if the compiler can find one operation for each of the functional unit internal to a processor (these instructions are usually RISC-like), which will be able to execute at the same time (that is, the data for their execution are statically determined to be available in registers), and none of the instructions depend on an instruction being issued in the same cycle, then you can execute them in parallel. All the sub-instructions will be issued by one long instruction. The name VLSI comes from the need that the instruction be long enough to hold multiple operation codes, one for each functional unit, which will be used, and the register identifiers, which they need. Unlike the three methods described previously, the compiler is responsible for finding instructions that do not interfere with each other and assigning the registers for these instructions [Rau93, Park97]. The compiler packs these instructions statically into the VLIW. The Intel iWarp can control a *floating point multiplier, floating point adder, integer adder, memory loader, increment unit*, and *condition tester* on each cycle [Cohn89]. The instruction is 96 bits long and can, with compiler support, execute nine instructions at once. The code for the following loop can be turned into a loop of just one VLSI instruction as opposed to a loop of at least nine RISC size instructions.

$$\text{for } I := 0 \text{ to } N - 1 \text{ do}$$
$$A(2*I) := C + B(I)*D;$$

It is difficult for a compiler to find instructions that can fill all the fields statically, so frequently some of the functional units go unoccupied. There are many techniques to find qualified instructions, and frequently the long instruction can be filled. One technique is to mine separate threads [Lam87, Bakewell91], another successful technique tries together several basic 0blocks into a *hyperblock*. The hyperblock has one entrance but may have several exits. This creates a long stream of code, which would normally be executed sequentially, and allows the compiler to choose instructions over this larger range. Roll-back code must be added to the hyperblock's exit to undo the affects of superfluous code that was executed, but would not execute sequentially. Loops are frequently *unrolled*, several iterations considered as straight code, to form hyperblocks. *Branch prediction* can also help create beneficial hyperblocks.

A newer approach is to dynamically pack the VLIW, using a preprocessor that accesses multiple queues, one for each functional unit. Realize that using queues is similar to *out of order execution*.

## Interconnection Network

An interconnection network is a necessary component of all parallel processing systems. Several features govern the choice of a network. A scalable interconnection network for parallel processor would be ideal if it meets the following requirements for a large range of system sizes. For instance, it may be scalable by reasonably small increments from $2^4$ to perhaps $2^{20}$ processors.

- Have a low average and maximum diameter (the distance between the furthest two nodes) to avoid communication latency.
- Minimize routing constraints (have many routes from *A* to *B*).
- Have a constant number of I/O port (channels) per node to allow for expansion without retrofit.
- Have a simple wire layout to allow for expansion and to avoid wasting VLSI space.
- Be inherently fault tolerant.
- Be sub-dividable for disjoint multiuser applications.
- Be able to handle a large range of algorithms without undo overhead.

The most popular parallel networks—hypercube, quad tree, fat-tree, binary tree, mesh, and torus—fail in one or more of these items.

Meshes have a major disadvantage: they lack support for long distance connections. Hypercubes have excellent connectivity by guaranteeing a maximum distance between any two nodes of log $N$ where $N$ is the number of nodes. Also, many paths exist between any two nodes making it fault tolerant and amenable to low contention. However, the number of I/O ports per node is log $N$. As a system scales, each node would need to be retrofit to add additional ports. In addition, the wire layout is complex, making this network expensive in space. Tree structures are popular and have a maximum long distance connection of $O(2 \log N)$. Communications on a tree, however, can be complicated by the fact that although many neighbors are close, many can only communicate through the root. This causes contention at the root. Fat-trees reduce this contention by increasing the bandwidth, as the network approaches the root [Leiserson85].

The extreme ideal network would allow all nodes to connect to all others. This is not practical for large system. However, one class of networks, the *multistage network*, uses an internal switching system and allows constant access time between any two nodes. Several arrangements are available for multistage networks. All are similar. One such network, the *baseline network*, is shown in Fig. 5.19. It can be proved that a $N$-by-$N$ network can be totally connected with log $N$ switches steps [Seigel89]. Each step is through a row of switches, with $N/2$ switches in each row. This requires quite a bit of hardware and does allow for a connection in log $N$ steps. This is not very scalable.

*Optical* technology [Yuan97] has shown to be promising for the implementation of all networks. Instead of a wire, an optical "beam" is used to make the connection. This is fast and has several advantages. One, a broadcast can be made from one node to many nodes at once (although, one node cannot receive many inputs at once), and two, the transmission can be sent through clear space.

## Conclusion

Parallel systems are going to become almost universal in computer systems. Desktop computers are now frequently being delivered with more than one CPU and definitely with more than one functional unit. The new models of SUN, MIPS, Intel, and Macintosh desktop computers currently are providing parallel

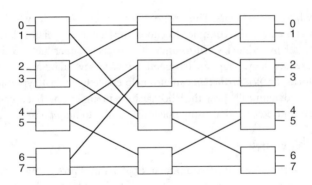

**FIGURE 5.19**   An 8 × 8 baseline network.

computing capabilities. This feature is no longer limited to just super computers. In order to use these systems efficiently, the consumer should be aware of how their programs are going to utilize the systems. Compilers, operating systems, and program design are all things that should be examined.

Most parallel processing is being aimed at hiding latency; however, embedded systems and super computing implementations also need the ability to execute separate lines of control running independently, which must communicate with each other. Embedded systems need this to assure the strict adherence to real-time deadlines. Super computer applications need the additional processing power.

This chapter section only briefly discussed this field. A full addressing of the field is covered in large volumes of books and journals. Topics, such as compiler techniques, dedicated languages, communication techniques, multi-user facilities, algorithms, memory hierarchies, I/O facilities, programming tools, fault tolerant, power consumption, and debugging technique, are only an abbreviated list of topics which need to be examined. Plus, each of these subtopics has many aspects. All computer users should certainly be aware of this field.

## References

[Arvind90] Ardvin and Nikhil, "Executing a Program on the MIT Tagged Dataflow Architecture," *IEEE Trans. Computer,* 1990.

[Bakewell 91] H. Bakewell, D. Quammen, and P. Wang, "Mapping Concurrent Programs to VLIW Processors" *Proc. Principles and Practices of Parallel Programming,* Williamsburg, Virginia, pp. 21–27, April 1991.

[Cintra00] M. Cintra, J. Martinez, and J. Torrellas, "Architectural Support for Scalable Speculative Parallelism in Shared-Memory Multiprocessors," *Int. Symp. Computer Architecture,* 2000.

[Cohn89] R. Cohn, T. Gross, M. Lam, and P. Tseng, "Architecture and Compiler Tradeoffs for a Long Instruction Word Microprocessor," *Third Int. Conf. on Architectural Support for Programming Languages and Operating Systems,* 1989.

[Cray92] Cray, *Cray/MPP Announcement,* Cray Research, Inc. Eagan, MN, 1991.

[Dennis91] J. Dennis, "The Evolution of Static Dataflow Architecture," in *Gaudiot and Bic., Advanced Topics in Dataflow Computing,* Prentice-Hill, Englewood Cliffs, NJ, 1991.

[Flynn72] M. J. Flynn, "Some Computer Organization and their Effectiveness," *IEEE Trans. Computer,* 21(9): 948–960, 1972.

[Gupta91] A. Gupta, J. Hennessy, et al., "Comparative Evaluation of Latency Reducing and Tolerating Techniques," *Proc. Int. Symp. Computer Architecture,* May 1991.

[Hwang93] Kai Hwang, *Advanced Computer Architecture,* McGraw-Hill, Inc, New York, 1993.

[Intel97] Intel Corporation, *Pentium(R) Pro Processor Developmer's Manual,* McGraw-Hill, New York, June 1997.

[Kessler99] R. E. Kessler, "The Alpha 21264 Microprocessor," *IEEE Micro,* 1999.

[Kirkman91] W. Kirkman and D. Quammen, "Packed Exponential Connections—A Hierarchy of 2D Meshes," *Proc. 5th Int. Parallel Proceedings Symposium,* Anaheim, pp. 464–470, California, April 1991.

[KSR91] KSR-1 *Overview*, Internal Report, Kendall Square Research Co.170 Tracer Lane, Waltham, MA 02154, 1991.

[Lam88] M. Lam Software Pipelining, "An Effective Scheduling Technique for VLIW Machines," *ACM Sigplan 1088 Conf. or Programming Language Design and Implementation*, 1988.

[Leiserson92] C. E. Leiserson, "The Network Architecture of the Connection Machine, CM-5," *Proc. ACM Symp. Computer Architecture*, 1992.

[Lo97] J. Lo, S, Eggers, et al., "Tuning Compiler Optimization for Simultaneous Multithreading," *Int. Symp. on Microarchitecture*, 1997.

[MasPar91] MasPar, "The MasPar Family of Data Parallel Computer," Technical summary, MasPar Computer Corporation, Sunnyvale, CA, 1991.

[May88] D. Pountain and D. May, *Occam Programming*, INMOS, Oxford England, 1988.

[Miller90] D. R. Miller and D. J. Quammen. "Exploiting Large Register Sets," *Int. J. Microprocessors and Microsystems*, pp. 333–340, August 1990.

[Park97] S. Park, S. Shim, and S. Moon, Evaluation of Scheduling Techniques on a SPARC-Based VLIW Testbed, Micro-30, 1997.

[Polychronopulos89] C. D. Polychronopulos, et al., "Paradrase 2: An Environment for Parallel zing, Partitioning, Synchronizing Programs on Multiprocessors," *Proc. Int. Conf. on Parallel Processing*, 1989.

[Quammen96] D. Quammen, J. Stanley, and P. Wang, "The Packed Exponential Connection Network," *Pre. Int. Symp. Parallel Arch. Algorithms and Networks*, 1996.

[Rau93] B. Rau and J. Fisher, "Instruction-Level Parallel Processing: History, Overview, and Perspective," *J. Supercomputing: Special Issue on Instruction-Level Parallelism*, 1993.

[Saulsbury95] A. Saulsbury, T. Wilkinson, et al., "An Argument for a Simple COMA," *Symp. Int. on High Perf. Computer Architecture*, 1995.

[Siegel89] H. J. Siegel, "A model of SIMD Machines and a Comparison of Various Interconection Networks," *IEEE Trans. Computer*, 28(12) 1989.

[Smith90] J. E. Smith, "Future General-Purposes Supercomputer Architecture," *Proc. ACM Supercomputing Conf.*, 1990.

[Tullsen95] D. Tullsen, et al., "Simultaneous Multithreading: Maximizing On-Chip Parallelism," *Proc. 23rd Int. Symp. on Computer Architecture*, 1995.

[Wolfe91] M. E. Wolfe and M. Lam, "A Loop Transformation Theory and an Algorithm to Maximize Parallelism," *IEEE Trans. Parallel Distri Systems*, 3(10), 1991.

[Yuan97] X. Yuan, R. Melhem, and R. Gupta, "Distributed Path Reservation Algorithms for Multiplexing All-Optical Interconnection Networks," *Proc. Symp. High-Performance Comp. Architecture*, 1997.

# 5.6   Virtual Memory Systems and TLB Structures

*Bruce Jacob*

## Virtual Memory, a Third of a Century Later

Virtual memory was designed in the late 1960s to provide automated storage allocation. It is a technique for managing the resource of physical memory that provides to the application an illusion of a very large amount of memory—typically, much larger than is actually available. In a virtual memory system, only the most often used portions of a process's address space actually occupy physical memory; the rest of the address space is stored on disk until needed. When the mechanism was invented, computer memories were physically large (one kilobyte of memory occupied a space the size of a refrigerator), they had access times comparable to the processor's speed (both were extremely slow), and they came with astronomical price tags. Due to space and monetary constraints, installed computer systems typically had very little memory—usually less than the size of today's on-chip caches, and far less than the users of the systems would have liked. The virtual memory mechanism was designed to solve this problem, by using a system's disk space as if it were memory and placing into main memory only the data used most often.

Since then, we have seen constant evolution (and revolution) in the computer industry. Typical microprocessors today have more on-chip cache than the core memory found in multimillion-dollar systems of yesterday and cost orders of magnitude less. Today, memory takes up very little space: you can easily hold a gigabyte of DRAM in your hand. In recent decades, processor designers have focused on improving speed while memory-chip designers have focused on improving storage size, and, as a result, memory is now extremely slow compared to processor speeds. Due to rapidly decreasing memory prices, it is usually possible to have enough memory in one's machine to avoid using the disk as a backup memory space. Many of today's machines generate 64-bit addresses, some even larger; most modern machines therefore reference 16 exabytes (16 giga-gigabytes) or more of data in their address space directly. The list goes on. In fact, one of the few things that has not changed since the development of virtual memory is the basic design of the virtual memory mechanism itself, and the one problem it was invented to solve—too little memory—is no longer a factor in most systems. However, the virtual memory mechanism has proven itself valuable in other areas besides extending the memory space. Today it is used in nearly every modern operating system because of the convenience offered by its features: It simplifies memory allocation and memory protection, and it provides an intuitive programming interface to the application—the "virtual machine" interface—that simplifies program design and provides a natural path to multitasking.

## Caching the Process Address Space

A process operates in its own little world; this is the *virtual machine* paradigm, illustrated in Fig. 5.20. Each running process generates addresses for loads and stores as if it has the entire machine to itself—as if the computer offers an extremely large amount of memory and no other processes are executing or consuming resources. This makes the job of the programmer and compiler much easier, because no details of the hardware or memory organization are necessary to build a program.

The operating system divides the process address space into equal-sized portions for ease of management; these divisions are called *virtual pages*. A page is usually a multiple of the unit of transfer that hard disks use, and in most operating systems ranges from several kilobytes to several dozen kilobytes. A page is never fragmented; if any data in a virtual page are in physical memory then all the data in that page are, and if any of the data in a virtual page are nonexistent or being held on disk then all the data are. When the word *page* is used in a verb form, it means to allow a section of memory to be virtual—to allow it

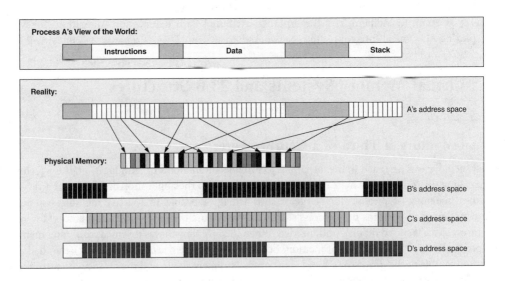

**FIGURE 5.20  The virtual machine paradigm.** A process operates in its own virtual environment, unaware that other processes are executing and contending for the same limited resources. The operating system views each process address space as a collection of pages that can be cached in physical memory, or left in backing store.

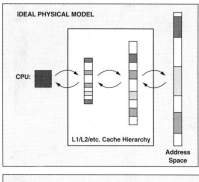

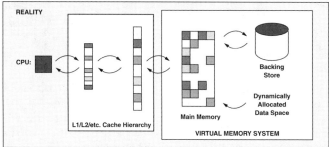

**FIGURE 5.21   Caching the process address space.** In the first view, a process is shown referencing locations in its address space. Note that all loads, stores, and fetches use virtual names for objects, and many of the requests can be satisfied by a cache hierarchy. The second view shows that the address space is not a linear object stored on some device, but is instead scattered across hard drives and dynamically allocated when necessary.

to move freely between physical memory and disk. This allows the physical memory to be used more efficiently: When a region of memory has not been used recently, the space can be freed up for more active pages, and pages that have been migrated to disk are brought back in as soon as they are needed again.

How is this done? The ultimate home for the process's address space is *backing store*, usually a disk drive; this is where the process's instructions and data come from and where all of its permanent changes go to. Every hardware memory structure between the CPU and the backing store is a cache for the instructions and data in the process's address space. This includes main memory—main memory is really nothing more than a cache for a process's virtual address space. A cache operates on the principle that a small, fast storage device can hold the most important data found on a larger, slower storage device, effectively making the slower device look fast. The large storage area in this case is the process address space, which can be many gigabytes in size. Everything in the address space initially comes from the program file stored on disk or is created on demand and defined to be zero. Figure 5.21 illustrates: There really is no linear array of data that houses the process address space. Its illusion is actually manufactured by the operating system through the virtual memory mechanism.

When a program first begins executing, the operating system copies a small portion of the process address space from the program file stored on disk into main memory. This typically includes the first page of instructions in the program and possibly a small amount of data that the program needs at startup. Then, as more instructions or data are needed, the operating system brings in pages from the process's address on demand. This process, called *demand paging*, is depicted in Fig. 5.22.

In step 1 of the figure, the operating system initializes a process address space and loads the first page of instructions into physical memory. The operating system then sets the hardware program counter to the first instruction in the program, which sets the process running. Assuming that one of the first few instructions references the initialized data area, the uninitialized data area, or the (so far nonexistent) stack, the operating system will have to bring in a page of data from the program file or create an

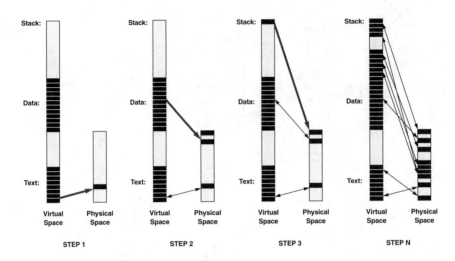

**FIGURE 5.22   Demand paging at process start-up.** In step 1, the operating system loads the first page of the process's instructions into physical memory, and sets the program counter to the first instruction in the program. This first instruction references a location in the process's data area, so in step 2 the operating system brings the corresponding data page into physical memory. The next instruction references a location on the process's stack, so in step 3 the operating system has allocated a stack page for the process and placed it into the process address space and main memory. Succeeding instructions reference more locations in the stack area, jump to instructions that lie outside of the initial page of instructions, and allocate extra data storage area on the heap. In step *N* (many steps later), these pages have been brought into main memory.

uninitialized-data page or stack page and link it into the process address space. This is shown in steps 2 and 3 of the figure. When a process references an item in its address space that is not currently in physical memory, the reference causes a *page fault*, and the operating system loads the necessary pages from backing store into main memory. Clearly, the term *demand paging* refers to the fact that pages are allocated or brought into physical memory on demand. Step *N* of the figure shows a process that has been executing for some time, as it has several pages of data in its stack area and several pages in its data area that were not there when the process began executing. All of these pages were dynamically allocated by the operating system as the process needed or asked for them.

As has been pointed out before, the process is unaware of the operating system activity that moves pages in and out of main memory on its behalf. It typically does not know whether or not any given page is memory-resident or where it is located if it is memory resident. Figure 5.20 at beginning of the section illustrates this by showing a process address space from two points of view. The first point of view is from the process itself; in most operating systems a process sees its address space as a contiguous span of memory locations from minimum to maximum. Somewhere in the address space is the program's instructions, or *text*; somewhere else is the program's data. Most operating systems also create a stack area, a heap area, and possibly one or more dynamically loaded libraries containing system-supplied utilities such as input/output routines or networking functions. The advantage of the virtual machine paradigm is that these can be arranged in physical memory, which is most convenient, rather than having to fit things together like the pieces of a puzzle, as would be the case without address translation.

The second point of view in the figure is from the operating system. In reality, the process address space is not a large contiguous segment in physical memory but is partially cached by physical memory. Portions of the process address space are scattered about physical memory and are likely to be not contiguous at all. The process is unaware of where in the system any particular portion of its address space is being held; some portions can be on disk (for example, the portions of the program that have not been used yet), some can be in main memory, and some can be in hardware caches. The operating system maintains a map for each address space so that, for every virtual page in the address space, it can tell where in memory or on disk the page can be found. As the figure suggests, the virtual machine

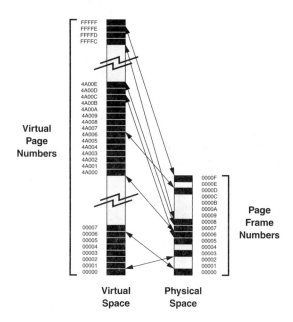

| Virtual Page Number (VPN) | Page Offset |
|---|---|
| 20 bits | 12 bits |

**FIGURE 5.23   Virtual addresses.** A Virtual address is divided into two components: the virtual page number and the page offset. The virtual page number identifies the page's location within the address space. The page offset identifies a byte's location within the page. Bit widths are shown for a 32-bit address and a 4 kbyte page size.

**FIGURE 5.24   Page numbers (for 32-bit virtual addresses).** Every page in an address space is given a virtual page number (VPN). Every page in physical memory is given a physical page number, called a page frame number (PFN).

paradigm allows each process to behave as if it owns the entire machine; each process is protected from all others and does not even know that other processes exist—for example, a process cannot spoof the identity of another process, and the resource-management mechanisms implemented by the operating system to support the illusion that each process own all physical resources means that no process may dominate system resources. One of the many benefits of this organization is that it makes facilities such as multitasking very easy to implement, because process protection, resource sharing, and a clean division of process identity are provided as side effects of the virtual machine paradigm by definition.

The mapping information that tells the location of pages in memory or on disk is organized into *page tables*, which are collections of *page table entries (PTEs)*. Virtual addresses (shown in Fig. 5.23) are mapped at the granularity of *pages*; at its simplest, virtual memory is then a mapping of *virtual page numbers (VPNs)* to *page frame numbers (PFNs)*, shown in Fig. 5.24. "Frame" in this context means "slot"—physical memory is divided into frames that hold pages. The page table holds one PTE for every mapped virtual page; an individual PTE indicates whether its virtual page is in memory, on disk, or not allocated yet. The logical PTE therefore contains the VPN and either the page's location in memory (a PFN), or its location on disk (a disk block number). Depending on the organization, some of this information is redundant; actual implementations do not necessarily require both the VPN and the PFN. Later developments in virtual memory added such things as page-level protections; a modern PTE usually contains protection information as well, such as whether the page contains executable code, whether it can be modified, and if so by whom.

The mapping is a function; any virtual page can have only one location. However, the inverse map is not necessarily a function; it is possible and sometimes advantageous to have several virtual pages mapped

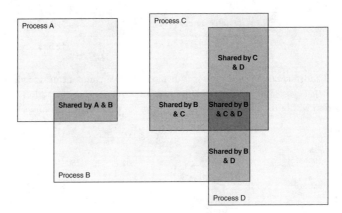

**FIGURE 5.25    Shared memory.** Shared memory allows processes to overlap portions of their address space while retaining protection for the nonintersecting regions; this is a simple and effective method for inter-process communication. Pictured are four process address spaces that have overlapped. The darker regions are shared by more than one process, while the lightest regions are still protected from other processes.

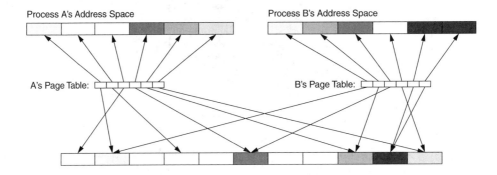

**FIGURE 5.26    How page tables support shared memory.** Two process address spaces are shown sharing several pages. Their page tables maintain information on where virtual pages are located in physical memory. The darkened pages are mapped to several locations; note that the darkest page is mapped at two locations in the same address space.

to the same page frame (to share memory between processes or threads, or to allow different views of data with different protections, for example). Shared memory is one of the more commonly used features of page tables. It is a mechanism whereby two address spaces that are protected from each other are allowed to intersect at points, still retaining protection over the nonintersecting regions. Several processes sharing portions of their address spaces are pictured in Fig. 5.25. The shared memory mechanism only opens up a pre-defined portion of a process's address space; the rest of the address space is still protected, and even the shared portion is only unprotected for those processes sharing the memory. For instance, in the figure, the region of A's address space that is shared with process B is unprotected from whatever actions B might want to take, but it is safe from the actions of any other processes. Shared memory is therefore useful as a simple, secure means for inter-process communication. Shared memory also reduces requirements for physical memory; for example, in most operating systems, the text regions of processes are shared whenever multiple instances of a single program are run, or when multiple instances of a common library are used in different programs.

The mechanism works by ensuring that shared pages map to the same physical page; this is done by simply placing the same page frame number in the page tables of two processes sharing a page. A simple example is shown in Fig. 5.26. Here, two very small address spaces are shown overlapping at several places, and one address space overlaps with itself; two of its virtual pages map to the same physical page.

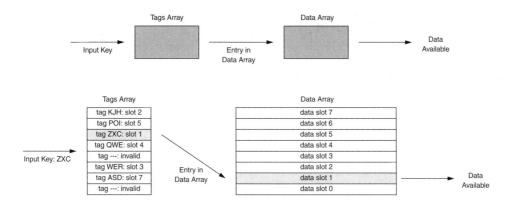

**FIGURE 5.27    An idealized fully associative cache lookup.** A cache is comprised of two parts: the tags array and the data array. The tags act as a database; they accept as input a key (a virtual address) and output either the location of the item in the data array, or an indication that the item is not in the data array. A fully associative cache allows an item to be located at any slot in the data array, thus the input key is compared against every key in the tags array.

This is not just a contrived example; many operating systems allow this, and it is useful, for example, in the implementation of user-level threads.

## An Example Page Table Organization

So now the question is: How do page tables work? If we think of main memory as the data array of a cache, then the page table is the cache's corresponding *tags array*—it is a lookup table that tells one what is currently stored in the data array. The traditional design of virtual memory uses a fully associative organization for main memory: Any virtual object can be placed at (more or less) any location in main memory, which reduces contention for main memory and increases performance. An idealized fully associative cache is pictured in Fig. 5.27. A data tag is fed into the cache; the first stage compares the input tag to the tag of every piece of data in the cache. The matching tag points to the data's location in the cache. The goal of the page table organization is to support this lookup function as efficiently as possible.

To access a page in physical memory, it is necessary to look up the appropriate PTE to find where the page resides. This lookup can be simplified if PTEs are organized contiguously so that a page number can be used as an offset to find the appropriate PTE. This leads to two primary types of page table organization: the *forward-mapped* or *hierarchical page table*, indexed by the virtual page number, and the *inverse-mapped* or *inverted page table*, indexed by the physical page number (page frame number). Each design has its strengths and weaknesses. The hierarchical table supports a simple lookup algorithm and simple sharing mechanisms and can require a significant fraction of physical memory. The inverted table supports efficient hardware table-walking mechanisms and requires less physical memory than a hierarchical table but inhibits sharing by not allowing the mappings for multiple virtual pages to exist in the table simultaneously, if those pages map to the same page frame. Detailed descriptions of these can be found elsewhere [Jacob & Mudge 1998a].

Instead of describing all possible page table organizations, we will look in some detail at a concrete example: the virtual memory implementation of one of the oldest and simplest virtual memory systems, 4.3BSD Unix [Leffler et al. 1989]. The intent is to show how mapping information is used by the operating system and how the physical memory layout is organized. Version 4.3 of Berkeley Unix provides support for shared text regions, address space protection, and page-level protection. There is a separate page table for every process, and the page tables cannot be paged to disk. As we will see, address spaces are organized to minimize memory requirements.

BSD defines segments to be contiguous regions of virtual space. A process address space is composed of five primary segments: the *text* segment, holding the executable code; the *initialized data* segment, containing those data that are initialized to specific nonzero values at process start-up; the *bss* segment,

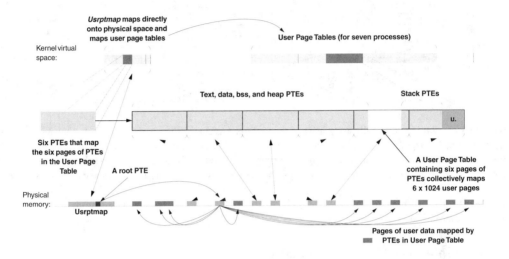

**FIGURE 5.28    The 4.3BSD per-process virtual address space.**

**FIGURE 5.29    User-process page tables in 4.3BSD Unix.**

containing data initialized as zero at process start-up; the *heap* segment, containing uninitialized data and the process's heap; and the *stack*. Beyond the stack is a region holding the kernel's stack (used when executing system calls on behalf of this process, for example) and the *user struct*, a kernel data structure holding a large quantity of process-specific information. Figure 5.28 illustrates the layout of these segments in a process's address space: The initialized data segment begins immediately after the text segment, the bss segment begins immediately after the initialized data segment, and the heap segment begins immediately after the bss segment. This is possible because the text, initialized data, and bss regions by definition cannot change size during the execution of a process. The heap segment can grow larger, as can the stack. Therefore, these two begin at opposite ends of the address space and grow towards each other. Beyond the 2 GB point, the address space belongs to the kernel; a user reference causes an exception.

This design makes sense for a number of reasons. When the operating system was designed, memory was at a premium. The choice was made to wire down the page tables. Given this, it makes most sense to restrict an address space to be composed of a minimal number of contiguous regions; this would ensure a compact page table (contiguous pages imply densely packed PTEs). The process model includes a single thread of execution per address space; 4.3BSD did not have multiple threads within an address space, nor did it use dynamically loaded libraries. Therefore, there was no need to support sparsely populated address spaces.

Figure 5.29 depicts the layout of process address spaces and the associated process page tables. The page tables are kept in the kernel's virtual address space and are relocatable even if wired down. As shown in the figure, each user-process page table mirrors the process's address space; the PTEs that map the text, data, bss, and heap segments are at the bottom end of a contiguous range of PTEs (which are held in the kernel's virtual pages), and the PTEs that map the user's stack are near the top of the range of PTEs. A user page table is therefore as compact as it can be, with no more than a page of wasted space; the empty space between the ranges of PTEs allows for expansion of the heap and stack segments.

When a process needs to expand its address space beyond the confines of its user page table, the operating system adds an additional page to the page table and shifts all following process page tables up by one virtual page. This is the advantage of placing the user page tables in virtual space; the displaced data need not be recopied. The disadvantage is that there needs to be another level of mapping to determine where in the physical memory the pages that comprise a process's user page table are located. The *Usrptmap* is a structure that mirrors the entire set of user page tables, and for every page in a process's user page table, there is one PTE in the *Usrptmap*.

When a user reference requires a lookup in the page table, the operating system first determines which process caused the fault; this identifies the appropriate page table within the region of user page tables. The operating system then determines whether the access was to the user's stack or one of the text, bss, or data segments. If the access is to the user's stack, the operating system indexes backward from the top of the appropriate user page table to find the PTE; if the access is to the text, data, bss, or heap segment, the operating system indexes forward from the bottom of the user page table.

The *usrptmap* begins at a known location in physical memory; therefore, any process address space can be mapped. The appropriate root PTE within the *usrptmap* can always be found, given a process ID, and each root PTE points to a page of PTEs in physical memory, each of which then points to a page in the user address space.

## Translation Lookaside Buffers: Caching the Page Table

There is an obvious question of performance to consider: If every memory access by a user program requires a lookup to the page table, how does anything ever get done? The answer is a familiar one: we cache things. Rather than perform a page-table lookup on every memory reference (which returns a PTE that gives us mapping information), we cache the most frequently used PTEs in hardware. The hardware structure is called a *translation lookaside buffer (TLB)*, and because it holds mapping information, the hardware can perform the address translations of those PTEs that are currently cached in the TLB without having to access the page table (see Fig. 5.30). If the appropriate PTEs are stored in hardware, a memory reference completes at the speed of hardware, rather than being limited by the speed of looking up PTEs in the page table.

Most architectures provide a TLB to support memory management; the TLB is a special-purpose cache that holds only virtual-physical mappings. When a process attempts to load from or store to a virtual address, the hardware searches the TLB for the virtual address's mapping. If the mapping exists in the TLB, the hardware can translate the reference to a physical address without the aid of the page table. If the mapping does not exist in the TLB (an event called a *TLB miss*), the process cannot continue until the correct mapping information is loaded into the TLB.

Translation lookaside buffers are fairly large; they usually have in the order of 100 entries, making them several times larger than a register file. They are typically fully associative, and they are often accessed every clock cycle. In that clock cycle they must translate both the I-stream and the D-stream. Thus, they are often split into two halves, each devoted to translating either instruction or data references. They can constrain the chip's clock cycle as they tend to be fairly slow, and they are also power hungry (both are a function of the TLB's high degree of associativity).

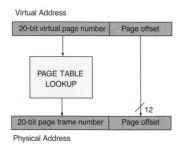
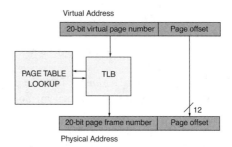

**FIGURE 5.30   Address translation with and without a TLB.** Address translation without a TLB is shown on the left; translation with a TLB is shown on the right. The only difference is that the TLB caches the most recently used entries in the page table, and the page table is only referenced when a lookup misses the TLB.

In general, if the necessary translation information is on-chip in the TLB, the system can translate a virtual address to a physical address without requiring an access to the page table. In the event that the translation information is not found in the TLB, one must search the page table for the translation and insert it into the TLB before processing can continue. This activity can be performed by the operating system or by the hardware directly; a system is said to have a *software-managed TLB* if the OS is responsible, or a *hardware-managed TLB* if the hardware is responsible. The classic hardware-managed design, as seen in the DEC VAX, GE 645, PowerPC, and Intel x86 architectures [Clark & Emer 1985, Organick 1972, IBM & Motorola 1993, Intel 1993], provides a hardware state machine to perform this activity; in the event of a TLB miss, the state machine would walk the page table, locate the translation information, insert it into the TLB, and restart the computation. Software-managed designs are seen in the Compaq Alpha, the SGI MIPS processors, and the Sun SPARC architecture [Digital 1994, Kane & Heinrich 1992, Weaver & Germand 1994].

The performance difference between the two is due to the page table lookup and the method of operation. In a hardware-managed TLB a hardware state machine walks the page table; there is no interaction with the instruction cache. By contrast, the software-managed design uses the general interrupt mechanism to invoke a software TLB miss-handler—a primitive in the operating system usually 10–100 instructions long. If this miss-handler is not in the instruction cache at the time of the TLB miss-exception, the time to handle the miss can be much longer than in the hardware-walked scheme. In addition, the use of the general-purpose interrupt mechanism adds a number of cycles to the cost by draining the pipeline and flushing a possibly large number of instructions from the reorder buffer; this can add up to something on the order of 100 cycles. This is an overhead that the hardware-managed TLB does not incur; when hardware walks the page table, the pipeline is not flushed, and in some designs (notably the Pentium Pro [Upton 1997]), the pipeline keeps processing, in parallel with the TLB miss-handler, those instructions that are not dependent on the one that caused the TLB miss. The benefit of the software-managed TLB design is that it allows the operating system to choose any organization for the page table, while the hardware-managed scheme defines an organization for the operating system. If TLB misses are infrequent, the flexibility afforded by the software-managed scheme can outweigh the potentially higher per-miss cost of the design. For the interested reader, a survey of hardware mechanisms is provided in [Jacob & Mudge 1998b], and a performance comparison of different hardware/operating system combinations is provided in [Jacob & Mudge 1998c].

Lastly, to put modern implementations in perspective, note that TLBs are not a necessary component for virtual memory, though they are used in every contemporary general-purpose processor. Virtually addressed caches would suffice because they are indexed by the virtual address directly, requiring address translation only on the (hopefully) infrequent cache miss. Such a scheme is detailed and evaluated in [Jacob & Mudge 2001].

## References

D. W. Clark and J. S. Emer. "Performance of the VAX-11/780 translation buffer: Simulation and measurement." *ACM Transactions on Computer Systems,* 3(1), 1985.

Digital. *DECchip 21064 and DECchip 21064A Alpha AXP Microprocessors Hardware Reference Manual,* Digital Equipment Corporation, Maynard, MA, 1994.

IBM and Motorola. *PowerPC 601 RISC Microprocessor User's Manual.* IBM Microelectronics and Motorola, 1993.

Intel. *Pentium Processor User's Manual.* Intel Corporation, Mt. Prospect, IL, 1993.

Bruce Jacob and Trevor Mudge. "Virtual memory: Issues of implementation." *IEEE Computer,* 31(6), pp. 33–43, June 1998a. <http://www.ece.umd.edu/~blj/papers/computer31-6.pdf>

Bruce Jacob and Trevor Mudge. "Virtual memory in contemporary microprocessors." *IEEE Micro,* 18(4), pp. 60–75, July/August 1998b. <http://www.ece.umd.edu/~blj/papers/micro18-4.pdf>

Bruce Jacob and Trevor Mudge. "A look at several memory management units, TLB-refill mechanisms, and page table organizations." In *Proc. Eighth International Conference on Architectural Support for Programming Languages and Operating Systems (ASPLOS '98),* pp. 295–306. San Jose, CA, October 1998c.

Bruce Jacob and Trevor Mudge. "Uniprocessor virtual memory without TLBs." *IEEE Transactions on Computers,* 50(5), May 2001. <http://www.ece.umd.edu/~blj/papers/ieeetc50-5.pdf>

G. Kane and J. Heinrich. *MIPS RISC Architecture.* Prentice-Hall, Englewood Cliffs, NJ, 1992.

Samuel J. Leffler, Marshall Kirk McKusick, Michael J. Karels, and John S. Quarterman. *The Design and Implementation of the 4.3BSD UNIX Operating System.* Addison-Wesley Publishing Company, Reading, MA, 1989.

E. I. Organick. *The Multics System: An Examination of its Structure.* The MIT Press, Cambridge, MA, 1972.

M. Upton. *Personal communication.* 1997.

D. L. Weaver and T. Germand, editors. *The SPARC Architecture Manual version 9.* PTR Prentice-Hall, Englewood Cliffs, NJ, 1994.

# 6
# System Design

**Mark Smotherman**
*Clemson University*

**Dezső Sima**
*Budapest Polytechnic*

**Kevin Skadron**
*University of Virginia*

**Tzi-cker Chiueh**
*State University of New York
at Stony Brook*

## 6.1   Superscalar Processors

*Mark Smotherman*

### Introduction

A superscalar processor is a computer designed to fetch, decode, and execute multiple instructions each clock cycle. The rationale for such a design can be illustrated by considering the basic computer performance equation, that is, execution time is a function of the path length (measured in number of instructions) multiplied by the cycles per instruction (CPI) multiplied by the clock cycle time. The goal of a pipelined processor is to strive towards a minimum CPI of 1.0, while simultaneously reducing or at least limiting any expansion of the path length or clock cycle time, and thus reduce the execution time. The goal of a superscalar design is to attain a fractional CPI, or, stated as the reciprocal, the goal is to attain instructions per cycle (IPC) greater than 1.0. With similar reductions or at least limits over the expansion of the path length and clock cycle time, the result is an even larger reduction in the execution time than for pipelining alone.

A VLIW (Very Long Instruction Word) processor is also designed for fetching, decoding, and executing multiple operations each clock cycle. The difference between a superscalar processor and a VLIW processor is one of implementation and architecture. Superscalar design can be applied as an implementation technique to an existing sequential instruction set, while VLIW design requires that the instruction set architecture, the implementation, and the compilers be specifically designed to support the packaging of multiple independent operations into long instruction words.

Proponents of the VLIW approach rightly contend that VLIW design reduces the control complexity within a processor; however, the corresponding drawbacks are a loss of program portability at the binary level and a lack of flexibility. With regard to portability, the control logic added by a superscalar processor is used to dynamically determine opportunities for parallel execution within a conventional instruction stream. Thus, superscalar processors dynamically schedule parallel execution of the instructions of existing executable program files, whereas recompilation into a static representation of parallel execution is a requirement for programs to run on VLIW processors. With regard to flexibility, superscalar processors can easily respond to dynamic events, such as cache misses. Dynamic events present a difficulty for VLIW designs. For example, early VLIW designs avoided data caches so that memory access time would be a known quantity for use in compiler scheduling.

The recent introduction of EPIC (Explicitly Parallel Instruction Computing) architectures, such as the IA-64 architecture of Intel and Hewlett-Packard, is an attempt to gain the best of both approaches. Explicit dependence information is incorporated into the instruction formats to reduce the control logic complexity, and some scheduling of dynamic behavior is incorporated to provide flexibility.

## Instruction-Level Parallelism

Superscalar processors attempt to identify and exploit parallelism in the instruction stream. That is, instructions that are independent should be executed in parallel. We briefly review the concept of dependencies. More details can be found in Mike Johnson's text on superscalar microprocessor design [1].

### Dependencies

Dependencies limit the parallelism between instructions because they must be enforced so that the results of program execution will be correct. Indeed, much of the control logic in a superscalar processor is devoted to identifying dependencies, so that execution will produce the same results as if the instruction stream was being executed on a purely sequential computer. Dependencies can be categorized in three ways.

#### Data Dependencies

Data dependencies exist between two instructions when the order between the two instructions must be maintained for execution to be correct. The most obvious data dependency is the true data dependency (or RAW: read-after-write dependency) in which the result of one instruction is used as an input operand for the second instruction. To preserve correctness, the first instruction must be executed prior to the second. The storage that is used first as a result and then as a source can be either a memory location or a CPU register.

Two other cases arise when the second instruction writes to a storage location. An output dependency (or WAW: write-after-write dependency) occurs when both instructions write to the same storage. To preserve correctness, the result of the second instruction must be the final value of the storage. An anti-dependency (or WAR: write-after-read dependency) occurs when the first instruction reads an input operand from the storage location that will be written with the result of the second instruction. To preserve correctness, the first instruction must obtain its input operand before that value is overwritten by a new value from the second instruction. Both of these cases are called false data dependencies because they arise from the reuse of storage locations.

#### Control Dependencies

A control dependency occurs when an instruction depends on a conditional branch instruction. It is not known whether the instruction is to be executed or not until the branch is resolved. Thus, the branch must be executed prior to the instruction.

#### Structural Dependencies

A structural dependency occurs when two instructions need the same resource. If the resource is not duplicated, the instructions must execute sequentially, one after the other, rather than in parallel. The resource for which the instructions contend might be an adder, a bus, a register file port, or some other component.

## Studies of Instruction-Level Parallelism

In the early 1970s, two studies on decoding and executing multiple instructions per cycle were published—one by Gary Tjaden and Mike Flynn on a design of a multiple-issue IBM 7094 [2] and the other by Ed Riseman and Caxton Foster on the effect of branches in CDC 3600 programs [3]. The conclusion in both papers was that only a small amount of instruction-level parallelism existed in sequential programs—1.86 and 1.72 instructions per cycle determined by the respective studies. Thus, these studies clearly demonstrated the limiting effect of data and control dependencies on instruction-level parallelism, and the result was to encourage researchers to look for parallelism in other arenas, such as vector processors and multiprocessors. However, the Riseman and Foster study did examine the effect of relaxing the control dependencies and found increasing levels of parallelism, up to 51 instructions per cycle, as the number of branches were eliminated (albeit in an impractical way). Later studies, in which false data dependencies were eliminated as well as control dependencies, found much more available parallelism, with the highest published estimate being 90 instructions per cycle by Alexandru Nicolau and Josh Fisher as part of their VLIW research [4].

## Techniques to Increase Instruction-Level Parallelism

Just as the limit studies indicated, performance can be increased if dependencies can be eliminated or reduced. Let us address the dependencies in the reverse order from their enumeration above. First, many structural dependencies can be avoided by providing duplicate copies of necessary resources. Even scalar pipelines provide two paths for memory access (i.e., separate instruction and data caches) and multiple adders (i.e., branch target adder and main ALU). Superscalar processors have even more resource requirements, and it is not unusual to find duplicated function units and even multiple ports to the data cache (e.g., true multiporting, multiple banks, or accessing a single-ported cache multiple times per cycle).

Control dependencies are eliminated by compiler techniques of unrolling loops and performing optimizations such as "if conversion" (i.e., using conditional or predicated execution of instructions so that a control-dependent instruction is transformed into a data-dependent instruction). However, the main approach to reducing the impact of control dependencies is the use of sophisticated branch prediction. For example, the Pentium 4 keeps the history of over 4000 branches [5]. Branch prediction techniques allow instructions from the predicted path to begin before the branch is resolved and execute in a speculative manner. Of course, if a prediction is incorrect, there must be a way to recover and restart execution along the correct path.

False data dependencies can be eliminated or reduced by better compiler techniques (e.g., register and memory allocation algorithms that avoid reuse) or by the use of register and memory renaming hardware on the processor. Register renaming can be accomplished in the hardware by incorporating a larger set of physical registers than are available in the instruction set architecture. Thus, as each instruction is decoded, that instruction's architectural destination register is mapped to a new physical register, and future uses of that architectural register will be mapped to the assigned physical register. Hardware renaming is especially important for older instruction sets that have few architectural registers and for legacy codes that for one reason or another will not be recompiled.

True data dependencies have been viewed as the fundamental limit for program execution; however, value prediction has been proposed in the past few years as somewhat of an analog of branch prediction, in which paths within the instruction stream, which depend on easily predicted source values, can be started earlier. As with branch prediction, there must be a way to recover from mispredictions. Another method that is currently being proposed to reduce the impact of true data dependencies is the use of simultaneous multithreading in which instructions from multiple threads are interleaved on a single processor; of course, instructions from different threads are independent by definition.

# Out-of-Order Completion

All processors that attempt to execute instructions in parallel must deal with variations in instruction execution times. That is, some instructions, such as those involving simple integer arithmetic or logic operations, will need only one cycle for execution, while others, such as floating-point instructions, will need multiple cycles for execution. If these different instructions are started at the same time, as in a superscalar processor, or even in adjacent cycles, as in a scalar pipelined processor, a simple instruction can complete earlier than a longer running instruction that appears earlier in the instruction stream. If we allow the simple instruction to write its result to storage before the longer running instruction completes, we may violate a data dependency. Dependency checking hardware can eliminate this problem; however, dependency checking will not solve the problem of an inconsistent state of storage (registers or memory) if the longer running instruction causes an exception. To handle this exception and to be able to resume the program we must know the precise state of the storage, that is, we must know which instructions, prior to the one causing the exception, have not completed and which instructions, after the one causing the exception, have completed. To resume the processor must restore the state and any uncompleted instructions. Two specific methods can accomplish this. The first is to not allow out-of-order completion and force all instructions to complete in-order. The second is to provide a form of buffering, usually called a reorder buffer, in which the instructions completing out-of-order can place their results and then retire the results out of this buffer in program order. If an exception (or for that matter, a branch or value misprediction) occurs, instructions prior to the one causing the exception (or misprediction) are allowed to complete and then the contents of the reorder buffer beyond that instruction are flushed. Execution can then be resumed with a consistent state of storage. See Johnson for more details [1].

## In-Order vs. Out-of-Order Issue

A superscalar processor can fetch multiple instructions and then issue (i.e., assign and route) as many instructions as are independent to the various function units, up to the width of the decoding logic and the issue pathways. If the decoding logic stops processing at the first dependent instruction, the instruction issue is said to be done in program order (or in-order). An alternative is to provide a buffer for decoded instructions and dynamically issue (or schedule) any of the buffered instructions that are ready to execute. The selected instructions may not be in program order (thus, out-of-order). The buffer for the instructions can take the form of a centralized "instruction window" or a decentralized set of "reservation stations," in which a subset of buffers are located at each function unit.

## Example Machines

### Historical Designs

The idea of a superscalar computer originated with John Cocke at IBM in the 1960s. Gene Amdahl, architect of the IBM 704 and one of the architects of the IBM S/360, postulated a bound on computer performance that included an assumption of a maximum decoding rate of one instruction per cycle on a single processor. John Cocke felt that this was not an inherent limit for a single processor. His ideas about multiple decoding became an important part of the IBM ACS-1 supercomputer design, which was started in 1965 but ultimately cancelled in 1969. In this design, up to 16 instructions would be decoded and checked for dependencies each cycle and up to seven instructions would be issued to function units [6].

After the ACS cancellation and the publication of [2] and [3], the idea of superscalar processing lay dormant until the early 1980s when further research at IBM revived the notion of multiple decoding and multiple issue. John Cocke teamed with Tilak Agerwala at IBM and worked on a series of designs that finally led to the IBM POWER (Performance Optimized With Enhanced RISC) instruction set architecture and the IBM RS/6000 workstation, which was announced in late 1989 and delivered in 1990. Agerwala is credited with coining the term superscalar during a series of talks in 1983–1984 in an effort to compare the performance available in these designs as compared to vector processors. These talks and the related IBM technical report [7] were influential in kindling interest in the approach. In 1989, Intel introduced the first single-chip superscalar microprocessor, the i960CA. Also around this time, LIW efforts, such as the Intel i860, the Apollo DN10000, and the National Semiconductor Swordfish, and VLIW efforts, such as those by Multiflow and Cydrome, were underway.

## Modern Designs

Most high-performance processors now incorporate some form of superscalar processing. Even many simple processors can decode and execute one integer instruction along with one floating-point instruction per cycle. We briefly survey three representative processors in the following subsections. Other notable superscalar designs include the Compaq Alpha 21264, HP 8000, and MIPS R10000. It should be noted that designers of IBM mainframes developed a superscalar implementation, the IBM ES/9000 Model 520, in 1992, but more recent implementations have reverted to scalar pipelines.

### UltraSPARC, 1995, [8]

The UltraSPARC is an example of an in-order superscalar processor. It provides four-way instruction issue to nine functional units. The design team extensively simulated many alternatives and concluded that an out-of-order approach would have required a 20% penalty in clock cycle time and increased the time to market by up to half a year. The final design involves a nine-stage pipeline. This includes a decoupled front-end pipeline (fetch and decode stages) that performs branch prediction and places decoded instructions in a 12-entry buffer. A grouping stage then selects up to four instructions in-order from the buffer to be issued in the next cycle. Precise exceptions are provided by padding out most function unit pipelines to four stages each (i.e., the required length for the floating-point pipelines) so that most four-instruction groups complete in-order. The final two stages resolve any exceptions in the groups and write back the results.

### PowerPC 750, 1997, [9]

The PowerPC 750 is an example of an out-of-order processor with distributed reservation stations and a reorder buffer (called the completion buffer in the 750). The 750 has six function units, including two integer units. Each unit has one reservation station, except the load/store unit, which has two. Instructions can issue, when ready, from these reservation stations. (This limited form of out-of-order execution is sometimes called "function unit slip.") The 750 also includes six rename registers for renaming the 32 integer registers and six rename registers for renaming the 32 floating-point registers.

The overall pipeline works as follows. A decoding stage is not needed since instructions are predecoded into a wider representation as they are filled into the instruction cache. Up to four instructions are fetched per cycle into a six-entry instruction buffer. Logic associated with the instruction buffer removes any nops or predict-untaken branches and overwrites predict-taken branches with target-path instructions so that no instruction buffer entries are required for nops or branches. (However, predicted branches are kept in the branch unit until resolution to provide for misprediction recovery.) Up to two instructions can be dispatched per cycle to the reservation stations and can be allocated entries in the six-entry completion buffer. The integer units require a single cycle for execution, while the load/store unit and the floating-point unit require two and three cycles, respectively. After execution, results are placed into the assigned entries in the completion buffer. Up to two entries per cycle can be written back from the completion buffer to the register files.

### Pentium 4, 2000, [5]

The Pentium 4 is the most recent 32-bit processor from Intel and is an example of a very aggressive out-of-order processor with a centralized instruction window and a reorder buffer. The original Pentium combines two integer pipelines, each similar in design to the pipeline of the 486, and can thus decode and execute up to two instructions in-order per cycle. Intel then developed the P6 core microarchitecture, which serves as the basis for the Pentium Pro, Pentium II, and Pentium III. After branch prediction and instruction fetch, the P6 core decodes up to three variable-length Intel IA-32 instructions each cycle and translates them into up to six fixed-length uops (microoperations). Up to three uops are processed by register renaming logic each cycle, and these are placed into the 20-entry centralized instruction window along with being allocated entries in the 40-entry reorder buffer. The window is scanned each cycle in a pseudo-FIFO manner in an attempt to issue up to four uops. Preference is given to back-to-back uops to reduce the amount of operand forwarding among the execution units. The actual scanning and issue requires two cycles, while most instructions require single-cycle execution. At maximum, the reorder buffer can receive up to three results per cycle and can start retirement of up to three uops per cycle. Retirement requires three cycles. Thus the overall pipeline has some 14 stages; but, because some of these stages can overlap, the effect is a minimum latency of 12 cycles per instruction.

The Pentium 4 is a redesign of the core microarchitecture. The translation of IA-32 instructions into uops is retained, but instead of repeatedly fetching, decoding, and translating recurring IA-32 instruction sequences, the uops are stored in a trace cache for repeated access. The trace cache can hold up to 12 K uops, and in a manner somewhat similar to the PowerPC 750 branch elimination logic, the trace cache stores frequently-traversed sequences (i.e., "traces") of uops with any predict-taken branches followed by instructions from the predicted path. The trace cache can provide up to three uops per cycle, which are then routed through reorder-buffer allocation logic, register-renaming logic, and then into uop queues for scheduling. Up to six uops can be issued per cycle, and up to three uops can be retired per cycle. Part of the aggressiveness of the design can be seen by the increase in the reorder buffer size from 40 entries in the P6 core to 126 entries for the Pentium 4. The clock rate can also be aggressively increased on the Pentium 4, since there are approximately double the number of pipeline stages in it as compared to the P6 core. By cascading ALUs, two dependent addition or subtraction operations can be performed in each cycle.

## References

1. Johnson, M., *Superscalar Microprocessor Design,* Prentice-Hall, Englewood Cliffs, NJ, 1991.
2. Tjaden, G., and Flynn, M., Detection of parallel execution of independent instructions, *IEEE Trans. Computers,* C-19, 889, 1970.
3. Riseman, E., and Foster, C., The inhibition of potential parallelism by conditional jumps, *IEEE Trans. Computers,* C-21, 1405, 1972.
4. Nicolau, A., and Fisher, J., Measuring the parallelism available for very long instruction word architectures, *IEEE Trans. Computers,* C-33, 968, 1984.
5. Hinton, G. et al., The microarchitecture of the Pentium 4 processor, *Intel Technology Journal,* available on-line, 2001.
6. Schorr, H., Design principles for a high-performance system, in *Proc. Symp. Computers and Automata,* New York, 1971, 165.
7. Agerwala, T., and Cocke, J., High performance reduced instruction set processors, Technical Report RC12434, IBM Thomas Watson Research Center, 1987.
8. Tremblay, M., Greenly, D., and Normoyle, K., The design of the microarchitecture of the UltraSPARC-I, *Proc. IEEE,* 83, 1653, 1995.
9. Kennedy, A., et al., A G3 PowerPC superscalar low-power microprocessor, in *Proc. COMPCON,* San Francisco, 1997, 315.

# 6.2   Register Renaming Techniques[1]

*Dezsö Sima*

## Introduction

Register renaming (or "renaming" for short) is a widely used technique in instruction level processors (ILP) to remove false data dependencies between register operands of subsequent instructions in a straight line code sequence.[1-3] As false data dependencies we designate read-after-write (RAW) and write-after-write (WAW) dependencies. If false data dependencies are removed, no related precedence requirements constrain the execution sequence of the instructions involved. Thus, on an average, more instructions are available for parallel execution per cycle, which increases processor performance.

---

[1]Portions of this chapter reprinted with permission from Sima, D., The design space of register renaming techniques, *IEEE Micro,* 20 Sept./Oct., 70, 2000. © 2000 IEEE

The *principle of register renaming* is straightforward. The processor removes false data dependencies by writing the results of the instructions first into dynamically allocated rename buffers, rather than into the specified destination registers. For instance, in the case of the following WAR dependency

$$i_1: \quad add \; ..., r_2, ...; \qquad [... \leftarrow (r_2) + (...)]$$

$$i_2: \quad mul \; r_2, ..., ...; \qquad [r_2 \leftarrow (...) * (...)]$$

the processor renames the destination register of $i_2$ ($r_2$), say to $r_{33}$. Then after the renaming of $r_2$, instruction $i_2$ becomes

$$i_2': \quad mul \; r_{33}, ..., ...; \qquad [33 \leftarrow (...) * (...)]$$

and the processor writes the result of $i_2'$ into $r_{33}$ instead of into $r_2$. This resolves the previous WAR dependency between $i_1$ and $i_2$. In subsequent instructions, however, references to the source register $r_2$ must be redirected to the rename buffer $r_{33}$ as long as the renaming remains valid. In the next section we give a detailed description of the whole rename process.

A precursor to register renaming was introduced in 1967 by Tomasulo in the IBM 360/91,[4] a scalar supercomputer of that time, which pioneered both pipelining and shelving. The 360/91 renamed floating point registers in order to preserve the logical consistency of the program execution, rather than to increase processor performance by removing false data dependencies.

Tjaden and Flynn[5] were the first to suggest the use of register renaming for removing false data dependencies. They proposed the renaming of load type instructions, but they did not yet use the term "*register renaming*." This specific term was introduced a few years later, in 1975, by Keller[6] who extended renaming to cover all instructions including a destination register. He also described a possible hardware implementation of this technique. Because of the complexity of its implementation, however, about two decades passed until register renaming came into widespread use in superscalars in the beginning of the 1990s.

Early superscalar models of significant processor lines, such as the PA 7100, SuperSparc, Alpha 21064, R8000, and the Pentium, typically did not yet use renaming as indicated in Fig. 6.1. Renaming appeared gradually, first in a restricted form, called *partial renaming*, in the beginning of the 1990s, in the IBM RS/6000 (Power1), Power2, PowerPC 601, and in NextGen's Nx586 processors, as depicted in Fig. 6.1. Partial renaming restricts renaming to one or to a few data types, such as floating point loads or floating point instructions, as detailed in the section "Scope of Register Renaming." *Full renaming* emerged later, beginning in 1992, first in the high-end models of the IBM mainframe family ES/9000, then in the PowerPC 603. Subsequently, renaming spread into virtually all superscalar processors with the notable exception of Sun's UltraSparc line. At present register renaming is considered to be a standard feature of performance oriented superscalar processors.

## Overview of the Rename Process

The rename process itself is considerably complex. It consists of a number of rename specific tasks—such as renaming the destination and the source registers, fetching renamed source operands, updating the rename buffers, releasing allocated rename buffers, recovery of the rename process from faultily executed speculative execution, etc. In addition, each of the rename specific tasks may be implemented in a number of different ways. Furthermore, the kind of the underlying microarchitecture affects how the rename process is carried out. Therefore, each concrete description of the rename process is related to a particular kind of the renaming technique employed and the underlying microarchitecture. Thus, before describing the rename process we need to be specific about both the renaming technique and the microarchitecture assumed.

As far as *the renaming technique* is concerned, in a subsequent section, we will show that eight *basic alternatives for renaming* are available. In our description of the rename process, we need to presume one

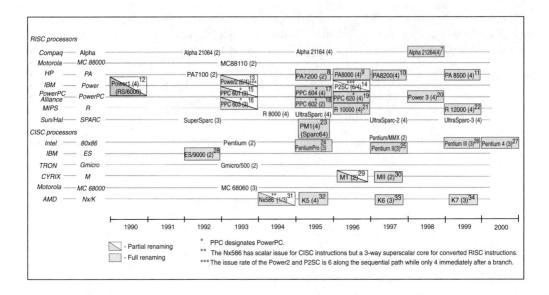

**FIGURE 6.1**   Chronology of the introduction of renaming in commercial superscalar processors. As date of intro-duction, we indicate the first year of volume production. Following the model designation, we also show the issue rate of the processors (in brackets). Concerning the issue rate of CISC processors we note that one x86 instruction can be considered to be equivalent of 1.3–1.9 RISC instructions.[38] In this figure, we give references to the processors that make use of renaming.

of them. Our choice is the one where (i) renaming is implemented by using *rename register files (RRF)*, and (ii) architectural registers are mapped to rename registers by means of *mapping tables*. Although both terms are explained later in the subsequent section, beforehand we note that rename register files, split to separate fixed-point (FX) and floating-point (FP) RRFs, store the instruction results produced by the execution units temporarily, while the FX- and FP-mapping tables hold the actual mappings of the FX- and FP-architectural registers to the associated rename registers, as indicated in the section on "Methods of Register Mapping."

Concerning the *underlying microarchitecture* there are two design aspects, which affect the implemen-tation of the rename process: (i) whether or not the processor uses shelving (dynamic instruction issue, queued issue; see related box) and (ii) assuming the use of shelving, what kind of operand fetch policy is employed (see related box). As recent superscalars predominantly make use of *shelving*, we take this design option for granted throughout this chapter section. Regarding the *operand fetch policy*, which is one design aspect of shelving, we take into account both alternatives, since superscalar processors make use of both policies. Thus, while we describe the rename process in the subsequent two sections, we do it in two scenarios, first assuming the *issue bound fetch policy* and then *the dispatch bound fetch policy*. In both the scenarios mentioned, we describe the rename process by focusing only on a small part of the microarchitecture, which is just enough to highlight the implementation of specific tasks of the rename process.

### The Process of Renaming, Assuming Issue-Bound Operand Fetching

The considered part of the microarchitecture executes FX-instructions and consists of an architectural register file (ARF) and of an execution unit (EU), as shown in Fig. 6.2.

We take for granted that shelving is implemented by providing dedicated buffers, called *reservation stations (RS)*, in front of the EU, and we assume that instructions are forwarded (dispatched ) from the RS to the EU in an in-order manner.

Our subsequent description of the rename process is embedded into the general framework of instruc-tion processing. Here, we distinguish the following four processing phases: (i) decoded instructions are

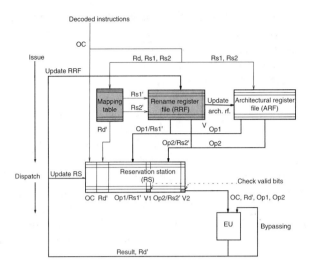

**FIGURE 6.2** The processor core providing shelving with issue bound operand fetching and renaming.

issued into the RS, (ii) executable instructions are dispatched from the RS to the EU, (iii) the EU performs the prescribed operation and generates its result. At this time the instruction is said to be *finished*, and finally, (iv) the processor *completes* (commits, retires) instructions in an in-order fashion, irreversibly updating the program state with the results of the EU.

Assuming the processor core as shown in Fig. 6.2 and issue bound operand fetching, the rename process is carried out as follows:

(i) *During instruction issue*, three rename-related tasks must be performed: (1) the destination registers of issued instructions (Rd) need to be renamed, (2) the source registers (Rs1 and Rs2) should be renamed in order to redirect the source references to the associated rename registers, and (3) the required source operands need to be fetched.

(a) In order *to rename the destination register* of an issued instruction, first a free rename register needs to be allocated to the issued instruction. This task is accomplished by means of the mapping table. The mapping table keeps track of the actual mappings of the architectural registers to the rename registers. Renaming of the destination register results in writing the identifier of the allocated rename register (Rd′) into the corresponding mapping table entry and forwarding this identifier also into the corresponding field of the RS. Typically, the processor uses the index of the allocated rename register as Rd′.

(b) *Source registers*, for which a valid renaming exists, *also need to be renamed*. This is carried out by accessing the mapping table with the source register identifiers ($Rs_1$, $Rs_2$) as indices, and fetching the identifiers of the allocated rename registers (designated as $Rs_1'$, $Rs_2'$). If for a particular source identifier there is no valid renaming, the required source operand will be accessed from the ARF by using the original source register identifier ($Rs_1$ or $Rs_2$).

(c) Finally, the *referenced source operands need to be fetched*. However, with renaming, requested source operands may be in one of two possible locations. If there is a valid renaming, the requested operand needs to be fetched from the RRF, else from the ARF. To fetch a requested operand, usually the processor accesses both the RRF and the ARF simultaneously. If only the ARF hits, the referenced source register is actually not renamed and the accessed value is the required one. If, however, for a particular source register a valid renaming exists, both register files hit and the processor will give preference to the response of the RRF. In this case, the RRF may deliver either a valid operand value ($Op_1/Op_2$), if it has already been produced by a preceding instruction, or the index of that rename register, which will hold the requested value after its generation ($Rs_1'/Rs_2'$), if the required result has not yet been calculated. Thus, for each referenced source register either the requested operand value ($Op_1/Op_2$) or the appropriate rename register identifier ($Rs_1'/Rs_2'$) will be written into the RS. The valid bits associated with the source operand fields ($V_1/V_2$) indicate whether the related operand field holds a valid source operand value ($Op_1/Op_2$) or a rename register identifier ($Rs_1'/Rs_2'$).

(ii) *Dispatching* is not at all rename specific. Assuming in-order dispatching, the processor inspects the valid bits of the source operands ($V_1$ and $V_2$) of the oldest instruction kept in the RS. If both valid bits of this instruction are set and the EU is also free, the instruction is forwarded to the EU for execution.

(iii) *After the EU has finished the execution of an instruction*, both the RS and the RRF need to be updated with the generated result. To *update the RS*, the generated results and their identifiers ($Rd'$) are broadcasted to all the source register entries held in the RS. Through an associative search, all source register identifiers ($Rs_1'$, $Rs_2'$) are located, which are waiting for the new result. The processor substitutes matching identifiers with the result value and sets the associated valid bits ($V_1$ or $V_2$) to indicate availability. We note that this task is performed basically in the same way with and without renaming. There is, however, a slight difference, with renaming the search key is the renamed destination register identifier ($Rd'$) rather than the original destination register identifier ($Rd$) that is used without renaming. The second task is to *update the rename register file*. This is done simply by writing the new result value into the RRF using the identifier accompanying the result produced ($Rd'$) and setting the associated valid bit ($V$) to signal availability.

(iv) *While an instruction completes, the processor permanently updates the ARF*, and thus the *program state*, with the content of the associated rename register. This is done by writing the result of the completed instruction from the associated rename register to the addressed destination register. At this stage of the instruction execution the established renaming becomes obsolete. Therefore, the related entry in the mapping table needs to be deleted and the rename register involved can be *reclaimed* for further use. This is so since (1) after completion, the result of the instruction, that is, the content of the rename register, has already been written into the addressed destination register, and (2) after finishing the instruction, the generated result has already been transferred to all instructions waiting for this operand in the RS.

During renaming, rename registers take on a sequence of states, as indicated in Fig. 6.3.

During initialization the processor sets all rename registers into the "*available*" state. When the processor allocates a rename register to an issued instruction, the state of the allocated register will be changed to "*allocated, not valid*" and its valid bit will be reset. When this instruction becomes finished, the newly produced result is written into the associated rename register, and its state is set to "*allocated, valid*." Finally, while the instruction completes, the result held temporarily in the rename register is written into the specified architectural register. Thus, the allocated rename register can be reclaimed. Its state is then changed to "*available*." Nevertheless, it can happen that an exception or faulty speculative execution gives rise to flush not yet completed instructions. In this case, a recovery procedure is needed, and the state of

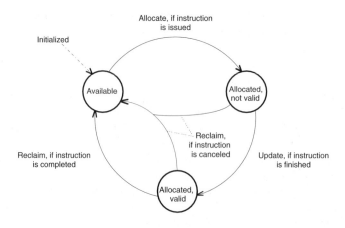

**FIGURE 6.3**   State transition diagram of the rename registers, assuming the use of a rename register file (RRF).

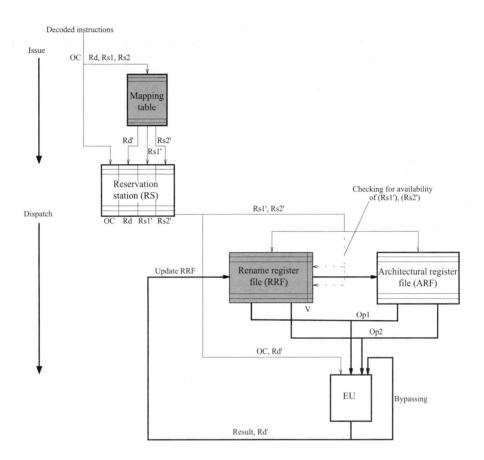

**FIGURE 6.4** The processor core providing shelving with dispatch-bound operand fetching and renaming.

the concerned rename registers will be changed from the "*allocated, not valid*" or "*allocated, valid*" state to the "*available*" state and the corresponding mappings between architectural and rename registers will be deleted.

### The Process of Renaming, Assuming Dispatch-Bound Operand Fetching

Assuming basically the same processor core as before, but using the *dispatch-bound operand fetching*, the *rename process* is carried out as follows (see Fig. 6.4).

(i) During instruction issue, both the destination register (Rd) and the source registers ($Rs_1$ and $Rs_2$) are renamed in the same way as described for issue bound operand fetching. But now, beyond the operation code (OC) and the renamed destination register identifier (Rd'), the renamed source register identifiers ($Rs_1'$ and $Rs_2'$) are written into the RS rather than the operand values ($Op_1$, $Op_2$, if available) as with issue bound operand fetching.

(ii) During dispatching two tasks need to be performed: (a) the instruction held in the last entry of the RS needs to be checked to see whether it is executable. If so and if the EU is also free, this instruction needs to be forwarded for execution to the EU. (b) During forwarding of the instruction, its operands need to be fetched either from the RRF or from the ARF in the same way as described in connection with the issue-bound operation.

(iii) When the EU finishes its operation, the generated result is used to update the RRF. Updating is performed by writing the result into the allocated rename register using the supplemented register identifier (Rd') as an index into the RRF and setting the associated valid bit (V-bit).

(iv) Finally, while the processor completes an instruction, the temporary result held in the associated rename register is written into the architectural register, which is specified in the destination field of the instruction. The only tasks remaining are to delete the corresponding entry in the mapping table and to reclaim the rename register associated with the completed instruction. Reclaiming of the rename register is, however, a far more complex task than with issue bound operand fetching. Notice that if operands are fetched issue bound, (a) issued instructions immediately access their operands and (b) missing operands are, after their generation, immediately forwarded from the EU to the instructions waiting for these operands in the RS. In this case, after completion of an instruction, the allocated rename register can immediately be reclaimed. However, if operands are fetched during dispatching, the RS is not automatically updated with the produced results. As a consequence, after an instruction completes, the RS may still contain instructions, which will require the contents of the rename register, which is allocated to the just completed instruction. Thus, while instructions complete, their allocated rename registers cannot be reclaimed immediately as in the case of the issue bound operand fetching. To resolve this problem one possible solution is to maintain a counter for each rename register, which keeps track of the number of references made to this register. The counter will be incremented each time if one of the source operands of an issued instruction addresses this particular rename register, and will be decremented during dispatching of the instructions each time when a source operand is fetched from this register. After all outstanding fetch requests for a particular rename register are satisfied, as indicated by the counter score of zero, and the associated instruction has been completed, the related register becomes eligible for reclaiming. At the first sight it may seem that this intricate reclaim process can be avoided if during completion the RS would have been searched for all renamed source operand identifiers ($Rs_1'$, $Rs_2'$), which refer to the rename buffer, allocated to the completing instruction ($Rd'$), and matching renamed source register identifiers would have been remapped to the associated architectural register ($Rd$). Unfortunately, this idea is not applicable, since there is no guarantee that the addressed architectural register would not be rewritten until instructions needing its content are dispatched.

During the rename process rename registers will take the same states and the same state transitions will also occur as described earlier in connection with Fig. 6.3. The only difference is that now rename registers are reclaimed according to modified conditions, as discussed previously.

We emphasize that other basic alternatives of register renaming differ mainly in two aspects: (1) the processor can hold renamed values in other structures than rename register files and (2) the processor can use a different scheme for mapping the architectural registers to rename registers as assumed above. In addition, the processor should be able to rename not just one instruction per cycle but all issued instructions. Nevertheless, despite these differences, the previous descriptions in the two characteristic scenarios give a good background about how the rename process is carried out in any of the possible implementation schemes.

## The Design Space of Register Renaming Techniques

### Overview

The *design space of register renaming* has four main dimensions: the scope of register renaming, the layout of the rename registers, the implementation technique of register mapping, and the rename rate, as indicated in Fig. 6.5. These aspects are discussed in the subsequent sections. For the presentation of the design space we make use of DS trees.[3,36]

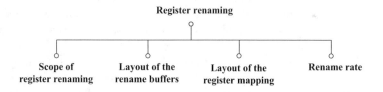

**FIGURE 6.5**  Design space of register renaming.

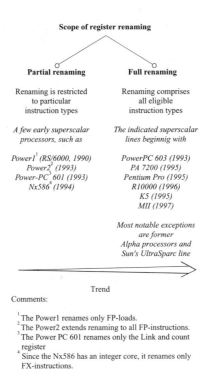

**FIGURE 6.6**    Scope of register renaming.

## Scope of Register Renaming

The *scope of register renaming* indicates how extensively the processor makes use of renaming. In this respect we distinguish between partial and full renaming. *Partial renaming* is restricted to one or to only a few instruction types, for instance only to FP-instructions. This incomplete form of implementation was typical for the introductory phase of renaming, at the beginning of the 1990s (see Fig. 6.1). Examples of processors using partial renaming are the Power1 (RS/6000), Power2, PowerPC 601, and the Nx586, as shown in Fig. 6.6. Of these, the Power1 (RS/6000) renames only FP-loads. As the Power1 has only a single FP-unit, it executes FP-instructions in sequence, so there is no need for renaming floating point register instructions. Power2 introduces multiple FP-units, consequently it extends renaming to all FP-instructions, whereas the PowerPC 601 renames only the Link and count register. In the Nx586, which includes an integer core, renaming is restricted obviously only to FX-instructions.

*Full renaming covers* all instructions including a destination register. As Fig. 6.6 demonstrates, virtually all recent superscalar processors employ full renaming. Noteworthy exceptions are Sun's UltraSparc line and Alpha processors preceding the Alpha 21264.

### Layout of the Rename Buffers

#### Overview
Rename buffers establish the actual framework for renaming. From their layout we point out three essential design aspects—the type and the number of the rename buffers provided as well as the number of the read and write ports, as shown in Fig. 6.7.

#### Types of Rename Buffers
The choice of which type of rename buffers to use in a processor has far reaching impact on the implementation of the rename process. Given its importance, we will outline the various design options. To simplify our presentation, we initially assume a common architectural register file for all data types processed. We later extend our discussion to the split register scenario that is commonly employed.

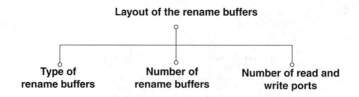

**FIGURE 6.7**   Layout of the rename buffers.

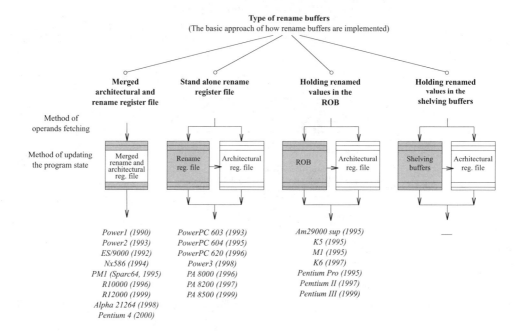

**FIGURE 6.8**   Generic types of rename buffers (rename buffers are indicated by shaded boxes).

As Fig. 6.8 illustrates, there are four fundamentally different ways to implement rename buffers. The range of choices include: (i) using a merged architectural and rename register file, (ii) employing a stand alone rename register file, (iii) keeping renamed values either in the reorder buffer (ROB), or (iv) in the shelving buffers.

(i) In the first approach, rename buffers are implemented along with the architectural registers in the same physical register file, called the *merged architectural and rename register file* or *the merged register file* for short. Here, both architectural and rename registers are dynamically allocated to particular registers of the same physical file.

Each physical register of the merged architectural and rename register file is at any time in one of four possible states.[28] These states reflect the actual use of a physical register as follows:

(a)  not committed ("*available*" state),
(b)  used as an architectural register ("*architectural register*" state),
(c)  used as a rename buffer, but this register does not yet contain the result of the associated instruction ("*rename buffer, not valid*" state), and finally
(d)  used as a rename buffer, and this register already contains the result of the associated instruction ("*rename buffer, valid*" state).

As part of the instruction processing, the states of the physical registers are changed as described below and indicated in the state transition diagram in Fig. 6.9.

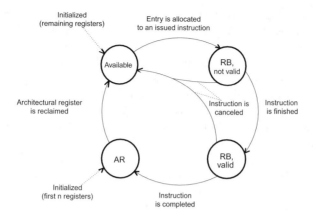

**FIGURE 6.9** State transition diagram of a particular register of the merged architectural and rename register file[28] (AR: architectural register, RB: rename buffer).

During initialization the first $n$ physical registers are assigned to the architectural registers, where $n$ is the number of the registers declared by the instruction set architecture. These registers are set to be in the "*architectural register (AR)*" state while the remaining physical registers take on the "*available*" state. When an issued instruction needs a new rename buffer, one physical register is selected from the pool of the available registers and is allocated to the destination register concerned. Accordingly, its state is set to the "*rename buffer, not valid*" state and its valid bit is reset. After the associated instruction finishes its execution, the produced result is written into the allocated rename buffer. Its valid bit is then set and its state is changed to "*rename buffer, valid.*" Later, when the associated instruction completes, the rename buffer, which is allocated to it will be declared to be the architectural register, which implements the destination register specified in the just completed instruction. Its state then changes to the "*architectural register*" state to reflect this. Finally, when an "old" architectural register is reclaimed, its state becomes again "*available*." Possible schemes for reclaiming "*old*" architectural registers are described for both issue bound and dispatch bound operand fetching in a previous section ("Overview of the Rename Process"). It can also happen that not yet completed instructions should be canceled due to exceptions or faultily executed speculative instructions. In this case allocated rename buffers in the states "*rename buffer, not valid*" or "*rename buffer, valid,*" are deallocated and their state are changed to "*available.*" In addition, the corresponding mappings, kept either in the mapping table or in the rename buffer (as discussed later), need to be canceled.

Note that merged architectural and rename register files do not require a physical data transfer to update architectural registers. All that is needed for updating is to change the status of the related registers. By contrast, separate rename register implementations need, for updating the architectural registers, a physical data transfer from the rename buffer file to the architectural register file. This requires additional read and write ports on the rename register file and on the architectural register file, respectively, as well as a dedicated data path. For this reason recent processors make increasing use of merged architectural and rename register files, e.g., the Alpha 21264, Pentium 4, or the K7 (for renaming floating point instructions).

Merged architectural and rename register files are employed furthermore, in the high end models (520-based models) of the IBM ES/9000 mainframe family, the Power and R1x000 lines of processors.

All other alternatives separate rename buffers from architectural registers. Their respective state transition diagram is depicted in Fig. 6.3 and has already been discussed in connection with the overview of the rename process.

(ii) In the first "separated" variant, a *stand alone rename register file (or rename register file* for short) is used exclusively to implement rename buffers. The PowerPC 603–PowerPC 620 and the PA8x00 line of processors are examples for using rename register files.

(iii) Alternatively, renaming can also be based on the *reorder buffer (ROB)*; see related box. The ROB has recently been widely used to preserve the sequential consistency of the instruction execution. When using a ROB, an entry is assigned to each issued instruction for the duration of its execution. Therefore, it is quite natural to use this entry for renaming as well, basically by extending it with a new field, which will hold the result of that instruction. Examples of processors, which use the ROB for renaming, are the Am 29000 superscalar, the K5, K6, the PentiumPro, PentiumII, and PentiumIII.

The ROB can even be extended further to serve as a central shelving buffer. In this case, the ROB is also occasionally designated as the DRIS (*Deferred Scheduling Register Renaming Instruction Shelve*). The Lightning processor proposal[37] and the K6 made use of this solution. As the Lightning proposal, which dates back to the beginning of the 1990s, was too ambitious in the light of the technology available at that time, it could not be economically implemented and never reached the market.

(iv) The last conceivable implementation alternative of rename buffers is to use the *shelving buffers* for renaming. In this case, each shelving buffer needs to be extended functionally to perform the task of a rename buffer as well. But this alternative has a drawback resulting from the different deallocation mechanisms of the shelving and rename buffers. While shelving buffers can be reclaimed as soon as the instruction has been dispatched, rename buffers can be deallocated only at a later time, not earlier than the instruction has been completed. Thus, a deeper analysis is needed to reveal the appropriateness of the use of shelving buffers for renaming. To date, no processor has chosen this alternative.

For simplicity's sake, we have so far assumed that all data types are stored in a common architectural register file. But usually, processors provide *distinct architectural register files* for FX- and FP-data, consequently they typically employ *distinct rename register files*, as shown in Fig. 6.10.

As depicted in this figure, when the processor employs the split register principle, distinct FX- and FP-register files are needed for both the merged files and the stand alone rename register files. In these cases separate data paths are also needed to access the FX- and the FP-registers. Recent processors typically incorporate split rename registers with one exception. When renaming takes place *within the ROB*, usually a *single mechanism* is maintained for the preservation of the sequential consistency of instruction execution. Then all renamed instructions are kept in the same ROB queue, despite using split architectural register files for FX- and FP-data. In this case, clearly, each ROB entry is expected to be long enough to hold either FX- or FP-data.

### Number of Rename Buffers
Rename buffers keep register results temporarily until instructions complete. As not every instruction produces a register result, in a processor up to as many rename buffers are needed as the maximum number of instructions that have been issued but not yet completed. Issued but not yet completed instructions are either (i) held in shelving buffers waiting for execution (if shelving is employed), or (ii) are just in processing in any of the execution units, or (iii) are in the load queue waiting for cash access (if there is a load queue), or finally (iv) are in the store queue waiting for completion and afterwards for forwarding them into the cache to execute the required store operation (if there is a store queue).

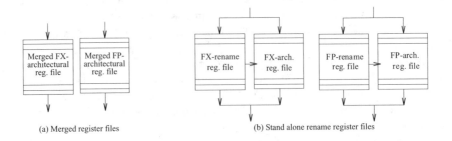

(a) Merged register files                    (b) Stand alone rename register files

**FIGURE 6.10**   Using split registers in the case of (a) merged register files, and (b) stand alone rename register files.

Thus, the maximal number of instructions that may have been issued but have not yet completed in the processor ($n_{\mathrm{pmax}}$) is

$$n_{\mathrm{pmax}} = w_{\mathrm{dw}} + n_{\mathrm{EU}} + n_{\mathrm{Lq}} + n_{\mathrm{Sq}} \qquad (6.1)$$

where $w_{\mathrm{dw}}$ is the width of the dispatch window (total number of shelving buffers), $n_{\mathrm{EU}}$ is the number of the execution units, which may operate in parallel, $n_{\mathrm{Lq}}$ is the number of the entries in the load queue, and finally $n_{\mathrm{Sq}}$ is the number of the entries in the store queue.

Assuming a worst case design approach, from Eq. (6.1) we can determine that the total number of rename buffers required ($n_{\mathrm{rmax}}$) is

$$n_{\mathrm{rmax}} = w_{\mathrm{dw}} + n_{\mathrm{EU}} + n_{\mathrm{Lq}} \qquad (6.2)$$

as instructions held in the store queue do not require rename buffers.

Furthermore, if the processor includes an ROB, the ROB needs to maintain an entry for every issued but not yet completed instruction. So, based on Eq. (6.1) the total number of ROB entries required ($n_{\mathrm{ROBmax}}$) is

$$n_{\mathrm{ROBmax}} = n_{\mathrm{pmax}} \qquad (6.3)$$

Nevertheless, if the processor has fewer rename buffers or fewer ROB entries than expected to have according to the worst case approach (as given by Eqs. (6.2) and (6.3), respectively), missing free rename buffers or ROB entries can cause issue blockages. With a decreasing number of entries provided we expect a smooth and a slight performance degradation. Hence, a stochastic design approach is also feasible, where the required number of entries is derived from the tolerated level of performance degradation.

Based on Eqs. (6.1)–(6.3), the following relations are typically valid concerning the width of the processor's dispatch window ($w_{\mathrm{dw}}$), the total number of the rename buffers ($n_{\mathrm{r}}$), and the reorder width ($n_{\mathrm{ROB}}$), which equals the total number of ROB entries available:

$$w_{\mathrm{dw}} < n_{\mathrm{r}} \leq n_{\mathrm{ROB}} \qquad (6.4)$$

In Table 6.1, we summarize the type and the number of rename buffers provided in recent RISC and x86 superscalar processors. In addition, we give four key parameters of the enlisted processors, (i) the issue rate, (ii) the width of the dispatch window ($w_{\mathrm{dw}}$), (iii) the total number of rename buffers provided ($n_{\mathrm{r}}$), and (iv) the reorder width ($n_{\mathrm{ROB}}$).

As the data in Table 6.1 shows, the interrelations Eq. (6.4) have been taken into account in the design of most processors; however, two obvious exceptions arise. First, the PowerPC 604 provides 20 rename buffers, four more buffers than the reorder width of the processor, which is 16. In the subsequent PowerPC 620, Intel corrected this by decreasing the number of rename buffers to 16. Second, the R10000 provides only 32 ROB entries. This number is far too low compared to the dispatch width (48) and to the number of available rename buffers (64). MIPS addressed this disproportion in its following model, the R12000, by increasing the reorder width of the processor to 48.

### Number of Read and Write Ports

By taking into account current practice, in our subsequent discussion we assume split register files.

First, let us focus on the *required number of read ports* (output ports). Clearly, as many read ports are required in the rename buffers as there are data items that the rename buffers may need to supply in any one cycle. In this respect, we should take into account that rename buffers supply required operands for the instructions to be executed and also forward the results of the completed instructions to the addressed architectural registers.

The number of operands, which need to be delivered in the same cycle, depends first of all on whether the processor fetches operands during instruction issue or during instruction dispatch.

**TABLE 6.1**    Type and Available Number of Rename Buffers in Recent Superscalars

| Processor Type/Year of Volume Shipment | Type of Rename Buffer | Number of Rename Buffers | | Issue Rate | Width of the Dispatch Window ($w_{dw}$) | Total Number of Rename Buffers ($n_r$) | Reorder Width ($n_{ROB}$) |
|---|---|---|---|---|---|---|---|
| | | FX | FP | | | | |
| *RISC Processors* | | | | | | | |
| PowerPC 603 (1993) | ren. reg. file | na. | 4 | 3 | 3 | na. | 5 |
| PowerPC 604 (1995) | ren. reg. file | 12 | 8 | 4 | 12 | 20 | 16 |
| PowerPC 620 (1996) | ren. reg. file | 8 | 8 | 4 | 15 | 16 | 16 |
| Power3 (1998) | ren. reg. file | 16 | 24 | 4 | 20(?) | 40 | 32 |
| R10000 (1996) | merged | 32 | 32 | 4 | 48 | 64 | 32 |
| R12000 (1998) | merged | 32 | 32 | 4 | 48 | 64 | 48 |
| Alpha 21264 (1998) | merged | 48 | 41 | 4 | 35 | 89 | 80 |
| PA 8000 (1986) | ren. reg. file | 56 | 56 | 4 | 56 | 112 | 56 |
| PA 8200 (1987) | ren. reg. file | 56 | 56 | 4 | 56 | 112 | 56 |
| PA 8500 (1989) | ren. reg. file | 56 | 56 | 4 | 56 | 112 | 56 |
| PM1 (1996) | merged | 38 | 24 | 4 | 36 | 62 | 62 |
| *x86 (CISC) Processors* | | | | | | | |
| Pentium Pro (1995) | in the ROB | 40 | | $3^2$ | $20^1$ | 40 | $40^1$ |
| Pentium II (1997) | in the ROB | 40 | | $3^2$ | $20^1$ | 40 | $40^1$ |
| Pentium III (1999) | in the ROB | 40 | | $3^2$ | $20^1$ | 40 | $40^1$ |
| Pentium 4 (2000) | merged | 120? | | $3^2$ | n.a. | 120? | $126^1$ |
| K5 (1995) | in the ROB | 16 | | $4^2$ | $11^1$(?) | 16 | $16^1$ |
| K6 (1996) | in the ROB | 24 | | $3^2$ | $24^1$ | 24 | $24^1$ |
| K7 (1999) | in the ROB /merged[3] | 72 | n.a. | $3^2$ | 54 | n.a. | 72 |
| M3 (2000exp.) | merged | 32 | n.a. | $3^2$ | $56^1$ | na. | $32^2$ |

*Note:* In this table we also indicate four related parameters of the enlisted processors.

[1] RISC operations.

[2] x86 instructions (On average x86 instructions produce 1.3–1.9 RISC operations).[38]

[3] The K7 renames FX operands in the ROB but FP operands in a merged architectural and rename register file, respectively.

? Designates questionable data.

If operands are fetched *issue bound*, the rename buffers need to supply the operands for all instructions, which are issued in the same cycle into the shelving buffers. If there are no issue restrictions, both the FX- and the FP-rename buffers are expected to deliver in each cycle all required operands for up to as many instructions as the issue rate. This means that in a recent four way superscalar processor the FX- and the FP-rename buffers typically need to supply eight and twelve operands respectively, assuming up to two FX- and three FP-operands in each FX- and FP-instruction, respectively. If, however, there are some issue restrictions, the required number of read ports is decreased accordingly.

By contrast, if the processor employs the *dispatch bound* fetch policy, the rename buffers should provide the operands for all instructions, which are forwarded from the dispatch window (instruction window) for execution in the same cycle. In this case, the FX-rename buffers need to supply the required FX-operands for the integer units and for the loadstore units (including register operands for the specified address calculations and FX-data for the FX-store instructions). As far as the FP-rename buffers are concerned, they need to deliver operands for the FP-units (FP-register data) and also for the load store units (FP-operands for the FP-store instructions). In the Power3, for instance, this implies the following read port requirements. The FX-rename buffers need to have 12 read ports (up to $3 \times 2$ operands for the three integer units as well as $2 \times 2$ address operands and $2 \times 1$ data operands for the two load store units). On the other hand, the FP-rename registers need to have eight read ports (up to $2 \times 3$ operands for the two FP-units and $2 \times 1$ operands for the two load store units).

In addition, if rename buffers are implemented separately from the architectural registers, the rename buffers need to be able to forward in each cycle as many result values to the architectural registers as the completion rate (retire rate) of the processor. As recent processors usually complete up to four instructions per cycle, this task increases the required number of read ports in the rename buffers typically by four.

We note here that too many read ports in a register file may unduly increase the physical size of the datapath and as a result the cycle time. To avoid this problem, a few high performance processors (such as the Power2, Power3, and the Alpha 21264) implement two copies of particular register files. The Power2 duplicates the FX-architectural register file, the Power3 doubles both the FX-rename and the FX-architectural files, and the Alpha 21264 has two copies of the FX-merged architectural and rename register file. As a result fewer read ports are needed in each of the copies. For example, with two copies of the FX-merged register file, the Power3 needs only ten read ports in each file, instead of 16 read ports in one FX-register file. A drawback of this approach is, however, that a scheme is also required to keep both copies coherent.

Now let us turn to the *required number of write ports* (input ports). Since rename buffers need to accept in each cycle all results produced by the execution units, they need to provide as many write ports as many results the execution units may produce per cycle. The FX-rename buffers receive results from the available integer-execution units and from the load/store units (fetched FX-data), whereas the FP-rename buffers hold the results of the FP-execution units and of the load/store units (fetched FP-data). Most results are single data items requiring one write port. However, there are a few exceptions. When execution units generate two data items they require two write ports as well; like the load/store units of PowerPC processors. After execution of the LOAD-WITH-UPDATE instruction, these units return both the fetched data value and the updated address value.

## Layout of the Register Mapping

### Overview
Register mapping includes three tasks, as depicted in Fig. 6.11: (1) The processor needs to allocate rename buffers to the destination registers of the issued instructions; (2) it also must keep track of the actually valid mappings; and (3) it needs to deallocate no longer used rename buffers.

### Allocation Scheme of Rename Buffers
As far as the *allocation scheme of rename buffers* is considered, processors usually allocate rename buffers to every issued instruction rather than only to those including a destination register in order to simplify logic. Although rename buffers are not needed until the results become available in the last execution cycle, rename buffers are typically allocated to the instructions as early as during instruction issue. This kind of register allocation leads to wasted rename register space. Delaying the allocation of rename buffers to the instructions until instructions finish[39] saves rename register space. Various schemes have been proposed for this, such as virtual renaming[39–42] and others.[43] In fact, a virtual allocation scheme has already been introduced into the Power3.[39]

### Method of Keeping Track of Actual Mapping
Two possibilities are available for *keeping track of the actual mapping* of particular architectural registers to allocated rename buffers. The processor can use a mapping table for this or can track the actual register

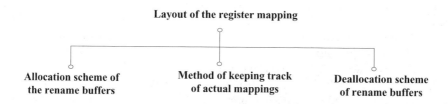

**Layout of the register mapping**

| Allocation scheme of the rename buffers | Method of keeping track of actual mappings | Deallocation scheme of rename buffers |

**FIGURE 6.11**   Layout of the register mapping.

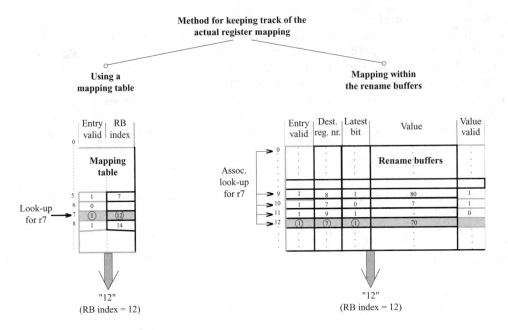

**FIGURE 6.12**  Methods for keeping track of the actual mapping of architectural registers to rename buffers. (RB designates rename buffer.)

mapping within the rename buffers themselves. In the following section we outline these methods, illustrated in Fig. 6.12.

A *mapping table* has as many entries as there are architectural registers in the instruction set architecture (ISA), usually 32. Each entry holds a status bit (called the entry valid bit in the figure), which indicates whether the associated architectural register is renamed. Each valid entry supplies the index of the rename buffer, which is allocated to the architectural register belonging to that entry (called the RB-index). For instance, the left side of Fig. 6.12 shows that the mapping table holds a valid entry for architectural register $r_7$, which contains the RB-index of 12, indicating that the architectural register $r_7$ is actually renamed to rename buffer number 12. As already indicated, usually each entry is set up during instruction issue while new rename buffers are allocated to the issued instructions. A valid mapping is updated when the architectural register belonging to that entry is renamed again, and it will be invalidated when the instruction associated with the actual renaming completes. In this way, the mapping table continuously holds the latest allocations. Source registers of issued instructions are renamed by accessing the mapping table with the register numbers as indices and fetching the associated rename buffer identifiers (RB-indices), as shown in Fig. 6.12.

We note that for split architectural register files obviously separate FX- and FP-mapping tables are needed.

Mapping tables should provide one read port for each source operand that may be fetched in any one cycle, and one write port for each rename buffer that may be allocated in any one cycle (as discussed earlier in the section on "Number of Read and Write Ports").

The other fundamentally different alternative for keeping track of the actual register mappings relies on an *associative mechanism* (see the right side of Fig. 6.12). In this case no mapping table exists but each rename buffer holds the identifier of the associated architectural register (usually the register number of the renamed destination register) and additional status bits as well. These entries are set up usually during instruction issue when a particular rename buffer is allocated to a specified destination register. As Fig. 6.12 shows, in this case each rename buffer holds five pieces of information: (1) a status bit, which indicates that this rename buffer is actually allocated (called the entry valid bit in the figure), (2) the identifier of the associated architectural register (Dest. reg. no.), (3) a further status bit, called the latest bit, whose role will be explained subsequently, (4) another status bit, called the value valid bit, which shows whether the actual value of the associated architectural register has already been generated, and finally (5) the value itself (value), provided that the "value valid" bit signifies an already produced result. The latest bit is needed to mark the last allocation of a given architectural register if it has more than one valid allocation due to repeated renaming. For instance, in our example, architectural register $r_7$ has two subsequent allocations. From these, entry number 12 is the latest one as its latest bit has been set. Thus, in our figure, renaming of the source register $r_7$ would yield the RB-index of 12. We point out that in this method source registers are renamed by an associative lookup for the latest allocation of the given source register.

If operands are fetched issue bound, source registers are both renamed and accessed during the issue process. Then processors usually integrate renaming and operand accessing, and therefore maintain register mapping within the rename buffers. For dispatch bound operand fetching, however, these tasks are separated. Source registers are usually renamed during instruction issue, whereas the source operands are accessed while the processor dispatches the instructions to the execution units. Therefore, in this case, processors typically use mapping tables.

### Deallocation Scheme of Rename Buffers

If rename buffers are no longer needed, they should be reclaimed (deallocated). The actual *scheme of reclaiming* depends on key aspects of the overall rename process. In particular, it depends on the allocation scheme of the rename buffers, the type of rename buffers used, the method of keeping track of actual allocations, and even whether operands are fetched issue bound or dispatch bound. Here, we do not go into details, but refer to the section on "Implementation of the Rename Process" for a few examples on how processors reclaim rename registers.

## Rename Rate

As its name suggests, the *rename rate* stands for the maximum number of renames that a processor is able to perform in a cycle. Basically, the processor should be able to rename all instructions issued in the same cycle in order to avoid performance degradation. Thus, the rename rate should equal the issue rate. This is easier said than done because it is not at all an easy task to implement a high rename rate (four or higher). This is true for two reasons. First, for higher rename rates the detection and handling of inter-instruction dependencies during renaming (as discussed later in the section on "Implementation of the Rename Process") becomes a more complex task. Second, higher rename rates require a larger number of read and write ports on register files and on mapping tables. For instance, the 4-way superscalar R10000 can issue any combination of 4 FX- and FP-instructions. Accordingly, its FX-mapping table needs 12 read ports and 4 write ports, and its FP-table requires 16 read and 4 write ports. This number of ports are needed since FX-instructions can refer up to three and FP-instructions up to four source operands in this processor.

Another example worth looking at is the PM1, also called Sparc64. This 4-way superscalar processor can issue any combination of 4 FX- and 2 FP-instructions, up to a maximum of 4 instructions. In this case, both the FX-mapping table and the merged register file have 10 read and 4 write ports while its FP-counterpart has 6 read and 3 write ports. According to Asato et al.,[44] this 14-port 116 word 64-bit merged register file needs 371 K transistors, far more than the entire Intel 8086 processor (about 30 K transistors) or slightly more than the i386 (about 275 K transistors).[45]

## Basic Alternatives and Possible Implementation Schemes of Register Renaming

In the design space of register renaming, theoretically each possible combination of the available design choices yields one possible implementation alternative. Instead of considering all possible implementation alternatives, it makes sense to focus only on those, which differ in relevant qualitative aspects from each other. We designate these alternatives the basic alternatives. Possible *basic alternatives* can be derived from the design space in two steps—first by identifying the relevant qualitative design aspects and then by

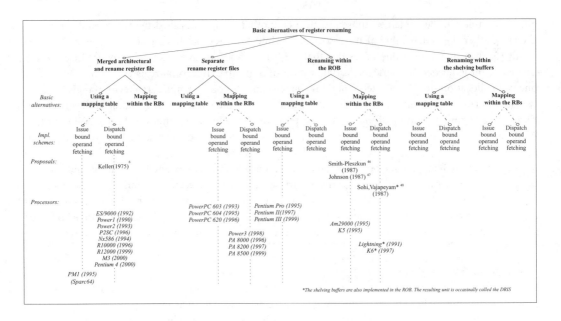

**FIGURE 6.13**  Basic implementation alternatives of register renaming.

composing their possible combinations. Concerning the selection of the *relevant qualitative design aspects*, we recall the design space of renaming, shown in Fig. 6.5. First, we can ignore two main aspects, the scope of register renaming, as recent processors typically implement full renaming, and the rename rate, because of its quantitative character. Thus, two main design aspects remain, the layout of the rename buffers and the implementation of register mapping. Furthermore, as Fig. 6.7 indicates, the layout of the rename buffers itself covers three design aspects: the type and the number of rename buffers, and the number of the read and write ports. Of these only the type of the rename buffers is of qualitative character. From the design aspect layout of the register mapping (Fig. 6.11) we consider the method of keeping track of actual mappings the only relevant aspect. It follows that the design space of register renaming includes only two relevant qualitative aspects: the type of the rename buffers and the method of keeping track of actual mappings.

The design choices available for these two relevant design aspects result in eight possible *combinations*, called the *basic alternatives* for register renaming, as shown in Fig. 6.13. In addition, as the operand fetch policy of the processor, which is a design aspect of shelving, significantly affects how the rename process is carried out, in this figure we also take into account this aspect. This splits the eight basic renaming alternatives into 16 feasible *implementation schemes*. In this figure we also indicate which implementation schemes are used in relevant superscalar processors, as well as give some hints about their origins.

As Fig. 6.13 indicates, out of the eight possible basic alternatives of renaming, relevant superscalar processors make use only of four. Moreover, we can recognize that the latest processors employ mostly the following three basic alternatives of renaming:

1. Use of merged architectural and rename register files and of mapping tables (R10000, R12000, M3)
2. Use of separate rename register files and mapping registers within the rename registers (PA8x00 line, Power3)
3. Renaming within the ROB and using mapping tables (Pentium Pro, Pentium II, Pentium III)

We note furthermore that it is also conceivable to use different basic alternatives for renaming FX- and FP-instructions, as is done in the K7. This processor uses the ROB for renaming FX-instructions and a merged architectural and rename register file for renaming floating point ones; however, as AMD did not disclose the method of register mapping, we have not included this processor into Fig. 6.13.

As Fig. 6.13 shows, the latest processors fetch operands predominantly dispatch bound due to the comparative advantage of this fetch policy.[49] The move away from the issue bound to the dispatch bound fetch policy is manifested in AMD's subsequent K5 and K6, in Intel's line of P6-based models (Pentium Pro, Pentium II, and Pentium III) compared to the Pentium 4, and by the fact that the PowerPC 620-based Power3 also made this transition.

## Implementation of the Rename Process

With reference to the section "Overview of the Rename Process" we emphasize that the rename process can be broken down into the following subtasks:

(a)  renaming the destination registers
(b)  renaming the source registers
(c)  fetching the renamed source operands
(d)  updating the rename buffers
(e)  updating the architectural registers with the content of the rename buffers
(f)  reclaiming of the rename buffers
(g)  recovery from wrongly performed speculative execution and handling of exceptions

These subtasks are carried out more or less differently in the 16 distinct implementation schemes of renaming.

Of these, in the section on "Overview of the Rename Process," we described the rename process presuming one particular basic alternative (assuming the use of rename register files and mapping tables) in both operand fetch scenarios, that is in two implementation schemes. Below, instead of pointing out all differences in all further implementation schemes of register renaming, we focus only on three particular tasks of renaming and point out significant differences encountered in different implementation schemes. In addition, we briefly discuss how inter-instruction dependencies are dealt with during renaming, how the processor recovers from misspeculation, and how it handles exceptions.

### Remarks on Renaming Destination Registers

The way how the processor allocates new rename buffers depends on the type of rename buffers used. If rename buffers are realized in the ROB, a new ROB entry, and thereby a new rename buffer will automatically be allocated to each issued instruction. Else rename buffers need to be allocated only to those issued instructions, which include a destination register.

### Remarks on Updating the Architectural Registers

As discussed previously, when instructions complete, their results need to be forwarded from the associated rename buffers into the originally addressed architectural registers. In cases where rename buffers are implemented separately from the architectural register file (as a stand alone rename register file, or they are in the ROB or in the shelving buffer file), this task instructs the processor to physically transfer the contents of the related rename buffers into the referenced architectural registers. By contrast, if the processor uses a merged architectural and rename file, no physical data transfer is required, instead only the status of the related registers needs to be changed, as indicated before and shown in Fig. 6.10.

### Remarks on Reclaiming Rename Buffers

The conditions for reclaiming no longer used rename buffers vary with the rename scheme employed. Thus, when operands are fetched issue bound, associated rename buffers may immediately be reclaimed after an instruction has been completed. On the other hand, if the processor fetches operands dispatch bound, associated rename buffers may only be reclaimed after the related instruction has been completed and, in addition, if it is also sure that no outstanding operand fetch requests are available to that rename buffer. The latter condition can be checked in different ways. One possibility is to use a counter for each rename buffer for checking outstanding fetch requests, as described in the section on "Overview of the Rename Process." Another option is applicable with merged architectural and rename register files.

In this case, however, during instruction execution a rename buffer becomes an architectural register and reclaiming is related to no longer used architectural registers, as discussed in the section on "Types of Rename Buffers." This method relies on keeping track of the most recent prior instance of the same architectural register, and on reclaiming it when the instruction giving rise to the new instance completes.[28]

### Renaming of Destination and Source Registers if Inter-Instruction Dependencies Exist between the Instructions Issued in the Same Cycle

As we know, shelving relieves the processor of the need to check for data- and control dependencies as well as for busy EUs during instruction issue. Nevertheless, despite shelving, instructions issued in the same cycle must still be checked for inter-instruction dependencies, and, in the case of dependencies, the rename logic must be modified accordingly. Let us assume, for instance, that there are RAW dependencies between two subsequent instructions issued in the same cycle, as in the following example:

$$i_1: \quad \text{mul} \quad r_2, ..., ...$$

$$i_2: \quad \text{add} \quad ..., r_2, ...$$

Here, $i_2$ needs the result of $i_1$ as $r_2$ is one of its source operands. We will also assume that the destination register of $i_1$ ($r_2$) will be renamed to $r_{33}$ as follows:

$$i_1': \quad \text{mul} \quad r_{33}, ..., ...$$

In this case the RAW-dependent source operand of $i_2$ ($r_2$) has to be renamed to $r_{33}$ rather than to the rename buffer allocated before renaming of $i_1$ to $r_2$.

Similarly, if WAW dependencies exist among the instructions issued in the same cycle, as for instance, between the instructions

$$i_1: \quad \text{mul} \quad r_2, ..., ...$$

$$i_2: \quad \text{add} \quad r_2, ..., ...$$

obviously, different rename buffers need to be allocated to the destination registers of $i_1$ and $i_2$, as shown below:

$$i_1': \quad \text{mul} \quad r_{34}, ..., ...$$

$$i_2': \quad \text{add} \quad r_{35}, ..., ...$$

### Recovery of the Rename Process from Wrongly Executed Speculation and Handling of Exceptions

If the processor performs speculative execution, for instance due to branch prediction, it may happen that the speculation turns out to be wrong. In this case the processor needs to recover from the misspeculation. This involves essentially two tasks: (i) to undo all register mappings set up, and (ii) to reclaim rename buffers allocated, as already discussed. *To invalidate established mappings* there are two basic methods to choose from, independently of the actual implementation of renaming. The first option is to *roll back* all register mappings made during speculative execution, by using the identifiers of the faulty instructions, supplied by the ROB. While using this alternative, the recovery process lasts several cycles, since the processor can cancel only a small number of instructions (two to four) per cycle. A second alternative is based on *checkpointing*. In this method, before the processor begins with speculative execution, it saves the relevant machine state, including also the actual mapping, in shadow registers. If the speculative execution turns out to be wrong, the processor restores the machine state in a single cycle by reloading the saved state. For instance, both the PM1 (Sparc64) and the R10000 use checkpointing for recovery. Both processors incorporate mapping tables for register mapping, while the R10000 provides four sets of shadow registers and the PM1 16 for subsequent speculations.

We note that beyond the two basic methods discussed above, there is also a third option in the case when the processor uses mapping tables and dispatch bound operand fetching. This method relies upon *shadow mapping tables*, which keep track of the actual mappings of the completed instructions. The entries of the shadow tables are set up when instructions complete and are deleted when allocated rename buffers are reclaimed. In the case of misspeculation, the correct state of the mapping table can be restored by loading the content of the shadow table. For example, Cyrix's M3 makes use of this recovery mechanism.

The second task to be done during misspeculation is *to reclaim rename buffers*, which are allocated to the faulty instructions. This task can easily be performed by changing the state of the rename buffers involved to "available," as indicated in Figs. 6.3 and 6.9.

A similar situation to the above described misspeculation arises when *exceptions* occur. In this case the exception request must wait until the associated instruction comes to completion to provide precise exceptions.[46] At this time, the processor accepts the exception and cancels all instructions, which have been issued after the failing one. For cancellation of the rename process the same methods can be used as discussed above. For example, in the event of an exception the R10000 rolls back all younger register mappings made, whereas the PM1 first restores the mapping state to the first checkpoint after the failing instruction in one cycle, and then rolls back the remaining mappings until the failing instruction is reached.

## Appendix A: Types of Data Dependencies[1–3]

Data dependencies are precedence requirements between operands of subsequent instructions. Data dependencies may occur in two different situations: either in straight line code segments, called *inter instruction dependencies,* or between operands of instructions occurring in subsequent loop iterations, designated as *recurrences* (see Fig. A). In both situations *either register operands* or *memory operands* may be involved.

Inter-instruction dependencies may be broken down into read-after-write (RAW), write-after-read (WAR), and write-after-write (WAW) dependencies, as depicted in Fig. B. In the following overview of these types of dependencies we confine ourselves to register operands, but the given interpretation can be applied to memory operands as well.

*RAW dependencies*, designated also as *flow dependencies*, are producer-consumer relations between operands, which can be bisected into load-use and define-use dependencies (see Fig. B). *Load-use dependencies*

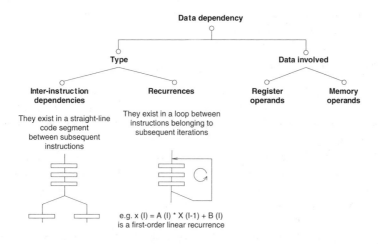

**FIGURE A.** Main aspects of data dependencies. (In this and in subsequent figures, relevant aspects and possible alternatives are illustrated by using DS-trees.[3,36])

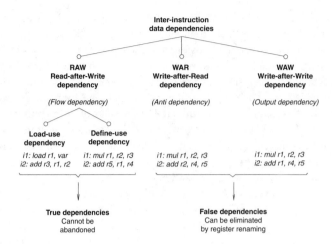

**FIGURE B.**    Terms relating to data dependencies occurring in straight line code (Instruction semantics is $r_1 \leftarrow r_2 * r_3$ etc.).

arise in scenarios when an instruction uses a register operand, which needs to have been loaded by a preceding load instruction from the memory, as shown in the example in Fig. B. If, however, the requested operand is produced by a preceding operational instruction, the arising dependency is called *define-use dependency*, as illustrated in Fig. B.

*WAR dependencies* or *anti-dependencies* arise between instructions if a given instruction reads an operand from a particular register and a subsequent instruction writes the same register, as depicted in Fig. B. If, for any reason, the subsequent instruction ($i_2$) would have written this register before it is read by the previous one ($i_1$), then the subsequent instruction would pick up an erroneous operand value.

Finally, two instructions are said to be *WAW dependent*, or *output dependent*, if they both write the same destination.

WAR and WAW dependencies are designated as *false dependencies*, since they can be removed by appropriate techniques (that is register renaming in the case of register operands). By contrast, RAW dependencies are *true dependencies*, since they cannot be eliminated.

Data dependencies may also occur in loops. This is the case if an instruction of the loop body is dependent on an instruction belonging to a previous loop iteration, as exemplified in Fig. A. This type of dependency is called *recurrence*, designated also as inter-iteration data dependency or loop carried dependency. In the above example the value of $X(I)$ depends on the value that is computed in the previous iteration. The recurrence shown is a first-order linear one.

## Appendix B: The Principle of Instruction Shelving

*Instruction shelving* (also known as indirect issue or dynamic instruction scheduling)[1–3,49] removes the issue bottleneck caused by control and data dependencies and by busy execution units. Its main idea is to "shelve" issued instructions and defer dependency checking until a subsequent processing step, designated as dispatching.

*Without shelving* (see Fig. C) the processor issues instructions from the so called *issue window* (instruction window), to the execution units (EU). Actually, the issue window comprises the last $n$ entries of the instruction buffer (I-buffer), where $n$ is the *issue rate*. The processor decodes the instructions kept in the window and checks for dependencies between the instructions in the window and those in execution, and also among the instructions held in the window. Dependent instructions are not issued, moreover, depending on the issue policy of the processor,[36] they can even block the issue of subsequent not dependent instructions. Occurring blockages heavily restrict the average number of instructions issued per cycle and thus also processor performance.

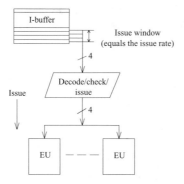

**FIGURE C.** The principle of direct issue.

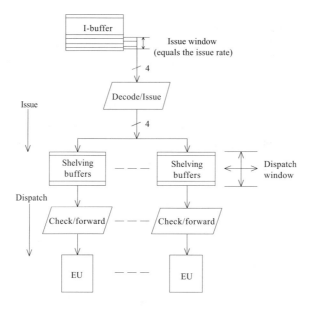

**FIGURE D.** The principle of shelving (indirect issue).

*Shelving* removes the issue bottleneck by decoupling instruction issue and dependency checking through buffering issued instructions, as indicated in Fig. D. There are various possibilities as to how shelving buffers can be implemented.[49] Of these in Fig. D we show shelving buffers provided in front of each execution unit (EU), also called individual reservation stations or simply reservation stations. With shelving, instructions are *issued* first to the shelving buffers, with no checks for data dependencies or busy execution units. In the second step, instructions held in the shelving buffers are *dispatched* for execution. During dispatching instructions are checked for dependencies and not dependent instructions are forwarded to free execution units. Concerning terminology we note that at the time being there is no consensus on the use of the terms instruction issue and instruction dispatch. Both terms are used in both possible interpretations.

Shelving not only removes the issue bottleneck but substitutes the *issue window* with the much wider *dispatch window* (instruction window), which is made up of all shelving buffers. Because the total number of the shelving buffers is usually an order of magnitude higher than the issue rate, with shelving the processor will find in each clock cycle on the average far more executable instructions than without shelving.

Thus, shelving substantially raises the sustained instruction throughput rate of the processor. Although conceived as early as in the middle of the 1960s for the first instruction level parallel (ILP) processors (the CDC6600[50] and the IBM 360/91),[4] because of the complexity of its implementation, shelving only came into widespread use more than two decades later in superscalars.

## Appendix C: Operand Fetch Policies[3]

If the processor uses the *issue bound fetch policy* it fetches referenced register operands during instruction issue, that is while it forwards decoded instructions into the shelving buffers.[3,36] In contrast, *the dispatch bound fetch policy* defers operand fetching until executable instructions are forwarded from the shelving buffers to the execution units. When the processor fetches operands issue bound, shelving buffers hold the source operand values. In contrast, in the case of dispatch bound operand fetching, shelving buffers have much shorter entries, as they contain only the register identifiers.

## Appendix D: The Principle of the Reorder Buffer (ROB)

It is implemented basically as a circular buffer whose entries are allocated and deallocated by means of two revolving pointers.[46] The ROB operates as follows. When instructions are issued, an ROB entry is allocated to each instruction strictly in program order. Each ROB entry keeps track of the execution status of the associated instruction. The ROB allows instructions to complete (commit, retire) only in program order by permitting an instruction to complete only if it has finished its execution and all preceding instructions are already completed. In this way, instructions update the program state in exactly the same way as a sequential processor would have done. After an instruction has completed, the associated ROB entry is deallocated and becomes eligible for reuse.

## References

1. Rau, B. R. and Fisher, J. A., Instruction level parallel processing: History, Overview and Perspective, *The Journal of Supercomputing*, 7, 9, 1993.
2. Smith, P. E. and Sohi, G. S., The microarchitecture of superscalar processors, *Proc. IEEE*, 83, 1609, 1995.
3. Sima, D., Fountain, T., and Kacsuk, P., *Advanced Computer Architectures*, Addison Wesley Longman, Harlow, 1997.
4. Tomasulo, R. M., An efficient algorithm for exploiting multiple arithmetic units, *IBM J. of Research and Development*, 11, 1, 25, 1967.
5. Tjaden, G. S. and Flynn, M. J., Detection and parallel execution of independent instructions, *IEEE Trans. on Computers*, C-19, 889, 1970.
6. Keller, R. M., Look-ahead processors, *Computing Surveys*, 7, 177, 1975.
7. Leibholz, D. and Razdan, R., The Alpha 21264: A 500 MIPS out-of-order execution microprocessor, in *Proc. COMPCON*, 1997, 28.
8. Kurpanek, G., Chan K., Zheng J., CeLano E., and Bryg W., PA-7200: A PA-RISC processor with integrated high performance MP bus interface, in *Proc. COMPCON*, 1994, 375.
9. Hunt, D., Advanced performance features of the 64-bit PA-8000, in *Proc. COMPCON*, 1995, 123.
10. Scott, A. P., et. al., Four-way superscalar PA-RISC Processors, *Hewlett-Packard Journal*, Aug., 1, 1997.
11. Lesartre, G. and Hunt, D., PA-8500: The continuing evolution of the PA-8000 Family, PA-8500 Document, Hewlett-Packard Company, 1998.
12. Grohoski, G. F., Machine organization of the IBM RISC System/6000 processor, *IBM J. of Research and Development*, 34, 1, 37, 1990.

13. White, S. and Reysa, J., *PowerPC and POWER2: Technical Aspects of the New IBM RISC System/6000*, IBM Corp. 1994.

14. Gwennap, L., IBM crams Power2 onto single chip, *Microprocessor Report*, 10, 11, 14, 1996.

15. Becker, M., et al., The PowerPC 601 microprocessor, *IEEE Micro*, 13, Oct., 54, 1993.

16. Burgess, B., et al., The PowerPC 603 microprocessor, *Comm. of the ACM*, 37, 6, 34, 1994.

17. Song, S. P., et al., The PowerPC 604 RISC microprocessor, *IEEE Micro*, 141, 8, 1994.

18. Ogden, D., et al., A new PowerPC microprocessor for low power computing systems, in *Proc. COMPCON*, 1995, 281.

19. Levitan, D., et al., The PowerPC 620 microprocessor: a high performance superscalar RISC microprocessor, in *Proc. COMPCON*, 1995, 285.

20. Song, S. P., IBM's Power3 to replace P2SC, *Microprocessor Report*, 11, 15, 23, 1997.

21. Gwennap, L., MIPS R10000 uses decoupled architecture, *Microprocessor Report*, 8, 18, 14, 1994.

22. Gwennap, L., MIPS R12000 to hit 300 MHz, *Microprocessor Report*, 11, 13, 1, 1997.

23. Patkar, N., et al., Microarchitecture of HaL's CPU, in *Proc. COMPCON*, 1995, 259.

24. Gwennap, L., Intel's P6 uses decoupled superscalar design, *Microprocessor Report*, 9, 2, 9, 1995.

25. Gwennap, L., Klamath extends P6 family, *Microprocessor Report*, 11, 2, 1, 1997.

26. Pentium III Processor, Product Overview, Intel Corp, 1999.

27. Hinton, G., The microarchitecture of the Pentium IV processor, *Intel Technology Journal*, 1.Q., 1, 2001.

28. Liptay, J. S., Design of the IBM Enterprise Sytem/9000 high-end processor, *IBM J. of Research and Development*, 36, 4, 713, 1992.

29. Burkhardt, B., Delivering next-generation performance on today's installed computer base, in *Proc. COMPCON*, 1994, 11.

30. "Cyrix 686MX," Cyrix Corporation, *Order No. 94329-00*, 1997.

31. Gwennap, L., NexGen enters market with 66-MHz Nx586, *Microprocessor Report*, 8, 4, 12, 1994.

32. Slater, M., AMD's K5 designed to outrun Pentium, *Microprocessor Report*, 8, 14, 1, 1994.

33. Shriver, B. and Smith, B., *The Anatomy of a High-Performance Microprocessor*, IEEE Computer Society Press, Los Alamitos, 1998.

34. Diefendorff, K., K7 challenges Intel, *Microprocessor Report*, 12, 14, 1, 1998.

35. Sima, D., The design space of register renaming techniques, *IEEE Micro*, 20, Sept./Oct., 70, 2000.

36. Sima, D., Superscalar instruction issue, *IEEE Micro*, 17, Sept./Oct., 29, 1997.

37. Popescu, V., Schultz, M., Spracklen, J., Gibson, G., Lightner, B., and Isaman, D., The Metaflow architecture, *IEEE Micro*, 11, June 10, 1991.

38. Gwennap, L., Nx686 goes toe-to-toe with Pentium Pro, *Microprocessor Report*, 9, 14, 1, 1995.

39. Monreal, T., et al., Delaying physical register allocation through virtual-psysical registers, in *Proc. MICRO-32*, 1999, 186.

40. Wallace, S. and Bagheryadeh, N., A scalable register file architecture for dinamically scheduled processors, in *Proc. Conf. Parallel Architectures and Compilation Techniques*, 1996, 179.

41. González, A., et al., Virtual registers, in *Proc. Third Int'l Symp. High-Performance Computer Architecture*, IEEE CS Press, 1997, 364.

42. González, A., González, J., and Valero, M., Virtual-physical register, in *Proc. Fourth Int'l symp. High-Performance Computer Architerture*, IEEE CS Press, 1998, 175.

43. Jourdan, S., et al., A Novel renaming scheme to exploit value temporal locality through physical register reuse and unification, in *Proc. MICRO-31*, IEEE CS Press, 1998, 216.

44. Asato, C., et al., A 14-port 3.8 ns 116 word 64b read-renaming register file, in *Proc. ISSC*, 1995, 104.

45. Crawford, H., The I486 CPU: executing instructions in one clock cycle, *IEEE Micro*, 10, Febr., 27, 1990.

46. Smith, J. E. and Pleszkun, A. R., Implementing precise interrupts in pipelined processors, *IEEE Trans. on Computers*, C-37, 562, 1988.

47. Johnson, M., *Superscalar Microprocessor Design*, Prentice-Hall, Englewood Cliffs, NJ. 1991.

48. Sohi, G. S. and Vajapayem, S., Instruction issue logic for high performance, interruptable pipelined processors, in *Proc. 14th ASCA,* 1987, 27.
49. Sima, D., The design space of shelving, *Journal of Systems Architecture,* 45, 863, 1999.
50. Thornton, J. E., *Design of a Computer: The CDC 6600,* Scott Foresman, Glenview III, 1970.

## 6.3   Predicting Branches in Computer Programs

*Kevin Skadron*

### What Is Branch Prediction and Why Is it Needed?

#### What Is Branch Prediction?

*Branch* instructions permit a program to control the flow of instruction execution within a program. Examples of high-level program constructs that translate into branches are "if-then" statements and "for" loops. They test some condition, and depending on the outcome, execution proceeds down one of two possible paths. In almost all instruction sets, branch instructions have exactly two possible outcomes: *not-taken,* the sequential or fall-through case, in which the condition is false and the program continues executing the instructions that immediately follow the branch; and *taken,* the nonsequential case, in which the condition is true and execution jumps to a target specified in the branch instruction. In the case of an "if" statement, the two outcomes are the "then" clause and the fall-through case, which may correspond to an "else" clause. In the case of a "for" loop, the two outcomes are an iteration of the loop body or the fall-through case, which corresponds to exiting the loop. For example, a typical loop structure in assembly code might look like this ("bnez" means "branch if the condition is not equal to zero"):

```
L:  (loop body)
    ...
    sub  r1, #1, r1    ; r1 is the loop counter
    bnez r1, L         ; if the loop count is not yet zero, branch back
                       ; to the top of the loop (label "L") and iterate
    (fall-through code) ; this code gets executed after the loop exits
```

Note that in all the assembly-language examples in this chapter, destination registers are listed last.

Branches create a problem because the identity of the proper path can only be known after the branch has finished testing its condition, a process that takes time. Due to the pipelined nature of almost all modern processors, this resolution latency necessitates branch prediction. Figure 6.14 shows the flow of a branch through a generic pipeline. Resolving the branch requires waiting until it proceeds through several stages and finally executes. If the fetching of subsequent instructions must wait until the proper path is known with confidence, stall time or a "bubble" results [1].

If branch outcomes are instead predicted and subsequent instructions are speculatively fetched and executed, this bubble is eliminated whenever the prediction is correct. This is shown in Fig. 6.15. If the prediction is incorrect, these speculative instructions must be squashed—removed from the pipeline—and no time has been wasted compared to the alternative of no prediction. Squashing can be accomplished simply by preventing the mis-speculated instructions from modifying any processor state. These squashed instructions, however, represent an opportunity cost: had the branch been correctly predicted, those instructions would have been correct, and would have performed useful work. This wasted time is called the *misprediction penalty* and is equal to the branch resolution time.

Other control-flow instructions exist that transfer execution to some other program location but are not conditional and do not branch. These *jump* instructions either jump to the target specified in the instruction (*direct* jumps), or jump to a target that has been computed and whose address is found in a register (*indirect* jumps). A procedure call is an example of the former, and a procedure return is an

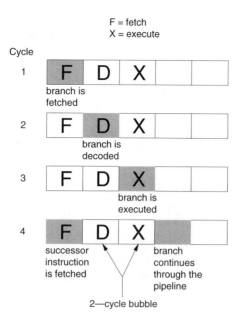

F = fetch
X = execute

FIGURE 6.14  A branch flowing through a generic pipeline with no prediction. The branch, the first gray box, flows from left to right. After being fetched, one or more cycles elapse (one cycle in this diagram) while the instruction is decoded and perhaps other manipulation takes place. Once the branch finally completes executing (i.e., testing its condition), the next instruction (the next gray box) can be identified and fetched. This figure shows that the resolution time introduces a delay during which the pipeline stalls. The corresponding "bubble" here is two cycles long. (From Skadron, K., "Characterizing and removing branch mispredictions." PhD thesis, Princeton Univ., June 1999. With permission.)

example of the latter. Jumps are also frequently used to jump around the else clause of an if-then-else construct. For example, the following C code on the left would be translated into the pseudo-assembly code on the right (bz: "branch if zero"):

```
                                                      ; r1 holds cond
if (cond)                      bz    r1, L1           ; if cond == 0, do else clause
        procedure1();          call  procedure 1      ; cond != 0
else    /* cond ==0 */         jump  L2               ; skip else clause
        procedure2();    L1:   call  procedure2       ; cond == 0
x = x +1;                L2:   add   r20, #1, r20     ; r20 holds x
```

As with branches, some time is required to determine jump targets. Direct jumps can be resolved early with proper hardware in the fetch stage to extract the jump target from the instruction, or the targets can be predicted (e.g., using a branch target address cache—see section on "Branch Target Address Caches"). Indirect jumps generally cannot be resolved early, and instead must proceed through the pipeline in order to read their target from the register file, just like any other instruction. Fortunately, their targets can also be predicted. Prediction of indirect jumps is an active research topic [2–5], but is beyond the scope of this treatment of branch prediction. Return instructions are a special case of indirect jumps, and are easily predicted using a simple structure known as a return-address stack [6,7].

The term "branch" is often used to refer to any type of control-flow instruction, giving us not only conditional branches but also direct and indirect (unconditional) *branches* instead of *jumps*. But the term *branch* is best reserved for conditional branches, because control truly "branches" at such instructions, and unconditional control-flow instructions are best called *jumps*.

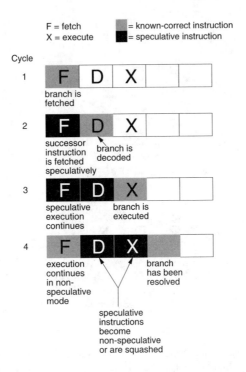

**FIGURE 6.15**   Pipeline behavior with branch prediction. In this diagram, the branch's outcome is predicted. Immediately in the next cycle, subsequent instructions are fetched and executed speculatively (black boxes). If the prediction is correct, the speculative instructions do useful work and the bubble has been eliminated. If the prediction is incorrect, the speculative instructions are squashed. (From Skadron, K., "Characterizing and removing branch mispredictions." PhD thesis, Princeton Univ., June 1999. With permission.)

### Why Is It Needed?

Branch prediction is necessary because branches are frequent, 15–25% of instructions in a typical program. Without prediction, the pipeline would stall for each branch's resolution (refer again to Fig. 6.14) and impose a substantial performance penalty. Even if the processor could issue only one instruction per cycle, and branch resolution stalled the pipeline for only one cycle, this would impose a performance penalty of 15–25%. But today's pipelines are substantially longer (to permit faster clock speeds) and wider (to exploit instruction-level parallelism or ILP), making the penalties much more severe in terms of wasted instruction-issue opportunities. Every additional stage in the pipeline between fetch and execute adds a cycle to the branch resolution delay. In addition, in today's wide-issue "superscalar" pipelines, the penalty is equal to the resolution delay times the issue width. The minimum resolution delay in the Compaq®[1] Alpha 21264—a four-wide superscalar processor—is seven cycles [8], and the minimum resolution delay in the Intel Pentium®[2] Pro—a three-wide superscalar organization—and its successors is eleven cycles [9]. The corresponding penalties are 28 and 33 instruction-issue slots. Of course, programs often do not exhibit enough ILP to use the full issue width all the time, so the actual penalties are not quite so severe. On the other hand, the resolution delays just specified are only the minimum delays. The out-of-order nature of many high-performance processors' execution engines means that instructions may spend an arbitrary amount of time in decoupling buffers, and this makes the pipeline seem longer and exacerbates the branch resolution delays. A correct branch prediction eliminates these stall cycles. A further problem

---

[1]Compaq Computer Corp., Houston, Texas.
[2]Intel Corp., Santa Clara, California.

is that mispredictions limit the processor's ability to build up a large window of instructions over which to expose ILP.

With the misprediction penalty so high in terms of wasted instruction-issue opportunities, not only is branch prediction necessary, but the highest possible prediction accuracy is necessary in order to minimize stall cycles and maximize the processor's ability to exploit ILP.

## Software Techniques

Branches can be predicted or otherwise managed by both software and hardware techniques. This section focuses on software techniques, and the section on "Hardware Techniques" focuses on hardware techniques.

### Branch Delay Slots

One early software technique that was able to eliminate the need for prediction in early processors is the *branch delay slot*. Instead of predicting the branch's outcome, the instruction-set architecture can be defined so that some number of instructions following a branch execute regardless of the branch's outcome. These instruction positions are called delay slot(s) and must be filled with instructions that are safe to execute regardless of the outcome of the branch, or with *nops* (but nops do no useful work). Instructions to fill the delay slot might come from positions that preceded the branch in the original code schedule but can safely be reordered, for example. Consider the sequence of code:

1. add   r1, r2, r3
2. add   r4, r5, r6
3. bnez  r6
4. (delay slot)

Instruction 1 can safely be moved into the delay slot, because doing so violates no data dependencies. Instruction 2, of course, cannot be moved into the delay slot, because it computes the value of r6 that the branch then examines. More aggressive techniques can analyze instructions from after the branch, identify a safe instruction, and hoist it into the delay slot. A more thorough treatment of branch delay slots and associated techniques can be found in [10].

Unfortunately, delay slots have drawbacks. Even the most aggressive techniques still leave some delay slots unfilled, wasting instruction-issue opportunities. Delay slots also have the problem that they expose processor implementation details that might change. Current instruction sets that use delay slots were defined when processors issued instructions in order, one at a time, and pipelines were short. The branch resolution delay was hence just one cycle and the corresponding penalty was only one instruction issue slot, so these instruction sets defined branches to have a single delay slot. Examples include the MIPS®[3] [11] and SPARC®[4] [12] instruction sets. Yet, later implementations made the pipeline longer and issued multiple instructions per cycle. This meant that the resolution delay corresponded to many issue slots, even though the number of delay slots was still fixed by the instruction set at one instruction. In addition, with multiple issue, a bundle of instructions being considered for issue in any particular cycle might consist of several instructions following a branch. Exactly one of these—the delay slot—must be issued unconditionally, while the others are control-dependent on the branch and their execution depends on the branch outcome. For these reasons, later instruction sets like Alpha AXP [13] do not include delay slots.

### Profiling and Compiler Annotation

An alternative software technique is to *profile* the program's behavior by gathering data about how individual branches behave. This involves gathering data while the program is running about its branches' behavior. This data can then be fed to a second compilation pass, which annotates the branches to indicate

---

[3]MIPS Technologies, Mountainview, California.
[4]SPARC International, Inc., Santa Clara, California.

the predominant direction. The hardware then predicts each branch according to the annotation. So for example, a branch that is taken 80% of the time and not taken 20% of the time would be annotated *predict-taken*. More sophisticated profiling and compiler analysis can even make multiple copies of segments of code so that the branches therein have more consistent behavior, or uncover branches whose behavior is correlated and thus capture some of the same behavior as global-history prediction. This is described by Young and Smith in [14].

## Predication

A third technique is *predication* or *if-conversion*, in which the branch is removed and instructions from both the taken and not-taken paths can be executed simultaneously. This eliminates the need to predict the branch, and converts code that was control-dependent into code that is data-dependent on the branch condition. This defers the dependence to the execution core and permits fetching to continue without risk of rollback due to mispredictions. If done judiciously and execution from the two paths is properly balanced, if-conversion can be done without any performance penalties. Correctness is ensured by modifying the instructions that were once controlled or "guarded" by the if-converted branch so that they can only commit if the branch condition would have permitted it.

If-conversion is accomplished in one of two ways. In *full* predication, each individual instruction is guarded by a condition. This *predicate value* is specified as a third operand register, usually from a dedicated register file. Clearly, this requires instruction-set support in every instruction. In *partial* predication, on the other hand, there is no support for guarding predicates. Instead, predication is accomplished using *conditional move* instructions (CMOVs), which can simply be added to retrofit to existing instruction sets. One branch path is executed unconditionally. The results for the other path are computed into temporary registers and then moved into their final destination with CMOVs. The CMOV only completes if the specified condition (the branch condition) holds true. The following code sequence gives an example:

| Original code | Full predication | Partial predication |
|---|---|---|
| if (cond) | pdef cond, p | add   a, b, x |
|    x = a + b; | add   a, b, x(p) | cmov a, x (cond) |
| else | mov  a, x (!p) | mul   x, x, y |
|    x = a; | mul   x, x, y | |
|  y = x *x; | | |

The "pdef" instruction defines a predicate; the condition is evaluated and the result placed in p. In all cases, "y = x * x" gets the correct value of x because y is data-dependent on x and can only use x once its final value is assigned. The final value of x, in turn, is either control-dependent (original code) or data-dependent (predicated code) on cond. Although in this example, the partially-predicated sequence is shorter, partial predication has two drawbacks. It requires a CMOV instruction for each destination register on the path being predicated, and each destination register requires a temporary register [15].

Research by Mahlke et al. [16] has shown that predication substantially reduces both the number of branches executed as well as the branch misprediction rate. Nevertheless, resource constraints mean that not all branches can be predicated, and so predication still requires the presence of branch prediction. This brings us to the hardware techniques, which can be used alone or in conjunction with the software techniques just described.

## Hardware Techniques

### Static Techniques

The simplest hardware technique is to simply stall after every branch until its outcome is known. As described above, the consequent delays lead to untenable performance penalties. A better yet still simple technique is to statically predict all branches to be either taken or not taken. A static not-taken policy is the easier of the two, because it corresponds to sequential execution. This eliminates the need for the fetch engine to identify which instructions are branches or to compute branch targets. Unfortunately, in most programs more than half of branches are taken [17], making the performance of static-not-taken usually quite poor. On the other hand, a static taken policy either requires the fetch engine to identify which instructions are branches and immediately identify their taken targets, or requires some delay while instructions are decoded and the target is computed.

A third policy takes advantage of the fact that backward conditional branches almost always correspond to loops, which tend to iterate multiple times, so these branches are likely to be taken. Non-backward branches, on the other hand, are less biased. Hennessy and Patterson [10] found that 85% of backward branches are taken while only 60% of forward branches are taken. This suggests a static policy of *backwards-taken, forwards-not-taken*, or BTFNT. The problem of computing branch targets remains.

These policies were described by Smith [17] along with the core, bimodal dynamic prediction technique described in the section on "Bimodal Prediction." Another seminal paper from this era is the exploration of branch predictor and branch target address cache design choices by Lee and Smith [18]. Both papers also survey the earliest literature on branch handling.

## Branch Target Address Caches

Not only static techniques, but in fact all branch-prediction techniques have the problem that on a predicted-taken branch, the branch's target must be computed. This requires extracting the offset field from the branch instruction and adding it to the PC; tasks which typically cannot be performed until the instruction-decode stage. If this is the case, some stall cycles result, called a "branch-taken bubble." A second type of predictor—a branch target predictor—can eliminate this problem. In its simplest form, this is simply a small on-chip memory in the fetch stage that serves as a table of recently seen branches, a *branch target address cache* or BTAC [19,20]. (The BTAC is also often referred to as a *branch target buffer* or BTB, but this latter term is too heavily overloaded.) The BTAC is indexed with the branch's address (in other words, the PC—program counter—used to fetch the branch). It may be direct-mapped or associative, and tagged or not tagged. Omitting tags reduces cost, but then a BTAC miss cannot be identified, the predicted-taken branch will use the wrong target, and this will not be discovered until the branch resolves. For this reason, BTACs are best tagged.

The dynamic hardware schemes described later in this section maintain tables in which they track state about conditional branch directions. These direction-prediction tables are often indexed using the branch address. Because the BTAC table is also indexed by branch address, it may be convenient with these dynamic schemes to store the direction-prediction information in the BTAC along with each branch's target. Aside from the convenience of integrating these different sources of information into one table, this confers the advantage that if the BTAC is tagged, any branch prediction state stored in the BTAC is also tagged. While some processors use this organization, Calder and Grunwald [21] point out that many branches are not taken and hence do not require the BTAC to store a target. Decoupling the direction-prediction state from the target-prediction state therefore permits a smaller BTAC. It also improves flexibility, as some predictors, such as global-history predictors (see the section on "Two-level Prediction") do not keep a one-to-one mapping between branch addresses and direction-prediction entries.

Instead of a BTAC, the processor might employ a *branch target instruction cache*, which stores some actual instructions from the branch target rather than merely the target address. This replicates quite a bit of state from the instruction cache, so this organization is rarely seen, although it does appear in the Motorola®[5] PowerPC®[6] G4 [22], for example.

The BTAC can also be integrated with the instruction cache. Each cache line can simply store the target address of one or more of its branches in case that branch is predicted taken. Alternatively, the I-cache can implement a *next-line* predictor [23]. Each cache line now stores the index of the next cache line to be fetched (and also the set if the cache is associative) [24]. If no branches are taken in the current line, the next-line address will be the next sequential address. If there is a taken branch, the next-line address

---

[5]Motorola, Inc., Schaumburg, Illinois.
[6]International Business Machines Corp., Armonk, New York.

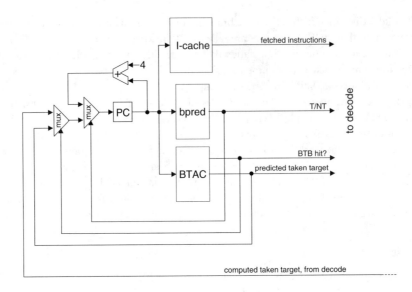

**FIGURE 6.16**   The placement of the branch prediction components in the pipeline.

will be the appropriate target address. As branches change their taken/not-taken behavior, this next-line address is updated accordingly. The next-line predictor is, therefore, a combination of the functionality of a BTB and a bimodal predictor (see the section on "Bimodal Prediction"). If a more sophisticated direction predictor is present, it overrides the next-line predictor. One motivation for using such an organization is to permit a larger, slower, but more accurate direction predictor that may not be able to be accessed in a single cycle. The Alpha 21264 takes such an approach [25], using as its slower but more accurate direction predictor the hybrid predictor described in the section on "Hybrid Prediction."

### Pipeline Issues

In the most efficient organization, both the BTAC and the branch direction predictor are consulted during the fetch stage as shown in Fig. 6.16. In this way, the PC can be updated immediately and the processor can fetch from the appropriate location (taken or not-taken) in the next cycle. This avoids introducing pipeline bubbles unless there is a BTAC miss or a branch misprediction.

Unfortunately, some problems occur with probing the branch-prediction hardware in the fetch stage. One concern is the branch-predictor and BTAC lookup times. These tables must be fast enough, and hence small enough, to permit the lookup to complete and the PC to be updated within a single cycle. Otherwise the fetch stage falls behind. Current processors use predictors as big as 32 kbits, but Jiménez et al. [26] argue that the feasible predictor size for single-cycle access will *shrink* in the coming years. The reason for this is that even though the feature size on a processor die continues to shrink with Moore's law [27], electrical RC delays are not shrinking accordingly, and hence wire delays are not shrinking as fast as logic delays. As feature size shrinks, large structures therefore seem to be getting relatively *slower*.

Another problem is that in a typical organization, the fetch stage cannot determine whether the instructions being fetched from the instruction cache contain any branches; that information must wait until the instructions are decoded. Several solutions are available. The first technique is for the instructions to be "pre-decoded" before they are installed into the instruction cache to indicate which instructions are branches. The predictor structures can then be indexed using the actual addresses of the branches. Note that this means either that the predictor must be multi-ported to cope with fetch blocks that contain more than one branch, or the predictor can only predict one branch at a time. This is not necessarily a major restriction, since if the predicted result is not-taken, the remaining instructions in

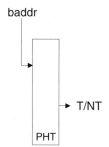

baddr

T/NT

PHT

**FIGURE 6.17** A schematic for a bimodal predictor. "Baddr" is the branch address or PC, which is used to index the PHT (pattern history table), select the corresponding two-bit counter, and make a prediction of taken or not-taken.

the fetch block after the branch are still valid and can still be passed on to decode. The second solution is for the branch predictor to just predict fetch-block successors instead of specific branches. In this case, the predictor simply predicts whether the next fetch block will be sequential (not-taken) or non-sequential (taken, in which case the target supplied by the BTAC is used). This is slightly better than the first choice, because it eliminates the need for pre-decode bits and can fetch past more than one not-taken branch in a fetch block. It does require the decode stage to identify how each branch in a fetch block was implicitly predicted. The third solution is for the BTAC and branch predictor to be indexed with the address of every instruction in the fetch block. Hits in the BTAC indicate which instructions are branches, and only the corresponding direction predictions are then used. The problem with this approach is that it requires as many ports into the BTAC and branch-prediction structures as there are instructions in the fetch block. These are the basic choices, although many variations and improvements have been proposed, e.g., [24,28–30].

## Bimodal Prediction

The simplest dynamic technique, introduced by Smith [17], is to maintain a small, on-chip memory with a table of saturating counters that is indexed by branch address. The saturating counters—typically two bits each—simply remember the predominant direction of previous outcomes for that branch. A schematic for a bimodal predictor appears in Fig. 6.17. As mentioned, the table—usually called the *pattern history table* or PHT—although logically a distinct entity, might actually be implemented as a unified structure with the BTAC. This prediction scheme goes by different names, often simply "two-bit prediction," but recent literature has often referred to it as "bimodal" prediction to distinguish it from other more sophisticated schemes that also use two-bit saturating counters.

Each time a branch resolves, its corresponding counter is incremented if the branch was taken, and decremented if not. Incrementing or decrementing has no effect if the counter is already at its maximum or minimum value, hence the term "saturating" counter and the name "bimodal." In the simplest case of a one-bit counter, the only possibilities are values of 0 and 1 and the predictor simply remembers the last outcome for each branch. In the case of two-bit counters, values of 00 and 01 correspond to strongly not-taken and weakly not-taken, and values of 10 and 11 corresponding to weakly taken and strongly taken. Two-bit counters give better performance because they exhibit some hysteresis that makes them less sensitive to infrequent occurrences of outcomes in the non-dominant direction. A state-transition diagram for the most common two-bit counter configuration appears in Fig. 6.18. Other configurations [18,31] are possible, however, for example, regardless of its current state, the counter might reset to 00 on a not-taken branch.

As an example of how two-bit counters improve over one-bit counters, recall that a loop branch will normally be taken. When the loop exits, a one-bit counter will only remember that most recent direction (not taken), even though the predominant direction is "taken." When this same loop is encountered again, and the loop branch will once again be taken until the loop exits, the first prediction with a one-bit counter will be "not taken." A two-bit counter, on the other hand, only changes its state from 11 to 10 upon loop exit, and still predicts taken when it returns to the loop, thus eliminating a misprediction compared to the one-bit counter.

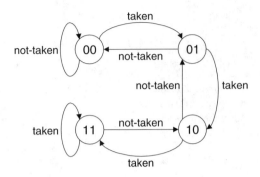

**FIGURE 6.18**   The state-transition diagram for a saturating two-bit counter.

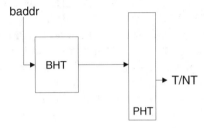

**FIGURE 6.19**   A schematic for a PAg local-history predictor. The branch address is used to index the table of per-branch histories (the BHT), select the appropriate history, and then this history is used to index the PHT.

Wider counters have been considered [17] but confer little benefit and take longer to adjust to a change in a branch's behavior.

The size of the PHT is of course not infinite, so the ideal of one entry per branch may not be realized. The table is indexed by the branch address modulo the table size, so some branches may collide. If these branches are biased in the same direction this is harmless, but if not, they will interfere with each others' attempts to update the counter, and these *destructive PHT conflicts* will lead to mispredictions. Sources of mispredictions are discussed in the section on "Sources of Misprediction."

### Two-Level Prediction

Bimodal prediction can be improved in two ways, both of which explicitly track prior branch outcomes and were introduced by Yeh and Patt. *Local-history* prediction [32] maintains a table of per-branch histories. Instead of tracking each branch's predominant direction, this *branch history table* or BHT tracks explicit history in order to detect patterns. For example, a local history can detect patterns like TNTN… that confound simple saturating counters. The predictor still keeps a PHT of two-bit counters, but these are now indexed using the local history pattern, and the counters now learn outcomes for each history pattern. A schematic of a local history predictor appears in Fig. 6.19. One apparent problem with local-history prediction is that it would seem to require two serial lookups: first the BHT to obtain the history pattern, then the PHT to obtain the actual prediction. This problem is solved by caching the most recent PHT value for a given BHT entry as an extra field in the BHT. The next time that BHT entry is indexed, it provides both the current history and the cached prediction. Fetching proceeds with that cached prediction while the PHT is probed with the history pattern. The PHT result overrides the cached result, so if the PHT disagrees with the cached prediction, the pipeline is flushed from the point of the "mispredicted" branch.

*Global-history* prediction [33] on the other hand, keeps a single history register—the global branch history register or GBHR—into which all branch outcomes are shifted, as seen in Fig. 6.20. It might seem that intermingling outcomes from different branches simply produces noise, but instead global-history

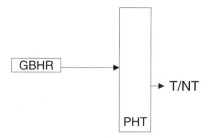

**FIGURE 6.20** A schematic for a GAg global-history predictor. The global history of recent branch outcomes, contained in the global branch history register (GBHR) is used to index the PHT.

prediction is extremely effective. The reason is that global history exposes correlation among branches (and hence these predictors are also called *correlating* predictors). Consider the following sequence of code.

$$
\begin{aligned}
&\text{B1:} \quad \text{if } (x) \\
&\qquad\qquad \cdots \\
&\text{B2:} \quad \text{if } (y) \\
&\qquad\qquad \cdots \\
&\qquad\quad z = x \,\&\&\, y; \\
&\text{B3:} \quad \text{if } (z) \\
&\qquad\qquad \cdots
\end{aligned}
$$

Even if B1 and B2 are entirely unpredictable because x and y have very random behavior, B3 can be predicted with *100% accuracy* if the outcomes of B1 and B2 are known, because the outcome of B3 is entirely correlated with the outcomes of B1 and B2. Global history is an admittedly crude way to expose this sort of correlation, because the GBHR also contains outcomes from other branches that provide no useful information. Yet as the section on "Comparison of Hardware Prediction Strategies" shows, global history is quite effective, and Evers et al. [34] have shown that many programs contain substantial degrees of correlated branch behavior. Unfortunately, no one has come up with a practical hardware technique for exposing correlation while avoiding the noise that unrelated branches introduce into the GBHR.

Both the local-history and global-history predictors described above have the problem that different branches may see the same prior history. All branches that see the same history will map to the same PHT entry. Especially with global prediction, equivalent history does not always mean the branches will behave the same way. To reduce the consequent destructive PHT conflicts, Pan, So, and Rahmeh [35] point out that bits from the branch address can be combined with the history bits in order to provide some degree of anti-aliasing—see Fig. 6.21, for example. The simplest technique is to concatenate the two bit sources. For $N$ bits of history and $M$ bits of branch address, this creates a configuration where each $M$-bit address pattern has its own $2^N$-entry PHT.

For a fixed table size and hence a fixed number of bits in the index, this necessitates a reduction in the number of history bits, so a balance must be found between the added prediction capability provided by history bits and the anti-aliasing capability provided by address bits. This balance is sensitive to the table size. In a study of the SPECint95 benchmarks [36], Skadron, Martonosi, and Clark [37] find that as a general rule of thumb, both global- and local-history predictors should use at least 6–7 bits of branch address, regardless of predictor size. Predictors with more aggressive anti-aliasing techniques, e.g., the bi-mode predictor of Lee, Chen, and Mudge [38], will need fewer address bits.

To classify the different possible two-level predictor organizations, Yeh and Patt [33,39] developed a naming scheme that uses three letters to characterize the different organizational choices. The first letter, G, P, or S, indicates the type of history, global, per branch (i.e., local), or per branch set. The last choice

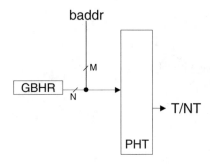

**FIGURE 6.21**    A schematic for a GAs global-history predictor. *N* global history bits are concatenated with M bits from the branch address to form the PHT index.

refers to a predictor that explicitly allocates groups of branches to particular BHT entries, and is only feasible with extensive profiling or compiler support and hence has received little study. Skadron, Martonosi, and Clark [37] added a fourth type, M, to this naming scheme to describe predictors that track a combination of global and local history. The second letter, A or S, indicates whether the PHT is adaptive, using a finite state machine based on saturating counters, or fixed, using statically assigned directions (a profiling pass might determine the best PHT value for each entry); almost all predictors proposed or under study, however, are A—adaptive. The third letter, g, s, or p, indicates the PHT organization. The PHT might be indexed purely by history (g); or indexed using some concatenated branch address bits, making it set-associative (s); or the predictor might have a separate PHT for each branch (p, for per-branch). This last choice eliminates aliasing among branches but is prohibitively large for all but small history sizes, and is therefore mainly of theoretical interest. A pure global-history predictor like that in Fig. 6.20 is, therefore, a GAg predictor and a pure local-history predictor like that in Fig. 6.19 is a PAg predictor. If either of these concatenate some address bits into the index, like the global-history predictor in Fig. 6.21, they become GAs or PAs predictors. Note that the GAs predictor has also sometimes been referred to as *gselect* [40]. Finally, a predictor that uses both global and per-branch history, such as the bi-mode predictor, would be an MAg or MAs predictor [37]. As for specifying the specific configuration of a predictor—how many bits, how many entries, etc.—so many notations are involved that it is better to just be explicit.

An alternative anti-aliasing approach is to XOR the history string and address string together; this approach, introduced by McFarling [40], is called *gshare*. This avoids the need to use a shorter history string—both strings can be as long as the index. Recent data by Sechrest, Lee, and Mudge [41], however, suggest that gshare confers little benefit over GAs.

Two-level prediction can seem like magic, especially global-history prediction. But it operates on the same principle as compression; a predictable sequence is also compressible. Indeed, two-level prediction is a simplified version of a Markov model, the same principle that underlies the *prediction by partial matching* (PPM) compression scheme [42].

### Hybrid Prediction

Because some branches do benefit from global history and others do not, McFarling [40] proposed *hybrid* branch prediction. Several different organizations have been proposed [43–45], but the common idea is to operate two different predictors in parallel, and for each branch select which predictor's output to actually use in making the prediction. The selector is itself a predictor and can be any of the structures described above, but the selector tracks predictor successes rather than branch outcomes. For each branch, the selector attempts to learn which predictor component is more effective. Figure 6.22 shows a high-level schematic of a hybrid predictor's organization. Note that both predictor components and the selector can all be accessed in parallel to minimize lookup time.

The Compaq Alpha 21264 [25] uses a hybrid predictor comprised of 12-bit GAg and 10-bit PAg predictors. The PAg component has a 1 K-entry BHT and, because it uses only history bits in indexing

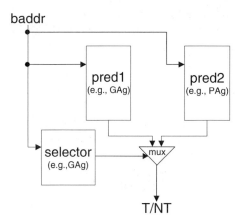

**FIGURE 6.22**  A schematic for a hybrid predictor. "Pred1" and "pred2" are configured as regular, standalone branch predictors (they might be a global-history and a local-history component, for example), but both components make a prediction and the selector then chooses one component prediction (via the multiplexor or "mux") to use as its final prediction. The selector is a predictor too, but tracks component outcomes rather than branch direction outcomes.

the PHT, the PHT is also 1 K entries. An unusual aspect of the PAg component is that it uses three-bit instead of two-bit saturating counters in order to achieve a stronger bias once the predictor has trained. The selector is also a 12-bit GAg predictor, but its PHT tracks which component has been more successful for each branch, rather than which direction the branch should take.

Hybrid prediction has also been called "tournament," "competitive," and "combining" branch prediction.

### Other Issues in Predictor Organization

The preceding sections have described the basic predictor organizations. Because prediction accuracy so strongly underpins processor performance, branch prediction remains an active area of research and a wealth of additional organizations have been proposed, primarily focusing on reducing mispredictions due to destructive aliasing. Interested readers should consult recent proceedings of the symposia and conferences in the list of works cited.

It is worth noting, however, that researchers have also considered how to adapt branch prediction to wider-issue machines. Such a machine must fetch past multiple, possibly-taken branches in order to exploit the wider fetch width. Otherwise the processor becomes fetch-bottlenecked and its effective width is restricted by the average basic block size.

Yeh, Marr, and Patt [29] describe a different branch address cache that learns segments of the control-flow graph and, in conjunction with a banked instruction cache, can fetch several blocks from non-contiguous cache lines in a single cycle. Conte et al. [28] describe a *collapsing buffer* that can also fetch past branches that are taken but whose target is in the same fetch block. Reinman, Austin, and Calder [46] decouple branch prediction from fetch, allowing the branch predictor to run ahead of fetch when possible, and they predict the length of fetch blocks so that not-taken branches do not unnecessarily limit fetching. The most aggressive proposal is the *trace cache* [30] of Rotenberg, Bennett, and Smith, which dynamically collapses noncontiguous fetch streams into contiguous *traces* that are stored in the trace cache and, which appears in the Intel Pentium® 4 [47] and the HAL Sparc64 V [48].

### Sources of Mispredictions

To better understand the behavior of branch predictors, it is helpful to examine some of the reasons a misprediction might occur. These reasons can be broken down into two broad categories: behavioral and structural. Behavioral mispredictions stem from the intrinsic behavior of a branch and are independent of the predictor's organization. Any irregular or random behavior by a branch will inhibit its predictability.

Structural mispredictions, on the other hand, stem from properties of the predictor's hardware organization. The major structural sources of mispredictions are described below and come from [37].

### Destructive PHT and BHT Conflicts

All predictors that track state can suffer when unrelated branches map to the same predictor entry and interfere with each others' state. In the predictor's PHT or in a hybrid predictor's selector PHT, destructive conflicts arise when branches map to the same 2-bit PHT counter and these branches go in opposite directions. In the BHT of a local-history predictor, destructive conflicts arise when branches map to the same history entry and hence the history of one branch displaces that of another branch. Note that *constructive* conflicts can also occur in all these structures when—for reasons of either luck or correlated behavior—the state of one branch causes a correct prediction by other branches. This means the expected gain from eliminating conflicts would eliminate both destructive and constructive conflicts, but the destructive behavior usually outweighs the constructive behavior.

### Training Time

Because dynamic predictors work by recognizing patterns of branch behavior, they take time to train. The training time comes from two sources. First, the predictor must see enough branches to observe any patterns that exist. Second, the predictor must reach steady state. Consider the simple pattern TN,TN… in a 6-bit history. After this branch has been seen twice, the history will contain xxxxTN, where "x" signifies that these history bits contain a random value. Unless by sheer luck the bits in the "xxxx" portion happen to be TNTN, this pattern is a transient that will not be seen again. This branch must therefore be seen four more times before the history is fully initialized. In addition, for both types of training, a pattern must be seen often enough not only to initialize the branch history, but also to put the corresponding counters in the PHT into the proper state. In the TN,TN…example and assuming two-bit counters in the PHT, this means that the history TNTNTN must be seen twice in order to ensure that the two-bit counter has crossed the threshold. (The counter's initial value might have been 00, but the correct prediction is T.) The larger the saturating counters, the longer this component of the training time.

The predictor must train not only when a program first starts executing, but must also retrain after every context switch and also when the program's behavior changes, either because it enters a new phase, or the nature of its input changes, etc.

### "Wrong" Type of History

Mispredictions can also occur because the predictor does not track the most useful type of history—global or local—for the branch in question. This has been called *wrong* history, even though it does not imply that the actual history bits contain any invalid information. Unfortunately, most programs have some branches that do well with global history *and* some branches that do well with local history. A predictor that only tracks one or the other type of history therefore penalizes some branches in each program. Evers et al. showed this to be important in [34]. Skadron, Martonosi, and Clark [37] found wrong-history mispredictions are especially severe in global-history predictors, comprising 35–50% of the total misprediction rate.

### History Length

Mispredictions might also arise even if the predictor tracks the correct type of history but it uses too short a history. For example, a history length of only two bits may not capture the full behavior of a pattern longer than 2 bits. Consider the pattern TNNN,TNNN…. A two-bit local history will learn that TN → N and this is always correct. But the problem arises for the pattern NN. The predictor will first learn NN → N, but on the fifth occurrence of the branch, this will cause a misprediction. On the other hand, there exist longer patterns for which short history is still sufficient. Consider two bits of history and the pattern TNNTT,TNNTT…. Although the overall pattern is longer than 2 bits, none of the distinct sub-patterns (TN, NT, and TT) are longer than two bits.

Alternatively, the history can also be too *long*. The problem here is that the history may contain many bits that are entirely uncorrelated with the behavior of the branch to be predicted. This means that every time this branch is seen, those bits may have a different value, and the predictor may potentially have to train on all possible combinations of those unrelated bits. This has the effect of smearing a particular branch's predictor state across a large portion of the PHT. In the absence of conflicts, this should, however, only be a problem for global history. This problem might also be called a training-time misprediction and was discussed by Evers et al. in [34].

### Update Timing

Depending on how the predictor is updated, mispredictions can also arise because the predictor contains *stale* state. If the predictor is not updated until a branch exits the pipeline, information about that branch's behavior does not appear in the predictor while the branch is in flight. Yet later branches that are fetched and predicted before the first branch retires may depend on that first branch's outcome [49]. Consider again the sequence of correlated branches:

$$
\begin{aligned}
&\text{B1:}\quad \text{if } (x) \\
&\qquad\qquad \dots \\
&\text{B2:}\quad \text{if } (y) \\
&\qquad\qquad \dots \\
&\qquad\qquad z = x \text{ \&\& } y; \\
&\text{B3:}\quad \text{if } (z) \\
&\qquad\qquad \dots
\end{aligned}
$$

In a global-history predictor, if B1 or B2 has not yet resolved, the predictor will use state and hence possibly incorrect global history when looking up the prediction for B3. A similar problem arises in a local-history predictor for branches with repeating patterns.

The solution is to speculatively update the branch history immediately after the branch has been predicted, using the just-predicted value. If the prediction is correct, all subsequent branches see the correct history. If not, the history must be repaired, or the predictor will accumulate bogus history. Fortunately, because all instructions after a misprediction are squashed and re-fetched, subsequent branches still see the correct history. This speculative-update-with-repair scheme therefore gives the illusion of omniscient history update. These mechanisms were first described by Jourdan et al. [50], who also found that in two-level predictors, it is only early update of the branch history that matters. Barring destructive conflicts, the prediction for a particular PHT index is fairly stable over time, so the two-bit saturating counters can be updated after the branch resolves.

## Comparison of Hardware Prediction Strategies

Figures 6.23 and 6.24 present the prediction accuracies of conditional-branch directions for static-not-taken, static-taken, BTFNT, bimodal, GAs, PAs, and hybrid predictors for the SPECint95 benchmarks [36] and for two different sizes: a small predictor configuration of 8 kbits, and a large configuration of 64 kbits. The specific configurations are presented in Table 6.2 and 6.3. Of course, static predictors have no size, so the data for these is simply replicated in both graphs. The configurations for GAs, PAs, and the hybrid predictor are taken from Skadron, Martonosi, and Clark [37], which explored the different possible combinations of history bits, address bits, and, for the hybrid predictor, different possible sizes of the three structures.

The data was gathered using a modified version of the simple, instruction-level branch-predictor simulator from SimpleScalar version 2.0 [51]. All the benchmarks were compiled using gcc version 2.6.3 for the SimpleScalar research instruction set (PISA), and with optimization set at −O3—funroll-loops (note that −O3 includes inlining). Simulation captures all user-level behavior, including libraries, but cannot capture any behavior in the kernel due to system calls. Data was gathered using the SPEC reference inputs. Some benchmarks come with multiple inputs, in which case one has been chosen. Go uses a playing level of 50 and a 21 × 21 board with the 9 stone 21 input. M88ksim uses the dhrystone input, gcc the cccp.i input, xlisp the 9-queens problem, ijpeg the vigo.ppm input, and perl the scrabble game.

**TABLE 6.2**    Predictor Configurations for an 8-kbit Hardware Budget

| Predictor | Index Bits (h = hist., a = addr.) | BHT Entries | PHT Entries |
|---|---|---|---|
| Static not-taken | — | — | — |
| Static taken | — | — | — |
| BTFNT | — | — | — |
| Bimodal | 12a | — | 4 K |
| GAs | 5h, 7a | — | 4 K |
| PAs | 4h, 7a | 1 K | 2 K |
| Hybrid (selector) | 3h, 7a | — | 1 K |
| (global) | 4h, 7a | — | 2 K |
| (local) | 2h, 7a | 512 | 512 |

**TABLE 6.3**    Predictor Configurations for a 64-kbit Hardware Budget

| Predictor | Index Bits (h = hist., a = addr.) | BHT Entries | PHT Entries |
|---|---|---|---|
| Static not-taken | — | — | — |
| Static taken | — | — | — |
| BTFNT | — | — | — |
| Bimodal | 15a | — | 32 K |
| GAs | 8h, 7a | — | 32 K |
| PAs | 8h, 6a | 4 K | 16 K |
| Hybrid (selector) | 6h, 7a | — | 8 K |
| (global) | 7h, 7a | — | 16 K |
| (local) | 8h, 4a | 1 K | 4 K |

**TABLE 6.4**    Branch and Fast-Forward Statistics for the SPECint95 Benchmarks

| | Fast-Forward Distance (million) | Static Conditional Branch Sites | Dynamic Conditional Branches Executed (million) |
|---|---|---|---|
| go | 925 | 5331 | 112 |
| m88ksim (m88) | 0 | 968 | 162 |
| gcc | 0 | 20,783 | 190 |
| compress | 1648 | 203 | 151 |
| xlisp | 0 | 676 | 154 |
| ijpeg | 823 | 1,415 | 58 |
| perl | 600 | 614 | 129 |
| vortex | 2450 | 3,203 | 124 |

*Note:* All benchmarks are run for one billion instructions in statistics-gathering mode after the fast-forward interval.

The reference inputs produce very long simulation times—on the order of days even for simpler instruction-level simulations—so the results here are taken for only a representative, 1-billion-instruction segment of each program's execution. A representative segment is reached by fast-forwarding past unrepresentative initial program behavior using a fast-simulation mode that updates the branch predictor state (so that the predictor state is accurate when the full-detail simulation starts) but does not gather branch-prediction statistics [52]. The fast-forward intervals are taken from [37] and are presented in Table 6.4, along with the observed number of static branch sites and the number of dynamic branches executed for each benchmark.

As can be seen from the data in Figs. 6.23 and 6.24, the static schemes all perform terribly, and different schemes are better for different benchmarks, usually by a significant margin. BTFNT is the best static scheme

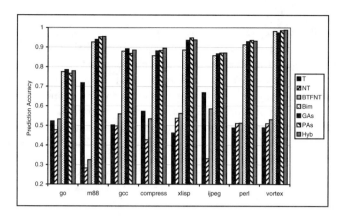

**FIGURE 6.23** Branch prediction accuracies for 8-kbit predictors for the SPECint95 benchmarks. "Bim" is the bimodal predictor, and "Hyb" is the hybrid predictor. Specific configurations appear in Table 6.3.

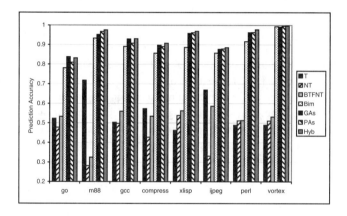

**FIGURE 6.24** Branch prediction accuracies for 64-kbit predictors for the SPECint95 benchmarks. Specific configurations appear in Table 6.4.

for five of the eight benchmarks, but performs terribly for m88ksim. (But keep in mind that BTFNT would look better for floating-point codes, which are heavily loop-oriented.) Always-taken is the best static scheme for m88ksim and ijpeg, but is the worst for three other benchmarks. This variability of the best scheme among different benchmarks makes it difficult to choose one static scheme to implement.

Among dynamic schemes, bimodal is worse than the more sophisticated dynamic schemes for all except go and vortex. Unlike the other schemes, however, bimodal is less sensitive to predictor size, with a mean difference between the 8-kbit and 64-kbit bimodal predictors of only 0.55%. The reason for this is that the bimodal predictor allocates only one entry to each branch site (i.e., a static branch location in the program), no matter how often that branch executes or how varied its behavior. Most of the programs have a fairly small number of branch sites, and of course the property of locality means that only a subset of these are active at any one time. A 4 K-entry (8 kbit) table is, therefore, sufficient to capture most of the static branch locations, and making the table larger has little effect.

Among two-level predictors, GAs is better than PAs about as often as PAs is better than GAs. As with the static schemes, this variability of the best scheme among benchmarks makes it difficult to choose which scheme to implement. This is strong motivation for use of the hybrid predictor, especially given the observation [34,37] that many programs have some branches that are much better predicted using global history, while other branches are much better predicted using local history. GAs, PAs, and hybrid, however, are all the more sensitive to predictor size than bimodal is. Go and gcc are particularly sensitive to predictor size, and so are xlisp and perl to some extent. The hybrid predictor is the most sensitive to size, because it must allocate the available hardware budget across four tables: the selector's PHT, the global-history component's PHT, and the local-history component's BHT and PHT. Each of these tables is therefore substantially smaller than in a single two-level predictor and therefore suffers more destructive interference. This especially affects the programs with large static branch footprints, like go and gcc. Yet a hybrid predictor also has an important advantage: in order to better control destructive conflicts, it can dynamically shift which component it uses to make a prediction for each branch.

Note that these results do not include the effects of predication, context switching, operating system behavior, or any profile-guided feedback. All of these effects might change the results.

## Summary

Branch prediction is important because otherwise every branch stalls the fetch engine. Some alternatives exist, like delay slots and predication, but delay slots are not compatible with modern, wide-issue super-scalar processors, and predication cannot remove all branches. Static prediction techniques that require no hardware support are also possible, but they are either very simple, or in the case of compiler directives, require instruction-set support. Static techniques also have the drawback that they cannot adapt to changing run-time conditions.

Dynamic branch-prediction techniques have evolved from the simple bimodal predictor to more sophisticated two-level and hybrid predictors that exploit patterns in branch behavior and correlation among branches. Refinements to these techniques, as well as new fetch organizations that permit fetching past multiple branches, continue to be active areas of research.

The massive effort to find better branch-handling techniques is motivated by the severe penalty imposed by mispredictions. Especially with the long and wide pipelines of modern processors, a very small misprediction rate can severely harm performance. Indeed, the fetch bottleneck remains one of the most severe limitations on faster processing, and Jouppi and Ranganathan [53] argue that it may become the most severe bottleneck in future processors, even more severe than memory latency or memory bandwidth.

## References

1. Skadron, K., Characterizing and removing branch mispredictions, PhD thesis, Princeton University Department of Computer Science, Princeton, NJ, 1999.
2. Calder, B. and Grunwald, D., Reducing indirect function call overhead in C++ programs, in *Proc. 21st ACM SIGPLAN-SIGACT Symp. on Principles of Programming Languages*, pp. 397–408, Jan. 1994.
3. Chang, P.-Y., Hao, E., and Patt, Y. N., Target prediction for indirect jumps, in *Proc. 24th Ann. Int. Symp. on Computer Architecture*, pp. 274–283, June 1997.
4. Driesen, K. and Hölzle, U., Accurate indirect branch prediction, in *Proc. 25th Ann. Int. Symp. on Computer Architecture*, pp. 167–178, July 1998.
5. Kalamatianos, J. and Kaeli, D. R., Predicting indirect branches via data compression, in *Proc. 31st Ann. ACM/IEEE Int. Symp. on Microarchitecture*, pp. 272–281, Dec. 1998.
6. Kaeli, D. R. and Emma, P. G., Branch history table prediction of moving target branches due to subroutine returns, in *Proc. 18th Ann. Int. Symp. on Computer Architecture*, pp. 34–41, May 1991.
7. Webb, C. F., Subroutine call/return stack, *IBM Technical Discl. Bull.*, 30(11), April 1988.
8. Gwennap, L., Digital 21264 sets new standard, *Microprocessor Report*, pp. 11–16, Oct. 28, 1996.
9. Gwennap, L., Intel's P6 uses decoupled superscalar design, *Microprocessor Report*, pp. 9–15, Feb. 16, 1995.
10. Patterson, D. A. and Hennessy, J. L., *Computer Architecture: A Quantitative Approach*, 2nd ed., Morgan Kaufmann, San Francisco, 1996.

11. Price, C., *MIPS IV Instruction Set,* Revision 3.1, MIPS Technologies Inc., Mountain View, CA, Jan. 1995.
12. SPARC International Inc., *The SPARC Architecture Manual,* version 8, Prentice Hall, Englewood Cliffs, NJ, 1992.
13. Digital Equipment Corp., *Alpha AXP Architecture Handbook,* Oct. 1994.
14. Young, C. and Smith, M. D., Static correlated branch prediction, *ACM Trans. Programming Languages and Systems,* 21(5):1028–1075, Sept. 1999.
15. Mahlke, S. A. et al., A comparison of full and partial predicated execution support for ILP processors, in *Proc. 22nd Ann. Int. Symp. on Computer Architecture,* pp. 138–149, June 1995.
16. Mahlke, S. A. et al., Characterizing the impact of predicated execution on branch prediction, in *Proc. 27th Ann. Int. Symp. on Microarchitecture,* pp. 217–227, Dec. 1994.
17. Smith, J. E., A study of branch prediction strategies, in *Proc. 8th Ann. Int. Symp. on Computer Architecture,* pp. 135–148, May 1981.
18. Lee, J. K. F. and Smith, A. J., Branch prediction strategies and branch target buffer design, *IEEE Computer,* 17(1):6–22, Jan. 1984.
19. Holgate, R. W. and Ibbett, R. N., An analysis of instruction fetching strategies in pipelined computers, *IEEE Trans. Computers,* C29(4):325–329, Apr. 1980.
20. Losq, J. J., Generalized history table for branch prediction, *IBM Technical Discl. Bull.,* 25(1):99–101, June 1982.
21. Calder, B. and Grunwald, D., Fast & accurate instruction fetch and branch prediction, in *Proc. 21st Ann. Int. Symp. on Computer Architecture,* pp. 2–11, May 1994.
22. Diefendorff, K., PowerPC G4 gains velocity, *Microprocessor Report,* pp. 10–15, Oct. 25 1999.
23. W. M. Johnson. *Superscalar Microprocessor Design.* Prentice Hall, Englewood Cliffs, NJ, 1991.
24. Calder, B. and Grunwald, D., Next cache line and set prediction, in *Proc. 22nd Ann. Int. Symp. on Computer Architecture,* pp. 287–296, June 1995.
25. Kessler, R. E., McLellan, E. J., and Webb, D. A., The Alpha 21264 microprocessor architecture, in *Proc. 1998 Int. Conf. on Computer Design,* pp. 90–95, Oct. 1998.
26. Jiménez, D. A., Keckler, S. W., and Lin, C., The impact of delay on the design of branch predictors, in *Proc. 33rd Ann. IEEE/ACM Int. Symp. on Microarchitecture,* pp. 67–77, Dec. 2000.
27. Moore, G. E., Cramming more components onto integrated circuits, *Electronics,* pp. 114–117, Apr. 1965.
28. Conte, T. et al., Optimization of instruction fetch mechanisms for high issue rates, in *Proc. 22nd Ann. Int. Symp. on Computer Architecture,* pp. 333–344, June 1995.
29. Yeh, T.-Y., Marr, D. T., and Patt, Y. N., Increasing the instruction fetch rate via multiple branch prediction and a branch address cache, in *Proc. 7th Int. Conf. on Supercomputing,* pp. 67–76, July 1993.
30. Rotenberg, E., Bennett, S., and Smith, J. E., Trace cache: a low latency approach to high bandwidth instruction fetching, in *Proc. 29th Ann. IEEE/ACM Int. Symp. on Microarchitecture,* pp. 24–34, December 1996.
31. Nair, R., Optimal 2-bit branch predictors, *IEEE Trans. Computers,* 44(5):698–702, May 1995.
32. Yeh, T.-Y. and Patt, Y. N., Two-level adaptive training branch prediction, in *Proc. 24th Ann. Int. Symp. on Microarchitecture,* pp. 51–61, November 1991.
33. Yeh, T.-Y. and Patt, Y. N., Alternative implementations of two-level adaptive branch prediction, in *Proc. 19th Ann. Int. Symp. on Computer Architecture,* pp. 124–134, May 1992.
34. Evers, M. et al., An analysis of correlation and predictability: What makes two-level branch predictors work, in *Proc. 25th Ann. Int. Symp. on Computer Architecture,* pp. 52–61, June 1998.
35. Pan, S.-T., So, K., and Rahmeh, J. T., Improving the accuracy of dynamic branch prediction using branch correlation, in *Proc. Fifth Int. Conf. on Architectural Support for Programming Languages and Operating Systems,* pp. 76–84, Oct. 1992.
36. Standard Performance Evaluation Corporation, SPEC CPU95 benchmarks, http://www.specbench.org/

37. Skadron, K., Martonosi, M., and Clark, D. W., A taxonomy of branch mispredictions, and alloyed prediction as a robust solution to wrong-history mispredictions, in *Proc. 2000 Int. Conf. on Parallel Architectures and Compilation Techniques*, pp. 199–206, Oct. 2000.

38. Lee, C.-C., Chen, I.-C. K., and Mudge, T. N., The bi-mode branch predictor, in *Proc. 30th Ann. Int. Symp. on Microarchitecture*, pp. 4–13, Dec. 1997.

39. Yeh, T. -Y. and Patt, Y. N., A comparison of dynamic branch predictors that use two levels of branch history, in *Proc. 20th Ann. Int. Symp. on Computer Architecture*, pp. 257–266, May 1993.

40. McFarling, S., Combining branch predictors, Tech. Note TN-36, Digital Equipment Corp. Western Research Laboratory, June 1993.

41. Sechrest, S., Lee, C.-C., and Mudge, T., Correlation and aliasing in dynamic branch predictors, in *Proc. 23rd Ann. Int. Symp. on Computer Architecture*, pp. 22–32, May 1995.

42. Chen, I.-C., Coffey, J. T., and Mudge, T. N., Analysis of branch prediction via data compression, in *Proc. Seventh Int. Conf. on Architectural Support for Programming Languages and Operating Systems*, pp. 128–137, Oct. 1996.

43. Chang, P.-Y., Hao, E., and Patt, Y. N., Alternative implementations of hybrid branch predictors, in *Proc. 28th Ann. Int. Symp. on Microarchitecture*, pp. 252–257, Dec. 1995.

44. Evers, M., Chang, P.-Y., and Patt, Y. N., Using hybrid branch predictors to improve branch prediction accuracy in the presence of context switches, in *Proc. 23rd Ann. Int. Symp. on Computer Architecture*, pp. 3–11, May 1996.

45. Grunwald, D., Lindsay, D., and Zorn, B., Static methods in hybrid branch prediction, in *Proc. 1998 Int. Conf. on Parallel Architectures and Compilation Techniques*, pp. 222–229, Oct. 1998.

46. Reinman, G., Austin, T., and Calder, B., A scalable front-end architecture for fast instruction delivery, in *Proc. 26th Ann. Int. Symp. on Computer Architecture*, pp. 234–245, May 1999.

47. Glaskowsky, P. N., Pentium 4 (partially) previewed, *Microprocessor Report*, pp. 1, 11–13, Aug. 2000.

48. Diefendorff, K., Hal makes Sparcs fly, *Microprocessor Report*, pp. 1, 6–12, Nov. 15 1999.

49. Hao, E., Chang, P.-Y., and Patt, Y., The effect of speculatively updating branch history on branch prediction accuracy, revisited, in *Proc. 27th Ann. Int. Symp. on Microarchitecture*, pp. 228–232, Nov. 1994.

50. Jourdan, S. et al., Recovery requirements of branch prediction storage structures in the presence of mispredicted-path execution, *Int. J. of Parallel Programming*, 25(5):363–383, Oct. 1997.

51. Burger, D. C. and Austin, T. M., The SimpleScalar tool set, version 2.0, *Computer Architecture News*, 25(3):13–25, June 1997.

52. Skadron, K. et al., Branch prediction, instruction-window size, and cache size: Performance tradeoffs and simulation techniques, *IEEE Trans. Computers*, 48(11):1260–1281, Nov. 1999.

53. Jouppi, N. P. and Ranganathan, P., The relative importance of memory latency, bandwidth, and branch limits to performance, in the *Wkshp. on Mixing Logic and DRAM: Chips that Compute and Remember*, June 1997.

# 6.4 Network Processor Architecture

*Tzi-cker Chiueh*

## Introduction

The explosive traffic growth on the Internet comes with an ever more demanding requirement on the available bandwidth and thus on the performance of the network devices that move network packets from sources to destinations. In the most general sense, network processors are those that are specifically designed to transport, order, and manipulate network packets as they move through the network. As network protocols are typically structured as a stack of layers, network processors can be classified into *physical-layer*, *link-layer*, and *network-layer* processors, depending on the protocol layer at which they operate. Physical-layer processors are responsible for electrical or optical signal generation and interpretation for transporting digital bits, whereas link-layer network processors deal with framing, bit error detection/correction and arbitration of concurrent accesses to shared media. Network-layer processors operate on individual packets and determine how to route packets from their senders to receivers in a particular order, and modify their headers or even payloads along the way if necessary. Because the Internet is largely based on the IP protocol, almost all state-of-the-art network-layer processors are designed to process IP packets only. The conspicuous exception is network-layer processors designed for ATM networks. The focus of this paper, however, is exclusively on network-layer processors, which can operate at from Layer 3 to Layer 7 in the ISO/OSI protocol stack model.

In general, three approaches are used for network processor design, which correspond to different design points in the programmability/performance spectrum. The *ASIC* approach takes a full customization route by dedicating specially-made hardware logic to specific network packet processing functionalities. Although this approach gives the highest performance, it is typically not programmable and therefore not sufficiently flexible to support a wide variety of network devices. Consequently, such processors are more expensive and tend to be outdated sooner because they cannot exploit economies of scale to keep up with technology advances. The *general-purpose CPU* approach either takes an existing processor for PCs or embedded systems as it is, or augments it with a small set of instructions specifically included to improve network packet processing. While this approach admits the most programming flexibility, the throughput of these processors is substantially lower than what modern network devices require. The main reason for this lackluster performance is that network device workloads are data movement-intensive, whereas traditional processors are designed to support computation-intensive tasks. The last approach to network processor design, *programmable network processor*, attempts to strike a balance between programmability and performance and achieves the best of both worlds. Instead of using general-purpose instruction set, a programmable network processor defines the set of instruction set primitives for network packet processing from scratch, and exposes these primitives to system designers so that they can tailor the processor to the requirement of different network devices. In the rest of this paper, we will concentrate only on programmable network processors, as they represent the most promising and commercially popular approach to network processor design.

In addition to the basic network processing function such as packet routing and forwarding, modern network processors are tasked with additional capabilities that support advanced network functionalities, such as differentiated quality of service (QoS), encryption/decryption, etc. For network processors that are to be used in *edge* network devices, they may need to perform even higher-level tasks such as firewalling, virtual private network (VPN) support, load balancing, etc. Given an increasing variety of features that network devices have to support, it is crucial for a network processor architecture to be sufficiently general that system designers can build newer functionalities on these processors without causing serious performance degradation. The challenge for network processor design is thus to identify the set of packet processing primitives that is elastic enough to support as many different types of network devices as possible, and at the same time is sufficiently customized so that the performance overhead due to "impedance mismatch" is minimized.

In the rest of this chapter section, we first discuss fundamental design issues related to network processor architecture in the "Design Issues" section, and then describe specific network processor architectural features that have been proposed in the "Architectural Support for Network Packet Processing" section. In the section on "Example Network Processors," we review the design of several commercially available network processors to contrast their underlying approaches. Finally, we outline future network processor research directions in the "Conclusion" section.

## Design Issues

To understand the network processor architecture, let us first look at what a programmable network processor is supposed to do. After receiving an IP packet from an input interface, the network processor first determines the output interface via which the packet should be forwarded toward its destination. In the case that multiple input packets are destined to the same output interface, the network processor also decides the order in which these packets should be sent out on the associated output link, presumably according to certain quality of service (QoS) policy. Finally, before the packet is forwarded to the next-hop router, the network processor modifies the packet's header or even payload according to standard network protocols or application-specific semantics. For IP packets, at least the TTL (time-to-live) field in the header must be decremented at each hop and as a result the IP packet header checksum needs to be re-computed. Other IP header fields such as TOS (type-of-service) may also need to be modified for QoS reasons. In some cases, even the packet body need to be manipulated, e.g., transcoding of a video packet in the presence of congestion. In summary, given an input packet, the network processor needs to identify its output interface, schedule its transmission on the associated output link, and make necessary modifications to its header or payload to satisfy general protocol or application-specific requirements.

Fundamentally, a network processor performs three types of tasks: *packet classification, packet scheduling,* and *packet forwarding.* Given an input IP packet, the packet classification module in the network processor decides how to process this packet, based on the packet's header and sometimes even payload fields. In the simplest case, the result of packet classification is the output interface through which the input packet should be forwarded. To support differentiated QoS, the result of packet classification becomes a specific output connection queue into which the input packet should be buffered. In the most general case, the result of packet classification points to the software routine that is to be invoked to process the input packet; possible processing ranges from forwarding the input packet into an output interface and a buffer queue, to arbitrarily complex packet manipulation. The design challenge of packet classification is that the number of bits used in packet classification is increasing due to IPv6 and/or multiple header fields, and varying because of application-level protocols such as URL in the HTTP protocol.

The packet forwarding module of a network processor physically moves an input packet from an incoming interface to its corresponding outgoing interface. The key design issues on packet forwarding are the topology of the switch fabric and the switch scheduling policy to resolve output contention, i.e., when multiple incoming packets need to be forwarded to the same output interface. State-of-the-art network devices are based on crossbar fabrics, which are more expensive but greatly reduce the implementation complexity of the switch scheduler. Given a crossbar fabric, the switch scheduler finds a match between the incoming packets and the output interfaces so that the switch fabric is utilized with maximum efficiency and the resulting matching is consistent with the output link's scheduling policy, which in turn depends on the QoS requirement. Algorithmically, this is a constrained bipartite graph matching problem, which is known to be NP-complete. The design challenge of switch scheduling is to find a solution that approximates the optimal solution as closely as possible and that is simple enough for efficient hardware implementation. One such algorithm is iterative random matching [1] and its optimized variant [2].

Traditionally, a FIFO queue is associated with each output link of a network device to buffer all outgoing packets through that link. To support fine-grained QoS, such as per-network-connection bandwidth guarantee, one buffer queue is required for each network connection whose QoS is to be protected from the rest of the traffic. After classification, packets that belong to a specific connection are buffered in the connection's corresponding queue. A link scheduler then schedules the packets in the per-connection queues that share the same output link in an order that is consistent with each connection's QoS requirement. A general framework of link scheduling is packetized fair queuing (PFQ) [3], which performs the following two operations for each incoming packet, *virtual finish time computation,* which is $O(N)$ computation, and *priority queue sorting,* which is $O(\log N)$ computation, where $N$ is the number of active connections associated with an output interface. Intuitively, a packet's virtual finish time corresponds to the logical time at which that packet should be sent if the output link is scheduled according to the fluid fair queuing model. After the virtual finish time for each packet is computed, packets are sent out in an ascending order of their virtual finish time. A nice property of virtual finish time is that an earlier packet's virtual finish time is unaffected by the arrival of subsequent packets. With per-connection queuing and output link scheduling, traffic shaping is automatic if packets are dropped when they reach a queue that is full. As the complexity of both operations in link scheduling depends

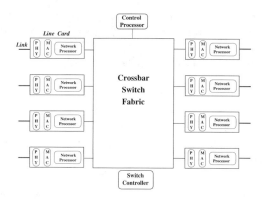

**FIGURE 6.25** The system architecture of a generic network device such as an IP packet router.

on *N*, they cannot readily scale to a large number of QoS-sensitive connections. Although there are various attempts to simplify PFQ, most hardware link schedulers use a much simpler weighted round-robin algorithm, which multiplexes connections on an output link according to weights that are proportional to the connections' QoS requirements.

In addition to the above three types of tasks, a network processor may need to support such higher-level functionalities as security, multicast, congestion control, etc., because more and more intelligence is moved from end hosts to the network. It is not clear what common primitives these high-level functions can share, as comprehensive workload characterization along this line is almost nonexistent. The entire *active network* field [4] is about the development of operating system and network procotols support for *programmable* network devices so that they can perform application-specific operations on an application's packets as they go through the network; however, until now the research on architectural support for active networking is almost nonexistent in the literature.

Figure 6.25 shows the generic architecture of an Internet router, which serves as an instance of a network device that is built on network processor. The line cards are input/output interfaces and are connected to external network links. Line cards typically include hardware for physical-layer and link-layer protocol processing, and a network processor that performs packet classification, queuing and output-link scheduling. The switch fabric controller determines when input packets should be forwarded to their corresponding output interface. The control processor is typically a standard RISC processor and is responsible for non-time-critical tasks such as routing table maintenance and traffic statistics collection and reporting.

## Architectural Support for Network Packet Processing

Given the network device system architecture in Fig. 6.25, in this section we present architectural features that were proposed previously to improve the performance of network processors. But first let's consider the performance requirements of a very high-speed router. Assuming the worst-case scenario, i.e., each packet is 64-byte long, an OC-768 or 40 Gbps network processor needs to handle 80 million packets per second, or one packet every 12.5 ns. Assume further that a packet is processed in a pipeline fashion, i.e., packet classification, packet forwarding, and packet scheduling. Therefore, this 12.5 ns corresponds to the pipeline cycle time, rather than the total packet latency within the network device. In packet classification, multiple memory accesses to the routing/classification table data structure are needed. For a static RAM with 2-ns cycle time, a 12.5-ns cycle time means that the network processor cannot access more than six memory words if the memory system is 32-bit wide. In packet forwarding, the output buffer queue memory should run at 1,250 MHz using a 128-bit-wide interface, because the rule of the thumb is that packet buffers need to operate at four times as fast the line rate. In packet scheduling, even assuming a modest number of active connections, say 1,000, the link scheduler logic needs to perform each primitive operation in virtual finish time calculation within 12.5 ps, or about one CMOS transistor delay.

The above analysis demonstrates that in all three cases, new architecture-level and circuit-level innovations are required to develop a network processor that meets the OC-768 performance goal.

Two basic approaches to speeding up network packet processing inside a network processor are pipelining and parallelization. A deeper pipeline reduces the cycle time of the pipeline and, therefore, improves the system throughput. However, because packet classification, packet forwarding, and packet scheduling each exhibit complicated internal dependencies and sometimes iterative structures, it is difficult to pipeline these functions effectively. Parallelization can be applied at different granularities. Finer granularity parallelism is more difficult to exploit but potentially leads to higher performance gain. In the case of network packet processing, because processing of one packet is independent of processing of another packet, packet-level parallelism appears to be the right granularity that strikes a good balance between performance gain and implementation complexity. Typically, a thread is dedicated to the processing of one packet, and different threads can run in parallel on distinct hardware engines. To reap further performance improvement by exploiting instruction-level parallelism, researchers and companies have proposed to run concurrent packet-processing threads on a simultaneous multi-threading processor [5,11] to mask as many pipeline stalls as possible. Such multithreading processors require the support of multiple hardware contexts and fast context switching.

Compared with generic CPU workloads, network packet processing requires much more frequent bit-level manipulation, such as header field extraction and header checksum computation. In a standard RISC processor, extracting an arbitrary range of bits from a 32-bit word requires at least three instructions, and performing a byte-wide summing of the four bytes within a word takes at least 13 instructions. Therefore, commercial network processors [6] include special bit-level manipulation and 1's complement instructions to speed up header field extraction and replacement, as well as packet checksumming computation.

Caching is arguably the most effective and most often used technique in modern computer system design. One place in network processor design to which caching can be effectively applied is packet classification. Since multiple packets travel on a network connection in its lifetime, in theory each intermediate network device only needs to perform packet classification once for the first packet and reuses the resulting classification decision for all subsequent packets. This corresponds to temporal locality if one treats the set of all possible values of the header fields used in packet classification as an address space. Empirical studies [7,8] show that network packet streams indeed exhibit substantial temporal locality but very little spatial locality. In addition, unlike CPU cache, the classification results for neighboring points in this address space tend to be identical. Therefore, network processor cache can be designed to cache address ranges rather than just address space points, as in standard cache. Chiueh and Pradhan [8] showed that caching ranges of classification address space can increase the effective coverage of a network processor cache by several orders of magnitude as compared to conventional caches that cache individual addresses.

Another alternative to speed up packet classification is through special content-addressable memory (CAM) [13]. Commercial CAMs support ternary comparison logic (0, 1, and X or don't-care). Classification rules are pre-stored in the CAMs. Given an input packet, the selective portion of its packet header is compared against all the stored classification patterns in parallel, and a priority decoder picks the highest priority among the matched rules if there are multiple of them. Although CAM can identify relevant packet classification rules at wire speed, two problems are associated with applying CAM to the packet classification problem. First, to support range match, e.g., source port number 130–202, one has to break a range rule to multiple range rules, each covering a range whose size is a multiple of 2. This is because CAMs only support don't-care match but not arbitrary arithmetic comparison. For example, the range 129–200 needs to be broken down into eight ranges: 130–130, 131–132, 133–136, 137–144, 145–160, 161–192, 193–200, and 201–202. For classification rules with multiple range fields, the need for range decomposition can significantly increase the number of CAM entries required. Second, because CAMs are hardwired memory with built-in width, it cannot easily support matching of variable-length fields such as URL, or accommodate changing packet classification rules after network devices are put into field use.

Finally, because the main task of network devices is to move packets from one interface to another, efficient data movement is of paramount importance. Because most packet buffer memory is implemented in DRAM, it is essential to exploit the fast access mode in modern DRAM chips to keep up with the line rate. In addition, it should support multiple DMA channels to allow multiple data transfer transactions to proceed in parallel without the attention of network processors.

## Example Network Processors

Intel's Internet exchange architecture (IXA) [6] includes an IXE component as the switching fabric, an IXF component for framing and formatting, an LXT component for physical-layer processing, and an Internet exchange processor (IXP) for packet processing. The IXP consists of a StrongARM core, six microengines and interfaces with the SRAM, SDRAM, the PCI bus, and a proprietary bus, the IX bus. The StrongARM core performs such supervisory processing as maintaining the routing table. Each of six microengines is a RISC core augmented with special instructions optimized for network processing such as bit extraction, table lookup, and single-cycle shifting, and with support for hardware multithreading. Each microengine has four program counters that allow four parallel threads to time-share a microengine's data path. There are two banks of single-ported general-purpose registers for ALU operations, and four single-ported transfer registers to read/write SRAM and SDRAM. The IX bus allows the IXPs to interface with IXFs and IXEs, and supports 5 Gbps at 80 MHz.

Agere's PayloadPlus architecture [9] includes a fast pattern processor (FPP), a routing switch processing (RSP), an agere system interface (ASI), and a functional programming language (FPL) for programming the FPP and RSP. The FPP sits between the physical interface and the RSP, and performs packet re-assembly, protocol recognition and associated computation, and calculation of checksums and CRC. The FPP is based on a pipelined and multithreaded architecture. It allocates a thread and a context to process each incoming packet, and operates on one 64-byte block at a time, each in the associated packet's context. To program the FPP, system designers use a declarative programming language, FPL, to specify the set of protocols to recognize and the set of actions to take for each specified protocol. Programs for the FPP are represented as trees, where nodes correspond to pattern recognition functions and leaves as actions. The RSP sits between the FPP and the switch fabric controller, and consists of three VLIW engines: Traffic Management Compute engine that enforces packet discarding policies and maintains queue statistics, Traffic Shaper Compute engine that ensures QoS and CoS for each connection queue, and Stream Editor Compute engine that performs necessary packet modifications. These three engines work on each packet together as a linear pipeline. The ASI interfaces with the host processor for configuration and program download, and in addition coordinates the data movement between the FPP and RSP.

C-Port's digital communications processor (DCP) [10] includes 16 channel processors (CP), five specialized processors, and a 160 Gpbs internal bus. Each CP interfaces with the physical link interface, and consists of a RISC core and two serial data processors (SDP). SDPs perform low-level bit manipulation task whereas the RISC core performs such high-level task as packet scheduling and traffic statistics collection. The five specialized processors perform classification table access, packet buffering, routing table look-up, interfacing with the switch fabric, and supervisory processing. C-Port supports a special communications programming interface called C-Ware to simplify system designers' task of programming DCP.

## Conclusion

In this chapter section, we present the set of tasks that a modern network processor needs to perform, describe a set of architectural features specifically designed for network packet processing, and survey several commercial network processor architectures as examples. Most of existing network processors include special instructions to speed up packet processing, and use a parallel multithreaded architecture to exploit multiple levels of parallelism; however, these architectures cannot scale to OC768 link rate and beyond, and, therefore, further research into network processor architecture is warranted. Here are several research directions that we believe are worth exploring:

- Scalable packet classification mechanism that supports variable-length application-level classification patterns
- Integrated packet scheduling for both switch fabric and output links to achieve per-connection QoS in an input queuing network device architecture
- Novel memory management scheme that exploits the abundant internal bandwidth of intelligent RAM architecture [12] to cost-effectively satisfy the memory bandwidth requirements of terabit links
- Architectural support for active networking and other high-level network functionalities

## References

1. Nick McKeown and Thomas E. Anderson. "A quantitative comparis on of scheduling algorithms for input-queued switches." *Computer Networks and ISDN Systems*, vol. 30, no. 24, pp. 2309–2326, December 1998.
2. Nick McKeown. "iSLIP: A scheduling algorithm for input-queued switches." *IEEE Transactions on Networking*, vol. 7, no. 2, April 1999.
3. Keshav, S., "On the efficient implementation of fair queueing." *Journal of Internetworking: Research and Experience*, Vol. 2, no. 3, September 1991.
4. Tennenhouse, D. and D. Wetherall. "Towards an active network architecture." *Computer Communication Review*, vol. 26, no. 2, p. 5–18, April 1996.
5. Patrick Crowley, Marc E. Fiuczynski, Jean-Loup Baer, and Brian N. Bershad. "Characterizing processor architectures for programmable network interfaces." In *Proceedings of the 2000 International Conference on Supercomputing*, Santa Fe, N. M., May, 2000.
6. Intel Internet Exchange Architecture, http://developer.intel.com/design/ixa/whitepapers/ixa.htm.
7. Tzi-cker Chiueh and Prashant Pradhan. "High-performance IP routing table lookup using CPU caching." In *Proceedings of IEEE INFOCOM 1999*, New York City, April 1999.
8. Tzi-cker Chiueh and Prashant Pradhan. "Cache memory design for internet processors." In *Proceedings of Sixth Symposium on High-Performance Computer Architecture (HPCA-6)*, Toulouse, France, January 2000.
9. Agere Systems. The PayloadPlus Architecture. http://www.lucent.com/micro/netcom/docs/fpppro-ductbrief.pdf.
10. David Husak and Robert Gohn "Network processor programming models: the key to achieving faster time-to-market and extending product life." http://www.cportcorp.com/products/pdf/net_proc_prog_models.pdf.
11. Xtream Logic Corporation. "Xstream logic packet processor core." http://www.xstreamlogic.com/architectural_files/v3_document.htm.
12. David Patterson, et al. "A case for intelligent DRAM: IRAM," *IEEE Micro*, April 1997.
13. Anthony J. McAuley, Paul F. Tsuchiya, and Daniel V. Wilson. "Fast multilevel hierarchical routing table using content-addressable memory." U.S. Patent serial number 034444. Assignee Bell Communications Research, Inc., Livingston, NJ, January 1995.

# 7

# Architectures for Low Power

Pradip Bose

*IBM T. J. Watson Research Center*

## 7.1 Introduction

Power dissipation limits have emerged as a key constraint in the design of microprocessors, even for those targeted for the high end server product space. At the low end of the performance spectrum, power has always dominated over performance as the primary design constraint; however, although battery life expectancies have shown modest increases, the larger demand for increased functionality and speed has increased the severity of the power constraint in the world of handheld and mobile systems. At the high end, where performance was always the primary driver, we are witnessing a trend where energy and power limits are increasingly dictating the high-level processing paradigms, as well as the lower-level issues related to clocking and circuit design.

Figure 7.1 shows the expected maximum chip power (for high performance processors) through the year 2014. The data plotted is based on the updated 2000 projections made by the International Technology Roadmap for Semiconductors [http://public.itrs.net]. The projection indicates that beyond the linear growth period (through the year 2005) there will be a saturation in the maximum chip power. This is ostensibly due to thermal/packaging and die size limits that are expected to kick in during that time frame. Beyond a certain power regime, air cooling is not sufficient to dissipate the heat generated; and, use of liquid cooling and refrigeration causes a sharp increase of the cost-performance ratio. Thus, power-aware design techniques, methodologies, and tools are of the essence at all levels of design.

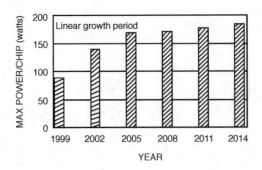

**FIGURE 7.1**    Maximum chip power projection (ITRS roadmap).

In this chapter, we first present a survey of some of the most promising ideas in power-aware design at the (micro)architecture level. We base this review on the currently available literature, with special emphasis on relevant work presented at recent architecture conferences and workshops. Where useful, we also refer to prior papers that deal with fundamental issues related to the performance, cost, and scalability of concurrent machine architectures. We show how the fundamentals of machine performance relate to the modern problem of architecting processors in a way that allows them to scale well (over time) in terms of joint power-performance metrics. In this context, we comment on and compare the viability and future promise of several microarchitectural paradigms that seem to be catching on in industry: e.g., clustered super scalars, various flavors of multithreading (e.g., SMT), and chip multiprocessors (CMP).

In Section 7.2, we review the fundamentals of pipelined and vector/parallel computation as they relate to performance and energy characteristics. We also touch briefly on the topic of defining a suitable set of metrics to measure power-performance efficiency at the microarchitecture level. In Section 7.3, we provide a survey of the most promising ideas and approaches in power-aware design at the microarchitecture level, with references to circuit design and clocking issues that are relevant in that discussion. This review is presented in the context of workloads and benchmarks that represent different markets. In Section 7.4, we compare the power-performance outlook of three emerging microarchitectural paradigms in the general purpose processor space: multicluster superscalars, multithreaded processors, and chip multiprocessors. We conclude, in Section 7.5, by summarizing the main issues addressed in this survey paper. We also point to a list of future research items that the architecture community needs to pursue in collaboration with the circuit design community in order to achieve the targets dictated by future cost and performance pressures. In passing, we refer briefly to LPX: a research processor prototype being designed at IBM Watson, to validate some key ideas in power-aware design.

## 7.2  Fundamentals of Performance and Power: An Architect's View

### Performance Fundamentals [1,2]

The most straightforward metric for measuring performance is the execution time of a given program mix on the target processor. The execution time can be written as:

$$T = \text{PL} \times \text{CPI} \times \text{CT} = \text{PL} \times \text{CPI} \times (1/f) \tag{7.1}$$

where PL is the dynamic path length of the program mix, measured as the number of machine instructions executed; CPI is the average processor cycles per instruction incurred in executing the program mix; and CT is the processor cycle time (measured in seconds per cycle) whose inverse determines the clock frequency *f*. Since performance increases with decreasing *T*, one may formulate performance, Perf as:

$$\text{Perf}_{\text{chip}} \sim= K_{\text{pf}} \cdot f \sim= K_{\text{pv}} \cdot V \tag{7.2}$$

where the *K*'s are constants for a given microarchitecture-compiler implementation and for a specific workload mix. The $K_{\text{pf}}$ value stands for the average number of machine instructions that are executed per cycle on the machine being measured; this is usually referred to as IPC, the inverse of CPI. Performance, $\text{Perf}_{\text{chip}}$, in this case is measured in units such as (millions of) instructions per second, or mips. In Eq. (7.2), *V* is the chip supply voltage (often written as $V_{\text{dd}}$). As stated below, and in [2,3], the operating frequency is often assumed to be roughly proportional to the supply voltage.

Selecting a suite of publicly available benchmark programs that everybody accepts as being "representative" of real-world workloads is difficult to begin with. Adopting a noncontroversial weighted mix is also not easy. For the commonly used SPEC benchmark suite (see http://www.specbench.org) the SPEC-marks rating (for each class: e.g., integer or floating point) is derived as a geometric mean of execution time ratios for the programs within that class. Each ratio is calculated as the speed up with respect to execution time on a specified reference machine. This method has the advantage that different machines can be ranked unambiguously from a performance viewpoint, if one believes in the particular benchmark suite. That is, the ranking can be shown to be independent of the reference machine used in such a formulation.

Even if one is able to fix the input workload mix to some known average characteristics, there is usually a large variation in workload behavior across different applications in the mix and in some cases, within even a single application. Thus, even though one can compute an average IPC (or $K_{\text{pf}}$ in Eq. (7.2)), it is possible to exploit the variations in IPC to reduce average power in architectures where the resources are dynamically adapted to match the IPC requirements (see the subsection "Adaptive Microarchitectures" in Section 7.3).

Let us now discuss the basics of power dissipation in a processor chip.

## Power Fundamentals [2–5]

At the elementary transistor gate (e.g., an inverter) level, total power dissipation can be formulated as the sum of three major components: switching loss, leakage, and short-circuit loss.

$$\text{Power}_{\text{device}} = \frac{1}{2} C \cdot V_{\text{dd}} \cdot V_{\text{swing}} a \cdot f + I_{\text{leakage}} \cdot V_{\text{dd}} + I_{\text{sc}} \cdot V_{\text{dd}} \tag{7.3}$$

where *C* is the output capacitance, $V_{\text{dd}}$ is the supply voltage, *f* is the chip clock frequency, and *a* is the activity factor ($0 < a \leq 1$), which determines the device switching frequency; $V_{\text{swing}}$ is the maximum voltage swing across the output capacitor, which in general can be less than $V_{\text{dd}}$; $I_{\text{leakage}}$ is the leakage current; and $I_{\text{sc}}$ is the short-circuit current. In the literature, $V_{\text{swing}}$ is often approximated to be equal to $V_{\text{dd}}$ (or simply *V* for short), making the switching loss $\sim(1/2)CV^2af$. Also, as discussed in [3], for today's range of $V_{\text{dd}}$ (say 1–3 V) switching loss: $(1/2)CV^2af$ remains the dominant component, assuming the activity factor to be above a reasonable minimum. So, as a first-order approximation, for the whole chip, we may formulate the power dissipation to be

$$\text{Power}_{\text{chip}} = \frac{1}{2} \left[ \sum_i C_i \cdot V_i^2 \cdot a_i \cdot f_i \right] \tag{7.4}$$

where $C_i$, $V_i$, $a_i$, and $f_i$ are unit- or block-specific average values in the most general case; the summation is taken over all blocks or units *i*, at the microarchitecture level (e.g., icache, dcache, integer unit, floating point unit, load-store unit, register files and buses [if not included in individual units], etc.). Also, for the voltage range considered, the operating frequency is roughly proportional to the supply voltage; and the capacitance $C$ remains roughly the same if we keep the same design but scale the voltage. If a single voltage and clock frequency are used for the whole chip, the above reduces to

$$\text{Power}_{\text{chip}} = V^3 \cdot \left( \sum_i K_i^v \cdot a_i \right) = f^3 \cdot \left( \sum_i K_i^f \cdot a_i \right) \tag{7.5}$$

If we consider the very worst-case activity factor for each unit $i$, i.e., if $a_i = 1$ for all $i$, an upper bound on the maximum chip power may be formulated as

$$\text{MaxPower}_{\text{chip}} = K_V \cdot V^3 = K_F \cdot f^3 \tag{7.6}$$

where $K_V$ and $K_F$ are design-specific constants. Note that an estimation of peak or maximum power is important, for the purposes of determining the packaging and cooling solution required. The larger the maximum power, the more expensive is the net cooling solution. Note that the formulation in Eq. (7.6) is overly conservative, as stated. In practice, it is possible to estimate the worst-case achievable maximum for the activity factors. This allows the designers to come up with a tighter bound on maximum power before the packaging decision is made.

The last Eq. (7.6) is what leads to the so-called "cube-root" rule [3], where redesigning a chip to operate at 1/2 the voltage (and frequency) results in the power dissipation being lowered to $(1/2)^3$ or 1/8 of the original. This implies the single-most efficient method for reducing power dissipation for a processor that has already been designed to operate at high frequency: namely, reduce the voltage (and hence the frequency). It is believed that this is the primary mechanism of power control in the Transmeta chip (see http://www.transmeta.com). There is a limit, however, of how low $V_{\text{dd}}$ can be reduced (for a given technology), which has to do with manufacturability and circuit reliability issues. Thus, a combination of microarchitecture and circuit techniques to reduce power consumption, without necessarily employing multiple or variable supply voltages, is of special relevance in the design of robust systems.

The formulation of performance and power, especially the abstractions expressed through Eqs. (7.2) and (7.4–7.6), can actually be improved quite a bit, based on more rigorous mathematics, backed by experimental evidence collected from real circuit-level simulations. This is reported separately for readers who want to delve into these issue in more detail [33].

## Power-Performance Efficiency Metrics

The most common (and perhaps obvious) metric to characterize the power-performance efficiency of a microprocessor is a simple ratio, such as mips/watt. This attempts to quantify the efficiency by projecting the performance achieved or gained (measured in millions of instructions per second) for every watt of power consumed. Clearly, the higher the number, the "better" the machine is. Dimensionally, mips/watt equates to the inverse of the average energy consumed per instruction. This seems a reasonable choice for some domains where battery life is important; however, strong arguments are against it in many cases, especially when it comes to characterizing higher end processors. Performance has typically been the key driver of such server-class designs and cost or efficiency issues have been of secondary importance. Specifically, a design team may well choose a higher frequency design point (which meets maximum power budget constraints) even if it operates at a much lower mips/watt efficiency compared to one that operates at better efficiency but at a lower performance level. As such, (mips)$^2$/watt or even (mips)$^3$/watt may be the metric of choice at the high end. On the other hand, at the lowest end, where battery-life (or energy consumption) is the primary driver, one may want to put an even greater weight on the power aspect than the simplest mips/watt metric, i.e., one may just be interested in minimizing the watts for a given workload run, irrespective of the execution time performance, provided the latter does not exceed some specified upper limit.

The "mips" metric for performance and the "watts" value for power may refer to average or peak values, derived from the chip specifications. For example, for a 1 GHz (=$10^9$ c/s) processor, which can complete up to 4 instructions per cycle, the theoretical peak performance is 4000 mips). If the average completion rate for a given workload mix is $p$ instructions per cycle, the average mips would equal 1000 times $p$; however, when it comes to workload-driven evaluation and characterization of processors, metrics are often controversial. Apart from the problem of deciding on a "representative" set of benchmark applications, there are fundamental questions which persist about how to boil down "performance" into a single ("average") rating that is meaningful in comparing a set of machines. Since power consumption varies, depending on the program being executed, the issue of benchmarking is also relevant in assigning an average power rating. In measuring power and performance together for a given program execution, one may use a fused metric like power-delay product (PDP) or energy-delay product (EDP) [5,6]. In general, the PDP-based formulations are more appropriate for low-power, portable systems, where battery-life is the primary index of energy efficiency. The mips/watt metric is an inverse PDP formulation, where delay refers to average execution time per instruction. The PDP, being dimensionally equal to energy, is the natural metric for such systems. For higher end systems (e.g., workstations) the EDP-based formulations are deemed to be more appropriate, since the extra delay factor ensures a greater emphasis on performance. The (mips)$^2$/watt metric is an inverse EDP formulation. For the highest performance, server-class machines, it may be appropriate to weight the "delay" part even more. This would point to the use of (mips)$^3$/watt, which is an inverse ED$^2$P formulation. Alternatively, one may use (cpi)$^3$.watt as a direct ED$^2$P metric, applicable on a "per instruction" basis (see [2]).

The energy$^*$(delay)$^2$ metric, or perf$^3$/power formula is analogous to the cube-root rule [3], which follows from constant voltage scaling arguments (see previous discussion, Eq. (7.6)). Clearly, to formulate a voltage-invariant power-performance characterization metric, we need to think in terms of perf$^3$/(power). When we are dealing with the SPEC benchmarks, one may therefore evaluate efficiency as (SPECrating)$^x$/watt, or (SPEC)$^x$/watt for short; where the exponent value $x$ (=1, 2, or 3) may depend on the class of processors being compared.

Brooks et al. [2] discuss the power-performance efficiency data [sources used are: http://www.bwrc.eecs.berkeley.edu/CIC/, http://www.specbench.org, *Microprocessor Report*, August 2000, and individual vendor Web sites] for a range of commercial processors of approximately the same generation. In each chart, the latest available processor is plotted on the left and the oldest one on the right. We have used SPEC/watt, SPEC$^2$/watt, and SPEC$^3$/watt as the alternative metrics, where SPEC stands for the processor's SPEC95 rating (see definition principles, earlier in this section or in [1]). For each category, such as SPEC$^2$/watt, the best performer is normalized to 1, and the other processor values are plotted as relative fractions of the normalized maximum. The data validates the assertion that depending on the metric of choice, and the target market (determined by workload class and/or the power/cost) the conclusion drawn about efficiency can be quite different. For performance-optimized, high-end processors, the SPEC$^3$/watt metric seems to be fairest, with the very latest Intel Pentium-III and AMD Athlon offerings (at 1 GHz) at the top for integer workloads; and, the older HP-PA 8600 (552 MHz) and IBM Power3 (450 MHz) still dominating in the floating point class. For "power-first" processors targeted toward integer workloads (such as Intel's mobile Celeron-333) spec/watt seems to be the fairest.

Tables 7.1 and 7.2 below show the explicit ranking of the processors considered in [2], from a power-performance efficiency viewpoint based on specint and specfp benchmarks. The only intent here is to illustrate the point that we tried to make earlier: that depending on the intended market (e.g., general purpose: server-class, workstation or low-power mobile, etc.) and application class (e.g., integer-intensive or floating-point intensive) different efficiency metrics may be suitable. Note that we have relied on published performance and "max power" numbers; and, because of differences in the methodologies used in quoting the maximum power ratings, the derived rankings may not be completely accurate or fair. As an example, the 33 W maximum power rating for the Intel PIII-1000 processor that we computed from the maximum current and nominal voltage ratings specified for this part in the vendor's Web page [http://www.intel.com/design/pentiumiii/datashts/245264.htm] is higher than that reported in the *Microprocessor Report* source cited previously. Actually, this points to the need of standardization of methods

**TABLE 7.1**   Rank Ordering Based on Specint95 and Alternate Performance-Power Efficiency Metrics

| Rank | SPECint/watt | SPECint^2/watt | SPECint^3/watt |
|------|--------------|----------------|----------------|
| 1 | Moto PPC7400 (450 MHz) | Intel PIII-1000 | Intel PIII-1000 |
| 2 | Intel Celeron (333 MHz) | Moto PPC7400-450 | AMD Athlon-1000 |
| 3 | Intel PIII (1000 MHz) | AMD Athlon-1000 | HP-PA8600-552 |
| 4 | MIPS R12000 (300 MHz) | HP-PA8600-552 | Moto PPC7400-450 |
| 5 | Sun USII (450 MHz) | Intel Celeron-333 | Alpha 21264-700 |
| 6 | AMD Athlon (1000 MHz) | Alpha 21264-700 | IBM Power3-450 |
| 7 | IBM Power3 (450 MHz) | MIPS R12000-300 | MIPS R12000-300 |
| 8 | HP-PA8600 (552 MHz) | IBM Power3-450 | Intel Celeron-333 |
| 9 | Alpha 21264 (700 MHz) | Sun USII-450 | Sun USII-450 |
| 10 | Hal Sparc64-III | Hal Sparc64-III | Hal Sparc64-III |

**TABLE 7.2**   Rank Ordering Based on Specfp95 and Alternate Performance-Power Efficiency Metrics

| Rank | SPECfp/watt | SPECfp^2/watt | SPECfp^3/watt |
|------|-------------|---------------|---------------|
| 1 | Moto PPC7400-450 | HP-PA8600-552 | HP-PA8600-552 |
| 2 | MIPS R12000-300 | IBM Power3-450 | IBM Power3-450 |
| 3 | IBM Power3-450 | MIPS R12000-300 | Alpha 21264-700 |
| 4 | Intel Celeron-333 | Alpha 21264-700 | MIPS R12000-300 |
| 5 | Sun USII-450 | Intel PIII-1000 | Intel PIII-1000 |
| 6 | HP-PA8600-552 | Moto PPC7400-450 | Sun USII-450 |
| 7 | Intel PIII-1000 | Sun USII-450 | Moto PPC7400-450 |
| 8 | Alpha 21264-700 | Hal Sparc64-III | AMD Athlon-1000 |
| 9 | Hal Sparc64-III | AMD Athlon-1000 | Hal Sparc64-III |
| 10 | AMD Athlon-1000 | Intel Celeron-333 | Intel Celeron-333 |

used in reporting maximum and average power ratings for future processors. It should be possible in future for customers to compare power-performance efficiencies across competing products in a given market segment, i.e., for a given benchmark suite.

## 7.3   A Review of Key Ideas in Power-Aware Microarchitectures

In this chapter, we limit our attention to dynamic ("switching") power governed by the $CV^2af$ formula. Recall that $C$ refers to the switching capacitance, $V$ is the supply voltage, $a$ is the activity factor ($0 < a < 1$), and $f$ is the operating clock frequency. Power reduction ideas must, therefore, focus on one or more of these basic parameters. In this section, we examine the key ideas that have been proposed in terms of (micro)architectural support for power-efficiency.

The effective (average) value of $C$ can be reduced by using: (a) area-efficient designs for various macros; (b) adaptive structures, that change in effective size, latency or communication bandwidth depending on the needs of the input workload; (c) selectively "powering off" unused or idle units, based on special "nap/doze" and "sleep" instructions generated by the compiler or detected via hardware mechanisms; (d) reducing or eliminating "speculative waste" resulting from executing instructions in mis-speculated branch paths or prefetching useless instructions and data into caches, based on wrong guesses.

The average value of $V$ can be reduced via dynamic voltage scaling, i.e., by reducing the voltage as and when required or possible (e.g., see the description of the Transmeta chip: http://www.transmeta.com). Microarchitectural support, in this case, is not required, unless the mechanisms to detect "idle" periods or temperature overruns are detected using counter-based "proxies," specially architected for this purpose.

Hence, in this paper, we do not dwell on dynamic voltage scaling methods. (Note again, however, that since reducing $V$ also results in reduction of the operating frequency $f$ net power reduction has a cubic effect; thus, dynamic voltage scaling, though not a microarchitectural technique *per se*, is the most effective way of power reduction).

The average value of the activity factor $a$ can be reduced by: (a) the use of clock-gating, where the normally free-running, synchronous clock is disabled in selected units or sub-units within the system based on information or predictions about current or future activity in those regions; (b) the use of data representations and instruction schedules that result in reduced switching. Microarchitectural support is provided in the form of added mechanisms to: (a) detect, predict, and control the generation of the applied gating signals or (b) aid in power-efficient data and instruction encodings. Compiler support for generating power-efficient instruction scheduling and data partitioning or special instructions for "nap/doze/sleep" control, if applicable, must also be considered under this category.

Lastly, the average value of the frequency $f$ can be controlled or reduced by using: (a) variable, multiple, or locally asynchronous (self-timed) clocks; (b) reduced pipeline depths.

We consider power-aware microarchitectural constructs that use $C$, $a$, or $f$ as the primary power-reduction lever. In any such proposed processor architecture, the efficacy of the particular power reduction method that is used must be assessed by understanding the net performance impact. Here, depending on the application domain (or market), a PDP, EDP, or $ED^2P$ metric for evaluating and comparing power-performance efficiencies must be used (see earlier discussion in Section 7.2).

## Optimal Pipeline Depth

A fundamental question that is asked has to do with pipeline depth. Is a deeply pipelined, high frequency ("speed demon") design better than an IPC-centric lower frequency ("brainiac") design? In the context of this chapter, "better" must be judged in terms of power-performance efficiency.

Let us consider, first, a simple, hazard-free, linear pipeline flow process, with $k$ stages. Let the time for the total logic (without latches) to compute one answer be $T$. Assuming that the $k$ stages into which the logic is partitioned are of equal delay, the time per stage and thus the time per computation becomes (see [7], Chapter 2)

$$t = T/k + D \tag{7.8}$$

where $D$ is the delay added due to the staging latch. The inverse of $t$ determines the clocking rate or frequency of operation. Similarly, if the energy spent (per cycle, per second, or over the duration of the program run) in the logic is $W$ and the corresponding energy spent per level of staging latches is $L$, then the total energy equation for the $k$-stage pipelined version is, roughly,

$$E = L \cdot k + W \tag{7.9}$$

The energy equation assumes that the clock is free-running, i.e., on every cycle, each level of staging latches is clocked to enable the advancement of operations along the pipeline. (Later, we shall consider the effect of clock-gating.) Equations (7.8) and (7.9), when plotted as a function of $k$, are depicted in Figs. 7.2(a,b), respectively.

As the number of stages increases, the energy or power consumed increases linearly; while, the performance also increases, but not as fast. In order to consider the PDP-based power-performance efficiency, we compute the ratio:

$$\frac{\text{Power}}{\text{Performance}} = (L \cdot k + W)(T/k + D) = L \cdot T + W \cdot D + (L \cdot D \cdot k^2 + W \cdot T)/k \tag{7.10}$$

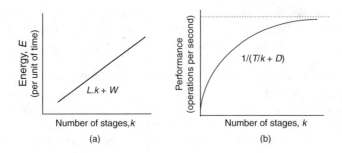

**FIGURE 7.2**    Power and performance curves for idealized pipeline flow.

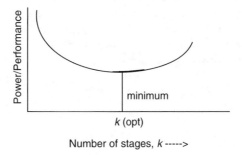

**FIGURE 7.3**    Power-performance ratio curve for idealized pipeline flow.

Figure 7.3 shows the general shape of this curve as a function of $k$. Differentiating the right hand side expression in Eq. (7.10) and setting it to zero, one can solve for the optimum value of $k$ for which the power-performance efficiency is maximized; i.e., the minimum of the curve in Fig. 7.2(b) can be shown to occur when

$$k(\text{opt.}) = \sqrt{(W \cdot T)/(L \cdot D)} \qquad (7.11)$$

Larson [8] first published the above analysis, albeit from a cost/performance perspective. This analysis shows that, at least for the simplest, hazard-free pipeline flow, the highest frequency operating point achievable in a given technology may not be the most energy-efficient! Rather, the optimal number of stages (and hence operating frequency) is expected to be at a point which increases for greater $W$ or $T$ and decreases for greater $L$ or $D$.

For real super scalar machines, the number of latches in a design tends to go up much more sharply with $k$ than the linear assumption in the above model. This tends to make $k$ (opt.) even smaller. Also, in real pipeline flow with hazards, e.g., in the presence of branch-related stalls and disruptions, performance actually peaks at a certain value of $k$ before decreasing [3,9] (instead of the asymptotically increasing behavior shown in Fig. 7.2(b)). This effect would also lead to decreasing the effective value of $k$(opt.). (However, $k$(opt.) increases if we use EDP or $ED^2P$ metrics instead of the PDP metric used.)

## Vector/SIMD Processing Support

Vector/SIMD modes of parallelism present in current architectures afford a power-efficient method of extending performance for vectorizable codes. Fundamentally, this is because: for doing the work of fetching and processing a single (vector) instruction, a large amount of data is processed in a parallel or pipelined manner. If we consider a SIMD machine, with $p$ $k$-stage functional pipelines (see Fig. 7.4) then looking at the pipelines alone, one sees a $p$-fold increase of performance, with a $p$-fold increase in power, assuming full utilization and hazard-free flow, as before. Thus, a SIMD pipeline unit offers the potential

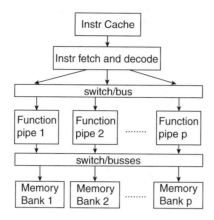

**FIGURE 7.4**   Parallel SIMD architecture.

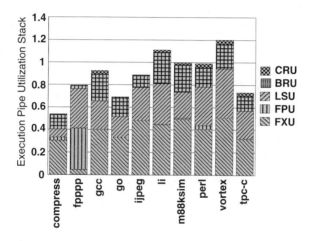

**FIGURE 7.5**   Execution pipe utilization component stack across workloads.

of scalable growth in performance, with commensurate growth in power, i.e., at constant power-perfor-mance efficiency. If, however, one includes the instruction cache and fetch/dispatch unit that are shared across the $p$ SIMD pipelines, then power-performance efficiency can actually grow with $p$. This is because, the energy behavior of the instruction cache (memory) and the fetch/decode path remains essentially invariant with $p$, while net performance grows linearly with $p$.

In a super scalar machine with a vector/SIMD extension, the overall power-efficiency increase is limited by the fraction of code that runs in SIMD-mode (Amdahl's Law).

## Clock-Gating: Power Reduction Potential and Microarchitectural Support

Clock-gating refers to circuit-level control (e.g., see [10,17]) for disabling the clock to a given set of latches, a macro, a bus or an entire unit, on a particular machine cycle. Microarchitecture-level analysis points to opportunities of power savings in a processor, since idle periods of a particular resource can be identified and quantified. Figure 7.5 depicts the execution pipe utilization of the various functional units (e.g., fixed point or integer unit, floating point unit, load-store unit, branch unit, condition register unit) within a current generation, out-of-order superscalar processor. This data is based on *simulation-based* data of a hypothetical processor, similar in complexity to that of current generation designs such as the Power4™ [11].

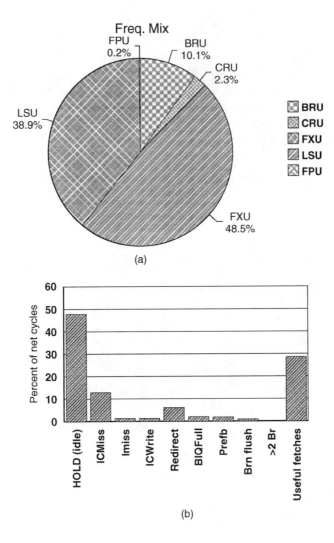

(a)

(b)

**FIGURE 7.6** (a) Instruction frequency mix for a typical commercial workload trace segment. (b) Stall profile in the instruction fetch unit (IFU) for the commercial workload.

We show the results for selected SPEC95 benchmarks and a large sample from a commercial TPC-C trace. The data shows that the pipe utilization attains a maximum of slightly over 50% only for the FXU; in many cases, the utilization is quite low, often 10% or less.

Figures 7.6(a) and (b) show the opportunities available within several units (and in particular, the instruction fetch unit, IFU) of the same example processor in the context of the TPC-C trace segment referred to above. Figure 7.6(a) depicts the instruction frequency mix of the trace segment used. This shows that the floating point unit (FPU) operations are a very tiny fraction of the total number of instructions in the trace. Therefore, with proper detection and control mechanisms architected in hardware, the FPU unit could essentially be "gated off" in terms of the clock delivery for the most part of such an execution. Figure 7.6(b) shows the fraction of total cycles spent in various modes within the instruction fetch unit (IFU). I-fetch was on hold for about 48% of the cycles; and the fraction of useful fetch cycles was only 28%. Again, this points to great opportunities: either in terms of clock-gating or dynamic ifetch throttling (see the subsection on "Dynamic Throttling of Communication Bandwidths below").

(Micro)architectural support for clock-gating can be provided in at least three ways: (a) dynamic detection of idle modes in various clocked units or regions within a processor or system; (b) static or dynamic prediction of such idle modes; (c) using "data valid" bits within a pipeline flow path to selectively enable/disable the clock applied to the pipeline stage latches. If static prediction is used, the compiler inserts special "nap/doze/sleep/wake" type instructions where appropriate, to aid the hardware in generating the necessary gating signals. Methods (a) and (b) result in coarse-grain clock-gating, where entire units, macros or regions can be gated off to save power; while, method (c) results in fine-grain clock-gating, where unutilized pipe segments can be gated off during normal execution within a particular unit, such as the FPU. The detailed circuit-level implementation of gated-clocks, the potential performance degradation, inductive noise problems, etc. are not discussed in this chapter; however, these are very important issues that must be dealt with adequately in an actual design.

Referring back to Figs. (7.2) and (7.3), note that since (fine-grain) clock-gating effectively causes a fraction of the latches to be "gated off," we may model this by assuming that the effective value of $L$ decreases when such clock-gating is applied. This has the effect of increasing $k$ (opt.); i.e., the operating frequency for the most power-efficient pipeline operation can be increased in the presence of clock-gating. This is an added benefit.

## Variable Bit-Width Operands

One of the techniques proposed for reducing dynamic power consists of exploiting the behavior of data in programs, which is characterized by the frequent presence of small values. Such values can be represented as and operated upon as short bit-vectors. Thus, by using only a small part of the processing datapath, power can be reduced without loss of performance. Brooks and Martonosi [12] analyzed the potential of this approach in the context of 64-bit processor implementations (e.g., the Compaq Alpha™ architecture). Their results show that roughly 50% of the instructions executed had both operands whose length was less than or equal to 16 bits. Brooks and Martonosi proposed an implementation that exploits this by dynamically detecting the presence of narrow-width operands on a cycle-by-cycle basis. (Subsequent work by Jude Rivers et al. at IBM has documented an approach to exploit this in PowerPC architectures, using a different implementation. This work is still not available for external publication).

## Adaptive Microarchitectures

Another method of reducing power is to adjust the size of various storage resources within a processor or system, with changing needs of the workload. Albonesi [13] proposed a dynamically reconfigurable caching mechanism, that reduces the cache size (and hence power) when the workload is in a phase that exhibits reduced cache footprint. Such downsizing also results in improved latency, which can be exploited (from a performance viewpoint) by increasing the cache cycling frequency on a local clocking or self-timed basis. Maro et al. [14] have suggested the use of adapting the functional unit configuration within a processor in tune with changing workload requirements. Reconfiguration is limited to "shutting down" certain functional pipes or clusters, based on utilization history or IPC performance. In that sense, the work by Maro et al. is not too different from coarse-grain clock-gating support, as discussed earlier. In recent work done at IBM Watson, Buyuktosunoglu et al. [15] designed an adaptive issue queue that can result in (up to) 75% power reduction when the queue is sized down to its minimum size. This is achieved with a very small IPC performance hit. Another example is the idea of adaptive register files (e.g., see [16]) where the size and configuration of the active size of the storage is changed via a banked design, or through hierarchical partitioning techniques.

## Dynamic Thermal Management

Most clock-gating techniques are geared towards the goal of reducing *average* chip power. As such, these methods do not guarantee that the worst-case (maximum) power consumption will not exceed safe limits. The processor's maximum power consumption dictates the choice of its packaging and cooling solution. In fact, as discussed in [17], the net cooling solution cost increases in a piecewise linear manner with respect to the maximum power; and the cost gradient increases rather sharply in the higher power regimes. This necessitates the use of mechanisms to limit the maximum power to a controllable ceiling, one defined by the cost profile of the market for which the processor is targeted. Most recently, in the high performance world, Intel's Pentium 4 processor is reported to use an elaborate on-chip thermal management system to ensure reliable operation [17]. At the lower end, the G3 and G4 PowerPC microprocessors [18,19] include a Thermal Assist Unit (TAU) to provide dynamic thermal management. In a recently reported academic work, Brooks and Martonosi [20] discuss and analyze the potential reduction in "maximum power" ratings without significant loss of performance, by the use of specific dynamic thermal management (DTM) schemes. The use of DTM requires the inclusion of on-chip sensors to monitor actual temperature; or proxies of temperature [20] estimated from on-chip counters of various events and rates.

### Dynamic Throttling of Communication Bandwidths

This idea has to do with reducing the width of a communication bus dynamically, in response to reduced needs or in response to temperature overruns. Examples of on-chip buses that can be throttled are: instruction fetch bandwidth, instruction dispatch/issue bandwidths, register renaming bandwidth, instruction completion bandwidths, memory address bandwidth, etc. In the G3 and G4 PowerPC microprocessors [18,19], the TAU invokes a form of instruction cache throttling as a means to lower the temperature when a thermal emergency is encountered.

### Speculation Control

In current generation high performance microprocessors, branch mispredictions and mis-speculative prefetches end up wasting a lot of power. Manne et al. [21,22] have described means of detecting or anticipating an impending mispredict and using that information to prevent mis-speculated instructions from entering the pipeline. These methods have been shown to reduce power by up to 38% with less than a 1% performance loss.

## 7.4  Power-Efficient Microarchitecture Paradigms

Now that we have examined specific microarchitectural constructs that aid power-efficient design, let us examine the inherent power-performance scalability and efficiency of selected paradigms that are currently emerging in the high-end processor roadmap. In particular, we consider: (a) wide-issue, speculative super scalar processors; (b) multi-cluster superscalars; (c) chip multiprocessors (CMP)—especially those that use single program speculative multithreading (e.g., multiscalar); (d) simultaneously multithreaded (SMT) processors.

In illustrating the efficiency advantages or deficiencies, we use the following running example. It shows one iteration of a loop trace that we consider in simulating the performance and power characteristics across the above computing platforms.

Let us consider the following floating-point loop kernel, shown below (coded using the PowerPC™ instruction set architecture):

### Example Loop Test Case

    [P] [A] fadd fp3, fp1, fp0
    [Q] [B] lfdu fp5, 8(r1)
    [R] [C] lfdu fp4, 8(r3)
    [S] [D] fadd fp4, fp5, fp4
    [T] [E] fadd fp1, fp4, fp3
    [U] [F] stfdu fp1, 8(r2)
    [V] [G] bc loop_top

The loop body consists of seven instructions, the final one being a conditional branch that causes control to loop back to the top of the loop body. The instructions are labeled A through G. (The labels P through V are used to tag the corresponding instructions for a parallel thread—when we consider SMT

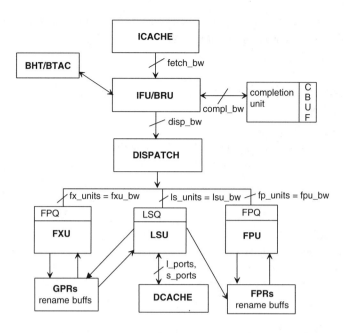

**FIGURE 7.7** High-level block-diagram of machine organization modeled in the eliot/elpaso tool.

and CMP). The lfdu/stfdu instructions are load/store instructions with update, where the base address register (e.g., r1, r2, or r3) is updated after execution by holding the newly computed address.

## Single-Core Superscalar Processor Paradigm

One school of thought anticipates a continued progression along the path of wider, aggressively superscalar paradigms. Researchers continue to innovate in an attempt to extract the last "ounce" of IPC-level performance from a single-thread instruction-level parallelism (ILP) model. Value prediction advances (pioneered by Lipasti et al. [23]) promise to break the limits imposed by true data dependencies. Trace caches (Smith et al. [23]) ease the fetch bandwidth bottleneck, which can otherwise impede scalability; however, increasing the superscalar width beyond a certain limit tends to yield diminishing gains in *net* performance (i.e., the inverse of CPI × CT; see Eq. (7.1)). At the same time, the power-performance efficiency metric (e.g., performance per watt or (performance)$^2$/watt, etc.) tends to degrade beyond a certain complexity point in the single-core superscalar design paradigm. This is illustrated below in the context of our example loop test case.

Let us consider a base machine that is a 4-wide superscalar, with two load-store units supporting two floating-point pipes (see Fig. 7.7). The data cache has two load ports and a separate store port. Two load-store unit pipes (LSU0 and LSU1) are fed by a single issue queue, LSQ; similarly, the two floating-point unit pipes (FPU0 and FPU1) are fed by a single issue queue, FPQ. In the context of the loop above, we essentially focus on the LSU-FPU sub-engine of the whole processor.

Let us assume the following high-level parameters (latency and bandwidth) characterizing the base super scalar machine model of width $W = 4$.

- Instruction fetch bandwidth, fetch_bw = $2 \times W$ = 8 instructions/cycle.
- Dispatch/decode/rename bandwidth, disp_bw = $W$ = 4 instructions/cycle; dispatch is assumed to stall beyond the first branch scanned in the instruction fetch buffer.
- Issue_bandwidth from LSQ (reservation station), lsu_bw = $W/2$ = 2 instructions/cycle.
- Issue_bandwidth from FPQ, fpu_bw = $W/2$ = 2 instructions/cycle.
- Completion bandwidth, compl_bw = $W$ = 4 instructions/cycle.

- Back-to-back dependent floating point operation issue delay, fp_delay = 1 cycle.
- The best-case load latency, from fetch to writeback is: 5 cycles.
- The best-case store latency, from fetch to writing in the pending store queue is: 4 cycles; (a store is eligible to complete the cycle after the address-data pair is valid in the store queue).
- The best-case floating point operation latency, from fetch to writeback is: 7 cycles (when the issue queue, FPQ is bypassed, because it is empty).

Loads and floating point operations are eligible for completion (retirement) the cycle after writeback into rename buffers. For simplicity of analysis let us assume that the processor uses in-order issue from the issue queues (LSQ and FPQ). In our simulation model, the superscalar width $W$ is a ganged parameter, defined as follows:

$$W = (\text{fetch\_bw}/2) = \text{disp\_bw} = \text{compl\_bw}$$

The number of LSU units, ls_units, FPU units, fp_units, data cache load ports, l_ports and data cache store ports are varied as follows as $W$ is changed:

$$\text{ls\_units} = \text{fp\_units} = \text{l\_ports} = \max[\text{floor}(W/2), 1]$$
$$\text{s\_ports} = \max[\text{floor}(\text{l\_ports}/2), 1]$$

For illustrative purposes, a simple (and decidedly naive) analytical energy model is assumed, where the power consumed is a function of the following parameters: $W$, ls_units, fp_units, l_ports, and s_ports. In particular, the power PW, in watts, is computed as: $\text{PW} = K \times [(W)^y + \text{ls\_units} + \text{fp\_units} + \text{l\_ports} + \text{s\_ports}]$, where $y$ ($0 < y < 1$) is an exponent that may be varied to see the effect on power-performance efficiency; $K$ is a constant. Figure 7.8 shows the performance and performance/power ratio variation with superscalar width, $W$; for this graph, $y$ has been set to 0.5 and the scaling constant $K$ is 2. The BIPS (billions of instructions per second) values are computed from the IPC (instruction per cycle) values, assuming a clock frequency of 1 GHz.

The graph in Fig. 7.8(a) shows that a maximum issue width of $W = 4$ could be used to achieve the best (idealized) BIPS performance. This idealized plot is obtained using a tool called eliot [24]. This is a parameterized, PowerPC super scalar model, that can operate either in cycle-by-cycle simulation mode, or, it can generate idealized bounds, based on static analysis of a loop code segment. The eliot model has now been updated to include parameterized, analytical energy models for each unit or storage resource within the processor. This new tool, called elpaso can be used to generate power-performance efficiency data for loop test cases. As shown in Fig. 7.8 (b), from a power-performance efficiency viewpoint

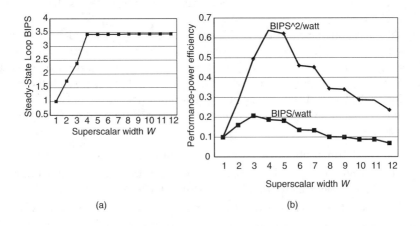

(a)                                                             (b)

**FIGURE 7.8**   Loop performance and performance/power variation with issue width.

(measured as a performance over power ratio), the best-case design is achieved for $W < 4$. Depending on the sophistication and accuracy of the energy model (i.e., how power varies with microarchitectural complexity), and the exact choice of the power-performance efficiency metric, the inflexion point in the curve in Fig. 7.8(b) changes; however, it should be obvious that beyond a certain superscalar width, the power-performance efficiency diminishes continuously. Fundamentally, this is due to the single-thread ILP limit of the loop trace being considered (as apparent from Fig. 7.8 (a)).

Note, by the way that the resource sizes are assumed to be large enough, so that they are effectively infinite for the purposes of our running example above. Some of the actual sizes assumed for the base case ($W = 4$) are: Completion (reorder) buffer size, cbuf_size = 32; load-store queue size, lsq_size = 6; floating point queue size, fpq_size = 8; pending store queue size, psq_size = 16.

The microarchitectural trends beyond the current superscalar regime, are effectively targeted towards the goal of extending the power-performance efficiency factors. That is, the complexity growth must ideally scale at a slower rate than the growth in performance. Power consumption is one index of complexity; it also determines packaging and cooling costs. (Verification cost and effort is another important index). In that sense, a microarchitecture paradigm that ensures that the power-performance efficiency measure of choice is a nondecreasing function of time: is the ideal, complexity-effective design paradigm for the future. Of course, it is hard to keep scaling a given paradigm beyond a few processor generations. Whenever we reach a maximum in the power-performance efficiency curve, it is time to invoke the next paradigm shift.

Next, we examine some of the promising new trends in microarchitecture that can serve as the next platform for designing power-performance scalable machines.

## Multicluster Superscalar Processors

As described in our earlier article [2], Zyuban et al. [25,26] studied the class of multicluster superscalar processors as a means of extending the power-efficient growth of the basic super scalar paradigm. One way to address the energy growth problem at the microarchitectural level is to replace a classical superscalar CPU with a set of clusters, so that all key energy consumers are split among clusters. Then, instead of accessing centralized structures in the traditional superscalar design, instructions scheduled to an individual cluster would access local structures most of the time. The main advantage of accessing a collection of local structures instead of a centralized one is that the number of ports and entries in each local structure is much smaller. This reduces the latency and energy per access. If the non-accessed substructures of a resource can be "gated off" (e.g., in terms of the clock), then, the net energy savings can be substantial.

According to the results obtained in Zyuban's work, the energy dissipated per cycle in every unit or sub-unit within a superscalar processor can be modeled to vary (approximately) as $IPC_{unit} \times (IW)^g$, where IW is the issue width, $IPC_{unit}$ is the average IPC performance at the level of the unit or structure under consideration; and, $g$ is the energy growth parameter for that unit. Then, the energy-delay product (EDP) for the particular unit would vary as:

$$EDP_{unit} = \frac{IPC_{unit} \times (IW)^g}{IPC_{overall}} \quad (7.12)$$

Zyuban shows that for real machines, where the overall IPC always increases with issue width in a sub-linear manner, the overall EDP of the processor can be bounded as

$$(IPC)^{2g-1} \leq EDP \leq (IPC)^{2g} \quad (7.13)$$

where $g$ is the energy-growth factor of a given unit and IPC refers to the overall IPC of the processor; and, IPC is assumed to vary as $(IW)^{0.5}$. Thus, according to this formulation, superscalar implementations that minimize $g$ for each unit or structure will result in energy-efficient designs. The eliot/elpaso tool does not model the effects of multi-clustering in detail yet; however, from Zyuban's work, we can infer that a carefully designed multicluster architecture has the potential of extending the power-performance efficiency scaling beyond what is possible using the classical superscalar paradigm. Of course, such extended scalability is achieved at the expense of reduced IPC performance for a given superscalar machine width. This IPC degradation is caused by the added inter-cluster communication delays and other power management overhead in a real design. Some of the IPC loss (if not all) can be offset by a clock frequency boost, which may be possible in such a design, due to the reduced resource latencies and bandwidths.

Current high-performance processors (for example, the Compaq Alpha 21264 and the IBM Power4) certainly have elements of multi-clustering, especially in terms of duplicated register files and distributed issue queues. Zyuban proposed and modeled a specific multicluster organization in his work. This simulation-based study determined the optimal number of clusters and their configurations, for the EDP metric.

## Simultaneous Multithreading (SMT)

Let us examine the SMT paradigm [27] to understand how this may affect our notion of power-performance efficiency. The data in Table 7.3 shows the steady-state utilization of some of the resources in our base super scalar machine in response to the input loop test case discussed earlier. Since, due to fundamental ILP limits, the IPC will not increase beyond $W = 4$, it is clear why power-performance efficiency will be on a downward trend beyond a certain width of the machine. (Of course, here we assume maximum processor power numbers, without any clock gating or dynamic adaptation to bring down power.)

With SMT, assume that we can fetch from two threads (simultaneously, if the icache is dual-ported, or in alternate cycles if the icache remains single-ported). Suppose two copies of the same loop program (see example at the beginning of this section, i.e., Section 7.4) are executing as two different threads. So, thread-1 instructions A-B-C-D-E-F-G and thread-2 instructions P-Q-R-S-T-U-V are simultaneously available for dispatch and subsequent execution on the machine. This facility allows the utilization factors, and the net throughput performance to go up, without a significant increase in the maximum clocked power. This is because, the issue width $W$ is not increased, but the execution and resource stages or slots can be filled up simultaneously from both threads. The added complexity in the front-end of maintaining two program counters (fetch streams), and the global register space increase alluded to previously, adds to the power a bit. On the other hand, the core execution complexity can be relaxed a bit without a performance hit. For example, the fp_delay parameter can be increased, to reduce core complexity, without any performance degradation. Figure 7.9 shows the expected performance and power-performance variation with $W$ for the 2-thread SMT processor. The power model assumed for the SMT machine is

**TABLE 7.3**  Steady-State Resource Utilization Profile for Base ($W = 4$) Superscalar Machine

| Resource Name | Steady-State Utilization (%) |
|---|---|
| Completion (reorder) buffer, CBUF | 53 |
| Load-store issue queue, LSQ | 0 |
| Load-store unit pipe-0, LSU-0 | 100 |
| Load-store unit-pipe1, LSU-1 | 50 |
| Floating point issue queue, FPQ | 0 |
| Floating point unit pipe-0, FPU-0 | 100 |
| Floating point unit pipe-1, FPU-1 | 50 |
| Data cache read port-0, C0 | 50 |
| Data cache read-port-1, C1 | 50 |
| Data cache store port, C2 | 50 |
| Pending store queue, PSQ | 12.5 |

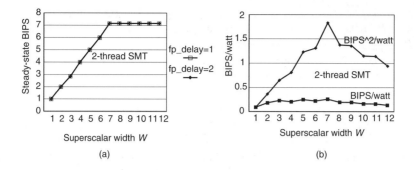

**FIGURE 7.9** Performance and power-performance variation with $W$ for 2-thread SMT.

the same as that of the underlying superscalar, except that a fixed fraction of the net power is added to account for the SMT overhead. (The fraction added is assumed to be linear in the number of threads, in an n-thread SMT). Figure 7.9 shows that under the assumed model, the performance-power efficiency scales better with $W$, compared with the base superscalar (Fig. 7.8).

Seng and Tullsen [28] presented analysis to show that using a suitably architected SMT processor, the per-thread speculative waste can be reduced, while increasing the utilization of the machine resources by executing simultaneously from multiple threads. This was shown to reduce the average energy per instruction by 22%.

## Chip Multiprocessing

In a multiscalar-like chip-multiprocessor (CMP) machine [29], different iterations of a single loop program could be initiated as separate tasks or threads on different core processors on the same chip. Thus, the threads A-B-C-D-E-F-G and P-Q-R-S-T-U-V, derived from the same user program would be issued in sequence by a global task sequencer to two cores, in a 2-way multiscalar CMP. Register values set in one task are forwarded in sequence to dependent instructions in subsequent tasks. For example, the register value in fp1 set by instruction E in task 1 must be communicated to instruction T in task 2; so instruction T must stall in the second processor until the value communication has occurred from task 1. Execution on each processor proceeds speculatively, assuming the absence of load-store address conflicts between tasks; dynamic memory address disambiguation hardware is required to detect violations and restart task executions as needed. In this paradigm also, if the performance can be shown to scale well with the number of tasks, and if each processor is designed as a limited-issue, limited-speculation (low complexity) core, it is possible to achieve better overall scalability of performance-power efficiency.

Another trend in high-end microprocessors is true chip multiprocessing (CMP), where multiple (distinct) user programs execute separately on different processors on the same chip. A commonly used paradigm in this case is that of (shared memory) symmetric multiprocessing (SMP) on a chip (see Hammond et al. in [23]). Larger SMP server nodes can be built from such chips. Server product groups such as IBM's high-end PowerPC division have relied on such CMP paradigms as the scalable paradigm for the immediate future. The Power4 design [11] is the first example of this trend. Such CMP designs offer the potential of convenient coarse-grain clock-gating and "power-down" modes, where one or more processors on the chip may be "turned off" or "slowed down" to save power when needed.

# 7.5 Conclusions and Future Research

In this chapter, we first discussed issues related to power-performance efficiency and metrics from an architect's viewpoint. We limited the discussion to dynamic power consumption. We showed that depending on the application domain (or market), it may be necessary to adopt one metric over another in comparing processors within that segment. Next, we described some of the promising new ideas in power-aware microarchitecture design. This discussion included circuit-centric solutions like clock-gating, where microarchitectural support is needed to make the right decisions at run time. Later, we used a simple loop test case to illustrate the limits of power-performance scalability in some popular paradigms that are being developed by various vendors within the high-end processor domain. In particular, we show that scalability of current generation super scalars may be extended effectively through multi-clustering, SMT, and CMP. Our experience in simulating these structures points to the need of keeping a single core (or the uni-threaded core) simple enough to ensure scalability in the power, performance, and verification cost of future systems. Detailed simulation results with benchmarks to support these conclusions were not provided in this tutorial-style paper. Future research papers from our group will present such data for specific microarchitectural paradigms of interest.

We limited our focus to a few key ideas and paradigms of interest in future power-aware processor design. Also, we did not consider methods to reduce static (leakage) power: a component of net processor power that is expected to grow significantly in future technologies. Many new ideas to address various aspects of power reduction have been presented in recent workshops (e.g., [30–32]). All these ideas could not be discussed in this chapter; but the interested reader should certainly refer to the cited references for further detailed study.

At IBM T. J. Watson Research Center, a project on power-aware microprocessor design, led by the author of this article, is currently engaged in designing a research processor prototype, called LPX (low-power issue-execute processor). This processor has many of the elements touched upon in this paper among other new innovations. By incorporating on-chip monitoring hardware, we shall attempt to measure power reduction benefits and performance degradations (if any) resulting from the various ideas that are being tried. This hardware prototype will also enable us to validate our power-performance simulation methodologies, e.g., the *PowerTimer* toolkit referred to in [2]. Details of the LPX design will be described in later publications.

## Acknowledgments

The author is indebted to his fellow researchers (including summer interns) who either have been or still are contributing to the power-aware microprocessor project at IBM Watson. In particular, the author thanks Victor Zyuban, David Brooks, Alper Buyuktosunoglu, Hans Jacobson, Stanley Schuster, Peter Cook, Jude Rivers, Daniel Citron, J-D Wellman, Prabhakar Kudva, and Phil Emma. The author also thanks to other colleagues in his organization's management chain, including Mike Rosenfield and Eric Kronstadt for their constant support and encouragement. In addition, the author expressses his gratitude to Prof. Margaret Martonosi at Princeton University and Prof. David Albonesi at University of Rochester for their active support and help in enabling the research work in this area within IBM Research.

## References

1. Hennessey, J. L. and Patterson, D. A., *Computer Architecture: A Quantitative Approach,* 2nd ed., Morgan Kaufmann Publishers, Inc. 1996.
2. Brooks, D. M., Bose, P., Schuster, S. E., Jacobson, H., Kudva, P. N., Buyuktosunoglu, A., Wellman, J.-D., Zyuban, V., Gupta, M., and Cook, P. W., "Power-aware microarchitecture: design and modeling challenges for next-generation microprocessors," *Proc. IEEE Micro,* vol. 20, no. 6, pp. 26–44, Nov./ Dec. 2000.
3. Flynn, M. J., Hung, P., and Rudd, K., "Deep-submicron microprocessor design issues," *Proc. IEEE Micro,* vol. 19, no. 4, pp. 11–22, July/Aug. 1999.
4. Borkar, S., "Design challenges of technology scaling," *Proc. IEEE Micro,* vol. 19, no. 4, pp. 23–29, July/Aug. 1999.
5. Gonzalez, R. and Horowitz, M., "Energy dissipation in general purpose microprocessors," *IEEE J. Solid-State Circuits,* vol. 31, no. 9, pp. 1277–1284, Sept. 1996.
6. Oklobdzija, V. G., "Architectural tradeoffs for low power," in *Proc. ISCA Workshop on Power-Driven Microarchitectures,* Barcelona, Spain, June 1998.
7. Kogge, P. M., *The Architecture of Pipelined Computers,* Hemisphere Publishing Corporation, 1981.

8. Larson, A. G., "Cost-effective processor design with an application to Fast Fourier Transform Computers," Digital Systems Laboratory Report SU-SEL-73-037, Stanford University, Stanford, Calif., August 1973; see also, Larson and Davidson, "Cost-effective design of special purpose processors: a Fast Fourier Transform Case Study," *Proc. 11th Ann. Allerton Conference on Circuits and System Theory,* University of Illinois, Champaihn-Urbana, pp. 547–557, 1973.

9. Dubey, P. K. and Flynn, M. J., "Optimal pipelining," *J. Parallel and Distributed Computing,* vol. 8, no. 1, pp. 10–19, Jan. 1990.

10. Tiwari, V. et al., "Reducing power in high-performance microprocessors," in *Proc. IEEE/ACM Design Automation Conference,* ACM, New York, pp. 732–737, 1998.

11. Diefendorff, K., "Power4 focuses on memory bandwidth," *Microprocessor Report,* pp. 11–17, Oct. 6, 1999.

12. Brooks, D. and Martonosi, M., "Dynamically exploiting narrow width operands to improve processor power and performance," in *Proc. 5th Int'l. Symp. on High-Performance Computer Architecture (HPCA-5),* Jan. 1999.

13. Albonesi, D., "Dynamic IPC/Clock Rate Optimization," in *Proc. 25th. Ann. Int'l. Symp. on Computer Architecture (ISCA),* pp. 282–292, Barcelona, 1998.

14. Maro, R., Bai, Y., and Bahar, R. I., "Dynamically reconfiguring processor resources to reduce power consumption in high-performance processors," in *Proc. Power Aware Computer Systems (PACS) Workshop,* held in conjunction with ASPLOS, Cambridge, MA, Nov. 2000.

15. Buyuktosunoglu, A. et al., "An adaptive issue queue for reduced power at high performance," in *Proc. ISCA Workshop on Complexity-Effective Design (WCED),* Vancouver, Canada, June 2000.

16. Cruz, J.-L., Gonzalez, A., Valero, M., and Topham, N. P., "Multiple-banked register file architectures," in *Proc. Int'l. Symp. On Computer Architecture (ISCA),* pp. 316–325, Vancouver, June 2000.

17. Gunther, S. H., Binns, F., Carmean, D. M., and Hall, J. C., "Managing the impact of increasing microprocessor power consumption," in *Proc. Intel Technology Journal,* March 2000.

18. Reed, P. et al., "250 MHz 5 W RISC microprocessor with on-chip L2 cache controller," in *Digest of Technical Papers, IEEE Int'l. Solid State Circuits Conference,* pp. 40:412, 1997.

19. Sanchez, H. et al., "Thermal management system for high performance PowerPC microprocessors," in *Digest of Papers, IEEE COMPCON,* p. 325, 1997.

20. Brooks, D. and Martonosi, M., "Dynamic thermal management for high-performance microprocessors," in *Proc. 7th Int'l. Symp. On High Performance Computer Architecture,* pp. 20–24, Jan. 2001.

21. Manne, S., Klauser, A., and Grunwald, D., "Pipeline gating: speculation control for energy reduction," in *Proc. 25th. Ann. Int'l. Symp. on Computer Architecture (ISCA),* pp. 132–141, Barcelona, 1998.

22. Grunwald, D., Klauser, A., Manne, S., and Pleszkun, A., "Confidence estimation for speculation control," in *Proc. 25th. Ann. Int'l. Symp. on Computer Architecture (ISCA),* pp. 122–131, Barcelona, 1998.

23. Theme issue, "The future of processors," *IEEE Computer,* vol. 30, no. 9, pp. 93–97, September 1997.

24. Bose, P., Kim, S., O'Connell, F. P., and Ciarfella, W. A., "Bounds modeling and compiler optimizations for superscalar performance tuning," *Journ. of Systems Architecture,* vol. 45, Elsevier, Amsterdam, pp. 1111–1137, 1999.

25. Zyuban, V., "Inherently lower-power high performance super scalar architectures," Ph.D Thesis, Dept. of Computer Science and Engineering, University of Notre Dame, 2000.

26. Zyuban, V. and Kogge, P., "Optimization of high-performance superscalar architectures for energy efficiency," in *Proc. IEEE Symp. on Low Power Electronics and Design,* ACM, New York, 2000.

27. Tullsen, D. M., Eggers, S. J., and Levy, H. M., "Simultaneous Multithreading: Maximizing On-Chip Parallelism," in *Proc. 22nd. Ann. Int'l. Symp. on Computer Architecture,* pp. 292–403, 1995.

28. Seng, J. S., Tullsen, D. M., and Cai, G., "The power efficiency of multithreaded architectures," invited talk presented at: ISCA Workshop on Complexity-Effective Design (WCED), Vancouver, Canada, June 2000.

29. Sohi, G., Breach, S. E., and Vijaykumar, T. N., "Multiscalar processors," in *Proc. 22nd Ann. Int'l. Symp. on Computer Architecture,* pp. 414–425, IEEE CS Press, Los Alamitos, California, 1995.

30. Talks presented at the 1998 ISCA Workshop on Power-Driven Microarchitecture: http://www.cs. colorado.edu/~grunwald/LowPowerWorkshop.
31. Talks presented at the 2000 ISCA Workshop on Complexity Effective Design (WCED-00), Vancouver, Canada, June 2000: http://www.ece.rochester.edu/~albonesi/WCED00/.
32. Talks presented at the Power Aware Computer Systems (PACS) Workshop, held in conjunction with ASPLOS, Cambridge, MA, Nov. 2000.
33. Zyuban, V. et al., "Power-performance efficiency metrics: an expanded and updated view," IBM Research Report (to appear), 2001.

# 8

# Performance Evaluation

Jozo J. Dujmović
*San Francisco State University*

Daniel Tomasevich
*San Francisco State University*

Ming Au-Yeung
*San Francisco State University*

Lizy Kurian John
*University of Texas*

Eric Rotenberg
*North Carolina State University*

## 8.1   Measurement and Modeling of Disk Subsystem Performance

*Jozo J. Dujmović, Daniel Tomasevich, and Ming Au-Yeung*

### Introduction

In queuing theory literature, many models describe the dynamic behavior of computer systems. Good sources of such information (e.g. [5,7]) usually include stochastic models based on birth-death formulas, the convolution algorithm [2], load independent and load dependent mean value analysis (MVA) models [10], and BCMP networks [1]. Theoretical queuing models presented in computer literature easily explain phenomena such as bottlenecks, saturation, resource utilization, etc.; however, it is very difficult to find sources that show a second level of modeling, which focuses on the ability of models to also achieve good numerical accuracy when modeling real computer systems running real workloads. Although the phenomenology is important in the classroom, it is the numerical accuracy that counts in engineering practice. The usual task of performance analysts is to measure system performance and then derive models that can describe and predict the behavior of analyzed systems with reasonable accuracy. Those who try to model the dynamic behavior of real computer systems running real workloads frequently find this to be a difficult task.

Our first goal is to develop load dependent models of disk units that have a moderate level of complexity suitable for engineering practice. The presented disk unit models describe disk access times, head movement optimization, and disk caching. These models are then used for creating MVA models of disk subsystems. Our second goal is to investigate and exemplify the limits of numerical accuracy of presented queuing models, and to propose indicators of predictive power of analyzed models. We present case studies of disk subsystem modeling of a VAX under VMS and a PC under Windows NT. They provide a good insight into the level of difficulty encountered in practical disk subsystem modeling and help establish realistic expectations of modeling errors. The relative simplicity of MVA models makes them attractive for practice. They can be easily combined with our disk unit models. However, our experiments with MVA models show that only the load dependent version of MVA generates results with reasonable accuracy.

## Description Errors and Prediction Errors of Disk Subsystem Models

Modeling errors are defined as differences between queuing theory results and experimental measurements. Simple queuing models of disk subsystems (such as load independent MVA) frequently generate modeling errors of 30–50% or more. In the majority of practical cases such low accuracy is not acceptable. Modeling errors below 5% are usually acceptable, but require detailed and more sophisticated models.

The accuracy of models can only be evaluated with respect to measurements performed for a specific system running a specific workload. Our approach to modeling and analysis of disk subsystems includes the following main steps:

- Specification of drive workload that can be used to create various levels of disk subsystem load.
- Measurement of system performance under a strictly increasing disk subsystem load.
- Development of an analytic model with adjustable parameters that describes the dynamics of a disk subsystem.
- Calibration of the analytic model by adjusting all model parameters to minimize the difference between the measured values and the values computed from the analytic model.
- Assessment of the predictive power of the analytic model.
- The use of the calibrated model for performance prediction of systems with different parameters and/or workload.

It is useful to identify two types of modeling errors: *description errors* and *prediction errors*. We define a description error as the mean relative error between the measured performance indicators of a real system and the performance indicators of a calibrated model. The description error is defined only within the range of measurements. By contrast, the prediction error is the error in predicting the values of performance indicators outside the range of measurements, or for different configurations of the analyzed system, or for a different workload. For example, if we measure the response time for the degree of multiprogramming from 1 to 8, then the description error is the mean error between eight measured values and eight computed values. The prediction error is the error between the computed response time for 20 jobs and the actual response time if it were measured. The prediction error is also the error between predicted and actual response times for a system with a different number of disks, processors, or for a different workload.

The basic problem of modeling is that the ratio between prediction errors and description errors can frequently be large, e.g., 2 to 10. Consequently, to provide reasonable prediction power, the description errors of analytic models must be small, typically just a few percent.

### A Simple Acceleration/Deceleration Model of Disk Access Time

The movement of the disk input/output (I/O) mechanism is usually modeled assuming that movement is caused by applying a constant force for both acceleration and deceleration. This is a simple and usually realistic assumption illustrated in Fig. 8.1. If the mass of the I/O mechanism is $m$, then force $f$ causes the acceleration $a = f/m$. After acceleration with force $f$ we apply deceleration with force $-f$. The I/O heads travel the total distance $x$ and the corresponding time $T$ is called the seek time. After accelerating for time $T/2$ the I/O heads attain the speed $v = aT/2$ and travel the distance $x/2 = a(T/2)^2/2$. Therefore, the

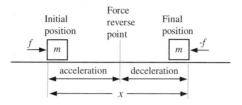

**FIGURE 8.1** Movement of the disk I/O mechanism (seek). (From Dujmovic, J., Tomasevich, D., and Au-Yeung, M., *Proc. CMG*, 1999, Reno, NV. With permission.)

seek time as a function of distance is $T(x) = 2\sqrt{x/a}$. If the maximum distance is $x_{max}$ then the maximum seek time is $T_{max}$, the acceleration is $a = 4x_{max}/T_{max}^2$, and $T(x) = T_{max}\sqrt{x/x_{max}}$. The distance $x$ can be expressed as a physical length, or as a number of cylinders traveled (in this case the dimension of acceleration is cylinder/s²). If the head moves from cylinder $y$ to cylinder $z$, the traveled distance is $x = |y - z|$. The seek time is $t(y, z) = T_{max}\sqrt{|y-z|/x_{max}}$. The initial position $y$ and the final position $z$ can be anywhere in the interval $[0, x_{max}]$. Assuming the uniform distribution of accesses to all cylinders the average seek time $T_{seek}$ can be computed as follows:

$$T_{seek} = \frac{1}{x_{max}^2}\int_0^{x_{max}}\int_0^{x_{max}} t(y, z)\,dy\,dz = \frac{T_{max}}{x_{max}^{5/2}}\int_0^{x_{max}}\int_0^{x_{max}}\sqrt{|y-z|}\,dy\,dz = \frac{8}{15}T_{max} = \frac{16}{15}\sqrt{\frac{x_{max}}{a}}$$

Consider the case where each cylinder has a fixed data capacity of $b$ bytes. For a large contiguous file of size $F$ the maximum distance the I/O mechanism can travel is $x_{max} = F/b$ cylinders. Consequently, the average seek time for this file is $T_{seek} = c\sqrt{F}$, where $c = 16/(15\sqrt{ab}) = $ const. If we access data in the range $0 \leq F \leq F_{max}$, the average seek time is the following function of the file size:

$$T_{seek}(F) = T_{max\,seek}\sqrt{F/F_{max}}, \qquad T_{max\,seek} = \frac{16}{15}\sqrt{\frac{F_{max}}{ab}}$$

Now the constant $T_{max\,seek}$ has a suitable interpretation of the maximum value of the average seek time for the file of size $F_{max}$.

When the I/O mechanism reaches a destination cylinder, it is necessary to wait the latency time until the desired sector reaches the read/write head. For a disk that rotates at $N_{rev}$ revolutions per minute, the total revolution time is $60/N_{rev}$. The latency time is uniformly distributed between 0 and $60/N_{rev}$. Therefore, the average latency is half of the revolution time, i.e., $T_{latency} = 30/N_{rev}$. The disk data transfer time for one sector is $T_{transfer} = 60/N_{rev}N_{sector} = 2T_{latency}/N_{sector}$. Therefore, the mean time to access and transfer disk data from a file of size $F$ is

$$\begin{aligned}
T_{access} &= T_{seek} + T_{latency} + T_{transfer} \\
&= T_{max\,seek}\sqrt{F/F_{max}} + 30(1 + 2/N_{sector})/N_{rev} \\
&\cong T_{max\,seek}\sqrt{F/F_{max}} + 30/N_{rev}
\end{aligned}$$

This is the simplest and idealized model of the mean disk access time. This model neglects phenomena such as differences between disk acceleration and deceleration, head settle time [15] (dominating short seeks), limited maximum velocity, nonuniformity of rotational latency for nonindependent requests, zoning, bus interface and contention [11], disk command overhead [4], as well as effects of caching and head movement optimization.

## A Fixed Maximum Velocity Model of Seek Time

A more realistic model of seek time can be derived if we assume that the maximum velocity of the I/O heads has a constant maximum value, as shown in Fig. 8.2. For small distances (exemplified by seek times $t_1$, $t_2$ and all other seek times $t \leq T^*$) we assume that the heads first linearly accelerate for some time and then decelerate exactly the same amount of time. For larger distances (seek times $t \geq T^*$) the

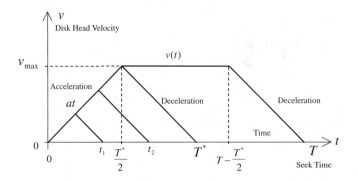

**FIGURE 8.2**   A simplified disk head velocity diagram. (From Dujmovic, J., Tomasevich, D., and Au-Yeung, M., *Proc. CMG*, 1999, Reno, NV. With permission.)

heads linearly accelerate until they achieve the maximum speed $v_{max}$, then travel at this constant speed, and eventually decelerate linearly.

The maximum time $T^*$ that the disk mechanism can travel without being limited by the maximum velocity is called the *critical seek time*. $T^*$ is the time to accelerate disk heads to the maximum speed and then to decelerate them to a standstill. In cases where disk heads travel at the constant maximum speed the critical seek time $T^*$ denotes the acceleration plus deceleration time, i.e. the total seek time minus the time heads spend traveling at the constant maximum speed. Assuming constant acceleration/deceleration, the critical seek time is $T^* = 2v_{max}/a$. During the critical seek time interval the mechanism travels the distance $x^*$, called the *critical distance*. In the case of constant acceleration/deceleration, we have $v = at$, $x(t) = at^2/2$, and $x^* = 2x(T^*/2) = v_{max}^2/a$.

Let us now investigate a general symmetrical case where the function $v(t)$ has the property that the acceleration time equals the deceleration time. We differentiate the small distance model ($T \leq T^*$) and the large distance model ($T \geq T^*$) as follows:

$$x(T) = \int_0^T v(t)dt$$

$$= \begin{cases} \underbrace{\int_0^{T/2} v(t)dt}_{\text{acceleration}} + \underbrace{\int_{T/2}^T v(t)dt}_{\text{deceleration}}, & T \leq T^* \\[2em] \underbrace{\int_0^{T^*/2} v(t)dt}_{\text{acceleration}} + \underbrace{\int_{T^*/2}^{T-T^*/2} v_{max}\, dt}_{\text{max velocity}} + \underbrace{\int_{T-T^*/2}^T v(t)dt}_{\text{deceleration}} = x^* + v_{max}(T - T^*), & T \geq T^* \end{cases}$$

$$x^* = \underbrace{\int_0^{T^*/2} v(t)dt}_{\text{acceleration}} + \underbrace{\int_{T-T^*/2}^T v(t)dt}_{\text{deceleration}}$$

The distance $x^*$ is the total distance for acceleration from 0 to $v_{max}$ and deceleration from $v_{max}$ to 0. In the constant acceleration case ($v(t) = at$), this model yields

$$x(T) = \begin{cases} \dfrac{aT^2}{4} = \dfrac{v_{max}}{2T^*}T^2, & T \leq T^* = \dfrac{2v_{max}}{a} \\[2em] v_{max}\left(T - \dfrac{v_{max}}{a}\right) = v_{max}\left(T - \dfrac{T^*}{2}\right), & T \geq T^* \end{cases}$$

The critical distance $x^*$ is

$$x^* = x(T^*) = \frac{a(T^*)^2}{4} = \frac{v_{max}T^*}{2} = \frac{v_{max}^2}{a}$$

Therefore, the acceleration and the maximum speed depend on the critical values $x^*$ and $T^*$:

$$a = 4x^*/(T^*)^2, \quad v_{max} = 2x^*/T^*$$

They can also be numerically determined from the linear segment of the seek time characteristic, using arbitrary points $(x_1, T_1)$ and $(x_2, T_2)$:

$$v_{max} = \frac{x_2 - x_1}{T_2 - T_1}, \quad a = \frac{(x_2 - x_1)^2}{(T_1 x_2 - T_2 x_1)(T_2 - T_1)}$$

The seek time characteristic follows from $x(T)$:

$$T(x) = \begin{cases} 2\sqrt{\dfrac{x}{a}} = 2\sqrt{\dfrac{xx^*}{v_{max}}} = T^*\sqrt{\dfrac{x}{x^*}}, & x \leq x^* \\[3mm] \dfrac{x + x^*}{v_{max}} = \dfrac{T^*}{2} + \dfrac{x}{v_{max}} = \dfrac{T^*}{2}\left(\dfrac{x}{x^*} + 1\right), & x \geq x^* \end{cases}$$

This function satisfies the following properties:

- The initial nonlinear segment, for $x \leq x^*$, is a square root function.
- The second segment, for $x > x^*$, is a linear function.
- At the critical point $x = x^*$, the first derivative of the square root function equals the first derivative of the linear function ($dT/dx = 1/v_{max}$).

From $T = T^*(1 + x/x^*)/2$ we can easily see that both $x^*$ and $T^*$ can be determined from the linear segment of the measured seek time characteristic using the following four steps, illustrated in Fig. 8.3:

1. Extend the linear segment of the measured seek time characteristic to the vertical axis. For $x = 0$ we get the point $T^*/2$ on the vertical axis.
2. Move vertically up to the point $T^*$ (this value is twice the distance between the origin and the intersection of the linear segment and the vertical axis).

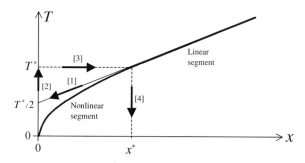

**FIGURE 8.3** Graphical method for determining $x^*$ and $T^*$. (From Dujmovic, J., Tomasevich, D., and Au-Yeung, M., *Proc. CMG*, 1999, Reno, NV. With permission.)

3. Move horizontally to the intersection with the linear segment.
4. Move down to the horizontal axis and determine the point $x^*$.

Because the linear segment of the seek time characteristic determines the values of $x^*$ and $T^*$ (as well as $a$ and $v_{max}$), it follows that the nonlinear segment must terminate exactly in the $(x^*, T^*)$ point. A numerical method for computing $x^*$ and $T^*$ can be based on any two points $(x_1, T_1)$ and $(x_2, T_2)$ taken on the linear segment. From the linear segment function $T = T_1 + (x - x_1)(T_2 - T_1)/(x_2 - x_1)$, it follows:

$$x^* = \frac{T_1 x_2 - T_2 x_1}{T_2 - T_1}, \quad T^* = 2\frac{T_1 x_2 - T_2 x_1}{x_2 - x_1}$$

The presented model is suitable for a qualitative description of the seek time behavior and for providing insight into disk characteristics, but its flexibility is limited because it has only two parameters. In addition to limited flexibility, this model is not appropriate for those disk units that do not satisfy the assumptions of constant acceleration/deceleration, and for units where the seek time for short distances is significantly affected by the head settling time. The accuracy of modeling can be improved using numerical models that fit the measured characteristic and use more than two adjustable parameters.

## Numerical Computation of the Average Seek Time

A simple numerical model can be based on three points: $(x_1, T_1)$, $(x^*, T^*)$, and $(x_2, T_2)$, where $x_1 < x^* < x_2$. Here, $(x_1, T_1)$ is the point from the initial nonlinear segment. Contrary to the approach presented in the section on "A Fixed Maximum Velocity Model of Seek Time," the middle point $(x^*, T^*)$ is not computed from the linear part of the measured characteristic, but directly selected from the seek time graph as the beginning of the linear segment. The point $(x_2, T_2)$ denotes the end of the linear segment (the maximum distance heads can travel). The corresponding model is

$$T(x) = \begin{cases} T^*\left(\dfrac{x}{x^*}\right)^r = tx^r, \quad t = \dfrac{T^*}{(x^*)^r}, & x \le x^* \\[2em] T^* + \dfrac{T_2 - T^*}{x_2 - x^*}(x - x^*) = Ax + B, & x \ge x^* \end{cases}$$

From $T_1 = tx_1^r$ and $T^* = t(x^*)^r$ it follows that $T^*/T_1 = (x^*/x_1)^r$. Therefore, the parameters are

$$r = \frac{\log(T^*/T_1)}{\log(x^*/x_1)}, \quad t = T_1/x_1^r = T^*/(x^*)^r$$

$$A = \frac{T_2 - T^*}{x_2 - x^*}, \quad B = T^* - Ax^*$$

Using this model it is possible to numerically compute the mean seek time. Suppose that a file occupies $N$ cylinders. The probability that the seek distance $x$ is less than or equal to a given value $z$ is

$$P_x(z) = P[x \le z] = (2Nz - z^2)/N^2$$

This probability distribution function yields the following probability density function:

$$p_x(z) = dP/dz = 2(N - z)/N^2$$

Hence, the average seek time for the $N$-cylinder file can be computed as follows:

$$\bar{T}_{\text{seek}} = \int_0^N T(z)p_x(z)dz = \frac{2}{N^2}\int_0^N T(z)(N-z)dz$$

Using the presented seek time model for $N \leq x^*$, we have

$$\bar{T}_{\text{seek}} = \frac{2t}{N^2}\int_0^N z^r(N-z)dz = \frac{2tN^r}{(r+1)(r+2)}$$

Similarly, for $N \geq x^*$, we get

$$\bar{T}_{\text{seek}} = \frac{2}{N^2}\left[\int_0^{x^*} T(z)(N-z)dz + \int_{x^*}^N T(z)(N-z)dz\right]$$

$$= \frac{2}{N^2}\left[\int_0^{x^*} tz^r(N-z)dz + \int_{x^*}^N (Az+B)(N-z)dz\right]$$

$$= \frac{2t(x^*)^{r+1}}{N^2}\left(\frac{N}{r+1} - \frac{x^*}{r+2}\right) + \frac{(N-x^*)[N(AN+3B+Ax^*)-x^*(3B+2Ax^*)]}{3N^2}$$

Therefore, the average seek time as a function of file size is given by the following function:

$$\bar{T}_{\text{seek}}(N) = \begin{cases} \dfrac{2tN^r}{(r+1)(r+2)}, & N \leq x^* \\[2ex] \dfrac{2t(x^*)^{r+1}}{N^2}\left(\dfrac{N}{r+1} - \dfrac{x^*}{r+2}\right) + \dfrac{(N-x^*)[N(AN+3B+Ax^*)-x^*(3B+2Ax^*)]}{3N^2}, & N \geq x^* \end{cases}$$

Advantages of the presented exponential model are: (1) parameters can be quickly computed from three selected points of the characteristic, and (2) parameter $r$ enables modeling of disk characteristics that are different from the square root model. From $T(1) = t$ it follows that $t$ is interpreted as the single cylinder seek time. The limitation of this model is that by determining $t$ and $r$ from points $(x_1, T_1)$ and $(x^*, T^*)$ it is not possible to have the exact value of $t$ and optimum modeling of the curvature. To improve this model we can introduce one more parameter as follows:

$$T(x) = \begin{cases} 0, & x = 0 \\ t + c(x-1)^r, & 1 \leq x \leq x^* \\ Ax + B, & x \geq x^* \end{cases}$$

This new model has a nonlinear part (for $x \leq x^*$) and a linear part (for $x \geq x^*$). Since $T(1) = t$ and $T(2) = t + c$ the parameter $t$ is the single cylinder seek time and the parameter $c$ is the difference $c = T(2) - T(1)$. The parameters of this model $(t,c,r,A,B,x^*)$ are not independent. First, for $x = x^*$ the nonlinear part must be connected to the linear part:

$$t + c(x^* - 1)^r = Ax^* + B.$$

In addition, to assure perfect continuity of this model, for $x = x^*$ the nonlinear and linear model must have the same first derivatives:

$$\left.\frac{dT}{dx}\right|_{x=x^*} = A = cr(x^* - 1)^{r-1}. \tag{8.1}$$

Inserting this value of $A$ in the connection relation, we have the expression for $B$:

$$B = t + c(x^* - 1)^r - cr(x^* - 1)^{r-1}x^*. \tag{8.2}$$

The linear function can now be written as

$$Ax + B = \frac{cr(x - x^*)}{(x^* - 1)^{1-r}} + t + c(x^* - 1)^r.$$

Therefore, using formulas (8.1) and (8.2) our exponential model is now

$$T(x) = \begin{cases} t + c(x - 1)^r, & 1 \leq x \leq x^* \\ \dfrac{cr(x - x^*)}{(x^* - 1)^{1-r}} + t + c(x^* - 1)^r, & x \geq x^* \end{cases}$$

The model has four independent parameters $t, c, r, x^*$ that can be determined using a calibration procedure. The objective of calibration is to make the model as close as possible to the measured values $(x_1, T_1), \ldots, (x_n, T_n)$. Optimum values of parameters can be computed from the measured values $(x_1, T_1), \ldots, (x_n, T_n)$ by minimizing one of the following criterion functions:

$$E_1(t, c, r, x^*) = \frac{1}{n}\sum_{i=1}^{n}(T(x_i) - T_i)^2$$

$$E_2(t, c, r, x^*) = \frac{1}{n}\sum_{i=1}^{n}|T(x_i) - T_i|$$

$$E_3(t, c, r, x^*) = \max_{1 \leq i \leq n}|T(x_i) - T_i|$$

$E_1$ is a traditional mean square error, $E_2$ is the mean absolute error and $E_3$ is used to minimize the maximum error ("minimax"). These criterion functions yield consistent or similar results and in this paper we primarily used $E_1$. For all the above criteria the most suitable minimization method is the Nelder-Mead simplex algorithm [8]. The resulting calibrated (optimum) values of parameters $t, c, r, x^*$ are those that yield the minimum value of the selected criterion function.

Experiments with modern disk units show that the four-parameter exponential model regularly achieves high accuracy. Typical average relative errors are between 2% and 3%. The quality of this model is illustrated in Fig. 8.4 for the Quantum Atlas III disk that has 8057 cylinders, and capacity of 9.1 GB. The optimum parameters of the model are $t = 1.55$ ms, $c = 0.32$ ms, $r = 0.387$, and $x^* = 1686$ cylinders. Note that the optimum value of the exponent $r$ is not $\frac{1}{2}$ as expected from constant acceleration/deceleration models, and frequently used in disk performance literature.

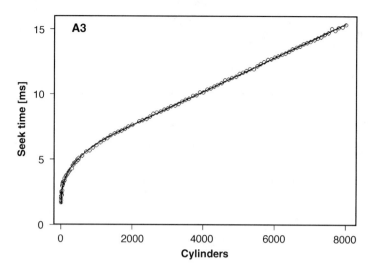

**FIGURE 8.4** Four-parameter exponential seek time model of the Quantum Atlas III disk (based on DiskSim measurements of G.R. Ganger available at http://www.ece.cmu.edu/~ganger.) (From Dujmovic, J. and Tomasevich, D., *Proc. CMG*, 2001, Anaheim, CA. With permission.)

The mean seek time for accessing a file (or database) occupying $N$ adjacent cylinders is

$$\bar{T}_{seek}(N) = \begin{cases} \dfrac{2}{N^2} \displaystyle\int_0^N T(z)(N-z)dz, & N \le x^* \\[3mm] \dfrac{2}{N^2}\left[\displaystyle\int_0^{x^*} T(z)(N-z)dz + \displaystyle\int_{x^*}^N T(z)(N-z)dz\right], & N \ge x^* \end{cases}$$

The final result is:

$$\bar{T}_{seek}(N) = \begin{cases} \dfrac{2(N-1)^2}{N^2}\left[\dfrac{t}{2} + \dfrac{c(N-1)^r}{(r+1)(r+2)}\right], & N \le x^* \\[3mm] \dfrac{2}{N^2}\left[\dfrac{t(x^*-1)(2N-x^*-1)}{2} + \dfrac{c(x^*-1)^{r+1}[N(r+2)-x^*(r+1)-1]}{(r+1)(r+2)} + \dfrac{(N-x^*)^2(AN+2Ax^*+3B)}{6}\right], & N \ge x^* \end{cases}$$

Here $A$ and $B$ are defined by formulas (8.1) and (8.2).

Numerical models based on best fit do not provide a direct correspondence between disk performance and physical attributes such as mass, force, acceleration, maximum speed, etc.; however, they are popular with many authors because of their low numerical errors. For example, Ruemmler and Wilkes [11] use the following simple model:

$$T(x) = \begin{cases} a + b\sqrt{x}, & \text{for short seeks} \quad (a, b = \text{const.}) \\ Ax + B, & \text{for long seeks} \quad (A, B = \text{const.}) \end{cases}$$

Similarly, Ng [9] uses the model

$$T(x) = a + b\sqrt{x} + c\log(d), \quad a, b, c = \text{const.}$$

where $d$ denotes the recording areal density in tracks per inch. Lee and Katz [6] propose a model having no linear segment:

$$T(x) = \begin{cases} 0, & x = 0 \\ A\sqrt{x-1} + B(x-1) + T_{\text{min seek}}, & x > 0 \end{cases}$$

In this model, $A$ and $B$ are constants and $T_{\text{min seek}}$ is the minimum seek time corresponding to the minimum nonzero number of cylinders $x = 1$. Finally, Shriver [12] suggests slightly higher model granularity:

$$T(x) = \begin{cases} 0, & x = 0 \\ a + b\sqrt{x}, & 0 < x \leq x_1 \\ c + d\sqrt{x}, & x_1 < x \leq x_2 \\ Ax + B, & x > x_2 \end{cases} \quad (a, b, c, d, A, B = \text{const.})$$

The accuracy of these models is less than the accuracy of the 4-parameter exponential model.

## A Simple Model of Cached Disk Access Time

Modern operating systems use the main memory as a disk cache. In such cases disk access is illustrated in Fig. 8.5. If data are not in the cache, it is necessary to fetch data from the disk. This causes one or more disk accesses, taking time $T_{\text{disk}}$. If data are already in the cache, access is very fast, $T_{\text{cache}} \ll T_{\text{disk}}$. The mean access time $T_a$ of a cached disk depends on the cache hit probability $p$:

$$T_a = pT_{\text{cache}} + (1-p)(T_{\text{cache}} + T_{\text{disk}}) = T_{\text{cache}} + (1-p)T_{\text{disk}}$$

Probability $p$ depends on the data access locality properties and for a large number of accesses, assuming $C < F$, it satisfies the inequality $p \geq C/F$. The lowest hit ratio, $p = C/F$, is obtained in the case of minimum locality, i.e., in the case of uniform distribution of disk accesses. If $T_{\text{disk}} = T_{\text{access}}$, the upper bound of the cached disk access time is a function of the disk file size $F$, which can be modeled as follows:

$$T_a(F) = \begin{cases} T_{\text{cache}}, & F \leq C \\ T_{\text{cache}} + \left(1 - \dfrac{C}{F}\right)\left[ T_{\text{max seek}} \left(\dfrac{F}{F_{\text{max}}}\right)^r + \dfrac{30}{N_{\text{rev}}} \right], & F \geq C \end{cases}$$

This model has four adjustable parameters: $T_{\text{cache}}$, $C$, $r$, and $T_{\text{max seek}}$. Two adjustable parameters ($T_{\text{cache}}$ and $C$) represent the disk cache, and two parameters ($T_{\text{max seek}}$ and $r$) represent the seek time model. The simple 2-parameter seek time model $T = T_{\text{max seek}}(F/F_{\text{max}})^r$ yields sufficiently good accuracy for the most frequent cases of relatively small databases where the seek time is nonlinear. For example, in the case of the Quantum Atlas III disk, the nonlinear segment corresponds to data sizes up to $(1686/8057) \cdot 9.1$ GB = 1.9 GB. For larger databases (that require the linear segment of the seek time characteristic) we can apply the 3- and 4-parameter models described in the previous section.

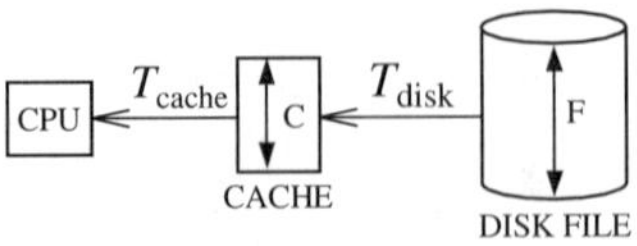

FIGURE 8.5    File access using a disk cache. (From Dujmovic, J., Tomasevich, D., and Au-Yeung, M., *Proc. CMG,* 1999, Reno, NV. With permission.)

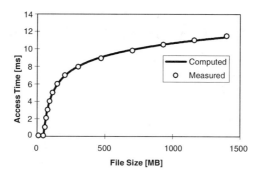

**FIGURE 8.6**   Measured and computed access times. (From Dujmovic, J., Tomasevich, D., and Au-Yeung, M., *Proc. CMG,* 1999, Reno, NV. With permission.)

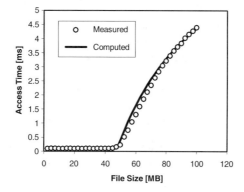

**FIGURE 8.7**   Measured and computed access times showing the cache size of 48 MB (magnified detail of Fig. 8.5). (From Dujmovic, J., Tomasevich, D., and Au-Yeung, M., *Proc. CMG,* 1999, Reno, NV. With permission.)

If we measure disk access times $T_1,\ldots,T_n$ for a sequence of file sizes $F_1,\ldots,F_n$, the calibration of the above model can be performed by selecting the optimum values of $T_{\text{cache}}$, $C$, $r$, and $T_{\text{max seek}}$, which minimize the criterion function

$$E(T_{\text{cache}}, C, r, T_{\text{max seek}}) = \sum_{i=1}^{n} |T_i - T_a(F_i, T_{\text{cache}}, C, r, T_{\text{max seek}})|^q$$

The exponent $q$ is usually selected in the range $1 \leq q \leq 4$, where larger values are selected in cases where the primary goal is to minimize large errors. The minimization can be performed using the traditional Nelder–Mead simplex method [8].

A verification of this model is shown in Figs. 8.6 and 8.7 for a 300 MHz PC with 64 MB of memory, Windows NT 4.5, and a 4-GB SCSI disk that has $N_{\text{nev}} = 7200$ rev/min. The resulting parameters are $T_{\text{cache}} = 96\ \mu s$, $C = 48$ MB, $r = 0.234$, and $T_{\text{max seek}}$ 7.51 ms for $F_{\text{max}} = 1400$ MB. In the majority of 245 measured points (only some of them shown in Fig. 8.6) the mean relative error of this model is less than 1%.

## Disk Access Optimization Model

The disk access time model described in the previous section assumes a single program that generates disk access requests. In such a case, all requests are served strictly in the order they are submitted and disk access optimization is not possible; however, in the case of multiprogramming, the disk queue contains multiple requests independently generated by various programs. It is possible to use a disk access optimization algorithm that increases the global disk throughput by minimizing the movement of I/O head mechanism. The simplest such an algorithm is the "shortest seek time first" (SSTF) [13,14], which can be easily analyzed.

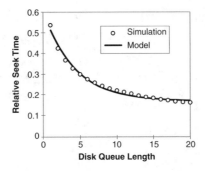

**FIGURE 8.8**  Comparing simulation and analytic models of seek time. (From Dujmovic, J., Tomasevich, D., and Au-Yeung, M., *Proc. CMG*, 1999, Reno, NV. With permission.)

A simulator for the SSTF technique can be easily written according to the following algorithm:

1. Create a disk queue with $n$ random requests.
2. Select an arbitrary initial position of disk heads.
3. Find the request that yields the shortest distance $x$.
4. Compute the relative seek time $t = \sqrt{x/x_{max}}$ (this is a normalized time with a maximum value of 1).
5. The position of the processed request becomes the new position of the disk head mechanism.
6. Replace the processed request with a new random request.
7. Repeat steps 3–6 many times and compute the average relative (normalized) seek time.

The results of the simulation yield a decreasing relative seek time function presented in Fig. 8.8. Taking into account this function, the optimized disk access time can be well approximated, using the following model:

$$T_a(n) = t_{min} + (t_{max} - t_{min})e^{\alpha(n-1)}$$

The parameter $t_{min}$ is introduced to reflect the mean latency time. The value of $t_{max}$ corresponds to the maximum seek distance. The quality of this approximation is rather good, as shown in Fig. 8.8. The exponent $\alpha$ has a negative value, which reflects the quality of the optimization algorithm (as the quality of optimization increases, so does the absolute value of the exponent $\alpha$).

## Disk Service Time Model

Generally, the mean disk access time is a decreasing function of the disk queue length and is an increasing function of file size. If we want to combine the disk cache access model and the disk access optimization model, the result can be the following formula for load dependent and cached disks:

$$T_d(F, n) = \begin{cases} T_{cache}, & F \leq C \\ T_{cache} + \dfrac{F-C}{F}\left[T_{max\,seek}\left(\dfrac{F}{F_{max}}\right)^r e^{\alpha(n-1)} + \dfrac{30}{N_{rev}}\right], & F \geq C \end{cases}$$

The disk service time is different from the mean disk access time. Disk service time is affected by caching and access optimization, but it includes only the cases of actual disk access, excluding the cases of fetching data from the cache without disk access. Consequently, we propose the following model of the load dependent cached disk service time:

$$S_d(F, n) = T_{max\,seek}\left(\dfrac{F}{F_{max}}\right)^r e^{\alpha(n-1)} + \dfrac{30}{N_{rev}} + t_0, \quad F > C$$

**TABLE 8.1**  Classification of Eight Basic Disk Workloads

| Workload Type | Access Method (S = Sequential, R = Random) | Operation (W = Write, R = Read) | Load balance (S = Symmetric, A = Asymmetric) |
|---|---|---|---|
| 0 | S | W | S |
| 1 | S | W | A |
| 2 | S | R | S |
| 3 | S | R | A |
| 4 | R | W | S |
| 5 | R | W | A |
| 6 | R | R | S |
| 7 | R | R | A |

From Dujmovic, J., Tomasevich, D., and Au-Yeung, M., *Proc. CMG,* 1999, Reno, NV. With permission.

The first term in this model reflects the optimized seek time, the second term is the latency time, and the third term reflects the data transfer time and related cache I/O operations. This model is successfully applied for the analysis of a cached system presented in the "MVA Models and Their Limitations" section. The presented load dependent service time model can also be developed using other seek time models described in the section on "Numerical Computation of the Average Seek Time."

## Disk Subsystem Benchmark Workload

Disk subsystem workloads always lie between two obvious extremes: sequential access and uniformly distributed random access. Sequential access is more frequent, but random access is more general because it includes seek operations. Similarly, benchmark workloads must balance write and read operations. This balance is based on two facts: (1) read operations are generally more frequent than write operations and (2) write operations are less desirable in benchmarking because performance results are rather sensitive to tuning of disk formats and/or blocking factors, which frequently yields questionable results. Finally, the benchmark workload can be symmetric (i.e., balanced load, where all disks have the same load) and asymmetric (usually with bottleneck disks). Symmetric loads are more desirable in benchmarking because they better expose the capabilities of disk controller(s) and central processor(s).

A simple classification of disk workloads is presented in Table 8.1. Workload type 0 or 1 can be used for creating files that are then processed by other workloads. Workload types 2 and 3 are used for benchmarking systems using sequential access. Similarly, workloads 6 and 7 are used for benchmarking, using random access. We use workload type 6 as the basic workload for measurement of disk subsystem performance. It consists of $n$ copies of a disk random access program DRAN that uniformly accesses files that are uniformly distributed over all disk units [3]. This is a simple balanced workload that should properly reflect disk subsystem performance and be suitable for both performance measurement and modeling. Typical results of running the DRAN workload type 6 are presented in Fig. 8.9.

The analyzed computer, VAX 8650, has 14 disk units (RA 81) and one or two disk controllers (HSC 50). Each program generates 7000 visits to the central processor, and 7000 visits to disks. Since the disk load is uniformly distributed, each program creates 500 accesses to each disk. In the case of a single program, the measured processor time for a single disk controller is 4.99 s and the total elapsed time is 163.16 s. The processor time can be interpreted as processor demand $D_p = 4.99$ s. A queuing model of this system, in the case of two disk controllers, is shown in Fig. 8.10. The next step is to develop an analytic model for the analysis of this system.

## MVA Models and Their Limitations

Let us introduce the following variables:

$N$ = degree of multiprogramming (number of jobs in the system)

$K$ = number of service centers (processors, disks, and disk controllers)

$P_k(j|n)$ = probability that there are $j$ jobs at the $k$th service center, if the total number of jobs in the system (degree of multiprogramming) is $n$

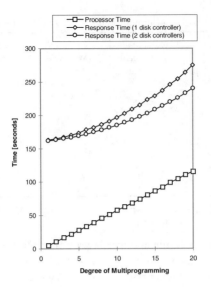

**FIGURE 8.9**  Measured response times for VAX 8650. (From Dujmovic, J., Tomasevich, D., and Au-Yeung, M., *Proc. CMG*, 1999, Reno, NV. With permission.)

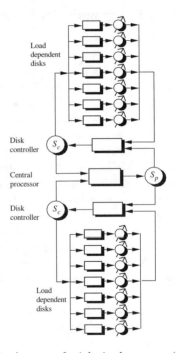

**FIGURE 8.10**  A queuing model of VAX 8650. (From Dujmovic, J., Tomasevich, D., and Au-Yeung, M., *Proc. CMG*, 1999, Reno, NV. With permission.)

$R_k(n)$ = response time of the $k$th service center in the case of $n$ jobs in the system ($n = 1, \ldots, N$)

$R(n)$ = response time of the whole system

$U_k(n)$ = utilization of the $k$th server

$Q_k(n)$ = queue length at the $k$th server

$S_k(j)$ = service time of the $k$th server if $j$ jobs are in the queue; if the $k$th server is load independent then $S_k(j) = S_k = \text{const.}$, $k \in \{1, \ldots, K\}$

$V_k$ = number of visits to the $k$th server per job

$D_k$ = service demand for the $k$th server; in the case of load-independent servers $D_k = V_k S_k$

$X(n)$ = system throughput (completed jobs per time unit)

$X_k(n)$ = throughput of the $k$th service center when there are $n$ jobs in the system: $X_k(n) = V_k X(n)$

The traditional load independent mean value analysis program (LIMVA) is based on assumption that the service times of all servers are constant. The goal of MVA models is to compute system response times, utilizations, and throughputs. Following is the traditional LIMVA model:

$$Q_k(0) = 0, \quad k = 1,\ldots,K$$

**for** $n = 1$ **to** $N$ **do**

$$R_k(n) = S_k[1 + Q_k(n-1)], \quad k = 1,\ldots,K$$

$$R(n) = \sum_{k=1}^{K} V_k R_k(n)$$

$$X(n) = n/R(n)$$

$$X_k(n) = V_k X(n), \quad k = 1,\ldots,K$$

$$U_k(n) = S_k X_k(n) = D_k X(n), \quad k = 1,\ldots,K$$

$$Q_k(n) = V_k X(n) R_k(n), \quad k = 1,\ldots,K$$

**end_for**

For perfectly balanced systems where all demands are equal ($D = V_1 S_1 = V_2 S_2 = \cdots = V_K S_K$), this algorithm yields equal distribution of jobs in service centers

$$Q_k(n) = n/K, \quad k = 1,\ldots,K$$

This is a consequence of equal residence times:

$$V_k R_k(n) = D_k[1 + Q_k(n-1)] = D[1 + (n-1)/K], \quad k = 1,\ldots,K$$

and their use for computing $Q_k(n) = V_k X(n) R_k(n)$. Furthermore, this yields linear response times, and other relations:

$$R(n) = KV_k R_k(n) = (n-1+K)D$$

$$R_k(n) = (n-1+K)S_k/K, \quad k = 1,\ldots,K$$

$$X(n) = n/(n-1+K)D$$

$$X_k(n) = n/(n-1+K)S_k, \quad k = 1,\ldots,K$$

$$U_k(n) = n/(n-1+K), \quad k = 1,\ldots,K$$

Of course, in a general case we have different demands, and the response time is no longer linear. Unfortunately, the nature of the LIMVA model is essentially quasi-linear. Even for different demands the response time curves remain similar to straight lines.

Limitations of the LIMVA model are exemplified in Fig. 8.11. In this case the processor service time obtained from measurements is $S_p = 825$ $\mu$s, the number of processor visits per job is $V_p = 7000$, yielding processor demand $D_p = 5.775$ s. The number of disks is 14 and the number of disk visits per job is $V_d = 7000/14 = 500$. The available resources include the central processor and 14 equally loaded disk units. A spectrum of LIMVA models can be obtained for disk service times varying in the range 12 ms $\leq S_d \leq$ 24 ms,

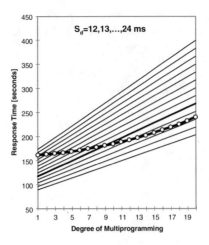

**FIGURE 8.11**   A family of LIMVA models and measured VAX 8650 response time. (From Dujmovic, J., Tomasevich, D., and Au-Yeung, M., *Proc. CMG,* 1999, Reno, NV. With permission.)

and yielding disk demands in the range, $6 \text{ s} \leq D_d \leq 12 \text{ s}$. The corresponding response times presented in Fig. 8.11 are, in the whole range, practically straight lines and obviously inadequate for representing the measured response time function. The best approximation would be obtained for $S_d = 16$ ms, but this approximation is equally poor as the attempt to use a straight line to approximate a parabola. The nature of the dynamic behavior of VAX 8650 is quite different from what can be modeled by LIMVA regardless how well we adjust its parameters. Thus, a more flexible model is needed. Taking into account that disks are never load-independent, because they regularly use either access optimization or access optimization and caching, we hope that better results should be expected from load dependent MVA models.

For batch systems we apply the load dependent mean value analysis model (LDMVA) introduced in [1] (see also [5,7]):

$$P_k(0|0) = 1, \quad k = 1,\ldots,K$$

**for** $n = 1$ **to** $N$ **do**

$$R_k(n) = \sum_{j=1}^{n} j S_k(j) P_k(j-1|n-1), \quad k = 1,\ldots,K$$

$$R(n) = \sum_{k=1}^{K} V_k R_k(n)$$

$$X(n) = n/R(n)$$

$$P_k(j/n) = \begin{cases} V_k S_k(j) X(n) P_k(j-1|n-1), & j = 1,\ldots,n \\ 1 - \sum_{i=1}^{n} P_k(j|n), & j = 0 \end{cases} \quad k = 1,\ldots,K$$

$$Q_k(n) = \sum_{j=1}^{n} j P_k(j|n), \quad k = 1,\ldots,K$$

$$Q_k(n) = 1 - P_k(0|n), \quad k = 1,\ldots,K$$

**end_for**

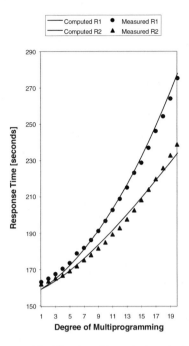

**FIGURE 8.12**    The results of LDMVA model calibration. (From Dujmovic, J., Tomasevich, D., and Au-Yeung, M., *Proc. CMG*, 1999, Reno, NV. With permission.)

## Experimental Results for LDMVA Model of a Disk Subsystem with Access Optimization

Let us now apply the LDMVA model for the VAX 8650 disk subsystem modeling. The measured response and processor times can be used to adjust parameters of the LDMVA model. This is called calibration of the queuing model. The calibration process is based on measured response times $T_{m1}(n)$ and $T_{m2}(n)$, which correspond to systems with one and two disk controllers. Suppose that the load dependent disk service time is approximated by $S_d(n) = t_{min} + (t_{max} - t_{min})e^{\alpha(n-1)}$. The parameters of the LDMVA model are $t_{min}$, $t_{max}$, $\alpha$, $S_p$, $S_c$. Let $R_{c1}(n, t_{min}, t_{max}, \alpha, S_p, S_c)$ and $R_{c2}(n, t_{min}, t_{max}, \alpha, S_p, S_c)$ be the response times computed from the LDMVA model, respectively using one and two controllers. The model calibration procedure is based on the minimization of the compound criterion function

$$C(t_{min}, t_{max}, a, S_p, S_c)$$

$$= \max\left(\sum_{i=1}^{n}[T_{m1}(n) - R_{c1}(t_{min} \cdot t_{max}, a, S_p, S_c)]^2, \sum_{i=1}^{n}[T_{m2}(n) - R_{c2}(t_{min} \cdot t_{max}, a, S_p, S_c)]^2\right)$$

The results of calibration performed using the Nelder-Mead simplex method [8] are the following values of parameters: $t_{min}$ = 11.5 ms, $t_{max}$ = 20 ms, $a$ = −4, $S_p$ = 0.822 ms, and $S_c$ = 0.89 ms. The mean relative error for all presented points is 1% (Fig. 8.12). At this level of description error it is realistic to expect good prediction results.

## Experimental Results for LDMVA Model of a Disk Subsystem with Caching and Access Optimization

In this experiment, we use the same 300 MHz PC presented in the "Numerical Computation of the Average Seek Time" section and Figs. 8.6 and 8.7. Its memory capacity is 64 MB with two disk units, and the disk cache size under Windows NT 4.5 is $C$ = 48 MB. The measured response times for DRAN

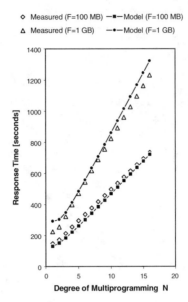

**FIGURE 8.13**   Measured response times and the results of the LDMVA model. (From Dujmovic, J., Tomasevich, D., and Au-Yeung, M., *Proc. CMG,* 1999, Reno, NV. With permission.)

benchmarks accessing a 100 MB file and 1 GB file are presented in Fig. 8.13. The LDMVA model we used is based on measured disk parameters reported in the "Numerical Computation of the Average Seek Time" section and on the disk service time model $S_d(F, n)$ proposed in the section on "Disk Access Optimization Model." Disk accesses to a file of size $F$ occur with the probability $(F - C)/F$ and cache accesses with the probability $C/F$. The number of disk visits $V_d$ now depends on the number of processor visits $V_p$ and the size of file. If the number of disks is $k$ then $V_d(F) = V_p(F - C)/kF$. Therefore, the disk cache causes both the disk service time and the number of visits to be functions of the file size. Processor service time is not constant. For cache accesses it can be expressed as $S_p = t_p^{prog} + t_p^{cache}$ and for disk accesses as $S_p = t_p^{prog} + t_p^{cache} + t_p^{disk}$, where the three components correspond to the processor activity for the benchmark program, cache access, and serving the file management system during the disk access. The mean service time is $S_p = t_p^{prog} + t_p^{cache} + t_p^{disk}(F - C)/F$. The calibrated model in Fig. 8.13 has the mean modeling error of 7.4%.

## Predictive Power of Queuing Models

All queuing models have adjustable parameters (e.g., the processor and disk service times). The default values of these parameters, taken from manufacturers specifications, regularly yield rather large prediction errors. These errors can be reduced by corrections of parameters in a calibration process. During the model calibration the parameters are adjusted to minimize the difference between the measured values and computed values from the model. In essence, this is just a standard curve fitting process, and the resulting low description error is not necessarily a proof of the quality of the model. The only way to assess the quality of the model is through the analysis of the prediction errors.

Let $n$ be the number of measured response times $R_1,\ldots,R_n$ and let us use the first $m$ measured values, $R_1,\ldots,R_m$, $m \leq n$, for the model calibration. The indicator $p = 100\ m/n$ shows the percent of values used for calibration. Let $e(p)$ denote the average relative error between the measured vales and the values of the calibrated model for the whole range of $n$ data points. Generally, $e(p)$ is expected to be a decreasing function, and three typical such functions are presented in Figs. 8.14 and 8.15.

In all cases, we measured the processor time and used this value in our LDMVA model. The calibration process included three parameters of the disk subsystem (minimum service time $t_{min}$, maximum service time $t_{max}$, and the exponent $\alpha$ introduced in the section on "A Simple Model of Cached Disk Access Time"). Consequently, the $e(p)$ function starts with $m = 3$ points.

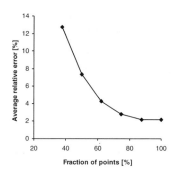

**FIGURE 8.14** Prediction errors $e(p)$ for VAX 11/785. (From Dujmovic, J., Tomasevich, D., and Au-Yeung, M., *Proc. CMG*, 1999, Reno, NV. With permission.)

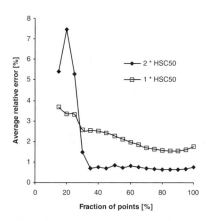

**FIGURE 8.15** Prediction errors $e(p)$ for VAX 8650. (From Dujmovic, J., Tomasevich, D., and Au-Yeung, M., *Proc. CMG*, 1999, Reno, NV. With permission.)

In the ideal theoretical case of a perfect model, we expect $e(p) = 0$ for all $m \geq 3$. Good predictive power of a model is indicated by $e(p)$, approaching a constant low value as soon as possible. Consequently, the predictive power is related to the smallest value of $p$ after which $e(p)$ remains in the $\delta$ neighborhood of the minimum $e_{\min} = \min\limits_{p \leq 100\%} e(p)$. Let us denote this value as $p^*(\delta)$. In other words

$$e(p) > (1 + \delta)e_{\min}, \quad \forall\, p < p^*(\delta)$$

Now, we can define the following predictive power quality indicator:

$$q(\delta) = \frac{1 - p^*(\delta)}{1 - p_{\min}} 100\%$$

where $p_{\min}$ denotes the minimum value of $p$ necessary for calibration (in our examples $p_{\min}$ corresponds to $m = 3$).

The case in Fig. 8.14 reaches the minimum error $e(100\%) = 2.16\%$. Let us take $\delta = 0.2$. Then we have $(1 + \delta)e_{\min} = 2.59\%$, $p^*(0.2) = 0.875(87.5\%)$, and the resulting predictive power is rather low:

$$q(0.2) = \frac{1 - 0.875}{1 - 0.375} 100\% = 20\%$$

In the case of Fig. 8.15, the model with 1 HSC50 disk controller yields $e_{min} = 1.53\%$, and for $\delta = 0.2$ we have:

$$(1 + \delta)e_{min} = 1.84\%, \quad p^*(0.2) = 0.7, \quad q(0.2) = 35.3\%$$

Finally, the predictive power in the case with two HSC50 disk controllers is much better: we have $e_{min} = 0.64\%$ yielding

$$(1 + \delta)e_{min} = 0.77\%, \quad p^*(0.2) = 0.35, \quad q(0.2) = 76.5\%$$

## Conclusions

Even in cases of fully controlled simple synthetic workloads, the performance modeling of disk subsystems is not a simple task. Basic popular load independent queuing models (load independent convolution algorithm or MVA) cannot be used for modeling modern disk subsystems, which use caching and disk access optimization. The use of load dependent MVA models is rather efficient and we proposed models for optimized disk access, cached disk access, and combined optimized and cached disk access. Presented models need a careful calibration procedure. In the majority of cases based on symmetric random disk accesses the modeling errors for optimized disk access were less than 2%. In more complex cases with optimized disk accesses and caching, our models regularly achieve errors below 10%. Experimental verification of our models has been successfully performed in both VAX/VMS and PC/NT environments.

## References

1. Basket, F., K. Chandy, R. Munz, and F. Palacios, Open, Closed, and Mixed Networks of Queues with Different Classes of Customers. *Journal of the ACM,* Vol. 22, No. 2, pp. 248–260, April 1975.
2. Buzen, J.P., Computational Algorithms for Closed Queueing Networks with Exponential Servers. *Communications of the ACM,* Vol. 16, No. 9, pp. 527–531, September 1973.
3. Dujmovic, J.J., Multiprogramming Efficiency Analysis for Computer Evaluation and Selection Studies. *Proceedings of the 11th International Symposium Computer at the University,* 1989.
4. IBM, *Hard disk drive specifications—Deskstar 60GPX.* S07N-4780-02, Publication #2818, February 1, 2001.
5. Jain, R., *The Art of Computer System Performance Analysis.* John Wiley, New York 1991.
6. Lee, E.K. and R.H. Katz, *An Analytic Performance Model of Disk Arrays.* Sigmetrics '93 Proceedings, pp. 98–109, 1993.
7. Menasce, D., V. Almeida, and L. Dowdy, *Capacity Planning and Performance Modeling.* Prentice-Hall, 1994.
8. Nelder, J.A. and R. Mead, *A Simplex Method for Function Minimization.* The Computer Journal, Vol. 7, No. 4, pp. 308–313, 1965.
9. Ng, S.W., *Advances in Disk Technology: Performance Issues.* Computer, pp. 75–81, May 1998.
10. Reiser, M. and S.S. Lavenberg, *Mean-Value Analysis of Closed Multichain Queueing Networks.* Journal of the ACM, Vol. 27, No. 2, pp. 313–322, 1980.
11. Ruemmler, C. and J. Wilkes, *An Introduction to Disk Drive Modeling.* Computer, pp. 17–28, March 1994.
12. Shriver, E., *Performance Modeling for Realistic Storage Devices.* PhD Thesis, Department of Computer Science, New York University, May 1997.
13. Silbershatz, A. and P.B. Galvin, *Operating System Concepts.* Addison–Wesley, Reading, MA 1994.
14. Worthington, B.L., G.R. Ganger, and Y.N. Patt, *Scheduling Algorithms for Modern Disk Drives.* Proceedings of SIGMETRICS'94, pp. 241–251, 1994.
15. Worthington, B.L., G.R. Ganger, Y.N. Patt, and J. Wilkes, *On-Line Extraction of SCSI Disk Drive Parameters.* Proceedings of SIGMETRICS'95, pp. 146–156, 1995.

# 8.2 Performance Evaluation: Techniques, Tools, and Benchmarks

*Lizy Kurian John*

## Introduction

State-of-the-art high performance microprocessors contain tens of millions of transistors and operate at frequencies close to 2 GHz. These processors perform several tasks in overlap, employ significant amounts of speculation and out-of-order execution, and other microarchitectural techniques, and are true marvels of engineering. Designing and evaluating these microprocessors is a major challenge, especially considering the fact that one second of program execution on these processors involves several billion instructions and analyzing one second of execution may involve dealing with tens of billion pieces of information.

In general, design of microprocessors and computer systems involves several steps (i) understanding applications and workloads that the systems will be running, (ii) innovating potential designs, (iii) evaluating performance of the candidate designs, and (iv) selecting the best design. The large number of potential designs and the constantly evolving nature of workloads have resulted in designs being largely adhoc. In this article, we investigate major techniques used in the performance evaluation process.

It should be noted that performance evaluation is needed at several stages of the design. In early stages, when the design is being conceived, performance evaluation is used to make early design tradeoffs. Usually, this is accomplished by simulation models, because building prototypes of state-of-the-art microprocessors is expensive and time consuming. Several design decisions are made before any prototyping is done. Once the design is finalized and is being implemented, simulation is used to evaluate functionality and performance of subsystems. Later, performance measurement is done after the product is available in order to understand the performance of the actual system to various real world workloads and to identify modifications to incorporate in future designs.

Performance evaluation can be classified into performance modeling and performance measurement, as illustrated in Table 8.2. Performance measurement is possible only if the system of interest is available for measurement and only if one has access to the parameters of interest. Performance measurement may further be classified into on-chip hardware monitoring, off-chip hardware monitoring, software monitoring, and microcoded instrumentation. Performance modeling is typically used when actual systems are not available for measurement or, if the actual systems do not have test points to measure every detail of interest. Performance modeling may further be classified into simulation modeling and analytical modeling. Simulation models may further be classified into numerous categories depending

**TABLE 8.2**  A Classification of Performance Evaluation Techniques

| | |
|---|---|
| Performance measurement | Microprocessor on-chip performance monitoring counters |
| | Off-chip hardware monitoring |
| | Software monitoring |
| | Micro-coded instrumentation |
| Performance modeling | Simulation |
| |    Trace driven simulation |
| |    Execution driven simulation |
| |    Complete system simulation |
| |    Event driven simulation |
| |    Software profiling |
| | Analytical modeling |
| |    Probabilistic models |
| |    Queuing models |
| |    Markov models |
| |    Petri net models |

on the mode/level of detail of simulation. Analytical models use probabilistic models, queueing theory, Markov models or Petri nets.

Performance modeling/measurement techniques and tools should possess several desirable features.

- They must be accurate. It is easy to build models that are heavily sanitized, however, such models will not be accurate.
- They must be noninvasive. The measurement process must not alter the system or degrade the system's performance.
- They must not be expensive. Building the performance measurement facility should not cost significant amount of time or money.
- They must be easy to change or extend. Microprocessors and computer systems constantly undergo changes and it must be easy to extend the modeling/measurement facility to include the upgraded system.
- They must not need source code of applications. If tools and techniques necessitate source code, it will not be possible to evaluate commercial applications where source is not often available.
- They should measure all activity including kernel and user activity. Often it is easy to build tools that measure only user activity. This was acceptable in traditional scientific and engineering workloads; however, in database, Web server, and Java workloads, significant operating system activity exists, and it is important to build tools that measure operating system activity as well.
- They should be capable of measuring a wide variety of applications including those that use signals, exceptions, and DLLs (dynamically linked libraries).
- They should be user-friendly. Hard-to-use tools often are underutilized. Hard-to-use tools also result in more user error.
- They should be fast. If a performance model is very slow, long-running workloads, which take hours to run, may take days or weeks to run on the model. If an instrumentation tool is slow, it can be invasive.
- Models should provide control over aspects that are measured. It should be possible to selectively measure what is required.
- Models and tools should handle multiprocessor systems and multithreaded applications. Dual and quad-processor systems are very common nowadays. Applications are becoming increasingly multithreaded especially with the advent of Java, and it is important that the tool handles these.
- It will be desirable for a performance evaluation technique to be able to evaluate the performance of systems that are not yet built.

Many of these requirements are often conflicting. For instance, it is difficult for a mechanism to be fast and accurate. Consider mathematical models. They are fast, although several simplifying assumptions go into their creation, and often they are not accurate. Similarly, it is difficult for a tool to be noninvasive and user-friendly. Many users like graphical user interfaces (GUIs), however, most instrumentation and simulation tools with GUIs are slow and invasive.

Benchmarks and metrics to be used for performance evaluation have always been interesting and controversial issues. There has been a lot of improvement in benchmark suites since 1988. Before that computer performance evaluation has been largely with small benchmarks such as kernels extracted from applications (e.g., Lawrence Livermore Loops), Dhrystone and Whetstone benchmarks, Linpack, Sorting, Sieve of Eratosthenes, 8-queens problem, Tower of Hanoi, etc. [1]. The Standard Performance Evaluation Cooperative (SPEC) consortium and the Transactions Processing Council (TPC) formed in 1988 have made available several benchmark suites and benchmarking guidelines to improve the quality of benchmarking. Several state-of-the-art benchmark suites are described in the "Workloads and Benchmarks" section.

Another important issue in performance evaluation is the choice of performance metric. For a system level designer, execution time and throughput are two important performance metrics. Execution time is generally the most important measure of performance. Execution time is the product of the number of instructions, cycles per instruction (CPI), and the clock period. Throughput of an application is a more important metric, especially in server systems. In servers that serve the banking industry, airline industry, or other similar businesses, what is important is the number of transactions that could be completed in unit time. Such servers, typically called transaction processing systems use transactions per minute (tpm) as a performance metric. Millions of instructions per second (MIPS) and million of floating point operations per second (MFLOPS) were very popular measures of performance in the past. Both of these are very simple and straightforward to understand and hence have been used often, however, they do not contain all three components of program execution time and hence are incomplete measures of performance. Several low level metrics are of interest to microprocessor designers, in order to help them identify performance bottlenecks and tune their designs. Cache hit ratios, branch misprediction ratios, number of off-chip memory accesses, etc. are examples of such measures.

Another major problem is the issue of reporting performance with a single number. A single number is easy to understand and easy to be used by the trade press. Use of several benchmarks also makes it necessary to find some kind of a mean. Arithmetic mean, geometric mean, and harmonic mean are three ways of finding the central tendency of a group of numbers; however, it should be noted that each of these means should be used in appropriate conditions depending on the nature of the numbers which need to be averaged. Simple arithmetic mean can be used to find average execution time from a set of execution times. Geometric mean can be used to find the central tendency of metrics that are in the form of ratios (e.g., speedup) and harmonic mean can be used to find the central tendency of measures that are in the form of a rate (e.g., throughput). Cragon [2] and Smith [3] discuss the use of the appropriate mean for a given set of data. Cragon [2] and Patterson and Hennessy [4] illustrate several mistakes one could possibly make while finding a single performance number.

The rest of this chapter section is organized as follows. "Performance Measurement" describes performance measurement techniques including hardware on-chip performance monitoring counters on microprocessors. "Performance Modeling" describes simulation and analytical modeling of microprocessors and computer systems. "Workloads and Benchmarks" presents several state-of-the-art benchmark suites for a variety of workloads. Due to space limitations, we describe some typical examples of tools and techniques and provide the reader with pointers for more information.

## Performance Measurement

Performance measurement is used for understanding systems that are already built or prototyped. Performance measurement can serve two major purposes: tune this system or systems to be built and tune the application if source code and algorithms can still be changed. Essentially, the process involves (i) understanding the bottlenecks in the system that has been built, (ii) understanding the applications that are running on the system and the match between the features of the system and the characteristics of the workload, and (iii) innovating design features that will exploit the workload features. Performance measurement can be done via the following means:

- Microprocessor on-chip performance monitoring counters
- Off-chip hardware monitoring
- Software monitoring
- Microcoded instrumentation

### On-Chip Performance Monitoring Counters

All state-of-the-art high performance microprocessors including Intel's Pentium III and Pentium IV, IBM's POWER 3 and POWER 4 processors, AMD's Athlon, Compaq's Alpha, and Sun's UltraSPARC processors incorporate on-chip performance monitoring counters, which can be used to understand performance of these microprocessors, while they run complex, real-world workloads. This ability has overcome a serious limitation of simulators, that they often could not execute complex workloads. Now, complex run-time systems involving multiple software applications can be evaluated and monitored very closely.

**TABLE 8.3**    Examples of Events That Can Be Measured Using Performance Monitoring Counters on an Intel Pentium III Processor

| Event | Description of Event | Event Number in Hex |
|-------|---------------------|---------------------|
| DATA_MEM_REFS | All loads and stores from/to memory | 43H |
| DCU_LINES_IN | Total lines allocated in the data cache unit | 45H |
| IFU_IFETCH | Number of instruction fetches (cacheable and uncacheable) | 80H |
| IFU_IFETCH_MISS | Number of instruction fetch misses | 81H |
| ITLB_MISS | Number of Instruction TLB misses | 85H |
| IFU_MEM_STALL | Number of cycles instruction fetch is stalled for any reason | 86H |
| L2_IFETCH | Number of L2 instruction fetches | 28H |
| L2_LD | Number of L2 data loads | 29H |
| L2_ST | Number of L2 data stores | 2AH |
| L2_LINES_IN | Number of lines allocated in the L2 | 24H |
| L2_RQSTS | Total number of L2 requests | 2EH |
| INST_RETIRED | Number of instructions retired | C0H |
| UOPS_RETIRED | Number of micro-operations retired | C2H |
| INST_DECODED | Number of instructions decoded | D0H |
| RESOURCE_STALLS | Number of cycles in which there is a resource related stall | A2H |
| MMX_INSTR_EXEC | Number of MMX Instructions Executed | B0H |
| BR_INST_RETIRED | Number of branch instructions retired | C4H |
| BR_MISS_PRED_RETIRED | Number of mispredicted branches retired | C5H |
| BR_TAKEN_RETIRED | Number of taken branches retired | C9H |
| BR_INST_DECODED | Number of branch instructions decoded | E0H |
| BTB_MISSES | Number of branches for which BTB did not predict | E2H |

**TABLE 8.4**    Software Packages for Performance Counter Measurement

| Tool | Platform | Reference |
|------|----------|-----------|
| VTune | IA-32 | http://developer.intel.com/software/products/vtune/vtune_oview.htm |
| P6Perf | IA-32 | http://developer.intel.com/vtune/p6perf/index.htm |
| PMON | IA-32 | http://www.ece.utexas.edu/projects/ece/lca/pmon |
| DCPI | Alpha | http://www.research.digital.com/SRC/dcpi/ |
|  |  | http://www.research.compaq.com/SRC/dcpi/ |
| Perf-mon | UltraSPARC | http://www.sics.se/~mch/perf-monitor/index.html |

All microprocessor vendors nowadays release information on their performance monitoring counters, although they are not part of the architecture.

For illustration of on-chip performance monitoring, we use the Intel Pentium processors. The microprocessors in the Intel Pentium contain two performance monitoring counters. These counters can be read with special instructions (e.g., RDPMC) on the processor. The counters can be made to measure user and kernel activity in combination or in isolation. A variety of performance events can be measured using the counters [50]. For illustration of the nature of the events that can be measured, Table 8.3 lists a small subset of the events that can be measured on the Pentium III. Although more than 200 distinct events can be measured on the Pentium III, only two events can be measured simultaneously. For design simplicity, most microprocessors limit the number of events that can be simultaneously measured to 4 or 5. At times, certain events are restricted to be accessible only through a particular counter. These steps are necessary to reduce the overhead associated with on-chip performance monitoring. Performance counters do consume on-chip real estate. Unless carefully implemented, they can also impact the processor cycle time.

Several tools are available to measure performance using performance monitoring counters. Table 8.4 lists some of the available tools. Intel's *Vtune* software may be used to perform measurements using the Intel processor performance counters [5]. The *P6Perf* utility is a plug-in for Windows NT performance monitoring [6]. The Compaq DIGITAL Continuous Profiling Infrastructure (DCPI) is a very powerful tool to profile programs on the Alpha processors [7,8]. The performance monitor *perf-mon* is a small hack that uses the on-chip counters on UltraSPARC-I/II processors to gather statistics [9]. Packages like Vtune perform extensive post-processing and present data in graphical forms; however, extensive post-processing can sometimes result in tools that are somewhat invasive. *PMON* [10] is a counter reading software written by Juan Rubio of the Laboratory for Computer Architecture at the University of Texas. It provides a mechanism to read specified counters with minimal or no perceivable overhead. All these tools measure user and operating system activity. Since everything on a processor is counted, effort should be made to have minimal or no other undesired process running during experimentation. This type of performance measurement can be done on binaries, and no source code is desired.

## Off-Chip Hardware Measurement

Instrumentation using hardware means can also be done by attaching off-chip hardware, two examples of which are described in this section.

### SpeedTracer from AMD

AMD developed this hardware tracing platform to aid in the design of its x86 microprocessors. When an application is being traced, the tracer interrupts the processor on each instruction boundary. The state of the CPU is captured on each interrupt and then transferred to a separate control machine where the trace is stored. The trace contains virtually all valuable pieces of information for each instruction that executes on the processor. Operating system activity can also be traced; however, tracing in this manner can be invasive, and may slow down the processor. Although the processor is running slower, external events such as disk and memory accesses still happen in real time, thus looking very fast to the slowed-down processor. Usually, this issue is addressed by adjusting the timer interrupt frequency. Use of this performance monitoring facility can be seen in Merten [11] and Bhargava[12].

### Logic Analyzers

Poursepanj and Christie [13] use a Tektronix TLA 700 logic analyzer to analyze 3D graphics workloads on AMD-K6-2-based systems. Detailed logic analyzer traces are limited by restrictions on sizes and are typically used for the most important sections of the program under analysis. Preliminary coarse level analysis can be done by performance monitoring counters and software instrumentation. Poursepanj and Christie used logic analyzer traces for a few tens of frames, which covered a second or two of smooth motion [13].

## Software Monitoring

Software monitoring is often performed by utilizing architectural features such as a trap instruction or a breakpoint instruction on an actual system, or on a prototype. The VAX processor from Digital (now Compaq) had a T-bit that caused an exception after every instruction. Software monitoring used to be an important mode of performance evaluation before the advent of on-chip performance monitoring counters. The primary advantage of software monitoring is that it is easy to do. The primary disadvantage is that the instrumentation can slow down the application. The overhead of servicing the exception, switching to a data collection process, and performing the necessary tracing can slow down a program by more than 1000 times. Another disadvantage is that software monitoring systems, typically, only handle the user activity.

## Microcoded Instrumentation

Digital used microcoded instrumentation to obtain traces of VAX and Alpha architectures. The ATUM tool [14] used extensively by Digital in the late 1980s and early 1990s uses microcoded instrumentation. This is a technique lying between trapping information on each instruction, using hardware interrupts (traps) or software traps. The tracing system essentially modified the VAX microcode to record all instruction and data references in a reserved portion of memory. Unlike software monitoring, ATUM could trace all processes including the operating system, but this kind of tracing is invasive, and can slow down the system by a factor of 10 without including the time to write the trace to the disk.

## Performance Modeling

Performance measurement as described in the previous section can be done only if the actual system or a prototype exists. It is expensive to build prototypes for early stage evaluation. Hence, one needs to resort to some kind of modeling in order to study systems yet to be built. Performance modeling can be done using simulation models or analytical models.

### Simulation

Simulation has become the de facto performance modeling method in the evaluation of microprocessor architectures for several reasons. The accuracy of analytical models in the past has been insufficient for the type of design decisions computer architects wish to make (for instance, what kind of caches or branch predictors are needed), therefore, cycle accurate simulation has been used extensively by architects. Simulators model existing or future machines or microprocessors. They are essentially a model of the system being simulated, written in a high-level computer language such as C or Java, and running on some existing machine. The machine on which the simulator runs is called the host machine and the machine being modeled is called the target machine. Such simulators can be constructed in many ways.

Simulators can be functional simulators or timing simulators. They can be trace driven or execution driven simulators. They can be simulators of components or that of the complete system. Functional simulators simulate functionality of the target processor, and in essence provide a component similar to the one being modeled. The register values of the simulated machine are available in the equivalent registers of the simulator. In addition to the values, the simulators also provide performance information in terms of cycles of execution, cache hit ratios, branch prediction rates, etc. Thus, the simulator is a virtual component representing the microprocessor or subsystem being modeled plus a variety of performance information.

If performance evaluation is the only objective, one does not need to model the functionality. For instance, a cache performance simulator does not need to actually store values in the cache; it only needs to store information related to the address of the value being cached. That information is sufficient to determine a future hit or miss. Although it is nice to have the values as well, a simulator that models functionality in addition to performance is bound to be slower than a pure performance simulator. Register transfer language (RTL) models used for functional verification may also be used for performance simulations, however, these models are very slow for performance estimation with real-world workloads and are not discussed in this article.

#### Trace Driven Simulation

Trace driven simulation consists of a simulator model whose input is modeled as a trace or sequence of information representing the instruction sequence that would have actually executed on the target machine. A simple trace driven cache simulator needs a trace consisting of address values. Depending on whether the simulator is modeling a unified instruction or data cache, the address trace should contain addresses of instruction and data references.

Cachesim5 and Dinero IV are examples of cache simulators for memory reference traces. Cachesim5 comes from Sun Microsystems along with its Shade package [15]. Dinero IV [16] is available from the University of Wisconsin, Madison. These simulators are not timing simulators. There is no notion of simulated time or cycles, only references. They are not functional simulators. Data and instructions do not move in and out of the caches. The primary result of simulation is hit and miss information. The basic idea is to simulate a memory hierarchy consisting of various caches. The various parameters of each cache can be set separately (architecture, mapping policies, replacement policies, write policy, statistics). During initialization, the configuration to be simulated is built up, one cache at a time, starting with each memory as a special case. After initialization, each reference is fed to the appropriate top-level cache by a single simple function call. Lower levels of the hierarchy are handled automatically. One does not need to store a trace while using Cachesim5, because Shade can directly feed the trace into Cachesim5.

Trace driven simulation is simple and easy to understand. The simulators are easy to debug. Experiments are repeatable because the input information is not changing from run to run; however, trace driven simulation has two major problems:

1. Traces can be prohibitively long if entire executions of some real-world applications are considered. The storage needed by the traces may be prohibitively large. Trace size is proportional to the dynamic instruction count of the benchmark.
2. The traces do not represent the actual stream of processors with branch predictions. Most trace generators generate traces of only completed or retired instructions in speculative processors. Hence, they do not contain instructions from the mispredicted path.

The first problem is typically solved using trace sampling and trace reduction techniques. Trace sampling is a method to achieve reduced traces; however, the sampling should be performed in such a way that the resulting trace is representative of the original trace. It may not be sufficient to periodically sample a program execution. Locality properties of the resulting sequence may be widely different from that of the original sequence. Another technique is to skip tracing for a certain interval, then collect for a fixed interval, and then skip again. It may also be needed to leave a warm-up period after the skip interval, to let the caches and other such structures to warm up [17]. Several trace sampling techniques are discussed by Crowley and Baer [18]. The QPT trace collection system [19] solves the trace size issue by splitting the tracing process into a trace record generation step and a trace regeneration process. The trace record has a size similar to the static code size, and the trace regeneration expands it to the actual full trace upon demand.

The second problem can be solved by reconstructing the mispredicted path [20]. An image of the instruction memory space of the application is created by one pass through the trace, and, thereafter, fetching from this image as opposed to the trace. Although 100% of the mispredicted branch targets may not be in the recreated image, studies show that more than 95% of the targets can be located.

### Execution Driven Simulation

Researchers and practitioners assign two meanings to this term. Some refer to simulators that take program executables as input as execution driven simulators. These simulators utilize the actual input executable and not a trace. Hence, the size of the input is proportional to the static instruction count and not the dynamic instruction count. Mispredicted branches can be accurately simulated as well. Thus, these simulators solve the two major problems faced by trace driven simulators. The widely used Simplescalar simulator [21] is an example of such an execution driven simulator. With this tool set, the user can simulate real programs on a range of modern processors and systems, using fast execution driven simulation. There is a fast functional simulator and a detailed, out-of-order issue processor that supports non-blocking caches, speculative execution, and state-of-the-art branch prediction.

Some others consider execution driven simulators to be simulators that rely on actual execution of parts of code on the host machine (hardware acceleration by the host instead of simulation) [22]. These execution driven simulators do not simulate every individual instruction in the application. Only the instructions that are of interest are simulated. The remaining instructions are directly executed by the host computer. This can be done when the instruction set of the host is the same as that of the machine being simulated. Such simulation involves two stages. In the first stage or preprocessing, the application program is modified by inserting calls to the simulator routines at events of interest. For instance, for a memory system simulator, only memory access instructions need to be instrumented. For other instructions, the only important thing is to make sure that they get performed and that their execution time is properly accounted for. The advantage of execution driven simulation is speed. By directly executing most instructions at the machine's execution rate, the simulator can operate orders of magnitude faster than cycle by cycle simulators that emulate each individual instruction. Tango, Proteus, and FAST are examples of such simulators [22].

### Complete System Simulation

Many execution and trace driven simulators only simulate the processor and memory subsystem. Neither I/O activity nor operating system activity is handled in simulators such as Simplescalar. But in many workloads, it is extremely important to consider I/O and operating system activity. Complete system simulators are complete simulation environments that model hardware components with enough detail to boot and

**TABLE 8.5**    Examples of Complete System Simulators

| Simulator | Information Site | Instruction Set | Operating System |
|---|---|---|---|
| SimOS | Stanford University http://simos.stanford.edu/ | MIPS | SGI IRIX |
| SIMICS | Virtutech http://www.simics.com http://www.virtutech.com | PC, SPARC, and Alpha | Solaris 7 and 8, Red Hat Linux 6.2 (both x86, SPARC V9, and Alpha versions), Tru64 (Digital Unix 4.0F), and Windows NT 4.0 |
| Bochs | http://bochs.sourceforge.net | x86 | Windows 95, Windows NT, Linux, FreeBSD |

run a full-blown commercial operating system. The functionality of the processors, memory subsystem, disks, buses, SCSI/IDE/FC controllers, network controllers, graphics controllers, CD-ROM, serial devices, timers, etc. are modeled accurately in order to achieve this. Although functionality stays the same, different microarchitectures in the processing component can lead to different performance. Most of the complete system simulators use microarchitectural models that can be plugged in and out. For instance, SimOS [23], a popular complete system simulator, provides a simple pipelined processor model and an aggressive superscalar processor model. SimOS and SIMICS [24,25] can simulate uniprocessor and multiprocessor systems. Table 8.5 lists popular complete system simulators.

### Stochastic Discrete Event Driven Simulation

It is possible to simulate systems in such a way that the input is derived stochastically rather than as a trace/executable from an actual execution. For instance, one can construct a memory system simulator in which the inputs are assumed to arrive according to a Gaussian distribution. Such models can be written in general purpose languages such as C, or using special simulation languages such as SIMSCRIPT. Languages such as SIMSCRIPT have several built-in primitives to allow quick simulation of most kinds of common systems. Built-in input profiles including resource templates, process templates, queue structures, etc., facilitate easy simulation of common systems. An example of the use of event driven simulators using SIMSCRIPT may be seen in the performance evaluation of multiple-bus multiprocessor systems in Kurian et. al [26,27].

### Program Profilers

Software profiling tools is a class of tools that is similar to simulators and performance measurement tools. These tools are used to generate traces, to obtain instruction mix, and a variety of instruction statistics. They can be thought of as software monitoring on a simulator. They input an executable and decode and analyze each instruction in the executable. These program profilers can be used as the front end of simulators. A popular program profiling tool is Shade for the UltraSparc [15].

### Shade

Shade is a fast instruction-set simulator for execution profiling. It is a simulation and tracing tool that provides features of simulators and tracers in one tool. Shade analyzes the original program instructions and cross-compiles them to sequences of instructions that simulate or trace the original code. Static cross-compilation can produce fast code, but purely static translators cannot simulate and trace all details of dynamically linked code. One can develop a variety of analyzers to process the information generated by Shade and create the performance metrics of interest. For instance, one can use shade to generate address traces to feed into a cache analyzer to compute hit-rates and miss rates of cache configurations. The Shade analyzer Cachesim5 does exactly this.

### Jaba

Jaba [46] is a Java Bytecode Analyzer developed at the University of Texas for tracing Java programs. Although Java programs can be traced using shade to obtain profiles of native execution, Jaba can yield profiles at the bytecode level. It uses JVM specification 1.1. It allows the user to gather information about the dynamic execution of a Java application at the Java bytecode level. It provides information on bytecodes executed, load operations, branches executed, branch outcomes, etc. Use of this tool can be found in [47].

A variety of profiling tools exist for different platforms. In addition to describing the working of Shade, Cmelik et. al [15] also compares Shade to several other profiling tools for other platforms. A popular one for the x86 platform is Etch [51]. Conte and Gimarc [52] is a good source of information to those interested in creating profiling tools.

## Analytical Modeling

Analytical performance models, while not popular for microprocessors, are suitable for evaluation of large computer systems. In large systems, where details cannot be modeled accurately for cycle accurate simulation, analytical modeling is an appropriate way to obtain approximate performance metrics. Computer systems can generally be considered as a set of hardware and software resources and a set of tasks or jobs competing for using the resources. Multicomputer systems and multiprogrammed systems are examples.

Analytical models rely on probabilistic methods, queuing theory, Markov models, or Petri nets to create a model of the computer system. A large body of literature on analytical models of computer exists from the 1970s and early 1980s. Heidelberger and Lavenberg [28] published an article summarizing research on computer performance evaluation models. This article contains 205 references, which cover all important work on performance evaluation until 1984. Readers interested in analytical modeling should read this article.

Analytical models are cost-effective because they are based on efficient solutions to mathematical equations; however, in order to be able to have tractable solutions, often, simplifying assumptions are made regarding the structure of the model. As a result, analytical models do not capture all the detail typically built into simulation models. It is generally thought that carefully constructed analytical models can provide estimates of average job throughputs and device utilizations to within 10% accuracy and average response times within 30% accuracy. This level of accuracy, while insufficient for microarchitectural enhancement studies, is sufficient for capacity planning in multicomputer systems, I/O subsystem performance evaluation in large server farms, and in early design evaluations of multiprocessor systems.

Only a small amount of work has been done on analytical modeling of microprocessors. The level of accuracy needed in trade off analysis for microprocessor structures is more than what typical analytical models can provide; however, some effort into this arena came from Noonburg and Shen [29] and Sorin et al. [30]. Those interested in modeling superscalar processors using analytical models should read Noonburg et al.'s work [29] and Sorin et al.'s work [30]. Noonburg et al. used a Markov model to model a pipelined processor. Sorin et al. used probabilistic techniques to processor a multiprocessor composed of superscalar processors. Queuing theory is also applicable to superscalar processor modeling, as modern superscalar processors contain instruction queues in which instructions wait to be issued to one among a group of functional units.

## Workloads and Benchmarks

Benchmarks used for performance evaluation of computers should be representative of applications that are run on actual systems. Contemporary computer applications include a variety of applications, and different benchmarks are appropriate for systems targeted for different purposes. Table 8.6 lists several popular benchmarks for different classes of workloads.

### CPU Benchmarks

**SPEC CPU2000** is the industry-standardized CPU-intensive benchmark suite. The System Performance Evaluation Cooperative (SPEC) was founded in 1988 by a small number of workstation vendors who realized that the marketplace was in desperate need of realistic, standardized performance tests. The basic SPEC methodology is to provide the benchmarker with a standardized suite of source code based upon existing applications that has already been ported to a wide variety of platforms by its membership. The benchmarker then takes this source code, compiles it for the system in question. The use of already accepted and ported source code greatly reduces the problem of making apples-to-oranges comparisons. SPEC designed CPU2000 to provide a comparative measure of compute intensive performance across the widest practical range of hardware. The implementation resulted in source code benchmarks developed from real user applications. These benchmarks measure the performance of the processor, memory, and compiler on the tested system. The suite contains 14 floating point programs written in C/Fortran and 11 integer

**TABLE 8.6**  Popular Benchmarks for Different Categories of Workloads

| Workload Category | Example Benchmark Suite |
| --- | --- |
| CPU benchmarks | |
|    Uniprocessor | SPEC CPU 2000 [31] |
| | Java Grande Forum Benchmarks [32] |
| | SciMark [33] |
| | ASCI [34] |
|    Parallel processor | SPLASH [35] |
| | NASPAR [36] |
| Multimedia | MediaBench [37] |
| Embedded | EEMBC benchmarks [38] |
| Digital signal processing | BDTI benchmarks [39] |
| Java | |
|    Client side | SPECjvm98 [31] |
| | CaffeineMark [40] |
|    Server side | SPECjBB2000 [31] |
| | VolanoMark [41] |
|    Scientific | Java Grande Forum Benchmarks [32] |
| | SciMark [33] |
| Transaction processing | |
|    OLTP (On-line transaction | TPC-C [42] |
|       processing) | TPC-W [42] |
|    DSS (Decision support systems) | TPC-H [42] |
| | TPC-R [42] |
| Web server | SPEC web99 [31] |
| | TPC-W [42] |
| | VolanoMark [41] |
| E-commerce | |
|    With commercial database | TPC-W [42] |
|    Without commercial database | SPECjBB2000 [31] |
| Mail-server | SPECmail2000 [31] |
| Network file system | SPEC SFS 2.0 [31] |
| Personal computer | SYSMARK [43] |
| | Ziff Davis WinBench [44] |
| | 3DMarkMAX99 [45] |

programs (10 written in C and 1 in C++). The SPEC CPU2000 benchmarks replace the SPEC89, SPEC92, and SPEC95 benchmarks.

**The Java Grande Forum Benchmark suite** consists of three groups of benchmarks—microbenchmarks that test individual low-level operations (e.g., arithmetic, cast, create), Kernel benchmarks which are the heart of the algorithms of commonly used applications (e.g., heapsort, encryption/decryption, FFT, Sparse matrix multiplication, etc.), and applications (e.g., Raytracer, Monte Carlo simulation, Euler equation solution, molecular dynamics, etc.) [48]. These are compute intensive benchmarks available in Java.

**SciMark** is a composite Java benchmark measuring the performance of numerical codes occurring in scientific and engineering applications. It consists of five computational kernels: FFT, Gauss-Seidel relaxation, Sparse matrix-multiply, Monte Carlo integration, and dense LU factorization. These kernels are chosen to provide an indication of how well the underlying Java Virtual Machines perform on applications utilizing these types of algorithms. The problems sizes are purposely chosen to be small in order to isolate the effects of memory hierarchy and focus on internal JVM/JIT and CPU issues. A larger version of the benchmark (SciMark 2.0 LARGE) addresses performance of the memory subsystem with out-of-cache problem sizes.

**ASCI**, the Accelerated Strategic Computing Initiative (ASCI) of the Lawrence Livermore laboratories contains several numeric codes suitable for evaluation of compute intensive systems. The programs are available from [34].

**SPLASH**, the SPLASH suite was created by Stanford researchers [35]. The suite contains six scientific and engineering applications, all of which are parallel applications.

**NAS Parallel** Benchmarks (NPB) are a set of eight programs designed to help evaluate the performance of parallel supercomputers. The benchmarks, which are derived from computational fluid dynamics (CFD) applications, consist of five kernels and three pseudo-applications.

## Embedded and Media Benchmarks

### EEMBC Benchmarks

The EDN Embedded Microprocessor Benchmark Consortium (EEMBC—pronounced "embassy") was formed in April 1997 to develop meaningful performance benchmarks for processors in embedded applications. EEMBC is backed by the majority of the processor industry and has therefore established itself as the industry-standard embedded processor benchmarking forum. EEMBC establishes benchmark standards and provides certified benchmarking results through the EEMBC Certification Labs (ECL) in Texas and California. The EEMBC's benchmarks comprise a suite of benchmarks designed to reflect real-world applications, while it also includes some synthetic benchmarks. These benchmarks target the automotive/industrial, consumer, networking, office automation, and telecommunications markets. More specifically, these benchmarks target specific applications that include engine control, digital cameras, printers, cellular phones, modems, and similar devices with embedded microprocessors. The EEMBC consortium dissected these applications and derived 37 individual algorithms that constitutes the EEMBC's Version 1.0 suite of benchmarks.

### BDTI Benchmarks

Berkeley Design Technology, Inc. (BDTI) is a technical services company that has focused exclusively on digital signal processing (DSP) since 1991. BDTI provides the industry standard BDTI Benchmarks™, a proprietary suite of DSP benchmarks. BDTI also develops custom benchmarks to determine performance on specific applications The benchmarks contain DSP routines such as FIR filter, IIR filter, FFT, dot-product, and Viterbi decoder.

### MediaBench

The MediaBench benchmark suite consists of several applications belonging to the image processing, communications and DSP applications. Examples of applications that are included are JPEG, MPEG, GSM, G.721 Voice compression, Ghostscript, ADPCM, etc. JPEG is the compression program for images, MPEG involves encoding/decoding for video transmission, Ghostscript is an interpreter for the Postscript language, and ADPCM is adaptive differential pulse code modulation. The MediaBench is an academic effort to assemble several media processing related benchmarks. An example of the use of these benchmarks may be found in [49].

## Java Benchmarks

**SPECjvm98**, the SPECjvm98 suite consists of a set of programs intended to evaluate performance for the combined hardware (CPU, cache, memory, and other platform-specific performance) and software aspects (efficiency of JVM, the JIT compiler, and OS implementations) of the JVM client platform [31]. The SPECjvm98 uses common computing features such as integer and floating point operations, library calls and I/O, but does not include AWT (window), networking, and graphics. Each benchmark can be run with three different input sizes referred to as S1, S10, and S100. The 7 programs are compression/decompression (compress), expert system (jess), database (db), Java compiler (javac), mpeg3 decoder (mpegaudio), raytracer (mtrt), and a parser (jack).

**SPECjbb2000** (Java Business Benchmark) is SPEC's first benchmark for evaluating the performance of server-side Java. The benchmark emulates an electronic commerce workload in a 3-tier system. The benchmark contains business logic and object manipulation, primarily representing the activities of the middle tier in an actual business server. It models a wholesale company with warehouses serving a number of districts. Customers initiate a set of operations such as placing new orders and checking the status of existing orders. It is written in Java, adapting a portable business oriented benchmark called pBOB written by IBM. Although it is a benchmark that emulates business transactions, it is very different from the

TPC benchmarks. There are no actual clients, but they are replaced by driver threads. Similarly, there is no actual database access. Data is stored as binary trees of objects.

**CaffeineMark 2.5** is the latest in the series of CaffeineMark benchmarks. The benchmark suite analyses Java system performance in eleven different areas, nine of which can be run directly over the internet. It is almost the industry standard Java benchmark. The CaffeineMark can be used for comparing applet-viewers, interpreters and JIT compilers from different vendors. The CaffeineMark benchmarks can also be used as a measure of Java applet/application performance across platforms.

**VolanoMark** is a pure Java server benchmark with long-lasting network connections and high thread counts. It can be divided into two parts: server and client, although they are provided in one package. It is based on a commercial chat server application, the VolanoChat, which is used in several countries worldwide. The server accepts connections from the chat client. The chat client simulates many chat rooms and many users in each chat room. The client continuously sends messages to the server and waits for the server to broadcast the messages to the users in the same chat room. VolanoMark creates two threads for each client connection. VolanoMark can be used to test both speed and scalability of a system. In speed test, it is run in an iterative fashion on a single machine. In scalability test, the server and client are run on separate machines with high-speed network connections.

**SciMark**, see subsection "CPU Benchmarks."

**Java Grande Forum Benchmarks**, see subsection "CPU Benchmarks."

## Transaction Processing Benchmarks (TPC)

The TPC is a nonprofit corporation founded in 1988 to define transaction processing and database benchmarks and to disseminate objective, verifiable TPC performance data to the industry. The term transaction is often applied to a wide variety of business and computer functions. Looked at it as a computer function, a transaction could refer to a set of operations including disk read/writes, operating system calls, or some form of data transfer from one subsystem to another. TPC regards a transaction as it is commonly understood in the business world: a commercial exchange of goods, services, or money. A typical transaction, as defined by the TPC, would include the updating to a database system for such things as inventory control (goods), airline reservations (services), or banking (money). In these environments, a number of customers or service representatives input and manage their transactions via a terminal or desktop computer connected to a database. Typically, the TPC produces benchmarks that measure transaction processing (TP) and database (DB) performance in terms of how many transactions a given system and database can perform per unit of time, e.g., transactions per second or transactions per minute. The TPC benchmarks can be classified into two categories, online transaction processing (OLTP) and decision support systems (DSS). OLTP systems are used in day-to-day business operations (airline reservations, banks), and are characterized by large number of clients who continually access and update small portions of the database through short running transactions. Decision support systems are primarily used for business analysis purposes, to understand business trends, and for guiding future business directions. Information from the OLTP side of the business is periodically fed into the DSS database and analyzed. DSS workloads are characterized by long running queries that are primarily read-only and may span a large fraction of the database. Four benchmarks are active: TPC-C, TPC-W, TPC-R, and TPC-H. These benchmarks can be run with different data sizes, or scale factors. In the smallest case (or scale factor = 1), the data size is approximately 1 GB. The earlier TPC benchmarks, namely TPC-A, TPC-B, and TPC-D have become obsolete.

### TPC-C

TPC-C is an OLTP benchmark. It simulates a complete computing environment where a population of users executes transactions against a database. The benchmark is centered around the principal activities (transactions) of a business similar to that of a worldwide wholesale supplier. The transactions include entering and delivering orders, recording payments, checking the status of orders, and monitoring the level of stock at the warehouses. Although the benchmark portrays the activity of a wholesale supplier, TPC-C is not limited to the activity of any particular business segment, but rather, represents any industry that must manage, sell, or distribute a product or service. TPC-C involves a mix of five concurrent transactions of different types and complexity either executed on-line or queued for deferred execution. There are multiple on-line terminal sessions. The benchmark can be configured to use any commercial database system such as Oracle, DB2 (IBM), or Informix. Significant disk input and output are involved. The databases consist of many tables with a wide variety of sizes, attributes, and relationships. The queries result in contention on data accesses and updates. TPC-C performance is measured in new-order transactions per minute. The primary metrics are the transaction rate (tpmC) and price per transaction ($/tpmC).

### TPC-H

The TPC Benchmark™ H (TPC-H) is a decision support system (DSS) benchmark. It consists of a suite of business oriented ad-hoc queries and concurrent data modifications. The queries and the data populating the database have been chosen to have broad industry-wide relevance. This benchmark is modeled after decision support systems that examine large volumes of data, execute queries with a high degree of complexity, and give answers to critical business questions. The benchmark contains 22 queries. The performance metric reported by TPC-H is called the TPC-H Composite Query-per-Hour Performance Metric (QphH@Size), and the TPC-H Price/Performance Metric, $/QphH@Size. One may not perform optimizations based on apriori knowledge of queries in TPC-H.

### TPC-R

The TPC Benchmark™R (TPC-R) is a decision support benchmark similar to TPC-H, but which allows additional optimizations based on advance knowledge of the queries. It consists of a suite of business oriented queries and concurrent data modifications. As in TPC-H, there are 22 queries. The performance metric reported by TPC-R is called the TPC-R Composite Query-per-Hour Performance Metric (QphR@Size), and the TPC-R Price/Performance Metric, $/QphR@Size.

### TPC-W

TPC Benchmark™ W (TPC-W) is a transactional web benchmark. The workload simulates the activities of a business oriented transactional Web server in an electronic commerce environment. It supports many of the features of the TPC-C benchmark and has several additional features related to dynamic page generation with database access and updates. Multiple on-line browser sessions and on-line transaction processing are supported. Contention on data accesses and updates are modeled. The performance metric reported by TPC-W is the number of Web interactions processed per second (WIPS). Multiple Web interactions are used to simulate the activity of a retail store, and each interaction is subject to a response time constraint. Different profiles can be simulated by varying the ratio of browsing and buying i.e., simulating customers who are primarily browsing and those who are primarily shopping.

## Web Server Benchmarks

**SPECweb99** is the SPEC benchmark for evaluating the performance of World Wide Web servers. It measures a system's ability to act as a Web server. The initial effort from SPEC in this direction was SPECweb96, but it contained only static workloads, meaning that the requests were for simply downloading web pages that do not involve any computation. But if one examines the use of the web, it is clear that many downloads involve computation to generate the information the client is requesting. Such Web pages are referred to as dynamic web pages. SPECweb99 includes dynamic Web pages. The file accesses are made to closely match today's real-world Web server access patterns. The pages also contain dynamic ad rotation using cookies and table lookups.

   **VolanoMark**, see the "Java Benchmarks" subsection.

   **TPC-W**, see the "Transaction Processing Benchmarks" subsection.

## E-commerce Benchmarks

See SPECjbb2000 in the subsection on "Java Benchmarks" and TPC-W in the subsection on "Transaction Processing Benchmarks."

## Mail Server Benchmarks

**SPECmail2001** is a standardized mail server benchmark designed to measure a system's ability to act as a mail server servicing e-mail requests. The benchmark characterizes throughput and response time of a mail server system under test with realistic network connections, disk storage, and client workloads. The benchmark focuses on the ISP as opposed to enterprise class of mail servers, with an overall user count in the range of approximately 10,000 to 1,000,000 users. The goal is to enable objective comparisons of mail server products.

## File Server Benchmarks

**System File Server Version 2.0** (SFS 2.0) is SPEC's benchmark for measuring NFS (network file system) file server performance across different vendor platforms. It contains a workload that was developed based on a survey of more than 1,000 file servers in different application environments.

## PC Benchmarks

A variety of benchmarks are available, primarily from Ziff Davis and Bapco to benchmark the Windows-based personal computer. Table 8.7 lists the most common PC benchmarks. Ziff Davis Winstone and Bapco SYSMARK are benchmarks that measure overall performance while the other benchmarks are intended to measure performance of one subsystem such as video or audio or one aspect such as power.

Techniques and tools for performance evaluation improve year by year. For instance, performance monitoring counters were not available to the public until 1997. Benchmarks get updated almost every year. Those interested in experimental performance evaluation should continuously monitor the state of the art.

**TABLE 8.7**  Popular Personal Computer Benchmarks

| Benchmark | Description |
| --- | --- |
| Business Winstone [44] | A system-level, application-based benchmark that measures a PC's overall performance when running today's top-selling Windows-based, 32-bit applications. It runs real 32-bit business applications through a series of scripted activities and uses the time a PC takes to complete those activities to produce its performance scores. The suite includes five Microsoft Office 2000 applications (Access, Excel, FrontPage, PowerPoint, and Word), Microsoft Project 98, Lotus Notes R5, NicoMak WinZip, Norton AntiVirus, and Netscape Communicator. |
| WinBench99 [44] | A subsystem-level benchmark that measures the performance of a PC's graphics, disk, and video subsystems in a Windows environment. |
| 3DwinBench [44] | Tests the bus used to carry information between the graphics adapter and the processor subsystem. Hardware graphics adapters, drivers, and enhancing technologies such as MMX/SSE are tested. |
| CD WinBench99 [44] | Measures the performance of a PC's CD-ROM subsystem, which includes the CD drive, controller, and driver, and the system processor. |
| Audio WinBench 99 [44] | Measures the performance of a PC's audio subsystem, which includes the sound card and its driver, the processor, the DirectSound and DirectSound 3D software, and the speakers. |
| Battery Mark [44] | Measures battery life on notebook computers. |
| I-bench [44] | A comprehensive, cross-platform benchmark that tests the performance and capability of Web clients. The benchmark provides a series of tests that measure both how well the client handles features and the degree to which network access speed affects performance. |
| Web Bench [44] | Measures Web server software performance by running different Web server packages on the same server hardware or by running a given Web server package on different hardware platforms. |
| NetBench [44] | A portable benchmark program that measures how well a file server handles file I/O requests from clients. NetBench reports throughput and client response time measurements. |
| 3Dmark MAX 99 [45] | From Futuremark Corporation. Is a nice 3D benchmark that measures 3D gaming performance. Results are dependent on CPU, memory architecture, and the 3D accelerator employed. |
| SYSMARK [43] | Measures a system's real-world performance when running typical business applications. This benchmark suite comprises the retail versions of eight application programs and measures the speed with which the system under test executes predetermined scripts of user tasks typically performed when using these applications. The performance times of the individual applications are weighted and combined into both category-based performance scores as well as a single overall score. The application programs employed by SYSmark 32 are: Microsoft Word 7.0 and Lotus WordPro 96 for word processing, Microsoft Excel 7.0 (for spreadsheet), Borland Paradox 7.0 (for database), CorelDraw 6.0 (for desktop graphics), Lotus Freelance Graphics 96 and Microsoft Powerpoint 7.0 (for desktop presentation), and Adobe Pagemaker 6.0 (for desktop publishing). |

**TABLE 8.8**    Benchmark Web Sites

| Example Benchmark Suite | Web Site for More Information |
| --- | --- |
| SPEC CPU 2000 | http://www.spec.org |
| Java Grande Forum Benchmarks | http://www.epcc.ed.ac.uk/javagrande/ |
| SciMark | http://math.nist.gov/scimark2 |
| ASCI | http://www.llnl.gov/asci_benchmarks/asci/asci_code_list.html |
| NASPAR | http://www.nas.nasa.gov/Software/NPB/ |
| MediaBench | http://www.cs.ucla.edu/~leec/mediabench/ |
| EEMBC benchmarks | http://www.eembc.org |
| BDTI benchmarks | http://www.bdti.com/ |
| SPECjvm98 | http://www.spec.org |
| CaffeineMark | http://www.pendragon-software.com/pendragon/cm3 |
| SPECjBB2000 | http://www.spec.org |
| VolanoMark | http://www.volano.com/benchmarks.html |
| TPC-C | http://www.tpc.org |
| TPC-W | http://www.tpc.org |
| TPC-H | http://www.tpc.org |
| TPC-R | http://www.tpc.org |
| SPECweb99 | http://www.spec.org |
| SPECmail2000 | http://www.spec.org |
| SPEC SFS 2.0 | http://www.spec.org |
| SYSMARK | http://www.bapco.com/ |
| Ziff Davis Benchmarks | http://www.zdnet.com/etestinglabs/filters/benchmarks |
| 3DMarkMAX99 | http://www.pcbenchmarks.com |

Table 8.8 provides sources for the benchmarks described in this article. The references at the end can provide new information on tools and benchmarks. Microprocessor vendors are inclined to show off their products in the best light, to projecting results for benchmarks that run well on their system, developing special optimizations within their compilers just for the sake of improving benchmark scores, and stretching the benchmark's behavior while staying within the "legal" limits of the benchmark guidelines. It is extremely important to understand benchmarks, their features and metrics used for performance evaluation to really understand the performance results.

## References

1. Reinhold P. Weicker, "An Overview of Common Benchmarks," *IEEE Computer*, pp. 65–75, Dec. 1990.
2. H. Cragon, *Computer Architecture and Implementation,* Cambridge University Press, Cambridge, 2000.
3. J. E. Smith, "Characterizing Computer Performance with a Single Number," *Communications of the ACM,* Oct. 1988.
4. Patterson and Hennessy, *Computer Architecture: The Hardware/Software Approach,* by Hennessy and Patterson, Morgan Kaufman Publishers, 2nd ed., 1998.
5. Vtune profiling software, http://developer.intel.com/software/products/vtune/vtune_oview.htm
6. P6perf utility, http://developer.intel.com/vtune/p6perf/index.htm
7. DCPI Tool home page, http://www.research.digital.com/SRC/dcpi/) and http://www.research.compaq.com/SRC/dcpi/
8. J. Dean, J. E. Hicks, C. A. Waldspurger, W. E. Weihl, and G. Chrysos, "Profile Me: Hardware Support for Instruction Level Profiling on Out of Order Processors," MICRO-30 proceedings, pp. 292–302, 1997.
9. Perf-monitor for UltraSparc, http://www.sics.se/~mch/perf-monitor/index.html
10. PMON http://www.ece.utexas.edu/projects/ece/lca/pmon
11. M. C. Merten, A. R. Trick, E. M. Nystrom, R. D. Barnes, and W. W. Hwu, "A Hardware-Driven Profiling Scheme for Identifying Hot Spots to Support Runtime Optimization," *Proceedings of the 26th International Symposium on Computer Architecture,* pp. 136–147, May 1999.

12. R. Bhargava, J. Rubio, S. Kannan, L. K. John, D. Christie, and L. Klaes, "Understanding the Impact of x86/NT Computing on Microarchitecture," in *Characterization of Contemporary Workloads*, pp. 203–228, Kluwer Academic Publishers, Dordrecht, the Netherlands, 2001.

13. Ali Poursepanj and David Christie, "Generation of 3D Graphics Workload for System Performance Analysis," *Presented at the First Workshop on Workload Characterization*, Also in *Workload Characterization: Methodology and Case Studies*, edited by John and Maynard, IEEE CS Press, 1999.

14. A. Agarwal, R. L. Sites, and M. Horowitz, "ATUM: A New Technique for Capturing Address Traces Using Microcode," *Proceedings of the 13th International Symposium on Computer Architecture*, pp. 119–127, June 1986.

15. B. Cmelik and D. Keppel, "Shade: A Fast Instruction-Set Simulator for Execution Profiling," Chapter 2 in *Fast Simulation of Computer Architectures*, by T. M. Conte and C. E. Gimarc, Kluwer Academic Publishers, Dordrecht, the Netherlands, 1995.

16. Dinero IV cache simulator, www.cs.wisc.edu/~markhill/DineroIV

17. P. Bose and T. M. Conte, "Performance Analysis and Its Impact on Design," *IEEE Computer*, pp. 41–49, May 1998.

18. P. Crowley and J.-L. Baer, "On the Use of Trace Sampling for Architectural Studies of Desktop Applications," Presented at the First Workshop on Workload Characterization, Also in *Workload Characterization: Methodology and Case Studies*, edited by John and Maynard, IEEE CS Press, pp. 15–24, 1999.

19. J. R. Larus, "Efficient Program Tracing," *IEEE Computer*, pp. 52–61, May 1993.

20. Ravi Bhargava, Lizy K. John, and Francisco Matus, "Accurately Modeling Speculative Instruction Fetching in Trace-Driven Simulation," *Proceedings of the IEEE Performance, Computers and Communications Conference (IPCCC)*, pp. 65–71, Feb. 1999.

21. The Simplescalar simulator suite, http://www.simplescalar.org or http://www.cs.wisc.edu/~mscalar/simplescalar.html.

22. B. Boothe, "Execution Driven Simulation of Shared Memory Multiprocessors," Chapter 6 in *Fast Simulation of Computer Architectures*, by T. M. Conte and C. E. Gimarc, Kluwer Academic Publishers, Dordrecht, the Netherlands, 1995.

23. The SimOS complete system simulator, http://simos.stanford.edu/

24. SIMICS www.simics.com

25. SIMICS, VIRTUTECH http://www.virtutech.com

26. L. Kurian, *Performance Evaluation of Prioritized Multiple-Bus Multiprocessor Systems*, M.S. Thesis, University of Texas at El Paso, Dec. 1989.

27. L. K. John, Yu-cheng Liu, "A Performance Model for Prioritized Multiple-Bus Multiprocessor Systems," *IEEE Transactions on Computers*, Vol. 45, No. 5, pp. 580–588, May 1996.

28. P. Heidelberger and S. S. Lavenberg, "Computer Performance Evaluation Methodology," *IEEE Transactions on Computers*, pp. 1195–1220, Dec. 1984.

29. D. B. Noonburg and J. P. Shen, "A Framework for Statistical Modeling of Superscalar Processor Performance," *Proceedings of the 3rd International Symposium on High Performance Computer Architecture (HPCA)*, pp. 298–309, 1997.

30. D. J. Sorin, V. S. Pai, S. V. Adve, M. K. Vernon, and D. A. Wood, "Analytic Evaluation of Shared Memory Systems with ILP Processors," *Proceedings of the International Symposium on Computer Architecture*, pp. 380–391, 1998.

31. SPEC Benchmarks, www.spec.org

32. Java Grande Benchmarks, http://www.epcc.ed.ac.uk/javagrande/

33. SciMark, http://math.nist.gov/scimark2

34. ASCI Benchmarks, http://www.llnl.gov/asci_benchmarks/asci/asci_code_list.html

35. S. C. Woo, M. Ohara, E. Torrie, J. P. Singh, and A. Gupta, "The SPLASH-2 Programs: Characterization and Methodological Considerations," *Proceedings of the 22nd International Symposium on Computer Architecture*, pp. 24–36, June 1995.

36. NAS Parallel Benchmarks, http://www.nas.nasa.gov/Software/NPB/

37. MediaBench benchmarks, http://www.cs.ucla.edu/~leec/mediabench/

38. EEMBC, www.eembc.org

39. BDTI, http://www.bdti.com/

40. The Caffeine benchmarks, http://www.pendragon-software.com/pendragon/cm3

41. VolanoMark, http://www.volano.com/benchmarks.html

42. Transactions Processing Council, www.tpc.org

43. SYSMARK, http://www.bapco.com/

44. Ziff Davis Benchmarks, www.zdbop.com or www.zdnet.com/etestinglabs/filters/benchmarks

45. PC Benchmarks, www.pcbenchmarks.com

46. The Jaba profiling tool, http://www.ece.utexas.edu/projects/ece/lca/jaba.html

47. R. Radhakrishnan, J. Rubio, and L. K. John, "Characterization of Java Applications at Bytecode and Ultra-SPARC Machine Code Levels," *Proceedings of IEEE International Conference on Computer Design*, pp. 281–284.

48. J. A. Mathew, P. D. Coddington, and K. A. Hawick, "Analysis and Development of the Java Grande Benchmarks," *Proceedings of the ACM 1999 Java Grande Conference*, June 1999.

49. C. Lee, M. Potkonjak, and W. H. M. Smith, "MediaBench: A Tool for Evaluating and Synthesizing Multimedia and Communication Systems," *Proceedings of the 30th International Symposium on Microarchitecture*, pp. 330–335.

50. D. Bhandarkar and J. Ding, "Performance Characterization of the Pentium Pro Processor," *Proceedings of the 3rd High Performance Computer Architecture Symposium*, pp. 288–297, 1997.

51. Ted Romer, Geoff Voelker, Dennis Lee, Alec Wolman, Wayne Wong, Hank Levy, Brian Bershad, and Brad Chen, "Instrumentation and Optimization of Win32/Intel Executables Using Etch," USENIX, 1997.

52. T. M. Conte and C. E. Gimarc, *Fast Simulation of Computer Architectures*, Kluwer Academic Publishers, Dordrecht, the Netherlands, 1995.

# 8.3   Trace Caching and Trace Processors

*Eric Rotenberg*

A superscalar processor executes multiple instructions in parallel each cycle. Because there are data dependences among instructions, finding multiple independent instructions that can execute in parallel requires examining an even larger group of instructions, called the *instruction window*. Figure 8.16 shows a high-level view of a superscalar processor, including instruction buffers that make up the window and the decoupled fetch and execution engines. The fetch engine predicts branches, fetches and renames instructions, and dispatches them into the window. Meanwhile, each cycle, the execution engine identifies instructions in the window whose operands are available, and issues them to parallel functional units (FUs).

Peak performance is increased by adding more parallel functional units. But adding more functional units has ramifications for other parts of the processor. First, instruction fetch bandwidth must be commensurate with peak execution bandwidth. Second, the window must be correspondingly larger. A larger window enables the processor to probe deeper into the dynamic instruction stream, increasing the chance of finding enough independent instructions each cycle to keep functional units operating at peak efficiency.

Next-generation, high-performance processors will need to issue 8, 12, or even 16 instructions per cycle. Unfortunately, at high issue rates, supporting mechanisms—instruction supply and the instruction window—are difficult to scale. This chapter section deals with *the instruction fetch bottleneck* and *inefficient execution mechanisms*, and surveys a next-generation microarchitecture, the *trace processor* [21,24,27,29, 31], that attacks these problems. A third problem, *control and data dependence bottlenecks*, is also covered; however, because this aspect is more involved, it is left to the reader to investigate the trace processor literature [24,25].

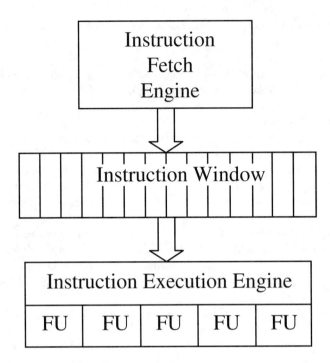

**FIGURE 8.16**    High-level view of a superscalar processor: instruction window and decoupled fetch and execute engines.

### Instruction Fetch Bottleneck

Taken branches in the dynamic instruction stream cause frequent disruptions in the flow of instructions into the window. The best conventional instruction cache and next-program-counter logic incurs a single-cycle disruption when a taken branch is encountered. At best, sustained fetch bandwidth is equal to the average number of instructions between taken branches, which is typically from 6 to 8 instructions per cycle for integer programs [2,19,32]. Moreover, conventional branch predictors predict at most one branch per cycle, limiting fetch bandwidth to a single basic block per cycle.

It is possible to modify conventional instruction caches and the next-program-counter logic to remove taken-branch disruptions, however, that approach is typically complex. Low latency is sacrificed for high bandwidth. A *trace cache* [8,14,18,20] changes the way instructions are stored to optimize instruction fetching for both high bandwidth and low latency.

### Inefficient High-Bandwidth Execution Mechanisms

The scheduling mechanism in a superscalar processor converts an artificially sequential program into an instruction-level parallel program. The scheduling mechanism is composed of register rename logic (identifies true dependences among instructions and removes artificial dependences), the scheduling window (resolves dependences near-optimally by issuing instructions out-of-order), and the register file with result bypasses (moves data to and from the functional units as instructions issue and complete, respectively). All of the circuits are *monolithic* and their speed does not scale well for 8 or more instructions per cycle [13].

*Trace processors* [21,24,27,29,31] use a more efficient, *hierarchical* scheduling mechanism to optimize for both high-bandwidth execution and a fast clock.

### Control and Data Dependence Bottlenecks

Most control dependences are removed by branch prediction, but branch mispredictions incur large performance penalties because all instructions after a mispredicted branch are flushed from the window, even control- and data-independent instructions. Exploiting *control independence* preserves useful instructions

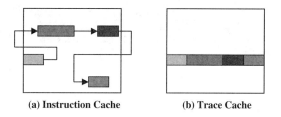

**(a) Instruction Cache**     **(b) Trace Cache**

**FIGURE 8.17**    Example dynamic sequence stored in an instruction cache and trace cache.

and their results [9], which would otherwise be thrown away due to branch mispredictions, but control independence mechanisms have numerous difficult implementation issues [22]. Moreover, a large instruction window does nothing to reduce the execution time of long data dependence chains, which ultimately limit performance if branch mispredictions do not. Value prediction and other forms of *data speculation* break data dependence chains [10], but difficult implementation issues must be resolved, such as providing high-bandwidth value prediction and high-performance recovery mechanisms.

The hierarchical organization of trace processors can be leveraged to overcome implementation barriers to data speculation and control independence. The interested reader may learn more about trace processor control independence mechanisms and data speculation from other sources [21,24,25].

## Trace Cache and Trace Predictor: Efficient High-Bandwidth Instruction Fetching

Conventional instruction caches are unable to meet future fetch bandwidth requirements because of taken branches in the dynamic instruction stream. A taken branch instruction and its target instruction reside in different cache lines, or in the same cache line with unwanted instructions in between, as shown in Fig. 8.17(a). Figure 8.17(a) shows a long dynamic sequence of instructions made up of four fetch blocks separated by taken branches. Ideally, to keep a 16-issue machine well-supplied, the entire sequence needs to be fetched in a single cycle. But, because the fetch blocks are noncontiguous, it takes at least four cycles to fetch and assemble the desired sequence.

The fundamental problem is instruction caches store instructions in their static order. A *trace cache* [8,14,18,20] stores instructions the way they appear in the dynamic instruction stream. Figure 8.17(b) shows the same sequence of four fetch blocks stored contiguously in one trace cache line. The trace cache allows multiple, otherwise noncontiguous fetch blocks to be fetched in a single cycle. A *trace* in this context is a dynamic sequence of instructions with a hardware-defined length limit (e.g., 16 or 32 instructions), containing any number of embedded taken and not-taken branches.

A trace cache can be incorporated in the fetch mechanism in several ways. One possibility is to replace the conventional instruction cache with a trace cache. More likely, both a trace cache and instruction cache are used. In trace processors, described in the next section, the trace cache is accessed first and, if it does not have the desired trace, the trace is quickly constructed from the back-up instruction cache. Early trace cache fetch units [14,20] access the trace cache and instruction cache in parallel, as shown in Fig. 8.18. If the trace exists in the trace cache, it supplies instructions and the instruction cache's instructions are discarded since they are subsumed by the trace. Otherwise, the instruction cache supplies a smaller fetch block.

A trace is uniquely identified by the program counter of the first instruction in the trace (start PC) and embedded branch outcomes (taken/not-taken bit for every branch; this assumes indirect branches terminate a trace, since taken/not-taken is insufficient for indirect branches). The start PC and branch outcomes are collectively called the *trace identifier*, or *trace id*. Looking up a trace in the trace cache is similar to looking up instructions/data in conventional caches, except the trace id is used instead of an address. A subset of the trace id forms an index into the trace cache and the remaining bits form a tag.

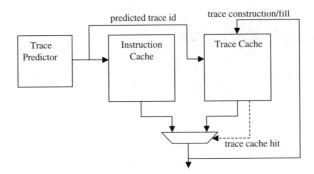

**FIGURE 8.18**   Instruction fetch unit with trace cache.

One or more traces and their identifying tags are accessed at that index (the number of traces depends on the trace cache's set-associativity). If one of the tags matches the tag of the supplied trace id, there is a trace cache hit. Otherwise, there is a trace cache miss. New traces are constructed and written into the trace cache either speculatively, as instructions are fetched from the instruction cache (as shown in Fig. 8.18), or non-speculatively, as instructions retire from the processor.

A new *predicted trace id* is supplied to the trace cache each cycle. Conventional branch prediction, with a throughput of only one branch prediction per cycle, is not designed to produce trace ids. Multiple-branch predictor counterparts of single-branch predictors have been proposed but they tend to be unwieldy [19]. A conceptually simpler approach is to not predict branches directly. *Explicit trace prediction* [6] predicts trace ids directly and, in doing so, implicitly predicts any number of embedded branches in a single cycle. The *trace predictor* shown in Fig. 8.18 supplies a predicted trace id—start PC and multiple branch predictions—to both the trace cache and instruction cache.

The trace cache design space is extensive. In addition to typical parameters such as size, set-associativity, and replacement policy, the design space includes: indexing methods (which PC bits and which, if any, branch prediction bits are used), path associativity (ability to simultaneously store different traces with the same start PC), partial matching (ability to use prefix of a trace if the trace id only partially matches), trace selection (policies for beginning and ending traces), trace cache fill policy, parallel or sequential accessing of the trace and instruction caches, and other aspects. The interested reader is referred to trace cache literature to gain an appreciation for the trace cache design space [4,5,7,14–20,23].

A problem of trace caches is they necessarily use storage less efficiently than instruction caches. A given static instruction appears exactly once in the instruction cache. In a trace cache, however, there may be multiple copies of the same static instruction. Redundancy within a trace is caused by dynamic unrolling of small loops. Redundancy among different traces is caused by partial overlap of different paths through a region. For example, two traces may start at the same program counter but diverge at a common branch, such that the two traces share a common prefix; the paths may reconverge before both traces end, causing even more redundancy.

Trace cache redundancy is the price paid for simplicity and a direct approach to high-bandwidth instruction fetching. There are other high-bandwidth fetch mechanisms that work solely out of the conventional instruction cache [2,3,26,32]. They all use the same basic approach. First, the branch predictor is modified to generate pointers to multiple noncontiguous fetch blocks. Second, the instruction cache is highly multiported so that pointers can access noncontiguous cache lines in parallel. Finally, a sophisticated instruction alignment network re-orders the blocks fetched in the previous step to construct the desired dynamic sequence of instructions. The approach is certainly high-bandwidth but the number of stages in the fetch pipeline is increased, and additional fetch unit latency impacts performance negatively [19]. The trace cache approach is less efficient in terms of storage. But other approaches are inefficient in terms of repeatedly constructing dynamic traces on-the-fly from the static instruction cache. The trace cache incurs the latency to construct a trace once and then efficiently reuses it many times.

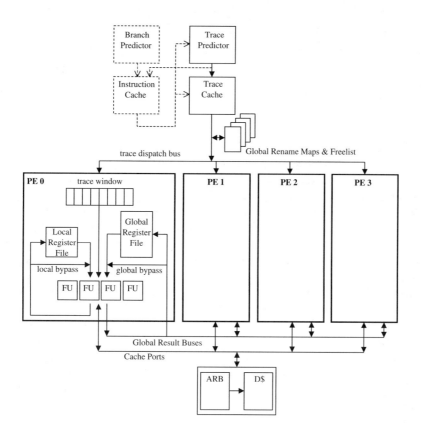

**FIGURE 8.19** Trace processor.

## Trace Processor: Efficient High-Bandwidth Instruction Execution

Instruction execution is inefficient in wide-issue superscalar processors because all data dependences are handled *uniformly*. When an instruction issues, its data dependent instructions wakeup with uniform latency, usually a single cycle, regardless of their location in the window. Resolving all dependences in a single cycle optimizes parallelism, but cycle time is extended to accommodate the full length of the window. Increasing processor cycle time penalizes the entire pipeline. A better alternative is to increase the number of cycles to resolve data dependences, e.g., two cycles instead of one, so other pipeline stages are unaffected. However, it still remains the case that *all data dependences are slow to resolve.*

Fortunately, there is a compromise between optimizing for parallelism and optimizing for cycle time if data dependences are handled *nonuniformly*. A *trace processor* [21,24,27–29,31] hierarchically divides the processor into smaller processing elements (PEs), as shown in Fig. 8.19. The approach preserves a fast clock and resolves many data dependences in one clock cycle (data dependences *within* PEs), at the expense of resolving some data dependences in two or more clock cycles (data dependences *among* PEs). The microarchitecture shown in Fig. 8.19 is described in the remainder of this section.

### Instruction Supply

The trace predictor and trace cache supply a single trace per cycle. The conventional branch predictor and instruction cache shown in Fig. 8.19 are secondary, back-up mechanisms for constructing traces that miss in the cache or that were mispredicted [21,23,24].

### Register Renaming

Register renaming determines data dependences among all newly-fetched instructions, and between newly-fetched instructions and other instructions already in the window. The first aspect—determining data dependences among 16 or 32 fetched instructions—almost certainly takes more than a single clock cycle.

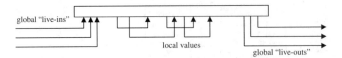

**FIGURE 8.20**  Data flow hierarchy of traces.

Each instruction compares its source registers to the destination registers of all logically preceding instructions. The second aspect—linking incoming instructions with previous and future instructions in the window—requires an impractical number of read and write ports to the register rename map table and high bandwidth to the register freelist.

The efficiency of register renaming and later execution stages is improved by hierarchically dividing data flow into intra-trace and inter-trace values [31], as shown in Fig. 8.20. *Local values* are produced and consumed solely within a trace and are not visible to other traces. *Global values* are communicated among traces. Global input values to a trace are called *live-ins* and global output values of a trace are called *live-outs*.

Local dependences in a trace are static because control flow is pre-determined. Thus, intra-trace dependence checking is performed only once, when the trace is first constructed and written into the trace cache. Furthermore, the local values that correspond to intra-trace dependences can be statically bound to registers in a local register file, a process called *pre-renaming* [31]. Each PE has a small private local register file, large enough to hold all local values produced by a trace. Local register files are private because their values do not need to be communicated to other PEs. Pre-rename information is computed once and stored along with the trace in the trace cache. Pre-renaming eliminates the first aspect of register renaming from the rename stage—dependence checking among newly fetched instructions.

The second aspect of renaming—linking fetched instructions with other instructions in the window—is still performed, but the hierarchical treatment of values makes this aspect efficient. The only linkages are inter-trace dependences. Live-in and live-out values are dynamically renamed to what is logically a single shared global register file. The global register file communicates values among traces.

Although the global register file, its map table, and its freelist are similar to a superscalar processor's monolithic register file and renaming structures, the trace processor's register file is more efficient because fewer values are processed. Reduced register file complexity is described below in the context of instruction issue logic. Global renaming structures are simplified in three ways. First, fewer read and write ports lead to the global rename map table because only live-ins/live-outs are renamed, and not local values. Second, bandwidth to the global register freelist is reduced since only live-outs consume free registers, and not local values. Third, to support trace misprediction recovery, the global rename map table is checkpointed only at trace boundaries instead of at every branch, so fewer shadow maps are required.

### Instruction Dispatch

Merging instructions into the window is also simplified. A single trace is routed to a single PE. A conventional processor routes multiple instructions to as many, possibly noncontiguous instruction buffers.

### Instruction Issue Logic, Register File, and Result Bypasses

The instruction issue mechanism is possibly the most complex aspect of current dynamically scheduled superscalar processors [13]. Each cycle, the processor examines the instruction window for instructions whose input values are available and are ready to issue (*wakeup logic*). Of the ready instructions, a number of them are selected for issue based on resource constraints (*select logic*). The selected instructions read values from the register file and are routed to functional units, where they execute and write results to the register file. Each result must also be quickly bypassed to functional units to be consumed by pipelined, data dependent instructions (*result bypasses*). The wakeup logic, select logic, register file, and result bypasses all grow in complexity as the size of the instruction window and the number of parallel execution units are increased [13].

The large trace processor instruction window is distributed among multiple smaller processing elements (PEs), as shown in Fig. 8.19. Each PE resembles a small superscalar processor and at any given time is allocated a single trace to process. A PE has (1) enough instruction issue buffers to hold an entire trace, (2) multiple dedicated functional units, and (3) a dedicated local register file for storing and communicating local values.

Logically, a single global register file stores and communicates global values. Each PE contains a copy of the global register file for private read ports. Write ports to the global register file are shared, however. All PEs are connected to shared global result buses, which write values simultaneously into all copies of the global register file.

A hierarchical instruction window simplifies the wakeup logic, select logic, register file, and result bypasses. Each aspect is described below.

Waiting instructions monitor fewer "tags" to determine when to wakeup. Tags are broadcast by producer instructions soon after issuing, to wakeup dependent instructions. Although each PE monitors both its own local tags and all global tags, overall, fewer tags are monitored than in an equivalent, nonhierarchical processor. The number of local tags is small, e.g., four tags for a four-issue PE. Even the number of global tags is small due to reduced global register traffic, e.g., typically two to four tags are sufficient [24]. Also, tags are broadcast on shorter wires—the length of a PE trace window instead of the length of the entire window (of course, global tags and values first incur one cycle of delay on the global result buses, as discussed below). The combination of fewer tags and a smaller wakeup window greatly reduces wakeup circuit delay, allowing a faster clock.

Instruction select logic is fully distributed. Each PE independently selects ready instructions from its trace and routes them to dedicated functional units. Here, fewer instruction candidates and fewer functional units reduce select circuit delay, allowing a faster clock.

The local register file is quite fast because it contains few registers (e.g., typically eight registers [24]) and has relatively few read and write ports, comparable to today's four-issue superscalar processors. The complexity of the global register file is reduced because much of the register traffic is off-loaded to the local register files. For an equivalent instruction window, the global register file requires far fewer registers and read/write ports than the monolithic file of nonhierarchical processors.

Finally, result bypasses, which are primarily long interconnect, are receiving much attention lately due to technology trends. In deep sub-micron technologies, interconnect delay improves less with technology scaling than logic delay does [1,13]. This trend highlights the importance of purposeful, nonuniform bypass latencies. Local values are bypassed quickly among functional units in a PE. Global values incur an extra cycle (or more) on the global result buses, but at least not all values are broadcast on global interconnect. In a conventional superscalar processor, all bypasses are effectively global.

## Summary via Analogy

Prior to superscalar processors, comparatively simple out-of-order processors fetched, dispatched, issued, and executed one instruction per cycle, as shown in the left-hand side of Fig. 8.21. The branch predictor predicts up to one branch each cycle and a single PC fetches one instruction from a simple instruction cache. The renaming mechanism, e.g., Tomasulo's algorithm [30], performs simple dependence checking by looking up a couple of source tags in the register file. And at most one instruction is steered to the reservation station of a functional unit each cycle. After completing, instructions arbitrate for a common data bus, and the winner writes its result and tag onto the bus and into the register file.

The superscalar paradigm "widens" each of these pipeline stages and increases complexity with each additional instruction per cycle. This is clearly manageable up to a point: high-speed, dynamically scheduled 4-issue superscalar processors currently set the performance standard in microprocessors. But there is a crossover point beyond which it becomes more efficient to manage instructions in groups, that is, hierarchically.

A trace processor manages instructions hierarchically. In the right-hand side of Fig. 8.21, the top-most level of the trace processor hierarchy is shown (the trace-level). The picture is virtually identical to the

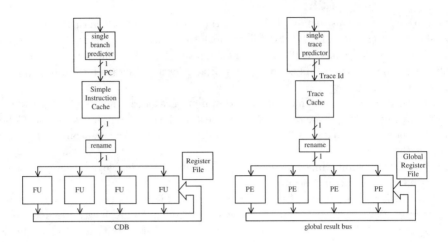

**FIGURE 8.21**    Analogy between a single instruction and a single trace.

single-issue, out-of-order processor on the left-hand side. The unit of operation has changed from one instruction to one trace, but the pipeline bandwidth remains 1 unit per cycle.

In essence, grouping instructions within traces is a reprieve. Complexity (cycle time) does not necessarily increase with each additional instruction added to a trace. Additional branches are absorbed by the trace cache and trace predictor, and additional source and destination operands are absorbed by handling data flow hierarchically. Also, complexity (cycle time) does not necessarily increase with one or two additional PEs. Hardware parallelism is allowed to expand incrementally—up to a point, at which time perhaps another level of hierarchy, and another reprieve, is needed.

Perhaps the most important thing to remember about trace processors is that the whole processor contributes to parallelism, but cycle time is influenced more by an individual processing element than the whole processor.

## References

1. M. Bohr. Interconnect Scaling—The Real Limiter to High Performance ULSI. *1995 International Electron Devices Meeting Technical Digest,* pp. 241–244, 1995.
2. T. Conte, K. Menezes, P. Mills, and B. Patel. Optimization of Instruction Fetch Mechanisms for High Issue Rates. *22nd International Symposium on Computer Architecture,* pp. 333–344, June 1995.
3. S. Dutta and M. Franklin. Control Flow Prediction with Tree-like Subgraphs for Superscalar Processors. *28th International Symposium on Microarchitecture,* pp. 258–263, November 1995.
4. D. Friendly, S. Patel, and Y. Patt. Alternative Fetch and Issue Policies for the Trace Cache Fetch Mechanism. *30th International Symposium on Microarchitecture,* pp. 24–33, December 1997.
5. D. Friendly, S. Patel, and Y. Patt. Putting the Fill Unit to Work: Dynamic Optimizations for Trace Cache Microprocessors. *31st International Symposium on Microarchitecture,* pp. 173–181, December 1998.
6. Q. Jacobson, E. Rotenberg, and J. E. Smith. Path-Based Next Trace Prediction. *30th International Symposium on Microarchitecture,* pp. 14–23, December 1997.
7. Q. Jacobson and J. E. Smith. Instruction Pre-Processing in Trace Processors. *5th International Symposium on High-Performance Computer Architecture,* January 1999.
8. J. Johnson. Expansion Caches for Superscalar Processors. Technical Report CSL-TR-94-630, Computer Systems Laboratory, Stanford University, June 1994.
9. M. S. Lam and R. P. Wilson. Limits of Control Flow on Parallelism. *19th International Symposium on Computer Architecture,* pp. 46–57, May 1992.
10. M. Lipasti and J. Shen. Exceeding the Dataflow Limit via Value Prediction. *29th International Symposium on Microarchitecture,* December 1996.

11. S. Melvin, M. Shebanow, and Y. Patt. Hardware Support for Large Atomic Units in Dynamically Scheduled Machines. *21st International Symposium on Microarchitecture*, pp. 60–66, December 1988.

12. S. Melvin and Y. Patt. Performance Benefits of Large Execution Atomic Units in Dynamically Scheduled Machines. *3rd International Conference on Supercomputing*, pp. 427–432, June 1989.

13. S. Palacharla, N. Jouppi, and J. E. Smith. Quantifying the Complexity of Superscalar Processors. Technical Report CS-TR-96-1328, Computer Sciences Department, University of Wisconsin-Madison, November 1996.

14. S. Patel, D. Friendly, and Y. Patt. Critical Issues Regarding the Trace Cache Fetch Mechanism. Technical Report CSE-TR-335-97, Department of Electrical Engineering and Computer Science, University of Michigan-Ann Arbor, 1997.

15. S. Patel, M. Evers, and Y. Patt. Improving Trace Cache Effectiveness with Branch Promotion and Trace Packing. *25th International Symposium on Computer Architecture*, pp. 262–271, June 1998.

16. S. Patel, D. Friendly, and Y. Patt. Evaluation of Design Options for the Trace Cache Fetch Mechanism. *IEEE Transactions on Computers* (special issue on cache memory), 48(2):193–204, February 1999.

17. S. Patel. Trace Cache Design for Wide-Issue Superscalar Processors. PhD Thesis, University of Michigan-Ann Arbor, 1999.

18. A. Peleg and U. Weiser. Dynamic Flow Instruction Cache Memory Organized around Trace Segments Independent of Virtual Address Line. U.S. Patent Number 5,381,533, January 1995.

19. E. Rotenberg, S. Bennett, and J. E. Smith. Trace Cache: A Low Latency Approach to High Bandwidth Instruction Fetching. Technical Report CS-TR-96-1310, Computer Sciences Department, University of Wisconsin-Madison, April 1996.

20. E. Rotenberg, S. Bennett, and J. E. Smith. Trace Cache: A Low Latency Approach to High Bandwidth Instruction Fetching. *29th International Symposium on Microarchitecture*, pp. 24–34, December 1996.

21. E. Rotenberg, Q. Jacobson, Y. Sazeides, and J. E. Smith. Trace Processors. *30th International Symposium on Microarchitecture*, pp. 138–148, December 1997.

22. E. Rotenberg, Q. Jacobson, and J. E. Smith. A Study of Control Independence in Superscalar Processors. *5th International Symposium on High-Performance Computer Architecture*, January 1999.

23. E. Rotenberg, S. Bennett, and J. E. Smith. A Trace Cache Microarchitecture and Evaluation. *IEEE Transactions on Computers* (special issue on cache memory), 48(2):111–120, February 1999.

24. E. Rotenberg. Trace Processors: Exploiting Hierarchy and Speculation. PhD Thesis, University of Wisconsin-Madison, August 1999.

25. E. Rotenberg and J. E. Smith. Control Independence in Trace Processors. *32nd International Symposium on Microarchitecture*, November 1999.

26. A. Seznec, S. Jourdan, P. Sainrat, and P. Michaud. Multiple-block Ahead Branch Predictors. *7th International Conference on Architectural Support for Programming Languages and Operating Systems*, October 1996.

27. J. E. Smith and S. Vajapeyam. Trace Processors: Moving to Fourth-Generation Microarchitectures. *IEEE Computer* (special issue on Billion-Transistor Processors), September 1997.

28. G. S. Sohi, S. Breach, and T. N. Vijaykumar. Multiscalar Processors. *22nd International Symposium on Computer Architecture*, pp. 414–425, June 1995.

29. K. Sundararaman and M. Franklin. Multiscalar Execution along a Single Flow of Control. *International Conference on Parallel Processing*, August 1997.

30. R. Tomasulo. An Efficient Algorithm for Exploiting Multiple Arithmetic Units. *IBM Journal of Research and Development*, 11(1):25–33, January 1967.

31. S. Vajapeyam and T. Mitra. Improving Superscalar Instruction Dispatch and Issue by Exploiting Dynamic Code Sequences. *24th International Symposium on Computer Architecture*, pp. 1–12, June 1997.

32. T.-Y. Yeh, D. T. Marr, and Y. N. Patt. Increasing the Instruction Fetch Rate via Multiple Branch Prediction and a Branch Address Cache. *7th International Conference on Supercomputing*, pp. 67–76, July 1993.

# 9

# Computer Arithmetic

Earl E. Swartzlander, Jr.
*University of Texas at Austin*

Gensuke Goto
*Yamagata University*

## 9.1  High-Speed Computer Arithmetic

*Earl E. Swartzlander, Jr.*

### Introduction

The speed of a computer is determined to a first order by the speed of the arithmetic unit and the speed of the memory. Although the speed of both units depends directly on the implementation technology, arithmetic unit speed also depends strongly on the logic design. Even for an integer adder, speed can easily vary by an order of magnitude while the complexity varies by less than 50%.

This chapter section begins with a brief discussion of binary fixed point number systems in the subsection on "Fixed Point Number Systems." The subsection on "Fixed Point Arithmetic Algorithms" provides examples of fixed point implementations of the four basic arithmetic operations (i.e., add, subtract, multiply, and divide). Finally, the "Floating Point Arithmetic" subsection describes algorithms for floating point arithmetic.

Regarding notation, capital letters represent digital numbers (i.e., $n$-bit words), while subscripted lower case letters represent bits of the corresponding word. The subscripts range from 0 to $n - 1$ to indicate the bit position within the word ($x_0$ is the least significant bit of $X$, $x_{n-1}$ is the most significant bit of $X$, etc.). The logic designs presented in this chapter are based on positive logic with AND, OR, and INVERT operations. Depending on the technology used for implementation, different logical operations (such as NAND and NOR) or direct transistor realizations may be used, but the basic concepts do not change significantly.

### Fixed-Point Number Systems

Most arithmetic is performed with fixed-point numbers, which have constant scaling (i.e., the position of the binary point is fixed). The numbers can be interpreted as fractions, integers, or mixed numbers, depending on the application. Pairs of fixed-point numbers are used to create floating-point numbers, as discussed in "Floating-Point Arithmetic" subsection.

At the present time, fixed-point binary numbers are generally represented using the two's complement number system. This choice has prevailed over the sign magnitude and one's complement number systems, because the frequently performed operations of addition and subtraction are easiest to perform on two's

**TABLE 9.1**    4-Bit Fractional Two's Complement Numbers

| Decimal Fraction | Binary Representation |
|:---:|:---:|
| +7/8 | 0111 |
| +3/4 | 0110 |
| +5/8 | 0101 |
| +1/2 | 0100 |
| +3/8 | 0011 |
| +1/4 | 0010 |
| +1/8 | 0001 |
| +0 | 0000 |
| −1/8 | 1111 |
| −1/4 | 1110 |
| −3/8 | 1101 |
| −1/2 | 1100 |
| −5/8 | 1011 |
| −3/4 | 1010 |
| −7/8 | 1001 |
| −1 | 1000 |

complement numbers. Sign magnitude numbers are more efficient for multiplication, but the lower frequency of multiplication and the development of the efficient modified Booth's two's complement multiplication algorithm have resulted in the nearly universal selection of the two's complement number system for most applications. The algorithms presented in this chapter section assume the use of two's complement numbers.

Fixed-point number systems represent numbers, say $A$, by $n$ bits: a sign bit, and $n-1$ data bits. By convention the most significant bit, $a_{n-1}$, is the sign bit, which is a ONE for negative numbers and a ZERO for positive numbers. The $n-1$ data bits are $a_{n-2}, a_{n-3}, \ldots, a_1, a_0$. In the section that follows fixed point fractions will be described for each of the three systems.

In the two's complement fractional number system, the value of a number is the sum of $n-1$ positive binary fractional bits and a sign bit which has a weight of $-1$:

$$A = -a_{n-1} + \sum_{i=0}^{n-2} a_i 2^{i-n+1} \qquad (9.1)$$

Examples of 4-bit two's complement fractions are shown in Table 9.1. A couple of significant points are shown in the table: first, there is only a single representation of zero (specifically 0, which is represented by 0000) and second, the system is not symmetric (there is a negative number, specifically −1, which is represented by 1000, for which there is no positive equivalent). The latter property means that negating a valid number can produce a nonrepresentable result.

Two's complement numbers are negated by complementing all bits and adding a ONE to the least significant bit position. For example, to form −3/8:

$$
\begin{array}{lll}
+3/8 & = 0011 & \\
\text{invert all bits} & = 1100 & \\
\text{add 1} & \quad 0001 & \\
& \quad 1101 & = -3/8 \\
\text{Check: invert all bits} & = 0010 & \\
\text{add 1} & \quad 0001 & \\
& \quad 0011 & = +3/8
\end{array}
$$

Truncation of two's complement numbers is shown in Fig. 9.1. This figure shows the relationship between an infinitely precise number $A$ and its representation with a two's complement fraction $T(A)$.

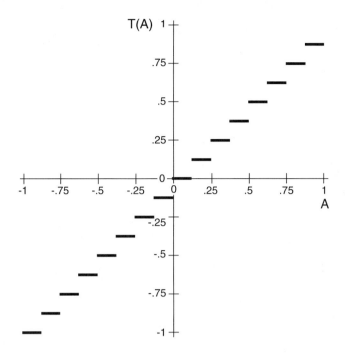

**FIGURE 9.1** Relationship between an infinitely precise number, A, and its representation by a truncated four-bit two's complement fraction $T(A)$.

As can be seen from the figure, truncation never increases the value of the number. The truncated numbers have values that are either unchanged or shifted toward negative infinity. If a large number of numbers are truncated, on the average there is a downward shift of one-half the value of a least significant bit (LSB). Summing many truncated numbers (which may occur in scientific, matrix, and signal processing applications) can cause a significant accumulated error.

## Fixed-Point Arithmetic Algorithms

This subsection presents a reasonable assortment of typical fixed point algorithms for addition, subtraction, multiplication, and division.

### Fixed-Point Addition

Addition is performed by summing the corresponding bits of the two $n$-bit numbers, including the sign bit. Subtraction is performed by summing the corresponding bits of the minuend and the two's complement of the subtrahend. Overflow is detected in a two's complement adder by comparing the carry signals into and out of the most significant adder stage (i.e., the stage which computes the sign bit). If the carries differ, the arithmetic has overflowed and the result is invalid.

#### Full Adder

The full adder is the fundamental building block of most arithmetic circuits. Its operation is defined by the truth table shown in Table 9.2. The sum and carry outputs are described by the following equations:

$$s_k = a_k \bar{b}_k \bar{c}_k + \bar{a}_k b_k \bar{c}_k + \bar{a}_k \bar{b}_k c_k + a_k b_k c_k \tag{9.2}$$

$$c_{k+1} = \bar{a}_k b_k c_k + a_k \bar{b}_k c_k + a_k b_k \bar{c}_k + a_k b_k c_k = a_k b_k + a_k c_k + b_k c_k \tag{9.3}$$

**TABLE 9.2**    Full Adder Truth Table

| Inputs | | | Outputs | |
|---|---|---|---|---|
| $a_k$ | $b_k$ | $c_k$ | $c_{k+1}$ | $s_k$ |
| 0 | 0 | 0 | 0 | 0 |
| 0 | 0 | 1 | 0 | 1 |
| 0 | 1 | 0 | 0 | 1 |
| 0 | 1 | 1 | 1 | 0 |
| 1 | 0 | 0 | 0 | 1 |
| 1 | 0 | 1 | 1 | 0 |
| 1 | 1 | 0 | 1 | 0 |
| 1 | 1 | 1 | 1 | 1 |

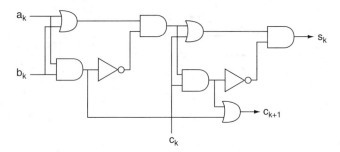

**FIGURE 9.2**    Nine gate full adder.

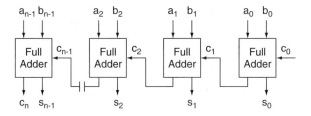

**FIGURE 9.3**    Ripple carry adder.

where $a_k$, $b_k$, and $c_k$ are the inputs to the $k$th full adder stage, and $s_k$ and $c_{k+1}$ are the sum and carry outputs, respectively.

In evaluating the relative complexity of implementations it is often convenient to assume a nine gate realization of the full adder, as shown in Fig. 9.2. For this implementation, the delay from either $a_k$ or $b_k$ to $s_k$ is six gate delays and the delay from $c_k$ to $c_{k+1}$ is two gate delays. Some technologies, such as CMOS, form inverting gates (e.g., NAND and NOR gates) more efficiently than the non-inverting gates that are assumed in this chapter. Circuits with equivalent speed and complexity can be constructed with inverting gates.

### Ripple Carry Adder
A ripple carry adder for $n$-bit numbers is implemented by concatenating $n$ full adders, as shown in Fig. 9.3. At the $k$th bit position, bits $a_k$ and $b_k$ of operands $A$ and $B$ and the carry signal from the preceding adder stage, $c_k$, are used to generate the $k$th bit of the sum, $s_k$, and the carry, $c_{k+1}$, to the next adder stage. This is called a ripple carry adder, since the carry signals "ripple" from the least significant bit position to the most significant. If the ripple carry adder is implemented by concatenating $n$ of the nine gate full adders, which were shown in Fig. 9.2, an $n$-bit ripple carry adder requires $2n + 4$ gate delays to produce the most significant sum bit and $2n + 3$ gate delays to produce the carry output. A total of $9n$ logic gates are required to implement the $n$-bit ripple carry adder. In comparing the delay and complexity of adders,

the delay from data input to most significant sum output denoted by DELAY and the gate count denoted by GATES will be used. These DELAY and GATES are subscripted by RCA to indicate ripple carry adder. Although these simple metrics are suitable for first order comparisons, more accurate comparisons require more exact modeling since the implementations may be effected with transistor networks (as opposed to gates), which will have different delay and complexity characteristics.

$$\text{DELAY}_{RCA} = 2n + 4 \qquad (9.4)$$

$$\text{GATES}_{RCA} = 9n \qquad (9.5)$$

### Carry Lookahead Adder

Another popular adder approach is the carry lookahead adder [1,2]. Here specialized logic computes the carries in parallel. The carry lookahead adder uses modified full adders (modified in the sense that a carry output is not formed) for each bit position and lookahead modules, which have carry outputs and block carry generate and propagate outputs that indicate that a carry is generated within the module, or that an incoming carry would propagate across the module. This is seen by rewriting Eq. (9.3) with $g_k = a_k b_k$ and $p_k = a_k + b_k$.

$$c_{k+1} = g_k + p_k c_k \qquad (9.6)$$

This helps to explain the concept of carry generation and propagation: At a given stage a carry is generated if $g_k$ is true (i.e., both $a_k$ and $b_k$ are ONEs), and a stage propagates an input carry to its output if $p_k$ is true (i.e., either $a_k$ or $b_k$ is a ONE). The nine gate full adder shown in Fig. 9.2 has AND and OR gates that produce $g_k$ and $p_k$ with no additional complexity. In fact, because the carry out is produced in the lookahead logic, the OR gate that produces the $c_{k+1}$ can be eliminated. The result is the eight gate modified full adder shown in Fig. 9.4.

Extending Eq. (9.6) to a second stage:

$$
\begin{aligned}
c_{k+2} &= g_{k+1} + p_{k+1} c_{k+1} \\
&= g_{k+1} + p_{k+1}(g_k + p_k c_k) \\
&= g_{k+1} + p_{k+1} g_k + p_{k+1} p_k c_k \qquad (9.7)
\end{aligned}
$$

Equation(9.7) results from evaluating Eq. (9.6) for the $(k+1)$th stage and substituting $c_{k+1}$ from Eq. (9.6). Carry $c_{k+2}$ exits from stage $k + 1$ if: (a) a carry is generated there or (b) a carry is generated in stage $k$ and propagates across stage $k + 1$ or (c) a carry enters stage $k$ and propagates across both stages $k$ and

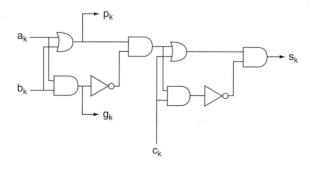

**FIGURE 9.4** Eight gate modified full adder.

$k + 1$, etc. Extending to a third stage:

$$c_{k+3} = g_{k+2} + p_{k+2}c_{k+2}$$

$$= g_{k+2} + p_{k+2}(g_{k+1} + p_{k+1}g_k + p_{k+1}p_kc_k)$$

$$= g_{k+2} + p_{k+2}g_{k+1} + p_{k+2}p_{k+1}g_k + p_{k+2}p_{k+1}p_kc_k \qquad (9.8)$$

Although it would be possible to continue this process indefinitely, each additional stage increases the fan-in (i.e., the number of inputs) of the logic gates. Four inputs (as required to implement Eq. (9.8)) is frequently the maximum number of inputs per gate for current technologies. To continue the process, block generate and block propagate signals are defined over four bit blocks (stages $k$ to $k + 3$), $g_{k:k+3}$ and $p_{k:k+3}$, respectively:

$$g_{k:k+3} = g_{k+3} + p_{k+3}\,g_{k+2} + p_{k+3}\,p_{k+2}\,g_{k+1} + p_{k+3}\,p_{k+2}\,p_{k+1}\,g_k \qquad (9.9)$$

and

$$p_{k:k+3} = p_{k+3}\,p_{k+2}\,p_{k+1}\,p_k \qquad (9.10)$$

Equation (9.6) can be expressed in terms of the 4-bit block generate and propagate signals:

$$c_{k+4} = g_{k:k+3} + p_{k:k+3}\,c_k \qquad (9.11)$$

Thus, the carry out from a 4-bit wide block can be computed in only four gate delays (the first to compute $p_i$ and $g_i$ for $i = k$ through $k + 3$, the second to evaluate $p_{k:k+3}$, the second and third to evaluate $g_{k:k+3}$, and the third and fourth to evaluate $c_{k+4}$ using Eq. (9.11)).

An $n$-bit carry lookahead adder requires $\lceil (n - 1)/(r - 1) \rceil$ lookahead blocks, where $r$ is the width of the block. A 4-bit lookahead block is a direct implementation of Eqs. (9.6)–(9.10), with 14 logic gates. In general, an $r$-bit lookahead block requires $\frac{1}{2}(3r + r^2)$ logic gates. The Manchester carry chain [3] is an alternative switch-based technique for the implementation of the lookahead block.

Figure 9.5 shows the interconnection of 16 adders and five lookahead logic blocks to realize a 16-bit carry lookahead adder. The sequence of events, which occur during an add operation, is as follows: (1) apply $A$, $B$, and carry in signals, (2) each adder computes $P$ and $G$, (3) first level lookahead logic computes the 4-bit propagate and generate signals, (4) second level lookahead logic computes $c_4$, $c_8$, and $c_{12}$, (5) first level lookahead logic computes the individual carries, and (6) each adder computes the sum outputs. This process may be extended to larger adders by subdividing the large adder into 16-bit blocks and using additional levels of carry lookahead (a 64-bit adder requires three levels).

The delay of carry lookahead adders is evaluated by recognizing that an adder with a single level of carry lookahead (for 4-bit words) has six gate delays, and that each additional level of lookahead increases the maximum word size by a factor of four and adds four gate delays. More generally [4, pp. 83–88], the number of lookahead levels for an $n$-bit adder is $\lceil \log_r n \rceil$ where $r$ is the maximum number of inputs per gate. Since an $r$-bit carry lookahead adder has six gate delays and there are four additional gate delays per carry lookahead level after the first,

$$\text{DELAY}_{\text{CLA}} = 2 + 4 \lceil \log_r n \rceil \qquad (9.12)$$

The complexity of an $n$-bit carry lookahead adder implemented with $r$-bit lookahead blocks is $n$ modified full adders (each of which requires eight gates) and $\lceil (n - 1)/(r - 1) \rceil$ lookahead logic blocks [each of which requires $\frac{1}{2}(3r + r^2)$ gates].

$$\text{GATES}_{\text{CLA}} = 8n + \frac{1}{2}(3r + r^2)\left\lceil \frac{n - 1}{r - 1} \right\rceil \qquad (9.13)$$

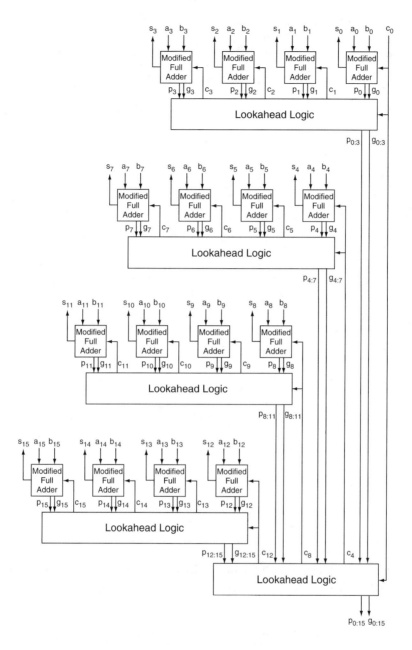

**FIGURE 9.5**  16-bit carry lookahead adder.

If $r = 4$

$$\text{GATES}_{\text{CLA}} \approx 12\frac{2}{3}n - 4\frac{2}{3} \tag{9.14}$$

The carry lookahead approach reduces the delay of adders from increasing linearly with the word size (as is the case for ripple carry adders) to increasing in proportion to the logarithm of the word size. As with ripple carry adders, the carry lookahead adder complexity grows linearly with the word size (for $r = 4$, this occurs at a 40% faster rate than the ripple carry adders).

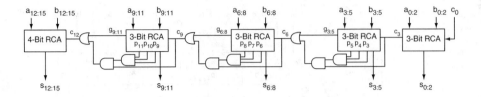

**FIGURE 9.6**    16-bit carry skip adder.

### Carry Skip Adder

The carry skip adder divides the words to be added into blocks (like the carry lookahead adder). The basic structure of a 16-bit carry skip adder is shown on Fig. 9.6. Within each block, a ripple carry adder produces the sum bits and the carry (which is used as a block generate). In addition, an AND gate is used to form the block propagate signal. These signals are combined using Eq. (9.11) to produce the carry signal for the next block.

For example, with $k = 3$, Eq. (9.11) yields $c_6 = g_{3:5} + p_{3:5}c_3$. The carry out of the second ripple carry adder is a block generate signal if it is evaluated when carries generated by the data inputs (i.e., $a_{3:5}$ and $b_{3:5}$ on Fig. 9.6) are valid, but before the carry that results from the $c_3$. Normally, these two types of carries coincide in time, but in the carry skip adder, the $c_3$ signal is produced by a 3-bit ripple carry adder, so the carry output is a block generate from nine gate delays after application of $A$ and $B$ until it becomes $c_6$ at 15 gate delays after application of $A$ and $B$.

In the carry skip adder, the first and last blocks are simple ripple carry adders while the $\lceil n/k \rceil - 2$ intermediate blocks are ripple carry adders augmented with three gates. The delay of a carry skip adder is the sum of $2k + 3$ gate delays to produce the carry in the first block, two gate delays through each of the intermediate blocks, and $2k + 1$ gate delays to produce the most significant sum bit in the last block. To simplify the analysis, the ceiling function in the count of intermediate blocks is ignored. If the block width is $k$:

$$\text{DELAY}_{\text{SKIP}} = 2k + 3 + 2\left(\frac{n}{k} - 2\right) + 2k + 1$$

$$= 4k + 2\frac{n}{k} \qquad (9.15)$$

where $\text{DELAY}_{\text{SKIP}}$ is the total delay of the carry skip adder with a single level of $k$-bit wide blocks. The optimum block size is determined by taking the derivative of $\text{DELAY}_{\text{SKIP}}$ with respect to $k$, setting it to zero and solving for $k$. The resulting optimum values for $k$ and $\text{DELAY}_{\text{SKIP}}$ are

$$k = \sqrt{\frac{n}{2}} \qquad (9.16)$$

$$\text{DELAY}_{\text{SKIP}} = 4\sqrt{2n} \qquad (9.17)$$

Better results can be obtained by varying the block width so that the first and last blocks are smaller and the intermediate blocks are larger, and by using multiple levels of carry skip [5,6].

The complexity of the carry skip adder is only slightly greater than that of a ripple carry adder because the first and last blocks are ripple carry adders and the intermediate stages are ripple carry adders with three gates added for carry skipping.

$$\text{GATES}_{\text{SKIP}} = 9n + 3\left(\left\lceil \frac{n}{k} \right\rceil - 2\right) \qquad (9.18)$$

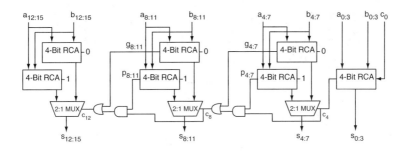

**FIGURE 9.7** 16-bit carry select adder.

### Carry Select Adder

The carry select adder divides the words to be added into blocks and forms two sums for each block in parallel (one with a carry in of ZERO and the other with a carry in of ONE). As shown for a 16-bit carry select adder on Fig. 9.7, the carry out from the previous block controls a multiplexer that selects the appropriate sum. The carry out is computed using Eq. (9.11), since the block propagate signal is the carry out of an adder with a carry input of ONE and the block generate signal is the carry out of an adder with a carry input of ZERO.

If a constant block width of $k$ is used, there will be $\lceil n/k \rceil$ blocks and the delay to generate the sum is $2k + 3$ gate delays to form the carry out of the first block, two gate delays for each of the $\lceil n/k \rceil - 2$ intermediate blocks, and three gate delays (for the multiplexer) in the final block. To simplify the analysis, the ceiling function in the count of intermediate blocks is ignored. The total delay is thus

$$\text{DELAY}_{\text{C-SEL}} = 2k + 2\frac{n}{k} + 2 \tag{9.19}$$

where $\text{DELAY}_{\text{C-SEL}}$ is the total delay. The optimum block size is determined by taking the derivative of $\text{DELAY}_{\text{C-SEL}}$ with respect to $k$, setting it to zero and solving for $k$. The result is

$$k = \sqrt{n} \tag{9.20}$$

$$\text{DELAY}_{\text{C-SEL}} = 2 + 4\sqrt{n} \tag{9.21}$$

As for the carry skip adder, better results can be obtained by varying the width of the blocks. In this case the optimum is to make the two least significant blocks are the same size and each successively more significant block is one bit larger. For this configuration, the delay for each block's most significant sum bit will equal the delay to the multiplexer control signal [7, p. A-38].

The complexity of the carry select adder is $2n - k$ ripple carry adder stages, the intermediate carry logic and $(\lceil n/k \rceil - 1)$ $k$-bit wide 2:1 multiplexers.

$$\begin{aligned}
\text{GATES}_{\text{C-SEL}} &= 9(2n - k) + 2(\lceil n/k \rceil - 2) + 3(n - k) + \lceil n/k \rceil - 1 \\
&= 21n - 12k + 3\lceil n/k \rceil - 5 \tag{9.22}
\end{aligned}$$

This is somewhat more than twice the complexity of a ripple carry adder.

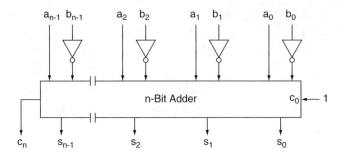

**FIGURE 9.8**   Two's complement subtracter.

## Fixed-Point Subtraction

As noted in previous subsection, subtraction of two's complement numbers is accomplished by adding the minuend to the inverted bits of the subtrahend and adding a one at the least significant position. Figure 9.8 shows a two's complement subtracter which computes $A - B$. The inverters complement the bits of $B$; formation of the two's complement is completed by setting the carry into the least significant adder stage to a ONE.

## Fixed-Point Multiplication

Multiplication is generally implemented either via a sequence of addition, subtraction, and shift operations or with direct logic implementations.

### Sequential Booth Multiplier

The Booth algorithm [8] is widely used for two's complement multiplication, since it is easy to implement. Earlier two's complement multipliers (e.g., [9]) required data dependent correction cycles if either operand is negative. To multiply $A$ $B$, the product, $P$, is initially set to ZERO. Then, the bits of the multiplier, $A$, are examined in pairs of adjacent bits starting with the least significant bit (i.e., $a_0 a_{-1}$) and assuming $a_{-1} = 0$:

- If $a_i = a_{i-1}$, $P = P/2$
- If $a_i = 0$ and $a_{i-1} = 1$, $P = (P + B)/2$
- If $a_i = 1$ and $a_{i-1} = 0$, $P = (P - B)/2$

The division by 2 is not performed on the last stage (i.e., when $i = n - 1$). All of the divide-by-two operations are simple arithmetic right shifts (i.e., the word is shifted right one position and the old sign bit is repeated for the new sign bit), and overflows in the addition process are ignored. The algorithm is illustrated in Fig. 9.9, which shows the formation of products for all combinations of $\pm 5/8$ times $\pm 3/4$ for 4-bit operands. The sequential Booth multiplier requires $n$ cycles to form the product of a pair of $n$-bit numbers, where each cycle consists of an $n$-bit addition and a shift, an $n$-bit subtraction and a shift, or a shift without any other arithmetic operation.

### Sequential Modified Booth Multiplier

The radix-4 modified Booth multiplier described by MacSorley [2] uses $n/2$ cycles where each cycle examines three adjacent bits, adds or subtracts 0, $B$, or $2B$ and shifts two bits to the right. Table 9.3 shows the operations as a function of the three bits $a_{i+1}$, $a_i$, and $a_{i-1}$. The radix-4 modified Booth multiplier takes half the number of cycles as the "standard" Booth multiplier, although the operations performed during a cycle are slightly more complex (since it is necessary to select one of five possible addends instead of one of three). Extensions to higher radices that examine more than three bits [10] are possible, but generally not attractive because the addition/subtraction operations involve non-power of two multiples (such as 3, 5, etc.) of $B$, which raises the complexity.

**TABLE 9.3**   Radix-4 Modified Booth Multiplication

| $a_{i+1}$ | $a_i$ | $a_{i-1}$ | Operation |
|---|---|---|---|
| 0 | 0 | 0 | $P = P/4$ |
| 0 | 0 | 1 | $P = (P + B)/4$ |
| 0 | 1 | 0 | $P = (P + B)/4$ |
| 0 | 1 | 1 | $P = (P + 2\,B)/4$ |
| 1 | 0 | 0 | $P = (P - 2\,B)/4$ |
| 1 | 0 | 1 | $P = (P - B)/4$ |
| 1 | 1 | 0 | $P = (P - B)/4$ |
| 1 | 1 | 1 | $P = P/4$ |

POSITIVE TIMES POSITIVE     $A = \frac{5}{8} = 0.101$     $B = \frac{3}{4} = 0.110$

| i | $a_i$ | $a_{i-1}$ | OPERATION | RESULT |
|---|---|---|---|---|
| 0 | 1 | 0 | $P = (P - B)/2$ | 1.1010 |
| 1 | 0 | 1 | $P = (P + B)/2$ | 0.00110 |
| 2 | 1 | 0 | $P = (P - B)/2$ | 1.101110 |
| 3 | 0 | 1 | $P = P + B$ | 0.011110 |

THUS: $P = 0.011110 = \frac{15}{32}$

NEGATIVE TIMES POSITIVE     $A = -\frac{5}{8} = 1.011$     $B = \frac{3}{4} = 0.110$

| i | $a_i$ | $a_{i-1}$ | OPERATION | RESULT |
|---|---|---|---|---|
| 0 | 1 | 0 | $P = (P - B)/2$ | 1.1010 |
| 1 | 1 | 1 | $P = P/2$ | 1.11010 |
| 2 | 0 | 1 | $P = (P + B)/2$ | 0.010010 |
| 3 | 1 | 0 | $P = P - B$ | 1.100010 |

THUS: $P = 1.100010 = -\frac{15}{32}$

POSITIVE TIMES NEGATIVE     $A = \frac{5}{8} = 0.101$     $B = -\frac{3}{4} = 1.010$

| i | $a_i$ | $a_{i-1}$ | OPERATION | RESULT |
|---|---|---|---|---|
| 0 | 1 | 0 | $P = (P - B)/2$ | 0.0110 |
| 1 | 0 | 1 | $P = (P + B)/2$ | 1.1010 |
| 2 | 1 | 0 | $P = (P - B)/2$ | 0.010010 |
| 3 | 0 | 1 | $P = P + B$ | 1.100010 |

THUS: $P = 1.100010 = -\frac{15}{32}$

NEGATIVE TIMES NEGATIVE   $A = -\frac{5}{8} = 1.011$     $B = -\frac{3}{4} = 1.010$

| i | $a_i$ | $a_{i-1}$ | OPERATION | RESULT |
|---|---|---|---|---|
| 0 | 1 | 0 | $P = (P - B)/2$ | 0.0110 |
| 1 | 1 | 1 | $P = P/2$ | 0.00110 |
| 2 | 0 | 1 | $P = (P + B)/2$ | 1.101110 |
| 3 | 1 | 0 | $P = P - B$ | 0.011110 |

THUS: $P = 0.011110 = \frac{15}{32}$

**FIGURE 9.9**   Example of sequential booth multiplication.

### Array Multipliers

An alternative approach to multiplication involves the combinational generation of all bit products and their summation with an array of full adders. The block diagram of a 6 by 6 array multiplier is shown in Fig. 9.10. It uses a 6 by 6 array of cells to form the bit products and five adders (at the bottom of the array) to complete the evaluation of the product. Three types of cells are used in the square array: gate cells (marked G in Fig. 9.10), which use a single gate to form the logic AND of the $x$ and $y$ inputs to the cell; half adder cells (marked HA), which sum the second input to the cell with the logic AND of the $x$

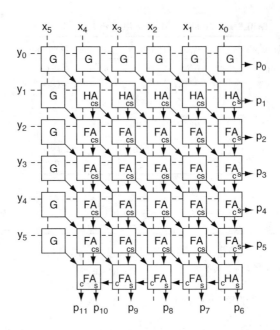

**FIGURE 9.10**  Unsigned 6 by 6 array multiplier.

and $y$ inputs to the cell; and full adder cells (marked FA), which sum the second and third inputs to the cell with the logic AND of the $x$ and $y$ inputs to the cell. Standard half adders and full adders are used in the 5 cell strip at the bottom. An $n$ by $n$ array multiplier requires $2n - 1$ gate cells, $n$ half adders, and $n^2 - 2n$ full adders. Of the half and full adder cells $(n - 1)^2$ have an extra AND gate.

The complexity of the array multiplier is $n^2$ AND gates, $n$ half adders, and $n^2 - 2n$ full adders. If a half adder comprises four gates and a full adder comprises nine gates, the total complexity of an $n$-bit by $n$-bit array multiplier is

$$\text{GATES}_{\text{ARRAY MPY}} = 10n^2 - 14n \qquad (9.23)$$

The delay of the array multiplier is evaluated by following the pathways from the inputs to the outputs. The longest path starts at the upper left corner, progresses to the lower right corner, and then across the bottom to the lower left corner. If it is assumed that the delay from any adder input (for either half or full adders) to any adder output is $k$ gate delays then the total delay of an $n$-bit by $n$-bit array multiplier is:

$$\text{DELAY}_{\text{ARRAY MPY}} = k(2n - 2) + 1 \qquad (9.24)$$

Array multipliers are easily laid out in a cellular fashion, making them suitable for VLSI implementation, where minimizing the design effort may be more important than maximizing the speed.

Modification of the array multiplier to multiply two's complement numbers requires inverting the bits of the multiplier and multiplicand in the most significant row and column while forming the bit product matrix and adding a few correction terms [11,12].

### Wallace Tree/Dadda Fast Multiplier

A method for fast multiplication was developed by Wallace [13] and refined by Dadda [14,15]. With this method, a three-step process is used to multiply two numbers: (1) the bit products are formed, (2) the bit product matrix is "reduced" to a two row matrix where the sum of the rows equals the sum of the bit products, and (3) the two numbers are summed with a fast adder to produce the product. Although this may seem to be a complex process, it yields multipliers with delay proportional to the logarithm of

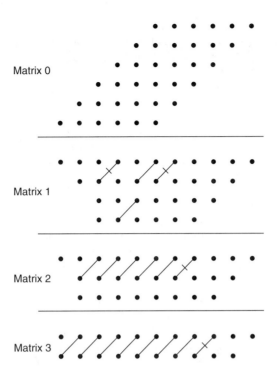

**FIGURE 9.11** Unsigned 6 by 6 Dadda multiplier.

the operand word size, which is "faster" than the Booth multiplier, the modified Booth multiplier, or array multipliers, which all have delays proportional to the word size.

The second step in the fast multiplication process is shown for a 6 by 6 Dadda multiplier on Fig. 9.11. An input 6 by 6 matrix of dots (each dot represents a bit product) is shown as matrix 0. Columns having more than four dots (or that will grow to more than four dots due to carries) are reduced by the use of half adders (each half adder takes in two dots and outputs one in the same column and one in the next more significant column) and full adders (each full adder takes in three dots from a column and outputs one in the same column and one in the next more significant column) so that no column in matrix 1 will have more than four dots. Half adders are shown by a "crossed" line in the succeeding matrix and full adders are shown by a line in the succeeding matrix. In each case the right most dot of the pair that are connected by a line is in the column from which the inputs were taken in the preceding matrix for the adder. In the succeeding steps reduction to matrix 2, with no more than three dots per column, and finally matrix 3, with no more than two dots per column, is performed.

The height of the matrices is determined by working back from the final (two row) matrix and limiting the height of each matrix to the largest integer that is no more than 1.5 times the height of its successor. Each matrix is produced from its predecessor in one adder delay. Since the number of matrices is logarithmically related to the number of rows in matrix 0, which is equal to the number of bits in the words to be multiplied, the delay of the matrix reduction process is proportional to $\log n$. Since the adder that reduces the final two row matrix can be implemented as a carry lookahead adder (which also has logarithmic delay), the total delay for this multiplier is proportional to the logarithm of the word size.

### Fixed Point Division

Division is traditionally implemented as a recurrence, which uses a sequence of shift, subtract, and compare operations, in contrast to the shift and add approach employed for multiplication. The comparison operation is significant. It results in a serial process, which is not amenable to parallel implementation.

### Digit Recurrent Division

The most common division algorithms are digit recurrent algorithms [16,17] based on selecting digits of the quotient $Q$ (where $Q = N/D$) to satisfy the following equation:

$$P_{k+1} = rP_k - q_{n-k-1} D \quad \text{for } k = 1, 2,..., n-1 \tag{9.25}$$

where $P_k$ is the partial remainder after the selection of the $k$th quotient digit, $P_0 = N$ (subject to the constraint $|P_0| < |D|$), $r$ is the radix, $q_{n-k-1}$ is the $k$th quotient digit to the right of the binary point, and $D$ is the divisor. In this section it is assumed that both $N$ and $D$ are positive, see [18] for details on handling the general case.

### Restoring Divider

The restoring division algorithm is similar to paper and pencil division. The basic scheme is shown in Fig. 9.12. Block 1 initializes the algorithm. In step 2, a trial dividend, $TP_{k+1}$, is computed based on the assumption that the quotient bit is a 1. In the third step, $TP_{k+1}$ is compared to 0. If $TP_{k+1}$ is negative, step 4 restores the trial dividend to what it would be if the quotient digit had been assumed to be 0. This restoring operation gives the algorithm its name. Step 5 is performed if $TP_{k+1}$ is zero or positive. Finally, step 6 tests whether all bits of the quotient have been formed and goes to step 2 if more need to be computed. Each pass through steps 2–6 forms one bit of the quotient. As shown in Fig. 9.12, each pass through steps 2–6 requires an addition in step 2, a comparison in step 3, and may require an addition in step 4. If half of the quotient bits are 0 and half are 1, computing an $n$-bit quotient will involve $3n/2$ additions and $n$ comparisons. This is the performing version of the restoring division algorithm, which means that the restoring operation is actually performed in step 4.

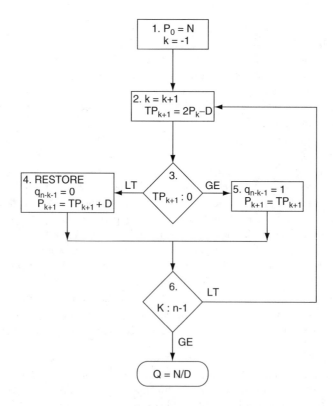

**FIGURE 9.12**   Restoring division.

$P_0 = N = \frac{5}{8}$

$D = \frac{7}{8}$

$n = 4$

$k = 0$, $TP_1 = 2\,P_0 - D = \frac{3}{8}$ Since $TP_1 > 0$, then $q_3 = 1$ and $P_1 = TP_1 = \frac{3}{8}$

$k = 1$, $TP_2 = 2\,P_1 - D = \frac{-1}{8}$ Since $TP_2 < 0$, then $q_2 = 0$ and $P_2 = TP_2 + D = \frac{3}{4}$

$k = 2$, $TP_3 = 2\,P_2 - D = \frac{5}{8}$ Since $TP_3 > 0$, then $q_1 = 1$ and $P_3 = TP_3 = \frac{5}{8}$

$k = 3$, $TP_4 = 2\,P_3 - D = \frac{3}{8}$ Since $TP_4 > 0$, then $q_0 = 1$ and $P_4 = TP_4 = \frac{3}{8}$

$Q = 0.1\ 0\ 1\ 1$

**FIGURE 9.13** Example of restoring division.

Figure 9.13 shows an example of the restoring division algorithm where the first 4-bits of quotient of 5/8 divided by 7/8 is evaluated.

The alternative non-performing version of the algorithm places $2P_k$ in a temporary register in step 2 and uses that value for $P_{k+1}$ in step 4. The nonperforming version computes an $n$-bit quotient in $n$ additions and $n$ comparisons.

### *Nonrestoring Divider*

In nonrestoring division, the quotient digits are constrained to be either $\pm 1$ (i.e., $q_k$ is selected from $\{1, \bar{1}\}$). The digit selection and resulting partial remainder are given for the $k$th iteration by the following relations:

$$\text{If } P_k \geq 0, \qquad q_{n-k-1} = 1 \quad \text{and} \quad P_{k+1} = rP_k - D \tag{9.26}$$

$$\text{If } P_k < 0, \qquad q_{n-k-1} = \bar{1} \quad \text{and} \quad P_{k+1} = rP_k + D \tag{9.27}$$

The basic scheme is shown in Fig. 9.14. Block 1 initializes the algorithm. In step 3, $P_k$ is compared to 0. If $P_k$ is negative, in step 4 the quotient digit is set to $\bar{1}$ and $P_{k+1} = 2P_k + D$. If $P_k$ is positive, in step 5 the quotient digit is set to 1 and $P_{k+1} = 2P_k - D$. Finally, step 6 tests whether all bits of the quotient have been formed and goes to step 2 if more need to be computed. Each pass through steps 2–6 forms one bit of the quotient. As shown in Fig. 9.14, each pass through steps 2–6 requires a comparison in step 3 and an addition in either step 4 or step 5. Thus, computing an $n$-bit quotient will involve $n$ additions and $n$ comparisons.

Figure 9.15 shows an example of the restoring division algorithm where the first four bits of quotient of 5/8 divided by 7/8 is evaluated.

The signed digit number (comprises $\pm 1$ digits) can be converted into a conventional binary number by subtracting, NEG, the number formed by the $\bar{1}$ (with ZEROs where there are +ONEs and ONEs where there are $\bar{1}$s in Q) from, POS, the number formed by the +ONEs (with ZEROs where there are $\bar{1}$s in Q). For the example of Fig. 9.15:

$$Q = 0\,.\,1\,1\ \bar{1},1)\ 1$$

$$POS = 0\,.\,1\,1\,0\,1$$

$$NEG = 0\,.\,0\,0\,1\,0$$

$$Q = 0\,.\,1\,1\,0\,1 - 0\,.\,0\,0\,0\,1$$

$$Q = 0\,.\,1\,1\,0\,1 + 1\,.\,1\,1\,1\,0$$

$$Q = 0\,.\,1\,0\,1\,1$$

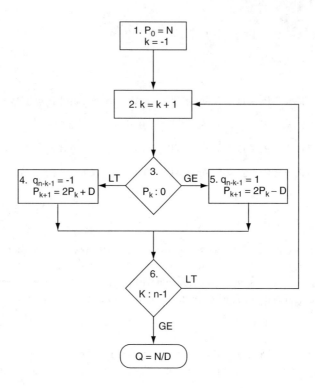

**FIGURE 9.14**   Nonrestoring division.

$$P_0 = N = \frac{5}{8}$$

$$D = \frac{7}{8}$$

$$n = 4$$

$k = 0$, Since $P_0 > 0$, then $q_3 = 1$ and $P_1 = 2P_0 - D = \frac{3}{8}$

$k = 1$, Since $P_1 > 0$, then $q_2 = 1$ and $P_2 = 2P_1 - D = \frac{-1}{8}$

$k = 2$, Since $P_0 < 0$, then $q_1 = \bar{1}$   and $P_3 = 2P_2 + D = \frac{5}{8}$

$k = 3$, Since $P_0 > 0$, then $q_0 = 1$ and $P_4 = 2P_3 - D = \frac{3}{8}$

$Q = 0.11\bar{1}1$   (SIGNED DIGIT FORM)

$Q = 0.1011$   (BINARY)

**FIGURE 9.15**   Example of nonrestoring division.

### *Binary SRT Divider*

The binary SRT division process is similar to nonrestoring division, but the set of allowable quotient digits is increased to $\{1, 0, \bar{1}\}$ and the divisor is restricted to $.5 \leq D < 1$. The digit selection and resulting partial remainder are given for the $k$th iteration by the following relations:

$$\text{If } P_k \geq .5, \qquad q_{n-k-1} = 1 \quad \text{and} \quad P_{k+1} = 2P_k - D \qquad (9.28)$$

$$\text{If } -.5 < P_k < .5, \qquad q_{n-k-1} = 0 \quad \text{and} \quad P_{k+1} = 2P_k \qquad (9.29)$$

$$\text{If } P_k \geq .5, \qquad q_{n-k-1} = \bar{1} \quad \text{and} \quad P_{k+1} = 2P_k + D \qquad (9.30)$$

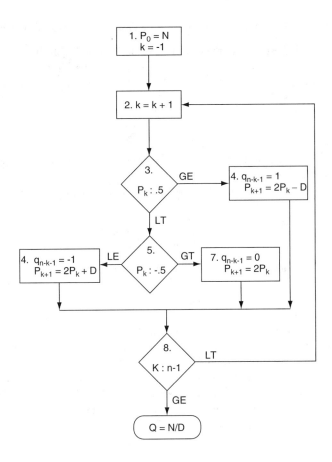

**FIGURE 9.16**    Binary SRT division.

The basic scheme is shown in Fig. 9.16. Block 1 initializes the algorithm. In steps 3 and 5, $P_k$ is compared to $\pm.5$. If $P_k \geq .5$, in step 4 the quotient digit is set to 1 and $P_{k+1} = 2P_k - D$. If $P_k \leq -.5$, in step 6 the quotient digit is set to $\bar{1}$ and $P_{k+1} = 2P_k + D$. If the value of $P_k$ is between $-.5$ and $.5$, step 7 sets $P_{k+1} = 2P_k$. Finally, step 8 tests whether all bits of the quotient have been formed and goes to step 2 if more need to be computed. Each pass through steps 2–8 forms one digit of the quotient. As shown on Fig. 9.16, each pass through steps 2–8 requires one or two comparisons in steps 3 and 5, and may require an addition (in step 4 or step 6). Thus computing an $n$-bit quotient will involve up to $n$ additions and from $n$ to $2n$ comparisons.

### Higher Radix SRT Divider
The higher radix SRT division process is similar to the binary SRT algorithms. Radix 4 is the most common higher radix SRT division algorithm with either a minimally redundant digit sets of $\{2, 1, 0, \bar{1}, \bar{2}\}$ or the maximally redundant digit sets of $\{3, 2, 1, 0, \bar{1}, \bar{2}, \bar{3}\}$. The operation of the algorithm is similar to the binary SRT algorithm shown on Fig. 9.16, except that $P_k$ and $Q$ are applied to a look up table or a programmable logic array (PLA) to determine the quotient digit. A research monograph provides a detailed treatment of SRT division [18].

### Newton–Raphson Divider
A second division technique uses a form of Newton–Raphson iteration to derive a quadratically conver-gent approximation to the reciprocal of the divisor which is then multiplied by the dividend to produce the quotient. In systems which include a fast multiplier, this process is often faster than conventional division [19].

The Newton–Raphson division algorithm to compute $Q = N/D$ consists of three basic steps:

(1) Calculating a starting estimate of the reciprocal of the divisor, $R_{(0)}$. If the divisor, $D$, is normalized (i.e., $\frac{1}{2} \leq D < 1$), then $R_{(0)} = 3 - 2D$ exactly computes $1/D$ at $D = .5$ and $D = 1$ and exhibits maximum error (of approximately 0.17) at $D = \sqrt{1/2}$. Adjusting $R_{(0)}$ downward to by half the maximum error gives

$$R_{(0)} = 2.915 - 2D \tag{9.31}$$

This produces an initial estimate, that is, within about 0.087 of the correct value for all points in the interval $\frac{1}{2} \leq D < 1$.

(2) Computing successively more accurate estimates of the reciprocal by the following iterative procedure:

$$R_{(i+1)} = R_{(i)}(2 - DR_{(i)}) \quad \text{for} \quad i = 0, 1, \ldots, k \tag{9.32}$$

(3) Computing the quotient by multiplying the dividend times the reciprocal of the divisor.

$$Q = NR_{(k)}, \tag{9.33}$$

where $i$ is the iteration count and $N$ is the numerator. Figure 9.17 illustrates the operation of the Newton–Raphson algorithm. For this example, three iterations (one shift, four subtractions, and seven multiplications) produces an answer accurate to nine decimal digits (approximately 30 bits).

With this algorithm, the error decreases quadratically, so that the number of correct bits in each approximation is roughly twice the number of correct bits on the previous iteration. Thus, from a $3\frac{1}{2}$-bit initial approximation, two iterations produce a reciprocal estimate accurate to 14-bits, four iterations produce a reciprocal estimate accurate to 56-bits, etc.

$A = .625$
$B = .75$

$R_{(0)} = 2.915 - 2 \cdot B$                                        1 Shift, 1 Subtract
       $= 2.915 - 2 \cdot .75$
$R_{(0)} = 1.415$

$R_{(1)} = R_{(0)}(2 - B \cdot R_{(0)})$                            2 Multiplys, 1 Subtract
       $= 1.414(2 - .75 \cdot 1.415)$
       $= 1.414 \cdot .95875$
$R_{(1)} = 1.32833125$

$R_{(2)} = R_{(1)}(2 - B \cdot R_{(1)})$                            2 Multiplys, 1 Subtract
       $= 1.32833125(2 - .75 \cdot 1.32833125)$
       $= 1.32833125 \cdot 1.00375156$
$R_{(2)} = 1.3333145677$

$R_{(3)} = R_{(2)}(2 - B \cdot R_{(2)})$                            2 Multiplys, 1 Subtract
       $= 1.3333145677(2 - .75 \cdot 1.3333145677)$
       $= 1.3333145677 \cdot 1.00001407$
$R_{(1)} = 1.3333333331$

$Q = A \cdot R_{(3)}$                                             1 Multiply
$Q = .83333333319$

**FIGURE 9.17**   Example of Newton–Raphson division.

The efficiency of this process is dependent on the availability of a fast multiplier, since each iteration of Eq. (9.32) requires two multiplications and a subtraction. The complete process for the initial estimate, three iterations, and the final quotient determination requires four subtraction operations and seven multiplication operations to produce a 16-bit quotient. This is faster than a conventional non-restoring divider if multiplication is roughly as fast as addition, a condition which may be satisfied for systems which include hardware multipliers.

## Floating-Point Arithmetic

Recent advances in VLSI have increased the feasibility of hardware implementations of floating point arithmetic units. The main advantage of floating point arithmetic is that its wide dynamic range virtually eliminates overflow for most applications.

### Floating-Point Number Systems

A floating point number, $A$, consists of a significand (or mantissa), $S_a$, and an exponent, $E_a$. The value of a number, $A$, is given by the equation:

$$A = S_a r^{E_a} \tag{9.34}$$

where $r$ is the radix (or base) of the number system. Use of the binary radix (i.e., $r = 2$) gives maximum accuracy, but may require more frequent normalization than higher radices.

The IEEE Std. 754 single precision (32-bit) floating point format, which is widely implemented, has an 8-bit biased integer exponent which ranges between 1 and 254 [20]. The exponent is expressed in excess 127 code so that its effective value is determined by subtracting 127 from the stored value. Thus, the range of effective values of the exponent is −126 to 127, corresponding to stored values of 1 to 254, respectively. A stored exponent value of ZERO ($E_{min}$) serves as a flag for ZERO (if the significand is ZERO) and for denormalized numbers (if the significand is non-ZERO). A stored exponent value of 255 ($E_{max}$) serves as a flag for infinity (if the significand is ZERO) and for "not a number" (if the significand is non-zero). The significand is a 25-bit sign magnitude mixed number (the binary point is to the right of the most significant bit and is always a ONE except for denormalized numbers). More detail on floating point formats and on the various considerations that arise in the implementation of floating point arithmetic units are given in [7,21]. The IEEE 754 standard for floating point numbers is discussed in [22,23].

### *Floating-Point Addition*

A flow chart for floating point addition is shown in Fig. 9.18. For this flowchart, the operands are assumed to be "unpacked" and normalized with magnitudes in the range [1/2, 1). On the flow chart, the operands are $(E_a, S_a)$ and $(E_b, S_b)$, the result is $(E_s, S_s)$, and the radix is 2. In step 1 the operand exponents are compared; if they are unequal, the significand of the number with the smaller exponent is shifted right in step 3 or 4 by the difference in the exponents to properly align the significands. For example, to add the decimal operands $0.867 \times 10^5$ and $0.512 \times 10^4$, the latter would be shifted right by one digit and 0.867 added to 0.0512 to give a sum of $0.9182 \times 10^5$. The addition of the significands is performed in step 5. Steps 6–8 test for overflow and correct, if necessary, by shifting the significand one position to the right and incrementing the exponent. Step 9 tests for a zero significand. The loop of steps 10–11 scales unnormalized (but non-ZERO) significands upward to normalize the result. Step 12 tests for underflow.

Floating point subtraction is implemented with a similar algorithm. Many refinements are possible to improve the speed of the addition and subtraction algorithms, but floating point addition and subtraction will, in general, be much slower than fixed-point addition as a result of the need for operand alignment and result normalization.

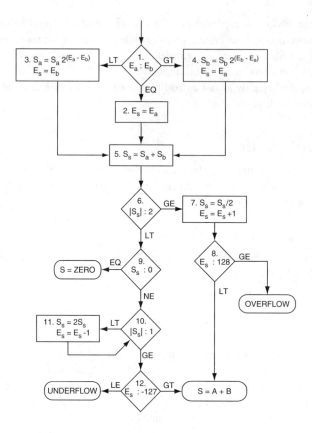

**FIGURE 9.18**    Floating-point addition.

### Floating-Point Multiplication

The algorithm for floating-point multiplication forms the product of the operand significands and the sum of the operand exponents. For radix 2 floating point numbers, the significand values are greater than or equal to 1 and less than 2. The product of two such numbers will be greater than or equal to 1 and less than 4. At most a single right shift is required to normalize the product.

### Floating-Point Division

The algorithm for floating-point division forms the quotient of the operand significands and the difference of the operand exponents. The quotient of two normalized significands will be greater than or equal to .5 and less than 2. At most a single left shift is required to normalize the quotient.

### Floating-Point Rounding

All floating-point algorithms may require rounding to produce a result in the correct format. A variety of alternative rounding schemes have been developed for specific applications. Round to nearest, round toward ∞, round toward −∞, and round toward ZERO are required for implementations of the IEEE floating point standard. Selection should be based on both static and dynamic performance [24], although round to nearest is appropriate for most applications.

## Conclusions

This chapter section has presented an overview of the two's complement number system, algorithms for the basic integer arithmetic operations of addition, subtraction, multiplication, and division, and a brief discussion of floating point operations. When implementing arithmetic units there is often an opportunity to optimize the performance and the complexity to the requirements of the specific application. In general, faster algorithms require more area or more complex control; it is often useful to use the fastest algorithm that will fit the available area.

# References

1. A. Weinberger and J. L. Smith, "A Logic for High-Speed Addition," *National Bureau of Standards Circular 591*, 1958, pp. 3–12.
2. O. L. MacSorley, "High-Speed Arithmetic in Binary Computers," *Proceedings of the IRE*, Vol. 49, 1961, pp. 67–91.
3. T. Kilburn, D. B. G. Edwards, and D. Aspinall, "A Parallel Arithmetic Unit Using a Saturated Transistor Fast-Carry Circuit," *Proceedings of the IEE*, Part B, Vol. 107, 1960, pp. 573–584.
4. Shlomo Waser and Michael J. Flynn, *Introduction to Arithmetic for Digital Systems Designers*, New York: Holt, Rinehart and Winston, 1982.
5. P. K. Chen and M. D. F. Schlag, "Analysis and Design of CMOS Manchester Adders with Variable Carry Skip," *IEEE Transactions on Computers*, Vol. 39, 1990, pp. 983–992.
6. S. Turrini, "Optimal Group Distribution in Carry-Skip Adders," *Proceedings 9th Symposium on Computer Arithmetic*, Santa Monica, CA, 1989, pp. 96–103.
7. D. Goldberg, "Computer Arithmetic," in D. A. Patterson and J. L. Hennessy, *Computer Architecture: A Quantitative Approach*, San Mateo, CA: Morgan Kauffmann, 1990, Appendix A.
8. A. D. Booth, "A Signed Binary Multiplication Technique," *Quarterly Journal of Mechanics and Applied Mathematics*, Vol. 4, Pt. 2, 1951, pp. 236–240.
9. R. F. Shaw, "Arithmetic Operations in a Binary Computer," *Review of Scientific Instrumentation*, Vol. 21, 1950, pp. 687–693.
10. H. Sam and A. Gupta, "A Generalized Multibit Recoding of Two's Complement Binary Numbers and Its Proof with Application in Multiplier Implementations," *IEEE Transactions on Computers*, Vol. 39, 1990, pp. 1006–1015.
11. C. R. Baugh and B. A. Wooley, "A Two's Complement Parallel Array Multiplication Algorithm," *IEEE Transactions on Computers*, Vol. C-22, 1973, pp. 1045–1047.
12. P. E. Blankenship, "Comments on 'A Two's Complement Parallel Array Multiplication Algorithm,'" *IEEE Transactions on Computers*, Vol. C-23, 1974, p. 1327.
13. C. S. Wallace, "A Suggestion for a Fast Multiplier," *IEEE Transactions on Electronic Computers*, Vol. EC-13, 1964, pp. 14–17.
14. L. Dadda, "Some Schemes for Parallel Multipliers," *Alta Frequenza*, Vol. 34, 1965, pp. 349–356.
15. L. Dadda, "On Parallel Digital Multipliers," *Alta Frequenza*, Vol. 45, 1976, pp. 574–580.
16. J. E. Robertson, "A New Class of Digital Division Methods," *IRE Transactions on Electronic Computers*, Vol. EC-7, 1958, pp. 218–222.
17. D. E. Atkins, "Higher-Radix Division Using Estimates of the Divisor and Partial Remainders," *IEEE Transactions on Computers*, Vol. C-17, 1968, pp. 925–934.
18. M. D. Ercegovac and T. Lang, *Division and Square Root: Digit-Recurrence Algorithms and Their Implementations*, Boston: Kluwer Academic Publishers, 1994.
19. D. Ferrari, "A Division Method Using a Parallel Multiplier," *IEEE Transactions on Electronic Computers*, Vol. EC-16, 1967, pp. 224–226.
20. *IEEE Standard for Binary Floating-Point Arithmetic*, IEEE Std 754–1985, Reaffirmed 1990.
21. J. B. Gosling, *Design of Arithmetic Units for Digital Computers*, New York: The Macmillan Press, 1980.
22. I. Koren, *Computer Arithmetic Algorithms*, Englewood Cliffs, NJ: Prentice Hall, 1993.
23. B. Parhami, *Computer Arithmetic: Algorithms and Hardware Designs*, New York: Oxford University Press 2000.
24. D. J. Kuck, D. S. Parker, Jr., and A. H. Sameh, "Analysis of Rounding Methods in Floating-Point Arithmetic," *IEEE Transactions on Computers*, Vol. C-26, 1977, pp. 643–650.

## 9.2 Fast Adders and Multipliers

*Gensuke Goto*

### Introduction

All the logic circuits used in an electronic computer are constituted of combinations of basic logic gates such as inverters, NAND or NOR gates. There exist many varieties of circuits that realize the basic arithmetic logic functions for addition and multiplication due to the difference in viewpoint of circuit optimization [1–4].

In this chapter section we will discuss an essence and an overview of recent high-speed digital arithmetic logic circuits. The emphasis is on fast adders and multipliers that are the most important logic units for high-speed data processing. Several types of these units are discussed and compared from various viewpoints of circuit simplicity, easiness of design and power consumption, in addition to high-speed capability.

### Adder

#### Principle of Addition

In the Boolean logic, numeral values are often represented as 2's complement numbers because it is easy to deal with negative values. Therefore, we assume that if not explicitly stated, numerals are represented in 2's complement numbers in this chapter section. It is to be noted, however, the previous works that appear in this chapter do not necessarily obey to this rule.

Let us consider the addition of two binary numbers $A$ and $B$ with $n$-bit width. $A$ is, for instance, represented by

$$A = -a_{n-1}\, 2^{n-1} + \sum_{i=0}^{n-2} (a_i\, 2^i)$$

(9.35)

where $a_{n-1}$ is the sign bit ($a_{n-1} = 1$ if $A$ has a negative value, and $a_{n-1} = 0$ if it has a positive value), and $a_i\,\{1, 0\}$ is the bit at the $i$th position counted from the least significant bit (LSB) $a_0$. The sum $S(S = A + B)$ is represented by an $(n + 1)$-bit binary number whose most significant bit (MSB) is the sign bit. An example of binary addition is shown in the following:

$$
\begin{array}{lll}
& 00101 & : A = 5 \text{ in decimal number} = 0101 \\
+ & 11001 & : B = -7 \text{ in decimal number} = 1001 \\
\hline
& 11110 & : S = -2 \text{ in decimal number} = 11110
\end{array}
$$

This is a case of adding $A = 5$ and $B = -7$ in decimal numbers that are represented by 4-bit binary numbers. The third bit positions of these operands in binary numbers are the sign bits $a_3 = a_s = 0$ and $b_3 = b_s = 1$, because $A$ is a positive number and $B$ is a negative number. Since the sum of these operands yields a 5-bit sum in principle, the fourth bit positions of these operands ($a_4, b_4$) have to be considered existent as sign bits in adding procedure (sign bit extension). Thus, the output signal $s_4$ at the sign bit position is obtained as 1. The effective number of bits in $S$ is 4 ($s_0$ to $s_3$), one-bit extension as a result of summation. These bits are represented in 2's complement form of a negative number.

#### One-Bit Full Adder

First we consider a 1-bit full adder (FA), which is a basic unit for constituting an $n$-bit adder. The sum ($s_i$) and carry ($c_i$) signals at the $i$th bit position in the $n$-bit adder are generated according to the operation defined by Boolean equations:

$$s_i = a_i \oplus b_i \oplus c_{i-1}$$

(9.36)

$$c_i = a_i b_i + (a_i + b_i)\, c_{i-1}$$

(9.37)

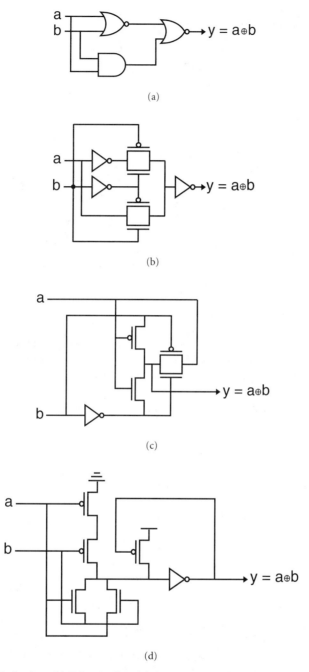

**FIGURE 9.19**    (a) XOR circuit-1, (b) XOR circuit-2, (c) XOR circuit-3, (d) XOR circuit-4.

where $c_{i-1}$ is the output carry signal of the 1-bit adder at the $(i-1)$th bit position, and $a_i \oplus b_i$ indicates an exclusive-OR (XOR) operation of $a_i$ and $b_i$. From the above equation, we can understand that two XOR logic gates are necessary to yield a sum signal $s_i$ in a 1-bit FA.

Many kinds of XOR gates implemented using CMOS transistors are proposed up to date. Some examples of such gates are shown in Fig. 9.19. Figure 9.19(a) is a popular XOR gate using a NOR gate and a 2-input AND-OR-inverter. The transistor count in this case is 10. Figure 9.19(b) is composed of two pass transistor switches, and this is another popular gate whose number of transistors is also 10. Figure 9.19(c) is of a six-transistor type [5]. Though this circuit is compact, driving ability of this gate

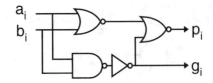

**FIGURE 9.20**   Half-adder circuit.

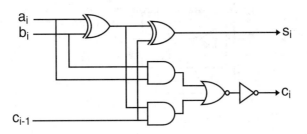

**FIGURE 9.21**   One-bit full adder.

is low because the output node has serial resistor to degrade the output signal [6], so the number of direct connection of this gate is practically limited to two. Figure 9.19(d) is of a 7-transistor type whose p-channel transistor is introduced to the gate of the output inverter to compensate for weak drivability to a high level when $a = b = 1$ (at high level) [7].

To control the carry propagation efficiently, the following signals are defined for long-word addition at each bit position $i$:

$$\text{carry-propagate signal } p_i = a_i \oplus b_i \tag{9.38}$$

$$\text{carry-generate signal } g_i = a_i b_i \tag{9.39}$$

Using these notations, Eqs. (9.36) and (9.37) are rewritten by

$$s_i = p_i \oplus c_{i-1} \tag{9.40}$$

$$c_i = g_i + p_i c_{i-1} \tag{9.41}$$

respectively. A carry is generated if $g_i = 1$, and the stage $i$($i$th bit position of an $n$-bit adder) propagates an input carry signal $c_{i-1}$ to its output if $p_i = 1$. These signals are generated in a gate called a half adder (HA) as shown in Fig. 9.20, and used to constitute a high-speed but complicated carry control scheme such as a carry lookahead adder as described in the later sections. FA is often implemented according to the Boolean equations (9.40) and (9.41). Though there exist many variations to constructing a FA, only one example is shown in Fig. 9.21. In this construction, the transistor count is 30. By using pass transistor switches, we can reduce it to 24.

### Ripple Carry Adder

A ripple carry adder (RCA) is the simplest one as a parallel adder implemented in hardware. An $n$-bit RCA is implemented by simple concatenation of $n$ 1-bit FAs. As the carry signal ripples bit by bit from the least significant bit to the most significant bit, the worst-case delay time is in proportion to the number $n$ of 1-bit full adders [1]. This is roughly equal to the critical path delay of RCA, if $n$ is large enough as compared with 1.

Manchester carry chain (MCC) is one of the simplest schemes for RCA that utilizes MOS technology [8,9]. The carry chain is constructed of series-connected pass transistors whose gates are controlled by the carry-propagate signal $p_i$ at every bit position $i$ of $n$ 1-bit FAs. This scheme can offer simple hardware implementation with less power as compared with other elaborate schemes. Because of distortion due to RC time constant, the carry signal needs to be regenerated by inserting inverters or true buffers at appropriate locations in the carry chain. Though this compensation needs additional transistors, the total power may be reduced appreciably if buffers are equipped with efficiently.

## Carry Skip Adder

If the carry-propagate signals $p_i$ that belong to the bit positions from the $m$th to $(m + k)$th are all 1, the carry signal at the $(m - 1)$th bit position can bypass through $(k + 1)$ bits to the $(m + k)$th bit position without rippling through these bits. A carry skip adder (CSKA) is a scheme to utilize this principle for shortening the longest path of the carry propagation. A fixed-group CSKA is such that the $n$ 1-bit FAs to construct an $n$-bit adder is divided equally into $k$ groups over which the carry signal can bypass if the condition to skip is fulfilled. The maximum delay of the carry propagation is reduced to a factor of $1/k$ as compared with RCA [1].

MCC is often used with several bypass circuits to speed up the carry propagation in longer word addition [10]. Figure 9.22(a) is a case of such implementation. Though this 4-bit bypass circuit may be considered to work well at a glance, it is not true because of the signal conflict during the transient phase from the former state to the new state to settle to, as shown in Fig. 9.22(c) with transition of the node voltage $Vs(A)$ at the node $A$ in Fig. 9.22(a) [11]. To avoid this unexpected transition delay, it is necessary to cut off all of other signal paths than expected logically as shown in Fig. 9.22(b). Under this modified scheme [11], the bypass circuit can function as expected like shown in Fig. 9.22(c), with change of the node voltage $Vs(B)$ at the node $B$ in Fig. 9.22(b).

A variable block adder (VBA) allows the groups to be different in size [12], so that the maximum delay is further reduced from the fixed group CSKA. The number of adders in a group is gradually increased from LSB toward the middle bit position, and then reduced toward MSB. This scheme may lead us to the total delay dependency on the carry propagation in the order of square root of $n$. Extension of this approach to multiple levels of carry skip is possible for further speeding up on a fast adder.

## Carry Lookahead Adder

A carry lookahead adder (CLA) [13] utilizes fully two types of signals $p_i$ and $g_i$ at the $i$th bit position of an $n$-bit adder to control carry propagation. For instance, the carry signals $c_i$, $c_{i+1}$, and $c_{i+2}$ can be estimated

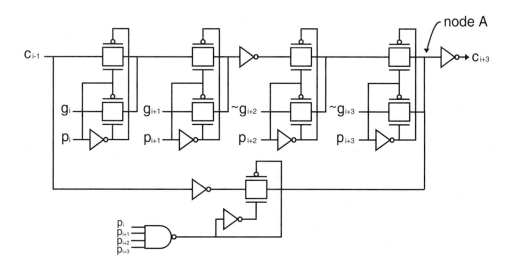

**FIGURE 9.22(a)**   Carry skip circuit that causes conflict during signal transient.

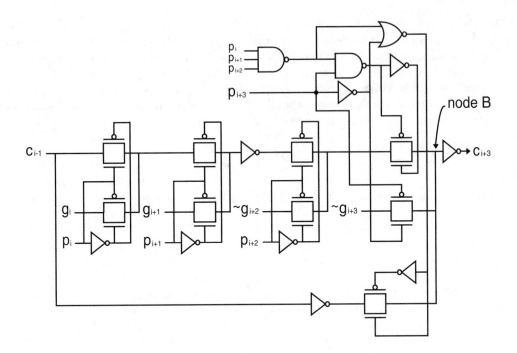

**FIGURE 9.22(b)**   Carry skip circuit that excludes conflict during signal transient.

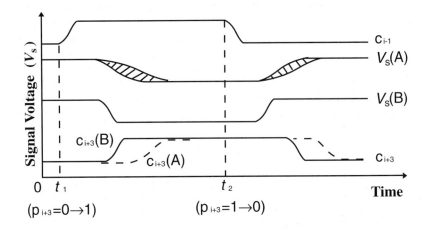

**FIGURE 9.22(c)**   Effect of signal conflict on circuit delay.

according to the following Boolean equations if the carry-in signal $c_{i-1}$ to the $i$th 1-bit full adder is determined:

$$c_i = g_i + p_i c_{i-1} \tag{9.42}$$

$$c_{i+1} = g_{i+1} + p_i g_i + p_{i+1} p_i c_{i-1} \tag{9.43}$$

$$c_{i+2} = g_{i+2} + p_{i+2} g_{i+1} + p_{i+2} p_{i+1} g_i + p_{i+2} p_{i+1} p_i c_{i-1} \tag{9.44}$$

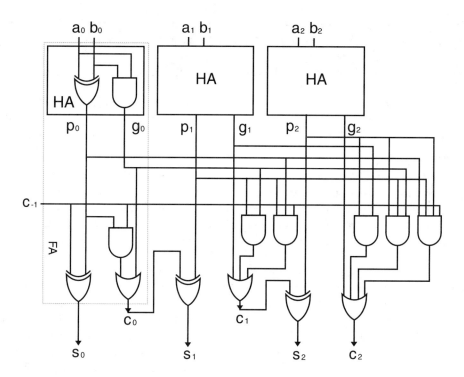

**FIGURE 9.23** 3-bit carry lookahead adder.

These three carry signals can be determined almost simultaneously after $c_{i-1}$ is input to the $i$th adder if hardware to yield the above signals is equipped with as shown in Fig. 9.23 for a case of $i = 0$. Within this scheme, a 1-bit full adder at each bit position ($i$) consists of a sum generator and a HA segment to yield $p_i$ and $g_i$ signals, and no carry generator is required at each bit position. Instead, the carry signals $c_i$, $c_{i+1}$, and $c_{i+2}$ are generated in a lookahead block whose Boolean expressions are given above.

Although the number $k$ of carry signals to be determined simultaneously in a lookahead block can be extended to more than 4, hardware to implement CLA logic becomes more and more complicated in proportion to $k$. This increases the necessary number of logic gates, power consumption, and the delay time to generate a carry signal at a higher bit position in a lookahead block. Considering this situation, a practically available number is limited to 4, and this limitation reduces much of the attractiveness on CLA as architecture of a high-speed adder. To overcome the inconvenience, group (or block) carry-generate ($G_j$) and carry-propagate ($P_j$) signals are considered for dealing with longer word operation. With these signals, the carry equation can be expressed by

$$c_j = G_j + P_j \, c_{i-1} \tag{9.45}$$

where

$$G_j = g_{i+k} + p_{i+k} \, g_{i+k-1} + p_{i+k} \, p_{i+k-1} \, g_{i+k-2} + \cdots + p_{i+k} \, p_{i+k-1} \cdots p_{i+1} \, g_i \tag{9.46}$$

and

$$P_j = p_{i+k} \, p_{i+k-1} \cdots p_{i+1} p_i. \tag{9.47}$$

In a recursive way, a group of groups can be defined to handle wider-word operands.

Assuming that a single level of the carry lookahead group generates $k$ carry signals simultaneously with two additional gate delays in the carry path, it can be shown that the total delay of an $n$-bit CLA is $2 \log_k n$-gate delay units [1]. Theoretically this may be considered one of the fastest adder structures, but the practical speed of CLA is not necessarily highest because of using complicated gates to implement a lookahead block in the carry path.

Recurrence solver-based adders are proposed with some popularity to systematically implement CLA blocks [14–16].

### Carry Select Adder

A carry select adder (CSLA) is one of the conditional-sum adder [1,17] that is based on the idea of selecting the most significant portion of the operands conditionally, depending on a carry-in signal to the least significant portion. This algorithm yields the theoretically fastest adder of two numbers [18]. In CSLA implementation, two operands are divided into blocks where two sum signals at each bit position are generated in parallel in order to be selected by the carry-in signal to the blocks. One is a provisional sum $s_i^0$ to be selected as a true sum signal $s_i$ at the $i$th bit position if the carry-in signal is 0, and the other provisional sum $s_i^1$ is selected as a true sum signal if the carry-in signal is 1. This provisional sum signal pair can be selected immediately after the carry-in signal is fixed.

In Fig. 9.24 where a 16-bit adder is constructed of CSLA, the provisional carry signal pair $(c_i^0, c_i^1)$ is generated at the highest bit position within each block, in addition to the provisional sum signal pairs generated at all bit positions within the block. This carry signal pair is used to generate a true carry signal in a carry-selector block (CS) along with similar signals located at the different blocks. The provisional sum signals within the block are selected by $c_{i-1}$ to yield true sum signals $s_{i+3:i}$. Figure 9.25 shows a combination of RCA and CSLA to construct a 16-bit adder. By such a combination, a high-speed and small size adder can be realized efficiently [19–21].

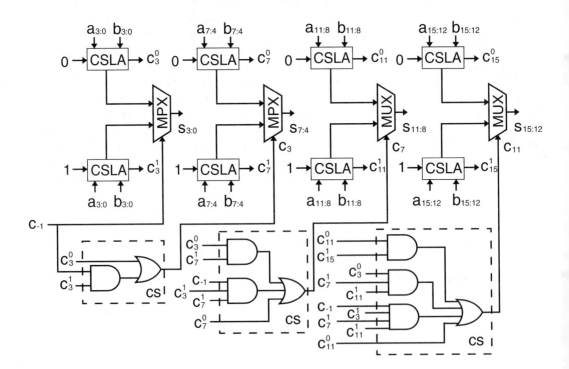

**FIGURE 9.24**   4-bit carry select adder.

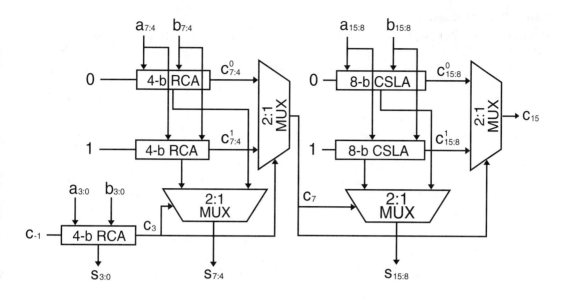

**FIGURE 9.25** 16-bit adder with combination of RCA and CSLA.

## Multiplier

### Algorithm of Multiplication

In the past when the scale of integration on VLSI was low, a multiplier circuit was implemented by a shift-and-add method because of simplicity in hardware. This method is, however, very time-consuming, so that the need of high-speed multiplication could scarcely be fulfilled in many practical applications. Now that a system-on-a-chip (SoC) with more than 10 million transistors has emerged with a rapid progress of the fine-pattern process technology of semiconductors, we are in a stage of using any parallel multipliers with full acceleration mechanisms for speeding up the processing.

In binary multiplication of an $n$-bit multiplicand $A$ and multiplier $B$, we begin to calculate partial products $p_j$ for implementation of a parallel multiplier, which is defined by

$$p_j = \sum_{i=0}^{n-1} \{(a_i 2^i)(b_j 2^j)\}$$

$$= \sum_{i=0}^{n-1} (p_{i,j} 2^{i+j}), \tag{9.48}$$

where $p_{i,j}$ is a partial product bit at the $(i+j)$th position. Each bit in a partial product $p_j$ is equal to 0 if $b_j = 0$, and $a_i$ if $b_j = 1$ for the case of multiplication of positive numbers. For multiplication of 2's complement numbers, the situation is a little complicated, because correction to sign-bit extension is necessary as described in the later section.

The product $Z(=A \times B)$ is expressed by using the partial products as follows:

$$Z = \sum_{j=0}^{2n-1} (z_j 2^j)$$

$$= \sum_{j=0}^{n-1} p_j. \tag{9.49}$$

## Array-Type Multiplier

The simplest parallel multiplier is such that pairs of an AND gate and a 1-bit full adder are laid out repetitively and connected in sequence to construct an $n^2$ array [1,22]. An example of a $4 \times 4$-bit parallel multiplier to manipulate two positive numbers is shown in Fig. 9.26. The operation time in this multiplier equals to sum of delays that consist of an AND gate, four FAs, and a 4-bit carry-propagate adder (CPA). The CPA may be consisted of a 4-bit RCA. It can be easily understood that the reduction process of partial products to two at each bit position dominates the operation time in this multiplier except for a CPA delay. Thus, the acceleration of the compression process for the partial product bits at each bit position is a key to obtain a fast multiplier. For the basic array-type multiplication in Fig. 9.26, this compression process constitutes ripple carry connection. The worst-case delay of this type is composed of 2n FA delays. For most recent high-speed data processing systems that deal with wider word than 32 bits, this delay time is too large to be acceptable. Therefore, some kinds of speeding-up mechanisms

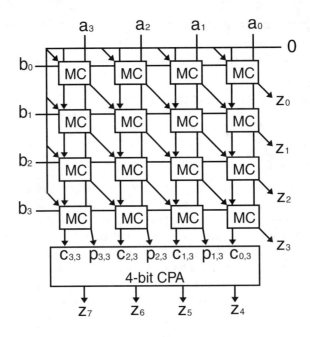

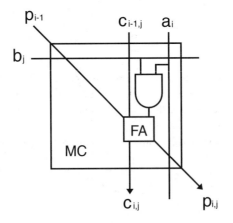

**FIGURE 9.26**  $4 \times 4$-bit array-type multiplier.

are necessary to satisfy requirement for recent high-speed systems. A modified-array approach is an example of such a speeding-up mechanism [23].

The carry signal generated in FA (contained in MC in Fig. 9.26) at each bit position is never propagated to a higher bit position within the same partial product, but it is treated as if it is a part of a partial product at one-bit higher position. This enables us to avoid the carry propagation from LSB to MSB in the same partial product, and this structure is called a carry-save adder (CSA) [1]. For this structure, whether the carry path or the sum path may constitute the critical path cannot be predicted beforehand. Therefore, not only the carry generator but also the sum generator must be designed as a fast path in order to constitute a fast multiplier.

## Wallace Tree

Summing the partial product bits in parallel using a carry-save adder tree is called a Wallace tree, which is introduced by Wallace [24] and later refined by Dadda [25,26]. In a case of using FA's as a unique constituent of CSA, the maximum parallelism can be reached by adding three partial product bits at a time in the same FA. The total delay time of CSA part for an $n \times n$-bit parallel multiplier in this case is $\log_{3/2} n$, thus the drastic reduction of the delay time is possible for large $n$ values as compared with a simple array-type multiplier. A multiplier with the Wallace tree is often called a tree-type one, in contrast with an array-type one shown in Fig. 9.26.

Although the Wallace tree can contribute much to realization of a fast long-word multiplier, its layout scheme is very complex as compared with the array-type because the wiring among FAs has little regularity. This is one of the reasons why this tree type had not been implemented widely as a long-word multiplier in the past. There exist many efforts that try to introduce regularity of layout on the Wallace tree [27–32], and now it is possible to implement it with higher regularity than ever.

## 4-2 Compressor

Weinberger disclosed a structure called "4-2 carry-save module" in 1981 [33]. This structure is considered to compress actually five partial product bits into three and is consisted of a combination of two FA's. The four of five inputs into this module come from the same bit position of the weight $m(=i+j)$ while the rest 1-bit, known as an carry-in signal, comes from the neighboring position of the weight $m-1$. This module creates three signals: two of which are a pair of carry and sum signals, and the rest is an intermediate carry-out signal that is input to a module at the neighboring position of the weight $m+1$. As the four signals are compressed at a time to yield a pair of carry and sum signals except for an intermediate carry signal, this module is called a 4-2 compressor.

The 4-2 compressor designed for speeding up the compression operation has speed of three XOR gate delays in series [34–36], and this scheme makes it possible to shorten the compression delay to three-fourths of the original one. Using this type of a 4-2 compressor, we can relieve the complicated wiring design among the modules in the Wallace tree with enhanced speed of processing. Some examples of 4-2 compressors are given in Fig. 9.27. Figure 9.27(a) represents a typical circuit composed of 60 transistors [34]. Figure 9.27(b) utilizes pass transistor multiplexers to enhance speed of compression by 18% compared with a FA-based circuit, and is composed of 58 transistors [35]. Figure 9.27(c) is an optimized one in view of both small number of transistors (48) and keeping high-speed operation [36]. This transistor count is comparable to using a pair of series-connected FAs, yet the speed is 30% higher.

## Booth Recoding Algorithm

For multiplication of 2's complement numbers, the modified Booth recoding algorithm is the most frequently used method to generate partial products [37,38]. This algorithm allows for the reduction of the number of partial products to be compressed in a carry-save adder tree, thus the compression speed can be enhanced. This Booth–MacSorley algorithm is simply called the Booth algorithm, and the two-bit recoding using this algorithm scans a triplet of bits to reduce the number of partial products by roughly one half. The 2-bit recoding means that the multiplier $B$ is divided into groups of two bits, and the algorithm is applied to this group of divided bits.

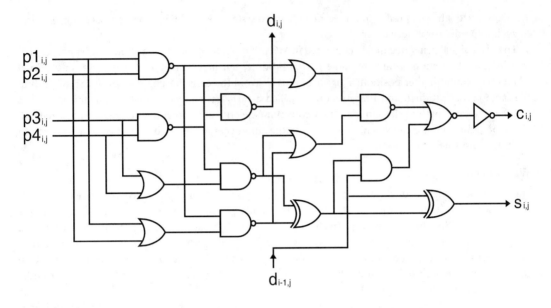

**FIGURE 9.27(a)**    4-2 compressor-1.

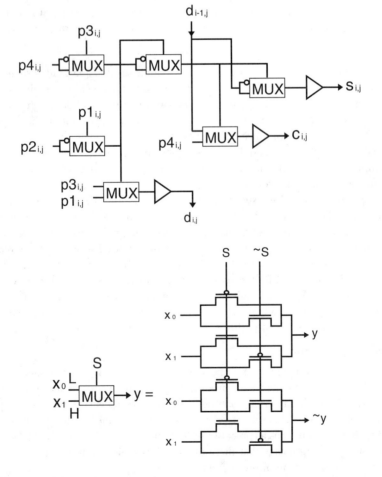

**FIGURE 9.27(b)**    4-2 compressor-2.

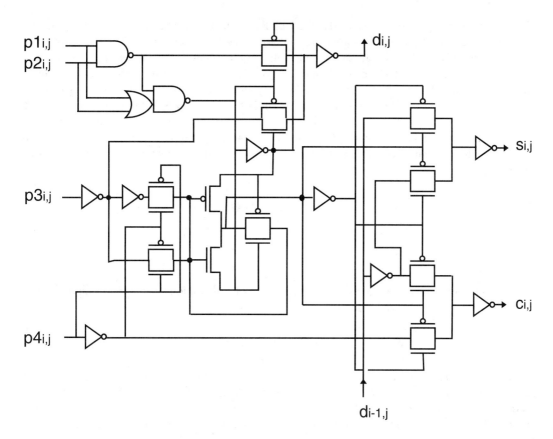

**FIGURE 9.27(c)** 4-2 compressor-3.

In general, the multiplier $B$ in 2's complement representation is expressed by

$$B = -b_{n-1}\, 2^{n-1} + \sum_{j=0}^{n-2} (b_j\, 2^j)$$

$$= (b_{n-3} + b_{n-2} - 2b_{n-1})\, 2^{n-2} + (b_{n-5} + b_{n-4} - 2b_{n-3})\, 2^{n-4} + \cdots$$

$$+ (b_{n-k-1} + b_{n-k} - 2\, b_{n-k+1})\, 2^{n-k} + \cdots + (b_{-1} + b_0 - 2b_{-1})\, 2^0$$

$$= \sum_{k=0}^{n/2-1} (b_{2k-1} + b_{2k} - 2\, b_{2k+1})\, 2^{2k}. \tag{9.50}$$

Assumption is made that $n$ is an even number, $b_{n-1}$ represents the sign bit $b_s$, and $b_{-1} = 0$. The product $Z( =A\,B)$ is then given by

$$Z = \sum_{j=0}^{n/2-1} (PP_j \quad A \quad 2^j) \quad \text{$j$: even number,} \tag{9.51}$$

where

$$PP_j = b_{j-1} \oplus b_j - 2\, b_{j+1} \tag{9.52}$$

The partial product $PP_j$ is to be calculated in the 2-bit Booth algorithm. Therefore, $n/2$ partial products and hence $n^2/2$ partial product bits are generated according to this algorithm. The partial product $PP_j$ has a value of one of 0, $\pm A$, and $\pm 2A$, depending on the values of the adjacent three bits on the multiplier ($b_{j-1}$, $b_j$, and $b_{j+1}$). The generation of $2A$ is easily realized by shifting each bit of $A$ to one-bit higher position. The negative value on the 2's complement system is realized by negating each bit of $A(=\bar{A})$ and adding 1 to the LSB position of $\bar{A}$. The latter is done by placing a new partial product bit ($M_j$) corresponding to 1 and adding it in a CSA. The Booth algorithm is implemented into two steps: Booth encoding and Booth selecting. The Booth encoding step is to generate one of the five values from the adjacent three bits $b_{j-1}$, $b_j$, and $b_{j+1}$. This is realized according to the following Boolean equations,

$$A_j = b_{j-1} \oplus b_j \tag{9.53}$$

$$2A_j = \sim(b_{j-1} \oplus b_j)(b_j \oplus b_{j+1}) \tag{9.54}$$

$$M_j = b_{j+1}. \tag{9.55}$$

The Booth selector generates a partial product bit at the $(i+j)$th position by utilizing the output signals from the Booth encoder and the multiplicand bits as follows:

$$p_{i,j} = (a_i A_j + a_{i-1} 2A_j) \oplus M_j \tag{9.56}$$

An example of a partial product bit generator is shown in Fig. 9.28(a). As is seen in the figure, a typical partial product bit generator requires 18 transistors in CMOS implementation as compared with 6 transistors for a case of generating it with a simple AND gate. Thus a part of the effect of reducing the number of partial product bits at the same bit position is compensated for because of the complexity of the circuit to generate a partial product bit in the Booth recoding.

Goto proposed a new scheme to reduce the number of transistors for generating a partial product bit. This scheme is called "sign-select Booth encoding" [36]. In this scheme, the Booth encoding is done so as to generate two sign signals $PL$ (positive) and $M$ (negative) that are selected depending on the logic of an input multiplicand bit in the Booth encoding step. The Boolean equations are shown in the following,

$$A_j = b_{j-1} \oplus b_j \tag{9.57}$$

$$2A_j = \sim(b_{j-1} \oplus b_j) \tag{9.58}$$

$$M_j = \sim(b_{j-1} \, b_j) \, b_{j+1} \tag{9.59}$$

$$PL_j = (b_{j-1} + b_j) \, (\sim b_{j+1}). \tag{9.60}$$

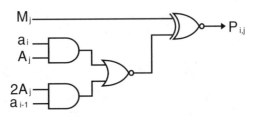

**FIGURE 9.28(a)**   Partial product bit generator-1.

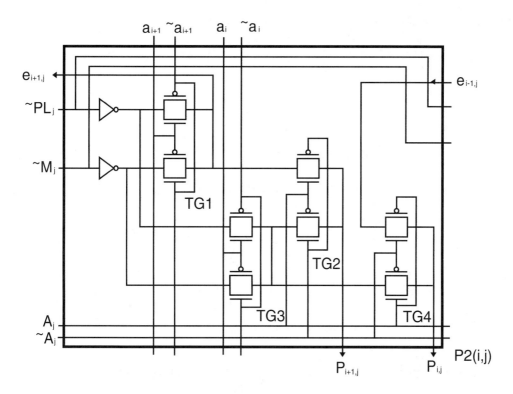

**FIGURE 9.28(b)** Partial product bit generator-2.

The Booth selector is constructed to select either $PL_j$ or $M_j$ depending on the multiplicand bit ($a_i$ or $\sim a_i$) according to the following Boolean equation:

$$p_{i,j} = (a_i\, PL_j + \sim a_i\, M_j)\, A_j + (a_{i-1}\, PL_j + \sim a_{i-1}\, M_j)\, 2A_j \tag{9.61}$$

In this modified Booth selector implemented with pass transistors, the transistor count per bit is as small as 10 as illustrated in Fig. 9.28(b). Thus it is reduced roughly to one-half as compared with that of the regular selector without the speed degradation.

As can be seen from the above explanations, the sign bit, unlike other approaches [39], need not be treated as a special case of partial product bit, but it is manipulated similarly to other bits. Thus the correction circuit need not be equipped with for the Booth algorithm.

The Booth algorithm can be generalized to any radix with more than two bits. However, a 3-bit recoding requires $\pm 3A$, which requires addition of $\pm A$ and $\pm 2A$, resulting in a carry propagation. The delay with such a mechanism degrades the high-speed capability of a 3-bit recoding. A 4-bit or higher bit recoding may be considered [40], but it requires very complex recoding circuitry. Eventually, only the 2-bit (radix 4) recoding is actually used.

## Sign Correction for Booth Algorithm

As mentioned in the former section on adders with 2's complement numbers, the sign bits of the operands need be extended to the MSB of the sum to correctly calculate these numbers. This sign extension can be simplified for addition of partial products based on the 2-bit Booth algorithm in the following way.

The sum SGN of the whole extended bits can be expressed by

$$SGN = (2^{2n-1} + 2^{2n-2} + \cdots + 2^{n})P_{s(0)} + (2^{2n-1} + 2^{2n-2} + \cdots + 2^{n+2})P_{s(2)}$$

$$+ \cdots + (2^{2n-1} + 2^{2n-2} + \cdots + 2^{n-j})P_{s(j)} + \cdots$$

$$+ (2^{2n-1} + 2^{2n-2})P_{s(n-2)}$$

$$= \{ - (2^{2n} + 1)\,2^0\,P_{s(0)} - (2^{2n} + 1)\,2^2\,P_{s(2)} - \cdots$$

$$- (2^{2n} + 1)\,2^j\,P_{s(j)} - \cdots - (2^{2n} + 1)\,2^{n-2}\,P_{s(n-2)}\}\,2^n$$

$$= \{-2^0 P_{s(0)} - 2^2 P_{s(2)} - \cdots - 2^j P_{s(j)} - \cdots - 2^{n-2} P_{s(n-2)}\}\,2^n$$

$$(\text{Mod } 2^{2n})$$

$$= \{\tilde{P}_{s(0)} + 2^1 + \tilde{P}_{s(2)} + 2^3 + \cdots + \tilde{P}_{s(j)} + 2^{j+1} + \cdots$$

$$+ \tilde{P}_{s(n-2)} + 2^{n-1} + 1\}\,2^n, \tag{9.62}$$

where $j$ is an even number and $P_{s(j)}$ indicates a sign bit of the partial product at the $j$th position. Considering the above result, the multiplication of $n$-bit 2's complement numbers are performed as illustrated in Fig. 9.29 for a case of $8 \times 8$-bit multiplication, where $M_j$ indicates a partial product bit introduced to add 1 at the LSB position in the $j$th partial product if the encoded result is a negative value. For the 2-bit Booth recoding, the maximum number of partial product bits at the same position is $n/2 + 1$ as the sign correction term or $M_j$ term has to be considered.

**Overall Design of Parallel Multiplier**

A high-speed but small-size parallel multiplier can be designed by devising recoding algorithm, arraying systematically well-configured components, and adopting a high-performance CPA. Most recent-day fast multipliers for mantissa multiplication of two double-precision numbers based on the IEEE standard [41] are designed according to the block diagram shown in Fig. 9.30. Under this standard, the mantissa

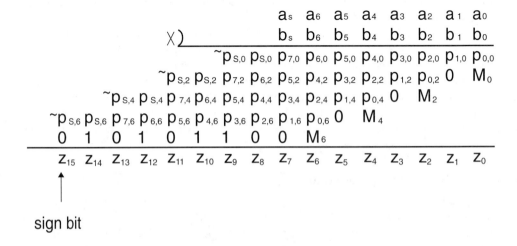

**FIGURE 9.29**  $8 \times 8$-bit multiplication with sign correction.

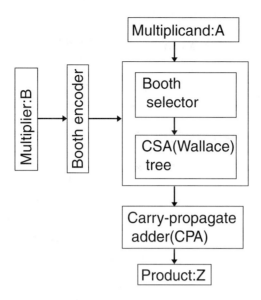

**FIGURE 9.30** Block diagram of high-speed parallel multiplier.

multiplication requires a $54 \times 54$-bit hardware multiplier, because the mantissa is represented by 52 bits internally, and a hidden bit and a sign bit must be added to manipulate 2's complement numbers.

A fast $54 \times 54$-bit parallel structured multiplier was developed by Mori, et al. in 1991 [7]. They adopted the 2-bit Booth algorithm and the Wallace tree composed of 58 transistor 4-2 compressors. By adopting the Wallace tree composed of the 4-2 compressors, only four addition stages suffice to compress the maximum number of the partial product bits at the same bit position. This design adopts an XOR gate that is a pseudo-CMOS circuit shown in Fig. 9.19(d) to increase the operation speed of 4-2 compressors and the final CPA. They obtained a $54 \times 54$-bit multiplier with a delay time of 10 ns and area of 12.5 mm$^2$ (transistor count is 81,600) in 0.5 $\mu$m CMOS technology.

Ohkubo, et al. implemented a $54 \times 54$-bit parallel multiplier by utilizing pass-transistor multiplexers [35]. The delay time constructed with them can be made smaller than that implemented in the conventional CMOS gates because of shorter critical path within the circuit. They constructed a CSA tree in Fig. 9.31 only by 4-2 compressors shown in Fig. 9.27(b). By combining a 4-2 compressor tree with a conditional carry-selection (CCS) adder [35], they obtained a fast multiplier with a delay time of 4.4 ns and area of 12.9 mm$^2$ (transistor count is 100,200) in 0.25 $\mu$m CMOS technology.

Goto proposed a new layout scheme named "Regularly Structured Tree (RST)" for implementing the Wallace tree in 1992 [34]. In this scheme, partial product bits with a maximum of 28 at the same bit position to be compressed into two for a $54 \times 54$-bit parallel multiplier are first divided into four 7-2 compressor blocks, as shown in Fig. 9.32. In this figure, a 4D2 block consists of two sets of four Booth selectors and a 4-2 compressor, and a 3D2 block consists of two sets of three Booth selectors and a FA. A 4W means a 4-2 compressor in the same figure. Thus, a 7D4 block constitutes four 7-2 compressors at the consecutive bit positions. Arranging this 7D4 block with regularity as shown in Fig. 9.33, the Booth selectors and the CSA part of a $54 \times 54$-bit parallel multiplier can be systematically laid out including the intermediate wiring among the blocks. This scheme simplifies drastically the complicated layout and wiring among not only the compressors in the CSA part but also the compressors and the Booth selectors. In a modified version of the RST multiplier, the delay time of 4.1 ns and as small size as 1.27 mm$^2$ (transistor count is 60,797) were obtained in 0.25 $\mu$m CMOS technology [36]. By adopting a 4-2 compressor with 48 transistors (Fig. 9.27(c)) and the sign-select Booth recoding algorithm as described earlier, the total number of transistors were reduced by 24% as compared with that of the earlier design.

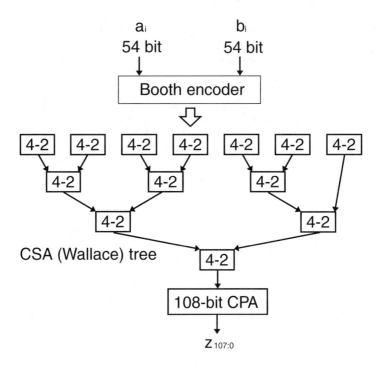

**FIGURE 9.31**  54 × 54-bit parallel multiplier composed of arrayed 4-2 compressors.

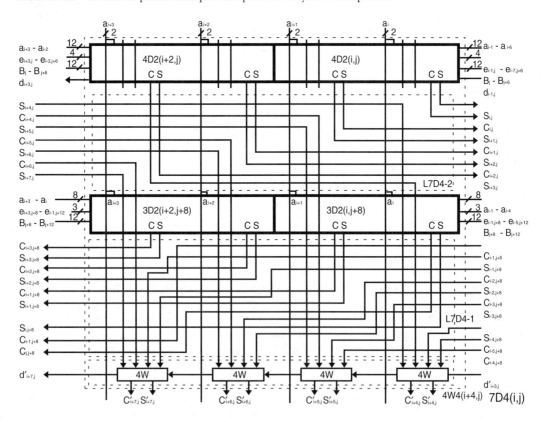

**FIGURE 9.32**  Layout of 7-2 compressors with Booth selectors for consecutive 4 bits.

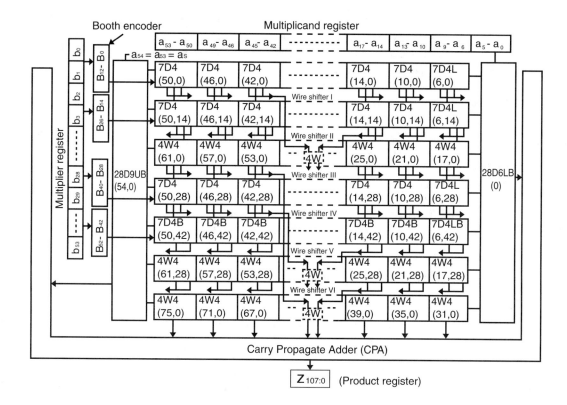

**FIGURE 9.33** 54 × 54-bit multiplier composed of arrayed 7-2 and 4-2 compressors.

## Conclusion

As has been mentioned in this chapter section, various attempts were tried and refined to implement fast adders and multipliers. The basic idea, however, is consistent among these studies in that the circuit components should be as simple as possible to shorten the critical path, and that the algorithm as a whole should be suitably refined for CMOS implementation. The well-prepared circuit components are in themselves valuable for easy implementation of fast and efficient arithmetic units.

The need for faster arithmetic logic units will be continually recognized for its importance among the application engineers of the up-to-date electronics systems, so that the design efforts will be continued to optimize the fast arithmetic algorithms in the advanced CMOS technology. With advance of the SoC technology, evaluating the merit of the algorithm and modifying it to fit to the execution model of the dedicated processor will increase its importance. The system-level performance optimization as a total system will be another subject for realization of the coming high-performance systems.

## References

1. Hwang, K., *Computer Arithmetic: Principles, Architecture and Design,* John Wiley & Sons, New York, 1979.

2. Weste, N. and Eshraghian, K., *Principles of CMOS VLSI Design: A System Perspective,* Addison-Wesley, Reading, MA, 1988, chap. 8.

3. Oklobdzija, V. G., *High-Performance System Design: Circuits and Logic,* IEEE Press, New York, 1999.

4. Chandrakasan, A., Bowhill, W. J., and Fox, F., *Design of High-performance Microprocessor Circuits,* IEEE Press, New York, 2001, chap. 10.

5. *Japanese Unexamined Patent Application,* No. 59-211138, Nov., 1984.

6. Svensson, C. and Tjarnstrom, R., Switch-level simulation and the pass transistor Exor gate, *IEEE Trans. Computer-Aided Design*, 7, 994, 1988.

7. Mori, J., et al., A 10-ns 54 × 54-b parallel structured full array multiplier with 0.5-$\mu$m CMOS technology, *IEEE J. Solid-State Circuits*, 26, 600, 1991.

8. Kilburn, T., Edwards, D. B. G., and Aspinall, D., Parallel addition in digital computers: a new fast "carry" circuit, *Proc. IEE*, 106, Pt. B, 464, 1959.

9. Mead, C. and Conway, L., *Introduction to VLSI systems*, Addison-Wesley, Reading, MA, 1980.

10. Oklobdzija, V. G. and Barnes, E. R., On implementing addition in VLSI technology, *J. Parallel and Distributed Computing*, 5, 716, 1988.

11. Sato, T., et al., An 8.5 ns 112-b transmission gate adder with a conflict-free bypass circuit, *IEEE J. Solid-State Circuits*, 27, 657, 1992.

12. Oklobdzija, V. G. and Barnes, E. R., Some optimal schemes for ALU implementation in VLSI technology, *Proc. 7th Symp. on Computer Arithmetic*, 5, 716, 1988.

13. Weinberger, A. and Smith, J. L., A logic for high-speed addition, *National Bureau of Standards*, Circulation 591, 3, 1958.

14. Kogge, P. M. and Stone, H. S., A parallel algorithms for the efficient solution of a general class of recurrence equations, *IEEE Trans. Computers*, C-22, 786, 1973.

15. Bilgory, A. and Gajski, D. D., Automatic generation of cells for recurrence structures, *Proc. 18th Design Automation Conf.*, Nashville, TN, 1981.

16. Brent, R. P. and Kung, H. T., A regular layout for parallel adders, *IEEE Trans. Computers*, C-31, 260, 1982.

17. Sklanski, J., Conditional-sum addition logic, *IRE Trans. Electron. Computers*, EC-9, 226, 1960.

18. Bedrij, O. J., Carry-select adder, *IRE Trans. Electron. Computers*, EC-11, 340, 1962.

19. Lynch, T. and Swartzlander, Jr., E. E., A spanning tree carry lookahead adder, *IEEE Trans. Computers*, 41, 931, 1992.

20. Dopperpuhl, D. W., et al., A 200 MHz 64-b dual-issue CMOS microprocessor, *IEEE J. Solid-State Circuits*, 27, 1555, 1992.

21. Suzuki, M., et al., A 1.5-ns 32-b CMOS ALU in double pass-transistor logic, *IEEE J. Solid-State Circuits*, 28, 1145, 1993.

22. Glasser, L. A. and Dobberpuhl, D. W., *The Design and analysis of VLSI circuits*, Addison-Wesley, Reading, MA, 1985.

23. Oowaki, Y., et al., A sub-10-ns 16 × 16 multiplier using 0.6-$\mu$m CMOS technology, *IEEE J. Solid-State Circuits*, SC-22, 762, 1987.

24. Wallace, C. S., A suggestion for a fast multiplier, *IEE Trans. Electron. Computers*, EC-13, 14, 1964.

25. Dadda, L., Some schemes for parallel multipliers, *Alta Frequenza*, 34, 349, 1965.

26. Stenzel, W. J., Kubitz, W. J., and Garcia, G. H., A compact high-speed parallel multiplication scheme, *IEEE Trans. Computers*, C-26, 948, 1977.

27. Cooper, A. R., Parallel architecture modified Booth multiplier, *IEE Proceedings*, 135, Pt. G., 125, 1988.

28. Stearns, C. C. and Ang, P. H., Yet another multiplier architecture, *IEEE Custom Integrated Circuits Conf.*, Boston, 24.6.1, 1990.

29. Nagamatsu, M., et al., A 15-ns 32 × 32-b multiplier with an improved parallel structure, *IEEE J. Solid-State Circuits*, 25, 494, 1990.

30. Hokenek, E., Montoye, R. K., and Cook, P. W., Second-generation RISC floating-point with multiply-add fused, *IEEE J. Solid-State Circuits*, 25, 1207, 1990.

31. Mou, Z. A. and Jutand, F., "Overturned-Stairs" adder trees and multiplier design, *IEEE Trans. Computers*, 41, 940, 1992.

32. Oklobdzija, V. G. and Villeger, D., Multiplier design utilizing improved column compression tree and optimized final adder in CMOS technology, *Int'l Symp. VLSI Tech., Systems & Appl.*, Taipei, Taiwan, 1993.

33. Weinberger, A., 4:2 carry-save adder module, *IBM Tech. Discl. Bulletin*, 23, 1981.

34. Goto, G., et al., A 54 × 54-b regularly structured tree multiplier, *IEEE J. Solid-State Circuits*, 27, 1229, 1992.

35. Ohkubo, N., et al., A 4.4 ns CMOS 54 × 54-b multiplier using pass-transistor multiplexer, *IEEE J. Solid-State Circuits*, 30, 251, 1995.

36. Goto, G., et al., A 4.1-ns compact 54 × 54-b multiplier utilizing sign-select Booth encoders, *IEEE J. Solid-State Circuits*, 32, 1676, 1997.

37. Booth, A. D., A signed binary multiplication technique, *Quarterly J. Mechan. Appl. Math.*, IV, 236, 1951.

38. MacSorley, O. L., High speed arithmetic in binary computers, *Proc. IRE*, 49, 1961.

39. Salomon, O., Green, J.-M., and Klar, H., General algorithm for a simplified addition of 2's complement numbers, *IEEE J. Solid-State Circuits*, 30, 839, 1995.

40. Sam, H. and Gupta, A., A generalized multibit recoding of two's complement binary numbers and its proof with application in multiplier implementations, *IEEE Trans. Computers*, 39, 1006, 1990.

41. *ANSI/IEEE Standard 754-1985 for Binary Floating-Point Arithmetic*, IEEE Computer Soc., Los Alamitos, CA, 1985.

# III

# Design Techniques

# 10

# Timing and Clocking

**John George Maneatis**
*True Circuits, Inc.*

**Fabian Klass**
*Sun Microsystems, Inc.*

**Cyrus (Morteza) Afghahi**
*Broadcom Corporation*

## 10.1   Design of High-Speed CMOS PLLs and DLLs

*John George Maneatis*

### Introduction

Phase-locked loops (PLLs), a set of circuits that include delay-locked loops, have found many applications within the realm of microprocessors and digital chips in the past 15 years. These applications include clock frequency synthesis, clock de-skewing, and high-bandwidth chip interfaces. A typical chip interface application is shown in Fig. 10.1 in which two chips synchronously send data to one another. To achieve high bandwidth, the data rate must be maximized with minimum data latency. Achieving this objective requires careful control over system timing in order to guarantee that setup and hold times are always satisfied.

Let us consider the requirements for receiving data by Chip 2. Chip 1 transmits this data synchronously along with a clock signal. Chip 2 would need to buffer this clock signal to drive all of the input latches and use it to sample the data. Buffering the clock signal will introduce a delay that will vary with process and environmental factors. The setup and hold time window for the input latches will then be shifted from the input clock edge by this varying delay amount. Such a delay can make it very difficult to insure that setup and hold times are always satisfied as the data rate is increased and this delay becomes a larger fraction of the clock cycle.

To alleviate the situation, it is desirable to eliminate this clock distribution delay and center the setup and hold time window on the input clock edge, which would remove any uncertainty in the window position relative to the clock signal. Such an approach also has the added benefit of avoiding the necessity for delay padding on the data wires to compensate for the clock distribution delay, which would increase the latency. It is also desirable to be able to multiply the frequency of the clock signal for use in the chip core so that the core logic can run with a higher clock frequency than available from the interface. These objectives can all be accomplished with a PLL [1,2].

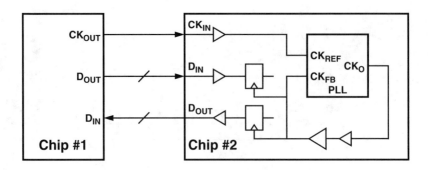

**FIGURE 10.1**  Typical chip interface.

The PLL generates an on-chip clock from the input clock to drive the clock distribution network and ultimately all of the latches and registers on the chip. By sensing the clock at the input of the receiving latches and adjusting its output phase until this latch clock aligns with the input clock, the PLL is able to subtract out the clock distribution delay and make it appear as though the input clock directly connects to all of the latches. The result is that the setup and hold time window is centered on the input clock edge with no process or environmental dependencies. The amount of setup and hold time can also be controlled relative to the clock cycle by centering the setup and hold time window relative to a different part of the clock cycle.

Although PLLs may seem to be the universal cure to all clock generation and interface problems, they do not come without problems of their own. PLLs can introduce time-varying offsets in the phase of the output clock from its ideal value as a result of internal and environmental factors. These time-varying offsets in the output clock phase are commonly referred to as jitter. Jitter can have disastrous effects on the timing of an interface by causing setup and hold time violations, which lead to data transmission errors.

Jitter was not a significant issue when PLLs were first introduced into digital IC interfaces. The techniques employed were fairly effective in addressing the jitter issue. However, designers often reapply those same PLL design techniques even though the nature of the problem has changed. IC technologies have improved, leading to decreasing cycle times. The number of input/output (I/O) pins and I/O data rates have increased leading to an increasing on-chip noise environment. An increasing aggressiveness in I/O system design has lead to a decreasing tolerance for jitter. The result is that PLL output jitter has increased while jitter tolerances have decreased, leading to significant jitter problems.

This chapter section focuses on the analysis and design of PLLs for interface applications in digital ICs with particular emphasis on achieving low output jitter. It begins by considering two basic PLL architectures in the section on "PLL Architectures." The next two sections perform a stability analysis for each architecture in order to gain insight into the various design tradeoffs and then present a comprehensive design strategy to establish the various loop parameters for each architecture. More advanced PLL architectures are briefly discussed in "Advanced PLL Architectures." "DLL/PLL Performance Issues" shifts gears to review the causes of output jitter in PLLs and examines circuit level techniques for reducing its magnitude. Circuits issues related to the implementation of the various PLL loop components are presented in the section on "DLL/PLL Circuits." "Self-Biased Techniques" briefly discusses self-biased techniques that can be used to eliminate the process and environmental dependencies within the PLL designs themselves. This chapter section concludes with a presentation of PLL characterization techniques in "Characterization Techniques."

## PLL Architectures

The basic operation of the PLLs considered in this chapter is the adjustment of the phase of the output so that no phase error is detected between the reference and feedback inputs. PLLs can be structured in a number of ways to accomplish this objective. Their structure can be classified based on how they react to phase errors and how they control the phase of the output. This chapter section focuses only on PLLs

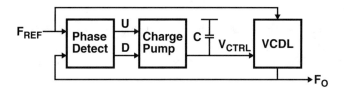

**FIGURE 10.2** Typical DLL block diagram (clock distribution omitted).

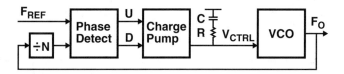

**FIGURE 10.3** Typical PLL block diagram (clock distribution omitted).

that integrate the phase error in the loop filter using charge pumps [3]. Charge pump PLLs have the property that in the locked state, the detected phase error is ideally zero.

In general, PLLs can control their output phases directly by delaying the reference signal or indirectly by changing the output frequency. The first is commonly referred to as a delay-locked loop (DLL) since it actually locks the delay between the reference input and the feedback input to some fraction of the reference input period. The second is referred to as a VCO-based PLL or simply as a PLL since it controls the frequency of a voltage-controlled oscillator (VCO) generating the output such that the feedback input is in phase with the reference input.

Figure 10.2 shows the general structure of a DLL. It is composed of a phase detector, charge pump, loop filter, and voltage-controlled delay line (VCDL). The negative feedback in the loop adjusts the delay through the VCDL by integrating the phase error that results between the periodic reference and delay line output. When in lock, the VCDL delays the reference input by a fixed amount to form the output such that the phase detector detects no phase error between the reference and feedback inputs. The clock distribution network, although not shown in the figure, is between the DLL output and the feedback input. Functionally, it can be considered as part of the VCDL.

Figure 10.3 shows the general structure of a PLL. It is composed of a phase detector, charge pump, loop filter, and VCO. Two key differences from the DLL are that the PLL contains a VCO instead of a VCDL and, as will be discussed below, requires a resistor in the loop for stability. The negative feedback in the loop adjusts the VCO output frequency by integrating the phase error that results between the periodic reference input and the divided VCO output. When in lock, the VCO generates an output frequency and phase such that the phase detector detects no phase error between the reference and feedback inputs. With no phase error between the reference and feedback inputs, the inputs must also be at the same frequency. If a frequency divider, which divides by N, is inserted between the PLL output and feedback input, the PLL output will be N times higher in frequency than the reference and feedback inputs, thus allowing the PLL to perform frequency multiplication.

The difference in loop structure between a DLL and a PLL gives rise to different properties and operating characteristics. DLLs tend to have short locking times and relatively low tracking jitter, but generally do not support frequency multiplication or duty cycle correction, have limited delay ranges, and require special lock reset functions. PLLs have unlimited phase ranges, support frequency multiplication and duty cycle correction, do not require special lock reset functions, but usually have longer lock times and higher tracking jitter. DLLs are less complex than PLLs from a loop architecture perspective, but are generally more complex from a design and system integration perspective.

## Loop Components

PLLs and DLLs share many common building blocks. These building blocks are the phase detector, charge pump, loop filter, voltage-controlled delay line, and voltage-controlled oscillator.

A phase detector, also known as a phase comparator, compares two input signals and generates "UP" and "DN" output pulses that represent the direction of the input phase error. There are many types of phase detectors; they differ in how they sense the input signals, what target input phase difference would cause them to detect no phase error, and how the phase error is represented in the output pulses.

For simplicity, we will initially only consider phase-frequency detectors. These detectors have the property that they are only rising or falling edge sensitive and, for each pair of input reference and feedback edges, produce a single pulse at either the UP or DN output, depending on which edge arrives first, with a duration equal to the time difference between the two edges or, equivalently, the input phase difference. When the reference and feedback edges arrive at the same time for zero input phase difference, the phase detector will effectively generate no UP or DN pulses; however, in actual implementation, the input phase difference may be represented by the phase detector as the difference between the pulse widths of the UP and DN outputs, where both are always asserted for some minimum duration in order to guarantee that no error information is lost due to incompletely rising pulses as the input phase difference approaches zero.

A charge pump, connected to the phase detector, sources or sinks current for the duration of the UP and DN pulses from the phase detector. The net output charge is proportional to the difference between the pulse widths of the UP and DN outputs. The charge pump drives the loop filter, which integrates and filters the charge current to produce the control voltage. The control voltage drives a VCDL in a DLL, which generates a delay proportional to the control voltage, or drives a VCO in a PLL, which generates a frequency proportional to the control voltage.

## Delay-Locked Loops

Before we consider a detailed analysis of the loop dynamics of a DLL, it is instructive to consider the control dynamics from a qualitative perspective as the loop approaches lock. Figure 10.4 illustrates the waveforms of signals and quantities inside a DLL during this locking process. Initially, the DLL is out of lock as the reference and output edges are not aligned.

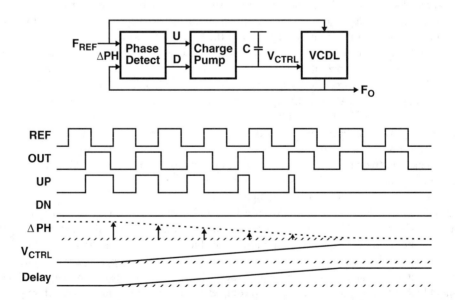

**FIGURE 10.4**   DLL locking waveforms.

Because the first output edge arrives before the first corresponding reference edge, the phase detector outputs a pulse at the UP output equal in duration to this phase error. A pulse at the UP output indicates that the delay needs to be increased. The charge pump generates an output charge proportional to the phase error, which increases the control voltage and thus the delay of the VCDL. After several cycles, the phase error is corrected.

The error is sampled only once per cycle, so the DLL is a sampled system as represented by the phase error impulses. However, if we limit the response time of the system to be a decade below the operating frequency, we can make a continuous time approximation. This approximation assumes that the phase errors are determined continuously as represented by the dashed line. Such a bandwidth limit will be required anyway to guarantee stability.

The magnitude of the delay correction per cycle is proportional to the detected phase error, therefore, the phase error, control voltage, and delay should change with an exponential decay toward their final values, rather than linearly as shown, for simplicity, in the figure. Also, it should be noted that there are different ways of configuring the charge pump in the DLL. Some DLLs, for example, output a fixed charge independent of the size of the phase error. This type of charge pump converts the DLL into a nonlinear system and as such will not be considered in the following DLL analysis.

## DLL Frequency Response

More insight into DLL design issues can be gained by determining the frequency response of the DLL. This frequency response can be derived with a continuous time approximation, where the sampling behavior of the phase detector is ignored. This approximation holds for response bandwidths that are a decade or more below the operating frequency. This bandwidth constraint is also required for stability due to the reduced phase margin near the higher-order poles that result from the delay around the sampled feedback loop. The mathematical symbols used in deviations for both the DLL and PLL are defined in Table 10.1.

Because the loop filter integrates the phase error, the DLL has a first order closed-loop response. The response could be formulated in terms of input phase and output phase. However, this set of variables is incompatible with the continuous time analysis since the sampled nature of the system must be considered. A better set of variables is input delay and output delay. The output delay is the delay between the reference input and the DLL output or, equivalently, the delay established by the VCDL. The input

**TABLE 10.1**  PLL Loop and Device Parameter Definitions

| Symbol | Definition | Unit |
|---|---|---|
| $F_{REF}$ | Reference frequency | Hz |
| $\omega_{REF}$ | Reference frequency | rad/s |
| $I_{CH}$ | Peak charge pump current | A |
| $K_{DL}$ | Voltage-controlled delay line gain (DLL) | s/V |
| $K_V$ | Voltage-controlled oscillator gain (PLL) | Hz/V |
| $G_O$ | Gain normalization factor (PLL) | — |
| $C$ | Loop filter capacitor | F |
| $C_2$ | Higher order roll-off capacitor (PLL) | F |
| $R$ | Loop filter resistor (PLL) | $\Omega$ (ohm) |
| $N$ | Feedback divider value (PLL) | — |
| $D(s)$ | Delay in frequency domain (DLL) | s |
| $P(s)$ | Phase in frequency domain (PLL) | rad |
| $H(s)$ | Response in frequency domain | — |
| $T(s)$ | Loop gain in frequency domain (PLL) | — |
| $\zeta$ | Loop damping factor (PLL) | — |
| $\omega_N$ | Loop bandwidth | rad/s |
| $\omega_C$ | Higher order cutoff frequency (PLL) | rad/s |
| $\omega_O$ | Unity gain frequency | rad/s |
| PM | Phase margin | rad |

delay is some fraction of the input clock period as determined by the phase detector. It is typically one, one half, or one quarter of the input clock period.

The output delay, $D_o(s)$, is related to the input delay, $D_I(s)$, by

$$D_O(s) = (D_I(s) - D_O(s)) \cdot F_{REF} \cdot I_{CH}/(s \cdot C) \cdot K_{DL}$$

where $F_{REF}$ is the reference frequency (Hz), $I_{CH}$ is the charge pump current (A), C is the loop filter capacitance (F), and $K_{DL}$ is the VCDL gain (s/V). The product of the delay difference and the reference frequency is equal to the fraction of the reference period in which the charge pump is activated. The average charge pump output current is equal to this fraction times the peak charge pump current. The output delay is then equal to the product of the average charge pump current, the loop filter transfer function, and the delay line gain.

The closed-loop response is then given by

$$D_o(s)/D_I(s) = 1/(1 + s/\omega_N)$$

where $\omega_N$, defined as the loop bandwidth (rad/s), is given by

$$\omega_N = I_{CH} \cdot K_{DL} \cdot F_{REF}/C$$

This response is of first order with a pole at $\omega_N$. Thus, the DLL acts as a single-pole low-pass filter to changes in the input reference period with cutoff frequency $\omega_N$. The delay between the reference and feedback signal will be a filtered version of a set fraction of the reference period. It is unconditionally stable as long as the continuous time approximation holds or, equivalently, as long as $\omega_N$ is a decade below $\omega_{REF}$ As $\omega_N$ increases above $\omega_{REF}/10$, the delay in sampling the phase error will become more significant and will begin to undermine the stability of the loop.

### DLL Design Strategy

With an understanding of the DLL frequency response, we can consider how to structure the loop parameters to obtain desirable loop dynamics. Using the bandwidth results from the DLL frequency response and, limiting it to a decade below the reference frequency, we can determine the constraints on the charge pump current, VCDL gain, and loop filter capacitance as

$$\omega_N/F_{REF} = I_{ch} \cdot K_{DL}/C \leq \pi/5$$

The VCDL also must be structured so that it spans adequate delay range to guarantee lock for all operating, environmental, and process conditions. The delay range needed is constrained by the lock target delay of the phase detector, $T_{LOCK}$, and the range of possible values for the clock distribution delay, $T_{DIST}$, and the reference period, $T_{CYCLE}$, with the following equations:

$$VCDL_{MIN} = (T_{LOCK} - T_{DIST\_MAX}) \text{ modulo } T_{CYCLE\_MIN}$$
$$VCDL_{MAX} = (T_{LOCK} - T_{DIST\_MIN}) \text{ modulo } T_{CYCLE\_MAX}$$

where $T_{LOCK}$ is 1 cycle for in-phase locks and 1/4 cycles for quadrature locks.

Also, special measures may be required to guarantee that the DLL reaches lock after being reset. These measures depend on the specific structure of the DLL. Typically, the VCDL delay is set to its minimum delay and the state of the phase detector is reset. However, for some DLLs, more complicated approaches may be required.

### Alternative DLL Structures

The complexity of designing a DLL is not so much in the control dynamics as it is in the underlying structure. Although the DLLs discussed in this chapter are analog-based, using VCDLs with analog control, many other approaches are possible that utilize different amounts of analog and digital control. These approaches can circumvent the problems associated with limited delay ranges and reaching lock. One possible structure is a rotating phase DLL that digitally selects and optionally interpolates with analog or digital control between intermediate output phases from a VCDL or VCO phase-locked to the clock period [4]. A related structure interpolates with analog control between quadratures phases generated directly from the clock signal [5]. Another even simpler structure with reduced jitter performance digitally selects intermediate outputs from an inverter chain-based delay line [6]. While digital control provides more flexibility, analog control requires less power and area.

## Phase-Locked Loops

Similar to a DLL, a PLL aligns the phase of the output to match the input. The DLL accomplishes this by appropriately delaying the input signal. The PLL accomplishes this by controlling an oscillator to match the phases of the input signal. The control for the PLL is more indirect, which requires it to have the resistor in the loop filter for stability.

Consider the typical PLL shown in Fig. 10.3 as it starts out from an unlocked state with a VCO frequency that is relatively close to but slightly higher than the reference frequency. To help understand the function of the resistor in the loop filter, let's first assume that it is zero valued making the loop filter equivalent to that of the DLL. Initially, the PLL is out of lock as the reference and feedback edges are not aligned. With the first feedback edge arriving before the first corresponding reference edge, the phase detector outputs a pulse at the DN output equal in duration to this phase error. A pulse at the DN output indicates that the VCO frequency needs to be reduced. The charge pump generates an output charge proportional to the phase error, which reduces the control voltage and thus the VCO frequency.

In order to reduce the phase error, the feedback edges need to arrive later and later with respect to the reference edges or, equivalently, the VCO frequency must be reduced below the reference frequency. After several cycles, the phase error is reduced to zero, but the VCO frequency is now lower than the reference frequency. This frequency overshoot causes the feedback edges to begin to arrive later than the corresponding reference edges, leading to the opposite error condition from which the loop started. The loop then begins to increase the VCO frequency above the reference frequency to reduce the phase error, but at the point when the phase error is zero, the VCO frequency is now higher than the reference frequency. Thus, in the PLL with a zero-valued resistor, the phase error will oscillate freely around zero, which represents unstable behavior.

This unstable behavior can be circumvented by adding an extra frequency adjustment that is proportional to the phase error and is therefore applied only for the duration of the phase error. This proportional control allows the loop to adjust the VCO frequency past the reference frequency in order to reduce the phase error without the frequency difference persisting when the phase error is eliminated. When the phase error reaches zero and the extra adjustment is reduced to zero, the VCO frequency should match the reference frequency leading to a stable result. This proportional control can be implemented by adding a resistor in series with the loop filter capacitor. This resistor converts the charge pump current, which is proportional to the phase error, into an extra control voltage component, which is added to the control voltage already integrated on the loop filter capacitor.

From another perspective, this resistor dampens out potential phase and frequency overshooting. The amount of damping depends on the value of the resistor. Clearly, with zero resistance, there will be no damping and the loop will be unstable as the output phase will oscillate forever around zero phase difference. As the resistor value is increased, the loop will become increasingly less underdamped as the oscillations will decay to zero at an increasing rate. For some resistor value, the loop will become critically damped as the oscillations will go away entirely and the phase will approach zero without overshooting. As the resistor value is increased further, the loop becomes overdamped as the phase initially approaches zero rapidly, then slows down, taking a long time to reach zero.

The overdamped behavior results when the damping is so high that it creates a large frequency difference between the VCO and reference that initially drives the phase error rapidly toward zero; however, this added frequency difference goes away when the phase error approaches zero. The VCO frequency that results from the voltage across the loop filter capacitor may still be different from the reference frequency. Unfortunately, the phase error has been reduced substantially so that there is little charge pump current to change the voltage on the loop filter capacitor very quickly. The phase will change rapidly to the point where the resultant phase error generates a proportional frequency correction that makes the VCO frequency match the reference frequency. As the proportionality constant, or, equivalently, the resistance, is increased, the rate at which the phase changes will also increase and the phase error after the initial phase change will decrease; however, as the initial phase error is reduced, the amount of time required to eliminate the phase error will increase because the charge pump current will also decrease.

### PLL Frequency Response

The different types of damping behavior can be quantified more carefully by deriving the frequency response of the PLL. As with the DLL, the frequency response of the PLL can be analyzed with a continuous time approximation for bandwidths a decade or more below the operating frequency. This bandwidth constraint is also required for stability due to the reduced phase margin near the higher-order poles that result from the delay around the sampled feedback loop. Because the loop filter integrates the charge representing the phase error and the VCO integrates the output frequency to form the output phase, the PLL has a second-order closed-loop response.

Considerable insight can be gained into the design of the PLL by first considering its open-loop response. This response can be derived by breaking the loop at the feedback input of the phase detector. The output phase, $P_O(s)$, is related to the input phase, $P_I(s)$, by

$$P_O(s) = P_I(s) \cdot I_{ch} \cdot (R + 1/(s \cdot C)) \cdot K_V/s$$

where $I_{CH}$ is the charge pump current (A), R is the loop filter resistor (ohms), C is the loop filter capacitance (F), and $K_V$ is the VCO gain (Hz/V). The open-loop response, H(s), is then given by

$$H(s) = P_O(s)/P_I(s) = I_{CH} \cdot K_V \cdot (1 + s \cdot R \cdot C)/(s^2 \cdot C)$$

The loop gain, T(s), which is the product of the gain through the forward path, H(s), and the gain through the feedback path, 1/N, is given by

$$T(s) = H(s)/N$$

The normalized loop gain magnitude and phase plots for the PLL are shown in Fig. 10.5. At low frequencies, the loop gain drops at 40 dB per decade where the phase is at $-180°$, since there are two poles at zero frequency. The zero caused by the resistor in the loop filter is at frequency $1/(R \cdot C)$ and causes the loop gain at higher frequencies to only drop at 20 dB per decade and the loop phase to "decrease" to $-90°$, which makes it possible to stabilize the loop.

The plotted loop gain magnitude is normalized with the gain normalization factor, $G_O$, given by

$$G_O = R^2 \cdot C \cdot I_{CH} \cdot K_V/N$$

The value of this factor will set the frequency at which the loop gain is unity. This frequency is significant because it determines the phase margin, which is a measure of the stability and the amount of damping for the PLL system. The phase margin is measured as $180°$ or $\pi$ radians plus the loop gain phase at the unity gain frequency or, equivalently, the frequency where the loop gain magnitude is unity. The unity gain level on the plot is the inverse of the gain normalization factor. No phase margin exists at unity gain frequencies below $0.1/(R \cdot C)$ because the loop gain phase is about $-180°$. The phase margin gradually increases with increasing unity gain frequency as a result of the zero at frequency $1/(R \cdot C)$.

The loop is critically damped with a phase margin of $76°$, corresponding to a normalized loop gain magnitude of 0.25, a gain normalization factor of 4, and a unity gain frequency of $4.12/(R \cdot C)$ (rad/s). The loop will be underdamped for smaller phase margins and overdamped for greater phase margins.

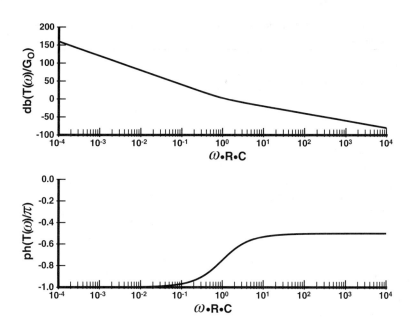

**FIGURE 10.5** PLL loop gain magnitude and phase (without $C_2$).

The closed-loop response can be derived from the open-loop response by considering the feedback signal. In the closed-loop system, the output phase, $P_O(s)$, is related to the input phase, $P_I(s)$, by

$$P_O(s) = (P_I(s) - P_O(s)/N) \cdot H(s)$$

where N is the feedback clock divider value. The closed-loop response is then given by

$$P_O(s)/P_I(s) = 1/(1/N + s/H(s))$$
$$= N \cdot 1 + s \cdot C \cdot R/$$
$$(1 + s \cdot C \cdot R + s^2/(I_{CH}/C \cdot K_V/N))$$

or, equivalently, by

$$P_O(s)/P_I(s) = N \cdot (1 + 2 \cdot \zeta \cdot (s/\omega_N)/$$
$$(1 + 2 \cdot \zeta \cdot (s/\omega_N) + (s/\omega_N)^2)$$

where $\zeta$, defined as the damping factor, is given by

$$\zeta = 1/2 \cdot (1/N \cdot I_{CH} \cdot K_V \cdot R^2 \cdot C)^{0.5}$$

and $\omega_N$, defined as the loop bandwidth (rad/s), is given by

$$\omega_N = 2 \cdot \zeta/(R \cdot C)$$

The loop bandwidth and damping factor completely characterize the closed-loop response. The PLL is critically damped with a damping factor of one and overdamped with damping factors greater than one.

Treating the PLL as a standard second order system makes it much easier to analyze. The time domain impulse, step, and ramp responses are easily derived from the frequency domain closed-loop response. Equations for these responses are summarized in Table 10.2. The peak values of these responses are very useful in estimating the amount of frequency overshoot and the amount of supply and substrate noise

**TABLE 10.2**   Equations for Second-Order PLL Impulse, Step, and Ramp Time Domain Responses

Define:

$$c_1 = -\zeta \cdot \omega_N + \omega_N \cdot (\zeta^2 - 1)^{0.5}$$
$$c_2 = -\zeta \cdot \omega_N - \omega_N \cdot (\zeta^2 - 1)^{0.5}$$
$$T_1 = C \cdot R = 2 \cdot \zeta/\omega_N$$

Note: $c_1 \cdot c_2 = \omega_N^2$

Impulse Response (Input is $\delta(t)$):

$\zeta > 1$:
$$h(t) = (N \cdot \omega_N/(2 \cdot (\zeta^2 - 1)^{0.5})) \cdot$$
$$((1 + T_1 \cdot c_1) \cdot e^{(c1 \cdot t)} - (1 + T_1 \cdot c_2) \, e^{(c2 \cdot t)}) \cdot u(t)$$
$\zeta = 1$:
$$h(t) = N \cdot \omega_N \cdot e^{(-\omega_N \cdot t)} \cdot (2 - \omega_N \cdot t) \cdot u(t)$$
$0 < \zeta < 1$:
$$h(t) = (N \cdot \omega_N/(1 - \zeta^2)^{0.5}) \cdot$$
$$e^{(-\zeta \cdot \omega_N \cdot t)} \cdot \cos (\omega_N \cdot (1 - \zeta^2)^{0.5} \cdot t - \phi) \cdot u(t)$$
where:
$$\phi = \tan^{-1} ((1 - 2 \cdot \zeta^2)/(2 \cdot \zeta \cdot (1 - \zeta^2)^{0.5}))$$

Step Response (Input is $u(t)$):

$\zeta > 1$:
$$s(t) = N \cdot (1 + (\omega_N/(2 \cdot (\zeta^2 - 1)^{0.5})) \cdot$$
$$((1/c_1 + T_1) \cdot e^{(c1 \cdot t)} - (1/c_2 + T_1) \cdot e^{(c2 \cdot t)})) \cdot u(t)$$
$\zeta = 1$:
$$s(t) = N \cdot (1 + e^{(-\omega_N \cdot t)} \cdot (\omega_N \cdot t - 1)) \cdot u(t)$$
$0 < \zeta < 1$:
$$s(t) = N \cdot (1 - (1/(1 - \zeta^2)^{0.5}) \cdot$$
$$e^{(-\zeta \cdot \omega_N \cdot t)} \cdot \cos (\omega_N \cdot (1 - \zeta^2)^{0.5} \cdot t + \phi')) \cdot u(t)$$
where:
$$\phi' = \sin^{-1} (\zeta)$$

Ramp Response (input is $t \cdot u(t)$):

$$r'(t) = r(t) - N \cdot t \cdot u(t) = P_O(t) - N \cdot P_1(t)$$
$\zeta > 1$:
$$r(t) = N \cdot (t - (1/(2 \cdot \omega_N \cdot (\zeta^2 - 1)^{0.5})) \cdot$$
$$(e^{(c1 \cdot t)} - e^{(c2 \cdot t)})) \cdot u(t)$$
$$r'(t) = -(N/(2 \cdot \omega_N \cdot (\zeta^2 - 1)^{0.5})) \cdot$$
$$(e^{(c1 \cdot t)} - e^{(c2 \cdot t)}) \cdot u(t)$$

$\zeta = 1$:
$$r(t) = N \cdot t \cdot (1 - e^{(-\omega_N \cdot t)}) \cdot u(t)$$
$$r'(t) = - N \cdot t \cdot e^{(-\omega_N \cdot t)} \cdot u(t)$$
$0 < \zeta < 1$:
$$r(t) = N \cdot (t - (1/(\omega_N \cdot (1 - \zeta^2)^{0.5})) \cdot e^{(-\zeta \cdot \omega_N \cdot t)} \cdot$$
$$\sin (\omega_N \cdot (1 - \zeta^2)^{0.5} \cdot t)) \cdot u(t)$$
$$r'(t) = -(N/(\omega_N \cdot (1 - \zeta^2)^{0.5})) \cdot e^{(-\zeta \cdot \omega_N \cdot t)} \cdot$$
$$\sin (\omega_N \cdot (1 - \zeta^2)^{0.5} \cdot t) \cdot u(t)$$

Slow Step Response ($d(t) = (r(t) - r(t - dt))/dt$):

$$d'(t) = d(t) - N \cdot (t \cdot u(t) - (t - dt) \cdot u(t - dt))$$
$$= r'(t) - r'(t - dt)$$
$$= P_O(t) - N \cdot P_1(t)$$
$0 < \zeta < 1$:
$$d'(t) = -(N/(dt \cdot \omega_N \cdot (1 - \zeta^2)^{0.5})) \cdot e^{(-\zeta \cdot \omega_N \cdot t)} \cdot$$
$$(\sin (\omega_N \cdot (1 - \zeta^2)^{0.5} \cdot t) \cdot u(t) - e^{(\zeta \cdot \omega_N \cdot dt)} \cdot$$
$$\sin (\omega_N \cdot (1 - \zeta^2)^{0.5} \cdot (t - dt)) \cdot u(t - dt))$$

**TABLE 10.3** Peak Values of Second-Order PLL Magnitude, Impulse, Step, and Ramp Responses

Magnitude Frequency Response (for all $\zeta$):

$\omega_1 = (\omega_N/(2 \cdot \zeta)) \cdot ((1 + 8 \cdot \zeta^2)^{0.5} - 1)^{0.5}$

$|H(j\omega_1)| = (N \cdot (1 + 8 \cdot \zeta^2)^{0.25})/$
$\qquad (1 + (1 - 1/(2 \cdot \zeta^2) - 1/(8 \cdot \zeta^4)) \cdot$
$\qquad ((1 + 8 \cdot \zeta^2)^{0.5} - 1) + 1/(2 \cdot \zeta^2))^{0.5}$

Step Response:

$\zeta > 1$:
$\qquad t_1 = (1/(\omega_N \cdot (\zeta^2 - 1)^{0.5})) \cdot$
$\qquad\qquad \log (2 \cdot \zeta \cdot (\zeta + (1 - \zeta^2)^{0.5}) - 1)$
$\quad s(t_1) = s(t = t_1)$

$\zeta = 1$:
$\qquad t_1 = 2/\omega_N$
$\qquad s(t_1) = N \cdot (1 + 1/e^2)$

$0 < \zeta < 1$:
$\qquad t_1 = (\pi - 2 \cdot \sin^{-1} (\zeta))/(\omega_N \cdot (1 - \zeta^2)^{0.5})$
$\qquad s(t_1) = N \cdot (1 + e^{((2 \cdot \sin^{-1} (\zeta) - \pi) \cdot (\zeta/(1-\zeta^2)^{0.5}))})$

Ramp Response:

$\zeta > 1$:
$\qquad t_1 = (1/(2 \cdot \omega_N \cdot (\zeta^2 - 1)^{0.5})) \cdot$
$\qquad\qquad \log (2 \cdot \zeta \cdot (\zeta + (1 - \zeta^2)^{0.5}) - 1)$
$\qquad r'(t_1) = r'(t = t_1)$

$\zeta = 1$:
$\qquad t_1 = 1/\omega_N$
$\qquad r'(t_1) = - N/(e \cdot \omega_N)$

$0 < \zeta < 1$:
$\qquad t_1 = \cos^{-1} (\zeta)/(\omega_N \cdot (1 - \zeta^2)^{0.5})$
$\qquad r'(t_1) = - N/\omega_N \cdot e^{(\cos^{-1} (\zeta) \cdot (\zeta/(1-\zeta^2)^{0.5}))}$

Slow Step Response:

$0 < \zeta < 1$:
$\qquad t_1 = (1/x) \cdot$
$\qquad\qquad \tan^{-1} ((-x + z \cdot y \cdot \sin (x \cdot dt) + z \cdot x \cdot \cos (x \cdot dt)) /$
$\qquad\qquad (-y + z \cdot y \cdot \cos (x \cdot dt) + z \cdot x \cdot \sin (x \cdot dt)))$
$\quad$ for $t_1 > dt$, otherwise given by $t_1$ for $r'(t)$
$\quad$ where:
$\qquad x = \omega_N \cdot (1 - \zeta^2)$
$\qquad y = \zeta \cdot \omega_N$
$\qquad z = e^{(\zeta \cdot \omega N \cdot dt)}$
$\quad d'(t_1) = d'(t = t_1)$

Note that $\omega_1$ or $t_1$ is the frequency or time where the response from Table 10.2 is maximized.

induced jitter for a set of loop parameters. The peak values and the point at which they occur are summarized in Table 10.3.

The closed-loop frequency response of the PLL for different values of $\zeta$ and for frequencies normalized to $\omega_N$ is shown in Fig. 10.6. This plot shows that the PLL is a low-pass filter to phase noise at frequencies below $\omega_N$. Phase noise at frequencies below $\omega_N$ passes through the PLL unattenuated. Phase noise at frequencies above $\omega_N$ is filtered with slope of –20 dB per decade. For small values of $\zeta$, the filter cutoff at $\omega_N$ is sharper with initial slopes as high as –40 dB per decade. However, for these values of $\zeta$, the phase noise is amplified at frequencies near $\omega_N$. This phase noise amplification or peaking increases, along with the initial cutoff slope, for decreasing values of $\zeta$. This phase noise amplification can have adverse affects on the output jitter of the PLL. It is important to notice that because of the zero in the closed-loop

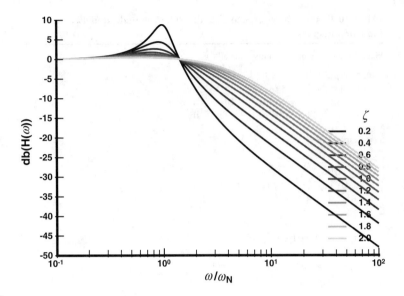

**FIGURE 10.6**   PLL closed-loop frequency response.

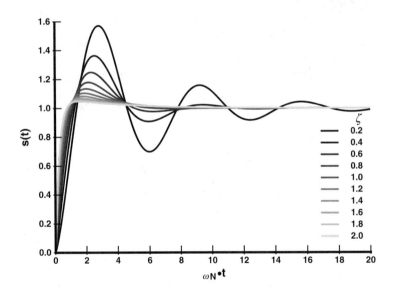

**FIGURE 10.7**   PLL closed-loop transient step response.

response, there is a small amount of phase noise amplification at phase noise frequencies of $\omega_N$ for all values of $\zeta$. However, for values of $\zeta$ less than 0.7, the amplification gain starts to become significant.

The closed-loop transient step response of the PLL for different values of $\zeta$ and for times normalized to $1/\omega_N$ is shown in Fig. 10.7. The step response is generated by instantaneously advancing the phase of the reference input by one radian and observing the output for different damping levels in the time domain. For damping factors below one, the system is underdamped as the PLL output overshoots the final phase and rings at the frequency $\omega_N$. The amplitude of the overshoot increases and the rate of decay for the ringing decreases as the damping factor is decreased below one. The fastest settling response is generated with a damping factor of one, where the system is critically damped. For damping factors

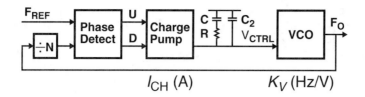

**FIGURE 10.8** Typical PLL block diagram with $C_2$ (clock distribution omitted).

greater than one, the system is overdamped as the PLL output initially responds rapidly but then takes a long time to reach the final phase. The rate of the initial response increases and the rate of the final response decreases as the damping factor is increased above one.

## PLL with Higher-Order Roll-Off

It is very common for an actual PLL implementation to contain an extra capacitor, $C_2$, in shunt with the loop filter, as shown in Fig. 10.8. This capacitor may have been introduced intentionally for filtering or may result from parasitic capacitances within the resistor or at the input of the VCO.

Because the charge pump and phase detector are activated once every reference frequency cycle, they can cause a periodic disturbance on the control voltage node. This disturbance is usually not an issue for loops with N equal to one because the disturbance will occur in every VCO cycle. However, the disturbance can cause a constant shift in the duty cycle of the VCO output. When N is greater than one, the disturbance will occur once every N VCO cycles, which could cause the first one or two of the N cycles to be different from the others, leading to jitter in the PLL output period. In the frequency domain, this periodic disturbance will cause sidebands on the fundamental peak of the VCO frequency spaced at intervals of the reference frequency.

Capacitor $C_2$ will help filter out this reference frequency noise by introducing a pole at $\omega_C$. It will decrease the magnitude of the reference frequency sidebands by the ratio of $\omega_{REF}/\omega_C$. However, the introduction of $C_2$ can also cause stability problems for the PLL since it converts the PLL into a third-order system. In addition, $C_2$ makes the analysis of the PLL much more difficult.

The PLL is now characterized by the four loop parameters $\omega_N$, $\omega_C$, $\zeta$, and N. The damping factor, $\zeta$, is changed by $C_2$ as follows:

$$\zeta = 1/2 \cdot (1/N \cdot I_{CH} \cdot K_V \cdot R^2 \cdot C^2/(C + C_2))^{0.5}$$

The loop bandwidth, $\omega_N$, is changed by $C_2$ through its dependency on $\zeta$. The added pole in the open-loop response is at frequency $\omega_C$ given by

$$\omega_C = (C + C_2)/(R \cdot C \cdot C_2)$$

This pole can reduce the stability of the loop if it is too close to the loop bandwidth frequency. Typically, it should be set at least a factor of ten above the loop bandwidth so as not to compromise the stability loop.

Because the stability of the loop is now established by both $\zeta$ and $\omega_C/\omega_N$, a figure of merit can be defined that represents the potential stability of the loop as

$$\zeta \cdot \omega_C/\omega_N = (C/C_2 + 1)/2$$

This definition is useful because it actually defines the maximum possible phase margin given an optimal choice for the loop gain magnitude.

Consider the normalized loop gain magnitude and phase plots for the PLL with different ratios of C to $C_2$ shown in Fig. 10.9. From these plots, it is clear that the added pole at $\omega_C$ causes the loop gain magnitude slope to increase to $-40$ dB per decade and the loop gain phase to "increase" to $-180°$ above the frequency of the pole. Between the zero at $1/(R \cdot C)$ and the pole at $\omega_C$ there is a region where the

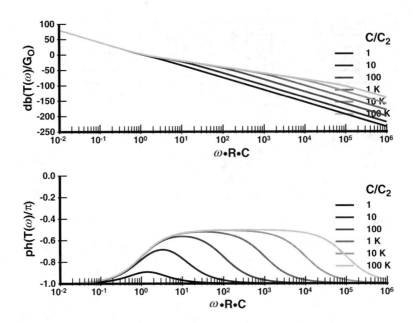

**FIGURE 10.9**   PLL loop gain magnitude and phase with $C_2$.

loop gain magnitude slope is −20 dB per decade and the loop gain phase approaches −90°. It is in this region where a unity gain crossing would provide the maximum possible phase margin. As the ratio of C to $C_2$ increases, this region becomes wider and the maximum phase becomes closer to −90°. Thus, the ratio of C to $C_2$, and, therefore, the figure of merit for stability, defines the maximum possible phase margin.

Based on the frequency response results for the PLL we can make a number of observations about its behavior. First, the continuous time analysis used assumes that the reference frequency is about a decade above all significant frequencies in the response. Second, both the second-order and third-order response are independent of operating frequency, as long as $K_V$ remains constant. Third, the resistor R introduces a zero in the open-loop response, which is needed for stability. Finally, capacitor $C_2$ can decrease the phase margin if larger than C/20 and can reduce the reference frequency sidebands by $\omega_{REF}/\omega_C$.

### PLL Design Issues

With a good understanding of the PLL frequency response, we can consider issues related to the design of the PLL. The design of the PLL involves first establishing the loop parameters that lead to desirable control dynamics and then establishing device parameters for the circuits that realize those loop parameters.

The loop parameters $\omega_N$, $\omega_C$, and $\zeta$ are often set by the application. The desired value for $\zeta$ is typically near unity for the fastest overdamped response and about 76° of phase margin, or at least 0.707 for minimal ringing and about 65° of phase margin. $\omega_N$ must be about one decade below the reference frequency for stability. For frequency synthesis or clock recovery applications, where input jitter filtering is desirable, $\omega_N$ is typically set relatively low. For input tracking applications, such as clock de-skewing, $\omega_N$ is typically set as high as possible to minimize jitter accumulation, as discussed in the sub-section on "PLL Supply/Substrate Noise Response." When reference sideband filtering is important, $\omega_C$ is typically set as low as possible at about a decade above $\omega_N$ to maximize the amount of filtering.

The values of the loop parameters must somehow be mapped into acceptable values for the device parameters R, C, $C_2$, $I_{CH}$, and $K_V$. The values of these parameters are typically constrained by the implementation. The value for capacitor $C_2$ is determined by all capacitances on the control voltage node if the zero is implemented directly with a resistor. If capacitor C is implemented on chip, which is desirable

**TABLE 10.4**  Proportionality Relationships between PLL Loop and Device Parameters

|  | $\omega_N$ | $\omega_C$ | $\zeta$ | $\omega_C/\omega_N$ |  |
| --- | --- | --- | --- | --- | --- |
| $I_{CH}$ | $I_{CH}^{0.5}$ | indep. | $I_{CH}^{0.5}$ | $1/I_{CH}^{0.5}$ |  |
| R | indep. | $1/R$ | R | $1/R$ |  |
| C | $1/C^{0.5}$ | indep. | $C^{0.5}$ | $C^{0.5}$ | $(C \gg C_2)$ |
| $C_2$ | indep. | $1/C_2$ | indep. | $1/C_2$ | $(C \gg C_2)$ |

**TABLE 10.5**  PLL Loop and Device Parameter Scaling Rules

Constant frequency scaling: Given x, suppose that

$$I_{CH} \cdot x \to I_{CH}$$
$$C_I \cdot x \to C_I$$
$$R/x \to R$$

Then all parameters, $G_O$, $\Omega_I$, and $\zeta$, remain constant

Proportional frequency scaling: Given x, suppose that

| | | |
| --- | --- | --- |
| $I_{CH} \cdot x \to I_{CH}$ | $I_{CH} \cdot x^2 \to I_{CH}$ | $I_{CH} \to I_{CH}$ |
| $C_I/x \to C_I$ | $C_I \to C_I$ | $C_I/x^2 \to C_I$ |
| $R \to R$ | $R/x \to R$ | $R \cdot x \to R$ |

Then,

$$G_O \to G_O$$
$$\omega \cdot x \to \omega_I$$
$$\omega_C/\omega_N \to \omega_C/\omega_N$$
$$\zeta \to \zeta$$

where $C_I$ represents all capacitors and $\omega_I$ represents all frequencies.

to minimize jitter, its size is constrained to less than about 1nF. The charge pump current $I_{CH}$ is constrained to be greater than about 10 $\mu$A depending on the level of charge pump charge injection offsets.

The problem of selecting device parameters is made more difficult by a number of constraining factors. First, $\omega_N$ and $\zeta$ both depend on all of the device parameters. Second, the maximum limit for C and minimum limit for $I_{CH}$ will impose a minimum limit on $\omega_N$, which already has a maximum limit due to $\omega_{REF}$ and other possible limits due to jitter and reference sideband issues. Third and most important, all worst-case combinations of device parameters due to process, voltage, and temperature variability must lead to acceptable loop dynamics.

Handling the interdependence between the loop parameters and device parameters is simplified by observing some proportionality relationships and scaling rules that directly result from the equations that relate the loop and device parameters. They are summarized in Table 10.4 and Table 10.5, respectively. The constant frequency scaling rules can transform one set of device parameters to another without changing any of the loop parameters. The proportional frequency scaling rules can transform one set of device parameters, with the resistance, capacitances, or charge pump current held constant, to another set with scaled loop frequencies and the same damping factor. These rules make it easy to make adjustments to the possible device parameters with controlled changes to the loop parameters.

With the many constraints on the loop and device parameters established by both the system environment and the circuit implementation, the design of a PLL typically turns into a compromise between conflicting design requirements. It is the job of the designer to properly balance these conflicting requirements and determine the best overall solution.

## PLL Design Strategy

Two general approaches can be used to determine the device parameters for a PLL design. The first approach is based on an open-loop analysis. This approach makes it easier to visualize the stability of the design from a frequency domain perspective. The open-loop analysis also easily accommodates more complicated loop filters. The second approach is based on a closed-loop analysis. This approach involves

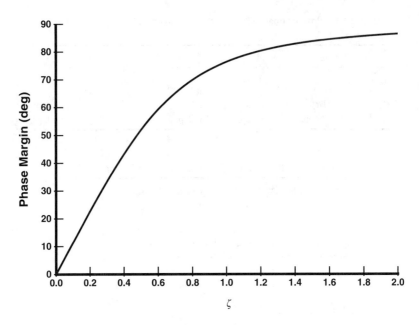

**FIGURE 10.10** PLL phase margin as a function of damping factor.

the loop parameters $\omega_N$ and $\zeta$, which are commonly specified by higher-level system requirements. The complexity of these approaches depends on whether $C_2$ exists and its level of significance.

If $C_2$ does not need to be considered, a simplified version of the open-loop analysis or second-order analysis can be used. For an open-loop analysis without $C_2$, we need to consider the open-loop response of the PLL in Fig. 10.5. The loop gain normalization constant, $G_o$, for the normalized loop gain magnitude plot is directly related to the damping factor $\zeta$ by

$$G_O = R^2 \cdot C \cdot I_{CH} \cdot K_V/N = 4 \cdot \zeta^2$$

This normalization constant is also the loop gain magnitude at the asymptotic break point for the zero at $1/(R \cdot C)$. An increase in the loop gain normalization constant will lead to a higher unity gain crossing, and therefore more phase margin. A plot of phase margin as a function of the damping factor $\zeta$ is shown in Fig. 10.10. In order to adequately stabilize the design, the phase margin should be set to 65° or more and the unity gain bandwidth should be set no higher than $\omega_{REF}/5$. It is easiest to first adjust the loop gain magnitude level to set the phase margin, then to use the frequency scaling rules to adjust the unity gain bandwidth to the desired frequency. Without $C_2$, the second-order analysis simply depends on the loop parameters $\omega_N$ and $\zeta$. To adequately stabilize the design, $\omega_N$ should be set no higher than $\omega_{REF}/10$ and $\zeta$ should be set to 0.707 or greater.

If $C_2$ exists but is not too large, an extension of the above approaches can be used. C should be set greater than $C_2 \cdot 20$ to provide a minimum of 65° of phase margin at the unity gain bandwidth with the maximum phase margin. For any $C/C_2$ ratio, the maximum phase margin is given by

$$PM_{MAX} = 2 \cdot \tan^{-1}(\sqrt{(C/C_2 + 1)}) - \pi/2$$

With the open-loop analysis, as before, the phase margin should be set to at least 65° or its maximum and the unity gain bandwidth should be set no higher than $\omega_{REF}/5$. With the second-order analysis, $\Omega_N$ should be set no higher than $\omega_{REF}/10$, $\zeta$ should be set to 0.707 or greater, and $\omega_C$ should be at least a decade above $\omega_N$.

If $C_2$ exists and is large enough to make it difficult to guarantee adequate phase margin, then a third-order analysis must be used. This situation may have been caused by physical constraints on the capacitor sizes, or by attempts to minimize $\omega_C$ in order to maximize the amount of reference frequency sideband filtering. In this case, it is desirable to determine the optimal values for the other device parameters that maximize the phase margin. The phase margin, PM, and unity gain bandwidth, $\omega_O$, where the phase margin is maximized, can be determined from the open-loop analysis as

$$PM = 2 \cdot \tan^{-1}(\sqrt{(C/C_2 + 1)}) - \pi/2$$
$$\omega_O = \sqrt{(C/C_2 + 1)/(R \cdot C)}$$

In order to realize the optimal value for $\omega_O$, the loop gain magnitude level must be appropriately set. This can be accomplished by determining $I_{CH}$ given R, or R given $I_{CH}$, using the equations

$$I_{CH} = N/K_V \cdot C_2/(R \cdot C)^2 \cdot (C/C_2 + 1)^{3/2}$$
$$R = \sqrt{(N/(K_V \cdot I_{CH}))} \cdot C_2 \cdot C^2 \cdot (C/C_2 + 1)^{3/2}$$

It is important to remember that all worst-case combinations of device parameters due to process, voltage, and temperature variability must be considered since they must lead to acceptable loop dynamics for the PLL to operate correctly under all conditions.

## Advanced PLL Architectures

PLL and DLL architectures each have their own advantages and disadvantages. PLLs are easier to use in systems than DLLs. DLLs typically cannot perform frequency multiplication and have a limited delay range. PLLs, however, are more difficult to design due to conflicting design constraints. It is difficult to assure stability while designing for a high bandwidth.

By using variations on the basic architectures many of these problems can be avoided. DLLs can be designed to perform frequency multiplication by recirculating intermediate edges around the delay line [7]. DLLs can also be designed to have an unlimited phase shift range by employing a delay line that can produce edges that completely span the clock cycle [4]. In addition, both DLLs and PLLs can be designed to have very wide bandwidths that track the clock frequency by using self-biased techniques [8], as discussed in "Self-Biased Techniques."

## DLL/PLL Performance Issues

To this point, this chapter section presents basic issues concerning the structure and design of DLLs and PLLs. While these issues are important, a good understanding of the performance issues is essential to successfully design a DLL or PLL. Many performance parameters can be specified for a DLL or PLL design. They include frequency range, loop bandwidth, loop damping factor (PLL only), input offset, output jitter, both cycle-to-cycle (period) jitter and tracking (input-to-output) jitter, lock time, and power dissipation; however, the biggest performance problems all relate to input offset and output jitter.

Input offset refers to the average offset in the phase of the output clock from its ideal value. It typically results from asymmetries between the circuits for the reference and feedback paths of the phase detector or from charge injection or charge offsets in the charge pump. In contrast, output jitter refers to the time-varying offsets in the phase of the output clock from its ideal value or from some reference signal caused by disturbances from internal and external sources.

### Output Jitter

Output jitter can create significant problems for an interface by causing setup and hold time violations, which lead to data transmission errors. Consider, for example, the measured jitter histogram in Fig. 10.11. It shows the traces of many PLL output transitions triggered from transitions on the reference input and

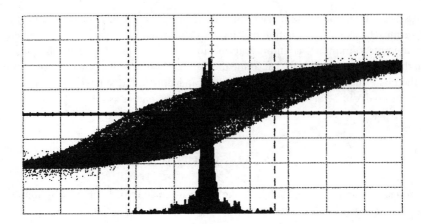

**FIGURE 10.11**    Measured PLL jitter histogram.

a histogram with the number of output transitions as a function of their center voltage crossing time. Most of the transition samples occur very close to the reference, while a few outlying transitions occur far to either side of the peak. These outlying transitions must be within the jitter tolerance of the interface. These few edges are typically caused by data dependent low frequency noise events with fast rise times.

Output jitter can be measured in a number of ways. It can be measured relative to absolute time, to another signal, or to the output clock itself. The first measurement of jitter is commonly referred to as absolute jitter or long-term jitter. The second is commonly referred to as tracking jitter or input-to-output jitter when the other signal is the reference signal. If the reference signal is perfectly periodic such that it has no jitter, absolute jitter and tracking jitter for the output signal are equivalent. The third is commonly referred to as period jitter or cycle-to-cycle jitter. Cycle-to-cycle jitter can be measured as the time-varying deviations in the period of single clock cycles or in the width of several clock cycles referred to as cycle-to-*N*th-cycle jitter.

Output jitter can also be reported as RMS or peak-to-peak jitter. RMS jitter is interesting only to applications that can tolerate a small number of edges with large time displacements that are well beyond the RMS specification with gracefully degrading results. Such applications can include video and audio signal generation. Peak-to-peak jitter is interesting to applications that cannot tolerate any edges with time displacements beyond some absolute level. The peak-to-peak jitter specification is typically the only useful specification for jitter related to clock generation since most setup or hold time failures are catastrophic to the operation of a chip.

The relative magnitude for each of these measurements of jitter depends on the type of loop and on how the phase disturbances are correlated in time. For a PLL design, the tracking jitter can be ten or more times larger than the period jitter depending on the noise frequency and the loop bandwidth. For a DLL design, the tracking jitter can be equal to or a factor of two times larger than the period jitter. However, in the particular case when the noise occurs at half the output frequency, the period jitter can be twice the tracking jitter for either the PLL or DLL due to the correlation of output edges times.

## Causes Of Jitter

Tracking jitter for DLLs and PLLs can be caused by both jitter in the reference signal and by noise sources. The noise sources include thermal noise, flicker noise, and supply and substrate noise. Thermal noise is generated by electron scattering in the devices within the DLL or PLL and can be significant at low bias currents. Flicker noise is generated by mobile charge in the gate oxides of devices within the DLL or PLL and can be significant for low loop bandwidths. Supply and substrate noise is generated by on-chip sources external to the DLL or PLL, including chip output drivers and functional blocks such as adders and multipliers, and by off-chip sources. This noise can be very significant in digital ICs.

The supply and substrate noise generated by the on-chip and off-chip sources is highly data dependent and can have a wide range of frequency components that include low frequencies. Substrate noise tends not to have as large low-frequency components as possible for supply noise since no significant "DC" drops develop between the substrate and the supply voltages. Under worst-case conditions, DLLs and PLLs may experience as much as 500 mV of supply noise and 250 mV of substrate noise with a nominal 2.5 V supply. The actual level of substrate noise depends on the nature of the substrate used by the IC process. To reduce the risk of latch-up, many IC processes use lightly doped epitaxy on the same type heavily doped substrate. These substrates tend to transmit substrate noise across large distances on the chip, which make it difficult to eliminate through guard rings and frequent substrate taps.

Supply and substrate noise affect DLLs and PLLs differently. They affect a DLL by causing delay shifts in the delay line output, which lead to fixed phase shifts that persist until the noise pulses subside or the DLL can correct the delay error, at a rate limited by its bandwidth (proportional to $\omega_{REF}/\omega_N$ cycles). They affect a PLL by causing frequency shifts in the oscillator output, which lead to phase shifts that accumulate for many cycles until the noise pulses subside or the PLL can correct the frequency error, at a rate limited by its bandwidth (proportional to $\omega_{REF}/\omega_N$ cycles). Because the phase error caused by period shifts in PLLs accumulate over many cycles, unlike the delay shifts in DLLs, the tracking jitter for PLLs that results from supply and substrate noise can be several times larger than the tracking jitter for DLLs; however, due to the added jitter from on-chip clock distribution networks, which typically have poor supply and substrate noise rejection, the observable difference is typically less than a factor of 2 for well designed DLLs and PLLs.

### DLL Supply/Substrate Noise Response

More insight can be gained into the noise response of DLLs and PLLs by considering how much jitter is produced as a function of frequency for supply and substrate noise. Figure 10.12 shows the output jitter sensitivity to input jitter for a DLL with a log-log plot of the absolute output jitter magnitude normalized to the absolute input jitter magnitude as a function of the input jitter frequency. Because the DLL simply delays the input signal, the jitter at the input is simply replicated with the same magnitude at the DLL output. For the same reason, the tracking jitter sensitivity to input jitter is very small at most frequencies; however, when the input jitter frequency approaches one half of the inverse of the delay line delay, the output jitter becomes 180° out-of-phase with respect to the input jitter and the observed tracking jitter can be twice the input jitter.

Figure 10.13 shows the output jitter sensitivity to sine-wave supply or substrate noise for a DLL with a log–log plot of the absolute output jitter magnitude as a function of the noise frequency. With the input jitter free, this absolute output jitter is equivalent to the tracking jitter. Also, since the DLL simply delays the input signal, the absolute output jitter is equivalent to the period jitter. This plot shows that the normalized jitter magnitude decreases at 20 dB per decade for decreases in the noise frequency below the loop bandwidth and is constant at one for noise frequencies above the loop bandwidth. This behavior results since the DLL acts as a low-pass filter to changes in its input period or, equivalently, to noise induced changes in its delay line delay. Thus, the jitter or delay error is the difference between the noise induced delay error and a low-pass filtered version of the delay error, leading to a high-pass noise response.

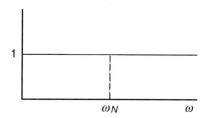

**FIGURE 10.12**   DLL output jitter sensitivity to input jitter.

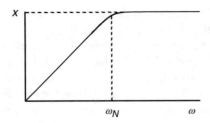

**FIGURE 10.13**   DLL output jitter sensitivity to sine-wave supply or substrate noise.

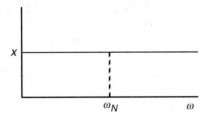

**FIGURE 10.14**   DLL output jitter sensitivity to square-wave supply or substrate noise.

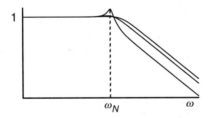

**FIGURE 10.15**   PLL output jitter sensitivity to input jitter.

Figure 10.14 shows the output jitter sensitivity to square-wave supply or substrate noise for a DLL with a log-log plot of the peak absolute output jitter magnitude as a function of the noise frequency. With fast rise and fall times, the square-wave supply noise causes the delay line delay to change instantaneously. The peak jitter is then observed on at least the first output transition from the delay line after the noise signal transition, independent of the loop bandwidth. Thus, the output jitter sensitivity is independent the square-wave noise frequency. Overall, the output jitter sensitivity to supply and substrate noise for DLLs is independent of the loop bandwidth and the reference frequency for the worst-case of square-wave noise.

### PLL Supply/Substrate Noise Response

Figure 10.15 shows the output jitter sensitivity to input jitter for a PLL with a log-log plot of the absolute output jitter magnitude normalized to the absolute input jitter magnitude as a function of the input jitter frequency. This plot shows that the normalized output jitter magnitude decreases asymptotically at 20 dB per decade for noise frequencies above the loop bandwidth and is constant at one for noise frequencies below the loop bandwidth. It also shows that for underdamped loops where the damping factor is less than one, the normalized jitter magnitude can be greater than one for noise frequencies near the loop bandwidth leading to jitter amplification. This overall behavior directly results from the fact that the PLL is a low-pass filter to input phase noise as determined by the closed-loop frequency response.

Figure 10.16 shows the tracking jitter sensitivity to input jitter for a PLL with a log-log plot of the tracking jitter magnitude normalized to the absolute input jitter magnitude as a function of the input

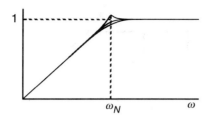

**FIGURE 10.16** PLL tracking jitter sensitivity to input jitter.

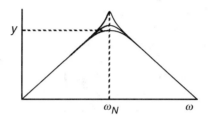

**FIGURE 10.17** PLL output jitter sensitivity to sine-wave supply or substrate noise.

jitter frequency. This plot shows that the normalized tracking jitter magnitude decreases at 40 dB per decade for decreases in the noise frequency below the loop bandwidth and is constant at one for noise frequencies above the loop bandwidth. Again, it shows that for underdamped loops, the normalized jitter magnitude can be greater than one for noise frequencies near the loop bandwidth. This overall behavior occurs because the PLL acts as a low-pass filter to input jitter and the tracking error is the difference between the input signal and the low-pass filtered version of the input signal, leading to a high-pass noise response.

Figure 10.17 shows the tracking jitter sensitivity to sine-wave supply or substrate noise for a PLL with a log-log plot of the tracking jitter magnitude as a function of the noise frequency. With the input jitter free, this tracking jitter is equivalent to absolute output jitter as with the DLL. This plot shows that the tracking jitter magnitude decreases at 20 dB per decade for decreases in the noise frequency below the loop bandwidth and decreases at 20 dB per decade for increases in the noise frequency above the loop bandwidth. It also shows that for underdamped loops, the tracking jitter magnitude can be significantly larger for noise frequencies near the loop bandwidth. This overall behavior results indirectly from the fact that the PLL acts as a low-pass filter to input jitter. Because a frequency disturbance is equivalent to a phase disturbance of magnitude equal to the integral of the frequency disturbance, the tracking jitter sensitivity response to frequency noise is the integral of the tracking jitter sensitivity response to phase noise or, equivalently, input jitter. Therefore, the tracking jitter sensitivity response to sine-wave supply or substrate noise should simply be the plot in Fig. 10.15 with an added 20 dB per decade decrease over all noise frequencies, which yields the plot in Fig. 10.17.

This tracking jitter sensitivity response to sine-wave supply or substrate noise can also be explained in less quantitative terms. Because the PLL acts as a low-pass filter to noise, it tracks the input increasingly better in spite of the frequency noise as the noise frequency is reduced below the loop bandwidth. Noise frequencies at the loop bandwidth are at the limits of the PLL's ability to track the input. The PLL is not able to track noise frequencies above the loop bandwidth. However, the impact of this frequency noise is reduced as the noise frequency is increased above the loop bandwidth since the resultant phase disturbance, which is the integral of the frequency disturbance, accumulates for a reduced amount of time.

Figure 10.18 shows the tracking jitter sensitivity to square-wave supply or substrate noise for a PLL with a log-log plot of the tracking jitter magnitude as a function of the noise frequency. This plot shows that the tracking jitter magnitude is constant for noise frequencies below the loop bandwidth and

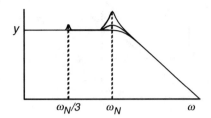

**FIGURE 10.18**   PLL output jitter sensitivity to square-wave supply or substrate noise.

decreases at 20 dB per decade for increases in the noise frequency above the loop bandwidth. Again, it shows that for underdamped loops, the tracking jitter magnitude can be significantly larger for noise frequencies near the loop bandwidth. This response is similar to the response for sine waves except that square-wave frequencies below the loop bandwidth result in the same peak jitter as the loop completely corrects the frequency and phase error from one noise signal transition before the next transition occurs; however, the number of output transition samples exhibiting the peak tracking jitter will decrease with decreasing noise frequency, which can be misunderstood as a decrease in tracking jitter. Also, the jitter levels for square waves are higher by about a factor of 1.7 compared to these for sine waves of the same amplitude.

Overall, several observations can be made about the tracking jitter sensitivity to supply and substrate noise for PLLs. First, the jitter magnitude decreases inversely proportional to increases in the loop bandwidth for the worst case of square-wave noise at frequencies near or below the loop bandwidth. However, the loop bandwidth must be about a decade below the reference frequency, which imposes a lower limit on the jitter magnitude. Second, the jitter magnitude decreases inversely proportional to the reference frequency for a fixed hertz per volt frequency sensitivity, since the phase disturbance measured in radians is constant, but the reference period decreases inversely proportional to the reference frequency. Third, the jitter magnitude is independent of reference frequency for fixed %/V frequency sensitivity, since the phase disturbance measured in radians changes inversely proportional to the reference period. Finally, the jitter magnitude increases directly proportional to the square root of N, the feedback divider value, with a constant oscillator frequency and if the loop is overdamped, since the loop bandwidth is inversely proportional to the square root of N.

### Observations on Jitter

The optimal loop bandwidth depends on the application for the PLL. For frequency synthesis or clock recovery applications, where the goal is to filter out jitter on the input signal, the loop bandwidth should be as low as possible. For this application, the phase relationship between the output of the PLL and other clock domains is typically not an issue. As a result, the only jitter of significance is period jitter and possibly jitter spanning a few clock periods. This form of jitter does not increase with reductions in the loop bandwidth; however, if the phase relationship between the PLL output and other clock domains is important or if the jitter of the PLL output over a large number of cycles is significant, then the loop bandwidth should be maximized. Maximizing the loop bandwidth will minimize this form of jitter since it decreases proportional to increases in loop bandwidth.

Because of the hostile noise environments of digital chips, the peak value of the measured tracking jitter from DLLs and PLLs will likely be caused by square-wave supply and substrate noise. For PLLs, this noise is particularly significant when the noise frequencies are at or below the loop bandwidth. If a PLL is underdamped, noise frequencies near the loop bandwidth can be even more significant. In addition, a PLL can amplify input jitter at frequencies near the loop bandwidth, especially if it is underdamped. However, as previously discussed, jitter in a PLL or DLL can also be caused by a dead-band region in phase detector and charge pump characteristics.

In order to minimize jitter it is necessary to minimize supply and substrate noise sensitivity of the VCDL or VCO. The supply and substrate noise sensitivity can be separated into both static and dynamic components.

The static components relate to the sensitivity to the DC value of the supply or substrate voltage. The static noise sensitivity can predict the noise response for all but the high-frequency components of the supply and substrate noise. The dynamic components relate to the extra sensitivity to a sudden change in the supply or substrate voltage that the static components do not predict. The effect of the dynamic components increases with increasing noise edge rate. For PLLs, the dynamic noise sensitivity typically has a much smaller overall impact on the supply and substrate noise response than the static noise sensitivity; however, for DLLs, the dynamic noise sensitivity can be more significant than static noise sensitivity. Only static supply and substrate noise sensitivity are considered in this chapter.

## Minimizing Supply Noise Sensitivity

All VCDL and VCO circuits will have some inherent sensitivity to supply noise. In general, supply noise sensitivity can be minimized by isolating the delay elements used within the VCDL or VCO from one of the supply terminals. This goal can be accomplished by using a buffered version of the control voltage as one of the supply terminals; however, this technique can require too much supply voltage headroom. The preferred and most common approach is to use the control voltage to generate a supply independent bias current so that current sources with this bias current can be used to isolate the delay elements from the opposite supply.

Supply voltage sensitivity is directly proportional to current source output conductance. Simple current sources provide a delay sensitivity per fraction of the total supply voltage change $((dt/t)/(dV_{DD}/V_{DD}))$, of about 10%, such that if the supply voltage changed by 10% the delay would change by 1%. This level of delay sensitivity is too large for good jitter performance in PLLs. Cascode current sources provide an equivalent delay sensitivity of about 1%, such that if the supply voltage changed by 10% the delay would change by 0.1%, which is at the level needed for good jitter performance, but cascode current sources can require too much supply voltage headroom. Another technique that can also offer an equivalent delay sensitivity of about 1% is replica current source biasing [9]. In this approach, the bias voltage for simple current sources is actively adjusted by an amplifier in a feedback configuration to keep some property of the delay element, such as voltage swing, constant and possibly equal to the control voltage.

Once adequate measures are taken to minimize the current source output conductance, other supply voltage dependencies may begin to dominate the overall supply voltage sensitivity of the delay elements. These effects include the dependencies of threshold voltage and diffusion capacitance for switching devices on the source or drain voltages, which can be modulated by the supply voltage. With any supply terminal isolation technique, all internal switching nodes will have voltages that track the supply terminal opposite to the one isolated. Thus, these effects can be manifested by devices with bulk terminals connected to the isolated supply terminal. These effects are always a problem for substrate devices with an isolated substrate-tap voltage supply terminal, such as for NMOS devices in an N-well process with an isolated negative supply terminal. Isolating the well-tap voltage supply terminal avoids this problem since the bulk terminals of the well devices can be connected to their source terminals, such as with PMOS devices in an N-well process with an isolated positive supply terminal. However, such an approach leads to more significant substrate noise problems. The only real solution is to minimize their occurrence and to minimize their switching diffusion capacitance. Typically, these effects will establish a minimum delay sensitivity per fraction of the total supply voltage change of about 1%.

## Supply Noise Filters

Another technique to minimize supply noise is to employ supply filters. Supply filters can be both passive, active, or a combination of the two. Passive supply filters are basically low-pass filters. Off-chip passive filters work very well in filtering out most off-chip noise but do little to filter out on-chip noise. Unfortunately, on-chip filters can have difficulty in filtering out low-frequency on-chip noise. Off-chip capacitors can easily be made large enough to filter out low-frequency noise, but on-chip capacitors are much more limited in size. In order for the filter to be effective in reducing jitter for both DLLs and PLLs, the filter cutoff frequency must be below the loop bandwidth.

Active supply filters employ amplifiers in a feedback configuration to buffer a desired reference supply voltage and act as high-pass filters. The reference supply voltage is typically established by a band-gap or control voltage reference. The resultant supply isolation will decrease with increasing supply filter bandwidth due to basic amplifier feedback tradeoffs. In order for the active filter to be effective, the bandwidth must exceed the inverse VCDL delay of a DLL or the loop bandwidth of a PLL. The DLL bandwidth limit originates because the VCDL delay will begin to be less affected by a noise event if it subsides before a signal transition propagates through the complete VCDL. The PLL bandwidth limit exists because, as higher-frequency noise is filtered out above the loop bandwidth, the VCO will integrate the resultant change in frequency for fewer cycles. Although the PLL bandwidth limit is achievable in a supply filter with some level of isolation, the DLL bandwidth limit is not. Thus, although active supply filters can help PLLs, they are typically ineffective for DLLs; however, the combination of passive and active filters can be an effective supply noise-filtering solution for both PLLs and DLLs by avoiding the PLL and DLL bandwidth constraints. When the low-pass filter cutoff frequency is below the high-pass filter cutoff frequency, filtering can be achieved at both low and high frequencies so that tracking bandwidths and inverse VCDL delays are not an issue.

Other common isolation approaches include using separate supply pins for a DLL or PLL. This approach should be used whenever possible. However, the isolated supplies will still experience noise from coupling to other supplies through off-chip paths and coupling to the substrate through well contacts and diffusion capacitance, requiring that supply noise issues be addressed. Also, having separate supply pins at the well tap potential can lead to increased substrate noise depending on the overall conductivity of the substrate.

### Minimizing Substrate Noise Sensitivity

Substrate noise sensitivity like supply noise sensitivity can create jitter problems for a PLL or DLL. Substrate noise can couple into the delay elements by modulating device threshold voltages. Substrate noise can be minimized by only using well-type devices for fixed-biased current sources, only using well-type devices for the loop filter capacitor, only connecting the control voltage to well-type devices, and only using the well-tap voltage as the control voltage reference. These constraints will insure that substrate noise does not modulate fixed-bias current source outputs or the conductance of devices connected to the control voltage, both through threshold modulation. In addition, they will prevent supply noise from directly summing into the control voltage through a control voltage reference different from the loop filter capacitor reference. Even with these constraints, substrate noise can couple into switching devices, as with supply noise, through the threshold voltage and diffusion capacitance dependencies on the substrate potential.

Substrate noise can be converted to supply noise by connecting the substrate-potential supply terminals of the delay elements only to the substrate [10]. This technique insures that the substrate and the substrate-potential supply terminals are at the same potential, however, it only works with low operating currents, because otherwise voltage drops will be generated in the substrate and excessive minority carriers will be dumped into the substrate.

### Other Performance Issues

High loop bandwidths in PLLs make it possible to minimize tracking jitter, but they can lead to problems during locking. PLLs based on phase-frequency detectors cannot tolerate any missing clock pulses in the feedback path during the locking process. If a clock pulse is lost in the feedback path because the VCO output frequency is too high, the phase-frequency detector will detect only reference edges, causing a continued increase in the VCO output frequency until it reaches its maximum value. At this point the PLL will never reach lock. To avoid losing clock pulses, which results in locking failure, all circuits in the feedback path, which might include the clock distribution network and off-chip circuits, must be able to pass the highest frequency the PLL may generate during the locking process. As the loop bandwidth is increased to its practical maximum limit, however, the amount that the PLL output frequency may overshoot its final value will increase. Thus, overshoot limits may impose an additional bandwidth limit on the PLL beyond the decade below the reference frequency required for stability.

A more severe limit on the loop bandwidth beyond a decade below the reference frequency can result in both PLLs and DLLs if there is considerable delay in the feedback path. The decade limit is based on the phase detector adding one reference period delay in the feedback path since it only samples clock edges once per reference cycle. This single reference period delay leads to an effective pole near the reference frequency. The loop bandwidth must be at least a decade below this pole to not affect stability. This bandwidth limit can be further reduced if extra delay is added in the feedback path, by an amount proportional to one plus the number of reference periods additional delay.

## DLL/PLL Circuits

Prior sections discussed design issues related to DLL and PLL loop architectures and low output jitter. With these issues in mind, this section discusses the circuit level implementation issues of the loop components. These components include the VCDL and VCO, phase detector, charge pump, and loop filter.

### VCDLs and VCOs

The VDCL and VCO are the most critical parts of DLL and PLL designs for achieving low output jitter and good overall performance. Two general types of VCDLs are used with analog control. First, a VDCL can interpolate between two delays through an analog weighted sum circuit. This approach only leads to linear control over delay, if the two interpolated delays are relatively close, which restricts the overall range of the VCDL. Second, a VCDL can be based on an analog delay line composed of identical cascaded delay elements, each with a delay that is controlled by an analog signal. This approach usually leads to a wide delay range with nonlinear delay control. A wide delay range is often desired in order to handle a range of operating frequencies and process and environmental variability. However, nonlinear delay control can restrict the usable delay range due to undesirable loop dynamics.

Several types of VCOs are used. First, a VCO can be based on an LC tank circuit. This type of oscillator has very high supply noise rejection and low phase noise output characteristics. However, it usually also has a restricted tuning range, which makes it impractical for digital ICs. Second, a VCO can be based on a relaxation oscillator. The frequency in this circuit is typically established by the rate a capacitor can be charged and discharged over some established voltage range with an adjustable current. This approach typically requires too much supply headroom to achieve good supply noise rejection and can be extra sensitive to sudden changes in the supply voltage. Third, and most popular for digital ICs, a VCO can be based on a phase shift oscillator, also known as a ring oscillator. A ring oscillator is a ring of identical cascaded delay elements with inverting feedback between the two elements that close the ring. A ring oscillator can typically generate frequencies over a wide range with linear control over frequency.

The delay elements, also known as buffer stages, used in a delay line or ring oscillator can be single-ended, such that they have only one input and one output and invert the signal, or differential, such they have two complementary inputs and outputs. Single-ended delay elements typically lead to reduced area and power, but provide no complementary outputs. Complementary outputs provide twice as many output signals with phases that span the output period compared to single-ended outputs, and allow a 50% duty cycle signal to be cleanly generated without dividing the output frequency by two. Differential delay elements typically have reduced dynamic noise coupling to their outputs and provide complementary outputs.

A number of factors must be considered in the design of the delay elements. The delay of the delay elements should have a linear dependence on control voltage when used in a VCDL and an inverse linear dependence on control voltage when used in a VCO. These control relationships will make the VCDL and VCO control gains constant and independent of the operating frequency, which will lead to operating frequency independent loop dynamics. The static supply and substrate noise sensitivity should be as small as possible, ideally less than 1% delay sensitivity per fraction of the total supply voltage change. As previously discussed, this reduced level of supply sensitivity can be established with current source isolation.

Figure 10.19 shows a single-ended delay element circuit for an N-well CMOS process. This circuit contains a PMOS common-source device with a PMOS diode clamp and a simple NMOS current source. The diode clamp restricts the buffer output swing in order to keep the NMOS current source device in saturation.

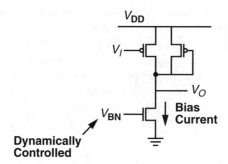

**FIGURE 10.19**   Single-ended delay element for an *N*-well CMOS process.

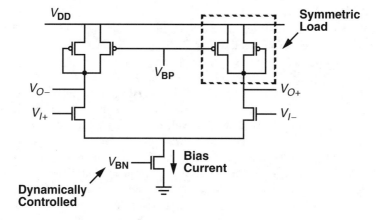

**FIGURE 10.20**   Differential delay element with symmetric loads for an *N*-well CMOS process.

In order to achieve high static supply and substrate noise rejection, the bias voltage for the simple NMOS current source is dynamically adjusted with changes in the supply or substrate voltage to compensate for its finite output impedance.

Figure 10.20 shows a differential delay element circuit for an N-well CMOS process [9]. This circuit contains a source-coupled pair with resistive load elements called symmetric loads. Symmetric loads consist of a diode-connected PMOS device in shunt with an equally sized biased PMOS device. The PMOS bias voltage $V_{BP}$ is nominally equal to $V_{CTRL}$, the control input to the bias generator. $V_{BP}$ defines the lower voltage swing limit of the buffer outputs. The buffer delay changes with $V_{BP}$ because the effective resistance of the load elements also changes with $V_{BP}$. It has been shown that these load elements lead to good control over delay and high dynamic supply noise rejection. The simple NMOS current source is dynamically biased with $V_{BN}$ to compensate for drain and substrate voltage variations, achieving the effective static supply noise rejection performance of a cascode current source without the extra supply voltage required by cascode current sources.

A block diagram of the bias generator for the differential delay element is shown in Fig. 10.21 and the detailed circuit is shown in Fig. 10.22. A similar bias generator circuit is used for the single-ended delay element. This circuit produces the bias voltages $V_{BN}$ and $V_{BP}$ from $V_{CTRL}$. Its primary function is to continuously adjust the buffer bias current in order to provide the correct lower swing limit of $V_{CTRL}$ for the buffer stages. In so doing, it establishes a current that is held constant and independent of supply and substrate voltage since the I-V characteristics of the load element does not depend on the supply or substrate voltage. It accomplishes this task by using a differential amplifier and a half-buffer replica. The amplifier adjusts $V_{BN}$, so that the voltage at the output of the half-buffer replica is equal to $V_{CTRL}$, the lower swing limit. If the supply or substrate voltage changes, the amplifier will adjust to keep the swing and thus the bias current constant.

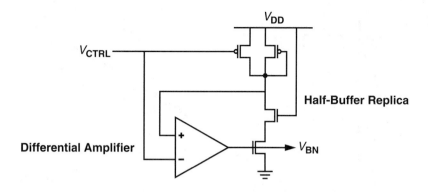

**FIGURE 10.21** Replica-feedback current source bias circuit block diagram.

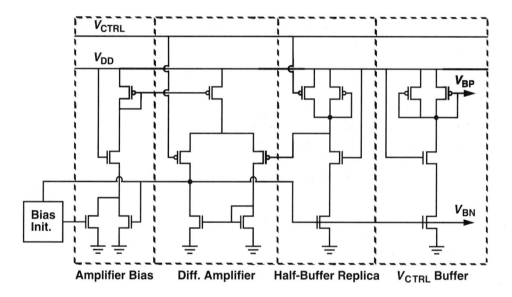

**FIGURE 10.22** Replica-feedback current source bias circuit schematic.

The bandwidth of the bias generator is typically set close to the operating frequency of the buffer stages or as high as possible without compromising its stability, so that the bias generator can track all supply and substrate voltage disturbances at frequencies that can affect the DLL and PLL designs. The bias generator also provides a buffered version of $V_{CTRL}$ at the $V_{BP}$ output using an additional half-buffer replica, which is needed in the differential buffer stage. This output isolates Vctrl from potential capacitive coupling in the buffer stages and plays an important role in self-biased PLL designs [8].

Figure 10.23 shows the static supply noise sensitivity of a ring oscillator using the differential delay element and bias generator in a 0.5 $\mu$m N-well CMOS process. With this bias generator, the buffer stages can achieve static frequency sensitivity per fraction of the total supply voltage change of less than 1% while operating over a wide delay range with low supply voltage requirements that scale with the operating delay. Buffer stages with low supply and substrate noise sensitivity are essential for low-jitter DLL and PLL operation.

## Differential Signal Conversion

PLLs are typically designed to operate at twice the chip operating frequency so that their outputs can be divided by two in order to guarantee a 50% duty cycle [2]. This practice can be wasteful if the delay elements already generate differential signals since the differential signal transitions equally subdivide

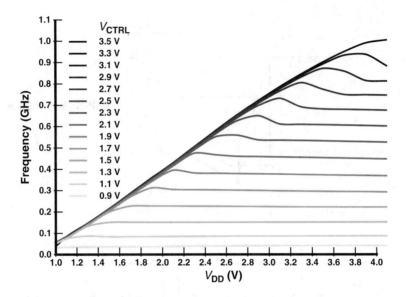

**FIGURE 10.23**    Frequency sensitivity to supply voltage for a ring oscillator with differential delay elements and a replica-feedback current source bias circuit in a 0.5 $\mu$m N-well CMOS process.

the clock period. Thus, the requirement for a 50% duty cycle can be satisfied without operating the PLL at twice the chip operating frequency, if a single-ended CMOS output with 50% duty cycle can be obtained from a differential output signal. This conversion can be accomplished using an amplifier circuit that has a wide bandwidth and is balanced around the common-mode level expected at the inputs so that the opposing differential input transitions have roughly equal delay to the output. Such circuits will generate a near 50% duty cycle output without dividing by two provided that device matching is not a problem; however, on-wafer device mismatches for nominally identical devices will tend to unbalance the circuit and establish a minimum signal input and internal bias voltage level below which significant duty-cycle conversion errors may result. In addition, as the device channel lengths are reduced, device mismatches will increase. Therefore, using a balanced differential-to-single-ended converter circuit instead of a divider can relax the design constraints on the VCO for high-frequency designs but must be used with caution because of potential device mismatches.

## Phase Detectors

The phase detector detects the phase difference between the reference input and the feedback signal of a DLL or PLL. Several types of phase detectors can be used, each of which will allow the loop achieve a different phase relationship once in lock. An XOR or mixer can be used as a phase detector to achieve a quadrature lock on input signals with a 50% duty cycle. The UP and DN outputs are complementary, and, once in lock, each will generate a 50% duty cycle signal at twice the reference frequency. The 50% duty cycle will cause the UP and DN currents to cancel out leaving the control voltage unchanged. An edge-triggered SR latch can be used as the phase detector for an inverted lock. The UP and DN outputs are also complementary, and, once in lock, each will generate a 50% duty cycle signal at the reference frequency. If differential inputs are available, an inverted lock can be easily interchanged with an in-phase lock. A sampling flip-flop can be used to sample the reference clock as the phase detector in a digital feedback loop, where the flip-flop is used to match the input delay for digital inputs also sampled by identical flip-flops. The output state of the flip-flop will indicate if the feedback clock is early or late. Finally, a phase-frequency detector (PFD) can be used as a phase detector to achieve an in-phase lock. PFDs are commonly based on two SR latches or two D flip-flops. They have the property that only UP pulses are generated if the frequency is too low, only DN pulses are generated if the frequency is too high, and to first order, no UP or DN pulses are generated once in lock. Because of this property, PLLs using PFDs will slew their control voltage with, on

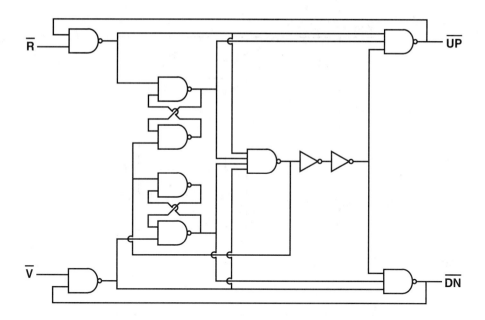

**FIGURE 10.24** Phase-frequency detector based on NAND gates.

average, half of the charge pump current until the correct frequency is reached, and will never falsely lock at some harmonic of the reference frequency. PFDs are the most common phase detectors used in DLLs and PLLs.

Phase detector can have several potential problems. The phase detector can have an input offset caused by different edge rates between the reference and feedback signals or caused by asymmetric circuits or device layouts between the reference and feedback signal paths. In addition, the phase detector can exhibit nonlinearity near the locking point. This nonlinearity can include a dead-band, caused by an input delay difference where the phase detector output remains zero or unchanged, or a high-gain region, caused by an accelerated sensitivity to transitions on both the reference and feedback inputs. In order to properly diagnose potential phase detector problems, the phase detector must be simulated or tested in combination with the charge pump.

A PFD based on SR latches [2], as shown in Fig. 10.24, can be implemented with NAND or NOR gates. However, the use of NAND gates will lead to the highest speed. The input sense polarity can be maintained as positive edge sensitive if inverters are added at both inputs. The layout for the PFD should be constructed from two identical pieces for complete symmetry. The basic circuit structure can be modified in several ways to improve performance.

One possible modification to the basic PFD structure is to replace the two-input NAND gates at the inputs with three-input NAND gates. The extra inputs can serve as enable inputs to the PFD by gating out positive pulses at the reference or feedback inputs. For the enable inputs to function properly, they must be low for at least the entire positive pulse in order to properly ignore a falling transition at the reference or feedback inputs.

**Charge Pumps**

The charge pump, which is driven by the phase detector, can be structured in a number of ways. The key issues for the structure are input offset and linearity. An input offset can be caused by a mismatch in charge-up or charge-down currents or by charge injection. The nonlinearity near the lock point can be caused by edge rate dependencies and current source switching.

A push-pull charge pump is shown in Fig. 10.25. This charge pump tends to have low output ripple because small but equal UP and DN pulses, produced by a PFD once in lock, generate equal current pulses at exactly the same time that cancel out with an insignificant disturbance to the control voltage.

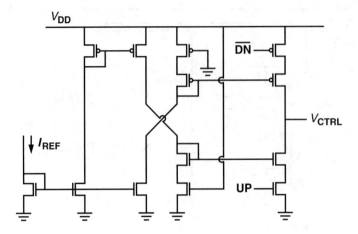

**FIGURE 10.25**   Push-pull charge pump.

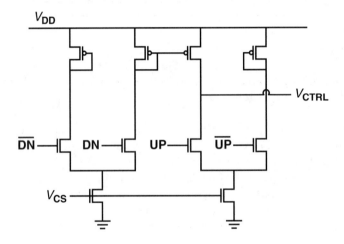

**FIGURE 10.26**   Current mirror charge pump.

The switches for this charge pump are best placed away from the output toward the supply rails in order to minimize charge injection from the supply rails to the control voltage. The opposite configuration can inject charge from the supply rails through the capacitance at the shared node between the series devices.

A current mirror charge pump is shown in Fig. 10.26. This charge pump tends to have the lowest input offset due to balanced charge injection. In the limit that a current mirror has infinite output impedance, it will mirror exact charge quantities; however, because the DN current pulse is mirrored to the output, it will occur later and have a longer tail than the UP current pulse, which is switched directly to the output. This difference in current pulse shape will lead to some disturbance to the control voltage.

Another combined approach for the charge pump and loop filter involves using an amplifier-based voltage integrator. This approach is difficult to implement in most IC processes because it requires floating capacitors. Any of the above approaches can be modified to work in a "bang-bang" mode, where the output charge magnitude is fixed independent of the phase error. This mode of operation is sometimes used with digital feedback loops when it is necessary to cancel the aperture offset of a high-speed interface receiver [11]; however, it makes the loop control very nonlinear and commonly produces dither jitter, where the output phase, once in lock, alternates between positive and negative errors.

## Loop Filters

The loop filter directly connects to the charge pump to integrate and filter the detected phase error. The most important detail for the loop filter is the choice of supply terminal to be used as the control voltage reference. As discussed in the section on "Supply Noise Filters," substrate noise can couple into delay elements through threshold modulation of the active devices. The substrate noise sensitivity can be minimized by using well-type devices for the loop filter capacitor and for fixed-biased devices. Also, care must be taken to insure that the voltage reference used by the circuitry that receives the control voltage is the same as the supply terminal to which the loop filter capacitor connects. Otherwise, any supply noise will be directly summed with the control voltage.

Some designs employ level shifting between the loop filter voltage and the control voltage input to the VCDL or VCO. Such level shifting is often the cause of added supply noise sensitivity and should be avoided whenever possible. Also, some designs employ differential loop filters. A differential loop filter is useful only if the control input to the VCDL or VCO is differential, as is often the case with a delay interpolating VCDL. If the VCDL or VCO has a single-ended control input, a differential loop filter adds no value because its output must be converted back to a single-ended signal. Also, the differential loop filter needs some type of common-mode biasing to establish the common-mode voltage. The common-mode bias circuit will add some differential mode resistance that will cause the loop filter to leak charge and will lead to an input offset for the DLL or PLL.

For PLLs, the loop filter must implement a zero in order to provide phase margin for stability. The zero can be implemented directly with a resistor in series with the loop filter capacitor. In this case, the charge pump current is converted to a voltage through the resistor, which is added to the voltage across the loop filter capacitor to form the control voltage. Alternatively, this zero can be formed by summing an extra copy of the charge pump current directly with a bias current used to control the VCO, possibly inside a bias generator for the VCO. This latter approach avoids using an actual resistor and lends itself to self-biased schemes [8].

## Frequency Dividers

A frequency divider can be used in the feedback path of a PLL to enable it to generate a VCO output frequency that is a multiple of the reference frequency. Since the divider is in the feedback path to the phase detector, care must be taken to insure that the insertion delay of the divider does not upset any clock de-skewing to be performed by the PLL. As such, an equivalent delay may need to be added in the reference path to the phase detector in order to cancel out the insertion delay of the divider. The best approach for adding the divider is to use it as a feedback clock edge enable input to the phase detector. In this scheme, the total delay of the feedback path, from the VCO to the phase detector, is not affected by the divider. As long as the divider output satisfies the setup and hold requirements for the enable input to the phase detector, it can have any output delay and even add jitter. As previously noted, an enable input can be added to both the reference and feedback inputs of an SR latch PFD by replacing the two-input NAND gates at the inputs with three-input NAND gates.

## Layout Issues

The layout for a DLL or PLL can have significant impact on its overall performance. Supply independent biasing uses many matched devices that must match when the circuit is fabricated. Typical device matching problems originate from different device layouts, different device orientations, different device geometry surroundings leading to device etching differences, and sensitivity to process gradients. In general, the analog devices should be arrayed in identical common denominator units at the same orientation so that the layers through polysilicon for and around each device appear identical. The common denominator units should use folding at a minimum to reduce the sensitivity to process gradients. Bias voltages, especially the control voltage, and switching nodes within the VCO or VCDL should be carefully routed to minimize coupling to the supply terminal opposite the one referenced. In addition, connecting the control voltage to a pad in a DLL or PLL with an on-chip loop filter should be avoided. At a minimum, it should only be bonded for testing but not production purposes.

### Circuit Summary

In general, all DLL and PLL circuits must be designed from the outset with supply and substrate noise rejection in mind. Obtaining low noise sensitivity requires careful orchestration among all circuits and cannot be added as an after thought. Supply noise rejection requires isolation from one supply terminal, typically with current source isolation. Substrate noise rejection requires all fixed-biased devices to be well-type devices to minimize threshold modulation. However, the best circuits to use depend on both the loop architecture and the IC technology.

## Self-Biased Techniques

Achieving low tracking jitter and a wide operating frequency range in PLL and DLL designs can be difficult due to a number of design trade-offs. To minimize the amount of tracking jitter produced by a PLL, the loop bandwidth should be set as high as possible. However, the loop bandwidth must be set at least a decade below the lowest desired operating frequency for stability with enough margin to account for bandwidth changes due to the worst-case process and environmental conditions. Achieving a wide operating frequency range in a DLL requires that the VCDL work over a wide range of delays. However, as the delay range is increased, the control becomes increasingly nonlinear, which can undermine the stability of the loop and lead to increased jitter. These different trade-offs can cause both PLLs and DLLs to have narrow operating frequency ranges and poor jitter performance.

Self-biasing techniques can be applied to both PLLs and DLLs as a solution to these design trade-off problems [8]. Self-biasing can remove virtually all of the process technology and environmental variability that affect PLL and DLL designs, and provide a loop bandwidth that tracks the operating frequency. This tracking bandwidth sets no limit on the operating frequency range and makes wide operating frequency ranges spanning several decades possible. This tracking bandwidth also allows the bandwidth to be set aggressively close to the operating frequency to minimize tracking jitter. Other benefits of self-biasing include a fixed damping factor for PLLs and input phase offset cancellation. Both the damping factor and the bandwidth to operating frequency ratio are determined completely by a ratio of capacitances giving effective process technology independence. In general, self-biasing can produce very robust designs.

The key idea behind self-biasing is that it allows circuits to choose the operating bias levels in which they function best. By referencing all bias voltages and currents to other generated bias voltages and currents, the operating bias levels are essentially established by the operating frequency. The need for external biasing, which can require special band-gap bias circuits, is completely avoided. Self-biasing typically involves using the bias currents in the VCO or VCDL as the charge pump current. Special accommodations are also added for the feed-forward resistor needed in a PLL design.

## Characterization Techniques

A good DLL or PLL design is not complete without proper simulation and measurement characterization. Careful simulation can uncover stability, locking, and jitter problems that might occur at the operating, environment, and process corners. Alternatively, careful laboratory measurements under the various operating conditions can help prevent problems in manufacturing.

### Simulation

The loop dynamics of the DLL or PLL should be verified through simulation using one of several possible modeling techniques. They can be modeled at the circuit level, at the behavioral level, or as a simplified linear system. Circuit-level modeling is the most complete, but can require a lot of simulation time because the loops contain both picosecond switching events and microsecond loop bandwidth time constants. Behavioral models can simulate much faster, but are usually restricted to transient simulations. A simplified linear system model can be constructed as a circuit from linear circuit elements and voltage-controlled current sources, where phase is modeled as voltage. This simple model can be analyzed not just with transient simulations, but also with AC simulations and other forms of analysis possible for linear circuits. Such models can include supply and substrate noise sensitivities and actual loop filter and bias circuitry.

Open-loop simulations at the circuit level should be performed on individual blocks within the DLL or PLL. The VCDL and VCO should be simulated using a transient analysis as a function of control voltage, supply voltage, and substrate voltage in order to determine the control, supply, and substrate sensitivities. The phase detector should be simulated with the charge pump, by measuring the output charge as a function of input phase different and possibly control voltage, to determine the static phase offset and if any nonlinearities exist at the locking point, such as a dead-band or high-gain region. The results of these simulations can be incorporated into the loop dynamics simulation models.

Closed-loop simulations at the circuit level should also be performed on the complete design in order to characterize the locking characteristics, overall stability, and jitter performance. The simulations should be performed from all possible starting conditions to insure that the correct locking result can be reliably established. The input phase step response of the loop should be simulated to determine if there are stability problems manifested by ringing. Also, the supply and substrate voltage step response of the loop should be simulated to give a good indication of the overall jitter performance. All simulations should be performed over all operating conditions, including input frequencies and divider ratios, and environmental conditions including supply voltage and temperature as well as process corners.

### Measurement

Once the DLL or PLL has been fabricated, a series of rigorous laboratory measurements should be performed to insure that a problem will not develop late in manufacturing. The loop should first be characterized under controlled conditions. Noise-free supplies should be used to insure that the loop generally locks and operates correctly. Supply noise steps at sub-harmonic of the output frequency can be used to allow careful measurement of the loop's response to supply steps. If such a supply noise signal is added synchronously to the output signal, it can be used as a trigger to obtain a complete time averaged response to the noise steps. The step edge rates should be made as high as possible to yield the worst-case jitter response. Supply noise steps swept over frequency, especially at low frequencies, should be used to determine the overall jitter performance. Also, supply sine waves swept over frequency will help determine if there are stability problems with the loop manifested by a significant increase in jitter when the noise frequency approaches the loop bandwidth.

The loop should then be characterized under uncontrolled conditions. These conditions would include worst-case I/O switching noise and worst-case on-chip core switching noise. These experiments will be the ultimate judge of the PLL's jitter performance assuming that the worst-case data patterns can be constructed. The best jitter measurements to perform for characterizations will depend on the DLL or PLL application, but they should include both peak cycle-to-cycle jitter and peak input-to-output jitter.

## Conclusions

DLLs and PLLs can be used to relax system-timing constraints. The best loop architecture strongly depends on the system application and the system environment. DLLs produce less jitter than PLLs due to their inherently reduced noise sensitivity. PLLs provide more flexibility by supporting frequency multiplication and an unlimited phase range. Independent of the chosen loop architecture, supply and substrate noise will likely be the most significant cause of output jitter. As such, all circuits must be designed from the outset with supply and substrate noise rejection in mind.

## References

1. M. Johnson and E. Hudson, "A Variable Delay Line PLL for CPU-Coprocessor Synchronization," *IEEE J. Solid-State Circuits,* vol. SC-23, no. 5, pp. 1218–1223, Oct. 1988.
2. I. Young, et al., "A PLL Clock Generator with 5 to 110 MHz of Lock Range for Microprocessors," *IEEE J. Solid-State Circuits,* vol. 27, no. 11, pp. 1599–1607, Nov. 1992.
3. F. Gardner, "Charge-Pump Phase-Lock Loops," *IEEE Trans. Communications,* vol. COM-28, no. 11, pp. 1849–1858, Nov. 1980.
4. S. Sidiropoulos and M. Horowitz, "A Semidigital Dual Delay-Locked Loop," *IEEE J. Solid-State Circuits,* vol. 32, no. 11, pp. 1683–1692, Nov. 1997.

5.  T. Lee, et al., "A 2.5V CMOS Delay-Locked Loop for an 18Mbit, 500Megabyte/s DRAM," *IEEE J. Solid-State Circuits,* vol. 29, no. 12, pp. 1491–1496, Dec. 1994.

6.  D. Chengson, et al., "A Dynamically Tracking Clock Distribution Chip with Skew Control," CICC 1990 Dig. Tech. Papers, pp. 13–16, May 1990.

7.  A. Waizman, "A Delay Line Loop for Frequency Synthesis of De-Skewed Clock," ISSCC 1994 Dig. Tech. Papers, pp. 298–299, Feb. 1994.

8.  J. Maneatis, "Low-Jitter Process-Independent DLL and PLL Based on Self-Biased Techniques," *IEEE J. Solid-State Circuits,* vol. 31, no. 11, pp. 1723–1732, Nov. 1996.

9.  J. Maneatis and M. Horowitz, "Precise Delay Generation Using Coupled Oscillators," *IEEE J. Solid-State Circuits,* vol. 28, no. 12, pp. 1273–1282, Dec. 1993.

10.  V. von Kaenel, et al., "A 600MHz CMOS PLL Microprocessor Clock Generator with a 1.2GHz VCO," ISSCC 1998 Dig. Tech. Papers, pp. 396–397, Feb. 1998.

11.  M. Horowitz, et al., "PLL Design for a 500MB/s Interface," ISSCC 1993 Dig. Tech. Papers, pp. 160–161, Feb. 1993.

# 10.2   Latches and Flip-Flops

*Fabian Klass*

## Introduction

This chapter section deals with latches and flip-flops that interface to complementary static logic and are built in CMOS technology. Two fundamental types of designs are discussed: (1) designs based on *transparent latches* and (2) designs based on *edge-triggered flip-flops*. Because conceptually flip-flops are built from transparent latches, the analysis of timing requirements is focused primarily on the former. Flip-flop-based designs are then analyzed as a special case of a latch-based design. Another type of latch, known as a *pulsed latch*, is treated in a special section also. This is because while similar in nature to a transparent latch, its usage in practice is similar to a flip-flop, which makes it a unique and distinctive type.

The chapter section is organized as follows. The first half deals with the timing requirements of latch- and flip-flop-based designs. It is generic and the concepts discussed therein are applicable to other technologies as well. The second half of the chapter presents specific circuit topologies and is exclusively focused on CMOS technology. Various latches and flip-flops are described and their performance is analyzed. A subsection on scan design is also provided. A summary and a historical perspective is finally presented.

### Historical Trends

In discussing latch and flip-flop based designs, it is important to review the fundamental concept behind them, which is *pipelining*. Pipelining is a technique that achieves parallelism by segmenting long sequential logical operations into smaller ones. At any given time, each stage in the pipeline operates concurrently on a different data set. If the number of stages in the pipeline is $N$, then $N$ operations are executed in parallel. This parallelism is reflected in the clock frequency of the system. If the clock frequency of the unsegmented pipeline is $F_{req}$, a segmented pipeline with $N$ stages can operate *ideally* at $N \times F_{req}$. It is important to understand that the increase in clock rate does not necessarily translate linearly into increased performance. Architecturally, the existence of data dependencies, variable memory latencies, interruptions, and the type of instructions being executed, among other factors, contribute to reducing the effective number of operations executed per clock cycle, or the effective parallelism [1]; however, as historical trends show, pipelines are becoming deeper, or correspondingly, the stages are becoming shorter. For instance, the design reported in [2] has a pipeline 15-stage deep. From a physical perspective, the theoretical speedup of segmentation is not attainable either. This is because adjacent pipeline stages need to be isolated, so independent operations, which execute concurrently, do not intermix. Typically, synchronous systems use *latches* or *flip-flops* to accomplish this. Unfortunately, these elements are not ideal and add overhead to each pipeline stage. This *pipeline overhead* depends on the specific latching style and the clocking scheme adopted. For instance, if the pipeline overhead in an $N$-stage design is 20%

of the cycle time, the effective parallelism achieved is only $N \times 0.8$. If the clock rate were doubled by making the pipeline twice as deep, e.g., by inserting one additional latch or flip-flop per stage, then the pipeline overhead would become 40% of the cycle time, or correspondingly, the achieved parallelism 2 $\times N \times 0.6$. So in such a case, a doubling of the clock rate translates into a 50% only increase in performance ($2 \times 0.6/0.8 = 1.50$). In practice, other architectural factors, some of them mentioned above, would reduce the performance gain even further.

From the above discussion, it becomes clear that in selecting a latch type and clocking scheme, the minimization of the pipeline overhead is key to performance; however, as discussed in detail throughout this chapter section, performance is not the only criterion that designers should follow in making such a selection. In addition to the pipeline overhead, latch- and flip-flop-based designs are prone to *races*. This term refers to fast signals propagating through contiguous pipeline stages within the same clock cycle, resulting in data corruption. Although this problem does not reflect directly in performance, it is the nightmare of designers because it is usually fatal. If it appears in silicon, it is extremely hard to debug, and therefore it is generally detrimental to the design cycle. Furthermore, since most of the design time is spent on verification, particularly timing verification, a system that is susceptible to races takes longer to design.

Other design considerations, such as layout area, power dissipation, power-delay product, design robustness, clock distribution, and timing verification, some of which are discussed in this chapter section, must also be carefully considered in selecting a particular latching design.

### Nomenclature and Symbols

The nomenclature and symbols used throughout this chapter are shown in Fig. 10.27. The polarity of the clock is indicated with a conventional bubble. The presence of the bubble means the latch is *transparent-low* or that the flip-flop samples with the *negative edge* of clock. Conversely, the lack of the bubble means the latch is *transparent-high*, or that the flip-flop samples with the *positive edge* of clock. The term *opaque*,

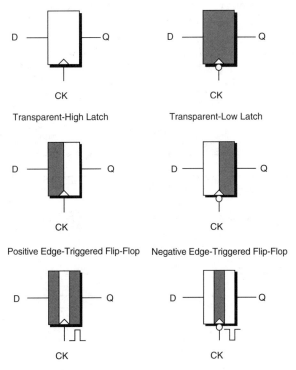

**FIGURE 10.27** Symbols used for latches, flip-flops, and pulsed latches.

introduced in [3], is used to represent the opposite to transparent. It is considered unambiguous in contrast to on/off or open/close. A color convention is also adopted to indicate the transparency of the latch. *White* means transparent-high (or opaque-low), while *shaded* means transparent-low (or opaque-high) (Fig. 10.27, top). Because most flip-flops are made from two transparent latches, one transparent-high and one transparent-low, a half-white half-shaded symbol is used to represent them (Fig. 10.27, middle). The symbol adopted for pulsed flops has a white band on a shaded latch, or vice versa, to indicate a short transparency period (Fig. 10.27, bottom).

To make timing diagrams easy to follow, relevant timing dependencies are indicated with light arrows, as shown in Fig. 10.28. Also, a coloring convention is adopted for the timing diagrams. Signal waveforms that are timing dependent are shaded. This eases the identification of the timing flow of signals and helps better visualize the timing requirements of the different latching designs.

### Definitions

The following definitions apply to a transparent-high latch; however, they are generic and can be applied to transparent-low pulsed latches, regular latches, or flip-flops. Most flip-flops are made from back-to-back latches, as will be discussed later on.

#### Blocking Operation

A *blocking* operation results when the input $D$ to the latch arrives during the *opaque* period of the clock (see Fig. 10.29). The signal is "blocked," or delayed, by the latch and does not propagate to the output $Q$ until clock CK rises and the latch becomes transparent. Notice the dependency between the timing edges, in particular, the *blocking* time from the arrival of $D$ until the latch opens. The delay between the rising edge of CK and the rising/falling edge of $Q$ is commonly called the *Clock-to-Q* delay ($T_{CKQ}$).

#### Nonblocking Operation

A *nonblocking* operation is the opposite to a blocking one and results when the input $D$ arrives during the *transparent* period of the clock (see Fig. 10.30). The signal propagates through the latch without being delayed by clock. The only delay between $D$ and $Q$ is the combinational delay of the latch, or latency, which is denoted as $T_{DQ}$.

In general, slow signals should not be blocked by a latch. As soon as they arrive they should transfer to the next stage with the minimum possible delay. This is equivalent to say that the latch must become

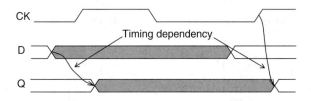

**FIGURE 10.28**   Timing diagram convention.

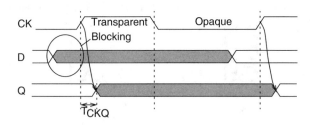

**FIGURE 10.29**   A blocking operation.

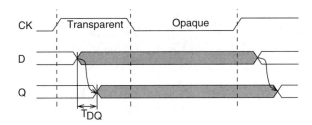

**FIGURE 10.30**  A nonblocking operation.

transparent before the slowest signal arrives. Fast signals, on the other hand, may be blocked by a latch since they do not affect the cycle time of the circuit. These two are the basic principles of latch-based designs. A detailed timing of latches will be presented later on.

## The Setup and Hold Time

Besides latency, setup and hold time are the other two parameters that characterize the timing of a latch. Setup and hold can be defined using the blocking and nonblocking concepts just introduced. The time reference for such definition can be either edge of the clock. For convenience, the falling edge is chosen when using a transparent-high latch, while the rising edge is chosen when using a transparent-low latch. This makes the definitions of these parameters independent of the clock period.

### Setup Time

It is the latest possible arrival of signal $D$ that guarantees nonblocking operation and optimum $D$-to-$Q$ latency through the latch.

### Hold Time

It is the earliest possible arrival of signal $D$ that guarantees a safe blocking operation by the latch.

Notice that the previous definitions are quite generic and that a proper criterion should be established in order to measure these parameters in a real circuit. The condition for *optimum latency* in the setup definition is needed because as the transition of $D$ approaches or exceeds a certain value, while the latch may still be transparent, its latency begins to increase. This can lead to a metastable condition before a complete blockage is achieved. The exact definition of optimum is implementation dependent, and is determined by the latch type, logic style, and the required design margins. In most cases, a minimum or near-minimum latency is a good criterion. Similarly, the definition of *safe* blocking operation is also implementation dependent. If the transition of $D$ happens too soon, while the latch is neither transparent nor opaque, small glitches may appear at $Q$, which may be acceptable or not. It is up to the designer to determine the actual criterion used in the definition.

The timing diagrams depicted in Fig. 10.31 show cases of signal $D$ meeting and failing setup time, and meeting and failing hold time. The setup and hold regions of the latch are indicated by the shaded area.

## The Sampling Time

Although the setup and hold time seem to be independent parameters, in reality they are not. Every signal in a circuit must be valid for a minimum amount of time to allow the next stage to sample it safely. This is true for latches and for any type of sampling circuit. This leads to the following definition.

### Sampling Time

It is the minimum pulse width required by a latch to sample input $D$ and pass it safely to output $Q$.

The relationship between setup, hold, and sampling time is the following:

$$T_{\text{setup}} + T_{\text{hold}} \geq T_{\text{sampling}} \tag{10.1}$$

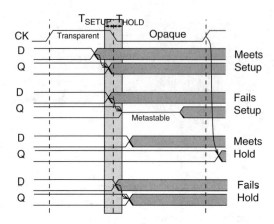

**FIGURE 10.31**   Setup and hold time timing diagrams.

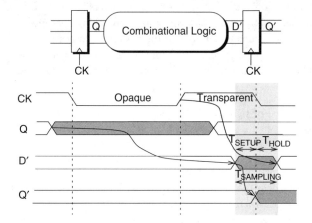

**FIGURE 10.32**   Relationship between setup, hold, and sampling time.

For a properly designed latch, $T_{setup} + T_{hold} = T_{sampling}$.

In contrast to the setup and hold time, which can be manipulated by the choice of latch design, the sampling time is an independent parameter, which is determined by technology. Setup and hold times may have positive or negative values, and can increase or decrease at the expense of one another, but the sampling time has always a positive value. Figure 10.32 illustrates the relationship between the three parameters in a timing diagram. Notice the lack of a timing dependency between the trailing edge of $D'$ and $Q'$. This is because this transition happens during the opaque phase of the clock. This suggests that the hold time does not determine the maximum speed of a circuit. This will be discussed more in detail later on.

## Timing Constraints

Most designers tend to think of latches and flip-flops as memory elements, but few will think of traffic lights as memory elements. However, this is the most appropriate analogy of a latch: the latch being transparent equals to a green light, being opaque to a red light; the setup time is equivalent to the duration of the yellow light, and the latency the time to cross the intersection. The hold time is harder to visualize, but if the road near the intersection is assumed to be slippery, it may be thought of as the minimum time after the light turns red that allows a moving vehicle to come to a full stop. Slow and fast signals may be thought of as slow and fast moving vehicles, respectively. Now, when electrical signals are stopped, i.e., blocked by a latch, their values must be preserved until the latch opens again. The preservation of the signal value, which may be required for a fraction of a clock cycle or several clock cycles, requires a form of storage or memory built into a latch. So in this respect a latch is both a synchronization and a memory element. Memory structures (SRAMs, FIFOs, registers, etc.) built from latches or flip-flops, use them primarily as memory elements. But as far as timing is concerned, the latch is a synchronization element.

### The Latch as a Synchronization Element

Pipelined designs achieve parallelism by executing operations concurrently at different pipeline stages. Long sequential operations are divided into small steps, each being executed at one stage. The shorter the stage, the higher the clock frequency and the throughput of the system. From a timing perspective, the key to such a design approach is to prevent data from different stages from intermixing. This might happen because different computations, depending on the complexity and data dependency, produce results at different times. So within a single stage, signals propagate at different speeds. A fast-propagating signal can catch up with a slow-propagating signal from a contiguous stage, resulting in data corruption. This observation leads to the following conclusion: if signals were to propagate all at the same speed (e.g., a FIFO), there would be no race through stages and therefore no need for synchronization elements. Designs based on this principle were actually built and the resulting 'latch-less' technique is called *wave-pipelining* [4]. A good analogy for wave-pipelining is the rolling belt of a supermarket: groceries are the propagating signals and sticks are the synchronization elements that separate a set of groceries belonging to one customer from the next. If all groceries move at the same speed, with sufficient space between sets, no sticks are needed.

### Single-Phase, Latch-Based Design

In viewing latches as synchronization elements, there are two types of timing constraints that define a latch-based design. One deals with the slow-propagating signals and determines the maximum speed at which the system can be clocked. The second deals with fast-propagating signals and determines race conditions through the stages. These timing constraints are the subject of this section. To make the analysis more generic, the clock is assumed to be asymmetric: the high time and the low time are not the same. As will be explained later on in the chapter, timing constrains for all other latching designs are derived from the generic case discussed below.

### Max-Timing Constraints

The max-timing problem can be formulated in the two following ways:

1. Given the maximum propagation delay within a pipeline state, determine the maximum clock frequency the circuit can be clocked at, or conversely,
2. Given the clock frequency, determine the maximum allowed propagation delay within a stage.

The first formulation is used when the logic partition is predefined, while the second is preferred when the clock frequency target is predefined. The analysis that follows uses the second formulation.

The circuit model used to derive the timing constraints is depicted in Fig. 10.33. It consists of a sending and receiving latch and the combinational logic between them. The logic corresponds to one pipeline stage.

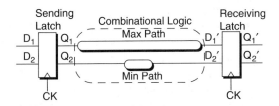

**FIGURE 10.33** Single-phase, latch-based design.

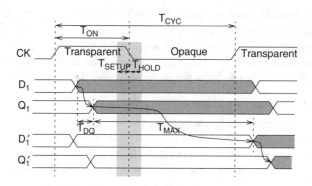

**FIGURE 10.34**   Max-timing diagrams for single-phase, latch-based design.

The model shows explicitly the slowest path, or *max path*, and the fastest path, or *min path*, through the logic. The two paths need not be independent, i.e., they can converge, diverge or intersect, although for simplicity and without losing generality they are assumed to be independent.

As mentioned earlier, the first rule of a latch-based design is that signals propagating through max paths must not be blocked. A timing diagram for this case is shown in Fig. 10.34. $T_{CYC}$ represents the clock period, while $T_{ON}$ represents the length of the transparent period. If max path signals $D_1$ and $D_1'$ arrive at the latch when it is transparent, the only delay introduced in the critical path is the latch latency ($T_{DQ}$). So, assuming that subsequent pipeline stages are perfectly balanced, i.e., the logic is equally partitioned at every stage, the maximum propagation delay $T_{max}$ at any given stage is determined by

$$T_{max} < T_{CYC} - T_{DQ} \tag{10.2}$$

So the pipeline overhead of a single-phase latch design is $T_{DQ}$.

Using the traffic light analogy, this would be equivalent to a car driving along a long road with synchronized traffic lights, and moving at a constant speed equal to the speed of the green light wave. In such a situation, the car would never have to stop at a red light.

## Min-Timing Constraints

Min-timing constraints, also known as *race-through* constraints, are not related to the cycle time, therefore they do not affect speed performance. Min-timing has to do with correct circuit functionality. This is of particular concern to designers because failure to meet min-timing in most cases means a nonfunctional chip regardless of the clock frequency. The min-timing problem is formulated as outlined below.

Assuming latch parameters are known, determine the minimum propagation delay allowed within a stage.

The timing diagram shown in Fig. 10.35 illustrates the problem. Signal $D_2$ is blocked by clock, so the transition of $Q_2$ is determined by the *CK-to-Q* delay of the latch ($T_{CKQ}$). The minimum propagation delay ($T_{min}$) is such that $D_2'$ arrives when the receiving latch is still transparent and before the setup time. Then, $D_2'$ propagates through the latch creating a transition at $Q_2'$ after a *D-to-Q* delay. Although the value of $Q_2'$ is logically correct, a timing problem is created because two pipeline stages get updated in the same clock cycle (or equivalently, a signal "races through" two stages in one clock cycle). The color convention adopted in the timing diagram helps identifying this type of failure: notice that when the latches are opaque, $Q_2$ and $Q_2'$ have the same color, which is not allowed.

The condition to avoid a min-timing problem now becomes apparent. If $T_{min}$ is long enough such that $D_2'$ arrives after the receiving latch has become opaque, then $Q_2'$ will not change until the latch becomes transparent again. This is the second rule of a latch-based design and says that a signal propagating

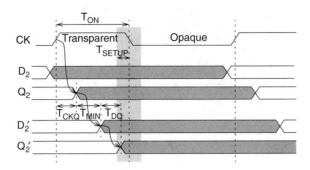

**FIGURE 10.35** Min-timing diagrams for single-phase, latch-based design showing a min-timing (or race-through) problem.

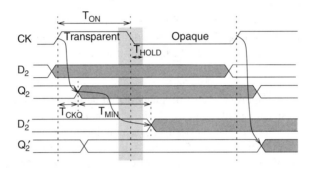

**FIGURE 10.36** Min-timing diagrams for single-phase, latch-based design showing correct operation.

through a min-path must be blocked. A timing diagram for this case is illustrated in Fig. 10.36 and is formulated as

$$T_{CKQ} + T_{min} > T_{ON} + T_{hold} \tag{10.3}$$

or equivalently

$$T_{min} > T_{hold} - T_{CKQ} + T_{ON} \tag{10.4}$$

Using the traffic light analogy again, a fast moving vehicle stopping at every red light on the average moves at the same speed as the slow moving vehicle.

Having defined max and min timing constrains, the valid timing window for a latch-based design is obtained by combining Eqs. (10.2) and (10.4). If $T_D$ is the propagation delay of a signal, the valid timing window for such signal is given by

$$T_{ON} + T_{hold} - T_{CKQ} < T_D < T_{CYC} - T_{DQ} \tag{10.5}$$

Equation (10.5) must be used by a timing analyzer to verify that all signals in a circuit meet timing requirements. Notice that this condition imposes a strict requirement on min paths. If $T_{ON}$ is a half clock cycle (i.e., 50% duty cycle clock), then the minimum delay per stage must be approximately equal to that value, depending on the value of ($T_{hold} - T_{CKQ}$). In practice, this is done by padding the short paths of the circuit with buffers that act as delay elements. Clearly, this increases not only area and power, but

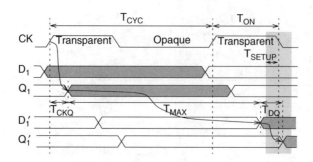

**FIGURE 10.37**  Time borrowing for single-phase, latch-based design.

also design complexity and verification effort. Because of these reasons, single latch-based designs are rarely used in practice.

Notice that the latch setup time is not part of Eq. (10.5). Consequently, it can be concluded that the setup time does not affect the timing of a latch-based design (although the latency of the latch does). This is true except when *time borrowing* is applied. This is the subject of the next subsection.

### Time Borrowing

Time borrowing is the most important aspect of a latch-based design. So far it has been said that in a latch-based design critical signals should not be blocked, and that the max-timing constraint is given by Eq. (10.2); however, depending on the latch placement, the nonblocking requirement can still be satisfied even if Eq. (10.2) is not. Figure 10.37 illustrates such a case. With reference to the model in Fig. 10.33, input $D_1$ is assumed to be blocked. So the transition of $Q_1$ happens a *CK-to-Q* delay after clock ($T_{CKQ}$) and starts propagating through the max path. As long as $D_1'$ arrives at the receiving latch before the setup time, the *D-to-Q* transition is guaranteed to be nonblocking. In this way, the propagation of $D_1'$ is allowed to "borrow" time into the next clock cycle without causing a timing failure.

The maximum time that can be borrowed is determined by the setup time of the receiving latch. The timing requirement for such condition is formulated as follows:

$$T_{CKQ} + T_{max} < T_{CYC} + T_{ON} - T_{setup} \qquad (10.6)$$

and rearranged as:

$$T_{max} < T_{CYC} + T_{ON} - (T_{setup} + T_{CKQ}) \qquad (10.7)$$

By subtracting Eq. (10.2) from Eq. (10.7), the maximum amount of time borrowing, $T_{borrow}$, can be derived and it is given by

$$T_{borrow} = T_{ON} - (T_{setup} + T_{CKQ}) + T_{DQ} \qquad (10.8)$$

Assuming that $T_{CKQ} \approx T_{DQ}$, Eq. (10.8) reduces to

$$T_{borrow} = T_{ON} - T_{setup} \qquad (10.9)$$

So the maximum time that can be borrowed from the next clock cycle is approximately equal to the length of the transparent period minus the latch setup time.

Because time borrowing allows signal propagation across a clock cycle boundary, timing constraints are no longer limited to a single pipeline stage. Using the timing diagram of Fig. 10.37 as a reference, and assuming that $T'_{max}$ is the maximum propagation delay from $Q'_1$, the following timing constraint, besides Eq. (10.7), must be met across two adjacent stages:

$$T_{max} + T'_{max} < 2T_{CYC} + T_{ON} - T_{setup} + T_{CKQ} - T_{DQ} \tag{10.10}$$

which again if $T_{CKQ} \approx T_{DQ}$, reduces to

$$T_{max} + T'_{max} < 2(T_{CYC} - T_{DQ}) + T_{ON} - T_{setup} \tag{10.11}$$

For $n$ stages, Eq. (10.11) can be generalized as follows:

$$\sum_n T_{max} < n(T_{CYC} - T_{DQ}) + T_{ON} - T_{setup} \tag{10.12}$$

where $\sum_n T_{max}$ is the sum of the maximum propagation delays across $n$ stages.

Equation (10.12) seems to suggest that the maximum allowed time borrowing across $n$ stages is limited to $T_{ON} - T_{setup}$ (see Eq. (10.9)); however, this is not the case. If the *average* $T_{max}$ across two or more stages is such that Eq. (10.2) is satisfied, then maximum time borrowing can happen more than once.

Although time borrowing is conceptually simple and gives designers more relaxed max-timing constraints, and thus more design flexibility, in practice timing verification across clock cycle boundaries is not trivial. Few commercial timing tools have such capabilities, forcing designers to develop their own in order to analyze such designs. A common practice is to disallow time borrowing as a general rule and only to allow it in exceptional cases, which are then verified individually by careful timing analysis.

The same principle that allows time borrowing gives transparent latches another very important property when dealing with clock skew. This is the topic of the next subsection.

### The Clock Skew

Clock skew refers to the misalignment of clock edges at the end of a clock distribution network due to manufacturing process variations, load mismatch, PLL jitter, variations in temperature and voltage, and induced noise. The *sign* of the clock skew is relative to the direction of the data flow, as illustrated in Fig. 10.38. For instance, if the skew between the clocks is such that CK arrives after CK′, data moving from left to right see the clock arriving *early* at the destination latch. Conversely, data moving in the opposite direction see the clock arriving *late* at the destination latch. The remainder of this chapter section assumes that the data flow is not restricted to a particular direction. Thus, the worst-case scenario of clock skew is assumed for each case: early skew for max-timing, and late skew for min-timing. How clock skew affects the timing of a single-phase latch design is discussed next.

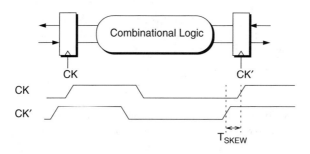

**FIGURE 10.38** Clock skew.

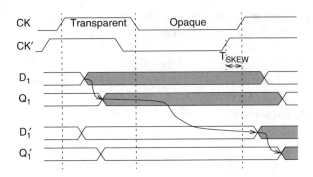

**FIGURE 10.39**   Max-timing for single-phase, latch-based design under the presence of *early* clock skew. $D_1$ transition is not blocking.

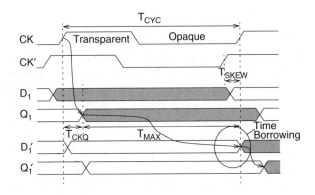

**FIGURE 10.40**   Max-timing for single-phase, latch-based design under the presence of *early* clock skew. $D_1$ transition is blocking.

### *Max-timing*

The max-timing of a single-phase latch-based design is, to a large extent, immune to clock skew. This is because signals in a max-path are not blocked. The timing diagram of Fig. 10.39 illustrates this case. Using Fig. 10.33 as a reference, the skew between clocks CK and CK' is $T_{skew}$, with CK' arriving earlier than CK. The transition of signals $D_1$ and $D_1'$, assumed to be critical, occur when latches are transparent or nonblocking. As observed, the receiving latch becoming transparent earlier than expected has no effect on the propagation delay of $Q_1$, as long as the setup time requirement of the receiving latch is satisfied. Therefore, Eq. (10.2) still remains valid.

Other scenarios where clock skew might affect max-timing can be imagined. However, none of these invalidates the conclusion arrived at in the previous paragraph. One of such scenarios is illustrated in the timing diagram of Fig. 10.40. In contrast to the previous example, the input to the sending latch ($D_1$) is blocked. If the maximum propagation delay is such that $T_{CKQ} + T_{max} = T_{CYC}$, the early arrival of CK' results in *unintentional* time borrowing. Although this reduces the maximum available *intentional* time borrowing from the next cycle (as defined earlier), no violation has occurred from a timing perspective. Another scenario is illustrated in Fig. 10.41. Similar to the previous example, $D_1$ is blocked and $T_{CKQ} + T_{max} = T_{CYC}$, but in this case the arrival of the receiving clock CK' is late. The result is that signal $D_1'$ gets blocked for the period of length equal to $T_{skew}$. Depending on whether the next stage receives a late clock or not, this blocking has either no effect on timing or may lead to time borrowing in the next clock cycle.

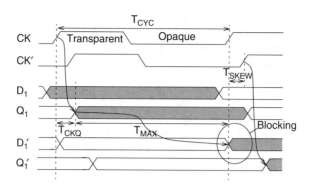

**FIGURE 10.41** Max-timing for single-phase, latch-based design under the presence of *late* clock skew. $D_1$ transition is blocked.

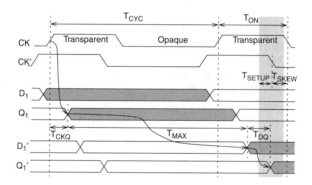

**FIGURE 10.42** Time borrowing for single-phase, latch-based design under the presence of *early* clock skew.

### Time Borrowing

The preceding max-timing discussion has indicated that the presence of clock skew may result in unintentional time borrowing. The timing diagram shown Fig. 10.42 illustrates how this could happen. Using Fig. 10.33 as a reference, the input to the sending latch ($D_1$) is assumed blocked. After propagating through the max path, the input to the receiving latch ($D_1'$) must arrive before its setup time to meet the max-timing requirement. The early arrival of clock CK′ may be interpreted as if the setup time boundary *moves* forward by $T_{skew}$, thus reducing the available borrowing time by an equivalent amount.

The condition for maximum time borrowing in this case is formulated as follows:

$$T_{CKQ} + T_{max} < T_{CYC} + T_{ON} - (T_{setup} + T_{skew}) \tag{10.13}$$

Again assuming that $T_{CKQ} \approx T_{DQ}$, in the same manner as Eq. (10.9) was derived, it can be shown that maximum time borrowing in this case is given by

$$T_{borrow} = T_{ON} - (T_{setup} + T_{skew}) \tag{10.14}$$

By comparing Eq. (10.14) against Eq. (10.9) (zero clock skew), it is concluded that the presence of clock skew reduces the amount of time borrowing by $T_{skew}$.

### *Min-Timing*

In contrast to max-timing, min-timing is not immune to clock skew. Figure 10.43 provides a timing diagram illustrating this case. With reference to Fig. 10.33, clock CK′ is assumed to arrive late. In order to insure that $D_2'$ gets blocked, it is required that:

$$T_{CKQ} + T_{min} > T_{ON} + T_{skew} + T_{hold} \tag{10.15}$$

After rearranging terms, the min-timing requirement is expressed as

$$T_{min} > T_{hold} - T_{CKQ} + T_{ON} + T_{skew} \tag{10.16}$$

Equation (10.16) shows that in addition to $T_{ON}$, $T_{skew}$ is added now. The clock skew presence makes the min-timing requirement even more strict than before, yielding a single-phase latch design nearly useless in practice.

### Nonoverlapping Dual-Phase, Latch-Based Design

As pointed out in the preceding subsection, the major drawback of a single-phase, latch-based design is its rigorous min-timing requirement. The presence of clock skew makes matters worse. Unless the transparent period can be made very short, i.e., a narrow pulse, a single-phase, latch-based design is not very practical. The harsh min-timing requirement of a single-phase design is due to the sending and receiving latches being both transparent simultaneously, allowing fast signals to race through one or more pipeline stages. A way to eliminate this problem is to intercept the fast signal with a latch operating on a complementary clock phase. The resulting scheme, referred to as a dual-phase, latch-based design, is shown in Fig. 10.44. Because the middle latch operates on a complementary clock, at no point in time

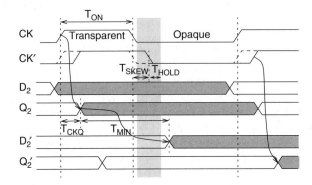

**FIGURE 10.43**   Min-timing diagrams for single-phase, latch-based design under the presence of *late* clock skew.

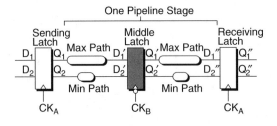

**FIGURE 10.44**   Nonoverlapping dual-phase, latch-based design.

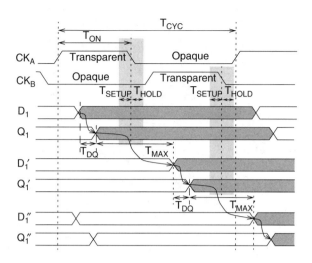

**FIGURE 10.45** Max-timing diagrams for nonoverlapping dual-phase, latch-based design.

a transparent period is created between adjacent pipeline stages, eliminating the possibility of races. Notice that the insertion of a complementary latch, while driven by the need to slow fast signals, ends up slowing down max paths also. Although, in principle, a dual-phase design is race free, clock skew may still cause min-timing problems. The clock phases may be nonoverlapping or fully complementary. The timing requirement of a nonoverlapping dual-phase, latch-based design is discussed below. A dual-phase complementary design is treated later as a special case.

### Max-timing

Because a signal in a max path has to go through two latches in a dual-phase latch-based design, the *D-to-Q* latency of the latch is paid twice in the cycle. This is shown in the timing diagram of Fig. 10.45. The max-timing constraint in a dual-phase design is therefore given by

$$T_{\max} < T_{\mathrm{CYC}} - 2T_{DQ} \qquad (10.17)$$

The above equation still remains valid under the presence of clock skew. By comparing it against Eq. (10.2), it is evident that as a result of the middle latch insertion the pipeline overhead ($2T_{DQ}$) becomes twice as large as in the single-latch design.

### Time Borrowing

Time borrowing does not get affected by the insertion of a complementary latch. Maximum time borrowing is still given by Eq. (10.9), or by Eq. (10.14) in the presence of clock skew.

### Min-timing

Min-timing is affected by the introduction of the complementary latch. As pointed out earlier, the complementary latch insertion is a solution to relax the min-timing requirement of a latch-based design. Figure 10.46 provides a timing diagram illustrating how a dual-latch design prevents races. Clock $CK_A$ and $CK_B$ are nonoverlapping clock phases, with $T_{\mathrm{NOV}}$ being the nonoverlapping time. With reference to Fig. 10.44, the input $D_2$ to the sending latch is assumed to be blocked. After a *CK-to-Q* and a $T_{\min}$ delay, signal $D_2'$ arrives at the middle latch while it is still opaque. Therefore, $D_2'$ gets blocked until $CK_B$ transitions and the latch becomes transparent. A *CK-to-Q* delay later, signal $Q_2'$ transitions. If the nonoverlapping time is long enough, the $Q_2'$ transition satisfies the hold time of the sending latch. The same phenomenon happens in the second half of the stage.

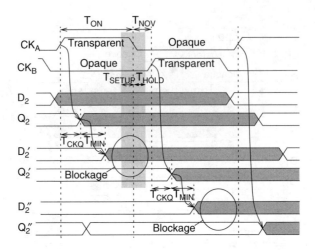

**FIGURE 10.46**   Min-timing diagrams for nonoverlapping dual-phase, latch-based design.

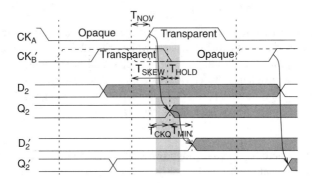

**FIGURE 10.47**   Min-timing diagrams for nonoverlapping dual-phase, latch-based design under the presence of *late* clock skew.

The presence of clock skew in this design makes min-timing worse also, as expected. The effect of late clock skew is to increase the effective hold time of the sending latch. This is illustrated in Fig. 10.47, where clock $CK_B'$ is late with respect to $CK_A$.

The min-timing condition is given by

$$T_{NOV} + T_{CKQ} + T_{min} > T_{skew} + T_{hold} \qquad (10.18)$$

which can be rearranged as

$$T_{min} > T_{hold} - T_{CKQ} + T_{skew} - T_{NOV} \qquad (10.19)$$

Comparing with Eq. 10.16, notice that the transparent period ($T_{ON}$) is missing from the right-hand side of Eq. (10.19), reducing the requirement on $T_{min}$, and that the nonoverlap time ($T_{NOV}$) gets subtracted from the clock skew ($T_{skew}$). The latter gives designers a choice to trade-off between $T_{ON}$ and $T_{NOV}$ by increasing $T_{NOV}$ at the expense of $T_{ON}$ (so the clock cycle remains constant), min-timing problems can be minimized at the cost of reducing time borrowing. For a sufficiently long $T_{NOV}$, the right hand side of Eq. 10.19 becomes negative. Under such assumption, this type of design may be considered *race free*. Furthermore, by making the nonoverlap time a function of the clock frequency, a manufactured chip is

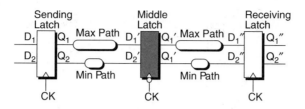

**FIGURE 10.48**   Complementary dual-phase, latch-based design.

guaranteed to work correctly at some lower than nominal frequency, even in the event that unexpected min-timing violations are discovered on silicon. This is the most important characteristic of this type of latching design, and the main reason why such designs were so popular before automated timing verification became more sophisticated.

Although min-timing constraints are greatly reduced in a two-phase, nonoverlapping latch-based design, designers should be aware that the introduction of an additional latch per stage results in twice as many potential min-timing races that need to be checked, in contrast to a single latch design. This becomes a more relevant issue in a two-phase, complementary latch-based design, as discussed next.

### Complementary Dual-Phase, Latch-Based Design

A two-phase, complementary latch-based design (Fig. 10.48) is a special case of the generic nonoverlapping design, where clock $CK_A$ is a 50% duty cycle clock, and clock $CK_B$ is complementary to $CK_A$. In such a design, the nonoverlapping time between the clock phases is zero. The main advantage of this approach is the simplicity of the clock generation and distribution. In most practical designs, only one clock phase needs to be globally distributed to all sub-units, generating the complementary clock phase locally.

#### *Max-timing*

Similar to a nonoverlapping design, the maximum propagation delay is given by Eq. (10.17), and it is unaffected by the clock skew. The pipeline overhead is $2T_{DQ}$.

#### *Time Borrowing*

Time borrowing is similar to a single-phase latch except that $T_{ON}$ is half a clock cycle. Therefore, maximum time borrowing is given by

$$T_{borrow} = T_{CYC}/2 - (T_{setup} + T_{skew})  \qquad (10.20)$$

So complementary clocks maximize time borrowing.

#### *Min-timing*

The min-timing requirement is similar to the nonoverlapping scheme except that $T_{NOV}$ is zero. Therefore,

$$T_{min} > T_{hold} - T_{CKQ} + T_{skew}  \qquad (10.21)$$

The simplification of the clocking scheme comes at a price though. Although Eq. (10.21) is less stringent than Eq. (10.16) (no $T_{ON}$ in it), it is not as good as Eq. (10.19). Furthermore, a min-timing failure in such a design cannot be fixed by slowing down the clock frequency, making silicon debugging in such a situation more challenging. This is a clear example of a design trade-off that designers must face when picking a latching and clocking scheme.

The next section discusses how a latch-based design using complementary clock phases can be further transformed into a edge-triggered-based design.

### Edge-Triggered, Flip-Flop-Based Design

The major drawback of a single-phase latch based design is min-timing. The introduction of dual-phase-latch-based designs greatly reduces the risk of min-timing failure; however, from a physical implementation perspective, the insertion of a latch in the middle of a pipeline stage is not free of cost. Each

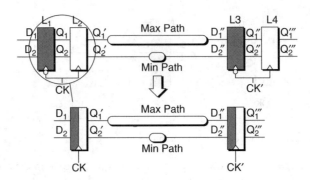

**FIGURE 10.49**   Edge-triggered, flip-flop-based design.

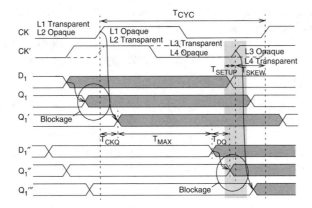

**FIGURE 10.50**   Max-timing diagrams for edge-triggered, flip-flop-based design.

pipeline stage has to be further partitioned in half, although time borrowing helps in this respect. Clock distribution and clock skew minimization becomes more challenging because clocks need to be distributed to twice as many locations. Also, timing verification in a latch-based design is not trivial. First, latches must be properly placed to allow maximum time borrowing and maximum clock skew hiding. Second, time borrowing requires multi-cycle timing analysis and many timing analyzers lack this capability. A solution that overcomes many of these shortcomings is to use flip-flops. This is discussed in the rest of this subsection.

Most edge-triggered flip-flops, also known as *master-slave* flip-flops, are built from transparent latches. Figure 10.49 shows how this is done. By collapsing the transparent-high and transparent-low latches in one unit, and rearranging the combinatorial logic so that it is all contained in one pipeline segment, the two-phase, latch-based design is converted into a positive-edge, flip-flop-based design. If the collapsing order of the latches were reverted, the result would be a negative-edge flip-flop. In a way, a flip-flop-based design can be viewed as an unbalanced dual-phase, latch-based design where all the logic is confined to one single stage. The timing analysis of flip-flops, therefore, is similar to latches.

### Max-timing

The max-timing diagram for flip-flops is shown in Fig. 10.50. Two distinctive characteristics are observed in this diagram: (1) the transparent-high latches ($L_2$ and $L_4$) are blocking, and (2) the transparent-low latches ($L_1$ and $L_3$) provide maximum time borrowing. The opposite is true for negative-edge flip-flops. The first condition results from the fact that the complementary latches are never transparent simultaneously, so a transparent operation in the first latch leads to a blockage in the second. The second condition is necessary to maximize the time allowed for logic in the stage. Because $L_2$ is blocking, unless time borrowing happens in $L_3$, only half a cycle would be available for logic.

The max-timing constraint is formulated as a maximum time borrowing constraint (see Eq. (10.13) for comparison), but confining it to one clock cycle because the sending latch ($L_2$) is blocking. With reference to Fig. 10.50, the constraint is formulated as follows:

$$T_{CKQ} + T_{max} < T_{CYC} - (T_{setup} + T_{skew}) \qquad (10.22)$$

which after rearranging terms gives

$$T_{max} < T_{CYC} - (T_{CKQ} + T_{setup} + T_{skew}) \qquad (10.23)$$

To determine the pipeline overhead introduced by flip-flops and compare it against a dual latch based design, Eq. (10.23) is compared against Eq. (10.17). To make the comparison more direct, observe that $T_{setup} + T_{CKQ} < 2T_{DQ}$. This is because as long as signal $D_1''$ meets the setup time of latch $L_3$, $Q_1''$ is allowed to *push* into the transparent period of $L_4$, adding one latch delay ($T_{DQ}$), and then go through $L_4$, adding a second latch delay. Therefore, Eq. (10.23) can be rewritten as

$$T_{max} < T_{CYC} - (2T_{DQ} + T_{skew}) \qquad (10.24)$$

By looking at Eq. (10.17), it becomes clear that the pipeline overhead is larger in flip-flops than in latches, and it is equal to $2T_{DQ} + T_{skew}$. In addition to the latch delays, the clock skew is now also subtracted from the cycle time, this being a major drawback of flip-flops. It should be noticed, however, that faster flip-flops with less than two latch delays can be designed.

### Min-timing

The min-timing requirement is essentially equal to a dual latch-based design and it is given by Eq. (10.21). An important observation is that inside the flip-flop this condition may be satisfied *by construction*. Since the clock skew is zero, it is only required that $T_{min} > T_{hold} - T_{CKQ}$. If the latch parameters are such that $T_{CKQ} > T_{hold}$ then this condition is always satisfied since $T_{min} \geq 0$. Timing analyzers still need to verify that min-timing requirements between flip-flops are satisfied according to Eq. (10.21), although the number of potential races is reduced to half in comparison to the dual latch scheme.

Timing verification is easier in flip-flop-based designs because most timing paths are confined to a single cycle boundary. Knowing with precision the departing time of signals may also be advantageous to some design styles, or may reduce iterations in the design cycle, resulting eventually in a simpler design (In an industrial environment, where design robustness is paramount, in contrast to academia, nearly 90% of the design cycle is spent on verification, including logic and physical verification, timing verification, signal integrity, etc.)

As discussed earlier, time borrowing in a flip-flop-based design is confined to the boundary of a clock cycle. Therefore, time borrowing from adjacent pipeline stages is not possible. In this respect, when choosing flip-flops instead of latches, designers have a more challenging task at partitioning the logic to fit in the cycle—a disadvantage. An alternative solution to time borrowing is *clock stretching*. The technique consists of the adjustment of clock edges (e.g., by using programmable clock buffers) to allocate more timing in one stage at the expense of the other. It can be applied in cases when logic partitioning becomes too difficult, assuming that timing slack in adjacent stages is available. When applied correctly, e.g., guaranteeing that no min-timing violation get created as by-product, clock stretching can be very useful.

### Pulsed Latches

Pulsed latches are conceptually identical to transparent latches, except that the length of the transparent period is designed to be very short (i.e., a *pulse*), usually a few gate delays. The usage of pulsed latches is different from conventional transparent latches though. Most important of all, the short transparency makes single pulsed latch-based design practical, see Fig. 10.51, contributing to the reduction of the pipeline overhead yet retaining the good properties of latches. Each timing aspect of pulsed latch-based design is discussed below.

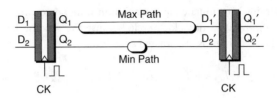

**FIGURE 10.51**    Pulsed latch-based design.

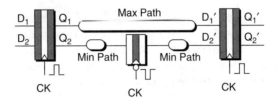

**FIGURE 10.52**    Pulsed latch-based design combining single- and dual-pulsed latches.

### Max-timing
Pulsed latches are meant to be used as one per pipeline stage, as mentioned earlier, so the pipeline overhead is limited to only one latch delay (see Eq. (10.2)). This is half the overhead of a dual-phase, latch-based design. Furthermore, logic partitioning is similar to a flip-flop-based design, simplifying clock distribution.

### Time Borrowing
Although still possible, the amount of time borrowing is greatly reduced when using pulsed latches. From Eq. (10.14), $T_{borrow} = T_{ON} - (T_{setup} + T_{skew})$. If $T_{ON}$ is chosen such that $T_{ON} = T_{setup} + T_{skew}$, then time borrowing is reduced to zero; however, the clock skew can still be hidden by the latch, i.e., it is not subtracted from the clock cycle for max-timing.

### Min-timing
This is the biggest challenge designers face when using pulsed latches. As shown by Eq. (10.16), the minimum propagation delay in a latch-based system is given by $T_{min} > T_{hold} - T_{CKQ} + T_{ON} + T_{skew}$. Ideally, to minimize min-timing problems, $T_{ON}$ should be as small as possible. However, if it becomes too small, the borrowing time may become negative (see above), meaning that some of the clock skew gets subtracted from the cycle time for max-timing. Again, this represent another trade-off that designers must face when selecting a latching strategy. In general, it is a good practice to minimize min-timing at the expense of max-timing. Although max-timing failures affect the speed distribution of functional parts, min-timing failures are in most cases fatal.

From a timing analyzer perspective, pulsed latches can be treated as flip-flops. For instance, by redefining $T'_{hold} = T_{hold} + T_{ON}$, min-timing constraints look identical in both cases (see Eqs. (10.16) and (10.21)). Also, time borrowing in practice is rather limited with pulsed latches, so the same timing tools and methodology used for analyzing flip-flop based designs can be applied.

Last but not least, it is important to mention that designs need not adhere to one latch or clocking style only. For instance, latches and flip-flops can be intermixed in the same design. Or single and dual-phase latches can be combined also, as suggested in Fig. 10.52. Here, pulsed latches are utilized in max paths in order to minimize the pipeline overhead, while dual-phase latches are used in min paths to eliminate, or minimize, min-timing problems. In this example, the combination of transparent-high and transparent-low pulsed latches works as a dual-phase nonoverlapping design. Clearly, such combinations require a good understanding of the timing constraints of latches and flip-flops not only by designers but also by the adopted timing tools, to ensure that timing verification of the design is done correctly.

**TABLE 10.6** Summary of Timing Requirements for Latch and Flip-Flop-Based Designs

| Design | $T_{overhead}$ | $T_{borrow}$ | $T_{min}$ |
|---|---|---|---|
| Single-phase | $T_{DQ}$ | $T_{ON} - (T_{setup} + T_{skew})$ | $T_{hold} - T_{CKQ} + (T_{skew} + T_{on})$ |
| Dual-phase Nonoverlapping | $2\,T_{DQ}$ | $T_{ON} - (T_{setup} + T_{skew})$ | $T_{hold} - T_{CKQ} + (T_{skew} - T_{NOV})$ |
| Dual-phase Complementary | $2\,T_{DQ}$ | $0.5\,T_{CYC} - (T_{setup} + T_{skew})$ | $T_{hold} - T_{CKQ} + (T_{skew})$ |
| Flip-flop | $\sim 2\,T_{DQ} + T_{skew}$ | $0$ | $T_{hold} - T_{CKQ} + (T_{skew})$ |
| Pulsed-latch | $T_{DQ}^{\ 1}$ | $T_{ON} - (T_{setup} + T_{skew})^2$ | $T_{hold} - T_{CKQ} + (T_{skew} + T_{ON})^3$ |

*Note*: 1. True if $T_{ON} > T_{setup} + T_{skew}$
   2. Equal to 0 if $T_{ON} = T_{setup} + T_{skew}$
   3. Equal to $T_{hold} - T_{CKQ} + (2 \times T_{skew})$ if $T_{ON} = T_{skew}$

## Summary of Latch and Flip-Flop-Based Designs

Table 10.6 summarizes the timing requirements of the various latch and flip-flop-based designs discussed in the preceding sections. In terms of pipeline overhead, the single latch and the pulsed latch appear to be the best. However, because of its prohibitive min-timing requirement, a single-phase design is of little practical use. Flip-flops appear the worst, primarily because of the clock skew. Although, as mentioned earlier, a flip-flop can be designed to have latency less than two equivalent latches. In terms of time borrowing, all latch-based designs allow some degree of it, in contrast to flip-flop based designs. From a min-timing perspective, nonoverlapping dual-phase is the best, although clock generation is more complex. It is followed by the dual-phase complementary design, which uses a simpler clocking scheme, and by the flip-flop design with an even simpler single-phase clocking scheme. The min-timing requirement of both designs is the same, so the number of potential races in the dual-phase design is twice as large as in the flip-flop design.

## Design of Latches and Flip-Flops

This sub-section covers the fundamentals of latch and flip-flop design. It starts with the most basic transparent latch: the pass gate. Then, it introduces more elaborated latches and flip-flops made from latches, and discusses their features. Next, it presents a sample of advanced designs currently used in the industry. At the end of the sub-section, a performance analysis of the different circuits described is presented.

Because often designers use the same terminology to refer to different circuit styles or properties, to avoid confusion, this sub-section adheres to the following nomenclature. The term *dynamic* refers to circuits with *floating* nodes only. By definition, a floating node does not see a DC path to either $V_{DD}$ or GND during a portion of the clock cycle, and it is, therefore, susceptible to discharge by leakage current, or to noise. The term *precharge logic* is used to describe circuits that operate in precharge and evaluation phase, such as Domino logic [5]. The term *skewed logic* refers to a logic style where only the propagation of one edge is relevant, such as Domino [5, 6], Self-Reset [7], or Skewed Static logic [8]. Such logic families are typically monotonic.

### Design of Transparent Latches

This sub-section explains the fundamentals of latch design. It covers pass and transmission gate latches, tristate latches, and true-single-phase-clock latches. A brief discussion of feedback circuits is also given.

#### Transmission-Gate Latches

A variety of transparent-high latches built from pass gates and transmission gates is shown in Fig. 10.53. Transparent-low equivalents, not shown, are created by inverting the clock. The most basic latch of all is the pass gate (Fig. 10.53(a)). Although it is the simplest, it has several limitations. First, being an NMOS transistor, it degrades the passage of a high signal by a threshold voltage drop, affecting not only speed but also noise immunity, especially at low $V_{DD}$. Second, it has dynamic storage: output $Q$ is floating when CK is low, being susceptible to leakage and output noise. Third, it has limited fanout, especially if input $D$ is driven through a long interconnect, or if $Q$ drives a long interconnect. Last, it is susceptible to input

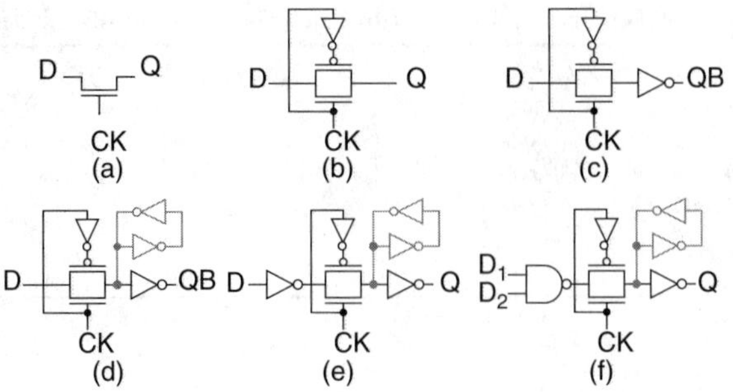

**FIGURE 10.53**   Transparent-high latches built from pass gates and transmission gates.

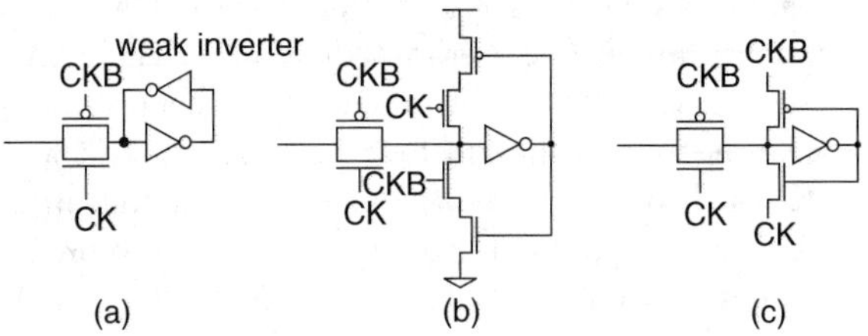

**FIGURE 10.54**   Feedback structures for latches.

noise: a noise spike can turn momentarily the gate on, or can inject charge in the substrate by turning the parasitic diode on, leading to a charge loss. To make this design more robust, each of the variants in Fig. 10.53(b-f) attempts to overcome at least one of the limitations just described. Figure 10.53(b) uses a transmission gate to avoid the threshold voltage drop, at the expense of generating a complementary clock signal [9, 10]. Figure 10.53(c) buffers the output to protect the storage node and to improve the output drive. Figure 10.53(d) uses a back-to-back inverter to prevent the storage node from floating. Avoiding node $Q$ in the feedback loop, as shown, improves robustness by completely isolating the output from the storage node, at the expense of a small additional inverter. Figure 10.53(e) buffers the input in order to: (1) improve noise immunity, (2) ensure the writability of the latch, and (3) bound the $D$-$to$-$Q$ delay (which depends on the size of input driver). Conditions 2 and 3 are important if the latch is to be instantiated in unpredictable contexts, e.g., as a library element. Condition 2 becomes irrelevant if a clocked feedback is used instead. It should be noted that the additional input inverter results in increased $D$-$to$-$Q$ delay; however, it need not be an inverter, and logic functionality may be provided instead with the latch. Figure 10.53(f) shows such an instance, where a NAND2 gate is *merged* with the latch. A transmission gate latch, where both input and output buffers can be logic gates, is reported in [11].

***Feedback Circuits***

A feedback circuit in latches can be built in more than one way. The most straightforward way is the back inverter, adopted in Fig. 10.53(d–f), and shown in detail in Fig. 10.54(a). Clock CKB is the complementary of clock CK. The back inverter is sized to be *weak*, in general by using minimum size transistors, or increasing channel length. It must allow the input driver to overwrite the storage node, yet it must provide enough charge to prevent it from floating when the latch is opaque. Although simple and compact layout-wise, this type of feedback requires designers to check carefully for writability, especially in skewed process corners (e.g., fast PMOS, slow NMOS) and under different temperature and voltage conditions. A more robust approach is shown in Fig. 10.54(b). The feedback loop is open when the storage node is driven, eliminating all contention. It requires additional devices, although not necessarily more area since the input driver may be downsized. A third approach is shown in Fig. 10.54(c) [12]. It uses a back inverter but connecting the rails to the clock signals CK and CKB. When the latch is opaque, CK is low and CKB

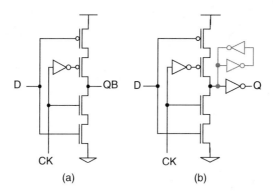

**FIGURE 10.55**   Transparent latches built from tristate gates.

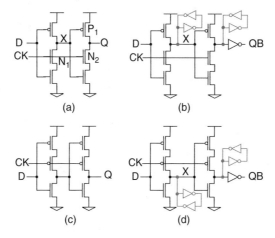

**FIGURE 10.56**   Complementary TSPC transparent-high and transparent-low latches.

is high, so it operates as a regular back inverter. When the storage node is being driven, the clock polarity is reverted, resulting in a *weakened* back inverter. For simplicity, the rest of circuits discussed in this section use a back inverter as feedback.

### Tristate Gate

Transparent-high latches built from tristate gates are shown in Fig. 10.55. The dynamic variant is shown in Fig. 10.55(a). By driving a FET gate as opposed to source/drain, this latch is more robust to input noise than the plain transmission gate of Fig. 10.53(c). The staticized variant with the output buffer is shown in Fig. 10.55(b). Similar to the transmission-gate case, transparent-low latches are created by inverting the clock.

## True Single-Phase Clock (TSPC) Latches

Transmission gate and tristate gate latches are externally supplied with a single clock phase, but in reality they use *two clock* phases, the second being the internally generated clock CKB. The generation of this complementary clock becomes critical when building flip-flops with these type of latches. For instance, unexpectedly large delay in CKB might lead to min-timing problem inside the flip-flop, as explained later on in the sub-section on "Design of Flip-Flops." To eliminate the need for a complementary clock, true single phase clock (TSPC) latches were invented [13,14]. The basic idea behind TSPC is the complementary property of CMOS devices in combination with the inverting nature of CMOS gates.

A complementary transparent-high TSPC latch is shown in Fig. 10.56(a). The latch operates as follows. When CK is high (latch is transparent), the circuit operates as a two-stage buffer, so output *Q*

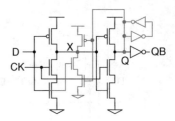

**FIGURE 10.57** Complementary TSPC transparent-high latch with direct feedback from storage node Q.

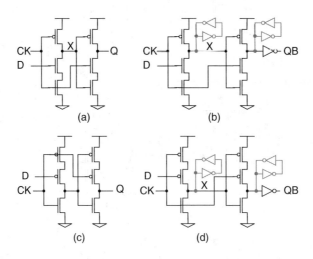

**FIGURE 10.58** Precharged TSPC transparent-high and transparent-low blocking latches.

follows input $D$. When CK is low (latch is opaque), devices $N_1$ and $N_2$ are turned off. Since node $X$ can only transition monotonically high, (1) $P_1$ is either on or off when $Q$ is high, or (2) $P_1$ is off when $Q$ is low. In addition to node $Q$ being floating if $P_1$ is off, node $X$ is floating also if $D$ is high. So the latch has two dynamic nodes that need to be staticized with back-to-back inverters for robustness. This is shown in Fig. 10.56(b), where the output is buffered also.

Contrary to the latches described in the previous sub-sections, a transparent-low TSPC latch cannot be generated by just inverting the clock. Instead, the complementary circuit shown in Fig. 10.56(c and d) is used (Fig. 10.56(c) is dynamic, Fig. 10.56(d) is static). The operation of the latch is analogous to the transparent-high case. A dual-phase complementary latch based design using TSPC was reported in [15].

As Fig. 10.56 shows, the conversion of TSPC latches into static ones takes several devices. A way to save at least one feedback device is shown in Fig. 10.57. If $D$ is low and $Q$ is high when the latch is opaque, this feedback structure results in no contention. The drawback is that node $X$ follows input $D$ when CK is low, resulting in additional toggling and increased power dissipation.

Another way to build TSPC latches is shown in Fig. 10.58. The number of devices remains the same as in the previous case but the latch operates in a different mode. With reference to Fig. 10.58(a), node $X$ is precharged high when CK is low (opaque period), while $Q$ retains its previous value. When CK goes high (latch becomes transparent), node $X$ remains either high or discharges to ground, depending on the value of $D$, driving output $Q$ to a new value. The buffered version of this latch, with staticizing back-to-back inverters, is shown in Fig. 10.58(b).

Because of its precharge nature, this version of the TSPC latch is faster than the static one. The clock load is higher also (3 vs. 2 devices), contributing to higher power dissipation, although the input loading is lower (1 vs. 2 devices). $X$ switches only monotonically during the transparent phase, so the input to the latch must either: (1) be monotonic, or (2) change during the opaque phase only (i.e., a blocking latch).

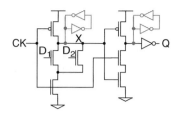

**FIGURE 10.59** Precharged TSPC transparent-high blocking latch with embedded NOR2 logic.

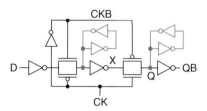

**FIGURE 10.60** A positive, edge-triggered flip-flop built from transmission gate latches.

One of the advantages of the precharged TSPC latch is that, similar to Domino, relatively complex logic can be incorporated in the precharge stage. An example of a latch with an embedded NOR2 is given in Fig. 10.59.

Although this latch cannot be used generically because of its special input requirement, it is the base of a TSPC flip-flop (discussed next) and of pulsed flip-flops described later on in this chapter section.

### Design of Flip-Flops

This sub-section explains the fundamentals of flip-flop design. It covers three types of flip-flops based on the transmission gate, tristate, and TSPC latches presented earlier. The sense-amplifier based flip-flop, with no latch equivalence, is also discussed. Design trade-offs are also briefly mentioned.

#### *Master-Slave Flip-Flop*

The master-slave flip-flop, shown in Fig. 10.60, is perhaps the most commonly used flip-flop type [6]. It is made from a transparent-high and a transparent-low transmission gate latch. Its mode of operation is quite simple: the master section writes into the first latch when CK is low, and the value is passed onto the slave section and propagated to the output when CK is high. As pointed out earlier, a flip-flop made this way has to satisfy the internal min-timing requirement. Specifically, the delay from CK to $X$ has to be greater than the hold time of the second latch. Notice that the second latch turns completely opaque only after CKB goes low. The inverter delay between CK and CKB creates a short period of time where both latches are transparent. Therefore, designers must pay careful attention to the timing of signals $X$ and CKB to make sure the design is race free. Setting the min-timing requirement aside, the master-slave flip-flop is simple and robust; however, for applications requiring very high performance, its long *D-to-Q* latency might be unacceptable.

A flip-flop made from tristate latches (see Fig. 10.55), that is free of internal races, yet uses complementary clocks, is shown in Fig. 10.61 [6]. The circuit, also known as $C^2MOS$ flip-flop, does not require the internal inverter at node $X$ because: (1) node $X$ drives transistor gates only, so there is no fight with a feedback inverter, and (2) there is no internal race: a pull up(down) path is followed by a pull down(up) path, and both paths see the same clock. The *D-to-Q* latency of the $C^2MOS$ flip-flop is about equal or better than the master-slave flip-flop of Fig. 10.60; however, because of the stacked PMOS devices, this circuit dissipates more clock power and is less area efficient. For the same reason, the input load is also higher.

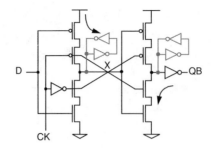

**FIGURE 10.61**    A positive, edge-triggered flip-flop built from tristate gates.

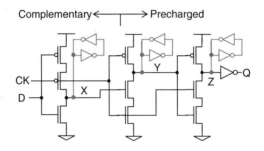

**FIGURE 10.62**    Positive, edge-triggered TSPC flip-flop built from complementary and precharged TSPC latches.

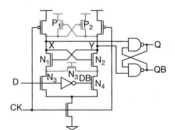

**FIGURE 10.63**    Sense-amplifier, edge-triggered flip-flop.

### TSPC Flip-Flop

TSPC flip-flops are designed by combining the TSPC latches of Figs. 10.56 and 10.58. There are several possible combinations. In an effort to reduce $D$-to-$Q$ delay, which is inherently high in this type of latches, a positive-edge flip-flop is constructed by combining a half complementary transparent-low latch (see Fig. 10.56(d)) and a full precharged transparent-high latch (see Fig. 10.58(b)). The resulting circuit is shown in Fig. 10.62. Choosing a precharged latch as the slave portion of the flip-flop helps reduce $D$-to-$Q$ delay, because (1) the precharged latch is faster than the complementary one, and (2) $Y$ switches monotonically low when CK is high, so the master latch can be reduced to a half latch because $X$ switches monotonically low also when CK is high. The delay reduction comes at a cost of a hold time increase: to insure node $Y$ is fully discharged, node $X$ must remain high long enough, increasing in turn the hold time of input $D$.

### Sense-Amplifier Flip-Flop

The design of a sense-amplifier flip-flop [10,17] is borrowed from the SRAM world. A positive-edge triggered version of the circuit is shown in Fig. 10.63. It consists of a dual-rail precharged stage, followed by a static SR latch built from back-to-back NAND2 gates. The circuit operates as follows. When CK is low, nodes $X$ and $Y$ are precharged high, so the SR latch holds its previous value. Transistors $N_1$ and $N_2$ are both on. When CK is high, depending on the value of $D$, either $X$ or $Y$ is pulled low, and the SR latch latches the new value. The discharge of node $X(Y)$ turns off $N_2(N_1)$, preventing node $Y(X)$ from

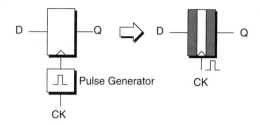

**FIGURE 10.64** A pulsed latch built from a transparent latch and a pulse generator.

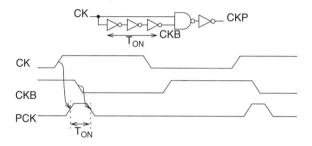

**FIGURE 10.65** A pulse generator.

discharging if, during evaluation, DB(D) transitions low-to-high. Devices $P_1$, $P_2$, and $N_3$ are added to staticize nodes $X$ and $Y$. Transistor $N_3$ is a small device that provides a DC path to ground, since either $N_1|N_4$ or $N_2|N_3$, and the clock footer device are all on when CK is high. While the *D-to-Q* latency of the flip-flop appears to comprise two stages only, in the worst-case it is four: the input inverter, the precharged stage, and two NAND2 delays. It should be noted that the precharge stage allows the incorporation of logic functionality. But it is limited by the dual-rail nature of the circuit, which required $2N$ additional devices to implement an $N$-input logic function. In particular, XOR/XNOR gates allow device sharing, minimizing the transistor count and the increase in layout area.

### Design of Pulsed Latches

This subsection covers the design of pulsed latches. It first discusses how this type of latch can be easily derived from a regular transparent latch, by clocking it with a pulse instead of a regular clock signal. It then examines specific circuits that embed the pulse generation inside the latch itself, allowing better control of the pulse width.

#### Pulse Generator and Pulsed Latch

A pulsed latch can be designed by combining a pulse generator and a regular transparent latch, as suggested in Fig. 10.64 [18, 19]. While the pulse generator adds latency to the path of the clock, this is not an issue from a timing perspective. As long as all clock lines see the same delay, or as long as the timing tool includes this delay in the timing analysis, the timing verification of a pulsed latch-based design should not be more complex than that of latch of flip-flop-based designs.

A simple pulse generator consists of the ANDing two clock signals: the original clock and a delayed and inverted version of it, as illustrated in Fig. 10.65. The length of the clock pulse is determined by the delay of the inverters used to generate CKB. In practice, it is hard to generate an acceptable pulse width less than three inverters, although more can be used.

This pulse generator can be used with any of the transparent latches described previously to design pulsed latches. Figure 10.66 shows two examples of such designs. The design in Fig. 10.66(a) uses the transmission gate latch of Fig. 10.53(e) [20], while the design Fig. 10.66(b) uses the TSPC latch of Fig. 10.56(b). As mentioned previously, designers should pay close attention to ensure that the pulse

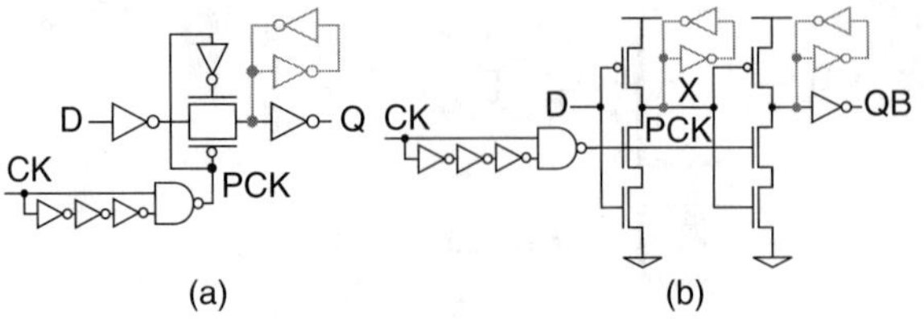

**FIGURE 10.66**   Pulsed latches.

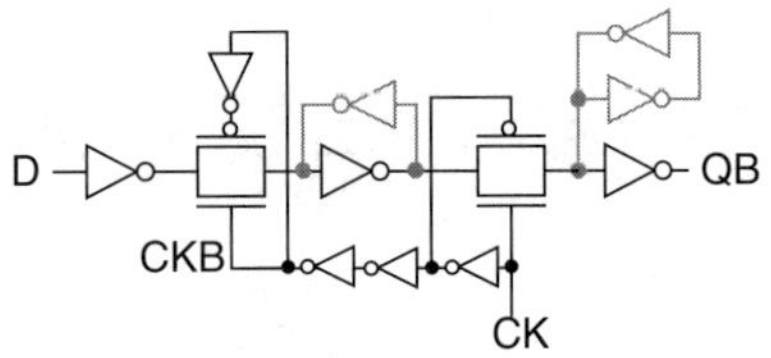

**FIGURE 10.67**   A pulsed latch built from transmission gates with embedded pulse generation circuitry.

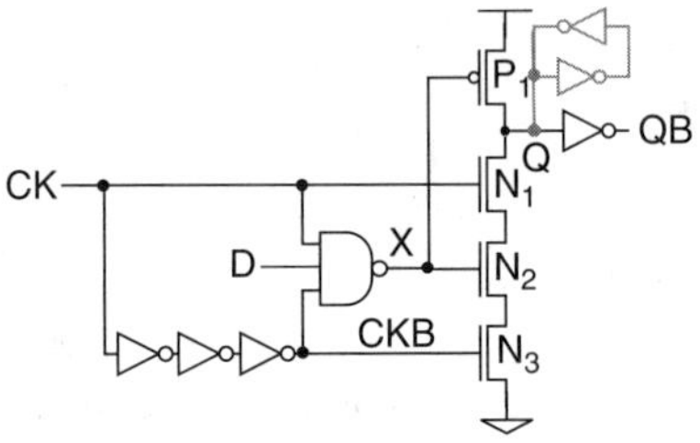

**FIGURE 10.68**   Hybrid latch flip-flop (HLFF).

width is long enough under all process corners and temperature/voltage conditions, so safe operation is guaranteed. On the other hand, a pulse that is too wide might create too many min-timing problems (see Eq. (10.4)). This suggests that the usage of pulsed latches should be limited to the most critical paths of the circuit.

### Pulsed Latch with Embedded Pulse Generation

A different approach to building pulsed latches is to embed the pulse generation within the latch itself. A circuit based on this idea is depicted in Fig. 10.67. It resembles the flip-flop of Fig. 10.60, with the exception that the second transmission gate is operated with a delayed CKB. In this way, both transmission gates are transparent simultaneously for the length of three inverter delays. The structure of Fig. 10.67 has longer *D-to-Q* delay compared to the pulsed latch of Fig. 10.66(a); however, this implementation gives designers a more precise control over the pulse width, resulting in slightly better hold time and more robustness. Compared with the usage of the circuit as a master slave flip-flop, this latch allows partial or total clock skew hiding, therefore, its pipeline overhead is reduced.

The hybrid latch flip-flop (HLFF) reported in [21] is based on the idea of merging a pulse generator with a TSPC latch (see Fig. 10.66(b)). The proposed circuit is shown in Fig. 10.68. The design converts the first stage into a fully complementary static NAND3 gate, preventing node $X$ from floating. The circuit operates as follows. When CK is low, node $X$ is precharged high. Transistors $N_1$ and $P_1$ are both off, so $Q$ holds its previous value. When CK switches low-to-high, node $X$ remains high if $D$ is low, or gets discharged to ground if $D$ is high. If $X$ transitions high-to-low, node $Q$ gets pulled high. Otherwise, it gets pulled down. After three inverter delays, node $X$ is pulled back high while $N_3$ is turned off, preventing $Q$ from losing its value. The NAND3 pull-down path and the $N_1 - N_3$ pull-down path are

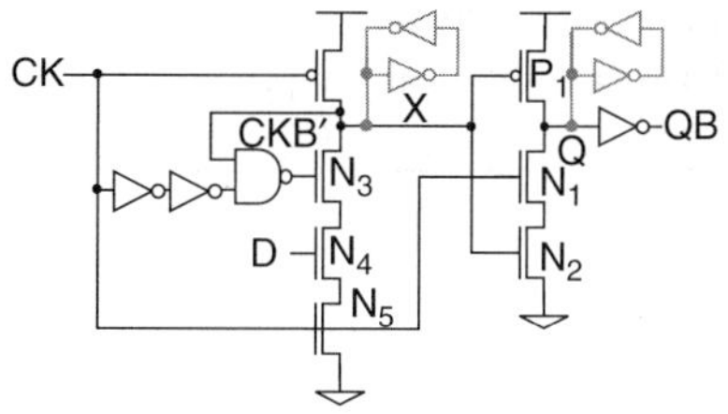

**FIGURE 10.69** Semi-dynamic flip-flop (SDFF).

both transparent for three inverter delays. This must allow node $X$ or node $Q$ to be fully discharged. If input $D$ switches high-to-low after CK goes high, but before CKB goes low (during the transparent period of the latch), node $X$ can be still pulled back high allowing node $Q$ to discharge. A change in $D$ after the transparent period has no effect on the circuit. To allow transparency and keep the *D-to-Q* delay balanced, all three stages of the latch should be designed to have balanced rise and fall delays. If the circuit is used instead as a flip-flop as opposed to a pulsed latch (i.e., not allowing $D$ to switch during the transparent period), then the *D-to-Q* latency can be reduced by skewing the logic in one direction.

A drawback of HLFF being used as a pulsed latch is that it generates glitches. Because node $X$ is precharged high, a low-to-high glitch is generated on $Q$ if $D$ switches high-to-low during the transparent period. Instead, a high-to-low glitch is generated on $Q$ if $D$ switches low-to-high during the transparent period. Glitches, when allowed to propagate through the logic, create unnecessary toggling, which results in increased dynamic power consumption.

The semi-dynamic flip-flop of Fig. 10.69 (SDFF), originally reported in [22] and used in [23], is based on a similar concept (here the term "dynamic" refers to "precharged" as defined in this context). It merges a pulse generator with a *precharged* TSPC latch instead of a static one. A similar design, but using an external pulse generator, is reported in [24]. Although built from a pulse generator and a latch, SDFF does not operate strictly as a pulsed latch. The first stage is precharged, so the input is not allowed to change during the transparent period anymore. Therefore, the circuit behaves as an edge-triggered flip-flop (it is included in this subsection because of its similar topology with other pulsed designs). The circuit operates as follows. When CK is low, node $X$ is precharged high, turning $P_1$ off. Since $N_1$ is also off, node $Q$ holds its previous value. Transistor $N_3$ is on during this period. When CK switches low-to-high, depending on the value of $D$, node $X$ remains either high or discharges to ground, driving $Q$ to a new value. If $X$ remains high, CKB' switches high-to-low after three gate delays, turning off $N_3$. Further changes in $D$ after this point have no effect on the circuit until the next clock cycle. If $X$ discharges to ground instead, the NAND2 gate forces CKB' to remain high, so the pull-down path $N_3 - N_5$ remains on. Changes in $D$ cannot affect $X$, which has discharged already. This feature is called *conditional shut-off* and it is added to reduce the effective width of the pulse without compromising the design safety. Having the characteristics of a flip-flop, the circuit does not allow time borrowing or clock skew hiding; however, by being precharged, transistors can be skewed resulting in a very short *D-to-Q* delay. Another major advantage of this design is that complex logic functions can be embedded in the precharge stage, which is similar to a Domino gate. Typical logic include NAND/NOR, XOR/XNOR, and AND-OR functions [25]. The merging of a complex logic stage, at the expense of a slight increase in *D-to-Q* delay, contributes to reducing the pipeline overhead of the design.

## Performance Analysis

This subsection attempts to provide a performance comparison of the diverse latching and flip-flop structures described in the previous sections. Because transistor sizing can be chosen to optimize delay, area, power, or power-delay product, and different fanout rules can be applied in the optimization process, a fair performance comparison based on actual transistor sizing and SPICE simulation results is not trivial. The method adopted here is similar to counting transistors in the critical paths, but it does so by breaking the circuit into source-drain interconnected regions. Each subcircuit is identified and a delay number is

**TABLE 10.7**  Normalized Speed (FO4 Inverter Delay) of Complementary and Skewed Logic, Where *Top* Refers to Device Next to Output, and *Bottom* to Device Next to $V_{DD}$ or GND

| Stack Depth | Input | Complementary Logic | | Skewed Logic | |
|---|---|---|---|---|---|
| | | NMOS | PMOS | NMOS | PMOS |
| 1 | Top | 1.00 | 1.20 | 0.50 | 0.60 |
| 2 | Top | 1.15 | 1.40 | 0.60 | 0.70 |
| | Bottom | 1.30 | 1.55 | 0.70 | 0.85 |
| 3 | Top | 1.30 | 1.55 | 0.70 | 0.85 |
| | Middle | 1.50 | 1.80 | 0.80 | 0.95 |
| | Bottom | 1.75 | 2.10 | 0.95 | 1.15 |

**TABLE 10.8**  Timing Characteristics, Normalized to FO4 Inverter Delay, for Various Latches and Flip-Flops

| Latch/Flip-Flop Design | Max D-to-Q | Min CK-to-Q | Hold Time | Pipeline Overhead (%) | Min Delay |
|---|---|---|---|---|---|
| Dual trans. gate latch w/o input buffer (Fig. 10.53(d)) | 1.50 | 1.75 | 0.75 | 15 | 0.00 |
| Dual trans. gate latch w/ input buffer (Fig. 10.53(e)) | 2.55 | 1.75 | −0.25 | 25.5 | −1.00 |
| Dual C$^2$MOS latch (Fig. 10.55(b)) | 2.55 | 1.75 | 0.75 | 25.5 | 0.00 |
| Dual TSPC latch (Fig. 10.56(b) and Fig. 10.56(d)) | 3.70 | 1.75 | 0.25 | 37 | 0.50 |
| Master-slave flip-flop w/ input buffer (Fig. 10.60) | 4.90 | 1.75 | −0.25 | 34.5 | −1.00 |
| Master-slave flip-flop w/o input buffer (not shown) | 3.70 | 1.75 | 0.75 | 28.5 | 0.00 |
| C$^2$MOS flip-flop (Fig. 10.61) | 3.90 | 1.75 | 0.75 | 29.5 | 0.00 |
| TSPC flip-flop (Fig. 10.62) | 3.85 | 1.75 | −0.05 | 29.2 | −0.80 |
| Sense-amplifier flip-flop (Fig. 10.63) | 3.90 | 1.55 | 1.40 | 29.5 | 0.85 |
| HLFF used as flip-flop (Fig. 10.68) | 2.90 | 1.75 | 1.95 | 24.5 | 1.20 |
| SDFF (Fig. 10.69) | 2.55 | 1.75 | 2.00 | 22.7 | 1.25 |
| Pulsed trans. gate latch (Fig. 10.66(a)) | 2.55 | 1.75 | 3.70 | 12.7 | 2.95 |
| Pulsed C$^2$MOS latch (not shown) | 2.55 | 1.75 | 3.70 | 12.7 | 2.95 |
| Pulsed transmission-gate flip-flop (Fig. 10.67) | 3.90 | 1.75 | 1.30 | 20.2 | 0.55 |
| HLFF used as pulsed latch (Fig. 10.68) | 3.90 | 1.75 | 1.95 | 19.5 | 1.20 |

*Note:*  The clock cycle is 20 FO4 inverter delays. Clock skew is 10% of the clock cycle for max-timing, and 5% (1 FO4 delay) for min-timing.

assigned, based on the subcircuit topology and the relative position of the driving transistor in the stack. The result, which is rather a measure of the logical effort of the design, reflects to a first order the actual speed of the circuit. Table 10.7 shows the three topologies used to match subcircuits. It corresponds to a single-, double-, and triple-transistor stack. Each transistor in the stack is assigned a propagation delay normalized to a FO4 inverter delay, with increasing delays toward the bottom of the stack (closest to $V_{DD}$ or $V_{SS}$). The table provide NMOS versus PMOS delay (PMOS stacks are 20% slower) and also skewed versus complementary static logic. Details on the delay computation for each design is provided in the "Appendix."

Table 10.8 provides a summary of the timing characteristics for most of the flip-flops and latches studied in this chapter section. The clocking scheme for latches is assumed to be complementary dual-phase. Values are normalized to a FO4 inverter delay, unless otherwise indicated. The first column is the maximum *D-to-Q* delay and is the value used to compute the pipeline overhead. The second and third column contain the minimum *CK-to-Q* delay and the hold time, respectively. The fourth column represents the overall pipeline overhead, which is determined according to Table 10.6. This establishes whether the latch delay is paid once or twice or whether the clock skew is added or not to the pipeline overhead. The overhead is expressed as a percentage of the cycle time, assuming that the cycle is 20 FO4 inverter delays, and that the clock skew is 10% of the cycle time. The fifth column represents the minimum propagation delay between latches, or between flip-flops, required to avoid min-timing problems. It is computed according to Table 10.6, and assuming that the clock skew is 5% of the cycle time. A smaller clock skew is assumed for min-timing because the PLL jitter, a significant component in max-timing, is not part of the clock skew in this case. From a max-timing perspective, Table 10.8 shows that pulsed latches have the minimum pipeline overhead, the winner being the pulsed transmission gate. The unbuffered transmission gate latch is a close second. But as pointed out earlier, unbuffered transmission gates are rarely allowed in practice. In the flip-flop group, SDFF is the best, while the buffered master-slave flip-flop is the worst. Merging a logic gate inside the latch or flip-flop may result in additional 5% or more reduction in the pipeline overhead, depending on the relative complexity of the logic function. Precharged designs such as SDFF or the sense-amplifier flip-flop are best suited to incorporate logic efficiently. From a min-timing perspective, pulsed latches with externally generated pulses are the worst, while the buffered master-slave flip-flop is the best. If the pulse is embedded in the circuit (like in SDFF or HLFF), min-timing requirements are more relaxed. It should be noticed that because of manufacturing tolerances, the minimum delay requirement is usually larger than what Table 10.8 (fifth column) suggests. One or two additional gate delays is in general sufficient to provide enough margin to the design.

Although pulsed latches are the best for max-timing, designers must keep in mind that max-timing is not the only criterion used when selecting a latching style. The longer hold time of pulsed latches may result in too many race conditions, forcing designers to spend a great deal of time in min-timing verification and min-timing fixing, which could otherwise be devoted to max-timing optimization. Ease of timing verification is also of great importance, especially in an industry where a simple and easily understood methodology translates into shorter design cycles. With the advancement of design automation, min-timing fixing (i.e., buffer insertion) should not be a big obstacle to using pulsed latches. Finally, notice that the selection of a latching technique can affect the cycle time of a design by 10–20%. It is important that designers look into all design trade-offs discussed throughout this chapter section in making the right selection of the latching scheme.

For a similar analysis of some of the designs included in this section but based on actual transistor sizing and SPICE simulation, including a power-delay analysis, the reader is referred to [26].

## Scan Chain Design

The previous sub-section covered the design of latches and flip-flops and presented a performance analysis of each of the circuits. In practice, however, these circuits are rarely implemented as shown. This is because in many cases, to improve testability, a widely accepted practice is to add scan circuitry to the design. The addition of scan circuitry alters both the circuit topology and the performance of the design. The design of scannable latches and flip-flops is the subject of this sub-section.

As mentioned previously, a widely accepted industrial practice to efficiently test and debug sequential circuits is the use of scan design techniques. In a scan-based design, some or all of the latches or flip-flops in a circuit are linked into a single or multiple scan chains. This allows data to be serially shifted into and out of the scan chain, greatly enhancing controllability and observability of internal nodes in the design. After the circuit has been tested, the scan mechanism is disabled and the latches of flip-flops operate independently of one another. So a scannable latch or flip-flop must operate in two modes: a *scan mode*, where the circuit samples the scan input, and a *data mode*, where the circuit samples the data input. Conceptually, this may be implemented as a 2:1 multiplexor inserted in the front of the latch, as suggested in Fig. 10.70. A control signal SE selects the scan input if asserted (i.e., scan mode) or the data input otherwise.

**FIGURE 10.70** A scannable latch.

A straightforward implementation of the scan design of Fig. 10.70 consists of adding, or merging, a 2-to-1 multiplexor to the latch. Unfortunately, this would result in higher pipelining overhead because of the additional multiplexor delay, even when the circuit operates in data mode, or would limit the embedding of additional logic. It becomes apparent that a scan design should affect as little as possible the timing characteristic of the latch or flip-flop when in data mode, specifically its latency and hold time. In addition, it is imperative that the scan design be robust. A defective scan chain will prevent data

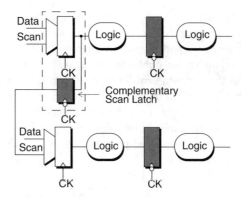

**FIGURE 10.71**   Scan chain for dual-phase, latch-based design.

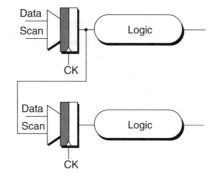

**FIGURE 10.72**   Scan chain for flip-flop-based design.

from being properly shifted through the chain and, therefore, invalidate the testing of some parts of the circuit. Finally, at current integration levels, chips with huge number of latches or flip-flops (>100 K) will become common in the near future. Therefore, a scan design should attempt to maintain the area and power overhead of the basic latch design at a minimum. The remainder of this section describes how to incorporate scan into the latches and flip-flops presented earlier.

Figure 10.71 shows a scan chain in a dual-phase, latch-based design. In such design, a common practice is to link only the latches on one phase of the clock. In order to prevent min-timing problems, the scan chain typically includes a complementary latch, as indicated in Fig. 10.71. The complementary latch, although active during scan mode only, adds significant area overhead to the design. Instead, in a flip-flop-based design, the scan chain can be directly linked, as shown in Fig. 10.72.

Similar to any regular signal in a sequential circuit, scan related signals are not exempt from races. To ensure data is shifted properly, min-timing requirements must be satisfied in the scan chain. Max-timing is not an issue because: (1) there is no logic between latches of flip-flops in the scan chain, and (2) the shifting of data may be done at low frequencies during testing.

To minimize the impact on latency, a common practice in scan design is to prevent the *data clock* from toggling during scan mode. The latch storage node gets written through a scan path controlled by a *scan clock*. In data mode, the scan clock is disabled instead and the data clock toggles, allowing the data input to set the value of the storage node. Figure 10.73(a) shows a possible implementation of a scannable transmission gate latch. For clarity, a dotted box surrounds all scan related devices. Either the data clock (DCK) or the scan clock (SCK) are driven low during scan or data mode, respectively. The scan circuit is a master-slave flip-flop, similar to Fig. 10.60, that shares the master storage node with the latch. To ensure scan robustness, the back-to-back inverter of the slave latch is decoupled from its output, and

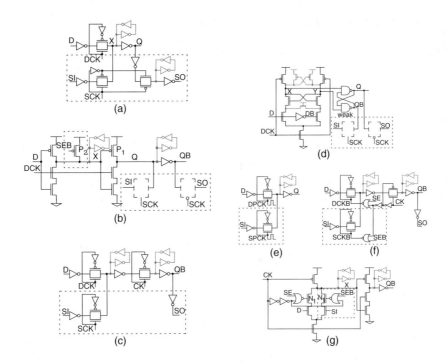

**FIGURE 10.73** Latches and flip-flops with scan circuitry.

both transmission gates are buffered. The circuitry that controls the DCK and SCK is not shown for simplicity. In terms of speed, drain/source and gate loading is added to nodes $X$ and $Q$. This increases delay slightly, although less substantially than adding a full multiplexor at the latch input. A similar approach to the one just described may be used with the TSPC latch, as suggested in Fig. 10.73(b). Since transistor $P_1$ is not guaranteed to be off when DCK is low, transistor $P_2$ is added to pull-up node $X$ during scan mode. Control signal SEB is the complement of SE and is set low during scan operation.

Figure 10.73(c) shows the scannable version of the master-slave flip-flop. This design uses three clocks: CK (free running clock), DCK (data clock), and SCK (scan clock). DCK and SCK, when enabled, are complementary to CK. Under data or scan mode, CK is always toggling. In scan mode, DCK is driven low and SCK is enabled. In data mode, SCK is driven low and DCK is enabled. While this approach minimizes the number of scan related devices, its drawback is the usage of three clocks. One clock may be eliminated at the expense of increased scan complexity. If CK and DCK are made fully complementary, and CK is set low during scan mode (DCK is set high), the same approach used in Fig. 10.73(a) may be used.

Figure 10.73(d) shows a possible implementation of an scannable sense amplifier flip-flop (see Fig. 10.63). In scan mode, DCK is set low forcing nodes $X$ and $Y$ to pull high. The output latch formed by the cross coupled NANDs is driven by the scan flip-flop. To ensure the latch can flip during scan, the NAND gate driving QB must either be weak or be disabled by SCK. Also for robustness, node QB should be kept internal to the circuit.

Figure 10.73(e) shows the scannable version of the transmission gate pulsed latch of Fig. 10.66(a). The circuit requires the generation of two pulses, one for data (DPCK) and one for scan (SPCK). It should be noticed that having pulsed latches in the scan chain might be deemed too risky because of min-timing problems. To make the design more robust, a full scan flip-flop like in Fig. 10.73(a) shall be used instead.

The disabling of the data (or scan) path in a pulsed latch during scan (or data) mode does not require the main clock to be disabled. Instead, the delayed clock phase used in the pulse generation can be disabled. This concept is used in the implementation of scan for the pulsed latch of Fig. 10.67, and it is shown in Fig. 10.73(f). As previously explained, this latch uses embedded pulse generation. Signals SE and SEB, which are complementary, control the mode of operation. In data mode, SE is set to low (SEB high), so SCKB is driven low disabling the scan path, and DCKB is enable. In scan mode, SE is set to high (SEB low), so DCKB is driven low, which disables the data path, and SCKB is enabled. The advantage of this approach is in the simplified clock distribution: only one clock needs be distributed in addition to the necessary scan control signals.

The disabling of the delayed clock is used in SDFF (see Fig. 10.69) to implement scan [27]. The implementation is shown in Fig. 10.73(g). For simplicity, the NAND gate that feeds back from node $X$ is not shown. Control signal SE and SEB determines whether transistor $N_1$ or $N_2$ is enabled, setting the flip-flop into data mode (when $N_1$ is on and $N_2$ is off) or scan mode (when $N_1$ is off and $N_2$ is on). Besides using a single clock, the advantage of this approach is in the small number of scan devices required.

For HLFF (see Fig. 10.68), the same approach cannot be used because node $X$ would be driven high when CKB is low. Instead, an approach similar to Fig. 10.73(b) may be used.

## Historical Perspective and Summary

Timing requirements of latch and flip-flop-based designs were presented. A variety of latches, pulsed latches, flip-flops, and hybrid designs were presented, and analyzed, taking into account max- and min-timing requirements.

Historically, the number of gates per pipeline stage has kept decreasing. This increases the pipeline clock frequency, but does not necessarily translate into higher performance. The pipeline overhead becomes larger as the pipeline stages get shorter. Clock skew, which is becoming more difficult to control as chip integration keeps increasing, is part of the overhead in flip-flop based designs. Instead, latch-based systems can absorb some or all of the clock skew, without affecting the cycle time. If clock skew keeps increasing, as a percentage of the cycle time, at some point in time latch based designs will perform better than flip-flop-based designs.

Clock skew cannot increase too much without affecting the rest of the system. Other circuits such as sense-amplifiers in SRAMs, which operate in blocking mode, get affected by clock skew also. The goal of a design is to improve overall performance, and access to memory is usually critical in pipelined systems. Clock skew has to be controlled also, primarily because of min-timing requirements. While some of it can be absorbed by transparent latches for max-timing, latches are as sensitive as flip-flops to clock skew for min-timing (with the exception of the nonoverlapping dual-phase design). While the global clock skew is most likely to increase as chips get bigger, local skews are not as likely to do so. PLL jitter, which is a component of clock skew for max-timing, may increase or not depending on advancements in PLL design. Because cycle times are getting so short, on-chip signal propagation in the next generation of complex integrated circuits (e.g., system on-chip) will take several clock cycles to traverse from one side of the die to the other, seeing mostly local clock skews along the way. Clocking schemes in such complex chips are becoming increasingly more sophisticated also, with active on-chip de-skewing circuits becoming common practice [28,29].

As for the future, flip-flops will most likely continue to be part of designs. They are easy to use, simple to understand, and timing verification is simple also. Even in the best designs, most paths are not critical and therefore can be tackled with flip-flops. For critical paths, the usage of fast flip-flops, such as SDFF/HLFF will be necessary. Pulsed latches will become more common also, as they can absorb clock skew yet provide smaller overhead than dual-phase latches. A combination of latches and flip-flops will become more common in the future also. In all these scenarios, the evolvement of automated timing tools will be key to verifying such complex designs efficiently and reliably.

## Appendix

A stage-by-stage $D$-to-$Q$ delay analysis of the latches and flip-flops included in Table 10.8 is shown in Fig. 10.74. The values per stage are normalized to a FO4 inverter delay. The delay per stage, which is defined as a source-drain connected stack, is determined by the depth of the stack and the relative position of the switching device, following Table 10.7. The delay per stage is indicated on the top of each circuit, with the total delay on the top high right-hand side. Transmission gates are added to the stack of the

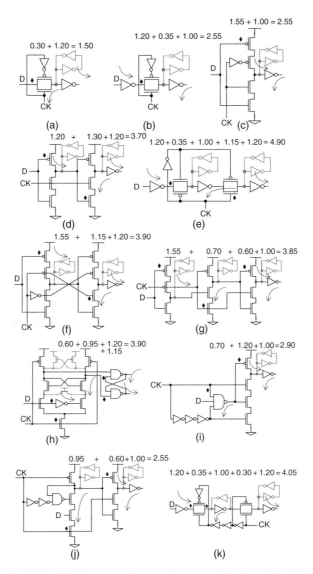

**FIGURE 10.74** Normalized delay (FO4 inverter) of various latches and flip-flops: (a) unbuffered transmission gate latch, (b) buffered transmission gate latch, (c) C²MOS latch, (d) TSPC latch, (e) master-slave flip-flop, (f) C²MOS flip-flop, (g) TSPC flip-flop, (h) sense-amplifier flip-flop, (i) hybrid latch flip-flop, (j) semi-dynamic flip-flop, and (k) pulsed transmission gate flip-flop.

driver to compute delay. For instance, a buffered transmission where CK is switching (Fig. 10.74(b)) is considered as a two-stack structure switching from top. If $D$ switches instead, it is considered as a two-stack structure switching from bottom. For each design, the worst-case switching delay is computed. In cases where the high-to-low and low-to-high delays are unbalanced, further speed optimization could be accomplished by equalizing both delays. A diamond is used to indicate the transistor in the stack that is switching. In estimating the total delay of each design, the following assumptions are made. Precharged stages (e.g., sense-amplifier flip-flop, TSPC flip-flop, SDFF) are skewed and therefore faster (see Table 10.7, skewed logic). Output inverters are complementary static in all cases. The input inverter in the sense-amplifier flip-flop (Fig. 10.74(h)) is skewed, favoring the low-to-high transition, because its speed is critical in that direction only. The SR latch is complementary static. In the case of HLFF (Fig. 10.74(i)), when used as a flip-flop, the NAND3 is skewed favoring the high-to-low transition, while the middle stack is complementary. This is because if the middle stack were skewed, favoring the low-to-high transition, the opposite transition would become critical. When the circuit is used as a transparent latch, all stages are static (i.e., both transitions are balanced). The worst-case transition in this case is opposite to that shown in Fig. 10.74: input $D$ is switching and the total delay is equal to $1.2 + 1.5 + 1.2 = 3.9$. In the case of SDFF (Fig. 10.74(j)), since the middle stack is shorter, both the first stage (precharged) and the middle stack are skewed.

A similar procedure to the one described above is followed to compute the minimum *CK-to-Q* delay. An additional assumption is that the output buffer has FO1 as opposed to FO4 as in max-timing, which results in shorter delay. The normalized FO1 pull-up delay of a buffer is 0.6 (PMOS), and the pull-down is 0.5 (NMOS).

To compute hold time the following assumptions are made. The inverters used in inverting or delaying clock signals, with the exception of external pulse generators (see Fig. 10.65), have FO1, so their delays are those of the previous paragraph. External pulse generators use three FO4 inverters instead (i.e., slower), because in practical designs it is very hard to create a full-rail pulse waveforms with less delay. For transparent-high latches, the hold time is defined as the time from CK switching high-to-low until all shutoff devices are *completely* turned off. To insure the shutoff device is completely off, 50% delay is added to the last clock driver. For instance, the hold time of the transparent-low transmission gate latch is 0.5 (FO1 inverter delay) × 1.5 = 0.75. For a positive edge-triggered flip-flop, the hold time is defined as the time from CK switching low-to-high until all shutoff devices are *completely* turned off. If there is one or more stages before the shutoff device, the corresponding delay is subtracted from the hold time. This is the case of the buffered master-slave flip-flop (Fig. 10.74(e)), which results in a negative hold time. An exception to this definition is the case of HLFF or SDFF. Here, the timing of the shutoff device must allow that the stack gets *fully* discharged. Therefore, the hold time is limited by the stack delay, which is again defined as 1.5 times the stage delay. For instance, for HLFF, the middle stage pull-down delay is 1.3, so the hold time is 1.5 × 1.3 = 1.95. SDFF, instead, has its hold time determined by the timing of the shutoff device because the precharged stage is fast.

# References

1. B. Curran, et al., "A 1.1 GHz first 64 b generation Z900 microprocessor," *ISSCC Digest of Technical Papers,* pp. 238–239, Feb. 2001.
2. G. Lauterbach, et al., "UltraSPARC-III: a 3rd-generation 64 b SPARC microprocessor," *ISSCC Digest of Technical Papers,* pp. 410–411, Feb. 2000.
3. D. Harris, "Skew-Tolerant Circuit Design," Morgan Kaufmann Publishers, San Francisco, CA, 2001.
4. W. Burleson, M. Ciesielski, F. Klass, and W. Liu: "Wave-pipelining: A tutorial and survey of recent research," *IEEE Trans. on VLSI Systems,* Sep. 1998.
5. R. Krambeck, et al., "High-speed compact circuits with CMOS," *IEEE J. Solid-State Circuits,* vol. 17, no. 6, pp. 614–619, June 1982.
6. N. Goncalves and H. Mari, "NORA: are race-free dynamic CMOS technique for pipelined logic structures," *IEEE J. Solid-State Circuits,* vol. 18, no. 6, pp. 261–263, June 1983.
7. J. Silberman, et al., "A 1.0 GHz single-issue 64 b PowerPC Integer Processor," *IEEE J. Solid-State Circuits,* vol. 33, no. 11, pp. 1600–1608, Nov. 1998.
8. T. Thorp, G. Yee, and C. Sechen, "Monotonic CMOS and dual Vt technology," *IEEE International Symposium on Low Power Electronics and Design,* pp. 151–155, June 1999.
9. P. Gronowski and B. Bowhill, "Dynamic logic and latches—part II," *Proc. VLSI Circuits Workshop, Symp. VLSI Circuits,* June 1996.
10. P. Gronowski, et al., "High-performance microprocessor design," *IEEE J. Solid-State Circuits,* vol. 33, no. 5, pp. 676–686, May 1998.
11. C. J. Anderson, et al., "Physical design of a fourth generation POWER GHz microprocessor," *ISSCC Digest of Technical Papers,* pp. 232–233, Feb. 2001.

12. M. Pedram, Q. Wu, and X. Wu, "A new design of double edge-triggered flip-flops," *Proc. of ASP-DAC*, pp. 417–421, 1998.

13. J. Yuan and C. Svensson, "High-speed CMOS circuit technique," *IEEE J. Solid-State Circuits*, vol. 24, no. 1, pp. 62–70, Feb. 1989.

14. Y. Ji-Ren, I. Karlsson, and C. Svensson, "A true single-phase-clock dynamic CMOS circuit technique," *IEEE J. Solid-State Circuits*, vol. SC-22, no. 5, pp. 899–901, Oct. 1987.

15. D. W. Dobberpuhl, et al., "A 200 MHz 64-b dual-issue CMOS microprocessor," *IEEE J. Solid-State Circuits*, vol. 27, no. 11, pp. 1555–1565, Nov. 1992.

16. G. Gerosa, et al., "A 2.2 W, 80 MHz superscalar RISC microprocessor," *IEEE J. Solid-State Circuits*, vol. 90, no. 12, pp. 1440–1452, Dec. 1994.

17. J. Montanaro, et al., "A 160 MHz 32 b 0.5 W CMOS RISC microprocessor," *ISSCC Digest of Technical Papers*, pp. 214–215, Feb. 1996.

18. S. Kozu, et al., "A 100 MHz, 0.4 W RISC processor with 200 MHz multiply-adder, using pulse-register technique," *ISSCC Digest of Technical Papers*, pp. 140–141, Feb. 1996.

19. A. Shibayama, et al., "Device-deviation-tolerant over-1 GHz clock-distribution scheme with skew-immune race-free impulse latch circuits," *ISSCC Digest of Technical Papers*, pp. 402–403, Feb. 1998.

20. L. T. Clark, E. Hoffman, M. Schaecher, M. Biyani, D. Roberts, and Y. Liao, "A scalable performance 32 b microprocessor," *ISSCC Digest of Technical Papers*, pp. 230–231, Feb. 2001.

21. H. Partovi, et al., "Flow-through latch and edge-triggered flip-flop hybrid elements," *ISSCC Digest of Technical Papers*, pp. 138–139, Feb. 1996.

22. F. Klass, "Semi-dynamic and dynamic flip-flops with embedded logic," *Symp. VLSI Circuits Digest of Technical Papers*, pp. 108–109, June 1998.

23. R. Heald, et al., "Implementation of a 3rd-generation SPARC V9 64 b microprocessor," *ISSCC Digest of Technical Papers*, pp. 412–413, Feb. 2000.

24. A. Scherer, et al., "An out-of-order three-way superscalar multimedia floating-point unit," *ISSCC Digest of Technical Papers*, pp. 94–95, Feb. 1999.

25. F. Klass, C. Amir, A. Das, K. Aingaran, C. Truong, R. Wang, A. Mehta, R. Heald, and G. Yee, "A new family of semi-dynamic and dynamic flip-flops with embedded logic for high-performance processors," *IEEE J. Solid-State Circuits*, vol. 34, no. 5, pp. 712–716, May 1999.

26. V. Stojanovic and V. Oklobdzija "Comparative analysis of master-slave latches and flip-flops for high-performance and low power systems," *IEEE J. Solid-State Circuits*, vol. 34, no. 4, pp. 536–548, April 1999.

27. Sun Microsystems, *Edge-triggered staticized dynamic flip-flop with scan circuitry*, U.S. Patent #5,898,330, April 27, 1999.

28. T. Xanthopoulos, et al., "The design and analysis of the clock distribution network for a 1.2 GHz Alpha microprocessor," *ISSCC Digest of Technical Papers*, pp. 402–403, Feb. 2001.

29. N. Kurd, et al., "Multi-GHz clocking scheme for Intel Pentium 4 microprocessor," *ISSCC Digest of Technical Papers*, pp. 404–405, Feb. 2001.

## 10.3  High-Performance Embedded SRAM

*Cyrus (Morteza) Afghahi*

### Introduction

Systems on-chip (SoC) are integrating more and more functional blocks. Current trend is to integrate as much memories as possible to reduce cost, decrease power consumption, and increase bandwidth. Embedded memories are the most widely used functional block in SoC. A unified technology for the memory and logic brings about new applications and new mode of operations. A significant part of almost all applications such as networking, multimedia, consumer, and computer peripheral products is memory. This is the second wave of memory integration. Networking application is leading this second

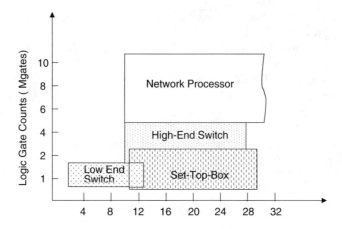

**FIGURE 10.75**   Integrated memory for some networking products (Mbit).

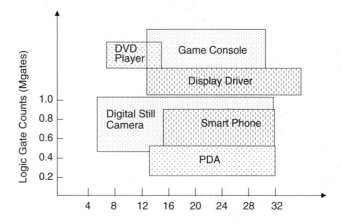

**FIGURE 10.76**   Integrated memory for some consumer products (Mbit).

wave of memory integration due to bandwidth and density requirements. Very high system contribution by this adoption continues to slow other solutions like ASIC with separated memories.

Integrating more memories extends the SoC applications and makes total system solutions more cost effective. Figure 10.75 shows a profile of integrated memory requirements for some networking applications. Figure 10.76 shows the same profile for some consumer product applications.

To cover memory requirements for these applications, tens of megabits memory storage cells needs to be integrated on a chip. In 0.18 $\mu$m process technology, 1 Mbits SRAM occupies around 6 mm$^2$. The area taken by integrating 32 Mbits memory in 0.18 $\mu$m, for example, alone will be ~200 mm$^2$. Adding logic gates to the memory results in very big chips. That is why architect of these applications are pushing for more dense technologies (0.13 $\mu$m and beyond) and/or other memory storage cell circuits.

In pursuing higher density, three main alternatives are usually considered, dense SRAM, embedded DRAM (eDRAM), and more logic compatible DRAM. We call this last alternative 2T-DRAM for the reason that soon becomes clear.

The first memory cell consists of two cross-couple inverters forming a static flip-flop equipped with two access transistors, see Fig. 10.77(a). This cell is known as 6T static RAM (SRAM) cell. Many other cells are derived from this cell by reducing the number of circuit elements to achieve higher density and bits per unit area. The one transistor cell (1T)-based dynamic memory, Fig. 10.77(b), is the simplest and also the most complex of all memories. To increase the cell density 1T-DRAM cell fabrication technology

**TABLE 10.9**  Comparison of Three Memory Cell Candidates for Embedded Application

|  | 1T-DRAM | 2T-DRAM | SRAM |
|---|---|---|---|
| Area | 1 | 3X | 5X |
| Active power | Low | Low | High |
| Standby power | High | High | Low |
| Speed | Low | Low | High |
| Yield | Low | Moderate | High |

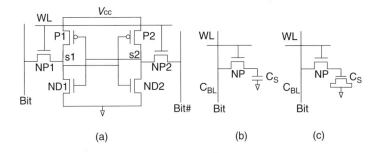

(a)   (b)   (c)

**FIGURE 10.77**  Cell circuits considered for embedded memory.

has become more and more specialized. As a consequence, adaptation of 1T-DRAM technology with mainstream logic CMOS technology is decreasing with each new generation. Logic CMOS are available earlier than technologies with embedded 1T-DRAM. 1T-DRAM is also slow for most applications and has a high standby current. For these and other reasons market for chips with embedded 1T-DRAM has shrunk and is limited to those markets, which have already adopted the technology. Major foundries have stopped their embedded 1T-DRAM developments. Another memory cell that has recently received attention for high density embedded memory uses a real MOS transistor as the storage capacitor, Fig. 10.77(c). This cell was also used in the first generation stand alone DRAM (up to 16 kbit). This cell is more compatible with logic process. Thus, availability will be earlier than 1T-DRAM, it is more flexible and can be used in many applications. This volume leverage helps in yield improvements and support from logic technology development.

Table 10.9 compares main performance parameters for these three embedded memory solutions. 2T-DRAM needs continuous refreshing to maintain the stored signal. This is a major contributor to the high 2T-DRAM standby power. SRAM and 2T-DRAM also differ in the way they scale with technology. To see this, consider again the Fig. 10.77.

The following equation summarizes the design criteria for a 2T-cell:

$$\Delta V + V_n = C_s V_s / 2(C_s + C_{BL}) \tag{10.25}$$

where $\Delta V$ is the minimum required voltage for reliable sensing (~100 mV); $V_n$ is the total noise due to different leakage, voltage drop, and charge transfer efficiency; $C_s$ is the storage capacitance; $C_{BL}$ is the total bit line capacitance; and $V_s$ is the voltage on the $C_s$ when a "1" is stored in the cell, $V_{cc} - V_{tn}$. Now the effect of process development on each parameter will be examined. $V_n$ includes sub-threshold current, gate leakage, which is becoming significant in 0.13 $\mu$m and beyond, the charge transfer efficiency, and voltage noises on the voltage supply. All these components degrade from one process generation to another. $V_s$ also scales down with technology improvements. We assume that $C_s$ and $C_{BL}$ scale in the same way. Then for a fixed $\Delta V$, for each new process generation, fewer numbers of cells must be connected to the bit line. This will decrease memory density and increase power consumption.

For SRAM the following equation may be used to study the effect of technology scaling:

$$\Delta V = (I_{sat} / C_{BL}) T \tag{10.26}$$

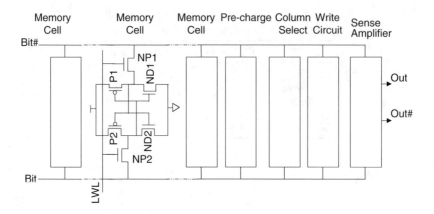

**FIGURE 10.78**    A basic column in a memory array.

New process generations are designed such that the current per unit width of transistor does not change significantly. So, although scaling reduces the size of the driving transistor $ND_1$, $I_{sat}$ remains almost the same. $C_{BL}$ consists mainly of two components, metal line capacitance and diffusion contact capacitance. Contact capacitance does not scale linearly with each process generation, but the metal bit lines scale due to smaller cell. This applies to Eq. (10.25) as well. To get the same access time, the number of cells connected to a column must be reduced. However, this trend is much more drastic for 2T-DRAM because $\Box V$ is proportional to $V_s$. For example, in a typical 0.18 $\mu$m technology to achieve access time <10 ns, the number of cells in a SRAM column is 256–512, while it is only 32 for 2T-DRAM. In 0.13 $\mu$m these numbers are reduced much slower for SRAM than for 2T-DRAM. Other factors like testing, experience and ease of design, standby current, soft error rate, foundry support, etc. are in favor of SRAM. For these reasons we concentrate on SRAM design.

## Embedded SRAM Design

To achieve high access and cycle time, low power and better noise immunity SRAM design is normally applied. To get the same speed and power performance, SRAM also results in more pact memory than 2T-DRAM. In this section we start with studying circuits involved in a column of memory cells. A memory column is used to build a memory array. Then we study the peripheral circuits for a memory array. Then techniques used to design a high-capacity memory with memory arrays will be presented. Embedded memories have different failure and testing requirements than commodity memories. Finally, these requirements and some techniques to increase yield will be discussed.

### A Memory Cell Column

Figure 10.78 shows the basic column of a SRAM memory array. For high-speed memory in 0.18 $\mu$m technology, usually 128–256 cells are hooked to Bit and Bit# lines. More memory cell per column improves the area efficiency of the memory. Area efficiency is the ratio of the cell array to the total array area.

#### *Memory Cell*
The SRAM memory cell is a cross-coupled CMOS inverter pair. The read and write to the cell is through N-pass transistors ($NP_1$ and $NP_2$). The absolute and relative sizes of the transistors in the cell must satisfy different, mostly conflicting, requirements. The general goal is to keep the transistors as small as possible to achieve high density. This may then conflict with high-speed requirements and radiation hardness. To explain the design guidelines in selecting the transistor sizes, write and read operations are presented briefly. Later these operations are presented in more details.

To write a data into the cell, Bit and Bit# are driven to the data and its complement. Then the LWL is activated for the selected row. The access transistors $NP_1$, $NP_2$ and the write drivers must be able to

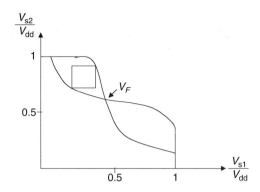

**FIGURE 10.79** Static noise margin of the memory cell.

provide sufficient current to flip the cell and latch the new data. Since access transistor is a single N-pass transistor, the bit line (Bit or Bit#), which is a logic "0", is most effective in the write (and read) operation. Inside the cell the logic "1" must be restore by the P-transistors. During read, Bit and Bit# are first pre-charged to "1" then the LWL is activated again for the selected row. Depending on the data stored in the cell, $ND_1$ (or $ND_2$) will pull the bit line down. The read operation must not destroy the stored data.

The NP transistor must be sized correctly with respect to driving ND transistor and restoring P-transistor. During the write a logic "0" on the bit line must be able to flip the cell. This means that NP transistor must be large enough to overcome the P-transistor. This transistor must also be large enough to decay the bit line for a fast read time; however, its size with respect to driver transistor $ND_1$ ($ND_2$) must be small enough such that during a read the internal node holding a "0" does not rise sufficiently to flip the cell. Other considerations, like sub-threshold leakage and glitches during a LWL transition, suggest to keep this transistor small.

The ND transistor drives the bit line down during a read. Since the bit line capacitance is high, for high-speed read this transistor must be large. Also it must be large enough to maintain the logic "0" in the cell while pulling down the pre-charged bit line during a read. However, to have some write margin this transistor must not be too large. When writing a "0" to one side of the memory cell (for example, $S_1$), the $ND_2$ transistor is fighting to maintain the old value. A large ND size requires the bit line to be pulled too close to $V_{ss}$. This limits the write margin. A large ND size also increases the standby current of the memory.

The restoring P-transistor pull up the high side of the cell to a logic "1" and maintain it at that level. Since the P-transistor only drives the internal cell nodes, it could be small. Smaller P-transistor also reduces the sub-threshold current. However, the P-transistor must be large enough to quickly restore a partially logic "1" written through N-pass transistor to a full level. Otherwise a read immediately following a write may not meet the access time. The P-transistor must also be large enough to reduce soft error rate.

These conflicting requirements on the absolute and relative size of transistors in the cell are summarized in a graphical analysis of the transfer curve of the memory latch, Fig. 10.79. To set up this graph, normalized transfer function of the inverter in the cell is overlapped with its mirror curve. The maximum square that fits these two characteristics defines the noise margin for read and write. This square is also an indication of the cell stability. This graph must be analyzed across the voltage, temperature, and process variations. In the next section some guidelines are given for these simulations.

### Memory Cell Stability and Noise Margin Analysis

Some parameters of a transistor are subject to variations during fabrication. These variations can be lumped and modeled in the transistor length and threshold. Figure 10.80(a) shows an ideal transistor that has a width of $W$ and length $L$. In a typical process, the transistor threshold voltage is $V_t$. A weak transistor is modeled by increasing the $L$ and threshold by $\Delta L$ and $\Delta V_t$, respectively. $\Delta V_t$ must be represented by a correct battery polarity in the schematic. A strong transistor is modeled by decreasing the $L$ and threshold by $\Delta L$ and $\Delta V_t$.

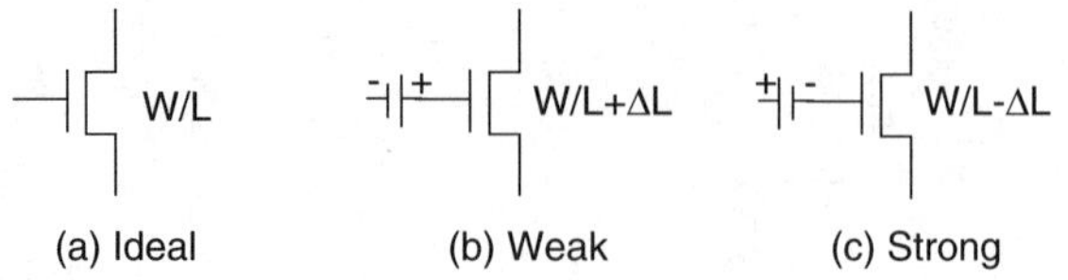

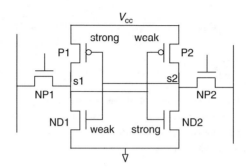

**FIGURE 10.80**   Modeling process variations in schematic.

**FIGURE 10.81**   Schematic model to simulate stability, read and write noise margin.

To estimate $\Delta L$ and $\Delta V_t$, use the 3-sigma figures for the specific process. These figures are usually obtainable from the process foundry. For example, in a typical 0.18 $\mu$m technology, 3-sigma for $L$ and $V_t$ are $\pm 0.01$ $\mu$m and $\pm 20$ mV. If 1 Mb memory is embedded in a die and you allow 1/1000 die to fail, the failure rate is 1E-9. This corresponds to 6.1-sigma. $\Delta V_t$ will be 40.6 mV. This mismatching is between two supposedly matched transistors in the same circuits. All $N$ and/or $P$ transistors on a die may shift from their typical characteristics to slower or faster corners. When simulating a circuit, all combination of process corners must be considered for the worst case.

The schematic model shown in Fig. 10.81 is used to study the memory cell stability, read and write margins. To initialize the cell, write a data into the cell and turn the word line (LWL) low. Then ramp the $V_{cc}$ from, say, $V_{cc} - 0.25V_{cc}$ to $V_{cc} + 0.25V_{cc}$. If the cell changes state, it is not stable. The lower and upper $V_{cc}$ levels used in this test are application dependent. For upper level the burn-in voltage may be used. This simulation must be carried out in all process corners. To improve stability, increase the width of the ND or/and decrease the width of the pass transistor.

A read operation starts with pre-charging the bit lines. During this phase no word line (LWL) is selected. Then a row will be selected for read. This will cause a charge sharing between the bit line and the low side of the cell. The memory cell read margin determines how far the upset side of the cell is from corrupting the stored data. To replicate a read operation, a current source is ramped up on the low side of the cell. The voltage at which the cell is flipped is called the trip point of the cell. The read margin is the trip point voltage minus 5–10% of $V_{cc}$. The percentage depends on the memory environment. This simulation must be carried out in all process corners. For good noise immunity, the read margin needs to be between 5–10% of $V_{cc}$. The same measures used to improve cell stability can also be used to improve the read noise margin.

As in the read operation a write also starts with pre-charging the bit lines. Then a row is selected and the bit line to write a "0" is driven low by the write circuitry. The write operation must be finished in a pre-specified time. The write margin is an indication of the write driver strength in writing an opposite data into a cell. For this purpose a transient simulation of the write driver, bit line, and a cell under test is required. A weak transistor must be used for the pass transistor (NP). Then the write margin is the trip point voltage (measured in the read operation) minus the bit line voltage at the end of the write period. For a good noise margin the write margin must be ~10% $V_{cc}$. Again, simulation must be carried

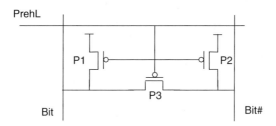

**FIGURE 10.82**   Bit-line, pre-charge circuit.

out in all process corners. To improve the write noise margin the write driver strength or/and the width of the pass transistor can be increased.

### Bit Line Pre-Charge Circuit

As mentioned earlier pre-charging precedes the read and write operations. If the write circuit drives both bit lines to full "0" and "1" logical level, pre-charging the bit lines before the write is not necessary; however, pre-charging the bit lines prior to write makes the write time more predictable and the write circuit less complex. Figure 10.82 shows a pre-charge circuit. P transistors pre-charge the bit lines to full $V_{cc}$. Static sense amplifiers used in some designs for read operation have very low gain at $V_{cc}$. In these designs either $N$ transistors is used to pre-charge the bit lines or level shifter is used to lower the voltage at the sense amplifier circuit. Using $N$ transistor results in unpredictable pre-charged level and variable read time. If a column is not selected for a long time, $N$ transistor leakage gradually raises the pre-charge level closer to $V_{cc}$.

The $P_1$ and $P_2$ transistors must be large enough to pre-charge the bit lines in the available time. But they must not be larger than required due to excessive gate to drain capacitance coupling and charge injection into the bit lines. $P_3$ is used to equalize the bit lines. Equalization is particularly important after a write as one of the bit lines is driven to "0". Any voltage mismatch between bit lines will reduce the read margin and slows down the read time if a static sense amplifier is used. In case of a sense amplifier with positive feedback, bit line voltage mismatch can cause wrong result.

### Column Select Circuit

The next element in the memory column to be considered is the column select circuit. In embedded applications, the number of bits per word can vary from as low as 3 bits to 512 or even higher. Column multiplexing gives some flexibility to handle this wide range of requirements. Multiplexing can vary from 1:1 to 1:32 or higher. Narrower multiplexing (1:1) creates difficulties in layout as the sense amplifier and write circuits must fit in a cell pitch. When the word is short, narrow multiplexing results in low memory area efficient. Wide multiplexing creates difficulties in matching Bit and Bit# lines. 1:4 and 1:8 are the usual ratio used.

In many designs read and write multiplexing are separated. This may be due to some system requirements. Figure 10.83 shows a 2:1 multiplexing with separated read/write column selects. In this circuit a single $N$ pass transistor is used for read select and a single P pass transistor is used for read. This circuit exploit the fact that the "0" is the most active in the write operation and pre-charge circuit have already charged the bit lines to "1". One must make sure that the "1" is not decayed below $V_{cc} - V_{tn}$ due to coupling, sub-threshold currents of nonselected memory cells in the column, and the charge sharing with the selected memory cell. During a read operation the bit line decays only a fraction of $V_{cc}$ (say ~100 mV). Thus, a single P transistor, instead of complementary gates, will be sufficient to transfer the bit line value to the sense amplifier input. In the Fig. 10.83 a simple write circuit is also shown. In more complex write circuit, explained later, the single multiplexing $N$ pass transistor should be replaced with a complementary transmission gate to pass both "0" and "1." It is also possible to use the same column select for both read and write. In this case the write circuit must be tri-stated during the read operation. In some systems, it is required to write or read only a part of a word. In these cases masking or two levels of decoding is may be used.

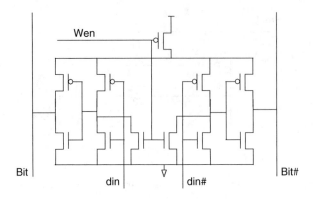

**FIGURE 10.83**  A column circuit.

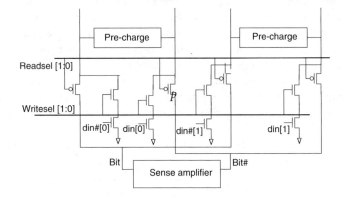

**FIGURE 10.84**  A write circuit.

### Write Circuit

In the previous sub-section, a simple and fast circuit was presented. The write *N* transistor (and write select transistor) are large enough to drive the highly capacitive bit line down and overcome the P pull-up transistor inside the memory cell in the available write time. In that circuit the bit line is not driven to "1". This is because the bit line can not write a "1" to the memory cell and the bit line is already pre-charged to "1". To make sure that the bit line maintains the pre-charge value or if the pre-charge is not complete prior to write, to save time, the write circuit must drive the "1" side also. Figure 10.84 is a more complex write circuit that has only one *N* transistor (in series with the *N* column select transistor) and drives the high side as well. During the read cycle, this circuit is in tri-state, so same column select might be used for both read and write. Wen signal is either the write enable signal or a derivation of it.

### Sense Amplifier

The sense amplifier is the last element considered in the column. In a read operation the bit lines are pre-charged first. Then a word line is activated to let the ND transistor in the cell pull either Bit or Bit#, depending on the data stored in the cell, down. The bit line is highly capacitive and the transistors in the memory cell are small for density purpose, so it may take a long time for the cell to completely discharge the bit line. The common practice is to let the cell develop only a limited differential voltage, about ~100 mV, on the bit lines and amplify it by a sense amplifier. Thus, reducing and matching the bit line capacitance is important for a fast and correct read. Power consumption of a memory is also mainly determined by the bit line capacitance.

Bit line capacitance components, contributed by each memory cell, include junction capacitance, bit line to bit line coupling, bit line to word line, and bit line to substrate capacitance. Thus, each cell connected

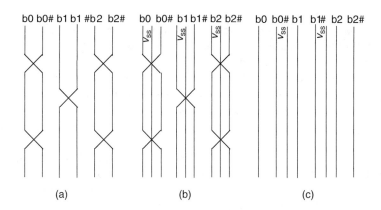

**FIGURE 10.85** Bit line twisting to reduce coupling capacitans and read time data dependency.

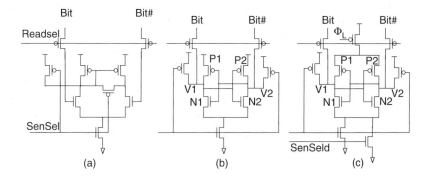

**FIGURE 10.86** Three popular sense amplifiers: (a) Current mirror based, (b) Latch with positive feedback, and (c) Dual slope or/and clocked $V_{cc}$.

to the bit line adds a certain amount of capacitance to the bit line. Junction capacitance is the main source of bit line capacitance. Choosing the number of cells per column is an important design decision as it determines the speed, power consumption, area efficiency, and hence, the architect of the memory. In a typical 0.18 $\mu$m technology 256–512 cells per bit line is a good compromise. Bit line to bit line coupling is a major source of mismatching. Its contribution to bit line capacitance is also significant and is the only component that circuit designers can influence.

Coupling capacitance between bit lines has two consequences. It increases the total capacitance and makes the read time data dependent. Adjacent cells to a cell may have different data for two reads of the same cell. The strategy to reduce the bit line coupling capacitance is to twist the bit line along long run of bit lines. Figure 10.85(a) shows a simple strategy in which the coupling between bit lines is completely cancelled; however, the coupling between Bit and Bit# of the same cell is not cancelled. But signal shifting due to this coupling is deterministic and limited. In modern CMOS process technologies, it is possible to use higher level of metals for bit lines to lower the line to substrate capacitance. It is also made possible that to run, in addition to bit lines, a supply line through the cell. This supply line not only helps to have a power mesh in the memory, it also can be used to cancel the Bit to Bit# coupling, see Fig. 10.85(b). Twisting the bit lines degrades the area efficiency of the memory. If the supply line is drawn outside the bit lines, the strategy in Fig. 10.85(c) may be used to increase the area efficiency and live with the known Bit to Bit# coupling capacitance.

Many different sense amplifiers circuits are used in memory design. Two most popular circuits are considered here. The miller current mirror sense amplifier, Fig. 10.86(a), is used in more conservative and slow designs. The SenSel signal is asserted after enough differential signals are developed on the bit lines. The main advantage of this circuit, compared to a circuit with positive feedback, is that it always resolves to right direction regardless of the initial amount of differential signals at the inputs. Thus it is not sensitive to the minimum delay of SenSel signal to word line. However, this circuit has many disadvantages. It is slow and consumes more power. The gain and speed of the circuit is very sensitive to the pre-charge value of the bit line. Because of the diode connected transistor in the circuit it is not suitable for low voltage operation and has structural offset. For these reasons the differential sense amplifier with positive feedback circuit, Fig. 10.86(b), is used in many designs.

This circuit is fast and consumes less power. The only disadvantage of this circuit is that it may latch in a wrong state. To avoid this, the SenSel signal must be activated after sufficient different voltage is developed on bit lines to overcome all worst-case offsets of the circuit. To calculate the worst-case offset, the schematic model in Fig. 10.81 can be used. $\Delta I$ and $\Delta V_t$ are smaller for sense amplifiers because bigger devices are used here. To reduce the offset, transistors used in the circuit must have at least 10–20% longer than the minimum length in the technology.

After sufficient differential voltage is developed between $V_1$ and $V_2$, the SenSel signal is activated. Initially, only two input N transistors, $N_1$ and $N_2$, are in saturation and two loading P transistors are off. This is a favorable case because N transistors normally have better matching characteristics than P transistors. Two cross-coupled N transistors increase the differential voltages further. Both $V_1$ and $V_2$ drop below pre-charge $V_{cc}$ voltage. When $V_1$ or $V_2$ are below $V_{cc} - V_{tp}$, the P transistors further increase the positive feedback and restore a full $V_{cc}$ on the side that is supposed to be a logic "1". To make the initial part of the operation longer, one may use a dual slope scheme or/and clock the $V_{cc}$ connection, Fig. 10.86(c). In the dual slope scheme first the weaker tail transistor is activated. This will cause the $V_1$ and $V_2$ to sink slowly. After a short delay the strong tail transistor is turned on by SenSel. In the clocked $V_{cc}$ connection the $\Phi_L$ is delayed with respect to SenSel. In some design the Bit and Bit# are not disconnected from the sense amplifier during sensing. This results in slower response and increased power consumption. Bit and Bit# can be disconnected by a column select transistors to increase speed and reduce power consumption.

## Memory Array

Now that main circuits comprising a column are presented, we can construct an array of columns. The goal is to organize $n \times n$ cells in such a way to meet the required access time, power budget, and high-area efficiency. In a flat organization, Fig. 10.87(a), all the cells are included in a single array. This architecture has many disadvantages for large memories. The main contributor to the power consumption

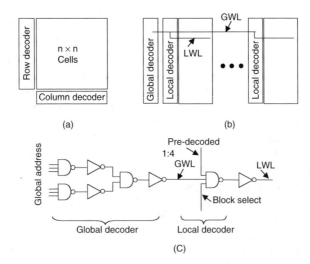

**FIGURE 10.87**   Memory organizations: (a) flat, (b) hierarchical, and (c) a hierarchical circuit solution.

is the bit line capacitance. The effect of bit line capacitance on the read access time is significant. It is thus desirable to have less number of cells per column. Having less number of cells per column also make the row decoder simpler. Row decoder time performance is also crucial for a fast access time because it is in the critical delay path; however, in a flat organization less number of rows means larger number of columns. This will increase the word lines delay, requires big word line drivers, and high column multiplexing ratio.

Partitioning of the memory array has been the subject of very creative challenges for many years. This challenge will continue, as the metal lines are becoming more resistive and new generation CMOS technologies offer multilayers of metals. This provides possibilities to introduce many layers of hierarchy in the memory organization to combat parasitics reduce power, access time, and to increase area efficiency. Figure 10.87(b) is an example of partitioning the array into sub-arrays and introducing hierarchy into the decoding and word lines. Assume you have 256 rows per sub-array. You need eight address bits to select each row. Out of these 8 bits, 6 bits are coded and driven across all the sub-arrays. These are global word lines, GWL. Although global word lines are long, they are not heavily loaded, as they are strapped only once per sub-array. The remaining 2 bits are pre-decoded in each sub-array. A sub-array is selected through sub-array decoder (block decoder). Block decoder is normally fast, as it has a smaller number of address bits to decode. The local decoder in each sub-array is a simple circuit that decodes GWL, pre-decoded signal, and block select. Figure 10.87(c) is a static circuit for the row decoder chain. For faster decoding pre-charge dynamic circuits may be used instead.

Column decoding is not as time critical as row decoder, as row decoding and bit sensing can be completed before the column decoder is finish. However, in a write operation there may be a race between row decoder and column decoder.

## Testing and Reliability

High-density and high-capacity memory cores are more vulnerable to physical defects than logic blocks. The higher defect is mainly caused by SRAM denser layout. Wafer yield can be assumed to be (SRAM yield) × (logic yield). In a logic chip with high density and capacity embedded SRAM, it is essential to enhance the SRAM yield to achieve better overall chip yield. In commodity SRAM redundancy is used to increase yield. This same methodology can be used to compensate for higher defect density of embedded SRAM. Redundancy is to replace a defected element by a redundant element. A pair of row(s) and column(s) are designed redundant to a memory block for this purpose. If any single memory block is denser than 0.5 Mbits, it is recommended to have redundant row and column. Columns fail more often than rows as they are more complex and include sense amplifier. At least use one redundant column per each 0.5 Mbits. For memories denser than 2 Mbits, both row and column redundancy is recommended.

Testing of embedded memories is more difficult than commodity memories due to the limitation in direct access, increase in data bus width, and increase in speed and flexibility in embedded memories configurations and specifications. It is, therefore, necessary to use a BIST for each memory block to run all standard test patterns. Address and data signals to embedded SRAMs may go through a long run. This can cause timing and signal integrity issues. Power supply voltage drop, flatuation and noise are another source of embedded memory failure. A well-designed power mesh together with sufficient and well-placed de-coupling capacitance is normally used in robust memory designs.

# 11

# Multiple-Valued Logic Circuits

K. Wayne Current
*University of California*

## 11.1 Introduction

Multiple-valued logic (MVL) is a hybrid of binary logic and analog signal processing: some of the noise advantages of a single binary signal are retained, and some of the advantages of a single analog signal's ability to provide greater informational content are used. Much work has been done on many of the theoretical aspects of MVL. The theoretical advantages of MVL in reducing the number of interconnections required to implement logical functions have been well established and widely acknowledged. Serious pinout problems encountered in some very large scale integrated (VLSI) circuit designs could be substantially influenced if signals were allowed to assume four or more states rather than only two. The same argument applies to the interconnect-limited IC design: if each signal line carries twice as much information, then only half as many lines are required. Four-valued logic signals easily interface with the binary world; they may be decoded directly into their two-binary-digit equivalent. Many logical and arithmetic functions have been shown to be more efficiently implemented with MVL, i.e., fewer operations, gates, transistors, signal lines, etc., are required. Yet, with all the theoretical advantages, MVL is not in wide use mainly because MVL circuits cannot provide these advantages without cost. The costs are typically reduced noise margins, slower raw switching speed due to increased circuit complexity and functionality, and the burden of proving MVL use improves overall system characteristics. As fabrication technologies evolve, MVL circuit designers adapt to the new technology-related capabilities and limitations and create new MVL circuit designs. Many MVL circuits have been proposed that use existing and proposed silicon and III-V fabrication technologies; that signal with flux, charge, current, voltage, and photons. A discussion of the extensive range of possible circuit-oriented MVL topics would be very

0-8493-0885-2/02/$0.00+$1.50

informative, but that is beyond the scope of this document. This discussion is intended to present a view of the state of the art in practical, realizable MVL circuits and of the trend expected in new MVL circuits. The reader is referred to the section on "Further Reading" below for references to additional literature and sources of information on MVL.

For most new chip designs that employ MVL to be useful and attractive, their inputs and outputs, and power supply voltages must be compatible with the signal swings and logic levels, and power supply voltages of the binary logic families with which they will be required to communicate. Looking at the potential of MVL realistically, in the near future, we expect few designers to risk using quaternary or other MVL logic signaling at the package pins (except possibly in a testing mode). The most likely situation in which MVL would be used is one in which binary signaling is done on the chip pads to be compatible with the rest of the system, some functions are realized with standard binary circuitry, and certain other functions are realized more advantageously with MVL. Rather than attempt to develop a general family of MVL circuits that is logically and computationally complete, we have examined the realization of specific MVL functions that we believe provide advantages now and may provide advantages in the future.

MVL has many theoretical advantages, but it is not widely used because MVL circuits do not provide overwhelmingly advantageous characteristics, in general. However, in many designs, overall system characteristics may be improved using specific MVL circuits in specific applications. For example, the most widely used commercial application of MVL is nonvolatile memory. The MVL nonvolatile memory provides greater memory density and decreased incremental memory cost. These circuits generate internal multiple-valued current signals that are interpreted and converted to binary voltage signals for interface out of the memory function. As system power supply voltages continue to decrease, current signaling can allow one to continue to use the advantages of MVL until subthreshold and leakage currents exceed the available noise margins. Thus, current-mode CMOS logic circuits are also seen as viable in the present and in the near future.

Several other MVL approaches may be potential candidates for MVL VLSI circuits. Current-mode, emitter-coupled, logic style circuits can be easily adapted to use multiple valued current signals and provide high-speed, high-packing-density MVL functions [1,2]. To take advantage of current-mode logic's series gating, power supply voltages must remain higher than the minimum projected for CMOS. Although the use of resonant tunneling diodes' and transistors' negative incremental resistance can be used for MVL and shows some promise [3,4], the series stacking of the multiple negative-resistance devices requires additional voltage overhead we are predicting will not be available, in general. Although interesting, these and other approaches to MVL circuits will not be discussed in detail here. Many MVL circuits that require enhancement- and depletion-mode NMOS and PMOS transistors with application-specific sets of designer-specified transistor threshold voltages have been proposed that are similar to or extend the ideas in [5,6]. We are not discussing those ideas in this document because the fabrication technologies required are too ambitious or because the circuit overhead required to maintain an MVL voltage-controlled-transistor-threshold voltage is excessive, and thus not as likely to be adopted by design engineers; however, it has been commonly observed that ideas that prove to be highly profitable can suddenly alter the vector of change in the electronics industry. If, for example, a highly capable, and highly profitable approach to photonic circuits were demonstrated that required a large power supply voltage, designers would not hesitate to reverse the power supply voltage reduction trend for the purpose of improved profit and enhanced performance. Yet, given the information now available about fabrication technology improvements and changes projected into the near future, the trend of reduced power supply voltages and minimized transistor dimensions will probably continue for some time. Under these conditions, we project current-mode MVL signals to be the most likely to be useful and advantageous.

In the next section, we discuss the use of MVL in nonvolatile memory circuits realized in CMOS technologies. Section 11.3 discusses current-mode CMOS circuits that can provide computational advantages because current summing requires no electronic components. A summary and conclusions are presented in section 11.4.

# 11.2  Nonvolatile Multiple-Valued Memory Circuits

The most widely used commercial application of MVL is in nonvolatile memory. Nonvolatile memory retains its stored information when there is no power supplied to the chip. Read only memory (ROM) is programmed in the manufacturing process and cannot be altered afterward. Programmable ROM (PROM) is programmed after manufacture only once, by the electrical means of blowing out, open circuiting, a fuse, or enabling, shorting, an "anti-fuse." Erasable PROM (EPROM) uses a floating-gate (FG) field effect transistor (FET) that has two separate, overlapping gates, one of which is electrically isolated or floating, as shown in Fig. 11.1. The floating gate lies on the thin gate oxide between the FET's channel and the top gate, which serves as the transistor's gate terminal that is driven to turn on or off the transistor's drain current. The transistor's effective threshold voltage can be changed by changing the number of electrons, the charge, stored on the floating gate. The difference between the applied gate voltage and the effective threshold voltage determines the drain current. The drain current represents the information stored in the FG transistor. The drain current is read by a column amplifier that converts the information to voltages compatible with the interfacing circuitry. All FG transistors in the EPROM are erased simultaneously by exposing the floating gates to ultraviolet light. Electrically Erasable PROM (EEPROM) uses floating gate transistors that are programmed and erased by electrical means. The FG transistor's effective threshold voltage, and resultant drain current, is programmed by placing charge on the floating gate. The arrangement of memory array transistors in nonvolatile memory can be in parallel as is done with a NOR gate, or in series as is done with a NAND gate, thus giving nonvolatile memory architectures NOR and NAND designations. The physical mechanism typically used in programming the floating gate is channel hot electron injection or Fowler–Nordheim tunneling, and for erasure Fowler–Nordheim tunneling [11]. Organizations of floating-gate transistors such that they can be electrically programmed one bit at a time and electrically erased a block, sector, or page simultaneously are called "Flash" memory. These nonvolatile memories usually have a single power supply, and generate the larger programming and erasure voltages on-chip. Floating gate transistors in these commercial products can typically be programmed in less than 1 ms, erased in less than 1 s, can retain data for more than 10 years, and can be erase/program cycled over 100,000 times. Binary and multiple-valued versions of flash memories can usually be realized in the same floating-gate FET fabrication technologies, and use the same memory cells. Differences are in binary and MVL read and write functions, and programming and erasure procedures.

MVL nonvolatile memory provides greater memory density and decreased incremental memory cost. In the next two sections, MVL ROM and MVL EEPROM memory, respectively, are discussed.

## Multiple-Valued Read Only Memory

Standard binary ROM circuits are programmed during the manufacturing process by making each cell transistor either operational or nonoperational. The programmed binary data is represented by either the presence or absence of drain current when the memory cell transistor is addressed. This can be accomplished in several ways. The memory cell transistor can be made nonoperational by having its

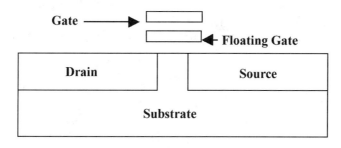

**FIGURE 11.1**  Floating-gate MOS FET.

drain omitted, its gate polysilicon over thin oxide omitted, and its threshold voltage increased to a value greater than the gate address voltage. For example, an additional mask and implant are used to increase the cell transistor's threshold voltage to a value large enough that the transistor remains "off" ($I_D = 0$) when the address voltage is applied to its gate. Thus, with all programming approaches, when the memory cell is addressed, those cell transistors that are operational conduct drain current, and those that are not operational do not conduct drain current. The binary information is in the presence or absence of drain current. Drain current is detected by the column read amplifier, and binary output voltages are created for communication out of the memory function. The column read amplifier can be a differential amplifier or a fixed reference comparator. MVL ROM uses multiple valued drain currents to represent the stored MVL data. MVL and binary ROM architectures are essentially the same except for sensing the multiple valued currents and the creation of the equivalent binary information for output out of the memory function. Four-valued ROM [7–10] have been successfully used in commercial products.

Four-valued ROMs can be programmed during manufacture using two approaches. One approach uses two additional masks and implants to create four possible memory cell transistor threshold voltages [8,10]. Drain current is nonlinearly proportional to the difference between the applied address gate voltage and the effective threshold voltage. Cell transistors with four possible effective threshold voltage values can be of minimum size and thus produce twice the cell bit density possible with the binary version. This approach uses additional processing steps and masks, and thus a more expensive fabrication technology. Another approach uses four different cell transistor channel widths or width-to-length ratios to set the four possible drain current values [7,9]. Drain current is directly proportional to the channel width. The spacing within the array of memory cell transistors must accommodate the largest of the four possible transistor sizes, and thus must be greater than that of the threshold programmable version. This geometry-variable approach requires additional silicon area and provides a bit density less than the threshold programmable approach, but greater than the binary version; however, no additional fabrication steps or masks are necessary for this geometry-variable cell.

Detection and interpretation of the four-valued memory cell transistor's drain current is an analog-to-two-bit digital conversion problem that has many solutions. Traditional analog-to-digital conversion design issues must be considered and all conversion approaches can be used. A simple approach uses as comparator threshold references three reference currents that lie between the four logical values of the drain current. This common "thermometer" arrangement of three comparators produces simultaneously three comparison results that are easily decoded into arbitrary two-bit binary output combinations. This simultaneous comparison of the data drain current to the references is the fastest approach to detecting the stored data. These column read amplifiers are more than twice as complicated as the binary versions. Because the number of read amplifiers is much smaller than the number of memory cells, this increase in the read amplifier overhead circuitry reduces only slightly the overall density improvement provided by the bit density increase of the large array of four-valued memory cells. Overall, four-valued ROM implementations reduce chip areas 30–40%. For example, in [7], a math co-processor uses a mask-gate-area-programmable quaternary ROM that provides an approximately 31% ROM area savings compared to a binary ROM. No system speed penalty was incurred because the slower MVL ROM is fast enough to respond within the time budgeted for ROM data lookup. In [9], the 256 K four-valued ROM is said to have minimal speed loss due to careful design of the ROM architecture, the sense amp operation, and the data decoder output circuit design. Chip area savings of this four-valued ROM is approximately 30%.

Both programming approaches provide significantly increased bit density compared to binary ROM. The speed of the four-valued ROM is inherently reduced because the increased complexity of the column read amplifiers, the increased capacitance of the larger memory cell transistors, and the reduced drain current created by the memory cell transistors with large threshold voltages. Designers have minimized the speed penalty with thoughtful chip architecture design and careful transistor level circuit performance optimization. The improved capabilities demonstrated in these four-valued ROM designs motivated the use of four-valued data storage in the EEPROM and flash memories discussed next.

## Multiple-Valued EEPROM and Flash Memory

Binary and multiple-valued EEPROM [11–13] circuits are used in successful commercial products. Many of them are organized for the simultaneous electrical erasure of large blocks of cells and are called "flash memory." Multiple-valued flash memory circuits provide greater memory density, at lower incremental cost, than the binary versions. The circuitry of multiple-valued ROM and multiple-valued EEPROM structures are very similar to each other and very similar to their binary counterparts. Development of commercially viable binary and MVL flash memory products has required extensive research in device physics and fabrication technology. That research continues and we see continual improvements in commercial flash memory products. Summary and overview discussions of flash memory [11] and multilevel flash memory [12] examine many of the inter-related effects and important tradeoffs that must be considered. Here, we discuss the principles of operation and do not attempt to explain in detail any of these evolving and complex issues.

In multiple-valued flash memory circuits, the floating gate of each EEPROM memory cell transistor is charged to one of the multiple values that creates one of the several memory cell transistor threshold voltages. Each memory cell transistor, when driven with the specified read gate voltage, generates one of the multiple logical drain current values. The multiple-valued drain currents are then decoded by a current sense amplifier column read circuit. The sense amplifier serves as an analog-to-digital converter that translates the multiple-valued drain current into an equivalent set of binary logical output signals with voltages compatible with the rest of the computing system. Four-valued signals are most commonly used. A few 16-valued EEPROM memory cells have been examined [13] and a 256-valued EEPROM "analog memory" has been used in a commercial analog audio storage product [14].

Precise control of the charge on the nonvolatile FET's floating gate is necessary to create one of the multiple distinct effective cell transistor threshold voltage values needed. Each nominal threshold voltage value will have a distribution of voltages around that target value. Noise margins, separations between adjacent threshold voltage value distributions, diminish as the number of logical values increases. It is necessary to keep the distribution narrow and to maintain adequate distances between the adjacent threshold voltage value distributions. Research is underway to develop a self-limiting programming technique, but at the present time programming of the floating gate is usually done with an iterative program and verify procedure. A programming voltage is applied for a fixed period of time, and the resultant programmed value is read by the column sense amp. If the desired threshold voltage is reached, then programming ends. If not, then another programming voltage pulse is applied and the programmed verified. The iterative procedure ends when the verify step indicates the correct programmed threshold voltage has been created.

Reading a stored multiple valued logical signal can be accomplished with any analog to digital process, such as that described above for the four-valued ROM. This simple approach uses as comparator threshold references three reference currents that lie between the four logical values of the drain current. This common "thermometer" arrangement of three comparators produces simultaneously three comparison results that are easily decoded into arbitrary two-bit binary output combinations. This simultaneous comparison of the data drain current to the references is the fastest approach to detecting the stored data. These column read amplifiers are more than twice as complicated as the binary versions. Another approach is to drive the memory cell's read signal from its minimum value to its maximum value with a series of steps or a ramp. Times when the read signal voltage exceeds each memory cell's possible programmed threshold voltages are known by design. When the single read amplifier comparator senses any current at the prescribed time, the programmed logical signal value has been detected. The column read amplifier used with this approach requires only one comparator, one threshold, and thus fewer devices, but requires more time than the simultaneous conversion described previously.

Compared with binary realizations, four-valued flash memory circuits have been shown to require 50% of the memory area, about 115% of the read circuit area, and have access times from about 100% to 150%. The fabrication technology is more complicated, requiring two additional memory cell threshold voltages. These 2 additional threshold voltages can be accomplished with only one additional implant.

Thus, four-valued flash memory can provide significantly increased memory density at a moderate increase in fabrication technology complexity.

For most new chip designs to be useful and attractive, they must be compatible with the signal swings and logic levels of standard binary logic families and use compatible power supply voltages. Thus, looking at the potential of MVL realistically, we expect few designers to risk using MVL logic signaling at the package pins (except possibly in a testing mode). The most likely situation in which MVL would be used is one in which binary signaling is done on the chip pads, some functions are realized with standard binary circuitry, and certain other functional modules are realized more advantageously with MVL. Rather than attempt to develop a family of MVL circuits that are logically and computationally complete, we have examined the realization of specific MVL functions that we believe provide advantages now and may provide advantages in the future. With the predominance of CMOS fabrication technologies and the continued decline of system and chip power supply voltages, signal processing with multiple-valued currents appears to be more naturally compatible with the evolving design environment than other approaches to MVL. Thus, current-mode CMOS MVL circuits are the focus of the remaining part of this presentation.

## 11.3  Current-Mode CMOS Multiple-Valued Logic Circuits

Current-mode CMOS circuits in general are receiving increasing attention. Current-mode CMOS MVL circuits [15] have been studied for over two decades and may have applications in digital signal processing and computing. Introduced in 1983 [16], current-mode CMOS MVL circuits were demonstrated that are compatible with the requirements for the VLSI circuits [17]. Various approaches to realizing current-mode CMOS MVL circuits have been discussed since then, and signal processing and computing applications of current-mode MVL have been evaluated. A convincing demonstration of the advantages of current-mode CMOS MVL is the $32 \times 32$ multiplier presented in [18]. This $32 \times 32$ multiplier chip is half the size of an equivalent all-binary realization, dissipates half the power, and has a multiply time within 5% of the fastest reported all-binary multiply time of a comparable design of that era. These advantages arise from the combination of two ideas. The authors use a signed-digit number system ($\pm 2$, $\pm 1$, $0$) and symmetric functions [19] to streamline the multiplier algorithm and architecture, and to limit the propagation of carrys. They then use multiple-valued bi-directional current-mode CMOS circuits to efficiently realize the function of addition. Addition of currents requires no components. Addition is the principal operation performed in the multiplier, so the current-mode MVL advantage in addition helps make the multiplier realization more area efficient. Thus, advantageous use of MVL usually requires finding its niche. For example, in the pipelined discrete cosine transform (DCT) chip designed using current-mode CMOS MVL circuits described in [20], it is the pipelined nature of the realization of the DCT and inverse DCT functions that makes using MVL potentially feasible. Since the maximum system clock is set by the longest delay required for any pipeline stage, as long as the slightly slower MVL current-mode CMOS adders and multipliers meet this timing requirement, then MVL circuits may be used to provide major area savings in realizing adders and multipliers.

Current-mode CMOS MVL circuits are often used to realize threshold functions. The two basic operations of a threshold function are: (1) the formation of a weighted algebraic sum-of-inputs, and (2) comparison of this sum to the multiple thresholds that define the MVL function to be realized. Current-mode CMOS MVL circuits use an analog current summing node to create the algebraic weighted-sum- or difference-of-input currents using Kirchoff's current law. This function is "free" because it requires no active or passive components. Uni- and bi-directional currents may be defined in each branch. The currents are usually defined to have logical levels that are integer multiples of a reference current. Currents may be copied, scaled, complemented, and algebraically sign changed with simple current mirror circuits realized in any MOS technology. Use of depletion-mode devices could sometimes simplify circuit design if they are available in the fabrication technology [18]. The weighted sum or difference of currents is then usually decoded into the desired MVL output function by: (1) comparing it to multiple current thresholds using some form of current comparator, and (2) using comparator-controlled switches to direct properly scaled and logically restored currents to the outputs. The variety of current-mode MVL circuits reported by various authors over the past decade use various combinations of these three operations (algebraic sum, compare to thresholds, and switch correct logical current values to the outputs) to realize all the circuit functions reported.

Most current-mode CMOS MVL circuits have the advantage that they will operate properly at proposed reduced CMOS power supply voltages. Critics of current-mode CMOS binary and MVL circuits worry that static current-mode circuits dissipate DC power. Dynamic current-mode CMOS circuits use additional clocked pairs of transistors and additional clock signals to reduce or eliminate DC power dissipation. Current-mode CMOS circuits have a fanout of only one, yet, if the loading is known in advance as is often the case in VLSI design, circuits may be designed very easily with the appropriate number of individual outputs. Given all the possible advantages and disadvantages of current-mode CMOS circuits, it is apparent that they warrant continued study. We do not propose that current-mode CMOS MVL circuits be used, in general, as a replacement for binary voltage-mode CMOS circuits. We do, however, claim that it may be advantageous in some situations to imbed current-mode CMOS MVL circuits in a binary design. In the discussions that follow, we review several of the input/output compatible current-mode CMOS MVL circuits that we have studied over the past decade. These current-mode CMOS circuits, reviewed in [15], include a simple current threshold comparator [16], MVL encoders and decoders, quaternary threshold logic full adders (QFAs), current-mode MVL latches, latched current-mode QFA circuits, and current-mode analog-to-quaternary converter circuits. Each of these circuits is presented and its performance described. In the next section, the simple current threshold comparator circuit is described.

## CMOS Current Threshold Comparator

A key component in the design of current-mode MVL threshold circuits is the current comparator [16], or current threshold detector. Performance limitations of the current comparator will determine our MVL threshold circuits' ability to discriminate between different input current levels. The current comparator's operation is now summarized. The simplest form of the current comparator circuit, shown in Fig. 11.2, is made up of the diode-connected input NMOS transistor $M_1$, and NMOS transistor $M_2$ connected to replicate this input current, a reference or threshold current generating pair of transistors $M_3$ and $M_4$, and a PMOS transistor $M_5$ that replicates the reference or threshold current. The current in the input mirror transistor $M_2$ limits at the threshold value as the comparator switches. The drains of the PMOS replicating transistor $M_5$ and NMOS replicating transistor $M_2$ are connected to generate the comparator circuit's output voltage. This comparator circuit is to provide a logical HIGH output voltage when the input current is less than the threshold current and a logical LOW output voltage when the input current is greater than the threshold current. (To make a current comparator that gives a logical HIGH output voltage when the input current is greater than the threshold current and a logical LOW output voltage when the input current is less than the threshold current we can simply reverse the roles of the NMOS and PMOS transistors.) Greatest comparator discrimination is obtained by using maximum comparator gain. This current comparator configuration converts the input current to a voltage, $V_{GS1}$, that drives a common-source amplifier with an active load. An equivalent way to describe the operation of this circuit is to consider it a current mirror that reproduces $I_{in}$ as $I_D$, and $I_D$ then drives a high-impedance active load to convert the current difference to an output voltage. We can analyze the comparator to find the transresistance amplifier gain, $R_o$, to be the parallel combination of the output resistances of the NMOS driver and PMOS load devices:

$$R_o = (I_D(\lambda_p + \lambda_N))^{-1}$$

where $\lambda$ represents the channel length modulation effect and has units of $V^{-1}$. A large gain is desired to provide a sharp comparator transition and greater noise margin. Lower threshold current values will increase the gain at the expense of greater comparator delay times when driving a constant load. Use of higher

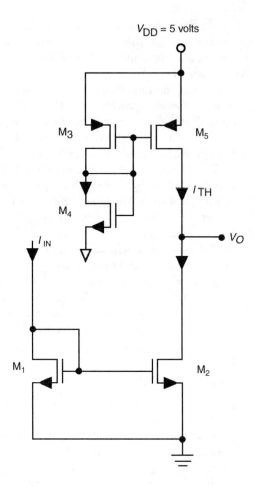

**FIGURE 11.2**    CMOS current comparator.

output impedance current sources improves the gain, but reduces the output voltage swing and increases the comparator delay. Our characterization of test circuits with threshold currents between 5 and 100 $\mu$A fabricated in 2-$\mu$m p-well CMOS shows best input-current/output-voltage propagation delays of approximately 2 ns. The best reported delay performance of a similar circuit that defines the output as the difference of the two drain currents, not the drain voltage, has been reported to be 500 ps in a ring oscillator [21] realized in 2-$\mu$m p-well CMOS.

To improve the delay performance of the comparator, we may provide a DC bias current to the input transistor to keep it biased in a conducting state. The change in input current then exceeds the bias-shifted reference threshold current. Delay improvements of more than 50% have been observed.

MVL circuits often realize threshold logic functions with several thresholds. This requires the comparison of the input current to several different threshold currents. It is possible to simply replicate the input current as many times as needed and compare these multiple copies of the input current to the set of increasingly larger threshold currents. Increased threshold current reduces the comparator gain. To keep gain higher, it is also possible to scale the input current to several different values (some of which may be smaller than the input) and then compare these scaled input currents to a set of smaller reference threshold currents. Design strategies that scale the input current and the threshold currents may be developed to optimize area, speed, and total current. For ease of explanation in this presentation, our discussions present the simplest approach: merely duplicating the input current and creating a set of linearly spaced, increasingly larger reference threshold currents.

Current comparators are a critical part of the current-mode MVL circuits presented here. This circuit with a standard CMOS inverter can also be used for current-to-voltage conversion when going from a current-mode MVL section back into a binary section of a chip. In the section that follows, we will describe the operation of CMOS current-mode binary/quaternary encoder/decoder circuits.

## Current-Mode CMOS Binary/Quaternary Encoders and Decoders

Quaternary-valued logic has the potential to increase the functional density of metal-limited digital integrated circuit layouts by reducing by almost 50% the number of signal interconnections required. The use of MVL input and output signals could also reduce the number of chip package pins required. It may be possible to use standard logical voltage swings at the package terminals during normal operation, and then use four-valued signaling during off-line testing. On-chip conversion from binary voltages to quaternary currents that would be used in a current-mode quaternary logic module can be done easily as shown below. With both on- and off-chip interfaces in mind, we have described current-mode [15] and voltage-mode CMOS circuits that perform the functions of encoding two binary signals into an equivalent four-valued (quaternary) signal for transmission to another location or use in a quaternary logic circuit like a multiplier, for example, and the decoding of this transmitted quaternary signal back into its equivalent two binary signals. Various encodings of the two binary signals are possible and several provide easier decoding. In this presentation of the encoder-decoder circuit combination we have assumed for simplicity of discussion that any two binary signals may be represented by a binary-weighted number. That two-bit number can then be encoded into a single-digit base-four equivalent number. The encoder-decoder circuit combination to be described is designed to serve both on-chip and off-chip interface functions. With proper scaling of device areas the encoder circuit can drive larger capacitive loads with reduced propagation delays and the decoder can maintain its high degree of logical discrimination.

Current-mode CMOS binary-to-quaternary encoder and quaternary-to-binary decoder circuits operate as follows. A schematic of the encoder circuit is shown in Fig. 11.3. A reference current is established and duplicated by transistors $M_1$–$M_4$. The current in $M_4$ is twice as large as that in $M_3$. The encoder's two binary CMOS logic signals that are to be encoded are input to the pass transistors $M_5$ and $M_6$, where the signal assigned the most significance is applied to the gate of $M_6$, which will pass the doubly-weighted current. The pass transistor sources are tied together to form the analog sum of the currents, the four-valued output current signal, $I_o$.

The encoder's quaternary output current is connected either on-chip or off-chip to the compatible current comparator section of the decoder circuit shown in a schematic in Fig. 11.4. The four-valued input current is applied to the drain of the decoder's input transistor $M_7$. $M_7$ then drives three current comparators [16] made up of transistor pairs $M_8$–$M_9$, $M_{10}$–$M_{11}$, and $M_{12}$–$M_{13}$. The common-drain connection of each current comparator transistor pair is labeled $A$, $B$, and $C$, respectively. Voltages $A$, $B$, and $C$ will remain HIGH as long as the input current is less than one-half the logical output current increment, $I$. For an input current greater than $0.5I$, $A$ will go LOW, while voltages $B$ and $C$ remain HIGH. For an input current greater than $1.5I$, $B$ will also go LOW and $C$ will remain HIGH. Input currents greater than $2.5I$ will drive $C$ to the LOW state and all three comparators will be LOW. The three CMOS-compatible logical voltages $A$, $B$, and $C$ then drive three standard CMOS decoding logic gates shown in Fig. 11.5. The decoding logic recreates the two binary logical voltages in the same order of significance that they were applied. Obviously there is a variety of possible encodings that require decoders of more or less complexity that may be chosen to satisfy a variety of different requirements. In this presentation we are, for simplicity, using binary- and quaternary-weighted number equivalents.

Transistors $M_{14}$ and $M_{15}$ in the decoder circuit schematic, Fig. 11.4, establish a reference current, $2I$, that is mirrored by factors 0.25, 0.75, and 1.25 by transistors $M_9$, $M_{11}$, and $M_{13}$, respectively, to establish the three threshold currents. For the $A$ logical output, the threshold current $I_{TH_A}$ is $0.5I$. For $B$ and $C$ outputs, the threshold currents are $I_{TH_B} = 1.51I$ and $I_{TH_C} = 1.51I$, respectively. In the encoder-decoder shown in the figures, we are using logical levels of 0, 10, 20, and 30 $\mu$A. Current comparator $C$ is to provide HIGH output voltage for input currents less than 25 $\mu$A and a logical LOW voltage for input currents greater than 25 $\mu$A. Thus, the threshold current for current comparator $C$ is 25 $\mu$A.

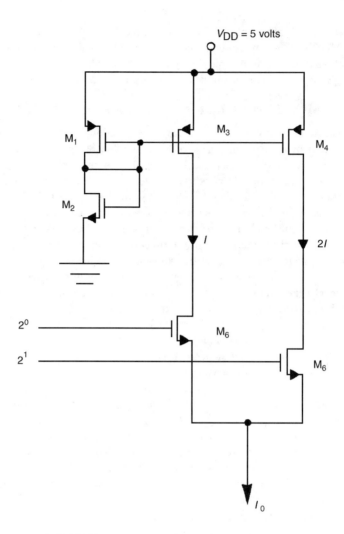

**FIGURE 11.3**    Current-mode CMOS binary-to-quaternary encoder.

One can increase the interface driving current, $I_{IN}$, by, for example, an order of magnitude to provide increased capacitive loading drive capability independently of the threshold currents and still maintain the same comparator current levels and gain by appropriately designing the width-to-length ratios of transistors $M_7$ and transistors $M_8$, $M_{10}$, and $M_{12}$. The comparators and decoder performance will be unchanged. For example, using $10I_{IN}$ instead of $I_{IN}$ for interfacing, we will need to increase the width of $M_7$ by a factor of 10. This feature allows considerable design flexibility. We could apply the same technique to each comparator to give them all the same low quantity of drain current and, thus, the same high value of gain and still detect the same three input current levels selected previously. The trade-off here is the reduced load driving current available in the scaled-down current comparators. If the comparator drives only an inverter, then this is not a significant problem. These scaled-down threshold currents are not used in the circuits discussed here. Decoders may also use an input bias current to speed-up the circuit's response [16]. When a bias current is used all the thresholds must also be shifted.

A variety of current-mode CMOS encoder/decoder pairs have been fabricated and characterized. One group was fabricated in 1985 in a standard 5-$\mu$m polysilicon-gate p-well CMOS technology. Large- and small-current current-mode, encoder–decoder circuit pairs with and without bias currents were included. Small-current, encoder–decoder pairs using nominal 10 $\mu$A incremental currents are realized with: (1) no bias current, and (2) a 5 $\mu$A bias current. Large-current, encoder–decoder pairs designed for driving off-chip

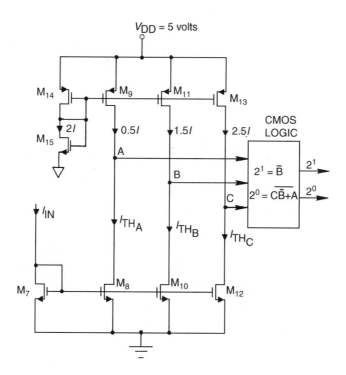

**FIGURE 11.4**   Current-mode CMOS quaternary-to-binary decoder.

loads of 100 pF that use nominal 3 mA incremental currents are realized with: (1) no bias current, and (2) a 50 $\mu$A bias current. The encoder and decoder circuits operated exactly as predicted. Propagation delay of binary/quaternary encoder-decoder circuits has been defined as the 50–50% delay time from the incidence of the simultaneous binary encoder inputs to the generation of the last binary decoder output. Worst-case propagation delay is experienced when the encoder output changes three full increments of output current. Propagation delays of our current-mode, encoder-decoder circuit pairs have been measured with the encoder output and decoder input package pins wired together on a breadboard. Thus, the encoder circuit drives off-chip, through the package, to a board, back through the package, on-chip, and lastly the decoder circuit. Typical values of CMOS-voltage-input-to-CMOS-voltage-output propagation delay exhibited by the small-current (intended for on-chip use) encoder-decoder pairs without and with bias current driving off-chip are about 375 and 275 ns, respectively. Because the large-current, encoder-decoder circuits were designed to drive PC board loads of 100 pF, we have examined the large-current, encoder-decoder circuit pairs loaded as outlined previously with an additional capacitance load of nominal value 100 pF connected from the I/O node to ground. Under this loading condition, typical values of delay exhibited by the large-current encoder-decoder circuits without and with bias current are about 48 and 30 ns, respectively. Although the use of large signaling currents may not be attractive to many designers, the option is available and may be of value in some situations.

One might use encoder/decoder circuits to increase the information on a signal line. Current summing at a node is a "free" computation that may be exploited in circuits that realize threshold logic functions as we will see in the next section where we summarize the quaternary threshold logic full adder.

## Current-Mode CMOS Quaternary Threshold Logic Full Adder

Some operations in digital signal processing and computing are more amenable than others to implementation with quaternary threshold logic. For example, by using the summing of logical currents, adding and counting may be efficiently implemented. The quaternary threshold logic full adder (QFA) adds the values of two quaternary inputs $A$ and $B$, and the value of a binary carry input, $C_i$, and produces a

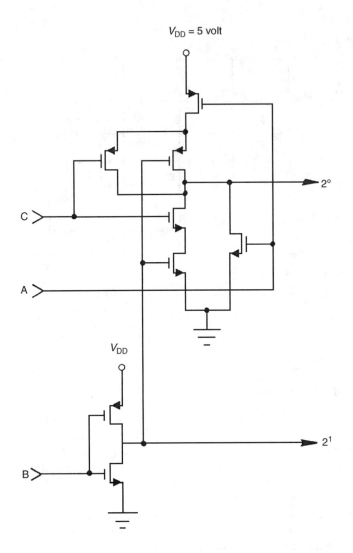

**FIGURE 11.5**   Current-mode CMOS quaternary-to-binary decoder logic.

two-quaternary-digit output, $CS$, that is the base-four value of this sum of the inputs. Logical currents have been used in QFA circuits realized with integrated injection logic ($I^2L$) (see, for example, [22]), current-mode logic (CML), and current-mode CMOS [15]. The well-known QFA function is summarized below.

The QFA circuit to be described implements threshold functions. The two basic operations of a threshold function are the formation of a weighted-sum-of-inputs and the comparison of that weighted-input-sum to the multiple thresholds. The QFA adds two quaternary inputs $A$ and $B$ and a binary input carry $C_i$ to produce a weighted-input-sum within the range 0–7. Representing this weighted sum in base-four with the two-digit output $CS$ requires the CARRY, $C$, output to assume only binary values ZERO and ONE, while the SUM, $S$, output will assume values ZERO, ONE, TWO, and THREE. The DC input-output transfer function for the ideal QFA is shown in Fig. 11.6. Several organizations of threshold detectors can be used to generate this two-digit output from the eight-valued weighted-sum-of-inputs. We will summarize the operation of two approaches to realizing this function with combinations of complementary MOS transistors serving as current sources and threshold detectors, and standard CMOS logic gates.

The first QFA discussed, shown in Fig. 11.7, is a direct implementation of the QFA definition. The input summing-node combines logical current inputs that are integer multiples of a reference current.

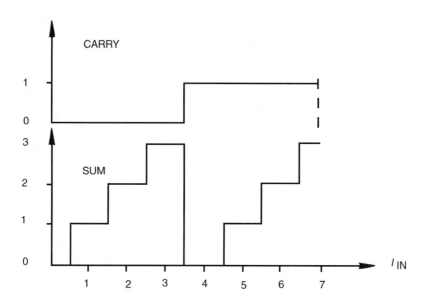

**FIGURE 11.6**   Current-mode CMOS quaternary threshold logic full adder I/O transfer characteristic.

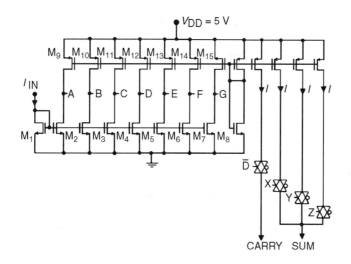

**FIGURE 11.7**   Current-mode CMOS quaternary threshold logic full adder schematic.

The sum-of-logical-inputs must lie between ZERO and SEVEN times the reference current. This sum-of-currents, $I_{in}$, is received and mirrored by input transistor $M_1$ to replicate the input current seven times by identical NMOS transistors $M_2$–$M_8$. These seven identical copies of the input current are the inputs to seven current comparators [15] that compare the input weighted sum to the seven thresholds. The other halves of these comparators are PMOS transistors $M_9$–$M_{15}$. The comparators generate seven binary voltage swings, $A$–$G$, that are capable of driving standard CMOS logic gates. Comparator output signal $\overline{D}$ controls the CMOS transmission gate that connects a unit value of logical current to the CARRY output line. The seven logical comparator output signals are combinationally reduced in groups of three variables with three standard CMOS logic gates to a set of control signals, $X$, $Y$, and $Z$ [$\overline{X} = (A + \overline{D})E$, $\overline{Y} = (B + \overline{D})F$, $\overline{Z} = (C + \overline{D})G$], that connect three current sources of unit reference value to the SUM output line through three CMOS transmission gates. Logical currents of 10, 20, and 30 $\mu A$ are used in the QFA presented in this paper, requiring threshold currents of 5, 15, 25, 35, 45, 55, and 65 $\mu A$. Gains of

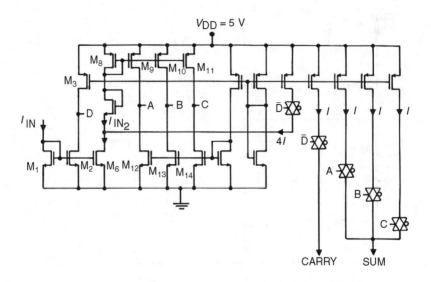

**FIGURE 11.8**  Current-mode CMOS quaternary threshold logic full adder with feedback schematic.

comparators realized with simple Widlar current mirrors of four-micron channel lengths and greater have been found to be adequate to resolve the eight-valued signals used in this circuit.

One potential problem with this QFA is the possible error accumulation involved with the analog summing of seven logical currents at a node; the higher the logical value of the weighted-sum-of-inputs, the greater error possible in the sum of currents. For increasing threshold current the current comparator circuits exhibit decreasing gain, and therefore reduced ability to discriminate the threshold function. The QFA has less accuracy in discriminating the presence of the higher valued weighted sums of inputs. To compensate for this decreasing gain with increasing threshold currents, we examine a feedback technique which eliminates the need to use the three largest values of threshold currents.

A schematic of one version of this QFA modified with feedback is shown in Fig. 11.8. In the figure we see that a current of four logical units in value is combined with a copy of the weighted-sum-of-inputs to create a new input current that is $I_{in2} = (I_{in} - 4)$ when the weighted sum of inputs exceeds logical four. The same three lowest threshold current comparators with greatest gain can now be used to generate the entire range of QFA SUM outputs. The QFA circuit with feedback operates as follows. The threshold current for the "$D$" comparator that controls the CARRY output is generated by PMOS transistor $M_3$. The input is first compared to this threshold to determine whether the input range is above or below 4. If the input is below 4, the output $D$ is in the HIGH state. $D$ is inverted to drive a pair of transmission gates; one controls the CARRY output current, the other controls the four units of logical current that are fed into the drain of $M_6$. At the drain of $M_6$, this feedback current is summed with a copy of the input current to form the total drain current of $M_6$. If the CARRY output is ZERO, no current is fed back and the $M_6$ drain current is equal to the input current. Let us assume for this discussion that the input current is, for example, logical six. The input current will be mirrored by $M_6$ to generate a total drain current of logical six. Since the $D$ comparator has switched to turn on the CARRY output, the feedback current transmission gate is also conducting the logical four feedback current into the node at the drain of $M_6$. The excess current (logical six minus logical four = logical two) must be provided by transistor $M_8$. $M_8$ is a diode connected PMOS transistor that serves as the input to the three current comparators that generate outputs $A$, $B$, and $C$. These comparators operate exactly as described previously except that the roles of the PMOS and NMOS transistors and thus the $A$, $B$, and $C$ voltage swings have been reversed. The PMOS devices $M_9$–$M_{11}$ serve as the input devices while the NMOS devices $M_{12}$–$M_{14}$ serve as the current reference devices. This feedback technique eliminates the CMOS logic stage that encodes the comparator outputs into controls signals for the transmission gates that then switch the logical current outputs onto the SUM output line. The three largest current mirror transistors are also eliminated. The propagation delays observed with these circuits are about 20% longer than those observed with the nonfeedback version of the QFA.

Several variations of the QFA circuits that used several different logical currents were fabricated in 1985 in a standard 5-$\mu$m polysilicon-gate p-well CMOS technology and others using 10 $\mu$A logical currents in MOSIS 2-$\mu$m p-well technology. These simple current-mode test circuits are intended to drive each other on-chip with small logical current increments; most examples use only 10 $\mu$A. Some individual test circuits are connected to input and output pads and package leads. This configuration allows examination of all important comparator and current signals and is intended for DC and low-frequency functional characterization, not for maximum operating speed evaluation. Gains of comparators realized with simple Widlar current mirrors of 4 $\mu$m channel lengths and greater have been found to be adequate to resolve the eight-valued signals used in this circuit. Since logical currents vary in only 10 $\mu$A increments, the circuits have insufficient capability to drive off-chip loads. Thus, meaningful on-chip delays can not be measured with these test circuits. Propagation delay is defined as the time between the midpoint of the transition between two adjacent input logic levels to the midpoint of the transition between two adjacent output logic levels. For example, if the output switches from logical ZERO to logical THREE, then the midpoint between TWO and THREE is used in the propagation delay measurement. To obtain realistic on-chip delays, we used a chain of $N$ cascaded QFA circuits connected between an input pad and an output pad. This configuration does not allow examination of internal signals. We also used a delay test path that is a direct on-chip connection between an input pad and an output pad. The delay through the I/O only path is subtracted from the total delay measured for the group of $N$ QFA circuits. This difference is approximately the total delay through $N$ latched QFA circuits. The average delay of an individual latched QFA circuit may then be calculated. Under these conditions, using test circuits with 4 $\mu$m channel lengths, propagation delay times for single logic level transitions (ZERO-ONE, ONE-TWO, etc.) of about 35 ns have been measured. In simulations of circuits with the same device sizes and using another QFA as a load, single logic level transitions were simulated to have delay times of about 10 ns, and worst-case propagation delay times were found to be about 60 ns for full-scale (ZERO-SEVEN, SEVEN-ZERO) input current signal transitions. To reduce delay times as much as 25%, we can include at the input a DC bias current source of one-half the logical current value to keep the input transistors always in the conducting mode, and shift the threshold currents by an equal amount.

## Current-Mode CMOS Multiple-Valued Latch

Although the use of current signals allows easy and area efficient formation of the multiple-valued sum of signals, storage of the information in this quantized analog signal might require storage of a set of binary signals if it were not for multiple-valued memory circuits [15] similar to that described next. A current-mode CMOS multiple-valued memory circuit organization is shown in a block diagram in Fig. 11.9. When clock signal $\phi$ is at a CMOS logical HIGH, the memory is in the SETUP mode. In the SETUP mode, the circuit accepts a multiple-valued input current $I_{in}$ and, with a quantizer, regenerates it as a feedback current, $I_F$, and an output current, $I_{out}$. When the clock signal $\phi$ goes to a CMOS logical LOW, the circuit goes into the HOLD mode. In the HOLD mode, the input current is disconnected from the quantizer and the regenerated current $I_F$ is switched to the input of the quantizer. This positive feedback circuit now holds the value of the input current that appeared during the preceding SETUP cycle. Changes in the input current $I_{in}$ during the HOLD mode do not alter the latch's output until a new SETUP cycle is entered. The memory circuit's quantizer is chosen to accommodate the range defined for the input current. We will summarize first the more easily described four-valued current-mode memory circuit [15]. An eight-valued, current-mode memory circuit will be presented in the discussion of the latched QFA.

A current-mode CMOS quaternary threshold logic latch circuit is shown in Fig. 11.10. Consider the situation in which the clock signal, $\phi$, is logically HIGH and the latch is in the SETUP mode. Transistor $M_1$ receives the input current, $I_{in}$, and in response generates a voltage $V_{GS1}$ that is coupled through pass transistor $M_{11}$ to the input of the quantizer portion of the latch. Under these conditions the input current

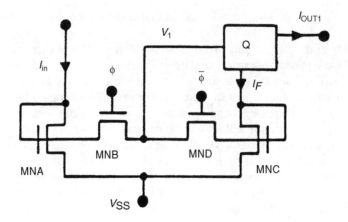

**FIGURE 11.9**   Current-mode CMOS quaternary latch block diagram.

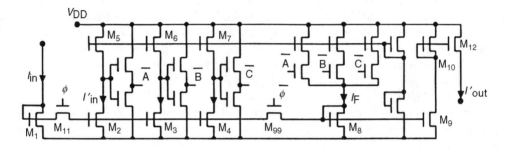

**FIGURE 11.10**   Current-mode CMOS quaternary latch schematic.

$I_{in}$ is reproduced as $I'_{IN}$ by transistors $M_2$, $M_3$, and $M_4$, the three NMOS current mirror inputs to the three current comparators in the quantizer. The current comparators' thresholds are set to detect input currents of logical values ONE, TWO, and THREE by the three PMOS current sources $M_5$, $M_6$, and $M_7$, respectively. As the input current exceeds the threshold of each comparator, each comparator output falls to a logical LOW and the current in each mirror transistor $M_2$, $M_3$, and $M_4$ limits at the threshold value. Each comparator drives a standard CMOS inverter, with output labels $\overline{A}$, $\overline{B}$, or $\overline{C}$ in the schematic, which, in turn, drives a pass transistor with input labels $\overline{A}$, $\overline{B}$, or $\overline{C}$. Each of these pass transistors, when activated, passes the appropriate quantity of current to the feedback summing node to form regenerated current $I_F$. Regenerated current $I_F$ is mirrored by transistors $M_8$, $M_9$, and $M_{10}$ to generate the latch output current, $I_{out}$. The $\overline{\phi}$ signal turns off pass transistor $M_{99}$, and the regenerated current is isolated from the comparator input.

Clock signal $\phi$ is then set LOW to HOLD the multiple-valued current data. With $\phi$ LOW and $\overline{\phi}$ HIGH, transistor $M_{11}$ is off, disconnecting input transistor $M_1$ from the quantizer, and transistor $M_{99}$ is on, connecting the regenerated current to the quantizer input. Because the quantizer and $I_F$ are in a positive feedback loop, the regenerated current, $I_F$, and the output current, $I_{out}$, remain stable at the value of the previous input current.

A variety of forms of the current-mode latched QFA circuit has been designed, fabricated in a standard 2-$\mu$m polysilicon-gate, double-metal CMOS process, and tested. These simple current-mode test circuits are intended to drive each other on-chip with small logical current increments of only 10 $\mu$A. Logical currents of 10, 20, and 30 $\mu$A are used in the quaternary latch, requiring threshold currents of 5, 15, and 25 $\mu$A. Gains of comparators realized with simple Widlar current mirrors of 2-$\mu$m channel lengths have been found to be adequate to resolve the four-valued signals used in the latch circuit. For purposes of oscilloscope display, the quaternary output current is driven into nominally 10 k$\Omega$ resistors connected

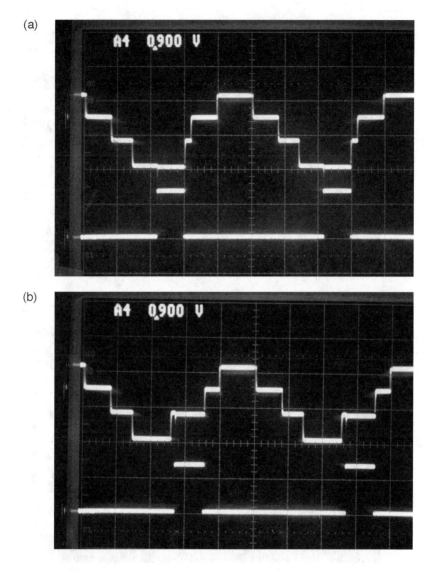

**FIGURE 11.11** Current-mode CMOS quaternary latch output waveforms: (a) Quaternary latch output and $\bar{\phi}$ holding a ZERO, (b) Quaternary latch output and $\bar{\phi}$ holding a ONE, (c) Quaternary latch output and $\bar{\phi}$ holding a TWO, and (d) Quaternary latch output and $\bar{\phi}$ holding a THREE.

on a standard prototyping board. The waveforms in Fig. 11.11 show a sequence of HOLD operations at times necessary to hold each of the four possible values of the output. In each photo, the pulse in the lower trace is $\bar{\phi}$, which goes HIGH to HOLD the value of the output signal at that time. SETUP and HOLD times have been inferred from measured experimental data to be about 10 ns for single level transitions and about 35 ns for ZERO-THREE and THREE-ZERO transitions.

## Current-Mode CMOS Latched Quaternary Logic Full Adder Circuit

The current-mode CMOS latched QFA circuit is described with the aid of the block diagram in Fig. 11.12. The single output quaternary quantizer shown in Fig. 11.9 is replaced by a modified QFA circuit that serves as the quantizer, creating the feedback current and the quaternary full adder outputs. Again, the latched QFA circuit is in the FOLLOW mode when $\phi$ is HIGH and $\bar{\phi}$ is LOW. The circuit is in the HOLD

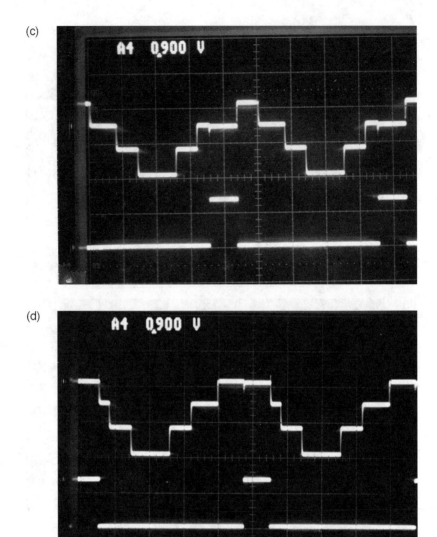

**FIGURE 11.11** (Continued)

mode when $\phi$ is LOW and $\bar{\phi}$ is HIGH. In the block diagram, an eight-valued weighted sum of input currents, $I_{in}$, enters the QFA's diode connected NMOS input transistor $MN_A$ generating a gate-to-source voltage $V_{GSA}$. When in the FOLLOW mode $\phi$ is high, turning on NMOS pass transistor $MN_B$, coupling $V_{GSA}$ to the input of the QFA block as input voltage $V_1$. In the FOLLOW mode, the input is converted by the combinational QFA circuit to the quaternary SUM and CARRY output currents. A quantized regenerated feedback current, $I_F$, is also created by the QFA block to logically replicate the input current. Simultaneously, the feedback current, $I_F$, generates $V_{GSC}$ in the diode-connected NMOS transistor $MN_C$. $\bar{\phi}$ is LOW disconnecting $V_{GSC}$ from the $V_1$ QFA input node. In the HOLD mode, with $\phi$ LOW and $\bar{\phi}$ HIGH, transistor $MN_B$, is off, disconnecting the effect of the input current from the input of the QFA. Transistor $MN_C$ is on, connecting the $V_{GSC}$ created by the regenerated feedback current, $I_F$, to the $V_1$ QFA input. Thus, in the HOLD mode $I_F$ regenerates itself with positive feedback through the nonlinear quantizer in the QFA block. The QFA block in Fig. 11.12 may be realized with a slight modification of the first QFA presented in this paper. The QFA section of the latched QFA is described next.

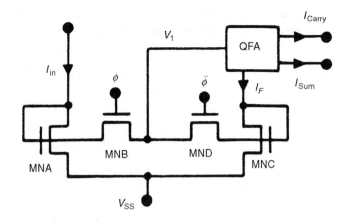

**FIGURE 11.12**   Current-mode CMOS latched QFA: block diagram.

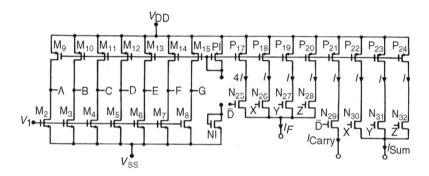

**FIGURE 11.13**   Current-mode CMOS latched QFA: QFA-block schematic.

A simple combinational QFA circuit [15] is shown in Fig. 11.13 that includes a sub-circuit that creates the regenerated feedback current, $I_F$, allowing the capability of latching the eight-valued input current. Notice in Fig. 11.13 that only four current sources and four transmission gates are used to create the regenerated feedback current that allows latching. The transmission gates are controlled by the same control signals that control the SUM and CARRY outputs. At the $I_F$ summing node, signals $X$, $Y$, and $Z$ each control one unit of current as is done at the SUM current summing node, thus reproducing the least significant digit of the two quaternary digit number represented by the pair of QFA output currents. The CARRY output is weighted four times the SUM output. In Fig. 11.13, we see that $\overline{D}$, the CARRY control signal, also controls the passage of four units of current to the $I_F$ summing node. Thus, at the $I_F$ summing node, the input current is requantized by the threshold current comparators and its logical value regenerated as $I_F$ by the current sources and transmission gates. The clock signal controls the input to the threshold current comparators. In the FOLLOW mode, the input current is converted by the QFA circuit to the quaternary SUM and CARRY output currents, and requantized to create regenerated feedback current, $I_F$. In the HOLD mode, $I_F$ regenerates itself and the QFA outputs with positive feedback through the nonlinear quantizer in the QFA circuit.

Logical currents of 10, 20, and 30 $\mu A$ are used in the latched QFA circuit presented here, requiring threshold currents of 5, 15, 25, 35, 45, 55, and 65 $\mu A$. Gains of comparators realized with simple Widlar current mirrors of 4 $\mu m$ channel lengths and greater have been found to be adequate to resolve the eight-valued signals used in this circuit.

A variety of forms of the current-mode latched QFA circuit has been designed, fabricated in a standard 2-$\mu m$ polysilicon-gate, double-metal CMOS process, and tested. These simple current-mode test circuits are intended to drive each other on-chip with small logical current increments of only 10 $\mu$A. Our individual test circuits are connected to input and output pads and package leads. This configuration allows examination of all important comparator and current signals and is intended for DC and low-frequency functional characterization, not for maximum operating speed evaluation. Since logical currents vary in only 10 $\mu$A increments, the circuits have insufficient capability to drive off-chip loads. Thus, meaningful on-chip delays must be inferred as described earlier. Test circuits with devices the same size as those used in the QFA yield SETUP about the same as the QFA delay times, and HOLD times of approximately zero. To reduce delay times as much as 25%, we can include at the input a DC bias current source of one-half the logical current value to keep the input transistors always in the conducting mode, and shift the threshold currents by an equal amount.

Maximum DC power required for the current-mode CMOS latched QFA circuit shown in Figs. 11.12 and 11.13 may be calculated as the product of the 5 V supply and the maximum DC current through the circuit. If we consider the input current, $I_{in}$, to be supplied by the output of another QFA, the maximum DC current occurs when $I_{in}$ and thus $I_F$ are at logical SEVEN. Using nominal logical current increments of 10 $\mu$A, the maximum DC current under these conditions is the sum of the following currents (in $\mu$A): 70 in $I_F$; 30 in SUM; 10 in CARRY; 5, 15, 25, 35, 45, 55, and 65 in the seven current comparators; and 20 in the current source bias circuit for a total current of 375 $\mu$A. The minimum total DC current occurs when $I_{in}$ is logical ZERO and essentially only the 20 $\mu$A bias current is used. Input bias currents must be added to these numbers if they are used, as well as the offset increases added to the threshold currents. A variety of approaches to reducing current requirements are being evaluated, including the obvious introduction of dynamic clocking of all current paths between power and ground and the reduction of the logical current increment. Both of these approaches require speed performance trade-offs.

Circuits nearly identical to those described above have been used for current-mode analog-to-digital conversion [23]. In the next section, we describe the use of our current-mode MVL circuits for analog-to-quaternary conversion.

## Current-Mode CMOS Algorithmic Analog-to-Quaternary Converter

Algorithmic (or cyclic or recirculating) analog-to-digital (A/D) (binary) data converters have been shown to be less dependent upon component matching and require less silicon area than other approaches. These data converters follow an iterative procedure of breaking the input range of interest into two sections and determining within which of the two sections the input signal lies. This process is repeated on each selected range of interest until the final bit of resolution is determined. This is summarized adequately in [23].

An algorithmic analog-to-quaternary (A/Q) data converter algorithm uses a procedure like that described in [23] for the algorithmic analog-to-digital (A/D) (binary) data converter except that the algorithmic A/Q procedure breaks the range-of-interest into quarters and determines within which quarter of the range-of-interest the signal lies at each decision step. This process is repeated on each selected range-of-interest until the final quaternary digit of resolution is determined. To accomplish this we may follow the procedure described below. The block diagram in Fig. 11.14 mimics the block diagram in [23] used to describe the algorithm used for binary converters. The quaternary comparator labeled *CQ* with four-valued output signal *Q* in Fig. 11.14 is used to convey the concept of breaking the range of interest into four sections (rather than two) and indicating the result with a four-valued "comparator" output signal (rather than a binary signal). Figure 11.14 is useful in visualizing the algorithm. The circuit that realizes the function is not organized exactly as shown in Fig. 11.14. The circuit schematic will be described later. Referring to Fig. 11.14 we see that the input IN is multiplied by 4 and the signal 4IN is compared to the full-scale reference signal REF in a quaternary comparator labeled *CQ*. This quaternary comparator *CQ* generates a quaternary-valued output signal *Q* that indicates which quarter of the full-scale range the input signal lies within. *Q* values ZERO, ONE, TWO, and THREE indicate that the signal lies within the bottom, second, third, and top quarter of the full-scale signal range, respectively. If this comparison is

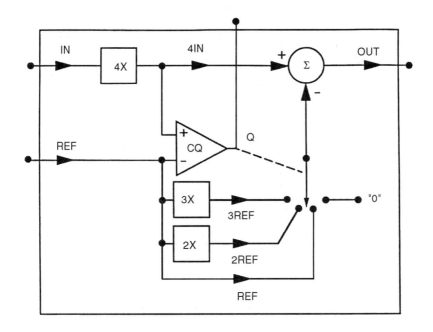

**FIGURE 11.14** Current-mode CMOS analog-to-quaternary converter block diagram.

the first done on the input, then the resultant $Q$ is the most-significant-digit (MSD) of the quaternary-valued output. Having identified the quarter-of-full-scale within which the input lies, we eliminate from further consideration the other regions by subtracting the number of full quarters above which the input lies from the input signal. Equivalently, we may subtract $Q \cdot$ REF from 4IN and obtain four times this desired difference. This factor of 4 weight of the difference signal is necessary to keep the bit significance correct as we continue to process the signal. The quaternary signal $Q$ controls the switch, which effectively subtracts $Q \cdot$ REF from 4IN. The output signal is thus

$$\text{OUT} = 4\text{IN} - Q \cdot \text{REF}.$$

After the appropriate quarter of full-scale that is now defined as the region-of-interest is identified, this new region-of-interest is then searched for the quarter within which the input signal lies. The signal OUT may be used as the input to another identical stage or the value of $Q$ may be stored and the signal OUT fed back to the input of this circuit for continued processing. Each pass through the procedure yields another digit of one lower level of significance until we reach the final least-significant-digit (LSD) decision. Thus, the MSD is determined first and the LSD determined last. The procedure may be implemented with some memory, control logic, and a single cell that performs the operations in Fig. 11.14, feeding the output back to the input. Or the procedure can be implemented by a cascade of $N$ cells, each using the same REF. In the next section, we describe the current-mode CMOS circuitry that implements this algorithmic analog-to-quaternary (A/Q) data converter function.

The schematic of the current-mode CMOS algorithmic A/Q data converter circuit is shown in Fig. 11.15. The circuit operates as follows. For our initial discussion, assume that the bias current $I_{\text{BIAS}}$ is zero and PMOS transistor $M_1$ is not used. The analog input current $I_{\text{IN}}$ into diode-connected input NMOS transistor $M_2$ is reproduced and multiplied by a factor of 4, 2, 2, and 4 by NMOS current mirror transistors $M_4$, $M_6$, $M_8$, and $M_{20}$, respectively. The full scale reference current $I_{\text{REF}}$ is brought into diode connected PMOS transistor $M_{21}$ and reproduced and multiplied by a factor of 1, 1, 1.5, 1, 1, and 1 by PMOS current mirror transistors $M_5$, $M_7$, $M_9$, $M_{12}$, $M_{13}$, and $M_{14}$, respectively. Transistors $M_4$ and $M_5$ form a current comparator circuit that compares $4I_{\text{IN}}$ to the full-scale reference current $I_{\text{REF}}$. Transistors $M_6$ and $M_7$ form a current comparator circuit that compares $2I_{\text{IN}}$ to the full-scale reference current $I_{\text{REF}}$. Transistors

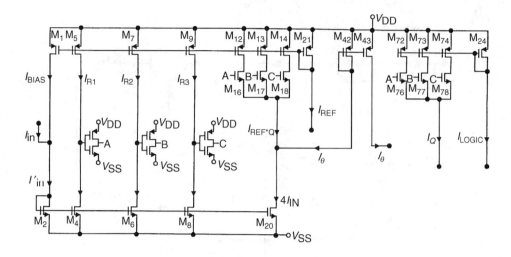

**FIGURE 11.15**   Current-mode CMOS analog-to-quaternary converter schematic.

$M_8$ and $M_9$ form a current comparator circuit that compares $2I_{IN}$ to the one and one-half times the full scale reference current, $1.5I_{REF}$. In each of these three current comparators, when the current in the input NMOS transistor is greater than the reference current in the PMOS transistor, the common drain connection of the transistors falls to a (low) voltage near $V_{SS}$. In each of these three current comparators, when the current in the input NMOS transistor is less than the reference current in the PMOS transistor, the common drain connection of the transistors rises to a (high) voltage near $V_{DD}$. These current comparator output voltages are inverted by standard CMOS inverters to yield signals $A$, $B$, and $C$ that drive NMOS switch transistors $M_{16}$, $M_{17}$, $M_{18}$, $M_{76}$, $M_{77}$, and $M_{78}$. The sum of signals $A$, $B$, and $C$ yield the value of $Q$. PMOS transistors $M_{12}$, $M_{13}$, and $M_{14}$ each provide one unit of $I_{REF}$ current to NMOS switches $M_{16}$, $M_{17}$, and $M_{18}$ that are controlled by signals $A$, $B$, and $C$, respectively. The signal $Q \cdot I_{REF}$ is created when signals $A$, $B$, and $C$ each switch one unit of $I_{REF}$ current to the summing node as the three thresholds are exceeded. This $Q \cdot I_{REF}$ current, the output current $I_\theta$, and $4I_{IN}$ current are summed at the drain of NMOS transistor $M_{20}$. Thus, the output current $I_\theta$ is $4I_{IN} - Q \cdot I_{REF}$. $I_\theta$ is mirrored by PMOS transistors $M_{42}$ and $M_{43}$ for delivery out of the cell. The full scale reference current, $I_{REF}$, is set externally based upon the particular application.

The logical output of the quaternary comparator, $I_Q$, is created by switching zero, one, two, or three units of logical current, controlled by comparator signals $A$, $B$, and $C$, to the logical output summing node through NMOS switches $M_{76}$, $M_{77}$, and $M_{78}$. PMOS transistors $M_{72}$, $M_{73}$, and $M_{74}$ mirror the reference logical current $I_{LOGIC}$ that is input to diode connected transistor $M_{24}$. The logical current reference, $I_{LOGIC}$, is set externally to be compatible with the rest of the current-mode logic used in the system. $I_{LOGIC}$ used here is 10 $\mu A$, making the logical currents 10, 20, and 30 $\mu A$.

A key component in this design, the current comparator, is described in [16]. Its gain will be greater when implemented with higher impedance current mirror driver and load circuits, such as the cascode current mirror. This higher impedance output node slows the circuit and the cascode mirror configuration reduces the voltage swing of the current comparator circuit; however, in this application, the additional current mirror accuracy provided by the cascode mirror outweighs the disadvantages as will be discussed later.

To improve the overall transfer and delay characteristics of the current mode A/Q, a bias current may be added to the input, each of the comparator thresholds, and the $Q \cdot I_{REF}$ signal. The small input bias current keeps the input transistor biased slightly on, allowing quicker mirror response and faster switching. The comparator thresholds and $Q \cdot I_{REF}$ must be offset by the same amount. The circuitry required to maintain bias level compatibility among cells is important but not discussed here.

A/Q decision circuit cells has been designed, fabricated, and tested in a variety of forms. We have studied circuits using simple Widlar and cascode current mirrors, with and without bias current. Experimental test results confirm the DC transfer functions and low frequency functional operation predicted in the simulations. Because of the replication and differencing of input currents used in these decision cells, it is important to use current mirrors with accuracy sufficient to provide correct conversion for the number of quaternary digits desired. It was observed that simple Widlar current mirrors were sufficient to provide three-quaternary-digit outputs using reference currents between 10 and 50 $\mu$A. To create a four-quaternary-digit output word, the additional accuracy of cascode current mirrors was found to be necessary. None of our test circuits would operate 100% correctly as a full five-quaternary-digit converter because of the accumulated error in the current signal transferred to the fifth decision cell.

Timing characteristics were evaluated using single decision cells and A/Q converter circuits made up of a cascade of five identical cells. We used $V_{DD}$ of 5 V, logical currents stated above, and reference currents, $I_{REF}$, ranging from 10 to 50 $\mu$A. The individual decision cell test circuits are in packaged parts and must be driven at their input with an external high resistance current source and loaded at the outputs with a 1 k$\Omega$ resistors. Thus, experimental delay measurements made on individual cells are dominated by the RC time constants of the voltage waveforms appearing at the package terminals. Using reference current of 10 $\mu$A, the delay between when the input crosses a threshold and the output's single level transition (the very best case delay) was measured to be of about 55 ns in both the Widlar and cascode realizations. Worst-case delay, which occurs when all the decision cell's comparators change state, was observed to be about 800 ns in the cascode realization. Worst-case delay through two cascaded cascode cells was observed to be about 2.44 $\mu$s and through four cascaded cascode cells to be about 5.2 $\mu$s.

## 11.4 Summary and Conclusion

MVL circuits that are presently used in commercial products and that have the potential to be used in the future were discussed in this chapter. Application of MVL to the design of nonvolatile memory is receiving a great deal of attention because the memory density of multilevel ROM and multilevel flash memory is significantly greater than that possible using binary signals using the same fabrication technology. In multilevel flash memory, the floating-gate memory cell transistor has multiple values of charge stored on its floating gate, which results in multiple values of the effective transistor threshold voltage that produces multiple values of cell transistor drain current when the memory cell transistor is addressed. This provides the potential for almost doubling the bit density of the memory when four valued signals are stored. Advantages and disadvantages of various memory architectures, memory cell layouts, addressing schemes, column read amplifier designs, and potential fabrication technologies changes for multilevel memory cell optimization are of current research interest.

Current-mode CMOS circuits can provide interesting performance characteristics, in some cases, improved characteristics [21], and are receiving increasing attention. Current-mode CMOS MVL circuits [15] have been reported that illustrate feasible circuit realizations of important functions. In this presentation, we have reviewed several of the current-mode CMOS MVL circuits that we have developed. It is widely acknowledged in the field of electronic design that multiple-valued-threshold-logic circuits will not, in general, supplant binary-logic circuits. However, situations exist in which the characteristics of certain multiple-valued-threshold-logic circuits will make their use advantageous; most likely when imbedded in a binary design. One possible situation in which current-mode CMOS MVL circuits may be advantageous involves pipelined signal processing in a DCT/IDCT chip [20]. A 32-bit multiplier [18] realized with signed-digit arithmetic, symmetric functions, and bi-directional current-mode CMOS plus depletion mode transistors MVL circuits has been shown to provide both speed and area advantages over voltage-mode binary logic. Our studies and those of other MVL circuits researchers attempt to identify and characterize circuitry that may feasibly be used advantageously in integrated systems. Similar system improvements may be possible by combining the characteristics of MVL with the potentials of other approaches to signal processing, such as pipelining, parallel processing, or artificial neural networks. Characteristics of artificial neural networks, such as fault tolerance, and increased system speed due to parallel processing, combined with the hybrid analog-digital circuitry used in many neural network realizations make neural networks an attractive potential application for MVL.

## Acknowledgment

This research was supported in part by grants from the National Science Foundation, the State of California MICRO program, IC Solutions, Inc. Data General Corporation, Hewlett Packard, Plessey Semiconductor, Ferranti-Interdesign, Gould-AMI, and Semiconductor Physics, Inc. Important contributions to research on multiple-valued logic circuits by Larry Wheaton, David Freitas, Doug Mow, and others are gratefully acknowledged.

## References

1. K. W. Current, "High density integrated computing circuitry with multiple valued logic," *IEEE Journal of Solid-State Electronics,* vol. SC-15, no. 1, pp. 191–195, Feb. 1980.
2. Brillman, et al., "A four-valued ECL encoder and decoder circuit," *IEEE Journal of Solid-State Electronics,* vol. 17, no. 3, pp. 547–552, June 1982.
3. F. Capasso, et al., "Quantum functional devices: Resonant-tunneling transistors, circuits with reduced complexity, and multiple-valued logic," *IEEE Transactions on Electron Devices,* vol. 36, no. 10, pp. 2067–2082, Oct. 1989.
4. T. Waho, K. J. Chen, and M. Yamamoto, "Resonant-tunneling diode and HEMT logic circuits with multiple thresholds and multilevel output," *IEEE Journal of Solid-State Circuits,* vol. 33, no. 2, Feb. 1998.
5. A. Heung and H. T. Mouftah, "Depletion/Enhancement CMOS for a low power family of three-valued logic circuits," *IEEE Journal of Solid-State Electronics,* vol. SC-20, no. 2, pp. 609–615, April 1985.
6. Y. Yasuda, Y. Tokuda, S. Zaima, K. Pak, T. Nakamura, and A. Yoshida, "Realization of quaternary logic circuits by n-channel MOS devices," *IEEE Journal of Solid-State Electronics,* vol. SC-21, no. 1, pp. 162–168, Feb. 1986.
7. M. Stark, "Two bits per cell ROM," *Proceedings of COMPCON,* pp. 209–212, Jan. 1981.
8. D. A. Rich, K. L. C. Naiff, and K. G. Smalley, "A four-state ROM using multilevel process technology," *IEEE Journal of Solid-State Circuits,* vol. SC-19, no. 2, pp. 174–179, April 1984.
9. B. Donoghue, P. Holly, and K. Ilgenstein, "A 256-K HCMOS ROM using a four-state cell approach," *IEEE Journal of Solid-State Circuits,* vol. SC-20, no. 2, pp. 598–602, April 1985.
10. D. A. Rich, "A survey of multivalued memories," *IEEE Transactions on Computers,* vol. xxx, no. 2, pp. 99–106, Feb. 1986.
11. P. Pavan, R. Bez, P. Olivo, and E. Zanoni, "Flash memory cells—an overview," *Proc. IEEE,* vol. 85, pp. 1248–1271, Aug. 1997.
12. B. Ricco, et al., "Nonvolatile multilevel memories for digital applications," *Proc. IEEE,* vol. 86, no. 12, pp. 2399–2421, Dec. 1998.
13. D. L. Kencke, R. Richart, S. Garg, and S. K. Banerjee, "A sixteen level scheme enabling 64 Mbit Flash memory using 16 Mbit technology," *IEDM 1996 Tech. Dig.,* pp. 937–939.
14. H. Van Tran, T. Blyth, D. Sowards, L. Engh, B. S. Nataraj, T. Dunne, H. Wang, V. Sarin, T. Lam, H. Nazarian, and G. Hu, "A 2.5 V 256-level nonvolatile analog storage device using EEPROM technology," *1996 IEEE ISSCC Dig. Tech. Pap.,* vol. 458, pp. 270–271.
15. K. W. Current, "Current-mode CMOS multiple valued logic circuits," *IEEE Journal of Solid State Circuits,* vol. 29, no. 2, pp. 95–107, Feb. 1994.
16. D. A. Freitas and K. W. Current, "A CMOS current comparator circuit," *Electronics Letters,* vol. 19, no. 17, pp. 695–697, Aug. 1983.
17. D. Etiemble, "Multiple-valued MOS circuits and VLSI implementation," presented at the Int. Symp. on Multiple-Valued Logic, May 1986.
18. S. Kawahito, M. Kameyama, T. Higuchi, and H. Yamada, "A 32 × 32-bit multiplier using multiple-valued MOS current-mode circuits," *IEEE J. Solid-State Circuits,* vol. 23, no. 1, pp. 124–132, Feb. 1988.

19. T. T. Dao, "Threshold I2L and its application to binary symmetric functions and multivalued logic," *IEEE Journal of Solid-State Circuits,* vol. 12, no. 5, pp. 463–472, Oct. 1977.

20. K. W. Current, "Application of quaternary logic to the design of a proposed discrete cosine transform chip," *International Journal of Electronics,* vol. 67, no. 5, pp. 687–701, Nov. 1989.

21. D. J. Allstot, G. Laing, and H. C. Yang, "Current-mode logic techniques for CMOS mixed-mode ASICs," *Proceedings of the 1991 Custom Integrated Circuits Conference,* pp. 25.2.1–25.2.4, May 1991.

22. T. T. Dao, E. J. McCluskey, and L. K. Russel, "Multivalued integrated injection logic," *IEEE Trans. Computers,* vol. C-26, no. 12, pp. 1233–1241, Dec. 1977.

23. D. G. Nairn and C. A. T. Salama, "Current-mode algorithmic analog-to-digital converters," *IEEE Journal of Solid-State Circuits,* vol. 25, no. 4, pp. 997–1004, Aug. 1990.

## Further Reading

This discussion is intended to present a view of the state-of-the-art in practical, realizable multiple-valued logic circuits, and of the trend expected in new multiple-valued logic circuits. The reader is referred to excellent survey and tutorial papers and books listed below and to special issues of journals and magazines that present the introductory, historical, background, and breadth material about MVL theory and circuitry that was not presented here.

K. C. Smith, "The prospects for multivalued logic: a technology and applications view," *IEEE Transactions on Computers,* vol. C-30, no. 9, pp. 619–632, Sep. 1981.

S. L. Hurst, "Multiple valued logic: its status and its future," *IEEE Transactions on Computers,* vol. C-33, no. 12, pp. 1160–1179, Dec. 1984.

K. C. Smith, "Multiple valued logic: A tutorial and appreciation," *Computer,* pp. 17–27, April 1988.

D. Etiemble and M. Israel, "A comparison of binary and multivalued ICs according to VLSI criteria," *Computer,* pp. 28–42, April 1988.

D. C. Rine, Ed., *Computer Science and Multiple-valued logic: Theory and Applications,* 2nd ed., North-Holland, Amsterdam, 1984.

J. C. Muzio and T. C. Wesselkamper, *Multiple-Valued Switching Theory,* Adam Hilger, Bristol and Boston, 1986.

J. T. Butler, Ed., *Multiple-Valued Logic in VLSI,* IEEE Computer Society Press, 1991.

Special issues of journals and magazines devoted to multiple-valued logic are listed below:

J. R. Armstrong, Ed., *IEEE Design and Test,* June 1990.

R. E. Hawkin, Ed., *International Journal of Electronics,* Nov. 1989.

R. E. Hawkin, Ed., *International Journal of Electronics,* Aug. 1987.

J. C. Muzio and I. C. Rosenberg, Ed., *IEEE Transactions on Computers,* Feb. 1986.

J. T. Butler and A.S. Wojic, Ed., *IEEE Transactions on Computers,* Sep. 1974.

R. Arrathoon, Ed., *Optical Computing,* Jan. 1986.

D. C. Rine, Ed., *IEEE Computer,* Sep. 1974.

J. T. Butler, Ed., *IEEE Computer,* Aug. 1988.

The annual International Symposium on Multiple Valued Logic sponsored by the IEEE Computer Society Technical Committee on Multiple Valued Logic, and *Multiple Valued Logic: An International Journal* (Gordon and Breach, London) are also excellent sources of information about the on-going developments in many theoretical and practical aspects of MVL. The IEEE Computer Society Technical Committee on Multiple Valued Logic maintains a website at http://www.computer.org/tab/tclist/tcmvl.htm.

# 12

# FPGAs for Rapid Prototyping

James O. Hamblen
*Georgia Institute of Technology*

## 12.1   Programmable Logic Technology

Digital systems can be implemented using several hardware technologies. As shown in Fig. 12.1, field programmable gate arrays (FPGAs), complex programmable logic devices (CPLDs), and application specific integrated circuits (ASICs), are integrated circuits whose internal functional operation is defined by the user. ASICs require a final customized manufacturing step for the user-defined function. Programmable logic devices such as CPLDs or FPGAs require user configuration or programming to implement the desired function. Full custom VLSI devices are internally hardwired and optimized to perform a fixed function. Examples of full custom very large scale integrated (VLSI) devices include the microprocessor and RAM chips used in computers.

### PALs, PLAs, CPLDs, FPGAs, ASICs, and Full Custom VLSI Devices

The different device technologies each have a different set of design tradeoffs as seen in Fig. 12.2. The design of a full custom VLSI device at the transistor level requires several years of engineering effort for design, testing, and fabrication [1,2]. This expensive development effort is only economical for the highest volume devices. Full custom VLSI devices will produce the highest performance, but they also have the highest development cost and the longest time to market.

ASICs are typically divided into two categories, gate arrays and standard cells. Gate arrays are built from arrays of pre-manufactured logic cells. A single logic cell implements only a few gates or a flip-flop. A final custom manufacturing step is required to interconnect the sea of logic cells on a gate array. This interconnection pattern is created by the user to implement a particular design. Standard cell devices contain no fixed internal structure. For standard cell devices, the device manufacturer creates a custom photographic mask to build the chip based on the user's selection of devices. These devices typically include communications and bus controllers, ALUs, RAM, ROM, and microprocessors from the manufacturer's standard cell library.

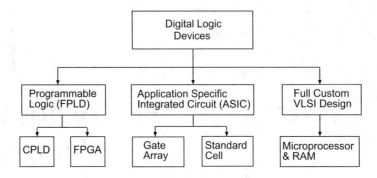

**FIGURE 12.1**   Device technologies used for implementation of digital systems.

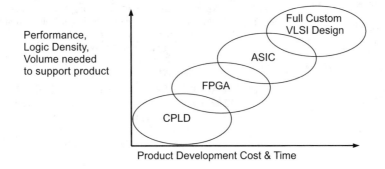

**FIGURE 12.2**   Comparison of device technologies used for digital systems.

ASICs will require additional time and development costs due to custom manufacturing. Several months are normally required to produce the device and substantial mask setup fees are charged. Additional effort in testing must be performed by the user, since chips can only be tested after the final custom-manufacturing step [3]. Any design error in the chip will lead to additional manufacturing delays and costs. For products with long lifetimes and large volumes, this approach has a lower cost per unit than CPLDs or FPGAs. Economic and performance trade-offs between ASICs, CPLDs, and FPGAs change constantly with each new generation of devices and design tools.

Several factors including higher densities, higher speed, and increased pressure to reduce time to market have enabled the use of programmable logic devices in a wider variety of designs. CPLDs and FPGAs are the highest density and most advanced programmable logic devices. These devices are also collectively called field programmable logic devices (FPLDs). Designs using a CPLD or FPGA typically require several weeks of engineering effort instead of months.

Because ASICs and full custom VLSI designs are hardwired and do not have programmable interconnect delays they provide faster clock times than CPLDs or FPGAs. ASICs and full custom VLSI designs do not require programmable interconnect circuitry so they also use less chip area and have a lower per unit manufacturing cost in large volumes. Initial engineering development costs for ASICs and full custom VLSI designs are higher. Initial prototypes of ASICs and full custom VLSI devices are often developed using CPLDs and FPGAs.

## Applications of FPGAs

FPGAs have become more widely used in the last decade. Higher densities, improved performance, and cost advantages have enabled the use of programmable logic devices in a wider variety of designs. A recent market survey indicated that there are over ten times as many CPLD and FPGA-based designs as ASIC-based designs. New generation FPGAs contain several million gates and can provide clock rates approaching 1 GHz. Example application areas include single chip replacements for old multichip technology designs, digital signal processing (DSP), image processing, multimedia applications, high-speed networking and communications equipment, bus protocols such as peripheral component interconnect (PCI), microprocessor glue logic, co-processors, and microperipheral controllers. RISC microprocessors are also starting to appear inside large FPGAs that are intended for system-on-a-chip (SOC) designs. For all but the most time critical design applications, CPLDs and FPGAs have adequate speed with maximum system clock rates typically in the range of 50–400 MHz. Clock rates up to 1 GHz have been achieved on new generation FPGAs.

Several large FPGAs with an interconnection network are used to build hardware emulators. Hardware emulators are specially designed commercial systems used to prototype and test complex hardware designs that will later be implemented on ASIC or custom VLSI devices. Several recent microprocessors including Intel and AMD x86 processors used in PCs were prototyped on hardware emulators. A new application area for FPGAs is reconfigurable computing. In reconfigurable computing, FPGAs are quickly reprogrammed or reconfigured during normal operations to enable them to perform different functions at different times for a particular application.

## Product Term (EEPROM and Fuse-Based) Devices

Simple programmable logic devices (PLDs), consisting of programmable array logics (PALs) and programmable logic arrays (PLAs), have been in use for over two decades. Simple PLDs can replace several older fixed function TTL-style parts in a design. Most PLDs contain a series of AND gates with fuse programmable inputs that feed into an array of fuse programmable OR gates. In PALs, the AND array is programmable but the OR array has a fixed input connection. In a PLA or PAL, a series of AND gates feeding into an OR gate are programmed to directly implement a sum-of-products (SOP) Boolean equation. An example SOP implementation using a PLA can be seen in Fig. 12.3. Note that inverters are provided so that every input signal is also available in normal or complemented form. A shorthand notation is used for the gate inputs in PLAs. A PLA's AND and OR gates have inputs where each horizontal and vertical line cross. Initially in a PLA, all fuses are intact so each AND gate ANDs every input signal and its logical complement. By blowing unwanted fuses or programming, the unwanted AND gate inputs are disconnected by the user and the required product term is produced. In PALs, different devices are

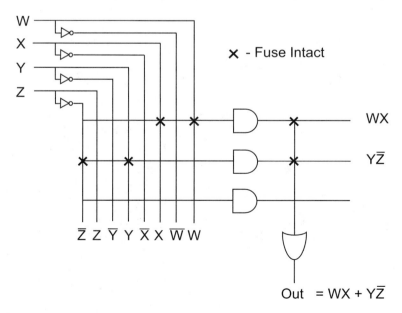

**FIGURE 12.3** Using a PLA to implement a sum of products equation.

selected depending on the number of product terms (i.e., inputs to OR gate) in the SOP logic equation. Some devices have one-time programmable fuses and others have fuses that can be erased and re-programmed. On many PLDs, the output of the OR gate is connected to a flip-flop whose output can then be fed back as an input into the AND gate array. This provides PLDs with the capability to implement simple state machines. A simple PLD can contain several of these AND/OR networks. The largest product term devices contain an array of PLAs with a simple interconnection network. This type of device is called a complex programmable logic device (CPLD). Product term devices typically range in size from several hundred to a few thousand gates.

## Lookup Table (SRAM-Based) Devices

FPGAs are the highest density and most advanced programmable logic devices. The size of CPLDs and FPGAs is typically described in terms of useable or equivalent gates. This refers to the maximum number of two input NAND gates available in the device. Different device manufacturers use different standards to determine the gate count of their device. This should be viewed as a rough estimate of size only. The gate utilization achieved in a particular design will vary considerably.

Most FPGAs use SRAM look-up tables (LUTs) to implement logic circuits with gates. An example showing how a LUT can model a gate network is shown in Fig. 12.4. First, the gate network is converted into a truth table. Because four inputs and one output are used, a truth table with 16 rows and one output is needed. The truth table is then loaded into the LUT's 16 by 1 high-speed SRAM when the FPLD is programmed. Note that the four gate inputs, *W, X, Y,* and *Z* are used as address lines for the RAM and that OUT, the output of the circuit and truth table, is the data that is stored in the LUT's RAM. Using this technique, the LUT's SRAM implements the gate network by performing a RAM-based truth table look-up instead of using actual logic gates. In some devices, LUTs can also be used directly to implement RAM or shift registers.

Internally, FPGAs contain multiple copies of a basic programmable logic element (LE), also called a logic cell (LC) or configurable logic block (CLB). A typical LE is shown in Fig. 12.5. Using one or more LUTs, the logic element can implement a network of several logic gates that then feed into a programmable flip-flop. The flip-flop can be bypassed when only combinational logic is needed. Some FPGA devices contain two similar circuits in each logic element or CLB. Numerous LEs or CLBs are arranged in a two

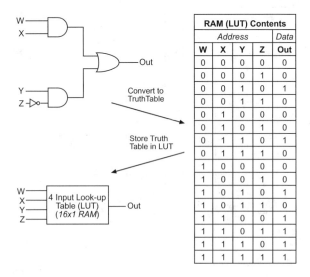

| RAM (LUT) Contents | | | | |
|---|---|---|---|---|
| Address | | | | Data |
| W | X | Y | Z | Out |
| 0 | 0 | 0 | 0 | 0 |
| 0 | 0 | 0 | 1 | 0 |
| 0 | 0 | 1 | 0 | 1 |
| 0 | 0 | 1 | 1 | 0 |
| 0 | 1 | 0 | 0 | 0 |
| 0 | 1 | 0 | 1 | 0 |
| 0 | 1 | 1 | 0 | 1 |
| 0 | 1 | 1 | 1 | 0 |
| 1 | 0 | 0 | 0 | 0 |
| 1 | 0 | 0 | 1 | 0 |
| 1 | 0 | 1 | 0 | 1 |
| 1 | 0 | 1 | 1 | 0 |
| 1 | 1 | 0 | 0 | 1 |
| 1 | 1 | 0 | 1 | 1 |
| 1 | 1 | 1 | 0 | 1 |
| 1 | 1 | 1 | 1 | 1 |

**FIGURE 12.4** Using an FPGA's look-up table (LUT) to implement a logic gate network.

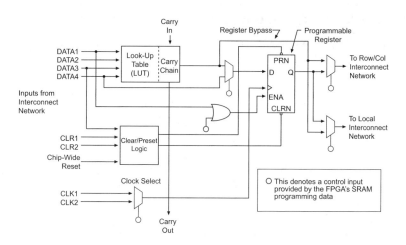

**FIGURE 12.5**   Typical FPGA logic element.

dimensional array on the chip. Current FPGAs contain a few hundred to over a hundred thousand logic elements. To perform complex operations, logic elements can be automatically connected to other logic elements on the chip using a programmable interconnection network. The programmable interconnection network is also contained in the FPGA.

The interconnection network used to connect the logic elements contains row and column chip-wide interconnects. In addition, the interconnection network usually contains shorter and faster programmable interconnects limited only to neighboring logic elements. The internal interconnect delays are an important performance factor since they are of the same order of magnitude as the logic element delay times. Using a shorter interconnect path means less delay time. So that high-speed adders can be produced, there is often a dedicated fast carry logic connection to neighboring logic elements.

Clock signals in large FPGAs must use special low-skew global clock buffer lines. These are dedicated pins connected to special internal high-speed busses. These special busses are used to distribute the clock signal to all flip-flops in the device at the same time to minimize clock skew. If the global clock buffer lines are not used, the clock is routed through the chip just like a normal signal. The clock signals could arrive at flip-flops at widely different times since interconnect delays will vary significantly in different parts of the chip. This delay time or clock skew may violate flip-flop setup and hold times. This causes metastability or unpredictable operation in flip-flops. Most large designs with clock signals that are used throughout the FPGA will require the use of the global clock buffers. Some CAD tools will automatically detect and assign clocks to the global clock buffers and others require designers to identify clock signals and assign them to one of the global clock buffers.

General purpose external I/O pins on CPLDs and FPGAs contain programmable bidirectional tristate drivers and flip-flops. Pins can be programmed for input, output, or bidirectional operation. The I/O signal can be loaded into the I/O pin's flip-flop or directly connected to the interconnection network and routed from there to internal logic elements. Multiple power and ground pins are also required on large CPLDs and FPGAs. FPGA internal core voltages range from 1.5 to 5 V. FPGAs using advanced package types such as pin grid array (PGA) and ball grid array (BGA) are available with several hundred pins.

When a design approaches the device size limits, it is possible to run out of either logic, interconnect, or pin resources when using a CPLD or FPGA. CPLD and FPGA families include multiple devices in a wide range of gates with varying numbers of pins available on different package types. To minimize cost, part of the design problem is selecting a device with just enough logic, interconnect, and pins. Another important device selection factor is the speed or clock rate needed for a particular design.

### Architecture of Newer Generation FPGAs

New generation FPGAs have continued to increase in size and are adding additional features. Several FPGAs now include a mix of both product term and LUT-based logic gate resources. Product term logic blocks are more efficient for the more complex control logic present in larger state machines and address decoders. Phase-locked loops (PLLs) are available in many newer FPGAs to multiply and shift clock signals.

Many recent generation FPGAs also contain internal or embedded RAM memory blocks. Although the RAM can be implemented using the FPGA's logic elements, it is more efficient to build dedicated memory blocks for larger amounts of RAM and ROM. These memory blocks are normally distributed throughout the chip and can be initialized when the chip is programmed. The capacity of these internal memory blocks is limited to a few thousand bits per block. Memory intensive designs may still require additional external memory devices.

Some new generation FPGAs also contain internal hardware multipliers. These offer higher performance than multipliers built using the FPGA's logic elements and are useful for many DSP and graphics applications that require intensive multiply operations. Several of the largest FPGAs are available with internal commercial RISC microprocessor cores.

Most recent FPGAs support a number of I/O standards on external input and output pins. This feature makes it easier to interface to external high-speed devices. Several different I/O standards are used on processors, memory, and peripheral devices. The I/O standard is selected when the device is programmed. These I/O standards have varying voltage levels to increase bandwidth, reduce emissions, and lower power consumption. One recently announced FPGA family also features selectable impedance on output drivers. This eliminates the need for external terminating resistors on high-speed signal lines.

The largest FPGAs have started to use redundant logic to increase chip yields. As any VLSI device gets larger, the probability of a manufacturing defect increases. Some devices now include extra rows or columns of logic elements. After the device is tested, bad rows of logic elements are automatically mapped out and replaced with an extra row. This occurs when the device is initially tested and is transparent to the user.

Presently, the two major FPGA manufacturers are Altera and Xilinx. Altera refers to their larger FPGA-like devices as CPLDs. Other companies include Actel, Atmel, Lucent Technologies, and Quicklogic. Extensive data on devices is available at each manufacturer's website. Currently available FPGA devices range in size from a few thousand to several million gates. Trade publications such as Electronic Design News periodically have a comparison of the available devices and manufacturers [4].

## 12.2 CAD Tools for Rapid Prototyping Using FPGAs

### Design Entry

Most FPGA CAD tools support both schematic capture and hardware description language (HDL) based design entry. With logic capacities of an individual FPGA chip approaching 10,000,000 gates, manual design of the entire system at the gate level is not a viable option. Rapid prototyping using an HDL with an automatic logic synthesis tool is quickly replacing the more traditional gate-level design approach using schematic capture entry. These new HDL-based logic synthesis tools can be used for ASIC-, CPLD-, and FPGA-based designs. The two most widely used HDLs at the present time are VHDL and Verilog. VHDL is based on ADA or PASCAL style syntax and Verilog is based on a C-like syntax. Historically, most ASIC designs used Verilog and most FPGA-based designs used VHDL. This has changed in the last decade. DoD funded design projects in the United States must use VHDL and most FPGA CAD tools now support both VHDL and Verilog [5,6]. Currently, most FPGA synthesis projects written in VHDL or Verilog specify the model at the register transfer level (RTL). RTL models list the exact sequence of register transfers that will take place at each clock cycle. It is crucial to understand that HDLs model parallel operations unlike the traditional sequential programming languages such as C or PASCAL.

Because synthesis tools do not support every language feature, models used for synthesis must use a subset of the HDL's features. In VHDL, signals should be used for synthesis models instead of variables. HDL models intended for synthesis should not include propagation delay times. After logic synthesis, actual delay times will be automatically calculated by the FPGA CAD tools for use in simulation. Initial values for variables or signals are not supported in HDL synthesis tools. This means that most HDL models originally written only for simulation use will not synthesize.

## Using HDLs for Design Entry and Synthesis

To illustrate and compare the features of the two most widely used HDLs, VHDL and Verilog, two example synthesis models will be examined. As seen in Table 12.1, VHDL and Verilog have a similar set of synthesis operators with VHDL operators based on PASCAL and Verilog operators based on C. Some shift operators are missing in Verilog, but they can be implemented in a single line of code with a few additional characters. In VHDL processes, concurrent statements and entities execute in parallel. Inside a process, statements execute in sequential order. In Verilog, modules and always blocks execute in parallel and statements inside an always block execute sequentially just like processes in VHDL. Processes and always blocks have sensitivity lists that specify when they should be reevaluated. Any signal that can change the output of a block must be listed in the sensitivity list. VHDL processes and Verilog always blocks with a clock signal sensitivity will generate flip-flops when synthesized.

**TABLE 12.1**   HDL Operators Used for Synthesis

| Synthesis Operation | VHDL Operator | Verilog Operator |
|---|---|---|
| Addition | + | + |
| Subtraction | − | − |
| Multiplication[*] | * | * |
| Division[*] | / | / |
| Modulus[*] | MOD | % |
| Remainder[*] | REM | |
| Concatenation—used to combine bits | & | { } |
| Logical shift left | SLL[**] | << |
| Logical shift right | SRL[**] | >> |
| Arithmetic shift left | SLA[**] | |
| Arithmetic shift right | SRA[**] | |
| Rotate left | ROL[**] | |
| Rotate right | ROR[**] | |
| Equality | = | == |
| Inequality | /= | != |
| Less than | < | < |
| Less than or equal | <= | <= |
| Greater than | > | > |
| Greater than or equal | >= | >= |
| Logical NOT | NOT | ! |
| Logical AND | AND | && |
| Logical OR | OR | \|\| |
| Bitwise NOT | NOT | ~ |
| Bitwise AND | AND | & |
| Bitwise OR | OR | \| |
| Bitwise XOR | XOR | ^ |

[*] Not supported in many HDL synthesis tools. In some synthesis tools, only multiply and divide by powers of two (shifts) are supported. Efficient implementation of multiply or divide hardware frequently requires the user to specify the arithmetic algorithm and design details in the HDL or call a FPGA vendor supplied function.

[**] Supported only in IEEE 1076–1993 VHDL.

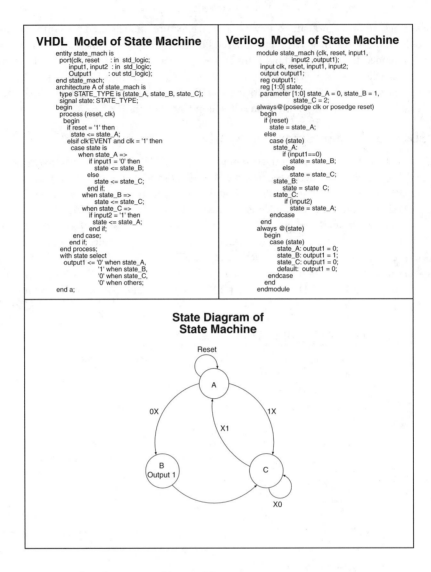

**FIGURE 12.6**    VHDL and Verilog state machine model.

   An example of a simple state machine is shown in Fig. 12.6. The state diagram shows that the state machine has three states with two inputs and one output that is active only in state B. The state machine resets to state A. Most FPGAs offer some advantages for Moore type state machines (i.e., output a function of state only) with one-hot encoding (i.e., one flip-flop per state) since they contain a register-rich architecture with limited gating logic. One-hot state machines are also less prone to timing problems and are the default encoding used in many FPGA synthesis tools. Since there are undefined states, a reset should always be provided to force the state machine into a known state. Most FPGAs automatically clear all flip-flops at power up. The first step in each model is to declare inputs and outputs. An internal signal, state, is then declared and used to hold the current state. Note that the actual encoding of the three states is not specified in VHDL, but it must be specified in the Verilog model. The first VHDL PROCESS and Verilog ALWAYS block are sensitive to the rising clock edge; so positive edge-triggered flip-flops are synthesized to hold the state signal. Inside the first PROCESS or ALWAYS block, if a synchronous reset occurs the state is set to state A. If there is no reset, a CASE statement is used to assign the next value of state based on the current value of state and the inputs. The new assignments to state will not take effect

```
                  VHDL  Model of ALU

entity ALU is
   port(ALU_control  : in std_logic_vector(2 downto 0);
       Ainput, Binput: in std_logic_vector(15 downto 0);
       Clock      : in std_logic;
       Shift_output: out std_logic_vector(15 downto 0));
end ALU;

architecture RTL of ALU is
signal ALU_output: std_logic_vector(15 downto 0);
begin
   process (ALU_Control, Ainput, Binput)
     begin
       case ALU_Control(2 downto 1) is
         when "00" => ALU_output <= Ainput + Binput;
         when "01" => ALU_output <= Ainput - Binput;
         when "10" => ALU_output <= Ainput and Binput;
         when "11" => ALU_output <= Ainput or Binput;
         when others => ALU_output <="0000000000000000";
       end case;
     end process;
   process
   begin
      wait until rising_edge(Clock);
      if ALU_control(0) = '1' then
        Shift_output <= ALU_output(14 downto 0) & "0";
      else
        Shift_output <= ALU_output;
      end if;
   end process;
end RTL;
```

```
                 Verilog  Model of ALU

module ALU ( ALU_control, Ainput, Binput,
                           Clock, Shift_output);
   input [2:0] ALU_control;
   input [15:0] Ainput;
   input [15:0] Binput;
   input Clock;
   output[15:0] Shift_output;
   reg [15:0] Shift_output;
   reg [15:0] ALU_output;
   always @ (ALU_control or Ainput or Binput)
     case (ALU_control[2:1])
       0: ALU_output = Ainput + Binput;
       1: ALU_output = Ainput - Binput;
       2: ALU_output = Ainput & Binput;
       3: ALU_output = Ainput | Binput;
       default: ALU_output = 0;
     endcase
   always @ (posedge Clock)
     if (ALU_control[0]==1)
       Shift_output = ALU_output << 1;
     else
       Shift_output = ALU_output;
endmodule
```

**Synthesized ALU Hardware**

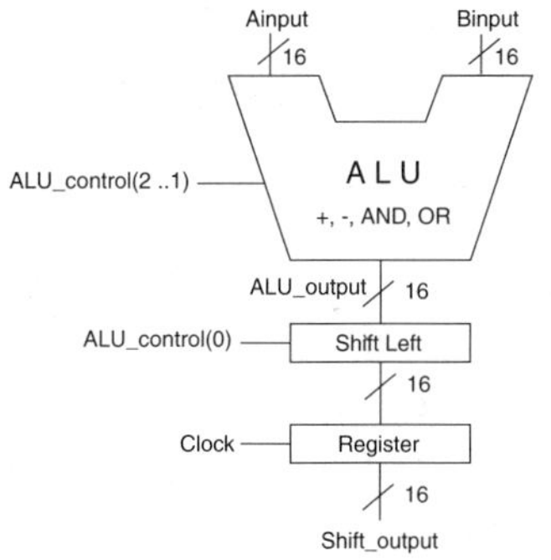

**FIGURE 12.7**  VDHL and Verilog ALU model.

until the next clock. In the second block of code in each model, a VHDL WITH SELECT concurrent statement and a Verilog ALWAYS block assigns the output signal based on the current state (i.e., a Moore state machine). This generates gates or combinational logic only with no flip-flops since there is no sensitivity to the clock edge.

In the second example seen in Fig. 12.7, the hardware to be synthesized consists of a 16-bit registered ALU. The ALU supports four operations, add, subtract, bitwise AND, and bitwise OR. The operation is selected with the high two bits of ALU_control. After the ALU operation, an optional shift left operation is performed. The shift operation is controlled by the low-bit of ALU_control. The output from the shift operation is then loaded in a 16-bit register on the positive edge of the clock.

At the start of each of the VHDL and Verilog ALU models, the input and output signals are declared specifying the number of bits in each signal. The top-level I/O signals would normally be assigned to I/O pins on the FPGA. An internal signal, ALU_output, is declared and used for the output of the ALU. Next, the CASE statements in both models synthesize a 4-to-1 multiplexer that selects one of the four ALU functions. The +, −, AND (&), and OR (|) operators in each model automatically synthesize a 16-bit adder/subtractor with fast carry logic, a bitwise AND, and a bitwise OR circuit. In most synthesis tools, the +1 operation is a special case and it generates a smaller and faster increment circuit instead of an adder. Following the CASE statement, the next section of code in each model generates the shift operation and selects the shifted or non-shifted value with a 16-bit wide 2-to-1 multiplexer generated by the IF statement. The result is then loaded into a 16-bit register. All signal assignments following the VHDL WAIT or second Verilog ALWAYS block will be registered since they are a function of the clock signal. In VHDL WAIT UNTIL RISING_EDGE(CLOCK) and in Verilog ALWAYS@(POSEDGE CLOCK) instructs the synthesis tool to use positive edge-triggered D flip-flops to build the register. A few additional Library and Use statements at the start of each VHDL model will be required in some VHDL tools to define the IEEE standard logic type. For additional information on writing HDLs for logic synthesis models, select an HDL reference text that includes example models intended for synthesis and not just simulation [6–15].

Behavioral synthesis tools using VHDL and Verilog behavioral level models have also been developed. Unlike RTL level models, behavioral level models do not specify states and the required sequence of register transfers. Behavioral compilers automatically design the state machine, allocate and schedule the logic and ALU operations, and register transfers subject to a set of constraints. These constraints are typically the number of clock cycles required to obtain selected signals [16]. By modifying these constraints, different design architectures and alternatives are automatically generated.

Newer system-level synthesis languages based on C and Java have also been recently developed but are not currently in widespread use in industry. These languages more closely resemble a traditional program that describes an algorithm without specifying register transfers at the clock level. Many of these tools output a VHDL or Verilog RTL description as an intermediate step. Some new tools are also appearing that automatically generate FPGA designs using other popular engineering design software such as MATLAB.

CAD tools for synthesis are available from the both the device manufacturers and third party vendors. Third party logic synthesis tools often provide higher performance and offer the advantage of supporting devices from several manufacturers. This makes it easier to retarget a design to a device from a different chip manufacturer. Following logic synthesis, many of the third party tools use the device manufacturer's standard place and route tools. Interfacing, configuring, and maintaining a design flow that uses various CAD tools provided by different vendors can be a complex task. Several academically oriented texts contain additional details on the logic synthesis and optimization algorithms used internally in FPGA CAD tools [17–20].

## IP Cores for FPGAs

Intellectual property (IP) cores are widely used in large designs. IP cores are commercial hardware designs that provide frequently used operations. These previously developed designs are available as commercially licensed products from both FPGA manufacturers and third party IP vendors. FPGA manufacturers typically provide several basic hardware functions bundled with their devices and CAD tools. These functions will work on their devices only. They include RAM, ROM, CAM, FIFO buffers, shift registers, addition, multiply, and divide hardware. A few of these device specific functions may be used by an HDL synthesis tool automatically, some must be called as library functions from an HDL, or entered using special symbols in a schematic. Explicitly invoking these FPGA vendor specific functions in HDL function calls or using the special symbols in a schematic may improve performance, but it also makes it more difficult to retarget a design to a different FPGA manufacturer.

Commercial third-party IP cores include microprocessors, communications controllers, standard bus interfaces, and DSP functions. IP cores can reduce development time and help promote design reuse by providing widely used hardware functions in complex hierarchical designs. For FPGAs, commercial IP cores are typically a synthesizable HDL model or in a few cases a custom VLSI layout that is added to the FPGA. Several large FPGA families are now available with multipliers or RISC microprocessor IP cores [21]. FPGAs with RISC microprocessors have additional support tools such as C compilers and design tools to configure the processor and I/O systems. In the near future, it is likely that a small operating system kernel will also be supplied with these tools. These new devices are a hybrid that contains both ASIC and FPGA features.

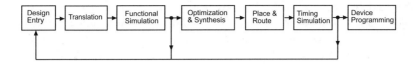

**FIGURE 12.8**    CAD tool flow for FPGAs and CPLDs.

## Logic Simulation and Test

A typical FPGA CAD tool design flow is shown in Fig. 12.8. First, the design is entered, using an HDL or schematic. Large designs are often simulated first using a faster running functional simulation tool that uses a zero gate delay model (i.e., it does not contain any gate level timing information). Functional simulation will detect logical errors but not synthesis related timing problems. Timing simulations are performed later after synthesis and mapping of the design onto the FPGA.

A test bench (also called a test harness or a test fixture) is a specially written module that provides input stimulus to a simulation and automatically monitors the output of the hardware unit under test (UUT) [8,22]. Using a test bench isolates the test-only code portion of a design from the hardware synthesis model. By running the same test bench code and test vectors in both a functional and timing simulation, it is possible to check for any synthesis related problems. It is common for the test bench code to require as much development time as the HDL synthesis model.

Following functional simulation of the design, the logic is automatically minimized, the design is synthesized, and saved as a netlist. A netlist is a text-based representation of a logic circuit's schematic diagram.

## FPGA Place and Route Tools

An automatic fitting or place and route tool then reads in the design's netlist and fits the design into the device. The design is mapped into the FPGA's logic elements, first by partitioning the design into small pieces that fit in an FPGA's logic element, and then by placing the design in specific logic element locations in the FPGA. After placement, the interconnection network routing paths are determined. Many logic elements must be connected to form a design, so the interconnect delays are a function of the distance between the logic elements selected in the place process. The place and route process can be quite involved and can take several minutes to compute on large designs. Combinatorial explosion prevents the tools from examining all possible place and route assignments for a design. Heuristic algorithms such as simulated annealing are used for place and route, so running the place and route tool multiple times may produce better performance. External I/O signals can be constrained to particular device pin numbers, but allowing them to be selected automatically by the place and route tools often results in improved performance. Many tools also allow the designer to specify timing constraints on critical signal paths to help meet performance goals. Most tools still include a floorplan editor that allows manual placement of the design into logic elements, but current generation tools, using automatic placement with appropriate timing constraints, are likely to produce superior performance. Place and route errors will occur when there are not enough logic elements, interconnect, or pin resources on the specified FPGA to support the design.

After partition, place, and route, accurate timing simulations can be performed using logic and interconnect time delays automatically obtained from the manufacturer's detailed timing model of the device. Although errors can occur at any step in the process, the most common step where errors are detected is during tests in an exhaustive simulation.

## Device Programming and Hardware Verification

After successful simulation, the final step is device programming and hardware verification using the actual FPGA. Smaller PLD and CPLD devices with fuses or EEPROM will only need to be programmed once since the memory is nonvolatile. Most FPGAs use volatile RAM memory for programming, so they need to be reprogrammed each time power is turned on. For initial prototyping, FPGA CAD tools can download the programming data to the FPGA, using a special cable attached to the development computer's parallel or serial port. For initial testing without the need for a custom printed circuit board, FPGA development boards are available from the device manufacturers and other vendors. The development boards typically contain an FPGA with a download cable, a small prototyping area, and I/O expansion connectors. In a final production system, FPGAs automatically read in their internal RAM programming data from a small external PROM each time power is turned on. Since FPGAs read in this programming data whenever they power up, it is possible to build systems that automatically install design updates by downloading the new FPGA programming data into an EEPROM or FLASH memory using a network connection.

## References

1. Rabaey, J. and Chandrakasan, A., *Digital Integrated Circuits,* Prentice Hall, Englewood Cliffs, 2001.
2. Oklobdzija, V., *High-Perfomance System Design: Circuts and Logic,* IEEE Press, 1999.
3. Smith, M., *Application-Specific Integrated Circuits,* Addison-Wesley, Reading, MA, 1997.
4. Dipert, B., Annual Programmable Logic Directory, *Electronic Design News,* August 17, 2000. http://www.ednmag.com
5. *MAX+PLUS II Getting Started,* Altera Corporation 1997. http://www.altera.com
6. *Synthesis and Simulation Design Guide,* Xilinx Corporation, 2000. http://www.xilinx.com
7. Smith, D., *HDL Chip Design,* Doone Publications, Madison, 1996. http://www.doone.com/hdl_chip_des.html
8. Hamblen, J. and Furman, M., *Rapid Prototyping of Digital Systems,* Kluwer Academic Publishers, Boston, MA, 2000. http://www.ece.gatech.edu/~hamblen/book/book.htm
9. Bhasker, J., *A VHDL Synthesis Primer,* Star Galaxy Press, Allentown, 1998.
10. Armstrong, J. and Gray, F., *VHDL Design Representation and Synthesis,* Prentice-Hall, Englewood Cliffs, NJ, 2000.
11. Brown, S. and Vranisic, Z., *Fundamentals of Digital Logic with VHDL Design,* McGraw-Hill, Boston, MA, 2000.
12. Salcic, Z. and Smailagic, A., *Digital Systems Design and Prototyping Using Field Programmable Logic and Hardware Description Languages,* Kluwer Academic Publishers, Boston, MA, 2000.
13. Yalamanchili, S., *Introductory VHDL: From Simulation to Synthesis,* Prentice-Hall, Englewood Cliffs, NJ, 2000.
14. Palnitkar, S., *Verilog HDL: A Guide to Digital Design and Synthesis,* Prentice-Hall, Englewood Cliffs, NJ, 1996.
15. Bhasker, J., *Verilog HDL Synthesis, A Practical Primer,* Star Galaxy Press, Allentown, 1998.
16. Knapp, D. W., *Behavioral Synthesis Digital System Design Using the Synopsys Behavioral Compiler,* Prentice Hall, Englewood Cliffs, NJ, 1996.
17. Gajski, D., Nikil, D., Wu, C., and Y. Lin, *High Level Synthesis: Introduction to Chip and System Design,* Kluwer Academic Publishers, Boston, MA, 1992.
18. Michel, P., Lauther, U., and Duzy, P., *The Synthesis Approach to Digital System Design,* Kluwer, Academic Publishers, Boston, MA, 1992.
19. De Micheli, G., *Synthesis and Optimization of Digital Circuits,* McGraw-Hill, New York, 1994.
20. Hactel and Somenzi, *Logic Synthesis and Verification Algorithms,* Kluwer Academic Publishers, Boston, MA, 1996.
21. Synder, C., FPGA Processor Cores Get Serious, *Microprocessor Report,* September 18, 2000.
22. Bergeron, J., *Writing Testbenches—Functional Verification of HDL Models,* Kluwer Academic Publishers, Boston, MA, 2000.

# 13

# Issues in High-Frequency Processor Design

Kevin J. Nowka
*IBM Austin Research Laboratory*

Successful design of high-frequency processors is predominantly the act of balancing two competing forces: striving to exploit the most advanced technology, circuits, logic implementations, and system organization; and the necessity to encapsulate the resulting complexity so as to make the task tractable. This chapter addresses some of the compelling issues in high-frequency processor design, both in taking advantage of the technology and circuits and avoiding the pitfalls.

Advances in silicon technology, circuit design techniques, physical design tools, processor organization and architecture, and market demand are producing frequency improvement in high-performance micro-processors. Figure 13.1 shows the anticipated global and local clock frequency of high-performance microprocessors from the SIA International Technology Roadmap for Semiconductors.[1,2] Because silicon technology continuously advances, it is necessary to either define high frequency at each time or define it in a technology-independent manner. For the remainder of this chapter, high frequency will be defined in terms of the technology-independent unit of fanout-of-4 (FO4) inverter delay.[3] Figure 13.2 presents the expected global clock frequency in terms of the ITRS gate delays.[1,2] From this figure, it is apparent that the local cycle time of high-performance microprocessors is expected to shrink by about a factor of two in number of gate delays. The ITRS gate delay is approximately a fanout-1 inverter delay, which is roughly a fixed fraction of one FO4. This cycle time improvement must be provided by improvements in the use of devices and interconnect, circuits, arithmetic, and organizational changes.

This chapter will concentrate on high-frequency designs, currently defined as less than 18 FO4 inverter delays for a 64-bit processor and 16 FO4 for a 32-bit processor. These break-points are chosen because (1) representative designs have been developed, which satisfy these criteria,[4–7] (2) they are sufficiently aggressive to demonstrate the difficulties in achieving high-frequency designs, and (3) they fall firmly within the expected targets of the high-performance microprocessor roadmaps.

In the remainder of this chapter, issues related to the design of processors for these high-frequency targets will be described. The ultimate dependence of the achievable cycle times on interconnect efficiency on low latency circuits will be discussed, and potential problems will be described.

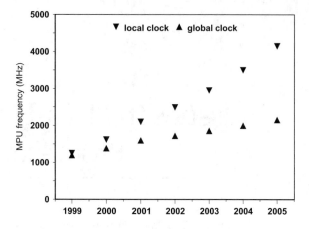

**FIGURE 13.1**   High-performance microprocessor frequency projection.[1,2]

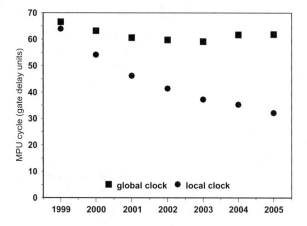

**FIGURE 13.2**   Frequency projection in ITRS gate delay units.

# 13.1   The Processor Implementation Performance Food-Chain

Performance of high-frequency processor designs is becoming increasingly centered around interconnect. Thus, designing for high frequency is largely a matter of interconnect engineering. The importance of optimizing designs by optimizing wiring will continue to accelerate.

Device placement determines interunit and global wiring. The electrical characteristics of this wiring and expected loads, in turn, determine the size of macro output drivers and global buffers. The sizes of these drivers and buffers coupled with the cycle time constraints determine the device sizes, transistor topologies, and combinational logic gate designs. These characteristics influence the size of the macros, which affects the placement. The combinational circuits also determine the topologies, size, and placement of latches. The latches and, in some designs, the combinational logic circuits determine the clock generation and distribution. The circuits drive the design of the power distribution. The delay, power, and noise susceptibility characteristics of the available topologies for logic circuits determine the arithmetic, which can be supported in a design. The same characteristics for memory circuits determine which latches, registers, SRAM arrays, and DRAM arrays can be supported in a design. Although the design of high-frequency processors is a complex process, one in which performance can be lost at any stage, the basis of the process is placement and routing.

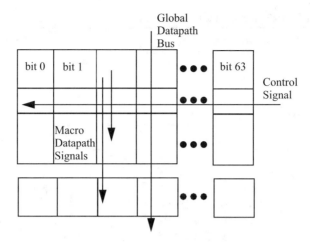

**FIGURE 13.3**   Custom or semi-custom macro cell placement and wiring.

## Placement and Routing: Distance and Wire Loads Are Performance

Custom and semi-custom design processes generally fix the dimension of one of the two wiring directions. This fixed dimension is most often in the direction of the width of the datapath. Each bit position in the datapath has a fixed number of available wiring tracks through the bit slice. The cross direction, or control direction, dimension varies with the complexity of the cells, the number of counter-datapath or control signals. In Fig. 13.3 the horizontal direction is fixed and the vertical dimension is variable. Thus, within a datapath, one dimension is determined by the maximum number of signals, which must travel within that bit position, and the cross dimension is determined by the sum of the individual cell dimensions, which are, in turn, determined by either the number of control signals which must pass through the cell or the size of the transistors and the complexity of the interconnections within the individual cells. From this simple analysis it is clear that the length of the wires, which drive control singles into the datapath, is determined by the datapath width, which is a function of the worst datapath-direction wiring needs. In the most general case, control signals must span all datapath bit positions.

Datapath signals are much more variable in length. Global datapath signals, including data span the entire dataflow stack. Some macro output datapath signals and forwarding busses may cross a significant portion of the dataflow stack. Other macro outputs will simply be driven back to the inputs of the macro for dependent operations or locally to an adjacent latch. In each of these cases, the wire lengths are determined primarily by the sum of the heights of the cells over which these signals must traverse. Important exceptions are for wide control buses and for cross wiring dominated structures like shifters and rotators whose height is determined by the cross, or control-direction, wiring.

Sizing the datapath bit width is performed by analyzing the interconnect needs for global buses and forwarding buses and local datapath interconnects. Once the maximum number of signals, which must travel through a bit position, is known and additional datapath wiring resources are allocated for power and ground signals, this dimension can be fixed.

Wire length analysis in the datapath direction is a more complex iterative process. It involves summing cross wiring needs for shifters and rotators and wide control buses and the lengths of spanned datapath circuits. The size of the spanned circuits are often estimated based upon scaling of previous designs and/or preliminary layout of representative cells. At this point, it is the length of the global and macro crossing signals which are important. Once the length of these signals is known, estimates of the size of global buffers and macro output drivers can be made. With repeated application of rather simple sizing rules, an analysis of the size and topologies of the macro circuits can then be performed. The wire and estimated sink gates form the load for the macro and global drivers, which determine the size of the drivers. Through straightforward rules, such as those presented by Sutherland, et. al.,[8] alternatives for

**TABLE 13.1**    Gigahertz PowerPC Delay Allocation

| Function | Delay (ps) | FO4 | Function | Delay (ps) | FO4 |
|---|---|---|---|---|---|
| Mux-latch Clk-Q | 200 | 2.9 | Mux-latch Clk-Q | 200 | 2.9 |
| Control logic | 470 | 6.8 | Datapath logic | 610 | 8.8 |
| Control distribution | 140 | 2.0 | Datapath distribution | 140 | 2.0 |
| Control latch setup | 140 | 2.0 | Datapath latch setup | 0 | 0 |
| Clock jitter/skew | 50 | 0.7 | Clock jitter/skew | 50 | 0.7 |

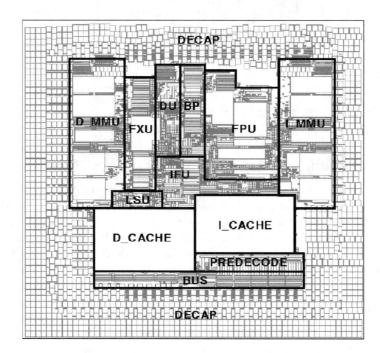

**FIGURE 13.4**    A 1 GHz PowerPC processor floorplan with representative global signal.

combinational logic circuits can be evaluated. In the end, final device sizings, placements, wire level assignments, buffer sizing and placement, and indeed some circuit designs will be adjusted, as the design becomes fixed. The final process is aided by device tuning, extraction, simulation, and static timing tools.

In high-frequency designs, the accurate analysis of the wiring becomes critical. Because the designer is only able to reduce to a limited extent the amount of the cycle time, which must be allocated to clock uncertainty, latching overhead, and the minimum required function (e.g., a 32-bit addition/subtraction and muxing of a logical result) pressure to minimize time in signal distribution, is intense. To date, the shortest technology-independent cycle time for a 64-bit processor, 14.5 FO4 inverter delays, has been an IBM research prototype.[5] The cycle time for this design was allocated according to the budget presented in Table 13.1.

The time available for distribution of results limits the placement of communicating macros. For results, which must be driven out of a macro through a wire into a remote receiving latch, an inverter was placed at the macro output to provide gain to drive the wire and another inverter was placed at the input of the latch to isolate the dynamic multiplexor from any noise on the wire.[9] Thus, the distribution wires could only be at most about 3.5 mm and thus the core of such a short cycle design with full forwarding must be quite small. For full-cycle latch-to-latch transfers, the wires were limited to about 10 mm. Figure 13.4 presents the floorplan of the processor with a representative full-cycle latch-to-latch transfer path of 6.5 mm from the fixed point instruction register to the floating-point decoder latches. Figure 13.5 presents a portion of the fixed point data-flow, FXU, with a representative maximum length forwarding wire of

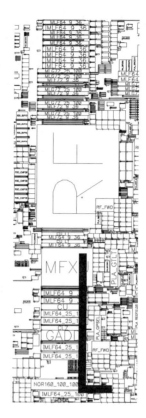

**FIGURE 13.5** Expanded view of fixed-point unit with macro distribution path.

3 mm from the output of the ALU to the operand latch of the load-store unit. In this technology, with a cycle time partitioning as presented, the scope of intracycle communication is small. As cycle times decrease, in terms of the FO4 technology-independent metric, either a greater portion of the cycle must be devoted to covering communication amongst units within the core, or this communication must be completed in subsequent cycles.

Distribution of results in subsequent cycles and forwarding path elimination would eliminate the signal distribution time from the cycle time, at the cost of increased cycles on adjacent dependent operations. Superpipelining of the datapath macro over multiple cycles can increase the throughput of the design, but affects the execution latency due to additional intra-macro latches. Again, the additional cycles to complete the operation are observed on adjacent dependent operations.

Although the interconnect performance is important, it must be tempered by the demands of reliable operation. Many of the noise mechanisms in a design are due directly or indirectly to the design of the interconnects. These effects will be revisited in section 13.2.

The thesis of this work is that there must be a balance between the pursuit of the ultimate exploitation of the technology and the management of the resulting explosion in design complexity. Wire engineering is fraught with such complexity traps. While it is recognized that, for example, inductance can be a concern for on-chip wires, not every wire needs to be modelled as a distributed RLC network. Complexity can be reasonable managed by (1) generating metrics for the classification of wires into modeling classes and (2) determining when individual wires (e.g., global clock nets, bias voltages, critical busses) need to be more carefully analyzed. For the 0.22 $\mu$m technology used in the IBM design,[5] Table 13.2 indicates the classification of general modeling classes for use in the preparation of detailed schematic simulation netlisting and schematic cross-section netlisting. For several wiring levels, the maximum wire length, where the application of each of the models resulted in approximately a 1% delay error, is presented. The T model placed the lumped capacitor to ground between two lumped resistors of value $R/2$. The multiple-T model divided the wires into four sections of T models. Use of these classes provides reasonably

**TABLE 13.2**  Wire Modeling Classes

| Wire Level | Model | Max Length ($\mu$m) |
|---|---|---|
| M1 | Ignore | 13.5 |
|  | Lumped C | 120 |
|  | Lumped RC | 200 |
|  | T | 450 |
|  | Multi-T | 2000 |
| M2 | Ignore | 13.5 |
|  | Lumped C | 180 |
|  | Lumped RC | 225 |
|  | T | 650 |
|  | Multi-T | 2500 |
| M5 | Ignore | 13.5 |
|  | Lumped C | 225 |
|  | Lumped RC | 450 |
|  | T | 900 |
|  | Multi-T | 4500 |

accurate wire modelling while limiting the complexity of the simulation and analysis. In the final design, more detailed analysis of global wiring is warranted. Extraction, including 3D extraction, and analysis of delays and noise are commonly included in a high-frequency design methodology.

From Fig. 13.5, several potential traps are exposed. It should be clear that signals should be produced as locally as possible. Round trip signalling into a datapath and back out in a single cycle consumes almost the entire cycle. In addition, multi-source (multi-sink) buses should have the sources (sinks) located such that the wire lengths are short.

One method of limiting the complexity of the signal distribution was used in an IBM research gigahertz microprocessor.[4,10] In this design, each circuit macro was connected locally to a source operand latch with an integrated data multiplexor and all control signals were required to meet the datapath data at either the input of the macro or at the multiplexor select inputs of the receiving latch. In this way, it was guaranteed that round-trip signals were avoided.

## Fast Wires and Fast Devices: Gain Is Performance

From the previous section, it is clear that the circuit topologies and the device sizes used in the design of macros are dependent upon the wires and device load, which the macro must drive. Macro output drivers can be sized to minimize the delay of driving the networks. The problem sizing CMOS inverters to drive a load is well established.[11] In general, fanout-3 (FO3) to fanout-6 (FO6) rules-of-thumb can be used to size arbitrary CMOS circuits.

As part of the high-frequency design process, logic is sized by stage from output to input. The macro load is the sum of the wire and estimated gate loads attached to the output. The size of the transistors, channel-connected to the output, is such that the current delivered is equivalent to an inverter, which has an input capacitance of 1/3 to 1/6 of an inverter, with an input capacitance equal to the gate's load. This process is repeatedly applied until the primary inputs are reached. These inputs then constitute the load on gates or latches, which drive these inputs. This sizing process can be conducted either manually with simple guidelines[8] or using sizing design automation tools.

The delay of each stage is approximately proportional to the capacitive load, which must be driven. Physical design techniques and technology improvements, which lower capacitance such as routing on higher and more widely spaced wires, low-k dielectrics, and the reduced junction capacitance of SOI technologies,[12–15] can improve the performance of these circuits. Technology improvements to raise the current of the driving transistors such as low-threshold devices, strained silicon, and high-k gate oxides will also improve the performance of these circuits. To the circuit designer, these improvements change not just the performance of the devices and interconnect, but the wiring density, noise margins, noise generation, and reliability characteristics of the wires and devices.

Although the capacitance of the wires and the capacitance of the gates associated with the signal sinks were summed to represent the loads on a macro output, these loads may actually be quite separable and may be sized independently. If the delay of a circuit is modelled by the charging or discharging of a capacitive load:

$$T_d = (C_{int}V_{dd} + C_{gate}V_{dd})/I_{ds\_avg}$$

where $C_{int}$ is the interconnect capacitance, $V_{dd}$ is the supply voltage, $C_{gate}$ is the gate capacitance of the load, and $I_{ds\_avg}$ is the average driver current, and $C_{gate} = const \times W$, and $I_{ds\_avg} = const \times W$, then the delay is minimized as $W$ approaches infinity. Or equivalently, as the $C_{gate}$ is made to fully dominate $C_{int}$. In practice, this relation does not hold; however, even if this were true, the energy consumed would also go to infinity. The ratio of gate capacitance to interconnect capacitance should be maintained at between 1:1 and 2:1 for power efficiency.[16] Driving interconnect significantly harder than this results in larger energy consumption and more severe coupled noise and power supply noise.

## Gate Design: Boolean Efficiency Is Performance

In the previous section, transistor topologies were abstracted as currents, which charged and discharged load capacitances. In this section, the constraints imposed by the short cycle time and the minimum allowable function to be completed in a cycle will be shown to determine the circuit topologies, which can be employed for high frequency designs.

When the clock and latch overhead presented in Table 13.1 is applied to a 64-bit processor with a cycle time target of 18 FO4, it is evident that addition and subtraction must be competed in less than 12.4 FO4. Achieving this target requires: (1) a selection of the true or complement value of all bits of one input, (2) the formation of the sums, of which the most significant bit is the most difficult:

$$S_0 = p_0 \text{ xor } G_{1\dots63}$$

where

$$p_i = A_i \text{ xor } b_i \qquad \beta_i = B_i \text{ xor subtract}$$

$$G_{1\dots63} = g_1 \text{ or } p_1g_2 \text{ or } p_1p_2g_2 \text{ or } p_1p_2p_3g_4 \text{ or } \dots p_1p_2p_3p_4\cdots p_{62}g_{63}$$

where $g_i = A_iB_i$, (3) the selection of the result of the add/subtract or a logical operation, and (4) the distribution of the result.

Very fast dynamic adders have been demonstrated, which perform the addition/subtraction in less than 10 FO4s.[17–19] These adders have achieved their high frequency through[9] (1) high degree of boolean complexity per logic stage, (2) aggressive sizing of device sizes, (3) ground interrupt NMOS elimination, and (4) high output inverter beta ratios.

Dynamic logic is well suited to complex boolean functions. The elimination of the PMOS pull-up network associated with static CMOS limits the amount of gate input capacitance, thereby increasing the capacitive gain of the gate. Thus, for a given input capacitance, domino logic can perform functions of greater boolean complexity. In addition, the dotting of the pull-down net-works allows for efficient implementation of wide OR functions. Finally, use of multiple-output domino allows for even greater boolean complexity for a given input capacitance.[20] Figure 13.6 is an example of a multiple-output, unfooted domino gate from a floating-point multiplier. This is a dual-rail output gate, which is generally required for domino logic as logical inversion cannot be performed within a traditional domino gate.

To illustrate the efficiency, in which complex boolean functions can be in domino logic, a series of carry merge structures were simulated. Carry merge gates perform a form of a priority encoding. The function implemented is:

$$G_{0\dots n} = g_0 + p_0g_1 + p_0p_1g_2 + \cdots + p_0p_1p_2p_3\cdots p_{n-1}g_n \qquad (13.1)$$

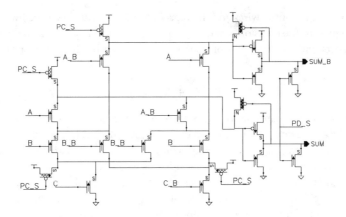

**FIGURE 13.6**  Dual-rail, multiple-output domino sum circuit.

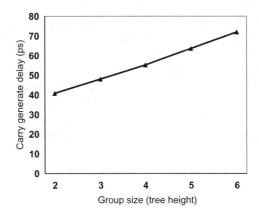

**FIGURE 13.7**  Carry merge delay vs. group size.

An implementation of this function contains an NMOS pull-down network, which is $n + 1$ transistors high and has $n + 1$ paths to ground. Delays for feasible, single level domino implementations for a 0.18 $\mu$m SOI technology are shown in Fig. 13.7. From Eq. (13.1), it can be shown that the higher order merging can be accomplished through the cascading of lower group size merge blocks and AND gates. From Fig. 13.7, however, it is clear that for merges up to group-6, a single level merge is more efficient than two group-3 or three group-2 merges.

Table 13.3 presents FO4 inverter normalized delays for a variety of custom, unfooted dynamic circuit units from the IBM 0.225 $\mu$m bulk-CMOS 1 GHz PowerPC.[5] To achieve these delays, particularly for the complex functions, dynamic gates with pull-down networks up to five NMOS transistors high were used.

As indicated earlier, increasing the width of the transistors in a design generally improves the propagation delay through the logic. Increasing the transistor widths, however, directly increases the energy consumed in the design. The power versus delay curve of a datapath macro is presented in Fig. 13.8. In this figure, the widths of all nonminimum width transistors were reduced linearly. The resulting macro power and delay including a fixed output load is presented. The nominal design was optimized for delay where about 4% marginal power was devoted to reduce the delay by 1%.

In addition to the use of relatively large transistor widths, performance of dynamic gates can be improved through the elimination of the ground interrupt NMOS. Figure 13.9 shows the ratio of footed domino gate delay to unfooted domino gate delay for a range of NMOS transistor pull-down network heights implemented in a 0.18-$\mu$m SOI process. In this graph the foot NMOS transistor is either two or four times the width of the logic NMOS transistors in the pull-down network.

**TABLE 13.3**    Dynamic Unit Delays

| Unit | No. of Dynamic Gate Levels | Delay (FO4) |
|---|---|---|
| 8:1 Mux latch | N/A | 2.9 |
| Carry save adder | 1 | 1.4 |
| Group-4 merge | 1 | 1.5 |
| AND6 | 1 | 2.3 |
| 53 × 53-bit multiplier reduction array | 9 | 16.5 |
| 161-bit aligner | 5 | 10 |
| 160-bit adder | 5 | 11.1 |
| 13-bit 3-operand adder | 5 | 9.3 |
| 53-bit increment | 4 | 7.5 |
| 130-bit shifter | 3 | 5.4 |
| 64-bit carry lookahead adder | 3 | 6.8 |
| 64 entry, 64-bit 6R4W register file | N/A | 8.3 |
| 64-kB sum addressed dual-port cache access | N/A | 16.4 |

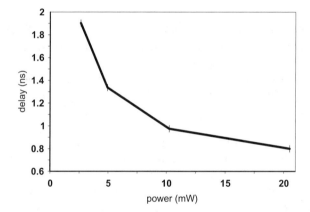

**FIGURE 13.8**    Power vs. delay of device sizings of condition code generator arithmetic macro.

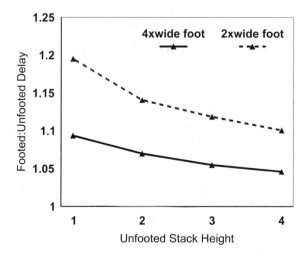

**FIGURE 13.9**    Performance potential of unfooted domino.

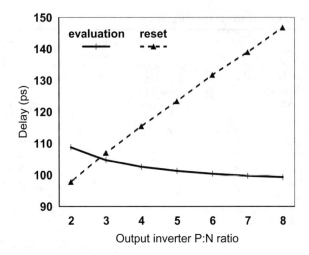

**FIGURE 13.10**   Effect of output inverter P:N size on delay.

In a very short-pipeline, high-frequency processor design, the 5–15% performance lost to the ground interrupt device was unacceptable. Unfooted domino also lowers the load on the clock, which, in turn, may lower the area and power required for generating and distributing the clock.

The delay of a domino gate can also be influenced by the sizing of the output inverter. The larger the ratio of PMOS to NMOS width, or beta ratio, the lower the delay for the output rising transition. The costs are an increase in the delay of the output reset operation and a decrease in noise-margin at the dynamic node.

Figure 13.10 shows the effect of the beta ratio on the output evaluate (rising) delay and output resetting (falling) delay. Adjusting the beta ratio of the output inverter can improve the delay of domino gates by 5–15% depending on the complexity of the gate. For the carry-merge gate used to derive Fig. 13.10, beta ratios of 3–6 provide most of the performance benefit without serious degradation of the delay of the reset operation or noise margins.

In the design of microprocessors with millions of logic transistors, it is of dubious value to do full analysis and optimization of the device topologies and sizings. To control the complexity of the design generation of simple guidelines for acceptable topologies and sizing, rules based upon simple device size ratios suffice for much of the design.

## 13.2   Noise, Robustness, and Reliability

The techniques described previously to improve performance cannot be applied indiscriminately. Performance can only be realized if sufficient noise margins are maintained. Dynamic circuits are subject to several potential noise events: Precharge-evaluation collisions, coupled noise on the input of the gates or onto the dynamic node, AC-noise or DC-offset in the $V_{dd}$ or ground power supplies, subthreshold leakage in the pull-down network or through the PMOS pre-charge device, charge sharing between the dynamic node and the parasitic capacitances in the NMOS pull-down network, substrate charge collection at the dynamic node, tunnelling current through the gates of the output inverter, and SER events at the dynamic node. Dynamic circuits in partially-depleted SOI technologies have the additional challenge of bipolar leakage currents through the pull-down network but have improved charge-sharing characteristics.

Dynamic circuits are more prone to these noise events primarily because of the undriven dynamic node. These noise events all tend to either remove charge from a precharged and undriven dynamic node or add charge to a discharged and undriven dynamic node. Increasing the capacitance of the dynamic node improves this problem, but generally slows the circuit. Alternative for most of these problems is to

(1) control the adjacency of noise sources, (2) limit the allowed topologies to those which have tolerable leakage, and (3) the introduction of additional devices onto the dynamic node, which either source or sink current in response to these noise events.

Precharge/evaluation collisions occur when the precharge transistor has not fully turned off prior to evaluation or when the pull-down paths have not been disconnected from the ground prior to initiation of precharge. As the pull-down paths are usually designed to overpower the pre-charge device, the result of these collisions is an increase in short-circuit power, a degradation of the noise margin on the dynamic node, and an increase in the delay of the gate. Careful timing of the precharge and the input signals can minimize the chance for these collisions.

Charge redistribution or charge sharing occurs when the charge is transferred from the dynamic node to parasitic capacitances within the pull-down network during the evaluation phase of operation. When the gate is not supposed to switch, the resulting transfer of charge and reduction of voltage on the dynamic node reduces noise margin and can potentially cause false evaluation of the gate. This is particularly problematic in dynamic gates with complex pull-down networks, with significant wiring in the pull-down network, and/or relatively small capacitance on the dynamic node when compared to the capacitance within the pull-down network. Because the voltage on the dynamic node is affected, both the noise margin and potentially the delay of the dynamic gate are affected. These events can be minimized through the increasing of the capacitance on the dynamic node through the increasing of the size of the output inverter, the introduction of a keeper device which helps maintain the precharged level, the introduction of pre-charge transistors within the pull-down network where capacitances are significant, and the maintenance of small beta ratio in the output inverter.

Coupled noise on the input of gates results in the increase in leakage current through the pull-down network and possibly a false evaluation. This effect can be minimized by avoiding routing hostile nets near the inputs, protecting the inputs to dynamic nodes by introducing high-noise margin gates between any long wires and the inputs to the dynamic gates, and/or introducing sufficiently large keeper devices on the dynamic node.

Coupled noise to the dynamic node, like coupled noise to the inputs, may result in a false evaluation. The coupled noise can degrade the voltage on the dynamic node, and thus, degrade the noise margin of the gate. As this changes the voltage on the dynamic node, it also can affect the delay of the gate. This effect can be minimized by avoiding routing hostile nets near the dynamic node, minimizing the wire associated with the dynamic node, and/or introducing sufficiently large keeper devices on the dynamic node. Critical signals may be required to be isolated or shielded by supply lines or power planes.

Subthreshold leakage through the pull-down network for precharged dynamic nodes and through the precharge and keeper PMOS transistors remove or introduce charge on the dynamic node of a dynamic gate. Use of higher threshold devices as precharge devices or integration of higher threshold devices in the pull-down network can minimize this problem. Other techniques include using nonminimum length devices and introducing appropriately sized keeper devices.

Power-supply and ground noise degrade the noise margins as they shift the transfer function of the gate. Ground offset in the gate driving an input to a dynamic node can lead to increased subthreshold leakage through the NMOS pull-down network. Supply variation also modifies the propagation delay through the dynamic gates. Careful design of the distribution network and correctly sized and placed decoupling to meet the DC and AC switching characteristics of the design avoids this problem. As in other failure modes keeper devices can protect the dynamic node from power supply induced failures.

Substrate charge collection and SER events can affect the voltage on the dynamic node of the dynamic gate. Increased dynamic node capacitance, keepers, and minimizing the occurrence of substrate current injection, and avoiding proximity to lead solder ball locations for critical dynamic circuits should be considered to avoid these problems.

Tunneling currents are increasingly becoming a concern for the circuit designer as gate oxide thicknesses are reduced. For dynamic circuits, tunneling currents can cause a degradation of the voltage on the dynamic node.

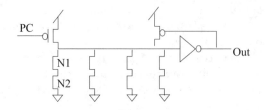

**FIGURE 13.11**    Unfooted dynamic 4:1 multiplexor.

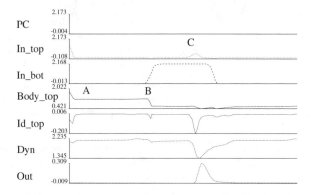

**FIGURE 13.12**    SOI noise simulation.

Because of the reduced junction capacitance of SOI devices, the charge redistribution problem presented earlier is significantly better in SOI than bulk technologies. Partially-depleted SOI has several other challenges for the circuit designer: bipolar leakage, the "kink effect" in the I-V characteristic, and the "history effect." Each of these effects is related to the body of the SOI device. Although the body can be terminated through a body contact,[21] the capacitive and delay overhead of the contact generally prevents them from being used for logic transistors. The voltage on the floating body of the device influences the on-current through the dynamic raising or lowering of the device threshold and the off-current through the flow of bipolar current and MOS leakage current due to the variation of the device threshold.

For the SOI 4-to-1 unfooted dynamic multiplexor circuit shown in Fig. 13.11 a noise event waveform is presented in Fig. 13.12. The waveform shows the voltages and the resulting currents through a leg of the mux which should be off. At location A in the waveform, the body of device $N_1$ has drifted to a relatively high steady-state voltage. At B, the device $N_2$ is made to conduct. This has the effect of coupling the body of device $N_1$ down as the source of $N_1$ is driven low; however, the body of $N_1$ is still sufficiently high to allow current to flow through the parasitic bipolar device. In addition, the voltage on the body of the device lowers the threshold of the MOS device $N_1$, making it particularly susceptible to noise at the gate of $N_1$. At C, a 300 mV noise pulse on the gate of $N_1$ results in the dynamic node discharging sufficiently low to produce an approximately 300 mV output noise pulse.

The failure mechanism is a leakage mechanism, therefore, this failure mode can be minimized through the introduction and proper sizing of keeper devices. In the previous example, the size of the keeper device helps determine the amplitude and duration of the noise output pulse. In addition, the predischarge of the internal nodes in the pull-down network can limit the excursion of the body voltages, thereby limiting the bipolar leakage current and the reduction in MOS threshold voltage due to the floating body. Limiting the number of potential leakage paths through pull-down network topology changes can also limit the floating body induced leakage effects.

Because both the current flow and thus the delay of the gate can be modified by the floating body, the delay of a circuit becomes time and state dependent. This "history effect" has been shown to lead to variations in delay of approximately 3–8% depending upon the technology, circuit, and time between activity.[22,23]

As is the case with sizing and topologies for performance, complexity in the analysis and optimization for robustness and reliability can be controlled through the generation of rather simple guidelines in sizing, wire length versus spacings, keeper size ratios, etc. In the case of reliability and robustness, however, verification that noise criteria are met is critical.

## 13.3   Logic Design Implications

As the technology-independent (FO4-based) cycle time shrinks, and signal distribution and clock and latch overhead shrink less quickly, the arithmetic and logic design must be more efficient. Linear depth arithmetic and logic structures quickly become impractical. Linear carry ripple addition, even on small group size, must be replaced with logarithmic carry-lookahead structures. Multiple arithmetic computations with a late selection, for example compound addition, may become necessary. In critical macros, additional logic may need to be introduced to avoid waiting for external select signals. For example, the carry-generation logic from a floating-point adder needed to be reproduced within the leading-zero-anticipator of a high-frequency, floating-point unit to avoid waiting for the sign of the add to be formed and delivered from the floating-point adder.[24]

Traditionally sequential events may need to be performed in parallel. For instance, to compute condition codes, rather than waiting for the result of the ALU operation and using additional levels of logic to form the condition codes, a parallel condition code generation unit, which formed the condition codes directly from the ALU input operands faster than the ALU result was required.[25] Sum-addressed caches have also been used to replace the sequential effective-address addition followed by cache access with a carry-free addition as part of the cache decoder.[26,27] Of more ubiquitous application, merging of logic with the latch is important as cycle times shrink. With increased pressure on cycle time, the latches and clocked circuits need a low skew and low jitter clock. Low jitter clock generation and low skew distribution require significant design, wiring, and power resource.[28,29]

## 13.4   Variability and Uncertainty

The wires and devices, which are actually fabricated in a design, may differ significantly from the nominal devices. In addition, the operating environment of the devices may vary widely in temperature, supply voltage, and noise. Usually delay analysis and simulation are performed at multiple corner conditions in which combinations of best and worst device and environmental conditions are used. For circuits in which the matching of individual transistors is required for correct operation such as current and voltage reference circuits and amplifiers, despite care being taken in the design and layout, mismatch does occur.[30] For timing chains, strobes, latches, and memories as well as the analog functions previously described, Monte Carlo analysis as well as worst-case analysis is often used to ensure correct operation and ascertain delays.

In the design of a high-frequency processor, performance gain can be made by minimizing the variation where possible and then taking advantage of systematic variation and only guard banding for random variations, variations which are time variant, and those for which the cost of taking advantage of the systematic variation exceeds the benefit. Methods of efficient models of the systematic and random components for device and interconnect can be used by the designer to optimize the design and determine what guard band is necessary to account for the random variations.[31,32]

## 13.5   Summary

Designing for the increasingly difficult task of high-frequency processors is largely a process of optimizing a design to within a reasonable distance of the constraints of (1) the ability of the interconnect to communicate signals, distribute clocks, and supply power, (2) the current delivering capabilities and noise margins of the devices, (3) the random or difficult to predict systematic variations in the processing, and

(4) the limit of designers to manage the resulting complexity. In technology-independent metrics, several high-frequency designs have been produced in this way.[5,6] Making better use of the technology should allow designers to meet or exceed cycle time expectations of the SIA International Technology Roadmap for Semiconductors.

## References

1. Semiconductor Industry Association, *The International Technology Roadmap for Semiconductors,* Technical Report, San Jose, California, 1997.
2. Semiconductor Industry Association, *The 2000 Updates to the International Technology Roadmap for Semiconductors,* Technical Report, San Jose, California, 2000.
3. Horowitz, M., Ho, R., and Mai, K., The Future of Wires, presented at *SRC Workshop on Interconnects for Systems on a Chip,* 1999.
4. Silberman, J., et al., A 1.0 GHz Single-Issue 64 b PowerPC Integer Processor, in *ISSCC Digest of Technical Papers,* 1998, 230–231.
5. Hofstee, P., et al., A 1 GHz Single-Issue 64 b PowerPC Processor, in *ISSCC Digest of Technical Papers,* 2000, 92–93.
6. Gieseke, B., et al., A 600 MHz Superscalar RISC Microprocessor with Out-of-Order Execution, in *ISSCC Digest of Technical Papers,* 1997, 76–177, 451.
7. Sager, D., et al., A 0.18 mm CMOS IA32 Microprocessor with a 4 GHz Integer Execution unit, in *ISSCC Digest of Technical Papers,* 2001, 324–461.
8. Sutherland, I. and Sproull, R., Logical Effort: Designing for Speed on the Back of an Envelope, in *Proceedings of Advanced Research in VLSI,* 1991, 1–16.
9. Nowka, K. and Galambos, T., Circuit Design Techniques for a Gigahertz Integer Microprocessor, in *Proceedings of the IEEE International Conference on Computer Design,* 1998, 11–16.
10. Silberman, J., et al., A 1.0 GHz single-issue 64-bit PowerPC integer processor, *IEEE J. Solid-State Circuits,* 33, 1600, 1998.
11. Mead, C. and Conway, L., *Introduction to VLSI Systems,* Addison-Wesley, Reading, MA, 1980.
12. Su, L., et al., Short-Channel Effects in Deep-Submicron SOI MOSFETS, in *Proceedings of IEEE International SOI Conference,* 1993, 112–113.
13. Assaderaghi, F., et al., A 7.9/5.5 psec Room/Low Temperature SOI CMOS, in *Technical Digest of IEDM,* 1997, 415–418.
14. Mistry, K., et al., A 2.0 V, 0.35 $\mu$m Partially Depleted SOI-CMOS Technology, in *Technical Digest of IEDM,* 1997, 583–586.
15. Chuang, C., Lu, P., and Anderson, C., SOI for digital CMOS VLSI: design considerations and advances, *Proceedings of the IEEE,* 86, 689, 1998.
16. Nowka, K., Hofstee, P., and Carpenter, G., Accurate power efficiency metrics and their application to voltage scalable CMOS VLSI design, submitted to *IEEE Transactions on VLSI,* 2001.
17. Stasiak, D., et al., A 2nd Generation 440 ps SOI 64-bit Adder, in *ISSCC Digest of Technical Papers,* 2000, 288–289.
18. Park, J., et al., 470 ps 64-bit Parallel Binary Adder, in *IEEE Symposium on VLSI Circuits, Digest of Technical Papers,* 2000, 192–193.
19. Ngo, H., Dhong, S., and Silberman, J., High Speed Binary Adder, U.S. Patent US5964827.
20. Hwang, I. and Fisher, A., A 3.1 ns 32 b CMOS Adder In Multiple Output Domino Logic, *ISSCC Digest of Technical Papers,* 1988, 140–333.
21. Sleight, J. and Mistry, K., A Compact Schottky Contact Technology for SOI Transistors, in *Technical Digest of IEDM,* 1997, 419–422.
22. Assaderaghi, F., et al., History Dependence on Non-Fully Depleted (NFD) Digital SOI Circuits, in *IEEE Symposium on VLSI Technology, Digest of Technical Papers,* 1996, 122–123.
23. Puri, R. and Chuang, C., Hysteresis Effect in Floating-Body Partially Depleted SOI CMOS Domino Circuits, in *Proceedings of the ISLPED,* 1999, 223–228.

24. Lee, K. and Nowka, K., 1 GHz Leading Zero Anticipator Using Independent Sign-bit Determination Logic, in *IEEE Symposium on VLSI Circuits, Digest of Technical Papers,* 2000, 194–195.
25. Nowka, K. and Burns, J., Parallel Condition-Code Generating for High Frequency PowerPC Microprocessors, in *IEEE Symposium on VLSI Circuits, Digest of Technical Papers,* 1998, 112–115.
26. Heald, R., et al., 64 kB Sum-addressed-memory cache with 1.6 ns cycle and 2.6 ns latency, *IEEE J. Solid-State Circuits,* 33, 1682, 1998.
27. Silberman, J., et al., A 1.6 ns Access, 1 GHz Two-Way Set-Predicted and Sum-Indexed 64- kbyte Data Cache, in *IEEE Symposium on VLSI Circuits, Digest of Technical Papers,* 2000, 220–221.
28. Restle, P., et al., A Clock Distribution Network for Microprocessors, in *IEEE Symposium on VLSI Circuits, Digest of Technical Papers,* 2000,184–187.
29. Bailey, D. and Benschneider, B. Clocking design and analysis for a 600-MHz Alpha microprocessor, *IEEE J. Solid-State Circuits,* 11, 1627, 1998.
30. Gregor, R., On the relationship between topography and transistor matching in an analog CMOS technology, *IEEE Transactions on Electronic Devices,* 39, 275, 1992.
31. Nassif, S., Delay Variability: Sources, Impacts and Trends, in *ISSCC Digest of Technical Papers,* 2000, 368–369.
32. Acar, E., et. al., Assessment of True Worst-Case Circuit Performance Under Interconnect Parameter Variations, in *Proceedings of Intnl Symp on Quality Electronic Design,* 2001, 431–436.

# IV

# Design for Low Power

# 14

# Low-Power Design Issues

Hemmige Varadarajan
*Intel Corporation*

Vivek Tiwari
*Intel Corporation*

Rakesh Patel
*Intel Corporation*

Hema Ramamurthy
*Intel Corporation*

Shahram Jamshidi
*Intel Corporation*

Snehal Jariwala
*Intel Corporation*

Wenjie Jiang
*Intel Corporation*

## 14.1 Introduction

Power consumption has emerged as one of the most important design constraints in today's systems. This is largely due to the rapid growth of mobile systems, which run on the limited energy available in batteries. In addition, increased power consumption implies increased heat dissipation, which leads to higher cooling and packaging costs. Increased power consumption is also detrimental to the reliability of integrated circuits (ICs). In addition, concerns about the environmental cost of electronic systems motivate the need to reduce their power requirements.

The increasing speed and complexity of today's designs implies that the power consumption is also increasing in the future. To meet this challenge, we need to develop design techniques for low power. The complexity of today's ICs with over 100 million transistors, clocked at over 1 GHz, demands computer-aided design (CAD) tools and methodologies for a successful design in time to market. Therefore, we also need low power techniques to be part of CAD tools. In addition, the overall system design, including software components needs to be power aware.

Figure 14.1 shows the historic power consumption for Intel CPUs. The X-axis shows the technology generation and the Y-axis the maximum power consumption. As indicated by the dashed line in the main part of the curve, power consumption has been increasing for each new CPU generation. The points to the side of the main curve indicate newer versions of each processor family. These are implemented in

**TABLE 14.1**   Compaq Alpha* Power Trends

| Alpha Model | Peak Power (W) | Frequency (MHz) | Die Size (mm$^2$) | $V_{dd}$ |
|---|---|---|---|---|
| 21064 | 30 | 200 | 234 | 3.3 |
| 21164 | 50 | 300 | 299 | 3.3 |
| 21264 | 72 | 667 | 302 | 2.0 |
| 21364 | 100 | 1000 | 350 | 1.5 |

*Alpha is a trademark of Campaq Inc.

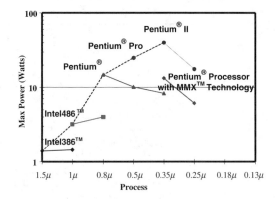

**FIGURE 14.1**   Historic trends for Intel CPU power consumption.

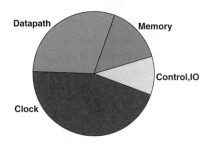

**FIGURE 14.2**   Power breakdown in a high-performance CPU.

newer semiconductor processes with smaller geometries than the lead processor in that family. Smaller feature sizes in conjunction with lower supply voltages lead to lower power consumption in the newer versions; however, moving to a new CPU generation in the same process is associated with an increase in the power consumption (Fig. 14.2).

Table 14.1 also depicts Compaq's Alpha* series in power, clock rate, die size, and supply voltage [1a]. Note the trend in increasing power though $V_{dd}$ the supply voltage, is decreased.

Why is this cause for concern? The reason is that increased power consumption directly impacts IC and system cost. This cost has two components. The first is *thermal* or *cooling cost*, which is associated with keeping the devices below the specified operating temperature limits. Maintaining the integrity of packaging at higher temperatures also requires expensive solutions. The second component of the cost of power consumption is the cost of power delivery, i.e., the on-chip, on-package, and on-board decoupling capacitances and interconnect associated with the power distribution network. Increased power consumption at lower voltages increases the magnitude of the current drawn by the IC. In addition,

---

*Alpha is a tradmark of Compaq Corp.

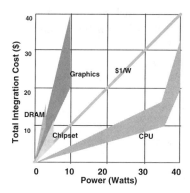

**FIGURE 14.3**    Cost of delivering power and cooling in a PC system.

today's design trends are such that the variability in the amount of current drawn from cycle to cycle is also increasing. These factors combine to make resistive and inductive noise a big problem. Dealing with this is becoming increasingly costly.

Figure 14.3 gives an idea of the range of dollar amounts associated with the above costs for different system components in a personal computer. As can be seen, when the CPU power is in the 35–40 W range, the cost of each additional watt goes above $1 per watt per chip. An interesting observation is that the power cost of the other system components (DRAM, chipsets, graphics) is on a steeper curve than the CPU. This is because the spatial layout of today's system chassis designs is such that these components are harder to cool. This is likely to change with new designs, further increasing the relative importance of the CPU power cost. Given the above trends, there is a clear need to analyze and optimize power consumption for all components of a given system.

This chapter is organized as follows. The need for reducing power consumption in systems is motivated in greater detail in the section on "The Need for Low Power." The sources of power consumption are reviewed in "Sources of Power Consumption," where a basic power model for complementary metal oxide semiconductor (CMOS) circuits is presented. "Reducing Power Consumption" provides a overview of basic power reduction methods. Section 14.2 deals with power estimation, which is a prerequisite for power aware design. Section 14.3 describes power reduction techniques at various levels of the design process in greater detail.

## The Need for Low Power

The different factors that have led to the increasing importance of the power metric are described in the following subsections.

### Heat Dissipation

The power consumed in an IC is dissipated as heat. Unless this heat is removed, the IC gets hot. The electrical properties of the devices on the chip are rated for specific temperature ranges, and exceeding the ranges shifts the parameters and the behavior of circuits. In addition, as an IC gets hot, catastrophic failure mechanisms become more likely. These include silicon interconnect and junction fatigue, package failure, thermal runaway, and gate dielectric breakdown. It has been estimated that each 10°C rise in operating temperature roughly doubles the component failure rate.

The power consumption in today's ICs has reached the point that expensive packaging and cooling mechanisms are needed to keep the operating temperature in check. The peak sustained power consumption in recent high-performance microprocessors is in excess of 70 W, as shown in Fig 14.1 and Table 14.1. Packaging and cooling costs are of direct concern even in the domain of lower performance and low power microprocessors and microcontrollers. The high volume nature of the market for these devices means that even slight reductions in cost can translate into large revenue increases for the manufacturer.

The cost impact of power consumption on packaging and cooling costs can be seen from the following data points. (The cost values are from the 1997 timeframe, but the relative trends still hold.)

If the power consumption of a chip is under 1 W, a plastic package can be used for it, at the cost of about 1 cent per pin. If the power consumption is between 1 and 2 W, a plastic package can still be used, but special heat conductors are required. The cost for a package of this kind is approximately 2–3 cents per pin. Exceeding 2 W, however, requires the use of ceramic packages. These packages cost between 5 and 10 cents per pin. Exceeding 10 W requires external cooling (air or liquid cooling) and a further increase in cost. The package cost for a 200-pin device would therefore be either $2, $4–6, or $10–20, depending on whether its power consumption is below 1 W, between 1 and 2 W, or above 2 W. Moving up from one power consumption range to another is therefore accompanied by significant cost increases, which are significant if the devices are manufactured in large volumes. A specific consideration in this regard is to keep the power consumption below 2 W. This allows the use of plastic packages, which are much cheaper than the ceramic packages that are otherwise needed.

### Portable Systems

The rising popularity of portable systems is primarily responsible for the upsurge in interest in power consumption in recent years. Portable systems include palmtop, laptop, notebook computers, telecommunication devices such as pagers, cellular phones, wireless modems, and consumer products such as audio players, video cameras, and electronic games. The defining characteristic of a portable system is that it is not connected to a fixed power source. It runs on the limited energy stored in a rechargeable battery. In any portable system, the length of battery driven operation (the *battery life*) is of prime importance. Longer battery life can provide a competitive advantage in the marketplace. In each of these applications, size, weight, and battery life are primary considerations. Low-power DSPs allow designers to extend battery life without the size and weight increases associated with more powerful batteries.

The trend in portable devices is towards increased computational requirements. Portable computer users desire performance levels that are comparable to those of desktop systems. In addition, personal communication applications, with multimedia access supporting full-motion digital video and speech recognition capabilities are being proposed. What this implies is that portability can no longer be associated with limited computational rates.

Meeting the increased energy requirements through use of larger and more batteries is not really an option. This increases the size and the weight—parameters that are also extremely important in portable systems. Increasing the amount of energy stored in the batteries (the *battery capacity*) is one way to solve the problem; however, growth in rechargeable battery capacity has been slow. Incremental improvements in nickel-cadmium (NiCd) technology, the mainstay of portable power, have led to about the doubling of capacity over the last 30 years. Newer battery chemistries, such as nickel-metal hydride (NiMH) are expected to have 20–30% higher capacity. Thus, battery capacity has increased by a factor of less than 4 over the last three decades. Recently, the ever-growing market for portable systems has motivated a faster rate of innovation in the battery industry. Lithium-ion, a newer technology, is rapidly gaining popularity since it allows lighter batteries with higher capacities. This may change with even newer battery technologies such as lithium-polymer, and zinc-air, which are claimed to have 2 and 10 times higher capacity than NiMH, respectively.

In any case, growth in battery capacity lags far behind the rapid growth in microprocessor power consumption, which has gone from under 1 W to over 50 W over the last 20 years. Thus, improvements in battery technology alone cannot be relied upon to meet the constraints of portable systems. The *energy demand* on the batteries has to be reduced.

A noteworthy research project was recently completed at UC Berkeley, California. A butane-powered Wankel internal combustion engine with a generator about as small as a chip-cooling fan was developed to power a laptop for longer durations while enabling a very small weight increase. Although it is amusing to note that an IC (internal combustion) engine is powering the IC (integrated circuit), it will be worth watching to see the evolution of practicality and application of this technology, in view of its safe and hazard-free use. The engine reportedly pollutes only as much as a human body.

## Data Center Issues

The growth of the Internet is driving increased awareness of power in the server, communication, and networking domains. The trend is to pack more and more computational resources in smaller spaces. A typical data center consists of racks of computation equipment, each rack with a maximum of 42 slots, each slot 1¾ inches high. Because data center space is at a premium, the desire is to pack more computational resources per rack and more racks per square yard. This drives the need for power efficiency mainly due to the following: First, when there are constraints on how much power a data center can draw from the public power grid, increasing computation density of a data center can only be done if the power efficiency of the equipment increases; second, it has been estimated that as much as 25% of the total cost of running a data center is directly related to power consumption (the cost of cooling, power delivery equipment, and the net consumption of electricity). Power has thus become a major design constraint for servers and high-performance communication and networking equipment.

## Reliability Issues

Certain issues related to reliable operation of ICs are directly related to the power drain of the on-chip circuits. Electromigration is one such issue. Under high electrical currents, the atoms in the metal power supply line may migrate, leading to electrical shorts and breakages. Reliable design of the power grid therefore requires a careful analysis of the current flow in different parts of the power grid. Reliable operation of ICs also requires verifiable electrical behavior. Some electrical verification problems are directly related to power consumption.

The first of these is voltage drops due to the resistance of power supply lines (also known as the *iR* problem). These drops lead to power supply DC voltage differences between the driver and receiver circuits. Thus, portions of the chip would receive a lower supply voltage than what they are designed for. In addition, transient currents drawn by one set of circuits causes transient *noise* in the supply rail of another and this noise can be only reduced by bulky capacitors. (But one cannot eliminate the perturbations.) The inductance of the power supply lines is the other problem. Rapid variation in the current flow on these lines can also lead to voltage variations (also known as the *supply bounce* or $L \cdot di/dt$ problem) that can affect the operation of the receiver circuits. The above problems necessitate specialized power analysis and design tools.

They also require tools to help avoid these problems, e.g., power line sizing tools. Increasing frequencies and device counts, coupled with shrinking feature sizes, will only exacerbate these problems [2]. Reduction in the total power consumption, on the other hand, helps to alleviate the impact of these problems.

## Environmental Considerations

Concerns about the environmental impact of the electricity consumed by computers are providing additional motivation for low power design. The U.S. Environmental Protection Agency (EPA) estimates that computers are a leading cause of the increased electricity demands in the U.S., accounting for about 5% of commercial demand (the figure is expected to reach 10% by the end of the decade). At present, PCs and their peripherals consume about $2 billion worth of electricity annually, and indirectly produce as much carbon-dioxide as 5 million cars. Also, of the total office equipment electricity consumption, 80% comes from PCs, monitors, and printers [2].

A large part of this is wasteful power consumption, coming from systems that are left turned on even when not in use. In order to encourage the development of power-saving systems, the EPA created the "Energy Star Program." The requirements of this program state that each of a PC's main elements (CPU unit, monitor, and printer) should consume less than 30 W when they are idle, i.e., not being used. In return, PC vendors can use the "Energy Star" logo and market their systems as being "Energy Star Compliant." It is expected that being identified as an energy-wise or "Green" PC will provide a competitive edge over otherwise comparable, but "non-Green," systems. There is even a political angle here. The President of the United States has declared a goal for the U.S. government to buy only PCs that qualify for the Energy Star Program.

In any case, the move toward "Green" desktop PCs implies that the technologies that would be otherwise meant for just portable computers have applications in the entire PC domain. The mindset for power efficient design is therefore starting to take hold within the industry. This provides additional justification for the consolidation of tested techniques, and continuous development of newer techniques.

## Sources of Power Consumption

The four sources of power consumption in digital CMOS circuits are [4]:

1. Capacitive switching power ($P_{switching}$)
2. Short circuit current ($I_{short-circuit}$)
3. Leakage current ($I_{leakage}$)
4. Static currents from specialized circuits ($I_{static}$)

The effects of these sources on the average power consumption ($P_{avg}$) can be summarized as:

$$P_{avg} = P_{switching} + (I_{short-circuit} + I_{leakage} + I_{static}) \times V_{dd} \qquad (14.1)$$

where $V_{dd}$ is the supply voltage. These sources of power consumption are explained in the next section.

### Switching Power

The dominant source of power consumption in a CMOS gate is the current due to the charging and discharging of the capacitance at the gate output. This capacitance, $C_{out}$, is the parasitic capacitance that can be lumped at the output of the gate. To understand this source of power consumption, consider the operation of a basic CMOS gate (an inverter), as its input goes through a high(1) to low(0) and a low to high transition (see Fig. 14.4). (In general, the bottom transistor (nMOS) can be replaced by a network of nMOS transistors, and the top transistor (pMOS) by a complementary network of pMOS transistors.) When the input goes low, the nMOS transistor is cut-off and the pMOS transistor conducts. This creates a direct path between the voltage supply and $C_{out}$. Current flows from the supply to charge up to the voltage level $V_{dd}$. The amount of charge drawn from the supply is $C_{out} \times V_{dd}$ and the energy drawn from the supply equals $C_{out} \times V_{dd}^2$. The energy actually stored in the capacitor $E_c$ is only half of this $E_c = {}^1/_2 \times C_{out} \times V_{dd}^2$. The other half is dissipated in the resistance represented by the pMOS transistor. During the subsequent low to high input transition, the pMOS transistor is cut-off and the nMOS transistor conducts. This connects $C_{out}$ to the ground, leading to the flow of current $I_n$. $C_{out}$ discharges and its stored energy $E_c$ is dissipated in the resistance represented by the nMOS transistor. Therefore an amount of energy equal to $E_c$ is dissipated (consumed) every time the output transitions.

If $N$ is the average number of transitions per clock cycle, the average energy consumed per clock cycle is $E_c \times N$. Power is the rate at which energy is consumed. Therefore, if $f$ is the clock frequency, the average

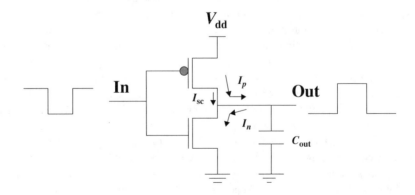

**FIGURE 14.4**   Dynamic power dissipation in a CMOS gate.

power consumption $P_{\text{switching}}$ is given by

$$P_{\text{switching}} = \frac{1}{2} \times C_{\text{out}} \times V_{\text{dd}}^2 \times N \times f \tag{14.2}$$

$C_{\text{out}}$ is the sum of three components [3] $C_{\text{int}}$, $C_{\text{wire}}$, $C_{\text{load}}$. Of these, $C_{\text{int}}$ represents the internal capacitance of the gate. This basically consists of the diffusion capacitance of the drain regions connected to the output. $C_{\text{load}}$ represents the sum of gate capacitances of the transistors fed by the output. $C_{\text{wire}}$ is the parasitic capacitance of the wiring used to interconnect the gates. It is a function of the placement of gates and the routing between them. $N$ is a measure of the switching activity of the circuit. It is a function of the logical behavior of the circuit and of the sequence of inputs applied to it. The three components of this interconnect capacitance are: The parallel plate capacitance between the wire and the substrate, the capacitance due to the (fringe effect) of electric fields, and the capacitance between neighboring wires.

## Short-Circuit Current

The capacitive switching power is independent of the rise and fall times (ramp times) of the input and output waveforms. There is, however, a transient source of power consumption that is dependent on these ramp times. As shown by the broken lines in Fig. 14.4, during the time that the input waveform is transitioning between its extreme values, a current flows from $V_{\text{dd}}$ to ground through both the nMOS and the pMOS transistors. This current, known as the *short-circuit* current, only occurs during the period of time when both the pMOS and the nMOS transistors conduct, i.e., when the input voltage $V_{\text{in}}$ is such that $V_{\text{tn}} < V_{\text{in}} < V_{\text{dd}} - V_{\text{tn}}$, where $V_{\text{tn}}$ and $V_{\text{tp}}$ are the threshold voltages of the nMOS and the pMOS transistors, respectively. The nMOS transistor conducts when $V_{\text{in}}$ exceeds $V_{\text{tn}}$, and the pMOS transistor conducts when $V_{\text{in}}$ is below $V_{\text{dd}} - V_{\text{tp}}$.

It has been shown that the impact of short-circuit current is reduced if the input ramp times are faster, relative to the output ramp times. This minimizes the time when significant short-circuit current can flow, but it also increases the gate delay. A good trade-off is to keep the input and output ramp times about equal. Careful design, including appropriate sizing of the transistors can keep the power contribution of short circuit current $I_{\text{short-circuit}} \times V_{\text{dd}}$ below 10% of the total power. So, while short-circuit current should not be completely ignored, it is reasonable to consider it as only a second order effect. It is even possible to eliminate short-circuit current altogether [5]. This happens if the chosen supply voltage $V_{\text{dd}}$ is such that $V_{\text{dd}} < V_{\text{tn}} + V_{\text{tp}}$. Under this condition, the nMOS and the pMOS transistors can never conduct simultaneously.

## Leakage Current

The previous two sources are dynamic sources of power consumption, i.e., they contribute to power only during transitions. It would seem that CMOS circuits should not consume any power at other times, since there are no available current paths when inputs are at stable logic levels.

There are, however, two types of leakage currents that also contribute to power consumption. These are:

- *Diode leakage current:* The source and drain regions of a metal oxide semiconductor field effect transistor (MOSFET) can form reverse biased parasitic diodes with the substrate. There is leakage current associated with these diodes. This current is very small and is usually negligible compared to dynamic power consumption.

- *Subthreshold leakage current:* This current occurs due to the diffusion of carriers between the source and drain even when the MOSFET is in the cut-off region, i.e., when the magnitude of the gate-source voltage $V_{\text{gs}}$ is below the threshold voltage $V_t$. In this region the MOSFET behaves like a bipolar transistor and the subthreshold current is exponentially dependent on $V_{\text{gs}} - V_t$. The significance of this current increases with technology scaling, as shown in Figure 14.9.

## Static Current

In certain designs, the pMOS network of a CMOS gate may be replaced by a single pMOS transistor that always conducts. This logic style, known as pseudo-nMOS, will lead to a constant current flow static at all times so that the output is at logic 0, i.e., when there is a direct path to ground through the nMOS network.

This static current is obviously undesirable, but it does not exist for true CMOS logic. This is one of the main reasons for the popularity of CMOS in low power applications.

Another situation that can lead to static power dissipation in CMOS is when a degraded voltage level (e.g., the "high" output level of a nMOS pass transistor) is applied to the inputs of a CMOS gate. A degraded voltage level may leave both the nMOS and pMOS transistors in a conducting state, leading to continuous flow of short-circuit current. This again is undesirable and care should be taken to avoid it in practice.

## Reducing Power Consumption

The capacitive switching power ($P_{switching}$), as given by the formula in Eq. (14.1), is the dominant source of power consumption in CMOS circuits today. Research and design efforts aimed at low power are therefore largely focussed on reducing $P_{switching}$. The parameters in its formula $V_{dd}, f, C, N$ provide avenues for power reduction. The idea is to either reduce each of the parameters individually without adversely impacting the others, or to trade them off against each other.

It should be noted that $f$ is also a measure of the performance (speed) of a system. Therefore, reduction in power through simply a reduction in $f$ is an option only if it is acceptable to trade off speed for power. Power is proportional to the square of $V_{dd}$. This makes reduction in $V_{dd}$ as the most effective way for power reduction. This has motivated the acceptance of 3.3 V as the standard supply voltage, down from 5 V. The downward trend in $V_{dd}$ continues, with processors with 1.5 V internal supply voltage and lower, already being shipped.

The problem with reducing $V_{dd}$ is that it leads to an increase in circuit delay. Circuit delay is inversely proportional to $V_{dd}$ as a first order of approximation. The increased delay can be overcome if device dimensions are also scaled down along with $V_{dd}$. In particular, in constant-field scaling, $V_{dd}$ and the horizontal and vertical dimensions of devices are scaled down by the same factor $k$. This is done in order to maintain constant electric fields in the devices. To the first order of approximation, the power consumption scales down by $k^2$, and the delays go up by $k$. Reducing device dimensions (or feature size reduction) is a very costly proposition, requiring changes in fabrication technology and semiconductor processes.

The other problem is that circuit delay actually rises rapidly as $V_{dd}$ approaches the threshold voltage $V_t$. As a general rule, $V_{dd}$ should be larger than $4V_t$, if speed is not to suffer excessively $V_t$ does not scale easily and, therefore, reducing $V_{dd}$ below $V_t$ will be difficult.

The speed degradation (increase in delay) may be reduced by circuit technologies that allow lower $V_t$; however, decrease in $V_t$ leads to a significant increase in subthreshold leakage current—every 0.1 V reduction in $V_t$ raises subthreshold leakage current by a factor of 10.

A tradeoff is involved in choosing a very low $V_{dd}$. Some design options in this regard are to either dynamically vary $V_t$ (lower $V_t$ when the circuit is active, higher when it is not) or using different $V_t$ for sub-circuits with different speed requirements. The speed degradation may also be compensated for by increasing the amount of parallelism in the system. This works well for applications such as digital signal processing, where throughput is used as the performance metric.

It is also worth noting that $V_{dd}$ reduction only provides temporary relief in the course of technological change. Please refer back to Fig. 14.1 and Table 14.1. These processors shown represent recent data points for a trend that has persisted for over 25 years—increased performance through higher clock frequencies or increased number of transistors, or both. This, however, directly increases the power consumption. Reductions in supply voltage and feature size do help to offset the effect of increased clock frequency and to reduce power.

For example, the original Intel Pentium processor had 0.8 $\mu$m feature size, 5 V supply voltage, 66 MHz clock frequency, and 16 W power consumption. Reduction in the feature size to 0.5 $\mu$m and voltage to 3.3 V, led to 10 W power consumption, even at 100 MHz. But such reductions are only temporary, since the march toward increased clock frequencies shows no signs of slowing. Thus, the power consumption of the 200 MHz Pentium climbed back to 17 W.

Also, the area made available from feature size reductions is immediately filled up with more transistors—for larger caches and increased instruction-level parallelism, in case of processors. For example, the Pentium Pro, the successor of the Pentium, has 70% more transistors and about 50% more power consumption at 200 MHz.

The trend in special purpose ICs is also to push the limits of integration by integrating as much functionality on a chip as possible. The goal of a host of multimedia capabilities on a single chip was being sought in earnest. These capabilities are now real but power consumption has gone up. Integration helps to reduce the overall power for the system. A rule of thumb stated is that four devices incorporated into an IC consume only half as much power as would be the case if they were configured as discrete components; however, it also implies that the power dissipation burden on the resulting single IC will increase. Thus, the current trends indicate that the voltage and feature size reduction notwithstanding, the power consumption problem in ICs will only get worse in the future. Therefore, it is important to explore other avenues of power reduction as described below.

### Reduction of Switched Capacitance

The parameters $N$ and $C_{out}$ in Eq. (14.2) provide the other set of avenues for power reduction. Their product $N \times C$ can be called the average switched capacitance per cycle (referred to as switched capacitance) of the circuit. Reduction in switched capacitance is in general orthogonal to the power reduction techniques described previously. It can therefore lead to power reductions beyond what is possible by voltage scaling alone. It may also be the only option if the large investments in time and money associated with the migration to newer processes and lower voltages are not feasible. Reduction in switched capacitance has thus been the subject of intense study in recent years since the last 10 years or so. Ideas and techniques at all levels of the design process are being developed. Figure 14.5 presents an overview of the salient directions that are being pursued in today's designs. Some of these are aimed specifically at reducing $N$ or $N \times C_{out}$. Others represent well-established design/synthesis problem domains, in which $N \times C_{out}$ can be considered as an additional target metric. The aim of all of these is to reduce $N \times C_{out}$. It should be kept in mind that these efforts are not isolated from one another. Thus, the impact of design decisions at any level cuts across other levels of the hierarchy too. Overviews of the published work in this area are available in several references [1,5,6].

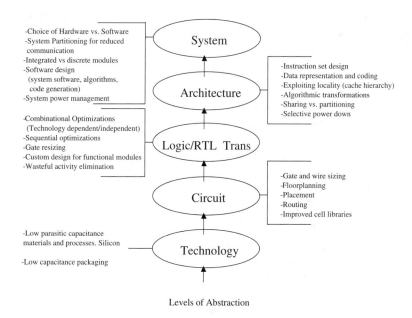

**FIGURE 14.5** Directions for reducing capacitance.

## 14.2    Power Estimation

As we saw in the last section, power dissipation in VLSI circuits is a major concern in the electronics industry. The rapid increase in the complexity and the decrease in design time have resulted in the need for efficient power estimation tools that can help in making important design decisions early in the design process. To accomplish this objective, the estimation tools must operate with a design description at the higher levels of abstraction; however, trade-offs exists between accuracy and speed in power estimation at various levels of a design hierarchy. In this section, an overview of the different power estimation tools and techniques are covered.

### Need for Power Estimation Tools

Low-power design requires good power analysis tools to evaluate the alternate choices in design. Consider modern high-performance CPUs, large portions of which are typically custom designed. These designs involve manual tweaking of transistors to upsize drivers in critical paths. If too many transistors are upsized, certain designs can lie on the steep part of a circuit's power-delay curve. The choice of logic family used, e.g., static versus domino logic, can also greatly influence the circuit's power consumption. Figure 14.6 illustrates these scenarios for a 32-bit adder. Suppose a designer has the data shown in the figure at his disposal. Knowledge of where on the power-delay curve the circuit operates can tell the designer whether he/she can trade a little performance for larger power savings. In this example, a total of 69% savings can be gained by transistor sizing and using domino instead of static logic. There is a 23% delay penalty. This extra delay penalty may be overcome by upsizing adjacent blocks at a much less power penalty and ending up with an overall power benefit. Experiments with this methodology have yielded 10% power savings with no delay increase in real designs. CAD tools that enable this kind of logic and circuit design exploration for custom circuits can thus have a significant impact at the full-chip level. Specifically, power analysis tools enable designers to:

1. Verify whether the power budgets are met by different parts of the design and identify the parts that do not satisfy the power requirements
2. Evaluate the effect of various optimizations and design modifications on power

A typical design flow has four steps. It starts with very high-level description of a design, called HLM (high-level modeling) or architectural description. Then the HLM is converted into RTL (register transfer level), and then RTL is synthesized into a gate level design. Finally, gates are replaced by transistors/layout

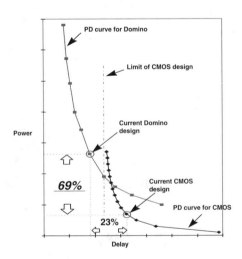

**FIGURE 14.6**    Power-delay curves for two different 32-bit adders.

and validated for design specs. As design flows into lower level of abstraction it becomes more complex and design changes become more difficult. So, it is advisable to start design trade-offs at the early stage of the design—HLM or RTL. Also, the higher level of abstraction allows greater impact on the design with less effort. So, power estimation tools are needed at all design levels. At the early stage they are needed to make smart decisions about power-performance trade-offs, and at lower levels to validate design changes and to quantify impact of design changes.

## Issues in Power Estimation

How do you know how much power your design will consume before plugging the chip into your board and measuring it? To perform these calculations, knowing the circuit's clock frequencies and the multiplicative constants (activity factors) provided by the vendor can help to some extent. But the more difficult parameter to be determined is the average number of flip-flops and routing nodes that transition during each clock edge. Determining this value is especially tough for hardware description language-based designs, as one may have little or no insight into the logic implementation of the chosen device. Some vendors suggest the use of a 12.5% usage estimate (refer to the section on "Switching Power," where this amounts to $N = 0.125$) corresponding to the average toggle percentage of a 16-bit counter. Others believe that a 25% estimate for an 8-bit counter is more typical. Some circuits, such as arithmetic units, have even higher toggle percentages. The choice can radically impact the accuracy of the estimate.

In general, the most effective design decisions can be derived from choosing and optimizing algorithms at the highest level of the design hierarchy. This dictates the need for an effective high-level power estimation tool. In the absence of a high-level power analysis tool, the designer has to first synthesize and validate the functionality of a lower-level netlist, and then run a logic or transistor-level power analysis tool to estimate power consumption. The large iteration times of lower-level power analysis tools, and the long time required to obtain and validate a gate-level or transistor-level netlist, makes this methodology inefficient to estimate power. At the same time, there is a penalty associated with high-level power estimation tools. The absolute accuracy of high-level power estimation tool tends to be lower than the accuracy provided by using low-level estimation tools. These are some of the issues in power estimation that need to be considered for a good design. In the following section, several power estimation tools operating at different levels of design abstraction are discussed.

## Power Estimation Techniques

Power estimation techniques can be broadly classified into statistical, probabilistic, and macromodeling techniques. In *statistical* techniques, the circuit is simulated using a timing or logic simulator, while monitoring the power being consumed. This procedure is repeated for various sets of input vectors until a desired level of accuracy is achieved. Eventually power converges to the average value. One example of accurate statistical analysis method is the activity-based control model. This model expresses the complexity of control units and input activities making it easy to analyze the power consumption of regular implementations, such as ROM and PLA-based structures.

In *probabilistic* techniques, the signals are represented with probabilities that substitute for the time consuming simulations; however, there is a loss in accuracy. The signal probability is defined as the probability of having a logic value of "1" on a signal and the transition probability represents the probability of the proportion of transitions on the signal. These probabilities lead to a simple computation of switching activity, the parameter that needs to be determined for power computation. The simplest way to propagate probabilities is to work at the gate-level description of the circuit. When the circuit is built from Boolean components that are not part of a predefined gate library, the signal probability can be computed by using a binary decision diagram (BDD) to represent the Boolean functions.

Another popular approach, mostly used for high level power estimation is the *macromodeling* technique. In this method, a macromodel is constructed by obtaining and characterizing a lower-level implementation. Based on the power consumption characteristics of the macroblock for various training sequences, a macromodel or function is then constructed that describes the power consumption of the block as a function of various parameters like the signal statistics of the block inputs, outputs, and states. A simplified example of macromodeling is the power factor approximation (PFA) technique. In this technique, the power consumption of a given type of functional block, implemented using a given design style that operates at frequency $f$ is estimated using the following equation,

$$P = KGf$$

where $K$ is the PFA constant and $G$ is a measure of the hardware complexity of the functional block. The PFA constant may be generated by characterizing one or a few implementations of the functional block.

## Examples of Power Estimation Tools

This subsection discusses practical implementations of different power estimation techniques.

### RT-Level/Gate-Level Techniques

At RT-level, power is estimated primarily in two ways: the top-down way and the bottom-up way. In the top-down approach, at first, power density (power/unit area) is calculated from the full-chip power and area estimates, where estimates are usually obtained from historical data. Then power values for the lower level blocks are calculated by scaling the estimated block area with the power density. This approach is good for a very quick power analysis. It suffers from very serious accuracy issues, it does not take into account the block's functionality, logic and circuit topologies, performance requirements or switching activities.

For better accuracy the bottom-up approach is used. It uses macromodeling technique, where analytical or table lookup models are built, using historical data or real simulation data, for each bottom level blocks. These models are usually parameterized for output load capacitances and input/output (I/O) switching activities for better accuracy. For power estimation, lower level blocks are first mapped to these precharacterized models. Then, a power value for each block is calculated by evaluating corresponding power models. The bottom-up roll-up is now done to generate power estimates for higher level blocks. Here, power estimate accuracy depends on the accuracy of models, which is typically good if simulation data is used for model building. This approach is advisable where design exploration is needed at the early stage.

### Transistor Level Power Estimation Techniques

At the transistor level, power per net is first estimated and then it is rolled up to generate block or system power. Two approaches to estimate power per net are used primerily: static and dynamic (simulation-based). In the static approach, capacitance ($C$) per net is first estimated (extracted if layout is available) then a blanket switching activity (AF) is used to calculate the switching component of power. The constant power component is then added to take leakage and short-circuit power into account. This approach is very quick and can be quickly automated and applied to very large designs. But its absolute accuracy is not high. Sometimes switching activity is varied based on net types—clock, CMOS, domino, gated clock, etc., to improve accuracy. This method is advisable for a large design and also where daily/weekly tracking of power is required.

For more accurate power estimate the dynamic approach is used. In this approach switching activity for each net is generated by simulating real test vectors on switch level or circuit simulation engines. Then the capacitive power component for each net is calculated using extracted/estimated capacitance data along with real switching activity data. For the short circuit and leakage power estimation, analytical models are used. These models are typically parameterized for transistor widths, rise/fall times, switching activity, etc., for better accuracy. This approach generates very accurate, test vector dependent, power estimates, but it takes very long run-time. Usage of this approach is limited by design size, length of test vectors, computing resources, and project timelines. This approach is typically used for transient power analysis and where absolute power estimates are a must, such as power-specing or power savings validation.

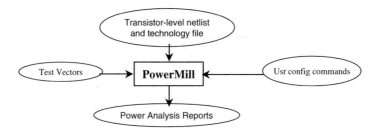

**FIGURE 14.7** PowerMill tool flow.

### *Examples of Commercial Power Estimation Tools*
A few examples of power estimation tools are provided here for reference. This is not a complete list, but only provides an example of what is available commercially. Power CAD is an active area of research.

WattWatcher is an RTL/gate-level, power-estimation tool from Sequence Design, Inc. It adopts a sophisticated bottom-up approach that focuses on the specific analysis methodology applicable to the major consumers of power such as memories on large ASIC, I/O pads, clock circuits, data path circuits, control logic, etc.

PowerMill is a circuit level power estimation tool from Synopsys, Inc. Its algorithm is based on fast circuit simulation employing table lookup of currents for a given transistor sizes (see Fig. 14.7).

## 14.3 Power Reduction Methodologies

The following subsections provide a brief overview of the concepts behind power reduction through various aspects of the design (process technology, circuit, tools, and system/software).

### Power Reduction through Process Technology

Power dissipation consists of a static component and a dynamic component. As described in section 14.1, dynamic power is due to charging and discharging of the load capacitance and is, by far, the dominant component in CMOS circuits. Static power is controlled by leakage currents of transistors and pn-junctions. Static power also arises from circuits that have a steady DC current source between the power supply rails (such as bias circuitry, analog circuits, pseudo-NMOS logic families).

Since dynamic power is proportional to the square of the supply voltage ($V_{dd}$), reduction of $V_{dd}$ is the most effective way for reducing power. The industry has thus steadily moved to lower $V_{dd}$. Indeed, reducing the supply voltage is the key to low-power operation, even after taking into account the modifications to the system architecture, which is required to maintain the computational throughput; however, the drive toward higher performance can sometimes outstrip the benefits of voltage scaling, as described in the section on "Reducing Power Consumption."

Another issue with voltage scaling is that to maintain performance, threshold voltage ($V_t$) also needs to be scaled down since circuit speed is roughly inversely proportional to ($V_{dd} - V_t$). Typically, $V_{dd}$ should be larger than $4V_t$ if speed is not to suffer excessively. As threshold voltage decreases, subthreshold leakage current increases exponentially. At present, $V_t$ is high enough such that subthreshold current is only a small portion of the total active current although it dominates the total standby current. However, with every 0.1 V reduction in $V_t$, subthreshold current increases by 10 times. In the future, with further $V_t$ reduction, subthreshold current will become a significant portion or even a dominant portion of the overall chip current. A first order analysis, using constant electric field scaling of the process parameters, illustrates this as shown in Fig. 14.9 [8]. At sub-0.1 $\mu$m feature sizes, the leakage power starts eating into the benefits for lower $V_{dd}$. In addition, design of dynamic circuits, caches, sense-amps, PLAs, etc., becomes difficult at higher subthreshold leakage currents. Lower $V_{dd}$ also exacerbates noise and reliability concerns. To combat subthreshold current increase, various techniques have been developed. Most techniques focus

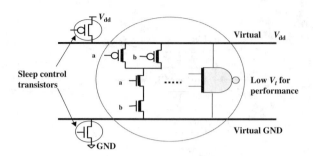

**FIGURE 14.8**   Sleep transistors to control circuit activity.

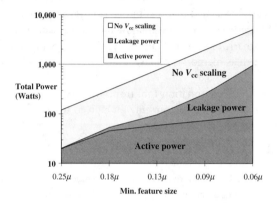

**FIGURE 14.9**   First-order analysis for leakage power trends.

on replacing low $V_t$ devices with high $V_t$ devices whenever and wherever it is possible in the design. High $V_t$ devices can be obtained either by an additional ion-implant with additional masks to the low $V_t$ devices or by back biasing the substrate of low $V_t$ devices. In addition, subthreshold leakage current can also be reduced by introducing special transistors called *sleep control transistors*. These are a pair of pass transistors, which act like circuit breakers through which current passes from $V_{dd}$ to ground. The gates of these transistors are controlled by signals, which can turn *both* devices of this $p$ and $n$ pair *off* (for inactive mode) or *on* for active mode. The concerned circuit operates between a *virtual* $V_{dd}$ rail and *virtual ground* rail between the pair of transistors (see Fig. 14.8).

As technology continues to scale down, oxide is becoming so thin that oxide tunneling current can also become a significant portion of the total chip power for feature size of 0.1 $\mu$m or below. Oxide tunneling current consists of gate leakage and decoupling capacitance leakage. Large gate leakage current not only increases the total chip power, it also imposes additional challenges for circuit design. Without effective solutions for subthreshold and gate leakage, CMOS LSI technology would eventually lose its low power advantage and face the same fate as bipolar LSI circuits.

In addition to the low power techniques that are discussed in this subsection and in the next few subsections many other novel high-speed and low-power techniques have been proposed [1]. Silicon-on-insulator (SOI) technology has been shown to improve delay and power through a ~25% reduction in total capacitance. SOI substrates are produced by either wafer bonding or separation by implantation of oxygen (SIMOX). Optimized SOI MOSFETs can have lower capacitance and slightly higher drive current because of the reduced body charge and slightly lower minimum acceptable $V_t$. Together with some improvement in layout density, this potentially can result in up to 40% improvement in speed [1]. This may be traded for lower $V_{dd}$ and hence a significant reduction in power.

Another way to reduce capacitance is to use the minimum possible width for metal interconnects that carry AC signals such as clock and data buses. A study in electromigration research indicates that AC interconnects can operate at much higher current density than design rules based on DC tests would allow. It has been shown that electromigration lifetime is orders-of-magnitude longer under AC stress than under DC stress. Similar behavior has also been reported for vias and other metal systems.

Yet another possible way to reduce metal capacitance would be to use insulators with lower permittivity for inter-metal dieletrics. Relative to $SiO_2$ which has $\varepsilon$ of ~4.2, SiOF has an $\varepsilon$ of ~3.3 and organic polymers may achieve an $\varepsilon$ of ~2.5.

There appears to be no revolutionary low power device/technology, such as quantum devices, that is manufacturable or compatible with mainstream circuit architectures today. The intrinsic speed-power benefit of galium arsenide technology (GaAs) is probably not sufficient to overcome the difference in cost and technology momentum with respect to silicon except for very high-speed circuits. Devices based on quantum tunneling or single electron effect have excellent intrinsic switching speed and energy, but they are not capable of driving the capacitance of long interconnects. In additon to the difficulty in manufacturing, there are no suitable circuit architectures that are compatible with the characteristic of these devices today. Fortunately, evolutionary innovations and optimization for low power plus continued device scaling in silicon CMOS technology have been sufficient to support the need for low power ULSI up to today, and hopefully for a long time into the future.

## Power Reduction through Circuit Design

In general, power spent in the clock network is the largest contributor to the total power on high-performance ICs such as a modern CPU, as indicated by the Fig. 14.2. The most effective impact for reducing the total power is accomplished by reduction of switching capacitance on the clock network. This is achieved through clock and data enabling (or gating). *Clock gating* is achieved by qualifying different clock partitions by enable signals. Figure 14.10 illustrates the mechanics of clock gating and clock networks. This in effect allows only the partitions that are active to toggle in each given cycle (Fig. 14.11).

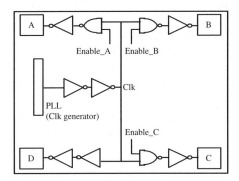

**FIGURE 14.10**  Clock gating and clock networks.

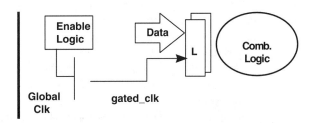

**FIGURE 14.11**  Clock enabling.

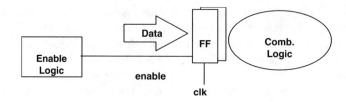

**FIGURE 14.12**   Data enabling.

In addition, this also helps the *di/dt* issues on the chip as sub-regions/blocks will be turned off selectively. Although this technique offers great power saving advantages, it also carries a few design challenges. Some of the concerns in clock gating are that the disabled block may not power up in time and also that modified clocks may generate glitches. As a result the enable signals will have a very strict timing requirement. In addition, at high frequencies, clock skew becomes a significant portion of cycle time and the gated clocks will add to the clock network skews, thus becoming undesirable. Therefore, the granularity at which clock gating can be applied becomes a tradeoff against overall clock network design time and complexity. Some other side effects of clock gating that a designer needs to consider are the area penalty due to generation of the enable signal, clock gating elements, and also the routing overhead to distribute enable signals.

An alternate method for power saving is through *data enabling*. Data enabling implementation is shown in Fig. 14.12. The enable signal generates a data enable signal that indicates whether the current data is valid or not. This prevents input data updates for invalid data or an idle condition. Thus it avoids unnecessary transitions within the design. One disadvantage of this implementation is that clock nodes are toggling during idle conditions. Due to low level of activity in static blocks, data enabling does not offer a large power saving advantage since clock nodes consume majority of the power. In high-frequency design, where aggressive circuit techniques such as domino logic are employed, this technique offers a great deal of power saving. In domino logic, data/non-clocked node activity factors are relatively high. In these cases, the "data enable" signal can be used to avoid evaluation of the first stage of a domino block or to set data inputs to a default state such that the domino gate does not discharge. It is also important to note that clock enabling (gating) for a block will save both clock and data power since the block will be turned off and there is no activity within the block unlike the data enabling.

Datapath circuits are the second highest power consuming category of circuits, after clock in modern high-performance designs. In such designs, datapath including register files fall in critical paths and hence they are custom designed (that is, carefully designed manually by expert designers). These designs involve manual tweaking of transistors and can lead to over-sizing of the devices, which become excessive power wasters. In addition, the choice of circuit family used, e.g., static versus domino can also influence the circuit's power consumption. To design a power-efficient circuit, the power-delay curve approach can be of great help, as described in the "Need for Power Estimation Tools" section (Fig. 14.6). CAD tools that enable a circuit family of this kind and design exploration for custom circuits can thus have a significant impact at full-chip level.

In the CPU arena, a lot of circuits, which are performance critical, get implemented as domino circuits. Wide datapaths such as adders, incrementors, and shifters are implemented in domino. In that case, specific optimizations on individual circuits can be done to reduce power. Consider an example of a domino mulitplexer, which usually appear in shifters, as shown in Fig. 14.13.

In this circuit, at least one of *SelA*, *SelB*, and *SelC* is high every cycle. The data inputs *A#*, *B#*, *C#* are mostly high (*A*, *B*, *C* have very low signal probability). In this situation, all the capacitances associated with the data nodes toggle almost every cycle. This total capacitance is almost three times that associated with the clocked nodes. Consequently, when the polarity of the data inputs is changed, as shown on the right, large power savings are seen.

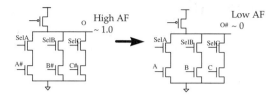

**FIGURE 14.13**   Domino AF reduction in a Mux.

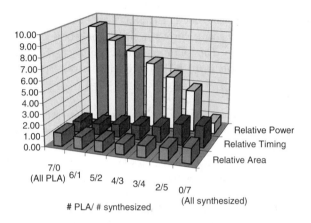

**FIGURE 14.14**   Power/area/delay trade-offs for PLA vs. synthesized logic.

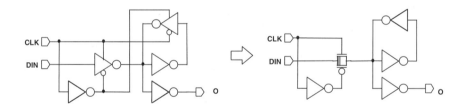

**FIGURE 14.15**   Latch redesign example.

Another example of power/performance trade-off is in the case of control logic, which can either be implemented in PLAs or synthesized gates. Figure 14.14 shows the results for a logic block whose seven sub-blocks can be implemented in PLAs or as synthesized random logic. Increasing the number of synthesized blocks leads to some increase in delay but with much larger power savings.

In library-based design, power savings from the design of the cell libraries can come from device sizing and from restructuring of the logical and physical schematics of the cell. Again, device sizing for optimizing switching energy versus delay ensures better power efficiency; however, resizing of the sequential cells requires extensive recharacterization for setup and hold times in addition to delays of clock to data output.

The second way to optimize a cell library is to change the schematics of the most commonly used and most power hungry cells in the design. These typically consist of latches and master slave flip-flops since these have clock nodes which switch on at every clock edge. Figure 14.15 shows an example of latch redesign that gets rid of clock nodes while still maintaining functionality and performance. Thus, it is advisable to replace more dissipative sequential cells by more efficient types. A small amount of redesign effort on some selected cells often can have a significant power impact for the full chip.

## Power Reduction through CAD Tools

Power estimation tools allow quantification of the power consumption of a whole system and the power contribution of its sub blocks. These help in identifying high power consuming blocks and power wasting blocks. The next step, after identifying the troubled areas is, to reduce power consumption of those blocks. Many techniques are discussed in this chapter, including clock gating, data gating, transistor sizing, and many other design techniques. To reduce time-to-market, designers want to make all the necessary modifications quickly without compromising the quality of the designs. This can be achieved by CAD tools. These tools can identify automatically those design areas where low power techniques can be applied and also perform feasibility of making design changes. CAD tools have limitations, especially dealing with complex clocked designs. So, not all techniques can be automated as quite a few need to go through very complex validation processes, which typically can only be done manually. These techniques were discussed in the circuits section. The following subsection discusses design techniques and CAD tools that help implement and validate many RTL, gate level, and transistor level techniques.

### Low-Power Design Rule Checker

Design rule checkers are usually implemented to look for violations of electrical design rules and layout guidelines. The design rule checking concept can also be applied to identify high impact areas for power savings as well as power wasting components. At different design levels, design rules are different. For example, at RTL, design rules can help us identify block level power optimization opportunities—such as clock gating, data gating, etc.—while at gate and transistor level they can identify over-sized drivers, wasted activity as that of glitches etc.

Two main design rules are: *static* and *dynamic*. Static design rules work on the raw design description and collect information about high power consuming design structures. A few examples of static design rules are: identify wide state buses controlled by a free running clock; identify wide buses driven by unmutexed multiple drivers, etc. Dynamic design rules need design simulation data, like toggle counts per cycle. Dynamic rules identify wasted activity. A few example of dynamic rules are: identify multiplexor blocks whose inputs are toggling even though they are not selected; identify nets toggling multiple times in a single clock cycle, etc. Design rule checking can also help by generating statistical data of the design—such as a list of clock controlled blocks, a list of gated clocks, a list of nets toggling above a specified range, etc. The idea here is that the tool identifies problem areas that the designer can fix to reduce power.

### Low-Power Synthesis

A lot of the CAD research in low power has been in the area of low power logic synthesis. Technology dependent phases of synthesis are particularly suited for practical applications, since they have access to low-level circuit information. It is possible to save power with these methods, even when they are constrained not to increase the delay of the circuit. Table 14.2 shows the results of applying these techniques on a couple of sample circuits from a high-performance CPU. Column 2 shows the power savings when only the combinational part of the circuit is allowed to be changed. Column 3 shows the results when the sequential elements are also allowed to be changed. The area impact is low (Column 5) and there is no increase in delay. The results show ~10% power savings for synthesized blocks, but this

**TABLE 14.2**  Low-Power Logic Synthesis Results (in percent)

| Circuit | After LP Synth. (%) | After Seq. dnsizing (%) | Total (%) | Area (%) |
|---------|---------------------|-------------------------|-----------|----------|
| 1       | 1.4                 | 7.39                    | 8.52      | −1.85    |
| 2       | 0.76                | 4.89                    | 5.65      | −0.69    |
| 3       | 8.40                | 1.53                    | 9.92      | 1.99     |
| 4       | 6.13                | 3.31                    | 9.44      | 7.12     |
| 5       | 11.03               | 1.07                    | 12.09     | 1.09     |
| Total   | 5.16                | 3.81                    | 8.97      | 0.53     |

translates into only 1% full-chip power savings. This is because only 10% of total power is from synthesized logic for CPUs such as the one whose power breakdown was shown in Fig. 14.13.

It is pertinent to note that the system power consumption problem also encompasses chipsets, i.e., devices such as the memory, I/O, and graphics controllers. These operate at a fraction of the CPU clock frequency, and large portions of these are well-suited to be implemented as ASICs. Low power synthesis thus has a much larger impact in this domain.

## Transistor Sizing

A large part of high-performance CPUs is typically custom designed. These designs typically involve manual tweaking of transistors to upsize drivers in critical paths. If too many transistors are upsized unnecessarily, certain designs can operate on the steep part of a circuit's power-delay curve. In addition, the choice of logic family used, e.g., static vs. dynamic logic, can also greatly influence the circuit's power consumption. Please see the "Need for Power Estimation Tools" subsection and Fig. 14.6.

Figure 14.14 shows an example of another kind of intelligent tradeoff for power/performance. It shows the results for a logic block whose seven sub-blocks can either be implemented as PLAs or as synthesized random logic. Increasing the number of synthesized blocks leads to some increase in delay but for much larger power savings.

The traditional emphasis on performance often leads to over-design, that is, wasteful for power. An emphasis on lower power, however, motivates identification of such sources of power wastage. An example of this is the case where paths that are designed faster than they ultimately need to be. For synthesized blocks, the synthesis tool can automatically reduce power by downsizing devices in such paths. For manually designed blocks, on the other hand, downsizing may not always get done. Automated downsizing tools can thus have a big impact. Transistor width savings (with no delay increase) from the use of one such tool are shown in Table 14.3. The benefit of such tools is power savings, as well as productivity enhancement over manual designs.

Many custom designers are now exploring dual-$V_t$ technique to take greater advantage of the transistor sizing. The main idea here is to use low-$V_t$ transistors in critical paths rather than upsizing high-$V_t$ transistors. The main issue with this technique is the increase in subthreshold leakage due to low-$V_t$. So it is very important to use low-$V_t$ transistor selectively and to optimize their usage to achieve a good balance between capacitive current and leakage current in order to minimize total current.

## Examples of Power Reduction Tools

A few examples of power reduction tools and their features are provided here for reference. This is not a complete list, but only provides an example of what is available commercially. Low-power CAD is thus an active area of research.

### PowerCompiler

It is a gate-level power optimization tool offered by Synopsys, Inc. It helps in achieving low power by identifying low power opportunites for clock gating, data-gating, logic restructuring, and downsizing. It also automatically checks feasibility of many low-power design techniques, such as low-power synthesis, clock gating, etc. and implements it. It also quantifies power savings.

### WattSmith

Wattsmith is an RTL power optimization tool offered by Sequence Design, Inc. It helps in identifying block level power reduction opportunities. It also does automatic implementation of many design techniques for low power, to name a few: memory banking, clock gating, etc.

**TABLE 14.3**  Transistor-Width Savings with a Sizing Tool

|                    | Ckt1  | Ckt2  | Ckt3  | Ckt4  |
|--------------------|-------|-------|-------|-------|
| No. of elements    | 4853  | 1953  | 18300 | 19756 |
| Width savings (%)  | 40.00 | 42.00 | 17.00 | 3.00  |

### AMPS

AMPS is a circuit power optimization tool from Synopsys, Inc. It optimizes existing transistor level netlist by downsizing individual transistors in noncritical parts of a given design. It has the capability to optimize designs for delay and area as well. It has configuration file commands to allow users more control on the optimization. AMPS has two major features: Downsize oversized transistor devices for area and power and upsize transistors selectively to fix critical paths. AMPs also performs power analysis, if toggle-count information is provided.

## Power Reduction Methodologies: System/Software

### System Level Power Reduction

The general design principles described in the previous subsections can also be extended at the higher-levels of design to obtain power reductions at the system level. Power should be used as a design constraint in the overall system interaction. System Power Management is a specific class of techniques that has been used effectively for power reduction. This is easiest to explain in the case of processor-based systems, but the ideas are applicable in other types of designs too.

The interaction of the processor (CPU) with the rest of the system provides avenues for reducing average power. Often the CPU is waiting for inputs from peripherals and its power is being wasted. To reduce this waste, CPUs are now provided with a hierarchy of power states. Each state defines a certain level of activity on the CPUs and a certain time penalty for it to get back into a fully active state. Memory and I/O devices often also have similar power states. It is the *system power management* mechanism that monitors the system activity and enforces the movement of the system components between different power states. System power management has its roots in mobile systems; however, EPA requirements under the Energy Star program motivated the migration of these techniques to desktop systems. A recent development in this area is a cross-company initiative called ACPI (advanced configuration and power interface) [1]. The recognition of the need to eliminate wasted power ensures that system power management will continue to be an area of high interest and active development.

### Software-Based Power Reduction

Traditionally, the focus on low-power design has been purely hardware based. This tends to ignore the fact that it is the software that executes on a CPU that determines its power consumption. The software perspective on power consumption has been the subject of recent work [9]. Here a detailed instruction-level power model of the Intel486DX2 was built. The impact of software on the CPU's power and energy consumption, and software optimizations to reduce these were studied. An important conclusion from this work was that in complex CPUs such as the 486DX2, software energy and performance track each other, i.e., for a given task, a faster program implementation will also have lower energy. This is because the CPU power consumption is dominated by a large cost factor (clocks, caches, etc.) that for the most part, does not vary much from one cycle to the other.

Some issues arise when this work is extended to recent CPUs. First, multiple-issue and out-of-order execution mechanisms make it hard to model power on a "per instruction" basis, and more complex power models are required. Also, increased use of clock gating implies that there is greater variation in power consumption from cycle to cycle; however, it is expected that the relationship between software energy and power that was observed before will continue to hold. In any case, it is important to realize that software directly impacts energy/power consumption, and thus, it should be designed to be efficient with respect to these metrics.

A classic example of inefficient software is "busy wait loops." Consider an application such as a spreadsheet that requires frequent user input. During the times when the spreadsheet is recalculating values, high CPU activity is desired in order to complete the recalculation in a short time. In contrast, when the application is waiting for the user to type in values, the CPU should be inactive and in a low-power state. However, a busy wait loop will prevent this from happening, and will keep the CPU in a high-power state. The power wastage is significant since the CPU is essentially fully active, even though it really is *not doing anything*. The Intel Power Monitor (IPM) is a publicly available [3] software analysis tool that monitors system activity to provide information about software that may be wasting power in this and other cases.

## 14.4 Conclusion

Power consumption has emerged as a key constraint in computing applications of almost all kinds. Today's design trends point to the fact that the importance of power consumption will grow in the future. The intent of this chapter was to explain the reasons why this is so and to introduce the reader to the basic concepts and ideas behind power reduction techniques. The interested reader can refer to the listed references for more in-depth information.

## References

1. Rabaey and M. Pedram. *Low Power Design Methodologies*. Kluwer Academic Publishers, Dordrecht, the Netherlands, 1996.
1a. Trevor Mudge. Power: A first-class architectural design constraint. *COMPUTER Magazine*, April 2001.
2. D. Singh, J. Rabaey, M. Pedram, F. Catthoor, S. Rajagopal, N. Sehgal, and T. Mozdzen. Power conspicuous CAD tools and methodologies: A perspective. *Proceedings of the IEEE*, 83(4):570–594, April 1995.
3. M. Nadel. The green machine. *PC Magazine*, 12(10), May 1993.
4. N. Weste and K. Eshraghian. *Principles of CMOS VLSI Design: A Systems Perspective*. Addison-Wesley Publishing Company, Reading, MA, 1985.
5. A. Chandrakasan and R. Brodersen. *Low Power Digital CMOS Design*. Kluwer Academic Publishers, Dordrecht, the Netherlands, 1995.
6. M. Pedram. Power minimization in IC Design. Principles and Applications. *ACM Transactions on Design Automation of Electronic Systems*, 1(1):3–56, December 1996.
7. Bellaouar and M. Elmasry. *Low Power Digital VLSI Design: Circuits and Systems*. Kluwer Academic Publishers, Dordrecht, the Netherlands, 1995.
8. V. Tiwari, et al., Reducing power in high-performance microprocessors. *Design Automation Conference*, June 1998.
9. V. Tiwari, S. Malik, A. Wolfe, and T. C. Lee. Instruction level power analysis and optimization software. *Journal of VLSI Signal Processing*, 13(2), August 1996.

# 15

# Low-Power Circuit Technologies

**Masayuki Miyazaki**
*Hitachi, Ltd.*

## 15.1 Introduction

Low-power complementary metal oxide semiconductor (CMOS) circuit design is required to extend the battery lifetime of portable electronics such as cellular phones or personal digital assistants. Table 15.1 shows a classification of various low-voltage and low-power approaches previously proposed. A system can be in one of two states. It can be active (or dynamic) performing useful computation, or idle (or standby) waiting for an external trigger. A processor, for instance, can transit to the idle state once a required computation is complete. The supply voltage ($V_{dd}$), the threshold voltage ($V_{th}$) and the clock frequency ($f_{clk}$) are parameters that can be dynamically controlled to reduce power dissipation.

In low-voltage systems, the use of reduced threshold devices has caused leakage to become an important idle state problem. There are several ways to control leakage. One approach is to use a transistor as a supply switch to cut off leakage during the idle state. Another approach to control leakage involves threshold voltage adaptation using substrate bias ($V_{bb}$) control. The use of multiple thresholds can be easily incorporated during the synthesis phase. The use of conditional (or gated) clocks is the most common approach to reduce energy. Unused modules are turned off by suppressing the clock to the module.

Low $V_{dd}$ operation is very effective for active-power reduction because the power is proportional to $V_{dd}^2$. Adapting the power supply dynamically is widely employed. A less aggressive approach is the use of multiple static supplies where noncritical path circuits are powered by lower voltages. Dynamic $V_{th}$ scaling by $V_{bb}$ control compensates for transistors' $V_{th}$ fluctuations caused by fabrication process variations. As a result, the technique suppresses the excess leakage power. When the $V_{th}$ of transistors is very low, the suppression of leakage current is useful in the total operating power savings. Conditional clocking also reduces the dynamic-power consumption since the clock signals are only distributed to operating modules. The multiple frequency method delivers several frequencies of clock signals in accordance with required performance in each module. The clock frequency is scheduled depending on data load, and

0-8493-0885-2/02/$0.00+$1.50
© 2002 by CRC Press LLC

**TABLE 15.1**    Classification of Low-Power Circuit Technologies

| Parameter | Idle State | Active State |
|-----------|------------|-------------|
| $V_{dd}$  | Supply switch | Voltage scaling<br>Multiple supply |
| $V_{th}$  | Substrate bias<br>Multiple threshold | Substrate bias |
| $f_{clk}$ | Conditional clocking | Conditional clocking<br>Multiple frequency<br>Frequency scheduling |

dynamic $V_{dd}$ scaling is usually applied with the frequency scheduling. These active-power controls can also be used as leakage reduction techniques during the idle state.

This chapter explores various circuit technologies for low-power systems grouped by the controllable parameters mentioned above.

## 15.2   Basic Theories of CMOS Circuits

In this section, a general analysis of a CMOS circuit is presented. The propagation delay and the power consumption are correlated in the circuit. The power dissipation of a CMOS circuit is described [1] as

$$P_{total} = P_{charge} + P_{leak} = af_{clk}C_L V_{dd}^2 + I_{l0} \times 10^{-(V_{th}/S)} \times V_{dd} \qquad (15.1)$$

where $a$ is the switching probability (transition activity), $C_L$ is the load capacitance, $I_{l0}$ is a constant, and $S$ is the subthreshold slope. Circuit operation causes dynamic charging and discharging power of load capacitance, represented as $P_{charge}$. Static leakage current resulting from subthreshold leakage of MOS transistors is represented as $P_{leak}$. Until recently, power consumption in CMOS circuits was dominated by $P_{charge}$ because of their high $V_{th}$ devices. In the idle state, the switching probability equals 0, and power is determined solely by $P_{leak}$.

The propagation delay of a CMOS circuit is approximately given in [2] by

$$T_{pd} = \beta C_L \frac{V_{dd}}{(V_{dd} - V_{th})^\alpha} \qquad (15.2)$$

where $\beta$ is a constant. The mobility degradation factor $\alpha$ is typically 1.3. With regard to performance, low $V_{dd}$ increases the delay, whereas low $V_{th}$ decreases it. Low $V_{dd}$ operation reduces $P_{charge}$, but increases $T_{pd}$. To maintain a low $T_{pd}$, $V_{th}$ must be reduced. As a result, $P_{leak}$ increases because of the low $V_{th}$ devices. In recent circuits developed for low $V_{dd}$ applications, $V_{th}$ is reduced to improve performance. $P_{leak}$ is becoming larger than $P_{charge}$ in devices with low $V_{th}$. $V_{th}$ is controllable by $V_{bb}$, and the relationship between them is described as

$$V_{th} = V_{th0} + \gamma(\sqrt{2\Phi_b - V_{bb}} - \sqrt{2\Phi_b}) \qquad (15.3)$$

where $V_{th0}$ is a constant, $\gamma$ is the substrate-bias coefficient and $\Phi_b$ is the Fermi potential. A substrate-bias current ($I_{bb}$) must be added to Eq. (15.1) when $V_{bb}$ is used to control $V_{th}$. This is necessary in the case of forward $V_{bb}$, which causes large substrate leakage because of p/n junctions and parasitic-bipolar transistors in the substrate.

## 15.3 Supply Voltage Management

### Supply Switch

A supply switch is one of the most effective means to cut off power in the idle state. Actually, the subthreshold leakage current caused by reduced $V_{th}$ devices is a major problem in that state. The supply switch realizes high-speed operation in the active state and low-leakage current in the standby state. The switch was originally applied to a dynamic random access memory (DRAM) to reduce its data-retention current [3]. As shown in Fig. 15.1, a switching transistor $W_s$ is inserted as the word drivers' supply switch. The transistor width of the switch $W_s$ is equal to the width of the driver $W_d$ because two or more word drivers will not be on at the same time. $W_s$ determines total leakage current in the data-retention mode. Without the switch, the total driver width is $n \times W_d$ and consumes large leakage. The supply switch is adopted to a microprocessor in [4].

A supply switch designed with high-$V_{th}$ MOS devices reduces leakage current, as represented by the multiple threshold-voltage CMOS (MT-CMOS) scheme [5]. The MT-CMOS circuit scheme is shown in Fig. 15.2. This technique combines two types of transistors: low-$V_{th}$ transistors for high-speed switching and high-$V_{th}$ transistors for low leakage. In the active state, SL is negated (low) and the high-$V_{th}$ supply switch transistors Q1 and Q2 supply $V_{dd}$ and GND voltage to the virtual $V_{dd}$ line ($V_{dd}V$) and to the virtual GND line (GNDV) respectively. The operating circuit itself is made of low-$V_{th}$ transistors to accelerate the switching speed of the gate. In the idle state, SL is asserted (high) and Q1 and Q2 disconnect the $V_{dd}V$ and GNDV to reduce leakage current when the circuits are in the idle state, with the asserted (high) SL signals. In a 0.5-$\mu$m gate-length technology, 0.6 V $V_{th}$ devices are used for high-$V_{th}$ switches and 0.3 V $V_{th}$ devices are used for low-$V_{th}$ circuits. When the $V_{th}$ difference between the two devices is 0.3 V, the switches reduce the circuit's idle current by three orders of magnitude.

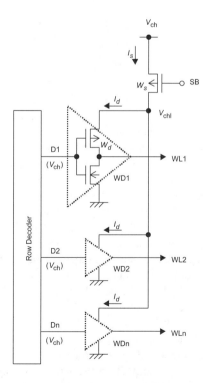

**FIGURE 15.1** Word driver with subthreshold-current reduction [3].

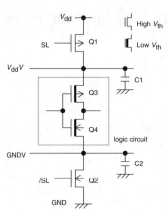

**FIGURE 15.2**  MT-CMOS circuit scheme [5].

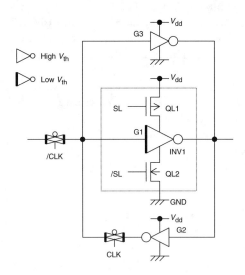

**FIGURE 15.3**  Latch circuit for the MT-CMOS flip-flop [5].

The size of the power switch is an important factor in MT-CMOS design [6]. To supply enough driving current to the circuit, the impedance of the switch must be low. To realize a reliable power supply, the capacitance of $V_{dd}V$ line must be large. Hence, the total gate width of the switch must be large. Here, it is assumed that the total width of all transistors in the logic circuit is $W_l$, the width of the supply switch is $W_h$. When $W_h = W_l$, the supply voltage drop across the switch becomes 15%, causing a 25% increase in gate propagation delay. In the case of $W_h = 10W_l$, the drop is 2.5% and the delay increase is 3.6%. Therefore, MT-CMOS with a large $W_h$ switch enables, at the same time, the high-speed operation of low-$V_{th}$ devices and the low-power consumption of high-$V_{th}$ devices.

When the MT-CMOS switches disconnect power, data stored in registers and memories disappears. Therefore, additional circuits are required to hold data in the idle state. There are several approaches to solve the problem: (a) the MT-CMOS latch [5], (b) the balloon circuit [7], (c) the intermittent power supply (IPS) scheme [8], and (d) the virtual rail clamp (VRC) circuit [9]. The MT-CMOS latch is a simple solution. As shown in Fig. 15.3, inverters G2 and G3 construct a latch circuit and are directly connected to $V_{dd}$. The local power switches $Q_{L1}$ and $Q_{L2}$ are applied to G1. This latch maintains the data in the idle state when G1 is powered down. To reduce the size of the local power switches and improve the latch delay, the balloon circuit is proposed in Fig. 15.4. In the active state, only TG3 is on and the balloon memory is disconnected from the logic circuit. Therefore, the balloon circuit does not degrade the low-$V_{th}$ circuit's performance. When the system goes to sleep, TG2 and TG3 briefly turn on so that data is

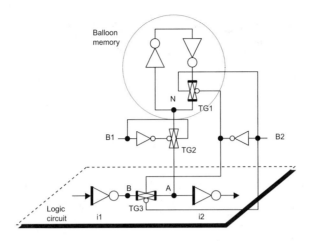

**FIGURE 15.4** MT-CMOS balloon circuit [7].

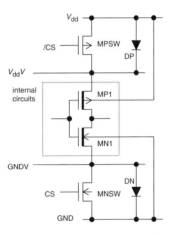

**FIGURE 15.5** The VRC scheme [9].

written into the balloon latch. During the standby state, TG1 is on to keep the information. When the system wakes up, TG1 and TG2 briefly turn on so that the held data can be written back into the low-$V_{th}$ circuit. The balloon can be made of minimum size transistors, so it can be designed to occupy a small area. The third method is IPS. The IPS supplies power in about 20 ms intervals in the idle state to maintain voltage on the $V_{dd}V$ line. The IPS acts similarly to the refresh operation of DRAM. The VRC circuit, as shown in Fig. 15.5, does not need extra circuits to maintain the data in the standby state. While the power switches MPSW and MNSW are disconnected, $V_{dd}V$ and GNDV voltage variations are clamped by the built-in potential of diodes DP and DN. The voltage between $V_{dd}V$ and GNDV keeps data in memories.

MT-CMOS has been applied to reduce the power consumed by a digital signal processor (DSP) [10]. The DSP includes a small processor named power management processor (PMP) that handles signal-processing computations for small amounts of data. Idle power is reduced to 1/37 of its original value by the MT-CMOS leakage reduction. Operating power is decreased by 1/2 because loads with small amount of data are processed by the PMP instead of the DSP. Therefore, total power is reduced to 1/9 of its original value.

## Dynamic Voltage Scaling

The active power is in proportion to $V_{dd}^2$, as shown in Eq. (15.1). The $V_{dd}$ reduction substantially reduces power. On the other hand, a low $V_{dd}$ increases the CMOS circuit propagation delay, as shown in Eq. (15.2). Fixed supply voltage reduction is applied to a DRAM [11]. The supply for the memory array is reduced

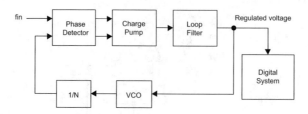

**FIGURE 15.6**    Principle of a supply voltage reducer [12].

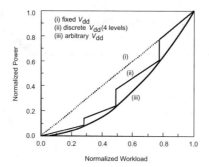

**FIGURE 15.7**    Power consumption with dynamic voltage scaling [13].

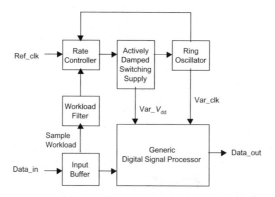

**FIGURE 15.8**    System diagram of variable supply-voltage processing [13].

to 3.7 V from a 5 V $V_{dd}$. It enables low-power operation and a high signal-to-noise ratio. Dynamic voltage scaling (DVS) in accordance with demanded performance is applied to a digital circuit [12]. This scheme can be realized with a phase-locked loop (PLL) system, as shown in Fig. 15.6. The voltage-controlled oscillator (VCO) is made of the critical path in the controlled digital system. This scheme provides a minimum $V_{dd}$ so that the digital system operates at clock frequency $f_{in}$.

$f_{clk}$ and $V_{dd}$ are controlled depending on the workload in [13]. This system is a combination of frequency scheduling and DVS. Depending on the workload, a frequency $f_{clk}$ is selected, and the DVS circuitry selects the minimum $V_{dd}$ in which a processor can operate at that frequency. The effect of DVS is shown in Fig. 15.7. Compared with a constant $V_{dd}$ case (i), DVS reduces power dissipation of a processor. The DVS method has two variations: discrete $V_{dd}$ scaling (ii) and arbitrary $V_{dd}$ scaling (iii). The arbitrary $V_{dd}$ scaling technique saves the most power among the three systems. Figure 15.8 shows an example of a complete DVS system [13]. The workload filter receives data and generates a signal to modulate the duty

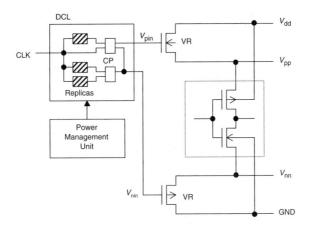

**FIGURE 15.9**  EVT-CMOS circuit design [19].

ratio of the reference clock. The actively damped switching supply provides the optimum $V_{dd}$ according to the duty ratio of input signal. The ring oscillator provides the clock, whose frequency depends on the $V_{dd}$ as given by a lookup table. DVS has been implemented on a DSP [14], an encryption processor [15], microprocessors [16,17], and I/Os [18]. DVS reduces the operating power to 1/5 in the DSP, 1/2 to 1/5 in the microprocessors, and 2/3 in the I/Os.

$V_{dd}$ control can also suppress process-induced performance fluctuations in CMOS circuits. The device characteristics have a distribution because of fabrication-process variations. $V_{dd}$ control reduces the range of the fluctuations. Such a technique is described in elastic $V_t$ CMOS (EVT-CMOS) [19], as shown in Fig. 15.9. EVT-CMOS changes $V_{dd}$, $V_{th}$ and the signal amplitude to reduce power and to raise operating speed. In the deviation compensated loop (DCL), signals $V_{pin}$ and $V_{nin}$ are generated by the charge pump (CP), so that the replica circuits operate at the given clock frequency. The voltage regulator (VR) is a $V_{dd}$ switch that cleans the power supplies for the inner circuits and ensures performance by source-biasing the inner circuits according to $V_{pin}$ and $V_{nin}$. The VR is a source-follower type to reduce the output impedance of the switch.

## Multiple Supply Voltage

If multiple supply voltages are used in a core of an LSI chip, this chip can realize both high performance and low power. The multiple supply system provides a high-voltage supply for high-performance circuits and a low-voltage supply for low-performance circuits. The clustered voltage scaling (CVS) [20] is another low-power method in which several $V_{dd}$s are distributed in the design phase. The CVS example shown in Fig. 15.10 uses two $V_{dd}$s. Between the data inputs and latches, there are circuits operated at high $V_{dd}$ and low $V_{dd}$. Compared to circuits that operate at only high $V_{dd}$, the power is reduced. The latch circuit includes a level-transition (DC-DC converter) if there is a path where a signal propagates from low $V_{dd}$ logic to high $V_{dd}$ logic.

For two supply voltages $V_{dd}H$ and $V_{dd}L$, there is an optimum voltage difference between the two $V_{dd}$s. If the difference is small, the effect of power reduction is small. If the difference is large, there are few logic circuits using the $V_{dd}L$. Two design approaches are used. One approach designs the entire device using high-$V_{dd}$ circuits at first. If the propagation delay of a circuit path is faster than the required clock period, the circuit is given a low-$V_{dd}$. The other approach allows the circuits to be designed as low-$V_{dd}$ circuits at first. If a circuit path cannot operate at a required clock speed, the circuit is given a high-$V_{dd}$. The dual $V_{dd}$ system is applied for a media processor chip providing MPEG2 decoding and real-time MPEG1 encoding. $V_{dd}H$ is 3.3 V and $V_{dd}L$ is 1.9 V. This system reduces power by 47% in the random module and 69% in the clock distribution [21].

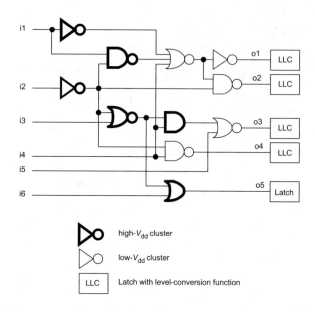

**FIGURE 15.10**   Clustered voltage scaling structure [20].

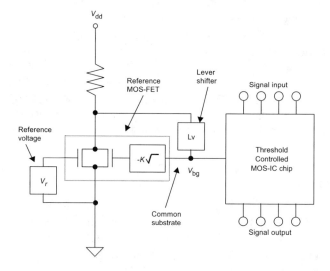

**FIGURE 15.11**   Schematic block diagram of threshold voltage controlling circuit for short channel MOS ICs [23].

## 15.4   Threshold Voltage Management

### Substrate Bias Control for Leakage Reduction

When a CMOS circuit is running in low $V_{dd}$ or is made of small technology devices, the $V_{th}$ fluctuation caused by the fabrication process deviations becomes large [22], and then, circuit performance is degraded. A $V_{bb}$ control scheme keeping the $V_{th}$ constant is presented in [23]. As shown in Fig. 15.11, the substrate bias is automatically produced and $V_{th}$ fluctuation caused by the short-channel effect is suppressed. If $V_{th}$ is lowered to improve performance, subthreshold leakage current grows too large in the standby state. Another $V_{bb}$ control method is proposed to solve the $V_{th}$ fluctuation and large-subthreshold leakage at the

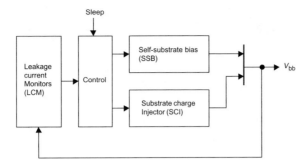

**FIGURE 15.12**   VT-CMOS block diagram [24].

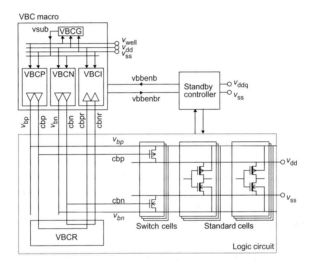

**FIGURE 15.13**   Switched substrate-impedance scheme [26].

same time. This method is the variable threshold-voltage CMOS (VT-CMOS) scheme [24]. The substrate bias to the $n$-type well of a pMOS transistor is called $V_{bp}$ and the bias to the $p$-type well of an nMOS transistor is called $V_{bn}$. The voltage between $V_{dd}$ and $V_{bp}$, or between GND and $V_{bn}$ is defined by $\Delta V_{bb}$. $\Delta V_{bb}$ controls $V_{th}$ as described by Eq. (15.3). This $V_{bb}$ control system raises CMOS circuit performance by compressing $V_{th}$ fluctuation in the active state, and reduces subthreshold leakage current by raising the MOS device $V_{th}$ in the idle state.

The system diagram of VT-CMOS is shown in Fig. 15.12. The control circuit enables the leakage current monitor (LCM) and the self-substrate bias (SSB) circuit in the active state. The LCM measures the leakage current of MOS devices. The SSB forces the leakage current to be constant at a given value. For example, suppose $V_{th}$ is designed at 0.1 ± 0.1 V initially. Applying a 0.4 V $\Delta V_{bb}$ increases the $V_{th}$ to 0.2 V ± 0.05 V. Therefore, the $V_{th}$ fluctuation is compensated from 0.1 to 0.05 V. In this way the $V_{bb}$ control system reduces $V_{th}$ fluctuation [25].

The SSB and the substrate charge injector (SCI) operate in the idle state. The SSB applies large $\Delta V_{bb}$ to reduce leakage current. The SCI enables $V_{bb}$ to drive the substrate quickly and accurately. $\Delta V_{bb}$ becomes about 2 V and then the $V_{th}$ is 0.5 V. The usage of the SSB and SCI results in low subthreshold leakage in the idle state. When applied to a discrete cosine transform processor, it occupies only 5% of the area. The substrate-bias current of $V_{bb}$ control is less than 0.1% of the total current, a small power penalty.

The Switched substrate-impedance (SSI) scheme [26], as shown in Fig. 15.13, is one solution for preventing the $V_{bb}$ noise. SSI distributes switch cells throughout a die that function as $V_{bb}$ supplies.

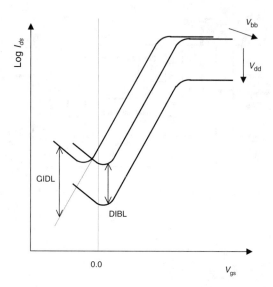

**FIGURE 15.14**   GIDL effect and DIBL effect.

The signals *cbp* and *cbn* turn the switch cells on during the active state. The switch cells connect $V_{dd}$ and GND lines with $V_{bp}$ and $V_{bn}$ lines, respectively, in the logic circuit. During the idle state, the switch cells turn off and the VBC macro scheme provides $V_{bb}$. The switch cells in a chip occupy less than 5% of the area. When the impedance of the switch is high, the substrate-bias lines are floating from the power-source lines, causing circuit-performance degradation. Hence, the size and layout of the switch are important issues. The switch cells are distributed uniformly, for instance, one per 100 gates.

When a MOS device shows a large gate-induced drain leakage (GIDL) effect, a large $V_{bb}$ increases the subthreshold leakage current, as shown in Fig. 15.14 [27]. In such a case, only a small substrate bias works as a leakage-reduction approach. Subthreshold leakage current in a MOS device is reduced for low $V_{dd}$ because of the drain-induced barrier lowering (DIBL) effect. So, the combination of small $V_{bb}$ and low $V_{dd}$ is useful for power reduction. In an experiment on a 360-MIPS RISC microprocessor, a 1.5-V $V_{bb}$ reduces the leakage current from 1.3 mA to 50 $\mu$A, and furthermore, lowering $V_{dd}$ from 1.8 to 1 V suppresses the leakage to 18 $\mu$A.

## Substrate Bias Control for Suppressing Device Fluctuations

As mentioned earlier, a small-size device and low $V_{dd}$ operation present device characteristic fluctuations and thus circuit performance variations [22]. $V_{bb}$ control reduces chip-to-chip leakage current variations; however, the situation is different for performance fluctuations. When the operating temperature is changed, the subthreshold leakage variation is not the same as the saturation current variation in a MOS transistor. The reason is that diffusion current is dominant in the subthreshold region while drift current is dominant in the saturation region. Therefore, when temperature rises, the subthreshold leakage current increases and the saturation current decreases. The propagation delay of a CMOS circuit depends on the saturation current. The operating speed and leakage current respond differently to temperature variation. However, there is another way to use $V_{bb}$ control to reduce speed fluctuations in CMOS circuits. Such a technique is applied to an encoder/decoder circuit in [28].

$V_{bb}$ is supplied to a whole LSI chip. $V_{bb}$ control is useful to suppress chip-to-chip variations. However, the reverse $V_{bb}$ raises the fluctuation *within* a chip [29]. In low $V_{dd}$ operation, performance degradation becomes significant. Substrate forward biasing is one technique to avoid such problems. A forward-bias $V_{bb}$ can be applied to CMOS circuits without latch-up problem [30]. A threshold scaling circuit named

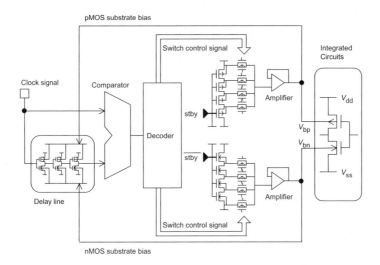

**FIGURE 15.15** SA-$V_t$ CMOS scheme with forward bias [31].

the speed-adaptive threshold-voltage CMOS (SA-VT CMOS) with forward bias for sub-1V systems is proposed in [31].

Figure 15.15 shows the SA-VT CMOS scheme, which realizes an automatic $V_{th}$ scaling depending on a circuit speed. It is constructed from a $V_{th}$-controlled delay line, a comparator, a decoder, a digital-to-analog (D/A) converter, and an amplifier. The comparator measures the timing difference between the $f_{clk}$ signal and a delayed signal from the delay line, and then, translates the difference into a digital word. After passing the delay information through the decoder, the D/A converter produces $V_{bb}$. The delay line is provided $V_{bb}$ to modify its delay. Therefore, this circuit realizes a feedback loop system. The loop locks when the delay of the delay line becomes the same as the $f_{clk}$ cycle. Once $V_{bb}$ is decided, the circuit delivers $V_{bb}$ to an LSI through the amplifier to set $V_{th}$ for the LSI. The delay line is made of circuits that imitate a critical path in the LSI. Hence, matching the delay line's delay to the $f_{clk}$ cycle ensures that the LSI's critical path completes within the clock period. The substrate biases $V_{bp}$ and $V_{bn}$ change discretely because the D/A converter in the SA-VT CMOS generates discrete voltages as substrate biases. $V_{bp}$ and $V_{bn}$ change symmetrically. Each transition time depends on the clock frequency. Therefore, the charging time of the delay line's substrate determines an upper bound on clock frequency. For high-speed circuits, the critical path replica must be divided to be used as the delay line to extend the maximum frequency.

The SA-VT CMOS keeps circuit delay constant by controlling $V_{bb}$. Because of this effect, it adjusts the optimum performance of an LSI along with the $f_{clk}$ and compensates the performance fluctuations caused by fabrication process deviations, $V_{dd}$ variations, and temperature variations. The performance degradations caused by fabrication process deviations are more critical in chip-to-chip distributions than within-chip distributions. This is because the degradations of circuit performance by within-chip distributions are statistically reduced when the circuit becomes larger. Therefore, it is sufficient to use one SA-VT CMOS control toward a whole VLSI substrate. The forward substrate biasing in SA-VT CMOS improves circuit delay degradation, especially at low $V_{dd}$. Although the performance variation caused by fabrication deviations becomes large with reverse substrate bias, it becomes small with forward bias.

## Multiple Threshold Voltage

Multiple $V_{th}$ MOS devices are used to reduce power while maintaining speed. Low-$V_{th}$ devices are delivered to high-speed circuit paths. High-$V_{th}$ devices are applied to the other circuit to reduce subthreshold-leakage current. In case of multiple $V_{th}$, the level converter is not required, as used in the multiple $V_{dd}$ technology.

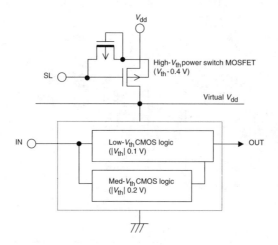

**FIGURE 15.16**  Triple-$V_{th}$ CMOS/SMOX circuit [33].

To make different $V_{th}$ devices, some steps of fabrication process are added. A fabrication process and the effects of dual $V_{th}$ MOS circuits are discussed in [32].

Figure 15.16 shows an example of a dual $V_{th}$ circuit with a high-$V_{th}$ power switch [33]. The high-$V_{th}$ transistor is used to cut off subthreshold leakage current. In the logic circuit, low-$V_{th}$ devices and medium-$V_{th}$ devices are used to make a dual-$V_{th}$ circuit system. In a 16-bit ripple-carry adder, the active-leakage current is reduced to one-third that of the all low-$V_{th}$ adder. Two design approaches are used for dual-$V_{th}$ circuit. One approach designs the entire device using low-$V_{th}$ transistors at first. If the delay of a circuit path is faster than the required clock period, the circuit is replaced to a high-$V_{th}$ transistor. The other approach allows all of circuits to be designed as high-$V_{th}$ transistors at first. If a circuit path cannot operate at a required clock speed, the circuit is replaced to a low-$V_{th}$ transistor. The synthesis algorithms are examined in [34,35].

## 15.5  Clock Distribution Management

### Conditional Clocking

A global clock network consumes 32% of the power in an Alpha 21264 processor [36]. This power is eliminated when clock distribution is suspended by gating during the idle state.

The operating power is also reduced with the conditional clocks, which deliver clock signals only to active modules. The Alpha 21264 uses conditional clocking in the data path as shown in Fig. 15.17. For instance, the control logic asserts the ADD CLK ENABLE signal when a floating-point addition is executed. The enable pulse propagates through latches to drive the AND gates. Other units are disabled while the adder is executed. When a datapath is not needed, the enable signal is negated, and the clock to that path is halted. The clock network reduces the power to 25% of the unconditional case when no floating-point instruction is executed.

### Multiple Frequency Clock

Multiple frequency clocks are used in the Super-H microprocessor [37]. This microprocessor has three kinds of clocks: I-clock for the internal main modules, B-clock for the bus lines, and P-clock for the peripheral circuits. Maximum frequencies of each clock are 200, 100, and 50 MHz, respectively. Compared to a 200 MHz single-clock design, it reduces the distribution power by 23%.

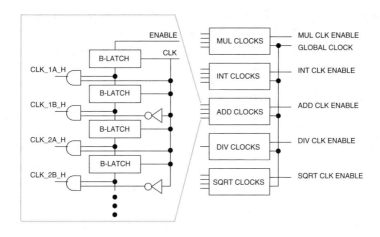

**FIGURE 15.17**    Floating-point datapath clocking of Alpha 21264 [36].

# References

1. Kuroda T. and Sakurai T., Overview of low-power ULSI circuit techniques, *IEICE Trans. Electronics,* vol. E78-C, no. 4, p. 334, 1995.
2. Sakurai T. and Newton A. R., Alpha-power law MOSFET model and its applications to CMOS inverter delay and other formulas, *IEEE J. Solid-State Circuits,* vol. 25, no. 2, p. 584, 1990.
3. Kitsukawa G., et al., 256 Mb DRAM technologies for file applications, *Int. Solid-State Circuits Conference Dig. Tech. Papers,* p. 48, 1993.
4. Horiguchi M., Sakata T., and Itoh K., Switched-source-impedance CMOS circuit for low standby subthreshold current giga-scale LSI's, *Symposium on VLSI Circuits Dig. Tech. Papers,* p. 47, 1993.
5. Mutoh S., et al., 1 V high-speed digital circuit technology with 0.5 $\mu$m multithreshold CMOS, *Proc. IEEE Int. ASIC Conference and Exhibit,* p. 186, 1993.
6. Mutoh S., et al., 1 V power supply high-speed digital circuit technology with multithreshold-voltage CMOS, *IEEE J. Solid-State Circuits,* vol. 30, no. 8, p. 847, 1995.
7. Shigematsu S., et al., A 1 V high-speed MTCMOS circuit scheme for power-down application circuits, *IEEE J. Solid-State Circuits,* vol. 32, no. 6, p. 861, 1997.
8. Akamatsu H., et al., A low power data holding circuit with an intermittent power supply scheme for sub-1V MT-CMOS LSIs, *Symposium on VLSI Circuits Dig. Tech. Papers,* p. 14, 1996.
9. Kumagai K., et al., A novel powering-down scheme for low $V_t$ CMOS circuits, *Symposium on VLSI Circuits Dig. Tech. Papers,* p. 44, 1998.
10. Shigematsu S., Mutoh S., and Matsuya Y., Power management technique for 1 V LSIs using Embedded Processor, *Proc. IEEE Custom Integrated Circuits Conference,* p. 111, 1996.
11. Itoh K., et al., An experimental 1 Mb DRAM with on-chip voltage limiter, *Int. Solid-State Circuits Conference Dig. Tech. Papers,* p. 282, 1984.
12. Macken P., et al., A voltage reduction technique for digital systems, *Int. Solid-State Circuits Conference Dig. Tech. Papers,* p. 238, 1990.
13. Gutnik V. and Chandrakasan A., An efficient controller for variable supply-voltage low power processing, *Symposium on VLSI Circuits Dig. Tech. Papers,* p. 158, 1996.
14. Sakiyama S., et al., A lean power management technique: the lowest power consumption for the given operating speed of LSIs, *Symposium on VLSI Circuits Dig. Tech. Papers,* p. 99, 1997.
15. Goodman J. and Chandrakasan A. P., A 1 Mbs energy/security scalable encryption processor using adaptive width and supply, *Int. Solid-State Circuits Conference Dig. Tech. Papers,* p. 110, 1998.
16. Suzuki K., et al., A 300MIPS/W RISC core processor with variable supply-voltage scheme in variable threshold-voltage CMOS, *Proc. IEEE Custom Integrated Circuits Conference,* p. 587, 1997.

17.  Burd T., et al., A dynamic voltage scaled microprocessor system, *Int. Solid-State Circuits Conference Dig. Tech. Papers,* p. 294, 2000.
18.  Wei G., et al., A variable-frequency parallel I/O interface with adaptive power supply regulation, *Int. Solid-State Circuits Conference Dig. Tech. Papers,* p. 298, 2000.
19.  Mizuno M., et al., Elastic-$V_t$ CMOS circuits for multiple on-chip power control, *Int. Solid-State Circuits Conference Dig. Tech. Papers,* p. 300, 1996.
20.  Usami K., et al., Low-power design technique for ASICs by partially reducing supply voltage, *Proc. IEEE Int. ASIC Conference and Exhibit,* p. 301, 1996.
21.  Igarashi M., et al., A low-power design method using multiple supply voltages, *Proc. Int. Symposium on Low Power Electronics and Design,* p. 36, 1997.
22.  Mizuno T., et al., Performance fluctuations of 0.10 $\mu$m MOSFETs—limitation of 0.1 $\mu$m ULSIs, *Symposium on VLSI Technology Dig. Tech. Papers,* p. 13, 1994.
23.  Kubo M., et al., A threshold voltage controlling circuit for short channel MOS integrated circuits, *Int. Solid-State Circuits Conference Dig. Tech. Papers,* p. 54, 1976.
24.  Kuroda T., et al., A 0.9 V, 150 MHz 10 mW 4 mm$^2$ 2-D discrete cosine transform core processor with variable threshold-voltage (VT) scheme, *IEEE J. Solid-State Circuits,* vol. 31, no. 11, p. 1770, 1996.
25.  Kobayashi T. and Sakurai T., Self-adjusting threshold-voltage scheme (SATS) for low-voltage high-speed operation, *Proc. IEEE Custom Integrated Circuits Conference,* p. 271, 1994.
26.  Mizuno H., et al., A 18 $\mu$m-standby-current 1.8 V 200 MHz microprocessor with self substrate-biased data-retention mode, *Int. Solid-State Circuits Conference Dig. Tech. Papers,* p. 280, 1999.
27.  Keshavarzi A., Roy K., and Hawkins C. F., Intrinsic leakage in low power deep submicron CMOS ICs, *Proc. Int. Test Conference,* p. 146, 1997.
28.  Burr J. B. and Shott J., A 200 mV self-testing encoder/decoder using Stanford ultra-low-power CMOS, *Int. Solid-State Circuits Conference Dig. Tech. Papers,* p. 84, 1994.
29.  Narendra S., Antoniadis D., and De V., Impact of using adaptive body bias to compensate die-to-die $V_t$ variation on within-die $V_t$ variation, *Proc. Int. Symposium on Low Power Electronics and Design,* p. 229, 1999.
30.  Oowaki Y., et al., A sub-0.1 $\mu$m circuit design with substrate-over biasing, *Int. Solid-State Circuits Conference Dig. Tech. Papers,* p. 88, 1998.
31.  Miyazaki M., et al., A 1000-MIPS/W microprocessor using speed-adaptive threshold-voltage CMOS with forward bias, *Int. Solid-State Circuits Conference Dig. Tech. Papers,* p. 420, 2000.
32.  Chen Z., et al., 0.18 $\mu$m dual $V_t$ MOSFET process and energy-delay measurement, *Int. Electron Devices Meeting Tech. Dig.,* p. 851, 1996.
33.  Fujii K., Douseki T., and Harada M., A sub-1 V triple-threshold CMOS/SIMOX circuit for active power reduction, *Int. Solid-State Circuits Conference Dig. Tech. Papers,* p. 190, 1998.
34.  Wei L., et al., Design and optimization of low voltage high performance dual threshold CMOS circuits, *Proc. ACM/IEEE Design Automation Conference,* p. 489, 1998.
35.  Kato N., et al., Random modulation: multi-threshold-voltage design methodology in sub-2 V power supply CMOS, *IEICE Trans. Electronics,* vol. E83-C, no. 11, p. 1747, 2000.
36.  Gowan M. K., Biro L. L., and Jackson D. B., Power consideration in the design of the Alpha 21264 microprocessor, *Proc. Design Automation Conference,* p. 726, 1998.
37.  Nishii O., et al., A 200 MHz 1.2 W 1.4GFLOPS microprocessor with graphic operation unit, *Int. Solid-State Circuits Conference Dig. Tech. Papers,* p. 288, 1998.

# 16

# Techniques for Leakage Power Reduction

Vivek De
*Intel Corporation*

Ali Keshavarzi
*Intel Corporation*

Siva Narendra
*Intel Corporation*

Dinesh Somasekhar
*Intel Corporation*

Shekhar Borkar
*Intel Corporation*

James Kao
*Intel Corporation*

Raj Nair
*Intel Corporation*

Yibin Ye
*Intel Corporation*

## 16.1  Introduction

Supply voltage ($V_{cc}$) must continue to scale down at the historical rate of 30% per technology generation in order to keep power dissipation and power delivery costs under control in future high-performance microprocessor designs. To improve transistor and circuit performance by at least 30% per technology generation, transistor threshold voltage ($V_t$) must also reduce at the same rate so that a sufficiently large gate overdrive ($V_{cc}/V_t$) is maintained. However, reduction in $V_t$ causes transistor subthreshold leakage current ($I_{off}$) to increase exponentially. Large leakage can (1) severely degrade noise immunity of dynamic logic circuits, (2) compromise stability of 6T SRAM cells, and (3) increase leakage power consumption of the chip to an unacceptably large value. In addition, degradation of short-channel effects, such as $V_t$ roll-off and drain induced barrier lowering (DIBL), in conventional bulk MOSFET's with low $V_t$ can pose serious obstacles to producing high-performance, manufacturable transistors at low cost in sub-100 nm $L_{eff}$ technology generations and beyond. To further compound the technology scaling problems, within-die and across-wafer device parameter variations are becoming increasingly untenable. This nonscalability of process tolerances is also a barrier to $V_{cc}$ and technology scaling.

To illustrate the barrier associated with excessive leakage power, one can estimate the subthreshold leakage power of future chips, starting with the 0.25 $\mu$m technology described in [1], and projecting subthreshold

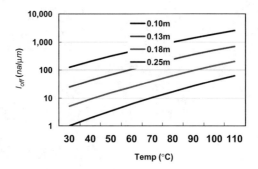

**FIGURE 16.1**   Projected off currents.

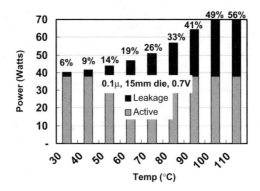

**FIGURE 16.2**   Projected leakage power in 0.1 $\mu$m technology.

leakage currents for 0.18 $\mu$m, 0.13 $\mu$m, and 0.1 $\mu$m technologies. Because subthreshold leakage is increasingly the dominant component of transistor leakage, it can be used to illustrate the excessive leakage power barrier. Assume that 0.25 $\mu$m technology has $V_t$ of 450 mV, and $I_{off}$ is around 1 nA/$\mu$m at 30°C. Also assume that subthreshold slopes are 80 and 100 mV/decade at 30°C and 100°C, respectively, $V_t$ scales by 15% per generation, and $I_{off}$ increases by 5 times each technology generation. Because $I_{off}$ increases exponentially with temperature, it is important to consider leakage currents and leakage power as a function of temperature. Figure 16.1 shows projected $I_{off}$ (as a function of temperature) for the four different technologies.

Next, we use these projected $I_{off}$ values to estimate the active leakage power of a 15 mm die (small die), and compare the leakage power with the active power. The total transistor width on the die increases by ~50% each technology generation; hence the total leakage current increases by ~7.5 times. This results in leakage power of the chip increasing by ~5 times each technology generation. Since the active power remains constant (per scaling theory) for constant die size, the leakage power will become a significant portion of the total power as shown in Fig. 16.2.

This chapter explores the various components of leakage currents at the transistor level, and also describes the effect of leakage currents at the circuit level. Finally, it concludes with a few techniques that can be used to help control subthreshold leakage currents in both sleep and active circuit modes.

## 16.2   Transistor Leakage Current Components

Transistor off-state leakage current ($I_{OFF}$) is the drain current when the gate-to-source voltage is zero. $I_{OFF}$ is influenced by threshold voltage, channel physical and effective dimensions, channel/surface doping profile, drain/source junction depth, gate oxide thickness, $V_{DD}$, and temperature; however, $I_{OFF}$ as defined above is not the only leakage mechanism of importance for a deep submicron transistor. Log($I_D$) versus $V_G$ is an important transistor curve in the saturated and linear bias states (Fig. 16.3). It allows measurement

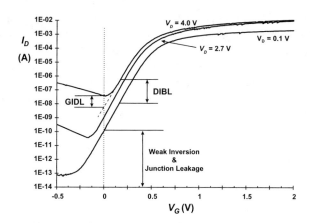

**FIGURE 16.3** *n*-channel $I_D$ vs. $V_G$ showing DIBL, GIDL, weak inversion, and p-n junction reverse bias leakage components in a 0.35 $\mu$m technology.

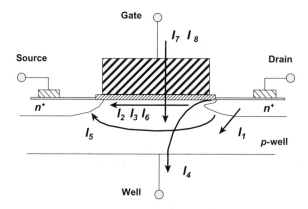

**FIGURE 16.4** Summary of leakage current mechanisms of deep submicron transistors [10].

of many device parameters such as $I_{OFF}$, $V_T$, $I_D$(SAT), $I_D$(LIN), $g_m$(SAT), $g_m$(LIN), and slope ($S_t$) of $V_G$ versus $I_D$ in the weak inversion state. $I_{OFF}$ is measured at the $V_G = 0$ V intercept. Measurements will illustrate all leakage current mechanisms and their properties in deep submicron transistors. The transistors in this study were from a 0.35 $\mu$m CMOS process technology with $L_{eff} \ll 0.25$ $\mu$m and nominal $V_{DD} \approx 2.5$ V [2].

We describe eight short-channel leakage mechanisms illustrating certain properties with measurements (Fig. 16.4). $I_1$ is reverse bias p-n junction leakage caused by barrier emission combined with minority carrier diffusion and band-to-band tunneling away from the oxide-silicon interface, $I_2$ is weak inversion, $I_3$ is DIBL, $I_4$ is gate induced drain leakage (GIDL), $I_5$ is channel punchthrough, $I_6$ is channel surface current due to narrow width effect, $I_7$ is oxide leakage, and $I_8$ is gate current due to hot carrier injection. Currents $I_1$–$I_6$ are off-state leakage mechanisms, while $I_7$ (oxide tunneling) occurs when the transistor is on. $I_8$ can occur in the off-state, but more typically occurs when the transistor bias states are in transition.

## p-n Junction Reverse Bias Current ($I_1$)

The reverse bias p-n junction leakage ($I_1$) has two main components: One is minority carrier diffusion/drift near the edge of the depletion region, and the other is due to electron-hole pair generation in the depletion region of the reverse bias junction [3]. If both n- and p-regions are heavily doped (this will be the case for advanced MOSFETs using heavily doped shallow junctions and halo doping for better short-channel effects), Zener and band-to-band tunneling may also be present. For a MOS transistor, additional leakage can occur between the drain and well junction from gated diode device action (overlap and vicinity of gate to the drain to well p-n junctions) or carrier generation in drain to well depletion regions with influences of the gate on these current components [4]. p-n reverse bias leakage ($I_{REV}$) is a function of junction area and doping concentration [3,5]. $I_{REV}$ for pure diode structures in our technology [2] was a minimal contributor to total transistor $I_{OFF}$. p-n junction breakdown voltage was >8 V.

## Weak Inversion ($I_2$)

Weak inversion or subthreshold conduction current between source and drain in a MOS transistor occurs when gate voltage is below $V_T$ [3,6]. The weak inversion region is seen in Fig. 16.3 as the linear portion of the curve. The carriers move by diffusion along the surface similar to charge transport across the base of bipolar transistors. The exponential relation between driving voltage on the gate and the drain current is a straight line in a semi-log plot. Weak inversion typically dominates modern device off-state leakage due to the low $V_T$ that is used.

## Drain-Induced Barrier Lowering ($I_3$)

DIBL occurs when a high voltage is applied to the drain where the depletion region of the drain interacts with the source near the channel surface to lower the source potential barrier. The source then injects carriers into the channel surface without the gate playing a role. DIBL is enhanced at higher drain voltage and shorter $L_{eff}$. Surface DIBL typically happens before deep bulk punchthrough. Ideally, DIBL does not change the slope, $S_t$, but does lower $V_T$. Higher surface and channel doping and shallow source/drain junction depths reduce the DIBL leakage current mechanism [6,7]. Figure 16.3 illustrates the DIBL effect as it moves the curve up and to the left as $V_D$ increases. DIBL can be measured at constant $V_G$ as the change in $I_D$ for a change in $V_D$. For $V_D$ between 0.1 and 2.7 V, $I_D$ changed 1.68 decades giving a DIBL of 1.55 V/decade change of $I_D$. DIBL may also be quantified in units of mV/V for at a constant drain current value.

The subthreshold leakage of a MOS device including weak inversion and DIBL can be modeled according to the following equation:

$$I_{subth} = A \times e^{\frac{1}{nv_T}(V_G - V_S - V_{TH0} - \gamma' \times V_S + \eta \times V_{DS})} \times \left(1 - e^{\frac{-V_{DS}}{v_T}}\right) \qquad (16.1)$$

where

$$A = \mu_0 C'_{OX} \frac{W}{L_{eff}} (v_T)^2 e^{1.8} e^{\frac{-\Delta V_{TH}}{\eta v_T}}$$

$V_{TH0}$ is the zero bias threshold voltage, $v_T = kT/q$ is the thermal voltage. The body effect for small values of source to bulk voltages is very nearly linear and is represented by the term $\gamma' V_S$, where $\gamma'$ is the linearized body effect coefficient. $\eta$ is the DIBL coefficient, $C_{OX}$ is the gate oxide capacitance, $\mu_0$ is the zero bias mobility, and $n$ is the subthreshold swing coefficient for the transistor. $\Delta V_{TH}$ is a term introduced to account for transistor-to-transistor leakage variations.

## Gate-Induced Drain Leakage ($I_4$)

GIDL current arises in the high electric field under the gate/drain overlap region causing deep depletion [7] and effectively thins out the depletion width of drain to well p-n junction. The high electric field between gate and drain (a negative $V_G$ and high positive $V_D$ bias for NMOS transistor) generates carriers into the substrate and drain from direct band-to-band tunneling, trap-assisted tunneling, or a combination of thermal emission and tunneling. It is localized along the channel width between the gate and drain. GIDL is at times referred to as surface band-to-band tunneling leakage. GIDL current is seen as the "hook" in the waveform of Fig. 16.3 that shows increasing current for negative values of $V_G$ (gate bias dependent specially observed at high $V_D$ curves). Thinner $T_{ox}$ and higher $V_{DD}$ (higher potential between gate and drain) enhance the electric field dependent GIDL. The impact of drain (and well) doping on GIDL is rather complicated. At low drain doping values, we do not have high electric field for tunneling to occur. For very high drain doping, the depletion volume for tunneling will be limited. Hence, GIDL is worse for drain doping values in between the above extremes. Very high and abrupt drain doping is preferred for minimizing GIDL as it provides lower series resistance required for high transistor drive current. GIDL is a major obstacle in $I_{OFF}$ reduction. As it was discussed, a junction related bulk band-to-band tunneling component in $I_1$ may also contribute to GIDL current, but this current will not be gate bias dependent. It will only increase baseline value of $I_4$ current component.

We isolated $I_{GIDL}$ by measuring source current $\log(I_s)$ versus $V_G$. It is seen as the dotted line extension of the $V_D = 4.0$ V curve in Fig. 16.3. $I_{GIDL}$ is removed since it uses the drain and substrate (well) terminals, not the source terminal. The GIDL contribution to $I_{OFF}$ is small at 2.7 V, but as the drain voltage rises to 4.0 V (close to burn-in voltage), the off-state current on the $V_D = 4.0$ V curve increases from 6 nA (at the dotted line intersection with $V_G = 0$ V) to 42 nA, for a GIDL of 36 nA. The pure weak inversion and reverse bias p-n junction current of 99 pA is approximated from the $V_D = 0.1$ V curve.

## Punchthrough ($I_5$)

Punchthrough occurs when the drain and source depletion regions approach each other and electrically "touch" deep in the channel. Punchthrough is a space-charge condition that allows channel current to exist deep in the subgate region causing the gate to lose control of the subgate channel region. Punchthrough current varies quadratically with drain voltage and $S_t$ increases reflecting the increase in drain leakage [8, p. 134]. Punchthrough is regarded as a subsurface version of DIBL.

## Narrow Width Effect ($I_6$)

Transistor $V_T$ in nontrench isolated technologies increases for geometric gate widths in the order of $\leq 0.5$ $\mu$m. An opposite and more complex effect is seen for trench isolated technologies that show decrease in $V_T$ for effective channel widths on the order of $W \leq 0.5$ $\mu$m [9]. No narrow width effect was observed in our transistor sizes with $W \gg 0.5$ $\mu$m.

## Gate Oxide Tunneling ($I_7$)

Gate oxide tunneling current $I_{ox}$, which is a function of electric field ($E_{ox}$), can cause direct tunneling through the gate or Fowler–Nordheim (FN) tunneling through the oxide bands [Eq. (16.1)] [8]. FN tunneling typically lies at a higher field strength than found at product use conditions and will probably remain so. FN tunneling has a constant slope for $E_{ox} > 6.5$ MV/cm (Fig. 16.5). Figure 16.5 shows significant direct oxide tunneling at lower $E_{ox}$ for thin oxides.

$$I_{OX} = A \cdot E_{OX}^2 \cdot e^{-\frac{B}{E_{ox}}} \tag{16.2}$$

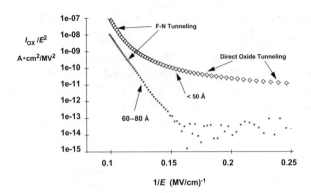

**FIGURE 16.5**   Fowler–Nordheim and direct tunneling in *n*-channel transistor oxide. The 60–80 Å curve shows dominance of FN tunneling while the <50 Å curve shows FN at high $E_{ox}$, but significant direct tunneling at low electric fields.

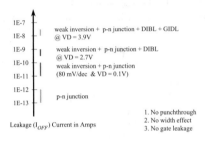

**FIGURE 16.6**   Components of $I_{OFF}$ for a 0.35 $\mu$m technology for a transistor of 20 $\mu$m wide. Currents from various leakage mechanisms accumulate resulting in a total measured transistor $I_{OFF}$ for a given drain bias.

Oxide tunneling current is presently not an issue for devices in production, but could surpass weak inversion and DIBL as a dominant leakage mechanism in the future as oxides get thinner.

### Hot Carrier Injection ($I_8$)

Short channel transistors are more susceptible to injection of hot carriers (holes and electrons) into the oxide. These charges are a reliability risk and are measurable as gate and substrate currents. While past and present transistor technologies have controlled this component, it increases in amplitude as $L_{eff}$ is reduced unless $V_{DD}$ is scaled accordingly.

Figure 16.6 summarizes relative contributions of main components of intrinsic leakage for a typical 0.35 micron CMOS technology. We can see that for a nominal drain voltage of 2.7 V (consistent with typical power supply voltage of the technology), DIBL is the dominant component of leakage (it elevates the amount of weak inversion subthreshold leakage current). At elevated burn-in voltage of 3.9 V, GIDL dominates; however, at low $V_D$, weak inversion is the primary leakage mechanism.

## 16.3   Circuit Subthreshold Leakage Current

Subthreshold leakage currents for a single device can be modeled as illustrated in Eq. (16.1), but in a CMOS circuit that contains multiple devices connected together, the net leakage effect will be highly dependent on the applied input vectors [11,12]. The underlying mechanisms are related to (1) transistor stack effect and (2) total effective width of NMOS and PMOS devices that are turned off. [13,14].

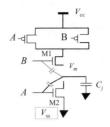

**FIGURE 16.7** Two-nMOS stack in a two-input NAND gate.

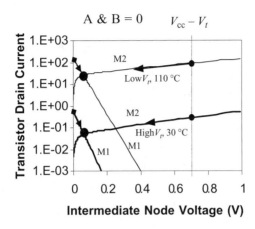

**FIGURE 16.8** DC solution of two-nMOS stack.

## Transistor Stack Effect

The "stack effect" refers to the leakage reduction effect in a transistor stack when more than one transistor is turned off. The dynamics of the stack effect can be best understood by considering a two-input NAND gate in Fig. 16.7. When both M1 and M2 are turned off, the voltage $V_m$ at the intermediate node is positive due to the small drain current. Thus, the gate-to-source voltage of the upper transistor M1 is negative, i.e., $V_{gs1} < 0$. The exponential characteristic of the subthreshold conductance on $V_{gs}$ greatly reduces the leakage. In addition, the body effect of M1 due to $V_M > 0$ further reduces the leakage current as $V_t$ increases.

The internal node voltage $V_M$ is determined by the cross point of the drain currents in M1 and M2. Since leakage current strongly depends on the temperature and the transistor threshold voltage, we consider two cases: (1) high $V_t$ and room temperature at 30°C and (2) low $V_t$ and high temperature at 110°C. Figure 16.8 shows the DC solution of nMOS subthreshold current characteristics from SPICE simulations. The leakage current of a single nMOS transistor at $V_g = 0$ is determined by the drain current of M1 at $V_M = 0$. It is clear that the leakage current through a two-transistor stack is approximately an order of magnitude smaller than the leakage of a single transistor. The voltage $V_M$ of the internal node converges to ~100 mV, as shown in Fig. 16.8. The small $V_M$ (= drain-to-source voltage of M2) reduces the DIBL, and hence increases $V_t$ of M2, which also contributes to the leakage reduction.

The subthreshold swing is proportional to $kT$. The slope decreases when the temperature $T$ increases, which moves the cross point (Fig. 16.8) upwards. Thus, the amount of reduction will be smaller at higher temperature. The amount of reduction is also dependent on the threshold voltage $V_t$, which is larger for higher $V_t$. For three- or four-transistor stacks, the leakage reduction is found to be 2–3 times larger in both nMOS and pMOS. Results are summarized in Fig. 16.9. Note that reductions are obtained at the room temperature, as we are only interested in standby mode.

The reduced standby stack leakage current is obtained under steady-state condition. After a logic gate has a transition, the leakage current does not immediately converge to its steady-state value. Let us again

|          | High $V_t$ | Low $V_t$ |
|----------|-----------|-----------|
| 2 NMOS   | 10.7X     | 9.96X     |
| 3 NMOS   | 21.1X     | 18.8X     |
| 4 NMOS   | 31.5X     | 26.7X     |
| 2 PMOS   | 8.6X      | 7.9X      |
| 3 PMOS   | 16.1X     | 13.7X     |
| 4 PMOS   | 23.1X     | 18.7X     |

**FIGURE 16.9**   Leakage current reduction by two-, three-, and four-transistor stacks at room temperature $T = 30°C$.

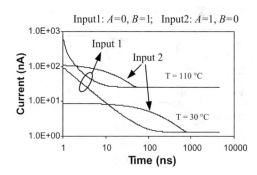

**FIGURE 16.10**   Temporal behavior of leakage current in transistor stacks for different temperatures and initial input conditions.

consider the NAND gate in Fig. 16.7. Assume that the inputs switches from $A = 0$, $B = 1$ to $A = 0$, $B = 0$ to turn off both transistors, the voltage $V_M$ of the internal node is approximately $V_{DD} - V_t$ after the transition. Due to the junction capacitance $C_j$, $V_M$ will "slowly" go down as it is discharged by the sub-threshold drain current of M2. In the other case, when the inputs switches from $A = 1$, $B = 0$ to $A = 0$, $B = 0$, $V_M$ is negative after the transition due to the coupling capacitance between the gate and drain of M2 (as shown in Fig. 16.7). It also takes certain amount of time for $V_M$ to converge to its final value as determined by the DC stack solution.

The time required for the leakage current in transistor stacks to converge to its final value is dictated by the rate of charging or discharging of the capacitance at the intermediate node by the subthreshold drain current of M1 or M2. The convergence of leakage current is shown in Fig. 16.10. We define the *time constant* as the amount of time required to converge to twice of its final stack leakage value. This time constant is, therefore, determined by (1) drain-body junction and gate-overlap capacitances per unit width, (2) the input conditions immediately before the stack transistors are turned "off," and (3) transistor subthreshold leakage current, which depends strongly on temperature and $V_t$. Therefore, the convergence rate of leakage current in transistor stacks increases rapidly with $V_t$ reduction and temperature increase. For $V_t = 200$ mV devices in a sub-1 V, 0.1 $\mu$m technology, this time constant in 2-nMOS stacks at 110°C ranges from 5 to 50 ns.

## Steady-State Leakage Model of Transistor Stacks

To investigate the leakage behavior of a stack of transistors, consider a stack of four NMOS devices. Such a structure would occur in the NMOS pull-down tree of a four input NAND tree as shown in Fig. 16.11. Let us assume that all four devices are OFF with the applied gate voltage VG1 through VG4 being zero. Additionally, the full supply voltage, 1.5 V in the figure, is impressed across the stack. After a sufficiently long time, the voltage at each of the internal nodes will reach a steady-state value. With the assumption that subthreshold leakage from the drain to the source of the MOS device is the dominant leakage component and source drain junction leakage is negligible, application of Kirchoff's current law (KCL)

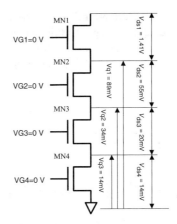

**FIGURE 16.11** Four-input NAND NMOS stack.

yields the current through each transistor being the same and being identically equally to the overall stack current.

To calculate the overall leakage of the stack we use Eq. (16.1) to determine the leakage through a transistor as a function of the drain to source voltage. This yields the voltage across second transistor from the top as

$$V_{DS2} = \frac{nv_T}{(1 + 2\eta + \gamma')} \ln\left(\left(\frac{A_1}{A_2}\right)e^{\frac{nV_{DD}}{nv_T}} + 1\right)$$

Additionally the voltage of the rest of the transistors can be expressed in a recursive fashion. The drain to source voltage of the *i*th transistor can be expressed in terms of the $(i - 1)$th transistor.

$$V_{DSi} = \frac{nv_T}{(1 + \gamma')} \ln\left(1 + \frac{A_{i-1}}{A_i}\left(1 - e^{\frac{-1}{v_T}V_{DS(i-1)}}\right)\right)$$

With the drain to source transistor voltages known, the leakage current through the stack can be computed by finding the leakage of the bottom transistor of the stack from the subthreshold equation. An identical method applies to the solution of leakage current for PMOS stacks. An estimate of leakage in transistor stacks was first presented by Gu and Elmasry [13]. The above analysis for transistor stack leakage was first presented by Johnson [14]. An early implementation of this idea for actively reducing leakage in word decoder-driver circuits for RAMs is presented by Kawhara [15]. The term "self-reverse biasing" used in this paper, gives a clear indication of the mechanism by which leakage of a stack of transistors is reduced.

## Transient Model of Transistor Stack Leakage

When stacked devices are turned off, the time required for the leakage currents to settle to the previously computed steady-state leakage levels can be large and can vary widely, ranging from microseconds to milliseconds. The settling time is important for determining if the quiescent leakage current model is applicable. The worst-case settling time for a stack occurs when all the internal nodes are charged to the maximum possible value $V_{DD} - V_T$ just before every transistor of the stack is turned off. We notice that a strong reverse gate bias will now be present for all devices except for the bottom-most device. In the figure, MN1 to MN3 will have a reverse gate bias and the leakage through them is small. Hence, we approximate the discharge current of the drain node of MN4 as being the leakage current of MN4 alone. Once the drain voltage of MN4 is sufficiently small, MN3 discharges its drain node with a discharge current, which is the leakage current of the two stacked devices MN3 and MN4. The discharge time of each internal node of the stack, $t_{disi}$, is sequential and the overall settling time is the sum of the discharge times.

To derive a closed form solution for the discharge time, it is assumed that the capacitance of the internal nodes is not dependent on voltage. Additionally it is assumed that we know the internal node voltages after the instant the devices are cut-off—this requires a determination of the voltage to which internal nodes are bootstrapped. By using the capacitor discharge equation for the internal nodes, the discharge time can be written as

$$t_{disi} = \frac{nC_iL_{eff}}{\mu_0 C_{OX} W v_T e^{1.8} \eta} \times e^{\frac{1}{nv_T}} [(1 + \gamma' + \eta)V_{qi+1} + V_{TH0}] \times \left( e^{\frac{-\eta V_{qi}}{\eta v_T}} - e^{\frac{-\eta V_{booti}}{\eta v_T}} \right)$$

# 16.4 Leakage Control Techniques

Many techniques have been reported in the literature to reduce leakage power during standby condition. Examples of such techniques are: (1) reverse body biasing, as discussed in another chapter of this book; (2) MTCMOS sleep transistor and variations of sleep transistor-based techniques; and (3) embedded multiple-$V_t$ CMOS design where low-$V_t$ devices are used only in the critical paths for maximizing performance, while high-$V_t$ devices are used in noncritical paths to minimize leakage power. In this section, we discuss two standby leakage reduction techniques: one through stack effect vector manipulation, and the other through embedded dual-$V_t$ design applied to domino circuits. We also discuss the applicability of reverse body biasing for improving performance and leakage power distribution of multiple die samples during active modes, as well as the impact of technology scaling on the effectiveness of this technique.

## Standby Leakage Control by Input Vector Activation

For any static CMOS gate other than the inverter, there are stacked transistors in nMOS or pMOS tree (e.g., pMOS stack in NOR, nMOS stack in NAND). Typically, a large circuit block contains high percentage of logic gates where transistor "stacks" are already present. Note that leakage reduction in a transistor stack can be achieved only when more than one device is turned off. Thus, the leakage current of a logic gate depends on its inputs. For a circuit block consisting of a large number of logic gates, the leakage current in standby mode is therefore determined by the vector at its inputs, which is fed from latches. For different vectors, the leakage is different. An input vector, which gives as small a leakage current as possible, needs to be determined. One of the following three methods can be used to select the input vector: (1) Examining the circuit topology makes it possible to find a "very good" input vector, which maximizes the stack effect, and hence minimizes the leakage current. (2) An algorithm can be developed for efficiently searching for the "best" vector. (3) Testing or simulating a large number of randomly generated input vectors, the one with the smallest leakage can also be selected and used in the standby mode. Method 1 is suitable for datapath circuits (e.g., adders, multipliers, comparators, etc.) due to their regular structure. For random logic, an algorithm in method 2 is required to find a vector with good quality. In [11], the input dependence of the leakage has been empirically observed and random search is used to determine an input vector; however, the fact that the dependence is due to the transistor stack effect has not been addressed.

Figure 16.12 shows the distribution of the standby leakage current of a 32-bit static CMOS Kogg-Stone adder generated by 1000 random input vectors, with two threshold voltages. The standby leakage power varies by 30–40%, depending on the input vector, which determines the magnitude of the transistor stack effect in the design. The best input vector for minimum leakage can be easily determined by examining the circuit structure. This predetermined vector needs to be loaded into the circuit during the standby mode. Figure 16.13 shows an implementation of the new leakage reduction technique where a "standby" control signal, derived from the "clock gating" signal, is used to generate and store the predetermined vector in the static input latches of the adder during "standby" mode so as to maximize the stack effect (the number of nMOS and pMOS stacks with "more than one 'off' device"). The desired input vector

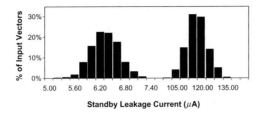

**FIGURE 16.12** Distribution of standby leakage current in the 32-bit static CMOS adder for a large number of input vectors.

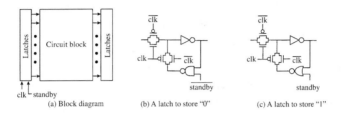

**FIGURE 16.13** An implementation of the standby leakage control scheme through input activation.

|  |  | % Reduction |
|---|---|---|
|  | Average | 35.4% |
| **High** $V_t$ |  |  |
|  | Worst | 60.7% |
|  | Average | 33.3% |
| **Low** $V_t$ |  |  |
|  | Worst | 56.5% |

**FIGURE 16.14** Adder leakage current reduction by the "best" input vector activation compared to average and worst standby leakage.

for leakage minimization is encoded by using a NAND or NOR gate in the feedback loop of the static latch, so minimal penalty is incurred in adder performance. As shown in Fig. 16.14, up to 2× reduction in standby leakage can be achieved by this technique. Note that the vector found by examining the design results in significantly smaller leakage than that obtained by any of the 1000 random vectors. In order that the additional switching energy dissipated by the adder and latches, during entry into and exit from "standby mode," be less than 10% of the total leakage energy saved by this technique during standby, the adder must remain in standby mode for at least 5 $\mu$s.

## Embedded Dual-$V_t$ Design for Domino Circuits

A promising technique to control subthreshold leakage currents during standby modes, while still maintaining performance, is to utilize dual $V_t$ devices. As previously described, two main dual $V_t$ circuit styles are common in the literature. MTCMOS, or multithreshold CMOS, involves using high $V_t$ sleep transistors to gate the power supplies for a low $V_t$ block [22]. Leakage currents will thus be reduced during sleep modes, but the circuit will require large areas for the sleep transistors, and active performance will be affected. Furthermore, optimal sizing of the sleep transistors is complex for larger circuits, and will be affected by the discharge and data patterns encountered [17,18].

The second family of dual $V_t$ circuits is one in which individual devices are partitioned to be either high $V_t$ or low $V_t$ depending on their timing requirements. For example, gates in the critical path would be

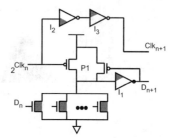

**FIGURE 16.15**  Dual threshold voltage domino logic gate.

chosen to have low $V_t$, while noncritical gates would have high $V_t$'s, with correspondingly lower leakage currents [19]. This technique in general is only effective up to a certain point (diminishes with more critical paths in the circuit), and determining which paths can be made high $V_t$ is a complex CAD problem [20].

An alternative application of dual $V_t$ technology that can be very useful in microprocessor design is dual $V_t$ domino logic [21]. In this style, individual gates utilize both high $V_t$ and low $V_t$ transistors, and the overall circuit will exhibit extremely low leakage in the standby mode, yet suffer no reduction in performance. This is achieved by exploiting the fixed transition directions in domino logic, and assigning a priori low-threshold voltages to only those devices in the critical charging/discharging paths. In effect, devices that can switch during the evaluate mode should be low $V_t$ devices, while those devices that switch during precharge modes should be high $V_t$ devices. Figure 16.15 shows a typical dual $V_t$ domino stage used in a clock-delayed domino methodology, consisting of a pull-down network, inverter ($I_1$), leaker device ($P_1$), and clock drivers ($I_2$, $I_3$), with the low $V_t$ devices shaded.

During normal circuit operation, critical gate transitions occur only through low $V_t$ devices, so high-performance operation is maintained. On the other hand, precharge transitions occur only through high $V_t$ devices, but since precharge times in domino circuits are not in the critical path, slower transition times are acceptable. By having high $V_t$ precharge transistors, it is possible to place the dual $V_t$ domino gate into a very low leakage standby state merely by placing the clock in the evaluate mode and asserting the inputs. In a cascaded design with several levels of domino logic, the standby condition remains the same, requiring only an assertion of the first-level inputs. The correct polarity signal will then propagate throughout the logic to strongly turn off all high $V_t$ devices and ensure low subthreshold leakage currents. In summary, dual $V_t$ domino logic allows one to trade-off slower precharge time for improved standby leakage currents. As a result, using dual $V_t$ domino logic can achieve the performance of an all low $V_t$ design, while maintaining the low standby leakage current of an all high $V_t$ design.

## Adaptive Body Biasing (ABB)

Another technique to control subthreshold leakage is to modulate transistor $V_t$'s directly through body biasing. With application of maximum reverse body bias to transistors, threshold voltage increases, resulting in lower subthreshold leakage currents during standby mode, but because the threshold voltage can be set dynamically, this technique can also be used to adaptively bias a circuit block during the active mode. Adaptive body biasing can be used to help compensate for large inter-die and within-die parameter variations by tuning the threshold voltage so that a common target frequency is reached. By applying reverse body bias to unnecessarily fast circuits, subthreshold leakage in the active mode can then be reduced as well. In order to use this technique, the initial process $V_t$ should be targeted to a lower value than desired, and then reverse body bias can be applied to achieve a higher threshold voltage mean with lower variation.

Adaptive body biasing can easily be applied to a die as a whole (single PMOS body and NMOS body bias values for the whole chip), which will tighten the distribution of chip delays and leakage currents for a collection of dies, but because die sizes and parameter variations are becoming larger with future scaling, within-die variation becomes a problem as well. ABB can be applied aggressively at the block level, where individual functional blocks within a chip, such as a multiplier or ALU, can be independently modulated to meet a common performance target. The following subsection, however, focuses on the

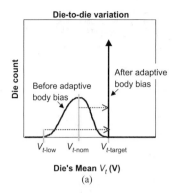
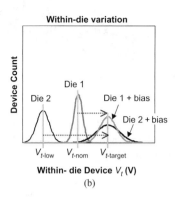

**FIGURE 16.16** (a) Adaptive body bias reduces die-to-die variation in mean $V_t$. (b) Within-die $V_t$ variation increases for die samples that require body bias to match their mean $V_t$ to the target $V_t$. $V_t$-target is the target saturation threshold voltage for a given technology. $V_t$-low and $V_t$-nom are the minimum and mean threshold voltages of the die-to-die distribution.

effectiveness of adaptive body biasing applied at the die level and further explores the limitations of technology scaling on this technique.

### Impact of ABB on Die-to-Die and Within-Die Variations

As illustrated in Fig. 16.16(a) adaptive body biasing technique matches the mean $V_t$ of all the die samples close to the target threshold voltage, when they were all smaller than the target to begin with. Hence, to use adaptive body bias we first need to retarget the threshold voltage of the technology to be lower than what it would have been if adaptive body bias weren't used. Also, short-channel effects of a MOS transistor degrades with body bias [6]. So as technology is scaled, this adverse effect of body biasing poses an increasingly serious challenge to controlling short-channel effects and results in (1) reduction in effectiveness of adaptive body bias to control die-to-die mean $V_t$ variation and (2) increase in within-die $V_t$ variation. As illustrated in Fig. 16.16(b), the die sample that requires larger body bias to match its mean $V_t$ to the target threshold voltage will end up with higher within-die $V_t$ variation. This increase in within-die $V_t$ variation due to adaptive body bias can impact clock skew, worst case gate delay, worst-case device leakage, and analog circuits.

### Short-Channel Effects

In this subsection, we describe short-channel effects, namely, $V_t$-roll-off and DIBL that are affected by body bias. In a long-channel MOS the channel charge is controlled primarily by the gate. As MOS channel length is scaled down, the source-body and drain-body reverse-biased diode junction depletion regions contribute a larger portion of the channel charge. This diminishes the control that gate and body terminals have on the channel, resulting in $V_t$-roll-off and body effect reduction [22]. Another short-channel effect of interest is reduction of the barrier for inversion charge to enter the channel from the source terminal with increase in drain voltage. This dependence of MOS threshold voltage on drain voltage is DIBL. Both $V_t$-roll-off and DIBL degrade further with body bias because of widening diode depletions. The threshold voltage equation for short-channel MOS that captures the two short-channel effects is given as

$$V_t = V_{fb} + |2\phi_p| + \frac{\lambda_b}{C_{ox}}\sqrt{2qN\varepsilon_s(|2\phi_p| + V_{sb})} - \lambda_d V_{ds}$$

$$\lambda_b = 1 - \left(\sqrt{1 + \frac{2W}{X_j}} - 1\right)\frac{X_j}{L}$$

$$\lambda_d = \left[\frac{L}{2.2\mu m^2 (T_{ox} + 0.012\,\mu m)(W_{sd} + 0.15\,\mu m)(X_j + 2.9\,\mu m)}\right]^{-2.7}$$

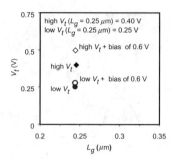

**FIGURE 16.17**  Body effect reduction for low-$V_t$ 0.25 $\mu$m device compared to a high-$V_t$ 0.25 $\mu$m device.

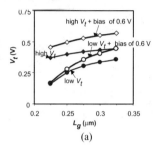
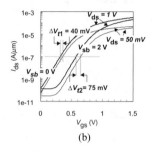

              (a)                         (b)

**FIGURE 16.18**  (a) Increase in $V_t$-roll-off due to $V_t$ lowering and body bias. (b) Increase in DIBL ($\Delta V_t/\Delta V_{ds}$) due to body bias, for a 0.25 $\mu$m NMOS.

$\lambda_b$ models the $V_t$-roll-off and body effect degradation with channel length reduction, and $\lambda_d$ models DIBL. This parameter is based on empirical fitting of device parameters and has been verified to be accurate down to 0.1 $\mu$m channel length [23].

### Effectiveness of ABB

We know that adaptive body bias requires (1) lower $V_t$ devices and (2) body bias to reduce die-to-die mean $V_t$ variation. We also know that as technology is scaled, body terminal's control on the channel charge diminishes. This is further aggravated if $V_t$ has to be reduced and/or if body bias has to be applied since both result in increased diode depletions. Figure 16.17 illustrates the shift in threshold voltage of two 0.25 $\mu$m MOS transistors. The two MOS transistors are identical in all aspects except in their threshold voltage values. The linear threshold voltages of the high-$V_t$ and the low-$V_t$ devices are 400 and 250 mV, respectively. It is clear from Fig. 16.17 that for 600 mV of body bias, the increase in threshold voltage for the high-$V_t$ device is significantly more than that of the low-$V_t$ device. The reasons for the reduced effectiveness of body bias for the low-$V_t$ device are (1) reduced channel doping required for $V_t$ reduction means these devices will have lower body effect to begin with, (2) low-$V_t$ devices have more diode depletion charge degrading body effect, and (3) body bias increases diode depletion even more resulting in added body effect degradation. It has been shown in [24] that with aggressive 30% $V_t$ scaling it will not be possible to match the mean $V_t$ of all the die samples for 0.13 $\mu$m technology.

### Impact of ABB on Within-Die $V_t$ Variation

Low-$V_t$ devices that are required for adaptive body bias schemes have worse short channel effects, and these effects degrade with body bias. As Fig. 16.18(a) illustrates, $V_t$-roll-off behavior is larger for low-$V_t$ device compared to high-$V_t$ device, and $V_t$-roll-off increases further with body bias, as expected. Also, body bias increases DIBL ($\Delta V_t/\Delta V_{ds}$) as expected, and this is depicted in Fig. 16.18(b).

    Within-die $V_t$ variation due to within-die variation in the critical dimension ($\Delta L$) will depend on $V_t$-roll-off ($\lambda_b$) and DIBL ($\lambda_d$). So, increase in $V_t$-roll-off and DIBL due to adaptive body bias will result in a larger within-die $V_t$ variation. It has been shown in [24] that this increase in within-die $V_t$ variation due to adaptive body bias worsens with scaling and is more pronounced under aggressive $V_t$ scaling. So, for effective use of adaptive body bias one has to consider the maximum within-die $V_t$ variation increase that can be tolerated. It should also be noted that adaptive body bias will become less effective with technology scaling due to increasing transistor threshold voltage variation and degrading body effect.

## Acknowledgments

The authors thank our colleagues K. Soumyanath, Kevin Zhang, Ian Young, and several others for providing insight into topics discussed in this paper. Bill Holt, Ricardo Suarez, Fred Pollack, and Richard Wirt provided continued support and encouragement.

## References

1. M. Bohr, et al., "A High Performance 0.25 $\mu$m Logic Technology Optimized for 1.8 V Operation," *IEDM Tech. Dig.,* p. 847, Dec. 1996.
2. M. Bohr, et al., "A High Performance 0.35 $\mu$m Logic Technology for 3.3 V and 2.5 V Operation," *IEDM Tech. Dig.,* p. 273, Dec. 1994.
3. A. Keshavarzi, S. Narendra, S. Borkar, C. Hawkins, K. Roy, and V. De, "Technology Scaling Behavior of Optimum Reverse Body Bias for Standby Leakage Power Reduction in CMOS ICs," *1999 Int. Symp. On Low Power Electronics and Design,* p. 252, Aug. 1999.
4. A. S. Grove, *Physics and Technology of Semiconductor Devices,* John Wiley & Sons, New York, 1967.
5. A. W. Righter, J. M. Soden, and R. W. Beegle, "High Resolution $I_{DDQ}$ Characterization and Testing-Practical Issues," *Int. Test Conf.,* pp. 259–268, Oct. 1996.
6. Y. P Tsividis, *Operation and Modeling of the MOS Transistor,* McGraw-Hill, New York, 1987.
7. J. R. Brews, "The Submicron MOSFET," Chapter 3 in S. M. Sze, editor, *High Speed Semiconductor Devices,* John Wiley & Sons, New York, 1990, pp. 155–159.
8. R. F. Pierret, *Semiconductor Device Fundamentals,* Addison-Wesley, Reading, MA, 1996.
9. J. A. Mandelman and J. Alsmeier, "Anomalous Narrow Channel Effect in Trench-Isolated Buried-Channel *p*-MOSFET's," *IEEE Elec. Dev. Ltr.,* vol. 15, no. 12. Dec. 1994.
10. A. Keshavarzi, K. Roy, and C. Hawkins, "Intrinsic Leakage in Low Power Deep Submicron ICs," *Int. Test Conf.,* p. 146, Nov. 1997.
11. J. P. Halter and F. Najm, "A Gate-level Leakage Power Reduction Method for Ultra-low-power CMOS Circuits," *Proc. IEEE CICC 1997,* pp. 475–478.
12. Y. Ye, S. Borkar, and V. De, "A New Technique for Standby Leakage Reduction in High-Performance Circuits," *1998 Symposium on VLSI Circuits,* June 1998, pp. 40–41.
13. R. X. Gu and M. I. Elmasry, "Power Dissipation Anlaysis and Optimization of Deep Submicron CMOS Digital Circuits," *IEEE Journal on Solid-State Circuits,* vol. 31, no. 5, pp. 707–713, May 1996.
14. M. C. Johnson, D. Somasekhar, K. Roy, "Deterministic Estimation of Minimum and Maximum Leakage Conditions in CMOS Logic," *IEEE Transactions on Computer-Aided Design of ICs,* June 1999, pp. 714–725.
15. T. Kawhara et.al., "Subthreshold Current Reduction for Decoded-driver by Self-reverse Biasing," *IEEE Journal of Solid-State Circuits,* vol. 28, no. 11, pp. 1136–1143, Nov. 1993.
16. S. Mutoh, T. Douseki, Y. Matsuya, T. Aoki, S. Shigematsu, J. Yamada, "1-V Power Supply High-Speed Digital Circuit Technology with Multithreshold-Voltage CMOS," *IEEE JSSC,* vol. 30, no. 8, pp. 847–854, Aug. 1995.
17. J. Kao, A. Chandrakasan, D. Antoniadis, "Transistor Sizing Issues and Tool for Multi-Threshold CMOS Technology," *34th Design Automation Conference,* pp. 409–414, June 1997.
18. J. Kao, S. Narendra, A. Chandrakasan, "MTCMOS Hierarchical Sizing Based on Mutual Exclusive Discharge Patterns," *35th Design Automation Conference,* pp. 495–500, June 1998.
19. W. Lee, et al., "A 1V DSP for Wireless Communications," *ISSCC,* pp. 92–93, Feb. 1997.

20. L. Wei, Z. Chen, M. Johnson, and K. Roy, "Design and Optimization of Low Voltage High Performance Dual Threshold CMOS Circuits," *35th Design Automation Conference,* pp. 489–494, June 1998.

21. J. Kao, "Dual Threshold Voltage Domino Logic," *25th European Solid State Circuits Conference,* pp. 118–121, Sep 1999.

22. H. C. Poon, L. D. Yau, and R. L. Johnston, "DC Model for Short-Channel IGFETs," *Int. Electron Device Meeting,* pp. 156–159, 1973.

23. K. K. Ng, S. A. Eshraghi, and T. D. Stanik, "An Improved Generalized Guide for MOSFET Scaling," *IEEE Trans. Electron Device,* vol. 40, no. 10, pp. 1895–1897, Oct. 1993.

24. S. Narendra, D. Antoniadis, and V. De, "Impact of Using Adaptive Body Bias to Compensate Die-to-die $V_t$ Variation on Within-die $V_t$ Variation," *Int. Symp. Low Power Electronics and Design,* pp. 229–232, Aug. 1999.

# 17

# Dynamic Voltage Scaling

Thomas D. Burd
*University of California, Berkeley*

## 17.1   Introduction

The explosive proliferation of portable electronic devices, such as notebook computers, personal digital assistants (PDAs), and cellular phones, has compelled energy-efficient microprocessor design to provide longer battery run-times. At the same time, this proliferation has yielded products that require ever-increasing computational complexity. In addition, the demand for low-cost and small form-factor devices has kept the available energy supply roughly constant by driving down battery size, despite advances in battery technology that have increased battery energy density. Thus, microprocessors must continuously provide more throughput per watt.

To lower energy consumption, existing low-power design techniques generally sacrifice processor throughput [1–4]. For example, PDAs have a much longer battery life than notebook computers, but deliver proportionally less throughput to achieve this goal. A technique often referred to as voltage scaling [3], which reduces the supply voltage, is an effective technique to decrease energy consumption, which is a quadratic function of voltage; however, the delay of CMOS gates scales inversely with voltage, so this technique reduces throughput as well.

This chapter will present a design technique that dynamically varies the supply voltage to only provide high throughput when required, as most portable devices require peak throughput only some fraction of the time. This technique can decrease the system's average energy consumption by up to a factor of 10, without sacrificing perceived throughput, by exploiting the time-varying computational load that is commonly found in portable electronic devices.

## 17.2 Processor Operation

Understanding a processor's usage pattern is essential to its optimization. Processor utilization can be evaluated in terms of the amount of processing required and the allowable latency for the processing to complete. These two parameters can be merged into a single measure, which is throughput or $T$. It is defined as the number of operations that can be performed in a given time:

$$\text{Throughput} \equiv T = \frac{\text{Operations}}{\text{Second}} \qquad (17.1)$$

Operations are defined as the basic unit of computation and can be as fine-grained as instructions or more coarse-grained as programs. This leads to measures of throughput of MIPS (instructions/sec) and SPECint95 (programs/sec) [5] that compare the throughput on implementations of the same instruction set architecture (ISA), or different ISAs, respectively.

### Processor Usage Model

Portable devices are single-user systems whose processor's computational requirements vary over time and typically occur in bursts. An example processor usage pattern is shown in Fig. 17.1, and demonstrates that the desired throughput varies over time, and the type of computation falls into one of three categories. These three modes of operation are found in most single-user processor systems, including PDAs, notebook computers, and even powerful desktop machines.

Compute-intensive and minimum-latency processes desire maximum performance, which is limited by the peak throughput of the processor, $T_{\text{MAX}}$. Any increase in $T_{\text{MAX}}$ that the hardware can provide will readily be used by these processes to reduce their latency. Examples of these processes include spreadsheet updates, document spell checks, video decoding, and scientific computation.

Background and high-latency processes only require some fraction of $T_{\text{MAX}}$. There is no intrinsic benefit to exceeding the real-time latency requirements of these processes since the user will not realize any noticeable improvement. Examples of these processes include video screen updates, data entry, audio codecs, and low-bandwidth input/output (I/O) data transfers.

The third category of computation is system idle, which has zero desired throughput. Ideally, the processor should have zero energy consumption in this mode and therefore be inconsequential; however, in any practical implementation, this is not the case. The section on "Dynamically Varying Voltage" will demonstrate how dynamic voltage scaling can minimize this mode's energy consumption.

### What Should Be Optimized?

Although compute-intensive and short-latency processes can readily exploit any increase in processor speed, background and long-latency processes do not benefit from any increase in processor speed above and beyond their average desired throughput since the extra throughput cannot be utilized. Thus, $T_{\text{MAX}}$ is

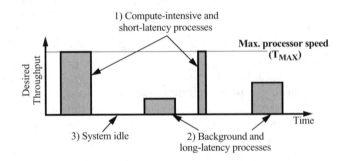

**FIGURE 17.1**   Processor usage model.

the parameter to be maximized since the user and/or operating environment determines the average throughput of the processor.

The run-time of a portable system is constrained by battery life. To maximize battery life, these systems require minimum energy consumption. Even for wired desktop machines, the drive toward "green" computers is making energy-efficient design a priority. Therefore, the computation per battery-life per watt-hour should be maximized, or equivalently, the average energy consumed per operation should be minimized.

This is in contrast to low-power design, which attempts to minimize power dissipation, typically to meet thermal design limits. Power relates to energy consumption as follows:

$$\text{Power} = \frac{\text{Energy}}{\text{Operation}} \times \text{Throughput} \qquad (17.2)$$

Thus, while reducing throughput can minimize power dissipation, the energy/operation remains constant.

## Quantifying Energy Efficiency

An energy efficiency metric must balance the desire to maximize $T_{\text{MAX}}$, and minimize the average energy/operation. A good metric to quantify processor energy efficiency is the energy-throughput ratio (ETR) [6]:

$$\text{ETR} = \frac{\text{Energy/Operation}}{\text{Throughput}} = \frac{\text{Power}}{\text{Throughput}^2} \qquad (17.3)$$

A lower ETR indicates lower energy/operation for equal throughput or equivalently indicates greater throughput for a fixed amount of energy/operation, satisfying the need to equally optimize $T_{\text{MAX}}$ and energy/operation. Thus, a lower ETR represents a more energy-efficient solution. The energy-delay product [7] is a similar metric, but does not include the effects of architectural parallelism when the delay is taken to be the critical path delay.

## Common Design Approaches

With the ETR metric, three common design approaches for processor systems can be analyzed, and their impact on energy efficiency quantified.

### Compute ASAP

In this approach, the processor always performs the desired computation at maximum throughput. This is the simplest approach, and the benchmark to compare others against. When an interrupt comes into the processor, it wakes up from sleep, performs the requested computation, then goes back into sleep mode, as shown in Fig. 17.2(a). In sleep mode, the processor's clock can be halted to significantly reduce idle energy consumption, and restarted upon the next interrupt. This approach is always high throughput, but unfortunately, it is also always high energy/operation.

### Clock Frequency Reduction

A common low-power design technique is to reduce the clock frequency, $f_{\text{CLK}}$. This in turn reduces the throughput, and power dissipation, by a proportional amount. The energy consumption remains un-changed, as shown in Fig. 17.2(b), because energy/operation is independent of $f_{\text{CLK}}$. This approach actually increases the ETR with respect to the previous approach, and is therefore more energy inefficient, because the processor delivers the same amount of computation per battery life, but at a lower level of peak throughput.

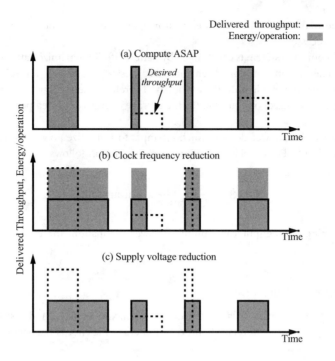

**FIGURE 17.2**    Throughput and energy/operation for three design approaches: (a) compute ASAP (b) clock frequency reduction, and (c) supply voltage reduction.

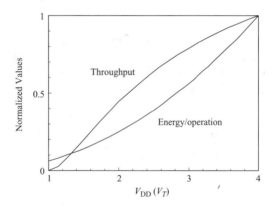

**FIGURE 17.3**    Throughput and energy/operation vs. supply voltage.

## Supply Voltage Reduction

When $f_{CLK}$ is reduced, the processor's circuits have a longer cycle time to complete their computation in. In CMOS, the common fabrication technology for most processors today, the delay of the circuits increases as the supply voltage, $V_{DD}$, decreases. Thus, with voltage scaling, which reduces $V_{DD}$, the circuits can be slowed down until they just complete within the longer cycle time. This, in turn, will reduce the energy/operation, which is a quadratic function of $V_{DD}$, as shown in Fig. 17.2(c).

Figure 17.3 demonstrates that the throughput and energy/operation can vary more than tenfold over the range of $V_{DD}$. The curves are derived from analytical sub-micron CMOS device models [6]. Because throughput and energy/operation roughly track each other, reducing $V_{DD}$ maintains approximately constant ETR, providing equivalent energy efficiency to the Compute ASAP approach. Thus, lower energy/operation can be achieved, but at the sacrifice of lower peak throughput.

# 17.3 Dynamically Varying Voltage

If both $V_{DD}$ and $f_{CLK}$ are dynamically varied in response to computational load demands, then the energy/operation can be reduced for the low computational periods of time, while retaining peak throughput when required. When a majority of the computation does not require maximum throughput, as is typically the case in portable devices, then the average energy/operation can be significantly reduced, thereby increasing the computation per battery life, without degradation of peak processor throughput. This strategy, which achieves the highest possible energy efficiency for time-varying computational loads, is called dynamic voltage scaling (DVS).

## Voltage Scaling Effects on Circuit Delay

A critical characteristic of digital CMOS circuits is shown in Fig. 17.4, which plots simulated maximum $f_{CLK}$ versus $V_{DD}$ for various circuits in a 0.6 $\mu$m CMOS process [8]. Whether the circuits are simple (NAND gate, ring oscillator) or complex (register file, SRAM), their circuit delays track extremely well over a broad range of $V_{DD}$. Thus, as the processor's $V_{DD}$ varies, all of the circuit delays scale proportionally making CMOS processor implementations very amenable to DVS, however, subtle variations of circuit delay with voltage do exist and primarily effect circuit timing, as discussed in the section on "Design Issues."

## Energy Efficiency Improvement

With DVS, peak throughput can always be delivered on demand by the processor, and remains a fixed value for the processor hardware. The average energy/operation, however, is a function of the computational load. When most of the processor's computation can be operated at low throughput, and low $V_{DD}$, the average energy/operation can be reduced tenfold as compared to the Compute ASAP design approach, which always runs the processor at maximum $V_{DD}$. This, in turn, increases the ETR tenfold, significantly improving processor energy efficiency.

Figure 17.5 plots the normalized battery run-time, which is inversely proportional to energy/operation, as a function of the fractional amount of computation performed at low throughput. Although a moderate run-time increase (22%) can be achieved with only 20% of the computation at low throughput, DVS yields significant increases when more of the computation can be run at low throughput, with an upper limit in excess of a tenfold increase in battery run-time, or equivalently, more than a tenfold reduction in energy/operation.

DVS can also significantly reduce a processor's energy consumption when it is idling. If the processor is put into its lowest performance mode before entering sleep mode, the energy consumption of all the circuits

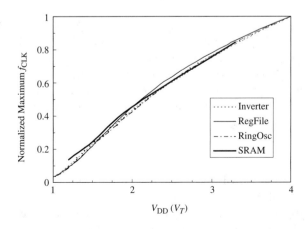

**FIGURE 17.4** Simulated maximum clock frequency for four circuits in 0.6 $\mu$m CMOS.

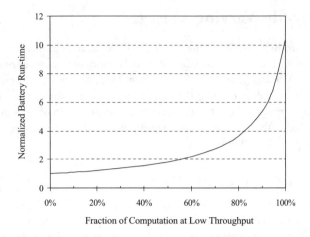

**FIGURE 17.5**   Battery run-time vs. workload.

that require continual operation (e.g., bus interface, VCO, interrupt controller, etc.) can be minimized. The processor can quickly ramp up to maximum throughput upon receiving an incoming interrupt.

## Essential Components for DVS

A typical processor is powered by a voltage regulator, which outputs a fixed voltage. However, the implementation of DVS requires a voltage converter that can dynamically adjust its output voltage when requested by the processor to do so. Programmable voltage regulators can be used, but they are not designed to continuously vary their output voltage and degrade the overall system energy efficiency. A custom voltage converter optimized for DVS is described further in the section on "A Custom DVS Processor System."

Another essential component is a mechanism to vary $f_{CLK}$ with $V_{DD}$. One approach is to utilize a look-up table, which the processor can use to map $V_{DD}$ values to $f_{CLK}$ values, and set the on-chip phase-locked loop (PLL) accordingly. A better approach, which eliminates the need for a PLL, is a ring oscillator matched to the processor's critical paths, such that as the critical paths vary over $V_{DD}$, so too will $f_{CLK}$.

The processor itself must be designed to operate over the full range of $V_{DD}$, which places restrictions on the types of circuits that can be used and impacts processor verification. Additionally, the processor must be able to properly operate while $V_{DD}$ is varying. These issues are described further in the "Design Issues" section.

The last essential component is a DVS-aware operating system. The hardware itself cannot distinguish whether the currently executing instruction is part of a compute-intensive task or a nonspeed critical task. The application programs cannot set the processor speed because they are unaware of other programs running in a multi-tasking system. Thus, the operating system must control processor speed, as it is aware of the computational requirements of all the active tasks. Applications may provide useful information regarding their load requirements, but should not be given direct control of the processor speed.

## Fundamental Trade-Off

Processors generally operate at a fixed voltage and require a regulator to tightly control voltage supply variation. The processor produces large current spikes for which the regulator's output capacitor supplies the charge. Hence, a large output capacitor on the regulator is desirable to minimize ripple on $V_{DD}$. A large capacitor also helps to maximize the regulator's conversion efficiency by reducing the voltage variation at the output of the regulator.

The voltage converter required for DVS is fundamentally different from a standard voltage regulator because in addition to regulating voltage for a given $f_{CLK}$, it must also change the operating voltage when a new $f_{CLK}$ is requested. To minimize the speed and energy consumption of this voltage transition, a small output capacitor on the converter is desirable, in contrast to the supply ripple requirements.

Thus, the fundamental trade-off in a DVS system is between good voltage regulation and fast/efficient dynamic voltage conversion. As will be shown in the "Voltage Converter" section, it is possible to optimize the size of this capacitor to balance the requirements for good voltage regulation with the requirements for a good dynamic voltage conversion.

## Scalability with Technology

Although the prototype system described next demonstrates DVS in a 3.3 V, 0.6 $\mu$m process technology, DVS is a viable technique for improving processor system energy efficiency well into deep sub-micron process technologies. Maximum $V_{DD}$ decreases with advancing process technology, seeming to reduce the potential of DVS, but this decrease is alleviated by decreases in the device threshold voltage, $V_T$. While the maximum $V_{DD}$ may be only 1.2 V in a 0.10 $\mu$m process technology, the $V_T$ will be approximately 0.35 V yielding an achievable energy efficiency improvement, $V_{DD}^2/V_T^2$, still in excess of a tenfold increase.

# 17.4 A Custom DVS Processor System

DVS has been demonstrated on a complete embedded processor system, consisting of a microprocessor, external SRAM chips, and an I/O interface chip [9]. Running on the hardware is a preemptive, multi-tasking, real-time operating system, which supports DVS via a modular component called the voltage scheduler. Benchmark programs, typical of software that runs on portable devices, were then used to quantify the improvement in energy efficiency possible with DVS on real programs.

## System Architecture

As shown in Fig. 17.6, this prototype system contains four custom chips in a 0.6 $\mu$m 3-metal $V_T \approx 1$ V CMOS process: a battery-powered DC-DC voltage converter, a microprocessor, SRAM memory chips, and an interface chip for connecting to commercial I/O devices. The entire system can operate at 1.2–3.8 V and 5–80 MHz, while the energy/operation varies from 0.54 to 5.6 mW/MIP.

The prototype processor, which contains a custom implementation of an ARM8 processor core [10], is a fully functional microprocessor for portable systems. The design contains a multitude of different

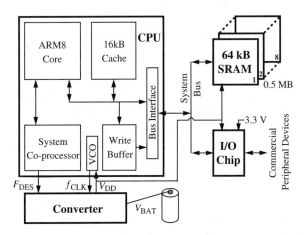

**FIGURE 17.6**  Prototype DVS processor system architecture.

circuits, including static logic, dynamic logic, CMOS pass-gate logic, memory cells, sense-amps, bus drivers, and I/O drivers. All these circuits have been demonstrated to continuously operate over voltage transients well in excess of 1 V/$\mu$s. While the voltage converter was implemented as a separate chip, integrating it onto the processor die is feasible [11].

To further improve the system's energy efficiency, not only was DVS applied to the processor, but the external SRAM chips and external processor bus, as well. While this system operates off of a single, variable $V_{DD}$, a future processor system could again increase energy efficiency by providing multiple, variable voltages sources. This would allow high-speed, direct-memory accesses to main memory, so that even when the processor core is operating at low speed, high-bandwidth I/O-memory transactions could still occur. Additionally, this would also enable DVS peripheral devices that can adapt their throughput to the processing requirements of the I/O data.

## Voltage Scheduler

The voltage scheduler is a new operating system component for use in a DVS system. It controls the processor speed by writing the desired clock frequency to a system control register, whose value is used by the converter loop to adjust the processor clock frequency and regulated voltage. By optimally adjusting the processor speed, the voltage scheduler always operates the processor at the minimum throughput level required by the currently executing tasks, and thereby minimizes system energy consumption.

The implemented voltage scheduler runs as part of a simple real-time operating system. Because the job of determining the optimal frequency and the optimal task ordering are independent of each other, the voltage scheduler can be separate from the temporal scheduler. Thus, existing operating systems can be straightforwardly retrofitted to support DVS by adding in this new, modular component. The overhead of the scheduler is quite small such that it requires a negligible amount of throughput and energy consumption [12].

The basic voltage scheduler algorithm determines the optimal clock frequency by combining the computation requirements of all the active tasks in the system, and ensuring that all latency requirements are met given the task ordering of the temporal scheduler. Individual tasks supply either a completion deadline (e.g., video frame rate), or a desired rate of execution in megahertz. The voltage scheduler automatically estimates the task's workload (e.g., processing an mpeg frame), measured in processor cycles. The optimal clock frequency in a single-tasking system is simply workload divided by the deadline time, but a more sophisticated voltage scheduler is necessary to determine the optimal frequency for multiple tasks. Workload predictions are empirically calculated using an exponential moving average, and are updated by the voltage scheduler at the end of each task. Other features of the algorithm include the graceful degradation of performance when deadlines are missed, the reservation of cycles for future high-priority tasks, and the filtering of tasks that cannot possibly be completed by a given deadline [13].

Figure 17.7 plots $V_{DD}$ for two seconds of a user-interface task, which generally has long-latency requirements. Clock frequency increases with $V_{DD}$, so processor speed can be inferred from this scope trace. The top trace demonstrates the microprocessor running in the typical full-speed/idle operation. A high voltage indicates the processor is actively running at full speed, and low voltage indicates system idle. This trace shows that the user-interface task has bursts of computation, which can be exploited with DVS. The lower trace shows the same task running with the voltage scheduler enabled. In this mode, low voltage indicates both system idle and low-speed/low-energy operation. The voltage spikes indicate when the voltage scheduler has to increase the processor speed in order to meet required deadlines. This comparison demonstrates that much of the computation for this application can be done at low voltage, greatly improving the system's energy efficiency.

## Voltage Converter

The feedback loop for converting a desired operating frequency, $F_{DES}$, into $V_{DD}$ is shown in Fig. 17.8, and is built around a buck converter, which is very amenable to high-efficiency, low-voltage regulation [14]. The ring oscillator converts $V_{DD}$ to a clock signal, $f_{CLK}$, which drives a counter that outputs a digital

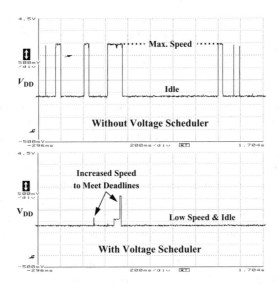

**FIGURE 17.7** DVS improvement for UI process.

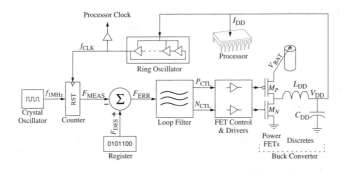

**FIGURE 17.8** Voltage converter negative-feedback loop.

measured frequency value, $F_{MEAS}$. This value is subtracted from $F_{DES}$ to find the frequency error, $F_{ERR}$. The loop filter implements a hybrid pulse-width/pulse-frequency modulation algorithm [9], which generates an $M_P$ or $M_N$ enable signal. The inductor, $L_{DD}$, transfers charge to the capacitor, $C_{DD}$, to generate a $V_{DD}$, which is fed back to the ring oscillator to close the loop.

The only external components required are a 4.7 $\mu$H inductor ($L_{DD}$) placed next to the converter, 5.5 $\mu$F ($C_{DD}$) of capacitance distributed near the chips' $V_{DD}$ pins, and a 1 MHz reference clock. The ring oscillator is placed on the processor chip, and is designed to track the critical paths of the microprocessor over voltage. A beneficial side effect is that the ring oscillator will also track the critical paths over process and temperature variations. The rest of the loop is integrated onto the converter die.

### New Performance Metrics

In addition to the supply ripple and conversion efficiency performance metrics of a standard voltage regulator, the DVS converter introduces two new performance metrics: transition time and transition energy. For a large voltage change (from $V_{DD1}$ to $V_{DD2}$), the transition time is:

$$t_{TRAN} \approx \frac{2C_{DD}}{I_{MAX}}|V_{DD2} - V_{DD1}| \tag{17.4}$$

where $I_{MAX}$ is the maximum output current of the converter, and the factor of two exists because the current is pulsed in a triangular waveform. The energy consumed during this transition is:

$$E_{TRAN} = (1 - \eta)C_{DD}\left|V_{DD2}^2 - V_{DD1}^2\right| \tag{17.5}$$

where $\eta$ is the efficiency of the DC-DC converter.

A typical capacitance of 100 $\mu$F yields a $t_{TRAN}$ of 520 $\mu$s and an $E_{TRAN}$ of 130 $\mu$J for a 1.2–3.8 V transition (for the prototype system: $I_{MAX} = 1$ A, $\eta = 90\%$). This long $t_{TRAN}$ precludes any real-time control or fast interrupt response time, and only allows very coarse speed control. For voltage changes on the order of a context switch (30–100 Hz), the 100 $\mu$F capacitor will give rise to 4–13 mW of transition power dissipation. In the prototype system, this was unreasonably large, since the average system power dissipation could be as low as 3.2 mW. To prevent the transition power dissipation from dominating the total system power dissipation, a converter loop optimized for a much smaller $C_{DD}$ was designed.

Increasing $C_{DD}$ reduces supply ripple and increases low-voltage conversion efficiency, making the loop a better voltage regulator, while decreasing $C_{DD}$ reduces transition time and energy, making the loop a better voltage tracking system. Hence, the fundamental trade-off in DVS system design is to make the processor more tolerant of supply ripple so that $C_{DD}$ can be reduced in order to minimize transition time and energy. The hybrid modulation algorithm of the loop filter maintains good low-voltage conversion efficiency to counter the effect of a smaller $C_{DD}$ [15].

### Limits to Reducing $C_{DD}$

Decreasing $C_{DD}$ reduces transition time, and by doing so increases $dV_{DD}/dt$. CMOS circuits can operate with a varying supply voltage, but only up to a point, which is process dependent. This is discussed further in the "Design Issues" section.

Decreased capacitance increases supply ripple, which in turn increases processor energy consumption as shown in Fig. 17.9. The increase is moderate at high $V_{DD}$, but begins to increase as $V_{DD}$ approaches $V_T$ because the negative ripple slows down the processor so much that most of the computation is performed during the positive ripple, which decreases energy efficiency. Loop stability is another limitation on reducing capacitance. The dominant pole in the system is set by $C_{DD}$ and the load resistance ($V_{DD}/I_{DD}$). The inductor does not contribute a pole because the buck converter operates in discontinuous mode; inductor current is pulsed to deliver discrete quantities of charge to $C_{DD}$ [9].

As $C_{DD}$ is reduced the pole frequency increases, particularly at high $I_{DD}$. As the pole approaches the sampling frequency, a 1 MHz pole due to a sample delay becomes significant, and will induce ringing. Interaction with higher-order poles will eventually make the system unstable.

Increasing the converter sampling frequency will reduce supply ripple and increase the pole frequency due to the sample delay. Thus, these two limits are not fixed, but can be varied; however, increasing the

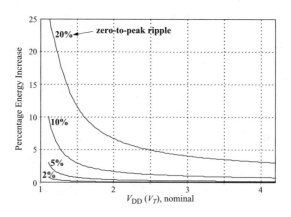

**FIGURE 17.9** Energy loss due to supply ripple.

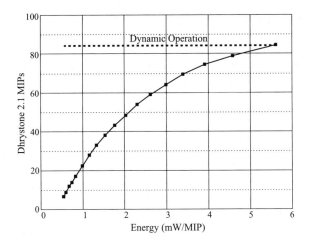

**FIGURE 17.10**   Measured throughput vs. energy/operation.

sampling frequency has two negative side effects. First, low-load converter efficiency will decrease, and $f_{CLK}$ quantization error will increase. These side effects may be mitigated with a variable sampling frequency that adapts to the system power requirements (e.g., $V_{DD}$ and $I_{DD}$). The maximum $dV_{DD}/dt$ at which the circuits will still operate properly is a hard constraint, but occurs for a much smaller $C_{DD}$ than the supply ripple and stability constraints.

## Measured Energy Efficiency

Figure 17.10 plots the prototype system's throughput versus its energy/operation for the Dhrystone 2.1 benchmark, which is commonly used to characterize throughput (MIPS), as well as energy consumption (watts/MIP), for microprocessors in embedded applications [16]. To generate the curve, the system is operated at constant $f_{CLK}$ and $V_{DD}$ to demonstrate the full operating range of the system. The throughput ranges 6–85 Dhrystone 2.1 MIPS, and the total system energy consumption ranges 0.54–5.6 mW/MIP. At constant $V_{DD}$, the ETR is 0.065–0.09 mW/MIP$^2$.

With DVS, peak throughput can be delivered upon demand. Thus, the true operating point for the system lies somewhere along the dotted line because 85 MIPS can always be delivered when required. When only a small fraction of the computation requires peak throughput, the processor system can deliver 85 MIPS while consuming, on average, as little as 0.54 mW/MIP. This yields an ETR of 0.006 mW/MIP$^2$, which is more than a tenfold improvement compared to when the system is operating with a fixed voltage.

To evaluate DVS on real programs, three benchmark programs were chosen that represented software applications that are typically run on notebook computers or PDAs. Existing benchmarks (e.g., SPEC, Dhrystone MIPS, etc.) are not applicable because they only measure the peak performance of the processor. New benchmarks were selected, which combine computational requirements with realistic latency constraints, and include video decoding (MPEG), audio decoding (AUDIO), and an address-book user interface program (UI) [9].

As expected, the compute-intensive MPEG benchmark only has an 11% energy reduction from DVS, but DVS demonstrates significant improvement for the less compute-intensive AUDIO and UI benchmarks, which have a 4.5 times and 3.5 times energy reduction, respectively. The voltage scheduler's heuristic algorithm has a difficult time optimizing for compute-intensive code, so it performs extremely well on nonspeed critical applications. Thus, DVS provides significant reduction in energy consumption, with no loss of performance, for real software that is commonly run on portable electronic devices.

## 17.5   Design Issues

By following a simple set of rules and design constraints, the design of DVS circuits moderately increases design validation and reduces energy-efficiency when measured at a fixed voltage; however, these constraints are heavily outweighed by the enormous increase in energy efficiency afforded by DVS.

### Design over Voltage

A typical processor targets a fixed supply voltage, and is designed for ±10% maximum voltage variation. In contrast, a DVS processor must be designed to operate over a much wider range of supply voltages, which impacts both design implementation and verification time. However, with a few exceptions, the design of a DVS-compatible processor is similar to the design of any other high-performance processor.

#### Circuit Design Constraints

To maximize the achievable energy efficiency, only circuits that can operate down to $V_T$ should be used. NMOS pass gates are often used in low-power design due to their small area and input capacitance [17], but they are limited by not being able to pass a voltage greater than $V_{DD} - V_T$, such that a minimum $V_{DD}$ of $2V_T$ is required for proper operation. Since throughput and energy consumption vary by a factor of 4 over the voltage range $V_T$ to $2V_T$, using NMOS pass gates restricts the range of operation by a significant amount, and are not worth the moderate improvement in energy efficiency. Instead, CMOS pass gates, or an alternate logic style, should be utilized to realize the full voltage range of DVS.

The delay of CMOS circuits tracks over voltage such that functional verification is only required at one operating voltage. The one possible exception is any self-timed circuit, which is a common technique to reduce energy consumption in memory arrays. If the self-timed path layout exactly mimics that of the circuit delay path as was done in the prototype processor, then the paths will scale similarly with voltage and eliminate the need to functionally verify over the entire range of operating voltages.

#### Circuit Delay Variation

Although circuit delay tracks well over voltage, subtle delay variations exist and do impact circuit timing. To demonstrate this, three chains of inverters were simulated whose loads were dominated by gate, interconnect, and diffusion capacitance respectively. To model paths dominated by stacked devices, a fourth chain was simulated consisting of 4 PMOS and 4 NMOS transistors in series. The relative delay variation of these circuits is shown in Fig. 17.11 for which the baseline reference is an inverter chain with a balanced load capacitance similar to the ring oscillator.

The relative delay of all four circuits is a maximum at only the lowest or highest operating voltages. This is true even including the effect of the interconnect's RC delay. Because the gate dominant curve is

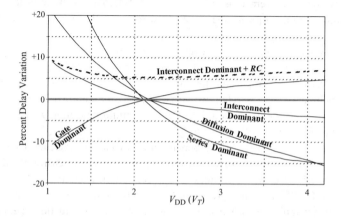

**FIGURE 17.11**   Relative CMOS circuit delay variation over supply voltage.

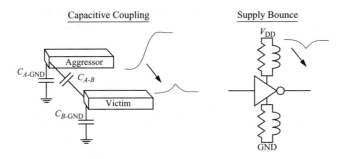

**FIGURE 17.12**   Sources of noise margin degradation.

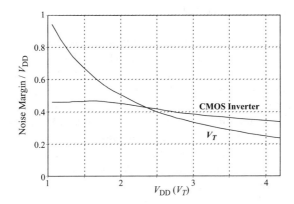

**FIGURE 17.13**   Noise margin vs. supply voltage.

convex, combining it with one or more of the other effects' curves may lead to a relative delay maxima somewhere between the two voltage extremes, but all the other curves are concave and roughly mirror the gate dominant curve such that this maxima will be less than a few percent higher than at either the lowest or highest voltage, and therefore insignificant. Thus, timing analysis is only required at the two voltage extremes, and not at all the intermediate voltage values.

As demonstrated by the series dominant curve, the relative delay of four stacked devices rapidly increases at low voltage, and larger stacks will further increase the relative delay [18]. Thus, to improve the tracking of circuit delay over voltage, a general design guideline is to limit the number of stacked devices, except for circuits whose alternative design would be significantly more expensive in area and/or power (e.g., memory address decoder).

### Noise Margin Variation

Figure 17.12 demonstrates the two primary ways that noise margin is degraded. The first is capacitive coupling between an aggressor signal wire that is switching and an adjacent victim wire. When the aggressor and victim signals have the same logic level, and the aggressor transitions between logic states, the victim signal can also incur a voltage change. Switching current spikes on the power distribution network, which has resistive and inductive losses, induces supply bounce. If a gate's output signal is the same voltage as the supply that is bouncing, the voltage spike transfers directly to the output signal. If the voltage change on the gate output for either case is greater than the noise margin, the victim signal will glitch and potentially lead to functional failure.

For the case of capacitive coupling, the amplitude of the voltage spike on the victim signal is proportional to $V_{DD}$ to first order. As such, the important parameter to analyze is noise margin divided by $V_{DD}$ to normalize out the dependence on $V_{DD}$. Figure 17.13 plots two common measures of noise margin versus $V_{DD}$,

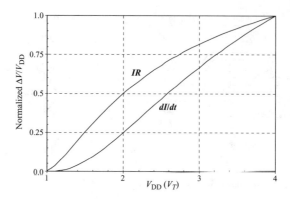

**FIGURE 17.14**   Normalized noise margin reduction due to supply bounce.

the noise margin of a standard CMOS inverter, and a more pessimistic measure of noise margin, $V_T$. The relative noise margin is a minimum at high voltage, such that signal integrity analysis to ensure there is no glitching only needs to consider a single value of $V_{DD}$. If a circuit passes signal integrity analysis at maximum $V_{DD}$, it is guaranteed to pass at all other values of $V_{DD}$.

Supply bounce occurs through resistive ($IR$) and inductive ($dI/dt$) voltage drop on the power distribution network both on chip and through the package pins. Figure 17.14 plots the relative normalized $IR$ and $dI/dt$ voltage drops as a function of $V_{DD}$. It is interesting to note that the worst-case condition occurs at high voltage, and not at low voltage, since the decrease in current and $dI/dt$ more than offsets the reduced voltage swing. Given a maximum tolerable noise margin reduction, only one operating voltage needs to be considered, which is maximum $V_{DD}$, to determine the maximum allowed resistance and inductance for the global power grid and package parasitics.

## Design over Varying Voltage

One approach to designing a processor system that switches voltage dynamically is to halt processor operation during the switching transient. The drawback to this approach is that interrupt latency increases and potentially useful processor cycles are discarded. Since static CMOS gates are quite tolerable of a varying $V_{DD}$, there is no fundamental need to halt operation during the transient. When the gate's output is low, it will remain low independent of $V_{DD}$, but when the output is high, it will track $V_{DD}$ via the PMOS device(s). Simulation demonstrated that for a minimum-sized PMOS device in our 0.6 $\mu$m process, the RC time constant of the PMOS drain-source resistance and the load capacitance is a maximum of 5 ns, which occurs at low voltage. Thus, static CMOS gates track quite well for a $dV_{DD}/dt$ in excess of 100 V/$\mu$s, and because all logic high nodes will track $V_{DD}$ very closely, the circuit delay will instantaneously adapt to the varying supply voltage. Since the processor clock is derived from a ring oscillator also powered by $V_{DD}$, its output frequency will dynamically adapt as well, as shown in Fig. 17.15.

Yet, constraints are necessary when using a design style other than static CMOS as well as limits on allowable $dV_{DD}/dt$. The prototype processor design contains a variety of different styles, including static CMOS logic, as well as dynamic logic, CMOS pass-gate logic, memory cells, sense-amps, bus drivers, and I/O drivers. The maximum $dV_{DD}/dt$ that the circuits in this 0.6 $\mu$m process technology can tolerate is approximately 5 V/$\mu$s, which is well above the maximum $dV_{DD}/dt$ (0.2 V/$\mu$s) of the prototype voltage converter.

### Dynamic Logic

Dynamic logic styles are often preferable over static CMOS as they are more efficient for implementing complex logic functions. They can be used with a varying $V_{DD}$, but require some additional design considerations. One failure mode can occur while the circuit is in the evaluation state and the gate inputs are low such that the output node is undriven at a value $V_{DD}$. If $V_{DD}$ ramps down by more than a diode drop by the end of the evaluation state, the drain-well diode will become forward biased. Current may

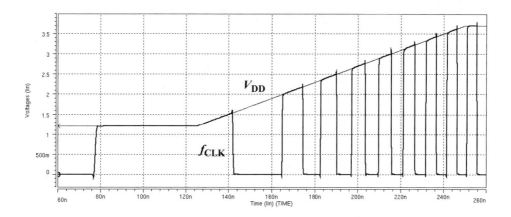

**FIGURE 17.15** Ring oscillator adapting to varying supply voltage (simulated).

be injected into the parasitic PNP transistor of the PMOS device and induce latch-up [19]. This condition occurs when

$$\frac{dV_{DD}}{dt} \leq \frac{-V_{BE}}{t_{CLK|AVE}/2} \tag{17.6}$$

where $t_{CLK|AVE}$ is the average clock period as $V_{DD}$ varies by a diode voltage drop, $V_{BE}$. Since the clock period is longest at lowest voltage, this is evaluated as $V_{DD}$ ranges from $V_{MIN} + V_{BE}$ to $V_{MIN}$, where $V_{MIN} = V_T + 100$ mV. For our 0.6 $\mu$m process, the limit is $-20$ V/$\mu$s. Another failure mode occurs if $V_{DD}$ ramps up by more than $V_{Tp}$ by the end of the evaluation state, and the output drives a PMOS device resulting in a false logic low, giving a functional error. This condition occurs when

$$\frac{dV_{DD}}{dt} \geq \frac{-V_{Tp}}{t_{CLK|AVE}/2} \tag{17.7}$$

and $t_{CLK|AVE}$ is evaluated as $V_{DD}$ varies from $V_{MIN}$ to $V_{MIN} + V_{Tp}$, since this condition is also most severe at low voltage. For our 0.6 $\mu$m process, the limit is 24 V/$\mu$s.

These limits assume that the circuit is in the evaluation state for no longer than half the clock period. If the clock is gated, leaving the circuit in the evaluation state for consecutive cycles, these limits drop proportionally. Hence, the clock should only be gated when the circuit is in the precharge state. These limits may be increased to that of static CMOS logic using a small bleeder PMOS device to hold the output at $V_{DD}$ while it remains undriven. The bleeder device also removes the constraint on gating the clock, and since the bleeder device can be made quite small, there is insignificant degradation of circuit delay due to the PMOS bleeder fighting the NMOS pull-down devices. A varying $V_{DD}$ will magnify the charge-redistribution problem of dynamic logic such that the internal nodes of NMOS stacks should be properly precharged [19].

### Tri-State Buses

Tri-state buses that are not constantly driven for any given cycle suffer from the same two failure modes as seen in dynamic logic circuits due to their floating capacitance. The resulting $dV_{DD}/dt$ can be much lower if the number of consecutive undriven cycles is unbounded. Tri-state buses can only be used if one of two design methods is followed.

The first method is to ensure by design that the bus will always be driven. Although this is done easily on a tri-state bus with only two drivers, this may become expensive to ensure by design for a large number of drivers, $N$, which requires routing $N$, or $\log(N)$, enable signals.

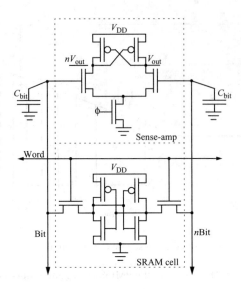

**FIGURE 17.16**   SRAM cell and basic sense-amp topology.

The second method is to use weak, cross-coupled inverters that continually drive the bus. This is preferable to just a bleeder PMOS as it will also maintain a low voltage on the floating bus. Otherwise, leakage current may drive the bus high while it is floating for an indefinite number of cycles. The size of these inverters can be quite small, even for a large bus. For our 0.6 $\mu$m process, the inverters could be designed to tolerate a $dV_{DD}/dt$ in excess of 75 V/$\mu$s with negligible increase in delay, while increasing the energy consumed driving the bus by only 10%.

### SRAM

SRAM is an essential component of a processor. It is found in the processor's cache, translation look-aside buffer (TLB), and possibly in the register file(s), prefetch buffer, branch-target buffer, and write buffer. Because all these memories operate at the processor's clock speed, fast response time is critical, which demands the use of a sense-amp. The static and dynamic CMOS logic portions (e.g., address decoder, word-line driver, etc.) of the memory respond to a changing $V_{DD}$ similar to the ring oscillator, as desired.

To first-order, the delay of both the six-transistor SRAM cell and the basic sense-amp topology (Fig. 17.16), track changes in $V_{DD}$ much like the delay of static CMOS logic. Second-order effects cause the SRAM cell behavior to deviate when $dV_{DD}/dt$ is in excess of 50 V/$\mu$s for our 0.6 $\mu$m process [20]. However, the limiting second-order effect occurs within the sense-amp because the common-mode voltage between *Bit* and *nBit* does not change with $V_{DD}$ as it varies during the sense-amp evaluation state.

Figure 17.17 plots the relative delay variation of the sense-amp compared against the relative delay variation for static CMOS for different rates of change on $V_{DD}$. It demonstrates that the delay does shift to first order, but that for negative $dV_{DD}/dt$, the sense-amp slows down at a faster rate than static CMOS. For the prototype processor design, the sense-amp delay was approximately 25% of the cycle time. The critical path containing the sense-amp was designed with a delay margin of 10%, such that the maximum increase in relative delay of the sense-amp as compared to static CMOS that could be tolerated was 40%.

This set the ultimate limit on how fast $V_{DD}$ could vary in our 0.6 $\mu$m process

$$|dV_{DD}/dt| \leq 5 \text{ V}/\mu\text{s} \tag{17.8}$$

This limit is proportional to the sense-amp delay, such that for improved process technology and faster cycle times, this limit will improve. What must be avoided are more complex sense-amps whose aim is

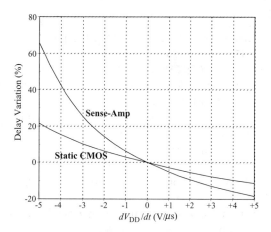

**FIGURE 17.17** Sense-amp delay variation with varying supply voltage.

to improve response time and/or lower energy consumption for a fixed $V_{DD}$, but fail for varying $V_{DD}$, such a charge-transfer sense-amp [21].

## 17.6 Conclusions

DVS is a powerful design technique that can provide a tenfold increase in the energy efficiency of battery-powered processors, without sacrificing peak throughput. DVS is amenable to standard digital CMOS processes, with a few additional circuit design constraints. Existing operating systems can be retrofitted to support DVS, with little modification, as the voltage scheduler can be added to the operating system in a modular fashion. The prototype system has demonstrated that when running real programs, typical of those run on notebook computers and PDAs, DVS provides a significant reduction in measured system energy consumption, thereby considerably extending battery life.

Although DVS was not even considered feasible in commercial products three or four years ago, the rapidly evolving processor industry has begun to adopt various forms of DVS

- In 1999, Intel introduced SpeedStep®*, which runs the processor at two different voltages and frequencies, depending upon whether the notebook computer is plugged into an AC outlet, or running off of its internal battery [22].
- In 2000, Transmeta introduced LongRun®*, which dynamically varies voltage and frequency over the range of 1.2–1.6 V and 500–700 MHz, providing a 1.8 times variation in processor energy consumption. Control of the voltage/frequency is in firmware, which monitors the amount of time the operating system is sleeping [23].
- In 2000, AMD introduced PowerNow!®*, which dynamically varies voltage and frequency over the range of 1.4–1.8 V and 200–500 MHz, providing a 1.7 times variation in processor energy consumption. Control of the voltage/frequency is implemented via a software driver that monitors the operating system's measure of CPU utilization [24].
- In 2001, Intel Inc. introduced the XScale®* processor, which is essentially the second generation StrongArm®* processor. It can dynamically operate over the voltage and frequency range of 0.7–1.75 V and 150–800 MHz, providing a 6.3 times variation in processor energy consumption, the most aggressive range announced to date. By further advancing the energy-efficiency of the original StrongArm, this device will be able to deliver 1000 MIPS with average power dissipation as low as 50 mW at 0.7 V, yielding an ETR as low as 0.05 $\mu$W/MIP$^2$ [25].

---

* Registered trademarks of Intel Inc., Transmetal Inc., and Advanced Micro Devices Inc.

## References

1. Montanaro, J., et al., A 160-MHz, 32-b, 0.5 W CMOS RISC processor, *IEEE J. Solid-State Circuits*, vol. 31, no. 11, pp. 1703–1714, Nov. 1996.
2. Vittoz, E., Micropower IC, *Proc. IEEE ESSCC*, pp. 174–189, Sep. 1980.
3. Chandrakasan, A., Sheng, S., and Brodersen, R. W., Low-power CMOS digital design, *IEEE J. Solid-State Circuits*, vol. 27, no. 4, pp. 473–484, April 1992.
4. Davari, B., Dennard, R., and Shahidi, G., CMOS scaling for high performance and low power—the next ten years, *Proc. IEEE*, pp. 595–606, April 1995.
5. Standard Performance Evaluation Corporation, *SPEC Run and Reporting Rules for CPU95 Suites*, Technical Document, Sep. 1994.
6. Burd, T. and Brodersen, R. W., Processor design for portable systems, *J. VLSI Signal Processing*, vol. 1, pp. 288–297, Jan. 1995.
7. Gonzalez, R. and Horowitz, M. A., Energy dissipation in general purpose microprocessors, *IEEE J. Solid-State Circuits*, vol. 31, pp. 1277–1284, Sept. 1996.
8. Hewlett Packard, *CMOS 14TA/B Reference Manual*, Document No. #A-5960-7127-3, Jan. 1995.
9. Burd, T., et al., A dynamic voltage scaled microprocessor system, *IEEE J. Solid-State Circuits*, vol. 35, pp. 1571–1580, Nov. 2000.
10. Advanced RISC Machines Ltd., *ARM8 data-sheet*, Document No. #ARM-DDI-0080C, July 1996.
11. Kuroda, T., et al., Variable supply-voltage scheme for low-power high-speed CMOS digital design, *IEEE J. Solid-State Circuits*, vol. 33, no. 3, pp. 454–462, March 1998.
12. Pering, T., Burd, T., and Brodersen, R. W., Voltage scheduling in the lpARM microprocessor system, in *IEEE ISLPED Dig. Tech. Papers*, July 2000, pp. 96–101.
13. Pering, T., *Energy-efficient operating system techniques*, Ph.D. dissertation, University of California, Berkeley, May 2000.
14. Stratakos, A., Brodersen, R. W., and Sanders, S., High-efficiency low-voltage dc-dc conversion for portable applications, in *IEEE Int. Workshop Low-Power Design*, April 1994, pp. 619–626.
15. Stratakos, A., High-efficiency, low-voltage dc-dc conversion for portable applications, Ph.D. dissertation, University of California, Berkeley, Dec. 1998.
16. Weicker, R., Dhrystone: a synthetic systems programming benchmark, *Communications of the ACM*, vol. 27, no. 10, pp. 1013–1030, Oct. 1984.
17. Yano, K., et al., A 3.8 ns CMOS 16 × 16 multiplier using complementary pass transistor logic, *Proc. IEEE CICC*, pp. 10.4.1–10.4.4, May 1989.
18. Burd, T. and Brodersen, R. W., Design issues for dynamic voltage scaling, in *IEEE ISLPED Dig. Tech. Papers*, July 2000, pp. 9–14.
19. Weste, N. and Eshraghian, K., *Principles of CMOS VLSI design*, 2nd ed., Addison-Wesley, Reading, MA, 1993.
20. Burd, T., *Energy-efficient processor system design*, Ph.D. dissertation, University of California, Berkeley, Document No. UCB/ERL M01/13, March 2001.
21. Kawashima, S., et al., A charge-transfer amplifier and an encoded-bus architecture for low-power SRAM's, *IEEE J. Solid-State Circuits*, vol. 33, no. 5, pp. 793–799, May 1998.
22. Intel Inc., *Mobile Intel®* Pentium® *III processor featuring Intel® SpeedStep™ technology performance brief*, Document No. 249560-001, 2001.
23. Klaiber, A., *The technology behind Crusoe™ processors*, Transmeta Inc. whitepaper, 2000.
24. Advanced Micro Devices Inc., *AMD PowerNow!™ Technology: dynamically manages power and performance*, Publication No. 24404, Dec. 2000.
25. Intel Inc., *Intel® XScale™ core*, Document No. 273473-001, Dec. 2000.

# 18

# Low-Power Design of Systems on Chip

Christian Piguet

*CSEM: Centre Suisse d'Electronique
et de Microtechnique SA and
LAP-EPFL*

## 18.1 Introduction

For innovative portable and wireless devices, systems on chip (SoCs) containing several processors, memories, and specialized modules are obviously required. Performance and also low power are main issues in the design of such SoCs. In deep submicron technologies, SoCs contain several millions of transistors and have to work at lower and lower supply voltages to avoid too high power consumption. Consequently, digital libraries as well as ROM and SRAM memories have to be designed to work at very low supply voltages and to be very robust while considering wire delays, signal input slopes, noise, and crosstalk effects.

Are these low-power SoCs only constructed with low-power processors, memories, and logic blocks? If the latter are unavoidable, many other issues are quite important for low-power SoCs, such as the way to synchronize the communications between processors as well as test procedures, online testing, software design and development tools. This chapter is a general framework for the design of low-power SoCs, starting from the system level to the architecture level, assuming that the SoC is mainly based on the reuse of low-power processors, memories, and standard cell libraries.

## 18.2   Power Reduction from High to Low Level

Design methodologies at different abstraction levels such as systems, architectures, logic design, basic cells as well as layout, have to take into account the power consumption. The main goals of such design methods are the $V_{dd}$ reduction, the activity reduction as well as the capacitance reduction [1–7]. One has to ask the following question: What are the results of several years of research, applications, industrial designs in low power?

Two ways to consider this:

- What are the new or effective design techniques to reduce power?
- What is the status of the CAD tools regarding low power, as it is well known that such tools are required today to layout several millions of transistors on a single chip?

### Design Techniques for Low Power

Future SoCs will contain several different processor cores on a single chip. It results in parallel architectures, which are known to be less power hungry than fully sequential architectures based on a single processor [8]. The design of such architectures has to start with very high-level models in languages such as System C, SDL, or MATLAB. The very difficult task is then to translate such very high-level models in application software in C and in RTL languages (VHDL, Verilog) to be able to implement the system on several processors. One could think that many tasks running on many processors require a multitask but centralized operating system (OS), but regarding low power, it would be better to have tiny OS (2 K or 4 K instructions) for each processor [9], assuming that each processor executes several tasks. Obviously, this solution is easier as each processor is different even if performances could be reduced due to the inactivity of a processor that has nothing to do at a given time frame.

One has to note that most of the power can be saved at the highest levels. At the system level, partition, activity, number of steps, simplicity, data representation, and locality (cache or distributed memory instead of a centralized memory) have to be chosen (Fig. 18.1). These choices are strongly application dependent. Furthermore, these choices have to be performed by the SoC designer, and he has to be power conscious.

At the architecture level, many low-power techniques have been proposed (Fig. 18.1). The list could be gated clocks, pipelining, parallelization, very low $V_{dd}$, several $V_{dd}$, variable $V_{dd}$ and $V_T$, activity estimation and optimization, low-power libraries, reduced swing, asynchronous, adiabatic. Some are used in industry, but some are not, such as adiabatic and asynchronous techniques. At the lowest levels, for instance a low-power library, only a moderate factor (about 2) in power reduction can be reached. At the logic and layout level, the choice of a mapping method to provide a netlist and the choice of a low-power library are crucial. At the physical level, layout optimization and technology have to be chosen.

| High level | LP systems, LP software, processor types, processors versus random logic, parallel machines, high-level power estimation | | |
|---|---|---|---|
| | Activity reduction | $V_{dd}$ reduction | Capacitance reduction |
| Architecture | LP Codes asynchronous | Parallelization adiabatic | Simplicity |
| Circuit layout | Gated clock | Low $V_T$ | Low-power library |

**FIGURE 18.1**   Overview of low-power techniques.

## Some Basic Rules

There are some basic rules that can be proposed to reduce power consumption at system and architecture levels:

- Reduction of the number $N$ of operations to execute a given task.
- Sequencing that is too high always consumes more than the same functions executed in parallel.
- Obviously, parallel architectures provide better clock per instruction (CPI), as well as pipelined and RISC architectures.
- The lowest $V_{dd}$ for the specific application has to be chosen.
- The goal is to design a chip that just fits to the speed requirements [10].

The main point is to think about systems, with power consumption reduction in mind. According to the mentioned basic rules, how to design a SoC that uses parallelism, at the right supply voltage, while minimizing the steps to perform a given operation or task.

The choice of a given processor or a random logic block is also very important. A processor results in a quite high sequencing while a random logic block works more in parallel for a same specific task. The processor type has to be chosen according to the work to be performed; if 16-bit data are to be used, it is not a good idea to choose a less expensive 8-bit controller and to work in double precision (high sequencing).

## CAD Tools

Each specialized processor embedded in a SoC will be programmed in C and will execute after compilation its own code. Low-power software techniques have to be applied to each piece of software, including pruning, inlining, loop unrolling, and so on. For reconfigurable processor cores, retargetable compilers have to be available. The parallel execution of all these task have to be synchronized through communication links between processors and peripherals. It results that the co-simulation development tools have to deal with several pieces of software running on different processors and communicating between each other. Such a tool has to provide a high-level power estimation tool to check which are the power hungry processors, memories or peripherals as well as the power hungry software routines or loops [11]. Such a tool is far from being commercially available. Embedded low-power software emerges as a key design problem. The software content of SoC will increase as well as the cost of its development.

Generally speaking, the available CAD tools for SoC chips have been designed for robust and reliable synchronous designs. It means that even gated clocks, low $V_{dd}$, several $V_{dd}$, are not or not yet supported, and that asynchronous and adiabatic will not be supported in the near future. It is a major problem because CAD tools are far behind (10 years) the 2000 year requirements. Furthermore, little money is invested in CAD tools. It could be a stopper for some low-power methods. One can conclude that if power can be saved at a high level (factor 10 to 100 or more!) while using conventional CAD tools, it could be the way to go; however, power conscious SoC designers are required [12].

# 18.3   Large Power Reduction at High Level

As mentioned previously, a large part of the power can be saved at high level. Factors of 10 to 100 or more are possible; however, it means that the resulting system could be quite different, with less functionality or less programmability. The choice among various systems is strongly application dependent. One has to think about systems and low power to ask good questions of the customers and to get reasonable answers. Power estimation at high level is a very useful tool to verify the estimated total power consumption. Before starting a design for a customer, it is mandatory to think about the system and what is the goal about performances and power consumption. Several examples will be provided because this way of thinking is application dependent.

## RF Devices

An FM radio can be designed with an analog FM receiver as well as with analog and digital (random logic) demodulations, but a software radio has also been proposed. Such a system converts the FM signal directly into digital with very high-speed ADCs and does the demodulation work with a microprocessor. Such a solution is interesting as the same hardware can be used for any radio, but one can be convinced that a very high-speed ADC is a very consuming block, as well as a microprocessor that has to perform the demodulation (16-bit ADC can consume 1–10 W at 2.2 GHz [13]). In [13], some examples are provided for a digital baseband processor, achieving 1500 mW if implemented with a DSP processor and only 10 mW if implemented with a direct mapped ASIC. The latter case provides a factor of 150 in power reduction.

The transmission of data from one location to another by RF link is more and more power consuming if the distance between the two points is increased. The power (although proportional to the distance at square in ideal case) is practically proportional to the distance at power 3 or even power 4 due to noise, interferences, and other problems. If three stations are inserted between the mentioned points, and assuming a power of 4, the power can be reduced by a factor 64.

## Low-Power Software

Quite a large number of low-power techniques have been proposed for hardware, but relatively fewer for software. Hardware designers are today at least conscious that power reduction of SoCs is required for most applications. However, it seems that it is not the case for software people. Furthermore, a large part of the power consumption can be saved while modifying the application software.

For embedded applications, it is quite often the case that an industrial existing C code has to be used to design an application (for instance, MPEG, JPEG). The methodology consists in improving the industrial C code by

1. pruning, some parts are removed.
2. clear separation of (a) the control code, (b) the loops, and (c) the arithmetic operations.

Several techniques can be used to optimize the loops. In some applications, the application is 90% of the time running in loops. Three techniques can be used efficiently, such as loop fusion (loops executed in sequence with the same indices can be merged), loop tiling (to avoid fetching all the operands from the data cache for each loop iteration, so some data used by the previous iteration can be reused for the next iteration), and loop unrolling.

To unroll a loop is to repeat the loop body $N$ times if there are $N$ iterations of the loop. The code size is increased, but the number of executed instructions is reduced, as the loop counter (initialization, incrementation, and comparison) is removed.

A small loop executed eight times, for instance an $8 \times 8$ multiplication, results in at least 40 executed instructions, while the loop counter has to be incremented and tested. If the loop is unrolled, the code size is larger, but the number of executed instructions is reduced to about 24 (Fig. 18.2). This example illustrates a general rule: less sequencing in the software at the price of more hardware, i.e., more instructions in the program memory. Table 18.1 also shows that a linear routine (without loops) is executed with fewer instructions than a looped routine at the price of more instructions in the program.

TABLE 18.1    Number of Instructions in the Code as well as the Number of Executed Instructions for an $N \times N$ Multiplication with a $2 \times N$ Result

| Number of Instructions 8-bit Multiply Linear | CoolRISC 88 in the Code 30 | CoolRISC 88 Executed 30 | PIC 16C5× in the Code 35 | PIC 16C5× Executed 37 |
| --- | --- | --- | --- | --- |
| 8-bit multiply looped | 14 | 56 | 16 | 71 |
| 16-bit multiply linear | 127 | 127 | 240 | 233 |
| 16-bit multiply looped | 31 | 170 | 33 | 333 |

**TABLE 18.2** Multiplication with and without Hardware Multiplier

| | CoolRISC 816 without Multiplier | CoolRISC 816 with Multiplier | Speed-Up |
|---|---|---|---|
| Looped 8-bit Multiply | 54–62 Executed Instructions | 2 Executed Instructions | 29 |
| Looped 16-bit multiply | 72–88 | 16 | 5 |
| Floating-Point 32-bit multiply | 226–308 | 41–53 | 5.7 |

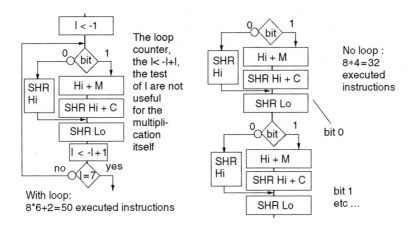

**FIGURE 18.2** Unrolled loop multiply.

## Processors, Instructions Sets, and Random Logic

A processor-based implementation results in very high sequencing. It is due to the processor architecture that is based on the reuse of the same operators, registers, and memories. For instance, only one step ($N = 1$) is necessary to up-date a hardware counter. For its software counterpart, the number of steps is much higher, while executing several instructions with many clocks in sequence. This simple example shows that the number of steps executed for the same task can be very different depending on the architecture.

The instruction set can also contain some instructions that are very useful but expensive to implement in hardware. An interesting comparison is provided by the multiply instruction that has been implemented in the CoolRISC 816 (Table 18.2). Generally, 10% of the instructions are multiplications in a given embedded code. Assume 4 K instructions, i.e., 400 instructions (10%) for multiply, resulting in 8 multiply (each multiply requires about 50 instructions), so a final code of 3.6 K instructions. This is why the CoolRISC 816 contains a hardware $8 \times 8$ multiplier.

## Processor Types

Several points must be fulfilled in order to save power. The first point is to adapt the data width of the processor to the required data. It results in increased sequencing to manage, for instance, 16-bit data on a 8-bit microcontroller. For a 16-bit multiply, 30 instructions are required (add-shift algorithm) on a 16-bit processor, while 127 instructions are required on a 8-bit machine (double precision). A better architecture is to have a $16 \times 16$ bit parallel-parallel multiplier with only one instruction to execute a multiplication.

Another point is to use the right processor for the right task. For control tasks, DSP processors are largely inefficient. But conversely, 8-bit microcontrollers are very inefficient for DSP tasks! For instance, to perform a JPEG compression on a 8-bit microcontroller requires about 10 millions of executed instructions for a $256 \times 256$ image (CoolRISC, 10 MHz, 10 MIPS, 1 s per image). It is quite inefficient. Factor 100 in energy reduction can be achieved with JPEG dedicated hardware. With two CSEM-designed

**TABLE 18.3**  Frequency and Power Consumption for a JPEG Compressor

| DCT Co-processor | No. of Cycles 3.6 per Pixel | Frequency 100 MHz | Power 110 $\mu$AMHz |
|---|---|---|---|
| Huffman co-processor | 3.8 per pixel | 130 MHz | 20 $\mu$AMHz |
| JPEG compression | 3.8 per pixel | 100 MHz | 130 $\mu$AMHz |

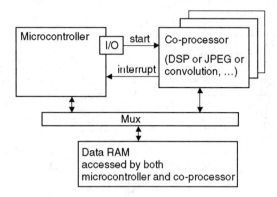

**FIGURE 18.3**  Microcontroller and co-processor.

co-processors working in pipeline, i.e., a DCT co-processor based on an instruction set (program memory based) and a Huffman encoder based on random logic, finite state machines, one has the following results (Table 18.3, synthesized by Synopsys in 0.25 $\mu$m TSMC process at 2.5 V) 400 images can be compressed per second with a 13 mA power consumption. At 1.05 V, 400 images can be compressed per second with a 1 mA power consumption, resulting in quite a large number of 80,000 compressed images per watt (1000 better than a programmed-based implementation).

Figure 18.3 shows an interesting architecture to save power. For any application there is some control that is performed by a microcontroller (the best machine to perform control). But in most applications, there is also a main task to execute such as DSP tasks, convolutions, JPEG, or other tasks. The best architecture is to design a specific machine (co-processor) to execute such a task. So this task is executed by the smallest and the most energy efficient machine. Most of the time, both microcontroller and co-processors are not running in parallel.

## Low-Power Memories

Memory organization is very important in systems on a chip. Generally, memories consume most of the power. So it comes immediately that memories have to be designed hierarchically. No memory technology can simultaneously maximize speed and capacity at lowest cost and power. Data for immediate use is stored in expensive registers, in cache memories, and less used data in large memories.

For each application, the choice of the memory architecture is very important. One has to think of hierarchical, parallel, interleaved, and cache memories (sometimes several levels of cache) to try to find the best trade-off. The application algorithm has to be analyzed from the data point of view, the organization of the data arrays, and how to access these structured data.

If a cache memory is used, it is possible, for instance, to minimize the number of cache miss while using adequate programming as well as a good data organization in the data memory. For instance, in inner loops of the program manipulating structured data, it is not equivalent to write (1) do i then do j or (2) do j then do i depending on how the data are located in the data memory.

Proposing a memory-centric view (as opposed to the traditional CPU-centric view) to SoC design has become quite popular. It is certainly of technological interest. It means, for instance, that the DRAM memory is integrated on the same single chip; however, it is unclear if this integration inspires any truly

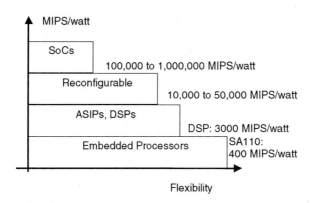

**FIGURE 18.4**  Energy-flexibility gap.

new architecture paradigms. We see it as more of a technological implementation issue [14]. It is, however, crucial to have most of the data on-chip, as fetching data off-chip at high frequency is a very high power consumption process.

### The Energy-Flexibility Gap

Figure 18.4 shows that the flexibility [13], i.e., to use a general purpose processor or a specialized DSP processor, has a large impact on the energy required to perform a given task compared to the execution of the same given task on dedicated hardware.

## 18.4  Low-Power and Reliability Issues in SoCs

For SoCs, very important design problems have to be solved. They are mainly the silicon complexity (reliability, power consumption, interconnect delays), the system complexity (logic, MPU, memories, RF, FPGA, RF, MEMS), the design procedures (300–800 people for the design of a single chip, IP reuse, design levels), verification and test. The total number of transistors on a single chip could be over one billion (predicted [15] to be between 4 to 19 billions in 2014 depending in the circuit type). Some partial answers have been given to the complexity problem, such as design reuse. The SIA Roadmap [15] predicts that in 2012 reuse of processors, logic blocks, and peripherals, would reach about 90% of the embedded logic on the chip.

### Low-Power SoC Architectures

Low-power SoCs will be based on low-power components, such as processor cores, memories, and libraries, that are available with good performances, i.e., 20,000–100,000 MIPS/watt [16] for some cores (using low-power techniques such as gated clocks); however, memories are the main consumers on a SoC and several techniques at the architecture and electrical levels have to be applied to reduce their power consumption (generally based on caches, DWL, bitline splitting, low swing).

The 1997 SIA Roadmap [15] recognizes that, in 2007, asynchronous design will be used in many designs. If $\partial$ is the distance travelled by a signal in one clock cycle, due to higher frequencies and increasing interconnect delays, a chip will contain several time zones of sizes $\partial \times \partial$. Due also to the increasing die size, this number of time zones will grow very rapidly with the new technologies, up to 10,000 zones in 2012. To synchronize 10,000 time zones is a true asynchronous problem [15]. This is why asynchronous design is strongly required for chip architectures in the future [17].

Asynchronous architectures are often presented as being capable of reducing significantly the power consumption [17]. Looking at the results from many papers, it turns out that the largest power savings are obtained with circuits or applications that present a very irregular behavior. An irregular behavior

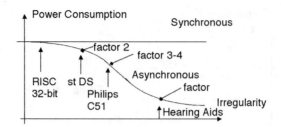

**FIGURE 18.5**   Comparison of the power consumption of asynchronous vs. synchronous architectures.

is, for instance, a processor that presents a tricky instruction set with multi-bytes instructions executed in a various number of cycles and phases. Or an application for which the controller has to very often stop and restart depending on the application. A very regular behavior is a 32-bit RISC core for which all instructions are always executed in one clock. Figure 18.5 illustrates this basic law [18]. Basically, SoCs will present more of an irregular behavior than a regular one.

At the architecture level, power and $V_{dd}$ management with behavior prediction of the user will be used extensively, as well as low-power communication protocols between the various processors on a single chip. These protocols have to be kept simple and will be asynchronous due to the fact that the various cores will be clocked (if not asynchronous cores) with many different frequencies.

## Low-Power Design and Testability Issue

At the low-level, low-power libraries and logic synthesis embedded with place and route are required, as well as estimation of interconnect delays with copper, low-k, and SOI; however, the main issue is $V_{dd}$ as low as 0.6 to 0.3 V in 2014. With very deep submicron technologies and very low $V_{dd}$, the static power will increase significantly due to low $V_t$. Several techniques with double $V_t$, source impedance, well polarization, dynamic regulation of $V_t$ are today under investigation and will be necessarily used in the future.

SoCs testability and debug, when the first silicon has been returned from the foundry, are important issues. Generally, the mean time to fix a bug is one week. Today, it is not possible do determine if more bugs will be present in a one-billion transistor chip, and if a one-week fix per bug is realistic or not; however, it has to be mentioned that it could be much more difficult to fix a bug in IP blocks that you have not designed. It is estimated that half of the total design effort will be devoted to verification tasks, including debugging of the embedded software [15].

## 18.5   Low-Power Microcontroller Cores

The most popular 8-bit microcontroller is the Intel 8051, but each instruction is executed in at least 12 clock cycles resulting in poor performances in MIPS (million of instructions per second) and MIPS/watt. MIPS performances of microcontrollers are not required to be very high. Consequently, short pipelines and low operating frequencies are allowed if, however, the number of CPI is low. Such a low CPI has been used for the CoolRISC microcontroller [19,20]. The CoolRISC 88 is an 8-bit core with eight registers and the CoolRISC 816 is an 8-bit core with 16 registers.

### CoolRISC Microcontroller Architecture

The CoolRISC is a 3-stage pipelined core. The branch instruction is executed in only one clock. In that way, no load or branch delay can occur in the CoolRISC core, resulting in a strictly CPI = 1 (Fig. 18.6). It is not the case of other 8-bit pipelined microprocessors (PIC, Nordic $\mu$RISC, Scenix, MCS-151, and 251). It is known that the reduction of CPI is the key to high performances. For each instruction, the first half clock is used to precharge the ROM program memory. The instruction is read and decoded in

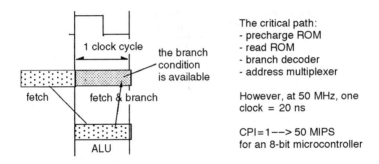

The critical path:
- precharge ROM
- read ROM
- branch decoder
- address multiplexer

However, at 50 MHz, one
clock = 20 ns

CPI = 1 --> 50 MIPS
for an 8-bit microcontroller

the branch
condition
is available

1 clock cycle

fetch          fetch & branch

ALU

**FIGURE 18.6**   No branch delay.

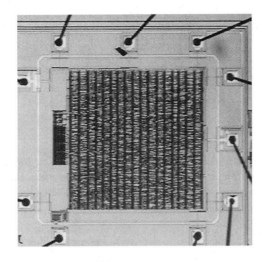

**FIGURE 18.7**   Microphotograph of CoolRISC 88.

the second half of the first clock. As shown in Fig. 18.6, a branch instruction is also executed during the
second half of this first clock, which is long enough to perform all the necessary transfers. For a load/store
instruction, only the first half of the second clock is used to store data in the RAM memory. For an
arithmetic instruction, the first half of the second clock is used to read an operand in the RAM memory
or in the register set, the second half of this second clock to perform the arithmetic operation, and the
first half of the third clock to store the result in the register set. Figure 18.7 is a CoolRISc 88 test chip.

Another very important issue in the design of 8-bit microcontrollers is the power consumption. The
gated clock technique has been extensively used in the design of the CoolRISC cores (Fig. 18.8). The
ALU, for instance, has been designed with input and control registers that are loaded only when an ALU
operation has to be executed. During the execution of another instruction (branch, load/store), these
registers are not clocked thus no transitions occur in the ALU (Fig. 18.8). This reduces the power consumption. A similar mechanism is used for the instruction registers, thus in a branch, which is executed only
in the first pipeline stage, no transitions occur in the second and third stages of the pipeline. It is interesting
to see that gated clocks can be advantageously combined with the pipeline architecture; the input and
control registers implemented to obtain a gated clocked ALU are naturally used as pipelined registers.

## IP "Soft" Cores

The main issue in the design of "soft" cores [21] is reliability. In deep submicron technologies, gate delays are
smaller and smaller compared to wire delays. Complex clock trees have to be designed using Synopsys
to satisfy the required timing, mainly the smallest possible clock skew, and to avoid any timing violations.

**TABLE 18.4** Power Consumption of the Same Core with Various Test Benches and Skew

| Skew | Test Bench A | Test Bench B |
| --- | --- | --- |
| 10 ns | 0.44 mW/MHz | 0.76 mW/MHz |
| 3 ns | 0.82 mW/MHz | 1.15 mW/MHz |

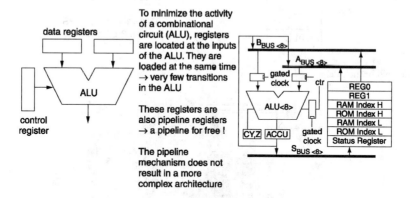

**FIGURE 18.8** Gated-clock ALU.

Furthermore, "soft" cores have to present a low power consumption to be attractive to the possible licensees. If the clock tree is a major issue to achieve the required clock skew, its power consumption could be larger than desired. Today, most IP cores are based on a single-phase clock and are based on D-flip-flops. As shown in the following example, the power consumption is largely dependent on the required clock skew.

As an example, a DSP core synthesized with the CSEM low-power library in TSMC 0.25 $\mu$m. The test bench A contains only a few multiplication operations, while the test bench B performs a large number of MAC operations (Table 18.4). Results show that if the power is sensitive to the application program, it is also quite sensitive to the required skew: 100% of power increase from 10 ns to 3 ns skew.

The clocking scheme of IP cores is therefore a major issue. Another approach other than the conventional single-phase clock with D-flip-flops (DFF) is presented in this paper. It is based on a double-latch approach with two nonoverlapping clocks. This clocking scheme has been used for the 8-bit CoolRISC microcontroller IP core [16] as well as for other cores, such as a DSP core and other execution units [22]. The advantages as well as the disadvantages will be presented.

## Latch-Based Designs

Figure 18.9 shows the double-latch concept that has been chosen for such IP cores to be more robust to the clock skew, flip-flop failures, and timing problems at very low voltage [16]. The clock skew between various $\varnothing 1$ (respectively $\varnothing 2$) pulses have to be shorter than half a period of CK. However, one requires two clock cycles of the master clock CK to execute a single instruction. It is why one needs, for instance, in technology TSMC 0.25 $\mu$m, 120 MHz to generate 60 MIPS (CoolRISC with CPI = 1), but the two $\varnothing i$ clocks and clock trees are at 60 MHz. Only a very small logic block is clocked at 120 MHz to generate two 60 MHz clocks.

The design methodology using latches and two nonoverlapping clocks has many advantages over the use of DFF methodology. Due to the nonoverlapping of the clocks and the additional time barrier caused by having two latches in a loop instead of one DFF, latch-based designs support greater clock skew, before failing, than a similar DFF design (each targeting the same MIPS). This allows the synthesizer and router to use smaller clock buffers and to simplify the clock tree generation, which will reduce the power consumption of the clock tree.

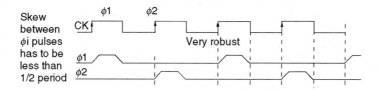

**FIGURE 18.9** Double-latch clocking schemes.

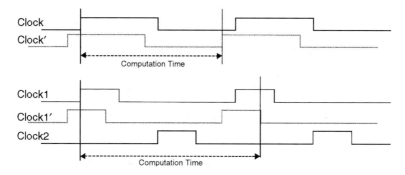

**FIGURE 18.10** Time borrowing.

With latch-based designs, the clock skew becomes relevant only when its value is close to the nonoverlapping of the clocks. When working at lower frequency and thus increasing the nonoverlapping of clocks, the clock skew is never a problem. It can even be safely ignored when designing circuits at low frequency, but a shift register made with DFF can have clock skew problems at any frequency.

Furthermore, if the chip has clock skew problems at the targeted frequency after integration, one is able, with a latch-based design, to reduce the clock frequency. It results that the clock skew problem will disappear, allowing the designer to test the chip functionality and eventually to detect other bugs or to validate the design functionality. This can reduce the number of test integrations needed to validate the chip. With a DFF design, when a clock skew problem appears, you have to reroute and integrate again. This point is very important for the design of a chip in a new process not completely or badly characterized by the foundry, which is the general case as a new process and new chips in this process are designed concurrently for reducing the time to market.

Using latches for pipeline structure can also reduce power consumption when using such a scheme in conjunction with clock gating. The latch design has additional time barriers, which stop the transitions and avoid unneeded propagation of signal and thus reduce power consumption. The clock gating of each stage (latch register) of the pipeline with individual enable signals, can also reduce the number of transitions in the design compared to the equivalent DFF design, where each DFF is equal to two latches clocked and gated together.

Another advantage with a latch design is the time borrowing (Fig. 18.10). It allows a natural repartition of computation time when using pipeline structures. With DFF, each stage of logic of the pipeline should ideally use the same computation time, which is difficult to achieve, and in the end, the design will be limited by the slowest of the stage (plus a margin for the clock skew). With latches, the slowest pipeline stage can borrow time from either or both the previous and next pipeline stage. And the clock skew only reduces the time that can be borrowed. An interesting paper [23] has presented time borrowing with DFF, but such a scheme needs a complete new automatic clock tree generator that does not minimize the clock skew but uses it to borrow time between pipeline stages.

Using latches can also reduce the number of MOS of a design. For example, a microcontroller has $16 \times 32$-bits registers, i.e., 512 DFF or 13,312 MOS (using DFF with 26 MOS). With latches, the master part of the registers can be common for all the registers, which gives 544 latches or 6528 MOS (using latches with 12 MOS). In this example, the register area is reduced by a factor of 2.

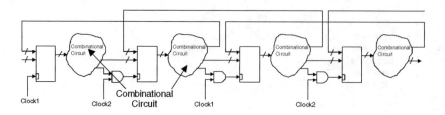

**FIGURE 18.11**   Latch-based clock gating.

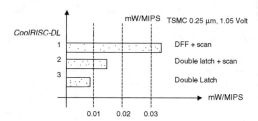

**FIGURE 18.12**   Power consumption comparison of "soft" CoolRISC cores.

## Gated Clock with Latch-Based Designs

The latch-based design also allows a very natural and safe clock gating methodology. Figure 18.11 shows a simple and safe way of generating enable signals for clock gating. This method gives glitch-free clock signals without the adding of memory elements, as it is needed with DFF clock gating.

Synopsys handles the proposed latch-based design methodology very well. It performs the time borrowing well and appears to analyze correctly the clocks for speed optimization. So it is possible to use this design methodology with Synopsys, although there are a few points of discussion linked with the clock gating.

This clock gating methodology cannot be inserted automatically by Synopsys. The designer has to write the description of the clock gating in his VHDL code. This statement can be generalized to all designs using the above latch-based design methodology. We believe Synopsys can do automatic clock gating for pure double latch design (in which there is no combinatorial logic between the master and slave latch), but such a design causes a loss of speed over similar DFF design.

The most critical problem is to prevent the synthesizer from optimizing the clock gating AND gate with the rest of the combinatorial logic. To ensure a glitch-free clock, this AND gate has to be placed as shown in Fig. 18.11. This can be easily done manually by the designer by placing these AND gates in a separate level of hierarchy of his design or placing a "don't touch" attribute on them.

## Results

A synthesizable by Synopsys CoolRISC–DL 816 core with 16 registers has been designed according to the proposed double latch (DL) scheme (clocks $\varnothing1$ and $\varnothing2$) and provides the estimated (by Synopsys) following performances (only the core, about 20,000 transistors) in TSMC 0.25 $\mu$m:

- 2.5 V, about 60 MIPS (but 120 MHz single clock) (It is the case with the core only, if a program memory with 2 ns of access time is chosen, as the access time is included in the first pipeline stage, the achieved performance is reduced to 50 MIPS.)
- 1.05 V, about 10 $\mu$W/MIPS, about 100,000 MIPS/watt (Fig. 18.12)

The core "DFF+Scan" is a previous CoolRISC core designed with flip-flops [19,20]. The CoolRISC-DL "double latch" cores [16] with or without special scan logic provide better performances.

## 18.6   Low-Power Memories

As memories in SoCs are larger and larger, the ratio between power consumption of memories to the power consumption of embedded processors is significantly increased. Several solutions have been proposed at the memory architecture level, such as, for instance, cache memories, loop buffers, and hierarchical memories, i.e., to store a frequently executed piece of code in a small embedded ROM memory and large but rare executed pieces of code in a large ROM memory [19,20]. It is also possible to read the large ROM in two or four clock cycles as its read access time is too large for the chosen main frequency of the microprocessor.

### Cache Memories for Microcontrollers

Cache memories are widely used for high-performance microprocessors. In SoCs, application software is stored in embedded memories, ROM, flash or EEPROM. If a conventional $N$-way set-associative cache is used, one has to compare the energy used for a ROM access and the energy for a SRAM cache access. While reading $N$ tags and $N$ blocks of the selected cache line just to select one instruction (hundreds of bits), one can see that a conventional cache consumes much more power than a ROM access.

The only way to save power is to use unconventional cache memories such as small L0 caches or buffers, which store only some instructions that are reused frequently from the cache. Such a scheme is used for some DSP processors to capture loops. Furthermore, the tags are read first and in case of a hit, only one way is accessed. So this mechanism avoids reading $N$ blocks in parallel and saves power. Before fetching a block in the cache, one has to check if the instruction is already in the buffer in order to stop the access to the cache or to the ROM if there is a buffer hit (Fig. 18.13). Obviously, the hit rate of such a cache cannot be as high as for a $N$-way set associative cache of the same size.

To improve the hit rate, one has a supplementary bit (flag) per instruction generated by the compiler (or manually generated) in the main memory indicating (if activated) that this instruction has to be stored in the L0 cache. If this bit is "0", the instruction, when fetched from L1 cache, is not stored in the L0 cache. It results in the fact that instructions not often used do not pollute the L0 cache (Fig. 18.13). Furthermore, with quite small caches (32–64 instructions), one has also to choose between cacheable instructions, which ones are the most useful to write in cache to reach the highest hit rate. Many algorithms working on program traces have been studied to maximize the number of instruction fetches per write in the cache. The results are strongly dependent on the applications, i.e., a scientific code is better than a control code (Table 18.5).

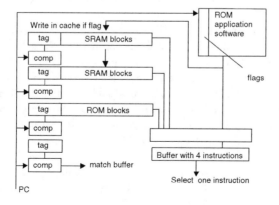

**FIGURE 18.13**   CoolCache for the CoolRISC microcontroller.

**TABLE 18.5**    CoolCache Results

| Cache Type | 1-way Standard Cache 64 Instructions | | CoolCache 64 Instructions | |
|---|---|---|---|---|
| | Hit Rate | Power Gain | Hit Rate | Power Gain |
| Program sinus | 89% | 6% | 89% | 64% |
| Watch application | 68% | −93% | 82% | 41% |

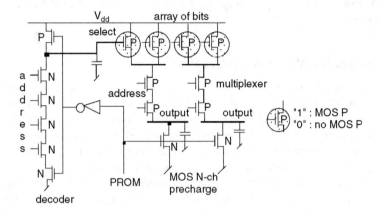

**FIGURE 18.14**    Old ROM memory structure.

Another idea is to search for instructions or routines that are obviously always in the cache during the program execution (or nearly always in the cache). So it is quite interesting to replace a part of the SRAM cache that is not written by a ROM structure (Fig. 18.13). In so doing, the power consumption is reduced, as a ROM access is less consuming than a RAM access. Furthermore, a ROM cell is smaller than a RAM cell, so there is no need to write something in the memory and a ROM memory is faster than a RAM. Another advantage is the fact that instructions stored in ROM are always in the ROM; it could be interesting for reactivity and real-time routines for which the execution time does not need to be dependent on the fact that this routine is already in or not in the cache.

## Electrical Design of Low-Power ROM Memories

Few papers describe very low-power ROM structures. A ROM memory is an array of transistors (a transistor means a logical bit "0"). Each bit is connected to a bitline to read the ROM and controlled by a wordline.

Figure 18.14 shows an old design of a ROM memory. Precharge techniques are used for both the decoder and bit array. After the address is provided, the decoder (NAND gates) is precharged to "1" and the bit array is precharged to "0" through the output multiplexer (PROM = 1). When PROM = 0, the ROM is read. If the P-MOS in the array is there, the bitline is charged to "1," otherwise it keeps its "0" value. Such a memory is very slow: NAND gates for the decoder, P-MOS for the array and long bitlines.

Existing ROM memories use a similar scheme: in a first step the bitlines are precharged to "1," and in the next step a wordline is selected. If there is a transistor (bit is "0") at the intersection of the selected wordline and a bitline, this bitline is discharged. The value of the selected word can therefore be read on the bitlines. Many techniques have been used to speed-up existing ROM memories: NOR gates, N-MOS for the array, to split the memory in several arrays, divided word lines (DWL), to divide the bit line, to precharge only the useful bitlines, partial swing with sense amplifiers. Two of these techniques are described in the following text.

Because a large part of the access time is due to the discharge of the bitline, split bitlines are generally used. Figure 18.15 presents the split bitlines principle. Each bitline is split in sub-bitlines that are

**TABLE 18.6**  ROM Memories Power Consumption Comparison

| Company | Techno ($\mu$m) | Size | Supply (V) | Access Time | Power ($\mu$AMHz) |
| --- | --- | --- | --- | --- | --- |
| Ref. [24] | 0.18 | 8K × 16 | 1.8 | NA | 110 |
| Ref. [24] | 0.18 | 64K × 32 | 1.8 | NA | 335 |
| CSEM | 0.25 | 64 Kbytes | 2.5 | 3 ns | 20 |

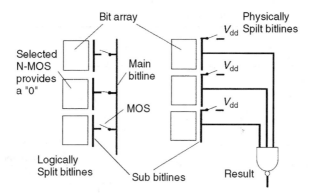

**FIGURE 18.15**   Split bitlines.

connected to the main bitline (only a wire) with an additional transistor. The selection of these transistors depends on address bits. Only one of the sub-bitlines can be connected to the main bitline. Since only a small fraction of the bit array transistor drains are connected to a given sub-bitline, the capacitance to be discharged is significantly reduced. The problem is that the capacitance of the main bitline is discharged through two transistors in series. Then, in order to have a speed gain, the additional transistors (which connect the sub-bitlines to the main bitlines) must be large. The number of large transistors is the same as the number of bitlines. So, for 1000 bitlines, one has to drive 1000 transistors. It is therefore quite difficult to reduce the access time and the power consumption.

Another solution is also shown in Figure 18.15. The drains of the bit array transistors are connected directly to a sub-bitline that is a single metal line. Figure 18.15 shows three metal lines and therefore three sub-bitlines. To access the ROM, one has to precharge to "1" the three metal lines, and when a transistor of a bit array is selected, only one of the three metal lines switch to "0" (if a "0" is read). A NAND gate can detect the read value. In this solution, each "read" bitline is split only "physically" in the layout, not "logically" as in other solutions.

The second technique aims at removing the sense amplifiers. It allows the ROM memory to be capable of working at any supply voltage. Noise problems are therefore removed, as sense amplifiers are very sensitive to noise. Furthermore, it is a very simple solution, as there is no need to detect when the read operation is finished to disable the sense amplifiers; however, if sense amplifiers are removed, bitlines switch with full swings. One could think that power consumption is largely increased, but the results show that power consumption is reduced. Table 18.6 shows the results in power and speed in a 0.25 $\mu$m process.

## Electrical Design of Low-Power SRAM Memories

Low power and fast SRAM memories have been described in many papers [24]. Very advanced technologies have been used with double $V_T$. RAM cells are designed with high $V_T$ and selection logic with low $V_T$ transistors. Some techniques such as low swing and hierarchical sense amplifiers have been used. One can also use the fact that a RAM memory is read 85% of the time and written only 15% of the time.

Low-power RAM memories designed by CSEM also use the split bitlines described for the ROM. However, the RAM cell is based on nonsymmetrical ways to read and to write the memory. The patented

**TABLE 18.7**   Performances of SRAM Memories

| Company | Techno ($\mu$m) | Size | Supply (V) | Access Time (ns) | Power ($\mu$AMHz) |
|---------|-----------------|------|-----------|------------------|-------------------|
| Mirage Logic | 0.25 | 2 K × 16 | 2.75 | 2.5 | 116 |
| CSEM | 0.25 | 4 K × 16 | 2.5 | 3 | 33 |
| ST | 0.25 | 8 K × 16 | 1.5 | 3 | 125 |
| CSEM | 0.25 | 4 K × 16 | 1.2 | 10 | 14 |
| ST | 0.25 | 8 K × 16 | 1.0 | 5.5 | 85 |
| NEC | 0.25 | 0.5 K × 16 | 0.9 | 10 | 16 |

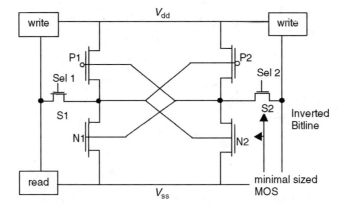

**FIGURE 18.16**   Asymmetrical SRAM cell.

idea is to write in a conventional way while using the true and inverted bitlines, but to read only through a single bitline (Fig. 18.16).

The advantages are the following:

- As it is the case in the conventional scheme, it is possible to write at low $V_{dd}$ since both true and inverted bitlines on both sides of the cell are used.
- The use of only one bitline for reading (instead of two) decreases the power consumption.
- The read condition (to achieve a read and not to overwrite the cell) has only to be effective on one side of the cell, so some transistors can be kept minimal. It decreases the capacitance on the inverted-bitline and the power consumption when writing the RAM. Furthermore, minimal transistors result in a better ratio between cell transistors when reading the memory, resulting in a speed-up of the read mechanism.
- Due to a read process only on one side of the cell, one can use the split bitlines concept more easily (Fig. 18.15).

Table 18.7 shows some results. As mentioned, the CSEM SRAM memory achieves a full swing without any sense amplifier.

## 18.7   Low-Power Standard Cell Libraries

At the electrical level, digital standard cells have been designed in a robust branch-based logic style, such as hazard-free D-flip-flops [7,25]. Such libraries with 60 functions and 220 layouts have been used for industrial chips. The low-power techniques used were the branch-based logic style that reduces parasitic capacitances and a clever transistor sizing. Instead, to enlarge transistors to have more speed, parasitic capacitances were reduced by reducing the sizes of the transistors on the cell critical paths. If several years ago, power consumption reductions achieved compared to other libraries were about a factor of 3–5, it

**TABLE 18.8** Delay Comparison

|  | Old Library Delay [ns] | $\mu m^2$ | New Library Delay [ns] | $\mu m^2$ |
|---|---|---|---|---|
| 32-b multiply | 16.4 | 907 K | 12.1 | 999 K |
| fp adder | 27.7 | 510 K | 21.1 | 548 K |
| CoolRISC ALU | 10.8 | 140 K | 7.7 | 170 K |

**TABLE 18.9** Silicon Area Comparison

|  | Old Library Delay [ns] | $\mu m^2$ | New Library Delay [ns] | $\mu m^2$ |
|---|---|---|---|---|
| 32-b multiply | 17.1 | 868 K | 17.0 | 830 K |
| fp adder | 28.1 | 484 K | 28.0 | 472 K |
| CoolRISC ALU | 11.0 | 139 K | 11.0 | 118 K |

is today only about a factor of 2 due to a better understanding of power consumption problems of library designers.

Today, logic blocks are automatically synthesized from a VHDL description while considering a design flow using a logic synthesizer such as Synopsys. Furthermore, deep submicron technologies with large wire delays imply a better robustness, mainly for sequential cells sensitive to the clock input slope. Fully static and branch-based logic style has been found as the best; however, a new approach has been proposed that is based on a limited set of standard cells. As a result, the logic synthesizer is more efficient because it has a limited set of cells well chosen and adapted to the considered logic synthesizer. With significantly less cells than conventional libraries, the results show speed, area, and power consumption improvements for synthesized logic blocks. The number of functions for the new library has been reduced to 22 and the number of layouts to 92. Table 18.8 shows that, for a similar silicon area, delays with the new library are reduced. Table 18.9 shows that, for a similar speed, silicon area is reduced for the new library. Furthermore, as the number of layouts is drastically reduced, it takes less time to design a new library for a more advanced process.

Overall, the main issue in the design of future libraries will be the static power. For $V_{dd}$ as low as 0.6–0.3 V in 2014, as predicted by the Roadmap [15], $V_T$ will be reduced accordingly in very deep submicron technologies. Consequently, the static power will increase significantly due to these low $V_T$ [3]. Several techniques with double $V_T$, source impedance, well polarization, dynamic regulation of $V_T$ [4] are today under investigation and will be necessarily used in the future. This problem is crucial for portable devices that are often in standby mode in which the dynamic power is reduced to zero. It results that the static power becomes the main part of the total power. It will be a crucial point in future libraries for which more versions of the same function will be required while considering these static power problems. A same function could be realized, for instance, with low or high $V_T$ for double $V_T$ technologies, or several cells such as a generic cell with typical $V_T$, a low-power cell with high $V_T$, and a fast cell with low $V_T$.

# References

1. A. P. Chandrakasan, S. Sheng, R. W. Brodersen, "Low-Power CMOS Digital Design" *IEEE J. of Solid-State Circuits*, Vol. 27, No. 4, April 1992, pp. 473–484.
2. R. F. Lyon, "Cost, Power, and Parallelism in Speech Signal Processing," *IEEE 1993 CICC*, Paper 15.1.1, San Diego, CA, USA.
3. D. Liu, C. Svensson, "Trading Speed for Low Power by Choice of Supply and Threshold Voltages," JSSC-28, No. 1, Jan. 1993, pp. 10–17.
4. V. von Kaenel et al. "Automatic Adjustment of Threshold & Supply Voltage Minimum Power Consumption in CMOS Digital Circuits," *1994 IEEE Symposium on Low Power Electronics*, San Diego, October 10–12, 1994, pp. 78–79.

5. J. Rabay, M. Pedram, "Low Power Design Methodologies," Kluwer Academic Publishers, Dordrecht, the Netherlands, 1996.

6. "Low-Power HF Microelectronics, a unified approach," Editor G. Machado, *IEE Circuits & Systems Series No. 8,* IEE Publishers, 1996.

7. "Low Power Design in Deep Submicron Electronics," *NATO ASI Series, Series E: Applied Sciences,* Vol. 337, Editors W. Nebel, J. Mermet, Kluwer Academic Publishers, 1997.

8. C. Piguet, "Parallelism and Low-Power," invited talk, SympA'99, Symposium Architectures de Machines, Rennes, France, June 8, 1999.

9. A. Jerraya, "Hardware/Software Codesign," Summer Course, Orebro, Sweden, August 14–16, 2000.

10. V. von Kaenel, P. Macken, M. Degrauwe, "A Voltage Reduction Technique for Battery-Operated Systems," *IEEE J. of Solid-State Circuits,* Vol. 25, No. 5, October 1990, pp. 1136–1140.

11. F. Rampogna, J-M. Masgonty, C. Piguet, "Hardware-Software Co-simulation and Power Estimation Environment for Low-Power ASICs and SoCs," DATE'2000, *Proc. User Forum,* pp. 261–265, Paris, 27–30, March 2000.

12. D. Singh et al., "Power Conscious CAD Tools and Methodologies: A Perspective," *Proc. IEEE,* Vol. 83, No. 4, April 1994, pp. 570–594.

13. J. M. Rabay, "Managing Power Dissipation in the Generation-after-Next Wireless Systems," *FTFC'99,* June 1999, Paris, France.

14. "Billion-Transistor Architectures," *IEEE Computer,* September 1997, Issue.

15. http://notes.sematech.org/ntrs/rdmpmem.nsf

16. C. Arm, J-M. Masgonty, C. Piguet, "Double-Latch Clocking Scheme for Low-Power I.P. Cores," *PATMOS 2000,* Goettingen, Germany, September 13–15, 2000.

17. M. Renaudin, "Asynchronous Circuits and Systems: a promising design alternative," MIGAS Summer School on Microelectronics for Telecommunications: Managing High Complexity and Mobility, June 28–July 4, 2000, Autrans, France.

18. C. Piguet et al., "Low-Power Digital Design and CAD Tools," invited talk, *Colloque CAO de circuits intégrés et systèmes, Aix en Provence,* May 10–12, 1999, pp. 108–127.

19. C. Piguet et al., "Low-Power Design of 8-bit Embedded CoolRISC Microcontroller Cores," *IEEE JSSC,* Vol. 32, No. 7, July 1997, pp. 1067–1078.

20. J.-M. Masgonty et al., "Low-Power Design of an Embedded Microprocessor," *ESSCIRC'96,* September 16–21, 1996, Neuchâtel, Switzerland.

21. M. Keating, P. Bricaud, "Reuse Methodology Manual," Kluwer Academic Publishers, 1999.

22. Ph. Mosch et al., "A 72 $\mu$W, 50 MOPS, 1 V DSP for a hearing aid chip set," *ISSCC'00,* San Francisco, February 7–9, Session 14, paper 5.

23. J. G. Xi, D. Staepelaere, "Using Clock Skew as a Tool to Achieve Optimal Timing," *Integrated System Magazine,* April 1999, webmaster@isdmag.com

24. A. Turier, Ph.D. Thesis, "Etude, Conception et Caractérisation de mémoires CMOS, faible consommation, faible tension en technologies submicroniques," University of Paris VI, Pierre and Marie Curie, France, December 13, 2000.

25. C. Piguet, J. Zahnd, "Signal-Transition Graphs-Based Design of Speed-Independent CMOS Circuits," *ESSCIRC'98,* September 21–24, 1998, Den Haag, The Netherlands, pp. 432–435.

# 19

# Implementation-Level Impact on Low-Power Design

Katsunori Seno
*SONY Corporation*

## 19.1  Introduction

Recently low-power design has become a very important and critical issue to enhance the portable multimedia market. Therefore, various approaches to explore low power design have been made. The implementation can be categorized into system level, algorithm level, architecture level, circuit level, and process/device level. Figure 19.1 shows the relative impact on power consumption of each phase of the design process. Essentially higher-level categories have more effect on power reduction. This section describes the impact of each level on low-power design.

## 19.2  System Level Impact

The system level is the highest layer. Therefore, it strongly influences power consumption and distribution by partitioning system factors.

Reference [1], InfoPad of University of California, Berkeley, demonstrated a low-power wireless multimedia access system. Heavy computation resources (functions) and large data storage devices such as hard disks are moved to the backbone server and InfoPad itself works as just a portable terminal device. This system level partitioning realizes Web browser, X-terminal, voice-recognition, and other application with low power consumption because energy hungry factors were moved from the pad to the backbone. And reference [2] demonstrates the power consumption of the InfoPad chipset to be just 5 mW.

## 19.3  Algorithm Level Impact

The algorithm level is the second to the system level, which defines a detailed implementation outline of a required original function. This level has quite a large impact on power consumption. It is because the algorithm determines how to solve the problem and how to reduce the original complexity. Thus, the algorithm layer is key to power consumption and efficiency.

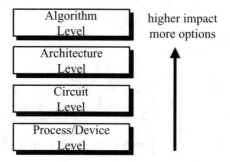

**FIGURE 19.1**   Each level impact for low-power design.

A typical example of algorithm contribution is motion estimation of MPEG encoder. Motion estimation is an extremely critical function of MPEG encoding. Implementing fundamental MPEG2 motion estimation using a full search block matching algorithm requires huge computations [3,4]. It reaches 4.5 teraoperations per second (TOPS) if realizing a very wide search range (±288 pixels horizontal and ±96 pixels vertical), on the other hand the rest of the functions take about 2 GOPS. Therefore motion estimation is the key problem to solve in designing a single chip MPEG2 encoder LSI. Reference [5] describes a good example to dramatically reduce actual required performance for motion estimation with a very wide search range, which was implemented as part of a 1.2 W single chip MPEG2 MP@ML video encoder. Two adaptive algorithms are applied. One is 8:1 adaptive subsampling algorithm that adaptively selects subsampled pixel locations using characteristics of maximum and minimum values instead of fixed subsampled pixel locations. This algorithm effectively chooses sampled pixels and reduces the computation requirements by seven-eighths. Another is an adaptive search area control algorithm, which has two independent search areas with H: ±32 and V: ±16 pixels in full search block matching algorithm for each. The center locations of these search areas are decided based on a distribution history of the motion vectors and this algorithm substantially expands the search area up to H: ±288 and V: ±96 pixels. Therefore, the total computation requirement is reduced from 4.5 TOPS to 20 GOPS (216:1), which is possible to implement on a single chip. The first search area can follow a focused object close to the center of the camera finder with small motion. The second one can cope with a background object with large motion in camera panning. This adaptive algorithm attains high picture quality with very wide search range because it can efficiently grasp moving objects, that is, get correct motion vectors. As shown in this example, algorithm improvement can drastically reduce computation requirement and enable low power design.

## 19.4   Architecture Level Impact

The architecture level is the next to the algorithm level, also in terms of impact on power consumption. At the architecture level there are still many options and wide freedom in implementation. The architecture level is explained as CPU (microprocessor), DSP (digital signal processor), ASIC (dedicated hardwired logic), reconfigurable logic, and special purpose DSP.

The CPU is the most widely used general-purpose architecture as shown in Fig. 19.2. Fundamentally anything can be performed by software. It is the most inefficient in power, however. The main features of the CPU are the following: (1) It is completely sequential in operation with instruction fetch and decode in every cycle. Basically this is not essential for computation itself and is just overhead. (2) There is no dedicated address generator for memory access. The regular ALU is used to calculate memory address. Throughput of data feeding is not, every cycle, based on load/store architecture via registers (RISC-based architecture). This means cycles are consumed for data movement and not just for computation itself. (CISC allows memory access operation, but this doesn't mean it is more effective; it is a different story, not explained in detail here.) (3) Many temporal storage operations are included in computation procedure.

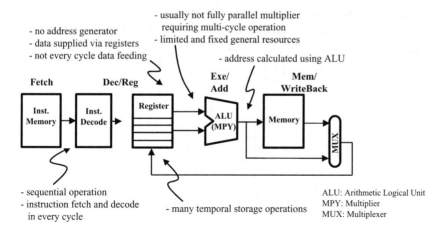

**FIGURE 19.2** CPU structure.

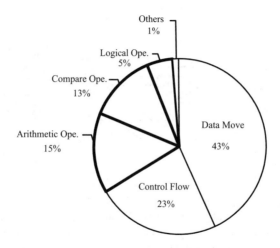

**FIGURE 19.3** Dynamic instruction statistics.

This is a completely justified overhead. (4) Usually, a fully parallel multiplier is not used, causing multi-cycle operation. This also consumes more wasted power because clocking, memory, and extra circuits are activated in multiple for one multiply operation. (5) Resources are limited and prefixed. This results in overhead operations to be executed as general purpose. Figure 19.3 shows dynamic run time instruction statistics [6]. This indicates that essential computation instructions such as arithmetic operation occupy just 33% of the entire dynamic run time instruction stream. The data moving and control-like branches take two-thirds, which is large overhead consuming extra power.

The DSP is an enhanced processor for multiply-accumulate computation. It is general-purpose in structure and more effective for signal processing than the CPU. But still it is not very power efficient. Figure 19.4 shows the basic structure and its features are as follows. (1) The DSP is also sequential in operation with instruction fetch and decode in every cycle similar to the CPU. It causes overhead in the same way, but as an exception DSP has a hardware loop, which eliminates continued instruction fetch in repeated operations, improving power penalty. (2) Many temporal storage operations are also used. (3) Resources are limited and prefixed for general purpose as well. This is a major reason for causing temporal storage operations. (4) Fully parallel multiplier is used making one cycle operation possible. And also accumulator with guardbits is applied, which is very important to accumulate continuously without accuracy degradation and undesired temporal storing to registers. This improves power efficiency for multiply-accumulate-based

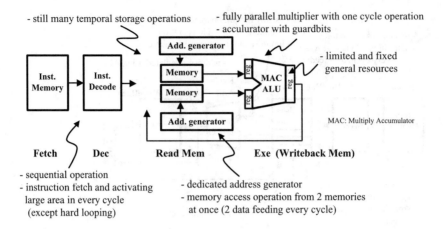

**FIGURE 19.4**   DSP structure.

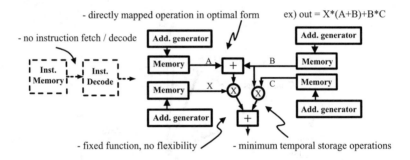

**FIGURE 19.5**   ASIC structure.

computations. (5) It is equipped with dedicated address generators for memory access. This realizes more complex memory addressing without using regular ALU and consuming extra cycles, and two data can be fed in every cycle directory from memory. This is very important for DSP operation. Features (4) and (5) are advantages of the DSP in improving power efficiency over the CPU.

We define the ASIC as dedicated hardware here. It is the most power efficient because the structure can be designed for the specific function and optimized. Figure 19.5 shows the basic image and the features are as follows: (1) Required functions can be directly mapped in optimal form. This is the essential feature and source of power efficiency by minimizing any overheads. (2) Temporal storage operation can be minimized, which is large overhead in general purpose architectures. Basically this comes from feature (1). (3) It is not sequential in operation. Instruction fetch and decode are not required. This eliminates fundamental overhead of general-purpose processors. (4) Function is fixed as design. There is no flexibility. This is the most significant drawback of dedicated hardware solutions.

There is another category known as reconfigurable logic. Typical architecture is field programmable gate array (FPGA). This is gate level fine-grained programmable logic. It consists of programmable network structure and logic blocks that have a look-up table (LUT)-based programmable unit, flip-flop, and selectors as shown in Fig. 19.6. The features are: (1) It is quite flexible. Basically, the FPGA can be configured to any dedicated function if integrated gate capacity is enough to map it; (2) Structure can be optimized without being limited to prefixed data width and variation of function unit like a general 32-bit ALU of CPU. Therefore, FPGA is not used only for prototyping but also where high performance and high throughput are targeted. (3) It is very inefficient in power. Switch network for fine-grain level flexibility causes large power overhead. Each gate function is realized by LUT programed as truth table, for example NAND, NOR, and so on. Power consumption of interconnect takes 65% of the chip, while logic part consumed only 5% [7]. This means major power of FPGA is burned in unessential portion.

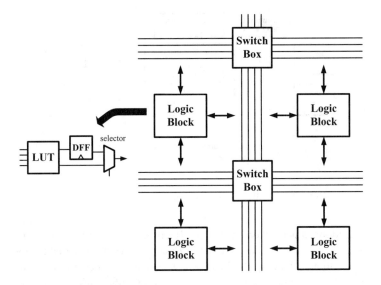

**FIGURE 19.6**   FPGA simplified structure.

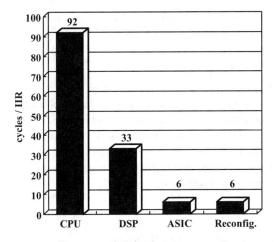

**FIGURE 19.7**   IIR comparison.

FPGA sacrifices power efficiency in order to attain wide range flexibility. It is a trade-off between flexibility and power efficiency. Lately, however, there is another class of reconfigurable architecture. It is coarse-grained or heterogeneous reconfigurable architecture. Typical work is Maia of Pleiades project, U.C. Berkeley [8–12]. This architecture consists of heterogeneous modules that are mainly coarse-grain similar to ALU, multiplier, memory, etc. The flexibility is limited to some computation or application domain but power efficiency is dramatically improved. This type of architecture might gain acceptance because of strong demand for low power and flexibility.

Figure 19.7 shows cycle comparison to execute fourth order infinite impulse response (IIR) for CPU, DSP, ASIC, and reconfigurable logic. ASIC and reconfigurable logic are assumed as two parallel implementations. CPU takes more overhead than DSP, which is enhanced for multiply computation as mentioned previously. Also, dedicated hardware structures such as ASIC and reconfigurable logic can reduce computational overhead more than others.

The last one is the special purpose DSP for MPEG2 video encoding. Figure 19.8 shows an example of programmable DSP for MPEG2 video encoding [13]. This architecture applied 3-level parallel processing of macro-block level, block level, and pixel level in reducing performance requirement from 1.1 GHz to

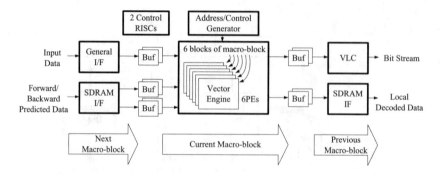

**FIGURE 19.8**  Special purpose DSP for MPEG2 video encoding.

81 MHz with 13 operations in parallel on an average. The macro-blocks are processed in 3-stage pipeline with MIMD controlled by two RISCs. The 6 blocks of macro-block are handled by 6 vector processing engines (PEs) assigned to each block with SIMD way. The pixels of block are computed by the PE that consists of extended ALU, multiplier, accumulator, three barrel-shifters with truncating/rounding function and 6-port register file. This specialized DSP performs MPEG2 MP@ML video encoding at 1.3 W/3 V/0.4 $\mu$m process with software programmability. The architecture improvement for dedicated application can reduce performance requirement and overhead of general-purpose approach and plays an important role for low-power design.

## 19.5  Circuit Level Impact

The circuit level is the most detailed implementation layer. This level is explained as module level such as multiplier or memory and basement level like voltage control that affects wide range of the chip. The circuit level is quite important for performance but usually has less impact on power consumption than previous higher levels. One reason is that each component itself is just a part of the entire chip. Therefore, it is needed to focus on critical and major factors (most power hungry modules, etc.) in order to contribute to power reduction for chip level improvement.

### Module Level

The module level is each component like adder, multiplier, and memory, etc. It has relatively less impact on power compared to algorithm and architecture level as mentioned above. Even if power consumption of one component is reduced to half, it is difficult to improve the total chip power consumption drastically in many cases. On the other hand, it is still important to focus on circuit level components, because the sum of all units is the total power. Memory components especially occupy a large portion of many chips. Two examples of module level are shown here.

Usually there occur many glitches in logic block causing extra power at average 15 to 20% of the total power dissipation [14]. Multiplier has a large adder-based array to sum partial products, which generates many glitches. Figure 19.9 is an example of multiplier improvement to eliminate those glitches [13]. There are time-skews between X-side input signals and Y-side Booth encoded signals (Booth select) creating many glitches at Booth selectors. These glitches propagate in the Wallace tree and consume extra power. The glitch preventive booth (GPB) scheme (Figure 19.9) blocks X-signals until Booth encoded signals (Y-signals) are ready by delaying the clock in order to synchronize X-signals and Y-signals. During this blocking period, Booth selectors keep previous data as dynamic latches. This scheme reduces Wallace tree power consumption by 44% without extra devices in the Booth selectors.

Another example is a memory power reduction [13]. Normally in ASIC embedded SRAM, the whole memory cell array is activated. But actually utilized memory cells whose data are read out are just part

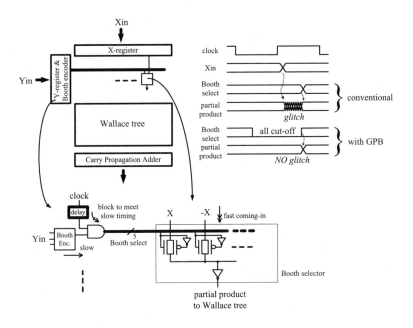

**FIGURE 19.9**   Glitch preventive booth (GPB) multiplier.

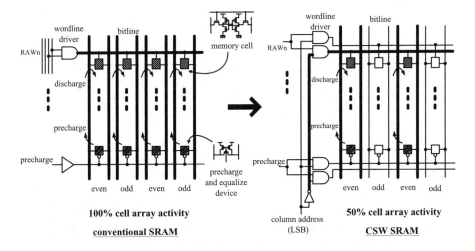

**FIGURE 19.10**   Column selective wordline (CSW) SRAM.

of them. This means large extra power is dissipated in memory cell array. Figure 19.10 shows column selective wordline (CSW) scheme. The wordline of each raw address is divided into two that are controlled by column address LSB corresponding to odd and even column. And memory cells of each raw address are also connected to wordline corresponding to odd or even column. Therefore, simultaneously activated memory cells are reduced to 50% and it saves SRAM power by 26% without using section division scheme.

## Basement Level

The basement level is another class. This is categorized as circuit level but affects all or a wide area of the chip like unit activation scheme as chip level control strategy or voltage management scheme. Therefore, it can make a much larger impact on the power than the module level.

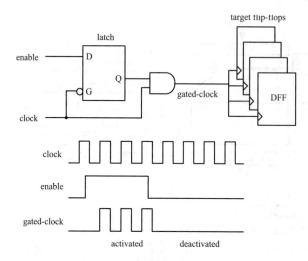

**FIGURE 19.11**    Gated-clock.

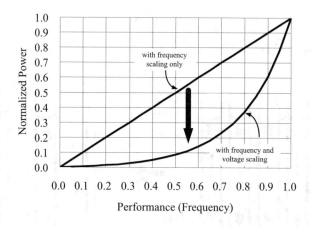

**FIGURE 19.12**    Frequency and voltage scaling.

Figure 19.11 describes the gated-clock scheme, which is very popular, and is the basic scheme to reduce power consumption. Activation of clock for target flip-flops is controlled by enable signal that is asserted only when needed. The latch of Fig. 19.4 prevents clock from glitch. This scheme is used to inactivate blocks or units when they are not used. Unless clocks are controlled on demand, all clock lines and inside of flip-flops are toggled and also unnecessary data propagate into circuit units through flip-flops, which causes large waste in power all over the chip. The gated-clock used to be handled manually by designer; today, however, it can be generated automatically in gate compilation and also static timing analysis can be applied without special care at latch by EDA tool. This means the gated-clock has become a very common and important scheme.

The operating voltage is conventionally fixed at the standard voltage like 5 V or 3.3 V. But when the system runs at multiple performance requirements, frequency can be varied to meet each performance. At this time, the operating voltage can be also changed to the minimum to attain that frequency. The power consumption is a quadratic function of voltage, therefore to control voltage has a very big impact and is quite an effective method of power reduction. Figure 19.12 shows an effect of scaling with frequency and voltage. Scaling with only frequency reduces power consumption in just proportion to frequency. On the other hand, scaling with frequency and voltage achieves drastic power saving because of quadratic effect of voltage reduction. It is really important to handle the voltage as a design parameter and not as a fixed given standard. References [15,16] are examples called dynamic voltage scaling (DVS), which demonstrated actual benchmark programs running on a processor system with dynamically varied frequency and voltage based on required performance, and indicate energy efficiency improvement by factor of 10 among audio, user interface, and MPEG programs.

## 19.6 Process/Device Level Impact

The process and device are the lowest level of implementation. This layer itself does not have drastic impact directly. But when it leads to voltage reduction, this level plays a very important role in power saving.

Process rule migration rate is about 30% (×0.7) per generation. And supply voltage is also reduced along with process shrinking after submicron generation, therefore capacitance scaling with voltage reduction makes good contribution on power.

Wire delay has become a problem because wire resistance and side capacitance are increasing along with process shrinking. To relieve this situation, inter-metal dielectric using low-k material and copper (Cu) interconnect have been utilized lately [17–19]. Still, however, dielectric constant of low-k is about 3.5–2.0 depending on materials while 4.0 for $SiO_2$, so this capacitance reduction does not a great impact on power because it affects just wire capacitance reduction as part of the whole chip. On the other hand, this can improve interconnect delay and chip speed allowing lower voltage operation at the same required speed. This accelerates power reduction with effect of quadratic function of voltage.

Silicon-on-insulator (SOI) is one of the typical process options for low power. The SOI transistor is isolated by $SiO_2$ insulator, so junction capacitance is drastically reduced. This lightens charge/discharge loads and saves power consumption. Partial depletion (PD)-type SOI and full depletion (FD)-type SOI are used. The FD type can realize a steep subthreshold slope of about 60–70 mV/dec while the bulk one is 80–90 mV/dec. This helps reduction of threshold voltage ($V_{th}$) at the same subthreshold leakage by 0.1–0.2 V, therefore operating voltage can be lowered while maintaining the same speed. References [20–22] are examples of PD type approach that demonstrate 20–35% performance improvement for microprocessor. Reference [23] is FD type approach also applied to microprocessor.

## 19.7 Summary

The impact on low-power design with each implementation classes of system level, algorithm level, architecture level, circuit level, and process/device level was described. Basically, higher levels affect power consumption more than lower levels because higher levels have more freedom in implementation. The key point for lower level to improve power consumption is its relationship with voltage reduction.

### References

1. Chandrakasan, A., and Broderson, R., Low Power Digital CMOS Design, Kluwer Academic Publishers, Norwell, 1995, Chap. 9.
2. Chandrakasan, A., et al., A low-power chipset for multimedia applications, *J. Solid-State Circuits*, Vol. 29, No. 12, 1415, 1994.
3. Ishihara, K., et al., A half-pel precision MPEG2 motion-estimation processor with concurrent three-vector search, in *ISSCC Dig. Tech. Papers*, Feb. 1995, 288.
4. Ohtani, A., et al., A motion estimation processor for MPEG2 video real time encoding at wide search range, in *Proc. CICC*, May 1995, 17.4.1.
5. Ogura, E., et al., A 1.2-W single-chip MPEG2 MP@ML video encoder LSI including wide search range motion estimation and 81-MOPS controller, *J. Solid-State Circuits*, Vol. 33, No. 11, 1765, 1998.
6. Furber, S., An Introduction to Processor Design, in ARM System Architecture, Addison-Wesley Longman, England, 1996, Chap. 1.
7. Kusse, E., and Rabaey, J., Low-energy embedded FPGA structures, in *1998 Int. Symp. on Low Power Electronics and Design*, Aug. 1996, 155.

8. Zhang, H., et al., A 1 V heterogeneous reconfigurable processor IC for embedded wireless applications, in *ISSCC Dig. Tech. Papers*, Feb. 2000, 68.

9. Zhang, H., et al., A 1 V heterogeneous reconfigurable DSP IC for wireless baseband digital signal processing, *J. Solid-State Circuits*, Vol. 35, No. 11, 1697, 2000.

10. Abnous, A., and Rabaey, J., Ultra-low-power domain-specific multimedia processors, in *Proc. IEEE VLSI Signal Processing Workshop*, San Francisco, California, USA, Oct. 1996.

11. Abnous, A., et al., Evaluation of a low-power reconfigurable DSP architecture, in *Proc. Reconfigurable Architectures Workshop*, Orlando, Florida, USA, March 1998.

12. Rabaey, J., Reconfigurable computing: the solution to low power programmable DSP, in *Proc. 1997 ICASSP Conference*, Munich, April 1997.

13. Iwata, E., et al., A 2.2 GOPS video DSP with 2-RISC MIMD, 6-PE SIMD architecture for real-time MPEG2 video coding/decoding, in *ISSCC Dig. Tech. Papers*, Feb. 1997, 258.

14. Benini, L., et al., Analysis of hazard contributions to power dissipation in CMOS ICs, in *Proc. IWLPD*, 1994, 27.

15. Burd, T., et al., A dynamic voltage scaled microprocessor system, in *ISSCC Dig. Tech. Papers*, Feb. 2000, 294.

16. Burd, T., et al., A dynamic voltage scaled microprocessor system, *J. Solid-State Circuits*, Vol. 35, No. 11, 1571, 2000.

17. Moussavi, M., Advanced interconnect schemes towards 01 $\mu$m, in *IEDM Tech. Dig.*, 1999, 611.

18. Ahn, J., et al., 1 GHz microprocessor integration with high performance transistor and low RC delay, in *IEDM Tech. Dig.*, 1999, 683.

19. Yamashita, K., et al., Interconnect scaling scenario using a chip level interconnect model, *Transactions on Electron Devices*, Vol. 47, No. 1, 90, 2000.

20. Shahidi, G., et al., Partially-depleted SOI technology for digital logic, in *ISSCC Dig. Tech. Papers*, Feb. 1999, 426.

21. Allen, D., et al., A 0.2 $\mu$m 1.8 V SOI 550 MHz 64 b PowerPC microprocessor with copper interconnects, in *ISSCC Dig. Tech. Papers*, Feb. 1999, 438.

22. Buchholtz, T., et al., A 660 MHz 64 b SOI processor with Cu interconnects, in *ISSCC Dig. Tech. Papers*, Feb. 2000, 88.

23. Kim, Y., et al., A 0.25 $\mu$m 600 MHz 1.5 V SOI 64 b ALPHA microprocessor, in *ISSCC Dig. Tech. Papers*, Feb. 1999, 432.

# 20

# Accurate Power Estimation of Combinational CMOS Digital Circuits

Hendrawan Soeleman
*Purdue University*

Kaushik Roy
*Purdue University*

## 20.1  Introduction

Estimation of average power consumption is one of the main concerns in today's VLSI (very large scale integrated) circuit and system design [18,19]. This is mainly due to the recent trend towards portable computing and wireless communication systems. Moreover, the dramatic decrease in feature size, combined with the corresponding increase in the number of devices in a chip, make the power density larger. For a portable system to be practical, it should be able to operate for an extended period of time without the need to recharge or replace the battery. In order to achieve such an objective, power consumption in portable systems has to be minimized.

Power consumption also translates directly into excess heat, which creates additional problems for cost-effective and efficient cooling of ICs. Overheating may cause run-time errors and/or permanent damage, and hence, affects the reliability and the lifetime of the system. Modern microprocessors are indeed *hot*: Intel's Pentium 4 consumes 50 W, and Digital's Alpha 21464 (EV8) chip consumes 150 W, Sun's UltraSPARC III consumes 70 W [14]. In a market already sensitive to price, an increase in cost

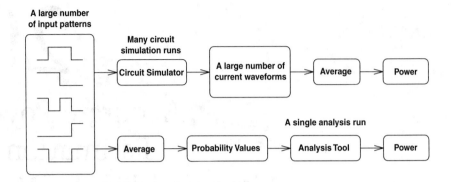

**FIGURE 20.1**  Probabilistic and simulation-based power estimation.

from issues related to power dissipation are often critical. Thus, shrinking device geometries, higher clocking speeds, and increased heat dissipation create circuit design challenges.

The Environmental Protection Agency's (EPA) constant encouragement for *green machines* and its Energy Star program are also pushing computer designers to consider power dissipation as one of the major design constraints. Hence, there is an increasing need for accurate estimation of power consumption of a system during the design phase so that the power consumption specifications can be met early in the design cycle and expensive redesign process can be avoided.

Intuitively, a straightforward method to estimate the average power consumption is by simulating the circuits with all possible combinations of valid inputs. Then, by monitoring power supply current waveforms, the power consumption under each input combination can be computed. Eventually, the results are averaged. The advantage of this method is its generality. This method can be applied to different technologies, design styles, and architectures; however, the method requires not only a large number of input waveforms combination, but also *complete and specific* knowledge of the input waveforms. Hence, the simulation method is prohibitively expensive and impractical for large circuits.

In order to solve the problem of input pattern dependence, *probabilistic techniques* [21] are used to describe the set of *all possible input combinations*. Using the probabilistic measures, the signal activities can be estimated. The calculated signal activities are then used to estimate the power consumption [1,3,6,12]. As illustrated in Fig. 20.1 [2], probabilistic approaches average all the possible input combinations and then use the probability values as inputs to the analysis tool to estimate power. Furthermore, the probabilistic approach requires only one simulation run to estimate power, so it is much faster than the simulation-based approaches, which require several simulation runs. In practice, some information about the typical input waveforms are given by the user, which make the probabilistic approach a *weakly pattern dependent* approach.

Another alternative method to estimate power is the use of *statistical techniques*, which tries to combine the speed of the probabilistic techniques with the accuracy of the simulation-based techniques. Similar to other simulation-based techniques, the statistical techniques are slower compared to the probabilistic techniques, as it needs to run a certain number of samples before simulation converges to the user-specified accuracy parameters.

This chapter is organized as follows. Section 20.2 describes how power is consumed in CMOS circuits. Probabilistic and statistical techniques to estimate power are presented in sections 20.3 and 20.4, respectively. Both techniques consider the temporal and spatial correlations of signals into account. Experimental results for both techniques are presented in section 20.5. Section 20.6 summarizes and concludes this chapter.

## 20.2  Power Consumption

Power dissipation in a CMOS circuit consists of the following components: static, dynamic, and direct path power. Static power component is due to the leakage current drawn continuously from the power supply. The dynamic power component is dependent on the supply voltage, the load capacitances, and the frequency of operation. The direct path power is due to the switching transient current that exists for a short period of time when both PMOS and NMOS transistors are conducting simultaneously when the logic gates are switching.

Depending on the design requirements, there are different power dissipation factors that need to be considered. For example, the peak power is an important factor to consider while designing the size of the power supply line, whereas the average power is related to cooling or battery energy consumption requirements. We focus on the average power consumption in this chapter. The peak power and average power are defined in the following equations:

$$P_{peak} = I_{peak} \cdot V_{supply} \quad \text{and} \quad P_{average} = \frac{1}{T} \int_0^T (I_{supply}(t) \cdot V_{supply}) \, dt$$

## Static Power Component

In CMOS circuit, no conducting path between the power supply rails exists when the inputs are in an equilibrium state. This is due to the complimentary feature of this technology: if the NMOS transistors in the pull-down network (PDN) are conducting, then the corresponding PMOS transistors in the pull-up network (PUN) will be nonconducting, and vice-versa; however, there is a small static power consumption due to the leakage current drawn continuously from the power supply. Hence, the static power consumption is the product of the leakage current and the supply voltage ($P_{static} = I_{leakage} \cdot V_{supply}$), and thus depends on the device process technology.

The leakage current is mainly due to the *reverse-biased parasitic diodes* that originate from the *source-drain* diffusions, the *well* diffusion, and the transistor *substrate*, and the *subthreshold current* of the transistors. Subthreshold current is the current which flows between the drain and source terminals of the transistors when the gate voltage is smaller than the threshold voltage ($V_{gs} < V_{th}$). For today and future technologies, the subthreshold current is expected to be the dominant component of leakage current. Accurate estimation of leakage current has been considered in [13].

Static power component is usually a minor contributor to the overall power consumption. Nevertheless, due to the fact that static power consumption is always present even when the circuit is idle, the minimization of the static power consumption is worth considered by completely turning off certain sections of a system that are inactive.

## Dynamic Power Component

Dynamic power consumption occurs only when the logic gate is switching. The two factors that make up the dynamic power consumption are the charging and discharging of the output load capacitances and the switching transient current. During the low-to-high transition at the output node of a logic gate, the load capacitance at the output node will be charged through the PMOS transistors in PUN of the circuit. Its voltage will rise from GND to $V_{supply}$. An amount of energy, $C_{load} \cdot V_{supply}^2$, is drawn from the power supply. Half of this energy will then be stored in the output capacitor, while the other half is dissipated in the PMOS devices. During the high-to-low transition, the stored charge is removed from the capacitor, and the energy is dissipated in the NMOS devices in the PDN of the circuit. Figure 20.2 illustrates the charging and the discharging paths for the load capacitor. The load capacitance at the output node is mainly due to the gate capacitances of the circuits that are being driven by the output node (i.e., the number of fanouts of the output node), the wiring capacitances, and the diffusion capacitances of the driving circuit.

Each switching cycle, which consists of charging and discharging paths, dissipates an amount of energy equals to $C_{load} \cdot V_{supply}^2$. Therefore, to calculate the power consumption, we need to know how often the gate switches. If the number of switching in a time interval $t(t \to \infty)$ is $B$, then the average dynamic power consumption is given by

$$P_{dynamic} = \frac{1}{2} \cdot C_{load} \cdot V_{supply}^2 \cdot B \cdot \frac{1}{t} = \frac{1}{2} \cdot C_{load} \cdot V_{supply}^2 \cdot A$$

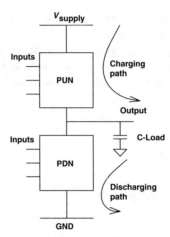

**FIGURE 20.2**   The charging and discharging paths.

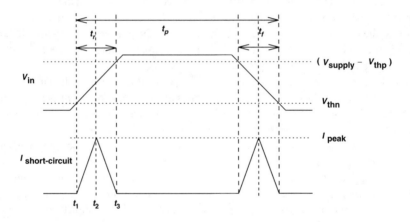

**FIGURE 20.3**   Switching current spikes.

where $A = B/t$ is the number of transitions per unit time.

During the switching transient, both the PMOS and NMOS transistors conduct for a short period of time. This results in a short-circuit current flow between the power supply rails and causes a direct path power consumption. The direct path power component is dependent on the input rise and fall time. Slow rising and falling edges would increase the short-circuit current duration. In an unloaded inverter, the transient switching current spikes can be approximated as triangles, as shown in Figure 20.3 [16]. Thus, the average power consumption due to direct-path component is given by

$$P_{\text{direct-path}} = I_{\text{avg}} \cdot V_{\text{supply}}$$

where

$$I_{\text{avg}} = 2\left[\frac{1}{T}\int_{t1}^{t2} I(t)\,dt + \frac{1}{T}\int_{t2}^{t3} I(t)\,dt\right]$$

The saturation current of the transistors determines the peak current, and the peak current is directly proportional to the size of the transistors.

## Total Average Power

Putting together all the components of power dissipation, the total average power consumption of a logic gate can be expressed as follows:

$$P_{\text{total}} = P_{\text{dynamic}} + P_{\text{direct-path}} + P_{\text{static}} = \frac{1}{2} \cdot C_{\text{load}} \cdot V_{\text{supply}}^2 \cdot A + I_{\text{avg}} \cdot V_{\text{supply}} + I_{\text{leakage}} \cdot V_{\text{supply}} \quad (20.1)$$

Among these components, dynamic power is by far the most dominant component and accounts for more than 80% of the total power consumption in modern day CMOS technology. Thus, the total average power for all logic gates in the circuits can be approximated by summing up all the dynamic component of each of the logic gate,

$$P_{\text{total}} = \frac{1}{2} \cdot V_{\text{supply}}^2 \cdot \sum_{i=1}^{n} C_{\text{load}_i} \cdot A_i$$

where $n$ is the number of logic gates in the circuit.

## Power Due to the Internal Nodes of a Logic Gate

The power consumption due to the internal nodes of the logic gates has been ignored in the above analysis, which causes inaccuracy in the power consumption result. The internal node capacitances are primarily due to the source and drain diffusion capacitances of the transistors, and are not as large as the output node capacitance. Hence, total power consumption is still dominated by the charging and discharging of the output node capacitances. Nevertheless, depending on the applied input vectors and the sequence in which the input vectors are applied, the power consumption due to the internal nodes of logic gates may contribute a significant portion of the total power consumption. Experimental results in section 20.5 show that the power consumption due to the internal nodes can be as high as 20% of the total power consumption for some circuits.

The impact of the internal nodes in the total power consumption is most significant when the internal nodes are switching, but the output node remains unchanged, as shown in Fig. 20.4. The internal capacitance, $C_{\text{internal}}$, is being charged, discharged, and recharged at time $t_0$, $t_1$, and $t_2$, respectively. During this period of time, power is dissipated solely due to charging and discharging of the internal node.

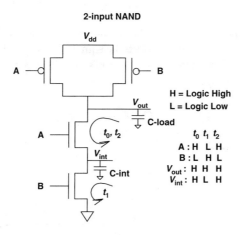

**FIGURE 20.4** Charging and discharging of internal node.

In order to obtain a more accurate power estimation result, the internal nodes have to be considered. In taking the internal nodes of the logic gates into consideration, the overall total power consumption equation is modified to

$$P_{total} = \sum_{i=1}^{n} \left( \frac{V_{supply}^2}{2} \cdot C_{load_i} \cdot A_i + \sum_{j=1}^{m} \frac{V_j^2}{2} \cdot C_{internal_j} \cdot A_j \right) \tag{20.2}$$

where $m$ is the number of internal nodes in the $i$th logic gate. Note that output node voltages can only have two possible values: $V_{supply}$ and GND; however, each internal node voltage can have multiple possible values ($V_j$) due to charge sharing, and threshold voltage drop. In order to accurately estimate power dissipation, we should be able to accurately estimate the switching activities of all the internal nodes of a circuit.

## 20.3  Probabilistic Technique to Estimate Switching Activity

Probabilistic technique has been used to solve the strong input pattern dependence problem in estimating the power consumption of CMOS circuits. The probabilistic technique, based on zero-delay symbolic simulation, offers a fast solution for calculating power. The technique is based on an algorithm that takes the switching activities of the primary inputs of a circuit specified by the users. The probabilistic analysis relies on propagating the probabilistic measures, such as *signal probability* and *activity*, from the primary inputs to the internal and output nodes of a circuit.

To estimate the power consumption, probabilistic technique first calculates the *signal probability* (probability of being logic high) of each node. The *signal activity* is then computed from the signal probability. Once the signal activity has been calculated, the average power consumption can then be obtained by using Eq. (20.2).

The primary inputs of a combinational circuit are modeled to be *mutually independent strict-sense-stationary (SSS) mean-ergodic 1-0 processes* [3]. Under this assumption, the probability of the primary input node $x$ to assume logic high, $P(x(t))$, becomes constant and independent of time, and denoted by $P(x)$, the *equilibrium signal probability* of node $x$. Thus, $P(x)$ is the average fraction of clock cycles in which the equilibrium value of node $x$ is of logic high.

The activity at primary input node $x$ is defined by

$$\lim_{n \to \infty} \frac{n_x(T)}{T}$$

where $n_x$ is the number of time the node $x$ switches in the time interval of $(-T/2, T/2)$. The activity $A(x)$ is then the average fraction of clock cycles in which the equilibrium value of node $x$ is different from its previous value ($A(x)$ is the probability that node $x$ switches). Figure 20.5 illustrates the signal probability and activity of two different signals.

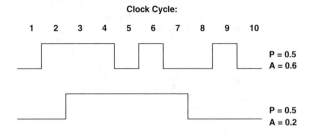

**FIGURE 20.5**  Signal probability and activity.

## Signal Probability Calculation

In calculating the signal probability, we first need to determine if the input signals (random variables) are independent. If two signals are correlated, they may never be in logic high together, or they may never be switching at the same time. Due to the complexities of the signals flow, it is not easy to determine if two signals are independent. The primary inputs may be correlated due to the feedback loop. The internal nodes of the circuit may be correlated due to the reconvergent fanouts, even if the primary inputs are assumed to be independent. The reconvergent fanouts occur when the output of a node splits into two or more signals that eventually recombine as inputs to certain nodes downstream. The exact calculation of the signal probability has been shown to be *NP-hard* [3].

The probabilistic method in estimating power consumption uses *signal probability* measure to accurately estimate *signal activity*. Therefore, it is important to accurately calculate signal probability as the accuracy of subsequent steps in computing activity depends on how accurate the signal probability calculation is. In implementing the probabilistic method, we adopted the general algorithm proposed in [4] and used the data structure similar to [5].

The algorithm used to compute the signal probability is given as follows:

- *Inputs*: Circuit network and signal probabilities of the primary inputs.
- *Output*: Signal probabilities of all nodes in the circuit.
- *Step1*: Initialize the circuit network by assigning a unique variable, which corresponds to the signal probability, to each node in the circuit network.
- *Step 2*: Starting from the primary inputs and proceeding to the primary outputs, compute the *symbolic probability expression* for each node as a function of its inputs expressions.
- *Step 3*: Suppress all exponents in the expression to take the spatial signal correlation into account [4].

### Example
Given $y = ab + ac$. Find signal probability $P(y)$.

$$
\begin{aligned}
P(y) &= P(ab) + P(ac) + P(abac) \\
&= P(a)P(b) + P(a)P(c) - P^2(a)P(b)P(c) \\
&= P(a)P(b) + P(a)P(c) - P(a)P(b)P(c)
\end{aligned}
$$

## Activity Calculation

The formulation to determine an exact expression to calculate *activity* of static combinational circuits has been proposed in [6]. The formulation considers spatio-temporal correlations into account and is adopted in our method. If a clock cycle is selected at random, then the probability of having a transition at the leading edge of this clock cycle at node $y$ is $A(y)/f$, where $A(y)$ is the number of transition per second at node $y$, and $f$ is the clock frequency. This normalized probability value, $A(y)/f$, is denoted as $a(y)$. The exact calculation of the *activity* uses the concept of *Boolean difference*. In the following sections, the Boolean difference is first introduced before applying it in the exact calculation of the activity of a node.

### Boolean Difference
The Boolean difference of $y$ with respect to $x$ is defined as follows:

$$
\frac{\partial y}{\partial x} = y|_{x=1} \oplus y|_{x=0}
$$

The Boolean difference can be generalized to $n$ variables as follows:

$$
\frac{\partial^n}{\partial x_1 \ldots \partial x_n} y|_{b_1 \ldots b_n} = y|_{(x_1=b_1)\ldots x=b_n} \oplus y|_{(x_1=b_{\bar{1}})\ldots x_i=b_{\bar{n}}}
$$

where $n$ is a positive integer, $b_n$ is either logic high or low, and $x_n$ are the distinct mutually independent primary inputs of node $y$.

## Activity Calculation Using Boolean Difference

Activity $a(y)$ at node $y$ in a circuit is given by [1]

$$a(y) = \sum_{i=1}^{n} P\left(\frac{\partial y}{\partial x_i}\right) \cdot a(x_i) \tag{20.3}$$

where $a(x_i)$ represents switching activity at input $x_i$, while $P(\partial y/\partial x_i)$ is the probability of sensitizing input $x_i$ to output $y$.

Equation (20.3) does not take simultaneous switching of the inputs into account. To consider the simultaneous switching, the following modifications have to be made:

- $P(\partial y/\partial x_i)$ is modified to $P(\partial y/\partial x_i | x_i^{\perp})$, where $x_i^{\perp}$ denotes that input $x_i$ is switching.
- $a(x_i)$ is modified to $\{a(x_i) \prod_{j \neq i, 1 \leq j \leq n} (1 - a(x_j))\}$

### Example

For a Boolean expression $y$ with three primary inputs $x_1$, $x_2$, $x_3$, the activity $a(y)$ is given by the sum of three cases, namely,

- when only one input is switching:

$$\sum_{i=1}^{3} P\left(\frac{\partial y}{\partial x_i}\Big|_{x_i^{\perp}}\right)\left(a(x_i) \prod_{j \neq 1, 1 \leq j \leq n} (1 - a(x_j))\right)$$

- when two inputs are switching:

$$\frac{1}{2}\left(\sum_{1 \leq i < j \leq 3}\left(P\left(\frac{\partial^2}{\partial x_i \partial x_j} y\Big|_{00}\Big|_{x_i^{\perp} x_j^{\perp}}\right) + P\left(\frac{\partial^2}{\partial x_i \partial x_j} y\Big|_{01}\Big|_{x_i^{\perp} x_j^{\perp}}\right)\right)\left(a(x_i)a(x_j) \prod_{k \in \{1,2,3\}-\{i,j\}} (1 - a(x_k))\right)\right)$$

- and when all three inputs are switching simultaneously:

$$\frac{1}{2^2}\left(P\left(\frac{\partial^3}{\partial x_1 \partial x_2 \partial x_3} y\Big|_{000}\Big|_{x_1^{\perp} x_2^{\perp} x_3^{\perp}}\right) + P\left(\frac{\partial^3}{\partial x_1 \partial x_2 \partial x_3} y\Big|_{001}\Big|_{x_1^{\perp} x_2^{\perp} x_3^{\perp}}\right) + P\left(\frac{\partial^3}{\partial x_1 \partial x_2 \partial x_3} y\Big|_{010}\Big|_{x_1^{\perp} x_2^{\perp} x_3^{\perp}}\right)\right.$$
$$\left. + P\left(\frac{\partial^3}{\partial x_1 \partial x_2 \partial x_3} y\Big|_{011}\Big|_{x_1^{\perp} x_2^{\perp} x_3^{\perp}}\right)\right)\left(\prod_{k=1}^{3} a(x_k)\right)$$

The activity calculation using Boolean difference can now be readily extended to the general case of $n$ inputs.

## Activity Calculation Using Signal Probability

The calculation of the activity of a node using the Boolean difference is computationally intensive. The complexity and computation time grow exponentially with the number of inputs. Hence, an alternative, and more efficient method to compute the activity using signal probability can be used instead.

Let $P(y(t))$ be the signal probability at time $t$. The probability of a given node $y$ is not switching at time $t$ is $P(y(t - T)y(t)) = P(y(t)) - \frac{1}{2}a(y) = P(y) - \frac{1}{2}a(y)$. Hence, $a(y) = 2(P(y) - P(y(t - T)y(t)))$. To calculate the activity $a(y)$ from the pre-computed signal probability $P(y)$, we must first calculate $P(y(t - T)y(t))$.

**Example**

Given $y = x_1 + x_2$. Find $P(y(t - T)y(t))$ and $a(y)$.

$$P(y) = P(x_1) + \overline{P(x_1)}P(x_2) \quad \text{and} \quad \overline{P(x_1)} = P(\bar{x}_1) = 1 - P(x_1)$$

$P(y(t - T)y(t))$ is given by the *product* of *two* terms, namely

$$P(x_1(t - T)) + \overline{P(x_1(t - T))}P(x_2(t - T)) \quad \text{and} \quad P(x_1(t)) + \overline{P(x_1(t))}P(x_2(t))$$

Expanding the product of these two terms, we obtain the following four terms:

$$P(x_1(t - T))P(x_1(t)) + P(x_1(t - T))\overline{P(x_1(t))}P(x_2(t)) + \overline{P(x_1(t - T))}P(x_1(t))P(x_2(t - T))$$

$$+ P\overline{(x_1(t - T))P(x_1(t))}P(x_2(t - T))P(x_2(t))$$

$$= P(x_1(t - T)x_1(t)) + P(x_1(t - T)\overline{x_1(t)})P(x_2(t)) + P(\overline{x_1(t - T)}x_1(t))P(x_2(t - T))$$

$$+ P(\overline{x_1(t - T)x_1(t)})P(x_2(t - T)x_2(t))$$

$$= P(x_1) - \frac{1}{2}a(x_1) + \frac{1}{2}a(x_1)P(x_2) + \frac{1}{2}a(x_1)P(x_2) + \left(1 - P(x_1) - \frac{1}{2}a(x_1)\right)\left(P(x_2) - \frac{1}{2}a(x_2)\right)$$

After rearranging the above equation, we obtain

$$a(y) = (1 - P(x_1))a(x_2) + (1 - P(x_2))a(x_1) - \frac{1}{2}a(x_1)a(x_2).$$

## Partitioning Algorithm

Accurate calculation of the *symbolic probability* is important to subsequent computation of the *activity* at internal node of a circuit; however, not only the *exact* calculation of the symbolic probability is *NP-hard*, but also the size of symbolic probability expression grows exponentially with the number of the inputs. Thus, a technique to partition the circuit network by utilizing the circuit topology information is used [6]. Using this partitioning scheme, the size of the probability expression is limited as each node in the circuit network is now only dependent upon its *minimum set of topologically independent inputs (MSTII)*. MSTII is a set of independent inputs (or internal nodes) that *logically* determines the logic function of a node. This partition scheme can trade off accuracy with computation speed and data storage size.

Figure 20.6 shows the MSTII of a logic gate Z. The MSTII of $y_1$, $x_4$, $w$, and $x_7$ are used instead of $x_1$, $x_2, \ldots, x_7$. Hence, we only deal with four inputs instead of the original seven.

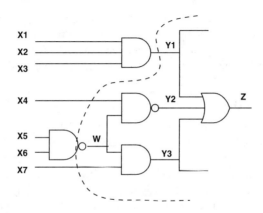

**FIGURE 20.6**  MSTII of a logic gate.

## Power Estimation Considering the Internal Nodes

In the previous analysis, we only considered the activity at the output of a logic gate; however, complex CMOS logic gates have internal nodes that are associated with capacitances that may charge/discharge based on the inputs applied to the logic gate. The power consumption due to the internal nodes in the logic gates may play an important role in determining the total power consumption for a certain sequence of input vectors. In order to improve the accuracy of the probabilistic, let us include the power consumed by the internal nodes of logic gates.

The algorithm to compute the power consumption due to the internal node is given as follows [7]:

- *Inputs*: Functional expression of the node in terms of its inputs, input signal probabilities, and activities.
- *Output*: Normalized power estimation measure, $\phi$ (described later in the section on "Normalized Power Measure").
- *Step 1*: Factorize the functional expression.
- *Step 2*: Determine the position of each internal node.
- *Step 3*: Compute the probability of the conducting path: from the internal node $i$ to $V_{supply}$ $(P^i_{V_{supply}})$, and to GND $(P^i_{V_{gnd}})$.
- *Step 4*: Compute the activity obtained from min $(P^i_{V_{supply}})(P^i_{V_{gnd}})$.
- *Step 5*: Compute the normalized power measure.

### Factorization of the Functional Expression

For a given functional expression of a node in term of its inputs, we need to factorize and simplify the expression to obtain a compact and optimal expression, and thus an optimal implementation of the logic gate. The functional expression is used to determine the position of the internal nodes of the logic gate. The output node of the logic gate will not be affected whether the factorized expression is used or not. However, the number of internal nodes of the logic gate depends on the functional expression used.

### Example
Given $X = \overline{AB}F + \overline{AB}E + \overline{DF} + \overline{CF} + \overline{DE} + \overline{CE}$.

If the expression is directly implemented as static CMOS complex gate, then a total of 13 internal nodes exist in the logic gate. Some of these internal nodes are redundant and can be eliminated if the factorized expression is used instead. The factorized expression is $X = (\overline{AB} + \overline{C} + \overline{D})(\overline{E} + \overline{F})$, and has only five internal nodes. Figure 20.7 shows the implementation of both the factorized and unfactorized expressions.

### The Position of the Internal Nodes

The position of the internal nodes can be determined while implementing the given functional expression of a node in static CMOS. Internal nodes exist whenever there is an AND or an OR function exist as both functions have at least two inputs. Inside an AND (OR) function, the internal nodes are found in the PUN (PDN). In both functions, the number of the inputs to the logic gate determines the number of the internal nodes. If there are $n$ inputs to the logic gate, then $(n-1)$ internal nodes must exist inside the logic gate. In implementing the functional expressions, the complemented input signals are assumed to be available.

### The Conducting Paths to the Supply Rails

After determining the position of the internal nodes inside the logic gate, the probabilities of the conducting paths from each internal node to the supply rails (both to $V_{supply}$ and GND) are then computed. The probability of the conducting path from an internal node to $V_{supply}$(GND) signifies the probability of charging (discharging) the capacitance in that internal node. The probability of charging and discharging the internal node capacitances is then used to calculate the *activity* of the internal nodes. The *signal probability* of each of the internal nodes is calculated using the algorithm outlined in the previous section, which takes spatio-temporal correlation among signals into account.

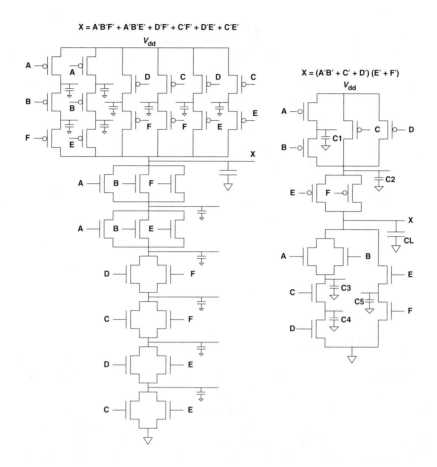

**FIGURE 20.7** Unfactorized and factorized functional expression.

*Example*

Given a 2-input NAND gate $Y = \overline{AB}$ as shown in Fig. 20.8. The probabilities of the conducting paths from the internal node to $V_{\text{supply}}$ and to GND are $P(\overline{AB})$ and $P(B)$, respectively.

## Internal Nodes Activity Computation

The activities of each internal node are calculated using the probabilities of the conducting paths from the internal nodes to the supply rails. The minimum of the two probabilities is used to compute the activity of the internal node because no effective charging/discharging will occur once this minimum threshold value is reached. For example, if within a period of 10 clock cycles, the probability of charging process is 0.5 (5 out of 10 clock cycles are conducting), and the probability of discharging process is 0.3, then the charging and discharging processes can only take place for 3 out of 10 clock cycles. The extra 2 charging cycles will have no effect on the outcome, as the internal node capacitance remains charged. Hence, only a previously charged (discharged) capacitance can be discharged (charged).

## Normalized Power Measure

The normalized power measure is computed from the activity of each of the internal nodes. At the logic gate output, the total normalized power measure is computed by $\phi = \Sigma_i fanout \times a(i)$ where $fanout_i$ is the number of gate being driven by the output node $i$ ($C_{\text{load-}i}$ is assumed to be proportional to $fanout_i$). At the internal nodes, the normalized power measure is computed by $\phi_{\text{internal}} = \Sigma_i C_{\text{int}_i} \times a_{\text{internal}}(i)$. The results for the power estimation using the probabilistic technique will be given in section 20.5.

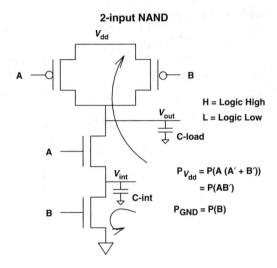

**FIGURE 20.8**   Charging and discharging paths of the internal node.

## 20.4   Statistical Technique

Statistical technique for estimating power consumption is a simulation-based approach. To improve the accuracy of this method, we need to run all possible sets of input combinations exhaustively for an indefinitely long period of time. Thus, this method is prohibitively expensive and impractical for very large circuits. The main advantage of this technique is that the existing simulators can be used readily. Furthermore, issues such as glitch generation and propagation, spatio-temporal correlations among signals are all automatically taken into account. The generality of this technique still attracts much interest, but Monte Carlo-based approaches [8,20] can be used to determine the number of simulation runs for a given error that can be tolerated.

We adopted a statistical sampling technique using Monte Carlo approach as proposed in [8], and included the internal node analysis to further improve the accuracy. To estimate the power consumption in the circuit, the statistical technique first generates random input vectors that conform to the user-specified signal probability and activity. The circuit is then simulated using the randomly generated input vectors. For each simulation run in time period $T$, the cumulative power dissipation is monitored by counting the number of transitions of each node (*sample*) in the circuit. The simulation run is then repeated $N$ times until the monitored power dissipation converges to the user-specified error and confidence levels. The average number of transitions (*sample mean*), $\bar{n}$, at each node is then obtained. The activity of each node is computed by $\bar{n}/\bar{T}$.

Because the signal probability and activity of the primary inputs are only needed, this technique is essentially *weakly pattern-dependent*. Monte Carlo method has an attractive property that it is *dimension independent*, meaning that the number of simulation runs needed does not depend on the circuit size. A good random input generator and an efficient stopping criterion are important for the Monte Carlo method. These issues are presented in the following sections.

### Random Input Generator

The input vector is considered to be a Markov process [9], meaning that the present input waveform only depends on the value of the waveform in the prior immediate clock cycle, and not on the values of the other previous clock cycles. The implementation is based on Markov process, so the length of time between successive transitions is a random variable with an *exponential* distribution [10]. Another implication of Markov process is that the pulse width distribution of the input waveform is a *geometric* distribution. The conditional probabilities of the input waveforms switching are then given as: $P(0|1) = T/\mu_1$ and $P(1|0) = T/\mu_0$ where $T$ is the clock pulse period, $\mu_1$ is the mean of high pulse width $(P(x)/a(x))$, and $\mu_0$ is the mean of low pulse width $(2[1 - P(x)]/a(x))$. Also, $P(0|0) = 1 - P(1|0)$ and $P(1|1) = 1 - P(0|1)$. The random number generator uses the above criteria to decide whether the input signals switch or not.

## Stopping Criteria

The number of simulation runs needed to converge the result determines the speed of the statistical technique. Hence, efficient stopping criteria are needed. The decision is made based on the mean and standard deviation of the monitored power consumption at the end of every simulation run.

For large sample $N$, the sample mean, $\bar{n}$ approaches $\eta$, the true average number of transitions in $T$, and the sample standard deviation, $s$, also approaches $\sigma$, the true standard deviation [10]. According to the *Central Limit Theorem*, $\bar{n}$ has the mean $\eta$ with the distribution approaching *normal* distribution for large $N(N \geq 30)$. It follows that for $(1 - \alpha)$ *confidence* level, $-z_{\alpha/2} \cdot \sigma \leq \eta - \bar{n} \leq z_{\alpha/2} \cdot \sigma$, where $z_{\alpha/2}$ is the point where the area to its right under the standard normal distribution curve is equal to $\alpha/2$.

Since $\sigma \approx s/\sqrt{N}$ for large $N$, and with confidence $(1 - \alpha)$, then

$$\frac{|\eta - \bar{n}|}{\bar{n}} \leq \frac{s \cdot z_{\alpha/2}}{\bar{n}\sqrt{N}} \tag{20.4}$$

If $\varepsilon_1$ is a small positive number and the number of sample is

$$N \geq \left(\frac{s \cdot z_{\alpha/2}}{\bar{n}\varepsilon_1}\right)^2 \tag{20.5}$$

then $\varepsilon_1$ sets the upper bound for Eq. (20.4):

$$\frac{|\eta - \bar{n}|}{\bar{n}} \leq \frac{s \cdot z_{\alpha/2}}{\bar{n}\sqrt{N}} \leq \varepsilon_1 \tag{20.6}$$

Equation (20.6) can also be expressed as the deviation percentage from the population mean $\eta$:

$$\frac{|\eta - \bar{n}|}{\bar{n}} \leq \varepsilon_1 \quad \text{translates into} \quad \frac{|\bar{n} - \eta|}{\eta} \leq \frac{\varepsilon_1}{1 - \varepsilon_1} = \varepsilon \tag{20.7}$$

where $\varepsilon$ is the user-specified percentage error tolerance.

Equation (20.5) thus provides the stopping criterion for the percentage error tolerance in Eq. (20.7) for $(1 - \alpha)$ confidence. The problem with this stopping criterion is that for small $\bar{n}$, a large number of samples $N$ are required, as shown in Eq. (20.5), so it becomes too expensive to guarantee percentage error accuracy in this case. The nodes with small $\bar{n}$ (or $\bar{n} < \eta_{min}$, where $\eta_{min}$ is the user-specified minimum threshold value) are called *low-activity* nodes. Large value of $N$ means that these low-activity nodes will take a much longer time to converge. Yet, these low-density nodes have the least effect on circuit power and reliability. To improve the convergence time without any significant effect in the overall result, an *absolute error bound*, $\eta_{min} \cdot \varepsilon_1$, is used instead of the *percentage error bound*, $\varepsilon$[9]. The absolute error bounds for low-density nodes are always *less than* the absolute error bounds for high-activity nodes.

Therefore, when dealing with low-activity nodes, instead of using Eq. (20.5), the following stopping criterion is used

$$N \geq \left( \frac{s \cdot z_{\alpha/2}}{\eta_{\min} \varepsilon_1} \right)^2 \tag{20.8}$$

For $(1 - \alpha)$ confidence level, the accuracy for the low-density nodes is given by $|\eta - \bar{n}| \leq s z_{\alpha/2} / \sqrt{N} \leq \eta_{\min} \varepsilon_1$.

During the simulation run, after $N$ exceeds 30, Eq. (20.5) is used as a stopping criterion as long as $\bar{n} \geq \eta_{\min}$. Otherwise, Eq. (20.8) is used instead.

## Power Estimation due to the Internal Nodes

We included the capability of estimating internal nodes power dissipation in the Monte Carlo technique. The algorithm to compute the internal nodes power is as follows [7]:

- *Inputs*: Functional expression of the node in terms of its inputs, and user-specified accuracy parameters
- *Output*: Normalized power measure $\phi$
- *Step 1*: Factorize the functional expression
- *Step 2*: Generate a graph to represent the expression
- *Step 3*: Simulate the circuit with random input
- *Step 4*: Update conducting path (event-driven process)
- *Step 5*: Sum all charges in the discharging path
- *Step 6*: Accumulate all the sum

The given functional expression of a node is expressed in terms of its inputs. The factorization process, the same as in the probabilistic technique, is to ensure that the expression is compact and does not contain any redundant items.

### Graph Generation

A graph to represent the factorized expression is generated to be used as the data structure in estimating power dissipation. The nodes of the graph represent all the nodes in the logic gate, such as supply rails, output node, and all the internal nodes inside the logic gate. The edges of the graph represent the inputs to the logic gate between the nodes. Information of the internal nodes capacitances and voltages are stored in nodes structure of the graph. Once the graph is generated, the circuit is simulated with randomly generated input vectors conforming to the user-specified input signal probability and activity.

Note that in the case of the probabilistic method, a graph is not used, as there is no need for such data structure. In the probabilistic method, the signal probability and activity of each node are calculated as we traverse level by level from primary inputs of the circuit network to the outputs. The calculated values are then stored in the data structure within the node itself. In the statistical technique, however, the graph is needed to store the simulation run results. An example of a generated graph for a given factorized functional expression $X = (\overline{AB} + \overline{C} + \overline{D})(\overline{E} + \overline{F})$ is shown in Fig. 20.9.

### Updating Conducting Paths

The path in the graph needs to be updated whenever a change in the input signals occurs. The change in the input signals is defined as an *event*. To improve the computation speed, the updating process of the path is being done only when an event occurs. Hence, the path updating process is said to be an *event-driven* process.

The path in the graph that needs to be updated may change from conducting to nonconducting or vice-versa, depending on the event which occurs. If the path becomes nonconducting, then the nodes at

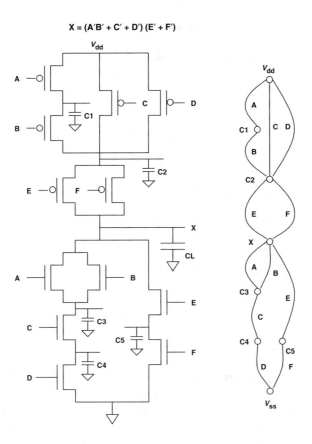

**FIGURE 20.9** A logic gate and its corresponding graph.

both ends of disjointed segments of the path become isolated and assumed to retain their voltage values. On the other hand, if a conducting path joins the disjointed segments, then all the nodes along the conducting paths must be updated to a new equilibrium value. If the conducting path to the $V_{supply}$ ($V_{gnd}$) exists, then all nodes along the path will be charged (discharged).

The algorithm for path updating process is as follows. When input node $i$ switches from OFF to ON:

1. If a conducting path from the internal node to Gnd exists:
   - collect all the node charges along the path
   - set all the node voltages to $V_{low}$ ($V_{low}$ for nodes in NMOS and PMOS are 0 and $V_{thp}$, respectively).
2. If a conducting path to $V_{supply}$ exists:
   - set all the node voltages to $V_{high}$ ($V_{high}$ for nodes in NMOS and PMOS are ($V_{supply} - V_{thn}$) and $V_{supply}$, respectively).

$V_{thp}$ and $V_{thn}$ are PMOS and NMOS threshold voltage, respectively. The internal nodes in PUN among PMOS devices will be fully charged to $V_{supply}$, but will only be discharged to $V_{thp}$. Similarly, the internal nodes in PDN among NMOS devices will be fully discharged to $V_{gnd}$, but will only be charged to ($V_{supply} - V_{thn}$). This is because the transistors will be cut-off when the gate to source voltage is less than the threshold voltage.

Along the discharging path (conducting path to the GND), all the charges in the internal nodes are added together. The sum of the charges is accumulated over all simulation runs. The normalized power measure is directly derived from this accumulated sum of charges as $\phi_{internal} = Q_{total} \cdot V_{supply}/$run-time.

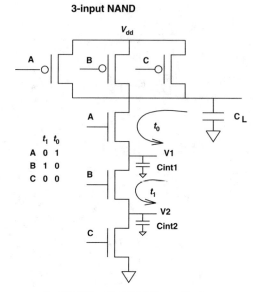

**FIGURE 20.10**    Charge-sharing.

### Charge-Sharing among the Internal Nodes

Charge-sharing among the internal nodes occurs when the conducting path that connects the nodes is not connected to either $V_{supply}$ or GND. The nodes along the path are then isolated from the supply rails, and will not be charged or discharged. These isolated nodes will come to a new equilibrium state, a value between $V_{supply}$ and GND. In the isolated state, the capacitances of the internal nodes are connected in parallel, and share the charges among themselves, thus the term charge-sharing. The new equilibrium voltage among the internal nodes is

$$V = \frac{\sum_{j=1}^{n} (C_j V_j)}{\sum_{j=1}^{n} C_j} \qquad (20.9)$$

where $n$ is the number of isolated nodes, and $V_j$ is the initial voltage across the internal node capacitance $C_j$. An example of the charge-sharing process is illustrated in Fig. 20.10. The event occurs when inputs $A$ and $B$ switch at time $t_1$. The internal nodes are then isolated from $V_{supply}$ and GND. The new equilibrium voltage between the two isolated internal capacitances is calculated to be

$$V = \frac{C_{int\,1} \cdot V_1 + C_{int\,2} \cdot V_2}{C_{int\,1} + C_{int\,2}}$$

## 20.5   Experimental Results

Both the probabilistic and the statistical techniques have been implemented in C within University of California at Berkeley's SIS [17] environment. SIS is an interactive tool for synthesis and optimization of logic circuits. The test circuits used in obtaining the results are the benchmarks presented at ISCAS in 1985 [11]. These circuits are combinational circuits and Table 20.1 shows the number of primary inputs, outputs, nodes, and circuit level of each benchmark circuit.

**TABLE 20.1**   The ISCAS-85 Benchmark Circuits

| Circuit | No. of Inputs | No. of Outputs | No. of Nodes | No. of Levels |
|---------|---------------|----------------|--------------|---------------|
| C1355   | 41            | 32             | 514          | 23            |
| C17     | 5             | 2              | 6            | 3             |
| C1908   | 33            | 25             | 880          | 40            |
| C2670   | 233           | 140            | 1161         | 32            |
| C3540   | 50            | 22             | 1667         | 47            |
| C432    | 36            | 7              | 160          | 17            |
| C499    | 41            | 32             | 202          | 11            |
| C5315   | 178           | 123            | 2290         | 49            |
| C6288   | 32            | 32             | 2416         | 124           |
| C7552   | 207           | 108            | 3466         | 43            |
| C880    | 60            | 26             | 357          | 23            |

**TABLE 20.2**   Results of Probabilistic Technique

| Circuit | CPU Time SPARCstation 5 (seconds) | Internal Nodes Power Measure | Total Power Measure ($\phi$) |
|---------|-----------------------------------|------------------------------|------------------------------|
| C1355   | 9.82                              | 40.9                         | 237.7                        |
| C17     | 0.03                              | 0.51                         | 3.77                         |
| C1908   | 72.92                             | 32.3                         | 343.97                       |
| C2670   | 34.36                             | 55.4                         | 505.7                        |
| C3540   | 86.14                             | 63.1                         | 590.3                        |
| C432    | 29.68                             | 8.92                         | 72.96                        |
| C499    | 12.98                             | 26.6                         | 118.79                       |
| C5315   | 398.74                            | 118.9                        | 1106.3                       |
| C6288   | 1786.44                           | 228.9                        | 1300.1                       |
| C7552   | 709.71                            | 172.3                        | 1516.8                       |
| C880    | 6.58                              | 22.3                         | 162.0                        |

## Results Using Probabilistic Technique

The signal probability and activity for the primary inputs are both specified to be 0.5. The load capacitance at the output nodes is specified to a unit capacitance and the internal node capacitances are specified to one-half unit capacitance. The maximum number of inputs allowed for each partition level is 10 inputs. The simulations are run on SPARCstation 5, and the results are shown in Table 20.2. Power dissipation due to the internal node ranges from 9.38% to 22.4% of the overall power consumption. Hence, the internal nodes power is a significant portion of the total power consumption. The result is given in term of power measure $\phi$ (switching activity $\times$ fanouts).

## Results Using Statistical Technique

Similar to the probabilistic technique, the signal probability and activity for the primary inputs are specified to be 0.5. The sample period of each simulation run is specified to be 100 unit clock cycles. The relative error is specified to be 30%, and the minimum threshold is specified to be 3%. In the simulation, 5 V power supply is used. The threshold voltages for both PMOS and NMOS devices are specified to be 1 V. The results are tabulated in Table 20.3.

The experiment shows that the percentage of internal nodes power consumption to overall power consumption ranges from 7.75% to 18.59%. The result of the same simulation with the charge-sharing option being switched off is shown in Table 20.4.

The computation time is faster by up to 10% for certain cases when the simulation is run with the charge-sharing option switched off. The percentage of internal power to overall power only changes by 0.1% to 0.2% when charge sharing is not taken into consideration, so neglecting the charge-sharing effect among the internal node capacitances will not affect the overall result significantly.

**TABLE 20.3**    Results of Statistical Technique with Charge-Sharing

| Circuit | CPU Time SPARCstation 5 (seconds) | Internal Nodes Power Measure | Total Power Measure ($\phi$) |
|---|---|---|---|
| C1355 | 194.13 | 33.0 | 228.7 |
| C17 | 3.28 | 0.38 | 3.67 |
| C1908 | 339.37 | 26.1 | 337.3 |
| C2670 | 453.76 | 49.9 | 497.0 |
| C3540 | 599.14 | 66.7 | 601.6 |
| C432 | 79.73 | 8.72 | 73.3 |
| C499 | 120.24 | 20.9 | 112.5 |
| C5315 | 1096.06 | 117.4 | 1113.0 |
| C6288 | 1102.43 | 183.1 | 1188.0 |
| C7552 | 1511.58 | 148.5 | 1497.2 |
| C880 | 161.87 | 18.1 | 157.6 |

**TABLE 20.4**    Results of Statistical Technique without Charge-Sharing

| Circuit | CPU Time SPARCstation 5 (seconds) | Internal Nodes Power Measure | Total Power Measure ($\phi$) |
|---|---|---|---|
| C1355 | 190.59 | 32.8 | 228.6 |
| C17 | 2.70 | 0.38 | 3.67 |
| C1908 | 328.75 | 25.5 | 336.6 |
| C2670 | 441.26 | 49.46 | 496.6 |
| C3540 | 590.87 | 66.46 | 601.3 |
| C432 | 71.64 | 8.64 | 73.3 |
| C499 | 117.42 | 8.64 | 112.4 |
| C5315 | 1052.83 | 115.65 | 1111.3 |
| C6288 | 1068.54 | 183.122 | 1188.1 |
| C7552 | 1485.76 | 147.18 | 1495.9 |
| C880 | 153.89 | 17.98 | 157.5 |

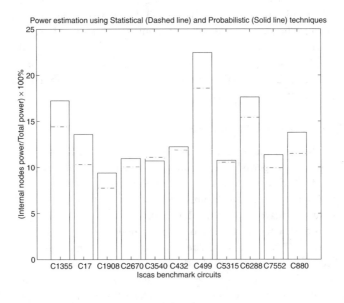

**FIGURE 20.11**    Percentage of total power due to internal nodes power.

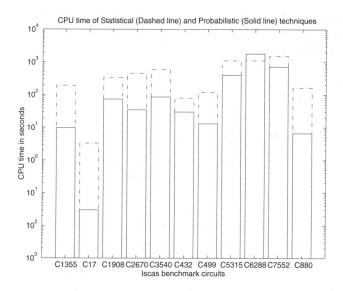

**FIGURE 20.12** Probabilistic and statistical run-time.

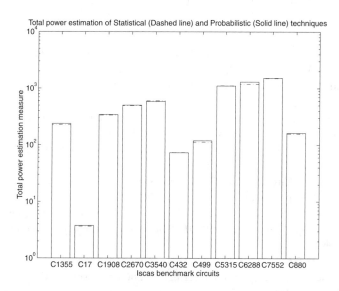

**FIGURE 20.13** Probabilistic and statistical total power consumption.

## Comparing Probabilistic with Statistical Results

Figure 20.11 illustrates the percentage total power consumption due to internal nodes as obtained from both probabilistic and statistical techniques [15]. A dashed line and a solid line for statistical and probabilistic techniques represent the results, respectively. On an average, the result from the statistical technique is slightly lower than the result obtained from the probabilistic approach. The discrepancy arises from various different sets of simplifying assumptions used in both techniques. Nevertheless, both results track one another closely.

Figure 20.12 illustrates the run time of the probabilistic and statistical techniques [15]. The vertical axis is in log scale. The probabilistic technique, as expected, runs one or two magnitude order faster than the statistical technique. The statistical technique needs a number of simulation runs before the result converges to the specified parameters, whereas the probabilistic technique only needs one run to obtain the result. This accounts for the difference in the computational time.

Figure 20.13 shows the total power consumption measure of both probabilistic and statistical techniques [15]. The results of both methods follow one another very closely. The vertical axis is plotted in log scale. The dashed line represents the result for statistical technique and the solid line represents the result for probabilistic technique.

## 20.6   Summary and Conclusion

In this chapter, estimation of activity and thus power consumption are presented. Probabilistic and statistical techniques, which take spatio-temporal correlations into account, are used. The probabilistic method uses a zero-delay model. If a nonzero model is used instead, the accuracy of the probabilistic method improves, but the underlying method and concept outlined for simplified zero-delay model still applies, i.e., the probability of some inputs switching simultaneously will change and thus causes a change in the calculated switching activity. The statistical method uses the inherent gate delay during the simulation run. Both probabilistic and statistical techniques include the effect of power consumption due to the internal nodes, which improves the accuracy of the methods by 7.75–22.4%. The power estimation methods allow circuit designers to analyze and optimize the designs for power consumption early in the design cycle. This is a critical requirement for today's demanding power-sensitive applications, such as portable computing and communication systems.

## References

1. F. Najm, "A survey of power estimation techniques in VLSI circuits," *IEEE Transactions on VLSI Systems*, pp. 446–455, December 1994.
2. F. Najm, "Feedback, correlation, and delay concerns in the power estimation of VLSI circuits," *ACM/IEEE 32nd Design Automation Conference*, pp. 612–617, 1995.
3. F. Najm, "Transition density, a new measure of activity in digital circuits," *IEEE Transactions on Computer-Aided Design*, vol. 12, no. 2, pp. 310–323, February 1993.
4. K.P. Parker and E.J. McCluskey, "Probabilistic treatment of general combinatorial networks," *IEEE Transactions on Computers*, vol. C-24, pp. 668–670, June 1975.
5. K. Roy and S. Prasad, "Circuit activity based logic synthesis for low power reliable operations," *IEEE Transactions on VLSI Systems*, pp. 503–513, December 1993.
6. T-L. Chou, K. Roy, and S. Prasad, "Estimation of circuit activity considering signal correlation and simultaneous switching," *Proceedings of the IEEE International Conference on Computer Aided Design*, pp. 300–303, 1994.
7. H. Soeleman, *Power Estimation of Static CMOS Combinational Digital Logic Circuit*, Master's Thesis, School of Electrical and Computer Engineering, Purdue University, 1996.
8. R. Burch, F. Najm, P. Yang, and T. Trick, "A Monte Carlo approach for power estimation," *IEEE Transactions on VLSI Systems*, vol. 1, no. 1, pp. 63–71, March 1993.
9. M. Xakellis and F. Najm, "Statistical estimation of the switching activity in digital circuits," *31st ACM/IEEE Design Automation Conference*, pp. 728–733, San Diego, CA, 1994.
10. A. Papoulis, *Probability, Random Variables, and Stochastic Processes*, 3rd edition, McGraw-Hill, New York, 1991.
11. F. Brglez and H. Fujiwara, "A neutral netlist of 10 combinational benchmark circuits and a target translator in Fortran," *IEEE International Symposium on Circuits and Systems*, pp. 695–698, June 1985.
12. Z. Chen and K. Roy, "A power macromodeling technique based on power sensitivity," *ACM/IEEE Design Automation Conference*, pp. 678–683, June 1998.
13. Z. Chen, M. Johnson, L. Wei, and K. Roy, "Estimation of standby leakage power in CMOS circuits considering accurate modeling of transistor stacks," *International Symposium on Low Power Electronics and Design*, pp. 239–244, 1998.

14. VLSI Microprocessors: A Guide to High-Performance Microprocessor Resources. http://www. micro-processor.sscc.ru/.

15. H. Soeleman, K. Roy, and T. Chou, "Estimating circuit activity in combinational CMOS digital circuits," *IEEE Design & Test of Computers,* pp. 112–119, April–June 2000.

16. N. Weste and K. Eshraghian, *Principles of CMOS VLSI Design, A systems Perspective,* 2nd edition, Addison-Wesley, Reading, MA.

17. http://www-cad.eecs.berkeley.edu/Software/sis.html.

18. M. Pedram, "Advanced power estimation techniques," in *Low Power Design in Deep Submicron Technology,* Edited by J. Mermet and W. Nebel. Kluwer Academic Publishers, 1997.

19. M. Pedram, "Power simulation and estimation in VLSI circuits," in *The VLSI Handbook,* Edited by W.-K. Chen. CRC Press, Boca Raton, FL, 1999.

20. C.-S. Ding, C.-T. Hsieh, and M. Pedram, "Improving efficiency of the Monte Carlo power estimation," *IEEE Trans. on VLSI Systems,* vol. 8, no. 5, pp. 584–593, October 2000.

21. C.-S. Ding, C.-Y. Tsui, and M. Pedram, "Gate-level power estimation using tagged probabilistic simulation," *IEEE Trans. on Computer Aided Design,* vol. 17, no. 11, pp. 1099–1107, Nov. 1998.

# 21

# Clock-Powered CMOS for Energy-Efficient Computing

Nestoras Tzartzanis
*Fujitsu Laboratories of America*

William Athas
*Apple Computer Inc.*

## 21.1 Introduction

Power dissipation is one of the most important design considerations for portable systems as well as desktop and server computers. For portable systems, long battery life is a necessity. There is only a fixed amount of energy stored in the battery; the lower the system dissipation, the longer the battery life. For desktop and server computers, cost is of utmost importance. Heat generation is proportional to power dissipation. Systems with high power dissipation require an expensive cooling system to remove the heat. CMOS is the technology used for implementing the vast majority of computing systems. In CMOS systems, dynamic power is the dominant dissipation factor, which is consumed for switching circuit nodes between 0 V and a voltage $V$ from a dc supply source. Dynamic power dissipation is generally denoted by $fCV^2$, where $f$ is the operating frequency and $C$ is the effective switching capacitance per cycle. As CMOS technology advances, both the operating frequency $f$ and the switching capacitance $C$ increase resulting in increasingly higher power dissipation. The typical approach to reduce power dissipation is to lower the supply voltage $V$ [1]. Despite the quadratic dependence of power to the voltage, the reduction of the voltage is not sufficient to surpass the increase of the frequency and capacitance [2].

Adiabatic charging [3] is an alternative approach to reduce energy dissipation below the $CV^2$ barrier. The basic idea of adiabatic charging is to employ an ac (i.e., time-varying) source to gradually charge and discharge circuit nodes. Examples of ac sources that can be used for adiabatic charging include a voltage-ramp source, a sinusoidal source, or a constant-current source. In time-varying supplies, energy dissipation is controlled by varying the charging time. For instance, if a capacitance $C$ is charged from

0 V to a voltage $V$ in time $T$ through a resistance $R$ from a voltage-ramp source, the energy dissipated in the resistance, $E_{vrs}$, is [4,5]:

$$E_{vrs} = \left(\frac{RC}{T} - \left(\frac{RC}{T}\right)^2 + \left(\frac{RC}{T}\right)^2 e^{-\frac{T}{RC}}\right) CV^2 \tag{21.1}$$

For $T \to 0$, the voltage-ramp source becomes equivalent to a dc source. Indeed, for $T \to 0$ Eq. (21.1) reduces to:

$$E_{dcs} = \frac{1}{2}CV^2 \tag{21.2}$$

which denotes the energy required to charge a capacitance $C$ from a dc source of voltage $V$. For $T \gg RC$, Eq. (21.1) can be approximated by [6,7]:

$$E_{ccs} = \left(\frac{RC}{T}\right)CV^2 \tag{21.3}$$

Equation (21.3) gives the energy dissipated in the resistance $R$ if a constant-current source is used to charge the capacitance $C$ to voltage $V$ in time $T$. It can be proved [8] that constant-current charging results in minimum energy dissipation for a given charging time $T$. Constant-current charging represents the ideal case. For practical purposes, it can be approximated with a sinusoidal source. In this case, although the energy dissipation increases by a constant shape factor [3], the inverse relationship between energy dissipation and charging time still holds.

The implementation of viable CMOS energy-recovery systems based on adiabatic charging has not been a trivial task. First, adiabatic charging is associated with some circuit overhead, which potentially cancels out the energy savings from adiabatic charging. Second, a key factor to implement an energy-recovery system is the efficiency of the time-varying voltage source. Proposals for exploiting adiabatic charging range from extreme reversible logic systems that theoretically can achieve asymptotically zero energy dissipation [3,9] to more practical partial adiabatic approaches [10–16]. The former requires the most overhead, both at the logic level and at the supply source level. The latter results in energy losses asymptotic to $CV_{th}^2$ or $CVV_{th}$ depending on the specific approach, where $V_{th}$ is the FET threshold voltage. Their overhead is mostly at the logic level. Some of them can operate from a single time-varying supply source [15,16].

In this chapter, we focus on clock-powered logic, which is a systematic approach for designing overall energy-efficient CMOS VLSI systems that use adiabatic charging and energy recovery. The motivation behind clock-powered logic is that the distribution of circuit nodes, excluding $V_{dd}$ and GND, for many VLSI chips can be relatively identified as either large capacitance or small capacitance. Clock-powered logic is a node-selective adiabatic approach, in which energy recovery through adiabatic charging is applied to only those nodes that are deemed to be large capacitance. The circuitry overhead for energy recovery and the adiabatic-charging process is amortized by the large capacitive load since energy savings is proportional to the load. Nodes that are deemed small capacitance can be powered as they usually are in CMOS circuits, e.g., precharging, pass-transistors networks, and static pull-up and pull-down networks that draw power from a dc supply.

This article is organized as follows: First, section 21.2 reviews clock-powered logic followed by a presentation of ac supply sources that can be used for adiabatic charging in section 21.3. In section 21.4, an energy-recovery (E-R) latch is presented. The E-R latch is a key circuit used to pass energy from the ac supply source to circuit data nodes and vice versa. Section 21.5 describes in detail how adiabatically-charged nodes interface with logic blocks powered from a dc supply voltage. In section 21.6, the drive part of the E-R latch is compared to conventional drivers for energy versus delay performance through HSPICE simulations. In section 21.7, two generations of clock-powered microprocessors are presented and compared against an equivalent fully dissipative design. Finally, section 21.8 presents the conclusions.

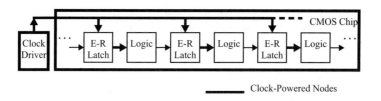

**FIGURE 21.1** Abstract block diagram for a clock-powered microsystem.

## 21.2 Overview of Clock-Powered Logic[1]

The overall organization for a clock-powered microsystem is shown in Fig. 21.1. Adiabatic charging requires a time-varying voltage signal as a source of ac power. Rather than introduce a new power supply, this power source can be naturally supplied in a synchronous digital system through the clock rails. Depending on the implementation, the E-R clock driver may or may not be on the same chip as the clock-powered logic. The clock phases that are generated by the clock driver synchronize the operation of the clock-powered logic as well as power the large-capacitance nodes through special latches, called E-R latches. E-R latches operate in synchrony with the clock phases, so their placement effects the timing and partitioning of logic functions into logic blocks. Placement of the E-R latches is determined not only by the location of the large capacitance nodes, but also by system-level factors such as circuit latencies and overall timing, e.g., pipelining.

Data representation is different between clock-powered and dc-powered signals. Nodes that are dc-powered are logically valid when their voltage levels are sufficiently close to the voltages supplied by the power rails, i.e., $V_{dd}$ and GND. Clock-powered signals are valid only when the clock phase is valid. The presence of a pulse that is coincident with a clock phase defines a logic value of one. The absence of a pulse defines a logic value of zero. When the clock phase is zero, the logical value of the clock-powered signal is undefined.

The co-existence of clock-powered and dc-powered nodes necessitates signal conversion from pulses to levels and vice versa. Levels are converted to pulses in the E-R latches, which receive dc-powered signals as inputs and pass clock pulses to the output. As discussed in detail later in this chapter, depending on the style of the logic blocks, either pulses are implicitly converted to levels, or, special pulse-to-level converters must be introduced between the E-R latches and the logic blocks.

The total average energy dissipation per cycle, $E_{tot}$, of clock-powered microsystems consists of two terms and is given by:

$$E_{tot} \sim \sum_i a_i \frac{R_i C_i}{T_s} C_i V_\varphi^2 + \sum_j a_j C_j V_{dd}^2 \qquad (21.4)$$

The first term models the clock-powered nodes that are adiabatically switched for $T_s \gg R_i C_i$. The second term models the dc-powered nodes that are conventionally switched. In Eq. (21.4), $a_i$ and $a_j$ denote the switching activity for clock- and dc-powered nodes, respectively; $C_i$ and $C_j$ denote the capacitance of clock- and dc-powered nodes, respectively; $R_i$ is the effective resistance of the charge-transfer path between the clock driver and the clock-powered nodes; $T_s$ is the transition time of the clock signal; $V_\varphi$ is the clock voltage swing; and $V_{dd}$ the dc supply voltage.

The benefit of applying clock-powered logic can be readily evaluated from Eq. (21.4). Capacitance information can be extracted from layout, assuming the various parasitic and device capacitances have been accurately characterized. Activity data for the different nodes can be determined for specified input data sets from switch-level and circuit-level simulation. As shown later, in clock-powered microprocessors,

---

[1]Portions in sections 21.2, 21.4, 21.6 and subsection "Static Logic" reprinted, with permission, from [23] © 1999 IEEE.

a small fraction of circuit nodes that are clock powered accounts for most of the power dissipation if they were powered from a dc supply voltage.

Equation (21.4) also defines the absolute maximum degree to which adiabatic charging can be used to reduce dissipation. As the clock transition time approaches infinity, the first term of Eq. (21.4) approaches zero and the dissipation is solely determined by the second term. $R_j$, the effective resistance of the charge-transfer path, is the difficult parameter to quantify. It depends upon the circuit topology of the E-R latch as shown in detail in section 21.4.

## 21.3  Clock Driver

Two known circuit types can be used as clock drivers in a clock powered system: *resonant* [3,17] and *stepwise* [8]. For the purposes of this text, only resonant drivers will be presented due to their superior energy efficiency.

A simple resonant clock driver can be built from an LRC circuit that generates sinusoidal pulses. Such a circuit can be formed with two nFETs ($M_1$ and $M_2$) and an inductor ($L$) (Fig. 21.2). The capacitor $C_\varphi$ represents the clock load. The resistance of the clock line is assumed negligible compared to the on-resistance of $M_1$. Two nonadiabatically-switched control signals drive $M_1$ and $M_2$. The circuit generates sinusoidal pulses if operated as follows. Assume that $\varphi$ is at 0 V, i.e., $C_\varphi$ is discharged and that both $M_1$ and $M_2$ are off. Then $M_1$ is turned on and $M_1$, $L$, and $C_\varphi$ form an LRC circuit that produces a sinusoidal pulse with width $2\pi(LC_\varphi)^{1/2}$ and amplitude approximately $2 \cdot V_{dc}$. $M_1$ should be turned off exactly at the end of the pulse. Then $M_2$ is turned on and fully discharges $\varphi$. Two such circuits can be synchronized to generate two nonoverlapping phases. If $T_s$ is the pulse switching time, it can be shown [3] that the energy for switching $\varphi$ scales as $T_s^{-1/2}$ instead of $T_s^{-1}$ solely because $M_1$ and $M_2$ are controlled by nonadiabatically-switched signals.

The LRC clock driver can be further simplified by eliminating the series nFET $M_1$ and using a single signal to control the pull-down nFET (Fig. 21.3). When the nFET is on, a current is built in the inductor while $\varphi$ is clamped at 0 V. When the nFET is turned off, the current flows to the load $C_\varphi$, generating a sinusoidal pulse. The energy dissipation for switching $C_\varphi$ still scales as $T_s^{-1/2}$ because the nFET is driven by a nonadiabatically-switched signal; however, two such circuits can combine as shown in Fig. 21.4 to form an all-resonant configuration [18] that generates two almost nonoverlapping clock phases (Fig. 21.5). The energy for switching the clock loads in the all-resonant configuration scales as $T_s^{-1}$ since the control signals are adiabatically switched.

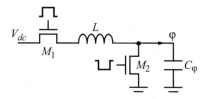

**FIGURE 21.2**   A simple LRC resonant clock driver ([18] © 1996 IEEE).

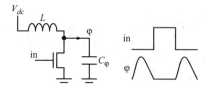

**FIGURE 21.3**   A single-phase resonant clock driver ([28] © 1997 IEEE).

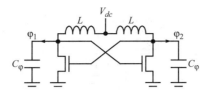

**FIGURE 21.4**    An all-resonant, dual-rail LC oscillator used as a clock driver ([18] © 1996 IEEE).

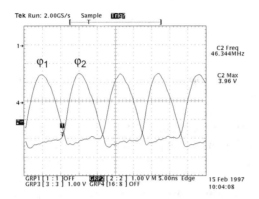

**FIGURE 21.5**    A scope trace of the almost nonoverlapping, two-phase clock waveforms ([28] © 1997 IEEE).

The main advantage of resonant clock drivers is their high energy efficiency since, for all-resonant configurations, the energy dissipation for driving the clock loads can scale as the inverse of the switching time. Nevertheless, these all-resonant configurations pose design challenges when frequency stability is important. Their frequency and, therefore, the system frequency depends on their loads. For the all-resonant two-phase clock driver, two types of potential load imbalances occur: between the two phases and between different cycles for the same phase. First, loads should be approximately evenly distributed between the two phases. Otherwise, inductors with different inductance and/or two different supply voltages should be used so that $\varphi_1$ and $\varphi_2$ have the same width and amplitude. Second, for clock-powered microsystems, clock loads are data dependent. Therefore, the load may vary from cycle to cycle for the same phase, resulting in a data-dependent clock frequency. A simple solution for this problem is to use dual-rail clock-powered signaling, which ensures that half of clock-powered nodes switch per cycle. The drawback of such a clock-powered system is its high switching capacitance. For the purposes of this research, the all-resonant clock driver (Fig. 21.4) has been sufficient and highly energy efficient. Resonant clock drivers can also be designed with transmission lines [17] instead of inductors.

## 21.4   Energy-Recovery Latch

The E-R latch serves two purposes: to latch the input data, and, conditionally on the latched datum, to transfer charge from a clock line to a load capacitance $C_L$ and back again. Consequently, the E-R latch consists of two stages: the *latch* and the *driver* (Fig. 21.6(a)). The latch-stage design is not important for clock-powered logic and can be chosen to meet other system requirements. Suitable latch designs are the 3-transistor dynamic latch consisting of a pass transistor and an inverter, and the doubled N-C$^2$-MOS latch [19]. The driver stage is based on the bootstrapped clocked buffer (CB) [20] implemented in CMOS. The driver choice is discussed later in this section. The E-R latch operates from a two-phase, nonoverlapping clocking scheme (Fig. 21.6(b)): the input is latched on $\varphi_L$ and the output is driven during $\varphi_D$. The two clock phases swing from 0 to voltage $V_\varphi$. A symbol used to denote the clocked buffer part of the E-R latch is shown in Fig. 21.6(c).

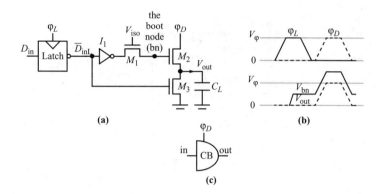

**FIGURE 21.6**   (a) E-R latch, (b) timing diagram when $D_{in}$ is high, and (c) symbol that denotes a clocked buffer pulsed on $\varphi_D$.

Without loss of generality, the latch-stage output $\overline{D}_{inL}$ is assumed in negative polarity. The latch stage and the inverter $I_1$ are powered from a dc supply with voltage $V_{dd}$. The gate of transistor $M_1$ connects to a dc supply with voltage $V_{iso}$. This dc supply dissipates no power since it is connected only to pass-transistor gates. $V_{iso}$ is equal to $V_{dd} + V_{tE}$, where $V_{tE}$ is the nFET effective threshold voltage, so that the boot node $bn$ can be charged close to the maximum possible voltage $V_{dd}$. During $\varphi_L$, $D_{in}$ is stored on the gate capacitance of $M_2$ (the boot node). If $D_{in}$ is low, then the clamp transistor $M_3$ holds the output to ground. If $D_{in}$ is high (Fig. 21.6b), then $bn$ charges to $V_{dd}$ through the isolation transistor $M_1$. When the positive edge of $\varphi_D$ occurs, the voltage of $bn$ bootstraps to well above $V_\varphi$ due to the gate-to-channel capacitance of $M_2$. Then the output charges to $V_\varphi$ from the clock line $\varphi_D$ through the bootstrap transistor $M_2$. Charge returns to the clock line through the same path at the end of $\varphi_D$. The timing sketch of Fig. 21.6(b) indicates $V_{dd}$ (i.e., the voltage that $V_{bn}$ is charged to) as being less than $V_\varphi$. Although this is possible and happens in certain cases, it is not necessary. Voltages $V_{dd}$ and $V_\varphi$ can be decided based on the logic style and the system requirements.

The dc supply $V_{iso}$ is introduced so that the transistor $M_2$ is always actively driven. Phase $\varphi_L$ could be used instead of $V_{iso}$ to drive the transistor $M_1$ [21]. If this were the case, when $\varphi_D$ occurred and $bn$ was at 0 V, the voltage of $bn$ would bootstrap to above 0 V and short-circuit current would flow from $\varphi_D$ to ground through the transistors $M_2$ and $M_3$.

The E-R latch is small in area. The size of $M_1$ is made small to minimize the parasitic capacitance of node $bn$. $M_3$ can also be small since it only clamps the output to ground to avoid coupling to the output when $bn$ is 0 V. It does not discharge the load capacitance. On the other hand, the size of the device $M_2$ is critical. Two criteria are used for sizing $M_2$. First, the ratio of the gate capacitance of $M_2$ to the parasitic capacitance of the node $bn$ should be large enough to allow the voltage of $bn$ to bootstrap to at least $V_\varphi + V_{tE}$. This criterion applies for small capacitance loads and/or slow systems. Second, the transistor $M_2$ should be large enough to meet the system frequency and energy savings specifications. A detailed analytical model for obtaining the on-resistance $R_b$ of the bootstrap transistor has been derived elsewhere [22,23]. This model can be used for sizing these transistors based on the load capacitance $C_L$ and the desired $R_bC_L/T_s$ ratio for a given switching time $T_s$.

The key feature of E-R latches for low power is that they pass clock power. Therefore, an energy-efficient charge-steering device is essential. In addition to a bootstrap transistor, other charge-steering topologies are a nonbootstrapped pass transistor and a transmission gate (T-gate). The pass transistor would require its gate to be overdriven, which would impose constraints on the allowable voltage levels. The pass-transistor gate would be powered from the dc supply $V_{dd}$, and $V_{dd}$ would need to be at least $V_\varphi + V_{tE}$. Otherwise the output would not be fully charged to $V_\varphi$. The T-gate would fully charge the output, but it would require a pFET connected in parallel to the nFET; however, since pFETs carry less current per unit gate area than nFETs, the combined nFET and pFET width of the T-gate would be larger than the width of an equal-resistance bootstrapped transistor. The larger gate capacitance of the charge-steering device translates directly into a higher, nonadiabatic, energy dissipated to control it.

The criterion for the charge-steering device is to minimize the dissipation by maximizing the energy that is recovered. The total dissipation required to operate the charge-steering device has two terms: one for the control charge and one for the controlled charge. For all the above CMOS charge-steering topologies, there exists an inverse dependency between the control energy and the loss in the switch. To reduce the total E-R latch dissipation, the charge-steering topology that experiences the smallest loss for a specified control energy should be selected. It was found [24] that bootstrapping is the most suitable charge-steering implementation in the CMOS technology. Effective bootstrapping makes the switch-transistor gate voltage rise high enough above the highest applied clock voltage to keep the channel conductance high, and consequently the instantaneous loss low, even for the maximum clock voltage. The output swing is thus fully restored to the clock amplitude.

## 21.5  Interfacing Clock-Powered Signals with CMOS Logic

This section shows how the E-R latch can be used in conjunction with the major CMOS logic styles (precharged, pass-transistor, and static logic) for the implementation of complete clock-powered microsystems. All three logic styles need to be modified so that they comply with the clock-powered approach requirements. First, logic should be operated from two nonoverlapping clock phases that are available only in positive polarity. To switch clock-powered nodes adiabatically, the two clock phases must have a switching time longer than the minimum obtainable from the process technology. Clock complements are not available, due to problems related to the efficiency of the clock driver. Second, clock-powered signals are pulses that need to be converted to levels. As we see next, this conversion happens inherently for precharged and pass-transistor logic, while pulse-to-level converters are required for static logic.

### Precharged Logic

Precharged logic works straightforwardly with clock-powered signals. These signals are valid during one clock phase and low during the other phase. Therefore, they can drive gates that are precharged during the other phase; however, precharging with pFETs is problematic for two reasons. First, the clock complements are not available. Second, the clock phases may have slow edges. Assume that the same clock phase $\varphi_1$ is used to precharge the gate through a pFET and power its inputs (Fig. 21.7a). The symbol "∧" indicates clock-pulsed signals in conjunction with the driving clock phase. Precharged gates driven by clock-pulsed signals do not need protection nFETs in their pull-down stacks since the input signals are low during precharge. Without loss of generality, assume that both pFETs and nFETs have the same threshold voltage magnitude $V_{th}$. Then, when $a_{in}$ is high, there will be a short-circuit current drawn while the clock phase transits from $V_{dd} - V_{th}$ to $V_{th}$. This current may be significant due to the slow clock edges, since it scales linearly to the input switching time [25]. The short-circuit current interval is marked in

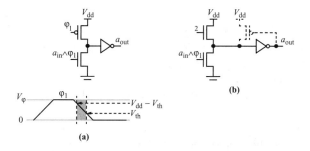

**FIGURE 21.7**  Precharging with (a) a pFET and (b) an nFET.

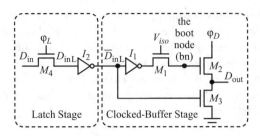

**FIGURE 21.8**   Potential E-R latch for precharged logic.

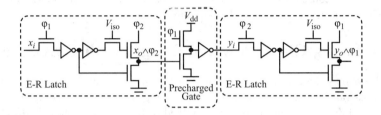

**FIGURE 21.9**   E-R latches used with precharged logic ([28] © 1997 IEEE).

the timing diagram of Fig. 21.7(a). Also note that the point $V_{dd} - V_{th}$ is chosen assuming that $V_{dd}$ is higher than $V_\varphi$, which may not be the case.

One solution to this problem is to set $V_{dd}$ to $2V_{th}$, which would impose restrictions on the system's operating voltage, and hence on its maximum frequency. Another solution is to precharge with an nFET driven by the other phase (Fig. 21.7(b)). This would require $V_\varphi$ to swing between 0 V and $V_{dd} + V_{th}$; otherwise, the inverter would experience a short-circuit current. A keeper pFET driven by $a_{out}$ (shown with dashed lines in Fig. 21.7(b)) can restore the voltage level of the precharged gate if necessary. The latter solution is more attractive because, despite the restrictions between the supply voltage $V_{dd}$ and the clock voltage swing $V_\varphi$, it provides a wider range of operating points. Moreover, it dictates that the clock-powered nodes be in higher energy levels than the dc-powered nodes, but the effect is mitigated when dissipation is considered because energy is recovered from the high-energy, clock-powered nodes.

If $V_\varphi$ swings from 0 V to $V_{dd} + V_{th}$, then a latch-stage that can be used for the E-R latch is the 3-transistor dynamic latch (Fig. 21.8). If necessary, the dynamic node $D_{inL}$ can be staticized with an inverter. Alternatively, a keeper pFET driven by $\overline{D}_{inL}$ can restore the voltage at node $D_{inL}$.

Figure 21.9 shows how an E-R latch drives a precharged gate and how the output of the gate is stored in an E-R latch. The gate precharges on $\varphi_1$ and evaluates on $\varphi_2$. Although for simplicity Fig. 21.9 shows a single gate, precharged gates can be arranged in domino style; the outputs of the final stage are stored in E-R latches. The precharged gates and the E-R latch inverters are powered from the same dc supply with voltage $V_{dd}$.

## Pass-Transistor Logic

The E-R latch design used with precharged logic (Fig. 21.8) can operate with pass-transistor logic as well (Fig. 21.10). As in precharged logic, the magnitude of clock voltage swing $|V_\varphi|$ is equal to $V_{dd} + V_{th}$. Pass-transistor gates are driven by clock-powered signals. Transistor chains can be driven either by clock-powered signals (i.e., signal $w_o$ in Fig. 21.10) or by dc-powered signals. When transistor chains are driven by clock-powered signals, the output of the first transistor (signal $u_i$ in Fig. 21.10) is a dc-level signal, due to the threshold voltage drop of the pass transistor. Therefore, dc-level signals are steered through transistor chains. The higher voltage swing of the clock-powered signals allows the dc-level signals to be passed at their full swing. Furthermore, some energy along the transistor-chain path can be recovered if the path is driven by a clock-powered signal; however, for typical pass-transistor gate configurations, HSPICE simulations indicate that most of the injected energy would be trapped in the path.

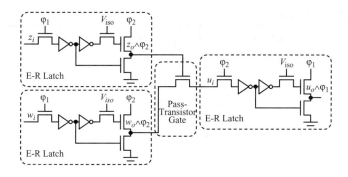

**FIGURE 21.10** E-R latches used with pass-transistor logic ([28] © 1997 IEEE).

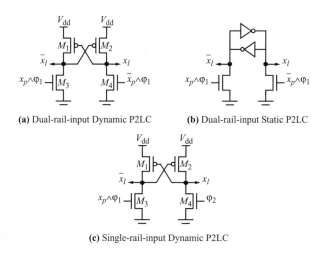

**(a)** Dual-rail-input Dynamic P2LC      **(b)** Dual-rail-input Static P2LC

**(c)** Single-rail-input Dynamic P2LC

**FIGURE 21.11** Various pulse-to-level converter designs.

## Static Logic

As was previously discussed, clock-powered signals can be used directly with precharged and pass-transistor logic. First, no pulse-to-level conversion is required; second, the latch-stage of the E-R latch consists of a 3-transistor dynamic latch. The limitation for these logic styles is that the clock voltage swing $V_\varphi$ should be equal to $V_{dd} + V_{th}$. This subsection investigates how clock-powered signals can operate with static logic. The main problem with static logic is that clock-powered signals may have long transition times. Therefore, they cannot drive static gates directly, because these gates would experience short-circuit current even if $V_\varphi$ were larger than $V_{dd}$. To solve this problem, pulse-to-level converters (P2LC) must be introduced between the E-R latches and the static logic blocks. A similar static-dissipation problem arises for conventional static-logic systems with multiple supply voltages; the outputs of low-supply-voltage gates cannot drive high-supply-voltage gates directly, because short-circuit current would be drawn in the high-supply-voltage gates. To solve this problem, low-to-high voltage converter designs have been proposed [26]. These low-to-high voltage converters can be slightly modified to operate as pulse-to-level converters (Fig. 21.11).

The first design (Fig. 21.11(a)) is a dual-rail-input, dynamic P2LC (DD P2LC). On every $\varphi_1$, exactly one of $x_p$ or $\bar{x}_p$ is pulsed, setting the outputs $x_l$ or $\bar{x}_l$ accordingly. Assume that $\bar{x}_l$ is high and $x_l$ is low. If $\bar{x}_p$ is pulsed, then $x_l$ and $\bar{x}_l$ remain unchanged. If $x_p$ is pulsed, then transistor $M_3$ turns on, discharging $\bar{x}_l$. This turns on $M_2$, which charges $x_l$ to $V_{dd}$, cutting off $M_1$. At the end of the operation, the outputs $x_l$ and $\bar{x}_l$ have been flipped. The second design (Fig. 21.11(b)) is a dual-rail-input, static P2LC (DS P2LC).

**TABLE 21.1**  Characteristics of Pulse-to-Level Converters

| Converter | Input Form | Output Timing | Description |
|---|---|---|---|
| DD P2LC | Dual rail | Valid on driving phase, stable on other phase | Nonrefreshed dynamic |
| DS P2LC | Dual rail | Valid on driving phase, stable on other phase | Nonrefreshed static |
| SD P2LC | Single rail | Valid on driving phase, reset on other phase | Refreshed dynamic |

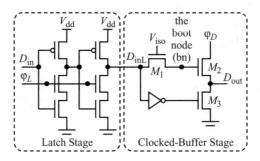

**FIGURE 21.12**  Potential E-R latch for static logic.

The only difference between the two designs is that the nodes $x_l$ and $\bar{x}_l$ of the DS P2LC are staticized. This converter can be used in cases where its inputs $x_p$ and $\bar{x}_p$ are not pulsed on every cycle. The third design (Fig. 21.11(c)) is a single-rail-input, dynamic P2LC (SD P2LC). In this case, $\varphi_2$ acts similar to a precharge phase, resetting the SD P2LC to low state (i.e., $x_l$ is low and $\bar{x}_l$ is high). On $\varphi_1$, if $x_p$ is high, the SD P2LC is set to high. Otherwise, it remains low. The SD P2LC converter does not need to be staticized because it is refreshed on every $\varphi_2$. If the output of the SD P2LC is required to be stable on $\varphi_2$, it should be latched on $\varphi_1$. This is not necessary for DD and DS P2LC since their outputs would not change until after the next $\varphi_1$.

Table 21.1 summarizes the characteristics of all three P2LC types. All three circuits inherently operate as level-to-level converters as well, which allows $V_\varphi$ and $V_{dd}$ to be independent from each other. Consequently, these voltages can be selected based solely on system and process specifications.

The 3-transistor dynamic latch, which is suitable for use with precharged and pass-transistor logic, requires that $V_\varphi$ depend on $V_{dd}$ (i.e., $V_\varphi$ must be at least equal to $V_{dd} + V_{th}$). This dependency is not important with precharged and pass-transistor logic because it is primarily imposed by these logic styles; however, static logic allows $V_\varphi$ and $V_{dd}$ to be independent from each other. Using the 3-transistor dynamic latch with static logic would impose unnecessary restrictions on the voltage levels of the clock phases and the dc supply.

Figure 21.12 shows a potential E-R latch design that is better suited to static logic. The latch stage consists of a 6-transistor dynamic latch [19]. During $\varphi_L$, the input $D_{in}$ gets propagated through the two latch gates. When $\varphi_L$ is low, propagation is blocked on either the first or the second latch gate, depending on the transition of $D_{in}$. The 6-transistor dynamic latch does not impose any voltage restrictions, although it is larger and slower than its 3-transistor counterpart. The clocked-buffer stage is slightly different from that of the E-R latch presented in Fig. 21.8 to accommodate the polarity change of its input.

## Clock-Powered Microsystems

This subsection shows how clock-powered microsystems can be built, investigates timing implications for the various styles of clock-powered logic, and discusses the energy dissipation of clock-powered microsystems.

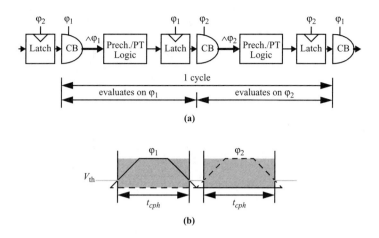

**FIGURE 21.13** (a) Clock-powered precharged and pass-transistor logic arranged in pipeline stages and (b) net computation time within a cycle.

Precharged and pass-transistor clock-powered logic microsystems are built in similar ways. Each logic block evaluates within a phase (Fig. 21.13(a)). Logic block outputs are latched at the same phase. Logic blocks start computing when the input clock-powered signals are charged to $V_{th}$. In order for the output to be latched in time, computation should finish before the falling edge of the clock phase crosses the $V_{th}$ voltage level (Fig. 21.13(b)). Therefore, precharged and pass-transistor logic blocks perform useful computations for less than half of the cycle time. However, precharged logic blocks are not totally idle the rest of the time, since these blocks are precharged during the phase in which they do not evaluate. Furthermore, clock-powered signals drive only the first gate level of precharged logic blocks. Precharged gates inside the logic blocks are arranged in domino form. During the evaluate phase, either the clock-powered block inputs are pulsed or they remain at 0 V, depending on their values. Therefore, once the computation is fired, these inputs are no longer needed. Thus, the energy return time of the pulsed inputs is totally hidden because of the nature of domino precharged logic. On the other hand, clock-powered signals that drive pass-transistor gates are required to remain valid throughout the entire computation time.

The way that static clock-powered logic is arranged into pipeline stages depends on the converters that are used. Both static and dynamic dual-rail-input converters (i.e., DD and DS P2LC) can drive static logic blocks directly. The inputs of these converters change once every cycle. Therefore, almost a full cycle is allotted for the static logic blocks to compute (Fig. 21.14(a)), disregarding the converter latency. Assuming that the inputs of the DS or DD converters are pulsed on $\varphi_1$, then the output of the static logic block is latched at the end of $\varphi_2$ (Fig. 21.14(b)).

As illustrated earlier, single-rail-input dynamic P2LCs operate like precharged gates because they are reset during the phase that their input is not valid. Therefore, the outputs of SD P2LCs are valid only for one phase, i.e., the phase in which their inputs are valid. One way to arrange them in pipeline stages is to latch their outputs, and then use the latch outputs to drive static logic blocks (Fig. 21.15(a)). Essentially, the SD P2LC output is transmitted through the latch at the beginning of the phase and remains stable when the phase goes away. The net computation time is as shown in Fig. 21.14(b). Alternatively, SD P2LC outputs can drive static logic blocks directly and the outputs of the static logic blocks can be latched at the end of the phase (Fig. 21.15(b)). This requires logic blocks to be split into smaller pieces with half latency. Operation is similar to the precharged clock-powered logic, and the net computation time is as shown in Fig. 21.13(b). The energy return time is totally hidden for static clock-powered logic, since clock-powered signals are not needed when they have been converted to levels.

For low-power operation, the rise and fall times of the clock phases must be longer than the practically obtainable minimum transition times. The consequence of stretching the rise time is that, within a clock cycle, the logic will activate later than it would from a minimal-transition-time input signal. A consequence

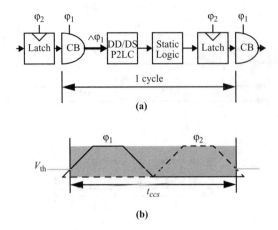

**FIGURE 21.14**   (a) Clock-powered static logic arranged in pipeline stages with DD/DS P2LC and (b) net computation time within a cycle.

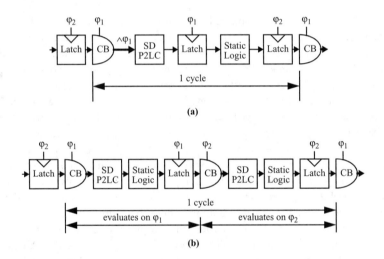

**FIGURE 21.15**   Clock-powered static logic arranged on pipeline stages with SD P2LC (a) for cycle- and (b) for phase-granularity computations.

of stretching the fall time is that the input cutoff voltage for the E-R latch will occur earlier in the clock phase. The net result is that for a fixed cycle time, the amount of computation that can be done during a cycle is decreased to reduce energy dissipation. For phase-granularity computations (i.e., mostly precharged and pass-transistor logic—Fig. 21.13(b)), the slow clock phase edges reduce the computation time four times within a cycle as opposed to twice per cycle for cycle-granularity computations (i.e., static logic—Fig. 21.14(b)). The benefit of phase-granularity computations is that more opportunities for energy recovery are available, since nodes can be clock-pulsed on both phases. This also results in balanced capacitance for both clock phases, which may be required for high-efficiency clock drivers; however, phase capacitance can be balanced for cycle-granularity computations if a phase-granularity computation is introduced in a sequence of pipeline stages. For example, assume a system with $N$ pipeline stages. Also assume that a phase-granularity computation is introduced after the $N/2$ pipeline stage while the rest of the stages are cycle-granularity computations. Then the clock-powered nodes of the first $N/2$ stages would be driven by one phase, whereas the clock-powered nodes of the final $N/2$ stages would be driven by the other phase.

## 21.6 Driver Comparison

In clock-powered logic, combinational logic blocks begin to switch as soon as clock-powered nodes are charged to $V_{th}$. For example, assume that a clock-powered signal drives a pulse-to-level converter. The converter starts operating as soon as the clock-powered signal voltage passes the threshold voltage $V_{th}$. Therefore, the switching time for charging the loads of clock-powered nodes to $V_\varphi$ is not as important as the delay for converting pulses to levels. With clock-powered logic, it is possible to overlap the time required for charge (and energy) recovery time with the computation time of the logic block. It is also possible, to a lesser degree, to overlap some of the charging time. The latter depends on many factors including clock and dc voltage levels, logic styles, and the CMOS technology.

In other E-R approaches (e.g., reversible logic [3,9], retractile cascade logic [27], and partially adiabatic logic families [10–16]), the signal switching time is important because the inputs of a logic block must be fully charged before the block starts operating. Furthermore, as in conventional CMOS circuits, voltage scaling is possible for clock-powered nodes at the expense of increased circuit latencies.

To investigate the effectiveness and the scalability of clock-powered logic, a simulation experiment was conducted to compare the driver stage of the E-R latch, i.e., the clocked buffer to a conventional driver. The two circuits were evaluated for energy versus delay and energy-delay product (EDP) versus voltage scaling.

### Experimental Setup

The goal of the experiment was to compare the clock-powered approach for driving high-capacitance nodes with a conventional, low-power approach. Because it is impractical to compare clock-powered logic against all low-power conventional techniques, a dual-supply-voltage approach in which high-capacitance nodes are charged to a lower voltage $V_{ddL}$ than the rest of the nodes was chosen. The dual-supply-voltage approach is similar to the clock-powered approach in that it attempts to reduce power dissipation in the high-capacitance nodes. Furthermore, like the clock-powered approach, the dual-supply-voltage approach requires that low-supply-voltage signals be converted to high-supply-voltage signals before they are fed to high-supply-voltage gates. Otherwise, these gates would suffer from short-circuit current, or may not work at all, depending on the two supply voltage levels, the logic style, and the technology process.

The dual-rail-input, static pulse-to-level converter (DS P2LC—Fig. 21.11(b)) is a converter circuit that operates simply with both approaches (Fig. 21.16). Two 150 fF capacitive loads were added to the converter

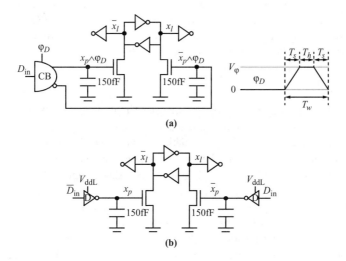

**(a)**

**(b)**

**FIGURE 21.16** Clocked buffer (a) and conventional drivers (b) connected to 150 fF capacitance loads and a DD P2LC.

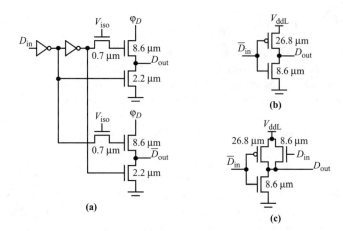

**FIGURE 21.17**  The three drivers used for the experiment: (a) clocked buffer, (b) inverter, and (c) inverter with pFET and nFET as pull-ups.

inputs $x_p$ and $\bar{x}_p$ to model the capacitance of the interconnect. Two inverters were added to the converter outputs $x_l$ and $\bar{x}_l$ to model the driving load of the converter.

A single-rail-input, dual-rail-output clocked buffer (Fig. 21.17(a)) was used for the clock-powered approach. This clocked buffer was derived from the single-rail-output buffer by duplicating the bootstrap, the isolation, and the clamp transistors. The two inverters of the clocked buffer, as well as the converter and its output inverters, were powered from the same supply voltage $V_{dd}$. The clock phase $\varphi_D$ swung to a voltage $V_{\varphi}$ (Fig. 21.17(a)). The input $D_{in}$ of the clocked buffer swung from 0 to $V_{dd}$.

For the dual-supply-voltage approach, two drivers, powered from the low-supply-voltage $V_{ddL}$, drove the converter (Fig. 21.16(b)). The converter and its output inverters were powered from the same supply voltage $V_{dd}$. The inputs $D_{in}$ and $\bar{D}_{in}$ of the two drivers swung from 0 to $V_{dd}$. Two different driver designs were used in the experiment. One was a regular inverter (Fig. 21.17(b)). The nFET of the inverter had the same width with the bootstrap transistors of the CB (Fig. 21.17(a)) and the pFET was set by the mobility ratio in the CMOS technology. The regular inverter becomes very slow as $V_{ddL}$ is scaled down. This is because the gate-to-source voltage of the pull-up transistor is equal to $V_{ddL}$ when the input is at 0 V. The operation of the pull-down nFET is not affected by $V_{ddL}$ scaling because when it is on, its gate-to-source voltage is equal to $V_{dd}$, i.e., the voltage that $D_{in}$ swings to. To mitigate this effect, a second driver design with both an nFET and a pFET as pull-ups was used (Fig. 21.17(c)). As $V_{ddL}$ decreases, the nFET pull-up can fully charge the output, given the significant voltage difference between $V_{ddL}$ and $V_{dd}$.

## Simulation Results

All circuits were laid out in Magic using the 0.5-$\mu$m Hewlett-Packard CMOS14B process parameters. The netlists extracted from the layout were simulated with HSPICE using the level-39 MOSFET models. The 150 fF load capacitances were added in the netlist as shown in Fig. 21.16. The delay to switch the DS P2LC output $x_l$ from zero to one and the required energy for switching the DS P2LC inputs (i.e., nodes $x_p$ and $\bar{x}_p$) were simulated for the clock-powered and dual-supply-voltage cases. For the clock-powered case, it was assumed that all return energy was recovered.

The supply voltage $V_{dd}$ was held constant at 3.3 V for all the simulations. The isolation voltage $V_{iso}$ of the clocked buffer was set to 4.5 V. This was found to be a near-optimum point through HSPICE simulations. If the isolation voltage is too low, the boot node will not charge to the maximum possible voltage. If the isolation voltage is too high, then during bootstrapping, the boot node voltage will reach a point at which the isolation transistor turns on and charge flows backward from the boot node, thus diminishing the bootstrapping effect.

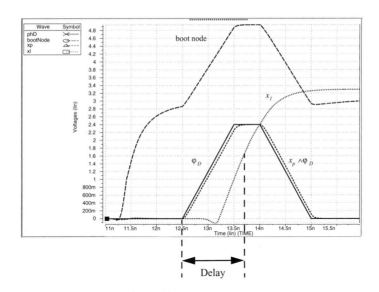

**FIGURE 21.18**    HSPICE waveforms for clock-powered approach when $V_\varphi$ is 2.4 V.

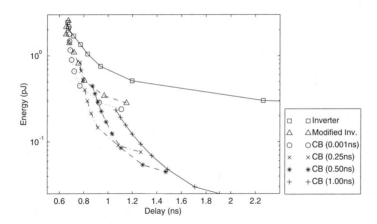

**FIGURE 21.19**    Energy vs. delay for the driver experiment. For comparison purposes, it should be noted that the delay of a minimum size inverter (nFET width 0.7 $\mu$m, pFET width 2.2 $\mu$m) was recorded at 150 ps by simulating a 15-stage ring oscillator in HSPICE (supply voltage 3.3 V).

The clock voltage swing, $V_\varphi$, of the clock-powered logic, was varied from 1.1 to 3.3 V. Specifically, simulations were performed for the following clock voltage swings: 1.1, 1.2, 1.5, 1.8, 2.1, 2.4, 2.7, 3.0, and 3.3 V. Switching time $T_s$ was varied from nearly 0 to 1 ns (0.001, 0.25, 0.50, and 1.0 ns). For all simulations the phase width $T_w$ was set to 2.5 ns, whereas the phase high time $T_h$ was equal to $T_w - 2T_s$ (see Fig. 21.16(a)). The delay was recorded from the point where the phase started switching until the output $x_l$ reached the 50% point (e.g., 1.65 V in Fig. 21.18). If the delays were evaluated from when the phase reached its 50% point, the clock-powered approach would be allowed a longer start time than the conventional case. To eliminate this advantage, the delay was evaluated as described previously (see Fig. 21.18). $V_{ddL}$ was varied identically to $V_\varphi$ for the conventional case. The switching time of the inputs $D_{in}$ and $\overline{D}_{in}$ was 1 ps. Delay was measured from the $D_{in}$ 50% point to the $x_l$ 50% point (i.e., 1.65 V).

The energy versus delay results (Fig. 21.19) show that the delay of the inverter increases significantly as $V_{ddL}$ is reduced. At 3.3 V, the delay is approximately 0.7 ns, whereas at 1.1 V, the delay is nearly 3.6 ns (not shown in Fig. 21.19). The conventional driver with the two pull-ups (Fig. 21.17(c)) has a performance

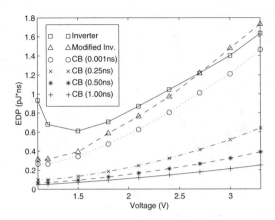

**FIGURE 21.20**    Energy-delay product (EDP) vs. driver operating voltage for the driver experiment.

similar to that of the clocked buffer when the clock transition time $T_s$ is 1 ps. The nearly zero transition time is equivalent to nonadiabatically switching nodes $x_p$ and $\bar{x}_p$. The performance of the clocked buffer indicates better scalability than conventional drivers. For a given transition time, delay can be traded efficiently for energy by reducing the clock voltage swing. When the point is reached where voltage scaling is no longer efficient, i.e., delay increases faster than energy decreases, then it is better to increase the transition time. For instance, when $T_s$ is 0.25 ns and $V_\varphi$ is 1.2 V, the energy dissipated is 91 fJ and the delay is 1.08 ns. If energy dissipation were to be reduced, it would be more energy efficient to increase the switching time to 0.50 ns rather than to scale the clock voltage swing to 1.1 V. The former would result in 54 fJ dissipation and 1.28 ns delay, whereas the latter would result in 76 fJ dissipation and 1.26 ns delay.

The pulse-to-level converter reaches its limits as the voltage swing of its inputs $x_p$ and $\bar{x}_p$ approaches $V_{th}$. For all cases, the converter would not switch during the allotted 5 ns cycle time when the driver operating voltage ($V_\varphi$ for the CB and $V_{ddL}$ for the conventional drivers) was 1.0 V. This is a limiting factor for conventional approaches. Energy cannot be reduced any further because the circuit would not work at lower voltages; however, energy can be reduced for the clocked-power approach simply by stretching out the switching time. The better scalability is a result of its energy dependency on both clock voltage swing and clock switching time.

The energy-delay product (EDP) versus driver operating voltage graph (Fig. 21.20) also indicates the scalability of the clock-powered approach. Moreover, the clocked buffer exhibits better EDP than the conventional drivers for all switching times. The point where energy is not efficiently traded for performance is clearly shown for the inverter to be around 1.5 V.

Some other important issues related to the nature of the two approaches should be pointed out. First, for the clock-powered approach, both $x_p$ and $\bar{x}_p$ are at 0 V before the CB passes a clock pulse to one of them. On the other hand, for the conventional approach, both $x_p$ and $\bar{x}_p$ switch simultaneously. This could potentially slow down the converter, since for a short time both pull-down devices would be on.

Second, in the clock-powered approach, the dual-rail-output CB used for this experiment has a switching activity of 1, meaning that one of its outputs is pulsed every cycle even if its input remains the same. CB designs with reduced output switching activity can be designed at the expense of increasing their complexity [22]. Nevertheless, conventional driver outputs switch only if their inputs change. Therefore, at a system level, energy dissipation would depend on the input switching activity factor. For instance, if inputs switch every other cycle, the conventional driver's average energy dissipation would be halved.

Third, although the internal dissipation of the clocked buffer and the conventional drivers was not presented, the conventional drivers have higher internal dissipation due to the wide pFETs [22]. Furthermore, the short switching time of the conventional driver inputs excluded short-circuit current. Typically, the conventional drivers would have some dissipation due to short-circuit current [25] for supply voltage $V_{ddL}$ higher than $2V_{th}$ (assuming that nFETs and pFETs have the same threshold voltage $V_{th}$).

## 21.7   Clock-Powered Microprocessor Design

General-purpose microprocessors represent a good application target for clock-powered logic for two reasons: First, they contain a mixture of different circuit types (i.e., function units, random logic, and register file). Second, high-capacitance nodes are a small percentage of the total node count and are easily identifiable (e.g., control signals, register file address, word, and bit lines, buses between function units, etc.). An example of a simple processor microarchitecture that shows potential clock-powered nodes is shown in Fig. 21.21. After identifying the high-capacitance nodes, it is decided on a case-by-case basis, which ones could be clock-powered. Factors to consider for this decision are system-level and timing implications, and associated overhead [22].

Two clock-powered microprocessors were successfully implemented: AC-1 [28] and MD1 [29]. In this section, first both these microprocessors are described followed by a presentation of their lab results. Finally, their performance is compared with an equivalent conventional implementation of the same processor architecture through circuit simulations.

### AC-1 Versus MD1

AC-1 and MD1 are extensively described in [28] and [29], respectively. The purpose of this section is to provide a brief description of each one and a summary of their comparison. As we see next, although both processors are based on similar instruction set architectures (ISAs), their implementations are radically different in terms of circuit style and physical design.

Both processors implement a RISC-type, 16-bit, 2-operand, 40-instruction architecture [30]. These instructions include arithmetic and logic operations that require an adder, a shifter, a logic unit, and a compare unit. In addition to the general-purpose instructions, MD1 supports another 20 microdisplay extension (MDX) instructions. These latter instructions operate on bytes that are packed in 16-bit words. The available function units were modified to support them along with general-purpose instructions. AC-1 and MD1 have similar five-stage pipelines.

Despite the fact that both AC-1 and MD1 are clock-powered CMOS microprocessors, they are based on two different design approaches. AC-1 is implemented with dynamic logic, i.e., precharged (Fig. 21.9) and pass-transistor logic (Fig. 21.10). As a result, clock phases were running a threshold voltage above the core supply voltage $V_{dd}$. Logic blocks were arranged in pipeline stages as shown in Fig. 21.13. Consequently, the available computation time was shortened by all four slow edges within a cycle. AC-1 was a full-custom layout implemented in the Hewlett-Packard CMOS14B process, which is a 0.5-$\mu$m, 3-metal-layer,

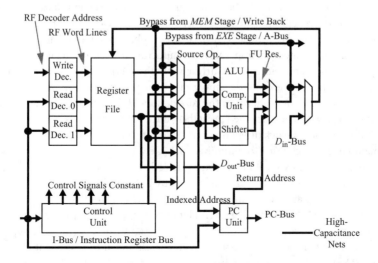

**FIGURE 21.21**   A simple processor microarchitecture that indicates high-capacitance nodes.

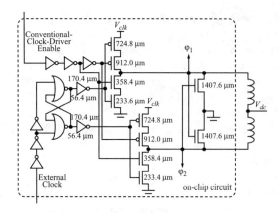

**FIGURE 21.22**   AC-1 clock-driver schematics ([28] © 1997 IEEE).

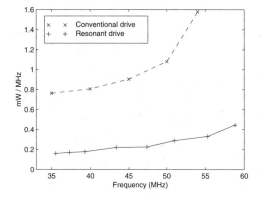

**FIGURE 21.23**   Lab measurements of AC-1 combined clock and core energy dissipation (mW/MHz) per clock cycle as function of frequency ([28] © 1997 IEEE).

3.3-V, *n*-well CMOS process. The core size is 2.63 mm by 2.63 mm. It contains 12.7 k transistors. The chip was packaged in a 108-pin PGA package.

Significant design effort was dedicated to implementing the clock driver and clock distribution network. AC-1 contains two clock drivers integrated together—a resonant clock driver like the one described previously (Fig. 21.4) and a conventional NOR-based, two-phase generator. The AC-1 clock circuitry (Fig. 21.22) was mostly integrated on-chip. Only the inductors for the resonant driver were externally attached. It is possible to enable either clock driver with an external control input. The conventional clock driver is powered from a separate dc supply ($V_{clk}$) for measurement purposes. Also, the voltage swing of the clock phases must be higher than the core dc supply. The clock phases are distributed inside the chip through a clock grid. The calculated resistance of the clock grid is less than 4$\Omega$. Each of the two large transistors of the resonant clock driver was partitioned in 306 small transistors that were connected in parallel throughout the clock grid. To minimize clock skew, the conventional clock driver was placed in the center of the grid. The extracted clock capacitance is 61 pF evenly distributed between the two phases. Approximately 20% of the clock capacitance is attributed to the clock grid.

The power measurements are plotted in Figs. 21.23 and 21.24. In resonant mode, the frequency was varied from 35.5 to 58.8 MHz by connecting external inductors that ranged from 290 nH down to 99 nH. The voltages for increasing frequencies ranged from 1.8 to 2.5 V for $V_{dd}$ (the core supply) and 1.0 to 1.4 V for $V_{dc}$ (the resonant clock driver supply), which corresponded to a resonant-clock voltage swing ($V_{\varphi}$) from 2.9 to 4.0 V. The combined power dissipation ranged from 5.7 to 26.2 mW. Under conventional drive, the external clock frequency was adjusted from 35 to 54 MHz and the power measurement

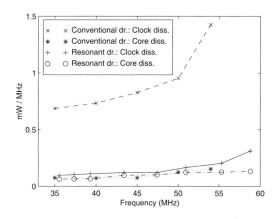

**FIGURE 21.24** Lab measurements of AC-1 clock and core energy dissipation (mW/MHz) per clock cycle as function of frequency.

procedure was repeated. The voltages for increasing frequencies ranged from 2.5 to 3.3 V for the supply voltage of the conventional clock driver ($V_{clk}$) and from 1.9 to 2.6 V for $V_{dd}$. The combined power dissipation ranged from 26.7 to 85.3 mW. The results show that in resonant mode, the dissipation is a factor of four to five less than in conventional mode. The clock power is approximately 90% of the total power under conventional drive and 60–70% under resonant drive. The core supply ($V_{dd}$) dissipation is about the same for both resonant and conventional modes.

The AC-1 results indicated two drawbacks on the dynamic-logic approach that was employed. First, the clock voltage swing was dependent on the core dc supply. Specifically, the clock voltage swing was a threshold voltage higher than the supply voltage $V_{dd}$. This made AC-1 a low-energy processor only when operated on energy-recovery mode, i.e., the energy savings were attributed mostly to the high-efficiency resonant clock driver. Second, the computation time was penalized for all slow clock edges within a cycle. These issues were addressed with MD1, the second generation clock-powered microprocessor. The key difference compared to AC-1 is that static logic was used instead of dynamic. As was discussed previously, with static logic and explicit pulse-to-level conversion, the clock voltage swing and core dc supply are independent from each other. Furthermore, it is possible to build pipeline stages that are slowed down by the slow clock edges twice per cycle instead of four times. Two options were available: (i) to use dual-rail pulse-to-level converters and arrange pipeline stages as shown in Fig. 21.14, or (ii) to use single-rail pulse-to-level convertors and arrange pipeline stages as shown in Fig. 21.15a. The latter was preferred because it considerably reduces bus wiring and switching activity of clock-powered nodes. In dual-rail signaling of clock-powered nodes, one node is pulsed every cycle regardless if the datum is a zero or a one. To further reduce the switching activity of clock-powered nodes, two other versions of clock buffers with a conditional enable signal were also used (Fig. 21.25). The output can either be clamped to ground or left floating.

The physical design approach for MD1 was different than AC-1. Individual cells were custom-made layouts. For larger blocks, a place-and-route CAD tool was used. The control unit was synthesized with standard cells from a Verilog description. MD1 was implemented in the same 0.5-$\mu$m, 3-metal-layer, 3.3-V, $n$-well CMOS process, but only two metal layers were available for routing. The top-level metal was reserved to be used as a ground shield to improve noise immunity. This was imposed by the MD1 application as a graphic processor closely placed to a microdisplay. The core size is 2.4 mm by 2.3 mm. It contains 28 k transistors. The chip was packaged in a 108-pin PGA package.

MD1 was tested with an external resonant clock driver for 8.5 and 15.8 MHz. The core dc supply voltage was set to 1.5 V. At 8.5 MHz, the dissipation of the core dc supply was 480 $\mu$W and the dissipation of the resonance clock driver was 300 $\mu$W. At 15.8 MHz, the dissipation of the core dc supply was 900 $\mu$W and the dissipation of the resonant clock driver was 2.0 mW. PowerMill simulations indicated that the

**TABLE 21.2**   AC-1 versus MD1 Summary

|  | AC-1 | MD1 |
|---|---|---|
| ISA | 16-bit RISC | 16-bit RISC plus MDX instr. |
| Word width | 16 bits | 16 bits |
| Pipeline structure | 5 Stages | 5 Stages |
| Logic style | Dynamic | Static |
| Pipeline style | As shown in Fig. 21.13(a) | As shown Fig. 21.15(a) |
| Transistor count | 12,700 | 28,000 |
| Cell design | Custom | Custom |
| Layout method | Custom | Synthesized |
| Clock-power nodes | 10% | 5% |
| Power accounted to clock-powered nodes at no energy recovery | 90% | 80% |
| Resonant clock driver FETs position | On-chip | Off-chip |
| Conventional clock driver | Yes | No |

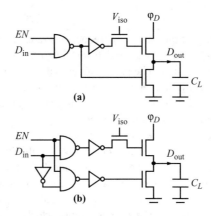

**FIGURE 21.25**   Clocked buffers with conditionally enabled outputs; when disabled, output is either clamped to ground (a) or is at high impedance (b) ([29] © 2000 IEEE).

clock-powered nodes accounted for 80% of the total dissipation when energy-recovery was disabled. Table 21.2 summarizes the characteristics for both AC-1 and MD1.

## Comparison Study

To compare the effectiveness of clock-powered logic against conventional CMOS, an equivalent fully dissipative microprocessor, DC1, was implemented. DC1 shares the same instruction set with AC-1, i.e., it does not include the MDX instructions. DC1 was implemented following the MD1 design flow for the same 0.5 $\mu$m CMOS process. All the three metal layers were available for routing. DC1 uses the same pipeline timing with MD1. Circuit-wise, DC1 is based on static CMOS as is MD1. The main difference compared to MD1 is that clocked buffers were replaced with regular drivers and latches were replaced with sense-amp, edge-triggered flip-flops [31]. DC1 uses a single-phase clock, which was distributed automatically by the place and route CAD tool following an H-tree. Clock is gated away from unused blocks. The DC1 core size is 1.8 mm × 1.9 mm. The core contains 21 k transistors.

The three processor cores were compared through PowerMill simulations since DC1 was not fabricated. All three SPICE netlists were extracted from physical layout using the same CAD tool and extraction rules. It was not possible to simulate the clock-powered processors operating in energy-recovery (i.e., resonant) mode due to limitations of the simulation software. Instead both of them were simulated operating in conventional mode. For AC-1, the conventional clock driver was used to generate the two

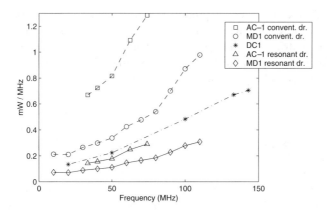

**FIGURE 21.26** Energy per cycle vs. frequency simulation results for all three processors (data combined from [28] © 1997 IEEE and [29] © 2000 IEEE).

clock phases. For MD1, conventional buffers were used to drive the two clock phases. These buffers were powered from a separate dc supply, so that clock power was recorded separately than the core power. For both AC-1 and MD1, the operating power under resonant mode was projected by dividing the clock power under conventional mode by 6.5. This factor indicates the efficiency of the all-resonant clock driver and was derived from laboratory measurements.

The simulation results are shown in Fig. 21.26. For DC1, the operating frequency ranged from 20 MHz at 1.5 V to 143 MHz at 3.3 V. Power dissipation ranged from 2.7 mW (at 20 MHz) to 100 mW (at 143 MHz). For AC-1, the top operating frequency was 74 MHz. For increasing frequency, clock voltage ranged from 2.4 to 3.3 V and core voltage ranged from 1.8 to 2.6 V. As discussed earlier, the AC-1 logic style requires that the clock voltage swing be a threshold voltage higher than the core voltage. Power dissipation under conventional mode was 22.3 mW at 33.3 MHz and 95.1 mW at 74 MHz. The projected power dissipation under resonant mode is 4.7 and 21.5 mW, respectively. For MD1, the top frequency was 110 MHz. For all operating points, clock and core voltages were maintained at the same level ranging from 1.4 V at 10 MHz to 2.7 V at 110 MHz. Power dissipation was 2.1 mW at 10 MHz and 108 mW at 110 MHz. The power dissipation in resonant mode would be 850 $\mu$W and 34 mW, respectively.

Simulation results show that MD1 is a more efficient design than AC-1 in terms of power dissipation and operating frequency especially under conventional mode. The significantly higher power dissipation of AC-1 under conventional mode is attributed to the higher clock voltage swing. Therefore, applying energy recovery has a greater effect on AC-1 than on MD1 since clock power is a larger portion of the total power for AC-1 when both processors operate in conventional mode. For MD1 under conventional mode, the clock-powered nodes (including the two clock phases) account for 80% of the total power dissipation. Clock-powered nodes are about 5% of the total nodes. Both AC-1 and MD1 would dissipate less power than DC1 when they operate under resonant mode. Specifically, the projected MD1 dissipation under resonant mode would be about 40% less than the dissipation of DC1.

## 21.8 Conclusions

In this chapter, clock-powered logic was discussed as a low-overhead, node-selective adiabatic style for low-power CMOS computing. The merit of clock-powered logic is that it combines the low-overhead of standard CMOS for driving low-capacitance nodes and the superior energy versus delay scalability of adiabatic charging for high-capacitance nodes. All the components of a clock-powered microsystem were presented in detail. Clock-powered logic is more effective for applications in which a small percentage of nodes accounts for most of the dynamic power dissipation (e.g., processors, memory structures [32], etc.).

Two generations of clock-powered microprocessors were presented in this article and compared against an equivalent standard CMOS design. For both processors, the results indicated that a small percentage of nodes (i.e., 5–10%) contributed most of the dynamic power dissipation (i.e., 80–90%) when operated in conventional mode. Compared to the standard CMOS design, the improved second-generation clock-powered microprocessor would dissipate approximately 40% less energy per cycle, assuming 85% efficiency of the clock driver.

DC1 is powered from a single supply voltage. Typically, microprocessors contain a few circuit critical paths. If such a system is powered from a single supply voltage, voltage scaling cannot provide a near-optimum dissipation versus speed trade-off, because the voltage level is determined by the few critical paths. The noncritical paths would switch faster than they absolutely need to. If a second dc supply voltage was used to power the high-capacitance nodes in conjunction with low-voltage-swing drivers [33], the DC1 dissipation would be decreased at the expense of reducing its clock frequency; however, clock-powered logic is inherently a multiple-supply-voltage system. As the driver experiment showed in section 21.6, energy dissipation for clock-powered nodes scales better than a dual-supply-voltage approach, since both the clock voltage swing and the switching time can be scaled. Another low-power approach is to dynamically adjust the system dc supply voltage and clock frequency based on performance demands [34]. Such a system resembles clock-powered logic. Voltage is dynamically varied to different constant dc levels, whereas in clock-powered logic, the supply voltage itself is statically time-varying, i.e., every cycle, it switches between 0 and $V_\varphi$.

Clock-powered logic is a low-power approach that does not rely solely on low-voltage operation. Therefore, it can be applied in CMOS processes without the need of low-threshold transistors that result in excessive leakage dissipation. Furthermore, the availability of high-energy signaling in clock-powered logic offers better noise immunity compared to low-voltage approaches.

To summarize, three conditions must be satisfied for applying clock-powered logic to a low-power system. First, the system should contain a small percentage of high-capacitance nodes with moderate to high switching activity. Second, the system should contain a few critical and many time-relaxed circuit paths. Third, the switching time of clock-powered nodes should be longer than the minimum obtainable switching time from the technology process. Controlling the speed of the energy transport to clock-powered nodes results in less energy dissipation. If the longer switching time of clock-powered nodes is made to be an explicit system-design consideration, conventional switching techniques can be used for nodes in critical paths while the other high-capacitance nodes are clock-powered.

## Acknowledgments

This work would not have been completed without contributions from many individuals from the ACMOS group at University of Southern California Information Sciences Institute over the last decade. Drs. Svensson, Koller, and Peterson helped in numerous aspects of the project. X.-Y. Jiang, H. Li, P. Wang, and W.-C. Liu contributed to the physical design of AC-1. Dr. Mao, W.-C. Liu, R. Lal, K. Chong, and J.-S. Moon were also members of the MD1 and DC1 design teams. The author is grateful to Fujitsu Laboratories of America for providing the time to write this manuscript and to B. Walker for reviewing it.

PowerMill and Design Compiler were provided by the Synopsys Corporation, HSPICE was provided by Avant!, and the Epoch place and route synthesis tool was provided by Duet Technologies.

## References

1. Chandrakasan, A. P. and Brodersen, R. W., *Low Power Digital CMOS Design,* Kluwer Academic Publishers, Norwell, 1995.
2. Gelsinger, P. P., Microprocessors for the new millenium: challenges, opportunities, and new frontiers, in *Proc. Int. Solid-State Circuits Conference,* San Francisco, 2001, 22.
3. Athas, W. C., Svensson, L. J., Koller, J. G., Tzartzanis, N., and Chou, E., Low-power digital systems based on adiabatic-switching principles, *IEEE Transactions on VLSI Systems,* 2, 398, 1994.

4. Koller, J. G. and Athas, W. C., Adiabatic switching, low energy computing, and the physics of storing and erasing information, in *Proc. Workshop on Physics and Computation, PhysComp '92*, Dallas, 1992.

5. Athas, W. C., Energy-recovery CMOS, in *Low Power Design Methodologies*, Rabaey, J. M. and Pedram, M., Eds., Kluwer Academic Publishers, Boston, MA, 1996, 65.

6. Watkins, B. G., A low-power multiphase circuit technique, *IEEE J. of Solid-State Circuits*, 2, 213, 1967.

7. Seitz, C. L., Frey, A. H., Mattisson, S., Rabin, S. D., Speck, D. A., and van de Snepscheut, J. L. A., Hot-clock NMOS, in *Proc. Chapel Hill Conference on VLSI*, Chapel Hill, 1985, 1.

8. Svensson, L. J., Adiabatic switching, in *Low Power Digital CMOS Design*, Chandrakasan A. P. and Brodersen, R. W., Eds., Kluwer Academic Publishers, Boston, MA, 1995, 181.

9. Younis, S. G. and Knight, T. F., Asymptotically zero energy split-level charge recovery logic, in *Proc. Int. Workshop on Low-Power Design*, Napa Valley, 1994, 177.

10. Denker, J. S., A review of adiabatic computing, in *Proc. Symp. on Low Power Electronics*, San Diego, 1994, 94.

11. Kramer, A., Denker, J. S., Avery, S. C., Dickinson, A. G., and Wik, T. R., Adiabatic computing with the 2N-2N2D logic family, in *Proc. Int. Workshop on Low-Power Design*, Napa Valley, 1994, 189.

12. Gabara, T., Pulsed power supply CMOS—PPS CMOS, in *Proc. Symp. on Low Power Electronics*, San Diego, 1994, 98.

13. De, V. K. and Meind, J. D., A dynamic energy recycling logic family for ultra-low-power gigascale integration (GSI), in *Proc. Int. Symp. of Low Power Electronics and Design*, Monterey, 1996, 371.

14. Moon, Y. and Jeon, D.-K., An efficient charge recovery logic circuit, *IEEE J. of Solid-State Circuits*, 31, 514, 1996.

15. Maksimovic, D., Oklobdzija, V. G., Nicolic, B., and Current, K. W., Clocked CMOS adiabatic logic with integrated single-phase power-clock supply: experimental results, in *Proc. Int. Symp. of Low Power Electronics and Design*, Monterey, 1997, 323.

16. Kim, S. and Papaefthymiou, M. C., Single-phase source-coupled adiabatic logic, in *Proc. Int. Symp. of Low Power Electronics and Design*, San Diego, 1999, 97.

17. Younis, S. G. and Knight, T. F., Non-dissipative rail drivers for adiabatic circuits, in *Proc. Conference on Advanced Research in VLSI*, Chapel Hill, 1995, 404.

18. Athas, W. C., Svensson, L. J., and Tzartzanis, N., A resonant signal driver for two-phase, almost nonoverlapping clocks, in *Proc. Int. Symp. on Circuits and Systems*, Atlanta, 1996, 129.

19. Yuan, J. and Svensson, C., High-speed CMOS circuit technique, *IEEE J. of Solid-State Circuits*, 24, 62, 1989.

20. Glasser, L. A. and Dobberpuhl, D. W., *The Design and Analysis of VLSI Circuits*, Addison-Wesley, Reading, MA, 1985.

21. Tzartzanis, N. and Athas, W. C., Clock-powered logic for a 50 MHz low-power datapath, in *Proc. Int. Solid-State Circuits Conference*, San Francisco, 1997, 338.

22. Tzartzanis, N., *Energy-Recovery Techniques for CMOS Microprocessor Design*, Ph.D. Dissertation, University of Southern California, Los Angeles, 1998.

23. Tzartzanis, N. and Athas, W. C., Clock-powered CMOS: a hybrid adiabatic logic style for energy-efficient computing, in *Proc. Conference on Advanced Research in VLSI*, Atlanta, 1999, 137.

24. Athas, W. C. and Tzartzanis, N., Energy recovery for low-power CMOS, in *Proc. Conference on Advanced Research in VLSI*, Chapel Hill, 1995, 415.

25. Veendrick, H. J. M., Short-circuit dissipation of static CMOS circuitry and its impact on the design of buffer circuits, *IEEE J. of Solid-State Circuits*, 19, 468, 1984.

26. Usami, K. and Horowitz, M. A., Clustered voltage scaling technique for low-power design, in *Proc. Int. Symp. on Low-Power Design*, Dana Point, 1995, 3.

27. Hall, J. S., An electroid switching model for reversible computer architectures, in *Proc. Workshop on Physics and Computation, PhysComp '92*, Dallas, 1992.

28. Athas, W. C., Tzartzanis, N., Svensson, L. J., and Peterson, L., A low-power microprocessor based on resonant energy, *IEEE J. of Solid-State Circuits*, 32, 1693, 1997.

29. Athas, W. C., Tzartzanis, N., Mao, W., Peterson, L., Lal, R., Chong, K., Moon, J.-S., Svensson, L. "J.", and Bolotksi, M., The design and implementation of a low-power clock-powered microprocessor, *IEEE J. of Solid-State Circuits*, 35, 1561, 2000.

30. Bunda, J. D., *Instruction-Processing Optimization Techniques for VLSI Microprocessors*, Ph.D. Dissertation, The University of Texas at Austin, Texas, 1993.

31. Montanaro, J. et al., A 160-MHz 32-b 0.5-W CMOS RISC microprocessor, *IEEE J. of Solid-State Circuits*, 31, 1703, 1996.

32. Tzartzanis, N., Athas, W. C., and Svensson, L. J., A low-power SRAM with resonantly powered data, address, word, and bit lines, in *Proc. European Solid-State Circuits Conference*, Stockholm, 2000, 336.

33. Zhang, H. and Rabaey, J., Low-swing interconnect interface circuits, in *Proc. Int. Symp. of Low Power Electronics and Design*, Monterey, 1998, 161.

34. Burd, T. D., Pering, T. A., Stratakos, A. J., and Brodersen, R. W., A dynamic voltage scaled microprocessor system, *IEEE J. of Solid-State Circuits*, 35, 1571, 2000.

# V

# Embedded Applications

# 22

# Embedded Systems-on-Chips

Wayne Wolf
*Princeton University*

## 22.1  Introduction

Advances in VLSI technology now allow us to build systems-on-chips (SoCs), also known as systems-on-silicon (SoS). SoCs are complex at all levels of abstraction; they contain hundreds of millions of transistors; they also provide sophisticated functionality, unlike earlier generations of commodity memory parts. As a result, SoCs present a major productivity challenge.

One solution to the SoC productivity problem is to use embedded computers.[1] An embedded computer is a programmable processor that is a component in a larger system that is not a general-purpose computer. Embedded computers help tame design complexity by separating (at least to some degree) hardware and software design concerns. A processor can be used as a pre-designed component—known as intellectual property (IP)—that operates at a known speed and power consumption. The software required to implement the desired functionality can be designed somewhat separately.

In exchange for separating hardware and software design, some elements traditionally found in hardware design must be transferred to software design. Software designers have traditionally concentrated on functionality while hardware designers have worried about critical delay paths, power consumption, and area. Embedded software designers must worry about real-time deadlines, power consumption, and program and data size. As a result, embedded SoC design disciplines require a blending of hardware and software skills.

This chapter considers the characteristics of SoCs built from embedded processors. The next section surveys the types of requirements that are generally demanded from embedded SoCs. Section 22.3 surveys the characteristics of components used to build embedded systems. Section 22.4 introduces the types of architectures used in embedded systems. Section 22.5 reviews design methodologies for embedded SoCs.

## 22.2 Requirements on Embedded SoCs

A digital system typically uses embedded processors to meet a combination of performance, complexity, and possibly design time goals. If the system's behavior is very regular and easy to specify as hardware, it may not be necessary to use embedded software. An embedded processor becomes more attractive when the behavior is too complex to be easily captured in hardwired logic.

Using embedded processors may reduce design time by allowing the design to be separated into distinct software and hardware units. In many cases, the CPU will be predesigned; even if the CPU and associated hardware is being designed for the project, many aspects of the hardware design can be performed separately from the software design. (Experience with embedded system designs does show, however, that the hardware and software designs are intertwined and that embedded software is prone to some of the same scheduling problems as mainframe software projects.)

But even if embedded processors seem attractive by reducing much of the design to "just programming," it must be remembered that embedded software design is much more challenging than typical applications programming for workstations or PCs. Embedded software must be designed to meet not just functional requirements—the software's input and output behavior—but also stringent nonfunctional requirements. Those nonfunctional requirements include:

- *Performance*—Although all programmers are interested in speed of execution, performance is measured much more precisely in the typical embedded system. Many embedded systems must meet real-time deadlines. The deadline is measured between two points in the software: if the program completely executes from the starting point to the end point by the deadline, the system malfunctions.
- *Energy/power*—Traditional programmers don't worry about power or energy consumption. However, energy and power are important to most embedded systems. Energy consumption is of course important in battery-operated systems, but the heat generated as a result of power consumption is increasingly important to wall-powered systems.
- *Size*—The amount of memory required by the embedded software determines the amount of memory required by the embedded system. Memory is often one of the major cost components of an embedded system.

Embedded software design resembles hardware design in its emphasis on nonfunctional requirements such as performance and power. The challenge in embedded SoC design is to take advantage of the best aspects of both hardware and software components to quickly build a cost-effective system.

## 22.3 Embedded SoC Components

### CPUs

As shown in Fig. 22.1, a CPU is a programmable instruction set processor. Instructions are kept in a separate memory—a program counter (PC) that points to the current instruction. This definition does not consider reconfigurable logic to be a programmable computer, because it does not have a separate instruction memory and a PC. Reconfigurable logic can be used to implement sequential machines, and

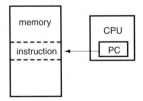

**FIGURE 22.1**   A CPU and memory.

so a CPU could be built in reconfigurable logic. But the separation of CPU logic and memory is an important abstraction for program design.

An embedded processor is judged by several characteristics:

- *Performance*—The overall speed of execution may be important in some systems, but in many cases we particularly care about the CPU's performance on critical sections of code.
- *Energy and power*—Processors provide different mechanisms to manage power consumption.
- *Area*—The area of the processor contributes to the total implementation cost of the SoC. The area of the memory required to store the program also contributes to implementation cost.

These characteristics are judged relative to the embedded software they are expected to run. A processor may exhibit very different performance or energy consumption on different applications.

RISC processors are commonly used in embedded computing. ARM[2] and MIPS[3] processors are examples of RISC processors that are widely used in embedded systems. A RISC CPU uses a pipeline to increase CPU performance. Many RISC instructions take the same amount of time to execute, simplifying performance analysis. However, many RISC architectures do have exceptions to this rule. An example is the multiple-register feature of the ARM processor: an instruction can load or store a set of registers, for which the instruction takes one cycle per instruction.

Most CPUs used in PCs and workstations today are superscalar processors. A superscalar processor builds on RISC techniques by adding logic that examines the instruction stream and determines, based on what CPU resources are needed, when several instructions can be executed in parallel. Superscalar scheduling logic adds quite a bit of area to the CPU in order to check all the possible conflicts between combinations of instructions; the size of a superscalar scheduler grows as $n^2$, where $n$ is the number of instructions that are under consideration for scheduling. Many embedded systems, and in particular SoCs, do not use superscalar processors and instead stick with RISC processors. Embedded system designers tend to use other techniques, such as instruction-set optimization caches, to improve performance. Because SoC designers are concerned with overall system performance, not just CPU performance, and because they have a better idea of the types of software run on their hardware, they can tackle performance problems in a variety of ways that may use the available silicon area more cost-effectively.

Some embedded processors are known as digital signal processors (DSPs). The term DSP was originally used to mean one of two things: either a CPU with a Harvard architecture that provided separate memories for programs and data; or a CPU with a multiply-accumulate unit to efficiently implement digital filtering operations. Today, the meaning of the term has blurred somewhat. For instance, version 9 of the ARM architecture is a Harvard architecture to better support digital signal processing. Modern usage applies the term DSP to almost any processor that can be used to efficiently implement signal processing algorithms.

The application-specific integrated processor (ASIP)[4] is one approach to improving the performance of RISC processors for embedded application. An ASIP's instruction set is designed to match the requirements of the application software it will run. On the one hand, special-purpose function units and instructions to control them may be added to speed up certain operations. On the other hand, function units, registers, and busses may be eliminated to reduce the CPU's cost if they do not provide enough benefit for the application at hand. The ASIP may be designed manually or automatically based on profiling information. One advantage of generating the ASIP automatically is that the same information can be used to generate the processor's programming environment: a compiler, assembler, and debugger are necessary to make the ASIP useful building blocks.

Another increasingly popular architecture for embedded computing is very long instruction word (VLIW). A VLIW machine can execute several instructions simultaneously but, unlike a superscalar processor, relies on the compiler to schedule parallel instructions at compilation time. A pure VLIW machine uses slots in the long, fixed-length instruction word to control the CPU's function units, with NOPs used to indicate slots that cannot be used for useful work by the compiler. Modern VLIW machines, such as the TI C6000[5] and the Motorola/Agere StarCore,[6] group single-operation instructions into execution packets; the packet's length can vary depending on the number of instructions that the compiler was able to schedule for simultaneous operation. VLIW machines provide instruction-level parallelism with a much smaller CPU than is possible in a superscalar system; however, the compiler must be able to extract parallelism at compilation time to be able to use the CPU's resources. Signal processing applications often have parallel operations that can be exploited at compilation time. For example, a parallel set of filter banks runs the same code on different data; the operations for each channel can be scheduled together in the VLIW instruction group.

## Interconnect

Embedded SoCs may connect several CPUs, on-chip memories, and devices on a single chip. High-performance interconnect systems are required to meet the system's performance demands. The interconnection systems must also comply with standards so that existing components may be connected to them.

Busses are still the dominant interconnection scheme for embedded SoCs. Although richer interconnection schemes could be used on-chip, where they are not limited by pinout as in board-level systems, many existing architectures are still memory-limited and not interconnect-limited. However, future generations of embedded SoCs may need more sophisticated interconnection schemes.

A bus provides a protocol for communication between components. It also defines a memory space and the uses of various addresses in that memory space, for example, the address range assigned to a device connected to the bus. Busses for SoCs may be designed for high-performance or low-cost operation. A high-performance bus uses a combination of techniques—advanced circuits, additional bus lines, efficient protocols—to maximize transaction performance. One common protocol used for efficient transfers is the block transfer, in which a range of locations is transferred based on a single address, eliminating the need to transfer all the addresses on the bus. Some recent busses allow split transactions—the data request and data transfer are performed on separate bus cycles, allowing other bus operations to be performed while the original request is serviced. A low-cost bus design provides modest performance that may not be acceptable for instruction fetching or other time-critical operations. A low-cost bus is designed to require little hardware in the bus itself and to impose a small hardware and software overhead on the devices connecting to the bus. A system may contain more than one bus; a bridge can be used to connect one bus to another.

The ARM AMBA bus specification[7] is an example of a bus specification for SoCs. The AMBA spec actually includes two busses: the high-performance AMBA high-performance bus (AHB) and the low-cost AMBA peripherals bus (APB). The Virtual Sockets Interface committee has defined another standard for interconnecting components on SoCs.

## Memory

One of the great advantages of SoC technology is that memory can be placed on the same chip as the system components that use the memory. On-chip memory both increases performance and reduces power consumption because on-chip connections present less reactive load than do pins and traces between chips; however, an SoC may still need to use separate chips for off-chip memory.

Although on-chip embedded memory has many advantages, it still is not as good as commodity memory. A commodity SRAM or DRAM's manufacturing process has been carefully tuned to the requirements of that component. In contrast, an on-chip memory's manufacturing needs must be balanced against the requirements of the logic circuits on the chip. The transistors, interconnections, and storage nodes of on-chip memories all have somewhat different needs than logic transistors.

Embedded DRAMs suffer the most because they need quite different manufacturing processes than do logic circuits. The processing steps required to build the storage capacitors for the DRAM cell are not good for small-geometry transistors. As a result, embedded DRAM technologies often compromise both the memory cells and the logic transistors, with neither being as good as they would be in separate, optimized processes. Although embedded DRAM has been the subject of research for many years, its limitations have kept its from becoming a widely used technology at the time of this writing.

SRAM circuits' characteristics are closer to those of logic circuits and so can be built on SoCs with less penalty. SRAM consumes more power and requires more chip area than does DRAM, but SRAM does not need refreshing, which noticeably simplifies the system architecture.

## Software Components

Software elements are also components of embedded systems. Just as pre-designed hardware components are used to both reduce design time and to provide predictions of the characteristics of parts of the system, software components can also be used to speed up software implementation time and to provide useful data on the characteristics of systems.

CPU vendors often supply software libraries for their processors. These libraries generally supply code for two types of operations. First, they provide drivers for input and output operations. Second, they provide efficient implementations of commonly-used algorithms. For example, libraries for DSPs generally include code for digital filtering, fast Fourier transforms, and other common signal processing algorithms. Code libraries are important because compilers are still not as adept as expert human programmers at creating code that is both fast and small.

The real-time operating system (RTOS) is the second major category of software component. Many applications perform several different types of operations, often with their own performance requirements. As a result, the software is split into processes that run independently under the control of an RTOS. The RTOS schedules the processes to meet performance goals and efficiently utilize the CPU and other hardware resources. The RTOS may also provide utilities, such as interprocess communication, networking, or debugging. An RTOS's scheduling policy is necessarily very different from that used in workstations and mainframes, because the RTOS must meet real-time deadlines. A priority-driven scheduling algorithm such as rate-monotonic scheduling (RMS)[9] is often used by the RTOS to schedule activity in the system.

# 22.4 Embedded System Architectures

The hardware architecture of an embedded SoC is generally tuned to the requirements of the application. Different domains, such as automotive, image processing, and networking all have very different characteristics. In order to make best use of the available silicon area, the system architecture is chosen to match the computational and communication requirements of the application. As a result, a much wider range of hardware architectures is found for embedded systems as compared with traditional computer systems.

Figure 22.2 shows one common configuration, a bus-based uniprocessor architecture for an embedded system. This architecture has one CPU, which greatly simplifies the software architecture. In addition to I/O devices, the architecture may include several devices known as accelerators designed to speed up

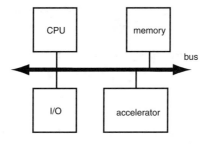

**FIGURE 22.2** A bus-based, single-CPU embedded system.

computations. (Though some authors refer to these units as co-processors, we prefer to reserve that term for units that are dispatched by the CPU's execution unit.) For example, a video operation's inner loops may be implemented in an application-specific IC (ASIC) so that the operation can be performed more quickly than would be possible on the CPU. An accelerator can achieve performance gains through several mechanisms: by implementing some functions in special hardware that takes fewer cycles than is required on the CPU, by reducing the time required for control operations that would require instructions on the CPU, and by using additional registers and custom data flow within the accelerator to more efficiently implement the available communication. The single-CPU/bus architecture is commonly used in applications that do not have extensive real-time characteristics and ones that need to run a wider variety of software. For example, many PDAs use this type of architecture. A single-CPU system simplifies software design and debugging since all the work is assumed to happen on one processing element. The single CPU system is also relatively inexpensive.

In general, however, a high-performance embedded system requires a heterogeneous multiprocessor—a multiprocessor that uses more than one type of processing element and/or a specialized communication topology. Scientific parallel processors generally use a regular architecture to simplify programming. Embedded systems use heterogeneous architectures for several reasons:

- *Cost*—A regular architecture may be much larger and more expensive than a heterogeneous architecture, which freed from the constraint of regularity, can remove resources from parts of the architecture where they are not needed and add them to parts where they are needed.

- *Real-time performance*—Scientific processors are desgined for overall performance but not to meet deadlines. Embedded systems must often put processing power near the I/O that requires real-time responsiveness; this is particularly true if the processing must be performed at a high rate. Even if a high-rate, real-time operation requires relatively little computation on each iteration, the high interrupt rate may make it difficult to perform other processing tasks on the same processing element.

Many embedded systems use heterogeneous multiprocessors. One example comes from telephony. A telephone must perform both control- and data-intensive operations: both the network protocol and the user interface require control-oriented code; the signal processing operations require data-oriented code. The Texas Instruments OMAP architecture, shown in Fig. 22.3, is designed for telephony: the RISC processor handles general-purpose and control-oriented code while the DSP handles signal processing. Shared memory allows processes on the two CPUs to communicate, as does a bridge. Each CPU has its own RTOS that coordinates processes on the CPU and also mediates communication with the other CPU.

The C-Port network processor,[11] whose hardware architecture is shown in Fig. 22.4, provides an example of a heterogeneous multiprocessor in a different domain. The multiprocessor is a high-speed bus. The RISC executive processor is C programmable and provides overall control, initialization, etc. Each of the 16 HDLC processors is also C programmable. Other interfaces for higher-speed networks are not general-purpose computers and can be programmed only with register settings.

Another category of heterogeneous parallel embedded systems is the networked embedded system. Automobiles are a prime example of this type of system: the typical high-end car includes over a hundred microprocessors ranging from 4-bit microcontrollers to high-performance 32-bit processors. Networks help to distribute high-rate processing to specialized processing elements, as in the HP DesignJet, but

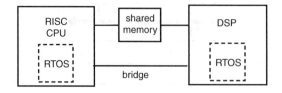

**FIGURE 22.3** The TI OMAP architecture.[10]

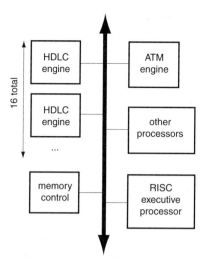

**FIGURE 22.4**  Block diagram of the C-Port network processor.[11]

they are most useful when the processing elements must be physically distributed. When the processing elements are sufficiently far apart, busses designed for lumped microprocessor systems do not work well. The network is generally used for data transfer between the processing elements, with each processing element maintaining its own program memory as well as a local data memory. The processing elements communicate data and control information as required by the application. I²C and CAN are two widely-used networks for distributed systems.

## 22.5  Embedded SoC Design Methodologies

### Specifications

As described in section 22.2, embedded computers are typically used to build systems with complex functionality. Therefore, capturing a functional description of the system is an important part of the design process. A variety of specification languages have been developed. Many of these languages were developed for software systems, but several languages have been developed over the past decade with embedded systems in mind.

Specification languages are generally designed to capture particular styles of design. Many languages have been created to describe control-oriented systems. An early example was Statecharts,[12] which introduced hierarchical states that provided a structured description of state machines. The SDL language[13] is widely used to specify protocols in telecommunications systems. The Esterel language[14] describes a reactive system as a network of communicating state machines.

Data-oriented languages find their greatest use in signal processing systems. Dataflow process networks[15] are one example of a specification language for signal processing. Object-oriented specification and design have become very popular in software design. Object-oriented techniques mix control and data orientation. Objects tend to reflect natural assemblages of data; the data values of an object define its state and the states of the objects define the state of the system. Messages providing communication and control. The real-time object-oriented Methodology (ROOM)[16] is an example of an object-oriented methodology created for embedded system design.

In practice, many systems are specified in the C programming language. Many practical systems combine control and data operations, making it difficult to use one language that is specialized for any type of description. Algorithm designers generally want to prototype their algorithms and verify them through experimentation; as a result, an executable program generally exists as the golden standard with

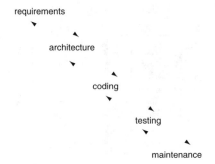

**FIGURE 22.5**    The waterfall model of software development.

which the implementation must conform. This is especially true when the product's capabilities are defined by standards committees, which typically generate one or more reference implementations, usually in C. Once a working piece of code exists in C, there is little incentive to rewrite it in a different specification language; however, the C specification is generally a long way from an implementation. Algorithmic designs are usually written for uniprocessors and ignore many aspects of I/O, whereas embedded systems must perform real-time I/O and often distribute tasks among several processing elements. Algorithm designers often do not optimize their code for any particular platform, and their code is certainly not optimized for any particular embedded platform. As a result, a C language specification often requires substantial re-engineering before it can be used in an embedded system.

## Design Flows

In order to better understand modern design methodologies for embedded SoCs, we can start with traditional software engineering methodologies. The waterfall model, one of the first models of software design, is shown in Fig. 22.5. The waterfall model is a top-down model with only local feedback. Other software design models, such as the spiral model, try to capture more bottom-up feedback from implementation to system design; however, software design methodologies are designed primarily to implement functionality and to create a maintainable design. Embedded SoCs must, as mentioned in section 22.2, satisfy performance and power goals as well. As a result, embedded system design methodologies must be more complex.

The design of the architecture of an embedded SoC is particularly important because the architecture defines the capabilities that will limit both the hardware and software implementations. The architecture must of course be cost effective, but it must also provide the features necessary to do the job. Because the architecture is custom designed for the application, it is quite possible to miss architectural features that are necessary to efficiently implement the system. Retrofitting those features back into the architecture may be difficult or even impossible if the hardware and software design efforts do not keep in sync.

Important decisions about the hardware architecture include:

- How many processing elements are needed?
- What processing elements should be programmable and which ones should be hardwired?
- How much communication bandwidth is needed in the system and where is it needed?
- How much memory is needed and where should it go in the system?
- What types of components will be used for processors, communication, and memory?

The design of the software architecture is just as important and goes hand-in-hand with the hardware architecture design. Important decisions about the software architecture include:

- How should the functionality be split into processes?
- How are input and output performed?

- How should processes be allocated to the various processing elements in the hardware architecture?
- When should processes be scheduled?

In practice, information required to make these decisions comes from several sources. One important source is previous designs. Though technology and requirements both change over time, similar designs can provide valuable lessons on how to (and not to) design the next system. Another important source is implementation. Some implementation information can come from pre-designed hardware or software components, which is one reason why intellectual-property-based design is so important. Implementation can also come from early design efforts.

A variety of CAD algorithms have been developed to explore the embedded system design space and to help automate system architectures. Vulcan[21] and Cosyma[22] were early hardware/software partitioning systems that implemented a design using a CPU and one or more custom ASICs. Other algorithms target more general architectures.[23,24]

Once the system architecture has been defined, the hardware and software must be implemented. Hardware implementation challenges include:

- finding efficient protocols to connect together existing hardware blocks,
- memory design,
- clock rate optimization,
- power optimization.

Software implementation challenges include:

- meeting performance deadlines,
- minimizing power consumption,
- minimizing memory requirements.

The design must be verified throughout the design process. Once the design progresses to hardware and software implementation, simulation becomes challenging because the various components operate at very different levels of abstraction. Hardware units are modeled at the clock-cycle level. Software components must often be run at the instruction level or in some cases at even higher levels of abstraction. A hardware/software co-simulator[19] is designed to coordinate simulations that run at different time scales. The co-simulator coordinates multiple simulators—hardware simulators, instruction-level simulators, behavioral software processes—and keeps track of the time in each simulation. The co-simulator ensures that communications between the simulators happen at the right time for each simulator.

Design verification must include performance, power, and size as well as functionality. Although these sorts of checks are common in hardware design, they are relatively new to software design. Performance and power verification of software may require cache simulation. Some recent work has developed higher-level power models for CPUs.

## Platform-Based Design

One response to the conflicting demands of SoC design has been the devlopment of platform-based design methodologies. On the one hand, SoCs are becoming very complex. On the other hand, they must be designed very quickly to meet the electronics industry's short product lifecycles.

Platform-based design tries to tackle this problem by dividing the design process into two phases. In the first phase, a platform is designed. The platform defines the hardware and software architectures for the system. The degree to which the architecture can be changed depends on the needs of the marketplace. In some cases, the system may be customizable only by reprogramming. In other cases, it may be possible to add or delete hardware components to provide specialized I/O, additional processing capabilities, etc. In the second phase, the platform is specialized into a product. Because much of the initial design work was done in the first phase, the product can be developed relatively quickly based on the platform.

Platform-based design is particularly well suited to products derived from standards. On the one hand, all products must meet the minimum requirements of the standard. On the other hand, standards committees generally leave room for different implementations to distinguish themselves: added features, lower power, etc. Designers will generally want to modify their design to add features that differentiate their product in the marketplace.

Platform-based design also allows designers to incorporate design experience into products. Each product derived from the platform will teach something: how to better design part of the system, unexpected needs of customers, etc. The platform can be updated as new products are developed from it so that successive designs will be easier.

Platforms are usually designed within a technology generation. A new VLSI technology generally changes enough design decisions that platforms must be rethought for each new generation of technology. Therefore, the platform itself must be designed quickly and each product based on the platform must be completed quickly in order to gain effective use of the platform design effort in the 18-month lifecycle of a manufacturing technology.

## Software Performance Analysis and Optimization

Although methods for hardware performance analysis and optimization are well-known, software techniques for optimizing performance have been developed only recently to meet the demands of embedded design methodologies.

The performance of an embedded system is influenced by several factors at different levels of abstraction. The first is the performance of the CPU pipeline itself. RISC design techniques tend to provide uniform execution times for instructions, but software performance is not always simple to predict. Register forwarding, which is used to enhance pipeline performance, also makes execution time less predictable. Branch prediction causes similar problems.

Superscalar processors, because they schedule instructions at execution time based upon execution data, provide much less predictable performance than do either RISC or VLIW processors. This is one reason why superscalar processors are not frequently used in real-time embedded systems.

The memory system is often an even greater source of uncertainty in embedded systems. CPUs use caches to improve average memory response time, but the effect of the cache on a particular piece of software requires complex analysis. In pathological cases, the cache can add uncertainty to execution times without actually improving the performance of critical software components. Cache simulation is often used to analyze the behavior of a program in a cache. Analysis must take into account both instructions and data. Unlike in workstation CPUs, in which the cache configuration is chosen by the CPU architect based on benchmarks, the designer of an embedded SoC can choose the configurations of caches to match the characteristics of the embedded software. Embedded system designers can choose between hardware and software optimizations to meet performance goals.

Analyzing the performance of a program requires determining both the execution path and the execution time of instructions along that path.[18] Both are challenging problems.[20] The execution path of a program clearly depends on input data values. To ensure that the program meets a deadline, the worst-case execution path must be determined. The execution time of instructions along the path depend on several factors: data values, interactions between instructions, and cache state.

## Energy/Power Analysis and Optimization

Many embedded systems must also meet energy and power goals as well as performance goals. The specification may impose several types of power requirements: peak power consumption, average power consumption, energy consumption for a given operation.

To a first-order, high-performance design is low-power design. Efficient implementations that run faster also tend to reduce power consumption, but trade-offs between performance and power in embedded system design. For example, the power consumption of a cache depends on both its size and the memory system activity.[25] If the cache is too small, too many references require expensive main memory accesses. If the cache is too large, it burns too much static power. Many applications exhibit a sweet spot at which the cache is large enough to provide most of the available performance benefit while not burning too much static power. Techniques have been developed to estimate hardware/software power consumption.[26]

System-level approaches can also help reduce power consumption.[27] Components can be selectively turned off to save energy; however, because turning a component on again may consume both time and energy, the decision to turn it off must be made carefully. Statistical methods based on Markov models can be used to create effective system-level power management methodologies.

## 22.6 Summary

Embedded computers promise to solve a critical design bottleneck for SoCs. Because we can design CPUs relatively independently of the programs they run and reuse those CPUs design across many chips, embedded computers help to close the designer productivity gap. Embedded processors, on the other hand, require that many design techniques traditionally reserved for hardware—deadline-driven performance, power minimization, size—must now be applied to software as well. Design methodologies for embedded SoCs must carefully design system architectures that will allow hardware and software components to work together to meet performance, power, and cost goals while implementing complex functionality.

## References

1. Wayne Wolf, *Computers as Components: Principles of Embedded Computer System Design*, San Francisco: Morgan Kaufman, 2000.
2. http://www.arm.com.
3. http://www.mips.com.
4. G. Goossens, J. van Praet, D. Lanneer, W. Geurts, A. Kifli, C. Liem, and P. G. Paulin, "Embedded software in real-time signal processing systems: design technologies," *Proceedings of the IEEE*, 85(3), March 1997, pp. 436–453.
5. http://www.ti.com.
6. http://www.lucent.com/micro/starcore/motover.htm.
7. ARM Limited, *AMBA(TM) Specification (Rev 2.0)*, ARM Limited, 1999.
8. http://www.vsi.com.
9. C. L. Liu and J. W. Layland, "Scheduling algorithms for multiprogramming in a hard real-time environment," *Journal of the ACM*, 20(1), 1973, pp. 46–61.
10. http://www.ti.com/sc/docs/apps/wireless/omap/overview.htm.
11. http://www.cportcorp.com/products/digital.htm.
12. D. Harel, "Statecharts: a visual formalism for complex systems," *Science of Computer Programming*, 8, 1987, pp. 231–274.
13. Anders Rockstrom and Roberto Saracco, "SDL—CCITT specification and description language," *IEEE Transactions on Communication*, 30(6), June 1982, pp. 1310–1318.
14. Albert Benveniste and Gerard Berry, "The synchronous approach to reactive real-time systems," *Proceedings of the IEEE*, 79(9), September 1991, pp. 1270–1282.
15. E. A. Lee and T. M. Parks, "Dataflow process networks," *Proceedings of the IEEE*, 83(5), May 1995, pp. 773–801.
16. Bran Selic, Garth Gullekson, and Paul T. Ward, *Real-Time Object-Oriented Modeling*, New York: John Wiley and Sons, 1994.
17. Henry Chang, Larry Cooke, Merrill Hunt, Grant Martin, Andrew McNelly, and Lee Todd, *Surviving the SOC Revolution: A Guide to Platform-Based Design*, Kluwer Academic Publishers, 1999.
18. Chang Yun Park and Alan C. Shaw, "Experiments with a program timing tool based on source-level timing scheme," *IEEE Computer*, 24(5), May 1991, pp. 48–57.

19. David Becker, Raj K. Singh, and Stephen G. Tell, "An engineering environment for hardware/software co-simulation," in *Proceedings, 29th Design Automation Conference*, IEEE Computer Society Press, 1992, pp. 129–134.

20. Yau-Tsun Steven Li, Sharad Malik, and Andrew Wolfe, "Performance estimation of embedded software with instruction cache modeling," in *Proceedings, ICCAD-95*, IEEE Computer Society Press, 1995, pp. 380–387.

21. Rajesh K. Gupta and Giovanni De Micheli, "Hardware-software cosynthesis for digital systems," *IEEE Design & Test*, 10(3), September 1993, pp. 29–41.

22. R. Ernst, J. Henkel, and T. Benner, "Hardware-software cosynthesis for microcontrollers," *IEEE Design & Test*, 10(4), December 1993, pp. 64–75.

23. Wayne Wolf, "An architectural co-synthesis algorithm for distributed, embedded computing systems," *IEEE Transactions on VLSI Systems*, 5(2), June 1997, pp. 218–229.

24. Asawaree Kalavade and Edward A. Lee, "The extended partitioning problem: Hardware/software mapping, scheduling, and implementation-bin selection," *Design Automation for Embedded Systems*, 2(2), March 1997, pp. 125–163.

25. Yanbing Li and Joerg Henkel, "A framework for estimating and minimizing energy dissipation of embedded HW/SW systems," in *Proceedings, 35th Design Automation Conference*, ACM Press, 1998, pp. 188–194.

26. W. Fornaciari, P. Gubian, D. Sciuto, and C. Silvano, "Power estimation of embedded systems: a hardware/software codesign approach," *IEEE Transactions on VLSI Systems*, 6(2), June 1998, pp. 266–275.

27. L. Benini, A. Bogliolo, and G. De Micheli, "A survey of design techniques for system-level dynamic power management," *IEEE Transactions on VLSI Systems*, 8(3), June 2000, pp. 299–316.

# 23

# Embedded Processor Applications

Jonathan W. Valvano
*University of Texas at Austin*

## 23.1 Introduction

This chapter overviews the field of embedded processors and their applications. Some basic concepts will be introduced, and examples of embedded systems will be given. Each topic will include a problem statement, definitions of terminology, fundamental hardware and software, and interfacing specific devices to create the desired functionality. A systems-level approach to microcomputer applications is achieved by presenting a few case studies that illustrate the spectrum of applications that employ microcomputers.

As shown in Fig. 23.1, the term embedded microcomputer system refers to a device that contains one or more microcomputers inside. To better understand the expression "embedded microcomputer system," consider each word separately. In this context, the word embedded means "hidden inside so one cannot see it." A computer is an electronic device with a processor, memory, and I/O ports. The processor executes software, which performs specific predefined operations. The processor includes registers (which are high-speed memory), an arithmetic logic unit or ALU (to execute math functions), a bus interface unit or BIU (which communicates with memory and I/O), and a control unit or CU (for making decisions.) Memory is a high-speed storage medium for software and data. Software consists of a sequence of commands that are usually executed in order. In an embedded system, we use read only memory (ROM) for storing the software and fixed constant data, and random access memory (RAM) for storing temporary information. The information in the ROM is nonvolatile, meaning the contents are not lost when power is removed. I/O ports allow information to enter via the input ports and exit via the output ports. The I/O devices (e.g., parallel ports, serial ports, timer, and ADC) are a crucial part of an embedded system because they

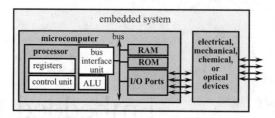

**FIGURE 23.1**   An embedded system includes a microcomputer with electrical, mechanical, chemical, and optical devices. A microcomputer includes a processor with memory, input, and output devices.

provide necessary functionality. The software together with the I/O ports and associated interface circuits give an embedded computer system its distinctive characteristics.

The term "microcomputer" means a small computer. Small in this context describes its size not its computing power, so a microcomputer can refer to a very wide range of products from the very simple (e.g., the PIC12C08 is a 8-pin DIP microcomputer with 512 by 12 bit ROM, 25 bytes RAM, and five I/O pins) to the most powerful Pentium. One typically restricts the term "embedded" to refer to systems that do not look and behave like a typical computer. Most embedded systems do not have a keyboard, a graphics display, or secondary storage (disk). Embedded systems can be developed in two ways. The first technique uses the microcomputers that are available as single chips. These devices are suitable for low-cost, low-performance systems. On the other hand, one can develop a high-performance embedded system around the PC architecture. These systems are first developed on a standard PC, and then the software and hardware are migrated to a stand-alone embedded-PC platform.

One can appreciate the wide range of embedded computer applications by observing existing implementations. Table 23.1 illustrates the breadth of applications that use an embedded microcomputer.

# 23.2   Embedded Processors

## Processor

In the last 30 years, the microprocessor has made significant technological advances. The term microprocessor refers to products ranging from the oldest Intel 8080 to the newest Pentium. The processor or CPU controls the system by executing instructions. It contains a BIU, which provides the address, direction (read data from memory into the processor or write data from processor to memory), and timing signals for the computer bus. The registers are very high-speed storage devices for the computer. The program counter (PC) is a register that contains the address of the current instruction that the computer is executing. The stack is a very important data structure used by computers to store temporary information. It is very easy to allocate temporary storage on the stack and deallocate it when done. The stack pointer (SP) is a register that points into RAM specifying the top entry of the stack. The condition code (CC) is a register that contains status flags describing the result of the previous operation and operating mode of the computer. Most computers have data registers that contain information and address registers that contain pointers. The ALU performs arithmetic (add, subtract, multiply, divide) and logical (and, or, not, exclusive or, shift) operations. The inputs to the ALU come from registers and/or memory, and the outputs go to registers or memory. The CC register contains status information from the previous ALU operation.

Software is a sequence of commands stored in memory. The control unit (CU) manipulates the hardware modules according to the software that it is executing. The CU contains an instruction register (IR) which holds the current instruction. The BIU contains an effective address register (EAR) which holds the effective address of the current instruction. The computer must fetch both instructions (op codes) and information (data). The BIU controls both types of access.

When an instruction is executed, the microprocessor often must refer to memory to read and/or write information. Often the I/O ports are implemented as memory locations. For example, on the Motorola

**TABLE 23.1**　Examples of Embedded Systems

| Category | Examples | What the Microcomputer Does |
|---|---|---|
| Consumer | Washing machines | Controls the water and spin cycles |
| | Exercise bikes | Monitors the workout |
| | TV remotes | Accepts key touches and sends IR pulses |
| | Clocks and watches | Maintains the time, alarm, and display |
| | Games and toys | Entertains the child |
| | Audio/video | Enhances performance |
| Communication | Answering machines | Saves and organizes messages |
| | Phones and pagers | Communication and security |
| | ATM machines | Security and convenience |
| Automotive | Automatic breaking | Stopping on slippery surfaces |
| | Noise cancellation | Improves sound quality |
| | Theft deterrent devices | Security |
| | Electronic ignition | Controls sparks and fuel injectors |
| | Windows and seats | Remember preferred settings |
| | Instrumentation | Collects and provides information |
| Military | Smart weapons | Does not fire at friendly targets |
| | Missile guidance | Directs ordnance at the target |
| | Global positioning | Where one is on the planet |
| Industrial | Set-back thermostats | Controls temperature and save energy |
| | Traffic control systems | Optimizes traffic |
| | Robot systems | Performs complex tasks |
| | Bar codes | Inventory control |
| | Sprinklers | Optimizes farming |
| Medical | Monitors | Measures and alarms |
| | Apnea | Alarms if the baby stops breathing |
| | Cardiac | Monitors heart functions |
| | Renal | Studies kidney functions |
| | Drugs | Automatic delivery |
| | Cancer treatments | Controls radiation, drugs, heat |
| | Pacemakers | Helps the heart beat regularly |
| | Prosthetic devices | Increases mobility |
| | Dialysis machines | Provides kidney functions |

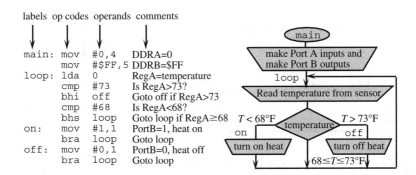

```
labels  op codes  operands  comments

main:  mov    #0,4    DDRA=0
       mov    #$FF,5  DDRB=$FF
loop:  lda    0       RegA=temperature
       cmp    #73     Is RegA>73?
       bhi    off     Goto off if RegA>73
       cmp    #68     Is RegA<68?
       bhs    loop    Goto loop if RegA≥68
on:    mov    #1,1    PortB=1, heat on
       bra    loop    Goto loop
off:   mov    #0,1    PortB=0, heat off
       bra    loop    Goto loop
```

**FIGURE 23.2**　A bang-bang temperature controller with hysteresis implemented using a Motorola 6808.

6808, I/O ports A and B exist as locations 0 and 1. Similar to most microcomputers, the I/O ports can be configured as inputs or outputs. The 6808 ports A and B have direction registers at locations 4 (DDRA) and 5 (DDRB), respectively. The software writes 0's to the direction register to specify the pins as inputs, and 1's to specify them as outputs. When the 6808 software reads from location 0 it gets information from Port A (`lda 0`). When the software writes to location 1, it sends information out Port B (`sta 1`). For example, the Motorola 6808 assembly language program, shown in Fig. 23.2, reads from a sensor that is connected to Port A, if the temperature is above 73°F, it turns off the heat (by writing 0 to Port B). If the temperature is below 68°F, it turns on the heat by writing 1 to Port B.

## Embedded Microcomputer

During the development phases of a project, we often would like the flexibility of accessing components inside the single-chip computer. In addition, during development, we are often unsure of the memory size and I/O capabilities that will be required to complete the design. Both of these factors point to the need for a single-board computer. This board has all of the features of the single-chip computer but laid out in an accessible and expandable manner. For some microcomputer systems, the final product is delivered using a single-board computer. For example, if the production volume is small and the project does not have severe space constraints, then a single-board solution may be cost-effective. Another example of final product delivered with a single-board occurs when the computer requirements (memory size, number of ports, etc.) exceed the capabilities of any single-chip computer.

## Choosing a Microcomputer

The computer engineer is often faced with the task of selecting a microcomputer for the project. In 1997 Motorola had 17.4% of the 4/8/16+ bit microcontroller market, Hitachi had 15.6%, and NEC had 13.2%. Table 23.2 breaks the 8-bit market share down by architecture, showing the 8051 architecture to be most popular. As of 1997, Motorola has shipped over 2 billion 68HC05 8-bit microcontrollers. This cumulative number on a unit level is more than all microprocessors from all other chip vendors. Table 23.3 lists major manufacturers and their web sites

Often, only those devices for which the engineers have hardware and software experience are considered. Fortunately, this blind approach often still yields an effective and efficient product, because many of the computers overlap in their cost and performance. In other words, if a microcomputer that you are familiar with can implement the desired functions for the project, then it is often efficient to bypass that perfect piece of hardware in favor of a faster development time. On the other hand, sometimes one wishes to evaluate all potential candidates. Sometimes, it may be cost-effective to hire or train the engineering

**TABLE 23.2**   1997 Market Share in Dollars of 8-bit Microcontrollers [1]

| μC | Company | Revenue (millions) |
|---|---|---|
| 8051 | Intel, Philips, Siemens, Dallas Semiconductor | 1027 |
| HC05 | Motorola | 864 |
| HC11 | Motorola | 643 |
| H8 | Hitachi | 505 |
| 78K | NEC | 497 |

**TABLE 23.3**   Web Sites of Companies That Make Microcontrollers

| Company | Products | Web Site |
|---|---|---|
| Motorola | HC05 HC08 HC11 HC12 HC16 683xx 68K MCORE Coldfire PowerPC | http://www.motorola.com/ |
| Hitachi | H8 | http://www.hitachi.com/ |
| NEC | 78K | http://www.nec.com/ |
| Intel | 8051 80251 8096 80296 | http://www.intel.com/ |
| Mitsubishi | 740 7600 7700 M16C | http://www.mitsubishichips.com/index.htm |
| Philips | 8051 | http://www.philips.com/home.html |
| Siemens | C500 C166 Tricore | http://www.siemens.de/en/ |
| Microchip | PIC12 PIC12 PIC16 PIC17 | http://www.microchip.com/ |

personnel so that they are proficient in a wide spectrum of potential computer devices. Many factors must be considered when selecting an embedded microcomputer. The labor costs include training, development, and testing. The material costs include parts and supplies. The manufacturing costs depend on the number and complexity of the components. The maintenance costs involve revisions to fix bugs and perform upgrades. The ROM size must be big enough to hold instructions and fixed data for the software. The RAM size must be big enough to hold locals, parameters, and global variables. The EEPROM size must be big enough to hold nonvolatile fixed constants that are field configurable. The speed must be fast enough to execute the software in real time. The I/O bandwidth affects how fast can the computer input/output data. The data size (8, 16, or 32 bit) should match most of the data to be processed. Numerical operations like multiply, divide, signed, and floating point may be needed. Special functions like multiply/accumulate, fuzzy logic, complex numbers are sometimes required. There must be enough parallel ports for all the I/O digital signals. The microcomputer needs enough serial ports to interface with other computers or I/O devices. The timer functions can be used to generate signals, measure frequency, and measure period. Pulse width modulation is convenient for the output signals in many control applications. An ADC is used to convert analog inputs to digital numbers. The package size and environmental issues affect many embedded systems. In order to meet manufacturing deadlines, the availability of a second source is advantageous. The availability of high-level language cross-compilers, simulators, emulators will facilitate software development. The power requirements will be important if the systems will be battery operated.

When considering speed, it is best to compare time to execute a benchmark program similar to your specific application, rather than just comparing bus frequency. One of the difficulties is that the microcomputer selection depends on the speed and size of the software, but the software can not be written without the computer. Given this uncertainty, it is best to select a family of devices with a range of execution speeds and memory configurations. In this way, a prototype system with large amounts of memory and peripherals can be purchased for software and hardware development, and once the design is in its final stages, the specific version of the computer can be selected now knowing the memory and speed requirements for the project.

# 23.3 Software Systems

## Assembly Language

An assembly language program, like the one shown in Fig. 23.2, has a 1-to-1 mapping with the machine code of the computer. In other words, one line of assembly code maps into a single machine instruction. The label field associates the absolute memory address with a symbolic label. The op code represents the machine instruction to be executed. The operand field identifies the data itself or the memory location for the data needed by the instruction. The comment field is added by the programmer to explain what, how, and why. The comments are not used by the computer during execution, but rather provide a means for one programmer to communicate with another, including oneself at a later time. This style of programming offers the best static efficiency (smallest program size), and best dynamic efficiency (fastest program execution). Another advantage of assembly language programming is the complete freedom to implement any arbitrary decision function or data structure. One is not limited to a finite list of predefined structures as is the case with higher level languages. For example, one can write assembly code with multiple entry points (places to begin the function).

## High-Level Languages

Although assembly language enforces no restrictions on the programmer, many software developers argue that the limits placed on the programmer by a structured language, in fact, are a good idea. Building program and data structures by combining predefined components makes it easy to implement modular software that is easier to debug, verify correctness, and modify in the future. Software maintenance is the debug, verify and modify cycle, and it represents a significant fraction of the effort required to develop products using embedded computers. Therefore, if the use of a high level language sacrifices some speed and memory performance, but gains in the maintenance costs, most computer engineers will choose reliability and ease of modification over speed and memory efficiency. Cross-compilers for C, C++, FORTH, and BASIC are available for many single-chip microcomputers with C being the most popular.

One of the best approaches to this assembly versus high-level language choice is to implement the prototype in a high level language, and see if the solution meets the product specifications. If it does, then leave the software in the high level language because it will be easier to upgrade in the future. If the software is not quite fast enough (or small enough to fit into the available memory), then one might try a better compiler. Another approach is to profile the software execution, which involves collecting timing information on the percentage of time the computer takes executing each module. The profile allows you to identify a small number of modules that, if rewritten in assembly language, will have a big impact on the system performance.

## Software Development

Recent software and hardware technological developments have made significant impacts on the software development for embedded microcomputers. The simplest approach is to use a cross-assembler or cross-compiler to convert source code into the machine code for the target system. The machine code can then be loaded into the target machine. Debugging embedded systems with this simple approach is very difficult for two reasons. First, the embedded system lacks the usual keyboard and display that assist us when we debug regular software. Second, the nature of embedded systems involves the complex and real time interaction between the hardware and software. These real-time interactions make it impossible to test software with the usual single-stepping and print statements.

A logic analyzer is a multiple channel digital oscilloscope. For the single-board computer that has external memory, the logic analyzer can be placed on the address and data bus to observe program behavior. The logic analyzer records a cycle-by-cycle dump of the address and data bus. With the appropriate personality module, the logic analyzer can convert the address and data information into the corresponding stream of executed assembly language instructions. Unfortunately, the address and data bus singles are not available on most single-chip microcomputers. For these computers, the logic analyzer can still be used to record the digital signals at the microcomputer I/O ports. The advantages of the logic analyzer are very high bandwidth recording (100 MHz to 1 GHz), many channels (16–132 inputs), flexible triggering and clocking mechanisms, and personality modules that assist in interpreting the data.

The next technological advancement that has greatly affected the manner in which embedded systems are developed is simulation. Because of the high cost and long times required to create hardware proto-types, many preliminary feasibility designs are now performed using hardware/software simulations. A simulator is a software application that models the behavior of the hardware/software system. If both the external hardware and software program are simulated together, even although the simulated time is slower than the actual time, the real time hardware/software interactions can be studied.

Once the design is committed to hardware, the debugging tasks become more difficult. One simple approach, mentioned earlier, is to use a single-board computer that behaves similarly to the single-chip. Another approach is to use an in-circuit emulator. An in-circuit emulator (ICE) is a complex digital hardware device, which emulates (behaves in a similar manner) the I/O pins of the microcomputer in real time. The emulator is usually connected to a personal computer, so that emulated memory, I/O ports, and registers can be loaded and observed. To use an emulator we first remove the microcomputer chip from the circuit then attach the emulator pod into the socket where the microcomputer chip used to be.

The only disadvantage of the in-circuit emulator is its cost. To provide some of the benefits of this high-priced debugging equipment, some microcomputers have a background debug module (BDM). The BDM hardware exists on the microcomputer chip itself and communicates with the debugging personal computer via a dedicated 2 or 3 wire serial interface. Although not as flexible as an ICE, the

BDM can provide the ability to observe software execution in real time, the ability to set breakpoints, the ability to stop the computer, and the ability to read and write registers, I/O ports, and memory.

## Memory Allocation

Embedded systems group together in physical memory information that has similar logical properties. Because the embedded system does not load programs off disk when started, allocation is an extremely important issue for these systems. Typical software segments include global variables, local variables, fixed constants, and machine instructions. For single chip implementations, different types of information are stored into the three types of memory. RAM is volatile and has random and fast access. EEPROM is nonvolatile and can be easily erased and reprogrammed. ROM is nonvolatile but can be programmed only once.

In an embedded application, structures that must be changed during execution are usually put in RAM. Examples include recorded data, parameters passed to subroutines, and global and local variables. We place fixed constants in EEPROM because the information remains when the power is removed, but can be reprogrammed at a later time. Examples of fixed constants include translation tables, security codes, calibration data, and configuration parameters. We place machine instructions, interrupt vectors, and the reset vector in ROM because this information is stored once and will not need to be reprogrammed in the future.

# 23.4   Interfacing

## Digital Logic

Many logic families are available to design digital circuits. Each family provides the basic logic functions (and or not), but differ in the technology used to implement these functions. This results in a wide range of parameter specifications. Basic parameters of digital devices can be found in references [1] and [2]. Because many microcomputers are high-speed CMOS, typical values for this family are given. In general, it is desirable to design digital systems using all components from the same family. There are three basic considerations when using digital logic: speed and signal loading.

One of the pressures that exists in the microcomputer embedded systems field is the need to implement higher and higher levels of functionality into smaller and smaller amounts of space using less and less power. Many examples of technology were developed according to these principles. Examples include portable computers, satellite communications, aviation devices, military hardware, and cellular phones. Simply using a microcomputer provides significant advantages in this faster-smaller race. The embedded system is not just a computer, so there must also be mechanical and electrical devices external to the computer. To shrink the size and power required of these external electronics, they can be integrated into a custom integrated circuit (IC) called an application specific integrated circuit (ASIC). An ASIC provides a high level of functionality squeezed into a small package. Advances in IC design allow more and more of these custom circuits (both analog and digital) to be manufactured in the same IC chip as the computer itself. In this way, single-chip solutions are possible.

The microcomputer typically responds to external events with an appropriate software action. The time between the external event and the software action is defined as the latency. If an upper bound on the latency can be guaranteed, the system is characterized as real-time, or hard real-time. If the system allows one software task to have priority over the others, then it is described as soft real-time. Because most real-time systems utilize interrupts to handle critical events, we can calculate the upper bound on the latency as the sum of three components (1) maximum time the software executes with interrupts disabled (e.g., other interrupt handlers, critical code); (2) the time for the processor to service the interrupt (saving registers on stack, fetching the interrupt vector); and (3) software delays in the interrupt handler before the appropriate software action is performed. Examples of events that sometimes require real-time processing include input, output, and alarms. When new input data is ready, the software must respond by reading the new input.

When the output device is idle, the software must respond by giving it more data to output. When an alarm condition occurs, the software must process the data until the time the alarm is processed.

Sometimes the software must respond to internal events. Many real time systems involve performing software tasks on a fixed and regular rate. For these systems, a periodic interrupt is employed to generate requests at fixed intervals. The microcomputer clock guarantees that the interrupt request is made exactly on time, but the software response (latency) may occur later. Examples of real-time systems that utilize periodic interrupts include: data acquisition systems where the software executes at the sampling rate, control systems where the software executes at the controller rate, and time of day clocks where the software maintains the date and time.

## Keyboard Interfacing

Individual buttons and switches can be interfaced to a microcomputer input port simply by converting the on/off resistance to a digital logic signal with a pull-up resistor. When many keys are to be interfaced, it is efficient to combine them in a matrix configuration. $n^2$ keys can be constructed as an $n$ by $n$ matrix. To interface the keyboard with $n^2$ keys, $2n$ I/O ports are needed, the rows to open collector (or open drain) microcomputer outputs and the columns to microcomputer inputs are connected. Open collector means the output will be low if the software writes a zero to the output port, but will float (high impedance) if the software writes a one. Pull-up resistors on the inputs will guarantee the column signals will be high if no key is touched in the selected row. The software scans the key matrix by driving one row at a time to zero, while the other rows are floating. If there is a key touched in the selected row, then the corresponding column signal will be zero. Many switches will bounce on/off for about 10 ms when touched or released. The software must read the switch position multiple times over a 20-ms time period to guarantee a reliable reading. One simple software method uses a periodic interrupt (with a rate slower than the bounce time) to scan the keyboard. In this way, the software will properly detect single key touches. One disadvantage of the matrix-scanned keyboard is the fact that three keys simultaneously pressed sometimes "looks" like four keys are pressed.

## Finite State Machine Controller

To illustrate the concepts of programmable logic and memory allocation consider the simple traffic light controller illustrated in Fig. 23.3. The finite state machine (FSM) has two inputs from sensors that identify the presence of cars. There are six outputs, red/yellow/green for the North road and red/yellow/ green for the East road. In this FSM, each state has a 6-bit output value, a time to wait in that state, and four next states depending on if the input is 00 (no cars), 01 (car on the North road), 10 (car on the East road) or 11 (cars on both roads). The software will output the pattern for the current state, wait the specified amount of time, input from the sensors, and jump to the next state depending on the input. The finite state machine data structure (linked list or table) will be defined in EEPROM, and the program will be stored in ROM. The software for this system exhibits the three classic segments. Since the variables have values that change during execution, they must be defined in RAM. One should be able to make

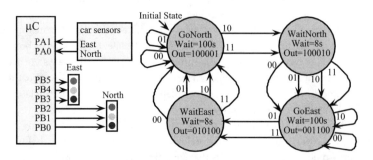

**FIGURE 23.3**   A simple traffic controller implemented using a finite-state machine.

minor modifications to the finite state machine (e.g., add/delete states, change input/output values) by changing the linked list data structure in EEPROM without modifying the assembly language controller in ROM. A C-level program written for a Motorola 6812 follows:

```
const struct State{          // const means put in EEPROM
  unsigned char Out;         // 6-bit Output
  unsigned char Time;        // Time to wait in seconds
  unsigned char Next[4];};   // Next state if input=00,01,10,11
typedef const struct State StateType;
#define GoN   0    // Green on North, Red on East
#define WaitN 1    // Yellow on North, Red on East
#define GoE   2    // Red on North, Green on East
#define WaitE 3    // Red on North, Yellow on East
StateType fsm[4]={                          //          EEPROM
  {0x21, 100, {GoN,  GoN,WaitN,WaitN}},   // GoN      EEPROM
  {0x22,   8, {GoE,  GoE,  GoE,  GoE}},   // WaitN    EEPROM
  {0x0C, 100, {GoE,WaitE,  GoE,WaitE}},   // GoE      EEPROM
  {0x14,   8, {GoN,  GoN,  GoN, GoN}}};   // WaitE    EEPROM
void main(void){                            //          ROM
  unsigned char Input;                      //          RAM
  unsigned int St;         // Current State            RAM
  St=GoN;                  // Initial State            ROM
  DDRA=0, DDRB=0xFF;       // Set direction registers  ROM
  while(1){                //                          ROM
    PORTB=fsm[St].Out;     // output for this state    ROM
    Wait(fsm[St].Time);    // wait in this state       ROM
    Input=PORTA&0x03;      // Input=00 01 10 or 11     ROM
    St=fsm[St].Next[Input];}}    //                    ROM
```

## Current-Activated Output Devices

Many external devices used in embedded systems activate with a current, and deactivate when no current is supplied. The control element can be either a diode or a coil (resistor and inductor combination). The microcomputer controls the device by passing current or no-current through the control element. Coil devices include electromagnetic relays, solenoids, DC motors, and stepper motors. Diode-based devices include LEDs, optosensors, optical isolation, solid state relays. Diode-based devices require a current limiting resistor. The value of the resistor determines the voltage ($V_d$), current ($I_d$) operating point. The coil-based devices require a snubber diode to eliminate the large back EMF (over 200 V) that develops when the current is turned off. The back EMF is generated when the large dI/dt occurs across the inductance of the coil. The microcomputer output pins do not usually have a large enough $I_{OL}$ to drive these devices directly, so an open collector gate (such as the 7405, 7406, 75492, 75451, or NPN transistors) can be used to sink current to ground or use an open emitter gate (like the 75491 or PNP transistors) to source current from the power supply. Darlington switches such as the ULN-2061 through ULN-2077 can be configured as either current sinks (open collector) or sources (open emitter). A device with an output current larger than the current required by the control element needs to be selected.

## Stepper Motors

A bipolar stepper motor has only two coils and four wires, as shown in Fig. 23.4. Using the full-step algorithm, current always passes through both coils. The computer controls a bipolar stepper by reversing the direction of the currents. If the computer generates the sequence (positive, positive) (negative, positive) (negative, negative) (positive, negative), the motor will spin. A unipolar stepper motor is controlled by

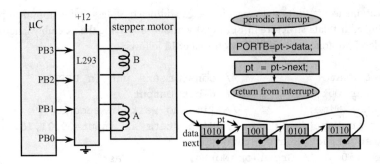

**FIGURE 23.4** A hardware interface of a bipolar stepper motor and the linked-list data structure used by the software to spin the motor.

passing current through four coils, exactly two at a time. There are five or six wires on a unipolar stepper motor. For both types of stepper motors, the software outputs the sequence 1010, 1001, 0101, 0110 to spin the motor. The software makes one change (e.g., change from 1001 to 0101) to affect one step. The software repeats the entire sequence over and over at regular time intervals between changes to make the motor spin at a constant rate. Some stepper motors will move on half-steps by outputting the sequence 1010, 1000, 1001, 0001, 0101, 0100, 0110, 0010. Assuming the motor torque is large enough to overcome the mechanical resistance (load on the shaft), each output change causes the motor to step a predefined angle. One of the key parameters that determine whether the motor will slip (a computer change without the shaft moving) is the jerk, which is the derivative of the acceleration (i.e., third derivative of the shaft position). Software algorithms that minimize jerk are less likely to cause a motor slip. If the computer outputs the sequence in the opposite order, the motor spins in the other direction. A circular linked list data structure, as shown in Fig. 23.4, is a convenient software implementation that guarantees the proper motor sequence is maintained.

## 23.5 Data Acquisition Systems

Before designing a data acquisition system (DAS) the system goals must be clearly understood. The system can be classified as a quantitative DAS, if the specifications can be defined explicitly in terms of desired range, resolution, precision, and frequencies of interest. If the specifications are more loosely defined, we classify it as a qualitative DAS. Examples of qualitative DASs include systems that mimic the human senses where the specifications are defined using terms like "sounds good," "looks pretty," and "feels right." Other qualitative DASs involve the detection of events. In these types of systems, the specifications are expressed in terms of specificity and sensitivity. For example, some premature infants stop breathing during sleep. If we can detect this event and "wake up the baby," it will start breathing again. An apnea monitor is attached to the baby as it sleeps to alert the parents to this life-threatening event. Other binary detection systems include the presence/absence of a burglar or the presence/absence of cancer. A true positive (TP) is defined when the condition exists (the baby stops breathing) and the system properly detects it (the alarm rings). A false positive (FP) is defined when the condition does not exist (the baby is breathing normally) but the system thinks it exists (the alarm rings). A false negative (FN) occurs when the condition exists (the baby stops breathing) but the system does not think it exists (the alarm is silent, and baby dies). Sensitivity, TP/(TP + FN), is the fraction of properly detected events (the baby stops breathing and the alarm rings) over the total number of events (the baby stops breathing). It is a measure of how well our system can detect an event. A sensitivity of 1 means the baby will not die. Specificity, TP/(TP + FP), is the fraction of properly detected events (the baby stops breathing and the alarm rings) over the total number of detections (number of alarms). It is a measure of how much we believe the system is correct when it says it has detected an event. A specificity of 1 means when the alarm rings, the parents will rush to the baby's crib and resuscitate the baby.

Many components are included in a data acquisition system. The transducer converts the physical signal into an electrical signal. The amplifier converts the weak transducer electrical signal into the range of the ADC (e.g., 0–5 V). The analog filter removes unwanted frequency components within the signal. The analog filter is required to remove aliasing error caused by the ADC sampling. A periodic interrupt is used to control the sampling process. The interrupt service routine will sample the ADC and store the data in a first-in-first-out queue. The data will be processed in the foreground by the main program. Examples of digital processing include digital filters, calibration calculations, event detection, and data display. Inherent in digital signal processing is the requirement that the ADC be sampled on a fixed time basis. Sampling at a known and fixed rate is particularly important when a digital filter is used.

The first decision to make is the ADC precision. Whether we have a qualitative or quantitative DAS, we choose the number of bits in the ADC so as to achieve the desired system specification. For a quantitative DAS, this is a simple task because the relationship between the ADC precision and the system measurement precision is obvious. For a qualitative DAS, experimental trials are often employed to evaluate the relationship between ADC bits and system performance.

The next decision is the sampling rate, $f_s$. The Nyquist theorem states we can reliably represent in digital form a band-limited analog signal if we sample faster than twice the largest frequency that exists in the analog signal. For example, if an analog signal only has frequency components in the 0–100 Hz range, then if sample are taken at a rate above 200 Hz, the entire signal can be reconstructed from the digital samples. One of the reasons for using an analog filter is to guarantee that the signal at the ADC input is band-limited. Violation of the Nyquist theorem results in aliasing. Aliasing is the distortion of the digital signal that occurs when frequency components above 0.5 $f_s$ exist at the ADC input. These high-frequency components are frequency shifted or folded into the 0–0.5 $f_s$ range.

# 23.6 Control Systems

## Digital Control Equations

A control system is a collection of mechanical and electrical devices connected for the purpose of commanding, directing, or regulating a physical plant. The real-state variables are the actual properties of the physical plant that are to be controlled. The goal of the sensor and data acquisition system is to estimate the state variables. Any differences between the estimated state variables and the real state variables will translate directly into controller errors. A closed loop control system uses the output of the state estimator in a feedback loop to drive the errors to zero. The control system compares these estimated state variables, $x(n)$, to the desired state variables, $x^*$, in order to decide appropriate action, $u(n)$. The terminology $(n)$ refers to the fact that these parameters are digital values sampled at finite-time intervals, where $n$ is the sample number. The actuator is a transducer, which converts the control system commands, $u(n)$, into driving forces, which are applied to the physical plant. The goal of the control system is to drive $x(n)$ to equal $x^*$. If the error is defined as the difference between the desired and estimated state variable:

$$e(n) = x^* - x(n) \qquad (23.1)$$

then the control system will attempt to drive $e(n)$ to zero. We usually evaluate the effectiveness of a control system by determining three properties: steady-state controller error, transient response, and stability. The steady state controller error is the average value of $e(n)$. The transient response is how long does the system take to reach 99% of the final output after $x^*$ is changed. A system is stable if steady state (smooth constant output) is achieved. An unstable system may oscillate.

## Pulse Width Modulation

Many embedded systems must generate output pulses with specific pulse widths. The internal microcomputer clock is used to guarantee the timing accuracy of these outputs. Many microcomputers have built-in hardware that facilitates the generation of pulses. One classic example is the pulse-width modulated motor controller. The motor is turned on and off at a fixed frequency (see the *Out* signal in Fig. 23.5).

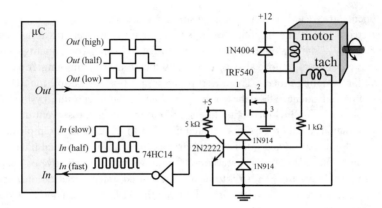

**FIGURE 23.5**   An interface to a DC motor that uses PWM to control the delivered power and period measurement to determine the rotation speed.

The value of this frequency is chosen to be too fast for the motor to response to the individual on/off signals. Rather, the motor responses to the average. The computer controls the power to the motor by varying the pulse width or duty cycle of the wave. The IRF540 MOSFET can sink up to 28 A. To implement pulse width modulation (PWM) the computer (either with the built-in hardware or the software) uses a clock. The clock is a simple integer counter that is incremented at a regular rate. The *Out* signal is set high for time $T_h$ then set low for time $T_l$. Since the frequency of *Out* is to be fixed, $(T_h + T_l)$ remains constant, but the duty cycle $T_h/(T_h + T_l)$ is varied. The precision of this PWM system is defined to be the number of distinguishable duty cycles that can be generated. Let $h$ and $l$ be integer numbers representing the number of clock counts the *Out* signal is high and low, respectively. We can express the duty cycle as $h/(h + l)$. Theoretically, the precision should be $h + l$, but practically the value may be limited by the speed of the interface electronics.

## Period Measurement

In order to sense the motor speed, a tachometer can be used. The AC amplitude and frequency of the tachometer output both depend on the shaft speed. It is usually more convenient to convert the AC signal into a digital signal (*In* shown in the Fig. 23.5) and measure the period. Again, many microcomputers have built-in hardware that facilitates the period measurement. To implement period measurement the computer (again either with the built-in hardware or the software) uses a clock. Period measurement simply records the time (value of the clock) of two successive rising edges on the input and calculates the time difference. The period measurement resolution is defined to be the smallest difference in period that can be reliably measured. Theoretically, the period measurement resolution should be the clock period, but practically the value may be limited by noise in the interface electronics. The software can calculate shaft speed, because the frequency is one over the period.

## Control Algorithms

There are many common approaches to designing the software for the control system. The simplest approach to the closed-loop control system uses incremental control. In this motor control example, the actuator command, $u$, is the duty cycle of the pulse-width-modulated system. An incremental control algorithm simply adds or subtracts a constant from $u$ depending on the sign of the error. To add hysteresis to the incremental controller, we define two thresholds, $x_H$ $x_L$, at values just above and below the desired speed, $x^*$. In other words, if $x < x_L$ (the motor is spinning too slow) then $u$ is incremented, and if $x > x_H$ (the motor is spinning too fast) then $u$ is decremented. It is important to choose the proper rate at which the incremental control software is executed. If it is executed too many times per second, then the actuator will saturate resulting in a bang-bang system like Fig. 23.2. If it is not executed often enough, then the system will not respond quickly to changes in the physical plant or changes in $x^*$.

A second approach, called proportional integral derivative (PID), uses linear differential equations. To simplify the PID controller, we break the controller equation into separate proportion, integral and derivative terms, where $p(n)$, $i(n)$, and $d(n)$ are the proportional, integral, and derivative components, respectively. In order to implement the control system with the microcomputer, it is imperative that the digital equations be executed on a regular and periodic rate (every $\Delta t$). The relationship between the real time, $t$, and the discrete time, $n$, is simply $t = n\Delta t$. If the sampling rate varies, then controller errors will occur. The proportional term makes the actuator output linearly related to the error. Using a proportional term creates a control system that applies more energy to the plant when the error is large.

$$p(n) = k_p e(n) \tag{23.2}$$

The integral term makes the actuator output related to the integral of the error. Using an integral term often will improve the steady state error of the control system. If a small error accumulates for a long time, this term can get large. Some control systems put upper and lower bounds on this term, called anti-reset-windup, to prevent it from dominating the other terms. The implementation of the integral term requires the use of a discrete integral or sum. If $i(n)$ is the present control output, and $i(n-1)$ is the previous calculation, the integral term is simply

$$i(n) = i(n-1) + k_i e(n) \qquad \text{where} \quad i_{\min} \le i(n) \le i_{\max} \tag{23.3}$$

The derivative term makes the actuator output related to the derivative of the error. This term is usually combined with either the proportional and/or integral term to improve the transient of the control system. The proper value of $k_d$ will provide for a quick response to changes in either the set point or loads on the physical plant. An incorrect value may create an overdamped (very slow response) or an underdamped (unstable oscillations) response. There are a couple of ways to implement the discrete time derivative. A simple approach is

$$d(n) = k_d(x(n) - x(n-1)) \tag{23.4}$$

In practice, this first order equation is quite susceptible to noise. More sophisticated calculations can be found in reference [1]. The PID controller software is also implemented with a periodic interrupt every $\Delta t$. The interrupt handler first estimates the state variable, $x(n)$, and then calculates $e(n)$. The next actuator output is calculated by combining the three terms.

$$u(n) = p(n) + i(n) + d(n) \tag{23.5}$$

A third approach uses fuzzy logic to control the physical plant. Fuzzy logic can be much simpler than PID. It will require less memory and execute faster. When complete knowledge about the physical plant is known, then a good PID controller can be developed, i.e., the physical plant can be described with a linear system of differential equations, an optimal PID control system can be developed. Because the fuzzy logic control is more robust (still works even if the parameter constants are not optimal), then the fuzzy logic approach can be used when complete knowledge about the plant is not known or can change dynamically. Choosing the proper PID parameters requires knowledge about the plant. The fuzzy logic approach is more intuitive, following more closely to the way a "human" would control the system. If there is no set of differential equations that describe the physical plant, but there exists expert knowledge (human intuition) on how it works, then a good fuzzy logic system can be developed. It is easy to modify an existing fuzzy control system into a new problem. So if the framework exists, rapid prototyping is possible. Examples of fuzzy logic implementations can be found in reference [1].

## 23.7  Remote or Distributed Systems

Many embedded systems require the communication of command or data information to other modules at either a near or a remote location. We will begin our discussion with communication with devices within the same room as presented in Fig. 23.6. A full-duplex channel allows data to transfer in both directions at the same time. In a half-duplex system, data can transfer in both directions but only in one direction at a time. Half-duplex is popular because it is less expensive (two wires) and allows the addition of more devices on the channel without change to the existing nodes. If the distances are short, half-duplex can be implemented with simple open collector TTL-level logic. Many microcomputers have open collector modes on their serial ports that allow a half-duplex network to be created without any external logic (although pull-up resistors are often used). Three factors will limit the implementation of this simple half-duplex network: (1) the number of nodes on the network, (2) the distance between nodes, and (3) presence of corrupting noise. In these situations a half-duplex RS485 driver chip, such as the SP483 made by Sipex or Maxim, can be used. The master-slave system connects the master transmit output to all slave receive inputs. This provides for broadcast of commands from the master. All slave transmit outputs are connected together using wire or open collector logic, allowing for the slaves to respond one at a time. The ring network is a simple distributed approach, because it can be constructed using standard serial ports, by chaining the transmit and receive lines together in a circuit, as shown in Fig. 23.6.

A very common approach to distributed embedded systems is called multi-drop. To transmit a byte to the other computers, the software activates the SP483 driver and outputs the frame. Since it is half-duplex, the frame is also sent to the receiver of the computer that sent it. This echo can be checked to see if a collision occurred (two devices simultaneously outputting.) If more than two computers exist on the network, address information is usually sent first, so that the proper device receives the data.

Within the same room, IR light pulses can be used to send and receive information. This is the technology used in the TV remote control. In order to eliminate background EM radiation from triggering a false communication, the signals are encoded as a series of long and short pulses that resemble bar codes.

A number of techniques are available for communicating across longer distances. Within the same building the X-10 protocol can be used. The basic idea is to encode the binary stream of data as 120 kHz pulses and mix them onto the standard 120 V 60 Hz AC power line. For each binary one, a 120 kHz pulse is added at the zero crossing of the 60 Hz wave. A zero is encoded as the absence of the 120 kHz pulse. Because there are three phases within the AC power system, each pulse is repeated also 2.778 ms, and 5.556 ms after the zero crossing. It is decoded on the receiver end. X-10 has the flexibility of adding or expanding communication capabilities in a building without rewiring. The disadvantage of X-10 is that the bandwidth is fairly low (about 120 bits/s) when compared to other techniques. A typical X-10 message includes a 2-bit start code, a 4-bit house code, and a 5-bit number code requiring 11 power line cycles to transmit. A second technique for longer distances is RF modulation. The information is modulated on the transmitted RF and demodulated at the receiver. Standard telephone modems and the Internet can also be used to establish long distance networks.

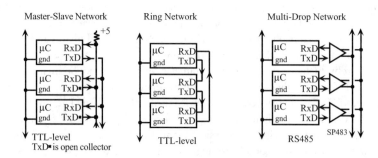

**FIGURE 23.6**   Three simple configurations for distributed embedded systems.

Two approaches are used to synchronize the multiple computers. In a master/slave system, one device is the master, which controls all the other slaves. The master defines the overall parameters that govern the functions of each slave and arbitrates requests for data and resources. This is the simplest approach but may require a high-bandwidth channel and a fast computer for the master. Collisions are unlikely in a master/slave system if the master can control access to the network.

The other approach is distributed communication. In this approach each computer is given certain local responsibilities and certain local resources. Communication across the network is required when data collected in one node must be shared with other nodes. A distributed approach will be successful on large problems that can be divided into multiple tasks that can run almost independently. As the interdependence of the tasks increase so will the traffic on the network. Collision detection and recovery are required due to the asynchronous nature of the individual nodes.

# References

1. J.W. Valvano, Real-Time Embedded Systems, Brooks-Cole, 2000.
2. C.H. Roth, Fundamentals of Logic Design, West Publishing, 1992.
3. H.M. Dietel, and P.J. Dietel, C++ How to Program, Prentice-Hall, Englewood Cliffs, NJ, 1994.
4. R.H. Barnett, The 8051 Family of Microcomputers, Prentice-Hall, Englewood Cliffs, NJ, 1995.
5. J.B. Peatman, Design with Microcontrollers, McGraw-Hill, New York, 1988.
6. J.B. Peatman, Design with PIC Microcontrollers, McGraw-Hill, New York, 1998.
7. J.C. Skroder, Using the M68HC11 Microcontroller, Prentice-Hall, Englewood Cliffs, NJ, 1997.
8. K.L. Short, Embedded Microprocessor Systems Design, Prentice-Hall, Englewood Cliffs, NJ, 1998.
9. P. Spasov, Microcontroller Technology The 68HC11, Prentice-Hall, Englewood Cliffs, NJ, 1996.
10. H.S. Stone, Microcomputer Interfacing, Addison-Wesley, Reading, MA, 1982.
11. R.J. Tocci, F.J. Abrosio, and L.P. Laskowski, Microprocessors and Microcomputers, Prentice-Hall, Englewood Cliffs, NJ, 1997.
12. W.C. Wray, and J.D. Greenfield, Using Microprocessors and Microcomputers, Prentice-Hall, Englewood Cliffs, NJ, 1994.

# VI

# Signal Processing

# IV

## Signal Processing

# 24
# Digital Signal Processing

Fred J. Taylor

*University of Florida*

## 24.1  Introduction

Signals are traditionally classified as being analog (continuous-time), discrete-time (sample-data), or digital. A continuous-time signal has infinite precision in both the time- and amplitude-domain. Discrete-time signals have infinite amplitude precision, but are discretely resolved in time (sampled). Digital signals are of finite precision in both the time (sampled) and amplitude (quantized). Digital signals are either synthesized by a digital system (e.g., computer), or digitized by quantizing the sample values of an analog signal using an analog-to-digital converter (ADC). A digital-to-analog converter (DAC) maps a digital signal into an analog signal. Signal processing refers to the science of analyzing, synthesizing, and manipulating audio, acoustic, speech, video, image, geophysical, radar, radio signals, plus a host of other signals, using mathematical and experimental methods. Signal may be scalars, of one, two, or $M$ dimensions, of finite or infinite duration. Digital signal processing (DSP) refers to the processing of digital or digitized signals using digital technologies. DSP system elements can be linear or nonlinear and perform in the time (e.g., filter) or transform domain (e.g., frequency). The processing agents range from mathematical and statistical abstractions or processes, to tangible software and hardware systems. DSP systems must often be designed to meet restrictive real-time speed, precision, dynamic range requirements in multisignal, multisystem environments. The design of a DSP solution, therefore, requires a concurrent knowledge of signal processing methods and technology.

   DSP is currently a major market force, consisting of semiconductor, hardware, software, methodology, application, and training sectors. The origins of DSP are open to debate, but a seminal moment surely occurred when Claude Shannon developed an understanding of sample-data signal processing in the middle of the 20th century. Shannon's sampling theorem states that if an analog signal, having a highest frequency bounded by $B$ Hz, is sampled at a rate in excess of $f_s > B$ Hz, then it can be perfectly reconstructed (exactly) from its sample values. The critical parameter $f_N = f_s/2$ is called the *Nyquist frequency* and represents a strict upper frequency bound on the highest baseband frequency allowed in the sampled signal (i.e., $B$). Most DSP solutions are over-sampled, operating at a sample frequency far in excess of its minimally required value. If a signal is under-sampled at a rate below the minimum rate of $2B$ Hz, *aliasing* errors can occur. An aliased signal is a baseband signal whose sample values impersonate those of a signal having frequency components in excess $B$ Hz. Another early enabler of the DSP revolution was the Cooley–Tukey fast Fourier transform (FFT) algorithm. The FFT made many signal-processing tasks practical for the first time using, in many instances, only software. Another defining DSP moment occurred when the first DSP microprocessors (DSP $\mu$p) made a marketplace appearance beginning in the late 1970s. These devices provided an affordable and tangible means of developing hardware and embedded solutions with a minimum risk and effort. Regardless of the origins, today's DSP objects and systems have become part of a pervasive technology, appearing in a myriad of applications, and supported with a rich and deep technological infrastructure. DSP is now a discipline unto itself, with its own professional societies, academic programs, trained practitioners, and industrial infrastructure.

## 24.2   Digital Signals and Systems

Digital systems process digital signals in the time or frequency-domain. Systems can be analyzed and characterized by the system's response to a pure impulse (i.e., $\delta[k]$), called the *impulse response* denoted $h[k] = \{h[0], h[1], h[2],\ldots\}$. The sequence of sample values $h[k]$, called a *time-series*, can also be mathematically represented using a *z-transform*. The z-transform of an arbitrary time-series $x[k]$, consisting of sample values $x[k] = \{x[0], x[1], x[2],\ldots\}$, is given by $X(z) = \sum_{k=0}^{\infty} x[k]z^{-k}$. The z operator is defined in terms of the Laplace transform delay operator, namely $z = e^{-sT_s}$, where $T_s$ is the sample period. The z-transforms of common signals are reported in standard table of z-transforms, such as those shown in Table 24.1. The common signals shown in Table 24.1 can be manipulated and combined, using the property list shown in Table 24.2, to synthesize higher-order and more complex signals. In addition to the properties listed in Table 24.2, the initial value theorem $x[0] = \lim_{z \to \infty} X(z)$ and the final value theorem $x[\infty] = \lim_{z \to \infty} (z - 1)X(z)$ provide a convenient means of evaluating two end points of a time-series. The mapping of a z-transformed signal $X(z)$ back into the time-domain is performed in a piecemeal manner. Specifically, the inverse z-transform $X(z)$ is normally expressed in partial fraction, or Heaviside expansion having the form $X(z) = \sum_{i=1}^{M} A_i X_i(z)$, where $X_i(z)$ is an element of Table 24.1 corresponding to a discrete-time signal $x_i[k]$, with $A_i$ is a Heaviside coefficient associated with the term $X_i(z)$. The inverse z-transform of $X(z)$ is given by $x[k] = \sum_{i=1}^{M} A_i x_i[k]$.

**TABLE 24.1**   z-Transforms of Primitive Time Functions

| Discrete-time signal $x[k]$ | z-transform $X(z)$ |
|---|---|
| $\delta[k]$ (impulse) | 1 |
| $u[k]$ (unit step) | $z/(z - 1)$ |
| $a^k u[k]$ (exponential) | $z/(z - a)$ |
| $\sin[bkT_s]u[kT_s]$ (sine wave) | $\sin(bT_s)z/(z^2 - 2z\cos(bT_s) + 1)$ |
| $\cos[bkT_s]u[kT_s]$ (cosine wave) | $(z - \cos(bT_s))z/(z^2 - 2z\cos(bT_s) + 1)$ |
| $a^k\sin(bkT_s)u[kT_s]$ (damped sine) | $a\sin(bT_s)z/(z^2 - 2az\cos(bT_s) + a^2)$ |
| $a^k\cos(bkT_s)u[kT_s]$ (damped cosine) | $(z - a\cos(bT_s))z/(z^2 - 2az\cos(bT_s) + a^2)$ |

**TABLE 24.2**   Properties of z-Transforms

| Property | Time-Series | z-Transform |
|---|---|---|
| Linearity | $x_1[k] + x_2[k]$ | $X_1(z) + X_2(z)$ |
| Real scaling | $ax[k]$ | $aX(z)$ |
| Complex scaling | $w^k x[k]$ | $X(z/w)$ |
| Time reversal | $x[-k]$ | $X(1/z)$ |
| Modulation | $e^{-ak}x[k]$ | $X(e^a z)$ |
| Summation | $\sum_{n=-\infty}^{k} x[n]$ | $zX(z)/(z - 1)$ |
| Shift delay | $x[k - 1]$ | $z^{-1}X(z) - zx[0]$ |

The output of a linear system having an impulse response $h[k]$ to an input $x[k]$ is denoted $y[k]=h[k] \times x[k]$, where $y[k]$ is defined by the discrete-time *linear convolution* sum

$$y[k] = -\sum_{m=1}^{N} a_m y[k-m] + \sum_{m=0}^{M} b_m x[k-m].$$

Computing the convolution sum is rare. Instead, a linear system is generally analyzed using simulation, emulation, or the $z$-transform. The *convolution theorem* states that the linear convolution $y[k] = h[k] \times x[k]$ of a $z$-transformable impulse response $h[k]$ (i.e., $H(z) = \sum_{k=-\infty}^{\infty} h[k]z^{-k}$) and input $x[k]$ (i.e., $X(z) = \sum_{k=-\infty}^{\infty} x[k]z^{-k}$), is given by the inverse $z$-transform of the product $Y(z)=H(z)X(z)$. This method is only viable in instances where the $z$-transform of $h[k]$ and $x[k]$ have been precomputed or tabled, and the inverse $z$-transform of $Y[z]$ can be computed. While $H(z)$ is generally known, most real signals are arbitrary and possibly noise contaminated, making the general availability of $X(z)$ questionable. Nevertheless, the importance of this equation has resulted in the elements being given specific titles and meaning. The $z$-transform of the impulse response $h[k]$, namely $H(z)$, is called the system's *transfer function* and has the general form

$$H(z) = Y(z)/X(z) = \sum_{m=0}^{M} b_m z^{-m} \Big/ \sum_{m=0}^{N} a_m z^{-m} = N(z)/D(z).$$

The filter's *poles* ($p_m$) and zeros ($z_m$) are the roots of $D(z)=0$ and $N(z)=0$, respectively. The system's steady-state frequency response can be determined by evaluating the transfer function $H(z)$ along the trajectory $z = e^{j\varpi}$, where $\varpi \in [-\pi, \pi]$ which represents a normalized baseband frequency range $[-f_s/2, f_s/2]$ ($\pm$Nyquist frequency). Specifically, the frequency response of a system in magnitude-phase form is $H(e^{j\varpi}) = |H(e^{j\varpi})| \angle \phi(e^{j\varpi})$.

## 24.3 Digital Filters

Transfer functions, when implemented in the time-domain, result in digital filters. The attributes of a digital filter can be specified in the time- or frequency-domain, or both. Digital filters can be grouped into three broad classes called finite impulse response (FIR), infinite impulse response (IIR), and multirate filters.

### Finite Impulse Response (FIR) Filters

An FIR filter possesses an impulse response that persists only for a finite number of sample values. The impulse response of an $N$th order FIR is given by $h[k] = \{h[0],...,h_{N-1}[k]\}$, and in the $z$-transform domain by $H(z) = \sum h_i z^{-i}$, $i \in [0, N-1]$. One of the attributes of an FIR is its simplicity, consisting of a string of multiply-accumulations (MACs), and shifts registers. The steady-state frequency response of an FIR $H(z)$ is given by $H(e^{j\varpi}) = |H(e^{j\varpi})| \angle \phi(e^{j\varpi})$. A system is said to possess a *linear phase response* if $\phi(e^{j\varpi}) = \alpha\varpi + \beta$ (i.e., linear in frequency). Linear phase filters are important in a number of applications including (1) synchronizing phase modulated data streams, (2) anti-aliasing filters placed in front of signal phase sensitive analysis subsystems (e.g., FFT), and (3) use in phase sensitive applications (e.g., image processing). Linear phase filtering can be guaranteed whenever the coefficients of an $N$th order FIR are symmetrically distributed about the filter's mid-point $L = (N-1)/2$ (i.e., $h_i = \pm h_{N-i}$, $i = 0,...,L$). The resulting phase response satisfies the linear phase equation $\angle \phi(\varpi) = -L\varpi + \{0, \pm\pi\}$. Another important phase response measure is called the group delay, given by $\tau_g = -d\phi(e^{j\varpi})/d\varpi$. For a linear phase FIR, $\tau_g = L$, which indicates that the filter propagation delay is always $L$ clock cycles regardless of the input signal frequency.

**TABLE 24.3**    Effects of Data Windows

| Window | Transition Width $f_s/N$ | Highest Sidelobe in dB |
|---|---|---|
| Rectangular | 0.9 | −13 |
| Hann | 2.07 | −31 |
| Hamming | 2.46 | −41 |
| Blackman | 3.13 | −58 |
| Kaiser ($\beta = 2.0$) | 1.21 | −19 |

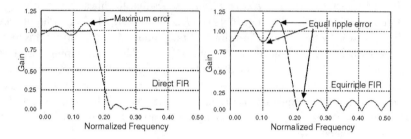

**FIGURE 24.1**    Comparison of direct and equirriple FIR designs.

FIR design methods are well known and well developed. The simplest design technique is called the direct, or window method. The design process begins with a specification of the desired filter frequency response $H(e^{j\omega})$. An $M$-harmonic ($M \gg 1$) inverse Fourier transform (IFFT) of $H(e^{j\omega})$ is computed, which defines an $M$-sample time-series $h'[k]$ that is an approximation to the desired FIR impulse response. Normally, the long $M$-sample symmetric time-series is symmetrically reduced to an $N$-sample impulse response $h[k]$, defined by the $N$ central values of $h'[k]$. The major weakness of the direct design paradigm is that the approximation errors in the frequency domain can be locally large about points of discontinuity of $H(e^{j\omega})$, as shown in Fig. 24.1. A commonly used design criteria that overcomes this weakness is based on a minimax error criterion. The minimax criterion requires that the maximum value of the approximation error be minimized. A minimax FIR is characterized by the frequency domain errors having an equirriple (equal ripple) envelope. Thus, this class of FIR is logically referred to as an equirriple filter and has a typical magnitude frequency response shown in Fig. 24.1.

Windows are tools that are sometimes used to improve the shape of an FIR's frequency domain envelope. An $N$-sample data window is applied to an $N$th-order FIR on a sample-by-sample basis according to the rule $h_w[k] = h[k]w[k]$, where $h[k]$ is an FIR's impulse response, $w[k]$ is a window function, and $h_w[k]$ is the windowed FIR impulse response. In the frequency domain, the effect of a window is defined by the convolution operation $H_w(n) = H(n) * W(n)$, which results in a tendency to smooth the envelope of the parent FIR's frequency response. The attributes of a window are defined by the width of the center (main) lobe and sideband suppression in the frequency domain (see Table 24.3). Common window functions are rectangular, Hann, Hamming, Blackman, Kaiser, and Flat Top. The effect of a window on the direct FIR frequency response shown in Fig. 24.1 is also displayed in Fig. 24.2.

## Infinite Impulse Response (IIR) Filters

Filters containing feedback are called IIR filters. With feedback, an IIR's impulse response can be infinitely long. The presence of feedback allows an IIR to achieve very high frequency selectivity and near resonance behavior. An $N$th-order constant coefficient IIR filter can be modeled by the transfer function

$$H(z) = N(z)/D(z) = \sum_{i=0}^{M} b_i z^{-i} \Big/ \sum_{i=0}^{N} a_i z^{-i} = K(z^{N-M}) \prod_{i=0}^{M-1}(z - z_i) \Big/ \prod_{i=0}^{N-1}(z - p_i)$$

where the filter's zeros $\{z_i\}$ are the roots of $N(z) = 0$, and the filter's poles $\{p_i\}$ are the roots of $D(z) = 0$.

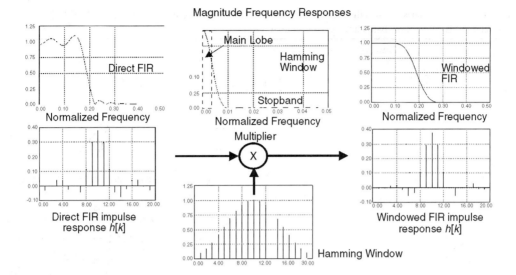

**FIGURE 24.2** Effects of windowing an FIR. Note that the windowed spectrum is smoothed and has an increased transition bandwidth.

The frequency response of an $N^{\text{th}}$-order IIR is given by

$$H(e^{j\varpi}) = \sum_{i=0}^{M} b_i e^{-j\varpi i} \Big/ \sum_{i=0}^{N} a_i e^{-j\varpi i} = (K e^{j\varpi(N-M)}) \prod_{i=0}^{M-1} (e^{j\varpi} - z_i) \Big/ \prod_{i=0}^{N-1} (e^{j\varpi} - p_i)$$

evaluated over the normalized frequency range $\varpi \in [-\pi \le \omega \le \pi)$, which defines the baseband frequency range bounded by $\pm f_{\text{Nyquist}}$.

The traditional IIR design strategy is based on converting classic analog filter models into their digital filter equivalents. Throughout the first half of the 20th century, analog radio filter engineers created classic Bessel, Butterworth, Chebyshev, and Elliptic (Cauer) filter instantiations whose magnitude frequency response emulates that of an ideal filter. To standardize the analog filter design procedures, a set of normalized −1 dB or −3 dB lowpass filter models, having a 1.0 rad/s passband were created. These models were reduced to tables, charts, and graphs and are called *analog prototype* filters. The prototype lowpass filters can be the frequency scaled to define an analog lowpass, highpass, bandpass, and bandstop filters $H(s)$, having desired frequency-domain attributes. The classic analog filter $H(s)$ can then be converted into a digital filter model $H(z)$ to define a classic digital filter (see Table 24.4). The basic domain conversion techniques (i.e., $H(s) \rightarrow H(z)$) are (1) the impulse-invariant and (2) bilinear $z$-transform methods.

The impulse invariance filter design method results in a digital filter having an impulse response $h[k]$ that agrees with that of the parent analog filter's impulse response $h_a(t)$, up to a scale factor ($h_d[k] = T_s\, h_a(kT_s)$). An impulse invariant design can be of significant value in applications, such as automatic control, where design objectives are defined in the time-domain (e.g., rise-time, overshoot, settling time). If the parent analog filter's impulse response $h_a(t)$, or transfer function $H_a(s)$ are known, then the impulse invariant digital filter is defined by

$$h_a(t) \Leftrightarrow H_a(s) = \sum_{i=1}^{N} \frac{a_i}{(s+p_i)} \overset{z}{\Leftrightarrow} \left(\frac{1}{T_s}\right)\sum_{i=1}^{N} \frac{a_i}{(1+e^{-p_i T_s}z^{-1})} = \left(\frac{1}{T_s}\right)H(z) \Leftrightarrow \left(\frac{1}{T_s}\right)h[k]$$

and in the frequency-domain by

$$H(e^{j\Omega}) = \left(\frac{1}{T_s}\right)\sum_{k=-\infty}^{\infty} H_a\left(j\left(\frac{\Omega}{T_s} - \frac{2\pi k}{T}\right)\right)$$

**TABLE 24.4** Comparisons of $N$th-Order Classic IIR Lowpass Filters Having $f_s$ = 50 kHz, a −3 dB 15 kHz Passband, 5 kHz Transition Band, and −50 dB Stopband

| Type | Order | Passband | Stopband | Magnitude Frequency Response |
|------|-------|----------|----------|------------------------------|
| Butterworth | High ($N$ = 8) | Smooth | Smooth | Generated ——— Desired ----- 1.000 / Frequency Response / Magnitude / 2.7E-17   6250.000   12500.000   18750.000   25000.000 |
| Chebyshev I | Medium ($N$ = 5) | Ripple | Smooth | Generated ——— Desired ----- 1.000 / Frequency Response / Magnitude / 2.7E-12   6250.000   12500.000   18750.000   25000.000 |
| Chebyshev II | Medium ($N$ = 5) | Smooth | Ripple | Generated ——— Desired ----- 1.000 / Frequency Response / Magnitude / 0.000   6250.000   12500.000   18750.000   25000.000 |
| Elliptic | Low ($N$ = 4) | Ripple | Ripple | Generated——— Desired ----- 1.000 / Frequency Response / Magnitude / 2.1E-06   6250.000   12500.000   18750.000   25000.000 |

This equation exhibits a weakness of the impulse invariant design method. For any physically meaningful sampling rate $f_s$ = $1/T_s$, aliasing errors can occur whenever the analog filter passes components at frequencies greater that $2f_s$. Typically, analog filters have a gain that is finite for all frequencies. The aliased filter energy can be mapped back into the baseband and can distort (sometime significantly) the frequency response of an impulse invariant filter. As a result, the impulse invariant method is generally only used to design frequency selective filters that are decidedly lowpass.

When meeting frequency domain specifications is the design objective, the *bilinear z-transform* method is normally used. The bilinear *z*-transform maps a classic analog filter $H_a(s)$ into a digital filter $H(z)$ without introducing aliasing errors. The bilinear *z*-transform establishes a relationship between the *s*- and *z*-domain, given by $s = (2/T_s)(z + 1)/(z - 1)$. The bilinear *z*-transform also defines an algebraic connection between the analog and digital frequency axis given by $\omega = (2/T_s)\tan(\varpi/2)$, where $\omega$ is the analog frequency, $|\omega| < \infty$, and $\varpi$ is the normalized digital frequency range $-\pi/2 \leq \varpi < \pi$, corresponding to the frequency range $\pm f_{\text{Nyquist}} = \pm f_s/2$. The mapping from analog frequencies $\omega$ to digital frequencies $\varpi$ is called *warping*, and *pre-warping* in the opposite direction. The bilinear *z*-transform design paradigm is a multistep process consisting of the following steps:

1. Define the digital filter's frequency-domain attributes (gains at critical frequencies).
2. Prewarp the critical digital frequencies $\varpi$ into analog frequencies $\omega$.
3. Design a prewarped classic analog filter $H_a(s)$ that meets specified passband and stopband gain requirements.
4. Apply the bilinear *z*-transform to convert $H_a(s)$ into a digital filter $H(z)$. In the process, the prewarped analog filter frequencies $\omega$ will be warped back to their original locations $\varpi$.

## Multirate Systems

DSP systems that contain multiple sample rates are called *multirate* systems. A signal $x[k]$, sampled at a rate $f_{\text{in}}$, is said to be *decimated* by $M$ if it is exported at a rate $f_{\text{out}} = f_{\text{in}}/M$, where $M > 1$. Mathematically, the decimated signal $x_d[k]$ can be expressed as $x_d[k] = x[Mk]$, indicating that only every $M$th sample of the fast sampled time-series $x[k]$ is retained in the decimated signal $x_d[k]$. Decimation can also be modeled in the *z*-transform domain as $X_d(z) = X(z^M)$ and $X_d(e^{j\phi}) = X_d(e^{jM\phi})$ in the frequency domain, as suggested in Fig. 24.3. In order to insure that a signal $x[k]$ can be reconstructed from its decimated samples of $x_d[k]$, Shannon's sampling theorem must be obeyed. Specifically, if the minimum sampling frequency is bounded by $f_s > 2B$ Hz, the maximum decimation rate must be bounded by $M \leq f_s/2B$. Decimation is routinely found in audio signal and video data transmission and signal compression applications, and interfacing equipment with dissimilar fixed sample rates. By reducing the system's sample rate by a factor $M$, arithmetic bandwidth requirements can often be reduced by a similar amount.

*Interpolation* is the antithesis of decimation. While decimation is used to reduce the sampling rate, interpolation is used to increase the sample rate. A signal $x[k]$, sampled at a rate $f_{\text{in}}$, is said to be inter-polated by $N$ if $x_i[k] = x[k]$ whenever $k \equiv 0$ modulo $(N)$, and zero elsewhere. The interpolated signal $x_i[k]$ is a time-series consisting of $N - 1$ zeros separated by the sample values $x[k]$ and $x[k + N]$ and is clocked at a rate $f_{\text{out}} = Nf_{\text{in}}$ $N > 1$. In the *z*-transform domain, $X_i(z) = X(z^N)$, and $X_i(e^{j\phi}) = X(e^{jN\phi})$ in the frequency-domain, as shown in Fig. 24.3. It can be noted that the interpolated spectrum contains multiple copies of the baseband spectrum $X(e^{j\phi})$, where the unwanted copies can be removed using a lowpass filter.

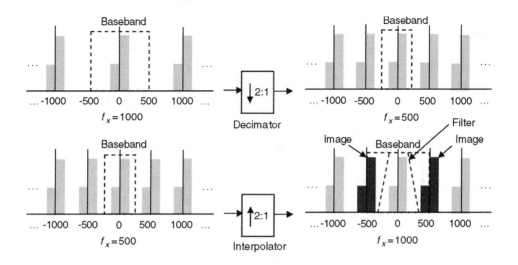

**FIGURE 24.3**   Multirate system elements showing decimation (top) and interpolation (bottom).

## Special Filter Cases

Besides baseline FIR, IIR, and multirate filters (which are based on FIR or IIR elements), other classes of digital filters are found in common use. One of the most important of these is the adaptive filter. An adaptive filter modifies the filter coefficients during run-time in order to respond to measurable changes in the signal and system environment. The adaptation rules and procedures, generally based on a squared error criteria, range from simple to sophisticated, establishing trade-offs between implementation simplicity and accuracy. Adaptive filters that contain nonlinear elements are called neural networks. Some filters classes are defined in terms of special features of their defining mathematical framework. Wavelets, for example, are basis functions that satisfy a formal set of scaling and dilatation rules. They often appear as a multirate solution consisting of collections of sub-filters defined by wavelet basis functions that have been selected to match signal-specific signal attributes or features.

## Digital Filter Architecture

The physical implementation of a particular FIR or IIR filter is called an *architecture*. Architectures specify how a digital filter is assembled using a collection of DSP primitive objects, such as shift-registers, multipliers, and adders. The choice of architecture has a direct influence on the performance, cost, power consumption, and precision of the design outcome. Common FIR architectures are the direct, transpose, and lattice implementations. Common IIR architectures include (1) direct I and II, (2) normal (optimized second-order section), (3) cascade ($H(z) = \prod H_i(z)$, $H_i(z)$ a first or second order direct II or normal subsystem), (4) parallel ($H(z) = \sum H_i(z)$, $H_i(z)$ a first- or second-order direct II or normal subsystem), (5) ladder-lattice, and (6) wave. Architectures are often instantiated in terms of a *state variable* model. The state variable model for a single-input single-output, $n$th order IIR, having an arbitrary architecture is given in terms of a state equation $\mathbf{x}[k+1] = A\mathbf{x}[k] + \mathbf{b}u[k]$, and output equation $y[k] = \mathbf{c}^T\mathbf{x}[k] + du[k]$, where $\mathbf{x}[k]$ is an $n$-vector, $y[k]$ and $u[k]$ are scalars, $A$ is an $n \times n$ matrix, and $\mathbf{b}$ and $\mathbf{c}$ are $n$-vectors, and $d$ is a scalar. The $i$th state of the digital filter, $\mathbf{x}_i[k]$ resides in the system's $i$th shift register. The coefficient $A_{ij}$ denotes the filter gain existing between the $i$th and $j$th shift register, $\mathbf{b}_i$ represents the gain between input and $i$th shift register, $\mathbf{c}_i$ the gain between $i$th shift register and output, and $d$ is the direct path gain between input and output. The state variable model is interpreted in Fig. 24.4, where the $n$ states of the system are stored in $n$ shift registers. The filter complexity and run-time dynamic range requirements of a system in state variable form can be mathematically computed or predicted. The dynamic range requirements are generally expressed in terms of the $l_p$ norm of the states, namely $\|\mathbf{x}_i[k]\|_p$, for $p = 1, 2,$ and $\infty$, where $\|\mathbf{x}_i[k]\|_p = (\sum |\mathbf{x}_i[k]|_p)^{1/p}$. These norms are used to scale a filter in order to protect it against run-time register overflow, a serious error condition. Errors of less severity, which can nevertheless adversely influence system performance, are coefficient and arithmetic roundoff errors. Another minor error source is called limit cycling, a phenomenon that relates to the least significant bits of the output being "toggling" (producing a dynamically changing output) while the input is zero. Of the common architectural choices, cascade is the most popular and generally provides a good balance between

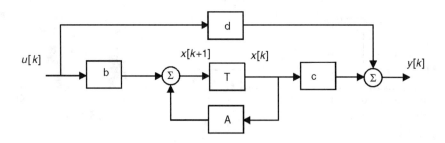

**FIGURE 24.4**  State variable system model where $x[k]$ is the state vector, $u[k]$ the input, and $y[k]$ the output.

performance, complexity, and precision. Direct II filters are known to be low-complexity, but often suffer from low precision. Parallel filters exhibit certain fault tolerance attributes, ladder-lattice have good coefficient roundoff error immunity, but are comparatively complex.

## 24.4 Fourier and Spectral Analysis

The frequency-domain analysis and representation techniques can provide invaluable information about a signal and a system's environment. The mapping between the time- and frequency-domain are traditionally defined by a Fourier transform. The historic difficulty in computing a Fourier transform of an arbitrary signal radically changed in 1965 when Cooley and Tukey introduced the now celebrated FFT algorithm. For over three decades, the FFT established that a time-series $x[k]$ can be efficiently mapped into a frequency-domain using a general purpose digital computer. The FFT is a special manifestation of a more general class of transform called the discrete Fourier transform (DFT). The DFT defines a mapping of an $N$-sample time-series $x_N[k]$ (possibly complex) into an $N$-harmonic complex frequency domain distribution $X[n]$, where $X[n]$ is called the $n$th harmonic. The DFT of the $N$-sample time-series $x_N[k]$ is given by the *analysis equation*

$$X[n] = \sum_{k=0}^{N-1} x_N[k] W_N^{nk}, \quad n \in [0, N-1]$$

where $W_N = e^{-j2\pi/N}$. The DFT is also known to be periodic with period $N$ (i.e., $X[n] = X[n \pm kN]$). The inverse transform is given by *synthesis equation*

$$x_N[k] = \frac{1}{N} \sum_{k=0}^{N-1} X[n] W_N^{-nk}, \quad n \in [0, N-1]$$

The DFT is parameterized in a manner shown in Table 24.5, and computes an $N$-harmonic spectrum using $N^2$ complex-multiply accumulates. The FFT algorithm significantly reduced the computational complexity of performing a DFT to $N \log_2(N)$. In general, a long FFT can be constructed from a collection of small DFTs. Using the Cooley–Tukey FFT ordering algorithm, a DFT of length $N = \Pi N_i$ can be created. Using the Good–Thomas ordering algorithm, a length $N = \Pi N_i$ ($N_i$ and $N_j$ relatively prime) transform result. For example, using a $N_1 = 15$, $N_2 = 16$, and $N_3 = 17$-point DFTs, an $N = 4080$-point DFT can be computed.

In addition to the classic FFT, there are other spectral analysis techniques found in common use. One is called the chirp-$z$ DFT that implements a DFT using linear convolution. The convolution filter has an

**TABLE 24.5** DFT Parameters

| DFT Parameter | Notation or Units |
|---|---|
| Sample size | $N$ samples |
| Sample period | $T_s$ seconds |
| Record length | $T = NT_s$ seconds |
| Number of harmonics | $N$ harmonics |
| Number of positive (negative) harmonics | $N/2$ harmonics |
| Frequency spacing between harmonics | $\Delta f = 1/T = 1/NT_s = f_s/N$ Hz |
| DFT frequency (one-sided baseband range) | $f \in [0, f_s/2)$ Hz |
| DFT frequency (two-sided baseband range) | $f \in [-f_s/2, f_s/2)$ Hz |
| Frequency of the $k$th harmonic | $f_k = kf_s/N$ Hz |

impulse response that is equivalent to a linearly swept FM signal. Other DFT forms include filter banks and number theoretic transforms (NTT) that can compete with the FFT only in narrowly defined applications. While not technically qualifying as a DFT, the discrete Cosine transform (DCT) has significance in image compression applications and, like the FFT, has been reduced to both software and hardware instantiations.

The DFT and its derivatives are an important signal analysis tool. They are sometimes used for offline signal processing, while in other applications they must operate at real-time speeds using dedicated hardware, firmware, or software. An $N$-sample time-series is often windowed (e.g., Hann) prior to being transformed in order to improve the interpretability of the resulting DFT. DFTs can also be used to convolve two time-series if the DFTs are suitably modified. The DFT assumes that the signals being transformed are periodic, with period $N$. As a result, the convolution theorem for DFT is expressed as the periodic outcome $y[k] = x[k] \otimes h[k] = \text{IDFT}(\text{DFT}(x[k]) \times \text{DFT}(h[k]))$, where $\otimes$ denotes *circular* (periodic) *convolution*, and IDFT denotes an inverse DFT. A circular convolution can be functionally converted to behave like a linear convolution by adding a string of $N$ zeros to the time-series $x[k]$ and $h[k]$ prior to performing the DFTs. This process, called *zero padding*, allows an efficient FFT replace an inefficient linear convolution sum. This advantage is exploited in high-order application, such as convolving two large, two-dimensional images.

One of the principle uses of a DFT or FFT is in performing *spectral analysis*. Spectral analysis pertains to the study of signals and systems based on their frequency-domain signatures and attributes. The frequency domain image of a signal or system is often interpreted in terms of a power spectrum that is a display of the power in a process on a per-harmonic basis. Spectral analysis methods generally fall into two classes, called parametric and nonparametric. Nonparametric spectral analysis methods are based on the DFT of one or more noise contaminated time-series records. The individual spectra can be averaged or combined in various ways to create a more interpretable frequency-domain image of the signal or system under study. Parametric methods attempt to build a mathematical model of a process that approximates the measured power spectrum of a signal or system. The moving-average (MA) method is a parametric spectral estimation method that constructs an FIR (all zero) model of a signal process or system. Another parametric method is called auto-regressive (AR) and produces an all-pole IIR model of a signal or system, combining the two results in the parametric auto-regressive moving-average (ARMA) method. Other parametric methods are based on an eigenvalue analysis and result in a highly frequency-selective signal or system model.

# 24.5   DSP System Implementation

The implementation of a digital filter is an iterative process requiring design trade-off choices be made in the statement of filter specifications, filter type, architecture, and technology to achieve a design that meets performance, precision, and complexity (cost/power) requirements. Numerous software packages are commercially available to automatically design a baseline FIR or IIR filter of DFTs. Fewer software packages automatically support architectural or design optimization activities that can quantify run-time errors and register overflow saturation events. Furthermore, the majority of hardware-enabled DSP filters and transforms are implemented in *fixed-point*, a point often ignored by existing design software tools. The range of an unsigned fixed-point number is given by $R = X_{max} - X_{min}$, and has a resolution given by $Q = R/2^N$, where $Q$ is called the quantization step-size and is the weighted value of the least significant bit (LSB). The quantization error is defined to be the difference between a number's real and fixed-point representation, specifically $e = X - X_Q$ (rounded). Statistically, the error is uniformly distributed over $[-Q/2, Q/2]$, with mean and variance is given as $E(e) = 0$ and $\sigma^2 = Q^2/12$, respectively. Of all the known fixed-point numbering systems, two's complement (2C) is by far the most popular and important. A 2C attribute, that makes it particularly attractive for DSP applications, is called the modulo $(2^N)$ wrap-around property. This property states that if a string of valid 2C numbers $\{X_i\}$ are added to form $S = \sum X_i$, and $S$ is a valid 2C number, then the final outcome will be correct regardless of possible overflows of intermediate sums. That is, as the final result is correct even though intermediate sums may be flawed.

For cases where higher dynamic ranges are needed, *floating point* solutions are employed. The floating point representation of a real number $X$ is given by $X \sim (-1)^S Mr^E$, where $M$ is the mantissa, $r$ the radix, $E$ is the signed exponent, and $S$ is the sign bit. The mantissa is usually normalized to a value $1/r \leq M < 1$, and the format is defined by published standards (e.g., IEEE). A variation on the floating-point theme is called *block floating point*, a format used by a number of DSP chips, especially FFTs. A block floating point representation of an array of numbers $\{x[k]\}$ is defined in terms of a maximum exponent $E$, where $|x[k]|_{max} = r^E$. A block floating point representation of the number $x[k]$ is given by $x[k] = \pm M[k]r^E$, where $E$ is the fixed maximum exponent and $M[k]$ is a fractional mantissa ($M[k] \leq 1$). Since the scale factor $r^E$ is known *a priori*, it need not be explicitly carried in number system representation.

The primary DSP arithmetic operation is the signed multiply accumulation (MAC). Fixed-point multipliers cover a wide range of speed, precision, and complexity tradeoffs. Compact low-complexity MACs can be designed using ripple adders. When adder area and power dissipation are not an issue, carry-lookahead adders can be used to accelerate wide wordlength adders and, therefore improve MAC speed. Carry-save adders (modified full adders) can also be an important element in implementing fast multipliers. Another fast multiplier architecture is based on Booth's algorithm and interprets strings of consecutive of "ones" as multiplicative NO-OP operations. Fast multipliers can also be constructed using arrays of small wordlength multipliers. These architectures are referred to as cellular array multipliers, or simply array multipliers.

General-purpose programmable DSP $\mu$ps make use of multipliers that map $X*Y \rightarrow P$, where $X$ and $Y$ are variables. Most DSP applications, however, are SAXPY ($S = A*X + Y$) intensive, which refers to multiplying a variable $X$ by a constant $A$ (e.g., filter coefficients), followed by an accumulation. Implementing SAXPY algorithms technically does not require general multiplication but rather an operation called scaling. Several techniques have been developed to exploit scaling in the implementation of DSP algorithms. They are particularly useful in implementing fixed-coefficient DSP algorithms with application specific integrated circuits (ASIC), application specific standard parts (ASSP), and field-programmable gate-arrays (FPGA) devices. One scaling technique is called the reduced adder graph (RAG) method. RAG arithemtic is based on the theory of the ternary-valued ($\{0, \pm 1\}$) canonical sign-digit numbers (CSD). For example, the 4-bit binary unsigned representation of the number 15 is $15_{10} \leftrightarrow 1111_2$, while the RAG representation is given by $15_{10} = 16_{10} - 1_{10} \leftrightarrow 100\bar{1}_{RAG}$, which can be implemented using one adder and a shift register. The cost of an RAG multiplier is measured in terms of the number of adders needed to complete a design. Another scaling method is called distribute arithmetic (DA) and is applicable only to the implementation of constant DSP coefficient algorithms. As a point of reference, an $N$th order FIR digital filter, having known coefficients $h_r$, $r \in [0, N)$, requires $N$ MAC operations be performed per cycle. The data is assumed to be coded as an $M$-bit 2C word, where

$$x[k] = -x[k:0] + x[k:1]2^{-1} + \cdots + x[k:N-1]2^{-(N-1)}$$

where $x[k:i]$ is the $i$th-bit of sample $x[k]$. The output $y[k]$ is given by

$$y[k] = -\sum_{r=0}^{N-1} h_i x[k-r:0] + \sum_{i=1}^{M-1} 2^{-i} \sum_{r=0}^{N-1} h_r x[k-r:i]$$

$$= \theta[\underline{x}[k]:0] + \sum_{i=1}^{M-1} 2^{-i} \theta[\underline{x}[k]:i]$$

where the mappings $\theta[\underline{x}[k]:i]$ are implemented using $2^N$-word memory lookups. The lookup table $\theta$ maps an array of binary valued digits $\underline{x}[k:i] = \{\underline{x}[k:i], x[k-1:i], \ldots, x[k-M-1:i]\}$, taken from the $i$th common-bit location from $x[s]$, $s \in [0,\ldots,N-1]$, under the rule

$$\theta[\underline{x}[k]:i] = \sum_{r=0}^{N-1} h_r x[k-r:i]; \; x[s:i] \in [0,1]$$

Weighting the lookup value $\theta[\underline{x}[k]:i]$ by a factor $2^{-i}$ is implemented using a shift register. The result is generally a high-speed compact design.

## 24.6  DSP Technology

The semiconductor revolution, which began in the 20th century, began to shape the field of DSP beginning in the late 1970s. Since then, DSP has been both a facilitating technology (replacing existing solutions) as well as an enabling technology (creating new solutions). The hallmark of the DSP technology revolution was the general purpose DSP microprocessor (DSP $\mu$p). The first generation DSP chips included on-chip ADC and DAC and large capable multiplier. The second generation DSP $\mu$ps overcame many of the first generation device memory and precision limitations, and also removed the noisy ADCs and DACs. Since then, third generation floating-point and fourth generation multiprocessors have been added to the list of general-purpose DSP products. Along with the DSP $\mu$p technology explosion came attendant improvements in software for both uni- and multiprocessor systems. High- and low-level software environments have been created to rapidly develop and test DSP solutions. Since DSP problems tend to be algorithmic, stressing real-time bandwidth, optimized solutions continue to be dominated by assembly language code solutions. Throughout these generational changes, DSP $\mu$ps have maintained their dependence on capable MACs, tightly coupled memory, and a modified Harvard architecture. These trends continue to differentiate DSP $\mu$ps from general-purpose microprocessors. Microprocessors emphasize (1) multiple data types, (2) multilevel cache memories, (3) paged virtual memory management in hardware, (4) support for hardware context management including supervisor and user modes, (5) large general-purpose register files, (6) orthogonal instruction sets, and (7) simple or complex memory addressing, depending upon whether the processor is RISC or CISC. DSP $\mu$ps, however, typically (1) have only one or two data types supported by the processor hardware, (2) limited data cache memory, (3) no memory management hardware, (4) no support for hardware context management, (5) exposed pipelines, (6) predictable instruction execution timing, (7) limited register files with special purpose registers, (8) nonorthogonal instruction sets, (9) enhanced memory addressing modes, (10) onboard fast RAM, ROM, and DMA, and (11) nonsequential access to data addressing modes (e.g., bit-reversed addressing). Techniques have also been developed to exploit opportunities for instruction level parallelism, superpipelining, and superscalar architectures. These innovations have led to very long instruction word (VLIW) architectures. Due to the upward spiral of software development costs a significant amount of the academic and commercial activities have been directed to automatic compiler-based optimization of high-level language code.

In parallel with the explosion of general-purpose DSP $\mu$p products, there has been a growing presence of DSP-centric ASICs, ASSPs, and FPGAs. Although DSP $\mu$ps enabled the DSP revolution, DSP technology innovations have become increasingly driven by intellectual property (IP) supplied by semiconductor houses, fabless semiconductor technology suppliers, and third-party IP providers. Their use and justification is based on performance, power dissipation, cost, and time-to-market considerations. At the beginning of the new millennium, the market value of ASICs and ASSPs exceeded that of general-purpose DSP $\mu$ps. The trend toward ASICs and ASSPs, over DSP $\mu$ps, is motivated by the need to achieve rapid system-on-a-chip (SOC) designs by integrating predefined DSP IP cores together using high-end electronic design automation (EDA) software. FPGAs are becoming an increasingly important DSP technology but continue to remain primarily prototype tools and useful in some low-volume applications.

# 24.7   Applications

"DSP" has become a well-known acronym, often appearing explicitly in the marketing vernacular of commercial electronic products. The sphere of influence and relevance of DSP continues to expand, often enabling solutions that could only be speculated a decade earlier. Modern DSP applications areas include general purpose DSP (filtering, signal detection/classification, spectral analysis, adaptive filtering), instrumentation (waveform analysis, transient analysis), information/communication systems (speech, audio, voice over Internet, facsimile, modems, cellular telephones, wireless LANS), control systems (servos, disks, printers, automotive, guidance, vibration, power systems, robots), entertainment (sound, video, music), defense (radar, sonar, object recognition, ordinance) plus other areas such as biomedical, transportation, and geophysical signal processing.

# References

1.  Blahut, R. (1985). Fast Algorithms for Digital Signal Processing, Addison-Wesley, Reading, MA.
2.  Brown, S. and Varnesic, Z. (2000). Fundamental of Digital Logic with VHDL Design, McGraw-Hill, New York.
3.  Koren, I. (1993). Computer Arithmetic Algorithms, Prentice-Hall, Englewood Cliffs, NJ.
4.  Mitra, S. (2001). Digital Signal Processing, 2nd edition, McGraw-Hill, New York.
5.  Oppenheim, A., ed. (1978). Application of Digital Signal Processing, Prentice-Hall, Englewood Cliffs, NJ.
6.  Oppenheim, A. and Schafer, R. (1998). Discrete-Time Signal Processing, 2nd edition, Prentice-Hall, Englewood Cliffs, NJ.
7.  Taylor, F. (1983). Digital Filter Design Handbook, Marcel Dekker, New York.
8.  Taylor, F. and Mellott, J. (1998). Hands-On Digital Signal Processing, McGraw-Hill, New York.

# 25

# DSP Applications

Daniel Martin
*Infineon*

## 25.1 Introduction

The story goes like this. In 1982, when Texas Instruments' (TI) engineers came up with their first general-purpose chip for DSP applications, they did not know how to call it. Terms like analog microprocessor or signal microprocessor sounded cumbersome for the user. Therefore, an engineer said, "why don't we confuse the chip and its application? In other words why don't we use the term DSP (digital signal processing) to describe our chip?" Hence, the DSP (digital signal processor) was born. Unfortunately, this still brings confusion 20 years later.

## DSP (Digital Signal Processor) or DSP (Digital Signal Processing)?

What do we mean by DSP applications?

  Applying the science of digital signal processing to the real world?
  An application that uses a digital signal processor?

Although the two areas largely overlap, they are not identical. For instance, a typical digital signal processing application such as V90 modem is performed by a general purpose DSP but also by a custom chip or a Pentium.

## A DSP Can Do More Than DSP Applications

A general purpose DSP can be efficient at many other tasks than pure processing of signals (Fig. 25.1). The reason is that a DSP is low cost and very efficient at processing in general. It is also good at processing math, bits, events, state-machines, etc. In addition, a DSP has a very deterministic behavior. Hence, it can precisely control hardware and multiple external events. It is the main reason that hard disk drives use a DSP as their main CPU. Disk drives and motor control represent one of the biggest applications for a DSP. They are classified under DSP applications, in reality they are more control-like; however, the "spread" of a general purpose DSPs into non-DSP applications is much less interesting than the discovery of new DSP applications.

  In the following paragraph, we will concentrate on describing applications, which recently opened new markets thanks to some DSP techniques.

## The Importance of DSP Applications

Over the last 20 years, the different market segments have made a different use of DSP applications (Fig. 25.2). The next 10 years will also bring its changes. For instance, the consumer market is likely to occupy more and more space in the life of DSP engineers.

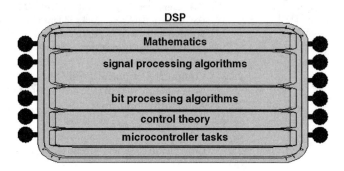

**FIGURE 25.1**    A general purpose DSP can do more than DSP.

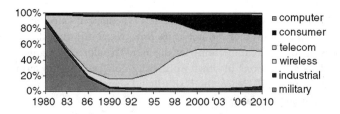

**FIGURE 25.2**    Relative importance of market segments for DSP applications.

## Classifying DSP Applications

It is usually to classify DSP applications following the market segments. For the purpose of this chapter, we conveniently classify the seven main areas of DSP applications without necessarily following the market segments of Fig. 25.1:

1. Military
2. Telecommunication terminals
3. Consumer products
4. Telecommunication infrastructure (including networking)
5. Computers, peripherals, and office automation
6. Automotive, industrial
7. Others, such as biometrics, biomedical, etc.

# 25.2   Military Applications

The first DSP applications were born in the 70s and were mainly military (radar, sonar). Today, the same applications exist with a much higher performance target. In addition, many military applications (vocoder) are taking advantage of "civilian" work. An interesting development for the military is the detection and disposal of mines [1]. It must be noted that, since the military community was the first DSP customer, strong links were created between DSP manufacturers and these pioneers. Despite its small size, the military community continues today to have a strong influence on the evolution of DSP architecture (floating-point, multiprocessing).

# 25.3   Telecommunication Terminals

By 1995, DSP has left its original circles (military, universities) and became a household name. The most popular DSP applications were telecommunications terminals such as cellular telephone, PC (modem), fax, and digital-answering machine (Table 25.1). Today, the quantity of telecom terminals that is produced per year reaches 450 M units for cell phones alone.

## Phones and Answering Machines

The plain old residential telephone has very little DSP inside it (maybe calling ID). This is the exception among voice communication devices. For instance, second generation cordless phones (DECT) use digital techniques. Also all "packet telephones" such as Internet (IP) phones, LAN phones, are using voice compression, echo cancellation, and modem techniques to receive/transmit voice. An extreme telephone application can cater for up to 12 voice conference channels. This requires 12 decompression channels and mixing. Voice compression is not new, since they allowed the development of cheap "solid-state" DAM (digital answering machines). All put together, a combo device including a multi-channel cordless + a DAM + a connection to IP is a very demanding DSP application.

**TABLE 25.1**   List of Telecom Terminals Using DSP Techniques

| Communication Function | List of Terminals |
| --- | --- |
| Voice (telephony) | Feature phone, DAM, cordless phone, Internet phone, business phone, LAN phone, DECT phone, combo products (LAN/POTS) |
| PC modem | (Voiceband) modem, DSL modem, cable modem |
| Fax | Color fax, fax/phone, fax/printer, fax/printer/scanner/copier |
| Web access | Web station, Web phone, Web pad |
| Videophony | Videophone |
| Cellular phone | Standard, voice + data cellular phone, smart phone, pager |

## PC as a Terminal (Modem)

The PC is the second most successful telecom terminal of all times. For that it requires a modem (most advanced voiceband modem is V90). The modem was the application that created a mass market for DSP devices (1982–1992). Today, all DSP devices are trying to implement broadband modems. Roughly five classes of broadband modems are available, which all use massive amount of DSP power:

- DSL, which is made of three classes in order of difficulty (SDSL, ADSL,VDSL)
- Cable modem, which is classified as a set-top box peripheral
- Broadband wireless modem (LMDS, MMDS), which is also called the "wireless DSL"
- Broadband satellite modems
- Gigabit Ethernet (and above), which positions itself as the cheapest technology

## Fax

A fax can be seen as medium range modem, plus a scanner writing bits into a graphics compression engine, and a decompression engine driving a printer. The three functions are all DSP-based. There is no reason why fax manufacturer will not develop DSL fax. Modern networks will allow a DSL fax to speak to a LAN fax. In fact, modern networks will allow "anything over everything" such as fax-over-IP and voice-over-DSL. You can bet that DSP will be in the middle of all that.

## Web Access Terminals

Not to be confused with an IP phone (which is limited to voice communication), a Web access device is targeted at Web browsing and e-mail. Today (2001), all these types of devices and the so-called "Internet appliances" are struggling to find a mass-market acceptance. Despite this, three classes exist: Web station, Web phone, and Web pad.

### Web Station

It is a $99–299 consumer device in the form factor of a small laptop. It allows web browsing, send/receive e-mail, and (maybe) JPEG decode. Web browsing requires a modem (more likely V90 than DSL), which means DSP. Since V90 is less than 30 DSP MIPS and today's DSPs give anything from 100 to 1500 DSP MIPS, the use of a full-blown DSP might not be required. On the other hand, the unused performance can be put to good use: multimedia decode.

### Web Phone

This is the same as the Web station with the addition of telephony. Note that in the IP world, phoning requires more DSP MIPS than Web browsing.

### Web Pad

This is a cordless web station with a form factor identical to the pentop of 1992–1994. The DSP functions are fifty/fifty shared between the base and the tablet. The big advantage of a Web pad is to be network independent or modem independent. The big disadvantage is the price of the display.

## Videophone

Videophone shares with speech recognition the honor of being the most promising 1971 DSP application. Thirty years later, many progresses have been made. The next 10 years will surely bring their annual series of breakthroughs.

## Cell Phones

The modem put DSP on the radar screen in the 80s. By comparison, cell phones put DSP in the stratosphere in the 90s. By the end 1999, the cell phone was the star of the electronics world with more than 300 million handsets a year, some containing multiple DSPs. Multiple DSPs are needed because a cell phone DSP function is traditionally divided into two parts: the speech coding and the channel coding.

**TABLE 25.2**   A List of Possible Wireless Devices

| | Cellular | Proximity (Bluetooth) | Home RF (Residential) | DECT (Cordless) | Wireless LAN | Broadband | Satellite |
|---|---|---|---|---|---|---|---|
| Phone | | | | | | | |
| Modem | | | | | | | |
| Fax | | | | | | | |
| Web access | | | | | | | |
| Videophone | | | | | | | |
| Digital camera | | | | | | | |
| Palm-top | | | | | | | |
| DVD player | | | | | | | |
| DVR | | | | | | | |
| Set-top | | | | | | | |
| Digital TV | | | | | | | |
| Games | | | | | | | |
| MP3 player | | | | | | | |
| Home theater | | | | | | | |
| DAB | | | | | | | |
| MP3 Juke-box | | | | | | | |
| E-book | | | | | | | |
| PC | | | | | | | |
| Printer | | | | | | | |
| Car | | | | | | | |

*Speech coding* is a traditional speech codec (compression/decompression) algorithm varying from 5 to 12 kbit/s depending on standards, economic forces, and target quality. Above that, several speech-quality enhancement features are added. This includes echo cancellation and noise suppression. A promising trend is the use of wideband codec. All together, the sum of all speech functions put in a modern cell phone can require up to 100 DSP MIPS.

*Channel coding* is working on bits in transmission and (supposedly) in reception. As such, it does not qualify as a pure DSP application; however, in the first place, the reception is mainly done on samples and secondly equalization and other heavy DSP techniques (Viterbi algorithm) are classified under channel coding. Finally, the channel coding problems represent DSP research at its best today.

## Wireless Terminals

The cell phone is the first of many types of wireless terminals that will come up over the next decade. In fact, wireless terminals are in a class of their own. Their rapid evolution differentiates them strongly from their wired cousins. Wireless is the technology with the most development potential over the next 10 years. It is easy to explain this statement by taking any existing equipment (from telephones to automobile) and turn it into a wireless device (Table 25.2). It is left to the reader to complete the table based on his or her own wishes.

# 25.4   Consumer Products

Section 25.3 proves that wireless will revolutionize many types of equipment. This is especially true for consumer devices. For instance, Bluetooth and GPS (both based on DSP) will be standard features on most consumer products described in the following subsections. In addition, consumer products have been traditionally nonconnected devices (camera, CD player) or passive devices (television). This is changing, in the form of access to the Web. This itself gives a big push to DSP applications.

## Digital Cameras (and Digital Pictures)

One of the most promising consumer DSP applications is the field of digital pictures. Its most common incarnation is the digital camera. This very large field can be segmented in many ways, following these characteristics:

- Fixed pictures versus moving pictures (example: digital camera versus digital camcorder)
- Picture production (camera) versus picture consumption (digital frame)
- Portable versus semi-fixed/fixed equipment (example: digital camcorder versus webcam)
- Equipment versus module (example: digital camera versus add-on to a palm-type device)

### Digital Camera

A digital camera is made of several functions: an image sensor, a processing part, and a storage element. The processing includes three main algorithms, front-end processing, image compression (DCT is mainly used here), and coding (Huffman coding).

In theory, a digital camera requires 10 DSP MIPS. Nevertheless, higher resolution, advanced algorithms (pixel by pixel) and sophisticated features such as the paparazzi effect turned the digital camera into a big DSP MIPS consumer. The paparazzi effect is when a series of pictures are taken at high speed (for example, 10 pictures in 1 s). In effect, we are not far from the performance of a video camera.

### Digital Video Camera (Camcorder)

Big brother to the still camera, the video camera follows the same principle. It approximates the behavior of a digital camera except it has a better resolution and a continuous automatic stream of pictures. Another key difference is that it is a slave to the television set. Hence, decompression of pictures is as important as compression.

### Web Camera

Not all video cameras need the sophistication of a camcorder. Common examples are surveillance cameras (slow speed, black and white) and Web cameras. The Webcam's block diagram is very similar to a digital (still) camera except the storage function has been replaced by a modem. Because the speed of the network is the bottleneck, there is no need to take more than one or two pictures every 5 s. Note also that a Web camera does not need any decompression algorithms.

### PC Camera

The PC is a $10 digital video camera put on top of PC and used for video telephony or college room broadcasting. Its consists of a very low sensor quality and a sub-dollar micro-controller. The PC has taken the role of a DSP.

### Modules and Toy Cameras

In the same spirit, any host can take the DSP role. For instance, there is the case of digital camera modules (host independent), add-on to a PDA (palm OS is the host), and toy cameras (PC is host).

### Digital Picture Frame

Not the most fascinating killer application of all times (sending baby pictures to grandparents), the digital picture frame is exactly the opposite of the Web camera. The image first goes through a modem function, then through decompression, and ends up its life on a picture frame display; however; contrary to a Web camera there are large problems due to the human interface and the way we (the grandparents) interact with this kind of device.

## PDAs (Handheld Devices, Palmtops)

PDA is not (yet) a big DSP platform. Still serious inroads are made. Two common ones are the use of a PDA as a common platform for digital camera and MP3 player. Also Web access (necessitating a modem) and wireless access (obviously necessitating a wireless link) are the two good classical DSP applications, which are being pushed into these devices.

## DVD Player (and Digital Storage Devices)

Storage devices such hard disk and CD-ROM players are basic sub-elements of the PC. The CD audio is also a well-known element of our life. The equipment, which really puts DSP into the consumer storage field, is the DVD player.

### DVD Player

A digital versatile disk (DVD) uses MPEG2 compression to store its video and audio tracks. A DVD player requires in the order of 200 DSP MIPS to decode the signal. Still, compared to some recent consumer platforms the function seems relatively straightforward, but this is only one-third of the DSP functions. The other two functions are the control of the disk (servo) and the reading and decoding of the stored data bits (channel coding).

### Universal Player/Recorder

Moreover, the DVD player is fast becoming a recorder device. MPEG2 coding algorithm necessitates many more DSP MIPS than decoding. Finally, the number of standards (in other words the number of DSP algorithms), which are currently supported by a DVD player, is mind-boggling. Effectively, the DVD player is the de facto universal home player/recorder. It can do nearly everything from recording MP3 audio to reading karaoke Chinese videodisk.

### DVR (Digital Video Recorder)

Further pushing this recording trend is the emergence of the DVR. Here there is no disk to read or to record. Or, more specifically, there is no BOUGHT disk; however, this is still a storage device (hard disk) on which television program can be stored (recorded) and read in nearly real-time. The DSP algorithm is the same as DVD (omnipresent MPEG2) but with the added complexity of simultaneous coding/decoding. In fact, there are two coding channels and one decoding channel requiring more than 700 DSP MIPS of DSP power.

## Digital Set-Top Box (and Digital Television Peripheral Devices)

The DVR function just described can also be integrated in a set-top device. We will call set-top devices any consumer devices, which sits at home between the TV operator(s) and the television set (hence the name set top). A Web TV fits neatly into this definition.

### Digital Set Tops

Two types of digital set-top boxes are currently used, the wired and the wireless. The wired is the well-known connection to a cable, the wireless is the satellite type. Both require a massive amount of DSP in the demodulation/error correction schemes, followed by the good old MPEG2 decode. It must be noted that the DSP functions have a relatively minor role to play in the whole software. Set-top boxes are considered more of an open platform similar to a PC, than a closed device such as a DVD player. This comment was to introduce the current evolution of set-top boxes from one-way device to two-way devices (up-link is added to down-link).

### Two-Way Set Tops—Cable Modems and Web TVs

But what about the amount of DSP functions? Intuitively both devices would require twice the number of DSP workload since they now receive and transmit information. This is not so. The up-link is only for data, consequently the need for compression is null and the modem speed relatively low. To summarize, DSP did not drive the recent evolution of set-top boxes; however, this might change if they evolve into multimedia home gateways.

## HDTV (and Digital Television)

If there is a domain in which DSP is bringing a lot, this is high definition TV (HDTV). This is not due to the high definition but to the use of digital techniques. Contrary to the current digital television, the digital functions (read MPEG2) are not put into a peripheral device but in the TV set. Even if there is still a lot of uncertainties in this market, there is no doubt about its massive use of DSP power.

## GAMES (and Toys)

Although it is not the obvious place where DSP can found, games and toys have more and more needs of DSP because of the need for communication.

### Games Consoles (3D)

Games have massive amount of CPU and hardware power devoted to the manipulation of 3D graphics. It is interesting to know the three reasons why this cannot be classified as DSP. The first one is that 3D graphics is executed in floating point (whereas DSP is 95% fixed point). Reason number two is that graphics is a synthesized object whereas DSP manipulates real signals. Finally, DSP is software whereas graphics is a pipelined hardware. It is obvious that a lot of DSP applications can be found, which corresponds to the three above criteria. What about a 33-stage hardware floating point multi-channel polyphase audio synthesizer. Also, there are a lot of graphics algorithms, which are *not* floating point for instance. The bottom line is that the world of gaming, the world of video communications, and the world of image processing are now very close:

- Mixing of synthesized and real images found in modern games
- The adoption of MPEG4 as a telecom standard (MPEG4 principles rely on objects commonly found in PC graphics)

### Game Consoles as an Universal Platform

The same story as for set-top box or PDA applies here. Web browsing, modem, DVD player, MP3 player are all good examples of DSP applications. All are finding their way into game consoles.

### Toys

The first consumer device based on DSP was the Texas Instruments' speak and spell learning aid (1981). In fact, it was a toy disguised as a learning aid. Another TI DSP milestone was the famous "Julie doll" (1987). For the future, a lot of toys will be based on sophisticated electronics, adaptive behavior, and connected to the PC (possibly Bluetooth). All these functions have strong DSP contents.

## MP3 Player (and Listening Musical Platforms)

Traditionally, the music industry was relying on very crude DSP in the consumer product (CD player). The explosion of MP3 portable devices is opening the doors to sophisticated DSP in mass-market audio devices.

### MP3 Player

When drawing a block diagram of a MP3 player, one can use the block diagram of a portable digital picture frame and replace the display by the connection to the speaker. This represents the simplicity of a MP3 player. The DSP MIPS number is low and the DSP functions pretty basic. Nevertheless, as for DVD, the difficulty is in the number of audio format to support (each one means a different DSP algorithm) and the security features. Note that a large number of MP3 players are built with a single DSP (no micro-controller host), which means than its 80% of its program is used for NON DSP work.

### Hi-Fi

A large number of high-fidelity equipment rely on DSP techniques. The most common is the Dolby standard, which can be found in cinema and home (5.1 channel) theater. The most exotic could be the digital speaker. The most difficult and resource intensive DSP application is the so-called 3D sound (PC games).

**TABLE 25.3** Consumer Equipment—How Big Is the Market and How Much DSP Is Required?

| Consumer Equipment | Units Sold per Year | DSP MIPS |
|---|---|---|
| Digital camera | 10 M | 10 → 1000 |
| Palm top | 10 M | 50 |
| DVD player | 60 M | 300 |
| DVR | <1 M | 700 |
| Set top | 50 M | 300 |
| Digital TV | <1 M | 1000++ |
| Games | 100 M | 100,000+ (graphics) |
| MP3 player | 10 M | 20 |
| Home theater | <1 M | 1000+ |
| DAB | <1 M | 80 |
| MP3 juke box | <1 M | 20 |
| E-book | <1 M | 5 |

Everyone knows about the difficulty of generating good 3D graphics. But one can appreciate the difficulty of generating 3D sounds when doing the comparison. An image is still displayed in a 2D world, whereas sound is really produced for a 3D world (by analogy: image will catch up with sound when it will be displayed as a hologram). In effect, we are speaking of thousands of DSP MIPS.

### Musical Instruments

In the professional musical world such as synthesizers, DSP first appeared as a label of quality. Music is a field where DSP can introduces massive improvements. For instance, adaptive techniques could make a good old country fiddle sounds like a Stradivarius. It does not sound like a very good idea, though.

## Home Networking and Multimedia

MP3 player is the top of iceberg. The iceberg is the "connected" home. The infrastructure of this connected home is partially described later (refer to home gateway heading). Here, the new "gizmos" that this infrastructure allows are briefly described:

*MPEG4 player:* This is the same as MP3, except it also allows viewing video clips.
*Internet radio:* listening to radio on the Internet.
*MP3 juke box:* listening to MP3 clips; they had been previously stored on a hard disk drive (from the Internet Web sites). Similarly, we can add MPEG4 juke box.
*Home Storage or Multimedia Storage Box:* hard disk drive containing multimedia files.
*E-book:* Electronic book. Presently downloaded from the Web; in the future, this will done in two passes: first to the home storage and then to the e-book.

Table 25.3 summarizes the DSP requirements of some consumer devices. Knowing that most of them are starting their commercial life, one is impressed by the amount of work remaining for DSP engineers.

## 25.5 The Telecom Infrastructure

The telecom infrastructure could be divided into three spheres of influence (wired, wireless, networking). The convergence of all networks renders this distinction illusory. A very interesting trend is that infrastructure equipment such as servers, gateways, switches, radio relays are now finding their way into the home.

### CTI (Computer Telephony Integration)

Before the net, CTI was the biggest infrastructure user of DSP. CTI means voice server, voice mail, and the infamous IVR (interactive voice response) machines "please hold on, etc." All these infrastructure equipment are built using standard software modules and boards. For years CTI was the lifeline of many DSP board manufacturers.

## Modem Banks

This is the first of the multi-channel DSP applications. Modem banks did not appear because of PC modems. They appeared because of the Internet (web servers) and remote workers (remote access servers). The number of required DSP MIPS is extremely high. For instance, a typical bank of 120 V90 modems requires 3600 DSP MIPS ($120 \times \sim 30$).

## DSL Modem Banks

This is nothing compared to DSL, where (for instance) 30,000 DSP MIPS ($120 \times \sim 250$) is required for a 120 channels S-HDSL modem bank.

## Broadband Line Card (Voice-over-Broadband)

The most likely example of broadband line card is a DSL line card, which fills the same function as modem banks plus the typical voiceband functions (echo cancellation, voice compression, DTMF detection, fax relay) found in gateways.

## Gateway (Voice-over-Broadband)

Under this heading are included all recent buzzword equipment such as voice-over-DSL, voice-over-IP, voice-over-Packet, etc. A gateway can be on the periphery of the network (access), in the center (core) or on customer premises (private). Its main use is to translate from a circuit network to a packet network and back. A state-of-the-art gateway SOC (System-on-Chip) targets 200 channels, which translates into 4000–10,000 DSP MIPS depending on the voice compression quality. The voice quality has been the subject of a lot of debate (and hard-learnt lessons) in the IP community over the last four years.

## Cellular Wireless Base Station

In wireless, voice quality is not a problem (relatively speaking) since compression algorithms are standardized. They require as low as 3 DSP MIPS (GSM full rate) to 30 DSP MIPS (third generation such as AMR) per channel. Cellular wireless base stations are half gateway (access to network) and half radio relay (air interface). It is this air interfaces, which presently (2001) presents a lot of challenges to the DSP world. Many MIPS-hungry techniques have been introduced (CDMA, turbo coder) and many more will be coming (smart antenna, multiple reception, software radio, etc.) over the next 20 years. In essence this is 25,000 DSP MIPS per channel. In other words, each channel requires a 25 GHz general purpose DSP. One can see the interest of application specific DSP and custom instruction set in this market.

## Home Gateways and "Personal Systems"

A residential cordless base station is now the most common example of a "personal system." A personal system is a device having both characteristics of telecom terminals and telecom infrastructure. It is a terminal because:

1. It is sold in retail stores.
2. It is targeted at a small entity (single person, family, SOHO).

It is a telecom infrastructure equipment because:

1. It has no human interface.
2. It very often acts as a point-to-multipoint access device.

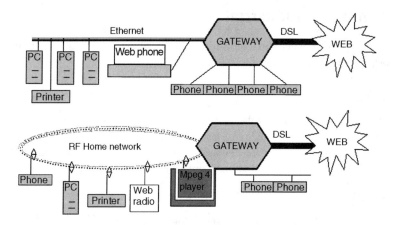

**FIGURE 25.3**   Two examples of residential gateways—SOHO and HOME.

### What is Residential Gateway?

This is the latest trend in "personal system." Two examples are given in Fig. 25.3. The first one is a DSL (external) to Ethernet/twisted pair (internal) gateway. It could be a typical SOHO scenario where phones are organized in star topology. Note that the LAN supports additional phones.

The second one is a HOME gateway, which differs by being driven more by entertainment than by work. It also uses an external DSL link but the internal communications are mainly wireless. The wireless network is used to avoid rewiring the house. The phones are organized in bus topology, which also corresponds to a typical home.

If the architecture of the home network evolves into thin-client terminals, home gateways are going to be a gold mine for DSP applications. DSP is required on all access points, DSP is required for voice compression, DSP can be required to do MP3 decompression (Internet radio), MPEG4 decompression (Internet clips), etc. The limit is one's wallet.

## 25.6   Computer, Peripherals, and Office Automation

### PC as a Home Gateway

Obviously, the home gateway market is not leaving the PC industry passive, especially after 10 years of multimedia hype. The more likely scenario will NOT see any major integration of "telecom personal systems" into PC; however, the home gateway is having several major impacts on PC: integration of wireless functions, still more performance for multimedia (such as the typical MPEG4 clip already mentioned).

### Printers

The benefit of a laser printer and color printer depends largely on the speed and quality of image processing. This is typical DSP task.

### Hard Disk Drive

In the last years, disk drives know-how has changed from complex control theory to sophisticated DSP coding techniques. The algorithms used have more to do with wireless telecommunications than servo control. In addition, the emergence of network attached storage requires communications, which in turn means DSP.

## 25.7   Automotive, Industrial

Although it is often forgotten when discussing advanced digital developments, the automotive industry could be the surprise of the decade for the DSP industry.

### Engine Control

Due to history and real-time constraints, the automotive industry uses the principle of table interpolation for engine control; however, the availability of faster CPUs and the development of sophisticated algorithms could change that in favor of more "classical" DSP techniques. In fact, automotive could become the first embedded mass-market where floating-point DSP is implemented.

### Navigation Platform

GPS/navigation: In automotive, GPS is part of the dashboard platform. How big will this market be?

### Industrial

A large application found in the industrial market segment is motor control. Quite a very different control from car engine control, the two applications are strongly related since they are the domain of microcontrollers. Identically to engine contol above, motor control is fast becoming a big DSP application.

## 25.8   Others

To finish, small many promising applications using DSP as their bases for new or more advanced features include:

*White appliances:* Refrigerators, washing machines, or any equipment requiring closed control will eventually be heavy DSP users.

*Biomedical:* A good example is the processing of image in medical equipment such as scanner.

*Audio aids:* This is a much larger application than previously thought. Gene FRANTZ [2] made a parallel between visual aids (glasses) and audio aids. Let us imagine the size of the market if everybody was wearing a hearing aid to cancel noise and unwanted conversation.

*Biometrics:* All recognition methods (fingerprint, retina, voice, etc.) rely on DSP.

## 25.9   Conclusions: General Trends

The time when a single application was driving DSP is finished. The next DSP application goal is now several thousands of DSP MIPS, and many applications are driving it:

- Smart and multiple antennae techniques in wireless base stations
- Third generation cellular wireless phones, smart-phones, and terminals
- Broadband access devices (VDSL modem, wireless broadband, gigabit Ethernet)
- Multi-channel application of the telecommunication infrastructure (typically: voice-over-broadband gateway).
- Multimedia home gateways, integrated access device (IAD), wireless Home/LAN access devices
- Streaming media devices (could be a MPEG4 player connected by Bluetooth to a home gateway)
- HDTV, high resolution cameras, 3D audio

Finally, even if no "broadband" applications existed, people would use DSP for cost reasons. When a very good sensor is needed, an imperfect sensor is a worthless commodity. By using DSP techniques (interpolation, adaptive behavior, etc.) a worthless commodity can be turned into a production device.

The author is eager to see the day where a 30-inch 2000 × 4000 color LCD matrix with 80% defects will be turned into a $100 HDTV screen. Only DSP can achieve that.

## References

Except for Will Strauss's unique (and expensive) monumental work, it is difficult to give a complete reference covering all those applications. Personal experience and key people from various conferences [3] were an invaluable tool. The author's recommendation is to go to the specialized electronics Web sites [4–12] and to type the keyword (e.g., e-book) in the search engine. Next, go to the Web sites of the principal DSP manufacturers [14–22] and look for products, white papers, and applications. The reader is encouraged to look into companies not so often associated with DSP, or smaller companies where the most innovative designs are found [23–45].

Finally, the author recommends the two INFINEON sites corresponding to the DSP chips on which he working or has recently worked: TriCore [46] and Carmel [47].

1. Strauss, Will (Aug., 1998) DSP strategies 2002—A study of markets driven by Digital Signal Processing Technology, Forward Concept. Website: www.forwardconcepts.com
2. Frantz, Gene (October 31, 2000) Techonline—Online Symphosium for Electronic Engineers— Digital logic Design—SOC: A system perspective. www.techonline.com
3. ICSPAT 1992, 1993, 1994, 1995, 1996, 1997, 1998, 1999, 2000
4. EE TIMES: www.eetimes.com
5. ICD magazine: icd.pennnet.com
6. Newsletters from INSTAT: www.instat.com
7. CHIP Center—electronics experts: www.chipcenter.com/eexpert
8. EDTN network: www.edtn.com
9. EDN magazine: www.ednmag.com/
10. ELECTONIC DESIGN magazine: www.elecdesign.com
11. ELECTRONIC NEWS online: http://www.electronicnews.com
12. VISION MAGAZINE: www.ce.org/vision_magazine/
13. ANALOG DEVICES: www.analog.com/industry/Industry_Solutions.html
14. INTEL: http://developer.intel.com/platforms/
15. IBM: www.chips.ibm.com
16. INFINEON: www.infineon.com.
17. LUCENT/AGERE: www.lucent.com/micro
18. MOTOROLA: http://e-www.motorola.com/solutions/index.html
19. PHILIPS: www.semiconductors.philips.com
20. STARCORE: www.starcore-dsp.com
21. TEXAS: www.ti.com/sc/docs/innovate/index.htm
22. TEXAS dsp village: http://dspvillage.ti.com/
23. ALTERA: www.altera.com/html/products/products.html
24. AMCC: www.amcc.com
25. ATMEL: www.atmel.com
26. ARM: www.arm.com
27. BOPS: www.bopsnet.com
28. C-CUBE: www.ccube.com/
29. CIRRUS: www.cirrus.com
30. CONEXANT: www.conexant.com/home.asp
31. EQUATOR: www.equator.com
32. IDT: www.idt.com/
33. JACOBS PINEDA: www.jacobspineda.com.
34. LSI logic: www.lsilogic.com
35. METALINK: www.metalink.co.il

36. MITEL Semiconductor: www.semicon.mitel.com
37. MORPHICS Technology: www.morphics.com
38. NS: www.national.com/
39. OAK TECHNOLOGY: www.oaktech.com
40. PMC-SIERRA: www.pmc-sierra.com
41. QUICKLOGIC: www.quicklogic.com
42. SHARP: www.sharpmeg.com
43. TERALOGIC: www.teralogic-inc.com
44. VIRATA: www.virata.com
45. XILINK: www.xilinx.com
46. INFINEON Universal Processor—TriCore: www.infineon.com/us/micro/tricore/
47. INFINEON Carmel DSP: www.carmeldsp.com

# 26
# Digital Filter Design

Worayot Lertniphonphun
*Georgia Institute of Technology*

James H. McClellan
*Georgia Institute of Technology*

## 26.1 Introduction

For computer and information technology (IT) applications, signal processing is an important tool. Nowadays, it is much more efficient and accurate to work with sampled (or digitized) signals rather than with analog (or electrical) signals. Once a signal has been sampled, it can be treated as a sequence of numbers that is a function of a discrete-time variable. When the sampling rate is greater than the Nyquist rate, the digital signal will completely represent the analog signal, because the analog signal can be reconstructed from the digital signal. Digital signal processing (DSP) implements various kinds of mathematical operations, so that physical electrical devices are replaced by computer software or hardware. Unlike analog systems, DSP can handle very sophisticated jobs with as much accuracy as needed. The theory of DSP can be found in three excellent references [1–3].

One very basic DSP operation is digital filtering. It is common to use many filters inside a larger DSP application. Digital filters have widely been used in the following applications:

- *Audio:* spectral shaping
- *Speech:* filter banks
- *Image:* de-blurring, edge-enhancement/detection
- *Communications:* bandpass filters
- *Radar:* matched filters

## 26.2  Digital Filters

The theory of digital filters can be found in references [4–6]. A digital filter is defined as a linear, time invariant operator on a discrete-time input signal, $x[n]$, that generates an output signal, $y[n]$. The filtering operation can always be written as a convolution

$$a[n] * y[n] = b[n] * x[n] \quad \text{(convolution)}$$

where $b[n]$ and $a[n]$ are the filter coefficients associated with the digital filter.

### Implementation

In order to implement the filter as a causal operation, the number of filter coefficients must be finite and the coefficients should be nonzero for only positive indices. Then the output signal can be computed via the difference equation:

$$y[n] = \sum_{k=0}^{M} b[k]x[n-k] - \sum_{k=1}^{N} a[k]y[n-k]$$

where $N$ and $M$ are the number of poles and the number of zeros, respectively, and $N + M$ is the total order of the filter. If any one of the feedback coefficients $a[k]$ is nonzero for $k > 0$, then the filter is called a recursive or infinite impulse response (IIR) filter. Otherwise, the filter is called a nonrecursive or finite impulse response (FIR) filter.

### Frequency Response

The filtering process for linear, time-invariant (LTI) systems can be characterized by the frequency response

$$H(\omega) = \sum_{n} h[n]e^{-j\omega n}$$

which shows how the filter processes sinusoidal inputs. The discrete-time Fourier transform (DTFT) decomposes a general input signal as a superposition of harmonic signals,

$$x[n] = \frac{1}{2\pi} \int_{-\pi}^{\pi} X(\omega)e^{j\omega n} \, d\omega,$$

where the complex amplitudes of those harmonic signals are computed by the DTFT sum:

$$X(\omega) = \sum_{n} x[n]e^{-j\omega n}.$$

Then the behavior of the system can be described as a multiplication in the frequency domain:

$$Y(\omega) = H(\omega)X(\omega)$$

where $Y(\omega) = H(\omega)X(\omega)$ is the DTFT of the output. In terms of the filter coefficients we get

$$Y(\omega) = \frac{B(\omega)}{A(\omega)}X(\omega)$$

where $A(\omega)$, $B(\omega)$, $X(\omega)$, and $Y(\omega)$ are the DTFT of $a[n]$, $b[n]$, $x[n]$, and $y[n]$, respectively. The difference between FIR and IIR filters can be summarized as follows:

**FIR filter:** An FIR filter has $A(\omega) = 1$, so its frequency response is formed as a linear combination of complex exponential functions that is equivalent to a polynomial. Hence, the design problem can be formulated on a linear vector space and very efficient mathematical optimization methods are available for approximating the desired frequency response. The design methods are simple, and often guarantee convergence to an optimal solution. Finally, since FIR filters do not have feedback they do not suffer stability and sensitivity problems.

**IIR filter:** In contrast to the FIR case, IIR filters are rational functions, so the design problem is inherently nonlinear. No elegant mathematical method can guarantee convergence to the global optimum. In addition to the difficulty of numerical design, IIR filters might exhibit instabilities where a finite input can generate infinite output and high sensitivity, and where roundoff noise can be amplified; however, IIR filter design has more design freedom, so IIR filters can have the same performance as FIR filters but with many fewer filter coefficients.

## FFT Implementation

It is possible to implement a digital filter in the frequency domain with the fast Fourier transform (FFT) algorithm [7]. The implementation requires one FFT of the input signal, one multiplication of vectors, and one inverse FFT. The length of the FFT determines a block length so the signal must be segmented into sections for both the input and output. The frequency domain implementation actually uses circular convolution, so some care is needed to get the correct outputs. The FFT-based method of convolution is used in special circumstances because it is only practical for real-time systems when the FIR filter length is rather long—the major drawback is that it requires a large amount of buffer memory for the block processing.

## Adaptive and Time-Varying Filters

Another important class of FIR filters is the class of adaptive filters [8], which find widespread application in areas such as equalizers for communication channels. The filter coefficients in an adaptive filter are continually changing as the input changes, so the filter design problem is quite different for these filters. The methods discussed in this chapter will not handle these cases where the coefficients are time varying.

# 26.3   Digital Filter Design Problem

## Design Specification

A digital filter is usually designed so that its output has a desired frequency content, i.e., the frequency response is frequency selective. The filter coefficients are then optimized so that the frequency response $H(\omega)$ will best approximate an ideal frequency response $I(\omega)$. The ideal response varies for different applications.

**Frequency selective filter:** The ideal frequency response is either one or zero.

$$(\omega) = \begin{cases} 1, & \omega \text{ in the pass band} \\ 0, & \omega \text{ in the stop bands} \\ \text{don't care}, & \omega \text{ in the transition bands} \end{cases}$$

The frequency selective filter is designed so that the actual frequency response $H(\omega)$ is close to 1 in the passband and nearly 0 in the stopband. An example of a frequency selective filter is shown in Fig. 26.1.

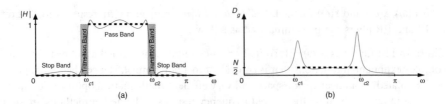

**FIGURE 26.1**  Frequency selective (bandpass) filter: (a) shows the ideal magnitude response (thick dashed line) and an example of an elliptic (with 6 poles, 6 zeros) bandpass filter (thin solid line.) The ideal filter has two cutoff frequencies, $\omega_{c1}$ and $\omega_{c2}$, that separate the two stop bands from the pass band; (b) shows the ideal group delay response (thick dashed line) and the group delay of the elliptic bandpass filter. Note that elliptic filters usually have severe phase distortion (i.e., a highly nonlinear group delay) in the passband.

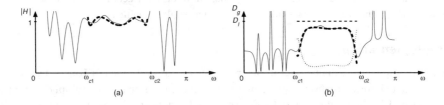

**FIGURE 26.2**  The phase equalizer is designed to equalize the passband of the elliptic filter in Fig. 26.1 so that the group delay is flat in the pass band: (a) shows the ideal equalizer response (thick dashed line) and a FIR (order 25) equalizer; (b) shows the group delay, $D_g\{\bullet\}$, where $D_g\{I_{Equal.}(\omega)\} = D_g\{I(\omega)\} - D_g\{H_{Elliptic}(\omega)\}$ is the ideal group delay (thick dashed line).

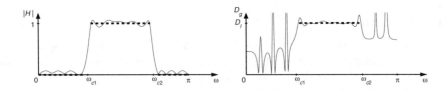

**FIGURE 26.3**  Equalized filter. The figures show the magnitude and the group delay of the elliptic filter (with 6 poles, 6 zeros) after being equalized by the FIR (order 25) equalizer. The ideal filter for the example is a flat group delay frequency selective filter.

**Equalizer:** Equalizers are applied to existing systems in order to remove distortion, or to improve the overall filter characteristic. Therefore, if the desired response of the system is $D(\omega)$, the ideal frequency response of the equalizer depends on the distortion filter $H_D(\omega)$, such that

$$I_{Eq}(\omega) = \frac{D(\omega)}{H_D(\omega)}$$

One example is shown in Fig. 26.2 where the equalizer is used to reduce the phase distortion of the filter in Fig. 26.1. The phase equalized filter is shown in Fig. 26.3.

**Filter bank:** A filter bank is a set of filters that sum to 1, the identity system:

$$I_k(\omega), \text{ for } k = 1,\ldots,P \quad \text{such that} \sum_{k=1}^{p} I_k(\omega) = 1$$

With actual filters, the sum might be approximately one. This property lets us decompose signals with a filter bank and then reconstruct perfectly. Filter banks are now widely used as analysis, storage, and compression tools for DSP.

**Differentiator:** The derivative operation is a filter whose ideal frequency response is

$$I_{\text{Diff.}}(\omega) = j\omega$$

Operators such as the first difference make poor filters because they do not work well for high-frequency signals. Filter design, however, can create high-order numerical differentiators that have excellent wideband characteristics by approximating the ideal frequency response, $I_{\text{Diff.}}(\omega) = j\omega$.

## Error Measurement

In order to have a filter whose frequency response is very close to a given ideal response, a norm for error measurement must be introduced. Then the filter design problem becomes a mathematical optimization problem. Many possible error norms can be used. For example, the most popular norms are:

- Maximal magnitude error, $\max \|\,|I| - |H|\,\|$ , for a frequency-selective filter
- Maximal phase error, $\max |\angle I - \angle H|$, for an allpass filter
- Weighted complex error, $\|W(I - H)\|$, for general filters where the function $W(\omega)$ is a positive weight function

The design problem is usually carried out by minimizing one of these norms, but it is also possible to add constraints on the error magnitude, on the pole locations, the transition band overshoot, the smoothness of the error, or the magnitude of the filter coefficients. These various criteria lead to many different filter design methods that offer trade-offs with respect to efficiency and flexibility.

## Filter Characteristics

Although many filter design papers and procedures have been published, only a few approaches have found widespread use in the 35-year history of DSP.

### Optimal Magnitude Response

IIR filters with optimal magnitude error are generally easy to design partially because they usually require low order; however, these IIR filters usually have severe phase distortion that, in turn, limits the filter's application to cases such as audio where phase does not seem to be important.

### Allpass Filters

The phase distortion of an optimal magnitude IIR filter is sometimes compensated by using an allpass equalizer, where the numerator and denominator of $H(\omega)$ have the same order, $M = N$, and the filter coefficients satisfy $a[k] = b^*[N - k]$. The allpass equalizer, however, is usually not an efficient way to implement filtering, because the equalizer usually has very high order compared to the original filter. This not only causes the filtering to become inefficient, but also causes a long delay in the output signal. Allpass filters can also be used for frequency selective filter design if a pair of allpass filters are connected in parallel. Details of this clever allpass design method can be found in [9–13].

### Filters Designed by Optimizing a General Weighted Norm

In the most general case, filter design can be treated as the process of approximating a complex-valued function $H(\omega)$, where the filter coefficients are the approximating parameters. This treatment gives the filter design problem more degrees of freedom in choosing the ideal response because both magnitude and phase can be approximated. Figure 26.4 shows an example using the general weighted norm. The filter has a much better response than the filter in Fig. 26.3 with the same order as summarized in Table 26.1.

**TABLE 26.1**   Filter Design Comparison

| Filter | # Zeros | # Poles | Mag. Error | GD. Error | RMS GD. Error |
|---|---|---|---|---|---|
| Elliptic (Fig. 26.1) | 6 | 6 | 0.082 | 13.90 | 3.57 |
| Equalized elliptic (Fig. 26.3) | 31 | 6 | 0.079 | 3.15 | 0.76 |
| IIR (Fig. 26.4) | 31 | 6 | 0.015 | 2.40 | 0.32 |

*Note:* The table shows three features: maximal magnitude error, maximal group delay error, and RMSs of the group delay error, of the optimal response of the filter in Figs. 26.3 and 26.4 designed under different approaches.

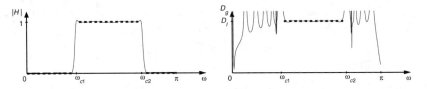

**FIGURE 26.4**   Filter with optimal general weighted norm. The figures show the magnitude and the group delay of an IIR frequency selective filter (31 zeros, 6 poles) with flat delay passband. The ideal filter is the same as in Fig. 26.3, and the filter order is the same as the equalized elliptic filter.

Several optimization techniques are available to solve these general problems. In addition, the error can be controlled by the selection of an error constraint, an error weight, or a design norm; however, the optimization of general norms is often a difficult problem, especially in the complex domain. Most recent research has studied these general norm problems in order to improve the design when the goal is a simultaneous approximation of the magnitude and phase.

## Filter Design as a Norm Problem

Filter design is usually done by minimizing either the worst-case error (Chebyshev norm), or the root mean squares (RMS) (least-squares norm) of the weighted error. Important norms from classical mathematics are listed below:

- Chebyshev norm: $\|E\|_\infty = \max_\omega |E(\omega)|$

- Least-squares norm: $\|E\|_2 = \left\{ \int_{-\pi}^{\pi} |E(\omega)|^2 \, d\omega \right\}^{1/2}$

- $p$-norm: $\|E\|_p = \left\{ \int_{-\pi}^{\pi} |E(\omega)|^p \, d\omega \right\}^{1/p}$ for $p \in [1, \infty]$

- Combined norm: $\|E\|_\alpha = \{ \alpha\|E\|_\infty^2 + (1 - \alpha)\|E\|_2^2 \}$ for $\alpha \in [0,1]$

where $E = W(I - H)$ is the weighted complex error. When optimizing the Chebyshev norm, the resulting optimal filters have the smallest maximal error, while filters with minimal least-squares norm have the smallest RMS error. Preference for one norm over the other will generally depend on the application. In many cases, where both norms need to be small, filters should be designed under either the $p$-norm or the combined norm. Along with the norm, the numerical optimization can be done under design constraints, e.g., the most obvious one is a constraint on the magnitude of the error

$$\min \|E\| \quad \text{such that} \quad |E(\omega)| \leq \varepsilon(\omega)$$

where $\varepsilon(\omega)$ is the error constraint.

Figure 26.5 shows the error of the filter with the same specification designed under four different norms. The RMS and maximal errors are summarized in Table 26.2.

**TABLE 26.2**  Error Measurements for Fig. 26.5

| Filter | RMS Error | Maximal Error in Passband | RMS Error in Stopband |
|---|---|---|---|
| (a) Least-squares | 0.0361 | 0.1793 | 0.0348 |
| (b) Chebyshev | 0.0657 | 0.0923 | 0.0660 |
| (c) Constrained least-squares | 0.0562 | 0.0959 | 0.0571 |
| (d) Least-squares stopband | 0.0584 | 0.0958 | 0.0374 |

*Note:* These are the passband and stopband errors in bandpass filters designed by a different norm problem.

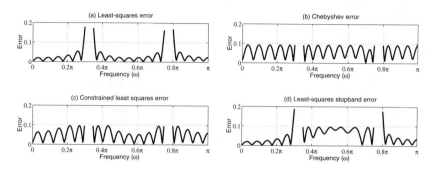

**FIGURE 26.5**  Different error norms. The four filters were designed to approximate the same bandpass filter of order 25 with four different norms. The filter in (c) was designed by minimizing the least-squares norm under the constraint that the maximal error be smaller than 0.0959. Note that the filter in (c) can also be designed by minimizing the unconstrained combined norm problem with the norm weighting $\alpha = 0.4$. The filter can also be designed so that both the distortion in the pass band and the power of the stopband error are small. The filter in (d) was designed by optimizing the combination of the Chebyshev error norm of the passband plus the least-squares norm of the stopband.

The norm optimization problem differs quite a bit for the FIR and IIR cases:

**FIR filter:** The problem is formed on a linear vector space and has been well studied. The optimal solution is unique by convexity. Many available design methods are not only elegant, but are also computationally efficient and have guaranteed convergence.

**IIR filter:** Although the IIR filter design problem does not have the same nice properties as the FIR filter design problem, optimizing the norm is relatively easy. One iterative approach to IIR filter design relies on a sub-procedure similar to the method for FIR filter design.

# 26.4  Conventional Design Methods

Although many filter design papers have been published in the 35 years of DSP, only a handful of filter design methods are widely used. Some of the older conventional methods can design filters with excellent magnitude response using a very simple procedure, but the variety of possible filter specifications and error norms are usually limited. More recent methods offer general design capabilities for both magnitude and phase approximation, but are based on numerical optimization.

## IIR Filters from Analog Filters

Originally digital filters were derived from analog filters [14] because analog filter design techniques had been studied for a long time and the design usually involved algebraic formulas that were simple to carry out. The two main design methods are impulse-invariance and the bilinear transformation.

### Impulse Invariance

The design is carried out by starting with an already designed analog filter that is bandlimited. Let $h_a(t)$ denote the impulse response of the analog filter. Then the impulse response of the digital filter is obtained by sampling, i.e., by setting $h[n] = T_d h_a(nT_d)$; however, no analog filter is truly bandlimited, so the actual frequency response involves some aliasing:

$$H(\omega) = \sum_{k=-\infty}^{\infty} H_a\left(j\frac{\omega}{T_d} + j\frac{2\pi}{T_d}k\right)$$

where $H_a(s)$ is the Laplace transform system function of the analog filter. The aliasing effect usually causes only a slight perturbation of the digital filter with respect to the analog filter. The system function of the analog filter can be expressed in partial fraction form

$$H_a(s) = \sum_{k=1}^{N} \frac{A_k}{s - s_k}$$

After sampling the digital filter has a frequency response that is also a rational form:

$$\text{DTFT:} \quad H(\omega) = \sum_{k=1}^{N} \frac{T_d A_k}{1 - e^{T_d s_k} e^{-j\omega}} = \frac{\sum_{k=0}^{N-1} b[n] e^{-j\omega n}}{1 + \sum_{k=1}^{N} a[n] e^{-j\omega n}}$$

where $b[n]$ and $a[n]$ are the coefficients of the designed filter. Impulse invariance is equivalent to a linear mapping of the analog frequency range $[-\pi/T_d, \pi/T_d]$ into the digital frequency range $[-\pi, \pi]$.

## Bilinear Transform

On the other hand, the bilinear transformation performs a nonlinear mapping of the whole analog frequency range $[-\infty, \infty]$ into the finite digital frequency range $[-\pi, \pi]$. The mapping of the $s$-plane to the $z$-plane is done by the bilinear transform:

$$s = \frac{2}{T_d}\left(\frac{1 - z^{-1}}{1 + z^{-1}}\right)$$

The resulting correspondence between the analog and digital frequency domains is a tangent function:

$$\omega_a = \frac{2}{T_d} \tan\left(\frac{\omega}{2}\right)$$

Despite the nonlinear nature of the mapping, it is relatively easy to turn the digital design specification into an analog design specification. The resulting filter is IIR and the filter coefficients can be computed with an algebraic form. The bilinear transform method is usually applied to four classical analog filter frequency selective filters: Butterworth, Chebyshev-I, Chebyshev-II, and elliptic filters. All these are well known for their frequency-selective behavior as lowpass, bandpass, or highpass filters. When using the bilinear mapping, elliptic IIR filters turn out to have the best magnitude response for given filter order, but elliptic filters have severe phase distortion, which can be a significant problem in advanced DSP applications such as telecommunications.

## Windowing

IIR filter designs have poor phase response, so interest in FIR filters has always been strong. If the coefficients of an FIR filter are real and symmetric $b[k] = b^*[M - k]$ then the filter will have perfectly linear phase. The first attempt to design FIR filters in the 1960s was to truncate the inverse DTFT of the ideal frequency response (which is the impulse response $h[n]$ of the ideal filter), so that the filter is symmetric and linear-phase. This requires the ideal filter to have linear-phase with slope $-\frac{1}{2}M$, where $M$

is the FIR filter order. This method of filter design turns out to give the optimal least-squares filter. However, the least-squares filter is not an acceptable filter, especially when the application calls for a frequency selective filter. The reason is that the least-squares approximation exhibits an overshoot called the *Gibbs' phenomenon*, which means that the magnitude of the error is large at the cutoff frequency regardless of the filter order. To reduce the magnitude error near the cutoff frequency, the strict truncation (done by applying a rectangular window) can be replaced by other windowing. Windowing for filter design involves the multiplication of a finite-length window shape times the ideal impulse response. For example, the ideal lowpass filter with delay $\mu = \frac{1}{2}M$ has an impulse response that is infinitely long:

$$h[n] = \frac{\sin(\omega_c(n - \mu))}{\pi(n - \mu)}, \quad -\infty < n < \infty$$

so the windowed filter coefficients are $b[n] = w[n]h[n]$ for $n = 0, 1, 2, \ldots, M$.

Different windows generate filter responses that allow a trade-off between the sharpness of transition region and the error magnitude. Popular windows are: Bartlett, Hamming, vonHann (or Hanning), and Kaiser, but for filter design the only important one is the Kaiser window, which is based on the modified Bessel function. The Kaiser window is defined as

$$w[n] = \frac{I_0(\beta\sqrt{1 - (n - \mu)^2/\mu^2})}{I_0(\beta)}, \quad n = 0, 1, 2, \ldots, M$$

where $I_0(x)$ is the modified Bessel function, and the parameter $\beta$ is chosen to control the ripple height in the stopband with the relationship:

$$\beta = \begin{cases} 0, & \delta_{dB} < 21 \\ 0.5842(\delta_{dB} - 21)^{0.4} + 0.07886(\delta_{dB} - 21), & 21 \leq \delta_{dB} \leq 50 \\ 0.1102(\delta_{dB} - 8.7), & \delta_{dB} > 50 \end{cases}$$

where $\delta_{dB} = -20\log_{10}(\delta_{stopband})$ is the ripple height in dB. The design of the Kaiser window is illustrated in Fig. 26.6. Examples of digital filters designed via windowing are shown in Fig. 26.7.

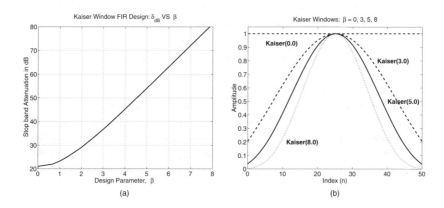

**FIGURE 26.6** The Kaiser window: (a) shows the relationship between $\beta$ and the ripple height in the stop band; (b) shows examples of length-51 Kaiser windows (i.e., filter order = 50) with different parameters $\beta$. Note that, with $\beta = 0$, the window is the rectangular window and, with $\beta = 5$, the window is very similar to the Hamming window.

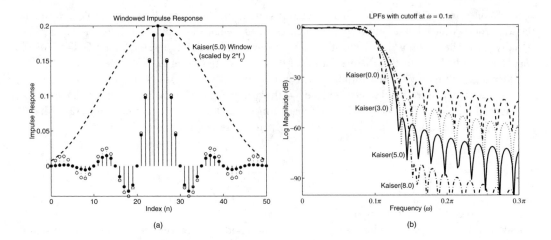

**FIGURE 26.7**  Digital filter design via Kaiser windowing: (a) shows the impulse response of an ideal lowpass filter (circles with dotted lines) and the filter designed by windowing (filled circles with solid lines). The windowed filter is the product of the ideal impulse response and the Kaiser window with $\beta = 5$ (dashed line); (b) shows the log magnitude of four filters designed using the Kaiser window with different parameters $\beta$.

### Frequency Sampling

Another common, but naive, approach to FIR design is the method of frequency sampling. In this case, the ideal frequency response is sampled over the range $-\pi < \omega \leq \pi$ at $M + 1$ points and then the inverse FFT is computed to get the order-$M$ impulse response, which then contains the coefficients of the FIR filter. It is possible to let a few of the frequency samples be free parameters for a linear program that will optimize the resultant $H(\omega)$. This, in turn, improves the filter characteristics by making the error smaller near the cutoff frequency.

### Weighted Least-Squares

Although frequency sampling filters and windowing designs have pretty good responses, neither one is an optimal filter. In the general optimization approach, the transition band of the frequency response should be treated as a "don't care" region. For common frequency selective filters, the optimal filter will have a smooth behavior in the transition band even though no optimization is done in that "don't care" region. The FIR filter can be designed by minimizing any norm with a guaranteed unique solution. The design can be generalized further by using a weighting function on the error. For example, the weight can be used in clever ways to control the error. Here is the weight definition for an inverse filter (or equalizer).

$$I_{Eq}(\omega) = \frac{D(\omega)}{H_{Sys}(\omega)}, \qquad W_{Eq}(\omega) = |H_{Sys}(\omega)| W(\omega)$$

The weighted design problem usually involves optimizing the norm of the error over the entire frequency domain, but that is done numerically by working on a dense frequency grid.

The easiest optimization problem is the least-squares norm minimization because the partial derivatives (which are the elements of the gradient) of the least-squares norm with respect to the filter coefficients are all linear combinations of the filter coefficients. This property implies that the optimal filter can be found by solving the set of linear equations obtained by setting all those partial derivatives to zero. The solution for the weighted least-squares FIR filter is

$$\frac{\partial}{\partial b[n]} \int_{\omega} |W(I - H)|^2 \, d\omega = 0, \quad \text{for} \quad n = 0, 1, \ldots, M$$

$$\int_{\omega} |W|^2 \left( I e^{j\omega n} - \sum_{k} b[k] e^{j\omega(n-k)} \right) d\omega = 0, \quad \text{for} \quad n = 0, 1, \ldots, M$$

For IIR filters, the problem is not nearly so easy because the denominator of the frequency response function makes the problem nonlinear. The solution can still be carried out by computing the partial derivatives and setting them equal to zero:

$$\int_\omega |W|^2 \left( \frac{e^{j\omega n}}{A^*} \left( I - \frac{B}{A} \right) \right) d\omega = 0, \quad \text{for } n = 0,1,\dots,M$$

$$\int_\omega |W|^2 \left( \frac{e^{j\omega n}}{A^*} \frac{B^*}{A^*} \left( I - \frac{B}{A} \right) \right) d\omega = 0, \quad \text{for } n = 0,1,\dots,N$$

The solution may not exist, however, but even if it does, it is often not unique. Furthermore, it is likely that only a locally optimal solution of the nonlinear equations can be found. Another approach is to use an iteration to find a close-to-optimal solution using the Steiglitz–McBride method [15]:

$$\min \left| W \left( I - \frac{B}{A} \right) \right| \rightarrow \min \left| \frac{W}{|A|} (IA - B) \right|$$

The solution can be realized by iteratively updating the rational functions $W/|A|$ and $B/A$.

## Remez Exchange

Least-squares filters are not desirable in many applications because they exhibit large worst-case error near the transition band. On the other hand, the worst-case error can be minimized by reformulating the design problem as a Chebyshev (or min-max) problem.

$$\min_{b[n],a[n]} \max_\omega |W(I - H)|$$

This min-max problem is usually difficult to solve unless the problem can be transformed into a real problem. To do this, the ideal filter needs to be a linear-phase filter with a group delay of $\frac{1}{2}M$. Then the problem becomes an approximation of a real function by a sum of sinusoidal functions. For the special case of an even-order FIR filter with symmetric coefficients, the real problem becomes:

$$\min_{c_k} \max_\omega \left| W(\omega) \left( I(\omega) e^{j\omega M/2} - \sum_{k=0}^{M/2} c_k \cos \omega k \right) \right|$$

where $a = [1]$ and $b = [\frac{1}{2} c_{N/2}, \dots, \frac{1}{2} c_1, c_0, \frac{1}{2} c_1, \dots, \frac{1}{2} c_{N/2}]$. This min-max problem can be solved by the Remez algorithm [16–19]. The algorithm exploits the famous Alternation Theorem, which gives the necessary and sufficient condition for an optimal real Chebyshev solution as one that has at least $M + 2$ alternating extremal points (i.e., points where the error is maximal). The operation of the algorithm involves an exchange that iteratively updates the extremal set and solves for the alternating error on that set. It turns out that the Remez Exchange algorithm is very efficient and always converges, so it has become a classical method for FIR filter design as the Parks–McClellan algorithm.

## Linear Programming

Filter design by optimizing the norm of the weighted error can be further improved by applying constraints. However, only the magnitude constrained problem seems to be easy to solve

$$\min \| W(I - H) \| \quad \text{or} \quad \min \| E \|$$
$$\text{subject to } |E(\omega)| < \varepsilon(\omega)$$

This constrained magnitude problem can be solved by Mathematical programming, which takes different forms depending on the norm. For the least-squares norm, the solution can be found by using quadratic programming.

Mathematical programming is also a tool for the nonlinear-phase Chebyshev problem [20], which can be rewritten as a constrained problem:

$$\min \delta$$

subject to

$$\Re\{E(\omega)e^{j\theta}\} < \delta, \quad \text{for all } \omega \text{ and } \theta$$

This problem is a semi-infinite linear minimization (SILM). Linear programming can then be applied to the problem by sampling the parameters $\omega$ and $\theta$. The algorithm is not efficient for high-order filters because dense parameter sampling is needed to design filters with high precision. In order to improve efficiency, the SILM can be rewritten in a *dual form* [21–24].

## 26.5  Recent Design Methods

Because conventional design methods are available for only special types of digital filters, e.g., linear-phase, researchers have proposed various new methods that use complex approximation in filter design. Among those, only a few are discussed because they are elegant and useful in various applications.

### Complex Remez Algorithm

The complex Chebyshev design problem is one of the most important approaches for designing digital filters. Unfortunately, it might need a general algorithm such as SILM, which requires a large number of frequency samples (with resulting high computation and high memory) when high precision is desired. For high order filters, linear programming is very inefficient for Chebyshev filter design. Instead, mod-ifications of the Remez Exchange algorithm would be more desirable. Therefore, the complex Remez algorithm (CRemez) [25,26] was proposed using an exchange method search that is similar to the Remez Exchange; however, the original CRemez is most efficient only for the special case where the extremal error alternates. In general, nonlinear-phase filters are not guaranteed to have this strict alternating property, so the exchange method does not converge to the optimum. In order to get the optimum filter in the case of nonalternating extremal errors, a second stage is needed for CRemez. This second stage has to be a general optimization method that ends up being as inefficient as the SILM method. As a result, some filters are designed very quickly by CRemez, but others take a long time when the general optimization step must be invoked.

### Constrained Least-Squares

Adams [27] suggested that Chebyshev digital filters do not always have the best overall characteristics. He found that by allowing the worst-case (Chebyshev) error to increase slightly, the least-squares error can be reduced significantly. To design this sort of filter, a constrained least-squares problem was intro-duced. The problem has been solved by [28–31] with an algorithm that is quite efficient for designing FIR filters.

### Generalized Remez Algorithm

The constrained least-squares methods have two design drawbacks: (1) error constraints are required to set up the problem, and (2) the existing methods only handle the FIR case. The first drawback is not severe, but it reduces the design efficiency because prior information such as a prior filter design procedure is needed to estimate the constraints; however, both drawbacks can be eliminated by using a different norm (called the combined norm) and by minimizing via the iterative reweighted least-squares (IRLS) technique.

## IRLS Technique

Lawson [32] proposed that the Chebyshev problem be turned into a weighted least-squares (WLS) problem. In fact, any general norm problem can also be turned into a WLS problem

$$\text{IRLS:} \quad \|E\| \to \|VE\|_2$$

The trick is to find the correct weight, $V$, which is an unknown that must be found by running an iterative update [32–34]. For example, the following iterations converge to the appropriate weight for the Chebyshev norm and the $p$-norm, respectively.

- Chebyshev update: $V^{(k+1)} = V^{(k)} \sqrt{|E|}$
- $p$-norm update: $V^{(k+1)} = \{ V^{(k)} \sqrt{|E|} \}^{\frac{p-2}{p-1}}$

The convergence of the weight is dependent on the number of points in the frequency grid, so IRLS alone usually converges slowly.

## Combined Norm

It can be shown that the solution of the combined norm problem is equivalent to a constrained least-squares problem. The solution has multiple extremals of the error similar to the Chebyshev solution. To solve the combined norm problem, the IRLS technique can be used after the problem is turned into a weighted least-squares problem:

$$\|E\|_\alpha \to \{ \alpha \|VE\|_2^2 + (1 - \alpha) \|E\|_2^2 \}^{1/2}$$

By iterating on the weight, $V$, the solution generally converges quickly unless $\alpha$ is large. The optimization procedure can be improved by exploiting the multiple extremal error property of the optimal combined norm solution.

## Generalized Remez Algorithm

The optimal filter design problem can be generalized further by considering the problem of minimizing the combined norm together with magnitude constraints. Using Lagrange multipliers, the problem can be turned into an unconstrained least-squares problem:

$$\min\{ \alpha \|VE\|_2^2 + (1 - \alpha) \|E\|_2^2 + \|\Lambda E\|_2^2 \}^{1/2}$$

where $\Lambda$ is the Lagrange multiplier. This problem can be solved by the basic IRLS technique, but often converges slowly. On the other hand, it can be shown that the weight, $V$, and the multiplier, $\Lambda$, are nonzero for only a finite number of points and those points are extremal points and points where constraints are reached. So, the multiple exchange in the Remez algorithm can be used to find those points. After the points are found, the IRLS technique is applied to compute the filter coefficients. The solution will converge much more quickly than the classical IRLS because it deals with less frequency points. The authors call this new algorithm the "generalized Remez algorithm" or GRemez because its structure is equivalent to the Remez algorithm for linear phase FIR filter design [35]. Note that the GRemez algorithm is similar to a multiple exchange algorithm for the Chebyshev problem by Tseng [36]. The GRemez algorithm is summarized as a block diagram in Fig. 26.8.

Not only can the GRemez be used for the general constrained norm problem, but IIR filters can also be designed by the GRemez with the least-squares techniques presented in the "Weighted Least-Squares" subsection to find either a close-to-optimal solution or a local optimal solution.

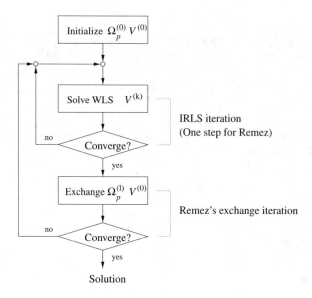

**FIGURE 26.8**   Block diagram of the generalized Remez algorithm.

# 26.6   Summary

## General Comment

This chapter has given a brief overview of various digital filter design methods. The theoretical ideas of frequency response and impulse response were reviewed in order to introduce the important design methods. In addition, the mathematical idea of optimizing with respect to a norm was discussed because many newer methods utilize numerical optimization to design general classes of filters. Readers are encouraged to find more details in the references that include many excellent DSP and digital filtering books [1–6].

Because digital filters must be designed for many diverse applications, a large number of design approaches are available; however, most filter applications can be addressed with an optimization algorithm when the general filter design problem is formed under the weighted norm of the complex error. This general problem can be difficult to solve in some cases. Fortunately, it is quite simple to design the most desirable filters, i.e., least-squares and Chebyshev FIR filters with linear-phase. Furthermore, filters with more general characteristics can be designed by methods presented in section 26.5. We introduce the generalized Remez algorithm in the "Weighted Least-Squares" section in order to design both FIR and IIR filters under the weighted norm formulation.

Filter design methods presented in this paper are usually quite efficient, but some still require a fair amount of computation. For example, even though the least-squares method requires an amount of computation proportional to the cube of the filter order, $O(M^3)$, it is considered to be a relatively efficient design method using a norm minimization. Fortunately, the design time is hardly noticed on today's desktop computers, which have very fast processors.

Many other important issues in filter design were not treated here. These include filter order selection, filter pole location sensitivity, effect of implementing filter with fixed-point arithmetic, and multidimensional filter design [37–39]. Some details about these issues can be found in the references. In addition, the design of two-dimensional (2-D) filters has not been treated. Some of the optimization methods discussed here will also work for the 2-D case, but much of the theory of Chebyshev approximation no longer applies, so methods that exploit special features such as the Alternation Theorem will no longer be efficient.

## Computer Tools

General filter design methods that are able to handle virtually all of the desired filter characteristics of common applications were discussed; however, most users would not want to be involved with details of programming the optimization algorithms. So, software applications have been built to help users skip the computer programming step and concentrate on entering the filter specifications for their application. Two types of interface for the design software are common: (1) allow users to set up the full design specification and (2) allow limited specifications.

The second type is generally implemented as a graphical user interface (GUI) that helps the user visualize all the steps of the design from creating the passband and stopband, setting the filter type (FIR or IIR), selecting the optimization tool, running the design program, and showing the designed filter responses. GUI software hides most of the design steps in the interest of simplicity, but it imposes a limitation on the amount of information that the user can see.

More advanced users probably need to design filters with more sophisticated specifications, more control on the error, or a wider variety of filter types. Therefore, they may need to enter the parameters manually in a command line to run the optimization function of the design algorithm. This normally requires some experience in the programming language and sometimes knowledge of the design program's source code.

One example of filter design programs can be found in the MATLAB© environment with its signal processing toolbox. Most of the design methods of filter design are available in the SP toolbox, and additional ones might be obtained by contracting the author who proposed the method. In MATLAB, the information for running the signal processing toolbox can be seen by typing "help signal." One attempt to make DSP simple to use is the MATLAB GUI program "sptool" that can upload and download signals, design and apply filters, and analyze the signal spectra. By pushing the button "New Design," the filter design GUI is called and the program gives the user an ability to design frequency selective filters by most of the conventional methods. Actually, the design GUI takes input parameters, changes them into the proper format, and then performs the design by calling design functions such as "butter," "cheby1," "cheby2," "ellip," "firls," and "remez." For more varieties of filter types, filters may be designed by calling "cremez," "fircls," etc., with appropriate parameters in the MATLAB command line. The authors have also developed the function "gremez" and "gremez_gui" as a MATLAB functions that can be downloaded from "http://users.ece.gatech.edu/mcclella/gremez".

## References

1. Oppenheim, A. V., Schafer, R. W., and Buck, J. A., *Discrete-time signal processing*, 2nd ed., Prentice-Hall, NJ, 1999.
2. McClellan, J. H., Schafer, R. W., and Yoder, M. A., *DSP first: a multimedia approach*, Prentice-Hall, NJ, 1998.
3. Proakis, J. G. and Manolakis D. G., *Digital signal processing: principles, algorithms, and applications*, Prentice-Hall, NJ, 1996.
4. Hamming, R. W., *Digital filters*, 3rd ed., Prentice-Hall, NJ, 1998.
5. Mersereau, R. M. and Smith, M. J. T., *Digital filtering: a computer laboratory textbook*, John Wiley & Sons, NY, 1994.
6. Parks, T. W. and Burrus, C. S., *Digital filter design*, John Wiley & Sons, NY, 1987.
7. Cooley, J. W. and Tukey J. W., An algorithm for the machine computation of complex Fourier series, *Math. Comput.*, 19, 297–301, April 1965.
8. Haykin, S. S., *Adaptive filter theory*, 3rd ed., Prentice-Hall, NJ, 1996.
9. Deczky, A. G., Recursive digital filter having equiripple group delay, *IEEE Trans. Circuits Syst.*, CAS-21, 131–134, Jan. 1974.
10. Deczky, A. G., Equiripple and minimax (Chebyshev) approximations for recursive digital filters, *IEEE Transactions on Acoust., Speech, Signal Processing*, ASSP-22, 98–111, April 1974.

11. Ikehara, M., Tanaka, H., and Kuroda, H., Design of IIR digital filters using allpass networks, *IEEE Trans. Circuits Syst. II*, 41, 231–235, March 1994.

12. Lang, M., Allpass filter design and applications, *IEEE Trans. Signal Processing*, 46, 2505–2513, Sep. 1998.

13. Zhang, X. and Iwakura, H., Design of IIR digital allpass filters based on eigenvalue problem, *IEEE Trans. Signal Processing*, 47, 554–559, Feb. 1999.

14. Weinberg, L., *Network analysis and synthesis*, R. E. Kreiger, Huntington, NY, 1975.

15. Steiglitz, K. and McBride, L. E., A technique for the identification of linear systems, *IEEE Trans. Automatic Control*, 10, 461–464, Oct. 1965.

16. Parks, T. W. and McClellan, J. H., Chebyshev approximation for nonrecursive digital filters with linear phase, *IEEE Trans. Circuit Theory*, CT-19, 189–194, March 1972.

17. McClellan, J. H. and Parks, T. W., A unified approach to the design of optimal FIR linear-phase digital filters, *IEEE Trans. Circuit Theory*, CT-20, 697–701, Nov. 1973.

18. McClellan, J. H., Parks, T. W., and Rabiner, L. R., A computer program for designing optimum FIR linear phase digital filters, *IEEE Trans. Audio Electroacoust.*, AU-21, 506–526, Dec. 1973.

19. Remez, E. Ya., General computational methods of Chebyshev approximation, *Atomic Energy Translation*, 4491, 1957.

20. Chen, X. and Parks, T. W., Design of FIR filters in the complex domain, *IEEE Trans. Acoust., Speech, Signal Processing*, ASSP-35, 144–153, Feb. 1987.

21. Alkhairy, A. S., Christian, K. G., and Lim, J. S., Design and characterization of optimal FIR filters with arbitrary phase, *IEEE Trans. Signal Processing*, 41, 559–572, Feb. 1993.

22. Komodromos, M. Z., Russell, S. F., and Tang, P. T. P., Design of FIR filters with complex desired frequency response using a generalized Remez algorithm, *IEEE Trans. Circuits Syst. II*, 42, 274–278, April 1995.

23. Burnside, D. and Parks, T. W., Optimal design of FIR filters with the complex Chebyshev error criteria, *IEEE Trans. Signal Processing*, 43, 605–616, March 1995.

24. Vuerinckx, R., *Design of Digital Chebyshev Filters in the Complex Domain*, Vrije Universiteit Brussel, Oct. 1997.

25. Karam, L. J., *Design of Complex Digital FIR Filters in the Chebyshev sense*, Georgia Institute of Technology, March 1995.

26. Karam, L. J. and McClellan, J. H., Chebyshev digital FIR filter design, *Signal Processing*, 76, 17–36, 1999.

27. Adams, J. W., FIR digital filters with least-squares stopbands subject to peak-gain constraints, *IEEE Trans. Circuits Syst.*, 39, 376–388, April 1991.

28. Sullivan, J. L. and Adams, J. W., Peak-constrained least-squares optimization, *IEEE Trans. Signal Processing*, 46, 306–321, Feb. 1998.

29. Sullivan, J. L. and Adams, J. W., PCLS IIR digital filters with simultaneous frequency response magnitude and group delay specification, *IEEE Trans. Signal Processing*, 46, 2853–2861, Nov. 1998.

30. Lang, M. C., An iterative reweighted least squares algorithm for constrained design of nonlinear phase FIR filters, *Proc. IEEE ISCAS*, 5, 367–370, 1998.

31. Lang, M. C., Multiple exchange algorithm for constrained design of FIR filters in the complex domain, *Proc. IEEE ICASSP*, 3, 1149–1152, 1999.

32. Lawson, C. L., *Contributions to the theory of linear least maximum approximations*, University of California, Los Angeles, 1961.

33. Lim, Y. C., Lee, J. H., Chen, C. K., and Yang, R. H., A weighted least squares algorithm for quasi-equiripple FIR and IIR digital filter design, *IEEE Trans. on Signal Processing*, ASSP-40, 551–558, March 1992.

34. Burrus, C. S., Barreto, J. A., and Selesnick, I. W., Iterative reweighted least-square design of FIR filters, *IEEE Trans. Signal Processing*, 42, 2926–2936, Nov. 1994.

35. Lertniphonphun, W. and McClellan, J. H., Unified design algorithm for complex FIR and IIR filters, *Proc. IEEE ICASSP*, 2001.

36. Tseng, C.-Y., An efficient implementation of Lawson's algorithm with application to complex Chebyshev FIR filter design, *IEEE Trans. Circuits Sys. II,* 42, 245–260, April 1995.

37. Dudgeon, D. E. and Mersereau, R. M., *Multidimensional digital signal processing,* Prentice-Hall, NJ, 1984.

38. McClellan, J. H., The design of two-dimensional digital filters by transformations, *Proc. 7th Annual Princeton Conf. on Inform. Sci. and Syst.,* 247–251, 1973.

39. McClellan, J. H., *On the design of one-dimensional and two-dimensional FIR digital filters,* Rice University, Houston, TX, April 1973.

# 27

# Audio Signal Processing

**Adam Dabrowski**
*Poznan University of Technology*

**Tomasz Marciniak**
*Poznan University of Technology*

## 27.1 Introduction

Information and communication systems play bigger and bigger role in our modern society—the so-called information society. Sound (audio and speech) is one of the most important signals in these systems and the growing need for audio and speech processing (transmission, storing, etc.) generates new scientific problems (e.g., formulates new questions about data acquisition, compression, and coding), stimulates new technologies and techniques, as well as creates new areas of science and technology in informatics, communications, artificial intelligence, psychoacoustics, etc.

Applications of digital audio processing systems are in audio production, storage, distribution, exchange, broadcasting, transmission, Internet services, etc. Modern multimedia coding standards (e.g., moving picture expert group (MPEG) standards: MPEG-4, MPEG-7, and MPEG-21) [3,18–20,34,36] cover the whole range of audio signals starting from high fidelity audio, through the regular quality of audio and speech, down to relatively low quality mobile-access and synthetic speech and audio.

In order to evaluate various audio coding systems it is necessary to qualify the audio quality they offer. Generally, three main parameters are used to describe the quality of audio: bandwidth, fidelity, and spatial realism.

For high-fidelity (wideband) audio a bandwidth of at least 20 kHz is needed. The acoustic signals with higher frequencies are not audible by human beings. Compact disc (CD)—the today's most popular standard for digital audio representation—offers a bandwidth of 20–20,000 Hz. Traditional (analog) radio covers the bandwidth of up to 15 kHz for frequency modulation (FM) and up to 4.5 kHz only for amplitude modulation (AM). Wideband speech standard has a bandwidth of 50–7000 Hz, while the telephone speech is reduced to a bandwidth of merely 300–3400 Hz.

Fidelity is a (subjective) measure of perceptibility of impairment (noise) present in the reproduced audio. Audio fidelity is usually determined subjectively by means of an averaged judgment called the mean opinion score (MOS). It is typically based on a 5-point grading scale: 5—impairment imperceptible, 4—perceptible but not annoying, 3—slightly annoying, 2—annoying, 1—very annoying [35].

Spatial realism of an audio representation system describes the naturalness and quality of directional information about places of particular sound sources contained in the reproduced sound. The spatial realism depends first of all on the number of audio channels. Typical configurations are: 1-channel audio (mono); 2-channel audio (stereo); multichannel audio (surround sound), e.g., 4-channel (3 front and 1 rear), 5-channel (3 front and 2 rear), or 8-channel (6 front and 2 rear). An additional low-frequency enhancement (LFE) or *subwoofer* channel, supplementing the low frequency content (in a bandwidth of approximately 15–150 Hz), can be added in any of these cases (e.g., a 5.1-channel format is a 5-channel configuration plus subwoofer).

## 27.2  Elements of Technical Acoustics

For the purpose of this chapter, sound can be defined as a mechanical oscillation of an elastic medium that potentially can be heard. If acoustic vibrations are too high in frequency to be heard, they are referred to as ultrasonic oscillations. Consequently, if they are too low in frequency, they are called infrasonic oscillations. The sound starts in approximately 20 Hz and extends up to 20 kHz (thus it covers a bandwidth of approximately 10 octaves) [32,54,55].

A source of sound undergoes rapid changes of position (and/or size, or shape) that disturb positions of adjacent molecules of the surrounding medium (in most cases the atmosphere). Thus, these molecules start to oscillate about their equilibrium positions. These disturbances propagate elastically to neighboring particles and then gradually to larger and larger distances, thus constituting an acoustic wave traveling through the medium. The acoustic wave speed in air equals

$$c = c_0\sqrt{1 + \frac{\vartheta}{273}} \tag{27.1}$$

where $\vartheta$ is the room temperature in degrees of celsius and $c_0 = 331$ m/s is the sound speed at $\vartheta_0 = 0°$C. At room temperature ($\vartheta = 20°$C) the speed of sound is calculated to be 343 m/s.

A sound wave compresses and dilates the elastic medium it passes through, generating associated pressure fluctuations. The minimum fluctuation to which the ear responds is extremely small, e.g., at a frequency of 1000 Hz the just noticeable effective air pressure amplitude is approximately 20 $\mu$Pa, i.e., less than $10^{-9}$ of the standard atmospheric pressure (equal to 1000 hPa = $10^5$ Pa). The limit of danger followed by the threshold of pain corresponds to effective air pressure amplitude one million ($10^6$) times larger, but still less than one-thousandth of the atmospheric pressure [24].

Because of this wide range of acoustic pressure amplitudes, it has become conventional to specify the sound pressure level (SPL), $L_p$, in terms of a decimal logarithm with the (dimensionless) unit of the decibel (dB)

$$L_p = 20 \log_{10} \frac{p}{p_0} \tag{27.2}$$

where $p_0 = 20$ $\mu$Pa.

Another quantity, which is often used, is the sound intensity level, $L_I$, defined in decibel as

$$L_I = 10 \log_{10} \frac{I}{I_0} \tag{27.3}$$

The reference in this case is the sound intensity $I_0 = 10^{-12}$ W/m$^2$. For a free progressive acoustic wave in air, sound pressure level and sound intensity level are approximately equal.

## 27.3 Parametric Modeling of Audio Signals

A natural representation of an audio signal is its waveform $x(t)$ describing the sound pressure changes in time. Signal $x(t)$ occurs at a microphone output, excites the speaker, and generally, represents sound in analog audio processing systems. On the other hand, in digital systems, in order to reduce the required bit rate, the physical signal $x(t)$ can be replaced by a number of parameters, e.g., describing the way the audio signal originates. The major problem, however, that immediately arises and has to be overcome, consists in a fact that there exists no unique plausible model for production of all kinds of audio signals. On the contrary, for different types of audio, only different models (if any) can be proposed [19,20,41].

For example, for speech efficient parametric description models can be developed by means of modeling of the human vocal tract [13]. Such parametric speech source models describe the speech production process by, first, modeling an excitation (noise for unvoiced speech and a periodic signal for voiced speech), and second, by representing the human voice tract by means of an appropriate infinite impulse response (IIR) filter. This is the so-called linear prediction coding (LPC) scheme [37].

Another signal example, for which an extremely efficient parametric description exists, is music. This description is the well-known musical score notation. Indeed, a kind of such a description has been applied in the musical instrument digital interface (MIDI). Although the musical score notation is extremely efficient and it does not probably exist any other representation for music that would be more efficient, the score as a means for audio coding has two major drawbacks. First of all, the whole information about the individual performer is lost. Second, an automatic transcription of audio into the musical score is very difficult. Thus, compromise solutions have to be searched for. Structured audio—a part of the MPEG-4 standard—uses such techniques. An audio signal is split into individual, meaningful source objects and is treated as a composition of them [18,34,35]. This approach is also used in the newest standards MPEG-7 and MPEG-21 [19,20,34].

One of the most promising approaches to the parametric description of a wide class of audio signals consists in removing the redundancy contained in the original audio signal representation $x(t)$. This can be done by splitting the signal into a number of almost uncorrelated components. The simplest and the most popular method is the time-to-frequency transformation by means of an appropriate analysis filter bank [52]. For example, in the MUSICAM standard the whole audio band, which is in this case 24 kHz wide, is split into 32 uniform subbands of the width $24,000/32 = 750$ Hz each. Another widely used uniform filter bank is based on a modified discrete cosine transform (MDCT) [40]. Nonuniform, e.g., octave filter banks can also be used. An optimized octave filter bank based on the so-called wave digital filters (WDFs) [11] is proposed in [43].

Efficient parametric description of audio signals, which is, in fact, a generalization of an octave filter bank approach and, in other words, is a simplified score-type representation, is the so-called discrete wavelet transformation (DWT). In order to introduce the DWT concept, it should first be noticed that the signal $x(t)$ can often be expressed as a linear expansion

$$x(t) = \sum_m c_m \psi_m(t) \tag{27.4}$$

where $m$ is an integer index, $c_m$ are the real-valued expansion coefficients (parameters describing the signal), and $\psi_m(t)$ is a set of real-valued functions of time $t$ called the expansion set. The expansion set is called *basis* if the representation (27.4) is unique, i.e., if functions $\psi_m(t)$ are linearly independent. The most interesting case is the orthogonal or even orthonormal basis. For example, for a Fourier series, the orthogonal basis functions $\psi_m(t)$ are $\cos k\omega_0 t$ and $\sin k\omega_0 t$, where $\omega_0$ is related to the signal period $T$ according to equation $\omega_0 = 2\pi/T$.

For the discrete wavelet expansion, called DWT, a two-dimensional set of coefficients $a_{kl}$ is constructed in such a way that

$$x(t) = \sum_{k=-\infty}^{\infty} \sum_{l=-\infty}^{\infty} 2^{k/2} a_{kl} \psi(2^k t - l) \qquad (27.5)$$

where the function $\psi(t)$, called *wavelet* (small wave), generates the expansion set $\psi(2^k t - l)$, which is an orthogonal basis. The wavelet $\psi(t)$ is an oscillating and quickly decaying function, which has its energy sufficiently well localized in time and in frequency. Several different wavelet classes have already been proposed [5].

Introducing another basic function $\varphi(t)$, called the *scaling function*, a multiresolution signal representation, starting from some resolution $k$, can be formulated:

$$x(t) = \sum_{l=-\infty}^{\infty} 2^{k/2} b_{kl} \varphi(2^k t - l) + \sum_{\kappa=k}^{\infty} \sum_{l=-\infty}^{\infty} 2^{\kappa/2} a_{\kappa l} \psi(2^\kappa t - l) \qquad (27.6)$$

Two fundamental self-similarity equations have to be fulfilled:

$$\varphi(t) = \sum_n \sqrt{2} h_0(n) \varphi(2t - n) \qquad (27.7a)$$

$$\psi(t) = \sum_n \sqrt{2} h_1(n) \varphi(2t - n) \qquad (27.7b)$$

where $h_0(n)$ and $h_1(n)$ are impulse responses of two discrete-time complementary filters—a lowpass filter and a highpass filter, respectively. For a finite even length $N$, responses $h_0(n)$ and $h_1(n)$ are related to each other by

$$h_1(n) = (-1)^n h_0(N - 1 - n), \quad n = 0,\dots,N-1 \qquad (27.8)$$

If resolution $k$ is large enough, $\kappa = k$ can only be taken into account in expansion (27.6). In other words, we can assume that

$$x(t) = \sum_{l=-\infty}^{\infty} 2^{k/2} b_{kl} \varphi(2^k t - l) + \sum_{l=-\infty}^{\infty} 2^{k/2} a_{kl} \psi(2^k t - l) \qquad (27.9)$$

Thus, from Eqs. (27.7a) and (27.7b) we conclude that $x(t)$ is a signal of resolution $k + 1$ and can be modeled as

$$x(t) = \sum_{n=-\infty}^{\infty} 2^{(k+1)/2} b_{(k+1)n} \varphi(2^{k+1} t - n) \qquad (27.10)$$

Assuming that functions $\varphi(2^k t - l)$ and $\psi(2^k t - l)$ in expansion (27.9) form an orthonormal basis, after some manipulations, we conclude that

$$b_{kl} = \sum_n h_0(n - 2l) b_{(k+1)n} \qquad (27.11a)$$

$$a_{kl} = \sum_n h_1(n - 2l) b_{(k+1)n} \qquad (27.11b)$$

If the signal $x(t)$ is of finite duration, the sums in expressions (27.9) and (27.10) are finite. The sets $\{b_{(k+1)n}\}$ and $\{b_{kl}, a_{kl}\}$ form alternative parametric descriptions for the signal $x(t)$. Although both sets have the same

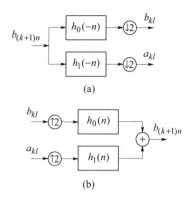

**FIGURE 27.1**  Two-band filter bank: (a) analysis bank, (b) synthesis bank.

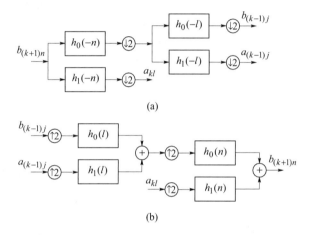

**FIGURE 27.2**  Discrete wavelet transformation (DWT): (a) two-band analysis tree, (b) two-band synthesis tree.

number of parameters, description $\{b_{kl}, a_{kl}\}$ is somehow more efficient because parameters $a_{kl}$ are less important than $b_{kl}$ and consequently $\{b_{(k+1)n}\}$. From Eqs. (27.11a) and (27.11b) we conclude that parameters $b_{kl}$ and $a_{kl}$ result from a lowpass and a highpass filtering of parameters $b_{(k+1)n}$, respectively, with a two-band splitting filter bank of impulse responses $h_0(-n)$ and $h_1(-n)$, respectively, followed by a down sampling with factor 2 (Fig. 27.1(a)). This procedure can be continued many times in order to obtain even more efficient parametric representation. If only parameters $b_{kl}$ are split, which is the case in the classical DWT, a kind of an octave signal analysis filter bank results (Figs. 27.2(a) and 27.3). If also parameters $a_{kl}$ are split (wavelet packet) and/or a multiband splitting filter bank is used (multiband wavelet system) [5], very flexible analysis filter banks can be realized (Fig. 27.4), e.g., those simulating along the frequency axis the distribution of a set of nonoverlapping *peripheral auditory filters* (cf., section 27.4).

Another quite efficient approach for the parametric description of audio is the so-called *sinusoidal modeling* often used for the analysis and synthesis of musical instrument sounds [41]. The audio signal $x(t)$ is modeled by a set of tones and noise.

$$x(t) = \sum_k a_k(t) \sin\left(\int_{\tau=0}^t \omega_k(\tau)\,d\tau + \phi_k\right) + \text{noise} \qquad (27.12)$$

The tones have slowly varying parameters: amplitude $a_k(t)$ and frequency $\omega_k(t)$. Additionally, an appropriate noise model has to be used. A perceptually acceptable noise model can be obtained by adding

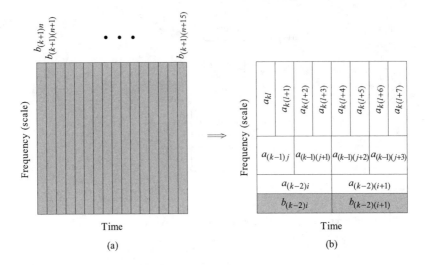

**FIGURE 27.3**   Time-frequency (scale) signal representation patterns: (a) an initial $(k+1)$-resolution scale pattern corresponding to expression (27.10); DWT pattern after three transformation steps (the first step is made according to Eq. (27.9)).

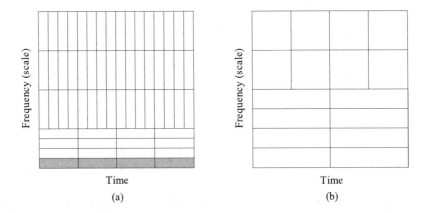

**FIGURE 27.4**   Time-frequency (scale) signal representation patterns: (a) a pattern after two transformation steps with a four-band wavelet basis, (b) an example of a two-band wavelet packet transformation.

some sinusoids with different frequencies and random phases. Alternative methods are based on the noise spectrum modeling.

An additional envelope model (with particular envelope attack and decay rates) can be added for some of the sinusoids in order to improve the sinusoidal model efficiency for highly nonstationary signals.

A dual approach to that described by Eq. (27.12) is also possible. The signal $x(t)$ is first transformed into the frequency domain, e.g., by means of the discrete cosine transform (DCT), and then the sinusoidal modeling is realized in the frequency domain [41].

## 27.4   Psychoacoustics and Auditory Perception

Understanding of psychoacoustics phenomena occurring during the auditory perception by humans is crucial for the design of efficient audio coding algorithms. An efficient audio coder (the so-called perceptual coder) should not only reduce redundant components in the audio representation, using an appropriate parametric audio model (cf., section 27.3), but it also should remove irrelevant components from the source signal, i.e., those, which are inaudible by humans (Fig. 27.17).

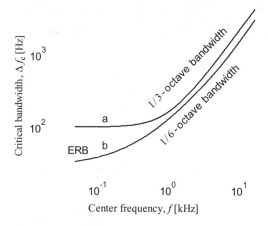

**FIGURE 27.5** Critical bandwidth and ERB as functions of the passband center frequency: (a) critical bandwidth according to Eq. (27.13), (b) ERB according to Eq. (27.14a).

Signal processing, which takes place in the human auditory system, can generally be divided into two stages: a preliminary phase realized in the acoustic auditory organs (ears) and the advanced phase done in auditory nervous system (in the brain). The auditory part of the inner ear, known as the cochlea because of its snaillike shape, performs a kind of the spectral analysis. The acoustic harmonic tones generate place selective oscillations distributed along the so-called basilar membrane, which extends down the cochlea. In result, the frequency is mapped into a place on the basilar membrane and a frequency scale can be laid out at the basilar membrane with low frequencies near the apex and high frequencies near the base of the cochlea. According to the authors' results the cochlear response is not a kind of a Fourier like transformation but, neglecting the nonlinearities, it is rather a kind of the continuous wavelet transformation (CWT) [5]. Consequently, the cochlear response can be interpreted as if it were produced by a filter bank composed of highly overlapping bandpass filters with increasing passbands. These filters are referred to as the *peripheral auditory filters*.

Two widely accepted approaches are used for estimation of the passbands of the peripheral auditory filters. The older approach is based on the notion of *critical bands* $\Delta f_c$ [12,45,56]. The widths of the critical bands vary from ca. 100 Hz for low frequencies (lower than 300 Hz) to about one-third of an octave for high frequencies (Fig. 27.5(a)). The critical bandwidth as a function of its center frequency can be estimated in Hertz using expression

$$\Delta f_c = 25 + 75(1 + 1.4f^2)^{0.69} \tag{27.13}$$

in which frequency $f$ is given in kilohertz [45].

The newer approach results from measurements of the frequency response shape of the peripheral auditory filters and uses a concept of equivalent rectangular bandwidth (ERB) [32,44]. ERB is a bandwidth of the equivalent ideal (rectangular) passband filter, which has the same center passband frequency as the respective peripheral auditory filter, transmits the same amount of power when excited with the same white noise, and has the passband gain equal to the maximum passband gain of the respective auditory filter. ERB as a function of frequency can be approximated in hertz as

$$ERB = 6.23f^2 + 93.3f + 28.52 \tag{27.14a}$$

where frequency $f$ is again given in kilohertz (cf. Fig. 27.5(b)). Sometimes, a slightly simpler formula is

**TABLE 27.1** Critical Bandwidth and Equivalent Rectangular Bandwidth (ERB) as Functions of the Respective Center Frequency

| Center Frequency $f_c$ (Hz) | Critical Bandwidth $\Delta f_c$ (Hz) | ERB (Hz) | $\Delta f_c$/ERB |
|---|---|---|---|
| 50 | 100 | 33 | 3.0 |
| 100 | 100 | 38 | 2.7 |
| 200 | 100 | 47 | 2.2 |
| 500 | 120 | 77 | 1.5 |
| 1000 | 160 | 128 | 1.3 |
| 2000 | 300 | 240 | 1.3 |
| 5000 | 900 | 651 | 1.4 |
| 10,000 | 2300 | 1585 | 1.5 |

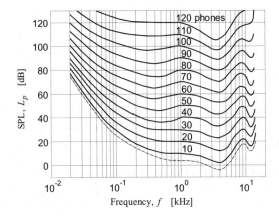

**FIGURE 27.6** Equal-loudness contours for pure tones.

used [32,44]

$$ERB = 24.7(4.37f + 1) \qquad (27.14b)$$

Chosen values of $\Delta f_c$ and ERB are listed in Table 27.1. Critical bandwidth is greater than ERB even three times for low frequencies but for higher frequencies, starting with ca. 500 Hz, it is 1.3–1.5 times larger only.

Approximately 24 nonoverlapping critical bands cover the whole audible frequency range, but it does not mean that there exist 24 peripheral auditory filters only. In fact, they occur as continuously distributed filters along the frequency axis and any audible tone creates an individual peripheral auditory filter centered on it.

The ear canal acts as a resonator and increases the sound pressure at the tympanic membrane in the frequency range of 1.5–5 kHz, with a maximum at 3.5 kHz by about 10–15 dB. The sensitivity of the ear varies strongly with the frequency and reaches the maximum exactly in this band. In Fig. 27.6 equal-loudness contours for pure tones are plotted. They are labeled in units of loudness called phones. By definition, the loudness in phones is numerically equal to SPL in decibels at the frequency $f = 1000$ Hz. The lowest curve in Fig. 27.6 represents the threshold of audibility (in quiet). This curve can be approximated [47] in decibels with expression

$$L_{ptq} = 3.64f^{-0.8} - 6.5e^{-0.6(f-3.3)^2} + 10^{-3}f^4 \qquad (27.15)$$

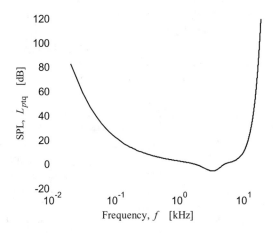

**FIGURE 27.7**  Threshold of audibility in quiet approximated by Eq. (27.15).

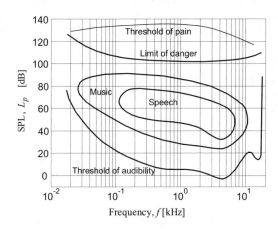

**FIGURE 27.8**  Region of audibility.

where frequency $f$ is as before given in kilohertz. The threshold of audibility computed with formula (27.15) is shown in Fig. 27.7.

A kind of positive feedback improves the sensitivity and selectivity of the basilar membrane oscillations. Its function can be compared with that of the so-called "reaction" used in early radio receivers to increase their amplification and to improve their frequency selectivity. The positive feedback effect decreases as sound intensity increases. Thus, the cochlea is less selective for intense sounds than for weak sounds. In result, the peripheral auditory filters are nonlinear, thereby extending the overall dynamic range of the hearing system to the range of approximately 120 dB (cf., Fig. 27.6).

Figure 27.8 shows the whole region of audibility extending from the threshold of audibility to the limit of danger (and further up to the threshold of pain). It also illustrates two important subregions: the speech region and the region of music. The rest of the audibility area is a reserve of the human hearing system. Speech covers the frequency band of ca. 200 Hz to 5 kHz and the dynamic range ca. 50 dB. Music occupies larger area, i.e., the frequency band of 50 Hz to 10 kHz and the dynamic range of ca. 70 dB. For the representation of high quality audio it is, however, necessary to cover and reproduce practically the whole region of audibility, i.e., the frequency band of 20 Hz to 20 kHz and the dynamic range of at least 80–90 dB.

Because of diffraction produced by the head, the sound that reaches the ears depends on the sound source direction. The difference between the arrival time of a sound at each of the two ears together with the difference in the intensity of the sound that reaches each ear is used by the auditory nervous system to determine the location of the sound source. This ability manifests mostly in the horizontal plane. In audio coding systems it is represented by stereo (2-channel) or more exactly by surround (multichannel) sound.

The spectral components of a sound are coded for intensity and time in the auditory nervous system, but not always all components are audible. This interesting phenomenon called *masking* is extremely important for efficient digital coding of audio. Masking is a kind of interference with the audibility of a sound (called probe or maskee) caused by the presence of another sound (called masker), if both these sounds are close enough to each other in frequency and occur simultaneously or closely to each other in time. If a lower level probe is inaudible, because of a simultaneous existence of a higher level masker, this effect is referred to as the *simultaneous masking*. If an inaudible probe precedes the masker or follows the masker, this phenomenon is called *temporal masking*. Masking is typically described by the minimum shift of the probe intensity level above its threshold of audibility in quiet, necessary for the probe to be heard in the presence of the masker.

Four different cases for masking can be distinguished: tone-masking-tone, noise-masking-tone, tone-masking-noise, and noise-masking-noise. The latter two cases are particularly important for the design of effective perceptual audio coders, because masking can be exploited to make the quantization noise inaudible. The first two cases were, however, so far, much more intensively investigated. In Fig. 27.9 a simultaneous tone-masking-tone effect relative to the threshold of audibility in quiet is illustrated. Masker is a pure harmonic tone of frequency 1.2 kHz and of three different sound pressure levels: 40, 50, and 60 dB. The following effects can be observed. First, the higher the level of the masker, the greater is the masking. Second, masking is largest for probe frequencies slightly above or below the masker frequency. Third, masking decreases as probe frequency gets closer to that of the masker. This phenomenon is observed for tone-masking-tone case only and is caused by audible beats between the two tones, which make the presence of the probe more apparent. Fourth, masking is greater on frequencies above the masker frequency than on frequencies below it. Fifth, due to a nonlinearity of the human hearing system, the masking curve has similar shape for various masker harmonics. This phenomenon is also typical for the tone-masking-tone case only.

Analyzing curves in Fig. 27.9 and taking the threshold of audibility in Fig. 27.6 or Fig. 27.7 into account, the maximum probe-to-masker ratios (PMRs) can be determined. For example, for a 40 dB SPL masker the maximum PMR is $15 + 3 - 40 = -22$ dB (the maximum level of the fully masked probe

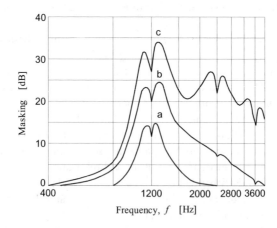

**FIGURE 27.9**  Simultaneous tone-masking-tone effect relative to the threshold of audibility in quiet with a masker of frequency 1.2 kHz and of three different levels (SPL): (a) 40 dB, (b) 50 dB, and (c) 60 dB.

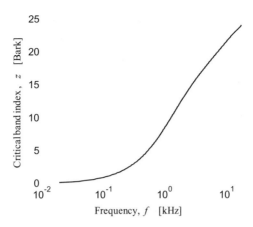

**FIGURE 27.10**   Critical band index in Bark according to Eq. (27.17).

relative to the threshold of audibility for the curve in Fig. 27.9(a) is almost 15 dB and the threshold of audibility for the tone of frequency 1.2 kHz is about 3 dB SPL). Similarly, for 50 and 60 dB maskers the maximum PMRs are calculated to be −22.5 and −23 dB, respectively.

Masking curves for tone-masking-noise are similar but smoother, because no audible bits occur in this case. In order to reduce the influence of audible bits also in the tone-masking-tone case, a tone-like narrow-band noise instead of a pure tone should be used as masker. In practical audio signals this situation is observed rather than appearance of audible bits. That is why both cases with the tone as masker can be reduced to only one: a tone-like masker. The maximum PMR can be approximated [14] in decibels by expression

$$PMR_t = -(14.5 + z) \tag{27.16}$$

in which $z$ is numerically equal to the critical band index in Bark [54] defined as

$$z = 13 \arctan(0.76f) + 3.5 \arctan(f/7.5)^2 \tag{27.17}$$

where frequency $f$ is in kilohertz. The curve determined by Eq. (27.17) is plotted in Fig. 27.10.

When a wideband flat noise is used to mask a pure tone, masking is much stronger than that just considered. It should, however, be stressed that only a narrow frequency band (the critical band) of the noise centered at the tonal frequency causes masking of this tone. If the bandwidth of the previously wideband masking noise is made narrower than the respective critical bandwidth (noise with the constant power spectral density is considered) and if the previous probe tone level was just below the masking threshold, then the intensity of this tone has to be lowered before it can be masked again. On the other hand, if the noise bandwidth is wider than this critical bandwidth, no significant change in the masking effect can be observed. In this case the maximum PMR, illustrated in Fig. 27.11, can be determined in decibels by expression [23]

$$PMR_n = -2.0 - 2.05 \arctan(f/4) - 0.75 \arctan(f^2/2.56) \tag{27.18}$$

where frequency $f$ is again given in kilohertz. Pessimistically, a constant value $PMR_n \approx -5.5$ dB can be used independently from frequency. Simultaneous noise-masking-tone effect relative to the threshold of audibility in quiet with a masker of center frequency $f_c = 1.2$ kHz, the critical bandwidth, and 40 dB SPL, is illustrated in Fig. 27.12.

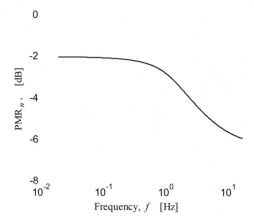

**FIGURE 27.11**    Maximum PMR for noise masker.

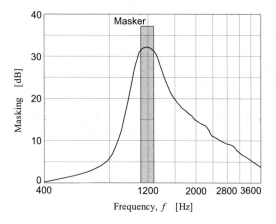

**FIGURE 27.12**    Simultaneous noise-masking-tone effect relative to the threshold of audibility in quiet with a masker of center frequency of 1.2 kHz, critical bandwidth, and 40 dB SPL.

Although masking is typically measured as a shift of the threshold level of hearing above the threshold level of audibility in quiet, its mathematical model should be based on the additivity of signal powers (linear scale) rather than on the additivity of levels (logarithmic scale). In this context a notion of psycho-acoustic excitation is widely used [32]. Particular excitations are approximately additive in terms of power; however, it is also convenient to introduce the excitation level (i.e., excitation described in the logarithmic scale), because the masking threshold level $L_{tm}$ can be modeled as the excitation level shifted by the PMR. In all masking cases the simplest mathematical description for the masking threshold level $L_{tm}$ is a triangular shape shown in Fig. 27.13. In the abscissa axis the critical band index $z$ in Bark is used. The masking threshold peak can be determined in decibel by the maximum PMR according to the following equation [14,22]:

$$PMR = \alpha PMR_t + (1 - \alpha)PMR_n \qquad (27.19)$$

where $0 \leq \alpha \leq 1$ is the masker tonality index defined in such a way that $\alpha = 0$ if the masker is a white noise and $\alpha = 1$ if the masker is a tone. Parameter $\alpha$ can be determined using the so-called spectral flatness measure (SFM) of the masker, defined as a decimal logarithm of the geometric average to the arithmetic average ratio of the masker power spectral density distribution in the masker frequency band.

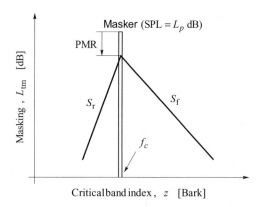

**FIGURE 27.13** Simplified model of the masking threshold level $L_{tm} = L_{tm}(z, z_c, L_p, \alpha)$.

$SFM_{max} = 0$ dB for a white noise masker and $SFM_{min} = -60$ dB for a pure tone masker. Parameter $\alpha$ could be computed as

$$\alpha = SFM/SFM_{min} \tag{27.20a}$$

but due to possible computational inaccuracies the result computed using expression (27.20a) could be greater than 1. Therefore, a slightly more complicated expression should be used

$$\alpha = \min(SFM/SFM_{min}, 1) \tag{27.20b}$$

The rising slope $S_r$ (dB/Bark) of the masking threshold triangle is approximately constant and equals [47]

$$S_r = (25 \div 27) \tag{27.21a}$$

The falling slope $S_f$ (dB/Bark) is smaller and depends on the masker SPL, $L_p$, in decibel and its center frequency, $f_c$, in kilohertz

$$S_f = -24 + 0.2L_p - 0.23f_c^{-1} \tag{27.21b}$$

In most typical situations, the falling slope can be approximated as $S_f \approx -10$ dB/Bark.

Consequently, the masking threshold level $L_{tm}$ is a function of the critical band index $z$, the masker center position $z_c$, the masker SPL, $L_p$, and the masker tonality index $\alpha$, i.e., $L_{tm} = L_{tm}(z, z_c, L_p, \alpha)$. If many simultaneous maskers occur together, the overall masking effect as a function of frequency can be determined by the global threshold of hearing $L_{ptg}$ (Fig. 27.14). In order to determine this threshold, additivity of signal powers or respective psychoacoustic excitations should be taken into account. Thus, the following approximate expression for the global threshold of hearing in decibel can be used

$$L_{ptg}(z) = 10\log_{10}\left(10^{L_{ptq}(z)/10} + \sum_i 10^{L_{tm}(z, z_{cj}, L_{pj}, \alpha_j)/10}\right) \tag{27.22}$$

where $L_{ptq}(z)$ is the threshold of audibility in quiet, $L_{tm}(z, z_{cj}, L_{pj}, \alpha_j)$ are particular masking threshold levels, and index $j$ indicates the $j$th masker.

Finally, the signal-to-mask ratio (SMR) can be computed in decibels as

$$SMR_j = L_{pj} - L_{ptg}(z_j) \tag{27.23}$$

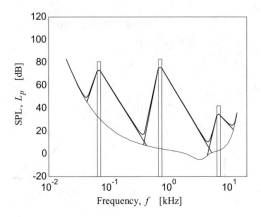

**FIGURE 27.14**   Global hearing threshold $L_{ptg}$ for several simultaneous maskers as a function of frequency.

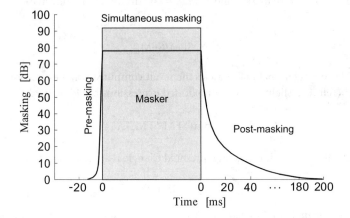

**FIGURE 27.15**   Temporal masking effect.

where $z_j$ corresponds to the smallest $L_{ptg}$ within the critical band of the $j$th masker. This is usually the left-hand side edge of this critical band.

Masking also occurs when the signal either precedes or follows the masker (Fig. 27.15). This is the already mentioned phenomenon of temporal masking. In backward masking (pre-masking) the signal precedes the masker, while in forward masking (post-masking) the signal follows the masker. The pre-masking effect appears in 10–20 ms before the masker, while the post-masking effect is by one order of magnitude longer, i.e., in the order of 50–200 ms after the masker ends. In order to take the post-masking into consideration, the signal power $P_j = 10^{L_{pj}/10}$ occurring in time $t$ should be seemingly increased according to equation

$$P_{sj}(t) \ = \ P_j(t) + c_j(\Delta t)P_j(t - \Delta t) \tag{27.24}$$

in which the post-masking coefficient $c_j(\Delta t)$ is given by

$$c_j(\Delta t) \ = \ \exp(-\Delta t / \tau_j) \tag{27.25}$$

but $\tau_j$ is a time constant depending on the $j$th critical band. In result, the simultaneous masking threshold rises according to the increased level $L_{psj} \ = \ 10 \log_{10} P_{sj}$.

All described masking effects are exploited for data compression in modern perceptual audio coders (e.g., in the MUSICAM procedure, MPEG standards, etc.).

## 27.5 Principles of Audio Coding

In order to digitally process audio, it is first necessary to sample and quantize the data, i.e., to convert the analog signal $x_c(t)$ into a digital form. This is realized in an analog-to-digital converter (ADC). The digital data can then be compressed and encoded in a digital audio coder (transmitter), transmitted through a communication channel, decoded in a receiver, and finally recovered in a digital-to-analog converter (DAC). A general scheme of a digital audio processing system is shown in Fig. 27.16.

Sampling of a continuous-time signal

$$x = x_c(t), \quad -\infty < t < \infty \tag{27.26}$$

is a process of time discretization. It consists in representing the signal $x_c(t)$ with a series of samples

$$x_n = x(n) = x_c(t_n), \quad n = 0, \pm 1, \pm 2, \ldots \tag{27.27}$$

referred to as the *discrete-time signal* or *sampled-data signal*. Uniform time discretization with sampling period $T_s > 0$ and rate

$$F_s = 1/T_s \tag{27.28}$$

is defined by

$$x_n = x(n) = x_d(nT_s) = x_c(t_n), \quad t_n = nT_s - \tau, \quad n = 0, \pm 1, \pm 2, \ldots \tag{27.29}$$

where $\tau > 0$ is some (usually unavoidable) system delay.

It should be stressed that scaling coefficients $b_{(k+1)n}$ in Eq. (27.10) approximate signal samples, i.e., $x_n \approx b_{(k+1)n}$, because for high enough scale $k + 1$ the scaling functions $\varphi(2^{k+1} t - n)$ act as "delta functions." Sampling period is in this case equal to $T_s = 1/2^{k+1}$.

According to the sampling theory, a low-band continuous-time signal $x_c(t - \tau)$, i.e., the signal, whose spectrum extends from zero to some maximum frequency, can be reconstructed on the basis of the discrete-time signal $x(n)$, if the sampling rate $F_s$ is greater or at least equal to the *Nyquist sampling rate*, which is twice as high as the greatest frequency contained in the continuous-time signal spectrum, or in other words, if the whole signal spectrum lies below $F_s/2$, called the *Nyquist frequency*. In practice, sampling rate $F_s$ has to be somewhat greater than the Nyquist sampling rate [37]. Typical sampling rates for audio are:

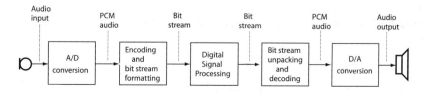

**FIGURE 27.16**   General scheme of a digital audio processing system.

8 ksamples/s for telephony (the signal spectrum extends up to 4 kHz, and thus covers most of the frequencies contained in speech), 32 ksamples/s for medium quality digital audio (audible frequency band up to 16 kHz is covered), 44.1 ksamples/s for a CD standard (audio frequency band up to 22.05 kHz is represented), 48 and 96 ksamples/s for high quality digital audio (the represented frequencies range up to 24 and 48 kHz, respectively).

An important generalization of the classic sampling theory applies to band signals [8]. A continuous-time signal, whose spectrum is limited to some frequency band

$$\Delta f = f_1 - f_2, \quad f_2 > f_1 \tag{27.30}$$

can be sampled with a sampling rate of at least $F_s = 2\Delta f$ only (i.e., critically sampled), if both spectrum border frequencies $f_1$ and $f_2$ in Eq. (27.30) are consecutive multiples of the Nyquist frequency $F_s/2$, i.e., if

$$f_1 = kF_s/2 \quad \text{and} \quad f_2 = (k+1)F_s/2 \tag{27.31}$$

where $k$ is an integer. Such a signal is referred to as the *integer-band signal*. Audio signals are not by themselves integer-band signals but they can be split with an analysis filter bank to some subband signals, which all are integer-band signals, and thus, can be critically sampled. This is indeed the case in many digital audio coders, e.g., in the MUSICAM standard the input audio signal, initially sampled with 48 ksamples/s, is split into 32 subbands with bandwidths of 24,000/32 = 750 Hz each. Signals in each subband are sampled with 48/32 = 1.5 ksamples/s sampling rate.

Another signal discretization process is quantization, i.e., the procedure of converting a signal with continuously distributed values into a signal with discrete values. Unlike sampling, which, under some conditions, can be considered lossless, i.e., the original signal can—at least theoretically—be perfectly recovered after sampling, quantization is an inherently lossy operation [8,37].

The error due to the quantization has a nature of noise and is referred to as the *quantization noise*. Although this noise is unavoidable and cannot be removed from the signal, it can be made inaudible by controlling its level and forcing it to lie under the threshold of audibility. Masking effects, discussed in section 27.4, can be very effectively exploited with this end in view.

The quantization noise is usually analyzed under the following simplifying assumptions:

- The quantization steps are uniform.
- The number of quantization levels is high.

The first assumption is not fulfilled in many quantization techniques for audio signals. This is because the perception of noise does not depend on its absolute power but on the signal-to-noise ratio (SNR). Thus, it is reasonable to quantize audio signals nonuniformly, with quantization steps proportional to the signal values. If the steps are not uniform, then the quantization error will be a function of the input signal, and consequently, it will not be an additive noise any more. Fortunately, in most procedures for the quantization of audio signals, quantization steps are at least range by range uniform and the first assumption can be considered as approximately valid. The second assumption is usually satisfactorily fulfilled. Due to this assumption the quantization noise has a uniform probability density distribution and is not correlated with the signal.

Denote by $Q$ the quantization step and by $p(x)$ the probability distribution function of the quantization error. Then

$$\int_{-Q/2}^{Q/2} p(x)\, dx = 1 \tag{27.32}$$

where

$$p(x) = \begin{cases} 1/Q & \text{for } x \in [-Q/2, Q/2] \\ 0 & \text{otherwise} \end{cases} \qquad (27.33)$$

From Eqs. (27.32) and (27.33), the average quantization noise power $p_q$ can be calculated as

$$P_q = \int_{-\infty}^{\infty} x^2 p(x) dx = \int_{-Q/2}^{Q/2} \frac{x^2}{Q} dx = \frac{Q^2}{12} \qquad (27.34)$$

The signal-to-noise ratio in decibels is then

$$\text{SNR} = 10 \log_{10} \left( \frac{P_s}{P_q} \right) \qquad (27.35)$$

where $P_s$ is the time-averaged signal power. Assume that the ADC has a full scale of $m$ bits. Then the maximum input signal amplitude is

$$A = (2^m - 1)Q \qquad (27.36)$$

and thus

$$P_s \propto [(2^m - 1)Q]^2 \qquad (27.37)$$

From Eqs. (27.34), (27.35), and (27.37) it follows that

$$\text{SNR}(m) = 20 m \log_{10} 2 + \text{const} \approx 6.02 m + \text{const} \qquad (27.38)$$

Thus, each additional bit in the quantized signal resolution means ca. 6 dB improvement in the SNR (or equivalently in the dynamic range). The "const" in expression (27.38) is of secondary importance. Its value depends on the signal probability density distribution and the ADC range. For instance, for an ADC range equal to $(-4\sqrt{P_s}, 4\sqrt{P_s})$, the respective value is const $\approx -7.3$ dB.

Representing a signal just as a stream of uniformly quantized samples is referred to as the pulse code modulation (PCM). Typical resolutions in bits per sample (bps) are 16 bps, 24 bps, and even 30 bps. For instance, for a CD standard with two stereo channels, 44.1 ksamples/s sampling rate and 16 bit resolution, the resulting audio bit rate is $2 \times 44,100 \times 16 = 1.41$ Mb/s. In reality, the CD standard has a large overhead bit rate due to 49-bit representation of every 16-bit sample. The resulting total bit rate is thus equal to $(49/16) \times 1.41 = 4.32$ Mb/s.

PCM representation is not an efficient method for high quality audio. In order to reduce the required bit rate, various data compression and coding techniques can be used. Simple but not very efficient approaches preserve the signal waveform and are therefore referred to as *lossless* coding techniques (section 27.8). Data compression facility of lossless audio coders is rather moderate. Average achievable bit per sample values are only slightly greater than 4.5 bps [35]. Sophisticated techniques, which are still subject of an intensive research, allow for a drastic reduction of this value—at least by one order of magnitude. These coding techniques are lossy in the sense that they corrupt the signal; however, this corruption, can be controlled in such a way that it is inaudible. Such audio coders are called *transparent* (section 27.9). In order to efficiently and transparently compress audio and/or speech, the knowledge about the speech and audio production (the parametric audio coding discussed in section 27.3) as well as the knowledge concerning the human auditory perception (discussed in section 27.4, resulting in the perceptual audio coding) should be exploited (Fig. 27.17).

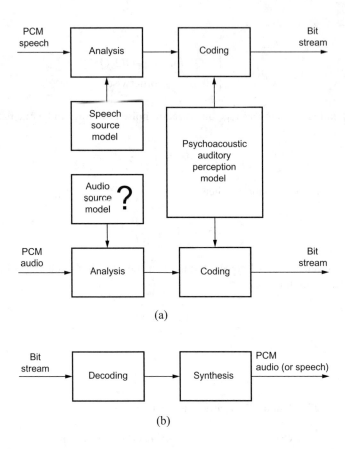

**FIGURE 27.17**    Efficient audio (and speech) compression by exploiting the knowledge about the audio (and speech) production and perception: (a) coder scheme, (b) decoder scheme.

## 27.6   Digital Audio Signal Processing Systems

Fast development of very large scale integration (VLSI) electronics chips (digital signal processors (DSPs), ADCs and DACs, audio codecs, etc.) gives the possibility of effective digital processing of audio signals. The general scheme of a digital audio processing system is shown in Fig. 27.16. Using novel facilities of DSPs, not only sophisticated digital filters and filter banks, but also whole audio codecs can usually be realized in real time with a single processor, i.e., without the necessity of using expensive multiprocessor systems.

Real-time implementation of DSP algorithms is possible due to new features of modern DSPs [7]. Among the most important are:

- Hardware multiplier and long accumulator
- Harvard type and multibus architecture
- An on-chip memory with no additional wait state cycles
- Time division multiplexed (TDM) port for communication between multiple DSPs
- Bit-reversed addressing used in fast Fourier transformation (FFT) algorithms
- Circular buffers—a key feature of many DSP routines (e.g., in the realization of finite impulse response (FIR) digital filters)
- Multiple data registers important, e.g., for storing of temporary data

New facilities of modern DSPs give the possibility for substantial reduction of the number of operations. A single DSP processor can be used for multichannel and/or multitasking applications, both realized in

**TABLE 27.2**   Main Features of Fixed-Point DSPs

| Processor Family | Bus Interface (bits) | Instruction Rate (MHz) | Core MIPS | RAM (bits) | ROM (KWords) |
|---|---|---|---|---|---|
| ADSP-218x | 16 | 33–75 | 33–75 | 128 K–1.6 M | — |
| DSP56300 | 24 | 66–160 | 66–160 | 120 K–1.2 M | 0–80 |
| DSP56600 | 16 | 60–104 | 60–104 | 384 K–1.2 M | 2–128 |
| TMS320C54x | 16 | 40–160 | 30–532 | 80 K–3.1 M | 0–48 |
| TMS320C55x | 16 | 160–200 | 320–400 | 2.5 M | 16 |
| TMS320C62x | 32 | 150–300 | 1200–2400 | 1–7 M | — |
| TMS320C64x | 32 | 400–600 | 3200–4800 | 8.5 M | — |

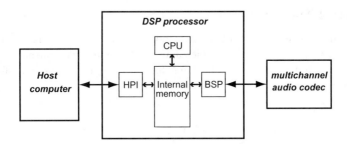

**FIGURE 27.18**   A digital audio signal processing system.

real-time. Although floating-point processors give very effective calculation performance, the fixed-point processors are also often used, because they are characterized by a much lower supply energy consumption (e.g., 0.05 mW/MIPS for the TMS320C55x processors) and are, moreover, much cheaper [50].

In order to facilitate communication with the host processor (computer), modern DSPs are equipped with a special interface—the host port interface (HPI) [49]. Using the HPI, the host processor has an access to the memory of the digital signal processor. Physical connection of processors uses 8- or 16-bit parallel data bus and several control lines. The HPI performs also a boot operation of the DSP. Due to this possibility an additional boot memory is not necessary. Selected DSPs provide also a glueless interface to the peripheral component interconnect (PCI) bus.

The next interesting feature of modern DSPs is the use of a buffered serial port (BSP) [49]. BSP makes a high-speed communication with external devices, e.g., ADCs and DACs, possible. In relation to a typical serial port, BSP offers enhanced features, which allow for a direct read/write operations from/to the memory connected to the signal processor without any participation of its central processing unit (CPU). The BSP interrupts to CPU are generated after filling halves of the buffer. This machanism makes it possible to effectively cooperate with multichannel ADCs and DACs or to accumulate samples for FFT analysis. The described features, such as the HPI and the BSP, can substantially simplify the audio digital signal processing system (cf., Fig. 27.18) [25,28].

Floating-point DSPs, with the support for the IEEE-754 standard of 32-bit floating-point format, are based on new architecture concepts in order to guarantee a very high computational efficiency. Among these concepts are:

- Texas Instruments' VelociTI, which is an advanced very long instruction word (VLIW) architecture [51],
- Analog Devices super Harvard architecture (SHARC) with a single instruction multiple data (SIMD) facility [1].

Effective utilization of these highly parallel architectures needs an efficient C-compiler and an assembly optimizer.

Comparison of selected fixed- and floating-point DSP processors is presented in Tables 27.2 and 27.3 [1,33,50,51].

**TABLE 27.3**   Main Features of Floating-Point DSPs

| Processor Name | Instruction Rate (MHz) | Peak MFLOPS | 1024-point Complex FFT (ms) | Accumulator Size (bits) | On-chip Memory (bits) |
|---|---|---|---|---|---|
| ADSP-2106x SHARC | 40–66 | 120–198 | 0.27 | 40 | 544 K–4 M |
| ADSP–21160 SHARC | 80–100 | 480–600 | 0.09 | 80 | 4 M |
| TMS320C67x | 100–167 | 600–1000 | 0.12 | 40 | 576 K–1 M |

## 27.7   Audio Processing Basics

### DFT and Related Transformations

Discrete Fourier transformation (DFT) is a powerful tool for the analysis of discrete-time signals. A block of $N$ samples $x(n)$, $n = 0, 1,...,N - 1$, is considered and its harmonic components are extracted under assumption that they also describe an infinitely long, block wise periodic extension of signal $x(n)$. DFT is defined as follows:

$$X(k) = \frac{1}{N}\sum_{n=0}^{N-1}x(n)W_N^{kn}, \quad k = 0, 1,...,N-1 \tag{27.39a}$$

where $W_N = e^{-j(2\pi/N)}$. The inverse discrete Fourier transformation (IDFT) is then given by

$$x(n) = \sum_{k=0}^{N-1}X(k)W_N^{-nk}, \quad n = 0, 1,...,N-1 \tag{27.39b}$$

Computation of DFT and IDFT is usually realized using the so-called FFT algorithms, which reduce the computational complexity of DFT from $\propto N^2$ to $\propto N \log N$ under assumption that $N = 2^K$, where $K$ is a natural number. Two main FFT types can be distinguished: decimation in time and decimation in frequency.

Assuming a typical DSP, realization of an FFT of the length $N = 512$, requires about 200 words of the program memory and $4N + 1050$ words of data memory. Using a fixed-point DSP, the number of necessary instruction cycles is about 33,000. Assuming a moderate instruction cycle period of 25 ns, sampling rate of 44.1 kHz ($T_s = 22.676 \ \mu s$). Accumulation time of 512 input samples is $512 \times T_s = 11.61$ ms. FFT analysis takes $33,000 \times 25$ ns $= 0.825$ ms only. This example shows that even a multichannel "online" audio range FFT analysis is easily possible with common DSPs [28,48].

A block of $N$ samples $x(n)$ can be mirrored before it is periodically extended. This results in the so-called discrete cosine transformation (DCT). Because of the mirroring symmetry, DCT gives sharper spectrum than DFT. This is the main advantage of this transformation.

In perceptual audio coders, signals are often mapped into the frequency domain by means of the so-called modified discrete cosine transformation (MDCT) [40]. This is a type of DCT with overlapped power complementary time windows (Fig. 27.19). By this means blocking and time aliasing effects are cancelled. Denote by $x_l(n)$, $n = 0, 1,...,N - 1$, time-domain signal samples in the $l$th block of $N$ samples. MDCT is defined as

$$X_l(k) = \sum_{n=0}^{N-1}w(n)x_l(n)\cos\left[\frac{\pi}{2N}\left(2n + 1 + \frac{N}{2}\right)(2k + 1)\right] \quad \text{for } k = 0, 1,...,\frac{N}{2} - 1 \tag{27.40a}$$

where $X_l(k)$ are samples in the frequency domain, $N$ is the number of input samples, $N/2$ is the frequency-domain blocklength, $w(k)$ is the time window function. Division of the input signal into MDCT block

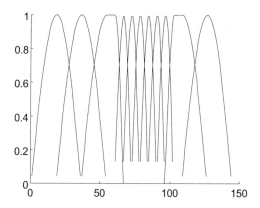

**FIGURE 27.19**  Overlapped, power complementary MDCT windows.

is quite flexible. A long block can be split into a shorter block. Figure 27.19 presents possible transitions MDCT windows between long and short block modes. The length of the block depends on stationarity of the input signal.

The respective inverse discrete cosine transform (IMDCT) is defined as

$$y_l(n) = w(n)\frac{N}{4}\sum_{k=0}^{N/2-1} X_l(k)\cos\left(\frac{\pi}{2N}\left(2n+1+\frac{N}{2}\right)(2k+1)\right) \quad \text{for } n = 0, 1,\dots, N-1 \quad (27.40b)$$

The input signal is recovered with an overlap add operation

$$\tilde{x}_l(n) = y_{l-1}\left(n+\frac{N}{2}\right) + y_l(n) \quad \text{for } n = 0, 1,\dots,\frac{N}{2}-1 \quad (27.40c)$$

which cancels the time-domain aliasing.

## FIR Filters

Basic operation in digital audio signal processing is frequency selective filtering. It can be realized in frequency domain, e.g., using FFT and in time domain using finite impulse response (FIR) and infinite impulse response (IIR) filters. Mostly FIR filters are used because they are always stable and can be easily designed with perfect linear phase characteristic.

Assuming an ideal filter frequency response given by

$$H_d(e^{j\omega}) = \sum_{n=-\infty}^{+\infty} h_d(n)e^{-j\omega n} \quad (27.41)$$

where

$$h_d(n) = \frac{1}{2\pi}\int_{-\infty}^{+\infty} H_d(e^{j\omega})e^{j\omega n}d\omega \quad (27.42)$$

the respective FIR filter impulse response is

$$h_{\text{FIR}}(n) = w_N(n)h_d(n) \quad (27.43)$$

**TABLE 27.4**    Impulse Response of Ideal Filters

| Filter Type | Impulse Response |
|---|---|
| Lowpass | $h_d(n) = \begin{cases} \dfrac{\sin(n\omega_c)}{n\pi} & n \neq 0 \\[2ex] \dfrac{\omega_c}{\pi} & n = 0 \end{cases}$ |
| Highpass | $h_d(n) = \begin{cases} -\dfrac{\sin(n\omega_c)}{n\pi} & n \neq 0 \\[2ex] 1 - \dfrac{\omega_c}{\pi} & n = 0 \end{cases}$ |
| Passband | $h_d(n) = \begin{cases} \dfrac{\sin(n\omega_2)}{n\pi} - \dfrac{\sin(n\omega_1)}{n\pi} & n \neq 0 \\[2ex] \dfrac{\omega_2 - \omega_1}{\pi} & n = 0 \end{cases}$ |
| Stopband | $h_d(n) = \begin{cases} \dfrac{\sin(n\omega_1) - \sin(n\omega_2)}{n\pi} & n \neq 0 \\[2ex] 1 + \dfrac{\omega_2 - \omega_1}{\pi} & n = 0 \end{cases}$ |

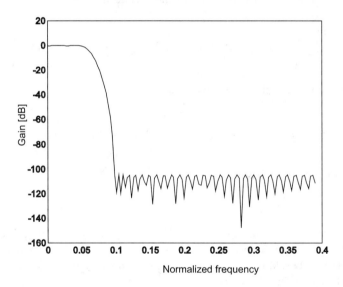

**FIGURE 27.20**    Frequency response of an FIR lowpass filter designed with the Parks–McClellan method.

where $w_N(n)$ is a specially selected time window (e.g., Hanning, Hamming, Blackman, or Kaiser window), used in order to reduce the so-called Gibbs phenomenon [37]. Depending on filter type, the ideal filter coefficients can be calculated using equations listed in Table 27.4 [9].

Another, more advanced, method for the design of FIR filters, is an optimization procedure developed by Parks and McClellan (also known as the Remez method) [9]. This method is implemented in the MATLAB environment with two functions: *remezord* to estimate the filter order and *remez* to compute the filter coefficients [30]. This optimization method should be used, if a relatively high stopband attenuation is required, e.g., with a 20-bit resolution for representation of signal samples, we usually need a stopband attenuation of approximately 120 dB. As a design example, Fig. 27.20 presents the frequency response of a lowpass FIR filter designed with the Parks–McClellan method, with the normalized cutoff frequency of $\pi/64$. This filter can be used as a prototype filter for the design of analysis and synthesis filter banks for audio coders, according, e.g., to the MUSICAM and MPEG-1 standards.

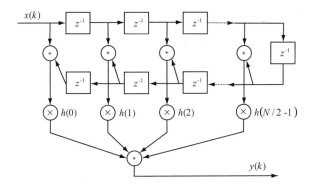

**FIGURE 27.21** Symmetrical FIR filter.

Using modern DSP's FIR filters can easily be implemented with the MACD instruction, which realizes multiplication, accumulation, and data move. When used with repeat next instruction (RPT) MACD becomes a single-cycle instruction once the RPT pipeline is started. The theoretical maximum length $L$ of the FIR filter can be computed as

$$L = \frac{T_s}{T_c k} \tag{27.44}$$

where $T_s$ is the sampling period, $T_c$ is the instruction cycle, and $k$ is the number of converted channels. Assuming sampling rate of 48 ksamples/s, 25 ns instruction cycle of the DSP and 6 output channels, we can realize FIR filters with the maximum length of about 138 [25].

Another method for the implementation of FIR filters in DSPs consists in the use of two further new features of modern DSPs, namely the circular addressing and the FIRS instruction. This possibility can be effectively used, if the filter has a symmetric impulse response $h(n)$ (cf., Fig. 27.21), i.e., if the filter output signal is given by

$$y(n) = \sum_{k=0}^{N/2-1} h(n)\{x(n-k) + x[n-(N-1-k)]\} \tag{27.45}$$

The FIRS instruction can add two data values (stored in a circular buffer) in parallel with the multiplication of this result by a filter coefficient. Once the repeat pipeline is started, this instruction becomes also a single-cycle instruction. A computational complexity is in this case reduced by half and makes it possible to realize FIR filters with the double length as compared with the programming technique previously described [48].

## IIR Filters

Although FIR filters have important advantages as linear phase, stability, robustness, easy design, and implementation, their infinite impulse response (IIR) counterparts will have complexity (order) reduced by some orders of magnitude. Therefore, IIR filters are advantageous over and above FIR filters in particular applications. IIR filters are typically designed starting with an analogue reference filter and then performing the bilinear transformation [8]. Denote by $H(s)$ transfer function of the analog reference filter. Then the resulting IIR filter transfer function $H(z)$ is calculated as

$$H(z) = H(s)\Big|_{s = \frac{2}{T_s}\frac{z-1}{z+1}} \tag{27.46}$$

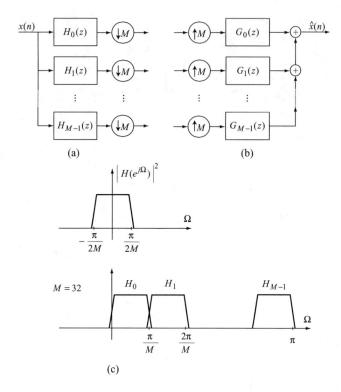

**FIGURE 27.22**   Filter banks: (a) analysis filter bank, (b) synthesis filter bank, (c) subband pattern.

where $T_s$ is the sampling period. The respective transformation of the analog frequency $\omega_a$ into the digital frequency $\omega_d$ is given by

$$\omega_d = \frac{2}{T_s} \arctan\left(\frac{T_s}{2}\omega_a\right) \tag{27.47}$$

## Filter Banks

A filter bank is a collection of digital filters with a multiple input and/or a multiple output [52]. The filter bank with one input and $M$ outputs is referred to as the *analysis filter bank*. On the other hand, the *synthesis filter bank* consists of $M$ inputs and one output (cf., Fig. 27.22). Splitting of the input signal into decimated subbands via an analysis filter bank and then reconstructing the initial signal from subband signals with a respective synthesis filter bank is referred to as the subband coding (SBC) technique commonly used for nearly lossless data compression.

A filter bank in the main path of the MPEG-1 audio coder [39] consists of 32 subband filters with a normalized bandwidth of $\pi/(32T_s)$, where $T_s$ is the input audio signal sampling period. The impulse responses of particular filters in this filter bank are defined as

$$H_i(n) = h(n)\cos\left[\frac{(2i+1)(n-16)\pi}{64}\right] \tag{27.48}$$

where $h(n)$ is an impulse response of the prototype lowpass filter. In the analysis filter bank case, the output signal in $i$th subband is defined as a convolution

$$S_i(m) = \sum_{n=0}^{511} x(m-n) * H_i(n) \tag{27.49}$$

In the MPEG-1 encoder an efficient polyphase filter bank realization is implemented, using the following steps:

1. Thirty-two new input samples $x(n)$ are shifted into a 512-point FIFO buffer.
2. Five hundred and twelve samples $x(n)$ are multiplied by the modified (the so-called analysis window) coefficients $C(n)$.

$$Z(n) = C(n)x(n) \qquad (27.50a)$$

where $C(n) = -h(n)$ if the integer part of $n/64$ is odd, otherwise $C(n) = h(n)$, $n = 0, 1,...,511$.

3. Intermediate result is calculated

$$Y(k) = \sum_{j=0}^{7} Z(k + 64j) \quad \text{for } k = 0, 1,..., 63 \qquad (27.50b)$$

4. Thirty-two new output samples are computed

$$S_i = \sum_{k=0}^{63} M_i(k)Y(k) \quad \text{for } i = 0, 1,..., 31 \qquad (27.50c)$$

where $M_i(k) = \cos\{[(2i + 1)(k - 16)\pi]/64\}$ are the modulation (or analysis) matrix coefficients.

## Sampling Rate Conversion

Currently, digital audio signals are used with various sampling rates. Typical values are 8, 16, 22.05, 32, 44.1, 48, and even 96 ksamples/s. Thus, an "online" sampling rate conversion is a very important task in digital audio signal processing algorithms. This, task can nowadays be realized using modern digital signal processors [6]. Generally, three different approaches are possible:

- Natural approach based on, first, interpolation with factor integer $M$, and then, decimation with factor integer $N$ (Fig. 27.23),
- Time-domain approach based on direct interpolation (or decimation) in time, i.e., on the realization of a sequence of noninteger delays (Fig. 27.24),

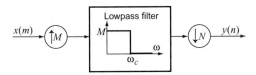

**FIGURE 27.23** Basic system for sampling rate conversion.

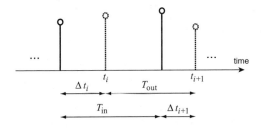

**FIGURE 27.24** Time relationships between input and output samples.

**FIGURE 27.25**  Sampling rate conversion with multistage oversampling.

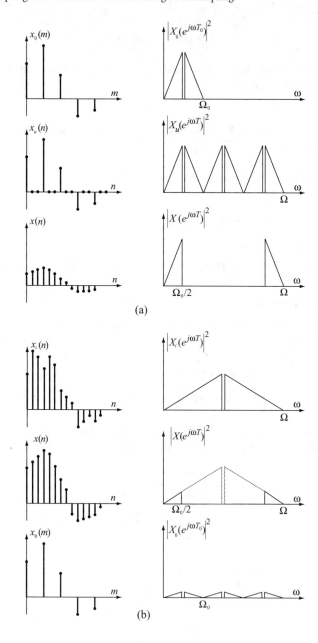

**FIGURE 27.26**  Sampling rate conversion in frequency domain: (a) interpolation, (b) decimation.

- Frequency-domain approach based on: first, a blockwise DFT; second, on respective spectrum modification in each block—a throw-in of zero spectral samples in the middle of the DFT spectrum for interpolation or cutting out of some of spectral samples in the middle of the DFT spectrum for decimation (cf., Fig. 27.26); and third, the backward blockwise IDFT transformation (cf., the *interpft* function in the MATLAB environment [30]).

**TABLE 27.5** Sampling Rate Conversion Factors

| Sampling Rate Conversion [ksamples/s] | Upsampling Coefficient $M$ | Downsampling Coefficient $N$ | Least Common Multiple of a Pair of Sampling Rates |
|---|---|---|---|
| $16 \to 48$ | 3 | 1 | 48,000 |
| $32 \to 48$ | 3 | 2 | 96,000 |
| $16 \to 44.1$ | 441 | 160 | 7,056,000 |
| $32 \to 44.1$ | 441 | 320 | 14,112,000 |
| $44.1 \to 48$ | 160 | 147 | 7,056,000 |

**TABLE 27.6** Sampling Rate Conversion to/from 44 ksamples/s

| Sampling Rate Conversion [ksamples/s] | Upsampling Coefficient $M$ | Downsampling Coefficient $N$ |
|---|---|---|
| $16 \to 44$ | 11 | 4 |
| $32 \to 44$ | 11 | 8 |
| $44 \to 48$ | 12 | 11 |

These first two approaches can be mixed, resulting in substantial reduction of the required intermediate sampling rate.

A scheme of the simplest system for the synchronic sampling rate conversion is shown in Fig. 27.23. The output samples are calculated using difference equations, which utilize the up- and downsampling and the filtering in between. Table 27.5 presents the respective up- and downsampling factors for the considered sampling rate conversions. These factors are equal to the least common multiple of a pair of sampling rates (the input sampling rate and the output sampling rate), divided by the respective sampling rate. Because the up- and downsampling factors for the rate conversion to/from 44.1 ksamples/s are inadmissibly large, a slightly lower sampling rate, namely 44 ksamples/s (cf., Table 27.6) can usually be accepted. This would introduce a small, not audible, error with a relative value of $\delta = 0.22676\%$.

The filtering operation between an interpolator and a decimator should be realized via a lowpass filter with gain $M$ and the normalized cutoff frequency $\omega_c = \min(\pi/M, \pi/N)$ [52]. The respective FIR filter can be designed, e.g., using the Parks–McClellan method. Depending on the converted rates and the desired signal resolution (16 or 20 bits, corresponding to the stopband attenuation of 96 or 120 dB, respectively) the required length $L$ of FIR filters varies between 154 and 198 [6]. Depending on the upsampling coefficient $M$, the number of effective filter taps, which have to be calculated, is reduced to $L/2M$.

Sampling rate alteration using the time domain approach can be applied in asynchronic systems. An output signal sample can be determined using the following relationship:

$$\Delta t_{i+1} = (\Delta t_i + T_{out}) \bmod T_{in} \tag{27.51}$$

where $T_{in}$ is the input sampling interval, $T_{out} = t_{i+1} - t_i$ is the output sampling interval, $t_{i+1}$ is the instant in which a new output sample should occur. The above relationships are illustrated in Fig. 27.24. Input samples are indicated with solid lines and output samples with dotted lines.

One of the simplest time domain sampling rate conversion methods is a high oversampling and then choosing appropriate output samples (those, which are the nearest to the required positions in time). A multistage approach of this type is illustrated in Fig. 27.25 [27].

Interpolators with factors 64 and 128 are controlled by a time-analysis unit, which measures the ratio between the input and the output sampling rates. An advantage of this method (in comparison with the natural method) is the possibility for the use of the same filter coefficients for different sampling rate conversion ratios, and thus, a simplified realization of the interpolation filters.

Time domain conversion can also be based on various numerical methods, e.g., on polynomial interpolation. Lagrange interpolation or spline interpolation can effectively be used [42,53]. In the case of an $N$th-order spline with a function defined in interval $[x_k,...,x_{k+m}]$ as

$$M_k^N(x) = \sum_{i=k}^{k+m} a_i \phi_i(x) \tag{27.52}$$

where

$$\phi_i(x) = (x - x_i)_+^N = \begin{cases} 0 & x < x_i \\ (x - x_i) & x \geq x_i \end{cases}$$

a 6th-order interpolation is used with a simple FIR filter to compensate $\text{sinc}^7$-distortion in the frequency domain caused by the spline interpolator [53].

## 27.8   Lossless Audio Coding

### Pulse Code Modulation

The most typical digital waveform coding is the pulse code modulation (PCM), in which a stream of uniformly distributed digitally coded samples, which represent a given analog continuous-time signal is used. Basic PCM coder consists of an antialiasing filter, sample device and a quantizer. In practice, in order to improve the subjective audio quality, the quantizer should have a nonlinear (logarithmic) characteristic based on, e.g., a 13-segment A-law or a 15-segment $\mu$-law used in telephone systems. The normalized characteristics are given by [2]

- A-law

$$f(x) = \begin{cases} \dfrac{Ax}{1 + \ln A} & 0 \leq x \leq \dfrac{1}{A} \\ \dfrac{1 + \ln Ax}{1 + \ln A} & \dfrac{1}{A} \leq x \leq 1 \end{cases} \tag{27.53}$$

- $\mu$-law

$$f(x) = \frac{\ln(1 + \mu x)}{\ln(1 + \mu)} \quad \text{for } 0 \leq x \leq 1 \tag{27.54}$$

For the compression from 16 bits to 8 bits typical values of the coefficients are $A = 87.6$ and $\mu = 255$.

In most cases, PCM bit stream has highly redundant information. Thus, using a number of previous samples of the input signal, we can predict the next sample with a relatively small error. This feature is used in differential pulse code modulation (DPCM), in which a difference between input sample and its estimation is coded. The prediction is realized with appropriate FIR filter. In the case in which the statistics of the input signal changes in time is unknown, the prediction should be made adaptive. An adaptive coding is realized in an adaptive difference pulse code modulation (ADPCM). The respective schemes, i.e., those of the ADPCM encoder and the ADPCM decoder are shown in Fig. 27.27.

A special case of the DPCM approach is delta modulation (DM). The DM encoder is very simple to implement because it uses a 1-bit quantizer and a first order predictor (cf. Fig. 27.28). The encoder is so strongly simplified, so high sampling rates are required. Among disadvantages of DM are: the possible

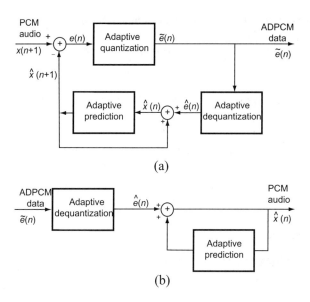

**FIGURE 27.27** ADPCM: (a) encoder, (b) decoder.

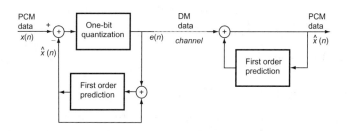

**FIGURE 27.28** Delta modulation system.

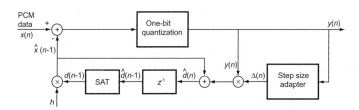

**FIGURE 27.29** CVSD encoder.

slope overload and granularity noise. They can, however, be easily reduced by adaptive versions of DM, i.e., ADM.

Continuous variable slope delta modulation (CVSD) is an example of the ADM. CVSD effectively reduces the DM slope overload [29]. An interesting advantage of this method is its resistance to transmission errors. Figure 27.29 presents structure of the CVSD encoder.

The output signal of the CVSD encoder is given by

$$y(n) = \text{sgn}\{x(n) - \hat{x}(n-1)\} \tag{27.55}$$

where $x(n)$ is the input PCM sample, $\hat{x}(n)$ is the estimated sample.

The parameter $\alpha$ depends on the signal slope, i.e., $J$ bits in $K$ output bits of $y(n)$:

$$\alpha = \begin{cases} 1 & J \text{ bits are the same} \\ 0 & \text{else} \end{cases} \tag{27.56}$$

The quantization step $\Delta(n)$ is increased or decreased using parameter $\alpha$:

$$\Delta(n) = \begin{cases} \min\{\Delta(n-1) + \Delta_{\min}, \Delta_{\max}\} & \text{for } \alpha = 1 \\ \max\{\beta\Delta(n-1), \Delta_{\min}\} & \text{for } \alpha = 0 \end{cases} \tag{27.57}$$

where

$\beta$ = step decreasing coefficient,
$\Delta_{\min}$ = minimum step size,
$\Delta_{\max}$ = maximum step size.

The estimated value $\hat{x}(n-1)$ is given by

$$\hat{x}(n-1) = hd(n-1) \tag{27.58}$$

where

$$d(n-1) = \begin{cases} \min\{\hat{d}(n-1), d_{\max}\} & \text{for } \hat{d}(n-1) \geq 0 \\ \max\{\hat{d}(n-1), d_{\min}\} & \text{for } \hat{d}(n-1) < 0 \end{cases}$$

$h$ is the accumulator decay coefficient.

### Entropy Coding Using Huffman Method

The entropy coding is a lossless bit stream reduction and can be used on its own or as a supplement to other methods, e.g., after the DPCM. This coding approach is based on the statistical redundancy, when the signal samples, or sequences (blocks) have different probabilities. The entropy of a signal is defined as the following average:

$$H(p_1,\ldots,p_n) = -\sum_{i=1}^{n} p_i \log_2 p_i \tag{27.59}$$

where $-\log_2 p_i$ is an information of the $i$th codeword and $p_i$ is the probability of its occurrence. The most popular method for the entropy coding is the Huffman coding method [15], in which the optimal code can be found using an iterative procedure based on the so-called *Huffman tree*. The Huffman coding is, e.g., used in MPEG-1 audio standard to reduce the amount of output data in layer III. The set of 32 Huffman tables are specially tuned for statistics of the MDCT coefficients divided into some regions and subregions [38].

## 27.9 Transparent Audio Coding

A need for reduction of bit rate required for the transmission of high quality audio signals draws a growing attention to lossy audio coding techniques. Lossy audio coding will be fully acceptable, if it is perceptually transparent, i.e., if the corruption of the audio signal waveform is inaudible. An efficient transparent audio coding algorithm (Fig. 27.17) should:

- remove redundancy contained in the original audio signal,
- remove the perceptual irrelevancy.

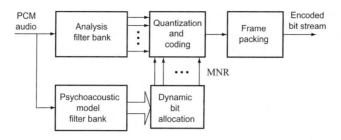

**FIGURE 27.30**   General scheme of the transparent audio coder.

The first task requires an efficient parametric description of audio, e.g., a plausible mathematical model of its production. Although this is a relatively simple task for speech, and at least a conceivable one for music, for general audio signals this is a very complex problem. Therefore, instead of a real audio production model, a compromise solution can be used, namely a general signal analysis model, e.g., in the frequency domain or in the scale-of-resolution domain (cf., section 27.3), reducing redundancy (correlation) of the signal components. In both cases, the signal is split into almost uncorrelated components with a proper analysis filter bank. At the receiver side these components are recombined via a corresponding synthesis filter bank. This procedure should allow perfect or at least nearly perfect signal reconstruction under ideal conditions.

The second task should be realized by means of a precise psychoacoustic hearing model, which should take all masking effects into account. This subject has been discussed in section 27.4. The hearing model provides information about the dynamic range, which is necessary for the proper representation of parameters (signal components) contained in the signal analysis model. Thus, it allows for efficient dynamic bit allocation to particular signal parameters or components.

A general scheme of the transparent audio coder is shown in Fig. 27.30. The input audio signal is first analyzed via an analysis filter bank. Taking different possible analysis filter banks into account, state-of-the-art coders can be divided into two historically relevant categories: subband coders (SBCs) and transform coders (TCs). TCs operate usually with much greater frequency resolution than SBCs. In typical SBCs uniform polyphase analysis filter banks are used (cf., section 27.7). On the other hand, TCs typically employ the MDCT [40]. Other types of analysis filter banks, e.g., octave filter banks, can also be very efficiently used. They can be realized with the discrete wavelet transformation (DWT) discussed in section 27.3 or with wave digital filters (WDFs) [43]. Another approach, which is implemented in MPEG-1 layer III audio coder, is a hybrid filter bank, which is combination of a coarse frequency resolution subband filter bank followed by a fine frequency resolution transformation (MDCT in this case).

Parallelly, the input signal is also analyzed with a psychoacoustic model filter bank. This filter bank should estimate a number of nonoverlapping peripheral auditory filters, which cover the whole audible frequency range. In those audio coders, which for parametric signal description exploit octave analysis filter banks, this can be just the same filter bank [43]; however, typically, the psychoacoustic model filter bank is realized separately with the FFT.

Using the psychoacoustic auditory model a global dynamic threshold of hearing is computed, e.g., by using the way shown in Eq. (27.22) or more precisely in Eq. (27.66b). Then in each analysis filter subband the respective $SMR_i$ is computed with Eq. (27.67). Finally, the mask-to-noise ratio (MNR) is computed as

$$MNR_i(m) = SNR(m) - SMR_i \qquad (27.60)$$

where, by $SNR(m)$, the signal-to-noise ratio determined by Eq. (27.38), resulting from an $m$-bit quantization, is denoted. Within the $i$th critical band the quantization noise will be inaudible as long as the $MNR_i(m)$ is positive. This observation can be used for efficient dynamic bit allocation, which can be realized, e.g., with the following procedure:

- The bit allocation unit searches for the analysis filter subband with the lowest MNR and allocates code bits to this subband; then the SNR($m$) value is updated for this subband and the actual MNR is computed with Eq. (27.60).
- The process is repeated until no more code bits can be allocated.

An important problem, resulting from the transformation of the audio signal (via an analysis filter bank) into the frequency domain, is the appearance of *pre-echoes*, occurring in silent signal periods followed by sudden sound attacks (e.g., of a percussive character). This phenomenon is caused by quantization errors, which are irrelevant in loud and stationary signal parts but are immediately audible in silent signal parts. In TCs, the inverse transform in the receiver distributes the quantization errors over the whole block of samples cut with the respective time window. In SBCs, this effect occurs due to transients. A possible method for suppression of pre-echos is the adaptive window switching (cf., Fig. 27.19) [46]. Windows of short lengths should be used in nonstationary parts of the signal, while in stationary signal parts wide windows (improving the overall coding efficiency) should be used. Typically, the block size vary between $N = 64$ and $N = 1024$.

Further reduction of audio bit rate is still possible by resignation from the full perceptual transparency. In many cases, especially in multimedia and/or in mobile-access applications, a not annoying reduction of fidelity of some audio components of secondary importance, is acceptable. The whole audio scene can be divided into a number of individual audio objects: a conversation, a background noise, a background music, sounds produced by particular sources, etc. These objects can be coded and transmitted separately. Furthermore, some of them may be added synthetically at the receiver. Such coding philosophy is used in the so-called *structured audio format* implemented in the MPEG-4 standard (cf., section 27.10). By this means, a very flexible scalability of audio quality can be realized. This is very useful when audio has to be transmitted through channels of varying capacity and/or is to be received with decoders of various quality and complexity.

## 27.10 Audio Coding Standards

### MUSICAM and MPEG Standards

Among standards for digital coding of high quality audio, the most important role play moving picture expert group (MPEG) standards designed for various communications and multimedia applications. They are elaborated as a result of efforts of the working group WG 11 within the International Organization for Standardization (ISO/IEC).

The first result was MPEG-1 standard IS 11172 designed (in its audio part) for a two-channel audio, approximately with a CD quality [16]. This standard consists of three layers I, II, and III, of increasing efficiency. For transparent transmission, they enable bit rates of 384, 192, and 128 kb/s, respectively. MPEG-1 supports sampling rates of 32, 44.1, and 48 ksamples/s. Layer II of MPEG-1 is based on the masking-pattern universal subband integrated coding and multiplexing (MUSICAM) standard designed for digital audio broadcasting (DAB) system. Layer III of MPEG-1 has become very popular in Internet due to *.mp3 audio files.

The next step of the standardization was MPEG-2 AAC (advanced audio coding) standard IS 13818 designed for high definition television (HDTV) [17]. It offers a multichannel (surround) sound for high spatial realism, provides low bit rate audio (below 64 kb/s), and also supports low sampling rates of 16, 22.05, and 24 ksamples/s.

The third generation standard MPEG-4 has been designed for a broad area of various communications (especially mobile access) and multimedia applications and is characterized by high flexibility, scalability, and universalism [18]. It supports bit rates between 2 and 64 kb/s and offers additional services as text-to-speech (TTS) conversion, structured audio format, and interface between TTS and synthetic moving face models (talking heads), which are driven from speech.

A new standard MPEG-7, named the *multimedia content description interface,* is aimed to support as broad range of communications and multimedia applications as possible [19]. MPEG-7 audio merges five different technologies: the audio description framework (scalable series, low-level descriptors, and uniform silence segments), musical instrument timbre descriptors, sound recognition tools, spoken content descriptors, and melody descriptors. In order to describe the low-level audio features, regions of similarity and dissimilarity within the sound are searched for. This can be done either using samples taken at regular intervals or segments of samples. The relevant samples are then further manipulated to form a scalable series, which allows to progressively down-sample the data contained in a series, according to the application, bandwidth, or storage requirements.

The scope of newest MPEG-21 standard is the integration of technologies enabling transparent and augmented use of multimedia resources across a wide range of networks and devices to support functions such as content creation, content production, content distribution, content consumption and usage, content packaging, intellectual property management and protection, content identification and description, financial management, user privacy, terminals and network resource abstraction, content representation and event reporting [20].

MUSICAM as well as MPEG-1 layers I and II coders have the same structure shown in Fig. 27.31. The input audio signal is transmitted via a 32-band polyphase analysis filter bank (Fig. 27.22(a)) with equally spaced passbands, according to Eqs. (27.50a–c). All subband filters with impulse responses $H_i(n)$, $i = 0$, $1,\ldots,31$, determined by Eq. (27.48), are obtained by modulation of a single prototype lowpass filter with the impulse response $h(n)$, as is illustrated in Fig. 27.22(c). Their output signals are critically decimated. For a 48 ksamples/s sampling rate, each subband filter has a passband width of 750 Hz. Although these filters are highly overlapping, they can guarantee a perfect (or at least a nearly perfect) signal reconstruction (via the synthesis filter bank in Fig. 27.22(b)) due to the power complementarity. For instance, at multiples of 750 Hz the respective filters, i.e., those with neighboring passbands exhibit a 3 dB attenuation.

Samples of subband signal components are quantized with a number of uniform midtread quantizers with 3, 5, 7,…, 65,535 possible levels. Blocks of samples are formed (e.g., blocks of 12 samples in layer I) and divided by a scalefactor $s_{sf}$ selected in such a way that the sample with the largest magnitude is scaled to 1. By this means a quite large overall dynamic range of approximately 126 dB is reached. Proper quantizers are selected with the dynamic bit allocation algorithm described in section 27.9, controlled

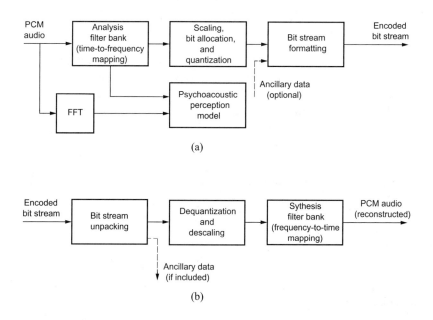

**FIGURE 27.31**  Structure of MUSICAM and MPEG-1 layer I and II coders: (a) encoder, (b) decoder.

by a psychoacoustic audibility model, in order to meet the bit rate and the global threshold of hearing requirements. The whole procedure is described below.

The psychoacoustic model filter bank is based on a 512-point FFT for layer I and on a 1024-point FFT for layers II and III. First, samples of the spectral power density $P(k)$ and the respective level $L_p(k)$ in decibels are computed:

$$P(k) = |X(k)|^2 \tag{27.61a}$$

$$L_P(k) = 10 \log_{10} P(k) \tag{27.61b}$$

where $X(k)$ are DFT spectrum samples defined by Eq. (27.39a). Next in each of $i = 0, 1, \ldots, 31$ subbands the signal SPL is computed as

$$L_{pi} = \max[L_{P\max i}, 20 \log_{10}(32768 s_{\text{sf max } i}) - 10] \tag{27.62}$$

where $L_{P\max i}$ is the maximum $L_p(k)$ value in $i$th subband.

Next, the relevant masker levels $L_{Pm}(z_j)$ are searched for: tone masker levels $L_{Ptm}(z_j)$, $j = 1, 2, \ldots, m_{\text{tm}}$, and noise masker levels $L_{Pnm}(z_j)$, $j = 1, 2, \ldots, m_{\text{nm}}$. Then, the masking indices are computed (in dB):

$$a_{\text{tm}}(z_j) = -1.525 - 0.275 z_j - 4.5 \tag{27.63a}$$

$$a_{\text{nm}}(z_j) = -1.525 - 0.175 z_j - 0.5 \tag{27.63b}$$

where by $z_j$ the $j$th critical band index in Bark is denoted.

Individual masking threshold levels are computed (in dB) as

$$L_{\text{ttm}}(z, z_j, L_{Pm}) = L_{Ptm}(z_j) + a_{\text{tm}}(z_j) + v(\Delta z, z_j) \tag{27.64a}$$

$$L_{\text{tnm}}(z, z_j, L_{Pm}) = L_{Pnm}(z_j) + a_{\text{nm}}(z_j) + v(\Delta z, z_j) \tag{27.64b}$$

for tone maskers and for noise maskers, respectively. The so-called masking function $v(\Delta z, z_j)$ is defined by

$$v(\Delta z, z_j) = \begin{cases} 17(\Delta z + 1) - 0.4 L_{Pm}(z_j) + 6 & \text{for } \Delta z < -1 \\ (0.4 L_{Pm}(z_j) + 6)\Delta z & \text{for } -1 \le \Delta z < 0 \\ -17\Delta z & \text{for } 0 \le \Delta z < 1 \\ (\Delta z - 1)(-17 + 0.15 L_{Pm}(z_j)) + 17 & \text{for } 1 \le \Delta z \end{cases} \tag{27.65}$$

where $\Delta z = z - z_j$. Expression (27.65) gives significant values in range $-3 \le \Delta z \le 8$ only. Outside this region we can assume that $v(\Delta z, z_j) \to -\infty$.

Using expression (27.22), the global threshold of hearing $L_{ptg}$ (Fig. 27.14) can now be computed (in dB):

$$L_{ptg}(z) = 10 \log_{10} \left( 10^{L_{ptq}(z)/10} + \sum_{j=1}^{m_{\text{tm}}} 10^{L_{\text{ttm}}(z, z_j, L_{Pm})/10} + \sum_{j=1}^{m_{\text{nm}}} 10^{L_{\text{tnm}}(z, z_j, L_{Pm})/10} \right) \tag{27.66a}$$

where $L_{ptq}(z)$ is the threshold of audibility in quiet. Consequently,

$$L_{ptg \min}(i) = \min(L_{ptg}(z_j)) \tag{27.66b}$$

for $i$th subband is computed over all critical bands $j$ contained in this subband. Now in each subband the signal-to-mask ratio $\text{SMR}_i$ can be computed (in dB):

$$\text{SMR}_i = L_{pi} - L_{ptg \min}(i) \tag{27.67}$$

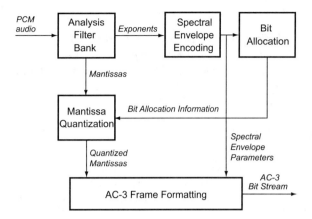

**FIGURE 27.32**   AC-3 encoder.

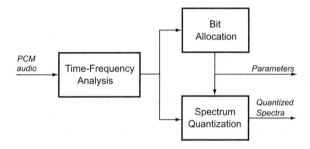

**FIGURE 27.33**   ATRAC encoder.

Finally, the dynamic bit allocation algorithm based on maximization of the mask-to-noise ratio $\text{MNR}_i(m)$ defined with Eq. (27.60) assign bits to each block and each subband.

## Dolby AC-3 Standard

Dolby AC-3 standard gives the possibility for multichannel audio compression (from 1 to 5.1 channels) [3]. The bit stream ranges from 32 to 640 kb/s. Coding operation in AC-3 format is realized using time division aliasing cancelation (TDAC) filter bank. The sample block of length 512 transformed into frequency domain and each sample block is overlapped by 256 samples. Spectral components are represented in floating-point format and the exponents and mantissas are coded separately. A set of exponents is coded into the spectral envelope. One AC-3 synchronization frame is composed for six audio blocks (1536 audio samples). Simplified AC-3 encoder is presented in Fig. 27.32. The psychoacoustic model used in the AC-3 standard divides the audio band (0–24 kHz) into 50 subbands.

## Adaptive Transform Acoustic Coding ATRAC Standard

An adaptive transform acoustic coder (ATRAC) is developed by Sony and is designed for the MiniDisk system [3]. The bit stream of 16-bit audio signal with sampling rate 44.1 ksamples/s (705.6 kbps) is reduced into 146 kbps. The input audio signal (512 samples per channel) is decomposed into spectral coefficients, which are grouped into 52 block floating units (BFUs). The spectral coefficients are normalized in each BFU, which are then quantized to the specified word length. Using QMF filters, the time-frequency analysis unit divides input signal into three subbands: 0–5.5 kHz, 5.5–11 kHz, and 11–22 kHz. Each subband is transformed into the frequency domain using the MDCT. Fig. 27.33 presents the general scheme of the ATRAC encoder.

# References

1. *Analog Devices DSP Selection Guide,* Analog Devices, Edition 2000.
2. Bellanger, M., *Digital signal processing—theory and practice,* 2nd ed., Teubner, Stuttgart, 1989.
3. Brandenburg, K. and Bosi, M., Overview of MPEG audio: current and future standards for low-bit-rate audio coding, *J. Audio Eng. Soc.,* 45(1/2), 1997, 4.
4. Brandenburg, K., MP3 and AAC explained, in *Proc. AES 17th Int. Conf. High Quality Audio Coding,* Erlangen, 1999.
5. Burrus, C. S., Gopinath, R. A., and Guo, H., *Introduction to wavelets and wavelet transforms,* Prentice-Hall, Upper Saddle River, NJ, 1998.
6. Dabrowski, A. and Marciniak, T., Conversion of digital audio signal formats using fixed-point signal processors, in *Proc. Int. Conf. on Signals and Electronic Systems,* Ustron, Poland, 2000, 555.
7. Dabrowski, A., Figlak, P., Golebiewski, R., and Marciniak, T., *Signal processing using signal processors* (in Polish), PUT Press, Poznan, 1997.
8. Dabrowski, A., *Multirate and multiphase switched-capacitor circuits,* Chapman and Hall, London, 1997.
9. DeFatta, D. J., Lucas, J. G., and Hodgkiss, W. S., *Digital signal processing: a system design approach,* John Wiley & Sons, New York, 1988.
10. Dehery, Y. F., Stoll, G., and Kerkhof, L. v. d., MUSICAM source coding for digital sound, in *Proc. 17th International Television Symposium,* Montreux, 1991, 612.
11. Fettweis, A., Wave digital filters: theory and practice, *Proc. IEEE,* 74(2), 1986, 270.
12. Fletcher, H., Auditory patterns, *Rev. Mod. Phys.,* 12, 1940, 47.
13. Gold, B. and Morgan, N., *Speech and audio signal processing—processing and perception of speech and music,* Wiley, New York, 2000.
14. Hellman, R. P., Asymmetry in masking between noise and tone, *Perception and Psychophys.,* 11, 1972, 241.
15. Huffman, D. A., A method for the construction of minimum redundancy codes, *Proc. IRE,* 40, 1952, 1098.
16. ISO/IEC JTC1/SC29, MPEG-1, Information technology—coding of moving pictures and associated audio for digital storage media at up to about 1.5 Mbit/s—IS 11172 (Part 3, Audio), 1992.
17. ISO/IEC JTC1/SC29, MPEG-2, Information technology—generic coding of moving pictures and associated audio informations—IS 13818 (Part 7, Audio), 1997.
18. ISO/IEC JTC1/SC29, MPEG-4 audio, Doc. N2431, 1998.
19. ISO/IEC JTC1/SC29, MPEG-7, Martínez, J. M. (Ed.), Doc. WG11, N4031, 2001.
20. ISO/IEC JTC1/SC29, MPEG-21, Bormans, J. and Hill, K. (Eds.), Doc. WG11 N4041, 2001.
21. Jayant, N. S. and Noll, P., *Digital coding of waveforms: principles and applications to speech and video,* Prentice-Hall, Englewood Cliffs, NJ, 1984.
22. Johnston, J. D., Transform coding of audio signals using perceptual noise criteria, *IEEE Journal on Selected areas in Communications,* 6(2), 1988, 314.
23. Kapust, R., A human ear related objective measurement technique yields audible error and error margin, in *Proc. 11th Int. AES Conf. Test and Measurement,* Portland, 1992, 191.
24. Kinsler, L. and Frey. A., *Fundamentals of acoustics,* Wiley, New York, 1962.
25. Kleczkowski, P., Marciniak, T., and Dabrowski, A., PC audio card for surround sound with real-time signal processing, in *Proc. 8th Int. Symp. on Sound Engineering and Mastering,* Gdansk, Poland, 1999, 65.
26. Kleczkowski, P., Marciniak, T., and Golebiewski, R., Multichannel DSP audio card for DVD applications, in *Proc. ECMCS '99 EURASIP, DSP for Multimedia Communications and Services,* Krakow, 1999, 65.
27. Lagadec, R., Pelloni, D., and Weiss, D., A 2-Channel, 16-Bit digital sampling frequency converter for professional digital audio, in *Proc. IEEE ICASSP-82,* Paris, 1982, 93.
28. Marciniak, T. and Dabrowski, A., Chosen aspects of audio processing using fixed-point digital signal processor, in *First Online Symposium for Electronics Engineers (OSEE),* www.osee.net, 2000.

29. Marven, C. and Ewers, G., *A simple approach to digital signal processing*, Texas Instruments, 1994.
30. MATLAB: *Signal processing toolbox for use with MATLAB*, The MathWorks Inc., 1999.
31. Mitra, S. K. and Kaiser, J. F., *Handbook for digital signal processing*, John Wiley & Sons, New York, 1993.
32. Moore, B. C. J., *An introduction to the psychology of hearing*, 4th ed., Academic Press, London, 1997.
33. Motorola DSP Products, www.mot.com/SPS/DSP/products/index.html, 2001.
34. MPEG home page, www.cselt.it/mpeg, 2001.
35. Noll, P. and Liebchen, T., Digital audio: from lossless to transparent coding, in *Proc. IEEE Signal Processing Workshop*, Dabrowski, A. (Ed.), IEEE Poland Section, Chapter Circuits and Systems, Poznan, Poland, 1999, 53.
36. Noll, P., MPEG audio coding standards, *IEEE Signal Processing Magazine*, 1997.
37. Oppenheim, A. and Schafer, R., *Discrete-time signal processing*, Prentice-Hall, Englewood Cliffs, NJ, 1989.
38. Pan, D. Y., A tutorial on MPEG/audio compression, *IEEE Multimedia Journal*, 1995.
39. Pan, D. Y., Digital audio compression, *Digital Technical Journal*, 5, 2, 1993.
40. Princen, J., Johnson, A., and Bradley, A., Subband transform coding using filter bank designs based on time domain aliasing cancellation, in *Proc. ICASSP*, 1987, 2161.
41. Purnhagen, H., Advances in parametric audio coding, in *Proc. 1999 IEEE Workshop on Applications of Signal Processing to Audio and Acoustics*, New Paltz, New York, 1999, W99-1.
42. Ramstadt, T. A., Digital methods for conversion between arbitrary sampling frequencies, *IEEE Transaction on Acoustics, Speech and Signal Processing*, ASSP-32, 3, 1984, 577.
43. Sauvagerd, U., *Bitratenreduktion hochwertiger Musiksignale unter Verwendung von Wellendigitalfiltern*, VDI Verlag, Düsseldorf, 1990.
44. Sek, A. P., An analysis of the peripheral auditory system based on the detection of modulation in sounds, Habilitation dissertation, Institute of Acoustics, A. Mickiewicz University, Poznan, 1995.
45. Scharf, B., Critical bands, in *Foundations of modern auditory theory*, Tobias, J. V. (Ed.), Academic Press, New York, 1970, 1,157.
46. Sporer, T., Brandenburg, K. and Edler, B., The use of multirate filter banks for coding of high quality audio, in *Proc. 6th EUSIPCO*, Amsterdam, 1992, 1, 211.
47. Terhardt, E., Calculating virtual pitch, *Hearing Res.*, 1, 1979, 155.
48. *TMS320C54x DSP—Applications guide—reference set*, 4., Texas Instruments, 1996.
49. *TMS320C54x DSP: CPU and peripherals*, 1, Texas Instruments, 1996.
50. *TMS320C5000 DSP Platform*, Texas Instruments, www.ti.com/sc/c5000, 2001.
51. *TMS320C6000 DSP Platform*, Texas Instruments, www.ti.com/sc/c6000, 2001.
52. Vaidyanathan, P. P., *Multirate systems and filter banks*, Prentice-Hall, Englewood Cliffs, NJ, 1993.
53. Zölzer, U., *Digitale Audiosignalverarbeitung*, Teubner, Stuttgart, 1997.
54. Zwicker, E. and Fastl, H., *Psychoacoustics*, Springer-Verlag, Berlin, 1990.
55. Zwicker, E. and Feldtkeller, R., *Das Ohr als Nachrichtenempfänger*, S. Hirzel Verlag, Stuttgart, 1967.
56. Zwicker, E., Flottrop, G., and Stevens, S. S., Critical bandwidth in loudness summation, *J. Acoust. Soc. Am.*, 1957, 29, 548.

# 28

# Digital Video Processing

Todd R. Reed
*University of California at Davis*

## 28.1 Introduction

Rapid increases in performance and decreases in cost of computing platforms and digital image acquisition and display subsystems have made digital images ubiquitous. Continued improvements promise to make digital video as widely used, opening a broad range of new application areas. In this chapter, some of the key aspects of this evolving data type are examined.

### Some Historical Perspective

The use of image sequences substantially predates modern video displays (see, e.g., [1]). As might be expected, the primary initial motivation for using these sequences was the depiction of motion. One of the earlier approaches to motion picture display was invented by the mathematician William George Horner in 1834. Originally called the Daedaleum (after Daedalus, who was supposed to have made figures of men that seemed to move), it was later called the Zoetrope (life turning) or the Wheel of Life. The Daedaleum works by presenting a series of images, one at a time, through slits in a circular drum, as the drum is rotated.

Although this device is very simple, it illustrates some important concepts. First and foremost, the impression of motion conveyed by a sequence of images is illusory. It is the result in part of a property

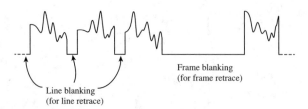

**FIGURE 28.1**  A noninterlaced video signal.

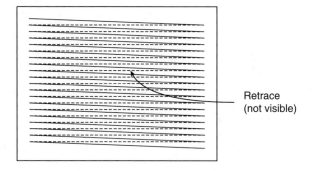

**FIGURE 28.2**  A noninterlaced scanning raster.

of the human visual system (HVS) referred to as persistence of vision. An image is perceived to remain for a period of time after it has been removed from view. This illusion is the basis of all motion picture displays. When the drum in the device is rotated slowly, the images appear (as they are) a disjoint sequence of still images. As the speed of rotation increases (the images are displayed at a higher rate), a point is reached at which motion is perceived, even though the images appear to "flicker." Further increasing the speed of rotation, a point is reached at which flicker is no longer perceived (the critical fusion frequency). Finally, the slits in the drum illustrate a critical aspect of this illusion. In order to perceive motion from a sequence of images, the stimulus the individual images represent must be removed for a period of time between each presentation. If not, the sequence of images simply merges into a blur, and no motion is perceived.

These concepts (rooted in the nature of human visual motion perception) are fundamental, and are reflected in all motion picture acquisition and display systems.

## Video

Unlike image sequences on film, video is represented as a 1-D signal, derived by scanning the camera sensor. The fact that the signal is derived by scanning imposes a particular signal structure, an example of which is shown in Fig. 28.1 for a noninterlaced system.

In principle, scanning can be done in many ways. The simplest in concept is noninterlaced line-continuous scanning (which yields the video signal just discussed). This approach is also referred to as progressive scanning. Viewed in the 2-D plane (either at the camera or display), this approach appears as shown in Fig. 28.2.

The bandwidth of the resulting video signal is relatively high. Transmitting a frame of 485 lines,[1] with a 4:3 aspect ratio (NTSC resolution), at 60 frames per second requires roughly twice the available channel bandwidth (6 MHz). Sixty updates per second are needed to avoid wide area flicker, dictated by the temporal response of the HVS. One approach to reducing the signal bandwidth is to send half as many samples (lines). This cannot be accomplished by reducing the frame rate to 30 frames per second, because

---

[1]NTSC consists of 525 lines, but only ~485 lines are active.

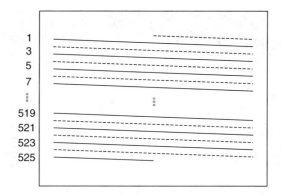

**FIGURE 28.3**   An NTSC frame, formed by interlacing two fields (2:1 interlace).

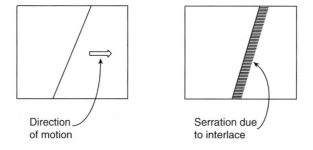

**FIGURE 28.4**   The effect of interlace on an edge in horizontal motion.

an unacceptable degree of flicker is introduced. Reducing the spatial resolution of each frame results in unacceptable blurring. Interlaced scanning is a compromise between the two approaches.

As used in NTSC television, each complete scan (a frame) contains 525 lines and occurs every 1/30 s. The frame consists of two fields (even and odd), $262\frac{1}{2}$ lines each. These fields are interlaced to form the frame. Fields are scanned every 1/60 s (reducing flicker). Because two fields are interlaced to form one frame, this is called 2:1 interlace. Two interlaced fields (NTSC) are shown in Fig. 28.3.

Image acquisition and display via scanning has several disadvantages. Nonideal aspects of the scanning system (e.g., nonzero spot size), and under some circumstances the act of scanning itself, lead to a reduction in vertical resolution below that predicted by the sampling theorem. The ratio of the actual to ideal resolution is called the Kell factor $k$, $0 \le k \le 1$. Typical values of $k$ are $.6 < k < .8$, with interlaced systems having lower $k$. Scanning also causes distortion when objects in the scene are in motion. For example, a vertical line in motion will result in a tilted scanned image (not due to the tilt of the scan line, but because points on the line at the bottom of the screen are reached later than points at the top). Finally, different points in space within the frame do not correspond to the same point in time. Viewed in the spatiotemporal volume, each frame is tilted, with the upper left corner of the frame corresponding to a significantly earlier time than the lower right corner. This can make the accurate analysis of the image sequence difficult.

Interlaced scanning has additional disadvantages. Interlaced display systems suffer from interline flicker (particularly in regions of the image with nearly horizontal structure). Interlacing results in reduced vertical resolution, which increases aliasing. It also increases the complexity of subsequent processing or analysis (such as motion estimation). Interoperability with other systems, such as computer workstations (which use noninterlaced displays), is made difficult. Still images extracted from interlaced video ("freeze frames") are generally of poor quality. Often only "freeze fields" are provided. This last point can be seen by considering the case of an edge in horizontal motion (Fig. 28.4). To merge two fields to get a still

**FIGURE 28.5**  An image sequence represented as a spatiotemporal volume, raytraced to exhibit its internal structure.

image of reasonable quality, or to get a good progressively scanned sequence from an interlaced one, is a nontrivial problem.

### Image Sequences as Spatiotemporal Data

As discussed previously, the scanning process makes the precise specification of an image sequence difficult (since every spatial point exists at a different time). Interlace complicates matters further. In the remainder of this chapter, the simplifying assumption will be made that each point in a frame corresponds to the same point in time. This is analogous to the digitization of motion picture film, or the sequence which results from a CCD camera with a shutter. It is a reasonable assumption in progressive or interlaced video systems when scene motion is slow compared to the frame rate. The series of frames are no longer tilted in the spatiotemporal domain and can be "stacked" in a straightforward way to form a spatiotemporal volume (see Fig. 28.5).

## 28.2  Some Fundamentals

Following are some notational conventions and basic principles used in the balance of this chapter. A continuous sequence is denoted as $u(x, y, t)$, $v(x, y, t)$, etc., where $x$, $y$ are the continuous spatial variables and $t$ is the continuous temporal variable. Similarly, a discrete sequence is denoted as $u(m, n, p)$, $v(m, n, p)$, etc., where $m$, $n$ are the discrete (integer) spatial variables and $p$ is the discrete (integer) temporal variable.

### A 3-D System

As in 1-D and 2-D, a 3-D discrete system can be defined as

$$y(m, n, p) = \mathcal{H}[x(m, n, p)] \tag{28.1}$$

where $\mathcal{H}$ is the system function. In general, this function need be neither linear nor shift invariant. If the system is both linear and shift invariant (LSI), it can be characterized in terms of its impulse response $h(m, n, p)$. The linear shift invariant system response can then be written as

$$y(m, n, p) = \sum_{m'=-\infty}^{\infty} \sum_{n'=-\infty}^{\infty} \sum_{p'=-\infty}^{\infty} x(m', n', p')h(m - m', n - n', p - p')$$
$$\equiv x(m, n, p) * h(m, n, p) \tag{28.2}$$

where '$*$' denotes (discrete) convolution. Similarly, for the continuous case,

$$g(x, y, t) = \int_{-\infty}^{\infty} \int_{-\infty}^{\infty} \int_{-\infty}^{\infty} f(x', y', t')h(x - x', y - y', t - t')\, dx'\, dy'\, dt' \tag{28.3}$$

## The 3-D Fourier Transform

The 3-D continuous Fourier transform can be expressed as

$$F(\xi_x, \xi_y, \xi_t) = \int_{-\infty}^{\infty} \int_{-\infty}^{\infty} \int_{-\infty}^{\infty} f(x, y, t)e^{-j2\pi(x\xi_x + y\xi_y + t\xi_t)}\, dx\, dy\, dt \tag{28.4}$$

where $\xi_x$, $\xi_y$, and $\xi_t$ are the spatiotemporal frequency variables and $f(x, y, t)$ is a continuous spatiotemporal signal. As in the 2-D case, the 3-D Fourier transform is separable:

$$F(\xi_x, \xi_y, \xi_t) = \int_{-\infty}^{\infty} \left[ \int_{-\infty}^{\infty} \left[ \int_{-\infty}^{\infty} f(x, y, t)e^{-j2\pi x\xi_x}\, dx \right] e^{-j2\pi y\xi_y}\, dy \right] e^{-j2\pi t\xi_t}\, dt \tag{28.5}$$

Also as in the 1-D and 2-D cases, if

$$g(x, y, t) = h(x, y, t) * f(x, y, t) \tag{28.6}$$

then

$$G(\xi_x, \xi_y, \xi_t) = H(\xi_x, \xi_y, \xi_t)F(\xi_x, \xi_y, \xi_t) \tag{28.7}$$

If $h(x, y, t)$ is the LSI system impulse response, then $H(\xi_x, \xi_y, \xi_t)$ is the frequency response of the system. The spatiotemporal discrete Fourier transform is defined as

$$v(h, k, l) = \sum_{m=0}^{N-1} \sum_{n=0}^{N-1} \sum_{p=0}^{N-1} u(m, n, p) W_N^{hm} W_N^{kn} W_N^{lp} \tag{28.8}$$

where $0 \le h, k, l \le N - 1$ and $W_N = e^{-j2\pi/N}$.
   The inverse transform is

$$u(m, n, p) = \frac{1}{N^3} \sum_{h=0}^{N-1} \sum_{k=0}^{N-1} \sum_{l=0}^{N-1} v(h, k, l) W_N^{-hm} W_N^{-kn} W_N^{-lp} \tag{28.9}$$

where $0 \le m, n, p \le N - 1$.

## Moving Images in the Frequency Domain

Following the discussion in [2], a moving monochrome image can be represented by an intensity distribution $f(x, y, t)$. The image is static if $f(x, y, t) = f(x, y, 0)$ for all $t$. The velocity of the image can be expressed via the image velocity vector

$$\vec{r} = (r_x, r_y) \tag{28.10}$$

If the (initially static) image translates at a constant velocity $\vec{r}$, then

$$f_r(x, y, t) = f(x - r_x t, y - r_y t, t) \tag{28.11}$$

Consider the case of a simple 2-D "image" $f(x, t)$. Let

$$\vec{a} = \begin{pmatrix} x \\ t \end{pmatrix} \quad \text{and} \quad \vec{b} = \begin{pmatrix} \xi_x \\ \xi_t \end{pmatrix} \tag{28.12}$$

where $\xi_x$ and $\xi_t$ are the spatial and temporal frequency variables. Then the transform pair can be written as

$$f(\vec{a}) \xrightarrow{\mathcal{F}} F(\vec{b}) \tag{28.13}$$

Now, translation can be represented as a coordinate transformation

$$\vec{a}' = \begin{pmatrix} x - r_x t \\ t \end{pmatrix} = \mathbf{A} \vec{a} \tag{28.14}$$

where

$$\mathbf{A} = \begin{bmatrix} 1 & -r_x \\ 0 & 1 \end{bmatrix} \tag{28.15}$$

and $r_x$ is the horizontal speed.

Using the expression for the Fourier transform after an affine coordinate transformation (any combination of scaling, rotation, and translation),

$$f(\vec{a}') \xrightarrow{\mathcal{F}} F[(\mathbf{A}^{-1})^T \vec{b}] \tag{28.16}$$

where

$$(\mathbf{A}^{-1})^T = \begin{bmatrix} 1 & 0 \\ r_x & 1 \end{bmatrix} \tag{28.17}$$

so that

$$f(x - r_x t, t) \xrightarrow{\mathcal{F}} F(\xi_x, \xi_t + r_x \xi_x) \tag{28.18}$$

### Example

Consider a simple static image with only two components (Fig. 28.6). As the image undergoes translation with horizontal speed $r_x$, all temporal frequencies are shifted by $-r_x \xi_x$. Spatial frequency coordinates remain unchanged. That is, all frequency components of an image moving with velocity $r_x$ lie on a line through the origin, with slope $-r_x$.

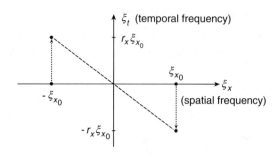

**FIGURE 28.6**   A two-component, 1-D signal in translational motion.

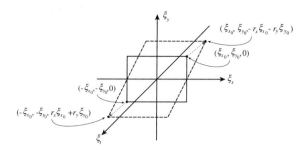

**FIGURE 28.7** A two-component, 2-D signal in translational motion.

Extending the analysis to the 3-D case ($f(x, y, t)$), let the velocity $\vec{r} = (r_x, r_y)$. Then

$$f(x - r_x t, y - r_y t, t) \xrightarrow{\mathcal{F}} F(\xi_x, \xi_y, \xi_t + r_x \xi_x + r_y \xi_y) \tag{28.19}$$

Each temporal frequency is shifted by the dot product of the spatial frequency vector $\vec{s} = (\xi_x, \xi_y)$ and the image velocity vector $\vec{r} = (r_x, r_y)$. If the image was originally static, then

$$\xi_t = -\vec{r} \cdot \vec{s} = -(r_x \xi_x + r_y \xi_y) \tag{28.20}$$

Geometrically, the image motion changes the static image transform (which lies in the ($\xi_x$, $\xi_y$) plane) into a spectrum in a plane with slope $-r_y$ in the ($\xi_y$, $\xi_t$) plane and $-r_x$ in the ($\xi_x$, $\xi_t$) plane. As in the 2-D case, the shifted points lie on a line through the origin. Note that this represents a relatively sparse occupation of the frequency domain (of interest for compression applications). A 3-D volume of data has been "compressed" into a plane. This compactness is not observed in the spatiotemporal domain.

In summary, the spectrum of a stationary image lies in the ($\xi_x$, $\xi_y$) plane. When the image undergoes translational motion, the spectrum occupies an oblique plane which passes through the origin. The orientation of the plane indicates the speed and direction of the motion. It is, therefore, possible to associate energy in particular regions of the frequency domain with particular image velocity components. By filtering specific regions in the frequency domain, these image velocity components can be detected. As will be seen shortly, other effects (such as the visual impact of temporal aliasing) can also be understood in the frequency domain.

## 3-D Sampling

In its simplest form (regular sampling on a rectangular grid, the method used here), 3-D sampling is a straightforward extension of 2-D (or 1-D) sampling (Fig. 28.8). Given a bandlimited sequence

$$f(x, y, t) \xrightarrow{\mathcal{F}} F(\xi_x, \xi_y, \xi_t) \tag{28.21}$$

with

$$F(\xi_x, \xi_y, \xi_t) = 0 \quad \text{whenever} \quad |\xi_x| > \xi_{x_0}, \; |\xi_y| > \xi_{y_0}, \; \text{or} \; |\xi_t| > \xi_{t_0} \tag{28.22}$$

the continuous sequence can be reconstructed from a discrete set of samples whenever

$$\xi_{x_s} > 2\xi_{x_0}, \; \xi_{y_s} > 2\xi_{y_0}, \; \text{and} \; \xi_{t_s} > 2\xi_{t_0} \tag{28.23}$$

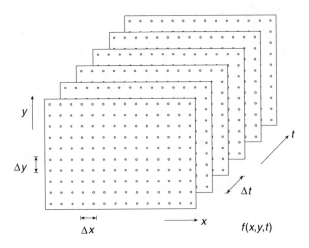

**FIGURE 28.8**  A sampled spatiotemporal signal (image sequence).

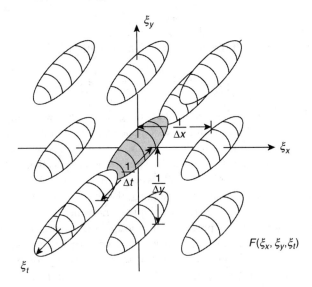

**FIGURE 28.9**  An image sequence with insufficiently high sampling in the temporal dimension.

where $\xi_{x_s}$, $\xi_{y_s}$, $\xi_{z_s}$ are the sampling frequencies. Equivalently, the sequence can be reconstructed if the intervals between samples are such that

$$\Delta x < \frac{1}{2\xi_{x_0}}, \quad \Delta y < \frac{1}{2\xi_{y_0}}, \quad \text{and} \quad \Delta t < \frac{1}{2\xi_{t_0}}. \tag{28.24}$$

If any of the sampling frequencies fall below the specified rates, the neighboring spectra (replications of the continuous spectrum, produced by the sampling process) overlap, and aliasing results. A case for which the temporal sampling frequency is too low is shown in Fig. 28.9. The appearance of aliasing in the spatial domain, where it commonly manifests as a jagged approximation of smooth high contrast edges, is relatively familiar and intuitive. The effect of sampling at too low a rate temporally is perhaps less so.

Consider the earlier simple example of a 1-D image with only two components, moving with velocity $r_x$. The continuous case, as derived previously, is shown in Fig. 28.10. $\xi_{x_0}$ is the frequency of the static image.

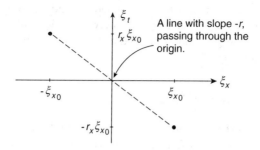

**FIGURE 28.10** A continuous, two-component, 1-D signal in translational motion.

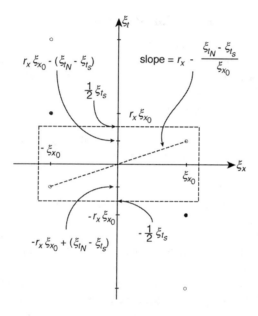

**FIGURE 28.11** A reconstruction of a sampled 1-D signal with temporal aliasing.

Suppose this image is sampled along the temporal dimension at a sampling frequency $\xi_{t_s}$ less than the Nyquist rate ($\xi_{t_N} = 2r_x\xi_{x_0}$), and the image is reconstructed via an ideal lowpass filter with temporal cutoff frequencies at plus and minus half the sampling frequency (Fig. 28.11). What is the visual effect of the aliased components?

As seen previously, the velocity of motion is reflected in the slope of the line connecting the components. For the situation shown, a sinusoidal grid (of the same frequency as the original) moving in the *opposite direction*, with speed $r_x\xi_{x_0} - (\xi_{t_N} - \xi_{t_s})$ is observed. As the sampling frequency drops, the velocity decreases, eventually reaching zero. Continued reduction in $\xi_{t_s}$ results in motion in the *same direction* as the original image, increasing in velocity until (at $\xi_{t_s} = 0$) the velocities of the two components are identical.

In the simple example just considered, the image was spatially homogeneous, so that the effects of aliasing were seen throughout the image. In general, this is not the case. As in the 1-D and 2-D cases, the temporal aliasing effect is seen in regions of the sequence with sufficiently high temporal frequency components to alias. Circumstances leading to high temporal frequencies include high velocity (large values of $r_x$ in our simple example) and high spatial frequency components with some degree of motion (high $\xi_{x_0}$ in our example). Higher spatial frequency components require slower speeds to cause aliasing.

A well-known example of temporal aliasing is the so-called "wagon wheel" effect, in which the wheels of a vehicle appear to move in a direction opposite to that of the vehicle itself. The wheels have both high spatial frequency components (due to their spokes) and relatively high rotational velocity. Hence, aliasing occurs (the wheels appear to rotate in reverse). The vehicle itself, however, which is moving more slowly and is also generally composed of lower spatial frequency components, moves forward (does not exhibit aliasing effects).

## 28.3   The Perception of Visual Motion

Visual perception can be discussed at a number of different levels: the anatomy or physical structure of the visual system; the physiology or basic function of the cells involved; and the psychophysical behavior of the system (the response of the system to various stimuli). Following is a brief discussion of visual motion perception. A more extensive treatment can be found in [3].

### Anatomy and Physiology of Motion Perception

The retina (the hemispherical surface at the back of the eye) is the sensor surface of the visual system, consisting of two major types of sensor elements. The rods are long and thin structures, numbering approximately 120 million. They provide scotopic ("low-light") vision and are highly sensitive to motion. The cones are shorter and thicker, and substantially fewer in number (approximately 6 million per retina). They are less sensitive than the rods, providing photopic ("high-light") and color vision. The cones are much less sensitive to motion.

The rods and cones are arranged in a roughly hexagonal array. However, they are not uniformly distributed over the retina. The cones are packed in the fovea (hence color vision is primarily foveal). The rods are primarily outside the fovea. As a result, motion sensitivity is higher outside the fovea, corresponding to the periphery of the visual field.

Visual information leaves each eye via the optic nerve. The nerves from each eye split at the optic chiasma, pass through the lateral geniculate nucleus, and continue to the visual cortex. Information is retinotopically mapped on the cortex (organized as in the original scene, but reversed). Note, however, that the mapping is not one-to-one (one retinal rod or cone to one cortical cell). As mentioned previously, approximately 120 million rods and 6 million cones are found in each eye, but only 1 million fibers in the associated optic nerve. This 126:1, apparently visually lossless compression, is one of the motivations for studying perceptually inspired image and video compression techniques, as discussed later in this chapter.

To achieve this compression, each cortical cell receives information from a set of rods and/or cones. This set makes up the *receptive field* for that cell. The response of a cortical cell to stimuli at different points in this field can be measured (e.g., via a moving spot of light) and plotted just as one might plot the impulse response of a 2-D filter.

Physiologically, nothing mentioned so far seems specifically adapted to the detection (or measurement) of motion. It might be reasonable to expect to find cells, which respond selectively to, e.g., the direction of motion. There appear to be no such cells in the human retina (although other species do have retinal cells that respond in this way); however, cells in the mammalian striate cortex exhibit this behavior (the complex cells).

How these cells come to act this way remains under study. However, most current theories fit a common organizational structure [4], shown in Fig. 28.12. The input receptive fields are sensitive both to the spatial location and spatial frequency of the stimulus. The role, if any, of orientation is not widely agreed upon. The receptive field outputs are combined, most likely in a nonlinear fashion, in the directionally sensitive subunits to produce an output highly dependent on the direction and/or velocity of the stimulus. The output of these subunits are then integrated both spatially and temporally.

Consider the hypothetical directionally sensitive mechanism in more detail for the case of rightward moving patterns (Fig. 28.13). For example, suppose the receptive fields are symmetric, and C is a comparator which requires both inputs to be high to output a high value. If a pattern, which stimulates receptive field 1 (RF1), moves a distance $\Delta x$ in time $\Delta t$ so that it falls within receptive field 2 (RF2), then the comparator will "fire."

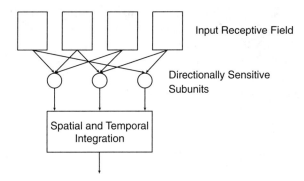

**FIGURE 28.12**   A common organizational structure for modeling complex cell behavior.

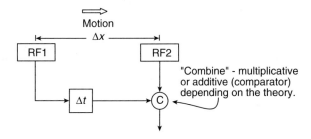

**FIGURE 28.13**   A mechanism for the directionally sensitive detection of motion.

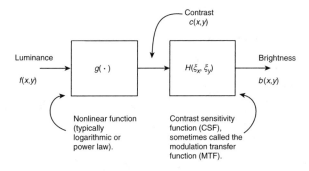

**FIGURE 28.14**   A simple block diagram modeling spatial vision.

Although it is simple, such a model establishes a basic link between moving patterns on the retina and the perception of motion. Additional insight can be obtained by considering the problem from a systems perspective.

## The Psychophysics of Motion Perception

### Spatial Frequency Response

In the case of spatial vision, much can be understood by modeling the visual system as shown in Fig. 28.14. The characteristics of the filter $H(\xi_x, \xi_y)$ have been estimated by determining the threshold visibility of sine wave gratings. The resulting measurements indicate visual sensitivity as a function of spatial frequency that is approximately lowpass in nature. The response peaks in the vicinity of 5 cycles/degree, and falls off rapidly beyond 10 cycles/degree.

If it were separable (that is, $H(\xi_x, \xi_y)$ could be determined by finding $H(\xi_x)$ and $H(\xi_y)$ independently), with $H(\xi_x) = H(\xi_y)$, or isotropic, the spatial response could be characterized via a single 1-D function. Although the assumption of separability is often useful, the spatial CSF of the human visual system is not, in fact, separable. It has been shown that visual sensitivity is reduced at orientations other than vertical and horizontal. This may be due to the predominance of vertical and horizontal structures in the visual environment, leading to the development or evolution of the visual system to be particularly sensitive at (or conversely, less sensitive away from) these orientations. This is referred to as the "oblique effect."

### Temporal Frequency Response

The most straightforward approach to extending the above spatial vision model to include motion is to modify the CSF to include temporal frequency sensitivity, so that $H(\xi_x, \xi_y)$ becomes $H(\xi_x, \xi_y, \xi_t)$.

One way to estimate the temporal frequency response of the visual system is to measure the flicker response. Although the flicker response varies with intensity and with the spatial frequency of the stimulus, it is again generally lowpass, with a peak in response in the vicinity of 10 Hz. The attenuation of the response above 10 Hz increases rapidly, so that at 60 Hz (the field rate of NTSC television) the flicker response is very low.

It is natural, as in the 2-D case, to ask whether the spatiotemporal frequency response $H(\xi_x, \xi_y, \xi_t)$ is separable with respect to the temporal frequency. There is evidence to believe that this is not the case. The flicker response curves for high and low spatial frequency patterns do not appear consistent with a separable spatiotemporal response.

### Reconstruction Error

To a first approximation, the data discussed above indicate that the HVS behaves as a 3-D lowpass filter, with bandlimits (for bright displays) at 60 cycles/degree along the spatial frequency axes, and 70 Hz temporally. This approximation is useful in understanding errors, which may occur in reconstructing a continuous spatiotemporal signal from a sampled one. Consider the case of an image undergoing simple translational motion. This spatiotemporal signal occupies an oblique plane in the frequency domain. With sampling, the spectrum is replicated (with periods determined by the sampling frequencies along the respective dimensions) to fill the infinite 3-D volume. The spectrum of a sufficiently sampled (aliasing-free) image sequence produced in this way is shown in Fig. 28.15.

The 3-D lowpass reconstruction filter (the spatiotemporal CSF) can be approximated as an ideal lowpass filter, as shown in Fig. 28.16. As long as the cube in Fig. 28.16 completely encloses the spectrum

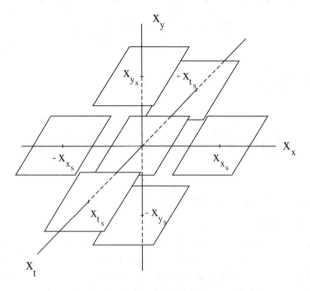

**FIGURE 28.15**   The spectrum of a sampled image undergoing uniform translational motion.

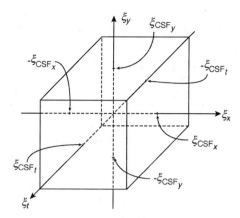

**FIGURE 28.16** An ideal 3-D, lowpass reconstruction filter, with cutoff frequencies determined by the spatiotemporal contrast sensitivity funtion.

centered at DC, without including neighboring spectra, there is no reconstruction error. This case included no aliasing. If aliasing is included (the sample rate during acquisition is too low), the aliased components will be visible only if they fall within the passband of the CSF filter.

The above frequency domain analysis explains some important aspects of human visual motion perception. Other observations are not as easily explained in this way, however. As observed in [5], perceived motion is local (different motions can be seen in different areas of the visual field) and spatial-frequency specific (individual motion sensors respond differently (selectively) to different spatial frequencies). These two observations suggest an underlying representation that is local in both the spatiotemporal and spatiotemporal-frequency domains. Examples of such representations will be discussed in the following subsection.

## The Effects of Eye Motion

The analysis of motion perception described previously assumed a "passive" view. That is, any change in the pattern of light on the retinal surface is due to motion in the scene. That this is not the case can be seen by considering the manner in which static images are viewed. They are not viewed as a whole, but in a series of "jumps" from position to position. These "jumps" are referred to as *saccades* (French for "jolt" or "jerk").

Even at the positions where the eye is "at rest" it is not truly static. It undergoes very small motions (microsaccades) of 1–2 min of arc. In fact, the eye is essentially never at rest. It has been shown that if the eye is stabilized, vision fades away after about a second. The relevance of this to the current discussion is that although the eye is in constant motion, so that the intensity patterns on the retina are constantly changing, when viewing a static scene no motion is perceived. Similar behavior is observed when viewing dynamic scenes [6]. Obviously, however, in the case of dynamic scenes motion is often perceived (even though the changes in intensity patterns on the retina are not necessarily greater than for static images).

Two hypotheses might explain these phenomena. The first is that the saccades are so fast that they are not sensed by the visual system; however, this does not account for the fact that motion is seen in dynamic scenes, but not static ones. The second is that the motion sensing system is "turned off" under some circumstances (the theory of corollary discharge). The basic idea is that the motor signals that control eye movement are also involved in the perception of motion, so that when intensity patterns on the retina change and there is a motor signal present, no motion is perceived. When intensity patterns change but there is no motor signal, or if there is no change in intensity patterns but there is a motor signal, motion is perceived. The latter situation corresponds to the tracking of moving objects (smooth pursuit).

The first hypothesis (the less plausible of the two) can be easily modeled with temporal linear filters. The second, more interesting behavior can be modeled with a simple comparator network.

## 28.4   Image Sequence Representation

### What Does "Representation" Mean?

The term "representation" may require some explanation. Perhaps the best way to do so is to consider some examples of familiar representations. For simplicity, 2-D examples will be used. Extension to 3-D is relatively straightforward.

### The Pixel Representation

The pixel representation is so common and intuitive that it is usually considered to be "the image." More precisely, however, it is a linear sum of weighted impulses:

$$u(m, n) = \sum_{m'=0}^{N-1} \sum_{n'=0}^{N-1} u(m', n') \delta(m - m', n - n') \tag{28.25}$$

where $u(m, n)$ is the image, $u(m', n')$ are the coefficients of the representation (numerically equal to the pixel values in this case), and the $\delta(m - m', n - n')$ play the role of basis functions.

### The DFT

The next most familiar representations (at least to engineers) is the DFT, in which the image is expressed in terms of complex exponentials:

$$u(m, n) = \frac{1}{N^2} \sum_{h=0}^{N-1} \sum_{k=0}^{N-1} v(h, k) W_N^{-hm} W_N^{-kn} \tag{28.26}$$

where $0 \leq m, n \leq N - 1$ and

$$W_N = e^{-j2\pi/N} \tag{28.27}$$

In this case $v(h, k)$ are the coefficients of the representation and the 2-D complex exponentials $W_N^{-hm} W_N^{-kn}$ are the basis functions.

   The choice of one representation over the other (pixel vs. Fourier) for a given application depends on the image characteristics that are of most interest. The pixel representation makes the spatial organization of intensities in the image explicit. Because this is the basis of the visual stimulus, it seems more "natural." The Fourier representation makes the composition of the image in terms of complex exponentials ("frequency components") explicit. The two representations emphasize their respective characteristics (spatial vs. frequency) to the exclusion of all others. If a mixture of characteristics is desired, different representations must be used.

### Spatial/Spatial-Frequency Representations

A natural mixture is to combine frequency analysis with spatial location. An example of a 1-D representation of this type (a time/frequency representation) is a musical score. The need to know not only what the frequency content of a signal is, but where in the signal the frequency components exist is common to many signal, image, and image sequence processing tasks [7]. A variety of approaches [8,9] can be used to develop a representation to facilitate these tasks. The most intuitive approach is the finite-support Fourier transform.

## The Finite-Support Fourier Transform

This approach to local frequency decomposition has been used for many years for the analysis of time-varying signals. In the 2-D continuous case,

$$F_{x,y}(\xi_x, \xi_y) = \int_{-\infty}^{\infty} \int_{-\infty}^{\infty} f_{x,y}(x', y') e^{-j2\pi(\xi_x x' + \xi_y y')} dx' dy' \qquad (28.28)$$

where

$$f_{x,y}(x', y') = f(x', y')h(x - x', y - y') \qquad (28.29)$$

$f(x', y')$ is the original image, and $h(x - x', y - y')$ is a window centered at $(x, y)$.

The properties of the transform depend a great deal on the properties of the window function. Under certain circumstances (i.e., for certain windows) the transform is invertible. The most obvious case is for nonoverlapping (e.g., rectangular) windows.

The windowed transform idea can, of course, be applied to other transforms, as well. An example that is of substantial practical interest is the discrete cosine transform, with a rectangular nonoverlapping window:

$$F(h, k) = \alpha(h)\alpha(k) \sum_{m=0}^{N-1}\sum_{n=0}^{N-1} f(m,n) \cos\left(\frac{(2m + 1)h\pi}{2N}\right) \cos\left(\frac{(2n + 1)k\pi}{2N}\right) \qquad (28.30)$$

where $h, k = 0, 1, \ldots, N - 1$,

$$\alpha(h) = \begin{cases} \sqrt{\dfrac{1}{N}} & \text{for } h = 0 \\[2mm] \sqrt{\dfrac{2}{N}} & \text{otherwise} \end{cases} \qquad (28.31)$$

$\alpha(k)$ is defined similarly, and the window dimensions are $N \times N$. This transform is the basis for the well-known JPEG and MPEG compression algorithms.

## The Gabor Representation

This representation was first proposed for 1-D signal analysis by Dennis Gabor in 1946 [10]. In 2-D [11], an image can be represented as the weighted sum of functions of the form

$$g(x, y) = \hat{g}(x, y)e^{j2\pi[\xi_{x_0}(x - x_0) + \xi_{y_0}(y - y_0)]} \qquad (28.32)$$

where

$$\hat{g}(x, y) = \frac{1}{2\pi\sigma_x\sigma_y} e^{-\frac{1}{2}\left[\left(\frac{x - x_0}{\sigma_x}\right)^2 + \left(\frac{y - y_0}{\sigma_y}\right)^2\right]} \qquad (28.33)$$

is a 2-D Gaussian function, $\sigma_x$ and $\sigma_y$ determine the extent of the Gaussian along the respective axes, $(x_0, y_0)$ is the center of the function in the spatial domain, and $(\xi_{x_0}, \xi_{y_0})$ is the center of support in the frequency domain. A representative example of a Gabor function is shown in Fig. 28.17.

Denoting the distance between spatial centers as $D$ and the distance between their centers of support in the frequency domain as $W$, the basis is complete if $WD = 2\pi$. These functions have a number of interesting aspects. They achieve the lower limits of the Heisenburg uncertainty inequalities:

$$\Delta x \Delta\xi_x \geq \frac{1}{4\pi}, \qquad \Delta y \Delta\xi_y \geq \frac{1}{4\pi} \qquad (28.34)$$

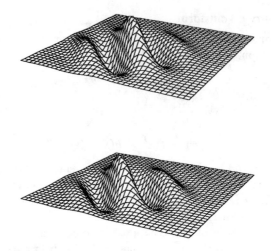

**FIGURE 28.17**   The real (top) and imaginary (bottom) parts of a representative 2-D Gabor function.

where $\Delta_x$, $\Delta_y$, $\Delta\xi_x$, and $\Delta\xi_y$ are the effective widths of the functions in the spatial and spatial-frequency domains. By this measure, then, these functions are optimally local. Their real and imaginary parts also agree reasonably well with measured receptive field profiles. The basis is not orthogonal, however. Specifically, the Gabor transform is not equivalent to the finite-support Fourier transform with a Gaussian window. For a cross-section of the state of the art in Gabor transform-based analysis, see [12].

### The Derivative of Gaussian Transform

In 1987, Young [13] proposed a receptive field model based on the Gaussian and its derivatives. These functions, like the Gabor functions, are spatially and spectrally local and consist of alternating regions of excitation and inhibition in a decaying envelope. Young showed that Gaussian derivative functions more accurately model the measured receptive field data than do the Gabor functions [14].

In [15], a spatial/spatial-frequency representation based on shifted versions of the Gaussian and its derivatives was introduced (the derivative of Gaussian transform (DGT)). As with the Gabor transform, although this transform is nonorthogonal, with a suitably chosen basis it is invertible. The DGT has significant practical advantage over the Gabor transform in that both the basis functions and coefficients of expansion are real-valued.

The family of 2-D separable Gaussian derivatives centered at the origin can be defined as

$$g_{0,0}(x, y) = g_0(x)g_0(y)$$
$$= e^{-(x^2+y^2)/2\sigma^2} \tag{28.35}$$

$$g_{m,n}(x, y) = g_m(x)g_n(y)$$
$$= \frac{d^{(m)}}{dx^{(m)}}g_0(x)\frac{d^{(n)}}{dy^{(n)}}g_0(y) \tag{28.36}$$

This set can then be shifted to any desired location. The variance $\sigma$ defines the extent of the functions in the spatial domain. There is an inverse relationship between the spatial and spectral extents, and the value of this variable may be constant or may vary with context.

The 1-D Gaussian derivative function spectra are bimodal (except for that of the original Gaussian, which is itself a Gaussian) with modes centered at $\pm\Omega_m$ rad/pixel:

$$\Omega_m = \frac{\sqrt{m}}{\sigma} \tag{28.37}$$

where $m$ is the derivative order. The order of derivative necessary to center a mode at a particular frequency is therefore

$$m = (\Omega_m \sigma)^2 \tag{28.38}$$

### The Wigner Distribution

The previous examples indicate that a local frequency representation need not have an orthogonal basis. In fact, it need not even be linear. The Wigner distribution was introduced by Eugene Wigner in 1932 [16] for use in quantum mechanics (in 1-D). In 2-D, the Wigner distribution can be written as

$$W_f(x, y, \xi_x, \xi_y) = \int_{-\infty}^{\infty} \int_{-\infty}^{\infty} f\left(x + \frac{\alpha}{2}, y + \frac{\beta}{2}\right) f^*\left(x - \frac{\alpha}{2}, y - \frac{\beta}{2}\right) e^{-j2\pi(\alpha\xi_x + \beta\xi_y)} \, d\alpha \, d\beta \tag{28.39}$$

where the asterisk denotes complex conjugation. The Wigner distribution is real valued, so does not have an explicit phase component (as seen in, e.g., the Fourier transform). A number of discrete approximations to this distribution (sometimes referred to as pseudo-Wigner distributions) have also been formulated.

## Spatial/Scale Representations (Wavelets)

Scale is a concept that has proven very powerful in many applications, and may under some circumstances be considered as fundamental as frequency. Given a set of (1-D) functions

$$W_{jk}(x) = W(2^j x - k) \tag{28.40}$$

where the indices $j$ and $k$ correspond to dilation (change in scale) and translation, respectively, a signal decomposition

$$f(x) = \sum_j \sum_k b_{jk} W_{jk}(x) \tag{28.41}$$

emphasizes the scale (or resolution) characteristics of the signal (specified by $j$) at specific points along $x$ (specified by $k$), yielding a multiresolution description of the signal.

A class of functions $W_{jk}(x)$ that have proven extremely useful are referred to as wavelets. A detailed discussion of wavelets is beyond the scope of this chapter (see [17–19] for excellent treatments of this topic); however, an important aspect of any representation (including wavelets) is the resolution of the representation, and how it can be measured.

## Resolution

In dealing with joint representations, resolution is a very important issue. It arises in a number of ways. In discussing the Gabor representation, it was noted that the functions minimized the uncertainty inequalities, e.g.,

$$\Delta x \, \Delta \xi_x \geq \frac{1}{4\pi} \tag{28.42}$$

Note that it is the product that is minimized. Arbitrarily high resolution cannot be achieved in both domains simultaneously, but can be traded between the two domains at will. The proper balance depends on the application. It should be noted that the "effective width" measures $\Delta x$, $\Delta\xi_x$, etc. (normalized second moment measures) are not the only way to define resolution. For example, the degree of energy concentration could

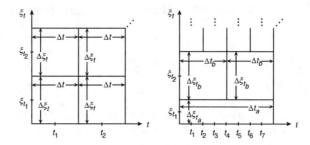

**FIGURE 28.18**  The resolution of a time/frequency representation and a wavelet representation in the time-frequency plane.

be used (leading to a different "optimal" set of functions, the prolate spheroidal functions). The appropriateness of the various measures again depends on the application. Their biological (psychophysical) relevance remains to be determined.

All the previously mentioned points are relevant for both spatial/spatial-frequency and spatial/scale representations (wavelets). Wavelets, however, present some special considerations. Suppose one wishes to compare the resolutions of time/frequency and wavelet decompositions? Specifically, what is the resolution of a multiresolution method? This question can be illustrated by considering the 1-D case, and examining the behavior of the two methods in the time-frequency plane (Fig. 28.18).

In the time/frequency representation, the dimensions $\Delta t$ and $\Delta \xi_t$ remain the same throughout the time-frequency plane. In wavelet representations the dimensions vary, but their product remains constant. The resolution characteristics of wavelets may lead one to believe that the uncertainty of a wavelet decomposition may fall below the bound in Eq. (28.42). This is not the case. The tradeoff between $\Delta t$ and $\Delta \xi_t$ simply varies. The fundamental limit remains.

A final point relates more specifically to the representation of image sequences. The HVS has a specific (bandlimited) spatiotemporal frequency response. Beyond indicating the maximum perceivable frequencies (setting an upper bound on resolution) it seems feasible to exploit this point further, to achieve a more efficient representation. Recalling the relationship between motion and temporal frequency, a surface with high spatial frequency components, moving quickly, has high temporal frequency components. When it is static, it does not. The characteristics of the spatiotemporal CSF may lead us to the conclusions that static regions of an image require little temporal resolution, but high spatial resolution, and that regions in an image undergoing significant motion require less spatial resolution (due to the lowered sensitivity of the CSF), but require high temporal resolution (for smooth motion rendition).

The first conclusion is essentially correct (although not trivial to exploit). The second conclusion, however, neglects eye tracking. If the eye is tracking a moving object, the spatiotemporal frequency characteristics experienced by the viewer are very similar to those in the static case, i.e., visual sensitivity to spatial structure is not reduced significantly.

## 28.5   The Computation of Motion

Many approaches are used for the computation of motion (or, more precisely, the estimation of motion based on image data). Before examining some of these approaches in more detail, it is worthwhile to review the relationship between the motion in a scene and the changes observed in an image of the scene.

### The Motion Field

The motion field [20] is determined by establishing a correspondence between the motion of points in the scene (the real world) and the motion of points in the image plane. This correspondence is found geometrically, and is independent of the brightness patterns in the scene (e.g., the presence or absence of surface textures, changes in luminance, etc.).

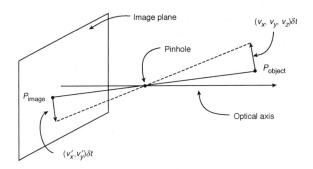

**FIGURE 28.19**  The motion field based on a simple pinhole camera model.

Consider the situation in Fig. 28.19. At a particular instant in time, a point $P_{\text{image}}$ in the image corresponds to some point $P_{\text{object}}$ on the surface of an object. The two points are related via the perspective projection equation. Now, suppose the object point $P_{\text{object}}$ has velocity $(v_x, v_y, v_z)$ relative to the camera. The result is a velocity $(v'_x, v'_y)$ for the point $P_{\text{image}}$ in the image plane. The relationship between the velocities can be found by differentiating the perspective projection equation with respect to time. In this way, a velocity vector can be assigned to each image point, yielding the motion field.

## Optical Flow

Usually, the intensity patterns in the image move as the objects to which they correspond move. Optical flow is the motion of these intensity patterns. Ideally, optical flow and the motion field correspond; but this is not always the case. For a perfectly uniform sphere rotating in front of an imaging system, there is shading over the surface of the sphere (due to the shape of the sphere), but it does not change with time. The optical flow is zero everywhere, while the motion field is not. For a fixed sphere illuminated by a moving light source, the shading changes with time, although the sphere is not in motion. The optical flow is nonzero, while the motion field is zero.

Furthermore, optical flow is not uniquely determined by local information in the changing image. Consider, for example, a region with uniform brightness which does not vary with time. The "most likely" optical flow value is zero, but (as long as there are corresponding points of equal brightness in both images) there are many "correct" flow vectors. What we would like is the motion field, but what we have access to is optical flow. Fortunately, the optical flow is usually not too different from the motion field.

## The Calculation of Optical Flow

Wide variety of approaches are used for the calculation of optical flow. The first, below, is a conceptually simple yet very widely used method. This approach is particularly popular for video compression, and is essentially that used in MPEG-1 and 2.

### Optical Flow by Block Matching

The calculation of optical flow by block-matching is the most commonly used motion estimation technique. The basic approach is as follows. Given two successive images from a sequence, the first image is partitioned into nonoverlapping blocks (e.g., $8 \times 8$ pixels in size, Fig. 28.20(left)). To find the motion vector for each block, the similarity (e.g., via mean-squared error) between the block and the intensities in the neighborhood of that block in the next frame (Fig. 28.20(right)) is calculated. The location that shows the best match is considered the location to which the block has moved. The motion vector for the block is the vector connecting the center of the block in frame $n$ to the location of the best match in frame $n + 1$.

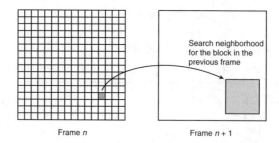

Frame *n*                                    Frame *n* + 1

**FIGURE 28.20**   Motion estimation by block matching.

The approach is simple, but a number of things must be consider. The size of the search neighborhood must be established, which in turn determines the maximum velocity that can be estimated. The search strategy must be decided, including the need to evaluate every potential match location and the precision with which the match locations must be determined (e.g., is each pixel a potential location? Is subpixel accuracy required?). The amount of computation time/power available is a critical factor in these decisions. Even at its simplest, block matching is computationally intensive. If motion estimates must be computed at frame rate (1/30 s) this will have a strong effect on the algorithm design. A detailed discussion of these and related issues can be found in [21].

### Optical Flow via Intensity Gradients

The calculation of optical flow via intensity gradients, as proposed by Horn and Shunck [22], is a classical approach to motion estimation.

Let $f(x, y, t)$ be the intensity at time $t$ for the image point $(x, y)$, and let $r_x(x, y)$ and $r_y(x, y)$ be the $x$ and $y$ components of the optical flow at that point. Then for a small time interval $\delta t$,

$$f(x + \underbrace{r_x \delta t}_{\delta x}, y + \underbrace{r_y \delta t}_{\delta y}, t + \delta t) = f(x, y, t) \tag{28.43}$$

This single equation is not sufficient to determine $r_x$ and $r_y$. It can, however, provide a constraint on the solution. Assuming that intensity varies smoothly with $x$, $y$, and $t$, the left hand side of equation 28.43 can be expanded in a Taylor's series:

$$f(x, y, t) + \delta x \frac{\partial f}{\partial x} + \delta y \frac{\partial f}{\partial y} + \delta t \frac{\partial f}{\partial t} + \text{higher-order terms} = f(x, y, t) \tag{28.44}$$

Ignoring the higher order terms, canceling $f(x, y, t)$, dividing by $\delta t$ and letting $\delta t \rightarrow 0$,

$$\frac{\partial f}{\partial x}\frac{dx}{dt} + \frac{\partial f}{\partial y}\frac{dy}{dt} + \frac{\partial f}{\partial t} = 0 \tag{28.45}$$

or

$$f_x r_x + f_y r_y + f_t = 0 \tag{28.46}$$

where $f_x$, $f_y$, and $f_t$ are estimated from the image sequence.

This equation is called the *optical flow constraint equation*, since it constrains $r_x$ and $r_y$ of the optical flow. The values of $(r_x, r_y)$ which satisfy the constraint equation lie on a straight line in the $(r_x, r_y)$ plane. A local brightness measurement can identify the constraint line, *but not a specific point on the line*. Note that this problem cannot really be *solved* via, e.g., adding an additional constraint. It is a fundamental aspect of the image data. A "true" solution cannot be guaranteed, but a solution can be found.

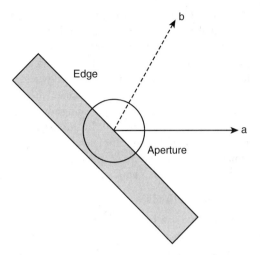

**FIGURE 28.21**   An instance of the aperture problem.

To view this limitation in another way, the constraint equation can be rewritten in vector form, as

$$(f_x, f_y) \cdot (r_x, r_y) = -f_t \tag{28.47}$$

so that the component of optical flow in the direction of the intensity gradient $(f_x, f_y)^T$ is

$$\frac{f_t}{\sqrt{f_x^2 + f_y^2}} \tag{28.48}$$

However, the component of the optical flow perpendicular to the gradient (along isointensity contours) cannot be determined. This is a manifestation of the *aperture problem*. If the motion of an oriented element is detected by a unit that is small compared with the size of the moving element, the only information that can be extracted is the component of motion perpendicular to the local orientation of the element. For example, looking at a moving edge through a small aperture (Fig. 28.21), it is impossible to tell whether the actual motion is in the direction of *a* or of *b*.

One way to work around this limitation is to impose an explicit smoothness constraint. Motion was implicitly assumed smooth earlier, when a Taylor's expansion was used and when the higher order terms were ignored. Following this approach, an iterative scheme for finding the optical flow for the image sequence can be formulated:

$$
\begin{aligned}
r_x(k, l)^{n+1} &= \overline{r_x(k, l)}^n - \frac{\lambda f_x^2 \overline{r_x(k, l)}^n + \lambda f_x f_y \overline{r_y(k, l)}^n + \lambda f_x f_t}{1 + \lambda (f_x^2 + f_y^2)} \\
&= \overline{r_x(k, l)}^n - \lambda f_x \frac{f_x \overline{r_x(k, l)}^n + f_y \overline{r_y(k, l)}^n + f_t}{1 + \lambda (f_x^2 + f_y^2)}
\end{aligned}
\tag{28.49}
$$

and

$$
r_y(k, l)^{n+1} = \overline{r_y(k, l)}^n - \lambda f_y \frac{f_x \overline{r_x(k, l)}^n + f_y \overline{r_y(k, l)}^n + f_t}{1 + \lambda (f_x^2 + f_y^2)}
\tag{28.50}
$$

where the superscripts $n$ and $n + 1$ indicate the iteration number, $\lambda$ is a parameter allowing a tradeoff between smoothness and errors in the flow constraint equation, and $\bar{r}_x(k, l)$ and $\bar{r}_y(k, l)$ are local averages of $r_x$ and $r_y$. The updated estimates are thus the average of the surrounding values, minus an adjustment (which in velocity space is in the direction of the intensity gradient).

The previous discussion relied heavily on smoothness of the flow field. However, there are places in image sequences where discontinuities *should* occur. In particular, the boundaries of moving objects should exhibit discontinuities in optical flow. One approach taking advantage of smoothness but allowing discontinuities is to apply segmentation to the flow field. In this way, the boundaries between regions with smooth optical flow can be found, and the algorithm can be prevented from smoothing over these boundaries. Because of the "chicken-and-egg" nature of this method (a good segmentation depends on a good optical flow estimate, which depends on a good segmentation ...), it is best applied iteratively.

## Spatiotemporal-Frequency-Based Methods

It was shown in section 28.2 that motion can be considered in the frequency domain, as well as in the spatial domain. A number of motion estimation methods have been developed with this in mind. If the sequence to be analyzed is very simple (has only a single motion component, for example) or if motion detection alone is required, the Fourier transform can be used as the basis for motion analysis, as examined in [23–25]; however, due to the global nature of the Fourier transform, it cannot be used to determine the location of the object in motion. It is also poorly suited for cases in which multiple motions exist (i.e., when the scene of interest consists of more than one object moving independently), since the signatures of the different motions are difficult (impossible, in general) to separate in the Fourier domain. As a result, although Fourier analysis can be used to illustrate some interesting phenomena, it cannot be used as the basis of motion analysis methods for the majority of sequences of practical interest.

To identify the locations and motions of objects, frequency analysis localized to the neighborhoods of the objects is required. Windowed Fourier analysis has been proposed for such cases [26], but the accuracy of a motion analysis method of this type is highly dependent on the resolution of the underlying transform, in both the spatiotemporal and spatiotemporal-frequency domains. It is known that the windowed Fourier transform does not perform particularly well in this regard. Filterbank-based approaches to this problem have also been proposed, as in [27]. The methods examined below each exploit the frequency domain characteristics of motion, and provide spatiotemporally localized motion estimates.

### Optical Flow via the 3-D Wigner Distribution

Jacobson and Wechsler [28] proposed an approach to spatiotemporal-frequency, based derivation of optical flow using the 3-D Wigner distribution (WD). Extending the 2-D definition given earlier, the 3-D WD can be written as

$$W_f(x, y, t, \xi_x, \xi_y, \xi_t) = \int_{-\infty}^{\infty} \int_{-\infty}^{\infty} \int_{-\infty}^{\infty} f\left(x + \frac{\alpha}{2}, y + \frac{\beta}{2}, t + \frac{\tau}{2}\right) \cdot f^*\left(x - \frac{\alpha}{2}, y - \frac{\beta}{2}, t - \frac{\tau}{2}\right)$$
$$\times e^{-j2\pi(\alpha\xi_x + \beta\xi_y + \tau\xi_t)} \, d\alpha \, d\beta \, d\tau \tag{28.51}$$

It can be shown that the WD of a linearly translating image with velocity $\vec{r} = (r_x, r_y)$ is

$$W_f(x, y, t, \xi_x, \xi_y, \xi_t) = \delta(r_x\xi_x + r_y\xi_y + \xi_t) \cdot W_f(x - r_x t, y - r_y t, \xi_x, \xi_y) \tag{28.52}$$

which is nonzero only when $r_x\xi_x + r_y\xi_y + \xi_t = 0$.

For a linearly translating image, then, the local spectra $W_{f_{x,y,t}}(\xi_x, \xi_y, \xi_t)$ contain energy only in a plane (as in the Fourier case) the slope of which is determined by the velocity. Jacobson and Wechsler proposed to find this plane by integrating over the possible planar regions in these local spectra (via a so-called "velocity polling function"), using the plane of maximum energy to determine the velocity.

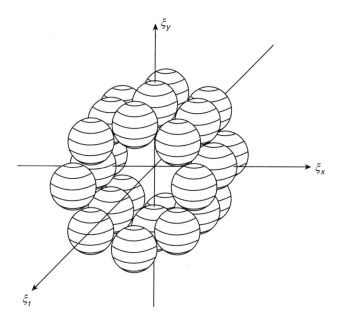

**FIGURE 28.22** The (stylized) power spectra of a set of 3-D Gabor filters.

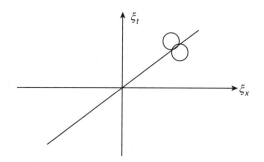

**FIGURE 28.23** Velocity estimation in the frequency domain via estimation of the slope of the spectrum.

### *Optical Flow Using 3-D Gabor Filters*

Heeger [29] proposed the use of 3-D Gabor filters to determine this slope. Following the definition discussed for 2-D, a 3-D Gabor filter has the impulse response

$$g(x, y, t) = \hat{g}(x, y, t)e^{j2\pi[\xi_{x_0}(x - x_0) + \xi_{y_0}(y - y_0) + \xi_{t_0}(t - t_0)]} \tag{28.53}$$

where

$$\hat{g}(x, y, t) = \frac{1}{(2\pi)^{3/2}\sigma_x\sigma_y\sigma_t}e^{-\frac{1}{2}\left[\left(\frac{x - x_0}{\sigma_x}\right)^2 + \left(\frac{y - y_0}{\sigma_y}\right)^2 + \left(\frac{t - t_0}{\sigma_t}\right)^2\right]} \tag{28.54}$$

To detect motion in different directions, a family of these filters is defined, as shown in Fig. 28.22.

In order to capture velocities at different scales (high velocities can be thought of as occurring over large scales, because a large distance is covered per unit time), these filters are applied to a Gaussian pyramidal decomposition of the sequence. Given the energies of the outputs of these filters, which can be thought of as sampling spatiotemporal/spatiotemporal-frequency space, the problem is analogous to that shown in Fig. 28.23. The slope of the line (corresponding to the slope of the plane which characterizes motion) must be found via a finite set of observations. In this method, this problem is solved under the assumption of a random texture input (the plane in the frequency domain consists of a single constant value).

### Optical Flow via the 3-D Gabor Transform

One shortcoming of a filterbank approach (if the filters are not orthogonal or do not provide a complete basis) is the possibility of loss. Using the 3-D Gabor functions as the basis of a transform resolves this problem. A sequence of dimension $N \times M \times P$ can then be expressed at each discrete point $(x_m, y_n, t_p)$ as

$$f(x_m, y_n, t_p) = \sum_{j=0}^{J-1}\sum_{k=0}^{K-1}\sum_{l=0}^{L-1}\sum_{q=0}^{Q-1}\sum_{r=0}^{R-1}\sum_{s=0}^{S-1} c_{x_q,y_r,t_s,\xi_{x_j},\xi_{y_k},\xi_{t_l}} \cdot g_{x_q,y_r,t_s,\xi_{x_j},\xi_{y_k},\xi_{t_l}}(x_m, y_n, t_p) \tag{28.55}$$

where $J \cdot K \cdot L \cdot Q \cdot R \cdot S = N \cdot M \cdot P$ for completeness, the functions $g_{x_q,y_r,t_s,\xi_{x_j},\xi_{y_k},\xi_{t_l}}(x_m, y_n, t_p)$ denote the Gabor basis functions with spatiotemporal and spatiotemporal-frequency centers of $(x_q, y_r, t_s)$ and $(\xi_{x_j}, \xi_{y_k}, \xi_{t_l})$ respectively, and $c_{x_q,y_r,t_s,\xi_{x_j},\xi_{y_k},\xi_{t_l}}$ are the associated coefficients. Note that these coefficients are not found by convolving with the Gabor functions, since the functions are not orthogonal. See [30] for a survey and comparison of methods for computing this transform.

In the case of uniform translational motion, the slope of the planar spectrum is sought, yielding the optical flow vector $\vec{r}$. A straightforward approach to estimating the slope of the local spectra [31,32] is to form vectors of the $\xi_x$, $\xi_y$, and $\xi_t$ coordinates of the basis functions that have significant energy for each point in the sequence at which basis functions are centered. From equation 20, the optical flow vector and the coordinate vectors $\vec{\xi}_x$, $\vec{\xi}_y$, and $\vec{\xi}_t$ at each point are related as

$$\vec{\xi}_t = -(r_x\vec{\xi}_x + r_y\vec{\xi}_y) = -\mathbf{S}\vec{r} \tag{28.56}$$

where $\mathbf{S} = (\vec{\xi}_x | \vec{\xi}_y)$. An LMS estimate of the optical flow vector at a given point can then be found using the pseudo inverse of $\mathbf{S}$:

$$\vec{r}_{\text{est}} = -(\mathbf{S}^T\mathbf{S})^{-1}\mathbf{S}^T\vec{\xi}_t \tag{28.57}$$

In addition to providing a means for motion estimation, this approach has also proven useful in predicting the apparent motion reversal associated with temporal aliasing [33].

### Wavelet-Based Methods

A number of wavelet-based approaches to this problem have also been proposed. In [34–37], 2-D wavelet decompositions are applied frame-by-frame to produce multi-scale feature images. This view of motion analysis exploits the multiscale properties of wavelets, but does not seek to exploit the frequency domain properties of motion. In [38], a spatiotemporal (3-D) wavelet decomposition is employed, so that some of these frequency domain aspects can be utilized. Leduc et al. explore the estimation of translational, accelerated, and rotational motion via spatiotemporal wavelets in [39–44]. Decompositions designed and parameterized specifically for the motion of interest (e.g., rotational motion) are tuned to the motion to be estimated.

## 28.6  Image Sequence Compression

Image sequences represent an enormous amount of data (e.g., a 2-hour movie at the US HDTV resolution of $1280 \times 720$ pixels, 60 frames/second progressive, with 24 bits/pixel results in 1194 Gbytes of data). This data is highly redundant, and much of it has minimal perceptual relevance. One approach to reducing this volume of data is to apply still image compression to each frame in the sequence (generally referred to as intraframe coding). For example, the JPEG still image compression algorithm can be applied frame by frame (sometimes referred to as Motion-JPEG or M-JPEG). This method, however, does not take advantage of the substantial correlation, which typically exists between frames in a sequence. Compression techniques which seek to exploit this temporal redundancy are referred to as interframe coding methods.

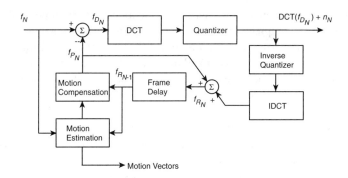

**FIGURE 28.24**   A hybrid (predictive/transform) encoder.

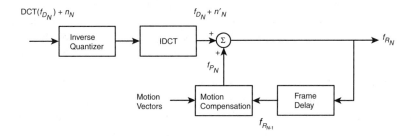

**FIGURE 28.25**   A predictive/transform decoder.

## Motion Compensated Prediction/Transform Coders

Predictive coding is based on the idea that to the degree that all or part of a frame in a sequence can be predicted, that information need not be transmitted. As a result, it is usually the case that the better the prediction, the better the compression that can be achieved. The simplest possible predicator is to assume that successive frames are identical (differential coding); however, the optical flow, which indicates the motion of intensity patterns in the image sequence, can be used to improve the predictor. *Motion compensated prediction* uses optical flow information, together with a reconstruction of the previous frame, to predict the content of the current frame.

Quantization (and the attendant loss of information) is inherent to lossy compression techniques. This loss, if introduced strategically, can be exploited to produce a highly compressed sequence, with good visual quality. Transforms (e.g., the DCT), followed by quantization, provide a convenient mechanism to introduce (and control) this loss. Following this approach, a hybrid (motion compensated prediction/transform) encoder and decoder are shown in Figs. 28.24 and 28.25. This hybrid algorithm (with the addition of entropy coders and decoders) is the essence of the H.261, MPEG-1, MPEG-2, and US HDTV compression methods [45].

## Perceptually Based Methods

Although algorithms such as MPEG exploit the properties of visual perception (principally in the formulation of quantization matrices), it is not especially central to the structure of the algorithm. There is, for example, no explicit model of vision underlying the MPEG-1 and 2 algorithms. In perceptually-based (sometimes called second generation) methods, knowledge of the HVS takes a much more central role. This view of the problem is particularly effective (and necessary) when designing compression algorithms intended to operate at very high compression ratios (e.g., over 200:1).

The methods in this subsection are inspired by specific models of visual perception. The first is an approach based on a very comprehensive vision model, performing spatial and temporal frequency decomposition via filters designed to reflect properties of the HVS. The second and third are techniques using visually relevant transforms (the Gabor and derivative of Gaussian transforms, respectively) in an otherwise conventional hybrid (predictive/transform) framework. Finally, a method based on spatiotemporal segmentation (following the contour/texture model of vision) will be discussed.

### The Perceptual Components Architecture

The perceptual components architecture [46] is a framework for the compression of color image sequences based on the processing thought to take place in the early HVS. It consists of the following steps. The input RGB image sequence is converted into an opponent color space (white/black (WB), red/green (RG), and blue/yellow (BY)). The sequence is filtered spatially with a set of frequency and orientation selective filters, inspired by the frequency and orientation selectivity of the HVS. Filters based on the temporal frequency response of the visual system are applied along the temporal dimension. The filtered sequences are then subsampled using a hexagonal grid, and subsampled by a factor of two in the temporal dimension. Uniform quantization is applied within each subband, with higher frequency subbands quantized more coarsely. The WB (luminance) component is quantized less coarsely overall than the RG and BY (chrominance) components. The first-order entropy of the result provides an estimate of the compression ratio.

Note that there is no prediction or motion compensation. This is a 3-D subband coder, where temporal redundancy is exploited via the temporal filters. For a 256 × 256, 8 frame segment of the "football" sequence (a widely used test sequence depicting a play from an American football game), acceptable image quality was achieved for about 1 bit/pixel (from 24 bits/pixel). Although this is not very high compression, the sequence used is more challenging than most. Another contributing factor is that the subsampled representation is 8/3 the size (in terms of bits) of the original, which must be overcome before any compression is realized.

### Very-Low-Bit-Rate Coding Using the Gabor Transform

In discussing the Gabor transform previously, it was stated that the basis functions of this transform are optimally (jointly) local. In the context of coding, there are three mechanisms that can be exploited to achieve compression, all of which depend on locality: the local correlation between pixels in the sequence; the bounded frequency response of the human visual system (as characterized by the CSF); and visual masking (the decrease in visual sensitivity near spatial and temporal discontinuities). To take advantage of local spatial correlation, the image representation upon which a compression method is based must be spatially local (which is why images are partitioned into blocks in JPEG, MPEG-1&2, H.261, etc.). If the CSF is to be exploited (e.g., by quantizing high frequency coefficients coarsely) localization in the spatial-frequency domain is required. To exploit visual masking, spatial locality (of a fairly high degree) is required.

The Gabor transform is inherently local in space, so the partitioning of the image into blocks is not required (hence no blocking artifacts are observed at high compression ratios). Its spatial locality also provides a mechanism for exploiting visual masking, while its spatial-frequency locality allows the bandlimited nature of the HVS to be utilized.

An encoder and decoder based on this transform are shown in Figs. 28.26 and 28.27 [47]. Note that they are in the classic hybrid (predictive/transform) form. This codec does not include motion compensation, and is for monochrome image sequences.

Applying this method to a 128-by-128, 8 bit/pixel version of the Miss America sequence resulted in reasonable image quality at a compression ratio of approximately 335:1.[2] At 24 frames per second, the associated bit rate is 9.4 kbits/s (a bitrate consistent, e.g., with wireless videotelephony).

---

[2]Not including the initial frame, which is intracoded to 9.1 kbits (a compression ratio of 14).

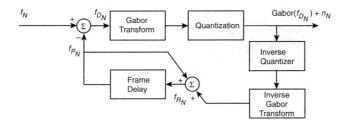

**FIGURE 28.26** A Gabor transform-based video encoder.

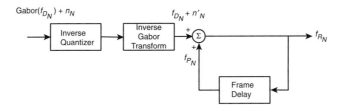

**FIGURE 28.27** The associated Gabor transform-based decoder.

## Video Coding Using the Derivative of Gaussian Transform

As mentioned previously, the derivative of Gaussian transform (DGT) has properties similar to the Gabor transform, but with the practical advantage that it is real-valued. This makes it particularly well-suited to video compression. In [48] the hybrid codec structure shown in Figs. 28.24 and 28.25 is adapted to the DGT, replacing the DCT (and IDCT), and adapting the quantization scheme to fit the visibility of the DGT basis, via a simple quantization mask.

Comparable results to those of the standard H.261 (DCT-based) codec are obtained for bitrates around 320 kbits/s (5 channels in the p*64 model).

## Object-Based Coding by Split and Merge Segmentation

Object-based coding reflects the fact that scenes are largely composed of distinct objects, and that these objects are perceived as boundaries surrounding fields of shading or texture (the contour/texture theory of vision). Encoding an image or sequence in this way requires segmentation to identify the constituent objects. This view of compression, which also facilitates interaction and editing, underlies the MPEG-4 video compression standard [49]. Although the method that will be described is different in detail from MPEG-4, as one of the earliest documented object-based systems, it illustrates many important aspects of such systems.

In this approach [50], 3-D (spatiotemporal) segmentation is used to reduce the redundant information in a sequence (essentially identifying objects within the sequence), while retaining information critical to the human observer. The sequence is treated as a single 3-D data volume, the voxels of which are grouped into regions via split and merge. The uniformity criterion used for the segmentation is the goodness-of-fit to a 3-D polynomial. The sequence is then encoded in terms of region boundaries (a binary tree structure) and region interior intensities (the coefficients of the 3-D polynomial).

The data volume is first split such that each region is a parallelepiped over which the gray level variation can be approximated within a specified mean squared error (Fig. 28.28). Regions are split by quadrants, following the octree strategy. A region adjacency graph is constructed, with nodes corresponding to each region and links between the nodes assigned a cost indicating the similarity of the regions. A high cost indicates low similarity. Regions are merged, starting with regions with the lowest cost, and the region adjacency graph is updated. The resulting regions are represented using a pyramidal (binary tree) structure, with the regions labeled so that adjacent regions have different labels.

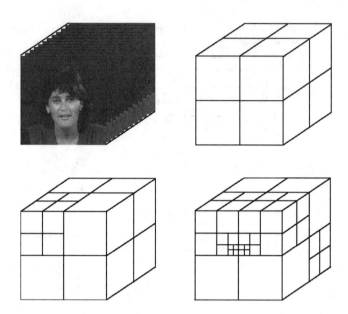

**FIGURE 28.28**   The split phase.

Using 16 frames from the "Secretary" sequence, the compression ratio achieved was 158:1 (a bitrate of 83 kbits/s). A total of 5740 parallelepipeds (1000 regions) were used.

## 28.7   Conclusions

In this chapter, some of the fundamental aspects and algorithms in the processing of digital video were examined. Continued improvements in computing performance make many methods that previously required specialized platforms (or were primarily of research interest due to computational requirements) practical. In addition to bringing high-end applications to the desktop, numerous new applications are thus enabled, in areas as diverse as medical imaging, entertainment, and human-computer interaction.

### References

1. John Wyver. *The Moving Image—An International Histoy of Film, Television and Video.* BFI Publishing, London, 1989.
2. A. B. Watson and A. J. Ahumada. A look at motion in the frequency domain. In *SIGGRAPH/ SIGART Interdisciplinary Workshop MOTION: Representation and Perception,* pp. 1–10, Toronto, Canada, April 4–6, 1983.
3. A. T. Smith and R. J. Snowden, editors. *Visual Detection of Motion.* Academic Press, San Diego, CA, 1994.
4. K. Nakayama. Biological image motion processing: a review. *Vision Research,* 25(5):625–660, 1985.
5. A. B. Watson and A. J. Ahumada. Model of human visual-motion sensing. *Journal of the Optical Society of America A,* 2(2), February 1985.
6. L. B. Stelmach, W. J. Tam, and P. Hearty. Static and dynamic spatial resolution in image coding: an investigation of eye movements. In *Proc. SPIE/SPSE Symp. on Electronic Imaging Science and Technology,* San Jose, CA, 1995.
7. T. R. Reed. Local frequency representations for image sequence processing and coding. In A. B. Watson, editor, *Digital Images and Human Vision.* MIT Press, Cambridge, MA, 1993.
8. L. Cohen. *Time-Frequency Analysis.* Prentice-Hall, Englewood Cliffs, NJ, 1995.

9. R. Tolimieri and M. An. *Time-Frequency Representations*. Birkhäuser, Boston, MA, 1998.

10. D. Gabor. Theory of communication. *Proceedings of the Institute of Electrical Engineers*, 93(26): 429–457, 1946.

11. J. G. Daugman. Complete discrete 2-D Gabor transforms by neural networks for image analysis and compression. *IEEE Transactions on Acoustics, Speech and Signal Processing*, 36(7):1169–1179, July 1988.

12. H. G. Feichtinger and T. Strohmer, editors. *Gabor Analysis and Algorithms*. Birkhäuser, Boston, MA, 1998.

13. R. A. Young. The Gaussian derivative model for spatial vision: I. Retinal mechanisms. *Spatial Vision*, 2:273–293, 1987.

14. R. A. Young. Oh say can you see? The physiology of vision. In *Proc. SPIE-Human Vision, Visual Processing, and Digital Display II*, vol. 1453, pp. 92–123, 1991.

15. J. A. Bloom and T. R. Reed. A Gaussian derivative-based transform. *IEEE Transactions on Image Processing*, 5(3):551–553, March 1996.

16. E. Wigner. On the quantum correction for thermodynamic equilibrium. *Physical Review*, 40:749–759, June 1932.

17. M. Vetterli and J. Kovačvic. *Wavelets and Subband Coding*. Prentice-Hall, Englewood Cliffs, NJ, 1995.

18. G. Strang and T. Nguyen. *Wavelets and Filter Banks*. Wellesley-Cambridge Press, Wellesley, MA, 1996.

19. S. Mallat. *A Wavelet Tour of Signal Processing*. Academic Press, San Diego, CA, 1998.

20. B. K. P. Horn. *Robot Vision*. MIT Press, Cambridge, MA, 1986.

21. G. Tziritas and C. Labit. *Motion Analysis for Image Sequence Coding*. Elsevier, Amsterdam, 1994.

22. B. K. P. Horn and B. G. Shunck. Determining optical flow. *Artificial Intelligence*, 17(1–3):185–203, 1981.

23. H. Gafni and Y. Y. Zeevi. A model for separation of spatial and temporal information in the visual system. *Biological Cybernetics*, 28:73–82, 1977.

24. A. Kojima, N. Sakurai, and J. Kishigami. Motion detection using 3D-FFT spectrum. In *Proc. IEEE Int. Conf. on Acoustics, Speech and Signal Processing*, vol. V, pp. 213–216, Minneapolis, Minnesota, April 27–30, 1993.

25. B. Porat and B. Friedlander. A frequency domain algorithm for multiframe detection and estimation of dim targets. *IEEE Transactions on Pattern Analysis and Machine Intelligence*, 12(4):398–401, 1990.

26. H. Gafni and Y. Y. Zeevi. A model for processing of movement in the visual system. *Biological Cybernetics*, 32:165–173, 1979.

27. D. J. Fleet and A. D. Jepson. Computation of component image velocity from local phase information. *International Journal of Computer Vision*, 5(1):77–104, 1990.

28. L. Jacobson and H. Wechsler. Derivation of optical flow using a spatiotemporal-frequency approach. *Computer Vision, Graphics, and Image Processing*, 38:29–65, 1987.

29. D. J. Heeger. Optical flow using spatiotemporal filters. *International Journal of Computer Vision*, pp. 279–302, 1988.

30. T. T. Chinen and T. R. Reed. A performance analysis of fast Gabor transforms. *Graphical Models and Image Processing*, 59(3):117–127, May 1997.

31. T. R. Reed. The analysis of motion in natural scenes using a spatiotemporal/spatiotemporal-frequency representation. In *Proc. IEEE Int. Conf. on Image Processing*, pp. I-93–I-96, Santa Barbara, California, October 26–29, 1997.

32. T. R. Reed. On the computation of optical flow using the 3-D Gabor transform. *Multidimensional Systems and Signal Processing*, 9(4):115–120, 1998.

33. T. R. Reed. A spatiotemporal/spatiotemporal-frequency interpretation of apparent motion reversal. In *Proc. Sixteenth Int. Joint Conf. on Artificial Intelligence*, vol. 2, pp. 1140–1145, Stockholm, Sweden, July 31–August 6, 1999.

34. J. Magarey and N. Kingsbury. Motion estimation using a complex-valued wavelet transform. *IEEE Transactions on Signal Processing*, 46(4):1069–1084, April 1998.

35. Y.-T. Wu, T. Kanade, J. Cohn, and C.-C. Li. Optical flow estimation using wavelet motion model. In *Proc. IEEE Int. Conf. on Computer Vision,* pp. 992–998, Bombay, India, January 4–7, 1998.

36. G. Van der Auwera, A. Munteanu, G. Lafruit, and J. Cornelis. Video coding based on motion estimation in the wavelet detail image. In *Proc. IEEE Int. Conf. on Acoustics, Speech and Signal Processing,* vol. 5, pp. 2801–2804, Seattle, WA, May 12–15, 1998.

37. C. P. Bernard. Discrete wavelet analysis: a new framework for fast optic flow computation. In *Proc. 5th European Conf. on Computer Vision,* vol. 2, pp. 354–368, Freiburg, Germany, June 2–6, 1998.

38. T. J. Burns, S. K. Rogers, M. E. Oxley, and D. W. Ruck. Discrete, spatiotemporal, wavelet multi-resolution analysis method for computing optical flow. *Optical Engineering,* 33(7):2236–2247, 1994.

39. J.-P. Leduc. Spatio-temporal wavelet transforms for digital signal analysis. *Signal Processing,* 60(1): 23–41, July 1997.

40. J.-P. Leduc, J. Corbett, M. Kong, V. Wickerhauser, and B. Ghosh. Accelerated spatio-temporal wavelet transforms: an iterative trajectory estimation. In *Proc. IEEE Int. Conf. on Acoustics, Speech and Signal Processing,* vol. 5, pp. 2781–2784, Seattle, WA, May 12–15, 1998.

41. J.-P. Leduc, J. R. Corbett, and M. V. Wickerhauser. Rotational wavelet transforms for motion analysis, estimation and tracking. In *Proc. IEEE Int. Conf. on Image Processing,* vol. 2, pp. 195–199, Chicago, IL, October 4–7, 1998.

42. J.-P. Leduc and J. R. Corbett. Spatio-temporal continuous wavelets for the analysis of motion on manifolds. In *Proc. IEEE-SP Int. Symp. on Time-Frequency and Time-Scale Analysis,* pp. 57–60, Pittsburgh, PA, October 6–9, 1998.

43. M. Kong, J.-P. Leduc, B. K. Ghosh, J. Corbett, and V. M. Wickerhauser. Wavelet-based analysis of rotational motion in digital image sequences. In *Proc. IEEE Int. Conf. on Acoustics, Speech and Signal Processing,* vol. 5, pp. 2777–2780, Seattle, WA, May 12–15, 1998.

44. J. Corbett, J.-P. Leduc, and M. Kong. Analysis of deformational transformations with spatio-temporal continuous wavelet transforms. In *Proc. IEEE Int. Conf. on Acoustics, Speech and Signal Processing,* vol. 6, pp. 3189–3192, Phoenix, AZ, March 15–19, 1999.

45. A. N. Netravali and B. G. Haskell. *Digital Pictures—Representation, Compression, and Standards.* Plenum Press, New York, 1995.

46. A. B. Watson and C. L. M. Tiana. Color motion video coded by perceptual components. In *SID '92 Digest of Technical Papers,* vol. XXIII, pp. 314–317, 1992.

47. T. R. Reed and A. E. Soohoo. Very-low-bit-rate coding of image sequences using the Gabor transform. *Journal of the Society for Information Display,* 3(2), September 1995.

48. J. A. Bloom and T. R. Reed. On the compression of video using the derivative of Gaussian transform. In *Proc. Thirty Second Annual Asilomar Conference on Signals, Systems, and Computers,* pp. 865–869, Pacific Grove, California, November 1–4, 1998.

49. R. Koenen, editor. *MPEG-4 Overview.* ISO/IEC JTC1/SC29/WG11 N3747, La Baule, October 2000.

50. P. Willemin, T. R. Reed, and M. Kunt. Image sequence coding by split and merge. *IEEE Transactions on Communications,* 39(12), December 1991.

# 29

# Low-Power Digital Signal Processing

Thucydides Xanthopoulos
*Caveo Networks Inc.*

## 29.1   Introduction

During the last few years, signal processing integrated circuits (programmable or not) have become primary experimentation grounds for low power digital design techniques. There have been two main motivating factors for this design trend. The first (and most significant) is the abundant proliferation and market penetration of cellular phones. During the first phase in the life cycle of cellular systems, programmable digital signal processings (DSPs) were used to implement the voice coding component. As DSPs became more powerful and flexible, they took over most of the baseband tasks within a cellular handset such as channel coding (convolutional coding and decoding), encryption/decryption, and demodulation/equalization [1]. Consumer preferences placed significant importance on handset size and battery life and this in turn created pressure in the design community to produce higher performance and lower power signal processors. The second motivating factor is the introduction of a new breed of consumer electronic devices such as digital cameras, portable digital video and audio players, wireless-enabled personal digital assistants that require substantial signal processing capability and at the same time are battery-powered and can benefit substantially from reduced energy consumption.

The low-power trends in the signal processing domain will definitely continue in the coming years with the introduction of 3G wireless and the corresponding wideband code-division multiple-access (WCDMA) physical transmission channel, and also with emerging wireless computing platforms such as sensor data processing systems [2].

In this chapter, an overview of commonly used low-power techniques in programmable digital signal processors, as well as embedded DSP subsystems for custom applications, are presented.

## 29.2   Power Dissipation in Digital Circuits

This section provides a brief overview of power dissipation basics to render this document self-contained. Four major sources of power dissipation are used in digital circuits:

- Switching or dynamic power ($P_{sw}$)
- Short-circuit or direct-path power ($P_{sc}$)
- Leakage power ($P_{leak}$)
- Static power ($P_{stat}$)

The total chip power is given by the following Eq. (29.1):

$$P_{total} = P_{sw} + P_{sc} + P_{leak} + P_{stat} \tag{29.1}$$

The switching power dissipation is the dominant component and is due to the charging and discharging of all capacitive nodes in the circuit. It is given by Eq. (29.2):

$$P_{sw} = aCV_{DD}^2 f \tag{29.2}$$

where $a$ is the switching activity ($0 \le a \le 1$), $C$ is the total capacitance of all capacitive nodes in the circuit, $V_{DD}$ is the supply voltage, and $f$ is the clock frequency. In case the internal nodes of the circuit do not experience a full voltage swing from 0 V to $V_{DD}$, Eq. (29.2) is modified as follows:

$$P_{sw} = aCV_{DD}V_{swing} f \tag{29.3}$$

where $V_{swing}$ is the low voltage swing.

Short-circuit power ($P_{sw}$) is dissipated when there is a transient direct path from $V_{DD}$ to ground during switching: During the rising (or falling) transition of static CMOS gates from $V_{TN}$ to $V_{DD} - V_{TP}$ ($V_{DD} - V_{TP}$ to $V_{TN}$) a direct path from $V_{DD}$ to ground exists through a PMOS and NMOS stack that are both in their ON region. If the rise and fall times of the digital circuit are kept well under control (a small fraction of the period), short-circuit power is rarely a design issue. A comprehensive analysis on short-circuit power in static CMOS circuits can be found in [3].

Two main types of leakage power are available. The first is subthreshold leakage and involves finite channel conductance in the NMOS and PMOS OFF regions. The second is reverse bias junction leakage and it involves source and drain-to-substrate PN junction leakage. Figure 29.1 shows the subthreshold and junction leakage components.

The subthreshold current is typically the dominant component of leakage power. Low-voltage process technologies that rely on reduced threshold voltages to maintain performance are especially susceptible to increased subthreshold leakage. Threshold reduction results in large increases in leakage currents as Idsat a percentage of device. Leakage currents can be especially important in low activity embedded DSP systems (i.e., pagers) that are mostly in standby mode. In such cases, system battery life is mainly dependent on Pleak. Techniques for reducing Pleak include the use of multiple $V_T$ devices (MTCMOS) [4] and substrate bias control variable threshold CMOS [5]. Commercial signal processors use such techniques for leakage reduction [6].

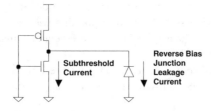

**FIGURE 29.1**   Leakage current components.

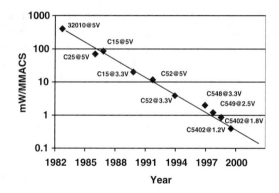

**FIGURE 29.2**    Power dissipation trends in TI DSPs (data reproduced from [1]).

## 29.3   Low-Power Design in Programmable DSPs

Programmable, general-purpose DSPs have experienced substantial reduction in power dissipation over the last 15–20 years. Figure 29.2 (data reproduced from [1]) shows an exponential reduction in power per million multiply-accumulate operations per second (MMACS) for a family of Texas Instruments' (TI) DSPs (TMS320). In this section, we examine several design trends that have contributed to increased power efficiency.

### Voltage Scaling

As shown in Fig. 29.2, the design supply voltage of programmable DSPs has been reduced substantially during the last 15–20 years. DSP performance is mostly driven by the sample data rate on which the processor operates as opposed to pure clock frequency, as is the case in the general-purpose microprocessor world. Adding multiple execution units in parallel to speed up DSP computational kernels with small code dependencies permits designers to reduce the required clock frequencies and in response reduce the supply voltage with important power benefits [7,8]. Voltage scaling may also be implemented without proportional performance degradation if the threshold voltages are scaled accordingly. In such case, techniques such as multiple-threshold CMOS (MTCMOS) are employed [6] to control leakage power. Voltage scaling has a dramatic effect on power efficiency due to the square law dependence on $V_{DD}$ in Eq. (29.2).

### Architectural Power Optimizations

Traditionally, programmable DSP chips have included support for frequently used DSP operations and addressing modes. Such operations include multiple parallel multiply-accumulate operations used to implement efficiently computation kernels such as FIR/IIR filters and linear transformation operations [9]. In the last few years, we have seen programmable DSPs that include native support for Vitterbi decoding [7]. The Vitterbi algorithm [10] is a computationally efficient maximum likelihood estimator for convolutional decoding used in cellular phone and modem applications. Programmable DSPs usually include hardware support for an Add Compare Select (ACS) operation used to eliminate the nonoptimal trellis paths during the decoding process [9]. The (TI) TMS320C54x architecture includes an explicit compare, select and store unit (CSSU), which decouples the path metric computation from the path selection process.

Maximum datapath efficiency and minimum control overhead has become of paramount importance in DSPs because of reduced power dissipation in addition to performance benefits [11]. Increased datapath parallelism can allow the DSP designer to reduce the clock frequency and power supply for additional power benefits. Efficient hardwired instructions can reduce control overhead and minimize communication among functional units thus reducing switched capacitance in Eq. (29.2).

General-purpose DSPs typically include instructions that place them in multiple levels of standby modes [6]. As an example, a DSP processor can be in full operational mode, in level 2 standby mode (computational units powered down, peripheral circuits and PLL on), in level 1 standby mode (only PLL on) or in sleep mode (everything including PLL is powered down except for a small sleep circuit capable of ramping up the PLL and powering on the rest of the units). Digital PLL designs help in the implementation of multiple idle states because they facilitate fast PLL frequency ramping sequences and fast switching between various standby modes. Depending on the application, such software-induced standby modes can provide substantial power savings.

DSP algorithms usually involve the repetitive execution of a small set of instructions (kernel). Most programmable DSPs include hardware support for tight loops. A standard software loop implementation requires the maintenance and update of a loop index, a compare instruction, and a conditional branch to the beginning of the loop. The loop overhead can easily slow down a DSP kernel by a substantial factor. DSPs include hardware support for both single and multiple instruction loops (i.e., REPEAT instruction) [11]. A single instruction loop repeats a single instruction multiple times without maintaining a loop index and by fetching it only once from memory. A multiple instruction loop on the other hand must repeatedly fetch the instructions from memory each time the processor executes the loop. Hiraki et al. [12] have proposed an interesting low power optimization for multiple instruction loops that has wide applicability in programmable DSPs. A small decoded instruction buffer (DIB) is provided that stores decoded instructions during the first iteration into the loop. Subsequent iterations do not engage the instruction memory and decode unit, but fetch the decoded instructions from the DIB. Case studies have indicated 40% power savings when a DIB is implemented in a DSP for certain multimedia applications.

Recently, the Berkeley Pleiades project [13] has introduced a 1-V heterogeneous reconfigurable DSP targeted to wireless baseband processing. The architecture consists of multiple "satellite" arithmetic processors, on-chip FPGA sections, on-chip memory banks, address generators, and an embedded ARM core. All these heterogeneous units are interconnected with a hierarchical reconfigurable network. The ARM core is responsible for the online reconfiguration through a dedicated bus. According to the Pleiades computation model, the embedded microprocessor core executes the high-level control and spawns arithmetic-intensive DSP kernels to the satellites. The flow of control is returned to the ARM core when all the satellite operations have completed. Run-time reconfiguration makes such an architecture very power-efficient compared to conventional programmable DSPs. A Pleiades silicon implementation is reported to implement baseband wireless functions at 10–100 MOPS/mW.

## Circuit Power Optimizations

Most of the DSPs available in the market today include some form of fine-grain, clock-gating mechanism for power reduction. DSPs are very well suited for clock-gating because of the regular datapath structure and the small control structures (which typically cannot employ fine-grain gated clocks). A typical datapath pipeline stage employing clock-gating is shown in Fig. 29.3. Signals EN0 and EN1 are the stage clock enables that are latched 180° ahead of time and computed by the control section. A master clock is distributed to the gating clock drivers, which are typically amortized across the entire datapath width of the pipeline. Clock-gating not only saves clock and flip-flop power, but also prevents the combinational logic between pipeline stages from switching. The main down side of clock-gating is that it can present some difficulties in static timing closure because of increased uncertainty during the calculation of setup and hold time constraints. Clock-gating reduces the switching activity factor *a* in Eq. (29.2).

On-chip memory blocks (SRAMs and ROMs) are typically optimized for low power: Memory blocks are partitioned in multiple banks so that a small fraction of the total memory array is activated during a memory access [6,8]. Moreover, address bits are typically allocated in such a fashion among row decoders and column decoders such that sequential memory accesses do not activate the row decoders during each cycle [8].

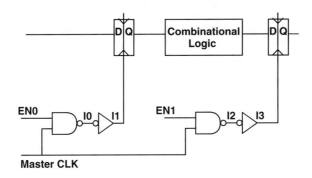

**FIGURE 29.3** Clock-gating.

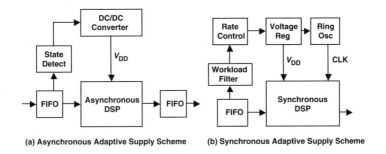

**FIGURE 29.4** Adaptive supply voltage schemes.

# 29.4  Low-Power Design in Application-Specific DSPs

Low-power design approaches in application-specific DSPs exhibit more breadth and innovation due to the fact that such designs target a well defined problem as opposed to a wide range of possible applications. Classification of such design techniques can by no means be complete due to continuous novelties in circuit and system designs improving DSP system power performance. In this section, technology and low-level circuit issues are not addressed because they were briefly addressed earlier and are also relevant to general-purpose DSP systems. Instead, the focus is on unique application-specific power reduction techniques that have been reported in the literature during the last few years.

## Variable Supply Voltage Schemes

Embedded adaptive supply scaling has been the focus of multiple investigators due to the potential for substantial power savings in both fixed and variable throughput systems.

Nielsen et al. [14] have demonstrated a self-timed adaptive supply voltage system that takes advantage of variable computational loads (Fig. 29.4(a)). The self-timed system operates in a synchronous environment and is enclosed between rate-matching FIFO buffers. The state detecting circuit monitors the state of the input FIFO, which is an indicator of remaining workload. If the buffer is relatively full, the supply voltage is increased and the circuit operates faster to keep up with the load. If the FIFO is relatively empty the supply voltage is reduced because the circuit operates too fast. In this way, the supply voltage is optimally adjusted to the actual workloads maintaining the throughput requirements at all times. Wei and Horowitz [15] have investigated techniques for low-power switching supplies for similar applications.

Gutnik [16] has demonstrated a synchronous implementation of a variable supply voltage scheme that uses FIFO state to generate both a supply voltage and a corresponding variable clock using a closed-loop ring oscillator (Fig. 29.4(b)). As the FIFO fills up the clock speed increases to sustain the higher workload and as the FIFO empties the clock slows and the supply voltage decreases for quadratic power reduction.

Power savings are higher than simple clock gating mechanisms due to the square law dependence of power dissipation on supply voltage. Buffering and workload averaging makes this scheme applicable to fixed throughput but variable algorithmic load applications (i.e., video compression/decompression and digital communication applications).

Goodman and Dancy [17] have demonstrated a low power encryption processor with an embedded high-efficiency DC-DC converter that takes advantage of the time-varying data rates found in wireless encryption applications. Power reduction varying from 1× up to 5.33× has been reported depending on data throughput variations.

## Nonstandard Arithmetic Structures

Fixed-function DSP VLSI implementations (i.e., digital filters with constant coefficients, frequency domain data transformations such as FFT and DCT) can benefit a lot from hardwired arithmetic structures, different from standard multipliers and adders. One such important structure is the distributed arithmetic (DA) implementation, which has found many applications in past chips [18,19].

DA [20,21] is a bit-serial operation that computes the inner product of two vectors (one of which is a constant) in parallel. In the DSP domain, this operation finds applications in FIR computations, linear transform computation, and any other DSP kernel which involves dot products. Its main advantage is the efficiency of mechanization and the fact that no multiplications are necessary. DA has an inherent bit serial nature but this additional latency can be hidden if the number of bits in each variable vector element is equal or similar to the number of elements in each vector. In other words, DA is very efficient in computing long dot products of relatively low precision numbers.

As an example of DA mechanization let us consider the computation of the following inner product of $M$-dimensional vectors $\mathbf{a}$ and $\mathbf{x}$ where $\mathbf{a}$ is a constant vector:

$$y = \sum_{k=0}^{M-1} a_k x_k \tag{29.4}$$

Let us further assume that each vector element $x_k$ is an $N$-bit 2's complement binary number and can be represented as

$$x_k = -b_{k(N-1)} 2^{N-1} + \sum_{n=0}^{N-2} b_{kn} 2^n \tag{29.5}$$

where $b_{ki} \in \{0, 1\}$ is the $i$th bit of vector element $x_k$. Note that $b_{k0}$ is the least significant bit (LSB) of $x_k$ and $b_{k(N-1)}$ is the sign bit.

Substituting Eq. (29.5) in Eq. (29.4) yields (after interchanging the double summation order):

$$y = -\sum_{k=0}^{M-1} a_k b_{k(N-1)} 2^{N-1} + \sum_{n=0}^{N-2} \left[ \sum_{k=0}^{M-1} a_k b_{kn} \right] 2^n \tag{29.6}$$

Let us consider the term in brackets:

$$q_n = \sum_{k=0}^{M-1} a_k b_{kn} \tag{29.7}$$

Because $b_{kn} \in \{0, 1\}$, $q_n$ has only $2^M$ possible values. Such values can be precomputed and stored in a ROM of size $2^M$. The bit serial input data ($\{b_{0i}, b_{1i}, \ldots, b_{ki}\}$ for $i = 0, 1, \ldots, N-1$) is used to form the ROM address, and the ROM contents can be successively added in an accumulation structure to form the outer sum of Eq. (29.6). Successive scalings with powers of 2 can be achieved with an arithmetic shifter in the accumulator feedback path. Some additional control circuit is necessary to ensure that the partial sum is subtracted as opposed to being added to the total at sign bit time (negative term in Eq. (29.6)).

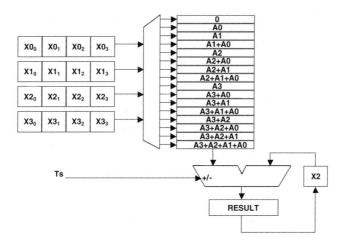

**FIGURE 29.5**  Distributed arithmetic ROM and accumulator (RAC) structure.

After $N$ cycles (where $N$ is the total bitwidth of the $x_k$ vector elements) the final result $y$ has converged to its final value in the accumulator.

Figure 29.5 shows a detailed example of a DA computation. The structure shown computes the dot product of a 4-element vector **X** and a constant vector **A**. All 16 possible linear combinations of the constant element vectors (**Ai**) are stored in a ROM. The variable vector **X** is forming the ROM address, MSB-first. The figure assumes that the **Xi** elements are 4-bit 2's complement integers (bit 3 is the sign bit.) Every clock cycle, the RESULT register adds 2× its previous value to the currently addressed ROM contents. In addition, the 4-shift registers that hold the variable vector **X** are shifted to the right. The sign timing pulse **Ts** is activated when the ROM is addressed by the sign bit (bit 3) of the vector elements. In this case, the accumulator subtracts the addressed ROM contents to implement the first negative term of Eq. (29.6). After four cycles, the dot product has been produced within the RESULT register.

The power advantages of DA versus multiply-accumulate can be summarized as follows:

1. ROM accesses can be more energy efficient than multiplications.
2. A ROM and accumulator (RAC) structure can be much more area efficient than a multiplier and accumulator (MAC) structure. In such case, wires tend to be shorter and less capacitive.
3. If the number of elements in the vectors forming the dot product is greater than the bit precision of the variable vector, then DA structure can be clocked slower than the sample rate and take advantage of voltage scaling techniques. Essentially, such a configuration is an interesting form of parallelism.
4. A DA RAC structure is an ideal arithmetic unit for approximate processing (trading off power dissipation vs. output quality). This property will be expanded upon in the subsection on "Power vs. Quality and Precision Trade-offs."

## Algorithmic/Architectural Exploitation of Data Distribution Properties

Fixed-function DSP systems typically operate on data streams that exhibit common distribution properties. Some examples are:

1. Data streams related to human aural and visual perception (uncompressed audio and video samples): Such streams typically exhibit large spatial and temporal correlation and reduced dynamic range.
2. Data streams of compressed video or image data in the frequency domain: Typically, such streams contain large numbers of zero-valued coefficients indicating the lack of high spatial frequencies in natural images.

A priori knowledge of data stream distribution can be exploited at the algorithmic and architectural level for computation minimization and power reduction.

Nielsen and Sparso [22] observed that 16-bit sampled speech data samples exhibit significant correlation, in addition to a predominance of small signal values. As a result, they have proposed a sliced datapath for a digital hearing aid filter bank to exploit the small magnitude of the input samples. The arithmetic datapath has been partitioned in an MSB and an LSB slice. The MSB slice is only engaged when the input bitwidth requires it. Activation of the slices is performed by using special data tags that indicate the presence of sign extension bits in the MSB input slice. Additional circuit overhead is required for the computation and update of the tags. Dynamic bitwidth adaptation is coarse and can only be performed on a slice basis. This scheme results in data-dependent power reduction and processing time.

Xanthopoulos [23] has demonstrated a DA-based dicrete cosine transform (DCT) [24] architecture that exploits correlation in the incoming image or video samples for computation minimization and power reduction. DCT is a frequency domain data transform widely used in video and still image compression standards such as MPEG [25] and JPEG [26]. The 8-point one-dimensional DCT transform is defined as follows:

$$X[u] = \frac{c[u]}{2} \sum_{i=0}^{7} x[i] \cos\left(\frac{(2i+1)u\pi}{16}\right) \qquad (29.8)$$

where $c[u] = 1/\sqrt{2}$ if $u = 0$ and 1 otherwise.

Image pixels are locally well correlated and exhibit a certain number of common most significant bits. These bits constitute a common-mode DC offset that only affects the computation of the DC DCT coefficient ($X[0]$ in Eq. (29.8)) and is irrelevant for the computation of the higher spectral (AC) coefficients ($X[1] \cdots X[7]$ in Eq. (29.8)). The DCT chip in [23] includes adaptive-bitwidth DA computation units that reject common most significant bits for all AC coefficent computations resulting in arithmetic operations with reduced bitwidth operands, thus reducing switching activity. The bit-serial nature of the DA operation allows very fine grain (1-bit) adaptation to the input dynamic range as opposed to the coarse slice-level adaptation in [22].

An interesting algorithmic adaptation to data distribution properties has been demonstrated in [27]. The chip computes the inverse discrete cosine transform (IDCT) and is targeted to MPEG-compressed video data. The 8-point, one-dimensional IDCT is defined as follows:

$$x[i] = \sum_{u=0}^{7} \frac{c[u]}{2} X[u] \cos\left(\frac{(2i+1)u\pi}{16}\right) \qquad (29.9)$$

where $c[u] = 1/\sqrt{2}$ if $u = 0$ and 1 otherwise.

Numerous fast IDCT algorithms can minimize the number of multiplications and additions implied by Eq. (29.9) [28,29]. Yet, the statistical distribution of the input DCT coefficients possesses unique properties that can affect IDCT algorithmic design. Typically, 64-coefficient DCT blocks of MPEG-compressed video sequences have only 5–6 nonzero coefficients, mainly located in the low spatial frequency positions due to the low pass characteristics of frame sequences [27]. The histogram of Fig. 29.6 shows the frequency of 64-coefficient block occurrence plotted versus the number of nonzero coefficient content for a typical MPEG sequence. The mode of such distributions is invariably blocks with a single nonzero spectral coefficient (typically the DC).

Given such input data statistics, we observe that direct application of Eq. (29.9) will result in a small average number of operations since multiplication and accumulation with a zero-valued coefficient $X[k]$ constitutes a NOP [30]. The chip in [27] uses such a direct coefficient-by-coefficient algorithm coupled with extensive clock-gating techniques to implement the implied NOPs. IDCT computation power of 4.5 mW for MPEG-2 sample rates has been reported.

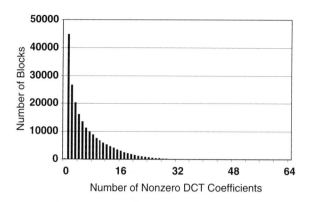

**FIGURE 29.6** Histogram of Nonzero DCT coefficients in sample MPEG stream.

## Power vs. Quality and Precision Trade-offs

In many DSP applications, lower quality in visual or audio output can be tolerated for reduced power dissipation. Recently, a number of researchers have resorted to approximate processing as a method for reducing average system power. Ludwig et al. [31] have demonstrated an approximate filtering technique, which dynamically reduces the filter order based on the input data characteristics. More specifically, the number of taps of a frequency-selective FIR filter is dynamically varied based on the estimated stopband energy of the input signal. The resulting stopband energy of the output signal is always kept under a predefined threshold. This technique results in power savings of a factor of 6 for speech inputs. Nikol et al. [32] have demonstrated an adaptive scheme for dynamically reducing the input amplitude of a Booth-encoded multiplier to the lowest acceptable precision level in an adaptive digital equalizer. Their scheme simply involves an arithmetic shift (multiplication/division by a power of 2) of the multiplier input depending on the value of the error at the equalizer output. They report power savings of 20%.

When the DA operation is performed MSB first ("Variable Supply Voltage Schemes" subsection), it exhibits stochastically monotonic successive approximation properties. In other words, each successive intermediate value is closer to the final value in a stochastic sense. An analytical derivation is presented in [33]. As an example, let us assume that we have a DA structure computing the dot product of two vectors. Each vector element is 8-bits 2's complement integer. If we clock the DA structure of Fig. 29.5 for eight full cycles, the full precision value of the dot product will form into the RESULT register. If instead we clock the DA structure for four cycles and perform a 4-bit arithmetic left shift of the output in the RESULT register (multiplication by $2^4$), we obtain an approximation of the actual dot product. If we clock the structure once more (total of five cycles) and then perform a 3-bit arithmetic left shift of the output (multiplication by $2^3$), we obtain a better approximation. In this way, a DA structure can implement a fine-grain trade-off between power and precision.

Xanthopoulos [23] is extensively using this property for power reduction in a DCT application. In image and video compression applications not all spectral coefficients have the same visual significance. Typically, a large number of high spatial frequencies are quantized to zero in a lossy image/video compression environment (i.e., JPEG and MPEG) with no significant change in visual quality. The DCT processor in [23] exploits such different precision requirements on a coefficient basis by reducing the number of iterations of the DA units that compute the visually insignificant spectral coefficients in a user-programmable fashion. Figure 29.7 plots average power chip dissipation vs. compressed image quality in terms of the image peak SNR (PSNR), a widely used quality measure in image processing. The data points in the graph have been obtained by chip power measurements at different RAC maximum iteration settings. The data implies that the chip can produce on average 10 additional decibels of image quality per milliwatt of power dissipation. Figure 29.8 displays the actual compressed images for three (power, PSNR) data points of Fig. 29.7 for visual appreciation.

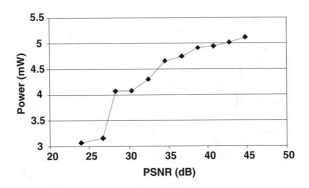

**FIGURE 29.7**    DCT Chip [my DCT] average power vs. compressed image quality.

**FIGURE 29.8**    Compressed image quality and power.

Amirtharajah et al. [34,36] use a similar DA-based approximate processing technique in a program-mable ultra-low-power DSP targeted to physiological monitoring. Reduced RAC iterations reduce the signal to noise ratio of the input signal (effectively increasing the quantization noise) and result in less reliable heart beat detection. Yet, the reduced performance results in linear power savings, which may be desirable in certain situations.

## 29.5   Conclusion

This chapter has presented a collection of power reduction techniques that applied in DSP applications during the last few years. Although presented in a categorized form to provide structure in the exposition, the author does not believe that true low-power design involves a laundry list of power reduction techniques and blind application to the problem in question. Instead, low-power design involves a vertical design process and a global optimization across algorithmic, architectural, circuit, and physical design boundaries. A designer must have a deep understanding of the DSP application under power optimiza-tion. The best algorithm must be selected, which minimizes a weighted average of the number of arithmetic operations, memory accesses, on-chip communication, and silicon area. The right boundary must be achieved between programmability and predefined functionality. Architectural, circuit, and physical design techniques must then be applied that fully support the algorithmic selection but at the same time should be allowed to influence such selection in order to achieve optimum results.

The author concludes by enumerating a few case studies, which demonstrate concurrent optimization across all design phases and as a result have achieved impressive results in a few key DSP application areas. Chandrakasan et al. [35] have demonstrated a low-power chipset for a portable multimedia terminal. This work was power optimized from a system perspective and performed a number of functions such as protocol conversion, synchronization, and video decompression, among others, while consuming under 5 mW of power. Amirtharajah [36] has demonstrated an ultra-low-power programmable DSP for physi-ological monitoring (heartbeat detection and classification). His techniques involved algorithmic design, a balanced hybrid architecture containing both customized and programmable units, and appropriate circuits supporting such architectural choices. The DSP consumes 220 nW at 1 V, 1.2 kHz and includes embedded support for harvesting energy from ambient sources. Simon [37] has demonstrated a low-power single chip video encoder with embedded dynamic memory. The compression is performed using wavelet filtering and a combination of zero-tree and arithmetic coding of filter coefficients. Hooks for motion estimation are also provided. The chip dissipates on the order of 0.5 mW while compressing an 8-bit gray scale 30 frames/sec, 128 × 128 video stream. Goodman [38] built a programmable reconfigurable public key processor that demonstrated 2–3 orders of magnitude of power reduction compared to software and programmable-logic based implementations while providing similar flexibility and freedom in algorithm selection. Finally, Mosch et al. [39] have demonstrated a DSP for a hearing aid chipset featuring 77 MOPS/mW. Algorithmic and architectural optimizations were heavily employed to achieve such a result.

# References

1. A. Gatherer, T. Stetzler, M. McMahan, E. Auslander. DSP-based architectures for mobile communications: past, present and future. *IEEE Communications Magazine,* 38(1), Jan. 2000, pp. 84–90.
2. R. Min et al. Low-power wireless sensor networks. In *Proceedings of the Fourteenth International Conference on VLSI Design,* 2001, pp. 205–210.
3. H. Veendrick. Short-circuit dissipation of static CMOS circuitry and its impact on the design of buffer circuits. *IEEE Journal of Solid-State Circuits,* Aug. 1984, pp. 468–473.
4. S. Mutoh et al. 1-V power supply high-speed digital circuit technology with multithreshold-voltage CMOS. *IEEE Journal of Solid-State Circuits,* Aug. 1995, pp. 847–854.
5. T. Kuroda et al. A 0.9-V, 150-MHz, 10-mW, 4 mm$^2$, 2-D discrete cosine transform core processor with variable threshold-voltage (VT) scheme. *IEEE Journal of Solid-State Circuits,* Nov. 1996, pp. 1770–1779.
6. W. Lee et al. A 1-V programmable DSP for wireless communications. *IEEE Journal of Solid-State Circuits,* Nov. 1997, pp. 1766–1776.
7. K. Ueda et al. A 16 b low-power-consumption digital signal processor. In *1993 IEEE International Solid State Circuits Conference Digest of Technical Papers,* Feb. 1993, pp. 28–29.
8. T. Shiraishi et al. A 1.8 V 36 mW DSP for the half-rate speech CODEC. In *Proceedings of the 1996 IEEE Custom Integrated Circuits Conference,* May 1996, pp. 371–374.
9. I. Verbauwhede and C. Nikol. Low power DSPs for wireless communications. In *Proceedings of the 2000 International Symposium on Low Power Electronics and Design,* July 2000, pp. 303–310.
10. B. Sklar. *Digital Communications.* Prentice-Hall, Englewood Cliffs, NJ, 1988.
11. P. Lapsley, J. Bier, A. Shoham, E. Lee. *DSP Processor Fundamentals.* IEEE Press, Piscataway, NJ, 1997.
12. M. Hiraki et al. Stage-Skip Pipeline: A low power processor architecture using a decoded instruction buffer. In *Proceedings of the 1996 International Symposium on Low Power Electronics and Design,* Aug. 1996, pp. 353–358.
13. H. Zhang et al. A 1-V Heterogeneous reconfigurable DSP IC for wireless baseband digital signal processing. *IEEE Journal of Solid-State Circuits,* Nov. 2000, pp. 1697–1704.
14. L. Nielsen et al. Low-power operation using self-timed circuits and adaptive scaling of the supply voltage. *IEEE Transactions on VLSI Systems,* Dec. 1994, pp. 391–397.
15. G. Wei, M. Horowitz. A low power switching power supply for self-clocked systems. In *Proceedings of the 1996 International Symposium on Low Power Electronics and Design,* Aug. 1996, pp. 313–318.
16. V. Gutnik, A. Chandrakasan. Embedded power supply for low-power DSP. *IEEE Transactions on VLSI Systems,* Dec. 1997, pp. 425–435.
17. J. Goodman, A. Dancy, A. Chandrakasan. An energy/security scalable encryption processor using an embedded variable voltage DC/DC converter. *IEEE Journal of Solid-State Circuits,* 33(11), Nov. 1998, pp. 1799–1809.
18. M. Sun, T. Chen, A. Gottlieb. VLSI Implementation of a 16 × 16 Discrete Cosine Transform. *IEEE Transactions on Circuits and Systems,* 36(4), April 1989.

19. S. Uramoto et al. A 100 MHz 2-D discrete cosine transform core processor. *IEEE Journal of Solid-State Circuits,* 36(4), April 1992.

20. A. Peled, B. Liu. A new hardware realization of digital filters. *IEEE Transactions on Acoustics Speech and Signal Processing,* ASSP-22, Dec. 1974.

21. S. White. Applications of distributed arithmetic to digital signal processing: a tutorial review. *IEEE ASSP Magazine,* July 1989.

22. L. Nielsen, J. Sparso. An 85 $\mu$W asynchronous filter bank for a digital hearing aid. In *1998 IEEE International Solid State Circuits Conference Digest of Technical Papers,* Feb. 1998, pp. 108–109.

23. T. Xanthopoulos, A. Chandrakasan. A low-power DCT core using adaptive bitwidth and arithmetic activity exploiting signal correlations and quantization. *IEEE Journal of Solid-State Circuits,* 35(5), May 2000, pp. 740–750.

24. K. Rao, P. Yip. Discrete Cosine Transform: Algorithms, Advantages, Applications. Academic Press, San Diego, 1990.

25. D. LeGall. MPEG: A video compression standard for multimedia applications. *Communications of the ACM,* 34(4), April 1991, pp. 46–58.

26. G. Wallace. The JPEG still picture compression standard. *Communications of the ACM,* 34(4), April 1991, pp. 30–44.

27. T. Xanthopoulos, A. Chandrakasan. A low-power IDCT macrocell for MPEG-2 MP@ML exploiting data distribution properties for minimal activity. *IEEE Journal of Solid-State Circuits,* 34(5), May 1999, pp. 693–703.

28. W. Chen, C. Smith, S. Fralick. A fast computational algorithm for the discrete cosine transform. *IEEE Transactions on Communications,* 25(9), Sept. 1977.

29. E. Feig, S. Winograd. Fast algorithms for the discrete cosine transform. *IEEE transactions on Signal Processing,* 40(9), Sept. 1992, pp. 2174–2193.

30. L. McMillan, L. Westover. A forward-mapping realization of the inverse discrete cosine transform. In *Proceedings of the 1992 Data Compression Conference, IEEE Computer Society Press,* March 1992, pp. 219–228.

31. J. Ludwig, S. Nawab, A. Chandrakasan. Low-power digital filtering using approximate processing. *IEEE Journal of Solid-State Circuits,* 31(3), March 1996, pp. 395–400.

32. C. Nikol, P. Larsson, K. Azadet, N. O'Neill. A low-power 128-tap digital adaptive equalizer for broadband modems. *IEEE Journal of Solid-State Circuits,* 32(11), Nov. 1997, pp. 1777–1789.

33. R. Amirtharajah, T. Xanthopoulos, A. Chandrakasan. Power scalable processing using distributed Arithmetic. In *Proceedings of the 1999 International Symposium on Low Power Electronics and Design,* Aug. 1999, pp. 170–175.

34. R. Amirtharajah, S. Meninger, O. Mur-Miranda, A. Chandrakasan, J. Lang. A micropower programmable DSP powered using a MEMS-based vibration-to-electric energy converter. In *2000 IEEE International Solid-State Circuits Conference Digest of Technical Papers,* Feb. 2000, pp. 362–363.

35. A. Chandrakasan, A. Burstein, R. Brodersen. A low-power chipset for a portable multimedia I/O terminal. *IEEE Journal of Solid-State Circuits,* Dec. 1994, pp. 1415–1428.

36. R. Amirtharajah. Design of low power VLSI systems powered by ambient mechanical vibration. PhD Thesis, Massachusetts Institute of Technology, May 1999.

37. T. Simon, A. Chandrakasan. An Ultra low power adaptive wavelet video encoder with integrated memory. *IEEE Journal of Solid-State Circuits,* 35(4), April 2000, pp. 572–582.

38. J. Goodman, A. Chandrakasan. An energy-efficient IEEE 1363-based reconfigurable public-key cryptography processor. In *2001 IEEE International Solid-State Circuits Conference Digest of Technical Papers,* Feb. 2001, pp. 330–331.

39. P. Mosch et al. A 660-$\mu$W 50-Mops 1-V DSP for a hearing aid chip set. *IEEE Journal of Solid-State Circuits,* 35(11), Nov. 2000, pp. 1705–1712.

# VII

# Communications and Networks

# 30

# Communications and Computer Networks

Anna Hać
*University of Hawaii*

## 30.1   Architecture

The set of layers and the corresponding set of protocols are called the architecture of a network. In designing a layered architecture there are problems that must be solved in several layers. These problems include addressing and connection establishment, connection termination, nature of channel (e.g., full or half-duplex), error control and sequencing, flow control, and multiplexing.

### OSI Reference Model

Open Systems Interconnect (OSI) Reference Model consists of seven layers: physical, data link, network, transport, session, presentation, and application.

The physical layer is responsible for transmitting bits over a communication channel.

The data link layer is responsible for providing an error-free line to the higher layers. It provides error and sequence checking, and implements a system of time-outs and acknowledgements that enables a transmitter to determine which frames need to be retransmitted due to error or drop out. In addition, flow control is provided in data link layer.

The network layer provides routing and congestion control services to higher layers. The network accounting function is obtained in this layer.

The transport layer accepts data in message form from the session layer above it, breaks it into smaller pieces, usually called packets, and passes the packets to the network layer. It must then ensure that the packets arrive correctly at the destination host. The transport layer is an end-to-end protocol, as opposed to layers below it, which are chained. The transport layer may multiplex several sessions over a single network connection, or it may utilize several connections to provide a high data rate for a session that requires it. The transport layer may provide either virtual circuit or datagram service to the session layer. In a virtual circuit, messages are delivered in the order in which they were sent, while in a datagram service there is no guarantee concerning order of delivery. The transport layer also has the responsibility for establishing and terminating connections between hosts across the network and for providing host-to-host flow control.

The session layer is responsible for establishing and managing connections between two processes. Session establishment typically requires authentication, billing authorization, and agreement on a set of parameters that will be in effect for the session. The session layer is also responsible for recovery from a transport failure and for providing virtual circuit service if the transport layer does not do so.

The presentation layer performs services that are commonly requested by users, such as text compression, code conversion, file formatting, and encryption.

The application layer contains routines specific to a particular application.

## Networks

### LAN

Local area network (LAN) is a privately owned network of up to a few kilometers in size. LANs are used to connect computers, workstations, and file servers, and attach printers and other devices. The restricted size of LANs allows for prediction of transmission time, and simplifies network management. Traditional LANs run at speeds of 10–100 Mbps and have low delay of tens of miliseconds.

Broadcast topologies include bus and ring. In a bus network, at any instant one machine is the master and is allowed to transmit. At the same time, all other machines are required to refrain from sending. IEEE 802.3, which is the Ethernet, is a bus-based broadcast network with decentralized control operating at 10 or 100 Mbps. Computers on an Ethernet can transmit at any time. If two or more packets collide, each computer waits for a random time and tries again later.

In a ring network, each bit propagates around on its own, not waiting for the rest of the packet to which it belongs. IEEE 802.5, which is the IBM token ring, is a ring-based LAN operating at 4 and 16 Mbps.

### WAN

Wide area network (WAN) covers a large area, a country or a continent. The hosts in WAN are used to run application programs and are connected by a communication subnet, which consists of transmission lines and switching elements. A switching element, also called router, is used to forward packets to their destinations.

### Cellular Network

The most widely employed wireless network topology is the cellular network. This network architecture is used in cellular telephone networks, personal communication networks, mobile data networks, and wireless local area networks (WLAN). In this network configuration, a service area, usually over a wide geographic area, is partitioned into smaller areas called cells. Each cell, in effect, is a centralized network, with a base station (BS) controlling all the communications to and from each mobile user in the cell. Each cell is assigned a group of discrete channels from the available frequency spectrum (usually radio frequency). These channels are in turn assigned to each mobile user, when needed.

Typically, BSs are connected to their switching networks using landlines through switches. The BS is the termination point of the user-to-network interface of a wireless cellular network. In addition, the BS also provides call setups, cell handoffs and various network management tasks, depending on the type of network.

## TCP/IP Protocol

Transmission control protocol/Internet protocol (TCP/IP) suite is used in the network and transport layers. TCP/IP is a set of protocols allowing computers to share resources across the network. Although the protocol family is referred to as TCP/IP, user datagram protocol (UDP) is also a member of this protocol suite.

TCP/IP protocol suite used as network and transport layers has the following advantages:

1. It is not vendor-specific.
2. It has been implemented on most systems from personal computers to the largest supercomputers.
3. It is used for both LANs and WANs.

Using TCP/IP also makes the network system portable, and program portability is one of the system design goals.

The network layer uses Internet protocol (IP). IP is responsible for routing individual datagrams and getting datagrams to their destination. The IP layer provides a connectionless and unreliable delivery system. It is connectionless because it considers each IP datagram independent of all others and any association between datagrams must be provided by the upper layers. Every IP datagram contains the source address and the destination address so that each datagram can be delivered and routed independently. The IP layer is unreliable because it does not guarantee that IP datagrams ever get delivered or that they are delivered correctly. Reliability must be provided by the upper layers.

Transport layer uses UDP and transmission control protocol (TCP). TCP is a connection-oriented protocol that provides a reliable, full-duplex, byte stream for the multimedia communication process. TCP is responsible for breaking up the message into datagrams, reassembling them at the other end, resending anything that got lost, and putting everything back in the right order. TCP handles the establishment and termination of connections between processes, the sequencing of data that might be received out of order, the end-to-end reliability (checksums, positive acknowledgments, timeouts), and the end-to-end flow control.

UDP is a connectionless protocol for user processes. Unlike TCP, which is a reliable protocol, there is no guarantee that UDP datagrams ever reach their intended destination. UDP is less reliable than TCP but transfers data faster because they are not held up by earlier messages awaiting retransmission. TCP protocol is used for file transfer that requires reliable, sequenced delivery, where real-time delivery may not be of utmost importance.

## Mobile IP Protocols

In TCP/IP an application is connected with another application through a router. Each host in Internet has a unique address. An IP address is a 32-bit binary number that can also be used in a dotted notation. IP addresses contain two parts: network address which identifies the network to which the host is attached, and local address which identifies the host. Local address can be separated into two parts, subnet address and local address.

The hierarchical address makes routing simple. A host that wants to send packets to another host only needs to send packets to the network to which the target host is attached. The host does not need to know the inside of the network; however, a computer's IP address cannot be changed during connection and communication. If the user wants to move the computer to the other area while using it, this will be difficult because the physical IP address of the computer must be changed in a different subnet. To solve this problem, a number of protocols have been proposed: virtual IP (VIP), loose source routing IP (LSRIP), and Internet engineering task force mobile IP (IETF-MIP).

### VIP

VIP uses two, 32-bit IP-style addresses to identify mobile hosts: one is named virtual IP (VIP) address, the other is named temporary IP (TIP) address. VIP address is the IP address that mobile hosts get from their home network. Mobile hosts always use VIP as their source address inside IP packet. When mobile hosts move to another network, they get another IP address from the foreign network, it is a TIP address. Each VIP packet contains information to combine VIP and TIP, so the packet target to VIP can be routed through general Internet to its temporary network by reading its TIP. VIP uses additional space inside packet to carry this information: a new IP option to identify VIP while original address fields carry TIP.

When a mobile host moves to a foreign network, the information about mobile host's current location is sent to the mobile host's home network. During the transmission, each intermediate router that supports VIP protocol can receive this information and update this router's cache. This cache is a database that stores information about mobile hosts' current location.

If a host wants to send a packet to a mobile host, it only knows the VIP address of the mobile host and does not know its TIP, which is its current location. The packet will be sent to the mobile host's home area. If any intermediate router that supports VIP receives this packet, it will modify this packet according to its cache so that the new packet will include information of TIP and can be routed to the mobile host's current location. If the packet does not reach any intermediate router that supports VIP and has cache information about the mobile host, the packet will be routed to mobile host's home network. The gateway in mobile host's home network can modify this packet according to this gateway's cache and route the packet to the mobile host's current network. This gateway always has the mobile host's current location, because each time when the mobile host moves to a new network, the mobile host notifies its home network about the mobile host's current location. The optimized path in VIP is mainly based on the number of intermediate VIP routers. If many intermediate routers support VIP, the optimized routing path should be obtained. The option VIP uses to carry information of VIP is an option of IP, and not all of the routers will support this option. Some computers even discard all of the options IP packets carry. VIP also needs many extra IP addresses for foreign network to assign to the mobile hosts.

## LSRIP

Loose source routing IP uses one of the IP options to cause the IP packets to be routed through a series of intermediate routers to the destination. This IP option is loose source and record route (LSRR). For example, if host A wants to send a packet to host C with LSRR option, the packet can reach host B through general IP routing. Then host B replaces the destination IP address in IP header with the first IP address C in LSRR option and routes the packet to a new destination C. Also host B puts the pointer to the second IP address in LSRR option. Host C can perform the same procedure: replace destination IP address with next IP address in LSRR option, increase pointer to next IP address in LSRR option, and reroute the packet to a new destination. Until the pointer points to the last IP address in LSRR option, the packet is sent to its destination address. LSRIP uses LSRR option to carry the information of a mobile host.

When a mobile host moves to a foreign network, the information about the mobile host's current location is sent to the mobile host's home network. During the transmission, each intermediate router that supports LSRIP protocol can receive this information and update this router's cache.

If a host wants to send a packet to a mobile host, which is not at its home area, the packet will be first sent to the mobile host's home network. During the path to the home network, if an intermediate router has the cache of the mobile host, this router can put the LSRIP option into the packet and cause it to be routed to the current network of the mobile host. The gateway of current network reads information from LSRIP option and can determine that the mobile host is the destination of this packet's destination. Thus, the gateway can route the packet to mobile host that is connected to current network.

If the packet does not reach any intermediate router that supports LSRIP and has cache information about the mobile host, the packet will be routed to mobile host's home network. The gateway in mobile host's home network can add the LSRIP option to this packet according to the gateway's cache and route the packet to the mobile host's current network. This gateway always has the mobile host's current location because each time when the mobile host moves to a new network, the mobile host notifies its home network about the mobile host's current location.

LSRIP needs more intermediate routers to achieve optimized routing path. Also, the option used by LSRIP is not compatible with current routers. This can be tested by sending a packet using traceroute, a tool to check the path one packet has passed. Traceroute uses LSRR option to record the path of the packet and the transmission time to each intermediate host. If any intermediate host does not support LSRR option, traceroute bypasses this host. After sending a packet, it can be found from the messages sent back that some sites are not displayed correctly, which means that these sites do not support LSRR option.

## IETF-MIP

IETF-MIP is the most usable protocol for mobile IP in the Internet. The basic idea is to use two agents to handle the job related to the mobile host. When the mobile host moves to the other networks, it will notify foreign network's agent, foreign agent, and its home agent about its current location. Then when the packet to mobile host is sent to home agent using general IP, the home agent will modify the header of IP packet: change the destination address to foreign agent's address and add some fields to the packet including the mobile host's permanent address. When the foreign agent receives this packet, it will know this is for one mobile host which is now at its location, the foreign agent will modify this packet again and send it directly to the mobile host through the local network. In IETF-MIP, there are cache agents to optimize the performance. A cache agent is a host that can maintain a database that stores the mobile hosts current location. This database can be changed according to the location change of the mobile host.

In this protocol it is difficult to achieve the optimized routing path, especially in a WAN. For example, a user in London wants to send a packet to a mobile host in London, whose home network is in New York. This packet will be first sent to New York, then modified by the home agent, and then sent back. This takes about one half of the circle of the whole earth. The optimized path can only be about 100 ft. Thus, the only solution for IETF-MIP is to set up as many cache agents as possible in the entire Internet. When the cache agents receive a packet, they can modify the packet instead of sending it to the home agent of the mobile host.

Mobile IP should be compatible with current IPs, that means the current protocols and applications do not need to be changed. Mobile IP also needs to have optimized routing path, that means the protocol should be efficient in routing packets. VIP and LSRIP use the option of IP to carry the information of mobile hosts. But some of the current hosts do not support an IP option. When these hosts receive a packet that includes options, they discard the options of the IP packet. Meanwhile, IETF-MIP only uses basic IP header and packet, and does not use any IP option. From the compatibility point, IETF-MIP is the best out of those three protocols. From the point of optimized routing path, all three protocols depend on intermediate cache hosts. If enough intermediate cache hosts are inside the Internet, the three protocols can find optimized routing path. The IETF-MIP is the best out of the three mobile IPs considering both the compatibility and optimized routing path. IETF-MIP is also the mobile IP protocol that is used in the Internet.

## 30.2   Technology

### Broadband Networks

Broadband integrated services digital network (B-ISDN) based on asynchronous transfer mode (ATM) is used for transport of information from multimedia services and applications.

### ATM

ATM is a cell-based, high-bandwidth, low-delay switching and multiplexing technology that is designed to deliver a variety of high-speed digital communication services. These services include LAN interconnection, imaging, and multimedia applications as well as video distribution, video telephony, and other video applications.

ATM standards define a fixed-size cell with a length of 53 bytes comprised of a 5-byte header and a 48-byte payload.

The virtual path identifiers (VPIs) and virtual channel identifiers (VCIs) are the labels to identify a particular virtual path (VP) and virtual channel (VC) on the link. The switching node uses these values to identify a particular connection and then uses the routing table established at connection set-up to route the cells to the appropriate output port. The switch changes the value of the VPI and VCI fields to the new values that are used on the output link.

### SONET

Synchronous optical network (SONET) is used for framing and synchronization at the physical layer. The basic time unit of a SONET frame is 125 $\mu$s. The basic building block of SONET is synchronous transport signal level 1 (STS-1) with a bit rate of 51.84 Mbps. Higher-rate SONET signals are obtained by byte-interleaving $n$ frame-aligned STS-1s to form an STS-$n$ (e.g., STS-3 has a bit rate of 155.52 Mbps).

Due to physical layer framing overhead, the transfer capacity at the user-network interface (UNI) is 155.52 Mbps with a cell-fill capacity of 149.76 Mbps. Because the ATM cell has 5 bytes of overhead, the 48 bytes information field allows for a maximum of 135.631 Mbps of actual user information. A second

UNI interface is defined at 622.08 Mbps with the service bit rate of approximately 600 Mbps. Access at these rates requires a fiber-based loop.

### ATM Services

Users request services from the ATM switch in terms of destination(s), traffic type(s), bit rate(s), and Quality of Service (QoS). These requirements are usually grouped together and categorized in different ATM traffic classifications. The ATM services are categorized as follows:

- *Constant Bit Rate (CBR):* Connection-oriented constant bit rate service such as digital voice and video traffic.
- *Real-Time Variable Bit Rate (rt-VBR):* Intended for real-time traffic from bursty sources such as compressed voice or video transmission.
- *Non-Real-Time Variable Bit Rate (nrt-VBR):* Intended for applications that have bursty traffic but do not require tight delay guarantee. This type of service is appropriate for connectionless data traffic.
- *Available Bit Rate (ABR):* Intended for sources that accept time-varying available bandwidth. Users are only guaranteed a minimum cell rate (MCR). An example of such traffic is LAN emulation traffic.
- *Unspecified Bit Rate (UBR):* Best effort service that is intended for noncritical applications. It does not provide traffic related service guarantees.

ATM networks are fixed (optical) point-to-point networks with high bandwidth and low error rates. These attributes are not associated with the limited bandwidth and error prone radio medium. While increasing the number of cables (copper or fiber optics) can increase the bandwidth of wired networks, wireless telecommunications networks experience a more difficult task. Due to limited usable radio frequency, a wireless channel is an expensive resource in terms of bandwidth. In order for wireless networks to support high-speed networks such as ATM, a multiple access approach is needed for sharing this limited medium in a manner different from the narrowband, along with the means of supporting mobility and maintaining QoS guarantees.

## Wireless Networks

Media access control (MAC) is a set of rules that attempt to efficiently share a communication channel among independent competing users. Each MAC uses a different media (or multiple) access scheme to allocate the limited bandwidth among multiple users. Many multiple access protocols have been designed and analyzed both for wired and wireless networks. Each has its advantages and limitations based on the network environment and traffic. These schemes can be classified into three categories: fixed assignments, random access, and demand assignment. The demand assignment scheme is the most efficient access protocol for traffic of varying bit rate in the wireless environment.

Due to the limited radio frequencies available for wireless communication, wireless networks have to maximize the overall capacity attainable within a given set of frequency channel. Spectral efficiency describes the maximum number of calls that can be served in a given service area. To achieve high spectral efficiency, cellular networks are designed with frequency reuse. If a channel with a specific frequency covers an area of a radius *R*, the same frequency can be reused to cover another area. A service area is divided into seven cell clusters. Each cell in the cluster, designated 1 through 7, uses a different set of frequencies. The same set of frequencies in each cell can be reused in the same service area if it is sufficiently apart from the current cell. Cells using the same frequency channels are called cocells. In principle, by using this layout scheme, the overall system capacity can be increased as large as desired by reducing the cell size, while controlling power levels to avoid co-channel interference. Co-channel interference is defined as the interference experienced by users operating in different cells using the same frequency channel. Smaller size cells called microcells are implemented to cover areas about the size of a city block. Research has been done on an even smaller cells called picocells.

## TDMA

Time-division multiple access (TDMA) and frequency-division multiple access (FDMA) are fixed assignment techniques that incorporate permanent subchannels assignments to each user. These traditional schemes perform well with stream-type traffic, such as voice, but are inappropriate for integrated multimedia traffic because of the radio channel spectrum utilization. In a fixed assignment environment, a subchannel is wasted whenever the user has nothing to transmit. It is widely accepted that most services in the broadband environment are VBR service (bursty traffic). Such traffic wastes a lot of bandwidth in a fixed assignment scheme.

## ALOHA

Typical random assignment protocols like ALOHA and carrier sense multiple access with collision detection (CSMA/CD) schemes are more efficient in servicing bursty traffic. These techniques allocate the full channel capacity to a user for short periods, on a random basis. These packet-oriented techniques dynamically allocate the channel to a user on a per-packet basis.

Although a few versions of the ALOHA protocol are used, in its simplest form it allows the users to transmit at will. Whenever two or more user transmissions overlap, a collision occurs and users have to retransmit after a random delay. The ALOHA protocol is inherently unstable due to the random delay, i.e., it is possible that a transmission may be delayed for an infinite time. Various collision resolution algorithms were designed to stabilize and reduce contention in this scheme.

Slotted ALOHA is a simple modification of the ALOHA protocol. After a collision, instead of retransmitting at a random time, slotted ALOHA retransmits at a random time slot. Transmission can only be made at the beginning of a time slot. Obviously, this protocol is implemented in time slotted systems. Slotted ALOHA is proven to be twice as efficient as a regular or pure ALOHA protocol.

## CSMA/CD

CSMA/CD, taking advantage of the short propagation delays between users in a typical LAN, provides a very high throughput protocol. In a plain CSMA protocol, users will not transmit unless it senses that the transmission channel is idle. In CSMA/CD, the user also detects any collision that happens during a transmission. The combination provides a protocol that has high throughput and low delay; however, carrier sensing is a major problem for radio networks. The signal from the local transmitter will overload the receiver, disabling any attempts to sense remote transmission efficiently. Despite some advances in this area, sensing still poses a problem due to severe channel fading in indoor environments. Similarly, collision detection proves to be a difficult task in wireless networks. Although it can be easily done on a wired network by measuring the voltage level on a cable, sophisticated devices are required in wireless networks. Radio signals are dominated by the terminal's own signal over all other signals in the vicinity preventing any efficient collision detection. To avoid this situation, a terminal transmitting antenna pattern has to be different from its receiving pattern. This requires sophisticated directional antennas and expensive amplifiers for both the BS and the mobile station (MS). Such requirements are not feasible for the low-powered mobile terminal end.

## CDMA

Code-division multiple access (CDMA) is a combination of both fixed and random assignment. CDMA has many advantages such as near zero channel access delay, bandwidth efficiency, and excellent statistical multiplexing, but it suffers from significant limitations such as limited transmission rate, complex BS, and problems related to the power of its transmission signal. The limitation in transmission rate is a significant drawback to using CDMA for integrated wireless networks.

### Demand Assignment

In demand assignment protocol, channel capacity is assigned to users on demand basis, as needed. Demand assignment protocols typically involve two stages: a reservation stage where the user requests access, and a transmission stage where the actual data is transmitted. A small portion of the transmission channel, called the reservation subchannel, is used solely for users requesting permission to transmit data. Short reservation packets are sent to request channel time by using some simple multiple access schemes, typically, TDMA or slotted ALOHA. Once channel time is reserved, data can be transmitted through the second subchannel contention-free. Unlike a random access protocol where collisions occur in the data transmission channel, in demand assignment protocols, collisions occur only in the small-capacity reservation subchannel.

This reservation technique allows demand assignment protocols to avoid bandwidth waste due to collisions. In addition, unlike fixed assignment schemes no channels are wasted whenever a VBR user enters an idle period. The assigned bandwidth will simply be allocated to another user requesting access. Due to these features, protocols based on demand assignment techniques are most suitable for integrated wireless networks.

Demand assignment protocols can be classified into two categories based on the control scheme of the reservation and transmission stages. They can be either centralized or distributed. An example of a centralized controlled technique in demand assignment is polling. Each user is sequentially queried by the BS for transmission privileges. This scheme, however, relies heavily on the reliability of the centralized controller.

An alternative approach is to use distributed control, where MSs transmit based on information received from all the other MSs. Network information is transmitted through broadcast channels. Every user listens for reservation packets and performs the same distributed scheduling algorithm based on the information provided by the MS in the network. Requests for reservation are typically made using contention or fixed assignment schemes.

## 30.3  Routing

### Routing in Terrestrial Networks

Routing refers to the determination of a set of paths to be used for carrying messages from a source node to all destination nodes. It is important that the routes used for such communications consume a minimal amount of resources. In order to use network resources as little as possible while meeting the network service requirements, the most popular solution involves the generation of a tree spanning the source and destination nodes.

Routing algorithms for constructing trees have been developed with two optimization goals in mind. Two measures of the tree quality are in terms of the tree delay and tree cost, and are defined as follows:

1. The first measure of efficiency is in terms of the cost of the tree, which is the sum of the costs on the edges in the tree.
2. The second measure is the minimum average path delay, which is the average of minimum path delays from the source to each of the destinations in the group.

Optimization objectives are to minimize the cost and delay, however, the two measures are individually insufficient to characterize a good routing tree. For example, when the optimization objective is only to minimize the total cost of the tree, a minimum cost tree is built. Although total cost as a measure of bandwidth efficiency is certainly an important parameter, it is not sufficient to characterize the quality of the tree, because networks, especially those supporting real-time traffic, need to provide certain QoS guarantees in terms of the end-to-end delay along the individual paths from source to destination node. Therefore, both cost and delay optimization goal are important for the routing tree construction. The performance of such a route is determined by two factors:

1. Bounded delay along the path from source to destination
2. Minimum cost of the tree, for example, in terms of network bandwidth utilization

The goal of the routing algorithm is to construct a delay constrained minimum cost tree. In order to provide a certain quality of service to guarantee end-to-end delay along the path from source to destination node, the algorithm sets the delay constraint on the path, instead of trying to minimize the average path delay. The two measures of the tree quality, the tree edge delay and tree edge cost, can be described by different functions. For example, edge cost can be a measure of the amount of buffer space or channel bandwidth, and edge delay can be a combination of propagation, transmission, and queuing delay.

The shortest path algorithm can be used to generate the shortest paths from the source to destination nodes; this provides the optimal solution for delay optimization. Routing algorithms that perform cost optimization have been based on computing the minimum Steiner tree, which is known to be an NP-complete problem.

## DDBMA

A heuristic algorithm called DDBMA (Dynamic Delay Bounded Multicasting Algorithm) is used for constructing minimum-cost multicast trees with delay constraints. The algorithm sets variable delay bounds on destinations and can be used to handle the network cost optimization goal: minimizing the total cost (total bandwidth utilization) of the tree. The algorithm can also be used to handle a dynamic delay-bounded minimum Steiner tree, which is accomplished by updating the existing multicast tree when destinations need to be added or deleted.

During the network connection establishment, DDBMA can be used to construct a feasible tree for a given destination set. For certain applications, however, nodes in the network may join or leave the initial multicast group during the lifetime of the multicast connection. Examples of these applications such as teleconferencing, mobile communication, etc., allow each user in the network to join or leave the connection at any time without disrupting network services to other users.

The DDBMA is based on a feasible search optimization method, which starts with the minimum delay tree and monotonically decreases the cost by iterative improvement of the delay-bounded tree. Then the algorithm starts to update the existing tree when nodes in the network request to join or leave. The algorithm will stay steady when there is no leaving or joining requests from nodes in the network.

Multimedia, multiparty communication services are supported by networks having the capability to setup/modify the following five basic types of connections: point-to-point, point-to-multipoint (also called multicast), multipoint-to-point (also called concast), multipoint-to-multipoint, and point-to-allpoint (also called broadcast).

Many types of communication require transmission of certain information from the source to a selected set of destinations. This could be the cast of multipoint video conference, the distribution of a document to a selected number of persons via a computer network or the request for certain information from a distributed database.

# Routing in Wireless Networks

Wireless personal communication networks use a general routing procedure, a rerouting procedure, and a handoff. Along with the features of wireless communication, the user mobility control function tracking locations of networks subscribers should be associated with routing schemes during communication connection. In wireless communications networks the network topology is established by virtual paths. Virtual paths are logical direct radio links between all switch nodes. The bandwidth of virtual path can consist of a number of virtual channels. Because of the features of wireless communications networks, the network topology is highly dynamic. The bandwidth of wireless communications networks is limited, the traffic increases quickly, and it is hard to schedule incoming traffic on time in the centralized approaches, which are not efficient when network size increases and the network services are enhanced.

The subscribers in wireless communications networks roam. To create connections between all communication parties to deliver incoming and outgoing calls, the first consideration is the current location of mobile users and hosts. In wireless communications networks, the key service for providing seamless connectivity to mobile hosts is creation and maintenance of a message forwarding path between two known locations of calling and called mobile hosts. A routing decision in wireless communications networks is made not only using the states of paths and internal switching nodes, but also using the location of available information.

Geographical area covered by wireless communication networks is partitioned into a set of cells. A routing path may be inefficient while a mobile host hands off to another cell coverage area. The connection paths need to be reestablished each time to continue communication. As a result, the network call processor can become involved many times during the lifetime of mobile connection. When wireless communications networks move toward smaller size cells to accommodate more mobile hosts or to provide higher capacity, the handoff becomes a more frequent part of communications. Conventional routing procedures for connecting mobile hosts fail due to frequent handoff when the network call processor becomes a bottleneck. Hence, routing efficiency in wireless communications networks depends critically on the propagation of location information into the network; however, excessive information propagation can waste network resources, while insufficient location information leads to inefficient routing.

Wireless communications networks can provide different personal communications services, which have different transmission time delay requirements. For cellular telephone communication, the shortest time delay or strict time delay to transmit voice message is required. In portable computer communications or other data communications, the requirements of transmitted time delay are not very strict. Transmitted data can be stored in buffers and be transmitted later when channels are available; however, in order to provide a high QoS, transmission time delay is an important factor in wireless communications networks. Routing procedure in wireless communications networks should depend on different requirements of transmission time delay, and on how to balance transmission load and find minimum cost transmission paths.

## 30.4   Applications Support

### Multimedia

Multimedia communications is the field referring to the representation, storage, retrieval, and dissemination of machine-processable information expressed in multimedia, such as voice, image, text, graphics, and video. With high-capacity storage devices, powerful and yet economical computer workstations, and high-speed integrated services digital networks, providing a variety of multimedia communication services is becoming not only technically but also economically feasible. Multimedia conference systems can help people to interact with each other from their homes or offices while they work as teams by exchanging information in several media, such as voice, text, graphics, and video. Multimedia conference system allows a group of users to conduct a meeting in real time. The participants can jointly view and edit relevant multimedia information, including text, graphics, and still images distributed throughout the LAN. Participants can also communicate simultaneously by voice to discuss the information they are sharing. This multimedia conference system can be used in a wide variety of cooperative work environment, such as distributed software development, joint authoring, and group decision support.

Multimedia is the integration of information that may be represented by several media types, such as audio, video, text, and still images. The diversity of media involved in a multimedia communication system impose strong requirements on the communication system. The media used in the multimedia communications can be classified into two categories: discrete media and continuous media.

Discrete media are those media that have time-independent values, such as text, graphics, or numerical data, bit mapped images, geometric drawings, or any other non-time-dependent data format. Capture, storage, transmission, and display of non-real-time media data does not require that it happen at some predictable and fixed time or within some fixed time period.

Continuous media data may include sound clips, video segments, animation, or timed events. Real-time data requires that any system that is recording or displaying be able to process the appropriate data within a predictable and specified time period. In addition, the display of real-time data may need to be synchronized with other data or some external (real-world) event.

Multimedia data can be accessed by the user either locally or remotely during multimedia communication. Locally stored data typically resides in conventional mass storage systems such as hard disk, CD-ROMs, optical disk, or high-density magnetic tape. It can also be stored to and recalled from analog devices that are under the control of the system, video tape disks, videodisk players, CD-audio disks, image scanners, and printers. In addition, media data can be synthesized locally by the systems or its peripherals. Multimedia data is typically recorded and edited on local systems for distribution on some physical media and is later played back using local devices.

Remotely stored multimedia data is accessed via a network connection to a remote system. The data is stored on that remote server and recalled over the network for viewing, editing, or storage on the user's system.

Multimedia communications cover a large set of domains including office, electronic publishing, medicine, and industry. Multimedia communication can be classified into real-time applications and non-real-time applications.

Multimedia conferencing represents a typical real-time multimedia communication. In general, high conductivity is needed for real-time multimedia communications. A guaranteed bandwidth is required to ensure real-time consistency, and to offer the throughput required by the different media. This bandwidth varies depending on the media involved in the application. There is also a need for synchronization between different users, and between different flows of data at a user workstation.

Non-real-time multimedia communications, such as multimedia mail are less demanding than real-time applications in terms of throughput and delay, but edition tools, exchange formats, and exchange protocols are essential. Multicast service and synchronization at presentation time has to be offered.

Local non-real-time multimedia characterizes most typical personal computer applications, such as word processing, and still image editing. Typical text-based telecommunications can be described as remote non-real-time. Database of text and still image may be interactively viewed and searched, and audio or video data (perhaps included in mail messages) can be downloaded for display locally.

Multimedia workstations are generally characterized by local real-time applications. Data from video and audio editing and annotations, interactive animated presentations, and music recording are stored on local devices and are distributed on physical media for use locally.

Networks that can provide real-time multimedia communication via a high-speed network connection enable the new generation of multimedia applications. Real-time remote workstation-based multimedia conferencing, video and audio remote database browsing, and viewing of movies or other video resources on demand are typical for these systems.

## Mobile and Wireless

The support for bandwidth intensive (multimedia) services in mobile cellular networks increases the network congestion and requires the use of micro/picocellular architectures in order to provide higher capacity in regard to radio spectrum. Micro/pico cellular architectures introduce the problem of frequent hand-offs and make resource allocation difficult. As a result, availability of wireless network resources at the connection setup time does not necessarily guarantee that wireless resources are available throughout the lifetime of a connection. Multimedia traffic imposes the need to guarantee a predefined QoS to all calls serviced by the network.

In microcellular networks supporting multimedia traffic, the resource allocation schemes have to be designed such that a call can be assured a certain QoS once it is accepted into the network. The resource allocation for multimedia traffic becomes quite complex for different classes of traffic comprising multimedia traffic. These classes of traffic have different delay and error rate requirements. Resource allocation schemes must be sensitive to traffic characteristics and adapt to rapidly changing load conditions. From a service point of view, multimedia traffic can be categorized into two main categories: real-time traffic with stringent time delays and relaxed error rates, and non-real-time traffic with relaxed time delays and stringent error rates.

It is important to note that provisioning of QoS to different classes of traffic necessitates a highly reliable radio link between the mobile terminal and its access point. This requires efficient communication techniques to mitigate the problems of delay sensitivity, multipath fading, shadow fading, and cochannel interference. Some methods such as array antennas and optimal combining can be used to combat these problems.

## CAC

Schemes have been proposed to address the problem of resource allocation for multimedia traffic support in microcellular networks. In these schemes, real-time traffic being more delay sensitive, is given priority over non-real-time traffic.

In these schemes, the central approach used is call admission control (CAC). CAC imposes a limit on the number of calls accepted into the network. Each cell site only supports a predetermined number of call connections. This call threshold is periodically calculated depending on the number of existing calls in the cell in which the call arrives and its adjoining cells and the resources utilized by all calls in the cell. Once the threshold is reached, all subsequent requests for new call connections are refused.

## AT

In an admission threshold (AT)-based scheme, resource management is done by periodically calculating the admission threshold and by blocking all new call connection requests once the threshold is reached. The call admission decision is made in a distributed manner whereby each cell site makes a decision by exchanging state information with adjoining cells periodically. A cell with a base station and a control unit is referred to as cell site.

## RS

In a resource sharing (RS)-based scheme to support traffic classes with different delay and error requirements, resource sharing provides a mechanism to ensure a different grade of service to each class of traffic. This scheme employs a resource sharing mechanism that reacts to rapidly changing traffic conditions in a cell. An adaptive call admission control policy that reacts to changing new call arrival rates can be used to keep the handoff dropping rate and forced call termination rate acceptably low.

The call admission control scheme differentiates the new call on the basis of its traffic class and a decision is based on traffic class of the new call connection request and number of call connections of each class already being serviced in the cell cluster.

For real-time call connections, a new call is blocked if no bandwidth is available to service the request. A similar algorithm is used to service a handoff request. The QoS metrics for real time calls are handoff dropping probability and forced call termination probability. For non-real-time calls, the available bandwidth is shared equally among all non-real-time call connections in the cell. Handoff queuing or delaying is not used in this scheme. CAC keeps the probability of a call being terminated before its lifetime acceptably low. Resource sharing algorithms provide better performance for a particular class of traffic.

## RRN

Resource reservation and renegotiation (RRN) scheme provides QoS guarantee to real-time traffic and at the same time guarantees a better performance to non-real-time traffic. The resource allocation scheme uses resource reservation in surrounding cells for real-time calls and renegotiation of bandwidth assigned to non-real-time calls. The resource allocation scheme is simple enough and can be implemented in a distributed manner to ensure fast decision making.

In RRN scheme, for service applications requiring smaller bandwidths, a shared pool of bandwidth is used for reservation. For applications requiring greater bandwidth, the largest of requested bandwidth is reserved. This helps in keeping the call blocking rate low and does not affect the handoff dropping rate.

In microcellular networks, calls require handoffs at much faster rates in comparison to networks with larger cells. On the other hand, microcellular networks provide a higher system capacity. The RRN scheme supports real-time calls and non-real-time calls along with a variety of service type for each class. Real-time calls are delay sensitive and hence cannot be queued or delayed. Resources must be available when a handoff is requested. In order to guarantee that real-time calls are not forced to terminate at the time of handoff, a resource reservation mechanism is used. Resource reservation guarantees acceptably low handoff dropping rate and forced call termination rate for real-time traffic.

For a real-time call, bandwidth is reserved in all cells adjacent to the cell in which the call arrives. When a call hands-off to another cell, if enough bandwidth is not available to service the handoff, it uses the bandwidth reserved in the target cell and thus the likelihood that a call will be dropped is reduced. When a call is successfully handed off to another cell, the bandwidth of old cell is released and reserved in the cell cluster of new cell.

Non-real-time calls are more tolerant to delay as compared to real-time calls. Delay tolerance is equivalent to accepting variable service rate. This property of data traffic makes resource renegotiation possible in microcellular networks. Non-real-time calls receive higher service rates under low traffic conditions while, under heavy traffic conditions, the service rate available to them is kept at a minimum. Thus, the resource renegotiation scheme adapts to changing traffic conditions in the network.

## References

1. A. Hać , Multimedia Applications Support for Wireless ATM Networks, Prentice-Hall, Englewood Cliffs, NJ, 2000.
2. A. S. Tanenbaum, Computer Networks, Prentice-Hall, Englewood Cliffs, NJ, 1996.

# VIII

# Input/Output

# 31

# Circuits for High-Performance I/O

Chik-Kong Ken Yang
*University of California*

The speed of off-chip I/O circuits plays a significant role in the overall performance of a computer system. To keep up with the increasing clock rates in processors, designers target I/O data rates that are exceeding gigabits per second per pin for memory busses [26], peripheral connections [29], and multiprocessor interconnection networks [17]. This chapter examines the issues and challenges in the design of these high-performance I/O subsystems.

As illustrated in Fig. 31.1, an I/O subsystem consists of four components: a transmitter, a transmission medium, a receiver, and a timing-recovery circuit. A transmitter converts the binary sequential bit stream into a stream of analog voltages properly sequenced in time. The medium such as a cable or PCB trace delays and filters the voltage waveform. The receiver recovers the binary values from the output of the medium. As part of the receiver, a clock samples the data to recover the bit sequence compensating for the arbitrary delay of the medium.

This chapter focuses on the transmission over an electrical medium[1] and begins by reviewing the electrical characteristics of transmission lines. The design issues and design techniques for each link component will be described, beginning with the transmitter (section 31.2) continuing with the receiver (section 31.3), and ending with the timing-recovery circuits (section 31.4).

## 31.1 Transmission Lines

A transmission medium confines the energy of a signal and propagates it [33]. The energy is stored as the electric and magnetic field between two conductors, the transmission line. The geometric configuration of the conductors for a segment of the transmission line determines the voltage and current

---

[1]Optical local interconnects are emerging as an alternative for short haul systems.

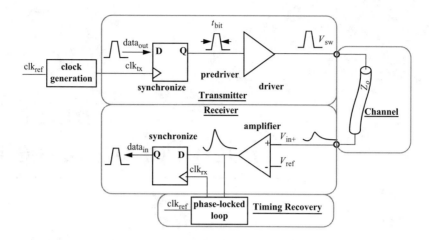

**FIGURE 31.1**   Components of an I/O subsystem.

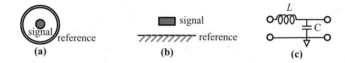

**FIGURE 31.2**   Cross-sectional view of transmission line: (a) coaxial, (b) microstrip (PCB), and (c) LC model of a transmission line.

relationship in that segment defining an effective impedance ($Z_o = V/I$). A signal source driving the segment only sees this impedance as a sink of the signal energy and has no immediate knowledge of other parts of the line.

The two conductors can be either two signals wires driven differentially or a single signal wire over a reference plane where an image current[2] flows in the plane coupled to the signal. A coaxial cable has a center conductor for the signal and the outer shield as the reference (Fig. 31.2(a)). Similarly a PCB trace forms a microstrip line with a ground plane as the reference (Fig. 31.2(b)).

An effective way to model a transmission line is to use capacitances and inductances to represent the electrical and magnetic energy storage and propagation. The entire line is modeled using multiple LC segments as illustrated in Fig. 31.2(c).[3] The impedance of the line and the propagation velocity can be represented as $Z = \sqrt{L/C}$ and $v = 1/(\sqrt{LC})$. An ideal transmission line propagates a signal with no added noise or attenuation. Imperfections in the construction of the line such as varying impedance or neglecting the image current path cause noise in the signal transmission.

## Reflections, Termination, and Crosstalk

When a signal wave encounters a segment with a different impedance, a portion of the signal power reflects back to the transmitter and can interfere with future transmitted signals. The reflection occurs because the boundary condition at a junction of two impedances must be preserved such that (1) the voltage is the same on both sides of the junction and (2) the signal energy into and out of the junction is conserved. For instance, if a lower impedance is seen by a signal, a lower voltage must be propagated along the new segment so that the propagated power is less than the original power. The lower voltage at the junction implies that a negative voltage wave is propagated in the reverse direction. Similarly, at the end of a transmission line, the receiver appears as an open circuit (high impedance) and would cause

---

[2]Image current, also called return current, is equal to the signal current.

[3]The *L*'s and *C*'s are per unit length.

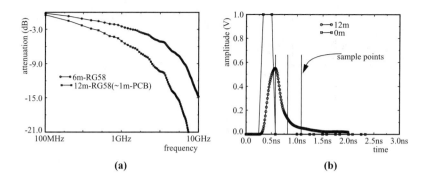

**(a)**                                                        **(b)**

**FIGURE 31.3**   Frequency (a) and time (b) domain of an RG-55U cable illustrating filtering and ISI.

a positive reflection of the entire signal energy. The equation

$$V_{reflect} = \Gamma V_{in} = \frac{Z_{out} - Z_{in}}{Z_{out} + Z_{in}} V_{in}$$

represents the reflected wave, where $\Gamma$ is the reflection coefficient.

Using a termination resistance at the end of the line that is equal to that of the transmission line impedance eliminates the reflection by dissipating the signal power. A reflection only poses a problem if the transmitter reflects the wave again causing the old signal energy from a previous bit to add to the signal of a newly transmitted data bit.[4] Allowing the entire signal to reflect at the receiver is acceptable as long as the line is properly terminated at the transmitter. So proper termination of a transmission line includes matching the resistance either at the receiver (end termination) or at the transmitter (source termination). Noise in the signal results either from imperfect termination at the ends of the line or from variations in the impedance along the line.[5]

A second source of noise is due to the leakage of signal energy from other transmission lines (aggressors) known as crosstalk. Improper design of transmission line often neglects the image current path. Image current can flow on closely routed signal traces on a PCB or nearby signal pins on a connector instead of the reference plane. The coupling appears as noise when the nearby signal transitions. The worst often occurs in the chip carrier where a reference plane is not readily available.

The noise source is modeled as either mutual inductance or capacitance in the LC model. The amount of noise is proportional to the aggressor's signal amplitude. Because the coupling is reactive, the noise is proportional to the frequency of the aggressor signal. This motivates the design of transmitters and receivers to filter frequencies above the data bandwidth, as will be discussed.

## Frequency Response and ISI

An ideal transmission-line segment delays a signal perfectly; however, real transmission media attenuate the signal because of the line conductor's resistance and the loss in the dielectric between the conductors. Both loss mechanisms of wires increase at higher signal frequencies. Hence, a wire low-pass filters and the filtering increases with distance. The transfer function of a 6-m and 12-m cable, shown in Fig. 31.3(a), illustrates increasing attenuation with frequency and distance. Figure 31.3(b) illustrates the effects of that frequency-dependent attenuation in the time-domain. The signal amplitudes are reduced and the energy of each bit is spread in time. If the bit time is short, the spreading causes interference between subsequent

---

[4]This noise can be compensated if the length of the delay and amount of reflection can be measured, but it adds significant complexity to the system.

[5]Impedance variations can be due to vias, changing of reference plane, connectors, etc.

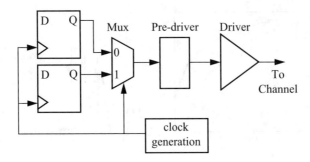

**FIGURE 31.4**   Transmitter components.

bits known as inter-symbol interference (ISI). As data rates increase beyond gigabits per second, the design of transmitters and receivers must incorporate additional filtering to compensate for this low-pass filtering.

## Methods of Signaling

The characteristics of the transmission medium influence the trade-off between various signaling methods. In DRAM or backplane applications where a data word connects between multiple chips, multi-drop busses save considerable pins over point-to-point connections; however, each drop of a bus structure introduces a splitting of a transmission line that causes reflections and increases noise. A similar trade-off exists with differential and single-ended signaling. Differential signaling is more robust to common-mode noise by using the second wire as the explicit image current path. A third trade-off involves whether or not signaling occurs in both directions on a pin simultaneously (full-duplex). Typically, an I/O link contains both a transmitter and a receiver on each end. Only one pair is operating at one time (half-duplex). Operating full-duplex halves the number of pins but degrades the signal amplitude and increases noise because the receiver must now compensate for the transmitted values. All three of these common choices are trading between the number of I/O pins and the signal-to-noise ratio (SNR). For high performance, system designers often opt for the more expensive options of point-to-point and differential links that are half-duplex. Some designers use single-ended signaling that has an explicit and dedicated ground pin for a signal's image current since perfectly differential structures are difficult to maintain in a PCB environment.

The following sections focus on the design of high-performance link circuitry in a high-performance system of point-to-point links. Many of the design techniques are applicable to busses and bidirectional links as well.

## 31.2   Transmitters

Transmitters convert the digital bits into analog voltages. Figure 31.4 illustrates the major pieces of a transmitter. Prior to the conversion by the output driver, transmitters commonly synchronize the data to that of a stable, noise-free clock so the resulting waveform has well-defined timing. Because I/Os often operate at a higher rate than the on-chip clock, the synchronization also multiplexes the data. The simplest and most commonly used is 2:1 multiplexing, using each half-cycle of the clock to transmit a data bit.[6] A pre-driver follows the multiplexing and provides any pre-conditioning of the data signal.

The output voltage range depends on the signaling specification. If the voltage range nears or exceeds that of the on-chip supply voltage, the design must convert the voltage and ensure the reliability to the over-voltage. In addition to protection against electrostatic discharge (ESD), transistors that are not built

---

[6]For memories, the 2:1 multiplexing is known as double-data rate (DDR). The duty cycle of the clock is critical in guaranteeing a constant width of each bit. Even higher multiplexing has been demonstrated using multiple clock phases [52].

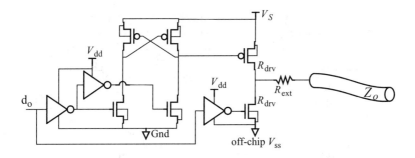

**FIGURE 31.5** Push-pull I/O driver with level shifting pre-drivers.

to handle large voltages across the gate oxide or source/drain junction must be appropriately protected by cascoding and well-biasing. This section begins with discussing these large output-swing transmitters. The section follows with low-swing transmitters, which are more common for high-performance designs.

Noise is the primary challenge. Techniques that reduce noise such as impedance matching, swing control, and slew-rate control are described next. The last part addresses techniques that can be used to reduce intersymbol interference due to a band-limiting transmission channel.

## Large-Swing Output Drivers

A simple push-pull architecture, as shown in Fig. 31.5, can drive a signal as large as the voltage provided for the I/O, $V_s$. When driving a transmission line, the initial output voltage is the result of a voltage division

$$V_o = V_s \left( \frac{R_o}{R_{drv} + R_o} \right)$$

where $R_{drv}$ is the on-resistance of the driving device. The initial voltage is also the final voltage if the line is terminated appropriately at the receiver. In which case, the driver draws continuous current even with the absence of signal transitions. With only source termination ($R_{drv}$ equal to $R_o$), the line voltage settles to $V_s$. The power dissipation is less since no current flows when the signal is constant. If the line is unterminated on either end, the signal will reflect several times before settling to $V_s$. Because the bit period must be long enough for the signal to settle, high-performance links avoid this penalty.

Impedance matching at the transmitter is challenging because (1) process, voltage, and temperature (PVT) varies, and (2) the impedance changes significantly as the device is switched from *on* to *off*. To minimize the net variation, designers over-design the size of the device for an impedance much lower than $R_o$. And then, by adding an external but constant resistance $R_{ext} = R_o - R_{drv}$, the net impedance varies within an acceptable tolerance.

Many chips are required to interface with chips that operate at different power supply voltages. As on-chip supplies lower with CMOS technology scaling, the disparity between on-chip and off-chip voltages increases. Unfortunately, for high reliability, the on-chip devices cannot tolerate excessive over-voltage. Catastrophic breakdown of gate oxide occurs at 12 MV/cm of oxide thickness.

Device technologists address the issue by providing transistors that are slower but high-voltage tolerant. One of the tasks of the pre-driver is to shift the level of the input so that the output-driver devices are fully turned *off*. Figure 31.5 illustrates an example of level-shifting using cross-coupled PMOS devices in the pre-driver.

To avoid over-voltage, circuit designers add a cascode transistor in series with the output switch to reduce the voltage drop [39]. Figure 31.6(a) shows a bottom device that switches with the data. The upper cascoding device uses a constant *high* gate voltage that is commonly the core $V_{dd}$. As long as the output voltage does not exceed $V_{dd} + V_{oxide(max)}$, the gate oxide is preserved. $V_x$ remains below $V_{dd} - V_{T(eff)}$,

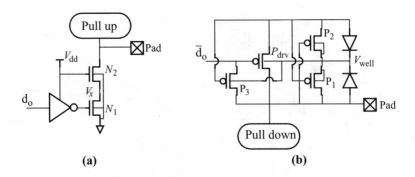

**FIGURE 31.6**   Cascoding (a) and well-biasing (b) to protect driving devices.

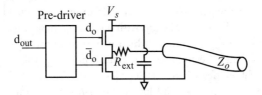

**FIGURE 31.7**   Low-swing, push-pull driver with supply bypassing.

hence avoiding source/drain punchthrough of $N_1$.[7] To avoid a source/drain punchthrough of $N_2$ during an output *high-low* transition, the size of the cascode device needs to be large enough so that $V_x$ does not fall too quickly.[8]

PMOS devices for the pull-up pose an additional challenge. In a half-duplex configuration, the system tri-states the transmitter by pulling the gate of the driving device to the I/O supply voltage, $V_s$; however, with reflections and inductive ringing, line voltages can exceed $V_s$. To avoid forward biasing the drain–well junction, designers leave the well floating, as shown in Fig. 31.6(b) [8]. Transistors $P_1$ and $P_2$ allow the well to be charged up to either the pad voltage or $V_s$ depending on which is higher. To avoid conduction of the driving device when pad voltage is *high*, $P_{drv}$, transistor $P_3$ pulls the gate input to the pad voltage.

## Small-Swing Output Drivers

I/O standards are migrating toward smaller output voltage swings due to several advantages. There is less concern regarding over-voltages on I/O devices. Using smaller devices and fewer over-voltage protection devices reduces output capacitance and improves bandwidth. The device stays in a single region of operation (either in triode or saturation) reducing impedance mismatches. The transmitter also dissipates less power because of the lower-swing and smaller drive devices; however, reducing signal swing directly reduces the SNR making the designs more sensitive to noise.[9] The following describes two commonly used driver architectures: low-impedance and high-impedance drivers.

A simple extension of the large-swing push-pull driver to low-swing is shown in Fig. 31.7, where $V_s$ is a low voltage that determines the signal swing. The transistors operate in the linear region of their I-V curve appearing as a low-impedance signal source. With signal swings under 1 V, a smaller NMOS device can have the same pull-up resistance as PMOS devices. The impedance matching is better than the large signal driver because the device impedance varies less with $V_{ds}$ [19].

However, with low-impedance drivers, power-supply noise appears directly on the signal. By connecting the power supply as the signal's return connection, the noise would appear as common-mode. Unfortunately,

---

[7]Feedthrough from output to the $V_{gate}$ of $N_2$ can dynamically elevate $V_x$ so $N_2$ cannot be excessively large.

[8]$N_2$ can often be a size 4× larger than $N_1$.

[9]Fortunately, many noise sources are proportional to the signal swing, so the SNR degradation is not overly severe.

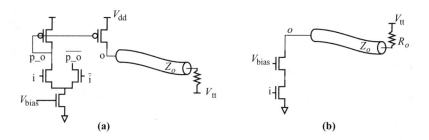

**FIGURE 31.8**    High-impedance drivers: PECL (a) and open-drain (b).

the connection is difficult because multiple I/Os (and sometimes the core logic) share the ground to minimize cost. Furthermore, signal current flows through two supplies. To reduce noise, designers trade-off area and pin by (1) bypassing $V_s$ to ground with a large capacitance, (2) limiting the number of I/Os sharing a single ground, and (3) carefully minimizing the inductive loop formed by the current return path (ground connection).

A second style of drivers, high-impedance drivers, switch currents instead of voltages. By keeping transistors in the saturated-current region, the devices appear as current sources. The current can be switched either differentially in PECL type drivers (Fig. 31.8(a)) or single-ended in open-drain type drivers (Fig. 31.8(b)). To provide source termination, a resistor ($R_o$) can be placed in parallel with the output. These drivers have several advantages over their low-impedance counterparts. The outputs have less noise because the high-impedance isolates the output from one of the power supplies, but it is critical for the current to remain constant. The output bandwidth is higher because the saturated device (with a higher $V_{ds}$) is smaller in size, for a given current than a triode device (with low $V_{ds}$); however, because of the higher $V_{ds}$, these drivers dissipate more power, $I \cdot V_s$.

For both high- and low-impedance drivers, switching currents inject noise onto the supply via di/dt. Instead of using purely single-ended drivers, complementary single-ended drivers approximates a constant current and reduces the noise. Differential drivers such as PECL force a constant current over time and eliminate the problem.[10]

## Impedance, Current, and Slew-Rate Control

Process, voltage, and temperature (PVT) variations can cause drive resistance (of low-impedance drivers) and currents (of high-impedance drivers) to deviate from the design target causing offsets and noise. For robust operation, control loops are often used to dynamically maintain the proper impedance or current. To minimize coupled and reflected noise, designers also limit the high-frequency spectral content of the output signal. This section describes these noise reduction methods.

Figure 31.9 illustrates the block diagram of a loop that controls the current of a high-impedance driver [28]. The output driver device is divided into binary-weighted segments. A digital control word, stored in a register, sets the number of transistors used by the driver. A replica driver determines the control word. The replica drives half the output impedance. A comparator compares the output voltage with a reference voltage set at $V_s - V_{sw}/2$, where $V_{sw}$ is the desired voltage swing of the output. The comparison result increments or decrements the control word until reaching the desired output current. A similar loop can control the output impedance by adjusting the resistance of driving devices using binary-weighted segments [7].

As mentioned earlier, filtering the high-frequency spectral content of the output signal reduces coupling noise. This is equivalent to limiting the output slew rate, but an excessively low slew rate may filter the signal's desired spectral frequencies and cause ISI. The difficulty arises when the slew rate is designed for

---

[10]The drawback is that differential drivers have slightly larger output capacitance because the differential input devices have smaller $V_{gs}$ and need to be larger to switch the output current.

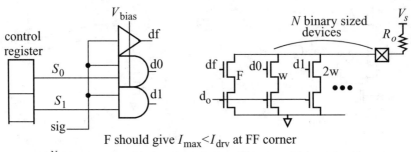

F should give $I_{max} < I_{drv}$ at FF corner

$(2^N-1) \times W + F$ should give $I_{min} > I_{drv}$ at SS corner ($S_0=..=S_N=1$)

**Setting the control register**

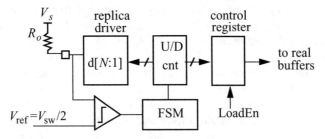

**FIGURE 31.9**  Current-control feedback loop.

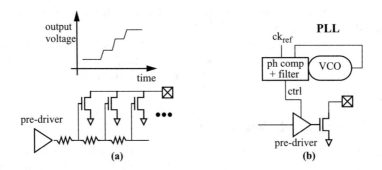

**FIGURE 31.10**  Slew-rate control using resistors (a) and controlled pre-driver (b).

the fastest operating condition. The slowest operating condition would cause excessive ISI. Early designs of drivers use devices that correlate inversely with transistor speed. In the example shown in Fig. 31.10(a), an output device can be broken into segments and each segment turns on sequentially [41]. The delay can be introduced using polysilicon resistors, which are not very sensitive to PVT. More recent methods (Fig. 31.10(b)) control the rate at which the pre-driver turns on the output device. By using a control voltage that tracks PVT,[11] the pre-driver resistance or current stays constant and consequently the slew-rate.

## Transmitter Pre-Emphasis

When the data rate exceeds the channel bandwidth, designers compensate for the filtering by equalization. Because of the ease of implementation, many high-speed links equalize at the transmitter by pre-distorting the signal to emphasize higher frequencies [6,14,50]. Early pre-emphasis designs were known as advanced pull up/down (APU/D) [12], which were applied to driving large capacitances. The technique turns on

---

[11]The control voltage can be the voltage of a VCO whose frequency is locked to an external reference clock via a PLL [49].

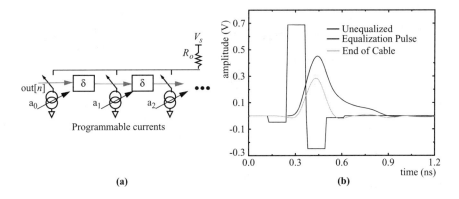

**FIGURE 31.11**  Transmitter pre-distorted waveform (a) and implementation (b).

the driver more strongly for a period immediately after a data transition so that the transmitter drives higher frequency components with more signal power. For more complex channel responses, a programmable filter precedes the actual line driver and inverts the effect of the channel. Figure 31.11(a) illustrates an example of an analog filter. The length of the optimal filter depends on the tail of the pulse response. For many cables (less than 10 m) one or two taps is sufficient [6,13,14]. Figure 31.11(b) shows the effect of transmitter equalization. The small, negative pulses before and after the original pulse eliminates the tails of the pulse response.

A digital-FIR filter would output a quantized word that represents the output voltage. Instead of transmitting two levels, the driver is a high-speed D/A converter. Because current or impedance control uses binary-weighted driver segments, designs for a D/A converter are not significantly different; however, a design with linearity of >6 bits at multi-GSamples/sec faces challenging issues: device mismatches limit linearity, transmit clock jitter limits the SNR, and the switching of output transitions induce glitches. Thermal noise for a 50-$\Omega$ environment is approximately $1\,\text{nV}/\sqrt{\text{Hz}}$ and only limits resolution at very high resolution. Recent research has demonstrated this potential with <6-bit D/A converters [10,13].

Two system issues must be considered when implementing transmitter pre-distortion. First, transmit power is limited, so the low-frequency signal energy must be attenuated to that of the worst-case attenuation of the channel. This leads to significant loss of SNR. Second, the channel characteristic is not known to the transmitter. Accurate filter coefficients are dynamically trained with loopback information sent from the receiver, which adds complexity to the system.

## 31.3  Receivers

The task of the receiver is to convert the analog waveform from the channel into a sequence of binary data. Figure 31.12 illustrates the common components of a receiver. First, an input amplifier conditions the signal. A sampling circuit follows and captures the analog value of each bit. A comparator amplifies the sampled value to digital values. Similar to the transmitter, the sampling block often demultiplexes the data so that the on-chip clock rate can be slower than the off-chip data rate. The most simple and common design uses two samplers operating on opposite edges of a digital clock for 2:1 demultiplexing.

The primary difficulty in high-performance receiver design is maintaining low noise, both static and dynamic. The noise of a signal at the receiver can be illustrated by an eye diagram (Fig. 31.13), which overlays the waveform of each bit of a random sequence. The transmitter design and the channel contributes the majority of the signal's amplitude and timing noise. The receiver should compare the signal with a proper reference voltage. Static offsets reduce the effective signal amplitude reducing the SNR. To minimize dynamic noise, the receiver should reject supply and common-mode noise, filter high-frequency input noise, and avoid any bandwidth limitation and ISI. Sampling the data at the optimal point will be addressed in the timing-recovery section. This section describes several examples of high-performance receiver designs. Then techniques to reduce noise and ISI are addressed.

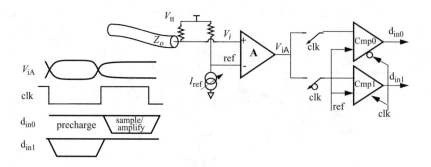

**FIGURE 31.12**   Receiver components.

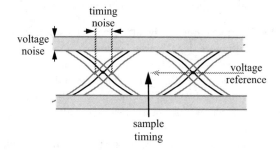

**FIGURE 31.13**   Eye diagram at the receiver.

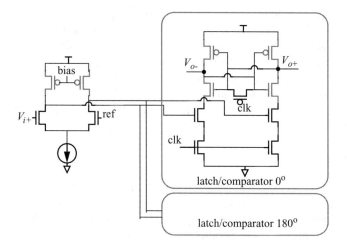

**FIGURE 31.14**   Receiver design with receiving amplifier.

## Receiver Designs

Figure 31.14 illustrates an example of a receiver design. The first stage performs several tasks: (1) filtering the noise, (2) level-shifting the output, and (3) amplifying the signal. An amplifier with appropriate bandwidth can filter input noise frequencies above the data bandwidth. Furthermore, using a differential structure improves the common-mode and supply noise rejection even though the input may be single-ended. The outputs of the first stage [5,9] are differential for good supply noise sensitivity and are

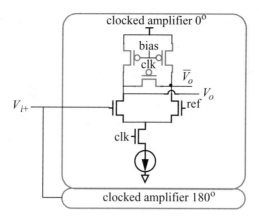

**FIGURE 31.15**  Receiver design using clocked amplifier/sampler as first stage.

level-shifted[12] to accommodate the clocked comparator that follows [34]. A *high* clock level resets the comparator shown in Fig. 31.14. The negative clock edge samples the data and starts a positive feedback that regeneratively amplifies the sampled value to digital values during the *low* clock phase. To demultiplex the data, the comparators operate on different clock phases. The amplification is exponentially dependent on the duration of the *low* phase. Because the comparator has high gain, the first stage does not need significant gain. Some gain reduces the effective input offset voltage since the contribution of the comparator's offset is divided by the gain. Mismatch in the feedback devices and clock coupling of the comparators can introduce significant offsets. For very high data rates, the drawback of the design is that the first stage must have sufficient bandwidth to minimize ISI. Furthermore, delay variation of the first stage can add timing noise.

A simple design can avoid ISI by eliminating the first stage and sampling/demultiplexing the input with comparators directly [24,52]. Because the comparators are reset before each sample, no signal energy from previous bits remains hence removing ISI; however, direct sampling is noisier and has larger static offsets. Figure 31.15 illustrates an alternate design that clocks the first stage to remove ISI but still conditions the signal [26,43]. During the low phase of the clock, the amplifier output is reset. During the high phase of the clock, the amplifier conditions the data. For demultiplexing, two clocked amplifiers loads the input. A comparator samples the amplifier output to further amplify to digital levels. The clock used for the clocked amplifier must be timed with the arriving signal to amplify the proper bit. The timing issue will be discussed in section 31.4.

## dc Offsets

Random dc offsets limit the voltage resolution of the receiver. These offset are due to random mismatches in the devices and scales inversely with the size of the device [35]. Because minimum size devices are often used to minimize pin capacitance and power dissipation, input-referred offset of amplifiers and comparators can be tens of millivolts.

To compensate for the error, devices are added that can create an offset in either the first amplifier or the comparator. The control can be open-loop where the compensation value is determined with an initial calibration [10]. Figure 31.16(a) shows a comparator with digitally controllable switches that differentially inject an error current. The open-loop compensation is commonly digital so the value does not drift in time. Alternatively, the control can be continuously operating and closed-loop [51]. As shown in Figure 31.16(b), a third nonoverlapping clock phase, $clk_1$, is added to the reset and amplify ($clk_0$) phases of operation. $Clk_1$ reconfigures the amplifier to short the inputs and to store the value of the offset on

---

[12]The input common-mode voltage depends on the transmitter and the I/O specification.

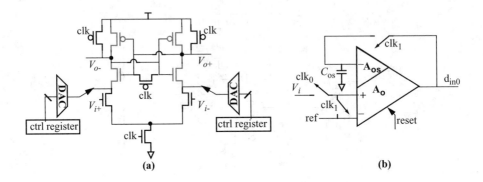

**FIGURE 31.16** Offset cancellation using digital controllable switchs (a) and using feedback control (b).

capacitors, $C_{os}$. If data is encoded so that averaged dc is a constant (dc-balanced), a similar technique finds the offset by averaging of the received data [22] instead of wasting a phase to short the inputs.

## Noise

The main sources of noise for a receiver are mutual coupling between I/O signals and differences between chip ground and board ground. Large image currents that flow through the supply pins to support the output drivers cause significant voltage differences.[13] Some of the supply noise inevitably appears at the input to the receiver. Signaling differentially and carefully routing the two signals together can effectively reduce noise to the order of tens of millivolts. Supply noise couple capacitively as common-mode noise. Furthermore, mutual coupling from other signals is at least partially compensated by coupling from its complement.

Single-ended signaling can achieve nearly the same performance if the return current supply connection is brought on-chip, tightly coupled to the signal through a separate pin. The receiver's reference can be derived from the return connection, but this requires the same number of pins as differential signaling. To save pins, most single-ended systems use the chip supplies ($V_{dd}$ and ground) to derive the reference. Or, several receivers share a single return current connection. Unfortunately, since the reference signal is shared, the capacitance between the supplies to the input pad and to the reference voltage differ. The larger capacitance to the reference couples more high-frequency supply noise [26,42,46]. Single-ended systems typically require larger input swings than differential systems for the same performance.

A band-limited receiving amplifier can filter some of the noise. One approach to control the bandwidth is to bias the effective load transistors with a control signal that tracks the bit time.[14] To maintain constant output swing, the bias current of the differential amplifier must also track. An ideal filter for square-wave inputs averages the input signal over the bit time with an integrator[15] [43]. An integrating receiver replaces the load elements with capacitors. The capacitors integrate the current that is switched by the input value. At the end of the bit time, a comparator samples and compares the values on the capacitors before the integrator is reset.

## Receiver Equalization

With data rates above the bandwidth of the channel, an alternative to transmitter pre-emphasis is to build the inverse channel filter at the receiver. Designers can increase the gain of the first amplifier at high-frequencies to flatten the system response [45]. The required high-pass filter can also be implemented

---

[13]On-chip bypass capacitance only reduces chip $V_{DD}$ to chip ground noise, and has no effect on the noise between chip ground and board ground.

[14]Similar to transmitter slew-rate control, one can leverage the fact that buffers in the clock generator have been adjusted to have a bandwidth related to the bit rate [49].

[15]Most signals are not perfect square waves. In addition to finite signal slew rate, bit boundaries contain timing uncertainty. Integrating over a portion of the bit-time ("window") can reduce noise.

digitally by first feeding the input to an analog-to-digital converter (ADC) and digitally post-processing the ADC's output. An ADC is commonly used in disk-drive read channels since it also allows one to implement more complex nonlinear receive filters. Although this approach works well at frequencies lower than 1 GHz, it is very challenging with gigahertz signals because of the required GSamples/sec converters. Recent research demonstrated a multi-GSamples/sec 4-bit ADC [10] (1 W of power), which indicates the potential of high data rate conversion albeit with high power dissipation. Instead of a digital implementation, for less area and power overhead at these high bit rates, a simple 1-tap FIR filter $(1 - \alpha D)$ has been implemented as a switched-current filter [13] or a switched capacitor filter [47].

## 31.4 Timing Generation and Recovery

The task of timing recovery essentially determines the timing relationship between the transmitter and the receiver so that the data can be received with minimal error. Typically, the burden of adjusting the timing relationship falls on the receiver. Transmitter clocking is much easier where one primarily needs a low-jitter clock source.[16] The receiver has a more difficult task of recovering the timing from the received signals.

The prior receiver discussion does not address how to generate the clock for the amplifiers and samplers. Recovering a clock signal with low timing noise (jitter) and with accurate phase position is the most difficult challenge for high data rates. The same eye diagram in Fig. 31.13 illustrates the timing margin of a receiver. To maximize the timing margin, the receiver should sample the data in the middle of the data-eye.[17] If clocked amplifiers are used, the clock should be in-phase with the data to maximize the settling time of the amplifier. Furthermore, designs should minimize the jitter of both the sampling clock and the clock used at the transmitter. Almost all clock recovery circuits use a feedback loop known as a phase-locked loop (PLL) to adjust the clock phase position and minimize jitter. This section discusses different PLL architectures and methods to reduce offsets from the ideal sampling position (static phase offsets) and jitter.

### Architectures

A PLL is often used to synchronize the transmitter clock's phase and frequency[18] to that of a system clock. In order to transmit phase information along with the data, two methods are commonly used. For short distances of a wide data bus, source synchronous clocking is a method that transmits a clock in-phase with the data. Otherwise, prior to transmission, data is encoded to contain periodic data transitions that can be used to align the receive clock [13,15]. In some systems, the receiver and the transmitter use clocks with slightly different frequencies. Then the timing recovery PLL has the additional task of recovering the frequency from the data transitions.

Figure 31.17 shows the architecture of a PLL. Two basic approaches are used: oscillator-based PLLs, and delay-line-based PLLs or delay-locked loops (DLLs). Both systems are similar feedback loops where a control voltage ($V_{ctl}$) adjust the phase of the periodic output signal ($clk_{int}$) to have a fixed phase relationship with the input signal ($inp_{ref}$). To distribute the clock to many receivers, a buffer chain drives the clock line, $clk_{samp}$.

DLLs control the output phase by directly adjusting the delay of a voltage-controlled delay line (VCDL) [25]. The control loop integrates the control voltage to drive the phase error to zero. This feedback loop is a first-order loop and is guaranteed stability, but it is constrained in that the frequency of the input clock ($clk_{ext}$ or $inp_{ref}$) determines the frequency of the output signal. Furthermore, the delay elements limit the maximum and minimum delay of the line. Designing the range to be large enough for all PVT and starting the loop at the correct delay often require auxiliary circuits. Using an oscillator-based PLL

---

[16]If data is multiplexed, clock phases must be properly positioned. For 2:1 multiplexing, the duty cycle needs to be 50%.

[17]The eye may not be symmetric. Off-center sampling may increase the amplitude of the sampled signal.

[18]PLLs are often used to generate a multiplied frequency.

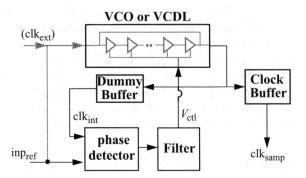

**FIGURE 31.17**    Phase-locked loop architecture using oscillator (a) and delay-line (b).

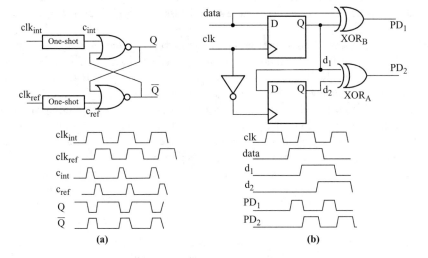

**FIGURE 31.18**    Phase-detection using SR-latch (a) or XOR (b) to detect data transition.

provides more flexible in frequency and phase. The oscillator is often implemented using a ring of controllable delay elements,[19] but an oscillator-based system is more complex to design. The phase of the output signal is adjusted by integrating the change in frequency of the oscillator. Thus, an oscillator-based PLL is a higher-order control system that has stability constraints [3,38].

Phase detector designs vary depending on whether the input reference is a clock or a data sequence. Recovering the phase from an input clock is easier because a transition is guaranteed every cycle. An example shown in Fig. 31.18(a) is an SR-latch where the Q and $\overline{Q}$ outputs have equal pulse widths when the input clocks are spaced 180° apart [44]. When the phases deviate from 180°, the difference in pulse width indicates the phase difference. For data input, the added difficulty is recovering the transitions. A common design technique shown in Fig. 31.18(b) uses XORs to compare consecutive bits [20]. When the XOR output is *high*, a phase difference is present. $PD_1$ is high starting on a transition of the input to the rising edge of the clock. $PD_2$ is high for half the clock period whenever data transitions. The phase difference is the difference between the pulse width of $PD_1$ and $PD_2$.[20]

---

[19]With the availability of on-chip inductors, LC-type oscillators often used in RF applications are being considered in large digital ICs.

[20]In order to recover frequency where the input data frequency is significantly different from the oscillator natural frequency, phase detection alone is often not sufficient. An entire class of circuits aids frequency acquisition [13,36,40].

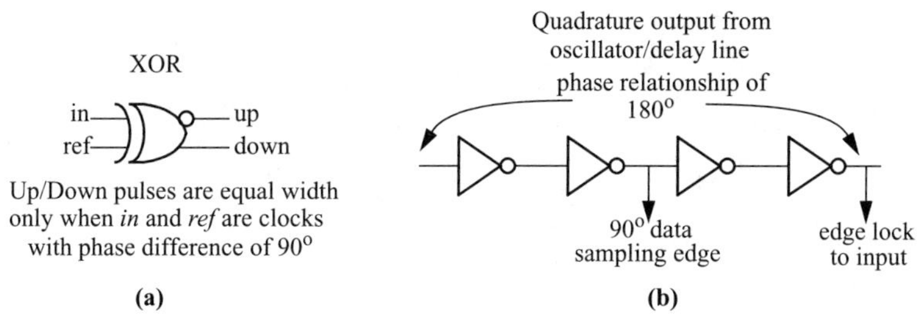

**FIGURE 31.19** 90° locking using XOR (a) and ring-oscillator (b).

## Minimizing Jitter

Jitter in the sampling clock is primarily due to the sensitivity of the loop elements to supply noise. Although the feedback system can correct for noise with frequencies below the bandwidth of the loop, high-frequency noise can appear as jitter on the output clocks. Loop elements, especially oscillator or delay-line buffer elements, are often differential and have high common-mode and supply rejection to minimize the noise. Oscillators in particular are carefully designed because noise causes errors in frequency [32]. Phase error accumulates because it is the integral of the frequency error.

Many clocks drive large capacitances. Clock buffers are typically CMOS inverters for power efficiency, but they have much higher supply sensitivity than the delay buffers[21] and cause over half of the total jitter of the output clock. Dummy clock buffers are often included in the feedback of the PLL (Fig. 31.17) to use the feedback loop to track out the low frequency portion of the noise [1,21]. A well-designed loop in a system with 5% supply noise will often have a jitter roughly 0.5 of the delay of a FO-4 inverter[22] of the clock period. Intrinsic jitter without supply noise can be more than three times less.

## Phase Detection and Static Phase Offsets

In addition to the jitter, dc phase offsets are equally important in maximizing the timing margin. Using a loop that integrates the phase error helps reduce any inherent offsets. The offset primarily depends on any errors in the time spacing between sampling clocks when demultiplexing, and the mismatch between the phase detector and the receiver.

In a 1:2 demultiplexing receiver, the clock (0°) and its complement (180°) are used. Duty cycle errors can cause one receiver to not sample at its optimal location. Typically, a correction loop is added to the PLL output to guarantee 50% duty cycle[23] [31]. The loop averages a clock waveform to determine the duty cycle. Using the information, the duty cycle can be adjusted by changing the logical threshold of a clock buffer.

To sample at the middle of a data bit, a clock must be 90° shifted with respect to the data. This shift can be achieved by either (1) using a phase detector that indicates zero error when the difference is 90° [42], or (2) locking to 0° and shifting the clock by 90°. The first method employs XORs in the design of the phase detector. Figure 31.19(a) illustrates a simple case, when the reference input and loop output are two clock waveforms. The XOR output has equal high and low durations when the clocks are 90° apart. In the second method shown in Fig. 31.19(b), reference and loop output are locked in-phase. Using a ring-oscillator with even number of stages, an internal clock phase in the ring can be tapped for the 90° clock [27,49].

A common error in phase locking is that the receiving comparator has a nonzero setup time. To optimally sample the data, the clock position should be adjusted for the setup time.[24] An additional delay

---

[21]A 1% change in supply yields roughly a 1% change in delay, which can be 10× that of delay buffers.

[22]For a figure relatively insensitive to PVT, the time can be normalized relative to the delay of a FO-4 inverter.

[23]A higher degree of demultiplexing requires multiple phases to be generated and tuning of each phase position [52].

[24]An error that is not easily dealt with is any data dependent setup time variations. This can be minimized by designing the receiver for low input-offset voltage and hysteresis.

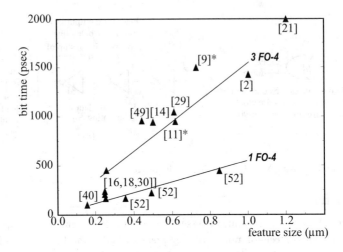

**FIGURE 31.20**   Scaling of link performance with process technology.

at the input of the phase detector can compensate for the setup delay. The most accurate compensation is to use a replica of the receiver as the phase detector since the setup time is inherent to the receiver; however, this poses challenge because a receiver does not give phase information proportional to the phase difference. The output only indicates that the loop clock is either earlier or later than an reference clock transition. An oscillator-based loop is not stable with this type of bang-bang control so only DLLs can be built. In order to also lock to the input frequency, a clever design uses a dual-loop architecture that locks to the input frequency using a core loop [21,27,44]. Coarsely-spaced clock phases from the core loop are interpolated[25] to generate a clock phase that can be finely controlled. This loop clock is locked to the input phase using a receiver replica phase detector. Using these techniques, phase offsets can be smaller than 2% of the bit time.

## 31.5   Conclusion

This chapter has described the design goals and challenges for high-performance I/O. Performance using 2:1 multiplexing of greater than 5 Gb/s has been demonstrated using a 0.18-$\mu$m CMOS technology [16,18,40]. Higher bit-rates have been shown using higher degree of multiplexing and demultiplexing. Because transistor speeds will scale with technology, link speeds are expected to scale as well. Unfortunately, noise coupling due to parasitic capacitances and inductances increases with frequency requiring designs to be even more robust to noise. Designs employ many of the noise reductions techniques described in this chapter and have continued to scale. Figure 31.20 illustrates the scaling so far. Future designs will need to improve these noise reducing and filtering techniques. Furthermore, wire bandwidth does not scale with technology scaling so the compensating for the low-pass filtering will be even more important.

Methods are being researched that can squeeze more bits into existing bandwidth. Given an SNR, Shannon's limit shows the maximum channel capacity to be Capacity/$f_{bw}$ = log(1 + SNR). Researchers are beginning to show that multilevel (4 + PAM) can be encoded in each bit period at the gigabits per second broadband data rate [10,13]. This and many techniques [37] that have been demonstrated in phone modems [4,23] can dramatically increase capacity to 10 bits/Hz in extremely noisy conditions, but all require accurate A/D and D/A converters. Research has shown that they are feasible but require extremely accurate timing. Low-jitter PLLs that lock accurately to the data phase are critical in maintaining the resolution at the gigahertz sampling rates.

---

[25]Interpolation takes two clock phases and performs a weighted average to generate an intermediate clock phase [32,52].

Power of these links is becoming an important issue. For many digital systems, the aggregate off-chip bandwidth is expected to exceed terabits per second in 2010. The data rate is not expected of a single link but over hundreds of I/Os. Each I/O cannot afford power more than a few tens of milliwatts.

These issues challenge the next generation of higher-performance link designs. The availability of faster and more abundant transistor as CMOS technology scales will help designers face the challenges.

# References

1. Alvarez, J. et al., "A wide-bandwidth low-voltage PLL for PowerPC microprocessors," *IEEE Journal of Solid-State Circuits,* vol. 30, no. 4, pp. 383–391, April 1995.
2. Banu, M., A. Dunlop, "A 660Mb/s CMOS clock recovery circuit with instantaneous locking for NRZ data and burst-mode transmission," in *1993 IEEE International Solid-State Circuits Conference. Digest of Technical Papers,* San Francisco, CA, pp. 102–103, Feb. 1993.
3. Best, R., *Phase-Locked Loops,* 3rd ed., McGraw Hill, New York, 1997.
4. Boxho, J. et al., "An analog front end for multi-standard power line carrier modem," in *1997 IEEE International Solid-State Circuits Conference. Digest of Technical Papers,* pp. 84–85.
5. Chappell, B. et al., "Fast CMOS ECL receivers with 100-mV worst case sensitivity," *IEEE Journal of Solid State Circuits,* vol. 23, no. 1, pp. 59–67, Feb. 1988.
6. Dally, W.J. et al., "Transmitter equalization for 4-Gbps signaling," *IEEE Micro,* vol. 17, no. 1, pp. 48–56, Jan.–Feb. 1997.
7. DeHon, A. et al., "Automatic impedance control," in *1993 IEEE International Solid-State Circuits Conference. Digest of Technical,* pp. 164–165, Feb. 1993.
8. Dobberpuhl, D. et al., "A 200-MHz 64 b dual-issue microprocessor," *IEEE Journal of Solid-State Circuits,* vol. 27, no. 11, p. 1555, Nov. 1992.
9. Donnelly, K.S. et al., "A 660 MB/s interface megacell portable circuit in 0.3 $\mu$m–0.7 $\mu$m CMOS ASIC," *IEEE Journal of Solid-State Circuits,* vol. 31, no. 12, pp. 1995–2003, Dec. 1996.
10. Ellersick, W. et al., "A serial-link transceiver based on 8 GSa/s A/D and D/A converters in 0.25-$\mu$m CMOS," in *2001 IEEE International Solid-State Circuits Conference. Digest of Technical,* pp. 58–59, Feb. 2001.
11. Enam, S.K., A.A. Abidi, "NMOS ICs for clock and data regeneration in gigabit-per-second optical-fiber receivers," *IEEE Journal of Solid-State Circuits,* vol. 27, no. 12, pp. 1763–1774, Dec. 1992.
12. Esch, G.L., Jr. et al., "Theory and design of CMOS HSTL I/O pads," *Hewlett-Packard Journal Hewlett-Packard,* vol. 49, no. 3, pp. 46–52, Aug. 1998.
13. Farjad-Rad, R. et al., "A 0.3-$\mu$m CMOS 8-GS/s 4-PAM serial link transceiver," *IEEE Journal of Solid-State Circuits,* vol. 35, no. 5, pp. 757–764, May 2000.
14. Fiedler, A. et al., "A 1.0625 Gbps transceiver with 2x-oversampling and transmit signal pre-emphasis," in *1997 IEEE International Solid-State Circuits Conference. Digest of Technical Papers,* pp. 238–239.
15. Franaszek, P., A. Widmar, "Byte oriented DC balanced (0,4) 8B/10B partitioned block transmission code," US Patent 4486739, Dec. 04, 1984.
16. Fukaishi, M. et al., "A 4.25-Gb/s CMOS fiber channel transceiver with asynchronous tree-type demultiplexer and frequency conversion architecture," *IEEE Journal of Solid-State Circuits,* vol. 33, pp. 2139–2147, Dec. 1998.
17. Galles, M. et al., "Spider: a high-speed network interconnect," *IEEE Micro,* vol. 17, no. 1, pp. 34–39, Jan.–Feb. 1997.
18. Gu, R. et al., "A 0.5–3.5 Gb/s low-power low-jitter serial data CMOS transceiver," in *1999 International Solid-State Circuits Conference. Digest of Technical Papers,* San Francisco, CA, pp. 352–353, Feb. 1999.
19. Gunning, B. et al., "A CMOS low-voltage-swing transmission-line transceiver," in *1992 International Solid-State Circuits Conference. Digest of Technical Papers,* San Francisco, CA, Feb. 1992.
20. Hogge, Jr., C.R., "A self-correcting clock recovery circuit," *IEEE Transation on Electron Devices,* vol. ED-32, pp. 2704–2706, Dec. 1985.

21. Horowitz, M. et al., "PLL design for a 500 MB/s interface," in *1993 IEEE International Solid-State Circuits Conference. Digest of Technical Papers,* pp. 160–161.

22. Hu, T.H. et al., "A monolithic 480 Mb/s parallel AGC/decision/clock-recovery circuit in 1.2-µm CMOS," *IEEE Journal of Solid-State Circuits,* vol. 28, no. 12, pp. 1314–1320, Dec. 1993.

23. Ishida, H. et al., "A single-chip V.32 bis modem," in *1994 IEEE International Solid-State Circuits Conference. Digest of Technical Papers,* pp. 66–67.

24. Johansson, H.O. et al., "Time resolution of NMOS sampling switches used on low-swing signals," *IEEE Journal of Solid-State Circuits,* vol. 33, no. 2, pp. 237–245, Feb. 1998.

25. Johnson, M.G. et al., "A variable delay line PLL for CPU-coprocessor synchronization," *IEEE Journal of Solid-State Circuits,* vol. 23, no. 5, pp. 1218–1223, Oct. 1988.

26. Kushiyama, N. et al., "A 500-megabyte/s data rate 4.5 M DRAM," *IEEE Journal of Solid-State Circuits,* vol. 28, no. 4, pp. 490–498, April 1993.

27. Larsson, P. et al., "A 2–1600 MHz 1.2–2.5 V CMOS clock-recovery PLL with feedback phase-selection and averaging phase-interpolation for jitter reduction," in *1999 IEEE International Solid-State Circuits Conference. Digest of Technical Papers,* pp. 356–357, Feb. 1999.

28. Lau, B. et al., "A 2.6 GB/s multi-purpose chip to chip interface," in *1998 IEEE International Solid-State Circuits Conference. Digest of Technical Papers,* pp. 162–163.

29. Lee, K. et al., "A jitter-tolerant 4.5 Gb/s CMOS interconnect for digital display," in *1998 IEEE International Solid-State Circuits Conference. Digest of Technical,* pp. 310–311, Feb. 1998.

30. Lee, M.J., W. Dally, P. Chang, "Low-power area-efficient high-speed I/O circuit techniques," *IEEE Journal of Solid-State Circuits,* vol. 35, no. 11, pp. 1591–1599, Nov. 2000.

31. Lee, T.H. et al., "A 2.5 V CMOS delay-locked loop for 18 Mbit, 500 megabyte/s DRAM," *IEEE Journal of Solid-State Circuits,* vol. 29, no. 12, pp. 1491–1496, Dec. 1994.

32. Maneatis, J.G. et al., "Low-jitter process-independent DLL and PLL based on self-biased techniques," *IEEE Journal of Solid-State Circuits,* vol. 31, no. 11, pp. 1723–1732, Nov. 1996.

33. Matick, R., "Transmission lines for digital and communication networks," 3rd ed., IEEE Press, 1997.

34. Montanaro, J. et al., "A 160-MHz 32-b 0.5-W CMOS RISC microprocessor," *IEEE Journal of Solid-State Circuits,* vol. 31, pp. 1703–1714, Nov. 1996.

35. Pelgrom, M.J., "Matching properties of MOS transistors," *IEEE Journal of Solid-State Circuits,* vol. 24, no. 10, p. 1433, Dec. 1989.

36. Pottbacker, A. et al., "A Si-bipolar phase and frequency detector IC for clock extraction up to 8Gb/s," *IEEE Journal of Solid-State Circuits,* vol. 27, pp. 1747–1751, Dec. 1992.

37. Proakis, J., Salehi, M., *Communication Systems Engineering,* Prentice-Hall, 1994.

38. Razavi, B. Editor, *Monolithic Phase Locked Loops and Clock Recovery Circuits,* IEEE Press, 1996.

39. Sanchez, H., et al., "A versatile 3.3 V/2.5 V/1.8 V CMOS I/O driver built in a 0.2-mm 3.5 nm tox 1.8 V technology," in *1999 IEEE International Solid-State Circuits Conference. Digest of Technical Papers,* p. 276.

40. Savoj, J., B. Razavi, "A 10 Gb/s CMOS clock data recovery circuit," *Symposium on VLSI Circuits (IEEE/JSAP). Digest of Technical Papers,* Honolulu, HI, pp. 136–139, June 2000.

41. Senthinathan, R. et al., "Application specific CMOS output driver circuit design techniques to reduce simultaneous switching noise," *IEEE Journal of Solid-State Circuits,* vol. 28, no. 12, pp. 1383–1388, Dec. 1993.

42. Sidiropoulos, S. et al., "A CMOS 500-Mbps/pin synchronous point to point link interface," in *Proceedings of 1994 IEEE Symposium on VLSI Circuits. Digest of Technical Papers,* pp. 43–44.

43. Sidiropoulos, S. et al., "A 700-Mb/s/pin CMOS signaling interface using current integrating receivers," *IEEE Journal of Solid-State Circuits,* vol. 32, no. 5, pp. 681–690, May 1997.

44. Sidiropoulos, S. et al., "A semi-digital DLL with unlimited phase shift capability and 0.08–400 MHz operating range," in *1997 IEEE International Solids-State Circuits Conference. Digest of Technical Papers,* pp. 332–333.

45. Song, B.S. et al., "NRZ timing recovery technique for band limited channels," in *1996 IEEE International Solid-State Circuits Conference. Digest of Technical Papers,* pp. 194–195.

46. Takahashi, T. et al., "A CMOS gate array with 600 Mb/s simultaneous bidirectional I/O circuits," *IEEE Journal of Solid-State Circuits,* vol. 30, no. 12, Dec. 1995.

47. Tamura, H. et al., "Partial response detection technique for driver power reductio in high speed memory-to-processor communications," in *1997 IEEE International Solid-State Circuits Conference. Digest of Technical Papers,* pp. 241–248.

48. Van de Plassche, R., *Integrated Analog-to-Digital and Digital-to-Analog Converters,* Kluwer Academic Publishers, Dordrecht, the Netherlands, 1994.

49. Wei, G. et al., "A variable frequency parallel I/O interface with adaptive supply regulation," *IEEE Journal of Solid-State Circuits,* vol. 35, no. 11, pp. 1600–1610, Nov. 2000.

50. Widmer, A.X. et al., "Single-chip 4 * 500-MBd CMOS transceiver," *IEEE Journal of Solid-State Circuits,* vol. 31, no. 12, pp. 2004–2014, Dec. 1996.

51. Wu, J.-T. et al., "A 100-MHz pipelined CMOS comparator," *IEEE Journal of Solid-State Circuits,* vol. 23, no. 6, pp. 1379–1385.

52. Yang, C.K.K. et al., "A 0.5-$\mu$m CMOS 4-Gbps serial link transceiver with data recovery using over-sampling," *IEEE Journal of Solid-State Circuits,* vol. 33, no. 5, pp. 713–722, May 1998.

# 32

# Algorithms and Data Structures in External Memory

Jeffrey Scott Vitter
*Duke University*

## 32.1  Introduction

In large applications, data sets are often too massive to fit completely inside the computer's internal memory. The resulting input/output (or I/O) communication between fast internal memory and slower external memory (such as disks) can be a major performance bottleneck. For example, loading a register takes on the order of a nanosecond ($10^{-9}$ s), and accessing internal memory takes tens of nanoseconds, but the latency of accessing data from a disk is several milliseconds ($10^{-3}$ s), which is about one million times slower.

0-8493-0885-2/02/$0.00+$1.50
© 2002 by CRC Press LLC

Many computer programs exhibit some degree of *locality* in their pattern of memory references: Certain data are referenced repeatedly for a while, and then the program shifts attention to other sets of data. Substantial gains in performance may be possible by incorporating locality *directly* into the algorithm design and by explicit management of the contents of each level of the memory hierarchy, thereby bypassing the virtual memory system.

## Overview of the Chapter

This chapter on the I/O communication between the random access internal memory and the magnetic disk external memory, where the relative difference in access speeds is most apparent. It surveys several paradigms for how to exploit locality and thereby reduce I/O costs when solving problems in external memory. The problems that are considered fall into two general categories:

1. *Batched problems*: No preprocessing is done and the entire file of data items must be processed, often by streaming the data through the internal memory in one or more passes.
2. *Online problems*: Computation is done in response to a continuous series of query operations and updates.

The approach is based upon the parallel disk model (PDM), which provides an elegant model for analyzing the relative performance of external memory (EM) algorithms and data structures. The three main performance measures of PDM are *the number of I/O operations, the disk space usage,* and *the CPU time.* For reasons of brevity, we focus on the first two measures. Most of the algorithms we consider are also efficient in terms of CPU time. In Section 32.4 we list four fundamental I/O bounds that pertain to most of the problems considered in this chapter. In Section 32.5 we discuss an automatic load balancing technique called disk striping for using multiple disks in parallel.

Section 32.6 examines canonical batched EM problem of external sorting and the related problems of permuting and fast Fourier transform. In Section 32.7, we discuss grid and linear algebra batched computations.

For most problems, parallel disks can be utilized effectively by means of disk striping or the parallel disk techniques of Section 32.6, and hence we restrict ourselves starting in Section 32.8 to the conceptually simpler single-disk case. In Section 32.8 we mention several effective paradigms for batched EM problems in computational geometry. In Section 32.9 we look at EM algorithms for combinatorial problems on graphs, such as list ranking, connected components, topological sorting, and finding shortest paths.

In Sections 32.10–32.12 we consider data structures based on hash tables and search trees in the online setting. We discuss some additional EM approaches useful for dynamic data structures, and we also consider kinetic data structures, in which the data items are moving. Section 32.13 deals with EM data structures for manipulating and searching text strings. In Section 32.14 we list several programming environments and tools that facilitate high-level development of efficient EM algorithms. In Section 32.15 we discuss EM algorithms that adapt optimally to dynamically changing internal memory allocations.

## 32.2 Parallel Disk Model (PDM)

EM algorithms explicitly control data placement and movement, and thus it is important for algorithm designers to have a simple but reasonably accurate model of the memory system's characteristics. Magnetic disks consist of one or more rotating platters and one read/write head per platter surface. The data are stored on the platters in concentric circles called *tracks*. To read or write a data item at a certain address on disk, the read/write head must mechanically *seek* to the correct track and then wait for the desired address to pass by. The seek time to move from one random track to another is often on the order of 3–10 ms, and the average rotational latency, which is the time for half a revolution, has the same order of magnitude. In order to amortize this delay, it pays to transfer a large contiguous group of data items, called a *block*. Similar considerations apply to all levels of the memory hierarchy.

Even if an application can structure its pattern of memory accesses to exploit locality and take full advantage of disk block transfer, there is still a substantial *access gap* between internal memory performance and external memory performance. In fact, the access gap is growing, because the latency and bandwidth of memory chips are improving more quickly than those of disks. Use of parallel processors further widens the gap. Storage systems such as RAID deploy multiple disks in order to get additional bandwidth [53,105].

The main properties of magnetic disks and multiple disk systems can be captured by the commonly used PDM introduced by Vitter and Shriver [202]:

$N$ = problem size (in units of data items)
$M$ = internal memory size (in units of data items)
$B$ = block transfer size (in units of data items)
$D$ = number of independent disk drives
$P$ = number of CPUs

where $M < N$, and $1 \le DB \le M/2$. The data items are assumed to be of fixed length. In a single I/O, each of the $D$ disks can simultaneously transfer a block of $B$ contiguous data items. When the problem involves queries, two more performance parameters are needed:

$Q$ = number of input queries (for a batched problem)
$Z$ = query output size (in units of data items)

It is convenient to refer to some of the above PDM parameters in units of disk blocks rather than in units of data items:

$$n = \frac{N}{B}, \quad m = \frac{M}{B}, \quad q = \frac{Q}{B}, \quad z = \frac{Z}{B} \tag{32.1}$$

It is assumed that the input data are initially "striped" across the $D$ disks, in units of blocks, as illustrated in Fig. 32.1, and we require the output data to be similarly striped. Striped format allows a file of $N$ data items to be read or written in $O(N/DB) = O(n/D)$ I/Os, which is optimal.

The three primary measures of performance in PDM are

1. the number of I/O operations performed,
2. the amount of disk space used,
3. the internal (sequential or parallel) computation time.

For reasons of brevity, this chapter focuses on only the first two measures. The reader can refer to [199] for discussion and references on more complex and precise disk models.

| | $\mathcal{D}_0$ | $\mathcal{D}_1$ | $\mathcal{D}_2$ | $\mathcal{D}_3$ | $\mathcal{D}_4$ |
|---|---|---|---|---|---|
| stripe 0 | 0  1 | 2  3 | 4  5 | 6  7 | 8  9 |
| stripe 1 | 10 11 | 12 13 | 14 15 | 16 17 | 18 19 |
| stripe 2 | 20 21 | 22 23 | 24 25 | 26 27 | 28 29 |
| stripe 3 | 30 31 | 32 33 | 34 35 | 36 37 | 38 39 |

**FIGURE 32.1** Initial data layout on the disks, for $D = 5$ disks and block size $B = 2$. The input data items are initially striped block-by-block across the disks. For example, data items 16 and 17 are stored in the second block (i.e., in stripe 1) of disk $\mathcal{D}_3$.

## 32.3 Related Memory Models, Hierarchical Memory, and Caching

The study of problem complexity and algorithm analysis when using EM devices began more than 40 years ago with Demuth's Ph.D. thesis on sorting [71,124]. In the early 1970s, Knuth [124] did an extensive study of sorting using magnetic tapes and (to a lesser extent) magnetic disks. At about the same time, Floyd [87,124] considered a disk model akin to PDM for $D = 1$, $P = 1$, $B = M/2 = \Theta(N^c)$, for constant $c > 0$, and developed optimal upper and lower I/O bounds for sorting and matrix transposition. Hong and Kung [108] developed a pebbling model of I/O for straightline computations, and Savage and Vitter [177] extended the model to deal with block transfer. Aggarwal and Vitter [15] generalized Floyd's I/O model to allow $D$ simultaneous block transfers, but the model was unrealistic in that the $D$ simultaneous transfers were allowed to take place on a single disk. They developed matching upper and lower I/O bounds for all parameter values for a host of problems. Because the PDM model can be thought of as a more restrictive (and more realistic) version of Aggarwal and Vitter's model, their lower bounds apply as well to PDM. The section on "A General Simulation" discusses a recent simulation technique due to Sanders et al. [176]; the Aggarwal–Vitter model can be simulated probabilistically by PDM with only a constant factor more I/Os, thus making the two models theoretically equivalent in the randomized sense. Deterministic simulations on the other hand require a factor of $\log(N/D)/\log[\log(N/D)]$ more I/Os [29].

Surveys of I/O models, algorithms, and challenges appear in [19,94,181,199]. Several versions of PDM have been developed for parallel computation [70,135,185]. Models of "active disks" augmented with processing capabilities to reduce data traffic to the host, especially during streaming applications, are given in [3,167]. Models of microelectromechanical systems (MEMS) for mass storage appear in [100].

Some authors have studied problems that can be solved efficiently by making only one pass (or a small number of passes) over the data [81,106]. One approach to reduce the internal memory requirements is to require only an approximate answer to the problem; the more memory available, the better the approximation. A related approach to reducing I/O costs for a given problem is to use random sampling or data compression in order to construct a smaller version of the problem whose solution approximates the original. These approaches are highly problem-dependent and somewhat orthogonal to our focus in this chapter.

The same type of bottleneck that occurs between internal memory (DRAM) and external disk storage can also occur at other levels of the memory hierarchy, such as between registers and level 1 cache, between level 1 and level 2 cache, between level 2 cache and DRAM, and between disk storage and tertiary devices. The PDM model can be generalized to model the hierarchy of memories ranging from registers at the small end to tertiary storage at the large end. Optimal algorithms for PDM often generalize in a recursive fashion to yield optimal algorithms in the hierarchical memory models [12,13,201,203]. Conversely, the algorithms for hierarchical models can be run in the PDM setting, and in that setting many have the interesting property that they use no explicit knowledge of the PDM parameters like $M$ and $B$. Frigo et al. [89] and Bender et al. [43] develop cache-oblivious algorithms and data structures that require no knowledge of the storage parameters.

However, the match between theory and practice is harder to establish for hierarchical models and caches than for disks. For reasons of focus, such hierarchical models and caching issues are not considered in this chapter. The reader is referred to the discussion and references in [199].

## 32.4 Fundamental I/O Operations and Bounds

The I/O performance of many algorithms and data structures can be expressed in terms of the bounds for the following four fundamental operations:

1. *Scanning* (a.k.a. *streaming* or *touching*) a file of $N$ data items, which involves the sequential reading or writing of the items in the file
2. *Sorting* a file of $N$ data items, which puts the items into sorted order

**TABLE 32.1** I/O Bounds for the Four Fundamental Operations

| Operation | I/O bound, $D = 1$ | I/O bound, general $D \geq 1$ |
|---|---|---|
| *Scan* ($N$) | $\Theta\left(\dfrac{N}{B}\right) = \Theta(n)$ | $\Theta\left(\dfrac{N}{DB}\right) = \Theta\left(\dfrac{n}{D}\right)$ |
| *Sort* ($N$) | $\Theta\left(\dfrac{N}{B}\log_{M/B}\dfrac{N}{B}\right) = \Theta(n\log_m n)$ | $\Theta\left(\dfrac{N}{DB}\log_{M/B}\dfrac{N}{B}\right) = \Theta\left(\dfrac{n}{D}\log_m n\right)$ |
| *Search* ($N$) | $\Theta(\log_B N)$ | $\Theta(\log_{DB} N)$ |
| *Output* ($Z$) | $\Theta\left(\max\left\{1, \dfrac{Z}{B}\right\}\right) = \Theta(\max\{1, z\})$ | $\Theta\left(\max\left\{1, \dfrac{Z}{DB}\right\}\right) = \Theta\left(\max\left\{1, \dfrac{z}{D}\right\}\right)$ |

*Note:* The PDM parameters are defined in Section 32.2.

3. *Searching* online through $N$ sorted data items
4. *Outputting* the $Z$ answers to a query in a blocked "output-sensitive" fashion

The I/O bounds for these four operations are given in Table 32.1. The special case of a single disk ($D = 1$) is emphasized, because the formulas are simpler and many of the discussions in this chapter will be restricted to the single-disk case.

## 32.5 Disk Striping for Multiple Disks

It is conceptually much simpler to program for the single-disk case ($D = 1$) than for the multiple-disk case ($D \geq 1$). *Disk striping* [122,169] is a practical paradigm that can ease the programming task with multiple disks: I/Os are permitted only on entire stripes, one stripe at a time. For example, in the data layout in Fig. 32.1, data items 20–29 can be accessed in a single I/O step because their blocks are grouped into the same stripe. The net effect of striping is that the $D$ disks behave as a single logical disk, but with a larger logical block size $DB$.

Therefore, the paradigm of disk striping can be applied to automatically convert an algorithm designed to use a single disk with block size $DB$ into an algorithm for use on $D$ disks each with block size $B$: In the single-disk algorithm, each I/O step transmits one block of size $DB$; in the $D$-disk algorithm, each I/O step consists of $D$ simultaneous block transfers of size $B$ each. The number of I/O steps in both algorithms is the same; in each I/O step, the $DB$ items transferred by the two algorithms are identical. Of course, in terms of wall clock time, the I/O step in the multiple-disk algorithm will be $\Theta(D)$ times faster than in the single-disk algorithm because of parallelism.

Disk striping can be used to get optimal multiple-disk algorithms for three of the four fundamental operations of Section 32.4—streaming, online search, and output reporting—but it is nonoptimal for sorting. If $D$ is replaced by 1 and then $B$ by $DB$ in the sorting bound $Sort(N)$ given in Section 32.4, an expression is obtained that is larger than $Sort(N)$ by a multiplicative factor of

$$\frac{\log(n/D)}{\log n}\frac{\log m}{\log(m/D)} \approx \frac{\log m}{\log(m/D)} \tag{32.2}$$

When $D$ is on the order of $m$, the $\log(m/D)$ term in the denominator is small, and the resulting value of (32.2) is in the order of $\log m$, which can be significant in practice.

It follows that the only way theoretically to attain the optimal sorting bound $Sort(N)$ is to forsake disk striping and to allow the disks to be controlled *independently*, so that each disk can access a different stripe in the same I/O step. In the next section, algorithms for sorting with multiple independent disks are discussed. The techniques that arise can be applied to many of the batched problems addressed later in the paper. Two such sorting algorithms—distribution sort with randomized cycling and simple randomized mergesort—have relatively low overhead and will outperform disk-striped approaches.

## 32.6  External Sorting and Related Problems

The problem of *external sorting* (or sorting in external memory) is a central problem in the field of EM algorithms, partly because sorting and sorting-like operations account for a significant percentage of computer use [124], and also because sorting is an important paradigm in the design of efficient EM algorithms, as shown in Section 32.9. With some technical qualifications, many problems that can be solved easily in linear time in internal memory, such as permuting, list ranking, expression tree evaluation, and finding connected components in a sparse graph, require the same number of I/Os in PDM as does sorting.

> **Theorem 32.6.1 [15,157]** *The average-case and worst-case number of I/Os required for sorting $N = nB$ data items using $D$ disks is*

$$Sort(N) = \Theta\left(\frac{n}{D}\log_m n\right) \tag{32.3}$$

From Section 32.5, efficient sorting algorithms can be constructed for multiple disks by applying the disk striping paradigm to an efficient single-disk algorithm. But in the case of sorting, the resulting multiple-disk algorithm does not meet the optimal $Sort(N)$ bound of Theorem 32.6.1. In the "Sorting by Distribution" and "Sorting by Merging" sections, some recently developed external sorting algorithms that use disks independently are discussed. The algorithms are based upon the important *distribution* and *merge* paradigms, which are two generic approaches to sorting.

### Sorting by Distribution

*Distribution* sort [124] is a recursive process in which we use a set of $S - 1$ partitioning elements to partition the items into $S$ disjoint buckets. All the items in one bucket precede all the items in the next bucket. We complete the sort by recursively sorting the individual buckets and concatenating them together to form a single fully sorted list.

One requirement is that we choose the $S - 1$ partitioning elements so that the buckets are of roughly equal size. When that is the case, the bucket sizes decrease from one level of recursion to the next by a relative factor of $\Theta(S)$, and thus there are $O(\log_S n)$ levels of recursion. During each level of recursion, we scan the data. As the items stream through internal memory, they are partitioned into $S$ buckets in an online manner. When a buffer of size $B$ fills for one of the buckets, its block is written to the disks in the next I/O, and another buffer is used to store the next set of incoming items for the bucket. Therefore, the maximum number of buckets (and partitioning elements) is $S = \Theta(M/B) = \Theta(m)$, and the resulting number of levels of recursion is $\Theta(\log_m n)$.

It seems difficult to find $S = \Theta(m)$ partitioning elements using $\Theta(n/D)$ I/Os and guarantee that the bucket sizes are within a constant factor of one another. Efficient deterministic methods exist for choosing $S = \sqrt{m}$ partitioning elements [15,156,202], which has the effect of doubling the number of levels of recursion. Probabilistic methods based upon random sampling can be found in [82]. A deterministic algorithm for the related problem of (exact) selection (i.e., given $k$, find the $k$th item in the file in sorted order) appears in [184].

In order to meet the sorting bound (3), the buckets at each level of recursion must be formed using $O(n/D)$ I/Os, which is easy to do for the single-disk case. In the more general multiple-disk case, each read step and each write step during the bucket formation must involve on the average $\Theta(D)$ blocks. The file of items being partitioned was itself one of the buckets formed in the previous level of recursion. In order to read that file efficiently, its blocks must be spread uniformly among the disks, so that no one disk is a bottleneck. The challenge in distribution sort is to write the blocks of the buckets to the disks in an online manner and achieve a global load balance by the end of the partitioning, so that the bucket can be read efficiently during the next level of the recursion.

Vitter and Shriver [202] develop two complementary randomized online techniques for the partitioning so that with high probability each bucket will be well balanced across the $D$ disks. Putting the methods together, they got the first provably optimal randomized method for sorting with parallel disks.

DeWitt et al. [72] present a randomized distribution sort algorithm in a similar model to handle the case when sorting can be done in two passes. They use a sampling technique to find the partitioning elements and route the items in each bucket to a particular processor. The buckets are sorted individually in the second pass.

An even better way to do distribution sort, and deterministically at that, is the BalanceSort method developed by Nodine and Vitter [156]. During the partitioning process, the algorithm keeps track of how evenly each bucket has been distributed so far among the disks. It maintains an invariant that guarantees good distribution across the disks for each bucket.

The distribution sort methods that we mentioned above for parallel disks perform write operations in complete stripes, which makes it easy to write parity information for use in error correction and recovery. But since the blocks written in each stripe typically belong to multiple buckets, the buckets themselves will not be striped on the disks, and we must use the disks independently during read operations. In the write phase, each bucket must therefore keep track of the last block written to each disk so that the blocks for the bucket can be linked together.

An orthogonal approach is to stripe the contents of each bucket across the disks so that read operations can be done in a striped manner. As a result, the write operations must use disks independently, since during each write, multiple buckets will be writing to multiple stripes. Error correction and recovery can still be handled efficiently by devoting to each bucket one block-sized buffer in internal memory. The buffer is continuously updated to contain the exclusive-or (parity) of the blocks written to the current stripe, and after $D - 1$ blocks have been written, the parity information in the buffer can be written to the final ($D$th) block in the stripe.

Under this new scenario, the basic loop of the distribution sort algorithm is, as before, to read one memoryload at a time and partition the items into $S$ buckets; however, unlike before, the blocks for each individual bucket will reside on the disks in contiguous stripes. Each block therefore has a predefined place where it must be written. If we choose the normal round-robin ordering for the stripes (namely, …, 1, 2, 3, …, $D$, 1, 2, 3, …, $D$, …), the blocks of different buckets may "collide," meaning that they need to be written to the same disk, and subsequent blocks in those same buckets will also tend to collide. Vitter and Hutchinson [200] solve this problem by the technique of *randomized cycling*. For each of the $S$ buckets, they determine the ordering of the disks in the stripe for that bucket via a random permutation of $\{1, 2,…,D\}$. The $S$ random permutations are chosen independently. If two blocks (from different buckets) happen to collide during a write to the same disk, one block is written to the disk and the other is kept on a write queue. With high probability, subsequent blocks in those two buckets will be written to different disks and thus will not collide. As long as there is a small pool of available buffer space to temporarily cache the blocks in the write queues, Vitter and Hutchinson show that with high probability the writing proceeds optimally.

The randomized cycling method or the related merge sort methods discussed at the end of the subsection on "Sorting by Merging" will be the methods of choice for sorting with parallel disks. Experiments are underway to evaluate their relative performance. Distribution sort algorithms may have an advantage over the merge approaches in that they typically make better use of lower levels of cache in the memory hierarchy of real systems, based upon analysis of distribution sort and merge sort algorithms on models of hierarchical memory, such as the RUMH model of Vitter and Nodine [201].

## Sorting by Merging

The *merge* paradigm is somewhat orthogonal to the distribution paradigm of the previous section. A typical merge sort algorithm works as follows [124]: In the "run formation" phase, the $n$ blocks of data are scanned, one memoryload at a time; each memoryload is sorted into a single "run," which is then output onto a series of stripes on the disks. At the end of the run formation phase, there are $N/M = n/m$ (sorted) runs, each striped across the disks. (In actual implementations, we can use the "replacement-selection" technique to get runs of $2M$ data items, on the average, when $M \gg B$ [124].) After the initial runs are formed, the merging phase begins. In each pass of the merging phase, we merge together groups of $R$ runs. For each merge, we scan the $R$ runs and merge the items in an online manner as they stream through internal memory. Double buffering is used to overlap I/O and computation. At most $R = \Theta(m)$ runs can be merged at a time, and resulting number of passes is $O(\log_m n)$.

To achieve the optimal sorting bound (32.3), each merging pass must be performed in $O(n/D)$ I/Os, which is easy to do for the single-disk case. In the more general multiple-disk case, each parallel read operation during the merging must on an average bring in the next $\Theta(D)$ blocks needed for the merging. The challenge is to ensure that those blocks reside on different disks so that they can be read in a single I/O (or a small constant number of I/Os). The difficulty lies in the fact that the runs being merged were themselves formed during the previous merge pass. Their blocks were written to the disks in the previous pass without knowledge of how they would interact with other runs in later merges.

For the binary merging case $R = 2$, can be devised a perfect solution, in which the next $D$ blocks needed for the merge are guaranteed to be on distinct disks, based upon the Gilbreath principle [92,124]: The first run is striped into ascending order by disk number, and the other run is striped into descending order. Regardless of how the items in the two runs interleave during the merge, it is always the case that we can access the next $D$ blocks needed for the output via a single I/O operation, and thus the amount of internal memory buffer space needed for binary merging is minimized. Unfortunately there is no analog to the Gilbreath principle for $R > 2$, and as we have seen above, we need the value of $R$ to be large in order to get an optimal sorting algorithm.

The Greed Sort method of Nodine and Vitter [157] was the first optimal deterministic EM algorithm for sorting with multiple disks. Each merge is done "approximately" so that items go relatively closely to their final destinations. A final application of Columnsort [133], using $O(n)$ extra I/Os, completes the merge.

Aggarwal and Plaxton [14] developed an optimal deterministic merge sort based upon the Sharesort hypercube parallel sorting algorithm [67]. To guarantee even distribution during the merging, it employs two high-level merging schemes in which the scheduling is almost oblivious. Similar to Greed Sort, the Sharesort algorithm is theoretically optimal (i.e., within a constant factor of optimal), but the constant factor is larger than the distribution sort methods.

One of the most practical methods for sorting is based upon the simple randomized merge sort (SRM) algorithm of Barve et al. [34,36], referred to as "randomized striping" by Knuth [124]. Each run is striped across the disks, but with a random starting point (the only place in the algorithm where randomness is utilized). During the merging process, the next block needed from each disk is read into memory, and if there is not enough room, the least needed blocks are "flushed" (without any I/Os required) to free up space. Barve et al. [34] derive an asymptotic upper bound on the expected I/O performance, with no assumptions on the input distribution. A more precise analysis, which is related to the so-called *cyclic occupancy problem*, is an interesting open problem. The expected performance of SRM is not optimal for some parameter values, but it significantly outperforms the use of disk striping for reasonable values of the parameters, as shown in Table 32.2. Experimental confirmation of the speedup was obtained on a 500-MHz CPU with six fast disk drives, as reported by Barve and Vitter [36].

**TABLE 32.2**    The Ratio of the Number of I/Os Used by Simple Randomized Merge Sort (SRM) to the Number of I/Os Used by Merge Sort with Disk Striping, During a Merge of $kD$ Runs, Where $kD \approx M/2B$

|          | $D = 5$ | $D = 10$ | $D = 50$ |
|----------|---------|----------|----------|
| $k = 5$  | 0.56    | 0.47     | 0.37     |
| $k = 10$ | 0.61    | 0.52     | 0.40     |
| $k = 50$ | 0.71    | 0.63     | 0.51     |

*Note:* The figures were obtained by simulation.

Further improvements can be obtained in merge sort by a more careful prefetching schedule for the runs. Barve et al. [35] and Kallahalla and Varman [114,115] have developed competitive and optimal methods for prefetching blocks in parallel I/O systems. Hutchinson et al. [112] have demonstrated a powerful duality between parallel writing and parallel prefetching, which gives an easy way to compute optimal prefetching and caching schedules for multiple disks. More significantly, they show that the same duality exists between distribution and merging, which they exploit to get a provably optimal and very practical parallel disk mergesort. Rather than use random starting points and round-robin stripes as in SRM, Hutchinson et al. order the stripes for each run independently, based upon the randomized cycling strategy discussed in Section "Sorting by Distribution" for distribution sort.

## A General Simulation

Sanders et al. [176] and Sanders [175] give an elegant randomized technique to simulate the Aggarwal–Vitter model of Section 32.3, in which $D$ simultaneous block transfers are allowed regardless of where the blocks are located on the disks. On the average, the simulation realizes each I/O in the Aggarwal–Vitter model by only a constant number of I/Os in PDM. One property of the technique is that the read and write steps use the disks independently. Armen [29] had earlier shown that deterministic simulations resulted in an increase in the number of I/Os by a multiplicative factor of $\log(N/D)/\log[\log(N/D)]$.

## Handling Duplicates

Arge et al. [23] describe a single-disk merge sort algorithm for the problem of *duplicate removal*, in which a total of $K$ distinct items are among the $N$ items. It runs in $O(n \max\{1, \log_m(K/B)\})$ I/Os, which is optimal in the comparison model. The algorithm can be used to sort the file, assuming that a group of equal items can be represented by a single item and a count.

A harder instance of sorting called *bundle sorting* arises when $K$ distinct key values are among the $N$ items, but all the items have different secondary information. Abello et al. [2] and Matias et al. [145] develop optimal distribution sort algorithms for bundle sorting using $BundleSort(N, K) = O(n \max\{1, \log_m \min\{K, n\}\})$ I/Os, and Matias et al. [145] prove the matching lower bound. Matias et al. [145] also show how to do bundle sorting (and sorting in general) *in place* (i.e., without extra disk space). In distribution sort, for example, the blocks for the subfiles can be allocated from the blocks freed up from the file being partitioned; the disadvantage is that the blocks in the individual subfiles are no longer consecutive on the disk. The algorithms can be adapted to run on $D$ disks with a speedup of $O(D)$, using the techniques described in the "Sorting by Distribution" and "Sorting by Merging" subsections.

## Permuting and Transposition

Permuting is the special case of sorting in which the key values of the $N$ data items form a permutation of $\{1, 2, \ldots, N\}$.

**Theorem 32.6.2** [15] *The average-case and worst-case number of I/Os required for permuting $N$ data items using $D$ disks is*

$$\Theta\left(\min\left\{\frac{N}{D}, Sort(N)\right\}\right) \tag{32.4}$$

The I/O bound (32.4) for permuting can be realized by using one of the sorting algorithms from Section 32.6 except in the extreme case $B \log m = o(\log n)$, in which case it is faster to move the data items one by one in a non-blocked way. The one-by-one method is trivial if $D = 1$, but with multiple disks there may be bottlenecks on individual disks; one solution for doing the permuting in $O(N/D)$ I/Os is to apply the randomized balancing strategies of [202].

Matrix transposition is the special case of permuting in which the permutation can be represented as a transposition of a matrix from row-major order into column-major order.

**Theorem 32.6.3** [15] *With D disks, the number of I/Os required to transpose a $p \times q$ matrix from row-major order to column-major order is*

$$\Theta\left(\frac{n}{D}\log_m\min\{M, p, q, n\}\right) \qquad (32.5)$$

*where $N = pq$ and $n = N/B$.*

When $B$ is relatively large (for instance, $1/2\,M$) and $N$ is $O(M^2)$, matrix transposition can be as hard as general sorting, but for smaller $B$, the special structure of the transposition permutation makes transposition easier. In particular, the matrix can be broken up into square submatrices of $B^2$ elements such that each submatrix contains $B$ blocks of the matrix in row-major order and also $B$ blocks of the matrix in column-major order. Thus, if $B^2 < M$, the transpositions can be done in a simple one-pass operation by transposing the submatrices one-at-a-time in internal memory.

Matrix transposition is a special case of a more general class of permutations called bit-permute/complement (BPC) permutations, which in turn is a subset of the class of bit-matrix-multiply/complement (BMMC) permutations. BMMC permutations are defined by a $\log N \times \log N$ nonsingular 0-1 matrix $A$ and a $(\log N)$-length 0-1 vector $c$. An item with binary address $x$ is mapped by the permutation to the binary address given by $Ax \oplus c$, where $\oplus$ denotes bitwise exclusive-or. BPC permutations are the special case of BMMC permutations in which $A$ is a permutation matrix, that is, each row and each column of $A$ contain a single 1. BPC permutations include matrix transposition, bit-reversal permutations (which arise in the FFT), vector-reversal permutations, hypercube permutations, and matrix reblocking. Cormen et al. [62] characterize the optimal number of I/Os needed to perform any given BMMC permutation solely as a function of the associated matrix $A$, and they give an optimal algorithm for implementing it.

**Theorem 32.6.4** [62] *With D disks, the number of I/Os required to perform the BMMC permutation defined by matrix A and vector c is*

$$\Theta\left(\frac{n}{D}\left(1 + \frac{\mathrm{rank}(\gamma)}{\log m}\right)\right) \qquad (32.6)$$

*where $\gamma$ is the lower-left $\log n \times \log B$ submatrix of $A$.*

An interesting theoretical question is to determine the I/O cost for each individual permutation, as a function of some simple characterization of the permutation, like number of inversions.

## Fast Fourier Transform and Permutation Networks

Computing the fast Fourier transform (FFT) in external memory consists of a series of I/Os that permit each computation implied by the FFT directed graph (or butterfly) to be done while its arguments are in internal memory. A permutation network computation consists of an oblivious (fixed) pattern of I/Os such that any of the $N!$ possible permutations can be realized; data items can only be reordered when they are in internal memory. A permutation network can be realized by a series of three FFTs [213].

**Theorem 32.6.5** *With D disks, the number of I/Os required for computing the N-input FFT digraph or an N-input permutation network is Sort(N).*

Cormen and Nicol [61] give some practical implementations for one-dimensional (1-D) FFTs based upon the optimal PDM algorithm of [202]. The algorithms for FFT are faster and simpler than for sorting because the computation is nonadaptive in nature, and thus the communication pattern is fixed in advance.

## Lower Bounds on I/O

The most trivial batched problem is that of scanning (a.k.a. streaming or touching) a file of $N$ data items, which can be done in a linear number $O(N/DB) = O(n/D)$ of I/Os. Permuting is one of several simple problems that can be done in linear CPU time in the (internal memory) RAM model, but require a nonlinear number of I/Os in PDM because of the locality constraints imposed by the block parameter $B$.

The proof of the permutation lower bound (32.4) of Theorem 32.6.2 is due to Aggarwal and Vitter [15]. A stronger lower bound is obtained from a more refined argument that counts input operations separately from output operations [111]. For the typical case in which $B \log m = \omega(\log N)$, the I/O lower bound, up to lower order terms, is $2n \log_m n$. For the pathological, in which $B \log m = o(\log N)$, the I/O lower bound, up to lower order terms, is $N/D$. Permuting is a special case of sorting, and hence, the permuting lower bound applies also to sorting. In the unlikely case that $B \log m = o(\log n)$, the permuting bound is only $\Omega(N/D)$, and the comparison model must be used to get the full lower bound (32.3) of Theorem 6.1 [15]. The reader is referred to [199] for further discussion and references on lower bounds for sorting and related problems.

## 32.7 Matrix and Grid Computations

Dense matrices are generally represented in memory in row-major or column-major order. Matrix transposition, which is the special case of sorting that involves conversion of a matrix from one representation to the other, was discussed in the subsection on "Permuting and Transposition." For certain operations such as matrix addition, both representations work well; however, for standard matrix multiplication (using only semiring operations) and LU decomposition, a better representation is to block the matrix into square $\sqrt{B} \times \sqrt{B}$ submatrices, which gives the upper bound of the following theorem:

**Theorem 32.7.1** [108,177,202,212] *The number of I/Os required for standard matrix multiplication of two $K \times K$ matrices or to compute the LU factorization of a $K \times K$ matrix is $\Theta(K^3/\min\{K, \sqrt{M}\}DB)$.*

Hong and Kung [108] and Nodine et al. [155] give optimal EM algorithms for iterative grid computations, and Leiserson et al. [134] reduce the number of I/Os of naive multigrid implementations by a $\Theta(M^{1/5})$ factor. Gupta et al. [102] show how to derive efficient EM algorithms automatically for computations expressed in tensor form.

If a $K \times K$ matrix $A$ is sparse, that is, if the number $N_z$ of nonzero elements in $A$ is much smaller than $K^2$, then it may be more efficient to store only the nonzero elements. Each nonzero element $A_{i,j}$ is represented by the triple $(i, j, A_{i,j})$. Unlike the dense case, in which transposition can be easier than sorting (e.g., see Theorem 32.6.3 when $B^2 \le M$), transposition of sparse matrices is as hard as sorting.

**Theorem 32.7.2** *For a matrix stored in sparse format and containing $N_z$ nonzero elements, the number of I/Os required to convert the matrix from row-major order to column-major order, and vice-versa, is $\Theta(Sort(N_z))$.*

The lower bound follows by reduction from sorting. If the $i$th item in the input of the sorting instance has key value $x \ne 0$, there is a nonzero element in matrix position $(i, x)$.

For further discussion of numerical EM algorithms, the reader is referred to the survey by Toledo [190]. Some issues regarding programming environments are covered in [59] and Section 32.14.

## 32.8 Batched Problems in Computational Geometry

Problems involving massive amounts of geometric data are ubiquitous in spatial databases [131,172, 173], geographic information systems (GIS) [131,172,194], constraint logic programming [119,120], object-oriented databases [215], statistics, virtual reality systems, and computer graphics [90]. NASA's Earth Observing System project, the core part of the Earth Science Enterprise (formerly Mission to Planet Earth), produces petabytes ($10^{15}$ bytes) of raster data per year [76]. Microsoft's TerraServer online database of satellite images is over one terabyte in size [188]. A major challenge is to develop mechanisms for processing the data, or else much of the data will be useless.[*]

For systems of this size to be efficient, fast EM algorithms and data structures are needed for basic problems in computational geometry. Luckily, many problems on geometric objects can be reduced to a small core of problems, such as computing intersections, convex hulls, or nearest neighbors. Useful paradigms have been developed for solving these problems in external memory.

**Theorem 32.8.1** *The following batched problems involving $N = nB$ input items, $Q = qB$ queries, and $Z = zB$ output items can be solved using*

$$O((n + q)\log_m n + z) \qquad (32.7)$$

*I/Os with a single disk:*

1. *Computing the pairwise intersections of $N$ segments in the plane and their trapezoidal decomposition,*
2. *Finding all intersections between $N$ nonintersecting red line segments and $N$ nonintersecting blue line segments in the plane,*
3. *Answering $Q$ orthogonal 2-D range queries on $N$ points in the plane (i.e., finding all the points within the $Q$ query rectangles),*
4. *Constructing the 2-D and 3-D convex hull of $N$ points,*
5. *Voronoi diagram and Triangulation of $N$ points in the plane,*
6. *Performing $Q$ point location queries in a planar subdivision of size $N$,*
7. *Finding all nearest neighbors for a set of $N$ points in the plane,*
8. *Finding the pairwise intersections of $N$ orthogonal rectangles in the plane,*
9. *Computing the measure of the union of $N$ orthogonal rectangles in the plane,*
10. *Computing the visibility of $N$ segments in the plane from a point,*
11. *Performing $Q$ ray-shooting queries in 2-D Constructive Solid Geometry (CSG) models of size $N$: The parameters $Q$ and $Z$ are set to 0 if they are not relevant for the particular problem.*

Goodrich et al. [97], Zhu [217], Arge et al. [27], Arge et al. [24], and Crauser et al. [64,65] develop EM algorithms for those problems using the following EM paradigms for batched problems:

*Distribution sweeping*—a generalization of the distribution paradigm of Section 32.6 for "externalizing" plane sweep algorithms.

*Persistent B-trees*—an offline method for constructing an optimal-space persistent version of the B-tree data structure (see the subsection "B-trees and Variants"), yielding a factor of $B$ improvement over the generic persistence techniques of Driscoll et al. [74].

*Batched filtering*—a general method for performing simultaneous EM searches in data structures that can be modeled as planar layered directed acyclic graphs; it is useful for 3-D convex hulls and batched point location. Multisearch on parallel computers is considered in [73].

*External fractional cascading*—an EM analog to fractional cascading on a segment tree, in which the degree of the segment tree is $O(m^\alpha)$ for some constant $0 < \alpha \le 1$. Batched queries can be performed efficiently using batched filtering; online queries can be supported efficiently by adapting the parallel algorithms of work of Tamassia and Vitter [187] to the I/O setting.

*External marriage-before-conquest*—an EM analog to the technique of Kirkpatrick and Seidel [123] for performing output-sensitive convex hull constructions.

*Batched incremental construction*—a localized version of the randomized incremental construction paradigm of Clarkson and Shor [56], in which the updates to a simple dynamic data structure

---

[*]For brevity, in the remainder of this chapter, only with the single-disk case $D = 1$ is presented. The single-disk I/O bounds for the batched problems can often be cut by a factor of $\Theta(D)$ for the case $D \ge 1$ by using the load balancing techniques of Section 32.6. In practice, disk striping (cf., Section 32.5) may be sufficient. For online problems, disk striping will convert optimal bounds for the case $D = 1$ into optimal bounds for $D \ge 1$.

are done in a random order, with the goal of fast overall performance on the average. The data structure itself may have bad worst-case performance, but the randomization of the update order makes worst-case behavior unlikely. The key for the EM version so as to gain the factor of $B$ I/O speedup is to batch together the incremental modifications.

## 32.9 Batched Problems on Graphs

The first work on EM graph algorithms was by Ullman and Yannakakis [192] for the problem of transitive closure. Chiang et al. [54] consider a variety of graph problems, several of which have upper and lower I/O bounds related to sorting and permuting. Abello et al. [2] formalize a functional approach to EM graph problems, in which computation proceeds in a series of scan operations over the data; the scanning avoids side effects and thus permits checkpointing to increase reliability. Kumar and Schwabe [128], followed by Buchsbaum et al. [49], develop graph algorithms based upon amortized data structures for binary heaps and tournament trees. Munagala and Ranade [151] give improved graph algorithms for connectivity and undirected breadth-first search, and Arge et al. [20] extend the approach to compute the minimum spanning forest (MSF). Meyer [148] provides some improvements for graphs of bounded degree. Arge [18] gives efficient algorithms for constructing ordered binary decision diagrams. Grossi and Italiano [101] apply their multidimensional data structure to get dynamic EM algorithms for MSF and 2-D priority queues (in which the *delete_min* operation is replaced by $delete\_min_x$ and $delete\_min_y$). Techniques for storing graphs on disks for efficient traversal and shortest path queries are discussed in [7,96,110,154]. Computing wavelet decompositions and histograms [205,206,208] is an EM graph problem related to transposition that arises in online analytical processing (OLAP). Wang et al. [207] give an I/O-efficient algorithm for constructing classification trees for data mining.

Table 32.3 gives the best known I/O bounds for several graph problems, as a function of the number $V = vB$ of vertices and the number $E = eB$ of edges. The best known I/O lower bound for these problems is $\Omega((E/V)Sort(V) = e\log_m v)$.

In the case of *semi-external graph problems* [2], in which the vertices fit in internal memory but not the edges (i.e., $V \leq M < E$), several of the problems in Table 32.3 can be solved optimally in external memory. For example, finding connected components, biconnected components, and minimum spanning forests can be done in $O(e)$ I/Os when $V \leq M$. The I/O complexities of several problems in the general case remain open, including connected components, biconnected components, and minimum spanning forests in the deterministic case, as well as breadth-first search, topological sorting, shortest paths, depth-first search, and transitive closure. It may be that the I/O complexity for several of these problems is $\Theta((E/V)Sort(V) + V)$. For special cases, such as trees, planar graphs, outerplanar graphs, and graphs of bounded tree width, several of these problems can be solved substantially faster in $O(Sort(E))$ I/Os [7,54, 141,142].

Chiang et al. [54] exploit the key idea that efficient EM algorithms can often be developed by a sequential simulation of a parallel algorithm for the same problem. The intuition is that each step of a parallel algorithm specifies several operations and the data they act upon. If the data arguments for each operation are brought together, which can be done by two applications of sorting, the operations can be performed by a single linear scan through the data. After each simulation step, sorting is again performed in order to reblock the data into the linear order required for the next simulation step. In list ranking, which is used as a subroutine in the solution of several other graph problems, the number of working processors in the parallel algorithm decreases geometrically with time, so the number of I/Os for the entire simulation is proportional to the number of I/Os used in the first phase of the simulation, which is $Sort(N) = \Theta(n\log_m n)$. The optimality of the EM algorithm given in [54] for list ranking assumes that $\sqrt{m}\log m = \Omega(\log n)$, which is usually true in practice. That assumption can be removed by use of the buffer tree data structure [17] (see Section 32.11 "B-trees and Variants"). A practical, randomized implementation of list ranking appears in [183]. Dehne et al. [69,70] and Sibeyn and Kaufmann [185] use a related approach and get efficient I/O bounds by simulating coarse-grained parallel algorithms in the BSP parallel model.

**TABLE 32.3**  Best Known I/O Bounds for Batched Graph Problems for the Single-Disk Case $D = 1$

| Graph Problem | I/O bound, $D = 1$ |
|---|---|
| List ranking, Euler tour of a tree, centroid decomposition, expression tree evaluation | $\Theta(Sort(V))$   [54] |
| Connected components, minimum spanning forest (MSF) | $O\left(\max\left\{1, \log\left(\log\dfrac{V}{e}\right)\right\}\dfrac{E}{V} Sort(V)\right)$<br><br>[20, 77, 151]  (deterministic)<br><br>$\Theta\left(\dfrac{E}{V} Sort(V)\right)$   [54]  (randomized) |
| Bottleneck MSF, biconnected components | $O\left(\min\left\{V^2, \max\left\{1, \log\dfrac{V}{M}\right\}\dfrac{E}{V} Sort(V), (\log B)\dfrac{E}{V} Sort(V) + e\log V\right\}\right)$<br><br>[2, 54, 77, 128]  (deterministic)<br><br>$\Theta\left(\dfrac{E}{V} Sort(V)\right)$   [54, 77]  (randomized) |
| Ear decomposition, maximal matching | $O\left(\min\left\{V^2, \max\left\{1, \log\dfrac{V}{M}\right\} Sort(E), (\log B)Sort(E) + e\log V\right\}\right)$<br><br>[2, 54, 128]  (deterministic)<br><br>$O(Sort(E))$   [54]  (randomized) |
| Undirected breadth-first search | $O(BundleSort(E, V) + V)$   [151] |
| Undirected single-source shortest paths | $O(e\log e + V)$   [128] |
| Directed and undirected depth-first search, topological sorting, directed breadth-first search, directed single-source shortest paths | $O\left(\min\left\{\dfrac{ve}{m} + V, (V + e)\log v\right\}\right)$ [49, 54, 128] |
| Transitive closure | $O\left(Vv\sqrt{\dfrac{e}{m}}\right)$   [54] |

*Note:* The number of vertices is denoted by $V = vB$ and the number of edges by $E = eB$. The terms *Sort* $(N)$ and *BundleSort* $(N, K)$ are defined in Sections 32.4 and 32.6.

## 32.10   External Hashing for Online Dictionary Search

This section focuses on online data structures for supporting the dictionary operations of insert, delete, and lookup. Given a value $x$, the lookup operation returns the item(s), if any, in the structure with key value $x$. The two main types of EM dictionaries are hashing, which we discuss in this section, and tree-based approaches, which is deferred until Section 32.11. The advantage of hashing is that the expected number of probes per operation is a constant, regardless of the number $N$ of items. The common element of all EM hashing algorithms is a predefined hash function:

$$hash : \{\text{all possible keys}\} \rightarrow \{0, 1, 2, \dots, K - 1\}$$

that assigns the $N$ items to $K$ address locations in a uniform manner. Hashing algorithms differ from one another in how they resolve the *collision* that results when there is no room to store an item at its assigned location.

The goals in EM hashing are to achieve an average of $O(Output(Z)) = O(\lceil z \rceil) I/Os$ per lookup, where $Z = zB$ is the number of items output, $O(1) I/Os$ per insert and delete, and linear disk space. Most traditional hashing methods use a statically allocated table and are thus designed to handle only a fixed

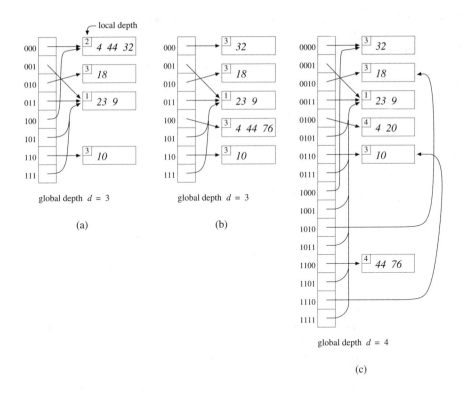

**FIGURE 32.2** Extendible hashing with block size $B = 3$. The keys are indicated in italics. For convenience of exposition, the hash address of a key consists of its binary representation. For example, the hash address of key 4 is "...000100" and the hash address of key 44 is "...0101100". (a) The hash table after insertion of the keys 4, 23, 18, 10, 44, 32, 9. (b) Insertion of the key 76 into table location 100 causes the block with local depth 2 split into two blocks with local depth 3. (c) Insertion of the key 20 into table location 100 causes a block with local depth 3 to split into two blocks with local depth 4. The directory doubles in size and the global depth $d$ is incremented from 3 to 4.

range of $N$. The challenge is to develop dynamic EM structures that can adapt smoothly to widely varying values of $N$.

EM hashing methods fall into one of two categories: *directory* methods and *directoryless* methods. Fagin et al. [79] proposed a directory scheme called *extendible hashing*, illustrated in Fig. 32.2: The directory, for a given $d \geq 0$, consists of a table (array) of $2^d$ pointers. Each item is assigned to the table location corresponding to the $d$ least significant bits of its hash address. The value of $d$, called the *global depth*, is set to the smallest value for which each table location has at most $B$ items assigned to it. Each table location contains a pointer to a block where its items are stored. Thus, a lookup takes two I/Os: one to access the directory and one to access the block storing the item. If the directory fits in internal memory, only one I/O is needed. Several table locations may have many fewer than $B$ assigned items, and for purposes of minimizing storage utilization, they can share the same disk block for storing their items by using a *local depth* smaller than the global depth. When new items are inserted and deleted, the blocks can overflow or underflow, and the local depths and global depth are changed accordingly.

The expected number of disk blocks required to store the data items is asymptotically $n/\ln 2 \approx n/0.69$; that is, the blocks tend to be about 69% full [147]. At least $\Omega(n/B)$ blocks are needed to store the directory. Flajolet [86] showed on the average that the directory uses $\Theta(N^{1/B}n/B) = \Theta(N^{1+1/B}/B^2)$ blocks, which can be superlinear in $N$ asymptotically; however, for practical values of $N$ and $B$, the $N^{1/B}$ term is a small constant, typically less than 2, and directory size is within a constant factor of optimal.

The resulting directory is equivalent to the leaves of a perfectly balanced trie [124], in which the search path for each item is determined by its hash address, except that hashing allows the leaves of the trie to be accessed directly in a single I/O. Any item can thus be retrieved in a total of two I/Os. If the directory fits in internal memory, only one I/O is needed.

A disadvantage of directory schemes is that two I/Os rather than one I/O are required when the directory is stored in external memory. Litwin [136] and Larson [130] developed a directoryless method called *linear hashing* that expands the number of data blocks in a controlled regular fashion. In contrast to directory schemes, the blocks in directoryless methods are chosen for splitting in a predefined order. Thus the block that splits is usually not the block that has overflowed, so some of the blocks may require auxiliary overflow lists to store items assigned to them. On the other hand, directoryless methods have the advantage that there is no need for access to a directory structure, and thus searches often require only one I/O.

## 32.11   Multiway Tree Data Structures

An advantage of search trees over hashing methods is that the data items in a tree are sorted, and thus the tree can be used readily for 1-D range search. The items in a range $[x, y]$ can be found by searching for $x$ in the tree and then performing an inorder traversal in the tree from $x$ to $y$. In this section we explore some important search-tree data structures in external memory.

### B-trees and Variants

Tree-based data structures arise naturally in the online setting, in which the data can be updated and queries must be processed immediately. Binary trees have a host of applications in the (internal memory) RAM model. In order to exploit block transfer, trees in external memory generally use a block for each node, which can store $\Theta(B)$ pointers and data values.

The well-known balanced multiway *B-tree* due to Bayer and McCreight [39,58,124] is the most widely used nontrivial EM data structure. The degree of each node in the B-tree (with the exception of the root) is required to be $\Theta(B)$, which guarantees that the height of a B-tree storing $N$ items is roughly $\log_B N$. B-trees support dynamic dictionary operations and 1-D range search optimally in linear space, $O(\log_B N)$ I/Os per insert or delete, and $O(\log_B N + z)$ I/Os per query, where $Z = zB$ is the number of items output. When a node overflows during an insertion, it splits into two half-full nodes, and if the splitting causes the parent node to overflow, the parent node splits, and so on. Splittings can thus propagate up to the root, which is how the tree grows in height. Deletions are handled in a symmetric way by merging nodes.

In the $B^+$-*tree* variant, pictured in Fig. 32.3, all the items are stored in the leaves, and the leaves are linked together in symmetric order to facilitate range queries and sequential access. The internal nodes store only key values and pointers and thus can have a higher branching factor. In the most popular variant of $B^+$-trees, called $B^*$-*trees*, splitting can usually be postponed when a node overflows, by "sharing" the node's data with one of its adjacent siblings. The node needs to be split only if the sibling is also full; when that happens, the node splits into two, and its data and those of its full sibling are evenly redistributed, making each of the three nodes about 2/3 full. This local optimization reduces how often new

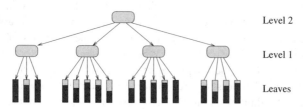

**FIGURE 32.3**   $B^+$-tree multiway search tree. Each internal and leaf node corresponds to a disk block. All the items are stored in the leaves; the darker portion of each leaf block indicates its relative fullness. The internal nodes store only key values and pointers, $\Theta(B)$ of them per node. Although not indicated here, the leaf blocks are linked together sequentially.

nodes must be created and thus increases the storage utilization. Because fewer nodes are in the tree, search I/O costs are lower. When no sharing is done (as in $B^+$-trees), Yao [214] shows that nodes are roughly ln 2 ≈ 69% full on the average, assuming random insertions. With sharing (as in $B^*$-trees), the average storage utilization increases to about 2 ln(3/2) ≈ 81% [32,129]. Storage utilization can be increased further by sharing among several siblings, at the cost of more complicated insertions and deletions. Some helpful space-saving techniques borrowed from hashing are partial expansions [33] and use of overflow nodes [186].

A cross between B-trees and hashing, where each subtree rooted at a certain level of the B-tree is instead organized as an external hash table, was developed by Litwin and Lomet [137] and further studied in [30,138]. O'Neil [158] proposed a B-tree variant called the SB-tree that clusters together on the disk symmetrically ordered nodes from the same level so as to optimize range queries and sequential access. Rao and Ross [165,166] use similar ideas to exploit locality and optimize search tree performance in internal memory. Reducing the number of pointers allows a higher branching factor and thus faster search.

Partially persistent versions of B-trees have been developed by Becker et al. [41] and Varman and Verma [195]. By persistent data structure, we mean that searches can be done with respect to any timestamp $y$ [74,75]. In a partially persistent data structure, only the most recent version of the data structure can be updated. In a fully persistent data structure, any update done with timestamp $y$ affects all future queries for any time after $y$. An interesting open problem is whether B-trees can be made fully persistent. Salzberg and Tsotras [171] survey work done on persistent access methods and other techniques for time-evolving data. Lehman and Yao [132], Mohan [149], and Lomet and Salzberg [140] explore mechanisms to add concurrency and recovery to B-trees.

Arge and Vitter [28] introduce a powerful variant of B-trees called *weight-balanced B-trees*, with the property that the weight of any subtree at level $h$ (i.e., the number of nodes in the subtree rooted at a node of height $h$) is $\Theta(a^h)$, for some fixed parameter $a$ of order $B$. By contrast, the sizes of subtrees at level $h$ in a regular B-tree can differ by a multiplicative factor that is exponential in $h$.

It is sometimes useful to augment B-trees with parent pointers. Order queries such as "Does leaf $x$ precede leaf $y$ in the total order represented by the tree?" can be answered using $O(\log_B N)$ I/Os by following parent pointers starting at $x$ and $y$. The update operations insert, delete, cut, and concatenate can be done in $O((1 + (b/B) \log_m n) \log_b N)$ I/Os amortized, for any $2 \le b \le B/2$, which is never worse than $O((\log_B N)^2)$ by appropriate choice of $b$.

Agarwal et al. [4] apply level-balanced B-trees in a data structure for point location in monotone subdivisions, which supports queries and (amortized) updates in $O((\log_B N)^2)$ I/Os. They also use it to dynamically maintain planar *st*-graphs using $O((1 + (b/B)(\log_m n) \log_b N)$ I/Os (amortized) per update, so that reachability queries can be answered in $O(\log_B N)$ I/Os (worst-case). (Planar *st*-graphs are planar directed acyclic graphs with a single source and a single sink.) An interesting open question is whether level-balanced B-trees can be implemented in $O(\log_B N)$ I/Os per update. Such an improvement would immediately give an optimal dynamic structure for reachability queries in planar *st*-graphs.

Arge [17] developed the elegant *buffer tree* data structure to support *batched dynamic* operations, such as in sweep line applications, where the queries do not have to be answered right away or in any particular order. The buffer tree is a balanced multiway tree, but with degree $\Theta(m)$ rather than degree $\Theta(B)$, except possibly for the root. Its key distinguishing feature is that each node has a buffer that can store $\Theta(M)$ items (i.e., $\Theta(m)$ blocks of items). Items in a node are pushed down to the children when the buffer fills. Emptying a full buffer requires $\Theta(m)$ I/Os, which amortizes the cost of distributing the $M$ items to the $\Theta(m)$ children. Each item thus incurs an amortized cost of $O(m/M) = O(1/B)$ I/Os per level, and the resulting cost for queries and updates is $O((1/B) \log_m n)$ I/Os amortized.

Buffer trees provide a natural amortized implementation of priority queues for *time-forward processing* applications like discrete event simulation, sweeping, and list ranking [54]. Govindrajan et al. [98] use time-forward processing to construct a well-separated pair decomposition of $N$ points in $d$ dimensions in $O(Sort(N))$ I/Os, and they apply it to the problems of finding the $K$ nearest neighbors for each point and the $K$ closest pairs. Brodal and Katajainen [48] provide a worst-case optimal priority queue, in the sense that every sequence of $B$ *insert* and *delete_min* operations requires only $O(\log_m n)$ I/Os. Practical implementations of priority queues based upon these ideas are examined in [47,174]. Further experiments on buffer trees appear in [109].

## 32.12  Spatial Data Structures and Range Search

A fundamental database primitive in spatial databases and GIS is range search, which includes dictionary lookup as a special case. An orthogonal range query, for a given $d$-dimensional rectangle, returns all the points in the interior of the rectangle. Various forms of 2-D orthogonal range search are pictured in Fig. 32.4. Other types of spatial queries include point location queries, ray shooting queries, nearest neighbor queries, and intersection queries, but for brevity we restrict our attention primarily to range searching.

Two types of spatial data structures are used: data-driven and space-driven. R-trees and kd-trees are data-driven since they are based upon a partitioning of the data items themselves, whereas space-driven methods like quad trees and grid files are organized by a partitioning of the embedding space, akin to order-preserving hash functions. In this section, primarily data-driven data structures are discussed. The goal is generally to perform queries in $O(\log_B N + z)$ I/Os, use linear storage space (namely, $O(n)$ disk blocks), and support dynamic updates in $O(\log_B N)$ I/Os.

### Linear-Space Spatial Structures

Grossi and Italiano [101] construct an elegant multidimensional version of the B-tree called the *cross tree*. Using linear space, it combines the data-driven partitioning of weight-balanced B-trees at the upper levels of the tree with the space-driven partitioning of methods like quad trees at the lower levels of the tree. For $d > 1$, $d$-dimensional orthogonal range queries can be done in $O(n^{1-1/d} + z)$ I/Os, and inserts and deletes take $O(\log_B N)$ I/Os. The O-tree of Kanth and Singh [121] provides similar bounds. Cross trees also support the dynamic operations of cut and concatenate in $O(n^{1-1/d})$ I/Os. In some restricted models for linear-space data structures, the 2-D range search query performance of cross trees and O-trees can be considered to be optimal, although it is much larger than the logarithmic bound of Criterion 1.

One way to get multidimensional EM data structures is to augment known internal memory structures, such as quad trees and kd-trees, with block-access capabilities. Examples include *kd-B-trees* [168], *buddy trees* [180], and *hB-trees* [78,139]. *Grid files* [107,127,152] are a flattened data structure for storing the cells of a 2-D grid in disk blocks. Another technique is to "linearize" the multidimensional space by imposing a total ordering on it (a so-called space-filling curve), and then the total order is used to organize the points into a B-tree [93,117,160]. Linearization can also be used to represent nonpoint data, in which the data items are partitioned into one or more multidimensional rectangular regions [1,159]. All the methods described in this paragraph use linear space, and they work well in certain situations; however, their worst-case range query performance is no better than that of cross trees, and for some methods, like grid files, queries can require $\Theta(n)$ I/Os, even if there are no points satisfying the query. The reader is referred to [10,91,153] for a broad survey of these and other interesting methods. Space-filling curves arise again in connection with R-trees, which is described next.

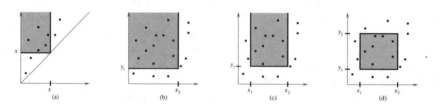

**FIGURE 32.4**    Different types of 2-D orthogonal range queries: (a) Diagonal corner 2-sided 2-D query equivalent to a stabbing query (cf., subsection "Specialized Structures for 2-D Orthogonal Range Search"), (b) 2-sided 2-D query, (c) 3-sided 2-D query, and (d) general 4-sided 2-D query.

## R-trees

The *R-tree* of Guttman [104] and its many variants are a practical multidimensional generalization of the B-tree for storing a variety of geometric objects, such as points, segments, polygons, and polyhedra, using linear disk space. Internal nodes have degree $\Theta(B)$ (except possibly the root), and leaves store $\Theta(B)$ items. Each node in the tree has associated with it a bounding box (or bounding polygon) of all the items in its subtree. A big difference between R-trees and B-trees is that in R-trees the bounding boxes of sibling nodes are allowed to overlap. If an R-tree is being used for point location, for example, a point may lie within the bounding box of several children of the current node in the search. In that case, the search must proceed to all such children.

In the dynamic setting, several popular heuristics are used to determine to insert new items into an R-tree and how to rebalance it; see [10,91,99] for a survey. The $R^*$-*tree* variant of Beckmann et al. [42] seems to give best overall query performance. New R-tree partitioning methods by de Berg et al. [68] and Agarwal et al. [9] provide some provable bounds on overlap and query performance.

In the static setting, in which there are no updates, constructing the $R^*$-tree by repeated insertions, one by one, is extremely slow. A faster alternative to the dynamic R-tree construction algorithms mentioned above is to bulk-load the R-tree in a bottom-up fashion [1,116,159]. The quality of the bottom-up R-tree in terms of query performance is generally not as good as that of an $R^*$-tree, especially for higher-dimensional data [45,118].

In order to get the best of both worlds—the query performance of $R^*$-trees and the bulk construction efficiency of Hilbert R-trees—Arge et al. [22] and van den Bercken et al. [193] independently devised fast bulk loading methods based upon buffer trees that do top-down construction in $O(n \log_m n)$ I/Os, which matches the performance of the bottom-up methods within a constant factor. The former method is especially efficient and supports dynamic batched updates and queries.

## Specialized Structures for 2-D Orthogonal Range Search

Diagonal corner 2-sided queries (see Fig. 32.4(a)) are equivalent to stabbing queries, which have the following form: "Given a set of 1-D intervals, report all the intervals 'stabbed' by the query value $x$." (That is, report all intervals that contain $x$.) A diagonal corner query $x$ on a set of 2-D points $\{(a_1, b_2), (a_2, b_2), \ldots\}$ is equivalent to a stabbing query $x$ on the set of closed intervals $\{[a_1, b_2], [a_2, b_2], \ldots\}$. Arge and Vitter [28,199] introduced a new paradigm we call *bootstrapping* to support such queries in optimal I/O bounds and space: The data structure uses $O(n)$ disk blocks, queries use $O(\log_B N + z)$ I/Os, and updates take $O(\log_B N)$ I/Os. In another example of bootstrapping, Arge et al. [25] achieve the same bounds for 3-sided orthogonal 2-D range searching (see Figure 32.4(c)).

The dynamic data structure for 3-sided range searching can be generalized using the filtering technique of Chazelle [51] to handle general 4-sided queries with optimal I/O query bound $O(\log_B N + z)$ and optimal disk space usage $O(n(\log n)/\log(\log_B N + 1))$ [25]. The update bound becomes $O((\log_B N)(\log n)/\log(\log_B N + 1))$, which may not be optimal.

## Other Types of Range Search

For other types of range searching, such as in higher dimensions and for nonorthogonal queries, different filtering techniques are needed. So far, relatively little work has been done, and many open problems remain.

Vengroff and Vitter [196] develop the first theoretically near-optimal EM data structure for static 3-D orthogonal range searching. They create a hierarchical partitioning in which all the points that dominate a query point are densely contained in a set of blocks. Compression techniques are needed to minimize disk storage. With some recent modifications [204], $(3 + k)$-sided 3-D range queries, where $k$ of the dimensions $(0 \le k \le 3)$ have finite ranges, can be done in $O(\log_B N + z)$ I/Os, which is optimal, and the space usage is $O(n(\log n)^{k+1}/(\log(\log_B N + 1))^k)$. The result also provides optimal $O(\log N + Z)$-time query performance for 3-sided 3-D queries in the (internal memory) RAM model, but using $O(N \log N)$ space.

By the reduction in [52], a data structure for 3-sided 3-D queries also applies to *2-D homothetic range search*, in which the queries correspond to scaled and translated (but not rotated) transformations of an arbitrary fixed polygon. An interesting special case is "fat" orthogonal 2-D range search, where the query rectangles are required to have bounded aspect ratio. For example, every rectangle with bounded aspect ratio can be covered by two overlapping squares. An interesting open problem is to develop linear-sized optimal data structures for fat orthogonal 2-D range search. By the reduction, one possible approach would be to develop optimal linear-sized data structures for 3-sided 3-D range search.

Agarwal et al. [6] consider halfspace range searching, in which a query is specified by a hyperplane and a bit indicating one of its two sides, and the output of the query consists of all the points on that side of the hyperplane. They give various data structures for halfspace range searching in two, three, and higher dimensions, including one that works for simplex (polygon) queries in two dimensions, but with a higher query I/O cost. They have subsequently improved the storage bounds for halfspace range queries in two dimensions to obtain an optimal static data structure satisfying Criteria 1 and 2 of Section 32.12.

The number of I/Os needed to build the data structures for 3-D orthogonal range search and halfspace range search is rather large (more than $\Omega(N)$). Still, the structures shed useful light on the complexity of range searching and may open the way to improved solutions. An open problem is to design efficient construction and update algorithms and to improve upon the constant factors.

Callahan et al. [50] develop dynamic EM data structures for several online problems in $d$ dimensions. For any fixed $\epsilon > 0$, they can find an approximately nearest neighbor of a query point (within a $1 + \epsilon$ factor of optimal) in $O(\log_B N)$ I/Os; insertions and deletions can also be done in $O(\log_B N)$ I/Os. They use a related approach to maintain the closest pair of points; each update costs $O(\log_B N)$ I/Os. Govindrajan et al. [98] achieve the same bounds for closest pair by maintaining a well-separated pair decomposition. For finding nearest neighbors and approximate nearest neighbors, two other approaches are partition trees [5,6] and locality-sensitive hashing [95]. Numerous data structures and lower bounds have been developed for range queries and related problems on spatial data. Refer to [10,91,153,199] for a broad survey.

## Dynamic and Kinetic Data Structures

The preceding sections have outlined cases of data structures in which the data items change dynamically. The bootstrapping paradigm discussed in the two previous subsections is a very useful approach for converting static data structures that are efficient in internal memory into dynamic ones that are efficient for external memory.

In another approach to dynamic data, Arge and Vahrenhold [26] obtain I/O bounds for dynamic point location in general planar subdivisions similar to those of [4], but without use of level-balanced trees. Their method uses a weight-balanced base structure at the outer level and a multislab structure for storing segments similar to that of Arge and Vitter [28]. They use an externalization of Bentley's logarithmic method [44,161] to construct a data structure to answer vertical rayshooting queries in the multislab structures. Arge et al. [8] apply the logarithmic method (in both the binary form and B-way variant) to get EM versions of kd-trees, BBD trees, and BAR trees.

In some applications, the data items are moving and their spatial coordinates change in a regular manner. Early work on temporal data generally concentrated on time-series data or multiversion data [171]. A question of growing interest in this mobile age is how to store and index continuously moving items, such as mobile telephones, cars, and airplanes (e.g., see [113,170,211]). Two main approaches are used for storing moving items: The first technique is to use the same sort of data structure as for nonmoving data, but to update it whenever items move sufficiently so far as to trigger important combinatorial *events* that are relevant to the application at hand [38]. A different approach is to store each item's location and speed trajectory, so that no updating is needed as long as the item's trajectory plan does not change. Such an approach requires fewer updates, but the representation for each item generally has higher dimension, and the search strategies are therefore less efficient.

Kollios et al. [126] developed a linear-space indexing scheme for moving points along a (1-D) line, based upon the notion of partition trees. Their structure supports a variety of range search and approximate nearest neighbor queries. For example, given a range and time, the points in that range at the indicated time can be retrieved in $O(n^{1/2+\epsilon} + k)$ I/Os, for arbitrarily small $\epsilon > 0$. Updates require $O((\log n)^2)$ I/Os. Agarwal et al. [5] extend the approach to handle range searches in two dimensions, and they improve the update bound to $O((\log_B n)^2)$ I/Os. They also propose an event-driven data structure with the same query times as the range search data structure of Arge and Vitter [25] discussed earlier, but with the potential need to do many updates. A hybrid data structure combining the two approaches permits a tradeoff between query performance and update frequency.

R-trees offer a practical generic mechanism for storing multidimensional points and are thus a natural alternative for storing mobile items. One approach is to represent time as a separate dimension and to cluster trajectories using the R-tree heuristics. However, the orthogonal nature of the R-tree does not lend itself well to diagonal trajectories. For the case of points moving along linear trajectories, Šaltenis et al. [170] build the R-tree upon only the spatial dimensions, but parameterize the bounding box coordinates to account for the movement of the items stored within. They maintain an outer approximation of the true bounding box, which they periodically update to refine the approximation. Agarwal and Har-Peled [11] show how to maintain a provably good approximation of the minimum bounding box with need for only a constant number of refinement events.

## 32.13   String and Text Algorithms

The simplest and most commonly used method to index text in large documents or collections of documents is the *inverted file*, which is analogous to the index at the back of a book. The words of interest in the text are sorted alphabetically, and each item in the sorted list has a list of pointers to the occurrences of that word in the text. In an EM setting, a hybrid approach makes sense, in which the text is divided into large chunks (consisting of one or more blocks) and an inverted file is used to specify the chunks containing each word; the search within a chunk can be carried out by using a fast sequential method, such as the Knuth–Morris–Pratt [125] or Boyer–Moore [46] methods. This particular hybrid method was introduced as the basis of the widely used GLIMPSE search tool [144]. Another way to index text is to use hashing to get small signatures for portions of text. The reader is referred to [31,88] for more background on the above methods.

In a conventional B-tree, $\Theta(B)$ unit-sized keys are stored in each internal node to guide the searching, and thus the entire node fits into one or two blocks; however, if the keys are variable-sized text strings, the keys can be arbitrarily long, and there may not be enough space to store $\Theta(B)$ strings per node. Pointers to $\Theta(B)$ strings could be stored instead in each node, but access to the strings during search would require more than a constant number of I/Os per node. In order to save space in each node, Bayer and Unterauer [40] investigated the use of prefix representations of keys. Ferragina and Grossi [83,84] recently developed an elegant generalization of the B-tree called the *String B-tree* or simply *SB-tree* (not to be confused with the SB-tree [158] mentioned in Section 32.11). The query time to search in an SB-tree for a string of $\ell$ characters is $O(\log_B N + \ell/B)$, which is optimal. Insertions and deletions can be done in the same I/O bound. Ferragina and Grossi [83,84] apply SB-trees to the problems of string matching, prefix search, and substring search. Ferragina and Luccio [85] apply SB-trees to get new results for dynamic dictionary matching; their structure even provides a simpler approach for the (internal memory) RAM model.

Tries and Patricia tries are commonly used as internal memory data structures for storing sets of strings. One particularly interesting application of Patricia tries is to store the set of suffixes of a text string. The resulting data structure, called a *suffix tree* [146,210], can be built in linear time and supports search for an arbitrary substring of the text in time linear in the size of the substring. A more compact (but static) representation of a suffix tree, called a *suffix array* [143], consisting of the leaves of the suffix tree in symmetric traversal order, can also be used for fast searching. (See [103] for general background.) Farach et al. [80] show how to construct SB-trees, suffix trees, and suffix arrays on strings of total length $N$ using $O(n \log_m n)$ I/Os, which is optimal. Clark and Munro [55] give a practical implementation of dynamic suffix trees that use about five bytes per indexed suffix. Crauser and Ferragina [63] present an extensive set of experiments on various text collections in which they compare the practical performance of some novel and known suffix array construction algorithms.

Arge et al. [21] consider several models for the problem of sorting $K$ strings of total length $N$ in external memory. They develop efficient sorting algorithms in these models, making use of the SB-tree, buffer tree techniques, and a simplified version of the SB-tree for merging called the *lazy trie*.

**Theorem 32.13.1 [21]** *The number of I/Os needed to sort $K$ strings of total length $N$, where there are $K_1$ short strings of total length $N_1$ and $K_2$ long strings of total length $N_2$ (i.e., $N = N_1 + N_2$ and $K = K_1 + K_2$), is*

$$O\left( \min\left\{ \frac{N_1}{B} \log_m \left( \frac{N_1}{B} + 1 \right), \ K_1 \log_M(K_1 + 1) \right\} + K_2 \log_M(K_2 + 1) + \frac{N}{B} \right) \qquad (32.8)$$

Lower bounds for various models of how strings can be manipulated are given in [21]. There are gaps in some cases between the upper and lower bounds for sorting.

## 32.14 The TPIE External Memory Programming Environment

Three basic approaches are used for supporting development of I/O-efficient code, which we call *access-oriented*, *array-oriented*, and *framework-oriented*. TPIE falls primarily into the third category with some elements of the first category. Access-oriented systems preserve the programmer abstraction of explicitly requesting data transfer. They often extend the read-write interface to include data type specifications and collective specification of multiple transfers, sometimes involving the memories of multiple processing nodes. Examples of access-oriented systems include the UNIX file system at the lowest level, higher-level parallel file systems such as Whiptail [182], Vesta [60], PIOUS [150], and the high-performance storage system [209], and I/O libraries MPI-IO [59] and LEDA-SM [66].

Array-oriented systems access data stored in external memory primarily by means of compiler-recognized data types (typically arrays) and operations on those data types. The external computation is directly specified via iterative loops or explicitly data-parallel operations, and the system manages the explicit I/O transfers. Array-oriented systems are effective for scientific computations that make regular strides through arrays of data and can deliver high-performance parallel I/O in applications such as computational fluid dynamics, molecular dynamics, and weapon system design and simulation. Array-oriented systems are generally ill-suited to irregular or combinatorial computations. Examples of array-oriented systems include PASSION [189], Panda [179] (which also has aspects of access orientation), PI/OT [164], and ViC* [57].

TPIE [22,191,197] provides a framework-oriented interface for batched computation as well as an access-oriented interface for online computation. Instead of viewing batched computation as an enterprise in which code reads data, operates on it, and writes results, a framework-oriented system views computation as a continuous process during which a program is fed streams of data from an outside source and leaves trails of results behind. TPIE programmers do not need to worry about making explicit calls to I/O routines. Instead, they merely specify the functional details of the desired computation, and TPIE automatically choreographs a sequence of data movements to feed the computation. The reader is referred to [199] for further discussion of TPIE and some examples of timing experiments in TPIE.

## 32.15 Dynamic Memory Allocation

The amount of internal memory allocated to a program may fluctuate during the course of execution because of demands placed on the system by other users and processes. EM algorithms must be able to adapt dynamically to whatever resources are available so as to preserve good performance [162]. The algorithms in the previous sections assume a fixed memory allocation; they must resort to virtual memory if the memory allocation is reduced, often causing a severe degradation in performance.

Barve and Vitter [37] discuss the design and analysis of EM algorithms that adapt gracefully to changing memory allocations. In their model, without loss of generality, an algorithm (or program) $\mathcal{P}$ is allocated internal memory in phases: During the $i$th phase, $\mathcal{P}$ is allocated $m_i$ blocks of internal memory, and this memory remains allocated to $\mathcal{P}$ until $\mathcal{P}$ completes $2m_i$ I/O operations, at which point the next phase begins. The process continues until $\mathcal{P}$ finishes execution. We say that $\mathcal{P}$ is *dynamically optimal*, no other algorithm can perform more than a constant number of sorts in the worst-case for the same sequence of memory allocations.

Barve and Vitter [37] define a precise model and give dynamically optimal strategies for sorting, matrix multiplication, and buffer tree operations. Previous work was done on memory-adaptive algorithms for merge sort [162,216] and hash join [163], but the algorithms handle only special cases and can be made to perform nonoptimally for certain patterns of memory allocation.

## 32.16    Conclusions

In this chapter, several useful paradigms for the design and implementation of efficient external memory (EM) algorithms and data structures were described. The problem domains we have considered include sorting, permuting, FFT, scientific computing, computational geometry, graphs, databases, geographic information systems, and text and string processing. Interesting challenges remain in virtually all these problem domains. One difficult problem is to prove lower bounds for permuting and sorting without an item indivisibility assumption. Another promising area is the design and analysis of EM algorithms for efficient use of multiple disks. Optimal bounds have not yet been determined for several basic EM graph problems like topological sorting, shortest paths, breadth-first and depth-first search, and connected components. There is an intriguing connection between problems that have good I/O speedups and problems that have fast and work-efficient parallel algorithms. Several problems remain open in the dynamic and kinetic settings, such as range searching, ray shooting, point location, and finding nearest neighbors.

A continuing goal is to develop optimal EM algorithms and to translate theoretical gains into observable improvements in practice. For some of the problems that can be solved optimally up to a constant factor, the constant overhead is too large for the algorithm to be of practical use, and simpler approaches are needed. In practice, algorithms cannot assume a static internal memory allocation; they must adapt in a robust way when the memory allocation changes.

Many interesting challenges and opportunities in algorithm design and analysis arise from new architectures being developed, such as networks of workstations and hierarchical storage devices. Active (or intelligent) disks, in which disk drives have some processing capability and can filter information sent to the host, have recently been proposed to further reduce the I/O bottleneck, especially in large database applications [3,167]. MEMS-based nonvolatile storage has the potential to serve as an intermediate level in the memory hierarchy between DRAM and disks. It could ultimately provide better latency and bandwidth than disks, at less cost per bit than DRAM [178,198].

### Acknowledgments

The author thanks the TPIE group and his colleagues for helpful comments and suggestions. This work was supported in part by Army Research Office MURI grant DAAH04-96-1-0013 and by National Science Foundation Research Grants CCR-9522047, EIA-9870734, CCR-9877133, and CCR-0082986.

### References

1. D. J. Abel. A B$^+$-tree structure for large quadtrees. *Computer Vision, Graphics, and Image Processing,* 27(1), 19–31, July 1984.
2. J. Abello, A. Buchsbaum, and J. Westbrook. A functional approach to external graph algorithms. In *Proceedings of the European Symposium on Algorithms,* volume 1461 of *Lecture Notes in Computer Science,* 332–343, Venice, Italy, Aug. 1998. Springer-Verlag.

3. A. Acharya, M. Uysal, and J. Saltz. Active disks: Programming model, algorithms and evaluation. *ACM SIGPLAN Notices,* 33(11), 81–91, Nov. 1998.

4. P. K. Agarwal, L. Arge, G. S. Brodal, and J. S. Vitter. I/O-efficient dynamic point location in monotone planar subdivisions. In *Proceedings of the ACM-SIAM Symposium on Discrete Algorithms,* volume 10, 11–20, 1999.

5. P. K. Agarwal, L. Arge, and J. Erickson. Indexing moving points. In *Proceedings of the ACM Symposium on Principles of Database Systems,* volume 19, 175–186, 2000.

6. P. K. Agarwal, L. Arge, J. Erickson, P. G. Franciosa, and J. S. Vitter. Efficient searching with linear constraints. In *Proceedings of the ACM Symposium on Principles of Database Systems,* volume 17, 169–178, 1998.

7. P. K. Agarwal, L. Arge, T. M. Murali, K. Varadarajan, and J. S. Vitter. I/O-efficient algorithms for contour line extraction and planar graph blocking. In *Proceedings of the ACM-SIAM Symposium on Discrete Algorithms,* volume 9, 117–126, 1998.

8. P. K. Agarwal, L. Arge, O. Procopiuc, and J. S. Vitter. A framework for index dynamization. In *Proceedings of the International Colloquium on Automata, Languages, and Programming,* volume 2076 of *Lecture Notes in Computer Science,* Springer-Verlag, Berlin, July 2001.

9. P. K. Agarwal, M. de Berg, J. Gudmundsson, M. Hammar, and H. J. Haverkort. Constructing box trees and R-trees with low stabbing number. In *Proceedings of the ACM Symposium on Computational Geometry,* volume 17, June 2001.

10. P. K. Agarwal and J. Erickson. Geometric range searching and its relatives. In B. Chazelle, J. E. Goodman, and R. Pollack (Eds.), *Advances in Discrete and Computational Geometry,* volume 23 of *Contemporary Mathematics,* 1–56. American Mathematical Society Press, Providence, RI, 1999.

11. P. K. Agarwal and S. Har-Peled. Maintaining the approximate extent measures of moving points. In *Proceedings of the ACM-SIAM Symposium on Discrete Algorithms,* volume 12, Washington, Jan. 2001, 148–157.

12. A. Aggarwal, B. Alpern, A. K. Chandra, and M. Snir. A model for hierarchical memory. In *Proceedings of the ACM Symposium on Theory of Computing,* volume 19, 305–314, New York, 1987.

13. A. Aggarwal, A. Chandra, and M. Snir. Hierarchical memory with block transfer. In *Proceedings of the IEEE Symposium on Foundations of Computer Science,* volume 28, 204–216, Los Angeles, CA, 1987.

14. A. Aggarwal and C. G. Plaxton. Optimal parallel sorting in multilevel storage. In *Proceedings of the ACM-SIAM Symposium on Discrete Algorithms,* volume 5, 659–668, 1994.

15. A. Aggarwal and J. S. Vitter. The Input/Output complexity of sorting and related problems. *Communications of the ACM,* 31(9), 1116–1127, 1988.

16.

17. L. Arge. The buffer tree: A new technique for optimal I/O-algorithms. In *Proceedings of the Workshop on Algorithms and Data Structures,* volume 955 of *Lecture Notes in Computer Science,* 334–345. Springer-Verlag, 1995. A complete version appears as BRICS technical report RS–96–28, University of Aarhus.

18. L. Arge. The I/O-complexity of ordered binary-decision diagram manipulation. In *Proceedings of the International Symposium on Algorithms and Computation,* volume 1004 of *Lecture Notes in Computer Science,* 82–91. Springer-Verlag, 1995.

19. L. Arge. External-memory algorithms with applications in geographic information systems. In M. van Kreveld, J. Nievergelt, T. Roos, and P. Widmayer (Eds.), *Algorithmic Foundations of GIS,* volume 1340 of *Lecture Notes in Computer Science,* 213–254. Springer-Verlag, 1997.

20. L. Arge, G. S. Brodal, and L. Toma. On external memory MST, SSSP and multiway planar graph separation. In *Proceedings of the Scandinavian Workshop on Algorithmic Theory,* July 2000.

21. L. Arge, P. Ferragina, R. Grossi, and J. Vitter. On sorting strings in external memory. In *Proceedings of the ACM Symposium on Theory of Computing,* volume 29, 540–548, 1997.

22. L. Arge, K. H. Hinrichs, J. Vahrenhold, and J. S. Vitter. Efficient bulk operations on dynamic R-trees. In *Workshop on Algorithm Engineering and Experimentation,* volume 1, 328–348, Baltimore, Jan. 1999.

23. L. Arge, M. Knudsen, and K. Larsen. A general lower bound on the I/O-complexity of comparison-based algorithms. In *Proceedings of the Workshop on Algorithms and Data Structures,* volume 709 of *Lecture Notes in Computer Science,* 83–94. Springer-Verlag, 1993.

24. L. Arge, O. Procopiuc, S. Ramaswamy, T. Suel, and J. S. Vitter. Theory and practice of I/O-efficient algorithms for multidimensional batched searching problems. In *Proceedings of the ACM-SIAM Symposium on Discrete Algorithms,* volume 9, 685–694, 1998.

25. L. Arge, V. Samoladas, and J. S. Vitter. Two-dimensional indexability and optimal range search indexing. In *Proceedings of the ACM Conference Principles of Database Systems,* volume 18, 346–357, Philadelphia, PA, May–June 1999.

26. L. Arge and J. Vahrenhold. I/O-efficient dynamic planar point location. In *Proceedings of the ACM Symposium on Computational Geometry,* volume 9, 191–200, June 2000.

27. L. Arge, D. E. Vengroff, and J. S. Vitter. External-memory algorithms for processing line segments in geographic information systems. *Algorithmica,* to appear. Special issue on cartography and geographic information systems. An earlier version appeared in *Proceedings of the Third European Symposium on Algorithms,* volume 979 of *Lecture Notes in Computer Science,* 295–310, Springer-Verlag, Sept. 1995.

28. L. Arge and J. S. Vitter. Optimal dynamic interval management in external memory. In *Proceedings of the IEEE Symposium on Foundations of Computer Science,* volume 37, 560–569, Burlington, VT, Oct. 1996.

29. C. Armen. Bounds on the separation of two parallel disk models. In *Proceedings of the Workshop on Input/Output in Parallel and Distributed Systems,* volume 4, 122–127, Philadelphia, May 1996.

30. R. Baeza-Yates. Bounded disorder: The effect of the index. *Theoretical Computer Science,* 168, 21–38, 1996.

31. R. Baeza-Yates and B. Ribeiro-Neto, (Eds.). *Modern Information Retrieval.* Addison Wesley Longman, 1999. Chapter 8.

32. R. A. Baeza-Yates. Expected behaviour of $B^+$-trees under random insertions. *Acta Informatica,* 26(5), 439–472, 1989.

33. R. A. Baeza-Yates and P.-A. Larson. Performance of $B^+$-trees with partial expansions. *IEEE Transactions on Knowledge and Data Engineering,* 1(2), 248–257, June 1989.

34. R. D. Barve, E. F. Grove, and J. S. Vitter. Simple randomized mergesort on parallel disks. *Parallel Computing,* 23(4), 601–631, 1997.

35. R. D. Barve, M. Kallahalla, P. J. Varman, and J. S. Vitter. Competitive analysis of buffer management algorithms. *Journal of Algorithms,* 36, Aug. 2000.

36. R. D. Barve and J. S. Vitter. A simple and efficient parallel disk mergesort. In *Proceedings of the ACM Symposium on Parallel Algorithms and Architectures,* volume 11, 232–241, St. Malo, France, June 1999.

37. R. D. Barve and J. S. Vitter. A theoretical framework for memory-adaptive algorithms. In *Proceedings of the IEEE Symposium on Foundations of Computer Science,* volume 40, 273–284, New York, Oct. 1999.

38. J. Basch, L. J. Guibas, and J. Hershberger. Data structures for mobile data. *Journal of Algorithms,* 31, 1–28, 1999.

39. R. Bayer and E. McCreight. Organization of large ordered indexes. *Acta Informatica,* 1, 173–189, 1972.

40. R. Bayer and K. Unterauer. Prefix B-trees. *ACM Transactions on Database Systems,* 2(1), 11–26, March 1977.

41. B. Becker, S. Gschwind, T. Ohler, B. Seeger, and P. Widmayer. An asymptotically optimal multiversion B-tree. *VLDB Journal,* 5(4), 264–275, Dec. 1996.

42. N. Beckmann, H.-P. Kriegel, R. Schneider, and B. Seeger. The R*-tree: An efficient and robust access method for points and rectangles. In *Proceedings of the ACM SIGMOD International Conference on Management of Data,* 322–331, 1990.

43. M. A. Bender, E. D. Demaine, and M. Farach-Colton. Cache-oblivious B-trees. In *Proceedings of the IEEE Symposium on Foundations of Computer Science,* volume 41, Redondo Beach, California, Nov. 12–14, 2000.

44. J. L. Bentley and J. B. Saxe. Decomposable searching problems I: Static-to-dynamic transformations. *Journal of Algorithms,* 1(4), 301–358, Dec. 1980.

45. S. Berchtold, C. Böhm, and H.-P. Kriegel. Improving the query performance of high-dimensional index structures by bulk load operations. In *Proceedings of the International Conference on Extending Database Technology,* volume 5, 216–230, 1998.

46. R. S. Boyer and J. S. Moore. A fast string searching algorithm. *Communications of the ACM,* 20(10), 762–772, Oct. 1977.

47. K. Brengel, A. Crauser, P. Ferragina, and U. Meyer. An experimental study of priority queues. In J. S. Vitter and C. Zaroliagis (Eds.), *Proceedings of the Workshop on Algorithm Engineering,* Lecture Notes in Computer Science, 345–359, London, July 1999. Springer-Verlag.

48. G. S. Brodal and J. Katajainen. Worst-case efficient external-memory priority queues. In *Proceedings of the Scandinavian Workshop on Algorithmic Theory,* volume 1432 of *Lecture Notes in Computer Science,* 107–118, Stockholm, Sweden, July 1998. Springer-Verlag.

49. A. L. Buchsbaum, M. Goldwasser, S. Venkatasubramanian, and J. R. Westbrook. On external memory graph traversal. In *Proceedings of the ACM-SIAM Symposium on Discrete Algorithms,* volume 11, Jan. 2000.

50. P. Callahan, M. T. Goodrich, and K. Ramaiyer. Topology B-trees and their applications. In *Proceedings of the Workshop on Algorithms and Data Structures,* volume 955 of *Lecture Notes in Computer Science,* 381–392. Springer-Verlag, 1995.

51. B. Chazelle. Filtering search: A new approach to query-answering. *SIAM Journal on Computing,* 15, 703–724, 1986.

52. B. Chazelle and H. Edelsbrunner. Linear space data structures for two types of range search. *Discrete and Computational Geometry,* 2, 113–126, 1987.

53. P. M. Chen, E. K. Lee, G. A. Gibson, R. H. Katz, and D. A. Patterson. RAID: high-performance, reliable secondary storage. *ACM Computing Surveys,* 26(2), 145–185, June 1994.

54. Y.-J. Chiang, M. T. Goodrich, E. F. Grove, R. Tamassia, D. E. Vengroff, and J. S. Vitter. External-memory graph algorithms. In *Proceedings of the ACM-SIAM Symposium on Discrete Algorithms,* volume 6, 139–149, Jan. 1995.

55. D. R. Clark and J. I. Munro. Efficient suffix trees on secondary storage. In *Proceedings of the ACM-SIAM Symposium on Discrete Algorithms,* volume 7, 383–391, Atlanta, GA, June 1996.

56. K. L. Clarkson and P. W. Shor. Applications of random sampling in computational geometry, II. *Discrete and Computational Geometry,* 4, 387–421, 1989.

57. A. Colvin and T. H. Cormen. ViC*: A compiler for virtual-memory C*. In *Proceedings of the International Workshop on High-Level Programming Models and Supportive Environments,* volume 3, 1998.

58. D. Comer. The ubiquitous B-tree. *ACM Computing Surveys,* 11(2), 121–137, 1979.

59. P. Corbett, D. Feitelson, S. Fineberg, Y. Hsu, B. Nitzberg, J.-P. Prost, M. Snir, B. Traversat, and P. Wong. Overview of the MPI-IO parallel I/O interface. In R. Jain, J. Werth, and J. C. Browne (Eds.), *Input/Output in Parallel and Distributed Computer Systems,* volume 362 of *The Kluwer International Series in Engineering and Computer Science,* chapter 5, 127–146. Kluwer Academic Publishers, 1996.

60. P. F. Corbett and D. G. Feitelson. The Vesta parallel file system. *ACM Transactions on Computer Systems,* 14(3), 225–264, Aug. 1996.

61. T. H. Cormen and D. M. Nicol. Performing out-of-core FFTs on parallel disk systems. *Parallel Computing,* 24(1), 5–20, Jan. 1998.

62. T. H. Cormen, T. Sundquist, and L. F. Wisniewski. Asymptotically tight bounds for performing BMMC permutations on parallel disk systems. *SIAM Journal on Computing,* 28(1), 105–136, 1999.

63. A. Crauser and P. Ferragina. On constructing suffix arrays in external memory. In *Proceedings of the European Symposium on Algorithms,* volume 1643 of *Lecture Notes in Computer Science.* Springer-Verlag, 1999.

64. A. Crauser, P. Ferragina, K. Mehlhorn, U. Meyer, and E. A. Ramos. Randomized external-memory algorithms for geometric problems. In *Proceedings of the ACM Symposium on Computational Geometry,* volume 14, 259–268, June 1998.

65. A. Crauser, P. Ferragina, K. Mehlhorn, U. Meyer, and E. A. Ramos. I/O-optimal computation of segment intersections. In J. Abello and J. S. Vitter (Eds.), *External Memory Algorithms and Visualization*, DIMACS Series in Discrete Mathematics and Theoretical Computer Science, 131–138. American Mathematical Society Press, Providence, RI, 1999.

66. A. Crauser and K. Mehlhorn. LEDA-SM: Extending LEDA to secondary memory. In J. S. Vitter and C. Zaroliagis (Eds.), *Proceedings of the European Symposium on Algorithms*, Lecture Notes in Computer Science, 228–242, London, July 1999. Springer-Verlag.

67. R. Cypher and G. Plaxton. Deterministic sorting in nearly logarithmic time on the hypercube and related computers. *Journal of Computer and System Sciences*, 47(3), 501–548, 1993.

68. M. de Berg, J. Gudmundsson, M. Hammar, and M. Overmars. On R-trees with low stabbing number. In *Proceedings of the European Symposium on Algorithms*, volume 1879 of *Lecture Notes in Computer Science*, 167–178, Saarbrücken, Germany, Sept. 2000. Springer-Verlag.

69. F. Dehne, W. Dittrich, and D. Hutchinson. Efficient external memory algorithms by simulating coarse-grained parallel algorithms. In *Proceedings of the ACM Symposium on Parallel Algorithms and Architectures*, volume 9, 106–115, June 1997.

70. F. Dehne, D. Hutchinson, and A. Maheshwari. Reducing I/O complexity by simulating coarse grained parallel algorithms. In *Proceedings of the International Parallel Processing Symposium*, volume 13, 14–20, April 1999.

71. H. B. Demuth. *Electronic Data Sorting*. Ph.D., Stanford University, 1956. A shortened version appears in *IEEE Transactions on Computing*, C-34(4), 296–310, April 1985, special issue on sorting, E. E. Lindstrom, C. K. Wong, and J. S. Vitter (Eds.).

72. D. J. DeWitt, J. F. Naughton, and D. A. Schneider. Parallel sorting on a shared-nothing architecture using probabilistic splitting. In *Proceedings of the International Conference on Parallel and Distributed Information Systems*, volume 1, 280–291, Dec. 1991.

73. W. Dittrich, D. Hutchinson, and A. Maheshwari. Blocking in parallel multisearch problems. In *Proceedings of the ACM Symposium on Parallel Algorithms and Architectures*, volume 10, 98–107, 1998.

74. J. R. Driscoll, N. Sarnak, D. D. Sleator, and R. E. Tarjan. Making data structures persistent. *Journal of Computer and System Sciences*, 38, 86–124, 1989.

75. M. C. Easton. Key-sequence data sets on indelible storage. *IBM Journal of Research and Development*, 30, 230–241, 1986.

76. NASA's Earth Observing System (EOS) Web page, NASA Goddard Space Flight Center, http://eospso. gsfc.nasa.gov/.

77. D. Eppstein, Z. Galil, G. F. Italiano, and A. Nissenzweig. Sparsification—A technique for speeding up dynamic graph algorithms. *Journal of the ACM*, 44(5), 669–696, 1997.

78. G. Evangelidis, D. B. Lomet, and B. Salzberg. The hB$^\Pi$-tree: A multi-attribute index supporting concurrency, recovery and node consolidation. *VLDB Journal*, 6, 1–25, 1997.

79. R. Fagin, J. Nievergelt, N. Pippinger, and H. R. Strong. Extendible hashing—a fast access method for dynamic files. *ACM Transactions on Database Systems*, 4(3), 315–344, 1979.

80. M. Farach, P. Ferragina, and S. Muthukrishnan. Overcoming the memory bottleneck in suffix tree construction. In *Proceedings of the IEEE Symposium on Foundations of Computer Science*, volume 39, 174–183, Palo Alto, CA, Nov. 1998.

81. J. Feigenbaum, S. Kannan, M. Strauss, and M. Viswanathan. An approximate l1-difference algorithm for massive data streams. In *Proceedings of the IEEE Symposium on Foundations of Computer Science*, volume 40, 501–511, New York, Oct. 1999.

82. W. Feller. *An Introduction to Probability Theory and its Applications*, volume 1. John Wiley & Sons, New York, 3rd ed., 1968.

83. P. Ferragina and R. Grossi. Fast string searching in secondary storage: Theoretical developments and experimental results. In *Proceedings of the ACM-SIAM Symposium on Discrete Algorithms*, volume 7, 373–382, Atlanta, June 1996.

84. P. Ferragina and R. Grossi. The String B-tree: a new data structure for string search in external memory and its applications. *Journal of the ACM*, 46(2), 236–280, March 1999.

85. P. Ferragina and F. Luccio. Dynamic dictionary matching in external memory. *Information and Computation*, 146(2), 85–99, Nov. 1998.

86. P. Flajolet. On the performance evaluation of extendible hashing and trie searching. *Acta Informatica*, 20(4), 345–369, 1983.

87. R. W. Floyd. Permuting information in idealized two-level storage. In R. Miller and J. Thatcher (Eds.), *Complexity of Computer Computations*, 105–109. Plenum, 1972.

88. W. Frakes and R. Baeza-Yates (Eds.). *Information Retrieval: Data Structures and Algorithms*. Prentice-Hall, 1992.

89. M. Frigo, C. E. Leiserson, H. Prokop, and S. Ramachandran. Cache-oblivious algorithms. In *Proceedings of the IEEE Symposium on Foundations of Computer Science*, volume 40, 1999.

90. T. A. Funkhouser, C. H. Sequin, and S. J. Teller. Management of large amounts of data in interactive building walkthroughs. In *Proceedings of the ACM Conference on Computer Graphics*, 11–20, Boston, March 1992.

91. V. Gaede and O. Günther. Multidimensional access methods. *ACM Computing Surveys*, 30(2), 170–231, June 1998.

92. M. Gardner. *Magic Show*, Chapter 7. Knopf, New York, 1977.

93. I. Gargantini. An effective way to represent quadtrees. *Communications of the ACM*, 25(12), 905–910, Dec. 1982.

94. G. A. Gibson, J. S. Vitter, and J. Wilkes. Report of the working group on storage I/O issues in large-scale computing. *ACM Computing Surveys*, 28(4), 779–793, Dec. 1996.

95. A. Gionis, P. Indyk, and R. Motwani. Similarity search in high dimensions via hashing. In *Proceedings of the International Conference on Very Large Databases*, volume 25, 78–89, Edinburgh, Scotland, 1999, Morgan Kaufmann Publishers.

96. R. Goldman, N. Shivakumar, S. Venkatasubramanian, and H. Garcia-Molina. Proximity search in databases. In *Proceedings of the International Conference on Very Large Databases*, volume 24, 26–37, Aug. 1998.

97. M. T. Goodrich, J.-J. Tsay, D. E. Vengroff, and J. S. Vitter. External-memory computational geometry. In *Proceedings of the IEEE Symposium on Foundations of Computer Science*, volume 34, 714–723, Palo Alto, CA, Nov. 1993.

98. S. Govindarajan, T. Lukovszki, A. Maheshari, and N. Zeh. I/O-efficient well-separated pair decomposition and its applications. In *Proceedings of the European Symposium on Algorithms*, Lecture Notes in Computer Science, Saarbrücken, Germany, Sept. 2000. Springer-Verlag.

99. D. Greene. An implementation and performance analysis of spatial data access methods. In *Proceedings of IEEE International Conference on Data Engineering*, volume 5, 606–615, 1989.

100. J. L. Griffin, S. W. Schlosser, G. R. Ganger, and D. F. Nagle. Modeling and performance of MEMS-based storage devices. In *Proceedings of ACM SIGMETRICS Joint International Conference on Measurement and Modeling of Computer Systems*, Santa Clara, CA, June 2000.

101. R. Grossi and G. F. Italiano. Efficient cross-trees for external memory. In J. Abello and J. S. Vitter (Eds.), *External Memory Algorithms and Visualization*, DIMACS Series in Discrete Mathematics and Theoretical Computer Science, 87–106. American Mathematical Society Press, Providence, RI, 1999.

102. S. K. S. Gupta, Z. Li, and J. H. Reif. Generating efficient programs for two-level memories from tensor-products. In *Proceedings of the IASTED/ISMM International Conference on Parallel and Distributed Computing and Systems*, volume 7, 510–513, Washington, D.C., Oct. 1995.

103. D. Gusfield. *Algorithms on Strings, Trees, and Sequences*. Cambridge University Press, Cambridge, UK, 1997.

104. A. Guttman. R-trees: A dynamic index structure for spatial searching. In *Proceedings of the ACM SIGMOD International Conference on Management of Data*, 47–57, 1984.

105. L. Hellerstein, G. Gibson, R. M. Karp, R. H. Katz, and D. A. Patterson. Coding techniques for handling failures in large disk arrays. *Algorithmica*, 12(2–3), 182–208, 1994.

106. M. R. Henzinger, P. Raghavan, and S. Rajagopalan. Computing on data streams. In J. Abello and J. S. Vitter (Eds.), *External Memory Algorithms and Visualization*, DIMACS Series in Discrete

Mathematics and Theoretical Computer Science, 107–118. American Mathematical Society Press, Providence, RI, 1999.

107. K. H. Hinrichs. *The grid file system: Implementation and case studies of applications.* Ph.D., Dept. Information Science, ETH, Zürich, 1985.

108. J. W. Hong and H. T. Kung. I/O complexity: The red-blue pebble game. In *Proceedings of the ACM Symposium on Theory of Computing,* volume 13, 326–333, May 1981.

109. D. Hutchinson, A. Maheshwari, J.-R. Sack, and R. Velicescu. Early experiences in implementing the buffer tree. Proceedings of the Workshop on Algorithm Engineering, 1997.

110. D. Hutchinson, A. Maheshwari, and N. Zeh. An external memory data structure for shortest path queries. In *Proceedings of the International Conference on Computing and Combinatorics,* volume 1627 of *Lecture Notes in Computer Science,* 51–60. Springer-Verlag, July 1999.

111. D. A. Hutchinson, P. Sanders, and J. S. Vitter. Duality between prefetching and queued writing with applications to integrated caching and prefetching and to external sorting. In Proceedings of the European Symposium on Algorithms, volume 2161 of *Lecture Notes in Computer Science,* Springer-Verlag, Berlin, August 2001.

112. D. A. Hutchinson, P. Sanders, and J. S. Vitter. The power of duality for prefetching and sorting with parallel disks. In *Proceedings of the ACM Symposium on Parallel Algorithms and Architectures,* volume 2076 of Lecture Notes in Computer Science, Crete, Greece, July 2001. Springer-Verlag.

113. D. P. C. S. Jensen and Y. Theodoridis. Novel approaches to the indexing of moving object trajectories. In *Proceedings of the International Conference on Very Large Databases,* volume 26, 395–406, Cairo, 2000.

114. M. Kallahalla and P. J. Varman. Optimal read-once parallel disk scheduling. In *Proceedings of the Workshop on Input/Output in Parallel and Distributed Systems,* volume 6, 68–77, Atlanta, GA, May 1999. ACM Press.

115. M. Kallahalla and P. J. Varman. Optimal prefetching and caching for parallel I/O systems. In *Proceedings of the ACM Symposium on Parallel Algorithms and Architectures,* volume 13, Crete, Greece, July 2001.

116. I. Kamel and C. Faloutsos. On packing R-trees. In *Proceedings of the International ACM Conference on Information and Knowledge Management,* volume 2, 490–499, 1993.

117. I. Kamel and C. Faloutsos. Hilbert R-tree: An improved R-tree using fractals. In *Proceedings of the International Conference on Very Large Databases,* volume 20, 500–509, 1994.

118. I. Kamel, M. Khalil, and V. Kouramajian. Bulk insertion in dynamic R-trees. In *Proceedings of the International Symposium on Spatial Data Handling,* volume 4, 3B, 31–42, 1996.

119. P. C. Kanellakis, G. M. Kuper, and P. Z. Revesz. Constraint query languages. In *Proceedings of the ACM Conference Principles of Database Systems,* volume 9, 299–313, 1990.

120. P. C. Kanellakis, S. Ramaswamy, D. E. Vengroff, and J. S. Vitter. Indexing for data models with constraints and classes. *Journal of Computer and System Sciences,* 52(3), 589–612, 1996.

121. K. V. R. Kanth and A. K. Singh. Optimal dynamic range searching in non-replicating index structures. In *Proceedings of the International Conference on Database Theory,* volume 1540 of *Lecture Notes in Computer Science,* 257–276. Springer-Verlag, Jan. 1999.

122. M. Y. Kim. Synchronized disk interleaving. *IEEE Transactions on Computers,* 35(11), 978–988, Nov. 1986.

123. D. G. Kirkpatrick and R. Seidel. The ultimate planar convex hull algorithm? *SIAM Journal on Computing,* 15, 287–299, 1986.

124. D. E. Knuth. *Sorting and Searching,* volume 3 of *The Art of Computer Programming.* Addison-Wesley, Reading, MA, 2nd ed., 1998.

125. D. E. Knuth, J. H. Morris, and V. R. Pratt. Fast pattern matching in strings. *SIAM Journal on Computing,* 6, 323–350, 1977.

126. G. Kollios, D. Gunopulos, and V. J. Tsotras. On indexing mobile objects. In *Proceedings of the ACM Symposium on Principles of Database Systems,* volume 18, 261–272, 1999.

127. R. Krishnamurthy and K.-Y. Wang. Multilevel grid files. Tech. report, IBM T. J. Watson Center, Yorktown Heights, NY, Nov. 1985.

128. V. Kumar and E. Schwabe. Improved algorithms and data structures for solving graph problems in external memory. In *Proceedings of the IEEE Symposium on Parallel and Distributed Processing*, volume 8, 169–176, Oct. 1996.

129. K. Küspert. Storage utilization in B*-trees with a generalized overflow technique. *Acta Informatica*, 19, 35–55, 1983.

130. P.-A. Larson. Performance analysis of linear hashing with partial expansions. *ACM Transactions on Database Systems*, 7(4), 566–587, Dec. 1982.

131. R. Laurini and D. Thompson. *Fundamentals of Spatial Information Systems*. Academic Press, 1992.

132. P. L. Lehman and S. B. Yao. Efficient locking for concurrent operations on B-Trees. *ACM Transactions on Database Systems*, 6(4), 650–570, Dec. 1981.

133. F. T. Leighton. Tight bounds on the complexity of parallel sorting. *IEEE Transactions on Computers*, C-34(4), 344–354, April 1985. Special issue on sorting, E. E. Lindstrom and C. K. Wong and J. S. Vitter (Eds.).

134. C. E. Leiserson, S. Rao, and S. Toledo. Efficient out-of-core algorithms for linear relaxation using blocking covers. In *Proceedings of the IEEE Symposium on Foundations of Computer Science*, volume 34, 704–713, 1993.

135. Z. Li, P. H. Mills, and J. H. Reif. Models and resource metrics for parallel and distributed computation. *Parallel Algorithms and Applications*, 8, 35–59, 1996.

136. W. Litwin. Linear hashing: A new tool for files and tables addressing. In *Proceedings of the International Conference on Very Large Databases*, volume 6, 212–223, Montreal, Quebec, Canada, Oct. 1980.

137. W. Litwin and D. Lomet. A new method for fast data searches with keys. *IEEE Software*, 4(2), 16–24, March 1987.

138. D. Lomet. A simple bounded disorder file organization with good performance. *ACM Transactions on Database Systems*, 13(4), 525–551, 1988.

139. D. B. Lomet and B. Salzberg. The hB-tree: A multiattribute indexing method with good guaranteed performance. *ACM Transactions on Database Systems*, 15(4), 625–658, 1990.

140. D. B. Lomet and B. Salzberg. Concurrency and recovery for index trees. *VLDB Journal*, 6(3), 224–240, 1997.

141. A. Maheshwari and N. Zeh. External memory algorithms for outerplanar graphs. In *Proceedings of the International Conference on Computing and Combinatorics*, volume 1627 of *Lecture Notes in Computer Science*, 51–60. Springer-Verlag, July 1999.

142. A. Maheshwari and N. Zeh. I/O-efficient algorithms for bounded treewidth graphs. In *Proceedings of the ACM-SIAM Symposium on Discrete Algorithms*, volume 12, Washington, D.C., Jan. 2001.

143. U. Manber and G. Myers. Suffix arrays: A new method for on-line string searches. *SIAM Journal on Computing*, 22(5), 935–948, Oct. 1993.

144. U. Manber and S. Wu. GLIMPSE: A tool to search through entire file systems. In USENIX Association, editor, *Proceedings of the Winter USENIX Conference*, 23–32, San Francisco, Jan. 1994. USENIX.

145. Y. Matias, E. Segal, and J. S. Vitter. Efficient bundle sorting. In *Proceedings of the ACM-SIAM Symposium on Discrete Algorithms*, volume 11, 839–848, San Francisco, Jan. 2000.

146. E. M. McCreight. A space-economical suffix tree construction algorithm. *Journal of the ACM*, 23(2), 262–272, 1976.

147. H. Mendelson. Analysis of extendible hashing. *IEEE Transactions on Software Engineering*, SE–8, 611–619, Nov. 1982.

148. U. Meyer. External memory BFS on undirected graphs with bounded degree. In *Proceedings of the ACM-SIAM Symposium on Discrete Algorithms*, volume 12, Washington, DC, Jan. 2001.

149. C. Mohan. ARIES/KVL: A key-value locking method for concurrency control of multiaction transactions on B-tree indices. In *Proceedings of the International Conference on Very Large Databases*, 392, Brisbane, Australia, Aug. 1990.

150. S. A. Moyer and V. Sunderam. Characterizing concurrency control performance for the PIOUS parallel file system. *Journal of Parallel and Distributed Computing*, 38(1), 81–91, Oct. 1996.

151. K. Munagala and A. Ranade. I/O-complexity of graph algorithms. In *Proceedings of the ACM-SIAM Symposium on Discrete Algorithms,* volume 10, 687–694, Baltimore, MD, Jan. 1999.

152. J. Nievergelt, H. Hinterberger, and K. C. Sevcik. The grid file: An adaptable, symmetric multi-key file structure. *ACM Transactions on Database Systems,* 9, 38–71, 1984.

153. J. Nievergelt and P. Widmayer. Spatial data structures: Concepts and design choices. In M. van Kreveld, J. Nievergelt, T. Roos, and P. Widmayer (Eds.), *Algorithmic Foundations of GIS,* volume 1340 of *Lecture Notes in Computer Science,* 153 ff. Springer-Verlag, 1997.

154. M. H. Nodine, M. T. Goodrich, and J. S. Vitter. Blocking for external graph searching. *Algorithmica,* 16(2), 181–214, Aug. 1996.

155. M. H. Nodine, D. P. Lopresti, and J. S. Vitter. I/O overhead and parallel VLSI architectures for lattice computations. *IEEE Transactions on Communications,* 40(7), 843–852, July 1991.

156. M. H. Nodine and J. S. Vitter. Deterministic distribution sort in shared and distributed memory multiprocessors. In *Proceedings of the ACM Symposium on Parallel Algorithms and Architectures,* volume 5, 120–129, Velen, Germany, June–July 1993.

157. M. H. Nodine and J. S. Vitter. Greed Sort: An optimal sorting algorithm for multiple disks. *Journal of the ACM,* 42(4), 919–933, July 1995.

158. P. E. O'Neil. The SB-tree. an index-sequential structure for high-performance sequential access. *Acta Informatica,* 29(3), 241–265, June 1992.

159. J. A. Orenstein. Redundancy in spatial databases. In *Proceedings of the ACM SIGMOD International Conference on Management of Data,* 294–305, Portland, OR, June 1989.

160. J. A. Orenstein and T. H. Merrett. A class of data structures for associative searching. In *Proceedings of the ACM Conference Principles of Database Systems,* volume 3, 181–190, 1984.

161. M. H. Overmars. *The Design of Dynamic Data Structures.* Lecture Notes in Computer Science. Springer-Verlag, 1983.

162. H. Pang, M. Carey, and M. Livny. Memory-adaptive external sorts. In *Proceedings of the International Conference on Very Large Databases,* volume 19, 618–629, Dublin, 1993.

163. H. Pang, M. J. Carey, and M. Livny. Partially preemptive hash joins. In P. Buneman and S. Jajodia (Eds.), *Proceedings of the ACM SIGMOD International Conference on Management of Data,* 59–68, Washington, DC, May 1993.

164. I. Parsons, R. Unrau, J. Schaeffer, and D. Szafron. PI/OT: Parallel I/O templates. *Parallel Computing,* 23(4), 543–570, June 1997.

165. J. Rao and K. Ross. Cache conscious indexing for decision-support in main memory. In M. Atkinson et al. (Eds.), *Proceedings of the International Conference on Very Large Databases,* volume 25, 78–89, Los Altos, CA 94022, USA, 1999, Morgan Kaufmann Publishers.

166. J. Rao and K. A. Ross. Making B$^+$-trees cache conscious in main memory. In W. Chen, J. Naughton, and P. A. Bernstein (Eds.), *Proceedings of the ACM SIGMOD International Conference on Management of Data,* 475–486, Dallas, Texas, 2000.

167. E. Riedel, G. A. Gibson, and C. Faloutsos. Active storage for large-scale data mining and multimedia. In *Proceedings of the International Conference on Very Large Databases,* volume 22, 62–73, Aug. 1998.

168. J. T. Robinson. The k-d-b-tree: A search structure for large multidimensional dynamic indexes. In *Proceedings of the ACM Conference Principles of Database Systems,* volume 1, 10–18, 1981.

169. K. Salem and H. Garcia-Molina. Disk striping. In *Proceedings of IEEE International Conference on Data Engineering,* volume 2, 336–242, Los Angeles, 1986.

170. S. Šaltenis, C. S. Jensen, S. T. Leutenegger, and M. A. Lopez. Indexing the positions of continuously moving objects. In W. Chen, J. Naughton, and P. A. Bernstein (Eds.), *Proceedings of the ACM SIGMOD International Conference on Management of Data,* 331–342, Dallas, Texas, 2000.

171. B. Salzberg and V. J. Tsotras. Comparison of access methods for time-evolving data. *ACM Computing Surveys,* 31, 158–221, June 1999.

172. H. Samet. *Applications of Spatial Data Structures: Computer Graphics, Image Processing, and GIS.* Addison-Wesley, Reading, MA, 1989.

173. H. Samet. _The Design and Analysis of Spatial Data Structures._ Addison-Wesley, Reading, MA, 1989.

174. P. Sanders. Fast priority queues for cached memory. In _Workshop on Algorithm Engineering and Experimentation,_ volume 1619 of _Lecture Notes in Computer Science,_ 312–327. Springer-Verlag, Jan. 1999.

175. P. Sanders. Reconciling simplicity and realism in parallel disk models. In _Proceedings of the ACM-SIAM Symposium on Discrete Algorithms,_ volume 12, Washington, Jan. 2001.

176. P. Sanders, S. Egner, and J. Korst. Fast concurrent access to parallel disks. In _Proceedings of the ACM-SIAM Symposium on Discrete Algorithms,_ volume 11, 849–858, San Francisco, Jan. 2000.

177. J. E. Savage and J. S. Vitter. Parallelism in space-time tradeoffs. In F. P. Preparata (Ed.), _Advances in Computing Research,_ volume 4, 117–146. JAI Press, 1987.

178. S. W. Schlosser, J. L. Griffin, D. F. Nagle, and G. R. Ganger. Designing computer systems with MEMS-based storage. In _Proceedings of the International Conference on Architectural Support for Programming Languages and Operating Systems,_ volume 9, Nov. 2000.

179. K. E. Seamons and M. Winslett. Multidimensional array I/O in Panda 1.0. _Journal of Supercomputing,_ 10(2), 191–211, 1996.

180. B. Seeger and H.-P. Kriegel. The buddy-tree: An efficient and robust access method for spatial data base systems. In _Proceedings of the International Conference on Very Large Databases,_ 590–601, 1990.

181. E. A. M. Shriver and M. H. Nodine. An introduction to parallel I/O models and algorithms. In R. Jain, J. Werth, and J. C. Browne (Eds.), _Input/Output in Parallel and Distributed Computer Systems,_ Chapter 2, 31–68. Kluwer Academic Publishers, 1996.

182. E. A. M. Shriver and L. F. Wisniewski. An API for choreographing data accesses. _Technical Report PCS-TR95-267,_ Dept. of Computer Science, Dartmouth College, Nov. 1995.

183. J. F. Sibeyn. From parallel to external list ranking. _Technical Report MPI–I–97–1–021,_ Max-Planck-Institute, Sept. 1997.

184. J. F. Sibeyn. External selection. In _Proceedings of the Symposium on Theoretical Aspects of Computer Science,_ volume 1563 of _Lecture Notes in Computer Science,_ 291–301. Springer-Verlag, 1999.

185. J. F. Sibeyn and M. Kaufmann. BSP-like external-memory computation. In _Proceedings of the Italian Conference on Algorithms and Complexity,_ volume 3, 229–240, 1997.

186. B. Srinivasan. An adaptive overflow technique to defer splitting in b-trees. _The Computer Journal,_ 34(5), 397–405, 1991.

187. R. Tamassia and J. S. Vitter. Optimal cooperative search in fractional cascaded data structures. _Algorithmica,_ 15(2), 154–171, Feb. 1996.

188. Microsoft's TerraServer online database of satellite images, available on the World Wide Web at http://terraserver.microsoft.com/.

189. R. Thakur, A. Choudhary, R. Bordawekar, S. More, and S. Kuditipudi. Passion: Optimized I/O for parallel applications. _IEEE Computer,_ 29(6), 70–78, June 1996.

190. S. Toledo. A survey of out-of-core algorithms in numerical linear algebra. In J. Abello and J. S. Vitter (Eds.), _External Memory Algorithms and Visualization,_ DIMACS Series in Discrete Mathematics and Theoretical Computer Science, 161–179. American Mathematical Society Press, Providence, RI, 1999.

191. TPIE user manual and reference, 1999. The manual and software distribution are available on the Web at http://www.cs.duke.edu/TPIE/.

192. J. D. Ullman and M. Yannakakis. The input/output complexity of transitive closure. _Annals of Mathematics and Artificial Intelligence,_ 3, 331–360, 1991.

193. J. van den Bercken, B. Seeger, and P. Widmayer. A generic approach to bulk loading multidimensional index structures. In _Proceedings of the International Conference on Very Large Databases,_ volume 23, 406–415, 1997.

194. M. van Kreveld, J. Nievergelt, T. Roos, and P. Widmayer (Eds.). _Algorithmic Foundations of GIS,_ volume 1340 of _Lecture Notes in Computer Science._ Springer-Verlag, 1997.

195. P. J. Varman and R. M. Verma. An efficient multiversion access structure. _IEEE Transactions on Knowledge and Data Engineering,_ 9(3), 391–409, May–June 1997.

196. D. E. Vengroff and J. S. Vitter. Efficient 3-d range searching in external memory. In *Proceedings of the ACM Symposium on Theory of Computing*, volume 28, 192–201, Philadelphia, PA, May 1996.

197. D. E. Vengroff and J. S. Vitter. I/O-efficient scientific computation using TPIE. In *Proceedings of NASA Goddard Conference on Mass Storage Systems*, volume 5, II, 553–570, Sept. 1996.

198. P. Vettiger, M. Despont, U. Drechsler, U. Dürig, W. Häberle, M. I. Lutwyche, E. Rothuizen, R. Stutz, R. Widmer, and G. K. Binnig. The "Millipede"—more than one thousand tips for future AFM data storage. *IBM Journal of Research and Development*, 44(3), 323–340, 2000.

199. J. S. Vitter. External memory algorithms and data structures: Dealing with MASSIVE data. *ACM Computing Surveys*, in press. Available via the author's web page http://www.cs.duke.edu/~jsv/.

200. J. S. Vitter and D. A. Hutchinson. Distribution sort with randomized cycling. In *Proceedings of the ACM-SIAM Symposium on Discrete Algorithms*, volume 12, Washington, Jan. 2001.

201. J. S. Vitter and M. H. Nodine. Large-scale sorting in uniform memory hierarchies. *Journal of Parallel and Distributed Computing*, 17, 107–114, 1993.

202. J. S. Vitter and E. A. M. Shriver. Algorithms for parallel memory I: Two-level memories. *Algorithmica*, 12(2–3), 110–147, 1994.

203. J. S. Vitter and E. A. M. Shriver. Algorithms for parallel memory II: Hierarchical multilevel memories. *Algorithmica*, 12(2–3), 148–169, 1994.

204. J. S. Vitter and D. E. Vengroff. Notes, 1999.

205. J. S. Vitter and M. Wang. Approximate computation of multidimensional aggregates of sparse data using wavelets. In *Proceedings of the ACM SIGMOD International Conference on Management of Data*, 193–204, Philadelphia, PA, June 1999.

206. J. S. Vitter, M. Wang, and B. Iyer. Data cube approximation and histograms via wavelets. In *Proceedings of the International ACM Conference on Information and Knowledge Management*, volume 7, 96–104, Washington, Nov. 1998.

207. M. Wang, B. Iyer, and J. S. Vitter. Scalable mining for classification rules in relational databases. In *Proceedings of the International Database Engineering & Application Symposium*, 58–67, Cardiff, Wales, July 1998.

208. M. Wang, J. S. Vitter, L. Lim, and S. Padmanabhan. Wavelet-based cost estimation for spatial queries, July 2001.

209. R. W. Watson and R. A. Coyne. The parallel I/O architecture of the high-performance storage system(HPSS). In *Proceedings of the IEEE Symposium on Mass Storage Systems*, volume 14, 27–44, Sept. 1995.

210. P. Weiner. Linear pattern matching algorithm. In *Proceedings of the IEEE Symposium on Switching and Automata Theory*, volume 14, 1–11, Washington, DC, 1973.

211. O. Wolfson, P. Sistla, B. Xu, J. Zhou, and S. Chamberlain. DOMINO: Databases fOr MovINg Objects tracking. In A. Delis, C. Faloutsos, and S. Ghandeharizadeh (Eds.), *Proceedings of the ACM SIGMOD International Conference on Management of Data*, 547–549, May 1999.

212. D. Womble, D. Greenberg, S. Wheat, and R. Riesen. Beyond core: Making parallel computer I/O practical. In *Proceedings of the DAGS Symposium on Parallel Computation*, volume 2, 56–63, Hanover, NH, June 1993. Dartmouth Institute for Advanced Graduate Studies.

213. C. Wu and T. Feng. The universality of the shuffle-exchange network. *IEEE Transactions on Computers*, C-30, 324–332, May 1981.

214. A. C. Yao. On random 2-3 trees. *Acta Informatica*, 9, 159–170, 1978.

215. S. B. Zdonik and D. Maier (Eds.), *Readings in Object-Oriented Database Systems*. Morgan Kauffman, 1990.

216. W. Zhang and P.-A. Larson. Dynamic memory adjustment for external mergesort. In *Proceedings of the International Conference on Very Large Databases*, volume 23, 376–385, Athens, Greece, 1997.

217. B. Zhu. Further computational geometry in secondary memory. In *Proceedings of the International Symposium on Algorithms and Computation*, volume 834 of *Lecture Notes in Computer Science*, 514 ff. Springer-Verlag, 1994.

# 33
# Parallel I/O Systems

Peter J. Varman
*Rice University*

## 33.1 Introduction

The I/O system is a critical bottleneck for many modern data-intensive applications. The demand for greater storage capacity and high-speed access to stored data is growing rapidly. Disks, the most common secondary-storage medium in use today, have shown remarkable improvements in capacity and performance over the past decade. Innovations in disk technology have resulted in higher recording densities, smaller form factors, increased spindle speeds, and the increased availability of multi-zoned disks with variable transfer rates. Nonetheless, the storage requirements of modern applications is growing at an even faster rate, exceeding the impressive capacity of modern disk drives, and necessitating the use of multiple storage devices. Simultaneously the I/O rates required by these applications has outstripped the data rates that can be provided by single disks, despite the very significant improvements that have been made.

Consider as one example the growing use of digital multimedia in diverse applications ranging from entertainment and education to medicine and commerce. Multimedia or multimedia-enhanced applications routinely manipulate digitized images and video and audio data, requiring tremendous amounts of storage capacity, and placing stringent real-time constraints on the delivery rate to ensure smooth playback. A single hour-long MPEG-compressed video stream recorded at a rate of 4 Mbits/s, would require almost 2 GB of storage. A storage system with hundred or thousands of such clips would require several storage devices, perhaps a combination of disks to keep the more popular clips online, and slower tertiary tape storage to archive less popular video streams. The data transfer rate of a single disk is able to support the real-time retrieval of at most a few tens of concurrent streams, and the capacity decreases with increased video resolution and playback speeds. Analogous issues arise in other applications like real-time databases [47] where large numbers of sensory inputs need to be continually monitored and logged in an event database; critical events in turn may trigger the execution of data analysis routines that need to be complete within stipulated time bounds, placing a tremendous strain on the I/O subsystem.

Spatial databases in geographic information systems [7], temporal and kinetic databases that track the evolution or movement of objects in time [2,47], Web and application servers, graphics and visualization, and data mining systems, are other examples of the growing list of data-centric applications requiring the use of parallel I/O [1]. Even in compute-intensive domains like scientific computing applications, the scale of problems being addressed necessitates the use of advanced data management techniques, including the use of concurrent I/O to achieve acceptable performance [41].

## 33.2 Parallel I/O Organization

In this chapter, a parallel I/O system will refer to a disk-based I/O subsystem, made up of multiple disk drives that can access their data in parallel. Within this broad framework, different parallel I/O organizations are conceivable and supported by different vendors. RAID (an acronym that now stands for redundant array of independent disks) systems provide increased storage capacity and bandwidth by incorporating multiple disk drives within a single storage unit, and employ fault-tolerance mechanisms to cope with the increased failure probability stemming from the use of multiple devices [15]. Different RAID organizations (traditionally referred to as RAID levels) using different redundancy techniques to achieve fault tolerance have been proposed. RAID 1 uses data mirroring, whereby the entire disk contents are mirrored on an additional disk. RAID 4 and RAID 5 systems (RAID 5 is probably the most popular organization used in practice), employ the concept of a parity block to achieve fault tolerance. The multiple-disk system is viewed as a collection of stripes. A stripe consists of a block from each disk. One block of each stripe is designated as a parity block; it stores the bitwise exclusive-or of the corresponding bits of each of the other blocks in that stripe. In the event of a single-disk failure, the blocks on the failed disk can be reconstructed from the blocks in the same stripe on the working disks. The storage overhead for fault-tolerance is much less than the 100% redundancy of RAID 1 systems. The penalty, however, is the increased time for a write, since an update to a data block requires a read-modify-write operation on the parity block as well. A RAID 4 system uses a single designated disk to hold the parity blocks of all the stripes. In RAID 5 the use of a roving parity block, that associates different parity disks for different stripes, alleviates the potential parity-disk bottleneck of a RAID 4 design. Other RAID organizations have been since proposed. RAID 6 systems permit the failure of up to two disks without incurring any loss of data; these systems either use two parity blocks with differently computed parities, or employ a two-dimensional arrangement of disks with associated row and column parities. RAID 0 does not provide any fault tolerance, but allows data to be striped across multiple disks thereby allowing high-bandwidth transfers to and from the disks. Hybrid combination like RAID 10 and RAID 53 attempt to combine the advantages of different RAID levels in a hybrid architecture [51].

The interconnection between the disk system and the server is also undergoing changes to facilitate the increasingly parallel and distributed nature of storage systems. Traditional disk architectures use bus-based interconnects like the small computer system interconnect (SCSI) to connect a set of devices to the host [53]. A SCSI interconnect permits only a small number (7 or 15 depending on the SCSI protocol level) of devices to be connected to a single controller using the shared bus. The maximum transfer rate is small, starting at 5 MB/s for the original SCSI-1 protocol up to 40 MB/s for UltraSCSI.

More scalable I/O architectures are based on the use of switched interconnections. The high performance parallel interface (HIPPI) [29] defines a point-to-point interconnection, with high speed peak data transfer rates of 100 MB/s (HIPPI-800) to 800 MB/s (HIPPI-6400). Multiple devices are interconnected using a cross-point switch. Fiber channel refers to a set of standards [25] being developed by the American National Standards Institute (ANSI) that allows for an active intelligent interconnection scheme, called a fabric, to connect devices. It attempts to combine both network-oriented communication methods and dedicated hardware-based channel communication into a single I/O interface for both channel and network users. Different fiber channel topologies are supported including point-to-point, cross-point switched, or an arbitrated loop (or ring topology) network. Fiber channel supports its own protocol, as well as higher level protocols such as the FDDI, SCSI, HIPPI, and IPI, enhancing its versatility, but increasing the potential compatibility problems as well. The fibre channel standard addresses the need for fast transfers, up to 1 Gbits/s, of large amounts of information. Other emerging interconnect standards include the switched InfiniBand architecture, a synthesis of formerly competing System I/O and NextGeneration I/O proposals, with projected peak bidirectional rates of up to 6 GB/s [30].

Another trend in I/O organizations is the decentralization of storage devices [24,45]. Storage area networks (SAN) and network-attached storage devices (NASD) are two such directions towards reducing the tight coupling between servers and devices in traditional I/O architectures. In a SAN, multiple servers and devices are connected together by a dedicated high-speed network different from, and in addition to, the local area network (LAN) connecting the servers and clients. Data transfer between a server and a device occurs over this dedicated back-end network. Networked storage architectures have several potential benefits. They facilitate sharing of disk-resident data between multiple servers by avoiding the three-step process (read I/O, network transfer, write I/O) required in transferring data on traditional server-hosted I/O architectures. Furthermore, they permit autonomous data transfer between devices simplifying backup and data replication for performance or reliability, and encourage the spatial distribution of devices on the network, while maintaining the capability for centralized management. A network-attached storage device [26] allows many of the server functions to be offloaded directly to the device. Once a request is authenticated by the server and forwarded to the device, data transfer to the network proceeds independently without further involvement of the server. In principle a NASD can be directly connected to the LAN or may serve as an independent module in a back-end SAN.

Highly parallel I/O organizations with high-bandwidth interconnections that have the capability of supporting hundreds of concurrent I/O transfers are a characteristic of current and evolving I/O architectures. The physical realization in terms of interconnection and communication protocols, redundancy and fault-tolerance, and balance between distribution and centralization of resources are a continuing topic of current research. Complex issues dealing with cost, performance, reliability, interoperability, security, and ease of configuration and management will need to be resolved, with perhaps different configurations suitable in different application domains.

Whatever the physical manifestation, managing hundreds of concurrent I/O devices in order to fully exploit their inherent parallelism and high interconnection bandwidth is a challenging problem. To study the issues at a high level, configuration-independent abstract models such as the parallel disk model (PDM) [58] have been proposed. Two extremes of logical I/O organizations based on the memory buffer can be identified: in a shared-buffer organization there is a centralized memory buffer shared by all the disks, and all accesses are routed through the buffer. In a distributed-buffer organization each disk has a private buffer used exclusively to buffer data from that disk. The shared configuration has the potential to make better use of the buffer space by dynamically changing the portion of the buffer devoted to any disk based on the load. In contrast, the performance of the distributed configuration can be limited by a few heavily loaded disks. Hybrid configurations are possible as in a logically shared but physically partitioned buffer. Such an architecture provides the scalability and modularity inherent in having distributed resources while providing increased resource utilization due to sharing.

## 33.3 Performance Model for Parallel I/O

Parallel I/O systems have the potential to improve I/O performance if one can exploit disk parallelism by performing multiple concurrent I/Os; however, it is a challenging problem to successfully exploit the available disk bandwidth to reduce application I/O latency. According to increasing evidence, traditional disk management strategies can severely under-utilize available bandwidth and therefore do not scale well, leading to excessive I/O service time. As a consequence, several new algorithms for managing parallel I/O resources, with the explicit intention of exploiting I/O parallelism have been recently advanced [5,11,32–36,50,57].

The performance of a parallel I/O system is fundamentally determined by the pattern of disk accesses. The simplest form of data access, sequential reading of a file, represents the canonical application that can benefit from parallel I/O. Disk striping provides the natural solution for such an access pattern. The file is broken into blocks, and the blocks are placed in a round-robin fashion on the $D$ disks, so that every $D$th block is placed on the same disk. A main memory buffer of $D$ blocks is used. In each I/O an entire stripe of D consecutive blocks, one block from each disk, is read into the memory buffer. The number of I/O steps is reduced by a factor of D over sequentially accessing the file from a single disk. Despite its simplicity, disk striping is not the best solution for most other data access problems. For instance, generalizing the above problem to concurrently read N sequential files, a disk-striping solution would read D blocks of a single file in each I/O. The total buffer space required in this situation is ND blocks. A more resource-efficient solution is to perform concurrent, independent read I/Os on the different disks. In one parallel I/O, blocks from D different files are fetched from the D disks; this requires only 1/Dth the buffer of a disk striping solution if the blocks are consumed at the same rates. In fact, if the blocks are consumed at a rate comparable to the I/O time for a block, then by using independent I/Os only $\Theta(D)$ blocks of buffer suffice.

In contrast to the uniform access patterns implied by the previous examples, a skewed data access pattern results in hot spots, in which a single disk is repeatedly accessed in a short time period. The bandwidth of the multiple-disk system is severely underutilized in this situation, and the performance degrades to that of a single disk. Consider, for instance, the retrieval of constant data length (CDL) video data, in which the frames are packed into fixed-size data blocks; the blocks are then placed on the disks using either striped, random, or other disk allocation policy. If a number of such streams are read concurrently, the access pattern consists of an interleaving of the blocks that depends on the playback times of the blocks. For constant-bit rate (CBR) video streams the playback time of a block is fixed, and (assuming striped allocation) the accesses are spread uniformly across the disks as in the example on multiple file access. In the case of variable bit rate (VBR) video data streams, the accesses are no longer uniformly distributed across the disks, but depend on the relative playback times of each of the blocks. Consequently, both the load on a disk and the load across the disks varies as a function of time. In this case, simply reading the blocks in the time-ordered interleaving of blocks, may no longer maximize the disk paral-lelism, and more sophisticated scheduling strategies are necessary to maximize the number of streams that can be handled by the I/O system [22].

The abstract model of the I/O system that will be used to analyze the quality of different schedules is based on the PDM [58]: the I/O system consists of D independent disks, which can be accessed in parallel, and has a buffer of capacity M, through which all disk accesses occur. The computation requests data in blocks—a block is the unit of disk access. The I/O trace of a computation is characterized by a reference string, which is an ordered sequence of I/O requests made by the computation. In serving a reference string the buffer manager determines which blocks to fetch and when to fetch them so that the computation can access the blocks in the order specified by the reference string. The computation waits for data from the I/O system only when the data are not available in the buffer. Additionally, when an I/O is initiated on one disk, blocks can be concurrently fetched from other disks. The number of parallel I/Os that are issued is a measure of performance in this model. Because the buffer is shared by all disks it is possible to allocate buffer space unevenly to different disks to meet the changing load on different disks. The PDM assumes unit time I/Os. In many applications like those dealing with streaming data, data logging or in several scientific computations, where large block sizes are natural, this is a viable and useful idealization. In these situations, the number of I/Os has a direct relationship to the I/O time. In other cases where requests are for small amounts of data and access times are dominated by the seek and rotational latency components, no analytical models are widely applicable. In these cases, empirical evaluations need to be employed in estimating performance [19,23].

# 33.4 Mechanisms for Improving I/O Performance

Prefetching and caching are two fundamental techniques that are employed for increasing I/O perfor-mance. Prefetching refers to the process of initiating a read from a disk before the computation demands the data. In a parallel I/O system, while a read progresses on one disk, reads can be started concurrently on other disks to prefetch data that are required later. These prefetched blocks are held in the I/O buffer till needed. In this way a temporary concentration of accesses to a small subset of the disks is tolerated by using the time to prefetch from the disks that are currently idle; when the locality shifts to the latter set of disks, the required data are already present in the buffer.

In contrast to prefetching that masks disk latencies by overlapping the access with that of I/Os to other disks, caching attempts to exploit temporal locality in the accesses. A selected subset of the recently accessed blocks are held in the I/O buffer in the expectation that they will be referenced again soon, thereby avoiding repeated disk accesses for the same block. Although both prefetching and caching are well-known techniques employed ubiquitously in computer systems and networking, deploying these mechanisms effectively in a parallel I/O system raises a unique set of challenges.

The I/O schedule determines the set of blocks that are fetched in each parallel I/O operation. The schedule is constructed dynamically so as to minimize the total number of parallel I/Os. This requires the scheduler to decide which blocks to prefetch, and, when the need for replacement arises, to decide which blocks in the buffer to cache and which to evict. Prefetching and caching in parallel I/O systems is fundamentally different from that in systems with a single disk, and requires the use of substantially different algorithms [11,32–36]. In a single-disk system, prefetching is used to overlap I/O operations with CPU computations. This is usually done using asynchronous I/O whereby a computation continues after making the I/O request without blocking. A stall model for analyzing the performance of overlapped I/O and computation was proposed in [17] for a single disk system; prefetching and caching algorithms to minimize stall time as a function of CPU and I/O speeds were presented in [5,17]. Disk scheduling algorithms that reorder I/O requests to minimize the disk seek times [59] can also be considered as a form of prefetching in single-disk systems.

In parallel I/O systems prefetching allows overlap between accesses on different disks thereby hiding the I/O latency behind the access latency on some other disk. The scheduler has to judiciously decide on questions like how much buffer to allocate for prefetching and how much for caching, which blocks to prefetch, and which blocks to cache. For instance, to utilize the available bandwidth, it may appear desirable to keep a large number of disks busy prefetching data during an I/O; however, excessive prefetching can fill up the buffer with blocks, which may not be used until much later in the computation. Such blocks have the adverse effects of choking the buffer and reducing the parallelism in fetching more immediate blocks. In fact, even when the problem does not involve the use of caching, the decisions of which blocks to prefetch and when to do so is not trivial.

Another issue needs to be addressed to employ prefetching and caching effectively. In order to prefetch accurately (rather than speculatively) some knowledge of future accesses is required. This is embodied in the notion of lookahead, which is a measure of the extent of knowledge about the future accesses that is available in making prefetching and caching decisions. Obtaining this lookahead has been the area of much active research [13,40,43,50]. In some applications like external sorting the lookahead can be obtained dynamically by using a sample of the data to accurately predict the sequence of block requests [10]. In video retrieval the sequence is determined by the playback times of blocks in the set of concurrently accessed streams; summary statistics of the streams are used to obtain the lookahead at run time [22]. Indexes in database systems can similarly be used to provide information about the actual sequence of data blocks that must be accessed. In broadcast servers the set of requests are prioritized by the system to maximize utilization of the broadcast channel [4]; the prioritized request sequence provides the lookahead for required I/O accesses. Access patterns can be revealed to the system either using programmer provided hints [50], or the system may attempt to uncover sequential or strided access patterns automatically at run time [40]. Speculative execution is another technique based on executing program code speculatively to determine the control path and the blocks accessed in the path [13].

## 33.5 Limitations of Simple Prefetching and Caching Strategies

In [11,32], the problem of scheduling read-once reference strings, in which each block is accessed exactly once, was considered. Such reference strings are characteristic of streaming applications like multimedia retrieval. Simple intuitive algorithms that work well in a single-disk scenario were analyzed and shown to have poor performance in the multiple-disk case. For instance, consider a natural scheduling algorithm that we refer to as *aggressive prefetching*. In each I/O, the next block required from each disk is fetched provided there is enough free buffer space; if not then only the block demanded immediately by the computation is read. Such an aggressive prefetching scheme, while intuitively attractive, can be shown to have poor worst-case as well as average-case performance. There exist worst-case reference strings for which aggressive prefetching can perform $\Theta(D)$ times as many I/Os as the optimal scheduling strategy [11]. In the average case, when the accesses are assumed to be randomly distributed across the disks with independent uniform probability, it has been shown that reading a reference string of length $N$ requires $\Theta(N/D)$ I/Os using a buffer of size $\Omega(D^2)$ blocks [48].

The problem with aggressive prefetching is that it prefetches too deep on some disks, holding up buffer space that could better be used in fetching more immediately required blocks. A simple heuristic to correct for this is to place a bound on the depth of prefetching. One such attractive policy is to always give priority to a block that is required earlier in the reference string over one that is accessed later, whenever there is insufficient buffer space to hold both blocks. Intuitively this scheme tries to keep all disks busy by fetching greedily, but prevents blocks that are prefetched very much earlier than their time of usage from holding up buffer space that can be used by other more urgently needed blocks. This greedy algorithm is referred to as earliest required first (ERF) prefetching.

Consider the following example of an I/O system with three disks and an I/O buffer of capacity 6. Let the blocks labeled $a_i$ (respectively $b_i$, $c_i$) be placed on disk A (respectively B, C), and the reference string be

$$a_1 \ a_2 \ a_3 \ a_4 \ b_1 \ c_1 \ a_5 \ b_2 \ c_2 \ a_6 \ b_3 \ c_3 \ a_7 \ b_4 \ c_4 \ c_5 \ c_6 \ c_7$$

Figure 33.1(a) shows the I/O schedule constructed by the ERF algorithm described above. In the first step blocks $a_1$, $b_1$, and $c_1$ are fetched concurrently in one I/O. When block $a_2$ is requested, blocks $a_2$, $b_2$, and $c_2$ are fetched in parallel in step 2. Subsequently the buffer contains five blocks: $a_2$, $b_1$, $b_2$, $c_1$, and $c_2$. Next when $a_3$ is requested, an I/O needs to be done to fetch it; however, there is buffer space for only one additional block besides $a_3$, and the choice is between fetching $b_3$, $c_3$, or neither. Fetching greedily in the order of the reference string means that we fetch $b_3$. Continuing in this manner we obtain a schedule of length 9. Figure 33.1(b) presents an alternative schedule for the same reference string. The first two steps in the schedule are identical to the previous case. In step 3, $c_3$ that occurs after $b_3$ is prefetched; and in step 4, $c_4$ is fetched by evicting $b_2$ even though $c_4$ is referenced only after $b_4$; however, by doing so the overall length of the schedule is reduced to 7, better than the previous schedule.

| Disk A | $a_1$ | $a_2$ | $a_3$ | $a_4$ | $a_5$ | $a_6$ | $a_7$ |  |  |
|--------|-------|-------|-------|-------|-------|-------|-------|--|--|
| Disk B | $b_1$ | $b_2$ | $b_3$ |  | $b_4$ |  |  |  |  |
| Disk C | $c_1$ | $c_2$ |  |  | $c_3$ | $c_4$ | $c_5$ | $c_6$ | $c_7$ |

(a)

| Disk A | $a_1$ | $a_2$ | $a_3$ | $a_4$ | $a_5$ | $a_6$ | $a_7$ |
|--------|-------|-------|-------|-------|-------|-------|-------|
| Disk B | $b_1$ | $b_2$ |  |  | $b_2$ | $b_3$ | $b_4$ |
| Disk C | $c_1$ | $c_2$ | $c_3$ | $c_4$ | $c_5$ | $c_6$ | $c_7$ |

(b)

**FIGURE 33.1**    (a) Greedy ERF schedule. (b) Optimal schedule.

The ERF algorithm was analyzed in [11]. It was shown that there exist reference strings for which ERF will perform $\Theta(\sqrt{D})$ times as many I/Os as the optimal schedule. For the average case, under the same assumptions as for aggressive prefetching, it can be shown that ERF can read an N block reference string in $\Theta(N/D)$ I/Os using a buffer of size $\Omega(D \log D)$ blocks [10]. Hence, although ERF improves upon aggressive prefetching, it does not construct the optimal-length schedule.

In the previous discussion all blocks were implicitly assumed to be distinct. Such reference strings are called read-once and are characteristic of streaming applications like multimedia retrieval. General reference strings where each block can be accessed repeatedly introduce additional issues related to caching. In particular, decisions need to be made regarding which blocks to evict from the buffer. In a single-disk system the optimal offline caching strategy is to use the MIN algorithm [12] that always evicts the block whose next reference is furthest in the future; however, it is easy to show that using this policy in a multiple-disk situation does not necessarily minimize the total number of parallel I/Os that are required. In fact, there exist reference strings for which the use of the MIN policy necessitates $\Theta(D)$ times as many I/Os as an optimal caching strategy [34].

## 33.6 Optimal Parallel-Disk Prefetching

In this section we present an *online* prefetching algorithm L-OPT for read-once reference strings. L-OPT uses L-block lookahead; at any instant L-OPT knows the next $L$ references, and uses this lookahead to determine blocks to fetch in the next I/O. It uses a priority assignment scheme to determine the currently most useful blocks to fetch and to retain in the buffer. As the lookahead window advances and information about further requests are made available, the priorities of blocks are dynamically updated to incorporate the latest information. When considered as an offline algorithm for which the entire reference string is known in advance, it has been shown that L-OPT is the optimal prefetching algorithm that minimizes the number of parallel I/Os [32].

L-OPT is a priority-controlled greedy prefetching algorithm. A priority-controlled greedy prefetching scheme provides a general framework for describing different prefetching algorithms. Blocks in the lookahead are assigned priorities depending on the scheduling policy in effect. The scheduler fetches one block each from as many disks as possible in every I/O, while ensuring that the buffer never retains a lower-priority block in preference to fetching one with a higher priority, if necessary by evicting the lower-priority blocks. Algorithm priority-controlled greedy I/O describes the algorithm formally using the definitions below.

Different prefetching policies can be implemented using this framework merely by changing the priority function. For instance, to implement the ERF prefetching algorithm the priority of blocks should decrease with their position in the reference string. This is easily achieved if the priority function assigns the $i$th block in the reference string a priority equal to $-i$. Similarly, prefetching strategies akin to aggressive prefetching can be emulated by assigning the $i$th referenced block from each disk a priority of $+\infty$ if it is the demand block and $-i$ otherwise.

### Definitions

1. Let $\Sigma = b_1, b_2, \ldots, b_n$ denote the reference string. If $b_i$ is a block in the lookahead, let *disk*$(b_i)$ denote the disk from which it needs to be fetched and let *priority*$(b_i)$ be the block's priority.
2. At the instant when $b_i$ is referenced, let $B_i$ denote the set of blocks in the lookahead that are present in the buffer.
3. When $b_i$ is referenced, let $H_i$ be the maximal set of (up to) $D$ blocks, such that if $b \in H_i$ then priority of b is the largest among all blocks from *disk*(b) in the lookahead but not present in the buffer.
4. Let $B_i^+$ be the maximal set of (up to) $M$ blocks with the highest priorities in $H_i \cup B_i$; in the case of ties the block occurring earlier in $\Sigma$ is preferred.

## Algorithm Priority-Controlled Greedy I/O

On a request for a block, $b_i$, the algorithm takes the following actions.

If $b_i$ is present in the buffer then no I/O is necessary.
If $b_i$ is not present in the buffer then
    update priorities of blocks using blocks revealed since the last I/O;
    accommodate the blocks to be read in, evict the blocks in $B_i - B_i^+$; and
    initiate an I/O to fetch the blocks in $H_i \cap B_i^+$.
Service the request for block $b_i$.

Implementing the priority-controlled greedy I/O algorithm can be done using a simple forecasting data structure similar to that in [10], to maintain the list of blocks with highest priority on each disk. On a hit in the buffer, the algorithm does not need to do any bookkeeping. When the requested block is not present in the buffer the algorithm needs to find the set of blocks to fetch and the corresponding set of blocks to evict from the buffer. If we have all the blocks in the buffer maintained and sorted in order of their priorities, then we can choose the $D$ blocks to fetch and evict in $O(M + D)$ time. With standard linked data structures, logarithmic update times are sufficient for these operations.

In contrast to the static priority assignments for ERF and aggressive prefetching, the priority function of the optimal algorithm L-OPT depends on the relative distribution of the load on different disks. Furthermore, as more lookahead is revealed, the previously assigned priorities of blocks may change as a result of the new information. At any time, the blocks in the lookahead are partitioned into two subsequences called the current and future window, respectively. At the start all blocks in the lookahead are in the current window and the future window is empty. As new blocks are revealed they are added to the future window. When the last block of the current window is referenced, the future window becomes the current window and a new (empty) future window begins. The priorities of blocks in the current window are fixed at the time the window became current, and do not change; however, the priorities of blocks in the future window are updated to reflect new additions. All blocks in the future window have priorities less than that of any block in the current window.

The priority assignment routine used by L-OPT to determine the priorities of blocks in a given piece of the reference string is described below. At any instant the priority of a block is a reflection of how urgently that block must be fetched. The lower the priority of a block, the later it can be fetched. The central idea is to set the priority of a block as low as possible, subject to two constraints. Blocks from the same disk are assigned priorities in order of their reference. Second, no block can have such a low priority that $M$ or more blocks referenced after it have a higher or same priority. In the routine below the variables *lowestPriorityOnDisk*[$d$] and *lowestPriority* track the smallest priority that can be assigned to a block without violating the two constraints. The former is incremented whenever a block is placed on disk $d$. The variable *lowestPriority* is incremented whenever $M$ blocks with priority *lowestPriority* or higher have been placed. A block is assigned the larger of these two priorities.

## L-OPT: Priority Assignment

Assign priorities to blocks $\langle b_1, b_2, \ldots, b_n \rangle$ of the reference string.
Initialize
    *lowestPriority* to 1
    *numberOfBlocksPlaced* to 0
    *lowestPriorityOnDisk*[1…$D$] to 0
    *blocksWithPriority*[1…$n$] to 0

for $i$ from $n$ down to 1
    if (*lowestPriority* > *lowestPriorityOnDisk*($disk$($b_i$))) then assign
        *lowestPriorityOnDisk*($disk$($b_i$)) ← *lowestPriority*
    assign *priority*($b_i$) ← *lowestPriorityOnDisk*($disk$($b_i$))

> increment *lowestPriorityOnDisk(disk(b$_i$))*
> increment *blocksWithPriority(priority(b$_i$))*
> increment *numberOfBlocksPlaced*
> if (*numberOfBlocksPlaced* = *M*) then
>> decrement *numberOfBlocksPlaced* by *blocksWithPriority(lowestPriority)*
>> increment *lowestPriority*

By using the priority assignment described here, it has been shown that L-OPT always creates a schedule that is within a factor $\Theta\sqrt{(MD/L)}$ times the length of the schedule created by the optimal *offline* algorithm, and that this is the best possible ratio. In addition, L-OPT's schedule is never more than twice the length of that created by any *online* algorithm (including algorithms that consistently make fortuitously correct guesses) that has the same amount of lookahead. Finally, note that if the entire reference string is known in advance, then L-OPT is the optimal offline algorithm [32].

## 33.7 Optimal Parallel-Disk Caching

For general reference strings where blocks may be repeatedly accessed, the buffer manager must decide which blocks to cache and which to evict. As noted earlier, the optimal single-disk caching policy embodied in the MIN algorithm can be decidedly suboptimal in the parallel I/O case. Prefetching and caching need to harmoniously cooperate in the multiple-disk situation. The caching problem has been studied by several researchers in the recent past for different I/O organizations. For a distributed-buffer configuration where each disk has its own private buffer, an algorithm P-MIN that generalizes MIN to multiple disks was shown to be optimal [57]. P-MIN uses the furthest forward reference policy on each disk independently to determine the eviction candidate for that disk. It initiates an I/O only on demand; in the ensuing I/O operation it prefetches aggressively from every disk unless the reference to the block to be prefetched is further than the references of all blocks currently in that buffer. For a shared-buffer configuration in the stall-model of computation, a sophisticated near-optimal algorithm called Reverse-Aggressive to minimize the stall time was proposed and analyzed in [36].

Recently, an optimal prefetching and caching algorithm, SUPERVISOR, for the parallel disk model was presented in [34]. Like the L-OPT algorithm for prefetching, SUPERVISOR uses the general framework of priority-controlled greedy I/O. The scheme for assigning priorities to references is, however, considerably more complex than that used by L-OPT for read-once reference strings. Just as a low priority with respect to prefetching indicates that an I/O for that block can be delayed, a low priority with respect to caching indicates that the block can be evicted from the buffer.

Intuitively, SUPERVISOR assigns priorities in accordance with two principles: issue prefetches for blocks close to their reference so that they do not wastefully occupy buffer space, and avoid caching a block if there is any later free I/O slot available, which can be used to fetch it. Among possible candidates for a block to cache, it is desirable to cache a block that will occupy the buffer for a smaller duration. Hence, the question to be answered is: Given that at some time we would like two previously referenced blocks in the buffer, which of these should have been cached and which should be fetched now? It is preferable to cache the block whose previous reference is closer to the current time, as this reduces the buffer pressure between the two previous accesses. SUPERVISOR uses this intuition to assign priorities to blocks for prefetching and caching.

The formal details of the priority assignment algorithm used by SUPERVISOR are presented in [34]. The routine examines subsets of the lookahead consisting of *M* distinct references and then assigns priorities to one block from each disk. The idea behind the assignment can be understood by considering the largest subsequence of the lookahead including the last reference and having at most *M* distinct references. All blocks which are assigned the smallest priority should belong to this set. Otherwise there will be some reference such that *M* or more blocks referenced after it have a higher, or same priority. Which among these blocks should have the lowest priority? The lowest priority can be assigned to, at most, one distinct reference from each disk. Additionally, among two blocks from the same disk, this priority is assigned to the block with the previous reference outside this subsequence is earlier, because we would rather not cache this block. It is shown in [34] that SUPERVISOR, which assigns priorities based on the above principle is the optimal offline algorithm for parallel prefetching and caching in the parallel disk model.

## 33.8   Randomized Data Placement

Randomizing the placement of blocks on the disks of a parallel I/O system is a method to reduce I/O serialization caused by hot spots [10,11,33,35,37,52,55]. If blocks are distributed on the disks randomly then the maximum number of accesses to a single disk in any sequence of requests can be bounded with high probability. There are two potential benefits of randomized placement: the amount of memory buffer required to smooth out the imbalance in disk accesses is greatly reduced, and good performance can be achieved using simpler prefetching and caching algorithms.

In a randomized data placement scheme each block is placed on any of the $D$ disks with a uniform probability $1/D$. The performance of two simple prefetching algorithms using randomized placement has been analyzed in [10,33]. Using the results of [46], aggressive prefetching was shown to read a reference string of $N$ blocks in an expected number $\Theta(N/D)$ I/Os using a buffer of size $\Theta(D^2)$ blocks [32]. Note that $\lceil N/D \rceil$ is the minimum number of I/Os needed to read $N$ blocks, so the scheme performs within a constant factor of the minimum possible number of I/Os. The performance of ERF that gives preference to blocks that occur earlier in the reference string was analyzed in [10] and shown to require an expected $\Theta(N/D)$ I/Os using a smaller buffer, of size $\Theta(D \log D)$ blocks. In an online situation the two prefetching algorithms require different lookahead information. The aggressive prefetching algorithm only needs to know the ordered sequence of accesses to be made from each disk independently. The greedy priority-based algorithm needs to know the global ordering of accesses across the disks. In some applications like external merging for instance, the global ordering can be inferred from the local ordering by using a small amount of preprocessing [10].

Recently, it was shown how randomized placement coupled with data replication can be used to improve I/O performance [37,50,55], particularly in [37] where two copies of each block are allocated randomly to the disks. A scheduling algorithm decides which of the copies should be read in an I/O. It was shown that $N$ blocks can be read in $\lceil N/D \rceil + 1$ I/Os with high probability, using only $\Theta(D)$ blocks of buffer storage [52].

For general reference strings a simple caching and prefetching algorithm that can be used in conjunction with randomized data placement was presented in [35]. The algorithm uses the ERF policy for prefetching and a variant of the least recently used buffer replacement policy to handle evictions. It was shown that the expected number of I/Os performed by this algorithm is within a factor $\Theta[\log D / \log(\log D)]$ of the number of I/Os performed by an optimal scheduling algorithm.

Randomized data placement can generally provide good expected performance using less buffer memory and simpler disk management algorithms than those required to deal with worst-case data placements.

## 33.9   Out-of-Core Computations

Out-of-core computation deals with the problems of solving computational problems that are too large for the entire data set to fit in primary memory. Although the virtual memory mechanisms of modern operating systems can handle the problem transparently by paging the required data in and out of main memory on demand, the performance of such a solution is usually poor. Improved performance is achieved by optimizing the algorithm to be sensitive to the constraints of the I/O subsystem. The computation should be structured to provide spatial locality using data clustering, accesses should be organized to expose temporal locality, and declustering should be used to exploit the parallelism provided by the underlying I/O system. In many cases traditional in-core algorithms that deal with minimizing the number of computations without explicit consideration of the data access costs perform poorly when the data is disk-resident, necessitating the development of new algorithms or requiring radical restructuring of the known algorithms to achieve good I/O performance.

External or out-of-core algorithms using parallel data transfers can be traced to the work by Aggarwal and Vitter [3], generalizing earlier models, which dealt with sequential or nonblocked data transfers. The model used in that work was more powerful than the PDM that models multiple-disk systems. A number of out-of-core algorithms for external sorting, computational geometry, FFT data permutations, linear algebra computations, scientific codes, and data structures for indexing complex multidimensional data have since been developed [1–3,9,20,21,27,46,56,58]. The reader is referred to [1] and the references therein for a comprehensive bibliography and discussion of these works.

Run-time environments to increase efficiency and simplify the programming effort in applications requiring parallel I/O has been addressed by several research groups [6,8,14,16,18,28,31,38,39,42,44,54]. For a detailed discussion of the different proposals the reader is referred to [41,49].

## 33.10  Conclusion

Parallel I/O systems consisting of multiple concurrent devices are necessary to handle the storage and bandwidth requirements of modern applications. Parallel I/O hardware and interconnection technology will continue to evolve to meet the growing demands. New algorithms and system software are essential to effectively manage the hundreds of richly interconnected concurrent devices. Caching and prefetching are two fundamental techniques to improve data access performance by exploiting temporal locality and latency hiding. In a parallel I/O system using these mechanisms effectively involve challenging issues, which have been extensively studied over the past few years. These have resulted in the design of optimal algorithms for prefetching and caching, techniques to obtain lookahead of the I/O accesses, external algorithms for important problems, and file system and I/O primitives to support parallel I/O. As systems grow larger and more complex, challenging problems to control and manage the parallelism automatically and effectively will continue to be explored. Building on the fundamental understanding of what works and the algorithms required to control them, tools to automatically perform configuration, dynamic declustering, replication, prefetching, and caching will continue to be developed. Finally, although this chapter deals primarily with disk I/O, it can be readily seen that many of the issues transcend device specificity and apply in more general contexts dealing with managing and processing multiple concurrent I/O streams, using limited storage and bandwidth resources, as in embedded system environments.

### Acknowledgment

Supported in part by NSF grant CCR-9704562.

### References

1. J. M. Abello and J. S. Vitter (Eds.). *External Memory Algorithms,* Volume 50 of DIMACS Series in Discrete Mathematics and Theoretical Computer Science. DIMACS, American Mathematical Society, Providence, RI, 1999.

2. P. K. Agarwal, L. Arge, and J. Erickson. Indexing moving points. In *Proceedings ACM SIGACT-SIGMOD-SIGART Symposium on Principles of Database Systems,* May 2000.

3. A. Aggarwal and J. S. Vitter. The input/output complexity of sorting and related problems. *Communications of the ACM,* 31(9): 1116–1127, Sep. 1988.

4. D. Aksoy and M. Franklin. RxW: A scheduling approach to large scale on-demand broadcast. *IEEE/ACM Transactions on Networking,* 7: 846–861, Dec. 1999.

5. S. Albers, N. Garg, and S. Leonardi. Minimizing stall times in single and parallel disk systems. In *Proceedings of the ACM Symposium on Theory of Computing,* pp. 454–462, 1998.

6. T. E. Anderson et al. Serverless network file systems. *ACM Transactions on Computer Systems,* 14(1): 41–79, Feb. 1996.

7. L. Arge. External-memory algorithms with applications in geographic information systems. In M. van Kreveld, J. Nievergelt, T. Roos, and P. Windmayer (Eds.). *Algorithmic Foundations of GIS,* volume 1340, Lecture Notes in Computer Science, Springer-Verlag, 1997.

8. R. H. Arpaci-Dusseau et al. Cluster I/O with river: making the fast case common. In *Proceedings 6th ACM Workshop on I/O in Parallel and Distributed Systems*, pp. 68–77, Atlanta, GA, 1999.

9. L. M. Baptist and T. H. Cormen. Multidimensional, multiprocessor out-of-core FFTs with distributed memory and parallel disks. In *Proceedings 11th ACM Symposium on Parallel Algorithms and Architectures*, June 1999.

10. R. D. Barve, E. F. Grove, and J. S. Vitter. Simple randomized merge-sort on parallel disks. *Parallel Computing*, 23(4): 601–631, June 1996.

11. R. D. Barve, M. Kallahalla, P. J. Varman, and J. S. Vitter. Competitive parallel disk prefetching and buffer management. *J. of Algorithms*, 36(2): 152–181, Aug. 2000.

12. A. Belady. A study of replacement algorithms for a virtual storage computer. *IBM Systems Journal*, 5(2): 78–101, 1996.

13. F. Chang and G. A. Gibson. Automatic I/O hint generation through speculative execution. In *Proceedings of Third Symposium on Operating Systems Design and Implementation*, pp. 1–14, Feb. 1999.

14. A. Choudhary et al. Data management for large-scale scientific computations in high performance distributed systems. In *Proceedings of the 8th IEEE Symposium on High Performance Distributed Systems*, Aug. 1999.

15. P. M. Chen et al. RAID: High performance and reliable secondary storage. *ACM Computing Surveys*, 26(2): 145–185, 1994.

16. Y. M. Chen et al. Automatic parallel I/O performance in Panda. In *Proceedings of the 10th ACM Symposium on Parallel Algorithms and Architectures*, pp. 108–118, June 1998.

17. P. Cao, E. Felten, A. Karlin, and K. Li. A study of integrated prefetching and caching strategies. In *Proceedings ACM SIGMETRICS Conference on Measurement and Modeling of Computer Systems*, 1995.

18. P. F. Corbett and D. G. Feitelson. The Vesta Parallel File System. *ACM Transactions on Computer Systems*, 14(3): 225–264, Aug. 1996.

19. T. H. Cormen and M. Hirschl. Early experiences in evaluating the parallel disk model with the ViC* implementation. *Parallel Computing*, 23(4–5): 571–600, June 1997.

20. T. H. Cormen and D. M. Nicol. Performing out-of-core FFTs on parallel disk systems. *Parallel Computing*, 24(1): 5–20, Jan. 1998.

21. T. H. Cormen, T. Sundquist, and L. F. Wisniewski. Asymptotically tight bounds for performing BMMC permutations on parallel disk systems. *SIAM Journal of Computing*, 28(1): 105–136, 1999.

22. O. Ertug, M. Kallahalla, and P. J. Varman. Real-time parallel disk scheduling for VBR video servers. In *Proceedings 5th International Conference on Computer Science and Informatics*, Feb. 2000.

23. S. Evgenia and D. A. Reed. Workload characterization of input/output intensive parallel applications. In *Proceedings of Modeling Techniques and Tools for Computer Performance Evaluation*, Volume 1245, Lecture Notes in Computer Science, Springer-Verlag, pp. 169–280, June 1997.

24. M. Farley. *Building Storage Networks*, Osborne/McGraw-Hill, 2000.

25. Fibre Channel Industry Association. See www.fibrechannel.com.

26. G. A. Gibson et al. A cost-effective, high-bandwidth storage architecture. In *Proceedings of the 8th Conference on Architectural Support for Programming Languages and Operating Systems*, 1988.

27. M. T. Goodrich, J.-J. Tsay, D. E. Vengroff, and J. S. Vitter. External-memory computational geometry. In *Proceedings of the IEEE Symposium on Foundations of Computer Science*, pp. 714–723, Nov. 1993.

28. R. L. Haskin. Tiger Shark—A scalable file system for multimedia. *IBM Systems Journal of Research and Development*, 42(2): 185–197, March 1998.

29. High Performance Networking Forum. See www.hnf.org

30. InfniBand Trade Association. See www.infinibandta.org

31. R. Jain, J. Werth, and J. C. Browne (Eds.). *Input/Output in Parallel and Distributed Computer Systems*. Kluwer Academic Publishers, Norwell, MA, 1996.

32. M. Kallahalla and P. J. Varman. Optimal read-once parallel disk scheduling. In *Proceedings 6th ACM Workshop on I/O in Parallel and Distributed Systems*, pp. 68–77, Atlanta, GA, 1999. (An expanded version is available at www.ece.rice.edu/~pjv).

33. M. Kallahalla and P. J. Varman. Randomized prefetching and caching. In *Randomization in Parallel and Distributed Systems,* S. Rajasekaran and S, Pardalos (Eds.), Kluwer Academic Press, Dordrecht, the Netherlands, 1999.

34. M. Kallahalla and P. J. Varman. Optimal prefetching and caching for parallel I/O systems. *Proceedings 13th ACM Symposium on Parallel Algorithms and Architectures,* July 2001.

35. M. Kallahalla and P. J. Varman. Analysis of simple randomized buffer management for parallel I/O, Online version available at www/ece/rice.edu/~pjv. (to be published in Information Processing Letters).

36. T. Kimbrel and A. R. Karlin. Near-optimal parallel prefetching and caching. *SIAM J. of Computing,* 5(3): 79–119, March 1988.

37. J. Korst. Random duplicate assignment: an alternative to striping in video servers. In *Proceedings ACM Multimedia Conference,* pp. 219–226, 1997.

38. D. Kotz. Disk-directed I/O for MIMD multiprocessors. *ACM Transactions on Computer Systems,* 15(1): 41–74, Feb. 1997.

39. W. B. Ligon III and R. B. Ross. Implementation and performance of a parallel file system for high performance distributed applications. In *Proceedings of the 5th IEEE International Symposium on High Performance Distributed Computing,* pp. 471–480, Aug. 1996.

40. T. Madyastha and D. A. Reed. Input/output access pattern classification using hidden Markov models. In *Proceedings of 5th Workshop on I/O in Parallel and Distributed Systems,* Nov. 1997.

41. J. M. May. *Parallel I/O for High-Performance Computing.* Morgan Kaufmann Publishers, Academic Press, San Diego, CA, 2001.

42. E. L. Miller and R. H. Katz. RAMA: An easy-to-use, high-performance parallel file system. *Parallel Computing,* 23(4–5): 419–446, June 1997.

43. T. C. Mowry, A. K. Demke, and O. Krieger. Automatic compiler-inserted I/O prefetching for out-of-core applications. In *Proceedings 2nd Symposium on Operating Systems Design and Implementation,* pp. 3–17, Oct. 1996.

44. S. A. Moyer and V. S. Sunderam. Scalable concurrency control for parallel file systems (in [1]).

45. National Storage Industry Consortium. See www.nsic.org.

46. M. H. Nodine and J. S. Vitter. Greed sort: An optimal sorting algorithm for multiple disks. *Journal of the ACM,* 42(4): 919–933, July 1995.

47. G. Ozsoyoglu and R. Snodgrass. Temporal and real-time databases: a survey. *IEEE Transactions on Knowledge and Data Engineering,* 7(4): 513–532, 1995.

48. V. S. Pai, A. Schaffer, and P. J. Varman. Markov analysis of multiple-disk prefetching strategies for external merging. *Theoretical Computer Science,* 128(1–2): 211–239, June 1994.

49. Parallel I/O Bibliography. See http://www.cs.dartmouth.edu/pario/bib/.

50. R. H. Patterson, G. Gibson, E. Ginting, D. Stodolsky, and J. Zelenka. Informed prefetching and caching. In *Proceedings 15th ACM Symposium on Operating System Principles,* pp. 79–95, Dec. 1995.

51. RAID Advisory Board. See www.raid-advisory.com.

52. P. Sanders, S. Egner, and J. H. M. Korst. Fast concurrent access to parallel disks. In *Proceedings of the SIAM Symposium on Discrete Algorithms,* pp. 849–858, Jan. 2000.

53. SCSI Trade Organization. See www.scsita.org.

54. R. Thakur et al. Passion: Optimized I/O for parallel applications. *Computer,* 29(6), June 1996.

55. R. Tewari, R. Mukherjee, D. Dias, and H. Vin. Design and performance tradeoffs in clustered video servers. In *Proceedings of the International Conference on Multimedia and Systems,* pp. 144–150, 1996.

56. S. Toledo. A survey of out-of-core algorithms in numerical linear algebra (in [1]).

57. P. J. Varman and R. M. Verma. Tight bounds for prefetching and buffer management algorithms for parallel I/O systems. *IEEE Transactions on Parallel and Distributed Systems,* 10: 1262–1275, Dec. 1999.

58. J. S. Vitter and E. A. M. Shriver. Optimal algorithms for parallel memory, I: Two-level memories. *Algorithmica,* 12(2–3): 110–147, 1994.

59. L. Zheng and Per-Ake Larson. Speeding up external mergesort. *IEEE Transactions on Knowledge and Data Engineering,* 8(2): 322–332, April 1996.

# 34

# A Read Channel for Magnetic Recording

Bane Vasić
*University of Arizona*

Miroslav Despotović
*University of Novi Sad*

Pervez M. Aziz
*Agere Systems*

Necip Sayiner
*Agere Systems*

Ara Patapoutian
*Maxtor*

Brian Marcus
*IBM*

Emina Šoljanin
*Lucent Technologies*

Vojin Šenk
*University of Novisad*

Mario Blaum
*IBM*

A steady increase in recording densities and data rates of magnetic hard drives during last 15 years are mostly due to advances in recording materials, read/write heads, and mechanical designs. The role of signal processing and coding has been to make the best use of the capacity and speed potentials offered by these advances. As the recording technology matures, the read channel is becoming more and more advanced, reaching the point where it uses equally or even more complicated signal processing, coding and modulation algorithms than any other telecommunication channel and where, due to the speed, power consumption, and cost requirements, the challenges in implementing new architectures and designs have been pushed to today's integrated circuit manufacturing technology limits.

This chapter reviews advanced signal processing, modulation, coding techniques, and architectures for magnetic recording read channel. In the most general terms, the *read channel* controls the reading and writing the data to/from magnetic medium (unjustifiably the "write" part has disappeared from its name). The operations performed in the data channel are: *timing recovery, equalization, data detection, modulation coding/decoding*, and limited *error control*. Besides this, so called *data channel*, a read channel also has a *servo channel*, which role is to sense head position information, and, together with the head positioning servo system, to regulate a proper position of the head above the track. This chapter gives an in-depth treatment of all of these subsystems.

We begin with the review of the magnetic recording principles. We describe basic recording physics and explain how the interactions among neighboring magnetic domains cause intersymbol interference (ISI). Then we introduce a partial response signaling as a method of controlling the ISI. The first section also describes physical and logical organization of data on a disk and methods of increasing recording density.

The second section gives a block diagram of a state-of-the-art read channel and explain its subsystems. We explain organization of data on the disc tracks, servo sectors and data sectors, seeking and tracking operations, and phase and frequency acquisition. The section on servo information detection explains sensing radial information and read channel subsystem used to perform this operation.

The treatment of the data channel begins with an in-depth treatment of partial response signaling and adaptive equalization-standard techniques used in today's read channels. The novel equalization approaches and *generalized* partial response polynomials are also discussed in this section. We continue with a maximum likelihood sequence detection algorithm—Viterbi algorithm—and a noise predictive Viterbi algorithm, which enhances the performance by exploiting the fact that noise is highly colored and can be therefore predicted to some extent. The data detection also includes error event correction through post-processing, a new technique used in latest generation of read channels, as well as novel soft decoding and iterative decoding techniques.

The fourth part of the chapter discusses modulation and error control coding. Modulation coding in a read channel serves a variety of important roles. Generally speaking modulation coding eliminates those sequences from a recorded stream that would degrade the error performance, for example, long runs of consecutive like symbols that impact the timing recovery, or/and sequences that result in a signal on a small Euclidian distance. We complete the coding section with error control coding—both traditional algebraic techniques such as Reed Solomon codes, as well as with new trends such as iterative decoding. The error control coding is not part of present read channel chips, but will be integrated in the next generation of so-called "super chips."

We conclude this chapter by the review of read channel technology including novel read channel architectures such as postprocessor, super chip, etc., as well as the issues of digital design, chip testing, and manufacturing.

# 34.1   Recording Physics and Organization of Data on a Disk

*Bane Vasić and Miroslav Despotović*

## Magnetic Recording Basics

The basic elements of a magnetic recording system are read/write head, which is an electromagnet with a carefully shaped ferrous core, and a rotating disk with a ferromagnetic surface. Since the core of the electromagnet is ferrous, the magnetic flux preferentially travels through the core. The core is deliberately broken at an air gap. In the air gap, the flux creates a fringing field that extends some distance from the core.

To record data on a surface of a disk, the modulated signal current, typically bipolar, is passed through the electromagnet coils thus generating a fringing magnetic field. The fringing magnetic field creates a remanent magnetization on the ferromagnetic surface, i.e., the ferromagnetic surface becomes permanently magnetic. The magnetic domains in the surface act like tiny magnets themselves and create their own fringing magnetic field above the ferromagnetic surface. The data are recorded in concentric tracks as a sequence of small magnetic domains with two senses of magnetization depending on a sign of writing current. In this, so-called *saturation recording*, the amplitude of two writing current signal levels are chosen sufficiently large so as to magnetize to saturation the magnetic medium in one of two directions. In this way, the nonlinear hysteresis effect does not affect domains recorded over previously recorded ones.

In a simple reading scenario the reading head flies over the disk-spinning surface (at head-to-medium velocity, $v$) and passes through the fringing magnetic fields above the magnetic domains. Depending on a head type, the output voltage induced in the electromagnet is proportional to the spatial derivative of the magnetic field created by the permanent magnetization in the material in the case of inductive heads, or is proportional to the fringing magnetic field in the case of magneto-resistive heads. Today's hard drives use magneto-resistive heads for reading, because of their higher sensitivity. Pulses sensed by a head in response to transition on the medium are amplified and then detected to retrieve back the recorded data. For both types of heads, it is arranged that the head readback signal responds primarily to transitions of the magnetization pattern. The simplest, single parameter model for an isolated magnetic *transition response* is the so-called Lorenzian pulse

$$g(t) = \frac{1}{1 + \left(\frac{2t}{PW_{50}}\right)^2}$$

where $t_{50}$ is a parameter representing the pulse width at 50% of the maximum amplitude. Simplicity and relatively good approximation of the channel response are the main reasons for attractiveness of this model. The family of $g(t)$ curves for different $t_{50}$ values is depicted in Fig. 34.3. The width at half amplitude

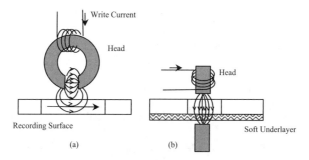

**FIGURE 34.1**   (a) Longitudinal recording. (b) Perpendicular recording.

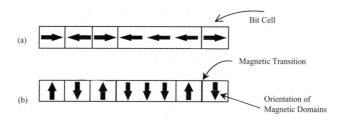

**FIGURE 34.2**   Magnetic domains representing bits.

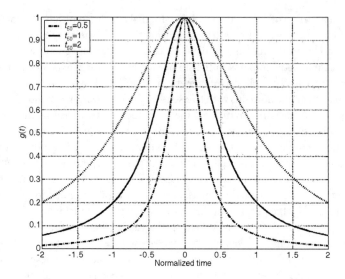

**FIGURE 34.3**    Transition response $g(t)$—mathematical model.

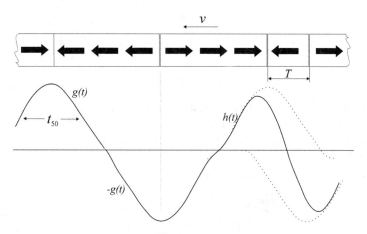

**FIGURE 34.4**    Sketch of a typical readback waveform in magnetic recording.

defines the recording process *resolution*, i.e., $PW_{50}$,* as a spatial, while $t_{50}$, as a temporal measure, is alternatively in use ($PW_{50} = vt_{50}$).

Ideal conditions for readback process would be to have head that is sensing the medium in an infinitely narrow strip in front of the head; however, head resolution is limited, so that the head output depends on "past" and "future" bit cell magnetization patterns. Such dependence causes superposition of isolated transition responses partly canceling each other. This phenomenon is known as intersymbol interference (ISI). The interference is largest for transitions at minimum spacing, i.e., a spacing of a single bit cell $T$. The response to two physically adjacent transitions is designated *dibit response* or *symbol response*, i.e., $h(t) = g(t) - g(t - T)$. Typical readback waveform illustrating these types of responses is depicted in Fig. 34.4.

Mathematically, the noiseless input-output relationship can be expressed as

$$y(t) = \sum_{i=-\infty}^{\infty} x_i h(t - iT) = \sum_{i=-\infty}^{\infty} (x_i - x_{i-1}) g(t - iT)$$

---

*This is not so strict because, contrary to this, some authors use $PW_{50}$ designating temporal resolution.

where $y$ and $\mathbf{x} \in \{-1, +1\}$ are readback and recorded sequences, respectively. Notice that every transition between adjacent bit cells yields a response $\pm 2g(t)$, while no transition in recorded sequence produces zero output.

Normalized measure of the *information density*[*] is defined as the ratio $D = t_{50}/T$ showing how many channel bits are packed "under" the dispersed pulse of duration $t_{50}$. Case in which we are increasing density ($D > 2$) is accompanied by an increase of duration of $h(t)$ expressed in units of $T$, as well as rapid decrease of the amplitude of dibit response, which is equivalent to lowering of signal-to-noise ratio in the channel. As a consequence, any given bit will interfere with successively more preceding and subsequent bits producing more severe ISI. At low normalized information densities, peaks of the transition responses are clearly separated, so it is possible to read recorded data in simple manner by detecting these peaks, i.e., *peak detectors*. Contrary to this, high-density detectors have to implement more sophisticated detection methods in order to resolve combination of these effects. One of the most important techniques to combat ISI in magnetic recording channels is partial-response (PR) signaling with maximum-likelihood (ML) sequence detection, i.e., PRML detection, Section 34.5. The applicability of this scheme in magnetic recording channels was suggested over 30 years ago [4], but the advance in technology enabled first disk detectors of this type at the beginning of nineties [2].

The basic idea of a PR system is that certain controlled amount of ISI, at the channel equalizer output, is left for a detector to combat with. The nature of controlled ISI is defined by a PR. This method avoids full channel equalization and intolerable noise enhancement induced by it in a situation when amplitude distortions, as a result of increased density, are severe. In magnetic recording systems the PR detector reconstructs recorded sequence from samples of a suitable equalized readback signal at time instants $t = iT$, $i \geq 0$. The equalization result is designed in a manner that produces just a finite number of *nonzero* $h(t)$ samples $h_0 = h(0)$, $h_1 = h(T)$, $h_2 = h(2T), \ldots h_K = h(KT)$. This is usually represented in a compact *partial-response polynomial* notation $h(D) = h_0 + h_1 D + h_2 D^2 + \cdots + h_K D^K$, where the dummy variable $D^i$ signifies a delay of $i$ time units $T$. Then the "sampled" input-output relationship is of the form

$$y(jT) = \sum_{i=j-K}^{j} x_i h(jT - iT)$$

For channel bit densities around $D \approx 2$, the target PR channels is usually the class-4 partial response (PR4), described by $h(D) = 1 - D^2 = (1 - D)(1 + D)$. At higher recording densities Thapar and Patel [6] introduced a general class of PR models with PR polynomial in the form $h_n(D) = (1 - D)(1 + D)^n$, $n \geq 1$ that is a better match to the actual channel discrete-time symbol response. Notice that the PR4 model corresponds to the $n = 1$ case. The channel models with $n \geq 2$ are usually referred to as "extended class-4" models, and denoted by $E^{n-1}$PR4 (EPR4, $E^2$PR4). Recently, the modified $E^2$PR4 (ME$^2$PR4) channel, $h(D) = (1 - D^2)(5 + 4D + 2D^2)$, was suggested due to its robustness in high-density recordings. Notice that as the degree of PR polynomials gets higher, the transition response, $g(t)$, becomes wider and wider in terms of channel bit intervals, $T$ (EPR4 response extends over 3-bit periods, $E^2$PR4 over 4), i.e., the remaining ISI is more severe.

The transfer characteristics of the Lorentzian model of the PR4 saturation recording channel (at densities $D \approx 2$), is close to transition response given by

$$g(t) = \frac{\sin\left(\pi \frac{t}{T}\right)}{\pi \frac{t}{T}} + \frac{\sin\left(\pi \frac{t-T}{T}\right)}{\pi \frac{t-T}{T}}$$

---

[*]When channel coding is introduced, this density is greater than the user information density because of added redundancy in the recorded channel sequence.

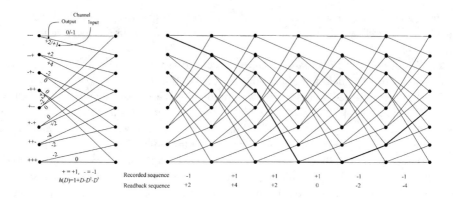

**FIGURE 34.5**   Trellis representation of EPR4 channel outputs.

generating the output waveform described by

$$y(t) = \sum_{i=-\infty}^{\infty} (x_i - x_{i-1})g(t-iT) = \sum_{i=-\infty}^{\infty} (x_i - x_{i-2})\frac{\sin\left(\pi\frac{t-iT}{T}\right)}{\pi\frac{t-iT}{T}}$$

Note that $g(t) = 1$ at consecutive sample times $t = 0$ and $t = T$, while at all other discrete time instants, its value is 0. Such transition response results in known ISI at sample times, leading to output sample values that, in the absence of noise, take values from the ternary alphabet $\{0, \pm2\}$. In order to decode the readback PR sequence it is useful to describe the channel using the *trellis state diagram*. This is a diagram similar to any other graph describing a finite-state machine, where states indicate the content of the channel memory and branches between states are labeled with output symbols as a response to the certain input (the usual convention is that for the upper branch leaving a state we associate input $-1$ and $+1$ for the lower). The EPR4 channel has memory length 3, its trellis has $2^3 = 8$ states, and any input sequence is tracing the path through adjacent trellis segments.

An example of the trellis diagram is given in Fig. 34.5 for the EPR4 channel. However, notice that in PR trellis there are also distinct states for which there exist mutually identical paths (output sequences) that start from those states, so that we can never distinguish between them (e.g., the all-zero paths emerging from the top and bottom states of the EPR4 trellis). Obviously, such a behavior can easily lead to great problems in detection in situations when noise can confuse us in resolving the current trellis state (e.g., the bottom one for the upper in the running example). Such a trellis is so-called *quasi-catastrophic* trellis and further details on this subject could be found in [3].

A common approach to studying the PR channel characteristics is to analyze its frequency spectra. Basically, when the recording density is low ($D \approx 0.5$) and readback pulses are narrow compared to the distance between transitions, such a signal contains a high-frequency component (highest frequency components correspond to the fastest edge of the signal). With the growth of density, the spectral energy distribution move towards lower frequency range. This means that for the system with $D = 2$, the signal spectrum is concentrated below half of the channel bit rate given by $1/T$. The power of the highest spectral components outside this half-bandwidth range is negligible. This means that for high-density recording we can limit the channel bandwidth to $1/2T$ without loss of information and filtering the high frequencies containing noise only.

Finding the Fourier transform of the dibit response we obtain the frequency response for the PR channel given by

$$H(w) = 1 - e^{i2wT}, \quad |H(w)| = 2\sin(wT), \quad 0 \le w \le \frac{\pi}{T}$$

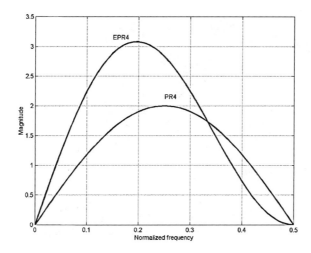

**FIGURE 34.6** Frequency response of PR4 and EPR4 channel.

For higher order PR channels we have different transition responses and accordingly different frequency responses calculated in a similar fashion as for the PR4 channel. The frequency response for these channels is shown in Fig. 34.6.

These lower frequency spectrum distributions of PR channels are closer to a typical frequency content of raw nonequalized pulses. Hence, equalization for extended PR channels can become less critical and requires less high frequency boost that may improve signal-to-noise ratio.

## Physical Organization of Data on Disk

In most designs, the head is mounted on a slider, which is a small sled-like structure with rails. Sliders are designed to form an air bearing that gives the lift force to keep the slider-mounted head flying at the small and closely controlled height (the so-called Winchester technology). A small flying height is desirable because it amplifies the readback amplitude and reduces the amount of field from neighboring magnetic domains picked by the head, thus enabling sharper transitions in the readback signal and recording more data on a disk; however, the surface imperfections and dust particles can cause the head to "crash." Controlling the head-medium spacing is of critical importance to ensure high readback signal, and stable signal range. It is also important during reading to keep the head center above the track being read to reduce magnetization picked up from neighboring tracks. The signal induced in the head as a result of magnetic transitions in a neighboring track is known as a cross-talk or inter-track interference. In order to position the head, special, periodic, wedge-like areas, the so-called *servo wedges*, are reserved on a disk surface for radial position information. They typically consume 5–10% of the disk surface available. An arch of a track laying in a servo wedge is called a *servo sector*. The area between servo wedges is used to record data, and a portion of a track between two servo sectors is referred to as a *data sector* or *data field*. In other words, the data and servo fields are time multiplexed, or using disk drive terminology, the servo field is *embedded* in the data stream. To estimate radial position a periodic waveform in a servo sector is detected, and the radial position error signal is calculated based on the current estimated position of a head and the actual position of the track to be followed, and then used in a head positioning servo system (Fig. 34.7).

## Logical Organization of Data on a Disk

On a disk, data are organized in *sectors*. For a computer system, the sector is a sequence of (8-bit) bytes within each addressable portion of data on a disk drive. The sector size is typically 512 bytes. For an error control system, the sector is a sequence of error control codewords or blocks. For interleaved error control systems, each sector contains as many blocks as there are interleave cycles. The block elements

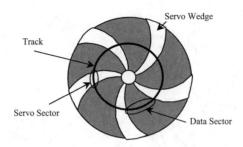

**FIGURE 34.7**   Data and servo sectors.

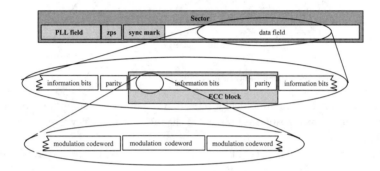

**FIGURE 34.8**   Format of data on a disk.

are symbols that are not necessarily eight bit long. In the most general terms, the symbols are used in the error control coidng (ECC) system to calculate and describe error locations and values.

A read channel sees a sector as a sequence of modulation codewords together with synchronization bits. Synchronization field is partitioned into a sector address mark, or sync mark, typically of length around 20 bits, and phase lock loop (PLL) field, a periodic pattern whose length is about 100 bits used for PLL synchronization. In addition to this, a secondary sync mark is placed within a data field and used for increased reliability. A zero-phase start pattern of length 8–16 bits is used for initial estimation of phase in the PLL. Figure 34.8 illustrates the format of user data on a disk.

## Increasing Recording Density

Increasing areal density of the data stored on a disk can be achieved by reducing lengths of magnetic domains along the track (increasing linear density) and by reducing a track width and track pitch (increasing radial density). Although the radial density is mostly limited by the mechanical design of the drive and ability to accurately follow the track, the linear density is a function of properties of magnetic materials and head designs, and ability to detect and demodulate recorded data.

As linear density increases, the magnetic domains on a surface become smaller and thus thermally unstable, which means that lower energy of an external field is sufficient to demagnetize them. This effect is known as a superparamagnetic effect [1]. Another physical effect is the finite sensitivity of the read head, i.e., at extremely high densities, since the domains are too small; the signal energy becomes so small as to be comparable with the ambient thermal noise energy.

The orientation of magnetization on a disk can be longitudinal, which is typical for today's systems, or perpendicular. The choice of the media influences the way the magnetization is recorded on the disk. Media with needle shaped particles oriented longitudinally tend to have a much higher remanent magnetization in the longitudinal direction, and favor longitudinal recording. The head design must support the favorable orientation of magnetization. Longitudinal orientation requires head shapes that promote longitudinal fields such as ring heads. Similarly, some media are composed of crystallites oriented perpendicularly to the field. Such media have a much higher remanent magnetization in the perpendicular direction, and favor perpendicular recording. If a head design promotes perpendicular fields, such as single pole heads, the result is perpendicularly recorded magnetization.

Some recent experiments have shown that media that favor perpendicular recording have better thermal stability. This is why, lately, perpendicular recording is attracting a considerable attention in magnetic recording community. Typically, in perpendicular recording a recording surface is made of a hard ferromagnetic material, i.e., material requiring large applied fields to permanently magnetize it. Once magnetized, the domains remain very stable, i.e., large fields are required to reverse the magnetization. The recording layer is made thick so that, since each magnetic domain contains a large number of magnetic particles, larger energy is required for demagnetization. The low remanence, low coercivity, materials (the so-called *soft materials*) are placed beneath hard ferromagnetic surface (soft underlayer) and used to conduct magnetic field back to another electromagnet pole. A pole-head geometry is used, so that the medium can effectively travel through the head gap, and be exposed to stronger magnetic field. A pole-head/soft-underlayer configuration can produce about twice the field that a ring head produces. In this way sharp transitions can be supported on relatively thick perpendicular media, and high frequencies (that get attenuated during readback) are written firmly. However, effects of demagnetizing fields are much more pronounced in perpendicular recording systems, because in longitudinal media the transitions are not that sharp.

## Physical Limits on Recording Density

At extremely high areal densities each bit of information is written on a very small area. The track width is small and magnetic domains contain relatively small numbers of magnetic particles. Because the particles have random positions and sizes, large statistical fluctuations or noise on the recovered signal can occur. The signal-to-noise ratio is proportional to the track width, and is inversely proportional to the mean size of the particle and the standard deviation of the particle size. Therefore, increasing the track size, increasing the number of particles by increasing media thickness, and decreasing the particle size will improve the signal-to-noise ratio. Uniaxial orientation of magnetic particles also gives higher signal-to-noise ratio; however, the requirement for thermal stability over periods of years dictates a lower limit to the size of magnetic particles in a magnetic domain because ambient thermal energy causes the magnetic signals to decay. Achieving both small particle size and thermal stability over time can be done by using magnetic materials with higher coercivity, but there is a strong practical upper limit to the coercivity that can be written, and it is determined by the saturation magnetization of the head material.

In addition to the basic physics, a number of practical engineering factors must be considered at extremely high densities. In particular, these factors include the ability to manufacture accurately the desired head geometries and control media thickness, the ability to closely follow the written tracks, to control head flying height, and the ability to maintain a very small, stable magnetic separation.

## The Future

The hard drive areal densities have grown at an annual rate approaching 100%. Recently a 20 Gbit/in.$^2$ has been demonstrated [5], and some theoretical indications of feasibility of extremely high densities approaching 1 Tbit/in.$^2$ have been given [8,9]. Although the consideration related to user needs including higher capacity, speed, error performance, reliability, environment condition tolerances, etc. are important, the factors affecting cost tend to dominate read channel architecture and design considerations. Thus, achieving highest recording density with lowest component costs at high manufacturing yields is the ultimate goal.

With areal densities growing at an annual rate approaching 100%, real concern continues to be expressed that we may be approaching a limit to conventional magnetic recording technology; however, as long as the read channel is concerned, large opportunities are available to improve on the existing signal processing, both with detectors better matched to the channel and by applying more advanced detection, modulation, and coding schemes.

## References

1. S. H. Charrap, P. L. Lu, and Y. He, "Thermal stability of recorded information at high densities," *IEEE Trans. Magn.*, pt. 2, vol. 33, no. 1, pp. 978–983, Jan. 1997.
2. J. D. Coker, et. al., "Implementation of PRML in a rigid disk drive," in *Digest of Magnetic Recording Conf.* 1991, paper D3, June 1991.
3. G. D. Forney and A. R. Calderbank, "Coset codes for partial response channels; or, coset codes with spectral nulls," *IEEE Transactions on Information Theory*, vol. IT-35, no. 5, pp. 925–943, Sept. 1989.
4. H. Kobayashi and D. T. Tang, "Application of partial response channel coding to magnetic recording systems," *IBM J. Res. Dev.*, vol.14, pp. 368–375, July 1970.
5. M. Madison, et al., "20 Gb/in.$^2$ Using a merged notched head on advanced low noise media," in *MMM Conference*, Nov. 1999.
6. H. Thapar and A. Patel, "A class of partial-response systems for increasing storage density in magnetic recording," *IEEE Trans. Magn.*, vol. MAG-23, pp. 3666–3668, Sept. 1987.
7. H. Osawa, Y. Kurihara, Y. Okamoto, H. Saito, H. Muraoka, and Y. Nakamura, "PRML systems for perpendicular magnetic recording," *J. Magn. Soc. Japan*, vol. 21, no. S2, 1997.
8. R. Wood, "Detection and capacity limits in magnetic media noise," *IEEE Trans Magn.*, vol. MAG-34, no. 4, pp. 1848–1850, July 1998.
9. R. Wood, "The feasibility of magnetic recording at 1 Tbit/in.$^2$," 36 *IEEE Trans. on Magnetics*, vol. 36, no. 1, pp. 36–42, Jan. 2000.

## 34.2   Read Channel Architecture

*Bane Vasić, Pervez M. Aziz, and Necip Sayiner*

The read channel is a device situated between the drive's controller and the recording head's preamplifier (Fig. 34.9). The read channel provides an interface between the controller and the analog recording head, so that digital data can be recorded and read back from the disk. Furthermore, it reads back the head positioning information from a disk and presents it to the head positioning servo system that resides in

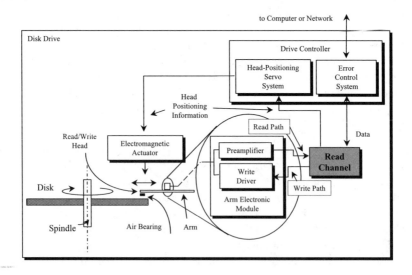

**FIGURE 34.9**   The block diagram of a disk drive.

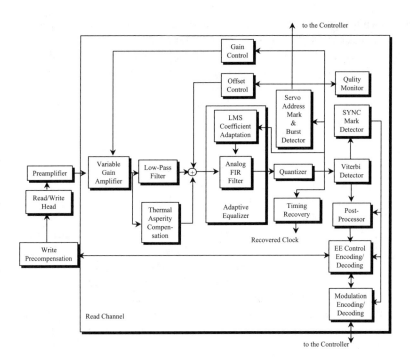

**FIGURE 34.10** A typical read channel architecture.

the controller. A typical read channel architecture is shown in Fig. 34.10. During a read operation, the head generates a pulse in response to magnetic transitions on the media. Pulses are then amplified by the preamplifier that resides in the arm electronics module, and fed to the read channel. In the read channel, the readback signal is additionally amplified and filtered to remove noise and to shape the waveform, and then the data sequence is detected (Fig. 34.10). The data to be written on a disk are sent from a read channel to a write driver that converts them into a bipolar current that is passed through the electromagnet coils. Prior to sending to read channel, user data coming from computer (or from a network in the network attached storage devices) are encoded by an error control system. Redundant bits are added in such a way to enable a recovery from random errors that may occur during reading data from a disk. The errors occur due to number of reasons including: demagnetization effects, magnetic field fluctuations, noise in electronic components, dust and other contaminants, thermal effects, etc. Traditionally, the read channel and drive controller have been separate chips. The latest architectures have integrated them into so called "super-chips."

## Analog Front End

As a first step, the read signal is normalized with respect to gain and offset so that it falls into an expected signal range. Variation of gain and offset is a result of variations in the head media spacing, variations in magnetic and mechanical and electronic components in the drive, preamplifier and read channel. The front end also contains a thermal asperity (TA) circuit compensation. Thermal asperity occurs when head hits a dust particle or some other imperfection on a disk surface. At the moment of impact, the temperature of the head rises, and a large signal at the head's output is generated. During TA a useful readback signal appears as riding on the back of a low frequency signal of much higher energy. The beginning of this "background" signal can be easily predicted and the TA signal itself suppressed by a relatively simple filter.

High-frequency noise is then removed with a continuous-time low pass filter to permit a sampling of the signal without aliasing of high-frequency noise back into the signal spectrum. The filter frequently includes programable cut-off frequency, which can be used to shape the signal to optimize data detection. A programmable cut-off frequency is essential since the disk rotates with constant angular velocity, and data rate varies by approximately a factor of two from the inner to outer radius of the disc. It is also important for the analog filter bandwidth to be switched to allow for low cut-off frequencies when processing servo sector information.

## Precompensation

Nonlinear bit shift in magnetic recording is the shift in position of a written transition due to the demagnetizing field from adjacent transitions. In a PRML channel, the readback waverofm is synchronously sampled at regular intervals, and the sample values depend on the position of written transitions. Therefore, nonlinear bit shift leads to error in sample values which, in turn, degrades the channel performance. The write precompensation is employed to counteract the nonlinear bit shift. However, determining the nonlinear bit shift is not simple and straightforward especially when one tries to fine tune each drive for its optimum precompensation. The precompensation circuit generates the write clock signal whose individual transition timing is delayed from its nominal position by the required precompensation amount. The amount of precompensation and the bit patterns requiring precompensation can be found using the extracted pulse shape [10,18]. Another approach is a frequency-domain technique that offers simple measurement procedure and a possible hardware implementation using a band-pass filter [32] or using PRML sample values [33].

## Partial-Response Signaling with Maximum Likelihood Sequence Estimation

After sampling with a rate $1/T$, the read signal is passed through an analog or digital front end filter and detected using a maximum likelihood sequence detector. The partial-response signaling with maximum likelihood (PRML) sequence estimation is proposed for use in magnetic recording by Kobayashi 30 years ago [15,16]. In 1990 IBM produced the first disk drives employing PRML detection. Today's all read channels are based on some version of the PRML. Cideciyan et al. [3] described a complete PRML systems including equalization, gain and timing control, and Viterbi detector. All basic functions of a PRML system have remained practically unchanged, until the introduction of a postprocessor that performs a special type of soft error correction after maximum likelihood sequence detection. Also, significant improvements in all the subsystems have been made during last 10 years. The term "partial response" comes from the fact that the sample of the equalized signal at, say, time $nT$ ($T$ is a signaling interval), contains information not only on data bits at time $nT$, but also on neighboring bits, i.e., magnetic transitions. The number of adjacent bits that determine the sample at $nT$ is referred to as *channel memory*. The channel memory is a parameter that can be selected in the process of defining a read channel architecture. The channel memory and the details of the partial response selection are made based on an attempt to have the partial response be as close a match to the channel as possible. Since the complexity of a maximum likelihood detector is an exponential function of a memory, it is desirable to keep the memory low, but, the equalization required to achieve this might boost the high-frequency noise, which result in decrease of a signal-to-noise ratio, called *equalization loss*. The typical value of channel memory in today's read channels is 4. The value of an equalized sample at time $nT$, $y_n$ can be written as

$$y_n = \sum_{k=0}^{L_h} h_k x_{n-k}$$

where $x_n$ is a user-data bit recorded at time $n$ ($x_n \in \{-1, +1\}$), and $L_h$ is a channel memory. The coefficients $h_k$ form, $h(D) = \sum_{k=0}^{L_h} h_k \cdot D^k$, a *partial response polynomial* or *partial response target* ($D$ is a formal, time-delay variable). The main idea in partial response equalization is to equalize the channel to a known and short target that is matched to the channel spectrum so that noise enhancement is minimum. Therefore, the deliberate inter-symbol interference is introduced, but since the target is known, the data can be recovered, as explained in the previous article.

## Adaptive Equalization

To properly detect the user-data it is of essential importance to maintain the partial response target during the detection. This implies that channel gain, finite-impulse response (FIR) filter coefficients, and sampling phase must be adaptively controlled in real-time. Continuous automatic adaptations allow the read channel to compensate for signal variations and changes that occur when drive operation is affected by changes in temperature or when the input signals are altered by component aging. Comparing the equalizer output samples with the expected partial response samples generates an error signal, which is used to produce adaptive control signals for each of the adaptive loops. For filter coefficients control, a least-mean square (LMS) algorithm is used [4]. LMS operates in the time domain to find filter coefficients that minimize the mean-squared error between the samples and the desired response. Initial setting of the filter coefficients is accomplished by training the filter with an on-board training sequence, and the adaptation is continued while chip is reading data. Adaptation can be in principle performed on all coefficients simultaneously at lower clock rate or on one coefficient at a time. Because disk channels variations are slow relative to the data rate, the time-shared coefficient adaptation achieves the same optimum filter response while consuming less power and taking up less chip area. Sometimes, to achieve better loop stability, not all filter coefficients are adapted during reading data. Also, before writing, data are scrambled to whiten the power spectral density and ensure proper filter adaptation.

The FIR filter also compensates for the large amount of group-delay variation that may be caused by a low-pass filter with a nonlinear phase characteristics. Filters with nonlinear characteristics, such as the Butter-worth filter, are preferred over, say, an equi-ripple design of the same circuit complexity, because they have much better roll-off characteristics. The number of FIR filter coefficients in practical read channels has been as low as 3 and as high as 10 with various trade-offs associated with the different choices, which can be made.

## Viterbi Detection

In many communications systems, a symbol-by-symbol detector is used to convert individual received samples at the output of the channel to corresponding detected bits. In today's PRML channels, a Viterbi detector is a maximum likelihood detector that converts an entire *sequence* of received equalized samples to a corresponding sequence of detected bits. Let $y = (y_n)$ be the sequence of received equalized samples corresponding to transmitted bit sequence $x = (x_n)$. Maximum likelihood sequence estimation maximizes the probability density $p(y|x)$ across all choices of transmitted sequence $x$ [7]. In the absence of noise and mis-equalization, the relationship between the noiseless equalized samples $z_n$ and the corresponding transmitted bits is known by the Viterbi detector and is given by

$$z_n = \sum_{k=0}^{L} h_k x_{n-k} \tag{34.1}$$

In the presence of noise and mis-equalization the received samples will deviate from noiseless values. The Viterbi detector considers various bit sequences and efficiently compares the corresponding expected PR channel output values with those actually received. For Gaussian noise at the output of the equalizer and equally probable input bits, maximizing $p(y|x)$ is equivalent to choosing as the correct bit sequence the one closest in a (squared) Euclidean distance sense to the received samples. Therefore, the following expression needs to be to minimized

$$\min_{x_k} \left( \sum_{n=0}^{P-1} \left[ y_n - \sum_{k=0}^{L} h_k x_{n-k} \right]^2 \right) \tag{34.2}$$

The various components of (34.3) are also known as branch metrics. The Viterbi detector accomplishes the minimization in an efficient manner using a trellis-based search rather than an exhaustive search. The search is effectively performed over a finite window known as the decision delay or path memory length of the Viterbi detector. Increasing the window length beyond a certain value leads to only insignificant improvements of the bit detection reliability or bit error rate (BER).

Despite the efficient nature of the Viterbi algorithm the complexity of a Viterbi detector increases exponentially with the channel memory of the PR target. A target with channel memory of $L-1$ requires for example a $2^{L-1}$ state Viterbi detector trellis. For a fully parallel Viterbi implementation, each Viterbi state contains an add-compare-select (ACS) computational unit, which is used to sum up the branch metrics of (34.4) and keep the minimum metric paths for different bit sequences. Also required for the hardware is a $2^{L-1} \cdot P$ bit memory to keep a history of potential bit sequences considered across the finite decision delay window.

## Timing Recovery

A phase-locked loop (PLL) is used to regenerate a synchronous clock from the data stream. The PRML detector use decision directed timing recovery typically with a digital loop filter. The digital loop filter parameters can be easily controlled using programmable registers and changed when read channel switches from acquisition to tracking mode. Because a significant pipelining is necessary in the loop logic to operate at high speeds, the digital loop filter architecture exhibits a relatively large amount of latency. It can affect considerably the acquisition time when the timing loop must acquire significant phase and frequency offsets. To ensure that only small frequency offsets are present, the synchronizer VCO is phase-locked to the synthesizer during nonread times. For fast initial adjustment of the sampling phase, a known preamble is recorded prior to user data. The time adjustment scheme is obtained by applying the stochastic gradient technique to minimize the mean squared difference between equalized samples and data signal estimates. To compensate for offset between the rate of the signal received and the frequency of the local timing source the loop filter design allows for a factor $\Delta T_n$ to be introduced, so that the sample at discrete time $n$ is taken $T + \Delta T_n$ seconds after the sample at discrete time $n-1$. In acquisition mode, in order to quickly adjust the timing phase, large values for loop gains are chosen. In tracking mode, the loop gains are lowered to reduce loop bandwidth.

## Read Channel Servo Detection

In an *embedded* servo system (introduced in the previous article), the radial position of the read head is estimated from two sequences recorded on servo wedges: *track addresses* and *servo-bursts*. The track address provides a unique number for every track on a disk, while a servo-burst pattern is repeated on each track or on a group of tracks. Determining the head position using only the track number is not sufficient because the head has to be centered exactly on a given track. Therefore, the servo-burst waveform is used in conjunction with the track address to determine the head position. Using the servo-burst pattern, it is possible to determine the off-track position of a head with respect to a given track with a high resolution. While positioning the head over a surface, the disk drive can be in either *seeking* or *tracking* operation mode. In a seeking mode, the head moves over multiple tracks, trying to reach the track with a desired address as quickly as possible, while in a tracking mode, the head tries to maintain its position over a track. The track addresses are therefore used mostly in the seeking mode, while servo-burst information is usually used in the tracking mode [25,30].

In read channels, periodic servo-burst waveforms are detected and used to estimate radial position. The radial position error signal is calculated based on the current estimated position and the position of the track to be followed, and then used in an external head positioning servo system. Generally, two types of position estimators are in use: maximum likelihood estimators based on a matched filtering and sub-optimal estimators based on averaging the area, or the peaks, of the incoming periodic servo-burst waveform. A variety of techniques have been used to demodulate servo bursts including amplitude, phase, and null servo detectors. Today, most read channels use an amplitude modulation with either peak or area detection demodulators.

Older generation channels generally implemented the servo functions in analog circuitry. The analog circuitry of these servo channels partially duplicates functions present in the digital data channel. Now, several generations of read-channel chips have switched from analog to digital circuits and digital signal processing [8,34]. These channels reduce duplication of circuits used for servo and data and provide a greater degree of flexibility and programmability in the servo functions.

Typically, a single analog-to-digital converter (ADC) or quantizer is used for both data datection and servo position error signal estimation [8,20,27,34], but quantizer requirements are different in data and servo fields. Compared to position error signal estimators, data detectors require a quantizer with higher sampling clock rate. On the other hand position error signal estimators require a quantizer with finer resolution. A typical disk drive has a data resolution requirement of around 6 bits, and a servo resolution requirement of around 7 or 8 bits. Furthermore, servo bursts are periodic waveforms as opposed to data streams. In principle, both the lower sampling clock rate requirement in the servo field and the periodicity property of servo-burst signals can be exploited to increase the detector quantization resolution for position error signal estimation. The servo field is oversampled asynchronously to increase the effective quantizer resolution.

Track densities in today's hard drives are higher than 25,000 tracks per inch, and the design of a tracking servo system is far from trivial. Some of the recent results include [Saks97], [2,24–26]. Increasing the drive level servo control loop bandwidth is extremely important. Typical bandwidth of a servo system is about 1.5 kHz, and is mainly limited by the parameters that are out of reach of a read channel designer, such as mechanical resonances of voice coil motor, arm holding a magnetic head, suspension, and other mechanical parameters.

Another type of disturbance with a mechanical origins, that has to be also detected and controlled in a read channel, is repeatable runout (RRO) in the position of the head with respect to the track center. These periodic disturbances are inherent in any rotating machine, and can be the result of an eccentricity of the track, offset of the track center with respect to the spindle center, bearing geometry, and wear and motor geometry. The frequencies of the periodic disturbances are integer multiples of the frequency of rotation of the disk, and if not compensated they can be a considerable source of tracking error. In essence the control system possesses an adaptive method to learn online the true geometry of the track being followed, and a mechanism of continuous-time adaptive runout cancellation [31].

## Postprocessor

Due to the channel memory and noise coloration, maximum likelihood sequence detector (Viterbi detector) produces some error patterns more often than others. They are referred to as *dominant error sequences*, or *error events*, and can be obtained analytically or through experiments and/or simulation. Relative frequencies of error events strongly depend on a recording density.

Parity check processors combine syndrome decoding and soft-decision decoding [35]. Error event likelihoods needed for soft decoding can be computed from a channel sequence by some kind of soft-output Viterbi algorithm. By using a syndrome calculated for a received codeword, a list is created of all possible *positions* where error events can occur, and then error event likelihoods are used to select the most likely position and most likely type of the error event. Decoding is completed by finding the error event position and type. The decoder can make two type of errors: it fails to correct if syndrome is zero or it makes a wrong correction if syndrome is nonzero, but the most likely error event or combination of error events do not produce right syndrome.

A code must be able to detect a single error from the list of dominant error events, and should minimize the probability of producing zero syndrome when more than one error event occur in a codeword.

Consider a linear code given by an $(n - k) \times n$ parity check matrix $H$, with $H$ capable of correcting or detecting dominant errors. If all errors from a list were contiguous and shorter than $m$, then a cyclic $n - k = m$ parity bit code could be used to correct a single error event; however, in reality, the error sequences are more complex, and occurrence probabilities of error events of lengths 6, 7, 8, or more are not negligible. Furthermore, practical reasons (such as decoding delay, thermal asperities, etc.) dictate using short codes, and consequently, in order to keep code rate high, only a relatively small number of parity bits is allowed, making the design of error event detection codes nontrivial.

The detection is based on the fact that we can calculate the likelihoods of each of dominant error sequences at each point in time. The parity bits serve to detect the errors, and to provide some localization in error type and time. The likelihoods are then used to choose the most likely error events (type and location) for corrections. The likelihoods are calculated as the difference in the squared Euclidean distances between the signal and the convolution of maximum likelihood sequence estimate and the channel partial response, versus that between the signal and the convolution of an alternative data pattern and the channel partial response. During each clock cycle, the lowest $M$ are chosen, and the syndromes for these error events are calculated. Throughout the processing of each block, a list is maintained of the $N$ most likely error events, along with their associated error types, positions, and syndromes. At the end of the block, when the list of candidate error events is finalized, the likelihoods and syndromes are calculated for each of six combinations of two candidate error events which are possible. After disqualifying those pairs of candidates, which overlap in the time domain, and those candidates and pairs of candidates which produced a syndrome, which does not match the actual syndrome, the candidate or pair, which remains and which has the highest likelihood, is chosen for correction.

## Modulation Coding

Modulation of constrained coding is used to translate an arbitrary sequence of input data to a channel sequence with special properties required by the physics of the medium [21]. Two large important classes of channel constraints are run-length and spectral constraints. The run-length constraints [12] bound the minimal and/or maximal lengths of certain types of channel subsequences, while the spectral constraints include dc-free [11] and higher order spectral-null constraints [6,23]. The spectral constraints also include codes that produce spectral zero at rational sub-multiples of symbol frequency as well as constraints that give rise to spectral lines. The most important class of runlength constraints is a $(d, k)$ constraint, where $d + 1$ and $k + 1$ represent minimum and maximum number of consecutive like symbols or space between the adjacent transitions. Bounding minimal length consecutive like symbols controls ISI in the excess bandwidth systems and reduces transition noise. Bounding the upper limits of the mark lengths improves timing recovery and automatic gain control. In order to keep code rate high, today's read channels employ only $k$ constrained codes. Typical code rates are: 16/17, 24/25, 32/34, 48/49. Modulation decodes can be either block-by-block or sliding-window. Block decoders determine data word by using a single codeword, while sliding-window decoders require so-called look-ahead, which means that the output data word is a function of several consecutive codewords. Due to inherent nonlinearity, a modulation decoder may produce multiple errors as a result of a single erroneous input bit. If a sliding-window decoding is used, an error can affect several consecutive data blocks. This effect is known as an *error propagation*. The block codes are favored because they do not propagate errors.

A mathematically rigorous code design approach based on symbolic dynamics was developed by Marcus and Siegel et al. [19,22]. The algorithm is known as the "state splitting algorithm" or Adler, Coppersmith, and Hassner (ACH) algorithm [1]. Another constrained coding approach, championed by Immink [14] emphasizes the low-complexity encoding and decoding algorithms [13]. Despite this nice mathematical theory, design of constrained codes remains too difficult to be fully automated, and in the art of designing efficient codes, human intervention and skill are still necessary.

## Error Control Coding

In a conventional hard disk drives the error control coding (ECC) system does not reside in a read channel; however, the ECC performance is linked to the performance of a detection algorithm, error propagation in a modulation code, and it is natural to try to expand the read channel functionality to error control as well. A new trend in industry is aimed toward designing an integrated circuit, so called *super chip* with a such expanded functionality.

In the most general terms, the purpose of ECC is to protect user data, and this is achieved by including redundant, so-called *parity* bits along with the data bits. The codes used in hard drives belong to a large class of ECC schemes, called block codes. A block code is a set of codewords (or blocks) of a fixed length $n$. The length is expressed in number of symbols, and a symbol is a binary word of length $m$. Other parameters of a block code are $k$-number of data symbols in the block, and $t$-number of symbols correctable by the ECC system [17,36].

Reed–Solomon (RS) codes [28] have been the class of codes most often used in the magnetic disk storage for the last 15 years. The reason is their excellent performance in presence of error events that exhibit burstiness, which is typical for magnetic recording channels, and lend themselves to high-speed encoding/decoding algorithms required for high-speed disk drives [5,9,37]. Very often RS codes are interleaved to reduce effect of long error burst, and to reduce the implementation cost by eliminating conversion of bytes to possibly longer code symbols used in encoding and decoding. The parameters of RS codes satisfy the following relations: $n \leq 2^m - 1$, number of parity symbols $n - k \geq 2t$, and code rate of the RS code $r = k/n$.

In today's hard drives typically, a part of ECC decoding is performed in hardware with a throughput equal to the data rate, and the other part is performed in firmware with much lower speed. In some cases, such as thermal asperities, no error control is sufficient to recover the data. In this case, it is necessary to retry reading the same sector. A choice between hardware or firmware correction depends on the application, the data transfer protocol, and the bus transfer rate. In applications such as single-user work-stations, short data transfers dominate, but streaming data transfers occasionally occurs (during boot, large file transfers, etc.). Additionally, data read from the disk drive can be transmitted to the host computer in a physically sequential or in any convenient order. If the bus transfer rate is higher than the ECC hardware throughput, and if sufficiently long ECC firmware buffer is available to store all the sectors, or if sectors are transmitted to the host computer in any convenient order all firmware error recovery can be performed in parallel with disk reads without interrupting streaming read operations. In the case of short packet transfers, it is better to perform read retry in parallel with firmware error correction. Retries in conjunction with hardware correction typically consume less time than firmware error correction. On the other hand, for long streaming transfers, correcting errors in firmware in parallel with reading the sector is better strategy, provided that the firmware ECC throughput is high enough to prevent buffer overflow. A detailed treatment of an error control system design considerations can be found in [29].

## The Effect of Thermal Asperites

As explained earlier, if a head hits a dust particle, a long thermal asperity will occur, producing a severe transient noise burst, loss of timing synchronization, or even off-track perturbation. Error events caused by TAs are much less frequent than random error events, but they exist and must be taken into account during read channel design. If there were no TA protection in the read channel, a loss of lock in timing recovery system would occur, causing massive numbers of data errors well beyond the error correction capability of any reasonable ECC system. Despite TA protection, the residual error cannot be completely eliminated, and many bits will be detected incorrectly; however, the read channel should be designed to enable proper functioning of timing recovery in the presence of bogus samples. Typically, the read channel estimates the beginning and length of TA and sends this information to the ECC system, which may be able to improve its correction capability using so-called erasure information; however, since the TA starting location is not known precisely, and the probability of random error in the same sector is not negligible, the ECC system can misscorrect, which is more dangerous than not to detect the error.

## Error Performance Measures

A commonly used measure of ECC performance is a BER, which is defined as a ratio of unrecoverable error events and total user data bits. An unrecoverable error event is a block that contains more erroneous symbols than the ECC system can correct, and it may contain as many as exist in a single data block protected by the ECC system. Various applications require different BERs, but they are typically in the range of $10^{-12}$–$10^{-15}$. Another ECC performance measure is undetected bit error rate (UBER), which is a number of undetected error events per total number of user bits. In some cases the ECC system detect that the sector contain errors, but is not able to correct them. Then a controller asks a read channel to retry reading the same sector. The *retry rate per bit* is a useful measure of a data throughput. The hard drive standards of a retry rate is $10^{-14}$. The performance measure used depends on the application. For example UBER is much more important for bank transactions than for multimedia applications ran on PC. All performance measures depend on a symbol length, number of correctable errors, and symbol error statistics. On the other hand symbol error statistics depend on the read channel error event distribution.

## References

1. R. L. Adler, D. Coppersmith, and M. Hassner, "Algorithms for sliding block codes: An application of symbolic dynamics to information theory," *IEEE Trans. Inform. Theory,* vol. IT-29, pp. 5–22, Jan. 1983.
2. D. Cahalan and K. Chopra, "Effects of MR head track profile characteristics on servo performance," *IEEE Trans. Magn.,* vol. 30, no. 6, Nov. 1994.
3. R. D. Cideciyan, F. Dolivo, R. Hermann, W. Hirt, and W. Schott, "A PRML system for digital magnetic recording," *IEEE J. Sel. Areas in Commun.,* vol. 10, no. 1, pp. 38–56, Jan. 1992.
4. J. M. Cioffi, W. L. Abbott, H. K. Thapar, C. M. Melas, and K. D. Fisher, "Adaptive equalization in magnetic-disk storage channels," *IEEE Comm. Magazine,* pp. 14–20, Feb. 1990.
5. E. T. Cohen, "On the implementation of Reed–Solomon decoders," Ph.D. dissertation, University of California, Berkeley, 1983.
6. E. Eleftheriou and R. Cideciyan, "On codes satisfying $M$th order running digital sum constraints," *IEEE Trans. Inform. Theory,* vol. 37, pp. 1294–1313, Sept. 1991.
7. G. D. Forney, "Maximum-likelihood sequence estimation of digital sequences in the presence of intersymbol interference," *IEEE Trans. Inform. Thoery,* vol. 18., no. 3, pp. 363–378, May 1972.
8. L. Fredrickson *et al.,* "Digital servo processing in the Venus PRML read/write channel," *IEEE Trans. Magn.,* vol. 33, pp. 2616–2619, Sept. 1997.
9. M. Hassner, U. Schwiegelshohn, and S. Winograd, "On-the-fly error correction in data storage channels," *IEEE Trans. Magn.,* vol. 31, pp. 1149–1154, March 1995.
10. R. Hermann, "Volterra model of digital magnetic saturation recording channels," *IEEE Trans. Magn.,* vol. MAG-26, no. 5, 2125–2127, Sept. 1990.
11. K. A. S. Immink, "Spectral null codes," *IEEE Trans. Magn.,* vol. 26, pp. 1130–1135, March 1990.
12. K. A. S. Immink, "Runlength-limited sequences," *Proc. IEEE,* vol. 78, pp. 1745–1759, Nov. 1990.
13. K. A. S. Immink and L. Patrovics, "Performance assessment of DC-free multimode codes," *IEEE Trans. Commun.,* vol. 45, pp. 293–299, March 1997.
14. K. A. S. Immink, *Codes for Mass Data Storage Systems,* Essen, Germany: Shannon Foundation Publishers, 1999.
15. H. Kobayashi and D. T. Tang, "Application of partial-response channel coding to magnetic recording systems," *Bell J. Res. and Develop.,* July 1970.
16. H. Kobayashi, "Correlative level coding and maximum-likelihood decoding," *IEEE Trans. Inform. Theory,* vol. IT-17, pp. 586–594, Sept. 1971.
17. S. Lin, *An Introduction to Error-Correcting Codes.* Englewood Cliffs, NJ: Prentice-Hall, 1970.
18. Y. Lin and R. Wood, "An estimation technique for accurately modeling the magnetic recording channel including nonlinearities," *IEEE Trans. Magn.,* vol. MAG-25, no. 5, pp. 4058–4060, Sept. 1989.
19. R. Karabed and B. H. Marcus, "Sliding-block coding for input-restricted channels," *IEEE Trans. Inform. Theory,* vol. 34, pp. 2–26, Jan. 1988.
20. H. Kimura, T. Nishiya, T. Nara, and T. Komotsu, "A digital servo architecture with 8.8 bit resolution of position error signal for disk drives," in *IEEE Globecom 97,* Phoenix, AZ, 1997, pp. 1268–1271.

21. B. Marcus, P. Siegel, and J. K. Wolf, "Finite-state modulation codes for data storage," *IEEE J. Select. Areas Commun.,* vol. 10, no. 1, pp. 5–37, Jan. 1992.

22. B. H. Marcus, "Sofic systems and encoding data," *IEEE Trans. Inform. Theory,* vol. IT-31, pp. 366–377, May 1985.

23. C. Monti, and G. Pierobon, "Codes with multiple spectral null at zero frequency," *IEEE Trans. Inform. Theory,* vol. 35, no. 2, pp. 463–472, March 1989.

24. A. Patapoutian, "Optimal burst frequency derivation for head positioning," *IEEE Trans. Magn.,* vol. 32, no. 5, pt. 1, pp. 3899–3901, Sept. 1996.

25. A. Patapoutian, "Signal space analysis of head positioning formats," *IEEE Trans. Magn.,* vol. 33, no.3, pp. 2412–2418, May 1997.

26. A. Patapoutian, "Analog-to-digital converter algorithms for position error signal estimators," *IEEE Trans. Magn.,* vol. 36, no. 1, pt. 2, pp. 345–400, Jan. 2000.

27. D. E. Reed, W. G. Bliss, L. Du, and M. Karsanbhai, "Digital servo demodulation in a digital read channel," *IEEE Trans. Magn.,* vol. 34, pp. 13–16, Jan. 1998.

28. I. S. Reed and G. Solomon, "Polynomial codes over certain finite fields," *J. Soc. Indust. Appl. Math.,* vol. 8, pp. 300–304, 1960.

29. C. M. Riggle and S. G. McCarthy, "Design of error correction systems for disk drives," *IEEE Trans. Magn.,* vol. 34 , 4 pt. 2, pp. 2362–2371, July 1998.

30. A. H. Sacks, "Position signal generation in magnetic disk drives," Ph.D. dissertation, Carnegie-Mellon University, Pittsburgh, PA, 1995.

31. A. H. Sacks, M. Bodson, and W. Messner, "Advanced methods for repeatable runout compensation [disc drives]," *IEEE Trans. Magn.,* vol. 31, no. 2 , pp. 1031–1036, March 1995.

32. Y. Tang and C. Tsang, "A technique for measuring nonlinear bit shift," vol. 27, no. 6, pp. 5326–5318, Nov. 1991.

33. Y. Tang, R. L. Galbraith, J. D. Coker, P. C. Arnett, and R. W. Wood, "Precompesation value determination in a PRML channel," *IEEE Trans. Magn.,* vol. 32, no. 3, pp. 2013–1014, May 1996.

34. G. T. Tuttle *et al.,* "A 130 Mb/s PRML read/write channel with digital-servo detection," in *Proc. IEEE Int. Solid State Circuits Conf. 96,* San Francisco, CA, Feb. 8–10, 1996, pp. 64–65.

35. J. L. Sonntag and B. Vasic, "Implementation and bench characterization of a read channel with parity check post processor," TMRC 2000, Santa Clara, CA, Aug. 2000.

36. S. B. Wicker, *Error Control Systems for Digital Communication and Storage.* Englewood Cliffs, NJ: Prentice-Hall, 1995.

37. D. L. Whiting, "Bit-serial Reed–Solomon decoders in VLSI," Ph.D. dissertation, California Inst. Tech., Pasadena, 1984.

# 34.3   Adaptive Equalization and Timing Recovery

*Pervez M. Aziz*

Adaptive signal processing plays a crucial role in storage systems. Proper detection of the readback signal by a Viterbi detector assumes that the signal has the right gain, is equalized to the partial response, and is sampled at the proper sampling instances. In this section, the focus is mainly on equalization and timing recovery. Some of the basic algorithms employed in equalization and timing recovery are reviewed. Various architectures and algorithms are presented, which have been used in state-of-the-art read channels. Finally, comparative performance data for some of these architectures are presented.

## Adaptive Equalization

What is equalization? It is the act of shaping the read back magnetic recording signal to look like a target signal specified by the partial response (PR). The equalized signal is made to look like the target signal in both the time and frequency domain. In this subsection, various equalization architectures and strategies are reviewed, which have been popular historically and still being used in present day read channels. A quick review of the well-known least mean square (LMS) algorithm used for adaptive equalizers is also provided. Finally, the performance implications of selecting several different equalizer architectures is explored. This performance is measured in terms of bit error rate (BER) at the output of the read channel's Viterbi detector.

## Equalization Architectures and Strategies

In PRML channels the read back signal will be sampled at some point in the data path for further digital signal processing. A continuous time filter (CTF) with a low-pass characteristic will be present as an anti-aliasing filter [1] prior to the sampling operation so that high-frequency noise is not aliased into the signal band. This same CTF may also play a role in equalizing the read back signal to the target partial response. Various architectures can be used to perform the required equalization. The equalizer architecture can consist of a CTF, a finite impulse response filter (FIR), or both. The CTF parameters may be fixed, programmable, or adaptive. The FIR filter coefficients may be fixed, programmable, or adaptive. In addition, the FIR operation may occur in the sampled data analog domain or digital domain. Following equalization, the data are detected using a Viterbi detector. Of course, quantization by an analog-to-digital converter (ADC) occurs at some point before the Viterbi detector.

Figure 34.11 shows some examples of various equalizer architecture configurations. The first architecture (Type 1) consists of a CTF-only equalizer. The CTF is comprised of an all-pole low-pass filter section whose purpose is to reject high-frequency noise for anti-aliasing. One key parameter in the CTF is its low-pass bandwidth determined by its cutoff or corner frequency, $f_c$. The type of CTF, $f_c$, and its order (or the number of poles it contains) will determine its low-pass rolloff characteristic. If the CTF is expected to take part in equalization, it must also be able to provide some boost and does so by typically having one or two real zeros at some frequency $f_z$ in its transfer function. These parameters are noted in the figure.

The second architecture (Type 2) is one where both the CTF and an analog FIR are involved in performing equalization. The third architecture (Type 3) is an analog FIR-only architecture in that the CTF design does not consist of any zeros, i.e., its main role is to perform anti-aliasing and not provide any boost for equalization. Finally, the last architecture (Type 4) is one where a CTF and FIR are both involved in equalization except that the FIR operation is done digitally.

In general, there is a clear trade-off between the degree of flexibility of the equalizer and implementation complexity. The read-back signal characteristics change across the disk surface as manifested by somewhat

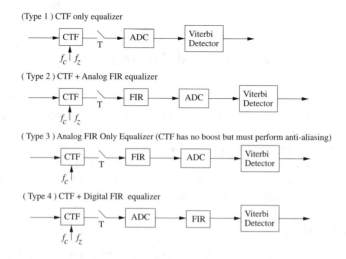

**FIGURE 34.11**   Various equalizer architectures.

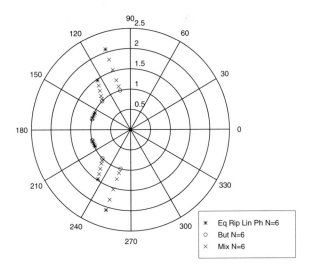

**FIGURE 34.12**  Normalized pole locations for sixth-order Butterworth and equiripple linear phase filters as well as mixed filters.

different channel bit densities (*cbd*s) or $pw_{50}/T$. Consequently, programmability of the equalizer parameters is a mimimum requirement for optimum performance. The signal or some of the equalizer parameters themselve may change with chip ageing and temperature variations [2]. Therefore, it is often desirable for some of the equalizer parameters to be continually adaptive to be able to compensate for these effects.

### CTF Configurations

Two common types of CTFs, which have been used in read channels are Butterworth filters and equiripple linear phase filters. Butterworth filters have a maximally flat  magnitude response but nonlinear phase response. Equiripple linear phase filters, as their name implies, have linear phase and constant group delay over the passband [3,4]. For a given order, the Butterworth filters will have sharper rolloff characteristics. One could also consider *mixed* filters whose poles are chosen to lie some percentage of the distance in between the poles of a Butterworth and equiripple linear phase filter. Figure 34.12 shows the normalized pole location on the *s* plane for a sixth-order Butterworth, a sixth-order equiripple linear phase filter, as well as the poles for various sixth order mixed filters, which are 25%, 50%, 75%, and 90% away from the poles of the equiripple filter. Note that the Butterworth poles lie on the unit circle. Figure 34.13 shows the corresponding magnitude responses for the filters, while Fig. 34.14 shows the group delay responses. As can be observed, the Butterworth has the sharpest lowpass rolloff and the equiripple filter has the shallowest rolloff but constant group delay over the passband.

The CTF parameters can be programmable or adaptive [5,6]; however, most CTFs that have been used in actual read channels have had programmable bandwidth and boosts any adaptivity being left to the FIR. Adaptive CTF systems face some challenging issues as discussed in [7]. Also, some work has been done to analytically determine the optimum CTF transfer functions [8,9].

The performance of equalizers involving several CTF configurations will be compared: fourth-order Butterworth (*b4*), sixth-order Butterworth (*b6*), seventh-order equiripple linear phase (*e7*) all with single zeros. We also examine a seventh-order equiripple linear phase CTF with two zeros (*e7tz*). The linear phase of the all pole section is kept in the *e7tz* filter. Another filter considered is the fourth-order 50% mixed filter with one zero (*em4*).

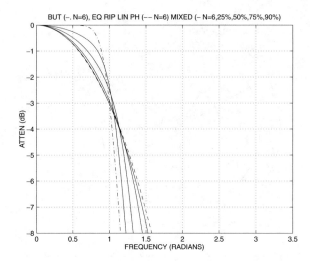

**FIGURE 34.13**    Magnitude response for sixth-order Butterworth and equiripple linear phase filters as well as mixed filters.

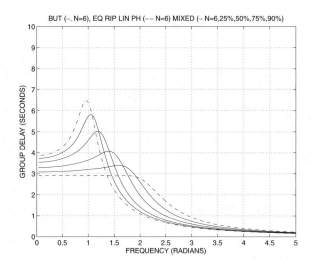

**FIGURE 34.14**    Group delay response for sixth-order Butterworth and equiripple linear phase filters as well as mixed filters.

## FIR Filter and the LMS Algorithm

The FIR filter is important for equalization. Whether implemented as an analog sampled data filter or a digital filter the FIR filter produces output samples $y(n)$ in terms of input samples $x(n)$ as

$$y(n) = \sum_{k=0}^{L-1} h(k)x(n-k) \qquad (34.3)$$

where $h(k)$ are the FIR filter tap weights. As noted, it is very desirable for the FIR to be adaptive. The FIR taps are adapted based on the well-known LMS algorithm [10,11]. Other adaptive algorithms can also be found in [12] and [13].

The basic idea is to minimize the mean squared error with respect to some desired or ideal signal. Let the desired or ideal signal be $\hat{y}(n)$ in which case the error is $e(n) = y(n) - \hat{y}(n)$. This minimization is achieved by adjusting the tap value in the direction opposite to the derivative (with respect to the tap values) of the expected value of the mean squared error. Dispensing with the expected value leads to the LMS or stochastic gradient algorithm. The stochastic gradient for the $k$th tap weight is

$$\Delta(k,n) = -\frac{\partial}{\partial h(k)}(e^2(n)) = -2e(n)\frac{\partial \hat{e}(n)}{\partial h(k)} = -2e(n)\left[\frac{\partial y(n)}{\partial h(k)} - \hat{y}(k)\frac{\partial \hat{y}(n)}{\partial h(k)}\right]$$

$$= -2e(n)\frac{\partial y(n)}{\partial h(k)} \tag{34.4}$$

where the partial derivative of $\hat{y}(n)$ with respect to $h(k)$ is zero. We can now expand $y(n)$ as in Eq. (34.3) to further obtain

$$\Delta(k,n) = -2e(n)x(n-k) \tag{34.5}$$

The gradient would actually be scaled by some tap weight update gain $t_{ug}$ to give the following tap update equation:

$$h(k,n+1) = h(k,n) - 2t_{ug}e(n)x(n-k) \tag{34.6}$$

The choice of this update gain depends on several factors: (a) it should not be too large so as to cause the tap adaptation loop to become unstable, (b) it should be large enough that the taps converge within a reasonable amount of time, (c) it should be small enough that after convergence the adaptation noise is small and does not degrade the BER performance. In practice, during drive optimization in the factory the adaptation could take place in two steps, initially with higher update gain and then with lower update gain. During the factory optimization different converged taps will be obtained for different radii on the disk surface. Starting from factory optimized values means that the tap weights do not have to adapt extremely fast and so allows the use of lower update gains during drive operation. Also, this means that the tap weights need not all adapt every clock cycle—instead a round-robin approach can be taken, which allows for sharing of the adaptation hardware across the various taps. A simpler implementation can also be obtained by using the signed LMS algorithm whereby the tap update equation is based on using 2- or 3-level quantized version of $x(n-k)$. For read channel applications, this can be done without hardly any loss in performance.

A few other issues should be emphasized about the adaptive FIR. During a read event, the FIR filter is usually adapted after the initial gain and timing recovery operations are performed over a preamble field. Nevertheless, during the rest of the read event, the FIR filter equalizes the signal at the same time that the gain and timing loops are operating. The adaptive gain loop uses an automatic gain control (AGC) block to apply the correct gain to the signal to achieve the desired partial response target values. Likewise the adaptive timing recovery loop works to adjust the sampling phase to achieve the desired PR target values. It is necessary to minimize the interaction between these adaptive loops. The FIR filter will typically have one tap as a "main" tap, which is fixed to minimize its interaction with the gain loop. Another tap such as the one preceding or following the main tap can be fixed (but allowed to be programmable) to minimize interaction with the timing loop [14]. In some situations it may be advantageous to have additional constraints to minimize the interaction with the timing loop [15].

## Performance Characterization

The performance of various equalizer architectures based on bit error rate simulations can now be characterized. The equalizer types (with reference to Fig. 34.11) actually simulated are of Types 2 (CTF + analog FIR) and 3 (anti-aliasing CTF + analog FIR). One can consider the case where there are very few taps as an approximation of the Type 1 (CTF only) equalizer. Although many actual read channel architectures do use digital FIRs (Type 4), we do not consider this type for simulations here. Although a digital FIR filter may be cost effective for implementation given a particular technology, it does have two disadvantages compared with the analog FIR. With the analog FIR, quantization noise is added *after* equalization and so is not enhanced through the equalizer whereas for the digital FIR the quantization noise does pass through the equalizer and could be enhanced. Consequently, fewer quantization levels can be used and this results in reduced chip area and power dissipation with the analog FIR. Also, the digital FIR is likely to have more latency in producing its final output and this extra latency may not hurt significantly but is nonetheless not beneficial for the timing loop.

### Simulation Environment and Optimization Procedure

The simulation environment, including two system simulation models, and the optimization methodology by which the optimum performance is obtained for each equalizer architecture can now be described. Finally, BER results quantifying the performance of the various architectures are presented.

To obtain a simulation bound for the performance of the best possible equalizer we use the system of Fig 34.15. The signal + noise is fractionally sampled at a rate of $T/5$ and filtered with a fractionally spaced FIR filter equalizer, which equalizes the signal to an EPR4 target. The channel bit period is $T$. The output of the equalizer is then sampled at the channel bit rate of $T$ and these samples are presented to the EPR4 Viterbi. The FIR has 125 taps (spanning $25T$). The FIR tap weights are adapted from zero starting values using the LMS algorithm. There is no quantization, AGC, or timing recovery. Therefore, the performance is solely determined by the noise.

Pseudo random data are 16/17 modulation encoded to generate a signal at various *cbd*s based on a Lorentzian pulse shape. For each *cbd*, the SNR needed by the "ideal" $T/5$ oversampled system of Fig 34.15 to produce a BER of $10^{-5}$ is determined. SNR is defined as the ratio of the isolated pulse peak to rms noise in the Nyquist band. The (*cbd*, SNR) pairs are used for performing simulations with the practical system of Fig. 34.16, which accurately models an actual read channel chip and a version of the $T/5$ system where the equalized samples are quantized before being detected with the Viterbi detector. Signals at

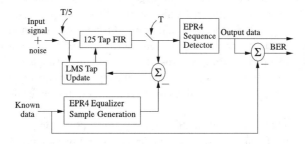

**FIGURE 34.15** Block diagram of system with five times oversampled equalizer.

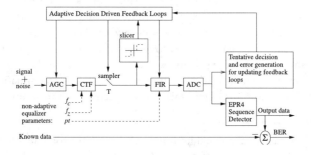

**FIGURE 34.16** Block diagram and simulation model of practical symbol rate sampled read channel system.

several *cbds* or *PW50/T* values 1.9, 2.4, and 2.8 are examined. The SNRs needed for 1e-5 BER for these densities are 21.66, 22.90, and 24.70 dB, respectively.

Let us now describe the simulation model for the actual read channel system. A block diagram of this system is shown in Fig. 34.16. The system consists of AGC, CTF, *T* rate sampled analog FIR equalizer, ADC quantizing the equalizer output, and an EPR4 Viterbi detector. Three decision directed adaptive loops are used: LMS tap update loop, AGC loop, and digital PLL (DPLL) timing recovery loop. Note that in this practical system the adaptive feedback loops are updated not based on known data but on tentative or preliminary decisions made by the read channel. The algorithm used for the tap update is the signed LMS algorithm as implied by the 3-level slicer shown in the figure.

Using the practical system model, BER simulations are performed for the various CTFs mentioned earlier and FIRs of various number of taps. The simulations are performed with this realistic system using the SNRs mentioned earlier. This allows the calculation of the BER degradation of the realistic system with respect to the *T*/5 system for a given *cbd* and SNR.

For each CTF type, *cbd*, and FIR length  we simulate the BER of the system across a space of equalizer parameters $f_c, f_z$ (which determines CTF boost), and the fixed programmable tap of the FIR, which is labeled as *pt* in Fig. 34.16. The parameters are varied across the following ranges: $f_c$ is varied between 20% and 38% of the channel bit rate, $f_z$ is varied to provide boosts between 2.6 and 8.6 dB, while the programmable tap is varied between 40% and 60% of the main tap value. For CTFs with two zeros the zeros are adjusted such that the total boost is in the above range. For the 10-tap FIR the fourth tap is chosen to be the fixed main tap while for the 6- and 3-tap filters the second tap is chosen as the main tap. For the other taps, the analog tap range was kept to be relatively large at ±80% of the main tap value. In a real system, one would choose smaller ranges based on tap settings fitting into the smaller range, which produced good results. For the equalizer configuration involving the FIR only equalizer, FIRs with 4–20 taps are examined. The programmable tap *pt* is re-optimized for each *cbd* and FIR filter length.

### Results

Before comparing BER results across different equalizers, some results from the equalizer optimization procedure are illustrated. Figure 34.17 shows a contour plot of the BER obtained with the *b4* CTF with a 10-tap FIR at a *cbd* of 2.4 and a SNR, which gives close to $10^{-5}$ BER. The horizontal axis is CTF corner frequency ($f_c$) and the vertical axis is CTF boost in decibel. The plot is for one particular value of the programmable FIR tap *pt*. The numbers on the contour plot are $10 \times \log10(\text{BER})$ so that $10^{-5}$ BER would correspond to 100. We observe that good BERs result for a large range of boosts and  range of $f_c$'s centered

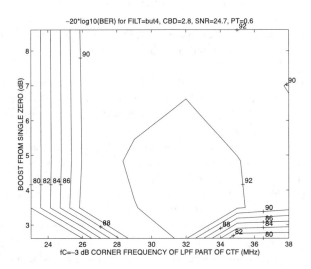

**FIGURE 34.17**  Boost bandwidth optimization.

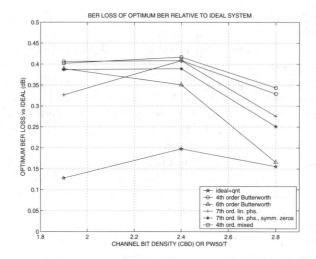

**FIGURE 34.18**   CTF BER performance degradation with respect to oversampled ideal system vs. *cbd* with 10-tap FIR.

in the plot. Upon examining contour plots for all the CTFs, we concluded that the *b*4 CTF achieves good BERs for $f_c$'s typically in the center of the range explored, while the *b*6 CTF the performance is better at somewhat higher $f_c$'s; however, the linear phase CTFs achieve good BERs at very low $f_c$'s. This is because CTFs with worse rolloff characteristics require a smaller $f_c$ to provide enough attenuation at the Nyquist frequency for anti-aliasing. We observe that the BER performance is mostly insensitive to the boost. This is because the adaptive FIR is able to provide any remaining equalization needed. In practice, there will be a trade-off in how much boost the CTF is able to provide and the corresponding analog tap ranges required by the FIR to provide any necessary remaining equalization—the more equalization the FIR has to provide, the larger tap ranges it will require.

Now compare the BER performance of various Type 2 (CTF + analog FIR) equalizers. Figure 34.18 shows the BER performance of different CTFs with a 10-tap FIR. The horizontal axis is *cbd* and the vertical axis is the BER degradation (in dB) of the optimum BER with respect to the BER of $10^{-5}$ achieved by the ideal oversampled system using the *T*/5 equalizer. The performance of the CTFs is similar across all *cbd*s—they perform within 0.15 dB of one another. All perform within 0.25–0.4 dB of the $10^{-5}$ BER achieved by the *T*/5 system. The linear phase of the seventh-order CTFs does not necessarily yield superior performance. A final comment is needed about the plot—one should not expect a fixed or monotonic relationship between *cbd* and the practical system BER in this plot. This is due to the finite resolution of the equalizer optimization search and the fact that BERs are based on observing 100 (vs. even larger number) bit errors.

As noted, the previous results were with a 10-tap FIR. Further simulations of the various CTFs with a 6-tap or even 3-tap show that the *optimum* BER performance is not very different than that with a 10-tap FIR. These results are presented in Fig. 34.19 where the BER degradation (again with respect to the $10^{-5}$ achieved by the ideal system) of the optimum BER obtained for the various CTFs is plotted versus the number of FIR taps for *cbd* = 2.4. This initially appears to be a surprising result, but this is not unreasonable when one observes that with fewer number of taps, a large percentage of the CTF programmings result in poor BER performance. This effect is shown in Fig. 34.20, which plots the percentage of CTF programmings (with respect to the total number of programmings producing convergent tap weights) producing BER worse than $4 \times 10^{-5}$. With more taps the percentage of poor programmings decreases. Thus, FIR filters with a few taps, with appropriately optimized CTF settings, can perform as well as a FIR with 10 taps; however, the difficulty in keeping the nonadaptive CTF parameters correct in the presence of realistic device conditions makes such a FIR with few taps impractical to use.

Finally, examine the performance of Type 3 equalizers. Here, the anti-aliasing CTF is a seventh-order linear phase filter. The performance of this equalizer is a function of the number of FIR taps. The BER

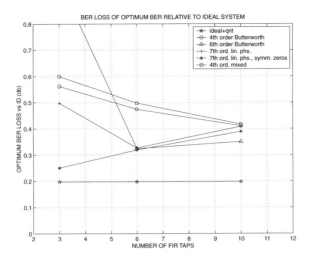

**FIGURE 34.19** CTF BER degradation with respect to oversampled ideal system vs. number of taps (*cbd* = 2.4).

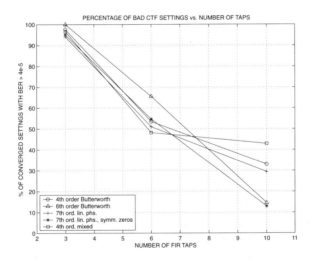

**FIGURE 34.20** Percentage of bad CTF settings vs. number of taps (*cbd* = 2.4).

performance are shown in Fig. 34.21. The vertical axis is again the degradation with respect to the ideal system BER of $10^{-5}$. The programmable tap of the FIR is optimized to yield the best performance in each case. The main tap is placed roughly in the center. There is benefit in increasing the number of taps from 4 to 6 to 10. Beyond 10 taps, however, there is more latency in the timing loop as the main tap position is more delayed. This causes increased phase errors to enter the timing loop and outweighs the benefit of enhanced equalization obtained with more taps. Although one could increase the number of taps while keeping the main tap location mostly fixed, the FIR will then not be able to cancel the precursor ISI as well with a CTF, which is not involved in equalization. Also shown (dashed plot) is the performance of a Type 2 equalizer (CTF, with its corner frequency optimized and with an optimized zero included to provide boost). Clearly the Type 2 equalizer outperforms the Type 3 equalizer.

### Actual Equalizer Architectures

Various equalization architectures and examined their performance have been considered. Let us now examine what actual architectures read channel vendors are using. Table 34.1 summarizes some of the most commonly used architectures. For example, Agere Systems (*Note*: storage products unit of AT&T was

**TABLE 34.1**  Examples of Equalizers Implemented on Read Channel Chips

| Company | CTF | | | FIR | | | Type (Fig. 34.11) | Ref/Yr | Comments |
|---------|-----|-----|-------|------|-----------|---------------|-------------------|--------|----------|
|         | Type | Order | Zeros | Taps | Adaptive? | Analog/Digital | | | |
| Agere | But | 4th | 2 | 10 | yes | analog | 2 | [16], 1995 | 8 adaptive taps |
| Cirrus | EqRip | 7th | 2 | 3 | no | digital | 2 | [17], 1995 | — |
| Cirrus | EqRip | 7th | 2 | 5 | no | digital | 2 | [18], 1996 | — |
| Datapath | EqRip | 7th | 2 | N/A | N/A | N/A | 1 | [19], 1997 | No FIR |
| Marvell | EqRip | 7th | ? | 7 | yes | digital | 2 | [20], 1997 | — |

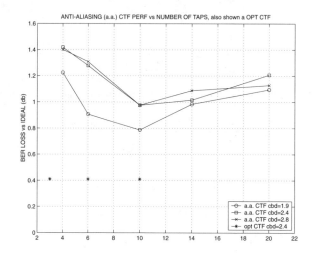

**FIGURE 34.21**  BER degradation with respect to oversampled ideal system vs. number of taps with anti-aliasing CTF (no boost).

spun off to Lucent Technologies in 1996 and again spun off to Agere Systems in 2001) has been using a Type 2 architecture with a fourth-order Butterworth CTF and 10-tap analog FIR. The CTF has a programmable corner frequency and zero for providing boost. This architecture is still in place now. Most other vendors have used Type 4 architectures (digital FIR) but with seventh-order equiripple linear phase filters. The linear phase filters typically have two programmable zeros to provide boost. In the examples of the Cirrus equalizers, the digital FIR does not appear to be adaptive. Some vendors such as Cirrus and Marvell seem to have increased the number of FIR taps or the number of adaptive (vs. only programmable) taps as the years have gone by. The Datapath equalizer cited is one of the few examples of an all CTF equalizer.

### Conclusions

The performance of various CTF + adaptive analog FIR (Type 2) equalizers in equalizing a signal to an EPR4 target has been quantified. It is shown that regardless of the number of taps in the FIR and CTF type, the BER performance of the CTF + FIR equalizers is approximately the same if the optimum fixed equalizer parameters (CTF corner frequency, boost, FIR fixed tap) are chosen.

Therefore, the choice of CTF type should be based on other constraints such as area, power, speed (data rate), as well the benefit of having one less analog block. It has also been shown that as the number of taps is increased, the space of CTF parameter programmings producing BERs close to the optimum increases significantly. Therefore, one can trade-off the cost of the FIR filter versus required accuracy in the CTF setting and the sensitivity of the resulting performance.

The performance of Type 3 equalizers consisting of a $T$ spaced FIR filter with only a Nyquist anti-aliasing CTF was also examined. Also, the Type 3 equalizer cannot approach the performance of a system whose CTF is involved in equalization and is optimized. Therefore, to make a valid comparison between FIR and CTF equalizers, one must include a reasonably optimum CTF prior to the FIR.

It has been demonstrated that a wide variety of optimized CTF + FIR equalizers can perform within 0.25 dB of the quantized system using the oversampled $T/5$ equalizer. As this 0.25 dB includes performance losses due to AGC and timing recovery, there is very little space left for improved equalization with any other equalizer architecture.

## Adaptive Timing Recovery

In storage systems such as PRML magnetic recording channels a clock is used to sample the analog waveform to provide discrete samples to symbol-by-symbol (s/s) and sequence (Viterbi) detectors. Improper synchronization of these discrete samples with respect to those expected by the detectors for a given partial response will degrade the eventual BER of the system. The goal of adaptive timing recovery is to produce samples for the s/s or sequence detector, which are at the desired sampling instances for the partial response being used. In this subsection, the basics of timing recovery as well as commonly used algorithms for timing recovery in magnetic recording channels are reviewed. Two classes of timing recovery algorithms are presented: symbol rate VCO-based and interpolation-based algorithms. After a discussion of the trade-offs between these two types of algorithms, the focus will be on the traditional symbol rate VCO algorithms for the rest of the discussion. One of these timing recovery algorithms from first principles will be derived. An analytical framework for comparing the performance of such algorithms using timing loop noise induced output jitter as the performance criterion is provided. Finally, quantitative comparative performance data for some of these algorithms based on the jitter analysis as well as simulations, which measure timing loop jitter and BER, is provided.

### Timing Recovery Basics

#### Symbol Rate VCO versus Interpolative Timing Recovery

Timing recovery schemes, which have been considered for magnetic recording channels, can be broadly classified into two groups: traditional symbol rate VCO-based schemes and interpolative schemes, [21,22], which sample slightly above the symbol rate. The key difference between the schemes is that the symbol rate VCO scheme adapts or adjusts the phase and frequency of the sampling clock to produce the desired samples whereas interpolative timing recovery samples the analog waveform using a uniformly sampled clock to produce samples from which the desired samples are interpolated.

Figure 34.22 shows high-level block diagrams of both approaches. Let us describe the VCO-based approach first. For the sake of the discussion the VCO approach is shown with an analog FIR equalizer. Consequently the sampling occurs at the input of the FIR equalizer. The noisy equalized output $y(k)$ must be used to detect the timing error present in these samples. This is done using a phase detector. The phase detector transforms an amplitude error in the samples to $\Delta(k)$, which is related to the desired change in the sampling phase. The phase detector output is also called the timing gradient.

The phase detector may require the use of the noisy equalized samples $y(k)$ or other signals derived from it. The other signals may be the preliminary or tentative decisions $\hat{d}(k)$s, decision directed estimates of $y(k)$, which are $\hat{y}(k)$ or other signals. These auxiliary signals are generated by the block labeled "Signal Generation for Phase Detector." The $y(k)$s are used to generate preliminary (tentative) decisions $\hat{d}(k)$ and an error signal $e(k)$, and a decision directed estimate of the ideal equalized sample value, $\hat{y}(k)$.

The phase detector output is filtered by a loop filter $T(z)$. The loop filter $T(z)$ is usually a second order DPLL with an additional delay term $z^{-L}$, which models any latency through the timing loop. Such latency arises from the group delay of the FIR, computations in the DPLL, calculating the signals needed by the phase detector, etc. The filtered phase detector output is the input to a VCO, which causes the actual

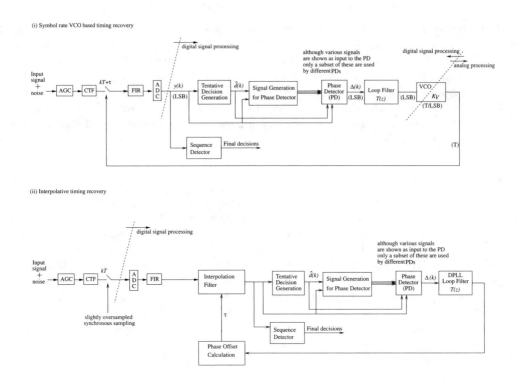

**FIGURE 34.22** (i) Symbol rate VCO-based timing recovery loop. (ii) Interpolative timing recovery loop.

sampling phase $\tau$ to change. The VCO is an analog circuit under digital control. The analog part can be a phase mixer, which is capable of adjusting the timing phase by small fractions of $T$ where $T$ is the channel bit period. In such a case, the VCO acts as an amplitude to time converter and so modeled as a simple gain. To give physical meaning to the system, the units of the signals are noted: the equalized output after quantization by the ADC is in amplitude units of LSBs, the timing gradient $\Delta(k)$ or phase detector output is proportional to an amplitude error and so is also in LSBs. The loop filter provides a frequency dependent gain, so the input of the VCO is LSBs. The VCO has a gain of $K_V$ in units of T/LSB, so the output of the VCO has units of time, $T$. The VCO gain can also be thought of as a clock update gain. For the specific system we will consider later, the phase mixer can make changes in the sampling phase in steps of 0, $\pm 1$, $\pm 2$ $T/64$ or more. The choice of this factor of 64 is such that the quantization of timing phase adjustment is well below the ADC quantization noise floor.

Let us now describe the interpolative timing recovery loop of Fig. 34.22. As noted, with this scheme, an asynchronous clock is used to sample the input to the ADC after which a FIR filter performs the necessary equalization. The asynchronous equalized samples are now used to interpolate samples at the correct sampling instances dictated by the partial response. This is done with the interpolation filter, which can be thought of as a filter which delays its input by an amount $\tau$, which is a fraction of the channel bit period $T$ [21]. Such an interpolation filter's transfer function is $z^{-\tau}$. The samples $y(k)$ at the output of the interpolation filter drive the phase detector and loop filter as in the VCO-based timing loop. The loop filter output after being processed by the phase offset calculator produces the required sampling phase change. For good operation, the loop must be able to produce a large number of fractional delays (such as 32 or 64) and correspondingly would require as many such filters for each of these delays. Figure 34.22 noted that the asynchronous sampling was performed at slightly above the Nyquist rate. The reasons for this is to accomodate a frequency offset between the written signal and the clock used to perform the asynchronous sampling. The magnitude of this frequency offset is usually limited in practical systems to 1% or less and so very little oversampling is required; however, oversampling ratios of up to 5% produce some improvement in performance by reducing the sensitivity of the aliasing with respect to the phase of the asynchronous sampling clock.

The advantages of the ITR-based timing loops are that they are all digital timing loops, which are more amenable for design, verification, and less susceptible to process variations. Also, for the ITR timing loop, the delays in the equalization filter and ADC do not contribute to the timing loop latency; however, the interpolation filter is not an extremely small piece of hardware and could make the ITR timing loop consume more chip area and power than a VCO-based loop. Practical design issues with the ITR-based system such as adaptation of the equalizer based on asynchronous samples [22] and design of the interpolation filter, have not been discussed. From a performance point of view, there is no significant difference between the ITR- or VCO-based approaches as indicated by simulation results in [21]. This also seems reasonable based on our observation in the subsection on adaptive equalization where it was noted that a read channel system with practical equalization and timing recovery performed within a few tenths of a decibel of the corresponding "ideal" system. Therefore, the choice between all digital ITR-based system or a conventional VCO-based system needs to be based on the relative merits of both systems from an ease of design and area/power standpoint.

### Timing Loop Modes

Let us now further describe the operation of the entire timing loop. The entire timing recovery process occurs in several steps: zero phase start (ZPS), acquistion mode (ACQ), and tracking mode (TRK). During the ZPS and ACQ modes the disk controller must guarantee that the read channel is reading a preamble signal known to the timing loop. The preamble signal for almost all magnetic recording channels is a $2T$ pattern, which is the periodic data sequence "…11001100…." The purpose of the ZPS is to obtain a good estimate of the initial phase error between the readback signal and the desired samples for the $2T$ pattern. Once this estimate is obtained the sampling clock's phase is changed by the calculated amount to approximate the desired sampling phase. The next step is the ACQ process where the sampling phase error is further reduced and the frequency offset between the input signal and the sampling clock is compensated for to produce even more accurately sampled preamble samples. Because the preamble is a known signal pattern, timing recovery is facilitated in that the preliminary decisions can be obtained more reliably with less loop latency. Consequently, high loop filter update gains can be used. Once this initial acquisition is complete, the timing loop transitions into a TRK, which is intended for tracking slow variations in timing. In this mode the signal may contain any excess preamble as well as random data, but no a priori assumption about the signal is made. The tentative decisions in the TRK mode are obtained with more loop latency and are not as reliable. The loop filter update gains are correspondingly lower. A summary of the operation described is provided in Fig. 34.23. More fine gradations of the loop filter gains (beyond the high/medium/low gains shown in Fig. 34.23 can be made across ACQ and TRK to produce improved performance [23]. Of course, there is a trade-off between improved performance and somewhat enhanced circuit complexity so that one would choose to increase the complexity only, until diminishing returns in performance is reached.

| Mode Name | ZPS | Acquisition (ACQ) | Tracking (TRK) |
|---|---|---|---|
| Assumed Data | Preamble | Preamble | Excess preamble / regular random data |
| Loop Filter Gains | Zero | High / medium | Medium / low |

**FIGURE 34.23** Timing loop operational modes: zero phase start, acquisition, and tracking.

## Symbol Rate Timing Recovery Schemes

Now consider in more detail the traditional symbol rate VCO-based schemes. A decision directed baud or symbol rate timing recovery algorithm was first proposed by Mueller and Muller [24]. Their technique relied on the concept of a "timing function." $f(\tau)$, which generates the proper amount of timing phase adjustment for a given phase shift, $\tau$, in the signal. The function should be monotonic, and have a zero output for zero sampling phase error. The Mueller and Muller (MM) technique provides a means to derive a timing function from a linear combination of samples of the channel's impulse response. In practice, one can design timing gradients where the expected value equals the suitably defined timing function. The timing gradients can be used to obtain the corresponding phase adjustment signal. In some magnetic recording systems using a PR4 target, a MM timing gradient with a second order DPLL was used to produce the necessary timing phase updates [8,25].

One can also derive timing recovery schemes based on other criteria such as the minimum mean square error (MMSE) criterion. MMSE methods seek to minimize the expectation of the square of an error signal $e(k,\tau)$ with respect to the timing phase. The error signal is obtained by subtracting the received equalized samples $y(k,\tau)$ from the corresponding "ideal" samples $\hat{y}(k)$. The minimization is done by adjusting the timing phase in the direction opposite to the derivative of the expected value of the squared error. In practice, one ignores the expected value and minimizes the squared error resulting in a stochastic gradient algorithm. MMSE timing recovery has been proposed in [26] and examined to some degree in [27] for PR magnetic recording channels. Another criterion, the maximum likelihood (ML) criterion, has also been used to derive a phase detector [28].

The derivation of the MMSE gradient is reviewed, and note that the MMSE gradient yields suitable timing functions. Also formulated is the MMSE timing recovery in the framework of a slope lookup table (SLT) instead of a discrete time filtered version of symbol rate spaced equalized samples $y(k,\tau)$. The SLT approach leads to an efficient implementation with slopes expressed directly in terms of a discrete time filtered version of the data bits $d(k)$ instead of the equalized signal samples.

A methodology for an analytical performance evaluation of the timing loop where the timing loop output noise jitter is the performance criterion. The analysis is described in detail for the SLT-based MMSE timing loop and also applied to the MM timing loop. The quantitative results from this technique are used to compare the SLT and MM timing loops. The ML loop is not considered further here as it has somewhat adverse jitter properties compared with the other two timing loops [29]. Finally, simulations results comparing the SLT and MM timing loops in terms of output noise jitter as well as BER performance are presented.

### *MMSE Slope Lookup Table (SLT) Timing Recovery*

Let us review MMSE timing recovery from first principles. The discussion is along the lines of [26] and [27]. The expectation of the square of the error, $e(k,\tau) = y(k,\tau) - \hat{y}(k)$, is minimized with respect to the timing or sampling phase. Here,

$$\hat{y}(k) = \sum_{p=0}^{P-1} h(p)\hat{d}(k-p) \tag{34.7}$$

and in the absence of any channel impairments we would have $\hat{d}(k) = d(k)$ and $\hat{y}(k) = y(k)$. The derivative of the expectation needs to be obtained with respect to $\tau$. Ignoring the expectation operator we obtain a stochastic gradient algorithm [26]:

$$\frac{\partial}{\partial \tau}(e^2(k,\tau)) = 2y(k,\tau)\frac{\partial y(k,\tau)}{\partial \tau} - 2\hat{y}(k)\frac{\partial y(k,\tau)}{\partial \tau} = -2e(k,\tau)\frac{\partial y(k,\tau)}{\partial \tau}$$

$$= -2e(k,\tau)\left[\frac{dy(t)}{dt}\right]_{t=kT+\tau} = -2e(k,\tau)s(k,\tau) \tag{34.8}$$

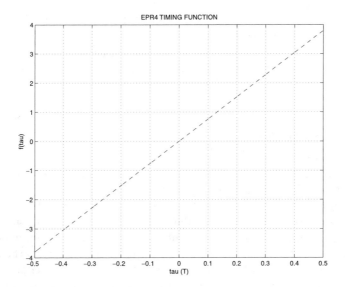

**FIGURE 34.24** Timing function for an EPR4 partial-response channel.

Note that the MM approach was to generate a timing gradient from a suitably defined timing function $f(\tau)$. Here, a timing gradient has been derived from the MMSE criterion; however, the resulting timing gradient should be a valid timing function, i.e., be monotonic, and have a zero-crossing for zero sampling phase error. This has been shown in [27]. An expression for the timing function in terms of the PR channel coefficients is [29]

$$f(\tau) = \sum_{l=-\infty}^{\infty} \left[ \underbrace{\sum_{\substack{p=0 \\ l \ne p}}^{P-1}}_{} h(p) \frac{(-1)^{l-p}}{(l-p)T} \right]^2 \tag{34.9}$$

The result of plotting $f(\tau)$ in Eq. (34.9) for EPR4 is shown in Fig. 34.24. Let us now consider a MMSE-based timing gradient or phase detector formulated in terms of a SLT. The signal slope is modeled in terms of a slope generating filter, which when used to filter the data $d(k)$ produces the slopes:

$$s(k) = d(k) \times \psi(k) = \sum_{c=-C_1}^{C_2} \psi(c)d(k-c) \tag{34.10}$$

where the negative coefficient index indicates that the slope at time $k$ depends on future bits (accomodated by delaying the slope and adding the delay into the model as additional latency). $C_1 + C_2 + 1$ is the number of nonzero coefficients of the slope filter's impulse response, $\psi$. The SLT output $\hat{s}(k)$ approximates $s(k)$, which depends on the data pattern. Such a SLT can be derived for any PR by correlating the data with the actual signal slopes. In practice, it is enough to use fewer terms from the filter. Therefore, the simplified SLT output can be represented as

$$\hat{s}(k) = \sum_{b=-B_1}^{B_2} \psi(b)d(k-b) \tag{34.11}$$

where $B = B_1 + B_2 + 1$ is the size of the slope table input i.e., the number of data bits used in calculating the slope. The SLT-based gradient is then,

$$\Delta(k) = e(k)\hat{s}(k) \tag{34.12}$$

where the factor of $-2$ in Eq. (34.8) can be absorbed in the lookup table. In our analysis we need the slope generating filter coefficients $\psi(c)$. These coefficients $\psi(c)$s are obtained in the process of numerically generating the signal slopes, which are correlated with the data.

*Phase Detector Properties*

Before computing the output noise jitter of the entire timing loop, the properties of the phase detector must be analyzed. Quantities important for the performance of the phase detector are its *KPD* and output noise standard deviation ratio $KPD/\sigma_{n_o}$. The *KPD* is the ratio of the mean phase detector output to a constant sampling phase error, $\tau$. The *KPD* can thus be thought of as the signal gain of the timing loop where the signal is the sampling phase error. The output noise $n_o(k)$ is the equivalent noise at the output of the phase detector for a given input noise $n(k)$ at the phase detector input. The error, $e(k)$, at the equalizer output is a combination of contributions from the sampling phase error, $\tau(k)$ and noise. Let $n(k)$ represent the noise at the equalizer output (intersymbol interference + filtered equalized noise). We then have,

$$e(k) = \tau(k)s(k) + n(k) \tag{34.13}$$

The phase detector output, $\Delta(k)$, is then

$$\Delta(k) = [\tau(k)s(k) + n(k)]\hat{s}(k) = \tau(k)s(k)\hat{s}(k) + n_o(k) \tag{34.14}$$

Figure 34.25 shows in detail the timing loop of Fig. 34.22 with the details of the SLT phase detector and the composition of the error signal from the sampling phase and noise per Eq. (34.13).

Now find the statistical properties of *KPD* and $n_o$ using $\mathcal{E}$ as the expectation operator. For a tractable analysis we assume $n(k)$ is AWG. To easily relate $\sigma_n$ to the error event rate (EER) at the output of the Viterbi detector, we assume that channel errors are dominated by a minimum distance error event (with distance $d_{min}$).

$$\sigma_n = \frac{d_{min}/2}{Q^{-1}(\text{EER})} \tag{34.15}$$

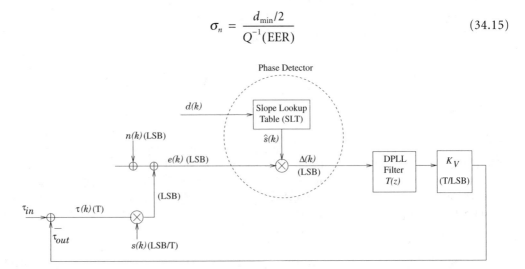

**FIGURE 34.25**   Timing loop with SLT phase detector.

The EER is the BER divided by the number of bit errors in the dominant error event. In Eq. (34.15) $Q$ refers to the well-known $Q$ function defined by

$$Q(x) = \frac{1}{2\pi} \int_x^\infty \exp\left(\frac{y^2}{2}\right) dy \tag{34.16}$$

*Signal Gain (KPD) of the Phase Detector*

Using the definition of KPD, for a constant sampling phase error $\tau$,

$$KPD = \frac{\mathcal{E}\{\tau \hat{s}(k)s(k) + n(k)\hat{s}(k)\}}{\tau} = \mathcal{E}\{\hat{s}(k)s(k)\} + \frac{\mathcal{E}\{n(k)\hat{s}(k)\}}{\tau} \tag{34.17}$$

Consider $\mathcal{E}\{n(k)\hat{s}(k)\}$, where $\hat{s}(k)$ is a linear function of the data bits, which can be realistically assumed to be uncorrelated with the noise $n(k)$. Therefore, this term is zero and as we should expect, the noise does not contribute to the mean phase detector output. Thus,

$$KPD = \mathcal{E}\{\hat{s}(k)s(k)\} = \sum_{b=-B_1}^{B_2} \sum_{c=-C_1}^{C_2-1} \psi(b)\psi(c)\mathcal{E}\{d(k-b)d(k-c)\} \tag{34.18}$$

If $d$ is uncoded, hence white, with zero mean, $\mathcal{E}\{d(k-b)d(k-c)\} = \sigma_d^2$ if $b = c$ and is 0 if $b \neq c$. Consequently, the KPD is

$$KPD = \sigma_d^2 \sum_{b=-B_1}^{B_2} \psi^2(b) \tag{34.19}$$

where it is assumed that slope table ouput is based on fewer than $C_1 + C_2 + 1$ terms to reduce the summation to be from $b = -B_1$ to $B_2$. We note that the KPD values obtained here are equivalent to the slopes of the $f(\tau)$ versus $\tau$ curve plotted in Fig. 34.24.

*Output Noise of the Phase Detector*
Computing the autocorrelation,

$$\mathcal{E}\{n_o(k)n_o(k+l)\} = \mathcal{E}\{n(k)\hat{s}(k)n(k+1)\hat{s}(k+l)\}$$

Because $\hat{s}(k)$ is a filtered version of $d(k)$, which is uncorrelated with $n$, $n$ and $\hat{s}$ are uncorrelated. Therefore,

$$\mathcal{E}\{n_o(k)n_o(k+l)\} = \mathcal{E}\{n(k)n(k+l)\}\mathcal{E}\{\hat{s}(k)\hat{s}(k+l)\}$$

$$= R_n(l)\mathcal{E}\{\hat{s}(k)\hat{s}(k+l)\}$$

$$\mathcal{E}\{\hat{s}(k)\hat{s}(k+l)\} = \sum_{b=-B_1}^{B_2} \sum_{b'=-B_1}^{B_2} \psi(b)\psi(b')\mathcal{E}\{d(k-b)d(k+l-b')\} \tag{34.20}$$

With $d$ being uncoded (hence white) and zero mean, $\mathcal{E}\{d(k-b)d(k+l-b')\} = \sigma_d^2$ if $b' = b+l$ and 0 if $b' \neq b+l$. Also assuming, $R_n(l) = \sigma_n^2 \delta[l]$, i.e., $n$ to be white, we need to consider only $l = 0$ in which case we have $b = b'$. In that case,

$$\mathcal{E}\{n_o(k)n_o(k+l)\} = \sigma_n^2 \sigma_d^2 \delta[l] \sum_{b=-B_1}^{B_2} \psi^2(b) \tag{34.21}$$

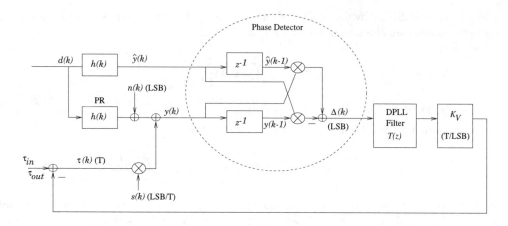

**FIGURE 34.26**   Timing loop with Mueller–Muller phase detector.

Observe that the noise at the phase detector output is indeed white with standard deviation,

$$\sigma_{n_o} = \sigma_n \sigma_d \sqrt{\sum_{b=-B_1}^{B_2} \psi^2(b)} \tag{34.22}$$

### Mueller and Muller (MM) Timing Loop

Now examine the properties of the MM timing gradient. This gradient is obtained as

$$\Delta(k) = y(k)\hat{y}(k-1) - y(k-1)\hat{y}(k) \tag{34.23}$$

in terms of the equalized signal $y(k)$ and its delayed version as well as the corresponding estimates of the "ideal" values $\hat{y}$ for these signals. A block diagram of a MM timing loop using this gradient is shown in Fig. 34.26. It is possible to evaluate this phase detector's *KPD* and noise performance. This is accomplished by writing $y(k)$ as $\hat{y}(k) + e(k)$, expanding $e(k)$ as in Eq. (34.13) from which $s(k)$ is further expressed in terms of the slope generating filter based on Eq. (34.10). Likewise, $\hat{y}(k)$ is expressed in terms of the PR coefficients as per Eq. (34.7). The analysis makes the usual assumptions about the data and noise $n(k)$ being white. The details of the analysis can be found in [29] which yields,

$$KPD = \sigma_d^2 \left( \underbrace{\sum_c \sum_m \psi(c)h(m)}_{m-c=-1} - \underbrace{\sum_c \sum_m \psi(c)h(m)}_{m-c=1} \right) \tag{34.24}$$

where the sum over $m$ is from 0 to $P-1$ and that over $c$ is from $-C_1$ to $C_2 + 1$.

The autocorrelation, $R_{n_o}(l)$ for the noise at the output of the phase detector, assuming the data to be white, is also computed in [29]. It is shown that even with AWG noise at the phase detector input, i.e., noise with autocorelation $R_n(l) = \sigma_n^2 \delta[l]$, noise at the phase detector output is not white; however, it is shown that if $R_n(l) = \sigma_d^2 \delta[l]$ the autocorrelation of $R_{n_o}(l)$ will be limited to only the first delay terms, i.e., $l = 1$ and $-1$ so we have,

$$R_{n_o}(0) = \sigma_{n_o}^2 = 2\sigma_d^2 \sigma_n^2 \sum_{p=0}^{P-1} h(p)^2 \tag{34.25}$$

and

$$R_{n_o}(1) = R_{n_o}(-1) = -\sigma_d^2 \sigma_n^2 \underbrace{\sum_{p=0}^{P-1} \sum_{m=0}^{P-1}}_{p-m=2} h(m)h(p) \qquad (34.26)$$

## Performance Comparison of Symbol Rate Timing Loops

So far, the properties of the SLT and MM timing gradients or phase detectors have been examined. If the noise at the phase detector output for both systems were white we could directly compare their performance by comparing their respective $KPD$ to $\sigma_{n_o}$ ratio as a kind of signal-to-noise ratio (SNR) of the phase detector. The ratio would measure a signal gain (experienced by sampling phase errors) to noise gain across the entire bandwidth. If the noise had been white for both systems this ratio would scale similarly for both systems when measured over the effective noise bandwidth determined by the loop filter; however, for the MM loop we observed that the noise at the phase detector output was not white. Therefore, we must examine the timing loop performance at the output of the loop filter not just at the output of the phase detector. Before continuing our analysis let us make some qualitative comments about the loop filter.

### Qualitative Loop Filter Description

A timing loop is a feedback control loop. Therefore, the stability/loop dynamics are determined by the "gain" (in converting observed amplitude error to a timing update) of the phase detector and the details of the loop filter. If the timing loop were needed to remove the effect of a sampling phase error, a first order DPLL would be sufficient; however, the timing loop must also recover the proper frequency with which to sample the signal. Therefore, the use of a second order DPLL loop filter is needed. This allows the timing loop to continually generate small phase updates to produce a clock, which not only has the correct sampling phase within a symbol interval $T$ but which also has the correct value for the symbol interval i.e., the correct clock frequency. DPLL here refers to the portion of the overall loop filter transfer function $T(z)$ without the fixed delay term $z^{-L}$. In addition, important to the performance of the loop is its noise performance, i.e., for a given level of input noise, the effect on the jitter in sampling phase updates. The jitter properties are determined by the noise gain of the phase detector as well as the loop filter properties. The loop filters out noise beyond the bandwidth of interest, this bandwidth being determined by how rapidly the loop is designed to react to timing changes. As mentioned earlier, the DPLL loop filter is a second order filter with an additional latency term. Its transfer function is given by:

$$T(z) = z^{-L} \left( \frac{f_g z^{-1}}{1 - z^{-1}} + p_g \right) \left( \frac{z^{-1}}{1 - z^{-1}} \right) \qquad (34.27)$$

where $f_g$ and $p_g$ are frequency and phase update gains for the second order and first order sections, respectively, while $L$ is the loop latency. A block diagram of $T(z)$ is also shown in Fig. 34.27(a).

### Noise Jitter Analysis of Timing Loop

Linearized $Z$ domain analysis of the DPLL is now performed by replacing the phase detector with its $KPD$ (denoted by $K_p$ in the equations for readability). In evaluating the SLT and MM DPLLs three sets or combinations of $p_g$ and $f_g$ will be used: "LOW", "MED", and "HGH" where the LOW gains, are relatively low update gains, which would be used in tracking mode, MED gains are moderate gains, and HGH gains, are high gains, which might be used during acquisition. For the SLT and MM DPLLs the $p_g$ and $f_g$ are scaled so that the same settings result in the about same transient response for a given sized phase or frequency disturbance.

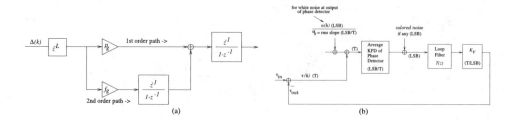

**FIGURE 34.27** Linearized model: (a) second-order DPLL loop filter, (b) timing loop with phase detector modeled by its average signal gain.

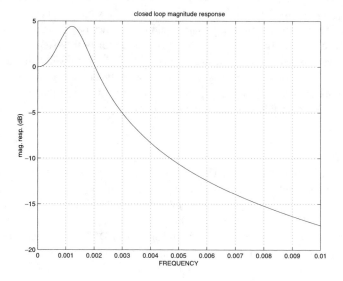

**FIGURE 34.28** Closed loop frequency response of SLT DPLL for low $p_g$ and $f_g$ update gains.

The open loop DPLL transfer function, $G(z)$, incorporating the loop filter $L(z)$ and clock update gain is

$$G(z) = K_V \left( \frac{f_g z^{-1}}{1 - z^{-1}} + p_g \right) z^{-L} \left( \frac{z^{-1}}{1 - z^{-1}} \right)$$

Referring to the timing loop model of Fig. 34.27(b), the *closed* loop transfer functiont $(T_{\text{out}}/T_{\text{in}}) = H(z)$ is

$$H(z) = \frac{K_p G(z)}{1 + K_p G(z)} \tag{34.28}$$

Note that $K_p$ has dimensions of LSB/T, $K_V$ and $G(z)$ have dimensions of T/LSB and $H(z)$ is a transfer function with respect to two time quantities. The effective noise bandwidth is then,

$$ENB = 2 \int_0^{0.5} |H(f)|^2 df$$

An example of a closed loop transfer function for the SLT DPLL is shown in Fig. 34.28 for LOW update gains. To find the effect of AWG noise, $n(k)$, first convert the $\sigma_n$ to an effective timing noise by dividing by the rms slope, $\sigma_s$, of the signal that is obtained during the numerical generation of the signal slopes and calculation of the slope generating filter coefficients. Now it can be multiplied by the square root of the *ENB* to determine the corresponding noise induced timing jitter $\sigma_j$ (units of T). Therefore,

$$\sigma_j = \frac{\sigma_n}{\sigma_s}\sqrt{ENB} \qquad (34.29)$$

The equivalent model for the above method of analysis is shown in Fig. 34.27(b).

For the SLT-based DPLL, the total jitter is simply the above $\sigma_j$. For the MM DPLL the phase detector output noise is colored; however, we know its properties here and can examine its effect from this point onwards. The only difference is that the closed loop transfer function seen by the MM phase detector output noise is,

$$F(z) = \frac{G(z)}{1 + K_p G(z)} \qquad (34.30)$$

The noise jitter is then obtained as,

$$\sigma_j = \sqrt{2\int_0^{0.5} P_n(f)|F(f)|^2 df} \qquad (34.31)$$

where $P_n(f)$ is the noise p.s.d. at the phase detector output.

Figure 34.29 plots the jitter performance of the SLT- and MM-based DPLLs for three sets of $(p_g, f_g)$: LOW, MED, HGH. Shown are the output, noise-induced timing jitter of the loop for four channel error event rates. Observe that the MM timing loop's output noise jitter is almost the same but slightly better than that of the SLT-based timing loop.

### Jitter and BER Simulation Results

Simulations on the SLT-based timing loop and the MM loop are run within the simulator framework described in Fig. 34.22. The same DPLL loop filter structure is used for both systems. Simulations are run at a channel bit density bit of 2.8 without noise and SNRs, which correspond with channel EERs of

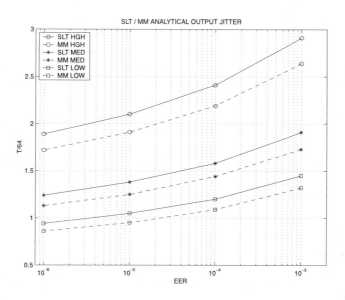

**FIGURE 34.29**  Analytically calculated output jitter for SLT and MM timing loops.

**TABLE 34.2**  Simulation-Based Timing Loop Output Jitter $\sigma_{jt}$ (Units of T/64)
Performance of SLT and MM Timing Loops for Final EERs of Zero (Noiseless),
$10^{-4}$, and $10^{-2}$

|  | SLT | | | MMPD | | |
|---|---|---|---|---|---|---|
| $p_g, f_g$ GAINS | EER 0 | EER $10^{-4}$ | EER $10^{-2}$ | EER 0 | EER $10^{-4}$ | EER $10^{-2}$ |
| LOW | 0.49 | 1.30 | 2.18 | 0.45 | 1.16 | 1.86 |
| MED | 0.49 | 1.69 | 2.99 | 0.46 | 1.56 | 2.51 |
| HGH | 0.67 | 2.67 | 4.86 | 0.70 | 2.67 | 4.38 |

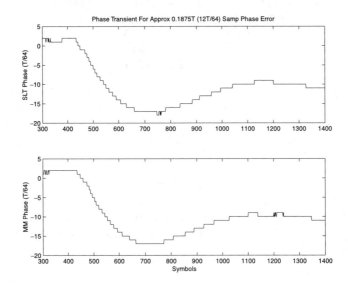

**FIGURE 34.30**  SLT and MM DPLL reaction to $0.1875T$ ($12T/64$) phase step. Low $p_g$, $f_g$ gains. No noise in this simulation.

$10^{-4}$ and $10^{-2}$. The steady-state jitter is examined in the DPLL output phase and the response of the timing loop to a phase step in the data field. Figure 34.30 shows the transient phase response plots of the SLT and MM DPLLs responding to a $0.1875T$ ($12T/64$) phase step in data field for the same LOW $p_g$ and $f_g$ settings. Note that they have very similar responses. Table 34.2 shows the steady-state output jitter of the two timing loops for various combinations of gains and noise levels corresponding to EERs of $10^{-4}$ and $10^{-2}$. The settled DPLL phases show some nonzero jitter without additive noise from quantization effects. Timing jitter at the DPLL output is measured by measuring the standard deviation of the DPLL phase. Again, observe that the two timing loops have very similar jitter numbers although the MM timing loop jitter is slightly lower.

Finally, the Viterbi detector BER performance is examined instead of the timing loop jitter performance for the read channel architecture of Fig. 34.31 employing the MM and SLT timing loops. Observe that the BERs of the two systems are practically indistinguishable.

## Conclusions

An overview of timing recovery methods for PRML magnetic recording channels, including interpolative and traditional symbol rate VCO-based timing recovery methods, was provided. Also reviewed was the MMSE timing recovery from first principles and its formulation in the framework of a SLT-based timing gradient. A framework for analyzing the performance of the timing loops in terms of output noise jitter was provided. The jitter calculation is based on obtaining linearized $Z$ domain closed loop transfer functions of the timing loop. Also compared was the output timing jitter, due to input noise,

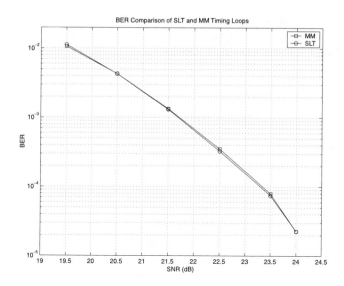

**FIGURE 34.31**  Simulated BERs of practical read channel using SLT and MM timing loops.

of the SLT and MM timing loops—two commonly used timing loops. The jitter performance of the MM loop is almost the same but very slightly better than that obtained with the SLT-based timing loop; however, the Viterbi BER performance of read channel systems employing the two timing loops are practically indistinguishable.

## References

1.  A. Oppenheim and R. Schafer, *Discrete Time Signal Processing*, Prentice-Hall, Englewood Cliffs, NJ, 1989.
2.  K. Fisher, W. Abbott, J. Sonntag, and R. Nesin, "PRML detection boosts hard-disk drive capacity" *IEEE Spectrum*, pp. 70–76, November, 1996.
3.  M. E. Van Valkenburg, *Analog Filter Design*, Holt Rinehart Winston, 1982.
4.  R. Schaumann, M. Ghausi, and K. Laker, *Design of Analog Filters*, Prentice-Hall, Englewood Cliffs, NJ, 1990.
5.  J. Park and L. R. Carley, "Analog complex graphic equalizer for EPR4 channels," *IEEE Transactions on Magnetics*, pp. 2785–2787, September, 1997.
6.  A. Bishop, et al., "A 300 Mb/s BiCMOS disk drive channel with adaptive analog equalizer," *Digests, Int. Solid State Circuits Conf.*, pp. 46–47, 1999.
7.  P. Pai, A. Brewster, and A. Abidi, "Analog front-end architectures for high speed PRML magnetic recording channels," *IEEE Transactions on Magnetics*, pp. 1103–1108, March 1995.
8.  R. Cideciyan and F. Dolivo, et al., "A PRML system for digital magnetic recording," *IEEE Journal on Selected Areas in Communications*, pp. 38–56, January, 1992.
9.  G. Mathew, et al., "Design of analog equalizers for partial response detection in magnetic recording," *IEEE Transactions on Magnetics*, pp. 2098–2107.
10. S. Qureshi, "Adaptive equalization," in *Proceedings of the IEEE*, September, 1973, pp. 1349–1387.
11. S. Haykin, *Communication Systems*, John Wiley & Sons, New York, 1992, pp. 487–497.
12. S. Haykin, *Adaptive Filter Theory*, Prentice-Hall, 1996.
13. J. Bergmans, *Digital Baseband Transmission and Recording*, Kluwer Academic Publishers, Dordrecht, the Netherlands, 1996.
14. P. Aziz and J. Sonntag, "Equalizer architecture tradeoffs for magnetic recording channels," *IEEE Transactions on Magnetics*, pp. 2728–2730, September, 1997.
15. L. Du, M. Spurbeck, and R. Behrens, "A linearly constrained adaptive FIR filter for hard disk drive read channels," in *Proceedings, IEEE Int. Conf. on Communications*, pp. 1613–1617.

16. J. Sonntag, et al., "A high speed low power PRML read channel device," *IEEE Transactions on Magnetics,* pp. 1186–1189, March, 1995.

17. D. Welland, et al., "Implementation of a digital read/write channel with EEPR4 detection," *IEEE Transactions on Magnetics,* pp. 1180–1185, March 1995.

18. G. Tuttle, et al., "A 130 Mb/s PRML read/write channel with digital-servo detection," *Digests, IEEE Int. Solid-State Circuits Conf.,* 1996.

19. J. Chern, et al., "An EPRML digital read/write channel IC," *Digests, IEEE Int. Solid State Circuits Conf.,* 1997.

20. N. Nazari, "A 500 Mb/s disk drive read channel in 0.25 $\mu$m CMOS incorporating programmable noise predictive Viterbi detection and trellis coding," *Digests, Intl. Solid-State Circuits Conf.,* pp. 78–79, 2000.

21. M. Spurbeck and R. Behrens, "Interpolated timing recovery for hard disk drive read channels," in *Proceedings, IEEE Int. Conf. on Communications,* 1997, pp. 1618–1624.

22. Z. Wu and J. Cioffi, "A MMSE interpolated timing recovery scheme for the magnetic recording channel", in *Proceedings, IEEE Int. Conf. on Communications,* 1997, pp. 1625–1629.

23. A. Patapoutian "On phase-locked loops and Kalman filters," *IEEE Transactions on Communications,* pp. 670–672, May, 1999.

24. K. Mueller and M. Muller, "Timing recovery in digital synchronous data receivers," *IEEE Transactions on Communications,* pp. 516–531, May, 1976.

25. F. Dolivo, W. Schott, and G. Ungerbock, "Fast timing recovery for partial response signaling systems," *IEEE Conf. on Communications,* pp. 18.5.1–18.5.4, 1989.

26. S. Qureshi, "Timing recovery for equalized partial-response systems," *IEEE Transactions on Communications,* pp. 1326–1331, December, 1976.

27. H. Shafiee, "Timing recovery for sampling detectors in digital magnetic recording," *IEEE Conf. on Communications,* pp. 577–581, 1996.

28. J. Bergmans, "Digital baseband transmission and recording," Kluwer Academic Publishers, Dordrecht, the Netherlands, pp. 500–513, 1996.

29. P. Aziz and S. Surendran "Symbol rate timing recovery for higher order partial response channels," *IEEE Journal on Selected Areas in Communications,* April, 2001 (to appear).

## 34.4   Head Position Sensing in Disk Drives

*Ara Patapoutian*

### Introduction

Data in a disk drive is stored in concentric tracks on one or more disk platters. As the disks spin, a magnetic transducer known as a read/write head, transfers information between the disks and a user [1]. When the user wants to access a given track, the head assembly moves the read/write head to the appropriate location. This positioning of the head is achieved by use of a feedback servo system as shown in Fig. 34.32. First, a position sensor generates a noisy estimate of the head location. Then by comparing the difference between this estimate and the desired location, a controller is able to generate a signal to adjust the *actuator* accordingly.

Two known approaches are used in sensing the head position. An external optical device can be used to estimate the head position by emitting a laser light and then by measuring the reflected beam. This approach is relatively expensive, may need frequent calibrations, and at present is limited to servo writers, which are discussed later. In the second approach, a read head, which is designed primarily to detect the recorded user data pattern, will itself sense position specific magnetic marks recorded on a disk surface. Using statistical signal-processing techniques, the read waveform is decoded into a head position estimate. At present this second approach is preferred for disk drives and is the topic of this article.

In an *embedded servo* scheme, as shown in Fig. 34.33, a portion of each platter, which is divided into multiple wedges, is reserved to provide radial and sometimes angular position information for the read

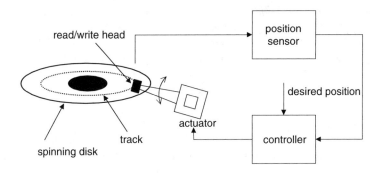

**FIGURE 34.32**   Position control loop for a disk drive.

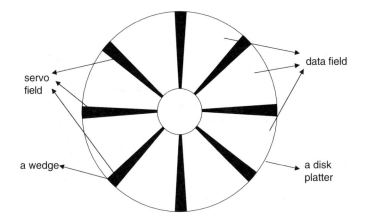

**FIGURE 34.33**   Data and servo fields on a disk drive.

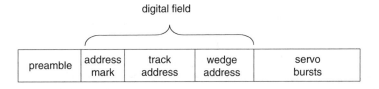

**FIGURE 34.34**   A generic composition of a servo field.

head. These reserved wedges are known as *servo fields*, and the number of wedges per surface varies significantly amongst different products. A generic servo wedge provides radial estimates in two steps. On a disk surface, each track is assigned a number known as the *track address*. These addresses are included in a servo field, providing complete radial position information with accuracy of up to a track. In other words, the information provided by a track address is complete but coarse. The positional error signal (PES) complements the track address by providing a more accurate estimate within a track. By combining these two estimates, a complete and accurate head position estimate can be obtained.

A wedge may also contain coarse information regarding angular position if a specific address is assigned to each wedge. The user data field, with its own address mark and timing capability, can complement the wedge address by providing finer angular position estimates.

A typical wedge will have multiple sub-fields, as shown in Fig. 34.34. A periodic waveform, known as a *preamble*, provides ample information to calibrate the amplitude of the waveform and, if necessary, to acquire the timing of the recorded pattern. Frame synchronization, or the start of a wedge, is recognized by a special sequence known as the *address mark*. This is followed by the track and wedge addresses, and finally by the servo burst that provides information regarding the PES. These multiple sub-fields can be divided into two distinct areas. Since the address mark, track address, and wedge address are all encoded as binary strings, they are referred to as the *digital field*, as shown in Fig. 34.34. By contrast, ignoring quantization effects of the *read channel*, the periodic servo burst field is decoded to a real number representing the analog radial position. Thus, the format designs as well as the demodulation techniques for the digital and burst fields are fundamentally different. The digital field demodulator is known as the *detector* while the servo burst field demodulator is known as the *estimator*.

Despite their differences, the two fields are not typically designed independently of each other. For example, having common sample rates and common front-end hardware simplifies the receiver architecture significantly. Furthermore, it makes sense to use coherent or synchronous detection algorithms with coherent estimation algorithms and vice versa.

Having a reserved servo field comes at the expense of user data capacity. A major optimization goal is to minimize the servo field overhead for a given cost and reliability target. Both the servo format design as well as that of the detectors/estimators in the read channel chip of a disk drive are optimized to minimize this overhead.

This chapter section reviews position sensing formats and demodulators. Because estimation and detection are well-known subjects, presented in multiple textbooks [2,3], issues that are particular to disk drive position sensors are emphasized. Furthermore, rather than the servo control loop design, the statistical signal processing aspects of position sensing are presented. For a general introduction to disk drive servo control design, the reader is referred to [4], where the design of a disk drive servo is presented as a case study of a control design problem. In general, because of the proprietary nature of this technology, the literature regarding head position sensing is limited to a relatively few published articles, with the exception of patents.

When a disk drive is first assembled in a factory, the servo fields have to somehow be recorded on the disk platters. Once a drive leaves the factory, these fields will only be read and never rewritten. Traditionally, an expensive external device, known as the *servo writer*, introduced in the subsection on "Servo Writers," records the servo fields. In general, the servo writing process constrains and affects the servo field format choices as well as the demodulator performance. In the next section, the digital field format and detection approaches are addressed, while in the subsection on "The Burst Field," the servo burst format and PES estimation approaches are introduced.

## Servo Writers

After a disk drive is assembled, the function of a servo writer is to record the servo wedges on a drive. While the disks are spinning, an *external* servo writer senses the radial position usually through the head assembly using the reflection of a laser beam. An external mechanical device moves the head assembly. Finally, an external read head locks on a clocking track on a disk to locate the angular position. By knowing both the radial and angular position, as well as controlling the radial position, the servo writer records the wedges, track by track, using the native head of the drive.

Servo writing has been an expensive process. The servo writing time per disk is an important interval that disk manufacturers try to minimize and is proportional to the number of tracks per disk surface, to the spin of the disk drive, and to the number of passes needed to record a track. Since the number of tracks per disk is increasing faster than the spin speed, the servo writer time becomes a parameter that needs to be contained. To this end, the disk drive industry has attempted to minimize both servo writer time and the servo writer cost.

Self-servo writing is a procedure where the wedges are written by the disk drive itself without using any external device [5,6]. Here, the servo writing time is increased but the process is less costly. Many hybrid proposals also use a combination of an external servo writer to record some initial marks and then complete the wedges by using the drive itself. An example of such a process is the printed media approach [7,8], where a master disk "stamps" each disk, and afterward the drive completes writing the wedges.

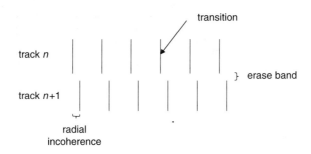

**FIGURE 34.35** Servo writer impairments: erase bands and radial incoherence.

In general, the servo writer cannot record an arbitrary wedge format. For example, it is very difficult for a servo writer that records wedges track-by-track to record a smooth angled transition across the radius. Furthermore, the wedges generated by a servo writer are not ideal. For example, servo writers that record wedges track-by-track create an *erase band* between tracks [9], where due to head and disk media characteristics, no transition is recorded in a narrow band between two adjacent tracks. Similarly, because of uncertainties in the angular position, two written tracks may not be aligned properly causing *radial incoherence* between adjacent tracks. These two impairments are illustrated in Fig. 34.35. In summary, the servo writer architecture affects both the wedge format design as well as the demodulator performance of a disk drive sensor.

## The Digital Field

The digital servo field has many similarities to the disk drive user data field [10] and to a digital communications system [2]. Each track in a digital field is encoded and recorded as a binary string similar to a data field. What differentiates a digital servo field from others is its short block length, and more importantly its off-track detection requirement.

Before discussing these differences, let us start by saying that a magnetic recording channel, for both the data and servo digital fields, is an intersymbol interference (ISI) channel. When read back, the information recorded in a given location modifies the waveform not only at that given location but also in the neighboring locations. Finite length ISI channels can be optimally detected using sequence detectors [11], where at least theoretically, all the field samples are observed before detecting them as a string of ones and zeros. For about a decade now, such sequence detectors have been employed in disk drives to detect the user data field.

The digital servo field length is very short relative to a data field. The present data sector length is around 512 bytes long, whereas the servo digital information string is only a few bytes long. So, whereas the percentage of overhead attributable to a preamble, address marks, and error correcting codes (ECC) is relatively small compared to the user data field, the overhead associated with a digital servo field can easily exceed one hundred percent. For example, it is well known that ECC coding efficiency increases with block length, i.e. codes with very short block lengths have weak error correction capability.

One strategy in minimizing the preamble field length is to use asynchronous detection, which usually trades performance for format, since it does not require exact timing information.

A simple strategy in minimizing the digital field is to write only partial information per wedge [12]. For example, with a smart controller, the absolute track or wedge address may not be needed, since it may be predicted using a state machine; however, such strategies improve format efficiency at the expense of performance robustness and complexity.

### Offtrack Detection

A primary factor that differentiates digital servo fields from other types of detection channels is the requirement to detect data reliably at any radial position, even when the read head is between two adjacent tracks. In contrast, a user data field is expected to be read reliably only if the read head is directly above

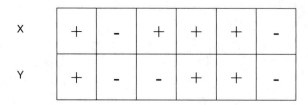

**FIGURE 34.36**   An example of two Gray-coded track addresses. The two addresses are different only in the third location.

that specific track. As will be discussed shortly, such a constraint influences the ECC as well as sequence detection strategies.

A related concern is the presence of radial incoherence, and the erase field introduced during servo writing that are present when the read head straddles two tracks. The detector performance will suffer from such impairments. Formats that tolerate such impairments are desired.

Because the recorded address mark and wedge address does not vary from one track to the next, the emphasis is on track addresses. When the read head is in the middle of two adjacent tracks, with track addresses X and Y, the read waveform is the superposition of the waveforms generated from each of the respective addresses. In general, the resulting waveform cannot be decoded reliably to any one of the two track addresses. A common solution is the use of a Gray code to encode track addresses, as shown in Fig. 34.36, where any two adjacent tracks differ in their binary address representation in only one symbol value. Hence, for the moment ignoring ISI, when the head is midway between adjacent tracks, the detector will decode the address bits correctly except for the bit location where the two adjacent tracks differ, that is, for the two track addresses labeled as X and Y, the decoder will decode the waveform to either track address X or Y, introducing an error of at most one track. By designing a radially periodic servo burst field, with period of at least two track widths, track number ambiguity generated by track addresses is resolved; however, as will be discussed next, Gray codes complicate the use of ECC codes and sequence detectors.

A Gray code restricts two adjacent tracks to differ in only a single position, or equivalently forcing the *Hamming distance* between two adjacent track addresses to be one. Adding an ECC field to the digital fields is desirable since reliable detection of track addresses is needed in the presence of miscellaneous impairments such as electronic and disk media noise, radial incoherence, erase bands, etc.; however, any ECC has a minimum Hamming distance larger than one. That is, it is not possible to have two adjacent track-addresses be Gray and ECC encoded simultaneously. If an ECC field is appended to each track address, it can be used only when the head is directly above a track. A possible alternative is to write the track addresses multiple times with varying radial shifts so that, at any position, the head is mostly directly above a track address [13]. Such a solution improves reliability at the expense of significant format efficiency loss.

Another complication of introducing Gray codes results from the interaction of these codes with the ISI channel. Consider an ISI free channel where the magnetic transitions are written ideally and where the read head is allowed to be anywhere between two adjacent Gray coded track addresses X and Y. As was discussed earlier, the track address reliability, or the probability that the decoded address is neither X nor Y, is independent of the read head position. Next, it is shown that for an ISI channel the detector performance depends on the radial position. In particular, consider the simple ISI channel with pulse response $1 - D$, which approximates a magnetic recording channel. For such a channel, events of length two are almost as probable as errors of length one (same distance but different number of neighbors). Now, as the head moves from track X to Y, the waveform modification introduced by addresses X and Y, at that one location where the two tracks differ, can trigger an error of length two. The detector may decode the received waveform to a different track address Z, which may lie far from addresses X or Y. In other words, in an ISI channel, whenever the head is between two tracks X and Y, the probability that the received waveform is decoded to some other address Z increases.

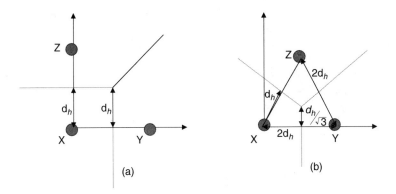

**FIGURE 34.37** Signal space representation of three codewords. Configuration (a) ISI free (b) with ISI.

For readers familiar with signal space representation of codewords, the ISI free and $1 + D$ channels are shown for the three addresses X, Y, and Z with their decision regions in Fig. 34.37. Let $d_h$ denote to the shortest distance from codeword X to the decision boundaries of codeword Z. As shown in Fig. 34.37, when the head is midway between tracks X and Y, the shortest distance to cross the decision boundaries of codeword Z is reduced by a factor of $\sqrt{3}$ (or 4.77 dB). Therefore, when the head is in the middle of two tracks, represented by addresses X and Y, the probability that the decoded codeword is Z increases significantly. For an arbitrary ISI channel this reduction factor in shortest distance varies, and it can be shown to be at most $\sqrt{3}$.

A trivial solution to address both the ECC and ISI complications introduced by the Gray code is not to use any coding and to write address bits far enough from each other to be able to ignore ISI effects. Then a simple symbol-by-symbol detector is sufficient to detect the address without the need for a sequence detector. Actually this is a common approach taken in many disk drive designs; however, dropping ECC capability affects reliability and forcing the magnetic recording channel to behave as ISI free requires additional format.

Another approach is to use symbol based codes, such as a bi-phase code, rather than sequence-based codes, that is, rather than maximizing the minimum distance between any two codewords, the distance between two symbols is maximized. For example, in a magnetic recording channel, a bi-phase code produces a positive pulse at the middle of the symbol for a symbol "1" and a negative pulse for a symbol "0," increasing symbol reliability [13,14]. In this example, it can be shown that the ISI related degradations are minimized and the detector performance is improved.

A fundamentally different approach would not make use of a Gray code at all. Instead, codes would be designed from scratch in such a way that for any two addresses X and Y the distance between X and Y would increase, as they are radially located further away from each other.

## The Burst Field

In the previous subsection, track addresses were introduced, which provide head position information to about single-track accuracy. To be able to read the data field reliably, it is essential to position the read head directly upon the desired track within a small fraction of a track. To this end the track number addresses are complemented with the servo burst field, where the analog radial position is encoded in a periodic waveform such as a sinusoid. Three ways to encode a parameter in a sinusoidal waveform are used: amplitude, phase, and frequency [3]. Servo burst fields are also periodic radially. Because the track address already provides an absolute position, such a periodicity does not create any ambiguity.

In a disk platter, information is recorded in one of two stable domains. Hence, a servo burst is recorded as a periodic binary pattern. The read back waveform, at the head output, is periodic and will contain both the fundamental and higher harmonics. The sinusoidal waveform is obtained by retaining only the fundamental harmonic. For a given format budget, it is possible to maximize the power of the read back

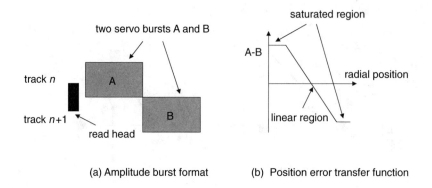

(a) Amplitude burst format          (b)  Position error transfer function

**FIGURE 34.38**    The amplitude burst format and its position error transfer function as the head moves from center-track *n* to center-track *n* + 1.

waveform by optimizing the fundamental period [15]. If recorded transitions get too close, ISI destroys most of the signal power. On the other hand, if transitions are far from each other, then the read back pulses are isolated and contain little power.

In this subsection, first the impairment sources are identified. Afterward, various servo burst formats and their performances are discussed [16,17]. Finally, various estimator characteristics and options are reviewed.

### Impairments

Here, impairments in a servo burst field are classified into three categories: servo-writer induced, read head induced, and read channel induced. Not all impairments are present in all servo burst formats.

As was discussed in the subsection on "Servo Writers", when the servo-writer records wedges track-by-track, erase band as well as radial incoherence may be present between tracks, degrading the performance of some of the servo burst formats. Also, the duty cycle of the recorded periods may be different than the intended 50%. Finally, write process limitations result in nonideal recorded transitions.

The read head element as well as the preamplifier, which magnifies the incoming signal, generate electronic noise, modeled by additive white Gaussian noise (AWGN). Also, in many situations the width of the read head element ends up, being shorter than the servo burst radial width as shown in Fig. 34.38 (a). As will be discussed shortly, for some formats, this creates saturated radial regions where the radial estimates are not reliable [9]. Finally, the rectangular approximation of the read head element shown in Fig. 34.38(a) is not accurate. More specifically, different regions of the read head may respond differently to a magnetic flux. Hence, the read head profile may be significantly different than a rectangle [18,19].

The read channel, while processing the read waveform, induces a third class of errors. Most present estimators are digitally implemented and have to cope with *quantization error*. If only the first harmonic of the received waveform is desired then suppressing higher harmonics may leave residues that may interact with the first harmonic inside the estimator. Furthermore, sampling a waveform with higher harmonic residues creates *aliasing effects*, where higher harmonics fold into the first harmonic. Many read channel estimators require that the phase, frequency, or both phase and frequency of the incoming waveform are known. Any discrepancy results in estimator degradation. Finally, estimator complexity constraints result in suboptimal estimators, further degrading the accuracy of the position estimate.

### Formatting Strategies

At present, the amplitude servo burst format, shown in Fig. 34.38(a), is the most common format used in the disk drive industry. Depending on the radial position of the read head, the overlap between the head and the bursts A and B varies. Through this overlap, or amplitude variation, it is possible to estimate the radial position. First, the waveforms resulting from the overlap of the read head and the burst fields

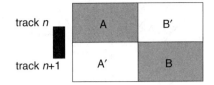

**FIGURE 34.39**    Alternative burst formats where A′ and B′ are either orthogonal to or of opposite polarity of A and B, respectively.

A and B are transformed into amplitude estimates. These amplitude estimates are then subtracted from each other and scaled to get a positional estimate. As the head moves from track center $n$ to track center $(n + 1)$, the noiseless positional estimate, known as *position error transfer function*, is plotted in Fig. 34.38(b). Here, since the radial width of the servo burst is larger than the read element, any radial position falls into either the *linear* region, where radial estimate is accurate, or in the *saturated* region, where the radial estimate is not accurate [9]. One solution to withstand saturated regions is to include multiple burst pairs, such that any radial position would fall in the linear region of at least one pair of bursts. The obvious drawback of such a strategy is the additional format loss. The amplitude format just presented does not suffer from radial incoherence since two bursts are not recorded radially adjacent to each other.

Because nonrecorded areas do not generate any signal, in Fig. 34.38(a) only 50% of the servo burst format is recorded with transitions or utilized. In an effort to improve the position estimate performance, the whole allocated servo area can be recorded. As a result, at least two alternative formats have emerged, both illustrated by Fig. 34.39.

In the first improved format, burst A is radially surrounded by an *antipodal* or "opposite polarity" burst A′. For example, if burst A is recorded as $++--++--\cdots$ then burst A′ is recorded as $--++--++\cdots$. For readers familiar with digital communications, the difference between the amplitude and antipodal servo burst formats can be compared to the difference between on-off and antipodal signaling. In on-off signaling, a symbol "0" or "1" is transmitted while in antipodal signaling 1 or −1 is transmitted. Antipodal signaling is 6 dB more efficient than on-off signaling. Similarly, it can be shown that the antipodal servo burst format gives a 6-dB advantage with respect to amplitude servo burst format under the AWGN assumption [17].

Instead of recording A′ to be the opposite polarity of A, another alternative is to record a pattern A′ that is orthogonal to A. For example, it is possible to pick up two sinusoids with different frequencies such that the two waveforms are orthogonal over a finite burst length interval. The resulting format is known as the *dual frequency* format [20]. Inside the read channel, two independent estimates of the head position can be obtained from two estimators, each tuned to one of the two frequencies. The final radial estimate is the average of the two estimates, resulting in a 3-dB improvement with respect to the amplitude format, again under AWGN assumption.

Unlike the amplitude format, these more sophisticated formats are in general more sensitive to other impairments such as erase band and radial incoherence.

A fundamentally different format is presented in Fig. 34.40. Here, the transitions are skewed and the periodic pattern gradually shifts in the angular direction as the radius changes. The radial information is stored in the phase of the period, so it is called the phase format. In Fig. 34.40 two burst fields A and B are presented where the transition slopes have the same magnitude but opposite polarities. An estimator makes two phase estimates, one from the sinusoid in field A and another one from the sinusoid in field B. By subtracting the second phase estimate from the first, and then by scaling the result, the radial position estimate can be obtained. Similar to the antipodal format, it can be shown that the phase pattern is 6 dB superior to the amplitude pattern [17] under AWGN. A major challenge for the phase format is successfully recording the skewed transitions on a disk platter without significant presence of radial incoherence and erase band.

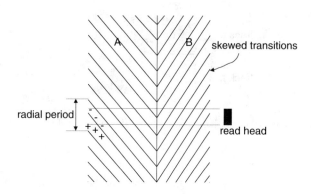

**FIGURE 34.40**  The phase format.

## Position Estimators

Estimating various parameters of a sinusoid is well documented in textbooks [3]. A decade ago position estimators were mostly implemented by analog circuitry, whereas at present, digital implementation is the norm and the one considered in this article [21–25]. One way of classifying estimators is to determine whether the phase and/or the frequency of the incoming waveform are known.

Assume that the amplitude of a noisy sinusoid needs to be determined. If the phase of this waveform is known, a matched filter can be used to generate the amplitude estimate. This is known as coherent estimation. Under certain assumptions and performance criteria such a filter becomes optimal. When the phase of the waveform is not known, but the frequency is known, then two matched filters can be used, one tuned to a sine waveform while the other filter is tuned to a cosine waveform. The outputs of the two filters are squared and added to give the energy estimate of the waveform. This is known as noncoherent estimation and is equivalent to computing the Fourier transform at the first harmonic. Other ad hoc estimators include the peak estimator and digital area estimators [26], which respectively estimate the averaged peak and the mean value of the unsigned waveform. Neither of these estimators requires the phase or the frequency of the waveform.

For the amplitude format, all the estimators mentioned here can be used. For the antipodal format, the phase of the waveform is needed and therefore a single matched filter is the required estimator. For dual frequency format, we need two estimators, each tuned to a different frequency. Since the two waveforms are orthogonal to each other, an estimator tuned to one of the waveforms will not observe the other waveform. Each estimator can utilize a single matched filter for coherent estimation or two matched filters for noncoherent estimation. Finally, for phase estimation, two matched filters are utilized, similar to noncoherent estimation; however, rather than squaring and adding the filter outputs, the inverse tangent function is performed on the ratio of the filter outputs.

## References

1. Comstock, R.L. and Workman, M.L., Data storage in rigid disks, in *Magnetic Storage Handbook*, 2nd ed., Mee, C.D. and Daniel, E.D., Eds., McGraw-Hill, New York, 1996, chap. 2.
2. Proakis, J.G., *Digital Communications*, 4th ed., McGraw-Hill, New York, 2000.
3. Kay, S.M., *Fundamentals of Statistical Signal Processing: Estimation Theory*, Prentice-Hall, Englewood Cliffs, NJ, 1993.
4. Franklin, G.F., Powell, D.J., and Workman, M.L., *Digital control of dynamic systems*, 3rd ed., Addison-Wesley, Reading, MA, 1997, chap. 14.
5. Brown, D.H., et al., Self-servo writing file, *US patent 06,040,955*, 2000.
6. Liu, B., Hu, S.B., and Chen, Q. S., A novel method for reduction of the cross track profile asymmetry of MR head during self servo-writing, *IEEE Trans. on Mag.*, 34, 1901, 1998.
7. Bernard, W.R. and Buslik, W.S., Magnetic pattern recording, *U.S. patent 03,869,711*, 1975.

8. Tanaka, S., et al., Characterization of magnetizing process for pre-embossed servo pattern of plastic hard disks, *IEEE Trans. on Mag.*, 30, 4209, 1994.

9. Ho, H.T. and Doan, T., Distortion effects on servo position error transfer function, *IEEE Trans. on Mag.*, 33, 2569, 1997.

10. Bergmans, J.W.M., *Digital Baseband Transmission and Recording*, Kluwar Academic Publishers, Dordrecht, 1996.

11. Forney, G.D., Maximum-likelihood sequence estimation of digital sequences in the presence of intersymbol interference, *IEEE Trans. on Info. Thy.*, 18, 363, 1972.

12. Chevalier, D., Servo pattern for location and positioning of information in a disk drive, *U.S. patent 05,253,131*, 1993.

13. Leis, M.D., et al., Synchronous detection of wide bi-phase coded servo information for disk drive, *U.S. patent 05,862,005*, 1999.

14. Patapoutian, A., Vea, M.P., and Hung, N.C., Wide biphase digital servo information detection, and estimation for disk drive using servo Viterbi detector, *U.S. patent 05,661,760*, 1997.

15. Patapoutian, A., Optimal burst frequency derivation for head positioning, *IEEE Trans. on Mag.*, 32, 3899, 1996.

16. Sacks, A.H., Position signal generation in magnetic disk drives, Ph.D. dissertation, Carnegie Mellon University, Pittsburgh, 1995.

17. Patapoutian, A., Signal space analysis of head positioning formats, *IEEE Trans. on Mag.*, 33, 2412, 1997.

18. Cahalan, D. and Chopra, K., Effects of MR head track profile characteristics on servo performance, *IEEE Trans. on Mag.*, 30, 4203, 1994.

19. Sacks, A.H. and Messner, W.C., MR head effects on PES generation: simulation and experiment, *IEEE Trans. on Mag.*, 32, 1773, 1996.

20. Cheung, W.L., Digital demodulation of a complementary two-frequency servo PES pattern, *U.S. patent 06,025,970*, 2000.

21. Tuttle, G.T., et al., A 130 Mb/s PRML read/write channel with digital-servo detection, *Proc. IEEE ISSCC'96*, 64, 1996.

22. Fredrickson, L., et al., Digital servo processing in the Venus PRML read/write channel, *IEEE Trans. on Mag.*, 33, 2616, 1997.

23. Yada, H. and Takeda, T., A coherent maximum-likelihood, head position estimator for PERM disk drives, *IEEE Trans. on Mag.*, 32, 1867, 1996.

24. Kimura, H., et al., A digital servo architecture with 8.8 bit resolution of position error signal for disk drives, *IEEE Globecom'97*, 1268, 1997.

25. Patapoutian, A., Analog-to-digital converter algorithms for position error signal estimators, *IEEE Trans. on Mag.*, 36, 395, 2000.

26. Reed, D.E., et al., Digital servo demodulation in a digital read channel, *IEEE Trans. on Mag.*, 34, 13, 1998.

# 34.5  Modulation Codes for Storage Systems

*Brian Marcus and Emina Šoljanin*

### Introduction

Modulation codes are used to constrain the individual sequences that are recorded in data storage channels, such as magnetic or optical disk or tape drives. The constraints are imposed in order to improve the detection capabilities of the system. Perhaps the most widely known constraints are the runlength limited (RLL($d,k$)) constraints, in which ones are required to be separated by at least $d$ and no more than $k$ zeros. Such constraints are useful in data recording channels that employ peak detection: waveform peaks, corresponding to data ones, are detected independently of one another. The $d$-constraint helps increase linear density while mitigating intersymbol interference, and the $k$-constraint helps provide feedback for timing and gain control.

Peak detection was widely used until the early 1990s. Although it is still used today in some magnetic tape drives and some optical recording devices, most high density magnetic disk drives now use a form of maximum likelihood (Viterbi) sequence detection. The data recording channel is modeled as a linear, discrete-time, communications channel with inter-symbol interference (ISI), described by its transfer function and white Gaussian noise. The transfer function is often given by $h(D) = (1 - D)(1 + D)^N$, where $N$ depends on and increases with the linear recording density.

Broadly speaking, two classes of constraints are of interest in today's high density recording channels: (1) constraints for improving timing and gain control and simplifying the design of the Viterbi detector for the channel and (2) constraints for improving noise immunity. Some constraints serve both purposes.

Constraints in the first class usually take the form of a PRML $(G, I)$ constraint: the maximum run of zeros is $G$ and the maximum run of zeros, within each of the two substrings defined by the even indices and odd indices, is $I$. The $G$-constraint plays the same role as the $k$-constraint in peak detection, while the $I$-constraint enables the Viterbi detector to work well within practical limits of memory.

Constraints in the second class eliminate some of the possible recorded sequences in order to increase the minimum distance between those that remain or eliminate the possibility of certain dominant error events. This general goal does not specify how the constraints should be defined, but many such constraints have been constructed; see [20] and the references therein for a variety of examples. Bounds on the capacities of constraints that avoid a given set of error events have been given in [26].

Until recently, the only known constraints of this type were the matched-spectral-null (MSN) constraints. They describe sequences whose spectral nulls match those of the channel and therefore increase its minimum distance. For example, a set of DC-balanced sequences (i.e., sequences of $\pm 1$ whose accumulated digital sums are bounded) is an MSN constraint for the channel with transfer function $h(D) = 1 - D$, which doubles its minimum distance [18].

During the past few years, significant progress has been made in defining high capacity distance enhancing constraints for high density magnetic recording channels. One of the earliest examples of such a constraint is the maximum transition run (MTR) constraint [28], which constrains the maximum run of ones. We explain the main idea behind this type of distance-enhancing codes in the subsection on "Constraints for ISI Channels."

Another approach to eliminating problematic error events is that of parity coding. Here, a few bits of parity are appended to (or inserted in) each block of some large size, typically 100 bits. For some of the most common error events, any single occurrence in each block can be eliminated. In this way, a more limited immunity against noise can be achieved with less coding overhead [5].

Coding for more realistic recording channel models that include colored noise and intertrack interference are discussed in the subsection on "Channels with Colored Noise and Intertrack Interference." The authors point out that different constraints, which avoid the same prescribed set of differences, may have different performance on more realistic channels. This makes some of them more attractive for implementation.

For a more complete introduction to this subject, the reader is referred to any one of the many expository treatments, such as [16,17,24].

## Constrained Systems and Codes

Modulation codes used in almost all contemporary storage products belong to the class of constrained codes. These codes encode random input sequences to sequences that obey the constraint of a labeled directed graph with a finite number of states and edges. The set of corresponding constrained sequences is obtained by reading the labels of paths through the graph. Sets of such sequences are called constrained systems or constraints. Figures 34.41 and 34.42 depict graph representations of an RLL constraint and a DC-balanced constraint.

Of special interest are those constraints that do not contain (globally or at certain positions) a finite number of finite length strings. These systems are called systems of finite type (FT). An FT system $X$

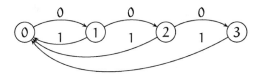

**FIGURE 34.41**   RLL (1,3) constraint.

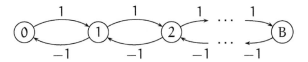

**FIGURE 34.42**   DC-balanced constraint.

over alphabet $\mathcal{A}$ can always be characterized by a finite list of forbidden strings $\mathcal{F} = \{w_1, \ldots, w_N\}$ of symbols in $\mathcal{A}$. Defined this way, FT systems will be denoted by $X_{\mathcal{F}}^{A}$. The RLL constraints form a prominent class of FT constraints, while DC-balanced constraints are typically not FT.

Design of constrained codes begins with identifying constraints, such as those described in the Introduction, that achieve certain objectives. Once the system of constrained sequences is specified, information bits are translated into sequences that obey the constraints via an *encoder*, which usually has the form of a finite-state machine. The actual set of sequences produced by the encoder is called a constrained code and is often denoted $\mathcal{C}$. A *decoder* recovers user sequences from constrained sequences. While the decoder is also implemented as a finite-state machine, it is usually required to have a stronger property, called sliding-block decodablility, which controls error propagation [24].

The maximum rate of a constrained code is determined by *Shannon capacity*. The Shannon capacity or simply *capacity* of a constrained system, denoted by $C$, is defined as

$$C = \lim_{n \to \infty} \frac{\log_2 N(n)}{n}$$

where $N(n)$ is the number of sequences of length $n$. The capacity of a constrained system represented by a graph $G$ can be easily computed from the *adjacency matrix* (or *state transition matrix*) of $G$ (provided that the labeling of $G$ satisfies some mildly innocent properties). The adjacency matrix of $G$ with $r$ states and $a_{ij}$ edges from state $i$ to state $j$, $1 \le i, j \le r$, is the $r \times r$ matrix $A = A(G) = \{a_{ij}\}_{r \times r}$. The Shannon capacity of the constraint is given by

$$C = \log_2 \lambda(A)$$

where $\lambda(A)$ is the largest real eigenvalue of $A$.

The *state-splitting algorithm* [1] (see also [24]) gives a general procedure for constructing constrained codes at any rate up to capacity. In this algorithm, one starts with a graph representation of the desired constraint and then transforms it into an encoder via various graph-theoretic operations including splitting and merging of states. Given a desired constraint and a desired rate $p/q \le C$, one or more rounds of state splitting are performed; the determination of which states to split and how to split them is governed by an approximate eigenvector, i.e., a vector $\mathbf{x}$ satisfying $A^q \mathbf{x} \ge 2^p \mathbf{x}$.

Many other very important and interesting approaches are used to constrained code construction—far too many to mention here. One approach combines state-splitting with look-ahead encoding to obtain a very powerful technique which yields superb codes [14]. Another approach involves variable-length and time-varying variations of these techniques [2,13]. Many other effective coding constructions are described in the monograph [17].

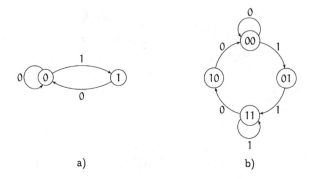

**FIGURE 34.43**   Two equivalent constraints: (a) $\mathcal{F} = \{11\}$ NRZI and (b) $\mathcal{F} = \{101, 010\}$ NRZ.

For high capacity constraints, graph transforming techniques, such as the state-splitting algorithm, may result in encoder/decoder architectures with formidable complexity. Fortunately, a block encoder/decoder architecture with acceptable implementation complexity for many constraints can be designed by well-known enumerative [6], and other combinatorial [32] as well as heuristic techniques [25].

Translation of constrained sequences into the channel sequences depends on the modulation method. Saturation recording of binary information on a magnetic medium is accomplished by converting an input stream of data into a spatial stream of bit cells along a track where each cell is fully magnetized in one of two possible directions, denoted by 0 and 1. Two important modulation methods are commonly used on magnetic recording channels: non-return-to-zero (NRZ) and modified non-return-to-zero (NRZI). In NRZ modulation, the binary digits 0 and 1 in the input data stream correspond to 0 and 1 directions of cell magnetizations, respectively. In NRZI modulation, the binary digit 1 corresponds to a magnetic transition between two bit cells, and the binary digit 0 corresponds to no transition. For example, the channel constraint which forbids transitions in two neighboring bit cells, can be accomplished by either $\mathcal{F} = \{11\}$ NRZI constraint or $\mathcal{F} = \{101, 010\}$ NRZ constraint. The graph representation of these two constraints is shown in Fig. 34.43. The NRZI representation is, in this case, simpler.

## Constraints for ISI Channels

This subsection discusses a class of codes known as codes, which avoid specified differences. This is the only class of distance enhancing codes used in commercial magnetic recording systems. Two main reasons for this are: these codes simplify the channel detectors relative to the uncoded channel and even high rate codes in this class can be realized by low complexity encoders and decoders.

### Requirements

A number of papers have proposed using constrained codes to provide coding gain on channels with high ISI (see, for example, [4,10,20,28]). The main idea of this approach can be described as follows [20]. Consider a discrete-time model for the magnetic recording channel with possibly constrained input $\mathbf{a} = \{a_n\} \, \mathcal{C} \in \subseteq \{0,1\}^\infty$, impulse response $\{h_n\}$, and output $\mathbf{y} = \{y_n\}$ given by

$$y_n = \sum_m a_m h_{n-m} + \eta_n \tag{34.32}$$

where $h(D) = \sum_n h_n D^n = (1 - D)(1 + D)^3$ (E$^2$PR4) or $h(D) = \sum_n h_n D^n = (1 - D)(1 + D)^4$ (E$^3$PR4), $\eta_n$ are independent Gaussian random variables with zero mean and variance $\sigma^2$. The quantity $1/\sigma^2$ is referred to as the signal-to-noise ratio (SNR). The minimum distance of the uncoded channel (34.32) is

$$d_{\min}^2 = \min_{\epsilon(D) \neq 0} \|h(D)\epsilon(D)\|^2$$

where $\epsilon(D) = \Sigma_{i=0}^{i-l} \epsilon_i D^i, (\epsilon_i \in \{-1,0,1\}, \epsilon_0 = 1, \epsilon_{l-1} \neq 0)$ is the polynomial corresponding to a normalized input error sequence $\epsilon = \{\epsilon_i\}_{i=0}^{l-1}$ of length $l$, and the squared norm of a polynomial is defined as the sum of its squared coefficients. The minimum distance is bounded from above by $\|h(D)\|^2$, denoted by

$$d_{\text{MFB}}^2 = \|h(D)\|^2 \tag{34.33}$$

This bound is known as the matched-filter bound (MFB) and is achieved when the error sequence of length $l = 1$, i.e., $\epsilon(D) = 1$, is in the set

$$\arg \min_{\epsilon(D)\neq 0} \|h(D)\epsilon(D)\|^2 \tag{34.34}$$

For channels that fail to achieve the MFB, i.e., for which $d_{\text{min}}^2 < \|h(D)\|^2$, any error sequences $\epsilon(D)$ for which

$$d_{\text{min}}^2 \leq \|h(D)\epsilon(D)\|^2 < \|h(D)\|^2 \tag{34.35}$$

are of length $l \geq 2$ and may belong to a constrained system $X_{\mathcal{L}}^{\{-1,0,1\}}$, where $\mathcal{L}$ is an appropriately chosen finite list of forbidden strings.

For code $\mathcal{C}$, the set of all admissible nonzero error sequences is written as

$$\mathcal{E}(\mathcal{C}) = \{\epsilon \in \{-1,0,1\}^\infty | \epsilon \neq 0, \, \epsilon = (\mathbf{a} - \mathbf{b}), \mathbf{a}, \mathbf{b} \in \mathcal{C}\}$$

Given the condition $\mathcal{E}(\mathcal{C}) \subseteq X_{\mathcal{L}}^{\{-1,0,1\}}$, the least restrictive finite collection $\mathcal{F}$ of blocks over the alphabet $\{0,1\}$ can be identified so that

$$\mathcal{C} \subseteq X_{\mathcal{F}}^{\{0,1\}} \Rightarrow \mathcal{E}(\mathcal{C}) \subseteq X_{\mathcal{L}}^{\{-1,0,1\}} \tag{34.36}$$

## Definitions

A constrained code is defined by specifying $\mathcal{F}$, the list of forbidden strings for code sequences. Prior to that one needs to first characterize error sequences that satisfy (34.35) and then specify $\mathcal{L}$, the list of forbidden strings for error sequences. Error event characterization can be done by using any of the methods described by Karabed, Siegel, and Soljanin in [20]. Specification of $\mathcal{L}$ is usually straightforward.

A natural way to construct a collection $\mathcal{F}$ of blocks forbidden in code sequences based on the collection $\mathcal{L}$ of blocks forbidden in error sequences is the following. From the above definition of error sequences $\epsilon = \{\epsilon_i\}$ we see that $\epsilon_i = 1$ requires $a_i = 1$ and $\epsilon_i = -1$ requires $a_i = 0$, i.e., $a_i = (1 + \epsilon_i)/2$. For each block $\mathbf{w}_\mathcal{E} \in \mathcal{L}$, construct a list $\mathcal{F}_{\mathbf{w}_\mathcal{E}}$ of blocks of the same length $l$ according to the rule:

$$\mathcal{F}_{\mathbf{w}_\mathcal{E}} = \{\mathbf{w}_C \in \{0,1\}^l | w_C^i = (1 + w_\mathcal{E}^i)/2 \text{ for all } i \text{ for which } w_\mathcal{E}^i \neq 0\}.$$

Then the collection $\mathcal{F}$ obtained as $\mathcal{F} = \cup_{\mathbf{w}_\mathcal{E} \in \mathcal{L}} \mathcal{F}_{\mathbf{w}_\mathcal{E}}$ satisfies requirement (34.36); however, the constrained system $X_{\mathcal{F}}^{\{0,1\}}$ obtained this way may not be the most efficient. (Bounds on the achievable rates of codes which avoid specified differences were found recently in [26].)

The previous ideas are illustrated in the example of the $E^2PR4$ channel. Its transfer function is $h(D) = (1 - D)(1 + D)^3$, and its MFB is $\|(1 - D)(1 + D)^3 \cdot 1\|^2 = 10$. The error polynomial $\epsilon(D) = 1 - D + D^2$ is the unique error polynomial for which $\|(1 - D)(1 + D)^3\epsilon(D)\|^2 = 6$, and the error polynomials $\epsilon(D) = 1 - D + D^2 + D^5 - D^6 + D^7$ and $\epsilon(D) = \Sigma_{i=0}^{l-1}(-1)^i D^i$ for $l \geq 4$ are the only polynomials for which $\|(1 - D)(1 + D)^3\epsilon(D)\|^2 = 8$ (see, for example, [20]).

```
          A              B              A              A
a:  0 1 0 1 0 0    1 1 0 1 0 0    0 1 0 1 0 1    1 1 0 1 0 1
b:  0 0 1 0 0 0    1 0 1 0 0 0    0 0 1 0 0 1    1 0 1 0 0 1

          A              A              B              A
a:  0 1 0 1 1 0    1 1 0 1 1 0    0 1 0 1 1 1    1 1 0 1 1 1
b:  0 0 1 0 1 0    1 0 1 0 1 0    0 0 1 0 1 1    1 0 1 0 1 1
```

**FIGURE 34.44** Possible pairs of sequences for which error event $+-+00$ may occur.

It is easy to show that these error events are not in the constrained error set defined by the list of forbidden error strings $\mathcal{L} = \{+-+00, +-+-\}$, where + denotes 1 and − denotes −1. To see this, note that an error sequence that does not contain the string $+-+00$ cannot have error polynomials $\epsilon(D) = 1 - D + D^2$ or $\epsilon(D) = 1 - D + D^2 + D^5 - D^6 + D^7$, while an error sequence that does not contain string $+-+-$ cannot have an error polynomial of the form $\epsilon(D) = \sum_{i=0}^{l-1}(-1)^i D^i$ for $l \geq 4$. Therefore, by the above procedure of defining the list of forbidden ode strings, we obtain the $\mathcal{F} = \{+-+\}$ NRZ constraint. Its capacity is about 0.81, and a rate 4/5 c code into the constraint was first given in [19].

In [20], the following approach was used to obtain several higher rate constraints. For each of the error strings in $\mathcal{L}$, we write all pairs of channel strings whose difference is the error string. To define $\mathcal{F}$, look for the longest string(s) appearing in at least one of the strings in each channel pair. For the example above and the $+-+00$ error string, a case-by-case analysis of channel pairs is depicted in Fig. 34.44. We can distinguish two types (denoted by A and B in the figure) of pairs of code sequences involved in forming an error event. In a pair of type A, at least one of the sequences has a transition run of length 4. In a pair of type B, both sequences have transition runs of length 3, but for one of them the run starts at an even position and for the other at an odd position. This implies that an NRZI constrained system that limits the run of 1s to 3 when it starts at an odd position, and to 2 when it starts at an even position, eliminates all possibilities shown bold-faced in Fig. 34.44. In addition, this constraint eliminates all error sequences containing the string $+-+-$. The capacity of the constraint is about .916, and rate 8/9 block codes with this constraint have been implemented in several commercial read channel chips. More about the constraint and the codes can be found in [4,10,20,28].

## Channels with Colored Noise and Intertrack Interference

Magnetic recording systems always operate in the presence of colored noise intertrack interference, and data dependent noise. Codes for these more realistic channel models are studied in [27]. The following is a brief outline of the problem.

The data recording and retrieval process is usually modeled as a linear, continuous-time, communications channel described by its Lorentzian step response and additive white Gaussian noise. The most common discrete-time channel model is given by Eq. (34.32). Magnetic recording systems employ channel equalization to the most closely matching transfer function $h(D) = \sum_n h_n D^n$ of the form $h(D) = (1 - D)(1 + D)^N$. This equalization alters the spectral density of the noise, and a better channel model assumes that the $\eta_n$ in Eq. (34.32) are identically distributed, Gaussian random variables with zero mean, variance $\sigma^2$, and normalized cross-correlation $E\{\eta_n\eta_k\}/\sigma^2 = \rho_{n-k}$.

In practice, there is always intertrack interference (ITI), i.e., the read head picks up magnetization from an adjacent track. Therefore, the channel output is given by

$$y_n = \sum_m a_m h_{n-m} + \sum_m x_m g_{n-m} + \eta_n \tag{34.37}$$

where $\{g_n\}$ is the discrete-time impulse response of the head to the adjacent track, and $\mathbf{x} = \{x_n\} \in \mathcal{C}$ is the sequence recorded on that track. Assuming that the noise is white.

In the ideal case (34.32), the probability of detecting **b** given that **a** was recorded is equal to $Q(d(\boldsymbol{\epsilon})/\sigma)$, where $d(\boldsymbol{\epsilon})$ is the distance between **a** and **b** given by

$$d^2(\boldsymbol{\epsilon}) = \sum_n \left( \sum_m \epsilon_m h_{n-m} \right)^2 \tag{34.38}$$

Therefore, a lower bound, and a close approximation for small $\sigma$, to the minimum probability of an error-event in the system is given by $Q(d_{\min,\mathcal{C}}/\sigma)$, where

$$d_{\min,\mathcal{C}} = \min_{\boldsymbol{\epsilon} \in \boldsymbol{\epsilon}_c} d(\boldsymbol{\epsilon})$$

is the channel minimum distance of code $\mathcal{C}$. We refer to

$$d_{\min} = \min_{\boldsymbol{\epsilon} \in \{-1,0,1\}^\infty} d(\boldsymbol{\epsilon}) \tag{34.39}$$

as the minimum distance of the uncoded channel, and to the ratio $d_{\min,\mathcal{C}}/d_{\min}$ as the gain in distance of code $\mathcal{C}$ over the uncoded channel.

In the case of colored noise, the probability of detecting **b** given that **a** was recorded equals to $Q(\Delta(\boldsymbol{\epsilon})/\sigma)$, where $\Delta(\boldsymbol{\epsilon})$ is the distance between **a** and **b** given by

$$\Delta^2(\boldsymbol{\epsilon}) = \frac{\left[ \sum_n \left( \sum_m \epsilon_m h_{n-m} \right)^2 \right]^2}{\sum_n \sum_k \left( \sum_m \epsilon_m h_{n-m} \right) \rho_{n-k} \left( \sum_m \epsilon_m h_{k-m} \right)}$$

Therefore, a lower bound to the minimum probability of an error-event in the system is given by $Q(\Delta_{\min,\mathcal{C}}/\sigma)$, where

$$\Delta_{\min,\mathcal{C}} = \min_{\boldsymbol{\epsilon} \in \mathcal{E}_C} \Delta(\boldsymbol{\epsilon})$$

In the case of ITI (Eq. 34.37), an important factor is the probability of detecting sequence **b** given that sequence **a** was recorded on the track being read and sequence **x** was recorded on an adjacent track. This probability is

$$Q(\delta(\boldsymbol{\epsilon},\mathbf{x})/\sigma)$$

where $\delta(\boldsymbol{\epsilon},\mathbf{x})$ is the distance between **a** and **b** in the *presence* of **x** given by [30]

$$\delta^2(\boldsymbol{\epsilon},\mathbf{x}) = \frac{1}{\left[ \sum_n \left( \sum_m \epsilon_m h_{n-m} \right)^2 \right]} \left[ \sum_n \left( \sum_m \epsilon_m h_{n-m} \right)^2 + \sum_n \left( \sum_m x_m g_{n-m} \right) \left( \sum_m \epsilon_m h_{n-m} \right) \right]^2$$

Therefore, a lower bound to the minimum probability of an error-event in the system is proportional to $Q(\delta_{\min,\mathcal{C}}/\sigma)$, where

$$\delta_{\min,\mathcal{C}} = \min_{\boldsymbol{\epsilon} \neq 0, \mathbf{x} \in \mathcal{C}} \delta(\boldsymbol{\epsilon},\mathbf{x})$$

Distance $\delta_{\min,\mathcal{C}}$ can be bounded as follows [30]:

$$\delta_{\min,\mathcal{C}} \geq (1 - \mathcal{M})d_{\min,\mathcal{C}} \qquad (34.40)$$

where $\mathcal{M} = \max_{n,\mathbf{x} \in \mathcal{C}} \sum_m x_m g_{n-m}$, i.e., $\mathcal{M}$ is the maximum absolute value of the interference. Note that $\mathcal{M} = \sum_n |g_n|$. We will assume that $\mathcal{M} < 1$. The bound is achieved if and only if there exists an $\boldsymbol{\epsilon}$, $d(\boldsymbol{\epsilon}) = d_{\min,\mathcal{C}}$, for which $\sum_m \epsilon_m h_{n-m} \in \{-1,0,1\}$ for all $n$, and there exists an $\mathbf{x} \in \mathcal{C}$ such that $\sum_m x_m g_{n-m} = \mp\mathcal{M}$ whenever $\sum_m \epsilon_m h_{n-m} = \pm 1$.

## An Example

Certain codes provide gain in minimum distance on channels with ITI and colored noise, but not on the AWGN channel with the same transfer function. This is best illustrated using the example of the partial response channel with the transfer function $h(D) = (1 - D)(1 + D)^2$ known as EPR4. It is well known that for the EPR4 channel $d_{\min}^2 = 4$. Moreover, as discussed in the subsection on "Constraints for ISI Channels," the following result holds:

**Proposition 1.** *Error events $\epsilon(D)$ such that*

$$d^2(\boldsymbol{\epsilon}) = d_{\min}^2 = 4$$

*take one of the following two forms:*

$$\epsilon(D) = \sum_{j=0}^{k-1} D^{2j}, \quad k \geq 1$$

*or*

$$\epsilon(D) = \sum_{i=0}^{l-1} (-1)^i D^i, \quad l \geq 3$$

Therefore, an improvement of error-probability performance can be accomplished by codes which eliminate the error sequences $\epsilon$ containing the strings $-1 +1 -1$ and $+1 -1 +1$. Such codes were extensively studied in [20].

In the case of ITI (Eq. 34.37), it is assumed that the impulse response to the reading head from an adjacent track is described by $g(D) = \alpha H(D)$, where the parameter $\alpha$ depends on the track to head distance. Under this assumption, the bound (34.40) gives $\delta_{\min}^2 \geq d_{\min}^2(1 - 4\alpha)^2$. The following result was shown in [30]:

**Proposition 2.** *Error events $\epsilon(D)$ such that*

$$\min_{\mathbf{x} \in \mathcal{C}} \delta^2(\boldsymbol{\epsilon}, \mathbf{x}) = \delta_{\min}^2 = d_{\min}^2(1 - 4\alpha)^2 = 4(1 - 4\alpha)^2$$

*take the following form:*

$$\epsilon(D) = \sum_{i=0}^{l-1} (-1)^i D^i, \quad l \geq 5$$

*For all other error sequences for which $d^2(\boldsymbol{\epsilon}) = 4$, we have $\min_{\mathbf{x} \in \mathcal{C}} \delta^2(\boldsymbol{\epsilon}, \mathbf{x}) = 4(1 - 3\alpha)^2$.*

Therefore, an improvement in error-probability performance of this channel can be accomplished by limiting the length of strings of alternating symbols in code sequences to four. For the NRZI type of recording, this can be achieved by a code that limits the runs of successive ones to three. Note that the set of minimum distance error events is smaller than in the case with no ITI. Thus, performance improvement can be accomplished by higher rate codes that would not provide any gain on the ideal channel.

Channel equalization to the EPR4 target introduces cross-correlation among noise samples for a range of current linear recording densities (see [27] and references therein). The following result was obtained in [27]:

**Proposition 3.** *Error events* $\epsilon(D)$ *such that*

$$\Delta^2(\boldsymbol{\epsilon}) = \Delta^2_{min}$$

*take the following form:*

$$\epsilon(D) = \sum_{i=0}^{l-1}(-1)^i D^i, \quad l \geq 3, \ l \ odd$$

Again, the set of minimum distance error events is smaller than in the ideal case (white noise), and performance improvement can be provided by codes which would not give any gain on the ideal channel. For example, since all minimum distance error events have odd parity, a single parity check code can be used.

## Future Directions

### Soft-Output Decoding of Modulation Codes

Detection and decoding in magnetic recording systems is organized as a concatenation of a channel detector, an inner decoder, and an outer decoder, and as such should benefit from techniques known as erasure and list decoding. To declare erasures or generate lists, the inner decoder (or channel detector) needs to assess symbol/sequence reliabilities. Although the information required for this is the same one necessary for producing a single estimate, some additional complexity is usually required. So far, the predicted gains for erasure and list decoding of magnetic recording channels with additive white Gaussian noise were not sufficient to justify increasing the complexity of the channel detector and inner and outer decoder; however, this is not the case for systems employing new magneto-resistive reading heads, for which an important noise source, thermal asperities, is to be handled by passing erasure flags from the inner to the outer decoder.

In recent years, one more reason for developing simple soft-output channel detectors has surfaced. The success of turbo-like coding schemes on memoryless channels has sparked the interest in using them as modulation codes for ISI channels. Several recent results show that the improvements in performance turbo codes offer when applied to magnetic recording channels at moderate linear densities are even more dramatic than in the memoryless case [12,29]. The decoders for turbo and low-density parity check codes (LDPC) either require or perform much better with soft input information which has to be supplied by the channel detector as its soft output. The decoders provide soft outputs which can then be utilized by the outer Reed–Solomon (RS) decoder [22]. A general soft-output sequence detection was introduced in [11], and it is possible to get information on symbol reliabilities by extending those techniques [21,31].

### Reversed Concatenation

Typically, the modulation encoder is the inner encoder, i.e., it is placed downstream of an error-correction encoder (ECC) such as an RS encoder; this configuration is known as standard concatenation (Fig. 34.45). This is natural since otherwise the ECC encoder might well destroy the modulation properties before

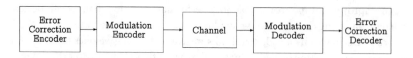

**FIGURE 34.45**   Standard concatenation.

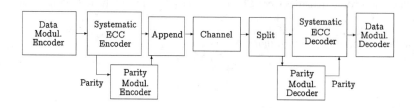

**FIGURE 34.46**   Reversed concatenation.

passing across the channel; however, this scheme has the disadvantage that the modulation decoder, which must come before the ECC decoder, may propagate channel errors before they can be corrected. This is particularly problematic for modulation encoders of very high rate, based on very long block size. For this reason, a good deal of attention has recently focused on a reversed concatenation scheme, where the encoders are concatenated in the reversed order (Fig. 34.46). Special arrangements must be made to ensure that the output of the ECC encoder satisfies the modulation constraints. Typically, this is done by insisting that this encoder be systematic and then re-encoding the parity information using a second modulation encoder (the "parity modulation encoder"), whose corresponding decoder is designed to limit error propagation; the encoded parity is then appended to the modulation-encoded data stream (typically a few merging bits may need to be inserted in between the two streams in order to ensure that the entire stream satisfies the constraint). In this scheme, after passing through the channel the modulation-encoded data stream is split from the modulation-encoded parity stream, and the latter is then decoded via the parity modulation decoder before being passed on to the ECC decoder. In this way, many channel errors can be corrected before the data modulation decoder, thereby mitigating the problem of error propagation. Moreover, if the data modulation encoder has high rate, then the overall scheme will also have high rate because the parity stream is relatively small.

Reversed concatenation was introduced in [3] and later in [23]. Recent interest in the subject has been spurred on by the introduction of a lossless compression scheme, which improves the efficiency of reversed concatenation [15], and an analysis demonstrating the benefits in terms of reduced levels of interleaving [8]; see also [9]. Research on fitting soft decision detection into reversed concatenation can be found in [7,33].

## References

1. R. Adler, D. Coppersmith, and M. Hassner, "Algorithms for sliding-block codes," *IEEE Trans. Inform. Theory,* vol. 29, no. 1, pp. 5–22, Jan. 1983.
2. J. Ashley and B. Marcus, "Time-varying encoders for constrained systems: an approach to limiting error propagation," *IEEE Trans. Inform. Theory,* 46 (2000), 1038–1043.
3. W. G. Bliss, "Circuitry for performing error correction calculations on baseband encoded data to eliminate error propagation," *IBM Tech. Discl. Bull.,* 23 (1981), 4633–4634.
4. W. G. Bliss, "An 8/9 rate time-varying trellis code for high density magnetic recording," *IEEE Trans. Magn.,* vol. 33, no. 5, pp. 2746–2748, Sept. 1997.
5. T. Conway, "A new target response with parity coding for high density magnetic recording," *IEEE Trans. Magn.,* vol. 34, pp. 2382–2386, 1998.
6. T. Cover, "Enumerative source encoding," *IEEE Trans. Inform. Theory,* pp. 73–77, Jan. 1973.

7.  J. Fan, "Constrained coding and soft iterative decoding for storage," PhD Dissertation, Stanford University, 1999.

8.  J. Fan and R. Calderbank, "A modified concatenated coding scheme, with applications to magnetic data storage," *IEEE Trans. Inform. Theory*, 44 (1998), 1565–1574.

9.  J. Fan, B. Marcus, and R. Roth, "Lossless sliding-block compression of constrained systems," *IEEE Trans. Inform. Theory*, 46 (2000), 624–633.

10. K. Knudson Fitzpatrick, and C. S. Modlin, "Time-varying MTR codes for high density magnetic recording," in *Proc. 1997 IEEE Global Telecommun. Conf. (GLOBECOM '97)*, Phoenix, AZ, Nov. 1997, pp. 1250–1253.

11. J. Hagenauer and P. Hoeher, "A Viterbi algorithm with soft–decision outputs and its applications," in *Proc. 1989 IEEE Global Telecommun. Conf. (GLOBECOM '89)*, Dallas, TX, Nov. 1989, pp. 1680–1687.

12. C. Heegard, "Turbo coding for magnetic recording," in *Proc. 1998 Information Theory Workshop*, San Diego, CA, Feb. 8–11, 1998, pp. 18–19.

13. C. D. Heegard, B. H. Marcus, and P. H. Siegel, "Variable-length state splitting with applications to average runlength-constrained (ARC) codes," *IEEE Trans. Inform. Theory*, 37 (1991), 759–777.

14. H. D. L. Hollmann, "On the construction of bounded-delay encodable codes for constrained systems," *IEEE Trans. Inform. Theory*, 41 (1995), 1354–1378.

15. K. A. Schouhamer Immink, "A practical method for approaching the channel capacity of constrained channels," *IEEE Trans. Inform. Theory*, 43 (1997), 1389–1399.

16. K. A. Schouhamer Immink, P. H. Siegel, and J. K. Wolf, "Codes for Digital Recorders," *IEEE Trans. Infor. Theory*, vol. 44, pp. 2260–2299, Oct. 1998.

17. K. A. Schouhamer Immink, *Codes for Mass Data Storage*, Shannon Foundation Publishers, The Netherlands, 1999.

18. R. Karabed and P. H. Siegel, "Matched spectral null codes for partial response channels," *IEEE Trans. Inform. Theory*, 37 (1991), 818–855.

19. R. Karabed and P. H. Siegel, "Coding for higher order partial response channels," in *Proc. 1995 SPIE Int. Symp. on Voice, Video, and Data Communications*, Philadelphia, PA, Oct. 1995, vol. 2605, pp. 115–126.

20. R. Karabed, P. H. Siegel, and E. Soljanin, "Constrained coding for binary channels with high intersymbol interference," *IEEE Trans. Inform. Theory*, vol. 45, pp. 1777–1797, Sept. 1999.

21. K. J. Knudson, J. K. Wolf, and L. B. Milstein, "Producing soft–decision information on the output of a class IV partial response Viterbi detector," in *Proc. 1991 IEEE Int. Conf. Commun. (ICC '91)*, Denver, CO, June 1991, pp. 26.5.1.–26.5.5.

22. R. Koetter and A. Vardy, preprint 2000.

23. M. Mansuripur, "Enumerative modulation coding with arbitrary constraints and post-modulation error correction coding and data storage systems," *Proc. SPIE*, 1499 (1991), 72–86.

24. B. Marcus, R. Roth, and P. Siegel, "Constrained systems and coding for recording channels," Chapter 20 of *Handbook of Coding Theory*, edited by V. Pless, C. Huffman, 1998, Elsevier.

25. D. Modha and B. Marcus, "Art of constructing low complexity encoders/decoders for constrained block codes," *IEEE J. Sel. Areas in Comm.*, (2001), to appear.

26. B. E. Moision, A. Orlitsky, and P. H. Siegel, "On codes that avoid specified differences," *IEEE Trans. Inform. Theory*, vol. 47, pp. 433–441, Jan. 2001.

27. B. E. Moision, P. H. Siegel, and E. Soljanin, "Distance Enhancing Codes for High-Density Magnetic Recording Channel," *IEEE Trans. Magn.*, submitted, Jan. 2001.

28. J. Moon and B. Brickner, "Maximum transition run codes for data storage systems," *IEEE Trans. Magn.*, vol. 32, pp. 3992–3994, Sept. 1996.

29. W. Ryan, L. McPheters, and S. W. McLaughlin, "Combined turbo coding and turbo equalization for PR4-equalized Lorentzian channels," in *Proc. 22nd Annual Conf. Inform. Sciences and Systems*, Princeton, NJ, March 1998.

30. E. Soljanin, "On–track and off–track distance properties of Class 4 partial response channels," in *Proc. 1995 SPIE Int. Symp. on Voice, Video, and Data Communications*, Philadelphia, PA, vol. 2605, pp. 92–102, Oct. 1995.

31. E. Soljanin, "Simple soft-output detection for magnetic recording channels," in *1998 IEEE Int. Symp. Inform. Theory (ISIT'00)*, Sorrento, Italy, June 2000.

32. A. J. van Wijngaarden and K. A. Schouhamer Immink "Combinatorial construction of high rate runlength-limited codes," *Proc. 1996 IEEE Global Telecommun. Conf. (GLOBECOM '96)*, London, U.K., pp. 343–347, Nov. 1996.

33. A. J. van Wijngaarden and K. A. Schouhamer Immink, "Maximum run-length limited codes with error control properties," *IEEE J. Select. Areas Commun.*, vol. 19, April 2001.

34. A. J. van Wijngaarden and E. Soljanin, "A combinatorial technique for constructing high rate MTR–RLL codes," *IEEE J. Select. Areas Commun.*, vol. 19, April 2001.

# 34.6 Data Detection

*Miroslav Despotović and Vojin Šenk*

## Introduction

Digital magnetic recording systems transport information from one time to another. In communication society jargon, it is said that recording and reading information back from a (magnetic) medium is equivalent to sending it through a time channel. There are differences between such channels. Namely, in communication systems, the goal is a user error rate of $10^{-5}$ or $10^{-6}$. Storage systems, however, often require error rates of $10^{-12}$ or better. On the other hand, the common goal is to send the greatest possible amount of information through the channel used. For storage systems, this is tantamount to increasing recording density, keeping the amount redundancy as low as possible, i.e., keeping the bit rate per recorded pulse as high as possible. The perpetual push for higher bit rates and higher storage densities spurs a steady increment of the amplitude distortion of many types of transmission and storage channels.

When recording density is low, each transition written on the magnetic medium results in a relatively isolated peak of voltage, and peak detection method is used to recover written information; however, when PW50 (pulse width at half maximum response) becomes comparable with the channel bit period, the peak detection channel cannot provide reliable data detection, due to intersymbol interference (ISI). This interference arises because the effects of one readback pulse are not allowed to die away completely before the transmission of the next. This is an example of a so-called baseband transmission system, i.e., no carrier modulation is used to send data. Impulse dispersion and different types of induced noise at the receiver end of the system introduce combination of several techniques (equalization, detection, and timing recovery) to restore data. This chapter section gives a survey of most important detection techniques in use today assuming ideal synchronization.

Increasing recording density in new magnetic recording products necessarily demands enhanced detection techniques. First detectors operated at densities at which pulses were clearly separated, so that very simple, symbol-by-symbol detection technique was applied, the so-called *peak detector* [30]. With increased density, the overlap of neighboring dispersed pulses becomes so severe (i.e., large intersymbol interference—ISI) that peak detector could not combat with such heavy pulse shape degradation. To accomplish this task, it was necessary to master signal processing technology to be able to implement more powerful *sequence detection* techniques. This chapter section will both focus on this type of detection already applied in commercial products and give advanced procedures for searching the detection trellis to serve as a tutorial material for research on next generation products.

## Partial-Response Equalization

In the classical peak detection scheme, an equalizer is inserted whose task is just to remove all the ISI so that an isolated pulse is acquired, but the equalization will also enhance and colorize the noise (from readback process) due to spectral mismatch. The noise enhancement obtained in this manner will increase

**FIGURE 34.47**  Maximum-likelihood sequence detector.

with recording density and eventually become intolerable. Namely, since such a full equalization is aimed at slimming the individual pulse, so that it does not overlap with adjacent pulses, it is usually too aggressive and ends up with huge noise power.

Let us now review the question of recording density, also known as packing density. It is often used to specify how close two adjacent pulses stay to each other and is defined as PW50/T (see Chapter 34.1 for definition). Whatever tricks are made with peak detection systems, they barely help at PW50/T ratios above 1.

Section 34.6 discusses two receiver types that run much less rapidly out of steam. These are the partial-response equalizer (PRE) and the decision-feedback equalizer (DFE). Both are rooted in old telegraph tricks and, just as is the case with peak detector, they take instantaneous decisions with respect to the incoming data. Section 34.6 will focus mainly on these issues, together with sequence detection algorithms that accompany partial-response (PR) equalization.

What is PR equalization? It is the act of shaping the readback magnetic recording signal to look like the target signal specified by the PR. After equalization the data are detected using a sequence detector. Of course, quantization by an analog-to-digital converter (ADC) occurs at some point before the sequence detector.

The common readback structure consists of a linear filter, called a whitened matched filter, a symbol-rate sampler (ADC), a PRE, and a sequence detector, Fig. 34.47. The PRE in this scheme can also be put before the sampler, meaning that it is an analog, not a digital equalizer. Sometimes part of the equalizer is implemented in the analog, the other part in the digital domain. In all cases, analog signal, coming from the magnetic head, should have a certain and constant level of amplification. This is done in a variable gain amplifier (VGA). To keep a signal level, VGA gets a control signal from a clock and gain recovery system. In the sequel, we will assume that VGA is already (optimally) performed. In the design of equalizers and detectors, low power dissipation and high speed are both required. The error perfor-mances need to be maintained as well. So far, most systems seek for the implementations in the digital domain, as is the case in Fig. 34.47, but it has been shown that ADC may contribute to the high-frequency noise during the PR target equalization, causing a long settling time in clock recovery loop, as well as degrading performance [33]. In addition, the ADC is also usually the bottleneck for the low-power high-speed applications. On the other hand, the biggest problem for an analog system is the imperfection of circuit elements. The problems encountered with analog systems include nonideal gain, mismatch, nonlinear hold step, offset, etc.

Let us now turn to the blocks shown in Fig. 34.47. The first of them, the whitened matched filter, has the following properties [7]:

*Simplicity:* a single filter producing single sample at the output is all that is needed. The response of the filter is either chosen to be causal and hence realizable, or noncausal, meaning some delay has to be introduced, yielding better performance.

*Sufficiency:* the filter is information lossless, in the sense that its sampled outputs are a set of sufficient statistics for estimation of the input sequence.

*Whiteness:* the noise components of the sampled outputs are independent identically distributed Gaussian random variables.

The whiteness and sufficiency property follow from the fact that the set of waveforms at the output of the matched filter is an orthonormal basis for the signal space.

The next block is PRE. What is PR? Essential to PR techniques is that the PR sequence is obtained from the channel sequence via a simple linear filter. More specifically, the impulse response of this filter is such that the overall response is modeled as having only a few small integer-valued coefficients, the condition actually considered crucial for the system to be called PR. This condition subsequently yields relatively simple sequence detectors. The correlative level coding [3], also known as PR [31] is adopted in digital communication applications for long time. Kobayashi [9] suggested in 1971 that this type of channels can be treated as a linear finite state machine, and thus can be represented by the state diagram and its time instant labeled counterpart, trellis diagram. Consequently, its input is best inferred using some trellis search technique, the best of them (if we neglect complexity issues) being the Viterbi algorithm [2] (if one is interested in maximizing the likelihood of the whole sequence; otherwise, a symbol-by-symbol detector is needed). Kobayashi also indicated that the magnetic recording channel could be regarded as the PR channel due to the inherent differentiation property in the readback process [8]. This is both present in inductive heads and in magnetoresistive (MR) heads, though the latter are directly sensitive to magnetization and not to its change (this is due to the fact that the head has to be shielded). In other words, the pulse will be read only when the transition of opposite magnet polarities is sensed.

Basic to the PR equalization is the fact that a controlled amount of ISI is not suppressed by the equalizer, but rather left for a sequence detector to handle. The nature of the controlled ISI is defined by a PR. A proper match of this response to the channel permits noise enhancement to remain small even when amplitude distortion is severe. In other words, PR equalization can provide both well-controlled ISI and spectral match.

PR equalization is based on two assumptions:

- The shape of readback signal from an isolated transition is exactly known and determined.
- The superposition of signals from adjacent transitions is linear.

Furthermore, it is assumed that the channel characteristics are fixed and known, so that equalization need not be adaptive. The resulting PR channel can be characterized using $D$-transform of the sequences that occur, $X(D) = I(D)H(D)$ [7] where $H(D) = \sum_{i=0}^{M-1} h_i D^i$, $D$ represents the delay factor in $D$-transform and $M$ denotes the order of the PR signals. When modeling differentiation, $H(D) = 1 - D$. The finite state machine (FSM) of this PR channel is known as the dicode system since there are only two states in the transition diagram.

The most unclear signal transformation in Fig. 34.47 is equalization. What does it mean that the pulse of voltage should look like the target signal specified by the PR (the so-called PR target)? To answer this question let us consider the popular Class IV PR, or PRIV system.

For magnetic recording systems with PW50/T approximately equal to 2, comparatively little equalization is required to force the equalized channel to match a class-4 PR (PR4) channel where $H(D) = (1 - D)(1 + D) = 1 - D^2$. Comparing to the Lorentzian model of Chapter 34.1, PR4 channel shows more emphasis in the high frequency domain. The equalizer with the PR4 as the equalization target thus suppresses the low frequency components and enhances the high frequency ones, degrading the performance of all-digital detectors since the quantization noise, that is mainly placed at higher frequencies, is boosted up.

The isolated pulse shape in a PR4 system is shown in Fig. 34.48. The transition is written at time instant $t = 0$, where $T$ is the channel bit period. The shape is oscillating and the pulse values at integer number of bit periods before the transition are exactly zeros. Obviously, it is this latter feature that should give us future advantage; however, at $t = 0$ and at $t = T$, i.e., one bit period later, the values of the pulse are equal to "1". The pulse of voltage reaches its peak amplitude of 1.273 at one half of the bit period. Assume that an isolated transition is written on the medium and the pulse of voltage shown in Fig. 34.48 comes to the PRML system. The PR4 system requires that the samples of this pulse should correspond to the bit periods. Therefore, samples of the isolated PR4 pulse will be 00…011000 … (of course, "1" is used for convenience, and in reality it corresponds to some ADC level).

Because the isolated transition has two nonzero samples, when the next transition is written, the pulses will interfere. Thus, writing two pulses adjacent to each other will introduce superposition between them,

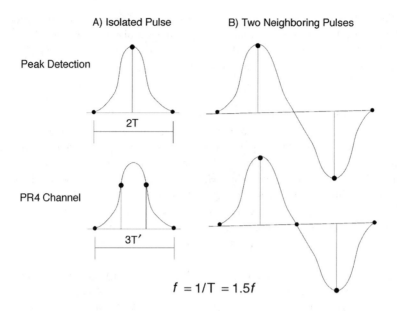

**FIGURE 34.48**  Capacity of PR4 channel.

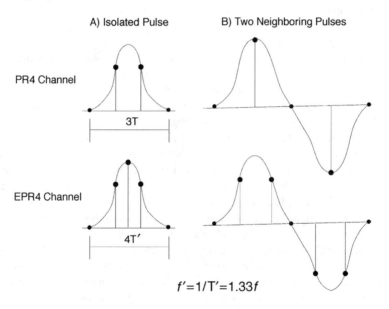

**FIGURE 34.49**  Capacity of EPR4 channel.

usually called a dipulse response, as shown in Fig. 34.49. Here, the samples are $[\ldots, 0, 0, 1, 0, -1, 0, 0, \ldots]$, resulting from

$$
\begin{array}{ll}
\phantom{+}0\ 0\ 0\ 1\ \phantom{-}1\ \phantom{-}0\ 0\ 0 & \text{from the first transition} \\
+\ 0\ 0\ 0\ 0\ -1\ -1\ 0\ 0 & \text{from the second transition} \\
\hline
\phantom{+}0\ 0\ 0\ 1\ \phantom{-}0\ -1\ 0\ 0 &
\end{array}
$$

Now, there is no concern about linear ISI; once the pulses can be reduced to the predetermined simple shape, the data pattern is easily recovered because superposition of signals from adjacent transitions is known.

In the above example, we see that sample "1" is suppressed by "−1" from the next transition. It is a simple matter to check that all possible linear combinations of the samples result in only three possible values {−1, 0, +1} (naturally, it is that all parts of the system are working properly, i.e., equalization, gain, and timing recovery, and that the signal is noise free). A positive pulse of voltage is always followed by a negative pulse and vice versa, so that the system can be regarded as an alternative mark inversion (AMI) code.

The higher bit capacity of the PR4 channel can best be understood from Fig. 34.48. It is observed that PR4 channel provides a 50% enhancement in the recording density as compared with the peak detection (fully equalized) one, since the latter requires isolation of single bits from each other. In the next figure, we see that the EPR4 channel (explained later) adds another 33% to this packing density. PR4 has another advantage over all the other PR systems; since $H(D) = 1 - D^2$, the current symbol is correlated to the second previous one, allowing the system to be modeled as two interleaved dicode channels, implying the use of simple dicode detectors for even and odd readback samples. RLL coding is necessary in this case, since nonideal tracking and timing errors result in a residual intermediate term (linear in $D$) that induces correlation between two interleaved sequences, and thus degrades systems that rely on decoupled detection of each of them.

RLL codes are widely used in conjunction with PR equalization in order to eliminate certain data strings that would render tracking and synchronization difficult. If PR4 target is used, a special type of RLL coding is used, characterized by $(0,G/I)$. Here, $G$ and $I$ denote the maximum number of consecutive zeros in the overall data string, and in the odd/even substrings, respectively. The latter parameter ensures proper functioning of the clock recovery mechanism if deinterleaving of the PR4 channel into two independent dicode channels is performed. The most popular is the $(0,4/4)$ code, whose data rate is 7/8, i.e., whose data loss is limited to 12.5%.

Other PR targets are used besides PR4. The criterion of how to select the appropriate PR target is based on spectral matching, to avoid introducing too much equalization noise. For instance, for PW50/T ≈ 2.25, it is better to model ISI pattern as the so-called EPR4 (i.e. extended class-4 partial response) channel with $H(D) = (1 + D)^2(1 - D) = 1 + D - D^2 - D^3$. As the packing density goes up, more low frequency components are being introduced (low compared to $1/T$, that also increases as $T$ is shortened, in reality those frequencies are higher than those met for lower recording densities, respectively greater $T$). This is the consequence of the fact that intersymbol interference blurs the boundary between individual pulses, flattening the overall response (in time domain). The additional $1 + D$ term in the target PR effectively suppresses the unwanted high frequencies. EPR4 enables even higher capacities of the magnetic recording systems than PRIV, observing the difference of 33% in the recording density displayed in Fig. 34.49; however, a practical implementation of EPR4 is much more complex than is the case with PR4. First, the deinterleaving idea used for PR4 cannot be implemented. Second, the corresponding state diagram (and consequently trellis) now has eight states instead of four (two if deinterleaving is used). Furthermore, its output is five-leveled, instead of ternary for the PR4 and the dicode channel, so that a 4.4 dB degradation is to be expected with a threshold detector. Naturally, if sequence detector is used, such as Viterbi algorithm (VA), this loss does not exist, but its elimination is obtained at the expense of a significantly increased complexity of the detector. Furthermore, if such a detector can be used, EPR4 has a performance advantage over PR4 due to less equalization noise enhancement, cf. Fig. 34.50.

Let us reconsider the PR equalizer shown in Fig. 34.47. Following the approach from Reference 44, its aim is to transform the input spectrum $Y'(e^{j2\pi\Omega})$ into a spectrum $Y(e^{j2\pi\Omega}) = Y'(e^{j2\pi\Omega})|C(e^{j2\pi\Omega})|^2$, where $C(e^{j2\pi\Omega})$ is the transfer function of the equalizer. The spectrum $Y(e^{j2\pi\Omega}) = I(e^{j2\pi\Omega})|H(e^{j2\pi\Omega})|^2 + N(e^{j2\pi\Omega})$ where $H(D)$ is the PR target. For instance, duobinary PR target $(H(D) = 1 + D)$ enhances low frequencies and suppresses those near the Nyquist frequency $\Omega = 0.5$, whereas dicode $H(D) = (1 - D)$ does the opposite: it suppresses low frequencies and enhances those near $\Omega = 0.5$.

In principle, the spectral zeros of $H(e^{j2\pi\Omega})$ can be undone via a linear (recursive) filter, but this would excessively enhance any noise components added. The schemes for tracking the input sequence to the system based on the PR target equalized one will be reviewed later in this chapter section. For instance,

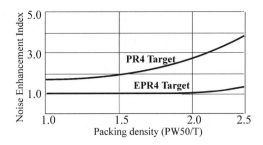

**FIGURE 34.50** Equalization noise enhancement in PR channels.

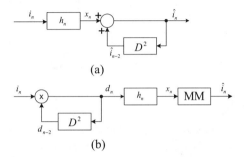

**FIGURE 34.51** (a) PR4 recursive restoration of information sequence and (b) precoder derived from it.

for a PR4 system, a second-order recursive filter can in principle be used to transform its input into an estimate of the information sequence, Fig. 34.51.

Unfortunately, if an erroneous estimate is produced at any moment, all subsequent estimates will be in error (in fact, they will no longer be in the alphabet $\{-1, 0, 1\}$, enabling error monitoring and simple forms of error correction [31]). To avoid this catastrophic error propagation, resort can be taken to a precoder.

Let us analyze the functioning of this precoder in the case of the PR4 channel $(1 - D^2)$ (generalization to other PR channels is trivial). Its function is to transform $i_n$ into a binary sequence $d_n = i_n d_{n-2}$ to which the PR transformation is applied, Fig. 34.51(b). This produces a ternary sequence

$$x_n = (d * h)_n = d_n - d_{n-2} = i_n d_{n-2} - d_{n-2} = (i_n - 1)d_{n-2}$$

Because $d_{n-2}$ cannot be zero, $x_n$ is zero iff $i_n - 1 = 0$, i.e., $i_n = 1$. Thus, the estimate $\hat{i}_n$ of $i_n$ can be formed by means of the memoryless mapping (MM)

$$\hat{i}_n = \begin{cases} 1, & x_n = 0 \\ 0, & \text{else} \end{cases}$$

This decoding rule does not rely on past data estimates and thereby avoids error propagation altogether. In practice, the sequences $i_n$ and $d_n$ are in the alphabet $\{0, 1\}$ rather than $\{-1, 1\}$, and the multiplication in Fig. 34.51(b) becomes a modulo-2 addition (where 0 corresponds to 1, and 1 to $-1$).

The precoder does not affect the spectral characteristics of an uncorrelated data sequence. For correlated data, however, precoding need not be spectrally neutral. It is instructive to think of the precoder as a first-order recursive filter with a pole placed so as to cancel the zero of the partial response. The filter uses a modulo-2 addition instead of a normal addition and as a result the cascade of filter and PR, while memoryless, has a nonbinary output. The MM serves to repair this "deficiency."

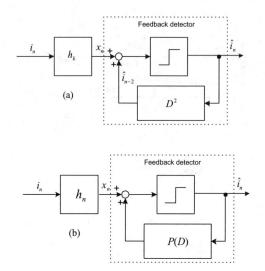

**FIGURE 34.52**   Feedback detector.

Catastrophic error propagation can be avoided without precoder by forcing the output of the recursive filter of Fig. 34.52 to be binary (Fig. 34.52(a)). An erroneous estimate $\hat{i}_{n-2} = -i_{n-2}$ leads to a digit

$$\hat{i}_n = x_n + \hat{i}_{n-2} = i_n - i_{n-2} + \hat{i}_{n-2} = i_n - 2i_{n-2}$$

whose polarity is obviously determined by $i_{n-2}$. Thus, the decision $\hat{i}_n$ that is taken by the slicer in Fig. 34.52(a) will be correct if $i_n$ happens to be the opposite of $i_{n-2}$. If data is uncorrelated, this will happen with probability 0.5, and error propagation will soon cease, since the average number of errors in a burst is $1 + 0.5 + (0.5)^2 + \cdots = 2$. Error propagation is thus not a serious problem.

The feedback detector of Fig. 34.52 is easily generalized to arbitrary partial response $H(D)$. For purposes of normalization, $H(D)$ is assumed to be causal and monic (i.e., $h_n = 0$ for $n < 0$ and $h_0 = 1$). The nontrivial taps $h_1, h_2, \ldots$ together form the "tail" of $H(D)$. This tail can be collected in $P(D)$, with $p_n = 0$ for $n \le 0$ and $p_n = h_n$ for $n \ge 1$. Hence, $h_n = \delta_n + p_n$, where the Kronecker delta function $\delta_n$ represents the component $h_0 = 1$. Hence

$$x_n = (i * h)_n = (i * (\delta + p))_n = i_n + (i * p)_n.$$

The term $(i * p)_n$ depends exclusively on past digits $i_{n-1}, i_{n-2}, \ldots$ that can be replaced by decisions $\hat{i}_{n-1}, \hat{i}_{n-2}, \ldots$. Therefore, an estimate $\hat{i}_n$ of the current digit $i_n$ can be formed according to $\hat{i}_n = x_k (\hat{i} * p)_n$ as in Fig. 34.52(b). As before, a slicer quantizes $\hat{i}_n$ into binary decisions $\hat{i}_n$ so as to avoid catastrophic error propagation. The average length of bursts of errors, unfortunately, increases with the memory order of $H(D)$. Even so, error propagation is not normally a serious problem [21]. In essence, the feedback detector avoids noise enhancement by exploiting past decisions. This viewpoint is also central to decision-feedback equalization, to be explained later.

Naturally, all this can be generalized to nonbinary data; but in magnetic recording, so far, only binary data are used (the so-called saturation recording). The reasons for this are elimination of hysteresis and the stability of the recorded sequence in time.

Let us consider now the way the PR equalizer from Fig. 34.47 is constructed. In Fig. 34.53, a discrete-time channel with transfer function $F(e^{j2\pi\Omega})$ transforms $i_n$ into a sequence $y_n = (i * f)_n + u_n$, where $u_n$ is the additive noise with power spectral density $U(e^{j2\pi\Omega})$, and $y_n$ represents the sampled output of a whitened matched filter. We might interpret $F(e^{j2\pi\Omega})$ as comprising two parts: a transfer function $H(e^{j2\pi\Omega})$ that captures most of the amplitude distortion of the channel (the PR target) and a function

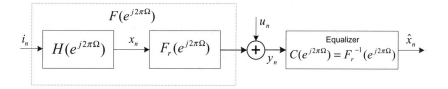

**FIGURE 34.53** Interpretation of PR equalization.

$F_r(e^{j2\pi\Omega}) = F(e^{j2\pi\Omega})/H(e^{j2\pi\Omega})$ that accounts for the remaining distortion. The latter distortion has only a small amplitude component and can thus be undone without much noise enhancement by a linear equalizer with transfer function

$$C(e^{j2\pi\Omega}) = \frac{1}{F_r(e^{j2\pi\Omega})} = \frac{H(e^{j2\pi\Omega})}{F(e^{j2\pi\Omega})}$$

This is precisely the PR equalizer we sought for. It should be stressed that the subdivision in Fig. 34.53 is only conceptual. The equalizer output is a noisy version of the "output" of the first filter in Fig. 34.53 and is applied to the feedback detector of Fig. 34.52, to obtain decision variables $\hat{\imath}'_n$ and $\hat{\imath}_n$. The precoder and MM of Fig. 34.51 are, of course, also applicable and yield essentially the same performance.

The choice of the coefficients of the PRE in Fig. 34.47 is the same as for full-response equalization and is explained in the subsection on "Adaptive Equalization and Timing Recovery." Interestingly, zero-forcing here is not as bad as is the case with full-response signaling and yields approximately the same result as minimum mean-square equalization. To evaluate the performance of the PRE, let us assume that all past decisions that affect $\hat{\imath}_n$ are correct and that the equalizer is zero forcing (see "Adaptive Equalization and Timing Recovery" for details). The only difference between $\hat{\imath}'_n$ and $\hat{\imath}_n$ is now the filtered noise component $(u * c)_n$ with variance

$$\sigma^2_{\text{ZFPRE}} = \int_{-0.5}^{0.5} U(e^{j2\pi\Omega})\left|C(e^{j2\pi\Omega})\right|^2 d\Omega = \int_{-0.5}^{0.5} \frac{U(e^{j2\pi\Omega})\left|H(e^{j2\pi\Omega})\right|^2}{\left|F(e^{j2\pi\Omega})\right|^2} d\Omega$$

Because $|H(e^{j2\pi\Omega})|$ was selected to be small wherever $|F(e^{j2\pi\Omega})|$ is small, the integrand never becomes very large, and the variance will be small. This is in marked contrast with full-response equalization. Here, $H(e^{j2\pi\Omega}) = 1$ for all $\Omega$, and the integrand in the above formula can become large at frequencies where $|F(e^{j2\pi\Omega})|$ is small. Obviously, the smallest possible noise enhancement occurs if $H(e^{j2\pi\Omega})$ is selected so that the integrand is independent of frequency, implying that the noise at the output of the PRE is white. This is, in general, not possible if $H(e^{j2\pi\Omega})$ is restricted to be PR (i.e., small memory-order, integer-valued). The generalized feedback detector of Fig. 34.52, on the other hand, allows a wide variety of causal responses to be used, and here $|H(e^{j2\pi\Omega})|$ can be chosen at liberty. Exploitation of this freedom leads to decision feedback equalization (DFE).

## Decision Feedback Equalization

This subsection reviews the basics of decision feedback detection. It is again assumed that the channel characteristics are fixed and known, so that the structure of this detector need not be adaptive. Generalizing to variable channel characteristics and adaptive detector structure is tedious, but straightforward.

A DFE detector shown in Fig. 34.54, utilizes the noiseless decision to help remove the ISI. There are two types of ISI: *precursor* ISI (ahead of the detection time) and *postcursor* (behind detection time). Feedforward equalization (FFE) is needed to eliminate the precursor ISI, pushing its energy into the postcursor domain. Supposing all the decisions made in the past are correct, DFE reproduces exactly the modified

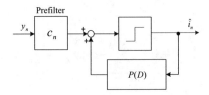

**FIGURE 34.54**   Decision feedback equalizer.

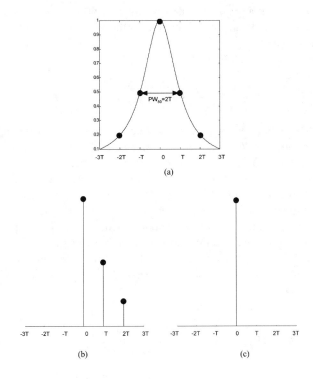

**FIGURE 34.55**   Precursor and postcursor ISI elimination with DFE (a) sampled channel response, (b) after feed-forward filter and (c) slicer output.

postcursor ISI (with extra postcursor ISI produced by the FFE during the elimination of precursor ISI), thus eliminating it completely, Fig. 34.55. If the length of the FFE can be made infinitely long, it should be able to completely suppress the precursor ISI, redistributing its energy into the postcursor region, where it is finally cancelled by feedback decision part. No spectrum inverse is needed for this process, so noise boosting is much less than is the case with linear equalizers.

The final decision of the detector is made by the memoryless slicer, Fig. 34.54. The reason why a slicer can perform efficient sequence detection can be explained with the fact that memory of the DFE system is located in two equalizers, so that only symbol-by-symbol detection can suffice. In terms of performance, the DFE is typically much closer to the maximum likelihood sequence detector than to the LE. If the equalization target is not the main cursor, but a PR system, a sequence detection algorithm can be used afterwards. A feasible way to implement this with minimum additional effort is the tree search algorithm used instead of VA [6]. The simple detection circuitry of a DFE, consisting of two equalizers and one slicer, makes implementation possible. The DFE may be regarded as a generalization of the PRE. In the DFE, the trailing portion of the ISI is not suppressed by a forward equalizer but rather canceled by a feedback filter that is excited by past decisions. Fortunately, error propagation is typically only a minor

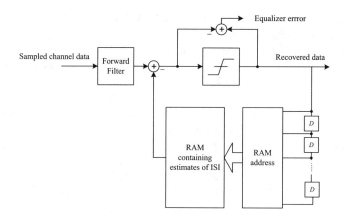

**FIGURE 34.56**   Block diagram of a RAM-based DFE.

problem and it can, in fact, be altogether avoided through a technique that is called Tomlinson/Harashima precoding.

Performance differences between zero-forcing and minimum mean-square equalizers tend to be considerably smaller in the DFE case than for the LE, and as a result it becomes more difficult to reap SNR benefits from the modulation code. It can be proved that DFE is the optimum receiver with no detection delay. If delay is allowed, it is better to use trellis-based detection algorithms.

### RAM-Based DFE Detection

Decision feedback equalization or RAM-based DFE is the most frequent alternative to PRML detection. Increase of bit density leads to significant nonlinear ISI in the magnetic recording channel. Both the linear DFE [12,26] and PRML detectors do not compensate for the nonlinear ISI. Furthermore, the implementation complexity of a Viterbi detector matched to the PR channel grows exponentially with the degree of channel polynomial. Actually, in order to meet requirements for a high data transfer rate, high-speed ADC is also needed. In the RAM-based DFE [19,24], the linear feedback section of the linear DFE is replaced with a look-up table. In this way, detector decisions make up a RAM address pointing to the memory location that contains an estimate of the post cursor ISI for the particular symbol sequence. This estimate is subtracted from the output of the forward filter forming the equalizer output. Look-up table size is manageable and typically is less than 256 locations. The major disadvantage of this approach is that it requires complicated architecture and control to recursively update ISI estimates based on equalizer error.

## Detection in a Trellis

A trellis-based system can be simply described as a FSM (Finite State Machine) whose structure may be displayed with the aid of a graph, tree, or trellis diagram. A FSM maps input sequences (vectors) into output sequences (vectors), not necessarily of the same length. Although the system is generally nonlinear and time-varying, linear fixed trellis based systems are usually met. For them,

$$F(a \cdot \mathbf{i}_{[0,\infty)}) = a \cdot F(\mathbf{i}_{[0,\infty)})$$

$$F(\mathbf{i}'_{[0,\infty)} + \mathbf{i}''_{[0,\infty)}) = F(\mathbf{i}'_{[0,\infty)}) + F(\mathbf{i}''_{[0,\infty)})$$

where $a$ is a constant, $\mathbf{i}_{[0,\infty)}$ is any input sequence and $F(\mathbf{i}_{[0,\infty)})$ is the corresponding output sequence. It is assumed that input and output symbols belong to a subset of a field. Also, for any $d > 0$, if $\mathbf{x}_{[0,\infty)} = F(\mathbf{i}_{[0,\infty)})$ and $\mathbf{i}'_l = \mathbf{i}_{l-d}$, $\mathbf{i}'_{[0,d)} = \mathbf{0}_{[0,d)}$ then $F(\mathbf{i}'_{[0,\infty)}) = \mathbf{x}'_{[0,\infty)}$, where $\mathbf{x}'_l = \mathbf{x}_{l-d}$, $\mathbf{x}'_{[0,d)}, = \mathbf{0}_{[0,d)}$. It is easily verified that $F(\cdot)$ can be represented by the convolution, so that $\mathbf{x} = \mathbf{i} * \mathbf{h}$, where $\mathbf{h}$ is the system impulse response (this is also valid for different lengths of **x** and **i** with a suitable definition of **h**). If **h** is of finite duration, $M$ denotes the system memory length.

Let us now consider a feedforward FSM with memory length $M$. At any time instant (depth or level) $l$, the FSM output $x_l$ depends on the current input $i_l$ and $M$ previous inputs $i_{l-1}, \ldots, i_{l-M}$. The overall functioning of the system can be mapped on a trellis diagram, whereon a node represents one of $q^M$ encoder states ($q$ is the cardinality of the input alphabet including the case when the input symbol is actually a subsequence), while a branch connecting two nodes represents the FSM output associated to the transition between the corresponding system states.

A trellis, which is a visualization of the state transition diagram with a time element incorporated, is characterized by $q$ branches stemming from and entering each state, except in the first and last $M$ branches (respectively called head and tail of the trellis). The branches at the $l$th time instant are labeled by sequences $x_l \in X$. A sequence of $l$ information symbols, $i_{[0,l)}$ specifies a path from the root node to a node at the $l$th level and, in turn, this path specifies the output sequence $x_{[0,l)} = x_0 \bullet x_1 \bullet \cdots \bullet x_{l-1}$, where $\bullet$ denotes concatenation of two sequences.

The input can, but need not, be separated in frames of some length. For framed data, where the length of each input frame equals $L$ branches (thus $L$ $q$-ary symbols) the length of the output frame is $L + M$ branches ($L + M$ output symbols), where the $M$ known symbols (usually all zeros) are added at the end of the sequence to force the system into the desired terminal state. It is said that such systems suffer a fractional rate loss by $L/(L + M)$. Clearly, this rate loss has no asymptotic significance.

In the sequel, the detection of the input sequence, $i_{(0,\infty)}$, will be analyzed based on the corrupted output sequence $y_{[0,\infty)} = x_{[0,\infty)} + u_{[0,\infty)}$. Suppose there is no feedback from the output to the input, so that

$$P[y_n | x_0, \ldots, x_{n-1}, x_n, y_0, \ldots, y_{n-1}] = P[y_n | x_n]$$

and

$$P[y_1, \ldots, y_N | x_1, \ldots, x_N] = \prod_{n=1}^{N} P[y_n | x_n]$$

Usually, $u_{(0,\infty)}$ is a sequence that represents additive white Gaussian noise sampled and quantized to enable digital processing.

The task of the detector that minimizes the sequence error probability is to find a sequence which maximizes the joint probability of input and output channel sequences

$$P[\mathbf{y}_{[0,L+M)}, \mathbf{x}_{[0,L+M)}] = P[\mathbf{y}_{[0,L+M)} | \mathbf{x}_{[0,L+M)}] P[\mathbf{x}_{[0,L+M)}]$$

Since usually the set of all probabilities $P[\mathbf{x}_{[0,L+M)}]$ is equal, it is sufficient to find a procedure that maximizes $P[\mathbf{y}_{[0,L+M)} | \mathbf{x}_{[0,L+M)}]$, and a decoder that always chooses as its estimate one of the sequences that maximize it or

$$\mu(\mathbf{y}_{[0,L+M)} | \mathbf{x}_{[0,L+M)}) = A \log_2 P[\mathbf{y}_{[0,L+M)} | \mathbf{x}_{[0,L+M)}]$$
$$-f(\mathbf{y}_{[0,L+M)}) = A \sum_{l=0}^{L+M} \log_2(P[\mathbf{y}_l | \mathbf{x}_l] - f(\mathbf{y}_l))$$

(where $A \geq 0$ is a suitably chosen constant, and $f(\cdot)$ is any function) is called a maximum-likelihood decoder (MLD). This quantity is called a metric, $\mu$. This type of metric suffers one significant disadvantage because it is suited only for comparison between paths of the same length. Some algorithms, however, employ a strategy of comparing paths of different length or assessing likelihood of such paths with the aid of some thresholds. The metric that enables comparison for this type of algorithms is called the Fano metric. It is defined as

$$\mu_F(\mathbf{y}_{[0,l)}|\mathbf{x}_{[0,l)}) = A \log_2 \frac{P[\mathbf{y}_{[0,l)}, \mathbf{x}_{[0,l)}]}{P[\mathbf{y}_{[0,l)}]}$$

$$= A \sum_{n=0}^{l} \left( \log_2 \frac{P[\mathbf{y}_n|\mathbf{x}_n]}{P[\mathbf{y}_n]} - R \right)$$

If the noise is additive, white, and Gaussian (an assumption that is not entirely true, but that usually yields systems of good performances), the probability distribution of its sample is

$$p[\mathbf{y}_n|\mathbf{x}_n] = \frac{1}{\sqrt{2\pi\sigma^2}} \exp\left( -\frac{(\mathbf{y}_n - \mathbf{x}_n)^2}{2\sigma^2} \right)$$

The ML metric to be used in conjunction with such a noise is the logarithm of this density, and thus proportional to $-(\mathbf{y}_n - \mathbf{x}_n)^2$, i.e., to the negative squared Euclidean distance of the readback and supposed written signal. Thus, maximizing likelihood amounts to minimizing the squared Euclidean distance of the two sequences, leading to minimizing the squared Euclidean distance between two sampled sequences given by $\Sigma_n(y_n - x_n)^2$.

The performance of a trellis-based system, as is the case with PR systems, depends on the detection algorithm employed and on the properties of the system itself. The distance spectrum is the property of the system that constitutes the main factor of the event error probability of a ML (optimum) detector, if the distance is appropriately chosen for the coding channel used.[45] For PR channels with additive white Gaussian noise, it is the squared Euclidean distance that has to be dealt with. Naturally, since the noise encountered is neither white, nor entirely Gaussisan, this is but an approximation to the properly chosen distance measure.

As stated previously, the aim of the search procedure is to find a path with the highest possible likelihood, i.e., metric. There are several possible classifications of detecting procedures. This classification is in-line with systematization made in coding theory, due to fact that algorithms developed for decoding in a trellis are general so that it could be applied to problem of detection in any trellis-based system as well. According to detector's strategies in extending the most promising path candidates we classify them into breadth-first, metric-first, and depth-first, bidirectional algorithms, and into sorting and nonsorting depending on whether the procedure performs any kind of path comparison (sifting or sorting) or not. Moreover, detecting algorithms can be classified into searches that *minimize* the *sequence* or *symbol* error rate.

The usual measure of algorithm efficiency is its complexity (arithmetic and storage) for a given probability of error. In the strict sense, arithmetic or computational complexity is the number of arithmetic operations per detected symbol, branch, or frame; however, it is a usual practice to track only the number of node computations, which makes sense because all such computations require approximately the same number of basic machine instructions. A node computation (or simply computation) is defined as the total number of nodes extended (sometimes it is the number of metrics computed) per detected branch or information frame $\mathbf{i}_{[0,L+M)}$. One single computation consists of determining the state in which the node is computing the metrics of all its successors. For most practical applications with finite frame length, it is usually sufficient to observe node computations since a good prediction of search duration can be precisely predicted. Nevertheless, for asymptotic behavior it is necessary to track the sorting requirements too. Another important aspect of complexity is storage (memory or space), which is the amount of auxiliary storage that is required for detecting memory, processors working in parallel, etc. Thus, space complexity of an algorithm is the size (or number) of resources that must be reserved for its use, while the computational, or more precisely time complexity, reflects the number of accesses to this resources taking into account that any two operations done in parallel by the spatially separated processors should be counted as one. The product of these two, the time-space complexity, is possibly the best measure of the algorithm cost for it is insensitive to time-space tradeoff such as parallelization or the use of precomputed tables, although it also makes sense to keep the separate track of these two. Finally, for selecting which algorithm to use, one must consider additional details that we omit here, but which can sometimes cause unexpected overall performance or complicate the design of a real-time detector. They include complexity of the required data structure, buffering needs, and applicability of available hardware components.

## Basic Breadth-First Algorithms

### The Viterbi Algorithm (VA)

The VA was introduced in 1967 as a method of decoding convolutional codes. Forney showed in 1972 [7] that the VA solves the maximum-likelihood sequence detection (MLSD) problem in the presence of ISI and additive white noise. Kobayashi and Tang [8] recognized that this algorithm is possible to apply in magnetic recording systems for detection purposes. Strategy to combine Viterbi detector with PR equalization in magnetic recording channel resulted with many commercial products.

The VA is an optimal decoding algorithm in the sense that it always finds the nearest path to the noisy modification of the FSM output sequence $\mathbf{x}_{[0, L+M)}$, and it is quite useful when FSM has a short memory. The key to Viterbi (maximum-likelihood, ML) decoding lies in the *Principle of Nonoptimality* [17]. If the paths $\mathbf{i}'_{[0,l)}$ and $\mathbf{i}''_{[0,l)}$ terminate at the same state of the trellis and

$$\mu(\mathbf{y}_{[0,l)}, \mathbf{x}'_{[0,l)}) > \mu(\mathbf{y}_{[0,l)}, \mathbf{x}''_{[0,l)})$$

then $\mathbf{i}''_{[0,l)}$ cannot be the first $l$ branches of one of the paths $\mathbf{i}_{[0, L+M)}$ that maximize the overall sequence metric. This principle which some authors call the *Principle of Optimality* literally specifies the most efficient MLD procedure for decoding/detecting in the trellis.

To apply VA as an ML sequence detector for a PR channel, we need to define the channel trellis describing the amount of controlled ISI. Once we define the PR channel polynomial, it is an easy task. An example of such trellis for PR4 channel with $P(D) = 1 - D^2$ is depicted in Fig. 34.57. The trellis for this channel consists of four states according to the fact that channel input is binary and channel memory is 2, so that there are four possible state values (00, 10, 01, 11). Generally, if the channel input sequence can take $q$ values, and the PR channel forms the ISI from the past $M$ input symbols, then the PR channel can be described by a trellis with $q^M$ states. Branches joining adjacent states are labeled with the pair of expected noiseless symbols in the form channel_output/channel_ input. Equalization to $P(D) = 1 - D^2$ results in ternary channel output, taking values {0, ±1}. Each noiseless output channel sequence is obtained by reading the sequence of labels along some path through the trellis.

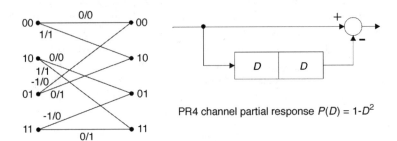

PR4 channel partial response $P(D) = 1\text{-}D^2$

**FIGURE 34.57**   PR4 channel trellis.

Now the task of detecting $\mathbf{i}_{[0,\infty)}$ is to find $\mathbf{x}_{[0,\infty)}$ that is closest to $\mathbf{y}_{[0,\infty)}$ in the Euclidean sense. Recall that we stated as an assumption that channel noise is AWGN, while in magnetic recording systems after equalization the noise is colored so that the minimum-distance detector is not an optimal one, and additional post-processing is necessary, which will be addressed later in this chapter.

The Viterbi algorithm is a classical application of dynamic programming. Structurally, the algorithm contains $q^M$ lists, one for each state, where the paths whose states correspond to the label indices are stored, compared, and the best one of them retained. The algorithm can be described recursively as follows:

1. *Initial condition:* Initialize the starting list with the root node (the known initial state) and set its metric to zero, $l = 0$.
2. *Path extension:* Extend all the paths (nodes) by one branch to yield new candidates, $l = l + 1$, and find the sum of the metric of the predecessor node and the branch metric of the connecting branch (ADD). Classify these candidates into corresponding $q^M$ lists (or less for $l < M$). Each list (except in the head of the trellis) contains $q$ paths.
3. *Path selection:* For each end-node of extended paths determine the maximum/minimum* of these sums (COMPARE) and assign it to the node. Label the node with the best path metric to it, selecting (SELECT) that path for the next step of the algorithm (discard others). If two or more paths have the same metric, i.e., if they are equally likely, choose the best one at random. Find the best of all the survivor paths, $\mathbf{x}'_{[0,l)}$, and its corresponding information sequence $\mathbf{i}'_{[0,l)}$ and release the bit $\mathbf{i}'_{l-\delta}$. Go to step 2.

In the description of the algorithm we emphasized three Viterbi-characteristic operations—add, compare, select (ADC)—that are performed in every recursion of the algorithm. So today's specialized signal processors have this operation embedded optimizing its execution time. Consider now the amount of "processing" done at each depth $l$, where all of the $q^M$ states of the trellis code are present. For each state it is necessary to compare $q$ paths that merge in that state, discard all but the best path, and then compute and send the metrics of $q$ of its successors to the depth $l + 1$.

Consequently, the computational complexity of the VA exponentially increases with $M$. These operations can be easily parallelized, but then the number of parallel processors rises as the number of node computations decreases. The total time-space complexity of the algorithm is fixed and increases exponentially with the memory length.

The sliding window VA decodes infinite sequences with delay of $\delta$ branches from the last received one. In order to minimize its memory requirements ($\delta + 1$ trellis levels), and achieve bit error rate only insignificantly higher than with finite sequence VA, $\delta$ is chosen as $\delta \approx 4M$. In this way, the Viterbi detector introduces a fixed decision delay.

## Example

Assume that a recorded channel input sequence $\mathbf{x}$, consisting of $L$ equally likely binary symbols from the alphabet $\{0, 1\}$, is "transmitted" over PR4 channel. The channel is characterized by the trellis of Fig. 34.57, i.e., all admissible symbol sequences correspond to the paths traversing the trellis from $l = 0$ to $l = L$, with one symbol labeling each branch, Fig. 34.58. Suppose that the noisy sequence of samples at the channel output is $\mathbf{y} = 0.9, 0.2, -0.6, -0.3, 0.6, 0.9, 1.2, 0.3, \ldots$ If we apply a simple symbol-by-symbol detector to this sequence, the fifth symbol will be erroneous due to the hard quantization rule for noiseless channel output estimate

$$\hat{y}_k = \begin{cases} -1 & y_k < -0.5 \\ 1 & y_k > 0.5 \\ 0 & \text{otherwise} \end{cases}$$

---

*It depends on whether the metric or the distance is accumulated.

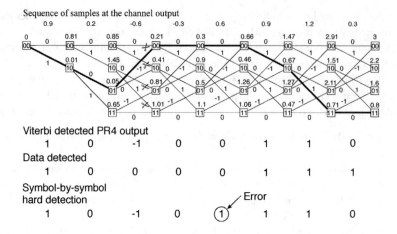

**FIGURE 34.58** Viterbi algorithm detection on the PR4 trellis.

The Viterbi detector will start to search the trellis accumulating branch distance from sequence **y**. In the first recursion of the algorithm, there are two paths of length 1 at the distance

$$d(\mathbf{y},0) = (0.9 - 0)^2 = 0.81$$
$$d(\mathbf{y},1) = (0.9 - 1)^2 = 0.01$$

from **y**. Next, each of the two paths of length 1 are extended in two ways forming four paths of length 2 at squared Euclidean distance from the sequence **y**

$$d(\mathbf{y},(0,0)) = 0.81 + (0.2 - 0)^2 - 0.85$$
$$d(\mathbf{y},(0,1)) = 0.81 + (0.2 - 1)^2 = 1.45$$
$$d(\mathbf{y},(1,0)) = 0.01 + (0.2 - 0)^2 = 0.05$$
$$d(\mathbf{y},(1,1)) = 0.01 + (0.2 - 1)^2 = 0.65$$

and this accumulated distance of four paths labels the four trellis states. In the next loop of the algorithm each of the paths are again extended in two ways to form eight paths of length 3, two paths to each node at level (depth) 3.

Node 00

$$d(\mathbf{y},(0,0,0)) = 0.85 + (-0.6 - 0)^2 = 1.21$$
$$d(\mathbf{y},(1,0,-1)) = 0.05 + (-0.6 + 1)^2 = 0.21 \quad \textit{surviving path}$$

Node 10

$$d(\mathbf{y},(0,0,1)) = 0.85 + (-0.6 - 1)^2 = 3.41$$
$$d(\mathbf{y},(1,0,0)) = 0.05 + (-0.6 - 0)^2 = 0.41 \quad \textit{surviving path}$$

Node 01

$$d(\mathbf{y},(0,1,0)) = 1.45 + (-0.6 - 0)^2 = 1.81$$
$$d(\mathbf{y},(1,1,-1)) = 0.65 + (-0.6 + 1)^2 = 0.81 \quad \textit{surviving path}$$

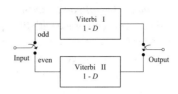

**FIGURE 34.59** Implementation of 1-$D^2$ Viterbi detector with two half-rate, 1-$D$ detectors.

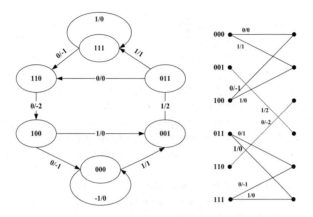

**FIGURE 34.60** (1,7) coded EPR4 channel.

Node 11

$$d(\mathbf{y},(0,1,1)) = 1.45 + (-0.6 - 1)^2 = 4.01$$

$$d(\mathbf{y},(1,1,0)) = 0.65 + (-0.6 - 0)^2 = 1.01 \quad surviving\ path$$

Four paths of length 3 are selected as the surviving most likely paths to the four trellis nodes. The procedure is repeated and the detected sequence is produced after a delay of $4M = 8$ trellis sections. Note, Fig. 34.58, that the symbol-by-symbol detector error is now corrected. Contrary to this example, a 4-state PR4ML detector is implemented with two interleaved 2-state dicode, $(1 - D)$, detectors each operating at one-half the symbol rate of one full-rate PR4 detector [35]. The sequence is interleaved, such that the even samples go to the first and the odd to the second dicode detector, Fig. 34.59, so the delay $D$ in the interleaved detectors is actually twice the delay of the PR4 detector. A switch at the output resamples the data to get them out in the correct order.

For other PR channels this type of decomposition is not possible, so that their complexity can become great for real-time processing. In order to suppress some of the states in the corresponding trellis diagram of those PR systems, thus simplifying the sequence detection process, some data loss has to be introduced. For instance, in conjunction with precoding (1,7) code prohibits two states in EPR4 trellis: [101] and [010]. This can be used to reduce the 8-state EPR4 trellis to 6-state trellis depicted in Fig. 34.60 and the number of add-compare-select units in the VA detector to 4. The data rate loss is 33% in this case. Using the (2,7) code eliminates two more states, paying the complexity gain by a 50% data rate loss.

Because VA involves addition, multiplication, compare and select functions, which require complex circuitry at the read side, simplifications of the receiver for certain PRs were sought. One of them is the dynamic threshold technique [22]. This technique implies generating a series of thresholds. The readback samples are compared with them, just as for the threshold detector, and are subsequently included in their modification. While preserving the full function of the ML detector, this technique saves a substantial fraction of the necessary hardware. Examples of dynamic threshold detectors are given in [30] and [6].

### *Noise-Predictive Maximum Likelihood Detectors*

Maximum likelihood detection combined with PR equalization is a dominant type of detection electronics in today's digital magnetic recording devices. As described earlier, in order to simplify hardware realization of the receiver, the degree of the target PR polynomial is chosen to be small with integer coefficients to restrict complexity of Viterbi detection trellis. On the other hand, if the recording density is increased, to produce longer ISI, equalization to the same PR target will result in substantial noise enhancement and detector performance degradation. Straightforward solution is to increase the duration of the target PR polynomial decreasing the mismatch between channel and equalization target. Note that this approach leads to undesirable increase in detector complexity fixing the detector structure in a sense that its target polynomial cannot be adapted to changing channel density.

The noise-predictive maximum likelihood (NPML) detector [20,32] is an alternative data detection method that improves reliability of the PRML detector. This is achieved by embedding a noise prediction/whitening process into the branch metric computation of a Viterbi detector. Using reduced-state sequence-estimation [43] (see also the description of the generalized VA in this chapter), which limits the number of states in the detector trellis, compensates for added detector complexity.

A block diagram of a NPML system is shown in Fig. 34.61. The input to the channel is binary sequence, **i**, which is written on the disk at a rate of $1/T$. In the readback process data are recovered via a lowpass filter as an analog signal $y(t)$, which can be expressed as $y(t) = \Sigma_n i_n h(t - nT) + u(t)$, where $h(t)$ denotes the pulse response and $u(t)$ is the additive white Gaussian noise. The signal $y(t)$ is sampled periodically at times $t = nT$ and shaped into the PR target response by the digital equalizer. The NPML detector then performs sequence detection on the PR equalized sequence **y** and provides an estimate of the binary information sequence **i**. Digital equalization is performed to fit the overall system transfer function to some PR target, e.g., the PR4 channel.

The output of the equalizer $y_n + i_n + \Sigma_{i=1}^{M} f_i x_{n-i} + w_n$ consists of the desired response and an additive total distortion component $w_n$, i.e., the colored noise and residual interference. In conventional PRML detector, an estimate of the recorded sequence is done by the minimum-distance criteria as described for the Viterbi detector. If the mismatch between channel and PR target is significant, the power of distortion component $w_n$ can degrade the detector performance. The only additional component compared to the Viterbi detector, NPML noise-predictor, reduces the power of the total distortion by

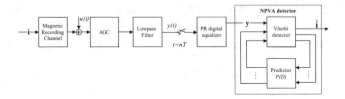

**FIGURE 34.61**    Block diagram of NPVA detector.

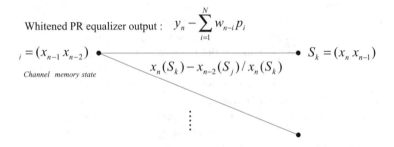

**FIGURE 34.62**    NPML metric computation for PR4 trellis.

whitening the noise prior to the Viterbi detector. The whitened total distortion component of the PR equalized output $y_n$ is

$$w_n - \hat{w}_n = w_n - \sum_{i=1}^{N} w_{n-i} p_i$$

where the $N$-coefficient MMSE predictor transfer polynomial is $P(D) = p_1 D^1 + p_2 D^2 + \cdots + p_N D^N$. Note that an estimate of the current noise sample $\hat{w}_n$ is formed based on estimates of previous $N$ noise samples. Assuming the PR4 equalization of sequence **y**, the metric of the Viterbi detector can be modified in order to compensate for distortion component. In this case, the equalizer output is $y_n = x_n - x_{n-2} + w_n$ and the NPML distance is

$$\left[ \left( y_n - \sum_{i=1}^{N} w_{n-i} p_i \right) - (x_n(S_k) - x_{n-2}(S_j)) \right]^2$$

$$= \left[ \left( y_n - \sum_{i=1}^{N} (y_{n-i} - \hat{x}_{n-i}(S_j) - \hat{x}_{n-i-2}(S_j)) p_i \right) - (x_n(S_k) - x_{n-2}(S_j)) \right]^2$$

where $\hat{x}_{n-i}(S_j)$, $\hat{x}_{n-i-2}(S_j)$ represent past decisions taken from the Vitrebi survivor path memory associated with state $S_j$. The last expression gives the flavor of this technique, but it is not suitable for implementation so that the interested reader can find details in [20] how to modify this equation for RAM look-up realization. Furthermore, in the same paper, a description of the general procedure to compute the predictor coefficients based on the autocorrelation of the total distortion $w_n$ at the output of a finite-length PR equalizer is given.

### Postprocessor

As explained earlier, Viterbi detector improves the performance of a read channel by tracing the correct path through the channel trellis [8]. Further performance improvement can be achieved by using soft output Viterbi algorithm (SOVA) [14]. Along with the bit decisions, SOVA produces the likelihood of these decisions, that combined create *soft information*. In principle, soft information can be passed to hard drive controller and used in RS decoder that resides there, but at the present time soft decoding of RS codes is still too complex to be implemented at 1 Gb/s speeds. Alternatively, much shorter inner code is used. Because of the nonlinear operations on bits performed by the modulation decoder logic, the inner code is used in inverse concatenation with modulation encoder in order to simplify calculation of bit likelihood. Due to the channel memory and noise coloration, Viterbi detector produces some error patterns more often than others [5], and the inner code is designed to correct these so-called *dominant error sequences* or *error events*. The major obstacle for using soft information is the speed limitations and hardware complexity required to implement SOVA. Viterbi detector is already a bottleneck and the most complex block in a read channel chip, occupying most of the chip area, and the architectural challenges in implementing even more complex SOVA would be prohibitive. Therefore, a postprocessor architecture is used [18]. The postprocessor is a block that resides after Viterbi detector and comprises the block for calculating error event likelihood and an inner-soft error event correcting decoder.

The postprocessor is designed by using the knowledge on the set of dominant error sequences $E = \{e_i\}_{1 \le i}$ and their occurrence probabilities $P = (p_i)_{1 \le i}$. The index $i$ is referred to as an *error type*, while the position of the *error event end* within a codeword is referred as an *error position*. The relative frequencies of error events will strongly depend on recording density [36]. The detection is based on the fact that we can calculate the likelihoods of each of dominant error sequences at each point in time. The parity bits detect the errors, and provide localization in error type and time. The likelihoods are then used to choose the most likely error events for corrections.

The error event likelihoods are calculated as the difference in the squared Euclidean distances between the signal and the convolution of maximum likelihood sequence estimate and the channel PR, versus that between the signal and the convolution of an alternative data pattern and the channel PR. During each clock cycle, the best $M$ of them are chosen, and the syndromes for these error events are calculated. Throughout the processing of each block, a list is maintained of the $N$ most likely error events, along with their associated error types, positions and syndromes. At the end of the block, when the list of candidate error events is finalized, the likelihoods and syndromes are calculated for each of $\binom{N}{L}$ combinations of $L$-set candidate error events that are possible. After disqualifying those $L$-sets of candidates, which overlap in the time domain, and those candidates and $L$-sets of candidates, which produce a syndrome which does not match the actual syndrome, the candidate or $L$-set of candidates, which remains and which has the highest likelihood is chosen for correction. Finding the error event position and type completes decoding.

The decoder can make two types of errors: it fails to correct if the syndrome is zero, or it makes a wrong correction if the syndrome is nonzero, but the most likely error event or combination of error events does not produce the right syndrome. A code must be able to detect a single error from the list of dominant error events and should minimize the probability of producing zero syndrome when more than one error event occurs in a codeword. Consider a linear code given by an $(n - k) \times n$ parity check matrix $H$. We are interested in capable of correcting or detecting dominant errors. If all errors from a list were contiguous and shorter than $m$, a cyclic $n - k = m$ parity bit code could be used to correct a single error event [16]; however, in reality, the error sequences are more complex, and occurrence probabilities of error events of lengths 6, 7, 8 or more are not negligible. Furthermore, practical reasons (such as decoding delay, thermal asperities, etc.) dictate using short codes, and consequently, in order to keep the code rate high, only a relatively small number of parity bits is allowed, making the design of error event detection codes nontrivial. The code redundancy must be used carefully so that the code is optimal for a given $E$.

The parity check matrix of a code can be created by a recursive algorithm that adds one column of $H$ at a time using the criterion that after adding each new column, the code error-event-detection capabilities are still satisfied. The algorithm can be described as a process of building a directed graph whose vertices are labeled by the portions of parity check matrix long enough to capture the longest error event, and whose edges are labeled by column vectors that can be appended to the parity check matrix without violating the error event detection capability [4]. To formalize code construction requirements, for each error event from $E$, denote by $s_{i,l}$ a syndrome of error vector $\sigma_l(e_i)$ ($s_{i,l} = \sigma_l(e_i) \cdot H^T$), where $\sigma_l(e_i)$ is an $l$-time shifted version of error event $e_i$. The code should be designed in such a way that any shift of any dominant error sequence produces a nonzero syndrome, i.e., that $s_{i,l} \neq 0$ for any $1 \leq i \leq I$ and $1 \leq l \leq n$. In this way, a single error event can be detected (relying on error event likelihoods to localize the error event). The correctable shifts must include negative shifts as well as shifts larger than $n$ in order to cover those error events that straddle adjacent codewords, because the failure to correct straddling events significantly affects the performance. A stronger code could have a parity check matrix that guaranties that syndromes of any two-error event-error position pairs $((i_1, l_1), (i_2, l_2))$ are different, i.e., $s_{i_1,l_1} \neq s_{i_2,l_2}$. This condition would result in a single error event correction capability. The codes capable of correcting multiple error events can be defined analogously. We can even strengthen this property and require that for any two shifts and any two dominant error events, the Hamming distance between any pair of syndromes is larger than $\delta$; however, by strengthening any of these requirements the code rate decreases.

If $L_i$ is a length of the $i$th error event, and if $L$ is the length of the longest error event from $E$, ($L = \max_{1 \leq i \leq I}\{L_i\}$), then it is easy to see that for a code capable of detecting an error event from $E$ that ends at position $j$, the linear combination of error events and the columns of $H$ from $j - L + 1$ to $j$ has to be nonzero. More precisely, for any $i$ and any $j$ (ignoring the codeword boundary effects)

$$\sum_{1 \leq m \leq L_i} e_{i,m} \cdot h_{j-L_i+m}^T \neq 0$$

where $e_{i,m}$ is the $m$th element of the error event $e_i$, and $h_j$ is the $j$th column of $H$.

# Advanced Algorithms and Algorithms under Investigation

This subsection gives a brief overview of less complex procedures for searching the trellis. It is intended to give background information that can be used in future development if it shows up that NPVA detectors and postprocessing are not capable of coping with ever-increasing storage densities and longer PRs needed for them. In such cases, a resort has to be made to some sort of reduced complexity suboptimal algorithms, whose performance is close to optimal. Explained algorithms are not yet implemented in commercial products, but all of them are a natural extension of already described procedures for searching the trellis.

## Other Breadth-First Algorithms

### The M-Algorithm

Since most survivors in the VA usually possess much smaller metrics than does the best one, all the states or nodes kept are not equally important. It is intuitively reasonable to assume that unpromising survivors can be omitted with a negligible probability of discarding the best one. The $M$-algorithm [10] is one such modification of the VA; all candidates are stored in a single list and the best $M \leq q^M$ survivors are selected from the list in each cycle. The steps of the $M$-algorithm are:

1. *Initial condition:* Initialize the list with the root node and set its metric to zero.
2. *Path extension:* Extend all the paths of length $l$ by one branch and classify all contenders (paths of length $l + 1$) into the list. If two or more paths enter the same state keep the best one.
3. *Path selection:* From the remaining paths find the best $M$ candidates and delete the others. If $l = L + M$, take the only survivor and transfer its corresponding information sequence to the output (terminated case, otherwise use the sliding window variation). Otherwise, go to step 2.

Defined in this way, the $M$-algorithm performs trellis search, while, when the state comparison in step 2 is omitted, it searches the tree, saving much time on comparisons but with slightly increased error probability. When applied to decoding/detecting infinitely long sequences, it is usual that comparisons performed in step 2 are substituted with the so-called ambiguity check [10] and a release of one decoded branch. In each step this algorithm performs $M$ node computations, and employing any sifting procedure (since the paths need not be sorted) perform $\sim Mq$ metric comparisons. If performed, the Viterbi-type discarding of step 2 requests $\sim M^2 q$ state and metric comparisons. This type of discarding can be performed with $\sim M \log_2 M$ comparisons (or even linearly) but than additional storage must be provided. The space complexity grows linearly with the information frame length $L$ and parameter $M$.

### The Generalized Viterbi Algorithm

In contrast to the VA, which is a multiple-list single survivor algorithm, the $M$-algorithm is a single-list multiple-survivor algorithm. The natural generalization to a multiple-list multiple-survivor algorithm was first suggested by Hashimoto [39]. Since all the lists are not equally important, this algorithm, originally called the generalized Viterbi algorithm (GVA), utilizes only $q^{M_1}$ lists (labels), where $M_1 \leq M$. In each list from all $q^{M-M_1+1}$ paths, it retains the best $M_1$ candidates. The algorithm can be described as follows:

1. *Initial condition:* Initialize the starting label with the root node and set its metric to zero.
2. *Path extension:* Extend all the paths from each label by one branch and classify all successors into the appropriate label. If two or more paths enter the same state keep the best one.
3. *Path selection:* From the remaining paths of each label find the best $M_1$ and delete the others. If $l = L + M$, take the only survivor and transfer its information sequence to the output (for the terminated case, otherwise use the sliding window variant). Go to step 2.

When $M_1 = M$, and $M_1 = 1$, the GVA reduces to the VA, and for $M_1 = 0$, $M_1 = M$ it reduces to the $M$-algorithm. Like the $M$-algorithm, GVA in each step performs $M_1$ node computations per label, and employing any sifting procedure $\sim M_1 q$ metric comparisons. If performed, the Viterbi-type discarding of step 2 requests $\sim M_1^2 q$ or less state and metric comparisons per label.

## Metric-First Algorithms

Metric-first and depth-first sequential detection is a name for a class of algorithms that compare paths according to their Fano metric (one against another or with some thresholds) and on that basis decide which node to extend next, which to delete in metric first procedures or whether to proceed with current branch or go back. These algorithms generally extend fewer nodes for the same performance, but have increased sorting requirements.

Sequential detecting algorithms have a variable computation characteristic that results in large buffering requirements, and occasionally large detecting delays and/or incomplete detecting of the received sequence. Sometimes, when almost error-free communication is required or when retransmission is possible, this variable detecting effort can be an advantage. For example, when a detector encounters an excessive number of computations, it indicates that a frame is possibly very corrupted meaning that the communication is insufficiently reliable and can ultimately cause error patterns in detected sequence. In such situations the detector gives up detecting and simply requests retransmission. These situations are commonly called erasures, and detecting incomplete. A complete decoder such as the Viterbi detector/decoder would be forced to make an estimate, which may be wrong. The probability of buffer overflow is several orders of magnitude larger than the probability of incorrect decision when the decoder operates close to the so-called (computational) cutoff rate.

The performance of sequential detecting has traditionally been evaluated in terms of three characteristics: the probability of sequence error, the probability of failure (erasure), and the Pareto exponent associated with detecting effort.

### The Stack Algorithm

The stack (or ZJ) algorithm was for the first time suggested by Zigangirov [1] and later independently by Jelinek [1]. As its name indicates, the algorithm contains a stack (in fact, a list) of already searched paths of varying lengths, ordered according to their metric values. At each step, the path at the top of the stack (the best one) is replaced by its $q$ successors extended by one branch, with correspondingly augmented metrics. The check whether two or more paths are in the same state is not performed. This algorithm has its numerous variations and we first consider the basic version that is closest to Zigangirov's:

1. *Initial condition:* Initialize the stack with the root node and set its Fano metric to zero (or some large positive number to avoid arithmetic with negative numbers, but low enough to avoid overflow).
2. *Path extension:* Extend the best path from the stack by one branch, delete it, sort all successors, and then merge them with the stack so that it is ordered according to the path metrics.
3. *Path selection:* Retain the best $Z$ paths according to the Fano metric. If the top path has the length $l = L + M$ branches, transfer its information sequence to the output (terminated case; otherwise, a sliding window version has to be used); otherwise, go to step 2.

It is obvious that this algorithm does not consider path merging since the probability that the paths of the same depth and the same state can be stored in the stack simultaneously is rather small. Nonetheless, some authors [1] propose that a following action should be added to the step 2: If any of the $2^K$ new paths merges with a path already in the stack, keep the one with the higher metric.

The stack algorithm is based on the nonselection principle [17]. If the paths $\mathbf{i}'_{[0,L+M)}$ and $\mathbf{i}''_{[0,L+M)}$ through the tree diverge at depth $j$ and

$$\min\{u(\mathbf{x}'_{[0,l)}, \mathbf{y}_{[0,l)})\}_{l \in [j+1,L+M)} > \min\{u(\mathbf{x}''_{[0,l)}, \mathbf{y}_{[0,l)})\}_{l \in [j+1,L+M)}$$

then $\mathbf{i}''_{[0,L+M)}$ cannot be the path at the top of the stack when the stack algorithm stops.

The computational complexity of the stack algorithm is almost unaffected by the code memory length, but well depends on the channel performance. Its computational complexity is a random variable and so is its stack size if not otherwise limited. The upper bound on the computational complexity is given by

$$P[C \geq \eta] < A\eta^{-\rho} \quad 0 < \rho \leq 1$$

where $A$ is a constant and $\rho$ is a power that goes to unity as $R \to R_0 < R_C$ and to zero as $R \to R_C$, where $R_C$ is the channel capacity and $R_0$ is the cutoff rate [17]. The distribution described previously is called a Pareto distribution, and $\rho$ a Pareto exponent.

Omit depth-first algorithms, such as the Fano algorithm, from consideration here, because they are not interesting for PR detection.

## Bidirectional Algorithms

Another class of algorithms are those that exploit bidirectional decoding/detection which is designed for framed data. Almost all unidirectional procedures have their bidirectional supplements since Forney showed that detecting could start from the end of the sequence provided that the trellis contains a tail. All bidirectional algorithms employ two searches from both sides. The forward search is performed using the original trellis code while the backward one employs the reverse code. The reverse trellis code is obtained from the original code by time reversing.

### The Bidirectional Stack Algorithm

This algorithm was independently proposed by Šenk and Radivojac [40–42], and Kallel and Li [38]. It uses two stacks F (forward) and B (backward, that uses the reverse code). It is based on notions of tunnel, tentative decision, and discarding criteria. The tunnel is the unique sequence $T$ ($0 \leq T \leq M$) branches long that connect two states in the trellis. The tentative decision is the sequence $L + M$ branches long that connects the known initial and terminal trellis states (direction does not matter here) that has the highest accumulated metric of all the sequences of that length analyzed so far. A set of discarding criteria is a means to tell beforehand whether a partly explored path is likely to be a part of the finally detected sequence or not (in the latter case, the path may be eliminated from the subsequent search). Because the version [30] of the algorithm is a special case of [41] (when $T = 0$), the steps of the BSA are:

1. Place the root node into F stack, and the unique terminal node into B stack, associating them the zero metric. Make one of these stacks active (e.g., the F one).
2. Choose the node with the largest metric (of length, say, $l$) from the active stack and eliminate it from the stack. Link it via a tunnel (if a tunnel is possible, i.e., if the states match) to each of the existing paths in the other stack whose lengths are $L - l + M - T$ (if a tunnel is $M$ branches long, then the best path from the active stack can be linked to all the paths from the other stack whose lengths are $L - l$). The total length of the paths obtained in this way is $l + T + (L - l + M - T) = L + M$ branches. Store the best one into the tentative decision register. If there is already a path in the register, keep the better. Prune the paths remaining in both stacks according to any of discarding criteria used. If both stacks are emptied in this way, output the tentative decision as the decoder's final decision and terminate the algorithm. Otherwise, evaluate the metrics of all the successors of the processed path, and eliminate all of them that do not conform to the discarding criteria established.
3. Sort the remaining successors into the active stack according to their metrics applying any tie-breaking rule. Change the active stack and return to step 2.

After each tentative decision, several discarding criteria can be applied. In [41] Šenk and Radivojac applied the nonselection principle and the maximum-likelihood criterion described. The algorithm can be easily performed by two processors, although one node computation lasts longer than in the original stack algorithm. Simulations showed [41] that the Pareto exponent of the BSA in the moment when the final decision is obtained is approximately doubled, but the discarding criteria used did not provide the termination at the same time. However, the algorithm may be stopped after the assigned time for its execution has elapsed, and in such cases the erasure probability is substantially decreased.

Two additional bidirectional algorithms are worth mentioning. Belzile and Haccoun [11] investigated the bidirectional *M*-algorithm. Since the *M*-algorithm inherently avoids erasures by its breadth-first nature it still suffers from the correct path loss in its unidirectional version. Another interesting algorithm is the bidirectional multiple stack algorithm [23]. It additionally decreases the erasure probability of the MSA without compromising the error performance.

### Algorithms That Minimize Symbol Error Rate

#### The BCJR Algorithm

So far, the algorithms that minimize the error probability of information sequence $\mathbf{i}_{[0,L+M)}$ have been considered. They accomplish it by searching for the "closest" sequence $\mathbf{x}_{[0, L+M)}$ according to the metric chosen; however, these algorithms do not necessarily minimize the symbol or bit error rate. The BCJR algorithm was independently proposed by Bahl et al. [25] and McAdam et al. [27], but a more detailed description can be found in [25]. The algorithm is a special case of a more general problem of estimating the *a posteriori* probabilities of the states and transitions of a Markov source observed through a DMC, i.e., the probabilities

$$P[s_l = i, s_{l+1} = j | \mathbf{y}_{[0,L+M)}] \tag{34.41}$$

or equivalently

$$\sigma_l(i,j) = P[s_l = i, s_{l+1} = j, \mathbf{y}_{[0,L+M)}] \tag{34.42}$$

where $s_l$ is the state of the trellis during *l*th branch. Introducing

$$\alpha_l(i) = P[s_l = i, \mathbf{y}_{[0,l)}]$$
$$\beta_l(i) = P[\mathbf{y}_{[l,L+M)} | s_l = i] \tag{34.43}$$
$$\gamma_l(i,j) = P[s_{l+1} = j, y_l | s_l = i]$$

it is not hard [25] to show that

$$\alpha_{l+1}(j) = \sum_{i=0}^{2^{KM}-1} \alpha_l(i)\gamma_l(i,j)$$

$$\beta_l(j) = \sum_{i=0}^{2^{KM}-1} \beta_{l+1}(i)\gamma_l(i,j) \tag{34.44}$$

$$\gamma_l(i,j) = \sum_{x_l} P[x_l | s_l = i, s_{l+1} = j]P[S_{l+1} = j | s_l = i]P[y_l | x_l]$$

$$\sigma_l(i,j) = \alpha_l(i)\gamma_l(i,j)\beta_l(j)$$

The known initial conditions are $\alpha_0(i = 0) = 1$, $\alpha_0(i \neq 0) = 0$, $\beta_{L+M}(i = 0) = 1$, $\beta_{L+M}(i \neq 0) = 0$. Assuming that the initial and terminating state in the trellis is the all zero state, the steps of the algorithm are

1. Initialize $\alpha_0(i)$, and $\beta_{L+M}(i)$, for $i = 0, 1, \ldots, q^M - 1$ according to (34.44).
2. As soon as $\mathbf{y}_l$ is received, compute $\alpha_l(i)$ and $\gamma_l(i,j)$. Store $\alpha_l(i,j)$ for all *l* and *i*.
3. When the complete sequence $\mathbf{y}_{[0,L + M)}$ is received, compute $\beta_l(i)$ using (34.44), and immediately the probabilities $\sigma_l(i,j)$. Group those $\sigma_l(i,j)$ that have the same information sequence $\mathbf{i}_l$, and choose the largest as the decoder estimate.

The basic problem with the algorithm is that it requires both large storage and great number of computations. All the values of $\alpha_l(i)$ must be stored, which requires almost $(L+M)q^{KM}$ memory locations. The number of multiplications required for determining the $\alpha_l(i)$ and $\beta_l(i)$ for each $l$ is $q^{M+1}$, and there are $q^M$ additions of $q^K$ numbers as well. The computation of $\gamma_l(i,j)$ is not costly and can be accomplished by a table look-up. Finally, the computation of all $\sigma_l(i,j)$ requires $q^{(M+1)+1}$ multiplications for each $l$, and $q-1$ comparisons in choosing the largest $\mathbf{i}_l$. Consequently, this is an algorithm with exponential complexity and in practice can be applied only when $M$ and $L$ are short. Nevertheless, it is used for iterative decoding where such requirements can be fulfilled, such as for turbo codes. The main advantage of the algorithm in such cases is its ability to estimate $P[s_{l+1} = j | s_l = i]$, which for the possible transitions equals $q^{-1}$ only in the first iteration.

### The SOVA Algorithm

The soft-output Viterbi algorithm (SOVA) [15] is a modification of the VA that was designed with the aim of estimating the reliability of every detected bit by the VA. It is applicable only when $q = 2$. The VA is used here in its sliding window form, which detects infinite sequences with delay of $\delta$ branches from the last received one.

The reliability (or soft value) of a bit $i$, $L(i)$, is defined as $L(i) = \ln(P[i=0]/P[i=1])$. The SOVA further extends the third step in order to obtain this value, in the following way:

*Path selection* (extension): Let $i_{[0,l-j)}^{(j)}, j \in \{0, 1, \ldots, \delta-1\}$ be the information sequences which merge with $i_{[0,l)}'$ at depths $l-j$. Their paths have earlier been discarded due to their lower metrics. Let the corresponding metric differences in the merging states be denoted $\Delta_j$, and let $J = \{j : i_{l-\delta}^{(j)} \neq i_{l-\delta}'\}$. Then $L(i_{l-\delta}') \approx (1 - 2i_{l-\delta}')\min_{j \in J} \Delta_j$.

Because VA detecting metric can be modified in a way to take into account a priori knowledge of input bit probabilities, the SOVA can be used as soft input-soft output (SISO) block in turbo decoding schemes.

## References

1. A. J. Viterbi and J. Omura, *Principles of Digital Communication and Coding*, McGraw-Hill, Tokyo, 1979.
2. A. J. Viterbi, "Error bounds for convolutional codes and asymptotically optimum decoding algorithm," *IEEE Trans. Inform. Theory*, vol. IT-13, pp. 260–269, 1967.
3. A. Lender, "Correlative level coding for binary-data transmission," *IEEE Trans. Commun. Technol.* (Concise paper), vol. COM-14, pp. 67–70, 1966.
4. B. Vasic, "A graph based construction of high-rate soft decodable codes for partial response channels," to be presented at ICC2001, Helsinki, Finland, June 2001, 10–15.
5. C. L. Barbosa, "Maximum likelihood sequence estimators, a geometric view," *IEEE Trans. Inform. Theory*, vol. IT-35, pp. 419–427, March 1989.
6. C. D. Wei, "An analog magnetic storage read channel based on a decision feedback equalizer," *PhD final report*, University of California, Electrical Eng. Department, July 1996.
7. G. D. Forney, "Maximum likelihood sequence estimation of digital sequences in the presence of intersymbol interference," *IEEE Trans. Inform. Theory*, vol. IT-18, pp. 363–378, May 1972.
8. H. Kobayashi and D. T. Tang, "Application of partial response channel coding to magnetic recording systems," *IBM J. Res. and Dev.*, vol. 14, pp. 368–375, July 1979.
9. H. Kobayashi, "Correlative level coding and maximum-likelihood decoding," *IEEE Trans. Inform. Theory*, vol. IT-17(5), pp. 586–594, 1971.
10. J. B. Anderson and S. Mohan, "Sequential coding algorithms: a survey and cost analysis," *IEEE Trans. Comm.*, vol. COM-32(2), pp. 169–176, Feb. 1984.
11. J. Belzile and D. Haccoun, "Bidirectional breadth-first algorithms for the decoding of convolutional codes," *IEEE Trans. Comm.*, vol. COM-41, pp. 370–380, Feb. 1993.
12. J. Bergmans, "Density improvements in digital magnetic recording by decision feedback equalization," *IEEE Trans. Magn.*, vol. 22, pp. 157–162, May 1986.

13. J. Hagenauer, "Applications of error-control coding," *IEEE Trans. Inform. Theory,* vol. IT-44(6), pp. 2531–2560, Oct. 1998.

14. J. Hagenauer and P. Hoeher, "A Viterbi algorithm with soft decision outputs and its applications," in *Proc. GLOBECOM 89,* Dallas, Texas, pp. 47.1.1–47.1.7, Nov. 1989.

15. J. Hagenauer, "Source-controlled channel decoding," *IEEE Trans. Comm.,* vol. COM-41, pp. 370–380, Feb. 1995.

16. J. K. Wolf and D. Chun, "The single burst error detection performance of binary cyclic codes," *IEEE Trans. Commun.,* vol. 42(1), pp. 11–13, Jan. 1994.

17. J. L. Massey, *Coding and Complexity,* CISM courses and lectures No. 216, Springer-Verlag, Wien, 1976.

18. J. L. Sonntag and B. Vasic, "Implementation and bench characterization of a read channel with parity check post processor," *Digest of TMRC 2000,* Santa Clara, CA, August 2000.

19. J. M. Cioffi, W. L. Abbott, H. K. Thapar, C. M. Melas, and K. D. Fisher, "Adaptive equalization in magnetic disk storage channels," *IEEE Communications Magazine,* pp. 14–29, Feb. 1990.

20. J. D. Coker, E. Eleftheriou, R. Galbraith, and W. Hirt, "Noise-predictive maximum likelihood (NPML) detection," *IEEE Trans. Magn.,* vol. 34(1), pp. 110–117, Jan. 1998.

21. J. J. O'Reilly and A. M. de Oliveira Duarte, "Error propagation in decision feedback receivers," *IEEE Proc.,* Pt. F, vol. 132(7), pp. 561–566, Dec. 1985.

22. K. Knudson et al., "Dynamic threshold implementation of the maximum likelihood detector for the EPR4 channel," *Conf. Rec. Globecom '91,* pp. 2135–2139, 1991.

23. K. Li and S. Kallel, "A bidirectional multiple stack algorithm," *IEEE Trans. Comm.,* vol. COM-47(1), pp. 6–9, Jan. 1999.

24. K. D. Fisher, J. Cioffi, W. Abbott, P. Bednarz, and C. M. Melas, "An adaptive RAM-DFE for storage channels," *IEEE Trans. Comm.,* vol. 39, no. 11, pp. 1559–1568, Nov. 1991.

25. L. R. Bahl, J. Cocke, F. Jelinek, and J. Raviv, "Optimal decoding of linear codes for minimizing symbol error rate," *IEEE Trans. Inform. Theory,* pp. 284–287, March 1974.

26. M. Fossorier, "Performance evaluation of decision feedback equalization for the Lorentzian channel," *IEEE Trans. Magn.,* vol. 32(2), March 1996.

27. P. L. McAdam, L. R. Welch, and C. L. Weber, "M.A.P. bit decoding of convolutional codes," in *Proc. of ISIT 1972,* Asilomar, USA.

28. P. R. Chevillat and D. J. Costello Jr., "A multiple stack algorithm for erasure free decoding of convolutional codes," *IEEE Trans. Comm.,* vol. COM-25, pp. 1460–1470, Dec. 1977.

29. P. Radivojac, V. Šenk, "The Generalized Viterbi-T algorithm," in *Proc. of XXXIX Conference on ETRAN,* vol. 2, pp. 13–16, Zlatibor, Yugoslavia, June 1995.

30. P. H. Siegel and J. K. Wolf, "Modulation and coding for information storage," *IEEE Comm. Magazine,* Dec. 1991, pp. 68–86.

31. P. Kabal and S. Pasupathy, "Partial response signaling" *IEEE Trans. Comm.,* vol. COM-23(9), pp. 921–934, Sept. 1975.

32. P. R. Chevillat, E. Eleftheriou, and D. Maiwald, "Noise-predictive partial-response equalizers and applications," *IEEE Conf. Records ICC'92,* pp. 942–947, June 1992.

33. P. K. Pai, A. D. Brewster, and A. A. Abidi, "Analog front-end architectures for high-speed PRML magnetic read channels," *IEEE Trans. Magn.,* vol. 31, pp. 1103–1108, 1995.

34. R. M. Fano, "A heuristic discussion of probabilistic decoding," *IEEE Trans. Inform. Theory,* vol. IT-9, pp. 64–74, April 1963.

35. R. D. Cideciyan et al, "A PRML system for digital magnetic recording," *IEEE J. Sel. Areas Communications,* vol. 10, pp. 38–56, Jan. 1992.

36. S. A. Altekar, M. Berggren, B. E. Moision, P. H. Siegel, and J. K. Wolf, "Error-event characterization on partial-response channels," *IEEE Trans. Inform. Theory,* vol. 45, no. 1, pp. 241–247, Jan. 1999.

37. S. J. Simmons, "Breadth-first trellis decoding with adaptive effort," *IEEE Trans. Comm.,* vol. COM-38(1), pp. 3–12, Jan. 1990.

38. S. Kallel and K. Li, "Bidirectional sequential decoding," *IEEE Trans. Inform. Theory,* vol. IT-43(4) pp. 1319–1326, July 1997.

39. T. Hashimoto, "A list-type reduced-constraint generalization of the Viterbi algorithm," *IEEE Trans. Inform. Theory*, vol. IT-33(6), pp. 866–876, Nov. 1987.

40. V. Šenk and P. Radivojac, "The bidirectional stack algorithm—simulation results," in *Proc. of TELSIKS '95*, pp. 349–352, Niš, Yugoslavia, Oct. 1995.

41. V. Šenk and P. Radivojac, "The bidirectional stack algorithm," in *Proc. of ISIT'97*, p. 500, Ulm, Germany, July 1997.

42. V. Šenk, "Bistack—a bidirectional stack algorithm for decoding trellis codes," in *Proc. of XXXVI Conference on ETAN*, pp. 153–160, Kopaonik, Yugoslavia, 1992.

43. V. M. Eyuboglu and S. U. Quereshi, "Reduced-state sequence estimation with decision feedback and set partitioning," *IEEE Trans. Comm.*, vol. 36(1), pp. 13–20, Jan. 1988.

44. J. Bergmans, *Digital Baseband Transmission and Recording*, Kluwer Academic, Dordrecht, the Netherlands, 1996.

45. M. Despotović and V. Šenk, "Distance spectrum of channel trellis codes on precoded partial response 1-D channel," *J. Facta Universitatis (Niš)*, vol. 1., pp. 57–72, 1995, http://factaee.elfak.ni.ac.yu.

## 34.7  An Introduction to Error-Correcting Codes

*Mario Blaum*

### Introduction

When digital data are transmitted over a noisy channel, it is important to have a mechanism allowing recovery against a limited number of errors. Normally, a user string of 0s and 1s, called bits, is encoded by adding a number of redundant bits to it. When the receiver attempts to reconstruct the original message sent, it starts by examining a possibly corrupted version of the encoded message, and then makes a decision. This process is called the decoding.

The set of all possible encoded messages is called an error-correcting code. The field was started in the late 1940s by the work of Shannon and Hamming, and since then thousands of papers on the subject have been published. Several very good books are available to touch different aspects of error-correcting codes, for instance, [1,3–5,7,8], to mention just a few.

The purpose of Section 34.7 is to give an introduction to the theory and practice of error-correcting codes. In particular, it will be shown how to encode and decode the most widely used codes, Reed–Solomon (RS) codes.

In principle, it will assumed that the information symbols are bits, i.e., 0s and 1s. The set $\{0, 1\}$ has a field structure under the exclusive-OR ($\oplus$) and product operations. This field is denoted as $GF(2)$, which means Galois field of order 2.

Roughly, two types of error-correcting codes are used—codes of block type and codes of convolutional type. Codes of block type encode a fixed number of bits, say $k$ bits, into a vector of length $n$. So, the information string is divided into blocks of $k$ bits each. Convolutional codes take the string of information bits globally and slide a window over the data in order to encode. A certain amount of memory is needed by the encoder; however, Section 3.7 concentrates on block codes only. For more on convolutional codes, see [3,8].

As stated previously, $k$ information bits are encoded into $n$ bits. So, we have a 1-1 function $f$,

$$f : GF(2)^k \rightarrow GF(2)^n$$

The function $f$ defines the encoding procedure. The set of $2^k$ encoded vectors of length $n$ is called a code of length $n$ and dimension $k$, and we denote it as an $[n, k]$ code. Codewords are called the elements of the code while words are called the vectors of length $n$ in general. The ratio $k/n$ is called the *rate* of the code.

The error-correcting power of a code is characterized by a parameter called the minimum (Hamming) distance of the code. Formally:

**Definition 1**  Given two vectors of length $n$, say $\underline{a}$ and $\underline{b}$, we call the Hamming distance between $\underline{a}$ and $\underline{b}$ the number of coordinates in which they differ (notation, $d_H(\underline{a}, \underline{b})$).

Given a code $C$ of length $n$ and dimension $k$, let

$$d = \min\{d_H(\underline{a}, \underline{b}): \underline{a} \neq \underline{b}, \underline{a}, \underline{b} \in C\}$$

$d$ is the minimum (Hamming) distance of the code $C$, and $C$ is an $[n, k, d]$ code.

It is easy to verify that $d_H(\underline{a}, \underline{b})$ satisfies the axioms of distance, i.e.,

1. $d_H(\underline{a}, \underline{b}) = d_H(\underline{b}, \underline{a})$,
2. $d_H(\underline{a}, \underline{b}) = 0$ if and only if $\underline{a} = \underline{b}$,
3. $d_H(\underline{a}, \underline{c}) \leq d_H(\underline{a}, \underline{b}) + d_H(\underline{b}, \underline{c})$.

A sphere of radius $r$ and center $\underline{a}$ are called the set of vectors that are at distance at most $r$ from $\underline{a}$. The relation between $d$ and the maximum number of errors that code $C$ can correct is given by the following lemma:

**Lemma 1** The maximum number of errors that an $[n, k, d]$ code can correct is $\lfloor (d-1)/2 \rfloor$, where $\lfloor x \rfloor$ denotes the largest integer smaller than or equal to $x$.

*Proof:* Assume that vector $\underline{a}$ was transmitted but a possibly corrupted version of $\underline{a}$, for instance $\underline{r}$, was received. Moreover, assume that no more than $\lfloor (d-1)/2 \rfloor$ errors have occurred.

Consider the set of $2^k$ spheres of radius $\lfloor (d-1)/2 \rfloor$ whose centers are the codewords in $C$. By the definition of $d$, all these spheres are disjoint. Hence, $\underline{r}$ belongs to one and only one sphere: the one whose center is codeword $\underline{a}$. So, the decoder looks for the sphere in which $\underline{r}$ belongs, and outputs the center of that sphere as the decoded vector. Subsequently, whenever the number of errors is at most $\lfloor (d-1)/2 \rfloor$, this procedure will give the correct answer.

Moreover, $\lfloor (d-1)/2 \rfloor$ is the maximum number of errors that the code can correct. For let $\underline{a}, \underline{b} \in C$ such that $d_H(\underline{a}, \underline{b}) = d$. Let $\underline{u}$ be a vector such that $d_H(\underline{a}, \underline{u}) = 1 + \lfloor (d-1)/2 \rfloor$ and $d_H(\underline{b}, \underline{u}) = d - 1 - \lfloor (d-1)/2 \rfloor$. We easily verify that $d_H(\underline{b}, \underline{u}) \leq d_H(\underline{a}, \underline{u})$, so, if $\underline{a}$ is transmitted and $\underline{u}$ is received (i.e., $1 + \lfloor (d-1)/2 \rfloor$ errors have occurred), the decoder cannot decide that the transmitted codeword was $\underline{a}$, since codeword $\underline{b}$ is at least as close to $\underline{u}$ as $\underline{a}$. $\qquad\square$

**Example 1** Consider the following 1-1 relationship between $GF(2)^2$ and $GF(2)^5$ defining the encoding:

$$00 \leftrightarrow 00000$$
$$10 \leftrightarrow 00111$$
$$01 \leftrightarrow 11100$$
$$11 \leftrightarrow 11011$$

The four vectors in $GF(2)^5$ constitute a $[5,2,3]$ code $C$. From Lemma 1, $C$ can correct one error.

For instance, assume that we receive the vector $\underline{r} = 10100$. The decoder looks into the four spheres of radius 1 (each sphere has six elements) around each codeword, finding that $\underline{r}$ belongs in the sphere with center 11100. If we look at the table above, the final output of the decoder is the information block 01. $\qquad\square$

Example 1 shows that the decoder has to make at most 24 checks before arriving to the correct decision. When large codes are involved, as is the case in applications, this decoding procedure is not practical, since it amounts to an exhaustive search over a huge set of vectors.

One of the goals in the theory of error-correcting codes is finding codes with rate and minimum distance as large as possible. The possibility of finding codes with the right properties is often limited by bounds that constrain the choice of parameters $n$, $k$, and $d$. Some of these bounds are given in the next subsection.

Let us point out that error-correcting codes can be used for detection instead of correction of errors. The simplest example of an error-detecting code is given by a parity code: a parity is added to a string of bits in such a way that the total number of bits is even (a more sophisticated way of saying this is that the sum modulo 2 of the bits has to be 0). For example, 0100 is encoded as 01001. If an error occurs, or, more generally, an odd number of errors, these errors will be detected since the sum modulo 2 of the received bits will be 1. Notice that two errors will be undetected. In general, if an $[n, k, d]$ code is used for detection only, the decoder checks whether the received vector is in the code or not. If it is not, then errors are detected. It is easy to see that an $[n, k, d]$ code can detect up to $d - 1$ errors. Also, one can choose to correct less than $\lfloor (d - 1)/2 \rfloor$ errors, say $s$ errors, by taking disjoint spheres of radius $s$ around codewords, and using the remaining capacity to detect errors. In other words, correct up to $s$ errors or detect up to $s + t$ errors when more than $s$ errors occur.

Another application of error-correcting codes is in erasure correction. An erased bit is a bit that cannot be read, so the decoder has to decide if it was a 0 or a 1. An erasure is normally denoted with the symbol "?". For instance, 01?0 means that we cannot read the third symbol. Obviously, it is easier to correct erasures than to correct errors, since in the case of erasures we already know the location, we simply have to find what the erased bit was. It is not hard to prove that an $[n, k, d]$ code can correct upto $d - 1$ erasures. One may also want to simultaneously correct errors and erasures. In fact, a code $C$ with minimum distance $d$ can correct $s$ errors together with $t$ erasures whenever $2s + t \le d - 1$.

## Linear Codes

The previous subsection showed that a binary code of length $n$ is a subset of $GF(2)^n$. Notice that, being $GF(2)$ a field, $GF(2)^n$ has a structure of vector space over $GF(2)$. A code $C$ is linear if it is a subspace of $GF(2)^n$, i.e.

1. $\underline{0} \in C$,
2. $\forall \underline{a}, \underline{b} \in C, \underline{a} \oplus \underline{b} \in C$.

The symbol $\underline{0}$ denotes the all-zero vector. In general, vectors will be denoted with underlined letters, otherwise letters denote scalars.

In the first subsection, it was assumed that a code had $2^k$ elements, $k$ being the dimension; however, a code of length $n$ can be defined as any subset of $GF(2)^n$.

Many interesting combinatorial questions can be asked regarding nonlinear codes. Probably, the most important question is the following: Given the length $n$ and the minimum distance $d$, what is the maximum number of codewords that a code can have? For more about nonlinear codes, the reader is referred to [4]. From now on, we assume that all codes are linear. Linear codes are in general easier to encode and decode than their nonlinear counterparts; hence they are more suitable for implementation in applications.

In order to find the minimum distance of a linear code, it is enough to find its minimum *weight*. The (Hamming) weight of a vector $\underline{u}$ is the distance between $\underline{u}$ and the zero vector. In other words, the weight of $\underline{u}$, denoted $w_H(\underline{u})$, is the number of nonzero coordinates of the vector $\underline{u}$. The minimum weight of a code is the minimum between all the weights of the nonzero codewords. The proof of the following lemma is left as an exercise.

**Lemma 2** Let $C$ be a linear $[n, k, d]$ code. Then, the minimum distance and the minimum weight of $C$ are the same.

Next, two important matrices are introduced that define a linear error-correcting code. A code $C$ is now a subspace, so the dimension $k$ of $C$ is the cardinality of a basis of $C$. Consider then an $[n,k,d]$ code $C$. A $k \times n$ matrix $G$ is a *generator* matrix of a code $C$ if the rows of $G$ are a basis of $C$. Given a generator matrix, the encoding process is simple. Explicitly, let $\underline{u}$ be an information vector of length $k$ and $G$ a $k \times n$ generator matrix, then $\underline{u}$ is encoded into the $n$-vector $\underline{v}$ given by

$$\underline{v} = \underline{u}G \tag{34.45}$$

**Example 2** Let $G$ be the $2 \times 5$ matrix

$$G = \begin{pmatrix} 0 & 0 & 1 & 1 & 1 \\ 1 & 1 & 1 & 0 & 0 \end{pmatrix}$$

It is easy to see that $G$ is a generator matrix of the $[5, 2, 3]$ code described in Example 1. $\qquad\square$

Notice that, although a code may have many generator matrices, the encoding depends on the particular matrix chosen, according to Eq. (34.45). We say that $G$ is a *systematic* generator matrix if $G$ can be written as

$$G = (I_k | V) \tag{34.46}$$

where $I_k$ is the $k \times k$ identity matrix and $V$ is a $k \times (n-k)$ matrix. A systematic generator matrix has the following advantage: given an information vector $\underline{u}$ of length $k$, the encoding given by Eq. (34.45) outputs a codeword $(\underline{u}, \underline{w})$, where $\underline{w}$ has length $n-k$. In other words, a systematic encoder adds $n-k$ redundant bits to the $k$ information bits, so information and redundancy are clearly separated. This also simplifies the decoding process, since, after decoding, the redundant bits are simply discarded. For that reason, most encoders used in applications are systematic.

A permutation of the columns of a generator matrix gives a new generator matrix defining a new code. The codewords of the new code are permutations of the coordinates of the codewords of the original code, therefore, the two codes are *equivalent*. Notice that equivalent codes have the same distance properties, so their error correcting capabilities are exactly the same.

By permuting the columns of the generator matrix in Example 2, the following generator matrix $G'$ is obtained:

$$G' = \begin{pmatrix} 1 & 0 & 0 & 1 & 1 \\ 0 & 1 & 1 & 1 & 0 \end{pmatrix} \tag{34.47}$$

The matrix $G'$ defines a systematic encoder for a code that is equivalent to the one given in Example 1. For instance, the information vector 11 is encoded into 11 101.

The second important matrix related to a code is the so-called *parity check* matrix. An $(n-k) \times n$ matrix $H$ is a parity check matrix of an $[n, k]$ code $\mathcal{C}$ if and only if, for any $\underline{c} \in \mathcal{C}$,

$$\underline{c} H^T = \underline{0} \tag{34.48}$$

where $H^T$ denotes the transpose of matrix $H$ and $\underline{0}$ is a zero vector of length $n-k$. The parity check matrix $H$ is in systematic form if

$$H = (W | I_{n-k}) \tag{34.49}$$

where $I_{n-k}$ is the $(n-k) \times (n-k)$ identity matrix and $W$ is an $(n-k) \times k$ matrix.

Given a systematic generator matrix $G$ of a code $\mathcal{C}$, it is easy to find the systematic parity check matrix $H$ (and conversely). Explicitly, if $G$ is given by Eq. (34.46), $H$ is given by

$$H = (V^T | I_{n-k}) \tag{34.50}$$

The proof of this fact is left to the reader.

For example, the systematic parity check matrix of the code, whose systematic generator matrix is given by Eq. (34.47), is

$$H = \begin{pmatrix} 0 & 1 & 1 & 0 & 0 \\ 1 & 1 & 0 & 1 & 0 \\ 1 & 0 & 0 & 0 & 1 \end{pmatrix} \tag{34.51}$$

Next is an important property of parity check matrices.

**Lemma 3**   Let $C$ be a linear $[n, k, d]$ code and $H$ a parity check matrix. Then, any $d - 1$ columns of $H$ are linearly independent.

*Proof:* Numerate the columns of $H$ from 0 to $n - 1$. Assume that columns $0 \leq i_1 < i_2 < \cdots < i_m \leq n - 1$ are linearly dependent, where $m \leq d - 1$. Without loss of generality, assume that the sum of these columns is equal to the column vector zero. Let $\underline{v}$ be a vector of length $n$ whose nonzero coordinates are in locations $i_1, i_2, \ldots, i_m$. Then,

$$\underline{v}H^T = \underline{0}$$

hence $\underline{v}$ is in $C$. But $\underline{v}$ has weight $m \leq d - 1$, contradicting the fact that $C$ has minimum distance $d$.  □

**Corollary 1**   For any linear $[n, k, d]$ code, the minimum distance $d$ is the smallest number $m$ such that there is a subset of $m$ linearly dependent columns.

*Proof:* It follows immediately from Lemma 3.  □

**Corollary 2 (Singleton Bound)**   For any linear $[n, k, d]$ code,

$$d \leq n - k + 1$$

*Proof:* Notice that, because $H$ is an $(n - k) \times n$ matrix, any $n - k + 1$ columns are going to be linearly dependent, so if $d > n - k + 1$ we would contradict Corollary 1.  □

Codes meeting the Singleton bound are called maximum distance separable (MDS). In fact, except for trivial cases, binary codes are not MDS. In order to obtain MDS codes, we will define codes over larger fields, like the so-called Reed Solomon codes, to be described later in the chapter.

A second bound is also given relating the redundancy and the minimum distance of an $[n, k, d]$ code the so-called Hamming or volume bound. Let us denote by $V(r)$ the number of elements in a sphere of radius $r$ whose center is an element in $GF(2)^n$. It is easy to verify that

$$V(r) = \sum_{i=0}^{r} \binom{n}{i} \tag{34.52}$$

We then have:

**Lemma 4 (Hamming bound)**   Let $C$ be a linear $[n, k, d]$ code, then

$$n - k \geq \log_2 V(\lfloor (d - 1)/2 \rfloor) \tag{34.53}$$

*Proof:*   Notice that the $2^k$ spheres with the $2^k$ codewords as centers and radius $\lfloor (d - 1)/2 \rfloor$ are disjoint. The total number of vectors contained in these spheres is $2^k V(\lfloor (d - 1)/2 \rfloor)$. This number has to be smaller than or equal to the total number of vectors in the space, i.e.,

$$2^n \geq 2^k V(\lfloor (d - 1)/2 \rfloor) \tag{34.54}$$

Inequality (34.53) follows immediately from Eq. (34.54).  □

A *perfect* code is a code for which inequality Eq. (34.53) is in effect equality. Geometrically, a perfect code is a code for which the $2^k$ spheres of radius $\lfloor (d - 1)/2 \rfloor$ and the codewords as centers cover the whole space.

Not many perfect codes exist. In the binary case, the only nontrivial linear perfect codes are the Hamming codes (to be presented in the next subsection) and the [23,12,7] Golay code. For details, the reader is referred to [4].

## Syndrome Decoding, Hamming Codes, and Capacity of the Channel

This subsection studies the first important family of codes, the so-called Hamming codes. As will be shown, Hamming codes can correct up to one error.

Let $C$ be an $[n, k, d]$ code with parity check matrix $H$. Let $\underline{u}$ be a transmitted vector and $\underline{r}$ a possibly corrupted received version of $\underline{u}$. We say that the syndrome of $\underline{r}$ is the vector $\underline{s}$ of length $n - k$ given by

$$\underline{s} = \underline{r}H^T \tag{34.55}$$

Notice that, if no errors occurred, the syndrome of $\underline{r}$ is the zero vector. The syndrome, however, tells us more than a vector being in the code or not. For instance, as before, that $\underline{u}$ was transmitted and $\underline{r}$ was received, where $\underline{r} = \underline{u} \oplus \underline{e}$, $\underline{e}$ an error vector. Notice that,

$$\underline{s} = \underline{r}H^T = (\underline{u} \oplus \underline{e})H^T = \underline{u}H^T \oplus \underline{e}H^T = \underline{e}H^T$$

because $\underline{u}$ is in $C$. Hence, the syndrome does not depend on the received vector but on the error vector. In the next lemma, we show that to every error vector of weight $\leq(d-1)/2$ corresponds a unique syndrome.

**Lemma 5**    Let $C$ be a linear $[n, k, d]$ code with parity check matrix $H$. Then, there is a 1-1 correspondence between errors of weight $\leq(d-1)/2$ and syndromes.

*Proof:* Let $\underline{e}_1$ and $\underline{e}_2$ be two distinct error vectors of weight $\leq(d-1)/2$ with syndromes $\underline{s}_1 = \underline{e}_1H^T$ and $\underline{s}_2 = \underline{e}_2 H^T$. If $\underline{s}_1 = \underline{s}_2$, then $\underline{s} = (\underline{e}_1 \oplus \underline{e}_2)H^T = \underline{s}_1 \oplus \underline{s}_2 = \underline{0}$, hence $\underline{e}_1 \oplus \underline{e}_2 \in C$. But $\underline{e}_1 \oplus \underline{e}_2$ has weight $\leq d - 1$, a contradiction.    $\square$

Lemma 5 gives the key for a decoding method that is more efficient than exhaustive search. We can construct a table with the 1-1 correspondence between syndromes and error patterns of weight $\leq(d-1)/2$ and decode by look-up table. In other words, given a received vector, we first find its syndrome and then we look in the table to which error pattern it corresponds. Once we obtain the error pattern, we add it to the received vector, retrieving the original information. This procedure may be efficient for small codes, but it is still too complex for large codes.

**Example 3**    Consider the code whose parity matrix $H$ is given by (34.51). We have seen that this is a [5, 2, 3] code. We have six error patterns of weight $\leq 1$. The 1-1 correspondence between these error patterns and the syndromes can be immediately verified to be

$$00000 \leftrightarrow 000$$
$$10000 \leftrightarrow 011$$
$$01000 \leftrightarrow 110$$
$$00100 \leftrightarrow 100$$
$$00010 \leftrightarrow 010$$
$$00001 \leftrightarrow 001$$

For instance, assume that we receive the vector $\underline{r} = 10111$. We obtain the syndrome $\underline{s} = \underline{r}H^T = 100$. Looking at the table above, we see that this syndrome corresponds to the error pattern $\underline{e} = 00100$. Adding this error pattern to the received vector, we conclude that the transmitted vector was $\underline{r} \oplus \underline{e} = 10011$.    $\square$

Given a number $r$ of redundant bits, we say that a $[2^r - 1, 2^r - r - 1, 3]$ Hamming code is a code having an $r \times (2^r - 1)$ parity check matrix $H$ such that its columns are all the different nonzero vectors of length $r$.

A Hamming code has minimum distance 3. This follows from its definition and Corollary 1. Notice that any two columns in $H$, being different, are linearly independent. Also, if we take any two different columns and their sum, these three columns are linearly dependent, proving our assertion.

A natural way of writing the columns of $H$ in a Hamming code, is by considering them as binary numbers on base 2 in increasing order. This means, the first column is 1 on base 2, the second column is 2, and so on. The last column is $2^r - 1$ on base 2, i.e., $(1, 1, \ldots, 1)^T$. This parity check matrix, although nonsystematic, makes the decoding very simple.

In effect, let $\underline{r}$ be a received vector such that $\underline{r} = \underline{v} \oplus \underline{e}$, where $\underline{v}$ was the transmitted codeword and $\underline{e}$ is an error vector of weight 1. Then, the syndrome is $\underline{s} = \underline{e}H^T$, which gives the column corresponding to the location in error. This column, as a number on base 2, tells us exactly where the error has occurred, so the received vector can be corrected.

**Example 4**  Consider the $[7, 4, 3]$ Hamming code $\mathcal{C}$ with parity check matrix

$$H = \begin{pmatrix} 0 & 0 & 0 & 1 & 1 & 1 & 1 \\ 0 & 1 & 1 & 0 & 0 & 1 & 1 \\ 1 & 0 & 1 & 0 & 1 & 0 & 1 \end{pmatrix} \tag{34.56}$$

Assume that vector $\underline{r} = 1100101$ is received. The syndrome is $\underline{s} = \underline{r}H^T = 001$, which is the binary representation of the number 1. Hence, the first location is in error, so the decoder estimates that the transmitted vector was $\underline{v} = 0100101$. $\qquad\qquad\square$

We can obtain 1-error correcting codes of any length simply by shortening a Hamming code. This procedure works as follows: assume that we want to encode $k$ information bits into a 1-error correcting code. Let $r$ be the smallest number such that $k \le 2^r - r - 1$. Let $H$ be the parity check matrix of a $[2^r - 1, 2^r - r - 1, 3]$ Hamming code. Then construct a matrix $H'$ by eliminating some $2^r - r - 1 - k$ columns from $H$. The code whose parity check matrix is $H'$ is a $[k + r, k, d]$ code with $d \ge 3$, hence it can correct one error. We call it a shortened Hamming code. For instance, the $[5, 2, 3]$ code whose parity check matrix is given by (34.51) is a shortened Hamming code.

In general, if $H$ is the parity check matrix of a code $\mathcal{C}$, $H'$ is a matrix obtained by eliminating a certain number of columns from $H$ and $\mathcal{C}'$ is the code with parity check matrix $H'$, we say that $\mathcal{C}'$ is obtained by shortening $\mathcal{C}$.

A $[2^r - 1, 2^r - r - 1, 3]$ Hamming code can be extended to a $[2^r, 2^r - r - 1, 4]$ Hamming code by adding to each codeword a parity bit, that is, the exclusive-OR of the first $2^r - 1$ bits. The new code is called an extended Hamming code.

So far, we have not talked about probabilities of errors. Assume that we have a binary symmetric channel (BSC), i.e., the probability of a 1 becoming a 0 or of a 0 becoming a 1 is $p < .5$. Let $P_{err}$ be the probability of error after decoding using a code, i.e., the output of the decoder does not correspond to the originally transmitted information vector. A fundamental question is the following: given a BSC with bit error probability $p$, does it exist a code of high rate that can arbitrarily lower $P_{err}$? The answer, due to Shannon, is yes, provided that the code has rate below a parameter called the capacity of the channel, as defined next.

**Definition 2**  Given a BSC with probability of bit error $p$, we say that the capacity of the channel is

$$C(p) = 1 + p \log_2 p + (1 - p) \log_2(1 - p) \tag{34.57}$$

**Theorem 1 (Shannon)**    For any $\epsilon > 0$ and $R < C(p)$, there is an $[n, k]$ binary code of rate $k/n \geq R$ with $P_{err} < \epsilon$.

For a proof of Theorem 1 and some of its generalizations, the reader is referred to [5], or even to Shannon's original paper [6].

Theorem 1 has enormous theoretical importance. It shows that reliable communication is not limited in the presence of noise, only the rate of communication is. For instance, if $p = .01$, the capacity of the channel is $C(.01) = .9192$. Hence, there are codes of rate $\geq .9$ with $P_{err}$ arbitrarily small. It also tells us not to look for codes with rate .92 making $P_{err}$ arbitrarily small.

The proof of Theorem 1, though, is based on probabilistic methods and the assumption of arbitrarily large values of $n$. In practical applications, $n$ cannot be too large. The theorem does not tell us how to construct efficient codes, it just asserts their existence. Moreover, when we construct codes, we want them to have efficient encoding and decoding algorithms. In the last few years, coding methods approaching the Shannon limit have been developed, the so-called *turbo codes*. Although great progress has been made towards  practical implementations of turbo codes, in applications like magnetic recording their complexity is still a problem. A description of turbo codes is beyond the scope of this introduction. The reader is referred to [2].

## Codes over Bytes and Finite Fields

So far, we have considered linear codes over bits. Next we want to introduce codes over larger symbols, mainly over bytes. A byte of size $v$ is a vector of $v$ bits. Mathematically, bytes are vectors in $GF(2)^v$. Typical cases in magnetic and optical recording involve 8-bit bytes. Most of the general results in the previous sections for codes over bits easily extend to codes over bytes. It is trivial to multiply bits, but we need a method to multiply bytes. To this end, the theory of finite fields has been developed. Next we give a brief introduction to the theory of finite fields. For a more complete treatment, the reader is referred to chapter 4 of [4].

We know how to add two binary vectors, we simply exclusive-OR them componentwise. What we need now is a rule that allows us to multiply bytes while preserving associative, distributive, and multiplicative inverse properties, i.e., a product that gives to the set of bytes of length $v$ the structure of a field. To this end, we will define a multiplication between vectors that satisfies the associative and commutative properties, it has a 1 element, each nonzero element is invertible and it is distributive with respect to the sum operation.

Recall the definition of the ring $Z_m$ of integers modulo $m$: $Z_m$ is the set $\{0, 1, 2, \ldots, m - 1\}$, with a sum and product of any two elements defined as the residue of dividing by $m$ the usual sum or product. It is not difficult to prove that $Z_m$ is a field if and only if $m$ is a prime number. Using this analogy, we will give to $(GF(2))^v$ the structure of a field.

Consider the vector space $(GF(2))^v$ over the field $GF(2)$. We can view each vector as a polynomial of degree $\leq v - 1$ as follows: the vector $\underline{a} = (a_0, a_1, \ldots, a_{v-1})$ corresponds to the polynomial $a(\alpha) = a_0 + a_1 \alpha + \cdots + \alpha_{v-1} \alpha^{v-1}$.

The goal is to give to $(GF(2))^v$ the structure of a field. We will denote such a field by $GF(2^v)$. The sum in $GF(2^v)$ is the usual sum of vectors in $(GF(2))^v$. We need now to define a product.

Let $f(x)$ be an irreducible polynomial (i.e., it cannot be expressed as the product of two polynomials of smaller degree) of degree $v$ whose coefficients are in $GF(2)$. Let $a(\alpha)$ and $b(\alpha)$ be two elements of $GF(2^v)$. We define the product between $a(\alpha)$ and $b(\alpha)$ in $GF(2^v)$ as the unique polynomial $c(\alpha)$ of degree $\leq v - 1$ such that $c(\alpha)$ is the residue of dividing the product $a(\alpha)b(\alpha)$ by $f(\alpha)$ (the notation $g(x) \equiv h(x)$ (mod $f(x)$) means that $g(x)$ and $h(x)$ have the same residue after dividing by $f(x)$, i.e., $g(\alpha) = h(\alpha)$).

The sum and product operations defined above give to $GF(2^v)$ a field structure. The role of the irreducible polynomial $f(x)$ is the same as the prime number $m$ when $Z_m$ is a field. In effect, the proof that $GF(2^v)$ is a field when $m$ is irreducible is essentially the same as the proof that $Z_m$ is a field when $m$ is prime. From now on, we denote the elements in $GF(2^v)$ as polynomials in $\alpha$ of degree $\leq v - 1$ with coefficients in $GF(2)$. Given two polynomials $a(x)$ and $b(x)$ with coefficients in $GF(2)$, $a(\alpha)b(\alpha)$ denotes

**TABLE 34.3** The Finite Field $GF(8)$ Generated by $1 + x + x^3$

| Vector | Polynomial | Power of $\alpha$ | Logarithm |
|--------|-----------|------------------|-----------|
| 000 | 0 | 0 | $-\infty$ |
| 100 | 1 | 1 | 0 |
| 010 | $\alpha$ | $\alpha$ | 1 |
| 001 | $\alpha^2$ | $\alpha^2$ | 2 |
| 110 | $1 + \alpha$ | $\alpha^3$ | 3 |
| 011 | $\alpha + \alpha^2$ | $\alpha^4$ | 4 |
| 111 | $1 + \alpha + \alpha^2$ | $\alpha^5$ | 5 |
| 101 | $1 + \alpha^2$ | $\alpha^6$ | 6 |

the product in $GF(2^v)$, while $a(x)b(x)$ denotes the regular product of polynomials. Notice that, for the irreducible polynomial $f(x)$, in particular, $f(\alpha) = 0$ in $GF(2^v)$, since $f(x) \equiv 0 \,(\mathrm{mod}\, f(x))$.

So, the set $GF(2^v)$ given by the irreducible polynomial $f(x)$ of degree $v$ is the set of polynomials of degree $\leq v - 1$, where the sum operation is the regular sum of polynomials, and the product operation is the residue of dividing by $f(x)$ the regular product of two polynomials.

**Example 5** Construct the field $GF(8)$. Consider the polynomials of degree $\leq 2$ over $GF(2)$. Let $f(x) = 1 + x + x^3$. Since $f(x)$ has no roots over $GF(2)$, it is irreducible (notice that such an assessment can be made only for polynomials of degree 2 or 3). Let us consider the powers of $\alpha$ modulo $f(\alpha)$. Notice that $\alpha^3 = \alpha^3 + f(\alpha) = 1 + \alpha$. Also, $\alpha^4 = \alpha\alpha^3 = \alpha\,(1 + \alpha) = \alpha + \alpha^2$. Similarly, we obtain $\alpha^5 = \alpha\alpha^4 = \alpha(\alpha + \alpha^2) = \alpha^2 + \alpha^3 = 1 + \alpha + \alpha^2$, and $\alpha^6 = \alpha\alpha^5 = \alpha + \alpha^2 + \alpha^3 = 1 + \alpha^2$. Finally, $\alpha^7 = \alpha\alpha^6 = \alpha + \alpha^3 = 1$.

Note that every nonzero element in $GF(8)$ can be obtained as a power of the element $\alpha$. In this case, $\alpha$ is called a *primitive* element and the irreducible polynomial $f(x)$ that defines the field is called a *primitive* polynomial. It can be proven that it is always the case that the multiplicative group of a finite field is cyclic, so there is always a primitive element.

A convenient description of $GF(8)$ is given in Table 34.3. The first column in Table 34.3 describes the element of the field in vector form, the second one as a polynomial in $\alpha$ of degree $\leq 2$, the third one as a power of $\alpha$, and the last one gives the logarithm (also called Zech logarithm): it simply indicates the corresponding power of $\alpha$. As a convention, we denote by $-\infty$ the logarithm corresponding to the element 0. □

It is often convenient to express the elements in a finite field as powers of $\alpha$; when we multiply two of them, we obtain a new power of $\alpha$ whose exponent is the sum of the two exponents modulo $2^v - 1$. Explicitly, if $i$ and $j$ are the logarithms of two elements in $GF(2^v)$, then their product has logarithm $i + j$ $(\mathrm{mod}\,(2^v - 1))$. In the example above, if we want to multiply the vectors 101 and 111, we first look at their logarithms. They are 6 and 5, respectively, so the logarithm of the product is $6 + 5\,(\mathrm{mod}\, 7) = 4$, corresponding to the vector 011.

In order to add vectors, the best way is to express them in vector form and add coordinate to coordinate in the usual way.

## Cyclic Codes

In the same way we defined codes over the binary field $GF(2)$, we can define codes over any finite field $GF(2^v)$. Now, a code of length $n$ is a subset of $(GF(2^v))^n$, but since we study only linear codes, we require that such a subset is a vector space. Similarly, we define the minimum (Hamming) distance and the generator and parity check matrices of a code. Some properties of binary linear codes, like the Singleton bound, remain the same in the general case. Others, such as the Hamming bound, require some modifications.

Consider a linear code $\mathcal{C}$ over $GF(2^v)$ of length $n$. We say that $\mathcal{C}$ is cyclic if, for any codeword $(c_0, c_1, \ldots, c_{n-1}) \in \mathcal{C}$, then $(c_{n-1}, c_0, c_1, \ldots, c_{n-2}) \in \mathcal{C}$. In other words, the code is invariant under cyclic shifts to the right.

If we write the codewords as polynomials of degree $<n$ with coefficients in $GF(2^v)$, this is equivalent to say that if $c(x) \in \mathcal{C}$, then $xc(x) \bmod (x^n - 1) \in \mathcal{C}$. Hence, if $c(x) \in \mathcal{C}$, then, given any polynomial $w(x)$, the residue of dividing $w(x)c(x)$ by $x^n - 1$ is in $\mathcal{C}$. In particular, if the degree of $w(x)c(x)$ is smaller than $n$, then $w(x)c(x) \in \mathcal{C}$.

From now on, we write the elements of a cyclic code $\mathcal{C}$ as polynomials modulo $x^n - 1$.

**Theorem 2**  $\mathcal{C}$ is an $[n, k]$ cyclic code over $GF(2^v)$ if and only if there is a (monic) polynomial $g(x)$ of degree $n - k$ such that $g(x)$ divides $x^n - 1$ and each $c(x) \in \mathcal{C}$ is a multiple of $g(x)$, i.e., $c(x) \in \mathcal{C}$ if and only if $c(x) = w(x)g(x)$, $\deg(w) < k$. We call $g(x)$ a generator polynomial of $\mathcal{C}$.

*Proof:* Let $g(x)$ be a monic (i.e., lead coefficient is 1) polynomial in $\mathcal{C}$ such that $g(x)$ has minimal degree. If $\deg(g) = 0$ (i.e., $g = 1$), then $\mathcal{C}$ is the whole space $(GF(2^v))^n$, so assume $\deg(g) \geq 1$. Let $c(x)$ be any element in $\mathcal{C}$. We can write $c(x) = w(x)g(x) + r(x)$, where $\deg(r) < \deg(g)$. Because $\deg(wg) < n$, $g \in \mathcal{C}$ and $\mathcal{C}$ is cyclic, in particular, $w(x)g(x) \in \mathcal{C}$. Hence, $r(x) = c(x) - w(x)g(x) \in \mathcal{C}$. If $r \neq 0$, we would contradict the fact that $g(x)$ has minimal degree, hence, $r = 0$ and $c(x)$ is a multiple of $g(x)$.

Similarly, we can prove that $g(x)$ divides $x^n - 1$. Let $x^n - 1 = h(x)g(x) + r(x)$, where $\deg(r) < \deg(g)$. In particular, $h(x)g(x) \equiv -r(x) \bmod (x^n - 1)$, hence, $r(x) \in \mathcal{C}$. Since $g(x)$ has minimal degree, $r = 0$, so $g(x)$ divides $x^n - 1$.

Conversely, assume that every element in $\mathcal{C}$ is a multiple of $g(x)$ and $g$ divides $x^n - 1$. It is immediate that the code is linear and that it has dimension $k$. Let $c(x) \in \mathcal{C}$, hence, $c(x) = w(x)g(x)$ with $\deg(w) < k$. Also, since $g(x)$ divides $x^n - 1$, $x^n - 1 = h(x)g(x)$. Assume that $c(x) = c_0 + c_1 x + c_2 x^2 + \cdots + c_{n-1} x^{n-1}$, then, $xc(x) \equiv c_{n-1} + c_0 x + \cdots + c_{n-2} x^{n-1} \pmod{x^n - 1}$. We have to prove that $c_{n-1} + c_0 x + \cdots + c_{n-2} x^{n-1} = q(x)g(x)$, where $q(x)$ has degree $\leq k - 1$. Notice that

$$
\begin{aligned}
c_{n-1} + c_0 x + \cdots + c_{n-2} x^{n-1} &= c_{n-1} + c_0 x + \cdots + c_{n-2} x^{n-1} + c_{n-1} x^n - c_{n-1} x^n \\
&= c_0 x + \cdots + c_{n-2} x^{n-1} + c_{n-1} x^n - c_{n-1}(x^n - 1) \\
&= xc(x) - c_{n-1}(x^n - 1) \\
&= xw(x)g(x) - c_{n-1} h(x)g(x) \\
&= (xw(x) - c_{n-1} h(x))g(x)
\end{aligned}
$$

proving that the element is in the code.                                                                        □

**Theorem 2**   gives a method to find all cyclic codes of length $n$, simply take all the (monic) factors of $x^n - 1$. Each one of them is the generator polynomial of a cyclic code.

**Example 6**   Consider the [7,4] cyclic code over $GF(2)$ generated by $g(x) = 1 + x + x^3$. We can verify that $x^7 - 1 = g(x)(1 + x)(1 + x^2 + x^3)$; hence, $g(x)$ indeed generates a cyclic code.

In order to encode an information polynomial over $GF(2)$ of degree $\leq 3$ into a codeword, we multiply it by $g(x)$.

Say that we want to encode $\underline{u} = (1, 0, 0, 1)$, which in polynomial form is $u(x) = 1 + x^3$. Hence, the encoding gives $c(x) = u(x)g(x) = 1 + x + x^4 + x^6$. In vector form, this gives $\underline{c} = (1\ 1\ 0\ 0\ 1\ 0\ 1)$.

It can be easily verified that the [7,4] code given in this example has minimum distance 3 and is equivalent to the Hamming code of Example 4. In other words, the codewords of the code given in this example are permutations of the codewords of the [7,4,3] Hamming code given in Example 4.          □

The encoding method of a cyclic code with generator polynomial $g$ is then very simple: we multiply the information polynomial by $g$. However, this encoder is not systematic. A systematic encoder of a cyclic code is given by the following algorithm:

**Algorithm 1 (Systematic Encoding Algorithm for Cyclic Codes)**   Let $\mathcal{C}$ be a cyclic $[n, k]$ code over $GF(2^v)$ with generator polynomial $g(x)$. Let $u(x)$ be an information polynomial, $\deg(u) < k$. Let $r(x)$ be the residue of dividing $x^{n-k} u(x)$ by $g(x)$. Then $u(x)$ is encoded into the polynomial $c(x) = u(x) - x^k r(x)$.

We leave as an exercise proving that Algorithm 2 produces indeed a codeword in $\mathcal{C}$.

**Example 7**  Consider the [7,4] cyclic code over $GF(2)$ of Example 6. If we want to encode systematically the information vector $\underline{u} = (1, 0, 0, 1)$ (or $u(x) = 1 + x^3$), we have to obtain first the residue of dividing $x^3 u(x) = x^3 + x^6$ by $g(x)$. This residue is $r(x) = x + x^2$. Hence, the output of the encoder is $c(x) = u(x) - x^4 r(x) = 1 + x^3 + x^5 + x^6$. In vector form, this gives $\underline{c} = (1\ 0\ 0\ 1\ 0\ 1\ 1)$. $\square$

## Reed Solomon Codes

Throughout this subsection, the codes considered are over the field $GF(2^v)$. Let $\alpha$ be a primitive element in $GF(2^v)$, i.e., $\alpha^{2^v - 1} = 1$, $\alpha^i \neq 1$ for $i \neq 0 \bmod 2^v - 1$. A Reed–Solomon (RS) code of length $n = 2^v - 1$ and dimension $k$ is the cyclic code generated by

$$g(x) = (x - \alpha)(x - \alpha^2) \cdots (x - \alpha^{n-k-1})(x - \alpha^{n-k})$$

Each $\alpha^i$ is a root of unity, $x - \alpha^i$ divides $x^n - 1$, hence, $g$ divides $x^n - 1$ and the code is cyclic.

An equivalent way of describing a RS code is as the set of polynomials over $GF(2^v)$ of degree $\leq n - 1$ with roots $\alpha, \alpha^2, \ldots, \alpha^{n-k}$, i.e., $F$ is in the code if and only if $\deg(F) \leq n - 1$ and $F(\alpha) = F(\alpha^2) = \cdots = F(\alpha^{n-k}) = 0$.

This property allows us to find a parity check matrix for a RS code. Say that $F(x) = F_0 + F_1 x + \cdots + F_{n-1} x^{n-1}$ is in the code. Let $1 \leq i \leq n - k$, then

$$F(\alpha^i) = F_0 + F_1 \alpha^i + \cdots + F_{n-1} \alpha^{i(n-1)} = 0 \tag{34.58}$$

In other words, Eq. (34.58) tells us that codeword $(F_0, F_1, \ldots, F_{n-1})$ is orthogonal to the vectors $(1, \alpha^i, \alpha^{2i}, \ldots, \alpha^{i(n-1)})$, $1 \leq i \leq n - k$. Hence, these vectors are the rows of a parity check matrix for the RS code. A parity check matrix of an $[n, k]$ RS code over $GF(2^v)$ is then

$$H = \begin{pmatrix} 1 & \alpha & \alpha^2 & \cdots & \alpha^{n-1} \\ 1 & \alpha^2 & \alpha^4 & \cdots & \alpha^{2(n-1)} \\ \vdots & \vdots & \vdots & \ddots & \vdots \\ 1 & \alpha^{n-k} & \alpha^{(n-k)2} & \cdots & \alpha^{(n-k)(n-1)} \end{pmatrix} \tag{34.59}$$

In order to show that $H$ is in fact a parity check matrix, we need to prove that the rows of $H$ are linearly independent. The next lemma provides an even stronger result.

**Lemma 6**  Any set of $n - k$ columns in matrix $H$ defined by Eq. (34.59) is linearly independent.

*Proof:*  Take a set $0 \leq i_1 < i_2 < \ldots < i_{n-k} \leq n - 1$ of columns of $H$. Denote $\alpha^{i_j}$ by $\alpha_j$, $1 \leq j \leq n - k$. Columns $i_1, i_2, \ldots, i_{n-k}$ are linearly independent if and only if their determinant is nonzero, i.e., if and only if

$$\det \begin{pmatrix} \alpha_1 & \alpha_2 & \cdots & \alpha_{n-k} \\ (\alpha_1)^2 & (\alpha_2)^2 & \cdots & (\alpha_{n-k})^2 \\ \vdots & \vdots & \ddots & \vdots \\ (\alpha_1)^{n-k} & (\alpha_2)^{n-k} & \cdots & (\alpha_{n-k})^{n-k} \end{pmatrix} \neq 0 \tag{34.60}$$

Let

$$V(\alpha_1, \alpha_2,\ldots,\alpha_{n-k}) = \det \begin{pmatrix} 1 & 1 & \cdots & 1 \\ \alpha_1 & \alpha_2 & \cdots & \alpha_{n-k} \\ \vdots & \vdots & \ddots & \vdots \\ (\alpha_1)^{n-k-1} & (\alpha_2)^{n-k-1} & \cdots & (\alpha_{n-k})^{n-k-1} \end{pmatrix} \tag{34.61}$$

We call the determinant $V(\alpha_1, \alpha_2,\ldots,\alpha_{n-k})$ a *Vandermonde determinant*—it is the determinant of an $(n-k)\times(n-k)$ matrix whose rows are the powers of vector $\alpha_1, \alpha_2,\ldots,\alpha_{n-k}$, the powers running from 0 to $n-k-1$. By properties of determinants, if we consider the determinant in (34.60), we have

$$\det \begin{pmatrix} \alpha_1 & \alpha_2 & \cdots & \alpha_{n-k} \\ (\alpha_1)^2 & (\alpha_2)^2 & \cdots & (\alpha_{n-k})^2 \\ \vdots & \vdots & \ddots & \vdots \\ (\alpha_1)^{n-k} & (\alpha_2)^{n-k} & \cdots & (\alpha_{n-k})^{n-k} \end{pmatrix} = \alpha_1\alpha_2\ldots\alpha_{n-k}V(\alpha_1,\alpha_2,\ldots,\alpha_{n-k}) \tag{34.62}$$

Hence, by Eqs. (34.60) and (34.62), since the $\alpha_j$'s are nonzero, it is enough to prove that $V(\alpha_1, \alpha_2,\ldots,\alpha_{n-k}) \neq 0$. A well-known result in literature states that

$$V(\alpha_1,\alpha_2,\ldots,\alpha_{n-k}) = \prod_{1\le i<j\le n-k}(\alpha_j - \alpha_i) \tag{34.63}$$

Because $\alpha$ is a primitive element in $GF(2^v)$, its powers $\alpha^l$, $0 \le l \le n-1$ are distinct. In particular, the $\alpha_i$'s, $1 \le i \le n-k$ are distinct; hence, the product in the right-hand side of (34.63) is nonzero. $\square$

**Corollary 3**   An $[n,k]$ RS code has minimum distance $d = n-k+1$.

*Proof:*   Let $H$ be the parity check matrix of the RS code defined by (34.59). Notice that, since any $n-k$ columns in $H$ are linearly independent, $d \ge n-k+1$ by Lemma 3.

On the other hand, $d \le n-k+1$ by the Singleton bound (Corollary 2), so we have equality. $\square$

Because RS codes meet the Singleton bound with equality, they are MDS (see second subsection).

**Example 8**   Consider the [7,3,5] RS code over $GF(8)$, where $GF(8)$ is given by Table 34.3. The generator polynomial is

$$g(x) = (x-\alpha)(x-\alpha^2)(x-\alpha^3)(x-\alpha^4) = \alpha^3 + \alpha x + x^2 + \alpha^3 x^3 + x^4$$

Assume that we want to encode the 3-byte vector $\underline{u} = 101\ 001\ 111$. Writing the bytes as powers of $\alpha$ in polynomial form, we have $u(x) = \alpha^6 + \alpha^2 x + \alpha^5 x^2$.

In order to encode $u(x)$, we perform

$$u(x)g(x) = \alpha^2 + \alpha^4 x + \alpha^2 x^2 + \alpha^6 x^3 + \alpha^6 x^4 + \alpha^4 x^5 + \alpha^5 x^6$$

In vector form the output of the encoder is given by 001 011 001 101 101 011 111. If we encode $u(x)$ using a systematic encoder (Algorithm 1), the output of the encoder is

$$\alpha^6 + \alpha^2 x + \alpha^5 x^2 + \alpha^6 x^3 + \alpha^5 x^4 + \alpha^4 x^5 + \alpha^4 x^6$$

which, in vector form, is 101 001 111 101 111 011 011. $\square$

Next we make some observations:

- The definition given above for an $[n, k]$ RS code states that $F(x)$ is in the code if and only if it has as roots the powers $\alpha, \alpha^2, \ldots, \alpha^{n-k}$ of a primitive element $\alpha$; however, it is enough to state that $F$ has as roots a set of *consecutive* powers of $\alpha$, say, $\alpha^m, \alpha^{m+1}, \ldots, \alpha^{m+n-k-1}$, where $0 \leq m \leq n - 1$. Although our definition (i.e., $m = 1$) gives the most usual setting for RS codes, often engineering reasons may determine different choices of $m$. It is easy to verify that with the more general definition of RS codes, the minimum distance remains $n - k + 1$.

- Given an $[n, k]$ RS code, there is an easy way to shorten it and obtain an $[n - l, k - l]$ code for $l < k$. In effect, if we have only $k - l$ bytes of information, we add $l$ zeros in order to obtain an information string of length $k$. We then find the $n - k$ redundant bytes using a systematic encoder. When writing, of course, the $l$ zeros are not written, so we have an $[n - l, k - l]$ code, called a shortened RS code. It is immediately verified that shortened RS codes are also MDS.

We have defined RS codes, proven that they are MDS and showed how to encode them systematically. The next step, to be developed in the next sections, is decoding them.

## Decoding of RS Codes: The Key Equation

Through this subsection, $\mathcal{C}$ denotes an $[n, k]$ RS code (unless otherwise stated). Assume that a codeword $F(x) = \sum_{i=0}^{n-1} F_i x^i$ in $\mathcal{C}$ is transmitted and a word $R(x) = \sum_{i=0}^{n-1} R_i x^i$ is received; hence, $F$ and $R$ are related by an error vector $E(x) = \sum_{i=0}^{n-1} E_i x^i$, where $R(x) = F(x) + E(x)$. The decoder will attempt to find $E(x)$.

Let us start by computing the syndromes. For $1 \leq j \leq n - k$, we have

$$S_j = R(\alpha^j) = \sum_{i=0}^{n-1} R_i \alpha^{ij} = \sum_{i=0}^{n-1} E_i \alpha^{ij} \tag{34.64}$$

Before proceeding further, consider Eq. (34.64) in a particular case.

Take the $[n, n - 2]$ 1-byte correcting RS code. In this case, we have two syndromes $S_1$ and $S_2$. So, if exactly one error has occurred, say in location $i$, by Eq. (34.64), we have

$$S_1 = E_i \alpha^i \quad \text{and} \quad S_2 = E_i \alpha^{2i} \tag{34.65}$$

Hence, $\alpha^i = S_2/S_1$, so we can determine the location $i$ in error. The error value is $E_i = (S_1)^2/S_2$.

**Example 9** Consider the $[7,5,3]$ RS code over $GF(8)$, where $GF(8)$ is given by Table 34.3.

Assume that we want to decode the received vector

$$\underline{r} = (101\ 001\ 110\ 001\ 011\ 010\ 100)$$

which, in polynomial form, is

$$R(x) = \alpha^6 + \alpha^2 x + \alpha^3 x^2 + \alpha^2 x^3 + \alpha^4 x^4 + \alpha x^5 + x^6$$

Evaluating the syndromes, we obtain $S_1 = R(\alpha) = \alpha^2$ and $S_2 = R(\alpha^2) = \alpha^4$. Thus, $S_2/S_1 = \alpha^2$, meaning that location 2 is in error. The error value is $E_2 = (S_1)^2/S_2 = (\alpha^2)^2/\alpha^4 = 1$, which, in vector form, is 100. The output of the decoder is then

$$\underline{c} = (101\ 001\ 010\ 001\ 011\ 010\ 100)$$

which, in polynomial form, is

$$C(x) = \alpha^6 + \alpha^2 x + \alpha x^2 + \alpha^2 x^3 + \alpha^4 x^4 + \alpha x^5 + x^6 \qquad \square$$

Let $\mathcal{E}$ be the subset of $\{0, 1,\ldots,n-1\}$ of locations in error, i.e., $\mathcal{E} = \{l : E_l \neq 0\}$. With this notation, (34.64) becomes

$$S_j = \sum_{i \in \mathcal{E}} E_i \alpha^{ij}, \quad 1 \leq j \leq n - k \qquad (34.66)$$

The decoder will find the error set $\mathcal{E}$ and the error values $E_i$ when the error correcting capability of the code is not exceeded. Thus, if $s$ is the number of errors and $2s \leq n - k$, the system of equations given by (34.66) has a unique solution. However, this is a nonlinear system, and it is very difficult to solve it directly.

In order to find the set of locations in error $\mathcal{E}$ and the corresponding error values $\{E_i : i \in \mathcal{E}\}$, we define two polynomials. The first one is called the *error locator polynomial*, which is the polynomial that has as roots the values $\alpha^{-i}$, where $i \in \mathcal{E}$. We denote this polynomial by $\sigma(x)$. Explicitly,

$$\sigma(x) = \prod_{i \in \mathcal{E}} (x - \alpha^{-i}) \qquad (34.67)$$

If somehow we can determine the polynomial $\sigma(x)$, by finding its roots, we can obtain the set $\mathcal{E}$ of locations in error. Once we have the set of locations in error, we need to find the errors themselves. We define a second polynomial, called the *error evaluator polynomial* and denoted by $\omega(x)$, as follows:

$$\omega(x) = \prod_{i \in \mathcal{E}} E_i \prod_{\substack{i \in \mathcal{E} \\ l \neq i}} (x - \alpha^{-l}) \qquad (34.68)$$

An $[n, k]$ RS code corrects at most $(n - k)/2$ errors, so we assume that $|\mathcal{E}| = \deg(\sigma) \leq (n - k)/2$. Notice also that $\deg(\omega) \leq |\mathcal{E}| - 1$, since $\omega$ is a sum of polynomials of degree $|\mathcal{E}| - 1$. Given a polynomial $f(x) = a_0 + a_1 x + \cdots + a_m x^m$ with coefficients over a field $F$, we define the (formal) derivative of $F$, denoted $f'$, as the polynomial

$$f'(x) = a_1 + 2a_2 x + \cdots + m a_m x^{m-1}$$

For instance, over $GF(8)$, if $f(x) = \alpha + \alpha^3 x + \alpha^4 x^2$, then $f'(x) = \alpha^3$ (since $2 = 0$ over $GF(2)$). The formal derivative has several properties similar to the traditional derivative, like the derivative of a product, $(fg)' = f'g + fg'$. Back to the error locator and error evaluator polynomials, we have the following relationship between the two:

$$E_i = \frac{\omega(\alpha^{-i})}{\sigma'(\alpha^{-i})} \qquad (34.69)$$

Let us prove some of these facts in the following lemma:

**Lemma 7**   The polynomials $\sigma(x)$ and $\omega(x)$ are relatively prime, and the error values $E_i$ are given by (34.69).

*Proof:*   In order to show that $\sigma(x)$ and $\omega(x)$ are relatively prime, it is enough to observe that they have no roots in common. In effect, if $\alpha^{-j}$ is a root of $\sigma(x)$, then $j \in \mathcal{E}$. By Eq. (34.68),

$$\omega(\alpha^{-j}) = \sum_{i \in \mathcal{E}} E_i \prod_{\substack{i \in \mathcal{E} \\ l \neq i}} (\alpha^{-j} - \alpha^{-l}), = E_j \prod_{\substack{i \in \mathcal{E} \\ l \neq j}} (\alpha^{-j} - \alpha^{-l}) \neq 0 \qquad (34.70)$$

Hence, $\sigma(x)$ and $\omega(x)$ are relatively prime.

In order to prove (34.69), notice that

$$\sigma'(x) = \sum_{i \in \mathcal{E}} \prod_{\substack{i \in \mathcal{E} \\ l \neq i}} (x - \alpha^{-l})$$

hence,

$$\sigma'(\alpha^{-j}) = \prod_{\substack{i \in \mathcal{E} \\ l \neq i}} (\alpha^{-j} - \alpha^{-l}) \tag{34.71}$$

By Eqs. (34.70) and (34.71), Eq. (34.69) follows. □

The decoding methods of RS codes are based on finding the error locator and the error evaluator polynomials. By finding the roots of the error locator polynomial, we determine the locations in error, while the errors themselves can be found using Eq. (34.69). We will establish a relationship between $\sigma(x)$ and $\omega(x)$, but first we need to define a third polynomial, the syndrome polynomial. We define the syndrome polynomial as the polynomial of degree $\leq n - k - 1$ where coefficients are the $n - k$ syndromes. Explicitly,

$$S(x) = S_1 + S_2 x + S_3 x^2 + \cdots + S_{n-k} x^{n-k-1} = \sum_{j=0}^{n-k-1} S_{j+1} x^j \tag{34.72}$$

Notice that $R(x)$ is in $\mathcal{C}$ if and only if $S(x) = 0$.

The next theorem gives the so-called *key equation* for decoding RS codes, and it establishes a fundamental relationship between $\sigma(x)$, $\omega(x)$, and $S(x)$.

**Theorem 3**    There is a polynomial $\mu(x)$ such that the error locator, the error evaluator and the syndrome polynomials verify the following equation:

$$\sigma(x)S(x) = -\omega(x) + \mu(x)x^{n-k} \tag{34.73}$$

Alternatively, Eq. (34.73) can be written as a congruence as follows:

$$\sigma(x)S(x) = -\omega(x)(\mathrm{mod}\ x^{n-k}) \tag{34.74}$$

*Proof:* By Eqs. (34.72) and (34.66), we have

$$
\begin{aligned}
S(x) &= \sum_{j=0}^{n-k-1} S_{j+1} x^j \\
&= \sum_{j=0}^{n-k-1} \left( \sum_{i \in \mathcal{E}} E_i \alpha^{i(j+1)} \right) x^j \\
&= \sum_{i \in \mathcal{E}} E_i \alpha^i \sum_{j=0}^{n-k-1} (\alpha^i x)^j \\
&= \sum_{i \in \mathcal{E}} E_i \alpha^i \frac{(\alpha^i x)^{n-k} - 1}{\alpha^i x - 1} \\
&= \sum_{i \in \mathcal{E}} E_i \frac{(\alpha^i x)^{n-k} - 1}{x - \alpha^{-i}}
\end{aligned}
\tag{34.75}
$$

because $\sum_{l=0}^{m} a^l = (a^{m+1} - 1)/(a - 1)$ for $a \neq 1$. Multiplying both sides of (34.75) by $\sigma(x)$, where $\sigma(x)$ is given by Eq. (34.67), we obtain

$$\sigma(x)S(x) = \sum_{i \in \mathcal{E}} E_i((\alpha^i x)^{n-k} - 1)\prod_{\substack{l \in \mathcal{E} \\ l \neq i}}(x - \alpha^{-l})$$

$$= -\sum_{i \in \mathcal{E}} E_i \prod_{\substack{l \in \mathcal{E} \\ l \neq i}}(x - \alpha^{-l}) + \left(\sum_{i \in \mathcal{E}} E_i \alpha^{i(n-k)}\prod_{\substack{l \in \mathcal{E} \\ l \neq i}}(x - \alpha^{-l})\right)x^{n-k}$$

$$= -\omega(x) + \mu(x)x^{n-k}$$

because $\omega(x)$ is given by (34.68). This completes the proof.                                      □

The decoding methods for RS codes concentrate on solving the key equation. In the next section we describe an efficient decoder based on Euclid's algorithm for polynomials. Another efficient decoding algorithm is the so-called Berlekamp–Massey decoding algorithm [1].

## Decoding RS Codes with Euclid's Algorithm

Given two polynomials or integers $A$ and $B$, Euclid's algorithm provides a recursive procedure to find the greatest common divisor $C$ between $A$ and $B$, denoted $C = \gcd(A, B)$. Moreover, the algorithm also finds two polynomials or integers $S$ and $T$ such that $C = SA + TB$.

Recall that we want to solve the key equation

$$\mu(x)x^{n-k} + \sigma(x)S(x) = -\omega(x)$$

In the recursion, $x^{n-k}$ will play the role of $A$ and $S(x)$ the role of $B$; $\sigma(x)$ and $\omega(x)$ will be obtained at a certain step of the recursion.

Let us describe Euclid's algorithm for integers or polynomials. Consider $A$ and $B$ such that $A \geq B$ if they are integers, and $\deg(A) \geq \deg(B)$ if they are polynomials. We start from the initial conditions $r_{-1} = A$ and $r_0 = B$.

We perform a recursion in steps $1, 2, \ldots, i, \ldots$. At step $i$ of the recursion, we obtain $r_i$ as the residue of dividing $r_{i-2}$ by $r_{i-1}$, i.e., $r_{i-2} = q_i r_{i-1} + r_i$, where $r_i < r_{i-1}$ for integers and $\deg(r_i) < \deg(r_{i-1})$ for polynomials. The recursion is then given by

$$r_i = r_{i-2} - q_i r_{i-1} \tag{34.76}$$

We also obtain values $s_i$ and $t_i$ such that $r_i = s_i A + t_i B$. Hence, the same recursion is valid for $s_i$ and $t_i$ as well:

$$s_i = s_{i-2} - q_i s_{i-1} \tag{34.77}$$

$$t_i = t_{i-2} - q_i t_{i-1} \tag{34.78}$$

Because $r_{-1} = A = (1)A + (0)B$ and $r_0 = B = (0)A + (1)B$, we set the initial conditions $s_{-1} = 1, t_{-1} = 0, s_0 = 0$ and $t_0 = 1$.

**TABLE 34.4**    Euclid's Algorithm for gcd(124,46)

| $i$ | $r_i$ | $q_i$ | $s_i = s_{i-2} - q_i s_{i-1}$ | $t_i = t_{i-2} - q_i t_{i-1}$ |
|-----|-------|-------|-------------------------------|-------------------------------|
| −1  | 124   |       | 1                             | 0                             |
| 0   | 46    |       | 0                             | 1                             |
| 1   | 32    | 2     | 1                             | −2                            |
| 2   | 14    | 1     | −1                            | 3                             |
| 3   | 4     | 2     | 3                             | −8                            |
| 4   | 2     | 3     | −10                           | 27                            |
| 5   | 0     | 2     | 23                            | −62                           |

Let us illustrate the process with $A = 124$ and $B = 46$. We will find gcd(124,46). The idea is to divide recursively by the residues of the division until obtaining a last residue 0. Then, the last divisor is the gcd. The procedure works as follows:

$$124 = (1)124 + (0)46$$
$$46 = (0)124 + (1)46$$
$$32 = (1)124 + (-2)46$$
$$14 = (-1)124 + (3)46$$
$$4 = (3)124 + (-8)46$$
$$2 = (-10)124 + (27)46$$

Because 2 divides 4, 2 is the greatest common divisor between 124 and 46.

The best way to develop the process above is to construct a table for $r_i$, $q_i$, $s_i$, and $t_i$, using the initial conditions and recursions in Eqs. (34.76)–(34.78). Table 34.4 provides such a table for 124 and 46.

From now on, let us concentrate on Euclid's algorithm for polynomials. If we want to solve the key equation

$$\mu(x)x^{n-k} + \sigma(x)S(x) = -\omega(x)$$

and the error correcting capability of the code has not been exceeded, then applying Euclid's algorithm to $x^{n-k}$ and to $S(x)$, at a certain point of the recursion we obtain

$$r_i(x) = s_i(x)x^{n-k} + t_i(x)S(x)$$

where $\deg(r_i) \leq \lfloor (n-k)/2 \rfloor - 1$, and $i$ is the first with this property. Then, $\omega(x) = -\lambda r_i(x)$ and $\sigma(x) = \lambda t_i(x)$, where $\lambda$ is a constant that makes $\sigma(x)$ monic. For a proof that Euclid's algorithm gives the right solution, see [1] or [5].

We illustrate the decoding of RS codes using Euclid's algorithm with an example. Notice that we are interested in $r_i(x)$ and $t_i(x)$ only.

**Example 10**    Consider the [3,7,5] RS code over $GF(8)$ and assume that we want to decode the received vector

$$r = (011 \quad 101 \quad 111 \quad 111 \quad 111 \quad 101 \quad 010)$$

which, in polynomial form, is

$$R(x) = \alpha^4 + \alpha^6 x + \alpha^5 x^2 + \alpha^5 x^3 + \alpha^5 x^4 + \alpha^6 x^5 + \alpha x^6$$

**TABLE 34.5**   Decoding of RS Codes Using Euclid's Algorithm

| $i$ | $r_i = r_{i-2} - q_i r_{i-1}$ | $q_i$ | $t_i = t_{i-2} - q_i t_{i-1}$ |
|-----|------------------------------|-------|-------------------------------|
| $-1$ | $x^4$ | | $0$ |
| $0$ | $\alpha^5 + \alpha x + \alpha^3 x^3$ | | $1$ |
| $1$ | $\alpha^2 x + \alpha^5 x^2$ | $\alpha^4 x$ | $\alpha^4 x$ |
| $2$ | $\alpha^5 + \alpha^2 x$ | $\alpha^2 + \alpha^5 x$ | $1 + \alpha^6 x + \alpha^2 x^2$ |

Evaluating the syndromes, we obtain

$$S_1 = R(\alpha) = \alpha^5$$

$$S_2 = R(\alpha^2) = \alpha$$

$$S_3 = R(\alpha^3) = 0$$

$$S_4 = R(\alpha^4) = \alpha^3$$

Therefore, the syndrome polynomial is $S(x) = \alpha^5 + \alpha x + \alpha^3 x^3$.

Next, we apply Euclid's algorithm with respect to $x^4$ and to $S(x)$. When we find the first $i$ for which $r_i(x)$ has degree $\leq 1$, we stop the algorithm and obtain $w(x)$ and $\sigma(x)$. The process is illustrated in Table 34.5.

So, for $i = 2$, we obtain a polynomial $r_2(x) = \alpha^5 + \alpha^2 x$ of degree 1. Now, multiplying both $r_2(x)$ and $t_2(x)$ by $\lambda = \alpha^5$, we obtain $\omega(x) = \alpha^3 + x$ and $\sigma(x) = \alpha^5 + \alpha^4 x + x^2$.

Searching the roots of $\sigma(x)$, we verify that these roots are $\alpha^0 = 1$ and $\alpha^5$; hence, the errors are in locations 0 and 2. The derivative of $\sigma(x)$ is $\sigma'(x) = \alpha^4$. By (34.69), we obtain $E_0 = \omega(1)/\sigma'(1) = \alpha^4$ and $E_2 = \omega(\alpha^5)/\sigma'(\alpha^5) = \alpha^5$. Adding $E_0$ and $E_2$ to the received locations 0 and 2, the decoder concludes that the transmitted polynomial was

$$F(x) = \alpha^6 x + \alpha^5 x^3 + \alpha^5 x^4 + \alpha^6 x^5 + \alpha x^6$$

which, in vector form, is

$$\underline{c} = (000\ 101\ 000\ 111\ 111\ 101\ 010)$$

If the information is carried in the first three bytes, the output of the decoder is

$$\underline{u} = (000\ 101\ 000) \qquad \qquad \square$$

## Applications: Burst and Random Error Correction

In the previous sections we have studied how to encode and decode RS codes. This subsection will briefly examine how they are used in applications, mainly for correction of bursts of errors. The two main methods for burst and combined burst and random error correction are interleaving and product codes.

In practice, errors often come in bursts. A burst of length $l$ is a vector whose nonzero entries are among $l$ consecutive (cyclically) entries, the first and last of them being nonzero. We consider binary bursts, and we use the elements of larger fields (bytes) to correct them. Below are some examples of bursts of length 4 in vectors of length 15:

$$0\ 0\ 0\ 1\ 0\ 1\ 1\ 0\ 0\ 0\ 0\ 0\ 0\ 0\ 0$$

$$0\ 0\ 0\ 0\ 0\ 0\ 1\ 1\ 1\ 1\ 0\ 0\ 0\ 0\ 0$$

$$1\ 0\ 0\ 0\ 0\ 0\ 0\ 0\ 0\ 0\ 0\ 0\ 1\ 0\ 0$$

Errors tend to come in bursts not only because the channel is bursty. Normally, both in optical and magnetic recording, data are encoded using a so-called modulation code, which attempts to match the data to the characteristics of the channel. In general, the ECC is applied first to the random data and then the encoded data are modulated using modulation codes (see the chapter on modulation codes in this book). At the decoding, the order is reversed; when data exits the channel, it is first demodulated and then corrected using the ECC. Now, the demodulator tends to propagate errors, even single-bit errors. Although most modulation codes used in practice tend to control error propagation, nevertheless errors have a bursty character. For that reason, we need to implement a burst-correcting scheme, as we will see next.

A well-known relationship between the burst-correcting capability of a code and its redundancy is given by the Reiger bound, to be presented next, and whose proof is left as an exercise.

**Theorem 4 (Reiger Bound)**   Let $C$ be an $[n, k]$ linear code over a field $GF(2^v)$ that can correct all bursts of length up to $l$. Then $2l \leq n - k$.

Cyclic binary codes that can correct bursts were obtained by computer search. A well known family of burst-correcting codes are the so-called Fire codes. Here, we concentrate on the use of RS codes for burst correction. There are good reasons for this. One of them is that, although good burst-correcting codes have been found by computer search, there are no known general constructions giving cyclic codes that approach the Reiger bound. Interleaving of RS codes on the other hand, to be described below, provides a burst-correcting code whose redundancy, asymptotically, approaches the Reiger bound. The longer the burst we want to correct, the more efficient the interleaving of RS codes is. The second reason for choosing interleaving of RS codes, and probably the most important one, is that, by increasing the error-correcting capability of the individual RS codes, we can correct multiple bursts, as we will see. The known binary cyclic codes are designed, in general, to correct only one burst.

Let us start with the use of regular RS codes for correction of bursts. Let $C$ be an $[n, k]$ RS code over $GF(2^b)$ (i.e., $b$-bit bytes). If this code can correct $s$ bytes, in particular, it can correct a burst of length up to $(s-1)b + 1$ bits. In effect, a burst of length $(s-1)b + 2$ bits may affect $s + 1$ consecutive bytes, exceeding the byte-correcting capability of the code. This happens when the burst of length $(s-1)b + 2$ bits starts in the last bit of a byte. How good are then RS codes as burst-correcting codes? Given a binary $[n, k]$ code that can correct bursts of length up to $l$, we define a parameter, called the *burst-correcting efficiency* of the code, as follows:

$$e_l = \frac{2l}{n - k} \tag{34.79}$$

Notice that, by the Reiger bound, $e_l \leq 1$. The closer $e_l$ is to 1, the more efficient the code is for correction of bursts. Going back to our $[n, k]$ RS code over $GF(2^b)$, it can be regarded as an $[nb, kb]$ binary code. Assuming that the code can correct $s$ bytes and its redundancy is $n - k = 2s$, its burst-correcting efficiency is

$$e_{(s-1)b+1} = \frac{(s-1)b + 1}{bs}$$

Notice that, for $s \to \infty$, $e_{(s-1)b+1} \to 1$, justifying our assertion that for long bursts, RS codes are efficient as burst-correcting codes (as a comparison, the efficiency of Fire codes asymptotically tends to 2/3); however, when $s$ is large, there is a problem regarding complexity. It may not be practical to implement a RS code with too much redundancy. Moreover, the length of a RS code is limited, in the case of 8-bit bytes, it cannot be more than 256 (when extended). An alternative would be to implement a 1-byte correcting RS code interleaved $s$ times.

An $[n, k]$ code interleaved $m$ times is illustrated in Fig. 34.63. Each column $c_{0,j}, c_{1,j}, \ldots, c_{n-1,j}$ is a codeword in an $[n, k]$ code. In general, each symbol $c_{i,j}$ is a byte and the code is a RS code. The first $k$ bytes carry information bytes and the last $n - k$ bytes are redundant bytes. The bytes are read in row order, and the

| $c_{0,0}$ | $c_{0,1}$ | $c_{0,2}$ | $\cdots$ | $c_{0,m-1}$ |
|---|---|---|---|---|
| $c_{1,0}$ | $c_{1,1}$ | $c_{1,2}$ | $\cdots$ | $c_{1,m-1}$ |
| $c_{2,0}$ | $c_{2,1}$ | $c_{2,2}$ | $\cdots$ | $c_{2,m-1}$ |
| $\vdots$ | $\vdots$ | $\vdots$ | $\ddots$ | $\vdots$ |
| $c_{k-1,0}$ | $c_{k-1,1}$ | $c_{k-1,2}$ | $\cdots$ | $c_{k-1,m-1}$ |
| $c_{k,0}$ | $c_{k,1}$ | $c_{k,2}$ | $\cdots$ | $c_{k,m-1}$ |
| $c_{k+1,0}$ | $c_{k+1,1}$ | $c_{k+1,2}$ | $\cdots$ | $c_{k+1,m-1}$ |
| $\vdots$ | $\vdots$ | $\vdots$ | $\ddots$ | $\vdots$ |
| $c_{n-1,0}$ | $c_{n-1,1}$ | $c_{n-1,2}$ | $\cdots$ | $c_{n-1,m-1}$ |

**FIGURE 34.63**    Interleaving $m$ times of code $\mathcal{C}$.

| $c_{0,0}$ | $c_{0,1}$ | $c_{0,2}$ | $\cdots$ | $c_{0,k_2-1}$ | $c_{0,k_2}$ | $c_{0,k_2+1}$ | $\cdots$ | $c_{0,n_2-1}$ |
|---|---|---|---|---|---|---|---|---|
| $c_{1,0}$ | $c_{1,1}$ | $c_{1,2}$ | $\cdots$ | $c_{1,k_2-1}$ | $c_{1,k_2}$ | $c_{1,k_2+1}$ | $\cdots$ | $c_{1,n_2-1}$ |
| $c_{2,0}$ | $c_{2,1}$ | $c_{2,2}$ | $\cdots$ | $c_{2,k_2-1}$ | $c_{2,k_2}$ | $c_{2,k_2+1}$ | $\cdots$ | $c_{2,n_2-1}$ |
| $\vdots$ | $\vdots$ | $\vdots$ | $\ddots$ | $\vdots$ | $\vdots$ | $\vdots$ | $\ddots$ | $\vdots$ |
| $c_{k_1-1,0}$ | $c_{k_1-1,1}$ | $c_{k_1-1,2}$ | $\cdots$ | $c_{k_1-1,k_2-1}$ | $c_{k_1-1,k_2}$ | $c_{k_1-1,k_2+1}$ | $\cdots$ | $c_{k_1-1,n_2-1}$ |
| $c_{k_1,0}$ | $c_{k_1,1}$ | $c_{k_1,2}$ | $\cdots$ | $c_{k_1,k_2-1}$ | $c_{k_1,k_2}$ | $c_{k_1,k_2+1}$ | $\cdots$ | $c_{k_1,n_2-1}$ |
| $c_{k_1+1,0}$ | $c_{k_1+1,1}$ | $c_{k_1+1,2}$ | $\cdots$ | $c_{k_1+1,k_2-1}$ | $c_{k_1+1,k_2}$ | $c_{k_1+1,k_2+1}$ | $\cdots$ | $c_{k_1+1,n_2-1}$ |
| $\vdots$ | $\vdots$ | $\vdots$ | $\ddots$ | $\vdots$ | $\vdots$ | $\vdots$ | $\ddots$ | $\vdots$ |
| $c_{n_1-1,0}$ | $c_{n_1-1,1}$ | $c_{n_1-1,2}$ | $\cdots$ | $c_{n_1-1,k_2-1}$ | $c_{n_1-1,k_2}$ | $c_{n_1-1,k_2+1}$ | $\cdots$ | $c_{n_1-1,n_2-1}$ |

**FIGURE 34.64**    Product code $\mathcal{C}_1 \times \mathcal{C}_2$.

parameter $m$ is called the depth of interleaving. If each of the individual codes can correct up to $s$ errors, the interleaved scheme can correct up to $s$ bursts of length up to $m$ bytes each, or $(m-1)b + 1$ bits each. This occurs because a burst of length up to $m$ bytes is distributed among $m$ different codewords. Intuitively, interleaving "randomizes" a burst.

The drawback of interleaving is delay. Notice that we need to read most of the information bytes before we are able to calculate and write the redundant bytes. Thus, we need enough buffer space to accomplish this.

Interleaving of RS codes has been widely used in magnetic recording. For instance, in a disk, the data are written in concentric tracks, and each track contains a number of information sectors. Typically, a sector consists of 512 information 8-bit bytes (although the latest trends tend to larger sectors). A typical embodiment would consist in dividing the 512 bytes into four codewords, each one containing 128 information bytes and six redundant bytes (i.e., each interleaved shortened RS codeword can correct up to three bytes). Therefore, this scheme can correct up to three bursts of length up to 25 bits each.

A natural generalization of the interleaved scheme described above is product codes. In effect, we may consider that both rows and columns are encoded into error-correcting codes. The product of an $[n_1, k_1]$ code $\mathcal{C}_1$ with an $[n_2, k_2]$ code $\mathcal{C}_2$, denoted $\mathcal{C}_1 \times \mathcal{C}_2$, is illustrated in Fig. 34.64. If $\mathcal{C}_1$ has minimum distance $d_1$ and $\mathcal{C}_2$ has minimum distance $d_2$, it is easy to see that $\mathcal{C}_1 \times \mathcal{C}_2$ has minimum distance $d_1 d_2$.

In general, the symbols are read out in row order (although other readouts, like diagonal readouts, are also possible). For encoding, first the column redundant symbols are obtained, and then the row redundant symbols. For obtaining the checks on checks $c_{i,j}$, $k_1 \leq i \leq n_1 - 1$, $k_2 \leq j \leq n_2 - 1$, it is easy to see that it is irrelevant if we encode on columns or on rows first. If the symbols are read in row order, normally $\mathcal{C}_1$ is called the outer code and $\mathcal{C}_2$ the inner code. For decoding, many possible procedures are used. The idea is to correct long bursts together with random errors. The inner code $\mathcal{C}_2$ corrects first. In that case, two events may happen when its error-correcting capability is exceeded: either the code will detect the error event or it will miscorrect. If the code detects an error event (that may well have been caused by a long burst), one alternative is to declare an erasure in the whole row, which will be communicated to the outer code $C_1$. The other event is a miscorrection, that cannot be detected. In this case, we expect that the errors will be corrected by the error-erasure decoder of the outer code.

Product codes are important in practical applications. For instance, the code used in the DVD (digital video disk) is a product code where $C_1$ is a $[208, 192, 17]$ RS code and $C_2$ is a $[182, 172, 11]$ RS code. Both RS codes are defined over $GF(256)$, where $GF(256)$ is generated by the primitive polynomial $1 + x^2 + x^3 + x^4 + x^8$.

# References

1. R. E. Blahut, *Theory and Practice of Error Control Codes*, Addison-Wesley, Reading, MA, 1983.
2. C. Heegard and S. B. Wicker, *Turbo Coding*, Kluwer Academic Publishers, Dordrecht, the Netherlands, 1999.
3. S. Lin and D. J. Costello, *Error Control Coding: Fundamentals and Applications*, Prentice-Hall, Englewood Cliffs, NJ, 1983.
4. F. J. MacWilliams and N. J. A. Sloane, *The Theory of Error-Correcting Codes*, North-Holland Publishing Company, 1978.
5. R. J. McEliece, *The Theory of Information and Coding*, Addison-Wesley, Reading, MA, 1977.
6. C. E. Shannon, "A mathematical theory of communication," *Bell Syst. Tech. Journal*, vol. 27, pp. 379–423 and 623–656, 1948.
7. W. Wesley Peterson and E. J. Weldon, *Error-Correcting Codes*, MIT Press, Cambridge, MA, second edition, 1984.
8. S. Wicker, *Error Control Systems for Digital Communications and Storage*, Prentice-Hall, Englewood Cliffs, NJ, 1995.

# Operating System

# 35

# Distributed Operating Systems

Peter Reiher
*University of California*

## 35.1 Definitions and Importance

A distributed operating system is software that runs on several machines whose purpose is to provide a useful set of services, typically to make the collection of machines behave more like a single machine. The distributed operating system plays the same role in making the collective resources of the machines usable that a typical single-machine operating system plays in making that machine's resources more usable.

Distributed operating systems are usually viewed as running cooperatively on all machines whose resources they control. These machines might be capable of independent operation, or they might be usable merely as resources in the distributed system. Unlike parallel operating systems, a distributed operating system typically runs on loosely coupled hardware. Parallel operating systems tend to focus on making all available resources usable by a single large task, while distributed operating systems focus on making the collection of resources usable by a set of loosely cooperating users. Network operating systems are sometimes regarded as systems that attempt merely to make the network connecting machines more usable, without regard for some of the larger problems of building effective distributed systems. The distinctions between parallel, distributed, and network operating systems are somewhat arbitrary, because all must handle similar problems.

Distributed operating systems are not in common use today. Altghough many interesting research systems have been built since the 1970s, and some systems have been in use for many years, they have not displaced more traditional operating systems designed primarily to support single machines; however, some of the components originally built for distributed operating systems have become commonplace in today's systems, the most notable example being services to access files stored on remote machines. Many researchers feel that the failure of distributed operating systems to capture a large share of the marketplace is primarily due to our lack of understanding on how to build them. An alternate point of view is that their lack of popularity stems from users not really needing many distributed services not already provided.

Distributed operating systems are also an important field for study because they have helped drive general research in distributed systems. Replicated data systems, authentication services such as Kerberos, agreement protocols, methods of providing causal ordering in communications, voting and consensus protocols, and many other distributed services have been developed to support distributed operating systems, and have found varying degrees of success outside of that field. Popular distributed component services like CORBA owe some of their success to leveraging hard lessons learned by researchers in distributed operating systems. The popularity of the World Wide Web suggests that users would desire a more global view of the resources available to them than is provided by today's operating systems.

Distributed operating systems are hard to design properly. They must solve inherently hard problems in system design. Further, they must properly trade-off issues of performance, user interfaces, reliability, and simplicity. The relative scarcity of such systems, and the fact that most commercial operating systems' design still focuses on single-machine systems, suggests that no distributed operating system yet developed has found the proper trade-off among these issues.

Research continues in distributed operating systems. Current directions are primarily towards the use of distributed operating systems in important specialized cases, such as providing high-performance clustered servers. The increasing popularity of portable and handheld computers is likely to lead to more distributed operating system research to support mobile computing. The emerging field of ubiquitous computing offers different hardware, networking, and application characteristics likely to spur further research on distributed operating systems. Future uses of the Internet are also likely to increase desire for more easily distributed systems.

## 35.2 Why Are Distributed Operating Systems Hard to Build?

This question touches directly on why distributed operating systems are not ubiquitous and also helps explain why research continues rapidly in certain areas, while it moves more slowly in others.

One core problem for distributed operating system designers is concurrency and synchronization. These issues arise in single-machine operating systems, but they are easier to solve there. Typical single-machine systems actually run only a single thread of control simultaneously, simplifying many synchronization problems. Further, they typically have access to memory, registers, or other useful physical resources that are directly accessible by all processes that they must synchronize. These shared resources allow use of simple and fast synchronization primitives, such as semaphores. Even modern machines that have multiple processors typically include hardware that makes it easier to synchronize their operations.

Distributed operating systems lack these advantages. Typically, they must control a collection of processors connected by some form of network, most often a local area network (LAN), but occasionally a network with even more difficult characteristics. The access time across this network is orders of magnitude larger than the access time required to reach local main memory and even more orders of magnitude larger than that required to reach information in a local processor cache or register. Further, such networks are not as reliable as a typical bus, so messages are more likely to be lost or corrupted. At best, this unreliability increases the average access time.

This imbalance means that running blocking primitives across the network is often infeasible. The performance implications for the individual component systems and the system as a whole do not permit widespread use of such primitives. Designers must choose between looser synchronization (leading to odd user-visible behaviors and possibly fatal system inconsistencies) and sluggish performance. The increasing gap between processor and network speeds suggests that this effect will only get worse.

Theoretical results in distributed systems are discouraging. Research on various forms of the Byzantine General problem and other formulations of the problems of reaching decisions in distributed systems has provided surprising results with bad implications for the possibility of providing perfect synchronization of such systems. Briefly, these results suggest that reaching a distributed decision is not always possible in common circumstances. Even when it is possible, doing so in unfavorable conditions is very expensive and tricky. Although most distributed systems can be designed to operate in more favorable circumstances than these gloomy theoretical results describe (typically by assuming less drastic failure modes or less absolute need for complete consistency), experience has shown that even pragmatic algorithm design for this environment is difficult.

A further core problem is providing transparency. Transparency has various definitions and aspects, but at a high level it simply refers to the degree to which the operating system disguises the distributed nature of the system. Providing a high degree of transparency is good because it shields the user from the complexities of distribution. On the other hand, it sometimes hides more than it should, it can be expensive and tricky to provide, and ultimately it is not always possible. A key decision in designing a distributed operating system is how much transparency to provide and where and when to provide it.

A related problem is that the hardware, which the distributed operating system must virtualize, is more varied. A distributed operating system must not only make a file on disk appear to be in the main memory, as a typical operating system does, but must make a file on a different machine appear to be on the local machine, even if it is simultaneously being accessed on yet a third machine. The system should not just make a multi-machine computation appear to run on a single machine, but should provide observers on all machines with the illusion that it is running only on their machine.

Distributed operating systems also face challenging problems because they are typically intended to continue correct operation despite failure of some of their components. Most single-machine operating systems provide very limited abilities to continue operation if key components fail. They are certainly not expected to provide useful service if their processor crashes. A processor crash in a distributed operating system should ideally allow the remainder of the system to continue operations largely unharmed. Actually achieving this ideal can be extremely challenging. If the topology of the network connecting the system's component nodes allows the network to split into disjoint pieces, the system might also need to continue operation in a partitioned mode and would be expected to rapidly reintegrate when the partitions merge.

The security problems of a distributed operating system are also harder. First, data typically moves over a network, sometimes over a network that the distributed operating system itself does not directly control. Second, access control and resource management mechanisms on single machines typically take advantage of hardware that helps keep processes separate, such as page registers. Distributed operating systems are not able to rely on this advantage. Further, distributed operating systems are typically expected to provide some degree of local control to users on their individual machines, while still enforcing general access control mechanisms. When an individual user is legitimately able to access any bytes stored anywhere on his own machine, preventing him from accessing data that belongs to others is a much harder problem, particularly if the system strives to provide controlled high-performance access to that data.

In many cases, distributed operating systems are expected to run on heterogeneous hardware. Although commercial convergence on popular processors has reduced this problem to some extent, the wide variety of peripheral devices and customizations of system settings provided by today's operating systems often makes supposedly identical hardware behave radically differently. If a distributed operating system cannot determine whether running the same operation on two different component nodes produces the same result, it will face difficulties in providing transparency and consistency.

All the previously mentioned problems are exacerbated if the system scale becomes sufficiently large. Many useful distributed algorithms scale poorly, because the number of messages they require faces combinatorial explosion, or because the delays required to include large numbers of nodes in computations become unreasonable, or because data structures grow in proportion to the number of participants. High scale ensures that partial failures will become more common, and that low probability events will begin to pop up every so often. High scale also often implies that the distributed operating system must operate away from the relatively friendly world of the LAN, leading to greater heterogeneity and uncertainty in communications.

## 35.3   Components of Distributed Operating Systems

Distributed operating systems consist of components that generally mirror those in their single-machine counterparts. Some of these components are typically little altered from single-machine operating systems. For example, many distributed operating systems schedule their tasks per machine, using standard scheduling mechanisms. Unless distributed shared memory is supported, components of the operating system that support virtual memory, paging, and swapping are typically similar to other operating systems. Support for devices and the use of device drivers is also common. Note that these similarities are merely the rule in distributed operating systems, and that some such systems handle even these components differently than in single-machine operating systems.

The components that tend to be most different are those related to file systems, interprocess communications, synchronization, reliability and recovery, and security. Also, some distributed operating systems include support for process migration, a facility that makes no sense in an operating system that limits its view to the boundaries of a single machine.

### File Systems

File systems were quickly recognized as one of the areas of a distributed operating system that required the most attention. Before the development of distributed operating systems, remote file access was limited to explicit copying, perhaps abetted by a program such as FTP. Distributed operating system designers instantly recognized the great value added to a computer on a network by giving it better access to files stored on other machines. The approach was generally to provide some integrated view of the collection of files stored on the various machines of the distributed system.

A key question in distributed file system design is the degree of transparency provided. At one extreme, services like FTP offer very little transparency. File locations must be explicitly named; the names effectively change if the file is moved to another machine, and files are accessed very differently if they are stored locally or remotely. Such services do not even allow all normal file operations to be performed on a remote file. At the other extreme, distributed operating systems like Locus tried to conceal the actual location of the file whenever possible. The most successful distributed file systems (NFS and the Windows file-sharing services) provide various intermediate points of transparency. NFS does not make file locations explicit in its naming conventions, but a single file may need to be accessed by different names on different machines. The Windows file-sharing service makes file locations explicit, requiring that users access remote files by looking under icons representing remote machines. But both services support their file access interface for both remote and local files, permitting these files to be read, written, and executed. This degree of transparency has proven to be the minimal acceptable amount that users demand. The World Wide Web provides this same amount of transparency, for example.

Other file system issues must be handled by the distributed operating system. Typically, remote access is slower than local access (though in modern systems, accessing data stored in the main memory of a remote machine may be faster than accessing data stored on a local hard disk drive). Many distributed file systems seek to conceal this speed difference, typically by providing a local copy of the data, thereby avoiding expensive remote access. Caching of data blocks from remote files is common, often using the same facilities that cache data blocks fetched from local disks. The Andrew File System [1] uses a different approach, caching whole files for extended periods (including over reboots) at client sites.

Cache consistency problems are caused by updates. When a local file is written, invalidating locally cached copies of the written block is straightforward and quick. Invalidating remotely cached copies is slower and more difficult, since the local operating system must signal the remote machine's system to perform the actual invalidation. Even being able to do so requires that the local machine keep track of remotely cached copies. If the local machine does keep track of these copies, the remote machine might need to signal the local machine if the cached copy is discarded. Handling all cases of partial and transient failures complicates the problem. The Andrew file system is one example of a system that has successfully handled these problems, aided in part by its use of reliable server machines that store the true permanent copy of all files. If writes are rare, ignoring the problem and accepting occasional reads of stale cached blocks may be a better solution than trying to maintain perfect consistency of the cached copies. The Sun Microsystems implementation of NFS improves on this approach at a reasonable cost by having caching clients periodically check to see if their cached copy is still fresh. This solution still allows use of stale data, but can be tuned to trade-off freshness versus cost. Not caching at all is another solution, but one with serious performance implications.

When file copies are to be permanently stored at a location, they switch from being cached to being replicated. Replicating files has several advantages, including superior fault tolerance, high performance for all file operations, and good support for disconnected operations, which is especially valuable for mobile computing. Replicating files has a significant cost, however. Beyond the mere storage costs of keeping multiple permanent copies of the same bits, maintaining consistency among replicated files is a difficult problem. Generally, replicated file systems must trade the consistency of the replicas against file system performance. Higher consistency is possible using conservative replication methods, which ensure that no inconsistent updates to files are possible. Conservative methods often have high costs and limit file availability, however. Optimistic replication reverses these advantages and disadvantages, offering lower cost and higher availability at the risk of permitting inconsistencies, which must then be handled by some method—typically a reconciliation process that tries to merge the results of conflicting updates. Sample replicated file systems include Coda (which uses optimistic client/server replication) [2] and Ficus (which uses optimistic peer replication) [3]. The systems in wide commercial use tend not to provide full functionality replicated file systems because of their cost and complexity.

File replication is widely used in an informal fashion. For example, programs that automatically distribute new versions of executables to all machines in an office are performing a limited form of file replication. Mechanisms like the Microsoft Briefcase offer limited forms of file replication for special cases, such as sharing files between a desktop and a portable computer, where typically only one machine is active at any given moment. By leveraging the special circumstances of such uses, many of the harder problems of file replication can be avoided. Such adoption of simple limited expedients for common circumstances is characteristic of much real-world use of distributed operating systems technology.

File migration is another alternative available to distributed file systems to avoid performance problems. Files move to the sites that use them. This paradigm requires a high degree of transparency, since all processes in the system must be able to access all files, local or remote, under the same names. Otherwise, applications might stop working when the file migrates from the remote to the local site. Further, such alternatives face difficulties in preventing popular files from moving constantly. This paradigm of remote data access has been more widely used and studied in the field of distributed shared memory.

## Interprocess Communications Services

Many distributed operating systems are designed to support distributed computations, where cooperating processes run on different nodes. Allowing the processes to cooperate implies that they can exchange information, which in turn implies a need for interprocess communications (IPC) services.

Single-machine systems have the same requirement, so a variety of IPC services exist for such environments, including remote procedure calls, messages, and shared memory. Generally, the implementation of these services in single-machine environments leverages shared hardware. For example, all three of these services are provided in most single-machine operating systems by writing information into main memory that can be read by all communicating processes, or by copying information from the memory of one process into the memory of another, or into buffers provided by the operating system. The shared hardware and the synchronization provided by the shared processor simplify many issues in making these IPC services work.

In a normal distributed system, the participating machines can only communicate by passing messages across a network. Such networks typically do not offer the guarantees available from the shared hardware of a single machine. Further, the participating machines are typically under the control of their local processor. No single processor controls the complete collection. These characteristics require different implementations of familiar IPC services.

Message-passing IPC shares many characteristics from the single-machine case. Bytes are gathered into an explicit message. Instead of merely being transferred from one buffer to another on the same machine, the message goes over the network. Failure of the network or the receiver introduces new problems. The issue of how long to block the sender is also different, since the time required to confirm delivery of the message in the remote case can be much longer than in the local case. Issues of message addressing must also be considered. In a single-machine system, all addressable processes are locally known. In a distributed system, some facility must be provided to allow the local process to discover the addressable names of remote processes and to send messages to those names.

Remote procedure call (RPC) faces similar challenges. In a single machine, remote procedures aren't that remote. Although they may have a different address space, the local operating system has access to all necessary facilities of both the calling and called processes. In distributed systems, the caller is on one machine and the called process on another. Further, the actual transfer of data must take place via messages crossing the network. One implication is that call-by-reference must be translated to call-by-return-value. Other complexities exist, including some similar to those for message passing. Another issue is handling partial failures. Either the caller or the called process can fail independently of the other, requiring the operating system on the surviving machine to recover.

Shared memory is the hardest common IPC mechanism to provide in distributed operating systems, because it relies most heavily on hardware characteristics not present in the distributed environment. Early distributed operating systems made no attempt to provide shared memory across the network; however, as LANs became more capable, researchers tackled the difficult problems of providing the semantics of shared memory across the network. This problem spawned vast amounts of research, which will not be covered in detail here. A slightly closer look at the concept of distributed shared memory will reveal why this research was necessary.

As before, the distributed system can only communicate via messages. Yet the distributed operating system must provide the illusion that two processes on different machines are sharing a single piece of physical memory. The basic approach is to give each process access to a local copy of the memory, then have the operating systems work behind the scenes to provide a consistent view between the processes. Another approach is to migrate the memory segments between machines, as needed. This approach can run into difficulties if processes frequently access the same memory locations. Also, because the overheads of handling shared memory at the word level are too extreme, distributed shared memory systems must aggregate words into shared blocks. If the aggregation is too large, *false sharing* occurs, where one process accesses the first part of a block while another process accesses the second part. Because the two parts are aggregated into a single block, the block must migrate back and forth, despite no actual commonly accessed memory locations.

Alternately, memory segments can be replicated. Doing so leads to problems when writes occur. Either the other copies of the segment must be updated (before they are accessed again), or they must be invalidated. Either approach requires much bookkeeping and incurs overheads when writes occur. False sharing effects can also play a role here, since writing to the first word of a block tends to invalidate or cause updates to the entire block.

Much inventive research has been performed on distributed shared memory, using various techniques to overcome its challenges. Although distributed shared memory has been demonstrated to be feasible, its performance, complexity, and limitations have prevented it from becoming popular. Few systems today provide this facility. Research continues on distributed shared memory, but not as widely as in the past.

## Naming Services

Names play an important role in operating systems. Many operating systems support several distinct name spaces for different purposes. For example, one name space might describe the file system, while another describes the processes running on a machine, and a third describes the users permitted to work on the machine. One legacy of Unix systems is that the file name space is used aggressively to provide name spaces for things that are not classically files, such as devices and interprocess communication services. (One distributed operating system, Plan 9, relies on this abstraction for all its naming needs [4].)

Distributed operating systems have similar naming needs, but now some of the entities that must be named are not located on the local machine. As before, these entities are of various types. The distributed nature of the system leads to different problems, however. For example, in a single machine, one directory can contain the names of all the entities in the system. Scaling and organizational concerns usually lead to breaking the single directory into hierarchical components, but there are relatively few difficulties with maintaining a single name space that describes the name-to-resource mappings of anything currently available in the system.

In a distributed system, independently operating nodes can create, destroy, and change names rapidly. These operations are local, so they are likely to appear instantly in the local name space. But how do the other machines in the system become aware of namespace changes?

One approach is to build a single global namespace for the entire distributed system. The Locus Operating System took this approach, for example. It extended the standard Unix file system naming convention across multiple machines. By providing a single hierarchical name space, the naming changes made by one machine were available to all machines. An advantage of this approach is high transparency. Files (and other nameable resources) had the same names on all machines, which provided an easier model for users. The difficulties with the Locus approach are that it scales poorly and only works well when all machines tend to be connected most of the time. Maintaining a global name space on multiple machines is very hard. Further, if replication is being used, name space changes in one replica can sometimes conflict with name space changes in other replicas.

The Andrew file system overcame some of these problems by storing all files on reliable servers. Whole file caching was used to provide fast access on machines that interacted directly with users. The Andrew file system has been operated at high scale, but usually in circumstances where one collocated set of servers can access all clients via a high-speed reliable network.

Windows file sharing and NFS provide a more limited form of global name space. In the Windows file sharing service, each machine has complete autonomy over its own name space, and exports that name space to remote machines explicitly, under its own machine name. NFS allows portions of one machine's name space to be spliced into the name spaces of other machines at fairly arbitrary points. Neither service is as transparent as a true global name space, but many control problems are avoided. As the World Wide Web has demonstrated, such a name space can scale well; however, the World Wide Web's name space also demonstrates some problems with the approach, such as poor results when a resource changes its location, since such a change implies a name change.

## Recovery, Reliability, and Fault Tolerance Services

Because distributed operating systems are more prone to partial failure, some such systems provide special facilities for recovery. The system itself must have internal mechanisms (typically hidden from normal users) that handle failure problems. These facilities ensure that system services like the file system and name spaces continue to exhibit reasonable behavior even in the face of failures. One common requirement was to provide transactional behavior in the face of failures and arbitrarily slow system components. The two-phase commit protocol is typically used for this purpose. The system might also provide checkpointing facilities for processes, services that allow cooperative processes on different machines to deal with failure of some of their components, or the ability to request replication or backup versions of important processes or data.

Arguably, such services are best provided transparently. Typical users and programmers are not experts in the complexities of distributed computations and failure handling, so few of them can make effective use of any such tools that the system provides. On the other hand, transparent recovery and reliability services are hard to provide.

## Process Migration

Some distributed operating system designers have foreseen value in permitting running processes to be migrated to other nodes, for load balancing, to achieve better performance for high-priority processes, to move processes closer to critical resources (typically files), or to provide improved reliability. Migrating a process at any arbitrary stage in its operations is difficult. The Locus Operating System provided such a facility, but handling all complex cases is tricky. A more common approach is to provide facilities that allow processes to enter migratable states where the more complex situations cannot arise. Typically, this means they are temporarily quiescent until the migration completes. Not providing process migration at all is even more common. Process migration has not been a popular capability in the systems that do provide it.

### Security Services

Single-machine operating systems provide some degree of security by relying on the characteristics of the hardware they run, and by leveraging the fact that the operating system trusts itself. Access control mechanisms for files, separation of data belonging to different processes, and authentication of users to the system work on these assumptions. In a distributed operating system, communications often go over insecure shared networks, and the remote operating systems might not be as fully trusted as the local system. The security problems are thus harder to solve, and distributed operating systems sometimes provide facilities to handle the problems.

The use of an insecure network is typically handled by either authenticating or encrypting network traffic. A properly designed cryptographic system can usually make it difficult for outsiders to improperly inject or alter traffic, or to read secret information in transit. Such a cryptographic approach does not solve all problems, since one system must still rely on a remote system to enforce security restrictions just as the local system would. For example, if a sensitive file is stored at node A, when node B requests access to the file, node A can check that the request was made by a user with the right to view the file; however, if in response node A provides blocks of the file to the proper user on node B, node A must trust that node B will not maliciously or accidentally also provide the blocks to improper users. Node B has concerns, as well, because it cannot determine if node A has properly applied access control to the file. If node A has not done so, node B might provide its user with data that should be inaccessible. These concerns make it relatively difficult to set up a distributed operating system in environments where all participant systems do not completely trust one another.

Assuming that the nodes are all trustworthy to the extent that they will properly handle data that they can properly access, the distributed system must still authenticate the requests from participants. Otherwise, one of the nodes in the distributed system might tag requests to remote nodes from user X with the identity of user Y, allowing X to access data improperly. The remote node must independently verify that the request really came from user Y. Many cryptographically based mechanisms can provide such authentication. One option is the Kerberos system, which allows machines in a distributed environment to authenticate identities and provide controlled access to services [5]. Security designers are generally happiest with heavily tested and used mechanisms, because they are less likely to have undiscovered security bugs, so Kerberos' long history and the amount of scrutiny applied to it make it popular.

## 35.4 Sample Distributed Operating Systems

### Locus

The Locus Operating System was an early ambitious attempt to build a distributed operating system that provided all users with a single system image [6]. It was developed at UCLA and the Locus Computing Corporation throughout the 1980s and into the 1990s. Locus was intended to be Unix-compatible, both in terms of the operating system interface provided and the experience of users. Ideally, a Locus user would be given the illusion of a single large Unix system vastly more powerful than any single machine could provide. In actuality, the distributed operating system would run on each component node of the system. The nodes worked together to maintain the single image.

The Locus system achieved some success, but ran into several problems that prevented it from becoming popular. The system demonstrated the value and feasibility of providing high transparency in a distributed operating system, and pioneered concepts such as file replication. But the challenges of providing a true single image were immense. Particularly, handling all of the difficult uncommon cases properly required much complexity. Further, one fundamental mechanism in achieving the single system image was to reach agreement on the set of participating nodes, a task that proved difficult and expensive. The final lesson from the Locus project was that, although transparency was valuable and attractive, too much obsession with providing complete transparency in all circumstances could be counterproductive.

## Amoeba

Amoeba provides service to a large community of users working at low-powered workstation systems. It does this by maintaining a pool of servers capable of working interchangeably with any of the work-stations, as well as some specialized servers [7]. When a user logs in to an Amoeba workstation, he is implicitly logging in to the entire distributed system. The Amoeba system software assigns user tasks to one or more machines in the server pool, handling all issues of communications and synchronization. Because any task can potentially run on any server in the pool, Amoeba must provide a high degree of transparency. Persistent data is typically stored remotely from both the workstation currently occupied by the user and the machines in the server pool working on the request, which also implies a need for high transparency.

Amoeba provides RPC and reliable multicast for interprocess communications. It handles issues of network security by using randomly assigned ports to obscure communications and by requiring cryptographic capabilities to access resources.

Amoeba provides a distributed file system with replication capabilities. An interesting aspect of the Amoeba file system is that it only permits creation of files, not their alteration. Instead of altering an existing file, a new file is created with the altered contents. This choice simplifies many replication issues, but requires users to adopt a different model of file behavior than is typical.

Amoeba was used for production purposes in several environments, and is available from Vrije Universiteit, where it was developed.

The design philosophy behind Amoeba and many other distributed operating systems is to support operations at one large, well-connected organization. Designers also assume that it is more economical to provide low-powered machines as a front end and perform the system's serious work on pools of servers. When a cheap workstation can provide all the computational and storage resources required by a particular user, there is less advantage in this approach; however, it still has some advantages because of system simplifications inherent in localizing important operations in well-connected, well-maintained servers. Also, this model is not well suited for integrating portable computers, because those machines can be disconnected from the network and are expected to continue providing service.

## Plan 9

Plan 9 is one of the more recent attempts to build a new distributed operating system [4]. Plan 9's approach to building a distributed operating system shares some similarities to Amoeba's. The system is designed primarily to support a single large organization, using a pool of CPU servers, file servers, and many terminal servers. All machines are connected by a high-speed LAN. All resources in Plan 9 are represented in a name space that resembles a Unix file system. A user at a terminal requests resources by mounting name space components representing those resources into his own name space. One standard protocol handles access to all resources, be they files, devices, or interprocess communications facilities. Plan 9 is still in use and being studied, but has not achieved widespread popularity.

## 35.5 Recent Research in Distributed Operating Systems

Although distributed operating systems have not become ubiquitous, their goals continue to be tempting, and the success and importance of some distributed operating system components suggest that further research and development is worthwhile. Further, changes in the use of computers, such as mobile computing and ubiquitous computing, demand new research to handle the problems of distribution encountered in these new environments.

Few attempts were made in the past decade to produce revolutionary new general-purpose distributed operating systems akin to Locus, Amoeba, and Plan 9. The focus has been on producing better distributed services and designing distributed operating systems for important special uses.

## Distributed File Systems

LAN speed and bandwidth now permit some remote file accesses to be cheaper than local accesses. Further, designating particular machines as file servers (as is commonly done with NFS and other similar systems) causes scaling problems when those machines become overloaded. The xFS project addressed these issues by striping files across the storage of all machines on a LAN [8]. By ensuring that commonly used files were in main memory at all participating machines, xFS allows most file accesses to proceed at network speeds, rather than disk speeds. The management responsibilities are spread across all participating nodes. By using RAID techniques, the failure of any individual machine does not cause unavailability of any files, unlike failure of an NFS server. Since RAID redundancy does not require full duplication of all bits of a file, this solution is less wasteful of storage than file replication. Other file systems, such as Zebra [9] and Frangipani [10] use similar methods to spread file data across multiple machines. This approach assumes that all machines are trustworthy, and is most suitable for use on a LAN, where partitioning of sets of the machines are rare. These limitations, the complexity of the implementations, and the lack of practical experience with their use have prevented this class of solution from being widely used, so far.

Striping files across multiple machines has particular advantages for video servers. Such services must move large quantities of data from persistent storage to a remote network location, quickly and predictably. Leveraging the capabilities of several cooperating servers simultaneously has proven advantageous for systems like the Tiger File System [11]. Such special purpose systems can often afford high-speed interconnection networks that avoid some performance problems.

Peer file-sharing services such as Gnutella have become popular recently. Such peer services seek to leverage the vast amount of storage available on machines connected to the Internet to make various kinds of files widely available to many users. These services spread requests out to other nearby machines running the service, with relatively little information distributed about what files are stored at which machines. Finding a particular file involves searching some of the participating machines to find the site (or sites) storing it. Such services can face scaling problems for a variety of reasons, especially if only a small number of participants actually store the files, since they can become overloaded. Also, machines connected via slow links can be quickly flooded by traffic generated by the system, rendering it ineffective for users at those machines and making the files they store hard to reach for other users.

## Networks of Workstations

The commercialization of the Internet has led to some high requirements for servers. Handling millions of Web page hits per day is vital to some companies, and other types of service can be equally stressful. One alternative to buying extremely expensive mainframes capable of handling such loads is to build a network of workstations, using commodity hardware connected by a dedicated high-speed network. This kind of hardware can be much less expensive than mainframes, and offers the promise of cheap expandability by merely adding more workstations to the network. The fundamental architecture is to farm out incoming requests to the workstations, balancing the load and leveraging their combined capabilities. This approach often requires special distributed systems support to handle problems of shared data access, reliability, and scalability.

The problem is relatively easy for loads like most web service, where almost all incoming requests are read-only. In such cases, the entire set of data required to respond to requests can be replicated at each machine in the system. The situation is trickier when writes are more common. One approach is to assign users or categories of requests to particular machines, but such approaches may face problems with load balancing and scaling when the pattern of work changes or large numbers of users are added. More sophisticated approaches have been investigated recently.

The DDS service provides tools for building distributed data structures to run on workstation clusters [12]. The DDS service must handle many of the problems of distributed systems in general, including performance and reliability; but by limiting its requirements to supporting particular types of carefully chosen data structures, the system can solve these hard problems and provide the necessary services. Porcupine uses a network of workstations to handle mail service, which requires significant amounts of writing and thus demands more sophisticated mechanisms to leverage the power of the distributed system [13]. Porcupine uses a set of nodes that can provide interchangeable services and replication techniques to build a high-performance mail server out of a network of workstation machines.

## Distributed Systems for Ubiquitous Computing

Many researchers predict that homes, offices, and other buildings of the future will contain large numbers of objects that have embedded processors and communications devices. For example, all appliances in a house might contain processing and communications capabilities. Also, humans may carry several computing and communications devices on their bodies, in much the same way that most people today wear a watch. The purposes and uses of machines in these environments are not yet clear, but they seem likely to differ from the way office workstations in a LAN or machines browsing the Web behave. Plausibly, they will require different sets of system services than today's distributed system services. Various researchers have started examining the requirements of these systems and designed distributed services for them.

One area of interest is naming in such systems. The publish/subscribe model of naming has been proposed and implemented in systems like the Jini service discovery system. In this model, devices on the network publish their capabilities, and other devices that hear the publications subscribe to the services they are interested in. Another proposed model of naming for this environment is intentional naming, where the system provides name resolution and request routing via a self-configured overlay network [14]. In such systems, users name objects by what they want to do with them, and the naming service takes responsibility for forwarding the request to some entity capable of fulfilling their need.

Ubiquitous computing systems also require access to persistent storage, both to access standard persistent data (e.g., files) and to allow the system to keep track of the state required to give users a consistent view of the world. Mobility, limited communications links, security concerns, and varying capabilities of participant machines make providing persistent data harder. One approach to solving the problem is provided by OceanStore, which postulates a utility-like model for providing persistent data handling in a ubiquitous environment [15]. OceanStore uses replication aggressively and relies on a combination of fast (but not always successful) search techniques and slow (but reliable) lookup algorithms.

## Security in Distributed Operating Systems

Some recent research has tried to tackle the problems of running a secure distributed operating system when not all participants are fully trusted. For example, recent enhancements to SFS have produced a secure read-only file system that allows remote clients to independently verify that the data provided to them by a server is indeed the true version of the data [16]. Another difficult security problem for distributed systems that span multiple administrative domains is proper authentication across those boundaries, particularly when the different domains use different authentication mechanisms. One recent approach to solving this problem is to build a logic of authentication and mechanisms for applying that logic to authentication information attached to remote requests [17]. The system can then determine if it should regard incoming requests as being legitimately made by the putative requestor.

## 35.6 Resources for Studying Distributed Operating Systems

Research appears frequently in the field of distributed operating systems. Some of the work is commercial, but much of it is described in the research literature. The principal conferences where distributed operating system research appears most often are the bi-annual Symposium on Operating Systems (SOSP), the bi-annual Conference on Operating Systems Design and Implementation (OSDI, held in alternate years with SOSP), and the annual Usenix Technical Conference. Interesting research on more specialized areas often appears in other venues. For example, mobile computing distributed system research often appears in the MOBICOM conference, and distributed systems security research will often appear in security conferences. A workshop called HotOS publishes early results on new areas of research in operating systems, including distributed operating systems.

The primary journals where distributed operating systems research appears are the ACM Transactions on *Computing Systems* journal and the *IEEE Transactions on Computers* journal. Again, research on specialized topics often appears in other journals, such as mobile computing research in Mobile Networks and Applications (MONET).

# References

1. Howard, J., et al., "Scale and performance in a distributed file system," *ACM Transactions on Computer Systems,* 6, 1, 1988.
2. Satyanarayanan, M., et al., "Coda: a highly available file system for a distributed workstation environment," *IEEE Transactions on Computers,* 39, 4, 1990.
3. Guy, R., et al., "Implementation of the Ficus replicated file system," in *Proceedings of the 1990 Usenix Summer Technical Conference,* June 1990.
4. Pike, R., et al., "The use of name spaces in Plan 9," *Operating Systems Review,* 27, 2, April 1993.
5. Steiner, J., Neuman, C., and Schiller, J., "Kerberos: an authentication service for open network systems," in *Proceedings of the Usenix Winter Conference,* 1988.
6. Popek, G. and Walker, B., *The Locus Distributed Operating System,* MIT Press, 1985.
7. Tannenbaum, A., et al., "Experiences with the Amoeba distributed operating system," *Communications of the ACM,* 33, 12, 1990.
8. Anderson, T., et al., "Serverless network file systems," *ACM Transactions on Computer Systems,* 14, 1, Feb. 1996.
9. Hartman, J. and Ousterhout, J., "The Zebra file system," *ACM Transactions on Computer Systems,* 13, 3, 1995.
10. Thekkath, C., Mann, T., and Lee, E., "Frangipani: a scalable distributed file system," in *Proceedings of the 16th Symposium on Operating System Principles,* Oct. 1997.
11. Bolosky, W., Fitzgerald, R., and Douceur, J., "Distributed schedule management in the Tiger video fileserver," in *Proceedings of the 16th Symposium on Operating System Principles,* Oct. 1997.
12. Gribble, S., et al., "Scaleable distributed data structures for internet service construction," in *Proceedings of the 4th Symposium on Operating Systems Design and Implementation,* Oct. 2000.
13. Saito, Y., Bershad, B., and Levy, H., "Manageability, availability, and performance in Porcupine: a highly scalable, cluster-based mail service," in *Proceedings of the 17th Symposium on Operating System Principles,* Dec. 1999.
14. Adjie-Winoto, W., et al., "The design and implementation of an intentional naming system," in *Proceedings of the 17th Symposium on Operating System Principles,* Dec. 1999.
15. Kubiatowicz, J., et al., "OceanStore: an architecture for global-scale persistent storage," in *Proceedings of the 9th International Conference on Architectural Support for Programming Languages and Operating Systems,* Nov. 2000.
16. Fu, K., Kaashoek, M. F., and Mazieres, D. "Fast and secure distributed read-only file system," in *Proceedings of the 4th Symposium on Operating Systems Design and Implementation,* Oct. 2000.
17. Howell, J. and Kotz, D., "End-to-end authorization," in *Proceedings of the 4th Symposium on Operating Systems Design and Implementation,* Oct. 2000.

# New Directions
# in Computing

# 36

# SPS: A Strategically Programmable System

M. Sarrafzadeh
*University of California*

E. Bozorgzadeh
*University of California, Los Angeles*

R. Kastner
*University of California, Los Angeles*

S. O. Memik
*University of California, Los Angeles*

## 36.1  Introduction

Programmability and reconfigurability are considered to be a key ingredient for future silicon platforms [1]. An increase in the complexity of integrated circuits and a shorter time-to-market requirement result in a need to develop hardware platforms shared across multiple applications. In the next generation of electronic systems, it is expected that the conventional embedded systems are unlikely to be sufficient to meet the timing, power, and cost of such systems. Diversity and increasing number of applications do not allow fully customized system design methodology for each application such as ASIC designs. One of the fundamental keys is integrating programmability and reconfiguration in the systems [1,2]. On the other hand, the current *general-purpose* fully programmable solutions cannot satisfy the future aggressive timing and power constraints. Therefore, a new design methodology has to be developed to combine reconfiguration into system design for future applications. One of the techniques to handle the increased complexity in integrated circuits is programmable system-on-a-chip (SoC) design methodology [1]. In this style, there is a combination of IP cores, programmable logic core, and memory blocks on a chip.

System design can be viewed in a variety of levels of granularity from architecture level to logic/interconnection level. Configuration can be applied in different hierarchy levels of a design [1]. For instance, programmability in logic/interconnect level of system is realized via a programmable module such as FPGA chip. Reconfigurable devices provide the necessary flexibility in such systems. FPGAs are mostly the reconfiguration cores. An FPGA is an array of logic blocks placed in an infrastructure of interconnections, which can be configured in logic functionality of logic blocks, interconnection between logic blocks, and input/output (I/O) interface (see Fig. 36.1). SRAM-based FPGAs allows reconfiguration of the device via string of bits loaded from external source once or several times. An FPGA is programmable at hardware level. Many high-performance operations, such as computationally intensive signal processing functions can be implemented very efficiently using FPGAs.

Xilinx™ first introduced FPGAs in mid-1980s. In the past, considerable research effort was made for developing programmable architectures in the past. Also, numerous commercial programmable devices

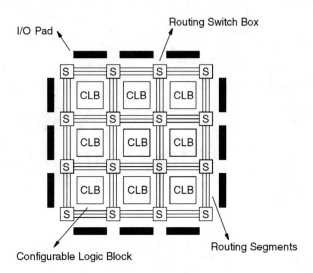

**FIGURE 36.1**

were introduced; however, not many works have been published on how those architectures were designed. The latest FPGA devices are provided by companies such as Xilinx™, Altera™, Actel™, and Lucent™. Industrial designers are increasingly capturing their designs using hardware description languages such as VHDL and Verilog. There are tools developed for FPGAs, which synthesize designs in VHDL format or other description format. Current synthesis tools for FPGAs are provided by companies Synopsys™, Synplicity™, and Leonado Spectrum™. Physical design tools perform placement and routing for FPGAs. Xilinx™ and Altera™ provide place/route tools for their own FPGA devices.

Today's high-volume applications require a fabric with higher complexity and better performance than FPGAs. Also, shorter development cost and more flexible reconfiguration are required. Several contributions have been made in FPGA devices toward this direction. Capacity of FPGAs has been increased. High-density FPGAs are available in the market offering competitive solutions to ASICs and programmable systems such as DSPs. Hierarchical features have been added into logic and routing architecture of FPGAs. The new generation of FPGAs have a trend towards embedding coarser grain units. Most applications require a large amount of storage. Architectural support for implementation of memory is crucial. Some FPGA devices have embedded memory (RAM, ROM). In addition, implementing general logic in these embedded arrays of memory blocks is viable. In order to support high repetitive and data intensive computation on FPGAs more efficiently, arithmetic resources have been developed. Examples of such enhancement are cascade chain, multipliers, and dedicated adders, etc. Fine-grain FPGA architectures are shifting towards new architectures where memory blocks, hard IPs, and even CPUs are being integrated into FPGAs. In these designs the traditional FPGA is not a co-processor, instead a reconfigurable fabric is embracing all the mentioned components and enabling a much tighter integration among them. Today, FPGA CAD tools provide integration of macro blocks into designs. Macro blocks are optimized for area, delay, or power consumption. In addition, placement of such macro blocks can be predefined in CAD tools such as CoreGEN@ integrated with Xilinx™ design implementation tool. MemGen@ and LogiBlox@ in Xilinx™ tool enable the implementation of embedded memory blocks. Hence, tool vendors are moving to higher-level optimization. There is better integration between synthesis and physical design tool.

Flexibility in reconfigurable systems comes at the expense of the reconfiguration time. The amount of time required to set the function to be implemented on the reconfigurable logic is the configuration time, which can become a serious bottleneck especially in systems where run-time reconfiguration is performed [3,4].

We have introduced a new architecture for a system that uses reconfigurable logic, which is referred as strategically programmable system (SPS) [5]. The basic building blocks of our architecture are parameterized functional blocks that are pre-placed within a fully reconfigurable fabric. They are called versatile parameterizable blocks (VPBs). When implementing an application, operations that can be mapped onto these fixed blocks will be performed by the VPBs; computational blocks that will be instantiated on the fully reconfigurable portion of the chip will perform the remaining operations. Properties of VPBs will be discussed in more detail in later sections. The motivation is to generate reconfigurable architectures that target a set of applications. Such architectures would contain VPBs to specially suit the needs of the particular family of applications. Yet the adaptable nature of our programmable device should not be severely restricted. The SPS will remain flexible enough to implement a very broad range of applications, thanks to the reconfigurable resources. These powerful features help our architecture maintain its tight relation to its predecessors, traditional FPGAs. At the same time the SPS is forming one of the first efforts in the direction of context-specific programmable devices.

Because the VPBs are custom made and fixed on the chip, they do not require configuration, hence there are considerably less switches to program as compared to the implementation of the same design on a traditional FPGA. More important, an instance of our SPS architecture is generated such that for a given set of applications the suitably selected fixed blocks provide the best performance.

In the proceeding sections, we introduce the basic concepts of our architecture and the notion of generating an instance of the SPS architecture for a given set of applications. We present a framework that provides tools for generating SPS instances and implementing applications once a fixed SPS architecture is given. In the following section, we present related work in the field of reconfigurable architecture. Examples of versatile programmable blocks are presented in Sections 36.3, 36.4 and 36.5 as well as details of our architecture. We complement our architecture with tools that perform the mapping of applications onto the architecture and the actual implementation and tuning for an application on our platform. These two major tasks will be discussed in Section 36.4. In Section 36.6 we present our preliminary results.

## 36.2 Related Work

With the current trend towards hybrid programmable architectures, new systems with embedded reconfigurable cores are also being developed. Among these architectures the basic distinction is due to the level of granularity of the reconfigurable logic.

Commercial FPGAs from several vendors such as Xilinx™, Altera™, and Actel™ are available in the market. Traditional FPGA chips like Xilinx™ 4000 series, or Altera™ Flex family all contain some form of an array of programmable logic blocks. Those blocks usually are not very complex and contain a few LUTs and a small amount of storage elements. They are designed for general-purpose use. Since they only contain fine-grain reconfigurable logic, for a new application to be implemented the whole chip goes through a configuration phase. Although newer devices such as Xilinx™ Virtex FPGA allow partial reconfiguration of selected rows or columns, this is still a critical issue.

Hybrid systems also contain reconfigurable cores as coprocessors. The Garp architecture developed at Berkeley combines a MIPS-II processor with a fine-grained FPGA coprocessor on the same die [6]. Unlike the Garp architecture the main load of hardware implementation lies on the coarse grain parameterized blocks in SPS architecture.

Chimaera [7] is a single chip integration of reconfigurable logic with a host processor. The reconfigurable coprocessor is responsible for performing the reconfigurable functional unit (RFU) instructions. An RFU instruction is any instruction from the program running on the host processor that is performed by the reconfigurable coprocessor. The Chimaera architecture is for a very specific class of data path applications and still requires a large amount of reconfiguration time.

Another reconfigurable architecture with fine granularity is the dynamically programmable gate array (DPGA) [8]. Although the logic structure is just like existing FPGAs, DPGAs differ from traditional

FPGAs by providing on-chip memory for multiple array configurations. The on-chip cache exploits high, local on-chip bandwidth to perform quick reconfiguration.

In addition, several systems with coarse-grain granularity exist, such as RaPiD [9], Raw [10], and Pleiades [11]. RaPiD is a configurable architecture that allows the user to construct custom application-specific architectures in a run-time configurable way. The system is a linear array of uncommitted functional units, which contain datapath registers, three ALUs, an integer multiplier, and some local memory. The RaPiD architecture targets applications that can be mapped to deep pipelines formed from the repeated functional units.

The Reconfigurable Architecture Workstation (Raw) is a set of replicated tiles, where each tile contains a simple RISC-like processor, small amount of bit-level configurable logic, and some memory for instructions and data.

The CS2112 reconfigurable communications processor (RCP) from Chameleon Systems, Inc.™ contains reconfigurable fabric organized in slices, each of which can be independently reconfigured. The CS2112 includes four slices consisting of three tiles. Each tile comprises seven 32-bit datapath units, two $16 \times 24$-bit single-cycle multipliers, four local store memories, and a control logic unit. The RCP uses a background configuration plane to perform quick reconfiguration. This reconfigurable fabric is combined with a 32-bit embedded processor subsystem.

The Pleiades architecture is a processor approach that combines an on-chip microprocessor with an array of heterogeneous programmable computational units of different granularities, connected by a reconfigurable interconnect network. The programmable units are MACs, ALUs, and an embedded FPGA.

Xilinx™ has recently introduced the Virtex-II® devices from the new Xilinx Platform FPGAs. The Virtex-II architecture includes new features such as up to 192 dedicated high-speed multipliers. Designers can use Virtex-II® devices to implement critical DSP elements of emerging broadband systems. This is somewhat a similar effort in the same direction that we are heading. The Virtex-II device is providing the dedicated high-performance multipliers for DSP applications like the VPBs on the SPS, which are intended to improve performance for a set of applications. SPS differs from a Virtex-II device in the following:

- The architecture can contain blocks of various complexities. Depending on the requirements of the applications fixed blocks can be as complex as an FFT block or as simple as an adder or multiplier. Examples of VPBs will be provided in the next section.

- The generation of an SPS instance is automated. Given a set of target applications an architecture generation tool determines the number and types of VPBs to be placed on the chip. Although the Virtex-II device is still general purpose, an instance of an SPS will be more context-defined according to a given set of applications.

## 36.3  Strategically Programmable System

Recently, reconfigurable fabric was integrated into SoCs forming hybrid (re)configurable systems. *Hybrid (re)configurable systems* contain some kind of computational unit, e.g., ALUs, intellectual property units (IPs) or even traditional general-purpose processors, embedded into a reconfigurable fabric (see Fig. 36.2).

One type of hybrid reconfigurable architecture embeds reconfigurable cores as a coprocessor to a general-purpose microprocessor, e.g., Garp [6] and Chimaera [7]. Another direction of new architectures considers integration of highly optimized hard cores and hardwired blocks with reconfigurable fabric. The main goal here is to utilize the optimized blocks to improve the system performance. Such programmable devices are targeted for a specific *context*—a class of similar applications, such as DSP, data communications (Xilinx Platform Series), or networking (Lucent's ORCA®). The embedded fixed blocks are tailored for the critical operations common to the application class. In essence, the programmable logic is supported with the high-density high-performance cores. The cores can be applied at various levels, such as the functional block level, e.g., fast Fourier transform (FFT) units, or at the level of basic arithmetic operations (multipliers).

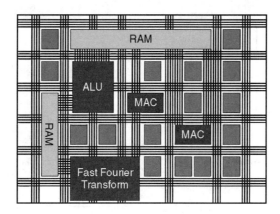

**FIGURE 36.2**

Presently, a context-specific architecture is painstakingly developed by hand. The SPS explores an auto-mated framework, where a systematic method generates context-specific programmable architectures.

The basic building blocks of the SPS architecture are parameterized functional blocks called VPBs. They are preplaced within a fully reconfigurable fabric. When implementing an application, operations can be performed on the VPBs or mapped onto the fully reconfigurable portion of the chip. An instance of our SPS architecture is generated for a given set of applications (specified by C or Fortran code). The function-ality of the VPBs is tailored towards implementing those applications efficiently. The VPBs are customized and fixed on the chip; they do not require configuration, hence there are considerably less configuration bits to program as compared to the implementation of the same design on a traditional FPGA.

The motivation is to automate the process of developing hybrid reconfigurable architectures that target a set of applications. These architectures would contain VPBs that specially suit the needs of the particular family of applications. Yet, the adaptable nature of our architecture should not be severely restricted. The SPS remains flexible enough to implement a very broad range of applications due to the reconfigurable resources. These powerful features help the architecture maintain its tight relation to its predecessors, traditional FPGAs. At the same time the SPS is forming one of the first efforts in the direction of context-specific programmable devices.

In general, two aspects are part of the SPS system. The first area involves generating a context-specific architecture given a set of target applications. Once there is a context-specific architecture, one must also be able to map any application to the architecture.

## 36.4   Overview of SPS

### Versatile Parameterizable Blocks (VPBs)

The main components of SPS are the VPBs. The VPBs are embedded in a sea of fine-grain programmable logic blocks. Consider a lookup table (LUT) based logic blocks commonly referred to as combinatorial logic blocks (CLBs), though it is possible to envision other types of fine-grain logic blocks, e.g., PLA-based blocks.

Essentially, VPBs are hard-wired ASIC blocks that perform a complex function. Because the VPB is fixed resource, it requires little reconfiguration time when switching the functionality of the chip.* Therefore, SPS is not limited by large reconfiguration times like current FPGAs. But, the system must strike a balance between flexibility and reconfiguration time. The system should not consist mainly of VPBs, as it will not be able to handle a wide range of functionality.

---

* By functionally, we mean the application of the chip can change entirely, e.g., from image detection to image restoration, or part of the application can change, e.g., a different image detection algorithm.

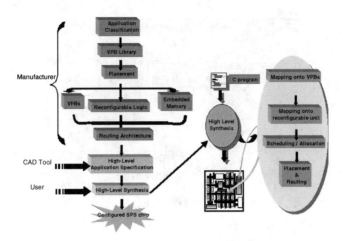

**FIGURE 36.3**

There is a considerable range of functionality for the VPBs. It ranges from high-level intensive tasks such as FFT to a "simple" arithmetic task like addition or multiplication. Obviously, there is a large range of complexity between these two extremes. Because we are automating the architecture generation process, we wish to extract common functionality for the given context (set of applications). The functionality should be as complex as possible while still serving a purpose to the applications in the context. An extremely complex function that is used frequently in only one application of the context would be wasted space when another application is performed on that architecture.

The past decade has brought about extensive research as to the architecture of FPGAs. As we previously discussed, many researchers have spent copious amounts of time analyzing the size and components of the LUT and the routing architecture. Instead of developing a new FPGA architecture, the SPS leverages the abundant body of FPGA architecture knowledge for our system. Embedding the VPBs into the programmable logic is the most important task for the SPS architecture generation.

## SPS Framework

In this section, the tools and algorithms that actually generate strategically programmable systems and perform the mapping of applications on the architecture are discussed. The architecture formation phase and the architecture configuration phase are the two major parts of the framework. The SPS framework is summarized in Fig. 36.3.

### Architecture Formation

This task can be described as making the decision on the versatile programmable blocks to place on the SPS chip along with the placement of fine-grain reconfigurable portion and memory elements, given an application or class of applications. In this phase, SPS architecture is customized from scratch given certain directives. This process requires a detailed description of the target application as an input to the formation process. A tool will analyze these directives and generate the resulting architecture. Again, the relative placement of these blocks on the SPS chip along with the memory blocks and the fully recon-figurable portions need to be done by the architecture formation tool.

Unlike a conventional fine-grain reconfigurable architecture, a uniform distribution of configurable logic blocks does not exist on the SPS. Hence, for an efficient use of the chip area as well as high performance, the placement of VPBs on the chip and the distribution of configurable logic block arrays and memory arrays among those are critical. The fact that the routing architecture supports such hybrid architecture is equally important and requires special consideration. If the routing architecture cannot provide sufficient routing resources between the VPBs and the configurable blocks, the hardware resources will be wasted. The type and number of routing tracks and switches need to be decided such that the resulting routing architecture can support this novel architecture most efficiently. The most important issues here is the routability of the architecture and the delay in the connections.

### Fixed Architecture Configuration

Another case to be considered is mapping an application onto a given architecture. At this point we need a compiler tailored for our SPS architecture. This SPS compiler is responsible for three major tasks.

The compiler has to identify the operations, groups of operations, or even functions in the given description of the input algorithm that are going to be performed by the fixed blocks. These portions will be mapped onto the VPBs and the information regarding the setting of the parameters of the VPBs will be sent to the SPS chip.

Second, the SPS compiler has to decide how to use the fully reconfigurable portion of the SPS. Based on the information on the available resources on the chip and the architecture, mapping of suitable functions on the fine-grain reconfigurable logic will be performed. Combining these two tasks the compiler will generate the scheduling of selected operations on either type of logic.

Finally, memory and register allocation need to be done. An efficient utilization of the available RAM blocks on the SPS has to be realized.

## 36.5 Target Applications

The first set of applications is DSP applications. Repetitive arithmetic operations on a large amount of data can be very efficiently implemented using hardware. The primary examples focus on several image-processing applications. This soon will be extended to cover other types of applications. First, algorithms that have common properties and operations are grouped together. Such algorithms can use a common set of VPBs for their implementation. The algorithms and the classes to which they belong are summarized in Table 36.1.

Image-processing operations can be classified into three categories. Those that generate an output using the value of a single pixel (point processing), those that take a group of neighboring pixels as input (local processing), and those that generate their output based upon the pixel values of the whole image (global operations) [12]. Point and local processing operations are the most suitable for hardware implementation, because they are highly parallelizable. We have designed three blocks, each representing one algorithm class. The blocks that we are currently considering are described in the following. Later, a reference will be made to the implementation of these blocks on fully reconfigurable logic versus the parameterized block realization and present the potential reduction in the number of configuration bits.

### Filter Operations Block

Many signal-processing algorithms are in essence filtering operations. Basically weighted sum of a collection of pixels indicated by the current position of the mask over the image is computed for each pixel.

The filter block is currently the most complex block we have designed. It is developed to cover an iterative image restoration algorithm, and several other filtering operations such as, mean computation, noise reduction, high pass sharpening, Laplace operator, and edge detection operators (e.g., Prewitt, Sobel). The block diagram is shown in Fig. 36.4.

**TABLE 36.1**  Classification of Algorithms

| Algorithms | Operations | Class |
|---|---|---|
| Image restoration, mean computation, noise reduction, sharpening/smoothing filter | Weighted sum, addition, subtraction, multiplication | Filter operations |
| Image half-toning, edge detection | Comparison | Thresholding |
| Image darkening, image lightening | Addition, subtraction | Pixel modification |

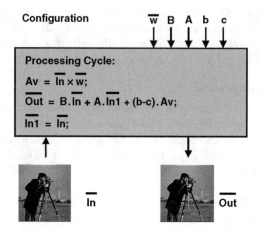

**FIGURE 36.4**

The general form of the computation that this block performs is given by the following equations:

$$\textbf{weighted\_sum} = \text{Sum}\{w_i \times \text{input\_pixel}_i\}$$
$$\textbf{output\_pixel\_value} = B \times \text{input\_pixel\_value} + A \times \text{pixel\_value\_from\_prev\_iteration} - b$$
$$\times \text{weighted\_sum} + c \times \text{weighted\_sum}$$

This block takes five parameters that define its operation. The mask coefficients array holds the values of the coefficients. The parameters $B$, $A$, and $c$ all take the value zero for all the functions except the iterative image restoration algorithm.

### Thresholding Block

The operators in this class produce results based on a single pixel's value. The computation is rather simple; it compares the value of the input pixel to a predetermined threshold value. The output pixel value is determined accordingly. The parameters of this block are the threshold value $T$ and the algorithm selection input. For the image halftoning application, the threshold value $T$ is set to be 127, where the pixel values range between 0 (black) and 255 (white). If the pixel value is above threshold, output is given as 255, otherwise it is 0. For the edge detection operation, the output is set equal to the input value if the pixel value is above threshold, and to 0 otherwise.

### Pixel Modification Block

Pixel modification operations are point-processing operations. This block performs darkening, lightening, and negation of images. It takes two parameters, $J$ and algorithm selection input ALG. For the darkening operation a positive value $J$ is added to the input pixel value. Lightening is achieved by subtracting $J$ from each input pixel. The negative of an image is achieved by subtracting the input pixel value from $J$, which takes the value 255 for this case.

## 36.6 Experiments

In this section, the author presents the experiments to estimate the potential gain in reconfiguration time that our SPS architecture will yield. This is an exploration of the reduction in reconfiguration bits that would follow as a result of providing preplaced computation blocks with our coarse grain architecture.

### Application Profiling

First, a profiling has been done on the image processing benchmarks in order to gain insight into what type of components are used more frequently. Such a profile can give directives to the architecture formation tool and guide it to employ certain blocks. Looking at the numbers and types of components that were selected by our scheduling tool, we have obtained the component usage profile as shown in Fig. 36.5.

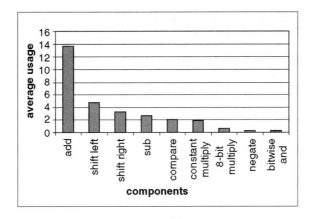

**FIGURE 36.5**

The first version of the experimental SPS architecture will be created, given the directives from the profiling information. According to Fig. 36.5 the most popular component is the adder with an average of approximately 14 adders per benchmark. Some components such as the 8-bit multiply and bit-wise could not average over 1. These components can be eliminated and we will focus on the rest and decide how many of each of the remaining ones to use on the SPS. If the numbers are normalized according to the constant multiplier, for each constant multiplier there would be one comparator, one subtractor, two right shifters, two left shifters, and seven adders. In the next section, this information will be used to estimate the gain of fixing different numbers of components on the chip. The start point will be the relative usage values given by our analysis.

## Reconfiguration Time

In the ideal case, the preplaced blocks should cover all the operations in our target applications such that we can fully exploit the benefits of the custom designed high-performance blocks and improved reconfiguration time. In reality it is not possible to create such an architecture that would support every operation that might be encountered in a wide variety of applications. Hence, in cases where provided blocks are not adequate, extra components are instantiated on the reconfigurable fabric. Here, we evaluate the gain that the VPBs would bring to the configuration process. Our scheduler uses the blocks that are made available and as many additional components as necessary for the best latency. As a result it produces an assignment of the operations to the hardware resources.

Compare the implementation of the same design on two architectures: a traditional fine-grain FPGA and a SPS. We are fixing certain blocks on the SPS assuming they are pre-placed blocks on the chip. These blocks will be the gain in reconfiguration time if they are used by the given application. The potential gain is modeled in configuration time by assuming that the number of configuration bits is proportional to the amount of logic to be implemented on the reconfigurable fabric. The higher the contribution of the preplaced blocks is to the total design, the more reduction in reconfiguration time is achieved.

Initially, an architecture is evaluated, which contains low-level blocks such as adders and subtractors. A set of functional blocks fixed on the chip is provided to the scheduler for operation assignment. The scheduler decides on the types and numbers of additional components, if they are needed. The first experiment fixes seven 8-bit adders, one 8-bit subtractor, two right shifters, two left shifters, and one constant multiplier. Then we have doubled the amount of hardware fixed in proportion at each step except the last one, where we have increased the fixed hardware 50% from the previous setup. Figure 36.6 presents the relative gains in configuration times for different setups. Observe how the gain in reconfiguration time improves with more logic provided, and how this trend saturates at a certain point. For the initial architecture setup the average reduction in reconfiguration time is 35%. Observe that, as resources available on the chip are duplicated, this reduction goes as high as 75%.

**TABLE 36.2**   Programming Bits Required Implementing the VPBs with Reconfigurable Logic

| Parameterizable Block | Size (CLBs) | Programming Bits |
|---|---|---|
| Pixel modification | 30 | 29,910 |
| Thresholding | 11 | 10,967 |
| Filtering | 99 | 98,703 |

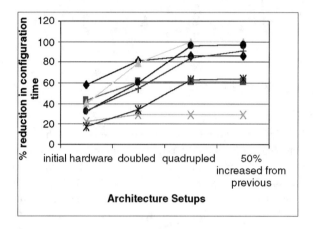

**FIGURE 36.6**

If a VPB can cover all operations of an application, then the largest gain can be obtained. Our image processing blocks presented in Section 36.5 will serve this purpose. They are capable of supporting several different image-processing applications. For the three blocks that we are initially considering, the potential savings in the number of programming bits is shown in Table 36.2. We have synthesized three parameterized designs for these blocks and obtained area information. Using the CLB count for these blocks we can estimate the number of programming bits required, proportional to the size of the designs just as we did for the first set of experiments. We assume that the reconfigurable fabric is similar to a Virtex chip. By using the numbers reported in [13] we derive the number of programming bits required per CLB and hence per parameterizable block.

## 36.7   Conclusion

A novel reconfigurable architecture was presented. The SPS can provide the degree of flexibility required in today's systems. Although offering high-performance for its application set and still a high degree of flexibility for other applications, the architecture promises a good performance and smaller reconfiguration time as well. Experiments indicate that a proper selection of common blocks among a fairly wide range of applications can yield an average reduction of 35% up to 100% in the number of programming bits that need to be transferred to the chip for configuration/reconfiguration. Because the VPBs eliminate a considerable amount of programming switches on the chip, the improvement in delay will be accompanied by improved power consumption as well. The individual VPBs will be designed targeting the best trade-off between delay and power consumption. Implementation of applications that are within the covering region of this system will highly benefit from these abilities.

# References

1. P. Schaumont, I. Verbauwhede, K. Keutzer, and M. Sarrafzadeh, "A quick safari through the reconfiguration jungle," in *Proceeding of Design Automation Conference,* June 2001.

2. K. Kuetzer, S. Malik, R. Newton, J. Rabaey, and A. Sangiovanni-Vincentelli, "System level design: orthogonalization of concerns and platform-based design," *IEEE Transactions on Computer-Aided Design of Ciruits and Systems,* Vol. 19, No. 12, Dec. 2000.

3. Ray Bittner and Peter Athanas, "Wormhole run-time reconfiguration," in *Proceedings of the 1997 ACM Fifth International Symposium on Field-Programmable Gate Arrays,* 1997, pp. 79–85.

4. J. G. Eldredge and B. L. Hutchings, "Run-time reconfiguration: a method for enhancing the functional density of SRAM-based FPGAs," in *Journal of VLSI Signal Processing,* Vol. 12, 1996.

5. S. O. Memik, E. Bozorgzadeh, R. Kastner, and M. Sarrafzadeh, "SPS: a strategically programmable system," in *Reconfigurable Architecture Workshop,* April 2001.

6. J. R. Hauser and J. Wawrzynek, "Garp: A MIPS processor with a re-configurable co-processor," in *Proceedings of the IEEE Symposium on FPGAs for Custom Computing Machines,* 1997.

7. S. Hauck, T. W. Fry, M. M. Hosler, and J. P. Kao, "The chimaera reconfigurable functional unit," *IEEE Symposium on FPGAs for Custom Computing Machines,* 1997.

8. E. Tau, D. Chen, I. Eslick, J. Brown, and A. DeHon, "A first generation DPGA implementation," *FPD95, Canadian Workshop of Field-Programmable Devices,* May 29–June 1, 1995.

9. C. Ebeling, D. Cronquist, and P. Franklin, "Configurable computing: the catalyst for high-performance architectures," in *Proceedings of the IEEE International Conference on Application-specific Systems, Architectures, and Proc.,* July 1997, pp. 364–372.

10. E. Waingold et al., "Baring it all to software: The Raw machine," *IEEE Computer,* Sept. 1997.

11. H. Zhang et al., "A 1V heterogenous reconfigurable processor IC for baseband wireless applications," ISSCC.

12. B. Wilkinson and M. Allen, *Parallel Programming,* Prentice-Hall, 1999.

13. Xilinx, Inc., "Virtex FPGA series configuration and readback," Application Note: Virtex Series.

# 37

# Reconfigurable Processors

John Morris
*University of Western Australia*

Danny Newport
*University of Tennessee*

Don Bouldin
*University of Tennessee*

Ricardo E. Gonzalez
*Tensilica, Inc.*

Albert Wang
*Tensilica, Inc.*

## 37.1 Reconfigurable Computing

*John Morris*

### Preamble

Architects of general-purpose processors face a herculean task: to design a processor that will run *every* application fast. However, applications vary widely in instruction mix, frequency, and patterns of data access, input and output bandwidth requirements, etc. A designer may incorporate elaborate and space-consuming circuitry that simulation shows will dramatically improve performance for one application but has no effect on another—or worse, slows it down. For example, designers will normally incorporate as large a cache as space allows on a die, since cache speeds up most applications; however, the data cache adds nothing to the performance of an application that copies data from one place to another.

Programmable hardware can be used to build systems in which the circuitry matches the structure of the problem. In particular, inherent parallelism in problems, which a general-purpose processor—despite multiple "go-fast" enhancements—cannot exploit, can be exploited in a system in which multiple circuits are used to speed up the computation.

### Programmable Hardware

Programmable hardware has evolved in capability and performance—tracking processor capabilities for many years now. Designers have a wide spectrum of devices that they can draw upon—from ones that provide a handful of gates and flip-flops to ones that provide well over a million gates.[1] In addition, modern devices provide:

- Considerable on-chip memory: this partially overcomes an inability of early devices to effectively solve problems that required more than a few memory bits
- Large numbers of I/O pins—permitting high data bandwidths between a custom processor and its environment
- Multiple I/O protocols, such as LVDS, GTL, and LVPECL—enabling high speed serial channels between the device and other components of a system

Programmability may be provided by a number of technologies:

- Fuses or anti-fuses, in which links are programmed open or closed
- EEPROM, in which a configuration bit is stored in nonvolatile read-only memory, and
- Static RAM cells, which store configuration bits, but, which need to be reloaded every time the device is powered up

Thus, a designer has a broad palette of devices on which to base a system design. All the usual trade-offs apply: in particular, the ability to change the circuit by reprogramming it invariably introduces a speed penalty. A configurable circuit is more complex and has longer propagation delays than a fixed one: this translates to a slower maximum clock frequency. This trade-off is discussed further when we consider whether an application is a good candidate for a reconfigurable processor compared to a general-purpose commodity processor.

A number of terms have been used to describe programmable devices. Simple early devices (ones with a simple programmable and-or array, coupled with ~10 flip-flops and ~20 I/O pins) were commonly called "programmable array logic" chips or PALs, but a host of other similar terms have been used for marketing purposes. The most important group of devices for building processors are now almost universally termed "field programmable gate arrays" (FPGAs)[2] and this chapter section will focus on them as the key building blocks of a reconfigurable system. As with general-purpose processors, designing a "universal" FPGA is essentially an impossible task and a number of different architectural styles have been proposed and manufactured. The following subsections will describe the key elements of some representative devices.

### FPGA Architectures

An FPGA's capability can usually be described in terms of three elements:

- *Logic blocks*: These are small blocks of logic, commonly consisting of a small number of simple and-or arrays, some multiplexers for steering signals, one or two flip-flops. Other features such as memory bits, lookup tables, special logic for handling the carry chains in adders, etc., may be present also. Marketing pressures have produced a bewildering array of names for these blocks: fortunately, most of them are readily understood. Examples are logic array blocks (Altera APEX 20k family), logic elements (Altera FLEX 10KE), macrocells (Altera MAX7000/MAX3000), configurable logic blocks (Xilinx), and programmable function units (Lucent ORCA).
- *Routing resources*: A typical FPGA will provide lines of various lengths to interconnect the logic blocks. Short lines provide low propagation delay paths between neighbouring blocks; longer lines connect more distant blocks with low delay. A small number of buffered low delay lines, which can interconnect large groups of logic blocks are usually provided for clocks.

---

[1]2001 value: apply Moore's Law for 2002 and forward.

[2]Market habits die hard, though: Altera persists in referring to its devices as programmable logic devices (PLDs).

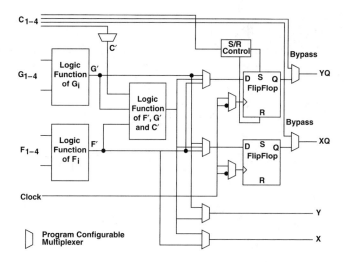

**FIGURE 37.1**  Simplified block diagram of the Xilinx XC4000 device control logic block. (The XC4000 CLBs have additional capabilities [1].)

- *I/O buffers*: Special purpose logic blocks provide interfaces to external circuitry. In modern devices, the I/O buffers provide a variety of electrical protocols eliminating the need to use special interface buffers. Reducing chip-to-chip connections provides greater data transfer bandwidth between the reconfigurable processor and its environment.

Recent devices include memory blocks, which may be configured in several ways.

### Xilinx 4000 and on

Xilinx' 4000 series devices [1] were not the first of their family, there were several antecedents; however, in order to avoid turning this chapter section into a history lesson, I will describe it first the author. It is a good representative of a number of commercially available devices.

*Control Logic Blocks*

Figure 37.1 shows the essential features of the 4000 series control logic blocks (CLBs). It contains three logic function blocks—each capable of implementing any arbitrarily defined boolean function of its inputs—and two flip-flops controlled by a common clock. "Programming" the device sets the logic functions in the logic function blocks, the signal steering multiplexors and the set/reset control. There are nine basic inputs: $F_{1-4}$, $G_{1-4}$ and $C_4$ (a direct data input to the flip-flops) and four outputs—two registered and two combinatorial. Paths can be chosen which bypass either or both flip-flops. Xilinx's designers have chosen to implement a moderately complex logic block. In contrast, Altera devices have simpler logic blocks with a single flip-flop[2] and Quicklogic's super cells are more complex [3]. Lucent refers to the ORCA logic block as a programmable functional unit (PFU) reflecting its complexity: 19 inputs and 4 flip-flops [4]. Additionally, the logic in the function blocks can be configured to act as a block of RAM, which can be configured as $16 \times 1$, $16 \times 2$, or $32 \times 1$ bit blocks. Without this capability, applications requiring memory are forced to use the CLB flip-flops, using a whole CLB for each 2 bits. This was a significant limitation of early devices, but newer ones, in addition to the 32 bits per CLB provided in the 4000 series, provide dedicated RAM blocks with significant capacities [2,5].

*Routing Resources*

A great challenge to FPGA designers is achieving a good balance in the allocation of die area to programmable logic (the CLBs) versus routing resources. The XC4000 designers provide a combination of short lines which connect each CLB to a programmable switch matrix adjacent to it, double and quad length lines which connect every second (or fourth) switch matrix, and long lines which run the entire length of a device (see Fig. 37.2). Connections through the switch matrices provide ultimate flexibility—any

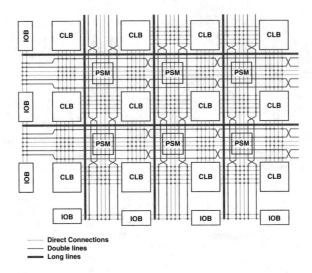

**FIGURE 37.2**  Conceptual view of the routing on an XC4000 device showing the pattern of logic blocks (CLBs) embedded in "channels" of routing resources. Direct connections to the programmable switch matrix (PSM) are shown as well as the patterns for double lines connecting every second PSM. Similarly, quad lines (omitted) connect every fourth PSM. Long lines run the length of horizontal and vertical channels. This is a concept diagram only: actual devices may differ in details [1].

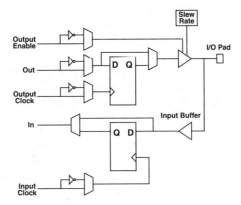

**FIGURE 37.3**  Simplified block diagram showing essential features of the Xilinx XC4000 input/output block (IOB). (The XC4000 IOBs have additional capabilities [1].)

CLB may be connected to any other; however, there is a penalty: the switch points are implemented with pass transistors which add to the propagation delay of any signal passing through them. Thus, the short lines through the switch matrices should not be used for critical signals connecting widely separated CLBs. The double, quad, or long lines need to be used to reduce delays. Predicting the optimal allocation for any application is obviously a hard task and many strategies may be seen in the commercially available devices. For example, Altera's Apex 20K devices employ a hierarchical structure, grouping basic logic elements (LEs) into logic array blocks (LABs), which are in turn grouped into MegaLABs [2]. Each block has appropriate internal routing resources. Copper is also used to reduce resistance and thus propagation delay.

*I/O Buffers*
I/O buffers provide circuitry to interface with external devices. Apart from input buffers and output drivers, the main additional feature is the ability to latch both inputs and outputs. The simplified diagram of an XC4000 I/O buffer (IOB) in Fig. 37.3 shows the output driver, input buffer, registers, several

inverters, and the programmable multiplexors. The inverters provide almost all combinations of normal and inverted direct output or latched signals synchronized with direct or inverted clocks: this avoids the need to use resources in the CLBs simply to invert signals. Limited slew rate control was also added to the output buffers—a precursor to the support for multiple electrical protocols now found in more modern designs.

### Additional Features

Adders, including counters, occur on the critical paths in many calculations, so the 4000 series, like most of its modern counterparts, provides "fast-carry" logic. Ripple carry adders are simple, regular, and use minimal logic, but they must wait until a carry bit has "rippled" through all the summing (full adder) blocks. By providing a fast, direct path for carry bits between blocks, the critical delay in a ripple carry adder is significantly reduced. The fast carry logic is so effective that there is no advantage to be gained from more complex adders, such as carry-lookahead ones. A carry-lookahead adder requires a much larger number of CLBs and the signal propagation times between these additional CLBs outweigh any benefit to be gained from a complex adder: trials with carry-lookahead adders show them to be slower than ripple carry adders that use the fast-carry logic [6].

The special needs of global clocks are addressed by providing "semi-dedicated" I/O pads connected to four primary global buffers designed for minimum delay and skew. The clocks of each CLB can be connected to these global buffers, a set of secondary buffers or any other internal signal. Thus multiple global and local clock domains can be established.

Problem diagnosis and boundary scan testing is facilitated through support for IEEE 1149.1 (JTAG) boundary scan logic attached to each I/O buffer.

The CLB structure lends itself to efficient implementation of functions of up to 9 inputs, but address decoders commonly require many more bits. Special decoders accepting up to 132 bits for large XC4000 devices are provided to ensure fast, resource-efficient decoding.

A simple internal oscillator and divider provides clock signals when precise frequencies are not required.

### Virtex

The Virtex family [5] are enhanced versions of the Xilinx 4000 series. Improved process technology has allowed the gate capacity to exceed one million ($4 \times 10^6$ are claimed for the largest member of the family, requiring 2 MB of configuration data). Supply voltages as low as 1.8 V allow internal clocks up to 400 MHz to be used.

### Memory

Blocks of dedicated memory are now provided, which can be programmed to a number of single- and dual-port configurations. This will allow considerable performance enhancements for designs which were previously forced to use external memory.

### I/O Buffers

One of the most dramatic additions to the newest devices from all manufacturers is the support of numerous electrical protocols at the I/O pins. For example, Virtex supports single-ended standards: LVTTL, LVCMOS, PCI-X, GTL, GTLP, HSTL, SSTL, AGP-2X and differential standards: LVDS, BLVDS, ULVDS, LDT, and LVPECL. Support for PCI-X means that a Virtex device can implement the industry-standard PCI interface, considerably reducing the complexity of PCI cards which can now combine interface logic, control logic, some memory, and external bus interfaces (e.g., LVDS) in a single chip.

Virtex devices are also partially reconfigurable: individual columns may be reprogrammed.

### Algotronix

Algotronix's approach to FPGA design was radically different from the Xilinx[3] approach. Cells were much simpler *and used for routing as well as logic*. The basic cell in shown in Fig. 37.4. By using a much simpler cell, it becomes possible to fit more logic per silicon die and the XC6264 device [7] was rated as containing

---

[3]However, Algotronix was taken over by Xilinx and its devices appeared as the Xilinx XC6200 series [7].

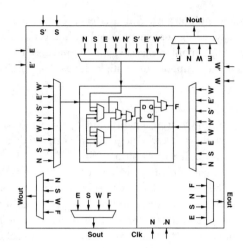

**FIGURE 37.4**   Block diagram of the cell in an XC6200 device. This cell is used for routing also.

$10^5$ gate equivalents early in 1997—about twice as many as devices with distinct logic blocks and routing resources at the same time. Routing—other than between neighboring cells—uses the logic cells programmed simply to route a signal from input to output. Signals routed in this way pass through transmission gates and suffer significant delays, so the XC6200 devices provided a hierarchy of "FastLANE" connections, which linked lines of 4 and 16 cells.

These devices also permitted fast reconfiguration: the SRAM cells that hold the configuration data can be directly addressed so that part of an operating circuit may be quickly reconfigured. (By contrast, the XC4000 devices are programmed cither with a serial bit stream or byte-by-byte from an EEROM—requiring milliseconds for a complete chip to be reconfigured.)

The "sea-of-gates" approach provided by the XC6200 devices may be viewed as one end of a spectrum stretching from simple cell/no dedicated routing devices to complex cell/dedicated routing devices such as the XC4000 and most other commercially available devices. Regular applications requiring large numbers of operations or very wide uniform data paths are likely to match a sea-of-gates device better. Less regular problems with complex control requirements—requiring functions of many signals—are likely to match the complex logic device devices better. The industry, however, appcars to have voted strongly for complex logic block devices and the XC6200 series is no longer commercially available.

## Reconfigurable Systems

Reconfigurable systems are easy to build: a designer has only to decide what interconnection patterns will best serve the needs of target applications and some systems, e.g., UWA's Achilles, even allow that to be deferred. The major proportion of the circuitry may be changed once the basic hardware system has been constructed. As a consequence, an enormous number of experimental and several commercial systems have been built: Guccione has compiled a list, it contains summaries of over 80 systems [8]. An attempt to cover all of these is clearly futile: a small representative sample has been chosen.

### SPLASH 2

One of the best known systems is SRC's SPLASH 2 [9]. It consists of an array of FPGAs and interface allowing the array to be attached to a SPARC host. The FPGA array itself was composed of a number of array boards, each containing 17 Xilinx XC4010 FPGAs—16 "computing" devices and one interface device. Typical of devices of its time (~1990), the XC4010 can provide limited amounts of memory itself, so 512 KB of conventional memory were attached to each FPGA. Apart from nearest neighbour connections, a crossbar switch permitted dynamic ("almost" tick-by-tick [9]) connection changes to be made.

## Programmable Active Memories (PAM)

A dozen copies of the variant named DECPeRLe-1 found their way into research centers around the world and were applied to a diverse set of problems [10]. The computing surface was a 4 × 4 array of XC3090 devices with seven additional FPGAs acting as memory and interface controllers. FPGAs in the array were connected directly to each of their four neighbours. Devices in each row and column shared common 16-bit buses, so that there were four 64-bit buses running the length of the array—one for each geographic direction N, S, E, and W. Static RAM was added to provide the storage lacking in the early devices used and FIFOs provided elasticity in a high-speed interface to a host processor. Vuillemin et al. discuss an extensive list of problems to which PAMs were applied [10]: long integer arithmetic, RSA cryptography, molecular biology, finite differences, neural networks, video compression, image classification, image analysis, cluster detection, image acquisition, stereo vision, sound synthesis, and Viterbi decoding.

They consistently applied the following rule in deciding what part of any problem should be allocated to the hardware:

"Cast the inner loop in PAM hardware; let software handle the rest [10]!"

PAM spawned a successor, PAMETTE, a PCI card with 5 Xilinx 4000 series devices on it [11]. One device served as the PCI interface with the remaining four arranged in a 2 × 2 matrix. SRAM and DRAM may be added and provision is made for external connections via a daughter board. A large number of similar boards—all with the same basic idea: place a number of FPGAs on a card, which may be inserted into the bus of a suitable host—have been designed by research groups. Several commercial products are also available.

## SPACE

The Scalable Parallel Architecture for Concurrency Experiments (SPACE) machine was developed at the University of Strathclyde [12]; it was followed by the SPACE-II, built at the University of South Australia [13]. Both variants used fine-grain FPGAs (Algotronix CAL1024s in SPACE and Xilinx XC6216s in SPACE 2) as the primary target was the simulation of highly concurrent systems such as digital circuits, traffic systems, particle flow, and electrical stimuli models of the heart. SPACE 2 processor boards contained 8 XC6216 processor FPGAs and an XC4025 providing a PCI interface to an Alpha host. On each board, the fine-grained processors are connected in a mesh in order to provide a seamless array of gates on the board. Additional memory (32 Mb of static RAM) was present on each board. A secondary backplane allowed high-bandwidth connections between SPACE 2 boards.

## Achilles

The Achilles architecture aims to provide much more flexible interconnection patterns: Figure 37.5 shows the 3-D arrangement in which small PCBs containing a single FPGA are arranged in a vertical "stack" [14,15]. A limited number of fixed bussed interconnections are provided at the base of the stack, committing only about one-third of the available I/O pins to fixed interconnect. A second side of the stack is used for programming and diagnostic connections: this enables the stack to be "gang" programmed—each FPGA is loaded with an identical program—or individually. The remaining two sides have uncommitted connections: connectors are provided for groups of eight signals and ribbon cables are used to connect FPGAs as the target application requires. This system offers wide variations in communication patterns at the expense of manual reconfiguration.

# Applications

The list of applications, which have been successfully implemented in reconfigurable hardware systems, is long; it includes applications from such diverse areas as:

- Image processing
- Cryptography

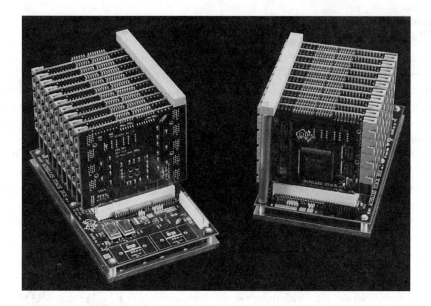

**FIGURE 37.5**   Achilles 3-D stack. Each small PCB contains one FPGA: connections are made by cabling between the connectors visible on each small PCB.

- Database and text searching
- Compression
- Signal processing

It is generally straightforward to transfer an algorithm from a general-purpose processor to reconfigurable hardware; synthesizers which convert VHDL or Verilog models into the bit streams necessary to program an FPGA-based system are available and efficient; however, a *successful* transfer must provide a solution which is more efficient, by some criterion, than the same algorithm running on fast commodity general-purpose processors. Reconfigurable hardware generally runs slower,[4] consumes more power, and costs more than commodity processors. This remains true at most points in the performance spectrum. At the low performance end, small processors, e.g., Motorola's HC11 series, are available at very low cost and very low power consumption and will thus perform simple control and data processing tasks effectively. Although a modern FPGA may outperform the relatively slow processors available at the low end of the performance spectrum, there are a host of general-purpose embedded processors, e.g., the PowerPC-based devices, which will provide the additional processing power while still consuming less power and costing less than an FPGA. At the high performance end of the spectrum, the internal clock speeds of FPGAs lag behind those of commodity processors and thus their sequential processing capability does not match that of, for example, a state-of-the-art Pentium or SPARC processor; however, although it is clear that reconfigurable hardware will not provide efficient solutions for all problems, there are areas in which it is extremely efficient.

The general characteristics of successful applications are

(a) *Sufficient parallelism:* The processing algorithm must have sufficient inherent parallelism to allow multiple processing pipelines to be created. This parallelism can be either *direct* or *pipelined*.

(b) *Low storage requirements:* Early FPGAs provided very few bits of memory—the flip-flops in logic blocks were an expensive way to provide memory. Later FPGAs have addressed this problem by allowing the configuration bits to be used as lookup tables and thus provides tens of bits per logic block. The newest generation of FPGAs provide blocks of dedicated memory but capacities are

---

[4]However, Tsu et al., argue that there is no inherent reason why an FPGA should be slower [16].

measured in megabits, not megabytes. Although external memory can always be added and wide buses employed to provide high bandwidth, this uses valuable I/O pins, the path to external memory is likely to become a bottleneck and limit performance.

(c) *"Decision-free" processing patterns:* Multiplexors in the data paths will readily handle simple decisions, which switch the dataflow between down-line functional blocks, but complex decision trees will generally not map efficiently to hardware. When large numbers of branches exist, inevitably many paths are little used and thus expensive to implement in fixed hardware relative to their benefit. In particular, error handling logic will generally be complex relative to its frequency of use. Complex decision logic is efficiently handled in high-performance modern processors, which move common logic to cache at the expense of little used code. When branches have similar probabilities, speculative execution ensures good average rates of instruction completion. However, this criterion for successful hardware implementation should be applied with caution: if high throughput for all possible processing paths is required, then the resources devoted to implementing all paths (including little used ones) may be justified. In the near future, dynamically reconfigurable logic may also provide effective solutions when there are complex decision trees.

(d) Ability to use local (i.e., between neighbouring devices) data paths in problems that are large enough to require multiple devices. Most systems provide high-bandwidth paths between nearest neighbors with lower-bandwidth multiple device buses and global interconnects. The 3-D Achilles design provides more device–device data path flexibility but at a cost—wiring patterns must be set up manually for each application [14].

(e) *Integer arithmetic:* Although it is possible to implement arbitrary precision floating-point processors in FPGAs, the number of logic blocks required and hence the delays introduced by data paths between logic blocks make them expensive in area and low in performance compared to those found in superscalar processors.[5] On the other hand, the ability to easily implement arbitrary precision integer arithmetic allows a reconfigurable system designer to pack more functional units of higher performance into a given area by choosing the minimum required word length.

### Image Processing

Real-time image processing presents a classic application for custom processors. A stream of pixels emanating from a camera can be passed through a wide deep pipeline—performing as many unrelated and complex operations on each pixel as needed. Unrelated operations (e.g., thresholding and masking) are performed in parallel and complex operations (e.g., masking) are performed in deep pipelines. For basic operations, little storage is required and the relatively inefficient memory on an FPGA suffices. A masking operation, such as applying a $3 \times 3$ mask to a group of neighboring pixels, requires the storage of two scanlines in a shift register and thus is feasible in large FPGAs. The reverse process, visualisation, or the processing of machine generated images for display is already the domain of special purpose processors, but market volumes have justified use of ASICs.[6]

### Stereo Vision

The matching problem dominates research into fully automated stereo vision systems; it requires the comparison of pixels (or regions of pixels) to determine matches between corresponding segments of two images. The distance between matching regions on the left and right images (the disparity) is combined with camera system geometry to determine the distance to objects in the field of view. Without the apparent ability of a human brain to "jump" to the obvious match, a machine must try all possible disparities in order to find candidate matches between pixels or to correlate regions. Objects close to the camera system

---

[5]Superscalar processor manufacturers are also prepared to invest large amounts in order to win benchmark competitions, which allows man-years of effort to be used to optimize individual circuits and layouts.

[6]However, prototyping designs which are destined for ASICs are a major application for reconfigurable processors. They can be used to ensure that a design is correct and that the silicon will function correctly first time. Some foundries will take FPGA-based designs and convert them directly to ASICs.

have disparities approaching infinity, but one of the major applications of stereo vision is collision avoidance in which it is possible to put a lower bound on the distances of objects from the camera.[7] In practical camera systems, this results in a need to consider objects with disparities from 0 pixels (i.e., at infinity) to of the order of 10–100 pixels at closest permissible approach. Thus this problem has all of the required attributes for an efficient pipeline parallel implementation:

- Parallelism of 10–100 or more
- Simple calculations (comparing pixel intensities)
- Regular computation (the same correlation operators are applied to each pixel)

Woodfill et al., using the census transform to reduce problems caused by intensity variations and depth discontinuities, programmed a PARTS engine [17] to calculate object depths from pairs of 320 × 240 pixel images. With a maximum disparity of 32, their system was able to compute depth at 42 frames per second [18]. They estimated that it was performing about $2.3 \times 10^9$ RISC equivalent operations per second. Piacentino et al. have built a video processing system (Sarnoff Vision Front End 200) in which reconfigurable processing elements are used not only for stereo computations, but for motion estimation and warping also [19]. They estimate that the VFE-200 can provide ~500 GOPS of processing power.

### Encryption/Decryption

Shand and Vuillemin have used RSA cryptography as a benchmark for their PAM machines; they were able to demonstrate an order of magnitude improvement in performance relative to the best software implementations of the time. In 1992, PAM achieved over 1 Mb/s for 512 bit keys compared to 56 kb/s on a 150 MHz Alpha processor [20]. This relative performance will not change; state-of-the-art FPGAs can now fit the entire PAM system in a single device, giving the reconfigurable hardware system additional speed as it no longer needs to use slower inter-device links or external memory.

Symmetric encryption algorithms are easily and efficiently implemented in FPGAs; they require a number of "rounds" of application of simple operations. Each round can be implemented as a pipeline stage. Thus, as an example, TwoFish [21] requires 16 rounds of lookup table accesses, which can be implemented as a 16-stage pipeline. This allows a stream of 32-bit input data words to be encrypted at very high input frequencies with a latency of 16 cycles. In a study of four AES candidates, Elbirt et al. report an order of magnitude difference between FPGA-based implementations and the best software ones [22]; however, they also note that for one AES candidate, CAST-256, FPGA implementations were slower than their software counterparts. This result highlights the fact that the performance advantage of commodity processors can only be overcome when the problem matches the capabilities of FPGA-based custom processors. By adding further pipeline stages within each round—24 for TwoFish, for example—Chodowiec et al. were able to achieve throughputs greater than 10 Gb/s for five of the AES candidate algorithms (12 Gb/s using a 95 MHz internal clock for Rijndael, the eventual winner of the AES competition) [23].

Secure communications systems require encryption hardware; placing the encryption subsystem in hardware makes it less susceptible to tampering and enables keys to be hidden in "write-only" registers. Reconfigurable hardware provides an additional capability, algorithm agility [24]. This not only enables an encryption algorithm which has become insecure to be replaced with a secure one, but permits an algorithm independent security protocol to use the hardware effectively, loading the appropriate algorithm on a transaction-by-transaction basis.

### Compression

Using a systolic array style implementation of the LZ algorithm, Huang et al. were able to obtain throughputs 30 times greater than those achievable with commodity processors [25]. This speedup was obtained even though their FPGAs (Xilinx XC4036s) were clocked at 16 MHz versus 450 MHz for the fastest software implementation. Huang et al. believe that even better relative performance would be obtained

---

[7]The vehicle carrying the camera system is expected to move away before this bound is violated.

from modern FPGAs, e.g., Altera's APEX 20K devices have built-in content addressable memories (CAMs), which would speed up the process of matching input strings with the dictionary.

## Arithmetic

When designing a reconfigurable system, the widths of arithmetic function units, and hence their propagation delays, can be constrained trivially to the number of bits actually required for the application. This saves space, logic resources, and time. Designers also have considerable flexibility when complex arithmetic expressions must be evaluated; they can choose a single-stage combinatorial circuit or increase throughput by adding registers and forming a pipeline. This can often be done at essentially no cost: the logic blocks contain flip-flops already, so there is no space penalty and negligible time penalty.

An application requiring floating point arithmetic may be a poor candidate for a reconfigurable system—to achieve performance comparable to that offered by a commodity processor will require significant effort; however, reconfigurable systems are excellent at processing streams of data from sensors: this data will be fixed point and readily handled by the same circuits used for integer arithmetic.

### CORDIC

Even trigonometric functions of fixed-point data are readily implemented using CORDIC arithmetic. CORDIC algorithms are iterative, but require only shifts and adds. Again, the designer has a large space in which to work [26]. Bit-serial designs are simple and compact, but require many cycles; this may not be a problem if the input data rate is relatively slow. An iterative bit-parallel design will require more space but fewer cycles. Finally, the iterative loop can be unrolled by one or more stages to produce the desired throughput/space balance.

## String and Text Matching

Genetic sequencing technology is just one technology that is producing enormous databases of data that must be searched. Thus, there has been considerable interest in hardware to accelerate the process of comparing new sequences with those in existing databases. Biologists use a measure known as the edit distance when comparing sequences. A simple implementation of a dynamic algorithm can compute the edit distance in $O(mn)$ time ($m, n$ = length of source and target sequences, respectively), but if the calculation is carried out on a processor array, then it can be seen that all operations on the diagonal may be performed in parallel. A single board Splash 2 machine achieved a factor of 20 speedup over a CM-2—a massively parallel processor [27]!

Similarly, full text searching of documents for relevance has sufficient parallelism to make FPGA-based hardware effective. When document content cannot be adequately described by keywords, a searcher will supply a list of relevant words and require that every word of every document be checked against the list in order to build a relevance score for each document. Gunther et al. demonstrated that the original SPACE machine was effective in this application [28]. They used a technique called "data folding" in which the data are built into the circuitry. Match circuitry is built for each of the words in the list of relevant words and incorporated into a fixed matching structure. This is an excellent example of the power of partial reconfiguration; circuit patterns corresponding to the relevant words are loaded for each new search. They demonstrate that matching in hardware does not need to be limited to direct character-by-character matching. It is possible to implement simple regular expressions allowing, e.g., matching on the root of a word only. Overall the system is able to test for each word in the relevant list in parallel and aggregate a weighted relevance score as the document is read, results become available at a rate which is basically limited by the rate at which documents can be read from disc.

## Simulations

Cellular automata map readily to reconfigurable systems. They involve arrays of cells: each cell is a simple finite state machine whose behavior depends only on its current state and the state of cells in its immediate environment. Milne extends the fundamental cellular automata concept by removing the restrictions on identical components, uniform update and synchronization of all updates to create generalized cellular automata (GCA); an example of traffic system simulation is described—digital circuits and forest fire development are further systems, which have suitable characteristics [13].

Petri net models are also used extensively in simulation studies; as with cellular automata, there is abundant low level parallelism to be exploited—the firability of each transition can be evaluated simultaneously. Petri net models are based on simple units—places and transitions. It is possible to create generic models in VHDL for these units [14], paving the way to automatic generation of VHDL code from natural visual representation of Petri nets, which can be compiled and downloaded to suitable hardware. A single Achilles stack is able to accommodate a model containing of the order of 200 transitions [14].

## Reconfigurable Processors vs. Commodity Processors

Any special purpose hardware has to compete with the rapid increase in performance of commodity processors. Despite the relative inefficiency of a general-purpose processor for many applications, if the special purpose hardware only provides a speedup of, say 2, then Moore's Law will ensure that the advantage of the special purpose hardware is lost in a year.[8] When assessing whether an application will benefit from use of a reconfigurable processor, one has to keep the following points in mind.

### Raw Performance

The raw performance of FPGA-based solutions will always lag behind that of commodity processors. This is superficially reflected in maximum clock speeds: an FPGA's maximum clock speed will typically be one-third or less of that of a commodity processor at the same point in time. This is inevitable and will continue: the reconfiguration circuitry loads a circuit and requires space, increasing its propagation delay and reducing the maximum clock speed.

### Parallelism

Thus, to realize a benefit from a reconfigurable system, the application must have a considerable degree of inherent parallelism which can be used effectively.

The parallelism may be exploited simply by deploying multiple processing blocks—each processing a separate data element at the same time—followed by some "aggregation" circuitry, which reduces results from the individual processing blocks in some way.

### Long Pipelines

Alternatively, a long pipeline may be employed in which the same data element transits multiple processing blocks in successive clock cycles. This approach trades latency for throughput: it may take many cycles—the latency—for the first result to appear, but after that new processed data are available on each clock cycle giving high throughput. Many signal processing tasks can effectively use long pipelines.

### Memory

FPGA devices do not provide large amounts of memory efficiently: recent devices (e.g., Altera's APEX 20K devices [2]) do attempt to address this deficiency and provide significant dedicated memory resources; however, the total number of memory bits remains relatively small and is insufficient to support applications which require large amounts of randomly accessible data. This means that, although preprocessing an image which is available as a pixel stream from a camera for edge detection is feasible, subsequent processing of the image in order to segment it is considerably more difficult. In the first case, to apply a $3 \times 3$ mask to the pixel stream, only two preceding rows of the image need be stored. The application of the $3 \times 3$ mask requires a maximum of nine basic multiply-accumulate operations. Thus, it can be effectively handled in a 9-stage pipeline—easily allowing an edge-detected image to be produced at the same rate as the original image is streamed into the FPGA (allowing for an 8-pixel clock latency before the first result is available). In the second, the whole image needs to be stored and be available for random access. Although an FPGA with auxillary memory might handle this task, it is less likely to offer a significant advantage over a general-purpose processor.

---

[8]The author has (somewhat arbitrarily) shortened the "break-even" point from the 18 months of Moore's Law, because the extra cost of additional hardware needs to be factored in versus using cheap commodity hardware.

### Regularity

A processing pipeline with large numbers of decisions (if .. then .. else blocks in a high-level language program) is also not likely to be efficiently implemented in reconfigurable hardware. In such a pipeline, there will generally be a large number of branches which are rarely taken, but all need to be implemented in hardware, taking up considerable space (or numbers of logic blocks). Paths with large numbers of blocks of variable size also present a problem for the fixed routing resources in a device.

### Power and Cost

FPGAs consume more power and cost more per gate than either commercial processors or custom ASICs. Although FPGA technology tracks processor technology and power consumption is being reduced through lower power supply voltages and reduced transistor size, it is unlikely that one will see reconfigurable technology in micro power applications such as wearable computers; however, experiments are underway to test their viability in spacecraft, where power is limited [29]. The cost factor is generally offset in low volume production by the significantly lower design cost, faster design cycles, and ease with which modifications can be incorporated.

## Dynamic Reconfiguration

There is considerable interest in the ability to reconfigure a running circuit. This would allow applications (or groups of applications) to load circuits on demand to meet the requirements of a current task. This would make a reconfigurable system a truly general purpose one: able to load processing tasks as demanded by the input data.

Although most commercial devices require a complete new configuration program to be loaded every time, usually by paths with limited bandwidths requiring thousands of cycles to completely reprogram a device, some commercially available devices have had limited dynamic reprogramming capabilities for some time, e.g., the original Algotronix CAL1024, its successor the Xilinx XC6200 (both now out of production), Atmel's AT6000 (now superceded), AT40K, and Xilinx's Virtex family.

These devices extend the standard device programming model by allowing a part of the configuration to be reloaded from an external source: an alternative has been proposed—the DPGA model [30]. A DPGA device would hold several configurations in the configuration memory for each logic block and allow the context to select one dynamically. The flexibility gained from this arrangement allows much more effective gate utilization—at the expense of the additional space for the configuration memory and context selection logic.

Noting some of the limitations introduced by conventional approaches to dynamic reloading of configuration data, Vasilko and Ait-Boudaoud have proposed an optical system for transferring new configuration data to a device [31]. Optical buses not only allow massively parallel data transfer but provide an additional dimension for information transfer and thus reduce the conflict for routing space between data paths and configuration nets. The advent of devices similar to their proposals would remove some of the practical limitations constraining effective dynamically reconfigurable systems.

One requirement for effective run-time reconfiguration is a model which allows a computation to be split into swappable computational blocks. Caspi et al. summarise several proposed models in introducing their SCORE (Stream Computations for Reconfigurable Extension) model [32]. SCORE divides a computation into fixed size pages, which can be swapped between the running hardware and backup store. A dataflow computation model is used, allowing the run-time system to manage resources: a dataflow model is "memory-less" as far as the programmer is concerned. Data flowing between pages is buffered transparently by the run-time system when necessary.

## Hybrid Systems

Hybrid systems couple a conventional processor and an area of uncommitted logic that may be configured to suit the demands of algorithms in which the conventional processor cannot exploit data or pipeline parallelism. Berkeley's Garp processor is an example of this approach [33]. Garp contains a RISC processor core (MIPS-II) and 32 × 23 array of logic blocks. A 24th column of logic blocks is responsible for

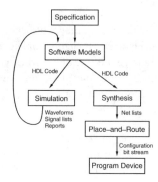

**FIGURE 37.6**  Design flow using an HDL (e.g., VHDL). Note the absence of a feedback loop in the synthesis branch: for a design verified in simulation, the synthesis process is a black box.

communication outside the array. Logic blocks take up to four 2-bit inputs and produce 2-bit outputs: a row of the array can thus process up to four 46-bit words. Garp's designers hypothesize that the reconfigurable section may be used effectively to implement the critical kernels found in most code: the ability to hard-wire the control logic will reduce instruction fetch bottlenecks and better exploit parallelism. Memory queues, which handle streaming of data to and from memory, were added because many applications which use reconfigurable systems effectively process streams of data.

Results from the Garp simulator on a wavelet image compression program showed an overall speedup of 2.9 compared to the MIPS processor. Individual kernels within this program showed speedups up to 12, observed when a kernel had high exploitable instruction level parallelism and the configuration loading time could be amortized over many compute cycles. Comparisons of Garp's performance with a 4-issue superscalar processor also showed significant speedups, indicating that Garp was able to exploit more instruction level parallelism, sustaining 10 instructions per cycle in many cases.

## Programming Reconfigurable Systems

### High-Level Hardware Design Languages

The design flow for a reconfigurable system is shown in Fig. 37.6; a high-level hardware design language (HDL) is usually used for the software modeling stage: VHDL and Verilog are widely used as excellent support tools are available. The design process is basically identical to that used for any software system: specifications are drawn up and validated, software models created and verified and the compiled "program" is loaded onto the target devices or burnt into ROMs. The only significant difference is that two compilers are generally used. A simulator compiles VHDL or Verilog source and produces diagnostic output not only as text to consoles or logged to files, but as waveforms or lists of changes in signal values. When the designer has verified that the models perform in accordance with their specifications under simulation, a synthesizer compiles the source again to a netlist—an intermediate representation of the final circuit. Device-specific place-and-route tools take netlists as input and place logic into logic blocks and configure the FPGA's routing resources to make the necessary connections between logic blocks and I/O pins. The output of this stage is a configuration file—a stream of bits which are loaded onto the device to program its internal registers, multiplexors, etc. For many designs, the whole process (synthesis → place-and-route → configuration bit stream) can be viewed as a single step black-box, which turns verified HDL models into configuration files. Whilst it may take several hours for a complex system, it does not require any input from the user. The designer will usually simply advise the tools whether speed or area is the primary constraint. Significant interaction with the place-and-route tools is needed only if there are performance constraints which cannot be met with default parameters: in this case, manual placement of logic blocks can assist in satisfying the constraints.

### Other Languages

Other routes from high-level languages are possible: Callahan et al. describe a tool which starts with C [34]: it is aimed at "dusty-deck" systems. Of more potential for effective use of reconfigurable systems are special purpose high-level languages such as Milne's process algebra, CIRCAL [35].

## Conclusions

In this chapter section, instead of providing a litany of praise for reconfigurable computing in all its forms, the author has tried to set out the general characteristics of problems, which a reconfigurable processor might be expected to solve efficiently. A key requirement is clearly sufficient exploitable parallelism, but that may appear either as raw or pipeline parallelism. Raw parallelism is a requirement to perform many simultaneous operations on a single item of data or the same operation on many data items, which may be presented to the reconfigurable hardware at the same instant. Pipeline parallelism, on the other hand, requires many operations to be performed on individual elements of a data stream, allowing a deep pipeline to process data at its arrival rate and produce results in real time, even if some latency penalty must be paid.

Reconfigurable systems are always competing against the inexorable rise in the power of general-purpose processors. Although reconfigurable devices track the performance gains due to better device technology, they inevitably lack the commercial drive that propels commodity processors forward in performance and thus lag behind their better funded cousins in raw performance. Thus, when considering a special purpose processor for any task, one must keep in mind the performance point at which commodity processors will be when the design is complete. With "multimedia extensions" such as MMX and Altivec, commodity processors even have limited parallel processing capabilities; however, these are limited to very regular computations and a reconfigurable system—with its ability to implement multiple parallel data paths—will generally be better at matching the "shape" of a multiple processing step algorithm. The use of high-level design languages, such as VHDL and Verilog, also shortens design cycles making time-to-completion for projects based on reconfigurable hardware considerably shorter than custom hardware designs.

Thus, although problems that fail to meet the criteria are set out here, and thus will be more effectively solved using commodity processors, the author has shown that many problem domains also exist in which large numbers of individual problems are well suited to reconfigurable processors.

In this chapter section, discussion of successes has, for the most part, focussed on systems in which reconfiguration times are long—requiring hours if the time for synthesis software to compile, analyze, and place and route a model expressed in a high-level design language is included; however, there is much active research into dynamically reconfigurable systems, which has the goal of producing hardware whose function may be altered as quickly and conveniently as the general-purpose processors. The significant problems with which researchers in this area are now grappling will be solved eventually. Thus, we can anticipate systems in which parallelism present at some level in virtually all problems, which cannot be exploited now, will be exploited by systems that have been configured on-the-fly. As with statically programmed systems, when data paths can be provided that match problem structures, we will obtain orders of magnitude larger processing powers efficiently. We will not need to use large processor arrays in which many processors are needed for a few vital steps but are idle for much of the time.

## References

1. Xilinx, Inc., XC4000 data book, 1997.
2. Altera Corp., APEX 20K Programmable Logic Device Family Data Sheet, http://www.altera.com/literature/lit-apx.html, 2001.
3. QuickLogic Corp., QuickLogic: Beyond Programmable Logic, Sunnyvale, California, 2001.
4. Lucent Technologies, Inc., ORCA Series 2 Field-Programmable Gate Arrays, June 1999.
5. Xilinx, Inc., Virtex-II 1.5 V Platform FPGA Family, http://www.xilinx.com/partinfo/ds013-2.pdf, 2001.

6. Baskoro, E. and Morris, J., Fast adders in FPGAs, Technical Report TR2001-01, Centre for Intelligent Information Processing Systems, University of Western Australia, 2001.

7. Xilinx, Inc., XC6200 Field Programmable Gate Arrays, 1997.

8. Guccione, S., List of FPGA-based computing machines, www.io.com/~guccione/HW_list.html, 1999.

9. Buell, D.A., Arnold, J.M., and Kleinfelder, W.J., *Splash 2: FPGAs in a Custom Computing Machine*, IEEE Computer Society Press, California, 1996.

10. Vuillemin, J., et al., Programmable active memories: reconfigurable systems come of age, *IEEE Trans. on VLSI Systems*, 4, 1, 56, 1996.

11. Moll, L. and Shand, M., Systems performance measurement on PCI Pamette, in *IEEE Symp. on FPGAs for Custom Computing Machines*, Pocek, K.L. and Arnold, J., Eds., Napa Valley, CA, p. 125, 1997.

12. Cockshott, W.P., Barrie, P., McCaskill, G., and Milne, G.J., Realising massively concurrent systems on the SPACE Machine, in *Proc. IEEE Workshop on FPGAs for Custom Computing Machines*, Buell, D. and Pocek, K., Eds., IEEE Computer Society Press, 1993.

13. Milne, G.J., Reconfigurable custom computing as a supercomputer replacement, in *Proc. 4th International Conference on High-Performance Computing*, Bangalore, India, p. 260, Dec. 1997.

14. Morris, J., Bundell, G.A., and Tham, S., A reconfigurable processor for Petri net simulation, in *Proc. HICSS-33*, El-Rewini, H. and Helal, S., Eds., Maui, HI, 2000.

15. Tham, S., Achilles: High bandwidth, low latency interconnection for parallel processors, PhD Thesis, Electrical and Electronic Engineering, University of Western Australia, 2001.

16. Motorola Semiconductor Products, MPC500, MPC800 microprocessors, http://e-www.motorola.com/index.html, 2001.

17. Woodfill, J., von Herzen, B., and Zabih, R., Real-time stereo vision on the PARTS reconfigurable computer, in *5th IEEE Symp on FPGAs for Custom Computing Machines*, Pocek, K.L. and Arnold, J., Eds., Napa Valley, CA, p. 201, 1997.

18. Woodfill, J., von Herzen, B., and Zabih, R., Frame-rate robust stereo on a PCI board, http://www.cs.cornell.edu/rdz/Papers/Archive/fpga.pdf, 1998.

19. Piacentino, M.R., van der Wal, G.S., and Hansen, M.W., Reconfigurable elements for a video pipeline processor, in *7th IEEE Symp on Field-Programmable Custom Computing Machines*, Pocek, K.L. and Arnold, J., Eds., p. 82, 1999.

20. Shand, M. and Vuillemin, J., Fast implementation of RSA cryptography, in *Proc 11th IEEE Symposium on Computer Arithmetic*, Windsor, Ontario, 1993.

21. Schneier, B. et al., Twofish: a 128-bit block cipher, http://www.counterpane.com/twofish-paper.html, 2001.

22. Elbirt, A.J. et al., An FPGA implementation and performance evaluation of the AES block cipher candidate algorithm finalists, in *The Third Advanced Encryption Standard Candidate Conference*, New York, April 13–14, 2000.

23. Chodowiec, P., Khuon, P., and Gaj, K., Fast implementations of secret-key block ciphers using mixed inner- and outer-round pipelining, in *9th ACM Intl Symp on Field-Programmable Gate Arrays*, Schlag, M., Ed., Feb. 2001.

24. Paar, C. et al., An algorithm-agile cryptographic co-processor based on FPGAs, in *Reconfigurable Technology: FPGAs for Computing Applications, Proc. SPIE*, Schewel, J. et al., Eds., 3844, p. 11, 1999.

25. Huang, W.-J., Saxena, N., and McCluskey, E.J., A Reliable LZ data compressor on reconfigurable coprocessors, in *8th IEEE Symposium on Field-Programmable Custom Computing Machines*, Pocek, K.L. and Arnold, J., Eds., p. 175, 2000.

26. Andraka, R., A survey of CORDIC algorithms for FPGA based computers, in *Proc 6th Intl Symp on Field Programmable Gate Arrays*, Kaptanoglu, S., Ed., p. 191, 1998.

27. Hoang, D.T., Searching genetic databases on Splash 2, in Buell, D.A., Arnold, J.M., and Kleinfelder, W.J., *Splash 2: FPGAs in a Custom Computing Machine*, IEEE Computer Society Press, California, 1996.

28. Gunther, B.K., Milne, G.J., and Narasimhan, L., Assessing document relevance with run-time reconfigurable machines, in *4th IEEE Symposium on FPGAs for Custom Computing Machines*, p. 10, 1996.

29. Bergmann, N.W., and Dawood, A., Adaptive interfacing with reconfigurable computers, in *Proc Australasian Computer Systems Architecture Conference*, Heiser, G., Ed., p. 11, 2001.

30. DeHon, A., DPGA utilization and application, in *Proc ACM/SIGDA 4th International Symposium on Field Programmable Gate Arrays*, Ebeling, C., Ed., 1996. Extended version available via anonymous FTP transit.ai.mit.edu:transit-notes/tn129.ps.Z

31. Vasilko, M. and Ait-Boudaoud, D., Optically reconfigurable FPGAs: Is this a future trend?, in *Proc 6th Intl Workshop of Field-Programmable Logic and Applications*, Darmstadt, LNCS, Hartenstein, R.W., and Glesner, M., Eds., 1142, p. 270, 1996.

32. Caspi, E., Chu, M., Huang, R., Yeh, J., Markovskiy, Y., Wawrzynek, J., and André DeHon, A., Stream computations organized for reconfigurable execution (SCORE), in *10th Intl Conference on Field Programmable Logic and Applications, LNCS*, Hartenstein, R.W. and Gruenbacher, H., Eds., p. 1896, 2000 also http://www.cs.berkeley.edu/projects/brass/documents/score_tutorial.html.

33. Callahan, T.J., Hauser, J.R., and Wawrzynek, J., The Garp architecture and C compiler, *IEEE Computer*, 33, 4, 62, 2000.

34. Callahan, T.J. and Wawrzynek, J., Instruction level parallelism for reconfigurable computing, in *8th International Workshop Field-Programmable Logic and Applications, LNCS*, Hartenstein, R. and Keevalik, A., Eds., p. 1482, 1998.

35. Tsu, W. et al., in *Proc. 7th International Symposium on Field Programmable Gate Arrays*, Trimberger, S., Ed., 1999.

36. Diessel, O. and Milne, G., Compiling process algebraic descriptions into reconfigurable logic, in *Proc 15th IPDPS Workshops, LNCS 1800*, Rolim, J. et al., Eds., p. 916, 2000.

# 37.2 Using Configurable Computing Systems

*Danny Newport and Don Bouldin*

## Definitions

**Configurable computing systems:** Systems that use reprogrammable logic components, typically field programmable gate arrays (FPGAs), to implement a specialized instruction set and/or arithmetic units to improve the performance of a particular application. These systems can be reconfigured, enabling the same hardware resource to be reused depending on its interaction with external components, data dependencies, or algorithm requirements.

**Configuration time:** Time required to program an FPGA or configurable computing system with a given configuration. This time varies from hundreds of nanoseconds to seconds depending on the system and the FPGAs that are used in the system.

**Field programmable gate array:** Integrated circuit containing arrays of logic blocks and programmable interconnect between these blocks. The logic blocks can be configured to implement simple or complex logical functions and can be changed as required. Example functions are registers, adders, and multipliers. The programmable interconnect permits the construction of even more complex functions and/or systems.

**FPGA:** Acronym for field programmable gate array.

**Reconfigurable computing systems:** Alternate term for "configurable computing systems." This term is usually used to indicate that the system can be "reconfigured" at any time for some desired function.

## Introduction

Configurable computing systems use reprogrammable logic components, which are now capable of providing more than a million logic gates on a single chip. These systems can be reconfigured at runtime, enabling the same hardware resource to be reused depending on its interaction with external components, data dependencies, or algorithm requirements.

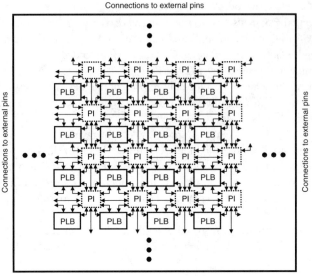

**FIGURE 37.7**    Basic internal structure of an FPGA.

In essence, a specialized instruction set and arithmetic units can be configured as desired by an application designer on an as-needed basis to achieve optimal performance. The location of configurable components within a computing system is one of the keys to achieving maximum efficiency and performance. A variety of architectures driven by the location of configurable components are described in a later section.

## Configurable Components

Before describing various architectures of configurable computing systems, an understanding of the internal structure of FPGAs, the major component of a configurable computing system is necessary. In 2001, the top two FPGA vendors were Altera Corporation and Xilinx, Inc. The FPGA products from these, and other vendors, differ in their internal structure and programming. However, the basic internal structure for FPGAs can be illustrated as shown in Fig. 37.7. Note that the "PLB" blocks are "programmable logic blocks" and the "PI" blocks are programmable interconnect. A current trend among the FPGA vendors is to also include RAM and/or a fixed microprocessor core on the same integrated circuit as the FPGA. This enables even greater system flexibility in a design.

The means by which the logic blocks and interconnect are configured for specific functions are of a proprietary nature and specific to each vendor's FPGA families. In general terms, the logic blocks and interconnect have internal structures that "hold" the current configuration and when presented with inputs will produce the programmed logic outputs. This "configuration" is FPGA-specific and contained in a vendor-specific file. A specific FPGA is programmed by downloading the information in this file through a serial or parallel logic connection.

The time required to configure an FPGA is known as the configuration time. Configuration times vary based on the FPGA family and the size of the FPGA. For a configurable computing system composed of several FPGAs, the configuration time is based not only on the configuration time of the individual FPGAs, but on how *all* the FPGAs are configured. Specifically, the FPGAs could be configured serially, in parallel, or a mixture of serial and parallel depending upon the design of the system. Thus, this time can vary from hundreds of nanoseconds to seconds. This directly impacts the types of applications that have improved performance on a particular configurable computing system. A configurable computing system that has a configuration time on the order of seconds is best suited for applications that do not

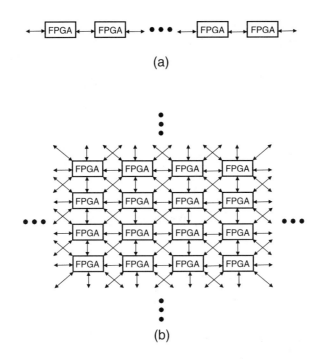

**FIGURE 37.8** Basic architectures for multiple FPGAs.

require reconfigurations "on-the-fly," i.e., applications with a single configuration associated with them or ones that are pipelined with slow pipeline stages. On the other hand, a configurable computing system that has a very short configuration time can be used for the same applications as one with a slower configuration time and applications that require "on-the-fly" reconfiguration.

As implied previously, the configurable component of a configurable computing system can be composed of a single FPGA or multiple FPGAs. Many architectures are used for a configurable component composed of multiple FPGAs. Figure 37.8 illustrates the basic architectures from which most of these architectures would be derived. Note that these architectures are very similar, or identical, to those used for parallel processing systems. As a matter of fact, many of the paradigms used in configurable computing systems are derived from parallel processing systems. In many cases, a configurable computing system is the hardware equivalent of a software parallel processing system. Figure 37.8(a) is a pipelined architecture with the FPGAs hardwired from one to the other. This type of architecture is well suited for functions that have streaming data at specific intervals. Note that variations of this architecture include pipelines with feedback, programmable interconnect between the FPGAs, and RAM associated with each FPGA. Figure 37.8(b) is an array of FPGAs hardwired to their nearest neighbors. This type of architecture is well suited for functions that require a systolic array. Note, as with the pipelined architecture, that variations of this architecture include arrays with feedback, programmable interconnect between the FPGAs, and RAM associated with each FPGA. Also note that an array of FPGAs is very similar to the internal structure of a single FPGA. Thus, one has a hierarchy of configurability.

## Configurable Computing System Architectures

The placement of one or more configurable components within a computing system is largely determined by the requirements of the application. Several architectures are shown in Fig. 37.9. In some cases as shown in Fig. 37.9(a), no additional computing power is required and the component can be utilized in a stand-alone mode. This situation occurs in Internet routing nodes and in some data acquisition systems as well as controllers for actuators. Note that the use of FPGAs to replace logic or to be used as state machines is this type of architecture. This type of application was the first widespread use of FPGAs.

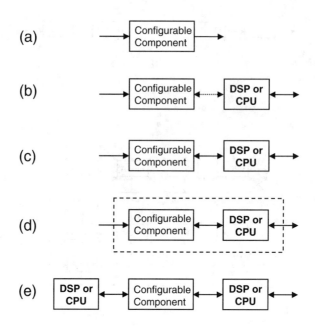

**FIGURE 37.9**   CPU/configurable computing architectures.

For configurable computing systems, configurable components are more commonly coupled with conventional DSPs or CPUs such that the processor can accomplish general purpose computing while acceleration of specialized functions can be performed by the configurable components. The type of general purpose computing required by the application determines the choice of a DSP or CPU. An application involving signal processing would naturally lead to the use of a DSP. Whereas, an application involving user interaction and/or user services (disks, etc.) would more likely lead to the use of a general purpose CPU. For this discussion on general configurable computing system architectures, the type of "general purpose" processor used is irrelevant; however, it is very relevant when an actual application and system are being developed.

Figures 37.9(b–e) depict architectures that have configurable components coupled with DSPs or CPUs. The communication requirements between the different types of processors determine the amount of bandwidth and latency provided. If infrequent communication is needed, a serial line or some other slow-speed connection may be sufficient as shown in Fig. 37.9(b). For higher bandwidth applications, placing the two types of components on a bus or some other high-speed connection as shown in Fig. 37.9(c) may be appropriate. In both of these cases, tasks best suited for a particular component can be delegated to that component and sharing of data and results are facilitated. Figure 37.9(d) depicts the tightest coupling with the lowest latency and highest bandwidth since both types of components are placed inside the same package. Often, the DSP or CPU manages the data, especially when disk storage is involved. When the data is being acquired at a high rate from a sensor, the configurable component is often used to perform initial operations to reduce the size of the data. Thus, the DSP or CPU has only a fraction of the data to be processed or stored. Note that the current trend to include RAM and a fixed microprocessor core on the same integrated circuit as the FPGA is an implementation of this architecture. Another variation of this theme of placing the configurable component within the system just where it is needed can be seen in a network of workstations as shown in Fig. 37.9(e). In this case, the configurable component can be inserted into the router itself to perform dedicated operations as the data is passed from processor node to processor node. The processing performed in this manner appears to be "free" because it occurs during message passing.

## Selected Applications

Several classes of applications have improved performance when implemented on configurable computing systems including image analysis, video compression, and molecular biology. In general, these applications exploit the parallel processing power of configurable computers.

### Image Analysis

Image analysis requires manipulating massive amounts of data in parallel and performing a variety of data interaction (e.g., point operations, neighborhood operations, and global operations). Many of these operations are ideally suited for implementation on a configurable computing system due to the parallel nature of the operations. Example implementations are image segmentation, convolution, automated target recognition (ATR ), and stereo vision. Image segmentation is often the first step in image analysis and consists of extracting important image features. For intensity images (i.e., those represented by point-wise intensity levels) four popular approaches are: threshold techniques, edge-based methods, region-based techniques, and connectivity-preserving relaxation methods. A systolic array of configurable components, similar to that depicted in Fig. 37.8(b), can be used to perform an edge-based image segmentation. Implementation results for various applications have shown that this approach is superior to the conventional digital signal processor approach.

Two-dimensional convolution is commonly used for filtering, edge detection, and feature extraction. The basic idea is that a window of some finite size and shape is scanned across the image. The output pixel value is the weighted sum of the input pixels within the window where the weights are the values of the filter assigned to every pixel of the window itself. Using a systolic array of configurable components, the convolution window can be applied in parallel with an output pixel value being produced as new pixel values are provided. The storage of intermediate pixel values within the window are inherent in the systolic array structure. Implementation results have shown impressive performance gains.

Automated target recognition (ATR) is a computationally demanding application in real-time image analysis problems. The objective of an ATR system is to analyze a digitally represented input scene to locate/identify all objects of interest automatically. Typically, algorithms begin with a preprocessing step to identify regions of interest in the input image. Next, template matching is performed to correlate these regions of interest with a very large number of target templates. The final identification step identifies the template and the relative offset at which peak correlation occurs. The template matching process is the most computationally intensive among these three steps and has the potential of being implemented in a parallel form. Therefore, the template matching is a good candidate to be mapped into a configurable computing system. Implementation results have shown significant performance improvements.

Stereo vision involves locating the same features in each of two images and then measuring the distances to objects containing these features by triangularization. Finding corresponding points or other kinds of features in two images, such that the matched points are the same projections of a point in the scene, is the fundamental computational task. Matching objects at each pixel in the image leads to a distance map. This is very similar to the template matching process in an ATR system and implementation results are similar.

### Image and Video Compression

Image and video compression are used in many current and emerging products. Image compression is widely used in desktop publishing, graphic arts, color facsimile, and medical imaging. Video compression is at the heart of digital television set-top boxes, DSS, HDTV decoders, DVD players, video conferencing, Internet video, and other applications. Compression reduces the requirements for storage of large archived pictures, less bandwidth for the transmission of the picture from one point to another, or a combination of both. Image and video processing typically require high data throughout and computational complexity. JPEG is widely used for compressing still pictures, and MPEG or wavelets are more appropriate for compressing videos or general moving pictures.

A configurable component using a pipelined approach, as depicted in Fig. 37.8(a), provides a much cheaper and more flexible hardware platform than special image compression ASICs, and it can efficiently accelerate desktop computers. A speed improvement over a modern workstation of a factor of ten or more can be obtained for JPEG image compression.

### Molecular Biology

Scanning a DNA database is a fundamental task in molecular biology. This operation consists of identifying those sequences in the DNA database that contain at least one segment sufficiently similar to some segment of a query sequence. The computational complexity of this operation is proportional to the product of the length of the query sequence and the total number of nucleic acids in the database. In general, segment pairs (one from a database sequence and one from query sequence) may be considered similar if many nucleotides within the segment match identically. This similarity search may take several hours on standard workstations when using common software that is parameterized for high sensitivity.

One method of performing DNA database searches is to use a dynamic programming algorithm for computing the edit distance between two genetic sequences. This algorithm can be implemented on a configurable computing system configured as two systolic arrays. Execution has been found to be several orders of magnitude faster than implementations of the same algorithm on a conventional computer. Another method is to use a systolic filter for speeding up the scan of DNA databases. The filter can be implemented on a configurable computing system, which acts as a coprocessor that performs the more intensive computations occurring during the process. An implementation of this system boosted the performances of the conventional workstation by a factor ranging from 50 to 400.

## Virtual Computing Power

Quantifying computing power is a challenging task due to differing computing architectures and applications. Vullemin et al. [13] define virtual computing power based on the number of programmable active bits (PABs) and the operating frequency. He defines a "reference" PAB as a 4-input Boolean function. These functions are essentially the core configurable elements of a configurable computing component; however, each vendor defines them differently. For example, Xilinx calls them "logic cells (LCs)" and organizes them into groups of four called "configurable logic blocks (CLBs)." Whereas, Altera calls them "logic elements (LEs)" and organizes them into groups of ten called "logic array blocks (LABs)." As newer and larger FPGAs with new architectures are constructed, the vendors will likely rename these logic blocks. But the configurable blocks can always be defined as Boolean functions.

Vullemin et al. define the virtual computing power of a configurable computing system with $n$ PABs operating at a frequency of $f$ Hz as the product $P = n \times f$ and is expressed in Boolean operations per second (BOPS). The frequency of operation for the PABs is taken to be the internal operating frequency of the component. Xilinx's largest component to date is the Virtex XCV2000E that has 43,200 LCs and a quoted "typical" internal operating frequency in excess of 100 MHz [3]. Based on this, the Virtex XCV2000E has a virtual computing power of 4.3+ TBOPS. Altera's largest available component is the APEX EP20K1500E, which has 54,720 LEs and a quoted "typical" internal operating frequency in excess of 100 MHz [1]. Based on this, the EP20K1500E has a virtual computing power of 5.4+ TBOPs. Note that both Xilinx and Altera quote a maximum internal operating frequency in excess of 200 MHz and have announced plans for even larger and faster components.

By comparison, an Intel Pentium III 32-bit microprocessor can execute two unrelated integer operations every clock cycle. When operating at 600 MHz, it has a virtual computing power of 38.4 GBOPs. Based on this analysis, a single, state-of-the-art configurable computing component has over 100 times the raw virtual computing power of a state-of-the-art microprocessor; however, taking full advantage of the virtual computing power of configurable computing systems is not trivial. The previous subsection listed a variety of application areas in which success has been achieved but the widespread use of these systems is presently hampered by the difficulty of programming them.

## Development Systems

Developing applications for microprocessor-based systems is currently far easier than developing applications for a configurable computing system. Microprocessor development systems have been optimized over years, even decades, while those for configurable computing systems are in their infancy. A design for a single FPGA is typically created using tools similar to those used for other digital systems, tools such as schematic capture, VHDL, etc. Due to the proprietary nature of FPGAs, however, a designer must typically use the design tools available from the FPGA vendor.

A software design environment that facilitates the rapid development of applications on configurable computing systems should permit high-level design entry, simulation, and verification by application designers who need not be familiar with the details of the hardware. Of course, on occasions, it may be necessary to expose to the application designer those hardware details deemed essential to ensure feasible and efficient implementations. Metrics and visualization are desirable to assist the application designer in achieving near-optimal system implementation rapidly. The tools available from the FPGA vendors are currently intended for digital systems designers not the application designer. Research efforts underway at various universities and startup companies are producing the first development systems for configurable computing systems similar to those for microprocessor systems.

## To Probe Further

More in-depth information on configurable computing systems is readily available. The first sources of information are the FPGA vendors. A few of these are

1. Altera Corporation, San Jose, CA. http://www.altera.com
2. Atmel Corporation, San Jose, CA. http://www.atmel.com
3. Xilinx, Inc., San Jose, CA. http://www.xilinx.com

Several sites on the World Wide Web are dedicated to configurable computing systems. A search using the terms "configurable computing systems" or "reconfigurable computing systems" via any of the search engines will yield a great number of hits. One of these sites is http://www.optimagic.com that provides not only information on configurable computing systems, but also information on programmable logic in general.

Currently, very few books focus specifically on configurable computing systems; however, many books about programmable logic provide excellent references for someone interested in configurable computing. Some of these are

4. *Digital Designing with Programmable Logic Devices,* John Carter, Prentice-Hall, Englewood Cliffs, NJ, 1996.
5. *Programmable Logic: PLDs and FPGAs,* Richard C. Seals and G.F. Whapshott, Macmillan, New York, 1997.
6. *FPGAs and Programmable LSI: A Designer's Handbook,* Geoff Bostock, Butterworth-Heinneman, 1996.
7. *Digital System Design Using Field Programmable Gate Arrays,* Pak K. Chan and Samiha Mourad, Prentice-Hall, Englewood Cliffs, NJ, 1994.

Many excellent conferences are held annually to provide the latest information on configurable computing systems from the FPGAs to development systems. Some of these conferences are

8. *Symposium on Field-Programmable Custom Computing Machines (FCCM).* http://www.fccm.org
9. *ACM/SIGDA International Symposium on Field-Programmable Gate Arrays (FPGA).*
10. *International Workshop on Field Programmable Logic and Applications (FPL).*
11. *Reconfigurable Architectures Workshop (RAW).*
12. *Design Automation Conference (DAC).* http://www.dac.com

The proceedings from these conferences contain many articles on not only configurable computing systems but applications for which configurable computing systems have been shown to be effective.

Other application areas that one may find configurable computing systems applied to are: cryptography, fingerprint matching, multimedia, and astronomy.

More in-depth information on virtual computing power and a list of applications of configurable computing system is

13. J. Vuillemin, P. Bertin, D. Roncin, M. Shand, H. Touati, and P. Boucard, Programmable active memories: reconfigurable systems come of age, *IEEE Trans. on VLSI Systems*, vol. 4, no. 1, pp. 56–69, March 1996.

More information on research and development into design tools for configurable computing may be obtained by visiting the web sites of the research groups involved. Some of these are

14. Brigham Young University, Configurable Computing Web page, http://splish.ee.byu.edu and the JHDL Web page, http://www.jhdl.org
15. University of Cincinnati, REACT Web page, http://www.ececs.uc.edu/~dal/acs/index.htm
16. Colorado State University, CAMERON Project Web page, http://cs.colostate.edu/cameron
17. Northwestern University, A Matlab Compilation Environment for Adaptive Computing Systems Web page, http://www.ece.nwu.edu/cpdc/Match/Match.html
18. University of Southern California, DEFACTO Web page, http://www.isi.edu/asd/defacto
19. University of Tennessee, CHAMPION Web page, http://microsys6.engr.utk.edu/~bouldin/darpa

# 37.3   Xtensa: A Configurable and Extensible Processor

*Ricardo E. Gonzalez and Albert Wang*

### Introduction

Until a few years ago, processors were only sold as packaged individual ICs. However, the growing density of CMOS circuits created an opportunity for incorporating the processor as part of a larger system on a chip. Initial processor designs for this market were based on the processor existing as a separate entity, and cores were handcrafted for each manufacturing process technology, resulting in costly and fixed solutions. Furthermore, it was not possible to modify these cores for the particular application, in much the same way that it was not possible to modify a stand-alone prepackaged processor.

Xtensa is a processor core designed with ease of integration, customization, and extension in mind. Unlike previous processors, Xtensa lets the system designer select and size only the features required for a given application. The configuration and generation process is straightforward and lets the designer define new system-specific instructions if preexisting features don't provide the required functionality. Furthermore, Xtensa fits easily into the standard ASIC design flow. Xtensa is fully synthesizeable, and designers can use the most popular physical-design tools during the place-and-route process.

### Processor Development

Application-specific processor development is an active area of research in the CAD, computer architecture, and VLSI design communities. Early attempts to add application-specific instructions to general-purpose computer engines relied on writable micro-code [1,2]. These techniques dynamically augmented the base instruction set with application-specific instructions.

More recent research focuses on automatic instruction set design [3,4] or on reconfigurable, also called retargetable, processors [5]. These groups, however, try to solve slightly different problems than those addressed by Xtensa. Automatic instruction set design systematically analyzes a benchmark program to derive an entirely new instruction set for a given microarchitecture. Our group—here referred to as "we"—focuses on how to generate a high-performance and low-power implementation of a given microarchitecture with application-specific extensions. In this respect, automatic instruction set design is a good complement to our work. Once the instruction set additions are derived automatically by analyzing the benchmark program, they can be given to the Xtensa processor generator to obtain a high-performance, low-power implementation. Reconfigurable or retargetable processors couple a general-purpose computer engine with various amounts of hardware-programmable logic. In the extreme, the entire processor is implemented using hardware-programmable logic. The technique, however, is limited by the large difference in operating frequency between programmable and nonprogrammable logic. Processors implemented entirely using programmable logic operate an order of magnitude slower than nonconfigurable processors implemented in a comparable process technology. Razdan and Smith present an interesting compromise [5]. Their approach couples a custom-designed high-performance processor with small amounts of hardware-programmable logic. Their system uses compiler-generated information to dynamically reconfigure a small amount of hardware-programmable logic to implement new application-specific functional units. This technique also has limitations due to the disparity in operating frequency of programmable and nonprogrammable logic. Thus, the new functional units must be extremely simple or be deeply pipelined.

The authors' approach is similar to that taken by Razdan and Smith except that we don't attempt to dynamically reconfigure the system. The Tensilica processor generator adds the application-specific functionality at the time the hardware is designed. Thus, the extensions are implemented in the same logic family as the rest of the processor. This eliminates the disadvantages of using programmable logic for implementing the extensions, but precludes modification of the extensions for different applications.

Due to a lack of automated tools, designers incorporated application-specific functionality in CPUs by adding specialized coprocessors [6,7]. This approach introduces communication overhead between the CPU and the coprocessor, making system design more arduous. Recently, with the advent of synthesizeable processors, some groups have proposed manual modification of the register-transfer level (RTL) description of the processor and the software development tools [8]. This approach is tedious and error prone. Furthermore, the extensions are only applicable to one implementation. If users want to add similar extensions to a future implementation of the same processor, they must modify the RTL again.

The authors' research differs from previous studies because we use a high-level language to express processor extension. This language, called Tensilica Instruction Extension (TIE), expresses the semantics and encoding of instructions. TIE can add new functionality to the RTL description and automatically extend the software tools. This lets the system developer code applications in a high-level language, such as C or C++. TIE imposes restrictions on functions that designers can describe, which greatly simplify verification of the processor and extensions. Because the extensions become an integral part of the processor, there is no communication overhead.

## Overview of Xtensa

We designed the Xtena instruction set architecture (ISA) to allow ease of extension and configuration. Furthermore, the ISA minimizes code size, reduces power dissipation, and maximizes performance.

The Xtensa ISA consists of a base set of instructions, which exist in all Xtensa implementations, plus a set of configurable options. The designer can choose, for example, to include a 16-bit multiply-accumulate option if it is beneficial to the application. The base ISA defines approximately 80 instructions and is a superset of traditional 32-bit RISC instruction sets [10]. The architecture achieves smaller code size through the use of denser encoding and register windows. The ISA defines 24- and 16-bit instruction formats, as opposed to 32-bit formats found in traditional RISC instruction sets. The Xtensa architecture provides a rich set of operations despite the smaller instruction size. These sophisticated instructions, such as single-cycle compare and branch, enable higher code density and improve performance.

The size of Xtensa instructions is encoded in the instruction, enabling 24- and 16-bit instructions to freely intermix at a fine granularity. The 16-bit instructions are a subset of the 24-bit instructions. Thus, the compiler optimization to reduce code size is trivial: replacing 24-bit instructions with their 16-bit equivalent. The compiler can reduce code size without sacrificing performance.

### Hardware Implementation

We built the first implementation of Xtensa around a traditional RISC five-stage pipeline, with a 32-bit address space. Many other characteristics of the processor implementation, however, are configurable. The configurability and extensibility of the implementation matches those of the architecture. Figure 37.10

**TABLE 37.1**    Xtensa Configuration Parameters

| Parameter | Legal Values |
|---|---|
| Instruction/data cache size | 1–256 KB |
| Instruction/data cache associativity | Direct-mapped, 2-way, 4-way |
| Instruction/data RAM size | 1 KB, 2 KB, 4 KB, 8 KB, 16 KB |
| Instruction/data ROM size | 1 KB, 2 KB, 4 KB, 8 KB, 16 KB |
| Size of windowed register file | 32, 64 |
| Number of interrupts | 0–32 |
| Interrupt levels | 0–3 |
| Timers | 0–3 |
| Memory order | Big-endian, little-endian |

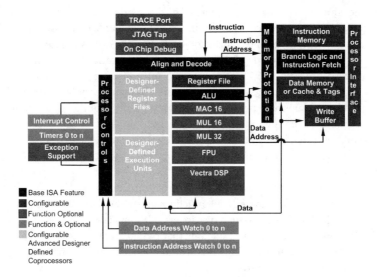

**FIGURE 37.10**    Block diagram of Xtensa.

shows a high-level block diagram of Xtensa. The base ISA features correspond to roughly 80 instructions. The designer can size or select configurable options, for example, how many physical registers to include in the implementation, or the size of the instruction and data caches. Optional features, shown as medium-gray in the figure, are selections the designer can make, such as whether to include a 16-bit multiply-accumulate functional unit. Optional and configurable functions let the designer select whether to include that feature and also to size it. For example, whether to include data watch-point registers and, if so, how many. Xtensa optionally supports several data formats such as fixed-point and floating-point. Vectra adds a configurable fixed-point vector coprocessor.

Table 37.1 shows a few of the configuration parameters and associated legal values available in the current Xtensa implementation. Unlike conventional processors, Xtensa gives designers a choice regarding the functionality of the processor.

## Configuration

The configuration process begins by accessing the Tensilica processor generator Web page at http://www.tensilica.com. Here, using a standard browser, the designer can select and size the desired features. The site's configuration page gives the designer instant feedback on whether a particular choice will affect the speed, power, or area of the core. The user interface warns the designer of conflicting options or requirements for a particular option.

The designer starts the generation process at the push of a button. The generation process produces the processor's configured RTL description and its configured software development tools. The software tools consist of an ANSI C/C++ compiler, linker, assembler, debugger, code profiler, and instruction set simulator.

The generation process takes approximately one hour to complete. After the process is complete, the designer can download and install the RTL and software development tools. At this point, the designer can either compile an application and measure the performance using the instruction set simulator, or start the hardware synthesis using the RTL description.

The software tools are built on top of the industry-standard GNU tools and include an optimizing C compiler enabling application development in a high-level language. The instruction set simulator and code profiler help the designer quickly identify bottlenecks in application performance. Optionally, the designer can recode the application to work around these bottlenecks or add new instructions to the processor designed to optimize this particular application.

The designer can map the RTL description to a gate-level netlist using industry-standard synthesis tools. Included with the RTL description are a set of synthesis scripts that help automate this process. These scripts let designers quickly obtain a fully optimized gate-level netlist of Xtensa. Tensilica also provides a set of scripts to automate the place-and-route process. It is common for new users to place and route Xtensa within a day or two of downloading the configured RTL.

## Instruction Set Extension

Hardware designers realized the advantages of extending a general-purpose processor with application specific functional units long time ago [6,7]. Until now, however, the only way to do this was to add the functional units as a coprocessor. This often meant there was some communication overhead between the processor and the application-specific logic. Also, often the coprocessor would require sophisticated control, which had to be implemented with finite state machines or with micro-sequencers.

The Tensilica processor generator provides a more flexible and powerful approach to processor extension. Using TIE the system designer can describe, at a high-level, the functionality of the new functional units. The TIE compiler will then automatically generate an efficient pipelined implementation. The system designer must specify only the functionality of the new hardware and the required (and architecturally visible) storage elements—register files and special-purpose state elements. The pipeline flip-flops and the bypass and interlock detection logic are then automatically generated by the TIE compiler. Furthermore, the TIE compiler (TC) will automatically extend the software tools so that the new hardware is accessible from C/C++.

Using TIE has many advantages over more traditional methods of extension. First, the sophisticated control can now be accomplished using software—making it easier to debug and optimize. Second, the system designer can quickly prototype different design alternatives enabling him (or her) to quickly converge to a good solution to the problem. Third, verification of the new hardware's functionality can be done using the instruction set simulator (ISS), which can simulate hundreds of thousands of instruction per second, rather than on the RTL model, which can only simulate hundreds of cycles per second.

Similar to most previous machine description languages [14], TIE is an instruction set architecture (ISA) description language. It relies on a tool, the TIE compiler, to generate an efficient hardware implementation and required additions to the software tools, including the compiler, ISS, and debugger. TIE is not intended to be a complete processor description language. Instead, the TIE language provides designers simple ways to describe a broad variety of computational instructions, yet allows the TIE compiler to generate efficient hardware. The language is simple enough for a wide range of designers to master, yet general enough to allow description of sophisticated ISAs. The rest of this section describes the capabilities of the TIE language.

TIE lets the designer specify the mnemonic, encoding, and semantics of new instructions. The designer uses a combination of `field`, `opcode`, `operand`, and `iclass` statements to describe the format and encoding of an instruction. The `field` statement gives a name to a group of bits in the instruction word.

The **opcode** statement assigns instruction fields with values. The **operand** statement specifies how an instruction's operand is encoded in an instruction field. The **iclass** statement describes the assembly format for an instruction and lists the input and output operands of the instruction. A large set of predefined instruction fields and operands (used to describe the base Xtensa ISA) can be used directly in the TIE description. The following example describes two instructions: A4 and S4. These instructions take two 32-bit operands from the core register file, perform four 8-bit additions and subtractions and store the result back to the core register file:

```
opcode    A4      op2 = 0 CUST0

opcode    S4      op2 = 1 CUST0

iclass    RR      {A4, S4} {out arr, in ars, in art}
```

The first two lines define the opcodes for **A4** and **S4** as sub-opcodes of a previously defined opcode CUST0 with the addition of field op2 equal to 0 and 1, respectively. The third line makes use of the predefined register operands **arr**, **ars**, and **art**, and defines two new assembly instructions,

```
A4 arr, ars, art

S4 arr, ars, art
```

### Customized Datapath

The computational part of an instruction is specified in a TIE **reference** block. The syntax of a **reference** block is very similar to the Verilog hardware description language. The variables used in the **reference** block are predefined (if they appear in the **iclass** statement), or locally declared variables. The **reference** block for the A4 and S4 instructions defined in the previous section are shown below,

```
reference A4 {

    assign arr = {

    ars[31:24] + art[31:24],

    ars[32:16] + art[23:16],

    ars[15:8] + art[15:8],

    ars[7:0] + art[7:0]};

}

reference S4 {

    assign arr = {

    ars[31:24] - art[31:24],

    ars[32:16] - art[23:16],

    ars[15:8] - art[15:8],

    ars[7:0] - art[7:0]};

}
```

The reference description for the two instructions is simple and direct, yet may not result in the best hardware implementation. For example, the logic for addition and subtraction could be shared between the two instructions. TIE allows the designer to describe this high-level hardware sharing between multiple instructions using the **semantic** block. The **semantic** block is similar to a **reference** block but allows multiple instructions to be described at the same time. The semantics of A4 and S4, for example, can be described as follows:

```
{semantic add sub {A4, S4}}
    assign arr = {
    ars[31:24] + (S4 ? ~art[31:24] : art[31:24]) + S4,
    ars[32:16] + (S4 ? ~art[23:16] : art[23:16]) + S4,
    ars[15:8] + (S4 ? ~art[15:8] : art[15:8]) + S4,
    ars[7:0] + (S4 ? ~art[7:0] : art[7:0]) + S4};
}
```

The **semantic** statements allow more efficient hardware implementation, while the **reference** statements are easier to write, are better suited for inclusion in documentation and are a better source for simulation code. Thus, TIE allows instructions to have either a **reference** block, a **semantic** block, or both. Most often, designers will write the reference description first. Once they have verified the correctness and usefulness of the instruction they write the semantics to optimize the hardware implementation. TIE allows formal equivalence checking between the semantic and reference description to ensure the implementation is identical.

## Multi-Cycle Instructions

To keep up with the speed of Xtensa, which is pipelined and runs at a high clock rate, instructions with complex computation may require multiple cycles to complete. Writing and verifying multi-cycle instructions is a challenging task for designer unfamiliar with the processor's pipeline, especially if the designer must add the appropriate data-forwarding and interlock detection logic. TIE provides a **schedule** statement that alleviates this problem. The schedule statement captures the timing requirements of the instruction. The designer can then rely on the TIE compiler to derive the implementation automatically. For example, a multiply-accumulate (MAC) instruction that performs the following operation: **acc = acc + (a\*b)** typically requires at least two cycles in a pipelined processor. In order to achieve one MAC per cycle throughput, the hardware must use (read) the **a** and **b** operands at the beginning of the first cycle, use **acc** at the beginning of the second cycle, and produce a new **acc** at the end of the second cycle. The timing of the instruction can be described in TIE as

```
schedule MAC_SCHEDULE {MAC} {
    use a = 1;
    use b = 1;
    use acc = 2;
    def acc = 2;
}
```

The rest of the implementation, including the efficient insertion of pipeline registers, interlock detection, result bypassing, and generation of good code schedules are all handled automatically by the TIE compiler.

## Register Files and State Registers

When adding new application-specific datapaths it is often necessary to add new storage elements. Two main reasons exist for adding new storage elements. First, algorithms often require specific bit widths, which may not be efficiently supported by the core register file. And second, some algorithms require higher bandwidth than the core register file provides. In the MAC instruction described in the previous subsection, for example, the machine would require a new state register to hold the value of the accumulator. Otherwise it would require an additional read port in the core register file (the accumulator value would be held in a register). Furthermore, the algorithm may require an accumulator value with more precision.

TIE states are extensions to the software visible programming model. They allow instructions to have more sources and destinations than provided by the read and write ports of the core register file. They can also be used as dedicated registers holding temporary values during program execution. When an application needs a large number of such sharable TIE states, it becomes more efficient to group the state into a register file and rely on the C compiler to assign the variables to register entries.

Describing instructions that use TIE states is simple. The designer must specify, in the `iclass` of the instruction, how the state is used. The state variable is then available in the instruction's `reference` and `semantic` blocks. The following example is a complete description of the MAC instruction,

```
state         acc 40       /* a 40-bit accumulator */

opode         MAC op2=0 CUST0

iclass        MAC_CLASS {MAC} {in ars, in art} {inout acc}

reference {

    assign acc = (ars * art) + acc;

}
```

Using a register file involves one more step: describing the register operands. The following TIE code, for example, adds a 24-bit register file:

```
regfile       GR 24 16                    /* 26 entries, 24-bits each*/

operand       gr r {GR[r]}

operand       gs s {GR[s]}

operand       gt t {GR[t]}
```

The three register operands use predefined instruction fields (`r, s, t`) as indices to access the register file contents. An instruction that uses these operands can be describes as,

```
iclass    RF {AVE} {out gr, in gs, in gt}
```

Using TIE it is possible to very quickly develop sophisticated hardware that can significantly enhance the application performance of the processor. Furthermore, the new hardware is easily accessible to the C/C++ programmer.

### Software Support

One key advantage of TIE is that it allows hardware and software to be extended together. This allows the programmer to access the new hardware from C or C++. This allows the programmer to focus on algorithmic optimization, rather than mapping the algorithm to a fixed processor architecture. Programmers often spend more time designing how to map the algorithm's data-types to the processor data-types than they do on optimizing the algorithm for their application. Using TIE it is possible to extend the hardware and software together so the mapping of the algorithm's data-types is more natural.

In order for this extension to be useful to the programmer, however, it must be complete. The compiler, assembler, simulator, debugger, real-time operating system, and application libraries must be extended to use the new hardware datapaths. The TIE compiler generates dynamically loadable libraries (DLLs) that are used to configure the software tools at runtime. Generation of the DLLs takes less than a minute (even for large TIE descriptions). This allows designers to quickly make changes to the TIE description and evaluate the performance of the system. TIE allows designers (or programmers) to define new C data-types that are mapped to TIE register files. The programmer must also specify, in the TIE description, instruction sequences to load and store these data-types from (to) memory. The programmer can then use these new data-types in C/C++ as if they were built-in data-types. Operations are described via instrinsics (every TIE instruction is available as an intrinsic in C/C++) but register allocation, variable saves and restores, addressing arithmetic, and control flow generation for the new data-types are handled automatically by the C compiler. The C compiler is also aware of any side-effects and pipelining of TIE instructions so it can efficiently schedule the instructions.

The TIE compiler also generates libraries to save and restore processor state on a context switch. The compiler uses the instruction sequences described by the programmer to load and store the new data-types. The libraries are used by commercial operating systems, such a WindRiver's VxWorks™. The operating system is delivered as a pre-built binary with hooks to call the context switch code generated by the TIE compiler.

The TIE compiler must also add knowledge of the new instructions and register files to the instruction set simulator and the debugger. The TIE compiler translates the reference block of each instruction to a C implementation that can be used by the simulator to model the execution of the instruction. The TIE compiler also extends the debugger to allow visualization of new register files and state registers.

## Application Examples

### DES

To demonstrate the potential of TIE, we extended Xtensa to improve the performance of the Data Encryption Standard (DES)—a popular encryption and decryption algorithm often used for secure Internet communication. We chose DES for two reasons: its growing popularity in embedded applications that require secure Internet transactions, and the relatively poor encryption and decryption performance of general-purpose processors.

A simple DES modification, known as Triple-DES, extends the key to 168 bits by iterating the DES algorithm three times with three different keys. Triple-DES has been specified as an encryption algorithm for both the secure shell tools[11] and the Internet protocol for security[12]. Both of these applications require high-speed encryption and decryption and are implemented as part of many of today's interesting embedded systems.

The DES algorithm requires extensive bit permutations, which are difficult to implement efficiently in software. However, designers can efficiently implement these permutations in hardware, since each corresponds to a simple renaming of the wires. The algorithm also specifies rotation on 28-bit boundaries. Even if the processor has a rotate instruction, it often is not usable since it most likely rotates on 32-bit boundaries. Finally, the algorithm requires bit packing, unpacking, and table lookups. These operations are slow in software but easy to implement with hardware. We modified the Xtensa processor to include special instructions to speed up these operations.

Based on run-time profile information, we defined four new instructions and reimplemented the application to use these instructions. We verified the implementation of the TIE instructions by comparing the output of the modified application, which uses the TIE-generated C description of the instructions, with the results of a reference implementation of DES written completely in C. In addition to four new instructions, we also added three new state registers to the processor. The registers hold intermediate values during the encryption and decryption process. Of the four new instructions, one performs the encryption and decryption step using values in the state registers. The other three instructions transfer data to (and from) the processor registers from (and to) the state registers, while concurrently permuting the data values. When compiled for the Xtensa architecture, the new application required only 154 bytes of object code and no static or dynamic data storage. Thus, the original implementation required 36 times more memory than this implementation.

Figure 37.11 shows the speedup of the DES-enhanced Xtensa core compared to an unmodified Xtensa core. The *X*-axis shows the block size used for encryption and decryption. The original DES implementation gains much of its speed by precomputing large tables of values from a fixed key, making key changes

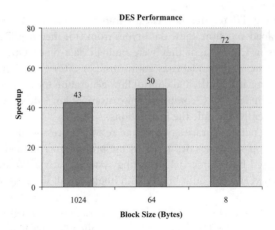

**FIGURE 37.11**   DES speedup using TIE.

very expensive. Thus, small blocks can attain speedup by a greater factor than large blocks (where key changes are less frequent). The modified Xtensa can encrypt and decrypt data at the rate of 377 MB/s. The hardware cost of the TIE instructions is roughly0 4,500 equivalent (NAND2) gates (measured in a 0.25-$\mu$m process technology). The reduced storage requirements of the application offset this hardware cost. In addition, the new TIE instructions did not increase the cycle time of the machine. DES is only one of the applications that can benefit from specialized hardware.

### Consumer Multimedia

The EEMBC consumer benchmarks contain a representative sample of multimedia applications of interest today. A baseline configuration of Xtensa contains many features suitable for these applications. At 200 MHz operation Xtensa delivers more than 11 times the performance of the reference processor (ST Microelectronics ST20C2™ at 50 MHz). Performance is measured as the geometric mean of the relative number of iterations per second for each algorithm compared to the reference processor; however, when we added instructions for image filtering and color-space conversion (RGB to YIQ and RGB to CYMB) the average performance increased by 17X (193 times faster then the reference). An AMD K6-III+ at 550 MHz, for comparison, is 34.2 times faster then the reference processor. The base configuration was optimized for 200 MHz operation in a 0.18-$\mu$m technology. The processr was configured with 16 KB two-way set associative caches, 256 KB local data RAM, 16-entry store buffer, and 32-bit multiplier. The total area of the processor was 57,600 NAND2-equivalent gates. The optimized TIE code cost an additional 64,100 NAND2-equivalent gates.

### DSP Telecommunications

The EEMBC "Telemark" benchmark suite includes many kernels representative of DSP applications. The performance of a base Xtensa processor in this suite is comparable to that of other 32-bit microprocessors (2.3 times faster than the reference). Performance was also measured as the geometric mean of the relative number of iterations per second for each algorithm compared to the reference processor (IDT 32334™ – MIPS32™ architecture at 100 MHz). Adding a fixed-point vector co-processor and a few more specialized instructions, the performance of Xtensa increases by 37X, or a speedup of 85.7X compared to the reference processor. The AMD K6-III+ at 550 MHz has a speedup of 8.7 compared to the reference, while a TI DSP (TMS320C6203) running hand-optimized code at 300 MHz has a 68.5 speedup compared to the reference processor. The base Xtensa configuration was also optimized for 200 MHz operation in 0.18-$\mu$m technology with 16 KB two-way set associative caches, and 16-entry write buffer. The vector co-processor and new TIE instructions add 180,000 thousand NAND2-equivalent gates.

## Conclusions

Configurable and extensible processors provide significant advantages compared to traditional hard-wired processors. To take full advantage of extensibility, however, requires a methodology that can extend both the hardware and the software together. We showed that TIE provides a methodology for extension that is complete, fast, and robust.

Using TIE can also help reduce design time by simplifing the hardware verification effort and also by allowing a more natural maping of the algorithm to the hardware implementation.

Furthermore, since the control flow is described in software it is much easier to verify and to enhance. We also showed the extension can significantly increase application performance. We showed that for two different set of application kernels an Xtensa procesor with application-specific extension was 20–40 times faster than a high-performance RISC processor.

## Acknowledgments

The authors thank the entire engineering staff at Tensilica. This article reflects their hard work and dedication. The authors are also grateful to Rick Rudell for the development of the DES TIE code and to Michael Carchia who did the EEMBC benchmarking.

## References

1. A. Abd-alla and D. Kartlgaard. Heuristic synthesis of microprogrammed computer architectures. *IEEE Transactions on Computers,* 23(8): 802–807, Aug. 1974.
2. P. Liu and F. Mowle. Techniques of program execution with a writable control memory. *IEEE Transactions on Computers,* 27(9): 816–827, Sept. 1978.
3. F. Haney. *Using a Computer to Design Computer Instruction Sets.* PhD thesis, Carnegie-Mellon University, Pittsburgh, PA, 1968.
4. B. Holmer. *Automatic Design of Computer Instruction Sets.* PhD thesis, University of California, Berkeley, CA, 1993.
5. R. Razdan and M. D. Smith. A high-performance microarchitecture with hardware-programmable functional units. In *Proc. of Micro-27,* Nov. 1994.
6. O. Nishii, F. Arakawa, K. Ishibashi, et al. A 200 MHz 1.2 W 1.4GFLOPS microprocessor with graphics unit. In *IEEE International Solid-State Circuits Conference,* vol. 41, pp. 288–289, IEEE, Feb. 1998.
7. S. Santhanam, A. Baum, D. Bertucci, et al. A low-cost 300 MHz RISC CPU with attached media processor. In *IEEE International Solid-State Circuits Conference,* vol. 41, pp. 298–299, IEEE, Feb. 1998.
8. http://www.arccores.com
9. S. Hesley, V. Andrade, R. Burd, et al. A 7th-generation x86 microprocessor. In *IEEE International Solid-State Circuits Conference,* vol. 42, pp. 182–183, IEEE, Feb. 1999.
10. J. L. Hennessy and D. A. Patterson. *Computer Architecture A Quantitative Approach.* First edition, Morgan Kaufmann Publishers, San Mateo, CA, 1990.
11. T. Ylonen, T. Kivinen, M Saarinen, et al. SSH protocol architecture. Internet-Draft, August 1998. *draft-ietf-secsh-architecture-02.txt.*
12. S. Kent, R. Atkinson, "Security architecture for the Internet protocol," RFC 2401, Nov. 1998.
13. G. Hadjiyiannis, S. Hanono, S. Devadas. IDSL: An instruction set description language for retargetability. In *Design Automation Conference,* 1997.
14. V. Zivojnovic, et al. LISA-machine description language and generic machine model for HW/SW co-design. In *IEEE Workshop on VLSI Signal Processing,* 1997.

# 38

# Roles of Software Technology in Intelligent Transportation Systems

Shoichi Washino
*Tottori University*

## 38.1   Background of Intelligent Transportation Systems

Today, one encounters a lot of traffic congestion and hears of people injured or killed by traffic accidents. Moreover, there has been no remarkable improvement in air pollution due to exhaust gases from vehicles inspite of the stringent regulation for vehicles. It is natural that frequent traffic congestion results in lower mean vehicle speed. Figure 38.1 shows an example of mean averaged vehicle speed in Japan. Vehicle speed in urban area like Tokyo and Osaka is very close to that of a bicycle. On the contrary, vehicle speed in countryside is faster than urban area. Therefore, average vehicle speed of the whole of Japan shows a little bit higher value, as shown in Fig. 38.1.

Traffic accidents are a more serious matter than vehicle speed. Figure 38.2 shows an example of the number of people killed due to traffic accidents in Japan. About ten thousand persons are still killed by traffic accidents. Moreover, the death rate of senior people has become higher in Japan.

A third example of traffic problems—the status of air pollution in Japan—is shown in Fig. 38.3. Both hydrocarbon (HC) and carbon monoxide (CO) have decreased gradually. On the contrary, nitric oxide (NOx) has not decreased. It has remained nearly constant in spite of the stringent Japanese exhaust gas regulation. These three examples are related to Japan. But the traffic situation of all countries is very much similar.

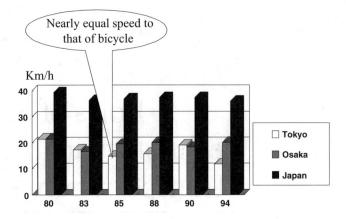

**FIGURE 38.1** Average vehicle speed.

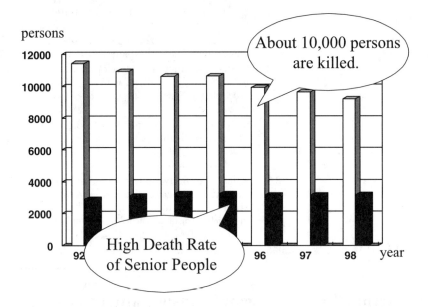

**FIGURE 38.2** Numbers of persons killed by traffic accidents.

In principle, these phenomena are eliminated by constructing new roads because it gives smoother traffic flow. The cost to construct them, however, has become very expensive in every country. So such a conventional way to solve these traffic problems is not available. On the other hand, information technology has progressed remarkably these days. As a result of this, many government officers have embraced an idea to solve these traffic problems by using information technology. Indeed the idea has led to a system image called Intelligent Transportation Systems (ITS), as shown in Fig. 38.4.

## 38.2 An Overview of Japanese ITS and the Nine Developing Fields of Japanese ITS

It was in 1995 that the second ITS World Congress was held at Yokohama. In Japan, several projects on ITS had been carried before 1995. Table 38.1 shows those projects. The first project was called comprehensive automobile traffic control system (CACS) proposed and lead by Ministry of Construction of the Japanese government at that time. Then the Ministry of Transport, Ministry of Post and Telecommunication,

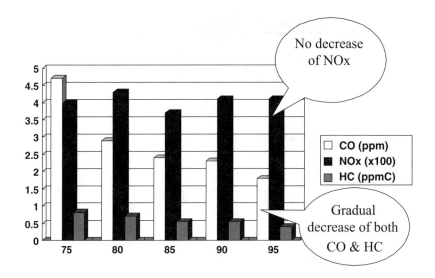

**FIGURE 38.3**  Air pollution.

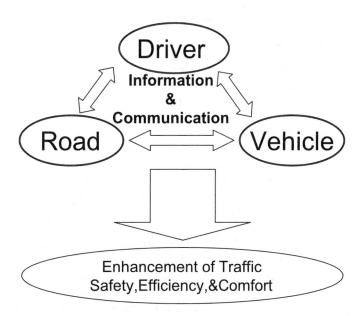

**FIGURE 38.4**  Concept of ITS.

Ministry of International Trade and Industry, National Police Agency, and Ministry of Construction proposed several projects on ITS and they had also promoted these projects. These are the major six projects to develop ITS in Japan, as shown in Table 38.1.

VICS means vehicle information & communication system. This mainly provides traffic information such as congestion, road construction, road restriction, traffic accidents, and parking information. VICS supposes an in-vehicle navigation system is loaded in a vehicle; this is already widespread in Japan as shown later.

ETC means electronic toll collection system. One often sees congestion in front of a tollgate due to "stop" and "go" at the tollgate. The aim of this project is to reduce such congestion using communication technologies between vehicle and road infrastructure.

**TABLE 38.1**    ITS Projects in Japan

- VICS (MOC, NPA, MPT)
  Vehicle Information & Communication System
- ETC (MOC, MPT)
  Electronic Toll collection System
- AHS (MOC)
  Advanced cruise-assist Highway System
- ASV (MOT)
  Advanced Safety Vehicle
- SSVS (MITI)
  Super Smart Vehicle System
- UTMS (NPA)
  Universal Traffic Management System

**TABLE 38.2**    Nine Developing Fields of Japanese ITS

1. Advances in navigation systems (ANS)
2. Electronic toll collection systems (ETC)
3. Assistance for safe driving (ASD)
4. Optimization of traffic management (OTM)
5. Increasing efficiency of road management (IERM)
6. Support for public transport (SPT)
7. Increasing efficiency in commercial vehicle operation (IECVO)
8. Support for pedestrians (SFP)
9. Support for emergency vehicle operation (SEVO)

AHS means advanced cruise-assist highway system originally from automated highway system. This system supposes advanced safety vehicle to enhance traffic safety and reduce accidents. This system is a kind of driving support system with collaborating road infrastructure and vehicle.

ASV is advanced safety vehicle to enhance traffic safety and reduce accidents. It has originally aimed to do so without any aid of road infrastructure. But now both ASV and AHS projects are collaborating because the collaboration is more effective from the point of view of both system performance and its cost.

SSVS means super smart vehicle system. Now, its main activity is related to the development of inter-vehicle communication technologies.

UTMS is an abbreviation of universal traffic management system. This project has an aim to develop ITS using two-way communication between road and vehicle, particularly using infrared light communication.

In 1995, the Japanese government set nine development fields to promote Japanese ITS. Both Fig. 38.5 and Table 38.2 show the nine development fields. In Fig. 38.5, those fields are expressed dividing the two categories of road infrastructure side and vehicle side.

Vehicle side includes only two fields. One is advances in navigation system (ANS) and the other is assistance for safe driving (ASD). For example, VICS is included in the field of ANS. Five of the nine fields belong to infrastructure side. For example, road maintenance by special cars like removal of snow on roads using snow shoveling car is in these five fields.

ETC and SFP, which means support for pedestrians, locate between infrastructure and vehicle because these systems are very effective only when both infrastructure and vehicle are collaborating.

## 38.3   Status of Japanese ITS Development

It is apparent that setting these developing fields shown in the above accelerates ITS development. As a result of this VICS has started its service to provide vehicles with real-time traffic information such as congestion, road construction, and accidents since 1996. Though this system assumes that in-vehicle navigation systems are loaded in a vehicle, VICS is the first system to be put into practical use all over the world. In 2001 ETC is also to be started at the several tollgates of highways in Tokyo and Osaka area.

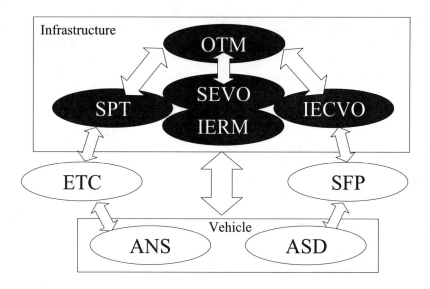

**FIGURE 38.5** Nine fields of Japanese ITS.

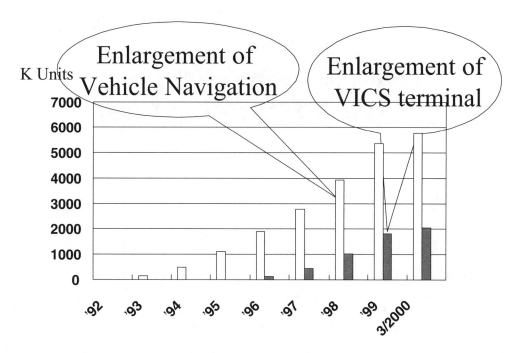

**FIGURE 38.6** Accumulated numbers of units.

As one can easily see, VICS is not likely to reduce traffic congestion and accidents in a direct way. But according to some statistics it is said that VICS also provides people with a kind of comfort when they drive. So VICS is very useful to reduce traffic problems.

At the time the VICS service started, Tokyo, Aichi, and Kansai were the only three available areas to receive the information provided by VICS service. But now the service areas have spread to almost all over Japan. Figure 38.6 shows how rapidly both in-vehicle navigation system and VICS terminals grow in Japan. White bars in Fig. 38.6 show the accumulated number of in-vehicle navigation units in Japan. At the end of the last year, the number reached to about 6 million units. Getting along the growth of in-vehicle

**TABLE 38.3**    Private Services of Information Provision

| Name | Information Provided & Function | Media | Start | Application Fee | Annual Fee |
|---|---|---|---|---|---|
| Intelligent traffic guidance system | 1. Optimum route to destination, travelling time<br>2. News, weather forecast<br>3. Leasure information | Cellular | April '97 | ¥5,000 | ¥36,000 |
| Moneh | 1. Conjesion, construction, traffic control<br>2. Parking, gas station, restaurant guide<br>3. News, weather forecast | Cellular | April '98 | ¥2,500 | ¥6,000 |
| Inter-navi system | 1. Setting of destination & course<br>2. Connecting to internet<br>3. Parking, gas station, restaurant guide | Cellular | July '98 | ¥2,500<br>Free 99/6 | ¥6,000<br>Free 99/6 |
| Compass link | 1. Parking, gas station, restaurant guide<br>2. News, weather forecast<br>3. Response by operators | Cellular | Sept. '98 | ¥3,500 | ¥30,000 |
| Mobile link | 1. Hotel, restrant, movies, news, TV guide | Cellular | Nov. '97 | Free | Free |

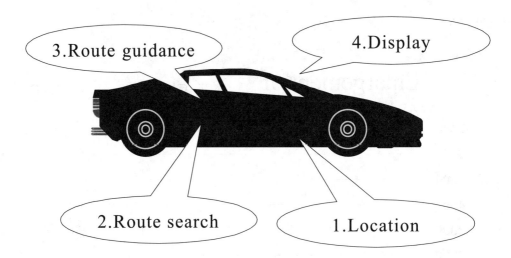

**FIGURE 38.7**    Major four functions of car navigation.

navigation systems VICS terminals also have grown very rapidly, as shown by the grey bars in Fig. 38.6 since 1996.

Besides VICS, five private companies shown in Table 38.3, Benz, Toyota, Nissan, Honda, and Sony, are also providing traffic information and other information such as parking area, weather forecast, sightseeing spots, and so on. Using the Internet, as Sony is doing, means no charge or fee to get information, except the media fee, to receive traffic information. In my opinion, it will be interesting to see which of the companies survive—the automakers or Sony.

## In-Vehicle Navigation System and VICS

First of all, the Japanese in-vehicle navigation system will be explained more minutely. Figure 38.7 shows the four main functions an in-vehicle navigation system can provide.

The first function is positioning of present vehicle location. Normally, global positioning system (GPS) and map matching technologies have been used to determine the present location of a car. The second function is route search between a present location of a vehicle and a driver's destination. One can easily get an optimum route between the present location and the destination when only the destination is

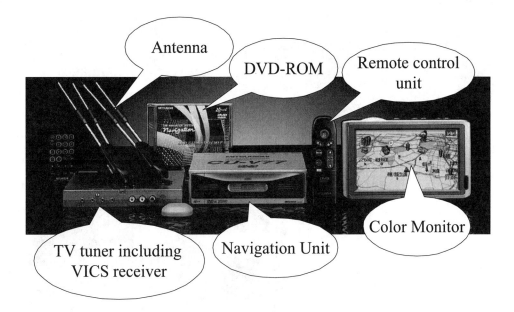

**FIGURE 38.8** Real configuration of in-vehicle navigation system.

input into an in-vehicle navigation system. The third function is route guidance to guide you to your destination along with the determined way by the route calculation function. Normally, this guidance is performed by both voice and display for driver's safety. The last important function is to display vehicle position, results of route search, and guidance so that drivers can understand them easily at a glance.

A real configuration of a typical in-vehicle navigation system is shown in Fig. 38.8. It normally consists of the six components shown in this picture. A color monitor for a navigation system is also used to display moving pictures from a TV set and a DVD player, as shown at the lower right of Fig. 38.9. An important issue is that VICS supposes an in-vehicle navigation system to be loaded in a vehicle. So, a TV tuner also includes a receiver for VICS, in general. As shown later, VICS uses three major media such as FM multiplex, electromagnetic beacon, and infrared light beacon.

Figure 38.10 is an example of a map display that often appears on a color display monitor of Japanese in-vehicle navigation system. It shows the three major basic results in the minute map: the display of the present vehicle position, the optimum route for the destination, and vehicle guidance. A simplified map in Fig. 38.10 helps drivers to understand the direction they have to follow at the next intersection. The large red triangle at the lower left of this figure shows the present vehicle position determined by the location identification technology. A row of small yellow triangles shows the optimum route calculated by a navigation system. The right simplified map in this picture enables a driver easily understand which way he or she should take at the next intersection.

Figure 38.11 is another example of map display of in-vehicle navigation system. The left map in this figure shows a real map showing the present vehicle position and the calculated optimum route to the destination. The right picture shows a 3-D, simplified map with several landmarks such as McDonald's, road messages, and a traffic signal. Normally, it is said that a 3-D representation is easily understandable for drivers regarding which way they have to go.

The situation is a bit different between Japan and other countries because of people's preferences for navigation displays are a bit different. For example, Japanese people like a map display as shown in Fig. 38.10, but people of other countries like only displays of the directions drivers have to take.

A block diagram of an in-vehicle navigation system is shown in Fig. 38.12. One can easily understand that essential configuration of an in-vehicle navigation system is the same as that of a personal computer excluding both the VICS unit and the sensors to be used to determine the vehicle location. In the CD-ROM,

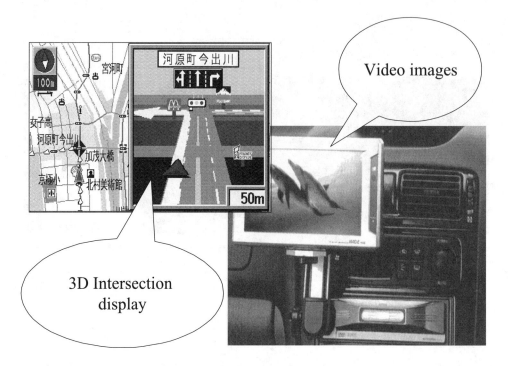

**FIGURE 38.9**   Examples of information display.

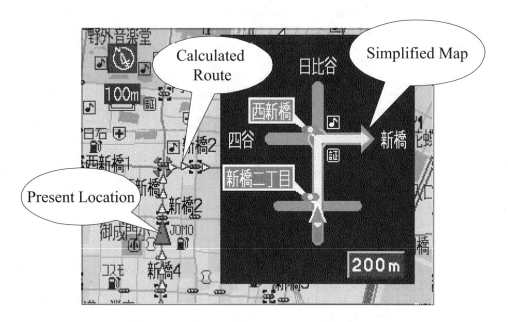

**FIGURE 38.10**   Example of a map display (1).

a map database is stored and accessed when a map is displayed, an optimum route is searched, and route guidance is performed. The software in the ROM in Fig. 38.12 provides the four functions—vehicle location, route search, route guidance, and display. For example, vehicle location is determined with processing signals from GPS, a vehicle speed sensor, and a gyro sensor. After vehicle location is fixed, a map database in the CD-ROM is accessed. Then, both the present vehicle location and a map near to the

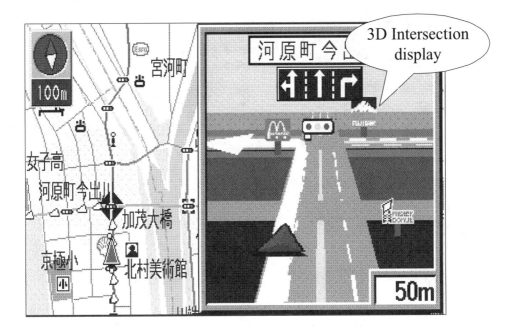

**FIGURE 38.11**    Example of a map display (2).

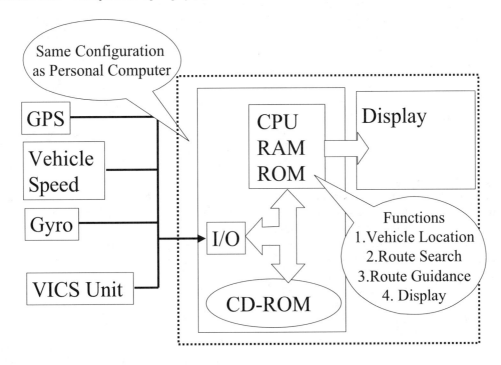

**FIGURE 38.12**    Vehicle navigation & VICS.

present vehicle location are displayed simultaneously on a color display moniter. If a driver inputs his or her destination to the navigation unit through the color monitor, the optimum route calculation is initiated and then the result is displayed. Along with the optimum route, the navigation unit guides the route to the driver in response to the vehicle movement. In addition to this, information such as the locations of restaurants, convenience stores, and gas stations near the vehicle's present location are also displayed.

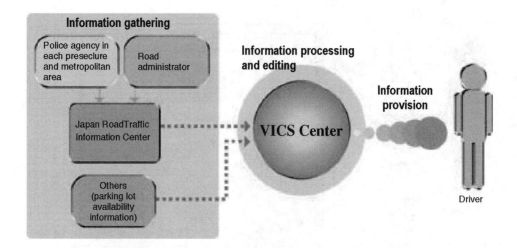

**FIGURE 38.13**  Configuration of VICS.

The four basic functions of an in-vehicle navigation system, including the required function by VICS, are performed by software implemented in a navigation system as previously mentioned. So the scale of the software of an in-vehicle navigation system has become very large, it needs about 10 MB memory. This means it is 100 times as much as that of the software scale of engine control system that can cope with emission regulation of the passenger cars by Japanese government. Therefore, the software development of an in-vehicle navigation system cannot be developed with a conventional way in a short time at low expense.

The whole system of VICS can be explained using Fig. 38.13. Traffic information is collected and edited in VICS center, then it transmitted with the three media—electromagnetic beacon, infrared light beacon, and FM multiplex. One can get information, such as traffic congestion, through display of in-vehicle navigation system with the VICS terminal. VICS is supported by three ministries of Japanese government: the Ministry of Construction, the Ministry of Post & Telecommunication, and the National Police Agency. Figure 38.14 shows an example of a display that shows several pieces of information such as traffic information sent by VICS service. The map display is performed using a map database of an in-vehicle navigation system in Fig. 38.12. A road next to one red line in the left part of Fig. 38.14 shows conjestion in only one direction. In this case up direction of this road is congested. Two red lines along a road shown at the right part in Fig. 38.14 means that the road is congested in two directions (up and down). One can easily detour these congested roads if with such real-time traffic information. VICS provides other information about road construction, road restrictions, and even about parking lots. VICS can also provide real-time information regarding traffic information and other useful information, and it gives a kind of comfort to drivers as a result.

## Electronic Toll Collection System

The electronic toll collection system (ETC) is an electronic fare collection system. This system was introduced in foreign countries earlier than in Japan. In Japan, the service of ETC starts this year. One of the aims of this system in Japan is to reduce the congestion at highway tollgates thereby resulting in less emission of exhaust. Figure 38.15 shows the whole system of Japanese ETC. Three major technologies are used: network in the infrastructure, automotive terminals for ETC, and road-to-vehicle communication. The infrastructure is composed of a huge network system into which personal information such as credit card numbers are flowing. Therefore, the information flowing into this network is written in code to ensure the security. Information from the automotive terminals for the ETC system is transmitted to the

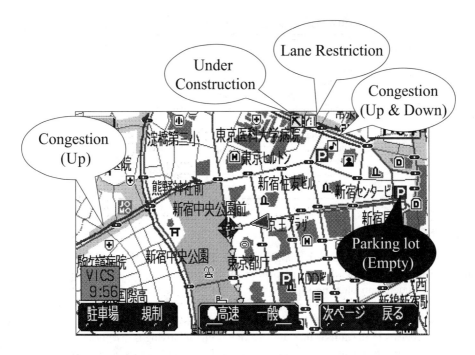

**FIGURE 38.14**   Examples of displayed information (VICS).

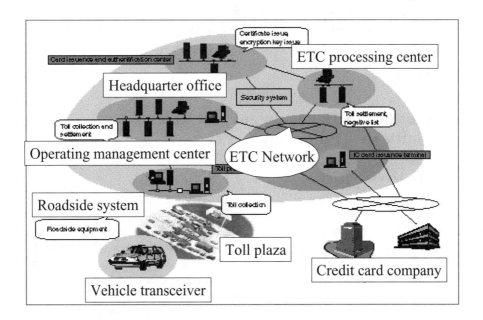

**FIGURE 38.15**   Network system for ETC.

network through road-to-vehicle communication known as dedicated short range communication (DSRC). Of course, it is also written in code to ensure the security. Specification of DSRC is shown in Table 38.4. In the same manner, information about road infrastructure, such as the location of the tollgate, is also transmitted to a vehicle from the infrastructure and through DSRC.

**TABLE 38.4**    Specification of DSRC

| Item | Description |
|------|-------------|
| Frequencies | Two pairs in the 5.8 GHz band |
| Bandwidth | 8 MHz max. |
| Transmitter output | 10 mW |
| Communication system | Active type with slotted Aloha |
| Maximum vehicle speed | 80 kph |
| Data transmission rate | 1.024 Mbps |
| Modulation method | Amplitude shift keying |
| Bit error rate | Less than 10 ppm |
| Communication error rate | Less than 1 ppm |
| Encoding method | Manchester encoding |

## Support of Safe Driving System

The support of safe driving system that appears in Fig. 38.5 is defined as the third development field of Japanese ITS has also been developed in Japan. In the early stages of the safe driving system, automatic driving was considered an ultimate support system. But many technical demonstrations on automatic driving from 1996 to 2000 gave people an impression that there were still many issues to be deployed from the point of view of both drivers and legal aspects. The author will demonstrate this more specifically later. So, recently it appears to the author that the idea of automatic driving is disappearing gradually. Instead of this, various warning systems and assistance systems have been considered. Demo2000 held at Japan last year shows effectiveness of those assistance systems such as AHS-I and ASV. "I" in the term of AHS-I means "information provision." AHS-I is a kind of concept to assure safe driving of vehicle by using information provision of both traffic information and road configuration through road-to-vehicle communication. Not only road-to-vehicle communication but inter-vehicle communication is also useful to ensure traffic safety. A demonstration showing the effectiveness of this technology was also shown in Demo2000 at Tsukuba, Japan. For example, it was shown to form platooning composed of running vehicles using inter-vehicle communication technology.

## 38.4  Issues of ITS Development and Roles of Software Technology

### Issues of ITS Development

The readers can easily think of technological issues to put into practical with the use of ITS, particularly an assist system of safe driving. Actually, the more important issues to deploy ITS are related to social, legal, and human issues, including responsibility, which are recognized with technical demonstration from 1996 to 2000 of the support system for safe driving. Table 38.5 shows the technical issues for deploying ITS. The importance of these technical issues will be easily understood. Figure 38.16 shows social, legal, and driver's issues summarized by Becker and the author.

Legal and driver's issues are composed of five terms, as shown in Fig. 38.16. The first is "product perception and use." This means how deeply users of the ITS-related system like the assist system for safe driving, can recognize the performance and the use of the system. For example, suppose you buy an air-bag system. You have to understand both its performance and how to use it very well. You have to know how it works depending on magnitude of the crash. If you do not know that, you will be overconfident about the air-bag system, and you may be injured by a traffic accident. In this process, sufficient explanation of a system by a salesman is very important for users to operate the system very well.

The second important issue is about "system safety and controllability" in Fig. 38.16. One can easily understand the importance of this issue if one compares control systems of a car with that of an aircraft. Pilots in an aircraft can operate the control system completely because pilots know how the control

**TABLE 38.5**    Technological Issues

---
1. Robust sensing technology
   (e.g., obstacles, road conditions, traffic flow, and so on)
2. Robust control technology
   (e.g., vehicle control, traffic control, platoon control, and so on)
3. Human technology
   (e.g., display, human I/F, drivers intention, and so on)
4. Information and processing technology
5. Communication technology
6. System integration technology

---

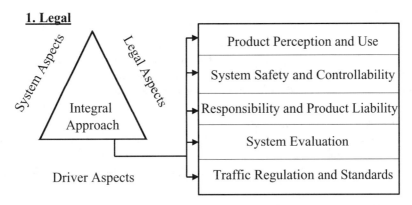

## 1. Legal

## 2. Social

1) Chicken-and-Egg Arguments
2) Persuasion of people who suspect effectiveness of ITS

**FIGURE 38.16**    Legal and social issues.

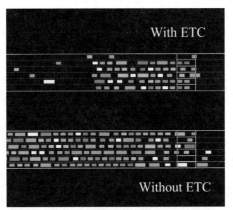

**ETC Simulation Result**

**FIGURE 38.17**    Simulation results with ITS simulator.

systems work well. Moreover, they know how to override the control systems in an emergency. Pilots are highly disciplined people, but drivers are not necessarily such people. So this issue becomes very important in case of drivers.

The third issue is related to "responsibility and product liability." Suppose a crash happens. Who has to be responsible for the crash? Which is more responsible, a control system or a driver? Is it the biggest issue to deploy the ITS properly?

System evaluation, the fourth issue, and traffic regulation and standard, the fifth issue, are also very important. So you can easily understand their importance without any explanation on these issues.

Two social issues are shown in Fig. 38.16. One is the chicken-and-egg argument and the other is persuasion of people who suspect effectiveness of ITS deployment. The chicken-and-egg argument holds in the spread of a system that is composed of both infrastructure and automotive equipments, which rely on infrastructure and vice versa. For example, we consider the case of ETC. There will be no incentive of spreading automotive terminal for ETC without preparation of infrastructure for ETC. On the other hand, there is no incentive for infrastructure to be prepared without automotive terminal of ETC. This is a so called a problem that is first infrastructure or automotive terminals.

Now many people say that ITS is necessary to make smoother traffic flow as well as decrease air pollution as a result. But some people are still suspicious as to the effectiveness of ITS. For example, is it true that ITS decreases traffic congestions? Even if it is true, less congestion makes more people use cars. As a result, less congestion cause more traffic demands. This will lead to more traffic flow. Therefore, only more vehicles can run, thanks to ITS. As a final result, they think that more cars can run on roads after ITS is deployed. So congestion will remain almost invariable even if ITS is introduced. It is a conclusion of the people who are suspicious about the effects of ITS and that traffic congestion will not decrease after ITS is introduced. In case of ETC deployment, several people do not believe the effect, and they say ETC will change only location of congestion. For example, suppose there is a junction in front of a tollgate. Before ETC is introduced, the tollgate was congested. After ETC is introduced, there will be congestion at the junction instead of the congestion in front of the tollgate. It seems that the location of the congestion shifts from the tollgate to the junction. This is a conclusion of the people who are suspicious as to the effect of ETC.

## Roles of Software Technology

As discussed earlier, ITS is making full use of both information technology and communication technology. Therefore, the importance of software technology does not need to be explained. For example, in-vehicle navigation system has a size of the software about 10 MB. This size is about one hundred times that of engine control software that meets the stringent exhaust gas regulation. This software can provide important performance, as shown in Fig. 38.7. Besides, this software technology has a great potential to solve these issues mentioned previously.

In advance, to explain the potential of software technology for solving the social and driver's issues, as shown in the preceding section, let us explain the concept to solve these issues. The first issue of "product perception and use" in Fig. 38.16 would be solved by showing both the performance of the product or system to be introduced into the market and how to use it. For this purpose, a simulation program that can simulate the performance is very effective and makes users understand it. For example, a simulation program of the performance of the air-bag system can show both its performance and how it works well. So users can easily understand the performance of an air-bag system or, in some cases, even the limitation of that system. In other words, the issue of product perception and use is realized by software technology.

In a similar way, the second issue of "system safety and controllability" is also solved by software technology. For example, you can very easily learn system safety and controllability if you have a simulation program. For a new aircraft, pilots can learn its control system and can be trained very well with a flight simulator.

As for the third issue of "responsibility and product liability," a simulation program is very helpful in solving this issue. Product liability (PL) is originally set for protecting users of product, but it sometimes makes manufacturers conservative about developing a new product. The solution for this issue, however, is obtained by assuring the safety of a product from the viewpoint of users. This can be done by showing users the safety of the product in every area where the product is supposed to be used. Only a simulation program of the performance of the product can perform this. For the third issue, software technology is also very effective.

The forth issue of "system evaluation" can also be supported with the use of a simulation program. It would not need to explain. The fifth issue of "traffic regulation and standards" is a little bit different compared with the four issues mentioned previously.

Social issues, including both the "chicken-and-egg argument" and persuasion of people who suspect effectiveness of ITS, are also solved by simulation. For example, people can learn about the effectiveness of ETC by a simulation program of ETC. Figure 38.17 is an example of a simulation of the effect of ETC with the ITS simulator that is under development. You can easily understand that the introduction of ETC decreases the congestion in front of a tollgate, as shown in the upper portion of Fig. 38.17. Even conservative people would agree to build ETC in order to see this result.

# 38.5   Practices of Software Development of Both In-Vehicle Navigation System and ITS Simulator

Software scales of both the in-vehicle navigation system and the ITS simulator are relatively large, but there is a difference in both properties between the navigation system and the ITS simulator. In the case of the navigation system it is embedded software that meets the needs of users. On the other hand, the ITS simulator is not embedded. In this section, both the software of the in-vehicle navigation system and the ITS simulator are explained briefly.

## In-Vehicle Navigation Systems

### Status of the Development of In-Vehicle Navigation System

One of the most severe issues in the development of the software for in-vehicle navigation is the short development time for the software, which meets customer requirements with low expense.

So some people say that only people who can develop in-vehicle navigation system software very quickly, at very low cost, would control the in-vehicle navigation system market.

As discussed earlier, in-vehicle navigation system software size is relatively large compared with other consumer products like a refrigerator, a washing machine, and an air conditioner. The size has reached nearly 10 MB. Cellular phones have almost the same software size. In general, this means that the cost to build the software has become very high and it needs a long time for development.

As you can easily understand, the market of the in-vehicle navigation system has two aspects. One is the aspect of consumer electronic products mainly sold at after-markets. The other aspect is that of the OEM market where the in-vehicle navigation system is sold and delivered directly to automakers from suppliers such as manufacturers of electric equipments. Table 38.6 shows three important issues to be maintanied or met by OEM suppliers of in-vehicle navigation system.

The first issue is customer satisfaction. Here, customer means automakers, not drivers themselves. That is, automakers decide which supplier's navigation system to buy. So, it is necessary for suppliers to meet the various needs of automakers.

The second important issue is keeping the delivery time set by automakers. Automakers have strategies to sell their cars. So the delivery time of navigation systems is set by automakers. The only thing that suppliers can do is to keep the delivery time very strictly. So the lead-time to develop an in-vehicle navigation system is normally very limited for suppliers.

The last important issue to keep in mind is reliability of an in-vehicle navigation system. Of course, reliability is also very important in the case of consumer electronic products; but in the OEM market, reliability is a more important issue because a sold car might have been returned due to the unreliability of the in-vehicle navigation system.

**TABLE 38.6**   Features of OEM Market as Customers

---

1. Customer satisfaction
     We have to meet the various needs of each automaker.
2. The date of delivery
     We have to keep it very strictly.
3. High reliability
     It may happen that a sold car is returned to automakers due to unreliability of car navigation system.

---

*Note:* Quick development of navigation software with high reliability.

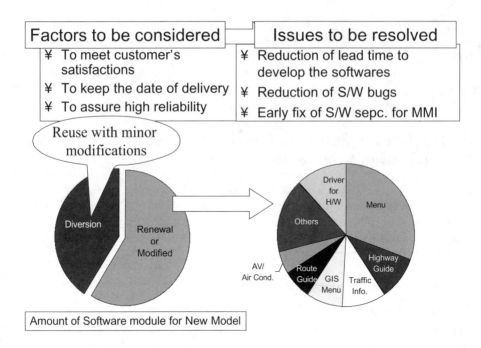

**FIGURE 38.18**    Issues of navigation software development.

Summarizing the three important issues, we can see a quick development of navigation software, with high reliability is a key point. Currently, many difficulties are present in navigation software development based on conventional methodology; however, as large as the software scale becomes, it does not have any problem if we can reuse the software in response to the needs of each automaker. But each auto-maker has many different needs, for example, different functions of a navigation system, man machine interfaces, desired price, and so on. On the other hand, normally the rate of reused software is relatively low, about 40%. Of the software, 60% has to be developed or modified profoundly in response to the needs of each automaker. Figure 38.18 shows the software volume ratio in developing the new navigation systems. About 60% of the software must be renewed for them, and the human-interface related software occupies a large part of all the renewed software. In addition to this, we have often encountered that software specification of each automaker has not been fixed until the end of development of the software.

To reduce both S/W bugs and lead-time to develop the navigation software, adoption of both middleware architecture and auto code generation is desirable. These techniques originate from the so-called object oriented development of software.

To promote determination of software specification of automakers, particularly man machine interface (MMI) portion of in-vehicle navigation system, it is suitable to introduce man machine builder tool that has already developed in another field, such as public infrastructure. The next subsection explains these two technologies realizing the issues stated earlier.

### New Methodology to Develop In-Vehicle Navigation Software

The first technology originated from object-oriented software development. Figure 38.19 shows the basic development flow along with the object-oriented software development. In the beginning, that is, the design stage of the object-oriented development model, customer requirements and system functions are decomposed of the object components that represent the basic or initial system. In this stage, various supplemental functions of automakers are decomposed of both each child component and the basic components that will incorporate features as additional components. Because all decomposed components including basic and child components are developed individually, their implementation and tests can be easily performed. For example, both the basic component and child components are implemented

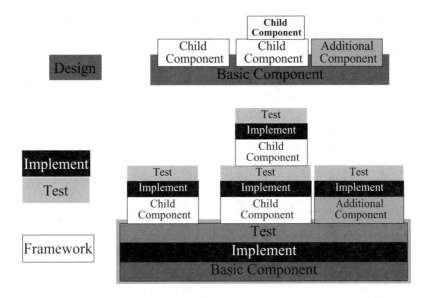

**FIGURE 38.19**  Object-oriented development model.

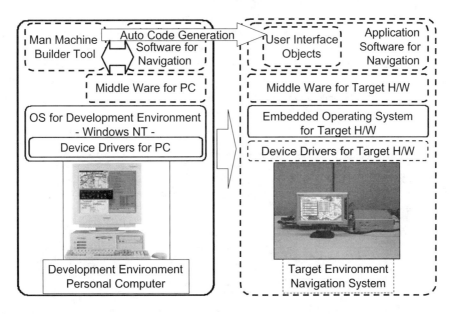

**FIGURE 38.20**  Hierarchical software architecture model.

and tested separately, and then both implementation and test as a whole system, such as system function, can be performed.

Child components and additional components are also given the same process to assemble the complete system, which meets the customers requirement. In object-oriented development we can easily modify with the addition of additional components. So this modification costs relatively less compared with the conventional waterfall software development. From the point of view of both easy debug and implementation to a target machine, we need another means besides adoption of object oriented development model. Moreover, we need a means to make automakers decide their specifications earlier.

Figure 38.20 shows the hierarchical software architecture models to make us debug easily and implement. The architecture has two distinct points. One is this middleware and the other, man machine builder tools serving to build MMI of in-vehicle navigation system. The middleware acts as a kind of separator between application software for navigation and hardware like personal computer (PC), and target machine. A detail of man machine builder tools will be shown later.

Generally speaking, it is desirable to use a PC as a software development environment because of its lighter weight, portability, and low price. The operating system (OS) for this environment is Windows NT. This OS includes device drivers for the hardware in the left picture of Fig. 38.20. Now let us explain the flow of navigation software development. In the beginning, application software of navigation system, composed of both child and basic components, is built with man machine builder on PCs as software development tools. Then the software is tested and debugged on the PCs. After that, the software is rewritten in terms of a target machine by using auto code generation and implemented. Then the application software is transferred to the target environment. This software definitely works well on the target machine because all necessary tests are already done by using PC and confirmed that the application software works well without any problem. So the remaining development that has to be done is to develop the device drivers for target hardware, which harmonizes the embedded OS with the hardware, as shown in the right picture of Fig. 38.20.

Also, it is necessary to modify the middleware for target hardware. After the modification of the middleware for target machine, the developed application software, excluding user interface objects, is tested to check how well it works. Thus, the application software for navigation can be easily applied onto the target environment by using this middleware.

The man machine builder tool automatically generates the software code for user interface object, and this software code is included into the application software. When one develops navigation software along with the above processes, one can indeed develop both software and hardware concurrently. This reduces the lead-time of developing new navigation system dramatically and enhances reliability of the software. Because the application software of the navigation system is developed on Windows OS, one can easily confirm its operation, in the early phase of development, even if the target hardware is still under development. CRT display in Fig. 38.21 shows an example of the software test in development phase. In this display, one can confirm how the functions of the navigation software work well, instead of the real

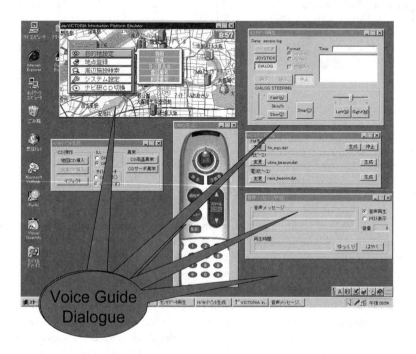

**FIGURE 38.21**   Confirmation of operation using PC.

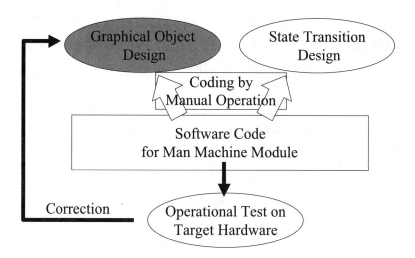

**FIGURE 38.22**   Conventional method for man machine module.

display device; that is, these functions of application software can operate and confirm with virtual operation panel with dummy signal dialog, and voice guide dialog.

The man machine builder tool is also used to make automakers decide the specification of the man machine interface in the early stage of the software development because man machine builder tool can give them virtual MMI and show how it works. For example, using the virtual display, drivers can input their destinations and their requests to search optimum routes or restaurants near their present locations. MMI serves drivers to do these interactively using several icons in Fig. 38.21. Generally speaking, the specification of man machine interface is often not determined until the end of development because the determination needs ergonomic studies. So it is desirable for providers to make a virtual environment to simulate the operation of man machine interface to be developed.

The man machine builder tool consists of both user interface design tool and state chart CASE tool. The missions of the user interface design tool are graphical object design, operation confirmation, and code generation.

On the other hand, the mission of the state chart CASE tool are production of operative transition, graphical confirmation of transition, and code generation of state transition.

Before explaining the function of the man machine builder tool briefly, we will explain about the conventional way to build MMI using Fig. 38.22. In the conventional method, the man machine module including graphical object design for user interface and state transition is designed from requirement analysis in the beginning. After both graphical object design and state transition are proceeded, software code of man machine module are coded separately by manual operation (hand coding).

Then the software code is combined with other application software. Finally, its operational test is performed on a display of target hardware. If some unexpected behavior or shape occurs in the user interface, its correction of design and coding are reprocessed. And, though this is a more important issue, additional requests by customers are often added to the specification to MMI. In order to cope with this, a new environment to build MMI differently from the conventional method is indispensable.

By using the new development environment of building MMI, one can generate the man machine module throughout from design to software code. With this tool, a graphical object is designed with the menu object editor, as shown in Fig. 38.23. This means both the graphic objects for MMI and the animation of their graphic objects are defined simultaneously with production of objects.

State transition is defined in the state chart editor in the right part of Fig. 38.23. In the state chart editor, both the animation parameters of graphic objects and navigation function behavior are defined following the state transition. After the graphical confirmation of both these graphic behaviors and state transition, these tools can generate the software code for man machine module automatically. Thus, you can show

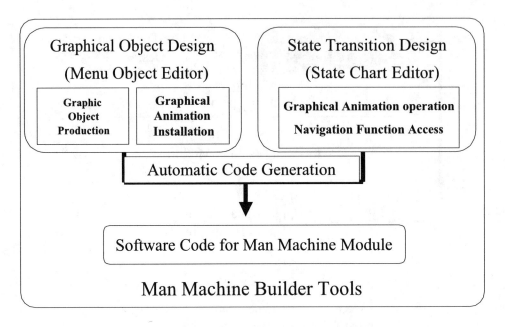

**FIGURE 38.23**  Development with man machine builder tool.

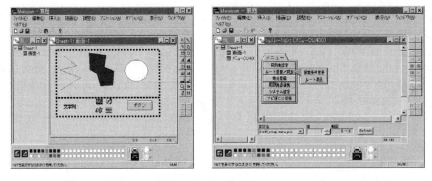

- ## Graphical Object production by basic/special components
  - Design Navigation menu objects by polygonal line, polygon, ellipse, character string, bit map, etc.

- ## "Operation" setting in diagram (Production of animation)
  - Transform each diagram in relation to its variable.

**FIGURE 38.24**  Function of menu object editor.

automakers how the user interface under development works well, using the virtual display. And you can get necessary suggestions including the additional needs from them. Thus, one can easily understand that this tool can accept various requests from customers interactively. So the specification of MMI is easily determined, unlike the conventional method, by using this tool.

The menu object editor in Fig. 38.23 has two main functions. One is the production of the graphical object of the user interface of the navigation system using the basic and special components. The other is the production of animation in the user interface. In Fig. 38.24 basic components, such as polygonal line, polygon and ellipse are shown in the upper dotted box of the left picture in Fig. 38.24. Special components are only needed for the navigation object, such as character strings, bitmaps representing

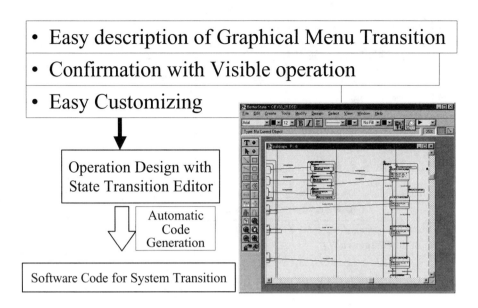

**FIGURE 38.25**    State transition design.

the specified functions of the system, and the button object for the menu interface are generated. In addition to the object design, animation of the object can also create its transition, and this animation can be simulated on this tool, as shown in Fig. 38.25. This menu object editor also has a function of automation code generation for designed object and animation.

Use of state chart CASE tool to state transition design has these major points. The first major point is the easy description of graphical menu transition. Designed transition can be visually confirmed with the visible state chart, which is the second major point. The third point is easy customizing of the state transition. It can be modified in the visual tool by moving the transition line in the design window in the right picture of Fig. 38.25. So one can introduce it to advanced environment for navigation software development. This CASE tool can also output the software code of the state transition with an automatic code generation function.

Here, we show the operation flow of making the entire software using the MMI builder tool. In Fig. 38.26, the man machine module provides the navigation software code. When the graphical object design is finished, the software code of the menu objects is generated automatically. The software code of the state transition is also generated in the same manner. Both the codes are included in man machine module, then the binary code of the navigation software is built to confirm its function on the PC. This sequence is continued until achievement of all requirements, and it builds for the target hardware to release the actual sample.

## ITS Simulator and Its Functions

ITS simulator is a kind of driving simulator. So real configuration of the ITS simulator is very similar to that of the driving simulator. Figure 38.27 shows the configuration that is composed of computer, screen, projector, and a half actual vehicle. Although the configuration of the ITS simulator is similar to a driving simulator, the functions are very different from those of a driving simulator. The ITS simulator can simulate both several effects and effectiveness of ITS deployment as a result of simulating the interaction between road infrastructure and vehicles. This is one of the greatest different points between a driving simulator and ITS simulator.

Figure 38.28 shows the architecture of ITS simulator. It consists of four major modules, vehicle dynamics simulator module, micro traffic simulator module, 3D road environmental simulator module, and system control module.

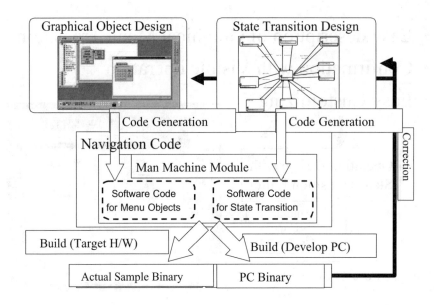

**FIGURE 38.26**  Operation flow with man machine builder.

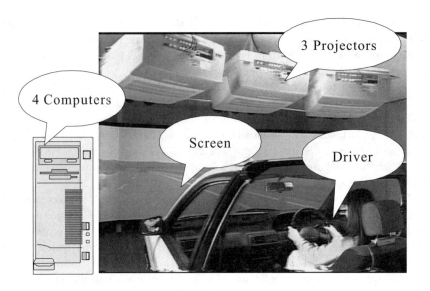

**FIGURE 38.27**  Physical configuration of ITS simulator.

The first module of vehicle dynamics simulator provides the movement of the half driving vehicle dynamics in real-time. This vehicle dynamics model has nine degrees of freedom of movements. Therefore, you can feel as if you were in a real car in the half vehicle of ITS simulator in the same manner of a driving simulator.

The second module of microscopic road traffic simulator, which is called MELROSE, generates a virtual road traffic environment based on an autonomous driving model. Every vehicle provided by this module acts as surrounded vehicles of the simulated vehicle of the vehicle dynamics simulator, and also every vehicle can run with its own origin and destination. So these vehicles can act as surrounded vehicles.

This third module is a 3D-computer graphics road environment simulator. This simulator creates actual geographical conditions and road configurations in response to the vehicle location of the simulated

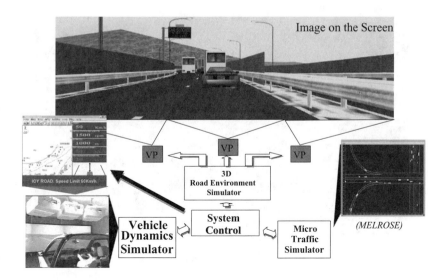

**FIGURE 38.28** Modules of ITS simulator.

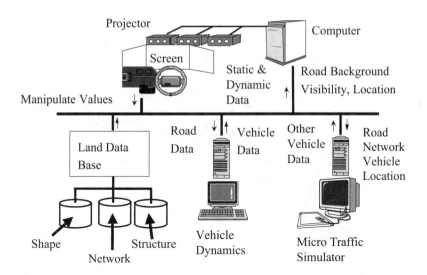

**FIGURE 38.29** Physical architecture of ITS simulator.

vehicle. For these, various road data like width, gradient, numbers of lane, road shape, and so on are stored in the memories of this module. In response to the vehicle movement the stored road data are accessed to form virtual road environment with 3D graphics based on real road data.

The final module is to control the operation of the above three module and to make the total modules operate as the ITS simulator. A representative action is to synchronize other three modules because all time units to compute are different in each module.

Figure 38.29 shows an architecture and data flow among all four modules. The land database means the stored data as shown before. The upper right computer in Fig. 38.29 means system control module and 3D graphic processing of road environment simulator.

A simulation result on how congestion is formed by a blocking vehicle is shown in Fig. 38.30. The reader can easily understand a process of congestion due to a blocking vehicle in a circle. A driving simulator cannot simulate such a situation. The next simulation result is shown in Fig. 38.31. It simulates

A blocking vehicle

**FIGURE 38.30**    Generation of congestion due to accident.

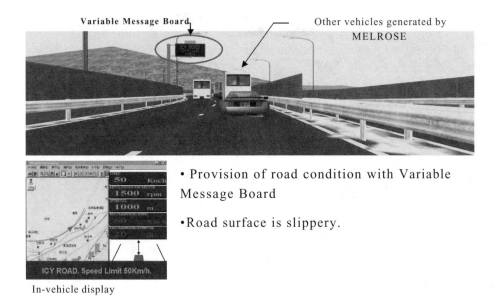

In-vehicle display

**FIGURE 38.31**    Simulation of effectiveness of AHS-i.

a kind of the interaction effects between provisions of traffic information and vehicles or drivers, that is, it simulates the differences of traffic flow rate with and without traffic information with a message board to drivers. For example, a roadside message board in the circle in Fig. 38.31 says that there is an icy road surface ahead, so please slow down. This message is also sent through road to vehicle communication to vehicle and shown in the in-vehicle display like in-vehicle navigation system in Fig. 38.31. Now a smart driver follows this advice to get smooth traffic flow. Some driver might not follow. As a result of this, congestion would occur to cause bad traffic flow. Therefore, traffic flow rates between these two cases are very different. ITS simulator can simulate such a situation and show the effectiveness of the provisions of traffic information.

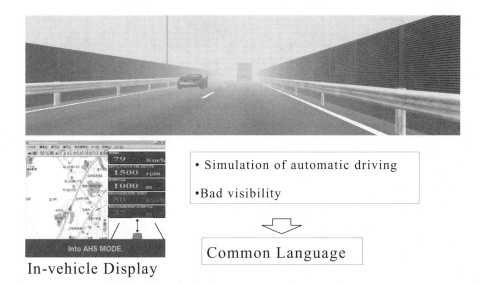

In-vehicle Display

**FIGURE 38.32** Simulation of effectiveness of AHS-a.

Figure 38.32 shows another example of the simulation with ITS simulator. A foggy situation with bad visibility is simulated. For example, a vehicle with an automatic driving system can run safely in spite of such a foggy condition. Though several modifications are needed, ITS simulator can simulate both every considerable traffic situation and considerable situation of use of control systems like automatic driving. As I mentioned earlier, this means that ITS simulator has a great advantage to show both the effects and the effectiveness of ITS deployment.

The microscopic traffic simulator, that is a part of the ITS simulator, alone can simulate several situations. For example, Fig. 38.17 shows the effects on congestion in front of a tollgate of a highway between with and without ETC. The upper case in Fig. 38.17 shows congestion in front of a tollgate with ETC. The lower shows the case without ETC. Each colored rectangle shows each vehicle. So the length of congestion is given by that of the row of the rectangles on each lane. You can easily see the difference between with and without ETC. Even people who suspect the effect of introducing ETC can understand the effect and would agree to the introduction of ETC.

## 38.6 Conclusion

We have the following conclusions:

1. In Japan in-vehicle navigation system are widespread and the VICS service to provide real-time traffic information is also widely spread. As for ETC, its service is about to start.
2. In the development of navigation software, adoption of both an hierarchical architecture and man machine builder into the development environment of navigation software is powerful enough to develop the software very quickly with high reliability.
3. ITS simulator is a powerful tool to solve the issues of ITS deployment.

### Acknowledgments

The author expresses his great thanks to Dr. Yukio Goto, Mr. Yoshihiko Utsui, Mr. Masahiko Ikawa, Mr. Akio Uekawa, Dr. Hiroyuki Kumazawa, Mr. Mitsuo Shimotani, Mr. Minoru Ozaki, Mr. Akira Sugimoto, and other many researchers and engineers at the Industrial Electronics and Systems Laboratory of Mitsubishi Electric Corporation, for their great assistance and encouragement.

## To Probe Further

In this field, there has been much rapid progress. So we cannot find comprehensive literature on Japanese ITS. Therefore, below is some literature about specific fields.

Japanese ITS in general:

"ITS Handbook" edited by 2000

and the following several website are available for your further study:

http//:www.vics.or.jp/;www.moc.go.jp/;www.mpt.go.jp/;www.npa.go.jp/;www.miti.go.jp/;www.mot.
go.jp/

In-vehicle navigation system:

For example, "Car-Navigation Systems" K. Yokouchi, H. Ideno, and M. Ota, Mitsubishi Electric Advance Vol. 91/Sep. 2000, 2000.

ITS deployment and ITS simulator:

1. "Driver Assistance Systems—industrial, psychological, and legal aspects" S. Becker, D. Randow, and J. Feldges, In *Proceeding of the Intelligent Vehicle Symposium,* 1998.
2. "Simulation environment for ITS—a real-time 3D simulator" M. Ikawa, H. Kumazawa, Y. Goto, H. Furusawa, and Y. Akemi, In *Proceeding of the 5th ITS World Congress,* 1998.
3. "A prototype of smart ways in ITS simulator" Y. Goto, M. Ikawa, and H. Kumazawa, In *Proceeding of the 6th ITS World Congress,* 1999.

# 39

# Media Signal Processing

**Ruby Lee**
*Princeton University*

**Gerald G. Pechanek**
*BOPS, Inc.*

**Thomas C. Savell**
*Creative Advanced Technology Center*

**Sadiq M. Sait**
*King Fahd University*

**Habib Youssef**
*King Fahd University*

## 39.1  Instruction Set Architecture for Multimedia Signal Processing

*Ruby Lee*

### Introduction

Multimedia signal processing, or media processing [1], is the processing of digital multimedia information in a programmable processor. Digital multimedia information includes visual information like images, video, graphics, and animation, audio information like voice and music, and textual information like keyboard text and handwriting. With general-purpose computers processing more multimedia information, multimedia instructions for efficient media processing have been defined for the instruction set architectures (ISAs) of microprocessors. Meanwhile, digital processing of video and audio data in consumer products has also resulted in more sophisticated media processors. Traditional digital signal processors (DSPs) in music players and recorders and mobile telephones are becoming increasingly sophisticated as they process multiple forms of multimedia data, rather than just audio signals. Video processors for televisions and video recorders have become more versatile as they have to take into account high-fidelity audio processing and real-time three-dimensional (3-D) graphics animations. This has led to the design

R<sub>a</sub>:

**FIGURE 39.1**   32-bit integer register made up of four 8-bit subwords.

of more versatile media processors, which combine the capabilities of DSPs for efficient audio and signal processing, video processors for efficient video processing, graphics processors for efficient 2-D and 3-D graphics processing, and general-purpose processors for efficient and flexible programming. The functions performed by microprocessors and media processors may eventually converge. In this chapter, some of the key innovations in multimedia instructions added to microprocessor ISAs are described, which have allowed high-fidelity multimedia to be processed in real-time on ubiquitous desktop and notebook computers. Many of these features have also been adopted in modern media processors and DSPs.

## Subword Parallelism

Workload characterization studies on multimedia applications show that media applications have huge amounts of data parallelism and operate on lower-precision data types. A pixel-oriented application, for example, rarely needs to process data that is wider than 16 bits. This translates into low computational efficiency on general-purpose processors where the register and datapath sizes are typically 32 or 64 bits, called the width of a word. Efficient processing of low-precision data types in parallel becomes a basic requirement for improved multimedia performance. This is achieved by partitioning a word into multiple *subwords*, each subword representing a lower-precision datum. A *packed data type* will be defined as data that consists of multiple subwords packed together. These subwords can be processed in parallel using a single instruction, called a *subword-parallel* instruction, a *packed* instruction, or a *microSIMD* instruction. SIMD stands for "single instruction multiple data," a term coined by Flynn [2] for describing very large parallel machines with many data processors, where the same instruction issued from a single control processor operates in parallel on data elements in the parallel data processors. Lee [3] coined the term microSIMD architecture to describe an ISA—where a single instruction operates in parallel on multiple subwords within a single processor.

Figure 39.1 shows a 32-bit integer register that is made up of four 8-bit subwords. The subwords in the register can be pixel values from a grayscale image. In this case, the register is holding four pixels with values 0xFF, 0x0F, 0xF0, and 0x00. The same 32-bit register can also be interpreted as two 16-bit subwords, in which case, these subwords would be 0xFF0F and 0xF000. The subword boundaries do not correspond to a physical boundary in the register file; they are merely how the bits in the word are interpreted by the program. If we have 64-bit registers, the most useful subword sizes will be 8-, 16-, or 32-bit words. A single register can then accommodate 8, 4, or 2 of these different sized subwords, respectively.

To exploit subword parallelism, packed parallelism, or microSIMD parallelism in a typical word-oriented microprocessor, new subword-parallel or packed instructions are added. (The terms "subword-parallel," "packed," and "microSIMD" are used interchangeably to describe operations, instructions and architectures.) The parallel processing of the packed data types typically requires only minor modifications to the word-oriented functional units, with the register file and the pipeline structure remaining unchanged. This results in very significant performance improvements for multimedia processing, at a very low cost (see Fig. 39.2).

Typically, packed arithmetic instructions such as **packed add** and **packed subtract** are first introduced. To support subword parallelism efficiently, other classes of new instructions such as subword permutation instructions are also needed. Typical subword-parallel instructions are described in the rest of this chapter, pointing out interesting arithmetic or architectural features that have been added to support this style of microSIMD parallelism. In the subsection on "Packed Add and Packed Subtract Instructions," **packed add** and **packed subtract** instructions described are, as well as several variants of these. These instructions can all be implemented on the basic Arithmetic Logical Units (ALUs) found in programmable processors, with minor modifications. Such partitionable ALUs are described in the subsection on "Partitionable ALUs." *Saturation arithmetic*—one of the most interesting outcomes of

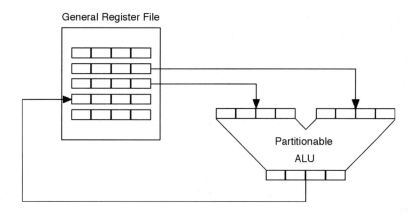

**FIGURE 39.2**    MicroSIMD parallelism uses packed data types and a partitionable ALU.

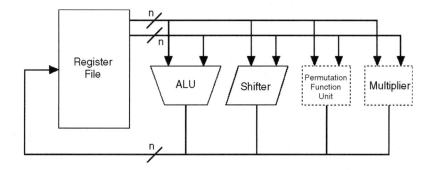

**FIGURE 39.3**    Typical datapaths and functional units in a programmable processor.

subword-parallel additions—for efficiently handling overflows and performing in-line conditional operations is also described. A variant of packed addition is the `packed average` instruction, where unbiased rounding is an interesting associated feature. Another class of packed instructions that can use the ALU is the `parallel compare` instruction where the results are the outcomes of the subword comparisons.

The subsection on "Packed Multiply Instruction" describes how packed integer multiplication is handled. Also described are different approaches to solving the problem of the products being twice as large as the subword operands that are multiplied in parallel. Although subword-parallel multiplication instructions generally require the introduction of new integer multiplication functional units to a microprocessor, the special case of multiplication by constants, which can be achieved very efficiently with `packed shift and add` instructions that can be implemented on an ALU with a small preshifter, is described.

The subsection on "Packed Shift and Rotate Operations" describes `packed shift` and `packed rotate` instructions, which perform a superset of the functions of a typical shifter found in microprocessors, in parallel, on packed subwords.

The subsection on "Subword Permutation Instruction" describes a new class of instructions, not previously found in programmable processors that do not support subword parallelism. These are subword permutation instructions, which rearrange the order of the subwords packed in one or more registers. These permutation instructions can be implemented using a modified shifter, or as a separate permutation function unit (see Fig. 39.3).

To provide examples and illustrations, the following first and second generation multimedia instructions in microprocessor ISAs are used:

- IA-64 [4,5], MMX [6,7], and SSE-2 [8] from Intel,
- MAX-2 [9,10] from Hewlett-Packard,

- 3DNow![1]1 [11,12] from AMD,
- AltiVec [13] from Motorola.

### Historical Overview

The first generation multimedia instructions focused on subword parallelism in the integer domain. These are described and compared in [14]. The first set of multimedia extensions targeted at general-purpose multimedia acceleration, rather than just graphics acceleration, was MAX-1, introduced with the PA-7100LC processor in January 1994 [15,16] by Hewlett-Packard. MAX-1, an acronym for "multimedia acceleration extensions," is a minimalist set of multimedia instructions for the 32-bit PA-RISC processor [17]. An application that clearly illustrated the superior performance of MAX-1 was MPEG-1 video and audio decoding with software, at real-time rates of 30 frames per second [18]. For the first time, this performance was made possible using software on a general-purpose processor in a low-end desktop computer. Until then, such high-fidelity, real-time video decompression performance was not achievable without using specialized hardware. MAX-1 also accelerated pixel processing in graphics rendering and image processing, and 16-bit audio processing.

Next, Sun introduced VIS [19], which was an extension for the UltraSparc processors. VIS was a much larger set of multimedia instructions. In addition to packed arithmetic operations, VIS provided very specialized instructions for accessing visual data, stored in predetermined ways in memory.

Intel introduced MMX [6,7] multimedia extensions in the dominant Pentium microprocessors in January 1997, which immediately legitimized the valuable contribution of multimedia instructions for ubiquitous multimedia applications.

MAX-2 [9] was Hewlett-Packard's multimedia extension for its 64-bit PA-RISC 2.0 processors [10]. Although designed simultaneously with MAX-1, it was only introduced in 1996, with the PA-RISC 2.0 architecture. The subword permutation instructions introduced with MAX-2 were useful only with the increased subword parallelism in 64-bit registers. Like MAX-1, MAX-2 was also a minimalist set of general-purpose media acceleration primitives.

MIPS also described MDMX multimedia extensions and Alpha described a very small set of MVI multimedia instructions for video compression.

The second generation multimedia instructions initially focused on subword parallelism on the floating-point (FP) side for accelerating graphics geometry computations and high-fidelity audio processing. Both of these multimedia applications use single-precision, floating-point numbers for increased range and accuracy, rather than 8-bit or 16-bit integers. These multimedia ISAs include SSE and SSE-2 [8] from Intel and 3DNow! [11,12] from AMD. Finally, the PowerPC's AltiVec [13] and the Intel-HP IA-64 [4,5] multimedia instruction sets are comprehensive integer and floating-point multimedia instructions. Today, every microprocessor ISA and most media and DSP ISAs include subword-parallel multimedia instructions.

## Packed Add and Packed Subtract Instructions

`Packed add` and `packed subtract` instructions are similar to ordinary `add` and `subtract` instructions, except that the operations are performed in parallel on the subwords of two source registers. Add (nonpacked) and `packed add` operations are shown in Figs. 39.4 and 39.5, respectively. The `packed add` in Fig. 39.5 uses source registers with four subwords each. The corresponding subwords from the two source registers are summed up, and the four sums are written to the target register. A `packed subtract` operation operates similarly.

### Partitionable ALUs

Very minor modifications to the underlying functional units are needed to implement `packed add` and `packed subtract` instructions. Assume that we have an ALU with 32-bit integer registers, and we want to extend this ALU to perform a `packed add` that will operate on four 8-bit subwords in parallel.

---

[1] 3DNow! may be considered as having two versions. In June 2000, 25 new instructions were added to the original 3DNow! specification. In this text, this extended 3DNow! architecture will be considered.

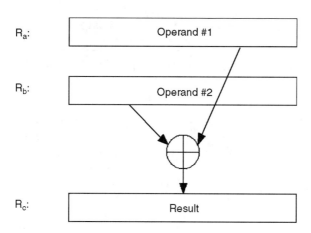

**FIGURE 39.4** ADD $R_c, R_a, R_b$ : Ordinary add instruction.

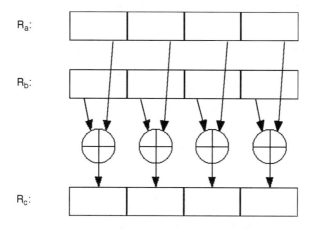

**FIGURE 39.5** PADD $R_c, R_a, R_b$ : Packed add instruction.

To achieve this, the carry propagation across the subword boundaries has to be blocked. Because each subword is interpreted as being independent of the neighboring subwords, by stopping the carry bits from affecting the neighboring subwords, the **packed add** operation can be realized.

In Fig. 39.6, the packed integer register $R_a$=[0xFF|0x0F|0xF0|0x00] is being added to another packed register $R_b$=[0x00|0xFF|0xFF|0x0F]. The result is written to the target register $R_c$. In an ordinary **add** instruction, the overflows generated by the addition of the second and third subwords will propagate into the first two sums. The correct sums, however, can be achieved easily by blocking the carry bit propagation across the subword boundaries, which are spaced 8-bits apart from one another.

As shown in Fig. 39.7, a 2-to-1 multiplexer placed at the subword boundaries of the adder can be used to control the propagation or the blocking of the carry bits. If the instruction is a **packed add**, the multiplexer control is set such that a zero is propagated into the next subword. If the instruction is an ordinary **add**, the multiplexer control is set such that the carry from the previous stage is propagated. By placing such a multiplexer at each subword boundary and adding the control logic, partitionable ALUs are achieved at insignificant cost.

By using 3-to-1 multiplexers instead of 2-to-1 multiplexers, we can also implement **packed subtract** instructions. The multiplexer control is set such that:

- For **packed add** instructions, zero is propagated into the next stage.
- For **packed subtract** instructions, one is propagated into the next stage.

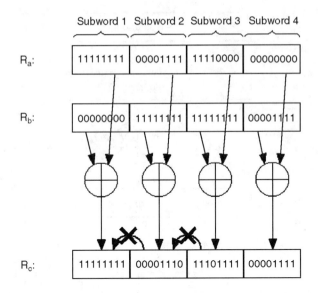

**FIGURE 39.6**  In the `packed add` instruction, the carry bits are not propagated.

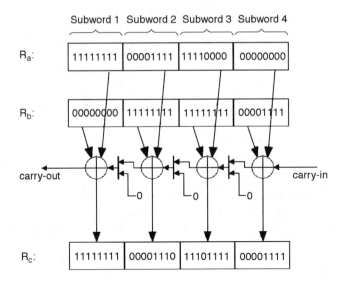

**FIGURE 39.7**  Partitionable ALU: In `packed add` instructions, the multiplexers propagate zero; in ordinary `add` instructions, the multiplexers propagate carry-out from the previous stage into the carry-in of the next stage.

- For ordinary `add/subtract` instructions, the carry/borrow bit from the previous stage is propagated into the next stage.

When a zero is propagated through the boundary into the next subword in the `packed add` instructions, we are essentially ignoring any overflow that might have been generated. Similarly, when a one is propagated through the boundary into the next subword in the `packed subtract` instructions, we are essentially ignoring any borrow that might have been generated. Ignoring overflows is equivalent to using modular arithmetic in `add` operations. Although modular arithmetic can be necessary or useful, other occasions arise when the carry bits should not be ignored and have to be handled differently.

## Handling Parallel Overflows

Overflows in `packed add/subtract` instructions can be handled in the following ways:

- The overflow may be ignored (modular arithmetic).
- A *flag* bit may be set if at least one overflow is generated.
- Multiple flag bits (i.e., one flag bit for each addition operation on the subwords) may be set.
- A software overflow trap can be taken.
- Saturation arithmetic: the results are limited to a certain range. If the outcome of the operation falls outside this range, the corresponding limiting value will be the result.

Most nonpacked integer `add/subtract` instructions choose to ignore overflows and perform modular arithmetic. In modular arithmetic, the numbers wrap around from the largest representable number to the smallest representable number. For example, in 8-bit modular arithmetic, the operation 254+2 will give a result of 0. The expected result, 256, is larger than the largest representable number, which is 255, and therefore is wrapped around to the smallest representable number, which is 0.

In multimedia applications, modular arithmetic frequently gives undesirable results. If the numbers in the previous example were pixel values in a grayscale image, by wrapping the values from 255 down to 0, white pixels would have converted into black ones. One solution to this problem is to use overflow traps, which are implemented in software.

A flag bit is an indicator bit that is set or cleared depending on the outcome of a particular operation. In the context of this discussion, an overflow flag bit is an indicator that is set when an **add** instruction generates an overflow. Occasions arise where the use of the flag bits are desirable. Consider a loop that iterates many times and in each iteration, executes many **add** instructions. In this case, it is not desirable to handle overflows (by taking overflow trap routines) as soon as they occur, because this would negatively impact the performance by interrupting the execution of the loop body. Instead, the overflow flag can be set when the overflow occurs, and the program flow continues as if the overflow did not occur. At the end of each iteration, however, this overflow flag can be checked and the overflow trap can be executed if the flag turns out to be set. This way, the program flow would not be interrupted while the loop body executes.

An overflow trap can be used to *saturate* the results so that the aforementioned problems would not occur. A result that is greater than the largest representable value is replaced by that largest value. Similarly, a result that is less than the smallest representable value is replaced by that smallest value. One problem with this solution will be its negative effects to performance. An overflow trap is handled in software and may take many clock cycles to resolve. This can be acceptable only if the overflows are infrequent. For nonpacked `add/subtract` instructions, generation of an overflow on a 64-bit register by adding 8-bit quantities will be rare, so a software overflow trap will work well. This is not the case for packed arithmetic operations. Causing an overflow in an 8-bit subword is much more likely than in a 64-bit register. Also, since a 64-bit register may hold eight 8-bit subwords, multiple overflows can occur in a single execution cycle. In this case, handling the overflows by software traps could easily negate any performance gains from executing packed operations. The use of saturation arithmetic solves this problem.

## Saturation Arithmetic

Saturation arithmetic implements in hardware the work done by the overflow trap described above. The results falling outside the allowed numeric ranges are saturated to the upper and lower limits by hardware. This can handle multiple parallel overflows efficiently, without operating system intervention. Two types of overflows for arithmetic operations are:

- A *positive overflow* occurs when the result is larger than the largest value in the defined range for that result
- A *negative overflow* occurs when the result is smaller than the smallest value in the defined range for that result

If saturation arithmetic is used in an operation, the result is clipped to the maximum value in its defined range if a positive overflow occurs, and to the minimum value in its defined range if a negative overflow occurs.

For a given instruction, multiple saturation options may exist, depending on whether the operands and the result are treated as signed or unsigned integers. For an instruction that uses three registers (two for source operands and one for the result), there can be eight different saturation options. Each one of the three registers can be treated as containing either a signed or an unsigned integer, which gives $2^3$ possible combinations. Not all of the eight possible saturation options are equally useful. Only three of the eight possible saturation options are used in any of the multimedia ISAs surveyed:

a) **sss** (signed result–signed first operand–signed second operand): In this saturation option, the result and the two operands are all treated as signed integers. The most significant bit is considered the sign bit. Considering $n$-bit subwords, the result and operands are defined in the range $[-2^{n-1}, 2^{n-1}-1]$. If a positive overflow occurs, the result is saturated to $2^n - 1$. If a negative overflow occurs, the result is saturated to $-2^{n-1}$. In an addition operation that uses the *sss* saturation option, since the operands are signed numbers, a positive overflow is possible only when both operands are positive. Similarly, a negative overflow is possible only when both operands are negative.

b) **uuu** (unsigned result–unsigned first operand–unsigned second operand): In this saturation option, the result and the two operands are all treated as unsigned integers. Considering $n$-bit integer subwords, the result and the operands are defined in the range $[0, 2^n - 1]$. If a positive overflow occurs, the result is saturated to $2^n - 1$. If a negative overflow occurs, the result is saturated to zero. In an addition operation that uses the *uuu* saturation option, since the operands are unsigned numbers, negative overflow is not a possibility; however, for a subtraction operation using the *uuu* saturation, negative overflow is possible, and any negative result will be clamped to zero as the smallest value.

c) **uus** (unsigned result–unsigned first operand–signed second operand): In this saturation option, the result and the first operand are treated as unsigned numbers, and the second operand is treated as a signed number. Although this may seem like an unusual option, it is very useful because it allows the addition of a signed increment to an unsigned pixel. It also allows negative numbers to be clipped to zero. Its implementation also has logical symmetry to the *sss* case.

In addition to the efficient handling of overflows, saturation arithmetic also facilitates several other useful computations. For instance, saturation arithmetic can also be used to clip results to arbitrary maximum or minimum values. Without saturation arithmetic, these operations could normally take up to five instructions for each pair of subwords. That would include instructions to check for upper and lower bounds and then to perform the clipping. Using saturation arithmetic, however, this effect can be achieved in as few as two instructions for all the pairs of packed subwords.

Saturation arithmetic can also be used for in-line conditional execution, reducing the need for conditional branches that can cause significant performance degradations in pipelined processors. Some examples are the `packed maximum` and `packed absolute difference` operations shown in Figs. 39.8(a, b).

Table 39.1 contains examples of operations that can be performed using saturation arithmetic [15]. All of the instructions in the table use three registers. The first register is the target register. The second and the third registers hold the first and the second operands respectively. `PADD` and `PSUB` denote `packed add` and `packed subtract` instructions. The three-letter field after the instruction mnemonic specifies which saturation option is to be used. If this field is empty, modular arithmetic is assumed. All the examples in the table operate on 16-bit integer subwords.

Table 39.2 contains a summary of the register and subword sizes and the saturation options found in different multimedia ISAs. Table 39.3 is a summary of the `packed add/subtract` instructions in several multimedia ISAs. The first column contains descriptions of common packed instructions. The symbols $a_i$ and $b_i$ represent the corresponding subwords from the two source registers. The symbol $c_i$ represents the corresponding subword in the target register.

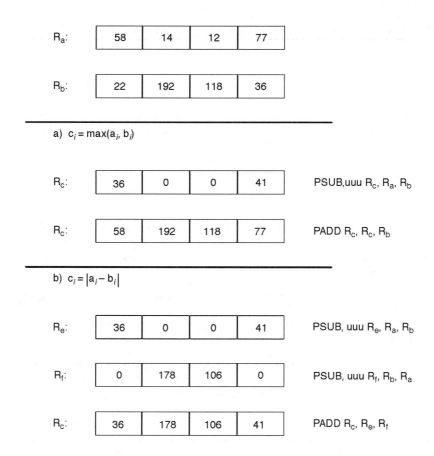

**FIGURE 39.8** (a) `Packed maximum` operation using saturation arithmetic. (b) `Packed absolute differ-`
`ence` operation using saturation arithmetic.

The IA-64[2] architecture has 64-bit integer registers. `Packed add` and `packed subtract` instructions
are supported for subword sizes of 1, 2, and 4 bytes. Modular arithmetic is defined for all subword sizes
whereas the saturation options (*sss, uuu,* and *uus*) exist for only 1 and 2-byte subwords.

The PA-RISC MAX-2 architecture also has 64-bit integer registers. `Packed add` and `packed sub-`
`tract` instructions operate on only 2-byte subwords. MAX-2 instructions support modular arithmetic,
and the *sss* and *uus* saturation options.

The IA-32 MMX architecture defines eight 64-bit registers for use by the multimedia instructions.
Although these registers are referred to as separate registers, they are aliased to the registers in the FP
data register stack. Supported subword sizes are 1, 2, and 4 bytes. Modular arithmetic is defined for all
subword sizes whereas the saturation options (*sss* and *uus*) exist for only 1- and 2-byte subwords.

The IA-32 SSE-2 technology introduces a new set of eight 128-bit FP registers to the IA-32 architecture.
Each of the 128-bit registers can accommodate four single-precision (SP) or two double-precision (DP)
numbers. Moreover, these registers can also be used to accommodate packed integer data types. Integer
subword sizes can be 1, 2, 4, or 8 bytes. Modular arithmetic is defined for all subword sizes whereas the
saturation options (*sss* and *uus*) exist for only 1- and 2-byte subwords.

The PowerPC AltiVec architecture has thiry-two 128-bit registers for multimedia instructions. `Packed`
`add/subtract` instructions are supported for 1-, 2-, and 4-byte subwords. Modular or saturation
arithmetic (*uuu* or *sss*) can be used, although *sss* saturation is only supported for `packed add`.

---

[2]All the discussions in this chapter consider Intel's IA-64 as the base architecture. Evaluations of the other
architectures are generally carried out by comparisons to IA-64.

**TABLE 39.1**    Examples of Operations That are Facilitated by Saturation Arithmetic

| Operation | Instruction Sequence | Notes |
|---|---|---|
| Clip $a_i$ to an arbitrary maximum value $v_{max}$, where $v_{max} < 2^{15} - 1$. | PADD.*sss* $R_a$, $R_a$, $R_b$ | $R_b$ contains the value $(2^{15} - 1 - v_{max})$. If $a_i > v_{max}$, this operation clips $a_i$ to $2^{15} - 1$ on the high end. |
| | PSUB.*sss* $R_a$, $R_a$, $R_b$ | $a_i$ is at most $v_{max}$. |
| Clip $a_i$ to an arbitrary minimum value $v_{min}$, where $v_{min} > -2^{15}$. | PSUB.*sss* $R_a$, $R_a$, $R_b$ | $R_b$ contains the value $(-2^{15} + v_{min})$. If $a_i < v_{min}$, this operation clips $a_i$ to $-2^{15}$ at the low end. |
| | PADD.*sss* $R_a$, $R_a$, $R_b$ | $a_i$ is at least $v_{min}$. |
| Clip $a_i$ to within the arbitrary range $[v_{min}, v_{max}]$, where $-2^{15} < v_{min} < v_{max} < 2^{15} - 1$. | PADD.*sss* $R_a$, $R_a$, $R_b$ | $R_b$ contains the value $(2^{15} - 1 - v_{max})$. This operation clips $a_i$ to $2^{15} - 1$ on the high end. |
| | PSUB.*sss* $R_a$, $R_a$, $R_d$ | $R_d$ contains the value $(2^{15} - 1 - v_{max} + 2^{15} - v_{min})$. This operation clips $a_i$ to $-2^{15}$ at the low end. |
| | PADD.*sss* $R_a$, $R_a$, $R_e$ | $R_e$ contains the value $(-2^{15} + v_{min})$. This operation clips $a_i$ to $v_{max}$ at the high end and to $v_{min}$ at the low end. |
| Clip the signed integer $a_i$ to an unsigned integer within the range $[0, v_{max}]$, where $0 < v_{max} < 2^{15} - 1$. | PADD.*sss* $R_a$, $R_a$, $R_b$ | $R_b$ contains the value $(2^{15} - 1 - v_{max})$. This operation clips $a_i$ to $2^{15} - 1$ at the high end. |
| | PSUB.*uus* $R_a$, $R_a$, $R_b$ | This operation clips $a_i$ to $v_{max}$ at the high end and to zero at the low end. |
| Clip the signed integer $a_i$ to an unsigned integer within the range $[0, 2^{16}]$. | PADD.*uus* $R_a$, 0, $R_a$ | If $a_i < 0$, then $a_i = 0$ else $a_i = a_i$. If $a_i$ was negative, it gets clipped to zero, else remains same. |
| $c_i = \max(a_i, b_i)$ Packed maximum operation | PSUB.*uuu* $R_c$, $R_a$, $R_b$ | If $a_i > b_i$, then $c_i = (a_i - b_i)$ else $c_i = 0$. |
| | PADD $R_c$, $R_b$, $R_c$ | If $a_i > b_i$, then $c_i = a_i$ else $c_i = b_i$. |
| $c_i = \lvert a_i - b_i \rvert$ Packed absolute difference operation | PSUB.*uuu* $R_e$, $R_a$, $R_b$ | If $a_i > b_i$, then $e_i = (a_i - b_i)$ else $e_i = 0$. |
| | PSUB.*uuu* $R_f$, $R_b$, $R_a$ | If $a_i <= b_i$, then $f_i = (b_i - a_i)$ else $f_i = 0$. |
| | PADD $R_c$, $R_e$, $R_f$ | If $a_i > b_i$, then $c_i = \lvert a_i - b_i \rvert$, else $c_i = \lvert b_i - a_i \rvert$. |

*Note:* $a_i$ and $b_i$ are the subwords in the registers $R_a$ and $R_b$, respectively, where $i = 1, 2, \ldots, k$, and $k$ denotes the number of subwords in a register. Subword size $n$, is assumed to be two bytes (i.e., $n = 16$) for this table.

**TABLE 39.2**    Summary of the Integer Register, Subword Sizes, and Subtraction Options Supported by the Different Architectures

| Architectural Feature | IA-64 | MAX-2 | MMX | SSE-2 | AltiVec |
|---|---|---|---|---|---|
| Size of integer registers (bits) | 64 | 64 | 64 | 128 | 128 |
| Supported subword sizes (bytes) | 1, 2, 4 | 2 | 1, 2, 4 | 1, 2, 4, 8 | 1, 2, 4 |
| Modular arithmetic | Y | Y | Y | Y | Y |
| Supported saturation options | *sss, uuu, uus* for 1, 2 byte | *sss, uus* for 2 byte | *sss, uuu* for 1, 2 byte | *sss, uuu* for 1, 2 byte | *uuu, sss* for 1, 2, 4 byte |

## Packed Average

Packed average instructions are very common in media applications such as pixel averaging in MPEG-2 encoding, motion compensation, and video scaling. In a packed average, the pairs of corresponding subwords in the two source registers are added to generate intermediate sums. Then, the intermediate sums are shifted right by one bit, so that any overflow bit is shifted in on the left as the most significant bit. The beauty of the average operation is that no overflow can occur, and two operations (add followed by a one bit right shift) are performed in one operation. In a packed average instruction, $2n$ operations are performed in a single cycle, where $n$ is the number of subwords. In fact, even more operations are performed in a packed average instruction, if the rounding applied to the least significant end of the result is considered. Here, two different rounding options have been used:

**TABLE 39.3**  Summary of the `packed add` and `packed subtract` Instructions and Variants

| Integer Operations | IA-64 | MAX-2 | MMX | SSE-2 | 3DNow! | AltiVec |
|---|---|---|---|---|---|---|
| $c_i = a_i + b_i$ | √ | √ | √ | √ | | √ |
| $c_i = a_i + b_i$ (with saturation) | √ | √ | √ | | | √ |
| $c_i = a_i - b_i$ | √ | √ | √ | √ | | √ |
| $c_i = a_i - b_i$ (with saturation) | √ | √ | √ | | | √ |
| $c_i = average(a_i, b_i)$ | √ | √ | | √ | √ | √ |
| $c_i = average(a_i, -b_i)$ | √ | | | | | |
| $[c_{2i}, c_{2i+1}] = [a_{2i} + a_{2i+1}, b_{2i} + b_{2i+1}]$ | | | | | | √ |
| $lsbit(c_i) = carryout(a_i + b_i)$ | | | | | | √ |
| $lsbit(c_i) = carryout(a_i - b_i)$ | | | | | | √ |
| $c_i = compare(a_i, b_i)$ | √ | | √ | | | √ |
| `Move mask` | | | | √ | √ | |
| $c_i = max(a_i, b_i)$ | √ | √[a] | | √ | √ | √ |
| $c_i = min(a_i, b_i)$ | √ | √[a] | | √ | √ | √ |
| $c = \Sigma\lvert a_i - b_i\rvert$ | √ | √[a] | | √ | √ | |

[a] This operation is realized by using saturation arithmetic.

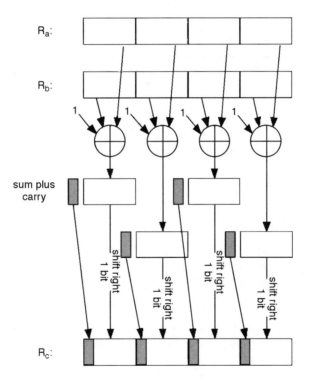

**FIGURE 39.9**  PAVG $R_c$, $R_a$, $R_b$: `Packed average` instruction using the *round away from zero* option.

- *Round away from zero:* A one is added to the intermediate sums, before they are shifted to the right by one bit position. If carry bits were generated during the addition operation, they are inserted into the most significant bit position during the shift right operation (see Fig. 39.9).
- *Round to odd:* Instead of adding one to the intermediate sums, a much simpler OR operation is used. The intermediate sums are directly shifted right by one bit position, and the last two bits of each of the subwords of the intermediate sums are ORed to give the least significant bit of the final result. This makes sure that the least significant bit of the final results are set to 1 (odd) if at least one of the two least-significant bits of the intermediate sums are 1 (see Fig. 39.10).

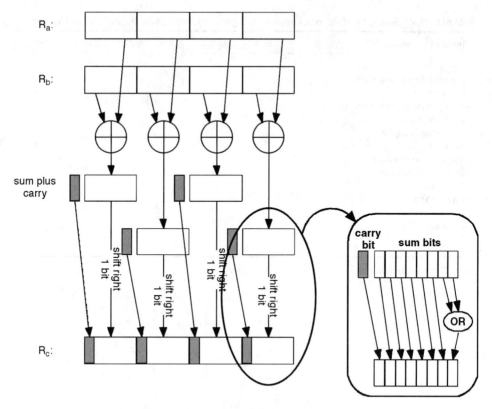

**FIGURE 39.10**   PAVG $R_c$, $R_a$, $R_b$: Packed  average instruction using the *round to odd* option. (From Intel, IA-Architecture Software Developer's Manual, Vol. 3, Instruction Set Reference, Rev. 1.1, July 2000. With permission.)

This rounding mode also performs *unbiased rounding* under the following assumptions. If the intermediate result is uniformly distributed over the range of possible values, then half of the time the bit shifted out is zero, and the result remains unchanged with rounding. The other half of the time the bit shifted out is one: if the next least significant bit is one, then the result loses −0.5, but if the next least significant bit is a zero, then the result gains +0.5. Because these cases are equally likely with a uniform distribution of the result, the *round to odd* option tends to cancel out the cumulative averaging errors that may be generated with repeated use of the averaging instruction.

### Accumulate Integer

Sometimes, it is useful to add adjacent subwords in the same register. This can, for example, facilitate the accumulation of streaming data. An accumulate integer instruction performs an addition of the subwords in the same register and places the sum in the upper half of the target register, while repeating the same process for the second source register and using the lower half of the target register (Fig. 39.11).

### Save Carry Bits

This instruction saves the carry bits from a packed add operation, rather than the sums. Figure 39.12 shows such a save carry bits instruction in AltiVec: a packed add is performed and the carry bits are written to the least significant bit of each result subword in the target register. A similar instruction saves the borrow bits generated when performing packed subtract instead of packed add.

### Packed Compare Instructions

Sometimes, it is necessary to compare pairs of subwords. In a packed compare instruction, pairs of subwords are compared according to the relation specified by the instruction. If the condition is true for a subword pair, the corresponding field in the target register is written with a 1-mask. If the condition is

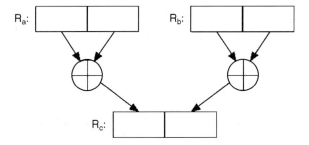

**FIGURE 39.11** ACC R$_c$, R$_a$, R$_b$: `Accumulate integer` working on registers with two subwords.

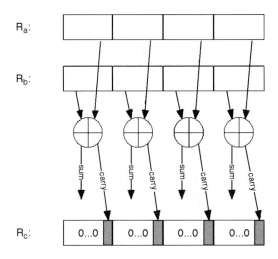

**FIGURE 39.12** `Save carry bits` instruction.

false, the corresponding field in the target register is written with a 0-mask. Alternatively, a true or false bit is generated for each subword, and this set of bits is written into the least significant bits of the result register. Some of the architectures have compare instructions that allow comparison of two numbers for all of the 10 possible relations,[3] whereas others only support a subset of the most frequent relations. A typical **packed compare** instruction is shown in Fig. 39.13 for the case of four subwords.

When a mask of bits is generated as in Fig. 39.13, often a **move mask** instruction is also provided. In a **move mask** instruction, the most significant bits of each of the subwords are picked, and these bits are placed into the target register, in a right aligned field (see Fig. 39.14). In different algorithms, either the subword mask format generated in Fig. 39.13 or the bit mask format generated in Fig. 39.14 is more useful.

Two common comparisons used are finding the larger of a pair of numbers, or the smaller of a pair of numbers. In the **packed maximum** instruction, the greater of the subwords in the compared pair gets written to the corresponding subword in the target register (see Fig. 39.15). Similarly, in the **packed minimum** instruction, the smaller of the subwords in the compared pair gets written to the corresponding subword in the target register. As described in the earlier section on saturation arithmetic, instead of special instructions for **packed maximum** and **packed minimum**, MAX-2 performs **packed maximum** and

---

[3] Two numbers *a* and *b* can be compared for one of the following 10 possible relations: equal, less-than, less-than-or-equal, greater-than, greater-than-or-equal, not-equal, not-less-than, not-less-than-or-equal, not-greater-than, not-greater-than-or-equal. Typical notation for these relations are as follows respectively: `=`, `<`, `<=`, `>`, `>=`, `!=`, `!<`, `!<=`, `!>`, `!>=`.

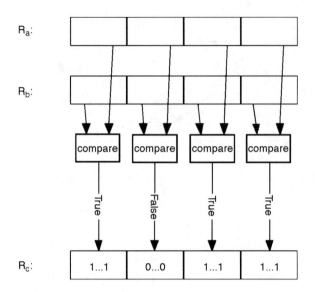

**FIGURE 39.13**   Packed compare instruction. Bit masks are generated as a result of the comparisons made.

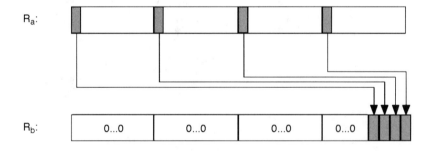

**FIGURE 39.14**   Move mask $R_b$, $R_a$.

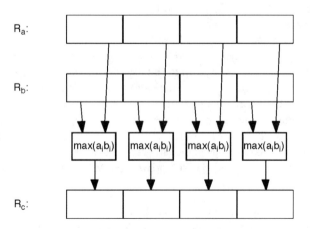

**FIGURE 39.15**   Packed maximum instruction.

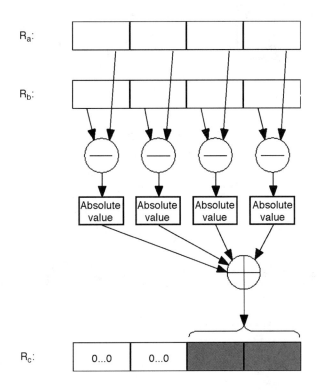

**FIGURE 39.16** SAD $R_c$, $R_a$, $R_b$: Sum of absolute differences instruction.

packed minimum operations by using packed add and packed subtract instructions with saturation arithmetic (see Fig. 39.8). An ALU can be used to implement comparisons, maximum and minimum instructions with a subtraction operation; comparisons for equality or inequality is usually done with an exclusive-or operation, also available in most ALUs.

### Sum of Absolute Differences

A more complex, multi-cycle instruction is the sum of absolute differences (SAD) instruction (see Fig. 39.16). This is used for motion estimation in MPEG-1 and MPEG-2 video encoding, for example. In a SAD instruction, the two packed operands are subtracted from one another. Absolute values of the resulting differences are then summed up.

Although useful, the SAD instruction is a multi-cycle instruction with a typical latency of three cycles. This can complicate the pipeline control of otherwise single cycle integer pipelines. Hence, minimalist multimedia instruction sets like MAX-2 do not have SAD instructions. Instead, MAX-2 uses generic packed add and packed subtract instructions with saturation arithmetic to perform the SAD operation (see Fig. 39.8(b) and Table 39.1).

## Packed Multiply Instructions

### Multiplication of Two Packed Integer Registers

The main difficulty with packed multiplication of two $n$-bit integers is that the product is twice as long as each operand. Consider the case where the register size is 64 bits and the subwords are 16 bits. The result of the packed multiplication will be four 32-bit products, which cannot be accommodated in a single 64-bit target register.

One solution is to use two packed multiply instructions. Figure 39.17 shows a packed multiply high instruction, which places only the more significant upper halves of the products into the target register.

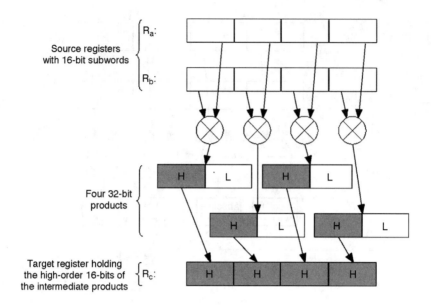

**FIGURE 39.17**  Packed multiply high instruction.

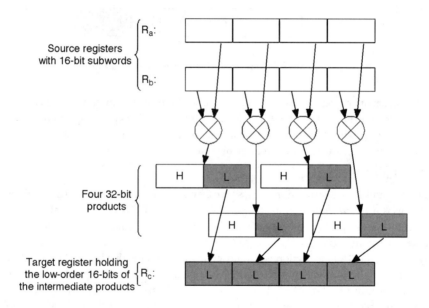

**FIGURE 39.18**  Packed multiply low instruction.

Figure 39.18 shows a packed multiply low instruction, which places only the less significant lower halves of the products into the target register.

IA-64 generalizes this with its packed multiply and shift right instruction (see Fig. 39.19), which does a parallel multiplication followed by a right shift. Instead of being able to choose either the upper or the lower half of the products to be put into the target register, it allows multiple[4] different 16-bit fields from each of the 32-bit products to be chosen and placed in the target register. Ideally, saturation

---

[4] In IA-64 the right-shift amounts are limited to 0, 7, 15, or 16 bits, so that only 2 bits in the packed multiply and shift right instruction are needed to encode the four shift amounts.

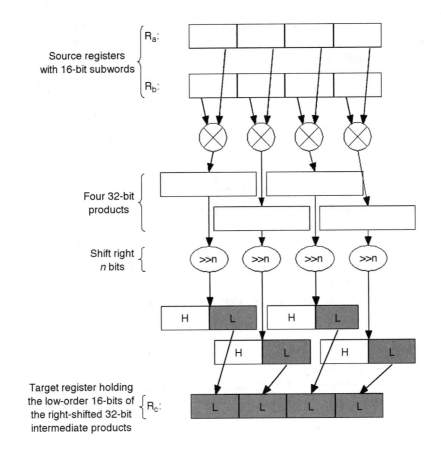

**FIGURE 39.19**  The generalized `packed multiply and shift right` instruction.

arithmetic is applied to the shifted products, to guard for the loss of significant "1" bits in selecting the 16-bit results.

IA-64 also allows the full product to be saved, but for only half of the pairs of source subwords. Either the odd or the even indexed subwords are multiplied. This makes sure that only as many full products as can be accommodated in one target register are generated. These two variants, the `packed multiply left` and `packed multiply right` instructions, are depicted in Figs. 39.20 and 39.21.

Another variant is the `packed multiply and accumulate` instruction. Normally, a `multiply and accumulate` operation requires three source registers. The `PMADDWD` instruction in MMX requires only two source registers by performing a `packed multiply` followed by an addition of two adjacent subwords (see Fig. 39.22).

Instructions in the AltiVec architecture may have up to three source registers. Hence, AltiVec's `packed multiply and accumulate` uses three source registers. In Fig. 39.23, the instruction `packed multiply high and accumulate` starts just like a `packed multiply` instruction, selects the more significant halves of the products, then performs a `packed add` of these halves and the values from a third register. The instruction `packed multiply low and accumulate` is the same, except that only the less significant halves of the products are added to the subwords from the third register.

### Multiplication of a Packed Integer Register by an Integer Constant

Many multiplications in multimedia applications are with constants, instead of variables. For example, in the inverse discrete cosine transform (IDCT) used in the compression and decompression of JPEG images and MPEG-1 and MPEG-2 video, all the multiplications are by constants. This type of multiplication can be further optimized for simpler hardware, lower power, and higher performance simultaneously by using

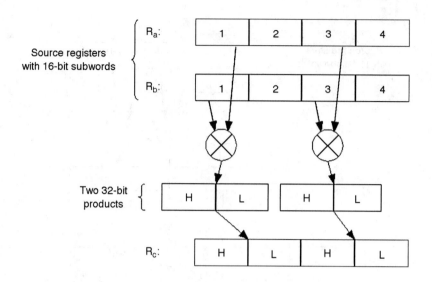

**FIGURE 39.20** Packed multiply left instruction where only the odd indexed subwords of the two source registers are multiplied.

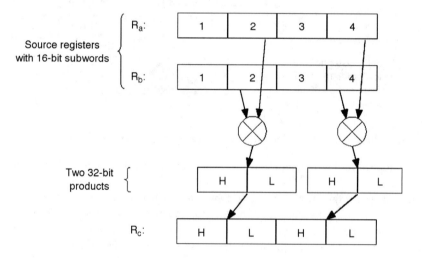

**FIGURE 39.21** Packed multiply right instruction where only the even indexed subwords of the two source registers are multiplied.

packed shift and add instructions [14,15,20]. Shifting a register left by $n$ bits is equivalent to multiplying it by $2^n$. Since a constant number can be represented as a binary sequence of ones and zeros, using this number as a multiplier is equivalent to a left shift of the multiplicand of $n$ bits for each $n$th position where there is a 1 in the multiplier and an add of each shifted value to the result register.

As an example, consider multiplying the integer register $R_a$ with the constant $C = 11$. The following instruction sequence performs this multiplication. Assume $R_a$ initially contains the value 6.

*Initial values:* $C = 11 = 1011_2$ and $R_a = 6 = 0110_2$

| Instruction | Operation | Result |
|---|---|---|
| Shift left 1 bit $R_b, R_a$ | $R_b = R_a \ll 1$ | $R_b = 1100_2 = 12$ |
| Add $R_b, R_b, R_a$ | $R_b = R_b + R_a$ | $R_b = 1100_2 + 0110_2 = 010010_2 = 18$ |
| Shift left 3 bit $R_c, R_a$ | $R_c = R_a \ll 3$ | $R_c = 0110_2 * 8 = 110000_2 = 48$ |
| Add $R_b, R_b, R_c$ | $R_b = R_b + R_c$ | $R_b = 010010_2 + 110000_2 = 1000010_2 = 66$ |

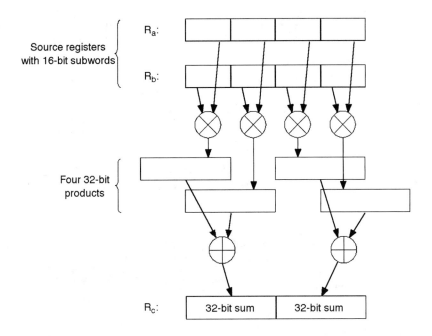

**FIGURE 39.22** Packed multiply and accumulate instruction in MMX.

This sequence can be shortened by combining the **shift left** and the **add** instructions into one new **shift left and add** instruction. The following new sequence performs the same multiplication in half as many instructions and uses one less register.

*Initial values:* $C = 11 = 1011_2$ and $R_a = 6 = 0110_2$

| Instruction | Operation | Result |
|---|---|---|
| Shift left 1 bit and add $R_b, R_a, R_a$ | $R_b = R_a \ll 1 + R_a$ | $R_b = 18$ |
| Shift left 3 bit and add $R_b, R_a, R_b$ | $R_b = R_a \ll 3 + R_b$ | $R_b = 66$ |

Multiplication of packed integer registers by integer constants uses the same idea. The **shift left and add** instruction becomes a **packed shift left and add** instruction to support the packed data types. As an example consider multiplying the subwords of the packed integer register $R_a = [1|2|3|4]$ by the constant $C = 11$. The instructions to perform this operation are:

*Initial values:* $C = 11 = 1011_2$ and $R_a = [1|2|3|4] = [0001|0010|0011|0100]_2$

| Instruction | Operation | Result |
|---|---|---|
| Shift left 1 bit and add $R_b, R_a, R_a$ | $R_b = R_a \ll 1 + R_a$ | $R_b = [3|6|9|12]$ |
| Shift left 3 bit and add $R_b, R_a, R_b$ | $R_b = R_a \ll 3 + R_b$ | $R_b = [11|22|33|44]$ |

The same reasoning used for multiplication by integer constants applies to multiplication by fractional constants. Arithmetic right shift of a register by $n$ bits is equivalent to dividing it by $2^n$. Using a fractional constant as a multiplier is equivalent to an arithmetic right shift of the multiplicand by $n$ bits for each $n$th position where there is a 1 in the multiplier and an add of each shifted value to the result register. By using a **packed arithmetic shift right and add** instruction, the **shift** and the **add** instructions can be combined into one to further speed such computations. For instance, multiplication of a

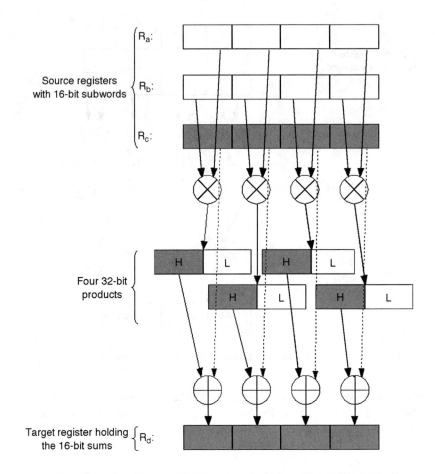

**FIGURE 39.23** In the packed multiply high and accumulate instruction in AltiVec, only the high-order bits of the intermediate products are used in the addition.

packed register by the fractional constant $0.011_2$ (=0.375) can be performed by using just two **packed arithmetic shift right and add** instructions.

*Initial values:* $C = 0.375 = 0.011_2$ and $R_a = [1|2|3|4] = [0001|0010|0011|0100]_2$

| Instruction | Operation | Result |
|---|---|---|
| Arithmetic shift right 3 bit and add $R_b, R_a, 0$ | $R_b = R_a \gg 3 + 0$ | $R_b = [0.125|0.25|0.375|0.5]$ |
| Arithmetic shift right 2 bit and add $R_b, R_a, R_b$ | $R_b = R_a \gg 2 + R_b$ | $R_b = [0.375|0.75|1.125|1.5]$ |

Only two single-cycle instructions are required to perform the multiplication of four subwords by a constant, in this example. This is equivalent to an effective rate of two multiplications per cycle. Without subword parallelism, the same operations would take at least four integer multiply instructions. Furthermore, the packed shift and add instructions use a simple ALU with a small preshifter, whereas the integer multiply instructions need a more complex multiplier functional unit. In addition, each multiplication operation takes at least three cycles of latency compared to one cycle of latency for a preshift and add operation. Hence, for this example, the speedup for multiplying four subwords by a constant is six times faster ($4 \times 3/2$), comparing implementations with one (non-pipelined) subword multiplier versus one partitionable ALU with preshifter.

MAX-2 in PA-RISC and IA-64 are the only multimedia ISAs surveyed that have these efficient packed shift left and add instructions and packed shift right and add instructions. The preshift

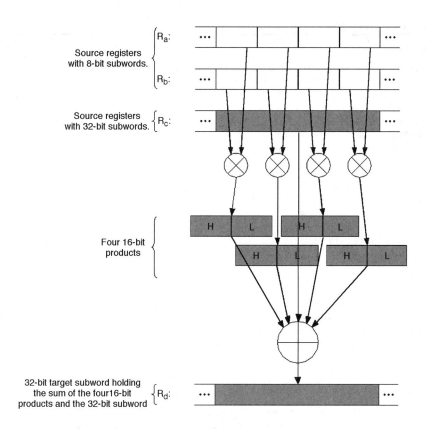

**FIGURE 39.24** AltiVec's `VSUMMBM` instruction: only one-fourth of the instruction is shown. Each box represents a byte. This process is carried out for each 32-bit word in the 128-bit source registers.

amounts allowed are by one, two, or three bits, and the arithmetic is performed with signed saturation, for 16-bit subwords.

## Vector Multiplication

So far, this chapter has examined relatively simple `packed multiply` instructions. These instructions all take about the same latency as a single `multiply` instruction, which is typically 3–4 cycles compared to an `add` instruction normalized to one cycle latency. For better or worse, some multimedia ISAs have included very complex, multiple-cycle operations. For example, AltiVec has a `packed vector multiply and accumulate` instruction, using three 128-bit packed source operands and a 128-bit target register (see Fig. 39.24). First, all the pairs of bytes within a 32-bit subword in two of the source registers are multiplied in parallel and 16-bit products are generated. Then, four 16-bit products are added to each other to generate a "sum of products" for every 32 bits. A 32-bit subword from the third source register is added to this "sum of products." The resulting sum is placed in the corresponding 32-bit subword field of the target register. This process is repeated for each of the four 32-bit subwords. This is a total of sixteen 8-bit integer multiplies, twelve 16-bit additions, and four 32-bit additions, using four 128-bit registers, in a single `VSUMMBM` instruction. This can perform a $4 \times 4$ matrix times a $4 \times 1$ vector multiplication, where each element is a byte, in a single instruction, but this single complex instruction takes many cycles of latency. While a multiplication of a $4 \times 4$ matrix with a $4 \times 1$ vector is a very frequent operation in graphics geometry processing, the precision required is usually that of 32-bit single-precision floating-point numbers, not 8-bit integers. Whether the complexity of such a compound `VSUMMBM` instruction is justified depends on the frequency of such $4 \times 4$ matrix-vector multiplications of bytes. Table 39.4 summarizes the packed integer multiplication instructions described.

**TABLE 39.4**  Packed Integer Multiplication Instructions

| Integer Operations | IA-64 | MAX-2 | MMX | SSE-2 | 3DNow! | AltiVec |
|---|---|---|---|---|---|---|
| $c_i = lower\_half(a_i * b_i)$ | √ | | √ | √ | √ | √ |
| $c_i = upper\_half(a_i * b_i)$ | √ | | √ | √ | √ | √ |
| $c_i = lower\_half[(a_i * b_i) \gg n]$ | √[a] | | | | | |
| Packed multiply left $[c_{2i}, c_{2i+1}] = a_{2i} * b_{2i}$ | √ | | | | | |
| Packed multiply right $[c_{2i}, c_{2i+1}] = a_{2i+1} * b_{2i+1}$ | √ | | | | | |
| Packed multiply and accumulate | | | | | | |
| $[c_{2i}, c_{2i+1}] = a_{2i} * b_{2i} + a_{2i+1} * b_{2i+1}$ | | | √ | | | |
| $d_i = upper\_half(a_i * b_i) + c_i$ | | | | | | √ |
| $d_i = lower\_half(a_i * b_i) + c_i$ | | | | | | √ |
| Packed shift left and add[b] | √ | √ | | | | |
| $c_i = (a_i \gg n) + b_i$, for $n = 1$, 2 or 3 bits. | | | | | | |
| Packed shift right and add[c] | √ | √ | | | | |
| $c_i = (a_i \ll n) + b_i$, for $n = 1$, 2 or 3 bits. | | | | | | |
| Packed vector multiply and accumulate (VSUMMBM) | | | | | | √ |
| $[d_{4i}, d_{4i+1}, d_{4i+2}, d_{4i+3}] =$ | | | | | | |
| $[c_{4i}, c_{4i+1}, c_{4i+2}, c_{4i+3}] + \Sigma_{j=1}^{4} a_{4i+j} * b_{4i+j}$ | | | | | | |
| VMSUMxxx instructions of AltiVec (general form) | | | | | | |
| $[d_{2i}, d_{2i+1}] = a_{2i} * b_{2i} + a_{2i+1} * b_{2i+1} + [c_{2i}, c_{2i+1}]$ | | | | | | √ |

[a] Shift amounts are limited to 0,7,15, or 16 bits.
[b] For use in multiplication of a packed register by an integer constant.
[c] For use in multiplication of a packed register by a fractional constant.

## Packed Shift and Rotate Operations

Most microprocessors have one or more shifters in addition to one or more ALUs (see Fig. 39.3). Just as the ALU is partitionable, so is the shifter, for subword-parallel operation. A packed shift instruction performs blocking shifts of the subwords packed in a register. Any bits shifted to the left are blocked from affecting the adjacent subword on the left; any bits shifted to the right are blocked from affecting the adjacent subword on the right.

For the packed shift instruction, the shift can be logical (zeros substituted for vacated bits) or arithmetic (zeros substituted for vacated bits on the right and sign-bit replicated for vacated bits on the left). The shift amount can be given by an immediate operand or by a register operand. When the shift amount is given by a register, each subword is usually shifted by the same amount, given by the least significant $\log_2 n$ bits of a second source register, for shifting the $n$ bits of a first source register (see Fig. 39.25). In a more complicated, but more versatile form, each subword in a packed register can be shifted by a different amount (see Fig. 39.26).

Similarly, the packed rotate instruction performs rotations on each subword in parallel. The amount to be rotated can be specified by an immediate in an instruction, by a single rotate amount in a register, or by different rotate amounts for each subword (see Fig. 39.27). Data-dependent rotations, where the single rotate amount is given in a register, have been proposed for symmetric cryptography algorithms like RC5.

Packed shift instructions may also be used to multiply or divide subwords by a constant that is a power of two. When used in this way, it may be necessary to apply saturation arithmetic with parallel left shifts used for multiplication. It may also be desirable to apply rounding with parallel arithmetic right shifts. Such saturation and rounding complicate the circuitry for the shifter functional unit, and is not implemented by any of the current multimedia ISAs. Hence, packed shift instructions should be used for multiplication or division only when no overflow can occur on left shifts, and sufficient precision can be preserved on right shifts. For multiplication by an integer or fractional constant, packed shift and add instructions, described in the subsection on "Multiplication of a Packed Integer Register by an Integer Constant," are preferable. These can better control accuracy in the multiplication.

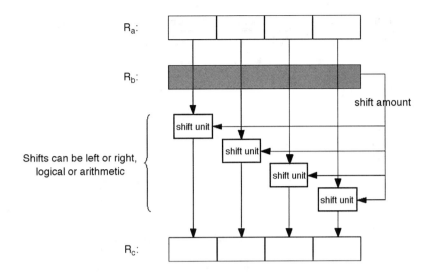

**FIGURE 39.25**  `Packed shift` instruction. Shift amount is given in the second operand. Each subword is shifted by the same amount.

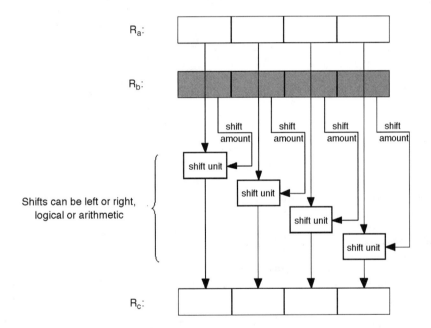

**FIGURE 39.26**  `Packed shift` instruction. Shift amount is given in the second operand. Each subword can be shifted by a different amount.

Table 39.5 summarizes the multimedia instructions involving `packed shift` and `packed rotate` operations. In the table, $n$ is used to represent a shift or rotate amount that is specified in the immediate field of an instruction. For example, in the operation denoted as $c_i = a_i \ll n$, each subword of $c$ is shifted to the left by the amount given in the immediate field of the corresponding instruction. Similarly, in the operation $c_i = a_i \ll b$, each subword of $c$ is shifted to the left by the amount specified in the source register $b$. In $c_i = a_i \ll b_i$, each subword of $c$ is shifted to the left by the amount specified in the corresponding subword of the source register $b$. Shift left is represented by $\ll$, shift right by $\gg$, and rotate by $\lll$.

**TABLE 39.5** Summary of `packed shift` and `packed rotate` Instructions

| Integer Operations | IA-64 | MAX-2 | MMX | SSE-2 | 3DNow! | AltiVec |
|---|---|---|---|---|---|---|
| $c_i = a_i \ll n$ | √ | √ | √ | | | |
| $c_i = a_i \ll b$ | √ | | √ | | | |
| $c_i = a_i \ll b_i$ | | | | | | √ |
| $c_i = a_i \gg n$ | √ | √ | √ | | | |
| $c_i = a_i \gg b$ | √ | | √ | | | |
| $c_i = a_i \gg b_i$ | | | | | | √ |
| $c_i = a_i \lll n$ | | | | | | |
| $c_i = a_i \lll b$ | | | | | | |
| $c_i = a_i \lll b_i$ | | | | | | √ |

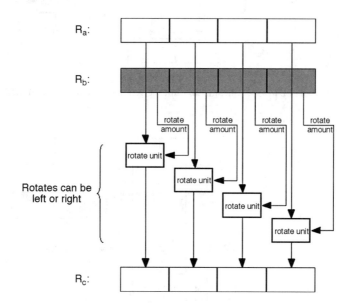

**FIGURE 39.27**　`Packed rotate` instruction. Rotate amount is given in the second operand. Each subword can be rotated by a different amount.

## Subword Permutation Instructions

Initially, the rearrangement of subwords in registers manifested only as packing and unpacking operations. MAX-2 first introduced general-purpose subword permutation instructions for more versatile reordering of subwords packed into one or more registers [9].

### Pack Instructions

`Pack` instructions convert from larger subwords to smaller subwords. If the value in the larger subword is greater than the maximum value that can be represented by the smaller subword, saturation arithmetic is performed, and the resulting subword is set to the maximum value of the smaller subword. Figure 39.28 shows how a register with smaller packed subwords can be created from two registers with subwords that are twice as large. `Pack` instructions differ in the size of the supported subwords and in the saturation options used.

### Unpack Instructions

`Unpack` instructions are used to convert smaller packed data types to larger ones. The subwords in the two source operands are written sequentially to the target register in alternating order. Because, only one-half of each of the source registers can be used, the `unpack` instructions come with two variants

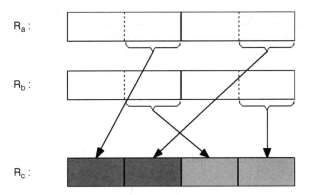

**FIGURE 39.28** Pack instruction converts larger subwords to smaller ones.

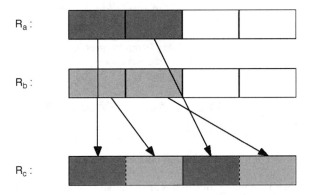

**FIGURE 39.29** Unpack high instruction.

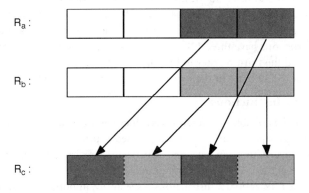

**FIGURE 39.30** Unpack low instruction.

unpack high or unpack low. The unpack high/low instructions select and unpack the high or low order subwords of a source register, when used with register zero as the second source register.[5]

### Subword Permutation Instructions

Ideally, it is desirable to be able to perform all possible permutations on packed data. This is only possible for small numbers of subwords. When the number of subwords increases, the number of control bits required to specify arbitrary permutations becomes too large to be encoded in an instruction. For the case of *n* subwords, the number of control bits used to specify a particular permutation of these *n* subwords

---

[5]Register zero gives a constant value of "zero" when used as a source register.

**TABLE 39.6**    Number of Control Bits Required to Specify an Arbitrary Permutation

| Number of Subwords in a Packed Data Type | Number of Control Bits Required to Specify an Arbitrary Permutation for a Given Number of Subwords |
|:---:|:---:|
| 2 | 2 |
| 4 | 8 |
| 8 | 24 |
| 16 | 64 |
| 32 | 160 |
| 64 | 384 |
| 128 | 896 |

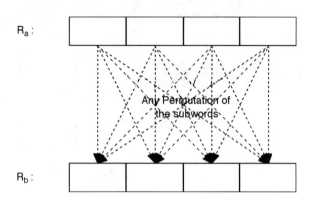

**FIGURE 39.31**    `Mux` instruction in IA-64 or `Permute` instruction in Max-2.

is $n \log_2(n)$. Table 39.6 shows how many control bits are required to specify any arbitrary permutation for different numbers of subwords. When the number of subwords is 16 or greater, the number of control bits exceeds the number of the bits available in the instruction, which is typically 32 bits. Therefore, it becomes necessary to use a second register[6] to contain the control bits used to specify the permutation. By using this second register, it is possible to get any arbitrary permutation of up to 16 subwords in one instruction.

Because AltiVec instructions have three 128-bit source registers, a subword permutation can use two registers to hold data, and the third register to hold the control bits. This allows any arbitrary selection and re-ordering of 16 of the 32 bytes in the two source registers in a **vperm** instruction.

### `Mux`, `Permute`, and `Mix` Instructions

Only a small subset of all the possible permutations is achievable with one subword permutation instruction, so it is desirable to select permutations that can be used as primitives to realize other permutations. A subword permutation instruction can have one or two source registers as operands. In the latter case, only half of the subwords in the two source operands may actually appear in the target register. Examples of these two cases are the **mux** and **mix** instructions respectively, in both IA-64 and MAX-2.

**Mux** in IA-64 operates on one source register. It allows all possible permutations of four packed 16-bit subwords, with and without repetitions (see Fig. 39.31). An 8-bit immediate field in the instruction is used to select one of the 256 possible permutations. This is the same operation performed by the **permute** instruction in the earlier MAX-2.

In IA-64, the **mux** instruction can also permute eight packed 8-bit subwords. For the 8-bit subwords, **mux** has five variants, and only the following permutations are implemented in hardware (see Fig. 39.32):

- **Mux.rev** (reverse): Reverses the order of bytes.
- **Mux.mix** (mix): Performs the **Mix** operation (see below) on the bytes in the upper and lower 32-bit halves of the 64-bit source register.

---

[6]This second register needs to be at least 64-bits wide to fully accommodate the 64 control bits needed for 16 subwords.

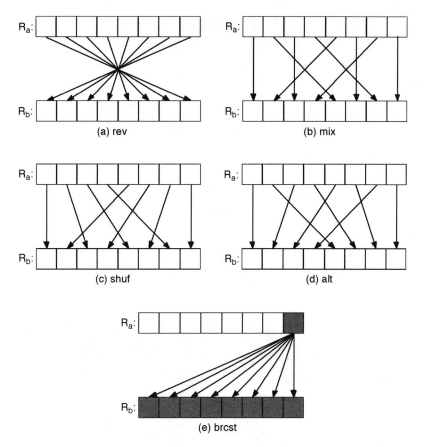

**FIGURE 39.32** `Mux` instruction in IA-64 has five permutation options for 8-bit subwords. (From Intel, IA-Architecture Software Developer's Manual, Vol. 3, Instruction Set Reference, Rev. 1.1, July 2000. With permission.)

- `Mux.shuf` (shuffle): Performs a perfect shuffle on the bytes in the upper and lower halves of the register.
- `Mux.alt` (alternate): Selects first the even[7] indexed bytes, placing them in the upper half of the result register, then selects the odd indexed bytes, placing them in the right half of the result register.
- `Mux.brcst` (broadcast): Replicates the least significant byte into all the byte locations of the result register.

`Mix` is a very useful permutation operation on two source registers. A `mix left` instruction picks even subwords alternately from the two source registers and places them into the target register (see Fig. 39.33). A `mix right` instruction picks odd subwords alternately from the two source registers and places them into the target register (see Fig. 39.34).

The versatility of `Mix` is demonstrated [9, 14], for example, in performing a matrix transpose. `Mix` can also be used to perform an unpacking function similar to that done by `Unpack High` and `Unpack Low`. The usefulness of `Mix` and `Mux` (or `Permute`) has also been validated in [21] as general-purpose subword permutation primitives for processing of two-dimensional data in microSIMD architectures.

### Extract, Deposit, and Shift Pair Instructions

A more sophisticated shifter can also perform `extract` and `deposit` bit-field operations, as in PA-RISC [17, 10]. An `extract` instruction picks an arbitrary contiguous bit-field from the source operand and places it right aligned into the result register (Fig. 39.35). `Extract` instructions may be limited to work

---

[7]The bytes indexed from 0 to 7. 0 corresponds to the most significant byte, which is on the left end of the registers.

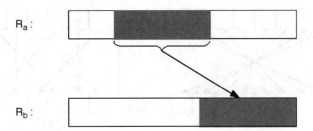

**FIGURE 39.33** Mix Left instruction.

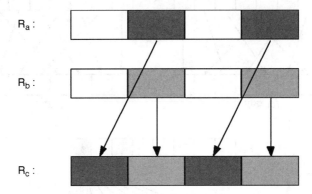

**FIGURE 39.34** Mix Right instruction.

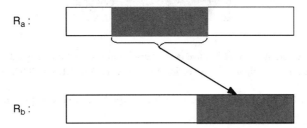

**FIGURE 39.35** Extract bit-field instruction.

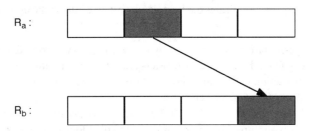

**FIGURE 39.36** Extract subword instruction.

on subwords instead of bit-fields (Fig. 39.36). Extract instructions clear the upper bits of the target register.

A deposit instruction picks a right-aligned contiguous bit-field from the source register and patches it into an arbitrary location in the target register (Fig. 39.37). The unpatched bits of the target register remain unchanged. Alternatively, they are cleared to zeros in a zero and deposit instruction [17]. Deposit instructions may be limited to work on subwords instead of arbitrarily long bit-fields and arbitrary patch locations (Fig. 39.38).

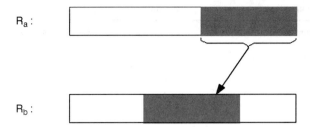

**FIGURE 39.37** `Deposit bit-field` instruction.

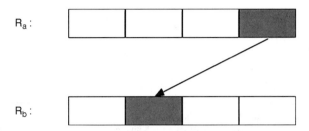

**FIGURE 39.38** `Deposit subword` instruction.

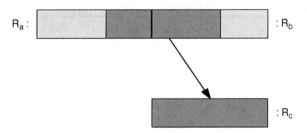

**FIGURE 39.39** `Shift pair` instruction in IA-64.

A very useful instruction for rearranging subwords from two registers is the `shift pair` instruction in IA-64 (see Fig. 39.39). This instruction, which was first introduced in the PA-RISC ISA [10,17], is essentially a `shift` instruction for bit-strings that span more than one register. `Shift pair` concatenates the two source registers to form a 128-bit intermediate value, which is shifted to the right by $n$ bits. The least significant 64 bits of the shifted value is written to the result register. If the same register is specified for both operands, the result is a `rotate` operation. Rotates can be realized this way, so IA-64 does not have a separate `rotate` instruction. This `shift pair` instruction is more general than a `rotate`, allowing flexible combination of two bit-fields from separate registers. Table 39.7 summarizes the subword permutation instructions on packed data types.

## Floating-Point MicroSIMD Instructions

High-fidelity audio and graphics geometry processing require the higher precision and range of floating-point numbers. Usually, single-precision (32-bit) floating-point (FP) numbers are sufficient, but 16-bit integers or fixed-point numbers are not. Double-precision (64-bit) floating-point numbers are not really needed for such multimedia computations.

Because floating-point registers are at least 64-bits wide in microprocessors to support double-precision (DP) FP numbers, it is possible to pack two single-precision (SP) FP numbers in a 64-bit register, to support subword parallelism, or packed parallelism, or microSIMD parallelism on the FP

**TABLE 39.7**    Subword Permutation Instructions

| Integer Operations | IA-64 | MAX-2 | MMX | SSE-2 | 3DNow! | AltiVec |
|---|---|---|---|---|---|---|
| Pack | √ | | √ | | | √ |
| Unpack low | √ | | √ | √ | | √ |
| Unpack high | √ | | | √ | | √ |
| Permute $n$ subwords | √ $(n=4)$ | √ $(n=4)$ | | √ $(n=4)$ | √ $(n=4)$ | √ $(n=16,32)$[a] |
| Mux.rev | √ | | | | | |
| Mux.mix | √ | | | | | |
| Mux.shuffle | √ | | | | | |
| Mux.alt | √ | | | | | |
| Mux.brcst | √ | | | | | |
| Mix left | √ | √ | | | | √ |
| Mix right | √ | √ | | | | √ |
| Extract bit-field | √ | √ | | | | |
| Extract subword | | | | | √ | |
| Deposit bit-field | √ | √ | | | | |
| Deposit subword | | | | | √ | |
| Shift pair $R_c,R_a,R_b$ | √ | √ | | | | |

[a] This is the **vperm** instruction, and it has some limitations for $n = 32$. See text for more details on this instruction. Subword size for this instruction is 8 bits regardless of whether $n$ is 16 or 32.

**TABLE 39.8**    Supported Precision Levels for the Packed FP Operations

| Architecture | IA-64 | SSE-2 | 3DNow! | AltiVec |
|---|---|---|---|---|
| FP register size | 82 bits | 128 bits | 128 bits | 128 bits |
| Allowed packed FP data types | 2 SP | 4 SP or 2 DP | 4 SP | 4 SP |

functional units and registers. The precision levels supported by different ISAs are shown in Table 39.8. SP and DP numbers are 32 and 64 bits long, respectively, as defined by the IEEE-754 FP number standard. Only SSE-2 supports packed DP FP numbers. MAX-2 and MMX do not support packed FP instructions.

## Packed Floating-Point Arithmetic Instructions

### Packed FP Add
Figure 39.40 shows a **packed FP add**, where four pairs of single-precision FP numbers in two 128-bit registers are added using floating-point addition. **Packed FP subtract** instructions are similar. While the packed FP instruction looks very similar to the packed integer equivalents (see Fig. 39.5), implementation of **packed FP add** is not as simple as blocking carries at the subword boundary as in packed integer addition (see Fig. 39.7). It is much more difficult to partition a FP functional unit for subword parallelism because of the nature of FP arithmetic acting on FP numbers represented in sign, mantissa, and exponent format. Another difference is that in floating-point number representation, considerations like modular arithmetic or saturation arithmetic are not applicable.

### Packed FP Multiplication
Multiplication of two packed FP registers involves multiplication of corresponding FP subwords from the source registers, where the products are written to the corresponding subword in the target register (see Fig. 39.41). In multiplication of two single-precision numbers, the product is also single-precision, and hence the same width. Therefore, **packed FP multiply** does not have the problem associated with **packed integer multiply** instructions, where the product is twice the width of the operands.

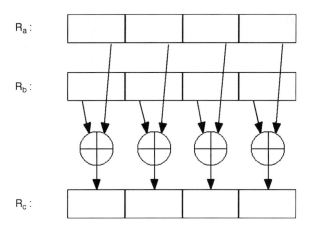

**FIGURE 39.40**  PFPADD R$_c$,R$_a$,R$_b$: Packed FP add instruction.

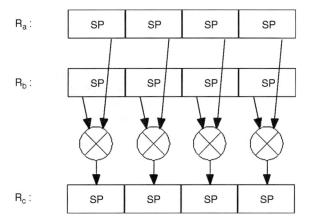

**FIGURE 39.41**  PFPMUL R$_c$,R$_a$,R$_b$: Packed FP multiply instruction.

### *Packed FP Multiply and Add*

The most important FP operation in audio, graphics, and digital signal processing is the FP multiply and accumulate operation. Recognizing this, many ISAs have implemented this as the basic FP operation, needing three source registers. For example, IA-64 implements packed FP multiply and add (FPMA), packed FP multiply and subtract (FPMS), and packed FP negative multiply and add (FPNMA). It then realizes packed FP add, packed FP subtract, and packed FP multiply operations by using FPMA and FPMS instructions. IA-64 architecture specifies 128 FP registers, which are numbered FR0 through FR127. Of these registers, FR0 and FR1 are special. FR0 always returns the value +0.0 when sourced as an operand, and FR1 always reads +1.0. When FR0 or FR1 are used as source operands, the FPMA and FPMS instructions can be used to realize packed FP add or packed FP subtract operations and packed FP multiply operations (see Table 39.9).

The format of the FPMA (Fig. 39.42) instruction is FPMA R$_d$,R$_a$,R$_b$,R$_c$ and the operation it performs is R$_d$ = R$_a$ * R$_b$ + R$_c$. If FR1 is used as the first or the second source operand, a packed FP add operation is realized. Similarly, a FPMS instruction can be used to realize a packed FP subtract operation. Using FR0 as the third source operand in FPMA or FPMS results in a packed FP multiply operation.

Table 39.10 is a summary of the packed FP instructions supported by multimedia ISAs. Several packed FP instructions operate like their packed integer equivalents, except that they operate on packed FP subwords

**TABLE 39.9**    IA-64 uses FPMA and FPMS Instructions for packed FP add, packed FP subtract, and packed FP multiply

| IA-64 Instruction | Operation | Equivalent Instruction |
|---|---|---|
| FPMA $R_d$,FR1,$R_b$,$R_c$<br>(packed FP multiply and add) | $R_d = FR1 * R_b + R_c$<br>$= 1.0 * R_b + R_c$<br>$= R_b + R_c$ | Packed FP add |
| FPMS  $R_d$,FR1,$R_b$,$R_c$<br>(packed FP multiply and subtract) | $R_d = FR1 * R_b - R_c$<br>$= 1.0 * R_b - R_c$<br>$= R_b - R_c$ | Packed FP subtract |
| FPMA $R_d$,$R_a$,$R_b$,FR0<br>(packed FP multiply and add) | $R_d = R_a * R_b + FR0$<br>$= R_a * R_b + 0.0$<br>$= R_a * R_b$ | Packed FP multiply |

Source registers
two SP FP subwords

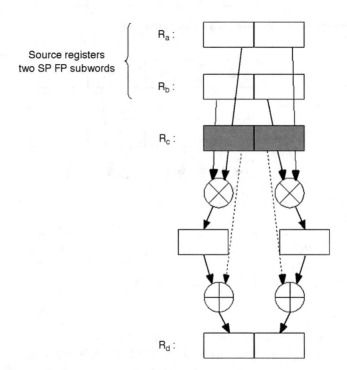

**FIGURE 39.42**    Packed FP multiply and add instruction in IA-64.

rather than packed integer (or fixed-point) subwords. These include packed FP add, packed FP subtract, packed FP multiply, packed FP negate, packed FP absolute value, packed FP compare, packed FP maximum, and packed FP minimum. IA-64 also has the packed FP maximum absolute value and the packed FP minimum absolute value. These put the larger or smaller of the absolute values of the pairs of FP subwords into the result subwords in the target register, respectively.

***Packed FP Compare***

The packed FP compare instruction compares pairs of FP subwords according to the relation specified by the instruction. If the condition is true for a subword pair, the corresponding field in the target register is written with a 1-mask. If the condition is false, the corresponding field in the target register is written with a 0-mask. The only difference is that two additional relations, ordered and unordered, are possible for floating-point numbers in addition to the 10 relations already specified for comparing integers (see

**TABLE 39.10**   Summary of FP microSIMD Instructions

| Packed FP Instructions | IA-64 | SSE-2 | 3DNow! | AltiVec |
|---|---|---|---|---|
| $c_i = a_i + b_i$ | $\sqrt{}^a$ | $\sqrt{}$ | $\sqrt{}$ | $\sqrt{}$ |
| $c_i = a_i - b_i$ | $\sqrt{}^b$ | $\sqrt{}$ | $\sqrt{}$ | $\sqrt{}$ |
| $c_i = a_i * b_i$ | $\sqrt{}^c$ | $\sqrt{}$ | $\sqrt{}$ | |
| $d_i = -a_i * b_i$ | $\sqrt{}$ | | | |
| $d_i = a_i * b_i + c_i$ (FPMA) | $\sqrt{}$ | | | $\sqrt{}$ |
| $d_i = a_i * b_i - c_i$ (FPMS) | $\sqrt{}$ | | | |
| $d_i = -a_i * b_i + c_i$ (FPNMA) | $\sqrt{}$ | | | $\sqrt{}$ |
| $c_i = -a_i$ | $\sqrt{}$ | | | |
| $c_i = |a_i|$ | $\sqrt{}$ | | | |
| $c_i = -|a_i|$ | $\sqrt{}$ | | | |
| $c_i = \text{compare}(a_i, b_i)$ | $\sqrt{}$ | $\sqrt{}$ | $\sqrt{}$ | $\sqrt{}$ |
| $c_i = \max(a_i, b_i)$ | $\sqrt{}$ | $\sqrt{}$ | $\sqrt{}$ | $\sqrt{}$ |
| $c_i = \min(a_i, b_i)$ | $\sqrt{}$ | $\sqrt{}$ | $\sqrt{}$ | $\sqrt{}$ |
| $c_i = \max(|a_i|, |b_i|)$ | $\sqrt{}$ | | | |
| $c_i = \min(|a_i|, |b_i|)$ | $\sqrt{}$ | | | |
| $c_i = \text{VCMPBFB}(a_i, b_i)^e$ | | | | $\sqrt{}$ |
| $c_i = \sqrt{a_i}$ | | $\sqrt{}$ | | |
| $c_i = 1/\sqrt{a_i}$ | $\sqrt{}$ | $\sqrt{}$ | | $\sqrt{}$ |
| $c_i = 1/a_i$ | $\sqrt{}$ | $\sqrt{}$ | | $\sqrt{}$ |
| $c_i = \log_2 a_i$ | | | | $\sqrt{}$ |
| $c_i = 2^{a_i}$ | | | | $\sqrt{}$ |
| `Permute` $n$ FP subwords | | $\sqrt{}$ $(n = 2,4)$ | | |
| `Swap` FP subwords (optionally negate left or right subword) | $\sqrt{}$ | | | |
| `Mix_Left, Mix_Right, Mix_Left_Right` | $\sqrt{}$ | | | |
| `Unpack_high, Unpack_low` | | $\sqrt{}$ | | |
| `Pack` | $\sqrt{}$ | $\sqrt{}$ | | |

[a] This operation is realized by using the **FPMA** instruction.
[b] This operation is realized by using the **FPMS** instruction.
[c] This operation is realized by using the **FPMA** or **FPMS** instruction.
[d] This operation is realized by using the **FPNMA** instruction.
[e] This is the **packed FP compare bounds** instruction, which is explained in the text.

subsection "Packed Compare Instruction"). Some ISAs have **packed FP compare** instructions that allow all the 12 possible relations,[8] whereas others support a more limited subset of relations.

### Packed FP Compare Bounds

An interesting comparison instruction is the **packed FP compare bounds** (**VCMPBFP**) instruction of AltiVec. This instruction compares corresponding FP subwords from the two source registers, and depending on the relation between the compared numbers, it generates a two-bit result, which is written to the target register. The resulting two-bit field indicates the relation between the two compared FP numbers. For instance, in **VCMPBFP** $R_c, R_a, R_b$, the FP number pairs $(a_i, b_i)$ are compared, and a two-bit field is written into $c_i$ such that:

- Bit 0 of the two-bit field is cleared if $a_i <= b_i$, and is set otherwise.
- Bit 1 of the two-bit field is cleared if $a_i >= (-b_i)$, and is set otherwise.
- Both bits are set if any of the compared FP numbers is a NaN.

---

[8]Two floating-point numbers a and b can be compared for one of the following 12 possible relations: equal, less-than, less-than-or-equal, greater-than, greater-than-or-equal, unordered, not-equal, not-less-than, not-less-than-or-equal, not-greater-than, not-greater-than-or-equal, ordered. Typical notation for these relations are as follows respectively: `=, <, <=, >, >=, ?, !=, !<, !<=, !>, !>=, !?`.

**TABLE 39.11** Result of the VCMPBFP
Instruction for Different Input Pairs

| Input | | Output | |
|---|---|---|---|
| $a_i$ | $b_i$ | Bit 0 | Bit 1 |
| 3.0 | 5.0 | 0 | 0 |
| −8.0 | 5.0 | 0 | 1 |
| 8.0 | 5.0 | 1 | 0 |
| 3.0 | −5.0 | 1 | 1 |

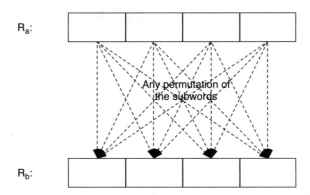

**FIGURE 39.43** FP permute $R_b$, $R_a$: FP permute instruction.

The two-bit result field is written to the high-order two bits of $c_i$; the remaining bits of $c_i$ are cleared to 0. Table 39.11 gives examples of input pairs that result in each of the four different possible outputs for this instruction.

The SSE-2 architecture also includes a **packed FP square root** instruction. This instruction operates on packed single-precision or double-precision numbers and computes the square roots to SP or DP accuracy. IA-64 has the **packed FP reciprocal square root** instruction and the **packed FP reciprocal** instruction. Both are very useful for graphics computations.

### FP Subword Permutation Instructions

#### FP Permutation Instructions

SSE-2 has an **FP permute** (see Fig. 39.43) instruction that allows any arbitrary permutation of the four 32-bit SP subwords in one of its 128-bit multimedia registers. This operates just like the **permute** instruction in MAX-2 and the **mux** instruction (2-byte subword version) in IA-64 (see Fig. 39.31).

IA-64 only has two single-precision subwords in its packed format, so all possible permutations of two subwords can be achieved with a much simpler operation, **FP swap**. This instruction just exchanges the two subwords. IA-64 also allows two variants of this: after swapping the subwords, the sign of either the left or the right FP value is negated.

**FP mix** is a useful operation that performs a permutation on two packed FP registers. A **FP mix** instruction picks alternating subwords from two source registers and places them into the target register. **FP mix** in IA-64 appears in three variants. The first one (Fig. 39.44) is called the **FP mix left** and uses the odd indexed FP subwords of the source registers in the permutation, starting from the leftmost subword. The second variant, **FP mix right** (Fig. 39.45) uses the even indexed FP subwords of the source registers, ending with the rightmost subword. The third variant, **FP mix left right** (Fig. 39.46) uses the odd indexed FP subword of the first source register, and the even indexed subword of the second

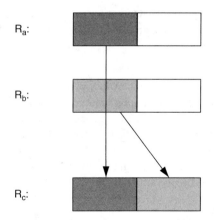

**FIGURE 39.44**  FP mix left R$_c$,R$_b$,R$_a$: FP mix left instruction in IA-64.

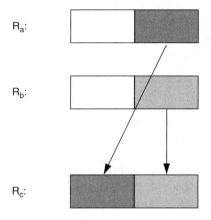

**FIGURE 39.45**  FP mix right R$_c$,R$_b$,R$_a$: FP mix right instruction in IA-64.

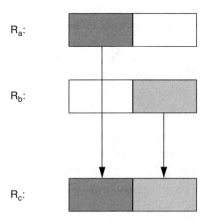

**FIGURE 39.46**  FP mix left right R$_c$,R$_b$,R$_a$: FP mix left right instruction in IA-64.

source register. These three FP mix instructions, together with the `Shift Pair` instruction described earlier, allow any one of the four combinations of the SP subwords packed into two IA-64 registers to be achieved with only one instruction.

### FP Unpack

Packing and unpacking subwords has a different interpretation for FP numbers than for integers. In general, there is sufficient precision in single-precision numbers, and there is no need to unpack it to a double-precision number; however, the `FP unpack` can be regarded as a useful subword permutation instruction like `FP mix`. It performs a `shuffle` by interleaving the subwords from two registers. The `FP unpack` instructions operate just like the equivalent integer unpack instructions (see Figs. 39.29 and 39.30). They come in two "flavors": `FP unpack high` and `FP unpack low`. Note that the SSE-2 employs `FP unpack`, after unpack in MMX, and IA-64 employs `FP mix`, after mix in MAX-2.

### FP Pack

In the integer domain, `pack` instructions are used to create smaller packed data types from larger data types. The `FP pack` instruction in IA-64 creates two packed SP numbers from two 82-bit source registers. All IA-64 FP registers are 82-bit extended precision FP format with two extra guard bits for computational accuracy. First, the two 82-bit numbers are converted to standard 32-bit SP representation. These two SP numbers are then concatenated and the result is stored in the significand field (which is 64 bits) of the 82-bit target FP register. The exponent field of the target register is set to the biased exponent for $2.0^{63}$, which indicates a packed FP format, and the sign bit is set to zero, indicating a positive number.

## Conclusions

Section 39.1 described multimedia instructions for programmable processors by broad classes according to the functional units used, first in the integer domain then in the floating-point domain. For integer subwords, `packed add` and `packed subtract` instructions, and different variants of these, use the ALU. `Packed multiply` instructions use the multiplier functional unit, although very efficient multiplication by constants can be implemented with `packed shift and add` instructions, which only need an ALU with a preshifter. `Packed shift` and `packed rotate` instructions use the shifter. Packed subword permutation instructions can either be implemented on a modified shifter or in a new permutation unit. For packed floating-point instructions, less leverage of hardware seems possible. The basic functional units are a floating-point adder, multiplier, and FP subword permutation unit. IA-64 combines the FP adder and multiplier into an FP multiply-add unit. For each of these instruction classes, interesting multimedia instructions introduced in current microprocessors were described, for example, in the IA-64, MMX, and SSE-2 from Intel; MAX-2 from Hewlett-Packard; 3DNow! from AMD; and AltiVec from Motorola.

The key feature in these multimedia instructions is the concept of subword parallelism, also called packed parallelism or microSIMD parallelism. This is implemented for packed integers or fixed-point numbers in the integer datapaths, and for packed floating-point numbers in the floating-point datapaths. Visual multimedia data like images, video, graphics rendering and animation involve pixel processing, which can fully exploit subword parallelism on the integer datapath. Higher-fidelity audio processing and graphics geometry processing require single-precision floating-point computations, which exploit subword parallelism on the floating-point datapath. Typical DSP operations such as `multiply and accumulate` have also been added to the multimedia repertoire of general-purpose microprocessors. These multimedia instructions have embedded DSP and visual processing capabilities into general-purpose microprocessors, providing native signal processing (sometimes referred to as NSP) for multimedia data. In fact, most DSPs and media processors have also adopted subword parallelism in their architectures, as well as other features often first introduced in microprocessors for multimedia signal processing.

More unusual computer arithmetic issues arising from subword-parallel multimedia instructions in microprocessors are saturation arithmetic, integer rounding alternatives, integer multiplication problems and solutions, and subword permutation instructions.

Some of the multimedia ISAs introduced in microprocessors adhere to the "less is more" minimalist architecture approach, defining as few instructions as necessary for high-performance, with each instruction executable in a single pipeline cycle. Others embody the "more is better" approach, where complex sequences of operations are represented by a single multimedia instruction, with such an instruction taking many cycles for execution. An example is the `packed vector multiply and accumulate` instruction in AltiVec (Fig. 39.24). These two trends represent different stylistic preferences, akin to reduced instruction set computer (RISC) and complex instruction set computer (CISC) architectural preferences. In fact, sometimes, RISC-like multimedia instructions have been added to CISC processor ISAs, and CISC-like multimedia instructions to RISC processor ISAs. The remarkable fact is that subword-parallel multimedia instructions have achieved such rapid and pervasive adoption in both RISC and CISC microprocessors, DSPs and media processors, attesting to their undisputed cost-effectiveness in accelerating multimedia processing in software.

To simplify software compatibility and interoperability of multimedia software across different processors, it is highly desirable to refine the best ideas from the different multimedia ISAs into a coherent set of subword-parallel instructions. If this is a small yet powerful set, it is more likely to be implemented in all future microprocessors and media processors, allowing algorithm and compiler optimizations to exploit microSIMD parallelism with confidence that benefits would be realized across almost all processors. While slight differences in multimedia instructions across processors may not affect the potential performance provided by each ISA, they make it difficult to design an optimal algorithm and a set of compiler optimizations that achieve the best multimedia performance for every processor. The challenge for the next phase of multimedia ISA design is to understand which ISA features are truly effective for multimedia signal processing, and encapsulate these insights into the design of third-generation multimedia ISA for both microprocessors and media processors.

## Acknowledgments

The author thanks her student, A. Murat Fiskiran, for surveying SSE-2, 3DNow! and AltiVec, and for his invaluable help in preparing the figures and tables.

## References

1. Ruby Lee and Michael Smith, "Media processing: a new design target," *IEEE Micro,* Vol. 16, No. 4, pp. 6–9, Aug. 1996.
2. Michael Flynn, "Very high-speed computing systems," *Proceedings of the IEEE,* No. 54, Dec. 1966.
3. Ruby Lee, "Efficiency of MicroSIMD architectures and index-mapped data for media processors," *Proceedings of IS&T/SPIE Symposium on Electric Imaging: Media Processors 99,* pp. 34–46, Jan. 1999.
4. Intel, "IA-64 architecture software developer's manual, volume 3: instruction set reference," Revision 1.1, July 2000, Order Code 245319-002.
5. Ruby Lee, Murat Fiskiran, and Abdulla Bubshait, "Multimedia instructions in IA-64," Invited paper. *Proceedings of the 2001 IEEE International Conference on Multimedia and Exposition,* Aug. 22–24, 2001.
6. Alex Peleg and Uri Weiser, "MMX technology extension to the intel architecture," *IEEE Micro,* Vol. 16, No. 4, pp. 10–20, Aug. 1996.
7. Intel, "Intel architecture software developer's manual, volume 2: instruction set reference," 1999, Order Code 243191.
8. Intel, "IA-32 intel architecture software developer's manual with preliminary willamette architecture information, volume 2: instruction set reference," 2000.
9. Ruby Lee, "Subword parallelism with MAX-2," *IEEE Micro,* Vol. 16, No. 4, pp. 51–59, Aug. 1996.
10. G. Kane, "PA-RISC 2.0 architecture," 1996, Prentice-Hall, Englewood Cliffs, NJ.
11. AMD, "3DNow! technology manual," March 2000, Order Code 21928G/0.
12. AMD, "AMD extensions to the 3DNow! and MMX Instruction Sets Manual," March 2000, Order Code 22466D/0.

13. Motorola, "AltiVec technology programming environments manual," Revision 0.1, November 1998, Order Code ALTIVECPEM/D.
14. Ruby Lee, "Multimedia extensions for general-purpose processors," Invited paper. *Proceedings of the IEEE Signal Processing Systems:Design and Implementation,* pp. 9–23. Nov. 1997.
15. Ruby Lee, "Accelerating multimedia with enhanced microprocessors," *IEEE Micro,* Vol. 15, No. 2, pp. 22–32, April 1995.
16. Ruby Lee, John Beck, Joel Lamb, and Ken Severson, "Real-time software MPEG video decoder on multimedia-enhanced PA7100LC processors," *Hewlett-Packard Journal,* Vol. 46, No. 2, pp. 60–68, April 1995.
17. Ruby Lee, "Precision architecture," *IEEE Computer,* Vol. 22, No. 1, pp. 78–91, Jan. 1989.
18. Vasudev Bhaskaran, Konstantine Konstantinides, Ruby Lee and John Beck, "Algorithmic and architectural enhancements for real-time MPEG-1 decoding on a general purpose RISC workstation," *IEEE Transactions on Circuits and Systems for Video Technology,* Vol. 5, No. 5, pp. 380–386, Oct. 1995.
19. Mark Tremblay, J. M. O'Connor, V. Narayanan, and H. Liang, "VIS speeds new media processing," *IEEE Micro,* Vol. 16, No. 4, pp. 10–20, Aug. 1996.
20. Zhen Luo and Ruby Lee, "Cost-effective multiplication with enhanced adders for multimedia applications," *Proceedings of ISCAS 2000, IEEE International Symposium on Circuits and Systems,* Vol. I, pp. 651–654, May 2000.
21. Ruby Lee, "Subword permutation instructions for two-dimensional multimedia processing in Micro-SIMD architectures," *Proceedings of the IEEE International Conference on Application-specific Systems, Architectures and Processors,* pp. 3–14, July 2000.

# 39.2   DSP Platform Architecture for SoC Products

*Gerald G. Pechanek*

### Introduction

The development of wireless, networking, communications, video, and consumer products has shifted toward low-power high-functionality systems-on-chip (SoC) semiconductors [1]. Driving this development is the availability of deep sub-micron technology allowing more complete system designs to be embedded in silicon. Some of these improvements include increasing on-chip memory capacity, the use of more fully programmable solutions using DSPs, and the inclusion of specialized interfaces and functions.

To make these high-value SoC products widely available at low cost requires the use of standard design practices that allow them to be fabricated at multiple semiconductor suppliers. This means that custom designed SoCs, optimized to a particular manufacturing process, cannot be used. Consequently, as the complexity and functionality of SoC products continues to increase with stringent power requirements, the standard approach of increasing clock speed on an existing design to meet higher performance requirements is infeasible.

The need to support multiple standards, and to quickly adapt to changing standards, has become a product requirement [2]. To satisfy this need, programmable DSPs and control processors are being increasingly used as the central SoC design component. These processors form the basis of the SoC product platform and permeate the overall system design including the on-chip memory, DMA, internal busses, etc. Consequently, choosing a flexible and efficient processor, which can be manufactured by multiple semiconductor suppliers, is arguably the most important intellectual property (IP) decision that needs to be made in the creation of an SoC product.

In recent years, a class of high-performance programmable processor IP has emerged that is appropriate for use in high-volume embedded applications such as digital cellular, networking, communications, and console gaming [3,4]. Section 39.2 briefly describes the ManArray thread coprocessor as an example of the architectural features needed for demanding SoC requirements. The next subsection provides a brief description of the ManArray thread coprocessor architecture. The subsection "The ManArray Thread

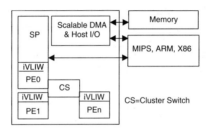

**FIGURE 39.47**   ManArray architectural elements.

Coprocessor Platform" describes how the ManArray architecture fulfills SoC application requirements, with focus on the implementation, compiler, and tools. "Performance Evaluation" presents performance results, and last subsection concludes the chapter section.

## The ManArray Thread Coprocessor Architecture

In numerous application environments there is a need to significantly augment the signal processing capabilities of a MIPS, ARM, or other host processor. In addition, many applications require low power consumption at very high performance levels to accomplish the tasks of emerging applications, such as wireless LAN (i.e., 802.11a) for battery-powered Internet devices. The BOPS SoC cores provide streamlined coprocessor attachment to MIPS, ARM, or other hosts for this purpose. Through selectable parallelism, the ManArray SoC cores achieve high performance at low clock rates, which minimizes power requirements. The compiler or programmer can select from packed data, indirect VLIW, PE array SIMD, and multiple threaded forms of parallelism to provide the best product solution. Further, BOPS provides a complete solution by providing a comprehensive top-down design methodology for delivering the SoC solutions.

The ManArray processor is an array processor using a sequence processor (SP) array controller and an array of distributed indirect VLIW processing elements (PEs) (see Fig. 39.47). By varying the number of PEs on a core, an embedded scalable design is achieved with each core using a single architecture. This embedded scalability makes it possible to develop multiple products that provide a linear increase in performance and maintain the same programming model by merely adding array processor elements as needed by the application. As the processing capability is increased, the memory-to-PE bandwidth is increased, and the system DMA bandwidth may be increased as well. Embedded scalability drastically reduces development costs for future products because it allows for a single BOPS software development kit (SDK) to support a wide range of products.

In addition to the embedded scalability, ManArray cores are configurable in the number and type of cores included on a chip, instruction subsetting for application optimization, the sizes of each SP's instruction memory, the distributed iVLIW memories, the PE/SP data memories, and the I/O buffers, selectable clock speed, choice of on-chip peripherals, and DMA bus bandwidth. The ManArray cores provide a lower cost, more optimized signal processing solution than reconfigurable processors designed using FPGA technology [5]. Multiple ManArray cores provide optimized scalable multiprocessing by including multiple BOPS cores on an SoC product. These multiple ManArray cores can be organized to provide data pipeline processing between SP/PE-array cores and the parallelization of sub-application tasks (thread parallelism) with a centralized host-based control to be described later in this chapter section.

Generally speaking, the ManArray processor combines PEs in clusters that also contain a SP, uniquely merged into the PE array, and a cluster-switch, Fig. 39.47. The SP provides program control, contains the instruction and data address generation units, and dispatches instructions to the processor array. In this manner, the ManArray processor is designed for scalability with a single architecture definition and a common tool set. The processor and supporting tools are designed to optimize the needs of a SoC platform by allowing a designer to balance an application's sequential control requirements with the application's inherent data parallelism. This is accomplished by having a scalable architecture that begins

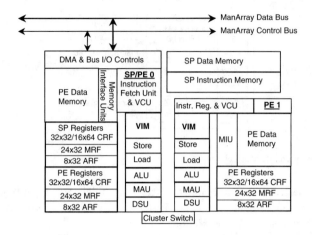

**FIGURE 39.48**   ManArray 1 ×2 core elements.

with a simple uniprocessor model and continues through multi-array processor implementations. In the design flow we ensured that the ManArray architecture supported a reasonably large array processor as well as a simple stand-alone uniprocessor that could act as an array controller. In more detail, a SP merged with PE0 (SP/PE0) and an additional PE (PE1), referenced as a 1 ×2, are shown in Fig. 39.48.

The ManArray architecture uses a distributed register file model where the SP and each PE contain their own independent register space, up to eight execution units (five shown), a distributed very long instruction word memory (VIM), local SP instruction memory, local data memories, and an application-optimized DMA and bus I/O control unit. In the Manta™ core, an available 2 × 2 implementation of the ManArray architecture, and its 1 × 1 and 1 × 2 subsets (available by software masking of selected PEs), a 64-entry register file space is used in the SP and each PE. The register space consists of a reconfigurable compute register file (CRF), which can act as a 32 × 32-bit or 16 × 64-bit register file for the execution units on a cycle-by-cycle basis, totally integrated into the instruction set architecture, an 8 × 32-bit address register file (ARF), and a 24 × 32-bit miscellaneous register file (MRF).

In the ManArray architecture, the address registers are separated from the compute register file. This approach maximizes the number of registers for compute operations and guarantees a minimum number of dedicated address registers. This approach does not require any additional ports from the compute register file to support the load and store address generation functions, and it still allows independent PE memory addressing for such functions as local data dependent table lookups. The Manta chip supports both 32-bit data types including quad byte, dual halfword, and word; and 64-bit data types including octal byte, quad halfword, dual word, and double word. The balanced architectural approach taken for the compute register file provides the high performance features needed by many applications. It supports octal byte and quad halfword operations in a logical 16 ×64-bit register file space without sacrificing the 32-bit data type support in the logical 32 × 32-bit register file. Providing both allows optimum usage of the register file space and minimum overhead in manipulating packed data items. By adding PEs, the packed data support grows such that a 1 × 2 effectively provides 128-bit packed data support, a 2 × 2 provides 256-bit packed data support, etc., growing the level of parallelism needed by appropriate choice of the selected core.

The ManArray instruction set is partitioned into four groups using the high two bits of the instruction format—a control group, an arithmetic group, a load/store group, and a reserved proprietary instruction group. Figure 39.49 shows 32-bit simplex instructions in groupings that represent the five execution unit slots of the Manta chip, the first ManArray implementation, plus a control group (01). The execution units include store and load units, an arithmetic logic unit (ALU), a multiply accumulate unit (MAU), and a data select unit (DSU). The load and store instructions support base plus displacement, direct, indirect, circular, and table addressing modes. The ALU, MAU, and DSU support basic add/subtract, multiply,

| Control | Store | Load | ALU | MAU | DSU |
|---------|-------|------|-----|-----|-----|
| Group 01 | Group 10 | Group 10 | Group 11 | Group 11 | Group 11 |
| Call | Base+Disp. | Base+Disp. | ADD/SUB | ADD/SUB | Copy |
| Jump | Direct | Direct | Butterfly | Butterfly | Shift/Rotate |
| EventPoint Loops | Indirect | Indirect | Compare | MPY/MPYA | Permute |
| Return | Circular | Circular | AbsoluteDiff | MPYCmplx | Bit operations |
| Load VLIW | Table | Table | Min/Max | MPYCmplxA | Divide |
| Execute VLIW | ARF group | ARF group | Logicals | SUM2P/SUM2PA | Communications PEeXchange |
| | | Immediate | | | |
| | | Broadcast | | | |

**FIGURE 39.49**

and data type manipulations such as shift, rotate, and permute, respectively. In addition, many application specific instructions are used for improved signal processing efficiency. An example of this are the multiply complex instructions for improved FFT performance described in reference [6].

The control and branch instructions are executed by the SP. It is also capable of indirectly executing VLIWs that are local to the SP and in each PE. To minimize the effects of branch latencies, a short variable pipeline is used consisting of Fetch, Decode, Execute, and ConditionReturn for non-iVLIWs and Fetch, PreDecode, Decode, Execute, and ConditionReturn for iVLIWs. The PreDecode pipeline stage is used to indirectly fetch VLIWs from their local VIMs. Note that VLIWs are stored locally in VIMs in each PE and in the SP and are fetched by a 32-bit execute VLIW (XV) instruction. In addition, an extensive scalable conditional execution approach is used in each PE and the SP to minimize the use of branches.

All loads/stores and arithmetic instructions execute in one or two cycles with no hardware interlocks. Further, all arithmetic and load/store instructions can be combined into VLIWs, stored locally in the SP and in each PE, and can be indirectly selected for execution from the small distributed VLIW memories (VIMs). Using the load iVLIW (LV) instruction, the programmer or compiler loads individual instruction slots with the 32-bit simplex instructions optimized for the algorithm being programmed. These VLIWs are used for algorithm performance optimization, are re-loadable, and require only the use of a 32-bit execute VLIW (XV) instructions in the program stored in the SP instruction memory.

A dedicated bit in all instruction formats controls whether an instruction is executed in parallel across the array of PEs or sequentially in the SP. To more optimally support a multiple PE array containing the distributed register files, the ManArray network is integrated into the architecture providing single-cycle data transfers within PE clusters and between orthogonal clusters of PEs. The DSU communications instructions can also be included into VLIWs, thereby overlapping communications with computation operations, which in effect reduces the communication latency to zero. The ManArray network operation is independent of background DMA operations, which provide a data streaming path to peripherals, such as a global memory.

The inherent scalability of the ManArray processor is obtained in part through the advanced ManArray network which interconnects the PEs. Consider by way of example, a two-dimensional (2D) $4 \times 4$ torus and the corresponding embedded 4D hypercube, written as a $4 \times 4$ table with both row, column, and hypercube node labels. (See Fig. 39.50A.)

In Fig. 39.50A, the $PE_{i,j}$ cluster nodes are labeled in gray-code as follows: $PE_{G(i),G(j)}$ where $G(x)$ is the gray code of $x$. First, columns 2, 3, and 4 are rotated one position down. Next, the same rotation is repeated with columns 3 and 4, and then with column 4. The resulting 4D ManArray table is shown in Fig. 39.50B.

Notice that the row elements in Fig. 39.50B, for example $\{(1,0), (0,1), (3,2), (2,3)\}$, contain the transpose PE elements. By grouping the row elements in clusters of four PEs each, and completely interconnecting the four PEs, connectivity among the transpose elements can be obtained. Notice also that, in the new matrix of PEs, the east and south wires, as well as the north and west wires, are connected between adjacent clusters. For example, using Fig. 39.50A note that node (2,3) connects to the east node (2,0) with wraparound

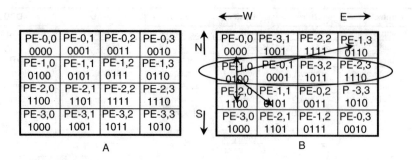

**FIGURE 39.50**    Hypercube interconnection scheme.

wires in a torus arrangement. Node (2,3) also connects to the south node (3,3). Now, using Fig. 39.50B, note that nodes (2,0) and (3,3) are both in the same cluster adjacent to the cluster containing node (2,3). This same pattern occurs for all nodes in the new matrix. This means that the east and south wires can be shared and, in a similar manner, the west and north wires can be shared between all clusters. This effectively cuts the wiring in half as compared to a standard torus, and without affecting the performance of any SIMD array algorithm.

The rotating algorithm maintains the connectivity between the PEs, so the normal hypercube connections still remain as shown in one example in Fig. 39.50B as PE (1,0/0100) can communicate to its nearest hypercube nodes {(0000), (0101), (0110), (1100)} in a single step. Note also that the longest paths in a hypercube, where each bit in the node address changes between two nodes, are all contained in the completely connected clusters of processors nodes. For example, the circled cluster contains node pairs {(0100), (1011)} and {(0001), (1110)}, which would take four steps to communicate between each pair in previous hypercube processors, takes only one step to communicate in the new ManArray network. These properties are maintained in higher dimensional ManArray networks containing higher dimensional tori, and thus hypercubes, as subsets of the ManArray connectivity matrix. We have also shown that the complexity of the ManArray network is small and that the diameter, the largest distance between any pair of nodes, is 2 for all $d$ where $d$ is the dimension of the subset hypercube [7].

Application-specific instructions are included in the various execution units, such as multiply complex [6] and other video, graphics, and communications unique instructions. Any of the four groups of instructions can be mixed on a cycle-by-cycle basis. The single ManArray instruction set architecture supports the entire ManArray family of cores from the single merged SP/PE0 $1 \times 1$ to any of the highly parallel multi-processor arrays ($1 \times 2$, $2 \times 2$, $2 \times 4$, $4 \times 4$, etc.), for more details see references [8] and [9].

## The ManArray Thread Coprocessor Platform

The ManArray thread coprocessors are designed to act as independent coprocessors to ARM, MIPS, or other hosts. The programmer's view is a shared memory sequentially coherent model where multiple processors operate on independent processes. With this model, an SoC developer can quickly utilize the signal processing capabilities of the ManArray core subsystem since the operating system already runs on the host processors. In its role as a digital signal coprocessor, the ManArray core is subservient to the host processor. A core driver running on the host operating system manages all the DSP resources on the core. The ManArray system interface allows multiple BOPS cores to be attached to a single host processor as shown, for example, in Fig. 39.51. For wireless and media processing applications the $1 \times 1$ MOCARay-I mobile communications accelerator and the $1 \times 2$ MICORay-I imaging communications engine are designed to work separately or jointly, as shown in Fig. 39.51, to provide ultra low-power baseband and media DSP services for 3G mobile products. Figure 39.51 shows a multimode Smart Phone or PDA with MOCARay-I providing the GPRS/EDGE and/or UMTS mode while MICORay-I provides support for video MPEG-4, JPEG 2000 photo imaging, speech decode/encode, sprite-based rendering in a gaming mode, audio processing MP3, etc.

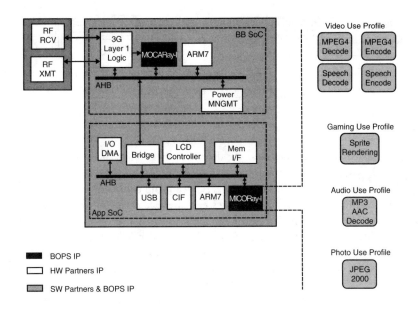

**FIGURE 39.51**   Application of multiple BOPS cores to 3G wireless.

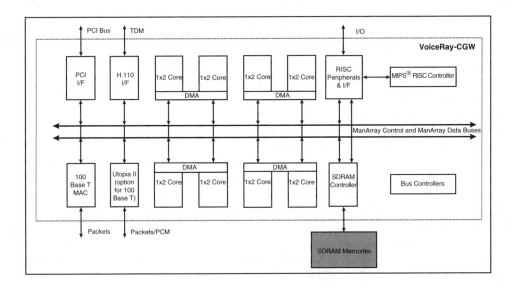

**FIGURE 39.52**   Application of multiple BOPS cores to VoIP.

Another example of the use of BOPS cores as thread coprocessors is in voice-over-Internet protocol (VoIP) products. For this application, an integrated dual $1 \times 2$ arrangement with a common DMA controller is used as the basic platform unit. One, two, or four of these dual $1 \times 2$ units are provided as an SoC DSP "farm" with an on-board host engine, e.g. MIPS.

Figure 39.52 illustrates the configuration with eight $1 \times 2$ cores. This system arrangement allows the workload to be partitioned appropriately allowing extant applications to run on existing host OSs in the MIPS controller. This lowers the risk of migrating an existing code base, and no new OS ports are required to support the ManArray cores. To complement the configurable hardware, there is a BOPS library of both DSP and control software routines to perform the desired VoIP gateway functions. In addition,

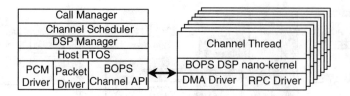

**FIGURE 39.53**   Host DSP software layers.

existing host optimized compilers are used for the sequential code that remains resident on the host allowing the parallel code to be optimized for the ManArray cores.

A driver API allows host applications to initialize, control, and communicate with multiple ManArray coprocessors attached to the host. A standard message interface exists for all coprocessors to/from the host. Specifically, the ManArray core DSPs are described as thread coprocessors because the host processor dispatches entire threads of execution to the cores. The host driver loads programs, schedules context switches, and manages data streams into and out of the various coprocessors. The high-performance DMA engine, scaled appropriately for the application, autonomously transfers data streams to and from the host. In addition, data streams can be "pushed/pulled" from one coprocessor to another, or to/from peripherals (such as an H.100 interface) and coprocessors, without host intervention, using the ManArray DMA-to-DMA interconnection protocol.

The DMA subsystem consists of the DMA controller, a ManArray control bus (MCB), and a ManArray data bus (MDB). The MDB provides the high-bandwidth data interface between the cores and other system peripherals including system memory. The MDB consists of multiple identical lanes and is scalable by increasing the number of lanes and/or increasing the width of the lanes. Specifically, the MDB uses time division multiplexing of multiple independent buses or lanes to transfer data. The MCB is a low latency coprocessor-to-coprocessor/peripheral messaging bus, which runs independently and in parallel with the MDB. This system of multiple independent application task-optimized cores is designed to have each core run an independent thread supported by the programmable DMA engines [10].

Figure 39.53 illustrates the host-DSP software layers. The multiple ManArray cores support the multiple independent program threads that are managed by the host OS through remote procedure calls (RPC) scheduled by the RTOS driver running in the host. The BOPS channel processing API provides a standard interface for allocating voice channel processing to the multiple 1 × 2 cores. On the ManArray core side, a thin DSP nano-kernel supports thread load/unload with DMA transfers overlapping computation. The RPC and DMA drivers provide standard host-DSP communication and data transfer support.

Supporting this scalable platform for VoIP solutions is BOPS SoC design flow as shown in Fig. 39.54. Four parallel processes are shown supporting both hardware and software design efforts for the thread coprocessors, peripherals, host software, and DSP software developments.

Once the SoC functional specification and a basic system design is determined the next development steps can be done in parallel. The ManArray core RTL and other peripheral RTL are done in parallel, being designed to the ManArray interface specifications. At the same time, due to the use of a cycle accurate system simulator and other supporting tools, the host CPU software and DSP software development are done in parallel.

To streamline development, verification and debug, BOPS provides a range of modeling and prototyping platforms to support system modeling, and software and hardware system development including:

- a cycle-accurate C-simulator, which can be used to develop ManArray DSP and system software. This can be used directly with other C simulations, or with control processor tools and bus models to provide a software simulation model of an entire system;
- a software development toolkit (SDK) including the BOPS ANSI-C Halo™ parallelizing C compiler;
- the Jordan™/Manta™ PCI card, which can be used to model and test DSP software at 100 MHz processor speeds and under actual DMA I/O conditions;

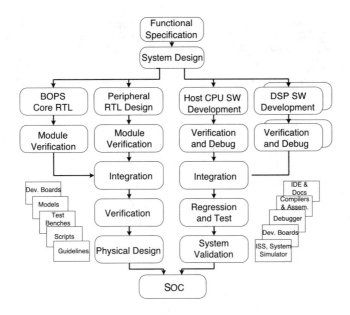

**FIGURE 39.54** BOPS SoC design flow.

- the Travis™/ Manta™ prototyping board, which can be used to prototype entire SoC systems at actual speeds;
- the Xemulator™ emulation board, which can be used to model RTL emulations of an entire SoC system.

The same DSP debugging GUI is shared by the C-simulator, Jordan, Travis, and Xemulator boards. The Jordan development and Travis prototyping boards are provided using a $2 \times 2$ Manta core that contains features needed in many applications. The Travis system prototyping board uses the standard configurations available on Manta cores $1 \times 1$, $1 \times 2$, and $2 \times 2$. All of the normal fixed resources such as host microcontroller, oscillators, memories, power supplies, configuration controls, debug, peripheral and PCI interfaces are also on board. In addition, a large FPGA accommodates all unique logic circuits allowing for rapid design, testing, and debug. The Jordan board with the Manta chip provides real time operation of standard cores in a MIPS host system with off board system prototyping. Also included on the Jordan board is a MIPS microcontroller with interrupts and boot ROM. With these development boards the software can be integrated and tested. BOPS also provides verification tools and supporting scripts and guidelines for the physical design.

The SoC emulator board, the Xemulator, allows MHz speed emulation in FPGAs of the many possible RTL hardware and software configurations of the scalable ManArray architecture. This is useful when bus sizes, bus protocols, and external interfaces are changed from the standard core configurations. Likewise, I/O and DMA controllers may need to be altered for certain applications. Additions, subsetting, and other changes to the instruction set can be explored on the Xemulator by modifying the downloaded core's FPGA description.

## Performance Evaluation

To illustrate the power of the highly parallel ManArray architecture, a simple example is presented: Two vectors are to be added and the result stored in a third vector.

$$\text{for } (i = 0; i < 256; i{+}{+})$$

$$A[i] = B[i] + C[i]$$

| Benchmark | Data Type | Performance |
|---|---|---|
| 256 pt. Complex FFT (2x2) | 16-bit real & imaginary | 383 cycles |
| 256 pt. Complex FFT (1x1) | 16-bit real & imaginary | 1115 cycles |
| 1024 pt. Complex FFT (2x2) | 16-bit real & imaginary | 1513 cycles |
| 1024 pt. Complex FFT (1x1) | 16-bit real & imaginary | 5221 cycles |
| 2048 pt. Complex FFT (2x2) | 16-bit real & imaginary | 3182 cycles |
| 2D 8x8 IEEE IDCT [11] (2x2) | 8-bit | 34 cycles |
| 2D 8x8 IEEE IDCT (1x1) | 8-bit | 176 cycles |
| 256 tap Real FIR filter, M samples (2x2) | 16-bit | 16*M + 81 cycles |
| 256 tap Real FIR filter, M samples (1x1) | 16-bit | 64*M + 78 cycles |
| 4x4 Matrix * 4x1 vector (2x2) | IEEE 754 Floating Point | 2 cycles / output vector |
| 3x3 Correlation (720col) (2x2) | 8-bit | 271 cycles |
| 3x3 Median Filter (720col) (2x2) | 8-bit | 926 cycles |
| 8x8 Block Motion Est. (H=64, V=32) (2x2) | 8-bit | 4611 cycles |
| Horizontal Wavelet (N Rows = 512) (2x2) | 16-bit | 1029 cycles |

**FIGURE 39.55**    Manta $2 \times 2$ thread coprocessor benchmarks.

In a sequential-only implementation there would be required a loop of four instructions, two loads to move a $B$ and a $C$ element to registers, an add of the elements, and a store of the result to register $A$. The sequential implementation takes (4*256) iterations = 1024 cycles, assuming single cycle load, add, and store instructions.

Assuming the data type is 16-bits and quad 16-bit packed data instructions are available, the vector sum would require (4*64) iterations = 256 cycles.

Further assuming an array processor of four PEs where each PE is capable of the packed data operations, then the function can be partitioned between the four PEs and run in parallel requiring (4*16) iterations = 64 cycles.

Finally, assuming a VLIW processor such as the ManArray processor, a software pipeline technique can be used with the VLIWs to minimize the instructions issued per iteration such that (2*16) iterations = 32 cycles are required. This represents a 32x improvement over the sequential implementation.

ManArray architecture allows a programmer or compiler to select the level of parallelism appropriate for the task at hand. This selectable parallelism includes packed data operations ($4 \times 16$-bits and $8 \times 8$-bits in one 64-bit operation on the Manta core), parallel array PEs (performance scales linearly with the addition of PEs), and instruction level parallelism (iVLIW concurrent store/load, ALU, MAU, and DSU instructions).

By use of the three levels of parallelism available on each core, including the use of single-cycle PE communications, scalable conditional execution, and background data streaming DMA, the following benchmarks, Fig. 39.55, can be obtained on the Manta $2 \times 2$ thread coprocessor, which can also function as subset array $1 \times 1$ and $1 \times 2$ array processors.

## Conclusions and Future Extensions

The pervasive use of processor IP in embedded SoC products for consumer applications requires a stable design point based on a scalable processor architecture to support future needs with a complete set of hardware and software development tools. The ManArray cores are highly scalable, using a single architecture definition that provides low power and high performance. Target SoC designs can be optimized to a product by choice of core type, $1 \times 1$, $1 \times 2$, $2 \times 2$, ... and by number of cores. The BOPS tools and SoC development process provides a fast path to delivering verified SoC products. Future plans include architectural extensions, representing a superset of the present design, which greatly improve performance in the intended applications.

## Acknowledgments

The author thanks Dr. Steve Walsh, Dr. Dave Strube, Dr. Sergei Larin, and Carl Lewis for their comments in preparing this paper. The author also thanks the BOPS, Inc. development team for their drive, excitement, and creative technical skills in developing the ManArray processor, tools, and their supporting functions, as well as for making BOPS, Inc. a fun place to work.

## Trademark Information

BOPS and ManArray are registered trademarks of BOPS, Inc. Manta, MoCARay, MICoRay, Jordan, Travis, Xemulator, and Halo are trademarks of BOPS, Inc. All other brands or product names are the property of their respective holders.

## References

1. The Design and Implementation of Signal-Processing Systems Technical Committee, edited by Jan M. Rabaey, with contributions from W. Gass, R. Brodersen, and T. Nishitani, "VLSI design and implementation fuels the signal-processing revolution," *IEEE Signal Processing Magazine,* pp. 22–37, Jan., 1998.
2. Alan Gatherer, Trudy Stetzler, Mike McMahan, and Edgar Auslander, "DSP-based architectures for mobile communications: past, present, and future," *IEEE Communications Magazine,* pp. 84–90, Jan., 2000.
3. Krishna Yarlagadda, "The expanding world of DSPs," *Computer Design,* pp. 77–89, March, 1998.
4. Ichiro Kuroda and Takao Nishitani, "Multimedia processors," *Proceedings of the IEEE,* Vol. 86, No. 6, pp. 1203–1227, June, 1998.
5. Bruce Schulman and Gerald G. Pechanek, "A 90k gate "CLB" for Parallel Distributed Computing," in *Proceedings of EHPC. IPDPS Workshops 2000,* pp. 831–838.
6. Nikos P. Pitsianis and Gerald G. Pechanek, "High-performance FFT implementation on the BOPS ManArray parallel DSP," *Advanced Signal Processing Algorithms, Architectures and Implementations IX,* Volume 3807, pp. 164–171, SPIE International Symposium, Denver, CO, USA, July, 1999.
7. Gerald G. Pechanek, Stamatis Vassiliadis, and Nikos P. Pitsianis, "ManArray interconnection network: an introduction," in *Proceedings of EuroPar '99 Parallel Processing,* Lecture Notes in Computer Science, Vol. 1685, pp. 761–765, Toulouse, France, Aug. 31–Sept. 3, 1999.
8. Gerald G. Pechanek and Stamatis Vassiliadis, "The ManArray embedded processor architecture," in *Proceedings of the 26th Euromicro Conference: "Informatics: inventing the future,"* Maastricht, The Netherlands, September 5–7, 2000, Vol. I, pp. 348–355.
9. BOPS, Inc. corporate Web site (www.bops.com).
10. David Baker, "BOPS DSPs as co-processors," BOPS Internal Technical Report, April 4, 2001.
11. Gerald G. Pechanek, Charles Kurak, and Bruce Schulman, "Design of MPEG-2 function with embedded ManArray cores," in *Proceedings of DesignCon 2000,* Jan. 31–Feb. 3, 2000.

## 39.3  Digital Audio Processors for Personal Computer Systems

*Thomas C. Savell*

### Introduction

The audio subsystem of the personal computer (PC), once an almost unnecessary component, has become an integral part of the operating systems and applications software that run on them. The evolution of the PC itself has led to a complex audio system; requiring simultaneous playback and recording while applying advanced signal processing. The best PC audio systems employ one or more specialized digital audio processors to offload the main processor and guarantee artifact-free audio.

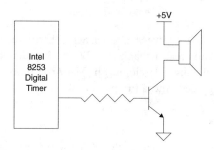

**FIGURE 39.56**    Simplified schematic of IBM-PC speaker circuit.

## Brief History and Evolution

The early PCs could only generate simple tones and beeps. In the early 1980s, the system designers of the original IBM-PC used the Intel 8253 digital timer to generate a series of pulses at a regular rate, usually a square wave within the audio range of less than 20 kHz. The output of this chip drove the base of a transistor to switch on and off a small speaker as shown in the schematic of Fig. 39.56. This simple, cost-effective solution effectively offloaded the 4.77 MHz Intel 8088 main processor from the task of generating a tone. The 8253 timer had three independent channels, and the system designers used channel 0 to keep track of the time of day and channel 1 to generate DRAM refresh cycles. Thus, the otherwise unused timer channel 2 provided an essentially cost-free audio processor.

Although the most common use of this primitive audio system was to alert the user to an event, clever programmers were able to play simple melodies using it. Eventually, they discovered how to use pulse-width modulation coupled with the reactance of the circuit to create a low-quality digital-to-analog converter (DAC), enabling the playback of digitally sampled waveforms. Audio created using this method, however, was very noisy and presented a significant load on the main processor.

Later in the 1980s, add-in cards appeared with an integrated music synthesizer capable of playing back polyphonic music. One such early card, the Adlib soundcard, used a form of music synthesis known as frequency modulation (FM) synthesis. As John Chowning described in 1973, FM synthesis creates complex sounds using simple sine waves to modulate the frequency of other sine waves [1]. The Adlib soundcard used the simple Yamaha OPL2 FM synthesis chip, which used only two sine waves per voice to synthesize complex waveforms. It could create satisfactory, yet unrealistic synthesis of natural musical instruments, as well as a limited spectrum of special sound effects.

The immensely popular Adlib-compatible SoundBlaster® (Creative Technology, Ltd.) was introduced in 1989 by Creative Labs. In addition to Adlib's FM synthesis capabilities, it added a simple method of playing and recording digital audio encoded as a pulse code modulated (PCM) stream. Perhaps as important to its success, Creative Labs provided software development support to computer game developers free of charge, resulting in widespread software support for the SoundBlaster. The new PCM audio capabilities added the possibility of using any sound as an effect in a game. This important enhancement led to the requirement for PCM audio on all future soundcards.

PCM audio was transferred to and from the soundcard using the Intel 8237 direct memory access (DMA) controller on the main system motherboard, as shown in Fig 39.57. The early SoundBlaster cards could only transfer 8-bit PCM audio, resulting in a dynamic range of only about 48 dB. Later, the Sound-Blaster 16 card added support for 16-bit PCM audio with a much better 96 dB dynamic range, using the 16-bit DMA controller of the newer computers.

As time progressed, wavetable synthesis replaced FM synthesis. Wavetable synthesis is capable of synthesizing musical instrument sounds that are nearly indistinguishable from real instruments except to the trained ear. It works by triggering digital recordings of notes played on actual instruments in response to keys played on a keyboard. To synthesize the sound of a piano, the wavetable synthesizer stores a series of digital recordings of a real piano, and plays them back on command. Although the sound

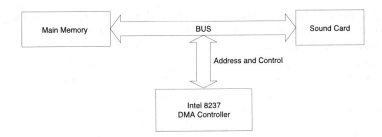

**FIGURE 39.57**   Slave DMA using the Intel 8237 DMA controller.

quality is far superior to that produced by the earlier FM soundcards, the high price of the early wavetable implementations was prohibitive to widespread market acceptance. The normal market forces eventually drove the price down, and soundcards that could only produce FM became obsolete.

An important force in the evolution of both graphics and audio in PCs is the computer game. The continually increasing realism of game graphics, with players able to navigate through virtual three-dimensional (3-D) environments, created demand for more realistic game audio. This demand led to the advent of 3-D positional audio, allowing accurate placement of sound sources within a virtual 3-D environment rendered on stereo speaker systems. It ultimately led to full environmental simulation, with the ability to simulate a sound in various environments such as a carpeted room, a large hall, and even underwater.

A 3-D audio experience is difficult to achieve using two speakers. The smallest head movement of the listener can often destroy the effect. Movie theaters overcame this problem using multi-speaker sound systems that placed speakers to the sides and rear of the listener. It eventually migrated to home theater systems and finally to computer gaming systems.

The best systems now have a 5.1 channel audio system such as Dolby Digital® (Dolby Laboratories) coupled to a 3-D rendering soundcard with environmental simulation capabilities. These systems provide an audio experience that immerses the listener in the environment, helping to create the illusion of realism.

## Today's System Requirements

Today's systems use a layered approach, with applications able to produce audio with little or no knowledge of the underlying hardware. Layers of software hide most of the hardware-specific features. Applications use a query mechanism to determine which features are present, enabling considerable freedom in hardware implementation. Many features of the audio system can also be rendered in software, guaranteeing the application developer a minimum feature set and performance level, nearly independent of the installed hardware. Thus, today's architecture is scalable, allowing the user to choose hardware acceleration for better performance, or software emulation for lowest cost.

Audio on a PC can be divided into several general categories, including operating system interaction, music, gaming, and voice applications. Each of these categories has unique properties, but with proper architecture, a single solution can apply to all of them.

Operating system interaction is generally limited to alerting the user to various events, such as starting up the system, selecting an invalid choice, or receiving new e-mail messages. In the early days of PCs, simple beeps communicated all of these items. Now, these events can be associated with any sound recording, and each association can be unique. Whenever an event occurs, the operating system instructs the soundcard to play back the associated sound recording.

Music applications are much more complex. The soundcard is required to provide a wavetable synthesizer responsive to musical instrument digital interface (MIDI) commands [2]. In addition, it must be able to play back streaming audio in various formats including PCM, MP3 (MPEG-1 Layer 3 Audio), and Dolby Digital (5.1-channel home theater audio). Finally, it must be capable of recording in CD quality, or 16-bit stereo PCM at a sample rate of 44.1 kHz. Each of these major features must be independent and operate simultaneously.

Gaming applications often require a very sophisticated audio system. Many games place sound sources in a virtual 3-D space. The user expects the system to render this 3-D space on any number of speaker systems, ranging from headphones to stereo speakers to 5.1-channel home theater systems. The virtual 3-D space includes not only positional cues, but environmental cues as well. A game player must be able to move a character from an open outdoor space into a small wooden room and seamlessly hear the environmental cues such as the short reverberation of a small room. Objects in motion produce the well-known Doppler effect increasing the apparent frequencies of the sounds emitted by objects moving toward the listener and decreasing those of objects moving away [3]. The most sophisticated audio systems can reproduce the Doppler effect on both the objects in motion and their reflections.

Voice applications, although not new, have yet to gain the widespread availability of operating system, music, and gaming applications. Because of the large memory requirements, voice recognition algorithms are better suited to the main processor and use limited, if any, preprocessing by the soundcard in the record path. Moreover, automatic voice recognition is still unreliable, except when restricted to isolated words from a limited vocabulary. Another class of voice applications is voice communication. The emergence of the Internet has brought with it the promise of low-cost worldwide telephony. The implementation of Internet telephony requires sophisticated noise-cancellation and echo-cancellation algorithms that are often best suited to run on the sound card.

## Hardware Architecture

The hardware of the PC audio system satisfies these system requirements with a simple model. Much like the entire computer system, it consists of three major subsystems: storage, processing, and input/output (I/O). The storage subsystem can include local memory, system memory, and disk storage such as hard drives and compact discs, but the audio processor does not usually interface directly with a disk storage device. The processing subsystem includes both the main processor and a processor located on the soundcard to provide hardware acceleration. The I/O subsystem usually consists of an analog interface such as the Audio CODEC '97 (AC97) standardized DAC and ADC. In addition, digital interfaces such as the Sony/Philips digital interface (S/PDIF) are often included. By dividing the audio system into three logical blocks, the system designer faces the simplified task of creating each block while optimizing the interfaces between them. The audio processor designer is concerned with the processing capabilities of the chip as well as the I/O system interface and the memory bus interface.

### Memory

Local memory connects directly to the audio processor. This includes both ROM and RAM of various types located on the soundcard, generally used to store wavetables for wavetable synthesis and digital delay lines for environmental simulation algorithms. Local memory provides the highest system performance for wavetable synthesis and environmental simulation since it need not share bandwidth with the main processor and other hardware such as disk, video, and networking interfaces; however, local memory costs money, and cost is often a major consideration in market driven engineering. The emergence of the RAM-less soundcard, which stores audio in system memory rather than local memory, is primarily due to the need to decrease costs.

Creation of a RAM-less soundcard requires that system memory store most audio data. A relatively small amount of RAM is still required on the audio processor chip for algorithms that require high-bandwidth access to memory. System memory connects to the main processor of the PC through bus bridging logic, and stores the programs and data that make up the operating system and application programs. When the audio processor requires access to system memory, it generates a memory access request on the add-in card bus. If the main processor or any other device is currently accessing system memory, the audio processor must wait.

The early PCs used a relatively low-performance add-in card bus known as ISA, or Industry Standard Architecture. The soundcards that plugged into the ISA bus accessed system memory through the Intel 8237 DMA controller. The 8237 DMA controller contains auto-incrementing address registers and uses a request/acknowledge handshake protocol to communicate with requesting devices. Because it generates the memory address and controls the direction of the transfer, it is the bus master.

The soundcard operates as a slave to the 8237 DMA controller, which is limited to a single address per requesting device and only performs single-word transfers. In addition, certain channels of the DMA controller are limited to 8-bit transfers, and others can perform 16-bit transfers. The soundcards that could support 16-bit samples had to allocate two DMA channels, one for 8-bit audio, and the other for 16-bit audio. These limitations were acceptable for soundcards that did not require system memory to store wavetables or digital delay lines. These soundcards either had local memory or supported only FM synthesis. They used this slave DMA system for streaming audio, which is generally a recording of music or other sounds.

Applications such as games that create virtual environments generate a continuous stream of audio; however, it is not as simple as playing a static recording. The content of the stream changes based on the actions of the user. As the user interacts with the virtual environment, virtual objects move in relation to the listener, and the sounds they produce may change over time. Each sound an object can make is usually stored as a short recording. The process of creating the continuous audio stream that represents the virtual environment entails summing all the sound sources within the listener's range. The use of slave DMA for these types of applications requires software to create the continuous audio stream. The software for positioning objects in a virtual 3-D space is nontrivial, so the applications generally simplify the problem when using an ISA bus soundcard.

A better solution is to place a powerful DMA controller directly on the soundcard. When the soundcard contains a DMA controller, it becomes the bus master, and can overcome the limitations of the 8237A DMA controller. For example, it can have a large number of independent address generators, enabling both wavetable synthesis and 3-D hardware acceleration for audio stored in system memory. A soundcard that supports wavetable synthesis or environmental simulation using system memory must have a bus mastering DMA controller.

The audio processor designer must consider the memory bandwidth requirements, bus bandwidth availability, and bus transfer latency to determine whether bus-mastering DMA is a viable design choice. Given the number of simultaneous audio channels, the sample rate of each channel, and the number of bytes in each sample, the designer can easily calculate the memory bandwidth requirements. For example, a processor supporting 64 audio channels with a sample rate of 48 kHz and 2 bytes (16-bit) per sample requires 6,144,000 bytes/s. The available bus bandwidth must be greater than that for it to be a viable design choice.

Calculating available bus bandwidth is much more difficult. It depends on the bus bandwidth capability, the reserved bandwidth for other transactions on the bus, and any transaction overhead not accounted for in the bus bandwidth capability. The bus bandwidth capability is straightforward to calculate. The simplest method is to use the data transfer rate times the bus width. For example, a 33.33 MHz PCI bus is 4-bytes wide, leading to a bus bandwidth capability of approximately 133 Mbytes/s.

This, however, ignores the per-transaction overhead required to arbitrate for the bus and begin a bus cycle. For example, a transaction with a single data transfer typically requires about five clocks to complete. If all transactions are single data transfers, the available bus bandwidth is only about 27 Mbytes/s. Burst data transfers reduce the effect of the per-transaction overhead. If 16 data transfers occur in a burst transaction that requires 20 clocks to complete, the available bus bandwidth increases to about 106 Mbytes/s. Computers represent a waveform as an array of numeric values in memory, so audio is well suited to burst transactions. Even so, the available bandwidth is generally much less than these theoretical amounts due to system overhead such as DRAM refresh and CPU cache access to main memory.

The least quantified of all the factors is the reserved bandwidth for other transactions on the bus. This includes bandwidth required by other devices on the bus and the bandwidth needed to program the audio processor itself. The bandwidth required by other devices is unknown since it depends on the add-in cards in each user's individual system. Even the bandwidth needed to program the audio processor is difficult to quantify, since it depends on the peculiarities of the software device driver, the operating system, and the application programs that ultimately generate the audio. Any method of determining the amount to reserve seems entirely arbitrary since variable quantities determine the optimal amount.

Instead of relying on an arbitrary decision based on a guess, one could make measurements of the bus bandwidth used by other devices on the bus in a typical system. Although measurements are by no means a guarantee that any particular system will provide enough bandwidth, one can assume that a similarly equipped typical system will provide a similar amount of bandwidth. The designer can also estimate the bandwidth needed to program the audio processor. Clearly, there is a known overhead to start up a single channel of audio. The bandwidth needed to program the processor includes at least this overhead multiplied by the number of channels. There is additional bandwidth required to maintain a channel of audio. For example, if an object in a virtual 3-D environment moves, the processor must reprogram the portion of the audio processor that positions the object. Numerous other facets are part of this problem, and the audio processor designer should consult with the software engineers to obtain a reasonable estimate of the true bandwidth needed to program the processor.

Given estimates of the memory bandwidth required for audio data transfer and the available bus bandwidth, the designer can determine the limits at which the system will fail. Based on this information, the processor implementation or the target system requirements may need to change.

## Mixing Multiple Sources

The basic system requirements and user expectations require that the sound system sum together multiple audio sources with an independent level control for each source. The audio term for this summation process is mixing. The operating system usually provides software for a simple audio mixer that enables the user to control the relative levels of the compact disc, line in, microphone, and various internally generated sound sources. The system often uses a small digitally programmable analog mixer for the analog sources such as line in and microphone; however, the wavetable synthesizer and 3-D gaming applications require mixing a relatively large number of channels under real-time software control, as shown in Fig. 39.58. These applications use an all-digital mixer due to the large number of channels.

On the surface, a digital audio mixer sounds like a trivial exercise in multiply-accumulate operations; however, in order to sum together sampled waveforms, they must all have the exact same sample rate. Consider two sampled waveforms, each 1-second in length. The first has a sample rate of 48 kHz and the second has a sample rate of 24 kHz. Although they both represent 1-second of time, the first waveform consists of 48000 points, and the second waveform consists of 24000 points. In order to mix them, they must have the same number of points representing the same amount of time.

The solution is to use a sample rate converter before the mixer. The sample rate converter has a fixed output sampling-rate and a variable input sampling-rate. This allows the digital mixer to operate on multiple waveforms of different sample rates. The software programs the sample rate converter with the ratio of input to output, also known as the pitch. Pitch is a musical term that relates to the frequency of

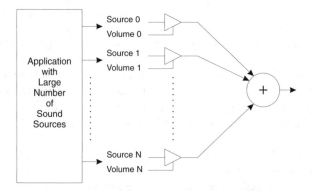

**FIGURE 39.58** Mixing a large number of sound sources under software control.

a note. A higher pitch corresponds to a higher frequency. The sample rate converter performs a double duty as a pitch shifter, enabling a single recorded note to reproduce many notes on the instrument. This provides effective data compression by reducing the number of recordings required to reproduce the sound of an instrument. In addition, it enables a variety of musical effects such as vibrato, pitch bend, and portamento. Finally, the pitch shifting effect of the sample rate converter emulates the Doppler effect needed by 3-D environmental audio. Thus, the sample rate converter is a fundamental building block used by nearly all facets of the digital audio system in the PC.

### Sample Rate Converters

Sample rate converters come in several varieties, offering different levels of conversion quality. Higher quality conversion requires more computation, and comes at a correspondingly higher cost. Drop-sample converters require almost no computation to implement and offer the lowest quality. Linear interpolation converters require more computation and offer reasonably good quality, especially for downward pitch shift. Multi-point interpolation converters require the most computation and memory bandwidth, but provide the highest quality; however, there can be considerable variation in the quality of multi-point interpolation converters.

To understand sample rate conversion, it is necessary to understand discrete-time sampling theory as described by Nyquist and Shannon [4,5]. In order to sample a signal properly, the sample rate must be at least twice the highest frequency component in the signal. The Nyquist frequency is one-half the sample rate, and indicates the highest frequency component that a particular sample rate can represent. Sampling of frequency components above the Nyquist frequency results in aliases in the sampled waveform that are not present in the original signal. Sampling systems such as digital recorders typically use a low-pass filter at the input of the analog to digital converter to avoid aliasing.

The relationship between the frequencies of the aliases and those of the original out-of-band signal is simple. A sine wave at a frequency $F$ between the Nyquist, $N$, and the sample rate, $2N$, will alias to a frequency of $2N - F$. Consider a signal consisting of two sine waves, one at 28,000 Hz and another at 45,000 Hz. Using a sample rate of 48,000 Hz, the resulting sampled waveform would consist of an alias of the 28,000 Hz sine wave at 20,000 Hz, and an alias of the 45,000 Hz sine wave at 3000 Hz. The sampling process has lost the original signal and created a new signal. Figure 39.59 illustrates the frequency domain spectrum of the original signal and the aliases created by sampling at too low of a rate.

In-band signals also create a type of alias, known as an image. Images and aliases are the converse of one another. A properly sampled sine wave at frequency $F$ has an image at $2N - F$. It also has images at $2N + F$, $4N - F$, $4N + F$, and so on up to infinity. Consider a signal consisting of two sine waves, one at 20,000 Hz, and the other at 3000 Hz. The spectrum of this signal is identical to the one generated by sampling sine waves at 28,000 Hz and 45,000 Hz, as shown in Fig. 39.60. One cannot determine by inspection whether the sampled waveform represents true in-band signals, aliases of out-of-band signals, or some combination of the two.

The images are quite important when performing sample rate conversion. At the original sample rate, the images fold back into the passband at exactly the same frequencies of the in-band signal; however, changing the sample rate causes the images to fold back onto different frequencies in the passband, creating

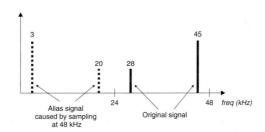

**FIGURE 39.59**     Aliasing caused by sampling at too low a rate.

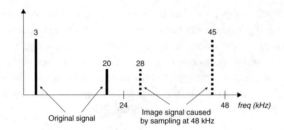

**FIGURE 39.60**   Images above the Nyquist frequency.

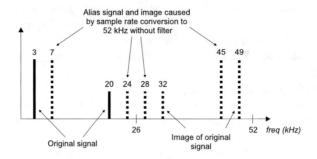

**FIGURE 39.61**   Aliases and images from sample rate conversion.

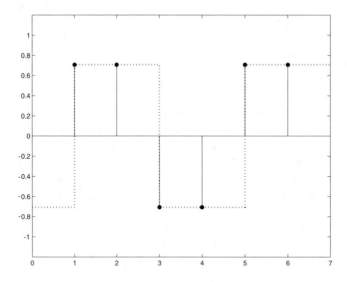

**FIGURE 39.62**   Simple time series that deceptively appears to represent a square wave.

aliasing distortion. Figure 39.61 illustrates the effect of changing the sample rate on the images of the in-band signal. The sample rate converter must remove these images in order to obtain high quality conversion.

It is easy to deceive a naïve observer by a sampled waveform. Consider the following time series:

$$0.707 \qquad 0.707 \qquad -0.707 \qquad -0.707 \qquad 0.707 \qquad 0.707 \qquad -0.707 \qquad -0.707$$

As shown in Fig. 39.62, the waveform might appear to represent a square wave of peak magnitude 0.707 at exactly one-half the Nyquist frequency. This is incorrect. A true square wave consists of an infinite

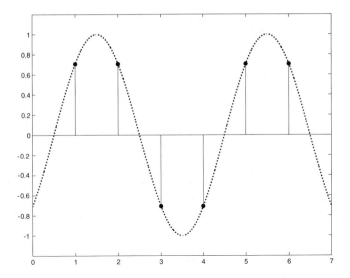

**FIGURE 39.63** True signal represented by simple time series.

series of frequencies at $F$, $3F$, $5F$, $7F$,…, $(2n+1)F$, where $n$ goes to infinity. However, the first partial, $3F$, is above the Nyquist frequency. Therefore, this must represent a sine wave. However, its peak magnitude is not 0.707, but is instead equal to 1.0, as shown in Fig. 39.63.

The ultimate goal of sample rate conversion is to create a new time series at a new sample rate that correctly represents the true original signal. An ideal sample rate converter creates a time series that is indistinguishable from that derived by resampling the original signal. Because it requires an infinite-length time series, no real sample rate converter achieves this ideal; however, it is possible to come arbitrarily close, given enough computation.

To create a new time series at a new sample rate, it is necessary to interpolate values between the input samples. To do this, the sample rate converter maintains an output phase that represents the time index of the output samples relative to the input samples. It maintains the phase by accumulating the pitch. To double the number of output samples, use a pitch of 0.5. On each output sample period, the sample rate converter adds the pitch to the phase accumulator. If the initial value for the phase accumulator is 0.0, the resulting phase over time will be the following:

$$0.0 \quad 0.5 \quad 1.0 \quad 1.5 \quad 2.0 \quad 2.5 \quad 3.0 \quad 3.5 \quad \dots$$

The integer portion of the phase accumulator is the address of the input sample(s) to convert, and the fractional portion is the interpolation factor that indicates how far between input samples to generate an output sample. In the previous example phase accumulator, the fraction alternates between 0.0 and 0.5. The fraction of 0.5 indicates that the output sample should be halfway between two input samples. This definition is somewhat imprecise when using multi-point interpolation, but in a logical sense, it still applies.

Usually, a hardware implementation of a sample rate converter uses a fixed-point representation for both the pitch and the phase accumulator. The fixed-point representation enables very simple extraction of both the integer and fractional portions, and minimizes the size of the adder used to maintain the phase accumulator. The number of integer bits in the phase accumulator limits the amount of memory addressable by the sample rate converter. Integer widths of at least 24-bit are common.

The number of integer bits required for the pitch is much smaller than the number required for the phase accumulator. Upward pitch shifting, which is equivalent to conversion to a lower sample rate requires filtering to a lower cutoff frequency than downward pitch shifting. Often, much more distortion occurs when performing upward pitch shifting. The additional filtering and distortion of upward pitch

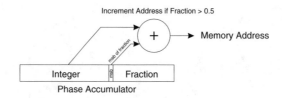

**FIGURE 39.64** Address generator for drop-sample interpolator.

shifting place limits on its usefulness. Upward pitch shifts of more than three octaves extend into the realm of special effects. When viewed as pure sample rate conversion, a three octave upward shift is equivalent to converting from a 48 to a 6 kHz sample rate. The lowest sample rate commonly used for audio is 8 kHz. Thus, it is usually acceptable to limit the number of integer bits in the pitch to two or three, providing a 2- to 3-octave upward shift capability.

The magnitude of the least-significant bit (LSB) of the pitch fraction, indicated by the number of fractional bits, determines the frequency ratio resolution. For example, the LSB of a 12-bit fraction is equal to 1/4096. The perceptual unit of measurement for pitch is cents, or 1/100 of a semitone. This is equal to a ratio of $2^{1/1200}$ or 1.00058. The just-noticeable-difference (JND) for pitch is around 8 cents, or 1.0046, indicating the acceptable frequency error [3]. Given this, it would seem that a 12-bit fraction is sufficient and even generous, since the ratio 4097/4096 is equal to 1.00024, much better than the JND of 1.0046; however, an effective method of data compression for sampled waveforms is to lower the sample rate such that the highest frequency of interest in the signal is near the Nyquist frequency of the lower sample rate. Consider a sine wave consisting of only four points. When played back at unity pitch on a system with a 48 kHz output rate, the frequency of the sine wave is 12 kHz. A more useful frequency in the human hearing range is 125 Hz. To generate this, the pitch must be 0.0104. The closest available ratio with 12-bits of fraction is 0.0105, generating a frequency ratio error of 1.0078, more than the JND. In practice, a minimum of 14-bits of fraction is required for acceptable results across a wide range of input rates and pitches. Ideally, the number of fractional bits in both the phase accumulator and the pitch should match.

### Drop-Sample Interpolation

Drop-sample interpolation, sometimes called nearest-neighbor interpolation, is the simplest type of sample rate converter. The drop-sample interpolator simply rounds the phase accumulator to the nearest integer and chooses the input sample at the resulting integer address to be the output sample. This requires very little hardware as illustrated in Fig. 39.64. It also requires access to only a single input sample to create an output sample, whereas all other forms of sample rate conversion require access to more than one input sample to create a single output sample, but the result can be very poor quality.

### Linear Interpolation

Linear interpolation may be the most common type of sample rate converter. The quality is good, and the cost is relatively low. It requires access to two input samples to create a single output sample. The computational cost is one multiply, one add, and one subtract. It is possible to implement the entire linear interpolator with a single adder, using a shift and add approach to the multiply. This is feasible as long as the clock rate is high enough to support the desired channel count and fractional accuracy. The following equation describes the linear interpolation process, where $x$ is the input waveform, $y$ is the output sample, $n$ is the integer part of the phase accumulator, and $f$ is the fractional part of the phase accumulator:

$$y = x_n + f \times (x_{n+1} - x_n)$$

One can clearly see that when the fraction is zero, the output sample is equal to the input sample at the address indicated by the phase accumulator. As the fraction approaches 1.0, the output follows a

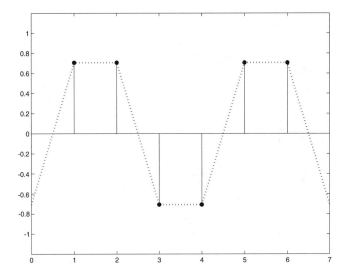

**FIGURE 39.65**  Linear interpolation of simple time series.

straight line drawn between adjacent input samples. Figure 39.65 illustrates the result of linearly interpolating a sine wave. The quality is quite good if the frequency of the sine wave is low relative to the
Nyquist, but the quality deteriorates significantly as the frequency approaches the Nyquist. The linear
interpolator has a low pass filtering effect that becomes noticeable above one half the Nyquist frequency.
In addition, the alias rejection is not very good for the images of signals above one-half the Nyquist
frequency. Thus, linear interpolation affects the quality in both the frequency response and aliasing
distortion for high frequencies.

### Multi-Point Interpolation

Multi-point interpolation can produce much better quality than linear interpolation in both frequency
response and aliasing distortion. The ideal interpolator has a frequency response that is perfectly flat
within the passband and attenuates all other frequencies to zero. Convolving the input waveform with a
*sinc* function that runs from negative to positive infinite time produces such a frequency response.
Unfortunately, we must work within the limits of finite time to build a real interpolator. In 1984, Gossett
and Smith showed an efficient way to use a finite-length, windowed *sinc* function as a finite-impulse-
response (FIR) filter for sample rate conversion over a wide range of pitches [6]. The definition of the
*sinc* function is $\sin t / t$.

The convolution equation is $\sum_{n=0}^{N-1} a_n x_{T-n}$, where $x$ is the input waveform and $a$ is a selected set of
coefficients, possibly a windowed *sinc* function.

The hardware implementation of a Gossett-Smith sample rate converter consists of a read-only-
memory (ROM) containing the filter coefficients, a linear interpolator to increase the resolution of the
filter coefficient set, and a multiply-accumulate unit to perform the convolution. Figure 39.66 shows a
block diagram of a typical Gossett-Smith interpolation system. Because the *sinc* function and other low-
pass FIR filters are symmetric about their centers, it is only necessary to store half of the points in the
ROM. Simple address mirroring makes the ROM appear to contain all the points.

Perceived quality is often more important than measured quality. That is, it is more important to sound
good to humans than to measure low distortion on laboratory instruments. Using a perceptual approach,
one can design sample-rate conversion filters that sound better [7]. For example, humans cannot hear
above 20 kHz, yet a 48 kHz sample-rate can represent frequencies up to 24 kHz. A filter that allows
distortion within this guardband between 20 and 24 kHz can achieve better quality within the audible
range of 20 Hz to 20 kHz.

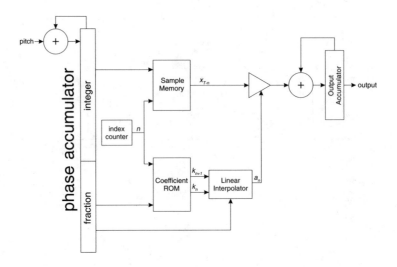

**FIGURE 39.66**  Gossett–Smith interpolator block diagram.

### Address Looping

The phase accumulator of the sample rate converter must have some provision for looping back to a lower address. Clearly, it cannot continue to increment to infinity. The finite number of bits used to represent the integer part of the phase precludes that possibility. In addition, it is not useful simply to rely on binary wraparound of the address from its maximum value back to zero. This would imply all channels of sample rate conversion are reading from the same input waveform. At a minimum, the phase accumulator contains a loop address and loop size for each channel. When the value of the phase accumulator crosses the loop address, it loops back by the loop size and continues from the beginning of the loop. This enables both streaming audio and wavetable synthesis.

Many natural musical instrument sounds can be characterized by an attack phase, sustain phase, and release phase. The attack phase is often a primary cue to the listener as to the identity of the instrument. Usually, it consists of a rapidly changing and nonrepeating waveform. Conversely, the sustain phase is often a steady state that can be easily described by a repeating waveform. This is also true of the release phase. During sustain and release phases, the phase accumulator can loop to create the repeating waveform, saving considerable memory. Besides, the length of the sustain phase is usually unknown because it is controlled by the length of time the musician presses the key.

When streaming audio, the software fills a circular buffer with a continuous waveform to play. The phase accumulator loops at the boundaries of the circular buffer and plays the stream. The software must be careful not to overwrite audio that the sample rate converter has not yet played.

### Envelopes and Modulation

It is often necessary to control various aspects of a sound, such as pitch, amplitude, and filter cutoff frequency with time-varying signals called envelopes. The audio system may use these envelopes to simulate the changes in sound that occur when a 3-D sound source moves, or as an integral part of the music synthesis process.

A typical music synthesizer envelope generator has four segments designated attack, decay, sustain, and release (ADSR) as shown in Fig. 39.67. These four segments are a reasonable approximation of the amplitude envelopes of real musical instruments. The first two segments are attack and decay, and are usually a fixed duration. During these segments, the sound is changing rapidly, often containing transients and wideband noise corresponding to the initial strike of a drum, or pluck of a string. The decay segment leads to the sustain segment, a variable duration, steady state corresponding to the portion of a note that is held for a length of time. The final segment, release, occurs after the musician releases the note.

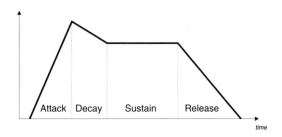

**FIGURE 39.67**    ADSR envelope.

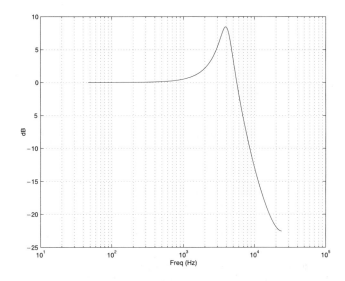

**FIGURE 39.68**    Frequency response of lowpass resonant filter.

Envelopes used for 3-D sound positioning do not have such a clearly defined set of segments. Instead, 3-D positional audio is often interactive. It is not possible to predict the movements of the user in advance. For these applications, a fixed segment envelope generator may not be useful. A more useful method is to set a target value to which the hardware will smoothly ramp from the current value, enabling the software to be event driven.

In addition to the ADSR envelopes used for music synthesis and ramp-to-target envelopes used for 3-D positioning, a complete system requires a low frequency oscillator, or LFO. The system uses the LFO to create slowly modulating effects such as vibrato and tremolo.

The final control signal is usually a weighted sum of one or more ADSR envelopes and one or more LFOs. The scaling applied to the envelopes and LFOs are often time varying signals as well. This enables, for example, vibrato to slowly increase during the sustain segment of a synthesized violin sound. It is important to note that the scaling and summation occurs in perceptual units such as decibels and pitch cents, not physical units such as voltage and Hertz. This means that the result of the summation goes through a perceptual to physical units transform function before it is useful to the destination process. Example transform functions are $10^{x/20}$ for decibels and $2^{x/1200}$ for pitch cents.

## Filters

The most common filters in music synthesis are low-pass resonators. The frequency response of these filters is generally flat from 0 Hz up, with a characteristic resonance just below the low-pass cutoff frequency, as shown in Fig. 39.68. It is most common to build these filters with an infinite impulse response, or IIR structure, such as that illustrated in Fig. 39.69. The software specifies the cutoff frequency and resonant

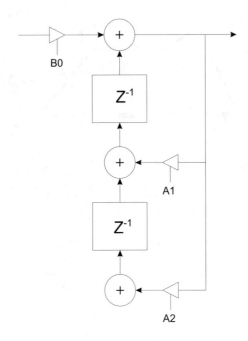

**FIGURE 39.69**   Two-pole IIR filter block diagram.

gain of the filter. It is possible to sweep these parameters in real time, so it is important to ensure filter stability under time-varying conditions. Stability criteria are outside the scope of this discussion, but it is not difficult to drive IIR filters to instability when varying coefficients in the presence of an input signal.

Three-dimensional positional audio and environmental simulation also demand the use of filters; however, low-pass resonators are not the ideal choice. The head-related transfer function (HRTF) describes the filtering performed by the shape of the human head, ear lobes, and ear canal [8]. In addition to loudness and inter-aural time delay, the brain uses cues provided by this filtering to determine the position of sound emitting objects. The most common implementation of an HRTF uses a FIR structure such as the Gossett–Smith interpolator filters; however, both the impulse response and the usage of HRTF filters are much different from that of Gossett–Smith interpolator filters.

Obstruction and occlusion are other filtering effects that occur when sound sources move in relation to other objects. For example, obstruction is the effect caused by an obstacle between the listener and a sound source in the same room. This applies a low-pass filtering effect on the direct sound, but not on the reverberation. In contrast, occlusion is the effect caused by a sound source located outside the same room as the listener. This applies a low-pass filtering effect on both the direct sound and the reverberation. Low-pass IIR filters are appropriate for these applications, although resonance is neither needed nor desired. The system can simulate these effects with the low-pass resonators used for music synthesis, but the typical −12 dB per octave attenuation slope is generally too steep. A gentle −3 or −6 dB per octave slope is more appropriate.

The audio system of the PC also performs the role of a typical component stereo system, playing prerecorded music from CD or other sources. Thus, the software distributed with soundcards often includes equalization, such as tone controls and graphic equalizers. Simple tone controls, such as bass and treble, often use shelving filters as shown in Fig. 39.70. Graphic equalizers can use a bank of either band-pass filters or parametric equalizers into a summation matrix.

It is the designer's choice whether to implement the filter types required by the digital audio system of the PC in hardware or software. The system often includes a programmable digital signal processor (DSP), enabling a software implementation. As the required filter count increases, it often becomes more

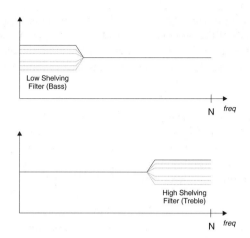

**FIGURE 39.70**   Bass and treble tone control filter shapes.

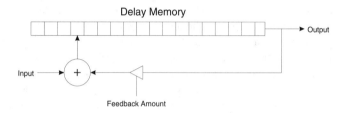

**FIGURE 39.71**   Delay line with feedback implementing a repeating echo.

efficient to implement them in hardware, especially if multiple filter types can use the same filter structure. Moreover, while FIR and IIR filter structures are quite different, a clever designer may find opportunities to reuse the same basic arithmetic hardware for both. For example, both structures can use a multiply-accumulate arithmetic unit. If each structure requires only one-half the available bandwidth, they can share the same math unit by time-division multiplexing the inputs. Because arithmetic units are generally costly, techniques such as this can significantly reduce the system cost.

### Effects

Music synthesis applications use effects such as reverb, delay, and chorus as sweeteners. They are not required, but tend to make the music sound more pleasing. In contrast, 3-D positional and environmental simulation applications require delay and reverb to achieve realistic results. The fundamental unit of many digital audio effects is the digital delay line. A simple echo effect may use only one delay line, whereas a reverb effect may use 20 or more delay lines. Even modulation effects such as chorus and flange use delay lines. Digital delay lines require one memory location per sample period of delay, an address generator, and arithmetic units to scale the inputs and outputs of the delay line. Figure 39.71 illustrates a typical delay line implementing a repeating echo through the use of feedback.

An obvious method of implementing a set of delay lines is to allocate memory buffers for each delay line and maintain circular address counters for each indicating the read and write locations. The delay time is equal to the difference between the read and write pointers, modulo buffer size. Maintaining circular address counters can easily use a large percentage of the total instruction bandwidth of a DSP. Many DSP implementations provide special instructions or self-maintaining address registers to reduce the load on the DSP.

To provide maximum flexibility in implementation of effects, most PC audio systems include a programmable DSP. The designer may choose to purchase an off-the-shelf DSP, either as a separate chip or as a core to integrate onto the same silicon as the rest of the solution. An alternative is to design a custom DSP to fit the particular needs of the system. The advantages of a custom design are the freedom to add or reduce features, easier integration, and often a lower cost. The disadvantages include possible increased time to market and the lack of standard development tools such as compilers.

## Digital Audio I/O

Eventually, the system must present the processed audio to the listener. A DAC outputs an analog voltage proportional to the value of a word of digital data written to it. The analog output voltage drives the input to an amplifier, and eventually the sound comes from a speaker. A DAC generally accepts serial digital data rather than parallel, so the processor must first perform a parallel to serial conversion. A DAC is usually stereo, so it accepts a time-multiplexed serial stream alternating between left and right channels. The serial protocols are usually synchronous, and come in a few varieties. The most common in use today are AC97 and $I^2S$, both of which are easily available and inexpensive.

In addition to audio output, the system must be capable of recording audio from microphones and external line-level devices such as CD players and tape decks. An ADC outputs digital data proportional to the magnitude of an analog voltage presented to its input. As in the case of a DAC, an ADC usually generates serial digital data consisting of time-multiplexed left and right channel data. The AC97 standard developed by Intel specifies a monolithic CODEC containing both a stereo DAC and a stereo ADC [9]. An AC97 implementation can sometimes be the most cost effective. Generally, devices that use the $I^2S$ protocol are of a higher quality but do not include both a stereo ADC and a stereo DAC.

For digital transmission of audio between the computer and an external device, the Sony/Philips Digital Interface (S/PDIF) protocol as specified in IEC-958 is the connection of choice [10]. It is a robust protocol intended for transmission over a 75-ohm coaxial cable. It uses Manchester encoding for the data, thus embedding a clock and making it insensitive to logical inversion. The ground is isolated, preventing hum and noise due to ground loops. Many consumer stereo components now have S/PDIF or its optical counterpart TOS-Link as integral connections.

## Emerging Applications

The basic digital audio system of a PC operates in stereo at 44.1 or 48 kHz sample rate with 16 bits of resolution. The current trend of audiophile systems is moving to a multichannel 96 kHz sample rate with 24 bits of resolution. Often, these audiophile trends trickle down to the mainstream systems as the cost comes down and demand rises. From a strict psycho-acoustical point of view, there is little value in increasing the sample rate to 96 kHz, since the range of human hearing is generally restricted to 20–20 kHz. In addition, a 96-kHz waveform requires twice the storage and twice the computation of the equivalent waveform at 48 kHz; however, there is some benefit to processing audio at 96 kHz, primarily in the response of filters over the human hearing range. It is easy to trade channel count for the higher sample rate. A system that can process 128 channels at 48 kHz can only process 64 channels at 96 kHz. The designer should weigh the cost versus the benefit, but often the market drives the decision. If the market demands 96 kHz, the designer must deliver it.

There is, however, a very real benefit to using 24 bits of resolution. The maximum dynamic range of human hearing is around 130–140 dB. The 96 dB dynamic range of 16-bit resolution is insufficient to cover this range. A 24-bit waveform has a dynamic range of 144 dB, more than sufficient to cover the range of human hearing. The design impact of 24 bits versus 16 bits is additional storage and larger arithmetic units, resulting in higher cost.

Likewise, there is a real benefit to multichannel audio beyond stereo. A real environment produces sounds from all directions instead of than only two points as in a stereo speaker system. But the processor should still support stereo as a minimum baseline system, since the majority of audio systems are stereo. To achieve this, the processor must have more than two separate outputs and be capable of sending different audio to the multiple outputs.

Data rate reduction is another important trend in digital audio processing. The majority of the popular techniques in use, including Dolby Digital and MP3, process the signal in the frequency domain.

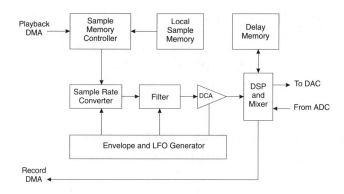

**FIGURE 39.72** Audio processor block diagram.

They employ a perceptual model that attempts to determine which frequency components are not perceivable by the human hearing system. By removing those components, the encoding process can reduce the amount of data required to represent the signal. For example, the MP3 encoding process achieves about a 10:1 compression ratio while maintaining a quality level high enough to satisfy most people.

## Conclusion

A digital audio processor for PCs consists of only a few components: a memory and host interface coupled to sample rate converters, filters, envelope generators, a mixer, and a programmable DSP. These components, as illustrated in Fig. 39.72, interact in various ways to become a variable-rate playback engine, a wavetable synthesizer, a 3-D positional audio processor, and an environmental audio simulator.

However, a digital audio system consists of both hardware and software. Given the wide range of possibilities, the designer has considerable freedom in choosing an implementation to meet particular market needs and price points. To meet the lowest price point, the designer chooses software implementations whenever possible. To achieve the highest performance, the designer chooses hardware; however, a hardware implementation may limit the flexibility of the end system. The task of partitioning the system into hardware and software components is one of the greatest hurdles to overcome. It requires a coordinated effort of strategic marketing with hardware and software engineering early in the design process. A proprietary chip is expensive to design and can take a long time from concept to production. The early involvement of strategic marketing and software engineering helps ensure the success of any new hardware design.

The customer purchases an audio system, not a chip. Thus, the designer must be aware of, yet look beyond the technical aspects of digital audio processors to create a system that provides the proper functionality at the right price.

## References

1. Chowning, J., The synthesis of complex audio spectra by means of frequency modulation, *Journal of the Audio Engineering Society*, 21, 526, 1973.
2. The Complete MIDI 1.0 Detailed Specification, MIDI Manufacturers Association, Los Angeles, 1996.
3. Rossing, T. D., *The Science of Sound*, Addison-Wesley, Reading, MA, 40, 1983.
4. Nyquist, H., Certain factors affecting telegraph speed, *Bell Systems Technical Journal*, 3, 324, 1924.
5. Shannon, C. E., A mathematical theory of communication, *Bell Systems Technical Journal*, 27, 379, 1948.
6. Smith, J. O. and Gossett, P., A flexible sampling-rate conversion method, *IEEE International Conference on Acoustics, Speech, and Signal Processing*, 19.4.1, March 1984.

7.  Rossum, D., Constraint based audio interpolators, *IEEE ASSP Workshop on Applications of Signal Processing to Audio and Acoustics (Mohonk)*, 1993.
8.  Zhang, M., Tan, K. C., and Er, M. H., Three-dimensional synthesis based on head-related transfer functions, *Journal of the Audio Engineering Society*, 46, 836, 1998.
9.  *Audio Codec '97 Revision 2.2*, Intel Corporation, San Jose, CA, 2000.
10. *IEC-958 Digital Audio Interface*, International Electrotechnical Commission, 1989.

# 39.4   Modern Approximation Iterative Algorithms and Their Applications in Computer Engineering

*Sadiq M. Sait and Habib Youssef*

## Introduction

This chapter section discusses one class of combinatorial optimization algorithms: approximation iterative algorithms. We shall limit ourselves to four of these algorithms, which are, in order of their popularity among the engineering community: (1) simulated annealing (SA), (2) genetic algorithm (GA), (3) tabu search (TS), and (4) simulated evolution (SimE).

GA and SimE are evolutionary algorithms, a term used to refer to any probabilistic algorithm whose design is inspired by evolutionary mechanisms found in biological species. Evolutionary algorithms, SA and TS have been found very effective and robust in solving numerous problems from a wide range of application domains. Furthermore, they are even suitable for ill-posed problems where some of the parameters are not known beforehand. These properties are lacking in all traditional optimization techniques. The four algorithms share the following properties:

1.  They are approximation algorithms, i.e., they do not guarantee finding an optimal solution. Actually, they are blind, in that they do not know when they reached an optimal solution. Therefore, they must be told when to stop.
2.  They are neighborhood search algorithms, which start from one suboptimal solution (or a population of solutions) and perform a partial search of the solution space for better solutions.
3.  They are all "general." They are not problem-specific and, practically, they can be tailored to solve any combinatorial optimization problem.
4.  They all strive to exploit domain specific heuristic knowledge to bias the search toward "good" solution subspace. The quality of subspace searched depends to a large extent on the amount of heuristic knowledge used.
5.  They are easy to implement. All that is required is to have a suitable solution representation, a cost function, and a mechanism to traverse the search space.
6.  They have *hill climbing* property, i.e., they occasionally accept uphill (bad) moves.

The goal in this chapter section is to briefly introduce these four powerful algorithms. It is organized into nine sections. In the next four subsections, an intuitive discussion of each of the four iterative algorithms is provided. The remaining sections briefly address convergence aspects of the heuristics, their parallel implementation, and examples of applications. The final subsection concludes the chapter section with a comparison among the heuristics and a glimpse at the notion of hybrids. This chapter section does not provide a full account of any of this important class of heuristics. For more details, readers should consult the numerous references cited in the body of this work.

## Simulated Annealing

*Simulated Annealing* (SA) is one of the most well-developed and widely used iterative techniques for solving optimization problems. It is a general adaptive heuristic and belongs to the class of nondeterministic algorithms [1]. It has been applied to several combinatorial optimization problems from various fields

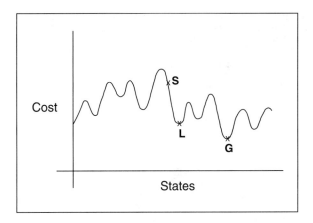

**FIGURE 39.73**  Local vs. global optima.

of science and engineering. The term *annealing* refers to heating a solid to a very high temperature (whereby the atoms gain enough energy to break the chemical bonds and become free to move), and then slowly cooling the molten material in a controlled manner until it crystallizes. By cooling the metal at a proper rate, atoms will have an increased chance to regain proper crystal structure with perfect lattices. During this annealing procedure, the free energy of the solid is minimized.

In the early 1980s, a correspondence between annealing and combinatorial optimization was established, first by Kirkpatrick, Gelatt and Vecchi [2] in 1983, and independently by Černy [3] in 1985. These scientists observed that a solution in combinatorial optimization is equivalent to a state in the physical system and the cost of the solution is analogous to the energy of that state. As a result of this analogy, they introduced a solution method in the field of combinatorial optimization. This method is thus based on the simulation of the physical annealing process, and hence the name *simulated annealing* [2,3].

Every combinatorial optimization problem may be discussed in terms of a *state space*. A *state* is simply a configuration of the combinatorial objects involved. For example, consider the problem of partitioning a graph of $2n$ nodes into two equal sized subgraphs such that the number of edges with vertices in both subgraphs is minimized. In this problem, any division of $2n$ nodes into two equal sized blocks is a configuration. A large number of such configurations exists. Only some of these correspond to global optima, i.e., states with optimum cost.

An iterative improvement scheme starts with some given state, and examines a *local neighborhood* of the state for better solutions. A local neighborhood of a state $S$, denoted by $N(S)$, is the set of all states which can be reached from $S$ by making a small change to $S$. For instance, if $S$ represents a two-way partition of a graph, the set of all partitions which are generated by swapping two nodes across the partition represents a local neighborhood. The iterative improvement algorithm moves from the current state to a state in the local neighborhood if the latter has a better cost. If all the local neighbors have larger costs, the algorithm is said to have *converged* to a *local optimum*. This is illustrated in Fig. 39.73. Here, the states are shown along the $x$-axis, and it is assumed that two consecutive states are local neighbors. It is further assumed that we are discussing a *minimization* problem. The cost curve is *nonconvex*, i.e., it has multiple minima. A greedy iterative improvement algorithm may start off with an initial solution such as **S** in Fig. 39.73, then slide along the curve and find a local minimum such as **L**. There is no way such an algorithm can find the global minimum **G** of Fig. 39.73, unless it "climbs the hill" at the local minimum **L**. In other words, an algorithm that occasionally accepts inferior solutions can escape from getting trapped in a local optimum. SA is such a hill-climbing algorithm.

During annealing, a metal is maintained at a certain temperature $T$ for a pre-computed amount of time, before reducing the temperature in a controlled manner. The atoms have a greater degree of freedom to move at higher temperatures than at lower temperatures. *The movement of atoms is analogous to the generation of new neighborhood states in an optimization process.* In order to simulate the annealing process,

**Algorithm** Simulated_annealing($S_0, T_0, \alpha, \beta, M, Maxtime$);
    (*$S_0$ is the initial solution *)
    (*BestS is the best solution *)
    (*$T_0$ is the initial temperature *)
    (*$\alpha$ is the cooling rate *)
    (*$\beta$ a constant *)
    (*$Maxtime$ is the total allowed time for the annealing process *)
    (*$M$ represents the time until the next parameter update *)

**Begin**
    $T = T_0$;
    $CurS = S_0$;
    $BestS = CurS$;/* $BestS$ is the best solution seen so far */
    $CurCost = Cost(CurS)$;
    $BestCost = Cost(BestS)$;
    $Time = 0$;
        **Repeat**
            Call Metropolis($CurS$, $CurCost$, $BestS$, $BestCost$, $T$, $M$);
            $Time = Time + M$;
            $T = \alpha T$;
            $M = \beta M$
        **Until** ($Time \geq MaxTime$);
        **Return** ($BestS$)
**End**. (*$of$ $Simulated\_annealing$*)

**FIGURE 39.74** Procedure for simulated annealing algorithm.

**Algorithm** Metropolis($CurS$, $CurCost$, $BestS$, $BestCost$, $T$, $M$);
**Begin**
    **Repeat**
        $NewS = Neighbor(CurS)$; /* Return a neighbor from $aleph(CurS)$ */
        $NewCost = Cost(NewS)$;
        $\Delta Cost = (NewCost - CurCost)$;
        **If** ($\Delta Cost < 0$) **Then**
            $CurS = NewS$;
            **If** $NewCost < BestCost$ **Then**
                $BestS = NewS$
            **EndIf**
        **Else**
            **If** ($RANDOM < e^{-\Delta Cost/T}$) **Then**
                $CurS = NewS$;
            **EndIf**
        **EndIf**
        $M = M - 1$
    **Until** ($M = 0$)
**End**. (*$of$ $Metropolis$*)

**FIGURE 39.75** The Metropolis procedure.

much flexibility is allowed in neighborhood generation at higher "temperature," i.e., many "uphill" moves are permitted at higher temperatures. The temperature parameter is lowered gradually as the algorithm proceeds. As the temperature is lowered, fewer and fewer uphill moves are permitted. In fact, at absolute zero, the SA algorithm turns greedy, allowing only downhill moves.

The SA algorithm is shown in Fig. 39.74 . The core of the algorithm is the *Metropolis* procedure, which simulates the annealing process at a given temperature $T$ (Fig. 39.75) [4]. The *Metropolis* procedure receives as input the current temperature $T$, and the current solution $CurS$, which it improves through local search. Finally, *Metropolis* must also be provided with the value $M$, which is the amount of time for which annealing must be applied at temperature $T$. The procedure *Simulated_annealing* simply invokes *Metropolis* at decreasing temperatures. Temperature is initialized to a value $T_0$ at the beginning of the procedure and is reduced in a controlled manner (typically in a geometric progression); the parameter

$\alpha$ is used to achieve this cooling. The amount of time spent in annealing at a temperature is gradually increased as temperature is lowered. This is done using the parameter $\beta > 1$. The variable *Time* keeps track of the time being expended in each call to the *Metropolis*. The annealing procedure halts when *Time* exceeds the allowed time.

The *Metropolis* procedure is shown in Fig. 39.75. It uses the procedure *Neighbor* to generate a local neighbor *NewS* of any given solution *S*. The function *Cost* returns the cost of a given solution *S*. If the cost of the new solution *NewS* is better than the cost of the current solution *CurS*, then the new solution is accepted, and we do so by setting *CurS = NewS*. If the cost of the new solution is better than the best solution (*BestS*) seen thus far, then *BestS* must be replaced by *NewS*. If the new solution has a higher cost in comparison to the original solution *CurS*, *Metropolis* will accept the new solution on a *probabilistic* basis. A random number is generated in the range 0 to 1. If this random number is smaller than $e^{-\Delta Cost/T}$, where $\Delta Cost$ is the change in costs, ($\Delta Cost = Cost(NewS) - Cost(CurS)$), and $T$ is the current temperature, the uphill solution is accepted. This criterion for accepting the new solution is known as the *Metropolis criterion*. The *Metropolis* procedure generates and examines $M$ solutions.

The probability that an inferior solution is accepted by the *Metropolis* is given by $P(RANDOM < e^{-\Delta Cost/T})$. The random number generation is assumed to follow a *uniform distribution*. Remember that $\Delta Cost > 0$ because it is assumed that *NewS* is uphill from *CurS*. At very high temperatures (when $T \to \infty$), $e^{-\Delta Cost/T} \approx 1$, and, hence, the above probability approaches 1. When $T \to 0$, the probability $e^{-\Delta Cost/T}$ falls to 0.

In order to implement SA, a suitable cost function needs to be formulated for the problem being solved. In addition, as in the case of local search techniques, the existence of a neighborhood structure is assumed, and the *perturb* operation or *Neighbor* function needs to generate new states (neighborhood states) from current states. And finally, a control parameter is needed to play the role of temperature and a random number generator. The actions of SA are best illustrated with the help of an example. For the solution of the two-way partitioning problem using SA, please refer to [5].

A quality SA implementation requires the careful setting of a set of parameters that govern the convergence of the algorithm, namely (a) the initial value of temperature, (b) the number of iterations of the inner loop, (c) the rate of temperature decrease, and (d) the number of global iterations (the stopping criterion or the final value of temperature). This set of parameters is commonly referred as the "cooling schedule" [2,6,7]. It is customary to determine the cooling schedule by trial and error. However, some researchers have proposed cooling schedules that rely on some mathematical rigor. For a discussion on cooling schedule, and SA requirements the reader is referred to [8].

## Genetic Algorithms

Genetic Algorithm (GA), is a powerful, domain-independent search technique that was inspired by Darwinian theory. It emulates the natural process of evolution to perform an efficient and systematic search of the solution space to progress toward the optimum. It is an *adaptive* learning heuristic that is based on the theory of *natural selection* that assumes that individuals with certain characteristics are more able to survive, and hence pass their characteristics to their offspring. Several variations of the basic algorithm (modified to adapt to the problem at hand) exist. Subsequently, this set will be referred to as genetic algorithms (in plural).

GAs were invented by John Holland and his colleagues [9] in the early 1970s. Holland incorporated features of natural evolution to propose a *robust*, computationally simple, and yet powerful technique for solving difficult optimization problems. The structure that encodes how the organism is to be constructed is called a *chromosome*. One or more chromosomes may be associated with each member of the population. The complete set of chromosomes is called a *genotype* and the resulting organism is called a *phenotype*. Similarly, the representation of a solution to the optimization problem in the form of an encoded string is termed as a *chromosome*. In most combinatorial optimization problems a single chromosome is generally sufficient to represent a solution, i.e., the genotype and the chromosome are the same. The symbols that make up a chromosome are known as *genes*. The different values a gene can take are called *alleles*.

The fitness value of an individual (genotype or a chromosome) is a *positive* number that is a measure of its goodness. When the chromosome represents a solution to the combinatorial optimization problem, the fitness value indicates the cost of the solution. In the case of a minimization problem, solutions with lower cost correspond to individuals that are more fit.

GAs operate on a *population* (or set) of *individuals* (or solutions) encoded as strings. These strings represent points in the search space. In each iteration, referred to as a generation, a new set of strings that represent solutions (called offspring) is created by crossing some of the strings of the current generation [10]. Occasionally, new characteristics are injected to add diversity. GAs combine information exchange along with *survival of the fittest* among individuals to conduct the search.

When employing GAs to solve a combinatorial optimization problem one has to find an efficient representation of the solution in the form of a chromosome. Associated with each chromosome is its *fitness value*. If we simulate the process of natural reproduction, combined with the biological principle of survival of the fittest, then, as each generation progresses, better and better individuals (solutions) with higher fitness values are expected to be produced.

Because GAs work on a population of solutions, an initial population constructor is required to generate a certain predefined number of solutions. The quality of the final solution produced by a genetic algorithm depends on the size of the population and how the initial population is constructed. The initial population generally comprises random solutions.

The population of chromosomes evolves from generation to the next through the use of two types of genetic operators: (1) unary operators such as mutation and *inversion*, which alter the genetic structure of a single chromosome, and (2) higher order operator, referred to as *crossover*, which consists of obtaining new individual by combining genetic material from two selected parent chromosomes. The resulting individuals produced when genetic operators are applied on the parents are termed as *offspring*. Then the new population is selected out of the individuals of the current population and its offspring.

The choice of parents for crossover from the set of individuals that comprise the population is probabilistic. In keeping with the ideas of natural selection, we assume that stronger individuals, i.e., those with higher fitness values, are more likely to mate than the weaker ones. One way to simulate this is to select parents with a probability that is directly proportional to their fitness values. Larger the fitness, the greater is chance of an individual being selected as one of the parents for crossover [10].

Several crossover operators have been proposed in the literature. Depending on the combinatorial optimization problem being solved some are more effective than others. One popular crossover that will also help illustrate the concept is the *simple crossover*. It performs the "cut-catenate" operation. It consists of choosing a *random* cut point and dividing each of the two chromosomes into two parts. The offspring is then generated by catenating the segment of one parent to the left of the cut point with the segment of the second parent to the right of the cut point.

*Mutation* ($\mu$) produces incremental random changes in the offspring by randomly changing allele values of some genes. In case of binary chromosomes it corresponds to changing single bit positions. It is not applied to all members of the population, but is applied probabilistically only to some. Mutation has the effect of perturbing a certain chromosome in order to introduce *new* characteristics not present in any element of the parent population. For example, in case of binary chromosomes, toggling some selected bits produces the desired effect.

*Inversion* is the third operator of GA and like mutation it also operates on a single chromosome. Its basic function is to laterally invert the order of alleles between two randomly chosen points on a chromosome.

A *generation* is an iteration of GA where individuals in the current population are selected for crossover and offspring are created. Due to the addition of offspring, the size of population increases. In order to keep the number of members in a population fixed, a constant number of individuals are selected from this set that consists of both the individuals of the initial population, and the generated offspring. If **M** is the size of the initial population and $N_0$ is the number of offspring created in each generation, then, before the beginning of next generation, **M** new parents from **M** + $N_0$ individuals are selected. A greedy

```
Procedure  (Genetic_Algorithm)
    M= Population size.                  (*# Of possible solutions at any instance.*)
    N_g= Number of generations.          (*# Of iterations.*)
    N_o= Number of offsprings.           (*To be generated by crossover.*)
    P_μ= Mutation probability.           (*Also called mutation rate M_r.*)
    P ← Ξ(M)                             (*Construct initial population P.
                                           Ξ is population constructor.*)
    For j = 1 to M                       (*Evaluate fitnesses of all individuals.*)
        Evaluate f(P[j])                 (*Evaluate fitness of P.*)
    EndFor
    For i = 1 to N_g
        For j = 1 to N_o
            (x, y) ← φ(P)                (*Select two parents x and y from current population.*)
            offspring[j] ← χ(x, y)       (*Generate offsprings by crossover of parents x and y.*)
            Evaluate f(offspring[j])     (*Evaluate fitness of each offsprings.*)
        EndFor

        For j = 1 to N_o                 (*With probability P_μ apply mutation.*)
            mutated[j] ← μ(y)
            Evaluate f(mutated[j])
        EndFor
        P ← Select(P, offsprings)        (*Select best M solutions from parents & offsprings.*)
    EndFor
    Return highest scoring configuration in P.
End
```

**FIGURE 39.76**  Structure of a simple genetic algorithm.

selection mechanism is to choose the best **M** individuals from the total of $\mathbf{M} + N_0$. The complete pseudo code of a simple GA is given in Fig. 39.76.

## Tabu Search

The previous subsection discussed simulated annealing, which was inspired by the cooling of metals, and genetic algorithms, which imitate the biological phenomena of evolutionary reproduction. In this section we present a more recent optimization method called tabu search (TS), which is based on selected concepts of artificial intelligence (AI).

Tabu search was introduced by Fred Glover [11–14] as a general iterative heuristic for solving combinatorial optimization problems. Initial ideas of the technique were also proposed by Hansen [15] in his *steepest ascent mildest descent* heuristic. TS is conceptually simple and elegant. It is a form of local neighborhood search. Each solution $S \in \Omega$ has an associated set of neighbors $N(S) \subseteq \Omega$. A solution $S' \in N(S)$ can be reached from $S$ by an operation called a *move* to $S'$. Normally, the neighborhood relation is assumed symmetric. That is, if $S'$ is a neighbor of $S$ then $S$ is a neighbor of $S'$. At each step, the local neighborhood of the current solution is explored and the best solution in that neighborhood is selected as the new current solution. Unlike local search that stops when no improved new solution is found in the current neighborhood, tabu search continues the search from the best solution in the neighborhood even if it is worse than the current solution. To prevent cycling, information pertaining to the most recently visited solutions are inserted in a list called *tabu list*. Moves to tabu solutions are not allowed. The tabu status of a solution is overridden when certain criteria (aspiration criteria) are satisfied. One example of an aspiration criterion is when the cost of the selected solution is better than the best seen so far, which is an indication that the search is actually not cycling back, but rather moving to a new solution not encountered before.

Tabu search is a *metaheuristic*, which can be used not only to guide the search in complex solution spaces, but also to direct the operations of other heuristic procedures. It can be superimposed on any heuristic whose operations are characterized as performing a sequence of *moves* that lead the procedure from one trial solution to another. In addition to several other characteristics, the attractiveness of tabu search comes from its ability to escape local optima.

Tabu search differs from SA or GA, which are *memoryless*, and also from branch-and-bound, $A^*$ search, etc., which are rigid memory approaches. One of its features is its systematic use of *adaptive*

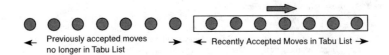

**FIGURE 39.77**   The tabu list can be visualized as a window over accepted moves.

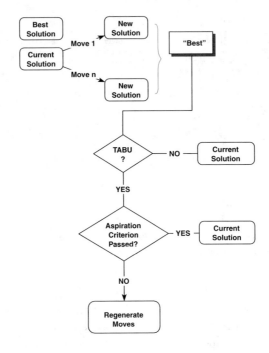

**FIGURE 39.78**   Flow chart of the tabu search algorithm.

(flexible) memory. It is based on very simple ideas with a clever combination of components, namely [16,17]:

1. A short-term memory component; this component is the core of the tabu search algorithm.
2. An intermediate-term memory component; this component is used for regionally **intensifying** the search.
3. A long-term memory component; this component is used for globally **diversifying** the search.

The central idea underlying tabu search is the exploitation of the above three memory components. Using the short-term memory, a *selective history* **H** of the states encountered is maintained to guide the search process. Neighborhood $N(S)$ is replaced by a modified neighborhood, which is a function of the history **H**, and is denoted by $N(\mathbf{H}, S)$. History determines which solutions may be reached by a move from $S$, since the next state $S'$ is selected from $N(\mathbf{H}, S)$. The short-term memory component is implemented through a set of *tabu* conditions and the associated *aspiration criterion*.

The major idea of the short-term memory component is to classify certain search directions as tabu (or *forbidden*). By doing so we avoid returning to previously visited solutions. Search is therefore forced away from recently visited solutions, with the help of a short-term memory (*tabu list* **T**). This memory contains *attributes* of some $k$ most recent moves. The size of the tabu list denoted by $k$ is the number of iterations for which a move containing that attribute is forbidden after it has been made. The tabu list can be visualized as a window on accepted moves as shown in Fig. 39.77. Moves that tend to undo previous moves within this window are forbidden. A flow chart illustrating the basic short-term memory tabu search algorithm is given in Fig. 39.78. An algorithmic description of a simple implementation of the tabu search is given in Fig. 39.79.

$\Omega$ : Set of feasible solutions.
$S$ : Current solution.
$S^*$ : Best admissible solution.
$Cost$ : Objective function.
$\aleph(S)$ : Neighborhood of $S \in \Omega$.
$\mathbf{V}^*$ : Sample of neighborhood solutions.
$\mathbf{T}$ : Tabu list.
$\mathbf{AL}$ : Aspiration Level.

**Begin**
1.  Start with an initial feasible solution $S \in \Omega$.
2.  Initialize tabu lists and aspiration level.
3.  **For** fixed number of iterations **Do**
4.      Generate neighbor solutions $\mathbf{V}^* \subset \aleph(S)$.
5.      Find best $S^* \in \mathbf{V}^*$.
6.      **If** move $S$ to $S^*$ is not in $\mathbf{T}$ **Then**
7.          Accept move and update best solution.
8.          Update tabu list and aspiration level.
9.          Increment iteration number.
10.     **Else**
11.         **If** $Cost(S^*) < \mathbf{AL}$ **Then**
12.             Accept move and update best solution.
13.             Update tabu list and aspiration level.
14.             Increment iteration number.
15.         **EndIf**
16.     **EndIf**
17. **EndFor**
    **End.**

**FIGURE 39.79** Algorithmic description of short-term tabu search (TS).

Intermediate-term and long-term memory processes are used to intensify and diversify the search, respectively, and have been found to be very effective in increasing both quality and efficiency [18,19].

The basic tabu search algorithm based on the short-term memory component is discussed first. Following this is a discussion on uses of intermediate and long-term memories.

Referring to Fig. 39.79, initially the current solution is the best solution. Copies of the current solution are perturbed with moves to get a set of new solutions. The best among these is selected and if it is not tabu then it becomes the current solution. If the move is tabu, its aspiration criterion is checked. If it passes the aspiration criterion, it becomes the current solution. If the move to the next solution is accepted, the move or some of its attributes are stored in the tabu list. Otherwise, moves are regenerated to get another set of new solutions. If the current solution is better than the best seen thus far, the best solution is updated. Whenever a move is accepted the iteration number is incremented. The procedure continues for a fixed number of iterations, or until some pre-specified stopping criterion is satisfied.

Tabu restrictions and aspiration criterion have a symmetric role. The order of checking for tabu status and aspiration criterion may be reversed, though most applications check if a move is tabu before checking for aspiration criterion. For more discussion on move attributes, types of tabu lists and the various tabu restrictions, the data structure to handle tabu-lists, and other aspiration criteria, the reader is referred to [8].

In many applications, the short-term memory component by itself has produced solutions superior to those found by alternative procedures, and usually the use of intermediate-term and long-term memory is bypassed; however, several studies have shown that intermediate and long-term memory components can improve solution quality and/or performance [19–22].

The basic role of the intermediate-term memory component is to *intensify* the search. By its incorporation, the search becomes more aggressive. As the name suggests, memory is used to intensify the search.

Intermediate-term memory component operates as follows. A selected number $m \gg |\mathbf{T}|$ (recall that $|\mathbf{T}|$ is the size of tabu list) of best trial solutions generated during a particular period of search are chosen and their features are recorded and compared. These solutions may be $m$ consecutive best ones, or $m$ local optimal solutions reached during the search. Features common to most of these are then taken and new solutions that contain these features are sought. One way to accomplish this is to restrict/penalize moves that remove such attributes. For example, in the TSP problem with moderately dense graphs, the number of different edges that can be included into any tour is generally a fraction of the total available edges (Why?). After some number of initial iterations, the method can discard all edges not yet incorporated into some tour. The size of the problem and the time per iteration now become smaller. The search therefore can focus on possibilities that are likely to be attractive, and can also examine many more alternatives in a given span of time.

The goal of long-term memory component is to *diversify* the search. The principles involved here are just the *opposite* of those used by the intermediate-term memory function. Instead of more intensively focusing the search with regions that contain previously found good solutions, the function of this component is to drive the search process into new regions that are different from those examined thus far.

Diversification using long-term memory in tabu search can be accomplished by creating an evaluator whose task is to take the search to new starting points [11]. For example, in the traveling salesman problem (TSP), a simple form of long-term memory is to keep a count of the number of times each edge has appeared in the tours previously generated. Then, an evaluator can be used to penalize each edge on the basis of this count; thereby favoring the generation of *other, hopefully good* starting tours that tend to avoid those edges most commonly used in the past. This sort of approach is viewed as a **frequency**-based tabu criterion in contrast to the **recency**-based (tabu list) discussed earlier. Such a long-term strategy can be employed by means of a long-term tabu list (or any other appropriate data structure) that is periodically activated to employ tabu conditions of increased stringency, thereby forcing the search process into new territory [23].

It is easy to create and test the short-term memory component first, and then incorporate the intermediate/long components for additional refinements.

Let a matrix entry $Freq(i,j)$ ($i$ and $j$ be movable or swappable elements) store the number of times swap $(i, j)$ was made to take the solution from current state $S$ to a new state $S^*$. We can then use this information to define a move evaluator $\varepsilon(\mathbf{H}, S)$, which is a function of both the cost of the solution, and the frequency of the swaps stored. Our objective is to diversify the search by giving more consideration to those swaps that have not been made yet, and to penalize those that frequently occurred, that is giving them less consideration [24]. Taking the above into consideration, the evaluation of the move can be expressed as follows:

$$\varepsilon(H,S^*) = \begin{cases} Cost(S^*) & Cost(S^*) \leq Cost(S) \\ Cost(S^*) + \alpha \times Freq(i,j) & Cost(S^*) > Cost(S) \end{cases}$$

$\alpha$ is a constant which depends on the range of the objective function values, the number of iterations, the span of history considered, etc. Its value ($\alpha$'s) is such that cost and frequency are appropriately balanced.

## Simulated Evolution (SimE)

The Simulated Evolution algorithm (SimE) is a general search strategy for solving a variety of combinatorial optimization problems. The first paper describing SimE appeared in 1987 [25]. Other papers by the same authors followed [26–28].

SimE assumes that there exists a population $P$ of a set $M$ of $n$ (movable) elements. In addition, there is a cost function *Cost* that is used to associate with each assignment of movable element $m$ a cost $C_m$.

**ALGORITHM** *Simulated_Evolution(M, L)*;
/* M: Set of movable elements; */
/* L: Set of locations; */
/* B: Selection bias; */
/* Stopping criteria and selection bias can be automatically adjusted; */
*INITIALIZATION*;
**Repeat**
   *EVALUATION*:
      **ForEach** $m \in M$ **Do** $g_m = \frac{O_m}{C_m}$ **EndForEach**;

   *SELECTION*:
      **ForEach** $m \in M$ **Do**
        **If** *Selection(m,B)* **Then** $P_s = P_s \cup \{m\}$
          **Else** $P_r = P_r \cup \{m\}$
        **EndIf**;
      **EndForEach**;
   *Sort the elements of $P_s$*;

   *ALLOCATION*:
      **ForEach** $m \in P_s$ **Do** *Allocation(m)* **EndForEach**;
**Until** *Stopping-criteria are met*;
**Return** *(BestSolution)*;
**End** *Simulated_Evolution.*

**FIGURE 39.80**  Simulated evolution algorithm.

The cost $C_m$ is used to compute the goodness (fitness) $g_m$ of element $m$, for each $m \in M$. Furthermore, Usually additional constraints must be satisfied by the population as a whole or by particular elements. A general outline of the SimE algorithm is given in Fig. 39.80.

SimE algorithm proceeds as follows. Initially, a population[1] is created at random from all populations satisfying the environmental constraints of the problem. The algorithm has one main loop consisting of three basic steps, *Evaluation*, *Selection*, and *Allocation*. The three steps are executed in sequence until the population average *goodness* reaches a maximum value, or no noticeable improvement to the population *goodness* is observed after a number of iterations. Another possible stopping criterion could be to run the algorithm for a prefixed number of iterations (see Fig. 39.80). Some details of the steps of the SimE algorithm are presented in the next subsection.

### Evaluation

The *Evaluation* step consists of evaluating the goodness of each individual $i$ of the population $P$. The *goodness* measure must be a single number expressible in the range $[0,1]$. *Goodness* is defined as follows:

$$g_i = \frac{O_i}{C_i} \tag{39.1}$$

where $O_i$ is an estimate of the optimal cost of individual $i$, and $C_i$ is the actual cost of $i$ in its current location. Equation (39.1) assumes a minimization problem (maximization of goodness). Notice that, according to the previous definition, the $O_i$'s **do not** change from generation to generation, and, therefore, are computed only once during the initialization step. Hence, only the $C_i$'s have to be recomputed at each call to the *Evaluation* function. Empirical evidence [29] shows that the accuracy of the estimation of $O_i$ is not very crucial to the successful application of SimE; however, the *goodness* measure must be strongly related to the target objective of the given problem.

---

[1] In SimE terminology, a population refers to a single solution. Individuals of the population are components of the solution; they are the movable elements.

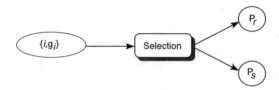

**FIGURE 39.81**   Selection.

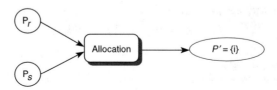

**FIGURE 39.82**   Allocation.

## Selection

The second step of the SimE algorithm is *Selection*. Selection takes as input the population $P$ together with the estimated *goodness* of each individual and partitions $P$ into two disjoint sets, a selection set $P_s$ and a set $P_r$ of the remaining members of the population (see Fig. 39.81). Each member of the population is considered separately from all other individuals. The decision whether to assign individual $i$ to the set $P_s$ or set $P_r$ is based solely on its *goodness* $g_i$. The operator uses a selection function *Selection*, which takes as input $g_i$ and a parameter $B$, which is a *selection bias*. Values of $B$ are recommended to be in the range [−0.2, 0.2]. In many cases a value of $B = 0$ would be a reasonable choice.

The *Selection* function returns *true* or *false*. The higher the *goodness* value of the element, the higher is its chance of staying in its current location, i.e., unaltered in the next generation. On the other hand, the lower the *goodness* value, the more likely the corresponding element will be selected for alteration (mutation) in the next generation (will be assigned to the selection set $P_s$). An individual with a high *fitness* (*goodness* close to one) still has a nonzero probability of being assigned to the selected set $P_s$. It is this element of nondeterminism that gives SimE the capability of escaping local minima.

For most problems, it is always beneficial to alter the elements of the population according to a deterministic order that is correlated with the objective function being optimized. Hence, in SimE, prior to the *Allocation* step, the elements in the selection set $P_s$ are sorted. The sorting criterion is problem specific. Usually there are several criteria to choose from [8].

## Allocation

*Allocation* is the SimE operator that has most impact on the quality of solution. *Allocation* takes as input the two sets $P_s$ and $P_r$ and generates a new population $P'$ that contains all the members of the previous population $P$, with the elements of $P_s$ mutated according to an *Allocation* function (see Fig. 39.82).

The choice of a suitable *Allocation* function is problem specific. The decision of the *Allocation* strategy usually requires more ingenuity on the part of the designer than the *Selection* scheme. The *Allocation* function may be a nondeterministic function, which involves a choice among a number of possible mutations (moves) for each element of $P_s$. Usually, a number of *trial-mutations* are performed and rated with respect to their *goodnesses*. Based on the resulting goodnesses, a final configuration of the population $P'$ is decided. The goal of Allocation is to favor improvements over the previous generation, without being too greedy.

The *Allocation* operation is a complex form of genetic *mutation* that is one of the genetic operations thought to be responsible for the evolution of the various species in biological environments; however, there is no need for a *crossover* operation as in GA since only one parent is maintained in all generations; however, because *mutation* is the only mechanism used by SimE for inheritance and evolution, it must be more sophisticated than the one used in GA.

*Allocation* alters (mutates) all the elements in the selected set $P_s$ one after the other in a predetermined order. For each individual $e_i$ of the selected set $P_s$, $W$ distinct trial alterations are attempted. The trial that leads to the best configuration (population) with respect to the objective being optimized is accepted and made permanent. The *goodness* of each individual element is also tightly coupled with the target objective, so the superior alterations are supposed to gradually improve the individual *goodnesses* as well. Hence, *Allocation* allows the search to progressively evolve toward an optimal configuration where each individual is optimally located.

### Initialization Phase

This step precedes the iterative phase. In this step, the various parameters of the algorithm are set to their desired values, namely, the maximum number of iterations required to run the main loop, the selection bias $B$, and the number of trial alterations $W$ per individual. Furthermore, similar to any iterative algorithm, SimE requires that an initial solution be given. The convergence aspects of SimE are not affected by the quality of the initial solution; however, starting from a randomly generated solution usually increases the number of iterations required to converge to a near-optimal solution.

## Convergence Aspects

One of the desirable properties that a stochastic iterative algorithm should possess is the convergence property, i.e., the guarantee of converging to one of the global optima if given enough time. The convergence aspects of the simulated annealing algorithm have been the subject of extensive studies. For a thorough discussion of simulated annealing convergence we refer the reader to [6,7,30].

For convergence properties of the GA heuristic based on Markovian analysis, the reader is referred to [31–37]. Fogel [38] provides a concise treatment of the main GA convergence results.

The tabu search algorithm as described in this article is known as *ordinary* or *deterministic tabu search*. Because of its deterministic nature, ordinary tabu search may never converge to a global optimum state. The incorporation of a nondeterministic element within tabu search allows the algorithm to lend itself to mathematical analysis similar to that developed for simulated annealing, making it possible to establish corresponding convergence properties. Tabu search with nondeterministic elements is called *probabilistic tabu search* [11,39]. Probabilistic tabu search has been shown to converge in the limit to a global optimum state. The proof is analogous to that of SA.

Proof of convergence of SimE can be found in [28,40]. For complete convergence analysis, the reader may refer to [8].

## Parallelization/Acceleration

Due to their iterative and blind nature, the heuristics discussed in this chapter section require large runtime, especially on large problems, and CPU-intensive cost functions. Substantial amount of work has been done to parallelize or design accelerators to run these time consuming heuristics. With respect to simulated annealing, which is inherently sequential, some ingenuity is required on the part of the designer to cleverly parallelize the annealing process. Several parallel implementations of SA have been reported in [6,41–47]. Hardware acceleration that consists of implementing time consuming parts in hardware is described in [48]. Parallel acceleration, where execution of the algorithm is partitioned on several concurrently running processors, is reported in [49–51]. Other approaches that have been applied to parallelize SA are found in [6,49,52,53]. The parallel accelerations follow two general strategies: (1) move acceleration, also called single-trial parallelism, and (2) parallel moves or multiple-trial parallelism.

The GA is highly parallel. The reported GA parallelization strategies fall into three general categories: the *island model* [54,55], the *stepping stone model* [56–59], and the *neighborhood model*, also called the cellular model [60,61].

Work on parallelization of the tabu search heuristic can be found in [8,62–66]. The heuristic has also been parallelized and executed on a network of workstations using PVM [67]. Techniques to accelerate the execution of SimE by implementing it on vector-processors [29] or on a network of workstations [68] are described in [8].

## Applications

The first applications of SA were on placement [2]. Furthermore, the largest number of applications of SA was on digital design automation problems [5]. A popular package that uses SA for VLSI standard-cell placement and routing is the TimberWolf3.2 package [46]. In addition to placement, SA has been applied successfully to several other problems. These include classical problems such as the TSP [2], graph partitioning, matching problem, Steiner problems [69], linear arrangement [1], clustering problem [70], quadratic assignment [71], various scheduling problems [72,73], graph coloring [74], etc. In the area of engineering SA has been applied extensively to solve various hard VLSI physical design automation problems [5]. In addition, it has been applied with success in other areas such as topology design of computer networks [75], image processing [76], test pattern generation, code design, etc. A comprehensive list of bibliography of some of the above applications and some details of their implementation such as cost function formulation, move set design, parameters, etc., is available in [6,8,77–79].

In addition to their application to classical optimization problems such as the knapsack problem [80], TSP [81,82], Steiner tree problem [83], set covering problem [84], N-queens problem [85], clustering problem [86], graph partitioning [87], etc., GAs have also been applied to several engineering problems. Some examples of these applications include job shop and multiprocessor scheduling [81,88,89], discovery of maximal distance codes for data communications [90], bin-packing [91], design of telecommunication (mesh) networks [92], test sequence generation for digital system testing [93], VLSI design (cell placement [5,94–96], floorplanning [97], routing [98]), pattern matching [99], technology mapping [100], PCB assembly planning [101], and high-level synthesis of digital systems [102,103]. The books by Goldberg (1989) [10], Davis (1991) [104], recent conference proceedings on evolutionary computation, and on applications of genetic algorithms discuss in detail the various applications of GAs in science and engineering. These range from optimization of pipeline systems and medical imaging to applications such as robot trajectory generation and parametric design of aircraft [10,104].

TS has also been applied to solve combinatorial optimization problems appearing in various fields of science, engineering, and business. Results reported indicate superior performance to other previous techniques. Examples of some hard problems to which tabu search has been applied with success include graph partitioning [105], clustering [106], TSP [107], maximum independent set problem [108], graph coloring [109,110], maximum clique problem [111], and quadratic assignment problem [62,112] to name a few. In the area of engineering, tabu search has been applied to machine sequencing [113], scheduling [22,114–118], fuzzy clustering [119], multiprocessor scheduling [120], vehicle routing [121–123], general fixed charge problem [17], bin-packing [124], bandwidth packing [24], VLSI placement [125], circuit partitioning [126], global routing [127], high-level synthesis of digital systems [128,129], etc. A good summary of most recent applications of tabu search can be found in [8,18,130].

The SimE algorithm has also been used to solve a wide range of combinatorial optimization problems. Kling and Banerjee published their results with respect to SimE in design automation conferences [25,27] and journals [26,28]. This explains the fact that most published work on SimE has been originated by researchers in the area of design automation of VLSI circuits [40,131–134]. The first problem on which SimE was first applied is standard cell placement [25,28]. A number of papers describe SimE-based heuristics as applied to the routing of VLSI circuits [131,135–140]. SimE was also successfully applied in high-level synthesis [141–143]. Other reported SimE applications are in micro-code compaction [144], automatic synthesis of gate matrix [134], and the synthesis of cellular architecture field programmable gate arrays (FPGAs) [145].

## Conclusion

This chapter section has introduced the reader to four effective heuristics that belong to the class of *general approximation iterative algorithms*, namely SA, GA, tabu search, and SimE. From the immense literature that is available it is evident that for a large variety of applications, in certain settings, these heuristics produce excellent results. All five algorithms are general iterative metaheuristics. A value of the objective function is used to compare results of consecutive iterations and a solution is selected based on its value.

All algorithms incorporate domain specific knowledge to dictate the search strategy. They also tolerate some element of nondeterminism that helps the search escape out of local minima. They all rely on the use of a suitable cost function, which provides feedback to the algorithm as the search progresses. The principle difference among these heuristics is how and where domain specific knowledge is used. For example, in SA such knowledge is mainly included in the cost function. Elements involved in a perturbation are selected randomly, and perturbations are accepted or rejected according to the *Metropolis* criterion, which is a function of the cost. The cooling schedule has also a major impact on the algorithm performance and must be carefully crafted to the problem domain as well as the particular problem instance.

For the two evolutionary algorithms discussed in the chapter, GA and SimE, domain specific knowledge is exploited in all phases. In the case of GA, the fitness of individual solutions incorporates domain specific knowledge. Selection for reproduction, the genetic operations, as well as generation of the new population also incorporate a great deal of heuristic knowledge about the problem domain. In SimE, each individual element of a solution is characterized by a goodness measure that is highly correlated with the objective function. The perturbation step (selection followed by allocation) affects mostly low goodness elements. Therefore, domain specific knowledge is included in every step of the SimE algorithm.

Tabu search is different from the above heuristics in that it has an explicit memory component. At each iteration the neighborhood of the current solution is partially explored, and a move is made to the best nontabu solution in that neighborhood. The neighborhood function as well as tabu list size and content are problem specific. The direction of the search is also influenced by the memory structures (whether intensification or diversification is used).

A classification of meta-heuristics proposed by Glover and Laguna [130] is based on three basic features: (1) the use of adaptive memory, where the letter $A$ is used if the meta-heuristic employs adaptive memory, and the letter $M$ is used if it is memoryless; (2) the kind of neighborhood exploration, where the letter $N$ is used if the meta-heuristic performs a systematic neighborhood search, and the letter $S$ is used if stochastic sampling is followed; and (3) the number of current solutions carried from one iteration to the next, where the digit 1 is used if the meta-heuristic maintains a single solution, and the letter $P$ is used if a parallel search is performed with a population of solutions of cardinality $P$. For example, according to this classification, GA is $M/S/P$, tabu search is $A/N/1$, SA is $M/S/1$, and SimE is also $M/S/1$.

It is also possible to make hybrids of these algorithms. The basic idea of hybridization is to enhance the strengths and compensate for the weaknesses of two or more complementary approaches. For the details about the hybridization the readers are referred to [8].

In this chapter section, it has not been the authors' intention to demonstrate the superiority of one algorithm over the other. Actually it would be unwise to rank such algorithms. Each one of them has its own merits. Recently, an interesting theoretical study has been reported by Wolpert and Macready in which they proved a number of theorems stating that the average performance of any pair of iterative (deterministic or nondeterministic) algorithms across all problems is identical. That is, if an algorithm performs well on a certain class of problems then it necessarily pays for that with degraded performance on the remaining set of problems [146]; however, it should be noted that the reported theorems assume that the algorithms do not include domain specific knowledge of the problems being solved. Obviously, it would be expected that a well-engineered algorithm would exhibit superior performance to that of a poorly engineered one.

## Acknowledgment

The authors acknowledge King Fahd University of Petroleum and Minerals, Dhahran, Saudi Arabia, for all support. This work is carried out under university-funded project number COE/ITERATE/221. Special thanks to Junaid Asim Khan and Salman Khan for their tremendous assistance and help in the preparation of this manuscript.

## References

1. S. Nahar, S. Sahni, and E. Shragowitz. Simulated annealing and combinatorial optimization. *International Journal of Computer Aided VLSI Design*, 1(1):1–23, 1989.
2. S. Kirkpatrick, Jr., C. Gelatt, and M. Vecchi. Optimization by simulated annealing. *Science*, 220(4598): 498–516, May 1983.
3. V. Černy. Thermodynamical approach to the traveling salesman problem: An efficient simulation algorithm. *Journal of Optimization Theory and Application*, 45(1):41–51, January 1985.
4. N. Metropolis et al. Equation of state calculations by fast computing machines. *Journal of Chem. Physics*, 21:1087–1092, 1953.
5. Sadiq M. Sait and Habib Youssef. *VLSI Design Automation: Theory and Practice*. McGraw-Hill, Europe (also co-published by IEEE Press), 1995.
6. Emile Aarts and Jan Korst. *Simulated Annealing and Boltzmann Machines: A Stochastic Approach to Combinatorial Optimization and Neural Computing*. John Wiley & Sons, New York, 1989.
7. R.H.J.M. Otten and L.P.P.P. van Ginneken. *The Annealing Algorithm*. Kluwer Academic Publishers, Boston, MA, 1989.
8. Sadiq M. Sait and Habib Youssef. *Iterative Computer Algorithms with Applications in Engineering: Solving Combinatorial Optimization Problems*. IEEE Computer Society Press, 1999.
9. J. H. Holland. *Adaptation in Natural and Artificial Systems*. University of Michigan Press, Ann Arbor, Michigan, 1975.
10. D. E. Goldberg. *Genetic Algorithms in Search, Optimization and Machine Learning*. Addison-Wesley, Reading, MA, 1989.
11. F. Glover. Tabu search—Part I. *ORSA Journal on Computing*, 1(3):190–206, 1989.
12. F. Glover. Tabu search—Part II. *ORSA Journal on Computing*, 2(1):4–32, 1990.
13. F. Glover, E. Taillard, and D. de Werra. A user's guide to Tabu search. *Annals of Operations Research*, 41:3–28, 1993.
14. F. Glover and M. Laguna. *Tabu Search*. Kluwer Academic Publishers, Boston, MA, 1997.
15. P. Hansen. The steepest ascent mildest descent heuristic for combinatorial programming. *Congress on Numerical Methods in Combinatorial Optimization*, 1986.
16. F. Glover. Artificial intelligence, heuristic frameworks and Tabu search. *Managerial and Decision Economics*, 11:365–375, 1990.
17. Minghe Sun and P. G. McKeown. Tabu search applied to the general fixed charge problem. *Annals of Operations Research*, 41:405–420, 1993.
18. F. Glover. Tabu search and adaptive memory programming-advances, applications and challenges. *Technical Report, College of Business, University of Colorado at Boulder*, 1996.
19. F. Dammeyer and Stefan VoB. Dynamic Tabu list management using the reverse elimination method. *Annals of Operations Research*, 41:31–46, 1993.
20. M. Malek, M. Guruswamy, M. Pandya, and H. Owens. Serial and parallel Simulated Annealing and Tabu search algorithms for the traveling salesman problem. *Annals of Operations Research*, 21:59–84, 1989.
21. J. Ryan, editor. *Heuristics for Combinatorial Optimization*, June 1989.
22. O. Icmeil and S. Selcuk Erenguc. A Tabu search procedure for the resource constrained project scheduling problem with discounted cash flows. *Computers & Operations Research*, 21(8):841–853, 1994.

23. J. P. Kelly, M. Laguna, and F. Glover. A study of diversification strategies for the quadratic assignment problem. *Computers & Operations Research*, 21(8):885–893, 1994.

24. M. Laguna and F. Glover. Bandwidth Packing; A Tabu search approach. *Management Science*, 39(4):492–500, 1993.

25. Ralph Michael Kling and Prithviraj Banerjee. ESP: A new standard cell placement package using Simulated Evolution. *Proceedings of 24th Design Automation Conference*, pp. 60–66, 1987.

26. R. M. Kling and P. Banerjee. ESP: Placement by Simulated Evolution. *IEEE Transactions on Computer-Aided Design*, 8(3):245–255, March 1989.

27. R. M. Kling and P. Banerjee. Optimization by Simulated Evolution with applications to standard-cell placement. *Proceedings of 27th Design Automation Conference*, pp. 20–25, 1990.

28. R. M. Kling and P. Banerjee. Empirical and theoretical studies of the Simulated Evolution method applied to standard-cell placement. *IEEE Transactions on Computer-Aided Design*, 10(10):1303–1315, October 1991.

29. R. M. Kling. *Optimization by Simulated Evolution and its Application to cell placement*. Ph.D. Thesis, University of Illinois, Urbana, 1990.

30. E. H. L. Aarts and P. J. N. Van Laarhoven. Statistical cooling: a general approach to combinatorial optimization problem. *Philips Journal of Research*, 40(4):193–226, January 1985.

31. D. E. Goldberg and P. Segrest. Finite Markov chain analysis of Genetic algorithms. *Genetic Algorithms and Their Applications: Proceedings of 2nd International Conference on GAs*, pp. 1–8, 1987.

32. A. E. Nix and M. D. Vose. Modeling Genetic algorithms with Markov chains. *Annals of Mathematics and Artificial Intelligence*, pp. 79–88, 1993.

33. A. H. Eiben, E. H. L. Aarts, and K. M. Van Hee. Global convergence of Genetic algorithms: A Markov chain analysis. In H. P. Schwefel and Männer, editors, *Parallel Problem Solving from Nature*, pp. 4–12. Springer-Verlag, Berlin, 1990.

34. T. E. Davis and J. C. Principe. A Simulated Annealing like convergence theory for the simple Genetic algorithm. *Proceedings of the 4th International Conference on Genetic Algorithm*, pp. 174–181, 1991.

35. T. E. Davis and J. C. Principe. A Markov chain framework for the simple Genetic algorithm. *Proceedings of the 4th International Conference on Genetic Algorithm*, 13:269–288, 1993.

36. S. W. Mahfoud. Finite Markov chain models of an alternative selection strategy for the Genetic algorithm. *Complex systems*, 7:155–170, 1993.

37. G. Rudolph. Convergence analysis of canonical genetic algorithms. *IEEE Transactions on Neural Networks*, 5:1:96–101, 1994.

38. D. B. Fogel. *Evolutionary Computation: Toward a New Philosophy of Machine Intelligence*. IEEE Press, 1995.

39. U. Faigle and W. Kern. Some convergence results for probabilistic Tabu search. *ORSA Journal on Computing*, 4(1):32–37, Winter 1992.

40. C. Y. Mao and Y. H. Hu. Analysis of convergence properties of Stochastic Evolution algorithm. *IEEE Transactions on Computer Aided Design*, 15(7):826–831, July 1996.

41. M. D. Huang, F. Romeo, and A. L. Sangiovanni-Vincentelli. An efficient general cooling schedule for Simulated Annealing. In *IEEE International Conference on Computer-Aided Design*, pp. 381–384, 1986.

42. H. Szu and R. Hartley. Fast Simulated Annealing. *Physics Letters, A*, 122:157–162, 1987.

43. J. W. Greene and K. J. Supowit. Simulated Annealing without rejected moves. *IEEE Tansactions on Computer-Aided Design*, 5:221–228, 1986.

44. P. J. M. Laarhoven and E. H. L. Aarts. *Simulated Annealing: Theory and Applications*. Reidel, Dordrecht, 1987.

45. F. Catthoor, H. DeMan, and J. Vandewalle. Samurai: A general and efficient Simulated-Annealing schedule with fully adaptive annealing parameters. *Integration*, 6:147–178, 1988.

46. C. Sechen and A. L. Sangiovanni-Vincentelli. Timberwolf3.2: A new standard-cell placement and global routing package. *Proceedings of 23rd Design Automation Conference*, pp. 432–439, 1986.

47. L. K. Grover. A new Simulated Annealing algorithm for standard-cell placement. In *IEEE International Conference of Computer Aided Design,* pp. 378–380, 1986.

48. A. Iosupovici, C. King, and M. Breuer. A module interchange placement machine. *Proceedings of 20th Design Automation Conference,* pp. 171–174, 1983.

49. Saul A. Kravitz and Rob A. Rutenbar. Placement by Simulated Annealing on a multiprocessor. *IEEE Transactions on Computer Aided Design,* CAD-6(4):534–549, July 1987.

50. F. Darema-Rogers, S. Kirkpatrick, and V. A. Norton. Parallel algorithms for chip placement by simulated annealing. *IBM Journal of Research and Development,* 31:391–402, May 1987.

51. F. Darema, S. Kirkpatrick, and V. A. Norton. Parallel techniques for chip placement by Simulated Annealing on shared memory systems. *Proceedings of International Conference on Computer Design: VLSI in Computers & Processors, ICCD-87,* pp. 87–90, 1987.

52. M. D. Durand. Accuracy vs. Speed in placement. *IEEE Design & Test of Computers,* pp. 8–34, June 1989.

53. Xin Yao. Global optimization by evolutionary algorithms. In *Proceedings of IEEE International Symposium on parallel algorithms architecture synthesis,* pp. 282–291, 1997.

54. T. Starkweather, D. Whitley, and K. Mathias. Optimization using distributed Genetic algorithm. In *Parallel problem solving from nature,* 1991.

55. M. Tanese. Distributed Genetic Algorithms. In J. D. Schaffer, editor, *Proceedings of the 3rd International Conference on Genetic Algorithms,* pp. 434–439. Morgan-Kaufmann, San Maeto, CA, 1989.

56. M. Gorges-Schleuter. Explicit parallelism of Genetic algorithms through population structures. In H. P. Schwefel and R. Männer, editors, *Problem Solving from Nature,* pp. 150–159. Springer-Verlag, New York, 1991.

57. N. Eldredge and S. J. Gould. *Punctuated Equilibrea: An alternative to phyletic gradualism. Models of Paleobiology,* T. J. M. Schopf, Ed. San Fransisco: CA, Freeman. Cooper and Co., 1972.

58. N. Eldredge. *Time Frames.* New York: Simon and Schuster, 1985.

59. J. P. Cohoon, S. U. Hegde, W. N. Martin, and D. S. Richards. Distributed Genetic algorithms for the floorplan design problem. *IEEE Transactions on Computer-Aided Design,* CAD-10:483–492, April 1991.

60. V. Scott Gordon and Darrell Whitley. A machine-independent analysis of parallel Genetic algorithms. *Complex Systems,* 8:181–214, 1994.

61. M. Gorges-Schleuter. ASPARAGOS-An asynchronous parallel Genetic optimization strategy. In J.D. Schaffer, editor, *Proceedings of the 3rd International Conference on Genetic Algorithms and their Applications,* pp. 422–427. Morgan-Kaufmann, San Maeto, CA, 1989.

62. E. Taillard. Robust Tabu search for the quadratic assignment problem. *Parallel Computing,* 17:443–455, 1991.

63. E. Taillard. Some efficient heuristic methods for the flow shop sequencing problem. *European Journal of Operational Research,* 417:65–74, 1990.

64. Bruno-Laurent Garica, Jean-Yves Potvin, and Jean-Marc Rousseau. A parallel implementation of the Tabu search heuristic for vehicle routing problems with time window constraints. *Computers & Operations Research,* 21(9):1025–1033, November 1994.

65. I. De Falco, R. Del Balio, E. Tarantino, and R. Vaccaro. Improving search by incorporating evolution principles in parallel Tabu search. In *Proc. of the first IEEE Conference on Evolutionary Computation-ICEC '94,* pp. 823–828, June 1994.

66. E. Taillard. Parallel iterative search methods for the vehicle routing problem. *Networks,* 23:661–673, 1993.

67. Sadiq M. Sait, Habib Youssef, H. Barada, and Ahmed Al-Yamani. A parallel Tabu search algorithm for VLSI standard-cell placement. *Proceedings of IEEE International Symposium on Circuits and Systems,* May 2000.

68. Ralph Michael Kling and Prithviraj Banerjee. Concurrent ESP: A placement algorithm for execution on distributed processors. *Proceedings of the IEEE International Conference on Computer-Aided Design,* pp. 354–357, 1987.

69. K. A. Dowsland. Hill climbing, Simulated Annealing, and the Steiner problem in graphs. *Eng. Opt.*, 17:91–107, 1991.

70. S. Selim and K. S. Al-Sultan. A Simulated Annealing algorithm for the clustering problem. *Pattern Recognition*, 24(10):1003–1008, 1991.

71. D. T. Connolly. An improved annealing scheme for the QAP. *European Journal of Operational Research*, 46:93–100, 1990.

72. I. H. Osman and C. N. Potts. Simulated Annealing for permutation flow-shop annealing. *OMEGA*, 17:551–557, 1989.

73. F. A. Ogbu and D. K. Smith. The application of the Simulated Annealing algorithm to the solution of the $n/m/c_{max}$ flowshop problem. *Computers & Operations Research*, 17:243–253, 1990.

74. M. Chams, A. Hertz, and D. de Werra. Some experiments with Simulated Annealing for coloring graphs. *European Journal of Operational Research*, 32:260–266, 1987.

75. C. Ersoy and S. S. Panwar. Topological design of interconnected LAN/MAN networks. *IEEE Journal on Selected Areas in Communications*, 11(8):1172–1182, 1993.

76. S. Geman and D. Geman. Stochastic relaxation, Gibbs distribution, and the Bayesian restoration of images. *IEEE Transactions on Pattern Analysis and Machine Intelligence*, PAMI-6:721–741, 1984.

77. K. A. Dowsland. Simulated Annealing. In C. R. Reeves, editor, *Modern Heuristic Techniques for Combinatorial Optimization Problems*. McGraw-Hill, Europe, 1995.

78. N. E. Collins, R. W. Eglese, and B. L. Golden. Simulated annealing: An annotated bibliography. *AJMMS*, 8:209–307, 1988.

79. R. W. Eglese. Simulated Annealing: A tool for operational research. *European Journal of Operational Research*, 46:271–281, 1990.

80. R. Spillman. Solving large Knapsack problems with a Genetic algorithm. In *International Conference on Systems, Man and Cybernetics*, pp. 632–637, 1995.

81. D. Whitley, T. Starkweather, and D'Ann Fuquay. Scheduling problems and traveling salesmen: the genetic edge recombination operator. In *Proceedings of the 3rd International Conference on Genetic Algorithms and their Applications*, pp. 133–140, 1989.

82. H. Tamaki et al. A comparison study of Genetic codings for the traveling salesman problem. In *Proceedings of the 1st IEEE Conference on Evolutionary Computation*, pp. 1–6, 1994.

83. J. Hesser, R. Manner, and O. Stucky. Optimization of Steiner trees using Genetic algorithms. In *ICGA '89*, pp. 231–236, 1989.

84. K. S. Al-Sultan, M. F. Hussain, and J. S. Nizami. A Genetic algorithm for the set covering problem. *Journal of the Operational Research Society*, 47:702–709, 1996.

85. A. Homaifar, J. Turner, and Samia Ali. The N-queens problem and Genetic algorithms. In *IEEE Proceedings of Southeastcon '92*, pp. 262–267, April 1992.

86. K. S. Al-Sultan and M. Maroof Khan. Computational experience on four algorithms for the hard clustering problem. *Pattern Recognition Letters*, 17:295–308, 1996.

87. H. Pirkul and E. Rolland. New heuristic solution procedures for uniform graph partitioning problem: Extensions and evaluation. *Computers & Operations Research*, 21(8):895–907, October 1994.

88. E. S. H. Hou, N. Ansari, and R. Hong. Genetic algorithm for multiprocessor scheduling. *IEEE Transactions on Parallel and Distributed Systems*, 5(2):113–120, February 1994.

89. M. S. T. Benten and Sadiq M. Sait. Genetic scheduling of task graphs. *International Journal of Electronics*, 77(4):401–415, 1994.

90. K. Dontas and K. De Jong. Discovery of maximal distance codes using Genetic algorithms. *Proceedings of the 2nd International IEEE Conference on Tools for Artificial Intelligence*, pp. 805–811, 1990.

91. E. Falkenauer and A. Delchambre. A genetic algorithm for bin packing and line balancing. *Proceedings of International Conference on Robotics and Automation*, pp. 1186–1192, May 1992.

92. King-Tim Ko et al. Using genetic algorithms to design mesh networks. *Computer*, pp. 56–60, 1997.

93. E. M. Rudnick, J. H. Patel, G. S. Greenstein, and T. M. Niermann. Sequential circuit test generation in a Genetic algorithm framework. In *Proceedings of the 31st Design Automation Conference*, pp. 698–704, 1994.

94. J. P. Cohoon and W. D. Paris. Genetic placement. *IEEE Transactions on Computer-Aided Design*, CAD-6:956–964, November 1987.

95. K. Shahookar and P. Mazumder. VLSI cell placement techniques. *ACM Computing Surveys*, 23(2):143–220, June 1991.

96. K. Shahookar and P. Mazumder. A genetic approach to standard cell placement using meta-genetic parameter optimization. *IEEE Transactions on Computer-Aided Design*, 9(5):500–511, May 1990.

97. Sadiq M. Sait et al. Timing influenced general-cell genetic foorplanner. In *ASP-DAC '95: Asia and South-Pacific Design Automation Conference*, pp. 135–140, 1995.

98. H. I. Han et al. GenRouter: A genetic algorithm for channel routing problems. In *Proceeding of TENCON 95, IEEE Region 10 International Conference on Microelectronics and VLSI*, pp. 151–154, November 1995.

99. N. Ansari, M-H Chen, and E. S. H. Hou. Point pattern matching by genetic algorithm. In *16th Annual Conference on IEEE Industrial electronics*, pp. 1233–1238, 1990.

100. V. Kommu and I. Pomeranz. GAFPGA: Genetic algorithms for FPGA technology mapping. In *Proceeding of EURO-DAC '93: IEEE European Design Automation Conference*, pp. 300–305, September 1993.

101. M. C. Leu, H. Wong, and Z. Ji. Genetic algorithm for solving printed circuit board assembly planning problems. *Proceedings of Japan-USA Symposium on Flexible Automation*, pp. 1579–1586, July 1992.

102. S. Ali, Sadiq M. Sait, and M. S. T. Benten. GSA: Scheduling and allocation using Genetic algorithms. In *Proceedings of EURODAC '94: IEEE European Design Automation Conference*, pp. 84–89, September 1994.

103. C. P. Ravikumar and V. Saxena. TOGAPS: A testability oriented genetic algorithm for pipeline synthesis. *VLSI Design*, 5(1):77–87, 1996.

104. L. Davis, editor. *Handbook of Genetic Algorithms*. Van Nostrand Reinhold, NY, 1991.

105. A. Lim and Yeow-Meng Chee. Graph partitioning using Tabu search. In *1991 IEEE International Symposium on Circuits and Systems*, pp. 1164–1167, 1991.

106. K. S. Al-Sultan. A Tabu search approach to the clustering problem. *Pattern Recognition*, 28(9): 1443–1451, 1995.

107. M. Malek, M. Heap, R. Kapur, and A. Mourad. A fault tolerant implementation of the traveling salesman problem. *Research Report, Department of EE and Computer Engineering, The University of Texas-Austin*, May 1989.

108. C. Friden, A. Hertz, and D. de Werra. TABARIS: An exact algorithm based on Tabu search for finding a maximum independent set in a graph. *Computers & Operations Research*, 19(1–4):81–91, 1990.

109. N. Dubois and D. de Werra. EPCOT: An efficient procedure for coloring optimally with Tabu search. *Computers Math Application*, 25(10/11):35–45, 1993.

110. A. Hertz and D. de Werra. Using Tabu search techniques for graph coloring. *Computing*, 39:345–351, 1987.

111. M. Gendreau, P. Soriano, and L. Salvail. Solving the maximum clique problem using a Tabu search approach. *Annals of Operations Research*, 41:385–404, 1993.

112. J. Skorin-Kapov. Tabu search applied to the quadratic assignment problem. *ORSA Journal on Computing*, 2(1):33–45, 1990.

113. C. R. Reeves. Improving the efficiency of Tabu search for machine sequencing problems. *Journal of Operational Research Society*, 44:375–382, 1993.

114. E. L. Mooney and R. L. Rardin. Tabu search for a class of scheduling problems. *Annals of Operations Research*, 41:253–278, 1993.

115. M. Dell'Amico and M. Trubian. Applying Tabu search to the job-shop scheduling problem. *Annals of Operations Research*, 41:231–252, 1993.

116. M. Widmer and A. Hertz. A new heuristic method for the flow shop sequencing problem. *European Journal of Operational Research*, 41:186–193, 1989.

117. J. W. Barnes and J. B. Chambers. Solving the job shop scheduling problem with Tabu search. *IIE Transactions*, 27:257–263, 1995.

118. M. Widmer. Job shop scheduling with tooling constraints: A Tabu search approach. *Journal of Operational Research Society*, 42(1):75–82, 1991.

119. K. S. Al-Sultan and C. A. Fedjki. A Tabu search based algorithm for the fuzzy clustering problem. *Pattern Recognition*, 1998.

120. R. Hubscher and F. Glover. Applying Tabu search with influential diversification to multiprocessor scheduling. *Computers & Operations Research*, 21(8):877–884, 1994.

121. I. H. Osman. Metastrategy Simulated Annealing and Tabu search algorithms for the vehicle routing problem. *Annals of Operations Research*, 41:421–451, 1993.

122. F. Semet and E. Taillard. Solving real-life vehicle routing problems efficiently using Tabu search. *Annals of Operations Research*, 41:469–488, 1993.

123. J. Renaud, G. Laporte, and F. F. Boctor. A Tabu search heuristic for the multi-depot vehicle routing problem. *Computers Ops Research*, 23:229–235, 1996.

124. F. Glover and R. Hubscher. Binpacking with a Tabu search. *Technical Report, Graduate School of Business Administration, University of Colorado at Boulder*, 1991.

125. L. Song and A. Vannelli. VLSI placement using Tabu search. *Microelectronics Journal*, 17(5):437–445, 1992.

126. S. Areibi and A. Vannelli. Circuit partitioning using a Tabu search approach. In *1993 IEEE International Symposium on Circuits and Systems*, pp. 1643–1646, 1993.

127. Habib Youssef and Sadiq M. Sait. Timing driven global router for standard cell design. *International Journal of Computer Systems Science and Engineering*, 1998.

128. Sadiq M. Sait, S. Ali, and M. S. T. Benten. Scheduling and allocation in high-level synthesis using stochastic techniques. *Microelectronics Journal*, 27(8):693–712, October 1996.

129. S. Amellal and B. Kaminska. Functional synthesis of digital systems with TASS. *IEEE Transactions on Computer-Aided Design*, 13(5):537–552, May 1994.

130. F. Glover and M. Laguna. Tabu search. In C. Reeves, editor, *Modern Heuristic Techniques for Combinatorial Problems*. McGraw-Hill, Europe, 1995.

131. Y. L. Lin, Y. C. Hsu, and F. H. S. Tsai. SILK: A Simulated Evolution router. *IEEE Transactions on Computer-Aided Design*, 8(10):1108–1114, October 1989.

132. A. Ly and Jack T. Mowchenko. Applying Simulated Evolution to high level-synthesis. *IEEE Transactions on Computer-Aided Design*, 12(3):389–409, March 1993.

133. C. Y. Mao and Y. H. Hu. SEGMA: A Simulated Evolution gate matrix layout algorithm. *VLSI Design*, 2(3):241–257, 1994.

134. C. Y. Mao. *Simulated Evolution Algorithms for Gate Matrix layouts*. Ph.D. Thesis, University of Wisconsin, Madison, 1994.

135. Ching-Dong Chen, Yuh-Sheng Lee, A.C.-H. Wu, and Youn-Long Lin. Tracer-FPGA: A router for RAM-based FPGA's. *IEEE Transactions on Computer-Aided Design of Integrated Circuits and Systems*, 14(3):371–374, March 1995.

136. T. Koide, S. Wakabayashi, and N. Yoshida an integrated approach to pin assignment and global routing for VLSI building-block layout. In *1993 European Conference on Design Automation with the European Event in ASIC Design*, pp. 24–28, Loss Alamitos, CA, USA, Feb 1993. IEEE Computer Society Press.

137. Yirng-An Chen, Youn-Long Lin, and Yu-Chin Hsu. A new global router for ASIC design based on Simulated Evolution. In *Proceedings of the 33rd IEEE Midwest Symposium on Circuits and Systems*, pp. 261–265, New York, NY, USA, May 1989.

138. Youn-Long Lin, Yu-Chin Hsu, and Fur-Shing Tsai. A detailed router based on Simulated Evolution. In *Proceedings of the 33rd Midwest Symposium on Circuits and Systems,* pp. 38–41, New York, NY, USA, Nov 1988. IEEE Computer Soc. Press.

139. Yuh-Sheng Lee and A.C.-H Wu. A performance and routability driven router for FPGAS considering path delays. *ANSI/IEEE Std 802.lb-1995,* pp. 557–561, March 1995.

140. Yung-Ching Hsich, Chi-Yi Hwang, Youn-Long, and Yu-Chin Hsu. LIB: A CMOS cell compiler. *IEEE Transactions on Computer-Aided Design of Integrated Circuits and Systems,* 10(8):994–1005, Aug 1991.

141. T.A. Ly. and J.T. Mowchenko. Applying Simulated Evolution to scheduling in high level synthesis. In *Proceedings of the 33rd Midwest Symposium on Circuits and Systems,* vol. 1, pp. 172–175, New York, NY, USA, Aug. 1990, IEEE Computer Soc. Press.

142. Yau-Hwang Kuo and Shaw-Pyng Lo. Automated synthesis of asynchronous pipelines. In *Custom Integrated Circuits Conference, Proceedings of the IEEE 1992,* vol. 2, pp. 685–688, New York, NY, USA, May 1992.

143. Yau-Hwang Kuo and Shaw-Pyng Lo. Partitioning and scheduling of asynchronous pipelines. In *Computer Systems and Software Engineering, CompEuro 1992 Proceedings,* pp. 574–579, Loss Alamitos, CA, USA, May 1992. IEEE Computer Soc. Press.

144. I. Ahmad, M.K. Dhodhi, and K.A Saleh. An evolutionary-based technique for local microcode compaction. In *Proceedings of ASP DAC '95/CHDL '95/VLSI with EDA Technofair,* pp. 729–734, Tokyo, Japan, Sept. 1995. Nihon Gakkai Jimu Senta.

145. A.K. Dasari, N. Song, and M. Chrzanowska-Jeske. Layout-driven factorization and fitting for cellular-architecture FPGAS. In *Proceedings of IEEE, NORTHCON '93 Electrical and Electronics Convention,* pp. 106–111, New York, NY, USA, October 1993.

146. D. H. Wolpert and W. G. Macready. No Free Lunch theorems for optimization. *IEEE Transactions on Evolutionary Computation,* 1(1):67–82, April 1997.

# 40

# Internet Architectures

Borko Furht
*Florida Atlantic University*

## 40.1 Introduction

### Computing Models for Internet-Based Architectures

The increasingly competitive global marketplace puts pressure on companies to create and deliver their products faster, with high quality and greater performance. To get the new products and technologies to consumers is through a new industry called application service providers (ASPs). Similar to Internet service providers, that linked businesses and consumers up to the Internet, ASPs lease software applications to businesses and consumers via the Internet. These applications range from word processing programs to payroll management software, document management systems, and many others. The major challenge is to develop an efficient Internet-based architecture, which will efficiently provide access to these software applications over the Internet.

Application architectures have traditionally followed software development architectures. The software development architectures can be classified into:

- traditional desktop computing model,
- client-server computing model,
- network computing model,
- server-based computing model.

*Traditional desktop computing model* assumes that the whole application is on the client and the application is executed locally. The client must be a "fat" client.

*Client-server computing model* assumes that clients are powerful and processing is centered around local execution on clients. Computer resources were split between a server and one or several clients.

This architecture allowed for larger, more scalable, applications to be brought to a larger number of clients; however, the key for this architecture was to successfully partition the complexity of overall application and determine correctly which part should reside on the server and which part should run on the client. As more and more functionality migrated to the client, it became harder for applications to be maintained and updated.

*Network computing model*, supported by Sun, Oracle, Netscape, IBM, and Apple, assumes that software applications are dynamically downloaded from the network into the client for execution by the client. This architecture requires that the clients are fat.

*Server-based computing model*, supported by Citrix, assumes that business applications reside on the servers and can be accessed by users without requiring them to be downloaded to the client. The client can be either "thin" or "fat."

## Server-Based Computing Model

The fundamental three elements of the server-based (or host-based) computing model are [1]:

- multi-user operating system,
- efficient computing technology,
- centralized application and client management.

*Multi-user operating system* allows multiple concurrent users to run applications in separate, protected sessions on a single server.

*Efficient computing technology* separates the application from its user interface, so only simple user's commands, received through keystrokes, mouse clicks, and screen updates, are sent via the network. As a result, application performance does not depend on network bandwidth.

*Centralized application and client management* allows efficient solution of application management, access, performance, and security.

A server-based computing model is very efficient for enterprise-wide application deployment, including cross-platform computing, Web computing, remote computing, thin-client device computing, and branch-office computing, as illustrated in Fig. 40.1 [1].

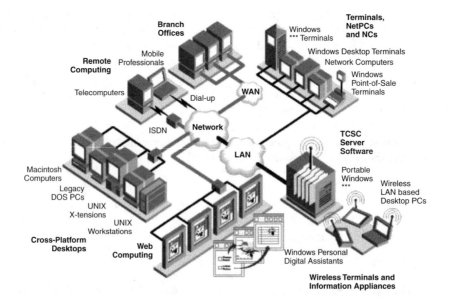

**FIGURE 40.1**    Server-based computing models can be used for enterprise-wide application deployment.

## 40.2 Evolution of Internet-Based Application Service Architectures

Similar to software development architectures, applications service architectures have emerged from the traditional client-server architectures to three-tier and multitier architectures.

The first generation of Internet-based application service architecture was based on delivery of information via public Web sites. This technology, sometimes referred to as the "first wave" Internet [2] employs the Web to present the information to the user and then allows the user to give some relevant information back. The primary focus of this architectural model is mass distribution of public information over the Internet. This architecture, which focuses on accessing information, consists of three levels (or three tiers)—presentation level, content level, and data and service level, as shown in Fig. 40.2 [2].

At the presentation level, there is the client system, which is used to view Web page information. The client contains both presentation and application logic components. At the content level, there is a Web server that provides interactive view of information from a relational database. Finally, at the data and service level, there is a relational database system, which provides data for the Web server. This architecture is also called three-tier architecture consisting of client tier, Web server tier, and database tier.

With the advancements of the Internet, the Web, and related technologies (such as Java and HTML), as well as acceptance of standard communication protocols (such as TCP/IP and HTTP), a new architecture has emerged. In this architecture, sometimes referred as to the "second wave" Internet [2] or network-based application architecture [3], focus is on highly targeted, private distribution of software services over Intranets and Extranets. In this architecture, the Web page is not only the agent for providing information but also offers a variety of application services to speed up business transactions and offer additional services. This architecture consists of $n$-tiers and offers maximum functionality and flexibility in a heterogeneous Web-based environment. An example of four-tier architecture is shown in Fig. 40.3.

At the presentation level, the client views Web pages for information as well as for a variety of application services. At the second, content level, the Web server provides an interactive view of information and supports client-initiated transactions. At the third, application level, there is an application server, which is used to find requested data and services, makes them available for viewing, and carries out transactions. At the fourth, data and service level, there is a variety of data and services accessible by the application server. This architecture, also called multitier architecture, consists of client tier, Web server tier, application server tier, and database tier.

Two-tier Internet architecture is typically limited for systems with a small number of users, a single database, and nonsecure network environments.

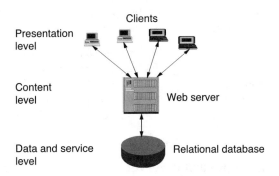

**FIGURE 40.2**    The three-tier architecture for application service providers (ASPs) is focused on accessing information.

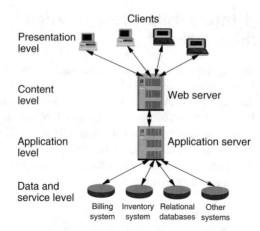

**FIGURE 40.3**   The multitier Internet-based architecture for ASPs is focused on accessing application services.

## 40.3   Application Server

In the second generation of Internet architectures, the focus has shifted to access to business services rather than to information only. The main component of the system is an application server, which searches for services and data—this is done in the background without involving the user.

The main challenges in developing the first generation of Internet architectures and application services were related to user interfaces and cross-platform interoperability. In developing the second generation of Internet architectures, the main challenge for service developers is to deliver their services seamlessly via the Internet, which in turn requires innovations in many areas. The following challenges need to be addressed in developing the second generation of Internet architectures:

- **Standards.** Many standards are used for developing Web pages, which causes difficulties for developers.
- **Increased programming complexity.** The implementation of business services on the Internet is a very complex programming task.
- **Network performance.** Business applications over Intranets and Extranets require very reliable and high-performance networks.
- **Security.** Business applications on the Internet require a very high level of security.
- **Web access to legacy applications.** As mentioned earlier, the new Internet architectures are focused on accessing various business applications rather than just information.
- **Database connection support across Web-based requestors.** Users should be able to access a variety of databases connected to the application server.

The majority of these functions, sometimes called *middleware*, are implemented in application servers that provide support for developing and deploying business applications located on the server or partitioned across client and server.

Application server offers support for developing and deploying business logic that may be located on the server or, more often, partitioned across client and server. Running business applications on the server provides many benefits [4].

### Key Technologies for Application Servers

Key technologies for developing contemporary application servers include:

- Java programming language and environment,

- JavaBeans—the Java-based component technology, which allows the development of new applications more rapidly and economically,
- ActiveX—the competing technology to JavaBeans, which is Windows platform-dependent and language-independent,
- Java Database Connectivity (JDBC)—the Java SQL that provides cross-platform database access for Java programs,
- Java servlets—small Java routines that service HTTP requests and dynamically generate HTML, and
- Common object request broker architecture (CORBA)—provides a standard architecture for distributed computing and interoperability on the Internet.

Java application servers have recently emerged as an efficient solution, with many features, for the application server tier. A Java application server:

- Makes it easy to develop and deploy distributed Java applications.
- Provides scalability, so hundreds to thousands of cooperative servers can be accessed from ten of thousands clients. Therefore, Java must be fully multithreaded and have no architectural bottlenecks that prevent scaling.
- Provides an integrated management environment for comprehensive view of application resources (e.g., Java Beans, objects, events, etc.), network resources (databases), system resources (ACLs, threads, sockets, etc.), and diagnostic information.
- Provides transaction semantics to protect the integrity of corporate data even as it is accessed by distributed business components.
- Provides secure communications.

CORBA and JavaBeans are open standards for component software development and deployment that allow writing small code objects that can be reused in multiple applications and updated quickly. They also allow developers to expose legacy system data and functionality as services available over the Web, and therefore most application servers are based on these technologies.

For example, the CORBA architecture makes it possible to find and use services over the Internet. Similarly, Enterprise JavaBeans is a standard server component model for Java application servers that provides services to network-enable applications, so that they may be easily deployed on Intranets, Extranets, and the Internet [5].

CORBA provides universal connectivity in broadly distributed environments as well as cross-platform interoperation of both infrastructures and applications. The object Web model based on CORBA and other standards is shown in Fig. 40.4 [7].

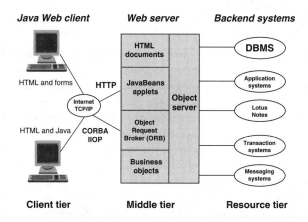

**FIGURE 40.4**  The object Web model based on CORBA and other standards provides universal connectivity in distributed environments.

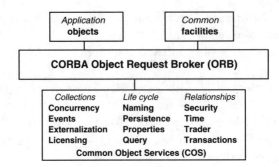

**FIGURE 40.5**    CORBA provides a standard for interoperability that includes many services required by object applications.

CORBA currently provides many services including naming, security, transactions, and persistence, as illustrated in Fig. 40.5 [7].

# 40.4    Implementations of Internet Architectures

In this section, four popular Internet architectures developed by Sun, Netscape, IBM, and Microsoft are presented.

## Sun's Architecture

Initially, Sun Microsystems defined, in Fall 1996, Java-based application development architecture, which consisted of three tiers: the client tier that provided user interface, the middle tier for business logic and database access, and the database tier, as illustrated in Fig. 40.6 [8].

Sun selected Java language for the client tier, which provided more sophisticated GUI capabilities than HTML implementation. Client applets did not perform significant business logic functions in order to keep clients as thin as possible. Java technology was also used for the middle tier and the middle tier servers were implemented as standalone Java applications.

Because both client and middle tiers are implemented using Java, client middle tier communication was performed using remote method invocation (RMI), where the middle tier servers created the necessary RMI objects and made them available to clients via the RMI object registry. The middle tier communicated with the database via the JDBC API. This architecture is based on client-server computing model, in which client resides on the user's desktop, and the middle and database tiers reside on one or more of five data centers around the company.

Recently, Sun has developed an enhanced multitier architecture, which includes an additional tier—the WebTop server tier, as shown in Fig. 40.7 [8].

In the three-tier architecture (Fig. 40.6), applets were dynamically downloaded at runtime to the users' locations from an application server. For remote locations and modem connections with constrained bandwidth, applet download time was a few minutes, which was unacceptable.

Another issue related to three-tier architecture was the access to network resources such as files and printers. Java prohibits applets from accessing any local or network resources. In addition, Java does not allow communications with any machine other than the one from which the applet was downloaded. As a result of these limitations, file access occurred at the middle tier. This meant that information might be sent from the client to the middle tier and then back to a file server near the client.

Introducing a new tier, WebTop server tier, has resolved the issues related to the three-tier architecture. The WebTop server runs the Java Web server and is located near the users it serves. This server is used as a cache for applets and static application data, so the first problem was resolved. The server also supports services that access network resources such as user files and printers, which are typically located near the users. Finally, the WebTop server is used to find the services that users need.

**FIGURE 40.6**   Sun's Java-based three-tier architecture for ASP.

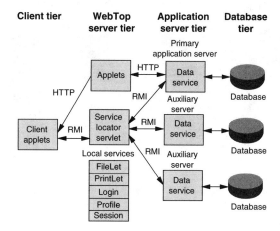

**FIGURE 40.7**   Sun's Java-based multitier architecture for ASP.

In the architecture in Fig. 40.7 the client is thin and typically includes a graphical user interface written as an applet that runs from a Web browser. The application server tier provides access to data and implements business logic and data validation. The application server is responsible for all database transaction handling.

For the communication between the client and WebTop server tier and between the WebTop server and the application server tier, HTTP and RMI are used. Communication between application servers and databases is performed via JDBC.

One of the main benefits of the multitier architecture is that it increases application scalability and performance by enabling clients to be connected concurrently. In a client-server model clients are directly connected to databases, while in a multitier architecture only application servers connect directly to databases. In this way, the application server can process multiple requests from many clients through a pool of preallocated database connections, thus reducing the database server load. Load on the application server tier can be balanced by using multiple application servers.

Another benefit of the multitier architecture is that it supports thinner clients, because most of the logic runs in the application server and database tiers. Thus, broad range of client platforms can run the applications.

## Netscape's Architecture

Similar to Sun's architecture, Netscape recently developed multitier architecture for application development and distributed computing, which is based on the separation of presentation logic from application logic, as illustrated in Fig. 40.8 [2].

In Netscape's multitier architecture, the client tier is typically based on an open-standard browser such as Netscape Navigator. The presentation logic and GUI is built using HTML pages that include Java applets. At the content level, a Web server primarily uses HTTP. It provides base-level information and content services as well as simple database information access via Java, JavaScript, and other high-level CGI scripting languages such as Perl.

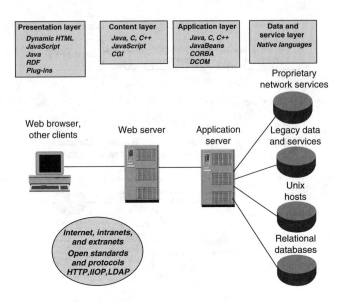

**FIGURE 40.8**   Netscape's multitier architecture for ASP.

The application server uses CORBA and JavaBeans components or objects. Transaction services enable access to relational databases and other legacy systems.

The first three levels in the multitier architecture in Fig. 40.8 are provided by Netscape technologies and products, while the last levels—back-end services and other legacy systems—are accessed through standard Internet interfaces.

## IBM's Architecture

IBM has developed the Component Broker, which is Internet middleware for distributed objects [7]. Component Broker is a software system that allows developers to build, run, and manage Web-enabled business objects, components, and applications. Component Broker consists of:

- tools for building distributed and business objects, and applications,
- a runtime that provides a distributed-object infrastructure on the middle tier, and
- a system management functions for the distributed object runtime and its resources.

Component Broker architecture, shown in Fig. 40.9, accepts inputs from any clients (Java or C++) transported via Internet InterORB Protocol, and ActiveX transported via a bridge. The object server consists of components that provide control, services, context, and connection resources.

The Component Broker receives client requests through the CORBA-compliant object request broker (ORB). Object services are supplied through the CORBA common object services (COS). These services provide object transaction services, database services, system services, and object management functions, as illustrated in Fig. 40.9.

Application adapters connect Component Broker object applications with existing software systems and applications.

## Microsoft's Architecture

Microsoft Internet architecture is a component-based architecture based on Windows DNA [14]. The heart of Windows DNA is the component object model (COM) that allows developers to build applications from binary software components at any tier of the application architecture. These components

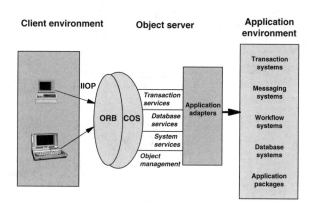

**FIGURE 40.9** Architecture of IBM's Component Broker at the middleware tier.

provide support for packaging, partitioning, and distributing application functionality [14]. Distributed COM (DCOM) enables communications between COM components that reside on different machines. DCOM is a competing model for distributed object computing to CORBA, described in section 40.3.

## 40.5  A Contemporary Architecture for Application Service Providers

In this section, ASP computing architecture using server-based computing model and the related ASP application architecture is presented.

### ASP Computing Architecture

Our computing architecture for application service providers is based on the server-based computing model, described in the subsection on "Computing Models for Internet-Based Architectures." As we indicated earlier, in server-based computing all applications and data are managed, supported, and executed on the server. This architecture provides the following benefits:

- Single-point management
- Predictable ownership costs
- High reliability
- Bandwidth-independent performance
- Universal application access
- Use of thousands of off-the-shelf applications
- Low-cost and fast application development
- Use of open standards
- Graphical and rich user interface
- Wide choice of client devices

The proposed server-based architecture uses two technologies developed by Citrix:

- Independent computing architecture (ICA)
- Windows-based terminal (WBT)

*Independent computing architecture* is a Windows presentation services protocol that turns any client device (thin or fat) into the thin client. The ICA consists of three components: server software, client software, and network protocol.

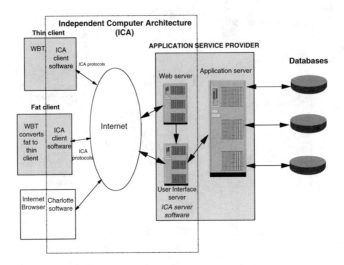

**FIGURE 40.10**   The proposed architecture for ASP uses server-based model. All applications are executed at the server or cluster of servers.

On the server, ICA separates applications from the user interface, while on the client users see and work with applications' interface. The application logic executes on the server. The ICA protocol transports keystrokes, mouse clicks, and screen updates over standard protocols requiring less than 20 kbps of network bandwidth.

*A Windows-based terminal* is a thin-client hardware device that connects to Citrix server-based system software. The WBT does not require downloading of the operating system or applications and there is no local processing of applications at the client, as in the case of other thin clients such as network computers or NetPCs. A WBT has the following features:

- An embedded operating system such as DOS, Windows CE, or any real-time operating system
- ICA protocol to transport keystrokes, mouse clicks, and screen updates between the client and the server
- Absolute (100%) execution of application logic on the server
- No local execution of application at the client device

The proposed architecture also allows consumers and business to access software applications from their Internet browsers. This is provided using Citrix's software *Charlotte*. In addition, software component *Vertigo* allows more interactive applications on the Web. This software allows customized Web pages such as electronic trading accounts to be updated automatically without hitting the refresh button on the computer.

The proposed architecture for ASP using server-based model and Citrix technologies is shown in Fig. 40.10.

The proposed architecture is platform independent and allows non-Windows and specialized ICA devises to run Windows applications residing and executing on application server farm. Application server farm is a group of application servers that are linked together as a single system to provide centralized administration and scalability.

The architecture in Fig. 40.10 allows ASPs to rapidly develop and deploy applications across complex computing environments. It also provides application access to all users, regardless of the their location, type of client device, or form of network connectivity. The architecture can be applied to any type of client hardware, and therefore requires no change in client hardware. The system significantly reduces requirements for network bandwidth compared to other architectures. Finally, the proposed architecture reduces the total cost of application, as analyzed in section 40.6.

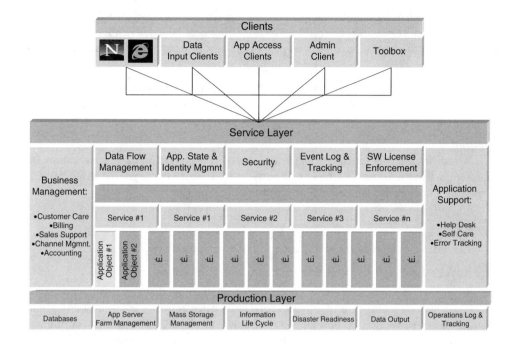

**FIGURE 40.11** Architecture of an ASP application.

## ASP Application Architecture

To take maximum advantage of ASP computing architecture, a new breed of applications needs to be developed. The key drivers of new distributed application architecture is a need for wide spectrum of thin clients, bandwidth usage optimization, application multi-identity shared back-end computing, reliable data flow management, security, legacy application integration, and long list of service operation requirements. The diagram shown in Fig. 40.11 can depict a desired architecture of an ASP application.

### Client Software

ASP application client software is in general very different from types of client software provided as part of traditional client-server applications available on the market today. To support ASP business model, client software must be "thin," i.e., requiring minimum computing power, installation and support effort, minimum communication bandwidth, and minimum version upgrade. Highly distributed nature of ASP service requires from client software ability to support versatile data inputs, highest level of user's security, and ability to support multiple communication protocols.

#### Data Input

ASP service architecture is in essence remote computing architecture, which requires capabilities to generate and import application data into the remote application. Data can be generated as part of specialized batch program or as by-product of third party software. Data input clients can be stand alone or integrated within other clients or legacy applications. Multistep data flow requires advanced information security, tracking, reporting, and above all ability to restore data in case that any stage system failure results in data loss. Data input clients may or may not be thin. The footprints of these clients are primarily defined by local functionality necessary to create the data at optimum cost.

#### Application Access

Application access clients are characterized by limited local computation capability and remote command capability to the server side application concentrated at service back end. These clients are the ones that should be as generic and as thin as possible. The smaller and simpler the client, the lesser the operational cost at the front end. The ideal application access client is plain Web browser. However, browser access is limited to very low level of functionality provided by HTML protocol. Function rich application computing requires specialized client software or plug-ins providing access to remote application at the back end.

### Toolbox

To bridge the existing legacy applications with ASP service, an ASP application software requires a comprehensive set of APIs or application enabling tools providing the system integration capabilities and customizations.

### Administration

This client should provide the end user with the ability to completely control its own application. Desired functions are: adding new users, setting up security profiles, managing application specific variables, usage tracking and reporting, and billing presentments and reporting.

### Security

Client software security capability must include ability to authenticate users on the front end and to create virtual private channel of communication with the service back end.

## Service Layer

Server side application is characterized by concentration of all computing and data intensive processes at back end, application multi-identity, sophisticated data flow management, and by its ability to integrate with business management, application support, and service production components. The ultimate goal of such application engineering is to create the fastest computing environment, economy of scale through all customers' sharing of common computing and data management infrastructure, and maximum operational readiness.

### Application Layer

At the core of service layer is the application layer of software providing actual computing application packaged as specific service, for example: Service #1. This service application can be either stand alone application or user interface into integrated solution based on several other independent third-party applications.

### Data Flow Management

Data generated through data input clients is managed by data flow management software. One can consider this software component as a data switch capable of accepting data input, decompressing and decoding data, identifying the owner of data and target data base, importing data in the target data base, cashing and mirroring data at each stage for disaster readiness reasons, and creating logs for data input tracking and reporting.

### Application State and Identity Management

An ASP provider will have many different applications for many different customers simultaneously. Also, each individual application will have many different users requiring different application setup and profile. Application state and identity management software acts as an application switch identifying individual users and applications and then assigning the appropriate user's profile. Therefore, ASP applications must support multiple identity capability. Ability to share the same computing and data management resources between many different users and applications is essential for reliable service delivery and economy of scale.

### Business Management

The ASP application should also integrate into business management software enabling automatic account creation and usage data feed into billing solution.

### Application Support

The ASP application should also integrate with application support solution that consists from customer self support site.

## 40.6 Evaluation of Various Architectures

Analysts and IT professionals have developed numerous models for estimating the total cost of IT services, sometimes called "total cost of ownership (TCO)." In the past, these models had the hardware-centric view because they analyzed the costs of owning and maintaining desktop computer hardware. In the age of the Internet, Web-based computing, and E-commerce, applications must be accessible across a wide variety of connectivity options, from low-speed, dial-up connections to wireless, WAN, and Internet connections. A contemporary cost analysis should consider the total cost of application ownership (TCA), rather than the total cost associated with specific computing devices. The Tolly Group has developed a model for comparing the TCA of different computing models, discussed earlier [9]. We present and discuss their results in this section.

In order to determine the cost of application deployment, four computing models introduced in section 40.1 can be analyzed from the following points of views:

- physical location of the application,
- execution location of the application,
- physical location of data,
- location of the user and means of connectivity.

The cost of complexity of deploying and managing an application strongly depends on physical location of the application. The cost of application distribution, installation, and managing of updates must be considered.

The choice of where an application is executed determines the hardware, network, and connectivity costs. An application can run on the server, on the client, or in a distributed server-client environment. In some cases, the application must be downloaded from a server to a client, which has an impact on performance and productivity.

The location of stored data determines the speed at which information is available. It also has an impact on the cost related to protecting and backing up critical corporate data.

The location of the user and the means of connectivity also have an impact on the cost and complexity of deploying an application.

Table 40.1 summarizes the application deployment characteristics for four computing models introduced in section 40.1 [9].

Tolly Group has analyzed and calculated the total cost of application ownership for a medium-size enterprise of 2500 users, with 175 mobile users working on the road. The calculated costs were divided into (a) Initial (first-year) cost (which includes hardware, software, network infrastructure, and user training) and (b) annual recurring costs (which includes technical support and application maintenance). The results of analysis are presented in Fig. 40.12.

Traditional desktop computing approach requires relatively high initial cost for hardware, software, network infrastructure, and training ($14,000) as well as very high annual recurring costs for technical support and application maintenance ($11,000 annually).

**TABLE 40.1** Computing Models and Application Deployment Characteristics

| | Application Location | Application Execution | Data Location | User Access | Network Requirements |
|---|---|---|---|---|---|
| Traditional desktop | Client | Client | Client | Local | None |
| Client-server | Client and server | Client and server | Client and server | Lan, WAN, Internet | High bandwidth |
| Network-based | Server | Client and server | Server or client | LAN, WAN, Internet | High bandwidth |
| Server-based | Server | Server | Server | LAN, WAN, Internet | Low bandwidth |

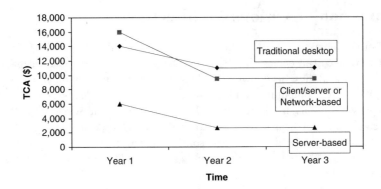

**FIGURE 40.12**    Analysis of total cost of application (TCA) for various computing approaches [9].

Client-server and network computing approaches require slightly higher initial investment ($16,000) in order to replace existing client hardware; however, annual recurring costs are reduced ($9,500). This model becomes less expensive than the traditional desktop model from the third year forward.

The server-based approach gives the best TCA both in terms of initial costs and annual recurring costs ($6,000 and $2,600, respectively). The reason for it is that this model allows any type of client to access any application across any type of connection. This model also provides single point for the deployment and management of applications.

In summary, the server-based model, which was applied in our architecture, is the most efficient and cost-effective solution to application deployment and management.

## 40.7   Conclusions

This chapter presented and evaluated contemporary multitier Internet architectures, which are well suited for distributed applications on the Internet including ASPs. The chapter also evaluated several computing models for Internet-based architectures and proposed a server-based computing model, which has a number of advantages over the other models.

### References

1. Citrix Systems, "Server-based computing," white paper, www.citrix.com, 1999.
2. P. Dreyfus, "The second wave: Netscape on usability in the services-based Internet," *IEEE Internet Computing*, Vol. 2, No. 2, March/April 1998, pp. 36–40.
3. Sun Microsystems, "Software development for the Web-enabled enterprise," white paper, 1999.
4. BEA WebLogic, "What is a Java application server?" weblogic.beasys.com, 1999.
5. A. Thomas, "Selecting enterprise JavaBeans technology," WebLogic, Inc., Boston, MA, July 1998.
6. R. Orfali, D. Harkey, and J. Edwards, *Instant CORBA*, John Wiley & Sons, New York, 1997.
7. C. McFall, "An object infrastructure for internet middleware: IBM on component broker," *IEEE Internet Computing*, Vol. 2, No. 2, March/April 1998, pp. 46–51.
8. Gupta, C. Ferris, Y. Wilson, and K. Venkatassubramanian, "Implementing Java computing: Sun on architecture and application development," *IEEE Internet Computing*, Vol. 2, No. 2, March/April 1998, pp. 60–64.
9. The Tolly Group, "Total cost of application ownership," Manasquan, NJ, white paper No. 199503, June 1999.
10. J.B. Eichler, R.Y. Roberts, K.W. Evans, and A.L. Carter, "The Internet: redefining traditional business and giving rise to new ones," Report, Stephens, Inc., Little Rock, AR, May 1999.
11. D. Rosenberg, "Bringing Java to the enterprise: Oracle on its Java server strategy," *IEEE Internet Computing*, Vol. 2, No. 2, March/April 1998, pp. 52–59.

12. M. Benda, "Internet architecture: its evolution from an industry perspective," *IEEE Internet Computing,* Vol. 2, No. 2, March/April 1998, pp. 32–35.

13. Sun Microsystems, "Enterprise JavaBeans technology: server component model for the Java platform," white paper, java.sun.com, 1999.

14. G.R. Voth, C. Kindel, and J. Fujioka, "Distributed application development for three-tier architectures: microsoft on Windows DNA," *IEEE Internet Computing,* Vol. 2, No. 2, March/April 1998, pp. 41–45.

15. C.J. Woodard and S. Dietzen, "Beyond the distributed object decision: using components and Java application servers as a platform for enterprise information systems," *Distributed Computing,* 1998.

16. G. Pour and J. Xu, "Developing 3-tier Web-based enterprise applications: integrating CORBA with JavaBeans and Java servlets," in *Proceedings of the 3rd International Conference on Internet and Multimedia Systems and Applications,* Nassau, Bahamas, October 1999.

17. L. Downes and Chunka Mui, "Unleashing the Killer App," Harvard Business School Press, Boston, MA 1998.

# 41

# Microelectronics for Home Entertainment

Yoshiaki Hagiwara

*Sony Corporation*

## 41.1  Introduction

The history of home entertainment consumer electronics begins in May 7, 1946, with the founding of Tokyo Tsushin Kogyou (Tokyo Telecommunication Engineering ) by Masaru Ibuka (36) and Akio Morita (25) in Tokyo, Japan. Had these two bright young men not met and combined their considerable resolve and talents, the home electronics business would not have accelerated so much as we see it today, and our semiconductor business efforts would have been aimed only for military purposes for a while.

In the Founding Prospectus, Ibuka eloquently stated his dreams for the company. Morita, together with the company's first directors headed by Kazuo Iwama, led employees to realize these goals. Throughout their work, the young force was inspired by the free and dynamic atmosphere of the "ideal" factory they were striving to create. From the onset, Ibuka, Morita, and Iwama endeavoured to develop unique and exciting products that fulfil their customers' dream.

Iwama was 35 when he visited Western Electric to study transistors in January 1954. Iwama was the first engineer in Japan who understood the concept of "electron fog" in the bipolar transistor device physics.

He worked as the leader of the bipolar transistor development project to realize the epoch-making portable bipolar transistor radio TR-55 introduced to the home entertainment electronics market in August 1955.

Seven years had passed since the invention of the bipolar transistor in Bell Lab in December 1947. I was only seven years old and had no idea about how a transistor works at that time.

I was a junior undergraduate at CalTech in Pasadena, California, in 1969 when I learned how the bipolar transistor and MOSFET work with the classical textbook by Grove. My class instructor was Prof. James McCaldin who was known as the co-inventor of basic planar passivation technology in modern MOS transistor fabrications.

In the summer of 1971, I visited Sony Atsugi plant right after I received a B.S. from CalTech and worked as a reliability engineer in Bipolar IC production line for Sony's Trinitron color TV sets.

In the fall of 1971, I returned to CalTech to pursue further my graduate work and learned how to design MOS LSIs from Professor Carver Mead. My Ph.D. thesis was about the buried channel CCD imagers, which can be applied to low light intensity solid state imagers. Prof. T.C. McGill was my Ph.D. thesis advisor.

After defending my Ph.D., in February 1975, I joined Sony at the Central Research Center in Yokohama, Japan, and engaged in further research on high-performance CCD imagers project headed by Iwama who was the pioneer engineer in the early bipolar technology development effort in Sony.

My first patent filed in Sony in November 1975 was about a simple pnp-substructure used as the light sensing device for imagers. The sensor structure is now called the HAD sensor in Sony's current video cameras and digital still cameras.

Sony put most of its engineering sources in CCD imagers and camera systems in 1970s. We engineers had to design signal processing and camera control chips by ourselves. Those experiences were useful to apply to other MOS LSI design applications, which made possible the current home entertainment LSI chip sets such as digital cameras, home robots, and games.

In this chapter, some basic semiconductor device concepts are first reviewed briefly. They are about the concept of "electron fog," the bipolar and MOSFET device model, the buried channel CCD imager structure, and the pnp-substructure which is used as the light sensing device, which is now universally adopted in most of high performance solid state imagers. Then, some general discussions on the product specifications and performance aspects of the home entertainment consumer LSI chip sets such as for digital cameras, home robotics, and games are presented in detail.

## 41.2 Basic Semiconductor Device Concepts

In this section, some introductory comments on the basic semiconductor device concepts are explained. They are strongly related to the microelectronics of the present home entertainment LSI chips.

### Concept of Electron Fog

Figure 41.1 shows the electron fog in metal and semiconductor. Electrons in metal are depicted in this picture as the moisture above the water surface in the container, while the electrons in the semiconductor are depicted as the moisture on the top of a floating box in water. If the box is heavy, the water surface is very close to the top of the box and there is a lot of moisture.

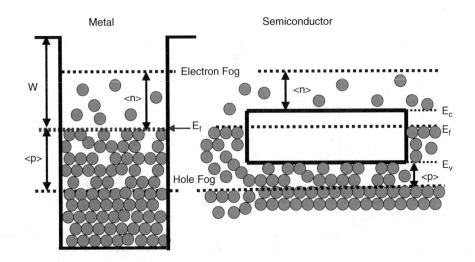

**FIGURE 41.1**    Electron fog model in metal and semiconductor.

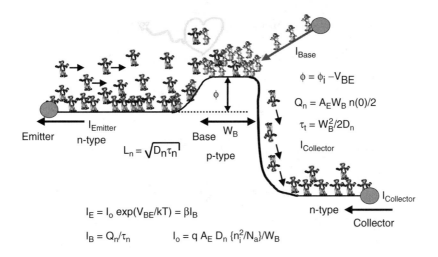

**FIGURE 41.2**   Bipolar transistor action.

This corresponds to the n-type semiconductor band diagram. If the box is relatively light, only a small bottom portion of the box is submerged into the water and the top of the box can be quite dry, and there will a lot of bubbles (holes) under the bottom of the box. This corresponds to the p-type semiconductor.

Applying these p- and n-type semiconductor box models, a diode behavior model can be constructed and the diode rectifying characteristics can be explained.

## Bipolar Transistor Device Model

Figure 41.2 shows energetic boys (electron fog in the emitter region) trying to climb a hill (base region) to catch the girls on the hill (hole fog, which is the majority carrier in the base region). Some of the boys can luckily catch girls on the hill, recombine, become happy and disappear as light or heat energy. But the hill width is very short and most of the boys will not have enough time to catch girls and fall down the cliff (the base-collector depletion region). The poor boys are now collected deep down the cliff in the collector region.

In the time interval $\Delta t$, $I_E \, \Delta t$ boys are jumping to the hill to catch girls on the hill. Some boys are lucky enough to catch girls on the hill. The number of girls caught by the energetic boys in $\Delta t$ is $I_B \, \Delta t$, which is proportional to the number of the average boys on the hill $Q_n$. The girls are supplied as the base current $I_B$. Other salient physical parameters normally used in the bipolar transistor device modeling are also given in the figure.

## MOSFET Model

Figure 41.3 shows a MOSFET structure. If you see how the electron fog moves from the left source n+ region to the right n+ region through the Si–SiO$_2$ surface under the MOS gate, one can see that it is also considered as an electron transportation along an npn-structure. In this case, however, the potential in the p-region is controlled by the gate voltage isolated by the thin oxide.

The figure shows the electron fog moving from the source to the region under the gate at the onset of strong inversion at the Si–SiO$_2$ surface. At this point the electron fog density at the channel is equal to the density of the majority "hole fog" in the p-type Si substrate, and the gate voltage at this point is defined to be the threshold voltage $V_{th}$ of the MOSFET.

Figure 41.4 shows water flowing from the right source region to the left drain region through the water gate. The depth of the channel $V_{ch}$ is given as $(V_g - V_{th})$, where $V_g$ is the applied gate voltage which induces the channel depth $V_{ch} = (V_g - V_{th})$. The amount of the water flow $I$ is proportional to the mobility $\mu$, the water amount $Q$ under the gate and the electric field $E$, i.e., $I = \mu Q E$ can be written in this rough approximation.

$$V_{th}(V_{BB}, V_S) = V_{FB} + \{B + V_S - V_{BB}\} + \gamma\sqrt{\{B + V_S - V_{BB}\}}$$

$$V_{FB} = V_{BB} - (kT/q)\ln\{N_c N_A/n_i^2\} - \{\chi_{si} - \phi_m\}/q + Q_{SS}/C_{OX}$$

$$K = q\,\varepsilon_{Si}\,N_A/C_{OX}^2 \qquad\qquad \gamma = \sqrt{2K} \qquad\qquad B = 2(kT/q)\ln(N_A/n_i)$$

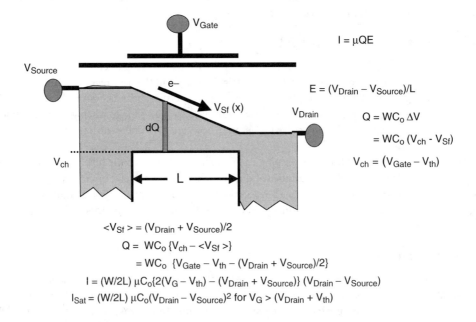

**FIGURE 41.3**    MOSFET at Onset $V_G = V_{th}$.

$$I = \mu QE$$

$$E = (V_{Drain} - V_{Source})/L$$

$$Q = WC_o\,\Delta V$$

$$= WC_o\,(V_{ch} - V_{Sf})$$

$$V_{ch} = (V_{Gate} - V_{th})$$

$$\langle V_{Sf}\rangle = (V_{Drain} + V_{Source})/2$$

$$Q = WC_o\{V_{ch} - \langle V_{Sf}\rangle\}$$

$$= WC_o\{V_{Gate} - V_{th} - (V_{Drain} + V_{Source})/2\}$$

$$I = (W/2L)\,\mu C_o\{2(V_G - V_{th}) - (V_{Drain} + V_{Source})\}(V_{Drain} - V_{Source})$$

$$I_{Sat} = (W/2L)\,\mu C_o(V_{Drain} - V_{Source})^2 \text{ for } V_G > (V_{Drain} + V_{th})$$

**FIGURE 41.4**    MOSFET I-V characteristics.

In the first approximation, take $E = (V_d - V_s)/L$, where $V_d$, $V_s$, and $L$ are the drain voltage, the source voltage, and the gate channel length. The total charge can be approximated as $Q = WC_o\Delta V$, where $W$ and $C_o$ are the channel width and the oxide capacitance of the actual corresponding MOSFET transistor, respectively. Now, $\Delta V$ corresponds to the voltage difference between the average water surface $(V_d + V_s)/2$ and the channel potential $V_{ch} = (V_g - V_{th})$.

That is, $\Delta V = (V_d + V_s)/2 - V_{ch}$. Hence, since $Q = WC_o\Delta V$, the equivalent amount $Q$ of the water (or charge) under the gate is given as $Q = WC_o[(V_d + V_s)/2 - V_{ch}]$, where $V_{ch} = (V_g - V_{th})$, $E = (V_d - V_s)/L$.

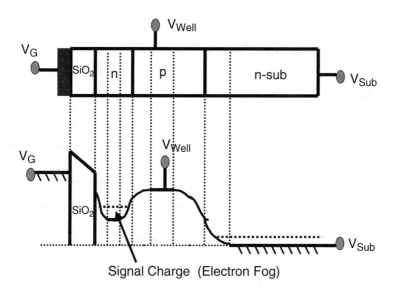

**FIGURE 41.5** Buried channel CCD structure.

Now if these relationships are put into the original equation $I = \mu QE$, this leads, without going through the calculations normally done in the classical gradual channel approximation, finally to the classical MOS I-V equation:

$$I = (W/2L)\, \mu C_o [V_d + V_s - 2V_{ch}]\, (V_d - V_s)$$
$$= (W/2L)\, \mu C_o [V_d + V_s - 2(V_g - V_{th})]\, (V_d - V_s)$$

## Buried Channel CCD Structure

Figure 41.5 shows the physical structure and the potential profile of a buried channel CCD. The signal charge is the electron fog in the lightly doped n-region at the surface. As you can see, these signal charges are isolated from the direct contact to the Si–SiO$_2$ interface and do not suffer the charge trapping. This structure gives a good CCD charge transfer efficiency of more than 99.9999% along the buried channel CCD shift register in the direction of this chapter. At very high light, excess charge can be drained into the substrate by lowering the well voltage $V_{well}$ or making the substrate voltage very deep and inducing the punch-through mode in the n-p-n(sub) structure.

High-density and high-performance, solid-state imagers became available applying this structure as the scanning system. The surface n-layer is completely depleted when there is no signal charge. It is dynamically operated.

It is considered as one extended application of dynamic MOS device operations. The most well-known dynamic operation of a MOS device application is the DRAM data storage operation.

## HAD Sensor, a pnp-substructure

The floating diode structure for image sensing unit was well known in early 1970s. The author simply proposed to use a pnp-substructure instead for the imaging element. Figure 41.6 shows the proposed structure.

It is a simple pnp bipolar transistor structure itself with a very lightly doped base region, operated in the strong cut-off mode with the base majority charge completely depleted.

It is the first practical application of the bipolar transistor in dynamic operation mode, which turned out to be the best structure and way to convert photons to electrons for imaging including the current MOS imagers applications. The sensor structure is now called the HAD sensor in Sony's current video cameras and digital still cameras.

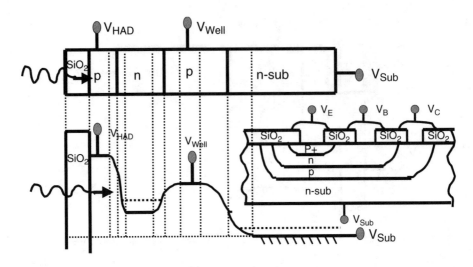

**FIGURE 41.6**   A typical PNP bip Tr structure in the early 1970s, and a proposed application as an image-sensing element in 1975.

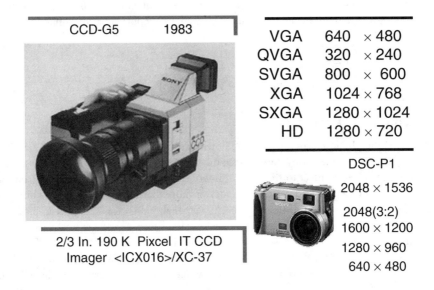

| | | |
|---|---|---|
| VGA | 640 | × 480 |
| QVGA | 320 | × 240 |
| SVGA | 800 | × 600 |
| XGA | 1024 | × 768 |
| SXGA | 1280 | × 1024 |
| HD | 1280 | × 720 |

DSC-P1

2048 × 1536

2048(3:2)
1600 × 1200
1280 × 960
640 × 480

CCD-G5          1983

2/3 In. 190 K  Pixcel  IT CCD
Imager  <ICX016>/XC-37

**FIGURE 41.7**   The world's first consumer CCD video camera for mass production 1983.

## 41.3   LSI Chips for Home Entertainment

### Digital Still Camera

The picture in the Fig. 41.7 shows a 2/3 in. 190 K pixel IT CCD imager, ICX016/XC-37, which the author designed when he was still a young CCD design engineer in early 1981. This model became the model of the world's first consumer CCD video camera for mass production in 1983.

The goal now is to become "Imaging Device No. 1!" Many applications of CCD and LCD are used, as seen in Fig. 41.8.

**FIGURE 41.8** Applications of CCD and LCD.

## AIBO, a Home Entertainment Robot

This subsection reviews the most popular product, the entertainment robot AIBO shown in Fig. 41.9. When you buy a brand new AIBO, it is like a baby, so it does not have any knowledge. It has a certain intelligence level that is preprogrammed. You can play with the AIBO and gradually your AIBO will recognize your gestures and voices. AIBO will remember the wonderful time you spent together with it. Actually the experience and knowledge AIBO accumulates during these memorable moments are stored in a chewing gum size NVRAM called a memory stick shown in Fig. 41.9.

This memory stick can be also used in other products such as PCs, digital audios, and DSCs. Unfortunately it is not used in PS and PS2 for generation compatibility as of now. But in one form or another, there is a definite need NVRAMs in PS, DSC, digital audio, PC, and the future home entertainment robots.

The twenty-first century will become an era of autonomous robots, which are partners of human beings. Autonomous robot will help and support people in the future. AIBO is designed to be the first product model of robot entertainment systems. The main application of this robot is a pet-style robot, which must be lifelike in appearance.

Although AIBO is not a nursing robot, the development of AIBO is the first step of the era of autonomous robots in the twenty-first century.

The following are some works done in the Digital Creation Laboratory at Sony. Most of the works were actually done by the pioneering engineers, Mr. Fujita, Mr. Kageyama, Mr. Kitano, and Mr. Sabe.

The epoch-making debut of AIBO, model ERS-110 in 1999, had the following features:

First of all, it has a CCD color camera with 180 K pixels. Of course, it does not have a mechanical shutter. It does not have any eyelid. It has an audio sensor called microphones, a pair of them for stereo audio pick-up. It also has an acceleration sensor, gyrometer, and also a tactile sensor. So, if you pat it on the head gently, it will show some happy gesture. If you strike it on the head, it will interpret it as your sermon. The moving joints have 18 degrees-of-freedom in total.

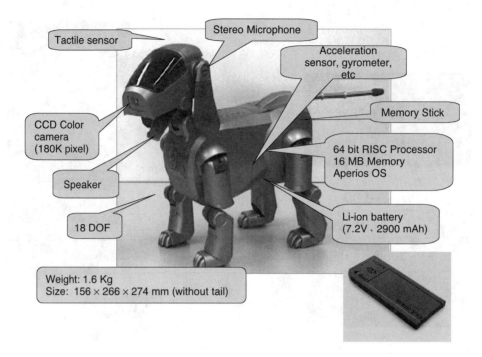

**FIGURE 41.9**  AIBO model ERS-110.

AIBO 2nd Generation, ERS-210                    Sony Dream Robot, SDR-3

**FIGURE 41.10**  New AIBO models: ERS-210 and SDR-3.

Before introducing this first AIBO model, ERS-110, the basic research period lasted about five years. Now we have the second generation AIBO model, ERS-210 and also another type of robot, Sony Dream Robot, SDR-3, as seen in Fig. 41.10.

The second generation AIBO model, ERS-210, has the following features:

Joint DOF: neck: 3, mouth: 1, ear: 2, legs: 3 × 4, tail: 2, total: 20
Sensors: color CMOS image

sensor (1100 K pixel)
Microphone × 2
Infrared sensor
Acceleration sensor × 3
Tactile sensor × 7
CPU: 64 bit RISC processor (192 MHz)
Memory: 32 MB DRAM
OS, Architecture: Aperios, OPEN-R1.1
IF: PCMCIA, memory stick

The model SDR-3 has the following features:

Joint DOF: neck: 2, body: 2, arms: 4 × 2, legs: 6 × 2, total: 24
Sensors: color CCD camera
1800 K pixel, microphone × 2
Infrared sensor, acceleration sensor × 2 gyrometer × 2, tactile sensor × 8
CPU: 64 bit RISC processor × 2
Memory: 32 MB DRAM × 2
OS, Architecture: Aperios, OPEN-R

It weighs 5.0 kg and its size is 500 × 220 × 140 mm.

It has an OPEN-R architecture. It is made of configurable physical components (CPCs). The CPU in the head recognizes the robot configuration automatically. The components are built for plug & play or hot plug-in use. The relevant information in each segment is memorized in each CPC.

Each CPS may have a different function such as behavior planning, motion detection, color detection, walking, and camera module. Each CPS is also provided the corresponding object oriented programming and software component.

With this OPEN-R architecture, the body can be decomposed or assembled anyway for plug & play or hot plug-in use. The diagram in Fig. 41.11 shows the details of the logical hardware block diagrams, which contain DMAC : FBK: CDT: IPE and HUB

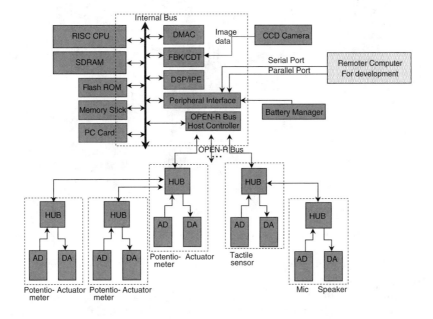

**FIGURE 41.11**  Logical hardware block diagram.

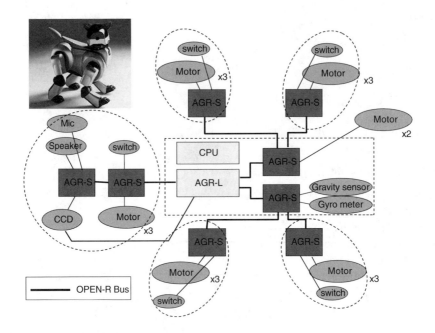

**FIGURE 41.12**   Topology of ERS-110.

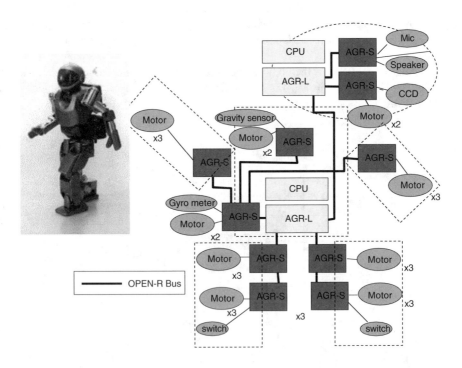

**FIGURE 41.13**   Topology of SDR-3x.

In the following two figures, Figs. 41.12 and 41.13, the topology of model ERS-110 and Model SDR-3x are shown, respectively.

At the same time, it is very important to have a powerful software platform that covers the top semantic layer to the deep bottom of the device driver objects codings. Careful design considerations are very important to make the middleware software components.

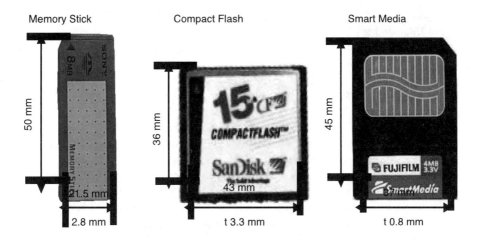

**FIGURE 41.14** Form comparison.

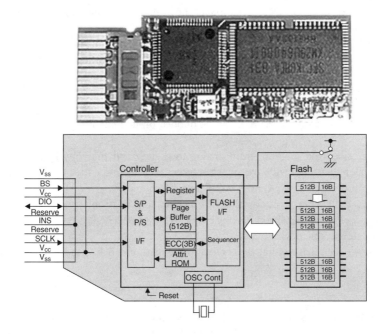

**FIGURE 41.15** Internal structure.

## Memory Stick

AIBO, VAIO PC, and other audio and video products now use memory sticks as digital data recording media.

In July 1997, Sony had a technical announcement. The following year, in January 1998, the VAIO center was inaugurated. On July 1998, Sony had a product announcement. The 4 Mbyte and 8 Mbyte memory sticks were on sale in September 1998. In February 1999, Sony announced Magic Gate, that is, memory sticks with copyright protection feature. Figure 41.14 shows the form comparison. The memory stick is unique in its chewing gum-like shape and it is much taller in length than other media. The difference in appearance of memory stick from other media is clear in size and features.

Figure 41.15 shows the internal structure. It is fool proof. It features a simple 10-pin connection and it is impossible to touch the terminals directly.

The shape was designed intentionally to make exchanging of media easy, without having to actually see them, and to guide the direction for easy and correct insertion. Much contrivance is made in the design.

In order to decrease the number of connector pins for ensuring reliability of the connectors, serial interface was adopted instead of parallel interface used in conventional memory cards. As a result, connector pins were reduced to 10. And as the structure is such that these pins do not touch the terminal directly, extremely high reliability is ensured. The length is same as AA size battery of 50 mm for further deployment to portable appliances. The width is 21.5 mm and the thickness is 2.8 mm.

The memory stick consists of Flash EEPROM and a controller, controlling multiple Flash EEPROM, flexible to their variations, and capable of correcting errors unique to different Flash EEPROMs used. The memory stick converts parallel to/from serial data with the controller designed in compliance with the serial interface protocol; any kind of existing or future Flash EEPROM can be used for the memory stick. The function load on the controller chip is not excessive, and its cost can be kept to a minimum.

It is light and the shape makes it easy to carry around and to handle. Also, the write-protection switch enables easy protection of variable data.

For still-image format, DCF standardized by JEIDA is applied. DCF stands for design rule for camera file system and JEIDA stands for Japan Electronic Industry Development Association. For voice format, ITU-T Recommendation G.726 ADPCM is adopted. The format is regulated for applications that convert voice data to text data by inserting a memory stick to a PC.

The memory stick can handle multiple applications such as still image, moving image, voice, and music on the same media. In order to do this, formats of respective application and directory management must be stipulated to realize compatibility among appliances. Thus, simply by specifying the "control information" format, one can have a new form of enjoyment through connecting AV appliances and the PC. This format, which links data handed in AV appliances, enables relating multiple AV applications. For example, voice recorded on IC recorder can be dubbed on to a still image file recorded by a digital still camera.

Presently, the music world is going from analog to digital, and the copyright protection issue is becoming serious along with the wide use of the Internet. The memory stick can provide a solution to this problem by introducing "Magic Gates (MG)," a new technology.

Open MG means (1) allowing music download through multiple electronic music distribution platforms, (2) enabling playback of music files and extracting CD on PCs (OpenMG Jukebox), (3) transferring contents securely from PCs to portable devices.

Figure 41.16 shows the stack technology applied to the memory stick with four stacked chips.

## PlayStation 2

PlayStation 2 was originally aimed at the fusion of graphics, audio/video, and PC. The chipset includes a 128-bit CPU called "Emotion Engine" with 300 MHz clock frequency with direct Rambus DRAM of 32 Mbyte main memory. The chipset also includes a graphic synthesizer chip with 150 MHz clock frequency. It has 4 MB video RAM as an embedded cache.

As SPUs, the chipset also has an I/O processor for X24 speed CR-ROM drive and X4 speed DVD-ROM. Figure 41.17 shows PlayStation 2 (SCPH-10000) system block diagram.

PlayStation 2, which Sony Computer Entertainment, Inc., released in March 2000, integrates games, music, and movies into a new dimension. It is designed to become the boarding gate for computer entertainment. PlayStation 2 uses an ultra-fast computer and 3-D graphics technology to allow the creation of video expressions that were not previously possible.

Although it supports DVD, the latest media, it also features backward compatibility with PlayStation CD-ROM so that users can enjoy the several thousand titles of PlayStation software. PlayStation 2 is designed as a new generation computer entertainment system that incorporates a wide range of future possibilities. The table shows the performance specifications of the graphic synthesizer chip, CXD2934.

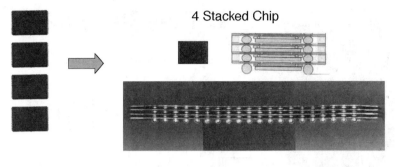

**FIGURE 41.16** Stack technology.

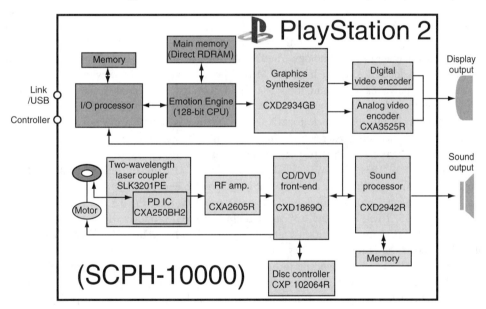

**FIGURE 41.17** PSX2 system block diagram.

| | |
|---|---|
| Clock Frequency | 150 MHz |
| Number of pixel engines | 16 parallel processors |
| Hybrid DRAM capacity | 4 MB@150 MHz |
| Total memory bandwidth | 48 GB/s |
| Maximum number of display colors | 2560 bits |
| Z buffer | 32 bits (RGBA: 8-bit each) |
| Process | |
| Technology | 0.25 $\mu$m |
| Total number of transistors | 43 M Tr'sPackage |
| 384-pin BGA image output formats | NTSC/PAL, D-TV, VESA (upto 1280 × 1024 dots) |

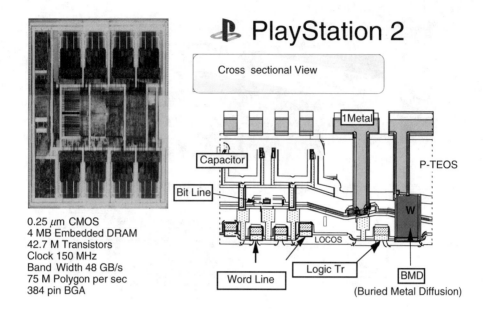

**FIGURE 41.18**    4 MB EmDRAM for PSX2.

In addition to the 128-bit CPU Emotion Engine™ and I/O processor, Playstation 2 adopts several advanced technologies. The graphics synthesizer graphic engine, CXD2934GB, takes full advantage of embedded DRAM system LSI technology. The Fig. 41.18 shows the chip photograph of Sony's 0.25 $\mu$m CMOS 4 MB embedded DRAM, which has 42.7 M Trs. The clock rate is 150 MHz, with 48 GB/s bandwidth. It can draw 75 M polygons per second. It has 384 pin in BGA. Its cross-sectional view is also shown here.

The semiconductor's optical integrated device technology contributes significantly to miniaturization and high reliability in the optical pickups, SLK3201PE, a two-wavelength laser coupler chip. PlayStation 2 also adopts the optical disc system chip solution which has a solid track record, CXD2942R, a sound processor chip, and has earned the trust of the optical disc system market.

It also includes CXD1869 (CD/DVD signal processor LSI), CXP102064R (disk controller), CXA2605R (Cd/DVD RD matrix amplifier), and CXA3525R (analog video encoder).

The first commercial product for use in consumer products were the 0.5 $\mu$m LSI chips for 8-mm camcorders in 1995. Then, Sony had 0.35 $\mu$m LSI chips for MD products with low voltage operation of 2.0 V. Now, the 0.25 $\mu$m PlayStation 2 graphics synthesizer has eDRAM with 48 GB/s bandwidth. Figure 41.19 shows the EmDRAM history.

Sony Em-DRAM has a high-band performance of 76.8 GB/s. See Fig. 41.20. In the following three figures, Figs. 41.21, 41.22, and 41.23, the memory cell size trend, some details of our embedded DRAM history, and the vertical critical dimensions between 0.25 and 0.18 $\mu$m EmDRAM process are shown, respectively.

Now, a few words on the feature and critical issues of 130 nm Emb-DRAM LSI process. The most advanced design rule to achieve high performance Tr –

Enhance resolution, and
refine OPC system (speed, accuracy)
Large variation in duty cycles
Reduce isolation—dense bias
High global step-> Enlarge D.O.F
High aspect hole process
Enhance etching durability
OPC = optical proximity correction
DOF = depth of focus

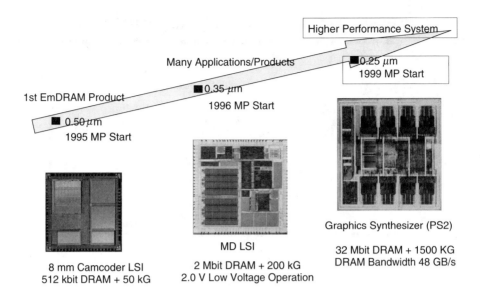

**FIGURE 41.19**  Embedded DRAM history.

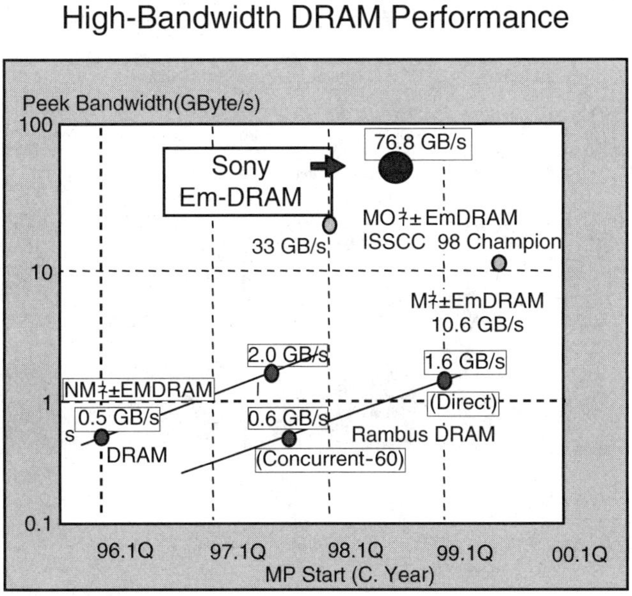

## High-Bandwidth DRAM Performance

**FIGURE 41.20**  Performance of embedded DRAM.

In the 0.18 $\mu$m EmDRAM process, the optical proximity correction (OPC ) technology and the phase-shift mask technology (PSM) were very important. See Figs. 41.24 and 41.25. Many high-performance manufacturing and measurement automatic machines, such as those shown in Fig. 41.26, are necessary.

Figure 41.27 shows the cross-sectional view of 0.18 $\mu$m EmDRAM, which was realized by utilizing all these technologies and high-performance machines.

Now some comments on key factors: technology extention such as optical extention and full flat process technology. KrF lithograpy optical extention features high NA, ultra-resolution, thin photo resist, and the OPC technology. Wirings are fully planarized interlayers of Cu/Dual Damascene. The EmDRAM features a fully planarized capacitor with the global step-less DRAM/logic structure by self-align process.

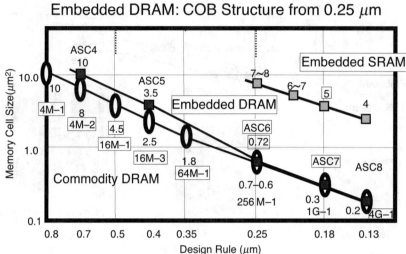

**FIGURE 41.21** CMOS memory cell size.

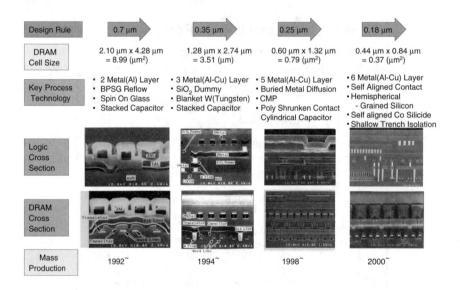

**FIGURE 41.22** Embedded DRAM history.

## 41.4 Conclusion

Some introductory comments on the basic semiconductor device concepts were given. They are strongly related to the microelectronics of the present home entertainment LSI chips. The chapter covered in detail some product specifications and performance aspects of the home entertainment LSI chip sets, such as those used in digital cameras, home robotics, and games. Cost of EmDRAM and its solutions by using EmDRAM are strongly related with new market creation such as PSX2. The EmDRAM technology for PS2/computer and some other future home entertainment electronics gadgets has a potential to be the technology driver in the years to come.

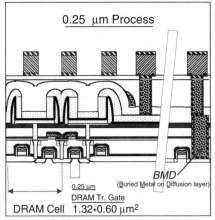
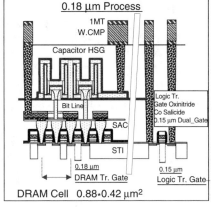

W-Policide Single Gate (L = 0.25 μm)
BMD(Buried Metal on Diffusion layer)

W-Policide DUAL Gate (L = 0.15 μm)
High Aspect Ratio 1st Metal Contact

**FIGURE 41.23** Em-DRAM process technology.

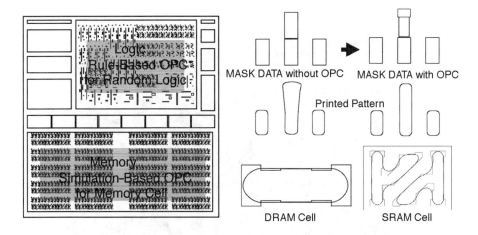

**FIGURE 41.24** Optical proximity correction.

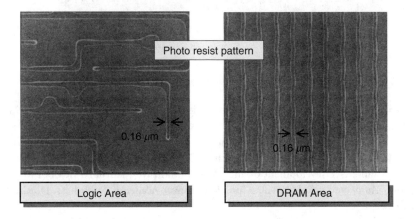

**FIGURE 41.25** Phase-shift mask (PSM) technology.

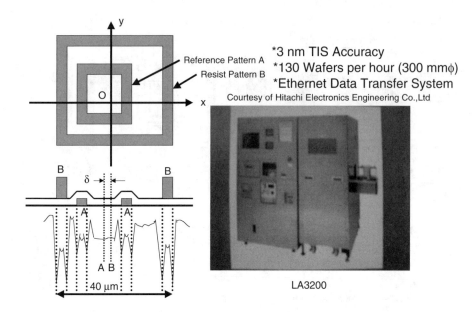

**FIGURE 41.26**   Overlay accuracy measurement system.

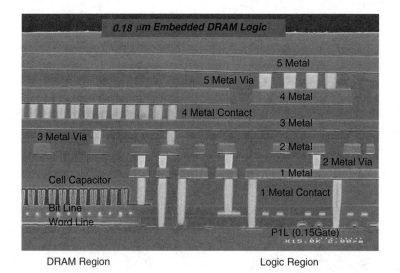

**FIGURE 41.27**   Cross-sectional view.

## References

1. Yoshiaki Hagiwara, "Solid State Device Lecture Series Aph/E183 at CalTech" in 1998–1999, http:www.ssdp.Caltech.edu/aphee183/

2. Yoshiaki Hagiwara, "Measurement technology for home entertainment LSI chips," Presentation at the Tutorial Session in ICMTS2001, Kobe, Japan, March 19–22, 2001.

3. M. Fujita and H. Kitano: "{{D}evelopment of and {A}utonomous {Q}uadruped {R}obot for {R}obot {E}ntertainment}," *Autonomous Robots,* vol. 5, pp. 7–8, Kluwer Academic Publishers, Dordrecht, the Netherlands, 1998.

4. Kohtaro Sabe, "Architecture of entertainment robot-development of AIBO –," *IEEE Computer Element MESA Workshop 2001,* Mesa, Arizona, Jan. 14–17, 2001.

5. JP 1215101 (a Japanese Patent #58-46905), Nov. 10, 1975 by Yoshiaki Hagiwara.

# 42
# Mobile and Wireless Computing

John F. Alexander
*University of North Florida*

Raymond Barrett
*University of North Florida*

Babak Daneshrad
*University of California,
Los Angeles*

Samiha Mourad
*Santa Clara University*

Garret Okamoto
*Santa Clara University*

Mohammad Ilyas
*Florida Atlantic University*

Abdul H. Sadka
*University of Surrey*

Giovanni Seni
*Motorola Human Interface Labs*

Jayashree Subrahmonia
*IBM Thomas J Watson Research
Center*

Ingrid Verbauwhede
*University of California, Los Angeles*

0-8493-0885-2/02/$0.00+$1.50
© 2002 by CRC Press LLC

## 42.1   Bluetooth—A Cable Replacement and More

*John F. Alexander and Raymond Barrett*

### What is Bluetooth?

Anyone who has spent the time and effort to connect a desktop computer to its peripheral devices, network connections, and power source knows the challenges involved, despite the use of color-coded connectors, idiot proof icon identification, clear illustrations, and step-by-step instructions. As computing becomes more and more portable, the problems are compounded in the laptop computer case, and the palmtop device case, let alone the cell phone case, where cabling solutions are next to impossible. The challenges associated with cabling a computer are tough enough for purposes of establishing the "correct" configuration, but are nearly unmanageable if the configuration must be dismantled each time a portable device is carried about in its portable mode.

Similar to a knight in shining armor, along comes Bluetooth; offering instant connectivity, intelligent service identification, software driven system configuration, and a myriad of other advantages associated with replacing cabling with an RF link. All of this good stuff is provided for a target price of $5 per termination, a cost that is substantially lower than the cost of most cables with a single pair of terminations. This miracle of modern communication technology is achieved with a 2.4-GHz frequency hopping trans-ceiver and a collection of communications protocols. At least, that is the promise. The participants who include such industrial giants as IBM, Motorola, Ericsson, Toshiba, Nokia, and over a thousand other consortium participants provide credibility for the promise.

There has been considerable interest in the press over the past few years in the evolution of the open Bluetooth® [1] specification for short-range wireless networking [2]. Bluetooth is one of many modern technological "open" specifications that are publicly available. The dream is to support Bluetooth short-range wireless communications (10–100 m) any where in the world. The 2.4 GHz frequency spectrum was selected for Bluetooth primarily because of its globally available free license. As we entered the twenty-first century there were already more than 1800 members of Bluetooth special interest group (SIG) [3]. Its reasonably high data rate (1 Mb/s gross data rate) and advanced error correction make it a serious consideration that is irresistible for hundreds of companies in a very diverse group of industries, all interested in ad hoc wireless data and voice linkages.

The Bluetooth specification utilizes a frequency hopping spread spectrum algorithm for the hardware and specifies rapid frequency hopping of 1600 times per second. As one might conclude 2.4 GHz digital radio transceivers that support this type of high frequency communication are quite complex, however, the hardware design and implementation is just the tip of the iceberg in understanding Bluetooth. The goal of this chapter is to provide the reader with a thorough overview of Bluetooth. An overview is detailed in the standard, but the Bluetooth specifications alone are thousands of pages.

Some of the proposed and existing Bluetooth usage models are the cordless computer, the ultimate headset, the three-in-one phone, the interactive conference (file transfer), the Internet bridge, the speaking laptop, the automatic synchronizer, the instant postcard, ad hoc networking, and hidden computing.

### Competing Infrared Technology

First, a brief digression will be taken into infrared wireless communication. With the advent of the personal digital assistant (PDA), it was obvious for the need of a low cost, low power means of wireless communication between user's devices and peripherals. At an Apple Newton users group one could see hundreds of enthusiasts "beaming" business cards back and forth. As other vendors came out with PDA each had its own proprietary infrared communication scheme. Eventually one "standard" method of communication between users applications came about as an outgrowth of the work of the Infrared Data Association. This specification became known as IrDA [4]. An international organization creates and promotes interoperable, low cost infrared data interconnection standards that support a walk-up, point-to-point user model. The standards support a broad range of appliances, computing, and communications devices.

Several reasons exist for mentioning the IrDA. First, many of the companies involved in the Bluetooth effort are members of the IrDA and have many products, which support IrDA protocols. Thus, much of the learning time in developing and attempting to implement a workable open standard for ad hoc short range wireless communication is *in house*. Also the IrDA has been one of the many well thought out high technology products that never gained much user acceptance. Many of the members of the Bluetooth SIG were anxious not to make the same mistake but to gain a way to profit from all the hard work invested in IrDA.

The proposed solution seemed simple. Just include more or less the entire IrDA software protocol stack in Bluetooth. Thus, the many already developed but seldom-used "beaming" applications out there could readily use Bluetooth RF connectivity. Whether this was a good idea, only time can tell. But it is important in understanding the Bluetooth specification because it is so heavily influenced by millions of hours of corporate IrDA experience and frustrations.

## Secure Data Link

Providing a secure data link is a fundamental goal for the Bluetooth SIG. One could envision the horror of walking through an airport with your new proprietary proposal on your laptop and having the competition wirelessly link to your machine and steal a copy. Without good security Bluetooth could never gain wide acceptance in virtually all cell phones, laptops, PDAs, and automobiles that the drafters envisioned.

Secure and nonsecure modes of operation are designed into the Bluetooth specification. Simple security is provided via authentication, link keys, and PIN codes, similar to bank ATM machines. The relatively high frequency hopping at 1600 hops/sec adds significantly to the security of the wireless link. Several levels of encryption are available if desired. In some cases, this can be problematic in that the level of encryption allowed for data and voice varies between countries and within countries over time. The Bluetooth system provides a very secure environment, eavesdropping is difficult. Bluetooth probably will be shown to be more secure than landline data transmission [5].

## Master and Slave Roles

The Bluetooth system provides a simple network, called a piconet, nominally 10 m in radius. This is the 1-mW power mode (0 dbm). There is also a 10-mW mode allowed, which probably could reach a 100 m in ideal cases, but it may not become widely implemented. One should think of a Bluetooth piconet as a 10 m personal bubble providing a moderately fast and secure peer-to-peer network. The specification permits any Bluetooth device to be either a master or a slave. At the baseband level, once two devices establish connection, one has to be a master and the other a slave. The master is responsible for establishing and communicating the frequency-hopping pattern based on the Bluetooth device address and the phase for the sequence based on its clock [6].

Up to seven active slaves are allowed all of which must hop in unison with the master. The Bluetooth specification allows for the direct addressing of up to 255 total slave units, but all but seven of the slaves must be in a "parked" mode. The master–slave configuration is necessary at the low protocol levels to control the complex details of the frequency hopping, however, at higher levels, the communication protocol is a peer-to peer and the connection established looks like point-to-point. The protocol supports several modes, which include active, sniff & hold, and park. Active uses the most power. While the master unit is in sniff mode, it conserves power by periodically becoming active. Additionally, the slave is in a hold mode but wakes up periodically based on timing from the master to "see" if any data is ready for it. While a slave is in park mode it consumes the least power, but the slave still maintains synchronization with the master.

A more complex Bluetooth communication topology is the scatternet. In one of the simpler scatternet schemes there are two masters with a common slave device active in two piconets. In another variation on the scatternet, one device is a slave in one piconet and the master in another. Using this scatternet idea some have speculated that an entire wireless network could be formed by having many piconets, each with one common node. Theoretically, this would work, but the rest of the original Bluetooth specification is not designed for making Bluetooth a wireless LAN. It is likely the newer SIG work group on personal area networking will be interested in expanding the definition and capability of Bluetooth scatternet capability. Currently there is lots of interest in forming location aware ad hoc wireless networks [7]. NASA has already approached this author for ideas for use of Bluetooth for ad hoc small area networks in space missions. The appeal of a wireless link made up of five dollar, very small, low-power, self-configuring, parts capable of connecting various sensors is irresistible for complex space missions where power and payload weight is at a premium.

## Bluetooth SIG Working Groups

To understand the Bluetooth specification it is important to understand how the very large Bluetooth SIG is organized. The actual work in producing the various specifications is done by the various SIG working groups. Given that the Bluetooth specification is thousands of pages of detailed technical documentation, it is not practical to just sit down and read the specification sheet. Briefly, five major groups compose the SIG including the air interface group, the software group, the interoperability group, the legal group, and the marketing group [3].

The software group contains three working subgroups primarily responsible for the Bluetooth protocol stack. These are the lower Transport Protocol Group, the Middleware Protocol Group, and the Application Group. The protocol stack follows the international origination of standardization (ISO) seven-layer reference model for open system interconnection [8].

## The Transport Protocol Group

The Transport Protocol Group includes ISO layers one and two, which are the Bluetooth radio, the link controller baseband, the link manager, the logical link controller and application protocol (L2CAP) layer, and the host controller interface. Collectively this set of protocol groups form a virtual pipe to move voice and data from one Bluetooth device to another. Audio applications bypass all of the higher level layers to move voice from one user to another [6].

The L2CAP layer prevents higher level layers from having to deal with any of the complexity of the frequency hopping Bluetooth radio and its complex control or special packets used over the Bluetooth air radio interface. The responsibility of the L2CAP layer is to coordinate and maintain the desired level of service requested and coordinate new incoming traffic. The L2CAP layer's concern is with asynchronous information (ACL packet) transmission [6]. This layer does not know about the details of the Bluetooth air interface such as master, slave, polling, frequency hopping, and such. Its job is to support the higher layer protocol multiplexing so multiple applications can establish connectivity over the same Bluetooth link simultaneously [9].

Device authentication is based on an interactive transaction from the link manager. When an unknown Bluetooth device request connectivity, the device requested ask the requester to send back a 16 byte random number key, which is similar to the familiar bank ATM PIN code procedure. Once a device is authenticated it is necessary for the device to store the authentication codes so this process can be automatic in future connections. Link encryption up to 128 bytes is supported and is controlled by desirability and governing legal issues of the area. Encryption applies only to the data payload and is symmetric.

Power management of connected devices is also handled at this level. In sniff mode the slave must wake up and listen at the beginning of each even-numbered slot to see if the master intends to transmit [6]. In hold mode the slave is suspended for a specified time. The API for hold mode puts the master in charge but provisions are available to negotiate the time. In Park mode, the slave dissociates itself from the piconet while still maintaining synchronization of the hopping sequence. Before going in to park mode the master informs the slave of a low-bandwidth beacon channel the master can use to wake the parked slave if there not already seven active slaves.

Paging schemes allow for a more repaid reconnection of Bluetooth devices. For example, paging is used in the event a master and a slave need to switch rolls to solve some problem such as forming some sort of local area network. Support for handling paging is optional in the Bluetooth specification. Another role of the link managers is to exchange information about each other to make passing data back and forth more efficient.

## The Bluetooth Transceiver

The Bluetooth systems operate in the industrial and scientific (ISM) 2.4 GHz band. This band is available license free on a global basis and is set a side for wireless data communications. In the United States the Federal Communication Commission (FCC) sets up rules for transmitters operating in the ISM band under section 15.247 of the Code of Federal Regulations. The frequency allocated is from 2,400 MHz to 2,483.5 MHz. The Bluetooth transceiver operates over 79 channels each of which is one megahertz wide. At least 75 of the 79 frequencies hoped to must be pseduo-random. Bluetooth uses all 79 channels and hops at a rate of 1600 hopes per second.

## The Middleware Protocol Group

The Middleware Protocol Group includes ISO layers three and six, which are made up of the RFCOMM protocol, the service discovery protocol (SDP), IrDA interoperability protocols, IrDA, and Bluetooth wireless protocol, and the audio and telephony control protocol. Fitting Bluetooth into the ISO model is really up to the developer. If you want to make it fit it makes sense, but there is lots of strange baggage imbedded protocols in Bluetooth that makes this difficult to see. First, we have already seen the voice communication connect down at the L2CAP layer. Now we are faced with how the toss in multiplexed serial port emulation, IrDA interoperability, and a bunch of protocols from telephony world. No wonder the standard goes on for thousands of pages and hundreds of companies around the world are struggling with comparability testing of various Bluetooth devices designed from this very complex specification.

## The Application Protocol Group

The Application Protocol Group includes ISO layer seven. This grouping contains the most extensive variety of special-purpose profiles all of which rely on the six lower levels for service. These include the generic profiles, the serial and object exchange profile, the telephony profiles, and the networking profiles.

The generic profiles includes the generic access profile and the service discovery application profile. The serial and object exchange profile contains the serial port profile, the generic object exchange profile, the object push profile, the file transfer profile, the synchronization profile, the networking profiles, the dial-up networking profile, the LAN access profile, the fax profile, the telephony profiles, the cordless telephony profile, the intercom profile, the headset profile, and the cordless telephony profile. Most of these applications profiles are self-explanatory and are only of detailed interest to the software developer when developing a specific application using the appropriate profile. This is not to say that they are not important, but they provide very detailed application programmer interfaces (API) [15].

The possible Bluetooth applications keep expanding. This stimulates interest in expanding the array of application profiles in the Bluetooth specification. Several of the newer application profiles are the car profile, a richer audio/video profile, and a local positioning profile.

## Bluetooth Development Kits

Given the obvious complexity of the Bluetooth hardware and software applications, having access to good development kits is essential to speed the implementation of the specification. The first inexpensive development kit to become widely available to universities was Ericsson's Bluetooth Application and Training Toolkit. This is a first generation Bluetooth kit that demonstrates important Bluetooth features and has a well defined, but extensive proprietary API in C++. Application development is possible, but is time-consuming and tedious requiring knowledge of C++ to learn a vast API. Newer kits, specifically for development, are more efficient.

Cambridge Silicon Radio (CSR) Bluetooth silicon radio has been very well publicized in the Bluetooth development and features "all CMOS" one chip solution. The CSR development kit includes software for CRR "BlueCore™" [11] IC with on-chip Bluetooth™ protocol and a PC development environment. Tools for embedded "1-chip" products are provided. Bluetooth BlueCore-to-host serial protocol and integrated Bluetooth protocol: BlueStack™. An innovative feature is that BlueCore devices enable users to configure the level of BlueStack that loads at boot time using software switches. SCR clams that running the full Bluetooth protocol locally on a BlueCore device significantly reduces the load on the host embedded processor, delivering major advantages to users of there Bluetooth system on a chip solution [12].

Many other development tools can be found currently at the http://www.bluetooth.com/product/dev_tools/development.asp. The above two are referenced because they have been around for a year or so and the authors have direct experience with them [2].

## Interoperability

There is a conflict with IEEE 802.11 Wireless Network Specification, which uses a direct sequence spread spectrum approach in the same frequency band. The direct sequence modulation is incompatible with the frequency hopping approach employed in Bluetooth. It is unlikely that an elegant interoperability solution can be found, without duplication of the entire hardware solutions for each; however, some early ad hoc reports in the trade press seem to point to the interoperability between 802.11 and Bluetooth to be minor [13,14].

Both operate in the 2.4 GHz ISM band, and both are a form of spread spectrum, but the 802.11 is direct sequence modulated spread spectrum and allows more power. Bluetooth is frequency hopping and low power.

## Bluetooth Hardware Implementation Issues

First, for Bluetooth to achieve the stated goals for widespread usage at low cost, there are severe hardware constraint issues to be addressed. Second, the environment into which Bluetooth is likely to be deployed is rapidly changing. Finally, the business models for adoption of Bluetooth technology are also impacted.

Broadly speaking, there are two classes of hardware implementation for Bluetooth, one employs discrete multiple chips to produce a solution, and a second in which Bluetooth becomes an embedded intellectual property (IP) block in a system-on-a-chip (SoC) product.

For the short run, the multiple chip strategy provides an effective implementation directed at prototype and assembly-level products. The strategy is effective during the initial period of development for Bluetooth, while the specification is still evolving and the product volumes are still low; however, a strong case can be made that the high volumes, low cost, and evolving environment make an IP block approach inevitable if Bluetooth is to enjoy wide acceptance.

In addressing the environmental issues, the most widely dispersed communications product today is the cell phone, with its service variants. The Internet connectivity of cell phones is soon to surpass the Internet connectivity of the desktop computer. The consequence of the cell phone driving the environment for all information processing connectivity under its constraints of low power, tight packaging, high volume, and low cost manufacturing forces examination of IP blocks for SoC solutions.

Bluetooth is highly attractive for cell phone products as a wire replacement, enabling many of the existing profiles from a cell phone, as well as providing expansion for future applications. The desktop computer embraces Bluetooth also as a wire replacement, but has a history of services supported by cabling. The cell phone cannot support many services with cabling, and in contrast to the desktop, service extensions for the raw communication capability of 3G and 4G cell phones must be addressed by wireless solutions.

Once Bluetooth IP block solutions exist, the market forces will drive high-volume products toward either embedded or single-chip Bluetooth implementations.

Technological hurdles must be overcome in the road toward Bluetooth IP block solutions. Presently, the RF front-end solutions for bluetooth are nearly all implemented in bipolar IC technology, implying at least a BiCMOS IC, which is widely recognized as too high cost for high-volume SoC products. As the lithography becomes available for denser CMOS IC products, the deep submicron devices provide the density and speed increases to support SoC solutions in the digital arena, and also improve the frequency response of the analog circuitry, enabling the possibility of future all-CMOS implementation.

In addition, communications system problems must be solved in order to ensure the feasibility of an all-CMOS implementation. For example, one of the more popular architectures for a modern communications receiver is the zero-IF (ZIF) approach. Unfortunately, the ZIF approach usually converts the RF energy immediately to baseband without significant amplification, which places the very small signal in the range of 1/f noise of the semiconductor devices employed. Typically, the only devices with substantially low enough noise are bipolar devices, which are to be avoided for system level considerations. Alternative architectures that are suitable include variants of super heterodyne architectures that usually require tuned amplifiers, which are also seldom suitable for integration. One approach that seems to meet all the requirements is one variant of the super heterodyne architecture known as low-IF, that places the energy high enough in the spectrum to avoid noise considerations, but low enough to be addressed by DSP processing to achieve the requisite filtering.

Regardless of the particular architecture chosen, the rapid channel switching involved in the frequency-hopping scheme necessitates frequency synthesis for local oscillator functions. There is considerable design challenge in developing a fully integrated voltage-controlled-oscillator (VCO) for use in a synthesizer that slews rapidly and still maintains low phase noise.

To compound the above issues, true IP block portability implies a level of process independence that is not currently enjoyed by any of the available architectures. Portability issues are likely to be addressed by intelligence in the CAD tools that are used to customize the IP blocks to the target process through process migration and shrink paths.

# References

1. Bluetooth is a trademark owned by Telefonaktiebolagent L M Ericsson, Sweden and licensed to the promoters and adopters of the Bluetooth Special Interest Group.
2. http://www.bluetooth.com/developer/specification/specification.asp Bluetooth Specification v1.1 core and v1.1 profiles.
3. http://www.bluetooth.com/sig/sig/sig.asp Bluetooth Special Interest Group (SIG).
4. Infrared Data Association IrDA http://www.irda.org.
5. Bray, J. and Sturman, C.F., Bluetooth, *Connectivity with our Cables,* Prentice-Hall, Englewood Cliffs, NJ, 2001.
6. Miller, B.A. and Bisdikian, C., *Bluetooth Revealed,* Prentice-Hall, Englewood Cliffs, NJ, 2001.
7. Tseng , Y., Wu, S., Liao, W., and Chao, C., Location Awareness in Ad Hoc Wireless Mobile Networks. [June 2001], *IEEE Computer,* 46,52.
8. International Origination of Standardization Information processing systems–Open Systems Interconnection–Connection Oriented Transport Protocol Specification, International Standard number 8825, ISO, Switzerland, May 1987.
9. Held, G., *Data Over Wireless Networks,* McGraw-Hill, New York, 2001.
10. http://www.comtec.sigma.se/Ericsson's Bluetooth Application and Training Tool Kit 200.
11. BlueCore™" and BlueStack™" are registered trademarks of Cambridge Silicon Radio, Cambridge, England, 2001.
12. http://www.csr.com/software.htm, Development software for BlueCore™ ICs Cambridge Silicon Radio, Cambridge, England, 2001.
13. Dornan, A., Wireless Ethernet: Neither Bitten or Blue. *Network Magazine,* May 2001.
14. Merritt, R., Conflicts Between Bluetooth and Wireless LANs Called Minor. *EE Times,* February 2001.
15. Muller, N.J., *Bluetooth Demystified,* McGraw-Hill, New York 2000.

## 42.2 Signal Processing ASIC Requirements for High-Speed Wireless Data Communications

*Babak Daneshrad*

### Introduction

To date, the role of application specific integrated circuits (ASICs) in wireless communication systems has been rather limited. Almost all of the signal processing demands of second generation cellular systems such as GSM and IS-136 (US TDMA) can be met with the current generation of general purpose DSP chips (e.g., TI TMS320, Analog Device's ADSP 21xx, or Lucent's DSP16xx families). The use of ASICs in wireless data communications has been limited to wireless LAN systems such as Lucent's WaveLAN and the front end, chip-rate processing needs of DSSS-CDMA based systems such as IS-95 (US CDMA).

Several major factors are redirecting the industry's attention towards ASICs for the realization of highly complex and power efficient wireless communications equipment. First, the move toward third generation (3-G) cellular systems capable of delivering data rates of up to 384 kbps in outdoor macro-cellular environments (an order of magnitude higher than the present second generation systems) and 2 Mbps in indoor micro-cellular environments. Second, the emergence of high-speed wireless data communications, whether in the form of high-speed wireless LANs [1] or in the form of broadband fixed access networks [2]. A third, but somewhat more subtle factor is the increased appeal of software radios. Radios that can be programmed to transmit and receive different waveforms and thus enable multi-mode and multi-standard operation. Although ASICs are by nature not programmable, they are parameterizable. In other words, ASIC designers targeting wireless applications must develop their architectures in such a way as to provide the user with features such as variable symbol rates and carrier frequency, as well as the ability to shut off parts of the circuit that may be unused under benign channel conditions. For DSSS systems the ASICs should provide sufficient flexibility to accommodate programmability of the chip-rate, spreading factor, and the spreading code to be used.

The next subsection further explores these elements and identify key signal processing tasks that are suited for ASIC implementation. In the subsection on "VLSI Architectures for Signal Processing Blocks" will present signal processing algorithms and ASIC architectures for the realization of these blocks. The chapter section ends with "Conclusions."

### Emerging High-Speed Wireless Systems

#### Third Generation (3-G) Cellular Networks

Second generation cellular systems such as IS-136, GSM, and IS-95 have mainly focused on providing digital voice services and low-speed data traffic. With the growing popularity of the Internet and the need for multimedia networking, standardization bodies throughout the world are looking at the evolution of current systems to support high-speed data and multimedia services. The technology of choice for all such 3-G systems is wideband code division multiple access (W-CDMA) based on direct sequence spread spectrum (DSSS) techniques [3,4]. The targeted chipping rate for these systems is 3.84 Mcps for the European UTRA standardization work, and a multiple of 1.2288 Mcps for the CDMA-2000 proposal.

In addition to providing higher data rates, which come about in part due to the increased bandwidth utilization of 3-G systems, a second and equally important aim of these systems is to increase the capacity of a cell (number of simultaneous calls supported by a cell). To this end, all the current proposals call for the use of sophisticated receivers utilizing multi-user detection and possibly smart antenna technologies.

In order to better appreciate the signal processing requirements of these receiver units, consider the block diagrams presented in Fig. 42.1. Figure 42.1(a) depicts the transmitter of a DSSS system, along with a candidate successive interference canceller (SIC) shown in Fig. 42.1(b) [5]. The details of the rake receiver are shown in Fig. 42.1(c).

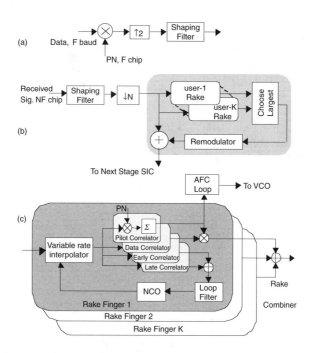

**FIGURE 42.1** Block diagram of (a) generic DSSS transmitter, (b) successive interference canceller for multiuser detection, and (c) rake receiver for a system with parallel pilot channel (i.e., IS-95).

The tremendous processing requirements of this architecture will become evident by considering a modest system operating at a chip rate of say, 4 Mcps using a 32-tap shaping filter, four rake fingers per user, four complex correlators per rake finger and 10 users in the cell, the number of operations (real multiply-adds) needed for a 5-stage SIC is upwards of 14 billion operations per second or giga-operations per second (GOPS). This amount of processing can easily overwhelm even the latest generation of general-purpose processors such as the TI TMS320C6x which delivers 1.6 giga-instructions per seconds (GIPS), but only 400 mega multiply-add operations per second [6]. At an anticipated power dissipation of 850 mW per processor, the overall power consumption of a SIC circuit based on such units will be quite large.

It is also worth noting that many operands are in the SIC or other MUD receiver that require only a few number of bits (i.e., multiplication with a 1-bit PN code sequence). This fact can be exploited in a dedicated ASIC datapath architecture but not in a general-purpose software programmable architecture.

### Broadband Wireless Networks

Emerging broadband fixed wireless access systems provide high-speed connectivity between a cellular base station and a home or office building at data rates of a few Mbps to a few tens of Mbps. On the other hand, standardization activities that are currently targeting high-speed wireless mico-cellular (wireless LAN) systems are looking at delivering 10–20 Mbps over the air data rates in the near future, with higher rates projected in the long term.

It is generally accepted that in order to achieve such high data rates, beam switching or beamforming techniques must be integrated into the development of the nodes. In addition, single carrier systems must include adaptive equalization to overcome time varying channel impairments, while multicarrier systems based on OFDM will require a large number of subcarriers [7]. The signal processing requirements for such high data rate systems could easily mount into the tens of GOPS range, thus necessitating the development of ASICs.

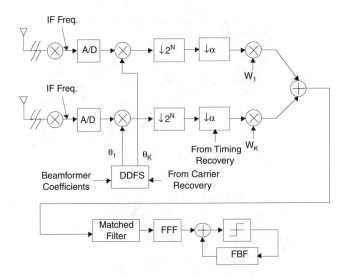

**FIGURE 42.2**   Block diagram of an all-digital receiver for a single carrier system (i.e., QAM) featuring digital IF sampling, beamforming, variable symbol rate, adaptive equalization, all digital timing, and carrier recovery loops.

Furthermore, the flexibility of digital implementation compared to an analog implementation of the down-conversion path makes a digital IF architecture more appealing. Figure 42.2 depicts the detailed block diagram of a single carrier high-speed wireless communication receiver complete with adaptive beamforming, adaptive equalization, and variable symbol rates. The flexibility offered by such an architecture can meet the demands of different systems requiring different levels of performance.

In this architecture, the direct digital frequency synthesizer (DDFS) serves three roles. First, it enables down-conversion of any carrier frequency up to half the sampling frequency of the analog-to-digital converter. Second, it can replace or complement a VCO for the purposes of carrier recovery, and third it can easily generate different phases needed by the beamforming circuit.

The variable rate decimator block is a key element in variable symbol rate systems where it is desired to maintain the same exact analog filtering, but yet accommodate user defined symbol rates. This is particularly important in wireless systems where a predefined data rate is difficult to guarantee due to statistical channel variations such as fading and shadowing. In such scenarios, the user can simply back-off on the symbol rate and provide connectivity albeit at a lower data rate.

The flexible decimation architecture depicted in Fig. 42.2 consists of two stages. The first is a course decimator block, which can decimate the signal by $2^N$ for $N = 0,1,2,\dots, M$. This section is realized using a cascade of $N$ decimate by two stages. The second part of the decimator is a variable rate interpolator block, which can change the sampling rate by any value in the range of 2–4. Not only can this block be used to change the sampling frequency of the signal, but it is the vital element in the realization of an all digital timing recovery loop.

The matched filter is typically a fixed coefficient fixed impulse response (FIR) filter. This block is followed by a decision feedback equalizer (DFE) that helps mitigate the effects of intersymbol interference (ISI) caused by the multipath nature of the channel. The DFE is made up of two adaptive FIR filters referred to as the feedforward filter (FFF) and the feedback filter (FBF).

The amount of processing (in terms of real multiply-adds per second) needed to realize these blocks can easily run into several GOPS. As an example, a baseband QAM receiver consisting of a 30-tap matched filter, a 10-tap FFF and a 5-tap FBF adapted using the least mean squares (LMS) algorithm, and running at 10 Mbaud requires close to 2.5 GOPS of processing. Once the processing needs of the DDFS, variable rate filters, and the beamforming network are also factored in, the processing requirements can easily reach 7–8 GOPS.

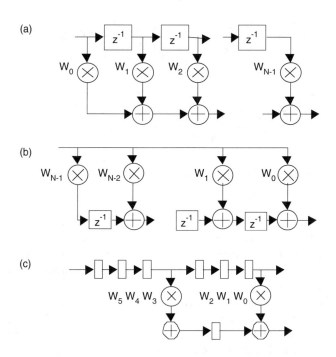

**FIGURE 42.3** Alternative FIR filter structures: (a) Direct form FIR structure, (b) Transposed form FIR structure, and (c) Hybrid FIR structure.

## VLSI Architectures for Signal Processing Blocks

### Fixed Coefficient Filters

The most intuitive means of implementing a FIR filter is to use the direct form implementation presented in Fig. 42.3(a) [12]. Applying the transposition theorem to this filter we get the transposed structure shown in Fig. 43.3(b). The two structures are identical in terms of I/O, however, the transposed form is ideal for high speed filtering operations since the critical path for an $N$ tap filter is always one multiplier delay plus one adder delay. The critical path of the direct form, however, is one multiplier delay plus $N$-1 adder delays. The fact is that the symbol rate for most wireless communication systems is a few tens of megahertz, whereas a typical multiplier in today's CMOS process technologies can easily reach speeds of 80–100 MHz. It is thus desirable to use the hybrid architecture shown in Fig. 43.3(c) where each multiplier accumulator is time-shared between several taps (three in this case) resulting in a more compact circuit for lower symbol rates.

The implementation of fixed coefficient FIR filters can be further simplified by moving away from the use of 2's complement number notation, and using a signed-digit number system in which each digit can take on one of three values {−1, 0, 1}. In general there are multiple signed-digit representations for the same number and a canonic signed-digit (CSD) representation can be defined for which no two nonzero digits are adjacent [8]. The added flexibility of signed-digit numbers allows us to realize the same coefficient using fewer nonzero coefficients than would be possible with a simple 2's complement representation. Using an optimization program, it is possible to design an FIR filter using CSD filters with as few as three or four nonzero digits for each coefficient. This could help significantly reduce the complexity of fixed coefficient multipliers since the number of partial products generated is directly proportional to the number of nonzero digits in the multiplier.

### Direct Digital Frequency Synthesizer (DDFS)

Given an input frequency word $W$, a DDFS will produce a frequency proportional to $W$. The most common techniques for realizing a DDFS consist of first accumulating the frequency word $W$ in a phase accumulator and then producing the sine and cosine of the phase accumulator value using a table lookup or a

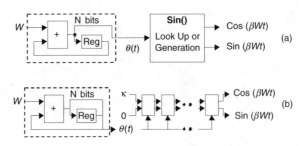

**FIGURE 42.4**   Two most common DDFS architectures: (a) Table lookup and (b) Coordinate rotation (CORDIC).

coordinate rotation (CORDIC) algorithm. These two approaches are depicted in Fig. 42.4. The two metrics for measuring the performance of a DDFS are the minimum frequency resolution Δf and the spurious free dynamic range (SFDR). The frequency resolution can be improved by increasing the wordlength used in the accumulator, while the SFDR is affected by the wordlengths in both the accumulator as well as the sine/cosine generation block.

One of the main challenges in the development of the table lookup DDFS has been to limit the size of the sine/cosine table. This has been accomplished through two steps [9]. First, by exploiting the symmetry of the sine and cosine functions it is only necessary to store $\beta$ of the period of a sine wave and derive the remainder of the period through manipulation of the saved portion. Second, the number of bits per entry can be reduced by dividing the sine table between a coarse ROM and a fine ROM with the final result obtained after simple post-processing of the values. Combining these two techniques can result in the reduction of the sine tables by an order of magnitude or better.

In the CORDIC algorithm, Fig. 42.4, sine and cosine of the argument are calculated using a cascade of stages, each of which rotates its input complex vector by $\delta/2^k$ ($\delta = \pi/2$) if the kth bit of W is 0 and $-\delta/2^k$ if the bit is a 1. Thus each stage performs the following matrix operation:

$$\begin{bmatrix} x_{out} \\ y_{out} \end{bmatrix} = \begin{bmatrix} \cos\theta & -\sin\theta \\ \sin\theta & \cos\theta \end{bmatrix} \begin{bmatrix} x_{in} \\ y_{in} \end{bmatrix} = \cos\theta \begin{bmatrix} 1 & -\tan\theta \\ \tan\theta & 1 \end{bmatrix} \begin{bmatrix} x_{in} \\ y_{in} \end{bmatrix}$$

In [10] a simplification of the CORDIC DDFS is presented in which for small $\theta$, $\tan(\theta)$ is simply approximated by $\theta$. In [11] a different modification to the CORDIC architecture is proposed that will facilitate low-power operation in cases where a sustained frequency is to be generated. This is achieved by calculating the necessary angle of rotation for each sampling clock period, and dedicating a single rotation stage in a feedback configuration to contiually rotate the phasor through the desired angle.

### Decimate/Interpolate Filters

Variable rate interpolation and decimation filters play a very important role in the development of highly flexible and self contained all-digital receivers. As previously mentioned, they are the critical element of all digital timing recovery loops as well as systems capable of operating at a host of user defined symbol rates. Additionally, digital resampling allows the ASIC designer to ensure that the clock frequency at all portions of the circuit are the minimum that they need to be to properly represent the signals. This could have significant impact on the size and power consumption of the resulting ASIC since power scales with the clock frequency and the square of the supply voltage. Thus, for a given circuit with a critical path of say $\tau$ seconds, if the data rate into the block is lowered by a factor K, then the frequency dependent portion of the dissipated power is also scaled by the same factor; however, additional power savings can be achieved by noting that the block now has $K\tau$ seconds to complete its task. Because the speed of a digital circuit is proportional to the supply voltage, we can reduce the supply voltage and still ensure that the circuit meets the speed constraints.

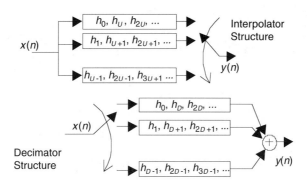

**FIGURE 42.5** Polyphase filter structures for interpolation and decimation.

**FIGURE 42.6** Variable rate interpolation.

Given the coefficients of an FIR decimation or interpolation filter, the structure of choice for the realization of a decimate by $D$ or an interpolate by $D$ filter is the polyphase structure [12] shown in Fig. 42.5. The attractiveness of this structure is in the fact that the filter is always operated at the lower sampling frequency.

In many cases it is desirable to resample the signal by a power of $2^N$. In which case $N$ decimate (interpolate) by two stages can be cascaded one after the other. Each decimator will consist of a halfband filter followed by a decimator. The halfband filter could be realized using the polyphase structure to simplify its implementation. Moreover, these filters are typically very small consisting of anywhere from 7 to 15 taps depending on the specified stopband attenuation and the size of the transition band. Their implementation can be simplified by exploiting the fact that close to half of the coefficients are zero and the remainder are symmetric about the main tap due to the linear phase characteristics of the halfband filter. Finally, since these are fixed-coefficient filters, they can be realized using CSD coefficients [13].

It is interesting to note that for the special case of a decimate (interpolate) by $2N$, it is possible to reuse the same hardware element and simply recirculate the data through it. In this architecture, the filter is run at the highest data sampling rate. The first pass through the filter will use up 1/2 of its computational resources, the second pass will use up 1/4 of the resources, and so on [14]. Although conceptually attractive, the clock generation circuit for such an architecture is quite critical and complex and this approach looses its appeal for recirculating factors greater than 3 or 4.

In cases where the oversampling ratio is large (e.g., narrowband signal) an alternative approach using a cascaded integrator-comb (CIC) structure can be used to implement a multiplierless decimator. The interested reader is referred to [15] for a brief overview of a CIC ASIC.

The continuously variable decimator block shown in Fig. 42.2 can resample the input signal by any factor $\alpha$ in the range of 2–4. The operation of this block is equivalent to that shown in Fig. 42.6, where the input data $x(n)$, originally sampled at $1/T_s$ is resampled to produce an output sequence $y(n)$ sampled at $1/T_i$. The entire operation is performed digitally.

To better understand the operation of this block, let us define the variable $\mu_k$, to be the time difference between the output sample $y(k)$ and the most recent input sample $x_1$. The job of the variable rate interpolator is to weight the adjacent input samples $(\ldots, x_0, x_1, \ldots)$, based on the ratio $\mu_k/T_s$, and add the weighted input samples to obtain the value of the output sample, $y(k)$. Mathematically, a number of interpolation schemes can perform the desired operation; however, many of them, such as sinc-based interpolation, require excessive computational resources for a practical hardware implementation. For real-time

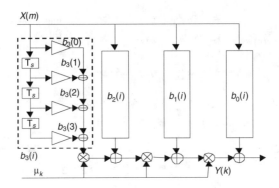

**FIGURE 42.7**   Farrow structure.

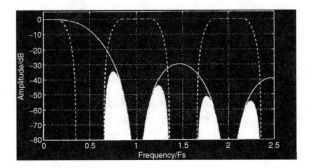

**FIGURE 42.8**   Frequency response of polynomial-based interpolator (from [18]).

calculation, Erup et al. [16] found polynomial-based interpolation to yield satisfactory results while minimizing the hardware complexity. In this approach, the weights of the input samples are given as polynomials in the variable $\mu_k$ and can be easily implemented in hardware using the Farrow structure [17] shown in Fig. 42.7. In this sructure, all the filter coefficients are fixed and polynomials in $\mu_k$ are realized by nesting the multipliers as shown in Fig. 42.7.

The signal contained in the imageband will cause aliasing after resampling; however, proper choice of the coefficients in the Farrow structure can help optimize the frequency response of the interpolator for a particular application. An alternative method to determine the filter coefficients is outlined in (see Fig. 42.8) [18].

## Conclusions

Section 42.2 reviewed trends in the wireless communications industry towards high speed data communications in both the macrocellular and the microcellular environments. The implication of these trends on the underlying digital circuits will move designers towards dedicated circuits and ASICs to meet these demands. As such the paper outlined the major signal processing tasks that these ASICs will have to implement.

## References

1.  K. Pahlavan, et. al., "Wideband local access: wireless LAN and wireless ATM," *IEEE Commun. Mag.*, pp. 34–40, Nov. 1997.
2.  J. Mikkonen, et. al., "Emerging wireless broadband networks," *IEEE Commun. Mag.*, vol. 36, no. 2, pp. 112–17, Feb. 1998.

3. E. Dahlman, Bjorn Gudmundson, M. Nilsson, and J. Skold, "UMTS/IMT–2000 based on wideband CDMA," *IEEE Commun. Mag.,* pp. 70–80, Sept. 1998.

4. Y. Furuya, "W-CDMA: an approach toward next generation mobile radio system, IMT–2000," *Proc. IEEE GaAs IC Symposium,* pp. 3–6, Oct. 1997.

5. A. Duel-Hallen, J. Holtzman, and Z. Zvonar, "Multiuser detection for CDMA systems," *IEEE Pers. Commun. Mag.,* pp. 46–58, April 1995.

6. http://www.ti.com/sc/docs/dsps/products.htm.

7. B. Daneshrad, et. al., "Performance and implementation of clustered OFDM for wireless communications," ACM MONET special issue on PCS, vol. 2, no. 4, pp. 305–14, 1997.

8. H. Samueli, "An improved search algorithm for the design of multiplierless FIR filters with powers-of-two coefficients," *IEEE TCAS,* vol. 36, no. 7, pp. 1044–1047, July 1989.

9. H. T. Nicholas, III and H. Samueli, "A 150-MHz direct digital frequency synthesizer in 1.25 $\mu$m CMOS with –90 dBc spurious performance," *IEEE JSSC,* vol. 25, no. 12, pp. 1959–969, Dec. 1991.

10. A. Madisetti, A. Kwentus, and A. N. Willson, Jr., "A sine/cosine direct digital frequency synthesizer using an angle rotation algorithm," *Proc. IEEE ISSCC '95,* pp. 262–63.

11. E. Grayver and B. Daneshrad, "Direct digital frequency synthesis using a modified CORDIC," *IEEE ISCAS,* June 1998.

12. J. G. Proakis and D. G. Manolakis, Introduction to Digital Signal Processing, Macmillan, London, 1988.

13. J. Laskowsky and H. Samueli, "A 150-MHz 43-tap halfband FIR digital filter in 1.2-$\mu$m CMOS generated by silicon compiler." *Proc. IEEE CICC '92,* pp. 11.4/1–4, May 1992.

14. T. J. Lin and H. Samueli, "A VLSI architecture for a universal high-speed multirate FIR digital filter with selectable power-of-two decimation/interpolation ratios," *Proc. ICASSP '91,* pp. 1813–816, May 1991.

15. A. Kwentus, O. Lee, and A. Willson, Jr., "A 250 Msample/sec programmable cascaded integrator-comb decimation filter," *VLSI Signal Processing, IX, IEEE,* New York, pp. 231–40, 1996.

16. L. Erup, F. M. Gardner, and R. A. Harris, "Interpolation in digital modems. II. Implementation and performance," *IEEE Trans. on Commun.,* vol. 41, no. 6, pp. 998–1008, June 1993.

17. C. W. Farrow, "A continuously variable digital delay element," *Proc. ISCAS '88,* pp. 2641–645, June 1988.

18. J. Vesma and T. Saramaki, "Interpolation filters with arbitrary frequency response for all-digital receivers," *IEEE ISCAS '96,* pp. 568–71, May 1996.

## 42.3 Communication System-on-a-Chip

*Samiha Mourad and Garret Okamoto*

### Introduction

Communication traffic worldwide is exploding: wired and wireless, data, voice, and video. This traffic is doubling every 100 days and it is anticipated that there will be a million people online by 2005. Today, more people are actually using mobile phones than are surfing the Internet. This unprecedented growth has been encouraged by the deployment of digital subscriber lines (DSL) and cable modems, which telephone companies have provided promptly and at a relatively low price. Virtual corporations have been created because of the availability and dependability of communication products such as laptops, mobile phones and pagers, which all support mobile employees. For example, vending machines may contact the suppliers when the merchandise level is low so that suppliers remotely vary the prices of the merchandise according to supply and demand.

With such proliferation in communication products and the need for a high volume, high speed transfer of data, new standards such as ATM and ITU-T are being developed. In addition, a vast body of knowledge, central to problems arising in the design and planning of communication systems, has been published; however, in fabricating products to meet these needs, the industry has continually attempted to use new design approaches that have not been fully researched or documented.

Communication devices need to be of small size and low power dissipation for portability and need to be operated at very high speed. Any of these devices, as other digital products, may consist of a single integrated circuit (IC) or more likely many ICs mounted on a printed circuit broad (PCB). Although the new technology (small feature size) has resulted in higher speed ICs, the transfer of data from one IC to another still creates a bottleneck of information. The I/O pads, with their increasing inductance, cause supply surges that compromise signal integrity. As an alternative to PCB design, another design approach known as multichip module (MCM) consists of placing more than one chip in the same package. The connections between modules have a large capacitive load that slows down communication among all of the modules. In the late 1990s, a new paradigm design called system-on-a-chip (SoC) has been successfully used to integrate the components of an entire system on one chip. This is in contrast to the traditional design where the components are implemented in separate ICs and then assembled on a PCB.

Section 42.3 describes the new design paradigm of a SoC and its beneficial attributes are outlined. The remainder of the paper concentrates on communication devices and the subsection on "Need for Communication Systems" emphasizes the need for these systems. Descriptions of communication SoCs and projections on their characteristics are given in "Communication SoCs." Latency, an important attribute, is the subject of "System Latency"; and "Communication MCMs" describes the integration of these systems with analog parts in MCM.

## System-on-a-Chip (SoC)

The shift toward very deep submicron technology has encouraged IC designers to increase the complexity of their designs to the extent that an entire system is now implemented on a single chip. To increase the design productivity and decrease time-to-market, reuse of previously designed modules is becoming common practice in SoC design; however, the reuse approach is not limited to in-house designs. It is extended to modules that have been designed by others as well. Such modules are referred to as *embedded cores*. This design approach has encouraged the founding of several companies that specialize in providing embedded cores to service multiple customers. It is predicted that in the near future, cores, of which 40% to 60% will be from external sources [Smith 1997], will populate 90% of a chip. Except for a very few, individual companies do not have the wide range of expertise that can match the spectrum of design types in demand today.

Core-based design, justified by the need to decrease time-to-market, has created a host of challenging problems for the design and testing community. First, there are legal issues for the core provider and the user, regarding the intellectual property (IP). Second, there are problems with integrating and verifying a mix of proprietary and external cores that are more involved than simply integrating ICs on a PCB.

A typical SoC configuration is shown in Fig. 42.9. It consists of several *cores* that are also referred to as *modules*, *blocks*, or *macros*. Often, these terms are used interchangeably. These cores may be DSP, RAM

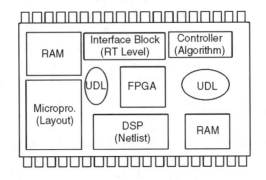

**FIGURE 42.9**   A system-on-a-chip (SoC).

**TABLE 42.1**　Categorizing Reusable Cores [Hunt 1996]

| Type | Flexibility | Design Flow | Representation | Libraries | Process Technology | Portability |
|------|-------------|-------------|----------------|-----------|--------------------|-------------|
| Soft | Very flexible Unpredictable | System design | Behavioral | Not applicable | Independent | Unlimited |
| | | RTL design | RTL | | | |
| Firm | Flexible | Floor planning | RTL, blocks Netlist | Reference | Generic | Library mapping |
| | | Placement | | Footprint, timing model | | |
| Hard | Inflexible Predictable | Routing Verification | Polygon data | Process specific library and design rules | Fixed | Process mapping |

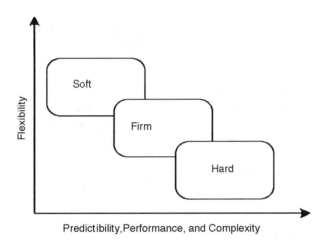

**FIGURE 42.10**　Trade-offs among types of cores　[Hunt 1996].

modules, or controllers. This same image of an SoC may be perceived as a PCB with the cores being the ICs mounted on it.

It also resembles standard cells laid on the floor of an IC. In the latter case, the blocks are of elementary gates of the same layout height. That is, they are all ICs in the PCB case or all standard cells in the IC case. For an SoC, they may consist of a several types, as described below. A UDL is a user defined logic that is basically equivalent to glue logic in microprocessors.

Cores are classified in three categories: hard, firm, and soft [Gupta 1997]. *Hard cores* are optimized for area and performance and they are mapped into a specific technology and possibly a specific foundry. They are provided as layout files that cannot be modified by the users. *Soft cores*, on the other hand, may be available as HDL technology-independent files. From a design point of view, the layout of a soft core is flexible, although some guidelines may be necessary for good performance. The flexibility allows optimization to the desired levels of performance or area. *Firm cores* are usually provided as technology-dependent netlists using library cells whose size, aspect ratio, and pin location can be changed to meet the customer needs. Table 42.1 summarizes the attributes of reusable cores. The table indicates a clear trade-off between design flexibility on one hand, and predictability and hence time-to-market performance complexity on the other. Soft cores are easily embedded in a design. The ASIC designers have complete control over the implementation of this core, but it is the designer's job to optimize it for area, test, or power performance.

Hard cores are very appropriate for time critical applications, whereas soft cores are candidates for frequent customization. The relationship between flexibility and predictability is illustrated in Fig. 42.10.

The cores can also be classified from a testing perspective. For example, there is typically no way to test a hard core unless the supplier provides a test set for this core, whereas a test set for the soft core needs to be created if not provided by the core provider. This makes hard cores more demanding when developing a test strategy for the chip. For example, it would be difficult to transport through hard cores a test for an adjacent block that may be another core or a UDL component. In some special cases, the problem may be alleviated if the core includes well described testability functions.

## Design and Test Flow

An integrated design and test process is highly recommended. This approach cannot be more appropriate than it is for core-based systems. Conceptually, the SoC paradigm is analogous to the integration of several ICs on a PCB, but there is a fundamental difference. Whereas in a PCB the different ICs have been designed, verified, fabricated, and tested independently from the board, fabrication and testing of an SoC are done only after integration of the different cores. This fact implies that even if the cores are accompanied by a test set, incorporation of the test sets is not that simple and must be considered while integrating the system. In other words, reuse of design does not translate to easy reuse of the test set. What makes this task even more difficult is that the system may include different cores that have different test strategies. Also, the cores may cover a wide range of functions as well as a diverse range of technologies, and they may be described using different HDL languages, such as Verilog, VHDL, and Hardware C to GDSII.

The basic design flow applies to SoC design in the sense that the entire system needs to be entered, debugged, modified for testability, validated, and mapped to a technology; but all of this has to be done in an *integrated framework*. Before starting the design process, an overall strategy needs to be chartered to facilitate the integration. In this respect, the specification phase is enlarged and a test strategy is included. This move toward more design on the system level and less time on the logic level.

The design must first be partitioned. Then decisions must be made on such questions as:

- Which partition can be instantiated by an existing core?
- Should a core be supplied by a vendor or done in-house?
- What type of core should be used?
- What is the integration process to facilitate verification and testing?

Because of the wide spectrum of core choices and the diversity of design approaches, SoC design requires a *meta-methodology*. That is, a methodology that can streamline the demands of all other methodologies used to design and test the reusable blocks as well as their integration with user defined logic. To optimize on the core-based design, an industry group deemed it necessary to establish a common set of specifications. This group, known as the virtual socket interface alliance (VSIA), was announced formally in September 1996. Its intent is to establish standards that facilitate communication between core creators and users, the SoC designers [IEEE 1999a].

An example of using multiple cores is the IBM-designed PowerPC product line, based on the PowerPC 40X chip series [Rincon 1997]. The PowerPC micro-controller consisted of a hard core and several soft cores. For timing critical components such as the CPU, a hard core was selected, while soft cores were used for peripheral functions such as the DMA controller, external bus interface unit (EBIU), timers, and serial port unit (SPU). The EBIU may be substituted by, say, a hard core from Rambus.

A change in the simulation and synthesis processes is required for embedded cores due primarily to the need to protect the intellectual property of the core provider. Firm cores may be encrypted in such a manner as to respond to the simulator without being readable by humans. For synthesis, the core is instantiated in the design. In the case of a soft core, sometimes the parameters are scaled to meet the design constraints. To preserve the core performance, the vendor may include an environment option to prevent the synthesis program from changing some parts of the design. This will protect the core during optimization, but the designer may remove such an option and make some changes in the design. A hard or a firm core is treated as a black box from the library and goes through the synthesis process untouched.

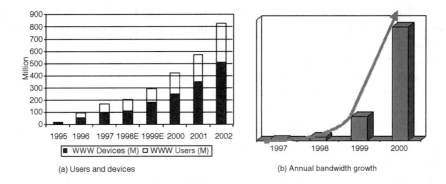

(a) Users and devices                    (b) Annual bandwidth growth

**FIGURE 42.11**    Internet growth.

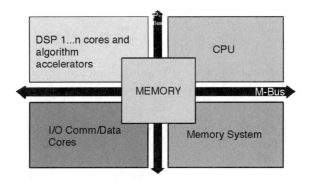

**FIGURE 42.12**    Components of a communication SoC.

### Advantages of SoCs

The overall size of the end product is reduced because manufacturers can put the major system functions on a single chip, as opposed to putting them on several chips. This reduces the total number of chips needed for the end product. For the same reason, the power consumption is reduced.

SoC products provide faster chip speeds due to the integration of the components/functions into one chip. Many applications such as high-speed communication devices (VoIP, MoIP, wireless LAN, 3G cellular phones) require chip speeds that may be unattainable with separate IC products. This is primarily due to the physical limitations of moving data from one chip to another, through bonding pads, wires, buses, etc. Integrating chip components/functions into one chip eliminates the need to physically move data from one chip to another, thereby producing faster chip speeds. Another important advantage of SoCs is the reuse of previously designed circuits, thereby reducing the design process time. This consequently translates into shorter time-to-market. In addition to decreasing time-to-market, it is very important to decrease the cost of packaging and testing, which are constantly increasing with the finer technology features. Instead of testing several chips and the PCB on which they are assembled, testing time is reduced to only one IC. SoCs are, however, very complex and standards are now being developed to facilitate their testing [IEEE 1995b]. In the remainder of this paper, we focus on communication systems that we will refer to as comm. SoC or simply SoC.

## Need for Communication Systems

Public switched telephone networks (PSTN) are becoming congested due to increasing Internet traffic as shown in Fig. 42.11. This drives the development of broadband access technology and high-speed optical networks. Another important factor is the convergence of voice, data, and video. As a consequence, there is a need for low and uniform latency devices for real time traffic. In addition, Internet service providers (ISP) and corporate Intranet are needed for voice and data IP gateways. Mobile users drive the development of wireless and satellite devices. In addition, there is an increasing demand for routers/switches, DSL modems, etc.

All needs mentioned above require smaller size and faster communication devices. Telephone calls that used to last an average of three minutes now exceed an hour or more when connected to the Internet. This has resulted in increasing the demand on DSL that transmit data over Internet protocols (IP) such as voice-over-IP (VoIP), mobile-over-IP (MoIP), and wireless requires speeds that may be unattainable with separate IC products. Examples of products:

1. 2G and 3G wireless devices (CDMA2000, WCDMA), etc.
2. DSL modems
3. Infrastructure, carrier, and enterprise circuit, packet switched and VoIP devices
4. Satellite modems
5. Cable modems and HFC routing devices
6. De/MUX for data stream on optical network
7. Web browsers (WAP) or short messaging systems (I-mode)
8. LAN telephony
9. ATM systems
10. Enterprise, edge network and media-over-IP switches and high-speed routers
11. Wireless LAN (IEEE 802.11 IEEE 802.11a, and IEEE 802.11b)
12. Bluetooth

Maybe the most important example of an emerging wireless communication standard is Bluetooth. This is a wireless personal area network (PAN) technology from the Bluetooth special interest group (SIG), founded in 1998 by Ericsson, IBM, Intel, Nokia, 3Com, Lucent, Microsoft, Motorola, and Toshiba. Bluetooth is an open standard for short-range transmission of digital voice and data between mobile devices (cellular phones, PDAs, laptops) and desktop devices. Bluetooth may provide a common standard to enable PDAs, laptop and desktop computers, cellular phones, thermostats, and virtually every other home and business electronic device to communicate with each other. Manufacturers will rely on SoC advances to help reach the target of $5 added cost to a consumer appliance by 2001. A study by Merrill Lynch projected that Bluetooth semiconductor revenue will reach $3.4 billion in 2005, with Bluetooth included in 1.7 billion devices that year, and the Bluetooth SIG estimated that the technology would be a standard feature in 100 million mobile phones by the end of 2001.

## Communication SoCs

The exponential growth of the Internet and the bandwidth shown in Fig. 42.11, indicate that more communication products are geared towards this technology, which requires a communication mode different than that used in traditional switching telephony. For example, in a PSTN, circuit switching is used and requires a dedicated physical circuit through the network during the life of a telephone session. In Internet and ATM technology, however, packet switching is used. Packet switching is a connectionless technology, where a message is broken into several small packets to be sent to a destination. The packet header contains the destination and source address, plus a sequence number so that the message can be reassembled.

There is a paradigm shift in digital communication motivated by the evolution of Internet as mission critical service that demands migration from circuit switch to packet switch. The older paradigm supported the data traffic part of the telephone networks. Whereas the new paradigm support the convergence of voice, data, and video and require a new class of media-over-IP systems voice traffic as part of the data network, thus requiring communication SoC for VoIP.

Most communication SoC consists of few components that are clustered around a central processing unit (CPU), which controls some or all of the following: (1) Packet processing, (2) Programmable DSP for data and signaling algorithm/protocol implementation, (3) I/O for interface with voice and data network such as ATM, PCI, Ethernet, H100/110, (4) memory system for intermediate storage of voice and data

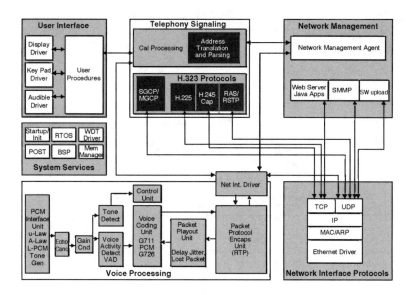

**FIGURE 42.13** Software for VoIP SoC.

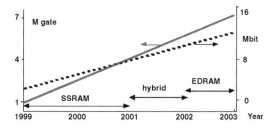

**FIGURE 42.14** Communications SoCs: Density and memory size.

streams, (5) hardwired DSP or accelerators for Codec and multi level mod/demod to increase system throughput, and (6) MPEG cores for media-over-IP MoIP processing.

Communication SoCs are actually a mix of software and hardware. Some of the circuits contain hardwired algorithms for code processing, but the software can be stored on the chip for protocols that process data. Figure 42.13 shows the software for a typical VoIP. This include several layers of software and IP such as:

1. *Telephony signaling:* Network interface protocol, which contains address translation and parsing and protocols such as H-3xx, media gateway control protocol (MGCP), and real time conferencing protocol (RTCP).
2. *Voice processing:* includes voice-coding unit using G.xx protocol, voice activation detection (VAD), comfort noise generation (CNG), which is used in fax-to-fax communication.
3. *User interface:* provides system services to the user such as key pad and display drivers and user procedures.
4. *Network management:* software upload and handling Java applets.
5. *Network Interface Protocols:* such as transmission control protocol (TCP), user datagram protocol (UDP), which is a TCP/IP, and Ethernet driver.

Other software and protocol may also be included such as packet processing and network management protocols, call control/signaling protocols/fax and modem tone detection, echo canceller, VAD, CNG, read to order systems (RTOS), and other software components for MoIP systems. Communication SoCs that accomplish the above tasks are expected to grow in size as projected in Fig. 42.14. The number of

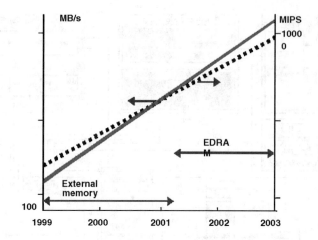

**FIGURE 42.15**    Communications SoCs processing power and memory handwidth.

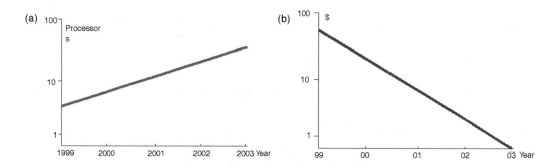

**FIGURE 42.16**    (a) Number of DSP processors per SoC. (b) Price per functional VoIP channel.

gates per chip will increase from one million in 1999 to 7 M in 2003. A major component in a communication SoC is the embedded memory banks, which is also expected to increase from 1 to 16 Mbit. The type of memory used will change from static RAMs (SRAM) to enhanced dynamic RAMs (EDRAM), which are much more compact.

The processing power of these SoCs is also expected to increase as illustrated in Fig. 42.15. The processing power is measured in million instructions per second (MIPs). It is predicted to grow from 100 to 1000 MIPs (dashed line) from 1999 to 2003. In same time period, the memory bandwidth (solid line) will increase from 100 to 1000 Mbits. The growth of the number of DSP processors by SoC is shown in Fig. 42.16(a). With all of this growth, it is interesting that the price of SoCs is estimated to decrease according to the trend shown in Fig. 42.16(b).

Several predictions were given to the bandwidth of communication chips. Two of these predictions are shown in Fig. 42.17. One assumes that the bandwidth will triple each year in the next 25 years as illustrated by the solid line [George Dilder-Telecosm]. The other shows that the growth will be at the rate of 8–16 times a year [SUN Microsystems]. In the 1990s, Bill Gates claimed that "we will have infinite bandwidth in a decade of time [Gates 1994]."

## System Latency

Latency is defined as the delay experienced a certain processing stage. The latency trends in Fig. 42.18 refer to the time taken to map the voice data into a packet to be transmitted. Three main types of latency are usually identified:

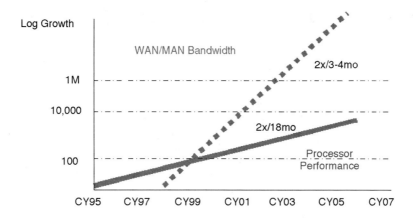

**FIGURE 42.17**   Bandwidth trends.

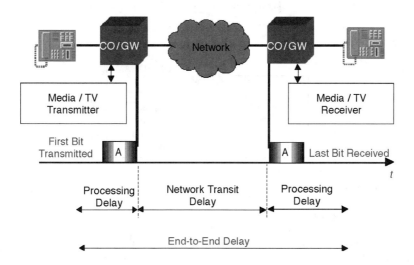

**FIGURE 42.18**   System latency.

- Frame/packetization Delay
- Media processing delay/complexity of the system
- Bridging delay, e.g., used for conferencing or multi SoC system

These delays may occur at different times in the life of the data in the communication system. A simplified communication system is shown in Fig. 42.18. It starts with the sender transmitting data through the network to a receiver at the other end. The total system latency is known as the end-to-end delay. It consists of the time taken to send the first bit of a packet to the time it takes to receive the last bit in the stream of data, i.e.,

- delay in processing the data at the sending end,
- transit delay within the network,
- delay in processing the data at the receiving end.

With the use of SoC, latency has been reduced and this reduction is projected to continue as the technology feature is getting finer. The trend is illustrated in Fig. 42.19. Several SoCs may themselves be integrated in one multichip module (MCM) as will be discussed next.

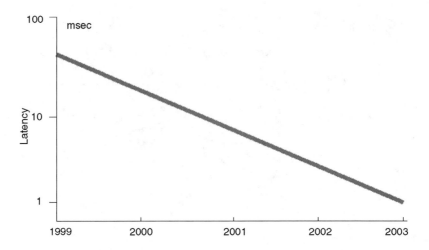

**FIGURE 42.19**     Latency for voice to packet in communication SoCs.

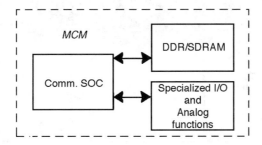

**FIGURE 42.20**     Communication MCMs.

## Communication MCMs

Digital communication SoCs are usually connected to external analog functions and I/O as depicted in Fig. 42.20. In order to optimize the interface between digital SoCs and analog functions, it is beneficial to integrate both designs in a MCM. The simplest definition for an MCM is a single electronic package containing more than one IC [Doanne 1993]. An MCM then combines high performance ICs with a custom-designed common substrate structure that provides mechanical support for the chips and multiple layers of conductors to interconnect them. Such an arrangement takes advantage of the performance of the ICs because the interconnect length is much shorter.

Multichip modules are not new, they preceded SoC. They have several advantages because they improve the maximum external memory bandwidth achieved, reduce size and weight of the product, increase the operating speed, and decrease power dissipation of the system; however, they are limited by wiring capacitance to frequencies below 150 MHz, e.g., Sony's HandyCam. Thus, they are limited by slower memory in comparison with the massive parallel processing power of an SoC with embedded memory.

MCM wide bus pin out is restricted by cost and yield in comparison with an SoC that provides high throughput data processing with wide 256–1024 bit on chip data bus. System configurability is harder to achieve in MCM than in SoC that are software configurable.

Analog and digital functions are separately optimized in MCM while in SoC many analog functions are optimized and their yield improved by using on chip integrated DSP algorithms. Multiple communication SoCs and analog functions can be packaged on a single MCM. The advantage of MCMs is even more pronounced when the package is enhanced. For example, flip-chips may be used or even more advanced package

The interconnections between the various SoCs and the memory chips are the major paths for crosstalk and other types of signal distortion. Reducing the routing length of the connection will help to increase the operation speed. This can be achieved with a chip-on-chip (CoC) module. The metal redistribution layers were fabricated on the top of the processor and the two memory chips, while the original bond pads still remained for the wire bonding to the substrate. The memory chips can be mounted on the top of the processor using flip-chip technology. Redistribution layers have been used to replace the bond wires and traces on the substrate to provide the interconnections between memory chip and processor. Since Know Good Die memory chips are usually used, testing only requires open/short test between the processor and memory chips. No burn-in and extensive memory tests are required, so the connection to the package ball can be removed as a new test program is implemented with the open/short test of the memory interface through other IO paths of the VGA processor.

## Summary

The broadband access, infrastructure, carrier, and enterprise Communication SoCs will demand higher MIPS, integration, and memory bandwidth. They will also demand lower latency, power dissipation, and cost/channel or function. Comm. SoC utilizes programmable DSP, hardwired DSP accelerators, and I/O to implement Comm. protocols and systems in a highly integrated form. Higher memory access frequency, DSP interface speeds, and specialized analog functions will demand the integration of Comm. SoCs on Comm. MCM

## References

Batista, Elisa, "Bluetooth Promises and Hurdles," Wired News, June 2000.

Doanne, D. A. and P. D. Franzon, Eds. (1993), *Multichip Module Technologies and Alternatives: The Basics,* Van Nostrand Reinhold, New York.

Gehring and Koutroubinas, "Designing cableless devices with the bluetooth specification," Communication Systems Design, February 2000.

Gupta, R. K. and Y. Zorian (1997), "Introduction to core—based system design," *IEEE Des. Test Comput.,* Vol. 14, No. 4, pp. 15–25.

Hunt, M. and J. A. Rowson (1996), "Blocking in a system on a chip," *IEEE Spectrum,* Vol. 36, No. 11, pp. 35–41.

IEEE (1999a), P1450 Web site *http//grouper.ieee.org/groups/1450/.*

IEEE (1999b), P1500 Web site *http//grouper.ieee.org/groups/1500/.*

Mourad, S. and Y. Zorian, Principles of testing electronic systems, Wiley, 2000.

Mourad, S. and B. Greene (2000), "Scan-path based testing of system on a chip," *Proc. IEEE International Conference of Electronics, Circuits and Systems,* Cyprus, pp. 1081–1084.

Murray, B. T. and J. P. Hayes (1996), "Testing ICs: getting to the core of the problem," *IEEE Computer,* Vol. 29, No. 11, pp. 32–38.

Okamoto, G, *Smart Antenna Systems and Wireless LANs,* Kluwer Academic Publishers, Boston, MA, 1999.

Okamoto, G., S.-S. Jeng, and G. Xu, "Evaluation of timing synchronization algorithms for the smart wireless LAN system," *Proceedings of the IEEE VTC '99 Conference,* May 1999, pp. 2014–2018.

Okamoto, G. and C.-W. Chen, "Capacity improvement of smart antenna systems via the maximum SINR beam forming algorithm," *Proceedings of the ICSPAT 2000 Conference,* October 2000.

Okamoto, G., et al., "An improved algorithm for dynamic slot assignment for the SWL system," *Proceedings of the Asilomar 2000 Conference,* Pacific Grove, CA, October 2000.

Smith, G. (1997), "Test and system level integration," *IEEE Des. Test Comput.,* Vol. 14, No. 4.

Varma, P. and S. Bhatia (1997), "A structured test reuse methodology for core-based system chip," *Proc. IEEE International Test Conference,* pp. 294–302.

Zorian, Y. (1993), "A distributed BIST control scheme for complex VLSI devices," *Proc. 11th IEEE VLSI Test Symposium,* pp. 6–11.

Zorian, Y. (1997), "Test requirements for embedded core-based systems and IEEE P-1500," *Proc. IEEE International Test Conference*, pp. 191–199.

Zorian, Y., et al. (1998), "Testing embedded-core based system chips," *Proc. IEEE International Test Conference*, pp. 135–149.

VSI (1998), VSI Alliance Web site *http:/www.vsi.org/*.

http://www.digianswer.com/bluetooth/.

## 42.4   Communications and Computer Networks

*Mohammad Ilyas*

The field of communications and computer networks deals with efficient and reliable transfer of information from one point to another. The need to exchange information is not new but the techniques employed to achieve information exchange have been steadily improving. During the past few decades, these techniques have experienced an unprecedented and innovative growth. Several factors have been and continue to be responsible for this growth. The Internet is the most visible product of this growth and it has impacted the life of each and every one. Section 42.4 describes salient features and operational details of communications and computer networks.

The contents of section 42.4 is organized in several subsections. "A Brief History" describes a brief history of the field of communications. The "Introduction" deals with the introduction of communication and computer networks. "Computer Networks" describes operational details of computer networks. "Resource Allocation Techniques" discusses resource allocation mechanisms. "Challenges and Issues" briefly describes the challenges and issues in communication and computer networks that are still to be overcome. The "Summary and Conclusions" subsection summarizes the article.

### A Brief History

Exchange of information (communications) between two or more entities has been a necessity since the existence of human life. It started with some form and shape of human voice that one entity can create and other(s) can listen and interpret. Over a period of several centuries, these voices evolved into languages. As the population of the world grew, more and more languages were born. For a long time, languages were used for face-to-face communications. If there were ever a need to convey some information (a message) over a distance, someone would be briefed and sent to deliver the message to a distant site. Gradually, additional methods were developed to represent and exchange the information. These methods included symbols, shapes, and eventually alphabets. This development facilitated information recording and use of nonvocal means for exchanging information. Hence, preservation, dissemination, sharing, and communication of knowledge became easier.

Until about 150 years ago, all communication was via wireless means and included smoke signals, beating of drums, and use of reflective surfaces for reflecting light signals (optical wireless). Efficiency of these techniques was heavily influenced by the environmental conditions. For instance, smoke signals were not very effective in windy conditions. In any case, as we will note later, some of the techniques that were in use centuries ago for conveying information over a distance, were similar to the techniques that we currently use. The only difference is that the implementation of those techniques is exceedingly more sophisticated now than it was centuries ago.

As the technological progress continued and electronic devices started appearing on the surface, the field of communication also started making use of the innovative technologies. Alphabets were translated into their electronic representations so that information may be electronically transmitted. Morse code was developed for telegraphic exchange of information. Further developments led to the use of telephone. It is important to note that in earlier days of technological masterpieces, users would go to a common site where one could send a telegraphic message over a distance or could have a telephonic conversation with a person at a remote location. This was a classic example of resource sharing. Of course, human help was needed to establish a connection with remote sites.

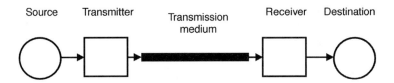

**FIGURE 42.21**   A typical communication system.

As the benefits of the advances in communication technologies were being harvested, the electronic computers were also emerging and making the news. The earlier computers were not only expensive and less reliable, they were also huge in size. For instance, the computers that used vacuum tubes, were of the size of a large room and used roughly about 10,000 vacuum tubes. These computers would stop working if a vacuum tube had burnt, and the tube would need to be replaced by using a ladder. On the average, those computers would function for a few minutes, before another vacuum tube's replacement was necessary. A few minutes of computer time was not enough to execute a large computer program. With the advent of transistors, computers not only became smaller in size, less expensive, but also more reliable. These aspects of computers resulted in their widespread applications. With the development of personal computers, there is hardly any side of our lives that has not been impacted by the use of computers. The field of communications is no exception and the use of computers has escalated our communication capabilities to new heights.

## Introduction

Communication of information from one point to another in an efficient and reliable manner has always been a necessity. A typical communication system consists of the following components as shown in Fig. 42.21:

- Source that generates or has the information to be transported
- Transmitter that prepares the information for transportation
- Transmission medium that carries the information from one end to the other
- Receiver that receives the information and prepares it for delivering to the receiver
- Destination that takes the information from receiver and utilizes it as necessary

The information can be generated in analog or in digital form. Analog information is represented as a continuous signal that varies smoothly in time. As one speaks in a microphone, an analog voice signal is generated. Digital information is represented by a signal that stays at some fixed level for some duration of time followed by a change to another fixed level. A computer works with digital information that has two levels (binary digital signals). Figure 42.22 shows an example of analog and digital signals. Transmission of information can also be in analog or in digital form. Therefore, we have the following four possibilities in a communication system [21]:

- Analog information transmitted as an analog signal
- Analog information transmitted as a digital signal
- Digital information transmitted as an analog signal
- Digital information transmitted as a digital signal

There may not be a choice regarding the form (analog or digital) of information being generated by a device. For instance, a voice signal as one speaks, a video signal as generated by a camera, a speed signal generated by a moving vehicle, and an altitude signal generated by the equipment in a plane will always be analog in nature; however, there is a choice regarding the form (analog or digital) of information being transmitted over a transmission medium. Transmitted information could be analog or digital in nature and information can be easily converted from one form to another.

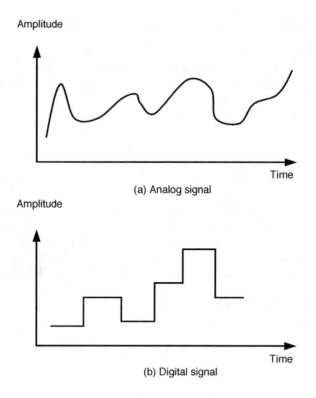

**FIGURE 42.22**   Typical analog and digital signals.

Each of these possibilities has its pros and cons. When a signal carrying information is transmitted, it looses its energy and strength and gathers some interference (noise) as it propagates away from the transmitter. If energy of signal is not boosted at some intermediate point, it may attenuate beyond recognition before it reaches its intended destination. That will certainly be a wasted effort. In order to boost energy and strength of a signal, it must be amplified (in case of analog signals) and rebuild (in case of digital signals). When an analog signals is amplified, the noise also becomes amplified and that certainly lowers expectations about receiving the signal at its destination in its original (or close to it) form. On the other hand, digital signals can be processed and reconstructed at any intermediate point and, therefore, the noise can essentially be filtered out. Moreover, transmission of information in digital form has many other advantages including processing of information for error detection and correction, applying encryption and decryption techniques to sensitive information, and many more. Thus, digital information transmission technology has become the dominant technology in the field communications [9,18].

As indicated earlier, communication technology has experienced phenomenal growth over the past several decades. The following two factors have always played a critical role in shaping the future of communications [20]:

- Severity of user needs to exchange information
- State of the technology related to communications

Historically, inventions have always been triggered by the severity of needs. It has been very true for the field of communications as well. In addition, there is always an urge and curiosity to make things happen faster. When electricity was discovered and people (scattered around the globe) wanted to exchange information over longer distances and in less time, telegraph was invented. Morse code was developed with shorter sequences (of dots and dashes) for more frequent alphabets. That resulted in transmission of message in a shorter duration of time. Presence of electricity, and capability of wires to carry information over longer distances, led to the development of devices that converted human voice into electrical signal, and thus led to the development of telephone systems. Behind this invention was also a need/desire to establish full-duplex (two-way simultaneous) communication in human voice. As the use of telephone became widespread, there was a need for a telephone user to be connected to any other user, and that led to the development of switching offices. In the early days, the switching offices were operated manually. As the state of the technology improved, the manual switching offices were replaced by automatic switching offices. Each telephone user was assigned a telephone number for identification purposes and a user able to dial the number for the purpose of establishing a connection with the called party. As the computer technology improved and the computers became easier to afford and smaller in size, they found countless uses including their use in communications. The computers not only replaced the automatic (electromechanical) switching offices, they were also employed in many other aspects of communication systems. Examples include conversion of information from analog to digital and vice versa, processing of information for error detection and/or correction, compression of information, and encryption/decryption of information, etc.

As computers became more powerful, there were many other applications that surfaced. The most visible application was the amount of information that users started sharing among themselves. The volume of information being exchanged among users has been growing exponentially over the last three decades. As users needed to exchange such a mammoth amount of information, new techniques were invented to facilitate the process. There was not only a need for users to exchange information with others in an asynchronous fashion, there was also need for computers to exchange information among themselves. The information being exchanged in this fashion has different characteristics than the information being exchanged through the telephone systems. This need led to the interconnection of computers with each other and that is what is called computer networks.

## Computer Networks

Computer networks is an interconnection of computers. The interconnection forms a facility that provides reliable and efficient means of communication among users and other devices. User communication in computer networks is assisted by computers, and the facility also provides communication among computers. Computer networks are also referred to as computer communication networks. Interconnection among computers may be via wired or wireless transmission medium [5,6,10,13,18].

There are two broad categories of computer networks:

- Wide area networks
- Local/metropolitan area networks

Wide area computer networks, as the name suggests, span a wider geographical area and essentially have a global scope. On the other hand, local/metropolitan area networks span a limited distance. Local area networks are generally confined to an industrial building or an academic institution. Metropolitan area networks also have limited geographical scope but it is relatively larger than that of the local area networks [19]. Typical wide and local/metropolitan area networks are shown in Fig. 42.23.

Once a user is connected to a computer network, it can communicate with any other user that is also connected to the network at some point. It is not required that a user must be connected directly to another user for communicating. In fact, in wide area networks, two communicating users will rarely be directly connected with each other. This implies that the users will be sharing the transmission links for exchanging their information. This is one of the most important aspects of computer networks. Sharing of resources improves utilization of the resources and is, of course, cost-effective as well. In addition to sharing the transmission links, the users will also share the processing power of the computers at the switching nodes, buffering capacity to store the information at the switching nodes, and any other resources that are connected to the computer network. A user that is connected to a computer network at any switching node will have immediate access to all the resources (databases, research articles, surveys, and much more) that are connected to the network as well. Of course, access to specific information may be restricted and a user may require appropriate authorization to access the information.

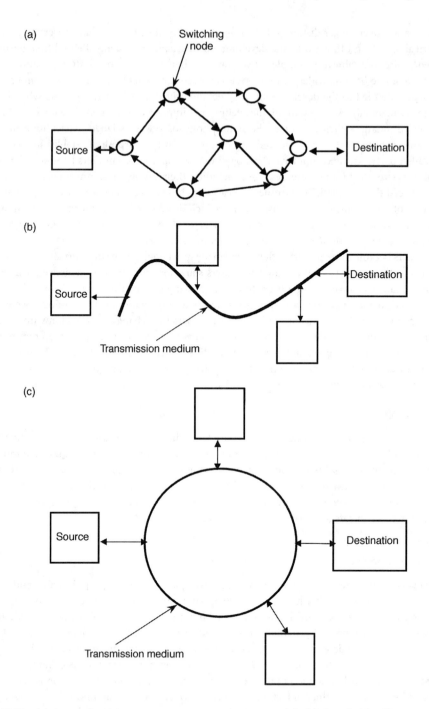

**FIGURE 42.23**    (a) A typical wide area computer communication network. (b) A typical local/metropolitan area communication bus network. (c) A typical local/metropolitan area communication ring network.

The information from one user to another may need to pass through several switching nodes and transmission links before reaching its destination. This implies that a user may have many options available to select one out of many sequences of transmission links and switching nodes to exchange its information. That adds to the reliability of information exchange process. If one path is not available, not feasible or is not functional, some other path may be used. In addition, for better and effective sharing of resources among several users, it is not appropriate to let any user exchange a large quantity of information at a time;

however, it is not uncommon that some users may have a large quantity of information to exchange. In that case, the information is broken into smaller units known as packets of information. Each packet is sent towards destination as a separate entity and all packets are assembled together at the destination side to re-create the original piece of information [2].

Due to resource sharing environment, users may not be able to exchange their information at any time they wish to because the resources (switching nodes, transmission links) may be busy serving other users. In that case, some users may have to wait for some time before they begin their communication. Designers of computer networks should design the network so that the total delay (including wait time) is as small as possible and that the total amount of information successfully exchanged (throughput) is as large as possible.

As can be noted, many aspects must be addressed for enabling networks to transport users' information from one point to another. The major aspects are listed below:

- Addressing mechanism to identify users
- Addressing mechanism for information packets to identify their source and destination
- Establishing a connection between sender and receiver and maintaining it
- Choosing a path or a route (sequence of switching nodes and transmission links) to carry the information from a sender to a receiver
- Implementing a selected route or path
- Checking information packets for errors and recovering from errors
- Encryption and decryption of information
- Controlling the flow of information so that shared resources are not over taxed
- Informing the sender that the information has been successfully delivered to the intended destination (acknowledgement)
- Billing for the use of resources
- Making sure that different computers that are running different applications and operating systems, can exchange information
- Preparing information appropriately for transmission over a given transmission medium.

This is not an exhaustive list of items that need to be addressed in computer networks. In any case, all such issues are addressed by very systematic and detailed procedures. The procedures are called communication protocols. The protocols are implemented at the switching nodes by a combination of hardware and software. It is not advisable to implement all these features in one module of hardware or software because that will become very difficult to manage. It is a standard practice that these features be divided in different smaller modules and then modules be interfaced together to collectively provide implementation of these features. International Standards Organization (ISO) has suggested dividing these features into seven distinct modules called layers. The proposed model is referred to as Open System Interconnection (OSI) reference model. The seven layers proposed in the OSI reference model are [2]:

- Application layer
- Presentation layer
- Session layer
- Transport layer
- Network layer
- Data link layer
- Physical layer

Physical layer deals with the transmission of information on the transmission medium. Data link layer handles the information on a single link. Network layer deals with the path or route of information from the switching node where source is connected to the switching node where receiver is connected. It also monitors end-to-end information flow. The remaining four layers reside with the user equipment. Transport layer deals with the information exchange from source to the sender. Session layer handles establishment of session between source and the receiver and maintains it. Presentation layer deals with the form in which information is presented to the lower layer. Encryption/decryption of information can also be performed at this layer. Application layer deals with the application that generates the information at the source side and what happens to it when it is delivered at the receiver side.

As the information begins from the application layer at the sender side, it is processed at every layer according to the specific protocols implemented at that layer. Each layer processes the information and appends a header and/or a trailer with the information before passing it on to the next layer. The headers and trailers appended by various layers contribute to the overhead and are necessary for transportation of the information. Finally, at the physical layer, the bits of information packets are converted to an appropriate signal and transmitted over the transmission medium. At the destination side, the physical layer receives the information packets from the transmission medium and prepares them for passing these to the next higher layer. As a packet is processed by the protocol layers at the destination side, its headers and trailers are stripped off before it is passed to the next layer. By the time information reaches the application layer, it should be in the same form as it was transmitted by the source.

Once a user is ready to send information to another user, he or she has two options. He or she can establish a communication with the destination prior to exchanging information or he can just give the information to the network node and let the network deliver the information to its destination. If communication is established prior to exchanging the information, the process is referred to as connection-oriented service and is implemented by using virtual circuit connections. On the other hand, if no communication is established prior to sending the information, the process is called connectionless service. This is implemented by using datagram environment. In connection-oriented (virtual circuit) service, all packets between two users travel over the same path through a computer network and hence arrive at their destination in the same order as they were sent by the source. In connectionless service, however, each packet finds its own path through the network while traveling towards its destination. Each packet will therefore experience different delay and the packets may arrive at their destination out of sequence. In that case, destination will be required to put all the packets in proper sequence before assembling them [2,10,13].

As in all resource sharing systems, allocation of resources in computer networks requires a careful attention. The main idea is that the resources should be shared among users of a computer network as fairly as possible. At the same, it is desired to maintain the network performance as close to its optimal level as possible. The fairness definition, however, varies from one individual to another and depends upon how one is associated with a computer networks. Although fairness of resource sharing is being evaluated, two performance parameters—delay and throughput—for computer networks are considered. The delay is the duration of time from the moment information is submitted by a user for transmission to the moment it is successfully delivered to its destination. The throughput is amount of information successfully delivered to its intended destination per unit time. Due to the resource sharing environment in computer networks, these two performance parameters are contradictory. It is desired to have the delay as small as possible and the throughput as large as possible. For increasing throughput, a computer network must handle increased information traffic, but the increased level of information traffic also causes higher buffer occupancy at the switching nodes and hence, more waiting time for information packets. This results in an increase in delay. On the other hand, if information traffic is reduced to reduce the delay, that will adversely affect the throughput. A reasonable compromise between throughput and delay is necessary for a satisfactory operation of a computer network [10,11].

## Wide Area Computer Networks

A wide area network consists of switching nodes and transmission links as shown in Fig. 42.23(a). Layout of switching nodes and transmission links is based on the traffic patterns and expected volume of traffic flow from one site to another site. Switching nodes provide the users access to a computer network and implement communication protocols. When a user is ready to transmit its information, the switching node, to which the user is connected to, will establish a connection if a connection-oriented service has been opted. Otherwise, the information will be transmitted in a connectionless environment. In either case, switching nodes play a key role in determining path of the information flow according to some well-established routing criteria. The criteria include performance (delay and throughput) objectives among other factors based on user needs. For keeping the network traffic within a reasonable range, some traffic flow control mechanisms are necessary. In late 1960s and early 1970s, when data rates of transmission media used in computer networks were low (a few thousands of bits per second), these mechanisms were fairly simple. A common method used for controlling traffic over a transmission link or a path was an understanding that sender will continue sending information until the receiver sends a request to stop. The information flow will resume as soon as the receiver sends another request to resume transmission. Basically the receiver side had the final say in controlling the flow of information over a link or a path. As the data rates of transmission media started increasing, this method was not deemed efficient. To control the flow of information in relatively faster transmission media, a sliding window scheme was used. According to this scheme, sender will continuously send information packet but no more than a certain limit. Once the limit has reached, the sender will stop sending the information packets and will wait for the acknowledgement of the packets that have been transmitted. As soon as an acknowledgement is received, the sender may send another packet. This method ensures that there are no more than a certain specific number of packets in transit from sender to receiver at any given time. Again the receiver has the control over the amount of information that sender can transmit. These techniques for controlling the information traffic are referred to as reactive or feedback based techniques because the decision to transmit or not to transmit is based on the current traffic conditions.

The reactive techniques are acceptable in low to moderate data rates of transmission media. As the data rates increase from kilobits per second to megabits and gigabits per second, the situation changes. Over the past several years, the data rates have increased manifold. Optical fibers provide enormously high data rates. Size of the computer networks has also experienced tremendous increase. The amount of traffic flowing through these networks has been increasing exponentially. Given that, the traffic control techniques used in earlier networks are not quite effective anymore [11,12,22]. One more factor that has added to the complexity of the situation is that users are now exchanging different types of information through the same network. Consider the example of Internet. The geographical scope of Internet is essentially global. Extensive use of optical fiber as transmission media provides very high data rates for exchanging information. In addition, users are using Internet for exchanging any type of information that they come across, including voice, video, data, etc. All these factors have essentially necessitated use of modified approach for traffic management in computer networks. The main factor leading to this change is that the information packets are moving so fast through the computer networks that any feedback-based (or reactive) control will be too slow to be of any use. Therefore, some preventive mechanisms have been developed to maintain the information traffic inside a computer network to a comfortable level. Such techniques are implemented at the sender side by ensuring that only as much information traffic is allowed to enter the network as can be comfortably handled by the networks [1,20,22]. Based on the users' needs and state of the technology, providing faster communications for different types of services (voice, video, data, and others) in the same computer network in an integrated and unified manner, has become a necessity. These computer networks are referred to as broadband integrated services digital networks (BISDNs). Broadband ISDNs provide end-to-end digital connectivity and users can access any type of communication service from a single point of access. Asynchronous transfer mode (ATM) is expected to be used as a transfer mechanism in broadband ISDNs. ATM is essentially a fast packet switching technique where information is transmitted in the form of small fixed-size packets called cells. Each cell is 53 bytes long and includes a header of 5 bytes. The information is primarily transported using connection-oriented (virtual circuit) environment [3,4,8,12,17].

Another aspect of wide area networks is the processing speed of switching nodes. As the data rates of transmission media increases, it is essential to have faster processing capability at the switching nodes. Otherwise, switching nodes become bottlenecks and faster transmission media cannot be fully utilized. When transmission media consists of optical fibers, the incoming information at a switching node is converted from optical form to electronic form so that it may be processed and appropriately switched to an outgoing link. Before it is transmitted, the information is again converted from electronic form to optical form. This slows down the information transfer process and increases the delay. To remedy this situation, research is being conducted to develop large optical switches to be used as switching nodes. Optical switches will not require conversion of information from optical to electronic and vice versa at the switching nodes; however, these switches must also possess the capability of optical processing of information. When reasonable sized optical switches become available, use of optical fiber as transmission media together with optical switches will lead to all-optical computer and communication networks. Information packets will not need to be stored for processing at the switching nodes and that will certainly improve the delay performance. In addition, wavelength division multiplexing techniques are rendering use of optical transmission media to its fullest capacity [14].

## Local and Metropolitan Area Networks

A local area network has a limited geographical scope (no more than a few kilometers) and is generally limited to a building or an organization. It uses a single transmission medium and all users are connected to the same medium at various points. The transmission medium may be open-ended (bus) as shown in Fig. 42.23(b) or it may be in the form of a loop (ring) as shown in Fig. 42.23(c). Metropolitan area networks also have a single transmission medium that is shared by all the users connected to the network, but the medium spans a relatively larger geographical area, upto 150 km. They also use a transmission medium with relatively higher data rates. Local and metropolitan area networks also use a layered implementation of communication protocols as needed in wide area networks; however, these protocols are relatively simpler because of simple topology, no switching nodes, and limited distance between the senders and the receivers. All users share the same transmission medium to exchange their information. Obviously, if two or more users transmit their information at the same time, the information from different users will interfere with each other and will cause a collision. In such cases, the information of all users involved in a collision will be destroyed and will need to be retransmitted. Therefore, there must be some well-defined procedures so that all users may share the same transmission medium in a civilized manner and have successful exchange of information. These procedures are called medium access control (MAC) protocols.

There are two broad categories of MAC protocols:

- Controlled access protocols
- Contention-based access protocols

In controlled access MAC protocols, users take turns in transmitting their information and only one user is allowed to transmit information at a time. When one user has finished its transmission, the next user begins transmission. The control could be centralized or distributed. No information collisions occur and, hence, no information lost due to two or more users transmitting their information at the same time. Example of controlled access MAC protocols include token-passing bus and token-passing ring local area networks. In both of these examples, a token (a small control packet) circulates among the stations. A station that has the token is allowed to transmit information, and other stations wait until they receive the token [19].

In contention-based MAC protocols, users do not take turns in transmitting their information. When a users becomes ready, it makes its own decision to transmit and also faces a risk of becoming involved in a collision with another stations who also decides to transmit at about the same time. If no collision occurs, the information may be successfully delivered to its destination. On the other hand, if a collision occurs, the information from all users involved in a collision will need to be retransmitted. An example of contention-based MAC protocols is carrier sense multiple access with collision detection (CSMA/CD) which is used in Ethernet. In CSMA/CD, a user senses the shared transmission medium prior to transmitting its information. If the medium is sensed as busy (someone is already transmitting the information), the user will refrain from transmitting its information; however, if the medium is sensed as free, the user transmits

its information. Intuitively, this MAC protocol should be able to avoid collisions, but collisions still do take place. The reason is that transmissions travel along the transmission medium at a finite speed. If one user senses the medium at one point and finds it free, it does not mean that another user located at another point of the medium has not already begun its transmission. This is referred to as the effect of the finite propagation delay of electromagnetic signal along the transmission medium. This is the single most important parameter that causes deterioration of performance in contention-based local area networks [11,19].

Design of local area networks has also been significantly impacted by the availability of transmission media with higher data rates. As the data rate of a transmission medium increases, the effects of propagation delay becomes even more visible. In higher speed local area networks such as Gigabit Ethernet, and 100-BASE-FX, the medium access protocols are designed such that to reduce the effects of propagation delay. If special attention is not given to the effects of propagation delay, the performance of high-speed local area networks becomes very poor [15,19].

Metropolitan area networks essentially deal with the same issues as local area networks. These networks are generally used as backbones for interconnecting different local area networks together. These are high-speed networks and span a relatively larger geographical area. MAC protocols for sharing the same transmission media are based on controlled access. Two most common examples of metropolitan area networks are fiber distributed data interface (FDDI) and distributed queue dual bus (DQDB). In FDDI, the transmission medium is in the form of two rings, whereas DQDB uses two buses. FDDI rings carry information in one but opposite directions and this arrangement improves reliability of communication. In DQDB, two buses also carry information in one but opposite directions. The MAC protocol for FDDI is based on token passing and supports voice and data communication among its users. DQDB uses a reservation-based access mechanism and also supports voice and data communication among its users [19].

## Wireless and Mobile Communication Networks

Communication without being physically tied-up to wires has always been of interest and mobile and wireless communication networks promises that. The last few years have witnessed unprecedented growth in wireless communication networks. Significant advancements have been made in the technologies that support wireless communication environment and there is much more to come in the future. The devices used for wireless communication require certain features that wired communication devices may not necessarily need. These features include low power consumption, light weight, and worldwide communication ability.

In wireless and mobile communication networks, the access to a communication network is wireless so that the end users remain free to move. The rest of the communication path could be wired, wireless, or combination of those. In general, a mobile user, while communicating, has a wireless connection with a fixed communication facility and rest of the communication path remains wired. The range of wireless communication is always limited and therefore range of user mobility is also limited. To overcome this limitation, cellular communication environment has been devised. In a cellular communication environment, geographical region is divided into smaller regions called cells, thus the name cellular. Each cell has a fixed communication device that serves all mobile devices within that cell. However, as a mobile device, while in active communication, moves out of one cell and into another cell, service of that connection is transferred from one cell to another. This is called handoff process [7,16].

The cellular arrangement has many attractive features. As the cell size is small, the mobile devices do not need very high transmitting power to communicate. This leads to smaller devices that consume less power. In addition, it is well known that the frequency spectrum that can be used for wireless communication is limited and can therefore only support a small number of wireless communication connections at a time. Dividing communication region into cells allows use of the same frequency in different cells as long as they are sufficiently apart to avoid interference. This increases the number of mobile devices that can be supported. Advances in digital signal processing algorithms and faster electronics have led to very powerful, smaller, elegant, and versatile mobile communication devices. These devices have tremendous mobile communication abilities including wireless Internet access, wireless e-mail and news items, and wireless video (through limited) communication on handheld devices. Wireless telephones are already available and operate in different communication environments across the continents. The day is not far when a single communication number will be assigned to every newborn and will stay with that person irrespective of his/her location.

Another field that is emerging rapidly is the field if ad hoc wireless communication networks. These networks are of a temporary nature and are established for a certain need and for a certain duration. There is no elaborate setup needed to establish these networks. As a few mobile communication devices come in one another's proximity, they can establish a communication network among themselves. Typical situations where ad hoc wireless networks can be used are classroom environment, corporate meetings, conferences, disaster recovery situations, etc. Once the need for networking is satisfied, the ad hoc networking setup disappears.

## Resource Allocation Techniques

As discussed earlier, computer networks are resource sharing systems. Users share the common resources as transmission media, processing power and buffering capacity at the switching nodes, and other resources that are part of the networks. A key to successful operation of computer networks is a fair and efficient allocation of resources among its users. Historically, there have been two approaches to allocation of resources to users in computer networks:

- Static allocation of resources
- Dynamic allocation of resources

Static allocation of resources means that a desired quantity of resources is allocated to each user and they may use it whenever they need. If they do not use their allocated resources, no one else can. On the other hand, dynamic allocation of resources means that a desired quantity of resources is allocated to users on the basis of their demands and for the duration of their need. Once the need is satisfied, the allocation is retrieved. In that case, someone else can use these resources if needed. Static allocation results in wastage of resources, but does not incur the overhead associated with dynamic allocation. Which technique should be used in a given a situation is subject to the famous concept of supply and demand. If resources are abundant and demand is not too high, it may be better to have static allocation of resources; however, when the resources are scarce and demand is high, dynamic allocation is almost a necessity to avoid the wastage of resources.

Historically, communication and computer networks have dealt with both the situations. Earlier communication environments used dynamic allocation of resources when users will walk to public call office to make a telephone call or send a telegraphic message. After a few years, static allocation of resources was adopted, when users were allocated their own dedicated communication channels and these were not shared among others. In late 1960s, the era of computer networks dawned with dynamic allocation of resources and all communication and computer networks have continued with this tradition to date. With the advent of optical fiber, it was felt that the transmission resources are abundant and can satisfy any demand at any time. Many researchers and manufacturers held the opinion in favor of going back to the static allocation of resources, but a decision to continue with dynamic resource allocation approach was made and that is here to stay for many years to come [10].

## Challenges and Issues

Many challenges and issues are related to communications and computer networks that are still to be overcome. Only the most important ones will be described in this subsection.

High data rates provided by optical fibers and high-speed processing available at the switching nodes has resulted in lower delay for transferring information from one point to another. However, the propagation delay (the time for a signal to propagate from one end to another) has essentially remained unchanged. This delay depends only on the distance and not on the data rate or the type of the transmission medium.

This issue is referred to as latency versus delay issue [11]. In this situation traditional feedback-based reactive traffic management techniques become ineffective. New preventive techniques for effective traffic management and control are essential for achieving the full potential of these communication and computer networks [22].

Integration of different services in the same networks has also posed new challenges. Each type of sexrvice has its own requirements for achieving a desired level of quality of service (QoS). Within the networks any attempt to satisfy QoS for a particular service will jeopardize the QoS requirements for other service. Therefore, any attempt to achieve a desired level of quality of service must be uniformly applied to the traffic inside a communication and computer network and should not be intended for any specific service or user. That is another challenge that needs to be carefully addressed and its solutions achieved [13].

Maintaining security and integrity of information is another continuing challenge. The threat of sensitive information passively or actively falling into unauthorized hands is very real. In addition, proactive and unauthorized attempts to gain access to secure databases are also very real. These issues need to be resolved to gain the confidence of consumers so that they may use the innovations in communications and computer networking technologies to their fullest [13].

## Summary and Conclusions

Section 42.4 discussed the fundamentals of communications and computer networks and the latest developments related to these fields. Communications and computer networks have witnessed tremendous growth and sophisticated improvements over the last several decades.

Computer networks are essentially resource sharing systems in which users share the transmission media and the switching nodes. These are used for exchanging information among users that are not necessarily connected directly. Transmission rates of transmission media have increased manifold and the processing power of the switching nodes (which are essentially computers) has also been multiplied. The emerging computer networks are supporting communication of different types of services in an integrated fashion. All types of information, irrespective of its type and source, is being transported in the form of packets (e.g., ATM cells). Resources are being allocated to users on a dynamic basis for better utilization. Wireless communication networks are emerging to provide worldwide connectivity and exchange of information at any time.

These developments have also posed some challenges. Effective traffic management techniques, meeting QoS requirements, and information security are the major challenges that need to be surmounted in order to win the confidence of users.

## References

1. Bae, J., and Suda, T., "Survey of traffic control schemes and protocols in ATM networks," *Proceedings of the IEEE*, Vol. 79, No.2, February 1991, pp. 170–189.
2. Beyda, W., "Data communications from basics to broadband," Third Edition, 2000.
3. Black, U., "ATM: foundation for broadband networks," Prentice-Hall, Englewood Cliffs, NJ, 1995.
4. Black, U., "Emerging communications technologies," Second Edition, Prentice-Hall, Englewood Cliffs, NJ, 1997.
5. Chou, C., "Computer networks in communication survey research," *IEEE Transactions on Professional Communication*, Vol. 40, No. 3, September 1997, pp. 197–208.
6. Comer, D., "Computer networks and internets," Prentice-Hall, Englewood Cliffs, NJ, 1999.
7. Goodman, D., "Wireless personal communication systems," Addison-Wesley, Reading, MA, 1999.
8. Goralski, W., "Introduction to ATM networking," McGraw-Hill, New York, 1995.
9. Freeman, R., "Fundamentals of telecommunications," John Wiley & Sons, New York, 1999.
10. Ilyas, M., and Mouftah, H.T., "Performance evaluation of computer communication networks," *IEEE Communications Magazine*, Vol. 23, No. 4, April 1985, pp. 18–29.

11. Kleinrock, L., "The latency/bandwidth tradeoff in gigabit networks," *IEEE Communications Magazine,* Vol. 30, No. 4, April 1992, pp. 36–40.

12. Kleinrock, L., "ISDN-The path to broadband networks," *Proceedings of the IEEE,* Vol. 79, No. 2, February 1991, pp. 112–117.

13. Leon-Garcia, A., and Widjaja, I., "Communication networks, fundamental concepts and key architectures," McGraw Hill, New York, 2000.

14. Mukherjee, B., "Optical communication networks," McGraw-Hill, New York, 1997.

15. Partridge, C., "Gigabit networking," Addison-Wesley, Reading, MA, 1994.

16. Rappaport, T., "Wireless communications," Prentice-Hall, Englewood Cliffs, NJ, 1996.

17. Schwartz, M., "Broadband integrated networks," Prentice-Hall, Englewood Cliffs, NJ, 1996.

18. Shay, W., "Understanding communications and networks," Second Edition, PWS, 1999.

19. Stallings, W., "Local and metropolitan area networks," Sixth Edition, Prentice-Hall, Englewood Cliffs, NJ, 2000.

20. Stallings, W., "ISDN and broadband ISDN with frame relay and ATM," Fourth Edition, Prentice-Hall, Englewood Cliffs, NJ, 1999.

21. Stallings, W., "High-speed networks, TCP/IP and ATM design principles," Prentice-Hall, Englewood Cliffs, NJ, 1998.

22. Yuan, X., "A study of ATM multiplexing and threshold-based connection admission control in connection-oriented packet networks," Doctoral Dissertation, Department of Computer Science and Engineering, Florida Atlantic University, Boca Raton, Florida 33431, August 2000.

## 42.5   Video over Mobile Networks

*Abdul H. Sadka*

### Introduction

Due to the growing need for the use of digital video information in multimedia communications especially in mobile environments, research efforts have been focusing on developing standard algorithms for the compression and transport of video signals over these networking platforms. Digital video signals, by nature, require a huge amount of bandwidth for storage and transmission. A 6-second monochrome video clip of QCIF (176 × 144) resolution and a frame rate of 30 Hz requires over 742 kbytes of raw video data for its digital representation where each pixel has an 8-bit luminance (intensity) value. When this digital signal is intended for storage or remote transmission, the occupied bandwidth becomes too large to be accommodated and thus compression becomes necessary for the efficient processing of the video content. Therefore, in order to transmit video data over communication channels of limited bandwidth, some kind of compression must be applied before transmission.

Video compression technology has witnessed a noticeable evolution over the last decade as research efforts have revolved around the development of efficient techniques for the compression of still images and discrete raw video sequences. This evolution has then progressed into improved coding algorithms that are capable of handling both errors and varying bandwidth availability of contemporary communication media. The contemporary standard video coding algorithms provide both optimal coding efficiency and error resilience potential. Current research activity is focused on the technologies associated with the provision of video services over the future mobile networks at user-acceptable quality and with minimal cost requirements. Section 42.5 discusses the basic techniques employed by video coding technology, and the associated most prominent error resilience mechanisms used to ensure an optimal trade-off between the coding efficiency and quality of service of standard video coding algorithms. The chapter section also sheds the light on the algorithmic concepts underlying these technologies and provides a thorough presentation of the capabilities of contemporary mobile access networks, such as general packet radio service (GPRS), to accommodate the transmission of compressed video streams at various network conditions and application scenarios.

## Evolution of Standard Image/Video Compression Algorithms

The expanding interest in mobile multimedia communications and the concurrently expanding growth of data traffic requirements have led to a tremendous amount of research work during a period of over 15 years for developing efficient image and video compression algorithms. Both International Telecommunications Union (ITU) and International Organization for Standardization (ISO) have released a number of standards for still image and video coding algorithms that employ the discrete cosine transforms (DCT) and the Macroblock (MB) structure of an image to suppress the temporal and spatial redundancies incorporated in a sequence of images. These standardized algorithms aimed at establishing an optimal trade-off between the coding efficiency and the perceptual quality of the reconstructed signal. After the release of the first still-image coding standard, namely JPEG [1], CCITT recommended the standardisation of the first video compression algorithm for low-bit rate communications at p × 64 kbit/s over ISDN, namely ITU-T H.261 [2] in 1990. In post 1990s, intensive work has been carried out to develop improved versions of the aforementioned ITU standard, and this has culminated in a number of video coding standards, namely MPEG-1 [3] for audiovisual data storage (1.5-2 Mbit/s) on CD-ROM, MPEG-2 [4] (or ITU-T H.262) for HDTV applications (4–9 Mbit/s), ITU-T H.263 [5] for very low bit rate (<64 kbit/s) communications over PSTN networks, and then the first content-based, object-oriented audiovisual compression algorithm, namely MPEG-4 [6], for multimedia communications over mobile networks in 1998. Recent standardization work resulted in recommending annexes to ITU-T H.263 standard, namely H.263+ [7] and H.263++ [8] for improved coding efficiency, bit rate scaleability, and error resilience performance. ITU-T is currently considering the standardization of H.26L, a new video compression algorithm expected to outperform H.263 at very low bit rate applications. Despite this remarkable evolution of digital video coding technology, the common feature for all the released standards so far is that they all employ the same algorithmic concepts and build on them for further improvement in both quality and coding efficiency. In this chapter section, the fundamental techniques that constitute the core of today's video coders are presented.

## Digital Representation of Raw Video Data

A video signal is a sequence of still images. When played at a high enough rate, the sequence of images (mostly referred to as video frames) gives the impression of an animated video scene. Video frames are captured by a camcorder at a certain sampling rate and processed as a sequence of still pictures correlated by motion dependencies. When adjacent frames are strongly correlated, smaller redundancy is found in the video signal if only the difference between successive frames is encoded. The process of exploiting temporal redundancies between adjacent frames by subtracting the prediction image (sometimes referred to as the motion compensated image) from the original input image and then coding the resulting residual is called INTER frame coding. If no motion prediction was employed in encoding a video frame and only spatial redundancies were exploited to compress a video frame, then the frame is said to be INTRA coded.

Each video frame is a two-dimensional matrix of pixels, each of which is represented by a luminance (intensity) component and two chrominance (color) components $Y$, $U$, and $V$, respectively. In block-based video coders, each frame is divided into groups of blocks (GOB). Each GOB is divided into a number of MBs (macroblock). A MB relates to 16 pixels by 16 lines of luminance $Y$ and the spatially corresponding 8 pixels by 8 lines of chrominance $U$ and $V$. A MB consists of four $Y$-blocks and two spatially corresponding color difference blocks. Figure 42.24 depicts the hierarchical layering structure of a video frame of Quadrature Common Intermediate Format (QCIF) resolution, i.e., 176 pixels by 144 lines.

## Basic Concepts of Block-Based Video Coding Algorithms

Despite their differences, the video coding standards have the same core structure. They all adopt the MB structure as described in the previous section and consist of the same major building blocks. The standard video coding algorithms employ one of the two coding modes, INTRA or INTER. A typical block diagram of a block-based transform video coder is depicted in Fig. 42.25.

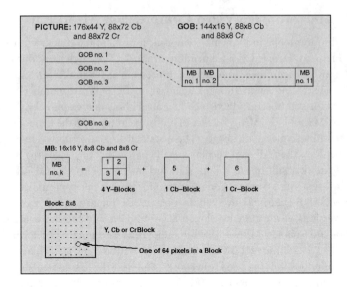

**FIGURE 42.24**   Hierarchical layering structure for a QCIF frame in block-based video coders.

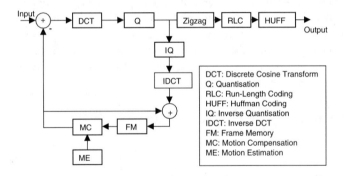

**FIGURE 42.25**   Block diagram of a block-based video coder.

## Discrete Cosine Transforms (DCT)

The 64 coefficients of an 8 × 8 block of data are passed through a DCT transformer. DCT extracts the spatial redundancies of the video block by gathering the biggest portion of its energy in the low frequency components that are located in the top left corner of the block. The transfer function of a two-dimensional DCT transformer employed in a block-based video coder is given in Eq. (42.1) below:

$$F(u,v) = \frac{1}{4}C(u)C(v)\sum_{x=0}^{7}\sum_{y=0}^{7}f(x,y)\cos\left[\pi(2x+1)\frac{u}{16}\right]\cos\left[\pi(2y+1)\frac{v}{16}\right] \qquad (42.1)$$

with $u, v, x, y = 0, 1, 2, \ldots, 7$, where $x$ and $y$ are the spatial coordinates in the pixel domain, $u$ and $v$ are the coordinates in the transform domain

$$C(u) = \frac{1}{\sqrt{2}} \qquad \text{for} \quad u = 0; \text{ 1 otherwise}$$

$$C(v) = \frac{1}{\sqrt{2}} \qquad \text{for} \quad v = 0; \text{ 1 otherwise}$$

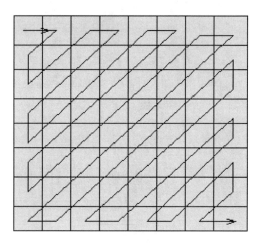

**FIGURE 42.26** Sequence of zigzag-coding coefficients of a quantised 8 × 8 block.

## Quantization

Quantization is a process that maps the symbols representing the DCT transformed coefficients from one set of levels to a narrower one in order to minimise the number of bits required to transmit the symbols. Quantization in block-based coders is a lossy process and thus it has a negative impact on the perceptual quality of the reconstructed video sequence. The quantization parameter (Qp) is a user-defined parameter that determines the level of distortion that affects the video quality due to quantization. The higher the quantization level, Qp, the coarser the quantization process. Quantization uses different techniques based on the coding mode employed (INTRA or INTER), the position of the coefficient in a video block (DC or AC coefficients), and the coding algorithm under consideration.

## Raster Scan Coding

It is also known as zigzag pattern coding. The aim of zigzag coding the 8 × 8 matrix of quantised DCT coefficients is to convert the two-dimensional array into a stream of indices with a high occurrence of successive 0 coefficients. The long runs of zeros will then be efficiently coded as will be shown in the next subsection. The order of a zigzag pattern encoder is depicted in Fig. 42.26.

## Run-Length Coding

The run-length encoder takes the one-dimensional array of quantised coefficients as input and generates coded runs as output. Instead of coding each coefficient separately, the run-length coder searches for runs of similar consecutive coefficients (normally zeros after the DCT and quantisation stages) and codes the length of the run and the preceding nonzero level. A 1-bit flag (LAST) is sent after each run to indicate whether or not the corresponding run is the last one in the current block. Run-lengths and levels are then fed to the Huffman coder to be assigned variable length codewords before transmission on the video channel.

## Huffman Coding

Huffman coding, traditionally referred to as entropy coding, is a variable length coding algorithm that assigns codes to source-generated bit patterns based on their frequency of occurrence within the generated bit stream. The higher the likelihood of a symbol, the smaller the length of the codeword assigned to it and vice versa. Therefore, Entropy coding results in the optimum average codeword size for a given set of runs and levels.

## Motion Estimation and Prediction

For each MB in a currently processed video frame, a sum of absolute differences (SAD) is calculated between its pixels and those of each 16 × 16 matrix of pixels that lie inside a window (in the previous frame) of a user-defined size called the search window. The 16 × 16 matrix, which results in the least

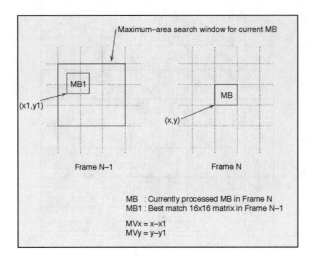

**FIGURE 42.27**    Motion estimation process in a block-based video coder.

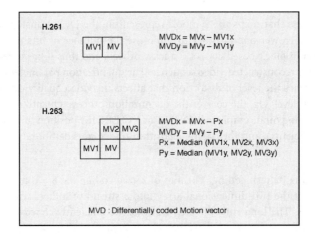

**FIGURE 42.28**    Motion prediction in 2 ITU-T video coding standards.

SAD, is considered to most resemble the current MB and referred to as the "best match." The displacement vector between the currently coded MB and the matrix that spatially corresponds to its best match in the previous frame is called the motion vector (MV) and the relative SAD is called the MB residual matrix. If the smallest SAD is less than a certain threshold then the MB is INTER coded by sending the MV and the DCT coefficients of the residual matrix, otherwise the MB is INTRA coded. The coordinates of the MV are transmitted differentially using the coordinates of one or more MVs corresponding to neighboring MBs (left MB in ITU-T H.261 or left, top, and top right MBs in ITU-T H.263 and ISO MPEG-4) within the same video frame. Figures 42.27 and 42.28 illustrate the motion estimation and prediction processes of contemporary video coding algorithms.

## Subjective and Objective Evaluation of Perceptual Quality

The performance of a video coding algorithm can be simply subjectively evaluated by visually comparing the reconstructed video sequence to the original one. Two major types of subjective methods are used to assess the quality of perceptual video quality. In the first, an overall quality rating is assigned to the image (usually last decoded frame of a sequence). In the second, quality impairment is induced on a standard type image until it is completely similar to the reference image or vice versa.

**FIGURE 42.29** 150th Frame of original: (a) "Suzie" sequence and its compressed version at 64 kbit/s using, (b) H.261, (c) baseline H.263, and (d) Full-option H.263.

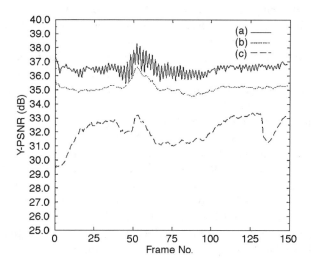

**FIGURE 42.30** PSNR values for Suzie sequence compressed at 64 kbit/s (a) baseline H.263 (b) Full-option H.263 (c) H.261.

Objectively, the video quality is measured by using some mathematical criteria, the most common of which is the peak-to-peak signal-to-noise ratio (PSNR) defined in Eq. (42.2).

$$PSNR = 10 \log_{10} \frac{255^2}{\frac{1}{M \times N} \sum_{i=0}^{M-1} \sum_{j=0}^{N-1} (x(i,j) - \hat{x}(i,j))^2} \qquad (42.2)$$

For a fair comparison of perceptual quality between two video coding algorithms, the objective and subjective results must be evaluated at the same target bit rates. Because the bit rate in kbit/s is directly proportional to the number of frames coded per unit of time, the frame rate (f/s) has also to be mentioned in the evaluation process.

Figures 42.29 and 42.30 show the subjective and objective results, respectively, for coding 150 frames of the sequence "Suzie" at a bit rate of 64 kbit/s and a frame rate of 25 f/s.

## Error Resilience for Mobile Video

Mobile channels are characterised by a high level of hostility resulting from high bit error ratios (BER) and information loss. Because of the bit rate variability and the spatial and temporal predictions, coded video streams are highly sensitive to transmission errors. This error sensitivity can be the reason for an ungraceful degradation of video quality, and hence the total failure of the video communication service. A single bit error could lead to a disastrous damage to perceptual quality. The most damaging effect of errors is that which leads to a loss of synchronisation at the decoder. In this case, the decoder is unable to determine the size of the affected variable-length video parameter and, therefore, drops the stream bits following the position of error until it resynchronises at the next synch word. Consequently, it is vital to employ an error resilience mechanism for the success of the underlying video communication service.

A popular technique used to mitigate the effects of errors is called error concealment [9]. It is a decoder-based zero-redundancy error control scheme whereby the decoder makes use of previously received error-free video data for the reconstruction of the incorrectly decoded video segment. A commonly used approach conceals the effect of errors on a damaged MB by relying on the content of the spatially corresponding MB in the previous frame. In the case where motion data is corrupted, the damaged motion vector can be predicted from the motion vectors of spatially neighboring MBs in the same picture. On the other hand, transform coefficients could also be interpolated from pixels in neighboring blocks.

However, error concealment schemes cannot provide satisfactory results for networks with high BERs and long error bursts. In this case, error concealment must be used in conjunction with error resilience schemes that make the coded streams more robust to transmission errors and video packet loss. In the literature, there are a large number of error resilience techniques specified in the standard ISO MPEG-4 [10] and the annexes to ITU-T H.263 defined in recommendations H.263+ [11] and H.263++ [12]. One of the most effective ways of preventing the propagation of errors in encoded video sequences is the regular insertion of INTRA-coded frames, which do not make use of any information from previously transmitted frames; however, this method has the disadvantage of making the traffic characteristics of a video sequence extremely bursty since a much larger number of bits are required to obtain the same quality levels as for INTER (predictively coded) frames. A more efficient improvement to INTRA-frame refresh consists of regular coding of INTRA MBs per frame, referred to as Adaptive INTRA Refresh (AIR), where the INTRA coded MBs are identified as part of the most active region in the video scene. The insertion of a fixed number of INTRA coded MBs per frame can smooth out the bit rate fluctuations caused by coding the whole frame in INTRA mode. In the following subsections, we present two major standard-compliant error resilience algorithms specified in the MPEG-4 video coding standard, namely data partitioning and two-day decoding with reversible codewords.

### Video Data Partitioning

The non error-resilient syntax of video coding standards suggests that video data is transmitted on a MB basis. In other words, the order of transmission is established such as all the parameters pertaining to a particular MB are sent before any parameter of the following MB is transmitted. This implies that a bit error detected in the texture data of an early MB in the video frame leads to the loss of all forthcoming MBs in the frame. Data partitioning changes the order of transmission of video data from a MB basis to a frame basis or a Visual Object Plane (VOP) basis in MPEG-4 terminology. Each video packet that corresponds to a VOP consists of two different partitions separated by specific bit patterns called markers (DC marker for INTRA coded VOPs and motion marker for INTER coded VOPs). The first partition contains the shape information, motion data, and some administrative parameters such as COD for INTRA frames and MCBPC of all the MBs in the VOP, while the second partition contains the texture data (i.e., the transform coefficients TCOEFF) of all the MBs inside the VOP and other control parameters such as CBPY. Using this partitioning structure as illustrated in Fig. 42.31, the errors that hit the data bits of the second partition do not lead to the loss of the whole frame since the error-sensitive motion data would have been correctly decoded upfront.

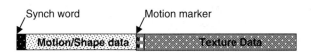

**FIGURE 42.31** Data partitioning for error resilient video communication.

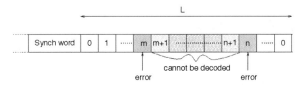

**FIGURE 42.32** One-way decoding of variable-length codes.

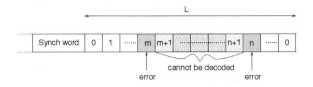

**FIGURE 42.33** Two-way decoding of variable-length codes.

### Two-Way Decoding and Reversible Variable-Length Codewords

Two-way decoding is used with reversible VLC words in order to reduce the size of the damaged area in a video bit stream. This error resilience technique enables the video decoder to reconstruct a part of the stream that would have been skipped in the ordinary one-way decoding due to loss of synchronisation. This is achieved by allowing the decoding of the variable-length codewords of the video bit stream in the reverse direction. The reversible codewords are symbols that could be decoded in both the forward and reverse directions. An example of reversible VLCs is a set of codewords where each one of them consists of the same number of the starting symbol, either 1 or 0. For instance, the set of variable-length codewords that is defined by 0100, 11001, 10101, 01010, 10011, 0010, consists of codewords that contain three 1s or 0s each, where the 1 or 0 is the starting symbol, respectively.

In conventional one-way decoding, the decoder loses synchronisation upon detection of a bit error. This is mainly due to the variable rate nature of compressed video streams and the variable-length Huffman codes assigned to various symbols that represent the video parameters. In order to restore its synchronisation, the decoder skips all the data bits following the position of errors until it falls on the first error-free synch word in the stream. The skipped bits are then discarded, regardless of their correctness, resulting in an effective error ratio that is larger than the channel BER by orders of magnitude. The response of the one-way video decoder to a bit error is depicted in Fig. 42.32.

With two-way decoding, a part of the skipped segment of bits can be recovered by enabling decoding in the reverse direction as shown in Fig. 42.33. Upon detection of a bit error, the decoder stops its operation searching for the next synch word in the bit stream. Upon gaining synchronization at the synch word, the decoder resumes its operation in the backward direction thereby rescuing the part of the bit stream, which has been discarded in the forward direction. If no error is detected in the reverse direction then the damaged area is confined to the MB where the bit error has been detected in the forward direction. If an error has also been flagged up in the backward direction, then the segment of bits between the positions of error in both the forward and backward directions is discarded as the error damaged area as shown in Fig. 42.33.

In many cases, a combination of error resilience techniques is used to further enhance the error robustness of compressed video streams to transmission errors of mobile environments. For instance, both data partitioning and two-way decoding can be jointly employed to protect the error-sensitive motion data of the first video partition. The motion vectors and the administrative parameters contained in the first partition are all coded with reversible VLC words. The detection of a bit error in the forward direction triggers the decoder to stop its operation, regain synchronisation at the motion marker separating the two partitions in the corresponding VOP, and then decode backwards to salvage some of the correctly received bits that were initially skipped in the forward direction.

## New Generation Mobile Networks

Packet-switched mobile access networks such as GPRS [13] and EGPRS [14] are intended to give sub-scribers access to a variety of mobile multimedia services that run on different networking platforms, let it be the core mobile network, i.e., UMTS, ATM, or even Internet. The packet-switched mobile access networks have a basic common feature in that they are all IP-based and allow time multi-slotting on a given radio interface. The multi-slotting capabilities enable the underlying networking platform to accom-modate higher bit rates by providing the end-user with a larger physical layer capacity.

The real-time interactive and conversational services are very much delay-critical, so the provision of these services over mobile networks can only be achieved by using a service class capable of guaranteeing the delay constraints with one-delays in the order of 200 msec being required. In order to achieve such delay requirements, it is necessary to avoid using any retransmissions or repeat-requests scenarios by oper-ating the RLC layer of the GPRS protocol stack in the unacknowledged mode of operations. Similarly, the transport layer protocol that must be employed is the user datagram protocol (UDP), which operates over IP and does not make use of any repeat-request system.

IP networks do not guarantee the delivery of packets and neither do they provide any mechanism to guarantee the orderly arrival of packets. This implies that not only does the inter-packet arrival time vary but it is also likely that packets may arrive out of order. Therefore, in order to transmit real-time video information, some transport-layer functionality must be overlaid on the network layer to provide timing information from which streaming video may be reconstructed. To offer this end-to-end network trans-port functionality, the IETF real-time transport protocol (RTP) [15] is used. RTP fulfills functions such as payload type identification, sequence numbering, timestamping, and delivery monitoring, and operates on top of IP and UDP for the provision of real-time services and video applications over the IP-based mobile networks.

On the other hand, the mobile access networks employ channel protection schemes that provide error control capabilities against multipath fading and channel interferers. For instance, GPRS employs four channel protection schemes (CS-1 to CS-4), offering flexibility in the degree of protection and data traffic capacity available to the user. Varying the channel coding scheme allows for an optimization of the through-put across the radio interface as the channel quality varies. The data rates provided by GPRS with the channel coding schemes enabled are 8 kbit/s for CS-1, 12.35 kbit/s for CS-2, 14.55 kbit/s for CS-3, and 20.35 kbit/s for CS-4; however, almost 15% of the bits in the payload of a radio block are used up by header information belonging to the overlying protocols. Therefore, the rates presented to the video source for each one of the channel coding schemes per time slot are 6.8 kbit/s for CS-1, 10.5 kbit/s for CS-2, 12.2 kbit/s for CS-3, and 17.2 kbit/s for CS-4. It is, however, envisaged that the CS-1 and CS-2 schemes will be used for video applications. Obviously, the available throughput to a single terminal will be multiples of the given rates per slot, depending upon the multi-slotting capabilities of the terminal. Conversely, EGPRS provides 9 channel coding schemes of different protection rates and capabilities and the choice of a suitable scheme is again a trade-off between the throughput and the error protection potential.

## Provision of Video Services over Mobile Networks

Taking into perspective the traffic characteristics of a coded video source employing a fixed quantiser, we observe that the output bit rate is highly variable with high peaks taking place each time an INTRA-coded frame is transmitted. INTRA frames require roughly three times on average the bandwidth required for transmitting a predictively coded frame. Therefore, if the frequency of INTRA frames is increased for error control purposes as discussed in the subsection on "Error Resilience for Mobile Video," the encoder will have to discard a number of frames following each INTRA coded frame until some bandwidth becomes available. Despite the fact that a fixed quantiser leads to a constant spatial quality, yet the frequent insertion of INTRA frames in the video sequence has a degrading effect on the temporal quality of the entire video sequence. In order to preventively cure this situation, it is advisable that a rate control mechanism be employed at the video encoder before the coded video bit stream is sent over the mobile channel. One method is to vary the used quantiser value in order to truncate the high-frequency DCT coefficients in accordance with the target bit rate of the video coder and the number of bits available to code a particular frame, VOP or MB. Coding an INTRA frame with a coarse quantiser results in a poor spatial quality but helps improve the temporal quality of the video sequence by maintaining the original frame rate and reducing the jittering effect caused by the disparity in size between INTRA and INTER coded frames.

The video delivery over mobile channels can take the form of real-time delay-sensitive conversational services, delay-critical (on-demand or live) streaming services, or delay-insensitive multimedia messaging applications. The latter requires guarantee on the error-free delivery of intended messages without placing any stipulation on the duration of transmission and therefore allows retransmissions of erroneous messages to take place. The former two categories of video services, however, are rather more delay-critical and necessitate the use of both application and transport layer end-to-end error control schemes for the robust transmission of compressed video in mobile environments.

The analysis of the GPRS protocol efficiency shows that a reduction of 15% in the data rate per time slot, as seen by the video encoder, is enough to compensate for all the protocol overheads. The video quality that can be achieved in video communications over the new generation mobile networks, is a function of the time slot/coding-scheme combination and the channel conditions during the time of video packet transmission. It is observed that in error-free conditions, CS-1 yields a sub-optimal quality due to the large overhead it places on the available bandwidth of each time slot; however, in error-prone conditions and for C/I ratios lower than 15 dB, CS-1 presents the best error protection capabilities and offers the best video quality as compared to other channel coding schemes. When eight time slots are used with CS-1, GPRS can offer a video payload data rate of 54.4 kbit/s. At this rate, it has been demonstrated that QCIF-resolution conversational MPEG-4 video services can be offered over GPRS for a frame rate of 10 f/s with fairly good perceptual quality, especially when frequency hopping is used; however, for highly detailed scenes involving a high amount of motion, the error-free video quality at high C/I ratios suffers both spatially and temporally because of the coarse quantiser used and the jitter resulting from the large number of discarded frames respectively. The error protection schemes of the GPRS protocol are used in conjunction with the application-layer error resilience techniques specified by the MPEG-4 video compression standard. Figure 42.34 shows the subjective video quality achieved

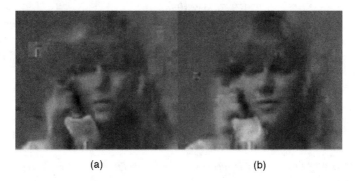

(a)　　　　　　　　　　　(b)

**FIGURE 42.34** One frame of Suzie sequence encoded with MPEG-4 at 18 kbit/s and transmitted over a GPRS channel with C/I = 15 dB, with CS-1 and 4 time-slots used: (a) no error resilience and (b) AIR.

by transmitting an MPEG-4 coded video sequence (at 18 kbit/s) over a GPRS channel with and without error resilience (AIR) when CS-1 and four time slots are used.

On the other hand, video services on EGPRS are less likely to encounter the same problems posed by the lack of bandwidth in the GPRS networks. When EGPRS employs the channel coding scheme MCS-9, the terminal can be offered a data rate of 402.4 kbit/s when 8 time slots are employed. Obviously, at this data rate, there exists a much higher flexibility in selecting the operating picture resolution and the video content intended for transmission over the mobile network.

## Conclusions

The provision of video services over the new generation mobile networks is made possible through the enabling technologies supported by the error protection schemes and the multi-slotting capabilities of the radio interface. Conversational video applications are delay-sensitive and thus do not support retransmissions of corrupted video data. To provide a user-acceptable video quality, the video application must employ an error resilience mechanism in conjunction with the physical layer channel coding schemes. A wide range of error resilience techniques have been developed in recent video compression algorithms and their annexed versions. The use of error resilience techniques for supporting the provision of video services over mobile networks helps enhance the perceptual quality, especially at times where the mobile channel is suffering from low C/I ratios resulting from high BERs and radio block loss ratios.

## References

1. ISO/IEC JTC1 10918 & ITU-T Rec. T.81: *Information Technology—Digital Compression and coding of continuous-tone still images: Requirements and guidelines,* 1994.
2. CCITT Recommendation H.261: *Video Codec for audiovisual services at p × 64 kbit/s,* COM XV-R 37-E, 1990.
3. ISO/IEC CD 11172: *Coding of moving pictures and associated audio for digital storage media at 1.5 Mbit/s,* December 1991.
4. ISO/IEC CD 13818-2: *Generic coding of moving pictures and associated audio,* November 1993.
5. Draft ITU-T Recommendation H.263: *Video coding for low bit rate communication,* May 1996.
6. ISO/IEC JTC1/SC29/WG11N2802: *Information technology—Generic coding of audiovisual objects—Part 2: Visual,* ISO/IEC 14496-2, MPEG Vancouver meeting, July 1999.
7. Draft ITU-T Recommendation H.263 Version 2 (H.263+): *Video coding for low bit rate communications,* January 1998.
8. Rapporteur for Q.15/16—*Draft for H.263++, Annexes U, V and W to Recommendation H.263,* ITU Telecommunication Standardisation Sector, November 2000.
9. Y. Wang, and Q. F. Zhu, "Error control and concealment for video communication: a review," *Proc. of the IEEE,* Vol. 86, No. 5, pp. 974–997, May 1998.
10. R. Talluri, "Error resilient video coding in the MPEG-4 standard," *IEEE Communications Magazine,* pp. 112–119, June 1998.
11. S. Wenger, G. Knorr, J. Ott, and F. Kossentini, "Error Resilience Support in H.263+," *IEEE Transaction on Circuit and Systems for Video Technology,* Vol. 8, No. 7, Nov. 1998.
12. G. Sullivan, "*Rapporteur for Q.15/16—Draft for H.263++, Annexes U, V and W to Recommendation H.263,*" ITU Telecommunication Standardisation Sector, November 2000.
13. Digital Cellular Telecommunications System (Phase 2+), "*General Packet Radio Service (GPRS); Overall description of the GPRS Radio Interface; Stage 2,*" ETSI/SMG, GSM 03.64, V. 5.2.0, January 1998.
14. Tdoc SMG2 086/00, "*Outcome of Drafting Group on MS EGPRS Rx Performance,*" EDGE Drafting Group, January 2000.
15. H. Schulzrinne, S. Casner, R. Frederick, and V. Jacobson, "*RTP: A Transport Protocol for Real-Time Applications,*" RFC1889, January 1996.

# 42.6   Pen-Based User Interfaces—An Applications Overview

*Giovanni Seni and Jayashree Subrahmonia*

## Introduction

A critical feature of any computer system is its interface with the user. This has led to the development of user interface technologies such as mouse, touch-screen, and pen-based input devices. They all offer significant flexibility and options for computer input; however, touch-screens and mice cannot take full advantage of human fine motor control, and their use is mostly restricted to data "selection," i.e., as pointing devices. On the other hand, pen-based interfaces allow, in addition to the pointing capabilities, for other forms of input such as handwriting, gestures, and drawings. Because handwriting is one of the most familiar communication media, pen-based interfaces appear to offer a very easy and natural input method.

A pen-based interface consists of a transducer device and a fine-tipped stylus so that the movement of the stylus is captured; such information is usually given as a time ordered sequence of *x-y* coordinates (*digital ink*) and an indication of "inking," i.e., whether the pen is up or down. Digital ink can be passed on to recognition software that will convert the pen input into appropriate computer actions. Alternatively, the handwritten input can be organized into ink documents, notes, or messages that can be stored for later retrieval or exchanged through telecommunications means. Such ink documents are appealing because they capture information as the user composed it, including text in any mix of languages and drawings such as equations and graphs.

Pen-based interfaces are desirable in mobile computing (e.g., Personal Information Appliances—PIAs) because they are scalable. Only small reductions in size can be made to keyboards before they become awkward to use; however, if they are not shrunk in size, they lose their portability. This is even more problematic as mobile devices develop into multimedia terminals with numerous functions ranging from agenda and address book to wireless web browser. Voice-based interfaces may appear to be a solution, but they entail all the problems that mobile phones already have introduced in terms of disturbing bystanders and loss of privacy. Furthermore, using voice commands to control applications such as a web browser can be difficult and tedious; by contrast, clicking on a link with a pen, or entering a short text by writing, is very natural and takes place in silence.

Recent hardware advances in alternative ink capture devices based on ultrasonic and optical tracking technologies have also contributed to the renewed interest in pen-based systems. These technologies avoid the need for pad electronics, thus reducing the cost and weight of a pen-enabled system. Furthermore, they can sometimes be retrofited to existing writing surfaces such as whiteboards [4] or used with plain paper [5].

Section 42.6 reviews a number of applications, old and new, where the pen can be used as a very convenient and natural form of input. Our emphasis will be on the user experience, highlighting limitations of existing solutions and suggesting ways of improving them. We start with a short review of currently available pen input hardware in the subsection on "Pen Input Hardware." We then, in "Handwriting Recognition," discuss handwriting recognition user interfaces for mobile devices and the need for making applications aware of the handwriting recognition process. In "Ink and the Internet" we present Internet related applications such as ink messaging. In "Extension of Pen-and-Paper Metaphor" we discuss functionality that extends the traditional pen and paper metaphor. Finally, in "Pen Input and Multimodal Systems," we present examples of synergistic interfaces that are being developed combining the pen with other input modalities.

## Pen Input Hardware

The function of the pen input hardware is to convert pen tip position over time into X,Y coordinates at a sufficient temporal and spatial resolution for handwriting recognition and visual presentation [25].

A pen input system consists of a combination of pen, pad, and in some cases, paper. Not all pen systems have a paper interface for capturing the position of the pen-tip. Examples of these include PIAs and some electronic tablets. Some of these have a glass surface on the pad that is the interface to capture and display ink. Others (like the electronic tablets) have an input device that is separate from the display. Although these are usable for small quantities of input and for navigating through applications using touch-selection, they are extremely difficult from a usability standpoint for entering large quantities of digital ink. Paper-based systems provide the best user interface for inputting digital ink and hence are the best user interface for large note-taking applications. They are also the highest resolution displays for ink available today and do not suffer from issues like tolerance to glare that glass surfaces do.

In systems that use paper, an additional challenge that needs to be addressed comes from the fact that pen tip contact with paper also needs to be sensed to establish when ink is deposited on paper.

Pen hardware platforms available today use one of the following four kinds of technologies:

**Magnetic Tracking** Here, sequentially energized coils embedded in the pad couple a magnetic field into a pen tank circuit (coil and capacitor). Neighboring coils pick up the magnetic field from the pen, and their relative strength determines pen location [22]. The magnetic field can also be generated in the pen, requiring a battery that increases pen weight and thickness [23].

**Electric Tracking** Here, the conductive properties of a hand and normal pen can be used for tracking [24]. A transmitter electrode in the pad couples a small displacement current through the paper to the hand, down through the pen, and back through the paper to an array of receiver electrodes. Pen location is calculated as the "center of mass" of the received signal strengths.

**Ultrasonic Tracking** Ultrasonic tracking is based on the relatively slow speed of sound in air (330 m/ sec). A pen generates a burst of acoustic energy. Electronics in the pad measure the time of arrival to two stationary ultrasonic receivers [4,5]. The ultrasonic transmission is either synchronized to the pad, typically with an infrared signal, or a third ultrasonic receiver is used [26].

**Optical Tracking Technology** Optical tracking systems can either provide relative tracking (like a mouse) or absolute position tracking (like a touch screen) [28,29].

Bar codes printed over an entire page can provide absolute position using a tiny camera mounted in a pen [30,31]. The bar codes can also encode page number, eliminating overwrites when a person forgets to tell the digitizer they have changed pages (a challenge that pen hardware systems with paper interfaces have to address). Another approach captures a sequence of small images of handwriting and assembles them to reconstruct the entire page [32].

### Discussion of Input Hardware

Magnetic tracking is the widest deployed system due to high spatial resolution (>1000 dpi), acceptable temporal resolution (>100 Hz), reliability, and modest cost [33].

Magnetic and electric tracking require pad electronics and shielding, making them thicker and heavier than a conventional clipboard. Electric tracking uses a normal pen but has no direct way to measure pen tip contact, and must rely on less reliable pen trajectory analysis [34].

Ultrasonic tracking does not require pad electronics, making it lower cost and weight. Relative tracking can reach 256 dpi, but absolute spatial resolution is limited to about 50 dpi due to air currents that cause Doppler shifts.

Optical tracking offers the highest spatial (>2000 dpi) and temporal (>200 Hz) resolution, and can utilize a self-contained pen that remembers everything written. Special bar code paper provides absolute position and page tracking. Optical methods based on CMOS technology lend themselves to low-power, low-cost, and highly integrated designs. These features suggest that optical tracking will play a significant role in future pen systems.

## Handwriting Recognition

Handwriting is a very well-developed skill that humans have used for over 5,000 years as means of communicating and recording information. With the widespread acceptance of computers, the future role of handwriting in our culture might seem questionable. However, as we discussed in introduction

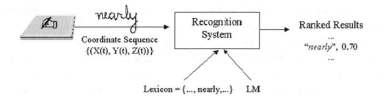

**FIGURE 42.35** The handwriting recognition problem. The image of a handwritten character, word, or phrase is classified as one of the symbols, or symbol strings, from a known list. Some systems use knowledge about the language in the form of dictionaries (or Lexicons) and frequency information (i.e., Language Models) to aid the recognition process. Typically, a score is associated with each recognition result.

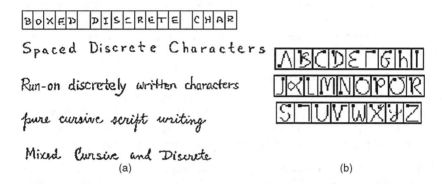

(a)                            (b)

**FIGURE 42.36** Different handwriting styles. In (a), Latin characters are used, from top to bottom, according to the presumed difficulty in recognition (adapted from Tappert,1984). In (b), the *Graffiti*™ unistroke (i.e., written with a single pen trace) alphabet which restricts characters to a unique pre-specified way that simplifies automatic recognition, the square dot indicates starting position of the pen.

section, a number of applications exist where the pen can be more convenient than a keyboard. This is particularly so in the mobile computing space where keyboards are not ergonomically feasible.

Handwriting recognition is fundamentally a pattern classification task; the objective is to take an input graphical mark, the handwritten signal collected via a digitizing device, and classify it as one of a pre-specified set of symbols. These symbols correspond to the characters or words in a given language encoded in a computerized representation such as ASCII (see Fig. 42.35). In this field, the term *online* has been used to refer to systems devised for the recognition of patterns captured with digitizing devices that preserve the pen trajectory; the term *offline* refers to techniques, which instead take as input a static two-dimensional image representation, usually acquired by means of a scanner.

Handwriting recognition systems can be further grouped according to the constraints they impose on the user with respect to writing style (see Fig. 42.36(a)). The more restricted the allowed handwritten input is, the easier the recognition task and the lower the required computational resources. At the highest restricted end of the spectrum, *boxed-discrete* style, users write one character at a time within predefined areas; this removes one difficult step, segmentation, from the recognition process. Very high levels of recognition accuracy can be achieved by requiring users to adhere to rules that restrict character shapes so as to minimize letter similarity (see Fig. 42.36(b)). Of course, such techniques require users to learn a "new" alphabet. At the least restricted end of the spectrum, *mixed* style, users are allowed to write words or phrases the same way they do on paper—in their own personal style—whether they print, write in cursive, or use a mixture of the two.

Recognition of mixed-style handwriting is a difficult task due to ambiguity in segmentation (partitioning the word into letters), and large variation at the letter level. Segmentation is complex because it is often possible to wrongly break up letters into parts that are in turn meaningful (e.g., the cursive letter "d" can be subdivided into letters "c" and "l"). Variability in letter shape is mostly due to *co-articulation* (the influence of one letter on another), and the presence of ligatures, which frequently give rise to unintended ("spurious") letters being detected in the script.

In addition to the writing style constraints, the complexity of the recognition task is also determined by *dictionary-size* and *writer-adaptation* requirements. The size of dictionary can vary from very small (for tasks such as state name recognition) to open (for tasks like proper name recognition). In open vocabulary recognition, any sequence of letters is a plausible recognition result and this is the most difficult scenario for a recognizer. In the writer-adaptation dimension, systems capable of out-of-the box recognition are called writer-independent, i.e., they can recognize the writing of many writers; this gives a good average performance across different writing styles; however, there is considerable improvement in recognition accuracy that can be obtained by customizing the letter models of the system to a writer's specific writing style. Recognition in this case is called writer-dependent.

Despite these challenges, significant progress has been made in the building of writer-independent systems capable of handling unconstrained text and using dictionary sizes of over 20,000 words [1,2,3]. Some of these systems are now commercially available. For a comprehensive survey of the basic concepts behind written language recognition algorithms see [14,21,37].

### User Interfaces on Mobile Devices

In Fig. 42.37, examples of user interfaces for handwritten text input are presented that are representative of those found on today's mobile devices. Because of the limited CPU and memory resources available on these platforms, handwritten input is restricted to the boxed-discrete style.

Additional highlights of the user interface on these text input methods are:

**Special Input Area.** Users are not allowed the fredom of writing anywhere on the screen. Instead, there is an area of the screen specially designated for the handwriting user interface, whether for text input or control. This design choice offers the following advantages:

(a)        (b)

**FIGURE 42.37** Character-based text input method on today's mobile devices. In (a), user interface for English character input on a cellular phone. In (b), user interface for Chinese character input on a 2-way pager.

- *No toggling between edit/control and ink mode.* Pen input inside the input method area is treated as ink to be recognized by the recognizer; pen input outside this area is treated as mouse events, e.g., selection, etc. Without this separation, special provisions, sometimes unnatural, have to be taken to distinguish among the two pen modes.

- *Better user control.* Within the specially designated writing window it is possible to have additional GUI elements that help the user with the input task. For instance, there might be buttons for common edit keys such as backspace, newline, and delete. Similarly, a list of recognition alternates can be easily displayed and selected from. This is particularly important because *top-n* recognition accuracy—a measure of how often the correct answer is among the highest ranked *n* results, is generally much higher than *top-1* accuracy.

- *Consistent UI metaphor.* Despite its ergonomic limitations, an on-screen keyboard is generally available as one of the text input methods on the device. Using a special input area for handwriting makes the user interface of alternative text entry methods similar.

**Modal Input.** The possibilities of the user's input are selectively limited in order to increase recognition accuracy. Common modes include "digits," "symbols," "upper-case letters," and "lower-case letters" in English, or "traditional" versus "simplified" in Chinese. By limiting the number of characters against which a given input ink is matched, the opportunities for confusion and mis-recognition are decreased, and recognition accuracy is improved. Writing modes represent another tradeoff between making life simpler for the system or simpler for the user.

**Natural Character Set.** It is possible to use any character writing style commonly used in the given language, no need to learn a special alphabet. Characters can be *multi-stroke*, i.e., written with more than one pen trace.

**Multi-boxed Input.** When multi-stoke input is allowed, end of writing is generally detected by use of a timer that is set after each stroke is completed; the input is deemed concluded if a set amount of time elapses before any more input is received in the writing area. This "timeout" scheme is sometimes confusing to users. Multiple boxes give better performance because a character in one box can be concluded if input is received in another, removing the need to wait for the timer to finish.

Of all the restrictions imposed on users by these character-based input methods, modality is the one where user feedback has been strongest: people want *modeless* input. The challenge lies in that distinguishing between letters which have very similar forms across modes is virtually impossible without additional information. In English orthography, for instance, there are letters for which the lower case version of the character is merely a smaller version of the upper case version; examples include "Cc," "Kk," "Mm," "Oo," "Ss," "Uu," "Ww," etc. Simple attempts at building modeless character recognizers can result in a disconcerting user experience because upper case letters, or digits, might appear inserted into the middle of lower case words. Such m1Xed CaSe w0rdS (mixed case words) look to users to be gibberish.

In usability studies, the authors have further found that as the text data entry needs on wireless PIA devices shifts from short address book or calendar items to longer notes or e-mail messages, users deem writing one letter at a time to be inconvenient and unnatural.

## More Natural User Interfaces

One known way of dealing with the character confusion difficulties described in section "User Interfaces on Mobile Devices" is to use contextual information in the recognition process. At the simplest level this means recognizing characters in the context of their surrounding characters and taking advantage of visual clues derived from word shape. At a higher level, contextual knowledge can be in the form of lexical constraints, e.g., a dictionary of known words in the language is used to restrict interpretations of the input ink. These ideas naturally lead to the notion of a *word-based* text input method. By "word" we mean a string of characters which, if printed in text using normal conventions, would be surrounded by white-space characters (see Fig. 42.38(a)).

**FIGURE 42.38**   Word-based text input method for mobile devices. In (a), a user interface prototype. In (b), an image of the mixed-case word "Wow," where relative size information can be used for distinguishing among the letters in the "Ww" pair. In (c), an image of the digit string "90187" where ambiguity in the identity of the first three letters can be resolved after identifying the last two letters as digits.

Consider the notion of a *mixed-case* word recognition context where the size and position of a character, relative to other characters in the word, is taken into account during letter identification (see Fig. 42.38(b)). Such additional information would allow us to disambiguate between the lower case and upper case version of letters that otherwise are very much alike. Similarly, Fig. 42.38(b) illustrates that relative position within the word would enable us to correctly identify trailing punctuation marks such as periods and commas. A different kind of contextual information can be used to enforce some notion of "consistency" among the characters within a word. For instance, we could have a *digit-string* recognition context that favors word hypotheses where all the characters can be viewed as digits; in the image example of Fig. 42.38(c), the recognizer would thus rank string "90187" higher than string "gol87."

In addition to the modeless input enabled by a word-based input method, there is a writing throughput advantage over character-based ones. In Fig. 42.39 we show the results of a timing experiment where eight users where asked to transcribe a 42-word paragraph using our implementation of both kinds of input methods on a keyboardless PIA device. The paragraph was derived from a newspaper story and contained mixed-case words and a few digits, symbols, and punctuation marks. The length of the text was assumed to be representative of a long message that users might want to compose on such devices. For comparison purposes, users were also timed with a standard on-screen (software) keyboard. Each timing experiment was repeated three times. The median times were 158, 185, and 220 s for the keyboard, word-based, and character-based input methods, respectively. Thus, entering text with the word-based input method was, on average, faster than using the character-based method.

Our current implementation of the word-based input method does not have, on average, a time advantage over the soft keyboard; however, the user who was fastest with the word-based input method (presumably someone for whom the recognition accuracy was very high and thus had few corrections to do) was able to complete the task in 141 s, which is below the median soft keyboard time.

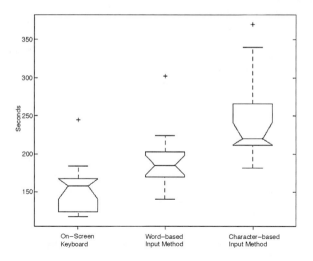

**FIGURE 42.39** Boxplots of time to enter a 42-word message using three different text input methods on a PIA device: an on-screen QWERTY keyboard, a word-based handwriting recognizer and a character-based handwriting recognizer. Median writing throughput were 15.9, 13.6, and 11.4 words-per-minute respectively.

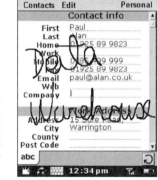

**FIGURE 42.40** Write-anywhere text input method for mobile devices. Example of an Address Book application with the *Company* field appearing with focus. Hand written input is not restricted to a delimited area of the screen but rather can occur anywhere. The company name "Data Warehouse" has been written.

Furthermore, the authors believe that the time gap between these two input methods will be reduced in the case of European languages that have accents, since they require additional key presses in the case of the soft keyboard.

As one can expect, the modeless and time advantage of a word-based input method over a character-based one comes at the expense of additional computational resources. Currently, the word-based recognition engine requires a 10× increment in MIPS and memory resources compared to the character-based engine. One should also say that, as evidenced by the range of the timing data shown in the above plots, there isn't a single input method that works best for every user. It is thus important to offer users a variety of input methods to experiment with and choose from.

### Write-Anywhere Interfaces

In the same way that writing words, as opposed to writing one letter at a time, constitutes an improvement in terms of "naturalness" of the user experience, we must explore recognition systems capable of handling continuous handwriting such as phrases. For the kind of mobile devices we've been considering, with very limited screen real estate, this idea leads to the notion of a "write-anywhere" interface where the user is allowed to write anywhere on the screen, i.e., on top of any application and system element on the screen (see Fig. 42.40).

|       |       |
|-------|-------|
| clog  | dog   |
| log   | dug   |
| lug   | lag   |
| clay  | *clug* |
| *clcrj* | *doij* |

(a)                              (b)

**FIGURE 42.41**  Inherent ambiguity in continuous handwriting recognition. In (a), a sample image of a handwritten word. In (b), possible recognition results, strings not in the English lexicon are in italics.

A write-anywhere text input method is also appealing because there is no special inking area covering up part of the application in the foreground; however, a special mechanism is needed to distinguish pen movement events intended to manipulate user interface elements such as buttons, scrollbars, and menus (i.e., edit/control mode) and pen events corresponding to longhand (i.e., ink mode). The solution typically involves a "tap and hold" scheme wherein the pen has to be maintained down without dragging it for a certain amount of time in order to get the stylus to act temporarily as a mouse.

An additional user interface issue with a write-anywhere text input paradigm is that there are usually no input method control elements visible anywhere on the screen. For instance, access to recognition alternates might require a special pen gesture. As such, a write-anywhere interface will generally have more appeal to advanced users. Furthermore, recognition in the write-anywhere case is more difficult because there is no implicit information on the word separation, orientation, or size of the text.

### Recognition-Aware Applications

Earlier in this section, the authors discussed how factors such as segmentation ambiguity, letter co-articulation, and ligatures make exact recognition of continuous handwritten input a very difficult task. To illustrate this point consider the image shown in Fig. 42.41 and the set of plausible interpretations given for it. Can we choose with certainty one of these recognition results as the "correct" one? Clearly, additional information, not contained within the image, is required to make such a selection. One such source of information that we have already mentioned is the dictionary, or lexicon, for constraining the letter strings generated by the recognizer. At a higher-level, information from the surrounding words can be used to decide, for example, among a verb and a noun word possibility. It is safe to say that the more constraints that are explicitly available during the recognition process the more ambiguity in the input that can be automatically resolved. Less ambiguity results in higher recognition accuracy and thus, improved user experience.

For many common applications in PIA devices, e.g., contacts, agenda, and web browser, it is possible to specify the words and patterns of words that can be entered in certain data fields. Examples of structured data fields are telephone numbers, zip codes, city names, dates, times, URLs, etc. In order for recognition-based input methods to take advantage of this kind of contextual information, the existing text input framework on PIA devices needs to be modified. Currently, no differentiation is made between text input made by tapping the "keyboard" and that of using handwriting recognition; i.e., applications are, for the most part, not aware of the recognition process. A possible improvement over the current state of the art for UI implementation would be for applications to make an encoding of the contextual constraints associated with a given field available to the recognition engine.

One typically uses a *grammar* to define the permitted strings in a language, e.g., the language of valid telephone numbers. A grammar consists of a set of rules or productions specifying the sequences of characters or lexical items forming allowable strings in the defined language. Two common classes of grammars are BNF grammar or context-free grammar and regular grammar (see [6] for a formal treatment). Grammars are widely used in the field of speech recognition and recently the W3C Voice

```
<rule id = "digits0-9" scope="private">    <rule id = "suffix" scope="private">
  <one-of>                                   <count number = "4">
    <item>0</item>                             <ruleref uri="#digit0-9"/>
    ...                                      </count>
    <item>9</item>                         </rule>
  </one-of>
</rule>
<rule-id = "area-code" scope="private">
  <token>(</token>                         <!-- Main rule -->
  <count number = "3">                     <rule id = "phone-num" scope="public">
    <ruleref uri="#digit0-9"/>               <count number = "0-1">
  </count>                                     <ruleref uri="#area-code"/>
  <token>)</token>                           </count>
</rule>                                      <ruleref uri="#prefix"/>
<rule id = "prefix" scope="private">        <count number = "0-1">
  <count number = "3">                         <token>-</token>
    <ruleref uri="#digit0-9"/>               </count>
  </count>                                    <ruleref uri="#suffix"/>
</rule>                                      </rule>
```

**FIGURE 42.42**  Example of an XML grammar defining telephone numbers and written as per the W3C Voice Working Group Specification. There are four "private" rule definitions that are combined to make the main rule called *phone-num*.

Browser Working Group has suggested an XML-based syntax for representing BNF-like grammars [7]. In Fig. 42.42 we show a fragment of a possible grammar for defining telephone number strings. In the extended text input framework that we are advocating, this grammar, together with the handwritten ink, should be passed along to the recognition engine when an application knows that the user is expected to enter a telephone number.

Information about how the ink was collected, such as resolution and sampling rate of the capture device, whether writing guidelines or other writing size hints were used, spatial relationships to nearby objects in the application interface, etc., should also be made available to the recognition engine for improved recognition accuracy.

## Ink and the Internet

Digital ink does not always need to be recognized in order for it to be useful. Two daily life applications where users take full advantage of the range of graphical representations that are possible with a pen are *messaging*, as when we leave someone a post-it note with a handwritten message, and *annotation*, as when we circle some text in a printed paragraph or make a mark in an image inside of a document. This subsection discusses Internet-related applications that will enable similar functionality. Both applications draw attention to the need for a standard representation of digital ink that is appropriate in terms of efficiency, robustness, and quality.

### Ink Messaging

Two-way transmission of digital ink, possibly wireless, offers PIA users a compelling new way to communicate. Users can draw or write with a stylus on the PIA's screen to compose a note in their own handwriting. Such an ink note can then be addressed and delivered to other PIA users, e-mail users, or fax machines. The recipient views the message as the sender composed it, including text in any mix of languages and drawings (see Fig. 42.43).

In the context of mobile-data communications it is important for the size of such ink messages to be small. There are two distinct modes for coding digital ink: raster scanning and curve tracing [8,9]. Facsimile coding algorithms belong to the first mode, and exploit the correlations within consecutive scan lines. Chain Coding (CC), belonging to the second mode, represents the pen trajectory as a sequence of transitions between successive points in a regular lattice. It is known that curve tracing algorithms result in a higher coding efficiency if the total trace length is not too long. Furthermore, use of a raster-base technique implies the loss of all time-dependent information.

**FIGURE 42.43**  Example of ink messaging application for mobile devices. Users can draw or write with a stylus on the device screen to compose an e-mail in their own handwriting; no automatic recognition is necessarily involved.

Message sizes of about 500 bytes have been recently reported for messages composed in a typical PIA screen size, using a CC-based algorithm known as multi-ring differential chain coding (MRDCC) [10]. MRDCC is attractive for transmission of ink messages in terms of data syntax, decoding simplicity, and transmission error control; however, MRDCC is lossy, i.e., the original pen trajectory cannot be fully recovered. If exact reconstructability is important, a lossless compression technique is required. This might be the case when the message recipient might need to run verification or recognition algorithms on the received ink, e.g., if the ink in the message corresponds to a signature that is to be used for computer authentication. One example of a lossless curve tracing algorithm proposed by the ITU is *zone coding* [11]. Our internal evaluation of zone coding, however, reveals there is ample room for improvement.

Additional requirements for an ink messaging application include support for embedded ASCII text, support for embedded basic shapes (such as rectangles, circles, and lines), and support for different pen-trace attributes (such as color and thickness).

### Ink and SMIL

SMIL, pronounced smile, stands for synchronized multimedia integration language. It is a W3C recommendation ([12]) defining an XML compliant language that allows a spatially and temporally synchronized description of multimedia presentations. In other words, it enables authors to choreograph multimedia presentations where audio, video, text, and graphics are combined in real-time. A SMIL document can also interact with a standard HTML page. SMIL documents might become very common on the web thanks to streaming technologies.

The basic elements in a SMIL presentation are (for a complete introduction see [13]): a **root-layout**, which defines things like the size and color of the background of the document; a **region**, which defines where and how a media element such as an image can be rendered, e.g., location, size, overlay order, scaling method; one or more media elements such as **text, img, audio**, and **video**; means for specifying a timeline of events, i.e., **seq** and **par** indicate a block of media elements that will all be shown sequentially or in parallel, respectively, **dur** gives an explicit duration, **begin** delays the start of an element relative to when the document began or the end of other elements; means for skipping some part of an audio or a video (**clip-begin** and **clip-end**); means for adapting the behavior of the presentation to the end-user system capabilities (**switch**); means for freezing a media element after its end (**fill**); and a mean for hyperlinking (**a**).

Digital ink is not currently supported as a SMIL native media type. One option would be to convert the ink into a static image, say in GIF format, and render it as an **img** element; however, this would preclude the possibility of displaying the ink as a continuous media (like an animation). Another option

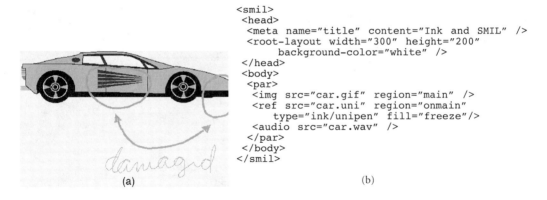

```
<smil>
 <head>
  <meta name="title" content="Ink and SMIL" />
  <root-layout width="300" height="200"
        background-color="white" />
 </head>
 <body>
  <par>
   <img src="car.gif" region="main" />
   <ref src="car.uni" region="onmain"
      type="ink/unipen" fill="freeze"/>
   <audio src="car.wav" />
  </par>
 </body>
</smil>
```

(a)                                          (b)

**FIGURE 42.44**   Example of the role of digital ink in SMIL documents. In (a), a diagram or photo taken with a digital camera can be annotated with a pen; the digital ink can be coordinated with a spoken commentary. In (b), a corresponding short SMIL document fragment assuming the existence of an appropriate MIME content-type called "ink" and a subtype called "unipen" for representing the ink.

is using the SMIL generic media reference **ref** (see Fig. 42.44); this option requires the existence of an appropriate MIME content-type/subtype.

In the near future, it is expected that a standard will be designed to allow SMIL documents to use animated or static digital ink content as a media component.

## Extension of Pen-and-Paper Metaphor

Use of the pen-and-paper paradigm dates back to almost 3000 BC. Paper, as we know of today, dates back to around 200 AD. Hence, the notion of writing with a pen on paper is a extremely natural way of entering handwritten information.

Archival and retrieval are two primary actions performed on handwritten information captured using traditional pen and paper. The problem, however, with regular pen and paper is that the process of retrieving information can be extremely inefficient. Retrieving information typically involves visually scanning the documents, which can be inefficient when the size of handwritten information becomes large. One way to make the process efficient is to tag the information in a useful way. For example, a yellow sticker on pages that relate to a certain topic, or entering information about different topics into different notebooks, can make the process of looking for information on a topic efficient, when using normal paper notebooks. The goal here is to extend the same functionality to electronic pen-and-paper systems.

Extending the pen-and-paper metaphor, one of the main applications for digital ink capture systems, aims to provide users with efficient ink archival/retrieval capabilities by providing users the tools to tag information captured on the devices in a useful way.

The need for efficient ink archival/retrieval is accentuated by devices like the IBM ThinkPad TransNote [27] and Anoto [30], which provide users the capability of using normal or special paper for capturing handwritten information. With paper, users of such devices tend to capture more handwritten information, which in turn increases the need for efficient ink archival/retrieval capabilities.

### Ink Archival and Retrieval

An example of a digital ink capture system that provides users the ability to efficiently archive/retrieve handwritten information is the ThinkPad TransNote system from IBM. The system combines a regular notebook PC with a digital notepad. Slider controls provided on the digital notepad allow users to assign handwritten notes to a particular page and to a specific topic. In addition, controls are provided on the digital notepad to mark blocks of handwritten ink as a keyword. Functions of the sliders and controls can be modified depending on the needs of the application.

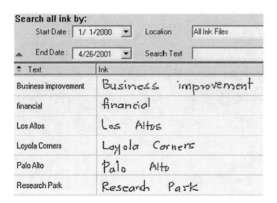

**FIGURE 42.45**   Ink retrieval using keywords. Example of an application that uses the ASCII tags associated with handwritten ink to retrieve information from handwritten documents.

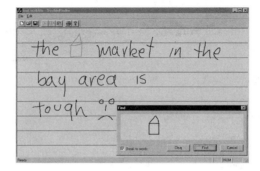

**FIGURE 42.46**   Ink searching example. Users can search for an ink pattern inside a longer ink document, or collection of documents.

Ink management software on the notebook PC allows users to archive handwritten notes and retrieve them, using either the time of creation of the handwritten notes or the tags associated with keywords. The tags are typically text strings created using a handwriting recognition system. Figure 42.45 shows an example of a piece of the ink management software that displays blocks of ink marked as keywords in the middle column and their tags in the left column. Users can retrieve handwritten documents by clicking on the keywords or typing a word in the search text box in the upper righthand-top corner of the application.

In the application shown in Fig. 42.45, all the tags are text strings; however, one can easily extend the retrieval paradigm to use graphical queries and retrieve documents containing graphics, using features extracted from the graphical query. An example of this is shown in Fig. 42.46.

### Gesture Recognition

A gesture is a set of handwritten ink that implies a certain action. In many cases, a gesture can be used to represent an action much more efficiently compared to enumerating the action through a set of keyboard events. An example is the task of moving a portion of text from one position to another. Using a keyboard would involve selecting the portion of ink to be moved, copying it into a clipboard, deleting the selection, moving the cursor to the place in the document where the user would like to place the ink, and finally pasting the ink. Using a pen would allow users to indicate the same action by drawing a selection area around the ink to be moved and an arrow indicating the position to move the selection to. An example of this is shown in Fig. 42.47.

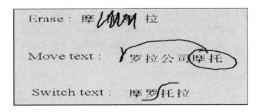

**FIGURE 42.47** Example of pen-and-paper-like editing. Users can perform erasing by scribbling directly on the unwanted text, moving text by circling and dragging, and transposing text by common gesturing.

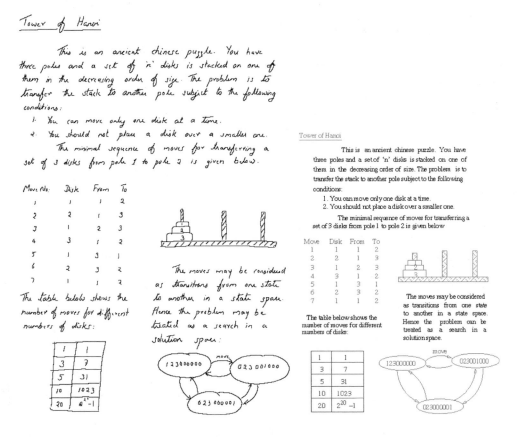

**FIGURE 42.48** Segmentation and recognition of on-line documents. Example of a typical handwritten page with text, tables and drawings; and the desired segmentation interpretation.

### Smart Ink

One can extend the gesture recognition system to allow users to associate more complex actions with groups of pen strokes as shown in Fig. 42.48. The handwritten document on the left side is a typical handwritten page with text, tables and drawings, and the one of the right side is a version of the same document after being automatically interpreted by a smart ink recognition scheme. This association allows users to work with handwritten documents in more efficient ways, which turn an electronic pen into a more effective way of entering information than a keyboard and mouse.

A successful implementation of these ideas led to the development of a tool, called SILK [35], which allows graphic designers to quickly sketch a user-interface with a electronic pen and stylus. The tool addresses the needs of designers who prefer to sketch early interface ideas on paper or whiteboard and concentrate on behavior. Existing interactive user interface construction tools make it hard for a user-interface designer to illustrate the behavior of an interface; these tools focus on specifying widgets and making it easy to manipulate details such as colors, alignment, and fonts, i.e., they can show what the interface will look like, but make it hard to show what it will do.

## Pen Input and Multimodal Systems

A multimodal interface is one that integrates multiple kinds of input simultaneously to achieve a desired result. With the increased availability of significant computing power on mobile devices and of efficient wireless connectivity enabling distributed systems, development of pen-based multimodal interfaces is becoming more and more feasible. The motivation is simple: create more robust, flexible, and user-friendly interfaces by integrating the pen with other input modalities such as speech. Higher robustness is achievable because cross-modal redundancy can be used to compensate for imperfect recognition on each individual mode. Higher flexibility is possible because users can choose from among various modes of achieving a task, or issuing commands, the mode that is most appropriate at the time. Higher user-friendliness will result from having computer interfaces that better resemble the multi-modality naturally present in human communication. In this section we review some successful multimodal systems that take advantage of the pen to produce very synergistic interfaces, highlighting their common features.

Cohen et al. [15] combined speech and pen gestures to interact with a 2D representation, like a map, of the entities in a 3D scene such as the one generated with a battlefield simulator. An interactive map is displayed on a handheld device where the user can draw or speak to control the system. For example, while holding the pen at some location in the map, the user may say "XXXX platoon"; this command will result in the creation of a platoon simulation element labelled "XXXX" at the desired location. The user can then assign a task to the new platoon by uttering a command like "XXXX platoon follow this route" while drawing a line on the map.

Heyer et al. [16] combined speech, pen gestures, and handwriting recognition in a travel planning application. Users interact with the map of a city, possibly displayed on a PIA device, to find out information about hotels, restaurants, and tourist sites. This information is accessed from a public database through the Internet. Pen and voice may be used by speaking a query such as "what is the distance from here to Fisherman's Wharf" while making a mark on the map. Pen-only gestures can also be used for control actions, such as moving the viewing area. Similarly, voice-only commands are allowed as in "show me all hotels with a pool."

Tue Vo et al. [17] prototyped a multimodal calendar application called Jeanie. This is a very common application on PIA devices and one having several tasks that can be simplified by the multimodal method of pointing to or circling objects on the screen in addition to speaking commands. For example, a command combining spoken and handwritten input is "reschedule this on Tuesday," uttered while holding the pen on a meeting entry in the appointment list. An example of a pen-only command is drawing an X on a meeting entry to cancel it.

Suhm et al. [18] have explored the benefits of multimodal interaction in the context of error correction. Specifically, they have integrated handwriting recognition in an automatic dictation system. Users can switch from continuous speech to pen-based input to correct errors. This work capitalizes on the fact that words that might be confused in one modality (e.g., sound similar) are not necessarily so in another one (e.g., with similar handwritten shape). Their study concluded that multimodal error correction is more accurate and faster than unimodal correction by re-speaking.

Multimodal applications such as these ones are generally built using a distributed "agent" framework. The speech recognizer, the handwriting recognizer, the gesture recognizer, the natural language under-standing module, the database access module, etc., might each be a different agent; a computing process that provides a specific service and which runs either locally on the PIA device or remotely. These agents cooperate and communicate in order to accomplish tasks for the user. One publicly available software environment offering facilitated agent communication is the open agent architecture (OAA) from SRI [19].

A special agent is needed for integrating information from all input sources to arrive at a correct understanding of complete multimodal commands. Such a unification agent is sometimes implemented using *semantic frames*, a knowledge representation scheme from the early A.I. days [36], consisting of slots specifying pieces of information about the command. Recognition results from each modality agent are parsed into partially filled frames, which are then merged together to produce a combined interpretation. In the merging process information from different input modes is weighted, meaningless command hypotheses are filtered out, and additional feedback from the user might be requested.

## Summary

As more electronic devices with pen interfaces have and continue to become available for entering and manipulating information, applications need to be more effective at leveraging this method of input. Pen is a mode of input that is very familiar for most users since everyone learns to write in school. Hence, users will tend to use this as a mode of input and control when available. Providing enhanced user-interfaces that will make it easier for users to use the pen interface in effective ways will make it easier for them to work with such devices.

Section 42.6 has given an overview of the pen input devices available today along with some of the applications that use the electronic pen either in isolation or in conjunction with other modes of input such as speech and the keyboard. The community has made great strides in addressing a number of the user-interface issues for capturing and manipulating information from electronic pens. A number of challenges still need to be addressed before such devices truly meet the needs of a user to a higher level of satisfaction.

## To Probe Further

**Pen Computing.** http://hwr.nici.kun.nl/pen-computing. A Web site hosted at the Nijmegen University with links related to practical issues in pen and mobile computing.

**Handhelds.** http://handhelds.org. A Compaq-hosted Web site created to encourage and facilitate the creation of open source software for use on handheld and wearable computers.

## Acknowledgment

The authors thank Thomas G Zimmerman, Research Staff Member with the Human/Machine Interface Gadgets at IBM Research, for his input on the subsection on "Pen Input Hardware," and Carlos McEvilly, Research Staff Member with the Motorola Human Interface Labs, for proofreading this manuscript.

## References

1. G. Seni, T. Anastasakos. Non-cumulative character scoring in a forward search for online handwriting recognition. In *IEEE Conf. on Acoustics, Speech and Signal Processing,* Istanbul, 2000.
2. K.S. Nathan, H.S.M. Beigi, J. Subrahmonia, G.J. Clary, M. Maruyama. Real-time on-line unconstrained handwriting recognition using statistical methods. In *IEEE Conf. on Acoustics, Speech and Signal Processing,* Michigan, 1995.
3. S. Jaeger, S. Manke, A. Waibel. NPEN++: An online handwriting recognition system. In *Proc. Workshop on Frontiers in Handwriting Recognition,* Amsterdam, The Netherlands, 2000.
4. www.mimio.com.
5. www.e-pen.com.
6. H.R. Lewis, C.H. Papadimitriou. Elements of the Theory of Computation. Prentice-Hall, Englewood Cliffs, NJ, 1981.
7. Speech Recognition Grammar Specification for the W3C Speech Interface Framework. W3C Working Draft. www.w3.org/TR/grammar-spec. 2001.
8. H. Freeman. Computer processing of line-drawing data. Computer Surveys. March 1974.
9. T.S. Huang. Coding of two-tone images. *IEEE Trans.* COM-25. November 1977.
10. J. Andrieux, G. Seni. On the coding efficiency of multi-ring and single-ring differential chain coding for telewriting application. To appear in *IEE Proceedings—Vision, Image and Signal Processing.*
11. ITU-T Recommendation T.150. Terminal Equipment and Protocols for Telematic Services. 1993.
12. Synchronized Multimedia Integration Language (SMIL) 1.0 specification. W3C Recommendation. www.w3.org/TR/REC-smil. 1998.

13. L. Hardman. A Smil Tutorial. www.cwi.nl/~media/SMIL/Tutorial. 1998.

14. R. Plamondon, S.N. Srihari. On-line and off-line handwriting recognition: a comprenhensive survey. *IEEE Trans. on Pattern Analysis and Machine Intelligence*, 22(1), 2000.

15. P.R. Cohen, D. McGee, S.L. Oviatt, L. Wu, J. Clow, R. King, S. Julier, L. Rosenblum. Multimodal interactions for 2D and 3D environments. *IEEE Computer Graphics and Applications.* July/August 1999.

16. A. Heyer, L. Julia. Multimodal Maps: An agent-based approach. In *Multimodal Human-Computer Communication, Lecture Notes in Artificial Intelligence*. 1374. Bunt/Beun/Borghuis Eds. Springer 1998.

17. M. Tue Vo, C. Wood. Building an application framework for speech and pen input integration in multimodal learning interfaces. In *IEEE Conf. on Acoustics, Speech and Signal Processing (ICASSP)*, 1996.

18. B. Suhm, B. Myers, A. Waibel. Model-based and empirical evaluation of multimodal interactive error correction. In *Proc. of the CHI 99 Conference*, Pittsburgh, PA, May 1999.

19. www.ai.sri.com/~oaa.

20. C.C. Tappert. Adaptive on-line handwriting recognition. In *7th Intl. Conf. on Pattern Recognition*, Montreal, Canada, 1984.

21. C.C. Tappert, C.Y. Suen, T. Wakahara. The state of the art in on-line handwriting recognition. *IEEE Trans. on Pattern Analysis and Machine Intelligence*, 12, 1990.

22. www.wacom.com/productinfo.

23. www.mutoh.com.

24. T. Zimmerman and F. Hoffmann, IBM Research, patent pending, 1995.

25. J. Subrahmonia, T. Zimmerman. Pen computing: challenges and applications. In *IEEE Conf. on Pattern Recognition*, Barcelona, Spain, 2000.

26. N. Yamaguchi, H. Ishikawa, Y. Iwamoto, A. Iida. Ultrasonic coordinate input apparatus. U.S. Patent 5,637,839, June 10, 1997.

27. www.ibm.com.

28. O. Kinrot and U. Kinrot. Interferometry: encoder measures motion through interferometry. In *Laser Focus Worlds*, March 2000.

29. www.goulite.com.

30. www.anoto.com.

31. M. Lazzouni, A. Kazeroonian, D. Gholizadeh, O. Ali. Pen and paper information recording system. US Patent 5,652,412. July, 1997.

32. S. Nabeshima, S. Yamamoto, K. Agusa, T. Taguchi. Memo-pen: A new input device. In *Proc. of the CHI 95 Conference*, 1995.

33. www.cross-pcg.com.

34. www.erc.caltech.edu/research/reports/munich1full.html.

35. M.W. Newman, J. Landay. Sitemaps, storyboards, and specifications: a sketch of Web site design practice. In *Designing Interactive Systems* DIS, NY, August 2000.

36. E. Charniak, D. McDermott. *Introduction to Artificial Intelligence.* Addison-Wesley, Reading, MA, 1987.

37. R. Plamandon, D. Lopresti, L. Schomaker, R. Srihari, *Online Handwriting Recognition*, Wiley. *Encyclopedia of Electrical and Electronics Engineering.* J.G. Webster Eds. John Wiley & Sons, 1999.

# 42.7   What Makes a Programmable DSP Processor Special?

*Ingrid Verbauwhede*

## Introduction

A programmable DSP processor is a processor "tuned" towards its application domain. Its architecture is very different from a general-purpose von Neumann architecture to accommodate the demands of real-time signal processing. When first developed in the beginning of the 1980s, the main application was filtering. Since then, the architectures have evolved together with the applications. Currently, the most stringent demands for low-power embedded DSP processors come from wireless communication applications: second, 2.5, and third generation (2G, 2.5G, and 3G) cellular standards. The demand for higher throughput and higher quality of source and channel coding keeps growing while power consumption has to be kept as low as possible to increase the lifetime of the batteries.

In this chapter section, first the application domain and its historical evolution will be described in the subsection on "DSP Application Domain." Then, in "DSP Architecture," the overall architecture will be described. In "DSP Data Paths," the specifics of the DSP data paths will be given. In "DSP Memory and Address Calculation Units," the memory architecture and its associated address generation units are described. In "DSP Pipeline," the specifics of the DSP pipeline will be explained. Finally, in "Conclusions and Future Trends," the conclusions will be given followed by some future trends.

## DSP Application Domain

DSP processors were originally developed to implement traditional signal processing functions, mainly filters, such as FIRs and IIRs [5]. These applications decided the main properties of the programmable DSP architecture: the inclusion of a multiply-accumulate unit (MAC) as separate data path unit and a Harvard or modified Harvard memory architecture instead of a von Neumann architecture.

### Original Motivation: FIR Filtering

The fundamental properties of these applications were (and still are):

- *Throughput driven calculations and real-time operation.* Signal processing applications, such as speech and video, can be represented as an "infinite stream" of data samples that need to be processed at a rate determined by the application [20]. The *sample rate* is a fundamental property of the application. It determines at what rate the consecutive samples arrive for processing. For speech processing, this is the rate of speech samples (kHz range), for video processing this might be the frame rate or the pixel rate (MHz range) [3]. The DSP has to process these samples at this given rate. Therefore, a DSP operates under worst-case conditions. This is fundamentally different from general-purpose processing on a micro processor, which operates on an average case base, but which has an unpredictable worst-case behavior.

- *Large amounts of computations, few amounts of control flow operations.* DSP processors were developed to process large amounts of data in a very repetitive mode. For instance, speech filtering, speech coding, pixel processing, etc., require similar operations on consecutive samples, pixels, frames, etc. The DSP processor has adapted to this, by providing means of implementing these algorithms in a very efficient way. It includes zero-overhead looping, very compact instruction code, efficient parallel memory banks, and associated address generation units.

- *Large amount of data*, usually organized in a regular or almost regular pattern. Because of the real-time processing and the associated "infinite" amount of data that is processed, DSP processors usually have several parallel memory banks; each bank has its own address generation unit and parallel reads and writes are supported by the DSP.

- *Embedded applications.* DSP processors are developed for embedded applications, ranging from cellular phones, disk drives, cable modems, etc. The result is that all the program codes have to reside on the processor (no external memory, no cache hierarchy). Thus, the code size has to be minimized, as a result of which, till today there is a lot of assembly code written. Secondly, the power consumption has to be minimized since many of these applications run from batteries or have tight cooling requirements such as the usage of cheap plastic packages or enclosed boxes.

### Modern Applications: Digital Wireless Communications

New applications drive the design of new DSP processors. State-of-the-art DSP processors will have more than one MAC, acceleration for Viterbi decoding, specialized instructions for Turbo decoding, and so on. Indeed, DSP processors have become the main workhorse for wireless communications for both the handsets and the base station infrastructure [22].

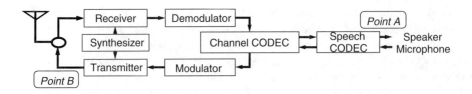

**FIGURE 42.49**  Fundamental building blocks in a communication system.

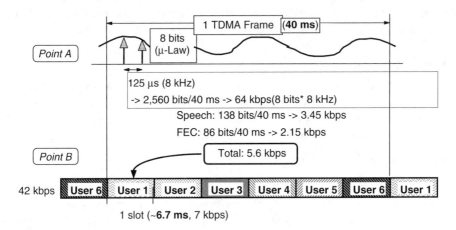

**FIGURE 42.50**  Relationship between speech signal and the transmitted signal.

Second generation (2G) cellular standards required the introduction of optimized instructions for speech processing and for communication algorithms used in the channel coding and modulation/demodulation. The fundamental components of a wireless system are shown on Fig. 42.49.

### Speech Coding
The source coder/decoder in 2G cellular standards (GSM, IS-136, IS-95 CDMA, Japanese PDC) is mainly a speech coder/decoder. The main function of a speech coder is to remove the redundancy and compress the speech signal and hence, reduce the bandwidth requirements for storage or transmission over the air. The required reduction in bit rate is illustrated in Fig. 42.50 for the Japanese PDC standard.

At point A, a "toll quality" digital speech signal requires the sampling of the analog speech waveform at 8 kHz. Each sample requires 8 bits of storage ($\mu$-law compressed) thus resulting in a bit rate of 64 kbits/s or 2560 bits for one 40 ms TDMA frame. This speech signal needs to be compressed to increase the capacity of the channel. One TDMA frame, which has a basic time period of 40 ms, is shared by six users. The bit rate at point B is 42 kbits/s. Thus, one user slot gets only 7 kbits/s. The 2560 bits have to be reduced to 138 bits, to which 86 bits are added for forward error correction (FEC), resulting in a total of 5.6 kbits/s.

The higher the compression ratio and the higher the quality of the speech coder, the more calculations, usually expressed in MIPS, are required. This is illustrated in Fig. 42.51. The first generation GSM digital cellular standard employs the Regular Pulse Excitation-Long Term Prediction (RPE-LTP) algorithm and requires a few thousand MIPS to implement it on a current generation DSP processor. For instance, it requires 2000 MIPS on the lode processor [21]. The Japanese half-rate coder Pitch Synchronous Innovation-Code Excited Linear Prediction (PSI-CELP) requires at least ten times more MIPS.

### Viterbi Decoding
The function of the channel codec is to add controlled redundancy to the bit stream on the encoder side and to decode, detect, and correct transmission errors on the receiver side. Thus, channel encoding and decoding is a form of error control coding. The most common decoding method for convolutional codes

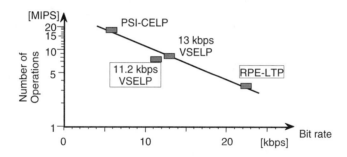

**FIGURE 42.51**   MIPS requirement of several speech coders.

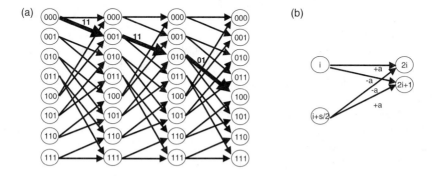

**FIGURE 42.52**   Viterbi trellis diagram and one butterfly.

is the Viterbi algorithm [4]. It is a dynamic programming technique as it tries to emulate the encoder's behavior in creating the transmitted bit sequence. By comparing to the received bit sequence, the algorithm determines the difference between each possible path through the encoder and the received bit sequence. The decoder outputs the bit sequence that has the smallest deviation, called the minimum distance, compared to the received bit sequence.

Most practical convolutional encoders are rate $1/n$, meaning that one input bit generates $n$ coded output bits. A convolutional encoder of constraint length $K$ can be represented by a finite state machine (FSM) with $K-1$ memory bits. The FSM has $2^{K-1}$ possible states, also called trellis states. If the input is binary, two next states are possible starting from the current state and the input bit. The task of the Viterbi algorithm is to reconstruct the most likely sequence of state transitions based on the received bit sequence. This approach is called the "most likelihood sequence estimation." These state transistions are represented by a trellis diagram. The kernel of the trellis diagram is the Viterbi butterfly as shown in Fig. 42.52(b).

### Next Generation Applications

Current generation DSP processors are shaped by 2G cellular standards, the main purpose of which is voice communication. 3G cellular standards will introduce new features: increased focus on data communication, e-mail, web browsing, banking, navigation, and so on.

2G standards can support short messages, such as the popular SMS messages in the GSM standard, but are limited to about 10 to 15 kbits/s. In the 2.5G cellular standards, provisions are made to support higher data rates. By combining GSM time slots, generalized packet radio services (GPRS) can support up to 115 kbits/s. But the 3G standards are being developed specifically for data services. Wideband CDMA (WCDMA) will support up to 2 Mbits/s in office environments, lowered to 144 kbits/s for high mobile situations [6,13].

The increased focus on data services has large consequences for the channel codec design. The traditional Viterbi decoder does not provide a low enough bit error rate to support data services. Therefore, turbo

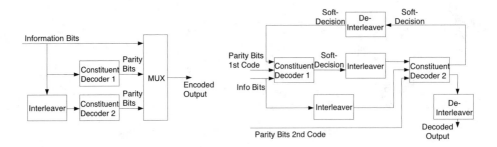

**FIGURE 42.53**   Turbo encoder and decoder.

codes are considered [2]. Turbo decoding (shown in Fig. 42.53) is a collaborative structure of soft-input/soft-output (SISO) decoders with the inclusion of interleaver memories between decoders to scatter burst errors [2]. Either soft-output viterbi algorithm (SOVA) [7] or maximum a posteriori (MAP) [1] can be used as SISO decoders. Within a turbo decoder, the two decoders can operate on the same or different codes. Turbo codes have been shown to provide coding performance to within 0.7 dB of the Shannon limit (after a number of iterations).

The log MAP algorithm can be implemented in a manner very similar to the standard Viterbi algorithm. The most important difference between the algorithms is the use of a correction factor on the "new path metric" value (the alpha, beta, and log-likelihood ratio values in Log MAP). This correction factor depends on the difference between the values being compared in the add-compare-select butterfly (as shown in Fig. 42.52). This means that the Viterbi acceleration units, that implement this add-compare-select operation, need to be modified. Turbo coding is one member of a large class of iterative decoding algorithms. Recently low density parity check codes (LDPC) that have gained renewed attention as another important class, which are potentially more easily translated to efficient implementations.

Other trends seem to place an even larger burden on the DSP processor. The Japanese i-Mode system includes e-mail, web browsing, banking, location finding in combination with the car navigation system, etc. Next generation phones will need to support video and image processing, and so on. Applications and upgrades will be downloadable from the Internet.

But at the same time, consumers are used to longer talk times (a couple of hours) and very long standby times (days or weeks). Thus, they will not accept a reduction of talk time nor standby time in exchange for more features. This means that these increased services have to be delivered with the same power budget because the battery size is not expected to grow nor is the battery technology expected to improve substantially.

## DSP Architecture

The fundamental property of a DSP processor is that it uses a Harvard or modified Harvard architecture instead of a von Neumann architecture. This difference is illustrated in Fig. 42.54.

A von Neumann architecture has one unified address space, i.e., data and program, are assigned to the same memory space. In a Harvard architecture, the data memory map is split from the program memory map. This means that the address busses and data busses are doubled. Together with specialized address calculation units, this will increase the memory bandwidth available for signal processing applications. This concept will be illustrated by the implementation of a simple FIR filter. The basic equation for an $N$ tap FIR equation is the following:

$$y(n) = \sum_{i=0}^{i=N-1} c(i) \cdot x(n-i)$$

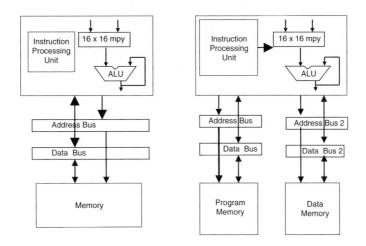

**FIGURE 42.54**   von Neumann architecture and Harvard/modified Harvard architecture.

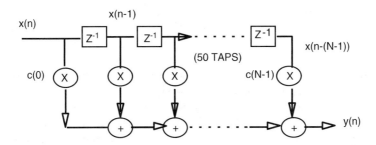

**FIGURE 42.55**   Finite impulse response filter.

Expansion of this equation results in the following pseudo code statements:

```
y(0) = c(0)x(0) + c(1)x(-1) + c(2)x(-2) + ... + c(N - 1)x(1 - N);
y(1) = c(0)x(1) + c(1)x(0) + c(2)x(-1) + ... + c(N - 1)x(2 - N);
y(2) = c(0)x(2) + c(1)x(1) + c(2)x(0) + ... + c(N - 1)x(3 - N);
...
 y(n) = c(0)x(n) + c(1)x(n - 1) + c(2)x(n - 2) + ... + c(N - 1)x(n - (N - 1));
```

When this equation is executed in software or assembly code, output samples $y(n)$ are computed in sequence. To implement this on a von Neumann architecture, the following operations are needed. Assume that the von Neumann has a multiply and accumulate instruction (not necessarily the case). Assume also that pipelining allows to execute the multiply and accumulate in parallel with the read or write operations. Then one tap needs four cycles:

1. Read multiply-accumulate instruction.
2. Read data value from memory.
3. Read coefficient from memory.
4. Write data value to the next location in the delay line (because to start the computation of the next output sample, all values are shifted by one location).

Thus even if the von Neumann architecture includes a single cycle multiply-accumulate unit, it will take four cycles to compute one tap.

Implementing the same FIR filter on a Harvard architecture will reduce the number of cycles to three because it allows the fetch of the instruction in parallel with the fetch of one of the data items. This was a fundamental property that distinguished the early DSP processors. On the TMS 320C1x, released in the early '80s, it took $2N$ cycles for a $N$ tap filter (without the shift of the delay line) [5].

The modified Harvard architecture improves this idea even further. It is combined with a "repeat" instruction and a specialized addressing mode, the circular addressing mode. In this case, one multiply-accumulate instruction is fetched from program memory and kept in the one instruction deep instruction "cache." Then the data access cycles are performed in parallel: the coefficient is fetched from the program memory in parallel with the data sample being fetched from data memory. This architecture is found in all early DSP processors and is the foundation for all following DSP architectures. The number of memory accesses for one tap are reduced to two and these occur in the same cycle. Thus, one tap can execute in one cycle and the multiply-accumulate unit is kept occupied every cycle.

Newer generation of DSP processors have even more memory banks, accompanying address generation units and control hardware, such as the repeat instruction, to support multiple parallel accesses. The execution of a 32-tap FIR filter on the dual Mac architecture of the Lucent DSP 1621, shown in Fig. 42.56, will take only 19 cycles. The corresponding pseudo code is the following:

```
do 14 { //one instruction !
    a0=a0+p0+p1
    p0=xh*yh p1=xl*yl
    y=*r0++ x=*pt0++
}
```

This code can be executed in 19 clock cycles with only 38 bytes of instruction code. The inner loop takes one cycle to execute and as can be seen from the assembly code, seven operations are executed in parallel: one addition, two multiplications, two memory reads, and two address pointer updates. Note that the second pointer update, `*pt0++`, updates a circular address pointer.

Two architectures which speed up the FIR calculation to 0.5 cycle per tap are shown in Fig. 42.56. The first one is the above mentioned Lucent DSP16210. The second one is an architecture presented in [9]. It has a multiply accumulate unit that operates at double the frequency from the memory accesses.

The difficult part in the implementation of this tight loop is the arrangement of the data samples in memory. To supply the parallel Mac data paths, two 32-bit data items are read from memory and stored in the $X$ and $Y$ register, as shown in Fig. 42.56. A similar split in lower and higher halfs occurs in the

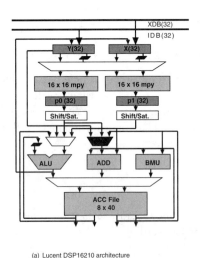

(a) Lucent DSP16210 architecture

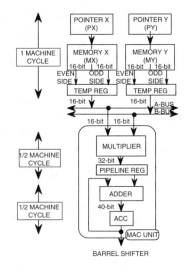

(b) MAC at double frequency [14]

**FIGURE 42.56**   DSP architectures for 0.5 cycle per FIR tap.

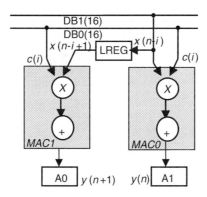

**FIGURE 42.57**   Dual Mac architecture with delay register of the Lode DSP core.

Intel/ADI Frio core [10]. Then the data items are split in an upper half and a low half and supplied to the two 16 × 16 multipliers in parallel or the left half and the right half of the TEMP registers in Fig. 42.56(b). It requires a correct alignment of the data samples in memory, which is usually a tedious work done by the programmer, since compilers are not able to handle this efficiently. Note that a similar problem exists when executing SIMD instructions on general purpose micro-processors.

Memory accesses are a major energy drain. By rearranging the operations to compute the filter outputs, the amount of memory accesses can be reduced. Instead of working on one output sample at a time, two or more output samples are computed in parallel. This is illustrated in the pseudo code below:

```
y(0) = c(0)x(0) + c(1)x(-1) + c(2)x(-2) + ··· + c(N-1)x(1-N);
y(1) = c(0)x(1) + c(1)x(0) + c(2)x(-1) + ··· + c(N-1)x(2-N);
y(2) = c(0)x(2) + c(1)x(1) + c(2)x(0) + ··· + c(N-1)x(3-N);
···
y(n) = c(0)x(n) + c(1)x(n-1) + c(2)x(n-2) + ··· + c(N-1)x(n-(N-1));
```

In the lode architecture [21] a delay register is introduced between the two Mac units as shown in Fig. 42.57. This halves the amount of memory accesses. Two output samples are calculated in parallel as indicated in the pseudo code of Table 42.3. One data bus will read the coefficients, $c(i)$, the other data bus will read the data samples, $x(N-i)$, from memory. The first Mac will compute a multiply-accumulate for output sample $y(n)$. The second multiply-accumulate will compute in parallel on $y(n+1)$. It will use a delayed value of the input sample. In this way, two output samples are computed at the same time.

This concept of inserting a delay register can be generalized. When the datapath has $P$ Mac units, $P-1$ delay registers can be inserted and only $2N/(P+1)$ memory accesses are needed for one output sample. These delay registers are pipeline registers and hence if more delay registers are used, more initialization and termination cycles need to be introduced.

The idea of working on two output samples at one time is also present in the dual Mac processor of TI, the TIC55x. This processor has a dual Mac architecture with three 16-bit data busses. To supply both Macs with coefficient and data samples, the same principle of computing two output samples at the same time is used. One data bus will carry the coefficient and supply this to both Macs, the other two data busses will carry two different data samples and supply this to the two different Macs.

A summary of the different approaches is given in Table 42.2. Note that most energy savings are obtained from reducing the amount of memory accesses and secondly, from reducing the number of instruction cycles. Indeed the energy associated with the Mac operations can be considered as "fundamental" energy without it, no $N$ tap FIR filter can be implemented.

Modern processors have multiple address busses, multiple data busses and multiple memory banks, including both single and dual port memory. They also include mechanisms to assign parts of the physical memory to either memory space, program, or data. For instance for the C542 processor the on-chip dual

**TABLE 42.2**  Data Accesses, Mac Operations, Instruction Cycles, and Instructions
for an $N$ Tap FIR Filter

| DSP | Data Memory Accesses | MAC Operations | Instruction Cycles | Instructions |
|---|---|---|---|---|
| von Neumann | $3N$ | $N$ | $4N$ | $2N$ |
| Harvard | $3N$ | $N$ | $3N$ | $3N$ |
| Modified Harvard with modulo arithmetic | $2N$ | $N$ | $N$ | 2 (repeat instruction) |
| Dual Mac or double frequency Mac | $2N$ | $N$ | $N/2$ | 2 (same) |
| Dual Mac with 3 data busses | $1.5N$ | $N$ | $N/2$ | 2 |
| Dual Mac with 1 delay registers | $N$ | $N$ | $N/2$ | 2 |
| Dual Mac with $P$ delay registers | $2N/(P+1)$ | $N$ | $N/(P+1)$ | 2 |

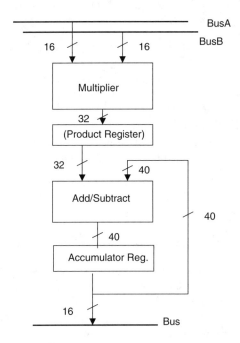

**FIGURE 42.58**  Multiply accumulate unit.

access RAM can be assigned to the data space or to the data/program space, by setting a specific control
bit (the OVLY bit) in a specific control register (the PMST register) [19].

## DSP Data Paths

The focus of the previous section was on the overall architecture of a DSP processor and its fundamental
properties to increase the memory bandwidth. This will keep the data paths of the DSP operating every
clock cycle. In this section, some essential properties of the DSP data paths will be described.

### Multiply-Accumulate Unit

The unit that is most associated with the DSP is the Mac. It is shown in Fig. 42.58. The most important
properties of the Mac unit are summarized below:

- The multiplier takes two 16-bit inputs and produces a 32-bit multiplier output. Internally the
  multiplication might be implemented as a $17 \times 17$ bit multiplier. This way the multiplier can
  implement both two's complement and unsigned numbers.

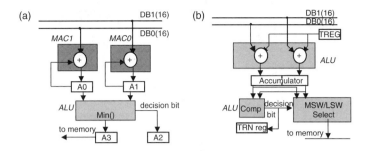

**FIGURE 42.59** Two data path variations to implement the add-compare-select operation.

- The product register is a pipelined register to speed up the calculation of the multiply-accumulate operation. As a result the Mac operation executes in most processors in one cycle effectively although the latency can be two cycles.
- The accumulator registers are usually 40 bits long. Eight bits are designated as "guard" bits [11]. This allows the accumulation of $2^8$ products before there is a need of scaling, truncation, or saturation. These larger word lengths are very effective in implementing DSP functions such as filters. The disadvantage is that special registers such as these accumulators are very hard to handle by a compiler.

## Viterbi Acceleration Unit

Convolutional decoding and more specifically the Viterbi algorithm, has been recognized as one of the main, if not the most, MIPS consuming application in current and next generation standards. The key issue is to reduce the number of memory accesses and secondly the number of operations to implement the algorithm. The kernel of the algorithm is the Viterbi butterfly as shown on Fig. 42.52. The basic equations executed in this butterfly are:

$$d(2i) = \min\{d(i) + a, d(i + s/2) - a\}$$

$$d(2i + 1) = \min\{d(i) - a, d(i + s/2) + a\}$$

These equations are implemented by the "add-compare-select (ACS)" instruction and its associated data path unit. Indeed, one needs to add or subtract the branch metric from states $i$ and $i + s/2$, compare them, and select the minimum. In parallel, state $2i + 1$ is updated. The butterfly arrangement is chosen because it reduces the amount of memory accesses by half, because the two states that use the same data to update the same two next states are combined.

DSP processors have special hardware and instructions to implement the ACS operation in the most efficient way. The lode architecture [21] uses the two Mac units and the ALU to implement the ACS operation as shown in Fig. 42.59(a). The dual Mac operates as a dual add/subtract unit. The ALU finds the minimum. The shortest distance is saved to memory and the path indicator, i.e., the decision bit is saved in a special shift register A2. This results in four cycles per butterfly.

The Texas Instruments TMS320C54x and the Matsushita processor described in [14,22] use a different approach that also results in four cycles per butterfly. This is illustrated in Fig. 42.59(b). The ALU and the accumulator are split into two halves (much like SIMD instructions), and the two halves operate independently. A special compare, select, and store unit (CSSU) will compare the two halves, will select the chosen one, and write the decision bit into a special register TRN. The processor described in [14] describes two ACS units in parallel. One should note that without these specialized instructions and hardware, one butterfly requires 15 to 25 or more instructions.

**TABLE 42.3**    Number of Parallel Address Generation
Units for a Few DSP Processors

| Processor | Generation Units | |
| | Data Address | Program Address |
|---|---|---|
| C5× [18] | 1 (ARAU) | 1 |
| C54× [19] | 2 (DAGEN has two units: ARAU0, ARAU1) | 1 |
| Lode [21] | 2 (ACU0, ACU1) | 1 |
| Frio [10] | 2 | 1 |

## DSP Memory and Address Calculation Units

Besides the data paths optimized for signal processing and communication applications, the DSP processors also have specialized address calculation units. As explained in section "DSP Architecture," the parallel memory maps in the Harvard or modified Harvard architecture are essential for the data processing in DSP processors; however, to avoid overload on the regular data path units, specialized address generation units are included. In general, the number of address generation units will be same as the maximum number of parallel memory accesses that can occur in one cycle. A few examples are shown in Table 42.3. Older processors, such as the C5× with a modified Harvard architecture, have one address generation unit serving the data address bus, and one program address generation unit serving the program address bus. When the number of address busses go up, so will the arithmetic units inside the address calculation unit. For instance the Frio [10] has two address busses served by two ALUs inside the data address generation unit.

The address generation units themselves are optimized to perform address arithmetic in an efficient way. This includes data paths with the correct word lengths. It also includes all the typical address modifications that are common in DSP applications. For instance indirect addressing with a simple increment can easily be done and expressed in the instruction syntax. More advanced addressing modes include circular buffering, which especially suits filter operations, and bit-reversed addressing, especially useful for fast Fourier transforms, and so on. There exist many good instruction manuals that describe the detailed operation of these specialized addressing modes, [11,18,19].

## DSP Pipeline

The pipeline of a DSP processor is different from the pipeline of a general purpose control-oriented micro-processors. The basic slots of the DSP pipeline and the RISC pipeline are shown in Fig. 42.60. In a DSP processor, the memory access stage in parallel with the address generation (usually "post-modification") occurs before the execute stage. An example is described in [10]. In a RISC processor the memory access stage follows the execute stage [8], because the execute stage is used to calculate the address on the main ALU. The fundamental reason for this difference in pipeline structure is that DSP processors are optimized for memory intensive number-crunching type of applications (e.g., FIRs), while RISC type processors, including micro-controllers and micro-processors, are optimized for complex decision making. This is explained in Figs. 42.61 and 42.62. Typical for real-time compute intensive applications, is the continuous memory accesses followed by operations in the data path units. A typical example is the execution of the FIR filter as shown in the FIR pseudo code above. On a DSP processor, the memory access and the multiply-accumulate operation are specified in one instruction and follow each other in the pipeline stage. The same operation on a RISC machine will need three instruction slots. The first instruction slot will read the value from memory and only in the third instruction slot the actual computation takes place. If these delays are not obeyed, a data hazard will occur [8]. Fixing data hazards will lead to a large instruction and cycle overhead.

Similarly, it can be argued that branches have a larger penalty on DSP processors than on RISC machines. The reason is explained on Fig. 42.62. If a data dependent branch needs to be executed, e.g., "branch if accumulator is zero," then it takes that this instruction cannot follow immediately after the

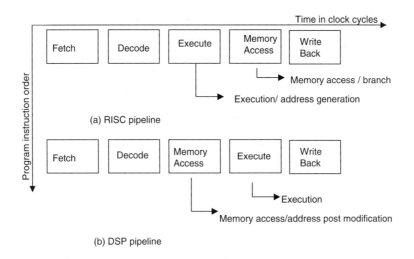

**FIGURE 42.60** Basic pipeline architecture for a RISC and a DSP processor.

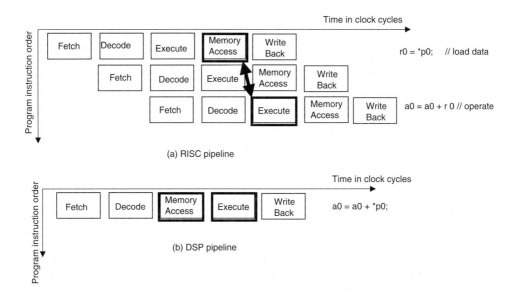

**FIGURE 42.61** Memory-intensive number crunching on a RISC and a DSP.

accumulator is set. In the simple examples of Fig. 42.62, there needs to be two, respectively three instruction cycles between the setting of the accumulator flag and the usage of it in the decode stage, by the RISC and DSP processor, respectively. Therefore, the RISC has an advantage for control dominated applications. In practice these pipeline hazards are either hidden to the programmer by hardware solutions (e.g., forwarding or stalls) or they are visible to the programmer, who can optimize his code around it. A typical example are the branch and the "delayed branch" instruction in DSP processor. Because an instruction is fetched in the cycle before it is decoded, a regular branch instruction will incur an unnecessary fetch of the next instruction in memory following the branch. To optimize the code in DSP processors, the delayed branch instruction is introduced. In this case, the instruction that follows the branch instruction in memory will be executed before the actual branch takes place. Hence, a delayed branch instruction takes effectively one cycle to execute while a regular branch will take two cycles to execute.

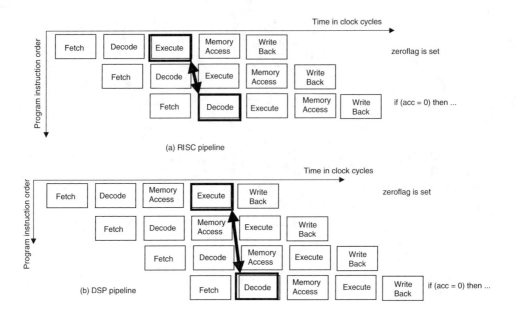

**FIGURE 42.62**   Decision making (branch) on a RISC and a DSP.

The delayed branch is a typical example on how DSP programmers are very sensitive to code size and code execution. Indeed, for embedded applications, minimum code size is a requirement.

## Conclusions and Future Trends

DSP processors are a special type of processors, very different from the general purpose micro controller or micro processor architectures. As argued in this chapter section, this is visible in all components of the processor: the overall architecture, the data paths, the address generation units, and even the pipeline structure.

The applications of the future will keep on driving the next generation of DSP processors. Several trends are visible. Clearly, there is a need to support higher level languages and compilers. Traditional compiler techniques do not produce efficient, optimized code for DSP processors. Compiler technology has only recently started to address the needs of low power embedded applications. But also the architectures will need changes to accommodate the compiler techniques. One drastic approach is the appearance of VLIW architectures, for which efficient compiler techniques are known. This results, however, in code size explosion associated with a large increase in power consumption. A hybrid approach might be a better solution. For example, the processor described in [10] has unified register files. Yet, it also makes an exception for the accumulators.

Another challenge is the increased demand for performance while reducing the power consumption. Next generation wireless portable applications will not only provide voice communication, but also video, text and data, games, and so on. On top of this the applications will change and will need reconfigurations while in use. This will require a power efficient way of runtime reconfiguration [16]. The systems on a chip that implement these wireless communication devices will include a large set of heterogeneous programmable and reconfigurable modules, each optimized to the application running on them. Several of these will be DSP processors and they will be crucial for the overall performance.

## Acknowledgments

The author thanks Mr. Katsuhiko Ueda of Matsushita Electric Co., Japan, for the interesting discussions and for providing several figures in this chapter section.

# References

1. Bahl L., Cocke J., Jelinek F., Raviv J., "Optimal decoding of linear codes for minimizing symbol error rate," *IEEE Trans. Information Theory*, vol. IT-20, pp. 284–287, March 1974.
2. Berrou C., Glavieux A., Thitimajshima P., "Near shannon limit error-correcting coding and decoding: turbo-codes (1)," *Proc. ICC '93*, May 1993.
3. Catthoor F., De Man H., "Application-specific architectural methodologies for high-throughput digital signal and image processing," *IEEE Transactions on ASSP*, Feb. 1990.
4. Forney G., "The viterbi algorithm," *Proceedings of the IEEE*, vol. 61, no. 3, pp. 268–278, March 1973.
5. Gass W., Bartley D., "Programmable DSPs," Chapter 9 in *Digital Signal Processing for Multimedia Systems*, Parhi K., Nishitani T. (Eds.), Marcel Dekker Inc., New York, 1999.
6. Gatherer A., Stetzler T., McMahan M., Auslander E., "DSP-based architectures for mobile communications: past, present, future," *IEEE Communications Magazine*, pp. 84–90, Jan. 2000.
7. Hagenauer J., Hoeher P., "A viterbi algorithm with soft-decision outputs and its applications," *Proc. Globecom '89*, pp. 47.1.1–47.1.7, Nov. 1989.
8. Hennessy J., Patterson D., *Computer Architecture: A Quantitative Approach*, 2nd Edition, Morgan Kaufmann Publ., San Francisco, CA, 1996.
9. Kabuo H., Okamoto M., et al. "An 80 MOPS peak high speed and low power consumption 16-bit digital signal processor," *IEEE Journal of Solid-State Circuits*, vol. 31, no. 4, pp. 494–503, 1996.
10. Kolagotla R., et al., "A 333 MHz dual-MAC DSP architecture for next-generation wireless applications," *Proceedings ICASSP*, Salt Lake City, UT, May 2001.
11. Lapsley P., Bier J., Shoham A., Lee E.A., *DSP Processor Fundamentals: Architectures and Features*, IEEE Press, 1996.
12. Lee E.A., "Programmable DSP architectures: Part I and Part II," *IEEE ASSP Magazine*, pp. 4–19, Oct. 1988, pp. 4–14, Jan. 1989.
13. McMahan M.L., "Evolving cellular handset architectures but a continuing, insatiable desire for DSP MIPS," *Texas Instruments Technical Journal*, Jan.–Mar. 2000, vol. 17, no. 1, reprinted as Application Report SPRA650-March 2000.
14. Okamoto M., Stone K., et al., "A high performance DSP architecture for next generation mobile phone systems," *1998 IEEE DSP Workshop*.
15. Oliphant M., "The mobile phone meets the internet," *IEEE Spectrum*, pp. 20–28, Aug. 1999.
16. Schaumont P., Verbauwhede I., Keutzer K., Sarrafzadeh M., "A quick safari through the reconfiguration jungle," *Proceedings 38th Design Automation Conference*, Las Vegas, NV, June 2001.
17. Strauss W., "Digital signal processing, the new semiconductor industry technology driver," *IEEE Signal Processing Magazine*, pp. 52–56, March 2000.
18. Texas Instruments, *TMS320C5x User's Guide*, document SPRU056B, Jan. 1993.
19. Texas Instruments, *TMS320C54x DSP CPU Reference Guide*, document SPRU131G, March 2001.
20. Verbauwhede I., Scheers C., Rabaey J., "Analysis of multidimensional DSP specifications," *IEEE Transactions on signal processing*, vol. 44, no. 12, pp. 3169–3174, Dec. 1996.
21. Verbauwhede I., Touriguian M., "Wireless digital signal processing," Chapter 11 in *Digital Signal Processing for Multimedia Systems*, Parhi K., Nishitani T. (Eds.), Marcel Dekker Inc., New York, 1999.
22. Verbauwhede I., Nicol C., "Low power DSP's for wireless communications," *Proceeding ISLPED*, pp. 303–310, Aug. 2000.

# 43
# Data Security

Matt Franklin
*University of California at Davis*

## 43.1  Introduction

Cryptography is the science of data security. This chapter gives a brief survey of cryptographic practice and research. The chapter is organized along the lines of the principal categories of cryptographic primitives: unkeyed, symmetric key, and asymmetric key. For each of these categories, the chapter defines the important primitives, give security models and attack scenarios, discuss constructions that are popular in practice, and describe current research activity in the area. Security is defined in terms of the goals and resources of the attacker.

## 43.2  Unkeyed Cryptographic Primitives

The main unkeyed cryptographic primitive is the cryptographic hash function. This is an efficient function from bit strings of any length to bit strings of some fixed length (say 128 or 160 bits). The description of the function is assumed to be publicly available. If $H$ is a hash function, and if $y = H(x)$, then $y$ is called the "hash" or "hash value" of $x$.

One desirable property of a cryptographic hash function is that it should be difficult to invert. This means that given a specific hash value $y$ it is computationally infeasible to produce any $x$ such that $H(x) = y$. Another desirable property is that it should be difficult to find "collisions." This means that it is computationally infeasible to produce two inputs $x$ and $x'$ such that $H(x) = H(x')$. The attacker is assumed to know a complete specification of the hash function.

A cryptographic hash function can be used for establishing data integrity. Suppose that the hash of a large file is stored in a secure location, while the file itself is stored in an insecure location. It is infeasible for an attacker to modify the file without detection, because a re-hash of the modified file will not match the stored hash value (unless the attacker was able to invert the hash function). We will see other applications of cryptographic hash functions when we look at asymmetric cryptographic primitives in Section 43.4.

Popular choices for cryptographic hash functions include MD-5 [1], RIPEMD-160 [2], and SHA-1 [3]. It is also common to construct cryptographic hash functions from symmetric key block ciphers [4].

0-8493-0885-2/02/$0.00+$1.50
© 2002 by CRC Press LLC

## Random Oracle Model

One direction of recent research is on the "random oracle model." This is a design methodology for protocols and primitives that make use of cryptographic hash functions. Pick a specific cryptographic hash function such as MD-5. Its designers may believe that it is difficult to invert MD-5 or to find collisions for it. However, this does not mean that MD-5 is a completely unpredictable function, with no structure or regularity whatsoever. After all, the complete specification of MD-5 is publicly available for inspection and analysis, unlike a truly random function that would be impossible to specify in a compact manner. Nevertheless, the random oracle model asserts that a specific hash function like MD-5 behaves like a purely random function. This is part of a methodology for proving security properties of cryptographic schemes that make use of hash functions.

This assumption was introduced by Fiat and Shamir [5] and later formalized by Bellare and Rogaway [6]. It has been applied to the design and analysis of many schemes (see, e.g., the discussion of optimal asymmetric encryption padding in the subsection on "Chosen Ciphertext Security for Public Key Encryption").

Recently, a cautionary note was sounded by Canetti, Goldreich, and Halevi [7]. They demonstrate by construction that it is possible for a scheme to be secure in the random oracle model and yet have no secure instantiation whatsoever when any hash function is substituted. This is a remarkable theoretical result; however, the cryptographic community continues to base their designs on the random oracle model, and with good reason. Although it cannot provide complete assurance about the security of a design, a proof in the random oracle model provides confidence about the impossibility of a wide range of attacks. Specifically, it rules out common attacks where the adversary ignores the inner workings of the hash function and treats it as a "black box." The vast majority of protocol failures are due to this kind of black box attack, and thus the random oracle model remains an invaluable addition to the cryptographer's tool kit.

## 43.3   Symmetric Key Cryptographic Primitives

The main symmetric key cryptographic primitives are discussed including block ciphers, stream ciphers, and message authentication codes.

## Symmetric Key Block Ciphers

A symmetric key block cipher is a parameterized family of functions $E_K$, where each $E_K$ is a permutation on the space of bit strings of some fixed length. The input to $E_K$ is called the "plaintext" block, the output is called the "ciphertext" block, and $K$ is called the "key." The function $E_K$ is called an "encryption" function. The inverse of $E_K$ is called a "decryption" function, and is denoted $D_K$.

To encrypt a message that is longer than the fixed-length block, it is typical to employ a block cipher in a well-defined "mode of operation." Popular modes of operation include output feedback mode, cipher feedback mode, and cipher block chaining mode; see [8] for a good overview. In this way, the plaintext and ciphertext can be bit strings of arbitrary (and equal) length. New modes of operations are being solicited in connection with the development of the Advanced Encryption Standard (see subsection "Advanced Encryption Standard (AES)").

The purpose of symmetric key encryption is to provide data confidentiality. Security can be stated at a number of levels. It is always assumed that the attacker has access to a complete specification of the parameterized family of encryption functions and to a ciphertext of adequate length. Beyond that, the specific level of security depends on the goals and resources of the attacker. An attacker might attempt a "total break" of the cipher, which would correspond to learning the key $K$. An attacker might attempt a "partial break" of the cipher, which would correspond to learning some or all of the plaintext for a given ciphertext. An attacker might have no resources beyond a description of the block cipher and a sample ciphertext, in which case he is mounting a "ciphertext-only attack." An attacker might mount a "known-plaintext attack," if he is given a number of plaintext-ciphertext pairs to work with (input-output pairs for the encryption function). If the attacker is allowed to choose plaintexts and then see the corresponding ciphertexts, then he is engaged in a "chosen-plaintext attack."

Symmetric key block ciphers are valuable for data secrecy in a storage scenario (encryption by the data owner for an insecure data repository, and subsequent decryption by the data owner at a later time), or in a transmission scenario (across an insecure channel between a sender and receiver that have agreed on the secret key beforehand).

Perhaps the most popular symmetric key block cipher for the past 25 years has been the Data Encryption Standard (DES) [9], although it may be near the end of its useful life. NIST recently announced the Advanced Encryption Standard (AES) block cipher, which we discuss in section "Advanced Encryption Standard (AES)."

Most modern block ciphers have an "iterated" design, where a "round function" is repeated some fixed number of times (e.g., DES has 16 rounds). Many modern block ciphers have a "Feistel structure" [10], which is an iterated design of a particular type. Let $(L_{j-1}, R_{j-1})$ denote the output of the $(j-1)$th round, divided into two halves for notational convenience. Then the output of the $j$th round is $(L_j, R_j)$, where $L_j = R_{j-1}$, and $R_j = L_{j-1}$ xor $f(R_{j-1}, K_j)$ for some function $f$. Here $K_j$ is the $j$th "round key," derived from the secret key according to some fixed schedule. Note that a block cipher with a Feistel structure is guaranteed to be a permutation even if the function $f$ is not invertible.

## Differential Cryptanalysis

Differential cryptanalysis is a powerful statistical attack that can be applied to many symmetric key block ciphers and unkeyed cryptographic hash functions. The first publication on differential cryptanalysis is due to Biham and Shamir [11], but Coppersmith [12] has described how the attack was understood during the design of the DES in the early 1970s.

The central idea of differential cryptanalysis for block ciphers is to sample a large number of pairs of ciphertexts for which the corresponding plaintexts have a known fixed difference $D$ (under the operation of bitwise exclusive-or). The difference $D$ leads to a good "characteristic" if the XOR of the ciphertexts (or of an intermediate result during the computation of the ciphertext) can be predicted with a relatively large probability. By calculating the frequency with which every difference of plaintexts and every difference of ciphertexts coincides, it is possible to deduce some of the key bits through a statistical analysis of a sufficiently large sample of these frequencies.

For a differential cryptanalysis of DES, the best attack that Biham and Shamir discovered requires $2^{47}$ chosen plaintext pairs with a given difference. They note that making even slight changes to the S-boxes (nonlinear substitution transformation at the heart of DES) can lead to a substantial weakening with respect to a differential attack.

## Linear Cryptanalysis

Linear cryptanalysis is another powerful attack that can be applied to many symmetric key block ciphers and unkeyed cryptographic hash functions. Consider the block cipher as being a composition of linear and nonlinear functions. The goal of linear cryptanalysis is to discover linear approximations for the nonlinear components. These approximations can be folded into the specification of the block cipher, and then expanded to find an approximate linear expression for the ciphertext output bits in terms of plaintext input bits and secret key bits. If the approximations were in fact perfect, then enough plaintext-ciphertext pairs would yield a system of linear equations that could be solved for the secret key bits; however, even when the approximations are far from perfect, they enable a successful statistical search for the key, given enough plaintext-ciphertext pairs. This is a known-plaintext attack, unlike differential cryptanalysis, which is chosen-plaintext.

Linear cryptanalysis was introduced by Matsui and Yamagishi [13]. Matsui applied linear cryptanalysis to DES [14]. In his best attack, $2^{43}$ known plaintexts are required to break DES with an 85% probability. See Langford and Hellman [15] for close connections between differential and linear cryptanalysis.

## Advanced Encryption Standard (AES)

In 1997, NIST began an effort to develop a new symmetric key encryption algorithm as a Federal Information Processing Standard (FIPS). The goal was to replace the DES, which was widely perceived to be at the end of its usefulness. A new algorithm was sought, with longer key and block sizes, and with increased resistance to newly revealed attacks such as linear cryptanalysis and differential cryptanalysis. The AES was to support 128-bit block sizes, and key sizes of 128 or 192 or 256 bits. By contrast, DES supported 64-bit block sizes, and a key size of 56 bits.

Fifteen algorithms were proposed by designers around the world. This was reduced to five finalists, announced by NIST in 1999: MARS, RC6, Rijndael, Serpent, and TwoFish. In 2000, Rijndael was selected as the Advanced Encryption Standard. Rijndael has a relatively simple structure; however, unlike many earlier block ciphers (such as DES), it does not have a Feistel structure.

The operation of Rijndael proceeds in rounds. Imagine that the block to be encrypted is written as a rectangular array of byte-sized words (four rows and four columns). First, each byte in the array is replaced by a different byte, according to a single fixed lookup table (S-box). Next, each row of the array undergoes a circular shift by a fixed amount. Next, a fixed linear transformation is applied to each column in the array. Last, the entire array is exclusive-or with a "round key." All of the round keys are calculated by expanding the original secret key bits according to a simple key schedule. Note that the only nonlinear component is the S-box substitution step. Details of Rijndael's operation can be found at [16].

## Symmetric Key Stream Ciphers

Stream ciphers compute ciphertext one character at a time, where the characters are often individual bits. By contrast, block ciphers compute ciphertext one block at a time, where the block is much larger (64 bits long for DES, 128 bits long for AES). Stream ciphers are often much faster than block ciphers. The typical operation of a stream cipher is to exclusive-or message bits with a "key stream." If the key stream were truly random, this would describe the operation of a "one-time pad." The key stream is not truly random, but it is instead derived from the short secret key.

A number of stream ciphers have been optimized for hardware implementation. The use of linear feedback shift registers is especially attractive for hardware implementation, but unfortunately these are not sufficiently secure when used alone. The Berlekamp–Massey algorithm [17] allows a hidden linear feedback shift register to be determined from a very short sequence of output bits. In practice, stream ciphers for hardware often combine linear feedback shift registers with nonlinear components to increase security. One approach is to apply a nonlinear function to the output of several linear feedback shift registers that operate in parallel ("nonlinear combination generator"). Another approach is to apply a nonlinear function to all of the states of a single linear feedback shift register ("nonlinear filter generator"). Still another approach is to have the output of one linear feedback shift register determine when a step should be taken in other linear feedback shift registers ("clock-controlled generator").

Some stream ciphers have been developed to be especially fast when implemented in software, e.g., RC5 [18]. Certain modes of operation for block ciphers can be viewed as symmetric key stream ciphers (output feedback mode and cipher feedback mode).

## Message Authentication Codes

A message authentication code (MAC) is a keyed cryptographic hash function. It computes a fixed-length output (tag) from an input of any length (message). When both the sender and the receiver know the secret key, a MAC can be used to transmit information with integrity. Without knowing the key, it is very difficult for an attacker to modify the message and/or the tag so that the hash relation is maintained. The MAC in the symmetric key setting is the analog of the digital signature in the asymmetric key setting. The notion of message authentication in the symmetric key setting goes back to Gilbert, MacWilliams, and Sloane [19].

Security for MACs can be described with respect to different attack scenarios. The attacker is assumed to know a complete specification of the hash function, but not the secret key. The attacker might attempt to insert a new message that will fool the receiver, or the attacker might attempt to learn the secret key. The attacker might get to see some number of message-tag pairs, either for random messages or for messages chosen by the attacker.

One popular MAC is the CBC-MAC, which is derived from a block cipher (such as DES) run in cipher block chaining mode. Another approach is to apply an unkeyed cryptographic hash function after the message has been combined with the key according to some pre-packaging transform. Care must be taken with the choice of transform; one popular choice is HMAC [20]. The UMAC construction [21] has been optimized for extremely fast implementation in software, while maintaining provable security. Jutla [22] recently showed especially efficient methods for combining message authentication with encryption, by using simple variations on some popular modes of operation for symmetric key block ciphers.

## 43.4  Asymmetric Key Cryptographic Primitives

Two asymmetric key cryptographic primitives are discussed in this section: public key encryption schemes and digital signature schemes.

### Public Key Encryption Schemes

A public key encryption scheme is a method for deriving an encryption function $E_K$ and a corresponding decryption function $D_K$ such that it is computationally infeasible to determine $D_K$ from $E_K$. The encryption function $E_K$ is made public, so that anyone can send encrypted messages to the owner of the key. The decryption function $D_K$ is kept secret, so that only the owner of the key can read encrypted messages. The functions are inverses of each other, so that $D_K(E_K(M)) = M$ for every message $M$. Unlike the symmetric key setting, there is no need for the sender and receiver to pre-establish a secret key before they can communicate securely.

Security for a public key encryption scheme relates to the resources and goals of the attacker. The attacker is assumed to have a complete description of the scheme, as well as the public encryption key $E_K$. Thus, the attacker is certainly able to encrypt arbitrary messages ("chosen-plaintext attack"). The attacker might be able to decrypt arbitrary messages ("chosen-ciphertext attack," discussed in more detail in subsection on "Chosen Ciphertext Security for Public Key Encryption"). The goal of the attacker might be to deduce the decryption function $D_K$ ("total break"), or simply to learn all or some information about the plaintext corresponding to a particular ciphertext ("partial break"), or merely to guess which of two plaintexts is encrypted by a given ciphertext ("indistinguishability").

The idea of public key encryption is due to Diffie and Hellman [23]. Most popular public key encryption schemes base their security on the hardness of some problem from number theory. The first public key encryption proposed remains one of the most popular today—the RSA scheme due to Rivest, Shamir, and Adleman [24]. Other popular public key encryption schemes are based on the "discrete logarithm problem," including ElGamal [25] and elliptic curve variants [26].

For efficiency purposes, public key encryption is often used in a hybrid manner (called "key transport"). Suppose that a large message $M$ is to be encrypted using a public encryption key $E_K$. The sender chooses a random key $k$ for a symmetric key block cipher such as AES. The sender then transmits $E_K(k)$, $AES_k(M)$. The first component enables the receiver to recover the symmetric key $k$, which can be used to decrypt the second component to recover $M$. The popular e-mail security protocol PGP uses this method (augmented with an integrity check).

It is also possible to use a "key agreement protocol" to establish a secret key over an insecure public channel, and then to use the secret key in a symmetric key block cipher. The idea is due to Diffie and Hellman [22], and the original Diffie–Hellman key agreement protocol is still widely used in practice.

### Digital Signature Schemes

A digital signature scheme is a method for deriving a signing function $S_K$ and a corresponding verification function $V_K$, such that it is computationally infeasible to derive $S_K$ from $V_K$. The verification function $V_K$ is made public, so that anyone can verify a signature made by the owner of the signing key. The signing function $S_K$ is kept secret, so that only the owner of the signing key can sign messages. The signing function and verification function are related as follows: If the signature of a message $M$ is $S_K(M)$, then it should be the case that $V_K(S_K(M)) =$ "valid" for all messages $M$.

Security for a digital signature scheme depends on the goals and resources of the attacker [27]. The attacker is assumed to know a complete specification of the digital signature scheme, and the verification function $V_K$. The attacker might also get to see message-signature pairs for random messages ("known message attack"), or for arbitrary messages chosen by the attacker ("chosen message attack"). The goal of the attacker might be to derive the signature function ("total break"), or to forge a signature on a particular message ("selected message forgery"), or to forge any message–signature pair ("existential message forgery").

In practice, a signing function is applied not to the message itself, but rather to the hash of the message (i.e., to the output of an unkeyed cryptographic hash function applied to the message). The security of the signature scheme is then related to the security of the hash function. For example, if a collision can be found for the hash function, then an attacker can produce an existential message forgery under a chosen message attack (by finding a collision on the hash function, and then asking for the signature of one of the colliding inputs).

One of the most popular digital signature schemes is RSA (based on the same primitive as RSA public key encryption, where $S_K = D_K$ and $V_K = E_K$). Other popular digital signature schemes include the digital signature algorithm (DSA) [28] and ElGamal [25].

## Advanced Topics for Public Key Cryptography

### Chosen Ciphertext Security for Public Key Encryption

As discussed earlier, a number of definitions for the security of a public key encryption scheme have been proposed. Chosen ciphertext security is perhaps the strongest natural definition, and it has emerged as the consensus choice among cryptographers as the proper notion of security to try to achieve. This is not to say that chosen ciphertext security is necessary for all applications, but instead of having a single encryption scheme, that is, chosen ciphertext secure will allow it to be used in the widest possible range of applications.

The strongest version of definition of chosen ciphertext security is due to Rackoff and Simon [29], building from a slightly weaker definition of Naor and Yung [30]. It can be described as a game between an adversary and a challenger. The challenger chooses a random public key and corresponding private key $[E_K, D_K]$, and tells the public key $E_K$ to the adversary. The adversary is then allowed to make a series of decryption queries to the challenger, sending arbitrary ciphertexts to the challenger and receiving their decryptions in reply. After this stage, the adversary chooses two messages $M_0$ and $M_1$ whose encryptions he thinks will be particularly easy to distinguish between. The adversary sends $M_0$ and $M_1$ to the challenger. The challenger chooses one of these messages at random; call it $M_b$, where $b$ is a random bit. The challenger encrypts $M_b$ and sends the ciphertext C to the adversary.

Now the adversary attempts to guess whether C is an encryption of $M_0$ or $M_1$. To help him with his guess, he is allowed to engage in another series of decryption queries with the challenger. The only restriction is that the adversary may never ask the challenger to directly decrypt C. At some point the adversary makes his guess for $M_b$. If the adversary can win this game with any nonnegligible advantage (i.e., with probability 1/2 plus $1/k^c$, where $k$ is the length of the private key and $c$ is any positive constant), then we say that he has mounted a successful chosen ciphertext attack. If no adversary (restricted to the class of probabilistic polynomial time turing machines) can mount a successful chosen ciphertext attack, then we say that the cryptosystem is chosen ciphertext secure.

This might seem like overkill for a definition of security. Unlimited access to a decryption oracle might seem like an unrealistically strong capability for the attacker. Merely distinguishing between two plaintexts might seem like an unrealistically weak goal for the attacker. Nevertheless, this definition has proven to be a good one for several reasons. First, it has been shown to be equivalent to other natural and strong definitions of security [31]. Second, Bleichenbacher [32] showed that a popular standard (RSA PKCS #1) was vulnerable to a chosen ciphertext attack in a practical scenario.

In the random oracle model, chosen ciphertext security can be achieved by combining a basic public key encryption scheme such as RSA with a simple "prepackaging" transform. Such a transform uses random padding and unkeyed cryptographic hash functions to scramble the message prior to encryption. The prepackaging transform is invertible, so that the message can be unscrambled after the ciphertext is decrypted.

The optimal asymmetric encryption padding (OAEP) transform takes an $m$-bit message $M$, a random bit string $R$ of length $s$, and outputs OAEP$(M, R) = ((M \parallel 0^s)$ xor $H(R)) \parallel (R$ xor $G((M \parallel 0^s)$ xor $H(R)))$. Here $G$ and $H$ are unkeyed cryptographic hash functions that are assumed to have no exploitable weaknesses (random oracles). This can be viewed as a two-round Feistel structure (e.g., DES is a 16-round round Feistel structure). Unpackaging the transform is straightforward. The OAEP transform is used extensively in practice, and has been incorporated in several standards. OAEP combined with RSA yields an encryption scheme that is secure against a chosen ciphertext attack [33,34].

Shoup [35] shows that OAEP+, a variation on OAEP, yields chosen ciphertext security when combined with essentially any public key encryption scheme: OAEP $+ (M, R) = ((M \parallel W(M, R))$ xor $H(R)) \parallel (R$ xor $G(M \parallel W(M, R))$ xor $H(R))$, where $G$, $H$, and $W$ are unkeyed cryptographic hash functions that behave like random oracles. Boneh [36] shows that even simpler prepackaging transforms (essentially one-round Feistel structure versions of OAEP and OAEP+) yield chosen ciphertext secure encryption schemes when combined with RSA or Rabin public key encryption.

Without the random oracle model, chosen ciphertext security can be achieved using the elegant Cramer–Shoup cryptosystem [37]. This is based on the hardness of the Decision Diffie–Hellman problem (see subsection "New Hardness Assumptions for Asymmetric Key Cryptography"). Generally speaking, constructions in the random oracle model are more efficient than those without it.

## Threshold Public Key Cryptography

In a public key setting, the secret key (for decryption or signing) often needs to be protected from theft for long periods of time against a concerted attack. Physical security is one option for guarding highly sensitive keys, e.g., storing the key in a tamper-resistant device. Threshold public key cryptography is an attractive alternative for safeguarding critical keys.

In a threshold public key cryptosystem, the secret key is never in one place. Instead, the secret key is distributed across many locations. Each location has a different "share" of the key, and each share of the key enables the computation of a "share" of the decryption or signature. Shares of a signature or decryption can then be easily combined to arrive at the complete signature or decryption, assuming that a sufficient number of shareholders contribute to the computation. This "sufficient number" is the threshold that is built into the system as a design parameter. Note that threshold cryptography can be combined with physical security, by having each shareholder use physical means to protect his individual share of the secret key.

Threshold cryptography was independently conceived by Desmedt [38], Boyd [39], and Croft and Harris [40], building on the fundamental notion of secret sharing [41,42]. Satisfactory threshold schemes have been developed for a number of public key encryption and digital signature schemes. These threshold schemes can be designed so as to defeat an extremely strong attacker who is able to travel from shareholder to shareholder, attempting to learn or corrupt all shares of the secret key ("proactive security"). Efficient means are also available for generating shared keys from scratch by the shareholders themselves, so that no trusted dealer is needed to initialize the threshold scheme [43,44]. Shoup [45] recently proposed an especially simple and efficient scheme for threshold RSA.

## New Hardness Assumptions for Asymmetric Key Cryptography

A trend has occurred in recent years toward the exploration of the cryptographic implications of new hardness assumption. Classic assumption include the hardness of factoring a product of two large primes, the hardness of extracting roots modulo a product of two large primes, and the hardness of computing discrete logarithms modulo a large prime (i.e., solving $g^x = y \bmod p$ for $x$).

One classic assumption is the Diffie–Hellman assumption. Informally stated, this assumption is that it is difficult to compute $(g^{ab} \bmod p)$ given $(g^a \bmod p)$ and $(g^b \bmod p)$, where $p$ is a large prime. This assumption underlies the Diffie–Hellman key agreement protocol. The "Decisional Diffie–Hellman Assumption" has proven to be useful in recent years. Informally stated, this assumption is that it is difficult to distinguish triples of the form ($g^a$ mod $p$, $g^b$ mod $p$, $g^{ab}$ mod $p$) and triples of the form ($g^a$ mod $p$, $g^b$ mod $p$, $g^c$ mod $p$) for random $a$, $b$, $c$. Perhaps most notably, the Cramer–Shoup chosen ciphertext secure encryption scheme is based on this new assumption.

The security of RSA is based on a root extraction problem related to the hardness of factoring: Given message $M$ and modulus $N = pq$ of unknown factorization and suitable exponent $e$, compute $M^{1/e}$ mod $N$. Recently, a number of protocols and primitives have been based on a variant of this assumption called the "Strong RSA Assumption:" Given $M$ and $N$, find $e$ and $M^{1/e}$ mod $N$ for any suitable $e$. For example, a provably secure signature scheme can be based on this new assumption without the need for the random oracle assumption [46].

The RSA public key scheme is based on arithmetic modulo $N$, where $N = pq$ is a product of two primes (factors known to the private key holder but not to the public). Recently, Paillier [47] has proposed a novel public key encryption scheme based on arithmetic modulo $p^2q$. His scheme has nice "homomorphic" properties, which enable some computations to be performed directly on ciphertexts. For example, it is easy to compute the encryption of the sum of any number of encrypted values, without knowing how to decrypt these ciphertexts. This has many nice applications, such as for secure secret ballot election protocols.

Lastly, the "Phi-Hiding Assumption" was introduced by Cachin, Micali, and Stadler [48]. This is a technical assumption related to prime factors of $p - 1$ and $q - 1$ in an RSA modulus $N = pq$. This assumption enables the construction of an efficient protocol for querying a database without revealing to the database what queries are being made. (Private Information Retrieval).

**Privacy Preserving Protocols**

Using the cryptographic primitives described in earlier sections, it is possible to design protocols for two or more parties to perform useful computational tasks while maintaining some degree of data confidentiality. Theoretical advances were well established with the "completeness theorems" of [49] and others; however, practical solutions have often required special-purpose protocols tailored to the particular problem.

One important example—both historically and practically—is the problem of conducting a secret ballot election [50,51]. This can be viewed as a cryptographic protocol design problem among three types of parties: voters, talliers, and independent observers. All types of parties have different security requirements. Voters want to guarantee that their individual ballots are included in the final tally, and that the contents of the ballots remain secret. Talliers want to produce an accurate final count that includes all valid ballots counted exactly once, and no invalid ballots. Independent observers want to verify that the tally is conducted honestly. One of the best secret ballot election protocol currently known for large-scale elections is probably [52], which is based on threshold public key encryption.

## 43.5 Other Resources

An excellent resource for further information is the CRC Handbook of Applied Cryptography [53], particularly the first chapter of that handbook, which has an overview of cryptography that is highly recommended. Ross Anderson's book on security engineering [54] is a recommended resource, especially for its treatment of pragmatic issues that arise when implementing cryptographic primitives in practice. See also the frequently asked questions list maintained by RSA Labs (www.rsa.com/rsalabs).

## References

1. Rivest, R., The MD5 message-digest algorithm, Internet Request for Comments, RFC 1321, April 1992.
2. Dobbertin, H., Bosselers, A., and Preneel, B., RIPEMD-160: a strengthened version of RIPEMD, in *Proc. Fast Software Encryption Workshop*, Gollman, D., Ed., Springer-Verlag, LNCS, Heidelberg, 1039, 71, 1996.

3. FIPS 180-1, Secure hash standard, Federal Information Processing Standards Publication 180-1, U.S. Dept. of Commerce/N.I.S.T., National Technical Information Service, Springfield, VA, May 11, 1993.

4. Preneel, B., Cryptographic hash functions, *European Trans. Telecomm.* 5, 431, 1994.

5. Fiat, A. and Shamir, A., How to prove yourself: Practical solutions to identification and signature problems, in *Advances in Cryptology—Crypto '93*, Springer-Verlag, LNCS, Heidelberg, 773, 480, 1994.

6. Bellare, M. and Rogaway, P., Random oracles are practical: a paradigm for designing efficient protocols, in *Proc. ACM Conf. Comput. and Comm. Security,* 62, 1993.

7. Canetti, R., Goldreich, O., and Halevi, S., The random oracle model revisited, in *Proc. ACM Symp. Theory Comput.,* 1998.

8. Davies, D. and Price, W., *Security for Computer Networks,* 2nd ed., John Wiley & Sons, New York, 1989.

9. FIPS 46, Data encryption standard, Federal Information Processing Standards Publication 46, U.S. Dept. of Commerce/N.B.S., National Technical Information Service, Springfield, VA, 1977 (revised as FIPS 46-1: 1988; FIPS 46-2:1993).

10. Feistel, H., Notz, W., and Smith, J., Some cryptographic techniques for machine-to-machine data communications, in *Proc. IEEE 63*, 1545, 1975.

11. Biham, E. and Shamir, A., Differential cryptanalysis of DES-like cryptosystems, *J. Cryptology*, 4, 3, 1991.

12. Coppersmith, D., The Data Encryption Standard (DES) and its strength against attacks, *IBM J. R&D,* 38, 243, 1994.

13. Matsui, M. and Yamagishi, A., A new method for known plaintext attack of FEAL cipher, in *Advances in Cryptology—Eurocrypt '92,* Springer-Verlag, LNCS, Heidelberg, 658, 81, 1993.

14. Matsui, M. Linear cryptanalysis method for DES cipher, in *Advances in Cryptology—Eurocrypt '93,* Springer-Verlag LNCS 765, 386, 1994.

15. Langford, S. and Hellman, M., Differential-linear cryptanalysis, in *Advances in Cryptology—Crypto '94,* Springer-Verlag, LNCS, Heidelberg, 839, 17, 1994.

16. National Institute of Standards and Technology, Advanced Encryption Standard (AES), http://csrc.nist.gov/encryption/aes/.

17. Massey, J., Shift-register synthesis and BCH decoding, *IEEE Trans. Info. Th.,* 15, 122, 1969.

18. Rivest, R., The RC5 encryption algorithm, in *Fast Software Encryption, Second International Workshop,* Springer-Verlag, LNCS, Heidelberg, 1008, 86, 1995.

19. Gilbert, E., MacWilliams, F., Sloane, N., Codes which detect deception, *Bell Sys. Tech. J.,* 53, 405, 1974.

20. Bellare, M., Canetti, R., and Krawczyk, H., Keying hash functions for message authentication, in *Advances in Cryptology—Crypto '96,* Springer-Verlag, LNCS, Heidelberg, 1109, 1, 1996.

21. Black, J., Halevi, S., Krawczyk, H., Krovetz, T., and Rogaway, P., UMAC: Fast and secure message authentication, in *Advances in Cryptology—CRYPTO '99,* Springer-Verlag, LNCS, Heidelberg, 1666, 216, 1999.

22. Jutla, C., Encryption modes with almost free message integrity, in *Advances in Cryptology—Eurocrypt 2001,* Springer-Verlag, LNCS, Heidelberg, 2045, 529, 2001.

23. Diffie, W. and Hellman, M., New directions in cryptography, *IEEE Trans. Info. Th.,* 22, 644, 1976.

24. Rivest, R., Shamir, A., and Adleman, L., A method for obtaining digital signatures and public-key cryptosystems, *Comm. ACM,* 21, 120, 1978.

25. ElGamal, T., A public key cryptosystem and a signature scheme based on discrete logarithms, *IEEE Trans. Info. Th.,* 31, 469, 1985.

26. Koblitz, N., Elliptic curve cryptosystems, *Math. Comput.,* 48, 203, 1987.

27. Goldwasser, S., Micali, S., and Rivest, R., A digital signature scheme secure against adaptive chosen-message attacks, *SIAM J. Comput.,* 17, 281, 1988.

28. Kravitz, D., Digital signature algorithm, U.S. Patent #5,231,668, July 27, 1993.

29. Rackoff, C. and Simon, D., Non-interactive zero-knowledge proof of knowledge and chosen ciphertext attack, in *Advances in Cryptology—Crypto '91,* Springer-Verlag, LNCS, Heidelberg, 576, 433, 1992.

30. Naor, M. and Yung, M. Public-key cryptosystems provably secure against chosen ciphertext attacks, in *Proc. ACM Symp. Th. Comput.,* 33, 1989.

31. Dolev, D., Dwork, C., and Naor, M., Non-malleable cryptography, *SIAM J. Comput.*, 30, 391, 2000.
32. Bleichenbacher, D., Chosen ciphertext attacks against protocols based on RSA encryption standard PKCS #1, in *Advances in Cryptology—CRYPTO'98*, Springer-Verlag, LNCS, Heidelberg, 1462, 1, 1998.
33. Bellare, M. and Rogaway, P., Optimal asymmetric encryption, in *Advances in Cryptology—Eurocrypt '94*, Springer-Verlag LNCS 950, 92, 1995.
34. Fujisaki, E., Okamoto, T., Pointcheval, D., and Stern, J., RSA-OAEP is secure under the RSA assumption, *Advances in Cryptology—Crypto 2001*, Springer-Verlag, LNCS, Heidelberg, 2139, 260, 2001.
35. Shoup, V., OAEP reconsidered., *Advances in Cryptology—Crypto 2001*, Springer-Verlag, LNCS, Heidelberg, 2139, 239, 2001.
36. Boneh, D., Simplified OAEP for the Rabin and RSA functions, *Advances in Cryptology—Crypto 2001*, Springer-Verlag, LNCS, Heidelberg, 2139, 275, 2001.
37. Cramer, R. and Shoup, V., A practical public key cryptosystem provably secure against adaptive chosen ciphertext attack, in *Advances in Cryptology—Crypto '98*, Springer-Verlag, LNCS, Heidelberg, 1462, 13, 1998.
38. Desmedt, Y., Society and group oriented cryptography: a new concept, in *Advances in Cryptology—Crypto '87*, Springer-Verlag, LNCS, Heidelberg, 293, 120, 1988.
39. Croft, R. and Harris, S., Public-key cryptography and re-usable shared secrets, in *Cryptography and Coding*, Beker, H. and Piper, F., Eds., Clarendon Press, Oxford, 189, 1989.
40. Boyd, C., Digital multisignatures, in *Cryptography and Coding*, Beker, H. and Piper, F., Eds., Clarendon Press, Oxford, 241, 1989.
41. Shamir, A., How to share a secret, *Comm. ACM*, 22, 612, 1979.
42. Blakley, R., Safeguarding cryptographic keys, in *Proc. AFIPS Nat'l Computer Conf.*, 313, 1979.
43. Pedersen, T., A threshold cryptosystem without a trusted party, in *Advances in Cryptology—Eurocrypt '91*, Springer-Verlag, LNCS, Heidelberg, 547, 522, 1992.
44. Boneh, D. and Franklin, M., Efficient generation of shared RSA keys, *J. ACM*, to appear.
45. Shoup, V., Practical threshold signatures, in *Advances in Cryptology—Eurocrypt 2000*, Springer-Verlag, LNCS, Heidelberg, 1807, 207, 2000.
46. Cramer, R. and Shoup, V., Signature schemes based on the Strong RSA assumption, *ACM Trans. Inf. Sys. Sec.*, to appear.
47. Paillier, P., Public key cryptosystems based on composite degree residuosity classes, in *Advances in Cryptology—Eurocrypt '99*, Springer-Verlag, LNCS, Heidelberg, 1592, 223, 1999.
48. Cachin, C., Micali, S., and Stadler, M., Computationally private information retrieval with polylogarithmic communication, in *Advances in Cryptology—EUROCRYPT '99*, Springer-Verlag, LNCS, Heidelberg, 1592, 402, 1999.
49. Goldreich, O., Micali, S., and Wigderson, A., How to play any mental game or a completeness theorem for protocols with honest majority, in *Proc. ACM Symp. Th. Comput.*, 218, 1987.
50. Cohen, J. and Fisher, M., A robust and verifiable cryptographically secure election scheme, in *Proc. IEEE Symp. Found. Comp. Sci.*, 372, 1985.
51. Benaloh, J. and Yung, M., Distributing the power of a government to enhance the privacy of voters, in *Proc. ACM Symp. Princ. Distrib. Comput.*, 52, 1986.
52. Cramer, R., Schoenmakers, B., and Genarro, R., A secure and optimally efficient multi-authority election scheme, *European Trans. Telecomm.*, 8, 481, 1997.
53. Menezes, A., van Oorschot, P., and Vanstone, S., *Handbook of Applied Cryptography*, CRC Press, Boca Raton, FL, 1997.
54. Anderson, R., *Security Engineering: a Guide to Building Dependable Systems*, John Wiley & Sons, New York, 2001.

# Testing and Design for Testability

# 44

# System-on-Chip (SoC) Testing: Current Practices and Challenges for Tomorrow

R. Chandramouli
*Synopsys Inc.*

## 44.1 Introduction

Rapidly evolving submicron technology and design automation has enabled the design of electronic systems with millions of transistors integrated on a single silicon die, capable of delivering gigaflops of computational power. At the same time, increasing complexity and time to market pressures are forcing designers to adopt design methodologies with shorter ASIC design cycles. With the emergence of system-on-chip (SoC) concept, traditional design and test methodologies are hitting the wall of complexity and capacity. Conventional design flows are unable to handle large designs made up of different types of blocks such as customized blocks, predesigned cores, embedded arrays, and random logic as shown in Fig. 44.1. Many of today's test strategies have been developed with a focus on single monolithic block of logic; however, in the context of SoC the test strategy should encompass multiple test approaches and provide a high level of confidence on the quality of the product. Design reuse is one of the key components of these methodologies. Larger designs are now shifting to the use of predesigned cores, creating a myriad of new test challenges. Since the end user of the core has little participation in the core's architectural and functional development, the core appears as a black box with known functionality and I/O. Although enabling designers to quickly build end products, core-based design requires test development strategies for the core itself and the entire IC/ASIC with the embedded cores.

This chapter begins with a discussion of some of the existing test methodologies and the key issues/ requirements associated with the testing of SoC. It is followed by a discussion on some of the emerging approaches that will address some of these issues.

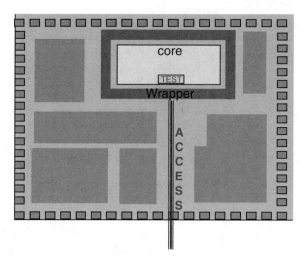

**FIGURE 44.1**    Core access through wrapper isolation.

## 44.2    Current Test Practices

Current test practices consist primarily of ATE-based external test approaches. They range from manual test development to scan-based test. Most of the manual test development efforts depend on fault simulation to estimate the test coverage. Scan-based designs are becoming very common, although their capacity and capability to perform at-speed test are being increasingly affected by physical limitations.

### Scan-Based Test

Over the past decade, there has been an increased use of the scan DFT methodology across a wide variety of designs. One of the key motivations for the use of scan is the resulting ability to automatically generate test patterns that verify the gate or transistor level structures of the scan-based design. Because test generation is computationally complex for sequential designs, most designs can be reconfigured in test mode as combinational logic with inputs and outputs from and to scannable memory elements (flip-flops) and primary I/O. Different types of scan design approaches include mux-D, clock scan, LSSD, and random access scan [1]. The differences are with respect to the design of the scannable memory elements and their clocking mechanisms.

Two major classes of scan design are full scan and partial scan. In the case of full scan, all of the memory elements are made to be scannable, while in the case of partial scan, only a fraction of the memory elements, based on certain overhead (performance and area) constraints, are mapped into scan elements. Because of its iterative nature, the partial scan technique has an adverse impact on the design cycle. Although full scan design has found wider acceptance and usage, partial scan is seen only in designs that have very stringent timing and die size requirements. A major drawback with scan is the inability to verify device performance at-speed. In general, most of the logic related to scan functionality is designed for lower speed.

### Back-End Scan Insertion

Traditional scan implementation depended on the "over-the-wall" approach, where designers complete the synthesis and hand off the gate netlist to the test engineer for test insertion and automatic test pattern generation (ATPG). Some electronic design automation (EDA) tools today help design and test engineers speed the testability process by automatically adding test structures at the gate level. Although this technique is easier than manual insertion, it still takes place after the design has been simulated and synthesized to strict timing requirements. After the completed design is handed over for test insertion, many deficiencies in the design may cause iteration back into module implementation, with the attendant risks to timing closure, design schedule, and stability.

These deficiencies may be a violation of full-scan design rules (e.g., improper clock gating or asynchronous signals on sequential elements not handled correctly). In some cases, clock domain characteristics in lower-level modules can cause compatibility problems with top-level scan chain requirements. In addition, back-end scan insertion can cause broken timing constraints or violate vendor-specific design rules that cannot be adequately addressed by reoptimization.

If back-end scan insertion is used on a large design, the reoptimization process to fix timing constraints violated by inserting scan can take days. If timing in some critical path is broken in even a small part of the overall design, and the violated constraint could not be fixed by reoptimization, the entire test process would have to iterate back into synthesis to redesign the offending module. Thus, back-end test, where traditionally only a small amount of time is budgeted compared to the design effort, would take an inordinately long time. Worse, because these unanticipated delays occur at the very end of the design process, the consequences are magnified because all the other activities in the project are converging, and each of these will have some dependency on a valid, stable design database.

### RT-Level Scan Synthesis

Clearly, the best place to insert test structures is at the RT-level while timing budgets are being worked out. Because synthesis methodologies for SoCs tend to follow hierarchical design flows, where subfunctions within the overall circuit are implemented earliest and then assembled into higher-level blocks as they are completed, DFT should be implemented hierarchically as well. Unfortunately, traditional full-scan DFT tools and methodologies have worked only from the top level of fully synthesized circuits, and have been very much a back-end processes.

The only way to simultaneously meet all design requirements—function, timing, area, power, and testability—is to account for these during the very earliest phases of the design process, and to ensure that these requirements are addressed at every step along the way. A tool that works with simulation and synthesis to insert test logic at this level will ensure that the design is testable from the start. It also ensures that adequate scan structures are inserted to meet the coverage requirements that most companies demand—usually greater than 95%. Achieving such high coverage is usually difficult once a design has been simulated and synthesized.

Tools that automatically insert test structures at the RT-level have other benefits as well. Provided that they are truly automatic and transparent to the user, a scan synthesis tool makes it easy for the designer to implement test without having to learn the intricacies of test engineering. Inserting scan logic before synthesis also means that designers on different teams, working on different blocks of a complex design, can individually insert test logic and know that the whole device will be testable when the design is assembled. This is especially important for companies who use intellectual property (IP) and have embraced design reuse. If blocks are reused in subsequent designs, testability is ensured because it was built in from the start. A truly automated scan synthesis tool can also be used on third party IP, to ensure that it is testable.

One of the key strengths of scan design is diagnosability. The user is able to set the circuit to any state and observe the new states by scanning in and out of the scan chains. For example, when the component/system fails on a given input vector, the clock can be stopped at the erring vector and a test clock can be used to scan out the error state of the machine. The error state of the machine is then used to isolate the defects in the circuit/system. In other words, the presence of scan enables the designer to get a "snap shot" of the system at any given time, for purposes of system analysis, debug, and maintenance.

## 44.3 SoC Testing Complexity

With the availability of multiple millions of gates per design, more and more designers are opting to use IPs to take advantage of that level of integration. The sheer complexity and size of such devices is forcing them to adopt the concept of IP reuse; however, the existing design methodologies do not support a cohesive or comprehensive approach to support reuse. The result is that many of these designs are created using ad hoc methodologies that are localized and specific to the design. Test reuse is the ability to provide access to the individual IPs embedded in the SoC so that the test for the IP can be applied and observed at the chip level. This ability to reuse becomes more complex when the IPs come from multiple sources with different test methods. It becomes difficult to achieve plug and play capability in the test domain. Without a standard, the SoC design team is faced with multiple challenges such as a test model for the delivery of cores, the controllability and observability of cores from the chip I/O, and finally testing the entire chip with embedded IPs, user defined logic, and embedded memories.

## Core Delivery Model

Core test is an evolving industry-wide issue, so no set standards are available to guide the testing of cores and core-based designs. Cores are often delivered as RTL models, which enable the end-users to optimize the cores for the targeted application; however, the current test practices that exist in the "soft core" based design environment are very ad hoc. To a large extent it depends on whether the "soft core" model is delivered to the end user without any DFT built into the core itself. The core vendors provide only functional vectors that verify the core functionality. Again, these vectors are valid only at the core I/O level and have to be mapped to the chip I/O level in order to verify the core functionality at the chip level. Functional testing has its own merits and demerits, but the use of functional tests as manufacturing tests without fault simulation cannot provide a product with deterministic quality. It can easily be seen that any extensive fault simulation would not only result in increased resources, but also an extended test development time to satisfy a certain quality requirement.

## Controllability and Observability of Cores

A key problem in testing cores is the ability to control and observe the core I/O when it is embedded within a larger design. Typically, an ASIC or IC is tested using the parallel I/O or a smaller subset of serial ports if boundary scan is used. In the case of the embedded core, an ideal approach would be to have direct access to its I/O. A typical I/O count for cores would be in the order of 300–400 signals. Using a brute-force approach all 300 signals could be brought out to the chip I/O resulting in a minimum of 300 extra multiplexers. The overhead in such a case is not only multiplexers, but also extra routing area for routing the core I/O to the chip I/O and most of all, the performance degradation of at least one gate delay on the entire core I/O. For most performance driven products, this will be unacceptable. Another approach would be to access the core I/O using functional (parallel) vectors. In order to set each core I/O to a known value, it may be necessary to apply many thousands of clocks at the chip I/O. (This is because, the chip being a sequential state machine, it has to be cycled through hundreds of states before arriving at a known state—the value on the core I/O signal).

## Test Integration

Yet another issue is the integration of test with multiple cores potentially from multiple sources. Along with the ability to integrate one or more cores on an ASIC, comes other design challenges such as layout and power constraints and, very importantly, testing the embedded core(s) and the interconnect logic. The test complexity arises from the fact that each core could be designed with different clocking, timing, and power requirement. Test becomes a bottleneck in such an environment where the designer has to develop a test methodology, either for each core or for the entire design. In either case, it is going to impact the overall design cycle. Even if the individual cores are delivered with embedded test, the end user will have to ensure testing of the interconnects between the multiple cores and the user logic. Although functional testing can verify most of these and can be guaranteed by fault simulation, it would be a return to resource-intensive ways of assuring quality.

Because many cores are physically distinct blocks at the layout level, manufacturing test of the cores has to be done independent of other logic in the design. This means that the core must be isolated from the rest of the logic and then tested as an independent entity. Conventional approaches to isolation and test impact the performance and test overhead. When multiple cores are implemented, testing of the interconnects between the cores and the rest of the logic is necessary because of the isolation-and-test approach.

## Defects and Performance

Considerable design and test challenges are associated with the SoC concept. Test challenges arise both due to the technology and the design methodology. At the technology level, increasing densities has given rise to newer defect types and the dominance of interconnect delays over transistor delays due to shrinking geometry's. Because designers are using predesigned functional blocks, testing involves not only the individual blocks, but also the interconnect between them as well as the user-created logic (glue logic). The ultimate test objective is the ability to manufacture the product at its specified performance (frequency) with the lowest DPM (defective parts per million).

As geometry's shrink and device densities increase, current product quality cannot be sustained through conventional stuck-at fault testing alone [2]. When millions of devices are packed in a single die, newer defect types are created. Many of these cannot be modeled as stuck-at faults, because they do not manifest themselves into stuck-at-like behavior. Most of the deep submicron processes use multiple layers, so one of the predominant defect types is due to shorts between adjacent layers (metal layers), or even between adjacent lines (poly or metal lines). Some of these can be modeled as bridging faults, which behave as the Boolean ANDing or ORing of the adjacent lines depending on the technology. Others do not manifest themselves as logical faults, but behave as delay faults due to the resistive nature of certain shorts. Unlike stuck-at faults, it becomes computationally complex to enumerate the various possible bridging faults since most of them depend on the physical layout. Hence, most of the practical test development is targeted towards stuck-at faults, although there has been considerable research in the analysis and test of bridging faults.

At the deep submicron level interconnect delays dominate gate delays and this affects the ability to test at speed the interconnect (I/O) between various functional blocks in the SoC design environment. Since manufacturing test should be intertwined with performance testing, it is necessary to test the interaction between various functional blocks at-speed. The testing of interconnects involves not only the propagation of signal between various blocks, but also at the specified timing. Current approaches to test do not in general support at-speed test because of a lack of accurate simulation model, limited tester capabilities, and very little vendor support. Traditional testing, which is usually at lower speed, can trigger failures of the device at the system level.

## 44.4   Emerging Trends in SoC Test

Two major capabilities are needed to address the major test challenges that were described earlier in this chapter: (1) making the core test-ready and (2) integration of test-ready cores and user logic at the chip level.

## Creation of Test-Ready Cores

Each core is made test-ready by building a wrapper around it as well as inserting appropriate DFT structures (scan, BIST, etc.) to test the core logic itself. The wrapper is generally a scan chain similar to the boundary scan chain [3] that helps the controllability and observability of the core I/O. The wrapper chain enables access to the core logic for providing the core test vectors from the chip boundary (Fig. 44.1). The wrappers also help in isolating the cores from other cores while the core is being tested, independent of the surrounding cores and logic. One of the key motivation for wrapper is test-reuse. When a test-ready core is delivered, the chip designer does not have to recreate the core test vectors but reuses the core test vectors. The wrappers also help in isolating the core electrically form other cores so that signals coming from other cores do not affect the core and vice versa.

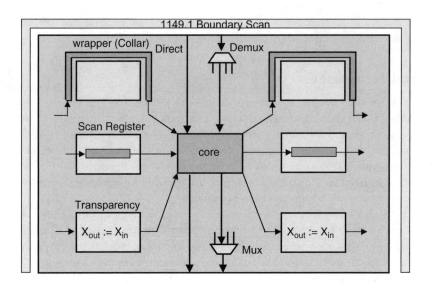

**FIGURE 44.2**   Core isolation techniques.

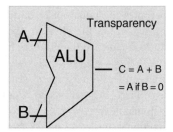

**FIGURE 44.3**   An example for transparency.

## Core Isolation

Many different approaches (Fig. 44.2) can be used to isolate a core from other cores. One common approach is to use multiplexers at each I/O of the core. The multiplexors can be controlled by a test mode so that external vector source can be directly connected to the core I/O during test. This approach is very advantageous where the core doesn't have any internal DFT structure and has only functional vectors which can be applied directly from an external source to the core I/O; however, this approach is disadvantageous when the number of core I/O exceeds that of the chip I/O and also impacts physical routing.

In contrast, other approaches minimize the routing density by providing serial access to the core I/O. The serial access can be through dedicated scan registers at the core I/O or through shared registers, where sharing can happen between multiple cores. The scan register is called a wrapper or a collar. The scan registers isolate the core from all other cores and logic during test mode. The wrapper cell is built with a flip-flop and multiplexor that isolates each pin. It can be seen that the wrapper-based isolation has impact on the overall area of the core. Sharing existing register cells at core I/O helps minimize the area impact. Trade-offs exist with respect to core fault coverage and the core interconnect fault coverage, between shared wrapper and dedicated wrappers.

Access to cores can also be accomplished using the concept of "transparency" through existing logic. In this case, the user leverages existing functionality of a logic block to gain access to the inputs of the core and similarly from the core outputs to the chip I/O through another logic block. Figure 44.3 shows an example of "transparency" in a logic block. Although this approach involves no hardware overhead, detection of transparency is not a simple automation process. In addition, the existence of transparency cannot be predicted a priori.

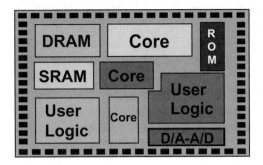

**FIGURE 44.4**　An SoC includes multiple cores with memory and user logic.

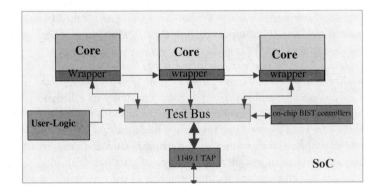

**FIGURE 44.5**　A high-level architecture for SoC test integration.

It becomes evident that the isolation approach and the techniques to make a core test-ready depends on various design constraints such as area, timing, power as well as the test coverage needs for the core, and the core interconnect faults.

## Core Test Integration

Testing SoC devices with multiple blocks (Fig. 44.4), each block embedding different test techniques, could become a nightmare without an appropriate test manager that can control the testing of various blocks. Some of these blocks could be user-designed and others predesigned cores. Given the current lack of any test interface standard in the SoC environment, it becomes very complex to control and observe each of the blocks. Two key issues must be addressed: sequencing of the test operations [4] among the various blocks, and optimization of the test interface between the various blocks and the chip I/O. These depend very much on the test architecture, whether test controllers are added to individual blocks or shared among many, and whether the blocks have adopted differing design-for-test (DFT) methodologies. A high-level view of the SoC test architecture is shown in Fig. 44.5, where the embedded test in each of the cores is integrated through a test bus, which is connected to a 1149.1 TAP controller for external access. Many devices are using boundary scan with the IEEE 1149.1 TAP controller not only to manage in-chip test, but also to aid at board and system-level testing. Some of the test issues pertain to the use of a centralized TAP controller or the use of controller in each block with a common test bus to communicate between various test controllers. In other words, it is the question of centralized versus distributed controller architecture. Each of these has implications with respect to the design of test functionality within each block.

Besides testing each core through their individual access mechanism such as the core isolation wrapper, the complete testing of the SoC also requires an integrated test which tests the interconnects between the cores and the user-defined-logic (UDL). The solution requires, first to connect the test facilities between all the cores and the UDL, and then connect it to a central controller. The chip level controller needs to be connected to either a boundary scan controller or a system interface. When multiple cores with different test methodologies are available, test scheduling becomes necessary to meet chip level test requirements such as test time, power dissipation, and noise level during test.

## 44.5   Emerging SoC Test Standards

One of the main problems in designing test for SoC is the lack of any viable standard that help manage the huge complexity described in this article. A complete manufacturing test of a SoC involves the reuse of the test patterns that come with the cores, and test patterns created for the logic outside the cores. This needs to be done in a predictable manner. The Virtual Socket Interface Alliance (VSIA) [5], an industry consortium of over 150 electronic companies, has formed a working group to develop standards for exchanging test data between core developers and core integrators as well as test access standards for cores. The IEEE Test Technology Committee has also formed a working group called P1500 to define core test access standards. As a part of the IEEE standardization effort, P1500 group [6,7] is defining a wrapper technology that isolates the core from the rest of the chip when manufacturing test is performed. Both the VSIA and IEEE standard are designed to enable core test reuse. The standards will be defining a test access mechanism that would enable access to the cores from the chip level for test application. Besides the access mechanism, the P1500 group is also defining a core test description language called core test language (CTL).

CTL is a language that describes all the necessary information about test aspects of the core such that the test patterns of the core can be reused and the logic outside the core can be tested in the presence of the core. CTL can describe the test information for any arbitrary core, and arbitrary DFT technique used in the core. Furthermore, CTL is independent of the type of tests (stuck-at, Iddq, delay tests) used to test the core. CTL makes this all possible by using protocols as the common denominator to make all the different scenarios look uniform. Regardless of what hardware exists in a design, each core has a configuration that needs to be described and the method to get in and out of the configuration is described by the protocol. The different DFT methods just require different protocols. If tools are built around this central concept namely CTL, then plug-and-play of different cores can be achieved on a SoC for test purposes. To make CTL a reality, it is important that tools are created to help core providers package their core with CTL and tools be developed that work off CTL and integrate the cores for successful manufacturing test of the SoC.

By documenting the test operation of the core in CTL reduces the test complexity and enables automation tools to use a black-box approach when integrating test at the SoC level. Black-boxed designs are delivered with documentation that describe the fault coverage of the test patterns, the patterns itself, the different configurations of the core, and other pertinent test information to the system integrator. The system integrator uses this information (described in CTL) possibly with the help of tools to translate the test patterns described in CTL at the boundary of the core to the chip I/O that is accessible by the tester. Furthermore, the system integrator would use the CTL to provide information on the boundary of the core to create patterns for the user defined logic (UDL) of the SoC outside the core. The methods used for system integration are dependent on the CTL information of the core, and the core's embedded environment. All these tasks can be automated if CTL is used consistently across all black-box cores being incorporated in the design. Figure 44.6 shows the tasks during the integration process.

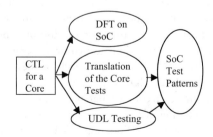

**FIGURE 44.6**   Core integration tasks with CTL.

SoC methodologies require synchronization between the core providers, system integrators, and EDA tool developers. CTL brings all of them together in a consistent manner. Looking ahead we can see the industry will create many other tools and methodologies for test around CTL.

## 44.6   Summary

Cores are the building blocks for the newly emerging core-based IC/ASIC design methodology and a key component in the SoC concept. It lets designers quickly build customized ICs or ASICs for innovative products in fast moving markets such as multimedia, telecom, and electronic games. Along with design, core-based methodology brings in new test challenges such as, implementation of transparent test methodology, test access to core from chip I/O, ability to test the core at-speed. Emerging standards for core test access by both VSIA and IEEE P1500 will bring much needed guidance to SoC test methodologies. The key to successful implementation of SoC test depends on automation and test transparency. A ready-to-test core (with embedded test and accompanying CTL, which describes the test attributes, test protocol, and the test patterns) provides complete transparency to the SoC designer. Automation enables the SoC designer to integrate the test at the SoC level and generate manufacturing vectors for the chip.

### References

1. Alfred L. Crouch, *Design for Test,* Upper Saddle River, NJ: Prentice-Hall, 1999.
2. R. Aitken, "Finding defects with fault models," in *Proc. International Test Conference,* pp. 498–505, 1995.
3. K.P. Parker, *The Boundary Scan Handbook,* Boston, MA: Kluwer Academic Publishers, 1992.
4. Y. Zorian, "A distributed BIST control scheme for complex VLSI devices," *VTS'93: The 11th IEEE VLSI Test Symposium,* pp. 4–9, April 1993.
5. Virtual Socket Interface Alliance, Internet Address: http://www.vsi.org
6. IEEE P1500, "Standards for embedded core test," Internet Address: http://grouper.ieee.org/groups/1500/index.html
7. Y. Zorian, "Test requirements for embedded core-based systems and IEEE P1500," in *Proc. International Test Conference,* pp. 191–199, 1997.

### To Probe Further

Core-based design is an emerging trend, with the result, test techniques for such designs are still in the evolutionary phase. While waiting for viable test standards, the industry has been experimenting with multiple test architectures to enable manufacturability of the SoC designs. Readers interested in these developments can refer to the following literature.

1. Digest of papers of IEEE International Workshop pf Testing Embedded Core-Based System-Chips, Amisville, VA, IEEEE TTTC, 1997, 1998, 1999, 2000, 2001.
2. *Proceedings of International Test Conference,* 1998, 1999, 2000.
3. F. Beenker, B. Bennets, L. Thijssen, *Testability Concepts for Digital ICs—The Macro Test Approach,* vol. 3 of Frontiers in Electronic Testing, Kluwer Academic Publishers, Biotin, USA, 1995.

# 45

# Testing of Synchronous Sequential Digital Circuits

U. Glaeser
*Halstenbach ACT GmbH*

Z. Stamenković
*University of Niš*

H. T. Vierhaus
*Bradenburgische Technische Universitat*

## 45.1  Introduction

Automatic test generation for combinational logic based on the FAN algorithm [1,2], relying on the D-algorithm [3] has reached a high level of maturity. FAN has also been modified for test generation in synchronous sequential circuits [4,5]. Because the shortcomings of the static stuck-at fault model in the detection of opens, dynamic faults, and bridging faults [6,7], became evident, interest has focused on refined fault modeling either using switch-level structures or dynamic gate-level fault models.

The authors have shown [8–10] that the potential fault coverage by stuck-at-based test patterns for transistor faults is potentially as high as 80% or above if the circuit consists of simple 2- and 3-input fully complementary static CMOS gate primitives (AND, NAND, OR, NOR) only, but may drop to 60% or below if complex gates and pass-transistor networks are used. The first solution to this problem is switch-level test generation [11], which is inherently slower than gate-level test generation. The need for test generation based on real transistor structures is also demonstrated by industrial work [12], which reported the first mixed-level test generation approach.

Advanced work in this area was reported more recently in [13–15]. The main problem associated with such methods is the adequate fault modeling based on the transistor circuitry for structures other than primitive logic gates. Cox and Rajski [16] have shown that also using a transition fault model in ATPG, transistor faults in fully complementary CMOS complex gates can be covered by gate-level networks.

This method, however, lacks the applicability to general pass-transistor networks and is also inefficient because the resulting networks have a very large number of gates.

Delay fault testing [17–21] based on gate or path delay fault models has recently emerged as the potentially most powerful method for functional testing. In order to achieve a high fault coverage, delay fault testing requires a detailed timing characterization of the circuit elements. Although this is usually satisfied for gate-level ATPG based on logic primitives, it is difficult to compute timing properties in a full-custom design style employing complex gates, transistor networks, and bidirectional switch-level macros. If no explicit timing information is available, a transition fault model [22] is the most convenient choice. Such a model checks for possible high-low and low-high transitions of all internal circuit nodes at gate-level. The system clock then sets the timing limit for transitions.

Recently, the detection of defects beyond functional faults by methods such as built-in overcurrent measurements (Iddq-testing) [23,24] has received considerable attention. Despite their potential coverage of transistor faults and bridging faults, these methods are static by nature and therefore they are a complement to, instead of a replacement for, dynamic testing.

The work introduced here is aimed at the generation of efficient test sets for conventional voltage-based tests as well as for Iddq tests. The method is based on the transition fault model and on available structural information at transistor-level and gate-level. Our software also supports various other fault models. The basic approach relies on relatively few but efficient modifications to the FAN algorithm in combination with adapted local switch-level test generation. The advantage over other approaches is that switch-level structures are only addressed where truly necessary, and fault propagation is essentially handled at gate-level. Test sets are kept short by using robust multipattern sequences where possible.

A sequential test pattern generation approach is presented in the second part of this paper. It is based on the new FOGBUSTER-algorithm. As opposed to the BACK-algorithm [25], which was built on basic theoretical work [26,27], FOGBUSTER uses a forward propagation and backward justification technique, which is in general more efficient than the exclusive reverse time processing BACK uses.

The advantage of all these test pattern generators over simulation-based approaches [28,29], which are generally much faster than these techniques, is that they are complete, i.e., for any given testable fault a test pattern is generated assuming sufficient time.

The overall approach is summarized in Table 45.1. Although MILEF (mixed-level FAN) is able to generate test patterns for combinational circuits using a modified FAN-algorithm, SEMILET can generate test patterns for synchronous sequential circuits using the FOGBUSTER-algorithm.

The rest of this chapter is organized as follows: The first part (Section 45.2) describes the mixed-level ATPG approach for combinational logic. The second part is devoted to sequential ATPG (Section 45.3). Results for the ISCAS '85 (combinational) and the ISCAS '89 (sequential) benchmark circuits are presented and compared to other approaches. The chapter ends with a summary (Section 45.4).

**TABLE 45.1**    The Relation between Test Generation Approaches

| ATPG Tool | MILEF | SEMILET |
|---|---|---|
| Circuit behavior | Combinational circuits or full scan circuits | Synchronous sequential circuits |
| Algorithm | Modified FAN | FOGBUSTER |
| Test generator for embedded switch-level macros | CTEST | CTEST |
| Voltage-based fault models | Stuck-at Stuck-open Transition | Stuck-at |
| Current-based fault models | Stuck-at Stuck-on | Stuck-at Stuck-on |

## 45.2 Mixed-Level Test Generation

The mechanism of mixed-level test generation technique is described as follows. An extraction algorithm is used for dividing the circuit into relatively small parts (1-stage complex gates, for instance) and extraction of primitive gates (NAND, NOR, INVERTER). The original FAN-algorithm can generate test patterns only for circuits that consist of primitive logic gates because FAN makes, exclusively, use of controlling and noncontrolling values. Thus the FAN-algorithm has to be modified to handle circuits, which consist of gates described by their logic behavior. These modifications and inter-level communication between gate- and switch-level are described in the following. Finally, additional heuristics like the robustness check supporting robust stuck-open test generation and the reconvergency analysis decreasing the number of backtracks between the two hierarchies are shown. The performance increase of the heuristics is pointed out by giving experimental results.

The overall MILEF approach is described in Fig. 45.1. If the circuit consists of complex gates or transistor networks, the logic extractor is called. Primitive gates can directly be handled by the FAN-algorithm. For complex gates and transistor networks, CMOS test pattern generator (CTEST) computes local test patterns. These local patterns are globally applied and propagated. Propagation of fault effects over a switch-level macro is done at gate-level.

### Basic Concepts

The MILEF system developed at GMD initially concentrated on the once popular stuck-open test [30]. MILEF has continuously been developed to cover other potentially more significant faults in an efficient way. MILEF is not restricted to a specific fault model. It is designed to also handle dynamic faults with the exception of explicit consideration of timing limits. Only transitions that are either impossible or delayed beyond the duration of a clock period are detected (gross delay faults).

The main objective in MILEF is to handle only the necessary structures at the switch-level and to perform all general path-tracing operations at the gate-level, thus obtaining an acceptable overall performance of the test generation system.

At the switch-level, a path-oriented ATPG approach as required for stuck-open tests is applied. At the gate-level, MILEF uses a transition fault model, which includes the restriction of single input transitions, e.g., the Hamming distance between init and test pattern is 1. Robust pattern pair requirements can be used as an option (see subsection "Robustness Check for Pattern Pairs"). With these extensions, stuck-open faults and stuck-at faults in primitive gates are safely covered. Stuck-on faults and local bridging faults are excited but not safely propagated.

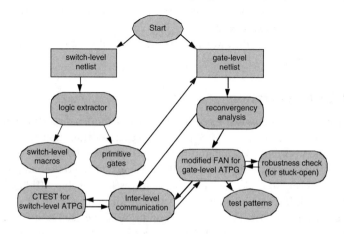

**FIGURE 45.1** Functionality of the MILEF A TPG system.

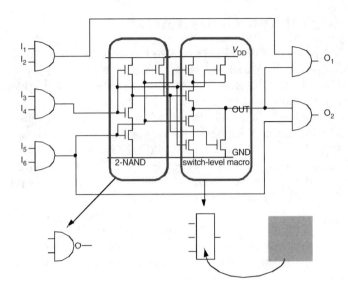

**FIGURE 45.2**   Logic extraction of switch-level macros.

Input formats of MILEF are ISCAS-benchmarks (for circuits with exclusive primitive gates) and SPICE for circuits including complex gates, transmission gates, and bus-structures.

Transistor-level information is actually reduced to a simplified switch-level structure for the test generation. All transistor-level networks are first analyzed by an advanced logic extraction program, which recognizes structures representing primitive gates such as NANDs, NORs, and inverters [31]. Transistor-level networks that contain only simple gates are shifted to the gate-level before any explicit test generation and are therefore not dealt with at the switch-level. Local test generation is done for nontrivial macros only and can mostly be limited to one-stage complex gates and smaller networks.

The example circuit in Fig. 45.2 consists of a number of primitive gates and one transistor netlist. This transistor netlist is divided into two parts by the extractor. The first part of this transistor netlist can be identified as a 2-input NAND and is therefore shifted to gate-level by the extractor. Test generation for this gate is done exclusively at gate-level. The second part of the transistor netlist representing a ANDNOR function could not be mapped to any primitive gate. Consequently, test generation for this gate is done at the switch-level. Fault propagation over this switch-level macro during the test generation is done at gate-level by using the 0- and 1-cubes of the switch-level macro. The idea of extracting gate-level modules from switch-level circuits was already proposed in [32].

To also handle sequential circuits, the extraction algorithm can also identify several sequential elements such as, for instance, flip-flops and D-latches.

## Switch-Level Test Generation

The local test patterns for the switch-level macros remaining after the extraction are generated by CTEST (CMOS test pattern generator) [30,33]. CTEST generates transition test pattern pairs with a hamming distance 1 between initialization and test. Therefore, the robust stuck-open test condition is satisfied for local test patterns since the switch-level macros extracted do not have internal path reconvergencies. To satisfy this condition also globally in as many cases as possible, MILEF avoids static hazards at the inputs of the switch-level macro with the actual fault whenever possible.

CTEST has a reasonable performance for circuits up to the size of 200 transistors. This is sufficient for the MILEF approach, because the switch-level macros left by the extractor are relatively small, in general, not exceeding 20 transistors [31]. The time spent for switch-level test generation measured in experimental results was less than 5% of the overall test generation time, even when the extraction process left around 30% of complex gates. The CPU time spent on global path tracing techniques of the FAN-algorithm was immensely larger.

In local mode, CTEST can also handle circuits including bi-directional transistors [34] and small sequential circuits like flip-flops and latches.

## Modified FAN Approach

MILEF is based on extensions of the de-facto standard FAN [1] for the test generation at the gate-level. The original FAN-algorithm is not able to generate test patterns for circuits, including switch-level macros, because FAN is exclusively based on controlling and noncontrolling values of the gates, which in general do not exist for switch-level macros. Consequently, the modified FAN in MILEF also handles Boolean functions of switch-level macros, i.e., multiple cubes [3]. Thus the main FAN functions such as implication, unique sensitization, and multiple backtrace are modified to handle switch-level macros. The modified FAN approach is described as follows (see also Fig. 45.1):

As a preprocess of the test generation process, gate-level netlists are analyzed for path reconvergencies. They have to be identified for the reconvergency analysis described in subsection on "Merging of Test Pattern Pairs." Most path reconvergencies in practical circuits are of a local nature, so this procedure is quite useful. Results are also transferred to the local switch-level test generator for specific macros in order to obtain globally applicable local test patterns from the beginning (see section "Reconvergency Analysis"). Furthermore, redundancies discovered during this initial step are included in the formal testability analysis. The constraint list is used later in conjunction with global implications in the FAN algorithm.

The second preprocessing step for the gate-level test generation is the formal testability analysis. In particular, the formal controllability and observability analysis guiding the path searching process in FAN was modified in order to also accommodate switch-level macros. Modified testability measures that can optionally be used are, for instance, COP [35], LEVEL [36], SCOAP [37], and EXTEST [8]. We got the best experimental results in MILEF by using COP.

Furthermore, the initial FAN-functions for implication, sensitization, and multibacktrace [1] are modified for handling switch-level macro cells described by multiple cubs [3]. Information for propagation over switch-level macros is described in a 9-valued logic, e.g., multiple cubes are used, and the good and faulty machine are described separately [10].

As MILEF is based on the transition fault model, pattern sequences instead of single vectors are generated. If possible, pattern pairs are merged into longer sequences to minimize initialization efforts and to save on the overall test length.

The path searching performed by MILEF differs from approaches known from gate delay fault test generation in three ways:

- Initialization is excited at a particular gate and test for a particular gate is propagated to primary outputs. The transition may not be observable directly as a transition at one output, which means it can also be observable because of a transition at an output in the faulty case. For example, in Fig. 45.3, the stuck-open fault at the n-transistor with the gate connected to $A_1$ in $g_1$ will cause a stable 1 at C and thus a rising transition at D while in the "good case" D has a "0" value.
- Hazard analysis concentrates on static hazards that can invalidate the test by switching other paths or elements to "conducting" (see subsection "Robustness Check for Pattern Pairs").
- For the generation of only overcurrent-related test vectors in combination with Iddq measurements, the propagation of faults to primary circuit outputs can be omitted. This results in a simplified path-tracing process and fewer patterns.

Three phases of test generation are used in MILEF. In the first phase, test patterns are computed for all easily detectable faults and no backtracking is allowed. No dynamic fault sensitization [2] and no dynamic learning [4] are used in this step. The user may give a backtrack limit for the second phase in which the extensions of SOCRATES [2] are used. For redundancy identification and generating test patterns for hard detectable faults, dynamic learning [4] is used in the third phase of test generation.

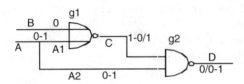

**FIGURE 45.3**    Stuck-open test in gate g1.

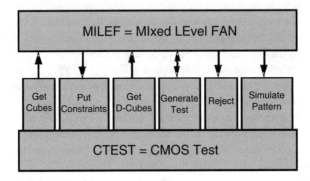

**FIGURE 45.4**    Communication between MILEF and CTEST.

## Robustness Check for Pattern Pairs

The understanding of "robustness" slightly differs between authors. We follow the robustness definition of Reddy et al., described in [38], avoiding static hazards in the input cone of the fault location.

Since MILEF has no information on timing conditions, a "worst case" analysis for static hazard occurrences is performed. Starting from the fault location backward to the primary inputs of the circuit, every constant signal is checked for a static hazard. If both a rising and a falling transition are found at one gate, the output of the gate is marked hazardous. If for a pattern the static hazard is propagated to the fault location, the corresponding pattern is marked nonrobust. By using a fault simulator that takes into account timing conditions such as FEHSIM [39], these nonrobust patterns possibly can be identified as robust.

## Inter-Level Communications

In the present version, MILEF works on two levels of hierarchy at the gate-level and the switch-level. Communication procedures between the gate-level and the switch-level are performed systematically during several steps of the program execution. The communication functions in Fig. 45.4 are described as follows:

- get_cubes: The logic function of a switch-level macro is computed and the corresponding values are prepared to be used at the gate-level.

- put_constraints: Constraints are computed on the gate-level for a block (e.g., by the reconvergency analysis described in the following section) and stored for a constraint driven ATPG at the switch-level.

- get_D_cubes: Propagation cubes are computed and prepared to be used for the propagation of fault effects over a switch-level macro during the test generation at the gate-level.

- generate_test: The previous local io-values of a switch-level macro are used locally as an init-pattern at the switch-level and the computed local test pattern is used at the gate-level for global propagation and application.

- reject: The actual local test pattern is not applicable at gate-level, e.g., the fault is redundant or aborted, an inter-level backtrack is performed. If possible a new local test pattern is generated for the same fault condition.
- simulate_pattern: A call of the local switch-level fault simulator for local simulation of the actual init/test-pattern pair is performed. A robustness check is included.

## Reconvergency Analysis

The reconvergency analysis is based on a learning technique at reconvergent paths. It is executed as a preprocess of the test generation. The learning technique is similar to SOCRATES [2]. The algorithm is described as follows:

For all switch-level macros M
    for all inputs S of M, which are part of a reconvergency in M
            assign all signals of the circuit to value X;
    (1)  assign S to value 0;
    (2)  implication;
            for all inputs I of M, which were set to any value 0 or 1 by the implication
            (a) store_constraint (S = 0 => I = value of I);
            assign all signals of the circuit to value X;
    (1)  assign S to value 1;
    (2)  implication;
            for all inputs I of M, which were set to any value 0 or 1 by the implication
            (a) store_constraint (S = 1 => I = value of I);

Every input of a switch-level macro M, which is part of a reconvergency in M, i.e., in one of the reconvergent paths reconverging in M, is set to both values 0 and 1 (1). By performing the implication of the modified FAN-algorithm (2) every resulting value of this assignment is computed. If any assignment is made at any other input of M, a local constraint at M is found. This constraint and its contraposition are stored by the function store_constraint (a).

Only simple constraints (dependencies between two signals) can be detected by this technique, e.g., if input A is 1, input B must be 1. By using these constraints at the switch-level and performing a constraint-based switch-level test generation, a large number of inter-level backtracks can be avoided, and thus the CPU time of switch-level test generation can be reduced. Since the constraints result from a simple FAN implication, no backtrack in test generation is required for computing the constraint behavior. For example, assume a constraint (a = 0 => b = 0) is detected by the reconvergency analysis. Thus, a simple implication with starting condition a = 0 will detect that b has to be assigned to 0. Since the same implication function is also performed during the test generation process whenever a is set to 0, b will be set to 0 by the implication. Thus no CPU time could be saved in the test generation at the gate-level. Experimental results showing the efficiency of the reconvergency analysis are illustrated in Table 45.2.

**TABLE 45.2**   Inter-Level Backtracks in Test Generation

| ISCAS-Benchmark Circuit Extracted from Layout | Inter-Level Backtracks with no Reconvergency Analysis | Inter-Level Backtracks with Reconvergency Analysis | Percentage of Saved Backtracks (%) |
|---|---|---|---|
| lay432 | 19 | 0 | 100 |
| lay880 | 29 | 2 | 93.1 |
| lay1355 | 65 | 2 | 96.9 |
| lay2670 | 254 | 31 | 87.8 |
| lay3540 | 147 | 89 | 39.5 |
| lay5315 | 336 | 40 | 88.1 |
| lay6288 | 542 | 0 | 100 |
| lay7552 | 221 | 46 | 79.2 |

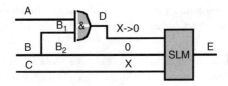

**FIGURE 45.5**   Reconvergency analysis of a simple circuit.

In Fig. 45.5 a simple example is shown. By performing the reconvergency analysis a constraint between the inputs of the macro SLM is detected. If $B_2$ is set to 0, by performing an implication D is set to 0. Thus the constraint ($B_2 = 0 \Rightarrow D = 0$) is found and stored at SLM by using the function put_constraints.

In Table 45.2 the number of inter-level backtracks without using the reconvergency analysis is compared to test generation while using the reconvergency analysis. Depending on the structure of the sequential benchmark circuits, between 39% and 100% of inter-level backtracks could be saved. The average saving in the ISCAS '85 benchmark circuits was about 85%.

These results are also important for hierarchical test generation on higher levels of abstraction (RT-level, behavior-level). The authors believe that using a simple constraint analysis on each abstraction level of the circuit could save a significant time. This requires a constraint-driven test generation technique at lower abstraction levels.

## Merging of Test Pattern Pairs

The test pattern set computed by MILEF is not a minimal set. A test set compaction method is implemented to reduce the number of test patterns as follows. Every generated test pattern is used as an initialization for the next undetected fault whenever possible. Experimental results with ISCAS '85 and ISCAS '89 benchmark circuits have shown that with this method between 30% and 45% of stuck-open patterns could be saved. This method is described in detail in [40].

## Comparative Results

MILEF was used for gate-level benchmark circuits, for mixed gate-level netlists, and for pure transistor netlists. Computations were performed on a Sun SPARC2 with a general limitation of 10 backtracks per fault. The computational effort for fault simulation, which is small in comparison to the test generation effort, is not included in the CPU times of the tables. MILEF was operated in the following modes:

1. Single-input robust transition fault generation including full stuck-open coverage and stuck-on/local bridging fault excitation.
2. Stuck-at test at gate-level including input/output stuck-at tests for switch-level macros.
3. Iddq-test patterns derived from stuck-at patterns, no propagation to outputs.

The fault coverage FC is computed by

$$\text{fault coverage} = \text{detected faults/total number of faults}$$

Table 45.3 gives results for switch-level circuits containing primitive and complex gates. The layouts of the ISCAS '85 circuits [41] were synthesized by MCNC, Raleigh, NC. For mixed-level netlists containing nontrivial switch-level primitives, no standard benchmarks could be used. The circuits in Table 45.3 contain several types of complex gates. The number of complex gates in these circuits was about 30–40% of the total number of gates in the circuit. This evaluation includes extraction and test generation on two levels with robustness checking.

**TABLE 45.3**    MILEF Performance on Pure Switch-Level Netlists (Robust Single-Input Transition Fault Model) Mode 1

| Circuit | Faults Redundant + Aborted | Robust Test Patterns | Non-Robust Test Patterns | Robust Fault Coverage (%) | CPU Time/s |
|---------|---------------------------|---------------------|-------------------------|--------------------------|------------|
| lay432  | 46 + 0   | 511  | 63  | 89.5 | 41   |
| lay499  | 8 + 0    | 1148 | 219 | 85.8 | 503  |
| lay880  | 0 + 4    | 491  | 43  | 97.2 | 30   |
| lay1355 | 5 + 1    | 1528 | 295 | 85.4 | 586  |
| lay1908 | 8 + 6    | 1056 | 93  | 95.6 | 146  |
| lay2670 | 65 + 22  | 1319 | 64  | 95.1 | 234  |
| lay3540 | 121 + 3  | 1858 | 166 | 92.6 | 487  |
| lay5315 | 33 + 2   | 3036 | 205 | 96.3 | 317  |
| lay6288 | 2 + 1    | 1282 | 63  | 91.1 | 4017 |
| lay7552 | 46 + 45  | 3079 | 258 | 95.7 | 1742 |

**TABLE 45.4**    Performance of MILEF (Stuck-at Fault Model) Mode 2

| Circuit | Faults Redundant + Aborted | Test Patterns | Fault Coverage (%) | CPU Time/s |
|---------|---------------------------|---------------|-------------------|------------|
| C432  | 4 + 0   | 77  | 99.2 | 9   |
| C499  | 8 + 0   | 90  | 98.9 | 34  |
| C880  | 0 + 0   | 120 | 100  | 2   |
| C1355 | 8 + 0   | 107 | 99.5 | 61  |
| C1908 | 9 + 0   | 142 | 99.5 | 42  |
| C2670 | 117 + 0 | 266 | 95.7 | 76  |
| C3540 | 137 + 0 | 222 | 96.0 | 58  |
| C5315 | 59 + 0  | 286 | 98.9 | 30  |
| C6288 | 34 + 0  | 41  | 99.6 | 133 |
| C7552 | 131 + 0 | 350 | 98.3 | 179 |

**TABLE 45.5**    Performance of MILEF (Stuck-at Patterns with Simplification for Overcurrent Tests) Mode 3

| Circuit | Faults Redundant + Aborted | Test Patterns | Fault Coverage (%) | CPU Time/s |
|---------|---------------------------|---------------|-------------------|------------|
| C432  | 0 + 0    | 14  | 100  | <1  |
| C499  | 0 + 0    | 44  | 100  | 2   |
| C880  | 0 + 0    | 22  | 100  | <1  |
| C1355 | 0 + 0    | 91  | 100  | 20  |
| C1908 | 0 + 0    | 45  | 100  | 9   |
| C2670 | 13 + 12  | 57  | 99.5 | 15  |
| C3540 | 1 + 0    | 66  | 99.9 | 20  |
| C5315 | 1 + 0    | 67  | 99.9 | 3   |
| C6288 | 17 + 1   | 59  | 99.9 | 463 |
| C7552 | 4 + 0    | 106 | 99.9 | 9   |

Table 45.4 shows that MILEF has a reasonable performance for large gate-level circuits. No aborted faults are left within a reasonable amount of time. The results presented in Tables 45.2–45.5 show that the number of redundancies and test patterns based on the different fault models is smallest when using overcurrent-based fault models. The CPU time and the number of test patterns required for overcurrent-based fault models is smaller (about 10% or less depending on the circuit structure) than for test pattern generation for the corresponding voltage-based fault models (exception C6288 where redundancies are

difficult to identify for overcurrent detection). Dynamic fault models require more test patterns than static fault models, but the effort for test pattern generation for dynamic fault models is tolerable. The highest effort in test pattern generation was spent for getting robust single input transition test patterns (Table 45.3) as expected. The time required for mixed-level test pattern generation is almost equal to the functional identical circuits described exclusively on the gate-level.

A further compaction of the test set, in addition to the compaction (described in the subsection on "Merging of Test Pattern Pairs") leading to a minimal test set, is not performed because long pattern sequences computed for transition fault models are difficult to compress with reordering methods as proposed in [2] for stuck-at pattern sets. With the use of an advanced fault simulator, which includes timing conditions such as FEHSIM [39,42], a further compaction of patterns is possible since MILEF performs a worst-case robustness check as described in the subsection on "Robustness Check for Pattern Pairs."

## 45.3 The Fogbuster Algorithm for Synchronous Circuits

To also handle mixed-level sequential circuits without or with a partial scan path, the sequential test generation system SEMILET (sequential mixed-level test generator) was developed as an extension to MILEF. To improve shortcomings of the state-of-the-art test generators such as HITEC [43] and GENTEST [44], the FOGBUSTER (forward propagation backward justification sequential test generator) algorithm was developed.

The only algorithm that uses exclusively forward time processing is the FASTEST approach [45]. The shortcomings of this algorithm are:

- The circuit is copied as often as needed for test generation, so it is very memory consuming.
- The test generation algorithm, in general, needs a large decision tree for fault excitation.

In this section, the FOGBUSTER algorithm for test generation for synchronous sequential circuit and the sequential test generator SEMILET, which makes use of this algorithm are described.

This section is organized as follows: Synchronous circuits that can be handled by our ATPG are characterized in subsection "Circuits." The main differences of FOGBUSTER and the BACK-algorithm are pointed out in subsection "General Approach in Comparison with Other Algorithms." The section "Test Generation Technique" describes FOGBUSTER, and subsection "Fault Propagation and Propagation Justification" gives a detailed description of the forward propagation technique. A solution for the over specification problem is presented in next subsection and finally, in next two subsections, the test generator SEMILET using the FOGBUSTER algorithm is described. Experimental results from the ISCAS '89 benchmark circuits [46] are given in subsection "Experimental Results."

### Circuits

FOGBUSTER and SEMILET can handle a superset of synchronous sequential circuits that HITEC [43] and GENTEST [44] accept. These circuits have to match the following characteristics:

- All feedback loops include at least one storage element.
- All storage elements have a clock input that is connected to one global clock signal, one data input, and one noninverting data output. It is assumed that the storage elements are master-slave flip-flops, or edge-triggered D-flip-flops.
- Global set and/or reset signals that affect all storage elements are allowed. The test generator can take advantage of them.
- The circuit may consist of primitive (AND, NAND, OR, NOR) and combinational complex gates.

The restriction concerning the types of storage elements seems to be severe at first, but if the design consists of storage elements with a local set and/or reset possibility or with multiple clocking phases,

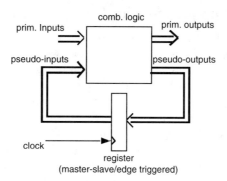

**FIGURE 45.6**    Finite state machine model.

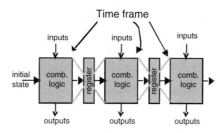

**FIGURE 45.7**    The iterative array model.

they can be substituted by circuits the algorithm can deal with. Basically FOGBUSTER can deal with finite state machines with just one clock depicted in Fig. 45.6.

Each circuit consists of a number of primary inputs and a number of primary outputs. In addition, the circuits have pseudo-inputs—the outputs of the sequential elements, and pseudo-outputs—the inputs of the sequential elements. Each sequential element can be handled as a register. They store the actual state of the circuit. In general, it is not possible to generate a test pattern directly from such a circuit because one special state is needed for the fault injection, and a synchronizing sequence to this state has at least length 1. It is also possible that more than one time frame is needed to propagate the fault effect to the primary outputs of the circuit. For instance, a binary counter may need $2n$ time frames for the propagation path depending on the fault location, where $n$ is the number of flip-flops in the counter.

Figure 45.7 shows the iterative array model used in sequential test generation. The combinational logic and the registers are copied as often as needed for the circuit, resulting in a number of copies equal to the test length. The pseudo-outputs of every time frame feed a register storing the state after execution of the time frame via the pseudo-outputs. Each register accesses a time frame feeding it with the state stored in the register. The first time frame is fed with the initial state of the circuit, which is in general the unknown state "xx…x." Patterns are applied via the inputs of every time frame, and the fault can be observed at the primary outputs of every time frame. For simplicity reasons, the inputs, the outputs, and the registers are left out in the following diagrams in the section on "General Approach in Comparison with Other Algorithms."

By giving as many time frames to the circuit as needed for the maximal test length, the circuits could be treated by a multi-fault combinational test generator as shown in [25]. This method is impractical because of the memory space required for copying circuit and register. Thus, a window is used, scrolling over the time frames. In most of test generation systems [4,5,44] the window size is one time frame. The only test generator operating also with larger window size is HITEC [43].

## General Approach in Comparison with Other Algorithms

As stated in the introduction, the most common approach in sequential test generation is based on the BACK-algorithm [25]. Starting from a target fault, BACK first selects a primary output, where the fault will be visible a number of time frames later. This selection is supported by a drivability measure, an additional approach to testability analysis [4,5]. After selecting a primary output, the fault propagation path starting from the selected primary output backward to the fault location is computed. Finally, the needed state at the fault location is generated in the backward direction.

In Fig. 45.8 a diagram for the BACK algorithm is shown. In this example, seven time frames are used for the test generation. It is visible that the pattern computing direction is reverse, e.g., the values of the time frame, where the fault effect occurs at a circuit output, are computed first, and the values for the time frame with the initial state are computed last. Thus, the fault propagation path and the fault justification are computed by reverse time processing.

Nearly all test pattern generators at the gate-level for sequential circuits [4,5,14,22,44,47,48] make use of a technique based on the BACK-algorithm. The only approaches that use different techniques are HITEC [43] and FASTEST [45]. FASTEST is a technique, which uses exclusively forward time processing. In HITEC, Niermann and Patel use a forward propagation backward justification technique, which means that the propagation is performed by forward processing and the line justification is done using reverse time processing. This technique is illustrated in Fig. 45.9.

The main advantages of forward propagation backward justification over the BACK algorithm are

- No drivability is needed for the test generation process, i.e., computing time is saved.
- In the BACK algorithm the selection of the output where the fault is finally visible requires a large search space, e.g., the initial decision tree is relatively large. Thus, if it is impossible to propagate the fault effect to this output, a backtrack to a different output has to be performed.
- It is possible to use efficient forward propagation techniques (unique sensitization, dominators), which are well known in combinational test generation; in the reverse time processing of the BACK algorithm these techniques are of no use.

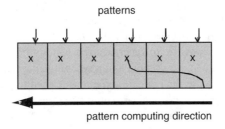

**FIGURE 45.8**   The BACK-algorithm.

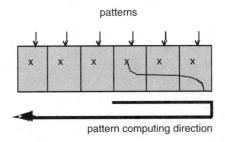

**FIGURE 45.9**   The forward propagation, backward justification technique.

A characteristic of HITEC is that it selects the best observable signal for the fault propagation leaving all others in a stack for backtracking possibility. The main disadvantage of HITEC is:

- In HITEC a large decision tree is built during the propagation by selecting one fanout branch when arriving at a fanout stem for driving the fault effect to a primary output. Thus, many backtracks requiring large CPU time are needed for redundancy identification.

An advantage of HITEC is that it can handle more than one time frame at the same time during propagation, because value assignment in later time frames can be performed. This should result in reduced CPU time required for the test generation. The main disadvantage of this technique is that much memory space is required for multiple storing of time frames.

To overcome the disadvantages of BACK and HITEC, an efficient test generator using forward propagation backward justification technique (FOGBUSTER) was implemented. FOGBUSTER and the corresponding test generation tool SEMILET are described in the following sections.

## Test Generation Technique

In this subsection, the different phases of FOGBUSTER are described. The algorithm proceeds in three main phases of computation:

1. Forward propagation phase
2. Propagation justification phase
3. Justification phase

In the first phase the fault is transported to at least one primary output of the circuit. Efficient heuristics for fault propagation are used in this phase, for instance, unique_sensitisation [1] with detection of dynamic dominators. In the second phase, the propagation path is justified, e.g., unjustified signals of the first phase, which are at the pseudo-outputs of the circuit, are justified. In the justification phase the initial state of the time frame of fault occurrence is confirmed, e.g., a synchronizing sequence for this state is computed.

If a fault is hard to detect, the computing time for finding a test pattern for this fault may be too large. To keep the computing time low, the maximal number of backtracks for one fault can be limited by the user. Hard faults are very often detected by a test pattern for a different fault. Therefore, after a test pattern for any fault is found, fault simulation for all remaining faults (which are not detected by any previous test pattern) of the test generation process is performed.

In Fig. 45.10, a simple diagram of the FOGBUSTER algorithm is shown. After selecting a fault and executing fault injection, the combinational FAN is started to compute a combinational test pattern for this fault. In this part of test generation, combinational redundancies can directly be identified. If a combinational test pattern is generated, the fault effect may be visible at least at one primary output. In this case the justification phase is directly started from here on. Otherwise, the fault effect must be visible at least at one pseudo-output, e.g., at one storage element of the circuit, and one or more time frames are needed to propagate this fault effect to a primary output. Then the forward propagation phase has to be entered.

In the forward propagation phase, a pattern sequence is computed to make the fault effect visible at a primary output of the circuit. For each time frame in the fault propagation, the FAN-algorithm for a multi-fault model is called. A multi-fault model is needed in the FAN-algorithm because the good machine and the bad machine are possibly different at least at one pseudo-input and at the fault location. If there is no path for fault propagation to a primary output for the computed combinational pattern, e.g., the combinational pattern is redundant, a backtrack has to be performed to the combinational FAN-algorithm. If a pattern sequence propagating the fault effect to a primary output is found, the propagation phase terminates, and the propagation justification phase is started.

In the propagation justification phase, all remaining unjustified bound lines [1] (at the sequential elements) of the propagation phase are justified. If justification is not possible, a backtrack to the first

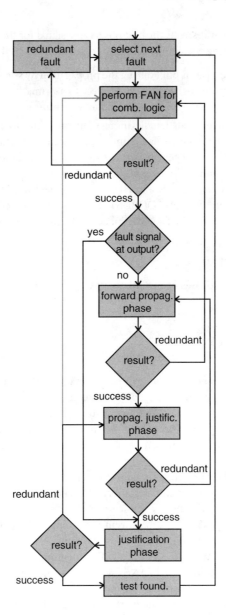

**FIGURE 45.10**    The FOGBUSTER algorithm.

phase—the propagation phase—is performed. Otherwise, after termination the justification phase is started. In the justification phase a synchronizing sequence to the initial state (the state required after the propagation justification process) with respect to fault location is computed. This means that the good and the bad machine both must justify a required state. On termination of this third phase, a test pattern sequence for the selected fault is found. If there is no synchronizing sequence for the initial state, a backtrack to the propagation justification phase or to the combinational FAN algorithm (if no propagation was required after the combinational FAN execution) is performed.

The justification phase of the FOGBUSTER-algorithm is equal to the BACK-algorithm after reaching the fault location. The main differences in FOGBUSTER are the D-propagation through the time frames and the propagation justification. These functions are described in the following subsection.

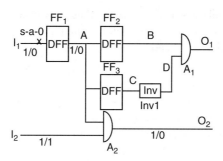

**FIGURE 45.11**  An example circuit.

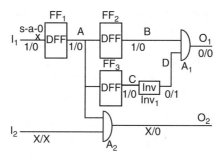

**FIGURE 45.12**  An example circuit.

## Fault Propagation and Propagation Justification

The fault propagation phase and the propagation justification phase are used to propagate a fault from the fault location to a primary output. The objective is to find an input-sequence resulting in a difference of at least one output of the good and the faulty machines, especially in the fault propagation phase where completeness of the algorithm can easily get lost. In HITEC completeness is guaranteed by the targeted D-front approach with optional decisions at every fanout of the circuit. In FOGBUSTER, as an alternative to the targeted D-front, the D-front is propagated through all fanout branches leaving a lower number of optional assignments. This method is motivated in Figs. 45.11 and 45.12 later in this subsection.

In each time frame the actual state is set to the pseudo-inputs of the circuit. The nonempty set of signals, which are on the propagation path, are added to the D-front [1], which is at any time built of the "end point signals" of all paths, transporting the fault effect in the multi-fault FAN-algorithm. The objective is to propagate the signals of the D-front until one output is included in the D-front, e.g., until the fault effect is visible at one output. The fault location is marked and added to the D-front, when a different value in the good machine is computed here. The multi-fault FAN terminates:

- If the D-front cannot be propagated through this time frame. A backtrack to the previous time frame has to be performed.
- If the D-front reaches a primary output. The propagation is finished and the propagation justification phase is started.
- If the D-front is completely propagated to pseudo-outputs (also partly dissolving of the D-front is possible). This is done because of two reasons. On one hand, for every pseudo-input, which is not included in the D-front by entering the time frame, the good and the faulty machine are equal. On the other hand, after reaching a pseudo-output of the circuit, a primary output and thus a

shorter test sequence could possibly be reached. If the propagation of the actual time frame would be stopped when reaching a pseudo-output, the completeness would also be lost. This will be illustrated later using Figs. 45.11 and 45.12.

In each time frame, some pseudo-inputs may have initial values X, because values here are not needed for fault propagation in the previous time frame. If these signals have value requirements in the actual time frame, they are marked as unjustified and prepared for justifying in the propagation justification phase. The latter has to be computed using reverse time processing.

In Fig. 45.11, a simple example circuit is shown. $I_1$ and $I_2$ are the prime inputs of the circuit and $O_1$ and $O_2$ are the prime outputs, respectively. Using the FOGBUSTER algorithm, two time frames are needed to generate a test for the stuck-at-0 fault at signal $I_1$. In the first time frame, the primary input $I_1$ is set to "1" to initialize the fault and thus propagate the fault to the D-flip-flop FF1.

In the second time frame, the values of all pseudo-outputs of the first time frame of the circuit are assigned to the pseudo-inputs, thus the signal A is set to "1/0," that means "1" in the good circuit and "0" in the faulty circuit. By using a simple implication the D-front consists of three signals, the fanout branches of A. Two of them are pseudo-outputs of the circuit, and the third signal of the D-front is at gate $A_2$. As the D-front has to be fully propagated, it is not possible to step to the next time frame in the test generation process. First, an optional assignment has to be performed at signal $I_2$ to propagate the D-front completely. In our example, $I_2$ is set to "1," and by performing an implication the D-front changes. Now $O_2$ is in the D-front, and thus the fault effect is propagated to a primary output of the circuit and the test pattern is generated.

Note that the assignment of signal $I_2$ to "1" is an optional assignment. It is also possible that $I_2$ was assigned to "0" instead. In this case the fault effect is not driven to the output $O_2$. Then, a third time frame has to be used with signals B and C in the initial D-front. As the fault effect cannot be propagated, neither to an output nor to a pseudo-output in the third time frame, a backtrack to the second time frame has to be performed. Thus, a backtrack is performed at $I_2$ setting $I_2$ to 1 and propagating the fault effect to the output $O_2$.

If the D-front was not completely propagated, the completeness of test generation would be lost. A completeness of algorithm means that for every testable fault, the algorithm can find a test pattern.

In Fig. 45.12 the effect of noncomplete D-front propagation is shown using the same example circuit. When the D-front reaches $FF_2$ and $FF_3$, a direct step into time frame 3 is executed, with signals B and C in the D-front. After performing a simple implication, the D-front is empty, and thus a backtrack has to be performed. As there was no optional assignment in the test generation process up to here, there is no backtracking possibility and the fault is marked redundant, although, as seen in Fig. 45.11, it is testable.

## The Over Specification Problem in Sequential Test Generation

A main problem of test generation for sequential circuits is the over specification problem. This problem results from mapping the backtracking technique of combinational test generation to sequential test generation. At worst-case, this problem may result in loosing completeness in test generation. Solutions of the problem are the consequent value model described in [5] and the use of a ternary decision tree described in [49], which both rely on increasing the logic used in the test generation. For completeness reason our algorithm uses the method described in [49].

## Detection of State Repetitions in Test Generation

To get a relatively short test sequence, state repetitions in the test sequence have to be avoided.

**Theorem:** *If a test sequence leading the good and the faulty machines to states* $q_1,...,q_i,...,q_j,...,q_r, i, j, r \in$ *IN,* $1 < i < j < r$, *with* $q_i = q_j$ *is a test for fault F, the test sequence leading the good and faulty machines to* $q_1,...q_i,q_{j+1},...,q_r$ *is also a test for fault F* [50].

A corollary [50] of this theorem is that a synchronizing sequence leading to a defined state (all storage elements store 0 or 1) of all storage elements is upper bounded by $3n - 2n$ ($n$ is the number of storage elements in the circuit) assuming that there is no global reset possibility. The reason is that a 3-valued logic is used starting from the undefined state. With $n$ storage elements, the number of states in the circuit is upper bounded to $3n$. Because no state repetition is allowed and the number of states where all storage elements have a defined state, is $2n$, the storage elements have a defined state after applying an input sequence with length at most $3n - 2n$. A second result is that all reachable states of the circuit can be reached by a sequence, which has a maximum length of $3n$.

Usually, the test generation results into a set of states after each considered time frame with $2y$ elements, $y$ is the number of $x$-values in the storage elements. For this reason, we use "set of states" instead of "state" as notation here.

To avoid long test sequences with state repetitions, SEMILET checks the propagation and the justification phases whether the actual set of states is a subset of a set of states, which occurred a number of time frames earlier in the test generation. For this purpose, the good and the faulty machines are considered during propagation while only the good machine is considered during justification. If the actual set of states is a subset of an earlier set of states, a backtrack to the previous time frame is performed and test generation is continued without loosing the completeness of the algorithm.

## Use of Global Set and Reset Signals in ATPG

If the circuits consist of global set and reset signals, test generation can take advantage of this. A global set signal effects that every flip-flop in the circuit is set to 1, and a global reset signal effects that every flip-flop is set to value 0. In the justification phase of the algorithm it is possible to make use of global set and reset signals:

- A set can be performed, if in the current state in ATPG there is no 0-requirement.
- A reset can be performed, if in the current state in ATPG there is no 1-requirement.

SEMILET can optionally use these features. The results with ISCAS-benchmark circuits in the subsection on "Experimental Results." Table 45.8 shows that use of global set- and/or reset-signals results in increased fault coverage and/or decreased CPU time as expected.

## Experimental Results

The authors have developed SEMILET for test generation for synchronous sequential circuits. SEMILET makes use of the FOGBUSTER-algorithm and has mixed level capabilities like MILEF. In the actual state of implementation, SEMILET can handle 3 fault models:

- Stuck-at with overcurrent detection (mode 1)
- Stuck-at with state propagation (mode 2)

SEMILET is programmed in C++ with about 30,000 lines of code. It is prepared for sequential test generation with two levels of hierarchy, the switch-level and the gate-level (see also [9]).

The overcurrent techniques are reported in [23,24]. Generation of test patterns for overcurrent techniques is in general easier in comparison with the test generation, which needs propagation techniques. The authors found that, if a stuck-at test is required, in many cases it makes sense to generate IDDQ patterns and simulate them like "intelligent random patterns" in a first phase of test generation. For all the faults that are not detected by these patterns, a "normal" stuck-at test pattern set is computed. Thus the test generation mode 3 is done in two phases. Table 45.9 shows experimental results of SEMILET with fault model mode 1 in comparison with results of GENTEST [44] for some ISCAS '89 benchmark [46] circuits. The times of GENEST, HITEC, and SEMILET were measured on a SUN 4/260. The efficiency is computed as follows:

$$efficiency = (redundant\ faults + detected\ faults)/total\ number\ of\ faults$$

**TABLE 45.6**   Performance of SEMILET and GENTEST in Comparison
(Stuck-at Patterns with Simplification for Overcurrent Tests) Mode 1

|  | GENTEST | | SEMILET | |
|---|---|---|---|---|
| Circuit | Efficiency (%) | CPU Time/s | Efficiency (%) | CPU time/s |
| s208 | 100 | 3 | 100 | 3 |
| s298 | 100 | 6 | 100 | 4 |
| s344 | 100 | 12 | 100 | 2 |
| s349 | 100 | 16 | 100 | 2 |
| s400 | 100 | 120 | 100 | 203 |
| s420 | 100 | 17 | 100 | 5 |
| s641 | 100 | 6 | 100 | 6 |
| s713 | 100 | 22 | 100 | 23 |
| s838 | 100 | 71 | 100 | 39 |
| s953 | 100 | 2 | 100 | 2 |
| s1196 | 100 | 7 | 100 | 5 |
| s1238 | 100 | 7 | 100 | 6 |
| s5378 | 98.4 | 27941[*] | 96.2 | 22113 |

[*] Results were computed on a Convex C-200.

**TABLE 45.7**   Performance of SEMILET, HITEC, and GENTEST in Comparison
(Stuck-at Fault Model) Mode 2

|  | GENTEST | | HITEC | | SEMILET | |
|---|---|---|---|---|---|---|
| Circuit | Fault Coverage (%) | CPU Time/s | Fault Coverage (%) | CPU Time/s | Fault Coverage (%) | CPU time/s |
| s208 | 63.7 | 15 | 63.7 | 24 | 63.7 | 9 |
| s298 | 85.7 | 2099 | * | * | 85.7 | 425 |
| s344 | 96.2 | 334 | 95.9 | 4775 | 96.2 | 628 |
| s349 | 95.7 | 489 | 95.7 | 3129 | 95.7 | 627 |
| s386 | 81.8 | 878 | 81.8 | 62 | 81.8 | 80 |
| s420 | 41.6 | 478 | 41.6 | 2701 | 41.6 | 280 |
| s510 | 0 | 1 | 0 | 2 | 0 | 0[**] |
| s641 | 86.5 | 11 | 86.5 | 737 | 86.5 | 15 |
| s713 | 81.4 | 438 | 81.9 | 84 | 81.9 | 18 |
| s1196 | 99.8 | 38 | 99.8 | 41 | 99.8 | 33 |
| s1238 | 94.7 | 61 | 94.7 | 183 | 94.7 | 58 |
| s5378 | 74.0 | 105[***] | * | * | 74.0 | 22603 |
| s9234 | 0.3 | 530 | 0.3 | 63 | 0.3 | 10 |

[*] No results known for this circuit.
[**] Test generation was not called for, and all redundancies were detected in the preprocess.
[***] Results were computed on a Convex C-200.

Looking at results of Table 45.6, it is visible that SEMILET has almost the same fault coverage and performance in comparison with GENTEST for IDDQ models. For some of the circuits (s344, s349, s838) SEMILET is a bit faster and for other circuits (s400, s713) SEMILET is a bit slower than GENTEST. This result was theoretically expected because only justification is used for computing test patterns for overcurrent related fault models since no fault propagation is required. Fault justification in FOGBUSTER is equal to fault justification in BACK.

Table 45.7 shows the stuck-at performance of SEMILET in comparison with HITEC and GENTEST. It is shown that the fault coverage of all approaches is equal (exception: for s344 the fault coverage of HITEC is a bit worse). In most cases the test generation time required for SEMILET was smaller in comparison with HITEC (except s386). The test generation times for GENTEST were sometimes a bit smaller (s344, s349, s641) but sometimes much larger (s298, s386, s713, s5378) than the SEMILET times.

**TABLE 45.8** Performance of SEMILET with and without Possibilities of Global Setting and Resetting (Stuck-at Patterns) Mode 3, CPU Times Computed on a Sparc10

| Circuit | Without Possibility of Setting and Resetting | | With Possibility of Setting and Resetting | |
|---|---|---|---|---|
| | Fault coverage (%) | CPU Time/s | Fault Coverage (%) | CPU Time/s |
| s208 | 63.7 | 3 | 78.1 | 17 |
| s298 | 85.7 | 142 | 87.7 | 106 |
| s344 | 96.2 | 257 | 99.4 | 56 |
| s349 | 95.7 | 251 | 96.2 | 114 |
| s386 | 81.8 | 32 | 81.8 | 21 |
| s420 | 41.6 | 112 | 58.8 | 237 |
| s510 | 0 | 0 | 100 | 109 |
| s641 | 86.5 | 6 | 94.4 | 55 |
| s713 | 81.9 | 7 | 87.6 | 74 |
| s1196 | 99.8 | 13 | 99.8 | 9 |
| s1238 | 94.7 | 23 | 94.7 | 13 |
| s5378 | 74.0 | 9042 | 74.9 | 6105 |
| s9234 | 0.3 | 4 | 6.3 | 22652 |

**TABLE 45.9** Comparison between Test Generation Phases in SEMILET

| Circuit | CPU Time/s | Percentage Prop. (%) | Percentage Prop-Just. (%) | Percentage Just. (%) |
|---|---|---|---|---|
| s208 | 3 | 15.8 | 16.5 | 67.7 |
| s298 | 142 | 16.7 | 55.2 | 28.1 |
| s344 | 257 | 10.0 | 19.5 | 70.5 |
| s349 | 251 | 7.4 | 17.4 | 75.2 |
| s386 | 32 | 5.6 | 5.6 | 88.8 |
| s420 | 112 | 9.0 | 29.6 | 61.4 |
| s641 | 6 | 7.1 | 4.7 | 88.2 |
| s713 | 7 | 10.8 | 6.7 | 82.5 |
| s1196 | 13 | 11.5 | 13.8 | 74.7 |
| s1238 | 23 | 21.7 | 10.0 | 68.3 |
| s5378 | 9042 | 7.6 | 14.8 | 77.6 |
| s9234 | 4 | 1.5 | 0 | 98.5 |

In many cases, it was measured in the experiments that if one of the test pattern generators HITEC or GENTEST is a bit faster than SEMILET the other test pattern generator is much slower (example: s344, s349, s386...). Thus, SEMILET had much better results than HITEC and GENTEST in the average. In the s510, no test pattern generation and fault simulation was necessary for SEMILET because all untestable faults could be identified in the preprocessing phase of the test generator.

In Table 45.8, "normal" test generation for the circuits is shown in comparison with test generation when using global set and reset signals in the circuit. For circuits that consist of noninitializable storage elements, the fault coverage increases rapidly. For instance, the s510 is completely untestable without use of global initialization, and by applying a global set and reset signal to all flip-flops it is completely testable. The stuck-at fault model was used for test generation here. The use of global set and reset signals results in increased fault coverage at reduced testing time. The fault coverage increased for s510 and s420. The testing time was reduced for s344 and s5378.

Table 45.9 shows the percentage of computation time in the three different phases of the algorithm. Most of the time was spent in the justification phase for almost all experiments (exception s298). This result is consistent with the HITEC analysis in [51].

## 45.4 Summary

Automatic test pattern generation yielding high fault coverage for CMOS circuits has received wide attention in industry and academia for a long time. Mixed-level test pattern generation offers advantages, since test generation from gate-level netlists has shortcomings regarding fault coverage in complex CMOS gates. A switch-level approach relying on the transistor structure only is too slow and impractical for larger circuits. The first part of this chapter describes automatic test pattern generation with a mixed switch-level and gate-level approach. It combines acceptable performance for large networks with a high fault coverage also for nontrivial transistor networks. Patterns generated this way are inherently capable to detect stuck-open faults and transition faults as well as various other fault models on different abstraction levels. In combination with local overcurrent detectors, also stuck-on and local bridging faults can be identified. To increase the efficiency of mixed-level test generation, a reconvergency analysis is performed and constraints are stored.

An original approach to test generation for synchronous sequential circuits was presented. Two levels of hierarchy, the switch-level and the gate-level are supported. Inter-level backtracks between these two hierarchies are implemented. The number of inter-level backtracks is minimized using simple heuristics for constraint identification, which is a promising method for hierarchical test generation also on higher levels (RT or behavior level). A new efficient algorithm called FOGBUSTER for the forward propagation backward initialization technique handles synchronous sequential circuits. A 4-valued logic and a two-staged backtracking mechanism are used to handle the over-specification problem and to achieve completeness. Experimental results for the ISCAS '85 and ISCAS '89 benchmark circuits are encouraging. In comparison to the BACK-algorithm and to the HITEC approach, FOGBUSTER on the average has a significantly better performance.

## References

1. H. Fujiwara, T. Shimono: On the acceleration of test generation algorithms, *IEEE Trans. on Computers (C-32)*, 1983, pp. 1137–1144.
2. M. H. Schulz, E. Trischler, T. M. Sarfert: SOCRATES: A highly efficient ATPG system, *IEEE Trans. CAD*, Vol. 7, Jan. 1988, pp. 126–137.
3. J. P. Roth: Diagnosis of Automata Failures: A calculus and a method, *IBM Journal*, 1966, pp. 278– 291.
4. M. H. Schulz, E. Auth: Essential: An efficient self-learning test pattern generation algorithm for sequential circuits, *Proc. IEEE Int. Test Conf.*, 1989, pp. 28–37.
5. N. Gouders, R. Kaibel: Advanced techniques for sequential test generation, *Proc. 2nd European Test Conf.*, Munich, 1991.
6. R. L. Wadsack: Fault modeling and logic simulation in CMOS and MOS integrated circuits, *Bell Systems Technical Journal*, May–June 1978, pp. 1449–1474.
7. F. Ferguson, J. Shen: Extraction and simulation of realistic CMOS faults under inductive fault analysis, *Proc. IEEE Int. Test Conf.*, 1988, pp. 475–484.
8. H. T. Vierhaus: Testability of CMOS faults under realistic conditions, *Microprocessing and Microprogramming*, Vol. 27, pp. 681–686, 1989.
9. U. Glaeser, U. Hübner, H. T. Vierhaus: mixed level hierarchical test generation for transition faults and overcurrent related defects, *Proc. ITC '92*, pp. 21–29.
10. U. Glaeser, H. T. Vierhaus: MILEF: an efficient approach to mixed level automatic test pattern generation, *Proc. EURODAC '92*, pp. 318–321.
11. K. W. Chiag, Z. G. Vranesic: on fault detection in CMOS logic networks, *Proc. IEEE Int. Test Conf.*, 1983, pp. 50–56.
12. C. Glover: Mixed mode ATPG under input constraints, *Proc. IEEE Int. Test Conf.*, 1990.
13. M. L. Flottes, C. Landrault et al.: Mixed level automatic test pattern generation for CMOS, *Proc. 2nd European Test Conf.*, Munich, 1991, pp. 273–282.

14. C.-H. Shen and J. A. Abraham: Mixed level sequential test generation using a nine valued relaxation algorithm, *Proc. ICCAD-90*, pp. 230–235.

15. K. J. Lee, C. A. Njinda, M. A. Breuer: SWITEST: a switch-level test generation system for CMOS combinational circuits, *Proc. DAC '92*, pp. 26–29.

16. H. Cox and J. Rajski: Stuck-open and transition fault testing in CMOS complex gates, *IEEE Int. Test Conf.*, 1988, pp. 688–694.

17. V. S. Iyengar, B. K. Rose, I. Spencer: Delay test generation I—concepts and coverage metrics," *Proc. Int. Test Conf.*, 1988.

18. E. S. Park, M. R. Mercer, T. W. Williams: Statistical delay fault coverage and defect level for delay faults, *Proc. Int. Test Conf.*, 1988.

19. K. Fuchs, F. Fink, M. H. Schulz: DYNAMITE: An efficient automatic test pattern generation system for path delay faults, *IEEE Trans. CAD*, Oct. 1991.

20. M. Geilert, J. Alt, M. Zimmermann: On the efficiency of the transition fault model for delay faults, *Proc. ICCAD-90*, pp. 272–275.

21. S. Devadas, K. Keutzer: Design of integrated circuits fully testable for delay faults and multifaults, *Proc. ITC '90*, pp. 284–293.

22. C. H. Chen, J. A. Abraham: Mixed-level sequential test generation using a nine-valued relaxation algorithm, *Proc. ICCAD '90*, pp. 230–233.

23. W. Maly, P. Nigh: Built-in current testing—a feasibility study, *Proc. IEEE ICCAD '88*, 1988, pp. 340–343.

24. T. Storey, W. Maly, J. Andrews, M. Miske: Comparing stuck fault and current testing via CMOS chip test, *Proc. 2nd European Test Conf.*, Munich, 1991, pp. 149–156.

25. W. Cheng: The BACK-algorithm for sequential test generation, *Proc. ICCD '88*, pp. 66–69.

26. R. Marlett: EBT: A comprehensive test generation technique for highly sequential circuits, *Proc. DAC '78*, pp. 335–339.

27. T. Ma, S. Devadas, A. R. Newton, A. Sangiovanni-Vincentelli: Test generation for sequential circuits, *IEEE Trans. Computer Aided Design*, 1888, pp. 1081–1093.

28. P. Camurati, F. Corno, P. Prinetto, M. Sonza Reorda: A Simulation-based approach to test pattern generation for synchronous sequential circuits, *IEEE VLSI Test Symposium*, 1992, pp. 263–267.

29. V. D. Agrawal, K. T. Cheng, P. Agrawal: A direct search method for test generation for sequential circuits, *IEEE Trans. Computer-Aided Design*, Feb. 1989, pp. 131–138.

30. U. Hübner, H. T. Vierhaus: Testmustergenerator für kombinatorische CMOS Schaltungen, GMD-Studie Nr. 155, GMD, St. Augustin, 1989, pp. 85–93.

31. U. Hübner, R. Camposano: Partitioning and analysis of static digital CMOS-circuits, Arbeitspapiere der GMD 761, July 1993.

32. D. T. Blaauw, R. B. Mueller-Thuns, D. G. Saab, P. Banerjee: SNELL: A switch level simulator using multiple levels of functional abstraction, *Proc. ICCAD '90*, pp. 66–69.

33. U. Hübner, H. Hinsen, M. Hofebauer, H. T. Vierhaus: Mixed level test generation for high fault coverage, *Microprocessing and Microprogramming*, Vol. 32, No. 1–5, Aug. 1991, pp. 791–796.

34. U. Hübner, H. T. Vierhaus: Built-in current testing vs. delay fault testing—a case study, *Proc. IEEE CompEuro '92*, Den Haag.

35. F. Brglez, P. Pownall, R. Hum: Applications of testability analysis: from ATPG to critical path tracing, *Proc. ITC '84*, pp. 705–712.

36. A. Lioy, M. Mezzalama: On parameters affecting ATPG performance, *Proc. CompEuro '87*, pp. 394–397.

37. L. H. Goldstein: Controllability/observability measure for logic testability, *IEEE Trans. Circuits and Systems*, Vol. CAS-26, pp. 685–693, 1979.

38. S. M. Reddy, M. K. Reddy, V. D. Agrawal: Robust tests for stuck-open faults in CMOS combinational logic circuits, *Proc. FTCS '84*, pp. 44–49.

39. W. Meyer, R. Camposano: Fast hierarchical multi-level fault simulation of sequential circuits with switch-level accuracy, *Proc. DAC '93*, pp. 515–519.

40. L. N. Reddy, I. Pomeranz, S. M. Reddy: COMPACTEST-II: a method to generate two-pattern test sets for combinational logic circuits, *Proc. ICCAD-92*, pp. 568–574.

41. F. Brglez, H. Fujiwara: A neutral list of 10 combinational benchmark circuits and a target translator in FORTRAN, *Proc. 1985 Int. Symp. Circuits and Systems,* pp. 671–674.

42. W. Meyer, H. T. Vierhaus: Switch-level fault simulation for non-trivial faults based on abstract data types, *Proc. IEEE CompEuro '91,* Bologna.

43. T. Niermann, J. H. Patel: HITEC: a test generation package for sequential circuits, *Proc. EDAC '91,* pp. 214–218.

44. W. Cheng, T. J. Chakraborty: GENTEST: An automatic test-generation system for sequential circuits, *IEEE Computer '89,* pp. 43–49.

45. T. P. Kelsey, K. K. Saluja, S. Y. Lee: An efficient algorithm for sequential circuit test generation, *IEEE Trans. Computers,* Nov. 1993, pp. 1361–1371.

46. F. Brglez, F. Bryant, D. Kozminski: Combinational profiles of sequential benchmark circuits, *Proc. 1989 Int. Symp. Circ. and Systems.*

47. H. Keung, T. Ma, et al.: Test generation for sequential finite state machines, *Proc. ICCAD '87,* pp. 288–291.

48. S. Mallela, S. Wu: A sequential circuit test generation system, *Proc. ITC '85,* pp. 57–61.

49. K. T. Cheng, T. Ma: On the over specification problem in sequential ATPG algorithms, *IEEE Trans. Computer Aided-Design,* 1993, pp. 1599–1604.

50. A. Miczo: The sequential ATPG: a theoretical limit, *Proc. DAC '83,* pp. 143–147.

51. T. E. Marchok, W. Maly, A. El-Maleh, J. Rajski: Complexity of sequential ATPG, *Proc. ED&TC '95,* pp. 252–261.

# 46
# Scan Testing

Chouki Aktouf
*Institute Universitaire*
*de Technologie*

## 46.1  Introduction

Given a design under test (DUT), a *test solution* is qualified as *efficient* if it allows the generation of test patterns, which enable the detection of most of possible physical faults that may occur in the design. Researchers talk about 99% of fault coverage and more. To reach such a test efficiency, the cost to pay is related to time which is necessary for test pattern generation and application, the area overhead for the added logic, the added number of pins, etc. These parameters are concerned through scan testing techniques, which are presented in the next section.

Some studies have shown that the testing phase can constitute a serious problem in the overall production time. For typical circuits, testing can take from the one-third to the half of the total time to market (TTM) [1]. In [2], it has been shown that a design-for-testability (DFT) technique such as full scan can reduce by more than a half the total engineering costs. Indeed, scan helps in detecting a fault quickly and in an efficient manner.

As shown in Fig. 46.1 the well-known "rule of ten" is true when scan is considered. Indeed, sooner a fault is detected the lower is the subsequent cost. This is explained by the fact that DFT helps in the generation of efficient test patterns. In other words, given in a short period of time, if a fault appears in a DFT-based design, a high probability exists to detect the fault. Furthermore, a DFT technique such as scan helps in the testing through the whole life cycle of the design including debug, production testing, and maintenance.

## 46.2  Scan Testing

Today, given strong time to market constraints on new products, only DFT is capable of ensuring the design of complex system-on-chips with a high testing quality. Scan is widely used in industry. It took almost 20 years to reach such a maturity, even if some designers still think that scan penalizes a design due to the required cost and performance degradation.

Scan testing is applied to sequential testing, i.e., testing of sequential designs. It relates to the ability of shifting data in and out of all sequential states. Regardless to the used scan approach, all flip-flops are interconnected into one or more shift registers that ensures the shifting in and the shifting out functions. The built shift register is fully controlled/observed from primary inputs/outputs as shown in Fig. 46.2 [3].

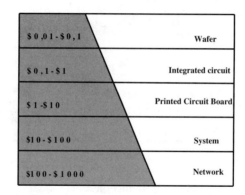

**FIGURE 46.1**    Rule of ten in testing economics.

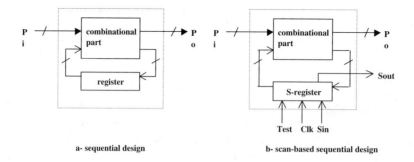

**FIGURE 46.2**    Sequential scan.

Hence, scan testing transforms the testing problem of a sequential design into a testing of a combinational design. The problem of testing combinational circuits problem is easier since classical test generation algorithms are more efficient (better testing results which mean an obtained fault coverage close to 100%). In fact, it is well known that the number of feedback cycles in a circuit can increase the complexity of sequential test generation. It is important to notice that the built shift register need to be tested too.

However, when scan is considered, the price to pay is related to the following parameters: logic overhead, which means more space, degradation of the production yield and the design performance since more logic is added to the original one, design effort, and usually more pins. As shown in Fig. 46.2, the "register" built on the flip-flops or the design memory cells is transformed into a *scannable* shift register (S-register). The complexity of the obtained register is more important since each memory cell might be used in both normal and test modes. This requires at least a *multiplexor* at each cell level and some additional wiring. As shown in the same figure, the normal and the test modes are controlled by the added input "Test."

One of the drawbacks when scan is used is the necessary time for scan-in (downloading test patterns) and scan-out (getting test results) operations. If the DUT includes thousands of memory cells, which is the case of nowadays integrated circuits (ICs), only one scan chain means shifting all test data serially through the whole "S-register." This is usually too long even if the frequency of the clock "Clk" is reasonably high. Dividing a scan chain into several scan chains is a good issue. Figures 46.3 and 46.4 illustrate each of the two concepts where one or several *scan paths* (called also *scan chains*) are considered. An example of a PCB (printed circuit board) of six ICs is considered.

To test this PCB, instead of using one scan chain as shown in Fig. 46.3, three scan chains are considered as illustrated in Fig. 46.4. It is noteworthy that more pins are required to allow the parallel use of the scan chains: three for scan-in and three for scan-out operations. In this case, two test pins are necessary for each scan path.

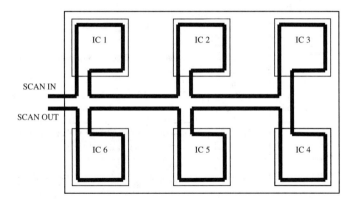

**FIGURE 46.3**    Scan architecture with a single path.

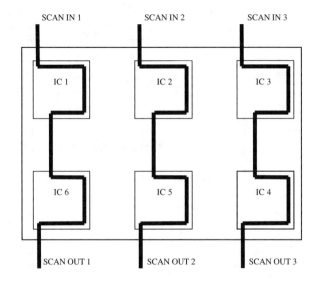

**FIGURE 46.4**    Scan architecture with several scan chains.

## Boundary Scan

As a widely used scan technique, boundary-scan (BS) provides an access to internal structures (blocks, IC, etc.) knowing that few logic is directly accessible from primary inputs and primary outputs. Probably one of the famous scan approaches is BS through the ANSI/IEEE 1149.1 standard. This standard is also known as JTAG (Join Action Test Group). A decade earlier, a group of test experts from industry and academia worked together in order to propose standardized protocols and architectures that help in the dissemination of the BS technique.

Given a DUT such as a PCB, BS consists of as a first step in making each input and output of a circuit as a memory element. Given all memory elements, the next step consists in linking all memory elements into a register called BS register. The access to this mandatory register is possible from four standard pins. Finally, in order to be conform with the boundary scan standard ANSI/IEEE Std. 1149.1, a controller called TAP (Test Access Port) and a set of registers are implemented within each circuit. This is shown in Fig. 46.5.

The BS register is mandatory in a JTAG compliant architecture. Figure 46.6 gives an example of a BS cell. Such a cell can be used as either an input or as an output cell. Such a cell supports four functional modes: normal mode (when *Mode_Control* = 0), where the BS cell is transparent during the normal use

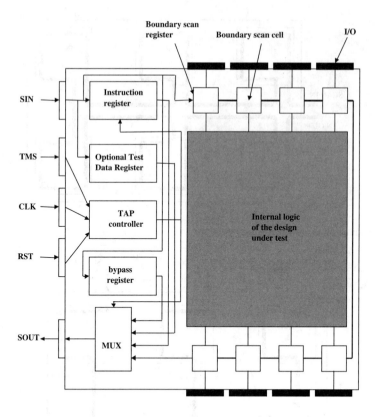

**FIGURE 46.5**   Overview of the ANSI/IEEE 1149.1 architecture.

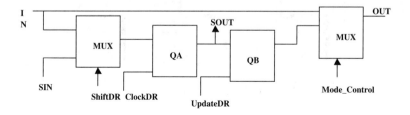

**FIGURE 46.6**   A BS cell.

of the DUT. In the second mode called scan mode, all BS cells are connected into a BS chain. In this mode *ShiftDR* = 1 and the necessary clock pulses are applied. The third mode is the capture mode where data are loaded through the input IN into the scan path. In this mode, *ShiftDR* = 0 and one clock pulse *ClockDR* is applied. The QA flip-flop serves as a snapshot cell. The final mode is called update mode. In this mode, *Mode_Control* = 1 and one pulse of the *UpdateDR* is activated.

These four functioning modes allow each of the instructions summarized below to be executed.

The main motivation for this standard is to overcome the problem of physical access to circuits that becomes more and more difficult. JTAG overcomes the need of bed-of-nails fixtures with a very fine resolution, if available.

As shown in Fig. 46.6, the BS architecture includes the following blocks:

- *TAP controller*: This block generates all clocks and signals that are necessary for the architecture.
- *Instruction register*: This register holds the instruction, which is related to the test that needs to be executed.

- *Test data register*: These registers hold test patterns that need to be run on the test logic. A specific register scanned BS register is mandatory; however, other registers can be added if necessary.

Based on the BS architecture, several tests can be executed: test logic, internal logic, and interconnection:

- *Test logic*: Before running the test of the circuit under test, the test logic must be checked through specific states of the TAP controller that can be used for that.
- *Internal logic testing*: This is ensured through the use of the specific instruction called *intest* presented below. Testing the internal test logic of a DUT means that each DUT block can be tested.
- *Interconnection testing*: It is related to the test of interconnection between two blocks. As summarized in the next paragraph, a specific instruction called *extest* is used.

The JTAG standard enables the application of several kinds of tests. This is summarized in the instructions proposed by the standard. These instructions are executed by the TAP controller. As explained in the following list, some of these instructions are mandatory and some are optional.

- *Bypass*: It is mandatory. This instruction allows a specific DUT to be tested by bypassing one or more other designs.
- *Extest*: This mandatory instruction allows the test of interconnection between two DUT. It is especially useful in the case of *integration testing*.
- *Intest*: This instruction is optional. It can be used to test the internal logic, a block, or a circuit.
- *Sample/Preload*: This instruction is mandatory. It helps in taking snapshots of useful data that run during normal operation of the DUT.
- *Icode and Usercode*: These two instructions are optional. They allow the access to a specific register known as the device-identification register.
- *RUNBIST*: This optional instruction allows the running of a BIST (built-in-self test) solution by using the TAP controller. BIST is explained later.

For more details regarding these instructions, please refer to [12].

## Partial Scan

The scan approach presented above is also called full scan because the built scan chain includes all the DUT memory elements; however, this might be costly for complex ICs where the number of memory elements exceeds thousands of cells. By cost, it is meant the area overhead that results from full scan (added multiplexors, wiring, pins, etc.), the performance degradation due to signal slowdown and test time due to very large scan chains. For a better trade-off performance/cost, a scan technique called partial scan is proposed [11]. Only a subset of memory elements are included in the considered scan chain. This decreases both the area overhead and the timing penalty.

The problem of partial scan is still open. No technique proposes how to effectively determine the appropriate subset of flip-flops to be scanned. Indeed, an effective partial scan technique is the one that selects the fewest flip-flops in the scan chain while achieving both a high fault coverage and an optimized physical design.

Knowing that DUT is modeled by a system graph called S-graph, the partial scan problem consists in finding the minimal feedback vertex set (MFSV). This is known as an NP-complete problem [4]. In an S-graph, the vertices are the DUT registers and the edges represent a combinational path from one register to another.

The proposed solutions are some heuristics, which are based on the following techniques: testability analysis, structural analysis, or test pattern generation. A testability analysis-based technique consists in predicting through measures of the problems faced during test pattern generation. The concept through structural analysis is some heuristics that try to break feedback cycles. Finally, when the selected flip-flops are based on test pattern generation (TPG), it generally means that a TPG program is used to

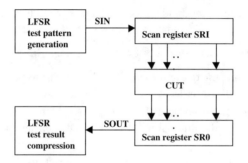

**FIGURE 46.7**    Example of merging scan and BIST.

generate tests for every fault and then the test patterns, which are selected, are those which necessitate the fewest number of flip-flops that are scanned.

## Scan and Built-in Test Solutions

A scan design can serve as a support for a complete built-in-test solution. Indeed, as assumed earlier (see Fig. 46.2), test patterns are supposed to be generated from outside and applied through the *Sin* pin. Furthermore, it is assumed that test results are scanned out through the *Sout* pin and compared one by one to the test results of a golden circuit. A *golden* circuit is a circuit, which is assumed to be fault-free.

A scan-based design can be used in order to implement both test pattern generation and test result verification functions within the DUT. Built-in-Self-Test (BIST) is a design-for-testability technique in which testing (test generation and test application) is accomplished through built-in hardware features [5–6]. When testing is built as a hardware it is very fast and very efficient.

The example in Fig. 46.7 shows how a basic scan design is considered for a BIST solution. The LFSR (linear feedback shift register) is used as an example of a test pattern generator. Pseudo-random test patterns, which can be very efficient in case of sequential designs, are generated using such a structure. For test results verification, a LFSR is used to compress test results and produce a signature which will represent the obtained test results.

## Tools and Languages for Scan Automation

Today, several CAD vendors include BS in their DFT test tool (Mentor Graphics, Teradyne, Jtag Technologies, Logic Vision, etc.). Tools which are available in the market propose scan testing solutions. The main functions that are proposed by such tools are: scan design rules checking, scan conversion, and the associated test pattern generation.

Through the IEEE standard 1149.1-1990, the BS technology is more and more embraced in electronic systems at several hierarchical levels: ICs, boards, subsystems, and systems. One of the key points that has helped in that is the availability of tools and languages that support such a technology. A subset of VHDL was proposed for this purpose [13]. The language is called BSDL (boundary scan description language). When a new standard is proposed many barriers may slow down its adoption. BSDL was proposed in order to speed up the implementation of the "dot one" standard through BSDL-based tools. This language helps in the description and the checking of the compliance of a design with BS technology. More precisely, BSDL helps in the implementation of testability features, which are related to the "dot one" technology. Hence, necessary simulation and verification of the BS technology can be performed. More precisely, testing if a DUT is compliant with the "dot one" technology means that devices that are mandatory to be implemented are checked. For example, the parameters that related to the TAP controller and the boundary scan register are described and checked out through such a language. Furthermore, BSDL serves as a support for IC vendors to automatically add BS logic through all design process of the design.

More information about BSDL can be found in [13].

# 46.3 Future of Scan: A Brief Forecast

## Scan for Analog and Mixed Designs

Boundary-scan was originally developed for digital circuits and systems. The motivations to use BS for analog designs is also true; however, in contrast to digital circuits and systems, analog components are specified by a continuous range of parameters rather than binary values 0 and 1. A new standard is coming called P1149.4. It consists in the development of a mixed signal test bus. The aim is to standardize to several possible tests in the case of analog DUT: interconnect test, parametric test, and internal test. Such tests should be fully compatible with the IEEE 1149.1 standard and helps in measuring the values of discrete components such as pull-up resistors and capacitors. Consequently, P1149.4 can be seen as an extension of IEEE 1149.1 where the BS cells presented above are replaced by analog boundary modules (ABM) at the level of each analog functional pin. Such pins can be accessed via internal analog test bus. Fig. 46.8 gives the structure of the P1149.4 bus.

As IEEE 1149.1 has proven its efficiency, P1149.4 is most likely a good DFT solution for analog circuits and systems. Furthermore, its compatibility with the IEEE 1149.1 will simplify the test of mixed DUT.

For more details regarding the standard, please refer to [7].

## RTL and Behavioral Scan

Scan techniques that have been presented until now have several drawbacks. First, they are highly related to the used design tools and target libraries. Moreover, in case of highly complex DUT, a high computation time is required because low-level descriptions (gate-level or lower) are considered. Furthermore, the added logic does not take advantage of the global *optimization* of the design, which can be performed by the used synthesis tools.

Recently, several techniques that improve the testability using high level descriptions [8-10], have been proposed. For example in [9], a technique which inserts a partial scan using the B-VHDL (behavioral VHDL) description has been presented. In [10], a technique that allows scan to be inserted at the B-VHDL description of a DUT has been presented. This has many advantages. The scan insertion problem is considered very early in the design process, which means that a fully testable design can be provided at the behavioral level, i.e., before any structural information is known. Compared to approaches that may include scan at the RTL or the logical level, inserting scan at the behavioral level is very promising since it takes fully advantage of design validation and test generation tools that might operate at the

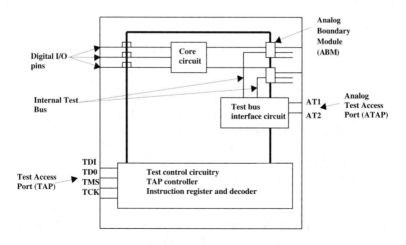

**FIGURE 46.8** Structure of the P1149.4 bus.

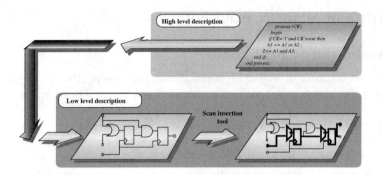

**FIGURE 46.9**   Low-level scan.

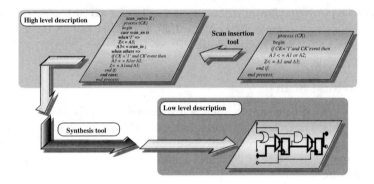

**FIGURE 46.10**   High-level scan.

behavioral level. Furthermore, the testable description can be synthesized using several libraries and tools. The testable design is consequently more *portable*. Moreover, when a scan chain is inserted at the high level of the DUT, the added logic used for the test is globally compiled and optimized during the synthesis process, which reduces the area overhead.

Fig. 46.9 shows the classical approach of scan insertion. Fig. 46.10 shows how scan can be inserted before the synthesis is performed.

To insert a scan register at a behavioral level (high-level scan), memory elements of the DUT need to be known. In fact, the scan insertion process is made up of two basic steps. First, memory elements are located. Then, the behavioral description of the design is modified in order to describe the behavior of the scan register.

Such a new scan insertion approach necessitates the development of the related tools. *Hiscan* (high-level scan) is a tool that allows scan insertion at the B-VHDL level. Given a synthesizable B-VHDL description, *Hiscan* generates a VIF (VHDL intermediate format) file, which contains necessary information of objects (signals and variables). *Hiscan* uses the VIF file to locate objects that correspond to memory elements once the synthesis is accomplished. Before constructing a B-VHDL scan chain, *Hiscan* considers constraints which can be used in the selection of the detected memory elements. Typically, constraints are related to testability measures at the B-VHDL level or ATPG-based constraints or both. During the last step, *Hiscan* generates a B-VHDL scannable description, which is ready for synthesis.

Given several examples of benchmarks, such a high-level scan insertion approach was shown efficient since the cost of inserting a scan design is significantly reduced when compared to classical scan techniques that operate at a low-level design. Please refer to [10] for more details.

# References

1. Parakevopoulos, D.E. and Fey, C.F., "Studies in LSI techonology economics III: Design schedules for application-specific integrated circuits," *Journal of Solid-State Circuits*, vol. sc-22, pp. 223–229, April 1987.

2. Dear, I.D. et al., "Economic effects in design and test," *IEEE Design & Test of Computers*, December 1991, pp. 64–77.

3. Williams, M.I.Y and Angell, J.B., "Enhanced testability of large scale integrated circuits via test points and additional logic," *IEEE Transactions of Computers*, C-22, no. 1, pp. 46–60, 1973.

4. Garey, M.R. and Johnson, D.S., *Computers and Intractability: A Guide to the Theory of NP-Completeness*, W.H. Freeman, San Francisco, 1979.

5. Agrawal, V.D., Kime, C.R., and Saluja, K.K., "A tutorial on built-in self test," *IEEE Design & Test of Computers*, Part 1, March 1993, pp. 73–82.

6. V.D. Agrawal, C.R. Kime, and K.K. Saluja, "A tutorial on built-in self test," *IEEE Design & Test of Computers*, Part 2, June 1993, pp. 69–77.

7. Parker, K.P., McDermid, J.E., and Oresjo, S., "Structure and metrology for analog testability bus," in *Proceedings of the International Test Conference*, 1993, pp. 309–317.

8. Wagner, K.D. and Dey, S., "High-level synthesis for testability: a survey and perspectives," in *Proceedings of 33rd Design Automation Conference*, pp. 131–136.

9. Chickermane, V., Lee, J., and Patel, J.H., "Addressing design for testability at the architectural level," *IEEE Transactions on Computer-Aided Design of Integrated Circuits and Systems*, vol. 13, no. 7, July 1994, pp. 920–934.

10. Aktouf, C., Fleury, H., and Robach, C., "Inseting scan at the behavioural level," *IEEE Design & Test of Computers*, July–September, pp. 34–44.

11. Abramovici, M., Breuer, M.A., and Friedman, A.D., *Digital Systems Testing and Testable Design*, Computer Science Press, 1990.

12. Maunder, C.M. and Tulloss, R.E., "An introduction to the boundary-scan standard: ANSI/IEEE Std 1149.1," *Journal of Electronic Testing, Theory and Applications (JETTA)*, vol. 2, no. 1, March 1991, pp. 27–42.

13. Parker, K.P. and Oresjo, S., "A language for describing boundary-scan devices," in *Proceedings of the International Test Conference*, September 1990, pp. 222–234.

# 47

# Computer-Aided Analysis and Forecast of Integrated Circuit Yield

Z. Stamenković
*University of Niš*

N. Stojadinović
*University of Niš*

## 47.1   Introduction

Yield is one of the cornerstones of a successful integrated circuit (IC) manufacturing technology along with product performance and cost. Many factors contribute to the achievement of high yield but also interact with product performance and cost. A fundamental understanding of yield limitations enables the up-front achievement of this technology goal through circuit and layout design, device design, materials choices, and process optimization. Defect, failure, and yield analyses are critical issues for the improvement of IC yield. Finally, the yield improvement is essential to success.

The coordination of people in many disciplines is needed in order to achieve high IC yield. Therefore, each needs to understand the impact of their choices and methods on this important technology goal. Unfortunately, very little formal university training exists in the area of IC yield. This chapter is intended to bring students, engineers, and scientists up to speed and enable them to function knowledgeably in this area.

Section 47.2 deals with IC yield and critical area models. Section 47.3 is dedicated to a local extraction approach for the extraction of IC critical areas. Finally, Section 47.4 presents an application of previously mentioned models and extraction approach in yield forecast.

## 47.2   Yield Models

This section is dedicated to IC yield analysis and modeling. Yield analysis includes the discussion of methods, models, and parameters for detecting which technology and design attributes are really yield relevant. Yield modeling mathematically expresses the dependence of yield on IC process defect characteristics and design attributes. Thus, correct yield models are essential for meaningful yield and cost projections.

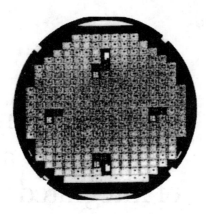

**FIGURE 47.1**    Defect clustering on semiconductor wafer.

This section describes a macroscopic approach to yield analysis and corresponding functional yield models and yield parameters.

## Classical Yield Models

Functional yield is the probability of zero catastrophic (fatal) defects. Catastrophic defects are defects that result in primitive electrical failures and, consequently, yield loss. Therefore, the yield is derived from Poisson's equation as follow [1]:

$$Y = \exp(-AD) \tag{47.1}$$

where $A$ is the area sensitive to defects (so-called critical area) [2–7] and $D$ is the defect density.

However, the simple Poisson yield formula is too pessimistic for IC chips on a wafer, because defects are often not randomly distributed, but rather are clustered in certain regions (Fig. 47.1). Defect clustering can cause large areas of a wafer to have fewer defects than a random distribution, such as the Poisson model, would predict, which in turn results in higher yields in those areas. Therefore, to tackle this nonrandom defect distribution, instead of using a constant defect density, Murphy introduced compound Poisson statistics [8]. The Poisson distribution is compounded with a function $g(D)$, which represents the normalized distribution of defect densities:

$$Y = \int_0^\infty \exp(-AD)g(D)dD \tag{47.2}$$

The function $g(D)$ is a weighting function that accounts for the nonrandom distribution of defects.

A number of distribution functions can be used to approximate the defect density distribution and analyze IC yield. Five of these are given below (Fig. 47.2) and corresponding yield models are described.

### Poisson Model

When defects are randomly and uniformly distributed over the wafer, the wafer defect statistics can be characterized by a constant $\bar{D}$, which is the average defect density. Therefore, $g(D)$ is a delta function centered at $D = \bar{D}$, resulting in the simple Poisson distribution and the yield given by

$$Y = \exp(-A\bar{D}) \tag{47.3}$$

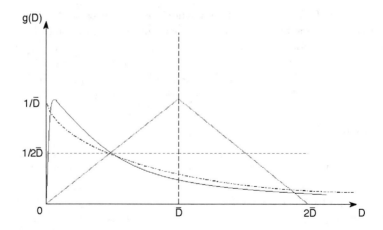

**FIGURE 47.2** Distribution functions for approximation of defect density distribution.

## Murphy's Model

The most preferred distribution function was a Gaussian; however, a Gaussian distribution gets difficult for integration most of the time. In order to carry out the integration in an easier way, Murphy [8] proposed using a symmetrical triangle weighting function for an approximation to a Gaussian distribution. Substituting this into formula (47.2) gives

$$Y = \left[ \frac{1 - \exp(-A\overline{D})}{A\overline{D}} \right]^2 \tag{47.4}$$

Murphy [8] also used a rectangle distribution function to represent the defect density distribution. This distribution function is constant between zero and $2\overline{D}$, and zero elsewhere. The meaning of this function, physically, implies that chip defect densities are evenly distributed up to $2\overline{D}$, but none have a higher value. Using the rectangle distribution function in Murphy's yield integral, we get

$$Y = \frac{1 - \exp(-2A\overline{D})}{2A\overline{D}} \tag{47.5}$$

## Price's Model

Price [9] applied an exponential distribution function to approximate the defect density distribution. The decaying form of the exponential function implies that higher defect densities are increasingly unlikely. Physically, this means that high defect densities are restricted to small regions of a wafer. The exponential distribution function can be used to represent severe clustering in small regions of a wafer. The resulting yield formula for this distribution function is as follow:

$$Y = \frac{1}{1 + A\overline{D}} \tag{47.6}$$

## Stapper's Model

Stapper [10] used a Gamma distribution, which led to the following yield formula

$$Y = \left[ 1 + \frac{A\sigma^2}{\overline{D}} \right]^{-\overline{D}^2/\sigma^2} \tag{47.7}$$

where $\sigma^2$ is the variance of Gamma distribution function. The parameter $\overline{D}^2/\sigma^2$ can be used to account for *defect clustering*. By varying this parameter, the model covers the entire range of yield predictions. The larger variance means more clustering of defects. If the parameter is equal to 1, this yield model reduces to the Price formula (exponential weighting). On the contrary, for $\sigma^2 = 0$, it becomes the Poisson formula (no clustering). The value of the clustering parameter must be experimentally determined. The smaller values reflect higher yield and occur with maturity of technology.

## Yield Distribution Model

Much work has been done in the field of yield modeling [11–30] and many results can be applied in yield analysis; however, there is too much indistinctness in a modeling approach and too many disputes about the correct model [16,17,19,23,24]. It appears that the main stumbling block was identification of the yield defined as a probability of failure-free IC chip (the chip yield) with the yield defined as a ratio between the number of failure-free chips $n$ and the total number of chips $N$ on a wafer (the wafer yield). There is a major difference between these two quantities: the chip yield is a probability and can be expressed by a number between 0 and 1, while the wafer yield is a stochastic variable and should be expressed by its distribution function.

The final goal of yield modeling must be to predict the wafer yield, so as to enable comparison with the production yield data. The authors have proposed a yield model that does not require any defect density distribution function but is completely based on the test chip yield measurement and can predict the wafer yield as a distribution [31].

### Chip Yield

Using corresponding in-line measurements of the test chip yields $Y_{ti}$, defined as a ratio between the number of failure-free test chips and the total number of test chips in a given wafer area, the IC chip yield, associated with the $i$th critical process step, can be directly predicted. A typical test chip containing MOS capacitors, diodes, transistors, long conducting lines, and chains of contacts is shown in Fig.47.3. The IC chip yield will differ from the test chip yield due to the difference in the critical area. So, if a ratio between the IC chip and test chip critical areas is given by $A_{ci}/A_{ti}$, and the wafer area can be divided into $m$ subareas with approximately uniform distribution of defects, the IC chip yield can be determined by [14,31]

$$Y_{cil} = Y_{til}^{A_{ci}/A_{ti}} \tag{47.8}$$

where $l$ denotes the corresponding subarea. If a control wafer area has been divided into subareas in the same way for each critical process step, the final IC chip yield is given by

$$Y_{cl} = \prod_{i=1}^{k} Y_{cil} \quad \text{for } l = 1, 2, \ldots, m \tag{47.9}$$

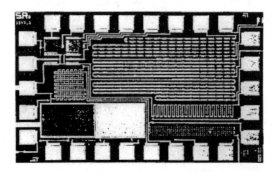

**FIGURE 47.3** Test chip containing test structures.

where $k$ is the total number of critical process steps, i.e., the total number of yield loss mechanisms; however, the chip yield is not enough for complete yield characterization, and the wafer yield $Y_i$ should be predicted as well.

## Wafer Yield

As far as only $i$th critical process step is considered, there is no need to explore the very yield distribution function, but it is enough to determine its parameters: the mean and variance. The parameters of wafer yield distribution function are given by [31]

$$\bar{Y}_i = \sum_{l=1}^{m} C_{il} Y_{cil} \tag{47.10}$$

$$\sigma_{Y_i}^2 = \frac{1}{N} \sum_{l=1}^{m} C_{il} Y_{cil} (1 - Y_{cil}) \tag{47.11}$$

where $C_{il}$ is equal to $l$th subarea divided by the total wafer area. At the end, the final wafer yield should be modeled as well. It is obvious that parameters of the final wafer yield distribution can be calculated by [31]

$$\bar{Y} = \sum_{l=1}^{m} C_l Y_{cl} \tag{47.12}$$

$$\sigma_Y^2 = \frac{1}{N} \sum_{l=1}^{m} C_l Y_{cl} (1 - Y_{cl}) \tag{47.13}$$

In the most complex case, summations should be done for each IC chip from the wafer separately, with $C_{il} = 1/N$; however, when there is a large number of chips on a wafer, this procedure is too cumbersome and the following approximations can be used:

$$\bar{Y} = \prod_{i=1}^{k} \bar{Y}_i \tag{47.14}$$

$$\sigma_Y^2 = \prod_{i=1}^{k} (\sigma_{Y_i}^2 + \bar{Y}_i^2) - \left( \prod_{i=1}^{k} \bar{Y}_i \right)^2 \tag{47.15}$$

The wafer yield distribution itself can be obtained by Monte Carlo simulation [12], with a simulation cycle consisting of:

- calculation of the final chip yield of each chip (Eq. (47.9)),
- decision of acceptance or rejection for each chip using a uniform pseudo-random number, and
- adding up of the number of failure-free chips on a wafer.

In some specific cases, the distribution of wafer yield can be approximated by known distribution functions. For example, if the total number of chips on a wafer is large ($N > 30$), a Gaussian (normal) distribution function can be used as an approximation:

$$f(Y) = \frac{1}{\sqrt{2\pi}\sigma_Y} \exp\left( -\frac{(Y - \bar{Y})^2}{2\sigma_Y^2} \right) \tag{47.16}$$

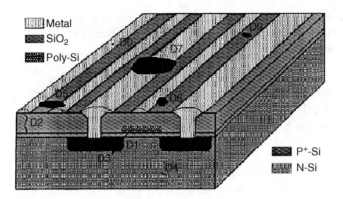

**FIGURE 47.4**   Point and lithographic defects in IC chip.

This distribution function cannot be used when the chip size increase is not accompanied by corresponding increase of the wafer size, and the total number of chips on a wafer is small. Then we can apply for approximation a binomial distribution function given by

$$f\left(Y = \frac{n}{N}\right) = \binom{N}{n} Y_c^n (1 - Y_c)^{N-n} \qquad (47.17)$$

where $Y_c$ is the value of final chip yield calculated by expression (47.9). Because of the small number of chips on a wafer, the clustering of defects cannot be recognized and the values of final chip yields $Y_{cl}$ are very close to each other.

## Critical Area Models

Yield models generally require the estimation of IC critical area associated with each type of catastrophic defects, i.e., each type of primitive failures. Examples of the defects include point defects (pinholes in insulator layers, dislocations, etc.) and lithographic defects (spots on IC chip). Some of these defects are shown in Fig. 47.4.

### Critical Area for Point Defects

Two most significant types of primitive failures in ICs related to their layer structure are a vertical short of two horizontal conducting layers through oxide (caused by a pinhole) and a leakage current increase (due to defects of silicon crystal lattice in the depletion region of p-n junction). The critical area for both of them can be defined as an overlap area of layout patterns from different IC conducting layers (silicon, polysilicon, or metal), i.e., IC mask layers [32]. Consider a domain shown in Fig. 47.5, where two layout patterns from two different mask layers are overlapping. If $(x_1, y_1)$ and $(x_2, y_2)$ denote canonical coordinates of overlap area, an overlap area $A_l$ is given by

$$A_l = (x_2 - x_1)(y_2 - y_1) \qquad (47.18)$$

In the case of defects in the depletion region of p-n junction, it is needed to calculate a vertical part of overlap area $A_v$ as well. The following expression is used for this calculation:

$$A_v = 2z[(x_2 - x_1) + (y_2 - y_1)] \qquad (47.19)$$

where $z$ is the depth of p-n junction. The total critical area for point defects $A_p$ is equal to a sum of the lateral part $A_l$ and the vertical part $A_v$.

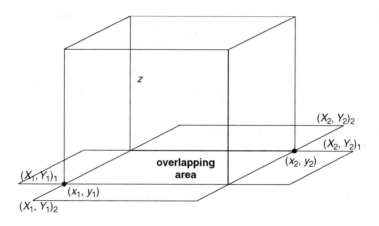

**FIGURE 47.5** Definition of IC critical area for point defects.

$$AB = x - s; \ GA = GC = \sin\alpha \ x/2; \ GE = \cos\alpha \ x/2$$
$$CD = CE = x/2; \ DF = s/2; \ |CF|^2 = x^2/4 - s^2/4$$
$$|2GA|^2 = |AC|^2 = \frac{(x-s)^2}{4} + \frac{x^2}{4} - \frac{s^2}{4} = \frac{x(x-s)}{2}$$

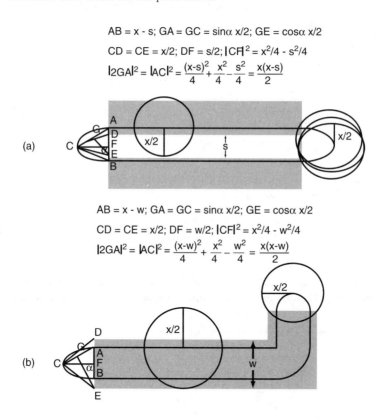

$$AB = x - w; \ GA = GC = \sin\alpha \ x/2; \ GE = \cos\alpha \ x/2$$
$$CD = CE = x/2; \ DF = w/2; \ |CF|^2 = x^2/4 - w^2/4$$
$$|2GA|^2 = |AC|^2 = \frac{(x-w)^2}{4} + \frac{x^2}{4} - \frac{w^2}{4} = \frac{x(x-w)}{2}$$

**FIGURE 47.6** Definition of IC critical area for lithographic defects.

## Critical Area for Lithographic Defects

Lithographic defects are extra and missing material spots on IC caused by particles and mask defects. The sizes of these defects are comparable to critical dimensions of IC layout patterns and, therefore, they can result in short and open circuits. The critical area for both of them can be defined as an area in which the center of a defect must fall to cause one of these failures. If the assumption of circular defects is valid, the critical area is a function of the defect diameter $x$. Consider the examples shown in Fig. 47.6. An example in Fig. 47.6(a) shows two geometrical objects of a circuit layout from the same mask layer and the equivalent critical area for shortening them. Moreover, an example in Fig. 47.6(b) shows a geometrical object of a circuit layout and the equivalent critical area for opening it. We have proposed the following expression [33]:

$$A_{s^0}(x) = \frac{x-s}{8}\sqrt{x^2 - s^2} + \frac{x^2}{4}\left(\arcsin\sqrt{\frac{x-s}{2x}} - \sqrt{\frac{x-s}{2x}}\cos\arcsin\sqrt{\frac{x-s}{2x}}\right) \tag{47.20}$$

for the definition of the circular part of the critical area for shortening two geometrical objects, and the expression [33]:

$$A_{o^0}(x) = \frac{x-w}{8}\sqrt{x^2 - w^2} + \frac{x^2}{4}\left(\arcsin\sqrt{\frac{x-w}{2x}} - \sqrt{\frac{x-w}{2x}}\cos\arcsin\sqrt{\frac{x-w}{2x}}\right) \tag{47.21}$$

for the definition of the circular part of the critical area for opening a geometrical object, where $x$ is the defect diameter, $s$ is the spacing between objects, $w$ is the width of an object, and $x \geq s, w$. The total critical areas can be calculated by

$$A_s(x) = L(x-s) + \frac{x-s}{2}\sqrt{x^2 - s^2} + x^2\left(\arcsin\sqrt{\frac{x-s}{2x}} - \sqrt{\frac{x-s}{2x}}\cos\arcsin\sqrt{\frac{x-s}{2x}}\right) \tag{47.22}$$

$$A_o(x) = L(x-w) + \frac{x-w}{2}\sqrt{x^2 - w^2} + x^2\left(\arcsin\sqrt{\frac{x-w}{2x}} - \sqrt{\frac{x-w}{2x}}\cos\arcsin\sqrt{\frac{x-w}{2x}}\right) \tag{47.23}$$

where $L$ is the length of objects.

The estimation of the critical area associated with lithographic defects requires averaging with respect to the defect size distribution as follows [3]:

$$A = \int_0^\infty A(x)h(x)\,dx \tag{47.24}$$

where $A(x)$ ($A_s(x)$ or $A_o(x)$) is the critical area associated with defects of a given size, and $h(x)$ is the defect size distribution. A Gamma distribution function (Fig. 47.7) is used to describe the defect size

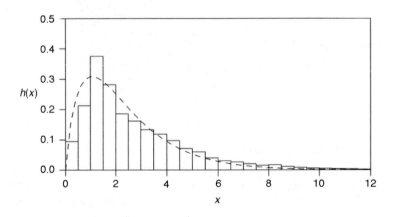

**FIGURE 47.7** Empirical defect size distribution (histogram) and defect size distribution approximated by Gamma distribution function (dashed line).

distribution [34,35]:

$$h(x) = \frac{x^{\alpha-1}\exp(-x/\beta)}{\Gamma(\alpha)\beta^{\alpha}} \qquad (47.25)$$

Parameters $\alpha$ and $\beta$ are the fitting parameters that can be determined from the measured data from the following expressions:

$$M(X) = \alpha\beta = \sum_{j=1}^{k} x_j f_j \qquad (47.26)$$

$$D(x) = \alpha\beta^2 = \sum_{j=1}^{k} x_j^2 f_j - \left(\sum_{j=1}^{k} x_j f_j\right)^2 \qquad (47.27)$$

where $M(x)$ and $D(x)$ are the mean and variance of the measured defect size distribution, $x_j$ is the middle of $j$th interval, and $f_j$ is the normalized number of defects with the size fallen into $j$th interval.

## 47.3 Critical Area Extraction

To facilitate failure simulations and IC yield predictions, the layout information such as minimum spacing and widths, and the critical areas for conducting layers must be extracted. An extractor to obtain the above layout information automatically is needed. Typical layout extraction approaches [36,37] extract the desired information for the entire circuit at once in a global way; however, due to the methodology requirements of the local failure simulators [38–56] as well as a visual inspection of the critical areas [45,47,55], it is convenient to have an extractor where performance is optimized for local layout extraction. To achieve this goal, the described critical area models and internal data structures are used for storing the geometrical objects (rectangles) of a circuit layout and these critical areas.

In this section, a local critical area extraction approach is described. Moreover, an extraction algorithm and implementation details for both the front-end and back-end of the extraction system are presented.

### Local Extraction Approach

The canonical coordinates of the critical area for point defects, i.e., overlap area of layout patterns from two IC conducting layers $A_l$ (Fig. 47.5) have already been defined. These coordinates can be simply extracted from the canonical coordinates of overlapping layout patterns (rectangles) as follow:

$$x_1 = \max(X_{1_1}, X_{1_2}) \qquad (47.28)$$

$$x_2 = \min(X_{2_1}, X_{2_2}) \qquad (47.29)$$

$$y_1 = \max(Y_{1_1}, Y_{1_2}) \qquad (47.30)$$

$$y_2 = \min(Y_{2_1}, Y_{2_2}) \qquad (47.31)$$

Canonical coordinates $(x_1, y_1)$ and $(x_2, y_2)$ are defined for a geometrical representation of the equivalent critical areas for lithographic defects by considering examples shown in Fig. 47.8. Consequently, canonical coordinates of the equivalent critical area for shortening two geometrical objects, in the case

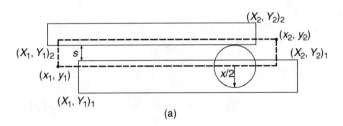

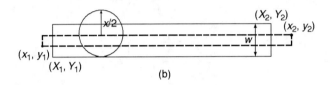

**FIGURE 47.8**   Definition of canonical coordinates of the equivalent critical area for shorts (a) and opens (b).

of $s = \max(Y_{1_1}, Y_{1_2}) - \min(Y_{2_1}, Y_{2_2})$, can be obtained by making use of the following expressions [33]:

$$x_1 = \max(X_{1_1}, X_{1_2}) - \frac{2A_s{}^0(x)}{x - s} \tag{47.32}$$

$$x_2 = \min(X_{2_1}, X_{2_2}) + \frac{2A_s{}^0(x)}{x - s} \tag{47.33}$$

$$y_1 = \min(Y_{2_1}, Y_{2_2}) - (x/2 - s) \tag{47.34}$$

$$y_2 = \max(Y_{1_1}, Y_{1_2}) + (x/2 - s) \tag{47.35}$$

but, in the case of $s = \max(X_{1_1}, X_{1_2}) - \min(X_{2_1}, X_{2_2})$, by making use of the expressions [33]:

$$x_1 = \min(X_{2_1}, X_{2_2}) - (x/2 - s) \tag{47.36}$$

$$x_2 = \max(X_{1_1}, X_{1_2}) + (x/2 - s) \tag{47.37}$$

$$y_1 = \max(Y_{1_1}, Y_{1_2}) - \frac{2A_s{}^0(x)}{x - s} \tag{47.38}$$

$$y_2 = \min(Y_{2_1}, Y_{2_2}) + \frac{2A_s{}^0(x)}{x - s} \tag{47.39}$$

Canonical coordinates of the equivalent critical area for opening a geometrical object, in the case of $w = Y_2 - Y_1$, are given by the expressions [33]:

$$x_1 = X_1 - \frac{2A_o{}^0(x)}{x - w} \tag{47.40}$$

$$x_2 = X_2 + \frac{2A_o{}^o(x)}{x - w} \tag{47.41}$$

$$y_1 = Y_1 - (x/2 - w) \tag{47.42}$$

$$y_2 = Y_2 + (x/2 - w) \tag{47.43}$$

and, in the case of $w = X_2 - X_1$, by the expressions [33]:

$$x_1 = X_1 - (x/2 - w) \tag{47.44}$$

$$x_2 = X_2 + (x/2 - w) \tag{47.45}$$

$$y_1 = Y_1 - \frac{2A_o{}^o(x)}{x - w} \tag{47.46}$$

$$y_2 = Y_2 + \frac{2A_o{}^o(x)}{x - w} \tag{47.47}$$

The simplest way to extract the critical area for shortening and opening geometrical objects is the comparison of a geometrical object to all the other geometrical objects. This is computationally prohibitive in the case of modern ICs that can contain millions of transistors due to its $O(n^2)$ performance, where $n$ is the total number of objects. Therefore, algorithms that enable efficient processing of geometrical objects and minimization of the number of comparisons between object pairs must be used. These algorithms are more complex than $O(n)$ and their complexity determines the CPU time and memory consumption.

Two main types of methods are used to scan objects in an IC layout: raster-scan based algorithm [57] and edge-based scan-line algorithm [58]. In raster-scan algorithms, the chip is examined in a raster-scan order (left to right, top to bottom) looking through an I-shaped window containing three raster elements. The main advantage is simplicity, but a lot of time is wasted scanning over grid squares where no information is to be gained. It further requires that all geometry be aligned with the grid. Edge-based scan-line algorithms divide the chip into a number of horizontal strips where the state within the strip does not change in the vertical direction. Change in state occurs only at the interface between two strips. At the interface, the algorithm steps through the list of objects touching the scan-line and makes the necessary updates to state. One of the main advantages of these algorithms over the raster-scan algorithms is that empty space and large device structures are extracted easily. Because scan-line algorithms are superior to raster-scan algorithms, a typical scan-line algorithm is used with a list for storing the incoming objects where the top edges coincide with the scan-line. Then every object in this list is sorted and inserted into another list called active list [32]. In the meantime, layout extractions are carried out by comparison of the object being inserted to other objects in the active list. An object then exits the active list when the scan-line is at or below its bottom edge.

## Data Structures

The choice of a data structure for efficient geometrical object representation plays an important role. The local extraction methodology is chosen, so a good candidate for the data structure requires a fast region query operation and reasonable memory consumption. Many data structures are suggested for the local extraction purposes. Among them, singly linked list, bin, k-d tree, and quad tree have been used most often [59–61]. A singly linked list is the most memory efficient but has the slowest region query performance. Conversely, a bin structure has the fast region query but consumes the most memory space. Both k-d tree and quad tree reside in the middle and have a trade-off between speed and memory space.

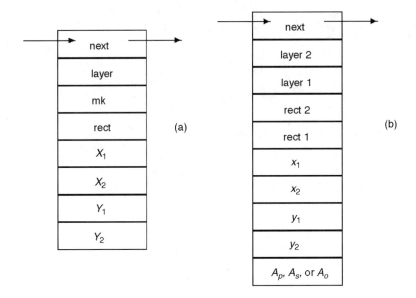

**FIGURE 47.9**   Data structure for a geometrical object representation in the active list (a) and data structure for critical area representation (b).

The layout information can be obtained by manipulating any efficient local extraction algorithm on the geometrical objects stored in internal data structure.

Two kinds of data structures are needed for the critical area extraction. The first one is used for efficient object representation in the active list. To minimize the number of comparisons between object pairs, a suitable structure should be developed so that extraction can be performed as locally as possible. A singly linked list is chosen for the active list not only for its simplicity, but also for its speed and memory efficiency [32,62]. The chosen singly linked list and corresponding data structure are described in Fig. 47.9(a). It contains fields $X_1$, $X_2$, $Y_1$, and $Y_2$, which represent the coordinates of the left, right, bottom, and top edges of a rectangle, respectively, and three additional fields called *layer*, *rect*, and *mk* used to indicate the layer number, the rectangle number, and the rectangles of the same pattern. The comparisons between active rectangles stored in the active list can be carried out as locally as possible by examining the sorted coordinates of rectangles. The second data structure is used for a list of coordinates of the critical areas (Fig. 47.9(b)). It contains fields $x_1$, $x_2$, $y_1$, and $y_2$, which represent the coordinates of the left, right, bottom, and top edges of the critical area, respectively, and a field $A_p$, $A_s$, or $A_o$, which represents the value of critical area itself. This data structure also includes four additional fields called *layer* 1, *layer* 2, *rect* 1 and *rect* 2 used to indicate the layer and rectangle numbers.

## Extraction Algorithm

The main tasks of described approach are to find out all pairs of overlapping rectangles from two IC mask layers, to determine canonical coordinates of their overlap areas $(x_1, y_1)$ and $(x_2, y_2)$, and to compute the critical areas by making use of Eqs. (47.18) and (47.19) or, in the case of extraction of the critical areas for lithographic defects, to find out all objects narrower than the largest defect with the diameter $x_{max}$, all pairs of objects with a spacing between them shorter than the largest defect diameter $x_{max}$, to determine canonical coordinates of the critical areas $(x_1, y_1)$ and $(x_2, y_2)$ for the largest defect diameter $x_{max}$, and to compute the critical areas by making use of the expression (47.24). Therefore, an algorithm has been developed for local critical area extraction based upon the scan-line method for scanning the sorted geometrical objects and the singly linked list for representation of the active list of geometrical objects. The main steps of the algorithm are as follows [32,62].

## Algorithm

- *Input:* a singly linked list of rectilinearly oriented rectangles sorted according to the top edges from top to bottom from two different IC mask layers (i.e., from the same IC mask layer in the case of extraction of the critical areas for lithographic defects).
- *Output:* overlap areas between rectangles from two different IC mask layers (i.e., the critical areas for opens and shorts between rectangles from the same IC mask layer).

1. Set the scan-line to the top of the first rectangle from input list.
2. WHILE (the scan-line $\geq$ the top of the last rectangle from input list)
   1. Update an active list called SOR;
   2. Fetch rectangles from input list whose the top coincides with the scan-line and store them in a singly linked list called TR;
   3. Update the scan-line;
   4. FOR each new rectangle in TR

      1. *Seek/Left* sorts the new rectangle and inserts it into SOR, computes $A_l$ and $A_v$ (i.e., $A_s^0$, $A_s$, $A_o^0$ and $A_o$) for the new rectangle and rectangles from SOR left to it, and computes and stores the coordinates of overlap areas in a singly linked list (i.e., the coordinates of critical areas for short and open circuits in two singly linked lists);
      2. *Seek/Right* computes $A_l$ and $A_v$ (i.e., $A_s^0$, $A_s$, $A_o^0$ and $A_o$) for the last inserted rectangle into SOR and rectangles from SOR right to it, and computes and stores the coordinates of overlap areas in a singly linked list (i.e., the coordinates of critical areas for short and open circuits in two singly linked lists);
   3. Write the critical areas into output files.

The scanning process starts with setting the scan-line to the top edge of the first rectangle from input list. The second step is a loop for updating the active list and moving the scan-line. To update rectangles in SOR, substep 2.1 of the above algorithm performs comparison between the current scan-line and the bottom edges of rectangles in SOR. If the bottom edge of a rectangle is above the current scan-line for a threshold value (in the case of critical areas for lithographic defects, the largest defect diameter $x_{max}$) or more, a rectangle will be deleted from SOR. This guarantees that the critical areas for short circuit between any two rectangles in the $y$-direction can be detected. Substep 2.2 makes a singly linked list TR contained rectangles with the same $y$-coordinates of the top edges. This step enables to sort rectangles according to the $x$-coordinate of the left edge. The $y$-coordinate of the next scan-line (substep 2.3) is equal to the top edge of the next rectangle in input list. Substep 2.4 sorts and inserts each new rectangle from TR into the SOR active list, and computes and stores the critical areas in output lists. The last step of the algorithm writes the content of output lists, i.e., coordinates of the critical areas $(x_1, y_1)$ and $(x_2, y_2)$, as well as values of the critical areas $A_p$, $A_s$ or $A_o$ in output files.

Procedure *Seek/Left* takes the new rectangle from TR and the SOR active list as inputs and reports the critical areas as output. Rectangles are sorted by the comparison of their left edge coordinates $X1$s. The sorted rectangles are stored in the active list SOR. Procedure *Seek/Right* takes the last inserted rectangle into SOR and SOR itself as input and reports the critical areas as output. In a loop of this procedure, the place of the last inserted rectangle *SOR is checked first by the comparison of its right edge coordinate $X2$ with the left edge coordinate $X1$ of the current SOR rectangle. It enables to end this loop earlier.

Note that geometrical objects (rectangles) from two IC mask layers have to be stored in the active list during extraction of the overlap areas. In the contrary, geometrical objects from only one IC mask layer have to be stored in this list during extraction of the critical areas for lithographic defects. A simple example illustrating the proposed algorithm is described in Fig. 47.10. The figure presents rectangles in the active list with scan-lines shown in sequence. When the scan-line reaches the position S1, the newest rectangle in SOR is the rectangle 6. In the meantime, the critical area for opening this rectangle and the critical areas for shortening it with the rectangles 3 and 4 are computed. As the scan-line moves down,

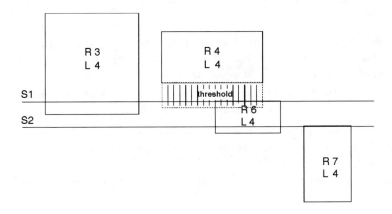

S1: (3,4) (4,4) (6,4)

S2: (3,4) (6,4) (7,4)

**FIGURE 47.10**  Scan-lines with rectangles in the active list.

**FIGURE 47.11**  Software system for extraction of IC critical areas.

its next stopping position is S2. Now the newest rectangle in the active list is the rectangle 7. In the same time, the rectangle 4 exits the active list because the spacing between its bottom edge and the current scan-line is greater than a threshold value ($x_{max}$). By making use of the described algorithm, the critical areas related to point and lithographic defects for any IC can be extracted.

## Implementation and Performance

The layout extraction starts from the layout description in CIF format and ends by reporting the critical areas for point or lithographic defects. In our case, this procedure is done through software system, which consists of three tools. The previous algorithm is only dedicated to the back-end of the entire system and is implemented in a program called EXACCA (EXtrActor of Chip Critical Area). The structure of this system is shown in Fig. 47.11.

### TRAnsformer of CIF (TRACIF)

The front-end of system is a technology-independent processor for transforming IC layout description from the unrestricted to a restricted format TRACIF [63]. The unrestricted format can contain overlapping rectangles, as well as rectangles making bigger rectangles from the same IC mask layer; however, an internal restricted geometric representation should contain a set of nonoverlapping rectangles that about only along horizontal edges. Two important properties are part of the restricted format:

- Coverage—Each point in the *x-y* plane is contained in exactly one rectangle. In general, a plane may contain many different types of rectangles.
- Strip—Patterns of the same IC mask layer are represented with horizontal rectangles (strips) that are as wide as possible, then as tall as possible. The strip structure provides a canonical form for the database and prevents it from fracturing into a large number of small rectangles.

**TABLE 47.1** Processing Time and Number of Objects Before and After Transformation of CIF File by TRACIF

| IC Cell | Rec. No. Before Processing | Rec. No. After Processing | CPU Time (s) |
|---|---|---|---|
| buf.CO | 394 | 394 | 1.164 |
| buf.ME | 58 | 37 | 0.014 |
| buf.NP | 203 | 14 | 0.033 |
| buf.NW | 102 | 2 | 0.014 |
| buf.PO | 44 | 41 | 0.017 |
| buf.PP | 200 | 14 | 0.031 |
| buf.TO | 414 | 40 | 0.130 |
| buf.VI | 11 | 11 | 0.006 |
| chi.CO | 2 | 2 | 0.006 |
| chi.ME | 199 | 108 | 0.108 |
| chi.PO | 4 | 4 | 0.006 |
| chi.VI | 67 | 67 | 0.021 |
| exo.CO | 63 | 63 | 0.027 |
| exo.ME | 3 | 3 | 0.006 |
| exo.NP | 35 | 2 | 0.006 |
| exo.NW | 21 | 1 | 0.006 |
| exo.PO | 45 | 21 | 0.009 |
| exo.PP | 35 | 2 | 0.006 |
| exo.TO | 73 | 18 | 0.012 |
| exo.VI | 2 | 2 | 0.006 |
| ful.ME | 30 | 9 | 0.007 |
| ful.PO | 4 | 4 | 0.006 |
| ful.VI | 6 | 6 | 0.006 |
| hal.CO | 2 | 2 | 0.006 |
| hal.ME | 88 | 58 | 0.025 |
| hal.PO | 5 | 4 | 0.006 |
| hal.VI | 27 | 27 | 0.008 |
| hig.ME | 7 | 3 | 0.006 |
| hig.PA | 1 | 1 | 0.006 |
| hig.VI | 1 | 1 | 0.006 |

TRACIF takes a CIF file as input and generates files containing geometrical objects (rectangles) defined by the canonical coordinates of each IC cell and mask layer as outputs. Thus, the outputs of TRACIF are lists of sorted rectangles according to the top edges from top to bottom. TRACIF can handle Manhattan shaped objects and consists of about 800 lines of C code. Therefore, TRACIF is capable to perform the layout description transformation hierarchically. Namely, TRACIF transforms a CIF file to the restricted format in a hierarchical way and makes different files for different cells and layers. This feature is desirable because most of the modern IC designs exploit the technique of design hierarchy. Within this design methodology, the layout extraction is only required once for each layout cell. Here, the results of transforming CIF file of IC *chip* that was designed using double metal CMOS process will be presented. The total number of rectangles before and after processing, as well as the CPU time needed for transforming this CIF file by TRACIF on Silicon Graphics Indy workstation are shown in Table 47.1.

## EXtrActor of Chip Critical Area (EXACCA)

EXACCA takes the sorted rectangles and starts the critical area extraction by using the proposed algorithm. EXACCA can handle Manhattan-type objects and consists of about 2000 lines of C code. The outputs of EXACCA are lists of the critical areas for point or lithographic defects. Software tool GRAPH performs the visual presentation of the critical areas. Pictorial examples of the layouts and snapshots of the corresponding critical areas are shown in Figs. 47.12. and 47.13. Precision of a visual presentation

**FIGURE 47.12**   Layout of two metal layers of operational amplifier and corresponding critical (overlap) areas.

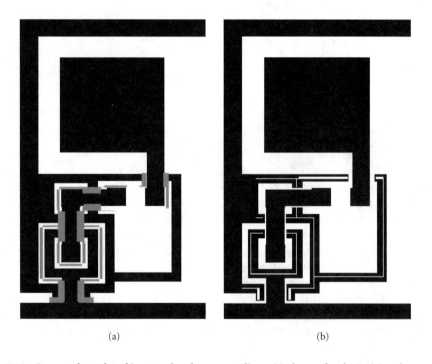

(a)                                                                      (b)

**FIGURE 47.13**   Layout of metal 1 of input pad and corresponding critical areas for shorts (a) and opens (b).

of the critical areas is limited by the error made in approximation of the circular parts by rectangular subareas.

To analyze the performance of the algorithm, an idealized model is used. If there are *n* uniformly distributed rectangles in a region of interest, there will be around √*n* rectangles, on an average, in each scan-line. Based upon this model, the time complexity of the algorithm is analyzed. Step 1 in the algorithm

**TABLE 47.2** Critical Area Extraction Time (in seconds) on Silicon Graphics Indy Workstation for Five Values of $x_{max}$

| Integrated Circuit | Number of Rectangles | 10 $\mu$m | 12 $\mu$m | 14 $\mu$m | 16 $\mu$m | 18 $\mu$m |
|---|---|---|---|---|---|---|
| chip | 4125 | 65.1 | 83.7 | 89.4 | 97.8 | 112.0 |
| counter4 | 11637 | 342.4 | 379.5 | 406.7 | 459.9 | 503.1 |
| counter6 | 19503 | 600.2 | 631.4 | 685.5 | 792.6 | 885.9 |
| counter8 | 24677 | 897.6 | 954.2 | 1083.6 | 1217.8 | 1399.8 |
| counter10 | 30198 | 1116.0 | 1338.1 | 1542.2 | 1689.5 | 1880.3 |

is trivial and takes a constant time. Step 2 is a loop with, on an average, $\sqrt{n}$ elements under which four substeps are required. Substeps 2.1 and 2.2 take $O(\sqrt{n})$ expected time due to the $\sqrt{n}$ length of elements in SOR and TR. Substep 2.3 takes a constant time. Substep 4 has $\sqrt{n}$ elements in a loop, under which sub-substeps 2.4.1 and 2.4.2 take $O(\sqrt{n})$. Hence, substep 4 takes $O(n)$ time. As a result, step 2 takes $O(n\sqrt{n})$ time. Note that the critical areas $A_s$ and $A_o$ are calculated using Simpson's method for numerical integration with the x-resolution 0.1 $\mu$m. Finally, step 3 takes a constant time. From the previous idealized analysis, the complexity of this algorithm is $CO(n\sqrt{n})$, where C is a constant. The approaches used in [41,42,44] promise $O(n \log n)$ performance, even though authors note that the actual consumption of CPU time is a very intensive.

Because today's VLSI circuits can contain up to 10 million transistors, the limitation of memory resources places an important role on extraction efficiency. To avoid running out of memory, special-coding techniques have to be employed. These techniques decrease the extraction efficiency, particularly for very big circuits. In general, this memory limitation problem affects the algorithms regardless of which data structure is used for the node representation of the active list. However, a singly linked list suffers the least due to its memory efficiency. Thus, a list structure is preferred as far as memory space is concerned. The memory consumption of EXACCA is proportional to $\sqrt{n}$.

Here, the simulated results of five examples, which were designed using double metal CMOS process, will be presented. The number of rectangles, as well as the CPU time of EXACCA on Silicon Graphics Indy workstation for these five IC layouts called *chip*, *counter4*, *counter6*, *counter8*, and *counter10* are shown in Table 47.2. The extraction speed is illustrated by the analysis of CPU times needed for the computation of critical areas for short and open circuits for five values of the largest defect diameter $x_{max}$. The extraction results show that a CPU time increases as the diameter of largest defect increases. Namely, the increase of the largest defect diameter means a greater threshold for updating the active list and, consequently, a greater number of rectangles in the active list. The increase of the number of comparisons between rectangle pairs causes a corresponding increase of the critical area extraction time. As can be seen from Table 47.2, one of the most important advantages of the proposed extraction algorithm and corresponding data structures is the ability to process large layouts in a relatively short CPU time.

## Applications

EXACCA ensures the microscopic layout information needed for more detailed analysis. Thus, the output of EXACCA may be used for any IC yield simulation system and design rule checking system. Also, our software system is useful for the classical yield models that require knowing the critical area of an IC chip. Caution should be taken in this case as the total critical area of a chip must be computed by finding the union of (not by adding) the critical areas. Regardless of the fact that this section has focused only on the extraction of critical areas, EXACCA can also be easily modified for the extraction of parasitic effects. Although the critical areas are required for the simulation of functional failures, the extraction of parasitic effects can be used for the simulation of performance failures.

This software system is capable to perform the critical area extraction hierarchically. Namely, TRACIF is capable to transform a CIF file to sorted lists in a hierarchical way. This feature is desirable since most of the modern IC designs exploit the technique of design hierarchy. Within this design methodology, the critical area extraction is only required once for each layout cell. Therefore, CPU time can be reduced significantly for extracting the critical areas of an IC with many duplicates of single cells. Following the design hierarchy, it can be used to predict and characterize yields of future products in order to decide about improvements in the corresponding layout cells that enable the desired yield.

## 47.4   Yield Forecast

By making use of the yield distribution model (see subsection "Yield Distribution Model") and the software system TRACIF/EXACCA/GRAPH (see subsection "Implementation and Performance"), yields associated with each defect type can be calculated and a sophisticated selection of IC types can be undertaken.

### Yield Calculations

An example of the characterization of IC production process is given in Table 47.3 (for point defects) and Table 47.4 (for lithographic defects). The critical processes listed in these tables were assumed to be responsible for the yield loss in double metal CMOS production process and were accompanied by in-line yield measurements made on the corresponding test structures, and the consequent yield analysis. The critical areas of test structures are in $mm^2$.

TRACIF/EXACCA/GRAPH system ensures, for the yield model, the critical area of IC (for given defect type) as a union of all local critical areas. Here, the simulated results for the IC chip, which was designed using double metal CMOS process, will be presented. The critical areas for five cells of this IC called *inpad, ota, buffer, selector,* and *exor* are shown in Tables 47.5 and 47.6. The numbers in parentheses denote how many times the corresponding cell appears in the circuit layout. As can be seen from Table 47.5, the critical areas for point defects (in $mm^2$) are defined as overlap areas of the corresponding mask layers. The first three are for defects of silicon crystal lattice in the depletion region of p-n junction and the second three are for pinholes in thin and CVD oxides.

**TABLE 47.3**  Yield Measurements for Point Defects

| Critical Process | $A_{ti}$ | $Y_{ti1}$ | $Y_{ti2}$ |
|---|---|---|---|
| NWI  | .4265 | .9754 | .9861 |
| PPI  | .0072 | .9960 | .9980 |
| NPI  | .0072 | .9980 | .9980 |
| TOX  | 1     | .9613 | .8547 |
| CVD1 | 1     | .9821 | .9654 |
| CVD2 | 1     | .9574 | .9203 |

**TABLE 47.4**  Yield Measurements for Lithographic Defects

| Critical Level | $A_{ti}$ | $Y_{ti1}$ | $Y_{ti2}$ |
|---|---|---|---|
| SPPI | .0042 | .8940 | .9168 |
| OPPI | .0042 | .8531 | .9328 |
| SNPI | .0042 | .9630 | .9842 |
| ONPI | .0042 | .9462 | .9750 |
| SCON | .0021 | .9351 | .9184 |
| OCON | .0021 | .9544 | .9076 |
| SPOL | .0042 | .8677 | .8559 |
| OPOL | .0042 | .9770 | .9642 |
| SME1 | .0042 | .8884 | .8520 |
| OME1 | .0042 | .9540 | .9397 |
| SME2 | .0042 | .7985 | .8220 |
| OME2 | .0042 | .8796 | .9081 |

**TABLE 47.5**   Critical Areas for Point Defects

| Cell Critical Area | inp (7) | ota (3) | buff (3) | selec (2) | exor (1) |
|---|---|---|---|---|---|
| NWI | .0060 | .0097 | .0168 | — | .0038 |
| PPI/NWI | .0007 | .0025 | .0019 | — | .0010 |
| NPI | .0005 | .0038 | .0021 | — | .0017 |
| POL/TOX | — | .0142 | .0013 | — | .0001 |
| ME1/POL | — | .0225 | .0002 | 0 | .0002 |
| ME2/ME1 | .0126 | .0118 | .0002 | 0 | 0 |

**TABLE 47.6**   Critical Areas for Lithographic Defects

| Cell Critical Area | inp (7) | ota (3) | buff (3) | selec (2) | exor (1) |
|---|---|---|---|---|---|
| SPPI | 31 | 0 | 14 | — | 0 |
| OPPI | 27 | 236 | 385 | — | 0 |
| SNPI | 0 | 59 | 16 | — | 0 |
| ONPI | 0 | 311 | 509 | — | 0 |
| SCON | 420 | 280 | 158 | — | 171 |
| OCON | 136 | 83 | 149 | — | 182 |
| SPOL | — | 127 | 145 | 0 | 138 |
| OPOL | — | 133 | 198 | 0 | 290 |
| SME1 | 214 | 916 | 858 | 80 | 519 |
| OME1 | 25 | 1194 | 880 | 17 | 531 |
| SME2 | 0 | 56 | 72 | 0 | 0 |
| OME2 | 176 | 321 | 387 | 0 | 28 |

**TABLE 47.7**   Yield Predictions for Point Defects

| Critical Process | $A_{ci}$ | $\bar{Y}_i$ | $\partial^2_{Y_i}$ |
|---|---|---|---|
| NWI | .1253 | .9943 | $6.51 \times 10^{-6}$ |
| PPI | .0191 | .9921 | $9.04 \times 10^{-6}$ |
| NPI | .0229 | .9936 | $7.25 \times 10^{-6}$ |
| TOX | .0466 | .9954 | $5.21 \times 10^{-6}$ |
| CVD1 | .0683 | .9982 | $2.08 \times 10^{-6}$ |
| CVD2 | .1242 | .9922 | $8.92 \times 10^{6}$ |
| Total | — | .9663 | $3.75 \times 10^{-5}$ |

Also, the critical areas for lithographic defects in Table 47.6 (in $\mu m^2$) can be divided into two groups. The first one consists of the critical areas for shorts and the second one contains the critical areas for opens.

The wafer yield predictions are shown in Table 47.7 (for point defects) and Table 47.8 (for lithographic defects). The total number of chips in a wafer was $N = 870$ and $C_{il} = C_l = 1/2$. The critical areas are calculated as a sum of the corresponding critical areas of all cells. Calculations needed for getting the mean and variance of the wafer yield related to each critical process step, as well as the mean and variance of the final wafer yield are carried out by means of Eqs. (47.8)–(47.15). The values of these parameters can now be used to decide about a possible corrective action.

## IC Type Selection

A usual approach to the IC production control needs estimating the defect density and does not give the opportunity for selection of IC types; however, the authors' approach uses both yield parameters, the mean and variance of the wafer yield distribution function, and enables sophisticated selection of IC types.

**TABLE 47.8**   Yield Predictions for Lithographic Defects

| Critical Level | $A_{ci}$ | $\bar{Y}_i$ | $\partial^2_{Y_i}$ |
|---|---|---|---|
| SPPI | .000259 | .9939 | $6.98 \times 10^{-6}$ |
| OPPI | .002052 | .9459 | $5.83 \times 10^{-5}$ |
| SNPI | .000225 | .9986 | $1.65 \times 10^{-6}$ |
| ONPI | .002460 | .9767 | $2.61 \times 10^{-5}$ |
| SCON | .004425 | .8520 | $1.45 \times 10^{-4}$ |
| OCON | .001830 | .9396 | $6.48 \times 10^{-5}$ |
| SPOL | .000954 | .9668 | $3.69 \times 10^{-5}$ |
| OPOL | .001283 | .9909 | $1.03 \times 10^{-5}$ |
| SME1 | .007499 | .7804 | $1.96 \times 10^{-4}$ |
| OME1 | .006962 | .9135 | $9.07 \times 10^{-5}$ |
| SME2 | .000384 | .9809 | $2.15 \times 10^{-5}$ |
| OME2 | .003384 | .9135 | $9.06 \times 10^{-5}$ |
| Total | — | .4490 | $2.84 \times 10^{-4}$ |

**TABLE 47.9**   Yield Prediction Results

| | Wafer Yield $Y_i$ | |
|---|---|---|
| Critical Process | Chip 1 | Chip 2 |
| 1. p$^-$-diffusion | 0.952 | 0.884 |
| 2. p$^+$-diffusion | 0.845/0.928[*] | 0.671/0.792[*] |
| 3. n$^+$-diffusion | 0.966 | 0.897 |
| 4. Gate oxide formation | 0.993 | 0.978 |
| 5. Photoprocess contacts | 0.984 | 0.949 |
| 6. Photoprocess metal | 0.958 | 0.867 |
| Final wafer yield $\bar{Y}$ | 0.727/0.799[*] | 0.428/0.505[*] |

[*]after investment in p$^+$-diffusion process

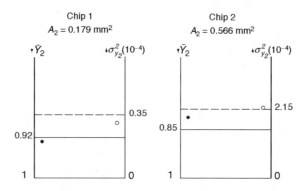

**FIGURE 47.14**   Example of IC type selection.

An example of the selection of CMOS IC types is given in Table 14.9 and Fig. 47.14. Six critical processes were assumed to be responsible for the yield loss, and were accompanied by in-line yield measurements and the consequent yield analysis. It can be seen from Table 14.9 that in this particular example, the yield associated with p$^+$-diffusion was much smaller than the yields of the other process steps and, therefore, was the main cause of the wafer yield loss. It is obvious that in this example an investment in the process of p$^+$-diffusion would be extremely beneficial. An investment made to improve the process of p$^+$-diffusion (enhancement of the process cleanliness, etc.) resulted in the final wafer yield increase of over 10%. Such a yield improvement could not be achieved by any investment in any other critical process step.

The usual approach to the IC production control is based on the defect or fault density measurements, and does not take into account the dependence on the complexity of a given IC type. Therefore, the lot of wafers may be stopped regardless of the IC type. Namely, a given defect density level can enable a decent yield (and price) of simpler IC chips, but it may not be sufficient to achieve the desired yield and price of more complex IC chips. The approach considered in this paper does not suffer of described disadvantage. Moreover, it can be used to forecast and characterize yields of future products in order to decide about investments that enable the desired final IC production yield.

In the considered example of production of IC *Chip*1, it is estimated that the mean and variance of the wafer yield associated with $p^+$-diffusion should be higher than 0.92 and lower than $3.5 \times 10^{-5}$, respectively, in order to ensure the acceptable value of the final wafer yield. It can be seen from Fig. 47.14 that the currently established $p^+$-diffusion process fulfills the imposed requirements; however, in the case of production of IC *Chip*2, the same defect density associated with the $p^+$-diffusion process has resulted in the mean of the wafer yield 0.792 and its variance $2.23 \times 10^{-4}$, both of them being out of estimated limits presented in Fig. 47.14. Therefore, in order to achieve the competitive price with a possible production of more complex IC *Chip*2, a further investment in $p^+$-diffusion process should be made.

## 47.5  Summary

Basic IC yield models (Murphy's approach) and yield parameters (test structure yield, chip yield, and wafer yield) are presented. Both defect density and defect size distributions are described. Using corresponding in-line measurements of the test structure yields, the chip yield, associated with the *i*th critical process step, is directly calculated; however, the chip yield is not sufficient for complete yield characterization, and the wafer yield, defined as a ratio between the number of failure-free chips and the total number of chips on a wafer, is predicted as well. We define the wafer yield as a distribution with two statistical parameters: the mean and variance.

A local layout extraction approach for hierarchical extraction of the IC critical areas for point and lithographic defects is described. The authors propose new expressions for definition of the circular parts of critical areas for shorts and opens between IC patterns. Also, the Gamma distribution is proposed as an approximation of the measured lithographic defect size distribution for estimating of the average critical area. It is shown that the Gamma distribution provides good agreement with the measured data, thus leading to a precise estimation of the critical area. Canonical coordinates $(x_1, y_1)$ and $(x_2, y_2)$ have been defined for a geometrical representation of the equivalent critical areas for shortening two geometrical objects and opening a geometrical object. Two kinds of data structures are used for the critical area extraction. The first one is used for efficient object representation in the active list. A singly linked list is chosen for the active list not only for its simplicity, but also for its speed and memory efficiency. The second data structure is used for a list of coordinates of the critical areas. The extraction of critical areas is carried out by an algorithm that solves this problem time proportional to $n\sqrt{n}$, on average, where $n$ is the total number of the analyzed geometrical objects (rectangles). This algorithm is a typical scan-line algorithm with singly linked lists for storing and sorting the incoming objects. The performance of the authors' algorithm is illustrated on five layout examples by the analysis of CPU time consumed for computing the critical areas applying a software tool system TRACIF/EXACCA/GRAPH.

The chip and wafer yields associated with each critical process step (i.e., each defect type) are determined by making use of the above-described approach. The final wafer yield predictions are made as well. An example of such a characterization of IC production process is described. It is shown that the proposed approach can be used for modeling yield loss mechanisms and forecasting effects of investments that are required in order to ensure a competitive yield of ICs. Our approach uses both wafer yield parameters, the mean and variance, and enables sophisticated selection of IC types.

# References

1. Hofstein, S. and Heiman, F., The silicon insulated-gate field-effect transistor, *Proc. IEEE*, 51, 511, 1963.
2. Stapper, C.H., Modeling of integrated circuit defect sensitivities, *IBM J. Res. Develop.*, 27, 549, 1983.
3. Stapper, C.H., Modeling of defects in integrated circuit photolithographic patterns, *IBM J. Res. Develop.*, 28, 461, 1984.
4. Ferris-Prabhu, A.V., Modeling the critical area in yield forecasts, *IEEE J. Solid-State Circuits*, 20, 874, 1985.
5. Ferris-Prabhu, A.V., Defect size variations and their effect on the critical area of VLSI devices, *IEEE J. Solid-State Circuits*, 20, 878, 1985.
6. Koren, I., The effect of scaling on the yield of VLSI circuits, in *Proc. Yield Modeling and Defect Tolerance in VLSI*, Moore, W., Maly, W., and Strojwas, A., Eds., Bristol, 1988, 91.
7. Kooperberg, C., *Circuit layout and yield, IEEE J. Solid-State Circuits*, 23, 887, 1988.
8. Murphy, B.T., Cost-size optima of monolithic integrated circuits, *Proc. IEEE*, 52, 1537, 1964.
9. Price, J.E., A new look at yield of integrated circuits, *Proc. IEEE*, 58, 1290, 1970.
10. Stapper, C.H., Defect density distribution for LSI yield calculations, *IEEE Trans. on Electron Devices*, 20, 655, 1973.
11. Seeds, R.B., Yield, economic, and logistic models for complex digital arrays, in *Proc. IEEE International Convention Record*, 1967, 61(6).
12. Yanagawa, T., Yield degradation of integrated circuits due to spot defects, *IEEE Trans. on Electron Devices*, 19, 190, 1972.
13. Okabe, T., Nagata, M., and Shimada, S., Analysis on yield of integrated circuits and a new expression for the yield, *Elect. Eng. Japan*, 92, 135, 1972.
14. Warner, R.M., Applying a composite model to the IC yield problem, *IEEE J. Solid-State Circuits*, 9, 86, 1974.
15. Stapper, C.H., LSI yield modeling and process monitoring, *IBM J. Res. Develop.*, 20, 228, 1976.
16. Hu, S.M., Some considerations on the formulation of IC yield statistics, *Solid-State Electronics*, 22, 205, 1979.
17. Hemmert, R.S., Poisson process and integrated circuit yield prediction, *Solid-State Electronics*, 24, 511, 1981.
18. Stapper, C.H. and Rosner, R.J., A simple method for modeling VLSI yields, *Solid-State Electronics*, 25, 487, 1982.
19. Stapper, C.H., Armstrong, F.M., and Saji, K., Integrated circuit yield statistics, *Proc. IEEE*, 71, 453, 1983.
20. Stapper, C.H., The effects of wafer to wafer defect density variations on integrated circuit defect and fault distributions, *IBM J. Res. Develop.*, 29, 87, 1985.
21. Stapper, C.H., On yield, fault distributions and clustering of particles, *IBM J. Res. Develop.*, 30, 326, 1986.
22. Stapper, C.H., Large-area fault clusters and fault tolerance in VLSI circuits: A review, *IBM J. Res. Develop.*, 33, 162, 1989.
23. Michalka, T.L., Varshney, R.C., and Meindl, J.D., A discussion of yield modeling with defect clustering, circuit repair, and circuit redundancy, *IEEE Trans. on Semiconductor Manufacturing*, 3, 116, 1990.
24. Cunningham, S.P., Spanos, C.J., and Voros, K., Semiconductor yield improvement: Results and best practices, *IEEE Trans. on Semiconductor Manufacturing*, 8, 103, 1995.
25. Berglund, C.N., A unified yield model incorporating both defect and parametric effects, *IEEE Trans. on Semiconductor Manufacturing*, 9, 447, 1996.
26. Dance, D. and Jarvis, R., Using yield models to accelerate learning curve progress, *IEEE Trans. on Semiconductor Manufacturing*, 5, 41, 1992.
27. Semiconductor Industry Association, *1978–1993 Industry Data Book*, 1994.

28. Corsi, F. and Martino, S., Defect level as a function of fault coverage and yield, in *Proc. European Test Conference*, 1993, 507.

29. Stapper, C.H. and Rosner, R.J., Integrated circuit yield management and yield analysis: Development and implementation, *IEEE Trans. on Semiconductor Manufacturing*, 8, 95, 1995.

30. Kuo, W. and Kim, T., An overview of manufacturing yield and reliability modeling for semiconductor products, *Proc. IEEE*, 87, 1329, 1999.

31. Dimitrijev, S., Stojadinovic, N., and Stamenkovic, Z., Yield model for in-line integrated circuit production control, *Solid-State Electronics*, 31, 975, 1988.

32. Stamenkovic, Z., Algorithm for extracting integrated circuit critical areas associated with point defects, *International Journal of Electronics*, 77, 369, 1994.

33. Stamenkovic, Z., Stojadinovic, N., and Dimitrijev, S., Modeling of integrated circuit yield loss mechanisms, *IEEE Trans. on Semiconductor Manufacturing*, 9, 270, 1996.

34. Stamenkovic, Z. and Stojadinovic, N., New defect size distribution function for estimation of chip critical area in integrated circuit yield models, *Electronics Letters*, 28, 528, 1992.

35. Stamenkovic, Z. and Stojadinovic, N., Chip yield modeling related to photolithographic defects, *Microelectronics and Reliability*, 32, 663, 1992.

36. Gupta, A., ACE: A circuit extractor, in *Proc. 20th Design Automation Conference*, 1983, 721.

37. Su, S.L., Rao, V.B., and Trick, T.N., HPEX: A hierarchical parasitic circuit extractor, in *Proc. 24th Design Automation Conference*, 1987, 566.

38. Maly, W., Modeling of lithography related yield loss for CAD of VLSI circuits, *IEEE Trans. on Computer-Aided Design of ICAS*, 4, 166, 1985.

39. Walker, H. and Director, S.W., VLASIC: A catastrophic fault yield simulator for integrated circuits, *IEEE Trans. on Computer-Aided Design of ICAS*, 5, 541, 1986.

40. Chen, I. and Strojwas, A., Realistic yield simulation for VLSIC structural failures, *IEEE Trans. on Computer-Aided Design of ICAS*, 6, 965, 1987.

41. Gyvez, J.P. and Di, C., IC defect sensitivity for footprint-type spot defects, *IEEE Trans. on Computer-Aided Design of ICAS*, 11, 638, 1992.

42. Allan, G.A., Walton, A.J., and Holwill, R.J., An yield improvement technique for IC layout using local design rules, *IEEE Trans. on Computer-Aided Design of ICAS*, 11, 1355, 1992.

43. Khare, J., Feltham, D., and Maly, W., Accurate estimation of defect-related yield loss in reconfigurable VLSI circuits, *IEEE J. Solid-State Circuits*, 28, 146, 1993.

44. Dalal, A., Franzon, P., and Lorenzetti, M., A layout-driven yield predictor and fault generator for VLSI, *IEEE Trans. on Semiconductor Manufacturing*, 6, 77, 1993.

45. Wagner, I.A. and Koren, I., An interactive VLSI CAD tool for yield estimation, *IEEE Trans. on Semiconductor Manufacturing*, 8, 130, 1995.

46. Gaitonde, D.D. and Walker, D.M.H., Hierarchical mapping of spot defects to catastrophic faults—design and applications, *IEEE Trans. on Semiconductor Manufacturing*, 8, 167, 1995.

47. Chiluvuri, V.K.R. and Koren, I., Layout-synthesis techniques for yield enhancement, *IEEE Trans. on Semiconductor Manufacturing*, 8, 178, 1995.

48. Khare, J. and Maly, W., Rapid failure analysis using contamination-defect-fault (CDF) simulation, *IEEE Trans. on Semiconductor Manufacturing*, 9, 518, 1996.

49. Mattick, J.H.N., Kelsall, R.W., and Miles, R.E., Improved critical area prediction by application of pattern recognition techniques, *Microelectronics and Reliability*, 36, 1815, 1996.

50. Nag, P.K. and Maly, W., Hierarchical extraction of critical area for shorts in very large scale ICs, in *Proc. IEEE Workshop on Defect and Fault Tolerance in VLSI Systems*, Lafayette, 1995, 19.

51. Allan, G.A. and Walton, A.J., Efficient critical area measurements of IC layout applied to quality and reliability enhancement, *Microelectronics Reliability*, 37, 1825, 1997.

52. Allan, G.A. and Walton, A.J., Critical area extraction for soft fault estimation, *IEEE Trans. on Semiconductor Manufacturing*, 11, 146, 1998.

53. Milor, L.S., Yield modeling based on in-line scanner defect sizing and a circuit's critical area, *IEEE Trans. on Semiconductor Manufacturing*, 12, 26, 1999.

54. Allan, G.A. and Walton, A.J., Efficient extra material critical area algorithms, *IEEE Trans. on Computer-Aided Design of ICAS*, 18, 1480, 1999.

55. Allan, G.A., Yield prediction by sampling IC layout, *IEEE Trans. on Computer-Aided Design of ICAS*, 19, 359, 2000.

56. Nakamae, K., Ohmori, H., and Fujioka, H., A simple VLSI spherical particle-induced fault simulator: Application to DRAM production process, *Microelectronics Reliability*, 40, 245, 2000.

57. Baker, C. and Terman, C., Tools for verifying integrated circuit designs, *VLSI Design*, 1, 1980.

58. Bentley, J.L. and Ottman, T.A., Algorithms for reporting and counting geometric intersections, *IEEE Trans. on Computers*, 28, 643, 1979.

59. Bentley, J.L., Haken, D., and Hon, R., Fast geometric algorithms for VLSI tasks, in *Proc. IEEE CompCon*, Spring 1980, 88.

60. Ousterhout, J., Corner stitching: A data-structuring technique for VLSI layout tools, *IEEE Trans. on Computer-Aided Design of ICAS*, 3, 87, 1984.

61. Rosenberg, J.B., Geographical data structures compared: A study of data structures supporting region queries, *IEEE Trans. on Computer-Aided Design of ICAS*, 4, 53, 1985.

62. Stamenkovic, Z., Extraction of IC critical areas for predicting lithography-related yield, *Facta Universitatis Nis, Series: Electronics and Energetics*, 12, 87, 1999.

63. Jankovic, D., Milenovic, D., and Stamenkovic, Z., Transforming IC layout description from the unrestricted to a restricted format, in *Proc. 21st International Conference on Microelectronics*, Niš, 1997, 733.

# Index